D0214350

THE
CAMBRIDGE
MEDIEVAL HISTORY

VOLUME IV. PART I

THE
CAMBRIDGE
MEDIEVAL HISTORY

VOLUME IV
THE BYZANTINE EMPIRE
PART I
BYZANTIUM AND ITS NEIGHBOURS

EDITED BY

J.M.HUSSEY

WITH THE EDITORIAL ASSISTANCE OF

D.M.NICOL AND G.COWAN

CAMBRIDGE UNIVERSITY PRESS

CAMBRIDGE
LONDON · NEW YORK · MELBOURNE

Published by the Syndics of the Cambridge University Press
The Pitt Building, Trumpington Street, Cambridge CB2 1RP
Bentley House, 200 Euston Road, London NW1 2DB
32 East 57th Street, New York, NY 10022, USA
296 Beaconsfield Parade, Middle Park, Melbourne 3206, Australia

© Cambridge University Press 1966

Library of Congress catalogue card number: 30–24288

ISBN: 0 521 04535 5

First published 1966
Reprinted 1975

Printed in Great Britain
at the
University Printing House, Cambridge
(Euan Phillips, University Printer)

PREFACE

This new edition is in a very real sense the outcome of N. H. Baynes' work for Byzantine studies in England and it is fitting that my acknowledgements should begin with a tribute to the distinguished scholar who continued the work of J. B. Bury, the original architect of the *Cambridge Medieval History*. The actual volumes would have been prepared with Baynes' help had not illness made this impossible. But in its early stages the project to replan the Byzantine volume in this series was long discussed with him and owes much to his guiding wisdom and discerning scholarship.

This is essentially the corporate enterprise of an international team of scholars and I am much indebted to their forbearance and generosity, particularly in undertaking the revision necessitated by unavoidable delays and in coming to the rescue in the face of unforeseen crises. When Professor Henri Grégoire was incapacitated by illness Professor R. J. H. Jenkins finished his chapter. One contributor withdrew at the last moment and Dr D. M. Nicol filled the gap at very short notice. Two contributors did not live to see their chapters in print and thanks are due to Professor R. J. H. Jenkins for his help with the proofs of the late Mr H. St L. B. Moss (chapter I) and to Father Joseph Gill, S.J., who dealt with those of the late Father Emil Herman, S.J. (chapter XXIV). I wish to record my special gratitude to Dr Janet Sondheimer. She translated a number of chapters, which in some cases had to be considerably adapted to reduce them to the required length, and she made many valuable comments on the text.

During the later stages of the work I was fortunate in being able to draw on Dr D. M. Nicol's expert advice and he gave most generous assistance in preparing the chapters for press and in many other ways. To Miss G. Cowan I am particularly indebted for help in proof reading both text and bibliographies and for making the Index; her wide knowledge and constant vigilance did much to reduce the errors and inconsistencies which so easily creep into a work of this complexity.

I have to thank Professor C. Toumanoff for drawing the maps of Armenia and Georgia (maps 10, 11 and 12), Professor D. Obolensky for help with the Slav territories (maps 8 and 9), and Professor B. Lewis and the late Dr D. E. Pitcher for suggestions in connection with Islamic lands and the eastern frontier (maps 13, 14 and 15).

I am also grateful to Dr D. M. Nicol for his general assistance in preparing the maps.

Among scholars who have assisted with the illustrations special thanks are due to Professor A. Grabar who was mainly responsible for their selection. I am most grateful for the advice which I have had from Professor H. Buchthal, Dr Alison Frantz, the late Mr H. St L. B. Moss, Dr D. M. Nicol, Professor D. Talbot Rice and Professor P. Underwood. Mr P. D. Whitting has generously provided the notes on the coins which were selected by him. For permission to publish I wish to thank the American School of Classical Studies at Athens, the Byzantine Institute of America, the Warburg Institute, the Dumbarton Oaks Research Library, the Agora Museum, the Corinth Museum, the British Museum, the Musée du Louvre, the Victoria and Albert Museum, Professor H. Buchthal, Dr Alison Frantz, Professor A. Grabar and Professor D. Talbot Rice.

Many other colleagues and friends have helped at all stages. I should like to record my gratitude to Mr J. S. F. Parker for editorial work on the first drafts, Dr D. I. Polemis for assistance with genealogies and proof reading, Professor P. Orgels for his work in connection with Professor Grégoire's chapter, Professor E. H. Sondheimer for help in translating the chapter on Byzantine Science, the late Dr C. M. Ady, Dr D. A. Bullough and Dr J. F. Fearns for advice on Italian history, the Rev. D. J. Chitty for a preview of his Birkbeck lectures and Dr A. D. Stokes for help with the transliteration of Slav words. And for various reasons I am also much indebted to the following: Miss E. Bickersteth, Mr P. Grierson, Miss J. L. Hurn, Professor D. M. Lang, Professor B. Lewis, Miss M. Pemberton, Professor K. M. Setton, Dr G. J. Whitrow and Miss A. Williams. I am most grateful to the secretariat of my own college for expert assistance in dealing during the past twelve years with an intractable mass of typescript. Finally it is a particular pleasure to acknowledge my debt to those of the staff of the Cambridge University Press who have helped with this enterprise, especially Mr P. G. Burbidge, whose magnificent efforts have made it possible to produce these volumes in the face of unending obstacles.

In accordance with the practice of this series, the Latin form of Greek names has generally been used, except for personal names where there is a familiar English version. In territories variously occupied by different races the same place-name may appear in more than one form, but it is hoped that the uninitiated will find some clue to such variants in the Index.

The typescript of both parts went to press in the autumn of 1961 and only a few bibliographical additions were possible after this date. The bibliographies vary in scope according to the subject-matter and the wishes of contributors. Those on Byzantium, the main concern of these volumes, may be supplemented by reference to the works cited in the General Bibliography.

J. M. H.

July 1964

INTRODUCTION

'Constantine sitting amongst the Christian bishops at the oecumenical council of Nicaea is in his own person the beginning of Europe's Middle Age.'[1] Baynes thus recognised the significance of the fourth century in the history of the Roman Empire and of Europe. Probably few scholars would still consider 717 to be the best starting point for a history of the Byzantine Empire. But unfortunately the original volume IV of the *Cambridge Medieval History* (*The Eastern Roman Empire 717–1453*) had to be revised in isolation without any foreseeable possibility of including volumes I and II which at present deal with early Byzantine history to 717 along with that of western Europe. Therefore the limiting dates of Bury's plan had to be adhered to. The most that could be done for the new volume IV was to provide two introductory chapters covering the vital years from Constantine the Great to the accession of Leo III in 717 and to ensure that such subjects as the secular church and monasticism, art and architecture, as well as political and administrative topics where necessary, included some reference to the formative period of the fourth to the seventh centuries.

Byzantine history is still in process of being written. Even so, work done since 1923 when the original volume IV appeared makes expansion possible and re-orientation inevitable. For this reason the old volume IV has been entirely replanned and rewritten (even though there could be no radical change in the limiting dates 717–1453). It was with great regret that it was decided to part with some of the brilliant contributions in the earlier volume IV, notably those of Charles Diehl on Byzantine civilisation and William Miller on the Latins in the Aegean. These still stand as memorials to Diehl's pioneer work in the Byzantine field and to Miller's historical insight based on his first-hand knowledge of Greece and the Aegean. But each generation must write its own histories: hence the complete abandonment of the old volume IV, except for J. B. Bury's Introduction.

The main emphasis in the two new volumes is placed on the history of Byzantium itself. Chapters have been added on administration, the church (including music), art, social life, literature and science, and the influence of Byzantium. Greater space has been given to the political history of the Empire. At the same time it has been possible to include (as before) a brief account of some of the near neighbours of Constantinople and their relations with Byzantium. The Balkan

[1] *CAH*, XII, p. 699.

and the Islamic countries of the near and middle East appear as in the 1923 volume; Hungary and the Caucasian lands, vital factors in the Byzantine political world, are all included. Venice, so closely linked with East Rome, has been retained as previously. On the other hand, Italy and the western European countries receive full attention in their own right in the other volumes of this series, though, as will be apparent, they do in fact impinge on the Byzantine story rather more than Bury would allow.

Perhaps the most marked advances of this century in Byzantine research have been in the field of music and in administrative and economic history. In Part II of these volumes music, with its close liturgical associations, is treated as an integral part of secular and ecclesiastical life. Administration is now shown to be a flexible system capable of organic development and adaptation, and the ancillary sciences, as for instance, numismatics, have contributed towards filling out administrative and prosopographical details. Even so, scholars are still reconstructing the work and personalities of Byzantine administrators and officials, and the full fruit of such investigations will not come in this generation. Another achievement of comparatively recent research is fuller knowledge of Byzantine land ownership and of various other aspects of economic life. As a result it is necessary to modify Bury's attribution of the Byzantine downfall to the evil effects of the Fourth Crusade.[1] Even before 1204, signs of internal difficulties were apparent. The development of vast landed estates threatened the central authority, while the marked antagonism between the civil aristocracy centred in Constantinople and the military landed magnates of the provinces was a feature of the Byzantine economy fully in evidence by the eleventh century. This threat to effective central control was certainly heightened by the disintegration of the Empire after 1204, but it must be admitted that Byzantine power had already been considerably weakened when this occurred, and was subsequently further undermined by civil wars, particularly during the fourteenth century.

Byzantium played an important role in the trade and industry of the medieval world, at least before it was supplanted by the Italian cities after 1204. The contribution of its merchants and its craftsmen is not however treated here in its own right. When these volumes were planned it was understood that this particular aspect of Byzantine life would be fully covered in the *Cambridge Economic History*, though this has in fact not proved to be the case. Economic, like administrative, history is still in process of investigation, but even so it is to be regretted that these volumes do not contain at least an

[1] See below, p. xvi.

interim report on commerce and industry. It also proved impracticable to provide chapters on military and naval defence and on the influence of geographical factors as had originally been intended.

The case for including some indication of the relations of Byzantium with its Caucasian, Muslim and Slav neighbours is self-evident. Both the Armenian and the Georgian principalities were near neighbours, and individual Armenians played a particularly significant role in the internal life of Byzantium. There were economic, and often cultural, relations with the Muslims, whether Umayyads, Abbasids, Fatimids or others. The Slavs in the Balkans also had specially close relations with Constantinople and although one might now hesitate to go as far as Bury did in saying that they 'owed absolutely everything' to the Empire,[1] their debt to Byzantium in many aspects of their medieval life is generally recognised.

Byzantium had its own integrated civilisation which was continuous throughout the middle ages, but it is being increasingly realised that the East Roman Empire cannot be viewed in isolation. Contacts were often casual and came about by chance, as in the case of Greek monks who settled in western communities and *vice versa*. Diplomatic and commercial intercourse was carefully regulated, but many other channels of communication existed. The manuscript or ivory which found its way into some royal or episcopal western treasury, or the active theological discussions between Latin and Greek theologians or the Greek tutors sent to the west to instruct some Byzantine bride-elect, all served to bring about exchange of knowledge and experience of different traditions. In the crusading period and the later middle ages contacts were perforce closer, and not always as hostile as is often imagined. Byzantium, though proudly aware of its former power, may have been only a pawn in the diplomatic game, but in other ways its influence was by no means negligible. The westerners who settled in Byzantine lands after the Fourth Crusade put down roots in Greek soil and came to know something of its civilisation. In the midst of what had once been Greek strongholds, Chios still bears witness to the Genoese occupation, and the Venetian Castro of Naxos to the Italian families who long flourished there. At the same time deeper knowledge of the classical and Hellenistic and Byzantine traditions passed to the West, where after many vicissitudes there has eventually grown up a fuller understanding of medieval Greek civilisation and the role of Byzantium, so that by now this has almost dispelled the myth of Gibbon's long and continuous decline and fall.   J.M.H.

---

[1] See below, p. xvi.

J.B.Bury's Introduction to the original volume IV published in 1923[1]

The present volume carries on the fortunes of a portion of Europe to the end of the Middle Ages. This exception to the general chronological plan of the work seemed both convenient and desirable. The orbit of Byzantium, the history of the peoples and states which moved within that orbit and always looked to it as the central body, giver of light and heat, did indeed at some points touch or traverse the orbits of western European states, but the development of these on the whole was not deeply affected or sensibly perturbed by what happened east of Italy or south of the Danube, and it was only in the time of the Crusades that some of their rulers came into close contact with the Eastern Empire or that it counted to any considerable extent in their policies. England, the remotest state of the West, was a legendary country to the people of Constantinople, and that imperial capital was no more than a dream-name of wealth and splendour to Englishmen, except to the few adventurers who travelled thither to make their fortunes in the Varangian guards. It is thus possible to follow the history of the Eastern Roman Empire from the eighth century to its fall, along with those of its neighbours and clients, independently of the rest of Europe, and this is obviously more satisfactory than to interpolate in the main history of Western Europe chapters having no connexion with those which precede and follow.

Besides being convenient, this plan is desirable. For it enables us to emphasise the capital fact that throughout the Middle Ages the same Empire which was founded by Augustus continued to exist and function and occupy even in its final weakness a unique position in Europe—a fact which would otherwise be dissipated, as it were, and obscured amid the records of another system of states with which it was not in close or constant contact. It was one of Gibbon's services to history that the title of his book asserted clearly and unambiguously this continuity.

We have, however, tampered with the correct name, which is simply *Roman Empire*, by adding *Eastern*, a qualification which although it has no official basis is justifiable as a convenient mark of distinction from the Empire which Charlemagne founded and which lasted till the beginning of the nineteenth century. This Western

[1 This is reprinted as a tribute to the distinguished Byzantinist who planned the *Cambridge Medieval History*. It remains unaltered except for the omission of Bury's references to chapters in the 1923 volume and the addition of editorial comments in square brackets. Ed.]

Empire had no good claim to the name of Roman. Charlemagne and those who followed him were not legitimate successors of Augustus, Constantine, Justinian, and the Isaurians, and this was tacitly acknowledged in their endeavours to obtain recognition of the imperial title they assumed from the sovrans of Constantinople whose legitimacy was unquestionable.

Much as the Empire changed after the age of Justinian, as its population became more and more predominantly Greek in speech, its descent from Rome was always unmistakably preserved in the designation of its subjects as Romans ('Ρωμαῖοι). Its eastern neighbours knew it as Rūm. Till the very end the names of most of the titles of its ministers, officials, and institutions were either Latin or the Greek translations of Latin terms that had become current in the earliest days of the Empire.[1] Words of Latin derivation form a large class in medieval Greek. The modern Greek language was commonly called *Romaic* till the middle of the nineteenth century. It is only quite recently that *Roumelia* has been falling out of use to designate territories in the Balkan peninsula. Contrast with the persistence of the Roman name in the East the fact that the subjects of the Western Empire were never called Romans and indeed had no common name as a whole; the only 'Romans' among them were the inhabitants of the city of Rome. There is indeed one district in Italy whose name still commemorates the Roman Empire—*Romagna*; but this exception only reinforces the contrast. For the district corresponds to the Exarchate of Ravenna, and was called Romania by its Lombard neighbours because it belonged to the Roman Emperor of Constantinople. It was at the New Rome, not at the Old, that the political tradition of the Empire was preserved. It is worth remembering too that the greatest public buildings of Constantinople were originally built, however they may have been afterwards changed or extended—the Hippodrome, the Great Palace, the Senatehouses, the churches of St Sophia and the Holy Apostles—by Emperors of Latin speech, Severus, Constantine, Justinian.

On the other hand, the civilisation of the later Roman Empire was the continuation of that of ancient Greece. Hellenism entered upon its second phase when Alexander of Macedon expanded the Greek world into the east, and on its third with the foundation of Constantine by the waters where Asia and Europe meet. Christianity, with

---

[1] Examples: (1) ἀσηκρῆτις (*a secretis*), δούξ, κόμης, μάγιστρος, πατρίκιος, δομέστικος, πραιπόσιτος, πραίτωρ, κουαίστωρ, κουράτωρ; ἰδίκτον, πάκτον; κάστρον, φοσσάτον, παλάτιον, βῆλον (*velum*); ἀπληκεύειν = (*castra*) *applicare*, παιδεύειν, δηριγεύειν; μοῦλτος = (*tu*)*multus*; (2) (ancient equivalents of Latin terms) βασιλεύς, αὐτοκράτωρ (*imperator*), σύγκλητος (*senatus*), ὕπατος (*consul*), ἀνθύπατος (*proconsul*), ὕπαρχος (*praefectus*), δρόμος (*cursus publicus*).

its dogmatic theology and its monasticism, gave to this third phase its distinctive character and flavour, and *Byzantine* civilisation, as we have learned to call it, is an appropriate and happy name....The continuity which links the fifteenth century A.D. with the fifth B.C. is notably expressed in the long series of Greek historians, who maintained, it may be said, a continuous tradition of historiography. From Critobulus, the imitator of Thucydides, and Chalcocondyles, who told the story of the last days of the Empire, we can go back, in a line broken only by a dark interval in the seventh and eighth centuries, to the first great masters, Thucydides and Herodotus.

The development of 'Byzantinism' really began in the fourth century. The historian Finlay put the question in a rather awkward way by asking, When did the Roman Empire change into the Byzantine? The answer is that it did not change into any other Empire than itself, but that some of the characteristic features of Byzantinism began to appear immediately after Constantinople was founded. There is, however, a real truth in Finlay's own answer to his question. He drew the dividing line at the accession of Leo the Isaurian, at the beginning of the eighth century. And, in fact, Leo's reign marked the consummation of a rapid change which had been going on during the past hundred years. Rapid: for I believe anyone who has studied the history of those centuries will agree that in the age of the Isaurians we feel much further away from the age of Justinian than we feel in the age of Justinian from the age of Theodosius the Great. Finlay's date has been taken as the starting point of this volume; it marks, so far as a date can, the transition to a new era.[1]

The chief function which *as a political power* the Eastern Empire performed throughout the Middle Ages was to act as a bulwark for Europe, and for that civilisation which Greece had created and Rome had inherited and diffused, against Asiatic aggression. Since the rise of the Sasanid power in the third century, Asia had been attempting, with varying success, to resume the role which it had played under the Achaemenids. The arms of Alexander had delivered for hundreds of years the Eastern coasts and waters of the Mediterranean from all danger from an Asiatic power. The Sasanids finally succeeded in reaching the Mediterranean shores and the Bosphorus. The roles of Europe and Asia were again reversed, and it was now for Byzantium to play on a larger stage the part formerly played by Athens and Sparta in a struggle for life and death. Heraclius proved himself not only a Themistocles but in some measure an Alexander. He not only checked the victorious advance of the enemy; he completely destroyed the power of the Great King and made him his vassal. But within ten

[1 For another view see above, p. ix. Ed.]

years the roles were reversed once more in that amazing transformation scene in which an obscure Asiatic people which had always seemed destined to play a minor part became suddenly one of the strongest powers in the world. Constantinople had again to fight for her life, and the danger was imminent and the strain unrelaxed for eighty years. Though the Empire did not succeed in barring the road to Spain and Sicily, its rulers held the gates of Europe at the Propontis and made it impossible for them to sweep over Europe as they had swept over Syria and Egypt. Centuries passed, and the Comnenians guarded Europe from the Seljuqs. The Ottomans were the latest bearers of the Asiatic menace. If the Eastern Empire had not been mortally wounded and reduced to the dimensions of a petty state by the greed and brutality of the Western brigands who called themselves Crusaders, it is possible that the Turks might never have gained a footing in Europe. Even as it was, the impetus of their first victorious advance was broken by the tenacity of the Palaeologi—assisted it is true by the arms of Timur. They had reached the Danube sixty years before Constantinople fell. When this at length happened, the first force and fury of their attack had been spent, and it is perhaps due to this delay that the Danube and the Carpathians were to mark the limit of Asiatic rule in Europe and that St Peter's was not to suffer the fate of St Sophia. Even in the last hours of its life, the Empire was still true to its traditional role of bulwark of Europe.

As a civilised state, we may say that the Eastern Empire performed three principal functions. As in its early years the Roman Empire laid the foundations of civilisation in the West and educated Celtic and German peoples, so in its later period it educated the Slavs of eastern Europe. Russia, Bulgaria, and Serbia owed it everything[1] and bore its stamp. Secondly, it exercised a silent but constant and considerable influence on western Europe by sending its own manufactures and the products of the East to Italy, France, and Germany. Many examples of its embroidered textile fabrics and its jewellery have been preserved in the West. In the third place, it guarded safely the heritage of classical Greek literature which has had on the modern world a penetrating influence difficult to estimate. That we owe our possession of the masterpieces of Hellenic thought and imagination to the Byzantines everyone knows, but everyone does not remember that those books would not have travelled to Italy in the fourteenth and fifteenth centuries, because they would not have existed, if the Greek classics had not been read habitually by the educated subjects of the Eastern Empire and therefore continued to be copied.

[1 This appears to do less than justice to the native contributions of these countries. Ed.]

Here we touch on a most fundamental contrast between the Eastern Empire and the western European states of the Middle Ages. The well-to-do classes in the West were as a rule illiterate, with the exception of ecclesiastics; among the well-to-do classes in the Byzantine world education was the rule, and education meant not merely reading, writing, and arithmetic, but the study of ancient Greek grammar and the reading of classical authors. The old traditions of Greek education had never died out. In court circles at Constantinople everyone who was not an utter parvenu would recognise and understand a quotation from Homer. In consequence of this difference, the intellectual standards in the West where book-learning was reserved for a particular class, and in the East where every boy and girl whose parents could afford to pay was educated, were entirely different. The advantages of science and training and system were understood in Byzantine society.

The appreciation of method and system which the Byzantines inherited both from the Greeks and from the Romans is conspicuously shewn in their military establishment and their conduct of war. Here their intellectuality stands out in vivid contrast with the rude dullness displayed in the modes of warfare practised in the West. Tactics were carefully studied, and the treatises on war which the officers used were kept up to date. The tacticians apprehended that it was stupid to employ uniform methods in campaigns against different foes. They observed carefully the military habits of the various peoples with whom they had to fight—Saracens, Lombards, Franks, Slavs, Hungarians—and thought out different rules for dealing with each. The soldiers were most carefully and efficiently drilled. They understood organisation and the importance of not leaving details to chance, of not neglecting small points in equipment. Their armies were accompanied by ambulances and surgeons. Contrast the feudal armies of the West, ill-disciplined, with no organisation, under leaders who had not the most rudimentary idea of tactics, who put their faith in sheer strength and courage, and attacked all antagonists in exactly the same way. More formidable the Western knights might be than Slavs or Magyars, but in the eyes of a Byzantine officer they were equally rude barbarians who had not yet learned that war is an art which requires intelligence as well as valour. In the period in which the Empire was strong, before it lost the provinces which provided its best recruits, its army was beyond comparison the best fighting machine in Europe. When a Byzantine army was defeated, it was always the incompetence of the general or some indiscretion on his part, never inefficiency or cowardice of the troops, that was to blame. The great disaster of Manzikert (1071), from which perhaps the decline of the Eastern Empire may be dated, was caused by the imbecility of the brave Emperor who was in command.[1] A distinguished student of the art of war has observed that Gibbon's dictum, 'the vices of Byzantine armies were inherent, their victories accidental', is precisely the reverse of the truth. He is perfectly right.

Military science enabled the Roman Empire to hold its own for many centuries against the foes around it, east and west and north. Internally, its permanence and stability depended above all on the rule of Roman law. Its subjects had always 'the advantage of possessing a systematic administration of justice enforced by fixed legal procedure'; they were not at the mercy of caprice. They could contrast their courts in which justice was administered with a systematic observance of rules, with those in which Mohammedan lawyers dispensed justice. The feeling that they were much better off under the government of Constantinople than their Eastern neighbours engendered a loyal attachment to the Empire, notwithstanding what they might suffer under an oppressive fiscal system.[2]

The influence of lawyers on the administration was always great, and may have been one of the facts which account for the proverbial conservatism of Byzantine civilisation. But that conservatism has generally been exaggerated, and even in the domain of law there was a development, though the foundations and principles remained those which were embodied in the legislation of Justinian.

The old Roman law, as expounded by the classical jurists, was in the East considerably modified in practice here and there by Greek and oriental custom, and there are traces of this influence in the laws of Justinian. But Justinianean law shows very few marks of ecclesiastical influence which in the seventh and following centuries led to various changes, particularly in laws relating to marriage. The lawbook of the Isaurian Emperor, Leo III, was in some respects revolutionary, and although at the end of the ninth century the Macedonian Emperors, eager to renounce all the works of the heretical Isaurians, professed to return to the pure principles of Justinian, they retained many of the innovations and compromised with others. The principal reforms of Leo were too much in accordance with public opinion to be undone. The legal status of concubinate for instance was definitely abolished. Only marriages between Christians were recognised as valid. Marriages between first and second cousins were forbidden. Fourth marriages were declared illegal and even third were discountenanced. It is remarkable however that in the matter of divorce, where the differences between the views of State and Church had been sharpest and where the Isaurians had given effect

[1 This judgement on Romanus IV Diogenes appears open to question. Ed.]
[2] Compare Finlay, *History of Greece*, II, 22–4; I, 411–12.

to the un-Roman ecclesiastical doctrine that marriage is indissoluble, the Macedonians returned to the common-sense view of Justinian and Roman lawyers that marriage like other contracts between human beings may be dissolved. We can see new tendencies too in the history of the *patria potestas*. The Iconoclasts substituted for it a parental *potestas*, assigning to the mother rights similar to those of the father....

In criminal law there was a marked change in tendency. From Augustus to Justinian penalties were ever becoming severer and new crimes being invented. After Justinian the movement was in the direction of mildness. In the eighth century only two or three crimes were punishable by death. One of these was murder and in this case the extreme penalty might be avoided if the murderer sought refuge in a church. On the other hand penalties of mutilation were extended and systematised. This kind of punishment had been inflicted in much earlier times and authorised in one or two cases by Justinian. In the eighth century we find amputations of the tongue, hand, and nose part of the criminal system, and particularly applied in dealing with sexual offences. If such punishments strike us today as barbaric (though in England, for instance, mutilation was inflicted little more than two centuries ago), they were then considered as a humane substitute for death, and the Church approved them because a tongue-less or nose-less sinner had time to repent. In the same way, it was a common practice to blind, instead of killing, rebels or un- successful candidates for the throne. The tendency to avoid capital punishment is illustrated by the credible record that during the reign of John Comnenus there were no executions.

The fact that in domestic policy the Eastern Empire was far from being obstinately conservative is also illustrated by the reform of legal education in the eleventh century, when it was realised that a system which had been in practice for a long time did not work well and another was substituted.... That conception of the later Empire which has made the word Byzantine almost equivalent to Chinese was based on ignorance, and is now discredited. It is obvious that no State could have lasted so long in a changing world, if it had not had the capacity of adapting itself to new conditions. Its administrative machinery was being constantly modified by capable and hardworking rulers of whom there were many; the details of the system at the end of the tenth century differed at ever so many points from those of the eighth. As for art and literature, there were ups and downs, declines and renascences, throughout the whole duration of the Empire. It is only in quite recent years that Byzantine literature and Byzantine art have been methodically studied; in these wide fields of research Krumbacher's *Byzantine Literature* and Strzygowski's *Orient oder*

Rom were pioneer works marking a new age. Now that we are getting to know the facts better and the darkness is gradually lifting, we have come to see that the history of the Empire is far from being a monotonous chronicle of palace revolutions, circus riots, theological disputes, tedious ceremonies in a servile court, and to realise that, as in any other political society, conditions were continually changing and in each succeeding age new political and social problems presented themselves for which some solution had to be found. If the chief interest in history lies in observing such changes, watching new problems shape themselves and the attempts of rulers or peoples to solve them, and seeing how the characters of individuals and the accidents which befall them determine the course of events, the story of the Eastern Empire is at least as interesting as that of any medieval State, or perhaps more interesting because its people were more civilised and intellectual than other Europeans and had a longer political experience behind them. On the ecclesiastical side it offers the longest and most considerable experiment of a State-Church that Christendom has ever seen.

The Crusades were, for the Eastern Empire, simply a series of barbarian invasions of a particularly embarrassing kind, and in the present volume they are treated merely from this point of view and their general significance in universal history is not considered. The full treatment of their causes and psychology and the consecutive story of the movement are reserved for Vol. v.

But the earlier history of Venice has been included in this volume. The character of Venice and her career were decided by the circumstance that she was subject to the Eastern Emperors before she became independent. She was extra-Italian throughout the Middle Ages; she never belonged to the Carolingian Kingdom of Italy. And after she had slipped into independence almost without knowing it—there was never a violent breaking away from her allegiance to the sovrans of Constantinople—she moved still in the orbit of the Empire; and it was on the ruins of the Empire, dismembered by the criminal enterprise of her Duke Dandolo, that she reached the summit of her power as mistress in the Aegean and in Greece. She was the meeting-place of two civilisations, but it was eastern not western Europe that controlled her history and lured her ambitions. Her citizens spoke a Latin tongue and in spiritual matters acknowledged the supremacy of the elder Rome, but the influence from new Rome had penetrated deep, and their great Byzantine basilica is a visible reminder of their long political connection with the Eastern Empire.

TABLE OF CONTENTS

CHAPTER I

THE FORMATION OF THE EAST ROMAN EMPIRE, 330–717

By the late H. ST L. B. MOSS

The first Christian Emperor	*page* 3
Advantages of site of Constantinople	5
Description of the city	7
New buildings and fortifications	9
Map	11
Constitutional position of the Emperor	13
Responsibilities of imperial power	15
Imperial victory. Church and State	17
The five Patriarchates	19
Arians and monophysites	21
Cleavage between Roman and Greek culture . . .	23
Strategic position of the Mediterranean	25
Invasions by Persians, Goths and Huns	27
Frontiers on the North and East	29
Expansion of Islam. Heraclian dynasty	31
Reorganisation of administration	33
Military recruitment. Anatolian themes	35
Centralised government and fiscal system	37
Power of great landowners	39
Trade and position of Constantinople	41

CHAPTER II

THE CHRISTIAN BACKGROUND

By G. MATHEW, O.P.

University Lecturer in Byzantine Studies in the University of Oxford

Transition from paganism to Christianity . . . *page* 43

Conception of imperial sovereignty 45

Continuity in system of education 47

Athanasius and the three Cappadocians 49

The Cappadocians and John Chrysostom 51

Theology of Cyril of Alexandria 53

Syria, Egypt and Asia Minor 55

Christology and monasticism 57

The ascetic ideal. *Corpus Dionysiacum* 59

CHAPTER III

ICONOCLASM AND IMPERIAL RULE 717–842

By M. V. ANASTOS

Professor of Byzantine Greek, University of California, Los Angeles

Reappraisal of Leo III 61

Leo III and the defeat of the Arabs 63

Theme system, taxation and the *Ecloga* 65

The beginnings of iconoclasm 67

Map 69

Transfer of dioceses to Constantinople 71

Constantine V's Arab campaigns 73

Bulgar wars. Negotiations with Italy 75

The Papacy and Pepin 77

The *Horos* and the theology of iconoclasm 79

Persecution of supporters of the images 81

Revolts against Irene. Arab wars . . . . . *page* 83

Deliberations of Seventh General Council 85

Christology and the question of images 87

Overthrow of Constantine VI by Irene 89

Irene overthrown by Nicephorus I 91

Reform of the army and of taxation 93

Studite opposition to Nicephorus I 95

Peace with Charlemagne. War with Krum 97

Leo V's iconoclastic policy 99

Wars and disputes under Michael II 101

The reign of Theophilus 103

CHAPTER IV

THE AMORIANS AND MACEDONIANS 842–1025

By the late H. GRÉGOIRE

Emeritus Professor of Greek and Byzantine History in the University of Brussels and President of the Centre Nationale de Recherches Byzantines, Brussels

Achievements of the regency 105

Career of Theoctistus 107

Conflict over Ignatius and Photius 109

Arabs defeated and Russians repelled 111

Rivalry with Rome over Bulgaria 113

Murder of Bardas and Michael III 115

Rise of Basil the Macedonian 117

Ignatian Council and the see of Bulgaria 119

Campaigns in Asia Minor and Calabria 121

Missionary work and the Slavonic liturgy 123

The Church in Moravia 125

Good relations with Rome restored 127

Bulgar and Arab attacks 129

Leo VI's four marriages . . . . . . *page* 131

The *Procheiron, Epanagoge* and *Basilica* 133

Diplomacy of the Patriarch Nicholas I 135

Zoe and the rise of Romanus Lecapenus 137

Peace with Bulgaria and war in the East 139

Russian attacks. Agrarian problems 141

Romanus I's land reforms and his fall 143

Property laws 145

War with the Arabs in Syria and Crete 147

Syrian campaigns of Nicephorus II 149

Capture of Antioch. Relations with Kiev 151

Sicilian campaigns. Agrarian laws 153

Nicephorus II and monastic policy 155

John Tzimisces and the Phocas family 157

Svjatoslav and his Russians in Bulgaria 159

The Russians attacked and defeated 161

Bulgaria subject to Byzantium 163

Tzimisces' Mesopotamian campaigns 165

Negotiations with Ashot III of Armenia 167

Campaigns against the Fatimids in Syria 169

Successes in Palestine and Syria 171

John Tzimisces' agrarian policy 173

The death of John Tzimisces 175

Revolt and defeat of Bardas Sclerus 177

Danger from Bulgaria. Civil war 179

Basil II's second Bulgarian campaign 181

Syrian campaign. Land reforms 183

Bulgarian campaigns 185

Victories over Samuel of Bulgaria 187

The Empire extended to north and east 189

Assessment of Basil II's achievements 191

CHAPTER V

THE LATER MACEDONIANS, THE COMNENI AND THE ANGELI 1025–1204

By J. M. HUSSEY

Professor of History in the University of London

Contrasts under the later Macedonians. . . . *page* 193

Failure to preserve Basil II's frontiers 195

Reigns of Romanus III and Michael IV 197

Michael V, the last of the Paphlagonians 199

Reorganisation of the university 201

Norman, Russian and Pecheneg attacks 203

Michael VI. Isaac I Comnenus 205

Isaac I's abdication. Constantine X 207

Loss of South Italy. Seljuq attacks 209

Reigns of Michael VII and Nicephorus III 211

Greece invaded by the Normans 213

The First Crusade 215

Alexius I's foreign and domestic policy 217

The *pronoia* and the *charisticium* 219

John II's relations with Hungary 221

The Normans in Sicily and in Syria 223

Struggle for control of Antioch 225

Manuel I and the Second Crusade 227

Expedition to South Italy 229

Plans for marriage alliances 231

Trouble with Venice, Rascia and Hungary 233

Surrender of Antioch to Manuel I 235

Defeat of Manuel I at Myriocephalum 237

Characteristics of Manuel I's policy 239

Weakening central auhority 241

Attempt to reconcile East and West 243

Andronicus I succeeded by Isaac II . . . . *page* 245

The Third Crusade 247

Decline of prestige in the Balkans 249

CHAPTER VI

VENICE TO THE EVE OF THE FOURTH CRUSADE

By R. CESSI

Emeritus Professor of Medieval and Modern History in the University of Padua

Venice as a Byzantine province 251

Separation of Istria and Venetia 253

End of the Exarchate of Ravenna 255

Factions and rivalries 257

Byzantine fleet in the Adriatic 259

Franco-Byzantine agreements over Venice 261

Growth of Venice as a mercantile city 263

Venice as a sovereign power 265

Peter I Orseolo and his successors 267

Dalmatian towns liberated from the Slavs 269

Alliance with Byzantium against Normans 271

Political institutions and legal codes 273

CHAPTER VII

THE FOURTH CRUSADE AND THE GREEK AND LATIN EMPIRES, 1204–61

By D. M. NICOL

Lecturer in Classics in University College, Dublin

Threats to Byzantium 275

Preparations for the Fourth Crusade 277

Arrival of Alexius, son of Isaac II 279

Diversion to Constantinople . . . . . . *page* 281

First attack on the capital 283

Preparations for the second attack 285

Sack of Constantinople by the crusaders 287

Partition of the Empire by the Latins 289

The Latins in Greece and Asia Minor 291

Attacks by Kalojan of Bulgaria 293

Byzantine Empire established at Nicaea 295

Venetians in Dyrrachium and Corfu 297

Career of Michael Ducas of Epirus 299

Achievements of the Latin Emperor Henry 301

The Greek Church under Latin rule 303

Theodore Ducas active in Epirus 305

Opposition of western Greeks to Nicaea 307

Capture of Thessalonica by the Greeks 309

Alliance between Nicaea and Bulgaria 311

Reappearance of Theodore Ducas 313

Thessalonica subject to Nicaea 315

John Vatatzes' gains in Macedonia 317

Respite for the Latin Empire 319

Byzantine culture in Nicaea 321

Revolt of Michael II of Epirus 323

The battle of Pelagonia 325

The recapture of Constantinople 327

Condition of the Empire after 1261 329

CHAPTER VIII

THE PALAEOLOGI

By G. OSTROGORSKY

*Professor of Byzantine History in the University of Belgrade and
Director of the Institute for Byzantine Studies, Belgrade*

Underlying weaknesses of Byzantium . . . . *page* 331

Gains in the Peloponnese and Bulgaria 333

Hostility of Sicily under the Angevins 335

Second Council of Lyons 337

Abandonment of plans for Church union 339

Power of the great landowners 341

Debasement of the coinage 343

Ecclesiastical and foreign policy 345

The Catalans in Asia Minor 347

The Catalan Company in Greece 349

Civil war between Andronicus II and III 351

Reorganisation of the judicial system 353

Turkish principalities in Asia Minor 355

Renewal of civil war 357

Class conflict and the Zealot party 359

Victory of John Cantacuzenus 361

Victory of hesychasm. Economic crisis 363

War with the Genoese 365

Abdication of John VI Cantacuzenus 367

John V's attempt at reunion with Rome 369

Byzantium a vassal of the Turks 371

Rebellion of Andronicus IV 373

The Turks in the Balkans and Greece 375

Bāyezīd defeated by Timur 377

Renewed Ottoman attacks 379

The Palaeologi in the Morea 381

Attacks on the Ottomans in the Balkans . . . *page* 383

Failure of Western help for Byzantium 385

The end of the Byzantine Empire 387

CHAPTER IX

THE LATINS IN GREECE AND THE AEGEAN FROM THE FOURTH CRUSADE TO THE END OF THE MIDDLE AGES

By K. M. SETTON

Henry Charles Lea Professor of History in the University of Pennsylvania

Latins established in central Greece 389

First parliament of Ravennika 391

Geoffrey I of Villehardouin in the Morea 393

The Greek Church under Latin rule 395

The Latin Church in the Morea 397

Geoffrey II of Villehardouin 399

Defeat of the Franks at Pelagonia 401

William of Villehardouin's successors 403

Angevin rule in Achaea 405

The Acciajuoli in the Morea 407

Otho de la Roche in Attica and Boeotia 409

End of the French duchy of Athens 411

The Catalan duchy of Athens 413

Administration of the Catalan duchy 415

Attempt to restore French rule in Athens 417

Advent of the Navarrese Company 419

Fighting between Catalans and Navarrese 421

The Florentine duchy of Athens 423

The Venetians in the Aegean islands 425

The Venetians in Crete 427

Relations between the Greeks and Latins 429

CHAPTER X

CONSTANTINOPLE AND ROME

By F. DVORNIK

*Emeritus Professor of Byzantine History, Dumbarton Oaks,
Center for Byzantine Studies, Trustees for Harvard University*

Christian Hellenism . . . . *page* 431

Primacy of honour of the Roman Church 433

Apostolicity 435

Justinian I and the primacy of Rome 437

Pope Gregory the Great 439

The monothelete heresy 441

Papal opposition to the Emperor Leo III 443

The Papacy and Pepin 445

Pope Leo III and Charlemagne 447

Carolingian views on Church and State 449

Pope Nicholas I and papal supremacy 451

Controversy between Photius and Ignatius 453

Papal intervention in Byzantine affairs 455

Idea of apostolicity in Constantinople 457

Reform of the Western Church 459

Michael Cerularius and Cardinal Humbert 461

Rift between Constantinople and Rome 463

Papal attempts to heal the schism 465

Urban II and the First Crusade 467

Innocent III and the Fourth Crusade 469

Attempts at reunion 471

CHAPTER XI

THE EMPIRE AND ITS NORTHERN NEIGHBOURS, 565–1018

By D. OBOLENSKY

Professor of Russian and Balkan History in the University of Oxford

Problems of imperial diplomacy . . . . . *page* 473

Justinian I's frontier policy 475

The Slavs. The Avars 477

Central Asian Turks and the silk routes . . . 479

Avar and Slav attacks on the Empire 481

Heraclius' frontier policy 483

Foundation of the Bulgarian state 485

Byzantine alliance with the Khazars 487

Slavs in the Balkans and the Peloponnese . . . 489

Conquests of Krum of Bulgaria 491

Missionary work among the Khazars 493

Southward migration of the Vikings 495

Mission to the Moravian Slavs 497

The Church in Bulgaria 499

Achievements of Cyril and Methodius 501

Symeon of Bulgaria 503

The Kievan state. Symeon of Bulgaria . . . 505

Symeon's imperial ambitions 507

Foundation of the Bulgarian Patriarchate . . . 509

Russia under Igor and Olga 511

Russian invasion of Bulgaria 513

Bulgaria annexed to the Byzantine Empire . . . 515

Conversion of Russia to Christianity 517

CHAPTER XII

THE BALKANS, 1018–1499

By M. DINIĆ

Emeritus Professor of Balkan History in the University of Belgrade

Byzantine domination challenged . . . . . *page* 519

Stephen Nemanja and Serbian independence . . . 521

Asen I and the Second Bulgarian Empire 523

Expansion of Bulgaria under Kalojan 525

Reigns of Boril and John Asen II 527

Byzantine influence in Bulgaria 529

The kingdom of Serbia and its Church 531

Serbian mining industry and trade 533

Serbia dominant in the Balkans 535

Decline of Bulgarian power 537

Stephen Dušan and the Serbian Empire 539

Break-up of the Serbian Empire 541

Bulgaria under the Šišman dynasty 543

Conquest of Bulgaria by the Turks 545

Bogomilism in the Bosnian Church 547

Expansion of Bosnian power 549

Defeat of the Serbs at Kossovo 551

Turkish occupation of Serbia 553

Final conquest of Serbia by the Turks 555

Turkish conquest of Bosnia 557

Fall of Zeta to the Turks 559

Principalities of Wallachia and Moldavia 561

Wallachia under Turkish control 563

Moldavia a Turkish vassal state 565

CHAPTER XIII

HUNGARY AND BYZANTIUM IN THE MIDDLE AGES

By GY. MORAVCSIK

Professor of Greek Philology in the University of Budapest

Origins of the Magyars . . . . *page* 567

Migrations and settlement in Hungary 569

Contacts with Byzantium 571

The Church in Hungary 573

Spread of Byzantine influence 575

The Crown of Constantine Monomachus 577

The Hungarian royal crown 579

Relations with the Comneni 581

Manuel I's plans for Béla (III) 583

Reign of Béla III 585

Greek Church and monasteries in Hungary 587

Relations with the Palaeologi 589

Byzantine appeals for help 591

CHAPTER XIV

ARMENIA AND GEORGIA

By C. TOUMANOFF

Professor of History and Director of the Russian Area Studies Programme in Georgetown University

The Caucasian polities 593

Conflict between Rome and Iran 595

Organisation of the Caucasian states 597

The partition of Armenia 599

Zoroastrianism and Christianity 601

End of monarchy in the Caucasian states . . . *page* 603

Overthrow of the Sassanids 605

Caucasia, Byzantium and the Arabs 607

Caucasia under Abbasid control 609

Rise of the Bagratids 611

Restoration of the monarchies 613

Caucasian architecture 615

Relations with the Byzantines 617

Annexations by the Byzantines 619

Armenia occupied by the Seljuq Turks 621

Bagratid rule in Georgia 623

The Golden Age in Georgia 625

Mongol invasions 627

Foundation of Lesser Armenia in Cilicia 629

Rubenid dynasty in Lesser Armenia 631

Prosperity of Cilicia under Leo II 633

Het'umid dynasty in Lesser Armenia 635

Mamluk occupation of Cilicia 637

CHAPTER XV

GOVERNMENT, SOCIETY AND ECONOMIC LIFE UNDER THE ABBASIDS AND FATIMIDS

By B. LEWIS

Professor of the History of the Near and Middle East in the University of London

Defeat of the Umayyads by the Abbasids 639

New capital built at Baghdad 641

The Caliphate and orthodox Islam 643

Rise of independent dynasties 645

The Buwayhids. Shī'ite expansion 647

The Fatimid Caliphate in Egypt 649

Administration. External enemies . . . . *page* 651

Turkic migrations. The Seljuq Turks 653

End of the Fatimid Caliphate 655

The Seljuq state. Shī'ism and Sunnism 657

Triumph of orthodox Islam 659

The Mongol attacks 661

CHAPTER XVI

MUSLIM CIVILISATION IN THE ABBASID PERIOD

By G. E. VON GRUNEBAUM

Professor of Near Eastern History and Director of the Near Eastern Center in the University of California

Cultural heritage of the Abbasids 663

Position of the Caliph 665

Persian influences 667

Manichaeism 669

The Mu'tazilite heresy 671

Traditionalism in religion 673

Islamic jurisprudence 675

Economic system 677

Structure of society 679

Shī'ism 681

Ismā'īlī revolts 683

Scientific studies 685

Literature. The Moderns 687

Ṣūfism 689

Development of Islamic theology 691

Influence of al-Ghazzālī 693

Character of Islamic society 695

CHAPTER XVII

BYZANTIUM AND THE MUSLIM WORLD TO THE MIDDLE OF THE ELEVENTH CENTURY

By M. CANARD

Emeritus Professor of the History of Islamic Civilisation in the University of Algiers

The Muslim Holy War . . . . *page* 697

Arab attacks on Constantinople fail 699

Abbasid Caliphate and revolts against it 701

Decline of the Abbasid Caliphate 703

Arab attacks on Asia Minor 705

Campaigns of Hārūn ar-Rashīd 707

Loss of Crete to the Arabs 709

Theophilus and Arab attacks on Anatolia 711

Byzantine successes under Bardas Caesar 713

Campaigns of Basil I 715

Operations under Leo VI and Romanus I 717

Campaigns of Sayf ad-Dawla 719

Campaigns of Nicephorus II Phocas 721

John Tzimisces in Mesopotamia and Syria 723

Basil II and the Fatimids 725

Fatimids and Seljuqs 727

Arab conquest of Sicily 729

Arabs in Sicily and South Italy 731

Trade relations 733

Cultural exchanges 735

CHAPTER XVIII

THE TURKS AND THE BYZANTINE EMPIRE
TO THE END OF THE THIRTEENTH CENTURY

By F. TAESCHNER

Emeritus Professor of Oriental Studies in the University of Münster

Early history of the Turks . . . . . . *page* 737

Seljuq Turks and the Holy War 739

The Seljuq Sultanate of Rūm 741

Seljuqs' victory over the Danishmends 743

Religion and culture under the Seljuqs 745

Expansion of the Seljuq Empire of Rūm 747

Mongol invasion of Asia Minor 749

Seljuqs of Rūm subject to the Mongols 751

CHAPTER XIX

THE OTTOMAN TURKS TO 1453

By F. TAESCHNER

Emeritus Professor of Oriental Studies in the University of Münster

The successors of the Seljuqs 753

Turkish principalities in Asia Minor 755

Gild system in Turkish principalities 757

The rise of the Ottomans 759

Expansion under Orkhan 761

Ottoman penetration into Europe 763

Murād I and Bāyezīd I 765

Ottoman defeat by the Mongols 767

Civil war and Karaman attacks 769

Campaigns of Hunyadi and Skanderbeg 771

The janissary corps 773

Capture of Constantinople by the Turks 775

LISTS OF RULERS

1. Byzantine Emperors . . . . . *page* 776
2. Epirus and Thessalonica 777
3. The Morea (Mistra) 778
4. Venice (to 1205) 778
5. Bulgaria 779
6. Serbia 780
7. Armenia and Georgia 780
8. Caliphs 786
9. Seljuqs 787
10. Ottomans (to 1481) 787

GENEALOGICAL TABLES

1. Dynasty of Heraclius 789
2. North Syrian or Isaurian Dynasty . . . 790
3. Amorian or Phrygian Dynasty 791
4. Macedonian Dynasty 792
5. Dynasty of Ducas 793
6. Dynasty of Comnenus 794
7. Dynasty of Angelus 795
8. Dynasty of Lascaris 796
9. Dynasty of Palaeologus . . . . *facing page* 796
10. Greek, Italian and Serbian Rulers of Epirus, Thessalonica and Thessaly . . . *facing page* 797

ECCLESIASTICAL LISTS

1. Popes, 314–1455 . . . . . *page* 798
2. Patriarchs of Constantinople, 381–1456 . . . 800

BIBLIOGRAPHIES

LIST OF ABBREVIATIONS 803

GENERAL BIBLIOGRAPHY 808

CHAPTER I: The formation of the East Roman Empire, 330–717 828

CHAPTER II: The Christian background . . . *page* 833

CHAPTER III: Iconoclasm and imperial rule, 717–842 . 835

CHAPTER IV: The Amorians and Macedonians, 842–1025 . 849

CHAPTER V: The Later Macedonians, the Comneni and the Angeli, 1025–1204 858

CHAPTER VI: Venice to the eve of the Fourth Crusade . 868

CHAPTER VII: The Fourth Crusade and the Greek and Latin Empires, 1204–61 880

CHAPTER VIII: The Palaeologi, 1261–1453 . . . 897

CHAPTER IX: The Latins in Greece and the Aegean from the Fourth Crusade to the end of the Middle Ages . . 908

CHAPTER X: Constantinople and Rome 938

CHAPTER XI: The Empire and its northern neighbours, 565–1018 952

CHAPTER XII: The Balkans, 1018–1499 966

CHAPTER XIII: Hungary and Byzantium in the Middle Ages 977

CHAPTER XIV: Armenia and Georgia 983

CHAPTER XV: Government, society and economic life under the Abbasids and Fatimids 1009

CHAPTER XVI: Muslim civilisation in the Abbasid period 1014

CHAPTER XVII: Byzantium and the Muslim world to the middle of the eleventh century 1028

CHAPTER XVIII: The Turks and the Byzantine Empire to the end of the thirteenth century 1039

CHAPTER XIX: The Ottoman Turks to 1453 . . . 1039

INDEX 1042

LIST OF MAPS

1. Constantinople . . . . . . *facing page* 6

2. Environs of Constantinople . . . . . *page* 11

3. Byzantine themes from the seventh to the ninth century 69

4. The Byzantine Empire, *c.* 1025 . . . *facing page* 192

5. The Empire of the Comneni 212

6. The Latins and the Byzantine Empire . . . 288

7. The Ottoman advance in the fourteenth century *facing page* 368

8. The northern neighbours of the Byzantine Empire . 474

9. The Balkans and Bulgaria in the tenth century . . 512

10. Caucasia from the fifth to the eighth century . . 598

11. Caucasia from the eighth to the eleventh century . 608

12. Caucasia from the twelfth to the fifteenth century . 624

13. Islamic lands of the Near and Middle East, *c.* 950 . 644

14. The eastern frontiers 698

15. Asia Minor in the early fourteenth century . . . 752

CHAPTER I

THE FORMATION OF THE EAST
ROMAN EMPIRE, 330-717

Eusebius of Caesarea is seldom thought of as a picturesque writer, but his description of the funeral of Constantine the Great brings the scene vividly to life. The soldier-Emperor died at Nicomedia on Whit Sunday, 337, about the hour of noon. Unofficial mourning by his personal attendants and guards, and lamentation in the streets, were succeeded by the ceremonial proper to the occasion. Enclosed in a golden coffin shrouded by purple draperies, the body was conveyed to the city which he had called by his own name. Here, in the central chamber of the palace, the dead ruler held his last audience. Each in his order of precedence, the officers of the household, the generals, senators and lesser dignitaries of the Empire performed their obeisance, or *proskynesis*, before the still figure, robed in purple and crowned with the diadem. The golden catafalque, placed impressively upon a lofty dais, was surrounded by burning lights and watched over day and night by the serried ranks of his bodyguard, while Constantine lay in state, and the endless throng of his subjects, men, women and children, filed through the hall to render their last homage. With the arrival of Constantius, the final obsequies began. Headed by the new Emperor, the funeral procession took its way through the streets till the shrine of the Holy Apostles was reached. At this point a dramatic and unprecedented change came over the proceedings. Constantius and his troops, together with the officials of the Roman state, withdrew. Their part in the ceremony was over. The clergy and the Christian community came forward to receive their brother in the faith. The burial prayers were recited, and the recently baptised Emperor was laid to rest in the mausoleum which he had built for himself. Flanked by memorial stelae of the Twelve Apostles, the sarcophagus of Constantine, himself the thirteenth of them, stood ready to receive through the centuries the devotions and veneration of the faithful.[1]

[1] Eusebius, *Vita Constantini*, IV, 65–70. Cf. A. Kaniuth, 'Die Beisetzung Konstantins des Grossen. Untersuchungen zur religiösen Haltung des Kaisers', *Breslauer Historische Forschungen*, XVIII (1941). The Eusebian authorship of the *Vita Constantini* has frequently been challenged. For the earlier literature on this question, see N. H. Baynes, *Constantine the Great and the Christian Church* (*Proc. Brit. Acad.* XV, 1929), pp. 40–56. References to more recent work may be found in J. Quasten, *Patrology*, III (Westminster, Maryland, 1960), pp. 322–4.

The dedication of Constantinople in 330 is generally taken as the starting-point of Byzantine history, and the details recounted by Eusebius with their curious, as yet unassimilated, mixture of old and new aptly symbolise the position at the death of Rome's first Christian Emperor. The momentous revolution which had taken place could hardly have been fully appreciated by contemporaries. The eastern capital, set up so recently by imperial decree, was still a parvenu city. Second in rank, and lacking in all the memories and prestige of Old Rome, it was destined perhaps, so it might have been thought, to become yet another Sirmium or Nicomedia, favoured by a particular ruler, but comparatively neglected by his successors. Who could have foreseen its millenary future, or the effect upon western Europe of the transference of the centre of imperial power? The privileged position of the Church, loaded with favours scarcely a generation after its fiercest persecution, was a more obvious threat to the old order; but other Emperors had privately followed strange cults, though none so well organised or so incompatible with the state religion. Even this incompatibility, however, was not always apparent. Nothing is more striking in the Eusebian account than the strongly pagan and traditional features of the ceremonial which attended the death of Constantine. The ritual which surrounded the 'sacred' palace and the Emperor's 'divine' person can be traced back to the ruler-worship of the ancient East, from which it had passed to the Hellenistic successors of Alexander the Great. Rome had already displaced these despots when Augustus founded the Empire, and their titles and attributes were inherited by the new masters. Fluid and emotional in content, the religious feelings of awe and reverence on the part of their subjects before the all-powerful dispensers of weal or woe had varied through intermediate stages, according to the cultural background and the level of education, from crude deification of the living Emperor to formal assumptions of the virtues which belonged to the imperial office. Refined by Greek thinking, the ruler-cult took on a Stoic colouring, and the concepts of the brotherhood of man, and of the controlling influence of the beneficent divine reason or Logos, combined with Roman imperialist ideals to support the universalist claims of the Emperors to the government, by divine right, of the οἰκουμένη, the inhabited world.

Christianity had grown up in this atmosphere. The translators of the Septuagint borrowed their vocabulary from the courts of the Diadochi to characterise the Kingdom of Heaven, just as Christian art, when called on to depict scenes and figures for which Judaism furnished no precedent, turned for its models to the classical iconography of late paganism. Thus not only Dionysiac imagery, but even the car of the Sun god had already been adopted as Christian funerary symbols, and Eusebius sees no incongruity in the commemorative coins representing Constantine, as in a pagan apotheosis, ascending to heaven in a solar chariot.[1] Furthermore, the Roman Empire was still officially a pagan state; its Emperor was still Pontifex Maximus, and would remain so for long after Constantine's death, while the army and officials, as well as the bulk of the population in the West, were still, so far as is known, predominantly pagan in their beliefs. Constantine's position was therefore a delicate one. The basis of his imperial authority was not only temporal but spiritual, and to discard the religious trappings of the ruler-cult would have shaken the very foundations of his power.

Nevertheless, the ambiguity of the situation was a surface appearance only; the revolution was already a reality. To the instructed Christian, the problem of Caesar-worship was an old story. Much of the earlier apologetic literature had centred round this difficulty, which had prevented many converts from entering the public service, and had at times formed the basis of persecution. The protracted symbiosis of the Church with the institutions of the Roman state had prepared the way for an eventual solution, and with the advent of a Christian ruler Eusebius was able to refashion the Hellenistic theory of kingship to suit the new conditions.[2] No longer a god among men, the Emperor is yet raised above his fellow-mortals by his divine commission to bring peace and justice to the world. As there is one God and one divine law in Heaven, so on earth one supreme governor, acting as God's vicegerent, must command the obedience and the devotion of the human race. Such, in brief, was the exalted position accorded to the first Christian Emperor, and such it remained to the end. Here, as in other respects, the decisive character of fourth-century developments can be observed; here the precedents were created which were to govern Byzantine history. Just as Augustus, founder of the Empire, had acquired his unique authority from the gratitude of the Mediterranean world to which he had brought peace and order after a generation of anarchy, so Constantine, the new Moses who had led the children of God out of the house of bondage, established over a grateful Church—emerging with incredulous joy from the severest of the persecutions to an honoured and privileged place in the community—an ascendancy which might well have been im-

[1] *Vita Constantini*, IV, 73. Cf. J. Maurice, *Numismatique Constantinienne*, I (Paris, 1908), p. 262 and pl. xviii, 19, and, generally, A. Grabar, *L'empereur dans l'art byzantin* (Paris, 1936), pp. 127 ff.

[2] See N. H. Baynes, 'Eusebius and the Christian Empire', *Mélanges Bidez* (= *AIPHO*, II, 1933–4), 13–18, reprinted in *Byzantine Studies and Other Essays* (London, 1955), pp. 168–72.

possible save at this peculiar conjuncture of events. The 'charismatic' aspect of the imperial office, which had itself grown in importance under the rule of Diocletian and Constantine, was thus not only retained unimpaired in its essential features, but materially strengthened by its Christian transformation. As defender of the orthodox faith, the Emperor acquired in course of time a new claim to the spiritual loyalty of his subjects, as well as a new principle of unity transcending national and racial differences, while Constantine's vital sense of his divine mission gave additional justification to his conviction that he had been chosen to bring all peoples under the rule of Christ.

The significance of the fourth century as a creative period is seen no less in the administrative and legal system of the Byzantine Empire, which bore to its last days, despite fundamental reforms carried out by later rulers, the stamp of the autocratic pattern introduced by Diocletian and remodelled by Constantine. But most decisive of all for the future was Constantine's personal choice of the new capital. Inferior at first to Old Rome not only in prestige but in ecclesiastical, cultural and economic importance, Constantinople was not slow to reap the benefits of its incomparable site. Even its relative obscurity—it could boast of no famous pagan sanctuary, no classical artists or philosophers, no Christian martyrs—aided the founder's intentions. It would have been impossible at Antioch or Alexandria, with their celebrated past and independent traditions, to realise that remarkable vision of a 'second Rome'[1] founded in the Greek-speaking East, with its seven hills, its senate-house and fora, its Great Palace adjoining the Hippodrome as the Palatine buildings overlooked the Circus Maximus, and, above all, its sense of continuity with the purely Roman sentiments and ideals associated with the city of Romulus on the Tiber.

The break-up of the Empire in the West only enhanced the superiority which the eastern provinces had always claimed as the home of communities wealthier and more civilised than their Italian conquerors. With the regression of trade and industry in western Europe, the decline of urban life, the cessation of revenues, and the disappearance, under the rule of the Germanic kings, of most of the organs of centralised government, East Rome became the City *par excellence*, the only survivor of the classical form of state, with its administrative, military and financial machinery, its Roman law, its controlled commerce, and its centrally directed provincial administration. Gradually Constantinople drew to itself the cultural activities of the eastern Mediterranean; the university of Athens, the law school of Beirut, the libraries of Alexandria found their successors in

[1] The nomenclature of Constantine's city is significant; see below, p. 18, note 1.

the capital city. The doctrinal controversies of the fifth and sixth centuries, and the imperial interventions which marked their course, raised the status of the Byzantine see at the expense of the ancient apostolic foundations, and its position was further strengthened when Syria and Egypt fell under Muslim rule. The economic advantages of the city and harbour, situated at the cross-roads of long trade-routes, had brought prosperity even in earlier times, and the factories and dockyards needed for the new centre of imperial administration gave an impetus to industrial expansion. But the most prominent feature of the site was its remarkable girdle of fortifications, behind which Byzantium could shelter from invasion. It was this impregnability, unique among ancient and medieval capitals, which gave to the Byzantines a visible symbol of the eternal destiny of the Empire, an ever-present assurance that their city was guarded by God and designed by Providence for the ultimate realisation of the Divine purpose. Within its walls were contained all the essential organs of the state, its imperial and noble residences, its finest monuments, its heaped-up treasures and saving relics. Even when the territory of the Empire had shrunk to a few square miles, recovery was possible, and was actually achieved, so long as the city remained intact. This extraordinary concentration within a small, confined area of all the forces making for survival was to prove the salvation of Byzantium in the recurrent crises of nine perilous centuries; and the fall of the city in 1204 was consequently a shattering blow from which its inhabitants never recovered.

The superb self-confidence which had for so long enabled a highly educated minority to control the resources, to absorb or replace the culture, and to a large extent to engage the loyalties of the hetero-geneous peoples of the Levant was derived from a closed circle of assumptions. Belief in the eternal destiny of East Rome and in the monopoly of Hellenic learning was fused with consciousness of ortho-doxy—right thinking—and of Divine favour continually manifested to the chosen people. The capture of Constantinople ended the legend of invincibility, and with the destruction of this article of faith the way was open for the disruptive and separatist tendencies, the doubts and questionings, which had hitherto been held in check. Similar tendencies had appeared in the anarchy of the third century and had been subdued, thanks to the consolidating work of the fourth-century Emperors. It says much for the durability of that work that the official Byzantine outlook, despite the increasing un-reality of its claims, could be maintained for yet another century after the capital had fallen to the crusaders. In the works of Theodore Metochites (1260–1332), scholar, disillusioned statesman, and benefactor of the famous Chora monastery, doubts of the accepted values of the earlier Byzantine world appear undisguised in a member of the ruling class.[1] The future of the Empire, the supremacy of Greek culture, confidence in the beneficent workings of Providence—all are implicitly questioned, and the questioning becomes overt in the writings of his successors. But by then the last act of the Byzantine drama had already begun.

I. CONSTANTINOPLE

Byzantium, as Constantine found it, resembled in general appearance those numerous Hellenistic cities of the Asian coast which despite temporary setbacks had grown to prosperity under the Roman peace. The street-plan of New Rome, buried beneath the modern Turkish city, is not yet recoverable, nor can the developments of its first four centuries be traced in detail. Sufficient, however, is known of the aspect of the capital in its early days to outline its principal features. The peninsular site, protruding eastwards into the Sea of Marmora where it narrows into the channel of the Bosphorus, is bounded on the north by the deep inlet which forms the majestic haven of the Golden Horn. The primitive settlement, dating from at least the twelfth century B.C.,[2] was grouped round the Acropolis, on the hill which rises from the north-eastern tip of the promontory, known later as Seraglio Point. Its buildings gradually spread westwards, and by the time of Septimius Severus already occupied the area which was to become the centre of the life alike of the imperial court and of the Byzantine populace. Constantine's land-wall, crossing the neck of the peninsula from the Sea of Marmora to the Golden Horn, trebled the size of the existing city; but throughout the fourth century its population continued to grow. A further westward extension, planned perhaps under Theodosius I,[3] was carried out in the time of his grandson Theodosius II (408–50), the building activities of whose reign entitle him to rank as the second founder. His great land-walls, a still extant masterpiece of Byzantine engineering, gave to Constantinople its final extent, save for subsequent modifications at the north-west angle, designed to protect the quarter of Blachernae, with its imperial palace and its famous shrine, where the Virgin's robe, the palladium of the city, was preserved.

The irregular contours of the site gave to Constantinople its monu-

[1] See H.-G. Beck, *Theodoros Metochites: die Krise des byzantinischen Weltbildes im 14. Jahrhundert* (Munich, 1952), pp. 76–95; cf. Ihor Ševčenko, 'The Decline of Byzantium seen through the Eyes of its Intellectuals', *DOP*, xv (1961), pp. 169–86.

[2] Cf. E. Mamboury, *B*, xxi (1951), p. 439.

[3] Themistius, *Or.* xviii (ed. Dindorf, Leipzig, 1832; repr. Hildesheim, 1961, p. 272/2–15).

mental beauty and determined the placing of its principal buildings, streets and squares. A series of hills, rising from sea-level to some 300 feet, and intersected by small ravines, formed the undulating plateau of the upper town, from which the ground dropped sharply to the Golden Horn, and more gradually to the Marmora coast-line. From Seraglio Point two long arcaded streets ran along the shore, inside the sea-walls which skirted the harbours on either side of the peninsula, until they reached the extremities of the landward defences. Numerous flights of steps or stone-paved ramps connected these lower roads with the streets and houses of the city above. Terraces were extensively used to provide foundations for the buildings which occupied the slopes and summits of the hills; their massive retaining walls, ranging from ten to thirty feet in height, often allowed for the construction of great underground cisterns.

South-west of the Acropolis with its cluster of temples was the main square of the Severan city, known as the Tetrastoön, or Fourfold Portico; adjoining it on the west were the Baths of Zeuxippus, south of which lay the great Hippodrome. Constantine enlarged and embellished the square, renaming it the Augusteum in honour of his mother Helena whom he had created Augusta, and whose statue, from the height of its porphyry column, dominated the scene. On the north side of the square the first church of St Sophia may already have begun to rise; on the south was the entrance-gate of the Great Palace, the buildings of which, connected by courts and arcades, stretched parallel to the Hippodrome towards the Marmora coast. From the north-west angle of the Augusteum the principal street and triumphal way, known later as the Mesē, began its course, skirting the Baths of Zeuxippus and passing through successive squares, or fora, till it reached the southernmost gate of the land-walls. The first of these squares was the Forum of Constantine, with its porphyry column bearing the famous statue of the Emperor, its triumphal arches, and its remarkable oval design, resembling in effect, though on a smaller scale, Bernini's colonnades in the Piazza di San Pietro at Rome.[1] This was the second centre of Constantine's city, and was regarded with special reverence. The street leading to it was bordered with two-storeyed arcades and luxurious shops and dwellings. The next square, the extensive Forum Tauri, completed in 393, commemorated the glories of the Theodosian house. At this point a main road diverged, leading north-west to the Adrianople Gate past the shrine of the Holy Apostles, the future resting-place of so many Emperors. The Mesē continued, in a south-westerly direction,[2]

[1] See R. Janin, *Constantinople byzantine* (Paris, 1950), p. 68.
[2] Cf. E. Mamboury, *B*, xxi (1951), 434.

through a series of later fora, to the wall of Constantine, and was finally extended to the Golden Gate in the Theodosian defences. Porticoes and basilicas marked its course, replacing the tombs of preceding centuries which had, as on Rome's Appian Way, lined the last stretches of the Via Egnatia, the imperial road from Dyrrachium across the Balkans, as it approached the outskirts of the old Byzantium.[1]

A remarkable feature of Constantinople was the wealth of statuary of every period and style which had been commandeered from all parts of the Empire. Pagan gods and heroes, biblical personages, single figures and groups of the reigning family, as well as numerous representations of animals, came eventually to people the streets and open spaces, and these, with the porticoes and isolated columns, gave to Constantinople a typically late antique aspect which she never lost. No churches of the pre-Constantinian period have been discovered, and only a few can with certainty be ascribed to the founder himself. Constantinople, however, was designed from the first not only as a Roman but as a Christian capital, and it is probable that the demolition of pagan temples, gradual though it must have been, met with fewer obstacles than at Rome. The fourth and fifth centuries saw the erection of many Christian basilicas, and domed churches with central plan were added by Justinian and his successors. The first orthodox monastery dates only from the late fourth century, but the number of monastic houses increased rapidly, especially in the outer regions and suburbs; at least eighty were in existence at the beginning of Justinian's reign.[2]

A steady expansion in public and private building marks the early centuries of Constantinople not only within the walls but along both shores of the Marmora and the Bosphorus, and across the Golden Horn in the settlements of Galata and Pera, which together formed an integral part of the city. Reconstruction on a large scale was also made necessary by frequent earthquakes, and by severe conflagrations which devastated whole quarters. The famous Nika Riot of 532, which lasted for five days, destroyed the centre of the city, and Justinian's subsequent rebuilding gave to the Augusteum its final form. On the north side rose the new St Sophia; on the east, as before, was the Senate House, while on the south the Chalce, or Brazen Gate,[3] which formed the principal entrance to the Great Palace, was restored. In the square itself, at the beginning of the Mese, stood the Milliarium (or Milion), an elaborate triumphal arch from which the roads

[1] Cf. E. Mamboury, *B*, xxi (1951), 434.
[2] See R. Janin, *REB*, ix (1951), 144.
[3] See C. Mango, *The Brazen House* (Copenhagen, 1959), pp. 30–4.

of the Empire took their course. The most striking monument, however, was the colossal equestrian figure, set on a massive pedestal, of Justinian himself in full armour, crowned with a strange, plumed head-dress, and with right hand extended towards the East, 'as if commanding the barbarians not to pass their frontiers'.[1] Accounts given by foreign visitors from the ninth to the fifteenth century bear witness to the lasting impression produced by this symbol of imperial power.[2]

Most of the Emperors were assiduous builders, and the Great Palace, in particular, received continual accretions. Justin II restored the small harbour which Julian had made on the Marmora shore;[3] Maurice constructed a new Praetorium; Heraclius drew the quarter of Blachernae within the circle of the city ramparts. But the constant preoccupation of rulers and citizens alike was the repair of the Theodosian land-walls on which the safety of the capital depended. Anastasius had built or restored[4] the 'Long Wall', spanning the isthmus some forty miles west of Constantinople, the defensive possibilities of which were once more exploited during the Balkan War of 1912–13, when the 'Chatalja Lines' were held by the Turks against modern Bulgarian invasion. But in Byzantine times the Long Wall was repeatedly overrun, since the resources of East Rome were insufficient to provide an adequate garrison. The Theodosian defences, on the other hand, with their formidable moat and glacis encompassing the double circuit of towers and curtain walls, were never breached by an external enemy until the crusaders' assault of 1204; and the fortunes of Byzantium repeatedly turned on their existence. In 408 a prolonged earthquake overthrew large parts of Constantine's wall, and this, together with the growing menace of the Huns, may well have prompted the advisers of Theodosius II to begin the new fortifications. Two years later, it may be noted in contrast, Old Rome fell to the Visigoths, and in the next two centuries she was to suffer the ignominy of repeated capture. Another severe earthquake at Constantinople in 447, when Attila was actually advancing on the city, led to desperate measures to repair the damaged walls, and ultimately to the construction of the second, or outer, circuit. The completed system now formed a barricade 190–270 feet in depth, and over a hundred feet high, when measured from the bed of the moat.[5] Essentially unaltered in its principal features, this masterpiece of late Roman military engineering challenged the

[1] Procopius, *De œdificiis*, I, 2, 12.
[2] See J. Ebersolt, *Constantinople byzantine et les voyageurs du Levant* (Paris, 1919).
[3] Cf. R. Janin, 'Les Ports de Constantinople', *B*, xx (1950), 73–9.
[4] Cf. E. Stein, *Histoire du Bas-Empire*, II (Paris, 1949), p. 89 and note 4.
[5] Cf. A. van Millingen, *Byzantine Constantinople* (London, 1899), p. 46.

infidel invader for a thousand years, until it succumbed to the
Turkish artillery of 1453.

The end of Justinian's reign (565) and the disorders under Phocas
(602–10) provoked further threats to the capital; but more sensational than any that had preceded them were the Avar attacks in
Heraclius' time, which culminated in the famous siege of 626. Here
the strategic value, both naval and military, of Constantine's site
becomes at last fully apparent. Heraclius could leave his city to be
defended by the patriarch Sergius while he raised troops in the distant
Caucasus for his adventurous Persian campaigns; and Constantinople,
strong in its reliance on the Virgin's protection, justified his confidence. The massed forces of Avars, Bulgars, Slavs and Gepids were
thrown back from the ramparts, while the Persian army, which had
marched overland to Chalcedon on the Asian side, was prevented
from joining its allies by the destruction of the Slav shipping in the
narrow seas. The high-water mark of Avar and Persian aggression
was thus registered on the Theodosian walls, and the flood tide of
their advance thereafter receded, never again to threaten East Rome.
Other and more formidable adversaries soon made their appearance:
but again the spearhead of the assault was shattered against its
impregnable bulwarks. The repulse of the Arab fleet in 678[1] saved not
only Constantinople but Europe from the initial impact of Muslim
aggression.[2] Forty years later, the attempt was renewed; and the
brilliant defence of the city by Leo the Isaurian—a victory no less
decisive in its consequences—opens the period with which this volume
is concerned.

II. THE EMPEROR

The position of the Emperor in the East Roman state was so overwhelming and affected so many aspects of Byzantine life that despite
all that has been written on the subject a brief outline is indispensable.
In appearance his rule was a personal autocracy, bounded by no
constitutional limits. This absolutism represents the stage reached
by the late third century in the evolution of the imperial office; it
was crystallised in the eastern half of the Empire, where it remained
essentially unaltered to the end. The despotic powers of the monarchy
had been gradually acquired, by peaceable or forceful means, at the
expense or by the control of the republican institutions on which
the principate of Augustus had been based—the standing army, the
senate, the sovereignty of the citizen body, the civil administration
and the Roman law. In earlier days the principal obstacle to the

---

[1] See below: p. 31.
[2] Cf. G. Ostrogorsky, *History of the Byzantine State* (Oxford, 1956), p. 112.

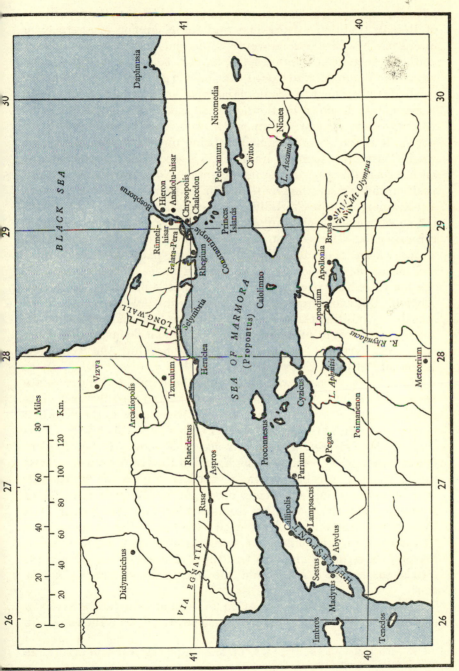

Map 2. Environs of Constantinople.

advance of despotism had been the senate, which was the repository of Roman traditions of freedom and the champion of aristocratic interests. No Emperor, however impatient, could ignore it, and neither a succession of purges and treason trials nor even the sharp weapon of the Praetorian Guard, stationed near at hand, could render it wholly subservient to the imperial will. Its central position in the Roman state is shown by the fact that the abolition of this inconvenient body was never proposed. Though shorn of many of its powers it nevertheless remained in being under the Dominate, and when Constantine founded East Rome a second senate was deemed an indispensable part of the new capital. No longer in regular opposition to the ruler, the senate of Constantinople continued to exert a restraining influence both by its conservative outlook and through the economic and social importance of the land-owning class which it represented. During an interregnum, moreover, it was accustomed to act as a sort of council of regency. The original senate on the Tiber was left as the guardian of pagan Roman tradition, and throughout the fourth century it carried on a losing battle in defence of the old religion. But as a threat to the monarchy its days were over. Constantius II, visiting the ancient city for the first time, could regard the senate almost in a romantic light, seeing in it no more, as had the envoy of Pyrrhus, 'an assembly of kings', but the venerated 'sanctuary of the entire world'.[1]

The sovereign people, whose name had been linked with the senate in the title of the Republic, had long surrendered the substance of its political rights. Its representative role in the election of the ruler had been taken over by the army,[2] and its voice was heard only in salutations of the Emperor. The same voice could, however, be raised in denunciation when feeling ran high, and in the Hippodrome, at least during the early centuries of the Byzantine Empire, the crowd realised its power to initiate a *coup d'état*. The tradition of παρρησία, of freedom of speech enjoyed by Romans when addressing their First Citizen, persisted far into Byzantine history, and the outspokenness of the earlier Cynic philosophers was inherited by the monks and hermits whose unceremonious treatment of the sacrosanct Emperor strikes so strange a note amid the solemnities of the Byzantine court.

The control of the administration now rested firmly in the hands of the autocrat. The older republican magistratures, from the consulate

---

[1] Ammianus Marcellinus, XVI, 10, 5. Cf. A. A. Christophilopoulou, Ἡ Σύγκλητος εἰς τὸ Βυζαντινὸν Κράτος (Athens, 1949).

[2] See J. B. Bury, *The Constitution of the Later Roman Empire* (Cambridge, 1910), pp. 4–9; reprinted in *Selected Essays* (Cambridge, 1930), pp. 101–3.

downwards, had been systematically degraded,[1] the power of the provincial governors checked, and the central direction of the civil service withdrawn behind the walls of the Great Palace. A more stubborn obstacle in the path of the despot was the Roman law itself, whose inviolable principles were hallowed by tradition; these were at once the driving force of the constitution and the abiding safeguard against arbitrary rule, which even the most tyrannical Emperor must respect. As in the development of English case-law, precedents, weighty though not formally binding, played a predominant part in the growth of the legal system at Rome, and during the early Empire such precedents were found in the *responsa prudentium*, the opinions of noted jurists whose authority could be cited in court. Gradually the doctrine enunciated by these jurists, who came increasingly to owe their advancement to the ruler himself, was brought into conformity with the climate of absolutism and the realities of the political situation. The Emperor was now acknowledged not only as the supreme court of appeal but as the actual *fons juris*, the source of law. The classical jurists had done their work; henceforth the lawyers who drafted the imperial enactments could remain anonymous.[2]

From what has been said, the position of the Byzantine Emperor might seem to differ little from that of an oriental monarch; and the impression of a hieratic, superhuman authority is heightened when one recalls the haloed and jewelled figures of the Ravenna mosaics, or the elaborate ceremonial of the Byzantine court, with its calendar of festivals and processions, its ritual use of vestments and chants, and its liturgy of prayers and obeisance before the sacred ruler.[3] The difference was in fact profound; and the contrast between the arbitrary character of Asian despotism and the legal authority of the Roman autocracy was fully recognised by contemporaries.[4] Apart from certain details apparently borrowed from Persian usage, the observances connected with the Emperor's person had their roots deep in the Roman past. The imperial cult was an organic growth, dating from the earliest days of the Empire, and the veneration of the imperial images at legionary headquarters and in provincial capitals continued for centuries after the Church's victory had destroyed the basis of emperor-worship. Pagan terminology was equally persistent; even in 425, and in a rescript limiting the honours paid to

---

[1] John Lydus, *De magistratibus*, ii, 6.

[2] Cf. H. F. Jolowicz, *Historical Introduction to the Study of Roman Law* (2nd ed., Cambridge, 1952), p. 372.

[3] Cf. L. Bréhier and P. Batiffol, *Les survivances du culte impérial romain* (Paris, 1920).

[4] E.g. John Lydus, *De magistratibus*, i, 3–4.

these *imagines*, the significant word *numen* could be officially employed to denote the imperial majesty.[1]

The favour of the gods concerned for the welfare of the human race had from the first been held to confer on the ruler, in recognition of his personal merit, the title to govern; and the Christianisation of this idea is the basis of Eusebius' political theory.[2] But the choice of Heaven must be confirmed by the acclamation of senate and people, for the Roman monarchy remained elective in principle, and this formal assertion of popular sovereignty was required at the beginning of each reign. The practical consequences were important. The acclamation itself bestowed a presumptive imperial status; and since the army, which was the deciding factor in the anarchic conditions of the third century, had by a constitutional fiction come to represent the will of the people,[3] it followed that a pretender to the throne, after being hailed as *imperator* by rebellious troops in the provinces, would thereafter be accepted as the rightful monarch, provided that his forces were sufficient to master the capital, secure the consent of the senate, and depose the existing ruler. His success, as in the story of David and Saul, was seen as a token of divine approval; and what to mortal eyes might initially have appeared an act of treason became manifest in its outcome as an act of God.

The advantages of hereditary succession were naturally not overlooked, least of all by the Emperors themselves, and from the time of Augustus onwards efforts were made to establish the continuity of the reigning house. The right of a ruler to nominate his successor was in fact recognised by custom, and during the earlier centuries of the Byzantine Empire three dynasties remained in power over long periods. Attempts to assert for the blood royal a supernatural claim to sovereignty were not without their effect, and legitimist feeling made headway under the Macedonian line; but the contradiction between this principle and that of the providential saviour, summoned by Heaven to rescue the state in its hour of crisis, was always too strong for any constitutional law of automatic succession to prove acceptable to the Roman people.

Once seated on the throne, the ruler was responsible only to God himself. But the Emperor-elect was in a different position, and pledges of orthodoxy and equitable government were sometimes exacted from him before final approbation was given. Other limitations

---

[1] *Cod. Theod.* xv, 4, 1. For the connection of *numen* and *maiestas* see W. Ensslin, *CAH*, xii, p. 359 and 'Der Kaiser in der Spätantike', *HZ*, clxxvii (1954), 452, 456. Cf. below: ch. ii, p. 45.

[2] See N. H. Baynes, 'Eusebius and the Christian Empire', cited above, p. 3, note 2 (*Byzantine Studies*, p. 170).

[3] See J. B. Bury, *loc. cit.*

on the imperial power must not be overlooked. Practical considerations of expediency prevented the monarch from resorting to measures which might seriously alienate public opinion or disturb the loyalty of his troops. Innovations in liturgy and doctrine, or even enforced agreement between warring sects, would be strongly resisted and might produce dangerous revolts. The wealthy senatorial class was always a force to be reckoned with, and in later centuries the great landowners entrenched in their Anatolian estates and surrounded by armed retainers could often defy the central power, and were a continual focus of insurrection until the coming of the Seljuq Turks. Even the civil servants, whose costly, oppressive but highly efficient administration kept the Empire solvent, were largely beyond the control of any individual ruler. However ardent might be his reforming zeal, the cumbrous machinery withstood all efforts to remove abuses; his interference was fiercely resented, and his threatening statutes, repeated in increasingly ferocious terms, indicate by their very persistence the failure of the imperial policy.

The force of tradition, the 'unwritten law' which governed men's lives in an intensely conservative civilisation, was even more powerful in limiting the actions of the Byzantine autocrat. Just as the Emperor's superhuman position and his claims to unquestioning obedience are proclaimed in his laws, his titles and his monuments,[1] so the responsibilities which corresponded to these lofty assumptions find their expression in the innumerable epigraphical and literary sources which indicate the behaviour expected of him by his subjects. Poets and orators, both Greek and Latin, political writers whether laudatory or critical, historians and theologians, all testify in the same sense, and the picture of the ideal governor which they combine to present is impressively consistent. The desired result is, in Psellus' phrase,[2] an 'imperial harmony' ($\dot{\alpha}\rho\mu o\nu i\alpha\ \beta\alpha\sigma\iota\lambda\iota\kappa\dot{\eta}$) in the body politic, sufficiently definite to be formulated in those 'mirrors of princes' which are a recurrent feature of Byzantine literature. Few Emperors, whatever their origin and antecedents, could remain unaffected by this all-embracing atmosphere, and some of them, consciously accepting their obligations, used them effectively to advertise the blessings of their rule. Never, perhaps, have the duties of the benevolent despot been placed so high. As successor of the saviour kings of the Hellenistic monarchies, the Roman Emperor is an earthly Providence, who must assist the lowliest of his subjects when natural catastrophes such as earthquake or famine overtake them:[3] the

---

[1] Cf. A. Grabar, *L'empereur dans l'art byzantin* (Paris, 1936).

[2] *Chronographia*, I, 22 (ed. Renauld, I, Paris, 1926, p. 14/9–10).

[3] Themistius, *Or.* XI, 107 (ed. Dindorf, p. 127/26–32).

peasantry, who are the economic foundation of the state, should be
his especial care.[1] Public works in the shape of roads, bridges and
aqueducts are incumbent upon him, just as much as the building of
frontier-castles; the endowment of schools and universities, no less
than the upkeep of famous temples, or in Christian times the erection
of hospitals, monasteries and churches. In all this the Emperor acts
not merely as a remotely benign influence: the semi-divine personage
is also a human individual, whose sympathies are directly engaged.
His features, depicted on coins and effigies, are familiar to the inhabitants of the farthest provinces, and his solicitude for his subjects
is constantly emphasised. Standing above the law, he graciously
submits to be governed by it, and his rule is therefore no tyranny,
but an ἔννομος ἀρχή:[2] his very freedom of action (since he is himself
the νόμος ἔμψυχος, the living law)[3] enables him to exercise a higher
justice, and to humanise the iron rigidity of the legal machine.[4] He
is thus the protector of the poor against the rich and powerful, against
the exactions even of his own officials. The list of imperial virtues is
long; it extends even to personal demeanour and habits. Impassive
dignity in public is required of the ruler,[5] and the magnificence of his
position must be matched by the lavish dispersal of gifts.[6]

Finally, the Roman *imperator* is no cloistered figure, but pre-
eminently, as his name implies, the leader in war. He is the ensurer
of victory for his people, and therefore of lasting peace.[7] 'The
Emperor's trade is fighting',[8] declared Synesius in blunt criticism of
the unwarlike Arcadius (395–408); and the fact was recognised when,
as so often, prominent generals were adopted into the reigning house.
The military basis of the ruler's power, which the rivalries of the third
century had so plainly demonstrated, was emphasised in the ceremonies of his accession; and the practical continuance of that power
was, as everyone knew, dependent on the loyalty of his troops. Such
was the harsh reality; but the 'theology of the imperial victory', as
it has been called, rested on deeper and more ancient foundations
than the ever-present possibility of the *coup d'état*. The Roman

---

[1] Libanius, ed. Foerster, III (Teubner, 1906), p. 486/1–11.

[2] Cf. F. Dölger, 'Die Kaiserurkunde der Byzantiner als Ausdruck ihrer politischen Anschauungen', *HZ*, CLIX (1938–9), 245 (reprinted in *Byzanz und die europäische Staatenwelt*, Ettal, 1953, p. 27).

[3] Themistius, *Or.* XVI, 212 (ed. Dindorf, p. 259/3).

[4] Themistius, *Or.* XIX, 228 (ed. Dindorf, p. 277/25–8).

[5] Ammianus Marcellinus, XVI, 10, 10 (Constantius II); XXV, 4, 18 (criticism of Julian).

[6] Cf. F. Dölger, *op. cit.* pp. 246–7.

[7] For the association of victory with peace, see *Digest*, Praefatio, I, and cf. G. Mauthey, *Rivista di archeologia cristiana*, XXVIII (1952), 45 ff.

[8] Περὶ βασιλείας, XIV: τεχνίτης ἐστὶν ὁ βασιλεὺς πολέμων ὥσπερ ὁ σκυτοτόμος ὑποδημάτων. Cf. tr. Lacombrade (Paris, 1951), p. 50, note 76.

Emperors had inherited the supreme command of the army, and with it the responsibility for all its successes and the sole right to celebrate triumphs. The primitive belief in the divinely predestined victory of the leader, which had formerly been exploited by Sulla and Julius Caesar, became an essential element of the imperial cult, and it can indeed be seen to permeate the ceremonial connected with the Byzantine Emperor.[1] The centre of this remarkable ritual was the Hippodrome, where not only the success of a campaign but even the victories of a charioteer were formally acclaimed as a personal triumph for the reigning prince. The chrism, the *labarum*, and subsequently the Cross might replace the likeness of Sol Invictus as the 'sign of victory' associated with the imperial images; but the *mystique* which surrounded the idea of the *Victoria Augusti* continued to operate as a living force, strengthening both the Emperor's position in the capital and the morale of his armies in the field.

III. THE CHURCH

If Constantine, realising the failure of the persecutions, had been content to allow Christianity to become merely a *religio licita*, competing on equal terms with the pagan cults, its superior organisation might well have given it the victory, but its institutional history would have followed very different lines. The close union, the *consonantia*[2] of Church and State which characterised the Byzantine Empire, would hardly have been possible without the personal conversion of Constantine to the Christian faith. The response of the Church to this unexpected development was shown in its willingness to accord him a controlling position in its affairs which his successors never equalled, but also never forgot. From it sprang the Emperor's right and duty not only to protect and further the interests of the Church, but to ensure the maintenance of sound doctrine and the suppression of heresy. The swift advance of ecclesiastical power and influence which resulted from the imperial favour altered the whole aspect of the Roman state. And the interpenetration of civil and religious institutions, together with the realisation of the economic and strategic dangers of sectarian revolt, made it inevitable that the ruler, whose constant preoccupation was the unity of the Empire, should concern himself increasingly with Church discipline and dogmatic disputes.

[1] J. Gagé, 'Σταυρὸς νικοποιός. La victoire impériale dans l'empire chrétien', *Revue d'histoire et de philosophie religieuses*, XIII (1933), 370–400; and cf. *RH*, CLXXI (1933), 1–43.

[2] Cf. *BZ*, XLVI (1953), 234.

The political background of the internal history of the Church during the formative centuries of the Byzantine Empire is the struggle for precedence between the see of Constantinople and the older centres of Christianity. Ecclesiastical administration, during the period when the West was overwhelmingly pagan, had been modelled on the civil organisation of Rome. The chief city of each district became the seat of the bishop, and the provincial capital the residence of the metropolitan. The authority of these dignitaries corresponded in large measure to the political importance of their sees, and this principle continued to be observed after the peace of the Church. Thus in Gaul the transference of the centre of government from Trier to Arles in the fifth century led to a claim for increased jurisdiction on the part of the Arlesian prelate, while in North Italy the change of the imperial residence from Milan to Ravenna diminished the status of the Ambrosian see. It was therefore natural, when Constantine had founded the new capital, that efforts should be made to exalt its ecclesiastical rank to a height commensurate with its secular pre-eminence. But Byzantium could boast of no noteworthy Christian past; her bishopric had been merely the suffragan see of Heraclea, and no change in its status seems to have been proposed at the First General Council of Nicaea in 325. All the more spectacular, then, was her demand, accepted by the Second General Council at Constantinople in 381, for the second place in the hierarchy of the whole Church, 'because Constantinople is the New Rome'.[1] Resistance to such pretensions came from several quarters. Three metropolitan sees in particular—Rome, Alexandria and Antioch—had long been accorded a special position which arose not only from their civic importance but from their claims to apostolic foundation. This last was the ground on which the Popes of the fourth century took their stand, and the Byzantine demand was repeatedly rejected at Rome until the day when a western bishop, after the Latin conquest, occupied the Constantinopolitan see. Nevertheless, despite the subsequent protests of Pope Leo I, the Fourth General Council, held at Chalcedon in 451, not only confirmed the position which Constantinople had secured in 381, but also reasserted, in its famous 28th canon, the political principle as the foundation of hierarchical precedence, and applied it to the bishopric of the old capital, conceding primacy of honour to the see of Rome 'because that is the imperial city'.[2]

---

[1] On the political and ecclesiastical significance of this claim, see F. Dölger, *Byzanz und die europäische Staatenwelt*, pp. 83 f.

[2] διὰ τὸ βασιλεύειν τὴν πόλιν ἐκείνην. For further discussion of this point, see Pt II, ch. XXIII, pp. 107 f., and cf. also F. Dvornik, *The Idea of Apostolicity in Byzantium* (Dumbarton Oaks Studies IV, Harvard, 1958), especially chapters 1, 2 and 6.

Henceforward the system of five 'Patriarchates' (Jerusalem, city of the Holy Places, had been added to the previous four) came to be recognised as the supreme institutional expression of Catholic unity. The limits of the Patriarchs' jurisdiction were defined, their powers were continually augmented by the growth of disciplinary procedure, and in the legislation of Justinian they take their place at the summit of the Church's constitution.

Some idea of the importance of the Patriarchs from the Emperor's point of view may be conveyed by a glance at their several spheres of influence. Rome, in addition to its unrivalled position in the West, and the respect accorded to it by the whole Church, possessed jurisdiction, until the iconoclast dispute in the eighth century, over Greece and most of the Balkans.[1] Alexandria, traditionally founded by St Mark, and famous for its contributions to Christian thought, seemed likely, until the sudden rise of Constantinople, to secure a corresponding hegemony in the East. Exercising immediate authority over the Egyptian bishops, its 'pope' had also at his command the formidable band of monks who made their voice heard in the background of so many Councils. Egypt was the granary of Constantinople, and a turbulent centre of disaffection. The Alexandrian Patriarch, backed by the anti-Roman sympathies of his people and by the material resources of a wealthy see, occupied a key position in imperial politics. The Patriarchate of Antioch, which claimed sisterhood with Rome in virtue of its Petrine origin, extended over Syria, Cilicia and Mesopotamia. It was less homogeneous in race than that of Alexandria, and less compact in its territory. Its political influence was accordingly less concentrated; but the proximity of the Persian frontier gave it a strategic significance that could not be overlooked. Like Alexandria it was a noted centre of theological studies, and the great controversies of the Church, which more than once originated in its schools, sharply divided the sees and monasteries which owed it allegiance. Jerusalem, though sharing fully in these disputes, occupied in some ways a position apart. Resort of pilgrims and recipient of benefactions from East and West, it maintained close though not always cordial relations with both Old and New Rome.

The Patriarchate of Constantinople, which ended by overshadowing all the Eastern Churches, was formally delimited at the Council of Chalcedon. Its territory lay principally in Asia Minor, where it displaced Ephesus, the old apostolic centre of Christianity, as the

---

[1] Cf. L. Duchesne, *Eglises séparées* (Paris, 1896), ch. VI, 'Illyricum ecclésiastique'. For recent literature see M. V. Anastos, 'The Transfer of Illyricum, Calabria, and Sicily to the Jurisdiction of the Patriarchate of Constantinople in 732–33', *SBN*, IX (1957), 14–31. See also below: ch. III, p. 71.

controlling authority, but it included also Thrace, the Crimea, and the Caucasus regions, which were to be of vital military importance. At the same time the Roman parts of Armenia, which had been converted to the faith from Caesarea in Cappadocia, became in theory subject to Constantinople; but this ancient state, so long a bone of contention between Rome and Persia, followed in ecclesiastical matters, whenever circumstances permitted, an independent line.

In the defeat of the Arian heresy Alexandria, in the person of Athanasius, had played a prominent part; and her ascendancy was maintained when in 404 her patriarch Theophilus, aided by the wavering policy of the Emperor Arcadius, secured the banishment from the capital of John Chrysostom. Nestorius, trained like Chrysostom in the school of Antioch, was the next victim, and the verdict of the Third General Council (Ephesus, 431), which deposed him from the see of Constantinople, was a personal triumph for Cyril of Alexandria. Dioscorus, Cyril's successor, was less fortunate. Once more, at the 'Robber' Council of Ephesus in 449, a bishop of Constantinople (Flavian) was overthrown by Egyptian influence; but two years later, at the Fourth General Council, held at Chalcedon, the situation was reversed. The death of Theodosius II in 450 had ended the period of imperial hesitancy; Dioscorus himself was condemned, and the hegemony of Alexandria was destroyed for ever.[1] From the political no less than the theological aspect the decision of Chalcedon was momentous in its effects. Arianism, proscribed at Nicaea in 325, had by the end of the fourth century lost its significance save as a continuing barrier between the orthodox Romans and the Germanic Arian converts. But the Christological controversy which was brought to a head by the Chalcedonian formula permanently divided not only the Church but the population of the Empire, and the resulting disorders preoccupied the rulers of Byzantium for over two hundred years. Only when the monophysite provinces of Syria and Egypt were finally in Muslim hands did the imperial task of reconciliation lose its urgency.

Rome, in the earlier stages of the struggle, had sided with Alexandria in its attacks on Constantinople; but the ambitious designs of Dioscorus, which challenged the position of both Pope and Emperor, brought the two powers together at Chalcedon to humble the Egyptian see. Marcian and his consort Pulcheria, grand-daughter of the strong-willed Theodosius I, guided the proceedings of the Council; but the all-important formula which was adopted as the final definition of the nature of Christ was essentially the work of Pope Leo

---

[1] See N. H. Baynes, 'Alexandria and Constantinople: A Study in Ecclesiastical Diplomacy', *Journal of Egyptian Archaeology*, XII (1926), 145–56 (reprinted in *Byzantine Studies and Other Essays*, pp. 97–115).

himself. The doctrinal breach was not, at the outset, irreparable. It is significant that Dioscorus was condemned not on grounds of heresy, but for offences against ecclesiastical discipline, and in the recrimination that followed, both sides could still appeal to the writings of Cyril of Alexandria. But the decision of Chalcedon, which was interpreted by its opponents as a surrender to Nestorianism, roused the East to fury. Violence was met by violence; separatist passion in Syria and Egypt was kindled, and in the fires of repression the anti-Chalcedonian movement crystallised into its historical monophysite shape. Rome, whose authority was involved in the Leonine definition, opposed all compromise, and steadily resisted the successive attempts of the Byzantine Emperors to render the hated formula acceptable to their dissident subjects.

These attempts varied with the political situation and the personal convictions of the ruler, whose will was paramount in the religious affairs of the Empire. The *Henoticon*, or Edict of Union, issued by the Emperor Zeno in 482, coincided with the temporary abandonment of Italy to Odoacer. Though it obtained considerable success among the more moderate monophysites, it resulted in the first major schism between Rome and Constantinople, which lasted for thirty-five years. The accession of the orthodox Justin in 518 restored communion with the West, which was to prove essential for the reconquest of Africa and Italy by his nephew Justinian. The disturbances in the eastern provinces caused by this anti-monophysite policy were met by an alternation of coercion and compromise, made necessary by the needs of the treasury and the exigencies of the Persian campaigns; but friction with Rome and the consolidation, at the hands of Jacob Baradaeus, of the persecuted monophysite church were the sole outcome of all these endeavours.

The seventh century witnessed a complete transformation of the scene of conflict. Syria and Egypt were overrun by Persia, reconquered by Heraclius, and shortly afterwards lost permanently to Islam. After the victory of Heraclius, fresh efforts had been made to conciliate the Eastern Churches, and the policy was continued by certain Emperors, with unfortunate effects in the West, long after the political reasons for it had disappeared. At the Sixth General Council, which Constantine IV summoned to Constantinople in 680, unity in the Church, on the basis of Chalcedon, was re-established. Full agreement with Rome was reached, and apart from a short-lived movement under Philippicus (711–13) no further approaches were made to the monophysites.

East Rome had at this time been practically reduced to its Greek-speaking provinces. By the exertions of the Heraclian dynasty the

Arab invaders had been halted at the Taurus, and the vital territory of Asia Minor was saved. Within its straitened boundaries, the Byzantine Empire assumed a more homogeneous form. Orthodoxy and Hellenic culture were the binding forces, the direction of which was concentrated increasingly in the capital. Relations with the West became correspondingly more distant. The divergence in language and ways of thought was sharply emphasised at the Quinisextum Council of Constantinople in 692, which endeavoured to impose uniform Greek practices in ecclesiastical ritual and discipline. Rome's uncompromising rejection of its decisions, and the ignominious failure of the attempts to coerce her, served only to demonstrate the strength and independence of the papacy. This independence must not be thought of as political separatism. Claims for ecclesiastical autonomy in spiritual matters might be raised at intervals, but Empire and Church were still generally regarded as indissoluble elements of the divinely appointed order of world government, and no alternative system was conceivable. The Pope was the Emperor's subject:[1] his election required the imperial assent,[2] and except in times of schism the Roman clergy, no less than that of Constantinople, prayed for the safety and well-being of the ruling house. Whatever differences of policy might arise, the interests of Pope and Emperor continued to coincide in the defence of Romania from the barbarian enemy.

IV. DEFENCE OF THE FRONTIERS

The most obvious contrast between the Empire of 330 and that of 717 lies in the drastic contraction of the Roman boundaries. A graph based on the extent of the territory controlled by Byzantium in the course of her millenary existence would depict this opening period as a double trough, separated by the peak of Justinian's reconquest of some of the lost western provinces. Among the causes which produced this physical transformation of the Byzantine Empire must be noted the geographical features which to a large extent shaped the forces threatening it with destruction, and which limited the measures adopted for its defence.[3]

Rome's unification of the ancient world rested on earlier foundations. The Greek city-states and trading stations which fringed the Mediterranean coast shared a common language, common cults and institutions, a common way of life based on intensive cultivation of

---

[1] Cf. E. H. Fischer, 'Gregor der Grosse und Byzanz. Ein Beitrag zur Geschichte der päpstlichen Politik', *ZSR*, LXVII, Kanon. Abt. XXXVI (1950), 15–144.

[2] E. Stein, *Histoire du Bas-Empire*, II, p. 675, note 1.

[3] Cf. A. Philippson, *Das byzantinische Reich als geographische Erscheinung* (Leiden, 1939), pp. 31–59.

the olive and vine, and, above all, a common dependence on maritime communications. Rome took over, enlarged and exploited this heritage; but in the arts of peace 'Greece took her fierce conqueror captive', and the expansion of the Empire led to the prevalence of a Graeco-Roman culture which overlay, without wholly extinguishing, the alien traditions of the subject peoples. The fusion of Greece and Rome was, however, incomplete. In the West, the work of Rome encountered no effective rival among the Iberians and Celts; but the inhabitants of the eastern Mediterranean basin could boast of a higher and more ancient civilisation, and despite the official use of Latin in administration, army and laws, the civic institutions, manners and education of these parts remained Greek. A potential line of cleavage thus persisted between the Hellenised Orient and the Romanised West, though the linguistic barrier was not yet apparent. A popular form of Greek was currently spoken in the trading quarters of western cities, and for the first two centuries it was the language of the scriptures and liturgy of the Western Church. Meanwhile, tutors from Greek lands had long been engaged in imparting Hellenic culture to the youth of the Roman upper class, some of whom completed their studies at the university of Athens. These were, however, a small minority. Roman education down to its last days remained bilingual, but a first-hand acquaintance with Greek thought became rare, and use was increasingly made of translations and epitomes.[1] The causes of this cultural decline are obscure, but it seems to have been accelerated by the disturbed conditions of the third century.

The restoration of order under Diocletian and Constantine did not reverse the process; instead, it gave a temporary impetus to the study of Latin in the East as a means of obtaining government posts; the official encouragement of Latin at the university of Constantinople and the law school at Beirut indicates the trend of imperial policy.[2] The earlier legislation of Justinian shows a similar purpose; but it is significant that most of the Novels were issued in Greek, and before the end of his reign the use of Latin had become exceptional. Military commands continued for centuries to be given in Latin, and many Roman technical terms were transliterated; but Greek had established itself as the speech of New Rome, and Greek culture and theology, becoming steadily more intransigent in their claims to superiority, were to be the test of patriotism and the bond of union between the heterogeneous peoples of the Byzantine Empire.

The foundation of Constantinople did not at first accentuate the

---

[1] See H. I. Marrou, *A History of Education in Antiquity* (London, 1956), pp. 255–64, and P. Courcelle, *Les lettres grecques en Occident de Macrobe à Cassiodore* (2nd ed., Paris, 1948). [2] Cf. E. Stein, *Histoire du Bas-Empire*, i, pp. 77 and 295–6.

division between East and West. The supremacy of Rome was not immediately challenged, nor its position as the heart of the Empire. The Emperor Julian was doubtless, whatever ulterior purpose may underlie the rhetorical emphasis, voicing the general sentiment of his time when he declared the new capital to be as far inferior to the old as it was superior to all other cities.[1] Still less must the repeated partitions which took place in the course of the fourth century[2] be taken as evidence of separatist tendencies. Needless to say, there was nothing which resembled a modern linguistic or national frontier. The grouping of the constituent parts of the single Roman Empire varied in accordance with the ambitions and military strength of the co-rulers. It is true that the relative importance of the eastern and western parts had changed. Economically as well as culturally the former centre of the Empire had been displaced; the agrarian decline and depopulation of Italy can be contrasted unfavourably with the more prosperous and stable condition of the commercial cities of the eastern Mediterranean. But questions of defence overshadowed all other considerations at this time. Internal developments may have prepared the way, but the menace from without must be held overwhelmingly responsible for the ultimate shape assumed by the frontiers of East Rome. The incidence of the barbarian invasions decided the differing fortunes of East and West, and it was the struggle for survival which transformed the partition of the Empire from an administrative convenience to a political necessity.

The Hellenic heritage which fell into the hands of the Roman republic during the last century of its existence was of course no longer a world of independent seaboard city-states. The conquests of Alexander had extended far into Asia, and the kingdoms of his successors, great and highly organised despotisms, embraced the Nile Valley, Syria and its desert fringes, parts of Mesopotamia and the mountainous interior of Asia Minor. The acquisition of these territories not only added to the Empire huge land-masses and complicated problems of frontier defence, but introduced exotic and unassimilable elements which had proved largely impervious to Hellenism and were to show themselves equally hostile to the political and religious traditions of Rome.[3] In the West, the defeat

---

[1] Julian, *Or.* I, 4 (ed. Bidez, I, i, Paris, 1932, p. 16/31–9). It may be noted that in the symbolic representation of the two capitals, shown as female figures confronting each other on coins, ivories, etc., Rome invariably occupies the place of honour on the left. See J. M. C. Toynbee, in *Studies presented to D. M. Robinson,* II (St Louis, Missouri, 1953), p. 275.

[2] Aurelius Victor, *De Caesaribus,* XXXIX, 30: 'quasi partito imperio'.

[3] Cf. K. Holl, 'Das Fortleben der Volkssprachen in Kleinasien in nachchristlicher Zeit', *Hermes,* XLIII (1908), 240–54.

of Carthage had been followed by the annexation of Africa, Spain, Gaul and finally Britain. Rhine, Danube and Euphrates thus constituted the limits of Rome's expansion in Europe and Asia, and a vast network of roads linked her distant provinces with the seat of government.

But this continental aspect of the Roman dominions must not obscure the fact that the heart of the Empire was the Mediterranean. On or near its shores stood the richest cities, the holiest shrines, the finest monuments, and the chief centres of learning, literature and art. Along its sea-lanes, during the early centuries, passed the heaviest traffic between East and West, Europe and Africa, carrying not only the multifarious raw materials and manufactured goods which supplied the complicated needs of a highly developed economy, but the corn-supplies for the provisioning of the capitals. The security of the coastal territories was therefore of vital importance; and even more essential, it would seem, was the command of the inland sea, though this view does not appear to have been held consistently by Roman strategists. As under the Republic, so in the days of the later Empire naval power was frequently neglected in favour of the land forces until a crisis compelled the government to adopt emergency measures. The growth of a Vandal fleet in the fifth century was felt as a disaster;[1] communications with the West were severed, and fears were even entertained of a raid on Alexandria.[2] Justinian's victory in 532 destroyed the Vandal sea-power, and Byzantine shipping was unmolested for nearly a century. The troubled period which followed the death of Heraclius coincided with the rise of a Muslim navy, operating from the Syrian ports, which cut the Mediterranean routes, already infested by Slav pirates in the Adriatic. More dangerous still was the seaward advance of the Arabs towards the capital, beginning with the capture of Rhodes and Cyprus and culminating in the five-year blockade of Constantinople (674–8). The repulse, with the aid of the famous 'Greek fire', of this formidable thrust marks a turning-point in Byzantine naval history, and in the following century improved methods of recruitment and organisation led to a more efficient use of maritime power.

Strategically, the central position of the Mediterranean should have secured to the Empire the advantage of interior lines; but the east–west axis was interrupted by the great promontories of Italy and Greece. Hence the importance of the Via Egnatia, the military road

---

[1] Cf. L. Schmidt, *Geschichte der Wandalen* (2nd ed., Munich, 1942), pp. 88 ff.

[2] See the *Life of St Daniel the Stylite*. Greek text in *AB*, xxxii (1913), 175/3–6: English translation in E. Dawes and N. H. Baynes, *Three Byzantine Saints* (Oxford, 1948), p. 40.

which by-passed the Helladic peninsula in its winding course over the Balkans from Dyrrachium (Durazzo) to Constantinople; but this became highly vulnerable once the line of the Danube had been broken. Long trade-routes, stretching far into the uplands of Asia and northern Europe, descended to the seaports of the Mediterranean at such points as Antioch or Aquileia, and brought wealth to the manufacturing and shipping industries of the Graeco-Roman world. But the same routes lured the invaders, and lack of manœuvring space made the coastal cities difficult to defend. North Africa presented a minor problem in this respect, since no centres of migration lay behind the Atlas mountains and the Sahara, and the tribes of the upper Nile confined themselves to troublesome raids. The eastern outposts required constant attention. Since 226 the aggressive Sassanid rulers of Persia had revived the ambitions of the Achaemenids, and the fortified zone which covered the approaches to Syria and Palestine, though successfully maintained till the seventh century, proved a heavy drain on Roman resources. Pressure on the Rhine and Danube frontiers, however, was of a different and more dangerous kind. The Germanic peoples sought not only plunder but permanent settlement, and barbarian colonisation of the border regions of the Empire had been the compromise followed by Roman policy since the time of Marcus Aurelius, with the object of supplying not only cultivators for the areas depopulated by war and pestilence, but also recruits for the Roman armies, to be used in repelling their German kinsfolk. During the fourth century this double process was intensified; stronger barbarian attacks and repopulation of the frontier districts were accompanied by progressive Germanisation of the imperial forces, which extended even to the higher command. The political consequences of the transfer of power to barbarian generals dominated the history of the early Byzantine Empire. The period of crisis, which lasted for over a century, began in 378, when the flower of the Roman army, led by the Emperor Valens, was slaughtered by the Goths at the disastrous battle of Adrianople in eastern Thrace. The situation was temporarily restored by Theodosius the Great. In accordance with previous practice, the invaders were assigned lands within the Danube frontier; many of them were enrolled in the Roman forces, or served as independent units under their own leaders (*foederati*). Once more, however, internal discord among the rulers of the Empire played into the hands of the barbarians. In 395 Theodosius was succeeded by his two young sons, Arcadius and Honorius. Rivalry between the two brothers, or between their advisers in East and West, prevented concerted action from being taken when Alaric, chief of the Visigoths, laid waste the Balkan provinces. The government in Constantinople came to terms with Alaric, and he was appointed supreme commander for the prefecture of Illyricum, while Gainas, also a Goth, occupied a similar position in the capital. The remarkable anti-German movement which in 400 led to the fall of Gainas saved the East from a German ascendancy; and a few years later, Alaric turned his attention to Italy, where in 410 he succeeded in capturing Rome.

Constantinople now enjoyed a period of comparative tranquillity. Theodosius I had concluded peace with Persia, at the price of a partition of Armenia between the two powers, and the eastern frontier caused no real anxiety for over a hundred years. Even the Hunnic raids, which began early in the fifth century, and came to a climax under Attila, though they devastated the Danube regions and more than once approached the capital, lost much of their importance after Attila moved westward in 451. But barbarians continued to occupy a preponderant place in the armies and at the court of East Rome. The Theodosian house was extinct, and Aspar, the Alan general, became the maker of Emperors in Constantinople just as Ricimer was in the West. It was the achievement of Leo I (457–74) and Zeno (474–91) to have broken, after a long struggle, the political power of the Gothic troops and their commanders by the use of mercenaries from Isauria, a mountainous district in south-west Asia Minor. These Isaurians in their turn were eventually brought under control in 497; but in the meantime a last and most formidable German threat had been removed when Theodoric, leader of the Ostrogoths, who had harassed the Balkans for several years, undertook to reconquer Italy for the Empire. The central administration of Constantinople had survived the most critical period of its existence, and the Emperor Anastasius (491–518), in the course of his long reign, laid the foundations for further recovery by the restoration of its shattered finances.

The barbarian kingdoms of the West were by this time fully established. Britain had long been lost; Gaul, Spain and Africa were in German hands, and no Roman Emperor of the western parts had existed since 476. The process, gradual and uneven in its incidence, by which the provinces were surrendered to the invaders was masked by the conception of the barbarians as allied mercenaries (*foederati*) quartered on Roman estates. The same principle, as we have seen, had been adopted in Illyricum; but the East, thanks to its greater stability and its favourable geographical position, had escaped the political consequences which had overtaken the West. Neglect of the Rhine frontier in the early fifth century was largely responsible for the widespread incursions of Vandals and other tribes in 406–7, which disorganised the administration of Gaul and Spain; and successive waves of invasion from the East prevented any real recovery. Constant dependence on the German *foederati* in staving off these crises and suppressing local disturbances made a consistent imperial policy impossible; and as the central authority weakened, independent Teutonic states arose on the ruins of western provincial organisation. Revenues ceased to flow to the capital, and inability on the part of the last puppet-Emperors to pay the armies of Italy,[1] now almost exclusively composed of barbarians, may have hastened the final development by which Odoacer, no longer content to act, like the generals who had preceded him, as the power behind the throne, deposed Romulus Augustulus and in 476 assumed the government of the West as independent viceroy of the ruler in Constantinople.

As in the time of Theodosius the Great, the Empire was once more in the hands of a single individual, whose rights over the whole extent of Rome's former dominions remained formally unimpaired. The ascendancy of the barbarians in the western provinces continued to be regarded in the East as a temporary phase, destined to give place to the restoration of direct Roman control. During the fifth century Constantinople had been preoccupied with her own survival, and occasional attempts to halt the German progress in the West, such as the naval expedition of 468 against the Vandals in Africa, had ended in failure. Nor were the prospects of intervention improved when Theodoric replaced Odoacer as the master of Italy. Like his predecessor, Theodoric was careful to observe his constitutional limitations; but he also contrived to safeguard his independence by dynastic alliances with the neighbouring Germanic kings. His death, and that of the monophysite Emperor Anastasius, which was followed by the reconciliation of the sees of Rome and Constantinople, left the way clear for the ambitious schemes of Justinian I (527–65). His aims, which included nothing less than the reconquest of all the lost provinces, were realised only in part; but Africa, Italy, the islands of the western Mediterranean and the south-eastern corner of Spain were, after wearisome and costly campaigns, restored to the Empire. These hard-won gains, which almost doubled the extent of his dominions, set the seal on the many-sided achievements of a glorious reign. But they exhausted the resources of East Rome, and created insoluble problems for his successors. Even before the death of Justinian cracks in the structure had appeared, and for the rest of the century the unwearying efforts of three conscientious rulers were devoted to saving the essential parts of an unstable edifice. To abandon the western conquests would have been an unthinkable

---

[1] Cf. E. Stein, *Histoire du Bas-Empire*, i (Paris, 1959), pp. 377–8.

betrayal of the Roman ideal; but there could be no question of further expansion. Merely to retain the existing territory was in itself an impossible task. Africa, under careful supervision, eventually regained some degree of prosperity, and in the days of Heraclius it emerged as a centre of imperial loyalties. By 578 the greater part of North Italy had been overrun by the Lombards; but Ravenna was held, connections with Rome were maintained, and South Italy and the islands continued for several centuries in Byzantine possession.

The vital frontiers, however, lay to the north and east; and for their defence all the available strength of the Empire was required. Justinian, whose eyes had been fixed on the West, had elsewhere been content to remain on the defensive; an elaborate system of fortresses covered the borderlands, and a precarious peace had been maintained by able diplomacy, backed by the payment of heavy subsidies to his hostile neighbours. This expensive policy could no longer be afforded, and in 572 a protracted struggle with Persia began, which ended only with the final victory of Heraclius in 629. A significant feature in this contest was the increasing importance attached to the control of Armenia, whose value to the Empire, not only as an economic and strategic asset, but also as a recruiting-ground for the Roman armies, was soon to be enhanced by the Muslim conquests. Meanwhile the Danube region, which had witnessed the westward movement of so many barbaric tribes, passing from the steppes of South Russia to the plains of central Europe, had now become subject to continual Slav incursions, forerunners of the permanent settlements which were to form the basis of the medieval Balkan states. Led by the Avars, who had established themselves in Hungary towards the middle of the sixth century, plundering Slavonic bands penetrated southwards into the Greek peninsula and even threatened the outskirts of the capital. The reign of Maurice (582–602) marks the last effective attempt to maintain the inheritance left by Justinian. The defence of the West was reorganised; viceroys, known as exarchs, who combined military and civil powers, were set up at Ravenna and Carthage, foreshadowing the seventh-century development of the theme-system. In 591 a favourable peace with Persia enabled Maurice to turn his attention to the neglected Balkan frontier, and the task of expelling the Slav and Avar intruders was begun. But this (as it proved) final opportunity of restoring the Danube line was not to be taken by East Rome. The successful revolt of Phocas, which cost Maurice his throne and life, spread disorder throughout the Empire, and internal anarchy invited attack from without. The Mesopotamian fortresses fell before the armies of Chosroes; the borders of Syria and Palestine were crossed, and Persian forces advanced into Asia Minor, occupying

Cappadocia, and even penetrating as far as Chalcedon. To meet this emergency Byzantine troops were withdrawn from the Balkan provinces, and Avars and Slavs resumed their work of destruction. Every element of cohesion in the Empire seemed to have disappeared. Phocas (602–10) had instituted a reign of terror in the capital, while the provinces were torn by religious and civil strife.

The advent of Heraclius (610–41) at the head of an army from North Africa did not end this tale of disaster; but the turn of the tide, when it came, was decisive, and his remarkable achievement reveals not only the personal genius of one of the greatest of Byzantine rulers but also the extraordinary recuperative powers of East Rome. The first ten years of his reign witnessed sensational Persian triumphs, unequalled since the days of the Achaemenids. Antioch fell in 611, Jerusalem in 614, and the conquest of Syria and Palestine was shortly followed by that of Egypt. Recovery from this desperate position was slow, and it is significant that at one point Heraclius contemplated a return to Carthage. But confidence was regained; the forces of Church and State were fused in a crusading ardour, and in a series of brilliant campaigns, based largely on the north-eastern regions of Asia Minor, Heraclius finally shattered the military might of Persia and in 629 restored to Jerusalem the Holy Cross, the most sacred relic of Christianity.

The moment of victory was short-lived. The declining years of Heraclius were darkened by the Arab conquests, which undid much of his life's work. The balance of power in the Near East, sustained for so many centuries by the rivalry of Rome and Persia, had been destroyed by the catastrophic events of his reign. Disorganised and exhausted by their internecine struggle, neither of the two ancient Empires was in a position to offer effective resistance to the fresh and vigorous forces of Islam, when a few years after the death of Muḥammad (632) hordes of fanatical warriors issued from the Arabian desert. Syria and Palestine, where long-standing disaffection had been intensified by the grievances of post-war taxation, were quickly overrun, and the reduction of these provinces was soon followed by the annexation of Egypt (641–2). The expansion of Islam continued. Persia was overwhelmed, and with the Mesopotamian strongholds in enemy hands a new and permanent threat to the vital territory of Asia Minor came into being, which necessitated a redistribution of the Byzantine defensive forces and led to radical changes in the provincial administration. Dynastic struggles in the Muslim world from 656 to 663 slowed down for a time the Arab advance, but the annual raids on Anatolia were soon resumed, and the successive capture by the infidel fleet of Cyprus, Rhodes and Chios revealed clearly the coming assault on the capital. By 674 an operational base had been established within the Marmora itself, and for four years Constantinople was blockaded throughout the summer months. The hour of decision came in 678. A great sea-fight before the walls ended in total defeat for the Saracens. The siege was raised, and many of the surviving vessels were wrecked in a storm. Naval supremacy in home waters was regained; military successes in Asia Minor completed the victory, and the Arabs were forced to sue for an ignominious peace. For the first time the challenge of Islam had been effectively answered; Rome's prestige was restored, and the effect of the triumph was soon manifest in the increased deference of her northern and western neighbours.[1]

As in the preceding century, three outstanding rulers were responsible for the preservation of Byzantium in its hour of need, and despite differences of approach the continuity of policy is plainly apparent. The paramount issue was the retention of Asia Minor, of which the military and economic resources formed the basis of Roman strength. The fulfilment of this task, together with the organisation of a permanent defensive scheme, was the greatest achievement of the Heraclian house. The West, however, was not forgotten. Constans II (641–68), whose visionary designs can only be conjectured, seems to have contemplated the overthrow of the Lombards and the restoration of Rome as a second capital; and his forcible treatment of Pope Martin, ill-judged though it was, proves his determination to reassert Byzantine authority in its western dominions. Constantine IV (668–85), more prudent in his ecclesiastical policy, ended the breach with Rome at the Sixth General Council in 680–1, and Justinian II (685–95 and 705–11), though his attempts to control the Papacy were a notable failure, displayed a continuous interest in the West. With the ending of the Heraclian dynasty came a change of outlook. Constans II's efforts to create a barrier in South Italy and Sicily against the Muslim advance were not repeated, and in 697 the African province fell to the invaders. Revolts in the Italian exarchate reflected the struggle for power in Constantinople, and by the early years of the eighth century ominous signs of the iconoclast dispute, the harbinger of fresh differences between East and West, were already apparent.

Steadily throughout this period the Slavs had increased their hold on the Balkan peninsula.[2] During the first half of the seventh century massive barbarian infiltration had taken place; civil and ecclesiastical

---

[1] Theophanes (ed. de Boor), p. 356/2–8.

[2] See P. Lemerle, 'Invasions et migrations dans les Balkans depuis la fin de l'époque romaine jusqu'au viiie siècle', *RH*, ccxi (1954), 265–308.

organisation had largely disappeared from the interior, and the provincials had been driven to seek refuge in the cities and islands of the coastal fringe. Under Avar leadership, plundering Slav bands harried the Dalmatian seaboard on the west, and penetrated as far south as the Peloponnese. With the break-up of the Avar confederacy, more permanent Slavonic settlements were established, and in Macedonia a *modus vivendi* seems to have been reached between Thessalonica—the great Byzantine trading city and provincial capital, whose walls had defied successive assaults—and the tribes which had taken possession of the Thracian hinterland. Preoccupied by the eastern danger, Constantinople fell back on passive defence or the payment of subsidies, and it was only in 658 that a temporary slackening of Arab pressure gave Constans II an opportunity to recover lost ground. As a result of his campaign in Macedonia, Slav tribes between the Strymon and the Vardar were induced to acknowledge Byzantine sovereignty, and a number of these were transplanted to Asia Minor, to fill the depleted ranks of the imperial army. Thirty years later an expedition with similar objects was carried out on a larger scale by Justinian II; but by this time a new threat had arisen still nearer home. Crossing the lower Danube about 670 the Bulgarians had established themselves in the Dobrudja, subduing the Slavs between the estuary and the Balkan mountains, and creating in the heart of the Empire an organised, aggressive state, with forces strategically placed to interrupt northern communications and (when occasion offered) to descend on the capital itself. Two of the principal problems which faced the reconstituted Empire of East Rome were thus already manifest by the end of the seventh century—the task of civilising its Slav neighbours and the standing menace of the Bulgarian kingdom.

V. ADMINISTRATION AND ARMY

Much of the old Roman world had vanished for ever during the chaos and anarchy of the third century, which had brought the state to the brink of destruction. Continuous civil war between the armies of rival Emperors had ruined the provinces; famine and plague had reduced the agricultural population, while barbarian pressure had been intensified on every frontier. Revenues had proved insufficient to meet the growing demands of the public services, and a debased currency led only to progressive inflation. The administrative reforms of Diocletian and Constantine must be judged in the light of these facts. In effect they prolonged the existence of the Roman Empire for a further millennium, while they imposed on its inhabitants the framework of an economic and social order which remained, in its essential features, the permanent basis of Byzantine life. The purpose of the reforms was practical and conservative. Safeguards were sought against the recurrence of the recent disorders, while abusive practices which it was too late to abolish were regulated and thus, it was hoped, brought under control. The security of the frontiers and the strengthening of the central authority were primary objectives, but financial solvency, the prerequisite of any ordered government, was perhaps the foremost consideration; and this, at a tremendous price in political and spiritual freedom, was eventually achieved.

At the head of the new system, which was brought to completion by Constantine's successors, stood a small number of high officials and commanders-in-chief, who were directly responsible to the Emperor. Of the central ministries in the capital, each with many departments and an extensive staff, the most important was that of the Master of Offices, whose miscellaneous duties included the super-vision of the imperial chanceries, the introduction of foreign em-bassies, the control of the palace guards, and the inspection of the arsenals. He played also a large part in the organisation of the postal system and its secret police. Foreign policy and state security, as well as the appointment to many senior posts in the civil service, were thus to a considerable extent in his hands.[1] Other high officials were the two finance ministers, the Count of the Sacred Largesse and the Count of the Private Estates. Equal to them in rank was the Lord Chamberlain, the eunuch who controlled the palace arrange-ments. It is significant of the new despotism and of the conditions of court life that the influence of this minister of the household, during the reign of feeble monarchs, often prevailed over that of the officers of state.[2]

Changes in the provincial administration were more radical. Efforts, not always successful, were made to establish a uniform pattern. Italy, and in some respects Egypt, lost their special position and were assimilated to the rest of the Empire. The provinces were reduced in size and their number was approximately doubled. They were grouped in dioceses, which were placed under the rule of *vicarii*, and by the end of the fourth century the Empire had been divided into four great prefectures, at the head of each of which stood a praetorian prefect, responsible to the Emperor alone. To these power-ful officials, whose dignity and privileges were in keeping with their

---

[1] See A. E. R. Boak, *The Master of the Offices in the Later Roman and Byzantine Empires* (New York, 1919).

[2] Cf. J. E. Dunlap, *The Office of the Grand Chamberlain in the Later Roman and Byzantine Empires* (New York, 1924), pp. 260–84.

position, were assigned the widest administrative, financial and judicial functions, which even tended to encroach upon those of the central ministries. They controlled both the *vicarii* and the provincial governors. They levied the principal tax, the *annona*, and provided not only for the salaries of their subordinates but the pay and rations of the armed forces. Edicts, though of limited application, issued from their chanceries; and from the decisions of their courts of ustice there lay no appeal.[1]

The risks inherent in such a complete delegation of authority were in some degree offset by the checks and balances which the system supplied. Thus the chain of command which stretched from the praetorian prefect to his subordinate administrators was linked at several points with the central government, since both the *vicarii* and the provincial governors could report independently to the Emperor. But far more fundamental as a restraining influence was the severance of military and civil powers which distinguished the new order alike from that of the earlier Empire and from the post-Heraclian developments. Over against the praetorian prefect stood now the master of soldiers, or commander-in-chief, and the danger of revolt was greatly diminished when provincial governors ceased to control local forces. The continued responsibility, on the other hand, of the civil administrators for provisioning the troops in their district served as a brake on the designs of ambitious generals.

The most striking feature of the new military system was the creation of a mobile field army, which the Emperor could use either to crush rebellion or to expel a barbarian invader. Personally attached to the ruler, these *comitatenses*, or 'troops of the retinue', became the regular army of the Empire, continually gaining in privilege and status at the expense of the garrisons permanently stationed under their *duces* in the border provinces, or the peasant militia (*limitanei*) who cultivated tax-free plots in the frontier zone in return for an hereditary obligation of service. It is the field army, small in numbers but highly efficient, which figures almost exclusively in the military annals of the earlier Byzantine Empire. Its organisation, which was due mainly to Constantine,[2] was preserved until the beginning of the seventh century, though changes in its composition, armament and tactics reflect the political developments of a troubled period. In response to barbarian methods of fighting, the cavalry arm gained steadily in importance; horses and their riders were clad

---

[1] Cf. E. Stein, *Untersuchungen über das Officium der Prätorianerpräfektur seit Diokletian* (Vienna, 1922).

[2] Cf. D. van Berchem, *L'armée de Dioclétien et la réforme constantinienne* (Paris, 1952), pp. 108–9.

in mail, and mounted archers played a prominent part in the campaigns of Justinian. Tactics were adapted to fresh adversaries; the *Strategicon* of Leo VI, dating probably from the early seventh century, seems to be based on recent experience, and recommends a more flexible line of battle, defence in depth, and carefully rehearsed manœuvres to counter the infiltration of fast-moving enemy skirmishers.[1]

Recruitment for the Roman forces was a permanent problem which taxed all the resources of imperial statesmanship. During the fifth century the barbarisation of the army and its generals had contributed largely to the loss of the western provinces, while the East, narrowly escaping a similar fate, was subsequently held to ransom by its Gothic *foederati*, tribal contingents under their own chiefs whom Theodosius I had engaged for the defence of the Danube. The expeditionary forces of Justinian also included large barbarian elements, though these were led by imperial officers. A fruitful source of indiscipline was the institution of *buccellarii*, or bands of retainers attached to a particular commander, on whom they depended for their equipment and pay. These troops, together with numbers of barbarian mercenaries, were still a conspicuous feature of Maurice's armies; but the bulk of the Byzantine forces was beginning to be drawn from within the frontiers, especially from Armenia and the Caucasus region.[2]

During the seventh century far-reaching changes began to take place in the military and civil administration of the Empire. The loss of Syria, Egypt and North Africa, together with the Slav occupation of the Balkans, transformed the problem of defending the frontiers. The safeguarding of the capital itself and the preservation of the vital provinces of Asia Minor were henceforth the primary considerations, before which all else must give way. The armed forces were accordingly organised and distributed on completely new lines. Apart from the regiments of picked troops stationed in and around Constantinople, the main strength of the imperial armies was concentrated in the Anatolian peninsula, the territory of which was divided into three great military districts. Each was garrisoned by an army corps (*thema*) under its *strategus*, and the word 'theme' was subsequently used to denote the military provinces, of varying size, which came into being when the system was extended to the rest of the Empire. Within these districts of Asia Minor the chief regiments

---

[1] *Strategicon*, XII, 1. See Gy. Moravcsik, *Byzantinoturcica*, 2nd ed., I, p. 417 and cf. *MPG*, CVII, 805 C–D, 808 B.
[2] Cf. E. Stein, *Studien zur Geschichte des byzantinischen Reiches* (Stuttgart, 1919), pp. 121, 123.

of the former field army appear to have been settled at the expense of the state, receiving grants of land in return for hereditary service. These farmer-soldiers, superior in quality and status to the old *limitanei*, formed the backbone of the imperial defensive system; as a tax-paying class of independent smallholders they proved themselves also a valuable element of stability in economic and social life.[1]

Gradually, in response to the altered conditions, the scheme of administration instituted by Diocletian and Constantine gave place to a new order. As the theme system developed, the principle of the separation of civil and military power, already abandoned in the case of the exarchates and some other special regions, was finally given up. What remained of the former provinces of East Rome became military districts in which the commanding officer exercised complete jurisdiction, and was responsible only to the Emperor. These changes, together with the great diminution of imperial territory, rendered obsolete the old pattern of provincial government and defence, with its dual hierarchy of civil and military officials; deprived of their functions, the Praetorian Prefects as well as the Masters of Soldiers eventually disappeared. A similar process can be observed in the central ministries: that of the Master of Offices, for example, was progressively dismembered, and the heads of most of its miscellaneous departments emerged as independent officials, directly subject to the Emperor's authority. The general effect of these administrative reforms, which were brought to completion under the Isaurian rulers, was, in Bury's phrase, 'to substitute the principle of co-ordination for that of subordination, and to multiply supreme offices instead of placing immense powers in the hands of a few'.[2]

The centralisation of the imperial government and the loss of such important cities as Antioch and Alexandria enhanced still further the political and commercial ascendancy of the capital, and increased the responsibilities of the city prefect, whose time-honoured office still retained something of the traditions of an earlier age. Constantinople, like Rome, enjoyed a privileged and largely autonomous status, which extended to the hundredth milestone from the centre of the city. Within this territory the prefect was the supreme civil authority. He represented the senate in its dealings with the Emperor, acted as the chief criminal judge, and controlled the urban police. The maintenance of law and order were in his hands, and the personal safety of the ruler, when threatened by popular uprisings, often depended on

[1] See G. Ostrogorsky, *History of the Byzantine State*, pp. 118–19. J. Karayannopoulos, *Die Entstehung der byzantinischen Themenordnung* (Byzantinisches Archiv, x; Munich, 1959), shows that the introduction of this system was gradual rather than revolutionary.

[2] *The Imperial Administrative System in the Ninth Century* (London, 1911), p. 20.

the loyalty of his prefect. Equally important were his duties in connection with the economic life of the city. Water and food supplies, regulation of markets and prices came under his jurisdiction, and the functions of his officials included detailed inspection of the working of the corporations, or guilds, which formed the prevailing system of Byzantine industry.

VI. TAXATION AND ECONOMIC LIFE

Even by modern standards, the Byzantine state was at all times expensive to run. The heads of its budget might vary with the strategic situation, the religious and social policy, or even the personal tastes of the ruler. But certain liabilities were permanent and inescapable. The first and supreme charge on the exchequer was the formidable cost of defence. Barbarian pressure at one point or another was continuous, and the security of the difficult frontier-line imposed on the Empire by its geographical position called for the maintenance of elaborate fortifications and an endless series of deterrent campaigns, with the alternative of danegeld or subsidies as the price of peace. Byzantine mercenaries were highly, though not always regularly, paid, and in addition to the sums lavished on equipment and supplies, frequent donatives were required to retain the loyalty of the standing armies. The upkeep of roads and bridges was a military as well as an economic necessity, and the vast building programme of an Emperor like Justinian constituted a further drain on the Empire's resources. Second only to the needs of defence came those of the enormously expanded civil service, itself the instrument which ensured a steady inflow of revenue. Lastly, the character of the monarchy, as we have seen, demanded the setting of a magnificent ritual, luxurious palaces, a court which numbered its dependants in thousands, and a tradition of imperial largesse which in certain reigns swelled to fantastic proportions.

It is a tribute to the work of Diocletian and Constantine that the fiscal machinery which they devised succeeded not only in meeting these onerous requirements but in restoring a stable economic system, backed by a sound currency, which enabled the administration of East Rome to weather the crises of its first three centuries. Of the multifarious sources of revenue, many had already a long past. The extensive imperial estates, augmented by confiscation and inheritance, continued to be a valuable asset, and to their produce must be added that of the state-owned mines, arsenals and factories which furnished clothing, weapons and equipment for the army. Indirect taxation, which affected chiefly the urban population and the trading

community, included substantial import duties, harbour dues and
market tolls. Of the direct taxes, far the most important was the
annona, or land tax, which formed the essential basis of the Byzantine
economy. Its origin must be sought in the inflationary conditions of
the third century, when the remuneration of soldiers and civil servants was made chiefly in kind, by means of supplies requisitioned
from the primary producers. This somewhat primitive practice, with
its obvious opportunities for extortion, was adapted and developed
by Diocletian. A complicated system was evolved, embodying certain
earlier forms of tribute, and the *annona* became a regular impost
covering the whole Empire.[1] The total requirements were estimated
by the government, and divided proportionately between the prefectures. Further subdivision by districts followed, until the quota of
each taxpayer was reached. Gradually, as a stable currency was
restored, money equivalents came to be fixed for the salaries of state
employees, and by the close of the fifth century contributions to the
annona itself had been largely commuted for money payments, the
rate of conversion being calculated according to an official tariff of
current prices.[2]

Byzantine rulers regarded the land primarily as a source of revenue,
and their financial policy did much to determine the pattern of
agricultural life. If the needs of the treasury were to be met, each
cultivable parcel of ground must be exploited to the fullest extent.
The later Roman Empire suffered from a perennial shortage of labour,
and the *coloni*, nominally free peasants, were therefore increasingly
bound to the soil on which they worked. The incidence of taxation
also furthered the growth of great rural estates. Many smallholders,
already at the mercy of bad harvests or accumulated debts, found the
additional burden too much to bear, and became the rent-paying
tenants of a wealthy landowner who could protect them from the
claims of the state. In face of this challenge to its authority the
administration was forced to compromise, and by the early fifth
century the great landowners had been entrusted with the responsibility of collecting the taxes for which their tenants were liable.
Steadily the power of these magnates increased, and the estates of the
Egyptian nobles came to resemble miniature kingdoms, equipped
with police, courts of justice, private armies, and elaborate postal and
transport services. Such *potentes* could afford to defy the agents of
the fisc, and an unceasing struggle to assert its control was carried

---

[1] On the system of assessment, many details of which are still obscure, see
A. Déléage, *La capitation du Bas-Empire* (Mâcon, 1945).
[2] Cf. F. W. Walbank, in *Cambridge Economic History of Europe*, II (Cambridge, 1952),
p. 67.

on by the central government. In the end financial considerations decided the issue; the co-operation of the landed proprietors was essential if the revenue was to be secured, and the *latifundia*, with all their abuses, continued to form the prevailing system of Byzantine rural economy.

The invasions of the Avars, Persians and Arabs produced a new situation. The great property-owners of Egypt, Syria and the Balkans were dispossessed; some of its most productive territory was lost to the Empire, and even Asia Minor was repeatedly ravaged by plundering bands. Now that the corn-fleets no longer sailed from Alexandria, fresh sources of supply for the capital had to be developed. Thrace and the Black Sea littoral became increasingly important, and an additional motive may have been given for the settlement of soldier-farmers in Anatolia, and the successive transplanting of Slav colonists to these parts. Most of our information on agricultural conditions comes from the Egyptian papyri, and it is only with reservations that this evidence can be applied to the Empire in general, especially for the period after the Arab conquest. It is unlikely, however, in view of later developments, that the system of *latifundia* was ever wholly abandoned in Asia Minor, while the 'free' village, to the survival of which the papyri bear ample witness, meets us again in the provisions of the 'Farmer's Law', a document variously attributed to the late seventh or the eighth century.[1] Even in the rural districts of Byzantine Egypt independent villages and country towns, populated by small proprietors, merchants and artisans, had in fact maintained a vigorous existence side by side with the scattered domains of the great nobles, and to this extent one may qualify the monotonous picture of oppression and misery which the denunciations of the imperial law-codes suggest.[2] In general, however, the social regime imposed on the Empire by Diocletian and his successors, though not without Hellenistic and earlier Roman precedent, represented a further curtailment of liberty for all except the richest class. Just as the peasant was tied to the soil, so the craftsmen and transport workers, especially those connected with the provisioning of the armies and urban centres, were organised in compulsory guilds, the members of which formed a series of hereditary castes, fixed by statute in their particular branch of the public service.

Similar coercion was applied to the *curiales*, or local senators, who constituted the bulk of the middle classes. Roman provincial admini-

[1] For recent literature on the Farmer's Law see F. Dölger and A. M. Schneider, *Byzanz* (Berne, 1952), pp. 34–5, and G. Ostrogorsky, *History of the Byzantine State*, pp. 82, 120; and see Pt II, ch. XXI, p. 64.

[2] Cf. M. Gelzer, *Studien zur byzantinischen Verwaltung Ägyptens* (Leipzig, 1909), p. 75, and G. Rouillard, *La vie rurale dans l'empire byzantin* (Paris, 1953), p. 50.

stration had from the first been based on the municipalities, and it was natural that the new fiscal system should assign to their governing bodies the task of producing for the treasury the quota of the revenue required from their districts. As in other spheres, the doctrine of corporate responsibility was ruthlessly employed by the central authority to cover deficits and evasions of tax, and the *curiales*, crushed by the load of increasing liabilities, and seeking by every means to escape from an impossible position, were, like their fellow-subjects in trade and industry, forced by successive enactments to remain at their post, deserters being actually apprehended like runaway slaves. But the decline of the cities, already far advanced by the end of the third century, could not be halted by legislation. Interprovincial trade had dwindled, and though certain countries, such as Britain and Spain, enjoyed a late summer of prosperity, no real revival was possible in the West. Private munificence no longer sufficed to maintain the baths and theatres of the municipalities; the rich landowners had retired to their country estates, and faced by the growing insecurity of the times the Gallic cities, rebuilt within a smaller circuit, huddled behind their defensive walls. The invasions of the fifth century destroyed the machinery of imperial administration over wide areas, and much of the state-controlled industry vanished with it. Italy, already impoverished, was reduced to her own resources, while the central government, deprived of its provincial revenues, lacked even the wherewithal to pay its barbarian mercenaries.

In the eastern half of the Empire, matters were very different. The cities of the Aegean seaboard lay for the most part off the main routes of invasion. Urban civilisation, with its Hellenistic traditions and stronger economic basis, had proved more resistant to the shocks of the third century, and municipal institutions continued to survive despite the pressure of heavier taxation and the increased interference of imperial officials. Justinian's policy favoured the conservation and growth of towns, and the enormous building activities of his reign have left traces still visible in every corner of the Byzantine world. At the beginning of the seventh century, as the incidents of the revolution which followed the death of Maurice vividly demonstrate, the life of the provincials still centred in their cities, and down to the Arab conquest the religious and political crises of the capital found their reflection in the struggles of the circus-parties at Antioch and Alexandria.

The economic preponderance of the eastern provinces, which became steadily more marked during the first centuries of the Byzantine Empire, had rested largely on the industry and commerce of Egypt and Syria. Renowned for their glassware, textiles and metalwork, these countries also dominated the carrying trade of the Mediterranean, and their merchants handled not only the products of the Aegean basin but the silks, spices, ivory and other exotic articles imported from Asia and Central Africa. The commercial rise of Constantinople which accompanied its political ascendancy created a rival to the older centres, and by the sixth century it was becoming the principal market for eastern wares.[1] Trade was regarded as a valuable adjunct of diplomacy, and Justinian's encouragement of the silk industry is well known. Control of the Straits enabled Constantinople to profit also from the Black Sea traffic, and the excellent road-system of Asia Minor provided access to the varied production of the Fertile Crescent as well as to the terminal points of the caravan routes across Central Asia. Further progress was cut short by the worsening situation on her northern and eastern frontiers, which culminated in the storms of the seventh century. The sweeping victories of Islam dislocated trading communications throughout the Near East, and Byzantium, after resisting the initial assault, entered upon a difficult period of recuperation. Equally decisive in its consequences was the westward extension of Muslim power. With the loss of Africa and Spain the economic unity of the Mediterranean, temporarily restored by Justinian, was broken for ever. The long history of Graeco-Roman development of this area had reached its conclusion, and when at length the revival came, the pattern of medieval commerce was drawn on new lines.

[1] Cf. L. Bréhier, *Le monde byzantin*, III: *La civilisation byzantine*, p. 184.

CHAPTER II

THE CHRISTIAN BACKGROUND

Much of the character of Byzantine religion was determined by the rapidity of the growth of Christianity in the eastern provinces of the Roman Empire during the fourth and fifth centuries. Few cultures have become so integrally Christian, yet East Rome was always to preserve a conscious continuity with the imperial Hellenistic world of the Severan age. The mass conversions of the literate Hellenised class, from which the civil service was recruited, were perhaps in many cases little more than a nominal acceptance of a new state religion; the conventional Graeco-Roman ideals of human virtue and of social and political duty remained almost unaffected by it and were quickly synthesised into the new doctrines, mainly through the work of Greek Christian philosophers and rhetoricians. The mass conversion in the city proletariate and in the unhellenised areas in Asia Minor, Syria and Egypt was perhaps more strictly a religious movement but even here the speed of the change ensured survivals in cult, in ritual and in the conception of the hero, the wonder-worker and the demi-god. Hagiography and the development of local shrines were to be the means by which these were incorporated throughout East Roman Christianity. The two movements blended. In the fifth century it is still possible to contrast literate and popular Christianity. By the seventh century they had interpenetrated each other. Byzantine Christianity became a single religious culture as well as a faith. Yet much of it remains unintelligible if the contrasted factors that led to its development are ignored.

The fourth-century religious transition had fallen into two main phases, particularly associated with the reigns of Constantius II and of Theodosius I. At the death of Constantine in 337, Christianity was still the religion of a relatively small minority in the Empire, even though it had been honoured by the personal choice of the Emperor and by the patronage of the imperial household; its exact legal position is suggested by Constantine's decree of 25 May 323 with its emphasis on the freedom of a Christian to follow the most Holy Law.[1] Under his son Constantius II (337–61) there is evidence of the new conception that Christianity, precisely because it was the personal religion of the Emperor, should be universally accepted by

---

[1] *Cod. Theod.* XVI, 2, 5 (ed. Th. Mommsen, P. M. Meyer (Berlin, 1905), I, 2, p. 836).

his subjects. The imperial enactment of 341 contains the phrase: 'May superstition cease and the madness of the sacrifices be abolished',[1] and the edicts of 346 and 356 prohibited the public worship of the gods.[2] It is probable that both the ability and the administrative success of Constantius II have been commonly underrated and it is certain that his reign coincides with a great increase in the numerical strength of Christianity, both in the higher ranks of the civil service and in the town proletariate. But it is clear that his religious edicts were only sporadically enforced and the strength of the conservative reaction under his successor Julian (361–3) suggests that his religious policy was premature.

The reigns of Constantine, Constantius and Julian belong ideologically to a single grouping; each Emperor was intent upon a *renovatio orbis*, even though each differed in his choice of means for the renewal. By the summer of 363 all three experiments had failed. It was the policy of Valentinian I and of his brother Valens to reorganise, not in order to innovate, but in order to conserve. Christianity was the religion of both Emperors. It was not the official religion of the Empire. Valentinian I had written in 371: 'The laws given by me at the beginning of my rule are witnesses that to each man is granted the free exercise to worship as he will.'[3] The fact that such tolerance was not extended to Manicheans, to astrologers or to magicians[4] further emphasised the traditional respect accorded to the Graeco-Roman cults and the new prestige possessed by the bishops of the Christian Church. For fifteen years the religious forces stayed in some form of equilibrium.

The real founder of the East Christian Empire was not Constantine but Theodosius I. The period of its formation stretched from his accession in 379 to the death of his son Arcadius in 408. The edict promulgated at Thessalonica on 27 February 380[5] established the Catholic Church as the state religion of the Empire:

We desire that all peoples who are governed by our Clemency should adhere to that religion which was taught by the divine apostle Peter to the Romans and which has been maintained in its traditional form to the present day, the religion which is now professed by the Pontiff Damasus and by Peter Bishop of Alexandria a man of apostolic sanctity.... We authorise the followers of this rule of faith to embrace the name of Catholic Christians.... We brand all others with the infamous name of heretic.

[1] *Cod. Theod.* xvi, 10, 2 (i, 2, p. 897).
[2] *Cod. Theod.* xvi, 10, 3–4, 6 (i, 2, p. 898).
[3] *Cod. Theod.* viii, 16, 9 (i, 2, p. 462).
[4] *Cod. Theod.* viii, 16, 7 and 8; xvi, 5, 3 (i, 2, pp. 462, 855).
[5] *Cod. Theod.* xvi, 1, 2 (i, 2, p. 833).

By the edict issued from Constantinople on 10 January 381[1] the Christian churches throughout the eastern provinces of the Empire were handed over to this state religion. The conception of imperial orthodoxy had at last been fully evolved. The Graeco-Roman cults were proscribed in a series of rescripts that culminate in the decree of 8 November 392.[2] A Christian calendar of state feasts was formulated as a symbol of the religious revolution,[3] and by the year 410 the profession of imperial orthodoxy had become a requisite throughout the Empire for any membership in the imperial civil service.[4]

Among well-educated fourth-century pagans it was fashionable to be syncretic and to be tolerant of all cults; 'not by one road alone does man reach so great a mystery'.[5] It could therefore be easy for a pagan official to accept somewhat superficially the now essential Christian rites. He could still pray to other gods while he was officially attending the Christian liturgy—as long afterwards Procopius was to report of John of Cappadocia.[6] A crypto-pagan element does indeed seem to have survived in the civil service at least until the reign of Justinian and perhaps for much longer. Open paganism certainly survived in academic circles. There were scholars who were publicly non-Christian until the end of the sixth century. For years to come temples were to be still open and sacrifices offered in country districts and even in small municipalities. But from 408 the hierarchical organisation of the Christian Church provided the religion of the majority of the population throughout the eastern provinces of the Empire.

Two factors had facilitated the religious transition among the literate: the religious movement associated with neoplatonism and the retention among the new Christians of the scale of social values explicit in Graeco-Roman education.

The new religious emphasis in neoplatonism, like the cult of *Summus Deus* and the worship of the Unconquered Sun, had been a symptom of a fundamental change in third-century non-Christian thought. The religious instinct was coming to find expression through a form of other-worldliness in which the Other World was conceived not merely as consecutive on this world but primarily as coincident with it. The emphasis on the transience of human life was now coupled

---

[1] *Cod. Theod.* xvi, 5, 6 (i, 2, p. 856).

[2] *Cod. Theod.* xvi, 10, 12 (i, 2, p. 900).

[3] *Cod. Theod.* ii, 8, 18–25 (i, 2, pp. 87–9).

[4] 'ut nullus nobis sit aliqua ratione coniunctus, qui a nobis fide et religione discordat.' *Cod. Theod.* xvi, 5, 42 (i, 2, p. 869); cf. *Cod. Theod.* xvi, 5, 48 (i, 2, p. 871).

[5] *Relatio Symmachi*, 10 (preserved in Ambrose, *Ep.* xvii (*MPL*, xvi, 969)).

[6] Procopius, *History of the Wars*, i, 25, 10 (ed. J. Haury, *Procopii Opera*, Leipzig, 1905, i, p. 135).

with an overwhelming sense of the presence of the transcendent and the immutable. All this was to become part of the Byzantine Christian background.

The love and worship of God for his own sake alone had become rooted in the Hellenistic tradition with the Stoics; it is patent in the Cleanthes hymn, sporadic in Epictetus. But the Stoic sense of worship was directed to an all-pervading divine force precisely because that force was conceived as immanent. The Plotinian One, on the other hand, is the object of desire precisely because it is transcendent. In the 6th Ennead the nature of transcendence is found to lie in complete otherness and in self-subsistence; the object apprehended as transcendent is so much above and beyond all other objects as to have quite a different mode of existence. This implies a judgement on the relative unimportance of all other objects. This was a prelude to Byzantine theories of contemplation. It was associated with a new emphasis on virginity, or at least abstinence from sex, as a necessary purification from the life of sense before attaining to the full vision of the Divine. Through the teaching of St Gregory of Nyssa this was to become part of Byzantine ascetic theory.

All this had synchronised with a changed emphasis on imperial divinity, first apparent in the *Virtus Augusti* series from the third-century mints, and symbolised by the new upward glance in imperial portraiture. The endurance and the tasks of Hercules are now used to convey the meaning of the imperial *Virtus*. The *Numen Augusti* is a Mercury, messenger from gods to men, and the genius of Rome is distinct from, and re-entering, his city. The imperial sovereignty is no longer strong through its own immanent divinity, but reflects by divine right another and transcendent and single Godhead; it is a link between two co-existing worlds yet isolated by very reason of that function. *Maiestas* lay as a radiate nimbus round *Auctoritas*, and the imperial bureaucracy was rendered sacred by its participation in sovereignty.

The symbols of the *Virtus Augusti* were to alter in the new official mythology. Mercury and Hercules were to be succeeded by Moses and by David. But while the second-century conception of immanent divine sovereignty could never have been Christianised, the third-century conception of the Sacred Emperor survived fundamentally unaltered into a Christian Empire. It was compatible not only with Christianity but with the theoretical assertion of the independence of the Church and priesthood from the civil power. The Emperor was to remain a link between human and divine. His sovereignty was a reflection of the omnipotence of God since it was derived from it, just as Divine Wisdom was reflected in his wisdom, Divine Care in his 'philanthropy'. He was the Anointed Shepherd of his people. But his prototypes were Moses and not Aaron, David and not Samuel.

One strand survived untouched through the third century to link Byzantine Christianity with an earlier Graeco-Roman world. The new religious movements had not affected the Graeco-Roman conception of education. It still remained the strongest single conservative force. It provided a moral as well as an intellectual training. It was designed primarily to perpetuate a uniform standard in social conduct and in literary expression; in the Ciceronian phrase it was the mistress 'et recte faciendi et bene dicendi'. Its prestige had never been higher than in the Greek-speaking provinces in the fourth century where, since society was neither an aristocracy nor a plutocracy, education had become the chief determinant of social status. It alone could provide entry into the expanding civil service, and in 357 a rescript of Constantius II had decreed that civil service promotion must be dependent on the degree of knowledge of 'good letters'.[1] Julian had noted in 362 that proper education consists in the acquisition of an attitude of mind and sound opinions,[2] and for many great officials who had accepted the new state religion it must have continued to provide the one unquestioned norm of taste and conduct.

In the East this education fell into three parts. Orthography implied the capacity to read and speak and write a standardised Greek. Grammar implied a study of Greek classical authors not only for their style but for their moral teaching, and finally there were the higher studies of rhetoric, law and philosophy. Rhetoric was the art of the use of words; law implied the conception of equity and the elements of jurisprudence; philosophy was conceived primarily as a *philosophia perennis* compiled from Platonist, Aristotelian and Stoic sources and divided into physics, ethics and dialectic. Early in the third century Diogenes Laertius had defined this already conventional division.[3] Physics was theoretical philosophy, the study of a hypothesis that could account for an ordered and intelligible universe. Ethics was practical philosophy, the study of the application of this hypothesis to human affairs. Dialectic was the study of an instrument of knowledge. For centuries this division was to provide the framework for the speculation of Greek Christian theologians.

During the fourth and fifth centuries a series of Christian Fathers transmitted to later Byzantine Christianity the common preconcep-

---

[1] 'Ne autem litteraturae, quae omnium virtutum maxima est, praemia denegentur ei qui studiis et eloquio dignus...', *Cod. Theod.* XIV, 1, 1 (I, 2, p. 771).

[2] Julian, *Ep.* XLII (ed. J. Bidez (Paris, 1924), *Opera*, I, 2, p. 73). Cf. *Cod. Theod.* XIII, 3, 5 (I, 2, p. 741).

[3] Diogenes Laertius, *Lives of the Philosophers*, I, 18 (ed. R. D. Hicks, London, 1950, p. 19).

tions of the educated class from which they came and by so doing gave them an ecclesiastical authority. The first of these was St Methodius of Olympus in Lycia. He wrote his *Dialogues* soon after the year 300, but his influence was at its strongest between the sixth and the eighth centuries when his opposition to Origenism had enhanced his reputation for orthodoxy and when the number of *spuria* attributed to him attest his recognised authority as a Father. His *Banquet of the Ten Virgins* presupposes the education and literary fashions of his contemporaries, and suggests some at least of the ideals of the third-century religious movement. It was consciously classical in inspiration. It is based on the *Symposium* as a central model. Its introduction is a mosaic formed from citations from the *Theaetetus* and the *Phaedrus*. It ends with an echo from the *Republic* following on an echo from the *Hippolytus* of Euripides. But it belongs to the new world of the embodied allegories and has links with the third-century Hellenistic romances that were to mean so much in the development of hagiography. Its motif lies in its repeated versicle 'I keep myself pure for thee, O Bridegroom, and holding a lighted torch I go towards thee'.

Unlike that of St Methodius, the authority of St Athanasius was to remain constant throughout Byzantine history. Athanasius, Bishop of Alexandria, was born between the years 293 and 296 and died in the spring of 373. It was never forgotten that in the Arian controversies he had been 'to the Church what the hair was to Samson'. To Photius he is still 'the Master' to be admired for 'his magnificence', 'his fecundity', 'his clear and sober style'.[1] Much that he had argued against became irrelevant when the controversy on the relation between the Father and the Son within the Godhead was eclipsed by that on the relation of the divine and human within God the Son. Yet his life and his sixteen years of exile almost as much as his writings deeply affected the East Roman conception of the Church, and perhaps more than any other factor determined the difference between the Constantinian and Theodosian settlements. He had taught that the visible unity of the hierarchic Church was the prolongation upon earth of the work of the Incarnate Word through its two great mysteries, Baptism and the Eucharist, and that its hierarchical organisation could function independently of imperial sovereignty because it was directly derived from the sovereignty of Christ.[2] He could write literary Greek and quote Euripides and

[1] Photius, *Bibl. Cod.* cxl (*MPG*, ciii, 420).

[2] In practice it was sometimes difficult to do without imperial help: Athanasius in the eastern provinces set an early precedent of an appeal to the Emperor from a judgement of a church council and the Emperor accepted the appeal. Cf. H. Berkhof, *Kirche und Kaiser* (Zürich, 1947).

Homer, but it is unlikely that his secular education had advanced beyond orthography and the elements of grammar. He seems to have been born, and was most probably educated, in a Christian milieu. It is improbable that he knew anything of the vital religious movements among his non-Christian contemporaries. But when he wrote 'The Word became Man so that we can become deified',[1] he was giving his authority to the only concept which could form a bridge between the Christian doctrine of grace and the neoplatonist doctrine of the effects of contemplation; a belief in the possibility of deification (*theosis*) was to become an essential part of Byzantine Christianity.

Yet though this concept would be acceptable to enlightened religious opinion among pagans, it was not for Athanasius pagan in its source. To him it was merely a gloss on phrases in the Psalter;[2] 'God standeth in the congregation of gods', 'I said, Ye are gods, and all sons of the Most High'. It was the effect, not of human endeavour, but of divine omnipotence; 'we are sons and gods by reason of the Word within us'.[3] It was the result of an historic act that had taken place in space and time when the Invisible Godhead became Visible. The powers that rendered it possible were transmitted through membership in a visible society, 'a single house' and 'a single sheepfold', 'a single faith' and 'a single tunic',[4] and by its nature that society was stronger than time and so remained unchanged by it.

The role of St Athanasius in the transition from Graeco-Roman culture to eastern Christianity had been essentially preparatory. It was of vital importance for the future that in a period of so much fluctuating change he had used phrases and concepts that non-Christian as well as Christian could understand and yet had emphasised for ever the ideal of an unchanging Christianity. 'This is the faith of the Catholic Church; this is the faith of the Fathers.'[5]

In contrast to St Athanasius the three Cappadocians, St Basil of Caesarea (329–79), St Gregory of Nazianzus (*c.* 329–*c.* 390) and St Gregory of Nyssa (*c.* 335–*c.* 395), completed their conventional higher education and were moulded by it. Basil had been born at Caesarea in Cappadocia and had studied rhetoric and philosophy for six years at Athens under the masters Himerius and Prohaeresius, and before he became a monk he had taught as a rhetorician at Caesarea. His younger brother, Gregory of Nyssa, was a professional rhetorician, while their friend Gregory of Nazianzus had studied not only at Athens but also at Alexandria and Constantinople. It is probable

---

[1] Athanasius, *Or. de Incarnatione Verbi*, 54 (*MPG*, xxv, 192).
[2] Psalm lxxxi. 1 and 6 (Septuagint).
[3] Athanasius, *Contra Arianos*, iii, 25 (*MPG*, xxvi, 376).
[4] Athanasius, *Ep. Heortastica*, v, 4 (*ibid*. 1382).
[5] Athanasius, *Ep. ad Epictetum*, 3 (*ibid*. 1056).

that both the closeness of their friendship and the unity of their theological thought has been over-stressed. The character of their contribution to East Christian theology was determined by the fact that they were trained rhetoricians. Through their rhetorical analysis of the exact meaning of words they created a theological terminology which made possible the exact formulation of Trinitarian doctrine and provided the setting of the Christological controversies of the next century. Their use of rhetorical images led to the development of the Christian conception of theological analogy. Just as they had treated Christian apologetics according to the rules of rhetoric, so their moral teaching fell naturally into the conventional philosophical division of physics and ethics. Their theology is the study of an underlying explanation of an intelligible and ordered nature, their moral theory is its corollary.

The Cappadocians have been described as Christian Platonists. But it would be an error to emphasise their Platonism. It is rather that they took for granted the truisms of the eclectic philosophy in which they had been bred and which they, like their contemporaries, regarded as a *philosophia perennis* to be safely assumed by all educated men. They gave conventional praise to Plato 'whose tongue is sweeter than honey'. They deliberately discarded the conception of 'a narrow jealous Jewish Godhead'.[1] Their teaching contains many elements from first- and second-century Platonism—the conception of evil as a privation, of punishment as a purification, of the double world of the intelligible and of the material, of man as the microcosm in which both mingle, and of the threefold division of the soul. Yet much of their phraseology and many of their concepts are purely Stoic—the nature of virtue and of vice and of passion and of emotion, the ideal of self-mastery. Behind all lay a conception of the unbroken rhythm of intelligible law, ultimately Stoic in its origin, but perhaps reaching them through the filter of the third-century jurists. All was linked by an Aristotelian emphasis on God as Final Cause, the Unmoved Mover of all desire.

They brought to Byzantine Christianity a cosmic conception of the nature and destiny of man and of the purpose and process of the Incarnation. Nazianzen in his 45th Oration had written of man that through him all creation grows articulate. 'Mind and sense remained distinct within their boundaries, bearing within themselves the magnificence of the Creator Logos, silent praisers. Not yet was there any mingling between them. Not yet were the riches of God's goodness known.' Then God placed Man on earth, 'a second world', a 'microcosm', a 'new angel', a 'mingled worshipper', the 'husbandman of

---

[1] Greg. Naz., *Or.* xxv (*MPG*, xxxv, 1197 f.).

immortal plants', 'visible and yet intelligible', a 'living creature in process of being deified'.[1] Thus through the act of Incarnation all the created world was joined to the Divine, and matter as well as spirit was transmuted. 'He united himself with our being that our being might become divine through intermingling with the Divine.' Nazianzen wrote in the 38th Oration, 'He came forth as God with that which he assumed. O new commingling, O strong conjoining. He assumes flesh that I might assume Godhead.'[2] Yet man retains his dual capacity, to sink as well as to rise. Through sin, that self-mutilation of the soul, he can be dragged down to lie self-buried and inarticulate in the swamp of the material. And education, as much as physical asceticism, can become the means to purify from dead matter and to keep the soul as master and as pilot.[3]

The two Gregorys had never queried the educational standards of their youth, as is constantly shown in their writings: 'all right-minded men know that education is the first of human goods, not only such as is our own but such as is profane';[4] 'for we also are Attics';[5] 'what is all Homer but the praise of the virtues?'[6] Discarding, like so many pagans, the classical mythology as factual record, they had proved to their Christian contemporaries that it was possible, in a characteristic phrase, 'to pluck the rose and to avoid the thorn'.[7]

St Basil of Caesarea had died within a year of the accession of Theodosius. The two Gregorys survived to write and preach through the crucial phase in the religious transition that followed. The teaching of all three became a part of the common heritage of Byzantine Christian speculation. For centuries Gregory Nazianzen was to be revered as 'the theologian' and Basil as 'master of the holy', while as late as the eleventh century the catechetical oration of St Gregory of Nyssa was the authoritative compendium of orthodox doctrine. Their writings ranked in authority only just below the Scriptures. They had come to include many *spuria*, but by this means the Cappadocians lent the prestige of their names to other Christian rhetoricians who had shared their preconceptions, such as their younger contemporary and disciple Amphilochius, Bishop of Iconium, who had studied rhetoric under Libanius at Antioch and had practised for six

---

[1] Greg. Naz., *Or.* XLV, 7–8 (*MPG*, XXXVI, 630 f.).

[2] Greg. Naz., *Or.* XXXVIII, 11 (*MPG*, XXXVI, 321–4). Cf. *Or.* XLV, 7–8 (*ibid.* 629–33).

[3] Greg. Naz., *Or.* XXXIX, 8–9 (*MPG*, XXXVI, 341–4). Cf. Amphilochius, *Ad Seleucum*, ll. 35–184 (*MPG*, XXXVII, 1579–89).

[4] Greg. Naz., *Or.* XLIII, 11 (*MPG*, XXXVI, 508).

[5] Greg. Naz., *Ep. ad Stagirium* (*MPG*, XXXVII, 307).

[6] Basil, *Ad adolescentes quomodo ex gentilium libris possint fructum capere*, cap. IV (*MPG*, XXXI, 572).

[7] Amphilochius, *Ad Seleucum*, l. 61 (*MPG*, XXXVII, 1581).

years as a jurist in the capital, and Nemesius, who would seem to have been a professional philosopher in fifth-century Emesa.

A generation later their influence was to be modified by that of St John Chrysostom. He was born at Antioch in 354, became Bishop of Constantinople in 397 and died in exile ten years later. He came from a different milieu from that of the three Cappadocians. Basil and Gregory of Nyssa were the sons of a sophist 'of repute throughout his province'. The father of Gregory Nazianzen had held an hereditary priesthood before he became a Christian bishop. Both fathers probably represented the higher middle class of the provincial towns which had provided for so long the strength of Hellenism in Asia Minor. But John as the son of a *magister militum orientis* came from the circle of the great officials, who were still at least as consciously Latin as Greek in their culture.[1] His secular education had finished when he was about sixteen, he had never shown interest in speculation, and he adapted the rhetoric that he had been taught to audiences that were partly illiterate. He had been acquainted with the classics, but he found his primary source within the Scriptures, and it has been calculated that he has more than 7,000 citations from the Old Testament and more than 11,000 from the New. His thought was dominated by a purely Christian conception of the personal compassion of God. He wrote in his 10th homily on Romans: 'Christ's payment is as much greater than our debt as an ocean is greater than a drop of water.'[2] It is characteristic that he should have been accused of 'multiplying the Church's pardon'. Yet it is arguable that the chief classical influence upon him was that of the jurists not of the philosophers. To him a bishop was a governor in Christ's Empire, an Empire that was one and universal, visibly united, indestructible, eternal.[3] But for that reason he was called on to be the champion of all equity, to be the *curator* and *defensor* of the people of his city. He put into practice the ideals that had long been reverenced among the great officials of the Stoic tradition: incorruptible integrity, public service, an impartial administration. He gave to each of these the lasting sanction of his personal holiness. There is much in his social teaching, as in that of Basil, which is common form in later classical thought and a Stoic heritage,[4] but it has become vitalised by charity and by a sense of the closeness of Christ. Faith had taught him to see in the Eucharist 'a deed of infinite love',[5] Christ 'coming to be

---

[1] For the survival of Latin culture in this milieu in the East cf. John Lydus, *De Magistratibus*, III, 68 (ed. R. Wuensch, Leipzig, 1903, pp. 158 f.).

[2] Chrysostom, *Hom. X in Ep. ad Romanos*, 2 (*MPG*, LX, 477).

[3] Chrysostom, *Hom. XI in Ep. ad Ephesios*, 5 (*MPG*, LXII, 87).

[4] Cf. Chrysostom, *Hom. XI De Divitiis et Paupertate* (*MPG*, LXIII, 637–45).

[5] Chrysostom, *Hom. XXIV in Ep. I ad Corinthios*, 4–5 (*MPG*, LXI, 204 f.).

touched and to be handled',[1] Christ's 'blood within the chalice'.[2] Faith made him conscious of another mode of presence: Christ still within the stable, Christ waiting to be freed from hunger or from the gaols, Christ present in the least of his own brethren. All his teaching focused on his conviction that the Incarnation, like the sacraments, its sequel, had been an act of personal love and personal compassion. 'He took flesh solely because of love, there is no other cause of the Incarnation except this.' 'He hungered, he thirsted, he was tortured, he died'; Christ lived and died for each. It is this that made his homilies a supplement to the writings of the Cappadocians with their more abstract speculation on the mingled worlds of matter and of thought. His authority came to rank with theirs. His manuscripts, with theirs and with the Scriptures, form the basis of most of such Byzantine monastic libraries of which record survives. For the fifth century saw the final development of the Eastern conception of the patristic canon: a group of treatises by Doctors of the Church which contained the authoritative exposition of the Church's teaching and an authoritative interpretation of the Scriptures.

Among such Doctors Cyril of Alexandria was pre-eminent. St Cyril was Bishop of Alexandria from 412 until his death in 444. In the controversies that followed on the Council of Chalcedon both factions claimed his authority. In the phrase of Anastasius of Sinai, he was held to be the 'seal of all the Fathers'. His influence on Byzantine theology long remained dominant, and, though his writings were less studied after the seventh century, his teaching was to be incorporated and popularised in the *De Fide Orthodoxa* of St John of Damascus. He was perhaps the greatest and the most original of all Greek patristic theologians. He owed much to Athanasius and much to Nazianzen, but in the last analysis his speculation remains integrally his own. For Cyril, man was the crowned image of the divine,[3] gifted with self-mastery,[4] marked out from all the brutes by his knowledge of Beauty.[5] He had learned from Nazianzen the Cappadocian theology of his fall. Turning from the Source of Light, the Source of Beauty, the image was uncrowned, self-darkened, man lost self-mastery and went clad in coats of skin, 'the coarser kinds of flesh, mortal and impatient of control'.[6] 'The mind follows the might of the flesh mourning the fatal tree and the ruin-bringing fruit.'[7] For

---

[1] Chrysostom, *Hom. LXXXII in Matthaeum*, 4 (*MPG*, LVIII, 743).

[2] Chrysostom, *Hom. XXIV in Ep. I ad Corinthios*, 1 (*MPG*, LXI, 199).

[3] Cyril, *Adversus Anthropomorphitas*, cap. 3 (*MPG*, LXXVI, 1081–4).

[4] Cyril, *Glaphyrorum in Genesim*, I, cap. 4 (*MPG*, LXIX, 24).

[5] Cyril, *ibid.* I, cap. 2 (*MPG*, LXIX, 20).

[6] Greg. Naz., *Or.* XLV, 8 (*MPG*, XXXVI, 633).

[7] For the conception of original sin in the writings of Cyril of Alexandria cf. *In*

Cyril, God's love and knowledge breaks through the darkness in a single free act[1] that is the coming of the Son, the Wisdom, the *dynamis* of the Father.[2] Since it is his touch that heals, he assumes human nature in its entirety. Only through utter union comes complete healing. It is this that is the key to the Christology of Cyril—the emphasis on the complete one-ness of divine and human in a single Christ[3]—and to his theology of the Eucharist, which is at once a sacrifice and a banquet at which Christ's Body and Blood are fused with our own to cleanse and to illuminate,[4] and thus become the leaven of our dough.[5] God being Love is also Mercy; 'there is no sin that he cannot remit, not even the sin against the Holy Ghost'.[6] 'He wills Iscariot to be saved as well as Peter.' Through the Church, the visible perpetuation of his coming, his mercy abides for ever. 'We also have the power to remit sins.'[7] In Cyril's writings the Church has become personalised, often in the feminine gender. She is the channel of all grace,[8] the New Jerusalem,[9] the Mother of the faithful.[10] In some fashion she possesses a prototype 'the God-bearer',[11] the Virgin,[12] unsoiled by any sin,[13] free of the Law.[14] All are called to enter into the Church. None are constrained. Christ seeks all. He invites all. He rejects none. He forces none.[15]

With Cyril, Greek patristic theology reaches a form that was definitive. East Roman theology had inevitably developed in a literary milieu and therefore within the frame of Graeco-Roman education. A conventional bitterness marks Cyril's anti-pagan apologetic, yet even for him late classical influences were inescapable. This is apparent in his citations: he quotes from Pindar, Euripides, Sophocles, Homer, Plutarch, Xenophon, Plotinus, Porphyry. It explains his rhetorical skill and his mastery of the dialogue form. It caused his theology to be conceived and planned in terms of third-century

Ep. ad Romanos, v, 12 (*MPG*, LXXIV, 784); *In Ioannis Evangelium*, I, 32–3 (122) (*MPG*, LXXIII, 205); *De adoratione in spiritu et veritate*, x, 332, 339 (*MPG*, LXVIII, 657, 670 f.).

[1] Cyril, *Contra Julianum*, VIII, 277 f. (*MPG*, LXXVI, 925 f.).
[2] Cyril, *Thesaurus*, 377 (*MPG*, LXXV, 637).
[3] Cyril, *Ep.* XVII, 71 f. (*MPG*, LXXVII, 112 f.).
[4] Cyril, *In Ioannis Evangelium*, VI, 27 (299) (*MPG*, LXXIII, 481).
[5] Cyril, *ibid.* VI, 57 (365) (*MPG*, LXXIII, 584).
[6] Cyril, *Comment. in Matthaeum*, 36 (*MPG*, LXXII, 409).
[7] Cyril, *Comment. in Lucam*, v, 24 (179) (*MPG*, LXXII, 568).
[8] Cyril, *Comment. in Ioelem*, XLIV (*MPG*, LXXI, 405).
[9] Cyril, *ibid.* XXXVIII (*MPG*, LXXI, 389).
[10] Cyril, *Comment. in Oseam*, XXXVIII (*MPG*, LXXI, 120).
[11] Cyril, *Ep. I, ad Monachos* (*MPG*, LXXVII, 20 D–21 A).
[12] Cyril, *Ep.* IV (*MPG*, LXXVII, 45).
[13] Cyril, *Adversus Nestorium*, I, cap. 1 (*MPG*, LXXVI, 17).
[14] Cyril, *De adoratione in spiritu et veritate*, XV (554) (*MPG*, LXVIII, 1005).
[15] Cyril, *Comment. in Lucam*, v, 23 (334) (*MPG*, LXXII, 792).

physics. Late Byzantine civilization maintained its continuity with a Hellenic past primarily through fourth- and fifth-century literary Christianity.

Yet Hellenism was never more than a segment of the background of Byzantine Christianity. For three generations there had been a parallel development in the gradual christianisation of the unhellenised populations of the eastern provinces of the Empire. It is easy to overestimate the extent of the effective hellenisation in the East Mediterranean world of the fourth century. The evidence both of epigraphy and of some of the papyri can be misleading, for it was natural that business and official formularies should be phrased in the official language of administration. It is probable that a contrast existed between Egypt and Syria, perhaps due originally to the different policies of the Ptolemies and Seleucids. From its foundation Alexandria had been cosmopolitan, a part of the Levant rather than a part of Egypt. Papyri suggest a considerable veneer of hellenisation in the small towns and villages of the Fayum. But southward down the valley of the Nile the policy of the Ptolemaic kings had enabled ancient Egyptian culture to survive, still centring in immemorial cults. Christianity had first grown strong in Alexandria. But already by the fourth century there were Egyptian Christians to whom Greek was unfamiliar. Coptic Christian literature begins in the fourth century, and it was necessary to translate into Sahidic the Paschal encyclicals of Athanasius for 364 and 367. It is probable that many of the founders of Egyptian monachism came from the unhellenised fellahin and it was largely through monachism that all the Nile Valley became christianised in the course of the fourth century. Through the same agency much Egyptian folk-lore, and echoes of pre-Greek Egyptian cults, became part of the Christian background of Byzantium, retold in the lives or sayings of the desert fathers. For a hundred years Egyptian Christianity grew increasingly Egyptian, as was shown by its awareness of the spirit world and of the world of animals, by its stories of conflicts with demons, of dreams and of the after-life. By the close of the fifth century Egypt was Christian and all Byzantine monachism and much Byzantine hagiography had been permanently affected by it.

In Syria on the other hand the policy of the Seleucids had favoured a more uniform hellenisation and this had been consistently supported by the Roman imperial administration. Yet, by the end of the third century, it must have been clear that this policy of hellenisation had failed. In the fourth century Greek culture was at its strongest in Antioch, in the coastal towns and in the south. But even here a knowledge of Greek was never universal; the life of St Porphyry by

Mark the Deacon shows that at Gaza the common people spoke only Syriac and the *Peregrinatio Etheriae* asserts that in Jerusalem the Greek homilies and lessons were translated 'siriste' so that all could understand. In North Syria and in Roman Mesopotamia there is much evidence for the existence of a considerable class who, though cultivated, wealthy and normally bilingual, were consciously Aramaean in their culture.[1] It was this class who were to create the Syriac Christian literature which in turn so profoundly influenced Byzantine developments, especially in hymnography. Still further to the north the emergence of an Armenian Christian literature in the fifth century, and of a very distinctive Georgian Christianity in what had been the kingdom of the Iberians, also affected Byzantium through the tales of martyr-saints and wonder-workers. The Iberian monks were in time to have a special significance as the carriers of influences from one monastic centre to another.

But this was to be a later development, and in the fifth century a far more crucial factor was the growing strength of Christianity in the country districts of Asia Minor. Here, though the town population and the landowners had been for long at least superficially hellenised, immemorial forces still survived, the cults of the Great Mother in many forms, the search for ecstasy and rebirth. These were to form recognisable elements in much Byzantine popular Christianity and were slowly blended with wonder tales from Egypt and from northern Syria. In the unhellenised countryside many such elements must have been grafted on to the new religion direct from primitive but elaborate forms of fertility cult, bearing with them almost unchanged conceptions. The Christian city proletariate has been described by Prudentius as 'all those who dwell in high garrets and run in the muddy streets of the city and eat the bread that is served out on the high steps'.[2] Even when these were Greek-speaking, at Constantinople, or Ephesus, or Antioch, the preconceptions of the unhellenised peasants must have blended more easily with theirs than did those of the more educated civil servant. The role played by the popular political party of the Greens throughout the monophysite controversy seems to illustrate this natural alliance. It has been customary to oversimplify the Christological controversy of the fifth century through a largely imaginary antithesis between Antiochene and Alexandrian schools of theology. The issue is the more complicated since neither Nestorians nor Chalcedonians nor monophysites admitted the views imputed to them by their opponents. But it is signifi-

---

[1] Cf. P. Peeters, *Le tréfonds oriental de l'hagiographie byzantine* (Brussels, 1950), pp. 46 f.
[2] Prudentius, *Contra Symmachum*, I, 581 f. (*MPL*, LX, 168–9).

cant that the prolonged controversies released passions among masses of the newly christianised population who can hardly have followed the exact nuances of the very philosophical terminology employed by the Greek disputants. It seems clear that within his lifetime Nestorius, Bishop of Constantinople, had become a symbol at least to those that hated him. By his apparent emphasis on the division between the divine and human natures within Christ, he seemed to be denying equally the worship of the divine Redeemer and the cult of the Mother of God. He could evoke sympathy from among some of the most cultivated members of the episcopate and from among leading members of the civil service. But to the mass of the monks, to the town proletariate and in the majority of the unhellenised areas of the Empire he would seem to have been considered primarily as the Blasphemer, and as the representative of all that was to be most abominated in the life of the capital. It is probable that the strength of anti-Nestorianism was due to sociological factors blended inextricably with outraged religious convictions. This may explain why the condemnation of Nestorius at Ephesus in 431 was followed by a search for possible Nestorian sympathisers that culminated with the condemnation of Flavian of Constantinople at Ephesus in 449. The final decision that Christ possessed two natures but a single person was officially formulated at Chalcedon in 451, but it was suspected by the intransigents throughout the East to be a compromise and a surrender to Nestorianism.

The Christological disputes within the Church remained vital until the Sixth General Council of 680 and 681. Besides the monophysite dissidents in northern Syria and in Egypt there was a considerable faction within the Greek Church itself which sympathised with their tenets and shared in their suspicions. The imperial government made persistent efforts to satisfy both bodies, by the compromise formula (the *Henoticon* or Letter of Union) of the Emperor Zeno in 484, by the ecclesiastical appointments of the Emperor Anastasius, by the posthumous condemnation under Justinian of the fifth-century moderates, Theodore, Theodoret and Ibas, and by the *Ecthesis* of Heraclius in 638, which attempted to reinforce the doctrine of a single person by that of a single energy and a single will. Throughout the struggle was confused by the existence of two other factions. There were those who combined Nestorian sympathies with a nominal acceptance of the decrees of Chalcedon. There were those who sincerely accepted the decrees of Chalcedon but consistently tended to emphasise the divinity rather than the humanity of Christ. It would seem to have been this last party that was finally triumphant. By the Sixth Council Byzantine Christology had assumed its definitive shape, so also had Byzantine Christianity. It was now no longer possible to distinguish between its literate and its popular forms. The two had completely interpenetrated each other. The influence of individual ascetics, a belief in wonder-tales, a complete acceptance of all the standards of current hagiography had become common to every social grouping in the Empire. Monasticism had helped towards this fusion for monks were recruited from every social milieu and exercised their influence upon them all. The legislation of the Novels of Justinian[1] had removed the only two obstacles that could have hindered the steady development of Byzantine monachism, since it regulated the relations of the monastery with the episcopate and attempted to clarify its relation to the hermit.

The real character of early monachism has been somewhat obscured by the attempt to import two later western categories of religious thought into its study: the antithesis between eremitical and coeno-bitic, contemplative and active. In the East these distinctions had long been recognised, but at least until the end of the medieval period they were never held to be antithetic. Action and contempla-tion were to be as closely mingled in the lives of many of the Byzan-tine monastic saints as they had been in the last years of John the Baptist. Behind all Byzantine monasticism there is the individual figure of the ascetic who has sold all that he has and given to the poor, taking up his cross and following Christ in his practical example as well as in his precepts. Such an ideal seemed explicit enough in the four Gospels, and it could appeal equally to the hellenised and un-hellenised elements among pagans and semi-pagans. It possessed an attraction for the sophisticated who had studied the *Life of Apol-lonius of Tyana* and its derivatives, while among the peasantry it fulfilled a need for local wonder-workers and for local shrines. Such an ascetic had conquered nature within him and was master of the animal passions, himself unmoved by them. It would seem to have been held that he had gained an intermittent control over the forces of nature itself. It was believed that he could heal disease and bring rain or drought, and that moving securely in the Spirit he could cast out demons, banish temptations and heal sin. Yet all this could be done not through his own power but through the power of God pass-ing through him as a channel, just as it was through God's grace that he had first gained self-mastery. So much had become possible to him through God's gifts, God's *charismata*. His new delegated powers bore testimony that he was God's athlete and champion; he had become God's voice against heresy, corruption and oppression; the

[1] *Nov. Just.* 133 (539), 137 (565) (ed. G. Kroll, R. Schoell, *Corpus Iuris Civilis*, III (Berlin, 1895), pp. 666–79, 695–9).

acknowledged heir to the Prophets of the old Law. Though he went out alone in the solitude to worship in the high places, inevitably disciples gathered around him, to be healed by him, to be taught by him, to join with him in his prayer of adoration.

But there were also other factors in determining the character of Byzantine monasticism, such as the Basilian conception of the religious life. The *Ascetica* attributed to Basil of Caesarea had perpetuated the memory of the community that he had founded at Annesi beside the river Iris. Further, and more vivid, details were preserved in the correspondence of Basil and Nazianzen. Its emphasis on the study of Divine Philosophy, on the intellectual approach to prayer, and on the due performance of each rite had been foreshadowed among neo-platonists. But the details of the life of this community and the memory of its careful discipline and moderation became an increasingly stabilising factor in Byzantine monasticism. It was perhaps primarily the example and the teaching of the Cappadocians which sanctioned the study of Divine Philosophy as a fit occupation for an ascetic.

It might have seemed in the fifth century that there would be an increasing tension within Byzantine Christianity between monks and bishops, monks and theologians. But this was not so. The upper hierarchy came to be recruited almost exclusively from the monks, primarily because of the ideal of a celibate episcopate and the practice of a married lower clergy. And it was in monasteries that the greatest theologians of the immediate future were to work. The lay grammarian theologian survived in sixth-century Alexandria with Stephen Gobarus and John Philoponus. But the acknowledged heir of Cyril of Alexandria was the sixth-century monk Leontius writing (*c.* 519–38) in the new Laura near Jerusalem. The great anthologies of patristic texts, 'the sacred parallels', first appear in North Syrian monasteries. The final codification of Greek patristic theology was carried out by the monk John of Damascus in the Palestinian house of St Sabas about 732–49.

It was this monastic influence that was mainly responsible for the authority attributed to the writings of the Pseudo-Dionysius. Some time between 614 and 641 St Maximus Confessor, abbot of a monastery in Chrysopolis, a suburb of the capital, composed scholia upon them and treated them without question as the work of a personal disciple of St Paul. They were to remain a primary source for Byzantine spirituality among the laity as well as among the ascetics. Their earlier history is obscure. They had certainly been in existence since the beginning of the sixth century when they were referred to by Severus of Antioch (d. 538). Their apparent dependence on the teach-

ing of Proclus (d. 485) makes it improbable that they had assumed
their present form much before the end of the fifth century.[1] One of
the causes of their quick success was perhaps the apostolic authority
which they gave to the tendencies that were most characteristic of
late fifth- and early sixth-century Byzantine monachism at the same
time as they reconciled these tendencies with episcopal authority.
The *Corpus Dionysiacum* consisted of eleven letters and four treatises
(*On the Celestial* and *Ecclesiastical Hierarchies, On Mystical Theology*
and *On the Names of God*). The eighth letter formulates the prerogatives
of the ascetic who by prayer and by austerity has at last become
πνευματικός, a temple of the Spirit, and to whom God has given the
power of forgiving sins. This was possible to him not through any
power of Order but through God's gifts, God's χαρίσματα. Such a
charismatic man was already a familiar figure in the Byzantine
Christian background. But such powers are set by Pseudo-Dionysius
in the context of an unbroken hierarchy of order. Just as in Heaven
nine choirs of angels transmitted the divine light downward from each
to each,[2] so here on earth the choirs of bishops, priests, deacons and
of monks, laity, catechumens, differed by the very nature of their
being.[3] The bishops stood parallel to the Seraphim.[4] Yet all were
linked in a single corporate unity. Life and reality streamed down
from God like light from the sun.[5] Each Christian could return to
him through purgation, through the ascent of illumination, and at
last in the ecstasy of union,[6] 'no longer learning but enduring the
divine'. Through the sudden intuitive prayer of contemplation the
ascetic becomes an initiate in mysteries, and, intent upon that real
world, moves securely in this world of shadows. Yet even in ecstasy
he could be blinded by excess of light, 'a ray of the divine darkness'.[7]
He was a night-bird caught and blinded by the sun. Among the rays
of that divine darkness the utter transcendence of eternal truth could
only be expressed by epithet and metaphor and analogy, all imperfectly revealing.[8] The *Corpus Dionysiacum* was specifically Christian, but it is again characteristic of Byzantine Christianity that it

[1] See B. Altaner, *Patrology* (New York, 1960), pp. 604 ff. Cf. E. Honigmann,
Pierre l'Ibérien et les écrits du pseudo-Denys l'Aréopagite (Acad. Roy. de Belgique,
Classe des lettres, et des sciences morales et politiques. Mém. XLVII, fasc. 3, Brussels,
1952), where it is suggested that they were the work of Peter the Iberian. This is not
generally accepted; cf. I. Hausherr, *OCP*, XIX (1953), 247–60.
[2] Ps.-Dionysius, *Celestial Hierarchy*, x, 2 (*MPG*, III, 273).
[3] Ps.-Dionysius, *Ecclesiastical Hierarchy*, I, 1 (*MPG*, III, 372).
[4] Ps.-Dionysius, *ibid.* v, 5 (*MPG*, III, 505).
[5] Ps.-Dionysius, *Divine Names*, IV, 4 (*MPG*, III, 700).
[6] Ps.-Dionysius, *Mystical Theology*, I (*MPG*, III, 997 f.); *Divine Names*, IV, 7
(*MPG*, III, 701).
[7] Ps.-Dionysius, *Mystical Theology*, I, 3 (*MPG*, III, 1001).
[8] Ps.-Dionysius, *Divine Names*, VII, 3 (*MPG*, III, 871).

possessed through so many strands a continuity with so much of the pre-Christian past : with a metaphysical conception of the descent and ascent of being, with the rhetorician's use of metaphor, with neoplatonist analyses of the process of contemplation and with the mystery cycles of birth, death and rebirth.

By the year 717 Byzantine Christianity had taken shape. Some aspects were to be challenged during the iconoclast controversies of the eighth and ninth centuries and for precisely that reason were to be emphasised intentionally during the reaction that followed— aspects of the cult of the Mother of God and of the saints, the freedom of the Church, the influence of the great monasteries, the significance of pilgrimage and shrine. But it is probable that the unorthodoxy of the iconoclast Emperors was exaggerated by their opponents and that, except on the development of secular art, their influence was transient. Under the Macedonian and Comnenian Emperors the Church was apparently identical with that of the late seventh century. The educated laity, both men and women, were perhaps more theologically minded, but however much they may have studied such later writers as Maximus the Confessor or Symeon the New Theologian, they were still dominated by third- and fourth-century forms of thought. The slowly widening schism with the Latins was to be occasioned and embittered by historical accidents. Yet some estrangement and much mutual misunderstanding arose inevitably as a result of the very different factors that had facilitated the triumph of the same faith in East and West. In the eastern provinces these factors were themselves often at first in apparent conflict, but by the early eighth century they had been blended within the framework of the creeds into a single cultural and religious synthesis: the Christian background to the Byzantine Empire.

CHAPTER III

ICONOCLASM AND IMPERIAL RULE 717–842

I. ICONOCLASM AND THE BYZANTINE VICTORIES OVER THE ARABS AND THE BULGARS 717–75

1. *The beginning of iconoclasm and the repulse of the Arabs*

The reign of Leo III (717–41) has been much misunderstood by both medieval and modern historians. The earliest extant chroniclers, who were iconophiles and for this reason hostile to Leo as an iconoclast, constantly imputed the worst of motives to him, and found little to admire in his administration of the affairs of state. Modern writers, on the other hand, taking Leo's denunciation of the images as proof of hostility to superstition and evidence of a spiritual approach to religion, have tended to regard him as a precursor of Martin Luther, and have also praised him as a versatile genius, who dedicated himself to a broad scheme of reform carried out in many fields—legal, military, agricultural, social and economic. This interpretation, in its way almost as misleading as that of the medieval sources, arose partly because of the attribution to Leo of four legal manuals: the *Ecloga*, the *Farmer's Law* (of the latter part of the seventh century or the beginning of the eighth), the *Rhodian Sea Law* (*c.* 600–800) and the *Military Code* (of undetermined date), of which only the first can with certainty be ascribed to him.[1] But the error stems principally from unwillingness to recognise that iconoclasm in the eighth and ninth centuries was primarily a religious phenomenon and must be understood as such.

It is an anachronism to dismiss the theological aspects of the question as unimportant and to interpret iconoclasm as a mere disguise or subterfuge for an economic or social programme designed, amongst other things, to liberate the peasants from bondage to large landowners, or to regain for the imperial exchequer valuable properties that had been absorbed by the Church or by monastic foundations. There is little information on such matters, although we do know that the Emperor could have seized or confiscated any kind of property, civil or ecclesiastical, at will, without hiding behind a theological mask. The Byzantines took theology very seriously, and the Emperors were willing to go to the greatest lengths for the sake of a

[1] See Pt II, ch. XXI, pp. 68 ff. and ch. XXVII, p. 238.

point of Christian dogma, since they looked upon themselves, and were regarded by their subjects, as divinely appointed guardians responsible to God no less for purity of doctrine and harmony in the Church than for the physical well-being of the state, which, it was felt, could never prosper if the Church were weakened by heresy or disorder. Hence, when the Emperors took action against the use of images (726–75, 815–42), they did not do so in order to increase their prerogatives or to assert the authority of the state over the Church, as some have maintained, but for the sake of what they thought to be theological propriety, with which they concerned themselves in the exercise of their normal functions, as understood by Constantine I or Justinian I, and in the Byzantine imperial tradition as a whole. Other objectives might become involved in an Emperor's decision to oppose icons or to favour them, but the decisive factor was of theological origin.

Nevertheless, when viewed in perspective Leo III was a figure of commanding stature. He was an energetic ruler, skilled in military science, diplomacy, and administration, who provided strong and effective leadership at a time of crisis. He delivered the Empire and the West from the Arabs, made an important contribution to Byzantine law, and established a new official policy on icons. His accession on 25 March 717 ended the period of anarchy begun in 685, and inaugurated a dynasty[1] that ruled for eighty-five years (717–802). He rose to prominence at court during the first reign of Justinian II (685–95). Then he was appointed general of the Anatolikon theme by Anastasius II (713–15), and in 715 favoured the latter against the usurper, Theodosius III (715–17). In this matter, as well as in his rise to power, he had the support of Artavasdus, general of the Armeniakon theme, to whom he gave his daughter Anna in marriage soon after his elevation to the throne. Leo gained the ascendancy without bloodshed by seizing Theodosius' son and the chief officers of the royal government and at the same time guaranteeing that Theodosius would suffer no bodily harm from the new regime. This agreement was negotiated with the approval of the Patriarch Germanus I (715–30), who compelled Leo to swear that he would make no innovation affecting dogma or the Church. Even his detractors had to admit that Leo had displayed considerable ingenuity in eluding the snares set for him by his enemies and in outwitting Maslama, the brother of the Umayyad Caliph Sulaymān (715–17), and other Arab generals. Leo managed to keep Amorium in Byzan-

---

[1] He was apparently a Syrian from Germanicea (Mar'ash), although, according to some authorities, he was a native of Isauria in southern Asia Minor; his family moved to Thrace during the first reign of Justinian II.

tine hands, but Maslama had seized Sardes and Pergamum, and the Arabs pillaged almost at will throughout Asia Minor.[1]

Determined to cut out the heart of the Empire, Maslama crossed the straits from Abydus and began to lay siege to Constantinople on 15 August 717 (or possibly a month earlier), after having assembled vast military stores, an army of 180,000 men, and a huge armada of more than 2,500 ships. But the imperial defences were in excellent shape, since the Arab attack had been anticipated from the time of Anastasius II. Moreover, Leo conducted a brilliant campaign behind the impregnable ramparts of the city and under the protection of the Byzantine navy, then at the peak of efficiency and equipped with the deadly 'Greek fire', the prototype of modern gunpowder. He made timely use of information received from Egyptian sailors who deserted from the Arabs after reaching the Bosphorus, and was able not only to obtain food for Constantinople, but also, for several months, to cut off the besiegers from access to urgently needed supplies. The Byzantine fleet prevented the enemy from making effective use of the seaways, and the infantry routed the Muslims under Mardasān in Bithynia. Hemmed in on all sides, the Arabs had to contend with famine, cold, and pestilence, and were set upon by a strong force of Bulgarian troops, whose intervention Leo had shrewdly arranged. At last on 15 August 718, after the lapse of exactly a year, when the situation had become hopeless, Maslama was ordered to retreat by the Caliph 'Umar II, who had succeeded Sulaymān in 717. On the return voyage, the Arabs were scattered over the Aegean Sea by a storm; of the ten vessels which escaped, five were captured by the Byzantines, and only five managed to reach Syria. Arab sources report that 150,000 of the attackers perished in the course of the campaign. In breaking the blockade of Constantinople Leo saved the Empire from destruction and inflicted upon the Arabs so over-whelming a defeat that they were never again able to threaten the capital. Leo's victory, one of the decisive battles of history, was even more significant than that of Charles Martel at Poitiers in 732, for it protected the main centres of Hellenic, Roman and Christian culture from inundation by the Arabs.

Crippled though they were by reason of the losses suffered in the campaign of 717–18, the Arabs still had power to damage the Empire, as they did in a series of almost annual raids upon Byzantine cities in Asia Minor, usually launched through the passes at Adata and Tarsus (near the north-eastern and south-western ends of the Taurus mountains, which served as an approximate frontier between the

---

[1] On the campaigns against the Arabs, see H. Ahrweiler, 'L'Asie Mineure et les in-vasions arabes (viie–ixe siècles)', *RH*, ccxxvii (1962), 1–32.

Christians and Muslims). Since these attacks were undertaken for the sake of booty and in order to eliminate important Byzantine bases that might threaten the security of the Caliphate, they involved little permanent loss of territory. But they were a constant burden and seriously disturbed the security and economic stability of an important segment of the Empire. Maslama took Caesarea in Cappadocia in 726. But Muʻāwiya and 100,000 men were repulsed at Nicaea in the same year; and Sulaymān's well-organised campaign of 740, though not a complete failure from the Arab point of view, ended in a brilliant victory for Leo and his son Constantine near Acroinon, which cleared western Asia Minor of the enemy. Leo's success is attributable in part to the valuable assistance of the Khazars, who harried the Arabs in the Caucasus. It was no doubt in order to retain the favour of these allies, as well as for dynastic reasons, that in 733 he married his son, Constantine V, then barely fourteen, and co-Emperor since 720, to a Khazar princess who took the name of Irene.

The prestige that Leo won as a result of his Arab wars was enhanced by his swift suppression of the two revolts that broke out in 717–19. The first of these, begun in the midst of the siege of Constantinople, was led by Sergius, the general of the theme of Sicily, who attempted to set up a rival Emperor named Tiberius. The second, which seems to have occurred a year after the Arab defeat, was headed by Nicetas Xylinites with the backing of the former Emperor Anastasius II. It was also supported by the Bulgarian Khan, Tervel, who, however, soon became reconciled to Leo and abandoned the rebels.

It was probably to avoid rebellions of this sort, as well as to increase the mobility and efficiency of his troops, that Leo decided to divide two of the most powerful of the themes into smaller units. For, from his own experience as general of the Anatolikon theme, he knew well how much power was concentrated in the hands of such commanders, who were in effect local rulers with full civil and military authority. Hence, *c.* 741, he set aside the western portion of his former command and designated it as the Thracesion theme, so called because of the Thracian origin of its troops. Somewhat earlier, between 710 and 732, the theme of the Carabisiani, the administrative unit comprising the provincial navies, was split into two sections: one formed the theme of the Cibyrraeots, while the other, the so-called drungariate (command) of the Aegean Sea, did not attain full status as an independent theme until the reign of Michael III (842–67).

Losses and military expenditure incurred in the course of conflict with the Arabs, with pretenders to the throne and other enemies of the state, seriously taxed the financial resources of the Empire. Leo met this emergency, not, as once believed, by 'doubling the indiction' (that is, by demanding double taxation for one year), but by an efficient system of taxation. He increased the capitation tax of Sicily and Calabria by one third. He also received additional revenue from other sources, including the confiscated papal patrimonies,[1] and the special *dikerata* tax (the equivalent of one *miliaresion* or one-twelfth of a *nomisma*), which was levied for the purpose of rebuilding the city walls and the public buildings destroyed by earthquakes and floods in 740–1.

Leo III was also responsible for initiating considerable legal activity. The code which he promulgated, known as the *Ecloga* (Selection), was issued in 726[2] under his name and that of his son Constantine; it was a revised, abridged, and simplified version in Greek of the *Corpus Iuris Civilis*, intended to facilitate the administration of justice.[3] It was the first law book based throughout upon Christian principles and, in this respect, as well as in many others, differed from the legislation of Justinian, which at numerous points was still dominated by the pagan spirit, especially in its treatment of what is now known as the law of probate and domestic relations. In the preamble to the *Ecloga*, the Emperors Leo and Constantine expressly state that they have attempted to make the laws more humane; and, in a passage of particular interest for political theory, they declare themselves to be, in effect, the successors of St Peter, charged by God to watch over the flock. The *Ecloga* limits the application of capital punishment chiefly to treason, desertion from military service, certain types of homicide and heresy (Manichaeanism and Montanism), and slander. The penalties substituted for the death sentence, and occasionally for the amercements of the older Roman law, are flogging, amputation, slitting of the nose, blinding, cutting out of the tongue, and emasculation. No provision is made for dealing with iconophiles. In an attempt to eliminate bribery and favouritism the *Ecloga* prescribes that judges should receive salaries and be forbidden to accept gifts. Much reviled in later generations because of the orthodox aversion to the iconoclasts, the *Ecloga* none the less exerted wide influence even upon the *Basilica*, which the Macedonian Emperors enacted to replace it.

Apart from Leo's military and diplomatic achievements, which even his enemies had to acknowledge, he is most celebrated as the originator of Byzantine iconoclasm. It is now agreed that official iconoclasm as a matter of imperial policy, apart from sporadic out-

---

[1] See below: p. 71.
[2] On this date see G. Ostrogorsky, *History of the Byzantine State*, p. 134, note 6, and also Pt II, ch. XXI, p. 62.
[3] *DR*, 304. See Pt II, ch. XXI, pp. 62 ff.

bursts against the use of icons, which had occurred frequently before, began in 726. Leo felt bound to condemn the images because he took them to be idols and as such forbidden by the Scriptures. It has been argued that objections on biblical grounds are insufficient to explain the iconoclast movement as a whole, and that it was in fact directly inspired by the Muslims, whom the iconoclasts hoped to conciliate by launching an attack upon 'idolatry'. The principal support for this argument is a famous document read in the fifth session of the Council of 787 by John the Presbyter, as representative of the three eastern Patriarchs (of Antioch, Jerusalem and Alexandria). According to this account a certain Jew of Tiberias named Tessarakontapechys ('forty cubits'), said by an Arab source to have been one of Leo's chief advisers from the beginning of his reign, promised the Caliph Yazīd II (720–4) long life and a reign of thirty years if he would order the immediate removal and utter destruction throughout his realm not only of all religious pictures ($\pi\hat{a}\sigma\alpha\nu$ $\epsilon\hat{i}\kappa o\nu\iota\kappa\grave{\eta}\nu$ $\delta\iota\alpha\zeta\omega\gamma\rho\acute{a}\phi\eta\sigma\iota\nu$) of every description to be found in Christian churches, but also of all representations ($\acute{o}\mu o\iota\acute{\omega}\mu\alpha\tau\alpha$) set up for the decoration and adornment of public squares.[1] Yazīd enforced this order in his territory, John says, before the evil [of iconoclasm] reached the Byzantine Empire. Nevertheless, Yazīd died two and a half years after his iconoclastic decree, and the new Caliph (Hishām, 724–43) allowed the Christians under his jurisdiction to restore the images. The numerous versions of this text differ in many details, but there is no doubt that Yazīd was an iconoclast.

It is not certain, however, that Leo was really influenced by the example of Arab iconoclasm, nor is it necessary to assume that some external, alien force was needed to give impetus to latent Byzantine iconoclastic tendencies, which had manifested themselves as recently as the seventh century in Constantinople and Armenia. Moreover, the iconoclast Theodosius, Archbishop of Ephesus, son of the former Emperor Tiberius III Apsimar (698–705), was said to have been Leo's close personal adviser; and the Emperor had probably discussed the merits of iconoclasm before 726 with Thomas, Bishop of Claudiopolis, as he undoubtedly had with Constantine, Bishop of Nacolea, whom the Patriarchs Germanus and Tarasius both branded as the originator of the iconoclastic heresy.[2] It is significant also that the monophysites and the Paulicians, both of whom were opposed to the use of images, were especially strong in Asia Minor and Syria, the regions in which Leo had spent his youth as well as part of his military career. He had already been exposed to non-Muslim iconoclasm; and his own

---

[1] Mansi, XIII, 197A ff.
[2] *MPG*, XCVIII, 77A; Mansi, XIII, 105, 108A.

hostility to images, to the doctrine of the intercession of the saints, and to the veneration of the relics of saints, coincided with the views of certain Paulicians, who, however, unlike the Byzantine iconoclasts, also objected to the use of the Cross. The visit of the Paulician leader, Gegnesius, to Constantinople some time before 726 may not have been without effect upon Byzantine iconoclasm.

Further, there is little doubt that the iconoclasm of Leo was directed against the 82nd canon of the Council in Trullo (692), which required that Christ be represented as a man and not as a lamb, in order to emphasise 'his life in the flesh, his passion, his saving death, and the ransom for the world that was won thereby'.[1] The immediate effect of this ordinance, which must have greatly increased the production of realistic portraits of Christ, can be illustrated by the coinage of Justinian II (685–95, 705–11), the first Emperor regularly to strike coins bearing the image of Christ. In the troubled periods 695–705 and 711–17, during which no less than five Emperors reigned, the figure of Christ was omitted from the coins, perhaps because it was associated with the dynastic claims of the family of Heraclius, but none of these five Emperors ruled long enough to deal with the problem of the theological implications of such representations. Leo, who had been the close friend and confidant of Justinian II, was the first of his successors with leisure to consider the subject. The frequent occurrence of Christ's likeness on coins was surely one of the factors which influenced Leo's attitude towards images, and provoked the agitated discussion of this topic (prior to 726) mentioned by the Patriarch Germanus in his letter to Thomas of Claudiopolis.[2]

On the other hand, it is hardly to be supposed that a Byzantine Emperor engaged in a deadly struggle for existence with the Arabs would deliberately adopt from the enemy a characteristically Muslim attitude towards an article of Christian theology. The fact that the iconoclasts were often called 'Saracen-minded' (σαρακηνόφρων) by their critics is not to be taken seriously at face value. The word was a term of reproach bandied about freely and without warrant. Even John of Damascus (d. *c*. 749), one of the earliest and most zealous apologists for the use of images, was condemned by the iconoclasts in 754 as 'Saracen-minded': for he was born of Arab parentage, the grandson of a man who is said to have betrayed Damascus to the Arabs in 635, and the son of Sargun ibn Manṣūr, who had held positions of responsibility at the Umayyad court for over sixty years. John himself

[1] Mansi, xi, 980.
[2] Mansi, xiii, 124D. On the coinage, see James D. Breckenridge, *Numismatic Iconography of Justinian II (685–695, 705–711 A.D.)*, *Numismatic Notes and Monographs*, 144 (New York, 1959); G. Zacos and A. Veglery, 'Marriage solidi of the fifth century', *Numismatic Circular*, April 1960.

served the Umayyads and ended his days as a monk in the monastery of St Sabas in Arab-held Palestine, while another champion of the images, Theodore Abū Qurra, Bishop of Harran (*c.* 740–820), his literary heir, wrote in Arabic as well as in Greek, if not also in Syriac. And when the second wave of iconoclasm arose in the reign of Leo V the Armenian (813–20), hostility to the images was obviously connected with monophysite currents of thought prevalent in the Emperor's native Armenia and not with Arab influence of any sort. Michael the Syrian, monophysite Patriarch of Antioch (1166–99), mentions the iconoclastic decrees of Constantine V but finds nothing in them to criticise, and even praises the Emperor's orthodoxy.

Even if the possibility of some Islamic influence upon Byzantine iconoclasm cannot be altogether excluded, as many authorities insist, it is obvious that Leo III's enemies grossly exaggerated its importance. The question of images would undoubtedly have arisen in Byzantium quite apart from Muslim or Semitic practice in such matters, because of the Christological issues involved, as the later history of the controversy indicates.[1] Moreover, given Leo's desire for religious harmony and unification, which led him to compel Jews and Montanists to be baptised (721–2), it is not at all improbable that he was first prompted to take action against the veneration of icons because, as Nicephorus says, he felt that divine disapproval of this cult was manifest in the great submarine volcanic eruption in the summer of 726 near Hiera, which cast cinders all over the Aegean, threw up a new island, and spread terror far and wide.

Whatever his motives, Leo began his attack on images in 726,[2] and a number of imperial officers were killed by an angry mob as they were removing the icon of Christ from above the Chalce (Bronze) Gate of the Great Palace. Many prominent iconophiles were punished by mutilation, flogging, exile, or confiscation of property, but apparently few, if any, were put to death. At the same time, Leo is said to have closed the imperial university because he could not persuade its teachers to join the iconoclastic movement; and a malicious legend has it that he even set fire to this institution, its library and its professors. In protest against Leo's measures, Pope Gregory II (715–31) withheld the Italian revenues normally paid to Constantinople, and wrote that the Emperor had no right to legislate on matters of faith or to make in-

---

[1] See below: p. 79.

[2] The present writer holds that there were two edicts against the icons, the first in 726, the second in 730. For the first see *Liber Pontificalis*, Gregorius II, 184, ed. Duchesne, I, p. 405/9–11; 'decreverat imperator ut nulla imago cuiuslibet sancti aut martyris aut angeli haberetur'; cf. *DR*, 291 and 298.

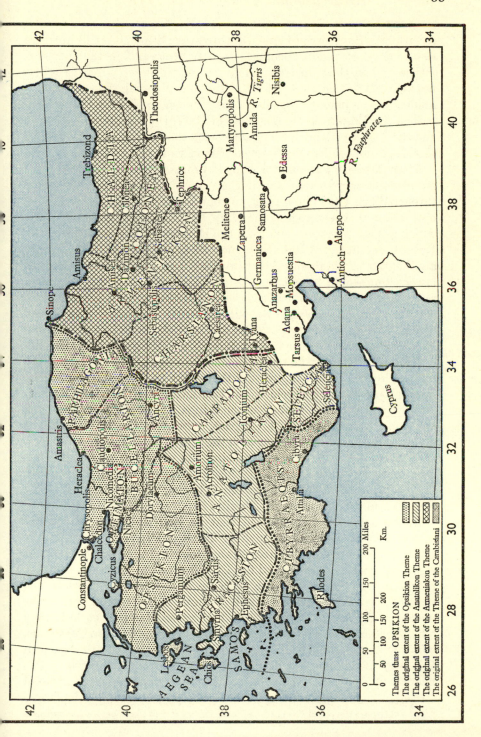

Map 3. Byzantine themes from the seventh to the ninth century.

novations in the doctrine handed down by the Fathers.[1] At this juncture a serious revolt against iconoclasm that broke out in the theme of Hellas and in the Cyclades ended in a naval disaster for the rebels near the capital on 18 April 727. But this outbreak, as well as subsequent developments, revealed a sharp cleavage between the western part of the Empire (including most of Italy, the mainland of Greece, and the Aegean islands), which supported the images, and the themes of Asia Minor, which championed iconoclasm.

After forbidding the use of icons in Constantinople, Leo also commanded Gregory to acquiesce in this ordinance or abdicate the papal throne. When the Pope refused to comply, he was encouraged in his opposition to the imperial mandate by the major cities of Italy, which rallied to protect him from the Emperor. They supplanted the Byzantine officials of Italy by men of their own choice, and not only anathematised Paul, the Exarch of Ravenna, together with his followers, but would have chosen a new Emperor, had they not been restrained by the Pope, who cherished the illusion that Leo might be led to reverse his policy. Rebellion against Byzantine rule spread widely, and imperial sympathisers and officials, including the Exarch Paul, were killed. Nevertheless, though the Emperor had allegedly ordered that Gregory be put to death, the Pope urged the Italians to remain loyal to the Empire. At this point (c. 729), Liutprand the Lombard king and Eutychius, the last Exarch of Ravenna, formed an alliance intended, among other things, to secure Rome and the Pope for Byzantium. But Gregory, who saw the advantages of maintaining friendly relations with the Byzantines and the Lombards simultaneously and thus neutralising the offensive power of both, managed to convert Liutprand's hostility into submission, and even helped the Exarch defeat a certain Petasius, who sought to become Emperor under the name of Tiberius.

In January 730 Leo decided that he had to secure patriarchal sanction for his iconoclastic policy. But the Patriarch Germanus of Constantinople refused to accept any doctrinal innovations without a general council, and begged the Emperor not to persist in hostility to the images or violate the oath he had taken to preserve the apostolic teaching of the Church without change. Leo then summoned a *silentium* (council of the highest secular and ecclesiastical officials), formally denounced the use of images, and forced Germanus, who remained adamant, to resign. For dismissing the Patriarch in this way Leo was condemned by a group of eastern ecclesiastics headed by John of Damascus, and also by Pope Gregory II, who at

---

[1] Theophanes, p. 404 (ed. C. de Boor); but the *Liber Pontificalis*, ed. Duchesne, I, pp. 403 f., puts the papal insubordination in the matter of taxes before Leo's decree.

the same time excommunicated the new Patriarch Anastasius, and detached 'Rome, Italy and all of the West from the political and ecclesiastical jurisdiction of Leo and the Empire'.[1] Unfortunately, Leo's reply to this papal pronouncement is no longer extant, but there are two letters ascribed to Gregory which seem to deal with the situation immediately preceding the resignation of Germanus. The authenticity of these two documents has been questioned; but whether or not they are genuine (as they appear to be except for some interpolations), they are at least close to the events described, and accurately portray the Byzantine theory that the Emperor was, as Leo expresses it, 'both Emperor and priest',[2] with full control over ecclesiastical as well as civil matters.

Leo's new Patriarch, Anastasius (elected on 22 January 730), and all other iconoclasts, presumably including the Emperor, were excommunicated in 731 by a Roman synod summoned by Pope Gregory III (731–41). Leo met the challenge implicit in the action the two Gregorys had taken against him by dispatching a large fleet under Manes, general of the Cibyrraeot theme. When this expedition was destroyed (732–3) by a storm in the Adriatic, Leo increased the capitation tax of Sicily and Calabria by a third, ordered that the patrimonies of the apostles Peter and Paul, amounting to three and a half talents of gold, previously paid to the Church of Rome, be transferred to the imperial treasury, and required that new-born males be registered for taxation.[3]

It was probably at the same time that the churches of Calabria, Sicily, eastern Illyricum (comprising the ancient dioceses of Dacia and Macedonia) and presumably Crete were transferred by Leo from the administrative sphere of the See of Rome to that of the Patriarchate of Constantinople.[4] The ecclesiastical government of eastern Illyricum had been severed in this way from that of the western part in 421 and also apparently, to some extent, during the Acacian schism (484–519), each time for only a brief interval. Thereafter, the Popes were again permitted to exercise surveillance over eastern Illyricum, and they retained this prerogative until the eighth century, when the Byzantine Church once more assumed control. But there is no Greek text which refers this change to the time of Leo III. For this reason and because of the evidence that can be cited for Gregory II's political loyalty to Leo, despite his disagreement in the matter of images, it has been argued that eastern Illyricum and the other areas mentioned above were not removed from papal jurisdiction

---

[1] Theophanes, pp. 408, 409, cf. p. 413 (ed. C. de Boor).
[2] Mansi, XII, 975D. See Pt II, ch. XXIV, pp. 104ff.
[3] *DR*, 300.   [4] *DR*, 301.

about 732–3 in reprisal for the Pope's intransigence, but during the pontificate of Stephen II (752–7). Nevertheless, the earlier date still seems preferable, chiefly because of the letter[1] of Pope Hadrian I to Charlemagne concerning the results of the Council of 787 (probably written just after the Council of Frankfurt in 794), in which Hadrian specifically states that the Roman Church had lost a number of arch-bishoprics together with its patrimonies at the time of Leo's attack upon the images.[2]

Whatever the date of this event, there is no doubt that Leo's attempt to enforce iconoclasm in the West was a failure and con-tributed, however indirectly, to the alienation of the Papacy and Italy from Byzantium. It also resulted in the aggrandisement of the Patriarchate of Constantinople, which now exercised a jurisdiction roughly co-terminous with the borders of the Empire, but operated under the direct supervision of the Emperor. The Roman Church, on the other hand, remote from the centres of imperial power, had greater freedom and was often to assert its independence of rulers seeking to control it. Henceforward, the Churches of Rome and Constan-tinople were to exert their influence in different directions, the former expanding in the West and in Central Europe, and the latter in the East and the North.

2. *Intensification of iconoclasm and Constantine V's successes against the Bulgars*

After Leo's death (18 June 741), his policies were carried out with even greater thoroughness and ardour by his son, Constantine V (741–75), who had been co-Emperor since 720. On account of his zeal against the icons, Constantine, the most maligned Emperor in Byzantine history, brought down upon himself the hatred of the iconophiles. Despite the lack of iconoclastic sources, which would have treated his reign more sympathetically, it is clear that he enjoyed great popularity among the people. Even forty years after his death, the Patriarch Nicephorus (806–15) found it difficult to refute the arguments of iconoclasts who maintained that Constantine had been a great general and a wise Emperor.

---

[1] Mansi, xiii, 808 d f.; xii, 1073 c; cf. xv, 167 (letter of Pope Nicholas [858–67] on the same subject). But cf. *Notitia Basilii*, ed. H. Gelzer, *Georgii Cyprii descriptio orbis Romani* (Leipzig, 1890), 27, 520–9; Georgius Monachus, ed. C. de Boor, ii, p. 744, 4 ff. (636); Cedrenus, i, p. 799/5–9; Zonaras, xv, 4, 1 (iii, p. 261); *Liber Ponti-ficalis*, 235, ed. Duchesne, i, p. 444.

[2] This same complaint was made in Hadrian's letter of 785 to Constantine and Irene, but was omitted in the Greek version of it read before the Council of Nicaea (Mansi, xii, 1071–6). For recent literature on this question see M. V. Anastos, 'The Transfer of Illyricum,'Calabria and Sicily to the Jurisdiction of the Patriarchate of Constantinople in 732–33', *SBN*, ix (1957), 14–31.

Resuming his father's campaign against the Arabs, he had set out to meet an invading force which had penetrated into Phrygia (June 742), when he was forced to turn back to deal with the revolt of his brother-in-law, Artavasdus, who set himself up as a champion of the images. Artavasdus seized power with the aid of the Thracian, Opsikion and Armeniakon themes, restored the images, and ruled in Constantinople until 2 November 743, when Constantine triumphantly entered his capital at the head of troops from the Thracesion, Anatolikon and Cibyrraeot themes. The usurper and his two sons were blinded; and all three were exhibited in the hippodrome, along with the Patriarch Anastasius, who had taken an active part in the rebellion. Anastasius, though flogged publicly and humiliated by being forced to ride backwards on an ass, was permitted to retain the patriarchal throne. Other partisans of Artavasdus were punished by execution, mutilation, or blinding.

Taking warning from this rebellion, Constantine split off the eastern portion of the Opsikion theme, which had supported Artavasdus, and established there the theme of the Bucellarii (767 or before). Likewise, he exercised the greatest care in the choice of generals, and succeeded in appointing men of unshakable loyalty, who accomplished much with small forces. Moreover, in an effort to achieve greater national unity, he curtailed the use of battalions from separate themes as distinct military entities, and employed instead armies made up of troops drawn from several of the themes merged together. Similarly, by a judicious transfer of populations, he not only made his northern and eastern boundaries more secure but also helped to diminish the intensity of the Thracian partisanship for images since the prisoners he moved to Thrace in 746 and 755 were iconoclasts, being Syrian monophysites from Germanicea and Doliche and Syrian and Armenian Paulicians from Melitene and Theodosiopolis. In the same way he repopulated Constantinople after the plague of 746–7 with people from Greece and the islands, presumably supporters of the images whom he probably preferred to keep in the capital under the watchful eyes of his troops (747–55).

When he had restored order within the Empire, Constantine returned to the work of strengthening his Arab borders, which had been interrupted by the insurrection of Artavasdus. He took the offensive against the enemy and achieved notable successes, aided in part by the incapacity of the Caliph al-Walīd II (743–4), who had been unable to profit from the Byzantine civil war, and also by the internal strife among the Arabs which followed the accession of Marwān II (744–50) to the Caliphate. The removal of the Arab capital from Damascus to Baghdad, which took place after the fall of the Umayyad dynasty in

750, was also to Byzantine advantage, for it shifted the major attention of the Arabs eastward. Constantine's objective was to attack the enemy in their own country, so as to prevent them from invading the Empire. He began by capturing Doliche and Germanicea in Arab-held Syria (746). Then, after destroying off the coast of Cyprus (747) all but three of 1,000 vessels which had put out from Alexandria, and thus nullifying the sea-power of the Arabs in the eastern Mediterranean for a generation, he pushed on to Melitene (in Mesopotamia) and Theodosiopolis (in Armenia), both of which he razed to the ground (751–2). The importance of Constantine's conquests beyond the confines of the Empire lies not in gain of territory, for the bastions he seized were retaken and refortified by the Arabs before his death, but in the new prestige gained for Byzantine arms in the East. In 756–7 the mere word that Constantine was on the march against them turned back the Arabs from Cappadocia. The Byzantines suffered some minor reversals after this, notably on the river Melas (759–60), at Laodicea Katakekaumene (770), and at Syke (771); but they had become masters of the situation, and were now able to prevent the Arabs from launching a major assault.

Having put the Arabs on the defensive (746–51) in this way, Constantine felt that Asia Minor was sufficiently secure for him to turn his attention to the Bulgars, allies of the Empire since 716, but, as he rightly foresaw, potentially dangerous enemies. Accordingly, in 755, he established a number of forts along the Thracian frontier. This apparently violated the treaty of 716, and provoked the Bulgarian Khan Kormisoš to descend in force to the very walls of Constantinople, where he demanded tribute and an indemnity. But Constantine drove the Bulgars off with heavy losses. Despite an apparent setback at Veregava in 759, he pressed his advantage so relentlessly that the Ukil dynasty, of which Kormisoš (d. 756) had been the leader, was overthrown and replaced in 761 by the warlike house of Ugain, led by the new Khan Telets, who was unwilling to make peace with Byzantium. In the ensuing conflict, 208,000 Slavs left Bulgaria to escape conscription into the Bulgarian army, and were settled in Bithynia by Constantine, in order to buttress the eastern front, and at the same time to remove from the European environs of his capital the kinsmen of the turbulent Macedonian Slavs he had been forced to subdue in 758.

Telets invaded Thrace with a huge army but was no match for Constantine, who attacked by land and sea and won a decisive victory near Anchialus on 30 June 763, which he celebrated gruesomely in Constantinople with the slaughter of his prisoners and with games in the Hippodrome. Telets was killed the following year by his disaffected people, and the house of Ukil was restored to power in the person of Sabinus, a son-in-law of the above-mentioned Kormisoš. The war continued intermittently, despite civil disorder in Bulgaria, until the year 773, when Constantine and his generals again forced the Bulgars, now under the Khan Telerig, to sue for peace. While terms were still under discussion, Telerig surreptitiously fitted out an army of 12,000 to invade Thessaly, but Constantine foiled him by a lightning descent into Bulgaria with a great force of 80,000 men, which he told the Bulgarian ambassador was being prepared for combat against the Arabs. The Bulgarians, taken completely by surprise, were routed at Lithosoria; and Constantine called the campaign 'the Noble War' because it had been won without the loss of a man. In 774, if Theophanes is to be believed, Telerig tricked Constantine into revealing the names of the Byzantine secret agents stationed in Bulgaria by pretending that he would need their aid in his contemplated flight to Constantinople.[1] The Byzantine spies were apparently put to death, and the Emperor set out immediately on a punitive expedition, which, however, came to nothing because of his sudden death at Fort Strongylus on 14 September 775. Though Constantine thus failed to subdue Bulgaria altogether, he seriously weakened the khanate and greatly increased the security of his northern borders.

While strengthening his eastern and northern frontiers by force of arms, Constantine was constrained, probably for lack of resources, to limit his operations in Italy to diplomatic manœuvres. At first this policy seemed to offer some hope of success, and he granted Pope Zacharias (741–52) the two valuable imperial properties of Ninfa and Norma, south of Rome, presumably at the end of 744 or early in 745,[2] after the papal chancery had discontinued giving the regnal year in the name of Artavasdus, who had been honoured in this way at least once in 743 and twice in 744.[3] Zacharias intervened successfully with the Lombard king Liutprand (743) and later with his successor, Ratchis (744–9), to save Ravenna for the Empire, but he was powerless against Ratchis' brother, Aistulf, who forcibly annexed a number of imperial possessions in 750, and by July 751 had occupied Ravenna itself, thus putting an end to the Exarchate. Venice, Sicily, Calabria, and part of Campania were now all that remained of Byzantine Italy.

Zacharias' successor, Pope Stephen II (752–7), was still willing to negotiate with the Lombards for the restoration of Ravenna. But

---

[1] *DR*, 336. [2] *DR*, 310.
[3] The *Liber Pontificalis* refers to Artavasdus only as a rebel (*Vita Zachariae*). Cf. E. Caspar, *Geschichte des Papsttums*, ii (Tübingen, 1933), p. 739.

instead of the armies he sought from Constantine he received only envoys with orders, which he was asked to transmit, commanding the Lombards to evacuate the territory they had occupied.[1] He therefore appealed to Pepin III, king of the Franks, who sent two ambassadors to conduct him northward across the Alps for a conference. The Pope stopped at Pavia, accompanied by Pepin's men and John the Silentiary from Byzantium. After failing to obtain any kind of satisfaction from Aistulf (November 753), Stephen went on without the Byzantine representative, and entered Frankish territory on 6 January 754. In the spring he consecrated Pepin together with his sons, Charlemagne and Carloman, in St Denis, and bestowed upon each of them the title of *patricius Romanorum*, which may have been intended as nothing more than an honorific distinction, without specific connotations, although it has been suggested that this was an imperial office properly conferred, and that the Byzantines were expecting thereby to obtain Frankish assistance against the Lombards. Others look upon it as constituting an act of treason against the Empire.[2]

Whatever the title was intended to mean, it is clear that, when Pepin set out to fulfil the promises which he had made to Stephen and to recover the territories seized by Aistulf, he regarded himself as acting on his own behalf and in the interests of the Papacy, and not for Byzantium. For when he was approached (756) by a Byzantine envoy, who promised huge rewards for the return of the former imperial possessions, he replied that he had presented these lands to St Peter and that nothing would induce him to take them back. By so doing he was in effect informing Constantinople that he had severed Ravenna, the Pentapolis, and Rome from the Empire, and that a pontifical state had been created. The precise frontiers of the new state are irrelevant here except for their connection with the notorious forgery, the so-called *Donation of Constantine*, which was apparently produced in Rome at this time expressly to reinforce the papal claims to temporal power. According to this document, the Emperor Constantine the Great, in gratitude to Pope Sylvester I for curing him of leprosy, allowed himself to be baptised by the latter and conferred upon the Popes many prerogatives normally reserved to the Emperor himself, together with primacy over the entire Christian Church, and sovereignty over Rome, Italy, and the whole of the West.

Even after the rebuff of 756, Constantine V did not altogether despair of winning concessions from the Franks, with whom he re-

---

[1] *DR*, 314.

[2] See F. Dölger, 'Europas Gestaltung im Spiegel der fränkisch-byzantinischen Auseinandersetzung des 9. Jahrhunderts', *Byzanz und die europäische Staatenwelt*, pp. 282 ff., 293 f.

mained, outwardly at least, on good terms. He even tried to arrange a marriage between his son, Leo, and Pepin's daughter, Gisela, who, however, eventually married Adalgisus, son of Desiderius, the last Lombard king. But there was definite hostility between the Emperor and the Popes, and the Byzantine imperial dating in papal documents appears to be used for the last time during the pontificate of Hadrian I (772–95).[1] The acts of the Frankish Council of Gentilly (767) have not survived, but a Roman synod under Pope Stephen III in 769 approved the veneration of images and denounced the iconoclasts. The Popes exerted themselves strenuously to prevent an alliance between Byzantium and the Franks; and when Constantine realised that it was impossible to detach Pepin from his allegiance to Rome, he decided to seek the assistance of disaffected elements in Italy, such as the Lombards, who were hostile to both the Franks and the Papacy. But Byzantine agents achieved little except to frighten the Popes; and the downfall of the Lombard kingdom after the victory of Pepin's son Charlemagne in 774 marks the termination of Byzantine rule in northern Italy.

The alienation of Italy and the Papacy from the Byzantine Empire was provoked in the first instance by the iconoclastic decrees of the Emperors. But it cannot be explained entirely in theological terms, as the failure of the Papacy to return to Byzantine allegiance after the restoration of the images in 787 and 843 clearly shows. On the contrary, the loss of Italy was the result of a combination of circumstances, chief amongst which were the inability of the Emperors to send to Italy forces sufficient to protect Byzantine interests there, the desire of the Popes to secure and to expand the boundaries of the papal state, the deeply rooted cultural differences between Greeks and Latins, and the growing power and national consciousness, not only of the Franks, but also of the Italian cities, which found it increasingly irksome to submit to the rule of a foreign power. This growing instinct for autonomy can be illustrated by the history of Venice, Naples, Gaeta, and Amalfi, which, if still nominally subject to Byzantine authority, were rapidly becoming free and independent states, loyal but not subservient to Constantinople.

In spite of the territorial readjustments brought about by the new situation in the West, which are not even mentioned by contemporary Greek sources,[2] it is by no means certain that the Empire actually suffered substantial losses thereby. The westward expansion of Byzantium had never been an unmixed blessing, and the greater cohesion of the Empire achieved by the expulsion from northern Italy and confine-

---

[1] For a different view, see below: ch. x, p. 446.
[2] But cf. Theophanes, p. 413.

ment within the limits of the Hellenic world may have released additional resources for the vital struggle against barbarian and infidel races, which it was the historic mission of Byzantium to lead.

At the time when Stephen II and Pepin were making their fateful decisions, Constantine was getting ready to strike a carefully planned blow against the images. Iconoclastic propaganda had been widely disseminated, iconophiles had been arrested, and the loyalty of the army and the people had been assured by the popularity of his great successes over the Arabs, when the death of the Patriarch Anastasius gave Constantine the opportunity in 754 of convoking a church council in the Palace of Hieria, south of Chalcedon on the Asian coast of the Sea of Marmora, under the presidency of Theodosius, Archbishop of Ephesus, and Pastillas, Bishop of Perga. No cleric of patriarchal rank attended, but the three hundred and thirty-eight bishops present regarded themselves as constituting the Seventh Oecumenical Council, although they were later forced to relinquish this title to the Second Council of Nicaea (787). From 10 February to 8 August 754, the Council conducted an exhaustive study of the propriety of the use of images and summarised its conclusions in its *Horos* (dogmatic definition), which is the only document of 754 to have escaped destruction by the iconophile party after their subsequent triumph. It owes its preservation to its having been quoted verbatim by the orthodox clergy at the Council of Nicaea in 787.

According to this *Horos*, the Emperors, described as 'the equals of the apostles (ἀποστόλων ἐφάμιλλοι), endowed with the...power of the Holy Spirit, not only to perfect and instruct mankind but also...to refute diabolical heresy', bade the bishops to undertake a scriptural examination of the 'deceptive art of painting images in colour that has seduced the mind of man from the exalted worship that is fitting for God to the gross and material worship of created things'[1] and to set forth their own views on this matter under divine inspiration. It is not suprising, therefore, that the deliberations of the bishops ended in the promulgation of a theology very similar to that of the Emperor, who himself seems to have been the guiding force and chief theologian of the iconoclasts. Nevertheless, the Council was not influenced by the Emperor's antipathy towards the doctrine of the intercession by the Virgin and by the saints, and unequivocally pronounced its approval of this article of faith. It would be interesting to determine to what extent their decision represented a concession or compromise on the part of the Emperor, who is said not to have repented of his attitude on this subject until the hour of his death.

It appears from their *Horos* that the iconoclasts objected to the use

[1] Mansi, XIII, 225D, 229D–E.

of icons for a number of reasons. They cited the scriptural[1] and patristic denunciations of graven images; they felt that the worship of physical and material objects was not only improper in itself but also unchristian and a mark of idolatry; they decried what seemed to them to be excessive worship of saints, holding that such veneration was too often an end in itself, and distracted the worshipper from the love and emulation of the saints, which was in their judgement the only valid standard of Christian conduct. They also made much of what might be called the ethical theory of images, according to which the virtues of the saints are the living images that the pious should reproduce in themselves. Finally, and most important, they attacked the icons on Christological grounds. Up to this time, official iconoclastic doctrine depended on scriptural prohibitions of the use of idols, and was directed against paganism and what were deemed to have been idolatrous practices. Constantine and his associates went a stage beyond this and gave iconoclasm a more developed theological basis. They assumed as their first premise that the divine nature is completely uncircumscribable (τὸ ἀπερίγραφον)[2] and hence cannot be portrayed or represented by artists in any medium whatsoever. They then applied this concept to Christology. Since the word Christ, they argued, means both God and man, an icon of Christ, if such a thing were possible, would have to be an image of God and man, inasmuch as his flesh is the flesh of the Logos, the Son of God. But this is impossible. For an image of Christ would either, in the manner of Nestorius,[3] completely sever the human nature or flesh of Christ (which, taken by itself, could conceivably be represented by an artist) from his divine nature (which is uncircumscribable, and therefore quite beyond the realm of pictorial representation); or, alternatively, it would try to circumscribe the uncircumscribable and, in the manner of the monophysites, would utterly destroy the independent entity of the two natures of Christ, the human and the divine, by commingling or confusing the one with the other.

Having rejected the conventional images for these reasons, the iconoclasts then formulated the theory that the only true image of Christ was to be found in the bread and wine of the Eucharist, which

---

[1] The chief texts were: Exod. xx. 4; Deut. v. 8; John i. 18; iv. 24; v. 37; xx. 29; Rom. i. 23, 25; x. 17; II Cor. v. 7, 16.

[2] Mansi, XIII, 252 A.

[3] According to the orthodox Christology, as formulated by the Fourth Oecumenical Council (Chalcedon, 451), Christ has two natures, the human and the divine, united without confusion or change, without separation or division, both of which together form one *prosopon* or *hypostasis* ('person'). Nestorius was condemned for dividing or separating the two and teaching that Christ had two separate *hypostases* or *prosopa*, one for each of his two natures, whereas the monophysites were attacked for insisting that Christ had only one nature.

they deemed to be the only form or figure that could properly be regarded as a representation of the Incarnation. They banned all dissent from the decrees of this *Horos* and sternly prohibited the production, worship, possession, or concealment of images under penalty of deposition for bishops, presbyters, or deacons, and anathematisation as well as prosecution by the imperial authorities for monks and laymen. It was after the Council of 754 that Constantine is said to have forbidden prayer to the Virgin or the saints, and to have banned the conventional entreaty: Θεοτόκε, βοήθει ('Help me, O Mother of God'); but this prohibition is not well authenticated. Similarly, it seems unlikely that he ever said that Christ was a mere man, and that for this reason Mary should not be described as the Mother of God.

Even after the clear decision of 754, and the unanimity of the bishops of the Council, Constantine at first made no attempt to force compliance with the measures against the images, now prohibited both by the imperial laws and the solemn mandate of the Church. Indeed the first execution for veneration of the icons did not take place until 762. Violence on a larger and hitherto unprecedented scale broke out in 765, when the Emperor ordered all his subjects to swear that they would not offer reverence (προσκυνῆσαι) to images.[1] In November of this year the monk Stephen of the monastery of Auxentius was murdered for not repudiating the condemned doctrine. In August of the following year, monks were forced to parade through the hippodrome, each holding a woman by the hand, and, four days later, nineteen imperial officials of high rank were humiliated publicly, allegedly because they had plotted against the Emperor, but possibly for theological reasons. Two of these were executed; the rest were blinded, exiled and sentenced to one hundred lashes a year. On 30 August 766 the Emperor removed the Patriarch Constantine, whom he had appointed at the Council of 754, for having been implicated in the conspiracy with the nineteen officials, and named Nicetas to take his place (16 November). A year later, the deposed Patriarch Constantine was tortured and executed. Theophanes says that the Emperor converted the shrine of the martyr St Euphemia into an armoury and storehouse for manure, and turned many monasteries into inns or military barracks. Yet as late as 768 the patriarchal palace contained a number of images in mosaic and wood, which had not been effaced or destroyed.

The persecutions in the capital were followed by similar acts of suppression in the provinces, notably under the leadership of Michael Lachanodracon, strategus of the Thracesion theme, who ordered

[1] Theophanes, p. 437/12.

monks to marry, and punished those who refused by blinding and deportation to Cyprus. Lachanodracon sold monastic property, burned manuscripts and relics, set fire to the beards and hair of monks, and attacked the monks so venomously that no one in his theme dared to wear the monastic habit. Although the chroniclers exaggerate the cruelty and ruthlessness of these measures, there is no doubt that many supporters of the images suffered barbarous treatment, and some were put to death. Works of religious art were destroyed; but another type of art, which was devoted to representing scenes from nature and the martial exploits of the Emperor, was assiduously cultivated; and the Emperor himself built churches.[1] Monks and monastic houses were often attacked as such, apparently not as part of a specifically anti-monastic programme, but because, as the controversy developed, it was the monks who turned out to be the most devoted to the use of images and the most inflexible in their opposition to iconoclasm. Nevertheless there were iconoclastic monks and monasteries, especially in the ninth century.

II. LEO IV, THE RESTORATION OF THE IMAGES AND THE COLLAPSE OF THE EMPIRE 775–813

With the death of Constantine V the first iconoclastic period comes to an end. Constantine's son, Leo IV the Khazar (775–80), so called because of the nationality of his mother, inherited a prosperous Empire, a full treasury and a system of defence efficiently organised against both the Bulgars, who had been reduced to impotence, and the Arabs, whose offensive power had been broken. Leo set out to continue in the footsteps of his two immediate predecessors, but his reign marks the transition from iconoclasm to the restoration of the images, which was brought about by his wife, Irene, and their son, Constantine VI. After a brief period during which he conciliated the monastic party, even to the extent of appointing monks to important metropolitan sees, he reverted to his father's principles; and in 780, after the death of the Patriarch Nicetas, a Slav eunuch, and the consecration of his successor, Paul of Cyprus (780–4), Leo resumed persecution of the iconophiles. He even went so far as to bar the Empress Irene from his bedchamber because she had two icons in her possession and had been involved in pro-image intrigue.

Concerned like his forbears for the perpetuation of the dynasty, Leo courted public favour by generous distribution of the ample public funds accumulated since 717, and readily responded to popular demand that he should make his son, Constantine VI, co-Emperor

[1] Cf. A. Grabar, *L'iconoclasme byzantin. Dossier archéologique* (Paris, 1957).

(776). At Constantine's coronation, Leo had the satisfaction of receiving written oaths in which the themes, the senate, the Constantinopolitan troops, and all the citizens and artisans swore 'that they would accept no Emperor but Leo, Constantine, and their descendants'.[1] Later in the same year this oath was put to the test, when a *coup d'état*, attempted by Leo's half-brother, the Caesar Nicephorus, was quickly suppressed. At the Emperor's request, an assembly of the people themselves pronounced judgement upon the conspirators and condemned them to exile. These incidents testify both to the efforts being made to create a tradition, not so far securely established, of orderly dynastic succession by the eldest son,[2] and also to the real personal popularity of the Emperor, whose capacity had been demonstrated in three successful campaigns against the Arabs in Asia Minor and Syria (777–80).

At the same time, profiting from dissension among the Bulgars, Leo gave Khan Telerig asylum in Constantinople (776–7) and a royal bride in the person of the Empress's cousin. Likewise, the Byzantine court refused to abandon the hope, always cherished by Constantine V, that the lost possessions in Italy might be recovered; and the fugitive Adalgisus (called Theodotus in Greek), son of the former Lombard king Desiderius, was so hospitably received at Constantinople in 775 as to lend colour to the Pope's fears of a Byzantino-Lombard campaign to restore the suzerainty of Constantinople in northern Italy and hence imperil the independence of the newly created papal state.

Leo's hopes of emulating his father came to nothing, and his death at the age of thirty (8 September 780) brought his widow Irene together with their son, Constantine VI, to the throne as joint sovereigns (780–97). Since Constantine was not quite ten, the initiative rested with Irene, an Athenian by birth and, perhaps for this reason, devoted to the images. She was ambitious, strong-willed, and capable, and might have furthered the interests of the Empire, had she not sacrificed all other considerations to her lust for power and passion for the restoration of the images.

Her first task was to consolidate her position, which was threatened barely forty days after Leo's death by what seems to have been an attempt by the iconoclasts to secure the throne for Leo's half-brother, the Caesar Nicephorus. But the plot was discovered, the ringleaders humiliated and exiled, and Leo's five half-brothers, around whom

---

[1] Theophanes, p. 449/27–32.

[2] Leo's half-brothers, though thus forced to give way to Constantine VI, figured frequently, and almost comically, in abortive usurpations; they were the Caesars Nicephorus and Christopher, and the Nobilissimi Nicetas, Anthimus, and Eudocimus.

intrigue principally revolved, were shorn, made priests, and compelled to distribute the elements of the Eucharist in St Sophia on Christmas Day 780, as if in public renunciation of all claims to the crown. In the following year, a more formidable revolt broke out in Sicily. Its leader, Elpidius, commander in Sicily and chief Byzantine official in the West, could not be overcome at once because of operations against the Arabs in Asia Minor, which ended in a resounding victory at Melon. Before proceeding in force against Elpidius, Irene arranged for the betrothal of the ten-year-old Constantine to Charlemagne's daughter Rotrud (Erythro in Greek), not merely to prevent Frankish intervention on behalf of the Sicilian rebels, but especially to secure a settlement in the West that would permit her to devote all her energy to domestic policy. After this diplomatic preparation, a Byzantine expedition to Sicily dislodged Elpidius, who fled to Africa and was there crowned king of the Romans by the Arabs (782).

But this effort had drawn off military forces badly needed in Asia Minor and was partly responsible for the crushing Byzantine defeat (782) which allowed Hārūn ar-Rashīd (775–85), son of the Caliph al-Mahdī, to penetrate as far as Chrysopolis, to the very shores of the Bosphorus, and enabled him to collect a tribute of 70,000 (or 90,000) dinars annually, in return for a truce of three years.[1] Actually, the imperial forces might have prevailed over the Arabs, except for the treachery of Tatzates, general of the Bucellarion theme, whose jealousy of Irene's favourite, the eunuch Stauracius, induced him to desert to the Arabs. Another factor was the stupidity of the Byzantine ambassadors, including Stauracius, who entered the Arab camp without a preliminary exchange of hostages and were held to ransom there. If Irene had made a determined effort, she might have been able to retrieve the situation. Instead, after allowing the Arabs to refortify Tarsus (786–8), retake Kamacha (793), and invade Cappadocia, Galatia, and Ephesus (797–8), she again consented to pay tribute (798).[2]

From Irene's point of view, however, the elimination of would-be usurpers, the abandonment of Italy to Charlemagne, and the ignominious truce with the Arabs all served her purpose equally well, for they left her free to transfer attention from what she regarded as extraneous matters to the important business of crushing the iconoclasts and restoring the images. Towards this end she was aided by the favourable circumstances consequent upon Stauracius' victory in 783 over the Slavs in Greece, for which he was rewarded with a splendid triumph. In the next year (784) the aged Patriarch Paul

[1] *DR*, 340.   [2] *DR*, 352.

(780–4), who seems to have been favourably disposed towards the images despite the iconoclastic oath which he had reluctantly sworn at his consecration,[1] abdicated and made a number of dramatic pronouncements against the iconoclasts.

Delighted by this turn of events, which she had probably engineered herself, Irene set out to seek a suitable Patriarch and at length settled upon an imperial official of scholarly inclinations named Tarasius, a man without experience in ecclesiastical affairs, whose selection by popular acclamation she ingeniously contrived. Since Tarasius required as a condition of acceptance that Irene convoke a general council, she willingly made the necessary preparations, and, with the approval of the other four Patriarchs (Rome, Alexandria, Antioch and Jerusalem), summoned the bishops to meet in the Church of the Holy Apostles on 31 July 786. But there were many iconoclasts amongst both the clergy and the imperial troops stationed in Constantinople, and they protested so vehemently against any attempt to review the results of the iconoclastic decisions of 754 or to abrogate the decrees of the popular Constantine V, that the Empress and her advisers were forced to postpone the proceedings until the following year. The government also took the precaution of ordering the army to leave the capital on the pretext that an expedition was being prepared against the Arabs. As soon as these iconoclastic military units had reached Malagina in Bithynia, however, they were demobilised and replaced by icon-venerating soldiers from Thrace, so as to ensure the success of Irene's schemes. To make doubly certain, the Empress reorganised the armed forces and appointed officers who were subservient to her wishes.

With the ground thus prepared, the Seventh General Council, the last recognized as oecumenical by the Orthodox Church, was finally convened on 24 September 787 in the Church of the Holy Wisdom at Nicaea, and was attended by approximately three hundred and fifty bishops, including two representatives (both named Peter) of the see of Rome, and two delegates of the three Patriarchs of the East, who were prevented by the Arab occupation from attending in person. The Council's deliberations lasted until 13 October, and were divided into eight sessions. In the first of these, the Council heard the retractions of a number of penitent iconoclasts, who were re-admitted to full standing in the Church and permitted to regain their episcopal thrones. It was also decided that clerics ordained by heretics should be recognised by the Church. In these discussions, as in the controversies of subsequent years, there was a sharp division between the monastic extremists, who insisted upon strict interpretation of the canons, and

[1] *DR*, 341.

the moderates, who took a more reasonable position. At Nicaea the moderates prevailed.

The fourth session of the Council, which was given over almost entirely to the recitation of stories about icons and the miracles associated with them, provides a survey of the chief characteristics of the cult of images and the features which both appealed to its adherents and scandalised its critics. The general attitude of those who favoured the use of images was that they recreated the events they portrayed for the instruction, inspiration, and spiritual improvement of their beholders. Many, however, stressed the miraculous power connected with certain images. The blood and water that gushed from a representation of Christ at Beirut, whenever it was pierced by a lance, were said to have cured a large number of Jews and thus to have converted the entire local synagogue. According to another witness, a certain devotee of Saints Cosmas and Damian covered the walls of her house with their portraits, and once, when desperately ill, scratched off the paint of the images with her finger nails, and dropped the scrapings into a glass of water. She drank the mixture, and was immediately restored to perfect health 'by the presence of the saints within her'.[1] Others believed also that images could punish iconoclasts, and several instances were reported of scoffers, both Christian and non-Christian, who suffered dire penalties for damaging them. But it should be noted that the argument based upon marvels of this sort is limited almost exclusively to the fourth session of the Council, and never obtrudes upon the dogmatic analysis of the iconoclastic doctrine, which was the principal subject of discussion. Indeed, at the conclusion of this session, Tarasius made a point of remarking that it was no longer necessary for the images to perform miracles because God had used them for this purpose only in order to win the pagans over to Christianity. Thus, the Council of Nicaea as a whole cannot be accused of entertaining superstitious notions about icons.

In the fifth session the Council examined and rejected the patristic authorities customarily cited by the iconoclasts, and in the sixth, which is the most important of all, refuted the iconoclastic *Horos* of 754 section by section. In the course of this refutation, the Nicene Council of 787 formulated a doctrine of the image which has considerable significance. The orthodox had an abundance of patristic passages to quote against the *Horos*, but they found it exceedingly difficult to answer the objection of the iconoclasts that there was no warrant for the use of images in the early history of the Church. They contended that images had been used in churches from the earliest times, and would not have been defended by the Fathers if

[1] Mansi, XIII, 68 c.

suitable precedents from the primitive Church had been lacking. They appealed frequently to the Old Testament,[1] but could cite no texts from the New Testament that were directly pertinent, and argued that the teaching on images was preserved in unwritten tradition and valid because of its acceptance by the Fathers.

Against the charge of idolatry, however, they easily defended themselves. They did not worship inanimate objects, they said,[2] for they distinguished carefully between the image and the prototype, offering to the former only reverence and honour (ἀσπασμὸν καὶ τιμητικὴν προσκύνησιν), and reserving true worship (τὴν κατὰ πίστιν ἡμῶν ἀληθινὴν λατρείαν) for the prototype alone. Defining their principles in these terms, they also championed the images of the saints, which the iconoclasts had repudiated, as reminders of the holy exploits that inspired men to emulation.

But the most important aspects of the orthodox doctrine are those which deal with Christology. To the contention of the iconoclasts that images presupposed a Nestorian Christology, the orthodox replied that an image of Christ was a representation of the incarnate Word, 'who was made flesh and dwelt among us', and who was subject to human limitations as a perfect man. A painting of a man, they argued, does not attempt to show his soul or his flesh, muscles, nerves, bones, blood, fluid, and bile. Nevertheless, no sensible person looking at a picture would think that the painter had separated the body of his subject from the soul. Similarly, the image of the incarnate Christ cannot be regarded as involving a separation of the human nature from the divine. When people contemplate an image of Christ, although they see only the human Christ, they do not separate his humanity from his divinity, but turn their thoughts at the same time to his uncircumscribable Godhead, which cannot be seen.

On the other hand, it was contended, images do not involve a monophysite confusion of the two natures, for they represent nothing but the human, visible manhood of Christ, and do not attempt to portray the divine, which is invisible and cannot be depicted. Christ is both man and God, but the image which is seen partakes of its prototype in name only and not in substance (οὐσία). Having disposed in this way of the Christology of their opponents, the Council then attacked the iconoclastic theory that the Eucharist constituted the only valid image of Christ, as being inconsistent with the words of the Gospel, which declare the bread and the wine of the Eucharist

---

[1] Gen. i. 26; xxiii. 7; xxviii. 18; xxxiii. 3; xlvii. 7; Exod. xxv. 18, 40; xxxi. 1–6; xxxv. 4–10; xxxvi. 37 f.; Josh. iv. 8, 21; I Kings vi. 25, 29; Ezek. xli. 18.

[2] Mansi, XIII, 377 D–E; cf. *ibid.* 100 B–104 E. This was often defined as a relative (σχετική) honour.

to be, not the image of Christ's body and blood, but his actual body and blood.

Throughout, the orthodox party laid stress on the reality of the Incarnation, and the decision of 787 in favour of images has for that reason an important place in the history of Christology. In 431, 553 and 681, in three oecumenical councils, the divinity of Christ had received greater attention than the humanity, and some theologians were going very far in the direction of monophysitism. This same monophysite tendency is to be found in the contention of the iconoclasts that the flesh of Christ, having been deified by union with the Logos, was just as free from human limitations after the Incarnation as it had been before. In resisting this movement, the defenders of images argued that to hold that the Christ whom men saw, touched and heard even after his Resurrection could not be represented was to affirm that he never really took flesh. This would be not only to repudiate the Gospel story, but also to deny mankind the salvation that had been won by the Resurrection.

The iconophiles had many faults; but, considered within the framework, and upon the premises, of Christology, they clearly had the better of the argument. Had they not prevailed, the great religious art of Byzantium, with its incalculable influence upon the civilisation of the West, would never have come into being.

The Latin translation of the acts of the Council of 787 grossly distorted the meaning of the original. Even apart from the inadequacies of the Latin version and the misunderstandings to which it gave rise, Charlemagne would never have endorsed the Nicene decision. For he had been estranged from Byzantium ever since the spring of 787 (or some time in 788) when Irene had broken off the betrothal of Constantine to Rotrud because of her fear that her son, with Charlemagne as father-in-law, would take the reins from her hand and rule as sole Emperor.[1] This estrangement, which led to war in 788, is reflected in the virulent attacks upon the Greeks made by the author (presumably Alcuin) of the *Libri Carolini*, who denounced both the iconoclasts and the orthodox and preferred the view of Gregory I (590–604), as expressed by Serenus, Bishop of Marseilles, that images should be neither adored nor destroyed. Pope Hadrian I approved the results of 787, but he could do nothing to annul the Frankish synod of Frankfurt, which formally condemned them (794), nor could he persuade the Byzantine court to restore ecclesiastical jurisdiction over Calabria, Sicily, Illyricum and Crete to

---

[1] *DR*, 345. According to the Franks, it was Charlemagne who annulled the agreement and provoked the outbreak of hostilities by withholding his daughter. *Einhardi Annales*, a. 788 (*MGH*, *Script.*, I, p. 175).

the Roman See, which had lost these provinces to the Byzantine patriarchate in 732–3. The East and the West were less widely separated dogmatically than Charlemagne and Alcuin realised. But there were essential differences, as can be seen, for example, in the Byzantine refusal to sanction the portrayal of the figure of God the Father, which occurs frequently in western medieval art.

Irene had achieved a personal triumph at the Council of Nicaea, but the Empire paid dearly for it. Her reorganisation of the army in 786–7, which had been undertaken for political rather than military reasons, was unwise and opened the way for the serious defeats which Byzantium suffered on the Arab and Bulgarian fronts in 788–9. Still worse, she rashly sent an army to Italy to assist the Lombard prince Adalgisus, whom she hoped to place on the Lombard throne, occupied since 781 by Charlemagne's son, Pepin. But the expedition was a disastrous failure (788) and finally ended (798) in the cession of Byzantine Istria and Benevento to Charlemagne,[1] who thus rudely shattered both the dream of regaining the Exarchate of Ravenna and the ineffective Byzantino-Lombard alliance.

In her reckless pursuit of power, to which these reverses and the disintegration of the Empire during her reign are directly to be ascribed, Irene not only ignored the imperial prerogatives of her son, whom she subjected to flogging and imprisonment (790), but also forced him to yield what should have been his place in the government to her favourite, the eunuch Stauracius, who was the *de facto* ruler of the Empire. Constantine finally rebelled against this treatment and in October 790 was proclaimed sole Emperor by the themes of Asia Minor, which had refused to take an oath requiring them to disregard his rights to the crown during Irene's lifetime, and to mention her name before his. He confined Irene to the palace of Eleutherius, in which she had concealed great sums of money, and exiled the eunuchs in her entourage. But he had neither ability nor determination. After being defeated by both the Arabs and the Bulgars in 791, he supinely recalled his mother to the palace as joint ruler on 15 January 792.

In July of the same year he suffered a shameful defeat at the hands of the Bulgars, to whom he was compelled to pay tribute, and vented his rage against his five uncles, who had been implicated once more in a plot against the crown. This time he blinded Nicephorus and cut out the tongues of the other four. Then recklessly following the far from disinterested advice of his mother, he provoked the men of the Armeniakon theme to rebellion by blinding their former commander, his benefactor, Alexius Musele, and thereupon ruthlessly cut them

[1] *DR*, 353.

down (26 May 793), heedless of their past devotion to his cause and their importance to the Empire. Two years later, in September 795, he alienated orthodox opinion by putting aside Maria, the innocuous Paphlagonian beauty he had been forced to marry, for Theodote, whom Irene had deliberately thrown into his path in order to take advantage of the public indignation which she knew would be provoked by a second marriage under these circumstances. The Patriarch yielded to the Emperor's wishes, and permitted a priest named Joseph to perform the ceremony. But the extremists, headed by Plato, abbot of the monastery of Saccudium, broke communion with Tarasius for tolerating a union which they regarded as adulterous. They were at length punished by the Emperor, who had tried at first to conciliate them. Plato was imprisoned, and the rest of his monastic followers, including his famous nephews, Theodore and Joseph, were exiled to Thessalonica, despite the favour they had won with Irene because of their attacks upon her son. The 'Moechian Schism' which thus arose was not easily healed and continued to disrupt the Church for many years to come, the Moechianists (from μοιχεία, adultery), as the defenders of Constantine's second marriage were called, being arrayed against the extremists.

Exploiting her son's mistakes to the full, Irene determined to remove him from the throne by force and persuaded a number of officials to help her do so in 796. But Constantine still had a large following and might have been saved from his mother, had it not been for traitors in his own inner circle, who imprisoned him in the Purple Chamber where he had been born twenty-seven years before. There on 15 August 797 his eyes were put out on the orders of his mother, who by this monstrous crime became the first woman in Byzantine history to rule the Empire in her own name.

Irene's reign (797–802) opened with another plot (797) centred around the sons of Constantine V, whom she exiled to Athens; the four younger brothers were blinded in 799 after a Slav official, Acamer of Belzetia, attempted to make one of them Emperor. Disregarding the national welfare as always, and thinking only of her personal interests, Irene sought to strengthen her position by distributing lavish gifts (799), by remitting the city tax paid by the people of Constantinople, by lowering (in 801) the import and export duties at Abydus and Hierus (the principal custom houses, which supplied a great part of the national income), and by other acts of benefaction and generosity that no prudent administrator could justify. She recalled the monks exiled by her son, and won praise from Theodore the Studite for her financial policy. But she was ill; and her two chief ministers, Aetius and Stauracius, neither of whom could succeed to the throne because they were eunuchs, each plotted to control the succession in his own interest. Stauracius died just as he was moving against Aetius in Cappadocia (800), and the arrogant behaviour of Aetius, who sought the crown for his brother Leo, was to cause his downfall two years later.

In the midst of these intrigues, Charlemagne received the crown from Pope Leo III on 25 December 800. According to the Latin sources and Theophanes (who actually uses the word βασιλεύς), he was proclaimed *Imperator Romanorum* (Emperor of the Romans). But he himself preferred to be described as *Imperator Romanum gubernans imperium*, either to placate the Byzantines, who would have looked upon the former designation as an intolerable usurpation of authority reserved exclusively to their own Emperors, or to indicate that he was not merely Emperor of the Romans of the city of Rome but of the entire Roman Empire.[1] Irene was in no position to dispute Charlemagne's new dignity by force of arms. Charlemagne, in turn, seems to have had no intention of asserting a claim to Constantinople and the Eastern Empire, as an ordinary usurper would have done; and the assault he is said to have contemplated making upon Sicily, one of the chief remaining Byzantine possessions in the West, was soon abandoned. Indeed, to judge from his conduct in later years, he sought nothing more than Byzantine recognition of his right to the imperial title. Nevertheless, he probably looked upon himself, or at least was often regarded, as in some sense the successor of the legitimate Emperors of Constantinople, since the western chroniclers considered the throne to be vacant, and refused to accept Irene as 'Emperor', as she styled herself.

Theophanes reports that Charlemagne had conceived the brilliant notion of marrying Irene in order to achieve the unity of the eastern and western portions of the Empire, which was still regarded as one and undivided. This ingenious project, which had Pope Leo's blessing, was opposed by Aetius. Irene was not unwilling, but the marriage, which might have greatly altered the course of history, never took place. Envoys from both Charlemagne and Pope Leo arrived to make preparations for signing the marriage contract. But soon after this in 802 the supporters of the logothete Nicephorus, Irene's minister of finance, obtained the imperial power for him by simply asserting that Irene herself had commissioned them to proclaim

---

[1] See F. Dölger, 'Europas Gestaltung im Spiegel der fränkisch-byzantinischen Auseinandersetzung des 9. Jahrh.', *Byzanz und die europäische Staatenwelt*; see also W. Ullmann, *The Growth of Papal Government in the Middle Ages* (London, 1955), pp. 87 ff.; W. Ohnsorge, *Abendland und Byzanz* (Darmstadt, 1958), pp. 1–49, 64–78, 79–130, and *passim*.

Nicephorus Emperor so as to exclude Aetius' brother Leo from the throne. Nicephorus promised Irene the right of asylum in the palace of Eleutherius if she would show him where she had hidden the royal treasury. She complied with his request. But her aptitude for intrigue was well known, and she appears to have made an actual attempt at a *coup d'état*. She was therefore banished, first to the island of Principo and then to Lesbos, where she died on 9 August 803.

Despite the hostility of Theophanes,[1] who, like most of the authorities for this period, resented the overthrow of the 'pious' Empress, it is obvious that the Emperor Nicephorus I, a descendant of an Arabian king, Jaballah of Ghassan, was a man of vigour and character, sincerely determined to repair the damage done to the Empire by Irene's selfishness and incompetence. A strong ruler and zealous exponent of Byzantine absolutism, he governed both Church and State with an iron hand. Although his reign (802–11) ended in a tragic defeat and the annihilation of a powerful Byzantine army, he made a valiant and intelligent effort to repair the borders of the Empire that Irene had allowed to crumble, and to institute a number of necessary reforms in administration and ecclesiastical policy.

But before he could turn to these matters he had, like most Emperors of Byzantium, to crush rival claimants to the throne, in his case two in number—Bardanes Turcus in 803, and Arsaber in 808. Taking advantage of popular sympathy after his overthrow of Bardanes Turcus, Nicephorus made his son Stauracius co-Emperor in December 803. Four years later he joined Stauracius in marriage to Theophano, an Athenian lady related to Irene, who had been chosen from among the loveliest women of the Empire in a 'bride show', regardless of the fact that she was not a virgin, and was reputedly less beautiful than two of the rival contestants whom Nicephorus had chosen for his own delectation.

From the beginning of his reign Nicephorus resolved to pay no more tribute to the enemies of the Empire. But he was no match for Hārūn ar-Rashīd, who invaded Asia Minor in 806 with over 135,000 men, took Heraclea, captured a number of other forts, including Tyana (where he erected a mosque), exacted an annual tribute of 30,000 (Arab sources say 50,000) *nomismata*, and raided Cyprus. He would have reaped an even greater harvest but for dissension within the Arab Empire, which gave peace to Byzantium on this front for

---

[1] Even the special court Nicephorus set up in the palace of Magnaura for the redress of grievances was condemned by Theophanes as a device to defraud the wealthy.

several years (808–29). Equally unsuccessful were Nicephorus' efforts to improve the situation in the West, which ended in the temporary loss to the Franks of Venice, Liburnia, and the Byzantine holdings on the Dalmatian coast (810).

Nicephorus was more fortunate in his campaign against the Slavs in the western Peloponnese, which they had invaded and partly dominated (possibly from 587, as the Chronicle of Monemvasia indicates). The length and importance of the Slav occupation of the Peloponnese has been disputed from the time of Fallmerayer (d. 1861), who contended that the Slav invasions of the sixth century resulted in the obliteration of the stock of ancient Greece, so that the modern Greeks are not of Hellenic origin at all, but descendants of the medieval Slavs. This radical hypothesis has been rejected, but the presence of a considerable number of Slavs in the Peloponnese during the middle ages cannot be doubted. A substantial force of them, aided by Muslims from Africa, strongly attacked Patras in 805, and were overwhelmingly defeated, probably in part with the aid of troops from the theme of the Peloponnese. This victory strengthened the position of the Greek population in the Balkan peninsula and enabled Nicephorus to continue the reorganisation of Greece which had been begun at the end of the eighth century with the creation of the themes of Macedonia (between 789 and 802) and the Peloponnese (between 783 and 805). Nicephorus made a contribution of his own by adding three themes, one of which was certainly Cephalonia (comprising the Ionian islands, in 809 or before) and the others probably Thessalonica and Dyrrachium. The result was a consolidation of Byzantine control over Greece, especially on the Aegean and Adriatic coasts.

Nicephorus' chief objective, however, to which his victory over the Slavs was a necessary prelude, was the conquest of Bulgaria, whose growing power gravely threatened the security of the Empire. He made two fruitless attempts to invade Bulgaria in 807 and 808, but Krum, the new and aggressive Bulgar Khan, destroyed the town of Sardica (Sofia). Nicephorus could only retaliate by a quick raid on Pliska, the Bulgarian capital, and by rebuilding Sardica (809). The Empire, in the state of collapse in which Irene had left it, was clearly too weak to deal decisively with the Bulgars or its other external enemies.

Nicephorus therefore resolved upon a programme of stern fiscal and military reform, which was bitterly denounced by the Byzantine chroniclers, though it seems to have been justified in the circumstances. About the year 810 he transferred large numbers of his subjects from every theme of the Empire to 'Sclavinia' (the area in the Balkans dominated by Slav population), and provided that poor men should be fitted out for military duty by their neighbours, who were required to pay 18½ *nomismata* for each soldier thus equipped and to assume responsibility jointly (ἀλληλεγγύως) for the taxes of the troops recruited.[1] Having dealt thus with the military situation, he proceeded to legislate on financial matters, which were his principal concern. He began by ordering a general review and increase of tax assessments, accompanied by a fee of two *keratia* (= one *miliaresion*, or one-twelfth of a *nomisma*), and cancelling all tax exemptions. Next he levied a hearth-tax (καπνικόν) upon each family,[2] which was to be paid, plus arrears from the first years of his reign, by all serfs, whether they were attached to property belonging to monasteries, charitable institutions, or churches, which Irene had presumably exempted from this levy. Moreover, he took over some of the richest ecclesiastical properties, but the foundations thus diminished in size were nevertheless compelled to pay the entire tax that would have been due before expropriation.

Then, to penalise the tax-delinquents of the provinces, he seized the wealth of subjects who had suddenly become affluent, and demanded payment from all who had found jars of any kind on their land within the last twenty years, on the assumption that these vessels had been filled with coins.[3] In addition, he taxed purchasers of domestic slaves who did not pay duty thereon at the customs house at Abydus at the rate of two *nomismata* per head (approximately 10 per cent[4]). As most of these provisions show, Nicephorus had resolved to prevent the accumulation of great riches in private hands. This purpose is even more clearly revealed in the legislation which forbade the lending of money at interest except by the state,[5] and compelled shipowners, especially on the coast of Asia Minor, not only to buy at officially determined prices some of the lands that had been confiscated by the crown, but also to borrow twelve pounds of gold from the government at 16⅔ per cent interest, plus certain other charges.[6] With the same ends in view, Nicephorus imposed strict regulation (and presumably taxation) upon sales of livestock and

---

[1] *DR*, 372, 373.

[2] *DR*, 374. This measure, now first mentioned in a Byzantine source, goes back in this form to the seventh century, and is nothing but a kind of head-tax, which is of even greater antiquity. Cf. Theophanes, pp. 486 f.; G. I. Bratianu, *Etudes byzantines d'histoire économique et sociale*, pp. 183 f.

In the article cited above (p. 63, n. 1), Ahrweiler contends (pp. 24 ff.) that, in economic policy, the iconoclasts favoured the lower classes and the rural areas, and that the iconophiles, on the contrary, granted special concessions to the urban merchants and the wealthy landowners. But the programme of the Emperor Nicephorus I, who was an iconophile, does not support this generalisation.

[3] *DR*, 376. [4] *DR*, 377.
[5] *DR*, 381. [6] *DR*, 379.

agricultural produce, harassed the wealthy by confiscation and penalties, instructed his officials in the themes to treat bishops and clergy 'like slaves', quartered troops in episcopal and monastic houses, and sequestered ecclesiastical silver and gold.

These and other measures bear witness to dire financial urgency and an Emperor of strong will who did not shrink from unpopular fiscal remedies in the national interest. They also demonstrate that an orthodox ruler could be as harsh to the Church and the monasteries as the iconoclasts, whose hostility to images, it has often been thought, was prompted by the desire to curb the power and limit the wealth of certain monastic institutions. Actually, the vast and expanding holdings of ecclesiastical foundations excited the envy and aroused the fears of iconoclast and orthodox alike, the latter of whom had as much reason to be apprehensive of the independent spirit and mighty forces at the disposal of the Studite monks, for example, as the most rabid iconoclast.

After allowing what he considered to be sufficient time for this programme to take effect, Nicephorus set out for Bulgaria (811) with a formidable array of troops from Thrace and Asia Minor. As soon as he saw them, Krum sued for peace, but Nicephorus ignored Krum's offer, easily took possession of Pliska and the Bulgarian palace, and again refused to discuss terms. This time, however, the Bulgarians sealed off the passes leading out of the mountain defile in which the Byzantine army had carelessly encamped, and managed this so effectively that Nicephorus was reported to have said, 'Even if we took wing, none of us could hope to escape destruction'.[1] They then swooped down upon the trapped Byzantines and butchered the entire force, including the Emperor and many of his chief officers. Krum cut off the Emperor's head, and after exhibiting it on a stake for several days, had the skull covered with silver and used it as a drinking bowl. The Byzantine army had not suffered such a disaster since the battle of Adrianople (378), which had cost the life of the Emperor Valens.

Although Nicephorus had had to concern himself primarily with the defence and rehabilitation of the Empire, he was by no means indifferent to theology. He loyally followed the decision of 787, but he was unsympathetic to the extremist Studites and their violent partisans. On the death of Tarasius in 806, therefore, the Emperor selected as Patriarch another moderate, the layman Nicephorus (806-15), despite the bitter but ineffective opposition of Theodore, abbot of the famous monastery of Studius. Similarly, he convoked a synod in 806, which rehabilitated the priest Joseph (who had

---

[1] Theophanes, p. 490.

been excommunicated by Tarasius about 797 for having married Constantine VI to Theodote in 795) and pronounced the marriage to have been valid. This decision was confirmed by the synod of 809, which authorised bishops to grant dispensation from the canons and decreed that the Emperor was not bound by the law of the Church.[1] But the Studites, who resisted every encroachment by the Emperor upon the ecclesiastical sphere, bitterly attacked these rulings and were therefore sent into exile. They could not charge Nicephorus with being an iconoclast, but they did criticise him for his unwillingness to convert iconoclasts by force, and for his friendly relations with the Paulicians and the Athingani, whose magical rites and incantations they accused him of having adopted in the course of his campaign against Bardanes Turcus. They even appealed to Pope Leo III to reverse the decrees of Nicephorus' councils.

Under Nicephorus, as these events show, it became even clearer than before that the extremists would oppose an orthodox Emperor just as energetically as if he were a heretic, unless he accepted their doctrine of the complete autonomy of the Church and yielded to their dictation in all ecclesiastical matters. Since they hardly ever found such complaisance on the part of an Emperor (Michael I, the sole exception in the period from 717 to 843, is practically unique in Byzantine history in this respect), they were driven increasingly to appeal for the intervention of the Pope, who represented the authority of the Church and was, it must be added, too remote to impose limitations upon them, even if he chose to do so. From the ecclesiastical point of view the Studite position was, perhaps, sounder than that of moderates like the Patriarchs Tarasius and Nicephorus, whose amenability to imperial dictation led them to a number of inconsistencies. For the extremists realised that a resolute Emperor, if unrestrained, could make substantial changes even in the fundamental creed of the Church. It has been argued that iconoclasm was overturned in the end because the defenders of the images (monks, women and devout folk) were in the majority. But this is difficult to prove, and the history of Byzantium shows that the Emperors had the power to initiate changes in the doctrine and practice of the Church. It was for this reason that the extremists struggled so intensely, and unsuccessfully, to impose limits upon the Emperor's sovereignty and to establish the principle that it did not extend to jurisdiction over the Church.

After the death of Nicephorus I, the Studites had a brief moment of ascendancy under Michael I Rangabe (811–13), who was proclaimed Emperor at the very time that his predecessor and brother-in-law,

[1] *MPG*, xcix, 1017D–1020A.

Stauracius, the short-lived son of Nicephorus, was planning to have him blinded. But the Patriarch and the chief men of the state had already decided to force Stauracius, who had been grievously wounded in Bulgaria and could not expect to live very long (he died on 11 January 812), to abdicate in favour of Michael, his sister Procopia's husband. Michael seemed to them more suitable because he was in good health and appeared more amenable to control.

The event proved them to have been good judges of Michael's character, for he submitted meekly to ecclesiastical direction and showed no independence of mind. At the request of the Patriarch Nicephorus, he signed a pledge to preserve the orthodox faith inviolate and to abstain from inflicting corporal punishment upon laymen or clergy.[1] Likewise, he annulled the councils which had rehabilitated the priest Joseph, and recalled Theodore the Studite from exile, along with the latter's uncle Plato and brother Joseph, the Archbishop of Thessalonica. Then, accepting the Studite line of reconciliation with Rome, he permitted the Patriarch Nicephorus, who had previously been forbidden to do so, to dispatch the customary synodical letter of enthronement to Pope Leo III, and sought a Frankish bride for his son Theophylact, whom he had crowned co-Emperor. He was even persuaded by Nicephorus to decree the death penalty for the Paulicians and Athingani in Phrygia and Lycaonia, although in the end he followed the counsel of those who urged mitigation of this harsh punishment, so that the heretics might have an opportunity for repentance. But he also placated the extremists by ordering some executions.

Finally he yielded, as Nicephorus had evidently been prepared to do at the time of his death, to Charlemagne's demands for recognition of the imperial title of 800.[2] He had no alternative, since the Byzantine forces, demoralised after the disaster of 811, and still under pressure from Krum, were in no position to contemplate a new naval expedition to Italy. Moreover, the Franks offered to return Venice, along with the maritime cities of Istria, Liburnia (i.e. Croatia), and Dalmatia to Byzantium and asked in exchange nothing but the right to use a single word, βασιλεύς (Emperor), in official documents. This was indeed a high price from the Frankish point of view, but so powerful was the medieval conception of the unity of the Roman Empire and of the legitimacy of the claim of the Byzantine Emperors to be its sole heirs and custodians that Charlemagne was eager to pay it in order to acquire formal endorsement of his right to the succession. The Byzantines accepted Charlemagne's terms, and Michael's envoys acclaimed Charlemagne as Emperor in both Greek and Latin

---

[1] *DR*, 384.   [2] *DR*, 385.

at Aachen in 812.[1] Thus the fiction of the unity of the Empire was outwardly preserved, just as if East and West did not really form two separate, dissimilar Empires,[2] with Charlemagne the undisputed monarch of all continental western Europe, except for the Iberian peninsula and the few Byzantine outposts in Italy. Still, the Byzantines never regarded him or his successors as the peers of the Byzantine Emperors, and designated their own ruler henceforth not merely as Emperor but as 'Emperor of the Romans' ($\beta \alpha \sigma \iota \lambda \epsilon \grave{\upsilon} s \ \tau \hat{\omega} \nu \ \text{'}\text{P} \omega \mu \alpha \acute{\iota} \omega \nu$).

Preoccupied with theological and dynastic matters, Michael expended vast sums in donatives to all classes of society, especially to the clergy. But these funds might better have been devoted to the defences of the Empire, which was at the mercy of the triumphant Krum, who in June 812 seized Develtus, a fortified town on the Gulf of Burgas facing across the Black Sea, a few miles south of Anchialus, and removed its population to Bulgaria. When Michael was prevented by a mutiny from pursuing Krum, panic spread through the cities of Thrace and Macedonia. The inhabitants of important citadels like Anchialus, Berroea and many others, though not attacked, were so intimidated by the spectre of the invincible Krum that they fled from their homes in terror, and the colonists settled along the Strymon (Sclavinia) by Nicephorus I took the opportunity to return to their homelands. Simultaneously, Michael had to face a new plot organized by admirers of Constantine V, who attributed the latter's victories to his iconoclastic policy, and the military disasters of the last few years to the restoration of the icons. Seeking a new repudiation of the images by an oecumenical council and a revival of the anti-monastic measures of the iconoclasts, the conspirators planned to establish one of Constantine's five blinded sons, at the time imprisoned on Panormus, one of the Princes Islands, upon the throne. But Michael quickly subdued the rebels and exiled the unfortunate sons of Constantine V once more, this time to Aphusia.

Krum demanded confirmation of a treaty that had probably been concluded between Constantine V and the Bulgarian Khan Kormisoš, and threatened that if the Byzantines did not meet his terms he would make an assault upon Mesembria, a strongly fortified city situated on a peninsula, a short distance north of Anchialus. While the Byzantine peace party, led by the Patriarch Nicephorus and the higher clergy, argued against the partisans of war, headed by Theodore the Studite and his monks, who were unwilling, on scrip-

---

[1] The exchange of treaties was not completed until the time of Leo V and Louis the Pious.

[2] In a letter to Michael I Charlemagne refers to his desire for 'pacem inter orientale atque occidentale imperium', *Ep. Merowingici et Karolini Aevi*, ii, p. 556/8f. (*MGH, Ep.* iv); cf. *ibid.* p. 547/15–18.

tural grounds, to hand back deserters as the treaty required, Krum took Mesembria (5 November 812), along with vast treasures, including great stores of gold and silver, thirty-six bronze tubes for the discharge of 'Greek fire', the chief weapon in the Byzantine armoury, whose composition was a closely guarded secret, and a great supply of the vital substance itself.

In the following year, after some successes, Michael suffered a defeat on 22 June 813 at Versinicia, near Adrianople, which was apparently engineered by Leo the Armenian, the general of the Anatolikon theme, who in this way forced the Emperor from the throne, which he himself then ascended.

III. THE SECOND ICONOCLASTIC CONTROVERSY (813–42) AND THE FINAL RESTORATION OF THE IMAGES (843)

Leo V the Armenian (813–20) was chosen as Emperor by the iconoclastic themes of Asia Minor to reorganise the defences of the Empire, which had been grossly neglected and mismanaged by his predecessors, and to overthrow the icons. In temperament and background he was much like Leo III, whom he consciously imitated, even to the extent of changing the name of his eldest son from Symbatius to Constantine, to emphasise the parallel. His first task was to meet a determined attack upon Constantinople launched by the Bulgarians six days after his coronation. Infuriated by Leo's treacherous attempt to assassinate him during an armistice, Krum pillaged, looted and burned at will in the suburbs of the city, though he could not penetrate the walls, and finally transferred his operations to Adrianople, which he captured. A Byzantine offer for peace was rejected, but Leo won a victory at Mesembria in the autumn of 813. The next year, as he was amassing a great force splendidly equipped with siege engines of the latest type, Krum died suddenly (14 April 814) of a ruptured blood vessel. A peace of thirty years was then arranged (815–16) with his son Omortag, a skilful warrior, who sought security on the Byzantine front so that he might go to the defence of his western provinces, then imperilled by Frankish expansion. The treaty between the two parties defined the Bulgaro-Byzantine border by a line, which the Bulgarians were empowered to fortify by a rampart and trench, the so-called Great Fence, running westward through Develtus to Macrolivada (between Adrianople and Philippopolis), and thence north to Mt Haemus.[1]

These arrangements in the Balkans and the preoccupation of the Arabs with their own domestic problems made it possible for Leo to

[1] *DR*, 393.

devote himself to the rebuilding of the cities in Thrace and Macedonia which the Bulgars had destroyed. He also turned to the revival of iconoclasm, for which his reign is chiefly memorable. He had apparently given the Patriarch Nicephorus some kind of assurance concerning his orthodoxy.[1] But, like many others, he was convinced that the iconoclastic policy of Leo and Constantine was pleasing in the sight of God and accounted for their success in warfare, and that the military failures of the 'orthodox' Emperors like Irene, Constantine VI, Nicephorus I and Michael I were proof of divine disapproval of the images. This notion was widespread, and in the spring of 814 Leo set up a commission headed by the scholar John the Grammarian (Hylilas) to prepare an exhaustive argument in favour of the iconoclastic theology. But Nicephorus, the Patriarch, refused to consider the question since the images had the irrevocable sanction of the Seventh General Council, nor would he yield to the Emperor's suggestion that those that were hung low should be removed. Leo attempted to persuade a convocation of bishops to proscribe the use of icons, and warned them that he would not tolerate disobedience; but many spoke out courageously, and Theodore the Studite protested that the Emperor had no right to intervene in ecclesiastical affairs, responsibility for which was reserved exclusively to the clergy.

After some further negotiation, a synod was convoked; Nicephorus was deposed in March 815, and on 1 April Theodotus Cassiteras was consecrated Patriarch. A second iconoclastic council then met in the church of St Sophia, revoked the decision of 787, reaffirmed the iconoclastic decrees of the Council of 754, and forbade the manufacture or use of images, which, however, it was agreed, should not be regarded as idols.[2] The iconoclasts advanced no new doctrine and only repeated the principal arguments of their predecessors, but there was some originality in the works of Nicephorus and Theodore the Studite, the two main champions of the use of images. Theodore annoyed Leo greatly by his attempts to secure papal intervention, and was banished along with many others. Some of his most refractory supporters were put to death.

On Christmas Eve 820 Michael, an old comrade in arms of the Emperor, was convicted of treason. Michael had fought with Leo on the side of the usurper Bardanes Turcus, and had then joined him in deserting Bardanes to support Nicephorus in 803. He was now sentenced by the Emperor to be bound to an ape and cast into the furnace which heated the baths of the palace. But as he lay in prison on the night before Christmas his friends acted swiftly. Dressed in clerical robes, they entered the palace chapel with the

---

[1] *DR*, 386.　　　　[2] *DR*, 394.

choristers on Christmas morning, and murdered Leo in the middle of the Christmas service.

Leo had proved to be an astute commander and shrewd administrator devoted to the welfare of the state, and the party which overthrew him did not object to him on theological grounds; Michael II (820–9) was also an iconoclast, though a moderate one. A rude professional soldier from Amorium in Phrygia, he had nevertheless considerable strength of character and much practical good sense. His family, the Amorian or Phrygian dynasty (820–67), served the Empire well, despite a number of military defeats, and laid the foundation, especially during the reign of his grandson Michael III (842–67), for the brilliant achievements of the Macedonians.

Michael II inherited a civil war, which had begun in Asia Minor during the last days of Leo V under the leadership of Thomas the Slavonian (820–3). Thomas, who was apparently of Slav origin, raised the standard of revolt, claiming to be Constantine VI, the son of Irene. Almost immediately he attracted a large following, which included some partisans of the images (but not the Studites or the people of Constantinople), the Paulicians, the lower social classes, the dissident and the oppressed, discontented racial and ethnic groups, the imperial tax-gatherers (who provided the necessary funds), and all the Byzantine military forces in Asia Minor, except for the Armeniakon and Opsikion themes, whose generals, Olbianus and Katakylas, remained faithful to Michael. In addition, the rebel leader concluded an alliance with the Caliph al-Ma'mūn (813–33), by which he secured a powerful army. Between 821 and 823 Thomas prevailed in Asia Minor and blockaded Constantinople by land and sea. But the capital put up a stout resistance, the imperial navy was victorious in two important engagements (822), and the Bulgarians under Khan Omortag shattered the rebel forces in a battle at Keduktos. These blows, especially the last, broke the spirit of Thomas' army, and the entire movement collapsed, but not until the strength and prosperity of the Empire had been gravely undermined.

It is not surprising therefore that Michael was unable to prevent the loss of Crete (*c.* 828), which fell to Arab refugees from persecution at the hands of al-Ḥakam, the Umayyad ruler of Spain. Similar weakness was also responsible for the success of Arabs from Africa in establishing themselves in Sicily (827–9) with the aid of a Byzantine admiral Euphemius, who had aspired to the purple but was murdered by the citizens of Castrogiovanni (Castrum Ennae) in 828. After considerable warfare, the Arabs had been confined to two towns, Mineo (Menae) and Mazara, at opposite ends of the island; but these, insignificant as they were in themselves, formed a foothold for subsequent conquest. These two strategic islands, Crete and Sicily, whose loss reveals the weakness of the Byzantine navy at this time, served the Arabs as bases for launching raids against Italy, the Balkans, and Asia Minor. The Byzantines made many counter-attacks, but Sicily was lost permanently, and Crete was not retaken until 961.[1]

Despite the support Thomas had received in Thrace from partisans of the images, Michael, though an iconoclast by personal conviction, was by no means moved to take violent measures against them, and even decided that persecution was unwise. He released all who had been imprisoned because of their devotion to the images, recalled the exiles, including the former Patriarch Nicephorus and Theodore the Studite, and granted complete freedom of conscience, especially outside Constantinople, so far as this could be arranged without any public manifestation of change. But he refused to remove the legal ban on the public use of images or to reappoint Nicephorus to the patriarchal throne, except on condition that there be no discussion for or against images, and no reference to the councils of 754, 787 and 815. This did not please the Studites, who refused to accept Michael's proposal for a conference at which the whole subject might be re-examined, and replied that the problem could best be solved by appeal to Rome. When Michael saw that the pro-image party was inflexible and that Nicephorus would not accept his terms, he appointed the bishop Antony Cassimatas, Leo's iconoclastic adviser, to fill the vacancy left by the death of Theodotus (815–21).

In 824 Michael once more suggested a meeting of the two theological parties. But Theodore rejected any compromise which did not contemplate a new general council or a synod to be held under Nicephorus as Patriarch, and stressed, as before, the primacy of the Roman See in the adjudication of all ecclesiastical and dogmatic questions, openly preferring in such matters the authority of Rome, as a sacerdotal institution, to that of the Emperor. The future Patriarch Methodius also represented this point of view and so infuriated Michael by actively sponsoring it that he was flogged and banished to a prison in Nicomedia, thus providing the sole instance of religious persecution in Michael's reign.

Michael then decided to approach Rome through Louis the Pious, to whom, in 824, he sent four ambassadors bearing gifts for the Pope and a long letter outlining his theological position. In this document, which is addressed condescendingly 'Hludovico glorioso regi Francorum et Langobardorum, vocato eorum imperatori' ('To Louis the glorious king of the Franks and of the Lombards, who is called their Emperor'),[2] he expressed his belief in the six general councils and

---

[1] For another view see below, p. 106.   [2] Mansi, xiv, 417–22; *DR*, 408.

veneration for the relics of the saints. He also summarised the abuses associated with the use of images, which, he objected, were honoured by candles and incense, prayed to, used as baptismal sponsors for children, and intimately associated with the celebration of the Eucharist, which was often dispensed from icons or mixed with scrapings therefrom. Taking no offence at Michael's reluctance to address him unequivocally as Emperor, Louis summoned a synod, which met in Paris in 825, condemned the worship of images, criticised Pope Hadrian I for approving the creed of 787, and also censured the iconoclasts for not tolerating the presence of images in the churches. This verdict, which merely ratified that of the Council of Frankfurt (794), must have been a disappointment for Michael. For he had no doubt hoped to persuade the West to sanction his attitude towards images and thus to undermine the position of the Studites. After his failure to do so, he seems to have taken no further steps to reach an understanding, and merely adhered to the policy of toleration which he had previously adopted.

Michael's son, Theophilus (829–42), unlike his uncultivated and somewhat boorish father, was a man of refinement with a taste for the arts, who had had the advantage of being tutored by the famous John the Grammarian, one of the leading scholars of his day. He had been associated with Michael as co-Emperor apparently as early as 821, and continued along the lines laid down by his father, except that he abandoned the latter's tolerant attitude and resumed active persecution. His military defeats were part of his inheritance, and the full meaning of the loss of Crete and Sicily became clear after his accession to the throne.

Though his reign was not distinguished by any achievement of outstanding significance, he seems to have been very sensitive to the demands of justice, and even went so far as to order the execution of the men who murdered Leo V, dissociating himself in this way from the crime to which, through his father, he owed his throne. He took pride in redressing grievances, and in the *Timarion*, a work of the twelfth century, he is represented as one of the judges of the underworld.

More significant than the Emperor's interest in judicial problems were the steps he took to strengthen the defences of the Empire. He made many notable additions to the walls of Constantinople, but his most important innovation was the creation of three new themes and three new military defence districts known as κλεισοῦραι (mountain passes). The new themes were constituted around the Black Sea, two on its southern shores, Paphlagonia and Chaldia (the north-eastern portions of the Bucellarion and Armeniakon themes respectively), and one on the north coast, Cherson, in South Russia, comprising the so-called *klimata*. The military defence districts (Charsianon, Cappadocia and Seleucia) were set up along the Arab frontier in the mountains, stretching south-west from the Armeniakon theme to the Mediterranean, just north of Cyprus, and later became themes. At about the time that Cherson became a theme (833), Byzantine engineers built a fort named Sarkel for their allies, the Khazars, at the mouth of the Don, which presaged increasing Byzantine interest in this region in the years to come.

On the field of battle Theophilus' record, apart from a few notable victories, was rather dismal. He was victorious in a number of operations against the Arabs in 831, and in 837 he captured Zapetra, Arsamosata, and Melitene. But Panormus (Palermo) in Sicily fell to the Arabs in 831, and the whole of the western part of the island was in enemy hands by 841. In 838 al-Mu'taṣim took Ancyra and Amorium, the birthplace of Michael II and a great citadel, which would not have fallen if it had not been betrayed. Literally sick with worry, Theophilus appealed to Louis the Pious and 'Abd ar-Raḥmān II, the Umayyad ruler of Spain, for aid against the western Muslims (839).[1] Both replied graciously but sent no reinforcements, and the Arabs not only captured Taranto in southern Italy (839), thus splitting Calabria in two, but defeated the Venetian fleet that had been sent out to dislodge them (840). In the following year, however, Byzantine troops occupied Adata, Germanicea and part of Melitene, and in this way got al-Mu'taṣim to consent to a truce.[2]

Despite the bitterness and intensity of the war with the Arabs, Theophilus was not hostile to their cultural influences and seems to have followed Arab models in the construction of the great palaces he built and splendidly adorned. But his fondness for the arts in no way disposed him to relax his father's opposition to the cult of images, against which he had a strong personal bias, intensified by his close association with the iconoclast John the Grammarian, who became Patriarch in 832. Theophilus made no changes in iconoclastic doctrine, but he issued an edict forbidding the production of images[3] and severely punished all who ignored it. The most celebrated martyrs of the period were Theodore and Theophanes, two Palestinian brothers, who had been persecuted under Leo V for their devotion to the images. They were so influential that, after having subjected them to imprisonment, flogging and exile, Theophilus recalled them to Constantinople in the hope of persuading them to denounce the use of icons. After failing to convince them, he had them beaten and caused twelve insulting iambic verses to be branded on their foreheads, which earned them the name of the *graptoi* (the 'inscribed'). Another

[1] *DR*, 438, 439. [2] *DR*, 441. [3] *DR*, 427.

of his victims, a monk called Lazarus, who was the most famous icon-painter of his day, had his hands burnt with red-hot rods for persisting in the manufacture of icons. It has been assumed that Theophilus limited the enforcement of his legislation against images to the city of Constantinople and that the iconoclastic movement had been losing strength since 815. These assumptions may be well founded, but they cannot easily be demonstrated, and do not account for the fact that iconoclasts were still active more than a generation after the final victory of the pro-image party.

Theophilus died on 20 January 842, and his wife Theodora and two regents assumed responsibility of government for the young Michael III (842–67). A little over a year later it was decided to revoke the iconoclastic decrees, and confirm the canons of the Second Council of Nicaea. This was done by a synod which met in March 843,[1] deposed the Patriarch John, who could not be made to accept the images, and elected Methodius. The new Patriarch had suffered for his views under both Michael II and Theophilus, but he was careful to omit from the list of heretics denounced by the new Council the name of the late Emperor, with whom after his imprisonment he had been on good terms. The restoration of the images was celebrated on the first Sunday of Lent (11 March 843) as the Feast of Orthodoxy. The iconoclasts did not disappear from the Church until the end of the ninth century, but they were never strong enough to secure a revival of the dogmatic decrees of 754 and 815.

The decision of the Council of 843 represents the defeat of the extremists no less than of the iconoclasts. The extremists had the satisfaction of witnessing the overthrow of their heretical opponents; but the moderates, like the new Patriarch Methodius, prevailed over zealots of both sides. Nevertheless, these results were achieved only by an autocratic act of the imperial authorities. Only in the matter of union with Rome were the Emperors never able to force their will on the Church, notwithstanding their most strenuous efforts. It is all the more significant, therefore, that this period ended with the triumph of the Hellenic pro-image theology over the iconoclastic doctrine of Asia Minor. For this triumph of the Greek spirit is the counterpart on the intellectual plane of the triumphant repulse of the Arabs in the eighth century. It symbolises the character of the Byzantine Church and Empire; for both, despite certain alien elements in their constitution, became more and more Greek in essence as they repudiated eastern influences, and both drew further away from their counterparts in the West, the Roman Church and the Carolingian Empire, neither of which they could any longer hope to control.

[1] *DR*, 446.

CHAPTER IV

THE AMORIANS AND MACEDONIANS 842-1025

It used to be customary to identify the epoch of the Macedonian dynasty with the apogee of Byzantium, contrasting its splendours with the 'poverty' of the time of the Amorians. But historians have at length revised this judgement. There can be no denying the glory of the Macedonians, but their achievement was in fact the fulfilment of a design conceived, and even in part realised, between 842 and 867.

I. AN UNAPPRECIATED GREAT STATESMAN: ST THEOCTISTUS THE LOGOTHETE

'Michael III reigned for a quarter of a century', wrote Bury in 1912, 'but he never governed. During the greater part of his life he was too young; when he reached a riper age he had neither the capacity nor the desire.' [1] It is, however, now admitted that one of the more serious failures of modern Byzantine historians has been the extent to which they have allowed themselves to be misled by sources substantially altered by historians biased in favour of the Macedonian dynasty, the Emperor Constantine Porphyrogenitus at their head. But it must be added that this falsification of the truth had begun well before 867; the men who were prominent during the personal rule of Michael III, and Bardas in particular, not content with the deposition of Theodora, sought also to disparage the achievements of the regency, showing especial animosity towards Theoctistus, Theodora's chief minister, whose rehabilitation must be our first concern. This might, in fact, have been achieved long since by church historians or *cultores sanctorum*, if the significance of a brief notice in the *Synaxarion* of Constantinople (under 20 November) concerning the martyrdom ($\check{\alpha}\theta\lambda\eta\sigma\iota\varsigma$) of 'Theoctistus, patrician and eunuch' under the Empress Theodora, had been perceived. It is known from the historians that Theoctistus, the powerful Logothete of the Drome and effective head of the council of regency under Theodora, was in fact both a eunuch and a patrician. His great authority in 842–3 had its origin not only in his record of loyal service under Theophilus but still more in the fact that it was he who had brought Michael II to the throne after the murder of Leo V, so that one might say that the

[1] J. B. Bury, *Eastern Roman Empire*, p. 154.

Amorians were indebted to him for their very creation as a dynasty. It was also due to him that the dynasty survived the ordeal, always a searching one at Byzantium, of the rule of a woman, as well as the reversal of imperial religious policy. But although Theoctistus' restoration of the icons was achieved without friction and with the acquiescence of the army (unlike Irene's which was hampered by military opposition), the history of this great deed has been obscured and distorted by Byzantine party quarrels, with the result that St Theodora, St Theoctistus and St Sergius Nicetiates have sometimes been denied credit for the decisive part they played in its execution. The surpassing skill with which the icons were restored, without any condemnation of the memory of Theophilus or of a largely heretical dynasty, was no doubt due to the wifely devotion of Theodora, who succeeded in getting the Patriarch to admit the repentance and pardon of her husband. But there was also the loyalty of Theoctistus, the servant of Michael II and Theophilus, who completely identified himself with the fortunes of the dynasty and of the army.

Theoctistus, in fact, hoped to save the dynasty by covering the army with glory. And this is the interpretation of the military events immediately following the first 'Feast of Orthodoxy' in March 843, given even by those sources most obviously poisoned by hatred and jealousy of the Logothete: Theoctistus' reconquest of Crete was to be a reparation for its loss by the Amorian heretics. But although this triumph is not disputed, the sources go on to say that Theoctistus forthwith returned to Constantinople, abandoning his army to the sword of the Saracens, and that his return was inspired by fear of a revolution against himself or Theodora. It is now known (the *Synaxarion* is once again the source) that on his return to Constantinople the Logothete left the *magister* Sergius Nicetiates behind as commander-in-chief. Moreover, it seems certain that the reconquest of Crete was no mere ephemeral and fruitless gesture, since a list of officers, which certainly belongs to the reign of Michael and Theodora, has mention of a governor of Crete (ἄρχων Κρήτης). So completely has the partisan spirit erased the memory of such undisputed triumphs that other naval and military operations of equal importance have also left no trace in Byzantine sources: the capture of Damietta on 22 May 853, for example, which is established beyond any doubt by two independent Arab sources, and is now further corroborated by a recently discovered papyrus, also of Arab origin.[1] And it is not merely

---

[1] The commander of the Byzantine fleet which captured Damietta was called Ibn Qatuna by the Arabs; he was not Sergius Nicetiates but the κοιτωνίτης or chamberlain (and eunuch) Damian—not to be confused with the Muslim admiral bearing the same name (see below, p. 130).

a question of the capture of Damietta, but also of the operations of three Byzantine fleets, comprising 300 vessels in all, which were in action in the Aegean and off the coast of Syria. Recent research has shed much light on the aggressive activities of Byzantine squadrons during the years 853–9; and the same administrative document which gives evidence of the reoccupation of the island of Crete also affords proof that the important island of Cyprus was in Byzantine hands in the time of Michael III and Theodora. It will thus be seen how far jealousy and partisanship succeeded down the centuries in depriving the epoch of Theodora, Theoctistus and Sergius, an epoch which can almost be described as a 'rule of the Saints', of its just title to fame.[1] In fact, Theoctistus must be credited with a quite prodigious activity: operations on a grand scale against the enemies of the Empire and a wise conduct of affairs in finance, administration and in religious and military matters. But this was not all; as was only to be expected, the magnificent and sophisticated Theophilus, himself an amateur of learning and literature, an artist in his own right and a lover of building, had interested his friend in advanced studies. It was Theoctistus who introduced into the palace and the patriarchal library the student of philosophy and philology who was later to be the instrument of Byzantium's greatest spiritual triumph, Constantine, the brother of Methodius, the two future apostles of the Slavs.

But this great minister who had such far-reaching plans was always in a precarious position, and from the time of the Cretan expedition of 843 there was continuous plotting against him at Constantinople. His enemies were to be found in many places. As between the parties, so long as the Patriarch Methodius was still alive, Theoctistus relied on the support of the moderates and like Methodius showed toleration towards the iconoclasts, under whom he had made his name. Later, however, like all insecurely established Byzantine rulers, together with Theodora he shifted to the right and brought to the patriarchal throne Ignatius, the eunuch son of Michael Rangabe, an ardent supporter of the icons, a patriarchal candidate at once imperial and ascetic, rigid in outlook and popular (Michael III called him 'the Patriarch of the people'). This appointment, although it made Theoctistus more acceptable in the eyes of some of the extremists, displeased Bardas, the leader of the moderate party. Bardas, a man of great intelligence and great ambition, was the brother of Theodora;

[1] The oft-repeated assertion that it was Basil who recaptured Cyprus from the Arabs is erroneous; the reoccupation in fact took place in 853, at the start of the attacks against Damietta and the Egyptian sea-board. On the Byzantine occupation of Cyprus, cf. Constantine VII, *De administrando imperio*, c. 47 (*DAI*, I, p. 225 and II, pp. 180–2).

since 843, Theoctistus had gradually been excluding him both from power and from the precincts of the palace. Still more serious, however, was the attitude of Ignatius towards Michael III. In 855 his mother was in the act of separating him from his mistress, Eudocia Ingerina, in order to marry him by force to another Eudocia, the daughter of Decapolites. The Patriarch Ignatius was also prepared to set himself up as an arbiter of morals, and publicly censured those of Bardas. There followed a series of *coups*, both in Church and State. Their chronology can now be clearly established, with the help of the *Synaxarion*, since the 'martyrdom' of St Theoctistus there noted at 20 November[1] must refer to the murder of Theoctistus by Bardas, authorised—even ordered—by Michael III on 20 November 855. Three or four months later Michael III was proclaimed Autocrator by a meeting of the Senate; his mother remained at the palace, dethroned but not yet enclosed in a convent.[2]

II. THE PERSONAL RULE OF MICHAEL III, 856–67

Michael III had as his advisers his two maternal uncles—Bardas, whom he created Caesar, and Petronas, whom he made Domestic of the Schools—as well as Photius, elevated to the Patriarchate in 858, and then in later years his great favourite and future murderer and successor, Basil the Macedonian. Despite his dynamic temperament, Michael in general contented himself with carrying out the programme bequeathed to him by Theodora and Theoctistus. And even when he appeared to be reversing their policy, as in ecclesiastical affairs where he favoured the moderate party and its distinguished leader Photius, it could be said that he was returning to the policy of 843–7, since Methodius, the Patriarch who had brought about the restoration of the icons, had been a member of the same party. It was only the fear of Bardas which had caused the regent to shift to the right and set the obstinate and bigoted monk Ignatius at the head of the Church. In this connection it can be said that the revolution in Church and State which took place from 855 to 858 represented a salutary reaction against extremism, all the more urgent in view of the fact that by his condemnation of Gregory Asbestas, the Bishop of Syracuse, and his following, Ignatius had created a danger-

---

[1] This date was uncertain until the discovery made by F. Halkin (cf. *B*, xxiv (1954), 11 ff.), and this has always been a source of confusion to historians of the period; cf. J. B. Bury, *Eastern Roman Empire*, app. vii, p. 469.

[2] The corrected chronology is as follows: murder of Theoctistus in 855, proclamation of Michael as sole Emperor in March 856, increasingly stringent measures against Theodora and her daughters in 856–7, expulsion of Theodora from the Palace in August–September 857, deposition of Ignatius in 858.

ous conflict within the Church and had provoked a still more serious disagreement with the Papacy. The election of Photius as Patriarch in 858 was in fact far from being intended as a further provocative gesture to Rome. In the judgement of those best qualified to judge, the election was canonical and the result of a compromise. No one protested against the fact that Photius, like his uncle the Patriarch Tarasius at the time of his election, was a layman or because he received all the orders of priesthood in the course of a single week. Moreover, Ignatius had resigned and had invited his friends to elect a successor. And although he later departed from this prudent position and allowed himself to be re-established as Patriarch by certain bishops and priests in the church of St Irene, this re-appointment was soon declared by a synod to be null and without effect. Moreover, in 861 the papal legates Radoald and Zacharias, sitting in judgement on Ignatius at Constantinople, declared his election irregular and that of Photius canonical. The fact that the Church of Constantinople recognised the right of the legates to judge Ignatius must have given pleasure to all supporters of the primacy of Rome. Had not a deputation of intransigent Ignatians arrived at Rome about 862, led by their fiery chief, Theognostus, and above all, had not Pope Nicholas suddenly resolved to make use of his power to reconsider the sentence of his legates in order to recover jurisdiction over Illyricum, it seems safe to assume that the cordial relations between Rome and Byzantium, between the Pope and the Patriarch, would never have been disturbed. 'The Photian affair' really only became shot through with venom later as a result of the rivalry between Rome and Byzantium for supremacy over the Bulgarian Church, and between 858 and 863 there was no reason to anticipate any serious quarrel between the Pope on the one side and the Emperor Michael and his Patriarch Photius on the other.

During the seven years between 856 and 863, in the military sense one of the most glorious epochs of Byzantine history, the military portion of the plan which Michael inherited from Theoctistus was carried out with brilliant effect: Amorium was indeed revenged. To appreciate this it is necessary once more to resort to the truthful— not to say candid—Arab sources, since the Greek sources have been systematically falsified.

The Continuator of Theophanes, speaking of the year 856, merely says: 'In this year the Domestic Petronas, *strategus* of the Thracesion theme, campaigned against the Arabs', making no mention of the outcome of the expedition. But Ṭabarī, whose account is fuller and more accurate than that of the Byzantines, admits that the Arabs and their Paulician allies met with a serious setback, and there is no reason to doubt him, since the Arabs were not in the habit of announcing imaginary defeats. Thus we learn that the army of Petronas, marching in the name of the young Emperor Michael III, not only reached the Euphrates, for the first time since the days of Theophilus, but even crossed the river, advancing a considerable distance beyond it, as far as Amida (Diyār-Bakr), and taking a large number of prisoners. Byzantium had indeed regained the offensive and the Byzantine general could deal with the enemy as he wished.

Three years later, says Ṭabarī, the Greeks made an incursion from the direction of Samosata and killed or captured about 500 persons. We know from the Byzantines that on this occasion the young Emperor himself was in command. This time the Macedonian 'historians' are not content with merely suppressing or masking information; they describe a defeat of Michael III which is sheer fabrication and which is related in terms identical with those describing a genuine defeat of Michael's father, Theophilus. But the truth, which is revealed by the Arabs, is also attested by the Greek popular epic. The first expedition, which reached the Euphrates and perhaps beyond it, was led by the young Michael riding at the head of his troops, a sight which must have fired one of his soldiers with the imagination which made him rightly see in these campaigns of 856–9 a glorious revenge for the shame of Amorium. There can be no doubt that the hero of one of the most famous ballads is called 'A(r)mouropoulos' in honour of the third representative of the house of Amorium. A poet of genuine inspiration describes, in the vernacular tongue which we know that Michael himself loved to speak, the victorious passage of the Euphrates in flood, contested by the Saracens, who were totally destroyed, with the exception of a man with one arm, an allusion to the familiar soubriquet of the Amir 'Amr Alaqta'. Moreover, inscriptions from Nicaea and Ancyra, dated 858 and 859 and already triumphal in tone, indicate that Michael III had made wise preparation for his victorious offensive by attending to the defences of the fortresses which would afford protection to the army in case of retreat. Simultaneously with these events, that is to say in June–July 859, the Byzantine fleet once more appeared before Damietta.

The final seal was set on the military superiority of Byzantium over the Arabs by the great and victorious encirclement achieved by Petronas in 863 which marks the apogee of the reign. The year 863 was, in fact, a year of two victories: the first was on 3 September, when 'Amr, Amir of Melitene, was slain in battle together with at least a thousand of his men, while the second took place between 18 October and 16 November, with the defeat at Mayyāfāriqīn of the Governor of Armenia, 'Alī ibn Yaḥyā, a battle which also ended in the death of the Arab commander.[1] These achievements greatly enhanced Michael III's prestige and had far-reaching effects: indeed the Byzantine triumph in Bulgaria in 864 would have been inconceivable had not the Muslim and Paulician armies been annihilated or hurled back into Cappadocia and beyond the Euphrates in the preceding year.

Just before these eastern campaigns the Empire had been threatened from the north when the first Russian attack on Constantinople was made, on 18 June 860. Michael, who had once more set out on campaign against the Arabs of Melitene and the Paulicians of Tephrice, received warning just in time from the Admiral Ooryphas and hastened back to the capital. The miraculous deliverance of the city from the Russian peril is well known. The homilies of Photius and one of his letters bear eloquent witness to the terror felt by the Byzantines at the approach of the fleet of *monoxyla* manned by the Scandinavian rulers of Kiev and their new Slav subjects, and to their pride in the preservation of the Christian Empire by the manifest intervention of the Mother of God. These sources also testify to the far-sighted wisdom of the great prelate who realised at once where the spiritual and political duty of State and Church now lay. The only answer to the danger presented by the barbarian enemies both old and new, the Bulgars and the Russians, emboldened as they were by the continuous warfare of the Empire with the Arabs and by the Paulician revolt, was in concentrated missionary effort, undertaken immediately, at the very moment when the reconquest of the Euphrates frontier, so auspiciously begun, was still in progress. This policy implied the application of the tried methods of Byzantine diplomacy. For centuries past the Empire had possessed potential allies in the region between the Volga and the Crimea in the Khazars, a Turkic people, who had on occasion even supplied Byzantine Emperors with their wives; the new Scandinavian rulers of Kiev were now trying to undermine the strength and influence of the Khazars by dissuading the Slavs from paying them tribute. It was to counter this move that Constantine,[2] philosopher and philologist and the most gifted of all the missionaries, was sent to Cherson and to the capital of the Khan of the Khazars. Constantine profited from his sojourn in a country which had been for more than half a century under predominantly Jewish influence by learning Hebrew and

---

[1] The exact locality of the battle of 3 September is obscured in the romantic versions of the Byzantine and Muslim historians, epic poets and hagiographers; but the principal engagement seems to have taken place at Marj al Usquf, between Nazianzus and Malakopia, in southern Cappadocia.

[2] Constantine is also known as Cyril; he took this name just before his death in a monastery in Rome in 869.

Syriac; he was also led by his perpetually alert curiosity to the discovery near Cherson of relics claimed to be those of Pope Clement, which in 867 or 868[1] he presented to Pope Hadrian II. He may not have achieved the political and religious objectives which were doubtless assigned to him on this mission, and the bishop who was dispatched to the Russians in the first seemingly auspicious dawn of Russian Christianity appears to have had little lasting success. But the fact remains that the conversion of the Bulgars by Byzantium was built on the solid foundations of the philological work carried out by the emissaries of Michael III and Photius, the 'Father translators' of the Slavonic Churches, all of them the spiritual offspring of Byzantium.

III. THE ADVERSE EFFECT OF THE BULGARIAN QUESTION ON THE QUARREL BETWEEN ROME AND BYZANTIUM

The ostensible purpose of the Council summoned by Photius in 861 was to effect the final condemnation of iconoclasm, with the implication that the credit for the final triumph of orthodoxy belonged to the period of the personal rule of Michael III, so that Theodora and Theoctistus were robbed of their chief title to fame, the re-establishment of orthodoxy in 843. But Photius' main objects in holding the Council were to consolidate his own position, to secure recognition from Rome and confirmation by Nicholas I's legates of the deposition of Ignatius. The legates readily lent themselves to these designs, and the Pope did not disavow their actions on their return; nevertheless, he reserved to himself the right of confirming their decision in the matter of Photius and Ignatius. The hardening of the Pope's attitude had a variety of causes: the arrival at Rome in 862–3 of Theognostus, the leader of the intransigent Ignatian party, and the pressing problem of Moravian and Bulgarian affairs, which for the Papacy implied the whole question of Illyricum.[2] The importunings of Theognostus, who pleaded the cause of Ignatius by furnishing information at variance with the account given by the legates; the hope of converting the Moravians, which seemed more likely to be achieved by the missionary works of Constantine (whom no one could consider an enemy of Rome) than by pressure exerted by German troops and the churches of Salzburg and Passau; and, finally, the attitude of Boris of Bulgaria, who was now in negotiation with Rome and in the act of allying himself with the Franks: all these considerations decided Nicholas against making a final ratifica-

---

[1] Ont he work of Constantine-Cyril and Methodius see also below: ch. XI, pp. 492 ff.
[2] On the Bulgarian problem see also below: ch. XI, pp. 496 ff.

tion of the decisions of the Council of Constantinople. At the Roman Council, held probably in August 863, Photius himself was deposed and Ignatius reinstated. But if, in 863, the Pope had thought that this aggressive attitude would undermine Photius' position or influence the policy of Michael III, he was seriously mistaken. Encouraged by the success of the Moravian mission, which seemed to give them an initial victory over the Franks, Michael and Photius settled the question of Illyricum by a brilliant *coup*. In 864, threatened by the Byzantine army and fleet, which the victory of 863 had made freely available, Boris capitulated, renounced his Frankish alliance and was baptised, Michael III standing as his god-father; in a letter written to the Pope in 865 Michael refused to reopen the case of Ignatius, denounced Theognostus and his fellow refugees, demanding their return to Constantinople, and altogether adopted a most haughty attitude, even going so far as to style Latin a barbarous and Scythian tongue. Nicholas' reply was equally insulting and contained a reassertion of the traditional and inalienable right of the Holy See to be governor 'super omnem terram, id est super omnem ecclesiam'. Only the end of the letter is more conciliatory, and the author no longer insists on the restitution of Illyricum. At that date Nicholas could not have anticipated the revolt of Boris against Byzantium, a revolt caused by Photius' obstinate refusal to grant the Bulgars a separate Patriarchate. This changed attitude of Boris, a change much in the interests of Rome, was only made known to the Pope in August 866, by the three boyar ambassadors Peter, John and Martin. To Nicholas, this turn of events seemed miraculous, and it was at this juncture that he sent to Bulgaria his skilfully composed *responsa*, a document revealing a perfect comprehension of the psychology and habits of neophytes; he sent also an embassy, which received the sworn oath of Boris to be for ever the faithful servant of St Peter. Encouraged by this striking success, Nicholas then wrote fresh letters to Michael III, Photius, Bardas, Theodora the Dowager-Empress, and Eudocia, Michael's wife.

Photius thought he could rely on spiritual weapons in his efforts to detach Boris from Rome. He decided to hold a Council. In his letter summoning the oriental Patriarchs, Photius announced that the object of the Council was first and foremost the condemnation of the false doctrines of the Frankish missionaries, in particular the Procession of the Holy Ghost from the Father and the Son, claiming that he had received from Italy a synodical letter of appeal against it. Finally, returning once again to the iconoclast question, the Council was to recognise the Second Council of Nicaea as the Seventh Oecumenical Council, a recognition hitherto consistently withheld by the West. Although the acts of the Council of 867 have not survived, we know that Pope Nicholas was tried and condemned and that at the last session Louis II and his wife Engelberga were given a great ovation, in the presence of Michael III and with his gracious acquiescence. This was the last official act of what might be called the personal policy of Michael III, which to the end followed the lead given by Photius. It is obvious that Michael III and Photius were trying to divide the West, setting the Emperor and the Empress against the Pope, and that they would even have liked to charge Louis II with the task of executing the sentence on Nicholas.[1] This adroit and audacious policy, which had the general effect of reconverting the Bulgars to their Byzantine allegiance, must certainly be attributed to Michael III and Photius rather than to Bardas, who was assassinated in April 866. As Dvornik has quite rightly pointed out, in rehabilitating Photius it is necessary also to rehabilitate Michael, at least politically, if not morally. Moreover, there can be no doubt that the more dramatic episodes in the Photian affair were materially affected by the vital problem of the relations between Byzantium and Bulgaria. A Christian but Roman Bulgaria, allied with the Franks, was a hundred times more dangerous to Byzantium than the pagan Bulgaria of the savage Krum. Even Ignatius himself, although the friend of Rome, was obliged to adopt towards Bulgaria the policy of his rival Photius. Nevertheless, Photius went too far. Today, the fatal importance attached for political reasons to the dangerous *Filioque* question appears quite misapplied. Nor was the condemnation of Nicholas sound diplomacy, for it brought Photius no advantage.[2] He would have done better to wait, since fate seemed to be on his side. Nicholas I died, and there was every prospect of a change of attitude at Rome, since Hadrian II, the new Pope, was seriously thinking of becoming more conciliatory towards Photius. But before any decision had been taken at Rome, a messenger arrived from Constantinople to announce that Michael III had been punished for his crimes by Basil I, and that the new Emperor had reinstated Ignatius on the patriarchal throne, following the instructions of Nicholas I.

IV. THE DOWNFALL OF MICHAEL III

Although the Roman army had reached and crossed the Euphrates, although the fleet dominated the waters of the Aegean and was threatening Egypt, it must not be forgotten that Crete, after its

---

[1] Cf. *GR*, 479, 482 and 484.
[2] Cf. F. Dvornik, *Photian Schism*, p. 130.

temporary occupation by Theoctistus and Sergius in 843, had been reconquered by the Arabs at a date now unknown. It seems that the Caesar Bardas was, quite justifiably, determined to repair this loss. In spring 866, after Easter (7 April), troops from various themes assembled at the mouth of the Meander. But Basil, who was now the great favourite with Michael, was jealous of the Caesar and was perhaps fearful lest this great campaign which was about to start should dangerously add to his prestige and authority, since Bardas was well loved by the soldiery. Basil, at Constantinople, had already won over the support of Symbatius, the Logothete of the Drome and son-in-law to Bardas, by promising him his father-in-law's title of Caesar. Rumours of Symbatius' promotion made Michael fear that it was Bardas who was plotting against him, with the result that he acquiesced in, or even encouraged, the murder of Bardas at Basil's own hands.

Constantinople learned the news of Bardas' murder (21 April 866) with stunned amazement; a month later (26 May) the capital witnessed the coronation of the favourite as Basileus. But this blood-stained tragedy was followed by an insurrection. Symbatius, who had not received his expected promotion to the rank of Caesar, himself headed the revolt, together with his friend Peganes. These events had greater repercussions, even outside the Empire, than one might believe merely from reading the Byzantine accounts. Mas'ūdī describes it as the last episode in the reign of Michael III and says that Michael's possession of the Empire was contested by an inhabitant of Amorium, one Ibn Bagrat, descendant of the ancient Emperors. It is alleged that Michael employed Muslim prisoners in the fight against him. According to the Greek sources the rebels had in fact risen only against Basil, which explains Michael's relative clemency, and also his displeasure with Basil, since he now had evidence of Basil's great unpopularity with the army, both officers and men.[1] Michael therefore now sought to rid himself of Basil; but he showed his disfavour too early, by investing a certain Basiliscianus with the purple boots. Basil lost no time in preparing for an ambush at St Mamas, a suburban imperial residence on the other side of the Golden Horn, in what is now Galata. Heavy with wine, Michael retired to his bedchamber. Slumber had hardly seized him when a band of men of threatening aspect forced their way into his apartment. They were a company of Armenians, led by Basil. The Emperor, who was still sodden with drink, roused himself, as though to witness in person the tragic ending of his life. The swords of the villains flashed and the

---

[1] On this revolt see N. Adontz, 'L'âge et l'origine de l'Empereur Basile Ier', *B*, IX (1934), 222 f. and 229.

unhappy victim fell. He had no proper obsequies until after the death of Basil, when his funeral was solemnly conducted at the Church of the Holy Apostles by the Emperor Leo VI.

V. THE ORIGINS OF BASIL I AND THE EARLY PART OF HIS REIGN

By the regicide of 24 September 867, Basil was firmly established on the throne to which he had just been elevated by his benefactor and victim, Michael III. Basil I, called 'the Macedonian', was the founder of a dynasty which was to last for almost two centuries, and which all writers during that long and glorious period covered with the incense of their praise. Basil himself had the good fortune of being lauded, in a suitably classical style, by the two most cultivated and learned of all the Byzantine Emperors, his son and successor, Leo, in a funeral oration, and his grandson Constantine Porphyrogenitus, in a biography which is famous. But neither Porphyrogenitus nor any other historian gives the name of Basil's father, nor is it to be found in any other record. This silence seems to prove that his origins were humble. His family was originally of Armenian descent settled near Adrianople, and was one of those taken prisoner by Krum, the Khan of the Bulgars, in 813, when he carried away ten thousand Armenian men, women and children captive to the Danube. This colony was then settled near the northern borders of Bulgaria, not far from the Hungarians; they took the name 'Macedonian' in memory of their birthplace, since this was the name given by the Byzantines to the theme which had Adrianople as its capital. During the reign of Theophilus, about 837–8, a Byzantine squadron which had penetrated up the Danube found that this northern march was temporarily denuded of Bulgar troops, and showed themselves willing to take the Macedonian captives back with them. The prisoners then rebelled against the Bulgar governor or *comes* and kept up a battle which lasted for three days; a curious detail, which confirms that the captives originally came from the region of Adrianople, is their invocation of Adrian as their patron saint. On the fourth day they emerged victorious and embarked on the Byzantine ships; they reached Constantinople in good order, where the Emperor welcomed them, but only to dispatch them immediately to Macedonia, that is to say Thrace. Among the returned prisoners was Basil, who took service with the *strategus* of the theme. Eventually he was commended to Theophilitzes, a favourite of the Emperor Michael, who took him to be chief of the equerries, or *protostrator*; in this capacity he was sent to the Peloponnese, where he made the valuable conquest of the rich and virtuous Danielis, owner of a silk factory at Patras. Basil had first attracted the notice of Michael on the occasion of an official festival at which the boasting of the Bulgar envoys over the prowess of their athletes so irritated Theophilitzes that he set Basil in combat against a Scythian opponent, whom he easily defeated. This was the beginning of Basil's extraordinary good fortune, since Michael treated him as a favourite from that time until the eve of his death. In 859 Basil accompanied Michael on his great expedition to Asia Minor; an inscription from Ancyra of that year gives Basil the rank of *spatharocandidatus*. After the assassination of Damian the *parakoimomenos*, Basil succeeded to this dignity; and after the murder of Bardas, in April 866, the favourite was rewarded with the title of Basileus, Michael himself still remaining as Autocrator. In 865 he had married his benefactor's mistress, Eudocia Ingerina. He had already one son, Constantine, his favourite, by his first wife; in September 866 Eudocia bore him Leo.

VI. REACTION IN RELIGIOUS POLICY: THE IGNATIAN COUNCIL

The revolt of Symbatius and Peganes had demonstrated to Basil, at whom the revolt was aimed, the extent of his unpopularity with the troops, particularly in Asia Minor. And, as has been shown, despite the success of the Photian Council of 867 (though the completeness of this success had its dangers), this serious military disaffection finally clouded the cordiality of Basil's relations with Michael, which had so long been harmonious. In striking down his benefactor, the audacious parvenu only added to the number of his enemies: if Bardas had been popular with the army, Michael 'the Armouropoulos' was its darling. On the morrow of the regicide, Basil must have realised his weakness. He looked for allies, and, logically enough, found them among the popular party of fanatics or extremists: had not Michael III, in one of his witticisms, already said 'Photius is the Patriarch of Bardas, Ignatius the Patriarch of the Christians'? This remark, incidentally, does credit to Michael's powers of observation and capacity to turn a phrase. The Ignatian party might have been subdued, but it could neither be exterminated nor reduced to impotence. On the contrary: it was the Ignatians, in fact, through their most active agents such as Theognostus, who had provoked the more dangerous of the Roman manœuvres and succeeded in poisoning the dispute between the Patriarch and the Pope until it reached the point of explosion in the anti-Roman Council of 867. It is true that Basil himself had presided at this Council, with Michael III, but he excused himself by pleading duress and resolutely ranged himself with the party plotting to remove Photius, Michael's bad angel. Basil was assured of the friendship and support of the Pope, now Hadrian II. The *coup d'état* was followed immediately by the deposition of Photius. Michael died on 24 September 867; Photius must have been deposed the next day and Ignatius was installed on 3 November, the anniversary of his first elevation to the Patriarchate. The Pope now congratulated Basil on his execution of the papal will concerning Photius and Ignatius. The way was being paved for the Ignatian Council of 869–70, which was to be the final revenge of the Ignatian extremists and of Rome. But the resolution of the matter was not as simple as was hoped. The first session of the Council took place on 5 October 869 and the last on 28 February 870. Basil made a great show of his submission to the Church. But, as soon as the question of the condemnation of Photius was raised, a matter regarded by the Roman legates as a *fait accompli*, the official spokesmen, who in general were expressing the opinions of Basil himself, at once asked how Photius could have been condemned in his absence. In fact, Basil and the officials of the Council were anxious for a second discussion and a second judgement on Photius, either to humour the moderates of the Photian party or else to forestall their probable protests. The Roman legates, however, won the day. Basil had preserved a strict neutrality. On 5 November, Photius and his supporters were finally anathematised. It would certainly have been better to follow Basil's wishes and reopen the case, both in order to reach a peaceful settlement and to bring the agitation to an end. But Basil had his revenge. The Council ended on 28 February 870; three days later an extra-conciliar meeting was called, consisting of some Bulgar legates who had just arrived, the Patriarch Ignatius, representatives of the eastern sees and the Roman legates, but without the librarian Anastasius, the Roman expert. The discussion was difficult, since Ignatius was torn between his desire to please the Roman legates and the Pope on the one hand, and the Emperor Basil, who wanted to retain an effective suzerainty over the Bulgars, on the other. Basil could not lay claim to the political supremacy over the Bulgars which would have arisen from a long war followed by a striking victory, but he had every intention of maintaining at least a moral authority, backed by the spiritual influence of the Byzantine Church. It was just such an allegiance which was now being offered to the new Emperor and Patriarch by the embassy from Boris, in protest against the harshness of Rome, which still refused the Bulgars any form of Bulgarian Patriarchate. And so, as soon as the Roman legates had withdrawn, the Patriarch Ignatius consecrated a pontiff for Bulgaria. Those present at this scene could scarcely have believed that they were witnessing the epilogue of a mighty deed consecrating the reunion of two Churches and the victory of the Pope, since the Bulgarian Archbishopric, the real object of the whole long embroilment, was even now being annexed to Byzantium, and that for ever. Although the Romans had quite fruitlessly humiliated Byzantium by claiming that the trial of Photius had long since been concluded, the final rebuff to the Pope in the Bulgarian affair was long to rankle in the West. By a strange twist of fate, St Ignatius, the protégé of Rome, was to end his days in excommunication, or at least under the grave threat of excommunication, as the despoiler of the Patrimony of St Peter by his violation of the *dioecesis Vulgarorum*. Basil had thus no further interest in persisting in his attitude towards Photius, since, even with Ignatius, he was now not reconciled to, but in conflict with, Rome. And thus it happened that Photius was able to recover his position. Moreover, he had lost none of his friends among the clergy, and in strength his party was in fact superior to that of Ignatius.

VII. BASIL'S WARS AND MISSIONARY ACTIVITIES

But this is to anticipate events. The return of Photius to the Patriarchate, the history of the Council rehabilitating him, the eastern policy of Pope John VIII and the ending of the glorious and tragic history of the Moravian apostles, Constantine-Cyril and Methodius, will find their natural place at the end of this section. Our present concern is to explain the various attitudes adopted by Basil in the early years of his reign in terms of the weakness of his position. Since he either could not or would not fight, he negotiated. This method had brought him only doubtful success in his dealings with Rome, and he succeeded no better with his enemies in Asia Minor. Admittedly, the Arabs, defeated in 863, seemed likely to be incapable of offensive action for a long time to come. But the Paulicians, although they had lost their great war leader Carbeas in 863, had found an even more daring and successful general in his nephew Chrysocheir. Basil's military weakness, which was his punishment for his two crimes, together with the probable disaffection of a large part of Asia Minor, where the passing of the glorious era of Michael III was deeply regretted, gave the Paulicians a great opportunity. Without apparently meeting any resistance, under their new leader they advanced to the sea at many points, reaching Nicomedia and Nicaea, the gateway to Byzantium, and Ephesus, where they turned the Church of St John into a stable. Basil's weakness and apparent readiness to compromise made Chrysocheir believe that he had only to ask for Asia Minor for it to be given him. At this moment the master of Tephrice was bold enough to contemplate advances beyond the narrow limits of his present conquests, and was extending his religious, and perhaps even his social, propaganda as far as Thrace and Bulgaria, where Paulicianism was to father Bogomilism.

Faced with this potentially dangerous and humiliating situation, Basil the meek once again became the valiant champion he had been in his earlier days. He made so bold as to march at the head of his troops on Tephrice. But Chrysocheir counter-attacked and took Ancyra. The military situation was only retrieved in 872, by Basil's son-in-law Christopher. A providential earthquake, which destroyed Tephrice, made possible the capture of Chrysocheir, who was beheaded. Basil, victor *in absentia*, triumphed at Constantinople in the autumn of 872. The defeated Paulicians were converted *en masse*. A number of them, however, went to reinforce the Arabs at Melitene. Basil was anxious to follow in the footsteps of Michael III and capture Melitene and Samosata; Porphyrogenitus, in his romanticised biography of Basil, devotes much attention to this campaign, which he depicts as victorious. In doing so, Porphyrogenitus perhaps hoped to silence for ever the ironic and cruel acclamation which greeted the sovereign after the murder of Bardas—'O Basil, what sort of a campaign have you carried out here?' But Basil was in fact defeated before Melitene. It was in an attempt to cover up his defeat that Basil on his return again invaded Paulician territory and destroyed a number of fortresses. He then made a second triumphal entry into Constantinople.

At all events the Paulicians had in fact been defeated, so thoroughly that they completely abandoned their holy war against the Empire and by slow degrees became reconciled to orthodoxy. The Tarsites had also experienced some serious defeats. First Andrew the Scythian, Domestic of the Schools, was victorious over them at the great battle of Podandus. Then a large Greek army (30,000 men) under five patricians penetrated into Cilicia as far as Adana, retiring after several days of pillage with a quantity of prisoners and booty. It is also to this period that the celebrated exploits of Nicephorus Phocas the Elder, ancestor of the Emperor of that name, must be assigned;[1] these exploits, closely connected with the victorious campaign in Cilicia, were Nicephorus' first experience of war, undertaken with his father, a Cappadocian, and in the presence of the Emperor Basil. Successively *manglavites*, *protostrator* and *strategus* of Charsianon,

[1] See H. Grégoire, 'La carrière du premier Nicéphore Phocas', Προσφορὰ εἰς Στ. Π. Κυριακίδην (= Ἑλληνικῶν Παράρτημα ιν, Thessalonica, 1953), pp. 232–54.

Nicephorus undoubtedly participated in the victorious march on Adana. He was then appointed *monostrategus* of five themes (Thrace, Macedonia, Cephalonia, Longobardia and Calabria), and with a legion of converted Paulicians was given in 885 (the date is known from Arab sources) the task of reconquering Calabria; this charge to Nicephorus was one of Basil's last acts.

This operation, which had been made all the more necessary by the disaster of the loss of Syracuse in March 878, had already been attempted on several occasions. In 880, after the admirals Nicetas and Adrian had tried and failed, Nasar, a most distinguished admiral, set out with a fleet of 140 vessels. He won a sea victory in October 880 off the islands of Lipari, and to the great joy of Pope John VIII disembarked a powerful army in Calabria. Five western themes were represented; special mention may be made of Sicily, which as long as Taormina held out was not officially abandoned as lost. Despite various setbacks, the campaign of 880 had one very important result, the recapture of Taormina and the surrounding countryside. In 883 the Basileus despatched an army composed of soldiers from the themes of Thrace, Macedonia, Cappadocia and Charsianon, under the command of the *strategus* Stephen Maxentius; despite its strength, this expedition was repulsed before Santa Severina and Amantea. But in 885 Nicephorus with his assemblage of Paulicians was successful. Only these magnificent soldiers from the marcher lands of the East, who had for so long guarded their independence between Byzantium and Islam, had impetus enough to break down the resistance of the Arabs in Calabria and capture fortress after fortress in this mountainous peninsula, which the Arabs had been prudent enough to occupy even before they had conquered Taormina and the last strongholds of the Greeks in Sicily. Whilst engaged on the siege of Amantea, the last of the Calabrian towns to be reconquered, Nicephorus heard of the death of Basil and the accession of Leo, who recalled him. Nicephorus concealed this important news from the besieged Arabs, in order that he might successfully treat with them; he allowed them to depart freely from this his last conquest, to rejoin, if they would, the Arabs of Africa or elsewhere. Nicephorus Phocas will reappear in this narrative as Domestic of the Schools, and in connection with the Bulgar war, in which he died; as already shown, his exploits in Asia Minor must be dated 879–80. Thanks to Nicephorus, the reign of Basil I, which had been clouded by so many reverses and tragedies, ended at least in a fugitive gleam of glory.

Basil's missionary fervour also brought some consolation by way of success and lasting profit to the Christian Empire. His project of converting the Paulicians, which had its origin in military weakness, was in general realised and it bore fruit in the reconquest of Calabria by the Paulician legion. He was concerned too with a wholesale conversion of the Jews, for which he was bitterly reproached by anti-semitic elements at Byzantium in later reigns. In connection with these pious activities it is instructive to re-read the chapters in the *Vita Basilii* of Constantine Porphyrogenitus concerning what the imperial panegyrist describes as the threefold mission of Basil: the conversion of the Jews, the Bulgars and the Russians. The conversion of Bulgaria can, however, only be credited to Basil if it is admitted, with Constantine VII,[1] that at the time of his accession the Bulgars were not firmly established in the faith. Porphyrogenitus is certainly thinking of the success of Ignatius in preserving the Bulgar diocese for Byzantium, to the great displeasure of Rome, and of his action in sending out bishops and an archbishop. Photius had already made a start with the Russian mission in 860 and further attempts were made by Basil and Ignatius. But in this case Basil could claim neither the initiative nor any measure of definite success. But this is no reason for denying that Basil's actual conversions were important and contributed to the consolidation of the Empire in the West. This work was greatly assisted by Basil's efforts, from the time of his accession, in re-establishing good relations with Rome, and also by the support he gave, during Ignatius' last years, to the movement for the restoration of Photius. Photius also had everything to gain from the consolidation of the *entente* with Rome, even though he might be required to make official renunciation of the 'diocese of the Bulgars' which was as important to John VIII as it had been to Nicholas I; but John VIII sought from Byzantium even more vital and costly favours, such as the succour of a naval rescue force, which was not denied him. As for the Serbian and Croatian missions which took place a little after 867, these were addressed to peoples who had in fact been baptised in the time of Heraclius and to peoples such as the Narentians in the mountains and remote parts of Croatia. This missionary activity was unleashed by a naval victory. Between 866 and 868 the Arabs had been besieging Ragusa; the population of Ragusa had asked for a fleet to relieve the city and the siege was raised in 868. This combined military and spiritual action brought the whole Balkan peninsula, with the exception of the Bulgar kingdom, under the hegemony of Byzantium. And the missionary work in the Balkans from the end of Basil's reign acquired a new impetus and powerful reinforcements with the arrival there of the disciples of the Archbishop of the Moravians, expelled from Moravia after the death of Methodius and the failure of his mission. Meanwhile the

[1] *Vita Basilii*, ch. 96 (Theoph. Cont., p. 342).

ecclesiastical history of the reign ended with the return of Photius to the Patriarchate, which was greatly assisted by the favourable attitude of John VIII, and with the part played by this great Pope, whose merits are too little appreciated, in conferring Roman approval on the Slavonic liturgy.

VIII. THE REHABILITATION OF PHOTIUS: THE MORAVIAN MISSION AND THE SLAVONIC LITURGY

John VIII, who had suffered disillusionment over the Bulgarian policy of Ignatius, the protégé of Rome, viewed without concern the return of Photius to imperial favour and to the patriarchal throne when Ignatius died in 877. He decided to recognise the old enemy of Rome on four conditions, the chief of them being the restitution of the diocese of the Bulgars to Rome and a patriarchal apology in the presence of a council. It is now accepted that the *acta* of this Council of 879–80 (the Eighth according to the Eastern reckoning, which discounts the preceding Ignatian Council) are not forgeries. It is true that the papal legates found that they had to accept modifications of some of the points contained in their instructions: in particular that there was to be no question of exacting an apology from Photius in the presence of the Council. But they kept closely to the most essential points—the restitution of Bulgaria and the Roman primacy. John VIII, in spite of some minor reservations, approved the Council and warmly thanked the Emperors Basil, Leo and Alexander, partly for having sent their fleet and for having put it 'at our service, for the defence of the land of St Peter', and partly 'for having, for the love of us, though it was only fair, allowed St Peter to re-enter into possession of the Bulgarian diocese....We also approve what has been mercifully done in Constantinople by the synodal decree of the very reverend Patriarch Photius' reinstatement, and if perchance at the same synod our legates have acted against apostolic instructions neither do we approve their action nor do we attribute any value to it.'[1]

In June of the same year 880 the Slav peoples derived from John VIII's eastern policy a glorious and outstanding benefit—papal consecration of the use of the Slavonic tongue in the liturgy. Tired of being the plaything of the German kings and bishops, John had the idea of annexing the diocese of the Moravians to the Papacy in perpetuity by a return to the policy of Hadrian II. He accordingly authorised the use of Slavonic not only for preaching and for certain prayers but also for all the liturgical offices. This shrewd and liberal

[1] *MGH, Ep.* vii, pp. 229 ff.

attitude towards the Archbishop of Moravia was indeed to be reversed by his successor Stephen V in 885; but as a result of John's gesture the Slavonic liturgy was adopted by the Bulgars as well as by all the eastern Slavs who were indebted for their conversion to Byzantium.

The Moravian mission had been begun in 863, even before the baptism of Boris. Meanwhile the conflict between Photius and Pope Nicholas I, which reached its climax in 867, made the position of the brothers Constantine and Methodius as envoys between Rome and Constantinople extremely delicate. Nicholas, in the last months of his life, was anxious to win them over to his side, especially as Boris was also at that moment again veering towards Rome. After spending several months at Venice the brothers did in fact come to Rome, where Hadrian II was now Pope, either towards the end of 867 or at the beginning of 868, bringing with them the relics of St Clement, which they had found near Cherson. Honigmann has suggested that when they left for Moravia, surreptitiously taking with them these precious relics, the brothers were given secret instructions concerning them by Photius. They were, perhaps, to await orders before presenting them to the Pope, in the hope that they might usefully prepare the way for a reconciliation with the Holy See. But after the fall of Photius, Constantine and Methodius no longer had any reason for withholding this pious offering: and Hadrian II gave the new Slavonic liturgy immediate approval. The relics of Clement, saint and Pope, had indeed wrought a miracle. Methodius and some of his pupils were then raised to the priesthood. After the death of Constantine-Cyril in Rome (14 February 869) and a visit by Methodius to the Slavs of Lake Balaton and their prince, Kocel, it was decided that a new ecclesiastical province should be created in what was once Roman Pannonia, with the addition of Slav tribes to the east and north, already conquered for Christianity or ripe for conversion. Methodius was made its first archbishop.

But the German response was swift and for a time successful, thanks to the treachery of Svatopluk, a nephew of Rastislav, who betrayed his uncle to the Germans. Rastislav, the prince who had introduced Christianity into Moravia, was blinded, and his archbishop was condemned by a council of German bishops held at Regensburg in the presence of Louis the German; Methodius was then held prisoner for at least two and a half years.[1] It was not until 873

[1] Methodius was perhaps still a prisoner at the time when a Byzantine embassy, led by a certain Archbishop Agathon, left Constantinople for Regensburg. Honigmann identifies this Agathon with Ἀγάθων Μωράβων, who signed the *acta* of 879–80. He advances the reasonable theory that Byzantium, or rather the Patriarch Ignatius, thought it necessary to fill the see of Methodius, now presumably vacant by reason of

that Pope John VIII, indignant at these proceedings, excommunicated the German bishops and insisted that Methodius should be set free and restored to his see. As for the Slavonic liturgy, the Pope resolved to wait until he had seen the Archbishop of Moravia at Rome before giving it his final recognition. His ultimate decision, taken in June 880, was as generous as Methodius could have wished. But unfortunately, when communicating this decision to Svatopluk, the Pope also announced that he had agreed to Svatopluk's wishes and appointed the German Wiching, Methodius' greatest enemy, as suffragan to the Moravian archbishopric. Less than six years later, in the very year of Methodius' death (6 April 885), Pope Stephen V, beguiled by Wiching and influenced by Svatopluk, took the step which cancelled out all that John VIII had achieved, acting in either real or feigned ignorance of John's solemn recognition of the Slavonic liturgy.

This catastrophe, as will be seen, was the result of the policy of Leo VI, Basil's successor, whose reign must now be considered. Basil died in a hunting accident on 29 August 886. He had never been consoled for the death of his elder and favourite son Constantine; and he had never been able to reconcile himself to the idea that Leo, whom he hated, would succeed him.

IX. THE REIGN OF LEO VI

Leo VI was probably born on 19 September 866;[1] he only became heir to the throne in 879, on the death of his elder brother Constantine, the son of Basil by his first wife. Basil certainly had no love for him; indeed, suspecting Leo of conspiring against him, Basil inflicted on his son a harsh imprisonment, from which he was delivered as he believed only by the protection of the Prophet Elijah. As a result of this tragic episode, Leo nursed a grievance not only against the Emperor but also, it seems, against Photius, although the Patriarch had intervened on his behalf. At his accession he was still gnawed by resentment. These circumstances help to explain his first actions: the interment of Michael's ashes, accompanied by solemn funerary rites, in the Church of the Holy Apostles, and the deposition of Photius. But there is also another explanation for this last action.

his imprisonment. This provides a further example of the rivalry between Rome and Byzantium over Illyricum in the time of Ignatius. Honigmann's suggestion is accepted here. This rivalry helps to explain why John VIII was so energetic in his efforts to restore Methodius to his see. Cf. E. Honigmann, 'Studies in Slavic Church History', *B*, XVII (1944–5), 165.

[1] On the question of Leo's paternity see G. Ostrogorsky, *History of the Byzantine State*, p. 207 and references.

Although none of the Popes who succeeded John VIII contested the validity of Photius' reinstatement, which was confirmed at the Council of 879–80, it appears that Stephen V did not consider that the Ignatian Council of 869–70 had been annulled, and moreover thought that Photius had been restored but not rehabilitated, since he had refused to make the apologies demanded by Rome. Such an attitude becomes more intelligible if it is set side by side with the Roman reversal of policy in the affair of the use of the Slavonic liturgy in Moravia in 885. In both cases, there is an obvious reaction against the eastern policy of John VIII. It is thus inaccurate to say that the deposition of Photius—or rather his forced resignation—at the beginning of the reign of Leo VI, had no connection with the earlier 'Photian affair'. On the contrary, the incident provides further proof of the power of the Ignatian party, whose favour was once again being courted at Rome. In sacrificing the Patriarch whom Basil had restored Leo was not merely giving vent to his malice towards the men of the preceding reign but also taking a step towards Rome, as though he had guessed that he would soon have need of the Pope's moral support. The 'Photian affair' was still not at an end. Admittedly, Leo did not replace Photius (whom he sent into exile) by one of the Ignatian partisans; but he profited by the vacancy to set his own brother Stephen on the patriarchal throne, an audacious innovation which was later to inspire Romanus Lecapenus to emulation and one which gave the Basileus direct control over the Church.

It is only right to point out at once that Leo did not persist in this hostile attitude towards the memory of his father and towards the great Patriarch and scholar. He well understood the full value of the legitimist principle. In the Funeral Oration over Basil, delivered on the second anniversary of his death, he was for dynastic reasons careful to proclaim his filial respect for his predecessor, and was indeed his first panegyrist; Leo thus at one stroke secured the future, the honour and the glory of the reigning family. As for Photius, Leo realised the power wielded by his party both in the Church and among the people and treated him lightly, leaving him in peace to complete his theological and literary work. This was a wise attitude to adopt. After the premature death of the Patriarch Stephen, an ascetic named Antony Cauleas was appointed Patriarch, a man of many excellent qualities; all the sources agree in affirming that he re-established, in 899, good relations between Byzantium and Rome and peace within the Byzantine Church, by winning over the last of the Ignatians, and in particular their leader Stylianus. There can be no doubt that this peace, which once more united the East and the West and healed the old ulcer of the schism, was only achieved with the co-operation of Rome and may even have taken the form of a General Council.[1] Here it is only necessary to observe that this marks the real ending of the Photian affair. Indeed, after the death of Antony Cauleas in 901, the Patriarchate was filled by Photius' own nephew Nicholas, a statesman and man of letters like his uncle, but in no sense a moderate. To a Basileus such as Leo, who by his too numerous marriages violated not only the religious but also the civil law, Nicholas must have appeared the incarnation of all the extremist principles recently supported by the Ignatians.

During the first ten years of Leo's reign, the Armenian Stylianus Zautzes was the outstanding political adjutor of the young Emperor and the inspiration of his legislative work, of which he was no doubt also the editor.[2]

One of Leo's first concerns was the Bulgar war.[3] The fact that there was a Bulgar war at all differentiates the reign of Leo from those of the last two Amorians and that of his father Basil. One might have thought that with the baptism of Boris there would be no further hostility between the Christian Empire and its wild neighbours, now converted by the Byzantines themselves to the faith of the civilised nations. But Boris-Michael had abdicated in 889; then Vladimir, his eldest son, who lapsed to paganism, was deposed, and the succession passed to Boris' third son Symeon (893–927). Brought up at Constantinople and full of native cunning and ambition, Symeon realised that his profession of Christianity opened up for him wide avenues of advancement denied to his ancestors, the pagan Khans; and he was indeed later proclaimed Basileus and from that eminence aspired even to the height of Empire itself, reaching it for one brief moment in 913. From the time of his first brush with Byzantium (894–6), in which victory was largely on his side, he proved to the world that the Bulgars had lost none of their military valour; the only alteration lay in their improved strategy and tactics. This first war of Symeon's was not a barbarian invasion but a commercial war, aimed at securing a free market. Two Byzantine

[1] The account in the *Cletorologion* of Philotheus (dated 899) of the reception given to the Roman legates on the occasion of the 'ecclesiastical union' perhaps describes the visit of papal legates to Constantinople in 907 (for which see below, pp. 131–2), rather than the act of union under Antony Cauleas. But see G. Ostrogorsky, *History of the Byzantine State*, p. 191, n. 3.

[2] His official titles were *magister officiorum* (μάγιστρος τῶν θείων ὀφφικίων) and Logothete of the Drome. In the spring of 894 he was created first holder of a new office, βασιλεοπάτωρ, which hints at the forthcoming second marriage of Leo with his daughter Zoe. But this marriage only took place in 898, and Stylianus died in 896. These dates were established by V. Grumel; cf. 'La chronologie des événements du règne de Léon VI', *EO*, xxxv (1936), 5–42.

[3] See also below: ch. xi, pp. 502–4.

merchants had been granted a monopoly of the Bulgar trade by the Byzantine government. They were in partnership with Stylianus Zautzes, the *magister* and Logothete of the Drome, and had transferred the staple for Bulgarian goods from Constantinople to Thessalonica, making gross overcharges. This exploitation of the Bulgar exporters to the profit of merchants who were protected by the imperial favourite, himself the father of the Emperor's favourite lady, might well be expected to arouse the moral indignation of the new converts. In 894 the Bulgars defeated the Byzantine army. Nicephorus Phocas, the best of the Empire's generals, who had been recalled from Calabria and Apulia in 886, replied by invading Bulgar territory; but he could not hope for reinforcements from the Byzantine–Arab front in Cilicia, which since the end of the reign of Basil I had already been denuded of a number of units for the defence of Sicily and the reoccupation of Calabria. Leo and Stylianus then had the idea of seeking aid from the Magyars, who had for some time been settled between the Dnieper and the Danube, where they were neighbours of the Bulgars. The Magyars responded to the imperial appeal and invaded Bulgaria, laying the country waste; meanwhile, Nicephorus Phocas introduced well-equipped mobile columns into southern Bulgaria, and the Byzantine fleet blockaded the mouth of the Danube. Symeon immediately concluded an armistice, but quickly followed it up by an astute stroke of diplomacy which revealed him as a worthy antagonist of Leo the Wise. Leo had mobilised the strength of the Magyars against Symeon; but Symeon well knew that beyond the Magyars and always ready to invade their kingdom in the region of the 'five rivers' there dwelt the Pechenegs, who only awaited a signal to strike. These fierce tribes took advantage of the absence of Magyar troops to conquer the whole vast region. The Magyars found their way back to the 'Atel Kuzu' barred by the Pechenegs; driven out of Bulgaria by Symeon and his new allies, they were forced to seek a new fatherland. Thus the first war between Byzantium and Christian Bulgaria, together with the rival diplomacies adopted by Symeon and Leo, changed the map of Central Europe; for the Magyars, crossing the passes over the Carpathians, broke the large Moravian kingdom in two and drove between the Northern and the Southern Slavs an ethnographic wedge which has not altered since the end of the ninth century.

The Bulgar–Byzantine war, which tends to get overlooked in view of this unexpected development, nevertheless continued. Disembarrassed both of the Magyars and of Nicephorus Phocas, who died between 894 and 896, Symeon was victorious over the Byzantines at Bulgarophygon (896). He imposed his own peace and forced Leo to pay him annual tribute. Symeon appears again eight years later, in 904, when he took advantage of the capture of Thessalonica by the Arabs to secure for himself a frontier well defined by stake-marks discovered about twelve miles from the Macedonian capital. This frontier saved the Empire from Bulgar occupation after the plundering by the Arabs, and was no doubt negotiated by the talented diplomat Leo Choerosphactes, who boasts in his letters of having been clever enough to recover forty fortified places occupied by the Bulgars and a very large number of prisoners. But the fact remains that both on sea and land, and both east and west, Leo's arms were generally lacking in success, especially if it is admitted, and the conclusion seems inescapable, that the exploits of Nicephorus Phocas in Asia Minor belong to the previous reign.[1]

It must also be admitted that the tale of military operations during Leo's reign includes more than one date of ominous significance. Leo showed a quite extraordinary reluctance to use his navy, perhaps because Basil's five or six major expeditions in the Adriatic and against Sicily and Italy had seriously weakened both the ships and their crews. This may explain the capture and sack of Demetrias or Volos in Thessaly, in 902,[2] and the catastrophe of 904, one of the most famous disasters in the whole history of Byzantium, when the Arab fleet, commanded by the renegade Leo of Tripoli, appeared suddenly before Thessalonica and captured it, after a three-day siege, on 31 July 904. The victors were able to take away with them, unpursued, more than 30,000 prisoners, some of whom were sold back again in Crete.[3] These terrible lessons were not lost on the Byzantines, particularly since, with the fall of Taormina (902), which finally sealed the loss of Sicily after seventy-five years of warfare, the Empire was given a chance to devote every effort to the struggle in the Aegean: South Italy itself was once again in firmer possession and the Asian front had been stabilised. The name of Himerius, a Byzantine admiral of the early tenth century, has gone down to fame and has even entered the province of hagiography; his popularity saved the military honour of Leo. Before his final defeat, this great sailor enjoyed an immense reputation in both the Byzantine and the Arab

---

[1] It has already been shown that the exploits rightly attributed to Nicephorus Phocas on the Arab front pre-date his reconquest of Calabria, and thus belong to the reign of Basil (see above, p. 120 and note 1). He was not, as is sometimes said, *strategus* of the Thracesion theme at the end of his career. He died before the battle of Bulgarophygon in 896. Cf. G. Ostrogorsky, *History of the Byzantine State*, pp. 227–8.

[2] This is the date given by Grumel and Ostrogorsky. I myself prefer 897. On this most complicated chronological problem of Byzantine history, see H. Grégoire, 'La vie de Saint Blaise d'Amorium', *B*, IV (1929), 391–414.

[3] See H. Grégoire, 'Le communiqué arabe sur la prise de Thessalonique', *B*, XXII (1952), 373–8.

worlds: and his naval triumph of 908[1] against the Muslims was set by Arethas, the Bishop of Caesarea, against Muslim claims that victory always went to the arms of Islam. Himerius' victory, and the success of Andronicus Ducas near Tarsus in November–December 904 are alluded to in Arethas' letter in colloquial Greek which undoubtedly reflects the state of popular opinion in the early tenth century. Indeed, Muslim defeats (or in fact the defeat of any enemy of Byzantium) were so rare during this disastrous period that the family of Ducas attracted to themselves not only much jealousy but also a name of immense renown in popular epic; on the death of Alexander, as will be seen, this family all but succeeded in usurping the place of his heir, having already threatened to seize the throne from the tetragamous Emperor himself.[2] The fame of Himerius, which survived his final defeat in 912, fortunately for us ensured the preservation of a text of great value for the study of Byzantine naval history, the section in the *De Cerimoniis* containing an inventory and description of all the equipment and manpower of this great armada, and an account of the cost of the several items. Himerius' fleet was however attacked by the two renegades, Damian and Leo of Tripoli, and destroyed by the Arabs off Chios in April or May 912.[3] But Leo, who rightly had much faith in the final triumph of the Byzantine navy, did not allow himself to be discouraged by this or any other reverse.[4]

At home one of Leo's major concerns had been to obtain the coronation of his son Constantine. In order to understand the difficulties which had to be overcome before this triumph of legitimism was achieved, a triumph which saved the dynasty and ushered in a glorious age, it is necessary to give a brief account of the affair of the tetragamy.

Leo, under pressure from his father Basil, had married a saint whom he did not love, Theophano, who died on 10 November 897. Leo's mistress, Zoe, the daughter of Stylianus Zautzes, has already been mentioned. He married her in 898 (her father had died in 896). In the following year Zoe died, without leaving him a male heir. In the summer of 900 the Emperor took a third wife, Eudocia Baiana,

---

[1] For the view that this took place in 805 see R. J. H. Jenkins, 'The Date of Leo VI's Cretan Expedition', *Προσφορὰ εἰς Στ. Π. Κυριακίδην* (= *Ἑλληνικά, Παράρτημα* IV, Thessalonica, 1953), pp. 277–81.

[2] For the later history of Andronicus Ducas after his victory see V. Grumel, 'La révolte d'Andronic Dux sous Léon VI, la victoire navale d'Himérius', *EO*, XXXVI (1937), 202–7.

[3] See R. J. H. Jenkins, *op. cit.*

[4] The present writer holds that Oleg did not raid Constantinople in 907. For another view, and for discussion of the trade treaty of 911 between the Russians and Byzantines, see below: ch. XI, pp. 504–5.

though a third marriage was forbidden by canon law and several years earlier Leo had expressed his own disapproval of the practice in a special law which even prohibited second marriage, and in strong terms. On 12 April 901, however, Eudocia also died. Leo, once again a widower, was anxious to marry the beautiful Zoe Carbonopsina. In view of the opposition shown by the Church to his third marriage he would not have persisted in his desire had she not borne him a son in 905. It was now a question of legitimising his heir. The first step was to have him baptised by the Patriarch, Nicholas Mysticus, an old fellow-student of Leo's and the nephew of Photius. The baptism took place on 6 January 906. But the Patriarch was supremely anxious to avoid the scandal of a fourth marriage. He only agreed to baptising the future Constantine VII on condition that the Emperor immediately separated himself from Zoe. But the parents of the infant in their turn were anxious to regularise their own position, and insisted that unless their union was blessed by the Church, Constantine would remain a bastard. A priest was found to perform the marriage ceremony, and on the same day Leo had his wife proclaimed Augusta. In the eyes of public opinion this was a great scandal, and to the Church an unheard of act of provocation. The Emperor found himself forbidden to enter St Sophia at Christmas and Epiphany 906–7.

But the Patriarch's rigorist attitude became untenable. It was at this juncture that the Emperor, apparently not without justification, accused the Patriarch of having entered into secret communication with Andronicus Ducas, the victor over the Arabs in 904, who had been accused of treason for having refused to co-operate with the Admiral Himerius and had later taken refuge at Kavalla, where he was being besieged by loyalist troops; Andronicus had already called in the Arabs for assistance and was preparing to flee to Baghdad. In these circumstances, Leo had every right to demand the deposition of the Patriarch, and to have him arrested and deported. But in order to legalise such a deposition it was necessary to summon a council to be attended by papal legates and representatives of the eastern Patriarchates. Leo approached Pope Sergius III and instructed Leo Choerosphactes, who had been sent on a mission to Baghdad, to bring back with him to Constantinople delegates from the Patriarchs of Alexandria, Antioch and Jerusalem. It was particularly necessary to secure the support of Rome. Now to the Pope (whose Church did not regard a fourth marriage with such distaste) it must have seemed that an appeal to Rome by an Emperor against his own Patriarch represented a considerable triumph for the Roman supremacy, particularly in view of the largely negative results, so far as Rome was concerned, of the Photian quarrel. The papal legates, therefore, like the representatives of the eastern Patriarchs, contented themselves with reaching a solution which would permit the Emperor to re-enter the Church as a penitent, and promised the vacant patriarchal throne to the pious Euthymius. There is something ironic in the spectacle of Rome authorising Leo to depose the Patriarch Nicholas, the nephew of Photius and his worthy pupil and yet an extremist more unyielding even than Ignatius, only to replace him, with all his heroic devotion to his moral and religious duty, by an accommodating monk (February 907). It must be added that at the Council which then took place formal assent was given to the proposition already made by the Roman legates: 'the Emperor guilty of tetragamy shall be received in the Church without being required to obtain a divorce, but this naturally does not imply that his marriage is recognised'. This prepared the way for what, without any shadow of irony, may be called the triumph of the legitimist principle, that is to say the coronation of the Porphyrogenitus.[1]

But the ex-Patriarch Nicholas and his supporters did not accept the *fait accompli*, and on the accession of Alexander, Leo's brother, the Augusta Zoe was relegated to a convent and the Patriarch Nicholas reinstalled.

X. THE LEGISLATIVE WORK OF BASIL I AND LEO VI[2]

It has already been shown that despite certain capricious actions at the beginning of his reign, which suggest a reaction against the methods of Basil and some of his colleagues, Leo seems to have understood the general trend of Basil's policy. This is demonstrated most clearly in Leo's legislative activity, in which he continued as a faithful collaborator the work of one who had felt himself a Roman Emperor indeed. As has been seen, Basil had markedly western interests; he was responsible for the liberation of Ragusa and the foundation of the theme of Dalmatia, and his chief claim to fame was to be the reconquest of Italy, prepared for by the operations of his fleet on both shores of the Adriatic. Basil's thoughts must often have turned to Justinian; above all he was ambitious to infuse fresh life into Roman law. He stands before us as one whose supreme contribution was to consolidate and to unify. Just as he tried by his missionary work to lead back into the fold of orthodoxy all the dissidents within his

---

[1] The date of Constantine VII's coronation has commonly been accepted as 9 June 911, but there is evidence to suggest that it was as early as 908; see the article by P. Grierson and R. J. H. Jenkins, *B*, XXXII (1962), 133 ff.

[2] See also Pt II, ch. XXI, pp. 65 ff.

frontiers, so he sought to impose on the peoples he had converted and civilised the blessings of the civil law, now brought within the reach of all by a great effort of codification and translation. Himself of little learning, he nevertheless sought to contribute to the renaissance symbolised by the university of Bardas and Photius, by the purification (as he put it) of the ancient law: and he must not be denied the credit of having taken on himself the truly imperial task of making a great legislative codification. He could neither complete nor publish his Ἀνακάθαρσις τῶν παλαιῶν νόμων, but he gathered together all the material which went to the making of the *Basilica*, finally published by Leo. Two manuals can be ascribed to Basil: the *Procheiron* (πρόχειρος νόμος), which appeared between 869 and 879 and stands in the names of the Emperors Basil, Constantine and Leo, and the *Epanagoge* (Ἐπαναγωγή), which must have been intended as an introduction to the *Basilica*.[1] The *Epanagoge* has been described, with justice and perception, as a new edition of the *Procheiron* and as the third edition of the Isaurian *Ecloga*, on which it leans even more heavily than does the *Procheiron*, particularly in the sections on marriage. But perhaps the chief interest of the *Epanagoge* lies in its exposition of the theory of the two powers, which is obviously the work of Photius. The rights and duties of Emperor and Patriarch are defined in a manner which must have been most acceptable at Rome, since the independence of the spiritual power is given an important place, an emphasis, indeed, which ill accords with the charges of Caesaropapism so long and so unjustly levelled against Byzantium.

Thanks to the material collected by his father, Leo was able to add to the *Procheiron* and the *Epanagoge* the sixty books of the *Basilica*, in six volumes, hence the name *Hexabiblos*. The editorial committee—or rather the committee of publication—worked with great speed and produced a veritable *summa utriusque iuris*. The three main sources used are the *Codex* of Justinian, the *Digest* and the Collection of 168 Novels. The original aims of the editors were to make a Greek translation of Roman law, prune away any repetitious matter and present the material in a systematic form. The *scholia*, or commentaries, only begin with Constantine Porphyrogenitus. The index, the famous *Tipoukeitos* (from τί ποῦ κεῖται), goes back only to the twelfth century. Leo also published 113 novels of his own, which deal in an unsystematic manner with a large number of topical problems. These Νεαραί have an official title which is reminiscent of one of Basil's formulae: αἱ τῶν νόμων ἐπανορθωτικαὶ ἀνακαθάρσεις. Novels 2–17 are addressed to the Patriarch Stephen, who died on 17 May 893, and nearly all the rest are addressed to Stylianus Zautzes the *basileopator*, who died in

---

[1] For a further discussion of these manuals see below: Pt II, ch. XXI, pp. 65 ff.

896, and who was their real instigator. It was in these novels of Leo VI that the disappearance of the curia and senate was finally confirmed. As supreme head of the state and of the army, supreme judge, sole legislator, protector of the Church and guardian of Orthodoxy, the power of the Emperor was in fact unlimited. But he was obliged to observe the moral law, of which the Church was the guardian, and it was thus that the old dyarchy, whereby power was shared between Emperor and senate, was reborn. The Patriarch of Constantinople was clearly determined, as the *Epanagoge* expresses it, to claim all that concerned the spiritual well-being of Christians as his province. Hence the great importance of the conflicts which arose between Church and state over questions of morals. Moreover, while the civil government and administration had now entirely lost their democratic character, Patriarchs could only be appointed or deposed by an ecclesiastical assembly, that is by a council. Gelzer was profoundly mistaken in applying the term 'Caesaropapism' to the Byzantine Empire, since the essence of Caesaropapism is the subordination of the Church to the state.

XI. THE REGENCY FOR CONSTANTINE VII: ZOE, SYMEON OF BULGARIA AND ROMANUS LECAPENUS

On Leo VI's death in 912 he was for a short time succeeded by his brother Alexander. Alexander reigned only from 12 May 912 until 6 June 913. He was a man given over entirely to pleasure, who regarded his brief period of personal rule merely as an occasion for the gratification of his own grievances and contrariness. By his attitude towards the Empress Zoe and the Patriarch Nicholas Mysticus he once again endangered the future of the dynasty, and by his refusal of the tribute promised to Symeon by Leo VI he reopened the Bulgar war and exposed the Empire to the greatest peril it had yet known. Zoe, whom he expelled from the palace, returned to be with him during his last hours. The Patriarch Nicholas, Zoe's enemy, was hopeful that his chance had now come to be rid of her entirely. But Alexander, *in extremis*, recognised the youthful Constantine, now seven years old, as his successor, and appointed a council of seven regents, with Nicholas, whom he had reinstated, as their president. Nicholas, the 'Richelieu' of Byzantium, was in a difficult position. He had every reason for feeling antagonistic towards the child he could think of only as a bastard and towards the mother who had so mortally offended him. Moreover, the Bulgar enemy, provoked to action by Alexander, was in the field and already threatening the capital. The one man capable of saving the situation was Constantine Ducas, Domestic of the Schools;

and Nicholas summoned him to help, just as he had summoned his father Andronicus in 907. Constantine Ducas was regarded by the people as the true Porphyrogenitus: he was also the candidate preferred by the party of the deposed Patriarch Euthymius. His attempt to profit from the circumstances by taking possession of the palace and the throne by force was consequently regarded with malevolent neutrality by Nicholas. He was killed in the confusion, and almost all the male members of his family were massacred.[1]

But though Nicholas might be rid of Ducas, the Bulgar problem still remained to be solved.[2] Symeon of Bulgaria was no ordinary enemy: he was another serious claimant to the imperial throne. He was a Christian, had been educated at Constantinople, was more than half-way to being hellenised and was convinced, like most of the Byzantines themselves, that the bastard Porphyrogenitus was incapable of ruling. What Symeon sought at Constantinople was the imperial crown itself. Nicholas set himself to flatter this naïve ambition. The Patriarch-regent and the young Emperor received Symeon with all solemnity. Constantine VII promised to marry his daughter and the Patriarch crowned him 'Emperor of the Bulgarians'. Symeon was now Basileus, admittedly of Bulgaria, but he expected to become the father-in-law of the Emperor, and all the indications were that one day soon he would become associated with him in power. Satisfied, Symeon agreed to withdraw. Nicholas, by a miracle of diplomacy, had temporarily charmed away the Bulgar peril. But public opinion was still vociferous against him because of the massacre of the Ducas family, and he was forced to find a support in legitimism. To do this he had to allow Zoe, whom he had himself tonsured and transformed into Sister Anna, to return to the palace. Zoe, in her turn, showed cunning: she did not insist on the reinstatement of the Patriarch Euthymius, who was in any case anxious to remain in his monastery. Nicholas' great merit was his acceptance of legitimism, even to the extent of acquiescing in the personal rule of the Augusta Zoe. The regents receded into the background and the authority of Nicholas was strengthened. The spectre of the co-regency, or even of the reign of the 'practically unwashed' Bulgar, had made it necessary to return completely to the legitimate house and the reconciliation of all true 'Romans'.

The project of the Bulgarian betrothal was repudiated as was also the validity (and even the fact) of Symeon's coronation. War again

---

[1] His epic popularity is perpetuated in the cantilenas of Andronicus and Constantine. See H. Grégoire, 'Etudes sur l'épopée byzantine', *REG*, XLVI (1933), 48 ff., and 'L'âge héroique de Byzance', *Mélanges Iorga* (Paris, 1933), pp. 382–97.

[2] For another account of the relations between Symeon and Byzantium see below: ch. XI, pp. 505–8.

broke out. Symeon took Adrianople and ravaged Thrace. But Zoe displayed great energy. She chose as commander-in-chief of her army Leo Phocas, the son of Nicephorus, who had the assistance of his brother Bardas. Her first minister was Constantine the *parakoimomenos*, a eunuch.[1] Nicholas, up to the time of the fall of Zoe, contented himself with the administration of the Church. The diplomatic and military successes of the years 915–17 can thus be credited to the Augusta herself. In Italy the Saracens were defeated at the Garigliano in 915 by the *strategus* of Longobardia, Nicholas Picingli, at the head of a great alliance composed of Pope John X, Gregory Duke of Naples, John Duke of Gaeta, and Landulph Prince of Benevento and Capua. By this victory the prestige of the Empire was re-established in Italy, and for a long time to come. But Zoe, who with the Pope had engineered this western crusade, was not forgetful of the East. Ashot, King of Armenia (the son of Smbat the Martyr), having fled from his country where the Muslims had played havoc and set up a rival to his throne, came to Byzantium in 914 to seek the aid of the great Christian Empire. In 915 Zoe was able to restore him to his throne. Nothing could have done more to raise the prestige of Byzantium: by this decisive and successful intervention a Byzantine protégé, the son of a famous martyr, had been restored, as it was hoped, to lead the Armenians back to orthodoxy, an event already announced, though a little prematurely, by Photius in 867.[2]

In contemplating this double military effort on the part of Byzantium at this period, achieved in spite of the Bulgar menace, it is impossible not to admire the energy, self-confidence and resolution of the Empress Zoe and of the forces of legitimism of which she was the embodiment. It must also be noted that Arethas of Caesarea, in his funeral oration over Euthymius (917), did not neglect to make a respectful reference to her, declaring her above reproach and blaming Alexander for her expulsion from the palace. Arethas had openly declared himself for her party and against the Patriarch Nicholas. Nevertheless, Zoe fell the victim of her commander-in-chief, Leo

[1] This was the man described with such hatred and prejudice by Arethas, in his funeral oration over the Patriarch Euthymius in 917, as 'the Slav eunuch' (*MPG*, cvi, 123). This speech, which is all too rarely cited, deserves careful consideration by anyone interested in Byzantine parties. It represents St Euthymius as a martyr of the tyrant Alexander, and Arethas couples his name with those of the other holy Patriarchs who, like him, were persecuted by the imperial power, such as Nicephorus and Photius.

[2] Admittedly, the restoration of Ashot II cannot be dated with absolute certainty although the Greek chroniclers, in speaking of his visit to Constantinople, make mention of a lady who must be Zoe. See N. Adontz, 'Ašot Erkat' ou de fer, roi d'Arménie de 913 à 929', *AIPHO*, iii (1935 = *Mélanges J. Capart*), 13–35, and the full note of M. Canard, *Histoire de la dynastie des H'amdanides de Jazīra et de Syrie*, Publications de la faculté des lettres d'Alger, sér. 2, xxi (Paris, 1953), p. 725, n. 15.

Phocas, whose armies were twice defeated by the Bulgars, first at Anchialus on 20 August 917 and then at Catasyrtae (near Constantinople) late in 917 or early in 918. Zoe was now more than ever anxious to marry the defeated general, and Leo himself hoped for the title of *basileopator*. But the fleet under its commander Romanus Lecapenus, with the acquiescence of Nicholas, frustrated this design: or rather it was Romanus who realised it, but in another way.

Romanus Lecapenus may have been only the son of an Armenian peasant,[1] but his father was singled out for distinction under Basil I, as was the father of Leo Phocas, and this in itself constituted a title to nobility. Romanus, however, retained a clearer memory than did the Phocas family of his humble origins: he was to be the Basileus of those peasant soldiers whom Leo the Wise had so little cherished. It was on 25 March 919 that Romanus disembarked at the capital to take possession of the palace. Nicholas was awaiting him. In April the young Emperor Constantine VII found himself betrothed not to a Bulgar but to Helena Lecapena. The marriage was celebrated; and Helena was proclaimed Augusta with Romanus as *basileopator*. Leo Phocas rebelled, but too late: he was captured and blinded.[2] But the most dangerous of the claimants to the Empire still remained— Symeon, who during the years 919 and 920 was fobbed off by Nicholas and Romanus with fair promises, when they were not occupying him in military activity by inciting the Serbs against him: for the Serbs presented the best foil to the Bulgar peril. While he was still biding his time, Nicholas thought fit to edify his most Christian adversary by proclaiming to him by letter the Peace of the Church. It was in June 920 (while Romanus was still *basileopator*) that a council which included Roman legates concluded the affair of the tetragamy by the publication of the τόμος ἐνώσεως. All the parties in the dispute had reason for satisfaction. Third marriages were still condemned, except on compassionate grounds in exceptional cases, and fourth marriages

---

[1] His name is derived from his birthplace, Lakape (Laqabin) between Melitene and Samosata. Cf. H. Grégoire, Διγενὴς Ἀκρίτας (New York, 1942), p. 119, and 'Le lieu de naissance de Romain Lécapène et de Digénis Akritas', *B*, VIII (1933), 572–4. Romanus' father was called Theophylact Abastactus. Like Nicephorus Phocas the Elder he served as an officer under the Emperor Basil I; according to the Continuator of Theophanes he once saved his imperial master's life when he was surrounded by the enemy during an expedition against the Saracens and the Paulicians of Tephrice. It is noteworthy that this Theophylact Abastactus is sung of in an epic poem which can be exactly dated, on account of a reference to the Emperor Alexander.

[2] The Empress Zoe, who had throughout remained at the palace, was now accused of having conspired with Leo against the new *basileopator*. She once again reverted to being Sister Anna, having played a notable part in the consolidation of the dynasty and of the prestige of the Empire, a part which deserves full-scale rehabilitation at the hands of the historians who have for so long neglected her.

were definitely prohibited. It can well be imagined that both Romanus Lecapenus and Nicholas were gratified at this belated triumph of the extremist cause. But Constantine's legitimacy was recognised, although with qualifications which weakened his dynasty to the advantage of the *basileopator*, who was thenceforth a candidate for the Empire: he became first Caesar, and then Emperor in that same year. Just as the quarrel between Ignatius and Photius had been followed by the appointment of a Patriarch from the imperial house, Stephen, so this act of union was followed, after two insignificant Patriarchs, by the elevation on 2 February 933 of the youthful Theophylact, son of Romanus, who, despite his inadequate preparation for his office, occupied the See of Constantinople until 956 with energy and success.

But Symeon of Bulgaria, who was persistent in his designs, had reopened hostilities. In 924 he marched on Constantinople. As in 913, once he was before the city he found that he was without allies, without a fleet, and without any means of forcing an entry. He was obliged, and this was evidence of his inferior position, to seek an interview with the Emperor and the Patriarch. This interview can perhaps be accounted the most impressive scene in the whole of Byzantine history. The chroniclers[1] give the text of the speech—or rather the sermon—made by Romanus Lecapenus, which can be epitomised as follows: 'You are a mortal, you await death and judgement. Today you live and tomorrow you are dead. One fever will quench all your pride. When you come before God what will you say of your unrighteous slaughter?' The exact date of this great and historic scene, which shows Byzantium, in all its immense superiority of moral authority in the ascendant over an enemy already penetrated with the Byzantine spirit, is unfortunately unknown.[2] In the event there was a compromise. Byzantium recognised Symeon's title of Βασιλεύς, but as Βασιλεύς of the Bulgars, and Romanus made an official protest against the title Βασιλεὺς Βουλγάρων καὶ Ῥωμαίων, and in particular against that of Βασιλεὺς Ῥωμαίων. But after eleven years of effort Symeon had at last been checkmated and his military power began all at once to crumble. Byzantine diplomacy had been very active among the Slav neighbours and rivals of the Bulgars. Symeon scored one more success in defeating and devastating Serbia in 924; but when he tried to deal as decisive a blow against Croatia, whose first king, Tomislav, had been recognised at Byzantium by the conferment of authority over the cities of Dalmatia, his army was

---

[1] Theophanes Cont., pp. 408–9; Symeon Magister, pp. 737–8.

[2] On this question of chronology see *DR*, 604, where Dölger says 'in the autumn of 924', rightly emphasising that a more precise dating is impossible. Ostrogorsky agrees; cf. *History of the Byzantine State*, p. 235, n. 1.

crushingly defeated. Symeon was forced to sue for peace through the mediation of the Pope. He died suddenly on 27 May 927. Serbia, which he had subjugated, revived under Byzantine sovereignty and its prince Časlav (927–8). The prince of Zachlumia was given the titles of *anthypatus* and *patricius*. Byzantine influence became completely dominant even in Bulgaria during the reign of Peter, Symeon's son, a humble and pious man of peace, who married Maria Lecapena.

The great Bulgarian crisis thus had a providential outcome, justifying the opinion of those who regard Romanus Lecapenus as perhaps the nearest to genius of all the Byzantine sovereigns. The concord in the Church, the achievement of good relations with Rome after such prolonged wrangling, and the peace with Bulgaria, were all magnificent deeds with which to mark his début. But his real glory lies elsewhere: he followed up and extended the work of expansion and reconquest whose progress under Michael III, Basil, Leo and Zoe has already been delineated. Romanus' ardour in pressing forward to the complete reconquest of the Euphrates march is explained by his origins, born as he was at Lakape, between Melitene and Samosata. He found a zealous instrument for the execution of this plan in his general John Curcuas, a native of Armenian Georgia, the hero of the reconquest. The reconquest had been vigorously resumed even before the final conclusion of peace with Bulgaria.[1] The Taurus frontier remained almost unaltered, the main fighting taking place on the Euphrates and in Armenia. On the Euphrates the chief event was the capture of Melitene (Malaṭiya), occupied by John Curcuas in 931 and 934. This made a great impression on contemporaries and led, moreover, to mass desertions and conversions. The Amir Abū Hafs of Melitene, grandson of the famous 'Amr, after surrendering to John Curcuas in 928, concluded a peace treaty with him by which he bound himself henceforth to take part with his men in all Byzantine military expeditions; and there is an Arab text which states that 12,000 horsemen were thus transferred to the enemy.[2] But the victorious progress of John Curcuas was retarded, despite the sudden decline of the Abbasid Caliphate of Baghdad, by the emergence of a foe worthy of his steel, the Hamdanid, Sayf ad-Dawla, Amir of Mosul and Aleppo. Byzantine diplomacy at once recognised that the jealousy felt by the

[1] The Byzantine chroniclers refer their readers to a book, now lost, recounting the many expeditions of John Curcuas. See Theophanes Cont., pp. 427–8.

[2] This episode is recognisable as the historical basis of the Byzantine epic which has as its main theme the conversion to the religious and political faith of Byzantium of a descendant of 'Amr and of the Paulicians who dwelt on the banks of the Euphrates, near Samosata, where Curcuas appeared on his conquering progress in 942. The epic, or rather one of its recensions, is dated by the reign of the Emperor Romanus, who is certainly Romanus Lecapenus. On the imperial names appearing in the Byzantine epic see H. Grégoire, Ὁ Διγενὴς Ἀκρίτας (New York, 1942), pp. 70 ff.

Baghdad Caliphate and the Ikhshīdids of Egypt towards this powerful feudatory could be exploited, and Romanus Lecapenus almost went so far as to ally himself with Baghdad and Egypt against the new amir. Sayf ad-Dawla's exploits between 936 and 940 had no lasting results, and he disappears from the Byzantine horizon during the rest of Romanus I's reign, summoned by political unrest to Baghdad. From 940 to 944 Curcuas' only adversary was the Amir of Tarsus, who was nominally a dependant of the Ikhshidids of Egypt.

After 940 the Byzantine armies were thus available for operations in other theatres of war: in Europe, against Igor's Russians, and even in Provence, against the Saracen fortress of Fraxinetum. This explains how it was that John Curcuas was able to take part in the defence of Constantinople against the Russians in 941. Like the first, in 860, this Russian attack stirred emotions deeply at Byzantium, as can be seen from the somewhat embroidered account in a very popular and representative work, the *Life of Basil the Younger*.[1] In 941 the commander of the Russian fleet was Igor, Grand Prince of Kiev, who reigned until 945. The attack of 941 is recorded in all the relevant Byzantine historical and hagiographical literature, and in one of the best of the western sources, the *Antapodosis* of Liutprand. The defence was very well organised by Theophanes the *protovestiarius*, who received as his reward the title of *parakoimomenos*. Three years later Prince Igor once again set out on campaign, on this occasion by the land route. The Byzantine government, warned in time, stopped the Russians at the Danube, by means of fair words and rich gifts. It was only in 944, after a further attack was threatened, that a commercial treaty was signed which reproduced, only with better terms for Byzantium, that of 911.[2]

In 941, however, as soon as the Russians had retreated, Curcuas resumed his conquests in Mesopotamia. He took Martyropolis, Amida (Diyār-Bakr), and then besieged Edessa. Edessa was not to be annexed to Byzantine territory until more than a hundred years later, by George Maniaces. The object of the attack in 944 was to win from

---

[1] This *Life*, written after the disgrace of Curcuas, robs him of the credit of defending Constantinople, setting in his place Panther or Pantherius, who succeeded him as Domestic of the Schools at the end of 944. This popular hero Panther is anachronistically invested with the dignity of Domestic, which he received after the recall of Curcuas. Theophanes the *protovestiarius*, the organiser of the victory against the Russians but also disgraced, probably in 946, is likewise displaced by the hagiographer—or rather transformed into Theodore 'the most saintly *strategus*', surnamed ὁ Σπογγάριος (corrupted from τὰ Σπωρακίου, the district where his chief shrine was). See H. Grégoire, 'Saint Théodore le Stratélate et les Russes d'Igor', *B*, XIII (1938), 291–300.

[2] For a more detailed account of relations with the Russians during the years 941–4 see below: ch. XI, pp. 510–11.

the inhabitants the miraculous picture of Christ (the μανδήλιον), which, according to legend, had been sent by the Saviour to King Abgar. After a now famous consultation of the highest authorities on Islamic doctrine, the people of Edessa held that they were justified in purchasing their freedom, as it were, by the surrender of the relic, especially as several copies of the image remained in the town. The translation of the relic, which was borne in triumph stage by stage to Constantinople, where it arrived on 15 August 944, gave rise to a new and glorious festival which Romanus Lecapenus had the honour of adding to the calendar.

The statesmanship of Romanus Lecapenus is particularly shown in his concern to defend the poorer soldiers, the πένητες στρατιῶται, against the powerful landed proprietors who were swallowing up their properties. This policy, and the very practical motives which inspired it, are not matters of conjecture, since Romanus himself puts them into words: 'The small landed proprietor is immensely valuable, since his existence implies that the state taxes will be paid and the obligations of military service observed: both of these things would completely founder if the number of small proprietors were diminished.'[1] It must be emphasised that no Byzantine Emperor before Romanus, nor indeed any Byzantine, had recognised, still less denounced, the danger which was threatening the economy and defence—even the life—of Byzantium. It was vital that the engrossing of the small properties of the peasant soldiers by the powerful proprietors should be prohibited and checked, whatever the cost. Digenis Akritas, in his discourse to the Emperor Romanus, makes use of the technical term πένητες στρατιῶται in admonishing him to protect the poorer soldiers; and we may be sure that the epic hero echoes faithfully both the groanings of the class whose survival was of such public importance and the intentions of the first Emperor to resolve to protect them. In this matter Romanus Lecapenus shows himself notably superior to his predecessor Leo VI who, far from resisting the landed aristocracy, recommended in the *Tactica* that the nobles and men of wealth should be entrusted with the functions of *strategi* and superior officers; he even went further and abolished the very ancient and wise ruling which prohibited office-holders from purchasing landed property or accepting legacies and gifts without imperial permission (*Cod. Just.* I. 53, 1, ann. 528). Leo removed the restriction completely in the case of office-holders at Constantinople; it was retained in a modified form in the provinces and in its full rigour only for the *strategi* of the themes; furthermore, Leo even revoked the right of pre-emption by neighbours, which had provided

[1] Zepos, *Jus graecoromanum*, I, p. 209.

an obstacle to the formation of large blocks of property. It can thus be held that Leo had systematically contributed towards the feudalisation of the Empire and the amassing of properties by the wealthy, while Romanus Lecapenus, to his great credit, put a brake on this fatal progress.

By his novel of 922, Romanus re-established pre-emption and increased the categories of small proprietors, neighbours or kinsmen, who were entitled to resist the alienation of property to a wealthy stranger. But he was forced to return to this capital point on several occasions, particularly after 927–8, a year which bore hardly on the peasantry by reason of its bad harvest, followed by a great famine. The novel of September 934 contains the famous invective of the 'socially minded' Emperor against the great engrossers, 'more merciless than famine or want'. The date of this novel shows, as might have been expected, that the agrarian policy of this Armenian Emperor ran strictly parallel to his strategy for the reconquest of the Euphrates *limes*, of which the Armenian peasant-soldiers and frontier fighters such as Mleh (Melias), the founder and *strategus* of the theme of Lycandus and one of the prototypes of Digenis Akritas, were the admirable executants. It was necessary to give these men courage and confidence at the time when they were making the definitive capture of Melitene, the key position on the Euphrates frontier, which took place in that very year 934.[1]

It is not possible to analyse here all the details of these legislative provisions; most of them stipulate the restoration of property without any indemnity when the price paid for the lands alienated was less than half the fair price. The novel of September 934 concludes: 'When we have done so much to repel the attacks of external enemies, how could we fail to extirpate also our domestic enemy, as one might describe him, the enemy from within, the enemy of nature, of creation and of all the beneficence of the rule of law? Our just intention is to let liberty reign, our keen-edged weapon this present liberating legislation, rooting out the insatiable passion for engrossment with wrath and loathing.' Naturally this by no means brought about the end of the struggle; three years after the fall of Romanus, Constantine Porphyrogenitus was forced to return to the charge. The will of the central government was being resisted by the will of a caste: a caste composed of members economically powerful and enjoying the prestige which always goes with membership of a superior class, πλούσιοι καὶ εὐγενεῖς. On occasion, moreover, the government had to defend its wise agrarian policy against the πένητες themselves,

---

[1] On the final capture of Melitene see the full account of M. Canard, *Histoire de la dynastie des H'amdanides, op. cit.* pp. 733–56. On the date of the novel, cf. *DR*, 628.

compelled by poverty to submit to the protection of powerful patrons.

The translation of the relic of Edessa to Constantinople was the last triumph of the reign of Romanus Lecapenus. Four months later, on 16 December 944, he was arrested by his rebellious sons and deported to the island of Prote. There he died on 15 June 948, having taken the monastic habit. His sons gained nothing, since Constantine Porphyrogenitus crushed the rebellion by seizing and banishing the imperial culprits.

The ending of the Lecapenids is difficult to explain. But one thing is certain: right up to the last Romanus continued to fulfil loyally his role as the protector of legitimism. Christopher, his eldest and favourite son, having died prematurely in 931, he would never have decided to set his other two sons, who had also been crowned co-Emperors, before Constantine Porphyrogenitus. Scylitzes is mistaken in attributing this intention to him. On the contrary, it seems that in September–December 944 he had made a solemn declaration concerning the imperial precedence announcing that Porphyrogenitus would succeed him.[1] It was this proclamation which provoked the revolt of Stephen and Constantine against their father on 16 December 944. But Porphyrogenitus' reply was prompt, for he felt that he had public opinion with him: on 27 January 945 he had Stephen and Constantine Lecapenus arrested, and sent them to die in exile. Liutprand, who got his information from Bishop Siegfried, the ambassador from Provence, recounts all the details of this legitimist revolution, which began with a popular movement in favour of Porphyrogenitus. It was witnessed by the diplomatic corps and enjoyed their full support, since the ambassadors from Rome and Provence, like the envoys of Gaeta and Amalfi, had actively upheld the son of Leo the Wise, who had waited thirty-three years for his hour to strike. With Romanus Lecapenus fell also the great general Curcuas. The sons of Lecapenus set in his place one of their own relatives, Panther or Pantherius. Pantherius must have been replaced almost immediately by Bardas Phocas, whose family was to cover itself with glory under Porphyrogenitus and Romanus II, and in the person of its most brilliant representative, Nicephorus, son of Bardas, to reach the imperial throne itself.

The disappearance of Romanus Lecapenus and John Curcuas at the height of their triumph might be considered as one of the major

---

[1] He thus confirmed the order in which the co-Emperors should be cited in acts and inscriptions. Cf. G. Rouillard, 'Note prosopographique et chronologique', *B*, VIII (1933), 109, and H. Grégoire, *ibid.* p. 758. Cf. also the novel of 934 and the act of 941, cited by G. Rouillard.

injustices of history. But the unpopularity of the younger Lecapenids, Stephen and Constantine, is well attested though their brother, the Patriarch Theophylact (who remained undisturbed until his death on 27 February 956), seems to have been an able and active head of the Church. Hagiography once again affords an insight if not into public opinion at least into the opinions held in influential circles, such as the great aristocratic families of Asia Minor, whose grievances against the enemy of their caste are understandable. Theophanes, the author of the *Life of St Michael Maleinus*, shows this saint prophesying the doom of the Lecapenids, to the great chagrin of Theophylact.[1] But it is clear that he does not include the father, whom he calls 'this very great Emperor Romanus', in his hatred of the ignoble or incapable sons. Linked to the fortunes of the Phocas family, whose greatest representative was to be the tutor of two Porphyrogeniti, St Michael no doubt knew full well the justice of the view presented here: the old *basileopator* had justified his title, even to his assumption of the boots of purple. The legitimate and tutelary usurper fell from the throne only because his tenacious loyalty had preserved it for the descendant of the first of the Macedonians.

XII. THE PERSONAL RULE OF CONSTANTINE VII PORPHYROGENITUS

It is too often forgotten that Porphyrogenitus had a reign of his own, a personal rule indeed, and that it lasted for fifteen years, from 944 to 959. The beginning of this may have been marked by a change in the governing personnel. Romanus Lecapenus had thrust himself forward for the good of the Empire by eliminating the Phocas family in the person of Leo, the son of Nicephorus Phocas the Elder; in 944 Curcuas had been dismissed. Under Constantine VII, Leo's brother Bardas Phocas, the Domestic of the Schools, held the supreme command. It could even be said that the Phocas dynasty had its origin at this moment, since Bardas was to become Caesar, and his son Emperor in 963. Nevertheless this period was characterised by the greatest possible continuity of both external and internal policy. The nature of this continuity can be precisely demonstrated. Constantine kept to the tenor of the novels of 922 and 934, which was indeed meritorious, for he writes in his *De administrando imperio*: 'The Emperor Romanus was a man lacking in culture and learning, and was not one of those who grew up in the imperial palace, to be educated in the Roman tradition. He was not of the imperial race and was not even

---

[1] See the edition by L. Petit, *ROC*, VII (1902), in particular pp. 755 f. The Maleini, whose immense domains shocked Basil II, were related to both Romanus Lecapenus and the Phocas family.

of noble family.'[1] Perhaps not, but he knew how to win victories in war and defended the rights of the small landowners who were the army's chief strength. Constantine, however, could compose laws as well as Romanus, though the pen was wielded for him, first, in March 947, by Theophilus, *patricius* and *quaestor*, and afterwards by the *patricius* and *quaestor* Theodore Decapolites, who continued in charge under Romanus II, the son of Constantine. One theme runs through these important laws: all peasant properties acquired by the wealthy landowners since the beginning of Constantine's personal rule (or to be acquired in the future) were to be restored immediately and without compensation. In principle, the rule requiring restitution of the purchase price was upheld, side by side with the right of pre-emption of the peasants, not merely, as under the novel of Romanus, in respect of the period anterior to 934, but also for the whole period since the great famine of 927 up to the accession of Constantine VII, which was a concession to the δυνατοί. However, the law of Constantine VII of 947 exempted sellers whose property was worth less than 50 gold *solidi* from making restitution of the purchase price.

The law which was drawn up by Theodore Decapolites was of capital importance for its pronouncement that the property of soldiers was absolutely inalienable and also for its statement of the revenues which such properties should secure: four gold pounds at least for the soldiers of the themes, including the three maritime themes of the Cibyrraeots, Aegean and Samos, and for ordinary seamen two gold pounds. There were very precise regulations forbidding prescription, or rather giving forty years as the period of long usage, which protected anyone who had acquired these inalienable properties against disturbance; and restitution of properties unlawfully alienated could be made not only to the former proprietor but also to his relatives to the sixth degree or to those who had owed military service in common with the old proprietor, or indeed to the meanest soldier (the formula of Digenis Akritas reappears here) who paid taxes jointly with him, or even to the poor peasant who formed part of the same fiscal community. This *patricius* and *quaestor* Theodore Decapolites, one of the heroes of social history, continued to work under Romanus II for the recovery of soldiers' lands alienated since the famine of 927, insisting that for those alienated since the accession of Constantine VII no indemnity should be paid. One more novel, that of Romanus II, March 962, should be mentioned; this was the most severe of all the novels against the engrossers, and distinguished between those who had acquired the property *bona fide*, who were allowed to extricate themselves by a simple restitution, and those

---

[1] Ch. xiii, *DAI*, i, p. 149.

who had acted *mala fide*, who were obliged to pay a penalty in addition to making restitution.

On the northern frontier at the very end of Romanus' reign and during the personal rule of Constantine VII there was comparative peace. The long reign of Peter of Bulgaria (927–69) guaranteed tranquillity in that quarter, while the Magyars only reached Thrace after the first impact of their attack had been weakened by their passage through Bulgaria, which had come to occupy the role of a buffer state. It seems that the Magyar attack of 958 was easily repulsed by the general Pothus Argyrus.

The Arab war, however, was renewed on all fronts. An expedition in the style of those of Leo VI was launched against Crete in 949, also without success. In October 944, Sayf ad-Dawla, the greatest of the Hamdanids, finally installed himself at Aleppo, whence he extended his authority over the whole of northern Syria. Relinquishing Armenia, and renouncing any idea of creating a fleet for himself, he concentrated instead on a seasonal rhythm of razzias (two, sometimes three, in a year). His chief adversary was Bardas Phocas, *magister* and Domestic, who had succeeded the ephemeral Pantherius. This warfare of audacious cavalry expeditions and devastating forays, conducted on both sides in the same spirit if not with the same dash, was also a conflict of dynasties, the Phocas family (Bardas and his three sons Nicephorus, Leo and Constantine) against the Hamdanids, Sayf ad-Dawla and his cousins, the sons of the amir of Mosul, Nāṣir ad-Dawla. It must be conceded that this war was less glorious for Byzantium than for Aleppo. Bardas was certainly not the equal of a Curcuas: he was, indeed, to be far surpassed by his own son Nicephorus. During the rout of 953 near Germanicea (Marʿash), which was continually changing hands, the Domestic was wounded in the face and let his youngest son Constantine be taken captive (he died at Aleppo some time later), an episode which has been immortalised in all its details by the poets of the court of Sayf ad-Dawla. This disaster, whose main effect was to consolidate the Hamdanid's hold on the frontier line running through Samosata–Germanicea–Ḥadath, was fatal to the ageing Greek general. He was replaced about 955 by his son Nicephorus, who resumed and triumphantly completed the work of Curcuas. Constantine VII lived to enjoy two triumphs: the capture of Ḥadath by Nicephorus (June 957) and the capture of Samosata by John Tzimisces (958). In 957 he himself assisted at another success, this time political, which brought the Empire within reach of the goal aimed at by Photius since 860, the baptism of the Russians.[1]

[1] See below: ch. XI, p. 511.

XIII. THE GREAT CONQUESTS: ROMANUS II, NICEPHORUS
PHOCAS AND JOHN TZIMISCES

Romanus II, a young man full of charm and grace, succeeded to the throne at his father's death on 9 November 959. His first wife was Bertha, the illegitimate daughter of Hugh of Provence, who took the Byzantine name of Eudocia and died very young. His second wife, whom he married in 956, was the notorious Theophano. She completely supplanted the Dowager-Empress Helena, and, with the assistance of the eunuch Joseph Bringas, Leo Phocas and John Tzimisces, upset the balance between the command of the army and navy and the civil government, although Bringas, like Theoctistus before him, aspired at least to the renown of having organised the victory, and had in fact instigated the expedition which led to the triumph of Nicephorus Phocas in Crete. At all events, whether or not the actions of Romanus II are to be attributed to the influence of Theophano or Bringas, or even to a desire to execute the plans made by Constantine VII, the fact remains that this short reign was marked by a very knowledgeable direction of military affairs. What has been called the dissociation of Romanus II from the wider interests of the Empire may well have been exaggerated; he was more active than is sometimes realised. He divided the office of Domestic of the Schools into two, primarily in the interests of the Cretan expedition, during which Leo Phocas, Nicephorus' brother, acted as Domestic of the East. He seems to have recognised not merely that the best commanders must be deployed to the best advantage, but also that they should not be allowed to remain in their commands too long—a principle which involved continual changes in the high command, though without depriving the generals of their usefulness. But although since the days of Michael III and Petronas many generals had distinguished themselves in the incessant warfare on the frontier of Asia Minor, everyone so far had failed when faced with the Arabs of Crete. The Muslims had held this important island for nearly a century and a half, and all efforts to dislodge them had failed: the iconoclast Theophilus, the 'orthodox' St Theodora and St Theoctistus (though they had succeeded for a brief moment), Michael III, Basil I, Leo VI, Romanus Lecapenus and Constantine VII had all been unsuccessful. The expedition of Nicephorus Phocas against Crete, 'the God-accursed', began in 960; and after a siege lasting throughout a very severe winter Chandax (Candia) fell in March 961.

After celebrating his well-deserved triumph at Constantinople, Nicephorus departed swiftly to Asia, where Sayf ad-Dawla was still not completely crushed. Here, reviving the exploits of his grandfather, Nicephorus invaded Cilicia and took Anazarbus. He reoccupied Germanicea, which had changed hands more than once, and other places on the frontier; then, in December 962, he captured Aleppo, the capital of Sayf ad-Dawla, which he had to recapture again in 969. But from that time his triumph over the Hamdanids was final. And this triumph, added to the reconquest of Crete and his dominance at sea, secured for Nicephorus the favour of the Empress Theophano, regent since the death of Romanus II (15 March 963). Nicephorus was first proclaimed by the army of Caesarea in Cappadocia, the cradle of his family. Theophano was intelligent enough to realise that her only chance of ensuring the rule of her infant sons, Basil II and Constantine VIII, lay in ratifying the pronouncement of the troops in favour of the man who had decisively defeated the hereditary enemy on two fronts. Nicephorus Phocas entered the capital on 14 August 963. The eunuch Joseph Bringas offered resistance and street warfare developed, in which, as on other battlefields, Nicephorus was victorious. Polyeuctus, the Patriarch, declared himself in his favour, and crowned him on 16 August in St Sophia. About a month later he married Theophano, and thus became the stepfather and protector of the two young Porphyrogeniti, whose rights were preserved intact. Once again, legitimism had triumphed, preserved by the recognition of the most worthy candidate as co-Emperor and by his marriage alliance with the Macedonian house. To rally the support of the Lecapenids, or more strictly speaking, the partisans of the great Emperor Romanus I, Nicephorus took the simple step of retaining in power Basil the *parakoimomenos*, the natural son of Romanus Lecapenus, to whom, indeed, he was indebted for his crowning victory at Constantinople.[1] Leo Phocas, who had distinguished himself during the preceding reign by a series of great victories over Sayf ad-Dawla, was given the title of *curopalates*. Nicephorus' father, Bardas Phocas, the former Domestic of the Schools, was created Caesar. He died in 969, more than ninety years old.

The general command of the armies of the East was entrusted not

[1] Constantine Porphyrogenitus, who was the brother-in-law of Basil the *parakoimomenos*, had created him in 944 *patricius* and then successively commander of the great *hetaireia*, and *parakoimomenos*. Basil was a eunuch, and like many other Byzantine eunuchs, a good general. In 958, with John Tzimisces, he took Samosata. In 963 he helped Nicephorus Phocas in the street fighting which gained him the Empire. In 968 he received the ambassador Liutprand and acted as official spokesman. Nevertheless, there is no ground for believing that he was responsible for the direction of internal policy under Nicephorus Phocas. The novels of Nicephorus were not composed by Basil (this is a commonly held error) but by Symeon the *protoasecretis*. His attitude to the conspiratorial movement which led to the murder of Nicephorus suggests that he was then in opposition to him. He cannot thus be held responsible for Nicephorus' agrarian policy which was contrary to that of Romanus Lecapenus and Constantine Porphyrogenitus.

to one of his relatives but to an Armenian noble who was as good a strategist as he was himself, John Tzimisces, the victor of Samosata. In the winter of 963–4, John Tzimisces, the new Domestic of the East, won the victory known as that of the Mount of Blood, before Tarsus. But it remained for Nicephorus, accompanied by the new *curopalates*, his brother Leo, to resume in Cilicia the offensive which was victorious and decisive; he was at the same time in negotiation with Sayf ad-Dawla who was preoccupied with affairs in Mesopotamia and southern Armenia and unable to send any effective help to the Cilicians. Nicephorus and Leo encamped before Adana, whose inhabitants had fled to Mopsuestia (Mamistra). Mopsuestia fell in July 965, in the presence of Nicephorus himself. A month later, on 16 August 965, Tarsus also fell, having surrendered on most humane terms to become once again a Christian city. The only Muslim prince who made any attempt at saving Tarsus was the Ikhshidid ruler of Egypt and his intervention came too late; his fleet bringing relief and supplies was partially destroyed. The most that Sayf ad-Dawla could do was to negotiate the exchange—or rather the ransom—of prisoners. The Amirate of Aleppo remained cut off from Cilicia, though Sayf ad-Dawla had now succeeded in reoccupying his capital. In October 966 Nicephorus acquired from the town of Manbij (Hierapolis) a relic similar to the image of Edessa, a brick on which the features of Christ were impressed. It was in vain that Sayf ad-Dawla offered the Emperor Nicephorus tribute money in return for a peace, and he died at Aleppo in February 967, which gave Nicephorus the opportunity of interrupting his eastern campaigns to march against the Bulgars.

But Nicephorus reappeared in Muslim territory in 968, and it was from that date that his campaign took on the nature of a crusade. The Muslims were divided and the prey of internal discords. The great champions of the Muslim holy war against Byzantium, the Hamdanids were now, and had been since Sayf ad-Dawla's declining years, seeking an *entente* with Byzantium, menaced as they were by the Buwayhids in the north and the Fatimids in the south. The Empire no longer needed to be on the defensive, and the time had come to envisage the reconquest of the provinces lost in the seventh century. The historian Kamāl ad-Dīn relates how Nicephorus, having entered the mosque of Tarsus, mounted the *minbar* and demanded of his followers 'Where am I now?' And when they replied, 'On the *minbar* of Tarsus', he cried, 'No, on the *minbar* of Jerusalem, for Tarsus alone barred the way to Jerusalem'. This incident well illustrates the crusading atmosphere which prevailed at that time at Byzantium, and which was to pervade the Syrian wars of Nicephorus, Tzimisces and Basil II. The feeling of superiority with which

Nicephorus Phocas regarded Islam and its moral and military resources is shown in his famous letter to the Caliph al-Mutʿī.[1] Even its form is remarkable and characteristic. It shows that the Christian Empire was able to call on the services of first-class Arab scholars. Despite its insolence, which must have been wounding to true believers, the Arabs preserved this document, together with a commentary on it which challenged, though mistakenly, the reality of some of the victories claimed by Nicephorus.

The Byzantine offensive had clearly stirred the Christian populations still subjected to Islam who felt that their deliverance was at hand. But the crusade of Nicephorus was not yet completed. Two great victories were yet to come, the second only after his death. On 28 October 969 the great city of Antioch fell to Michael Burtzes and the eunuch Peter Phocas the *stratopedarches*, who came from Cilicia to assist him. Immediately afterwards Peter marched on Aleppo, which had cut loose from the Hamdanids and was now being governed by Karguyah, who in December–January 969–70 signed with the *stratopedarches* the treaty which made Aleppo a simple vassal of the Empire. It was only right that the Byzantine epic in its latest redaction should record this capitulation by the hereditary enemy, although Karguyah, who is called Karois, is confused with the Paulician Karbeas. Thus, what had been merely a series of marauding expeditions round Adana in the time of Nicephorus the Elder had developed, under the guidance of his grandson, into a firm occupation of Cilicia and a great part of Syria. The island of Cyprus also, which had remained in a state of ambiguous neutrality, had been reclaimed for the Empire in 965. No terms could be too strong in which to emphasise the achievement of the reconquest of Syria and its great metropolitan city Antioch, the 'city of God', the seat of the orthodox Patriarchate, an ambition which no Emperor had dared to dream of for the past three centuries. The strength and prestige of Byzantium must have been fully in evidence when Liutprand of Cremona, the ambassador of Otto the Great, who had restored the Western Empire, appeared at Constantinople in 968.

The new Emperor of the West was seeking a marriage alliance between his son and a Byzantine princess, who would bring as her dowry all the remaining Byzantine possessions in Italy. Never was any diplomatic proposal so ill-received. Unfortunately for the West, the proposal was made at a time when the Eastern Empire had become almost miraculously rejuvenated, so much so that the Byzantines felt themselves perfectly capable of achieving the reconquest of

---

[1] G. von Grunebaum, 'Eine poetische Polemik zwischen Byzanz und Bagdad im X. Jahrhundert', *Studia Arabica*, I, in *Analecta Orientalia*, XIV (Rome, 1937).

Palestine without any assistance from the West. In these circumstances, Nicephorus could not but feel deeply vexed at Otto's various activities: his assumption of the imperial crown, his subjugation of Rome and the Roman Church, his alliance with the princes of Capua and Benevento, who were vassals of the Empire, and his tentative attack against Bari. His ambassador was curtly told that there could be no question of a marriage between a barbarian king and a Porphyrogenita. Nor had the Bulgars realised that Byzantium had reached its apogee. In 965 they were foolish enough to lay claim to the payment, with arrears, of the tribute they had once been promised. The throne of Bulgaria was still occupied by Peter (927–69), but his prudence and moderation—and his sincere devotion to Byzantium— had by this time no doubt been overborne by the influence of his heir, Boris II (969–72). Nicephorus had the Bulgarian envoys whipped and sent home without vouchsafing any reply; but so long as Antioch remained uncaptured he did not condescend to allow himself to become completely immersed in a war with Bulgaria. Instead, he called on the assistance of Svjatoslav, prince of Kiev and son of Olga, who twice invaded Bulgaria, taking captive the new Tsar, Boris II. But this appeal to an overmighty ally was a mistake. On the eve of his assassination Nicephorus was preparing to make good the damage and planned a reversal of alliances: that is, he intended that there should be a Bulgar–Byzantine expedition against Svjatoslav.[1] The projected alliance with the Bulgars permitted the marriage of the two Porphyrogeniti Emperors with two Bulgar princesses.

Nicephorus Phocas was assassinated on 10 December 969, six weeks after his military and political achievement had been crowned by the conquest of Antioch. Attempts have been made to explain the crime by reference to the sacrifices imposed on the country by a government bent on conquest, heavy taxation and inflation,[2] and to the resulting discontent. But although Nicephorus was not always popular, his murder was generally deplored, and few lines of Byzantine poetry have found as sympathetic an echo as the third iambic trimeter of his epitaph by John Geometres:

> O Nicephorus, well-named indeed, since thou wast
> Conqueror of all thine enemies, except thy wife.

---

[1] It is well known that Liutprand, the envoy of Otto the Great in 968, complained greatly at being placed lower at table than the Bulgarian ambassadors, whom he considered unwashed barbarians. This display of favour towards the Bulgars only becomes explicable if it is assumed that Nicephorus was already planning the reversal of alliances, while the date of Liutprand's embassy cannot be other than 968 (see G. Ostrogorsky, *History of the Byzantine State*, p. 259, and D. Anastasijević, *Glasnik Skopskog Naučnog Društva*, XI (1932), 51 ff.).

[2] On the difficult question of the *tetarteron*, see below: p. 155, n. 2.

The unpopularity of Nicephorus Phocas, in Constantinople at least, is proved by the hostility of the crowd towards him, particularly during the episode of the 'Armenian frenzy', as it might be called. There exists a curious passage in an eyewitness account of this affair, that of Leo the Deacon, who is otherwise very favourable to Nicephorus, and who refrained from reproducing the accusations against the merciless exactions of a ruler who was primarily concerned with the payment of his troops, accusations which are repeated by chroniclers such as Scylitzes-Cedrenus and Zonaras. Leo the Deacon related how whilst he was still very young he witnessed an explosion of popular discontent which was met by Nicephorus with an intrepid and impassive composure. The Armenians had started a quarrel with the marines, which caused a general flight of the populace from the capital. This curious incident is not the only one of its kind reported.[1] On another occasion, the crowd of spectators at the Hippodrome imagined that the soldiers, who had been ordered to enact a mock battle, were preparing a massacre of the citizens. And, as with the 'Armenian attack' (αἱ ἔφοδοι τῶν Ἀρμενίων), there was once again panic. This time Leo the Deacon lays the blame on the ignorance of the urban crowd who, he says, had no understanding of military spectacles.[2] Admittedly, with all the many triumphs they were privileged to witness thanks to Nicephorus' magnificent series of conquests, the Byzantine populace could satisfy themselves that the financial aid demanded of them had not been wasted. But they also had cause to regret certain disasters, such as the Sicilian expedition. Without detracting from the glory of the conqueror of Crete, it must be remembered that Nicephorus dreamed of inaugurating his reign by the reconquest of a still greater prize, Sicily, and that this campaign, commanded by the eunuch and *patricius* Nicetas, admiral of the fleet, and by another patrician, Manuel, commander of the cavalry, had a disastrous ending. The campaign began well: so well, in fact, that the Greeks reoccupied Syracuse, Himera, Taormina and Leontini without spilling a drop of blood. But Manuel was incapable of profiting from his victory and of keeping what he had gained. He dispersed his forces, which were probably in any case inadequate for the occupation of the whole island, and the adventure which had begun so gloriously ended with a series of partial defeats followed by

[1] This 'flight from the Armenians' figures in a curious narrative which in some manuscripts forms the concluding portion of the *Synaxarion* of Constantinople.

[2] Leo the Deacon gives the date of these disturbances as 966 and puts the 'Armenian frenzy' in the following year. Between his account of these two affairs, both of which illustrate the unpopularity of Nicephorus, Leo denounces the engrossing of corn by the Emperor's brother, Leo the *curopalates*, and also the excessive and unprecedented taxes which Nicephorus demanded from his subjects to pay his troops.

a total catastrophe.[1] Liutprand, who because of his anti-Byzantine attitude, generated by his visit of 968, was prompt to record anything which seemed to detract from the glory of Nicephorus, does not fail to recall this disaster in his malicious account of his second embassy, which fixes the date of the expedition: it took place three years before the summer of 968, thus in 965.[2] Leo the Deacon, however, praises the stoical calm with which Nicephorus bore the failure of the Sicilian expedition. He ransomed the prisoners and in 967 made a peace with the Amir of North Africa. But all this testimony proves that the populace were murmuring their discontent, not without reason, and that they were put harshly to the test by a policy of indisputable but costly grandeur.

On the other hand, it cannot be deduced from Nicephorus' legislation on the subject of military landholdings that he lost the sympathy of the 'poor' soldiers by ceasing to protect them from the encroachments of the 'powerful'. It is true that in his Novel xx of 967 he withdrew the right of the poor to pre-empt over the property of the wealthy, and accused previous Emperors of having showed themselves partial towards the πένητες, whereas in the name of justice they should have held the scales equal in their dealings with their subjects. It is also true that forty years after the great famine of 927 the Emperor decreed that there should be no further appeals against alienations in favour of the wealthy made before that year. But the great principle laid down by Romanus Lecapenus was still observed; the wealthy were not to acquire the property of the poor. As for Novel xxii, although its date is not so well established as is that of Novel xx, it must also certainly be ascribed to the very last period of the reign,[3] since it introduced a new principle into the legislation, a principle of such importance that it could hardly have escaped mention in, for example, the novel of 967. After reaffirming the right of restitution without compensation in respect of all military

---

[1] The unfortunate Nicetas was taken prisoner; he was a highly educated person, and a manuscript written by him whilst he was in captivity in Africa has been preserved. The *Life* of St Nicephorus, later Bishop of Miletus, who was chaplain-general to the expedition, reveals the commotion produced among the populace by this fresh Sicilian disaster; cf. *AB*, xiv (1895), 133–61.

[2] Cf. *Legatio*, p. 361 (*MGH*, ed. Bekker), where Liutprand speaks of a terrible famine, in addition to other misfortunes of the Empire, which weakened Nicephorus' troops; this famine, he says, was reigning in the capital in July 968, at the time of the Emperor's departure for the East.

[3] It is interesting that the preceding novels and one of Romanus the Younger were inspired by Symeon the *protoasecretis*, while Novel xxii owes its inspiration to a functionary otherwise unknown, Basil the *protospatharius* ὁ ἐπὶ τῶν δεήσεων, who cannot readily be identified with Basil the *parakoimomenos*. It may be recalled that Symeon the *protoasecretis* played an important role in one of the most curious episodes of Liutprand's embassy in July 968.

property which did not yield more than the minimum revenue of four gold pounds and the right of pre-emption of the *stratiotes* over all land which exceeded the fixed minimum in value, the legislator raised the minimum value of inalienable soldiers' holdings from four to twelve gold pounds; it was stated that this was done in view of the formation of a new military category, that of the armed horsemen (οἱ κλιβανοφόροι καὶ ἐπιλωρικοφόροι), who would naturally have to be richer than the old infantrymen.

This new legislation forms a natural accompaniment to an era of great expeditions in which a heavy cavalry was 'the queen of battles' and to an era of reoccupation and settlement, such as that which saw the reconquest of Cilicia and Syria, where the victor freely distributed the lands vacated by the Muslims to soldier-colonists of every race, and particularly to 'Romans' and Armenians. In this way was created a reservoir of excellent mounted troops, who distinguished themselves by their triumphs on every field of battle, particularly against the Russians under Svjatoslav and during the crusade of John Tzimisces. Novel XXII was the foundation statute of the Byzantine army of this great epoch (975–1025). It would be unjust and somewhat undiscerning to read anything hostile to the πένητες into this novel. On the contrary, this law must have been very popular with the new army that the men of the *reconquista* had had the foresight to create. Indeed it must be considered as the expression of clever diplomacy, designed to satisfy and soothe the discontent in an army for which the advent of new perils, such as the Russian and Bulgarian dangers, was to provide new tasks. Again, Nicephorus, himself an ascetic and devout man, had certainly no hatred for monasteries, and appears as patron of the development of monasticism on Mt Athos. But, like many Christian sovereigns of all periods, he thought it his duty to purge monasteries of abuses. His great novel against their enrichment and pointless multiplication (Novel XIX) was one of his first legislative acts (924).[1] Nicephorus did not hesitate to resort to radical means in order to remedy so regrettable a condition. Henceforth any new monastic foundation was forbidden and the prohibition applied also to the foundation of new hospices for strangers (ξενῶνες) and old people (γηροκομεῖα), to prevent any evasion of the order.

Furthermore, in future, hospices and almshouses were not to receive any benefactions, except in the case of establishments which as a result of bad administration would be without means of survival.

---

[1] See the analysis of this remarkable document in A. Ferradou, *Des biens des monastères à Byzance* (Bordeaux, 1896), pp. 145 ff., and P. Charanis, 'The Monastic Properties and the State in the Byzantine Empire', *DOP*, IV (1948), 55 ff.

In such cases, the Emperor reserved to himself the right of deciding whether the conditions laid down for the receipt of a grant had been fulfilled. The reasons which (religious considerations apart) impelled Nicephorus Phocas to this energetic offensive against the rapid accumulation of property held in mortmain, a campaign which was aimed at augmenting the resources of the Empire, are too obvious to need any reiteration here. It would be almost as superfluous to mention that each of these actions, 'which seem to reveal the man behind them as a genuine statesman, far in advance of his time, created new groups of malcontents at Byzantium, and alienated the new privileged classes from the Basileus'.[1] Moreover, and this is curious, he had bitter critics even among the ascetics whom he favoured. It is well known that Nicephorus, the nephew of the monk Michael Maleinus, hermit of Kyminas in Bithynia, whom he venerated throughout his life, was the real founder of the monastic republic of Mt Athos, and that his greatest favourite, the monk who fulfilled his ideal, was St Athanasius, who, thanks to his benefactions, built the Great Lavra. In the *typikon* of Athanasius, Nicephorus is even classed among the martyrs and, although he does not figure in the *Synaxarion*, an *acolouthia* was composed in his honour. But this reputation for saintliness did not prevent Nicephorus from being the object of grave accusations, even in the monastic circles which he had favoured and which were so devoted to him. His zeal was such that whilst he was in Crete he had even promised Athanasius that he would shortly retire from the world to finish his days on Mt Athos. Athanasius was therefore indignant and disillusioned to hear of his accession and marriage to a woman so suspect, actions which to him seemed like the breaking of a vow, a veritable betrayal. This perjury, which could alienate even one of his most privileged partisans, in other monastic circles must certainly have reinforced the bad impression produced by Nicephorus' legislation concerning ecclesiastical property.

Finally, it must be mentioned that the sources accuse Nicephorus of a debasement of the coinage, which aggravated the distress of the people, already weighed down by taxation and suffering from dearth. It seems that the debased coinage, which was below the legal weight, was called the *tetarteron*.[2] These measures, to which the glorious and victorious Basileus was reduced in order to finance his policy of victory, reaped him such a harvest of discontent that his enemies

[1] G. Schlumberger, *Nicéphore Phocas*, p. 536.
[2] See R. S. Lopez, 'La crise du besant au Xe siècle et la date du Livre du Préfet', *Mélanges Henri Grégoire*, II (1950), 403 ff. and the bibliography cited by G. Ostrogorsky, *History of the Byzantine State*, pp. 192, n. 1 and 260, n. 1.

both in the army and at court could strike at him with impunity at the very moment when the reoccupation of Bulgaria by Svjatoslav imposed a fresh and terrible ordeal on Byzantium. It must be mentioned that Nicephorus, doubtless on account of his austerity, had lost the affections of his wife, who had taken as her lover the Domestic of the East, the Armenian John Tzimisces. John, together with Michael Burtzes, the conqueror of Antioch, and many others who were more or less actively implicated in the plot (for example, Basil the *parakoimomenos*), were the instruments of Nicephorus' assassination, on the night of 10 or 11 December 969.

XIV. THE REIGN OF JOHN TZIMISCES

In spite of all the discontent produced in certain circles by Nicephorus Phocas, events were to show that his family retained faithful and even fanatical adherents throughout the Empire, who up to the end of the reign of Basil II did not despair of restoring to the throne this dynasty which from the time of the first Nicephorus Phocas had been distinguished by generations of heroes of genuine popularity. In fact, the plot of 10–11 December 969, the murder of Nicephorus Phocas and the accession of John Tzimisces, came as a complete surprise. The explanation for it is to be found in the split in the aristocratic and military party which, in conjunction with the Empress Theophano and Basil the *parakoimomenos*, had brought Nicephorus Phocas to the throne on 16 August 963. This split was the work of a coalition of malcontents, and its chief cause was the deep and not unjustified rancour felt by the Armenian John Tzimisces, the prime instigator and author of the earlier *coup d'état* of 963. It is clear that Nicephorus had but ill rewarded the author of his imperial fortunes. Tzimisces had received from him the title of Domestic of the Schools. But in fact, throughout the reign of Nicephorus, he found himself refused the opportunity, which he sought, of directing decisive operations.[1] He was only second in command, and his secondary role became all the more conspicuous after the last attack on Tarsus. His name is not mentioned in connection with any Byzantine conquest in Cilicia or Syria after 965. He was not among those who had the honour of capturing either Antioch[2] or Aleppo. This

---

[1] It seems that Nicephorus prevented him from marching against Mayyāfāriqīn in 966; cf. G. W. Freytag, *Zeitschrift der deutschen morgenländischen Gesellschaft*, xi (1857), 208.

[2] Kamāl ad-Dīn (1193–1282) is alone in making John Tzimisces a participant in the capture of Antioch. But since he does not mention Burtzes it seems clear that he has substituted the more famous name of the future Emperor for his. See the translation of the passage from Kamāl ad-Dīn in Leo the Deacon, p. 391.

might cause some surprise were it not for the fact that Scylitzes tells us in categorical terms that Tzimisces was deprived of his functions as Domestic of the Schools.[1] The sources are not in agreement concerning the results of Theophano's action in demanding the return of Tzimisces to the court, since Scylitzes tells us that the Empress could only meet him in secret. What does appear obvious is that Tzimisces was suspect in the eyes of Nicephorus, doubtless not without reason. There can be little doubt of the truth of the allegations concerning the relations between Tzimisces and Theophano. But the ease with which Tzimisces abandoned his accomplice once he had become Emperor suggests that he had accepted her help in order to re-enter the palace without feeling as strongly for her as she did for him.

As Tzimisces had not himself inflicted the mortal blow on Nicephorus he appears to have been able to meet the requirements of the Patriarch Polyeuctus, who laid down three conditions for the recognition and coronation of the new Basileus: he was to punish the assassin (or the two assassins—the sources disagree on this point), to exile Theophano, according to popular rumour the real instigator of the murder, and to repeal the law of Nicephorus which limited episcopal rights over ecclesiastical property. In addition to satisfying these conditions Tzimisces also made numerous charitable gifts. He was crowned by Polyeuctus on Christmas Day 969.

Immediately after the murder, Basil the *parakoimomenos*, the natural son of Romanus Lecapenus, took it on himself to conduct the revolution and organise the new regime, just as he had in 963. His first task was to remove the members of the Phocas family. Leo Phocas and his son Nicephorus were exiled to the islands. Bardas Phocas, Leo's other son, the governor of the themes of Chaldia and Colonea, was ordered not to move outside Amasea. The greatest weakness in John Tzimisces' position lay not unnaturally in the resentment felt in the powerful Phocas family, whose adherents were numerous and whose popularity was to some extent enhanced by the

---

[1] Scylitzes-Cedrenus, II, p. 375. Zonaras, III, p. 516, is the only authority to maintain that in exchange Tzimisces was given the office of Logothete of the Drome. As for the recall of Tzimisces, this is affirmed by Cedrenus (*loc. cit.*). It is difficult to date Tzimisces' disgrace with certainty. After his victory at the Mount of Blood in 963–4 and an unsuccessful attempt to take Mopsuestia (a disaster celebrated by the poet Mutanabbi), Tzimisces took part in the siege of Tarsus in 965 where, according to Leo the Deacon, he commanded the left wing of the troops brought up to assist Leo Phocas, while Nicephorus Phocas commanded the right wing. It is after this year 965 that Tzimisces seems to have ceased to play any part in military affairs. It must have been shortly after the events of 964–5 that he began his period in disgrace, during which he was deprived of his military command and reduced to civil functions and finally to exile from the capital.

martyrdom of one who had been at once general, Emperor and monk. The new Emperor's strength lay in his military genius and in his Armenian origin. He was born in a small Armenian town in the region of Khozan (Χόζανον θέμα)[1] which later adopted his name (Tshmishkatzak), and was a descendant of the family which had also given the Empire the great general of the reconquest, John Curcuas (Tzimisces' grandfather Theophilus was a brother of the Domestic). Tzimisces was related through his mother to the Phocas family, but it is his Armenian ancestry which explains his close alliance with the Lecapenid Basil the *parakoimomenos*, himself the offspring of an Armenian Emperor, who had already made two Emperors and on whose abilities Tzimisces greatly relied. Both men were undoubtedly in agreement in keeping a close watch on the Phocas family and also in attempting to win them over. The first step was to enlist the services of Peter Phocas the *stratopedarches* who had captured Antioch: he, together with the half-Armenian Bardas Sclerus, who was very popular in the East and was the brother-in-law of John Tzimisces, was at once charged with the task of mounting guard over the Russians, the masters of Bulgaria, and of making preparations in Thrace for a victorious offensive, while Tzimisces was establishing his power and gathering his forces.[2] There was thus complete continuity in government, policy and strategy.

Bardas Sclerus was wonderfully successful in his mission. By an adroit strategic withdrawal, he lured the Russians and their allies the Pechenegs into an ambush near Arcadiopolis (now Lüleburgaz); the Russian chronicle transformed the engagement into a victory, but the invaders were in fact contained, although the Byzantines could not prevent the enemy from making raids which thrust as far forward as Constantinople. But Svjatoslav then evacuated Thrace and negotiations were begun. This was all the more opportune since Bardas Phocas had meanwhile proclaimed himself Emperor in Asia Minor, and Tzimisces had been obliged to recall Bardas Sclerus from the Bulgar front. This first revolt of the Phocas family was fairly easily subdued, thanks to the skilful diplomacy of Bardas Sclerus in winning over one by one almost all the military men who had joined Bardas Phocas. Bardas Phocas finally capitulated, to be transported, together with his family, to Chios. They were deliberately spared mutilation, since it was hoped that they might be persuaded to support the new regime.

The *pronunciamiento* of Bardas Phocas in 970 determined the Em-

---

[1] See E. Honigmann, *Ostgrenze*, pp. 75 ff.
[2] Leo the Deacon (p. 107) is alone in mentioning two Greek corps whose commanders were Bardas Sclerus and Peter Phocas.

peror to take steps to consolidate his position by marriage with a Porphyrogenita. In November 970 John Tzimisces, whose first wife had belonged to the Sclerus family, married Theodora, a daughter of Constantine Porphyrogenitus and aunt to the two Porphyrogeniti Basil and Constantine: she was a lady already mature in years and, according to Leo the Deacon, more wise than beautiful.

The offensive against the Russians could now be resumed. Attempts at negotiation had proved fruitless. Svjatoslav, greedy for loot and victories, as Leo the Deacon puts it, and in disregard of the example set by his mother, the regent Olga, who had been baptised and had visited Constantinople in state in 957,[1] reverted to the aggressive policies of Igor and his predecessors, taking full advantage of Nicephorus Phocas' mistake in calling him into Bulgaria. 'I have no pleasure in living in Kiev; I would sooner dwell at Perejaslavec on the Danube, for that is the centre of my territories. Riches are continually pouring into Perejaslavec: gold, cloth, wine, and a variety of fruits from Greece; silver and horses from Bohemia and Hungary; skins, wax, honey and slaves from Russia.' These are the words put into his mouth by the Russian chronicle. When a Byzantine peace mission offered him the sum already promised him by Nicephorus Phocas on condition that he would withdraw from the territory he had occupied,[2] he replied in provocative terms. He demanded an enormous ransom for the prisoners he held and inordinate compensation in money for the conquered territories; and he ended with these words: 'If the Romans do not want to pay, the only course open to them is to withdraw from Europe, where they have no right to be, and to retire to Asia. There can be no other way of establishing peace between the Romans and the Russians.' The Byzantines replied by demanding the immediate and complete evacuation of the territories occupied by the Russians, and by threatening Svjatoslav with the tragic fate of his father Igor, who had also dreamed of the conquest of Constantinople, but had been reduced to an ignominious retreat. The Greek threats could not immediately be put into execution in that year (970), because of the rising of Bardas Phocas; but once that had been suppressed Bardas Sclerus resumed his command.

In the war of Tzimisces against Svjatoslav the military skill and the personal courage of the Basileus were both displayed to their best advantage. The chronology of Tzimisces' Russian campaign, for long disputed, now appears to have been firmly established, both

---

[1] On this controversial question see also below: ch. XI, p. 511, note 4.

[2] Leo the Deacon (p. 103), Scylitzes-Cedrenus (II, p. 384) and the *Russian Primary Chronicle* (ed. Cross and Sherbowitz-Wetzor, p. 87) are all in complete agreement concerning these conditions of peace.

as regards its duration and the year when it took place.[1] Early in the spring of 971, a fleet of more than 300 ships was sent to the mouth of the Danube to cut off the Russian retreat.[2] At the same time, the Emperor, who now had all his land forces once more at his disposal, left the capital for Adrianople, where his troops probably joined up with those under John Curcuas. The Greeks crossed the Balkan mountain-range without difficulty and on 12 April poured into the plain which contained Preslav, the Bulgar capital. On the evening of 13 April this great city and its royal *aoul*, transformed by the Russians into a last stronghold of desperate resistance, fell into Byzantine hands. The Tsar Boris was taken prisoner but Tzimisces treated him with respect, declaring that he had come not to enslave his country but to liberate it from the Russians. It was at Dorystolum that Svjatoslav learned of the fall of Preslav. The Russian prince set out to meet Tzimisces, who was waiting for him in a plain twelve miles south of the city. On St George's day, 23 April, a great battle was joined, in the course of which, it is said, the advantage passed a dozen times from one army to the other. In the event, the Russians were put to flight, though they had succeeded in upsetting both wings of the Greek army; their defeat was brought about by the valour of the Armenian infantry and the personal intervention of the Emperor.[3] Once arrived at Dorystolum, Tzimisces prepared to blockade the place, since he could not hope to take such a powerfully defended position by storm.

Meanwhile, however, whilst the siege of Dorystolum was still in progress, Constantinople became the scene of an event which might have had disastrous consequences for Tzimisces. Profiting by the absence of the Emperor, Leo Phocas the *curopalates* and his son Nicephorus, the rebels who had once received generous treatment from Tzimisces, now secretly re-entered the capital. But the con-

---

[1] On the chronology and duration of Tzimisces' Russian campaign see principally: F. Dölger, 'Die Chronologie des grossen Feldzuges des Kaisers Johannes Tzimiskes gegen die Russen', *BZ*, xxxii (1932), 275–94; H. Grégoire, 'La dernière campagne de Jean Tzimisces contre les Russes', *B*, xii (1937), 267–76. See also P. O. Karyškovskij, 'O chronologii russkovizantijskoj vojny pri Svjatoslave', *VV*, v (N.S.) (1952), 127–38.

[2] It is usually claimed that the fleet was commanded by Leo the *drungarius*, though no text says so explicitly. If it was, then Tzimisces must shortly afterwards have ordered Leo to return to the capital, since Leo was certainly there before hostilities had come to an end; see below: p. 161.

[3] The decisive role played by the corps of Armenian infantry in the battle of 23 April 971 emerges from a passage in the *Universal History* of Stephen Asoļik of Taron (ch. viii, trans. F. Macler, ii, p. 45), where the Armenian author describes a fight between the troops of Tzimisces and those of Svjatoslav, which, thanks to certain features which are common to this narrative and that of Scylitzes-Cedrenus (ii, p. 399), can be identified as referring to this battle. C. Göllner, however (*RHSE*, xiii (1936), 356), exaggerates the extent of these resemblances.

spiracy was betrayed and was immediately scotched, thanks to the energy of the two men entrusted by Tzimisces with the defence of the city, Leo the *drungarius* and Basil the *rector*.[1] Leo Phocas and his son were arrested in St Sophia and deported to the island of Calonymus,[2] where, on the Emperor's orders, they were blinded.

The struggle for Dorystolum was pursued with unabated tenacity right up to the end. Finally, on 20 July the Russians, whose situation was becoming more and more critical, made a supreme effort at raising the blockade. A lengthy battle ensued. In this decisive conflict of 21 July both sides fought with a fervour born of despair. For a long time the battle remained undecided. But at the end of the day a violent storm broke, raising clouds of dust which blinded the Russians soldiers, and the Greeks claimed that they saw an unknown horseman, mounted on a white horse, at the head of their formations, who spread disorder and terror among the enemy ranks. They saw this mysterious ally as none other than St Theodore the Stratelates 'whose feast we are accustomed to celebrate on this day'. The Emperor was the first to credit the glorious martyr with the laurels of victory: on his return to Constantinople, he changed the name of Dorystolum to Theodoropolis.[3]

After this fresh defeat, there was no choice for the Russians but to sue for peace. Svjatoslav offered to surrender Dorystolum, return all his prisoners, and evacuate Bulgaria. In exchange, he asked for permission to return home with the remnants of his army and for supplies. He further asked that the Russians might be recognised as

[1] It is tempting to identify this Basil with the famous Basil the *parakoimomenos* (cf. G. Schlumberger, *Epopée*, I, p. 130). The functions of *rector* would have suited this individual to perfection, and there is nothing to prove that Tzimisces kept him at his side throughout the whole of his campaign in Bulgaria. Moreover, the conduct of Leo the *drungarius* and Basil the *rector* in dragging Leo Phocas and his son Nicephorus from their refuge in St Sophia is strikingly reminiscent of the conduct of Basil the *parakoimomenos* towards Joseph Bringas and the Empress Theophano: and one could also add the fact that later on, during the first revolt of Bardas Sclerus, Basil the *parakoimomenos* called on the services of the ex-*drungarius* Leo, who was now *protovestiarius* (Scylitzes-Cedrenus, II, p. 424). But since the sources never give the *parakoimomenos* the title of *rector* the identification of the two Basils must remain merely an attractive hypothesis.

[2] Leo the Deacon, p. 147; Scylitzes-Cedrenus (II, p. 404) has it that they were sent to the island of Prote.

[3] This is the account of Leo the Deacon, and clearly correct. Scylitzes-Cedrenus (II, p. 411) and Zonaras (III, p. 534) state that the town whose name was changed was not Dorystolum but Euchaneia (Εὐχάνεια ἢ Εὐχάϊτα). The Pontic town of Euchaneia was the centre of the cult of St Theodore the Stratelates, and Tzimisces built there a new basilica to replace the old *martyrion* of the Saint. He was also on very good terms with its Metropolitan Theophilus (or Philotheus) (see below: p. 162, n. 1). For the locality and identification of Euchaneia–Euchaïta (= Avkhat), see H. Grégoire, *BZ*, XIX (1910), 59 ff.; J. G. C. Anderson, F. Cumont and H. Grégoire, *Studia Pontica*, III (Brussels, 1910), 205 ff.; H. Delehaye, *AB*, XXX (1911), 326.

one of the peoples friendly to the Empire and allowed, as in the past, to sell their merchandise at Constantinople. These proposals, as has been remarked, were indeed those of a defeated people. Tzimisces hastened to accept them. It is also said that the Emperor, at the request of Svjatoslav, sent an embassy to the Pechenegs:[1] he proposed a treaty of friendship, demanded that they should cease making incursions into Bulgar territory and requested a free passage of their country for the Russian prince and his troops. The Pechenegs agreed to everything except this last request. In the spring of 972, Svjato-slav, who had been forced by this hostile attitude on the part of his former allies to winter at the foot of the cataracts of the Dnieper, was attacked by Kurya, the Pecheneg prince, and perished miserably at the hands of this nomadic people.

Tzimisces took the Bulgarian royal family, together with spoils of every kind, back with him to Constantinople, where he celebrated a triumph. On the chariot drawn by four white horses, the rightful place of the Emperor, was set in his stead a greatly venerated icon of the Virgin, which he had brought from Bulgaria, while Tzimisces made his entry into the city following devoutly behind. Before entering the imperial palace, he led forth Boris, the young Bulgar Tsar, who had followed the triumph on foot, and in the presence of the crowd assembled in the forum of Constantinople[2] he first ordered him to remove his insignia of sovereignty and then raised him to the rank of *magister*.[3] There could have been no more impressive demon-

---

[1] Scylitzes-Cedrenus (II, p. 412) says that the ambassador was Bishop Theophilus of Euchaïta, almost certainly to be identified with the Bishop Philotheus of Euchaïta who had acted as negotiator for Nicephorus Phocas in 963 and 969 (see S. Runciman, *History of the First Bulgarian Empire*, p. 214), and with the *syncellus* Theophilus who appears as author of the Russo-Byzantine treaty of 971 in the Nestorian Chronicle (see *DR*, 739): for it is known that the title of *syncellus* was granted to a number of the Bishops of Euchaïta, purely as a mark of the Emperor's esteem and not in the official sense of secretary. See V. Grumel, *REB*, III (1945), 92 ff.

[2] Not, as has been said (cf. G. Schlumberger, *Epopée*, I, p. 176), the 'Forum Augustéon'. According to Scylitzes-Cedrenus (II, p. 413) the deposition of Boris took place ἐν τῷ λεγομένῳ φόρῳ, according to Zonaras (III, p. 536), κατὰ τὴν πλακωτὴν λεγομένην ἀγοράν. The use of these expressions proves that the forum in question is that of Constantine, the forum *par excellence* (ὁ φόρος), also known as the πλακωτὸς φόρος or πλακωτόν (cf. R. Janin, *Constantinople byzantine*, pp. 67 f.). Leo the Deacon (p. 158) places the scene of the deposition inside the imperial palace, which is less spectacular and, for that reason, less likely to be correct.

[3] It was probably at this time that Boris' brother Romanus was made a eunuch (cf. G. Schlumberger, *Epopée*, I, p. 178). Scylitzes-Cedrenus (II, p. 435) attributes the mutilation of Romanus to Joseph Bringas the *parakoimomenos* in 963: but at that time he was merely a hostage. In 972 he was a prisoner, and at the mercy of the imperial government who had decided to make an end of the Bulgarian monarchy. The mutilation of Romanus (attributable then to the *parakoimomenos* Basil Lecapenus, not Bringas) was the complement to the deposition of his brother Boris, since eunuchs were permanently debarred from reigning.

stration of the victory which at one stroke deflected the terrible danger threatening the capital, reconquered the old frontier of the Danube and recovered Bulgaria as a province of Byzantium. The loss of political independence necessarily entailed also a loss of religious independence for the Bulgar kingdom: the Patriarchate of Bulgaria was suppressed and the Bulgar bishops were once again placed under the direct authority of the Patriarch of Constantinople.

Tzimisces had thus consolidated his power and warded off the Russian danger. It remained for him to settle the problem of relationships with the Western Empire, which had been aggravated in the last years of Nicephorus Phocas and had brought the two Christian Empires into serious collision. John Tzimisces was an adroit diplomat as well as a brilliant general. He now consented to the marriage of a Byzantine princess to the son of the Emperor Otto I. She was not the princess 'born in the purple' that Liutprand had requested, but probably the Emperor's niece Theophano; but Tzimisces' own marriage with a genuine Porphyrogenita permitted the Ottos to accept a union so auspicious for Byzantine prestige in the West.[1] The marriage was celebrated in Rome on 14 April 972, and it put an end for the time being to the dangerous crises which had threatened relations between the two states.

Tzimisces was now free to turn to the great enterprise which he had, as it were, inherited from his predecessor Nicephorus Phocas: to confirm and expand Byzantine conquests on the eastern frontier, and reduce the Hamdanid Amir of Mosul to the position of vassal, as Nicephorus had done with the Amir of Aleppo. The weakening of Mosul would then allow him to strike a mortal blow at the Caliph of Baghdad, and to frustrate the ambitions of a new enemy, the Fatimid Caliph, who was rapidly becoming more of a menace than Baghdad. During 970–1 Antioch had for five months been besieged by an African (Egyptian) army sent from Damascus, and Tzimisces, occupied in Europe by the Russian danger, had sent the *strategus* of Mesopotamia with his troops as well as the *patricius* Nicholas, a eunuch of the imperial household, with further reinforcements, to the rescue of the great city. Thanks to this help Antioch had been able to hold out, and the enemy were finally compelled to withdraw because of a Carmathian invasion in Syria. By the spring of 972 circumstances seemed to favour a renewal of the Byzantine advance in the East.

It was in this same year that Tzimisces began his campaign against

[1] See the references cited by G. Ostrogorsky, *History of the Byzantine State*, p. 263, n. 1. Theophano has long passed as Romanus II's daughter, but it is now recognised that she was almost certainly Tzimisces' niece.

the Arabs. It is clear that the Emperor himself directed operations in Mesopotamia. But the Greek and Arab sources are at variance as to the events of his campaign. Leo the Deacon and Yaḥyā of Antioch both describe a campaign in Mesopotamia: but there the similarity ends. Leo dates the operations to the year after the Emperor's defeat of Svjatoslav (that is, 973 according to his chronology): Yaḥyā dates them to 972. Leo says that Tzimisces forced Amida and Mayyāfāriqīn to surrender before entering Nisibis, which he found deserted: Yaḥyā maintains that he took Nisibis first, before proceeding to Mayyāfāriqīn and that, far from finding it deserted, he massacred or took prisoner its inhabitants. Then, after failing to subdue Mayyāfāriqīn, he retired to Constantinople, leaving one of his officers, the Armenian Mleh, to conduct new and ill-fated operations in the east. Leo, on the other hand, records that Tzimisces, having taken Nisibis, marched on Ecbatana (or Baghdad), but finding himself in a desert region and in want of provisions, abandoned the project and went back to Constantinople. There is no mention in Leo's account of Mleh the Armenian. The two historians are clearly describing different expeditions, and it would appear that Leo has confused the campaign of 972 with the second Mesopotamian campaign of Tzimisces in 974, about which the Arab historians are silent.

It is then from the Arab historian Yaḥyā that we derive our information about the first Mesopotamian expedition of Tzimisces. In September–October 972 the Emperor crossed the Euphrates near Melitene (Malatya), entering Nisibis on 12 October. There 'he massacred, burnt, took prisoners' and stayed in the town until the Hamdanid Amir of Mosul, Abū Taghlib, agreed to pay him an annual tribute. From Nisibis he advanced on Mayyāfāriqīn but failed to take it. He then left one of his 'servants' (*ghulām*) in Batn Hanzith as Domestic of the East and apparently returned to Constantinople. If he did celebrate a triumph in the city, it was probably not that which Leo the Deacon mentions, which was during the winter of 974–5 after his second Mesopotamian campaign. The Arab chronicler also relates the effect which this first expedition had on the Muslim world. The news of the sack of Nisibis caused a profound sensation in Mosul and led to serious trouble in Baghdad. This sudden reappearance of the Byzantine army in the Euphrates region created widespread fear and discontent amongst all the Caliph's subjects.

The Domestic of the East whom Tzimisces appointed before his departure does not figure in the Greek sources; but he is mentioned by the oriental writers, particularly his fellow-countryman Matthew of Edessa. His name Mleh betrays his Armenian origin. He had formerly been an officer under Nicephorus Phocas and appears to have been promoted by Tzimisces to the important position of commander-in-chief of the Anatolian troops. During the winter of 972–3 he assembled a large army in the district of Hanzith and in the following spring marched on Amida. The Amir of Mosul, Abū Taghlib, sent out an army under his brother Hibāt Allāh, to oppose him; and on 4 July 973 a fierce battle took place near Amida. The Domestic was completely defeated and was himself wounded and taken prisoner. Many of his men and a vast amount of booty fell into Muslim hands. The heads of the enemy killed were sent to Baghdad to quieten the restive populace who were fulminating against the Caliph's inactivity. In February or March 974 Mleh died as a result of his wounds, still a prisoner of Abū Taghlib, who seems to have treated him well. Matthew of Edessa gives in his *Chronicle* a letter which the Domestic sent to the Emperor. In this he invoked 'terrible curses' upon him, and charged him with being responsible for the fate of the unhappy prisoners who had been killed, or who would perish in captivity in infidel lands, and he threatened him with having to answer for this at the Last Judgement should he fail to avenge their deaths. Whatever Tzimisces thought of this he could not but realise the imperative need for following up with all the resources at his command the eastern drive begun in 972, and so disastrously checked by the defeat of his general in 973. This clearly needed serious preparation and the Emperor did not take the field in the east until the spring of 974.

The Arab sources, as has been noted, make no mention of this second expedition of Tzimisces. Fortunately the gap can be filled from Leo the Deacon, though his account has to be supplemented on one important point from another quarter. For Leo has nothing to say about the episode which formed, as it were, the prelude to the second campaign against the Muslims. This curious affair, which concerns Byzantine relationships with Armenia, is retailed by Matthew of Edessa. In 973 Armenia, usually so incurably divided between its warring feudal lords, underwent an experience rare enough in its history. The Armenian princes of the royal blood and the chief barons of the 'Eastern nation', with all their armies, united and rallied round their King, Ashot III. The assembly point was the district of Harq to the north-east of Taron, which had recently become a Byzantine province. Here an army of some 80,000 men, according to Matthew of Edessa, gathered round the King of Kings, 'the whole Armenian nation under arms', as he says. He does not explain the reason for this impressive rally and we are thrown back on conjecture. But the facts speak for themselves. Total mobilisation of this kind points to an acute awareness of threatened danger, the nature of which can be more precisely defined when it is observed that the place of the rally was admirably situated to protect both Vaspurakan and Bagratid Armenia against an invader coming from the direction of Taron. It is clear that in 973 Tzimisces was preparing for a major campaign in Asia and equally certain that he meant to begin this by marching towards the Armenian frontier. This explains why the Armenian princes and feudatories, already alarmed at the increasing advance of Byzantium on their eastern frontiers, and particularly by the annexation of Taron, were moved by growing apprehension. Whatever Tzimisces really had in mind (and we shall return to this later) the Armenians thought that their independence was threatened and did not hesitate to support the King of Kings. The Emperor soon learnt of this move and was considerably annoyed. Imperial envoys commissioned to make inquiries arrived in Armenia and brought back to Constantinople a delegation of confederate princes. These were warmly received by Tzimisces, whose envoys had evidently been successful. Matthew of Edessa writes: 'The Emperor made a treaty of peace and alliance with Ashot.' This was concluded towards the end of 973. It did not prevent Tzimisces from setting out in the next year with an enormous army and marching in the direction of Armenia. He penetrated into the province of Taron, which resented its annexation, in spite of the wise imperial policy of conciliating the local magnates; and while there he received a delegation of the confederates bringing him a letter from Vahan, the former Katholikos of Armenia who, deposed in 969 by reason of his pro-Byzantine sympathies, had taken refuge in Vaspurakan. This ardent philhellene was reasonably sure of a favourable reception by the Emperor, and it is not surprising that the Armenian princes used him as their intermediary. Matthew of Edessa reports that his letter was well received by Tzimisces, who confirmed his treaty of alliance with the Armenians. But he made a request: he demanded that Ashot's troops should go with him on his campaign against the Muslims. The King of Kings was quick to supply him with a contingent of 10,000 Armenians, completely equipped and from his best soldiers. Ashot also provided the Emperor with the provisions which he had asked for. The Emperor then richly rewarded the envoys and sent them back while he himself moved south. And so the curtain went up on what may be described as the opening act of the great Byzantine crusade.

Historians have been somewhat puzzled as to what lay behind this advance of Tzimisces towards Armenia in 974. Possibly he began with the thought of attacking his former homeland and perhaps even incorporating it into the Empire. The Armenian princes evidently feared something of this kind. But it is unlikely that Tzimisces had this in mind at a time when he was desperately anxious to retrieve the defeat of Mleh and drive forward in a crusade against the Arabs. It would have been a difficult task to break Armenian independence, even though the country was rent by perpetual rivalries. In any case, even if he had dreamt of this, the resolute and united stand taken by Ashot and his vassals would have shaken his determination. As it was, his demonstration of force on the borders of Armenia was probably aimed at gaining the support of Ashot in his coming campaign against the Muslims. This was a normal manœuvre, similar to that of Nicephorus Phocas against the Bulgarians in 966. Tzimisces knew the value of Armenian support—none better, for he himself had often commanded the warriors of Huyastan and he owed to them one of his signal victories in 971. And so the tension between Byzantium and Armenia was relaxed, and the two Christian powers found themselves in alliance in the first crusade against the infidel.

Tzimisces then left the Armenian borders and penetrated into upper Mesopotamia. It has been thought that the importance of this new campaign has been overstated by Leo the Deacon and Matthew of Edessa; and indeed one cannot accept all that they say, nor all that the Emperor himself says in a document which will shortly be referred to. Nevertheless, even though the Emperor had in the end to abandon his objective and made no territorial gain, there is undoubted evidence that he made an expedition on a considerable scale.

The imperial army left the region of Mus, the chief town of the province of Taron, and went down to Amida and Mayyāfāriqīn. Both towns were spared pillage and sack at the cost of immense quantities of gold and other valuables. Tzimisces then marched south and reached Nisibis, which he found deserted. The inhabitants feared treatment similar to that inflicted in 972 and had fled. Nowhere was serious resistance offered. Abū Taghlib was in conflict with the Amir Cuwalhide of Baghdad and perhaps even wanted an understanding with the Emperor: he showed no sign of opposing the Byzantine advance. The plains of Mesopotamia, denuded of inhabitants who had either fled or taken refuge in their walled towns, were at the disposal of the invader. The Caliph's power was already tottering, and it looked as though the time was ripe for striking a mighty blow at his authority by attacking him in his very capital, that mysterious city, inviolate, crammed with wealth, whose conquest seemed like some fabulous adventure to the soldiers of Rum. What prevented Tzimisces from attempting this? According to Leo the Deacon, the Emperor was on his way towards Ecbatana, that is towards Baghdad, the Abbasid capital, as this historian explicitly states; and Matthew of Edessa says that he got very near to it. Leo suggests that he was forced to retreat because of the arid nature of the country and lack of provisions. But he could not have been in the desert of Carmania, that ἔρημος of Persia, as Leo says, but in Mesopotamia. The question remains as to whether these were the real reasons for his retreat when he was so near to his objective, and if so whether this was the final episode in the campaign of 975.

Some light is thrown on this by a letter addressed by Tzimisces in the autumn of 975 to King Ashot of Armenia, the text of which is preserved almost complete in Matthew of Edessa's *Chronicle*.[1] The letter begins with a brief reference to the military operation of 974, and before embarking on a detailed account of the expedition of 975 the Emperor writes:

The aim of our campaign was to chasten the pride and arrogance of the Amir al-Mumenin, ruler of the Africans, called the Maghrib Arabs, who have attacked us with considerable forces. First they placed our army in danger, but then we conquered them thanks to our irresistible strength and the help of God, and they retreated in disgrace like our other enemies. We then attacked the interior of the country and put to the sword the peoples of many provinces; and finally we made a prompt withdrawal to our winter quarters.

It has been supposed that the whole of the first part of this letter refers to the campaign of 974. Such an interpretation would imply that Leo the Deacon was guilty of an incomplete if not inaccurate account of this campaign; for he says nothing of the Emperor's operations against the Maghrib Arabs immediately after the Mesopotamian expedition. Rather the 'interior of the country' referred to by the Emperor must mean Syria, which was partly occupied, as he had just indicated, by Fatimid troops. In other words this passage, which has been taken as a brief account of the campaigns of 974, is in reality a summary of the events which preceded and provoked the intervention of Tzimisces in Syria, namely the operations of the Fatimids in this part of the Empire; and it serves as an introduction to the detailed account of the campaign of 975 which was the subject of the Emperor's letter. The 'danger' in which the imperial army was placed must refer back to the five-month siege of Antioch in 970–1; and the 'withdrawal to winter quarters' refers to the conclusion of the campaign of 975, and not of the expedition of 974. It was to Antioch that the Emperor withdrew (as is clear from the end of this letter) and it was from Antioch that the letter was written.

There is thus no warrant for supposing that Leo the Deacon's account of the Mesopotamian campaign is incomplete. But one may

[1] Matthew of Edessa, *Chronicle* (ed. E. Dulaurier, Paris, 1858), p. 17.

still ask whether Leo provides the real and only reason why so intrepid and experienced a general as Tzimisces, better equipped than any other to conduct operations in such a theatre of war, stopped short of attaining his objective. It was in fact in that very year 974 that the Egyptian Arabs, finally delivered from the onslaughts of the Carmathians and assisted by the quarrels between the Amir of Aleppo and his lieutenants, renewed their offensive in Syria. In June one of the generals of al-Muʿizz occupied Damascus; and at the end of 974 and the beginning of 975 other Fatimid officers captured Tripoli and Beirut and attacked the local Greek troops. The year 974 therefore marked the beginning of a period of intensive activity on the part of the Egyptians; and it was the news of these alarming events, reaching him in the course of his victorious progress over the plains of Jazira, that persuaded the Emperor to abandon his march on Baghdad and to return with all speed to Constantinople to prepare a counter-offensive and obviate the threat to Antioch. Thus, after the long march which had taken him from the borders of Armenia to the frontiers of Babylonia, Tzimisces, leaving his army in Antioch, returned to his capital in 974 with an immense quantity of booty, there to celebrate the triumph recorded by Leo the Deacon (which has generally been dated to 972). The Emperor must have spent at least a part of the winter of 974–5 in Constantinople, but the serious events in Syria required that he should resume his command without delay, and by April 975 he had rejoined his troops at Antioch.

The circumstances of the campaign (or rather the crusade) which opened in the spring of 975—the third and the most famous of the eastern campaigns of Tzimisces—are well enough known; and the inaccuracies and the deficiencies of the other sources can be corrected and supplied by the letter referred to above which the Emperor himself wrote to his ally King Ashot III of Armenia in 975. In April of that year Tzimisces left Antioch at the head of his army to drive out 'the accursed Africans' from Syria and Palestine. Following the course of the Orontes he arrived first at Emesa, where he was honourably received according to the terms of his treaty of 969–70 with the inhabitants, and then at Baalbek ('also called Heliopolis'), which he entered on 29 May after a short resistance. According to Leo the Deacon he also captured Manbij (Μέμπετζε, the ancient Bambyke) and Apamea; but Leo is here guilty of a confusion with the campaign of Nicephorus Phocas in 966, and neither town is mentioned in Tzimisces' own letter. From Baalbek the imperial army marched on Damascus. The town had recently fallen into the possession of one Aftakīn, a refugee amir from Baghdad who, despite the fact that he had already made submission to the Fatimids, quickly came to terms with the Emperor, became his vassal and agreed to pay him tribute. Damascus was therefore spared, and Tzimisces continued his march towards Galilee. According to the account contained in his own letter (which need not be condemned as 'fantasy' simply because the other sources are silent or at variance) Tzimisces intended to liberate Jerusalem and to pray in the Holy Places. But once again he was obliged to stop short of his objective.

From Damascus he proceeded to Tiberias, and then to Nazareth, both of which, for reasons of piety, were spared destruction. They were placed in the charge of Greek commanders, as indeed were all the conquered territories, notably Acre ('Arguea, also called Ptolemais') which made its surrender in writing. At Mt Thabor the Emperor received delegations from Ramleh and Jerusalem offering the submission of both towns and requesting Byzantine governors for them. Finally, Caesarea was taken. This marked the most southerly point of the Emperor's rapid conquest of the territory of Palestine. For in the meantime the African garrisons, fleeing before the troops of Tzimisces, had been entrenching themselves in the fortresses on the coast, thus constituting a dangerous concentration of the enemy's forces in the rear of the imperial army. Tzimisces himself expressly states that it was this circumstance which made him decide to abandon his march to Jerusalem, just as in the preceding year, when equally close to Baghdad, he had elected to withdraw. The 'Egyptian peril' prevented him from reaching his goal and fulfilling the symbolic object of his expedition. Once again he turned off to the north and made his way along the sea-coast. One by one the coast fortresses were besieged and captured, with one exception. First Beirut and then Sidon fell into the Emperor's hands—in that order, as both the letter to Ashot and the Arab sources relate; for Tzimisces, although coming from the south, left Sidon to be dealt with after Beirut. Whatever the reason for this strategy, his victory at Beirut, which was strongly defended, was one of the outstanding events of his campaign. From Sidon he continued his triumphal progress along the coast, conquering town after town—Byblos especially, which was taken by assault; and everywhere he set up commanders of his own choice, as in Palestine. His return, however, was marked by one serious check. Having forced a passage with his cavalry through the defile which Matthew of Edessa calls K'urercs (= $\Lambda\iota\theta o\pi\rho\acuteo\sigma\omega\pi o\nu$, 'stone-faced'), Tzimisces arrived in sight of Tripoli, a vital stronghold whose natural position and powerful defences rendered it almost impregnable. Schlumberger, despite the testimony of the Greek and Arab sources to the contrary, maintained that the Emperor captured Tripoli, basing his argument on the purely rhetorical statement of

Tzimisces in his letter that no place offered him any resistance.[1] On the other hand, had he in fact taken Tripoli he would hardly have neglected to say so; but after reporting that he had ravaged the whole region round about the town he merely adds: 'The Africans in these parts dared to advance against us; but immediately we fell upon them and exterminated them to the last man.' The Arab sources seem to complement this account with their version of a 'complete defeat' suffered by the Greeks in the province of Tripoli at the hands of a Fatimid officer who had contrived to regroup some of the remnants of the garrison of Beirut. Doubtless the possession of Tripoli was fiercely contested and the battle claimed as a victory by both sides; but its effects persuaded Tzimisces that he must relinquish the hope of gaining the town, solidly defended as it was by the Amir's soldiers.

Continuing his journey north along the coast, Tzimisces captured Balamea and then Gabala ('Coueln' in the Armenian text, 'called also Gabauon', a name which, as has been observed, recalls that of a tribe of Benjamin, to the north of Jerusalem). The whole coast-line of Phoenicia and Syria, from Caesarea to the borders of the duchy of Antioch, was thus reclaimed, with the important exception of Tripoli and the surrounding area. This brilliant campaign of reconquest was completed by 'mopping-up operations' in the hinterland which gave the Emperor possession of the castles of Burzuya (the Βορζῶ of Leo the Deacon) and Saḥyūn, the one on the heights of Lebanon, the other in the territory of Antioch. Burzuya was apparently handed over to the Emperor by its governor, a renegade Muslim called Kulayb, secretary of the Mamluk Ruytash. Since it formed a part of the territory ceded to the Greeks by terms of the treaty of 969–70 its occupation by the Emperor was a legitimate act of recovery. But Kulayb, whose adventurous career was not yet over, received his due reward. Tzimisces gave him the title of *patricius* and designated him *basilikos* or imperial commissioner (not governor, as has been suggested) at Antioch.

These operations were the last of the campaign. In September 975 the Emperor led his victorious army back to Antioch from which he had set out five months before. The re-establishment of Byzantine rule over lands in which no Emperor had set foot for many centuries was a brave enterprise. The fact that the reconquests achieved by Tzimisces proved, despite all his precautions, to be ephemeral must not obscure the audacity, the energy and the skill of an undertaking which was, in a sense, the crowning episode of what has so justly been called the epic glory of tenth-century Byzantium. Before the

---

[1] G. Schlumberger, *Epopée*, I, p. 307.

premature death which cut short his brilliant career the Emperor had
been able at least to lay the foundations of the great work of which
he seems to have dreamed, and which he outlined so well himself in
his letter to the Armenian king: the restoration of the authority of
the Empire and the domination of the Cross in those eastern lands
which were his great preoccupation. In this Tzimisces, the Armenian
on the throne, appears as the continuator, in the fullest sense of the
term, of the work of Nicephorus Phocas, the great feudatory of
Anatolia, whose mind was likewise dominated by the East, by strenuous preparations for its recovery, and by the thought of a Byzantine
crusade. As will shortly appear, the case was by no means the same
with their successor Basil II.

The Emperor returned to Constantinople in the last months of 975
—and there he died shortly afterwards, the victim of an apparently
mysterious malady, the exact nature of which can scarcely have been
obscure to his contemporaries. Leaving aside Matthew of Edessa,
whose account of the end of Tzimisces is imaginary though not without interest, all the sources, Arab as well as Greek, attribute the
death of Tzimisces to poisoning and almost all accuse the *parakoimomenos* Basil. The most authoritative witnesses, Leo the Deacon on
the one hand, Scylitzes and Zonaras on the other, give the following
account. While passing through Cilicia and Cappadocia on his way
back from Antioch the Emperor admired certain rich and fertile lands
in the district of Anazarbus and Podandus, and inquired to whom
they might belong. He was informed that they were all the property
of the famous *parakoimomenos*, his first minister. The state, in fact,
had retained nothing of a productive stretch of territory which the
Byzantine armies had wrested from the enemy at the price of much
blood and toil in the reign of his predecessor. The sacrifices of the
inhabitants and the soldiers of the Empire, the self-imposed hard-
ships of the Emperors and their officers, not least of Tzimisces himself, had served in the end only to enrich an avaricious eunuch. The
Emperor was furious and vented his feelings in bitter imprecations
against this insatiable expropriator of state property. The incident
was reported to the *parakoimomenos* who, sensing the danger to his
position, resolved from that moment to bring about the death of the
Emperor. He succeeded by promises in gaining the help of the
imperial cup-bearer, and through his offices administered a slow but
certain poison to the Emperor while he was being entertained by one
of his great vassals in Bithynia. The Emperor's strength at once
began to decline. He hastened to return to Constantinople; but by
the time he arrived he was in a pitiful condition, completely exhausted and breathing only with difficulty. He had already ordered

the tomb, which he had previously prepared in the oratory of Christ of the Chalke, to be made ready; and it was not long before he died, after distributing largesse to the poor and most devoutly making his confession.

It is unfortunately impossible to know to what extent this detailed account of the illness and death of Tzimisces can be trusted. The circumstances of the discovery by the Emperor of the illegal acquisitions made by the *parakoimomenos* at the expense of the state are plausible enough. They recall the discovery by his successor Basil II of similar expropriations made by the 'powerful' (δυνατοί) at the expense of the poor, in particular Basil's dealings with Eustathius Maleinus, the extent of whose power and landed property was brought to the Emperor's notice when he was returning from his first Syrian expedition. Maleinus was brought to Constantinople and there held prisoner until his death. His property was then confiscated, and Basil passed a law forbidding the large-scale acquisition of land by the 'powerful', comparable to the measures already taken by Romanus Lecapenus and Constantine Porphyrogenitus to combat the same abuse. There can be no doubt that Tzimisces was no less energetically opposed than Romanus and Basil II to such accumulations of landed property. Two recently found documents, of September 974 and September 975, show that Tzimisces issued a decree expressly forbidding soldiers and peasants from establishing themselves on the estates of the great proprietors, whether lay or ecclesiastical, as their *paroikoi* (*coloni*) and thus divesting themselves of their obligations to the state.[1] The serious conflict in society in the tenth century was a conflict not between rich and poor but between two rival powers, the imperial government and the wealthy landed aristocracy, who disputed the possession not so much of the soil as of the occupants of the soil, reduced to choosing between two forms of servitude. In this conflict Tzimisces acted with no less firmness and energy than the other Emperors of the period: his two decrees of 974 and 975 are, as has been pointed out, clearly in direct line with the legislation of the Macedonian rulers forbidding the expropriation of small-holdings by the great. It is now evident in fact that Tzimisces was more than a brilliant soldier; he was a statesman as well. In his political capacity he did not hesitate to track down those with obligations to the exchequer (οἱ δημοσιάριοι) who took refuge on the estates of great landowners, nor to condemn the injury done to the state by the cupidity of his own first minister. The account of the manner of his death thus acquires a fresh interest and may to some extent be

[1] Cf. G. Ostrogorsky, *Quelques problèmes d'histoire de la paysannerie byzantine,* pp. 12 ff.

confirmed in the light of our new understanding of Tzimisces the statesman.

Whether or not the *parakoimomenos* Basil was as directly responsible for the Emperor's death as the Byzantine historians suggest is another question. But to appreciate the lengths to which Basil would go when he felt his ambitions thwarted or his position threatened it is enough to glance at his career. Heaped with honours under Nicephorus Phocas, but denied the high office which he considered his due, he joined in the conspiracy of malcontents pledged to overthrow the Emperor. The events immediately following the deed leave no doubt about the part played, however indirectly, by Basil in the assassination of Nicephorus Phocas and the elevation of Tzimisces, whose first care was to grant him the title of *parakoimomenos*. Again, ten years after the death of Tzimisces, when Basil II deprived the *parakoimomenos* of his office and sent him into exile, it was not simply the act of an authoritarian and ungrateful young Emperor. The account of Yaḥyā (here, as so often, complementary to the Greek sources) makes it clear that the *parakoimomenos* was the life and soul of the vast plot against Basil II engineered by the great military leaders like Bardas Phocas and Leo Melissenus, which threatened not only the Emperor's independence but also his life. The Emperor forestalled the danger by humiliating the ambitious and unscrupulous eunuch who was its inspiration. In the light of these facts it is plausible enough that the *parakoimomenos* Basil should stand condemned at least of implication in the death of Tzimisces. And there is the added circumstance that his personal relationships with the Emperor must have deteriorated as a result of Tzimisces' legislation to defend the interests of the state against the great landed proprietors. After 974 Basil (who can have had no part in this legislation) was no longer, as he had been in the early years, the acceptable pillar of the Emperor's authority; and the Emperor's discovery of his properties and consequent anger might well seem to portend imminent disgrace. It seems difficult then to accept the hypothesis of Schlumberger that Tzimisces probably died of typhus. The character of Basil, the motives and the circumstances all seem to combine to substantiate the truth of the accounts of Leo the Deacon and Scylitzes concerning the end of John Tzimisces, namely that he died of poisoning. That Basil should have contrived to remain in power after the death of Tzimisces, even though 'publicly accused' of the Emperor's murder, is not so unlikely or surprising as Schlumberger imagined. For as the same historian justly observed, the sudden disappearance of Tzimisces left the *parakoimomenos* master of the situation in the capital. The only potential rival, Bardas Sclerus, appears to have been absent. Given this tremendous advantage Basil was able to devote his skill and energy to restoring his compromised position and acquiring a greater power than he had ever known before. Who, in Constantinople at that moment, would have cared to level a 'public accusation' against the murderer?

John Tzimisces, the conqueror of the Russians in 971, the glorious crusader of 975, died on 10 January 976, at the age of fifty-one years and after a reign exactly computed by Leo the Deacon and Yaḥyā as six years and one month.

XV. THE REIGN OF BASIL II

On the death of John Tzimisces, the two sons of Romanus II, Basil II, aged eighteen, and his brother Constantine VIII, aged sixteen, inaugurated a joint reign of nearly fifty years (fifty-two years if one adds to Basil's reign the years 1025–8 during which Constantine ruled alone). This return to the legitimate Macedonian succession seemed to put an end to the line of legitimised usurpers which had become almost a constitutional tradition. The work of these co-Emperors had been of great consequence for Byzantium; for a succession of three powerful rulers, Romanus Lecapenus, Nicephorus Phocas and John Tzimisces, had enriched the Empire with some brilliant military successes and immense prestige. These usurpations had become so familiar that it was generally expected that the two young princes, absorbed in the pleasures of their age, would remain under the guardianship of a minister of state, the *parakoimomenos* Basil, who, being a eunuch, could present no threat to the dynasty, and as the son of Romanus Lecapenus stood for a beneficent and glorious policy. Tzimisces himself had left no children; but the head of his family was Bardas Sclerus, his brother-in-law and his most competent general, who after defeating the Russians at Arcadiopolis had suppressed the first rebellion of the Phocas family and made an outstanding contribution to the great victory over Svjatoslav.

It was the *parakoimomenos*, however, who, without aspiring to the throne, longed to hold in his own hands the real power of the state. He lost no time in removing Bardas Sclerus, who was deprived of his title of Domestic of the East and sent off with the title of *dux* as commander of the theme of Mesopotamia. His lieutenant Michael Burtzes, also under suspicion, was separated from his former general and dispatched, also as *dux*, to Antioch. The eastern military command was entrusted to Peter Phocas the *stratopedarches*, who had shown himself an energetic and resourceful soldier, and being a eunuch could, like the *parakoimomenos* himself, present no danger to the claims of the young Emperors.

Bardas Sclerus, however, would not accept his disgrace. He proclaimed himself Emperor (probably in the spring of 976), and inevitably he was sooner or later supported by all the relations, friends and allies of his late brother-in-law. To begin with he could count on the sympathy of the Armenians, on the assistance of the Arab amirates and the Arabs, Christian or Muslim, who served in great numbers in the Byzantine army, and on the support of all the enemies of the hated *parakoimomenos*, of whom, perhaps like Tzimisces, he was the victim. He was surrounded by capable generals, he had a fleet at his disposal, and his own military talent secured his success on many fields of battle. He went from victory to victory, from his triumph at Lapara-Lycandus in the valley of Pyramus (or Jeyhan) in the autumn of 976, which threw open to him the gates of Cappadocia, the first and decisive step towards his conquest of Asia Minor, to his triumph at Rhageas to the east of Caesarea in the autumn of 977. Early in 978, despite a courageous and skilful defence by Manuel Comnenus, Sclerus captured the great city of Nicaea and was in a position to threaten the capital by land and sea. The imperial government seemed in a desperate situation. All the generals who had opposed the pretender had been defeated one after the other. Peter Phocas had been killed at Rhageas: Burtzes, after the battle at Lapara, had gone over to the side of his former commander and secured the recognition of his claim in Antioch.

In these critical circumstances the Emperors and the *parakoimomenos* resolved to call on the services of the disgraced Bardas Phocas, son of the *curopalates* Leo and nephew of the Emperor Nicephorus Phocas, whom Sclerus himself, in the defence of the authority of Tzimisces, had once besieged and captured. The rebel Phocas had been banished to Chios and there taken the monastic habit. He was now brought out of his captivity and required to swear loyalty to the Porphyrogeniti; and his personal rancour against his former conqueror kept him true to his word. As the new commander-in-chief he succeeded in joining the imperial forces at Caesarea, with a view to reorganising them under the command of Eustathius Maleinus and Michael Burtzes, who had again changed sides; and there he regrouped an army with a speed which can only be explained by the tremendous prestige enjoyed by the families of Phocas and Maleinus in that part of the world. Bardas Phocas then led his troops to the west to take Sclerus from behind. This clever stratagem forced the pretender to abandon his positions on the Asian side of the Bosphorus in order to crush the army which had been reconstituted in his rear. Phocas advanced as far as Amorium; and it was near here, in the plain of Pancalia, that the two armies met on 19 June 978. Once again the victory went to Bardas Sclerus. But for Phocas the defeat was not dishonourable, and he was able to retire in good order to the Halys. Sclerus, however, followed him up, and a second battle was fought at Basilica Therma in the autumn of 978. Again Phocas was defeated, but for the last time. It was another anxious moment for the young Emperors. But the resourcefulness and the diplomatic skill of Phocas could yet repair the damage inflicted on the imperial cause by these two defeats. Without delay he made the long trek to Iberia, to seek the help of the *curopalates* David, the strongest of the princes of Taïk, with whom he had struck up a friendship during his term as *strategus* of the theme of Chaldia. David received him warmly, and gave him an auxiliary company of 72,000 men under the command of John Tornik (Tornicius—another soldier-monk who was to end his days at Iviron, the Georgian monastery on Mt Athos).

Early in the following year Phocas marched on his enemy at the head of his combined forces. A third battle was fought on 24 March 979 at 'Aquae Saravenae' in the theme of Charsianon, near the Halys. From Scylitzes' account it would appear that the issue was decided by single combat between the two commanders. Sclerus was worsted and knocked out in this heroic duel, and recovered consciousness only to join the stampede of his troops who had supposed him dead. At all events Sclerus was defeated, and this time irremediably. The Georgians took the credit for this decisive victory, as can be seen from the famous inscription of Zarzma, set up by a member of Tornik's auxiliary corps. Sclerus sought refuge with a small number of his men in the territory of his ally Abū Taghlib, the Hamdanid Amir of Mosul. But the Amir, himself a refugee, could offer no help. He then managed to reach Mayyāfāriqīn before being captured and transferred, on orders from the Caliph's palace, to Baghdad, where he languished in captivity for seven years.

Thus the Empire was saved—by the skill of a Phocas and the alliance of the Georgians, the natural enemies of the Armenians and Arabs on whom Sclerus had relied for support. Basil II was not to forget this lesson: the heroic family and the national state founded by the *curopalates* David were to engage his attentions right up to the last years and the last battles of his life. For the moment he might have enjoyed the peace which it had cost so much to achieve, had not this first civil war left him at the mercy of two men whose services he was obliged to employ—the *parakoimomenos* Basil and the Domestic Bardas Phocas, commander-in-chief of the eastern armies. There was the added worry of interminable negotiations with the court of Baghdad, conducted through the mediation of the *vestes* Nicephorus Uranus, to secure the extradition of Bardas Sclerus; for the Emperor was uneasily aware of the possible danger of an *entente* between the Caliph and his prisoner. Lastly, as a result of the civil war and the Empire's embarrassments, there was trouble in Bulgaria. The Bulgarians, bereft of their king Boris, the son of Peter, appeared at first to have accepted the fact of their annexation. Boris, like his brother Romanus (who had been made a eunuch), was held prisoner in Constantinople. But the events of the years 976–9 inspired the Bulgarians with the hope of freedom. They found provisional leaders for their liberation in the four 'Comitopuli', David, Aaron, Moses and Samuel (of Armenian origin).[1] Their lawful rulers, whose return they awaited, escaped or were released by the imperial government in the hope of forestalling sedition. But Boris was accidentally killed by the Bulgars themselves and the eunuch Romanus, after meeting Samuel at Vodena, joined himself to the cause of the four brothers to organise and spread the national rebellion.

The years 985–6 were critical. Basil II, suspecting the *parakoimomenos* of hatching a plot against him with some of the military leaders such as Bardas Phocas and Leo Melissenus, called him to account and banished him to Bosporus in the Crimea (985). Bardas Phocas himself, though remaining *dux* of Antioch, lost his rank of Domestic of the Schools. Experience had matured the young Emperor: since the end of the civil war he had shown increasing evidence of awakening to his own independence, thereby, it would seem, provoking the plot against him; and now he felt able to proclaim the commencement of his personal rule, dating it, in a famous edict, from the humiliation of his hated guardian. To inaugurate the new regime he would suppress the revolt of Bulgaria, which he no doubt considered to be merely a provincial insurrection of no great seriousness. His march on Sardica, ill-prepared, commanded by mediocre or quarrelsome generals, ended in a precipitate retreat, the famous rout of 'Trajan's Gate' (17 August 986). This resounding reverse placed the imperial house in even greater peril than the first civil war. In Bulgaria itself its consequences were certainly disastrous. It led indeed to a war of thirty years. In Baghdad, on the other hand, it confirmed the Caliph's resolve not to send back Bardas Sclerus to a young Emperor whose weakness was so manifest. Instead, in return for certain territorial concessions, Sclerus was allowed to return to Byzantine territory, and there, at the beginning of 987, resumed the insignia of Empire. The civil war began again, but this time there was a new

[1] Cf. G. Ostrogorsky, *History of the Byzantine State*, p. 267 and references.

factor which gravely aggravated the situation. For Bardas Phocas, re-established in his high military command and sent once again to fight the pretender, turned traitor. He began by coming to terms with Sclerus on the basis of a partition of the Empire; but then, feeling himself to be the stronger party, he interned Sclerus in his stronghold at Tyropoion under the guardianship of his wife. Phocas then proclaimed himself Emperor, on 14 September 987.

Bardas Phocas could not, like Sclerus, count on the alliance of the Armenians and the Arabs, but he was certainly the man whom all the Greek-speaking Byzantines wanted as their Emperor. His revolt, which extended far and wide, cost him no fighting: it was in the nature of a triumphal march across the whole of Anatolia. The literature of the people, the Byzantine epic, in some famous verses sung to this day, shows how the House of Phocas, to which Byzantium owed the recovery of Calabria, its finest victories on the Asia Minor front, and such trophies of war as Crete, Cyprus, Antioch and Aleppo, was and would remain the most popular of all the dynasties —even though it produced but one Emperor recognised as such, Nicephorus Phocas. If Byzantium, to defeat Bardas Sclerus, had fallen back on the support of one of those very heroes of its epic and his Georgian auxiliaries (who now remained loyal to him), the imperial government in its new hour of crisis could find but one possible ally when the armies of Bardas Phocas were already at Chrysopolis and Abydus. This was the Grand Prince of Kiev, Vladimir, son of Svjatoslav; and his price was the promise of the hand of a genuine Porphyrogenita, the sister of the Emperors Basil and Constantine, the princess Anna. The Russians guaranteed, in accord with the terms of the treaty imposed on them by John Tzimisces, to dispatch a *družina* of 6000 men. These arrived in Byzantium in the spring of 988, and thanks to them Bardas Phocas was defeated first at Chrysopolis in the summer of 988 and finally on 13 April 989 at Abydus, where he died in mysterious circumstances. His end came not a moment too soon; for his Georgian allies, led by his son Nicephorus 'the wry-necked', had in 988 defeated the *magister* Taronites who had been sent to Trebizond to create a diversion in the rear of the pretender's army. Thus, thanks to Russian help, the Empire was saved in 989 in a manner as providential as that in which it had been saved, by Georgian help, ten years before.

But the disasters of the year 989 were not yet over. The victory at Abydus had barely been announced when news reached the capital of the capture of Verria (Berroea) by the Bulgarians. Thessalonica, the first city of the Empire, was in grave danger. About the same time further news arrived to add to the consternation in the Sacred

Palace. The Russian prince Vladimir, annoyed at the imperial government's dilatoriness in sending him the promised Porphyrogenita, had occupied Cherson and so threatened to deprive Byzantium of the last shreds of its possessions on the northern shores of the Black Sea. Cherson was important commercially no less than strategically. But its capture by Vladimir was rendered doubly disquieting in that it opened up the possibility of a rapprochement between Vladimir and Samuel of Bulgaria. At best it could only mean that Russian support would be withdrawn, and that at a moment when the civil war was threatening to break out again. Realising the urgency of taking prompt action to stem the menacing tide of the Bulgarian advance, Basil II sought means to free himself as quickly as possible from his other anxieties. The Emperors resigned themselves at length to sending their sister Anna to Cherson: and there, in 989, there took place in quick succession the baptism and the marriage of Vladimir. In this way Russia entered into the orbit of Byzantine influence, an event destined to exercise a decisive effect on her future history.

It remained for Basil, if his hands were to be free, to put an end once and for all to the threat of civil war. Its renewed outbreak had occurred in a quite unforeseen manner: on the news of the death of Bardas Phocas his widow had set her prisoner Bardas Sclerus at liberty; and Sclerus for the third time assumed the purple. He was now an old man; he had tasted defeat and seen the end of his none too loyal partner. But he did not lack partisans, among them naturally enough the two sons of Bardas Phocas, Nicephorus 'the wry-necked' and Leo, who had been made commander of Antioch by his father, and there, with the help of his Arab and Armenian auxiliaries, raised an energetic resistance to the loyalists. But the imperial government handled the situation skilfully and diplomatically. On the initiative of the Basileus Constantine, who no doubt resented the somewhat subordinate role allotted to him by his elder brother and wished to assert himself, negotiations were instituted between the court and the pretender, with Manuel Comnenus, who had formerly defended Nicaea, acting as intermediary. Sclerus was offered the most reassuring guarantees, including full pardon for himself and all his partisans. On such generous terms he had the good sense to give in. Experience had taught him wisdom; he was spent with age and in danger of going blind. On 11 October 989 he laid aside the emblems of the imperial power, and soon afterwards made his solemn submission to Basil II at a meeting which set the seal on the reconciliation between the Emperor and the old rebel.[1]

Nothing could better illustrate the unquenchable spirit and vigour

[1] From this point onward the contributor is Professor R. J. H. Jenkins.

of the young Emperor than his conduct at this conjuncture. As soon as Bardas Phocas was dead, and while Sclerus was still in arms, he dispatched a powerful force under John of Chaldia to chastise the Georgian princes who had succoured the chief rebel. David, the prince of Tao, who in 978, while he was aiding the then-loyal Bardas, had been granted temporary possession of the Roman territories of Phasiane, Harq and Apachounis, had continued to support Bardas when the latter had himself revolted in 987. He was now to make atonement. Basil's terms, accepted in 990, were characteristically far-sighted. David might retain the lands ceded to him in 978, and be invested with the title of *curopalates*, but at his death, all his lands, including his native Tao, were to lapse to the Byzantine crown. By this politic settlement Byzantium was assured of her title to all, and much more than all, her former domains on her north-eastern frontier.

At the end of the same year (990) Basil embarked on his second Bulgarian campaign, which occupied him almost without intermission until 995. In 991 he restored the position at Thessalonica by the recapture of Verria; and then began a systematic pacification of the enemy's territory. Details are wholly lacking; yet there is reason to think that he devoted special attention to establishing a firm hold on the area about Sardica, the importance of which was to be demonstrated during the years 998–1003. A vivid impression of his general strategy is conveyed by a brief passage of Yaḥyā of Antioch: 'During four years [that is, 991–5] Basil made war on the Bulgarians and invaded their country. In winter time he marched upon the most remote provinces in the Bulgarian territory, assailed their inhabitants and took them prisoner. During this time he stormed a number of fortresses, retaining some and destroying others which he thought he had not means to hold.' It was in these years that Basil himself developed from the irresolute youth who had fled from Trajan's Gate into the wary and ruthless slayer of the Bulgars; and perfected that scheme of warfare which made him invincible whenever he took the field. This scheme was the annihilating progress through a specific area by an overwhelming force, perfectly equipped and perfectly disciplined, which could be neither openly encountered nor surprised. Such a method of warfare called not so much for brilliant generalship as for meticulous organisation: and here Basil was in his element. His exactitude and attention to detail were phenomenal. Nothing more was needed. His soldiers grumbled to his face at his minute punctilio; but he blandly assured them that by such means, and by such alone, could they hope to return safe to their families and homesteads.

At the same time the Emperor was busily engaged in strengthening his position in the enemy's rear by diplomatic means. In March 992 a treaty, long in preparation, was concluded with Venice, whereby the tolls payable on Venetian bottoms trading with the empire, and the method of their exaction, were regulated on terms highly favourable to the republic. Venice, for her part, undertook police and carrying duties for Byzantium in the Adriatic. In the same year, while still encamped in Bulgaria, Basil negotiated an agreement with the Serbs, which probably had the effect of drawing to his side John Vladimir, the powerful ruler of Dioclea.

The progress of these necessarily protracted operations was interrupted during the winter of 994–5, when they were still far short of completion. A disaster on the Syrian frontier compelled the Emperor to proceed thither in person. Since 992 the Hamdanid Amir of Aleppo, a Byzantine protectorate, had been under pressure from the encroaching power of the Fatimid Caliph al-'Azīz. The Amir appealed to Basil, who in 994 sent reinforcements to Antioch, with instructions to its governor to intervene. The governor, Michael Burtzes, was old and incompetent. He advanced languidly to the Orontes. The Fatimid commander, Manjūtakīn, hurried westwards from Aleppo to meet him. On 15 September he forced the ford of the Orontes, turned the Byzantine position and routed the Roman army with great slaughter. Burtzes fled back to Antioch. The Amir of Aleppo dispatched a second appeal to Basil, who was wintering in Bulgaria. The Emperor was quick to see the danger, which now menaced Antioch itself. He gathered some levies, which included newly recruited Bulgarians, and, travelling by forced marches, crossed his Empire from west to east in twenty-six days. At the end of April 995 he appeared unannounced beneath the walls of Antioch, at the head of 17,000 men. At the mere report of his presence Manjūtakīn threw up the siege of Aleppo and retreated in haste to Damascus. Basil received the homage and thanks of Aleppo; then, turning south, sacked Rafaniya and Emesa, and penetrated as far as Tripoli, burning and pillaging as he went. On his return he garrisoned Tortosa, and, after appointing Damian Dalassenus to govern Antioch, with instructions to continue the policy of annual demonstrations in force, made his way back to Constantinople. In less than six months the eastern situation was restored.

His homeward journey could be taken more leisurely; and he was able for the first time to see for himself the vast encroachments which during the past century the Anatolian aristocracy had made on the lands of the village communes and on the estates of the crown. Eustathius Maleinus, the old rebel, whose properties spread mile after mile over the provinces of Charsianon and Cappadocia, received his sovereign much in the style of a powerful independent prince. Basil saw, as his predecessors had seen, that while this immense and growing influence was wielded by military magnates jealous of and hostile to the crown, the legitimate Emperor could never be master of his own soldiers and his own revenues. But where Basil differed from his predecessors was in his ability to apply a practical remedy. He was now the head of the strongest military force in Christendom; and his remedy was soon forthcoming. On 1 January 996 was promulgated a comprehensive law for the repression of landed estates. This celebrated edict combines a searching demand for titles to landed properties which is reminiscent of the *Quo Warranto*, with a ban on the alienation of estates to the church which is reminiscent of *Mortmain*. As the law then stood, forty years of undisputed tenure were required to establish rights of ownership and disposal. But it was easy enough for a powerful proprietor, whether by bribery or brute force, to suppress any claims for restitution during the period of suspense. The provision was openly derided; and estates held by no legal title whatever were handed on from father to son as though they had been the real properties of the testators. This provision was now repealed. Estates which had been held, and could by properly authenticated documents be shown to have been held, during seventy-five years or more, were confirmed on the possessors. The rest were to be handed back, without compensation, to the original proprietors. But for crown lands seized and held through bribery of government inspectors, no time limit less than one thousand years was to be valid. Documents emanating from the Treasury and purporting to make grants of such land in the imperial name were revoked. In particular, a demand was made for the revision of all deeds of grant issued between the years 976 and 985 in the name of the *parakoimomenos* Basil. These were submitted to the personal scrutiny of the sovereign; and all which were not accorded his 'endorsement', written in his own hand, were declared invalid.

The effects of this radical enactment were felt even before its formal promulgation. Maleinus was expropriated and imprisoned for life. The estates of the Phocae were drastically curtailed. The grasping *protovestiarius* Philokales was evicted and humbled to the status of a peasant. The Musele family was reduced to beggary. These were examples *in terrorem*: 'so that', as the Emperor bluntly expressed it, 'the powerful may take note of it, and not leave this sort of inheritance to their children'. The law was thereafter enforced during thirty years with unceasing rigour; and all the great properties, whether military, civil or ecclesiastical, suffered substantial diminution if not wholesale extinction. Yet even this was insufficient. Eight years later (1003–4) the terrible Emperor imposed a yet more crushing burden on the estates of the 'powerful'. The groups or communes of villages were assessed at an annual sum which all the proprietors were jointly held liable for subscribing. This system had borne harshly on the 'poor', and Basil determined to relieve them. The *allelengyon* (as it was called) now became the sole responsibility of the 'powerful' landowner. This final blow fell most heavily on the church properties, which had fewer resources to meet it. The 'ministers of God', who, says the chronicler, 'were reduced to the extreme of penury', urged the Patriarch Sergius to repeated protests (1004, 1019); but these were dismissed with contempt.

Basil remained at home during the unusually long period of two years and a half (January 996–midsummer 998). The wide application of his land law demanded his presence: for his draconian measures provoked serious disaffection. Ecclesiastical and diplomatic affairs of grave import also claimed his attention. In 996, after the Patriarchate had been four years vacant, he appointed to the see a layman, the well-known physician Sisinnius, and set him to work towards a rupture with the Papacy. At almost the same time a yet bolder design occurred to him: of placing a Greek prelate on the Throne of St Peter. Bishop John Philagathus, a Greek-speaking native of Calabria and a protégé of the late Empress of the West, Theophano, was sent to Constantinople in the summer of 996 to negotiate the betrothal of Basil's niece Zoe to the young Emperor Otto III. The tenor of these negotiations is unknown; but the result is notorious. On his return to Italy Philagathus, trusting to the anti-German reaction in Rome fostered by the patrician Crescentius, allowed himself to be chosen anti-Pope in opposition to the German Gregory V, the cousin and nominee of Otto himself. The manœuvre miscarried disastrously. After a few months of ineffectual presidency, the upstart was seized by the Ottonians, horribly mutilated and thrown into prison. Thereafter, negotiations between Basil and Otto were indecisive during four years.

Meanwhile Basil's withdrawal from the west in 995 had led to a dangerous revival of the power of Samuel. In 996 he ambushed and killed the governor of Thessalonica, Gregory Taronites, and took prisoner successively Gregory's son Ashot and his *remplaçant* John of Chaldia. Samuel then swept south into the defenceless province of Hellas, and ravaged it down to the Isthmus of Corinth. Basil, preoccupied at home, could not intervene. But he sent to Thessalonica, which still held out, the ablest and most fortunate of his marshals, Nicephorus Uranus, who, in 997, encountered the returning Bulgars on the river Spercheius, and inflicted on them a bloody defeat.

Samuel himself was wounded, and barely escaped. Nicephorus seized the opportunity to advance into the centre of Bulgaria; and such was the completeness of his victory that during a progress of three months he met no opposition. From 997 until 1001 Samuel's arms were not seen in eastern Bulgaria or Macedonia. Indeed, he seems for a moment to have thought of submission. But events of the same year caused him to think again.

In 997 died the Croat ruler Stephen Držislav, to whom the Byzantine government had granted the title of king and entrusted the protection of their province of Dalmatia. His death inspired Samuel with the grand design of carving out a fresh and unassailable Empire in the west. From this time may be dated the truly imperial policy of Samuel. He proclaimed himself Tsar. He seized and garrisoned Dyrrachium. He invaded Dioclea and took prisoner its prince, John Vladimir, whom he married to his daughter Kosara. He advanced up Dalmatia, where, though its maritime cities repulsed him, he was soon master of the hinterland, hitherto under Croat protection. He then turned north-eastwards into Bosnia; and in or about the year 1000 he set the seal on his triumph by concluding a marriage alliance between his son and heir Gabriel Radomir and a daughter of St Stephen of Hungary.

His power in the west of the Balkan peninsula was now enormous. But Basil was more than a match for him. The Emperor's first counter-stroke was the transfer of the protectorate over Dalmatia from the feeble successors of Držislav to Venice. The Doge's eldest son, John Urseolo, hastened to Constantinople (997–8), and the bargain was soon struck. John returned to Venice with the promise of a wife from the imperial house; and in 1000 the Doge himself, in a splendid progress down the Adriatic, received the grateful homage of his new protectorate. Meanwhile Samuel had virtually abandoned his territories east of a line from Vidin through Sardica to Vodena, and Basil was not slow to take advantage of the respite. When Samuel returned eastwards in 1001, it was too late.

Basil's strategy in the Bulgarian war from 998 to 1003 is clear enough. It was a steady progress outwards from the centre, each advance being secured by the garrisoning of strong-points along the route. Philippopolis was first made into a strong base camp, with a permanent governor. Next, the forts about Sardica had to be occupied, for they commanded the route north-westward up the valley of the Isker to the Danube, and the route south-westward through Pernik and Radomir to Skoplje. If the centre were firmly held, each of these routes could be pursued in turn. A chain of Byzantine garrisons on the Danube would prevent the crossing of any reinforcements from

Hungary or Patzinakia,[1] a danger always present to imperial governments of that time. An advance on Skoplje would menace any
Bulgarian thrust south-eastwards, and would concentrate Bulgarian
defences on the threatened capital at Ochrida. Basil took the field
in the summer of 998, and had carried out the first part of his programme, the reduction of fortresses about Sardica, by the following
spring. In 999 he was urgently recalled to the Syrian frontier, in
circumstances precisely similar to those of 995. But this time he
could safely leave western operations in the hands of his marshals. In
1000 Xiphias and Theodorocanus overran the Dobrudja, and established the Byzantine arms firmly on the lower Danube. They returned
without loss.

In July 998 the energetic governor of Antioch, Dalassenus, was
accidentally slain during a campaign against Apamea. His troops at
once broke, and were massacred. Basil saw that it would be necessary
to repeat the lesson administered four years before. He arrived in
Syria in September 999, at the head of the invincible Russian troops
of his household, and during three months spread devastation far and
wide, though once again he had to fall back before the impregnable
defences of Tripoli. He appointed Nicephorus Uranus to succeed
Dalassenus at Antioch, and in January 1000 went into winter
quarters at Tarsus.

But he had other work to do in the east, and this was the time to
do it. In April, as he lay at Tarsus, came news, not unexpected by
him, of the murder on Easter Day of the *curopalates* David, prince of
Tao, whose rich legacy to the Emperor must now be occupied in
force. Without delay Basil, at the head of his army, pushed north-
eastwards through Melitene and Hanzith and Erez, settling local
affairs by the way. At Hafjij, a fortress on the south bank of the
Phasis river, the Georgian and Armenian potentates were gathered
to receive him. A bloody encounter between the Emperor's Russians
and the Iberian levies, which may have been accidental but was
certainly impressive, preceded the assize. The chief of the despots to
be reckoned with was Bagrat, King of Abasgia and Prince of Karthli,
whose southern frontier marched with that of Tao, now annexed
to the Empire. He was given the title of *curopalates* in succession
to his deceased cousin, and his borders were carefully defined
and agreed upon. The assize, which included a tentative towards
the annexation of Vaspurakan, was followed by a progress through
the recovered territories north of Lake Van, and thence into the
heart of the new province of Tao itself. Late in the year Basil
returned by way of Theodosiopolis to Constantinople. In the

---

[1] The Pechenegs were known in the Byzantine sources as 'Patzinaks'.

following year, 1001, the Fatimid caliphate signed a ten years' truce with the Empire.

Matters being thus satisfactorily settled in the east, the Emperor at once resumed his interrupted campaign in Bulgaria. In the spring and autumn of 1001 he made two short but fruitful forays into the southern area, capturing Verria and Servia in the first, and rooting out Bulgarian garrisons from Thessaly in the second. Samuel, now effectually roused by the Byzantine menace, advanced eastwards and made an attempt to recapture Servia, but was repulsed. Late in the year Basil returned to Constantinople, to renew and this time to complete the negotiations for the marriage of his niece with the Western Emperor. But here, once again, his western diplomacy miscarried. The princess, magnificently escorted, set out for Italy in January 1002, only to learn, on her arrival at Bari, that her betrothed, in the flower of his 'sweet years', had passed away.

This year (1002) Basil devoted to extending the work of his marshals on the Danube. He hastened to the north-west, and, probably in March or April, laid siege to Vidin. The town, defended strongly by art and nature, resisted during eight months. Samuel tried to relieve it by a destructive raid far in the Emperor's rear. Basil was not to be deflected; and at last the fortress surrendered. Samuel was now forced to make a serious attempt to stem the tide of Byzantine invasion. In the spring of 1003 Basil advanced to the Vardar and menaced Skoplje. The Bulgarians lay in strength on the opposite bank of the swollen river. Samuel repeated the blunder which had cost him the battle at the Spercheius six years before. He trusted too much to the natural barrier, and kept slack guard. Basil forded the river by night, and massacred his army. This was the turning-point in the war, and even Samuel's allies saw that it was so. Nothing could now prevent the final and total victory of the Byzantine arms, however long it might be in coming; and the navy of Venice presented an insuperable barrier to Samuel's establishing an Adriatic power. In the summer of 1004 the grand Veneto-Byzantine alliance was confirmed by the marriage in Constantinople of John Urseolo with Basil's second cousin, Maria Argyrou, at which the imperial brothers acted as groomsmen. In the spring of 1005 the bridal pair returned in triumph to Venice; and in the same year Dyrrachium, Samuel's all important outlet on the western sea, was surrendered by his own father-in-law to a Byzantine fleet.

The last sparks of Bulgarian resistance were not finally trampled out until 1019. This was partly due to the tenacious spirit of the Bulgarian people and to the natural strength of many of their fortresses, impervious to any siege which even Basil could mount against them; and partly to the fact that, now Samuel was incapable of serious resistance in the field, the occupation could be slower and more methodical and more time be given to consolidating the revolutionary progress made both at home and abroad in the years 996–1004. For these reasons, we have almost no details, apart from scattered and unreliable hints, about the annual incursions into Bulgaria during the next decade. It is certain only that many or most of them were undertaken in winter-time, when the flocks were down from the hills and the peasant at his fireside; and that they were accompanied by systematic destruction, pillage and mass deportation. When the curtain rises again in 1014, the aspect of the war has changed, very much to Samuel's disadvantage. Northern and central Bulgaria were now firmly held; and Basil, in his gradual progress towards the heart of Samuel's dominion, had during successive campaigns entered Bulgaria from the south, by way of Serres, the pass of Rupel and the long plain, the Campulungu, of the Strymon valley, between the mountain barriers of Ogražden and Belasica. The Tsar, in this year, made a final and desperate effort to halt the ruinous advance. With 15,000 men he blocked the pass near Kleidion, the modern village of Ključ; and sent another force across the mountain to Doiran, in order to menace Thessalonica. Both manœuvres failed. The latter force was cut to pieces by Theophylact Botaneiates, the governor of Thessalonica; while from the Long Plain Basil sent a detachment over the Belasica which, on 29 July, fell suddenly on Samuel's rear. The Tsar himself got clear away to Prilep. His army fell, almost to a man, into Basil's hands. Then was committed the savage crime which has left a lasting stain on the memory of that great Emperor. The number of the prisoners was 14,000. Basil put out the eyes of ninety-nine in every hundred, leaving the hundredth wretch one eye to guide his fellows back to their prince. This fearful instance of severity has been received with scepticism by some writers in our own age; but nothing we know of Basil's character or of his conduct on similar occasions gives us any reason to doubt it. The punishment was inflicted, as always, with a politic end in view, and this end was achieved. The sight of his mutilated host as it stumbled towards him broke Samuel's heart. He fell down in a seizure, and died two days afterwards (6 October 1014).

The end of the whole gigantic undertaking was now in sight. Sporadic and unorganised opposition was encountered from Samuel's son Gabriel Radomir (d. 1016), and from his murderer John Vladislav (d. 1018), who was said to be his cousin, but who may in fact have been heir to the old legitimate house of Symeon and Peter. Basil never relaxed. He was everywhere, mopping up resistance, storming and garrisoning fortresses, disposing of the royal and noble personages who fell into his hands, riveting the chains of Byzantine control and administration on one area after another. By 1019 the whole, or nearly the whole, of the vast domain reaching from the Euxine to the Adriatic was an integral part of the Byzantine Empire. It was parcelled out into the three provinces of Bulgaria in the centre and Sirmium and Paristrium on the upper and lower Danube. These, as imperial provinces, were now entitled to the imperial philanthropy; and they were administered, especially in the collection of revenue, with a leniency demanded by their ravaged and ruinous condition. Serbia (Dioclea, Rascia, Bosnia) and Croatia were allowed to remain self-governing dependencies; but their proximity to the Byzantine provinces of Dyrrachium, Dalmatia and Sirmium, as well as to the Adriatic power of Venice, rendered them powerless to do harm.

Basil's ambitions were directed toward the west; but during the past five years the unquiet state of affairs on his Georgian borders had disturbed the settlement of 1000, and led him in 1021 to undertake his third and last progress in the east. In 1014 died the *curopalates* Bagrat of Abasgia, and his son George at once broke the agreement. With Armenian aid, he invaded and occupied Tao and Phasiane. Basil had no time to deal with him personally, though in 1016, as a preliminary step, he sent a naval force to occupy the Khazar ports in the rear, that is, to the north-west, of George's dominions. In 1021 the Emperor's hands were free. He recovered Phasiane, and pushed on beyond the frontiers of Taïk into inner Iberia. A drawn battle was fought near Lake Palakatzio; but after it George abandoned his gains in Tao and fled northwards into Abasgia. In the following year, though he was able to incite Basil's trusted marshal Xiphias to an abortive revolt in the Emperor's rear, he was finally defeated in September near the Phasis river. Menaced both by land and sea, he left his infant son a hostage in Basil's hands, and retired, this time for good, beyond his frontier. Basil, as was his wont, improved the occasion by making a wider settlement of the east. He compelled John Smbat, King of Armenia, as he had once compelled David of Tao, to bequeath his lands about Ani to the Byzantines, a legacy which fell to them in 1045. He then turned south and occupied the territory of Vaspurakan, to the east of Lake Van, whose ruler Sennacherib, alarmed by the first ripple of the swelling Seljuq inundation, had in the winter of 1021–2 ceded his lands to the Empire.

When Basil returned to his capital early in 1023, the Byzantine Empire had, through the energy and resolution of one man, achieved a territorial extent combined with internal security which it had

never known before and was never to know again. From Azerbaijan
to the Adriatic the Emperor was absolute master. In southern Italy
a dangerous Lombard revolt, which broke out in 1011 and was
rendered yet more dangerous by the adhesion of the earliest Norman
invaders, had been crushed in a second *clades Cannensis* (1018) by
the catepan Basil Boiannes. Four years later the same Normans,
now prudently enrolled in the imperial service, repulsed from Byzantine territory the last of the Saxon Emperors, Henry II. At home the
land-holding aristocracy, though seething with resentment, was held
powerless in an iron grip; and the old system of 'free' peasant communes and soldiers' estates, relieved of the crushing burdens of taxation which had ruined them in the past, was enjoying a halcyon
interlude of prosperity and devotion to the central government.
Moreover, the solid strength of the Empire had, as was natural,
enormously enhanced its political influence beyond its borders, of
which the most spectacular symptom was the firm establishment of
the imperial religion and culture in Christian Russia. The achievement was so splendid and astonishing that it demands a brief review
of the circumstances which made it possible.

Of all the Emperors of Byzantium Basil II, in his own person, came
nearest to the imperial ideal of boundless power and boundless providence. He seemed to have been sent by Heaven to show that, in a
set of highly exceptional circumstances, it was humanly possible to
put the age-old theory into practice. He was the supreme, exclusive
pantocrat; over the army, over the civil administration, over the
Church. His fiat seemed to be invested with a godlike omnipotence
and inexorability. At his nod, Russians and Slavs threw back his
enemies in south Italy: Armenians fought on the Danube: Bulgarians
were settled in Vaspurakan. His treatment of the Church is especially
worthy of notice, in view of a modern tendency to misconceive the
nature and extent of its authority at Byzantium. Basil appointed
three Patriarchs of Constantinople, of whom one was a layman and
the other two were ciphers. They were wholly subservient to his
policies, especially where these concerned his relations with the West.
Before the first and second of these appointments he allowed the see
to remain vacant during a total of more than seven years, for no
better reason than that he was absent from the capital and could not,
or would not, make time to nominate. He rusticated the Patriarch
of Antioch (989) and seven years later deposed him, nominating as his
successor a creature of his own. He detained the Patriarch of Jerusalem at Constantinople from the year 1000 until his death in 1004. His
ambition, as we have seen, did not stop short of appointing a Greek
Pope of Rome. His ecclesiastical settlement of conquered Bulgaria

degraded its Patriarchate to an archbishopric, the appointment to which was in the Emperor's own personal gift, without reference to the Patriarch of Constantinople. His legislation bore as hardly on church as on lay property, and he was deaf to all remonstrance against it. There was, plainly, no room for a Polyeuctus or Cerularius in the economy of this sovereign autocrat.

In his diplomacy he was not less independent and despotic. His dynastic marriage of a Porphyrogenita to Vladimir of Russia has often been cited as a breach with tradition, committed under duress; but the marriage of Maria Argyrou to John Urseolo and the betrothal of the Porphyrogenita Zoe to Otto III were not different in principle. Of the Byzantine tradition of learning and education, which his own ancestors had done so much to foster, he was openly contemptuous. To the end of his life he spoke and wrote, plainly and forcibly indeed, but without the smallest regard to grace or propriety. Extravagant ceremonies and pageants he disliked in themselves and because they cost money: his own apparel when he was in his capital was ostentatiously sober and shabby. Some money he did spend on architecture; but this was from political rather than from aesthetic or pious motives. In these departments, as in all others, his word was absolute. The unity of the world under the elect of Christ, which the sovereigns of the ninth and tenth centuries had postulated, and for which they had striven, was finally consummated in the person of their prodigious offspring.

Yet the very qualities required to achieve this consummation—the unswerving resolution of a dedicated ruler, the strategic grasp of a commander-in-chief united to the meticulous precision of a drill-sergeant, the practical talent and far-sightedness of a statesman, the laborious fidelity of an administrator, above all, perhaps, the physical toughness and endurance of a body insensible to fatigue and privation —were so various that they could never again be found in a single frame. The flaw in the noble structure built by Basil, as in many of the structures of Byzantine architecture, was that it was built for the day without regard to the morrow. The internal forces which threatened disruption were held in check by his arm alone. The military aristocrats he could humble by economic oppression; and he could and did submit their rash and hot-headed methods of warfare to the iron discipline of his imperial military machine. But even he could not do without them. If he had found it as easy to recruit capable general officers from the ranks as to recruit capable clerks for administration, he would have dispensed with the services of the military even more readily than he did with those of the bureaucratic grandees. But this was impossible; and throughout his reign Dalasseni,

Melisseni, Argyri, Comneni, even Phocae, are found in high command. Abroad, Normans and Seljuqs were by his death already on the western and eastern borders of his Empire. The inevitable result of his being succeeded by his brother and his nieces must have been clear to eyes far less sharp than his. Yet he 'put out no roots for the throne'. He probably never married, and certainly left no heirs of his body. He was and remained a unique phenomenon.

Bulgaria, Georgia, Armenia had not sated that thirst for conquest. In 1025 he sent his marshal Boiannes into Sicily, to prepare his way. He was about to follow, at the head of his invincible army; but, on 15 December, in his sixty-ninth year, he died.

CHAPTER V

THE LATER MACEDONIANS, THE COMNENI AND THE ANGELI 1025-1204

I. THE LATER MACEDONIANS AND THEIR IMMEDIATE SUCCESSORS, 1025–81

The years between the death of Basil II in 1025 and the accession of Alexius I Comnenus in 1081 were at once fruitful and disastrous. Historiography, poetry, spirituality and religious life, painting and architecture, flourished. But imperial authority dwindled; military defences were to some extent neglected; considerable incentive was given to separatism. It thus proved impossible to make any effective stand against rising forces on every front. Particularly dangerous were the Seljuqs to the East, the Balkan principalities and the Pechenegs[1] and other Turkic raiders to the North, and the Normans to the West, while added complications were to arise from the crusading movement led by a reinvigorated Papacy and Latin barons moved by secular ambition as well as Christian devotion. The contrast between these years and the reign of Basil II was all the more marked since that tough old warrior had kept firm check on wealthy military land-owners and on financial resources and had himself led his troops to victory in a series of ruthless campaigns. He appeared to have had no ambition to found a dynasty though he must have been aware that the next in the Macedonian line, his brother Constantine VIII, was hardly suited to continue his own hard-won policy of relentless control and unceasing military vigilance, and still less could he expect anything of Constantine's heirs apparent, a trio of comparatively elderly daughters.

The character of Constantine VIII is graphically portrayed in the early pages of Psellus' *Chronographia*. Though not a fool, he lacked good judgement and a sense of proportion; he was quick-tempered, unreliable, fond of his creature comforts, with a passion for the theatre and horse-racing, a gambler and something of a glutton. He had no sons, and his daughters were now getting on in years. Eudocia was a calm and gentle woman who asked no more than to be allowed to enter a convent; Theodora, the youngest, was tall like her father, abrupt and quick in speech, not particularly beautiful, and she evi-

---

[1] The 'Patzinaks' of the Byzantine sources.

dently did not get on well with Zoe, the middle sister and the best known of the three. Zoe has been immortalised by Psellus in his history of his own age—the old scholar and politician had every opportunity to know her well—and also by the artist who has left her portrait in a mosaic panel in the women's gallery in St Sophia in Constantinople. Zoe was beautiful, vain and ambitious, credulous and gullible, drinking in the promises of soothsayers and quacks, no judge of character and without any glimmering of statesmanship. Attractive even in old age, as her mosaic portrait shows, with her clear smooth skin, her make-up and her amiable expression, she had to put away her high hopes of an heir of her body, and finally to resign herself to being relegated to the women's quarters of the palace until her death in 1050, apparently contentedly sharing the honours accorded to women of the imperial family with the young and beautiful mistresses of her last husband, Constantine IX.

During the previous century and a half of the Macedonian dynasty, the throne had from time to time been occupied by minors, by studious and lettered men, even for a short space by a young hothead. The age had nevertheless been one of vigorous development and, on the whole, effective government. One explanation lies in the opportune appearance of strong co-Emperors just when they were most needed, and another in the outlet provided for the landed military families in a series of successful military drives followed by the expansion of the frontiers. Under the later Macedonians and their successors, the luck turned: these factors no longer held. Zoe's second husband Michael IV, and later Isaac I Comnenus and Romanus IV, were brave and vigorous generals, but they could not stem the turbulent Slavs or the Seljuq hordes. George Maniaces proved himself an able military leader, but he was not of aristocratic origin and he roused fierce antagonism from the old established families, and the deep suspicions of Zoe's third husband, Constantine IX; he might have gained the throne but he was killed on his way to Constantinople. For the most part control during the years 1025–81 lay with rulers who were not competent to deal with military matters. The landed magnates were now in a difficult position. Far from continuing their victorious expansion, they now saw the frontiers ominously contracting in Italy, in the Balkans, and above all in the eastern reaches. They had already been ruthlessly penalised and weakened by the enmity and confiscations of Basil II. It was therefore a matter of life and death for them to gain control of the government and inaugurate sound measures for imperial defence. Hence the bitterness of the underlying struggle during the period between the death of Basil II and the accession of Alexius I in 1081; and while the civil and military aristocracy were at each others' throats it was impossible to concentrate on stabilising the frontiers.

It is against this background that palace dramas and the brilliant intellectual life of the capital during the lifetime of the later Macedonians must be viewed. Constantine VIII was already elderly when his brother Basil died, and the three years of his reign were marred by his reliance on a group of eunuchs and his acute fear of political rivals. In Antioch and in the Caucasus there were already uneasy stirrings; the Pechenegs to the north were restive; Basil II's plans for the reconquest of the Italian lands were not carried out. Then, 'surprised by death and reminded by old age that he must die',[1] Constantine VIII hurriedly provided for the succession by marrying his second and most beautiful daughter Zoe to Romanus Argyrus, the prefect of the city. The Church objected because Romanus was already married, but the difficulty was met by tricking his wife into entering a nunnery. A further obstacle connected with the prohibited degrees (for the respective great-grandfathers of the couple had married the two daughters of Romanus I) was smoothed over by the Patriarch Alexius, who wished to avoid any possibility of a disputed succession.

Romanus III (1028–34) is painted by Psellus in the *Chronographia* as a poseur, a mediocre Emperor, ineffectively emulating first one, then another, great man of the past, imagining himself to be outstanding as a philosopher, as a general or as a pious builder of churches. He inaugurated his reign by measures designed to placate. He released certain prisoners, and made increased grants to the cathedral of St Sophia, where he himself had been *oeconomus*. He carried out a measure which was apparently contemplated by Constantine VIII,[2] and abolished the *allelengyon*, the system whereby the well-off had to pay the taxes due from uncultivated land, thus making a concession to the substantial landowners whom Emperors such as Romanus I or Basil II had tried to check.

On the eastern frontier recent brilliant successes were imperilled by the weak duke of Antioch and by the rising power of Aleppo. Romanus appointed his brother-in-law Constantine Carantenus as the new duke of Antioch, and himself took the field, crossing the Taurus and Amanus mountains in 1030. He was defeated and hurriedly retreated to Antioch, and then returned to Constantinople. The Muslims were emboldened to raid up to the Taurus range, but the situation was redeemed by the exploits of the *strategus* of the frontier theme of Teluch who was rewarded by being appointed military commander of the Upper Euphrates cities with his seat at Samosata. He was the

---

[1] Michael Psellus, *Chronographia*, Constantine VIII, ch. 9 (ed. Renauld, I, p. 30).
[2] Scylitzes-Cedrenus, II, p. 486 (*CSHB*).

renowned and audacious George Maniaces, a soldier, probably of central Asian origin, who had worked his way up from the ranks and was regarded as a parvenu by established Byzantine families. Maniaces restored Byzantine prestige, and in 1032 added to his reputation by taking Edessa, an important strategic and economic centre. According to Scylitzes, Romanus III himself also undertook a fresh campaign in Syria in this year but was recalled by news of a conspiracy. He had already married one of his nieces to the king of Georgia and Abasgia in 1030, and another to John Smbat, and Byzantine policy was directed towards further securing its position in the Caucasian lands.

At home Romanus proved quite incapable of countering attempts to undermine his authority. Once he realised the futility of hoping to establish his own dynasty, he unwisely ignored his wife and restricted her expenditure. Zoe, though elderly, was still active and self-assertive. She was evidently jealous of her sister Theodora, whom she had sent to a nunnery. Neglected by her husband, she then began an active intrigue with a young Paphlagonian of humble origin, Michael, whose brother, the capable eunuch John, already held office. Romanus either could not, or would not, perceive this, though warned by his sister, 'a woman of great spirit who had contributed a good deal to her brother's success'. When her vigilant eye was removed, the Emperor fell ill, perhaps poisoned by Zoe and Michael, as Psellus hints. On the evening of 11 April 1034 he died in his bath, some asserting that he was forcibly held under the water. As he lay dying, Zoe came into the room, gave him one look, and then at once took control. Though faced by strong opposition, she immediately married Michael.

At the Empress Zoe's insistence Michael the Paphlagonian was at once proclaimed Emperor (12 April 1034). Behind Michael IV stood his four brothers, in particular the eunuch John the Orphanotrophus, a man of keen intelligence, a shrewd administrator, perpetually vigilant, determined to build the fortunes of his family. Michael IV was already afflicted with epilepsy when he came to the throne and this grew rapidly worse. If he appeared in public, red curtains were hung on either side of him, ready to be drawn at the first sign of his illness. Nevertheless, during the seven years of his rule (1034–41) Michael, though he appears to have debased the coinage, showed himself in many respects to be a reasonably capable Emperor who held his own against opposition from the Byzantine military aristocracy. Even so, he was scarcely able to check the rising forces on the frontiers. On the north the Pechenegs crossed the Danube in 1033 and ravaged the Balkans, and again in 1036. The Slavs settled there rose in rebellion with the reversal of Basil II's concession that their taxes might be paid in kind. This revolt, led by Peter Deljan, probably the grandson of the West Bulgarian ruler, Samuel, was quelled by 1041, but the Byzantines failed in their struggle to compel the Prince of Zeta, Stephen Vojislav, to acknowledge their suzerainty.

In South Italy an attempt was made to strengthen the Byzantine position, both by allying with Salerno and by using Norman mercenaries. An attack was launched on Sicily to stop the Saracens from menacing the mainland. George Maniaces was sent and with him the almost legendary Norwegian hero Harold Hardraga, who was then serving with the Byzantine forces. The capture of Messina (1037) was followed by progress to the west and the capture of Syracuse in 1040. Unfortunately, Maniaces was recalled, ostensibly on a charge of treason, but probably because in a burst of temper he had offended one of the Emperor's relatives, Stephen the Admiral. His gains were rapidly lost by incompetent leaders. This affected the position in South Italy where Guaimar V of Salerno was steadily growing in power. Anti-Byzantine agitation and discontent in Apulia was however stemmed by Argyrus who won back Bari in 1040. But the Normans were in the ascendant; in March 1041 they captured Melfi, the key to Apulia, and the Byzantines found themselves with difficulty retaining control over the strongholds in the south, as Taranto or Brindisi.

On the east the uncertain struggle continued against the levies of Mesopotamia and northern Syria; Byzantium was continually contesting with the Caliph of Egypt for control over Aleppo. On the Armenian frontier Percri was recaptured from the Seljuqs in 1037. But there were perpetual difficulties with both Armenians and Georgians. The situation was complicated by the reluctance of the Byzantine military families to co-operate with the Paphlagonian upstarts, and by the innumerable local feuds and rebellions in the Caucasian regions. When in 1040 the Bagratid ruler John Smbat III died, a year after his brother Ashot IV, Michael IV claimed Ani as promised to Basil II, but in spite of Byzantine expeditions, there was a strong nationalist reaction and Ashot's fourteen-year-old son Gagik II was made king, thus postponing for a few years the incorporation of the kingdom into the East Roman Empire.

Michael IV had excellent qualities, as Cecaumenus pointed out.[1] But his disease grew apace and when it was clear that he had only a short time to live, he retired to the monastery of the Anargyri, St Cosmas and St Damian, which he had built, and put on the monk's habit and was tonsured. He died on 10 December 1041 and was buried there. His brother John the Orphanotrophus had already

[1] Cecaumenus, *Strategicon*, ch. 250 (ed. B. Wassiliewsky–V. Jernstedt, St Petersburg, 1896, p. 99).

made preparations to retain political control within the family circle. By urging Michael IV to provide for the succession he had gained the Emperor's reluctant support for a plan whereby Zoe was induced to adopt his nephew, another Michael, his sister's son. This young man was made Caesar, and when his uncle died he was brought forward by Zoe, in whom supreme control was vested by hereditary right, and on the same day (10 December 1041) was crowned as Michael V.

Before he came to the throne Michael V (known as Calaphates) had to some extent concealed his dislike of his family, and he had been kept in the background, for Michael IV does not seem to have liked him. Once he became Emperor he was able to act on his own initiative, and Scylitzes says that his success went to his head.[1] He began by exiling his uncles. John was sent to the monastery of Monobatae; Constantine was however allowed to return and was made *nobilissimus*. Maniaces was released from prison and created catepan and magister of the Italian provinces; and Constantine Dalassenus, an old enemy, was also set free, perhaps in an attempt at conciliation. But Michael ruled only for four months. His major blunder was not his shabby treatment of John the Orphanotrophus, but his attitude towards the old Macedonian Empress Zoe. Psellus says that he was jealous of her popularity and he evidently found her tedious and boring. Strict surveillance—which indeed she had suffered under Michael IV—was succeeded by a fatal attempt to remove her altogether from the field of practical politics: she was charged with plotting to poison the Emperor and on the night of Easter Day 1042, evidently accompanied only by one lady-in-waiting, was exiled to the island of Principo in the Sea of Marmora. On the Easter Monday both the senate and the people were given the story of the plot. In a proclamation read by the prefect of the city, accusations were brought against Zoe, and also the Patriarch Alexius, who was disliked by the Paphlagonian family. For a short time Michael V enjoyed his apparent triumph. Then there was a rising in the city, graphically described by Psellus, who, as secretary to the Emperor, was in the imperial palace. The rising was directed against the Emperor and also his family. His uncle Constantine, aware of the danger, armed his household and rushed with his retinue to assist his nephew in the palace. The Empress was recalled and displayed to the mob from the balcony of the Great Theatre, but apparently still in her nun's habit and not in the imperial robes. It was clear that she was still under the control of Michael. The leaders of the opposition could count on the support of the Patriarch Alexius, whom John the Orphanotrophus had wished to depose and Michael V had confined to his monastery

---

[1] Scylitzes-Cedrenus, II, p. 532 (*CSHB*).

on the Bosphorus and may have planned to kill. They were determined to exploit the violent popular reaction against the young Emperor, and they went to fetch Zoe's sister Theodora, a nun in the monastery of the Petrion, who was also of the Macedonian house. Dragged against her will from the sanctuary on Easter Tuesday, she was taken to St Sophia and proclaimed Empress.

This alarmed Michael Calaphates, and on the Wednesday he fled by boat from the palace to the Studite monastery with his uncle. Both were found at the altar facing the inflamed mob, and eventually they were dragged away and that night they were blinded by officials sent for this purpose, and then exiled to monastic houses. As Psellus, who was present, acutely observes, Theodora's supporters knew that it was unsafe to allow Michael V to remain on the throne because so bitter was Zoe's jealousy of her sister that she would have been likely to prefer ill-treatment from Michael rather than share the throne with Theodora. As it was, Zoe had to bring herself to accept Theodora as co-Empress, though she insisted on taking precedence of her sister.

Behind the dramatic rise and fall of the Paphlagonians during the years 1034–42 certain trends emerge. Like Romanus III, they lacked the support of the important military families in Asia Minor. Unlike Romanus III, they were of humble origin and they had enemies among powerful elements in Constantinople. It was therefore essential to establish control through their own family; hence the policy of John the Orphanotrophus who apparently wanted to become Patriarch himself, thus antagonising the Patriarch Alexius and the Church. When Michael V came to the throne any pretence at family solidarity broke down, and this, together with the ill-judged attempt to eliminate Zoe, gave dissident elements their opportunity. The Patriarch was amongst those who supported the legitimist principle and pressed home the attack against Michael V. The opposition seems to have regarded Zoe and Theodora as pawns, using popular feeling for the established dynasty in order to supplant a parvenu family.

The legitimist principle had its drawbacks. It was impossible for two elderly women to guide the Empire, even though Psellus says that during their brief joint reign both civil and military elements managed to work together harmoniously. In reality, both parties were playing for time, waiting to seize any opportunity to gain control. Meanwhile Zoe was looking round in the court circle for a third husband, and she chose Constantine Monomachus, a man of good family, who had been imprisoned on Mitylene as a political suspect in Michael IV's reign. He married the old Empress and was crowned on 12 June 1042. Psellus was in his service and writes at length on his reign, wishing that he could have claimed that his favourite Emperor was perfect, only historical facts did not fit in with his desire.[1] Constantine IX occupies a central position in the *Chronographia*: again and again Psellus is at pains to point out some good quality, some virtue, reluctantly mentioning some defect or mistake. Nor is he alone, for Attaleiates considered that until the last years of his reign, Constantine IX had his points as a ruler.[2] But he was not outstanding for his statesmanship. He is shown in the *Chronographia* as a good-natured man, kindly, humorous, even frivolous, quick-tempered, erratic and over-indulgent. He enjoyed his imperial position, spent freely, satisfied his whims and his desires. His mistresses, his indiscriminate pardonings, his expensive building programme, all helped to empty the treasury. Additional appointments to office and the expansion of the bureaucracy, which followed the ascendancy of the civil party, also meant increased expenditure. Psellus may be right in referring to the successful and economical way in which Constantine ran his estates, but it is a fact that his reign, like that of Michael IV, saw a debasement of the nomisma, which continued to deteriorate in varying degrees during the years 1025–81.

At home Constantine IX was served by able men—his first minister, Constantine Leichudes, was politician, orator, scholar, well-versed in public affairs and in civil law. Michael Psellus, John Xiphilinus and John Mauropous were at court, and whatever charges may be levelled against Psellus, none could deny the high moral standards of Leichudes, Xiphilinus and Mauropous. The two first were later on to fill the office of Patriarch, the last-named was the humane and scholarly Archbishop of Euchaïta. This group of men was passionately interested in promoting higher education; the younger men had been tutored by John Mauropous and together they must almost certainly have strongly influenced the Emperor. In 1045 the university of Constantinople was reorganised, and evident rivalry between the humanists and the jurists was resolved by the creation of a Faculty of Law and a Faculty of Philosophy. The guardian of the laws (*nomophylax*) was to be John Xiphilinus, and the head of philosophical studies was Michael Psellus. Details about the Law Faculty are given in its constitution (commonly attributed to Mauropous but possibly drafted in part by Xiphilinus).[3] There appears to be no surviving constitution of the Faculty of Philosophy, but something of its teaching and its teachers can be learnt from Psellus. His old friends, John Mauropous and Nicetas, as well as he himself, all lectured. Their syllabus included literature, rhetoric and dialectic, mathematics,

---

[1] Michael Psellus, *Chronographia*, Constantine IX, ch. 28 (ed. Renauld, I, p. 131).
[2] Michael Attaleiates, *Historia*, pp. 49–50 (*CSHB*).
[3] Cf. J. Cvetler, *Eos*, XLVIII, II (1957), 297–328.

music, geometry and astronomy, and it culminated in philosophy. In his *Chronographia* Psellus describes his search for philosophical instruction, and his own journey back to Plato and Aristotle, and thence forward again to Plotinus, Porphyry, Iamblichus and Proclus. His metaphysical writings bear out his declaration that his own philosophy was not simply derived from the ancient systems, but, as he says, it transcended them, for it was based on Christian principles. And Psellus' work, in more ways than one, was continued by his follower John Italus. He took over the office of chief (*hypatos*) of the philosophers when Psellus left Constantinople intending to enter a monastery, and he gave lectures explaining the books of Aristotle and Plato. The reorganisation of the university of Constantinople, financed by the Emperor, reflects the keen activity in legal, literary and philosophical studies which is evident throughout this period.

Later generations, particularly in the Latin West, look back to Constantine IX's reign as the time when, for various reasons, the age-long differences between Rome and Constantinople came to a head in 1054. This event is not mentioned in Byzantine histories, but there are graphic accounts of the episode by the two dominating protagonists, Cardinal Humbert and Michael Cerularius, and it is clear that Humbert's attitude and excommunication had made it impossible for the arrogant Cerularius even to consider the Roman point of view.[1] Indeed, in Cerularius' eyes Rome was the aggressor. The breach between the two churches still remains unhealed and for that reason undue stress is sometimes placed on the events of 1054. Differences between Rome and Constantinople had long been recognised, and to some extent accepted. It was unfortunate for Byzantium and for the Papacy that there should have been an aggressive Patriarch, Michael Cerularius, and an equally difficult legate, Cardinal Humbert, at precisely the moment when, if only for political needs, it was imperative to work together.

During Constantine IX's reign the Byzantine position in Italy steadily deteriorated. Michael V had released the able general George Maniaces from prison and appointed him in Italy as magister and catepan. He had taken up his command during the brief joint rule of Zoe and Theodora, arriving in Taranto at the end of April 1042. Unfortunately, his campaigns against the Normans and the rebellious Apulian cities were cut short. His enemy and neighbour in Asia Minor, Romanus Sclerus, attacked his estates and his wife and stirred up feeling against him in Constantinople. He was recalled by Constantine IX in October 1042. Enraged by this double injustice and acclaimed Emperor by his troops, he crossed to Dyrrachium in

[1] For details of the schism see below: ch. x.

February 1043, gained allies amongst the Slavs, and took the Via Egnatia to the capital. In panic, Constantine sent all his available resources to meet him. These were defeated at Ostrovo in upper Macedonia, but in the moment of victory a stray arrow killed the usurper, and Constantine IX was able to celebrate a triumph which he certainly did not deserve. But the Empire had lost a general it could ill spare.

This left the Greeks in South Italy in a precarious position. Here the Lombards in alliance with certain of the Normans were vigorously contesting Byzantine authority. After the departure of Maniaces in September 1042, one of the Lombard leaders, Argyrus, son of Melo of Bari, went over to the Greek side and directed the Byzantine forces, attempting to counter the Normans of Melfi and Aversa in alliance with the prince of Salerno. In 1046 Robert Guiscard arrived, and in 1047 the German Emperor Henry III, though he limited Guaimar of Salerno's power, agreed to recognise the Norman Rainulf as Count of Aversa. Argyrus tried by various methods to drive the Normans out of South Italy. In 1051 he did succeed in regaining Bari, which had been in the hands of a pro-Norman party. Pope Leo IX also attempted to build up an alliance against the Normans. In 1052 he tried to negotiate with the Byzantines and in 1052–3 with the German Emperor. Argyrus meanwhile had been defeated at Bari in 1052 and had left this city by sea. Leo IX was himself defeated by the Normans at Civitate on 23 June 1053, but he still hoped for help from Henry III and Constantine IX.

At this critical juncture Leo, Archbishop of Ochrida, possibly at the instigation of Michael Cerularius, chose to launch his attack on certain usages and teaching of the Latin Church, sending a provocative letter to John, Bishop of Trani, a friend of Argyrus. Knowledge of the defeat of Pope Leo at Civitate, followed by his death in the following year (19 April 1054), did not make the aggressive behaviour of his legate, Cardinal Humbert, any the more palatable. By now the projected political alliance between the West and Constantinople had already fallen to the ground and the Normans were consolidating their position in South Italy at the expense of the Byzantines. Even Psellus admits that Maniaces suffered injustice during his lifetime, though it is not clear whether he is implying criticism of Constantine IX's decision to recall him from Italy. Had Maniaces lived he might have gained the throne and given effective military leadership to the Empire, though it is by no means certain that he would have been *persona grata* with the landed magnates of Asia Minor.

The rebellion of Maniaces was not the only internal attack which

Constantine IX surmounted. Simultaneously, a revolt led by Theophilus Eroticus broke out in Cyprus but was quickly suppressed. There were also conspiracies nearer home. Romanus Boilas, whom Psellus misleadingly portrays as a court buffoon, though he was in fact a person of standing and substance, plotted to kill the Emperor, but was betrayed and forgiven. Much more dangerous was the revolt of the Armenian Leo Tornicius in 1047. Leo was descended from the Armenian royal family and was offended by Constantine IX's capricious attitude towards him. He found support in discontented military circles in Macedonia and Thrace, and he was proclaimed Emperor at Adrianople. He then approached Constantinople and encamped outside the city walls. And once again, as in the case of Maniaces, it was only by lucky chance that Constantine gained control of the situation. For on the failure of the imperial sortie, Tornicius did not press home his advantage and enter the open city gates, but chose to wait until the next day. Meanwhile the gates were closed, the guards rallied, and the eastern army arrived. The rebels had to capitulate and on 24 December the leaders Leo Tornicius and John Vatatzes were blinded. Constantine had been saved, this time first by good fortune, and then by the latent rivalry between the European and Asian troops which ensured him the support of the latter.

On two other occasions during Monomachus' reign, Constantinople and its Balkan hinterland were threatened. In 1043 the Russians under Vladimir of Kiev sailed into the Bosphorus, allegedly to revenge the death of a Russian merchant in a broil in Constantinople, but their fleet was defeated. Then from 1048 onwards the Pechenegs, nomadic Turkic tribes from beyond the Danube, flooded over the northern frontier and scourged the Balkans. Constantine IX tried various expedients: he stirred up strife between the Pechenegs and their enemies, the Uzes; he enlisted Pechenegs into his army to fight the Turks in Asia Minor, but they were said to have panicked, deserted, and swum back across the Bosphorus to rejoin their fellow tribesmen in the Balkans; he rallied an army against them and under Nicephorus Bryennius' command in 1051 it made some attempt to stem the raids; and finally, as the attacks eased off, Constantine allowed some of the invaders to settle in the Bulgarian provinces.

In the east, the Byzantines had the twofold problem of controlling the troubled Caucasian lands and of stemming the raids of the Turks. None of Constantine's immediate predecessors had been able to implement the terms of the treaty of 1022 which Basil II had made with the Armenian Bagratids. In spite of this agreement, Armenian nationalist feeling supported John Smbat III and his brother Ashot IV, and then in 1040 Ashot's son Gagik II. In 1044

Constantine IX allied with the Muslim amir of Tovin in Persarmenia, and Gagik was first lured to Constantinople, and then induced to accept estates in Cappadocia, where he lived until his death in 1079. The Bagratid lands were thus surrendered to Constantinople in 1045 and incorporated into the Empire as the theme of Armenia. But from 1045 to 1047 border warfare continued because the Byzantine ally, the amir of Tovin, refused to return the fortresses which he had captured.

The possession of Armenia brought Byzantium face to face with the Seljuq Turks who had for some time been establishing themselves in the Middle East. Contemporary writers comment on the failure of imperial policy towards the Caucasian vassal states and the eastern themes. Constantine's attempt to turn internal Georgian feuds to his advantage was neutralised by his inability to provide the promised funds for Georgian troops. Cecaumenus notes that in Georgia and in the theme of Mesopotamia taxes were so oppressive that certainly on one occasion whole families preferred to go over to the Muslims.[1] From 1048 onwards Turkish raids on the provinces increased. The wealthy city of Erzerum, said to have had 800 chapels and churches, was sacked and burnt. In 1049 a brief respite was afforded but only because the Sultan Tughril-Bey was occupied by internal affairs. In 1052 attacks on Armenia and Georgia were renewed, though they met with fierce resistance. On the extreme southern frontier the position was easier: the border amirs here were themselves being harassed by the Seljuqs, while the Muslim power in the south, the Fatimids of Egypt, were for the moment at peace with Constantinople.

Constantine IX died on 11 January 1055. He had apparently given some thought as to who might succeed him but without consulting the old Empress Theodora, the only surviving member of the Macedonian house. Hearing of this, she returned to the palace, won over the imperial bodyguard and at once took up the reins of power. The attempt of the Macedonian general, Bryennius, to gain control proved abortive. Once again the army was thwarted. Not only was Bryennius punished, but to the indignation of military circles Isaac Comnenus was deprived of his command of the Eastern troops. Theodora made a determined attempt at ruling. She took no husband, but appointed the *syncellus* Leo Paraspondylus as her minister. He was hard-headed and hard-working and inaugurated a policy of economy at home and peace abroad. Michael Cerularius, who had at first supported Theodora, found that he failed to get control of the administration of the property of St Sophia as he wished, and had Theodora lived longer, there might have been an open rift between the Empress and Patriarch. Unexpectedly, Theodora fell ill. Her

---

[1] Cecaumenus, *Strategicon*, ch. 50 (*op. cit.* p. 18).

ministers persuaded her to agree to the accession of an elderly and undistinguished soldier, the patrician Michael Stratioticus. On her death on 21 August 1056[1] the Patriarch reluctantly crowned him as her successor.

The extinction of the Macedonian house did not remove the weakness in the central government. Psellus, commenting on the accession of Michael VI, the Aged, as he was called, frankly pointed out that Emperors of recent memory had relied on the civil element, and had therefore set out to placate the people and the senate, while neglecting the third factor on which imperial power also rested, namely, the army. From 1056 to 1081 when Alexius I firmly established the Comnenian dynasty, the rule of the civil aristocracy continued, broken only by the brief interludes of the military Emperors Isaac I Comnenus (1057–9) and Romanus IV Diogenes (1068–71). It is during this period that adverse rising forces begin to show, both within and without.

Michael VI ruled only a year. His unbelievably foolish mistakes drove the Norman soldier Hervé Francopulus to enter the service of the Turks, and he antagonised the eastern army and its leaders who now planned to overthrow the civil party. Isaac Comnenus advanced across Asia Minor towards the capital. In this dilemma Psellus gave Michael VI sound advice: he counselled him to win over the Patriarch Michael, to temporise, and if possible to sow dissension, by sending an embassy to Isaac, while he himself mobilised the European armies and allied with neighbouring barbarians. Michael, however, neglected to placate Cerularius which, as Psellus shrewdly observed, was in itself sufficient to cause his downfall. Two embassies went from the capital to Isaac and they are described in detail by Psellus who took part in them. Michael finally abdicated on 31 August 1057, and Isaac, already proclaimed Emperor by his army in Asia Minor on 8 June, was crowned on 1 September 1057. His accession marked the victory of the Asian military party in opposition to the European army, the bureaucracy and the senate.

Psellus, though long connected with the civil party (and indeed at the time of the crisis in some trepidation as to whether he might not have his throat slit), gives a very fair and pithy account of Isaac's attempt to purge the state of its unhealthy and rotten elements. As commander-in-chief of the army, Isaac knew 'why our neighbours prospered while our affairs declined'. But, adds Psellus, he went too far and acted too quickly, thus antagonising those who found themselves affected by his schemes for economy, including some of the army. But in particular he alienated the Church by diverting certain

---

[1] Scylitzes-Cedrenus, II, p. 612 (*CSHB*), gives the date as 31 August.

of their revenues to public funds. An open rift between Isaac and the Patriarch broke out, and in November 1058 Michael Cerularius was arrested. He refused to abdicate and Psellus drew up a list of charges against him, set out in a document known as the *Accusation*. These range from treason and heresy to supporting soothsayers and dabbling in magic. Scylitzes seems to suggest that the Patriarch had challenged the position of the Emperor and threatened to reverse the customary interdependence of Church and State, and a bitter struggle ensued.[1] Cerularius died while on his way to be tried in a synod summoned to meet in Madytus. He was succeeded as Patriarch by Constantine Leichudes in February 1059. Michael, who seems to have had a vision just before his death, was highly venerated by the people of Constantinople, and his body was brought back to be buried in the capital. Seen in this context, it is not surprising that Isaac gained many enemies by his action against Cerularius, or that Psellus was later impelled to write an oration in praise of the dead Patriarch.

Isaac, by reason of his character and his experience, even in his short reign of little over two years, was able to give energetic direction to Byzantine foreign policy, ably combining the traditional weapons of diplomacy and military force. Firmness in the face of attack, abstention from further expansion, consolidation of present boundaries, careful attention to native defences, alliances with neighbours and if necessary their recruitment as mercenaries—these were the guiding principles of his foreign policy. Peace with Egypt was maintained. On the eastern frontier, it is true, Isaac could do little to quell the inroads of the Seljuqs who ravaged the Armenian provinces and penetrated beyond into Asia Minor. In the spring of 1059 the Emperor had to lead an expedition north against the Hungarians, and then against the Pechenegs. He had not yet had time to turn his attention to South Italy, where the Normans were by now firmly established and recognised by the Papacy.

Isaac's reign was cut short for reasons which are not entirely clear. He was an ardent hunter, and there is a tradition which says that he had a terrible supernatural experience while pursuing a wild boar, which plunged into the sea and disappeared, while an apparition of fire rose up.[2] Psellus says that he caught a chill and became seriously ill. During this illness he abdicated on 25 December 1059; he became a Studite monk and died not long afterwards (1061). His abdication may have been partly due to the growing hostility of the Church and of the civil party who brought pressure to bear on him; it is also clear that his measures of economy had roused general opposition from all

[1] Scylitzes-Cedrenus, II, p. 643 (*CSHB*).
[2] Scylitzes-Cedrenus, II, p. 647 (*CSHB*).

ranks and parties. In such circumstances it is understandable that he was not succeeded by a member of his family though he is said first to have offered the crown to his brother, John Comnenus. The new Emperor was the president of the senate, Constantine X Ducas, whose wife Eudocia Macrembolitissa was the niece of the now venerated Cerularius.

If any one event can be singled out as peculiarly disastrous for the Byzantine Empire in the eleventh century, it is the accession of Constantine X. He continued and accentuated the policy of the civil aristocracy. In the *Chronographia* there is a warm tribute to his impartiality, his care for justice, his humaneness in never inflicting corporal punishment, his lavish dispensation of rewards, even raising manual workers to the dignity of senators, his delight in studying the Scriptures and in conversing with his friend Psellus, his happy family circle and, in short, his glorious, tranquil and contented reign.[1] This is however far from the whole truth. The accession of an Emperor who was the tool of the civil nobility meant an anti-military policy. Constantine's effort to win over and placate ever-increasing numbers of the civil population, by such measures as the extension of senatorial rank, or the expansion of the civil service, was expensive. The central government was further undermined by selling offices, farming out taxes, in short—by unwise delegation of its functions. Unpopular measures of economy such as Isaac Comnenus had resorted to were out of the question. Such funds as could be raised, by however short-sighted a method, were needed to ensure the continued support of the Church and the civil element, and to buy the friendship of foreign powers. Even Psellus has to admit the folly of Constantine's foreign policy and frankly says that it was due partly to a reluctance to spend anything on the army and partly to a personal desire not to be embroiled in wars, or any activity which might disturb the even tenor of his own life.

The effect during Constantine's reign (1059–67) and the succeeding years was twofold. In their desperation at being deliberately starved of military and naval resources by the central government the provincials organised their defence as best they could. They were driven to support rival claimants to the throne, or leaders of various nationalities who were trying to set up little independent principalities, and on occasion they even went to the invading Turks, especially in Asia Minor. On the other hand, the enemies of Byzantium, particularly the

---

[1] Michael Psellus entirely omits to state that as the supporter of Isaac Comnenus and the author of the *Accusation* against Cerularius he was for several years confined to the monastery τὰ Ναρσοῦ until he succeeded in placating the Ducas family. See P. Joannou, *BZ*, XLIV (1951), 283–90.

Seljuqs, were encouraged to adopt a policy of deliberate conquest, whereas they had previously been indulging in raids as a profitable side-line rather than with permanent settlement in view. It is now that imperial defences really break down. Moreover, from the mid-eleventh century onwards a succession of nomadic Turkic tribes had been continually threatening the northern frontier. The Pechenegs were now joined by the Uzes, who fled south before the Cumans, and in Constantine X's reign this whole tribe surged into the Balkans, ravaging Thrace and Macedonia and Greece in 1064, even threatening the capital. According to Attaleiates, the terrified inhabitants thought that they would have to abandon Europe.[1] From time to time an uneasy peace was bought by means of bribes and tribute. Some attempt was made to use these warlike nomads as mercenaries, but in the absence of a strong hand they proved an unreliable element, prone to desert to their kinsmen in the ranks of the enemy, or to go over to the rival faction in time of civil war, and they were not brought under control until the time of the Comneni. In the Balkans during the third quarter of the eleventh century the situation was further endangered by the undercurrent of hostility felt by the Bulgars towards their Greek masters. In Serbia, Croatia and the Dalmatian coast the ties between Constantinople and the Slav rulers were daily weakened to the profit of western powers, such as the Papacy, the Normans, Venice and Hungary.

In South Italy the Byzantine position was extremely precarious. In 1059 the Papacy had recognised Robert Guiscard's claim to the duchy of Apulia and Calabria and Sicily, and in 1060 he had captured Reggio, Brindisi and Taranto. But expeditions were sent in the autumn of 1060 and succeeding years which restored imperial control of the important maritime cities of Otranto, Taranto and Bari, and gained the support of Guiscard's opponents. But divided interests prevented the Byzantines from following up their successes, and after a number of prolonged sieges Guiscard was at last master of the land. Bari, the one remaining Byzantine stronghold, fell in 1071 after being invested for three years.

During the last four years of the struggle for South Italy (1067–71) the Byzantine Empire was handicapped by an internal struggle for control of the government and by war on its eastern front against the Seljuq Turks. Constantine X died on 21 May 1067 after commending his family first to his brother the Caesar John Ducas, and then a little later on to his wife, Eudocia Macrembolitissa. The Empress took control of the government, acting on behalf of her sons Michael, Andronicus and Constantine. Then after a few months she faced

---

[1] Michael Attaleiates, *Historia*, p. 84.

Psellus and other members of the civil party with a *fait accompli*.
She decided to marry Romanus Diogenes, a member of the military
aristocracy of Cappadocia, and she only revealed her plans to her
immediate circle as Romanus arrived to be crowned on the morrow
(1 January 1068). She defended her action on grounds of urgent
military necessity. Psellus, her son the Emperor Michael VII, and
her brother-in-law the Caesar John Ducas apparently concealed their
feelings at the time, though Psellus' hostility towards Romanus IV
is clear from his biased account of this Emperor's reign and it was
shared by the Ducas family. John Ducas, the centre of the opposition, was suspected by Romanus but according to Psellus he did not
carry out his intention to put him to death.

Though obviously harassed by the civil aristocracy Romanus, who
belonged to an old Asia Minor family, knew only too well where his
main task lay. He led a series of expeditions against the Seljuq Turks
who were attacking the Asian provinces. Psellus maliciously carica-
tures his efforts, and gives him no credit for getting together an
army and conducting campaigns based on provinces which had been
ravaged by tax collectors, by military requisitioning and by enemy
inroads. The Turkish attacks had grown in number from the mid-
eleventh century onwards, but they were still in the nature of raids
led by different Turkish leaders acting independently, and often with
the concurrence of the discontented native Christians in the Caucasian regions, in Mesopotamia and Armenia. In the course of such
attacks Caesarea, once the seat of St Basil, was sacked in 1067; Cilicia
and the country round Antioch were ravaged, as well as Amorium
in the heart of Anatolia. In 1068 Romanus IV led his army from
Cappadocia southwards, and achieved some success in northern
Syria. In 1069 he sent help to Melitene and was himself in Armenia,
but his resources were inadequate to deal effectively with the scattered and uncontrolled bands of Turks, who evaded Byzantine defences and sacked towns as far west as Iconium and Chonae. Alp
Arslan, the leader of the Seljuqs who were rapidly emerging as the
dominating element amongst the Turks, was more anxious to establish his position in the Islamic world than to attack Byzantium. He
had designs therefore on Syria and Egypt, and with this in mind he
showed himself willing to negotiate with Romanus in 1070. But in
the following year Romanus took the offensive in Armenia and was
defeated and taken prisoner at Manzikert. Contributory factors to
his defeat were the desertion of a corps of Turkish mercenaries, and
the deliberate treachery of the Caesar John Ducas' son Andronicus,
who was serving with the army. The terms offered by Alp Arslan again
showed that he wished for the alliance, or at any rate the neutrality,

of the Byzantine Empire: he demanded tribute and assistance when needed, the recognition of the Muslim claim to Edessa and Antioch, a ransom and a marriage alliance. Romanus was set free to return to Constantinople to implement these terms.

News of the defeat of the Emperor and his capture gave the civil party in Constantinople their opportunity. The Caesar John Ducas who had been exiled in Bithynia was recalled. It was decided that the Empress Eudocia and her eldest son Michael should rule jointly. These plans were imperilled by a letter announcing the Emperor Romanus' liberation and imminent return to the capital. John Ducas and his sons, together with leaders of the civil party such as Psellus, determined to oppose Romanus by force. The Empress Eudocia was excluded from the government since she was known to be attached to Romanus; Michael VII was proclaimed sole ruler (24 October 1071) and expeditions led by the two Ducas sons were sent to Asia Minor to capture Romanus, who had invoked the aid of the Turks. At Adana in Cilicia he agreed to surrender, and his personal safety was guaranteed by the archbishops of Chalcedon, Heraclea and Colonea. John Ducas broke this promise with Psellus' approval, and Romanus was savagely blinded and exiled to the island of Prote in the sea of Marmora where he died soon afterwards in 1072.

It was the deposition of Romanus IV by the civil party, not his defeat at Manzikert, which opened the doors to a series of civil wars and usurpers and to the systematic conquest of Asia Minor by the Seljuqs which resulted in the establishment of the Sultanate of Rum. In Romanus' day it might still have been possible for a strong ruler to hold at least Asia Minor intact with the Armenian uplands. Now Alp Arslan swore to avenge his wronged ally. At the same time the Norman mercenary Roussel of Bailleul proclaimed his independence in Asia Minor in 1073. The imperial army sent against him under the Caesar John Ducas was defeated and the Caesar, taken prisoner, was then proclaimed Emperor by Roussell. But the Byzantine government appealed to the Turks for help and the rebels were defeated. Roussel was ransomed by his wife and fell into the hands of the general Alexius Comnenus who allowed him again to take service in the Byzantine army. The Caesar, whose influence over Michael VII had already been undermined by a certain Nicephorus, or Nicephoritzes, was ransomed by his nephew and retired to monastic life. But he still kept in touch with the political world and worked unceasingly to promote the interests of his own family. Perhaps foreseeing the weakness of the regime which he had helped inaugurate, he astutely induced Alexius Comnenus to marry his granddaughter Irene in spite of the opposition of Alexius' mother Anna Dalassena and of John's imperial nephews, Michael VII and Constantine.

Michael VII, the pupil of Psellus, who warmly praises his studious nature and love of philosophy, had none of the qualities needed for guiding the Empire at a time when even Psellus admitted that it had reached its lowest ebb. Michael soon listened only to Nicephoritzes whom he made logothete. But the new minister set flame to widespread hostility in attempting to create a state monopoly in corn. This touched the interests of the great secular and ecclesiastical proprietors. The rise in the price of corn also meant a rise in the cost of living, affecting not only the very poor, but various classes of civil servants, who demanded an increase in salary which would only have defeated the whole aim of the measure. Michael's unpopular and ineffective government was challenged by two rival claimants to the throne. Both belonged to the military party, but one was from Europe, the other from Asia Minor. The old hostility between the eastern and western provinces still held. In the west Nicephorus Bryennius, *dux* of Dyrrachium, was proclaimed Emperor; he reached Adrianople in November 1077 and his troops marched on the capital. Nicephorus Botaneiates, *strategus* of the Anatolikon theme and a member of the Asian military party, while still in Asia Minor was proclaimed Emperor by the populace in St Sophia in Constantinople on 7 January 1078. A revolt broke out against Michael VII, and the unpopular Nicephoritzes was put to death. On 31 March Michael abdicated and became a monk and for three days the city had no ruler.

Nicephorus Botaneiates, who had also been acclaimed Emperor at Nicaea on 25 March, entered Constantinople on 3 April, and was invested by the Patriarch, though his formal coronation does not appear to have taken place until July. Later on, after the death of his wife, he married Mary the Alan, the wife of the abdicated Emperor Michael, though this caused some scandal as Michael VII was still living. He adopted as his successor the young son of Michael, Constantine Ducas, though he later decided on one of his own nephews, to the dismay of the old Caesar John Ducas. The rival claimant, Nicephorus Bryennius, as well as a subsequent pretender, Nicephorus Basilacius, Bryennius' successor as *dux* of Dyrrachium, were defeated with the help of Alexius Comnenus. Yet another usurper, Nicephorus Melissenus, then appeared in Nicaea in 1080, and like Botaneiates before him, attempted to get the help of the Seljuqs of Rūm. The constant disputes within the Empire after Romanus IV's forced abdication had enabled the Seljuq Sulaymān to establish a principality in Asia Minor, most of which was now lost to the Byzantines. Nicephorus was too old to save what remained of the Empire, or to subdue the dissident forces within. It fell to a younger representative of the military aristocracy to placate the Ducas family, to win over Nicephorus Melissenus, and to gain control of the capital. In late March 1081 Alexius Comnenus, the husband of Irene Ducas, entered Constantinople and Botaneiates abdicated.

II. THE COMNENI AND ANGELI 1081–1204

In April 1081 Alexius I Comnenus was crowned. The bitter stand of Basil II against the landed magnates had failed; the long eleventh-century struggle between the military and civil aristocracy had been decided in favour of the former. Alexius I's accession inaugurated the hundred years of Comnenian rule during which the fortitude, tenacity and statesmanship of three outstanding rulers did much to maintain Byzantine prestige amongst European rulers. At the same time this regime was marked by significant internal developments which were to alter the character of Byzantine policy and eventually played into the hands of western rivals. This is particularly true of agrarian changes and increasing separatist tendencies.

Alexius I had come to the throne as a result of a series of astute manœuvres and he had to watch his own position at home. At the same time he had to meet attacks on all fronts. The Seljuqs were established in the central and eastern areas of Anatolia and had also penetrated into the province of Bithynia, thus depriving the Empire of economic resources and manpower. The Normans were entrenched in Italy and were antagonistic to the Comneni; fast-developing cities, particularly Genoa and Pisa, envious of Venice's rich trade in the East Mediterranean were ready to insinuate themselves into any new openings. Slav principalities in the western Balkans were prepared to play off Latin against Greek if it were to their advantage, and Bulgarian provinces were restive under Byzantine rule. Beyond the Danube the Pechenegs and Cumans still constituted a threat, while Hungary, with its ambitions in the north-west Balkans and Dalmatia, was a power which imperial policy could not afford to neglect.

It was then scarcely an exaggeration when Anna Comnena wrote that Alexius on his accession found the Empire surrounded by enemies on all sides. His most dangerous enemy was the Norman Robert Guiscard, whose real aims were nothing so peaceful as the marriage which had been negotiated between his daughter and Constantine the son of the now deposed Michael VII Ducas. Guiscard clearly wanted a foothold on Greek soil and in 1081 took possession of Corfu and attacked the mainland: in order to free his hands to deal with

Guiscard one of Alexius' first moves was to come to terms with the Seljuq ruler in Asia Minor. In June 1081 peace was made with Sulaymān, the Sultan of Iconium: it was agreed that he was to keep the lands already held with the river Dracon as the boundary but should not encroach on Bithynia. At the same time Alexius was negotiating with the Papacy, with Venice, and with the German Emperor Henry IV; he also obtained mercenaries from Sulaymān. As well as the Norman attack, he had to face opposition stirred up in the Balkans and in Dalmatia, where Bulgarians, Serbs and Ragusans were supporting a pro-Norman Ducas party led by a pretender claiming to be Michael VII. In the autumn of 1081 Guiscard had taken Dyrrachium; he then advanced into the mountainous Macedonian territory and his next objective was Thessalonica. Alexius' brother, the Sebastocrator Isaac, meanwhile raised funds by a forced loan from ecclesiastical treasure. The Emperor's personal participation in John Italus' trial for heresy at this juncture (early 1082) may have been partly due to political motives, for the philosopher was a well-known friend of the Ducas family. In the spring of 1082 Guiscard was however checked by troubles in Italy and in April or May he returned. But his son Bohemond was left in command, and his forces retained their hold on western Macedonia, Epirus, and northern Thessaly. In 1083 Alexius, making full use of discontent amongst the Normans due to lack of pay, successfully counter-attacked in Thessaly and retook Dyrrachium. Guiscard prepared for a fresh expedition in 1084. With the help of the Venetian fleet, the Byzantines defeated him off Corfu, and his unexpected death in 1085 followed by the evacuation of Greek territory brought temporary relief. But the danger remained, for his policy was continued by his successors and their ambitions in the East Mediterranean were something which Byzantine diplomats had to reckon with even after the Norman dynasty had perished.

During the years 1085–96 Alexius surmounted further dangers. Sulaymān of Iconium died in 1086; this removed a strong ruler, but it also released various dissident forces who allied with Byzantine enemies, particularly the Turkic nomads north of the Danube. Of these, the Pechenegs were the scourge of the Balkans, and were all the more dangerous since they found ready allies amongst the discontented Bogomil heretics in the Bulgarian provinces. Their invasion in the spring of 1087 was only defeated by playing off one barbarian against another, in this case by inciting the Cumans to quarrel with the Pechenegs over booty. A truce was agreed on in 1089. In the next year the Pechenegs again advanced in alliance with the Turkish amir of Smyrna, Tzachas, who had naval resources. Alexius defeated Tzachas, and waged desperate war on the Pechenegs. He allied with the Cumans; he appealed to the Pope for help and may have hoped for Norman mercenaries. Finally, on 29 April 1091, the Pechenegs were crushed at Mt Levunium.

Alexius then turned to Asia Minor and the eastern frontier. Malik-Shāh, who had approached him in 1091 with a view to an alliance, died in 1092, and the ensuing dissensions amongst the Seljuqs gave a breathing space to the Byzantines. But Alexius I clearly saw that his first eastern offensive must be nearer home. Affairs in Iconium had become more settled and Sulaymān's son Kilij Arslan had established himself and had shown himself willing to ally with Alexius against dissident Turkish elements, such as Tzachas. But once Alexius had secured his position in the Balkans by suppressing the Pechenegs and the ambitious and rebellious Serbs, and had quashed signs of a conspiracy at home, as well as putting down the revolts in Cyprus and Crete, he felt sufficiently sure of himself to attempt to regain ground in northern Asia Minor. He successfully recaptured territory along the coastal strip on the sea of Marmora, including the city of Cyzicus. But his plan of turning his attention to Asia Minor where there was ample scope for playing off one Muslim power against another was abruptly halted by the First Crusade.

In the past Alexius I had certainly asked for, and used, mercenaries from the Latin west, as also from Muslim territories. But it is difficult to believe that he ever appealed to Urban II for a crusade in the western sense—that is, a concerted Christian offensive whose immediate aim would be the reconquest of Jerusalem.[1] Crusading zeal as such had been known in Byzantium since the rise of Islam, but it had been related to the practical military needs of Empire. War with some branch of the infidel had long been an everyday concern, but it was conducted on a realistic basis. It was useless to go direct to Jerusalem while the greater part of Asia Minor remained in Muslim hands, and it was recognised by Byzantine diplomats that circumstances, such as revolts in the Balkans or attacks from the Normans, might make it expedient to ally from time to time with Muslim rulers. Contemporary accounts of Urban II's appeal to the west differ, but he appears to have coupled recovery of the Holy Places with aid to the Christian brethren in the east, without realising the underlying difficulties in combining these two aims. As events were to prove, western devotion placed Jerusalem in the foreground and western ambitions found an outlet in Syria and Palestine, so that there was an inevitable clash between Byzantine and Latin policy.

Alexius I dealt admirably with this situation. Faced with the

---

[1] For a different view see *History of the Crusades*, gen. ed. K. M. Setton, I, p. 219; cf. G. Ostrogorsky, *History of the Byzantine State*, p. 321.

passage through his provinces of the uncontrolled, and often unarmed, rabble under the leadership of Peter of Amiens (called Peter
the Hermit), he provided provisions and guides, and shipped them to
Asia Minor where they were almost wiped out by the Seljuq Turks
near Nicomedia. Alexius' real trial came with the arrival of the
feudal contingents whose leaders were by no means disposed to accept
Byzantine control. At this stage they were however dependent on
Alexius for guides and provisions, a consideration which may have
persuaded them to concede Alexius' demand that they should take
an oath of allegiance to him and promise to restore to him any former
Byzantine territory which should be recaptured. All save Count Raymond of Toulouse, and the Norman Tancred of South Italy who had
avoided Constantinople, took this oath. In return Alexius promised
supplies and military support under his own leadership. Initial successes in Asia Minor where the Latin crusaders captured Nicaea in
June 1097 were followed by the Latin march south-eastwards towards Antioch and the Byzantine concentration on re-establishing
control over western Asia Minor.[1] The parting of the ways came with
the Latin capture of Antioch in 1098. This city had been in Byzantine
hands as recently as 1085, yet in clear violation of his oath the
Norman Bohemond, the son of Alexius' old enemy Guiscard, outmanœuvred his fellow crusaders and settled down to build up for
himself an independent Latin principality in Syria. This was followed
by the establishment of the Latin kingdom of Jerusalem and the
county of Edessa, and later on, the county of Tripoli. These successes
marked an obvious set-back in Muslim fortunes, but they could not
be exploited to the full for lack of unanimity in the Christian ranks.

Alexius' main concern was to counter Norman hostility, directed
against the Empire from Antioch and from Italy. Bohemond's quarrel-
someness and temerity resulted in his defeat by the Turkish Danishmends in 1100. Meanwhile the Byzantines were re-establishing
themselves in the coastal regions of Cilicia and northern Syria.
Therefore Bohemond went back to Italy to organise an attack on
Alexius. His campaign of anti-Byzantine propaganda in the west
shows the superficiality of Christian unity. According to Bohemond,
the Byzantine Emperor was the crusaders' worst enemy, and the
capture of Constantinople was even put forward as an essential
preliminary in any effective western crusading programme. In 1107
Bohemond landed on the west coast of Greece at Avlona, planning to
advance into Byzantine territory. Alexius, now in a stronger position

[1] For more detailed accounts of the crusades in the eleventh and twelfth centuries,
see S. Runciman, *A History of the Crusades*, and *A History of the Crusades*, gen. ed.
K. M. Setton.

than he had been in 1081, easily defeated him and in 1108 exacted the treaty of Devol, whose terms are reported by Anna Comnena. By this treaty Bohemond was forced to recognise Alexius and his son John as overlords; he was to hold Antioch from them as an imperial fief, and was to give them military service as their vassal. Further—and this reveals how the appointment of a Latin patriarch in Antioch had offended Byzantine susceptibilities—the Patriarch of Antioch was to be 'one whom your Majesties shall appoint from among the Great Church [that is, St Sophia] of Constantinople'. This treaty was never fully implemented. Bohemond had never gone back to Antioch, and Tancred, who governed Antioch during his uncle's absence and retained control after his death in 1111, proved obdurate. Antioch remained a problem for Alexius' son and grandson and one of the major obstacles to united action against the infidel.

Nevertheless, Alexius had checked Norman aggression in his western provinces, and his own prestige and strength steadily increased. In the Balkans the Byzantine ruler's astute diplomacy enabled him to hold the balance between the rival Slav principalities of Zeta and Rascia. His son John was married to a Hungarian princess, thus giving him an alliance with a rising country which was already establishing its control over Croatia and Dalmatia. He had also succeeded in pacifying the rival maritime Italian cities, whose ambitions were finding an outlet in the East Mediterranean, whether in the service of the Latin principalities or of the Byzantine Empire. Venice was an old ally of Byzantium and its maritime resources had proved indispensable during Alexius' reign. As early as 1082 it had been rewarded by generous commercial privileges. Later, in 1111, at the time when Alexius was turning to his Asia Minor campaign, he was threatened by hostilities from Genoa and Pisa, and had to make serious trading concessions to Pisa. In Asia Minor intermittent campaigns against the Sultan of Iconium during the years 1111–15 were crowned by the defeat of Malik-Shāh of Iconium and a treaty. Anna Comnena's claim that the Empire was restored to its former bounds under Romanus IV Diogenes goes too far, but Alexius had at any rate kept Iconium in check. By the end of his reign he had control over the lands bordering on the Black Sea and the Sea of Marmora, as well as the territory in western Asia Minor and the coastal strip south of the Taurus mountains extending round towards the principality of Antioch in Syria.

It would clearly be an exaggeration to regard his achievements in the field of foreign policy as marking a return to the comparative security of tenth- and early eleventh-century Byzantium with its victorious extension of its frontiers beyond Asia Minor in the east and up to the Danube in parts of the Balkans. Factors which were to mark the later medieval period and to bring about the downfall of Byzantium were already in evidence. Of these, the continual infiltration of the various branches of the Turks was on the whole a less dangerous threat in the twelfth century than the rising ambitions of the South Italian Normans and the Hohenstaufen, and the ruthless economic policy of Venice. All that Alexius' astuteness, vigilance and statesmanship could establish was an uneasy equilibrium.

Alexius' policy at home was wholly directed towards fulfilling his imperial responsibilities as he understood them. In the ecclesiastical sphere tradition largely determined his actions. In time of financial stringency he was not above allowing the temporary appropriation of church treasure, for which he was severely censured. But on major issues his attitude was above reproach. He took the lead in attempting to exterminate heresies. The most dangerous of these was the dualism rampant in the Bulgarian provinces of the Empire where it was closely allied to political discontent. This Bogomilism, as it was called, was even rearing its head in the capital and hostile sources rumoured that it had claimed Alexius' mother, Anna Dalassena. Anna Comnena describes how her father used military force as well as theological argument against the various forms which this dualism took. His measure of success was only temporary and this heresy was still to be found in the Balkans at the time of the Ottoman conquest in the fifteenth century. Alexius also presided over rather more domestic problems of heresy which were to occur from time to time under the Comnenian rulers. The impetus given to philosophical studies in the eleventh century, particularly by scholars such as Michael Psellus and John Italus, had evidently resulted in discussion which appeared on occasion to overstep the bounds of orthodoxy. Even Psellus himself had to make a profession of faith in Constantine IX's reign. In Michael VII's reign *c.* 1077 there was an ecclesiastical tribunal set up which considered the dissemination of non-Christian views. In 1082 Alexius summoned a synod to deal with specific charges brought against John Italus, Psellus' disciple and successor, and also, it may be added, a strong supporter of his patrons, the Ducas family, who were old enemies of Alexius, whence it has been suggested that the trial at this particular juncture may have had political as well as religious motives. According to Anna Comnena and the account given in the Church's official statement against heresies called the *Synodicon*, John Italus publicly abjured his erroneous metaphysical views and repented of his errors.

Throughout the stress of eleventh-century movements within the Empire, from time to time a certain antagonism between the claims of humanism and asceticism comes to the surface. Both elements flourished. The scholarly and artistic achievements of the eleventh and twelfth centuries were paralleled by the full flowering of Byzantine spirituality and steady support for monasticism in which the imperial house took the lead. Alexius dealt with problems of discipline on the great monastic peninsula of Mt Athos, and he regulated and supported foundations elsewhere, particularly in the region of the island of Patmos where a prominent part was taken by the house of St John under the austere guidance of the monk Christodulus. Alexius' wife Irene founded and patronised a convent in Constantinople, carefully regulating its life in her *Typicon*. There was in this respect no imperial deviation from the traditional veneration of monasticism rooted in the unshakeable Byzantine belief in the efficacy of prayer.

Much of Alexius' work at home aimed at strengthening defence and finance, two of the weakest points in administration during the years 1025–81. While introducing no radical changes of policy, he attempted to check debasement and inflation. His ruling that the nomisma should be stabilised at a third of its original value bore hardly on the poorest classes who were now for the first time liable to taxation. Labour services and billeting as well as the tax farmer's extortion added to their burden. The central government, its revenue depleted by loss of land and by earlier mismanagement, its liabilities increased by urgent calls on its diplomacy (always expensive) and its defences, had to resort to every device to pay its soldiers and reward its supporters. Alexius relied heavily on mercenaries, drawing on all available foreign sources from the English to the Pechenegs and Cumans. He also recruited native levies, especially of light-armed infantry, from the great estates of Byzantine nobles and ecclesiastics. Themes were each responsible for providing a certain number of men. Alexius took a keen interest in military matters, and attempted to strengthen his depleted cavalry, buying throroughbred horses as far afield as Damascus, Edessa and Arabia. He found the fleet as neglected as the land forces, and when attacked by the Normans in 1081 had to rely on the Venetians. Anna Comnena relates his various attempts at strengthening the navy and by the later years of his reign he had to some extent built up his maritime resources.

One of the most significant internal developments during Alexius' reign was closely connected with the problem of military defence. This was the granting of estates, usually in return for military service. These grants in *pronoia* had been known from the mid-eleventh century onwards, but it is not until Alexius I's reign that they are found associated with military obligations. They were at first inalienable and for a limited time, and the military nature of the grant was reflected in the name *stratiotes* (στρατιώτης) which was usually given to the recipient or pronoiar. The particular attraction of the grant lay in the enjoyment of the revenue from the estate, including the right to collect the taxes and dues of its tenants (πάροικοι). Alexius also made frequent use of the *charisticium*, which he found a convenient method of reward. This was the handing over of monastic property to the care of a layman, and it had in the past been used by churchmen as a means of ensuring the economic use of monastic land. The community was granted an income sufficient for its needs and the *charisticarius* kept the rest. Churchmen were divided in their attitude towards this practice; some, as Eustathius of Thessalonica, regarded it as promoting the sound development of monastic property while others saw only the obvious opportunities for abuse. In different ways, both the *pronoia* and the *charisticium* foreshadowed future lines of development. The *pronoia* became an ineradicable feature of the Byzantine polity and on the whole it strengthened the position of the military landed families. It was essentially an indigenous growth and not due to western influence,[1] and it marked the failure of the attempt to check the magnates in the middle Byzantine period. In the imperial use of the *charisticium* there was perhaps reflected the view that the extensive property of the Church could be made to serve the needs of the state. Alexius' grants of *charisticia* are not so far removed from the use of ecclesiastical property in the mid-fourteenth century which roused the wrath of Nicholas Cabasilas in his discourse[2] on illegal acts of officials.

However successfully Alexius repaired Byzantine fortunes, drove the Normans out of Greece, made substantial gains in Asia Minor, he could never restore to the central authority the position which it had had before 1025 and before the prolonged struggle between the civil and military aristocracy. Alexius himself belonged to one of the military families, and he was essentially a realist. Both tradition and necessity led him to recognise and make full use of these landed magnates. And so, in spite of appearances to the contrary, his reign saw the steady growth of local and separatist elements which in the long run seriously undermined imperial authority and led to the civil wars of the fourteenth century.

Alexius was succeeded by his son John who made good his claim with the support of his dying father, in spite of the intrigues of his

---

[1] See G. Ostrogorsky, *Pour l'histoire de la féodalité byzantine*, and P. Lemerle, 'Recherches sur le régime agraire à Byzance: la terre militaire à l'époque des Comnènes', *Cahiers de civilisation médiévale*, II (1959), 265–81.

[2] The so-called 'Anti-Zealot' Discourse; see I. Ševčenko, *DOP*, XI (1957), 79–171.

mother Irene and his sister Anna, who coveted the throne for her husband Nicephorus Bryennius. He was crowned on 16 August 1118. Unlike his father and his son, John II Comnenus was never the central figure of any contemporary history. Anna obviously disliked him and offers only a few disparaging remarks in passing. But John Cinnamus and Nicetas Choniates, though they view his reign only as a prelude to later events, make it clear that he was a man of fine personal qualities and a far-sighted statesman. The moral principles of his daily life were openly declared in private and in public; he was equally distinguished for the prudence and tenacity with which he continued Alexius' policy both at home and abroad.

Though the records for his domestic policy are somewhat sparse, they show him maintaining the normal imperial tradition as his father before him had done. His right hand was his Grand Domestic, John Axuch, originally a Muslim who had been captured young at the time of the First Crusade and brought up with him. John Axuch was an able administrator, and he was also keenly interested in Christian metaphysics and in close touch with contemporary scholars and theologians. John II's wife, by whom he had four boys and four girls, was Irene, the Hungarian princess, a devout woman who died in 1134. True to tradition, the Emperor John established in October 1136 the splendid foundation of the Pantocrator, where the duties of the monastic community included the supervision of hospitals and various forms of social work for which detailed provision was made. Watchful vigilance was evidently maintained in the preservation of orthodoxy, and in 1140 the monks of the monastery of St Nicholas and other houses were condemned by an ecclesiastical synod for allowing the circulation of manuscripts containing the heretical writings of the recently deceased Constantine Chrysomalus, said to have been strongly influenced by Massalian and Bogomil teaching.

It is understandable that during the years 1118–43 military needs were in the foreground at home as well as abroad. John's agrarian policy closely resembled that of his father: prisoners of war (as Serbs or Pechenegs) were settled on the land in return for military service, and estates were granted in *pronoia* on the same condition. Mercenaries were perforce still largely employed, and Nicetas Choniates says that separate corps were now formed, each consisting entirely of one or other of the different tribes or races enlisted. So pressing were the military needs of Empire that John had to make heavy demands on his troops, and he became well known as an austere disciplinarian.

John's foreign policy was a successful combination of diplomacy and force. The underlying thread in events during his reign, and indeed throughout the twelfth century, was the increasing extent to which Latin powers were becoming involved in the Mediterranean world. John could build on the advantages secured by Alexius during his thirty-seven years—firm establishment of his dynasty, the strengthening of defences, certain territorial gains, and the expulsion of the Normans from some Byzantine provinces, though not from Antioch. But unlike Alexius in 1081, he had to face a complex international situation, due mainly to the conflicting ambitions of Hungary, Venice, Pisa and Genoa, the rise of the kingdom of Sicily, and the intermittent hostility of the Latin crusading principalities in Syria and Palestine. John realised that he must protect his flank if he wished to concentrate on establishing his authority in Antioch as a first step to taking control in the East Mediterranean. In particular, it was clear that the growing power of the Normans in Sicily and South Italy was a potential danger to Constantinople.

John therefore began by looking for allies in the west and in the Balkans, neither of which could be considered in isolation. In the western Balkans, and particularly in Dalmatia, there was keen rivalry between Venice and Hungary over their respective spheres of influence. Hungarian influence and encroachment south of the Danube had for some time been steadily increasing, and Alexius Comnenus judged it wise to come to an understanding with Hungary. John II, whose wife was Hungarian, resorted to active intervention in Hungarian politics which eventually led to a declaration of war by Stephen II in 1128. Stephen was checked by Byzantium, but after his death Béla II the Blind (1131–41) came to an understanding with both the German Conrad III and the Balkan principality of Rascia, evidently thus insuring himself against possible Venetian, or further Byzantine, attacks. As Conrad III was pro-Byzantine, Béla may on this account have refrained from hostilities against Constantinople. John Comnenus, like Alexius, attempted to intervene in disputed elections in the Balkan principalities. Although he defeated Rascia and tried to get recognition of his suzerainty, when its Župan Uroš married Helen the daughter of Béla II, it was drawn into the orbit of Hungary and was antagonistic to Constantinople. Bosnia appeared to be under Hungarian suzerainty; in 1137 it was given as an appanage to the son of Béla II. Zeta still recognised Byzantine overlordship, but it was Rascia which was the growing force. Thus in the Balkans the Byzantine Emperor was by no means the dominating power and was indeed to some extent dependent on an understanding either with Hungary, or with Hungary's rival, Venice.

Venice had taken advantage of Alexius I's difficulties to obtain extremely advantageous trading concessions which John was at first reluctant to renew. But Venetian attacks on Byzantine islands during the years 1122–6 made him realise the inexpediency of antagonising this strong maritime power, and in 1126 he agreed to confirm its privileges. In 1127 Sicily and South Italy were united under Roger II who in 1130 successfully took the royal title. John realised the threat implicit in this consolidation of the Norman position. Both for this reason, and as a counterpoise to Venice, in 1136 he renewed the trading privileges granted by his father to Pisa. In 1142 the Genoese were in Constantinople for diplomatic reasons, possibly also to negotiate a treaty of this kind. Similarly, John could not afford to neglect either Germany or the Papacy. He first approached Lothair in 1135, hoping to form a coalition with him in view of their common interest in the Sicilian threat, for as St Bernard wrote to Lothair, 'He who makes himself king of Sicily is attacking the Emperor',[1] a remark which applied equally well to the East or to the West. The aim of the Byzantine embassy of 1135 was to induce Lothair to attack Roger of Sicily and it promised subsidies for this purpose, to which Lothair agreed. When Lothair died shortly afterwards (1138), John turned to his successor Conrad III, proposing in 1140 a marriage alliance between his son Manuel and Conrad's sister-in-law, Bertha of Sulzbach. This was designed to strengthen his hand against Roger and to give him support in the west while he was carrying out his eastern campaigns. Further, throughout his reign John kept in touch with the Papacy. Hope of conciliation and understanding between Rome and Constantinople was a constant factor in Byzantine diplomacy, though continually opposed by the Orthodox Church solidly supported by the mass of the people. The Papacy, faced by the growing power of the Norman Roger II, was open to Byzantine advances. At one point John Comnenus held out the offer of union between the two Churches and even suggested an understanding between *sacerdotium* and *regnum* whereby the Pope was accorded spiritual, and the Byzantines (the *Romaioi*) secular, supremacy. This was set out in the second of two letters from John *ad sanctissimum papam*,[2] and to a Byzantine Emperor it could still seem a practical possibility. Tensions and cross-currents amongst the Christians in the East Mediterranean were to demonstrate the futility of any such hope. Even the Pope was at heart antagonistic to John's desire to restore a Greek Patriarch to Antioch, as Innocent II showed

---

[1] *Ep.* 139; *MPL*, CLXXXII, 294.
[2] These were originally dated 1124 (Calixtus II), and 1126 (Honorius II), but they have more recently been ascribed to the years 1139–41 (Innocent II). See G. Ostrogorsky, *History of the Byzantine State*, p. 341, and P. Lamma, *Comneni e Staufer*, I, pp. 28–9; cf. *DR*, 1302 and 1303.

by his express warning to the Latins in the kingdom of Jerusalem to beware of an Emperor who took any such action.

Though he could never relax hold on the threads of his Balkan and western diplomacy, the greater part of John's time was occupied in Asia Minor and Syria. He had to guard his borders from Iconium, and more particularly from the growing power of the Danishmends who under the amir Ghāzī III were expanding westwards and southwards. They captured Melitene in 1124; they drove west as far as Ancyra; and then south across the Taurus mountains into Cilicia in 1129. They forced the Armenian Rupenians to pay tribute, and then further south in 1130 defeated the Normans of Antioch. This threatened John's plans for the implementation of the treaty of Devol as the first step towards full control in the East Mediterranean. As a preliminary he took steps to safeguard his frontiers against the Danishmends and from 1130 onwards he led expeditions against them. In 1134 the amir Ghāzī III died, which brought a temporary relief. John then turned his attention towards the Armenian principality of Lesser Armenia which lay across his route to Antioch. Its ruler, the Rupenian Leo, took refuge in the Taurus mountains in 1137. Thus in control of Lesser Armenia, John felt free to approach Antioch.

In Antioch as in Jerusalem, the throne had passed in 1131 to the female line and internal problems of succession were already weakening the Latin principalities. There were also rifts amongst the Latins in Antioch where a pro-Byzantine party urged making common cause against Zengi, the formidable ruler of Mosul. John reached Antioch in August 1137 and in his camp outside the city Raymond of Poitiers, the husband of the Norman princess Constance, had to swear allegiance to him. Antioch was to be returned to the Byzantines and in return Raymond was to receive a principality centred in Aleppo, provided that the Greeks and Franks could capture this from the Muslims. John's claims were resented by many of the Latins and he did not get full support for his campaign against the amir of Shaizar on the Orontes. He therefore came to terms with Shaizar in May 1138 and returned to make his ceremonial entry into the city. This was followed by a request for control of the citadel, but at this anti-Greek riots threatened and John judged it expedient to leave the city.

There were various other reasons for this move. John could not afford to neglect Asia Minor where the Danishmend amir Muḥammad was again attacking in the Black sea coastal area. He also had to reinforce his western alliances. Pope Innocent II, no doubt fearing that he meant to replace the Latin by a Greek Patriarch in Antioch, had sent a warning in 1138 to Latin Christians not to tolerate any attempt of this kind. His German ally Lothair III had died in the same year. Roger II's ambitions were known to include an interest in Antioch which conflicted with Byzantine policy, for he had already put forward claims to the succession on the death of Bohemond II in 1130. John's second letter to the Papacy proposing a division of authority between the *sacerdotium* and the *regnum* may well belong to this period and represent an attempt to come to terms with Innocent II before the next bid to gain control of Antioch. He also approached Lothair's successor, Conrad III, and in 1140 opened negotiations with a view to gaining support against Roger II and arranging a marriage alliance between Conrad's sister-in-law, Bertha of Sulzbach, and his fourth son, Manuel. This approach was favourably received and discussed during the next two years, and the German princess arrived in Constantinople some time before the summer of 1142.

During 1139–41 John had been on campaign in Asia Minor against the Danishmend amir Muḥammad with only intermittent success. But the death of Muḥammad followed by a disputed succession gave him the opportunity to follow up his Syrian project. He left Constantinople in the spring of 1142. His terms to Raymond of Poitiers had already shown that he intended to take control of Antioch. John Cinnamus suggests that he had in mind the creation of a frontier principality for his son Manuel.[1] This was to include Attalia in southern Asia Minor, Antioch and Cyprus, and would have provided a Byzantine base for campaigns against the Muslims and a safeguard against the half-hearted, and often treacherous, attitude of the Franks. John travelled south *via* Sozopolis and Lake Karalis where he hoped to re-establish control over the Christian natives who were being drawn into Muslim ways of life in this frontier area separating Byzantium and Iconium. He then reached Attalia where his heir Alexius died. He sent the corpse to Constantinople in the charge of his sons Andronicus and Isaac, and moved on through Cilicia to Antioch with his fourth son, Manuel.

Since his last departure in 1138 the Franks in Syria had made no effective headway against either the amir of Aleppo or Zengi of Mosul, who was attacking Damascus (though it is true that Fulk of Jerusalem had temporarily saved this city by his alliance with the Damascenes in 1139). Toward the end of September 1142 John reached northern Syria. Joscelin of Edessa quickly came to terms. Raymond of Poitiers in Antioch was faced with a demand for the surrender of the entire city including all the defences and the citadel. In return for this he was offered a principality in regions still to be regained from the infidel. Raymond took refuge behind the anti-Byzantine

---

[1] John Cinnamus, *Historia*, I, 10, p. 23 (*CSHB*).

party within the city. The Latin Patriarch was strongly opposed to recognising an authority who had in mind his replacement by a Greek ecclesiastic and he could support his attitude by quoting the papal warning of 1138. The Norman vassals summoned to give their views laid down that Raymond had exceeded his authority in recognising Byzantine claims in 1137 and had no right to hand over the inheritance of his wife, the heiress Constance. For the Latin clergy and the Latin lords a repudiation of the agreement of 1137 was clearly the lesser evil. All that the Normans were prepared to concede to the Byzantine Emperor was another ceremonial entry into the city. John therefore realised that he could only establish his claim to Antioch by force and laid his plans accordingly. It was by now autumn and he wintered near Mopsuestia. From here in the following spring he wrote to the king of Jerusalem expressing his wish to come south in person to visit the Holy Places and to discuss concerted action against the Muslims, presumably after he had subdued Antioch. But in April 1143 John died unexpectedly of a wound perhaps incurred while hunting, perhaps at the hand of an enemy,[1] and Fulk of an accident in November 1143. It is possible that the kingdom of Jerusalem had in the past temporised and even recognised the Byzantine Emperor's claims to overlordship and to control of Antioch. In 1137 Fulk was reported as advising Raymond that Constantinople had a valid claim to Antioch.[2] And according to a Byzantine source, Michael Italicus, he appeared to acknowledge John's overlordship, stating that only the Byzantine Emperor could wear the diadem and bear the name of Basileus.[3] Such professions were never put to the test, though Fulk's apprehensiveness is reflected in his reply to John in 1143 that he could only provide hospitality in Palestine for a limited imperial retinue. In any case in the following year the situation was radically altered for Greeks and Franks alike by Zengi's capture of Edessa (1144).

The year before his death John Comnenus had lost both his eldest and his second son. When he realised that his poisoned wound would be fatal he decided to pass over his third son Isaac, choosing as his successor his youngest son Manuel who was with him in his hunting camp in the Taurus mountains. The dying Emperor announced his decision to his entourage including his faithful friend and servant Axuch, who was inclined to support the absent Isaac, and he said that he acted thus because he considered that of the two Manuel was the

---

[1] See R. Browning, 'The death of John II Comnenus', *B*, XXXI (1961), 229–35.
[2] See authorities cited by S. Runciman, *History of the Crusades*, II, p. 213, n. 1.
[3] See P. Lamma in *Mem. dell' Acc. delle Sc. di Bologna*, cl. sc. mor., vol. IV, s. V, ff. 89 r–89 v, cited in his *Comneni e Staufer*, I, pp. 26–7.

better qualified to serve the state. He placed the crown upon Manuel's head, and then the young Emperor was acclaimed by the surrounding troops.

Manuel Comnenus was renowned for his powers of physical endurance and he shared the toils of his soldiers on campaigns or during military exercises; he was devoted to hunting and he delighted to take part in the jousts of his western contemporaries. There was too another side to him: he enjoyed a full and luxurious court life and unlike his father John II was by no means austere in his private life. He was also well able to take his place in the cultivated circles of Constantinople. Though not a scholar or theologian, he enjoyed discussing philosophical and doctrinal matters. But at least one of his contemporaries, John Cinnamus, considered that in spite of his alert and quick intelligence, he had no really profound grasp of such problems. He was also a man of considerable personal charm who seemed to be as much at home with westerners as with his own subjects. His first wife was Bertha of Sulzbach (who took the name of Irene), and his second was Mary of Antioch, daughter of the Norman princess Constance of Antioch; his mother had been a Hungarian princess. Inclination, and perhaps deliberate policy, encouraged contacts with Latins who found a ready welcome at the Byzantine court and were often provided for either by a grant of lands or by appointment to some official post. It has been suggested that Manuel attempted by such means to break down the barriers between the Greek and Latin world and to introduce vigorous western blood into Byzantium.[1]

Manuel's accession had been unexpected and the eastern campaign was interrupted. The young Emperor travelled back to Constantinople and with the help of his father's faithful friend the Grand Domestic Axuch he made good his claim to the throne. Manuel's policy was a sound one. He attempted to strengthen his position in Asia Minor against the constant inroads of the Seljuqs of Iconium. He did this in various ways: he built up a line of fortifications; he allied with the Danishmends, and he led expeditions against the Sultan Masud. Manuel himself marched on Iconium in 1146, but did not besiege it. He made a treaty with Masud in 1147, perhaps because of the approaching Second Crusade. At the same time his generals had vigorously counter-attacked in Cilicia where Raymond of Antioch had been taking advantage of John's death. Now with renewed Byzantine activity and the rise to power of the ruler of Mosul, Raymond found himself threatened on two sides.

Norman antagonism in Antioch, as well as the knowledge of opposi-

[1] See P. Lamma, *Comneni e Staufer*, i, pp. xii ff.; ii, pp. 320 ff. and *passim*.

tion at home, made it imperative for Manuel to renew the alliances with the West which his father had built up. Manuel's policy is however characterised by a boldness and originality and a readiness to experiment. He might even be called an opportunist. The pivot of John's western policy had been his alliance with the German rulers, first Lothair III, and then Conrad III. Manuel from time to time considered the possibility of an understanding with Sicily. At the very opening of his reign his ambassador Basil Xeres was negotiating with Roger who had asked for a Greek princess as wife for his son. This came to nothing; the reported terms of the agreement included a clause that Roger should be recognised as the equal of the Basileus which could not be ratified by Constantinople. Manuel fell back on the German alliance with Conrad. His marriage to Bertha of Sulzbach took place in 1146 and Conrad renewed his promise of military assistance if needed, either in the form of German knights or personal intervention. Manuel's plans both for Italy and for Asia Minor and Syria were however hampered by the unfortunate Second Crusade of 1147.

The capture of Edessa by Zengi of Mosul in 1144 had stirred the West to activity, though hardly to concerted effort. The Second Crusade, led by the kings of France and Germany, created a difficult situation for the Byzantines. The crusade was preached by St Bernard of Clairvaux first in France and then at Conrad's court in Germany, where Manuel's ambassadors were in December 1146. St Bernard's hope of a united Christian offensive, perhaps led by Manuel, was the dream of a visionary. Manuel promised support, provisions and guides for the land route provided that the Latin crusaders would take the same oath to him as their predecessors had to Alexius. Roger of Sicily also made his bid to control the expedition: he offered to provide shipping for the sea route. But both Conrad III and Louis VII refused and travelled by land. Manuel therefore had to deal with the vast forces converging on Constantinople. He himself had made a truce with Iconium in 1147, and he was of necessity engaged elsewhere. For while the crusading armies were being shipped into Asia Minor and given directions to follow the safer coastal route, Roger of Sicily in the autumn of 1147 was attacking Corfu and Greece.

The western crusaders, particularly the Franks, bitterly reproached Manuel for the failure of the Second Crusade and their anger at his treaty with Iconium is understandable. Nevertheless, Byzantine safety depended on careful balancing of forces. Manuel dared not neglect his western provinces, particularly as there was evidently some support for the Normans in Corfu, while elsewhere, as at Corinth, there appears to have been little effective means of local defence. Manuel had to rely on mercenaries; he also secured Venetian help in recapturing Corfu by extending its trading privileges to Cyprus and Rhodes in the chrysobulls of 1147 and 1148. At the same time he had to meet a Cuman attack from the north and his drive against the Normans was temporarily halted. When Conrad III returned from the Second Crusade he sailed to Thessalonica and renewed his friendship with Manuel, spending the Christmas of 1148 in Constantinople where the marriage between Manuel's niece Theodora and Conrad's half-brother Henry of Babenburg, first duke of Austria, was celebrated. Manuel had concluded an alliance with Conrad in the treaty of Thessalonica. This was directed against Roger of Sicily and appears to have included an agreement to cede some Italian territory to the Byzantine Emperor. The text of the treaty is not extant, but Cinnamus says that Manuel reminded Conrad that he had previously promised to restore to him 'Italia' as the dowry of his kinswoman, the Empress Irene.[1]

The proposed joint Italian expedition of Manuel and Conrad resulted in something in the nature of an anti-Byzantine coalition. Manuel found himself hampered by disturbances in Serbia fostered by Hungary. Conrad was temporarily held up by the revolt in 1150 of Welf VI, the uncle of Henry the Lion and dispossessed duke of Bavaria, who in return was receiving an annual subsidy from Roger of Sicily. Roger himself had concluded a four-year truce with Pope Eugenius III in 1149. There was even a suggestion supported by Louis VII of France that a European league should launch a new crusade against the Emperor who was 'Christian only in name',[2] with the capture of Constantinople as its first objective. This project (to be realised later in 1204) came to nothing at the time, partly because of Conrad III's staunch support of his Byzantine ally, partly because the Pope did not wish to increase the power of Roger II. In 1151 Conrad and Manuel were both getting ready for the Italian expedition according to plan, and Roger was in a dangerous position. But Conrad's preparations, now warmly supported by Eugenius III, failed to materialise because of his illness, followed by his death in February 1152. He had been Manuel's most loyal western ally and indeed the two men had developed a genuine personal liking for each other.

Frederick I was crowned at Aachen on 9 March 1152. In an agreement between the German ruler and Pope Eugenius III in March 1153 (the treaty of Constance) it was explicitly stated that no territory 'on this side of the sea' was to be ceded to the king of the Greeks should

---

[1] John Cinnamus, II, 19, p. 87 (*CSHB*).
[2] Odo of Deuil, *MPL*, CLXXXV, 1223.

he presume to invade it,[1] and in such a case both agreed to take steps to expel Manuel from Italy. This did not by any means imply open rupture. On the contrary. From just after the treaty of Constance to the end of 1154 or early 1155 there appear to have been five diplomatic exchanges. Frederick's first marriage to Adela of Vohburg had been annulled at the Council of Constance in March 1153, and he was now seeking the hand of a Byzantine princess, Manuel's niece Mary, the daughter of his brother the Sebastocrator Isaac. The marriage did not however materialise and he married Beatrice of Burgundy later in 1156. These negotiations may have been designed to keep Manuel in play while Frederick was preparing to go to Italy and Manuel probably realised this. The death of Roger II in February 1154 gave both their opportunity.

In 1155 Frederick came south and was crowned in Rome on 18 June, but the Germans refused to support any further expeditions in Italy and to his disappointment he had to go north again. In Sicily William I had succeeded in 1154 to a difficult situation. He was beset by feudal rebels within his kingdom and he had reason to fear the intentions of both Frederick and Manuel. He first approached the Byzantine ruler, as his father had done before him. When Manuel rejected his overtures he turned to Venice, then on bad terms with Byzantium, and in 1155 he at least obtained a promise of neutrality. Manuel, though uncertain of Frederick's intentions and in difficulties with Hungary, at that time secretly plotting with his treacherous cousin Andronicus Comnenus to attack the Empire, had sent his agents to Italy with large subsidies to win support and maintain troops. They set to work among the discontented Normans. His cousin Michael Palaeologus apparently came to an understanding with Ancona, a convenient base, and he successfully approached Genoa and Pisa. These negotiations were followed by Byzantine successes in gaining a foothold in South Italy. Bari was taken and Trani. Pope Hadrian IV (Eugenius III had died in July 1153) was on bad terms with William and therefore susceptible to Manuel's overtures. He was, at this time, engaged in correspondence with Byzantine ecclesiastics and so may also have been influenced by the hope of union between the two Churches. But Manuel's successes in Apulia were short-lived. He had no really secure base and no powerful and reliable allies. William I grew in strength and after crushing the Byzantines at Brindisi in May 1156 he moved north to Benevento and in June forced the Pope to come to terms with him. Frederick I in Germany clearly had no intention of giving Manuel any support, and an embassy in the spring of 1156 had failed to obtain from him any help against Hun-

---

[1] *MGH, Legum Sectio* IV, *Const.* I, p. 202.

gary. Manuel did not at first accept the defeat at Brindisi as decisive. He sent the *protostrator* Alexius on a further mission, but, in spite of some initial success, this ended in failure. After negotiations William I and Manuel signed a thirty-years peace in 1158 and Byzantine troops were withdrawn from South Italy. This treaty probably suited Hadrian, for, in view of the growing rift between the Papacy and Barbarossa after the events of Besançon, he obviously hoped to unite Sicily and the Byzantine Empire against the western Emperor.

For Manuel the year 1158 marked an epoch. He never again attempted to use direct military intervention in Italy. He did not abandon his western projects but he concentrated on other methods. During the years 1158–77 the threads of international diplomacy and political circumstances drew him to the eastern as well as the northern and western peripheries of the Empire where for nearly twenty years he was markedly successful. Manuel's policy during this period brought him into contact with Frederick Barbarossa whose position in Germany, Burgundy and North Italy, and designs in the rest of Italy, made him a formidable opponent and whose imperial pretensions clashed with the Byzantine claim to universal empire. It cannot however be maintained that Manuel deliberately reorientated his policy and threw over the German alliance on which his father had built. He exploited unforeseen circumstances, such as the western schism, but he kept open the possibility of an understanding with Germany and as late as 1172–4 still had hopes of a marriage alliance.

The papal schism which was caused by the election in 1159 of an anti-Pope Victor IV in opposition to Alexander III was a major factor in European diplomacy. Manuel maintained cordial relations with Alexander and the problems of ecclesiastical reunion and the restoration of imperial unity were in the forefront of their discussions. Manuel's plan was to receive the imperial crown from the Pope in return for the union of the two Churches. He also promised Alexander substantial financial aid and had in mind a coalition against Barbarossa who was behind the anti-Pope. He therefore negotiated with France and Sicily (now the strongest supporter of the Pope). In 1163 Byzantine envoys were in France, but nothing came of this proposal for a concerted attack on Frederick I for Louis VII appeared to have inexplicably withdrawn. In 1166 Manuel made another bold bid to turn circumstances to his advantage. On 7 May 1166 William I of Sicily died leaving a minor, his son William II, as his heir. According to the Archbishop of Salerno, Manuel at once proposed to the council of regency that the young king should marry Mary, then his only child and heiress (born in 1152), and should succeed to the imperial

throne on his (Manuel's) death.[1] This proposal to cement the Sicilian–
Byzantine alliance was made at the time when Frederick I was preparing his fourth Italian expedition (1166), which may be the reason
why Manuel was prepared to throw over his understanding with
Hungary, for he had already betrothed Mary to Béla the heir-
apparent to the Hungarian throne. But Sicily did not favour the
proposal. Precise reasons why are not given, but it must have been
clear that it would, for the time being at any rate, considerably
strengthen Manuel's own position in Italy, especially as he was also
planning to secure from the Papacy his coronation and recognition
as sole Roman Emperor. With this in view Manuel sent ambassadors
to the curia in late 1167. He may have hoped that the West would
accept the setting aside of Frederick as a schismatic and excommunicate. But strong Latin feeling against the Byzantines as responsible
for crusading disasters, and equally strong resistance to papal claims
on the part of Byzantine clergy and people, made it unlikely that
any such plan could succeed. And even Manuel refused to agree to
the papal demand—if Cinnamus can be believed—that the seat of
Empire be transferred from Constantinople to Rome.[2] The position
of the Pope grew steadily stronger after the formation of the Lombard
League and he was therefore less dependent on Byzantine help, while
Manuel became more and more involved in his eastern projects,
where his very successes, as in the principality of Antioch, roused
further western hostility to him.

But in spite of the failure of Manuel's negotiations with the Papacy
he still maintained relations with Sicily. In 1169, probably in September, his son Alexius was born. This meant breaking off the betrothal
of his daughter Mary to Béla of Hungary who up to now had been
destined to succeed him. Almost at once proposals for a marriage
between William II and Mary were again made and this time accepted, probably in 1170. Various embassies were exchanged between
the two courts and the news almost certainly reached Frederick I.
If so, this may account for the dispatch of Christian of Mainz to
Constantinople in 1170. Frederick's counter-attack was apparently a
proposal conveyed by the Chancellor Christian that Mary should
marry his son Henry. In 1171 Byzantine envoys in Cologne were
concerned with this same proposal. It would thus appear that Manuel
was carrying on two sets of negotiations simultaneously, resolved to
accept the greater prize, that is, Henry. This would account for the
failure to send Mary to William, who went to Taranto in 1172 to meet
a bride who never arrived. As it happened, Manuel seems to have

---

[1] Romuald of Salerno, *MGH, Script.* xix, p. 436.
[2] John Cinnamus, vi, 4, p. 262 (*CSHB*).

been outwitted by Frederick who broke up the Sicilian project and then failed to implement his own proposal. Byzantine ambassadors came to Regensburg in June 1174 in connection with the marriage but they were not received by Frederick. Mary eventually married Renier of Montferrat in 1179, and it was Frederick's son Henry VI who obtained the Sicilian kingdom through his marriage to the heiress Constance.

During the second phase of Manuel's policy it was not only the great western powers, as the Papacy or the rulers of France, Sicily and Germany, whom he approached. His agents and his gold were well known in many Italian cities, including Rome. Major maritime trading centres, long-established Venice, the rapidly expanding Pisa and Genoa, all played an important role, particularly in East Mediterranean regions where they had strong commercial interests. In the opening years of Manuel's reign Venice had given maritime assistance which enabled the Byzantines to recover Corfu from the Sicilian Normans during the year 1148–9. But Venice obviously did not wish to see Manuel established in South Italy and was therefore inclined to ally with William I at the time of the Byzantine expedition to Apulia. Manuel therefore approached Pisa and Genoa, concluding treaties with them in 1170 and 1169–70 respectively. All three cities were granted trading concessions including quarters in Constantinople and elsewhere. All were bitterly jealous of each other, and at the same time their privileged position within the Empire roused the bitter hostility of the Byzantine merchants. In 1162 the Genoese were attacked in Constantinople by the Pisans and Venetians (and also the Byzantines), and they left the capital and had to be placated by Manuel who opened negotiations with Genoa in 1164 and signed treaties with them in 1169 and 1170. Venice, growing uneasy at Manuel's policy in Italy and in Dalmatia, was further antagonised by a well-organised attack on all Venetians throughout the Empire on 12 March 1171 when they were arrested and their goods were confiscated. Hatred of the arrogant and wealthy Venetians was widespread, and the Emperor himself may still have resented the Venetian parody of Byzantine imperial ceremonies at the recapture of Corfu from the Normans in 1148–9. On that occasion Manuel (well known for his immense stature and dark skin) was represented by an enormous negro. As a result of the attack the indignant Venetians compelled the Doge, who still wished to maintain diplomatic relations, to send a fleet to attack Dalmatia and the islands. Manuel opened negotiations which, despite Nicetas Choniates' statement to the contrary, were probably not concluded until the reign of Andronicus I.[1]

---

[1] Nicetas Choniates, v, 9, p. 225 (*CSHB*). Cf. the Venetian sources cited by G. Ostrogorsky, *History of the Byzantine State*, p. 346, n. 1.

The episode was not forgotten and the need to secure its economic position in the East Mediterranean was one of the underlying causes for Venice's part in diverting the Fourth Crusade to Constantinople.

In view of Venetian, and also Hohenstaufen, ambitions the Dalmatian coast, the Balkan principalities and Hungary were vital links in the network of Byzantine foreign policy. Here to the north and north-west Manuel scored notable successes.[1] Rascia in particular was open to Latin overtures, and Manuel was engaged in dealing with his unruly Serbian vassals in 1149 and 1150 when he was being attacked by the Normans elsewhere. Stephen Nemanja who succeeded to the throne of Rascia *c.* 1167[2] was lukewarm in his support of Constantinople and therefore ready to listen to the suggestions of Germany and Hungary. When Manuel was fighting Hungary in 1163 it was with difficulty that he obtained from Rascia the military contingent owed him and its ruler submitted to Manuel with great reluctance after a campaign against him in 1165. Manuel further strengthened his position by his conquest of Dalmatia. In 1168 he again had to tame Stephen Nemanja who had attacked Zeta, and then Ragusa where the ruler of Zeta had fled. After further expeditions against Stephen in 1172, he defeated him and took him in triumph to Constantinople. Later Stephen was set at liberty and he caused no more trouble during Manuel's reign.

Hungary, by reason of its geographical position, was something of a buffer state between Byzantium and Germany. Its interests in Croatia and Dalmatia clashed with those of both Venice and Constantinople. In the opening years of Manuel's reign, Hungary was suspicious of the alliance between Conrad and Manuel. It was also allied by marriage to the Kievan house where rival claimants to the throne were supported by Byzantium. It was therefore ready to negotiate with the Normans of Sicily. Growing bolder after the death of Conrad III, Géza II threatened to attack Byzantine territory, and there was intermittent warfare until peace was made in 1156 at a time when Manuel no doubt wished to concentrate on retrieving the situation in South Italy. After his defeat in Apulia and treaty with William I in 1158, Manuel turned again to the north. On the death of Géza II in 1162, Manuel's candidate, Stephen IV (the brother of Géza), was unsuccessful, but the Byzantine Emperor came to terms with Stephen III (Géza's son) and proceeded to embark on a bold scheme which might have united Hungary and the Empire. In 1162

---

[1] See also below: chs. XII and XIII.

[2] In 1166 or 1167; on the chronology see G. Ostrogorsky, *History of the Byzantine State*, p. 345, n. 1. Cf. V. Grumel, *La Chronologie*, p. 391; and see also below: ch. XII, p. 520.

Géza's brother Béla, the heir-apparent, was surrendered to Manuel as hostage, and Croatia, Sirmium and Dalmatia were to be his appanage. He was betrothed to Manuel's only child and heiress, Mary, and was to succeed to the thrones of Hungary and Byzantium. That Manuel was ready to throw over this agreement in 1166 for the more advantageous Sicilian marriage alliance has already been shown. When the Sicilian project failed he apparently reverted to his Hungarian plan, though this did not necessarily ensure peace between the two countries. Stephen III took the offensive again in 1165, and hostilities ended in 1167 with Manuel in possession of Dalmatia, Bosnia, Sirmium and part of Croatia. When his son Alexius was born in 1169 the betrothal of Béla and Mary was dissolved; Béla was demoted to the rank of Caesar and married to Manuel's sister-in-law Anne, the daughter of Constance of Antioch. On Stephen III's death in 1172 Béla succeeded to the throne of Hungary, apparently acquiescing in Byzantine possession of the lands which were his appanage. He remained loyal to Manuel and it was only after 1180 that attempts were made to regain the lost territory coveted not only by Hungary but by its rival Venice. Thus although Manuel's bold project of incorporating Hungary into the Empire fell through, during his lifetime he kept his hold on the Dalmatian lands.

Manuel's activities in South Italy, his preoccupation with his northern frontier, and his unceasing attempt at building up a series of alliances with western powers did not cause him to neglect either Muslim or Christian rulers in Asia Minor and farther east. He could not indeed afford to do so, for most diplomatic threads led east as well as west, and although he is most often remembered for his 'western design', he was in fact markedly successful in the east, like his father before him. His failure in Italy and enforced truce with William I in 1158 contrast with his spectacular successes shortly afterwards in Cilicia and Antioch. In this year Manuel turned first to Cilicia where the lands regained by John had been lost, and at his approach the Armenian prince Thoros fled. At Mopsuestia (Mamistra) he received the apprehensive Reynald of Châtillon, husband of Constance of Antioch, who came barefooted. Reynald, together with Thoros, had in 1156 led a devastating and unprovoked attack on Cyprus, still a Byzantine province. This had brought on him the displeasure not only of Manuel but of Baldwin of Jerusalem, and his only hope lay in abject surrender. He had to agree to Manuel's demands which included the surrender of the citadel of Antioch, and the appointment of a Greek, instead of a Latin, Patriarch. Then in 1159 Manuel entered Antioch on horseback, his horse decorated with imperial insignia, his bridle held by Reynald walking on foot. Behind followed Baldwin III of Jerusalem who had married Manuel's niece Theodora and had now come north to greet him and to acknowledge his sovereignty. Manuel, who generally got on well with westerners, made an excellent impression during the week of festivities in Antioch and it looked as though Byzantine leaders might give some unity to the Christian cause in the East. But Manuel could not concentrate all his forces and his energies on a single frontier. At this juncture he appears to have had disquieting news from Constantinople and it suited him for the moment to make a treaty with Nur-ad-Din the ruler of Aleppo instead of undertaking a campaign against him. He then took his army back to Constantinople, travelling by the most direct route *via* Iconium, though not without some brushes with the Seljuqs.

Manuel had thus successfully reasserted Byzantine authority over the Christian principalities and had secured the alliance of Nur-ad-Din, a clever move from Manuel's point of view, since it gave some security to the crusaders without increasing their power as a decisive defeat of Nur-ad-Din would have done, and at the same time it served as an additional check to the Sultan of Iconium. In December 1161 Manuel further strengthened his links with Antioch by marrying as his second wife Mary, daughter of Constance of Antioch. And in 1165 the crowning sign of Byzantine authority over Antioch was the appointment of a Greek ecclesiastic to the ancient Patriarchate, though this was of short duration for Patriarch Athanasius II was killed in 1170 by an earthquake (a sign of divine displeasure according to the Franks) and the Latin Aimery was promptly reinstated. But the position was a precarious one and with difficulties on other and widely separated fronts Manuel could only give intermittent attention to the east. In 1162 Byzantine authority in Cilicia was again challenged by the Armenian prince Thoros, who in 1159 had been pardoned his share in the raid on Cyprus and given territory in the mountains. This offensive was taken as a result of the murder of Thoros' brother at Tarsus. Manuel sent reinforcements to Cilicia, and appointed his cousin Andronicus as the new governor, an unfortunate choice for Andronicus proved eminently unsuitable. On the death of Thoros in 1168 Rupen II's succession was disputed by his uncle Mleh supported by Nur-ad-Din and again Cilicia was attacked. During the last years of Manuel's reign the Byzantine position in Cilicia was insecure, not only because of the perpetual troubles in the Armenian house, but by reason of the growing insecurity of the Christian cause.

Nur-ad-Din had strengthened his position by taking advantage of troubles in the Taurus and anti-Taurus region in the north. He was also well aware of the strategic importance of Egypt in the south. In 1160 the new caliph in Egypt was a minor. Muslim and Christian powers competed with each other in trying to exploit this situation by responding to calls for help from rival viziers. Almaric of Jerusalem realised that it would be fatal to allow Nur-ad-Din to gain control of Egypt, and from 1165 onwards he sought a military alliance with Manuel. His own campaigns in Egypt in 1168–9 failed. Worse still, he was outmanoeuvred by Nur-ad-Din's contingent under Shirkuh and his nephew Saladin who successfully asserted control over the Egyptian government. A combined Greek and Latin siege of Damietta late in 1169 ended in disaster, and Saladin (for Shirkuh had died in March 1169) was left in possession. A renewed treaty between Almaric and Manuel on the occasion of the former's visit to Constantinople in the spring of 1171 bore witness to their realisation of the common danger, but the further expedition suggested did not materialise. Though Nur-ad-Din died in 1174 (with important repercussions on the political situation in Asia Minor), Saladin kept his hold on Egypt and prepared to encircle the Latin principalities by extending his authority northwards.

In Asia Minor since the eleventh century the real protagonist had been the Sultan of Iconium. His conquests in central and western Anatolia bordered on the coastal Byzantine lands and it was essential to keep him in check and be assured of his neutrality. Hence the frequent treaties between Byzantium and Iconium which were often bitterly criticised by the western powers, as for instance at the time of the Second Crusade. Manuel also fostered the rivalry between Iconium and the neighbouring Muslim state of the Danishmends in eastern Asia Minor. The Danishmends in turn were supported by Nur-ad-Din in their stand against any eastward expansion of Iconium and this may have been in Manuel's mind when he himself made a treaty with Nur-ad-Din in 1159. Thus Kilij Arslan II was kept in check after a successful Byzantine campaign in the region of the Meander valley, and he sought peace with Manuel in 1161, agreeing to restore Greek cities captured and to provide military contingents for the imperial army. In the following year he visited Constantinople and was splendidly received. During the years 1162–74 there were the usual raids and spasmodic attacks along the marches of Byzantium and Iconium, but Manuel was engaged on other frontiers in Europe. Kilij Arslan II took this opportunity to consolidate his position and to advance eastwards at the expense of the Danishmends who sought the help of Nur-ad-Din. Seeing a possible threat to himself in the Seljuq attacks on Melitene, Nur-ed-Din put himself at the head of Kilij Arslan's enemies in 1171, and after a series of inconclusive campaigns a treaty was arranged in 1173. One of its clauses was an undertaking by Kilij Arslan that he would make war on the Greeks. Nur-ad-Din, who had to some extent taken Manuel's place as supporter of dissident elements and refugee Muslim princes, died in 1174, with the consequence that the Danishmend Dhū'n-Nūn and Kilij's brother Shahinshah turned again to Constantinople, and Kilij Arslan recaptured the eastern cities of Cappadocia which he had recently been forced to evacuate.

On the whole relations between Iconium and Byzantium had been reasonably good, hence Nur-ad-Din's reproach to Kilij Arslan that he chose to attack Muslims rather than his near Christian neighbours. And Manuel began to realise that although a treaty had been made in 1161 and Kilij Arslan had duly sent his troops for the Hungarian campaign, he had for some time been building up his own position, taking advantage of Manuel's preoccupation elsewhere, and possibly also urged on by Frederick Barbarossa. In 1173 Manuel was himself in Asia Minor and advanced to Philadelphia. Kilij preferred to renew his understanding with Manuel rather than risk an open breach in accordance with the wishes of his ally Nur-ad-Din. Manuel undertook more strenuous fortification of his frontiers; he rebuilt Dorylaeum and he renewed his demands for the restoration of captured cities. He wintered in Constantinople during 1175–6. An embassy from Kilij Arslan reached him there, seeking the renewal of the peace treaty. This was refused and in the spring of 1176 expeditions set out against Kilij Arslan. The attack against Neocaesarea, led by Andronicus Vatatzes and Dhū'n Nūn, was a failure. Manuel himself led his army against Iconium, travelling by way of Laodicea and the upper Meander valley until he reached the mountainous region near the frontier. Here Kilij Arslan again renewed his request for a peace treaty. Manuel refused. Against the advice of his seasoned generals he and his army advanced through the pass of Myriocephalum and were trapped by the Turks. Manuel turned and fled and was only restrained from further flight by his officers. The massacre of the Byzantine troops was halted by Kilij Arslan who surprisingly offered terms to Manuel. Peace was made, according to Nicetas Choniates,[1] on condition that Manuel destroyed his two newly built fortresses of Dorylaeum and Sublaeum. Manuel then retreated, destroying the fortifications of Sublaeum, but leaving those of Dorylaeum, and with his shattered forces he re-entered Constantinople. It seems extraordinary that Kilij Arslan did not press home his advantage, but, even so, the defeat at Myriocephalum was a disaster for the Christian cause, whether Greek or Latin. After this only minor expeditions

---

[1] Nicetas Choniates, vi, 4, p. 245 (*CSHB*).

were undertaken in Asia Minor. Worse still Manuel's prestige had suffered and his enemies did not hesitate to stress his humiliating defeat. It was on this occasion that Frederick I wrote as heir of the Roman Emperors to demand the submission of the Greek ruler. However much the flexibility of twelfth-century Mediterranean diplomacy is emphasised, it is difficult not to regard this as manœuvring for position as far as Manuel and Frederick were concerned. As the reign advanced their rivalry became intensified. What the German Emperor desired was 'the destruction of the whole of Greece and the establishment of his control over the Greeks'.[1]

For the four remaining years of Manuel's life he still pursued an active policy as far as depleted military resources would allow, though William of Tyre says that he never regained his former good health or peace of mind.[2] Activities on a minor scale against Iconium continued in the disputed region of the Meander valley. When he was able, Manuel struck with his customary boldness. In 1177 he provided naval support for a joint expedition with Jerusalem against Egypt. The expedition never set sail, largely through the non-cooperative attitude of Philip Count of Flanders, newly arrived from Europe. With his old Latin friends in the crusading states there is ample evidence that Manuel maintained good relations; his capacity for breaking down barriers between Greek and Latin was one of his greatest gifts and the felicitous personal relationships of this period do to some extent compensate for the acrimonious political wrangles and undercurrents of religious antagonism. The Latin William of Tyre shows in his *History* the affection and esteem in which Manuel was held by many Latins in the crusader states. William himself visited Constantinople on his return from the third Lateran council in Rome in 1179, and there he was present at the spendid celebrations for the marriages of Manuel's daughter Mary to Renier of Montferrat, and his young son Alexius to Louis VII's daughter, Agnes of France. He speaks of the lavish games in the hippodrome, the glorious shows of various kinds, the magnificence of the imperial robes and vestments decorated with a profusion of precious stones, the solid gold and silver furniture in the palace.[3] This was the impression made by the Empire before it was looted by the crusaders in 1204.

The dramatic catastrophe of Myriocephalon in 1176 was however a significant pointer. It symbolises as it were the failure to make any decisive headway in the Anatolian lands near at hand, largely because

---

[1] *Historia Ducum Veneticorum, MGH, Script.* xiv, 77, cited by P. Lamma, *Comneni e Staufer*, ii, p. 210.
[2] William of Tyre, Bk. xxi, ch. 12.
[3] William of Tyre, Bk. xxii, ch. 4.

of energy, men and money lavished in Italy. The northern frontier, or Cilicia and Antioch in the south-east, might be allowed as legitimate spheres of influence, as well as the Asia Minor provinces nearer at hand. But to attempt to restore the old imperial control over even a part of Italy was to ignore forces such as the Italian cities, the Hohenstaufen, the Papacy, as well as the by now traditional suspicion of the Greeks current in western circles.

Manuel's policy was marked by much that was traditional while containing certain bold and unusual features. His conception of the Byzantine imperial office was essentially that of his forbears. But his mode of meeting his responsibilities was often original and experimental, as for instance his plan to unite the thrones of Constantinople and Hungary by betrothing his only child, Mary, to Béla-Alexius, or even to marry her to William II thus joining Sicily and Byzantium. The same flexibility of outlook is found in other aspects of his work at home. There was the usual concentration on needs of defence, the steady growth in the power of the landowning classes and in grants of *pronoia*, the continued cultural and ecclesiastical life of a civilised polity. But in the midst of such familiar activities there intruded another and more alien element. This was the increasing settlement of Latins within the Empire, partly due to Manuel's deliberate encouragement, though partly the inevitable result of commercial concessions granted, not only by Manuel, but by his father and grandfather.

The Comnenian rulers, in contrast to the civil aristocracy in the previous century, concentrated on restoring the efficiency of imperial defences. Under Manuel the military forces were well organised, though recruitment always remained a problem. Hence the importance of the system of granting land in *pronoia* often in return for the provision of troops. It was equally vital to ensure payment of mercenaries, even if this meant resorting to the extreme measure of handing over to soldiers the privilege of collecting revenue from the tenants (*paroikoi*) on an estate, as Manuel seems to have done. Mercenaries still remained a vital source of manpower, and these were provided in various ways, either on a temporary basis, or as enrolled corps, or in the form of contingents furnished by arrangement with allies or vassal states, as Iconium or Rascia. The navy was stronger than it had been in Alexius I's day, in spite of Manuel's policy of permitting the islands and maritime provinces to commute their naval service and duties. Venetian help was still welcome, as in the recapture of Corfu, but even at the end of Manuel's reign he could still send a substantial naval contingent to Acre. The expenses of defence and of foreign policy had always been a major item in the

Byzantine budget, and this as always fell heavily on the lower classes. But it is clear that Byzantium still had impressive resources. Manuel's agents in Italy drew freely on imperial gold in a way that would have been impossible in the impoverished days of the Empire in the late fourteenth and fifteenth centuries when Emperors had to pawn their few remaining jewels and were even held prisoner in Venice for unpaid debts. Byzantium had lost rich provinces in Anatolia to the Turks and customs revenue to Venice, Genoa and Pisa, but its own merchants still carried on a lucrative trade, its wealthy citizens lived in palatial style, and its Emperors fittingly maintained the imperial dignity.

One of the most striking contrasts between the Empire of this period and the middle Byzantine state was the perceptible weakening of the central authority, and the loosening of its links with the periphery. This was partly due to the internal troubles of the eleventh century, from which the Empire never recovered, partly to external pressure on all fronts. It was also accelerated by the frequent grants of various kinds which the Emperors made to individuals. The *pronoia* was the most usual, and by the end of the twelfth century was an accepted, expedient of the Byzantine government. It gradually changed its character and instead of a carefully limited non-heritable grant for a specified time, it developed into something very like the Latin *feudum* which could be passed from father to son. From the point of view of the pronoiar, the value of the grant lay in the rights which it carried with it of collecting taxes and dues from any tenants (*paroikoi*) who went with the property. This system was applied not only to landed wealth; it might concern flocks and herds. It was not granted only to men of standing, nor indeed reserved exclusively for Byzantines. Manuel I made grants in *pronoia* to foreigners and 'half-barbarians' and to men of humble origin, which Nicetas Choniates considered to be most discouraging to good Greek soldiers who felt that such rewards should be reserved for them.[1] Such 'half-barbarians' may have been Cumans in the Balkans whose wealth was in their flocks, or the Latins who were encouraged to settle in the Empire, as well as the Emperor's many western relations and friends. Quite apart from the foreign merchants with their quarters in the big cities and their privileges regulated by treaty, there was a marked influx of Latins during Manuel's reign, due largely to what appears to be deliberate imperial policy. It has been suggested that Manuel sought in this way to invigorate conservative Byzantine society and

---

[1] Nicetas Choniates, VII, 4, p. 273 (*CSHB*). Cf. G. Ostrogorsky, *La féodalité byzantine*, pp. 28–31 and p. 53; and for a different view on grants and military recruitment see P. Lemerle, 'Recherches sur le régime agraire à Byzance', *loc. cit.*

to bridge the difference in tradition and outlook between the two worlds. But Orthodoxy in both the ecclesiastical and the secular sense was antagonistic to any such policy.

Although Manuel tried to graft Latins on to Byzantine life and to use different Greek social classes, he could not halt the strengthening of the feudal element. Some of his measures even supported the interests of secular landowners. In 1158 he permitted alienation of property only to the senatorial and the military (i.e. pronoiar) classes, while monasteries were not allowed to acquire land or increase the number of their tenants. On the other hand tenants were freely assigned to the secular pronoiars. At the same time there was no relaxation in the struggle to control the state tenants (*demosiakoi*), who had special obligations to the imperial fisc. Thus when charters of confirmation were granted, the imperial bull would state the number of tenants (*paroikoi*) on the estate, and the number of new tenants who might be acquired provided that they were free of obligations to the exchequer. Though limiting the rights of monasteries to acquire new property, Manuel was in no way hostile to the Church. Amongst his administrative rulings there are a number concerning ecclesiastical discipline and problems of ownership of church property. He was a liberal patron of the Church, particularly monasteries: 'The fellowship of the saints will always hold his memory blessed because of his almsgiving and generous benefactions.'[1] Manuel, like Nicephorus II, thought that the true monk should make his home in the isolated countryside and not in large cities.

During Manuel's reign there were a number of theological disputations and some trials for heresy which may have had political as well as religious implications. Distinguished churchmen from the west, as Anselm of Havelberg, took part in some of the discussions, as that on the nature of the Sacrifice of the Mass, and Manuel himself liked to argue and also to make his point of view prevail, though it was not always strictly orthodox. His attitude towards the Muslims provoked his subjects' criticism. The Patriarch refused to allow Kilij Arslan II to accompany Manuel in the procession to St Sophia when he visited Constantinople in 1162 and regarded the earthquake of that year as a divine rebuke at such a suggestion. Manuel did succeed in getting the wording of the abjuration made by Muslims modified, so that the convert no longer had to anathematise the God of Muḥammad. His own cosmopolitan outlook and his desire to press his point of view sometimes led him into theological difficulties, and both Cinnamus and Nicetas Choniates note that he laid himself open to the charge of heresy, though it was felt that this should not be

---

[1] William of Tyre, Bk. XXII, ch. 5.

pressed until after his death.[1] Manuel's policy towards the dualist heresies was not however open to any such criticism. Bogomil, Massalian and Paulician teaching still persisted within the Empire and elsewhere, and like his grandfather Alexius, Manuel tried to root this out. There is some suggestion that it had affected the imperial family, though it is difficult to disentangle this from an element of political opposition involving Manuel's brother Isaac as well as the Patriarch Cosmas Atticus. In 1143 in Constantinople two bishops and a monk called Niphon, who evidently had the support of the Patriarch, were condemned for holding Bogomil doctrines. These men had worked in Asia Minor where the sect still existed, particularly in Cappadocia. It was also strongly rooted in Macedonia and Bulgaria, though here Manuel could do little to eradicate it.[2] Such heretical movements were fed by popular Slav antagonism to Byzantine influence and they introduced an additional problem into an already complex situation at the time of the Latin Empire in Constantinople.

Desire to promote union between the various Christian churches was in keeping with Manuel's conception of his imperial office. He wanted for instance to win over the separated churches such as the Armenian, and with this in mind a number of embassies were exchanged, but without any lasting success, for in both churches the majority remained intolerant of each other's point of view. Manuel was also concerned with ecclesiastical reunion with the West. Here, as in the case of other Christian churches, and even the Muslim creed, political and ecclesiastical motives were closely interwoven.[3] In the Byzantine polity it could not indeed be otherwise. In the case of Manuel's approach to Pope Alexander III, the Greek sources are not explicit on the ecclesiastical aspect. It is Cardinal Boso in his life of Alexander who says that Manuel was anxious 'to unite his Greek Church with the venerable Roman Church, the mother of all the churches'.[4] In return, Alexander was to declare Frederick deposed as a schismatic and to crown Manuel as the sole Roman Emperor, but to the Byzantines this was simply to restore to him what was his by right. Cinnamus, while conceding to the Pope 'the right of laying on of hands, as far as consecration is concerned, for this is a spiritual matter', makes it clear that, in his view, the Pope had not any power

[1] John Cinnamus, vi, 2, pp. 251 ff. (*CSHB*) and Nicetas Choniates, vii, 5, pp. 274 ff. (*CSHB*).

[2] On chronology see *GR*, iii, 1013 ff.

[3] See above: pp. 230 ff.

[4] *Liber Pont.* (ed. L. Duchesne, Paris, 1957), ii, p. 415; this is Boso's account of the first embassy. Cf. *DR*, 1480, where it is suggested that there was in fact only one embassy.

'to grant the imperial majesty'.[1] The Pope, though affirming his desire for reunion, found it impossible to comply with the conditions attached. The papal demand for imperial residence in Rome (which only Cinnamus mentions) may simply have been in the nature of a deliberate diplomatic stalemate. And even had Alexander been willing to recognise Manuel's imperial claims, there is no evidence to suggest that the Byzantine Emperor would have been able to implement the ecclesiastical side of the agreement, as specified in Boso's account of the second embassy, that is, to recognise a single head of the Church and to be bound by the same observances of divine law.[2] Most Byzantines would have found it as impossible to accept papal supremacy in the twelfth century as in 1274 or 1439.

Manuel may have misjudged the temper of his age both at home and abroad. Even his charm and vitality could not reconcile the Greek and Latin worlds. His bold and original policy failed to gain him any permanent foothold in Italy; his plans for Syria and Palestine were frustrated by crusading dissensions and hostility; in the Aegean, the Balkans and Asia Minor, the most his diplomacy could achieve was a precarious balancing of opposing forces. Within the Empire he left a minor and an unpopular regency. The aristocracy were antagonised by his attempts to mobilise all resources and make use of other social classes. Everyone was incensed by his policy towards the Latin foreigners—merchants, adventurers, relations and friends who thronged the Empire. For almost a hundred years the Byzantine Empire was ruled by the three outstanding Emperors of the Comnenian house. All three were respected in military and diplomatic circles but they could not control feudal tendencies at home, nor could they restore authority in provinces lost to the Muslims and the westerners. And it was beyond their power to stem the upsurge of the growing western and Slav forces and to bridge the gulf between Greek and Latin.

The years 1180–1204 clearly demonstrated that the East Roman Empire had lost the supremacy of the middle Byzantine period. Manuel I died on 24 September 1180, refusing almost until the last to make arrangements for the regency during his son's minority, so confident was he in the astrologers' prediction that he was not yet to die. Finally, upbraided by the Church he appointed his wife, the Norman Mary of Antioch, as regent, and took before his death the monk's habit as was customary. His son Alexius II was eleven years old on his accession. There followed two uneasy years during which the Dowager-Empress virtually entrusted the government to an

---

[1] John Cinnamus, v, 7, pp. 219–20 (*CSHB*).
[2] *Liber Pont.* II, p. 419.

unpopular member of the Comnenian family, Manuel's nephew, the *protosebastus* Alexius, thus playing into the hands of her opponents by her unwise policy. A critical situation developed in which general hatred of the Latins and the increasingly disruptive attitude of the landed families were the predominant factors. This was the opportunity for which Andronicus Comnenus had been waiting. He was the son of John II's brother Isaac and had long proved a trial to his cousin, the Emperor Manuel. A man of charm and ability, yet treacherous and unstable, he had wandered in restless exile throughout the Middle East. At this time he had made his peace with Manuel and was living as governor in Pontus. On hearing of the rising in the capital against the regency he marched to the Bosphorus and camped at Chalcedon. He was supported by all the dissident elements in Asia Minor and in the capital, and by the admiral the *megas dux* Andronicus Contostephanus. The regency's defence broke down; the *protosebastus* Alexius was imprisoned and blinded; and the populace of Constantinople made a savage attack on all foreigners in the city. In September 1182 Andronicus Comnenus crossed the Bosphorus and entered the capital. At first he only claimed to take over the regency in the interests of Byzantium, but by September 1183 he was sufficiently established to be crowned as co-Emperor. He had already executed his major opponents including the Dowager-Empress Mary and Manuel I's daughter Mary. Shortly after his coronation Alexius II was strangled and Andronicus married his cousin's widow, the little French princess Agnes-Anna.

Andronicus I was a man of violent contrasts, as his contemporaries noted. He passionately desired to purge the administration of corruption and to protect the oppressed poorer classes. He therefore saw that officials were adequately paid and he ruthlessly punished extortion. He tried to strike at the power of the provincial landowners. The privilege of alienating imperial grants of land permitted only to the senatorial and military classes by Manuel I's bulls of 1158 and 1170[1] was revoked as early as December 1182. His policy roused the opposition of both the officials and the landed magnates, and in antagonising the latter Andronicus made a major error. In the twelfth century it was impossible to subdue the powerful feudal elements in the state. As it was, Andronicus lived in perpetual fear of conspiracies and attempted to root out opposition by exterminating his opponents. But a policy of constant executions and terrorism failed to secure his position and it also deprived the state of military leaders at a time when it was called upon to face grave external dangers. During the chaotic times after Manuel's death, his

[1] On the dates, see G. Ostrogorsky, *History of the Byzantine State*, p. 348, n. 6.

system of alliances broke down and the hostile ring closed in upon the weakened Empire. The Grand Župan of Serbia, Stephen Nemanja, shook off his allegiance and set about increasing his territory. Hungary's ruler, Béla III, claimed vengeance for the death of his sister-in-law, Mary of Antioch, and in 1181 he regained Dalmatia, part of Croatia and Sirmium. In 1183 he allied with Stephen Nemanja to make further attacks on the imperial provinces in the Balkans. Andronicus tried to safeguard his position by re-establishing relations with the western powers, particularly Venice, and by making a treaty with Saladin. But the Normans of Sicily, true to tradition, took Corfu, invaded the imperial mainland and then in August 1185 captured and sacked Thessalonica. When this news reached the capital, it was the signal for another rising. Andronicus was cruelly killed by the mob, and his cousin Isaac Angelus was proclaimed Emperor.

Isaac II had not the statesmanlike qualities of the three great Comnenian rulers of the twelfth century, nor had he the individuality of his immediate predecessor, Andronicus. He did not attempt to swim against the current as Andronicus had done, and he had no exalted ideas of imperial responsibility. Administrative abuses rapidly reappeared and the tax-collector and the official reverted to their normal practice. The predominance of the landed classes went unchecked and in the provinces the local magnate, as in later Palaeologian times, was the predominant figure. In 1185 centrifugal forces had already shown to what lengths they could go when Isaac Comnenus, the grandnephew of Manuel I, had proclaimed himself the independent ruler of Cyprus, henceforth to be lost to the Empire and soon to pass out of Greek hands altogether. Faced by a desperate situation, with the Normans still on Byzantine territory and the ferment of rebellion in the Bulgarian provinces, Isaac did at least attempt to build up his position. In 1185 he tried to gain the support of Hungary by treaty and he married Margaret the daughter of Béla III. The Normans were driven out of Macedonia and Epirus and their fleet sailed away from the Sea of Marmora. Isaac himself in 1186–7 led expeditions against the rebels in Bulgaria and Wallachia. But here long-standing resentment against Byzantine rule could not be quelled and under the leadership of two local nobles, Peter and Asen, an independent kingdom, the Second Bulgarian Empire, was once again established, composed of all three racial groups, Bulgar, Vlach and Cuman.[1] Asen was crowned by the newly constituted Archbishop of Trnovo, and Isaac had to acquiesce in the loss of the provinces. Byzantine authority was constantly being diminished throughout the Balkans. Serbia, for instance, continued the policy of consolida-

[1] See also below: ch. XII.

tion which it had pursued as soon as Manuel I died, and it was quick to support the Bulgarians against Byzantium and later on to make the most of western hostility towards the Empire.

The Latin threat to Constantinople now took a double form: the marriage of Frederick Barbarossa's son Henry to Constance, the heiress of Sicily, heralded the union of two kingdoms hostile to the Greeks, and the envious glances of Latin crusaders were increasingly cast in the direction of the East Roman Empire. For a number of reasons it looked as though Constantinople would be attacked. Commercial rivalry and bitter memories of recent Byzantine attacks on westerners, the constant deterioration of the Christian position in Palestine and Syria, the schism between the two churches, widespread envy of the apparent wealth of the Greeks and perhaps the desire to share in some of the holy relics accumulated within the walls of the capital—all these were contributing factors in hastening the downfall of the Empire. There were also political ambitions. The Third Crusade of 1189, ostensibly provoked by Saladin's capture of Jerusalem from the Christians, was led by the old enemy Frederick I. He had negotiated with the Sultan of Iconium who was busy expanding in Asia Minor at Byzantium's expense, and he took full advantage of the hostility felt towards the Greeks by the various Balkan principalities, including the newly formed Bulgaria. He had also approached Isaac on the question of the crusading passage through imperial territory. Isaac, apprehensive of Frederick's intentions, renewed in 1189 the alliance which Andronicus had made with Saladin, an action which was interpreted by the Latins as treating with their arch-enemy. As Frederick approached Constantinople friction between the Germans and Byzantines was intensified by Isaac's folly in imprisoning Frederick's ambassadors sent to negotiate for the passage across to Asia Minor. Enraged, Frederick showed his hand. He had already occupied Philippopolis and he wrote to his eldest son Henry for a fleet to attack Constantinople. He also asked for the papal blessing on this enterprise, urging that it was a necessary preliminary to any crusade against the Muslims. He himself had meanwhile occupied Thrace and was advancing on Constantinople. Isaac was therefore forced to come to terms with him and in February 1190 the treaty of Adrianople was made and Byzantine hostages given. In March 1190 the Germans were shipped across the Hellespont to Asia Minor and they began their journey south. Frederick's unexpected death soon afterwards in June 1190 brought a further brief respite to Byzantium. But it did not prevent Cyprus, then under the independent control of Isaac Comnenus, from falling into the hands of Richard of England who had joined the Third Crusade and travelled to Palestine by the sea route. Richard shortly afterwards passed it to the Templars and then in 1192 to the Lusignan house. Apart from the capture of Cyprus the Third Crusade did little to help the Latin cause.

In Byzantium Isaac had too many problems near at hand to be able to think of regaining Cyprus or maintaining the Greek cause against the Muslims as John II and Manuel I had done. Taking advantage of the death of the German ruler he hurriedly set about restoring Byzantine authority in the Balkans. He led a campaign against the recalcitrant Serbs and defeated Stephen Nemanja who was then forced to relinquish at least his most recent conquests. A treaty was made between the two rulers and the Serbian king's second son Stephen married Eudocia, the daughter of Isaac's brother Alexius, and was given the Byzantine title of Sebastocrator. Thus the Byzantine Emperor still tried to maintain his position at the apex of the Christian hierarchy and linked lesser lights to him by devices of this kind, though it was clear that Serbia could no longer be regarded as anything but an independent state. With Bulgaria Isaac was less successful. His campaign of 1190 ended in disaster. He could not take the Bulgarian capital Trnovo and he was ambushed in retreating over the Balkan mountains and barely escaped with his life. Undaunted he embarked on fresh expeditions and encountered fresh defeats. In 1194 he gained help from his Hungarian father-in-law Béla III, but his plans were cut short in April 1195 when he was deposed and blinded by his brother who was crowned Emperor as Alexius III.

Isaac had his shortcomings: he lacked good judgement and was no statesman. But he had made some effort to uphold Byzantine prestige by means both of diplomacy and warfare, and to defend the Empire at least from its enemies near at hand. Alexius III was weak and greedy and his *coup d'état* had far-reaching political consequences. Both the western powers and the Balkans were quick to press home their advantages. By 1194 Henry VI of Germany had made good his claim through his wife to the Sicilian lands, and had already demanded from Isaac II the restoration of the Greek territory invaded by William II. His brother Philip of Swabia was married to Irene the daughter of the deposed Isaac II. Henry himself was the true heir of Hohenstaufen and Norman ambitions and he planned a far-reaching policy of conquest which would force the Greek Emperor as well as the crusading princes and the other Christian rulers of the East Mediterranean to submit to western imperial overlordship. Alexius III prepared to stave off the worst of Henry's demands by agreeing to pay a crushing tribute. This was known as the 'German' tax, and when the already exhausted countryside could not produce the requisite amount, Alexius had to supplement it by stripping the imperial tombs in the Church of the Holy Apostles of their precious ornaments. Henry, though not supported by the Papacy in his proposed attack on Constantinople, pressed on and had secured his recognition from the rulers of Cyprus and Lesser Armenia when once again the Byzantine Empire was saved by unexpected death. Henry died in September 1197.

In the Balkans Alexius III had opportunities for extending his influence, but failed to use them. His daughter Eudocia was married to Stephen Nemanja's son, and the year after Alexius' succession, Nemanja abdicated in favour of this particular son, the Sebastocrator Stephen, possibly due to imperial pressure. But the new ruler soon found Byzantium an ineffective ally in his wars with his eldest brother Vukan, who resented being passed over in the succession. Stephen divorced his Byzantine wife, was driven to appeal to Rome, and even so he temporarily lost his throne in 1202 to Vukan who had forestalled him in allying with Hungary and recognising papal supremacy. And when Stephen managed to regain his throne it was with Bulgarian, and not Byzantine, aid. The decline of Byzantine prestige and the ineffectiveness of Alexius III were generally recognised. Bosnia acknowledged papal authority. Byzantine campaigns against Bulgaria met with defeat in 1195 and 1196. Byzantium then adopted underground methods and after the murder of Asen in 1196 and Peter in 1197, the old expedient of setting up a Byzantine protégé was attempted. But this time the central government could not control its allies and subordinates; civil war, rebellion, the rise of small virtually independent principalities in Macedonia were followed by the establishment of Kalojan, the youngest brother of Asen and Peter, as ruler of an enlarged Bulgaria (1197–1207). He himself had been a hostage in Constantinople, but he did not value Byzantine support: he turned to Rome, recognised papal supremacy, and was crowned by Archbishop Basil of Trnovo who had been consecrated by Cardinal Leo, the papal legate.

Thus Innocent III lost no opportunity for extending his authority in the Balkans at the request of princes who recognised the weakness of the Empire and were therefore ready to turn from Constantinople to Rome. But he was also anxious to effect the reunion of the two Churches by peaceful means and had corresponded with Alexius III on this subject. And he took the lead in directing a new crusade having Egypt as its immediate objective, though here events turned out other than he had planned.[1] Hostile Latin forces were eager to

---

[1] On the Fourth Crusade, see below: ch. VII.

take advantage of the obvious weakness of the Byzantine Empire, and control passed into the hands of the old Venetian Doge, Enrico Dandolo. During the twelfth century Venice had recognised the obvious reluctance of Byzantium to guarantee its commercial privileges in the Empire and had seen the dangerous growth of its rivals Genoa and Pisa. It was also aware of the intense hatred felt by the Greeks towards the Latins. At this moment the condition of the Empire presented an unrivalled opportunity. The reigning dynasty was ineffective and hopelessly divided amongst itself. The central authority was continually being undermined by separatism and by centrifugal forces. The Latin attack on Constantinople and its tragic outcome could have been no surprise to contemporaries.

CHAPTER VI

VENICE TO THE EVE OF THE FOURTH CRUSADE

Venetia was the name of a region long before it became the name of a city situated on a group of islands. The territorial integrity of the old Italian province of *Venetia et Histria* (*regio* XI of Italy as re-organised by Augustus), bounded as it was by the Adda and the Adriatic to west and east and by the Po and the eastern ranges of the Alps to the south and north, remained unaffected by the successive barbarian invasions of the fifth and early sixth centuries, and it was taken over intact in the course of the laborious Byzantine attempt at reconquest. But when the Lombards, who were more numerous and better organised than their barbarian predecessors, poured into Italy after 568 and spread east and west, they not merely put an end to the territorial unity of Italy; they broke up the old Venetian region, transforming it in a way that was both radical and permanent. Mainland Venetia became *Langobardia* and its former inhabitants, taking with them the old name of the province, went to live on the sandbanks and islands of the lagoons: here they began the work of drainage and cultivation and made permanent homes for themselves where hitherto there had only been the huts of fishermen or boatmen. Although still called *Venetia et Histria*, the process of migration had given the province a completely new character. Seriously reduced in size, it still clung firmly to the mainland on the east, where it embraced the Istrian peninsula, and, more precariously, on the west also, where it included areas of no great size in the territories Padua, Altino and Oderzo. Soon these too were to be engulfed by the irresistible Lombard advance, until in the end there remained only narrow strips of coast round Altino and Oderzo and round Ilario and Cavarzere: direct contact by land with the rest of Byzantine territory farther south was now severed, and the link with Istria became more and more tenuous until finally it too ceased to exist.

Despite these losses Venetia, with or without Istria, was still a province of the Byzantine Empire in the early seventh century, with the normal administrative organisation of such a province; this continued to be true after the loss in 639 of Oderzo, the last centre of Byzantine rule on the mainland. A *dux* or *magister militum* was the Byzantine official at the head of the administration; he was directly responsible to the Exarch of Ravenna, the representative of the Emperor in Byzantine Italy. Later tradition attempted to obliterate the memory of this dependence. Venice was supposed to have arisen by itself, independent of its neighbours and destined by God for a special purpose; Byzantium was forgotten. But such historical fantasies are rudely shattered by the simple yet eloquent language of one piece of rough stone. An inscription, dated 639, commemorates the building of the basilica of the Virgin, either at Torcello or at Cittanova, and gives the names of the political and administrative rulers of the province. The small church, for which a greater future was perhaps intended, arose, we are told, under the patronage of the Emperor Heraclius himself, at the command of the Exarch of Ravenna, Isaac, and through the endeavours of the *magister* Maurice, the local governor, who chose it as his last earthly resting-place.

The province, then, with its rulers and its administration, was Byzantine. When Oderzo in 639 fell to the Lombards the exiles in the lagoon willingly gave hospitality to the now fugitive government on an island to which was given the name of *Civitas nova*: the place was rebuilt and then received (in honour of the reigning Emperor) the name of *Civitas Heracliana*. But the exiles had brought with them to the lagoons not only the memory of their former homes but also the habits and manners of their ancestors which their first conquerors had respected and which their latest ones had not had time to alter. Their traditions were soundly Roman, and it was in this spirit—free from foreign influences, whether German or Byzantine—that the Venetians undertook the work of reconstruction on virgin soil, whither they had been forced by circumstances, long before the organs of civil and ecclesiastical government crossed from the mainland also. The basis of Venice's spiritual and material life was that popular *romanità* which had survived the collapse of the old aristocratic orders.

Churches, the symbols of the undying spirituality of the people, arose before there was an ecclesiastical hierarchy; the life of the civic community was re-established around its traditional representatives, the *tribuni*, thus pointing the way to the reorganisation of a properly constituted administration: and the foundations for the new institutions of civil and ecclesiastical government which duly emerged were thus laid by the people themselves, through their own effort and at their own desire. There can be no doubt that even through so many upheavals the forms proper to Byzantine provincial organisation were respected and that the authority of the *magister militum*, now based on Cittanova, had not been diminished; but between his office and that of the tribunes there existed, unrecognised, a gulf sufficient to explain how a later chronicler came to ignore the former and lay great stress on the latter.

Meanwhile the metropolitan ecclesiastical authority which had its seat at Grado had undergone a similar development in the process of withdrawing in the face of Lombard pressure. Paulinus, a bishop of Aquileia, had about the year 569 moved the treasures of his church to Grado, about six miles to the south, to keep them safe from the Lombards. When the threat passed he returned to his episcopal see, and several of his successors maintained their position there. In 579 Elias built the basilica of St Euphemia at Grado and held a synod to consecrate it at which the clergy of Aquileia reaffirmed its determined opposition to the decisions of the Fifth Oecumenical Council held at Constantinople in 553. The clergy of Aquileia protested against Rome's support of this Council. They were accused of rebellion and schism, and measures were taken against them with the aid of the secular arm. In 590 Pope Gregory I began the attack on the schismatic Severus, an attack which led to protests, and later to revolt in the area of Lombard occupation. Finally, there was a split between the 'Roman' party and the 'schismatics', and two rival metropolitans came into being, the 'Roman' Candidianus at Grado, and the 'schismatic' John at Aquileia, or rather Cormons.

These ecclesiastical divisions, which owed their origin to a delicate political situation and to the territorial division between Lombards and Byzantines, were to play their part in shaping many later events, and acted as a disturbing factor in the evolution of political life in this extreme corner of the Byzantine world. It was almost inevitable that it should happen, but it was only made irrevocable by the events which followed: the synod of ten 'Lombard' bishops which met at Marano in 591, and the intransigence of Gregory the Great who called on the secular arm to impose the creed of Constantinople on the 'schismatic' bishops (that is, the Metropolitan Severus himself and the bishops of Istria, who were brought to Ravenna as prisoners). Even the appeal and protest made at Marano, Severus' abjuration and the resistance of the majority of the clergy could do nothing to stop the process. The next vacancy, in 606 (or 607), led to the double election which confirmed the schism. Nor was the problem merely a religious one, for the political strife between Grado and Aquileia survived the conclusion of a religious peace at the synod of Pavia in 695. These events marked the beginnings of the age-long conflict between Venice and the mainland, which was to become serious after the definitive split between Istria and the area of the lagoons.

There were now two metropolitan sees, one situated (in theory at least) at Aquileia in the area of Lombard influence, with jurisdiction over the sees of the Venetian and Tridentine provinces, the other at Grado, with jurisdiction only over the bishoprics of Istria, until Istria fell to the Lombards in the time of Desiderius (middle of the eighth century) and later to the Franks.

It is difficult to say exactly when Istria and the province of Venetia became politically separate. It is possible that the military and territorial conditions which led to a separation *de facto* (brought about by the need to face a rapidly changing situation) may have existed as early as the late sixth century. At the time when the Lombard occupation of the area began there was already a great difference, politically, between Istria and Venetia, and the division was to be strengthened by ecclesiastical schism.

When external pressure gave a definitive frontier to the new province of Venetia, it was confined to the islands and *lidi* of the lagoons, except for a few very narrow strips of ground on the mainland. It was almost cut off from the rest of Byzantine territory both to north and south, and though subordinate to Byzantine authority it had already acquired certain elements peculiar to itself, the beginnings of that personality which was to characterise its development as a self-governing and sovereign power. Though it may be accepted that the belief in Venice's primitive autonomy was a later invention, and that her assumption of independence originated and developed in the same way as that of other provinces, it is none the less true that the final outcome of the process was entirely different.

The later chronicler John the Deacon says that the province on the lagoons existed independently under its own tribunes for a century and a half after the Lombard invasion (569), which is untrue. Such officials undeniably existed, but they were subordinate to the Byzantine authorities. The story of how such an institution gave way to the dogeship is equally untrue, and is the result of a curious manipulation of the sources. According to this version of events, after 150 years of liberty the exiles chose a doge to protect them against the Lombard menace; the doge then succeeded in restoring peace by making a treaty which established neighbourly relations with King Liutprand.

It is unnecessary to discuss here the disputes that have raged around this event, which used to be considered the very foundation of the independent dogeship. The *dux* Paulicius who appears on this occasion was not a native, nor was he the first of the series of Venetian doges: nor did his treaty with King Liutprand ever exist except in the distorted version of later writers. What the sources say is that the *dux* Paulicius and Marcellus the *magister militum* drew up a unilateral definition of the boundaries of Venice's territory on the mainland near Cittanova. This occurred in Liutprand's time, 712–39, and the Byzantine authorities marked their boundary with stone landmarks. Later the same frontier was accepted (again without any bilateral agreement) by the Lombard Aistulf. No doubt Paulicius and Marcellus were officials of the Byzantine government, and it is not difficult to identify the former with an Exarch of Ravenna of the same name and the latter with the provincial governor. It is natural to find these two officials thus associated in performing one of the most delicate of sovereign functions. They were living in the most crucial moment of Italian history when a general revolt of the local population had broken out against the Greek authorities on account of threats to apply the iconoclastic decrees. This rising was also the result of a long-standing hatred of the Byzantines; and the garrisons (which had been recruited locally) revolted and chose their own commanders. The Venetian armies played their part in this movement; the leader chosen was not Paulicius but Orso, who figures second or third in the late list of doges. Paulicius, who is first in this list, was Exarch of Ravenna, as has been said, and not *dux* of the Venetian province. He was put to death in 727 by the rebels who, when a general insurrection broke out in Italy, were aided by the Lombards.

The province of Venice, then, played its part in the revolt, which had been largely instigated by the Pope. Here as elsewhere the movement was quelled with much bloodshed after the defection of its own leaders, and Venice returned to her Byzantine obedience. In 741 the city even gave support and hospitality to the Exarch of Ravenna when temporary persecution by the Lombards drove him into exile.

The revolt, however, had not been in vain. Its tangible results were the development of local autonomy and the recognition of Venice's right to choose her own local governors or *duces*. These governors recognised the sovereignty of Byzantium and owed their powers to it, but they were chosen from the ranks of the local armies and in fact were often nominated by these armies without the consent of higher authority. From Orso's time onwards *duces* chosen illegally on the spot alternated with *magistri militum* sent from Ravenna. In this way control from Ravenna was progressively weakened, and as the power of local factions increased, so hatred grew between island and island and between family and family, often ending in civil war.

When the government of the Exarchate finally collapsed in 751 the province of Venice was, like the others, dominated by party faction. In 742 Malamocco had risen against Cittanova, the old seat of the provincial government, possibly because the Byzantine bureaucracy was still the dominant element at Cittanova. Malamocco chose as its leader a certain Deusdedit who embarked on a long struggle against the rival centre.

Is it possible that the real independence of Venice dates from this time? It may be so, but the question is one which at that time was perhaps not consciously formulated. It would be rash, too, to see in the struggles between island and island, and within each island, the effect of the opposed interests of landowners on the one hand and merchants and sailors on the other.

The collapse of the Exarchate centred in Ravenna and the severe contraction of Byzantine power in Italy made the relations between the central government and what remained of its Italian territory a difficult matter. The provincials were obliged to supply their own wants and regulate their everyday affairs independently; they were too far distant for effective control, and the process of disintegration was hastened by the claims and violence of local loyalties. Yet it would seem that all control was not abandoned, that the province did not become an independent entity. The outlying parts of the great Empire may have had to fend for themselves, but under the firm rule of the *dux* Maurice and his family (765–802)—after a brief period of disorganisation under Monegarius—we find the province of Venetia recognising the link with Byzantium and acting as a faithful subject. When the Lombards and Franks invaded Istria, Venice took a share in its defence. Later she opposed the agreements of Pavia and Pepin's donations whereby Byzantine territory was handed over to the Papacy under Frankish control, and it joined in the Byzantino-Lombard coalition against the Franks. The policy followed was a very cautious one, but it certainly showed that the province still felt itself part of the Byzantine family. Were other forces at work in the formulation of this policy? Venice, so poor materially yet so rich in promise, was destined to be the meeting-point in the struggle for Empire between two powers. Yet to see this struggle simply as the opposition of two fundamentally different civilisations, Byzantine and Franco-Germanic, is an oversimplification; for if the Franks found supporters among the population of the lagoons, this pro-Frankish party came of the same stock as its opponents and derived from the same traditions. Above all, it is important to realise that Venice was not merely an active participant in this great drama, but to some extent its involuntary author.

The rule of the Maurices, though at times violently opposed, lasted from 765 to 802. At first sight their policy appears to have been pro-Byzantine, opposed to local autonomy. But it may be doubted whether their cautious co-operation with Byzantine designs in the Adriatic, together with the existence of some Greek names among the ecclesiastical hierarchy, provides sufficient evidence to suggest an active pro-Byzantine policy. The situation was in fact more complicated. When the Maurices and their supporters began a policy of violent repression directed against their enemies, were they really being 'pro-Byzantine'? And were these enemies supporters or tools of the Franks, so that Venetian politics were subordinated to the interests of the greater powers? It is not easy to find answers to these questions. The war of Malamocco against Cittanova and Grado, the merciless destruction of these old centres, and the persecution of what were perhaps opposition groups, may have arisen from the existence of two great parties, supported or at least inspired by outside influences. But it is at least equally possible that the causes were domestic ones, such as the ambitions of rival families, or questions of jealously defended prerogative. It would be no safer to call Cittanova and Grado the centres of a pro-Frankish and anti-Byzantine movement than to suppose them the enemies of the dominant Maurician party.

The rivalry between Cittanova and Malamocco was a long-standing matter of insular and family jealousies. That between Grado and Malamocco was more recent and arose over disputed ecclesiastical authority. Sometime between 780 and 790 the first diocese in the lagoon came into being, at Olivolo, under the protection of the doge. It is not known whether this came about in response to genuine spiritual needs or in an attempt to provide a counterbalance to Grado. Nor is it known whether it was the cause or the effect of open conflict between Malamocco and Grado. In any case the event played a big part in what was destined to be a serious and extensive struggle.

The fact that the first bishops of Olivolo bore a Greek name, Christopher, is not sufficient to prove that Byzantium was responsible for the new foundation which was opposing Grado. The civil and ecclesiastical opponents of the party in power were brought together by their hostility to a common adversary and after their defeat all went into exile. But they had no common ideal; some, like Obelerius and Beatus, were merely anxious to overthrow the government and take over control, while Fortunatus, bishop of Grado, was fighting a battle in defence of his own ecclesiastical claims.

Meeting at first with defeat, the leaders of the opposition went into exile on the nearest part of the mainland to prepare for a new assault; this was a process which was destined to be repeated many times in Venetian history. Bishop Fortunatus' wanderings led him to the Frankish court, but his allies under Obelerius and Beatus remained near Venice in order to organise their revenge. Each party operated separately and in its own interests. There was no direct collaboration between them, and Bishop Fortunatus was not successful in obtaining aid from the Franks. As for the exiles on the Italian mainland, they secured no more than a benevolent toleration of their presence while they evolved their schemes for a rising which was to bring them to power. Each partner could rely only on his own sources of strength, within and outside Venice: the bishop on ecclesiastical solidarity and his own cunning, the political leaders on their companions in exile and on those of their faithful followers who had stayed behind.

The plans of these two parties came to fruition at the same time, but their actions were entirely uncoordinated, and in fact one of them met with much greater success than the other. Under the pressure of discontent at home, combined with a violent attack from without, the regime of the Maurices collapsed. Obelerius and Beatus returned triumphant, were acclaimed as liberators and the restorers of Venetian fortunes, and installed their followers in the leading offices of the state. The bishop met with much less success. He was unable to abolish the *fait accompli* of the bishopric of Olivolo, though the unpopular occupant of the see was removed; Fortunatus returned to Grado, but the new regime was distrustful of him.

A greater drama had begun in Rome with the coronation of Charlemagne at Christmas 800, and was only to end with the uncertain peace of 814, but the state of political crisis in Venice was by no means unusual, and can only be ascribed to these greater events by an arbitrary interpretation of the inadequate evidence available. It is possible that the exiled Venetians made use of the increasing tension between Franks and Byzantines which followed the imperial restoration of 800, while the suspicions, misunderstandings and struggles aroused by their intrigues may have served to complicate and intensify the situation elsewhere. But in the main the Venetian crisis of 800–10 was a matter of local interest and its connection with the larger struggle was tenuous and intermittent.

Byzantium was distant, and was incapable of defensive, still less of offensive, action in the area. The new Empire of the West, on the other hand, pressed insistently against the very frontier of Venice, and contacts with the neighbouring territory were essential to the city's existence. Under the continuous pressure of Frank and Slav the Adriatic territories sought compensation for their abandonment by Byzantium in co-operation with Frankish rule, rather than submission to the loss of their independence. When in 805 the dukes of Dalmatia and Venetia did homage to the Frankish Emperor they had not suddenly changed sides; they were merely attempting to protect their own interests in a situation where either of the two great powers might take action against what it regarded as territory subject to its opponent.

Unfortunately, the gesture was ill-timed and served only to increase the tension that had arisen. At Byzantium it was considered, rightly or wrongly, as an act of defiance which could not go unchallenged. The reaction of Byzantium was prompt. A Byzantine fleet (the first to appear for a very long time) came to the northern Adriatic with orders to restore the situation and to reaffirm Byzantine control on land and sea over this distant province which had never been intentionally abandoned.

In 807 a squadron under the admiral Nicetas passed along the Dalmatian coast and cast anchor in the Venetian lagoon. The Byzantine flag again flew in the Adriatic to affirm the unaltered rights of Constantinople over the province and its waters. The little Frankish flotilla based on Comacchio put up no opposition, and indeed there is no reason why it should have done so. The local rulers had done homage to the Franks purely to suit their own interests, not in anticipation of any schemes of Frankish conquest, and there is no reason to suppose that their act aroused great interest at the Frankish or Italian courts.

In view of the indifference of the Franks it was not difficult for Nicetas to bring the supposed rebels back to the Byzantine obedience. He reaffirmed the suzerainty of the East in the area and at the same time succeeded in coming to an 'amicable' agreement with the Frankish kingdom in Italy; this was intended as the prelude to a formal treaty which was to settle the main problem of the relations between the two Empires. The most important thing was to eliminate the factors that had poisoned good relations between the powers in a particularly disturbed frontier zone. Exiles had been, and still were, the greatest source of trouble. It was in the interest of both parties to put an end to their intrigues, for both had suffered from them. King Pepin, Charlemagne's eldest son, and Admiral Nicetas therefore gave mutual guarantees, the Byzantines not to leave the way open for Slav raids on the Frankish lands in Istria, the Franks to prevent the formation on their territory of any coalition aimed against the Byzantine provinces.

It is not known why this agreement, made at Ravenna, was not at once ratified, for in the same year a similar truce was made which assured peace in the Adriatic and the maintenance of the *status quo*. A firm agreement was not in the interests of all parties, however, and probably elements which felt that such an agreement threatened Venice's position as an arbiter succeeded in delaying it. The doges of Venetia saw in Nicetas' conduct a check on their freedom of action, and in the agreement of Ravenna a blow to their policy and ambitions. A peace which militated against their interests appeared to them intolerable and they did everything in their power to oppose it. When a Byzantine fleet under the patrician Paul returned to the upper Adriatic and the lagoons rather over a year later, the atmosphere had become much more difficult and possible sources of tension and misunderstanding were now manifold. The clever schemes of those who planned to destroy good relations as well as the ineffectiveness of Paul himself probably played their part in the events that followed. In any case Paul failed to act calmly in the face of artificially organised 'incidents' and allowed himself to be provoked into threatening both Franks and the local political leaders. They in turn opposed him and he was compelled to quit the Adriatic (809).

This inglorious episode had serious consequences. The area of the lagoons was again in an unsettled state and the Franks had now been antagonised. King Pepin was provoked by the unsuccessful attack on his naval base at Comacchio and was inclined to enter on an anti-Byzantine policy, while the Venetian doges now found themselves threatened by internal strife as well as by the danger from without. They sought a desperate remedy in this serious crisis and invited King Pepin to garrison the coast and occupy the province. In an evil hour for him he accepted.

In 810 Pepin undertook an ill-prepared expedition. He was unaware of the military and political difficulties and he relied on the vague and inconsistent promises that had been made to him. The result was failure and disgrace. The majority of the population fought for their independence against the invaders and won a resounding victory over them. Beatus and Obelerius, whose actions had led to the invasion, were not saved by a last-minute repentance. They were condemned to a life of exile, in which their only comfort was the fond hope of revenge.

The cost of this deliverance was heavy, but it was not paid in vain. The self-sacrifice and tenacity of the local inhabitants, with no outside help, had preserved their liberty. Only later did the Byzantines come on the scene to reap the benefit of what the Venetians had achieved. The danger of foreign domination had for once put an end to recriminations and even to legitimate grievances. The victims of persecution, who had fled from Cittanova, Equilo, Malamocco, Grado and other places, gathered on the uncultivated island of Rialto. Here they forgot their wrongs, undertook the defence of their country, and later set about repairing the material damage caused by the war and (what was equally serious) the moral harm done by a policy which had exposed Venice to much destruction and had almost deprived her of her liberty.

They believed that their task was still incomplete and they planned to attract more settlers and to build up new institutions capable of representing the whole population and not merely a selfish faction. Rialto was the obvious centre for such a task. Its position and its marked fertility (now utilised by its new inhabitants) made it a natural capital; so did the feeling of fraternity that had sprung up among a population which though of varied origin had gathered round the only really national ecclesiastical centre (Olivolo) and had shared a common experience. The exile of the men who had been responsible for so many troubles eradicated an important source of discord, while the removal of the government from Malamocco to Rialto helped to cancel out the sad memories of the past.[1]

After the liberation, a Byzantine representative, called Arsafius the *spatharius*, was sent to take a share in the new government, but his arrival made no substantial difference. Venetia was still a Byzantine province, but events had given it independence; the recent happenings had strengthened its autonomy and this could not now be taken away. Arsafius had come as an emissary of the Emperor to give official recognition to this state of affairs. He had also been entrusted with a wider mission. He was to try to achieve a general pacification, not merely an agreement on the status of Venetia. The events of the previous years had taught much to all who had played a part in them, directly or indirectly. The gravity of the crisis in Venetia had brought home to the Byzantine government the dangers inherent in a prolongation of the greater crisis which overshadowed the whole Mediterranean world.

After the fighting had ceased Arsafius went to Pavia to offer the hand of friendship to the defeated enemy and to resume the negotiations which had been so rashly broken off. The Frankish representative had been Pepin, the ruler of the former Lombard kingdom. Now Pepin was dead, and in any case Byzantium sought not merely an 'Italian peace' with a king but an 'imperial peace' with the Emperor himself. Whatever Arsafius' instructions may have been, he had no hesitation in crossing the Alps and going to the imperial court at Aachen, where he suggested to Charlemagne that formal negotiations should take place to put an end to the deadlock between the two Empires. The offer was accepted, discussions took place and in the spring of 811 an agreement was reached, and finally ratified in 814.[2] The results of Charlemagne's coronation were tacitly and implicitly

---

[1] On the episode of Pepin's attack and on Venetian origins cf. Constantine Porphyrogenitus, *De administrando imperio*, caps. 27–8, *DAI*, I, pp. 116–21 and II, pp. 91–3.

[2] On the chronology adopted here and throughout in this chapter see R. Cessi, *Venezia Ducale*, I (Venice, 1940, new edition in press; II is in preparation).

recognised. Each of the specific problems which had embittered relations between the two powers was settled in detail. A series of fortuitous events had concentrated the crisis in the area of the upper Adriatic, around the Dalmatian and Venetian provinces. The new agreement was based on that reached with Pepin, and its spirit was the same, but it was strengthened by additional clauses which dealt in detail with frontier problems, such as rights of transit, the question of extradition, and customs. Thus the factor that had done most to embitter feelings between the two Empires was removed, and henceforth normal relations were restored.

By the terms of this agreement the province of Venetia was guaranteed support against any external aggression and its highly prized rights over surrounding territory, which had often been threatened, were recognised. At the same time its maritime supremacy—for Venice had already begun her prosperous maritime career—was also recognised. The Franco-Byzantine agreements of 814 and of 824 had been brought about by Byzantium, under whose suzerainty the Venetian provinces would now be able to develop their resources on land and sea, secure from external attack.

Venice thus remained a Byzantine province, retaining the status which had brought her so many benefits in the past. There was no fear that she might lose her real autonomy. Rather was this strengthened by her position, for the distant government of Constantinople came to take less and less interest in the Adriatic, leaving its affairs more and more to the energies of the Italian population. In any case, Venice had the support of the new guarantees.

Outwardly the machinery of government was little changed by the removal of the ducal administration to Rialto and the presence of an official representative of Byzantium. This was in fact the last occasion on which Byzantium intervened solemnly in the affairs of Venice. There was something almost ostentatious about the nominal nature of its overlordship, yet beneath these superficialities the relationship between the two powers exerted a profound influence upon Venice and upon the development of her institutions.

The position of the doge had altered little. The Maurices and the Obelerii at Malamocco and the new dynasty of Partecipazi at Rialto were all Byzantine officials, and the doges were to remain so for a long time. They may even have received pay from Byzantium for in addition to their honorary titles (*consul, protospatharius, protoedrus* and so on) they drew a salary, the *roga magistratus* which was the sign of their link with the suzerain power. But more important than such symbols, which had lost all substantial importance, was the reappearance of that phenomenon which had brought so much tragedy to Venice, i.e. family factions. Once again Venice became the scene of plots and counter-plots. To some extent this was the work of figures from the past. Obelerius succeeded in escaping from enforced exile at Constantinople and in making a daring return to Venice, where he was favourably received by his last sympathisers at Malamocco. But at the first sign of opposition he was abandoned and left to his own devices; he paid for his daring with his life. His former associate Bishop Fortunatus fared no better. After intriguing with Franks and Byzantines, and betraying them both, he died miserably in exile, his appeals for clemency unheard.

A new poison had worked its way into the veins of Venice's political life. To the hatred of island against island was added the still more furious civil strife of family against family, and of one member of a family against another. These troubles were a far more serious menace to the first dynasty of Rialto than any pro-Byzantine sympathisers. Not even an event of the first importance in the spiritual life of the nation, the acquisition of the body of St Mark (828), could save the new regime from these internal troubles. This symbol of increasing national consciousness, which was destined to be the emblem of Venice's greatness, came to the city at a vital moment (the truth of the story of its theft from Alexandria is immaterial). Its possession played an important part in the struggle against the decision of the synod of Mantua (827), which had abolished the patriarchal authority of the See of Grado, placing Venice under the jurisdiction of Aquileia and thereby (perhaps unintentionally) threatening her independence. In this struggle Venice was led by the different generations of Partecipazi, Agnellus, Justinian and John. Though her claims naturally gave a national significance to the dispute, there was nothing anti-Byzantine in the aims of such leaders. But this new stage in the independence of a Venice torn by internal strife was reached at a time when Byzantine interest in the Adriatic had disappeared and a fresh set of problems was on the horizon.

The local agreements made with the Carolingian rulers were respected by the successors of the original signatories (which on one side meant the doges, as heirs to the Byzantine Emperor) and they guarded Venice against any threat from the mainland. Henceforth a greater danger had to be faced, the inundation of the Adriatic area by the tide of Slav invasion. In 840 and 841 Lothair I confirmed the previous agreements and thereafter the problem for Venice was the security of her sea routes, for the land ones were now safe. The expansion of her interests in the Adriatic and Mediterranean was being rapidly intensified under both the rival families of Partecipazi and Badoer, and the presence of the Slavs on the opposite shore was a greater danger than the troublesome raids of the Saracens. The Venetian merchant had already shown that he could overcome the difficulties that faced him. He was not overawed by the trials and surprises that he encountered in distant markets, but he had to be sure that he would be able to reach them and that he would not be cut off when he was there. This was the most important problem that Venice had to confront during the period of her great mercantile expansion in the ninth and tenth centuries.

Meanwhile internal conditions were far from peaceful. Venice was becoming a city, and islands which had once been deserted were now a great emporium swarming with people and with businesses of every size, but the tale of jealousy and party strife, of subtle plot and violent counter-plot, continued unchanged. In one sense this can be regarded as a necessary part of the political education of the Venetian people, for they thus learnt the need to play a bigger part in civic life. As the pace of this life quickened they came to realise that it could not be entrusted to one clique, one family or one individual, intent only on acquiring power which it had not the strength or resources to maintain. Fresh elements came into play to make good the failings of their predecessors and to round off their work, but the city needed stability and order as well. Certainly the factions gave birth to the great period of the Partecipazi, as well as Doge Peter (832–64) and Doge Orso (864–81), a time marked by considerable activity and progress and by the intelligent and benevolent policy of the government. But the danger of a conspiracy was a constant threat to such a regime and often impeded or put an end to its achievements. There came a time when it was essential to give stability to the organs of government, and this could best be done by going to the source of national life, the people themselves. Hitherto public affairs had been the plaything of chance and of intrigue between rival interests; the intention was that their direction should now be placed under a direct popular control.

In theory the people were supposed to give their approval to all decisions affecting the state, but too often their rights had been overruled by a small clique which through violent means assumed and exercised power in its own interests until overthrown by the secret machinations of its rivals. The unlimited personal control of the Doge and the growth of his despotic powers (for which there was no constitutional justification) as well as the decline of the tribunate, which had also become the monopoly of a few, were a hindrance to Venice's progress in the hard struggle for expansion. At the same time the Venetian Church had also become the monopoly of successive victorious factions. The hard-working Doge Orso I (864–81) attempted to remedy this situation by a series of reforms in the civil and ecclesiastical administration. The first step in the process of restricting the arbitary power of the government was the institution of judges, with judicial and consultative duties, as a check on the authority of the doge. The creation of five new bishoprics, Equilo, Caorle, Cittanova, Torcello and Malamocco (the story of their translation from former sees is a legend), served to free the spiritual government of Venice from the control of Grado, which had in the past threatened even her political independence.

Yet the roots of this crisis went deeper still, as Orso's successor John (881–8) discovered. Threatened by Slav pressure from without and by the political crisis within, John failed to maintain the continuity of the dogeship. In 887 a sudden popular rising put in his place Peter Candiano; John was allowed to remain as nominal co-regent, but actual power lay with the new doge. As the people's choice, Peter Candiano was faced with the double task of restoring political order at home and defending the interests of Venice abroad. The work of checking the Slav advance was extremely formidable. Peter Candiano met his death on the battlefield (887) before he had been able to achieve much, yet he had had time to contribute to the solution of Venice's two great problems; he struck a telling, though not a decisive, blow against the Slavs, and he strengthened the popular element in the Venetian constitution by introducing electoral methods in the choice of the doge. This conquest was not always respected, but the ground gained could never be entirely lost.

After Peter Candiano's sudden and premature death the people elected as his successor Peter Tribuno (888–920). He it was who raised the cradle of Venice's greatness to the rank of a city, the *civitas Venetiarum*. Henceforward this city was Venice in name and fact, the symbol of her unity and the guardian of her national spirit. Venetian patriotism was concentrated around the name of St Mark, whose cult was organised with loving care in the very heart of the ducal palace. Thus Venice had emerged from her minority to become a sovereign power, even if her theoretical subordination to the Eastern Empire had not yet officially ended. It is not clear whether the frequent demands of Constantinople for help against the Saracens were orders to a subject power or appeals to a friendly one. The Venetians responded, but we cannot tell what was the official opinion of either power with regard to their relations. In practice Venetian independence was now complete in domestic politics and almost complete in external affairs.

Henceforward the city presents a spectacle of ceaseless activity. There is a period of apparent decadence in public life in the early decades of the tenth century when the honest but rather colourless Orso II (912–32) succeeded the vigorous Peter Tribuno. Political apathy was to lead to a renewal of the factions, with their plots and histories of family revenge and the factions in their turn to a new series of dictatorships. Such episodes were by now contrary to the traditions as well as to the interests of Venice, but the great work of commercial advance continued without interruption.

It is questionable whether the government of the later Candiani doges was a move towards monarchical absolutism and a reaction against the popular tendencies represented by the first Candiano doge half a century before. The parallel between the rise of the *signorie* elsewhere in Europe and the policy of the tenth-century Candiani and their successors, the Orseoli, is hardly a convincing one. The new situation should rather be ascribed to a resurgence of the old factions, intensified now by increasing self-consciousness and by external influences, for the Orseoli showed themselves as willing to intrigue with outside forces in the East as the Candiani had been with those of the West. It was not simply a question of personal ambitions, for the strife between the family confederacies took on new forms as it came to draw its sustenance from a far wider sphere.

The dogeship of Peter Badoer (930–9) was followed by the harsh struggle between father and son (the third and fourth of the line) in the Candiano family. Peter (IV)'s exile was the result of family factions and interests rather than political issues, but external forces became involved in the crisis and it thus acquired wider political significance. In the event, this exile proved to be most influential in the important and possibly unpremeditated changes during the three decades 939–72. When Peter left Venice he came into contact with a way of life quite different from the simplicity of his homeland. He became convinced that new methods of rule could prevail over the instability of Venice's constitution and at the same time make life there more polished and attractive.

Thus the Peter IV who returned on the death of his father was inspired by quite different motives from those of the men who recalled him. By fighting on behalf of others when in exile he had won the gratitude of his hosts and this encouraged him in his determination to transform the austerity of the Venetian court. He had ambitious visions of greatness and conquest, and he sought alliances on the mainland, judging such links to be more profitable than oriental ones. After wedding Waldrada, a niece by marriage of Otto I and a product of the cultivated feudal society that he so greatly admired, he began to realise how much hostility had been aroused by his innovations. His reaction to this was to convert his court into a fortress and surround himself with foreign mercenaries of the type he had known during his exile. At the same time his unwise policy of power and aggrandisement involved him in repressive and extortionate measures which increased his unpopularity. He failed to understand the reality of the dangers in which his actions involved him. He waited until the crisis broke, then found that his supposedly faithful bodyguard had deserted him. By the time that he had repented, coming on bended knee to ask forgiveness for himself, for his evil genius of a wife, and their child, it was too late. His strongly fortified palace was burnt down by the populace, and he himself was murdered by them.

A new line of doges now began with Peter Orseolo (976–8), whose mild and religious character typified the common desire to re-establish an atmosphere of serenity and concord. But the vital importance of maintaining internal harmony was not yet sufficiently appreciated. Faction broke out again yet more strongly, both within the city and outside. A party of exiles came into being, headed by another Candiano, Vitale, Patriarch of Grado. This party sought revenge through an alliance with the internal and external enemies of the popular party. For the first time since the signature of the Carolingian agreement, imperial assistance was solicited against Venice. The prudence both of the Emperor Otto II and the doge prevented an open conflict from breaking out, but Orseolo's temperate firmness and good humour were inadequate to stamp out the recurrent disease of faction. A man of great piety, his election to the dogeship seems at first to have been very popular. Opposition, however, soon developed, and sought to attain his removal from office by means which, if ingenious, were certainly unscrupulous. Twice an obscure monk, the abbot of St Michael of Cusa in Aquitaine, was used to persuade the doge to abandon worldly cares and yield to his religious inclinations. Faced with the choice between his duty towards his fellow-citizens and the scruples roused by the man of God, Orseolo for a long time stood firm, then finally gave up the struggle and disappeared (1 September 978). It is an open question whether his abdication was really prompted by conscience or by his inability to stand the relentless pressure exerted on him from so many quarters, but at least it is clear that Orseolo's disappearance put an end to the process of restoration and opened the gates of Venice to the party of exile.

Whether or not they were allies of the Candiani, Orseolo's successors, the little-known Vitale Candiano (978–9) and Tribuno Menio (979–91), attempted to resolve the crisis by granting a generous amnesty. The leaders in the bloody events of 976 were pardoned and allowed to return to Venice. Yet this generous act was not enough to restore peace. The factions broke out again under new names; this time the parties were Morosini and Colopini, and once again Venice's mercantile expansion was hindered by domestic war. Deaths, mourning, tears and exile: the tragic cycle continued. Nor was the subtle Tribuno Menio the right man to put an end to Venice's troubles, for his dexterous manœuvring between the rival parties finally made him the enemy of both. Money rather than power was his passion, and this led him to follow a policy which neglected the city's vital interests and made him enemies among those who suffered most by this neglect. In the end he too paid the penalty of his errors, as so many of his predecessors had done; the last days of his life were spent in the silence of a monastery.

The first Orseolo's attempt at reconstruction had ended in failure, while his successor's programme of conciliation led to a worsening of the political and even the economic situation. Two great issues were at stake, Venice's relations with the Ottonian emperors in the West, and her position in the Mediterranean; in particular her situation *vis-à-vis* Constantinople had been dangerously compromised by the policy of Tribuno Menio. At home Tribuno had attempted to play off one faction against the other until both turned against him together. His foreign policy was similar, for he first proposed that Venice should submit to the Western Empire on humiliating terms, then, when he found himself faced by the prospect of an imperial onslaught (which was prevented only by Otto II's death in 983) and a revolt of his exiled enemies, he solicited intervention from the Eastern Empire by offering to renew the old ties of Byzantine overlordship. In both cases he had sacrificed the city's most vital interests. His intrigues came to nothing, but the suspicions that they aroused worsened Venice's internal situation and helped to precipitate a crisis.

The second Orseolo, Peter (991–1008), the heir to his father's tradition, attempted to meet this crisis by modifying the family programme in the light of the experience gained in his father's time. The versatility of the new doge and his skill as a negotiator combined with an improvement in internal affairs to produce an atmosphere in which a satisfactory agreement could be reached with the Western Empire (992); Venice's sovereignty could no longer be in question, the fear of intervention in her affairs was removed, and old grievances might now be forgotten. The same year saw an agreement with the Eastern Empire which recognised Venice's privileged position in trade with Byzantium and omitted any explicit suggestion that Venice was still a subject power.

These agreements both strengthened the constitutional position of the doge and served to safeguard Venice's mercantile activity on the continent of Europe and in the Mediterranean. Amalfi and the Apulian ports were losing ground to her in the Mediterranean and she was even assuming a share of the functions of the Byzantine navy. Moreover, she now had guarantees which gave her freedom to develop her trade with the Saracen states as well as with Byzantium.

There remained the problem of the Adriatic, where Slav pressure was still serious, though the periodic Islamic raids had no lasting results. Peter (Trasdominico), Orso I, Peter I Candiano, Orso II, Peter II and III Candiano had all tackled the Slav question, some by diplomatic and some by military methods, but it remained unsolved. In the last years of the tenth century the situation grew worse through the clash of Slav and Venetian expansion in Istria and Dalmatia. Agreements made in 932 and 933 had given Venice a position of preponderance in Istria, which was a necessary prelude to direct rule, while in Dalmatia extensive trading connections and much immigration had confirmed Venetian control over local raw materials and secured the sea-route. The Slavs were already drawing tribute from parts of Dalmatia which were still politically autonomous, and they were now hoping to extend this authority to Venetian subjects resident in Dalmatia. Hitherto the appeals of natives and Venetian citizens had only moved the doges to diplomatic action. Now military force took the place of threats; Doge Orseolo decided to meet violence with violence.

In 1000 Peter II Orseolo organised an expeditionary force which was to bar the road to further Slav expansion and at the same time alter fundamentally the balance of power in the Adriatic. The Slavs were driven out of much of the territory they had overrun and the payment of tribute was abolished. A number of Dalmatian towns and islands (Ossero, Veglia, Arbe, Pasman, Zara, Traù, Curzola and Lagosta) were liberated and a new epoch began in their history. It is not clear whether the act of homage performed by their representatives to the doge was regarded as a submission to the Venetian government and justified the doge's addition to his official title of the words *dux Dalmatie*. The terms of the Dalmatian *promissiones* were not those of a real submission, for the juridical status of the cities remained unchanged; their domestic affairs were unaffected and their independence was not curtailed. The relations between Venice and these cities were determined by the offer of *fidelitas* in exchange for a promise of protection; other Adriatic cities had sworn the same oath in return for a promise to defend their liberties, and their relationship was not one of subjection. There is no evidence for the statement (which has sometimes been made) that the doge acted in Dalmatia as a subject and agent of the Eastern Empire and on behalf of the interests not of Venice but Byzantium. The name of the Emperor was officially honoured and respected, but he was not obeyed, for he never gave any orders. It was normal to ignore the existence of any link with Byzantium in the past as well as the present; this was true both of inner political circles and public opinion, and its consequences may be seen in the confident but incorrect version of Venetian history given by John the Deacon.

Venice's Dalmatian triumphs had an influence on her foreign relations, and especially on those with the Western Empire. Mystery envelops the secret meeting between Peter II Orseolo and Otto III in the ducal palace (1001), which had been skilfully prepared by John the Deacon in the face of much fear and suspicion. It is clear, however, that the meeting marks the beginning of a new era in the relations between the two powers; a lasting settlement was reached, based on the mutual recognition of spheres of influence.

This was Peter II Orseolo's great achievement; his policy had given new confidence to Venice in all her activities. Yet his success had gone to his head and was to have consequences which overshadowed his triumphs. Just as the last Candiano had been seduced by the glittering temptations of luxury, so Orseolo tired of a virtuous career and exchanged it for the vanities of excessive worldliness. Whereas Candiano had been charmed by the customs of the western courts, Orseolo was ensnared by the sumptuosity of the orient; he chose a wife whose refined manners were those of Constantinople, not of feudal society. The results were the same. The Venetians were opposed to luxury in dress, food, celebrations and ornaments, and in both cases a different way of living served to estrange the ruler from the ideas and ideals of his subjects. In the eyes of his countrymen the 'father of his country' became a tyrant, a stranger and an enemy in his own land. Such a change might have been a prelude to catastrophe, but thanks to his great achievements in the past Orseolo II was spared the grim fate that had befallen so many of his predecessors.

Otto Orseolo was expelled in 1022 as the result of a rising, and Poppo of Treffen, the rapacious Patriarch of Aquileia, realised that this was his opportunity to emerge from his den and to seize the See of Grado with its revenues, a prize which he had long coveted. He relied upon the approval of Rome, which was refused in 1024 but was granted in 1027 by two successive synods, with the consent of John XIX and the Emperor Conrad II. On a previous occasion internal concord had been miraculously restored by a threat from without, and the former government had returned. This time the government was too weak, but the demagogic regime of Domenico Flabianico and Domenico Barbolano Centranico (with the latter as a puppet doge) was unable to find a solution to the crisis. The Patriarch of Aquileia failed to suppress the metropolitan see of Grado but the old Patriarch of Grado, Orso Orseolo, failed equally to make the brief period of his restoration the occasion of an Orseolo revival. The dynasty came to an end and the dogeship was occupied by the representative of a new generation, Domenico Flabianico.

It has been suggested that Flabianico's accession to the dogeship (1032) closed an era of servitude (under the Orseolo coterie) and began an era of liberty. Certainly there was a change, but it was less radical than such an interpretation would imply. The assertion that a new constitution and a new social structure were introduced to replace an outworn system is a great exaggeration. Flabianico's 'reform' consisted in putting into practice the representative functions of the popular assembly and the elective system in the choice of the doge; both of these had existed in principle for a century, though they had not been effective. Now that these changes were respected the practice whereby the doge co-opted a co-regent came to an end. This had strengthened the system of family parties and retinues which itself had made the government of Venice a quasi-tyrannical or monarchical regime subordinated to the rule of a dynasty. Henceforward the wishes of the people were effective and this meant that the sovereign powers of the assembly were reaffirmed; for this no new legislation was required.

It was the great merit of Flabianico and succeeding doges that they used what was good in the work of their predecessors while eliminating what was harmful. Through their labours the constitution was moulded and the nation formed. In the description of Venice given by Domenico Tino (1072) we find the people in possession of the sovereign power within the state.

The doge as the executive representative of the popular will was also the guardian of Venetian autonomy, and under Flabianico (1032–43) and Domenico Contarini (1043–70) Venice had to face a new series of external probems which tended to involve her in the great struggle between Rome, Byzantium and the Western Empire. The trouble over the Patriarchate of Grado did not end on the death of the Patriarch Poppo, indeed it became more serious. The Patriarch of Aquileia's claims to metropolitan status, put forward at synods convened in 1044 and 1053, had aroused the opposition of the Emperor and the Roman Curia. The situation was further complicated by the growing reform movement in the Western Church. As a monk, Hildebrand had defended the authority of the doges against their powerful opponents; but when he became Pope as Gregory VII his attitude altered. He still praised the liberty of Venice and likened it to that of ancient Rome, but he now opposed the very Venetian rights that he had previously advocated. There were three reasons for this change. The Patriarch of Grado was a supporter of the Hildebrandine programme of reform, and Venice was said to have flouted his authority; Venice's intervention in Dalmatia was also believed to be contrary to papal interests; and finally, Venice was supposed to have been sympathetic to Henry IV during the period of his excommunication.

The papal accusations against Venice were without foundation. In actual fact Venetian policy at this time was determined by her vigilant hostility to Norman expansion in the Adriatic, both in Dalmatia and at the expense of Byzantium. As the guardian of his people's interests Domenico Silvo (1070–84) had to remain neutral between Hildebrand and Henry IV, but he could not afford to see the Normans in Dalmatia (whence he expelled Count Ami) nor on the Greek coast. When Robert Guiscard invaded Albania and Epirus (1082–5), Venice immediately allied herself with the Emperor Alexius in the bitter struggle against the Normans.[1] From the fierce battle of Dyrrachium to the great victory won off Corfu, Venice had to bear the brunt of the conflict, and her efforts were repaid by a Byzantine guarantee securing all the markets that she needed on imperial territory, in the Adriatic, the Aegean, and the Sea of Marmora. One has only to compare the terms of the chrysobull of 1082 with that of 992 to realise the extent of Venetian expansion in the Mediterranean and the East in less than a century. The outward signs of this expansion (such as the doge's assumption of the title of *dux Dalmatiae et Chroatiae*) were a recognition not of Venetian claims but of a completely altered situation.

Urban II's call to Christendom to deliver the Holy Land (1095) at first had little effect on the Venetians, for they were intent on the defence of their interests in Dalmatia, where, the Slav menace being over, they were now threatened by the Magyars, and on the consolidation of their pre-eminence in the East. Venice played a cautious and tardy part in the First Crusade; she would commit herself to no rash schemes in Syria. Under the doges Vitale Michiel, Ordelaffo Faliero and Domenico Michiel, her major preoccupation was the safeguarding of her interests in Dalmatia against rising national feeling and growing Magyar opposition and in the Mediterranean against the competition of Pisa and Genoa and temporary Byzantine hostility at the beginning of the reign of John II (1118–26). Ordelaffo Faliero

[1] See also above: ch. v.

was not entirely successful in repressing the Dalmatian revolt (1115), but he left to his successor, Domenico Michiel, an improved situation in the Adriatic. In consequence Michiel could deal successfully with Venice's problems in the Mediterranean. The emporium of the Rialto had been rebuilt in 1099 and an ever greater volume of trade flowed into it now that military successes had assured Venice's enjoyment of the new privileges granted her, in Syria (1124) and in the Byzantine Empire (1126).

The city's military enterprises had the backing of popular support at home. Her people, who had accomplished so much, now played their part in the discussion of public affairs which affected their own future. The *patria* was too vague a nucleus for their loyalty, and they felt the need for some more definite institutions to serve as a focus for their patriotic instincts. Hence, around the middle of the twelfth century, the first representative bodies began to emerge from the popular assembly. As more political and administrative organs came into existence, Venice became a *Comune*, and the arbitrary powers of the doge were abolished and the authority of the popular assembly curtailed.

In 1143 Peter Polani instituted a council, the *Consilium sapientium*, with delegative, consultative and deliberative powers. This small reform was the beginning of wide constitutional and administrative changes. In the next half-century Venice's internal organisation altered fundamentally in the face of great external problems. It was a time too of spectacular increase in private activities, and Venice's new institutions had to face an entirely new situation.

Venice needed to possess political organs capable of regulating her vast interests by land and sea. Moreover, she could not afford to hold aloof from the extensive acquisition of territory and markets by the western powers in the Mediterranean, attracted as they often were by greed and ambition rather than by religious motives. The hostilities between Byzantium and the Sicilian Norman kingdom, and the later friction between the Empires of East and West in the reign of Manuel I afforded to the city opportunities of enlarging her power and influence that the doges could hardly be expected to ignore.

Before the imperial crisis became serious, Venice played a part in its prelude, the anti-Norman coalition of 1147–8. Thereafter she was poised uneasily between Constantinople and Aachen, hardly an ally of the latter, but suspicious of the former's obviously hostile attitude. Byzantine support of Venice's rivals in the Adriatic and Tyrrhenian, such as Ancona and Genoa, and her open hostility to Venetian traders resident at Constantinople, were the most frequent sources of discord. Another factor that cannot have been without influence was the development of municipal liberty in the towns of the Italian mainland, the result of economic expansion and a new political spirit.

The republic had its setbacks. Barbarossa showed no gratitude for the aid that the doge had voluntarily offered him, while Byzantine anger at this offer showed itself in the fierce attack on Venetians at Constantinople and indeed throughout the Empire which occurred in 1171. Even Venice's masterly negotiation of a satisfactory peace to end the bloody Italian conflict (1177) seems to have earned her no thanks from the newly arisen communes. Whatever the price might be, the doge had no alternative but to intervene when Venice's interests were at stake. Problems arose in plenty. The city encountered trading difficulties on foreign markets or on the mainland. Routes by land, sea or river were blocked. Her merchants in the East were ill-treated and a rash punitive expedition organised by an incautious doge, Vitale Michiel, met with a humiliating defeat (1171). The atmosphere at Constantinople grew increasingly oppressive, due partly to the pretensions of the huge Latin colonies in the city (whose inhabitants numbered some 80,000), partly to the jealousy and intrigues of the other rival republics of Genoa and Pisa.

The situation was not a happy one. Certainly the government had been much strengthened by the elaboration of new constitutional forms. A *Maggior Consiglio* of thirty-five and a *Minor Consiglio* of three, with six councillors, had emerged from the old *Consilium sapientium*, and a large number of new offices had come into being to regulate and control Venice's multifarious activities at home and abroad. The work of legal codification was just beginning; the first regulations (*promissiones*), collected volumes of jurisprudence (the *ratio de lege Romana* and *iudicia*) and statutes (Dandolo's *statutum parvum*) had all been issued. Sebastiano Ziani had improved Venice's political and constitutional organisation, while Enrico Dandolo had revised her economic and mercantile institutions and issued the first Venetian coins.

Yet bad relations with Byzantium continued as a constant problem after the events of 1171. Michiel paid for his mistakes with his life, but his successor Sebastiano Ziani, for all his skill in diplomacy, could not improve things. There was so much in the situation that tended to make for conflict, however moderate the policy followed by the two sides. In particular the presence of a large and powerful body of foreigners at Constantinople was a source of continual discord, and the Byzantines bitterly resented the privileged position which the Venetian merchants enjoyed in the Empire. Friction in Constantinople flared up again in a massacre of the Latins in 1182, though Andronicus I Comnenus appears to have made some attempt to conciliate Venice. The Angeli, who succeeded Andronicus in 1185, also tried to ameliorate the situation, but the pressure of factors making for conflict was too much for them. But solemn and repeated promises and highly favourable terms were not enough to protect aliens who were hated for their supposed arrogance and greed. The signature of Alexius III Angelus (1198) was no better guarantee of security than that of his deposed brother Isaac. In fact the increasingly advantageous terms granted had the opposite effect and tended to exasperate Byzantine public opinion, which blamed this endless crisis at Constantinople entirely on the shameless avarice of the foreign traders. The Venetians, as the richest, largest, most powerful (and therefore perhaps the most arrogant) of these foreign colonies, were the most hated of all.

It was then not surprising that at the beginning of the next century under Venetian inspiration the Fourth Crusade was diverted to Constantinople. The crusaders put forward the pretext of restoring the deposed Angeli and punishing the usurper Alexius III Angelus. But behind this intervention in the domestic quarrels of the Byzantines, the Franks and Venetians regarded themselves as the defenders of the economic interests of the West, now seriously threatened by the collapse of Christian rule in Syria. The Fourth Crusade, summoned to redeem the Holy Land, was led by an inevitable chain of events to Constantinople, and thus inaugurated a new epoch in the history of the Mediterranean.

CHAPTER VII

THE FOURTH CRUSADE AND THE GREEK AND LATIN EMPIRES, 1204-61

In April 1195 the Emperor Isaac II was blinded and thrown into prison with his young son by his brother Alexius, who ascended the throne as Alexius III. The reign of Isaac II had not been enlightened; that of Alexius III was disastrous; and the enemies of Byzantium saw various ways to profit from the declining authority and prestige of the Empire. In Bulgaria the revolt that had broken out under Isaac II became more than a mere nationalist uprising under the powerful leadership of Kalojan, who took control in 1197. Kalojan, like his predecessor Symeon in the tenth century, conceived of a Bulgarian Empire which would absorb the universal Empire ruled from Constantinople. In Serbia too Byzantine influence ceased to count for much. Stephen II Nemanja, who came to the throne in 1196, divorced his wife Eudocia, a daughter of Alexius III, and looked for allies elsewhere. It is significant that both Kalojan and Nemanja sought ratification of their sovereignty not from Constantinople but from Rome.

In the western world, when Alexius III came to the throne, the most dangerous enemies of Byzantium were Venice and the German Emperor Henry VI. Henry had inherited from his father the dream of a universal Empire, and from the Norman rulers of Sicily the ambition to conquer Constantinople. He died in 1197, but he bequeathed his ideas to his brother Philip of Swabia, who had married Irene, a daughter of the deposed Emperor Isaac II. Philip's interest in the affairs of Byzantium was enhanced by the desire to right the wrong done to his father-in-law. But his hands were tied by the activities of his rival, Otto of Brunswick.

The interests of Venice in the Byzantine world did not depend upon imperial dreams or family ties, but upon the hard facts of commerce. For over a century Venetian merchants had enjoyed special trade concessions in Constantinople and the chief ports of the Empire. It was an arrangement that the Emperors and their subjects found increasingly irksome, and there were ugly incidents between Greeks and foreigners in the capital and elsewhere. From time to time the Emperors had tried to break what had become a stranglehold on their trade by granting similar concessions to the merchants of Genoa and Pisa. But such measures only deepened the mistrust of the Venetians. The Doge of Venice at the turn of the twelfth century was Enrico Dandolo. He was blind and, at the most conservative estimate, over eighty. But age had added to the wealth of his experience rather than sapped his vitality; and blindness had merely sharpened his insight. He was convinced that the only sure way of protecting the interests of the Republic would be to place the Byzantine Empire under Venetian management.

In February 1198 Innocent III was enthroned as Pope. The idea of a new crusade was dear to his heart. If properly organised it would help to give the Christian world a fresh sense of purpose and unite it in obedience to the supreme pontiff. One of his first acts as Pope, in August 1198, was to instruct his clergy to preach the crusade for the recovery of Jerusalem. The kings of France and England were busy with their own affairs, and Germany was distracted by civil war between Philip and Otto. But in France the emotions of men were fired by the eloquence of an itinerant preacher, Fulk of Neuilly, whom Innocent had commissioned to preach the Cross; and their resolve was strengthened by the offer of plenary indulgences made by a crusading cardinal from the Curia. In November 1199, at his castle at Écry on the Aisne, Count Tibald of Champagne held a tournament.[1] Among the many guests were Count Louis of Blois, Geoffrey of Villehardouin, Marshal of Champagne, and his nephew. In a great outburst of enthusiasm the whole company took the Cross. The Fourth Crusade was inaugurated. Geoffrey of Villehardouin was one of the few then present who followed the movement to its bitter end; and his account remains, for all its ambiguities, the most coherent version of how it all took place. Fulk of Neuilly continued the good work in other parts of France, and the Abbot Martin of Pairis in Germany. The enthusiasm spread. In February 1200 the Cross was taken at Bruges by Tibald's brother-in-law, Baldwin IX of Hainault, Count of Flanders, by Henry his brother, and by a host of others. It was agreed that the leader of the Crusade should be Tibald of Champagne, a choice acceptable to Innocent III.

There were many arrangements to be made before the crusaders could fulfil their vows. In the following months the leading counts and barons held several meetings to debate the strategy of their campaign. They decided to make first for Egypt rather than Palestine, in the hope of outflanking the Saracens; and six envoys were appointed to go to Venice to negotiate the hire of troopships. The

---

[1] A different chronology of these events has been suggested by E. John, 'A note on the preliminaries of the Fourth Crusade', *B*, XXVIII (1958), 95–103.

Venetians were hard bargainers, but there was no alternative. The overland route to the East was too hazardous, and the crusaders had almost no ships of their own. The fact that they were intent on invading Egypt was unfortunate, for Venice had hopes of negotiating a trade agreement with the Sultan's viceroy in Cairo. But the Venetians were more cynical than the Franks. There was profit to be made out of the transaction; and once the contract had been signed the object of the expedition might be open to reconsideration.

In April 1201 Geoffrey of Villehardouin, on behalf of the crusaders, signed an agreement with the Doge Dandolo. For the sum of 94,000 silver marks Venice contracted to supply ships and provisions for an estimated total of 4500 knights with their horses, 9000 esquires and 20,000 infantry. The fleet would be ready to sail from Venice by 29 June 1202; and, 'for the love of God', the Doge promised to supplement it with fifty galleys, on condition that Venice should have the right to one half of any conquests made by the crusaders. A first instalment of at least 2000 marks was paid to the Doge; the contract was ratified by the Pope; and Villehardouin with his colleagues returned to Champagne.

They arrived to find Count Tibald mortally ill. He died soon after, and the crusade was suddenly without a leader. After some deliberations the barons decided, on the proposal of Villehardouin, to appoint as Tibald's successor Boniface, Marquis of Montferrat. Boniface was invited to Soissons, and there accepted the leadership of the Fourth Crusade with a readiness which suggests that the invitation had not been entirely unforeseen. From many points of view he was an admirable candidate. His family had been closely connected with the fortunes of the Latin kingdom of Jerusalem, which gave him a special prestige in the eyes of the crusaders; and, though it may not have seemed particularly relevant to the object of the crusade at the time, his family connections with Byzantium were equally strong. His brother Renier had married a daughter of the Emperor Manuel, and had received the title of Caesar and an estate, or as it was called in western sources a 'kingdom', in Thessalonica. Conrad, another of his brothers, had also married into the Byzantine imperial family and been honoured at court. Both brothers, however, had been treated with the perfidy which, in western eyes, was characteristic of the Greeks. Conrad had fled to Syria; Renier had been murdered. Boniface therefore had cause for resentment against the Byzantines, which might in some measure be satisfied if he could reclaim his brother's property in Thessalonica. Such considerations may not have been in the forefront of his mind when the Cross was fixed to his shoulder by Fulk of Neuilly at Soissons in September 1201.

But he left France almost at once to pay his respects to his friend and suzerain Philip of Swabia, who had rather more compelling reasons for laying the Byzantine Empire under obligation to the West.

Thus at the outset there were three men concerned with the fate of the crusade, Philip, Boniface and the Doge Dandolo, who were as much interested in Byzantium as they were in the Holy Land. But it was the Doge whose motives were the most clear-cut, calculated, and, in the circumstances, practicable. In the interminable controversy over the diversion of the Fourth Crusade, many have doubted the ulterior motives of Philip of Swabia, of Boniface of Montferrat, and of Innocent III. But few have tried to exonerate the Venetians. At worst the Doge of Venice stands out as the villain of the piece; at best as the only realist in a tale of confused aims and misdirected ideals.

The appointment of Boniface as leader of the crusade was not welcomed by Innocent III. Boniface, though a model of the chivalrous virtues, was not noted for his piety; and his friendship with Philip of Swabia was most undesirable. When he heard that Boniface was spending the winter of 1201 with Philip, the Pope must have felt that the arrangements for his crusade were slipping from his grasp. His suspicions must have been further aroused when Boniface and Philip were joined by a third party. For it was during this lull before the storm that the young Alexius Angelus, son of the dethroned Emperor Isaac II, arrived in western Europe. He had been released from prison to accompany his uncle, Alexius III, on a campaign against the rebel Manuel Camytzes, who had taken sides with the Bulgarians. He escaped from the Emperor's camp, boarded a ship from Pisa which was anchored in the Sea of Marmora, and was carried to Ancona, hoping to find support in the West for the restoration of his father Isaac. After an unsatisfactory interview with Innocent III, he went on to see his sister Irene, the wife of Philip of Swabia. On his journey north through Italy he stopped at Verona, and met there a contingent of crusaders on their way to the assembly-point at Venice. It was then that the idea seems first to have entered his mind that the Fourth Crusade might be of service to him; and his arrival in Germany at a time when the leader of the crusade was plotting its course at Philip's court opened up new possibilities.

The main body of the crusade began to converge on Venice after Easter 1202, and by June they were ready to embark. But they could not sail until the Venetians had been paid for the hire of their ships; and though the leaders of the army set a good example by turning in all their gold and silver plate, the sum of 34,000 marks had still to be found. In these circumstances the Doge suggested that, since the crusaders had put the Republic to so much trouble, they might be willing to perform a service for him by capturing the port of Zara on the Dalmatian coast, which the king of Hungary had appropriated some years before. If they agreed he would postpone settlement of their debt, and the crusade might then go on its way. Some dissented from this shabby arrangement. But the expedition as a whole was at the mercy of the Venetians; and the crusaders, who had been cooped up on an island in the lagoons, welcomed a move in any direction. In September 1202 Dandolo ostentatiously took the Cross in St Mark's; in November the fleet sailed for Zara; and after a fierce assault the city surrendered. Dandolo then informed the leading knights that it was too late in the year to continue their voyage. They would do better to wait at Zara until the spring.

The sack of Zara, which he had expressly forbidden as soon as he heard of the project, confirmed Innocent's fears that the management of the Fourth Crusade was now beyond his control. He excommunicated all those who had defied his orders. Boniface, however, the leader of the crusade, could plead absence if not ignorance. For he had, as Villehardouin says, 'remained behind for some business that detained him', and only reached Zara two weeks after the event.[1] Villehardouin may not have known, or may have preferred not to enlarge upon the nature of the Marquis's business affairs. But a fortnight later Boniface was followed by messengers from Germany bringing a firm proposal from Alexius Angelus, backed by the recommendation of his brother-in-law Philip. If the crusaders would help him to recover his inheritance in Constantinople and restore the Empire to his father, Alexius promised to pay what they still owed to Venice, to subsidise their expedition to Egypt, to swell their numbers by 10,000 men for one year, and to maintain a permanent garrison of 500 troops in the Holy Land. In addition he promised that 'the whole Empire of Romania' would recognise the supremacy of the See of Rome.

It is hard to be certain how far the Doge had been directly implicated in the plans already laid by Boniface, Philip and Alexius. But when the proposal was submitted to the crusaders, he strongly supported Boniface in urging its acceptance. A minority disagreed, on the ground that they had enlisted to fight the infidel and not to interfere in the politics of a Christian state. Some of them left the army at Zara to make their own way to Syria. But the majority were persuaded that there was no harm in the proposal, and that it might even be of great advantage for the future of the Holy War. Jerusalem, it was said, could only be recovered by way of Egypt, or

[1] Villehardouin, *La Conquête de Constantinople*, ed. E. Faral, I (Paris, 1938), p. 81.

by way of Greece; and if the Greeks would now renounce the schism and throw their vast resources into the common cause then ultimate victory over the infidel would be assured. To the more high-minded the decision rested on a point of honour; they would be ashamed to refuse their help to this young and evidently devout prince. To the more realistic there was the prospect of a campaign that might be immensely lucrative; while the ordinary crusaders, who regarded themselves as pilgrims, thought of the benefits to be gained from a pilgrimage to the city of Constantinople, so famous for its relics.[1] But in the end the decision rested with the Doge of Venice; for without his ships the crusade could sail nowhere. An agreement was drawn up; and the messengers from Germany, who had been empowered to sign it in the name of Alexius, returned to their master.

The Pope's reaction to this new development in the course of his crusade was curiously hesitant. The evidence suggests that it was not until the decision to make for Constantinople had been taken that the knights and barons begged him to lift the excommunication laid upon them for the attack on Zara. Innocent took the view that the crusaders had been the victims of Venetian greed, and forgave them; but the Venetians themselves remained excommunicated. It is apparent that the idea of a temporary diversion of the crusade to Constantinople did not come as a surprise to the Pope. But this was a different matter from the wanton assault on Zara, a city which belonged to the king of Hungary, the only monarch who had shown any interest in the crusade. Innocent had not been very sympathetic towards Alexius when he met him, having little confidence in Alexius' ability to bring the Greek Church over to Rome. He pinned his own hopes of healing the schism rather on the reigning Emperor Alexius III, to whom he mentioned the possibility of the diversion of the crusade in a letter in November 1202.[2] But the elaborate promises made by the young Alexius at Zara may have convinced him that an unparalleled opportunity presented itself for securing the union of the Churches and the active co-operation of the Greeks in the Holy War. The whole expedition might well disintegrate if further cause for disagreement was given to its members. It was better to sanction what he could no longer control, for fear that his outright condemnation would leave matters entirely in the hands of those whose motives were the least Christian. It may be said, therefore, that the Fourth Crusade set out for Constantinople with the connivance if not with the blessing of Innocent III. In June 1203, when they were already

---

[1] Cf. A. Frolow, *Recherches sur la déviation de la IVe Croisade vers Constantinople* (Paris, 1955), pp. 46–71.

[2] *MPL*, ccxiv, 1123–5.

well on their way, he wrote forbidding the crusaders to launch another attack upon a Christian country. But by then, as he must have known, it was too late to prevent them; and in any case there was some doubt in the minds of the crusaders as to whether schismatics, who had so often thwarted and betrayed the course of the Holy War in the past, could really be accounted Christians.

At the beginning of April 1203 the advance party of the crusade sailed from Zara. Dandolo and Boniface waited for Alexius to arrive from Germany, and towards the end of the month put out to Corfu, where they had agreed to assemble. On the way they stopped at Dyrrachium, which became the first Greek city to accept Alexius as Emperor. At Corfu his agreement with the crusaders was solemnly ratified; and on 24 May, a fine, clear day with a favourable breeze, the whole fleet set sail. Rounding the Peloponnese, they proceeded by way of the islands of Euboea and Andros to Abydus on the Hellespont, where those who had gone ahead waited for the rest to catch up. On 23 June they came within sight of Constantinople, and marvelled at the glory of the city spread before their eyes. Next morning they coasted under the walls, and made for Chalcedon and Scutari on the other side of the Bosphorus, where they disembarked and set up camp.

Alexius III, who had had ample notice of the approach of the crusade, had made few preparations to defend his capital. There was in fact little that he could do. The Byzantine fleet was reduced to a few antiquated vessels. The army was Byzantine only in name, being mainly composed of foreign mercenaries. But the huge walls of the city had held off all comers in the past. There was no reason to think that the crusaders would succeed where so many had failed before. The young Alexius had boasted that his return to Constantinople would be greeted with joy by the inhabitants. But no one came out to welcome him. On the contrary, a messenger came from Alexius III bringing both threats and promises; and the crusaders' attempt to inspire a popular demonstration by parading the legitimate heir to the throne in the Doge's ship before the walls was greeted only with derision.

It became clear that the crusade would have to fight to achieve the purpose for which it had come. On 5 July the fleet crossed the Bosphorus and forced a landing at Galata. On the following day a Venetian ship rammed and broke the iron chain that closed the mouth of the harbour, and the fleet sailed up the Golden Horn. The army meanwhile repaired the bridge over the river at the head of the Golden Horn, which the Greeks had destroyed, and marched unopposed to encamp by the land walls on the north side of the city, near enough to the Blachernae Palace to be able to shoot their arrows through its windows. The final assault was to be a combined operation. The Venetians prepared scaling-ladders and erected platforms on the masts of their ships, from which the soldiers could fire over the walls, and covered the boards of the ships with hide to protect them against the Greek fire. Seldom can a besieging army have been so out-numbered. But the crusaders were inspired by an enthusiasm lacking in the defenders of the city, and also by a sense of desperation. For their rations were short, and their survival depended on their success. On 17 July, when all was ready, the attack was launched. On the land side a party of soldiers who had mounted a ladder near the Bla-chernae Palace were beaten off in hand-to-hand fighting with the Varangian guards. But by sea the Venetians managed to bring their ships in a long line close under the walls. The first to leap to shore was the Doge himself, clutching the banner of St Mark. The resistance which had at first been strong weakened before the general assault which then took place. Suddenly the Venetians found themselves scaling the walls and masters of twenty-five of the towers. To cover their movements they created a smoke screen by setting fire to some houses. The wind fanned the flames away from the walls and made the conflagration more disastrous than had been intended. But it served its purpose.

Alexius III was finally induced to lead his troops out against the army encamped beyond the land walls. But when he saw that the crusaders had drawn up in purposeful line of battle, he lost heart and withdrew. That night he packed together as many of his jewels as he could carry and fled from the city with his daughter Irene. The Venetians, who had left their positions on the walls when they heard of the impending attack on the crusaders' camp, knew nothing of what was taking place in the city. But in the morning they dis-covered to their surprise that the Greeks, bereft of their Emperor, had brought Isaac II out of prison and set him on the throne, blind and senile though he was, thus presenting them with a *fait accompli*. Messengers came to their camp before dawn to announce that the object for which they had diverted their crusade had been peacefully achieved.

The shock was as great to the young Alexius as it was to the crusaders. According to Byzantine tradition blindness unfitted a man to be Emperor. Alexius had perhaps kept this secret to himself. But he had not expected that his prospective subjects would ignore it. The crusaders too felt that they had come all this way on behalf of Alexius and not on behalf of his aged father, whom they had never seen. They insisted therefore on sending envoys into the city to make sure that if they recognised Isaac as Emperor he in his turn would recognise Alexius as co-Emperor, and also honour all the terms of the agreement that Alexius had made with them. Isaac hesitated, but consented; and Alexius was escorted into the city by his benefactors. On 1 August 1203 he was crowned co-Emperor as Alexius IV.

It now remained for Alexius to fulfil all the promises that he had so liberally made when far from home. But the citizens of Constantinople, who had chosen to reinstate his father rather than admit their indebtedness to the Latins, were in no mood to help him. The atmosphere was so tense that he had to ask the crusaders to keep to the other side of the Golden Horn. They were only allowed to come across as visitors and tourists; but the mere sight of the arrogant westerners strutting through the streets and poking into the churches was enough to annoy the Greeks. Alexius soon found that the imperial treasury was unable to provide the vast sum of money that he had guaranteed to the Venetians. He played for time, begging his creditors to be patient and to wait until the following spring. His attempts to raise the money by imposing new taxes made him more unpopular than ever; and his efforts to bully his clergy into accepting submission to the Papacy branded him as a traitor who had sold Byzantium to the West. The fact that he melted down church plate to pay his debts was of small account compared to the enormity of trying to force his people to accept a creed in which the Holy Spirit proceeded from the Father *and* the Son and a liturgy in which unleavened bread was used. In these circumstances time was not on the side of the Emperor Alexius IV. The longer the crusaders stayed the more likely it was that some incident would lead to open war. In August, while he and Boniface were in Thrace hunting for Alexius III, some of the resident Latins in Constantinople, whose piety had no doubt been excited by the arrival of the crusade, tried to burn down a mosque. When the Emperor returned in November he found that a whole quarter of the city had been devastated by fire.

As the winter drew on, Alexius began to resign himself to the fact that he would never be able to fulfil his agreement, and to hope that the crusaders would simply go without bothering him further. There were those among them who felt that this was the wisest course and longed to be on their way to Egypt. But once again they could do nothing without the consent of the Venetians; and the Doge was determined to extract his due from the Greeks, and to make the most of the situation by adding to the Emperor's embarrassments. Towards the end of 1203 the crusaders sent a deputation to Isaac and Alexius with an ultimatum, which only roused the fury of the Greeks still further; the messengers were lucky to escape with their lives. The way was open not only for war between Greeks and Latins, but also for a revolution among the Greeks directed against the Emperor who had brought them to this pass. Skirmishes took place in the harbour; the Greeks tried unsuccessfully to set fire to the Venetian fleet; and a conspiracy was formed for the election of another Emperor, who would redeem the betrayal of the Byzantine Church and people. The ringleader of the conspiracy was the *protovestiarius* Alexius Ducas Murtzuphlus, a son-in-law of Alexius III. In January 1204, however, a rioting mob in St Sophia took the law into their own hands and proclaimed as their Emperor a young and reluctant nobleman called Nicholas Canabus. Some of them then tore down the great statue of Athena Promachos, the work of Phidias which had once graced the Acropolis at Athens, because the goddess appeared to be beckoning the westerners into the city. Seeing that the situation was out of control, Alexius sought the protection of the crusaders, offering to hand over the Blachernae Palace. But he was injudicious enough to entrust the message to Alexius Murtzuphlus, who promptly revealed its contents and took over the palace, arresting the unfortunate Canabus. Alexius IV was thrown into prison and strangled on 8 February 1204. His father Isaac, who had already withdrawn into a world of his own, died a few days later either of fright or of old age. Murtzuphlus came to the throne as Alexius V.

It was the declared intention of the new Emperor to disclaim every item of the agreement which his predecessor had made with the Latins, and to clear them from the scene as soon as possible. In one way this made things simpler for the crusaders. With Alexius and his father gone they were now free of moral obligations towards the Greeks. They need have no further scruples about following the advice which the Doge had for long been giving them, to settle the matter by helping themselves to Byzantium and all its wealth and appointing an Emperor of their own. The capture of Constantinople and the conquest of the Byzantine Empire became the object of the Fourth Crusade. To the Venetians it was a matter of realistic policy and cool calculation; to the crusaders a matter of righteous indignation and moral fervour. Their clergy assured them that a war against the Greeks would be a just war, since its aim would be to avenge the murder of Alexius IV and to place the Byzantine Church and Empire under obedience to Rome. But the scheme was also born of desperation. For the crusaders could expect no supplies and no protection from the new regime in Constantinople. Even to escape might be difficult. Once again they must fight or perish.

Having made their decision they turned to anticipating its outcome. In March 1204 a new treaty was drawn up concerning the management of the city and the Empire which they hoped to conquer.

It was made between the Doge Dandolo on behalf of the Venetians, and Boniface of Montferrat, Baldwin of Flanders and two other French knights on behalf of the crusaders, and it provided for the division of the booty, the election of an Emperor and the distribution of the provinces. First and foremost the Venetians must be paid the debt for which they had waited so long. The Doge was therefore to be allowed to have first pick of the spoils, up to three-quarters of the amount taken. The election of a Latin Emperor of Constantinople was to rest with a committee of six Franks and six Venetians. The successful candidate, whether Frank or Venetian, was to have possession of one-quarter of the city and Empire and the imperial palaces; while the disappointed party was to be consoled with the possession of St Sophia, and their clergy were to have the right to elect a cathedral chapter and a Latin Patriarch. The remaining three-quarters of the Empire would be equally divided between Venetians and Franks, who would hold their acquisitions as fiefs from the Emperor, whom all parties must agree to serve until March 1205; but the Doge himself would not be obliged to render military or other service to the Emperor for his portion of the Empire. Whatever eventualities this treaty may have failed to envisage, whatever defects it may have had, it was above all designed to protect and enlarge the interests of Venice. The interests of the Greeks, who were to be ruled by a foreign Emperor, were not considered; and in the excitement of the moment all but the most conscientious of the crusaders forgot about the Holy Land.

Preparations were hurried on for the attack. It was decided to stake all on an assault from the sea, against the walls along the line of the Golden Horn. The first attempt was made at dawn on 9 April. Alexius V, who had set up his headquarters on a hill from which he could look down on the fleet, fought with more spirit than his predecessor; and by midday, after fierce fighting all along the walls, the crusaders were forced to retire with heavy losses. Three days later, however, they returned to the attack, doubling the line of their ships to accommodate a greater number of assault troops. Towards noon, when things were going badly, a wind got up which blew their ships closer to the shore. Some of the bolder knights clambered on to the walls, and four of the towers were soon taken. But the first to enter the city was Aleaume, brother of the historian of the crusade, Robert of Clari, who, under heavy fire, fought his way in through a postern gate. Before long three more gates had been forced, and the knights were pouring in on horseback. The Emperor retreated to the Bucoleon Palace; and Boniface with Baldwin and Henry of Flanders took up their stations in different parts of the city, to continue the struggle on the following day. Some of their soldiers, afraid of being surprised in the darkness, lit a fire which got out of hand and burnt down still more buildings. In the night Alexius V slipped away, to take refuge with his father-in-law in Thrace. Constantine Lascaris, who like his brother Theodore had distinguished himself in the defence of the city, was hurriedly proclaimed Emperor in St Sophia. But it was already too late to reorganise the defences. Not even the Varangian guard could be inspired to prolong the fight. Constantine, Theodore and his wife joined the crowd of refugees at the palace harbour, and sailed to the other side of the Bosphorus.[1]

On the morning of 13 April Boniface of Montferrat received the submission of the remaining soldiers, clergy and people. Those who could afford or contrive to do so had already fled with their belongings. But the common people crowded the streets and hailed the Marquis as their new Emperor with the words 'Hagios vasileas, marchio!' While their leaders moved in to the imperial palaces, the soldiers of the crusade were given leave to pillage the city. Regulations had been made about the disposition of the booty and forbidding excesses. But in the event there was neither order nor discipline. The city of Constantinople, like the Empire of which it was the capital, never fully recovered from the treatment that it received at the hands of the crusaders. Three disastrous fires, one of which was still smouldering on 13 April, had already swept away 'more houses than stood in the three largest towns of France'. But the violence of the western knights and soldiers, unleashing their inhibited envy and resentment against the perfidious Greeks, did more deliberate and lasting damage. Open murder was incidental to the more profitable activities of plunder and robbery. Perhaps no more than 2000 of the inhabitants were slaughtered. But lust and avarice raged through the streets. The treasured monuments of antiquity, which Constantinople had sheltered for nine centuries, were overthrown, carried off, or melted down. Private houses, monasteries and churches were emptied of their wealth. Chalices, stripped of their jewels, became drinking-cups; icons became gaming-boards and tables; and nuns in their convents were raped and robbed. In St Sophia the soldiers tore down the veil of the sanctuary and smashed the gold and silver carvings of the altar and the ambon. They piled their trophies on to mules and horses which slipped and fell on the marble pavement, leaving it running with their blood; and a prostitute sat on the Patriarch's throne singing bawdy French songs. Nicetas Choniates, who was an eye-witness,

---

[1] That Constantine rather than Theodore Lascaris was proclaimed Emperor in 1204 was established by B. Sinogowitz, 'Über das byzantinische Kaisertum nach dem vierten Kreuzzuge (1204–1205)', *BZ*, XLV (1952), 345–56.

contrasts the savagery of these 'forerunners of Antichrist' in Constantinople with the restraint of the Saracens in Jerusalem, who had respected the Church of the Holy Sepulchre and molested neither the persons nor the property of the conquered Christians. A sense of racial pride or national disaster might well have driven the Greeks to exaggerate their accounts and paint the picture of the sack of Constantinople in too lurid colours. Yet Nicetas gives a sober and sometimes verifiable list of the Greek statues and works of art destroyed in those terrible days; and the most horrifying account of all comes from the pen not of a Greek but of Innocent III, who was quick to condemn what he might have foreseen but had been powerless to prevent.

After three days a halt was called to the looting and destruction, and the proceeds were collected together in three of the churches. Never, says Villehardouin, since the world was created had so much booty been seen in any city. Although no one could assess the extent of its real value, and although much was withheld, it was estimated to be worth at least 400,000 silver marks, more than four times what the Venetians had demanded for the transport of the Fourth Crusade. When the Doge had been paid the sum of 50,000 marks, the rest of the spoil was divided according to the treaty.

It remained to elect an Emperor from among themselves and to divide and conquer the Empire. For the position of Emperor there were really only two candidates—Boniface of Montferrat and Baldwin of Flanders. The Doge Dandolo was prepared to forego the doubtful honour of becoming a feudal monarch on the throne of Constantinople; but he was determined to have his say in the election. For the future of the Latin Empire the appointment of Boniface might have been the more promising. The Greeks might have co-operated more willingly with a ruler whose family was already connected with Byzantium. Boniface himself had high hopes of being chosen, and lost no time in improving his prospects by marrying Maria or Margaret, widow of the Emperor Isaac II and sister of the king of Hungary, and installing himself in the Bucoleon Palace. The Doge, however, favoured Baldwin. Feelings ran so high among the crusaders when it came to appointing their electors that they decided to nominate six churchmen. It was agreed that the unsuccessful candidate should be given the provinces of Asia Minor and the Peloponnese. In the end Baldwin, Count of Flanders and Hainault, was elected Emperor; and eight days later, on 16 May 1204, his coronation was performed in St Sophia by the bishops of the crusade. Boniface, who had been obliged to move out of the palace, nobly held the crown at the ceremony and did homage to his rival.

But his pride had been wounded, and his supporters encouraged him to make things embarrassing for the new Emperor. He called upon Baldwin to honour the agreement made before the election by handing over Asia Minor and the Peloponnese. Baldwin agreed so readily that Boniface asked him if he would exchange these provinces for the city and province of Thessalonica, partly because it was nearer the territory of the king of Hungary, whose sister he had just married, but partly no doubt because it was in Thessalonica that his late brother Renier had owned his estate. But Thessalonica had still to be taken from the Greeks, and as events turned out Baldwin was the first to get there, having started for Adrianople in pursuit of Alexius III. It was Baldwin and not Boniface who received the submission of the city and, as Emperor, confirmed the privileges granted to it by the Byzantine Emperors in the past. Boniface, who had pleaded with him not to interfere in what he regarded as his own province, took to arms; and a civil war, which might have split the Latin Empire at its outset, was only averted by the intervention of the Doge. A *parliamentum* at Constantinople decided in favour of Boniface; Baldwin admitted his mistake and conferred on Boniface the title to the kingdom of Thessalonica.

It had fallen to Baldwin, now 'by the grace of God, Emperor of the Romans', to notify the western world of the achievement of the Fourth Crusade. In a letter addressed to the Pope and to the whole of Christendom he related the events that had led to the capture of Constantinople and his own coronation. Innocent III, who had remained sceptical about the first attack on the city, now expressed his overwhelming joy at what must surely be accounted a miracle wrought by God and took the new Empire and its pious ruler under his protection. His joy turned sour, however, when he heard the full details of the plunder of the city, and of the arrangements which the Venetians had made behind his back for the administration of the Church of Constantinople. But for the moment, once peace had been restored between Baldwin and Boniface, the crusaders were happy to have their adventure blessed, and looked forward with excitement to plucking and enjoying its fruits.

In October, when Baldwin returned to the capital, they addressed themselves to the distribution of the provinces of the Empire. A commission of twelve Venetians and twelve crusaders, working on the lines laid down in the previous March, drew up a treaty of partition. Since the Venetians alone, through the operations of their merchants, had any first-hand knowledge of the geography of the Empire, it may be supposed that their advice was followed; and indeed it seems that the partition treaty was much indebted to the text of the last commercial agreement made between the Doge and Alexius III. The capital was divided between the Emperor and the Doge, Baldwin taking five-eighths, Dandolo three-eighths of the city. Beyond the capital, much of Thrace had already been conquered. What remained to be conquered consisted of the Byzantine provinces in Asia Minor, Macedonia, northern and central Greece, the Peloponnese and the Ionian and Aegean islands. To avoid any further embarrassment, the territories thought to belong to Thessalonica were left out of account. For the rest the division was threefold, between the Emperor, the Venetians and the crusaders. Around Constantinople itself, the parts of Thrace east of Mosynopolis, which was taken to be the western limit of the kingdom of Thessalonica, were divided into three; the Emperor received the territory up to Agathopolis on the Black Sea and Tzurulum near the Sea of Marmora, the Venetians the country from Adrianople to the Sea of Marmora and the Hellespont, and the crusaders what remained. Asia Minor with the offshore Aegean islands, including Imbros, Lesbos, Chios and Samos, passed to the Emperor. The continent of Greece was to be shared between Venice and the crusaders. In the north the partition followed the natural barrier of the Pindus mountains. To the west of that line the Venetians claimed everything from Dyrrachium to Naupactus, comprising what the Greeks called New Epirus and Old Epirus, Acarnania and Aetolia, with Corfu and the other Ionian islands, as well as most of the Peloponnese, or the Morea as the Latins called it, from the Gulf of Corinth down to the ports of Modon and Coron and Cape Malea, and also Salamis and Aegina. To the east of the Pindus range Greece was to belong to the crusaders, from Lake Prespa and the Vardar river in the north, through Thessaly and Boeotia down to Attica and the Argolid in the south. The island of Euboea or Negroponte was at first divided between Venetians and crusaders; the title to Crete had already been acquired by the Doge, who had seized the opportunity to buy it from Boniface earlier in the year.[1]

These claims had now to be substantiated by conquest, and the land distributed in fiefs to be ruled according to feudal law. The Venetians were satisfied; they had acquired the right to the whole of the Adriatic coast line, the west coast of Greece and the islands which would be most useful to them on the trade route between Venice and Constantinople. They were content to leave the work of conquering the rest of the Empire to the crusaders. Baldwin and his feudal lords knew almost nothing about the Empire whose management they

---

[1] The text of the *Partitio Romaniae* is in G. L. F. Tafel and G. M. Thomas, *Urkunden zur älteren Handels- und Staatsgeschichte der Republik Venedig* (Fontes rerum Austriacarum, II, XII), I (Vienna, 1856), pp. 464–88.

were to undertake. They knew still less about its potential friends and enemies. In Asia Minor their piety led them to regard with righteous hostility the Seljuq Turks, who might have served them well as allies. The Sultan Kaykhusraw I, in exile from his throne at Konya, gave them the opportunity. But his offer was rejected; and by the time he was restored to his capital in 1205 it was too late. In Europe the Latins found themselves face to face with Kalojan of Bulgaria, whose Empire lay to the north of the strip of coast which they had acquired between Constantinople and Thessalonica. Kalojan had just succeeded in having himself recognised by the Pope as king of the Bulgars and Vlachs; his Archbishop of Trnovo had been made Primate of All Bulgaria; and he was confident that the new Latin Emperor would receive him at least as an equal ally. But he was given a rude shock. Baldwin informed him that, far from being the equal of the Latins, he was nothing but a vassal whose dominions were legally the property of Byzantium, and so of the Empire of Constantinople. This diplomatic blunder deprived the Latin Empire at the start of a powerful supporter. Kalojan turned from massacring his Greek neighbours to inciting them against the common enemy.

Towards the Greeks themselves Baldwin showed a similar lack of tact and understanding. The decentralisation of the Byzantine Empire, resulting from the policy of recent Emperors, had led to the growth of a type of feudal structure in many parts of the provinces which must have seemed familiar to the Latins. Members of the imperial family or other aristocratic landlords ruled their *pronoiai* in Greece or Asia Minor without much reference to the government in Constantinople. In several cases such Greek landlords, some of whom were already connected with French or Italian families, were at first prepared to co-operate with the Latins, acknowledging Baldwin as their suzerain so long as they were allowed to retain their property. But the Latins, as conquerors, were usually more interested in acquiring the land themselves than in working out ways of promoting the form of feudalism that already existed in the Byzantine Empire. As a result, many of the pronoiars of Byzantium, who might have lent their military and economic resources to the new regime, turned against it, and sought means of using those resources for the organisation of resistance and the perpetuation of the Byzantine Empire in exile. Their resolve was strengthened by the dispersal of refugees from the capital, who had already tasted the gall of Latin occupation.

At the end of 1204 the conquest began. Baldwin, with his brother Henry and Count Louis of Blois, set out from Constantinople to invade Asia Minor, while Boniface descended upon Greece from Thessalonica. The coast of the Black Sea to the west of Trebizond had been allotted to Baldwin in the partition treaty. Trebizond itself, however, was held by two grandsons of Andronicus I, David and Alexius Comnenus, who, supported by Thamar, Queen of Georgia, at whose court they had been brought up, had taken the opportunity to capture it in April 1204. There, styling themselves the Grand Comneni, they and their descendants were to establish the Empire of Trebizond. By the time that Baldwin arrived, Alexius had already been acclaimed Emperor, and David had extended his territory along the coast as far west as Sinope. In other parts of the country several landlords had taken the occasion to transform their estates into independent principalities. At Philadelphia Theodore Mancaphas set himself up; at Sampson near Miletus, Sabas Asidenus; and in the Meander valley, Manuel Mavrozomes, who had diplomatically married a daughter of the Sultan Kaykhusraw. But the most determined and, as it proved, the most successful adversary of the Latins in Asia Minor was Theodore Lascaris, whose brother Constantine had been offered the crown on the fateful night when Murtzuphlus deserted his capital. Theodore was a brave soldier who had already crossed swords with the Latins; like Murtzuphlus, he was a son-in-law of Alexius III, who had honoured him with the title of Despot. He had fled from Constantinople with his wife Anna, their three daughters, and his brother Constantine. He had hoped to take refuge in Nicaea, but the inhabitants at first refused to admit him. At Brusa, however, he managed to establish himself and soon gathered round him a large number of refugees. But the army that he was able to collect was not strong enough to stem the first invasion of the Latins. In December 1204, near Poimanenon, he was routed by Baldwin's knights, who continued their victorious advance as far south as Adramyttium, where Henry of Flanders defeated Theodore Mancaphas in March 1205. For a few months the Latins carried all before them, and Theodore Lascaris was condemned to fight a losing battle. It was in the course of this campaign that a French knight surprised and arrested the fugitive Alexius V Murtzuphlus. He was taken to Constantinople and there executed in a manner fitting, by the standards of chivalry, to one who was of imperial rank and yet had murdered his lord. He was thrown to his death from the top of the column of Theodosius.

While Baldwin and his men were carving out their fiefs in Asia Minor, Boniface of Montferrat assumed command of the army of crusaders which was to conquer Greece. The conquest proved easy enough. The great landlords of Thessaly were prepared to be co-operative; in Halmyros and around the Gulf of Volos, Latin, and especially Venetian and Jewish, merchants were already familiar figures; and at Thebes the citizens flocked out to welcome Boniface. The Greeks had been harshly taxed by their own Emperors and by the local archons or dynasts who lorded it over them. They hoped that a change of rulers might bring them some relief; but they were soon to be disappointed. The only effective resistance was offered by Leo Sgouros, the archon of Corinth and the Argolid, who, in an attempt to hold the invaders at bay, had advanced as far north as Thermopylae and Larissa, where the Emperor Alexius III had at length found refuge. Alexius hoped that Sgouros might be the saviour of the realm and gave him a daughter in marriage. But both of them were forced to withdraw before Boniface and his army. Sgouros retired to Corinth to continue resistance there; and the Latins swept on through Boeotia to Athens, and over to Euboea.

The Dowager-Empress Maria, whom Boniface had married, had many friends in Greece, and among those who set out from Thessalonica with the Marquis in 1204 was one Michael Ducas Angelus Comnenus, a cousin of Isaac II and Alexius III. He was the illegitimate son of a *sebastocrator* John Ducas,[1] and had earlier served as *dux* and tax-collector in the Meander valley in Asia Minor. While he was accompanying Boniface through northern Greece, Michael received a call for help from his relative Senacherim, the governor of Nicopolis in Epirus. He promptly disappeared across the Pindus mountains, married the widow of Senacherim, who had been assassinated, and took command of the district of Arta. Meanwhile the conquest of the Peloponnese was begun from the south. A chance adventure brought Geoffrey of Villehardouin, nephew of the chronicler, to Messenia; and from there, with the help of William of Champlitte and one of the local archons, he set about establishing the Latins in the south. One last stand, however, was made by the Greeks of Arcadia, who invited Michael Ducas to come to their aid. Michael crossed the Gulf of Corinth with an army, only to be beaten by the French cavalry at Koundoura in Messenia. He returned to Arta to lay the foundations of a more lasting resistance to the Latins. The battle of Koundoura was the Hastings of the Morea. Leo Sgouros held out grimly in Corinth and the Argolid for a few more months, and the rock of Monemvasia had still to be won. But by the beginning of 1205 the Emperor Baldwin and the crusaders could congratulate themselves that they had achieved the conquest of a large part of the Byzantine Empire in Greece and in Asia Minor. The completion of that conquest seemed only a matter of time.

But in February 1205 Kalojan of Bulgaria, incensed at Baldwin's

---

[1] John Ducas the *sebastocrator* was a brother of Andronicus, father of the Emperors Isaac II and Alexius III.

rude refusal of his alliance, attacked Adrianople in support of the
Greek inhabitants of Thrace. The whole countryside was up in arms.
Baldwin had cause to regret his tactlessness, and also that his armies
were scattered over so wide an area. Most of the troops campaigning
in Asia Minor had to be hastily recalled to defend Constantinople
against Kalojan and his savage Cuman auxiliaries. But they suffered
heavy casualties and a serious defeat. Louis of Blois was killed,
Baldwin himself was captured. His brother Henry arrived with
reinforcements from Asia Minor, but it was too late to save the day.
It was due mainly to the aged Dandolo that even the remnants of the
army were collected and brought to safety. But the exertion proved
too much for a nonagenarian, and at the end of May he died. This was
the first great crisis of the Latin Empire, and it was now deprived of
two of the leaders who had been its main inspiration.

It was some months before there was any certainty about Baldwin's fate, but his brother Henry was appointed bailie or regent of
the Empire. Henry appealed to the West for help, asking the Pope
to grant to those who would come out the indulgences offered to
crusaders to the Holy Land. But Kalojan pressed on, devastating all
that lay in his path, and capturing the city of Serres on the road to
Thessalonica. Boniface, who was engaged in the conquest of the
Argolid, had to hurry back to defend his kingdom. Kalojan withdrew
at the end of the summer, but at the beginning of 1206 he returned in
force. Almost the whole of Thrace fell before his Vlach and Cuman
troops, who massacred Greeks and Latins indiscriminately, and
marched to the very walls of Constantinople. The defence of Adrianople and Didymotichus had been entrusted to the Greeks under the
command of Theodore Branas, whom the Venetians were only too
glad to regard as a tributary vassal if he could hold these towns
against the Bulgars. Branas successfully thwarted Kalojan's assaults
upon them; and in July Kalojan withdrew once again into Bulgaria,
pursued by Henry's troops.

A party of French knights who had been isolated at Stenimachus
and who were rescued by Henry confirmed the rumour that Baldwin
had died in captivity. The Empire desperately needed an Emperor,
and Henry of Flanders, already its regent, was the obvious choice.
He was crowned by the new Latin Patriarch, Thomas Morosini, who
had recently arrived from Venice, in St Sophia on 20 August 1206,
and swore to honour all the agreements that had been made between
the Venetians and the crusaders. With the death of Dandolo the
Venetian community in the Latin Empire had also suffered a change
of rulers. In June 1205 the Venetians in Constantinople had elected
Marino Zeno, Dandolo's nephew, as their Podestà, with the proud

title of *quartae partis et dimidiae totius imperii Romaniae Dominator*.[1] It was assumed that the Venetian territories within the Empire would fall under his jurisdiction. But the new Doge of Venice, Pietro Ziani, who was elected in August 1205, quickly disillusioned the Podestà on this point, and required him to sign an agreement ceding to the direct control of Venice the whole of the north-west of Greece which had been assigned to the Venetians in the partition treaty. The Republic was alarmed that its colonists overseas might gain too great a measure of independence. It was safer to circumscribe the authority of their Podestà and his council and have them all directly answerable to the Doge. It soon became the rule that each new Podestà of Constantinople was sent out from Venice instead of being elected on the spot; he had to swear obedience to the Doge as his loyal agent; and even the title of *Dominator* passed to the Doge.

In August 1206, only a few days after Henry's coronation, Kalojan returned to the attack. There was little left for his troops to plunder, since they had already reduced Thrace to a desert. But he was determined to have Adrianople. Theodore Branas was unprepared; the city was destroyed and its inhabitants carried off. The Emperor Henry, however, again pursued Kalojan's army, and contrived to release the prisoners before marching on to attack Anchialus on the Black Sea. This was the first successful act of vengeance on the part of the Latins, and it marked the turn of the tide. There was one more disaster that they had to endure. Boniface of Montferrat, who had paid his homage to Henry, had been confirmed as king of Thessalonica. In February 1207 he gave Henry his daughter Agnes in marriage; and in the summer he joined him in Thrace to plan a campaign against Kalojan. In September, while making a reconnaissance near Mosynopolis, he was ambushed by the Bulgars and killed. Kalojan had done his work well. Within three years he had accounted for the deaths of Baldwin, Dandolo and Boniface. But he had little time to rejoice, for within a matter of weeks, while preparing an attack on Thessalonica, he died himself in October 1207, on the feast of St Demetrius, patron of the city. It seemed logical to both Greeks and Latins at the time that the great Kalojan had been struck down by the saint who had so often defended his city in the past. His death led to confusion in the Bulgarian Empire, and brought a welcome relief to his late enemies.

Kalojan's activities in Thrace had diverted the attention and the forces of the Latins from other parts of the Empire and rendered great service to the cause of the Greeks who had resolved to fight on.

[1] On the use of the word 'Romania' to describe the Empire, see R. L. Wolff, 'Romania: the Latin Empire of Constantinople', *SP*, XXIII (1948), 1–34.

In Asia Minor Theodore Lascaris was given a breathing-space in which to recover from his initial defeat by the crusaders and to contend with his Greek rivals. The people of Nicaea agreed, after all, to accept him; and it was there that he gathered together the up-rooted elements of the Byzantine Church and Empire and trans-planted them in the soil of Bithynia. David Comnenus of Trebizond, who found his westward advance blocked by Lascaris at Heraclea Pontica, allied himself with the Latins and became a vassal of the Emperor Henry. Theodore Mancaphas and the other dynasts who had proclaimed their independence were gradually defeated. Early in 1207 Lascaris made an alliance with Kalojan to draw the net tighter around Constantinople. Henry was obliged to make a truce; and soon afterwards Lascaris wrote to Innocent III, asking him to use his influence to enforce the terms of the truce, and proposing a permanent settlement on the basis of a partition between a Latin Europe and a Greek Asia Minor. The Pope was unimpressed, feeling that the Greeks, being in schism, had brought their own troubles on themselves. But he no doubt found it useful to have a spokesman for their cause, and promised to send a legate to Nicaea.

As his confidence and his territory grew, Theodore Lascaris became determined to make of Nicaea something more substantial than the centre of a mere resistance movement, and to have himself acknow-ledged as the legitimate successor to the Byzantine throne. His brother Constantine, who had ably assisted him in his early successes, seems to have died in 1205. Many of those who had hailed Constan-tine as Emperor in April 1204 were now in Nicaea and ready to accord the same honour to his brother. Theodore invited the Greek Patriarch, John Camaterus, who had taken refuge in Didymotichus, to come and settle in Nicaea; for if he were to be Emperor it would be necessary to have the Patriarch to crown him. Camaterus declined; but in 1206 he died, and the Patriarchate was vacant. In March 1208 Theodore assembled as many of the Greek hierarchy as he could find and bade them appoint a new Patriarch. The choice fell on Michael Autorianus, and it was he, as the Patriarch Michael IV, who crowned Theodore Lascaris as Emperor in Holy Week in 1208. The Byzantine Empire was born again in Nicaea; and for the eastern Greeks, at least, there was a new rallying-point and new hope.

But the new Empire had to fight to survive. Its principal enemies at first were the Seljuq Turks rather than the Latins. The Emperor Henry, hard-pressed in Europe and more realistic than his late brother Baldwin, sank his moral scruples and made an alliance with the Sultan Kaykhusraw, even sending a contingent of Latin troops to help the Sultan make war on Theodore Lascaris. The Sultan found a more demanding ally in the Emperor Alexius III, who arrived at his court at Konya. When abandoned in Thessaly by Leo Sgouros, Alexius had been arrested by some of Boniface's soldiers and detained in Thessalonica. His cousin Michael Ducas of Epirus, however, had paid Boniface a ransom for his release; and for a while Alexius and his wife Euphrosyne lived as refugees in Arta. It was in the expectation of recovering his lost Empire that Alexius sailed to Asia Minor, hoping that the Sultan would befriend one who had befriended him in similar circumstances in the past. He incited Kaykhusraw to attack the upstart in Nicaea, who had had the audacity to proclaim himself Emperor; and the Sultan, having failed to persuade Lascaris to abdicate in favour of his father-in-law, invaded his territory in force in the spring of 1211. A pitched battle was fought near Antioch on the Meander, the Sultan's Latin troops fighting valiantly on the side of the infidel. Victory was almost in their grasp when, if the Greek sources are to be believed, the Sultan was unhorsed and killed by Lascaris in single combat in the thick of the fray. His army fled and Lascaris entered Antioch in triumph. Alexius III, who was among the prisoners taken, was confined for the rest of his days to a monastery in Nicaea. It was a double victory for the Greek Emperor. At one blow he had silenced the last surviving Greek claimant to the Empire and disposed of his nearest and most dangerous enemy. The new Sultan Kaykāwūs I came to terms with him; and Lascaris could now concentrate his attention on the Latins. After the battle he sent letters to all the Greek provinces, announcing his triumph and foretelling the day when, if all the Greeks would but support him as their Emperor, he would liberate their land from the 'Latin dogs'.

Meanwhile in Europe the Latin Empire was in serious difficulties, and the Greeks were given their opportunity. At Arta, in the wide plain of the river Arachthus which flows down to the Ambracian Gulf, Michael Ducas set out to play the part played by Theodore Lascaris at Nicaea. The temporary settlement there of the Emperor Alexius III may have added to his prestige, but there is no evidence that Michael was granted any title or that he regarded himself as a claimant to the throne.[1] His half-brother Theodore had attached

---

[1] L. Stiernon, 'Les origines du Despotat d'Epire', *REB*, xvii (1959), 90–126, has shown that the contemporary sources do not refer to Michael as Despot, so that he cannot be accounted the founder of the Despotate of Epirus, as has been generally supposed. Nor does he seem to have used the name Angelus, which he inherited from his grandfather Constantine Angelus, perhaps because he preferred the more reputable names of Ducas and Comnenus. The nature of his authority seems hard to define. But John Cantacuzenus (i, p. 520 (*CSHB*)), justifying his own invasion of Epirus in 1340, remarks that 'the Angeli did not acquire the rule of Acarnania by liberating it from barbarians, but by being the subjects of the Roman Emperors and having been by them entrusted with an annual command (ἐτήσιον ἀρχήν) of the country'.

himself to the cause of Theodore Lascaris. But Michael soon asked that he might be allowed to join him in Greece; and in 1205 Theodore left Asia Minor. It was recalled in later days, when Theodore had come to be the ambitious rival of the Empire at Nicaea, that Lascaris had obliged him to swear loyalty to him and his successors before he left. It was to Theodore that Michael entrusted the defence against the Latins of the few remaining Greek strongholds in the Morea. But it was a hopeless cause; and though Theodore, taking over where Leo Sgouros had left off, held out in Corinth and then in Argos for a few years, by 1212 he had abandoned his charge and joined his brother Michael in Epirus.

The problems that faced Michael Ducas in north-western Greece were different from those that faced Theodore Lascaris in Bithynia. The country from Dyrrachium to Naupactus had passed to the Venetians in the partition treaty, and it seemed unlikely that it would be subject to any large-scale military invasion. Moreover, surrounded as it was by mountains, Epirus was easily defended and naturally fitted for the establishment of an independent state. The Venetians were determined, however, to substantiate their claim to the more important harbours and islands. In the spring of 1205 the fleet from Venice, which was taking the first Latin Patriarch to Constantinople, attacked Dyrrachium and then Corfu. A Venetian governor was installed in Dyrrachium; but the Corfiotes fought back, and it was not until 1207 that the island finally submitted, to be governed by a decarchy of Venetian nobles in the interests of the Republic. The adjacent Ionian islands of Cephalonia, Ithaca and Zacynthus had been appropriated before the Fourth Crusade by an Italian adventurer, Matthew Orsini, who was a vassal of the kingdom of Sicily. He now diplomatically sought the protection of the Pope and accepted the suzerainty of Venice. The contract made in 1205 between the Doge and the Podestà of the Venetians in Constantinople made things easier for Michael Ducas, for it had been agreed that the Venetian territories in Epirus should be directly under the control of the Doge. This made it seem even less likely that they would be invaded by the armies of the Latin Empire. Michael made doubly sure by imitating the example of Matthew Orsini and asking for the protection of the Pope. He may have given his sister Anna in marriage to Orsini. Diplomacy rather than force was the weapon which Michael at first chose to preserve his independence.

The death of Boniface of Montferrat in 1207 led to a situation in Greece which was as dangerous to the Latin regime as it was to Michael of Epirus. The latent rivalry between the house of Montferrat and the house of Flanders, which had almost split the Latin Empire after its foundation, came to a head. The kingdom of Thessalonica passed to Demetrius, the infant son of Boniface, under the regency of his mother Maria. But the Lombard barons who owed their positions to Boniface refused to do homage to the Emperor Henry, and claimed that the kingdom belonged not to Demetrius but to his half-brother, William of Montferrat. They invited William to come from Italy to take over his inheritance which, in their view, comprised the whole continent of Greece, including the land owned by 'Michael and his barons in Epirus'. Henry, with characteristic energy, took immediate action to suppress this rebellion. In the winter of 1208 he marched on Thessalonica, outmanœuvred Count Hubert of Biandrate, who was the ringleader of the revolt, and crowned Demetrius as king with his own hands. Then, early in 1209, he dealt with the barons who remained in revolt, first in the district of Serres, and then in Thessaly and Greece. Resistance was finally narrowed down to Thebes, where the die-hards barricaded themselves in the citadel. In May they surrendered, and Henry marched in triumph to Athens, where he took the opportunity to receive the homage of Geoffrey of Villehardouin as prince of Achaea. Hubert of Biandrate had managed to escape, but Henry crossed over to Euboea on his way back to Thessalonica and caught up with him. The Lombard rebellion was over, and Henry's position as Emperor was stronger than ever before. There was nothing to stop him invading north-western Greece and completing his triumph by making Michael Ducas, whom he already regarded with the deepest mistrust, his vassal. Michael forestalled him, however, by offering to negotiate. A conference took place not far from Thessalonica, at which Michael ingeniously turned the crisis to his own advantage. He offered the hand of his eldest daughter in marriage to Henry's brother Eustace, and promised one-third of his territory as her dowry. Henry was naïve enough to accept the offer, and returned to Constantinople, leaving Eustace as one of the two guardians of the young King Demetrius in Thessalonica.

The history of the career of Michael Ducas derives almost wholly from hostile sources. But his treachery can hardly be denied. He regarded all the agreements that he made with the Latins simply as matters of convenience, binding only so long as it suited his own purposes. The year after his alliance with Henry he made a treaty with Venice, and became the faithful servant of the Doge. The Venetians must have been surprised at the claims made first by the rebellious Lombards and then by the Latin Emperor to the part of northern Greece which belonged by right to them. It was not their policy to go to the trouble of conquering what they could acquire by diplomatic means. They therefore asked Michael Ducas whether he would agree to govern Epirus, Acarnania and Aetolia as their agent or vassal, as Orsini had already agreed to govern Cephalonia. In the circumstances Michael was glad to accept such a proposal. On 20 June 1210 he signed a contract with the Doge, Pietro Ziani, acknowledging the concession by Venice to himself and his heirs of all the country from the limits of the new Venetian Duchy of Dyrrachium in the north to Naupactus in the south. For the moment this seemed to Michael a convenient arrangement. By guaranteeing the immunity of Venetian merchants it might help the prosperity of Epirus; and it gave him a new confidence with regard to his Latin neighbours in the kingdom of Thessalonica. He could afford to take the offensive.

Almost at once, in the summer of 1210, he made a raid into Thessaly, capturing and crucifying the Constable of the Latin Empire, Amadeo Buffa, storming the Emperor's camp, and destroying a number of Latin-occupied towns. This gross breach of faith horrified the Emperor as well as the Pope, who was scandalised to learn that there were Latin soldiers serving in Michael's army. He excommunicated them as well as Michael. Michael was undeterred. He found a useful ally in a Bulgarian chieftain called Dobromir Strez. When Kalojan died in 1207 his son John Asen was still a boy, and the throne had been usurped by his nephew Boril. Two of Boril's relatives had seized the moment to set up principalities of their own. His cousin, Alexius Slav, occupied the fortress of Melnik above the Strymon valley; his brother, Strez, took over the impregnable rock of Prosek in the Vardar valley above Thessalonica. Slav was content to make friends with the Latins, and married an illegitimate daughter of the Emperor Henry, who gave him the Byzantine title of Despot. Strez, however, preferred to join forces with Michael Ducas in harrying the Latin kingdom of Thessalonica. Towards the end of 1210 Henry had to go out of his way to defend the kingdom against their combined attacks, and bound both of them under oath. The alliance was broken soon after, and Strez was defeated in 1211 by Eustace, regent of Thessalonica, with the help of his father-in-law Michael. This was the first and last service that Michael, the 'traditor potentissimus' among Henry's enemies, rendered to the Latin cause.

In the following years Michael campaigned with increasing success against the Latins on all sides. Latin soldiers, lured by the prospect of higher pay, continued to swell the numbers of his army; the Venetians ran a recruiting agency and shipped mercenaries direct to Epirus from Venice. In 1212 he drove the remaining Lombard barons out of central Thessaly, and occupied Larissa and the surrounding district, thus severing communications between Thessalonica and the French Duchy of Thebes and Athens. He then turned on his Venetian protectors, attacked and captured Dyrrachium, and occupied the island of Corfu, which seems to have been in his hands at least by 1214. But his career of conquest, which had made the whole of Epirus free of dependence upon Venice and of domination by the Franks, was cut short; for he was murdered by one of his servants, perhaps in 1215.

Michael's victories in the last years of his life had been snatched while the Latins were otherwise occupied. Boril of Bulgaria repeatedly rose to the attack. Theodore Lascaris, temporarily freed from the necessity of fighting the Turks, made considerable advances in Asia Minor, and even meditated an attack on Constantinople itself. In 1211 Henry made a bold effort to subdue the Empire of Nicaea. After a striking victory over the army of Lascaris on the Rhyndacus river, not far from Brusa, on 15 October, he drove on triumphantly to the south to capture Pergamum, Nymphaeum and other places. On 13 January 1212, elated by his success, Henry addressed a letter from Pergamum to all his friends in the West, to announce his victories over his four principal enemies, Boril and Strez of Bulgaria, Lascaris of Nicaea and Michael of Epirus. If these victories were to be consolidated, however, the Latin Empire must have many more troops at its disposal. For with the forces that he had Henry could hardly maintain a line of defence that stretched from the Morea to the Black Sea, from Bulgaria to the Turkish frontier in Asia. But the western world did not respond to his appeal with much enthusiasm; and in the end Henry decided to cut his losses and come to a working agreement with Theodore Lascaris. In December 1214, if not before, the two Emperors signed a treaty.[1] The Latins were to retain the north-west coast of Asia Minor as far south as Adramyttium, while the Greeks should have the rest, including what Henry had recently occupied, up to the boundaries of the Seljuq Sultanate. The treaty of 1214 was a triumph for Lascaris rather than Henry, for the establishment of a recognised frontier implied the recognition by the Latins of a rival Empire. Lascaris made the most of his advantage by turning on Henry's allies, the Grand Comneni of Trebizond, advancing along the Black Sea coast from Heraclea to Amastris and as far as Sinope. But there his progress was stopped by the intervention of the Sultan. It was to the Sultan and not to Lascaris that

---

[1] J. Longnon, 'La campagne de Henri de Hainaut en Asie Mineure en 1211', Acad. Roy. de Belgique, *Bull. de la cl. des Lettres*, xxxiv (1948), 442–52, argues that this treaty was arranged in 1214 and not in 1212. Cf. A. Gardner, *The Lascarids of Nicaea* (London, 1912), pp. 84–6; *DR*, 1684.

Sinope fell. David Comnenus was killed, and his brother Alexius of Trebizond, isolated from his allies, saved his Empire from destruction by becoming the vassal of the Turks and paying an annual tribute to the Sultan.

The triumph of Boril of Bulgaria over the Latin Emperor was of another kind. Seeing that Kalojan's son, John Asen, was already asserting his right to the throne, Boril somewhat unexpectedly offered his daughter in marriage to Henry, who was now a widower. Henry was understandably reluctant to take the grand-niece of Kalojan to wife; but his barons persuaded him that the interests of the Empire came first. This strange alliance of Franks and Bulgars led, according to Serbian tradition, to Henry being involved in a campaign with Boril, Strez and King Andrew of Hungary against Stephen Nemanja of Serbia, which came to an indecisive end at Niš. Henry must have felt that he had enough to do without being dragged into dynastic conflicts in the distant Balkans.

On 11 June 1216 Henry died suddenly at Thessalonica. He was barely forty years of age and at the height of his powers. In the ten years of his reign the Latin Empire had been transformed from a lost cause into a workable reality. Much of his time and energy had been spent in securing what had already been acquired, but at least he had achieved a balance of power between the Latins and the Greeks in the east and west. It is a measure of his success that his death was lamented by many of his Greek subjects, who could contrast his tolerance and understanding with the intolerance and bigotry of his brother Baldwin. The Greeks admired him as a soldier and as a man with a sense of honour, a virtue which, as Henry ruefully noted, was sadly lacking among some of their own leaders. Henry of Flanders was the greatest of the Latin Emperors; he was also the only one under whom the Greeks might have been content to live. For he was prepared to treat them as partners rather than subjects; he respected their rights, and above all he respected their religion.

Only a few weeks later, on 16 July 1216, Pope Innocent III died. It was as if the wind of the Fourth Crusade had blown itself out. Innocent, although deeply shocked by the manner in which the crusaders had set up their Empire in Constantinople, had long since decided that the advantages gained for the Church outweighed the crime against humanity, and that the Latin Empire was perhaps God's way of restoring the schismatic Greeks to the fold. He had been shocked too by the conduct of the Venetians, who, acting in accordance with the terms of the partition treaty, had appointed their own clergy to the cathedral chapter of St Sophia, who in their turn had elected the Venetian, Thomas Morosini, as the first Latin

Patriarch. The title of 'Patriarch of Constantinople' had dangerous associations. It must not be allowed to become a Venetian monopoly. Innocent protested, as a matter of principle, at what was, after all, an uncanonical appointment, before confirming Morosini's election. But once its incumbent had received his sanction, he was ready to acknowledge the eminent position in the Church of the Patriarchate of Constantinople, even to the extent of admitting what the Byzantines had believed and the Popes had denied ever since the Second Oecumenical Council in 381, that it ranked second after Rome among the five primatial sees.[1]

The Greeks themselves were bewildered by this sudden adoption and distortion by the Papacy of their own inherited view of the order of the Church. For they believed that the Roman Church was in heresy on the question of the *filioque* and misguided in many other ways; and they could not conceive by what authority the Pope could claim to be able to appoint a Patriarch of Constantinople, whether Greek or Latin. It was the first time that the Greeks had been treated to the direct application of the papal theory of universal supremacy. The exiled Greek Patriarch, John Camaterus, wrote an indignant letter to Innocent III. John Mesarites and his brother, the learned Nicholas, soon to become Metropolitan of Ephesus, defended the Greek position in debates with Morosini himself and with the papal legate Benedict, Cardinal of Santa Susanna, who was sent to Constantinople in 1205.[2] The Greeks argued reasonably enough that their Patriarch should be a Greek; and when Camaterus died in 1206 they appealed to the Emperor Henry and then to the Pope to be allowed to elect a successor. But the appeal went unanswered, and the successor, Michael Autorianus, was elected not in Constantinople but in Nicaea. Benedict also held discussions in Athens and in Thessalonica, where he was received by Michael Choniates, brother of the historian and Metropolitan of Athens, who had fled from his beloved city rather than live there under Latin rule.

Innocent III, while he could not respect the theology of the Greeks, wanted to respect their feelings and to convert them by persuasion rather than by force. But the Venetian Patriarch and the Latin hierarchy made things difficult for him partly by unseemly quarrels

---

[1] Cf. R. L. Wolff, 'Politics in the Latin Patriarchate of Constantinople, 1204–1261', *DOP*, VIII (1954), 225–304. The theory of the pentarchy of Patriarchates was enshrined in the Fifth Canon of the Lateran Council in 1215. Mansi, XXII, 990.

[2] The letter of John Camaterus to Innocent III, unpublished, is given in extract by M. Jugie, *Theologia dogmatica Christianorum orientalium*, IV (Paris, 1931), pp. 341–2. For the discussions of the Mesarites brothers with Benedict, see A. Heisenberg, *Neue Quellen zur Geschichte des lateinischen Kaisertums und der Kirchenunion* I, II (*SBAW*, Munich, 1922, 1923).

among themselves, and partly by antagonising the Greek clergy who refused to accept the Roman creed. Innocent allowed that the Latin form of consecration should only be insisted upon in the case of Greek bishops not already consecrated. But all Greek bishops were required to declare their loyalty and obedience to the Holy See, and to respect and assist the papal legate to the Empire.[1] Only one or two of them saw fit to accept these terms. The rest, driven from their sees, sought refuge in Epirus or in Nicaea, and there encouraged resistance to the Latins as a spiritual obligation for the Greeks. If Michael of Epirus murdered every Latin priest he could lay his hands on, as Innocent complained, it was because he believed it to be his moral as well as his patriotic duty to do so. Orthodoxy became synonymous with nationalism. The ordinary parish priests had little option but to obey and pay taxes to their new Latin superiors, putting up with whatever changes might be made in the extent and status of each diocese, since their livelihood depended on their parishes. But many of the monks were driven into exile when their houses were requisitioned and made over to western orders; and the monks of Athos suffered much, even though taken directly under the protection of the Papacy.

The Spanish Cardinal Pelagius, who came to Constantinople as papal legate in 1213, made matters worse. Morosini had died in 1211, and there was the chance for the Papacy to reconsider the whole question of a Latin Patriarch. The Greeks in Constantinople, who had the sympathy of the Emperor Henry, were ready to acknowledge the supremacy of the Pope and to honour his name by acclamation in their services. But Pelagius had no patience with the schismatic Greeks. He ordered their churches to be closed, and threw many of their priests and monks into prison. Once again the spokesman for the Greeks was Nicholas Mesarites, who led a deputation from Nicaea in 1214. The Greeks of Nicaea were sensitive, as was fitting to the heirs of Byzantium, about their dignity. They were annoyed that the Pope refused to address Theodore Lascaris as Emperor, and that his legate, a mere bishop, thought himself grander than Mesarites, Metropolitan of Ephesus and Exarch of All Asia, and referred to the Oecumenical Patriarch in Nicaea only as Archbishop of the Greeks. The discussions all but foundered at the start on matters of protocol. As it was they drifted into a sea of theology in which there was no hope of agreement. Finally, in December 1214, two of the legate's retinue accompanied Mesarites to Heraclea Pontica, where Lascaris was encamped on an expedition against Alexius Comnenus of Trebizond.

---

[1] For the problems facing the Greek clergy in Latin-occupied territory, cf. R. L. Wolff, 'The Organisation of the Latin Patriarchate of Constantinople', *Trad.*, VI (1948), 33–60.

There the treaty was arranged recognising the partition of Asia Minor between the two Empires. Otherwise, the best that can be said is that the Greeks and Latins parted on friendly terms. Indeed Mesarites was scolded on his return to Nicaea by the new Patriarch, Theodore Irenicus, for having made himself too amenable to the enemy. The religious differences between Greeks and Latins became increasingly identified with the political separation implicit in the recognition by the Emperor Henry of a Greek Empire in Nicaea.

It is true that as the years went on the Emperor at Nicaea began to look on some kind of ecclesiastical rapprochement as a means of recovering Constantinople. But the Greeks in Greece, who bore the brunt of the Latin occupation, would tolerate no compromise. The Lateran Council summoned by Innocent III for 1215 was boycotted by the Greek hierarchy. Basil Pediadites, Metropolitan of Corfu, who had recently been restored to his see by Michael Ducas, replied to the Pope's invitation by asking him how he could expect any members of the Greek clergy, whom he had himself evicted from their churches and replaced by heretics, to attend a council in Rome. For all the efforts of Innocent III to make triumph out of disaster, the situation was such that both Greeks and Latins thought it necessary to purify the altar of any church that had been desecrated by the rival faith before it was fit to be used. It is to the credit of some of the more enlightened Latins, however, that they incurred trouble in high ecclesiastical quarters through trying to be fair to the Greeks in religious matters. The Emperor Henry earned the respect of his Greek subjects by handing back to its rightful owners the monastery of Chortaitou near Thessalonica, which had been taken over by Cistercians, and still more by openly defying the cardinal legate Pelagius and reopening the Orthodox churches in Constantinople. But such westerners were, as the Greeks discovered, exceptional; nor could the Latins restrain the bigotry of their clergy, who despised the bearded, foreign priests with their wives and children, and were in their turn despised as barbarous, arrogant and avaricious.

When Henry died in 1216 he had reached a *modus vivendi* with the Empire of Nicaea. In Greece, however, the situation was more ominous. Michael Ducas of Epirus was succeeded by his half-brother Theodore.[1] Theodore's ambitions extended far beyond the maintenance of a Byzantine province in the mountains of north-western Greece. He dreamt of the conquest of Thessalonica, which would be the stepping-stone to Constantinople itself. He laid the ground

---

[1] Contemporary sources, including Theodore's own chrysobulls and coins, refer to him as Theodore Ducas, or Theodore Comnenus Ducas, rarely adding the name of Angelus.

by making his peace with the chieftains of Albania to the north of Epirus, and with Stephen, ruler of Serbia, who in 1217 was at length honoured with a crown by the new Pope Honorius III. The state of civil war prevailing in Bulgaria between Boril and John Asen gave Theodore the opportunity to invade the parts of western Macedonia that had been overrun by Kalojan, and to capture the towns of Ochrida and Prilep. The death of Henry gave him the chance to extend his conquests into the kingdom of Thessalonica; it also gave him an unexpected opportunity to bring himself to the notice of a wider public. Since Henry died without immediate heir, the barons elected as Emperor his brother-in-law, Peter of Courtenay, who was then in France. Early in 1217 Peter set out for Constantinople, stopping at Rome to receive his crown from the Pope. Honorius III, fearful of granting him a title to the Western as well as the Eastern Empire, performed the coronation in San Lorenzo, outside the walls of the city, on 9 April 1217. Shortly afterwards he embarked for Dyrrachium with a papal legate and an army of 5500 soldiers on Venetian ships. His wife Yolanda was to proceed by sea, while Peter and his army recovered the city of Dyrrachium from Theodore Ducas and then marched overland to Constantinople. It was an ill-conceived scheme from which only Venice could hope to benefit. The siege of Dyrrachium was a failure, and Peter and his retinue were ambushed and captured in the mountains of Albania by Theodore Ducas. Whatever the ultimate fate of Peter of Courtenay, and no one in the West was sure whether he was alive or dead for some years to come, his disappearance was no less complete and mysterious than that of his predecessor Baldwin. It was as encouraging to the Greeks as it was disastrous to the Latins. Chastened by the angry reaction of Pope Honorius, who threatened him with a crusade of vengeance, Theodore in the end released the papal legate, John Colonna, and sent him on his way to Constantinople in 1218. The Venetians, who had rather hoped that a crusade against Epirus would materialise, had to content themselves with signing a five-year treaty with Theodore.

The Empress Yolanda had meanwhile reached the capital, and had been delivered of a son, the future Emperor Baldwin II. Her eldest son, Philip of Namur, obstinately refused to leave France, and for two years Yolanda reigned as regent. Her one act of diplomacy was to stem the tide of the Greek advance in Asia Minor by giving one of her daughters in marriage to Theodore Lascaris. It was a marriage that disgusted the Greeks of Epirus, who, under the able leadership of Theodore Ducas, were becoming less disposed than ever to regard Lascaris as the lawful heir to the Byzantine throne.

It was unfortunate for the Latin Empire that both Constantinople and Thessalonica should have been left in the hands of women at the same time. Maria, widow of Boniface, still reigned as regent for her son Demetrius, who retained the title to the kingdom of Thessalonica; but it was known that Peter of Courtenay had invested William of Montferrat with the rights of that kingdom. Theodore of Epirus was hopeful that he could dispossess both of them. In 1218 he began the campaign, first in Thessaly and then in Macedonia, which was to end in the recapture of Thessalonica by the Greeks. To the south of Larissa, Neopatras and Lamia fell to his troops; to the north, Plata- mona and Servia. The collapse of Thessalonica seemed imminent; it was confidently predicted by his supporters, who also began to hint that the master of the second city of the Byzantine Empire would have a better claim to the title of Emperor than one who ruled at Nicaea.

This suggestion was voiced particularly by the Greek clergy in Epirus. The prolific correspondence of John Apocaucus, Metropolitan of Naupactus, gives an idea of the extent and rapidity of Theodore's conquests from the Latins. It also demonstrates the growing feeling among the western Greeks that they owed nothing to the Emperor at Nicaea. The clergy who were restored to their churches in Thessaly and elsewhere by Theodore's victories felt little sense of allegiance to a Patriarch in distant Bithynia, whose apostolic succession was in any case doubtful; and Theodore, like Michael before him, appointed bishops in his territory without any reference to that Patriarch. These acts of defiance were hotly challenged by the Patriarchs of Nicaea; but Theodore found an eloquent champion in the erudite canonist and theologian Demetrius Chomatianus, whom he had him- self raised to the See of Ochrida in 1217. It was true, as Chomatianus liked to emphasise, that the Archbishopric of Ochrida could lay claim to certain exceptional prerogatives bestowed upon it many centuries before by Justinian and Pope Vigilius. It was not true, as he also claimed, that it took precedence over the recently constituted Pri- mates of Bulgaria and Serbia. But it was certainly an important see; and its incumbent had some justification for thinking himself more exalted than the Bishop of Nicaea who wished to be called Patriarch. Demetrius Chomatianus readily supplied for Theodore the spiritual sanction for declaring himself independent both of the Emperor and of the Patriarch of Nicaea. In 1219, when Theodore Lascaris, to strengthen his position with regard to the Latins, proposed that a council of Greek and Latin clergy should meet in Nicaea to discuss once again the union of the Churches, the clergy of Epirus were loud and unanimous in their condemnation. Negotiations of any kind with the Latins, let alone intermarriage which they deplored, were mere treachery to the cause of the Greeks. Their own ruler, 'appointed and protected by God' as Apocaucus described him, was fighting for the victory of Orthodoxy and would countenance no compromise with the faith of his fathers. Spurred on by Chomatianus, the Greek Church was soon divided between those who acknowledged the Patriarch in Nicaea and those who did not; and the division was reflected in the growing division of loyalties between Theodore Ducas and Theodore Lascaris.

The Empress Yolanda died in 1219, and the Latin Empire passed to her second son, Robert of Courtenay. On 25 March 1221 he was crowned in Constantinople by the new Latin Patriarch, Matthew, who had just been appointed by the Pope. Robert was young and self-indulgent. He had none of the adventurous spirit, however misdirected, which had fired the leaders of the Fourth Crusade. His accession may be said to mark the beginning of the decline and fall of the Latin Empire, a process which was to be prolonged for forty years. Through the international matrimonial policy of King Andrew of Hungary, Robert had family connections with John Asen, who had finally defeated Boril and entered upon his inheritance in Bulgaria. Asen had allowed him to travel through his country to reach Constantinople. With Theodore Lascaris, who had returned to the attack in 1219, he renewed his mother's treaty. But Lascaris knew who were the real masters of the Latin Empire. In August 1219 he had made a five-year agreement with the Venetian Podestà, granting to the merchants of Venice complete freedom of access to Nicaea, and undertaking not to allow his warships to approach Constantinople without the Podestà's consent; the Greeks of Nicaea were to be permitted access to Venetian territory, though on less favourable terms. A state of peaceful co-existence, foreshadowed by the Emperor Henry's treaty with Lascaris, seemed to have been established between the two Empires. As soon as the new Emperor arrived, Lascaris proposed a marital alliance to bring Nicaea and Constantinople still more closely together. He offered his daughter Eudocia as wife to Robert of Courtenay. But the Greek Patriarch, who had been unhappy about Lascaris marrying Yolanda's daughter, was quick to appeal to the objections of canon law against the daughter of Lascaris marrying Yolanda's son. Negotiations were still proceeding when Theodore Lascaris died in 1222.

The founder of the Empire of Nicaea left no sons to succeed him. But by general agreement his son-in-law, John Ducas Vatatzes, husband of his eldest daughter Irene, was proclaimed and crowned Emperor by the Patriarch Manuel. It was a wise choice, for John III Vatatzes proved to be the most successful of all the Emperors at

Nicaea and one of the ablest of all Byzantine rulers. The two eldest brothers of Lascaris, however, took offence at the appointment, deserted to the Latins, and incited Robert to make war on Nicaea. It was not until 1225 that Vatatzes was able, in a battle at Poimanenon, to defeat the Latin armies that marched upon him in support of Theodore I's rebellious brothers. But the defeat was decisive; and the subsequent treaty deprived the Latin Empire of all its former territory in Asia Minor except Nicomedia and the coast opposite Constantinople.

The dispute over the succession to the throne of Nicaea in 1222 and the feebleness of the new Latin Emperor gave Theodore of Epirus the opportunity that he needed to achieve the conquest of Thessalonica. At the end of 1221 his soldiers had occupied the city of Serres, thus isolating Thessalonica from Constantinople and completing its encirclement. The Queen-mother Maria fled to Hungary. The young Demetrius of Montferrat left for Italy, and persuaded Pope Honorius to preach a crusade for the defence of his kingdom. It was to be led by his step-brother William, and to be supported by the Latin Emperor and all the Latin princes in Greece. But at the end of 1224, after a long siege, Thessalonica fell to the Greeks. William of Montferrat, who finally reached Greece in 1225, died of dysentery in the plain of Thessaly, and his crusade dispersed.

The capture of Thessalonica was the culminating triumph of Theodore Ducas. To the western Greeks it seemed as if the Byzantine Empire had been born again in Greece. To them Theodore Ducas, who had defeated a Latin Emperor and conquered a Latin kingdom, was himself Emperor in all but name. Only the act of coronation was needed. The Greek Metropolitan of Thessalonica, Constantine Mesopotamites, whom Theodore had reinstated in his see, was reluctant to perform the ceremony. But a synod of the western Greek clergy, presided over by John Apocaucus, delegated the task to Demetrius Chomatianus of Ochrida, who already saw himself in the role of Patriarch and believed that one of the many prerogatives of his archbishopric was the right of anointing kings. It was he who placed the crown on Theodore's head—the crown not, as John Vatatzes would have liked to think, of the kingdom of Thessalonica, but of the one true Emperor of the Romans.[1] From being the leader of the western Greeks, appointed by God, Theodore became the Emperor of all the Greeks, 'crowned and defended by God'. A new Byzantine

---

[1] The only known chrysobulls signed by Theodore Ducas as Emperor date from 1228, which may indicate that his coronation was not performed before that year. One confirmed the rights and privileges of the Metropolis of Naupactus, the other those of Corfu. See D. M. Nicol, *The Despotate of Epiros* (Oxford, 1957), pp. 56, 105–6 and references.

court was set up at Thessalonica; Theodore gave the title of Despot to his brothers Manuel and Constantine, and showered lesser dignities upon the courtiers and officials of his Empire. The Greeks at Nicaea mocked at the provincial character of Theodore's court; but they had to reckon with the fact that they were now no longer the sole claimants to the Byzantine inheritance. Even the Latins were forced to acknowledge Theodore's title as 'imperator Graecorum'. George Bardanes, Metropolitan of Corfu, renowned for his literary talent no less than his theological learning, addressed a long apologia of the Emperor Theodore to the Patriarch of Nicaea, Germanus II, suggesting that the two Greek Empires might live in peace and harmony. It would have been better still if they could have co-operated. But as it was neither co-existence nor co-operation proved possible; and it was due mainly to the jealousy among the Greeks, which had ultimately to be resolved in open warfare, that the Latins were allowed to maintain their tenuous hold on Constantinople for so long.

By 1225 the Latin Empire was almost confined to Constantinople and its suburbs. The Morea, Athens and Thebes, and some of the Aegean islands remained under its control, and Venetian ships maintained communications. But John Vatatzes had all but driven the Latins from Asia Minor, and was already attacking the coast of Gallipoli in Europe. When the Greeks of Adrianople sent to him for help he seized the chance to instal a garrison of his troops in their city. But it was here, at Adrianople, that the two Greek Empires first came into collision. For Theodore Ducas, who had already occupied the whole of Thrace as far as Mosynopolis, persuaded the Greeks of Adrianople to dismiss the soldiers of Vatatzes, and the city changed hands. Theodore's army was within striking distance of Constantinople, and he began to make preparations for the conquest of what he now regarded as his capital. But John Asen of Bulgaria also had designs on Constantinople; and the Latin Emperor Robert, having nowhere else to turn, looked to him for protection. Moreover, Theodore himself had made an alliance with Bulgaria, cemented by the marriage of his brother, the Despot Manuel, to Asen's illegitimate daughter Maria. The fate of Constantinople hung in the balance, but it was John Asen who held the scales.

At the critical moment, in 1228, the Latin Empire was once again without an Emperor. Robert, having incurred the chivalrous wrath of his barons by his profligacy and by an amorous adventure in his palace, had fled to Italy to be comforted by Pope Gregory IX. Gregory persuaded him to return, but he died in the Morea on his way back. His brother Baldwin was but eleven years old. A regent had to be appointed. The first to offer his services was John Asen, who proposed that Baldwin should marry his daughter Helen, in which case he would formally take the Empire under his protection and recover for it all its former territories, including Thessalonica. But the barons turned him down, and appointed as regent and Emperor the aged warrior John of Brienne; Baldwin was to marry his daughter Maria. After the ineffectual reign of Robert of Courtenay the Latin Empire needed a soldier at its head. John of Brienne was over eighty, but his military prowess was undiminished. As king of Jerusalem he had led the Fifth Crusade, until dispossessed of his title by his son-in-law Frederick II, when he became the champion of the Papacy against the godless Hohenstaufen. It was agreed that he should be Latin Emperor so long as he lived, and that when Baldwin reached the age of twenty they should rule as co-Emperors. The agreement was ratified by Pope Gregory in April 1229, but John had to settle his accounts with Frederick II before he could leave Italy; and it was not for another two years that he reached Constantinople.

The way was still open for Theodore Ducas to close in on the city from Adrianople. The Latin barons expected that he would, and in December 1228 hurriedly made a truce of one year. The truce ran its course. But in the spring of 1230, instead of marching on Constantinople, Theodore invaded Bulgaria. The later Byzantine historians, whose loyalties lay with Nicaea, point to Theodore's unprovoked attack on Bulgaria as another instance of the perfidy of the western Greeks. But Theodore himself had reason to complain of the duplicity of his supposed ally John Asen, who had so recently offered to conquer Thessalonica for the Latins. He could hardly undertake what might be a long siege of Constantinople with so treacherous an ally in the background. Asen, however, played the part of an injured friend, and went out to defend his Empire with the text of Theodore's alliance pinned to his standard. The Greek and Bulgarian armies met at Klokotnica, on the road from Adrianople to Philippopolis, in April 1230, and Theodore suffered his first defeat. He was taken prisoner and his army destroyed. The Latin Empire was saved by the ruler whose services it had spurned; the Empire of Thessalonica was deflated; and the western Greeks were for the moment no longer serious rivals either of Bulgaria or of Nicaea.

John Asen followed up his victory by pouring troops into Thrace and Macedonia; and within a few months Adrianople, Didymotichus, Serres, Ochrida, Prilep and even Dyrrachium were in Bulgarian hands, and Asen's authority was recognised from the Black Sea to the Adriatic, from Thessaly to Albania. Only the ghost of the Empire of Thessalonica survived. Theodore's brother Manuel, Asen's son-in-law, was allowed to reign in the city with the title of Despot. The fact that he signed his decrees in the cinnabar ink reserved to an Emperor was thought a great joke in Nicaea, where John Vatatzes had cause to be grateful to Asen for removing his rival from the scene. In the Cathedral of the Forty Martyrs which he built at Trnovo, Asen set up an inscription to record his victories. The Franks, he claimed, were now confined to the city of Constantinople, and ruled even that only at his pleasure. The claim was justified, for the initiative which had lain with Theodore Ducas had now passed to John Asen.

In the following years he proposed a grand alliance of the Orthodox powers against the common enemy, the Latins. In 1232, having quarrelled with Pope Gregory, he renounced the dependence of the Bulgarian Church upon Rome; and three years later he signed a treaty with John Vatatzes. Asen's daughter Helen, who had been rejected as a bride for the Latin Emperor Baldwin II, was to marry the son of Vatatzes, Theodore II Lascaris. The wedding took place at Lampsacus early in 1235; and Vatatzes officially recognised the autonomy and patriarchal status of the now Orthodox Bulgarian Church. Manuel of Thessalonica, who had toyed with the idea of putting himself under the protection of the Pope, quickly changed his mind and became a party, though a subordinate one, to the agreement made between his protector in Bulgaria and his rival in Nicaea. Thus, once again, as in the days of Kalojan, Greeks and Bulgars had been driven into each others' arms by the Latins.

That Vatatzes saw fit to reach this agreement with Bulgaria was due rather to his failure to reach agreement with the Papacy than to his fear of John of Brienne. In 1233 John had made a half-hearted raid over the Hellespont to Lampsacus, while most of the army and navy of Nicaea was otherwise occupied. Vatatzes had sent them to conquer the island of Rhodes, which had been held since 1204 by a Greek adventurer, Leo Gabalas, who had preserved his independence by favouring the commercial interests of Venice. He was reduced to a vassal of Nicaea, with the title of Caesar. Meanwhile, Vatatzes, though with inferior forces, had prevented the Latins from penetrating into his Empire; and John of Brienne, having missed his chance, withdrew. Nicaea could more than hold its own against the Latins. But Vatatzes, like Lascaris before him, had hopes that, as the Latin Empire grew manifestly weaker, the Pope would be ever more prepared to consider the restoration of Constantinople to the Greeks, if he could be assured that they for their part would renounce the schism.

Some Franciscans who happened to be passing through Nicaea in 1233 were able to convey this suggestion to Pope Gregory IX, who replied by sending to Vatatzes early in 1234 a delegation of two Franciscan and two Dominican friars, to discuss the problems involved. The Patriarch Germanus had recently sent an Exarch to reassert his authority over the Orthodox Church in Epirus, whose pretensions to autonomy had suffered with the collapse of the Empire of Thessalonica. His own Church was united, and he thought in terms of convening a general council. But the Pope's legates had no warrant for taking part in such a gathering, and the discussions that took place, first in Nicaea and then in Nymphaeum, soon came up against the familiar theological obstacles. Vatatzes offered to accept the Latin position on the use of unleavened bread in the Eucharist if the Latins would leave out the *filioque* from the Creed. On such conditions it was idle for the papal legates to hold out the hope that the Patriarchate might be restored to the Greeks if only they would recognise obedience to Rome. For, as later Byzantine Emperors were to discover to their cost, the theological differences were always dearer to the hearts of their clergy than any political advantages that might be gained by the union of the Greek and Roman Churches. The conference ended in anger and abuse; each side accused the other of heresy; and the Latin monks were lucky to get away without injury. At best they were able to take back to Pope Gregory a first-hand account of the desperate plight of the Latin Empire.

The coalition of Bulgaria and Nicaea, strengthened by the marriage of the young Theodore Lascaris to Helen Asen, was not as effective as it might have been. In 1235 the two rulers joined forces in Thrace and fought their way to the walls of Constantinople to besiege it by land and sea. But the city was saved, as it had been conquered, by Venetian ships, and by the courage of John of Brienne, who, though greatly outnumbered, fought like Hector at the walls of Troy. In 1236 Asen and Vatatzes tried again, only to be thwarted by the intervention of Geoffrey II of Villehardouin, who hurried from the Morea to add his resources to the defence of the city. But the Latins were almost at the end of their endurance. In the same year Baldwin II, then aged nineteen, left for Italy to seek help. Gregory IX appealed to the conscience of the western world to rescue Constantinople from the impious alliance of schismatics which threatened it, and warned Vatatzes of his impending destruction—to which Vatatzes replied, as before, that he would recognise the rights of the Papacy if the Pope would recognise his rights as Emperor. But John of Brienne died in March 1237, leaving an Empire which consisted of little more than a city, and that ever more impoverished and depopulated. A number of French knights responded to the call of Baldwin and the Pope; but most of the western world had lost interest in a dying cause, or had more important things in mind. The invasion of Europe by the Mongols portended greater disaster than the loss of Constantinople.

The alliance of Greeks and Bulgars soon broke up, however, as it had done before. John Asen quarrelled with Vatatzes, and sent ambassadors to Nicaea to retrieve his daughter. Feeling that a Greek Emperor restored to Constantinople would be the greater of two evils, he changed sides and went to the rescue of the Latin Empire. In 1237 he allowed a band of Cumans, fleeing from the Mongols, to cross the Danube and enter the service of the Latins; and at the end of the year he led an army of Bulgars, Cumans and Latins to lay siege to Tzurulum, one of the key strongholds of Vatatzes in Thrace. In the course of the campaign, however, the vengeance of God for his treachery to Nicaea visited him. His wife, his son and his Patriarch were all swept away by an epidemic. Asen was chastened into renewing his alliance with Vatatzes. The Pope was bitterly disappointed in him, and tried to persuade King Béla of Hungary to lead a crusade against Bulgaria. But the king of Hungary soon had enough to do in keeping the Mongols out of his country.

The alliance between Bulgaria and Nicaea produced no further fruits. But the death of Asen's wife led to the re-appearance of an older rival of Nicaea. Theodore Ducas, once Emperor in Thessalonica, who had been a prisoner in Bulgaria since 1230, suggested that Asen should marry his daughter Irene. Theodore had chafed in captivity; Asen had been forced to blind him when he was caught plotting against the throne. But now he had his way. He became the father-in-law of John Asen, and was allowed to make his way back to the scene of his former triumphs in Thessalonica. Having entered the city in disguise he soon dislodged his brother Manuel, and invested his reluctant son John with all the trappings of an Emperor. The unfortunate Manuel fled to Asia Minor, where the Seljuq Sultan was as interested as Vatatzes in helping him take his revenge on Theodore. Both supplied him with money and ships with which to return to Greece; and in 1239 he landed in Thessaly, which was controlled by his brother Constantine. But Theodore at once changed his tactics and persuaded Manuel to come to terms. A defensive alliance against Nicaea was formed by Theodore, Manuel, Constantine and John, the puppet Emperor in Thessalonica; and the three brothers made a treaty with the Latin princes of the Morea and Euboea. It looked as if almost the whole of Greece was now ranged against Nicaea.

In the north-west of Greece, however, there was yet another claimant to be considered. During the years when Theodore was a prisoner,

Michael II, son of the first Michael Ducas of Epirus, who had fled to the Morea when his father was murdered, had returned to Arta to take over what he regarded as his heritage.[1] He appears to have been established, with the consent of his uncle Manuel, as ruler of Epirus by 1231; he was certainly in possession of Corfu by 1236, for in December of that year he confirmed by chrysobull the privileges granted to the Corfiotes by his father Michael and his uncle Manuel, signing himself as Michael the Despot. He does not seem to have been included in the Greek and Latin coalition sponsored by his uncle Theodore, preferring perhaps to preserve his independence both from Thessalonica and from Nicaea. But his hour was soon to come.

John Vatatzes was discouraged by the re-emergence of his old enemy in Thessalonica. But he was patiently biding his time for another attempt on Constantinople. With John of Brienne gone and the Emperor Baldwin II still in the West, it seemed as if the Latin Empire might die a natural death, although Pope Gregory was doing his best to keep it alive. The barons longed for their Emperor to come back with an army. In desperation they had pawned the Crown of Thorns, the most sacred relic of the chapel of the Bucoleon Palace, to Venice. Unable to redeem it themselves, they gave the option to St Louis of France, who satisfied their creditors; and the relic was transported with fitting solemnity to Paris. Baldwin's return was delayed by his domestic affairs in France, and deliberately thwarted by Frederick II. But in the summer of 1239 he was at length able to set out by land for Constantinople at the head of a crusade of not less than 30,000 men. John Asen generously allowed him to lead them through Bulgaria, and he arrived in his capital at the end of the year. The Latin Empire enjoyed a brief moment of renewed glory. Baldwin secured the friendship of the invaluable Cumans by taking part in a curiously savage ceremony of alliance and encouraging his barons to marry their pagan daughters. Latins and Cumans together besieged and captured Tzurulum in 1240. Things had changed since the days when the first Baldwin had piously refused to parley with the infidel. His successor not only made a treaty with the new Seljuq Sultan Kaykhusraw II, who had been helped to his throne by Latin troops in 1237; he even tried to find him a wife from among his own relations in France. But he was hard put to it to pay his own troops

---

[1] Michael I of Epirus, in his treaty with Venice in 1210, refers to his son and heir by the name of Constantine. It is possible that Constantine and Michael II are to be identified. The principal source for his early career is the biography of his wife, St Theodora of Arta, by the monk Job, ed. A. Mustoxidi, Ἑλληνομνήμων (1843), pp. 42–59; J. A. Buchon, *Nouvelles recherches historiques sur la principauté française de Morée*, II (Paris, 1843), pp. 401–6; *MPG*, cxxvii, 901–6.

let alone those of his allies. The Cumans began to go over to Nicaea; and in 1241 Baldwin accepted a two-year truce with Vatatzes.

The year 1241 marks a turning point in the history of the Latin and Greek Empires. John Asen, who had successfully fished in troubled waters for twenty-three years, died in June, leaving Bulgaria in the hands of his infant son Koloman, whose regents promptly renewed his father's alliance with Nicaea. Pope Gregory IX, always a devoted supporter of the Latin Empire, died in August; and shortly before, Manuel of Thessalonica, who had tried to steer a middle course between Bulgaria and Nicaea, died, leaving northern Greece to be divided between his blind but restless brother Theodore, who maintained his son John as Emperor in Thessalonica, and his no less ambitious nephew Michael II of Epirus, who marched into Thessaly.

John Vatatzes was a methodical man who laid his plans carefully. He realised that the power behind the scene in Thessalonica was Theodore Ducas, and that his way towards the recovery of Constantinople could never be clear until he had eliminated the rival claimant to the Empire. In 1241 he invited Theodore to Nicaea as his guest. Theodore unwisely accepted, and found that he was detained as a prisoner. It remained to dispose of his son John. In 1242 Vatatzes led an army to Thessalonica, taking Theodore with him. He had barely arrived when news came from the East that the Mongols had invaded the Seljuq Sultanate on the very borders of Nicaea. Vatatzes withheld the news from his enemies, in case it would seem that he was acting under duress, and sent Theodore to negotiate a treaty with his son. John, who wanted to be a monk and might willingly have handed over the city, was persuaded by his father to surrender no more than was necessary. He agreed to be content with the title of Despot in place of that of Emperor, and to acknowledge the suzerainty of Nicaea over Thessalonica. Having thus humiliated the rival Empire, Vatatzes hurried back to Asia to defend his frontiers. But his work in Greece was only half done so long as Theodore Ducas remained at large; and he had given himself no time to come to terms with Theodore's nephew, the Despot Michael of Epirus.

Four years were to elapse before he was able to return to Greece. The Mongol invasion of Asia Minor threatened the existence of Greeks and Turks alike. In June 1243 Kaykhusraw II was defeated in battle by the Mongol general Baichu, and made to pay tribute to the Khan; and fearful of a worse fate he turned for support to Nicaea. In face of the common danger Vatatzes and the Sultan signed a treaty of alliance. Manuel Comnenus, Emperor at Trebizond, who, as a vassal of the Turks, had fought on the losing side, discreetly went over and was accepted as a vassal of the Mongols, who regarded Trebizond as a useful outlet to the Black Sea rather than as the capital of an Empire. But the Mongols withdrew as swiftly as they had appeared; and although Vatatzes had made great preparations to repel an invasion, the Empire of Nicaea survived unscathed and indeed stronger than before as a result of the damage that had been done to its neighbours.

Soon afterwards Vatatzes added greatly to the prestige of his Empire by securing an influential friend in the West. The Emperor Frederick II, at war with the Papacy, found himself in sympathy with the Greeks. The Greeks of Epirus were nearer neighbours than those of Nicaea, and he had come to regard them as allies who might one day be useful. Theodore Ducas and his brother Manuel had both sent embassies to him; and Michael, Despot of Epirus, followed their example in 1239. John Vatatzes too had already been in correspondence with him. Frederick was related by marriage to the Latin Emperor Baldwin and felt sorry for him. He had helped to arrange the truce between Baldwin and Vatatzes in 1241. But he felt also that Constantinople belonged by right to the Greeks, and hoped that if he supported them he would acquire a controlling interest in the city himself. In 1244 he gave his illegitimate daughter Constance, or Anna as the Greeks called her, in marriage to Vatatzes, and at the same time arranged for the truce between Nicaea and the Latin Empire to be extended for another year. Constance of Hohenstaufen was never happy in Nicaea. Her husband was fifty-two and she was only twelve; and he soon deserted her for one of her ladies-in-waiting. The marriage scandalised Pope Innocent IV. The treatment that Vatatzes gave his young wife scandalised his own clergy. But the friendship between the Eastern and the Western Emperors survived unbroken until Frederick's death in 1250.

By 1245 the patient diplomacy and careful strategy of Vatatzes was bearing its fruit. His truce with the Latins was running out; and Baldwin had left again for western Europe. He had weathered the storm of the Mongols, and had little to fear from the Turks. In the summer of 1246 he crossed over to inspect his garrisons in Thrace. While he was encamped by the Marica river word reached him that Koloman of Bulgaria had died, leaving the throne to his young brother Michael Asen. The temptation to invade Bulgaria was too strong to resist. Vatatzes led his army to Serres, which quickly surrendered, and from there overran all the country between the Strymon and the Marica, and much of western Macedonia, from Skoplje down to Prilep and Pelagonia. In November 1246 he signed a treaty with Michael Asen confirming his conquests. In Thessalonica the Emperor's triumphant progress created much excitement. Two years before, the Despot John had died, and his father Theodore had replaced him by his younger son Demetrius, who had tactfully sought recognition of his title as Despot from Nicaea. Demetrius was a dissolute and feckless youth. A plot was hatched to be rid of him. The conspirators went to see Vatatzes while he was encamped at Melnik on the Strymon, and obtained an assurance confirmed by chrysobull that if they succeeded and handed over the city to the Emperor he would guarantee its ancient rights and privileges. The plot matured, and before the end of 1246 Vatatzes was master of Thessalonica, and the Despot Demetrius was his prisoner. In the space of a few months the territory of the Empire of Nicaea had been doubled, and the ghost of the Empire of Thessalonica seemed to have been laid. Vatatzes returned in triumph to Asia Minor early in 1247, congratulating himself that he had now eliminated the last rival for the prize of Constantinople.

But he was rash enough to leave his oldest rival behind him. Theodore Ducas, blind, elderly and isolated, was allowed to stay in retirement in his castle at Vodena. Nor had Vatatzes yet come to terms with the Despot of Epirus. He might have guessed that Theodore would nourish the ambitions of his nephew Michael, and spur him on to the recovery of Thessalonica. For Michael too had profited from the weakness of Bulgaria and regained much of the territory that had been lost to John Asen in 1230. In the region of Ochrida and Prilep his boundaries for the first time now marched with those of Nicaea. He began to see himself as the only surviving heir to the title of Emperor in Greece.

But Vatatzes hoped for the best. He left strong garrisons in Thessalonica and the towns of Macedonia, and trusted that he would be master of Constantinople before the danger in Greece materialised. On his way back to Nicaea in 1247 he recaptured Tzurulum and drove the Latins out of Vizya, confining them even more closely to the suburbs of their capital. Baldwin was still in the West, dividing his hopes and attentions between Pope Innocent IV and his relative Frederick II. He was given an honourable seat at the Council of Lyons in 1245, at which Frederick was excommunicated; and the Council voted that a sum of money should be allotted for the relief of the Latin Empire and Patriarchate. He was sympathetically received at the court of St Louis, busy though Louis was with preparations for his own crusade which was destined for Syria; and he travelled to London to see Henry III, who grudgingly gave him some financial help. But the bankruptcy of the Latin Empire was now chronic. When he got back to Constantinople in October 1248,

Baldwin was reduced to selling the lead from the roof of his palace, and then to putting his only son, Philip of Courtenay, in pawn to the Venetians, the only Latins who contrived to remain solvent.[1]

But, as it happened, Constantinople was to receive yet another respite. A Genoese fleet attacked the island of Rhodes during the absence of its governor John, brother of the late Caesar, Leo Gabalas. Their enterprise was supported by William of Villehardouin, the prince of Achaea; and in 1249 Vatatzes had to take immediate action to avoid losing control of this strategic position. Much of his army and navy had to be diverted before the Genoese were driven out and Rhodes was restored. At the same time Pope Innocent IV put forward a new proposal for the solution of the problem of Constantinople. He had heard the facts from Baldwin and drawn his own conclusions. The union of the Churches might after all be better realised through Nicaea than through the now doomed experiment of a Latin Empire. Vatatzes was willing to reopen negotiations, for he would prefer if possible to win Constantinople by diplomacy rather than by force. For once both sides were ready to make concessions. The Pope would agree to sacrifice the Latin Empire and recognise the Greek Patriarchate if Vatatzes would guarantee the submission of the Greek Church to the Papacy. It was a bargain made between two political realists. But it left out of account the theological issues which would certainly have to be debated if the project were ever to be put into practice, and which would equally certainly generate such feeling that the project would come to grief. As it was, however, the preliminary discussions dragged on until both Vatatzes and Innocent IV died in 1254. It may be said that it was partly these negotiations which saved the Latin Empire from destruction by Vatatzes in the last few years of his reign.

But the Latins also owed their salvation to the mounting discord among the Greeks. In 1249 Vatatzes had proposed to protect his European frontier by arranging a diplomatic marriage with the Despot of Epirus. His grand-daughter Maria should marry Michael II's eldest son, Nicephorus. Michael's wife, Theodora Petraliphina, a lady renowned for her humility and piety, preferred peace to glory, and was doubtful about her husband's ambition to revive the Empire of Thessalonica. It was she who took her son to the court of Vatatzes, and made sure that the betrothal was solemnised and a treaty signed. But the aged Theodore Ducas, though confined to his castle at Vodena, regarded a liaison between Epirus and Nicaea as a betrayal

---

[1] On the fate of Philip of Courtenay see R. L. Wolff, 'Mortgage and redemption of an Emperor's son: Castile and the Latin Empire of Constantinople', *SP*, xxix (1954), 45–84.

of his life's work. He soon persuaded Michael to reject the treaty, and the last hope that the Greeks of east and west might combine forces for the restoration of their Empire was shattered.

In 1251 Michael, encouraged by Theodore, crossed his frontier in Macedonia, captured Prilep and advanced as far as the Vardar valley. Vatatzes had to bring a large army over to Europe and spend valuable months campaigning in the mountains behind Thessalonica. Early in 1253 he persuaded Michael to come to terms. Prilep was to be restored to him, and the frontier between the Empire of Nicaea and the Despotate of Epirus respected by both parties. Michael's Albanian allies, who had changed sides during the fighting, were rewarded with privileges which, it was hoped, would keep them loyal to Nicaea. But Theodore Ducas, condemned as the chief instigator of the 'revolt' of his nephew against the Emperor, was arrested and carried off to end his tumultuous career in prison. Later in the year 1253 Vatatzes returned to Nicaea, convinced that he had now finally stifled the pretensions of the western Greeks and could give his undivided attention to recovering Constantinople from the Latins. In Vodena, the last outpost of one who had never ceased to regard himself as Emperor, he left as one of his officers a young man of equally restless ambition called Michael Palaeologus.

It was John III Vatatzes who laid the ground and made it possible for the Greeks to restore the Byzantine Empire. But it was not given to him to reap the harvest of his labours. He died at Nymphaeum on 3 November 1254. The Empire that he left was a worthy successor of Byzantium. When he took it over thirty-two years before, the foundations of a sound administration and a solid defence had already been laid by Theodore Lascaris. Lascaris had shown that Nicaea could become a faithful copy of the Byzantine Empire; Vatatzes proved that, in many ways, the copy was more successful than the original as it had existed in the previous century. The economy of his Empire was essentially rural. There were few large cities, but much land; and it was on the distribution of that land that Vatatzes, like Lascaris before him, based his economic and military administration. The cartulary of the monastery of Lembos, rebuilt by Vatatzes in 1224, provides a fund of information in this respect for the parts of the Empire centred around Smyrna.[1] There, as no doubt elsewhere, the Emperors took over the estates which had formerly been held by proprietors in Constantinople, and divided them among the members of the aristocracy who had left the capital, either as *pronoiai* held in fief from the state, or as hereditary properties. The

[1] H. Glykatzi-Ahrweiler, 'La politique agraire des Empereurs de Nicée', *B*, XXVIII (1958), 51–66.

dispossessed members of the Byzantine aristocracy were well content to work loyally for Emperors who rewarded them so handsomely. The attempt of his cousin, Andronicus Nestongus, to organise a conspiracy against him is an isolated incident in the long reign of Vatatzes.

Along the vulnerable frontiers of his Empire, Vatatzes wisely revived the practice of earlier Emperors by granting small properties to his soldiers and establishing military *pronoiai*. The Cumans were eager to enter the service of Nicaea when they were offered small-holdings on which to settle along the Empire's boundaries in Thrace or in the Meander valley. The eastern frontier defences of Byzantium, strengthened by new fortifications, were better guarded in the time of Vatatzes than they had been for generations; and thanks to his sound economic policy he was never at a loss to pay for the hire of mercenaries, particularly Latins, who came to form a special corps in the army of Nicaea. Diplomacy too was a weapon in the hands of the Emperors of Nicaea, who, in the best Byzantine traditions, played off their enemies one against the other. Lascaris made friends with King Leo II of Lesser Armenia, just as in later years Vatatzes exchanged embassies with the Mongols, in order to embarrass the Turks, and annoyed the Despot of Epirus by granting privileges to the Albanians.[1] But Vatatzes liked to keep reminding his people that they lived in a constant state of emergency. He encouraged them to be self-sufficient by promoting agriculture and the breeding of cattle, and set the example himself by managing his own farm. The proceeds from the sale of the Emperor's eggs were enough to pay for a jewelled coronet which he gave to his first wife Irene, as an advertisement for what could be achieved by careful management. The trade in cattle and food between Nicaea and the Turks, especially after the devastation of the Sultanate by the Mongols, added greatly to the Empire's prosperity. But Vatatzes tried to shake off the dependence upon foreign, and particularly Venetian, trade which had begun to cripple the Byzantine economy in the twelfth century, and to make his subjects content with the products of their own soil and their own craftsmanship. No doubt the laws that he passed to repress extravagance and luxury were none too popular with an aristocracy that yearned for the bright lights of Constantinople. But Vatatzes worked hard to make the city of Nicaea a microcosm of the Queen of Cities. His wife Irene supported him in the foundation and patronage of hospitals and orphanages, the endowment of monasteries and churches, and the relief of the poor; and Nicaea provided a centre also for the perpetua-

[1] Theodore I Lascaris married Philippa, a niece of Leo II of Armenia, in 1214, by whom he had a son; but the marriage ended in divorce after only one year; see George Acropolites, ed. A. Heisenberg, I, pp. 26, 305.

tion of Byzantine art and literature. Men like George Pachymeres and Manuel Holobolus were born there during the years of exile, and Byzantine learning, culture and civilisation continued in unbroken tradition in Nicaea between the fall of Constantinople and its recovery. George Acropolites indeed, who came there as a youth, could see no reason for regarding the history of the Empire of Nicaea as anything but an integral part of the history of the Byzantine Empire.[1]

It was this sense of their own exclusiveness that led Acropolites and the other historians of Nicaea to belittle the achievements of the western Greeks, and to accuse them of having salvaged nothing from the wreck of Byzantium and contributed nothing to its revival. They liked to forget that the city of Arta, like Nicaea, was a flourishing offshoot of the Byzantine tradition, endowed with churches and monasteries by its rulers, not least the Despot Michael and his saintly wife Theodora. They might grudgingly allow that Theodore's capture of Thessalonica was a remarkable victory; but they could never regard him or his successors as anything but rebels against the divinely appointed Emperors in Nicaea. Finally, one searches in vain in the pages of Acropolites for any reference to the literary activities of John Apocaucus, George Bardanes or Demetrius Chomatianus, for all of whom it might be claimed that they played no less a part than the scholars of Nicaea in preserving and handing on the heritage of Byzantine learning and culture.

When Vatatzes died in 1254, his son, Theodore Lascaris, whom he had already made co-Emperor, was crowned as his successor. Theodore II had taken little part in the strategy or diplomacy of his father. He had been educated by the learned doctor Nicephorus Blemmydes, and had grown up preferring literature and theology to warfare and statesmanship. He was an epileptic, and his affliction made him vacillate between the extremes of nervous diffidence and blind self-confidence. Morbidly suspicious of the aristocracy, he surrounded himself with dependable civil servants of less exalted birth, of whom the chief was George Muzalon, who became his Grand Domestic; and he antagonised his clergy by appointing as Patriarch a narrow-minded ascetic called Arsenius. Theodore II was not the man to organise the recovery of Constantinople; but at least he was determined not to lose the territory or the prestige which his father had won for Nicaea.

[1] It is a measure of the affection and honour that John Vatatzes enjoyed in his own country that he was canonised soon after his death and revered as a local saint in Nymphaeum, where he died, and in Magnesia, where he was buried. See the fourteenth-century *Life of St John the Merciful* in A. Heisenberg, 'Kaiser Johannes Batatzes der Barmherzige', *BZ*, xiv (1905), 160–233.

At the start of his reign he announced his accession to the Sultan Kaykāwūs II and renewed the alliance between Greeks and Turks. No doubt he intended to perpetuate the alliances created by his father in other quarters. But he was forestalled; for early in 1255 Michael Asen of Bulgaria broke the bounds that Vatatzes had set to his territory, and invaded Thrace and Macedonia. It was not until May 1256, after two hard-fought campaigns, that Lascaris managed to restore his European frontiers and compel Asen to sign a treaty. The death of Vatatzes inspired Michael of Epirus also to rebellious thoughts. But when Asen was unexpectedly defeated he prudently changed his mind, and sent his wife Theodora with his son Nicephorus to see the Emperor in his camp on the Marica river, to conclude the arrangements made seven years before for the marriage of Nicephorus to the Emperor's daughter Maria. The wedding took place in October 1256. But Lascaris foolishly tried to exploit his advantage by demanding the surrender of Dyrrachium and Servia as a condition of the marriage. They were the most important towns on the east and west of the Despotate of Epirus, the one controlling the overland route from the Adriatic to the east, the other guarding the main road to Thessalonica from the south. Theodora, alone and defenceless, had to agree for fear of being taken prisoner. But Lascaris soon had cause to regret his unchivalrous diplomacy.

Like his father only three years before, he returned to Nicaea at the end of 1256 confident that he had settled affairs on his European frontiers. With regard to Bulgaria his confidence was justified, for Michael Asen was murdered in 1257; his cousin Kalojan II who usurped the throne was deposed; and a half-Serbian boyar, a nephew of Uroš I called Constantine Tich, was proclaimed tsar. His first act was to repudiate his wife and marry a daughter of Theodore Lascaris. But by then the storm had broken in the west. The Despot of Epirus, furious at the conditions deceitfully imposed on the marriage of his son, launched a campaign against Thessalonica. He incited the Albanians to break into revolt against Nicaea; his Serbian allies came to help him. The towns of western Macedonia were lost in quick succession; and in the summer of 1257, George Acropolites, whom Lascaris had left as Praetor of the western provinces, besieged in Prilep and cut off from Thessalonica, was sending urgent messages to Nicaea for reinforcements.

The best soldier that Lascaris could find was Michael Palaeologus, though he had a disquieting record of treachery. In 1253 he had been accused but acquitted of conspiracy by Vatatzes. Since then he had risen to be Grand Constable and commander of the Latin mercenaries of the Empire; and during the Bulgarian war Lascaris had made him governor of Nicaea. He had deserted to the Turks, only to return and ask for pardon with many protestations of unswerving loyalty to the Emperor and his son. Lascaris was torn between his well-merited mistrust of Michael Palaeologus and his faith in him as a general. In the end he compromised, and sent him to Thessalonica with an army which was too small to be effective. Palaeologus fought bravely with the forces that he had; but Michael of Epirus stormed his way into Prilep, captured Acropolites, and by the end of 1257 was master of most of western Macedonia and the approaches to Thessalonica. It was then that Lascaris, for reasons best known to himself, recalled Palaeologus to Nicaea and put him in prison without trial. The defence of Thessalonica was left in feeble hands; and several of the Emperor's officers, disgusted at his conduct, went over to the enemy.

For the last few years of its existence the Latin Empire of Constantinople, bankrupt and on the verge of collapse, was almost forgotten by the Greeks as the struggle for ascendancy was fought out between Epirus and Nicaea. Pope Alexander IV sent a legate to Nicaea in 1256 with powers to repeat the offer made by Innocent IV. But the legate never arrived. Lascaris instructed George Acropolites to waylay him in Macedonia and send him home. There was no longer any need to compromise the independence of the Byzantine Church in order to win the Byzantine throne. It was far more urgent for Lascaris to ensure that that throne was won from Nicaea and not from Epirus.

The situation became more ominous as Michael of Epirus began to build up a formidable chain of alliances. In the winter of 1257–8, while Michael was otherwise engaged, Manfred, the bastard son of Frederick II who had come into possession of the kingdom of Sicily, invaded Dyrrachium and other towns on the coast of Epirus. Michael, who had already reached the Vardar valley, was not to be discouraged from pressing on to Thessalonica. Instead he proposed to settle his accounts with Manfred by becoming his ally. Manfred, like earlier rulers of Sicily, had his own designs on Constantinople; and he had personal reasons for disliking the Greeks of Nicaea, for his half-sister Constance, widow of John Vatatzes, was being detained against her will at the court of Theodore Lascaris. Michael therefore suggested that Manfred should marry his eldest daughter Helena, offering as her dowry Corfu and many of the places on the Epirote mainland which Manfred had already appropriated. It was an arrangement convenient to both parties; and although the wedding did not take place at once, Michael was tactful enough not to dispute the terms of the dowry.

The third party in Michael's grand alliance was William of Villehardouin, the highly successful prince of Achaea. He was a fine soldier who enjoyed fighting. To join in battle against Nicaea would be for him to defend the lost cause of the Latin Empire. In the summer of 1258 he married Michael's second daughter Anna, who brought him a handsome dowry which included valuable estates in southern Thessaly. It seemed once again as if the whole continent of Greece was ranged against Nicaea.

The last months of the life of Theodore II Lascaris were overshadowed by the military and diplomatic victories of his rival in Greece. In a fit of impotent rage he ordered his Patriarch Arsenius to excommunicate Michael and all his people. But in August 1258 he died, leaving his Empire to his eight-year-old son John, under the regency of the Patriarch and his trusted adviser George Muzalon. The aristocracy of Nicaea, prominent among them Michael Palaeologus, swore to be loyal to the regent and his ward. But their pent-up bitterness against Muzalon and the *novi homines* whom Lascaris had favoured broke out only nine days after the Emperor's death. A conspiracy was formed, and in September Muzalon was murdered at the altar during a memorial service for the late Emperor. Michael Palaeologus became the hero of the hour. He seemed the man best able to defend the Empire. He was an illustrious member of its slighted aristocracy; for he could claim connections with the families of Ducas, Angelus and Comnenus, had married Theodora, a grand-niece of the Emperor Vatatzes, and came of parents who were both of the house of Palaeologus. He was popular with the army, not least with the Latin mercenaries, whose pay had been docked by Lascaris, and with the clergy; and the very fact that Lascaris had looked on him with such suspicion was now in his favour. He was appointed Grand Duke, and then, being careful to seek the Patriarch's approval, became regent for the young John Lascaris, with the title of Despot. The ease and rapidity of his rise to power suggests that Palaeologus knew what he wanted and had prepared the ground well in advance. In December 1258 he was proclaimed Emperor, and then, perhaps on Christmas Day, the Patriarch performed the double coronation of Michael VIII Palaeologus and John IV Lascaris.

As soon as he became regent Palaeologus posted reinforcements to Thessalonica under the command of his own brother John, the new Grand Domestic. In December 1258 he sent ambassadors to Michael of Epirus, and also to Manfred of Sicily and William of Achaea, hoping to break up the coalition by persuasion. But his diplomacy failed; and at the beginning of 1259 he made preparations for war. In March a large army, supplemented by Cuman and Turkish mercenaries, with contingents also from Hungary and Serbia, assembled in Thrace and set out for Thessalonica. John Palaeologus, however, had meanwhile scored an unexpected victory by surprising Michael of Epirus and his troops in the region of Castoria, driving them across the mountains and capturing the town of Berat in Albania. At Avlona on the Albanian coast Michael reassembled his army and called on the help of his allies. Arrangements were hastily concluded for the marriage of his daughter Helena to Manfred of Sicily, and an escort arrived to take her over to Trani in Apulia, where the wedding took place on 2 June 1259. Manfred promptly honoured his alliance by sending four hundred German knights to fight for his new father-in-law.

After an unsuccessful attempt to recover Berat, Michael joined forces with William of Villehardouin who had brought his own army over from the Morea, and with his son John Ducas, who was gathering an army of Vlachs in Thessaly. John Palaeologus had meanwhile regrouped his forces at Ochrida and was marching south. The armies met in the plain of Pelagonia. For a moment the fate of the Empire of Nicaea and the Byzantine throne seemed once again to hang in the balance. But in the tense excitement of that moment the army of Nicaea, composed of Greek soldiers and mercenaries under unified command, held firm, while the international alliance fighting for Epirus collapsed on the battlefield as its leaders fell out with each other. The Despot Michael's son John, personally insulted by Villehardouin and his knights, went over to the enemy. Michael himself, with his other son Nicephorus, deserted his allies in the night. What battle there was at Pelagonia was fought between John Palaeologus and the French and German cavalry of Villehardouin and Manfred. They fought with the desperation of men betrayed. But the Cumans mowed down the horses with their arrows. Manfred's knights were rounded up and surrendered. Villehardouin was found hiding near Castoria and taken prisoner. John Palaeologus followed up his victory by marching down into Thessaly, while his colleague, Alexius Strategopulus, invaded Epirus and captured Arta. Michael with his son Nicephorus took refuge with Matthew Orsini in Cephalonia.[1]

The victory of Pelagonia set the stage for the recovery of Constantinople. The only serious rival of Nicaea had been humiliated, and the capture of William of Villehardouin had deprived the Latin Empire of its only capable soldier. The Latins knew that their days were numbered. Even before his coronation they had made haste to

---

[1] A special study of the battle of Pelagonia has been made by D. J. Geanakoplos, 'Greco-Latin relations on the eve of the Byzantine restoration: The Battle of Pelagonia—1259', *DOP*, VII (1953), 99–141. Cf. D. M. Nicol, 'The date of the Battle of Pelagonia', *BZ*, XLIX (1956), 68–71.

ask for a truce with Michael Palaeologus, bargaining away their few remaining assets to play for time. But Michael refused to listen; and Baldwin II sheltered behind the walls of Constantinople and pinned his hopes on the only two powers who still showed any interest in his fate, the Papacy and Venice. Pope Alexander IV had no help to offer. But the Venetian fleet was still a potent factor in the defence of the city. So long as it patrolled the Bosphorus, Michael VIII could hardly fight his way in by sea. In the spring of 1260 there seemed a chance that the city might be delivered to him by treachery. One of Baldwin's knights called Anseau, perhaps the Anseau of Toucy who had been captured at Pelagonia, offered to have a gate opened from inside to permit the entry of the Emperor's troops. Michael VIII took an army over to Thrace and up to the outskirts of the city. But Anseau failed to fulfil his promise. The attempt ended in a futile attack on Galata; and Baldwin seized the moment to arrange a truce for another year.

The next attempt must be made by more open-handed methods; and there was no time to lose. For the news from Greece was disturbing. The Despot Michael, rejoined by his repentant son John, had fought his way back to Arta earlier in the year. His other son, Nicephorus, had been to see Manfred in Italy and had come back to Epirus with a company of Italian soldiers. Alexius Strategopulus, but lately made Caesar for his part at Pelagonia, had allowed himself to be captured by Nicephorus in a battle in the hills behind Naupactus, and was released only after signing a treaty. The Emperor hastily sent his brother John, whom he had now made Despot, back to Thessalonica to take control of the situation.

In the winter of 1260 he made sure of his other frontiers by renewing his alliances with the Sultan Kaykāwūs II, with the Mongols and with Constantine Tich of Bulgaria. It remained to find allies who could help him break the Venetian defences of Constantinople by sea. The problem was soon solved. The Genoese, ever the rivals of Venice, and only recently driven out of their profitable quarter in Acre, eagerly offered their services; and a treaty between Michael VIII and Genoa was drawn up at Nymphaeum on 13 March 1261. In return for the help of their fleet, and in the event of victory, the merchants of Genoa were to become heirs to all the concessions hitherto enjoyed by the Venetians in Byzantine waters, to have their own commercial quarter in Constantinople and the other major ports of the Empire, and to have free access to the harbours of the Black Sea. The treaty was ratified at Genoa on 10 July. Its consequences were disastrous for the future economy and peace of Byzantium; for Venice and Genoa were gradually to usurp almost all the commerce of the eastern

Mediterranean and the Black Sea, and fought out their perennial conflict over the paralysed body of the Empire. But at the time it seemed providential. For Michael VIII was not to know that, only a few weeks later, Constantinople would fall to him without the help of any fleet at all.

The recovery of Constantinople, which had so often seemed in sight in the last fifty years, and which had led to so much jealousy and bloodshed between the Greeks of the east and the Greeks of the west, was achieved in the end almost by accident. While waiting for his truce with Baldwin to expire in August 1261, Michael VIII had sent his general Alexius Strategopulus with a small army over to Thrace to guard the Bulgarian frontier and sound the defences of Constantinople. The Latins had long since abandoned their land beyond the walls and made it over to Greek farmers who had free access to the city. They called themselves *thelematarioi* or Voluntaries, to describe the kind of neutrality that they enjoyed. It was from them that Strategopulus, having reached Selymbria, learnt that almost the whole of the Latin garrison was at that moment absent from the city. The new Venetian Podestà, Marco Gradenigo, had persuaded Baldwin to allow him to take them away in ships to attack the island of Daphnusia in the Black Sea off the Bithynian coast. The Voluntaries also knew of an underground passage into the city and of a spot where scaling-ladders could safely be erected. The opportunity was too good to miss. In the dead of night some of Strategopulus' troops made their way, with the help of the Voluntaries, under or over the walls, surprised the guard at the Gate of the Fountain, and hacked it open from inside before the alarm could be sounded. On 25 July 1261 a Greek army marched once more into Constantinople.

There was some fighting in the streets, but by the break of day it was seen that the Greeks had taken possession of the land walls. As they advanced on the imperial palace, the Emperor Baldwin escaped to the harbour, where he boarded a Venetian merchant ship and fled to Euboea. His crown and sceptre were found abandoned in the palace. To forestall the return of the garrison from Daphnusia, Strategopulus was advised to set fire to the Venetian quarter of the city; and when the Venetians, hearing of the disaster, returned with the soldiers, it was to find their homes and properties in flames and their families crowded on the quays. All that they could do was to salvage what remained and sail away. The refugees swarmed aboard their ships and the fleet made for Euboea; but many died of hunger or thirst before they reached safety.

Michael VIII was asleep in his camp at Meteorium some two hundred miles away when the good news was brought to him. His sister Eulogia woke him. At first he refused to believe the story; but when a courier from Strategopulus arrived bringing the regalia of the Latin Emperor, Michael joyfully accepted the fact that Christ had delivered Constantinople to him. When he had made fitting preparations for so great an occasion he crossed the Sea of Marmora; and on 15 August 1261, with the icon of the Hodegetria held aloft, he entered the Golden Gate and walked in solemn procession along the ancient triumphal way to the cathedral of St Sophia. There, when he had given thanks to God, a second coronation ceremony was performed by the Patriarch Arsenius. But this time Michael Palaeologus was crowned alone. The legitimate Emperor, John IV Lascaris, was left neglected in Nicaea. Within the year he had been blinded and confined to a castle on the Black Sea. The tale ended as it had begun, with a usurper on the throne and a blinded Emperor in prison.

The Latin Empire had run its course. There is little to be said in its favour. But it seemed that only when it was too late did the western world realise the value of the jewel that had been let slip, and cast about for means of recovering it. Baldwin II found help and comfort at the court of Manfred of Sicily. Manfred's successor, Charles of Anjou, almost succeeded in launching what some of the Popes were still prepared to define as a crusade for the benefit of the Church and the Holy Land. For many generations the Byzantine Emperors had to be constantly on their guard against the efforts of the Latin claimants to their Empire to stage a repetition of the Fourth Crusade.

The Greeks returned to find their capital desolate and in ruins. Whole districts had been devastated by fire, and even the imperial palaces were so dilapidated as to be scarcely habitable. The damage to the city could be repaired. But the damage to the Byzantine Empire was irreparable. Constantinople, once the capital of an Empire that claimed to embrace the *oikoumene*, was reduced to the status of an overgrown city quite disproportionate in size to the extent of its dominions. Many provinces remained in the hands of French or Italian colonists, or what was worse, in the hands of Greeks who refused to recognise Michael VIII and his successors as Emperors. The Emperors of Trebizond maintained their independence to the last. Though cut off by Seljuqs, Mongols and finally Ottomans, the heirs of David and Alexius the Grand Comneni, embarrassed Michael VIII and his successors by refusing to revoke their claim to the title of Emperor, and built up a microcosm of Byzantium on the shores of the Black Sea. The walls and churches of Trebizond, with their frescoes of the thirteenth to fifteenth centuries, still testify to the preservation of an outpost of Greek culture and Christianity in an alien world for over two and a half centuries. For the Empire of Trebizond had the distinction of being the last Greek Empire. It outlived Byzantium itself, and did not finally succumb to the Turks until 1461. The Despots of Epirus, who could never forget their years of glory, also went on fighting for what they still considered to be their rights, making friends with all the foreign enemies of Byzantium and keeping open house for all the Greeks who, for reasons of Church or state, fell foul of Michael VIII. The habit of independence proved too strong to be eradicated. The heirs of the first Michael of Epirus and his half-brother Theodore, once Emperor at Thessalonica, held out in Arta and in Thessaly for over half a century after the recovery of Constantinople. The many richly decorated Byzantine churches and monasteries which they built and endowed are still to be seen in the town and district of Arta; and the memory of the Blessed Theodora, wife of Michael II, is still revered. The reconquest for Byzantium of the long-lost provinces of Epirus and Thessaly was reckoned among the greatest achievements of Andronicus III. But they fell an easy prey to the Serbs in 1348 and to the Turks some fifty years later. The Fourth Crusade accelerated the process of the decentralisation of the Empire, and made it impossible for the Byzantines ever again to present a united front to the growing danger from the East. It was the Greeks in Nicaea and not the Latin Emperors who kept the Seljuq Turks at bay during the years of exile. But when the Ottoman Turks directed their immense power against Byzantium in later years, the Empire was too divided to fulfil its traditional function of defending the eastern wall of Christendom.

Perhaps the greatest victim of the Fourth Crusade was Christendom itself. The Popes, who had made themselves believe that the Latin Empire would be the means of uniting eastern and western Christians in faith and action against the infidel, were loth to admit that the experiment had failed. But after the experience of Latin pillage and Latin occupation it was no longer possible for the Christians of the East to think dispassionately or in rational terms about the Christians of the West. The union of the Churches was again proposed from time to time; it was forced on his unwilling subjects by Michael VIII, with unhappy consequences. But the proposal was made as a matter of policy and not as a matter of faith. The Greeks, who had suffered what they considered to be the effects of papal ambition, were inclined to think that this was all that could be expected from foreigners who tampered with the traditions and the creed of the councils of the Church. It was not simply dogma or doctrine that separated the Greek East from the Latin West after

1204. Many years later the monk Barlaam of Calabria spoke for the Greeks when he pointed out to Pope Benedict XII 'that a difference of dogma does not so much divide the hearts of the Greeks from you as the hatred of the Latins which has entered into their spirit, as a result of the many and great evils which the Greeks have suffered from the Latins at various times, and are still suffering day by day'.[1]

[1] Barlaam, *Oratio pro unione habita, MPG,* CLI, 1336.

CHAPTER VIII

THE PALAEOLOGI

I. AFTER THE RESTORATION

The two hundred years (1261–1453) during which the Palaeologi occupied the throne of Constantinople are marked by the steady decline of the Byzantine Empire. At a time when western Europe saw vigorous national development and the evolution of new forms of society, the strength of East Rome was withering away. Its history during this period can show no real parallel to the youthful vitality of the western cities, caused by the rise of new social forces; on the contrary, signs of old age become ever more apparent. The growing internal weakness of the Byzantine State continually lessened its power to resist external foes, and this was the real cause of its ultimate collapse.

The origins of decline can be traced far back into the past. As early as the eleventh century there are signs that the power of Byzantium was on the wane. Under the weak rule of the later Macedonians and the Ducas family the economic strength of the Empire declined and its administration began to crumble. Under the Comneni, Byzantium lost her naval supremacy to Venice. During the early middle ages the Empire had been the leading Christian power in the economic, political and cultural life of the Mediterranean world; now it was pushed into the background by the ascendancy of the western powers, above all the Italian city-states, and was eventually overthrown by the crusading army of the West and the fleet of Venice (1204). Driven back into Asia Minor, the Byzantines created there a state of greater internal strength and soundness than the old Empire which had broken down. From Asia Minor they gradually succeeded in regaining the status of a great power, and in 1261 they re-entered Constantinople. Thus a situation was re-established which once before had already proved to be untenable. Moreover, the position in Asia Minor was now weakened, and the way prepared for the rise of the Ottoman Turks.

It is true that after the restoration of 1261 the general prestige of the Byzantine Empire was at first strongly enhanced. For a time Byzantium once more exerted definite influence on the political life of the European states, and once again became the focus of Mediterranean politics. This revival was, however, deceptive, and although the political skill of the first of the Palaeologi secured some triumphs,

they were followed by even severer setbacks. To maintain the renewed status of a great power, more strength and more resources
were required than the Empire could muster; all the more so as the
era of Latin rule in Constantinople had left many serious after-effects.
The wounds in the body politic could not be healed simply by the
restoration of its head, for the supporting but enfeebled frame was
open to attack from all sides. The Italian maritime cities controlled
Byzantine waters, their colonies were scattered all over the Empire,
the most important islands of the eastern Mediterranean were subject
to them. Southern and central Greece were still dominated by the
Franks. Under Greek leadership, Epirus, together with Thessaly,
had withdrawn from the Byzantine Empire and stubbornly resisted
its policy of unification. The north of the Balkan peninsula was held
by the Slav states of the Bulgars and Serbs which had grown at
the expense of the Byzantine Empire; their tendency to expand
threatened it with further losses. None of these powers was yet strong
enough to start an action on a major scale, but they were all ready to
support any western enterprise hostile to Byzantium. And the restored Empire certainly had western enemies, particularly among
those same powers who had been interested in maintaining the Latin
Empire. An attack could thus be expected at any time, and an
alliance between the enemies of Byzantium in the West and those in
the Balkans would mean mortal danger.

This threat could only be averted by skilful diplomacy. Michael
VIII, an unrivalled master in political manœuvring, was faced by a
double task. The aggressive plans of the West had to be thwarted by
diplomatic means, and Byzantine rule in the Balkan countries to be
re-established by force of arms.[1] This led to hard fighting on several
fronts, making severe demands on imperial resources.

In his relations with Frankish Greece, Michael VIII seemed at first
to be in a favourable position for, since the battle of Pelagonia in
1259, William of Villehardouin had been his prisoner. Thus the
Emperor could dictate terms before allowing him to return to the
Morea late in 1261 to resume his rule. William of Villehardouin
received the honorary title of Grand Domestic, took the oath of
fealty to the Emperor, and had to cede to him the important fortresses
of Monemvasia, Mistra, Maina and Geraki.[2] Thus Byzantium gained
a strong base for operations in the Peloponnese, from which an offensive was mounted in the following spring, for William of Ville-

---

[1] On the policy of Michael VIII towards the western powers see D. J. Geanakoplos,
Emperor Michael Palaeologus and the West.

[2] Geraki (Hierakion) is mentioned only by Pachymeres, I, p. 88 (*CSHB*), and not in
the *Chronicle of Morea* (ed. J. Schmitt), ll. 4329 ff., or by Sanudo, *Istoria del regno di
Romania* (ed. C. Hopf, *Chroniques gréco-romanes*), p. 103.

hardouin deserted his overlord soon after his return. William had been absolved by the Pope from the oath of loyalty which he had sworn at Constantinople. He also obtained strong backing from the Venetian Republic whose interests the Emperor had seriously menaced in destroying the Latin Empire, virtually created by Venice, and in concluding a treaty of alliance with its rival Genoa.

The war started with the victorious advance of Byzantium, whose armies, supported by strong auxiliary forces of Seljuqs, penetrated deep into the interior of the Peloponnese. At the same time, the combined fleets of Byzantium and Genoa attacked the Frankish islands. Apart from the campaign in Frankish Greece, there was also fighting against Epirus and Bulgaria. The operations in Epirus were at first unsuccessful, but in 1264 the Byzantines gained an important victory, whereupon the Despot Michael II had to acknowledge the suzerainty of the Emperor. His son and heir Nicephorus, who had once been married to a daughter of Theodore II Lascaris, now married a niece of Michael VIII. The establishment of dynastic unions by marriage was an instrument of diplomacy which Michael Palaeologus used frequently and with particular skill.

Then, with comparatively little effort, Byzantine power was further extended at the expense of the weakened Bulgarian Empire, which was forced to surrender the territories of Philippopolis and Stenimachus as well as the seaports of Sozopolis, Develtus, Anchialus and Mesembria on the west coast of the Black Sea (1263). Contention over these important harbours, particularly Anchialus and Mesembria, disturbed relations between Byzantium and Bulgaria as long as the Empire lasted.

Meanwhile the fighting in the Peloponnese, after initial successes, took an unfavourable turn. Frankish resistance stiffened, and as the war continued, Byzantine difficulties increased. The Seljuq auxiliaries, failing to receive regular pay, went over to the Franks and in 1264 the Byzantines were severely defeated at Makry-Plagi.

Their allies at sea fared no better; in the spring of 1263 the Genoese fleet was beaten at Settepozzi by the Venetians. The defeat caused the Emperor to change his policy towards the Italian maritime republics: he temporarily severed his alliance with the Genoese, sent their ships home, and took up negotiations with the superior power of Venice. On 18 June 1265 a treaty was drafted according to which the Venetians were again to enjoy extensive privileges in the Empire. Venice, however, delayed the ratification of the treaty, and since the situation in the West was becoming more and more threatening, Michael VIII once again approached Genoa. The Genoese, who had suffered a further defeat in their war with Venice (1266), readily accepted the Emperor's offer. They were again to enjoy freedom of trade in the Empire and were assigned quarters in Galata, the suburb of Constantinople on the Golden Horn (1267). Here they remained until the Turkish conquest, and Galata soon developed into a flourishing Genoese trading community. The recall of the Genoese to Byzantium ended Venetian vacillation: on 4 April 1268 the treaty between Byzantium and Venice was ratified, although the clause dealing with the expulsion of the Genoese was omitted. It is significant that for the time being the treaty was concluded for five years only; Venice introduced a new system of agreements which could be annulled at short notice. As it was, by establishing contact with Venice as well as with Genoa, the Emperor was in a position to shift his policy between the two maritime republics and to play off one against the other.

It was outside the Empire, however, in southern Italy that the most decisive and for the Byzantines the most disastrous events occurred. Sicily was the centre of aggression against Byzantium, and therefore the policy of Michael VIII throughout his reign revolved round his relations with the Sicilian kingdom. Sicilian plans of conquest only began to be dangerous when supported by the Pope; Michael Palaeologus therefore made it his chief concern to prevent an alliance between the Sicilian kingdom and Rome. This was easy as long as King Manfred ruled over Sicily, because the ancient papal feud with the Hohenstaufen stood in the way of a union between the Curia and Manfred. But the situation was radically changed when, at the Pope's invitation, Charles of Anjou, the Count of Provence and brother of the French king Louis IX, came to Italy and overthrew the rule of the Hohenstaufen in the battle of Benevento, on 26 February 1266. The danger that the Pope would favour Sicilian projects of conquest then became immediate and acute. In fact, Charles of Anjou had hardly become master of Sicily when his anti-Byzantine intentions became manifest, and the papal attitude was made equally obvious. At Viterbo on 27 May 1267, in the presence of the Pope, the new king of Sicily concluded a treaty of friendship with the Latin Emperor Baldwin II who had been expelled from Constantinople. The treaty envisaged a marriage between Charles's daughter Beatrice and Baldwin's son Philip, and culminated in an agreement to conquer and partition the Byzantine Empire. The agreement was also joined by William of Villehardouin who had gone in person to Viterbo. He put his country under the suzerainty of Charles of Anjou, and gave his daughter and heiress Isabella in marriage to Charles's son Philip. Thus after his death the principality of the Morea would fall to the house of Anjou.

In order to avert the danger threatening his realm, Michael VIII had already begun to negotiate with Urban IV (1261–4) about reunion between the Greek and Roman Churches. After the situation in southern Italy had changed, he approached Clement IV (1264–8) with new promises of a reunion, and once again the bait which Byzantine diplomacy held out to Rome and which had always worked, produced the desired effect. For Rome sought to extend papal influence over the eastern Christians by the removal of the Greek schism and the liberation of the Holy Land. Papal plans, unlike those of the king of Sicily, did not include the conquest of the Byzantine Empire. In fact, events from 1204 onwards had already shown that the cause of ecclesiastical reunion was not to be advanced simply by occupying Byzantine territory. A far-sighted papal policy in the East could not be well served by association with the aggressive plans of Charles of Anjou. If Clement IV pretended to support those plans, he did so with the intention of exerting pressure on the Byzantine Emperor and of forcing him into submission to the Church, in order to achieve the papal, not the Angevin, policy.[1] After the death of Clement IV a prolonged vacancy of the Holy See occurred. The versatile Palaeologus then approached St Louis; the French king, zealous as always for a crusade, did in fact prevent his aggressive brother from waging war against the Greek Christians and compelled Charles to join his expedition to Tunis in the summer of 1270. Thus at a decisive moment the enterprise planned against Byzantium came to a standstill. The Tunisian crusade, however, was but a brief interlude; soon after his arrival in Africa Louis IX succumbed to an epidemic. After a short and victorious campaign Charles returned to Sicily, again prepared for an expedition against Byzantium, and once more sent troops to Greece. In September 1271 the vacancy in the Roman See was at last filled, and in spite of the opposition of Charles of Anjou, Gregory X, an ardent champion of the idea of a united Church, became Pope. More than ever before, plans for a crusade and reunion were made the centre of Rome's eastern policy.[2]

In the Balkans, Michael VIII sought to strengthen his position by dynastic marriages. The western Greek realm had disintegrated after the death of the Despot Michael II (1271): in Epirus, Nicephorus I, the legitimate heir who was married to a niece of the Emperor of Byzantium, took control; in Thessaly however, John, an illegitimate son of Michael II, maintained his rule. He was awarded the title of *sebastocrator* by the Emperor who also made his nephew

---

[1] Cf. the argument of W. Norden, *Das Papsttum und Byzanz*, pp. 443 ff., which, though often criticised, has never been surpassed in the acuteness of its analysis.

[2] On Gregory X see I. Gatto, *Il Pontificato di Gregorio X (1271–1276)*.

Andronicus Tarchaniotes marry John's daughter. This turned out to be an insufficient safeguard. The energetic and bellicose ruler of Thessaly soon became a relentless enemy of the Empire, and Tarchaniotes made common cause with his father-in-law. It was all the more difficult for Byzantium to reach agreement with the separatist Greek states, since the destruction of these states was one of the chief aims of the Emperor. Indeed the same difficulties stood in the way of closer relations with the countries of the southern Slavs as they too were included in Michael VIII's irredentist plans. The project of a marriage alliance with the ruling Serbian house did not materialise. Instead Michael VIII managed to ally with Hungary, thus counterbalancing Serbia's preference for the Angevins, and his heir and successor Andronicus was married to a Hungarian princess (1273). In Bulgaria the tension seemed to be lessening; the Tsarina Irene Lascarina, who had been bitterly hostile to Palaeologus, had died and the Bulgarian Tsar Constantine Tich had married a niece of the Emperor. Michael VIII, however, did not hand over the ports of Anchialus and Mesembria which he had promised as dowry. Another war broke out and the Bulgars invaded Byzantine territory; but under pressure from the Tatars they were forced to withdraw and to give up the disputed cities. For Michael VIII had come to an understanding with Nogaj, the great leader of the Golden Horde, to whom he gave his illegitimate daughter Euphrosyne in marriage together with valuable presents. The ring of hostile powers surrounding Byzantium was itself encircled by another ring which was to keep in check the enemies of the Empire. Michael VIII had for some time past maintained friendly relations with Hülegü, the powerful Khan of the Mongols in the Near East, as a counter-balance to the sultanate of Rūm in Asia Minor; in the same way the Mongols of the Golden Horde now exerted pressure on Bulgaria. In the rear of the Serbs stood Hungary as an ally of the Empire, and Charles of Anjou, the chief enemy of Byzantium, was restrained from attacking the Empire by a Papacy inspired by the hope of ending the schism.

But mere promises of reunion, which Michael had dangled before the Curia for over a decade, could no longer satisfy Gregory X. He set before the Emperor a clear-cut alternative, promising him full security against action by the Catholic powers if he submitted to the Roman Church; otherwise he declared himself unable to restrain Charles of Anjou any longer. When the treaty between Byzantium and Venice expired, the Pope used this added opportunity to exert strong pressure on the Emperor, exhorting the Venetians not to renew the treaty before reunion had been achieved.

Charles of Anjou, for his part, put up a great display of political and diplomatic activity. In 1273 he sent more troops to the Morea than ever before. He already held a commanding position in Albania, gateway for the invasion of Byzantium, since his authority was recognised by the Catholic part of the country. It was also easy for him to win over the ruler of Thessaly who was such a bitter opponent of the Emperor. Furthermore, Charles succeeded in making contact with the rulers of the southern Slavs. In 1273 ambassadors of the Bulgarian tsar and the Serbian king arrived at his court. All the enemies of the Byzantine Empire—Latins and Greeks, Slavs and Albanians—rallied under the leadership of Charles of Anjou. He was preparing for a major attack on the Empire, supported by the titular Latin Emperor of Constantinople and the ruler of Frankish Greece, to both of whom he was allied and related by marriage. In these circumstances Gregory X's ultimatum had a crushing effect. Nothing was left to the Emperor but submission to the papal will. At the Second Council of Lyons, on 6 July 1274, the Grand Logothete George Acropolites took the oath and accepted papal primacy and the Roman faith in the name of his master. The Union of the Church, which for more than two centuries had been one of the chief aims of Rome's eastern policy and the subject of frequent but always unsuccessful negotiations, had become a reality.

The Emperor could now avail himself of the political advantages accruing from the ecclesiastical submission. Papal pressure forced Charles of Anjou to give up the campaign against Byzantium and to commit himself to an armistice until 1 May 1276. Venice renewed her treaty with the Emperor in March 1275, though for two years only. Byzantium, which had but recently been precariously on the defensive, had now regained the initiative and could take the offensive on all sides. Even while the Council of Lyons was still in session, the Angevin troops were being hard pressed in Albania; the Byzantines occupied Berat and Butrinto, laid siege to Dyrrachium and Avlona, and did not raise it even after the conclusion of the armistice. On the other hand, the campaign against Thessaly, which under the *sebastocrator* John Angelus had become a centre of hostility to the Emperor, failed after initial successes (1275 and 1277). But at sea the Empire gained some important acquisitions. The successful naval operations of the Italian Licario, who had been promoted *megas dux*, culminated in the occupation of Euboea and several of the Aegean islands; thus Byzantium again controlled the sea-route from Constantinople to Monemvasia. At the same time, Byzantine rule was considerably extended in the Peloponnese. After the death of William of Villehardouin in 1278, it is true that the Latin principality of the Morea came under the direct rule of Charles of Anjou, but this did in fact weaken the system of Frankish rule. All told, the position of Byzantium was greatly strengthened by sea and land.

These successes, however, were gained at the cost of grave internal disturbances. The large majority of the Byzantine clergy and people had always regarded Orthodoxy as their most sacred possession, and hatred of the Latins was in their very blood; they flatly refused to submit to Rome and put up a strong resistance to the Emperor. The relations of Michael VIII with the Greek Church had been seriously disturbed before. After the young John Lascaris had been blinded, Michael was excommunicated by the Patriarch Arsenius. After great efforts, the Emperor eventually succeeded in deposing the rigid and ascetic Patriarch (1265), but part of the clergy and the people remained loyal to the banished Arsenius. A new party, the Arsenites, came into being which stubbornly opposed the Emperor and the new leaders of the Church. There was an outcry of indignation when Michael VIII submitted to the Pope and asked his Church to recognise the supremacy of Rome. The situation became even more difficult when the Patriarch Joseph could not be induced to accept the Union. It was therefore necessary to make a complete break and appoint a new head of the Church. In 1275 the Chartophylax John Beccus was installed as Patriarch, a very gifted and many-sided man, who after initial opposition had accepted the Union. Two hostile camps now confronted each other: the elimination of the Greco-Roman schism, imposed as it was from above, created a deep schism within the Byzantine Empire. Moreover, the Emperor's policy of Union gave rise to serious complications in the Orthodox countries outside the frontiers of Byzantium. Michael's sister, Eulogia, who was strongly opposed to the Union, joined her daughter Maria, the Tsarina of the Bulgars. Under the influence of the two women, the Bulgarian court became a focus of activity against the Emperor. The tension soon lessened, if only temporarily, as a long civil war broke out in Bulgaria. In 1279 the Byzantines succeeded in forcibly placing on the Bulgarian throne John Asen III, a Hellenised descendant of the Asen family, who was married to Michael's daughter Irene. In the separatist Greek states hostility against an Emperor who had accepted the Union led to particularly disastrous repercussions. Even the peaceful Nicephorus of Epirus rose against Michael and occupied Butrinto which had only recently been taken by the Byzantines; later he handed it over to Charles of Anjou (1279). John of Thessaly, the Emperor's old enemy, and for many years an ally of the western powers, now made himself the champion of Greek Orthodoxy, and at a Council in 1277 even had the Emperor condemned as a heretic.

At Rome itself there were critical developments in the policy of ecclesiastical reunion. On 22 February 1281, Martin IV, a Frenchman and a mere tool in the hands of Charles of Anjou, was elected to the Holy See. A sudden change of policy ensued. The Curia renounced the supreme right of arbitration which it had hitherto striven to exercise in the political struggles of the great powers. Under the patronage of the Pope, Charles of Anjou on 3 July 1281 concluded a treaty at Orvieto with the titular Latin Emperor Philip, the son of Baldwin II who was now dead, and with the republic of Venice, for the purpose of destroying Byzantium and restoring the Latin Empire. Indeed Martin IV, blindly following Charles's instructions, deviated from the policy of his predecessors to such an extent that he condemned as schismatic the Byzantine Emperor who had upheld the Union and had for that reason encountered bitter opposition from his own people. The Pope proclaimed Michael's deposition and ordered all Christian rulers to sever relations with him.

Thus Michael VIII's policy of Union had suffered complete shipwreck. Even Rome abandoned it. The western powers united to fight Byzantium; Venice lent Charles her fleet, and the Pope gave moral support. The rulers of the Balkan states joined the front against the Eastern Empire. John of Thessaly and the Serbian King Milutin made a joint attack on Macedonia (1282). In Bulgaria, John Asen III, the Byzantine favourite, had lost his crown in 1280 and George I Terter, who had deprived him of his throne, naturally turned against Byzantium and formed an alliance with Charles of Anjou and John of Thessaly. Never before had Charles of Anjou been nearer his goal, and never before had the situation been so desperate for Michael VIII.

At that crucial moment a complete change took place. Michael's diplomatic skill achieved its greatest triumph. Through the mediation of the famous adventurer John of Procida, Michael VIII seems to have made contact with King Peter of Aragon, son-in-law of Manfred. Peter was to attack Charles from the rear and wrest from him the kingdom which he had taken from King Manfred. The Byzantine Emperor put at his disposal the means for the building of a fleet. Simultaneously, the Emperor's partisans in Sicily stirred up rebellion against the foreign rule of the Angevins. Success was assured; there was deep discontent among the exhausted populace because Charles of Anjou was continuously arming and his officials abused their authority. On 31 March 1282 a revolt broke out at Palermo and rapidly spread over the whole island. Charles of Anjou's domination of Sicily came to a sudden and bloody end in the Sicilian Vespers.[1] In August, Peter of Aragon arrived with his fleet and at Palermo he

---

[1] Cf. S. Runciman, *The Sicilian Vespers.*

received the crown of Manfred. Charles of Anjou barely saved his possessions on the Italian mainland.

A campaign for the conquest of Byzantium was now out of the question: the kingdom of South Italy was in ruins, Charles of Anjou vanished from the scene and the Pope also was severely affected by the consequences of this catastrophe; the titular Latin Emperor was no longer taken seriously, and Venice sought an alliance with Peter of Aragon and the Byzantine Emperor.

II. THE BEGINNING OF THE DECLINE

Thus the struggle against western aggression had been successfully carried through. But the strain of that struggle and of continuous warfare in the Balkans had completely exhausted the Empire. Michael VIII's desire to play the part of a great power placed too heavy a burden on the ageing state. Its military and financial strength was drained and its capacity for warding off new enemies was undermined. The heavy overstrain during Michael VIII's reign was followed by a serious relapse and Byzantine power began rapidly to decay without any prospect of recovery. The state, internally exhausted and suffering from incurable ailments, was never again sufficiently resilient to recover from a severe crisis, while the growing pressure from without drove the Empire towards the inevitable catastrophe. Only as a centre of civilisation did Byzantium retain its importance undiminished. Art and scholarship flourished during the age of the Palaeologi and, in spite of political decline, Constantinople remained one of the cultural centres of the world. Politically, however, the Empire sank to the position of a minor state, and eventually became the prey of more powerful neighbours. Nevertheless, by reason of its geographical position and its great traditions, the Byzantine Empire remained a particularly important and desirable object of conquest in the eyes of surrounding countries. It is for this reason that it still retained some political significance in international diplomacy.

The contrast between its outstanding cultural achievements and its political decline is especially characteristic of the period of Andronicus II (1282–1328). His long reign was a period of decisive events and heavy losses; the restored Empire sank from illusory heights to a state of exhaustion and chaos, partly brought about by suicidal internal conflicts.

During the reign of his father Michael VIII, Andronicus II as his co-Emperor had enjoyed far-reaching powers. His own son and co-Emperor Michael IX (d. 1320) was to play under him an even more important part. The growing significance of the position of the co-Emperor was typical of the age of the Palaeologi.[1] The centralised monarchy was beginning to be transformed into the joint rule of the imperial house over the centrifugal forces of the Empire. In fact the structure of the state became more and more unstable, and the ties between the centre and the provinces were increasingly weakened. The provinces were actually bound to the central government only by the person of the governor. It was for that reason that provincial governors were usually chosen from relations of the Emperor or members of his household. They changed quickly, as confidence in them was often rapidly undermined. When these remaining feeble ties were broken, provinces fell under the influence of the local landlords.

The installation of the dynasty of the Palaeologi was a victory for the greater aristocracy. The process of feudalisation was given a powerful impetus and reached its height from the fourteenth century onwards. Secular and ecclesiastical landlords extended their possessions and acquired more and more important privileges. They frequently enjoyed legal as well as financial immunity, that is to say they not only had rights of taxation over their lands, but sometimes also rights of jurisdiction. Detaching themselves more and more from the central authority, they led their own life of comparative luxury in the midst of general misery. On the other hand, not only did the property of the peasantry decay, but also the non-privileged landed property of the lesser aristocracy whose lands and peasantry were absorbed by the great landowners. This process undermined not only the political and financial, but also the military resources of the state. As the great magnates increasingly evaded taxation, and in addition consumed the property of the smaller landowners who did pay their taxes, the revenues of the state were severely reduced.

Like other estates, the landed property granted as *pronoia* received new privileges. Originally, the *pronoia* fiefs were not in principle heritable as they were conditional possessions granted for a fixed time; but now the *pronoiarii* were frequently accorded the right to bequeath fiefs and their incomes to their heirs. Michael VIII, on his accession, had already changed the *pronoia* fiefs of his supporters into hereditary possessions.[2] As time went by, the imperial government proved increasingly ready to agree to applications of the *pronoiarii* for hereditary rights, although these fiefs remained possessions of a

[1] This is shown by the identity of title given to senior Emperor and co-Emperor. Not only the ruling Emperor, but with his consent the first co-Emperor, as the heir-presumptive (and he alone and no other co-Emperor), could also hold the title of Basileus as well as of Autocrator. Cf. Ps.-Codinus, *De officiis*, XVII, pp. 86f. (*CSHB*).

[2] Pachymeres, I, p. 97 (*CSHB*).

special kind. For even where they were hereditary, the lands of the *pronoiarii* could not be sold; the duty of military service remained attached to the fief and went with it.[1] Yet although the hereditary *pronoia* fiefs always remained inalienable possessions owing service, the original system was somewhat weakened as bequests of *pronoia* property became more frequent. This shows clearly the increasing weakness of the central government and its growing compliance with the requests of the feudal aristocracy which by then had become all-powerful.

How inadequate the *pronoia* system was in the days of the Palaeologi is clearly indicated by the fact that the Byzantine army, which as early as the Comneni already consisted largely of foreign mercenaries, now relied on them almost exclusively. This laid an extremely heavy financial burden on the state. The maintenance of strong mercenary forces, as necessitated by Michael VIII's desire to play the part of a great power with consequent military activity, had financially ruined the Empire. Thus the armed forces had to be severely curtailed; this was done by Andronicus II, though at first he went too far. He believed that by relying on the maritime power of his ally Genoa he could do without the fleet altogether;[2] thereby he tied the Empire to both economic and political dependence on Genoa. The land forces were also severely reduced, and the Byzantine army sank to such a low level that it became the laughing-stock of contemporaries.[3] In fact after the late thirteenth century there was rarely an army of more than a few thousand men. This alone makes it plain why Byzantium lost her status of a great power and why the Empire was helpless in face of the onslaught of the superior Ottoman forces.

An important symptom of the financial crisis was the heavy decline in the value of the Byzantine gold coin owing to debasement. The Byzantine *hyperpyron* had gradually recovered to some extent from its fall during the eleventh century, but from the thirteenth century it was again debased, and this new and irrevocable devaluation was also the end of its reputation. The widespread confidence earlier placed in the Byzantine coinage was now everywhere superseded by growing distrust. As early as the middle of the thirteenth century the Byzantine gold coin which had once dominated international trade unrivalled was increasingly displaced by the new gold coins of the Italian republics. This is readily understandable since even in the Empire of Nicaea under John Vatatzes the standard of the Byzantine

[1] Cf. G. Ostrogorsky, *Pour l'histoire de la féodalité byzantine*, pp. 133 ff.
[2] Nicephorus Gregoras, I, pp. 174 f. (*CSHB*).
[3] Nicephorus Gregoras, I, p. 223 (*CSHB*).

hyperpyron was only 16 carat, that is, two-thirds of its nominal value, only 15 carat after the reconquest of Constantinople under Michael VIII, and only 14 carat during the first years of the reign of Andronicus II. At the time of the new troubles in the beginning of the fourteenth century the *hyperpyron* sank to only half of its original value.[1] The devaluation of the coinage proceeded proportionately to the continuous deterioration of the general situation and the increasing economic distress, and resulted in a steep rise in prices. The high cost of food frequently meant famine for the masses. Henceforth, until the fall of the Empire, the food crisis weighed relentlessly and ever more heavily on the Byzantine capital.[2]

In order to increase the revenues of the state, which had shrunk considerably, Andronicus II carried out a reform of taxation and succeeded in achieving a substantial increase in returns. The yearly income from the taxes rose to 1,000,000 *hyperpyra*. Compared with the past, this was but a modest amount and the fact that it seemed very large to contemporaries reveals the extent of Byzantine impoverishment. Thus the burden of taxation grew, and the conditions of the people were ever worsened, all the more as taxation in kind was increased as well. A new tax was introduced, the so-called σιτόκριθον; every peasant had to give the state part of his harvest in kind, namely six *modioi* of wheat and four *modioi* of barley per *zeugarion*.[3] Revenue, however, was increased not only by higher taxation but also by Andronicus II's attempt to restrict the excessive tax privileges of the great landlords. Certain taxes, above all the land-tax, were often excluded from immunities granted and had to be paid even by those who held charters of immunity from taxation.[4] This may have contributed a certain amount to the rise in the state revenues.

The increased income was to cover current administrative expenses as well as payments to neighbouring powers, and also the maintenance of a fleet of twenty triremes and a standing army of 3000 horsemen of whom 2000 were to be stationed in Europe and 1000 in

---

[1] Pachymeres, II, pp. 493 f. (*CSHB*). These developments are correctly interpreted by D. A. Zakythinos, *Crise monétaire et crise économique à Byzance du XIIIe au XVe siècle*, pp. 8 ff.

[2] Pachymeres, II, p. 494 (*CSHB*). Athanasius, Patriarch of Constantinople (1289–93; 1304–10), in his letters provides striking details of the misery and famine of the Byzantine population. Cf. the extracts in R. Guilland, 'La correspondance inédite d'Athanase, Patriarche de Constantinople', *Mélanges Ch. Diehl*, I (Paris, 1930), pp. 138 f. In addition G. I. Bratianu, 'Etudes sur l'approvisionnement de Constantinople et le monopole du blé à l'époque byzantine et ottomane', *Études byzantines d'histoire économique et sociale*, pp. 163 ff.; D. A. Zakythinos, *op. cit.* pp. 109 f.

[3] Pachymeres, II, p. 493 (*CSHB*).

[4] Cf. G. Ostrogorsky, 'Pour l'histoire de l'immunité à Byzance', *B*, XXVIII (1958), 205 ff.

Asia.[1] Thus the Emperor tried to rectify the rash reduction of the armed forces which he had carried through under pressure of financial emergency on his accession to the throne. But the measures he had in mind were quite inadequate for his needs. Small wonder that payments to foreign powers were one of the most important items of expenditure in the Byzantine economy. As enemies could not be warded off by force of arms, the Emperor sought to buy peace. Restriction and deprivation became the watchwords of Byzantine policy.

In ecclesiastical matters also there was a reaction against the policy of Michael VIII; here too circumstances demanded a complete reversal. It was useless to support reunion with Rome. The Union was dead, if not since the beginning of the pontificate of Martin IV, at any rate since the Sicilian Vespers. Immediately after his accession to the throne Andronicus II solemnly renounced the Union and embarked on a distinctly Orthodox course. Thus the main cause of the grave spiritual crisis and the internal split which had disrupted the Empire since the days of the Second Council of Lyons was removed, though it was some time before the Byzantine Church could recover its equilibrium. Within the Church itself, the old struggle broke out again between the moderate party willing to collaborate with the government, and the more extremist party of the Zealots; the latter still adhered to the views of Arsenius who had died in 1267, and opposed both the ecclesiastical authority and the government. Yet however violent these dissensions, they ultimately came to nothing. At the beginning of the fourteenth century the Arsenites, with the exception of a few fanatics, made their peace with the leading ecclesiastics.

The Orthodox Church gained new and growing influence on the Byzantine state. Public life in Byzantium increasingly showed theocratic trends. The monasteries, above all those on Mt Athos, the most venerated centre of Orthodoxy, exerted a powerful influence. After the crises precipitated by Latin rule and the policy of Union, Byzantine monasteries began a period of rapid advance. They received lavish grants of land; their material wealth increased simultaneously with their spiritual authority. Under the orthodox Emperor Andronicus II the monasteries enjoyed their golden age.

Foreign policy was at that time, by reason of the military weakness of the Empire, cautious and moderate. The Emperor tried to safeguard his position on all sides by concluding alliances which included even the western powers interested in the East, although after the Sicilian Vespers serious danger from the West had been averted, at any rate for the time being. After the premature death of his first

---

[1] Nicephorus Gregoras, I, pp. 317 f. (*CSHB*).

wife, Anne of Hungary, the Emperor married Irene, the daughter of the Marquis of Montferrat. In consequence the claims of the house of Montferrat to the royal crown of Thessalonica expired, as the marquis, who was titular king of Thessalonica, renounced his rights in favour of his daughter who had become Empress of Byzantium; those rights, it is true, had never been very real. A similar policy was adopted by the Emperor when he tried to marry his son and heir, Michael IX, to Catherine of Courtenay, the daughter of Philip and granddaughter of Baldwin II, who in the West was regarded as the titular Empress of Constantinople. Although negotiations for this project, begun in 1288, went on for many years, the marriage was not concluded, and Michael IX eventually married an Armenian princess. In the West the old plans against the Byzantine Empire were still alive. They had their strongest backing in France and in the kingdom of Naples. Their most active champions were Philip of Taranto, son of Charles II, king of Naples, and Charles of Valois, brother of the French king, Philip the Fair. But the efforts of these two princes were only a feeble reflection of the vigorous aggressive policy of Charles of Anjou.

In fact, the foreign policy of the Empire was really determined by its relations with the growing Serbian kingdom in the Balkans, with the all-powerful Italian city-states at sea, and with the Turkish tribes who were rapidly advancing in Asia Minor. As early as 1282 the Serbian king Milutin (1282–1321) had occupied Skoplje and this important town was lost to Byzantium for ever. From now on Serbian attacks in the Macedonian borderland continued incessantly. In order to put an end to the exhausting struggle and to secure peace on that front, the Emperor had to give his small daughter Simonis in marriage to the Serbian ruler, and to cede to him, by way of dowry as it were, the territory north of Ochrida–Prilep–Štip (1299).

By sea Byzantium was more and more harassed by the Italian city-states and seriously involved in their mutual struggles. In the Black Sea, Genoa had supplanted Byzantium as supreme naval power. The Genoese owned prosperous colonies there and dominated the very lucrative trade with the countries of the East, successfully eliminating the competition of Pisa. But the Venetians also tried to maintain their commercial interests and to break the Genoese hegemony in Pontus; to this end they concluded an alliance with the Mongols of the Golden Horde. A long and hard war followed, a colonial war of the Italian maritime republics into which Byzantium as an ally of Genoa was soon drawn. When the Venetian fleet attacked Genoese Galata (1296), the Emperor granted his allies protection behind the walls of the capital, and when the Venetians plundered and destroyed the abandoned Genoese quarter, the Venetian inhabitants of Constantinople were taken prisoner in retaliation and their possessions seized. This brought the conflict to a head, and soon the war between Venice and Genoa became a war between Venice and Byzantium. Although the Genoese gained an important victory over the Venetian fleet in a naval battle between the Dalmatian coast and the island of Korčula (1298), the two opponents, exhausted by the prolonged struggle, concluded a peace treaty in May 1299. Thus the Empire, deserted by her allies and herself weakened, was in the most perilous position. For reasons of prestige, Byzantium opposed Venetian demands for compensation for the losses sustained in 1296, but when attacked by Venetian ships in the Golden Horn, was compelled to bow to superior force and to pay the sum demanded. Eventually an armistice was concluded in 1302 for a period of ten years: the Venetians were granted their former trading privileges and a number of new colonies in the Archipelago. The Genoese on the other hand, as a result of their experiences during the war, surrounded Galata by a strong wall; thus a powerful Genoese fortress arose close to the Byzantine capital. Furthermore, in 1304 the Genoese Benedetto Zaccaria, who had already during the reign of Michael VIII occupied the territory of Phocaea and amassed enormous wealth from its alum mines, seized the island of Chios. Thus the two maritime republics once more succeeded in strengthening their positions at the expense of the Byzantine Empire.

The most important historical events, however, took place in Asia Minor, and it was there that the Empire was hit hardest. As a result of the Mongol invasion which in the mid-thirteenth century brought upheaval to the whole of the Near East, numerous Turkish tribes were driven into Asia Minor. Fresh peoples moved towards the Byzantine–Seljuq frontier, and the migrants in search of land and booty invaded Byzantine territory in western Asia Minor. As time went on, the Turkish invasions became increasingly violent and Byzantine resistance conspicuously feeble. The system of frontier defences, which had been erected in the Nicaean period, had decayed, and the country lay unprotected and open to hostile attacks. There can be no doubt that the Byzantine position in Asia Minor had been considerably weakened by the restoration of 1261. The new tasks which the restored Empire had to face in the Balkans, and the dangers threatening from the West, required the concentration of all forces in the European part of the Empire. For the defence of Asia both military and financial resources were lacking. The Turkish conquest spread over the whole territory, and though the cities resisted the enemy here and there, it would appear that no opposition whatsoever was offered in the open country. By about 1300 almost the whole of Asia Minor had fallen to the Turks. Soon only a few fortresses such as Nicaea, Nicomedia, Brusa, Sardes, Philadelphia, Magnesia and a few ports such as Heraclea on the Pontus, and Smyrna and Genoese Phocaea on the Aegean shore, stood out surrounded by the Turkish flood. The Turkish chieftains carved up the conquered territories amongst themselves, and western Asia Minor was divided into a number of Turkish principalities. Osman, the founder of the Osmanli dynasty, held ancient Bithynia.

Asia Minor, once the core of Byzantium, was lost to the Empire for ever. Bereft of all her military power, the Empire was helpless in the face of this disaster. At this crucial moment, the Emperor was given an unexpected chance. Roger de Flor, leader of the famous Catalan Company, offered him his services against the Turks. This capable army of Catalan mercenaries had assisted King Frederick III of Aragon against Charles II of Anjou in the struggle for Sicily, and had helped him through to victory. After the peace of Caltabellotta (1302) which had secured Aragon rule over Sicily, the Catalan mercenaries were unemployed and looking for new fields of action. The Byzantine Emperor most readily accepted their offer and by the end of 1303 Roger de Flor with about 6500 men arrived in Constantinople.[1] As had been agreed, the Catalans received high pay for four months in advance; their leader married a Byzantine princess and was made *megas dux* and later even Caesar. At the beginning of the following year the Catalans crossed over to Asia Minor and marched against the Turks who were besieging Philadelphia. The enemy were beaten and the victorious Roger de Flor entered the liberated city. This shows that it needed only a small but determined army to master the situation. It was the tragedy of the Byzantine Empire that it had no such army and was no longer able to acquire one except by enrolling mercenaries. An army consisting of foreigners was, however, a two-edged weapon, in particular when it was autonomous and could at any moment evade the control of an Empire lacking the means of coercion.

After their victory, the Catalans took to marauding and indiscriminately attacked Byzantines as well as Turks; nobody was safe. Eventually, instead of fighting the Turks, the mercenaries attacked Byzantine Magnesia. Relief was felt in Constantinople when towards the end of the year the Catalans were induced to return to Thrace. They spent the winter of 1304–5 at Gallipoli; they were supposed to return to Asia in the spring. But tension between the imperial government and the Catalan company increased; in Byzantium

[1] Cf. K. M. Setton, *Catalan Domination of Athens*, and see below: ch. IX.

indignation was growing against their insolence, and the co-Emperor Michael IX was particularly opposed to them. The Catalans themselves were disgruntled because they were not being paid regularly, and they used this grievance as an excuse for all their outrages. In April 1305 Roger de Flor was murdered in the palace of Michael IX. It was hoped thus to get rid of these troublesome mercenaries, but the worst was yet to come. In revenge the Catalans began to campaign against the Empire and open war broke out.

For Byzantium, this war against their former mercenaries took a most unfortunate course. The inadequate imperial forces were disastrously defeated by the Catalans at Aprus in 1305; and the Byzantines had then to confine themselves to defending the most important cities of Thrace, while the open country was abandoned to the fury of the enemy. For two whole years the Catalans mercilessly pillaged and ravaged Thrace. Then they left and crossed the Rhodope mountains; in the autumn of 1307 they settled at Cassandrea. From there they continued their raids. Even the monasteries on Mt Athos had to endure their savagery, though the attack on the strong fortress of Thessalonica failed.

The misfortunes brought on Byzantium by the Catalans were exploited by Theodore Svetoslav, the Bulgarian tsar. He advanced the frontiers of his country south of the Balkan mountains and occupied several fortresses and harbours, among them the hotly disputed strongholds of Anchialus and Mesembria. The government of Constantinople had to accept these losses; it concluded a peace treaty with the Bulgarian ruler, leaving him in possession of all his conquests (1307).

The Catalans then moved on from Cassandrea to Thessaly, where John II (1303–18), a grandson of the *sebastocrator* John Angelus, was ruler. John at first tried to get support from the neighbouring Duchy of Athens and later from the Byzantine Empire; but he was young and in poor health, and the government of his country was in fact in the hands of feudal magnates. As a state Thessaly was dying, and resistance to the Catalans was impossible. For a whole year the company lived on the rich produce of the fertile countryside. In the spring of 1310, they proceeded to central Greece and took service with Walter of Brienne, duke of Athens. But the Catalans quarrelled with the Franks as they had done with the Byzantines, and in the end here, too, the result was open warfare. On the river Cephissus in Boeotia they gained an overwhelming victory over superior Frankish forces (15 March 1311). Duke Walter, as well as most of his knights, fell in battle. The power of the Franks in Athens and Thebes was broken, and in its place a Catalan principality arose. Athens, which had been under French rule for a century, was now to be ruled by the Catalans for almost eighty years. The ravages of the Catalans in Asia Minor, Thrace and Macedonia, north and central Greece, and their victorious campaigns against the Turks, the Byzantines and the Franks, show most clearly the weakness of the Byzantine Empire and the Greek and Latin separatist states. The Catalan company reached the East at a time when there was a vacuum of power: the power of Byzantium had come to an end, that of the Turks was only at its beginning.

The departure of the Catalans to Frankish Greece brought considerable relief to the Byzantines. Equally, the plans of the West for a new aggressive campaign against Byzantium, which seemed to gain momentum during the years of the Catalan plague, were frustrated. The ambitious Charles of Valois, husband of the titular Latin Empress Catherine of Courtenay, had seemed to be near the fulfilment of his plans; but the ground had now been cut from under his feet. The intentions of Philip of Taranto were likewise thwarted; and the projects of the two princes for the restoration of Latin rule thus came to nothing. Venice, which had supported the Valois, realised that the game was up and as early as 1310 concluded with Byzantium a treaty for twelve years. The Serbian king Milutin, who had also entered into an alliance with the French prince, turned once again to Byzantium.

Even more rapid than the decline of Byzantium proper was that of the separatist states of Greece. In 1318 the dynasty of the Angeli came to an end both in Epirus and in Thessaly. The Despot Thomas was murdered by his nephew Nicholas Orsini of Cephalonia. Nicholas, an enemy of the Angevins, embraced the Greek Orthodox faith, and maintained himself in Epirus as successor of the murdered Despot and married his widow Anna, a daughter of Michael IX. Joannina and several other fortresses in Epirus fell to the Emperor of Byzantium. The change in Thessaly was even more decisive. After the death of John II, it ceased to exist as an independent state. The Emperor Andronicus claimed the province as a forfeited fief; but he could establish his rule only in the northern part of the country, and even that rendered him only nominal obedience. The most powerful of the Thessalian magnates, above all the ancient house of the Melisseni, tried to make themselves independent and to found principalities of their own. The most important part of the late principality, however, with its capital Neopatras, was seized by the Catalan Duchy of Athens, and the harbour of Pteleum fell to the Venetians.

The respite after the departure of the Catalans came to a sudden end, however, and the first beginnings of an improvement were frustrated by the internal strife into which the Empire was thrust by the feud between the old Emperor and his grandson Andronicus III.

III. THE CIVIL WARS: SERBIAN PREDOMINANCE IN THE BALKANS

The dispute between Andronicus II and Andronicus III resulted in a series of civil wars which contributed much to the disruption of the Byzantine Empire. The old Emperor certainly had personal reasons for depriving his grandson of his right to the succession. But this private family quarrel soon turned into a long-drawn-out civil war which drained away the last strength of the Empire and facilitated the advance of its enemies in Asia Minor and the Balkans.

The young Andronicus had many supporters among the younger generation of the Byzantine aristocracy and a strong opposition was formed against the unpopular old Emperor. This was headed by John Cantacuzenus, a wealthy young magnate and great friend of Andronicus III; by Syrgiannes, an ambitious adventurer descended from the Cumans on his father's side, but related to the imperial family through his mother; by Theodore Synadenus, another member of the great Byzantine nobility and a friend of the late co-Emperor Michael IX; and last, but not least, by the energetic upstart Alexius Apocaucus. Taking advantage of provincial discontent due to heavy taxation, the supporters of the young Andronicus were able to stir up a rising against the government of Constantinople in Thrace and Macedonia. In the spring of 1321 Andronicus III left the capital and joined the army which his friends had got together near Adrianople. In the struggle which followed he had a distinct advantage over the old Emperor. Under the pressure of financial necessity Andronicus II had been compelled to adopt drastic economic measures, including the unpopular step of raising the taxes. Andronicus III, unhampered by responsibility, was free to make lavish promises and generous gifts of land and privileges. He is even said to have remitted all taxes in Thrace.[1] It was this, rather than his military strength, that influenced the outcome of the civil war. It is not surprising that Thrace rallied to the generous young Emperor. His army, commanded by Syrgiannes, marched on Constantinople, and Andronicus II, fearing a rising in the city, hastened to come to terms.

An agreement was made dividing the territory of the Empire. Andronicus III received the whole of Thrace and certain lands in Macedonia which he had already granted to his supporters. The rest,

[1] Nicephorus Gregoras, I, p. 319 (*CSHB*).

including the capital, remained under the rule of the old Emperor. Peace, however, did not last long and by 1322 civil war had again broken out. Misunderstandings arose in the camp of the young Andronicus due, amongst other things, to the rivalry between the *megas dux* Syrgiannes and the Grand Domestic Cantacuzenus. Andronicus sided with his friend Cantacuzenus, and Syrgiannes, up to then the real leader of the enterprise, went over to the service of the old Emperor and took the lead in the struggle against his former master and protégé. But support for Andronicus III continued to grow, and after several towns in the immediate neighbourhood of Constantinople had acclaimed him, the old Emperor once more gave in and peace was made on the same terms as before. A longer interval of peace followed. On 2 February 1325 Andronicus III was crowned as co-Emperor with his grandfather.

No major battles were fought during this civil war, but in spite of this it had the most serious repercussions on both internal and external political affairs. Warfare and continual movement of troops hindered agriculture and generally impeded economic life, particularly in Thrace. Central authority was undermined even in those districts which by the terms of the peace were controlled by the old Emperor. In 1326 the governor of Thessalonica, the *panhypersebastus* John Palaeologus, a nephew of the Emperor and son-in-law of the Grand Logothete Theodore Metochites, decided to secede from the central authority and was supported by Metochites' two sons who were in command of Strumica and Melnik. This was particularly dangerous as he appealed for help to the king of Serbia Stephen Uroš III Dečanski, his son-in-law. The harassed government hurriedly offered him the title of Caesar, but he died soon after while at the Serbian court. In Asia Minor the Turks systematically continued their conquests. On 6 April 1326 hunger forced the besieged town of Brusa to surrender and Osman's son Orkhan made it his capital.

Meanwhile in the spring of 1327 war broke out between the two Emperors for the third time, and from now on the southern Slavs played an increasingly important part in the internal disputes of Byzantium. Antagonism between Serbia and Bulgaria was reflected in alliances with the two Byzantine parties whose quarrels rent both dynasty and Empire. Andronicus II, thanks to his old connections with the Nemanjids, allied himself with Serbia, and Andronicus III had an understanding with the Bulgarian Tsar Michael Šišman, who divorced his wife, the sister of the king of Serbia, and married his predecessor's widow, Theodora, the sister of the younger Andronicus. Once more fortune favoured Andronicus III, since the hopeless situation aggravated discontent in the Empire, and increased the numbers of the adversaries of the old Emperor. Even Thessalonica recognised Andronicus III and gave him a royal reception in January 1328. In the capital itself the opposition grew at an alarming rate and Andronicus II was considering fresh negotiations for peace when the Bulgarian Tsar Michael Šišman suddenly changed his attitude and sent him an auxiliary force of Bulgars and Tatars. This gave the old Emperor fresh confidence, though it also moved the young Andronicus to still more energetic action. By negotiation and threat he managed to persuade the Bulgarian tsar to recall the forces sent and at the same time he got into touch with his supporters in Constantinople. On 24 May 1328 he forced his way into the capital and made his grandfather abdicate.

The reign of Andronicus III (1328–41) brought a temporary lull in this age of civil war and allowed the Empire to breathe again. The policy of the State was directed by the Grand Domestic John Cantacuzenus. He had been leader of the rebellion in its later years and after its success became the real authority in the state and showed considerable political ability. On the other hand, the economic and financial distress caused by the civil war was a heavy burden, and the fatal weakness of the Empire, confronted by powerful enemies, inevitably led to fresh losses. Yet the new government was not lacking in energy and initiative and managed to obtain considerable success, at least against its weaker adversaries, while showing itself capable of making important decisions in affairs of state.

Andronicus II had already tried to reorganise the judicial system by appointing a panel of twelve judges in Constantinople in 1296. This supreme court of justice consisted of high ecclesiastics and lay dignitaries, but it soon fell into disrepute and was suspended. Andronicus III inaugurated another reform of the judiciary. In 1329 he set up a new supreme court which consisted of only four members: two ecclesiastics and two laymen. Endowed with almost absolute authority these four 'General Justices of the Romans' (καθολικοὶ κριταὶ τῶν 'Ρωμαίων) were responsible for justice throughout the Empire. Their verdicts were final and irrevocable. But Andronicus III, like his grandfather, was to be greatly disappointed in his chief justices. By 1337 three of them had been found guilty of taking bribes, and they were dismissed from office and exiled. In spite of this the institution of chief justices continued to exist right down to the dissolution of the Empire, although in the course of time it underwent various changes in response to practical needs. In the provinces it was often impracticable for all four judges to participate simultaneously in the sessions of the court and the verdict of one of them, given in the name of all four, was accepted as binding. From the middle of the fourteenth century onwards, it was increasingly evident that the links between the different parts of the Empire were weakening. Consequently, the over-centralised system of jurisdiction had to be modified in order to introduce greater flexibility. In addition to the 'General Justices of the Romans' in the capital, local chief justices were appointed. In the later period Thessalonica, the Morea and Lemnos all had their own local supreme judges. It is characteristic of the age of the Palaeologi that the clergy took an active part in the secular administration of justice. The influence of the Church on the jurisdiction of the Empire was further increased by the existence of an ecclesiastical court of justice at the Patriarchate. This officiated side by side with the imperial court which it supported and supplemented, and on occasion even opposed. But in times of crisis it was competent to act in place of the imperial court.[1]

The outstanding characteristic of external politics was the continual progress of the Ottomans in Asia Minor and of the Serbs in Macedonia. The crushing victory of the Serbs over the Bulgarians in the battle near Velbužd in 1330 had far-reaching repercussions on developments in the Balkans and consequently also affected Byzantium. The Bulgarian Tsar Michael Šišman lost his crown and life, and his widow Theodora, the sister of Andronicus III, had to take refuge in flight, while the victorious Serbian king Stephen Uroš III restored his sister Anna and her son John Stephen to the Bulgarian throne. The battle of Velbužd decided the struggle for Macedonia and laid the foundation stone of the Serbian predominance which in the following years was to affect the whole course of Balkan history. Andronicus III did at least try to gain some advantage from the Bulgarian collapse. Under pretence of avenging his sister Theodora, he occupied several fortresses on the Byzantino-Bulgarian border, as well as the much-contested ports of Mesembria and Anchialus. Soon after, however, changes took place on the thrones of both Bulgaria and Serbia and the two Slav countries came to an understanding. The new Serbian monarch, the great Stephen Dušan (1331–55), married the sister of the new tsar of the Bulgarians, John Alexander (1331–71). Bulgaria managed to win back the towns occupied by Andronicus and to secure its former frontier by treaty (1332). Under Dušan's leadership the growing strength of the Serbian aristocracy found an

---

[1] On the history of Byzantine legislation in the age of the Palaeologi cf. P. Lemerle, 'Le juge général des Grecs et la réforme judiciaire d'Andronic III', *Mémorial L. Petit* (Bucharest, 1948), pp. 292–316; 'Recherches sur les institutions judiciaires à l'époque des Paléologues. I: Le tribunal impérial', *Mélanges H. Grégoire*, I = *AIPHO*, IX (1949), 369–84; 'II: Le tribunal du patriarcat ou tribunal synodal', *Mélanges P. Peeters*, II = *AB*, LXVIII (1950), 320–33.

outlet for its capacity for expansion at the cost of the Byzantine Empire. The internal complications of Byzantium were turned to great advantage by the rising power of the Serbs. Syrgiannes, who had taken the lead, first on one side, then on the other, during the Byzantine civil war, had fled from Constantinople and had gone over to Dušan. This energetic and experienced soldier gave considerable help to the king of Serbia until an agent of the Emperor succeeded in assassinating him. But by that time the most important Byzantine fortresses in western and middle Macedonia had fallen. Only the strong walls of Thessalonica halted the advance of the victorious Serbian armies, and in August 1334, after a personal meeting with Andronicus III, Dušan concluded a peace treaty with Byzantium by which he confirmed his right to some of the conquered towns.

While in the Balkans catastrophe was only beginning to reveal itself, in Asia the last act of the tragedy was being played. Andronicus III and John Cantacuzenus did indeed attempt to oppose the overwhelming strength of the Turks. In 1329 they had advanced against the Ottomans with an army of 2000 warriors to relieve the siege of Nicaea, but were defeated in an unequal battle near Philocrene, and on 2 March 1331[1] Orkhan took the town which two generations earlier had been the centre of the Byzantine state. Six years later the town of Nicomedia also fell to the Ottomans. All that remained of the Empire in Asia Minor were isolated and widely separated towns such as Philadelphia, and Heraclea on the Black Sea. After the conquest of the Bithynian coast the Ottomans were well placed to continue the attacks on the European shores of the Empire, attested as early as 1321.

While the Ottomans were crossing the northern Aegean, the Turks of the coastal principalities in Asia Minor were penetrating its southern waters. Their attacks were especially aimed at the Latins who controlled this area, and did little harm to the Byzantines whose possessions were confined to the islands off the Thracian and Asia Minor coasts. This led to an understanding between the Empire and these amirs arising out of their common hostility to the Ottomans and the Latins. Indeed the collaboration between the amirs and the Grand Domestic John Cantacuzenus was characteristic of the latter's policy. This alliance and the hurried building of ships were to free the Empire from the grip of the Genoese and to restore its naval and economic independence at sea. In 1329 the newly built Byzantine fleet attacked the important island of Chios, then

---

[1] See Lampros–Amantos, Βραχέα Χρονικά, no. 26, 4. Cf. B. T. Gorjanov, *VV*, n.s. II (1949), 283–6, where the date of the battle is given as 1 March 1331; see also V. Laurent, *REB*, VII (1950), 209.

under the rule of the Genoese family of the Zaccaria. Chios had at first recognised the imperial authority but had later asserted its complete independence: it was now recovered for the Empire. With the help of the Turks, Phocaea, also under the rule of this same Genoese family, was forced to acknowledge Byzantine sovereignty, and Lesbos was saved from invasion by the so-called league of Christian powers. This league, which had been founded to fight the Turkish pirates, attacked the island in spite of the fact that the Byzantine Emperor was himself formally one of its members. He now had to call on the amirs to help him defend his possessions against his Christian colleagues, and after a hard-fought battle he was successful.[1]

But the most important Byzantine victories were won in Thessaly and Epirus. After the death in 1333 of the most powerful of the Thessalian rulers, Stephen Gabrielopulus, the country was at once thrown into complete chaos. A Byzantine army was thus able without great difficulty to annex the northern half of Thessaly down to the borders of the Catalan Duchy. With Thessaly restored to the Empire the annexation of Epirus now became a matter of some urgency. The endless party struggles, the conflicting claims to power and the continual inroads of neighbours, had caused such upheavals in the territory of Epirus that its collapse as an independent state was only a question of time. It was precipitated by the triumph of the Byzantine party in Arta, and the death of the Despot John II Orsini (1323–35), poisoned by his wife Anna Palaeologina. Anna took over the government with her son Nicephorus II and opened negotiations with the Byzantine Emperor. Andronicus III and Cantacuzenus crossed Thessaly at the head of an army whose *élite* consisted of Turkish mercenaries. They quelled an insurrection in Albania and then received the submission of Epirus and Acarnania which were joined to the Empire without any fighting (1337). The *protostrator* Theodore Synadenus was installed as imperial governor, while Anna and Nicephorus were assigned a residence in Thessalonica.

The western powers with an interest in Epirus tried to snatch back from the Empire this all too easily won territory and the slighted Nicephorus was used as a tool for the restoration of Angevin suzerainty over the despotate. The Angevin governor of Dyrrachium, who was in the service of the titular Latin Empress Catherine of Valois, incited a revolt in favour of the dethroned despot. Nicephorus II was proclaimed in Arta and the *protostrator* Synadenus was thrown into prison. But only a few towns joined the

---

[1] On the Turkish amirates in Asia Minor in the fourteenth century see also below: ch. xix.

movement and most of the country remained loyal to the Greek Emperor. In the spring of 1340 Andronicus and Cantacuzenus appeared with a small army and the revolt was soon quelled. Nicephorus returned to his honourable exile in Thessalonica and had to content himself with the title of *panhypersebastus* and accept the honour of betrothal to a daughter of Cantacuzenus as compensation for his lost rights as ruler. John Angelus, a nephew of Cantacuzenus, who had distinguished himself in putting down the revolt, was made governor of Epirus, while Synadenus became governor of Thessalonica. Thus one of the most serious consequences of the Byzantine collapse of 1204 seemed at last to have been rectified. There were indeed still Latin principalities in Greece, but there were no longer any independent Greek units: the former separatist states were once more provinces of the Empire. Cantacuzenus gives high praise to this success which all the efforts of former governments had failed to achieve.[1]

This achievement, however, was due not so much to Byzantine armed strength as to the internal weakness of the separatist states, which had once been able to defy all the might of Michael VIII but now surrendered almost without a struggle to a comparatively feeble Empire. Moreover, it was an achievement which proved to be of little permanent value for Byzantium: for at the very moment when the separated provinces were at last reunited with the Empire, they became the object of the Serbian desire for expansion. By 1346 Dušan had already conquered Albanian territory as well as Joannina and two years later Epirus and Thessaly were overrun by the armies of the great Serbian tsar. Given favourable circumstances, Byzantium was still capable of achieving a measure of success by means of wise statesmanship and judicious diplomacy, but it was no longer capable of holding its gains permanently. And indeed the Empire had hardly recovered from the civil war of the twenties when it was again overtaken by a similar and even greater disaster. After the death of Andronicus III a new civil war broke out, which was far more terrible and of far greater significance than the previous dynastic struggle: and from this second civil war the Empire was never to recover.

When Andronicus III died on 15 June 1341, his son John V was not yet ten years old.[2] The Grand Domestic John Cantacuzenus, who had controlled the government under Andronicus III, claimed the

---

[1] Cantacuzenus, i, p. 504 (*CSHB*).

[2] He was born in November 1331: see Lampros–Amantos, Βραχέα Χρονικά, no. 47, 11, and also P. Charanis, 'An Important Short Chronicle of the Fourteenth Century', *B*, XIII (1938), 344.

regency as the nearest friend of the late Emperor. But he was strongly opposed by the party which supported the dowager Empress Anna of Savoy and the Patriarch John Calecas. The cunning Alexius Apocaucus, once Cantacuzenus' follower and favourite, now became his most dangerous enemy. Taking advantage of the absence of Cantacuzenus from the capital, his opponents achieved a *coup d'état*. He was declared an enemy of the Empire, his house was destroyed and his possessions plundered. Those of his followers who had not been able to fly from Constantinople in time were thrown into prison. The Empress Anna and the Patriarch John took over the regency; Apocaucus, raised to the rank of *megas dux*, was made governor of the capital and the neighbouring cities and islands. Cantacuzenus accepted the challenge and had himself proclaimed Emperor in Didymotichus on 26 October 1341. Strictly observing the principle of legitimacy, he ordained that the names of the Empress Anna and of the young Emperor John V Palaeologus should be proclaimed before the names of himself and his wife. It was important to him to emphasise that he was not fighting against the legitimate imperial family but against the usurpation by Apocaucus who soon rose to virtual dictatorship in Constantinople. As Andronicus III had done before him in the fight against his grandfather, Cantacuzenus relied mainly on the support of the Thracian aristocracy in his fight against the regency in Constantinople, and once again the province was to be victorious over the capital.

Byzantium was faced by one of the gravest crises of its history. The civil war of the twenties had seriously weakened the Empire, but the civil wars of the forties deprived it of its little remaining vitality. Foreign powers interfered in this internal dispute to a much greater extent than previously and what began as a political struggle was complicated by the different social and religious affinities of either side. For Byzantium was undergoing a grave social crisis, and at the same time it was rent by the most significant of all religious conflicts in the later period of its history—the hesychast controversy.

The mystical and ascetic teaching of the hesychasts was enthusiastically welcomed in the monasteries, especially on Mt Athos, but it also met with fierce opposition, and the hesychast techniques and methods of contemplation were particularly ridiculed. Hesychasm thus became the centre of a bitter dispute within the Byzantine Church.[1] The Patriarch John Calecas was the determined opponent of the hesychast movement and so was Anna of Savoy. After the revolution of 1341 the ecclesiastical as well as the secular authorities

[1] On the hesychast movement cf. especially J. Meyendorff, *Introduction à l'étude de Grégoire Palamas*.

in Constantinople turned against the hesychasts. Their leader Gregory Palamas was imprisoned. The result was that the hesychasts allied themselves even more closely with John Cantacuzenus; and the Empire was divided into two hostile camps on issues of religious as well as political controversy.

The division in society was no less radical. Indeed it was the social conflict in the Empire that aggravated and prolonged the violence of the civil war. Growing economic impoverishment had sharpened the contrasts between different social classes. As the Empire declined, so the poverty and misery of the populace increased. Property was concentrated in the hands of a comparatively small class of nobles and this roused the envy and hatred of the people. The dispute between the regency in Constantinople and the leader of the magnates, Cantacuzenus, caused the smouldering social hatred to burst into flame. In his fight for power against Cantacuzenus, Alexius Apocaucus depended on the populace, whom he incited against the aristocratic followers of his opponent. A rising against the local magnates broke out in Adrianople and soon spread to the other Thracian towns. Members of the aristocracy and the property-owning classes and the supporters of the magnate Cantacuzenus were everywhere annihilated.

The bitterness of this class conflict reached its height in Thessalonica, the great port with its heterogeneous population, where opulence and extreme poverty lived side by side. Thessalonica had a strong popular party, well organised and with a more or less clearly defined political ideology, the party of the Zealots. Here the anti-aristocratic movement was more than a sudden outburst of popular emotion, and for a time the Zealots took control of the city's government. Cantacuzenus' followers had fled from the town headed by the governor Synadenus; and in 1342 the Zealots set up their own regime in Thessalonica. The wealthy classes in Thessalonica were expropriated.[1] The Zealots also stood in sharp opposition to the hesychasts, the allies of Cantacuzenus. Yet they combined their revolutionary social policy with a certain respect for dynastic legitimacy. As opponents of Cantacuzenus they recognised John Palaeologus as the legitimate Emperor, and one at least of the most

---

[1] The information on the programme of the Zealots and the measures taken under their rule is very meagre. The oration of Nicholas Cabasilas on the alienation of church property, which was considered as the main source on this subject, was in fact directed not against the Zealots but against the imperial government's measures of secularisation, which aimed at granting monastic property as *pronoia*. This has been shown by I. Ševčenko, 'Nicholas Cabasilas' "Anti-Zealot" Discourse: a reinterpretation', *DOP*, xi (1957), 81–171, and 'The Author's Draft of Nicholas Cabasilas' "Anti-Zealot" Discourse in *Parisinus Graecus 1276*', *DOP*, xv (1960), 179–201.

prominent leaders of this extremely anti-aristocratic party, Michael Palaeologus of Thessalonica, was by marriage a member of the Palaeologian family. The administration of Thessalonica was shared between a governor appointed by Constantinople and the leader of the Zealots; but the influence of the latter predominated in the city, which lived according to its own laws and was virtually independent.

From Thessalonica to Constantinople the power of the aristocrats was everywhere broken. Deprived of all support in the Empire, Cantacuzenus retreated to the Serbian frontier with about 2000 men and begged Stephen Dušan for help. Intervention in the Byzantine civil war suited Serbian plans, and in 1342 an alliance between Cantacuzenus and Dušan was concluded, by means of which both parties were trying to pursue their own aims. But the allied campaigns against the strongly fortified town of Serres were, however, unsuccessful. The retinue of Cantacuzenus dwindled to a bare 500 men. On the other hand his position in the Empire was strengthened when Thessaly joined his cause. This land of great estate-owners acknowledged the leader of the Greek aristocracy as Emperor, and Cantacuzenus appointed his old friend and relative John Angelus as governor of the province. Though loyally recognising the sovereign rights of his lord, Angelus was now a virtually independent ruler; he controlled Epirus, Acarnania, Aetolia and Thessaly, and was soon able to extend his considerable realm still further at the expense of the Catalan possessions in the south. Although Cantacuzenus had been forced to leave the old imperial territory, he was supported by the recently regained Greek lands; he had always treated these with special consideration and they had indeed been reunited with the Empire largely through his efforts.

This success of the rival Byzantine Emperor hastened the break between him and the Serbian king. For it was certainly not Dušan's intention to allow either of the Byzantine parties to achieve success, nor did it please him to see Cantacuzenus established in just those lands which he himself coveted and which he was indeed to annex a few years later. He therefore abandoned Cantacuzenus and negotiated with the regency in Constantinople, which was only too anxious to gain his friendship. So instead of a partner, Cantacuzenus now had a powerful enemy in the Serbian ruler. But he had another ally, the Amir Omur, with whom he had been in close contact as early as the days of Andronicus III. At the end of 1342 Omur had come to his assistance and from then on he had continual support from the Turks—first from the Seljuqs and then from the Ottomans—which turned the balance in his favour, and from the military point of view this virtually decided the Byzantine civil war.

But even with Omur's support he was unable to take Thessalonica. The city bitterly resisted him, and the threat to its existence from outside increased the radicalism of the Zealot regime within. Cantacuzenus therefore had to abandon Thessalonica and the rest of Macedonia to Dušan, but with the support of the Seljuqs he began to subdue Thrace: and in the autumn of 1343 he made a triumphal entry into Didymotichus. But his success was achieved only at the cost of terrible devastation of the countryside by the Turkish troops in his service.

On the other hand the regency in Constantinople was trying to strengthen its position with the aid of the southern Slavs. In addition to Dušan, the Bulgarian Tsar John Alexander had been won over, and also the adventurer Hajduk Momčilo, a former ally of Cantacuzenus who had settled on the Byzantino-Bulgarian frontier with his own troops. But the friendship of the Slav rulers was of little help to the legitimate Emperor and was achieved only at great cost to the Byzantine state. While the allies of Cantacuzenus were devastating the Byzantine provinces, the allies of the Empress Anna were seizing great stretches of territory from the Empire. Dušan continued his conquests, keeping what he had won from the rival Emperor and incorporating it into his kingdom. The cession of considerable territory on the upper Marica, with Philippopolis and Stenimachus, was the price claimed by the Bulgarian tsar for his friendship, but he gave no practical assistance to the government which had rashly agreed to his terms. The daring Momčilo founded a principality of his own in the Rhodope, and terrorised the whole countryside until in 1345 he was eventually overcome by Omur in the service of Cantacuzenus.

By the summer of 1345 Cantacuzenus had subdued almost the whole of Thrace, and in Constantinople his opponents had suffered a serious reverse. Their strongest supporter, the *megas dux* Alexius Apocaucus, was murdered on 11 June 1345 by some of his political prisoners. Reaction against Zealot rule began to emerge even in Thessalonica, though its first consequence was an even more violent outburst on the part of the revolutionary forces. It is significant that the attempted reaction was promoted by the imperial governor who was none other than the *megas primicerius* John Apocaucus, a son of the dictator in Constantinople. He quarrelled with the Zealots, had their leader Michael Palaeologus murdered, took control of the government of the city and, after his father's murder in Constantinople, openly sided with Cantacuzenus. But the Zealots led by Andrew Palaeologus counter-attacked. John Apocaucus was overpowered, and there ensued a terrible reckoning for the members of the aristocracy. The Zealot government was re-established and remained in power for several years, in a state of almost complete independence. The links binding Thessalonica to the rest of the Empire became weaker than before.

In spite of these events there was no doubt about the issue of the civil war, especially after the overthrow of the *megas dux* Alexius Apocaucus. Backed by the most influential social and economic elements, supported by the powerful spiritual movement of the hesychasts, Cantacuzenus' victory was certain, while the authority of the regency at Constantinople rapidly declined. But Cantacuzenus could not count on the continued support of the Seljuq Omur, and he was soon to lose it altogether: for war with the league of the western powers increasingly claimed Omur's attention, and during this long fluctuating struggle he finally met his death (1348). But in the meantime, during the winter of 1344–5, Cantacuzenus had made an alliance with the Ottoman Sultan Orkhan and thenceforth could call on the help of this effective if dangerous ally. He even consented to give one of his daughters in marriage to the Sultan. Times had indeed changed: once the greatest rulers in Christendom were not considered worthy to marry a Byzantine princess; now a Byzantine princess could grace the harem of a Turkish Sultan.

Certain of victory, Cantacuzenus allowed himself to be crowned Emperor as John VI in Adrianople on 21 May 1346. The coronation ceremony, which was performed by the Patriarch of Jerusalem, gave legal sanction to his proclamation as Emperor in Didymotichus in 1341, which had precipitated the civil war. The war itself was now coming to an end. All the last minute measures of the Empress Anna failed to save the situation, and on 3 February 1347 Constantinople opened its gates to Cantacuzenus. He was recognised as Emperor; he was to rule over the Empire for ten years and only after that time was the young legitimate Emperor, John V Palaeologus, to take his part in the affairs of government. Cantacuzenus gave him his daughter Helen in marriage. On 13 May another coronation ceremony took place: Cantacuzenus now received the imperial crown from the hands of the Patriarch of Constantinople, for only a coronation performed by the bishop of the capital was completely valid. A spiritual relationship was established between Cantacuzenus and the family of the Palaeologi, designed to legalise the position of the new ruler. Cantacuzenus stepped, as it were, into the place of Andronicus III; he was regarded as the 'spiritual' brother of Andronicus, and as the 'common father' of John Palaeologus and of his own children, and therefore as the head of the dynasty.

The Zealots were still in control in Thessalonica, and stubbornly refused to acknowledge the new Emperor or to accept orders from

Constantinople. But after the victory of Cantacuzenus, sensing that their hour had come, they began negotiations with Stephen Dušan, for they would have preferred to surrender the town to the Serbs rather than to the rival party. But the rule of the Zealots collapsed at the beginning of 1350. Their leader Andrew Palaeologus fled to the Serbs and the governor Alexius Metochites appealed to Cantacuzenus for help. Towards the end of the year, the latter, accompanied by John Palaeologus, made his triumphant entry into the city which had defied him so long and so stubbornly. Gregory Palamas, who had been elected Metropolitan of Thessalonica but had been refused admission by the Zealots, now entered the city of St Demetrius.

The victory of Cantacuzenus was also the victory of hesychasm. At a council convened in 1351 in the palace of the Blachernae the orthodoxy of the hesychasts was recognised and their opponents anathematised. Although opposition still continued, the teaching of the hesychasts was now recognised as the official doctrine of the Greek Orthodox Church and permanently influenced the development of Byzantine spirituality. The acceptance of hesychasm had for Byzantium a cultural as well as a religious significance. After the strong Latin influence of the twelfth and thirteenth centuries, the fourteenth century saw the predominance of the conservative Greek tradition which was strongly opposed both to the Roman Church and to western culture.

The chief beneficiary of the Byzantine civil war was the Serbian king Stephen Dušan. Except for Thessalonica, the whole of Macedonia almost as far as the Nestos had been conquered by him; and after repeated attacks, on 25 September 1345 the strongly fortified town of Serres capitulated. Soon afterwards Dušan adopted the imperial title and from now on styled himself 'Emperor of the Serbs and Greeks'. The coronation ceremony took place in Skoplje on Easter Sunday, 16 April 1346, and was designed to inaugurate a new Serbo-Greek Empire in place of the old Byzantine Empire. Like Symeon of Bulgaria before him, Dušan now indicated the climax of his struggle with Byzantium by laying claim to the imperial title, the supreme symbol of the spiritual and political pre-eminence of Byzantium.

The lull in the Byzantine civil wars did not stay his advance. On the contrary, during the first years of John VI's reign Dušan completed his conquest of Albania and Epirus, occupied Acarnania and Aetolia and finally took Thessaly. Cantacuzenus, after taking Zealot-controlled Thessalonica, again invaded Macedonia and managed to secure possession of several towns, but he soon lost these again to Dušan. Thus the authority of the Serbian ruler now reached from the Danube to the Gulf of Corinth and from the Adriatic to the Aegean.

The Byzantine Empire was now limited to Thrace and the islands in the northern part of the Aegean together with its possessions in the distant Peloponnese and Thessalonica, which was isolated by the Serbian conquests. These areas were not very considerable and they were moreover separated from each other and controlled by virtually independent authorities. It is characteristic of the later Byzantine period that the single imperial sovereignty had been replaced by a many-headed regime of members of the dynasty. Under John Cantacuzenus this appanage system of government became the regular practice. He granted the Byzantine lands in the Morea to his second son Manuel. His elder son, Matthew, received a principality of his own in western Thrace stretching from Christopolis to Didymotichus. In this way Cantacuzenus no doubt intended to strengthen his own new dynasty against the legitimate ruling house of the Palaeologi. But of even greater importance was the fact that owing to increasing separatist tendencies the different parts of the Empire could only be held together by building up a strong dynastic system of government. Cantacuzenus' method was therefore continued and developed by his successors of the house of Palaeologus.

But far worse than the loss of territory and the partition of the Empire were the economic and financial straits of the Byzantine government. The population could not pay their taxes, for in Thrace, the chief possession of the Empire, agriculture had come to a complete standstill during the civil wars; territory which had endured the horrors of internal struggles, followed by the frightful devastations of the Turkish troops, was reduced to the condition of a desert.[1] Byzantine trade had shrunk considerably and even in the capital was being eclipsed by its flourishing competitors, the Italian city-states: while the Genoese customs authorities in Galata drew a revenue of 200,000 *hyperpyra* a year, the annual customs revenues in Constantinople had sunk to a bare 30,000 *hyperpyra*.[2] The *hyperpyron* itself had no fixed value, for its purchasing power diminished daily.[3] There was a gaping deficit in the treasury, and any expenditure above the normal could only be met by private donations from the propertied classes or by loans and gifts from abroad. At the beginning of the civil war the Empress Anna had had to pawn the crown jewels in Venice to raise a loan of 30,000 ducats: this debt was never paid and the jewels of the Empire remained among the ecclesiastical treasure

---

[1] Nicephorus Gregoras, II, p. 683 (*CSHB*); Cantacuzenus, II, p. 302 (*CSHB*).
[2] Nicephorus Gregoras, II, p. 842 (*CSHB*).
[3] Nicephorus Gregoras, III, p. 52 (*CSHB*).

of St Mark's.[1] About 1350 the Grand Duke of Moscow sent money for the renovation of St Sophia; it was humiliating enough to have to accept money from abroad for such a purpose, but the pious offering of the Russian Grand Duke was embezzled by the Byzantine government and lavished on the infidel: it was used for the recruiting of Turkish auxiliary troops.[2] All this shows how great the distress of Byzantium was. Even in the imperial palace where wealth and splendour once abounded, there was now such poverty that the Emperor himself had to save every farthing. In the reign of Cantacuzenus only a tenth of former expenditure could be spared for the imperial household.[3] Everything valuable had been either pawned or already used. At the coronation festivities of Cantacuzenus the goblets were of lead and clay instead of gold and silver.[4]

By land the Empire stood in complete and humiliating impotence between the Ottomans and Serbs; by sea it was likewise hemmed in between Genoa and Venice and here it had also suffered new losses during the civil wars. In 1346 the Genoese recaptured Chios, and the island soon became a base for the trading activities of the Giustiniani in whose possession it remained until the middle of the sixteenth century. However energetically Cantacuzenus tried to free himself from the clutches of Genoa, he was not successful. To undermine the Genoese predominance it was essential to have a strong fleet. As the state was too poor to finance the building of such a fleet, the Emperor appealed to those with private means. But private resources had also shrunk considerably and the propertied class did not show much inclination to make any sacrifices. With great difficulty the sum of 50,000 *hyperpyra* was raised to be spent on shipbuilding.[5] The Emperor also aspired to put an end to the deplorable and humiliating situation whereby the Genoese claimed almost nine-tenths of the customs duties on the Bosphorus. He introduced new customs regulations, lowering the tariffs in Constantinople for most imports, with the result that incoming merchant ships put in at the Byzantine harbour and avoided the Genoese Galata.[6] But as might have been expected, the Genoese, hard-hit by these measures, took up arms and, in spite of the preparations which had been made, the Byzantine fleet was destroyed, and all the Emperor's efforts and sacrifices were proved to have been in vain.

[1] Miklosich–Müller, III, pp. 124 and 140.
[2] Nicephorus Gregoras, III, p. 199 (*CSHB*).
[3] Nicephorus Gregoras, II, p. 811 (*CSHB*).
[4] Nicephorus Gregoras, II, p. 788 (*CSHB*).
[5] Cantacuzenus, III, p. 80 (*CSHB*).
[6] Cantacuzenus, III, pp. 68 ff. (*CSHB*); see W. Heyd, *Histoire du commerce du Levant*, I, pp. 498 ff.

The war between Byzantium and Galata was hardly over when fresh hostilities in Byzantine waters broke out between Genoa and Venice. For some time rivalry between the two Italian city-states had been intensified by the desire of Genoa to control all trade in the Black Sea. It attempted to ban the transit of foreign ships and several Venetian ships which had evaded the naval patrols were seized at Kaffa (1350). Venice then entered into an alliance with King Peter IV of Aragon and after some hesitation due to uncertainty about the outcome of the war, John Cantacuzenus joined them. On 13 February 1352 a great naval battle took place in the Bosphorus. On one side were the Genoese, on the other the Venetian and Aragonese fleets, with the small contingent of fourteen ships which the Emperor had equipped with Venetian aid. The battle lasted until nightfall and was indecisive, so that both sides could claim the victory. The war was carried on in western waters until the belligerents were so exhausted that they had to make peace in 1355. After the battle of the Bosphorus the Venetian and the Aragonese navies departed and thus put Cantacuzenus into a difficult position. His isolation forced him to come to an understanding with the Genoese, especially as they had made an agreement with Orkhan. But these diplomatic changes forced the Venetians to ally with John V Palaeologus. Palaeologus then received a loan of 20,000 ducats as a subsidy for resisting Cantacuzenus, in return for which he promised to cede the island of Tenedos to the Venetian Republic. The mighty Serbian tsar also pressed the young Emperor to break with Cantacuzenus offering him military and financial aid. Byzantium thus stood on the threshold of a new civil war.

The relegation of the young legitimate Emperor to the background was a further threat to the very precarious peace of the Empire, a danger which only increased as he grew older and which stimulated opposition to the Cantacuzenus regime. John Cantacuzenus tried to relieve the growing tension by arrangement. The territory in Rhodope ruled by Matthew Cantacuzenus was given to Palaeologus, while Matthew received more important lands in the district of Adrianople. But this settlement did not last long. The inevitable break came and hostilities took the form of a war between the autonomous principalities of John Palaeologus and Matthew Cantacuzenus. In the autumn of 1352 John V led a small army into the territory of his brother-in-law. He nowhere met with strong resistance and Adrianople opened her gates to the legitimate Emperor, while Matthew shut himself up in the acropolis of the city. John Cantacuzenus hurried to his aid with Turkish troops and soon retrieved the situation. Adrianople, like the other towns which had revolted against the

Cantacuzeni, was punished by having to endure a terrible plundering by the Turks. Hard pressed, Palaeologus appealed to the Serbs and Bulgarians for help. Cantacuzenus countered this by turning once more to his friend Orkhan. So the outcome of the dispute between the two Byzantine Emperors really rested with the Ottomans and Serbs. The superior military resources of the Turks were victorious; the Bulgarians retreated before the advance of the powerful Turkish army and the Serbians together with John's forces were defeated.

The final break with the Palaeologi, which John Cantacuzenus had for so long tried to avoid, was now clear to everyone and there was no longer any point in supporting the principle of legitimacy. Cantacuzenus therefore allowed his son Matthew to be proclaimed co-Emperor and John Palaeologus was deprived of his imperial rights and was no longer to be commemorated in the liturgy or in proclamations. This move was opposed by the Patriarch Callistus, but he was shortly after deposed by a synod, and in 1354 Matthew received the imperial crown at the hands of his father and the new Patriarch Philotheus in the Church of the Blachernae. But the triumph of the house of Cantacuzenus did not last long. The opposition grew stronger and the alliance with the Turks, which gave Cantacuzenus the upper hand over his internal adversaries, eventually proved disastrous not only for the Empire but also for him. The days of haphazard Turkish depredations were ending; the period of Ottoman colonisation on European territory was beginning. By 1352 they had already established themselves in the fortress of Tzympe near Gallipoli and on 2 March 1354, after a severe earthquake which made all the Byzantine population leave the neighbourhood, Orkhan's son Sulaymān took possession of Gallipoli.[1] It was no use for Cantacuzenus to appeal to Orkhan's friendship or to offer the Sultan large sums for the evacuation of the town. The Ottomans kept the fortress, which provided a splendid base for further conquests in Thrace. In Constantinople the population was panic stricken; they already believed that the capital was in danger of immediate attack by the Turks. It was this which undermined Cantacuzenus' position and prepared the way for his overthrow.

Meanwhile John V had allied with Cantacuzenus' old enemies the Genoese and had won their goodwill and their support without difficulty. A Genoese corsair, Francesco Gattilusio, the owner of two galleys with which he crossed the Aegean in search of booty and

---

[1] On the chronology, see Lampros–Amantos, Βραχέα Χρονικά, no. 52, 22, and P. Charanis, *B*, XIII (1938), 347 ff. G. Georgiades Arnakis, *SP*, XXVI (1951), 111 ff. and *B*, XXII (1952), 310 ff., is wrong in dating the fall of Gallipoli in March 1355, since it is known that the city was conquered under Cantacuzenus' rule.

adventure, agreed to help Palaeologus to regain the throne. In return John V promised him the hand of his sister with the island of Lesbos as a dowry, the largest and most important of the islands which still belonged to the Empire. In November 1354 the conspirators penetrated into Constantinople; John Cantacuzenus was forced to abdicate and became a monk. As the monk Joasaph he lived for nearly thirty years longer (he died on 15 June 1383); the period of his retirement was almost as long as that of his active political life. He passed the time writing his famous history and some theological works in which he defended the hesychast doctrines.

The historical role of the house of Cantacuzenus did not end with the abdication of John VI. It is true that Matthew Cantacuzenus did not manage to assert himself for long in his Thracian principality. Defeated by the Serbs, he fell into the hands of John V and had to abdicate (1357). But Manuel Cantacuzenus managed to maintain his rule in the Morea and all attempts of the Palaeologi to deprive him of it failed. The able Despot continued to rule over the Byzantine possessions in the Peloponnese until he died in 1380. His elder brother Matthew, who had taken refuge in the Morea after his abdication as co-Emperor, then succeeded him until 1382. During his long rule, Manuel Cantacuzenus had done much to promote law and order in the Morea, he had strengthened the economic position of the country and had successfully defended it against Turkish attacks. In a time of hopeless decline this more constructive work in the Greek Morea appears as the one ray of light on the Byzantine horizon. But as the country remained under the autonomous rule of the Cantacuzenus dynasty it was for a considerable period virtually cut off from the central authority of the Palaeologi.

But taken as a whole the weakness of the Byzantine Empire was now greater than when Cantacuzenus had ascended the throne of Constantinople; the fragmentation of the Empire continued and economic and financial distress was even worse than before. The Byzantine Empire, which had experienced three civil wars in the course of a single generation, could not hope to retrieve so desperate a situation. The decline was long drawn out, for to the end Byzantium remained a marvel of tenacity. But the last hundred years of Byzantine history is nevertheless the story of increasing decay.

IV. THE OTTOMAN ADVANCE: BYZANTIUM AS A
VASSAL STATE OF THE TURKS

John V opens the line of the later Palaeologian Emperors, each of
whom appears to have been more powerless and unfortunate than his
predecessor. John's childhood and youth were passed in civil wars,
his long rule in incessant and invariably fruitless appeals for aid. He
first turned for assistance to the Roman Church, promising the
reunion of the Greek and Latin Churches—a policy which had been
pursued tenaciously by the founder of the Palaeologian dynasty.
But the circumstances were now entirely different. In the reign of
Michael VIII the Empire had been threatened by a western power
over whom the Papacy had been able to exercise spiritual authority,
but now Constantinople was threatened by infidels against whom
only military force could hope to be effective. The earlier activities of
the league of Christian princes in the Aegean sponsored by the Papacy
hardly augured well for any such effort. The promise of reunion had
always been the trump card of the imperial government, to be produced over and over again. After the Union of Lyons had failed,
negotiations with Rome lapsed for a good forty years; but even in the
difficult days of civil war Andronicus II reopened this question. Again
during the rule of Andronicus III and especially that of the Empress
Anna, and in the critical times of John VI Cantacuzenus, the government had approached the Papacy with this in view, though without
any success worth mentioning. But John V really did try to achieve
an agreement. With great energy he worked to bring about union
with the Roman Church to which he may in all probability have been
genuinely attached, since he had grown up under the influence of his
Catholic mother.

In a detailed and somewhat naïve letter dated 15 December 1355,
he asked the Pope to send him five galleys and fifteen transport ships
together with 1000 soldiers and 500 knights. In return he undertook
to convert his people within six months to the Roman faith and
offered astonishingly wide guarantees for this rash promise. He was
prepared to send his second son Manuel, at that time a child of
five or six years, to Avignon as a hostage to be brought up by the
Pope; should he be unable to keep his promise, he would abdicate in
favour of his son Manuel, the papal ward, who would have his
guardian the Pope as regent of the Empire until he came of age.
These exuberant offers were apparently not taken seriously by Innocent VI and the only people to arrive were papal legates, un-
accompanied by galleys or warriors. Soon the Emperor had to inform
the Pope that in these circumstances he was in no position to make

his subjects accept reunion for many of them would not listen to his ruling in this matter. As in the case of earlier negotiations so once again the overwhelming majority of both clergy and people refused to acknowledge the doctrines of the Roman Church. The Emperor and his small group of supporters who were in favour of reunion were no match for them. The great orator Demetrius Cydones tried in vain to convince the Byzantine people that the Empire's security depended on western help; his fiery speeches fell on deaf ears and hardened hearts, especially as the longed-for western aid was only wishful thinking on the part of the friends of the union.

Meanwhile thunder-clouds were gathering over the Byzantine Empire. Soon after they had taken Gallipoli, the Ottomans began their advance into Balkan lands. Neither Byzantium nor the south Slav countries could offer effective opposition to the superior forces of the Turks. The Empire of Dušan fell to pieces after his death in 1355. Bulgaria had also been split into various principalities and the country was almost paralysed by serious economic impoverishment and religious disturbances. By 1359 Ottoman troops appeared under the walls of Constantinople, and even if the fortifications were strong enough to prevent immediate danger to the capital, the rest of the country quickly surrendered to the enemy. One by one the principal towns of Thrace were captured: Didymotichus (1361), Adrianople (1362),[1] Philippopolis (1363). The Turkish advance was accompanied by comprehensive measures for colonisation. The local population was deported in great numbers to Asia Minor as slaves, and Turkish colonists settled in the conquered areas. The Sultan soon moved his court to Thrace; Adrianople became the residence of Murād I.

Disappointed in his hopes of any help from Rome, John V tried to ally himself with the Italian city-states or with the southern Slavs against the Turks. But negotiations with Genoa and Venice failed. The Patriarch Callistus himself went to Serres to interview the widow of Stephen Dušan, but the discussions were terminated by the sudden death of the Patriarch. Negotiations with Bulgaria proved even less successful and a most untimely armed conflict broke out, in which the Byzantines had at least the satisfaction of taking the port of Anchialus from the Bulgarians (1364), who proved to be even weaker than the Empire.

Once more the Emperor appealed to Avignon. It now seemed that the West really was preparing for a crusade, and an expedition led by King Peter of Cyprus actually took place in the autumn of 1365, but it headed for Egypt and so John V was again dis-

---

[1] On the chronology see G. Ostrogorsky, *History of the Byzantine State*, p. 478, n. 3.

appointed. So he energetically went himself to Hungary in the spring of 1366 to procure the help of Louis the Great. For the first time a Byzantine Emperor entered a foreign country, not as commander-in-chief at the head of his army, but as a suppliant for aid. But without result; the Roman principle was insisted upon: 'first conversion, then assistance'.[1] John V left Hungary with empty hands and fresh misfortune befell him on the way home. When he arrived in Vidin which was occupied by the Hungarians, he had to break his journey because the Bulgarians refused to allow him to pass through their country. Only through the intervention of the 'Green Count' Amadeo of Savoy was the unhappy Emperor rescued in his need. The 'Green Count', a cousin of the Emperor, had appeared in the summer of 1366 in Byzantine waters with a crusading army. He began by taking Gallipoli from the Turks. Then he attacked Bulgaria and not only compelled the liberation of the Emperor, but also forced the Bulgarians to surrender Mesembria and Sozopolis to Byzantium. Thus the Byzantine position on the west coast of the Black Sea was unexpectedly strengthened.

However, for Amadeo of Savoy as well the crusading expedition was closely connected with plans for reunion, while his military operations against the Turks remained limited mainly to the capture of Gallipoli. In Constantinople he had various conferences with his imperial cousin and not without result for he persuaded John V to go to Rome in person. There was great opposition to this in the Empire, so that John did not reach Rome until August 1369. It was significant that his retinue contained many high dignitaries of the Empire but not one representative of the Greek Church. Thus John V's conversion to Roman belief which took place with great ceremony in October 1369 was only an individual act affecting him alone. Union between the Churches had not been achieved.[2] Nor did the journey result in any political gain, for the Emperor's hope of western aid proved deceptive. On the return journey the unhappy ruler suffered yet another humiliation which throws a vivid light on the poverty of the Byzantine Empire and the decline of imperial prestige. His pressing need for money led him to Venice. He agreed to sell the island of Tenedos to the Venetians who promised, in their turn, to give him 25,000 ducats and six transport ships. The matter seemed settled, and the

---

[1] See the well-known letter of Urban V to King Louis of 23 June 1366 in A. Theiner and F. Miklosich, *Mon. spect. ad unionem eccles. Graecae et Romanae* (Vienna, 1872), II, pp. 74 f. (no. 142). O. Halecki, *Un empereur de Byzance à Rome*, pp. 129 ff., tried without success to minimise the significance of this document for Byzantine–Hungarian negotiations. But compare the pertinent remarks of W. Norden, *Papsttum und Byzanz*, p. 703.

[2] As O. Halecki, *op. cit.* p. 205, rightly shows.

unfortunate Emperor got an advance of 4000 ducats. But his eldest son, Andronicus, who was acting as regent in Constantinople during his father's absence, refused to hand over the island which, on account of its position at the entrance to the Dardanelles, was ardently desired by his friends the Genoese, as well as by the Venetians. So the Emperor found himself in a desperate situation. He was in fact a captive in Venice since he had no money for the return to his country, nor could he pay his debts to the city of Venice. But he could indeed be thankful that his plans of 1355 had never come to anything and that he had not sent young Manuel as he had then intended as a hostage to Avignon. For Manuel, now ruling in Thessalonica, extricated his father from this unpleasant situation as quickly as possible.[1] In October 1371 the sorely tried Emperor returned to Constantinople after an absence of almost two years, having achieved nothing.

The urgency of the Byzantine need for help which John V's unceasing effort had failed to get was clearly demonstrated in September 1371 when the Turks won their great victory at the famous battle on the Marica. In this battle King Vukašin, the ruler of the most powerful of the Serbian principalities, and his brother, the Despot John Uglješa, who ruled in Serres, were both killed. This new Turkish victory, the greatest and most important before 1453, was not only a catastrophe for the Macedonian territory which had been governed by the two brothers, but also for the rest of the Balkans. Macedonia lost her independence, the Byzantine Empire itself became an Ottoman tributary state soon afterwards, and the same fate was shared by Bulgaria.[2]

Immediately after the battle of the Marica, Manuel of Thessalonica marched into the territory of the fallen Despot Uglješa and occupied Serres (November 1371). For all their straitened circumstances—and they had no illusions about this—the Byzantines could not resist the temptation to exploit the misfortune of their stricken neighbour. The imperial government was so well aware of the gravity of the situation that, as Manuel himself states in a later document 'after the death of the Serbian Despot', it made the grave decision to seize half the lands of the Byzantine monasteries to grant them out as *pronoiai* in order to strengthen the military forces of the Empire. It was hoped that an improvement in conditions would permit the return of the alienated lands; but as Manuel admits, as time went on

---

[1] The circumstances of John V's stay in Venice, which had provoked many controversies, have been clarified by R.-J. Loenertz, 'Jean V Paléologue à Venise (1370–1371)', *REB*, xvi (1958), 217 ff.

[2] Cf. G. Ostrogorsky, 'Byzance, État tributaire de l'Empire turc', *Zbornik radova Vizantološkog instituta*, v (1958), 49 ff.

the situation only grew worse, and soon the lands that were still owned by the monasteries had to bear additional burdens.[1]

By the spring of 1373 the Emperor John V, fulfilling his duties as a vassal, accompanied the Sultan on campaign in Asia Minor. During his absence Andronicus took the opportunity to rebel against his father (May 1373). He joined forces with the Ottoman prince, Saudži Čelebi, whom Murād had left behind in Thrace, and so there arose the unusual sight of the Byzantine and Ottoman princes joining forces against their respective fathers. But Murād quickly quelled the rebellion, had Čelebi blinded and insisted that John V should punish his son in the same manner. Čelebi died of his cruel injuries, but the punishment of Andronicus and his little son John was evidently not so rigorously carried out for later events show that they did not entirely lose their sight. Andronicus was imprisoned and deprived of his rights to the succession and in his place Manuel now became heir to the throne, and was crowned co-Emperor on 25 September 1373.

Soon afterwards the dispute in the Byzantine imperial house was caught up in the Genoese–Venetian contest for possession of Tenedos. As John V had promised this most strategically placed island to the Venetians, the Genoese decided to prevent this by instigating a change of government. They helped the imprisoned Andronicus to escape to Galata and allowed the usurper to take up arms against his father John V, an action which implied hostility to Venice. On 12 August 1376 Andronicus entered Constantinople and took his father and brother prisoner. His intention of ceding Tenedos to Genoa did not, however, materialise, and in October 1378 the Venetians actually succeeded in taking possession of the island.[2] On the other hand, Andronicus tried to win Turkish support by handing over Gallipoli which ten years previously had been recaptured by Amadeo of Savoy.

It was now the turn of John V and Manuel to escape from prison, this time with Venetian help, and with Turkish consent they were reinstated in their imperial position. Byzantium was by now a mere pawn in the political game of the great powers who shared the east Mediterranean, that is, the two Italian republics and the Ottoman Empire. In their rivalry for the throne John V and Andronicus IV were only tools being used to further the interests of Venice and

[1] Compare V. Mošin, 'Akti iz svetogorskih arhiva', *Spomenik*, XCI (1939), 165, who gives the *prostagma* of Manuel II of December 1408. On the secularisation of monastic lands and their distribution to the *pronoiarii*, see G. Ostrogorsky, *Pour l'histoire de la féodalité byzantine*, pp. 161 ff.

[2] Cf. F. Thiriet, 'Venise et l'occupation de Ténédos au XIVe siècle', *Mélanges d'Archéologie et d'Histoire*, LXV (1953), 219 ff.

Genoa. In the end it was the Sultan who had the final say. With Turkish support John V and Manuel II entered the city on 1 July 1379 on condition that they again became vassals of the Sultan, swore allegiance to him and paid him tribute.

The Venetians and Genoese themselves finally came to terms. After a long and hard struggle they made peace in Turin (1382) through the mediation of Count Amadeo of Savoy. Tenedos was to be given neither to Genoa nor to Venice, its fortifications were to be demolished, and the island itself handed over to the Count of Savoy. No mention was made of Byzantium, as though the island had never belonged to her.

On his restoration John V had had to recognise Andronicus IV and his son John VII as his rightful heirs again, and to hand over to Andronicus Selymbria, Heraclea, Rhaedestus and Panidus. And so what remained of the Byzantine Empire was split up into a number of separate parts: John V ruled in Constantinople; the cities still remaining to the Byzantines on the coast of the Sea of Marmora were governed by Andronicus IV, dependent on the Sultan rather than on his father; Manuel II once more resumed control of Thessalonica; in the Morea the Emperor's third son, Theodore I, ruled as Despot of Mistra. The only success that the Palaeologi had managed to achieve in those unhappy days had been the recovery of the Byzantine lands in the Peloponnese from the house of Cantacuzenus. Theodore I (1382–1406) had to recognise the Sultan's suzerainty and as his submissive vassal he at first enjoyed Turkish support against his enemies at home and abroad.[1] By campaigning against the local aristocracy and small adjacent Latin states he was able to strengthen Byzantine rule. In the capital, however, the situation was desperate. External pressure increased and the patched-up peace in the imperial house soon broke down. Andronicus once more took up arms, but John V succeeded in defeating him in a hard battle in which the Emperor almost lost his life.[2] Andronicus IV's death in 1385 put an end to his subversive activities and Manuel again replaced him as heir to the throne.

Resistance to Ottoman advance in the Balkan peninsula was certainly not due to Byzantine effort. Byzantium took no part in the decisive battles which marked the main stages of that advance. As on the Marica, so at the historic battle on the field of Kossovo on 15 June 1389, it was the Turks and Serbs who stood face to face; but

---

[1] See the important investigation by R.-J. Loenertz, 'Pour l'histoire du Péloponnèse au XIVᵉ siècle (1382–1404)', *EB*, ɪ (1943), 152–96.

[2] See R.-J. Loenertz, 'Manuel Paléologue et Démétrius Cydonès', *EO*, xxxvɪ (1937), 477 ff. and 'Fragment d'une lettre de Jean V à la commune de Gênes', *BZ*, ʟɪ (1958), 39 ff.

in the case of both battles the defeat struck a crushing blow at Balkan lands as well as at Constantinople itself. After heroic fighting, Prince Lazar with his Serbian and Bosnian troops was overwhelmed by the Ottomans and his country was forced to become a tributary state. This meant that the last real centre of resistance was broken and the Turkish conquest from now onwards spread with still greater rapidity.

The powerful Bāyezīd (1389–1402), who succeeded his father Murād I on his death in battle at Kossovo, was in an overwhelmingly strong position. Not only did the Sultan control the surrounding territory but he could impose his will on the very capital itself and forestall any indication of independent imperial action. His tool was the young John VII who as a true son of Andronicus IV played into the Sultan's hands in his attempts to assert his claim to the throne. Since Manuel was not sufficiently submissive Bāyezīd allowed the rival claimant to take action and on 14 April 1390 he gained possession of Constantinople and the imperial throne.[1] But five months later on 17 September Manuel managed to drive out John and to restore his own and his father's rule. But it was now all too plain in Constantinople that only he who was entirely submissive to the Sultan could wear the imperial crown. While John V continued to rule as figurehead in Constantinople, Manuel remained at the court of the Sultan complying with all his overlord's demands as an obedient vassal should. Both he and his father had accompanied Murād I on campaign, but at first they had supported the Sultan against the Seljuqs. Now Manuel was forced to fight on the side of Bāyezīd against Byzantine Philadelphia and to help him conquer the last Byzantine town in Asia Minor with Byzantine troops.[2] Similar humiliation was suffered by the old Emperor John V then in Constantinople. At the Sultan's order, he had to demolish the new fortifications which he had built for the defence of the capital. His troubled life ended on 16 February 1391.

On the news of his father's death Manuel escaped from Brusa and hurried to Constantinople to anticipate any move on the part of his ambitious nephew, John VII, and to secure his own possession of the

[1] Lampros–Amantos, Βραχέα Χρονικά, no. 52, 41. Cf. F. Dölger, 'Johannes VII. Kaiser der Rhomäer', *BZ*, xxxi (1931), 27 ff.; P. Charanis, 'The Strife among the Palaeologi and the Ottoman Turks, 1370–1402', *B*, xvi (1942–3), 303 ff. On the usurpation of John VII see G. Kolias, ''Η ἀνταρσία 'Ιωάννου Ζ΄ ἐναντίον 'Ιωάννου Ε΄ Παλαιολόγου (1390)', 'Ελληνικά, xii (1951), 34–64, which for the first time makes use of the eye-witness account of Ignatius of Smolensk.
[2] The capture of Philadelphia must in any case have taken place between 17 September 1390 and 16 February 1391, and most probably at the end of 1390. See P. Charanis, *op. cit. B*, xvi (1942–3), 304 ff.; P. Wittek, *Das Fürstentum Mentesche* (Istanbul, 1934), pp. 78 ff.; cf. also F. Babinger, *Beiträge zur Frühgeschichte der Türkenherrschaft in Rumelien* (Brno–Munich–Vienna, 1944), p. 9, n. 37.

throne. The responsibility of the imperial office was indeed far more of a burden than a privilege. Each day brought fresh humiliations, new misery and terror for the Emperor of the Romans. Ottoman pressure steadily increased, the danger of final subjection became more threatening. The dramatic meeting in Serres, in the winter of 1393–4, which Bāyezīd commanded his Greek and Slav vassals to attend, seemed to announce the last act of the tragedy. The Sultan did in fact impose a blockade on Constantinople. Distress in the Byzantine capital and the lack of food which had increasingly oppressed her for years now reached its climax, while territories farther afield were subject to new devastation and conquest.

Thessalonica, the second city of the Empire, after capitulating in 1387 after a long siege, had apparently once again freed itself, but it was now stormed and captured by the Turks on 12 April 1394. About the same time Thessaly was also occupied and the Ottomans then turned to central and southern Greece. Here their work was made easy by lack of co-operation among the Christian rulers. The Catalan regime in Greece was already a thing of the past. By 1379 the Navarrese Company had taken Thebes from them. In Attica the Florentine Nerio I Acciajuoli (1388–94) had just begun to rule as duke of Athens. Nerio and the Despot Theodore Palaeologus, his son-in-law, were on good terms. But a disadvantage was that both princes were often on bad terms with Venice, and the Byzantine Despot of Mistra was constantly fighting against the Navarrese of Achaea. When Nerio died in September 1394 almost all his possessions went to his second son-in-law, the Count Carlo Tocco of Cephalonia, and Theodore, feeling slighted, quarrelled with the fortunate heir and tried to take Corinth from him by force. Carlo Tocco appealed to the Ottomans for help. They defeated Theodore beneath the walls of Corinth, invaded the Byzantine Morea and with the efficient support of the Navarrese occupied the Byzantine fortresses Leontarion and Akova at the beginning of 1395.

The Ottoman conquest of the northern part of the Balkan peninsula continued with equal vigour. By 1393 the Bulgarian Empire had been finally subjected. After a severe siege the town of Trnovo capitulated on 17 July. For almost five hundred years Bulgaria was to be a province of the Ottoman Empire.

The Wallachian Prince Mircea the Old, strongly supported by Hungary, proved however a much tougher proposition. A fierce battle was fought on 17 May 1395 on the plain of Rovine.[1] The military

---

[1] See Dj. Radojičić, 'La chronologie de la bataille de Rovine', *RHSE*, v (1928), 136 ff., which stands in spite of F. Babinger, *Beiträge zur Frühgeschichte der Türkenherrschaft in Rumelien*, pp. 3 ff. See also M. Dinić, 'Hronika sendeniskog kaludjera

victory appears to have gone to Mircea but he had nevertheless to submit to the Sultan and to pay tribute. Moreover, the Dobrudja fell into Ottoman hands and Ottoman troops controlled the bridges of the Danube.

These latest successes of the Ottomans made a tremendous impression on the West. When Bulgaria was occupied Hungary seemed directly threatened, while the Latin principalities in Greece had themselves already felt the full force of the Turkish advance. Byzantine appeals for help in the past may have fallen on deaf ears, but now Christendom realised the urgency for combined action. Sigismund king of Hungary called for help and this was answered by companies of knights from several European countries in particular by the knights of France who were specially susceptible to any crusading appeal. After wavering for a time, Venice also joined the coalition and sent a small fleet to the Dardanelles. This promising enterprise was a complete failure. In the battle near Nicopolis on 25 September 1396 the strong but all too ill-coordinated army was annihilated by the victorious Turks.

After this new catastrophe the situation of the Balkan lands became still more hopeless and its effects were even felt in Greece. In 1397 Athens was temporarily occupied by the Ottomans. The Byzantine Morea experienced another devastating invasion. The Ottomans crossed the Isthmus, besieged Argos, which had been held by the Venetians since 1388, defeated the army of the Byzantine Despot, and passed through Byzantine territory burning and pillaging as far as the south coast.

In desperation Constantinople sent out an agonised cry to the world for help. The city was blockaded by the Turks and its capitulation seemed imminent. The Emperor Manuel appealed to the Pope, to the Doge of Venice, to the Grand Duke of Moscow, the kings of France, England and Aragon. At the same time John VII tried to sell his claim to the Byzantine imperial throne to the French king—which is equally indicative of the desperate situation of the Empire. He asked in return for a castle in France and a yearly pension of 25,000 florins. Charles VI, however, does not appear to have been very interested in the imperial rights offered for sale. But he listened to Manuel's appeal for help and sent Marshal Boucicaut with a picked army of 1200 soldiers. The bold marshal was able to force his way through to Byzantium and fought bravely against the Turks. Although successful as a raiding party, so small an army could not free the Empire from the Turkish danger. Manuel therefore decided to go to the West

kao izvor za bojeve na Kosovu i Rovinama', *Prilozi za književnost, jezik, istoriju i folklor*, XVII (1937), 51 ff.

to plead in person for help for his unfortunate Empire. Boucicaut had persuaded him to make this decision and he also managed to bring about an understanding between the two rival Byzantine Emperors. During Manuel's absence John VII was to reign as Emperor in Constantinople. But Manuel had no illusions about the city's position and despite the reconciliation had so little faith in the regent left behind that he thought it wise to leave his wife and children in the safer keeping of his brother Theodore in the Morea.

At the end of 1399 Manuel set out on his journey.[1] He went first to Venice and also visited several other Italian cities; then he took the road to Paris and from there went on to London. Everywhere he was well received and his arresting personality made a great impression. The stay of the enlightened Emperor and his retinue in the capitals of western Europe was of considerable cultural significance as it facilitated closer contacts between the Byzantine and western worlds in the age of the early Renaissance. But Manuel failed to achieve his immediate object, receiving only vague promises which were never made good. He remained absent from his Empire for an extraordinarily long time during which his rival, John VII, ruled as he pleased and became increasingly dependent on the Sultan. On his return Manuel broke his journey in Paris and stayed there almost two years. It was here that he received the good news that the power of Bāyezīd had been broken by the Mongols of Timur and that Byzantium was now freed from the Turkish danger.

Timur is one of the greatest conquerors of world history. Descended from a side-line of a small Turkish dynasty, after lengthy and bitter fighting he created a mighty empire comparable with that of Jenghiz Khan. After subjugating central Asia and the Golden Horde in south Russia, he undertook a campaign to India in 1398. When he had overrun Persia, Mesopotamia and Syria, he finally attacked the Ottoman principality in Asia Minor. His campaigns were accompanied by fearful devastations. After his hordes had passed through, the countryside was like a lifeless desert, 'one heard neither the barking of a dog, nor the crow of a cock, nor yet the cry of a child'.[2] This violent urge for conquest now crushed the power of Bāyezīd. In the memorable battle near Ankara (Ancyra) on 28 July 1402 Timur, after a long and hard fight, defeated the Ottoman army. Bāyezīd fell into the hands of the victor and died in Mongolian imprisonment. By the spring of 1403 Timur had left Asia Minor and two years later the old conqueror died on an expedition to China.

---

[1] Cf. A. Vasiliev, 'Putešestvie vizantijskogo imperatora Manuila II Paleologa po zapadnoj Evrope', *ZMNP*, n.s. xxxix (1912), 41–78, 260–304.
[2] Ducas, p. 77 (*CSHB*).

Nevertheless, his short and violent invasions were of great importance for the Near East. The power of the Ottomans was severely shaken and at the eleventh hour the Byzantine Empire was saved from certain destruction.

V. THE DOWNFALL OF THE EMPIRE

The defeat of the Ottomans near Ankara prolonged the life of the Byzantine Empire for half a century. Within the defeated Ottoman Empire there was great confusion. In spite of this, the Byzantine Empire was too far gone in internal decay to possess any recuperative powers. The situation in the east had however fundamentally altered and this in itself brought with it considerable relief to Byzantium. Bāyezīd's eldest son, Sulaymān, had established himself in European territory and was at loggerheads with his brothers who were in control in Asia Minor. He came to terms with Byzantium, the Serbian prince Stephen Lazarević and the sea powers of Venice, Genoa and Rhodes. Thessalonica with the adjacent region as well as the cities on the Sea of Marmora were returned to Byzantium and tribute was no longer exacted. But by reason of this pact with Sulaymān the Byzantines were involved in the internal quarrels of the rival claimants to the Turkish throne. After a long struggle Sulaymān was defeated by his brother Mūsa (1411) and the Byzantine Empire was again threatened by a serious crisis, for Mūsa took cruel reprisals on Sulaymān's allies and even besieged Constantinople. But the final victor in the Ottoman civil war was Muḥammad. With the support of the Emperor Manuel and the Despot Stephen Lazarević, he overpowered Mūsa in 1413 and ascended the throne. This put an end to the Ottoman dissension and the way was clear for the rebuilding of the Turkish power.

It was, however, some time before this power once again constituted a real threat to the existence of the Byzantine Empire. Muḥammad I (1413–21) concentrated mainly on the internal consolidation of his kingdom and the strengthening of his power in Asia Minor and he was therefore anxious to maintain the friendship of the Byzantine Emperor. So convinced was he of the new Sultan's desire for peace that Manuel II left Constantinople and remained for some time in Thessalonica, going on to the Peloponnese where he arrived on 29 March 1415. While the core of the Empire was slowly withering away, even though external pressure was somewhat relaxed, life in the Greek Morea was flourishing. The distinguished humanist George Gemistus Plethon was then living in Mistra hoping for the rebirth of Hellenism in southern Greece. He dreamed of a Utopia and drafted a new constitution for it after the model of Plato's *Republic*. Thus on the eve of the downfall of the Empire there was in the Byzantine Peloponnese the will to survive and to create new forms of life. The Morea was indeed the refuge of Hellenism which not only maintained but even seemed able to extend its influence here.

To protect this vital possession, Manuel II had a strong wall built on the Isthmus of Corinth, the so-called Hexamilion. Manuel's stay was not without effect on the internal government of the country, for he strengthened the central authority against the centrifugal tendencies of the local nobility. The Emperor left Mistra in March 1416 and was succeeded by his eldest son, John VIII, who arrived in the Morea in the autumn of the same year to help his younger brother, the Despot Theodore II, in the government of the country. Under John's command Byzantine troops victoriously advanced against the Navarrese in Achaea. Prince Centurione Zaccaria lost the greater part of his possessions and only the intervention of Venice postponed the final collapse of his rule.

With the death of Muḥammad I and the accession of his son Murād II (1421–51) Byzantium's breathing space was ended. The Ottomans had reconsolidated their position and the new Sultan returned to the aggressive policy of Bāyezīd. The situation was therefore much the same as it had been before the battle of Ankara. It was useless for the Byzantines to support the rival claimant to the Ottoman throne who was then in rebellion against Murād II and had promised them lavish reward in the event of his success. Murād II defeated his rival and then made a great drive on Constantinople. On 8 June 1422 a full-scale siege began. Once again the Byzantine capital was saved by its strong fortifications and when another claimant to the throne, this time his young brother Muṣṭafā, rebelled against Murād, he had to abandon the siege. The decisive blow was to fall thirty years later but it is true to say that when Constantinople was besieged in 1422 the death agony of the Byzantine Empire had begun.

In the spring of 1423 the Turks again invaded southern Greece. The Hexamilion wall, which had been built across the Isthmus at great cost, was demolished and the whole Morea devastated. In the end the Byzantine government was successful in coming to terms with Murād II, but they were forced to pay tribute once again and to cede to the Ottomans in 1424 several of the towns they had retaken after the battle of Ankara.

At the same time the fate of Thessalonica was sealed. The starving city, severely harassed by the Turks, was governed by Manuel's third son, the Despot Andronicus. In the face of almost unbearable difficulties and an apparently hopeless situation he ceded the city to the Venetians in the summer of 1423. Venice promised to uphold the rights and customs of the citizens and took over its defence and provisioning.[1] This agreement, however, thwarted the Sultan's plans for he had regarded the city as his certain booty. The Venetians continually attempted to come to terms with him and their offers became more and more generous as Turkish pressure without and famine within the city increased. It was with some hesitation that they had at first offered to take on the yearly payment of 100,000 *aspra* which the Byzantine Despot had been paying the Ottomans, but they raised this sum to 150,000 and finally even to 300,000 *aspra*. All bargaining and negotiation were however useless and after a brief rule of seven years the Venetians lost Thessalonica. Murād II himself arrived with a large army and seized the city after a short attack on 29 March 1430.

Manuel II ended his eventful and unhappy life as the monk Matthew, on 21 July 1425. His eldest son John VIII (1425–48), as Basileus and Autocrator of the Romans, had nothing to rule over except Constantinople and its suburbs. What was left of the Byzantine Empire on the Black Sea and in the Peloponnese was controlled by his brothers as independent rulers. The partitioned and exhausted Empire was in total economic and financial ruin. In Manuel II's day gold coins had been rarely minted. In the reign of John VIII the minting of gold in Constantinople ceased altogether and only silver coinage was used.

The only redeeming feature in the Byzantine situation was the Morea, whose government was shared by the three imperial brothers, Theodore, Constantine and Thomas. Undaunted by the devastating Turkish invasion of 1423, the Byzantine principality continued its successful advance against the neighbouring Latin states. Count Carlo Tocco was defeated by the Byzantines in a naval battle in 1427 and he came to an understanding with them whereby he gave his niece in marriage to the Despot Constantine with the rest of his possessions in the Peloponnese as dowry (1428). In the spring of 1430 Constantine entered Patras after a long siege and two years later the Latin principality of Achaea had ceased to exist. With the exception of the Venetian colonies of Coron and Modon in the south and Nauplia and Argos in the east, the whole of the Peloponnese was now under Greek rule. The struggle here between

---

[1] The story of the sale of the city by the Despot Andronicus for 50,000 ducats originates from the so-called *Chronicon Maius* of G. Sphrantzes, which the most recent research has shown to be a later compilation. Cf. especially R.-J. Loenertz, 'Autour du Chronicon Maius attribué à George Phrantzès', *Miscellanea G. Mercati*, III (Vatican, 1946), pp. 273 ff. That this story is in fact a later fable is clearly shown by K. Mertzios, Μνημεῖα Μακεδονικῆς Ἱστορίας (Thessalonica, 1947), pp. 34 ff., citing important documents from the Venetian archives.

the Greeks and Latins which had begun in the days of Michael VIII and continued almost without interruption, had ended on the very eve of the Turkish conquest with the victory of the Greeks—a telling instance of the marked contrast between the vigorous capacity of the principality of southern Greece to expand and the steady decline in power of the Byzantine capital.

In a last attempt to save the city, Byzantium decided once more to open negotiations for reunion with Rome in return for the frequently promised western aid against the infidel. It is true that earlier experiences could hardly be considered encouraging. Whenever Constantinople and Rome negotiated they seemed inevitably to move in a circle. They deceived each other and also themselves. The Byzantine Empire expected Rome to save her from the Turkish threat and promised in return the union of the churches, but the promise could not be fulfilled as it was angrily rejected by the Byzantine people. Rome on the other hand demanded the recognition of her supremacy as an essential preliminary and promised in return aid against the Turks which she could scarcely provide even for the Roman Catholic powers in the east. But although the general feeling of the Byzantines still strongly resisted reunion, there was also an influential party in Constantinople in its favour. As difficulties increased they saw Byzantium's only hope in union with Rome, and this movement was now headed by John VIII. Negotiations were of long duration until it was finally decided to call a council in Italy which the Emperor would attend in person.

In November 1437 John VIII left the capital for Italy as his father had done almost forty, and his grandfather almost seventy, years ago. But he did not go like Manuel only to plead for help; he went to follow the example of John V and to accept the Roman faith, and, moreover, to do so in the name of all his people and the Greek clergy. Accompanied by his brother Demetrius, the Patriarch Joseph and a number of secular and ecclesiastical dignitaries, he reached Ferrara early in 1438. The urgency of the Byzantine plight was such that the outcome was a foregone conclusion, but all the same there were lengthy debates in Ferrara and then in Florence. These were marked by violent disputes, due to the keen opposition of Mark Eugenicus, the Metropolitan of Ephesus, to the Roman Church and the Byzantine supporters of the union. This opposition was eventually repressed. Several anti-unionists allowed themselves to be overruled, others remained steadfast and left Florence with the Despot Demetrius and the great humanist George Gemistus Plethon, fully determined not to subscribe to the decrees of the council. On 6 July 1439 the union was proclaimed in both Greek and Latin in the cathedral of

Florence by the Cardinal Julian Cesarini and the Archbishop Bessarion of Nicaea. The statement about papal primacy was made in deliberately vague terms; the Greeks were to keep the rites of their Church, but all controversial points were settled in a sense favourable to Rome.

The movement for union thus seemed to have won a still greater victory than in the days of the Second Council of Lyons, for this time the Emperor had appeared in person at the Council and together with the highest dignitaries of the Greek Church had accepted the Roman position. But in actual fact nothing had been gained at the Council of Florence. On the contrary, its decrees only incited anti-Roman feeling in Byzantium and the Byzantines rejected the Florentine settlement with fanatical passion. The Union of Florence was in actual fact less effective than the Union of Lyons; for Michael VIII had managed to force his will upon the opposition to a far greater extent than John VIII, and the union of 1274 which aimed at protecting the Byzantine Empire from western aggression did achieve a certain political success. It was, however, quite impossible for the union of 1439 to save Byzantium from the Turkish danger. Instead of bringing help against an external enemy, it fostered internal dissension and sowed seeds of enmity and hatred among the Byzantine population. Moreover the Empire lost what was left of her prestige in Slav lands beyond her frontiers. The Muscovite Empire, far removed from the harassed Byzantine world, had been trained by the Byzantines themselves to hate Rome and regarded the conversion of the Emperor and the Patriarch as an inexplicable betrayal. The Greek Isidore who had been appointed Metropolitan of Russia was one of the foremost supporters of union; on his return from Florence he was deposed by the Grand Duke Basil II and imprisoned. From now on Russia elected her Metropolitans herself. She turned her back on an apostate Byzantium which had betrayed the Orthodox faith and forfeited the right to be the leader of the Orthodox world. Moreover, the much desired help from the West did not arrive, nor was the union consummated in Constantinople. A Roman Catholic and a Greek Orthodox Church continued to confront each other as before. The Byzantine people firmly supported their faith while the most eminent pro-unionists consistently became Roman Catholics. The leader of the Greek unionists, the learned Bessarion, and Isidore, who had fled from Russia, became cardinals of the Roman Church. In spite of the union's lack of any positive political success, Murād II was suspicious about the council held in Ferrara and Florence and John VIII had to conciliate the Sultan by attempting to convince him that these negotiations were of a purely religious nature.

The Ottomans had however to meet real difficulty from another source. As once before during Bāyezīd's reign, the Turkish advances in the Balkans induced Hungary to enter the war. The bold Voivode of Transylvania, John Corvinus Hunyadi, aroused great enthusiasm and fresh hope by his brilliant victories over the Turks in Serbia and Wallachia. The Pope sent an appeal to Christian peoples to undertake a crusade and soon a motley army of 25,000 men gathered in south Hungary, led by King Vladislav III, the young Jagellon and king of Poland and Hungary, together with Hunyadi and the Serbian Despot George Branković, who had been forced by the Turks to leave his country. In the autumn of 1443, while Murād II was fighting against the Amir of Karamania in Asia Minor, the crusaders crossed the Danube near Semendria (Smederevo). They passed rapidly through Serbian territory, and Hunyadi who led the vanguard crushed the army of the governor of Rumelia in an overwhelming victory above Niš. Without meeting any resistance the Christian army entered Bulgaria and occupied Sofia, and then advanced into Thrace. But here they met with strong Turkish resistance and were forced by the severity of the winter to retreat. But in so doing they inflicted a severe defeat on the Ottomans at a battle fought on the mountain of Kunovica in the early days of 1444.

The tide seemed to have turned. The Ottomans, until now usually the victors, saw themselves forced on to the defensive on several fronts. In Albania, where rebellion had been smouldering for several years, the heroic Skanderbeg (George Castriota) revolted and under his leadership the movement for independence gained considerable success. For a number of years (1443–68) he fought as 'Captain of Albania' against the superior forces of the Ottomans, to the great admiration of surrounding countries. The Despot Constantine took the offensive in southern Greece. After the rebuilding of the Hexamilion wall on the Isthmus of Corinth, demolished by the Turks a few years before, he advanced into central Greece and occupied Athens and Thebes. The Duke Nerio II Acciajuoli, hitherto a Turkish vassal, recognised the overlordship of the Byzantine Despot and was forced to pay him tribute.

In view of the changed situation, Murād II tried to come to terms with his opponents. In June 1444 he received the representatives of King Vladislav, George Branković and Hunyadi in Adrianople and they agreed to an armistice for ten years.[1] The Serbian Despot was

---

[1] An entirely new light is thrown on the events of the year 1444 and especially on the agreement of Adrianople by the collection of letters of the humanist Cyriacus of Ancona, made available by F. Pall, 'Ciriaco d'Ancona e la crociata contro i Turchi', *Bull. hist. de l'Acad. Roumaine*, xx (1937), 9–60; see also O. Halecki, *The Crusade of Varna* (New York, 1943), who has reprinted them in a new sequence.

to have his lands returned to him while greater independence was granted to Wallachia. After the Sultan had affirmed an oath to maintain these terms, he left for Asia Minor and sent his plenipotentiary to Hungary to ratify the treaty with King Vladislav who at the end of July signed the treaty at Szegedin and in turn swore to adhere to it. No doubt Ottoman control in the Balkans was considerably restricted by the treaty, and it gave the Christians a longer respite. On the other hand there was disappointment in the Christian world, especially at the Roman Curia, for recent successes had given rise to the hope that the Turks would be completely driven out of the Balkans. There was a demand for the continuance of the war which had such an auspicious beginning. Cardinal Julian Cesarini absolved the hesitant young king of Hungary from the oath which he had just taken, and by September the Christian army was on the march. But it was not as strong as before and above all it no longer had the help of Serbia, since George Branković was satisfied by the terms which he had got from the Turks and therefore refrained from joining the enterprise. Hoping to receive help from the Venetian fleet, the Christian army made its way laboriously through Bulgarian territory towards the Black Sea and finally reached the coast. But Murād II hastened to meet them and the fierce battle fought on 10 November near Varna put a sudden end to the proud hopes of Christendom. After a hard struggle the Christian army was annihilated. King Vladislav fell in battle as well as Cesarini, the real instigator of this unfortunate crusade.[1] This defeat of the Christians was of still greater significance than that of Nicopolis; it was the last effort of a concerted Christian action against the Turks and it had failed. Depression in the Christian world was greater than ever before. The unfortunate Emperor of Constantinople hastened to offer congratulations and presents to the victor.

The Sultan soon took revenge on the Despot Constantine who had been advancing from success to success and had extended his authority in Greece to the Pindus mountains. In 1446 Murād II invaded Greece with a strong force and moved rapidly through central Greece. It was not until he reached the Hexamilion wall that the Despot was able to put up any real resistance to him, and even so the Turkish

---

[1] O. Halecki, *op. cit.* maintains that King Vladislav did not sign the Peace Treaty with the Sultan and that the Treaty of Szegedin is only a legend, but in my view this cannot be accepted. Cf. F. Pall, 'Autour de la croisade de Varna: la question de la paix de Szeged et sa rupture', *Bull. hist. de l'Acad. Roumaine*, XXII (1941), 144 ff., and 'Un moment décisif de l'histoire du Sud-Est européen: la croisade de Varna', *Balcania*, VII (1944), 102 ff., who rightly rejects any doubts as to the historical facts of the Treaty of Szegedin and its breaking. A detailed account of the controversy is given by F. Babinger, 'Von Amurath zu Amurath. Vor- und Nachspiel der Schlacht bei Varna', *Oriens*, III (1950), 229 ff.

artillery proved irresistible. On 10 December 1446 the Hexamilion was taken by storm and the outcome of the struggle was a foregone conclusion. The Turks invaded the Morea, devastated the Byzantine towns and villages and took a great number of prisoners. The Byzantine Despot only secured peace by recognising the overlordship of the Ottomans and agreeing to pay tribute.

Soon after this the Despot Constantine ascended the imperial throne of Constantinople. The Emperor John VIII died childless on 31 October 1448, and Theodore had also died shortly before. So the brave Despot Constantine Dragases, so called after his mother Helena, daughter of prince Constantine Dragaš in east Macedonia, succeeded John VIII as Byzantine Emperor. He was crowned Emperor in the Morea on 6 January 1449 and two months later arrived in the capital.

But not even the courage and self-sacrifice of the last Emperor of Byzantium could delay the certain fate of the Empire. In February 1451 Murād II died and with the accession of his son Muḥammad II the last hour of the Byzantine Empire had come. Byzantine Constantinople was now situated in the heart of Ottoman territory, thus separating the European and Asian possessions of the Turks. The new Sultan's first aim was to remove this alien element and to provide the growing Ottoman Empire with a central capital in Constantinople. With great prudence and energy he laid his plans for the conquest of the imperial city that he might thus bring to fruition the work of his predecessors. The Byzantine court was left in no doubt as to the intentions of the Ottomans, especially as the Sultan had a strong outer fort (Rümeli ḥiṣār) built on the Bosphorus quite close to the city. The Emperor Constantine XI pinned all his hope on western help as his brother had done before him, and at the eleventh hour he tried to revive the union which had been such a complete failure. Cardinal Isidore, formerly Metropolitan of Russia, came to Constantinople as papal legate and on 12 December 1452, five months before the fall of the imperial city, he announced the union and celebrated Roman Mass in St Sophia. The Byzantine people, clinging still more tenaciously to their faith in the hours of their great distress, protested more passionately than ever at this violation of their religious feelings.

But the hostility of the Byzantine people towards any question of reunion was certainly not the only reason why western help for Constantinople was not forthcoming. The conflicting interests and ambitions of the western powers had always precluded any effective aid for Byzantium. In the last years before the fall of the Empire, Alfonso V of Aragon and Naples, at that time the most powerful ruler in the Mediterranean world, was pursuing the policy towards Byzantium which he had inherited from his Norman, German and

French predecessors in south Italy. He attempted to set up a new Latin Empire in Constantinople and he wanted the imperial crown for himself. The very modest subsidy which Pope Nicholas V (1447–55) had meant to use for the defence of Constantinople against the Turks was swallowed up by the ambitious plans of the king of Naples whose incessant demands for money were met without protest by Rome. Had the West really embarked on active intervention in Constantinople, its aims would certainly not have been to save the Byzantine Empire. But it was not the time for the establishment of a new Latin Empire in the East. It was no longer an open question whether the remains of the Byzantine Empire would fall to the Turks or the Latins. The die was cast and the Byzantines themselves had little part in this. The significant events which decided the fate of Byzantium took place outside the Empire which for so long had been little more than a political pawn in the hands of foreign powers. Exhausted internally and reduced to a city-state, it now fell to the Turks.

Early in April 1453 Muḥammad II assembled a great army under the walls of the city. The Byzantines had only a small number of Greek and a still more limited number of Latin soldiers: the main contingent of the Latins consisted of 700 Genoese commanded by Giustiniani who had arrived in two galleys just before the siege began. It is safe to assume that the aggressor had about twenty times as many troops as the defender. The strength of Constantinople did not however lie in its defending troops who were brave but numerically quite inadequate, but in the unique situation of the city and the solidity of its walls. Its extraordinarily strategic position and the strength of its city walls had often saved Byzantium, and in the past these advantages had been combined with Byzantine superiority in military technique. Now the technical superiority was on the Turkish side. Muḥammad II had assembled powerful armaments and with the help of western technicians had created a strong artillery. The Turks used this new weapon at the storming of Constantinople to an extent never yet experienced, and according to the words of a contemporary 'the cannons decided everything'.[1] The little cannons which were available in Constantinople were no match against the new Turkish artillery.

On 7 April the real siege began. The storm was directed against the wall of the town on the landward side, especially the Pempton Gate, which the Turks had found to be the weakest spot in the Byzantine defence. The Golden Horn was blocked by a heavy iron chain which the Turks tried in vain to blast. At one of these blasting attempts a naval battle took place on 20 April and the imperial fleet was victorious. This gave new courage to the defenders but brought the

---

[1] Critobulus, ed. C. Müller, *FHG*, v, p. 80.

city no relief. Two days later the Turks were able to drag a great number of ships overland into the Golden Horn and the city was now bombarded both by land and by sea. With great courage the small band of defenders fought off inevitable defeat. Several attacks had failed, the confidence of the enemy was beginning to dwindle, but after a seven weeks' attack the walls of the city showed serious breaches. The final hour had come.

Muḥammad planned his general assault for 29 May. The onslaught began in the early hours of the morning; the city was stormed simultaneously on all three sides. But for a long time its courageous defenders drove back all attacks. The Sultan then brought up his picked troops, the Janissaries, and after a bitter struggle they managed to scale the walls and get into the city. Constantine XI fought on to the end and died fighting. The conquered city was given over to the unrestrained plundering of the Turkish army. Innumerable treasures and masterpieces, icons and priceless church jewels, unique works of art and irreplaceable manuscripts were destroyed. The Sultan made his solemn entry into the city and Constantinople became the capital of the Ottoman Empire. The Byzantine Empire had ceased to exist.

The principality of Mistra in southern Greece and the Empire of Trebizond survived the fall of Constantinople for a few years. But their subjection created no special problem for the Turks. The conquest of Constantinople had made a strong bridge between the Asian and the European possessions of the Ottomans. It united their Empire and gave a new stimulus to their capacity for conquest and expansion. The mighty Ottoman Empire rapidly annexed the remaining Greek, Latin and Slav possessions in the Balkans. In 1456 Athens fell to the Ottomans, and the Parthenon which had been for a thousand years a church of the Mother of God was now turned into a Turkish mosque. In 1460 the Greek principality of the Morea was overrun; Thomas fled to Italy, while the anti-Latin Demetrius joined the court of the Sultan. In September 1461 the Empire of Trebizond also fell, bringing the last remnants of Greek territory under Turkish rule. Before the end of the century all the Balkan lands had been annexed by the Ottomans.

Once more an Empire stood, reaching from Mesopotamia to the Adriatic and having Constantinople as its capital. The Empire of the Ottomans rose from the ruins of the East Roman Empire and for several centuries again united the former lands of Byzantium.

CHAPTER IX

THE LATINS IN GREECE AND THE AEGEAN FROM THE FOURTH CRUSADE TO THE END OF THE MIDDLE AGES

The imposing remains of Latin castles in Greece and the Aegean which have resisted the destruction of time and the Turk still remind us of the Fourth Crusaders and the states they founded. The crusaders were a hardy lot. Everyone who has made the steep, winding ascent to the walled crown of Acrocorinth, or has struggled up the slope of Arcadian Orchomenus to view the medieval tower at its summit, has thought of the endurance of the men and horses to whom such a climb was an almost daily occurrence. The crusaders were no strangers to the Byzantine Empire where under the Comneni many westerners had found their fortunes. Byzantine territory in the Balkans had been seriously diminished during the generation which preceded the catastrophe of 1204. The Serbs were establishing a state which, a century and a half later, Stephen Dušan was to elevate to a position of great power, and the Bulgars were embarking on the history of the Second Bulgarian Empire, which was to prove a most formidable enemy to the new Latin Empire of Constantinople, and to exhaust the crusaders' strength on the Bosphorus in the three decades which followed the conquest. There was already a Latin state in the Ionian Greek islands of Cephalonia and Zante, where young Matthew Orsini of Apulia had set up a county that was to play a most conspicuous role in the history of Latin dominion in Greece. Centrifugal currents were tearing the Empire to pieces, and of the last two decades before the crusade, when the Angeli were ruling (1185–1204), the contemporary Nicetas Choniates wrote that 'there were those who revolted in one place or another, again and again, and it is not possible to say how many times this happened'.[1] The crusaders knew well the manifold weaknesses of the Empire.

After the establishment of a Latin regime in Constantinople, Greek rulers seized certain areas for themselves. Long-lived states were set up in Nicaea, Trebizond and Epirus. Leo Sgouros, the hereditary archon of Nauplia, entertained similar ambitions in the Morea. According to Nicetas, Sgouros had already 'seduced Argos and stolen

[1] Nicetas Choniates, *De Isaacio Angelo*, III, no. 2, p. 553 (*CSHB*).

Corinth'. He now sought further acquisitions in continental Greece. Early in 1204 he invaded Attica, and if he was unable to take the Acropolis, the ashes turned up in the Athenian Agora by the American excavators attest the extent of his destruction in the lower city. From Athens Sgouros went on to occupy Thebes. Farther north, at Larissa, he met the fallen Emperor Alexius III Angelus, and married the Emperor's daughter Eudocia. Before the approach of the small army of Boniface of Montferrat, who had established himself as King of Thessalonica by September 1204, Sgouros fell back upon Thermopylae, but the famous pass did not inspire him with the will to play Leonidas' heroic part. One look at the Frankish cavalry was enough to send him, in terrified haste, southward over the Corinthian isthmus to the rocky height of Acrocorinth. In October or November 1204 Boniface overran Boeotia and Attica, meeting little resistance. Athens was taken and a Latin garrison installed on the Acropolis. Acrocorinth was put under a siege which lasted about five years, falling to the Latins early in 1210—although two years before, in 1208, unable to tolerate the narrow confinement of his fortress, Sgouros in despair had leaped on horseback from the high walls, and crashed to his death upon the rocks below.

The many Greek towns and strongholds which fell to Boniface of Montferrat in his southward march were promptly granted as fiefs to his followers. Among the most important was the town of Boudonitza, the modern Mendenitza, commanding the pass at Thermopylae; it was bestowed upon the Marquis Guy Pallavicini, whose descendants long ruled over it, and where the extensive remains of their castle still bear witness to the watch they kept over the road into Greece. Farther south and west, on a height above the ancient town of Amphissa, Thomas d'Autremencourt (Stromoncourt) built the castle of Salona, overlooking one of the most beautiful valleys in Greece. The Burgundian Otho de la Roche became the lord of Athens, and possibly of Thebes, in late October or November 1204. Although there is some reason to believe that Thebes was first granted to Albertino and Rolandino of Canossa, who became involved in the rebellion against the Latin Emperor Henry in 1209, the city of Epaminondas was certainly being ruled after 1211 by Otho and his nephew Guy de la Roche as *domini Thebarum*. While Boniface and Otho de la Roche pushed on into the Morea late in the year 1204, the island of Euboea, which the Franks called Negroponte, was quickly overrun by the Fleming James of Avesnes, whose rapid success allowed him to join Boniface and Otho in besieging Sgouros's strongholds of Acrocorinth, Argos and Nauplia. In the meantime one of the epic adventures of the Fourth Crusade was beginning.

Geoffrey of Villehardouin, nephew of the chronicler of the Fourth Crusade, had been among the many crusaders who had gone directly to Syria. When news of the fall of Constantinople reached him there, he desired to share in the spoils. He left Syria in the late summer of 1204, but adverse winds drove him westward, to land at Modon in the extreme south-west of the Peloponnese. Here he spent the winter, entering into a compact with the Greek lord of Messenia to conquer as much of the western Peloponnese as they could. The Greek lord soon died, however, and his son discontinued the alliance, seeking to retain all the profits. It was at this point that Geoffrey learned of the appearance of Boniface of Montferrat before Nauplia, whence he determined to seek aid. Boniface received him well, and sought to retain him in his service; but at Nauplia Geoffrey also found his friend William of Champlitte, grandson of Count Hugh I of Champagne. Geoffrey explained to Champlitte that he had just come from a very rich land 'called the Morea', which name had been given to Elis for two or three generations, and was soon to be given to the whole Peloponnese. 'Let us go, with God's help, and conquer. And that which you shall wish to give me from the conquests, I will hold of you, and I will be your liege man.' So the elder Villehardouin reports his nephew's offer, and with the permission of Boniface, the great adventure was begun.

Champlitte and Villehardouin set out in the spring of 1205, with 100 knights and 400 mounted men-at-arms. From Nauplia they made their way north to Corinth, and thence to Patras, where they took the city and the castle. They continued down the coast to Andravida, the fall of which meant the easy occupation of Elis. Farther down the coast Pundico Castro, 'Mouse Castle' (*Pontikocastro*), at the base of the small Cape of Katakolo, was taken, and a strong garrison was left there. The conquerors met their first serious obstacle in the sea-board fortress of Arcadia, the ancient Kyparissia, which had to be by-passed, and Champlitte and Villehardouin pushed on to Modon. Finally, the Greeks were moved to concerted action. The natives of Nikli, Veligosti and Lacedaemonia, together with some of the Slav Melings of the Taygetus, formed an army, from four to six thousand strong, to oppose the Frankish advance; and Michael Ducas, the enterprising ruler of Epirus (1204–14), crossed the straits of Naupactus, to lead the embattled Greeks, and to add the western Morea to his newly won dominions in Epirus, Acarnania and Aetolia. This was the crisis. But the Greeks, said to have outnumbered the Franks by almost ten to one, were stopped in an olive grove called Koundoura, presumably in north-eastern Messenia. Victory once again attended the efforts of the Latin adventurers, and Michael Ducas returned

to Arta with narrower ambitions.[1] Coron was besieged and surrendered; Kalamata was occupied. The Morea had not been entirely
overrun by the Franks but, on 19 November 1205, Pope Innocent III,
in a letter to the new Latin Patriarch of Constantinople, could refer
to William of Champlitte as 'princeps totius Achaiae provinciae'.[2]

Events were occurring in the north which had an important bearing
on the affairs of the new principality of Achaea. The Latin Emperor
Baldwin I had been captured in April 1205 by the terrible Kalojan,
King of the Vlachs and the Bulgars. Baldwin never regained his
freedom, and it was only after a year of dangerous uncertainty that
his brother Henry of Hainault could succeed him (August 1206).
Boniface of Montferrat now fell into a Bulgarian ambush, and was
killed in western Thrace (September 1207); his death did irreparable
damage to the Latin cause in Greece. The ambitious Count Hubert
of Biandrate, guardian of Boniface's younger son, Demetrius, heir to
the crown of Thessalonica, organised a cabal of the Lombard nobles
in northern Greece to set Demetrius' half-brother, the Marquis
William of Montferrat, on the throne of Thessalonica. Hubert and
the Lombards rejected the claims of the Emperor Henry to suzerainty
over the disputed kingdom. Henry was thus forced to take the
field against the insurgents in December 1208. In the struggle that
followed Henry successfully established his suzerainty over Thessalonica, put the young Demetrius on the throne, and managed to
take Hubert into custody. He summoned a great parliament to
assemble on the plains of Ravennika, near Zeitounion (the ancient
Lamia), to which some sixty barons came on 1–2 May 1209, but many
of the Lombard lords refused to appear, taking their defiant stand
behind the ample walls of the Cadmea at Thebes. There Henry arrived
on Friday, 8 May, to be warmly greeted in the outer city by the
Greek inhabitants' repeated cries of 'Many years!' (πολλὰ χρόνια).
In the face of Henry's determination to take the Cadmea, and his
apparent means to do so, the resolution of the Lombards dissolved,
and the Emperor generously allowed them to retain their fiefs, as his
vassals, on the surrender of the Cadmea. He had succeeded in
restoring imperial power and prestige in Greece.

The year 1208 was probably far advanced when William of Cham-

---

[1] For the career of Michael Comnenus Ducas, often wrongly described as the
founder of the 'despotate' of Epirus, and his successors, see above: ch. VII, pp. 296 ff.

[2] Innocent III, *Epp.* VIII, no. 153 (*MPL*, CCXV, 728); A. Potthast, *Regesta Pontificum Romanorum*, I, no. 2608. Champlitte's 'principality' thus seems to begin as an
ecclesiastical circumscription, as the 'province' under the metropolitical authority
of Patras; the vernacular title soon became 'Prince of the Morea' (cf. J. Longnon,
L'empire latin de Constantinople, pp. 74–5). The ecclesiastical term 'province' was
dropped, at least generally, and Achaea quickly became a lay 'principality'.

plitte learned of the death of his elder brother Louis in Burgundy. Louis had left an inheritance which William set out to claim, but died himself some time early in 1209. William had put his conquests in the Morea in the charge of a nephew, who also died very shortly, and so by the beginning of May 1209, when Geoffrey of Villehardouin had appeared at the (first) parliament of Ravennika in response to the summons of the Emperor, he had come as the ruler of the Morea. The Venetians also had a claim to much of the Morea, arising out of the partition treaty of 1204, and by now had occupied and fortified both Modon and Coron. The relations of Venice and Villehardouin had undoubtedly been discussed at Ravennika, and in June 1209 a treaty between the two saw Geoffrey acknowledge Venetian suzerainty for his holdings from the region of Navarino as far as Corinth, in return for Venetian citizenship for himself and his successors. The Venetians received exemption from all levies on their commerce, and were to have a church, a market and a court in whatever of Villehardouin's cities they might wish. They reserved the southern end of the Messenian promontory, including Modon and Coron, for themselves. It was a satisfactory arrangement. The Frankish ruler of the Morea kept his lands, castles and revenues; Venice, her strategic ports; and the army of the one might aid the navy of the other against their common enemies in the years that lay ahead.

The partition treaty of 1204 had not only awarded Venice most of the Morea, but also, among other territories, Euboea (Negroponte), as well as Epirus, Acarnania and Aetolia. After the treaty with Villehardouin the Venetians made similar agreements in 1209–10 both with Ravano dalle Carceri, successor to the late James of Avesnes, and now sole lord of Euboea, and with Michael Ducas, the ruler of Epirus, who also possessed Acarnania and Aetolia. Michael had been most impressed with the Emperor Henry's show of force against the Lombard barons in 1208–9, and so had made obeisance to him, and now acknowledged himself the Republic's vassal for his disputed lands. The ink was scarcely dry, however, upon the drafts of the treaty before he attacked both the Latin kingdom of Thessalonica and the principality of the Morea, and Venetian suzerainty over his dominions became merely another document in the rich archives of the Republic. By the agreement negotiated with Ravano dalle Carceri, however, Venetian suzerainty over the island of Euboea was made to endure. James of Avesnes's great seignory had been divided by Boniface of Montferrat in August 1205 into three great fiefs, to be held by 'triarchs' (*terzieri*, *terciers*), and these had been given to Ravano dalle Carceri and two other Veronese, of whom one died and the other went back home; after Ravano's own death (in 1216) the

Venetian bailie in Euboea superintended the division of these three fiefs among six heirs, and, in the decades that followed, Venetian influence was to grow and to remain paramount in Euboea until the fall of the island to the Turks in 1470.

The *Chronicle of the Morea* tells how William of Champlitte had designated his cousin Robert as his Moreote heir, provided the latter arrived in the East within a year and a day to claim the succession; how the regent Geoffrey of Villehardouin managed to put off Robert until the allotted time had expired; and how the high court of Achaea adjudged Robert to have forfeited the principality, which was now formally awarded to Villehardouin. This account seems to contain less fact than fancy, although the heir or heirs of Champlitte apparently did have to abandon their rights to the exigencies of the time, which made the strong and experienced Villehardouin a proper ruler for that newly conquered land. In any event Villehardouin seems to have assumed the title Prince of Achaea before the close of the year 1209: he is so addressed by Innocent III in letters dated on and after 22 March 1210. Villehardouin had summoned his wife from Champagne, and she came with their young son Geoffrey II, who was to succeed to the principality about 1228.[1] They took up their residence in the fine castles of La Crémonie (Lacedaemonia) and Kalamata, in the latter of which Villehardouin's second son, William (II), was born to become his brother Geoffrey's successor in 1246. Some ruins of the Villehardouin's castle still stand on a hill in the northern part of the modern town of Kalamata.

After the departure of Champlitte from the Morea in 1208, Villehardouin went on with the task of organising the newly won state and of effecting its division into fiefs to be held by the Latin conquerors. A commission, which included Greeks, had already been appointed to establish the new fiefs; the results of its work had been set down in a feudal register, called by the Greek *Chronicle of the Morea* (vv. 1908–9), τὸ βιβλίο, ὅπου ἦτο ἡ μερισία ἐγράφως...τοῦ καθενός..., in accordance with which the assignment of fiefs was accepted by a great baronial parliament assembled by Villehardouin at Andravida, the Elian capital of the principality. Twelve great baronies had been or were soon to be established, the barons of which made up, with their liegemen, the High Court of Achaea. These twelve baronies, commonly identified by their (later) castles, were: Matagrifon, in Arcadia, near the modern town of Dimitzana (worth 24 knights' fees); Karytaina, in the region of Skortá, in the valley of

---

[1] For the date of Geoffrey I's death, see J. Longnon, 'Problèmes de l'histoire de la principauté de Morée', *Journal des Savants* (1946), pp. 158–9, and cf. *L'empire latin*, pp. 164, 166.

the Alpheus (22 knights' fees); Patras, probably worth some 24 knights' fees, and ruled by its archbishop from about 1266; Passavá or Passavant, on the gulf of Laconia, at the base of the peninsula of Maina (4); Vostitza, the classic Aegium, on the gulf of Corinth (8); Kalavryta (12) and Chalandritza (4), just south of Vostitza and Patras respectively; Veligosti, near the ancient Megalopolitan plain (4); Nikli, near Tegea and the once famous temple of Athena Alea (6); Geraki, on a western ridge of Mt Parnon, overlooking the Laconian plain (6); Gritzena, which had very little Frankish history (4), near Kalamata; and, finally, the Villehardouin's fiefs of Kalamata, on the gulf of Messenia, and Arcadia (Kyparissia),[1] on the so-called gulf of Arcadia. The original families of the conquest did not long survive; the men led too robust lives, and warfare and the climate took their toll. When William of Villehardouin, Geoffrey's second son, died in 1278, only the baronies of Vostitza and Chalandritza were still in the possession of the founding families, and by this time Passavá, Geraki, and Kalavryta had already been retaken by the Greeks, now established in Mistra.

After the conquest of continental Greece and the Morea Pope Innocent III and the Roman Curia were faced with the task of organising the religious life of the new Latin colonies. Innocent acted as common sense required under the circumstances, and took over the existing structure of the Greek Church. As time passed, however, experience suggested alteration of this structure. Greek bishops were given an opportunity to retain their sees by accepting papal authority, the *azymes*, and the *filioque* clause, but a succession of conferences between Latin and Greek ecclesiastics to discover some mutual accommodation of their beliefs and practices achieved nothing. On 2 August 1206, in reply to a series of questions addressed to him by the Latin Patriarch Thomas Morosini, Innocent III outlined the policy to be followed in Greece. Greek bishops who submitted to the authority of the Pope and the Latin Patriarch might continue as pastors of their flocks, but those who persisted in contumacious refusal of such authority were to receive three separate admonitions; if these were unavailing—and, for the most part, they were to be so—the Patriarch and the Cardinal legate Benedict might suspend from office and excommunicate the recalcitrant Greek bishops, who could then be replaced by Latins.

Very few Greek bishops, however, deserted the faith of their fathers for that of their conquerors. Even where lack of conscience or conviction made the spiritual compromise possible, the hostility of their

---

[1] The name 'Arcadia' was used for both the region of the central Peloponnese and the town of Kyparissia.

Greek congregations, the contempt of their Orthodox confrères, and the suspicions of their new Latin colleagues were almost insurmountable barriers. In Greece proper apparently only one important Greek bishop accepted papal supremacy and rendered canonical obedience thereto; this was Theodore of Euboea (Negroponte), the friend and former suffragan of the Athenian Metropolitan Michael Choniates. Theodore had abundant trouble with his new superior, the Latin Archbishop Bérard of Athens, who was anxious to remove him from his island see, and papal intervention was necessary to retain him therein. Everywhere in continental Greece and the Morea, however, most of the parish priests who administered the sacraments, especially in the smaller villages, were and continued to be Greek.

Meanwhile there had been much friction between the Church and the new Latin rulers of the Byzantine Empire ever since the autumn of 1204. The crusaders had agreed, subject to certain restrictions and qualifications, to grant the Latin clergy one-fifteenth of their new lands and possessions located outside the walls of Constantinople.[1] Dissension had continued, however, over payment by the parochial clergy of the old Byzantine land-tax, called the *crustica* or *akrostichon* (ἀκρόστιχον), to the lay lords of the territories in which their parishes were located. A further source of grievance lay in the fact that, while the Latin barons had insisted upon collecting the land-tax from Greek and even Latin priests, they had themselves been very remiss in paying tithes. A concordat was now arranged, on 2 May 1210, at the second parliament of Ravennika. According to its terms the barons in continental Greece granted exemption from all feudal jurisdiction to ecclesiastical persons and properties, from the borders of the Latin kingdom of Thessalonica to the city of Corinth, except that the land-tax was to be paid to their lay lords by both the Latin and Greek clergy, at the rate paid by Greeks on those lands 'at the time of the capture of the imperial city of Constantinople'. Young Greeks, whether of lay or clerical parentage, were liable to feudal or manorial service according to the custom of the region in which they lived, unless and until they were themselves ordained as priests, after which they were to enjoy the same privileges with respect to such service as Roman Catholic clerics. These were eminently fair provisions. Unfortunately for the future relations of the Church with the Latin feudatories of the Morea, however, Geoffrey of Villehardouin, Prince of Achaea, was not represented at the parliament of 1210, nor a party

---

[1] The settlement had been reached on 17 March 1206, with papal confirmation on 4 August following: Innocent III, *Epp.* IX, no. 142 (*MPL*, ccxv, 967); G. L. F. Tafel and G. M. Thomas, *Urkunden zur älteren Handels- und Staatsgeschichte der Republik Venedig*, II (Vienna, 1856), no. clxiii, pp. 31–4.

to its proceedings. Otho de la Roche, the lord of Athens, although he was represented and his seal affixed to the agreement, was not to abide by it. Its terms were not forgotten by the Curia, however, and in the years that followed, both Villehardouin and de la Roche were to find themselves, for considerable periods, under the ban of excommunication and their lands laid under the interdict.

The first organisation of the Latin hierarchy in the Morea consisted of seven episcopal sees, presided over by the Archbishop of Patras and the six suffragans under him: the Bishop of Olena (near the modern Pyrgos), who resided in the capital city of Andravida, together with the Bishops of Veligosti, Amyclae, and Lacedaemonia, and of the Venetian stations of Modon and Coron. The Hospitallers, Templars, and Teutonic Knights also received some lands and built some strongholds. Only part of the Morea, however, had thus been brought under the control of the Roman Catholic Church. When Corinth fell in 1210, its church was immediately organised by the Latins as a second metropolitan see, also with seven suffragan bishoprics: the island sees of Cephalonia and Zante; Damala, near the ancient Troezen; Monemvasia, which remained in Greek hands until 1248; together with Argos, Helos (*Gilas* in the documents) in Laconia, and Zemena (*Gimenes*) near Corinth. Much of this organisation was merely on paper, however, and time, necessity and further knowledge of the Morea led the Roman Curia to introduce many changes into this structure. By the middle of the thirteenth century, in the time of Prince William of Villehardouin, the Latin hierarchy in the Morea consisted of the Archbishop of Patras, with his suffragans of Olena, Coron, Modon and Cephalonia, together with the Archbishop of Corinth and the Corinthian suffragans of Argos, Monemvasia, Lacedaemonia and Maina. Thus some sees, which had been found to be too poor to support a bishop or to be without Latin inhabitants enough to require one, had been abolished or, as the case might be, combined with some nearby see, which was more prosperous or had a larger Latin population.

For some twenty years Prince Geoffrey I of Villehardouin ruled over most of the Morea as an almost independent state. His suzerains were the Latin Emperor in Constantinople and the Venetian republic, but after the death of the Emperor Henry in 1216, the imperial power on the Bosphorus counted for little, and the Venetians did not interfere in the affairs of the Moreote principality so long as their own interests were in no way endangered. Geoffrey was an able prince who knew how to preserve the state he had helped to found by his enterprise and imagination. He appears, by and large, to have dealt justly with the native Greeks, but he did not get along well with the Latin clergy. He had delayed acceptance of the concordat of Ravennika, and when the Latin clergy of the Morea refused to render military service for their fiefs, according to the *Chronicle of the Morea*, he expropriated their revenues to build the great castle of Chloumoutsi, called by the French Clermont and by the Italians Castel Tornese. Together with Otho de la Roche, lord of Athens and Thebes, he resisted the claims and unwarranted usurpations of the Latin Patriarch Gervase (1216–19), who excommunicated the two princes while a patriarchal legate laid an interdict upon their lands, contrary to the express limitations of the Lateran Council. On 31 March 1218 Pope Honorius wrote to the Patriarch rebuking him severely for overreaching himself and demanding the relaxation of the bans pronounced by the Patriarch against the prince of Achaea and the lord of Athens. But if the former was presumptuous, so too were the latter, and less than a year later Honorius acceded to the formal petition of the Latin episcopacy in Greece to maintain the bans of excommunication and the interdict directed against the rulers of that alien land where an alien Church could never find the peace and security it sought.

In 1218–19 Villehardouin and de la Roche again fell under the ban of the Church for their contumacious retention of certain abbeys, churches and other properties, together with their reduction to serfdom of Greek rural priests, contrary to the provisions of the concordat of Ravennika. These sentences of excommunication endured for about five years, until 4 September 1223, when they were relaxed by Pope Honorius in a compromise based upon the terms of Ravennika. The independence of the Latin Church in the Morea, except for just and due land-taxes (*akrosticha*), was again asserted. As at Ravennika in 1210, the lower Greek clergy was not ungenerously protected by the Pope, and there were now established for each village, depending on its size, the numbers of Greek priests (*papades*) who could enjoy the clerical immunity from lay jurisdiction which meant also freedom from feudal and manorial service: a village having from 25 to 70 homes (*lares*) might have two such priests; a village of from 70 to 125 homes, four priests; and those containing more than 125 might have six priests. Such priests were to pay the *akrostichon* if it was due from their lands. Villehardouin was himself to pay tithes; so were his subjects, both Latin and Greek; but he was to keep the treasures and movable properties of the Church which he had already expropriated, in return, however, for an annuity of 1000 *hyperpyra* to be paid by him and divided among certain churches in the Morea. A similar arrangement was made also with Otho de la Roche, who was to pay to the Church an annuity of 500 *hyperpyra* for the property and revenues which he had seized. The Pope and the chief Latin rulers in Greece had reason to come to terms with each other. Towards the end of the year 1224 the Latin kingdom of Thessalonica had come to an end with the capture of its capital by Theodore Ducas, now ruler of Epirus, who now set up the almost equally short-lived Greek Empire of Thessalonica (1224–46). The terrible danger in which the Latin Empire of Constantinople now stood made the Pope anxious to enlist the prince of Achaea and the lord of Athens and Thebes in the cause of Latin Christendom and Constantinople.

About 1228 Prince Geoffrey I of Villehardouin died, and was succeeded by his distinguished son Geoffrey II, who ruled with courage and justice through very critical years. The eyes of the Greek world had become fastened upon Theodore Ducas of Epirus, who having taken Thessalonica, assumed the title 'King and Emperor of the Romans'. Theodore launched the Greek Empire of Thessalonica upon a violent history which, after his own defeat and capture by the Bulgars at Klokotnica in 1230, was continued under his brother Manuel (1230–41), and finally under his feeble sons John and Demetrius, until its fall in 1246 to the Greek Emperor of Nicaea, John Ducas Vatatzes. A Latin expedition to recover Thessalonica had been led into Greece in 1225 by the Marquis William of Montferrat, accompanied by his half-brother, the titular King Demetrius, but it had come to grief in Thessaly, where William had died, some said of poison. The fate of the Latin Empire was now of much concern in France, Italy and Greece. The fall of Thessalonica had interposed formidable enemies between Constantinople and Greece, but the Bulgarian Tsar John Asen II's decisive victory at Klokotnica in 1230 had freed the rulers of both Athens and Achaea from the dangers inherent in the great concentration of power in the hands of Theodore Ducas.

In 1228 the inept Latin Emperor Robert of Courtenay had died in the Morea; his brother Baldwin II was a boy; and so the next year John of Brienne, former King of Jerusalem, was elected Emperor for his lifetime and regent until Baldwin should attain his majority. He arrived in Constantinople in the autumn of 1231, and from this time Prince Geoffrey II of Achaea is said by a contemporary source to have sent John 22,000 *hyperpyra* each year with which to hire auxiliary troops to help defend the capital. The Latins on the Bosphorus had two determined enemies, the Bulgarian Tsar John Asen II and the Greek Emperor of Nicaea, John Ducas Vatatzes, who came together in an alliance in 1234. In the following year Vatatzes drove the Venetians from Gallipoli, swept across the Chersonese, and conquered everything of importance to the river Marica, including the strong fortress of Tzurulum (Tchorlu), in south-eastern Thrace. John Asen plundered the north. Small victories were won by John of Brienne on land and by the Venetians on the sea, but in 1236 Geoffrey II of Achaea sailed to Constantinople and compelled the Greeks to raise their siege of the city. As a reward for this spectacular service Baldwin II is said to have given Geoffrey suzerainty over the duchy of Naxos in the Archipelago, over the island of Euboea, and probably over the marquisate of Boudonitza. Two years later Geoffrey's fleet again conducted operations against that of Nicaea.

Geoffrey II was at the pinnacle of his career. During most of his eighteen years of rule peace obtained in the principality of Achaea. He seems to have made little or no effort to subdue the Slavs of Mt Taygetus and the Tzakones of Mt Parnon. He did not undertake the reduction of the great fortress town of Monemvasia, although it was a menace to Latin shipping. He maintained sometimes close relations with John Ducas Vatatzes, and apparently avoided serious conflict with Epirus. Geoffrey died in 1246, much lamented, and was succeeded by his brother William of Villehardouin.

By playing off the despotate of Epirus against the Empire of Nicaea, while committing himself to neither side, William of Villehardouin might have enlarged his principality and made his influence predominant in the affairs of Greece. Already in 1236, however, the astute Michael II, a bastard of the first ruler, Michael Ducas, had made himself ruler of Epirus, Acarnania and Aetolia; and by marrying Michael's daughter, William was to become involved disastrously in the unrelenting hostility between Epirus and Nicaea. He was one of the greater soldiers and less fortunate diplomats of his age.

William is the hero of the *Chronicle of the Morea*; born at Kalamata, he spoke Greek almost with the ease of a native. He began his long and colourful reign (1246–78) with the successful siege of Monemvasia (1246–8), in which he was assisted by Guy I de la Roche, the second lord of Athens, his vassal for the Moreote fiefs of Argos and Nauplia, and also by the triarchs of Euboea, Duke Angelo Sanudo of the Archipelago, some of the lesser lords of the Aegean, and Count Matthew Orsini of Cephalonia. William granted the Monemvasiotes the franchise, left the chief archontic families undisturbed in their possessions, and built castles to extend his sway in the central and southeastern parts of the Morea. The Tzakones of Mt Parnon, the ancient Laconians, were made to submit to his authority, and during the winter of 1248–9 he began the famous castle on the steep height of Mistra, some four miles west of Sparta. (Mistra was destined to have a great future, but not under Latin hegemony.) William next built the castle of Old Maina ('le Grand Magne'), on the Laconian Gulf near Cape Matapan, and another castle called Beaufort, in Greek 'Levtro', on the eastern shore of the Messenian Gulf, just across from the Venetian station of Coron. These fortresses produced a more submissive attitude among the Slavic tribe of the Melings of Taygetus and among the natives of Maina.

William of Villehardouin, Prince of Achaea, was at the height of his power and prestige during the first half dozen or more years which followed the taking of Monemvasia. Marino Sanudo the Elder has borne witness to the magnificence of William's court, the fame of his warriors, and the well-being of his subjects; but his love of splendour was excessive, and *hybris* played its part in yet another drama soon to be enacted in that land of great tragedians. William's second wife, Carintana dalle Carceri, of the family of the triarchs of Euboea, died in 1255, leaving him a somewhat dubious claim, which ambition prompted him to press, to the great northern barony of Oreos. The other two triarchs, William of Verona and Narzotto dalle Carceri, fearing to have so powerful a neighbour, opposed Villehardouin's claim, although he was their suzerain. Narzotto and William of Verona now secured as allies the Venetians in Euboea; Guy I de la Roche, the lord of Athens, who held Argos and Nauplia as a vassal of the Prince of Achaea; and Guy's brother William, who was also the prince's vassal for the Moreote fiefs of Veligosti and Damala (Troezen). Villehardouin captured and imprisoned William of Verona and Narzotto, but the Venetian bailies of Euboea were left to carry on the struggle against him; this they did in conjunction with Geoffrey of Bruyères ('de Briel'), lord of Karytaina; Thomas II d'Autremencourt, lord of Salona (Amphissa); and Hubert Pallavicini, the marquis of Boudonitza (Thermopylae). Other northern barons, fearing the power of the Prince of Achaea, joined the league against him; some of these also, like the lords of Karytaina and Boudonitza, were vassals of the prince. The Genoese aided William of Villehardouin, glad of a legal chance to strike at the Venetians, and in May 1258 William defeated Guy de la Roche of Athens and some of the allies at the pass of Mt Karydi, on the old road from Megara to Thebes, whither the vanquished barons now fled to the refuge of the Cadmea. William's victory more or less ended the 'war of the Euboeote succession', but owing to the tragedy about to befall him there was to be no opportunity to re-establish peace with the Venetians until 1262.

The death of William's second wife, Carintana dalle Carceri, had caused his unwise entry into the war with the northern barons and Venice. It was now, in 1258, that he married Anna Comnena Ducaena, daughter of the Despot Michael II of Epirus, and it was this marriage which involved him in the conflict between Epirus and

Nicaea. The death of John Ducas Vatatzes, four years before, had tempted Michael to invade the European possessions of Nicaea up to the Vardar valley, and when in 1258 Vatatzes' son Theodore II Lascaris died, leaving a boy as his successor, the Despot decided that the time had come for Epirus to take over the lands and leadership in northern Greece which Vatatzes had won for Nicaea. Michael allied himself with King Manfred of Sicily by bestowing upon him another daughter, Helena, and awaited, with confidence in his own strength and that of his new sons-in-law, the armed response which his territorial ambitions were certain to evoke from Michael VIII Palaeologus, who had just been crowned Emperor at Nicaea. William of Villehardouin led an army of Frankish knights and Moreote natives into northern Greece, and Manfred of Sicily sent a German cavalry force of 400 heavily armed knights. The Nicaean general John Palaeologus, brother of Michael VIII, commanded a polyglot army of Greeks, Germans and Hungarians, Serbs and Bulgars, Turks, Cumans and others. Just before the battle John Ducas, lord of Neopatras (the modern Hypate), bastard son of the Despot Michael, deserted the allied army, in animus against the arrogant Franks, whereupon the Despot himself fled, and the Frankish army which had gathered on his behalf met the enemy alone in the plains of Pelagonia, in western Macedonia, in the summer of 1259. The Franks suffered an overwhelming defeat; Villehardouin was captured, and so were many others, among them Geoffrey of Karytaina. Michael Palaeologus was to spend the winter at Lampsacus, and the Latin prisoners were now sent thither to wait upon his pleasure. Pelagonia marks the turning-point, the dramatic *peripeteia*, not only in the career of William of Villehardouin, but also in the history of the Frankish principality of Achaea.

For more than two years Prince William remained a prisoner, refusing to pay the price of his freedom, the surrender of the Morea in return for a money indemnity. The principality of Achaea was a feudal state; its usages were enshrined in the *Assizes of Romania* (to be written down something over half a century later); and the rights of the baronial families of the conquest were still fresh in mind. The fall of Constantinople in July 1261, however, moderated William's intransigence and also inclined the triumphant Emperor Michael to compromise. William was now released by guaranteeing the surrender of the three great Moreote fortresses of Mistra, Old Maina, and Monemvasia.[1] William had built Mistra and Maina himself; he had taken Monemvasia, after a three years' siege, in 1248; thus the rights

---

[1] Pachymeres, I, p. 88 (*CSHB*) adds the fortress of Geraki; see above: ch. VIII, p. 332, n. 2.

of the Latin barons of Achaea and the usages and customs of the principality were not violated when William surrendered these products of his own enterprise. He also became, according to a Greek source, the Emperor's vassal for the principality of Achaea, as previously he had held his great fief of the Latin Emperor, but soon after William's release Pope Urban IV freed him from any such obligations on the grounds that they had been incurred under duress. The cession of the Moreote castles had to be confirmed, before William's release, by a 'parliament of dames', representing their imprisoned husbands, which the Princess Anna (of Epirus), William's Greek wife, had summoned to Nikli, because the *Assizes of Romania* provided, 'if the prince has a castle on an enemy frontier, he cannot pledge it to the enemy or destroy it without the counsel and consent of his liegemen' (art. 19). The lonesomeness of the women prevailed over the dictates of military prudence, and the prince's concessions to the Greek Emperor were ratified, despite the objections of Guy I of Athens. William of Villehardouin returned to his principality late in the year 1261.

After the fatigue and expense of another war with Villehardouin in 1263–4, Michael VIII became embroiled with his former allies, the Genoese; he therefore made peace with the Venetians by restoring to them the rights and privileges they had lost with the fall of the Latin Empire of Constantinople. Michael also had recourse to the customary device of offering to discuss Church union, which led Pope Urban IV, now seeking to destroy the Hohenstaufen King Manfred of Sicily and southern Italy, to cease his endeavours against the restored Byzantine Empire. The Pope helped to establish an uneasy peace between the Emperor and the Prince of Achaea. But on 26 February 1266 the Hohenstaufen were crushed, and Manfred killed, at Benevento; Charles of Anjou, the brother of St Louis, became King of Sicily, and inherited with his throne the Norman-Hohenstaufen designs upon the capital city on the Bosphorus. Villehardouin welcomed the advent of a powerful French monarchy in southern Italy, a few days from his own domains, and he naturally sought its protection. At Viterbo, on 24 May 1267, with the agreement of the titular Latin Emperor Baldwin II, William of Villehardouin surrendered the principality to Charles of Anjou; William, however, was to retain it for his lifetime, and his daughter Isabella was to marry Charles's son Philip. Failing the birth of a son to Isabella and her Angevin husband (and they were to have no son), the Villehardouin principality was to pass to the Neapolitan house of Anjou; if William should have a son, the latter was to receive, as a fief under Angevin suzerainty, only one-fifth of his father's lands. Charles of Anjou, in return, was to help

William to recover his lost possessions in the Morea and to hold final dominion over the entire principality, under the conditions stipulated. The alternative for William, it was felt, was the ultimate loss of the Morea to the Palaeologi. The principality of Achaea had passed, for the duration of its existence, within the orbit of Neapolitan politics, warfare and intrigue, and most of those who served the Angevins in Greece were ill rewarded for their efforts.

For the restored Palaeologian Empire, the acquisition of Mistra, Maina and Monemvasia was pregnant with far-reaching consequences. From this triangle of Greek fortresses the influence of the Palaeologi extended throughout the south-eastern Morea. In 1348 the Greek despotate of Mistra was established to rule over these lands; the first Despot was Manuel Cantacuzenus (d. 1380), son of the Emperor John VI; and under the Cantacuzeni and the Palaeologi who succeeded them Mistra became, after Constantinople, the chief centre of Greek political strength and culture. Despite the growing power of the Byzantine government, however, which took over the Latin baronies of Passavá, Geraki and Kalavryta, William of Villehardouin maintained his principality almost to the extent that he had inherited it from his elder brother. It was a large realm.

Prince William's son-in-law and heir, Philip of Anjou, died between January and March 1277; it was a blow to William, who had expected his daughter Isabella to share the Moreote succession with her husband, but the latter's death had effected her disherison, though a generous chance was again to bring her the princely title of Achaea. When William himself died, on 1 May 1278, the principality of Achaea became the direct possession of the Angevins. Charles of Anjou now added to his many other titles (King of Jerusalem and Sicily, Duke of Apulia, Prince of Capua, and so on) that of Prince of Achaea, retaining the authority it signified until his death in January 1285. As far as we know, he never went into the Morea. He ruled the principality by a bailie and vicar-general, the first incumbent of which office, Galeran d'Ivry, Grand Seneschal of the kingdom of Sicily, provoked by his lordly airs and arbitrary decisions the keen resentment of the independent barons of the Morea, who appealed to Charles, and the latter was obliged to caution his bailie and confirm the barons' rights and the customs of the principality in April 1280. The good old days of a prince always resident in the Morea, peer of his vassals, were gone; the ruler was now an absentee lord; his military forces were chiefly mercenaries, who sometimes pillaged the country; and the Morea became the victim of the bureaucratic whims of officials in the highly centralised kingdom of Naples, which paid it sometimes too much attention, sometimes too little. The principality possessed henceforth the weakness of a feudal state; it was almost a political anachronism by the close of the thirteenth century, and had none of the strength of the centralised monarchy upon which it depended. The rights of William's daughter Isabella, signed away by her father in the treaty of Viterbo (1267), were to be restored for a time by Charles II of Naples (1289), perhaps at the intervention of Philip the Fair on Isabella's behalf. In any event Isabella was to reign as Princess of Achaea with her two later husbands—Florent of Hainault (1289–97), a great-grandson of the Latin Emperor Baldwin I, and Philip of Savoy (1301–7), a nephew of Count Amadeo V—but the glorious past of the Villehardouin did not return to the Morea.

Following the Sicilian Vespers (1282), the principality was generally neglected by its Angevin suzerains. For twenty years, until the peace of Caltabellotta in 1302, the Angevin kingdom required all its strength for the struggle with the house of Barcelona, which had seized and held the island kingdom of Sicily (*Trinacria*). Many Moreote knights fought in the Angevin armies against the Catalans, Aragonese, Sicilians and Italian Ghibellines, who opposed the re-establishment of French rule in the island. Fortunately for the principality, however, Michael VIII Palaeologus had died (in December 1282), and the Latins in Greece and the Aegean profited from the weakness of his successor Andronicus II.

The rule of Florent of Hainault in the Morea was wise, his administration for the most part just and humane. Florent established peace with the Byzantine governor (κεφαλή) of Mistra, and refused to allow minor incidents to lead to war; security of life and property brought back some economic well-being to the Morea. His death at Andravida in 1297 was much regretted by Latins and Greeks alike. Thereafter, at the insistence of Pope Boniface VIII, King Charles II unwillingly accepted Isabella's marriage to young Philip of Savoy, and invested her new husband with the principality of Achaea in February 1301. With more ambition than integrity, more cupidity than capacity, Philip of Savoy failed to establish a satisfactory regime during the three years he spent in the Morea (1301–4); he was thus the more vulnerable to the slings of Angevin policy; for Philip of Savoy, who was Count of Piedmont, was also at odds in northern Italy with Charles II, who possessed the nearby counties of Provence and Forcalquier. Disagreement arose between them, and in June 1306 Charles II declared that Philip of Savoy had forfeited the principality of Achaea. In May 1307 Philip relinquished his unenforceable claims to the principality in return for certain concessions in Italy, and Charles II's son Philip of Taranto was now recognised as the Prince of Achaea (1307–13). Isabella finished her life in exile, mostly in Hainault, in the lands of her second husband. Her unhappy daughter Matilda, who had four husbands, did become in after years the Princess of Achaea (1313–18), but finally died in 1331, in prison at Aversa, a victim of Angevin greed.

The dynastic history of the titular and actual rulers of the Achaean principality was of considerable political importance, but we cannot trace here the half-dozen marriage alliances which produced claims and counter-claims to the principality, some of which were only to be extinguished in blood. In any event Angevin intrigue was not enough to defend the Morea against the growing power of the Greeks of Mistra, who occupied, between 1318 and 1320, the important Arcadian castles of Matagrifon, near the modern Dimitzana, and of Karytaina, which looks down into the valley of the Alpheus. The Greeks took other castles too, and of the dozen baronies organised after the conquest only three now remained intact, the archiepiscopal barony of Patras, Chalandritza, and Vostitza. Most of the great families of the conquest had become extinct. The French declined in numbers and influence, and Italians came to predominate. Feudalism declined. The barons became great landholders, who commuted their military service to the prince in money. From this period of political disintegration in the Morea, and very likely in consequence of it, have come both the *Assizes of Romania*, called the 'Book of the Usages and Statutes of the Empire of Romania', and the original version, no longer extant, of the *Chronicle of the Morea*, called the 'Book of the Conquest'.[1] The *Assizes* seem to have been codified and written down about 1322, perhaps for the instruction of the Angevin court of Naples, whose high-handed sons and officials were in grave need of instruction in the feudal rights and usages which had obtained in the Morea since the first years of the conquest. The original version of the *Chronicle* dates from about the same time as the *Assizes*, the prologue of which refers to it as 'lo libro della conquista'. The *Chronicle* sought to supply the Angevins with the historical, as the *Assizes of Romania* sought to supply the legal, traditions of the once brilliant principality of the Morea.

The death of Charles II did not dispel the uncertainty in Naples as to what disposition to make of the Latin Morea. Robert the Wise, however, secured the principality for his younger brother John of

---

[1] The *Chronicle* survives in four versions in as many languages; but disagreement still obtains as to the language in which the original was written. The French version ends with events in the year 1304; the Greek, in jog-trot verse, in 1292; these two versions are older and fuller than the others. The Aragonese version comes all the way down to 1377, and was prepared for Juan Fernández de Heredia, grand master of the Hospitallers, in 1393. The approximately fifty-page Italian version is clearly a prose résumé of the Greek *Chronicle*.

Gravina (1322–33), who made an expedition against Mistra in 1325–6, the last considerable Latin offensive against the Moreote Greeks. He achieved nothing more than great expenditure, some of which was met by the Florentine banking house of the Acciajuoli, who were soon repaid for their loans by grants of Lechena and La Mandria in the north-western Morea. In 1332–3 John of Gravina's claims to the Moreote principality were surrendered for various lucrative considerations to his nephew Robert of Taranto (1333–64), son of Philip (I) of Taranto and the titular Latin Empress Catherine of Valois, the great granddaughter of Baldwin II. The Morea was the cause of much anxiety in Naples. The independent Archbishops of Patras claimed to hold their great ecclesiastical barony directly from the Pope. The Latin baronage hardly concealed its distrust of Angevin emissaries. The Byzantines of Mistra had become perilously strong. The Catalans, who had occupied the duchy of Athens, were always adventurous, and Turkish corsairs terrorised the Aegean islands and did not spare the Moreote coasts.

The Latin Empress Catherine of Valois now went into the Morea herself, with her family, accompanied by the famous Niccolò Acciajuoli, who had received many fiefs by this time in the north and west of the peninsula (1331–8). Catherine remained for more than two years in the Morea (November 1338–June 1341). Her genuine interest in the land, together with Niccolò's energy and astuteness, accomplished something. More was done by Acciajuoli money, but not enough, and certain Moreote feudatories appealed, in 1341, to John (VI) Cantacuzenus, then the Grand Domestic: they were willing to accept the suzerainty of Byzantium for security in their possessions. A large group of barons next appealed to James II of Majorca, who also had a claim to the principality through his grandmother, Margaret, second daughter of William of Villehardouin. Nothing came of these overtures, for the principals were otherwise engaged. In France the Hundred Years War had come; the Hungarians invaded the kingdom of Naples; and the Frankish Morea was left to shift for itself.

In April 1358 Robert of Taranto, who had become the Latin Emperor upon his mother Catherine's death (in 1346), granted Niccolò Acciajuoli, now Grand Seneschal of the kingdom of Naples, the great castellany of Corinth with its eight dependent castles, for he alone could furnish protection against Turkish depredation and Byzantine ambition. Niccolò was a tower of Latin strength in the Morea. He died in 1365, a year after Robert of Taranto, whose widow, Maria of Bourbon, now claimed to be Princess of Achaea (1364–70), which caused much dissension and war yet again in the principality, since Philip (II) of Taranto, younger brother of Robert, also asserted his right to the succession (1364–73). Niccolò Acciajuoli, however, had left his family singularly well established in the Morea. A list of the Moreote feudatories and their tenures, from this period, identifies a total of some fifty-one castles (*castelli*) and two other districts less strongly defended: of these, fifteen are attributed to Maria of Bourbon as Princess of Achaea, and about twenty to Niccolò and other members of his family. When Niccolò's son Angelo succeeded to his lands and titles (1365), he made his cousin Nerio Acciajuoli, to whom he owed money, vicar of the lands and castles in the great Corinthian barony, and for almost thirty years Nerio figures prominently in the history of the Morea and that of continental Greece.

Late in the year 1373 Philip (II) of Taranto was succeeded in his claims to the Latin Empire and the principality of the Morea by his nephew, Jacques des Baux, whose suzerain, Joanna I of Naples, promptly contested his rights and claimed the Morea for herself. After a disturbed administration of almost three years in the Morea, Joanna I leased the principality, apparently in early August 1376, for five years, at 4000 ducats a year, to the Hospitallers. About a year later Juan Fernández de Heredia, friend and adviser of kings and popes, one of the most interesting and cultured *grands seigneurs* of his age, was elected Grand Master of the Hospitallers, who seem to have held the principality for the full length of their lease, involving Heredia very deeply in the troubled affairs of Greece. Although undoubtedly self-seeking, Heredia had much ability. Soon the 'Navarrese Company' (or rather Companies) arrived in the Morea, however, and after serving the Hospital of St John for a while looked for lands for themselves, finally recognising Jacques des Baux as their prince and suzerain (1381–3).[1] The Navarrese Company will be considered below in connection with the Catalan history of Athens. Suffice it to say at this point that a state of constant hostility obtained between the Navarrese Company and the Greek Despot Theodore I Palaeologus of Mistra (1383–1407). The Turks used the opportunity to pillage, and the Morea suffered much.

When Jacques des Baux died in July 1383, four or five pretenders laid claim to the title Prince of Achaea. One of them, Amadeo of Savoy, planned an ambitious expedition to take over his alleged inheritance (1390–1), but nothing came of these plans. At length, the then commander of the Navarrese Company in the Morea, Pedro Bordo de San Superano, declared himself twentieth Prince of Achaea (1396–

---

[1] Cf. in general R.-J. Loenertz, 'Hospitaliers et Navarrais en Grèce', *OCP*, xxii (1956), 319–60.

1402); he was fraudulently succeeded by his wife's nephew, Centurione II Zaccaria (1404–32), who finally lost the now much-diminished principality in 1430 to the Greek Despots of the Morea. Thirty years later, in 1460, the Despots Thomas and Demetrius Palaeologus, brothers of the last Byzantine Emperor, lost the peninsula to the Turks under the redoubtable Muḥammad II 'the Conqueror', to whom Constantinople had fallen seven years before.

In the autumn of 1204 Otho de la Roche had been invested with the lordship of Athens, and therewith began more than a century of Burgundian rule in Boeotia and Attica. In late May 1209, after the Emperor Henry's suppression of the Lombard rebellion, Otho entertained the Emperor for two days in Athens, and accompanied him when the imperial entourage moved on to Euboea. Otho assisted Prince Geoffrey I in the prolonged siege of Acrocorinth, which finally fell early in 1210; Nauplia was taken later; and early in 1212 Argos also; Geoffrey I then granted both Argos and Nauplia to Otho as fiefs. After 1210–11 Otho shared Thebes with his nephew Guy de la Roche. Some time after the grant of one half of Thebes to Guy, the latter's sister Bonne received the other half which she brought, by marriage in the 1230's, into the powerful Flemish family of the St Omer, who built a few decades later a great castle on the Cadmea, of which there still remains the square 'Santameri Tower'.

Although a faithful and not ungenerous son of the Church, Otho was anxious to exploit to the full the fine opportunities for enrichment which the conquest had given him. Like Geoffrey I of Achaea, Otho was under the ban of excommunication and his lands placed under the interdict for lengthy periods. He refused to relinquish his asserted right to collect the old Byzantine land-tax (akrostichon), although after the second parliament of Ravennika had recognised this right, he could remit part of the tax to the grateful chapter of Thebes (1211). Otho's name is so constantly associated with that of Geoffrey I in papal documents that we are inclined to describe their relations with the Roman Curia pari passu, but it is possible that there may have been in actual fact less similarity between the ecclesiastical history of Achaea and that of Athens than appears from the documents.

The Latin successor to the famous Athenian Metropolitan Michael Choniates was a Frenchman named Bérard, who was confirmed by Pope Innocent III on 27 November 1206. The Pope took the Athenian church under his protection, and granted it the customs of Notre Dame of Paris; on 13 February 1209 he also sent Bérard a long statement and renewed confirmation of his rights, immunities and properties, apparently based upon the metropolitical jurisdiction of Bérard's Greek predecessors. Bérard exercised authority over eleven suffragan bishoprics, which were said to have been, despite some changes, the pastoral responsibility of the Archbishop of Athens 'since ancient times': (1) Euboea (Negroponte), (2) Thermopylae, (3) Daulia, (4) Aulon, (5) apparently Oreos (*Zorconensis*), (6) Carystus, (7) Coronea, (8) Andros, (9) Megara, (10) Skyros, and (11) Ceos. Some twenty monasteries and twenty-five towns and villages are mentioned in the papal declaration; a few of the monasteries, like Kaisariane and St John the Hunter, were famous in their day. A few years after the conquest Otho de la Roche gave the beautiful monastery of Daphni, not far from Athens, to the Cistercian monks of the Burgundian abbey of Bellevaux, an establishment dear to Otho and his family.

For some twenty years Attica and Boeotia owned the sway of Otho de la Roche, who was apparently not unpopular among his Greek subjects, but in 1225 he returned with his wife and two sons to his home in Burgundy. He left his lands in Greece and the castles on the Acropolis and the Cadmea to his nephew Guy, who was to rule for almost forty years (1225–63). The prosperity of the lordship of Athens and Thebes increased under Guy de la Roche; both Thebes and Athens, especially the former, were centres of the silk industry, with a Genoese community and many Venetians in each city.

Guy became involved, as we have seen, in the 'war of the Euboeote succession' (1256–8), and was the leader of those knights and barons whom Prince William of Achaea defeated at the pass of Mt Karydi. The High Court of Achaea, sitting at Nikli in Laconia, refused to pass judgement on Guy for his part in the war, for the assembled bishops and barons decided that they were not Guy's peers: he held only Argos and Nauplia of their common lord, Prince William, but the Athenian lordship was an hereditary possession, held by right of conquest, wherein Guy de la Roche was sovereign. The High Court therefore referred the case to St Louis of France. In 1260 Guy appeared before the king in Paris, where a parliament decided that, since he had never done homage to Prince William, he should not even forfeit the fiefs he held of the prince. William was declared to have received sufficient satisfaction in having sent him to France, 'a land so far from Romania'. According to the *Chronicle of the Morea* it was at this time that Guy received from St Louis, as a boon, the title Duke of Athens—a title borne by Theseus in the works of Dante and Boccaccio, Chaucer and Shakespeare. Contemporaries had already, unofficially, sometimes given both Otho and Guy the title of Duke during the years since the conquest. There is no evidence, however, that either Guy or his son and successor John (1263–80) ever used the title: in fact, John's younger brother and successor, William (1280–7), seems first to have styled himself Duke, and those who succeeded him also used the title, which appears on coins as *Dux Atenes* and *Dux Actenar'*.

When the long rule of Guy de la Roche had come to an end, his son John followed him. Like his father, John was a ruler of wisdom and ability, although he was sometimes almost incapacitated by gout. In 1276 he was captured by the Latin adventurer Licario, who commanded the fleet of the Emperor Michael VIII Palaeologus in an attack upon Euboea. Michael found the lord John of Athens to be a worthy person; he offered him his daughter in marriage, but John refused the princess' hand owing to his very bad health; and so he was freed upon payment of a ransom of 30,000 *solidi*. He was succeeded in 1280 by his brother William de la Roche, already lord of Livadia, who had married a daughter of John Ducas of Neopatras. John Ducas had bestowed upon William, as a dowry, the important towns of Gravia and Siderocastron, Gardiki and Zeitounion (Lamia), which were now incorporated into the duchy of Athens, of which Thebes remained the capital. William's lands and power thus extended north into Thessaly; the marquisate of Boudonitza was almost surrounded by the Athenian ducal domain. In the Morea William also possessed the Larissa of Argos and the harbour fortress of Itsh Kaleh at Nauplia, fiefs held of the Prince of Achaea. In 1285 William was appointed bailie and vicar-general of the Moreote principality, but the once great state of the Villehardouin had already entered upon the long period of its decline under the dominance of the absent Angevins, and the Athenian court, resident mostly at Thebes, became increasingly conspicuous as the school of Latin chivalry in Greece.

When Duke William died in 1287, he left as heir his little son, Guy II de la Roche, called 'Guyot', whose mother Helena Comnena Ducaena refused to recognise the suzerainty of Florent of Hainault and the Princess Isabella of Villehardouin of Achaea. Her opposition thereto was strengthened when she married, in 1291, her brother-in-law, Hugh of Brienne, Count of Lecce, whose first wife had been the late Isabella de la Roche, sister of Duke William. Hugh of Brienne became bailie of the duchy during the remainder of Guy II's minority (1291–4); a proud and independent baron, he wished to render the ducal homage directly to King Charles II of Naples. The ill feeling between Frankish Athens and Achaea was ended only with the betrothal, in 1299, of Duke Guy II to the tiny Matilda of Hainault, the five-year-old daughter of Florent and the Princess Isabella. Guy II's life was marked and marred by undue magnificence; charming and courteous, he was the most important local figure in the Greek politics of his day. In May 1304 he participated with dash and vigour in a brilliant parliament which met on the isthmus of Corinth, where the Latin knights of Greece in full panoply jousted for three weeks in long-remembered encounters under the approving eyes of lovely ladies. When Philip (I) of Taranto became Prince of Achaea, in 1307, he appointed Guy II as his bailie in the principality, but Guy, the last of his line, died in his twenty-eighth year, on 5 October 1308. He was buried in the Cistercian abbey of Daphni, on the road from Athens to Eleusis.

The successor of Guy II, and the last French Duke of Athens, was Hugh of Brienne's son Walter I (V), whose claims to the duchy were preferred by the High Court of Achaea to those of a female cousin. On 15 March 1311, however, Walter of Brienne was killed together with, it was claimed, seven hundred knights recruited from all the Latin states in Greece, in the battle of the river Cephissus in Boeotia. Victory went to the Catalan Grand Company, which had first come into the Levant in the employ of the Byzantine government to serve against the newly risen power of the Ottoman Turks in Asia Minor (1303). The Palaeologi, however, had murdered the Catalans' too ambitious leader Roger de Flor (1305), and for two years the Company had remained encamped at Gallipoli in a state of war with the Byzantine Empire (until June 1307). Then, rather suddenly, the Company had moved westward, pillaging Thrace and Macedonia for some months, stopping on Mt Athos and before Thessalonica, and finally descending into the plains of Thessaly in the spring of 1309. The next year they had entered the service of Duke Walter, who soon sought to be rid of them when they had served his purpose. But they refused to go, and there was no recourse but to arms. Walter lost the battle of the Cephissus and the Company promptly occupied and sacked Thebes, and then Athens, from which Walter's wife, daughter of a constable of France, fled for safety with their small son. The Catalan Grand Company settled down in the Athenian duchy where its members and their descendants remained for more than three-quarters of a century.

The Company was now composed of some seven thousand Catalans and Aragonese. The Greek natives of Livadia had almost welcomed the Catalans, who obviously looked no worse to them than the French. The heirs of Walter of Brienne, whose son was also named Walter, continued to hold Argos and Nauplia in the Morea, whither the Catalans did not succeed in extending their possessions. After failing to find adequate leadership in Greece, the Catalan Company turned, with reluctance according to Marino Sanudo, to King

Frederick II of Sicily (1296–1337), for whom they had fought against the Angevins before their great Levantine adventure. Frederick appointed at their behest his second son, the five-year-old Don Manfred, as their duke. The Company's victory on the Cephissus had earned them a multiplicity of enemies—in Constantinople and Mistra, Epirus and Thessaly, the principality of Achaea, Venice, Naples, Paris and Avignon, where papal authority was exercised in behalf of French rights and Latin legitimacy everywhere. Quite understandably, therefore, the Catalans now turned to Sicily for the support which King Frederick II was very willing to give, since the Athenian duchy would add substantially to his dominions.

The document is still extant which sets forth the terms whereby the 'Corporation of the Army of Franks in Romania' (*Universitas exercitus Francorum in Romanie partibus existentis*), as the Company officially called itself, recognised the Infante Don Manfred as their 'true, legitimate, and natural lord': the young Manfred and, on his behalf, Frederick II of Sicily were to exercise all right, dominion, power and jurisdiction over the members of the Company and their possessions; the Company swore perpetual allegiance to their new ruler, 'in accordance with the laws of Aragon and the customs of Barcelona', and the authority thus granted was accepted by the Crown in accordance with these laws and customs.[1] Frederick II sent Don Berenguer Estañol of Ampurias as the new duke's vicar-general; he ruled well from 1312 to 1316. Under him the Catalans maintained themselves against the hostility of the Greek rulers in Thessaly and Epirus, the Venetians in Negroponte, and the Briennist retainers in Argos and Nauplia. After Estañol's death, Frederick II sent his natural son, Don Alfonso Fadrique of Aragon, into Greece as vicar-general. On 9 November 1317 the young Duke Manfred died in Trapani, and his younger brother succeeded him as Duke William of Athens. In 1319 the Vicar-General Alfonso Fadrique added, by conquest, the duchy of Neopatras to that of Athens; he held the high command in Greece for some fourteen years (1317–30), and during this period the prowess of the Catalan Company was most feared, and their reputation, however sinister, most respected.

At the beginning of his residence in Thebes Alfonso Fadrique married Marulla (Maria), daughter of Boniface of Verona, triarch of Euboea. When Boniface died in the summer of 1317, Alfonso seized what he could of his wife's inheritance, most notably the important castles of Carystus and Larmena, where the Venetian colony was

[1] A. Rubió i Lluch, *Diplomatari de l'Orient català (1301–1409)* (Barcelona, 1947 [1948]), no. LIII, pp. 67–9. For the history of Catalan enterprise in Greece, see in general K. M. Setton, *Catalan Domination of Athens (1311–1388)*.

much distressed to acquire such a dangerous neighbour. (The Venetians were not able, however, to secure Carystus from the Fadrique family until 1365–6.) Besides the seizure of Neopatras (1319), Alfonso took the castle town of Siderocastron (near the ancient Heraclea), Loidoriki, Domokos, Liconia and Pharsalus; he occupied the castle of Zeitounion and the town of Gardiki in Thessaly, to both of which his wife possessed a claim from her father. Alfonso also became Count of Salona (Amphissa), which may have escheated to the Company upon the death of its rulers. We do not know why Alfonso was removed from the office of vicar-general about 1330 although in November of this year he was made Count of Malta and Gozo in the mid-Mediterranean, fiefs held of his father, the Sicilian king. Marulla bore Alfonso at least five sons who were destined to play leading roles in the history of the Attica and Boeotia of their generation.

The organisation of the Catalan duchy of Athens well illustrates certain aspects of the medieval theory of contract between the ruler and his people. The Company had won their new lands by force of arms and now held them by right of conquest. From the time of their early establishment in Greece the Company possessed written Articles or Statutes (*Capitula*), an actual constitution, written in Catalan, and largely based upon the *Constitutions of Catalonia* and the *Customs of Barcelona*. The text of the Statutes of the Company has not come down to us, unfortunately, although here and there a fragment appears in the documents. The Company had its own chancellor, who affixed to important documents the Company's seal, which showed St George slaying the dragon, and bore the legend 'Felix Francorum exercitus in Romanie finibus comorans'. St George was patron of Catalonia as well as of England. An excellent example of this seal is still extant. The vicar-general, *vicarius generalis*, the chief executive officer in the Catalan states in Greece, was appointed by the royal duke, to whom he swore fealty; upon arriving in Athens or Thebes, he took another oath before representatives of the Company to fulfil the duties of his office in conformity with the Statutes of the Company. The duke also acquired the right of appointment to the most important military position in his new dominions overseas, that of marshal of the duchies (*marescalcus exercitus ducatuum*), but the Catalans in Greece looked with disapproval upon the appointment of any but their own leaders to the chief offices of state. The capital of the Athenian duchy was Thebes, 'civitas nostra Thebana', as King Frederick III of Sicily, who was also Duke of Athens (1355–77), once called the city, 'quae in ipsis ducatibus quasi caput est et magistra'.[1] The Catalans in Athens were organised into a municipal

[1] Rubió, *Diplomatari*, no. CCLIII, p. 336, dated 16 August 1363.

corporation ('la universitat de Cetines'), with their own civil and military officials ('capità e veguer, castelià') and with their own syndics, chief citizens, and municipal council ('sindichs, prohomens e consell dela dita universitat'). The city of Neopatras, the modern Hypate, was the capital of the northern duchy to which it gave its name; within the borders of the duchy of Neopatras was located the important castle and town of Zeitounion (in Catalan 'la Citó'), the ancient Lamia. Over the city of Neopatras a captain (*capità*) presided, and a castellan (*castellà*) commanded the garrison in the hilltop fortress. Neopatras had been won less by the united effort of the Company than by the enterprise of the duke's vicar-general Alfonso Fadrique, and so ultimate authority over the northern duchy could be retained in the hands of the duke in Sicily and, after 1378–9, in Catalonia and Aragon.

Thebes and Athens, Livadia, Siderocastron and Neopatras were located on the ducal domain. They were organised as town corporations or municipalities, with notaries, clerks, judges and bailiffs. We do not know the extent to which similar municipal corporations existed in the lands of the great feudatories. The municipalities were presided over by their local syndics and councillors, headed by their own veguers and captains (*vigerii et capitanei*), and protected from external enemies by their own local military commandants (*castellani*). There was no castellan in Thebes where the vicar-general resided. The documents reveal Greeks as serving on the municipal councils in Athens, Livadia and Neopatras. At the time of the conquest in 1311, the *Assizes and Customs of Romania*, presumably the feudal code of the Burgundian duchy of Athens, had given way to the famous *Customs of Barcelona*, which now became the bases of public and even private law in the Athenian duchy as in Catalonia. The ducal revenues were administered by the vicar-general, and included certain crown rents and fees, taxes levied in the cities and country districts, various tolls and commercial imposts, and the incidents and profits from the domain. There was a land-tax (*ius terragii*), which was paid annually to the royal fisc. Ground rents were collected in wax each year in Thebes (*census cere civitatis Thebarum*), to which the Armenian commercial colony in the city contributed heavily. The sale of wax seems to have been a crown monopoly. The Crown also collected house rents and taxes, and confiscated the property of Greeks who, having accepted Roman Catholicism, had reverted to the faith of their fathers. Nevertheless, the Greek dominions of the Catalan-Sicilian crown were doubtless more a source of prestige than of profit.

Before the close of the first decade of their rule in Greece the

Catalans were much heartened by the diminution in the numbers of their active enemies. In 1318 the Ducae became extinct both in Thessaly and in Epirus; Neopatras fell to Alfonso Fadrique (in 1319), and the Despotate of Epirus was appropriated by the Orsini family of Cephalonia. After 1318–21 the Emperor Andronicus II was involved in intermittent civil war with his grandson and eventual successor Andronicus (III); and in addition the Ottoman Turks and the Serbs were becoming ever more formidable. The Byzantine government, despite its increasing strength in the Morea, was therefore obliged to curtail its acts of hostility against the Catalans. Most important of all, however, the Catalans now succeeded in establishing peace with the Venetians of Euboea. A pact was signed between the Catalan Company and the Venetian captain and bailie in 1319; this pact was renewed in 1321 and in 1331, and on several occasions in the years that followed. By its terms the Catalans agreed not to maintain armed vessels in the Saronic Gulf or in the waters off Euboea, but Catalan merchantmen might, if unarmed, enter and leave the (Theban) port of Livadostro, in the north-east corner of the Corinthian Gulf. Although the Catalans did not adhere to these hard terms without occasional infractions, they were sufficiently observant of their undertakings to prevent Athens from becoming, to any considerable extent, a depot in transit in the Catalan trade with the Byzantine Empire, Asia Minor, Syria and Egypt.

At the time of the Catalan conquest in Greece the Papacy was beginning its long residence in Avignon (which belonged to the Angevins of Naples until its purchase by Clement VI in 1348) where the Popes were excessively subject to the influence of the French kings. The dispossessed Brienne were a French family of ancient ancestry, loyal Guelfs, vassals of the Angevins of Naples and Achaea, and beloved sons of his Holiness in Avignon. As long as young Walter II (VI) of Brienne sought to vindicate his claim to the duchy which his father had lost with his life in the swamps of the Cephissus, the Popes tried to aid him. Complaints were constantly lodged at the Curia; the Latin clergy in Greece told sad stories of Catalan depredation. The Popes wrote many letters denouncing the Catalan Company. The Angevins and Brienne appealed for help to Venice. After the Republic and the Company came to terms in 1319, however, there was little likelihood of the Venetians assisting the Brienne to regain the duchy of Athens. In the dozen years that followed, moreover, the Catalans enjoyed their greatest security, until the attempt by Walter II of Brienne in 1331 to drive them from the Athenian duchy.

For twenty years young Walter of Brienne had dreamed of regaining his lost duchy of Athens. His family had never ceased to importune the Pope, the kings of Naples and France, and the doge. When Walter was at last ready to make trial of arms with the Catalans, Pope John XXII directed that a crusade be preached against those 'schismatics, sons of perdition, and pupils of iniquity, devoid of all reason and detestable'.[1] In July 1330 King Robert of Naples granted permission to his feudatories to join Walter of Brienne's coming expedition, and even remitted certain feudal service due the Neapolitan crown to those who would do so. In late August 1331 Walter assembled at Brindisi a large force which included some 800 French knights and 500 Tuscan foot; he occupied the island of Santa Maura (Leucas), the mainland stronghold of Vonitza, and the Epirote capital of Arta, forcing Count John II Orsini of Cephalonia to acknowledge the suzerainty of King Robert. He pushed across the peninsula to Boeotia and Attica. The vicar-general of the Catalan Company was now Nicholas Lancia (1330–5). The Catalans destroyed most of the great castle of St Omer in Thebes with its famous frescoes of crusading scenes in Syria, for the Cadmea was hard to defend. They refused to meet Walter in the open field; the months passed; Walter ravaged the land in vain; and his funds ran out. The Venetians watched serene and unassisting; in April 1331 they had renewed their pact with the Catalans. The Greeks made no effort to assist Walter, which may indicate that Catalan rule cannot have borne too harshly upon them. The expedition was an expensive failure, and Walter returned to Brindisi in the late summer of 1332. He had secured the island of Leucas and the town of Vonitza; restored, for a time, the Angevin suzerainty over Epirus; and doubtless made more certain his hold upon his fine castles at Argos and Nauplia. The game, however, had not been worth the candle, and he never returned to Greece.[2]

After the failure of Walter of Brienne's expedition the Catalan states in Greece enjoyed some three decades of relative peace. The Papacy continued its ban of excommunication and interdict which were occasionally removed for brief periods when hope was entertained in Avignon of employing the Catalans against the increasing menace of the Turks. Catalan relations with the Venetian colony of Negroponte improved after the removal of Alfonso Fadrique from the vicariate-general about 1330, and became more amicable still, apparently, when Alfonso died in 1338. During the fifth decade of the century the Catalans had need of Venetian support and of whatever friendly neighbours they could find, for in 1348 the great Serbian Tsar Stephen Dušan annexed Thessaly and Epirus to the northern Empire

---

[1] Rubió, *Diplomatari*, no. CL, pp. 189–91 and cf. pp. 193–4, dated 14 June 1330.
[2] In after years Walter of Brienne became the tyrant of Florence (1342–3); he fought at Crécy in 1346; and died as constable of France at Poitiers in 1356.

he was building. The Catalans lost the fortress towns of Pharsalus, Domokos, Gardiki and Liconia, acquired by Alfonso Fadrique thirty years before, and never had a chance to recover them. They held on to Neopatras, however, the capital of their northern duchy. When King Pedro IV of Aragon-Catalonia joined the Venetians in the renewal of their long-continued war with Genoa (1350–5), the Catalans and Aragonese in the Athenian duchy did what little they could to assist the cause of Venice.

In the midsummer of 1355 Frederick III 'il Semplice' became the Duke of Athens and Neopatras, and a few months later also King of Sicily (1355–77). Among his first known acts as Duke of Athens was that confirming the rights of James Fadrique, second son of Alfonso, to the county of Salona and the lordship of Loidoriki. Shortly thereafter he made James vicar-general of the duchies (1356–9). The loss of many registers from the Sicilian archives has left some twenty years (1335–54)[1] of the internal history of the duchies in a darkness but little dispelled by papal, Venetian and other documents; from the sixth decade of the century, however, our knowledge of Catalan affairs in Greece increases considerably, and after the annexation of the duchies to the crown of Aragon (1379), which followed Frederick's death, we know a good deal, owing to the preservation of many documents relating to Greece in the archives of the crown of Aragon in Barcelona.

There were many disturbances in the political and social life of the duchies of Athens and Neopatras during the last decades of their existence. When Matthew of Moncada, Grand Seneschal of the Sicilian kingdom (*Trinacria*), left the Greek duchies, where he had spent something over a year (1360–1) as the vicar-general (1359–61), he left behind him as his successor one Pedro de Pou, a Catalan long resident in Thebes. Pedro de Pou became involved with the former vicar James Fadrique; he expelled James and the Fadrique family from the castles of Salona, Loidoriki and Veteranitza, and not only refused, apparently, a royal order to restore James's castles to him, but also defrauded him of the sum of 5000 *hyperpyra*. The tyranny which the weak Frederick III could not check from distant Sicily was abruptly terminated by strong-willed Catalan feudatories in Greece. Roger de Lluria, who had been the marshal since about 1354, led an uprising in Thebes early in 1362. Pedro de Pou and a number of his

---

[1] When Frederick (III) 'il Semplice', Duke of Athens (from 11 July 1355), succeeded his elder brother Louis as King of Sicily (on 16 October 1355), the so-called ducal chancery of Athens and Neopatras was merged with the royal chancery of Sicily, assisting thus in the preservation of a number of 'sovereign acts' relating to the duchies in the Archivio di Stato di Palermo (cf. R.-J. Loenertz, 'Athènes et Néopatras', *Arch. Praed.* xxv [1955], 110).

followers were killed.[1] The government of the duchies now passed to some extent into the hands of James Fadrique, who appears as vice-regent in 1365, and above all into those of the powerful Marshal Roger de Lluria, who was virtual ruler from 1362 until his death in 1369. In 1362, owing to their seizure of the property of certain Venetians in the Athenian duchy, connected somehow with the fall of Pedro de Pou, the Catalans found themselves at war with Pietro Gradenigo, Venetian bailie of Negroponte. Roger de Lluria made an alliance with some Anatolian Turks, whom he admitted into Thebes (1363–4); the Turks were soon repulsed, however, and Lluria made peace with the Venetians in 1365. Indeed from 1362 until 1365 the Greek duchies were more or less isolated from the royal court in Sicily, and contemporary documents reflect the confusion of the period; it is only too clear, however, that Frederick III secured final recognition of his authority, in May 1367, by accepting accomplished facts which it was quite beyond his capacity to alter.

During the last decade or so of his reign Frederick III tried to increase his power in Greece by appointing Sicilians to important positions in the duchies. From 1370 to 1374 the King's vicar-general was Don Matteo de Peralta, of the noble Catalan-Sicilian family of the Counts of Caltabellotta, whose young relative Galcerán de Peralta was made, for about three years, castellan of the Acropolis (1371) and veguer and captain of the city of Athens (1372). These Sicilian appointments caused much vexation to the Catalan colony in Thebes. There appear to have been Catalan and Sicilian parties in Greece not unlike those which harassed Frederick in his Sicilian realm. Frederick's overseas dominions were beset by internal 'dissensions and discords', as a contemporary document states, partly caused by his appointments to office, which sometimes ran beyond the statutory limit of three years fixed by the revered *Customs of Barcelona.*

After the death of Roger de Lluria, at the end of 1369, the chief Catalan feudatory in Greece was Don Luis Fadrique, the 'last Count of Salona' (1365–82), who became vicar-general of the duchies of Athens and Neopatras in April 1375 and held office during a critical and unfortunate period in the Catalan history of Greece (1375–81). There were serious problems to face. When the Turks were not allies, they were enemies, and the rule of Frederick III was so ineffective that it is no wonder his Catalan subjects in the imperilled duchies

---

[1] For the events of 1362 see R.-J. Loenertz, 'Athènes et Néopatras', in *Arch. Praed.* xxv (1955), 101, 114–17, 122, 127, cf. 189 ff., and Rubió, *Diplomatari*, esp. nos. CCC–CCCVI, properly dated 28 May 1362 (not 1368); nos. CCLXVII–LXX, properly dated 29 July 1362 (not 1366); no. CCLII, dated 26 August 1362; nos. CCLXXI–II, dated 3 August 1366; and no. CCXC, dated 18 May 1367.

should have asked Queen Eleanora of Aragon, wife of King Pedro IV and sister of Frederick, 'on many and diverse occasions...that she might be willing to receive them as vassals', and in June 1370 Eleanora of Aragon had offered to take over the duchies of Athens and Neopatras in return for certain grants to her brother of Sicily totalling some 100,000 florins. It was only, however, after the death of Frederick on 27 July 1377 that Pedro IV was able to annex the duchies directly to the 'sacrosanct Crown of Aragon' (1378–9), and then not without opposition from the Sicilian faction in Greece. The Catalan duchy of Athens was thus, for the last decade of its history, under Aragonese rule. In the meantime Nerio Acciajuoli, Florentine lord of Corinth, had seized Megara (in 1374), southern outpost of the Athenian duchy. This had much weakened the Isthmian defences of the Catalans, and factional strife had rendered them even more vulnerable to the heavy blow which descended in the spring of 1379 —the invasion of the duchy by the Navarrese Company under its bold captain John de Urtubia.

This Company had fought in the war between France and Navarre which had ended in 1366, and had thereafter been reorganised for service under Louis of Evreux, brother of King Charles II of Navarre. Louis was preparing an expedition to conquer the 'kingdom of Albania', to which he had acquired the title by marriage with the Duchess Joanna of Durazzo, granddaughter and heiress of John of Gravina, who had exchanged the principality of Achaea for, among other grants, Albania and the duchy of Durazzo (1332). In 1368, however, Albania, together with Durazzo, had fallen to the Albanian lord Charles Topia, who took the title of king, and so, if Louis of Evreux would rule over the kingdom he had thought to secure by marriage to the Angevin heiress, he must begin by conquering it.

The Navarrese Company succeeded in occupying Durazzo, apparently in the midsummer of 1376. But Louis died about this time, and when his wife Joanna promptly remarried, the four leaders of the Company regarded their Albanian contract as terminated. These leaders were Pedro de la Saga and Mahiot de Coquerel, both chamberlains of the Navarrese king, and John de Urtubia and a certain Garro or Guarro, called squires in the documents. The Company spent two or three very difficult years in Durazzo (1376–8). Of the four leaders only two were to play a conspicuous role in the medieval history of Greece, John de Urtubia as the conqueror of Thebes and Boeotia and Mahiot de Coquerel as conqueror of Achaea and the Argolid, Elis and Messenia. Free-lance contractors, each held a separate command.

Although we do not know any details of the Navarrese withdrawal from Durazzo (still held by the Duchess Joanna) John de Urtubia, apparently the first Navarrese captain to arrive in the Morea, may have entered the service of Nerio Acciajuoli by April 1378. When Mahiot de Coquerel arrived in the Morea, Urtubia joined him for eight months in the service of the Hospitallers, who more than once contemplated the transfer of their high commandery from Rhodes to the Morea. Coquerel had no interest in continuing to work for St John, and later accepted the commission of Jacques des Baux, Angevin Prince of Achaea and last titular Latin Emperor of Constantinople, in whose name he and his lieutenants held the Moreote principality (1381–3). There is no evidence, however, that the members of the Navarrese Company who served under Coquerel participated in any way in Urtubia's expedition against Thebes or that they ever attacked Athens. The traditional view that the Navarrese Company under Coquerel, allegedly serving Jacques des Baux, was the force which took Thebes is quite wrong. The traditional date of 1380 for the expedition is also wrong.[1]

It was conceivably in May 1379 that John de Urtubia and a so-called 'Navarrese Company' of some three or four hundred men, among whom must have been many Gascons and Italians, set out from the Morea, possibly from the headquarters of the Hospitallers at Sta Maria de Zonklon (Navarino) and Kalamata. They passed through Corinthia and the Megarid, obviously with the permission of Nerio Acciajuoli, who appears to have promoted their assault upon Thebes.

---

[1] G. T. Dennis, 'The Capture of Thebes by the Navarrese', *OCP*, xxvi (1960), 45–7, has published an interesting 'short chronicle' from Cod. Paris, gr. 445, fol. 126ᵛ, which places the Navarrese occupation of Thebes 'at the ninth hour of the night' on Friday, 6 March 1378. Aside from the fact that this date fell on a Saturday, 1378 seems most unlikely as the year in which the Catalans lost Thebes, in view of the data to be culled from documents of the period 1379–81 in Rubió's *Diplomatari*. King Pedro IV of Aragon could not have remained in ignorance of the loss of Thebes for twenty months, and yet it is clear that his first news of the Navarrese occupation came in September 1379 (cf. Setton, *Catalan Domination of Athens*, esp. p. 146; Loenertz, in *Arch. Praed.* xxv [1955], *passim.*, and *OCP*, xxii [1956], *passim*; and note Rubió, *Diplomatari*, nos. ccclxxii–xxx, ccclxxxii–iv, and cf. cccxci–ii, cccxcvi, cccxcviii, cd, cdii, cdvi, cdxvii, cdxxiv–v, cdlvii, cdlix, and cdlxxvi). On 19 October 1379 Pedro IV wrote that he had been informed that Thebes had been *recently* captured by the Navarrese Company, '...nuper...civitas nostra Thebarum per illam cohortem gencium armigerarum Navarrensium capta fuit...' (no. ccclxxxiv, p. 465). The word 'recently' (*nuper*) is curiously retained in a document dated 8 May 1381, to add vividness to an event now two years in the past: 'Informati quod antequam civitas d'Estives [i.e. Thebes] nuper fuisset per Navarros hostes nostros expugnata et capta,...Rogerius de Puntinyano tenebat et possidebat [quedam] bona...' (no. cdlxxvi, p. 537). The Greek 'short chronicles' are often unreliable.

Concerning what follows, it should be noted that if Nerio Acciajuoli acquired Thebes before the beginning of the year 1381, Pedro IV had apparently not been so informed by 31 April [*sic*] (Rubió, *Diplomatari*, nos. cdlviii, cdlxviii). The Navarrese must have taken Livadia late in 1380 or at the beginning of 1381 (nos. cdlxxvii ff.).

The Catalans in the Athenian duchy were not prepared to withstand any such attack in strength, and Thebes fell to Urtubia after a quick investment and violent encounter, aided by traitors within the walls. Many of the inhabitants, both Frankish and Greek, fled to Euboea. Galcerán de Peralta, veguer, captain and castellan of Athens and the Acropolis, appeared with a force under the walls of Thebes and was wounded and captured by Urtubia, who held him to ransom. Athens also had traitors within its walls, but the Acropolis was to remain in Catalan hands for another decade. The great Catalan castle of Livadia, however, was betrayed to the Navarrese in 1380; years later, in 1393, the Gascon soldier Bertranet Mota, 'captain of the duchy of Athens', was said to be in possession of Livadia, which he had at that time only recently captured, but of Bertranet's career we know little.

The Catalans never regained their capital city of Thebes, and although Bertranet Mota may have secured Livadia, he does not appear to have regarded himself as holding the city by warrant of the King of Aragon. Thebes was already a Florentine possession, and Livadia was too, or soon to become so, for both cities were bequeathed by Nerio Acciajuoli to his son Antonio I in 1394. Thebes seems to have been surrendered to Nerio, for whatever cause or consideration, by the Navarrese captain Urtubia, who may have been in his employ, and Livadia must have been taken over from Bertranet, who was also associated with the enterprising Nerio. When Pedro IV of Aragon in 1379 began the last decade of Catalan rule in continental Greece, his sovereignty was recognised only in the capital cities of the two duchies, now Athens itself and Neopatras, together with some of their dependencies, and the county of Salona, where Don Luis Fadrique held sway. After the death of Don Luis in 1382, destruction hovered over the Catalan states of Greece in the person of Nerio Acciajuoli, who held the barony of Corinth.

After the danger from the Navarrese had subsided, a parliament was summoned in Athens, meeting on 20 May 1380, possibly in the Parthenon. This parliament prepared, for submission to Pedro IV of Aragon, the important document which Rubió i Lluch has named the 'Articles of Athens' ('els Capítols d'Atenes'), a general petition, written in Catalan, containing some fourteen specific requests, of which only four are concerned with the welfare of the state and the common necessities of the inhabitants. The other ten are in behalf of individuals, who, having served the cause of Aragon in Greece against John de Urtubia and the Navarrese, now demanded their rewards, although they emphasised 'the desperate conditions that obtain in Athens and the poverty of the people'. On 1 September (1380) Pedro IV granted most of their requests, pleading for unity and

reminding the Catalans in Athens that they were but few in number.[1]
He assured them that his newly appointed vicar-general Philip Dalmau, Viscount of Rocaberti, was being sent to Greece (to replace Luis
Fadrique) with forces strong enough to regain the lost territories of
the Athenian duchy.

During the years of their rule and residence in Athens there had
been Catalans who had come to love the historic city and the glorious
buildings on the Acropolis, then perfectly preserved. Pedro IV's own
appreciative interest is reflected in the order to his treasurer, dated
11 September 1380, providing a guard for the Acropolis, which he
describes as the richest jewel in all the world, the like of which all the
kings of Christendom might seek in vain to match! Although Don
Pedro was doubtless impressed by the apparent impregnability of the
Acropolis, there is more to his description, and Gregorovius and Rubió
i Lluch have both emphasised that this is perhaps the first aesthetic
eulogy of the Acropolis spoken by anyone in western Europe after
about a thousand years of silence and of ignorance.

The Viscount of Rocaberti spent only a year in Greece (1381–2);
he accomplished little, and upon departing left as his lieutenant in
the duchies Ramón de Vilanova, who accomplished little more
(1382–6). Although the Crown of Aragon abated no whit its claims
to Boeotia, such claims were in vain; Thebes was never recovered by
the Catalans, and the last years of their history in Greece are largely
associated with Athens. On 20 April 1387, King John I, who had
just succeeded his father Pedro IV as Duke of Athens, promised to
visit Greece, assuring the officers and syndics of Athens that he had
not forgotten the renowned city. The lower city, however, had been
occupied for some time by Nerio Acciajuoli, who already called himself 'Lord of the Duchy of Athens' (1385). John I sent no aid to the
Catalan garrison on the Acropolis, and, of course, he made no effort
to come himself. Athens was too far away. Rocaberti, who had been
removed and reappointed as vicar-general, remained in Catalonia; his
lieutenant in Athens was Pedro de Pau (1386–8), a noble but little
known soldier, who addressed a desperate appeal to the king for aid.
The Florentine siege was now pressed in deadly earnest, and the
Acropolis fell to Nerio Acciajuoli on 2 May 1388.

Nerio had already secured possession of Thebes, and two years
later, in 1390, the Catalan captain of Neopatras, Andrés Zavall, was
forced to surrender the northern capital to one 'Micer Aner', who
would appear to be Nerio himself, for when the latter acknowledged

[1] The population of Athens in the later fourteenth century has been estimated at
about 9000 persons, of every age and of all conditions, of whom fewer than 3000 were
Catalans and Aragonese.

Amadeo of Savoy as Prince of Achaea and as his suzerain for the fief of Athens (29 December 1391), Nerio called himself 'Lord of Corinth and the Duchy of Athens and Neopatras' (*dominus Corinti, ducatus Athenarum et Neopatrie*). In any event Neopatras was permanently lost to the Catalans, and if Nerio's authority really obtained in the city, it was not for long: Neopatras was soon lost to the Turks, and Salona shortly after, both places being seized by the Sultan Bāyezīd I (1393–4). On 11 January 1394 King Ladislas of Naples, who still preserved the Angevin claim to suzerainty over the principality of Achaea, upon which the Athenian duchy had rested in feudal dependence at the time of the Catalan conquest, recognised Nerio Acciajuoli as Duke of Athens. Nerio had attained to a lofty dignity; he had founded a new dynasty in Greece; but his near neighbour in the Athenian duchy was the Turk, now established in southern Thessaly and in Salona.

Less than nine months, however, after he had thus become Duke of Athens Nerio died, on 25 September 1394, leaving by his last will and testament 'to the Church of Santa Maria di Athene [the Parthenon] the city of Athens with all its appurtenances and effects'. Nerio placed the executors of his will under the supervision of the Venetian Signoria, while his Venetian castellan, Matthew of Montona, remained in control of Athens and the Acropolis. Nerio had made his daughter Francesca, wife of Carlo Tocco, Duke of Leucadia and Count Palatine of Cephalonia, the chief beneficiary of his will; to his elder daughter, the beautiful Bartolomea, Despina of Mistra, wife of Theodore I Palaeologus, Nerio left only 9700 ducats of gold which Theodore had owed the Venetians and which Nerio had been obliged to pay for him. To his son Antonio, whom time and Antonio's own energy were finally to make his heir, Nerio left Thebes and the fortress town of Livadia. Carlo Tocco and Theodore Palaeologus fought over Corinth, which had been left to Carlo's wife. Theodore won. The times were critical, and to secure the city of Athens against the Turks, whose establishment on the Acropolis and in Piraeus would have been a terrible danger to the Venetian colony in Negroponte, the Venetian senate voted to take over the city and citadel of Athens 'according to the form of the testament of the lord Nerio Acciajuoli' (18 March 1395): this was done at the behest of Montona, the Venetian castellan of Athens. In 1397 the lower city seems to have been occupied by the Turks; Montona held the Acropolis, and the danger passed. The Venetians soon found a more successful enemy in the late Nerio's son Antonio, lord of Thebes and Livadia. Antonio seized the lower city of Athens, and laid siege to the Acropolis; he intercepted and defeated a large Venetian field force being sent against Thebes;

and resuming his attack upon the Acropolis, finally effected its occupation about January or February 1403. The siege had lasted seventeen months, and the Venetian garrison had consumed every horse except those in the sculptures on the Parthenon. It took the Venetians more than two years to recognise Antonio's forcible re-establishment of the rule of the Acciajuoli in Athens.

For some thirty-three years Antonio I Acciajuoli ruled as Duke of Athens (1403–35), peacefully, prosperously, and many of his Florentine relatives came to visit him and even live with him. He was succeeded in 1435 by two sons of his cousin Franco (or Francesco), the latter being a son of Nerio I's brother Donato: Nerio II ruled from the Acropolis for a few years (1435–9?), and was expelled by his brother Antonio II, who died after two years (1439?–41); Nerio II then returned to Athens, and prolonged his weak and inconspicuous rule through the remaining decade of his life (1441–51). Nerio II had spent his exile in 1439–40 in Florence. He should have been an object of some interest to the Florentine philhellenists, but they do not mention him.

The last years of the Latin history of Athens are much like a tragic opera. Upon the death of Nerio II, his little son Francesco I bore the title Duke of Athens (1451–4), but his mother, the Duchess Chiara Zorzi (Giorgio), a daughter of the Venetian house of Boudonitza, ruled the Athenian duchy with her lover Bartolomeo Contarini, who murdered his wife in Venice in order to live with Chiara in Athens. Their scandalous rule, however, was terminated by the Sultan Muḥammad II, who set the young Franco Acciajuoli, son of Antonio II, upon the throne which his father had usurped from the second Nerio. Franco ruled in Athens only a year (1455–6), for the Turkish Pasha Omar occupied the Acropolis, at the command of the Sultan, on 4 June 1456, leaving to Franco, however, the city of Thebes and a precarious rule over Boeotia. This was almost the end, and Franco knew it. On 10 February 1460 he wrote to Francesco Sforza, lord of Milan, offering to enter his service for a proper stipend, to spend 10,000 ducats of his own on the establishment of a condotta, and to join his excellency in Milan as soon as the latter might wish. After the loss of the Morea later in the same year, 1460, by the Greek Despots Demetrius and Thomas, brothers of the last Byzantine Emperor, Franco was ordered to participate in a Turkish campaign against Leonardo III Tocco of Cephalonia; a little later, having become an object of suspicion to the Sultan, Franco was murdered by the Turks, and the rule of the Acciajuoli now came to its inglorious end in Greece, Franco being the last of his family to hold sway on the Acropolis (1456) and on the Cadmea (1460).

The history of Latin dominion in the islands of the Aegean begins shortly after the Fourth Crusade, with the capture of Naxos by the enterprising Venetian Marco Sanudo. With a fleet of eight galleys loaned him by the Venetian authorities, Sanudo cast anchor in the harbour of Potamides, in the south-west of the island of Naxos, and advanced upon the inland Greek fortress of Apalire, which fell to him after a five weeks' siege, despite the aid rendered to the Greeks by the Genoese. A little later, while the Latin Emperor Henry was engrossed in his struggle with Theodore Lascaris of Nicaea, and the Venetian government was much occupied with the conquest of Crete, Sanudo, with some adventurous companions, most of whom apparently paid their own expenses, undertook the reduction of the other islands of the Aegean. Sanudo's islands were organised as a duchy, with Naxos as its capital; and here the conqueror ruled as Duke Marco I for twenty years (1207–27). As a result of several similar expeditions a dozen noble Venetians acquired, as fiefs, more than two dozen islands in the Aegean, for which some of them did homage to the Duke of Naxos, or of the Archipelago, as the islands and the duchy were later called (that is, *Egeo pelago*).[1] Now began the long and little-read annals of the Latin Archipelago, filled with the names of the Sanudi and Ghisi, Crispi and Sommaripa, Quirini, Barozzi and Gozzadini.

Besides the capital island of Naxos, Marco Sanudo himself took over about eleven islands, including nearby Paros, Antiparos, Ios (Nio) and Amorgos, as well as Cythnos (Thermia), Siphnos, and Melos. Marco's cousin, Marino Dandolo, was enfeoffed with the important island of Andros. The brothers Andrea and Geremia Ghisi, relatives of the Doge Enrico, acquired Tenos, Mykonos, and the northern Sporades, Skyros, Skopelos and Skiathos, to which they soon added shares in Seriphos and in Ceos (Zia), where the Greek Metropolitan of Athens, Michael Choniates, was then living in exile, within sight of his beloved Attica. Jacopo Barozzi became lord of the volcanic island of Thera, called Santorin (that is, St Irene), and Leonardo Foscolo of adjoining Anaphe (Namfio). Giovanni Quirini took over the neighbouring island of Astypalaea, called by the Latins Stampalia, which was added to the Quirini family name, and is preserved to this day in Venice in the Campiello, Palazzo, and Pinacoteca Quirini-Stampalia (near the Church of Sta Maria Formosa). Marco Venier received Cythera (Cerigo), and Jacopo Viaro

---

[1] The Venetians acquired the Aegean islands by a number of contemporaneous but probably little co-ordinated expeditions, the earliest taking place in the summer of 1206 presumably, on which cf. R.-J. Loenertz, 'Marino Dandolo, seigneur d'Andros', *OCP*, xxv (1959), 165–8. The well-known genealogical tables of the Italian dynasts of the Aegean, which form the last part of C. Hopf's *Chroniques gréco-romanes* (Berlin, 1873), contain numerous errors.

the island of Cerigotto, while entirely on his own initiative Filocalo Navigaioso took possession of Lemnos, of which the Latin Emperor Henry made him grand duke (*megadux*). In the islands as on the mainland Latin feudalism supplied, in good part, the political and social structure under which Greeks of high estate and low now lived as vassals and serfs. The introduction of the feudal system was easy here, as in continental Greece, because the inhabitants were familiar with the Byzantine *pronoia*, which resembled the western fief. Certain feudal rights of Latin origin survived in the island of Naxos and elsewhere until their abrogation in 1720 by the Turks.

After Marco I Sanudo the ducal sceptre of the Archipelago was borne by his heirs for more than a century and a half. They were succeeded, violently, by the Crispi in 1383. Twenty-one dukes of the two dynasties ruled, first as vassals of the Latin Emperors, next of the Villehardouin Princes of Achaea, and thereafter of the Angevins of Naples and Taranto; in 1418 they became vassals of the Serene Republic of Venice, and later tributaries of the Sublime Porte. The last Latin Christian duke, Jacopo IV Crispo, was deposed in 1566 by the Sultan Selim II, who appointed a rich Jew, Joseph Nasi, the last Duke of the Archipelago (1566–79). Even now, however, Latin Christian rule was not entirely extinguished, for the Gozzadini, a family of Bolognese origin, survived, with many vicissitudes of fortune, as lords of Siphnos (Sifanto), Cythnos (Thermia), and five other little islands in the Cyclades until 1617, and the island of Tenos remained Venetian until 1714.

In the years following 1206–7 Marco Sanudo built on a hill, on the west side of the island of Naxos, the castle (*Castro*), where a Roman Catholic colony still lives; below the Castro there quickly appeared a walled town (known as the *Borgo*); and below the Borgo there grew up, along the coast, the modern town of Neochori. A large influx of westerners into the aristocratic colony on the hill caused Sanudo to build a Latin cathedral in the Castro beside his own palace; a full complement of canons was appointed to the new cathedral, and the name of Naxos was added by papal scribes to the *Provinciale Romanum*. The Archbishop of Naxos had under him the four suffragans of Melos, Santorin, Tenos and Syra. Throughout the thirteenth century and much of the fourteenth the duchy of the Archipelago and the island of Naxos, and the capital city in particular, enjoyed a prosperity such as it had seldom known since the ancient Naxiotes had been members of the Delian League. From the later fourteenth century, however, war and piracy again disrupted the economy of the Aegean, destroyed much commerce, rendered agriculture unprofitable, and sapped the strength and hope of the inhabitants. Rhodes fell to the

Turks in January 1523, and Chios in 1566, the same year in which the Naxiote duchy of the Crispi came to an end. With the return of some slight measure of orderly rule under the Ottoman government just before the mid-sixteenth century, a little of the prosperity which the Aegean islanders had known under the Sanudi was theirs again, and the population, sadly depleted in the fifteenth and earlier sixteenth centuries, grew again in numbers and in confidence.

On 12 August 1204 Venice had purchased Boniface of Montferrat's claims, granted to him by Alexius (IV) Angelus fifteen months before, to the island of Crete, which had still, however, to be conquered from the Greeks. The Venetian occupation of Crete was rendered difficult by the Genoese, who also aspired to its possession, and it cost the Venetians a good deal to secure the island for themselves, against the determined opposition put up, until 1211–12, by the Genoese lord Enrico Pescatore, Count of Malta and Gozo, who coveted the island for himself and the Genoese. Pescatore was defeated; the Venetians established themselves in Crete, and Giacomo Tiepolo was sent out as the first Venetian Duke of Candia. His was the responsibility of subduing in 1212 the first of many Greek uprisings against the Venetians. The Duke of Candia generally held office for two years; he was assisted by two special councillors and two councils. Venice gave lands in Crete and fiefs to various of her citizens who rendered military service to the duke.

Crete was rich in natural products, and situated on the main sea lanes of the eastern Mediterranean. The Catalans and French, bound for Syria and Egypt, generally used the southern route, passing the island on their left, a shorter voyage for them when they sailed south of Sicily; but the Genoese and Pisans, going through the straits of Messina, found it most advantageous to stop at Crete, which explains the great efforts of the Genoese to secure the island for themselves. The Venetians sailed down the Adriatic, past Durazzo and Corfu, in which they were interested, regularly stopping at their well-fortified ports of Modon and Coron, 'the chief eyes of the Commune' ('oculi capitales Communis'). On their way to Syria they sometimes took the more northern route, stopping in the Cyclades, Rhodes and Cyprus, thus passing the island of Crete on their right, although they might also put in at Candia, where great Venetian walls and the fortress still bearing the leonine escutcheon of St Mark stand in the harbour of modern Heraklion. On their way to Egypt they preferred to stop at Candia rather than attempt the voyage from Modon direct to Alexandria. Crete also lay athwart the routes between Constantinople and Alexandria. Cretan exports included wheat, honey, wax, cheese, minerals, sugar, silk and wines—as well as the editors and proof-readers of some of the first Greek texts printed during the Italian Renaissance.

From the port of Halmyros, on the Gulf of Volos, north of the island of Negroponte (Euboea), was exported the wheat grown in the rich fields of Thessaly. Wine was shipped from nearby Pteleum. The chief products of Negroponte were grain from the fertile Lelantine plain, wine, olive oil, honey and wax, as well as both raw and worked silks. In the north Aegean, Thracian grain was loaded for export in the Venetian harbour of Rodosto. In continental Greece, figs and vines were cultivated at Larissa. The olive and the vine were still the twin staples of Attica and Boeotia; Attic wine was resinated (*retsina*), as it is today. Oil was very important, not only for food, but also for making soap, for tanning leather, and for softening wool in the combing process. Even when soap was not applied to the person, it was essential for scouring wool. The Morea was rich in natural products. The dried raisins of Corinthia and the Argolid were much in demand in Europe. Wine was exported from Monemvasia ('Malmsey'). Olive oil was produced, figs, honey and wax, scarlet dye (*kermes*), a little sugar, and a fair amount of silk, Corinth indeed being a centre of silk manufactures. Although the Morea was actually not a land of great or even very good silk production, silk was worked in Patras as well as Corinth; it was shipped from Glarentza, especially to Ancona and Ragusa; and was cultivated and woven at Mistra, where the mulberry still thrives. In his great marauding expedition of 1147 Roger II of Sicily removed silk workers from Corinth and Thebes and sent them to Palermo; Michael Choniates, the Metropolitan of Athens, informs us, in a letter written after 1185, that the rich clothes of lords and ladies in Constantinople were woven by 'Theban and Corinthian fingers'. Thebes was indeed the chief silk-manufacturing centre in Greece. Some years after the Norman attack, Benjamin of Tudela still found Thebes 'a large city...with about two thousand Jewish inhabitants...the most eminent manufacturers of silk and purple cloth in all Greece'. The silk industry was profitable in Greece and continued to be so, with some ups and downs, until the first half of the nineteenth century.

Greeks and Latins had grown accustomed to each other during the many years that followed the conquest. The first barons, intending to remain in Greece, had dealt with the natives fairly, and some of them had grown to love the land and its people. Later comers sometimes caused trouble by their arrogance and their exactions. Prince William of Villehardouin might marry an Epirote princess; and his namesake, Duke William of Athens, her niece of Neopatras; but most of the Latin settlers remained separated from the Greeks by the threefold barrier of race, religion and culture. At best there must have been much tension which now and then manifested itself in dangerous ways, but the lapse of time and the advent of the Turk tended to bring the Greeks and Latins more closely together. The long reign of the wise Despot Manuel Cantacuzenus of Mistra (1348–80), except for occasional forays on one side or the other, was marked by the political peace and social accommodation which had finally come about between the Moreote Greeks and the Latins of the principality. The passage of years also saw the basic concept of the Crusade altered: hopes for the reconquest of Jerusalem were generally abandoned; even the re-establishment of the Latin Empire was deemed impracticable. The Crusade, as conceived by Count Amadeo VI of Savoy and the Emperor Sigismund, Count John of Nevers and the Marshal Boucicault, was rather to support the Byzantine capital against the Turks, Latin recognition at long last that the Greek state was a Christian bulwark against Islam. Since there was less theological rancour in continental Greece and the Morea than in Constantinople, the turban was not often preferred to the Latin tiara.

If the Greeks preferred Latins to Turks, however, they were merely choosing the lesser of two evils. Although some of the Aegean islanders came to have the highest respect for the justice and forbearance of the great Venetian Republic, the Greeks lavished little love upon the Latins. This was well understood in the West. On 10 April 1330, for example, Marino Sanudo addressed a long and instructive letter to Bertrand, Cardinal Bishop of Ostia and Velletri, wherein he summarised a hundred and twenty-five years of Latin experience in Greece: 'The land of Cyprus, which is inhabited by Greeks, and the island of Crete, and all the other lands and islands, which belong to the principality of the Morea and the duchy of Athens, are all inhabited by Greeks, and although they are obedient in words, they are none the less hardly obedient in their hearts, although temporal and spiritual authority is in Latin hands.'

As the foregoing pages have shown, the strong period of Latin rule in Greece and the Aegean islands lies in the thirteenth and fourteenth centuries. In Constantinople during this time the Italian dialects and French, Catalan, Latin and other western languages were spoken as well as Greek. There was a Lombard court in Thessalonica until the fall of the Latin kingdom to the Epirote Greeks in 1224; in the island of Euboea, in the Cyclades and the Sporades Italian barons lived; French, Catalan and Tuscan were successively spoken on the Acropolis and the Cadmea; and in the principality of Achaea a French court was held which appeared in the eyes of a contemporary 'greater than the court of a great king'. With the advent of the Turk, however, in the course of the fifteenth and sixteenth centuries, the Latin states in Greece and the islands gradually disappeared. The Latin regimes in Greece had renewed in some small measure the military and political, if not the cultural, glories of antiquity;[1] and indeed not since antiquity had Greece and the Peloponnese seen cities as lively and courts as splendid as those of the Villehardouin and the de la Roche; but the Turks had come, and the greatness of Greece, even of medieval Greece, had gone. Only monuments were left and memories, which, as Michael Choniates might have said, were beyond the envy and destruction of time.

---

[1] On the intellectual interests of the Latins in Greece and the islands, see K. M. Setton, 'The Byzantine Background to the Italian Renaissance', *Proceedings of the American Philosophical Society*, c, 1 (1956), 31–40.

CHAPTER X

CONSTANTINOPLE AND ROME

The names of the two cities, Constantinople and Rome, both claiming the heritage of ancient Rome, became the symbols of two interpretations of Christian thought and life: the eastern, rooted in Hellenistic traditions, deriving from the Greek spirit, enriched by the remnants of ancient eastern civilisations; and the western, rooted in old Roman traditions but only partially fertilised by eastern Hellenism. The interpenetration of these two traditions, so similar in some respects and so different in others, forms the central theme of the centuries-old relationship between Constantinople and Rome. It was not the intention of Constantine to create a *new* Rome—he called his foundation after himself—but only a *second* Rome, and it would be wrong to regard the founding of Constantinople as the creation of a new Christian centre after the failure to win over to Christianity the Old Rome with all its pagan associations. Yet the fact that the eastern part of the Roman Empire was more deeply penetrated by Christianity than the West assured to it a preponderant position in the Christian Church, and opened fresh possibilities of growth to the new imperial city in the East.

Thanks to the preparatory work of the first Christian political theorists, Clement of Alexandria and Eusebius of Caesarea, the Christians were able to accommodate to their own creed the main ideas of Hellenistic political philosophy which had already been accepted by the Roman Emperors. The Emperor, who was thus regarded as the representative of God on earth, retained in Christian political writings his Hellenistic titles of benefactor of mankind, pilot providing for its material and spiritual needs, and supreme lord, surrounded with almost divine glory. He was also invoked as father and harmoniser of the different groups of his subjects.

Julian the Apostate tried in vain to arrest this development and to hark back not only to the old Roman religion, but also to the old Roman political ideas. But the new course in politics and religion was too strong, especially in the eastern provinces, and swept away the last vestiges of Julian's bold attempt. During the reign of the dynasty of Valentinian and Theodosius the Great, the triumph of Christian Hellenism became complete.

The consequences of this development were most portentous for the further relationship between Constantinople and Rome. The victory of Christian Hellenism brought Church and State into a close relationship illustrated by the adaptation of Church organisation to the administrative division of the Empire. This principle was approved by the Council of Nicaea (325). It was further developed in the East and was also accepted by the Church in the western provinces. The Hellenistic conception of the Emperor as representative of God on earth made it a sacred duty for the Emperor to care for the purity of the faith and to decide finally, as Constantine declared during the Donatist controversy, 'which divine worship should be used and in what manner'.

The adoption by Constantine and his successors of the conciliar practice as it had developed in the Church during the third century, and the further assimilation of this practice to the Roman senatorial procedure, preserved theoretically the independence of the bishops and the Church. Following the practice established in the senate, the Emperor did not vote in the assemblies. But the right of convoking the Church assembly, of preparing the agenda and of presiding over it—derived again from the senatorial procedure—gave the Emperors opportunity to excess of imposing their own will on the bishops. The spell of Christian Hellenism over the bishops of the eastern part of the Empire weakened among them the spirit of opposition to imperial interventions in matters of faith. On the other hand the fact that the western co-Emperors preferred to reside in Milan and Ravenna, as being more central than the old capital, gave more freedom and greater prominence to the Roman Bishop.

Christian Hellenism was accepted by Rome also as the only possible political system for Church and State. The Bishop of Rome had profited from the principle of adaptation to the administrative division of the Empire. Since from the latest period of the Republic onwards all inhabitants of Italy were Roman citizens, and all Italian cities Roman *municipia*, it was natural for the Christians of Italian towns to regard themselves as members of the Christian community of Rome. So it happened that the Bishops of Rome were acknowledged as Metropolitans of all Italy, and their prestige helped them to extend their direct influence over Africa, Gaul and Illyricum. But it was not only their episcopal position in the capital of the *orbis Romanus* which gave such prominence to the Roman Bishops. They were also the successors of St Peter, the head of the Apostles, and this prerogative was recognised voluntarily outside Italy as is attested by St Cyprian of Carthage.

This idea of apostolicity did not need to be stressed by the Bishops of Rome as long as their city was the only centre of the *orbis Romanus*. The situation changed, however, when it became clear that the transfer of the imperial residence to Constantinople was to become permanent. It was during the reign of Pope Damasus (336–84) that the expression *sedes apostolica* became synonymous with the See of Rome or of Peter.

Damasus is also believed to have been responsible for the first open clash between Constantinople and Rome. Canon three of the Council of Constantinople of 381 accorded to the see of that imperial city the honour of precedence before that of Alexandria and of Antioch. The following year a Roman council is said to have protested against this measure, stating that the first see of the Church was that of Rome, and attributing the second place in church organisation to Alexandria and the third to Antioch. There is, however, no evidence that the Council of Rome under Damasus had dealt with the recent promotion of Constantinople. The Council of 381 was originally a synod to which only the prelates of the eastern part of the Empire were invited and its third canon was not inspired by any anti-Roman bias. It was intended to apply only to the Eastern Church. This and other reasons favour the opinion that the so-called Damasian canon originated only in the fifth or sixth century.

In any event, from Damasus on the apostolic and Petrine character of the Roman see was increasingly stressed by its Bishops, who found in the idea of apostolicity a mighty weapon against the encroachments of the Emperors in matters of faith and against the pretensions of the Bishops of the residential city. In the East, the apostolic idea did not find as ready a response as in the West, and the importance of the episcopal sees in church organisation continued to be measured by that of their cities in the Empire.

But again, the predominance of this mentality in the East assured to Rome the first place in the Church, because Rome was the first capital, and had given its name to the Empire, often identified with the Church. To deny the primacy in the Church to Rome would have meant abandoning the very basis on which the Empire and its Church were built. This was inconceivable to the Emperors, to the Bishops of Constantinople and to all easterners.

The Bishops of Rome could, however, not be satisfied with such a basis for their primacy. In their correspondence with the East, and through their legate at the Councils of Ephesus (431) and of Chalcedon (451), they insisted constantly and stubbornly on the apostolic and Petrine character of their see. They obtained, however, little response from the East. And this difference between the Roman and eastern conceptions is responsible for the violent clash between Rome and Constantinople at the two closing sessions of the Council of Chalcedon.

It should be stressed that the vote of the so-called twenty-eighth canon confirming canon three of the Council of 381 was not inspired

by anti-Roman sentiment. Its wording discloses, however, the extent
to which the easterners were still under the spell of the principle of
adapting ecclesiastical organisation to the political division of the
Empire and how little understanding they had for the apostolic and
Petrine character of the Roman See. It was a great mistake not to
have mentioned it in the canon, and this is the more to be wondered
at, as the apostolic character of Rome was often recognised in the
acta of the Council, and Roman leadership in defining the faith was
readily accepted.

What frightened the legates and Pope Leo the Great (440–61) was
not so much that the second place in the Church was assigned to
Constantinople as the subordination of the minor dioceses—Thrace,
Pontus and Asia—to its jurisdiction. Although there are signs that
Rome was ready to grant honorary precedence to the Bishops of the
imperial residence over the other two major sees in the East, it was
not willing to sanction the promotion of Constantinople to the role
of the most powerful and influential see in the East.

Leo the Great objected that this new promotion violated the
stipulations of canon six of the Council of Nicaea, which recognised
only three major sees in the Church—Rome, Alexandria and Antioch.
Disregarding the fact that these sees originally owed their prominence
in Church organisation to the circumstance that they were the greatest
political and cultural centres in the Empire, Leo further extended
the importance of the idea of apostolicity in Church organisation by
stating that the three sees owed their prominence only to the teaching
there of St Peter and his close disciple St Mark. The See of Constantinople was denied a place among the major sees, because it was
not founded by an apostle.

The fact that the contested canon was not officially counted among
the decisions of the Council marked an apparent victory for Leo in
the controversy. This could not, however, prevent Constantinople from
maintaining its jurisdiction over the three minor dioceses. In the end
Leo of Rome and Anatolius of Constantinople became allies against
Timothy of Alexandria who was urging the convocation of a new
council. The fear that the new council would endanger the dogmatic
decisions of Chalcedon and question the validity of the twenty-eighth
canon brought the two rivals together. However, the heretical
tendencies manifested by the Bishops of Alexandria and Antioch had
shattered Leo's hopes of finding in them allies against Constantinople.

It is possible that a compromise between Rome and Constantinople
would have been found if this collaboration between the two sees
had lasted longer. Unfortunately, the Acacian schism (484–519),
provoked by the acceptance by Acacius of Constantinople of the

Emperor Zeno's *Henoticon*—a new declaration of faith making some concessions to the monophysites—shattered all such hopes.

During this controversy Pope Gelasius (492–6) extended the claims made by his predecessors on the basis of the Petrine tradition. He was emboldened in his attitude by political changes in the western parts of the Empire. Italy, ravaged by invading Germans and Huns, found a new master in 476 in the person of the Rugian Odoacer. He was replaced in 491, with the help of high Italian clerics, by the Ostrogoth Theodoric. Certain of support from Theodoric, whose relations with the Emperor Anastasius I (491–518) were strained, Gelasius boldly challenged the right of intervention in religious affairs, claimed by the Emperor, and exalted the authority of the priesthood almost to the level of the imperial power: 'There are two things by which this world is governed: the sacred authority of the pontiffs and the royal power. Of these, priests carry a weight all the greater, as they must render an account to the Lord even for kings before the divine Judgment.'

The Pope's declaration was destined to become the source of a new current in political speculation. This, finally, elevated the spiritual power above the temporal, and definitely terminated, in the West, the surviving remnants of Christian Hellenism, while it stretched the last ties between Rome and Constantinople to breaking point.

This development could not have been foreseen in the fifth and sixth centuries. The stress laid by Gelasius and his successors on the apostolic and Petrine principle in Church administration, however, caused this principle to find increasing appreciation in the East and in Constantinople, at least among the orthodox prelates, deprived of their sees because they opposed Anastasius' religious policy. Slowly, the apostolic see was being recognised, even in the East, as a providential factor destined to keep the imperial power within its due limits.

On the other hand, in spite of the refusal of Gelasius and of Symmachus to give the See of Constantinople *de jure* recognition as a metropolis, Rome was forced to negotiate with Constantinople as if it were a major see. So it happened that, when the schism was concluded, Constantinople was recognised, at least *de facto*, as a major see, taking precedence over those of Alexandria and Antioch.

This state of things was sealed by Justinian (527–65) who was also mainly responsible, as adviser to his uncle Justin I (518–27), for the liquidation of the schism. On becoming Emperor, Justinian concentrated all his efforts on the realisation of his dream: the restoration of the Roman Empire within its old limits. After destroying the armies of the Goths in Italy, and of the Vandals in Africa, Justinian brought the Western Church back into the confines of the Empire.

It was his intention to make this union enduring and to end the jealousy between the two capitals of his Empire.

It is against this background that Justinian's classic definition in the edict of 6 March 535 (Novel 6, pr.) of the function of the *Basileia* and of the priesthood must be viewed: 'God's greatest gifts to men derive from His infinite goodness—the *sacerdotium* and the *imperium*, the first serving divine interests, the second human interests and watching over them: both come from the same principle and perfect human life. Hence nothing claims the Emperor's care so much as the honour of the priests, since these continually pray God for them. If the priesthood is sound and trusts completely in God and if the Emperor rules the polity entrusted to him with justice and honour, mutual harmony will arise which can only prove useful to the human race. God's true dogmas and the priests' honour are therefore our first care.'

This is a definition of Christian Hellenism as it had developed in the East, the insistence on the greatness of the priesthood being a concession to the growing self-consciousness of the *sacerdotium* which had manifested itself recently in Rome.

Justinian's insistence on harmonious collaboration between *imperium* and *sacerdotium* is entirely in the spirit of old Hellenism, and it was not mere coincidence that Justinian should have insisted on the *imperium* supporting the decisions of the *sacerdotium*, thus 'judiciously harmonising things human and divine', in Novel 42, published in August 536. He announced the condemnation of the Patriarch Anthimus, engineered by Pope Agapetus during his visit to Constantinople as envoy of the Gothic King Theodatus, and confirmed by a local synod.

If the Roman Empire was to be more than a fiction, Justinian felt that Rome should recover its prestige as the source of Roman power and law: it should be the centre of Christianity as it had been the centre of the Empire and also the imperial residence. It was in this sense that in the introduction to his Novel 9 in May 535 he exalted Rome in the following words: 'Old Rome enjoys the honour of being the mother of law and none will doubt that she is the head of the supreme pontificate. For these reasons we too have deemed it necessary to honour the cradle of law and the source of the priesthood by a special law of our sacred will....'

In his letter to Pope John II the Emperor called the Church of Rome 'caput omnium sanctarum ecclesiarum' and in a letter to the Patriarch Epiphanius, which was included in Justinian's Constitution on the Blessed Trinity, he declared: 'We have condemned Nestorius and Eutyches, preserving in every way the unity of the sacred

Churches with the holy Pope and Patriarch of Old Rome....For we cannot tolerate that anything concerning the ecclesiastical order should be settled independently of his Holiness, since he is the head of all the sacred priests of God, and because, whenever heretics have arisen in these parts, they have been checked by the sentence and the fair judgement of that venerable see.'

To stabilise this position and to end the strife between Rome and Constantinople, Justinian issued, in 545, the famous Novel 131: 'In accordance with the definitions (of the four councils) we declare the holy Pope of the see of Rome to be the first of all priests and the blessed Archbishop of Constantinople—the New Rome—to be second after the holy apostolic see of Rome though with precedence over all the other sees.' Thus Justinian admitted and confirmed the primacy of the Bishop of Rome in the Church—he seems also to have initiated the tradition that Emperors should address the Bishop of Rome as 'their spiritual Father'. But he had no intention of prejudicing the Emperor's rights in the Christian commonwealth. He remained the supreme master, the representative of God on earth, taking care of the material and spiritual needs of his subjects; only in purely doctrinal matters did he leave the last word to the Bishop of Rome.

It looked as if a new era had started in the relationship between Rome and Constantinople. Justinian's conception of his imperial duties was approved by Pope John II in a letter which strongly echoes Hellenistic court style. Pope Agapetus I also congratulated Justinian on his orthodoxy and his desire to bring all his subjects to the true faith, although he cautiously mentioned that it was the business of the clergy to teach the faith. Pope Vigilius thanked the Lord that he had given to Justinian 'not only an imperial but also a priestly soul'.

In spite of this ecclesiastical approval, Justinian was to learn that the new current of speculation on relations between Church and State, which had started in Rome and had spread over the West, was stronger than it appeared. His most glaring intrusion into theology was the condemnation of the so-called Three Chapters. Although well inspired, Justinian carried matters too far, making his decision without convoking a council and trying to force his edict on the bishops. The strongest protest against this high-handed imperial action was voiced by the Church of Africa. The African bishop Facundus insisted that the definition of the faith was the preserve of the priesthood, and threatened Justinian with God's punishment for 'discussing the essentials of the Christian faith which he cannot do, or for enacting new canons, which is the privilege of the priests of the first order, when a number of them are gathered together'.

Justinian was obliged to recognise his mistake, and in the end, to extricate himself from the impasse, he had to resort to the customary procedure of summoning a council. In his letter to the Fifth Oecumenical Council he defined as follows the role of the *imperium* and of the *sacerdotium* in similar cases: 'It has always been the practice of our orthodox and imperial forefathers to counter every heresy as it arose through the instrumentality of the most zealous priests assembled in council and to keep the Holy Church of God in peace by the sincere preaching of the true faith.' The final acceptance by Pope Vigilius of the synodal decisions concluded this tedious incident.

In spite of the criticism heaped by many historians on Justinian's political ideas and achievements, it must be admitted that his policy would have contributed to a better understanding between Constantinople and Rome if his work had lasted longer.

Unfortunately, at the very moment when Constantinople and Rome needed a respite in order to find a basis of understanding, obstacles arose in the shape of new barbarian invasions of Illyricum and Italy, bringing Justinian's renovation of the Roman Empire to an untimely end.

The conquest of the north of Italy by the Lombards and the foundation of a new Germanic kingdom in Italy are generally held responsible for the fateful new development. Not less important, however, was the destruction of the Latin and Greek civilisation of Illyricum by the Avars and Slavs and the foundation of new Slav principalities in the province which had formed for centuries a bridge between the Latin and Greek worlds. The destruction of this land bridge between Constantinople and Rome, and the control which the Arabs achieved over the Mediterranean, made communication between Constantinople and Rome extremely difficult. The Byzantines were forced by the Persians and then by the Arabs to look increasingly towards the East, whence came the vital danger.

On the other hand, Christianity in the western part of the Roman Empire lost many of its old Roman traditions and customs as a result of the Germanic invasions. In order to win over the Germanic nations, Rome had to respect and accept their national traditions in so far as they were not directly anti-Christian. Thus, Constantinople and Rome came to follow divergent courses of development.

The first serious consequences were not felt until the second half of the seventh and in the eighth centuries. In the meantime Justinian's reorganisation of Church affairs continued to be respected. Rome was lucky to find in Gregory the Great (590–604) a Pope who was both able to maintain the prestige of his see in the Empire and also energetic and diplomatic enough to reduce the danger arising from the progress of the Lombards. In reorganising the administration of the vast *patrimonia*—the land and property belonging to his see— he created a solid economic basis for his enterprises in Italy and among the new nations. Although Gregory had sometimes to act as if he were the real master of Rome, he remained loyal to the Emperor Maurice (582–602) in Constantinople. He did not continue to develop Gelasius' theory of the two powers, but contented himself with the political order established by Justinian, while stressing the necessity for harmonious co-operation between the two powers. The Roman Empire remained for Gregory the only political expression of Church universality. Thus he asked the Emperor's permission to send a pallium to the Bishop of Autun when this was requested by the Frankish Queen Brunhilda, and thought it his duty to inform the Emperor of the conversion of the Anglo-Saxons which he had instigated. Although energetic in defence of what he considered his rights against imperial interventions, he forged a principle which gives a clear insight into his views on these matters. In his letter to the deacon Anatolius (*Ep.* II, 29 of February 601) Gregory confessed: 'Whatever he (the Emperor) should do, we follow, if it is in accord with canon law; when, however, it is not in accord with canon law, we tolerate it in so far (as we can do so) without committing a sin.'

Constantinople continued to be regarded, at least *de facto*, as a major see, second in rank to Rome, although Gregory did not modify the Papacy's negative attitude to the contested canon. The fact that the anonymous author of the *Prisca*, the first Latin collection of canon law, and Dionysius Exiguus had included the third canon of the Council of 381, giving the second place in the Church to the Bishop of Constantinople, illustrates the confusion of thought in Rome in this respect. This, however, helped the Westerners to reconcile themselves to an accomplished fact which could not be undone.

Gregory himself defended the right of appeal to his see and expressed the contemporary relationship between Rome and Constantinople thus, in his letter to Gregory, Bishop of Syracuse (*Ep.* IX, 26 of 598): 'As concerns the See of Constantinople, what do they say, who doubt that it is subject to the Roman See? This is continuously recognised equally by the most pious Emperor and master, and by our brother, the Bishop of that city.'

It is in this light that the controversy provoked between Rome and Constantinople by the use of the title Oecumenical Patriarch by John IV the Faster should be examined. This title seems to have been in use in Constantinople from the time of Acacius on. It appears to have been a further elaboration, in line with the principle of adaptation

to actual political circumstances, expressive of the supreme position of Constantinople in the East. In view of Gregory's declaration in his letter to the Bishop of Syracuse, it must be concluded that
the introduction of this title had no direct anti-Roman bias. The
Byzantines seem to have been logical in this matter, and, as there
were, in some ways, two capitals of the Empire, it is most interesting
that at the very time when this title began to be used in Constantinople, some Byzantine documents gave the same title also to the
Popes.

The strong reaction on the part of Rome against the use of this
title is to be explained by the fear that its wrong interpretation might
include the negation of Rome's primacy in the Church. The title of
'servant of the servants of God' was not, however, instituted by
Gregory the Great as an antidote to it. He had already so called
himself when he was a simple monk and deacon, and this later became
one of the official papal titles.

The controversy about the use of this patriarchal title seems to
have disturbed the hitherto peaceful relations between Constantinople and Rome to such an extent that the Emperor Phocas
(602–10) thought it necessary to intervene and to redefine the status
of Rome and Constantinople in the Church. The *Liber Pontificalis*
reports that one of Gregory's successors, Boniface III (607), had
obtained from the Emperor Phocas a declaration 'that the see of the
senior of the apostles, Peter, is to be the head of all Churches, while
the Church of Constantinople calls itself the first of all Churches'.
Contrary to some interpretations of this edict, it should only be seen
as a reiteration of Justinian's decision on the status of both sees with
a new confirmation of Rome's primacy.

Nevertheless, Constantinople took the initiative in doctrinal matters. The Patriarch Sergius promoted the doctrine of one will in
Christ—monotheletism—and succeeded, for a short time, in deceiving
the vigilance of Rome, when Honorius I (625–38), although himself
professing the orthodox doctrine, gave the impression in his answers
to Sergius of being favourable to the Patriarch's views. The Emperor
Heraclius (610–41), anxious in the face of the Persian danger to bring
the monophysites in Egypt and Syria back to orthodoxy, published
his *Ecthesis* (638) and this monothelete profession of faith was
generally accepted in the East. The opposition which this new
doctrine had provoked in the West induced Constans II (641–68) to
replace Heraclius' edict by his own, the *Typus*, in which he forbade
the discussion of this subject (648).

Pope Martin I (649–55) protested against this, defined the orthodox
doctrine of two wills in Christ and condemned the heresy. The

Emperor, already offended by the fact that Martin had omitted to wait for the imperial approval of his election, had the Pope arrested and brought to Constantinople where he was accused of supporting the insurrection of Olympius and was condemned as a traitor. The unfortunate Pope died in exile in the Crimea (656).

This was the deepest shadow which the imperial power threw over Rome. There were other irritating interventions into Roman affairs by the Emperors or their Exarchs of Ravenna. More and more signs indicated that in Italy, disturbed by the penetration of the Lombards, the spirit of solidarity with the Roman Empire, which Justinian had tried to strengthen, was vanishing. The decision of the Emperor Constantine IV (668–85) to hark back to the definitions of Chalcedon was therefore timely. Pope Agatho (678–81) resumed the role of Leo the Great and prepared the convocation of the Sixth Oecumenical Council (680–1) by the dogmatic missives which he dispatched to the East. The council condemned the monothelete heresy and added the name of Pope Honorius to the list of condemned heretics. In the profession of faith which the elected Popes had to sign, this condemnation of Honorius' memory was maintained. The *Liber Diurnus*, which contains this profession and which received its definitive form after the Sixth Oecumenical Council, also gives a clear picture of the diplomatic relationship between Rome and Constantinople in its formulas concerning the election of the Popes and letters to be sent to the Emperor or to the Exarch of Ravenna.

The peaceful conclusion of this new controversy between Constantinople and Rome ended, however, with a dissonant note. Another council was convoked by Justinian II (685–95, 705–11) in the imperial hall called Trullos (692) in order to supplement the last two general councils. It condemned, among its 102 canons, some usages current in the West. This condemnation not only indicated that the estrangement between Rome and Constantinople was growing, but also bore witness to Constantinople's mounting self-confidence evident in its attempt to impose its eastern customs on the whole Church. Pope Sergius I (687–701) refused to sign the *acta*, and when the Emperor attempted to have the Pope arrested and sent to Constantinople, the growing Italian national resentment against the Emperor manifested itself for the first time in an open revolt. The militia of Ravenna, of Pentapolis and of Rome hastened to the aid of the Pope, and the Emperor's envoy only escaped death through the intervention of the Pontiff. Similar events were witnessed in Italy when Tiberius III attempted to punish the rebels. Pope John VI (701–5), however, remained loyal to the Emperor and calmed the rebellious militia.

Similar sentiments of loyalty towards Constantinople were manifested by Popes John VII (705–7) and Constantine I (708–15). Constantine boldly accepted the invitation of the Emperor to come to Constantinople in 710, in order to settle the dispute. It was a courageous act which was well rewarded. The conflict ended peacefully, and Rome seems to have received from the Emperor a new confirmation of its primacy in doctrinal matters, similar to that given by Justinian and Phocas. It is in this sense that the words of the *Liber Pontificalis*, that the Emperor 'had renewed all privileges of the Church', should be explained.

Only when Philippicus had usurped the throne and returned to the monothelete heresy did Constantine I, supported by his faithful Romans, refuse obedience to the usurper.

These events testify to the important transformation through which Rome and Italy were passing from the end of the sixth century on. The influence of the aristocracy and of the militia was making itself increasingly felt during the elections of new Popes. On the other hand, the bureaucratic element also grew in size and importance, comprising both clerics and laymen. All this contributed to a certain laicisation of the Papacy, which was also illustrated by the development of the papal court ceremonial. The descriptions of the papal processions from the *Patriarchium Lateranense* to the *stationes* by contemporary Roman *ordines* show too how the importance of the Popes had grown in the eyes of the Roman populace, which often looked upon them as its sole protectors and benefactors.

The election of so many Popes of Greek origin also testifies to the strength of pro-imperial and pro-Byzantine tendencies in Rome. On the other hand, however, Roman and Italian national sentiments were gaining in strength and permeating the *Patriarchium* of the Lateran.

The Popes of this so-called Byzantine period of Roman history were still able to maintain a balance between these two influences and remained loyal to Constantinople in spite of the mounting tension. During the reign of the Emperor Leo III the Isaurian (717–41) and Pope Gregory II (715–31), however, the situation deteriorated and reached breaking point. The Pope did not support the rebels in Italy during the troubled period preceding Leo's accession. But he emerged as the protector of Italian national interests when Leo III, having saved Constantinople from the Arabs (717–18), and anxious to affirm the imperial authority in Italy, imposed heavy taxes on the western provinces. This open obstruction of an imperial order by Gregory II was regarded by the Emperor as meriting the punishment meted out to Martin I. But the situation in Rome had changed. The executors of the Emperor's order were lynched by the populace and when the Exarch Paul of Ravenna with his militia was approaching Rome, he was stopped by the Roman militia and the troops of the neighbouring Lombard dukes.

Gregory II was well aware of the strength of his position in Italy and this explains the bold tone of his letters in reply to the imperial missive (726) ordering him to accept the new iconoclast creed proclaimed by Leo III. Neither this letter nor that which the Emperor sent in 730/1 is preserved. However, their main contents can be reconstructed from Gregory's answers which, as E. Caspar has shown,[1] should be regarded as genuine with only minor interpolations.

Mindful of the recent events in Italy, Gregory II boldly told the Emperor that in case of attack the Pope had only to penetrate a few miles into the Campagna in order to be perfectly secure. Rome's authority and prestige were, however, not limited to Italy. 'The whole West casts its eyes towards our humility and although we are now in such a situation, they have nevertheless great confidence in us, and in him whose image you are threatening to put down and to destroy, whom all the kingdoms of the West regard as if he were God on earth.'

When writing this, the Pope was reviewing the results of the great missionary work done by Rome among the Germanic nations since the time of Gregory the Great. The Pope further assured the Emperor that all the letters and orders he had sent to Rome had been made available to the western kings in a manner exalting and commending the imperial authority. This shows that the idea of the universal Church in a universal Empire was still alive in Rome and this admonition was intended to remind the Emperor of the services which Rome could render to Constantinople among the new nations.

In order to vindicate his iconoclastic decree, the Emperor had written signing himself 'Emperor and Priest'.[2] The Pope—still accepting the main principles of Christian Hellenism—pointed out that such a title could rightly be given to the Emperors who, in perfect accord with the priests, had convoked councils in order that the true faith might be defined. But Leo III had transgressed the decisions of the Fathers. 'Dogmas do not concern Emperors but priests....As the priest has no right to supervise the affairs of the palace and to propose ⟨the distribution of⟩ imperial dignities, so also the Emperor has no right to supervise the Church and to judge the

---

[1] E. Caspar, 'Papst Gregor II und der Bilderstreit', *ZKG*, LII (1933), 29–89; see also G. Ostrogorsky, *History of the Byzantine State*, p. 134, n. 1.

[2] This declaration may be genuine because in the introduction to his new law book, the *Ecloga*, Leo III averred that the Lord bade him 'as he bade Peter, the supreme Head of the Apostles, to feed his most faithful flock'.

clergy, or to consecrate and to handle the symbols of the holy sacraments.... We admonish you to be ⟨a true⟩ Emperor and priest.'[1]

In spite of this very energetic condemnation of the Emperor's interference in doctrinal matters, the Pope's letters show clearly that Gregory II intended to remain loyal to Constantinople. In his words a strong echo may be detected of Gelasius' thesis on the division of the two powers. But these words also provide evidence that the theses of Gelasius and Symmachus had not yet eliminated in Rome the main principles of Christian Hellenism.

Although the Pope was sure of the support of the militia in case of an open conflict, he used his influence to calm the revolutionary agitation which broke out in Italy against the Emperor and helped the Exarch Eutychius to defeat an anti-Emperor in Tuscany. Hoping that events might take a better turn, he contented himself by admonishing the Emperor once again and by refusing to recognise the iconoclastic Patriarch installed in Constantinople in 730.

The situation deteriorated however under his successor Gregory III (731–41). The Emperor simply imprisoned all papal envoys bearing the sentence of excommunication against iconoclasts, imposed new taxes on the population in Calabria and in Sicily, confiscated the revenues of papal patrimonies in these provinces and detached them like Illyricum from Rome, subordinating them to the jurisdiction of the Patriarch of Constantinople. This latter measure had most serious consequences because it enforced the isolation of the West from the East, strengthened the position of Constantinople in the Church and destroyed in Illyricum the last bridge between East and West.

One of Gregory II's reasons for seeking to avoid a break with the Emperor lay in the Lombard danger. The Lombard King Liutprand had great ambitions and aimed at the subjection of all Italy by a clever exploitation of the confused situation there. In 728 he had appeared before Rome as the Exarch's ally and Gregory II had had to appeal to the king's veneration for St Peter to prevent him from entering the city. Having re-established his authority over the southern Lombard duchies, Liutprand took Ravenna in 731. Gregory III begged the Venetians to help bring Ravenna 'back to the old union with the holy *respublica*', which was accomplished in 735. In 739 Liutprand occupied the duchy of Spoleto and invaded the duchy of Rome. Gregory III appealed to the Franks for help but in vain, because Charles Martel had concluded a pact with the Lombards.

Gregory's successor Zacharias (741–52) managed to keep Ravenna within the Empire by concluding an agreement with Liutprand, and protected Rome by a treaty with Liutprand's successor Ratchis,

[1] See also above: ch. III, p. 71.

which ended the attacks against imperial possessions in Italy. But Zacharias could only look on hopelessly when the new King Aistulf put a definite end to the Exarchate of Ravenna in 751. With Zacharias' death the Byzantine period of Rome's history ended.[1] He was also the last Pope to announce his election to the Emperor and to ask for confirmation.

It was this Greek Pope who unwittingly inaugurated a new period in Rome's history by his intervention in Frankish affairs. By giving his moral sanction to the deposition of the last Merovingian king and the elevation of Pepin to the Frankish throne, he placed the new dynasty under an obligation to Rome and facilitated the inauguration of a pro-Frankish policy by Stephen II (752-7).

The latter still acted as the Emperor's subject in requesting Constantine V to send troops to Italy to protect Rome against Aistulf's threats, and to reconquer Ravenna. On the Emperor's order, Stephen II, accompanied by an imperial envoy, went in vain to Pavia to request Aistulf to restore Ravenna to the Empire. Thereupon the Pope set out alone on his journey to the Franks, which had been well prepared by secret negotiations. At Ponthion the Pope begged King Pepin 'to arrange the affairs of St Peter and of the Roman republic'. Pepin promised help and, peaceful negotiations having failed, he defeated Aistulf in battle. In accordance with his promise at the national assembly of Kiersey (754) where the Lombard war had been decided on, Pepin donated the Exarchate and the duchy of Rome to St Peter and his successors.

This was the beginning of the papal state in Italy, although the relationship between Rome and Constantinople remained somewhat vague. Pepin maintained good relations with the Eastern Empire and it is quite probable that the title of *Patricius Romanorum*, bestowed on him and his sons at Ponthion by the Pope, was conferred with the Emperor's authority. It is noteworthy that the offices of Exarch of Ravenna and of Dux of Rome—both of whose titularies enjoyed the title of *patricius*—were not renewed, as if to show that these functions had been transferred to the new *Patricius Romanorum*.

This new vague relationship between Rome and Constantinople must have worried some legalistic Roman clerics. In this atmosphere there originated the legend according to which Constantine the Great, before moving to Constantinople, had bestowed on the Pope all the imperial possessions in Italy, had given him the right to use imperial insignia, and had declared that the priests of the Church were patricians and consuls, although the articulation of this legend as the

[1] See above: ch. III, p. 75.

'Donation of Constantine' only seems to have taken place between about 804 and 806.

The Emperor's authority continued to be recognised, at least outwardly, in the territory presented by Pepin to St Peter. Papal letters and the documents issued by the senate and other Roman offices continued to be dated according to the years of the Emperor's reign. The Roman mint also went on issuing money with the Emperor's effigy. This was certainly the case during the pontificates of Paul I (757–67), Stephen III (768–72) and Hadrian I (772–95). The suggestion put forward that Hadrian discontinued these practices in 781 is most doubtful.[1]

It was natural that the new state structure should soon be involved in political entanglements which threatened to compromise the prestige of the Popes. Paul I looked for support amongst the Franks against a strong pro-Byzantine party led by the archdeacon Theophylact. Stephen II, victorious over an opponent who was supported by the aristocracy, finally abandoned the Franks for the Lombard King Desiderius, and only Hadrian I returned to the Frankish alliance. When Desiderius attacked Roman territory in 774, Hadrian appealed to King Charlemagne who finally abolished the Lombard kingdom. On his Roman expeditions in 781 and 787, Charlemagne transferred to the Pope the duchy of Rome, the Pentapolis and the Exarchate, considerably enlarged.

An important test for the nature of the relationship between Rome and Constantinople at this period is provided by the letters exchanged between the two cities on the occasion of the Seventh Oecumenical Council (787). The letter addressed by the Empress Irene and her son Constantine VI to Hadrian gives the impression that, after the impetuous declarations on kingship and priesthood by the iconoclast Emperors, Irene was coming back to Justinian's definition of the great gifts vouchsafed by God to humanity. The letter begins with the words: 'Those who receive from our Lord Jesus Christ, true God, either the imperial dignity or the honour of supreme priesthood, have to think of and care for that which pleases Him and have to direct and govern the people entrusted to them by Him, according to His will.... From Him we have received the *imperium* and you the dignity of supreme priesthood.' The primacy of Rome in matters of faith also seems to be acknowledged quite clearly in the letter, when the Empress calls the Pope 'truly first priest, who presides instead of the holy and all-praised Apostle Peter in his very chair'.

Hadrian's answer, of course, stresses Roman primacy and protests

[1] But see also above: ch. III, p. 77.

against the title of Oecumenical Patriarch, but contains words addressed to the Emperors which suggest quite clearly that he had not yet broken with the basic principles of Christian Hellenism. The Patriarch Tarasius, who renewed the practice of sending synodical letters announcing his consecration, also paid homage to the apostolic and Petrine character of the Roman See. He is called 'Patriarch' by the Pope and this shows that Constantinople was, at last, regarded in Rome as a major see. However, when the Pope's letter was read at the Council, his demand for the return of Illyricum and of the patrimonies and his protest against the consecration of a layman, Tarasius, to the patriarchal dignity were omitted. This showed clearly that Constantinople was determined to keep all Greek territories under its jurisdiction and to regulate its own affairs in its own way.

The open break between Constantinople and Rome should therefore be dated from the reign of Pope Leo III (795–816). He also regarded himself as a subject of the Emperor, but the violent accusations launched against him by his adversaries, led by the Roman aristocracy, threw him completely into the arms of Charlemagne (771–814), who was at that time approaching the apex of his power. Leo was probably influenced by the Constantinian legend which had put under his control the three factors—army, senate and people— which, according to the Roman constitution, elected an Emperor. And, having need of an Emperor—in accordance with the Byzantine lawbook, the *Ecloga*—in order to free himself definitively from serious accusations, and regarding the imperial throne as vacant after the deposition of Constantine VI by Irene, Leo III took the initiative into his own hands and proclaimed Charlemagne Emperor of the Romans on Christmas Day in the year 800.

This event changed profoundly the relationship between Rome and Constantinople. The coronation performed by the Pope would have been regarded as valueless—and in fact Theophanes ridiculed the ceremony in his history. But there was a solemn acclamation by the Roman people, including probably the representatives of the militia and the senate, and this characterised the event in the eyes of the Byzantines as a rebellion against the lawful Emperor.

Charlemagne was well aware of the complications created by the Pope's action and this may have been one of the reasons for his displeasure at it, as recorded by his biographer Einhard. Not wishing to offend the Byzantines further, he refused to use the title of *Imperator Romanorum*—contenting himself with the title *Imperator Romanum gubernans imperium*—and he initiated negotiations with Irene with a view to regularising his position. But the deposition of

Irene by Nicephorus I (802–11) put an end to these plans, and when negotiations with the new Emperor failed, Illyricum became the battlefield on which Byzantine and Frankish armies clashed. But Nicephorus' successor Michael I Rangabe (811–13) ended the conflict with a compromise: Charlemagne handed over Istria and Venice which he had conquered in return for the recognition of his title as co-Emperor. A year before his death Charlemagne had the satisfaction of being greeted in Aachen by Michael's envoys as *Imperator-Basileus*.[1]

Leo III seems to have been aware of the danger which might emanate from the new master of Italy. He hoped, however, that the Donation of Constantine would keep the Franks at a safe distance, ready to come to Rome only when the Pope might need them. This may have been his secret wish when, in 806, he presented Charlemagne with a copy of the forgery.

In this respect, however, Leo III was not successful. The oriental conception of the Priest-King had also found its way into the West and reached the primitive courts of the new Christian princes. Several Merovingian kings had been hailed by prominent ecclesiastics as Priests and Kings. And, as their heir, Charlemagne visualised himself likewise, charged with the supreme control over all secular and spiritual matters and as the builder of the City of God, an ideal borrowed from St Augustine. Viewing with disfavour the new Roman spirit revealed in the document, Charlemagne went on ruling Church and State in his own way. In 813 he designated his son as co-Emperor, without the intervention of the Pope, but employing every Roman formality of designation, acclamation and coronation, the Frankish nobles taking the place of the Romans. The *Annals of Lorsch* defended Charlemagne's right to the imperial title, not because he was crowned by the Pope but on the ground that he was master of Rome and of all imperial residences in Italy, Gaul and Germany.

In spite of this, the curial notions of the forged Donation soon took root in western minds, because the Franks, unlike the Romans and the Byzantines for whom the coronation was of minor importance, laid emphasis on the coronation ceremony performed by the head of Christendom. Louis II (855–75), when rebuked by Basil I of Byzantium for his use of the imperial title, retorted that he had been crowned and anointed by the Pope, an argument which the Byzantines must have found ridiculous.

The western imperial conception soon underwent other changes.

---

[1] On Charlemagne's relations with Constantinople see also above: ch. III, pp. 90 and 96–7.

Charlemagne's successor Louis the Pious (814–40) already dropped his royal title and called himself *Imperator Augustus*, later adopting the title of *Imperator Francorum* and calling his realm the *Imperium Francorum*. This was the first step to the conception of a western Roman Empire, unknown to the Romans and their heirs. On the other hand, the intimate association of the Popes with the Emperors prepared the medieval assumption that through the instrumentality of Leo III imperial power had passed from the Greeks to the Germans.

In spite of the great respect manifested by the Franks for St Peter and his successors, Charlemagne regarded Rome only as the first see of his Empire, incorporating it into his imperial church. The *respublica Romanorum*, which had hitherto existed as an autonomous part of the Roman Empire under the political leadership of the Popes, be-came a part of the Carolingian Empire. It may well be asked whether it would not have been more profitable for the Papacy to content itself with the defeat of the Lombards and to continue recognising the nominal suzerainty of Constantinople over the *respublica Romanorum* without creating a rival and much nearer Emperor in the West.

In any event, the conclusion of peace between Charlemagne and Michael I restored the theoretical unity of the universal Roman Empire. The first consequence of it was that the Patriarch Nicephorus (806–15) was now allowed to send the customary synodical letter to Leo III. The Patriarch's praise of the Roman Church whose faith was spread over the whole world might have been inspired by the courageous defence of the Seventh Oecumenical Council by Hadrian I against objections voiced by Charlemagne and the Frankish Church, of which echoes had certainly reached Constantinople. Leo III, on his side, averted a new misunderstanding between Rome and Constantinople by his defence of the Nicene Creed as it stood, and his refusal to add the words *Filioque* to it, at the request of Charlemagne and the Franks.

The decadence of the Carolingian Empire, beginning under Louis I, saved Rome from the danger which had appeared under Charlemagne. But the rapid succession of Popes during the first part of the ninth century prevented Rome from taking full advantage of the situation. With Nicholas I (858–67), however, a new period opened in the evolution of the medieval Papacy and in the relationship between Rome and Constantinople. Like Gregory I, Nicholas did not propound any new theory on the relationship between the spiritual and the temporal power. But he gave expression in his letters to his predecessors' ideas on the divine origin of the Roman primacy, and of its Petrine and apostolic character. He did this so clearly, precisely and self-consciously, that his declarations, more than those of

Gelasius and Symmachus, helped Gregory VII and his successors to develop the medieval papal theory, so fraught with consequences, of the superiority of the spiritual over the temporal.

As the representative of God on earth, Nicholas claimed supreme jurisdiction over all bishops, in East and West, declaring himself the supreme judge over Patriarchs and bishops, hearing appeals from the whole world and giving decisions which were final. Nicholas also believed in the separation of the two powers ruling over mankind—the *sacerdotium* and the *imperium*—but he was more determined than any other Pope before him not to admit any trespassing by the *imperium* into the field strictly reserved for the *sacerdotium*. The protection of the Church and especially of the Roman See remained, however, in his eyes, the foremost duty of the *imperium*. When he stressed the submission of the princes to ecclesiastical judgement in morals, he was preparing, unwittingly, the papal thesis later expressed so openly by Boniface VIII, that the princes were subject to the Pope 'ratione peccati'.

Several circumstances helped Nicholas to try out his ideas successfully. The Carolingian Empire was disintegrating and there were signs that the era of national kingdoms was coming. The Emperor Louis II who was mainly responsible for Nicholas' election was poor and weak. The idea of universality implicit in the imperial dignity was replaced therefore by Nicholas' programme of Pseudo-Isidore's decretals, intended to protect the clergy against their metropolitans and exalting the papal power, which helped Nicholas considerably in his subjugation of the mighty rival of Ravenna and of the leader of the Frankish Church, Hincmar of Reims. His defence of the sanctity of Christian marriage against Lothair, although not altogether successful, impressed his pious contemporaries and enhanced his prestige.

Constantinople was unaware of this development. However, Rome's supremacy in the Church was still recognised there, as was demonstrated by the appeal to Rome of Bishop Gregory Asbestas and his associates against the sentence of deposition pronounced against them by the Patriarch Ignatius (847–58, 867–78). Both parties had sent delegates to the first Patriarch and Rome had some doubts concerning the legality of Ignatius' judgement. It was a welcome opportunity for Nicholas to act as judge over a Patriarch, but, before he could make a final decision, Ignatius had resigned because of difficulties with the new regime inaugurated by Bardas.

The latter terminated Theodora's regency and started to direct affairs for his nephew, Michael III (842–67). The troubles which forced this issue to a head were an aftermath of iconoclasm and were caused by the rivalry of two factions—the extremists and the moderates—so named from their views on the treatment of heretics.[1] Bardas and Asbestas were the political and religious leaders respectively of the moderates.

Although the election of Photius (858–67, 878–86) as successor to Ignatius was also sanctioned by the extremists, the latter soon revolted against the new Patriarch and proclaimed that Ignatius was still the legitimate holder of the see. Only when these new disturbances were quelled did Photius send to the Pope the synodical letter announcing his nomination. As the recent troubles had shown that some excesses on the part of the extremists were liable to give rise to the danger of an iconoclastic revival, Michael III decided to convoke a new anti-iconoclastic council in 861 and invited the Pope and the other Patriarchs to send their delegates to Constantinople.

Nicholas I saw in this move an opportunity to reassert his authority in the East. He refused to acknowledge Photius as the legitimate Patriarch before his legates should have examined on the spot the circumstances of Ignatius' dismissal and he reserved the final decision to himself. The papal decision was not welcomed in Constantinople. Ignatius' case was regarded as conclusively settled by a local synod and it was feared that a new investigation of the case would only give the intransigents a pretext for further intrigues. The legates—Bishops Radoald and Zacharias—soon perceived that the Pope's fears were ill-founded and, faced by the dilemma of cancelling the synod or of judging Ignatius in Constantinople in the Pope's name, they consented to judge the case on the spot. They saw clearly that the Pope's prestige would gain immensely in the East if a Patriarch were to be judged in the Pope's name in his city. In spite of Ignatius' declaration that he had not appealed to Rome, the legates investigated his case and Ignatius was suspended because of the irregularity of his appointment, without the procedure of a synod. The legates also settled Asbestas' appeal, and the synod voted a series of canons directed against abuses introduced by the extremists.

Nicholas seems to have had some misgivings about events in Constantinople. But he did not blame the legates, because the condemnation of a Patriarch corresponded with his ideas of supreme jurisdiction over the whole Church and because—as can be seen from the extract of the *acta* which has survived in Deusdedit's *Collectio canonum*—the Byzantine prelates had expressed a great reverence for Rome and a readiness to acknowledge the right of appeal to the Pope as the first Patriarch.

---

[1] For discussion of these ecclesiastical problems in their more specifically Byzantine historical framework see above: ch. IV *passim*.

One card was left to Nicholas, the right he had reserved to himself to confirm the verdict of his legates, and this he was determined to play for the recovery of western jurisdiction over Illyricum. But although the Emperor's envoy, who brought the *acta* of the synod with Michael's and Photius' letters, had informed his master of the Pope's desire, Nicholas waited in vain for a reply to his demand. Constantinople regarded Ignatius' case as definitely closed.

So it happened that Nicholas listened readily to the accusations of the monk Theognostus, one of the leaders of the extremists. This man had appeared in Rome pretending to be an envoy of Ignatius bringing his appeal to Nicholas' judgement, although in fact Ignatius did not appeal to the Pope. The refugees gave the Pope the impression that the opposition to the new Patriarch was formidable and their display of zeal for, and subservience to, the apostolic see seemed to guarantee that Ignatius' party would be better disposed towards the papal claims. In a Roman synod (August 863) Nicholas decided for Ignatius, denounced his legates, and announced to Constantinople the solemn deposition and excommunication of Photius and his followers.

The Emperor and the Patriarch were deeply offended by Nicholas' decision, provoked by the intrigues of intransigent refugees in Rome, as can be gathered from the Pope's answer to an imperial letter which he got in 865. The Emperor seems to have defended the right of the Byzantine Church to administer its own affairs without the intervention of the Pope. He regarded Ignatius' case as a purely disciplinary matter which had been regulated by a local synod, and considered that the Pope should have appreciated the concession granted to his legates of investigating the case and judging it in the Pope's name.

Nicholas' answer shows also how far the estrangement between Rome and Constantinople had progressed. The old arguments against the claim of Constantinople to the second place in the Church hierarchy are brought forward, and the Pope had to protest against the Emperor's description of Latin as a barbarian and Scythian language.

The Bulgarian affair added fuel to the flames. Boris of Bulgaria was forced by the Byzantines to abandon his intention of receiving baptism from the Franks and accepted Byzantine missionaries in 864. But, dissatisfied with Photius' refusal to give him a Patriarch, Boris turned to the Pope (866) and expelled the Greek clergy. In competition for Bulgaria the Latin and Greek missionaries must have attacked certain customs of each other's Churches. The Pope was alarmed by this, especially when his legates were refused admittance to Byzantine territory.

In Byzantium misgivings were also aroused by the Latin success in Bulgaria, and it was decided to convoke a Council of eastern Patriarchs in order to impress Boris by a condemnation of Latin usages and of the Pope. The Council met in 867, condemned among other usages the addition of the words *Filioque* to the Creed by the Franks, and accused Nicholas of disregarding the customs of the Church of Constantinople and of abusing his rights. Nicholas was deposed and it was hoped that Louis II would be persuaded by the recognition of his imperial title to carry out the sentence.

Nicholas I died before he learned of what had happened. His successor Hadrian II (867–72) seriously considered the adoption of a more benevolent attitude towards Photius, but before steps could be taken, a messenger arrived with the news that Michael III had been assassinated by his co-Emperor Basil I (867–86) and that the latter had restored Ignatius to the patriarchal throne. Knowing little about the rivalry between the extremists and the moderates in Byzantium and ignoring the fact that Basil I, after having assassinated Bardas and Michael III, had to look for support among the extremists, the Romans regarded the sudden change in Constantinople as a vindication of the oriental policy of Nicholas I.

Thus Hadrian stiffened his attitude towards Photius, who was once more condemned by a Roman synod. The sentence was to be made public before a synod in Constantinople. However, it was at this juncture that Basil's interests clashed with the Pope's orders. Having no desire to exasperate the party of the moderates, the Emperor wished the synod to pass a second judgement on Photius in order to rally the whole clergy to the cause of Ignatius. But the legates, especially the deacon Marinus, persistently maintained that the case had already been judged in Rome and that the bishops had simply to submit. Such obstinacy exasperated both the Emperor and Ignatius, and this was aggravated by the insistence of the legates that every member of the synod should sign a document proclaiming the Roman primacy in a manner too blunt for Byzantine susceptibilities. The synod (869–70) left Basil sadly disappointed. Most of the bishops remained loyal to Photius and Ignatius found himself unable to provide for the needs of his flock. He had to send Photian clerics to Bulgaria, which had again returned to the Byzantine obedience.

The intransigent policy towards Constantinople, inaugurated by Nicholas and followed by Hadrian, ended in complete disaster when Basil turned to the moderates, recalled Photius from exile and reinstated him in his previous function at the imperial university. Soon after there followed the reconciliation between Photius and Ignatius. The peace had to be sealed by a new council and to this Rome was asked to send legates.

Unfortunately, Ignatius died in 877 before the legates of John VIII (872–82) reached Constantinople and, according to a previous arrangement between the Emperor and the late Patriarch, Photius was again promoted to the patriarchal see. John VIII was informed by the legates and the Emperor of what had happened, but still believed that the previous condemnation of Photius was well founded. In his instruction to the legates and in his letters to the Emperor, to Photius and to the Council, John therefore declared his readiness to acknowledge Photius as the legitimate Patriarch on condition that he should apologise to the Council for his past conduct and renounce jurisdiction over Bulgaria.

The legates realised the hopelessness of the first condition, laid down in complete ignorance of the situation in Byzantium. It was easy for them to see that the opposition to Photius was insignificant and that he could not possibly comply with the Pope's wish without *ipso facto* approving the unjust attitude of the extremists towards himself. In order to save the Pope's prestige they were willing to drop John VIII's insistence on an apology and consented to modify the pontifical letters that were to be read before the Council. All reference to apology was suppressed, and other alterations were made, but the fact that Photius left most of the Pope's statements about the Roman primacy untouched proves that the alterations were not made in a spirit hostile to Rome, and that Photius was not opposed in principle to the idea. Because Basil I was in mourning for the death of his son Constantine, Photius was commissioned to take the Emperor's place as chairman at the debates. The Council solemnly confirmed the rehabilitation of Photius and of his clergy and declared the Council of 869–70 to be null and void. The Emperor signed the decrees in a session which was held in the palace.

In Rome John VIII had to face strong opposition, led by the former legate Marinus, against his new policy towards Photius. In a carefully worded letter John VIII accepted the reinstatement of Photius by the Council, but he was not willing to declare that Nicholas' attitude in this case had been wrong. The anti-Byzantine and pro-Nicolaite party in Rome was still strong and few there accepted the argument of Radoald, the papal legate to the synod of 861, condemned by Nicholas, that the great Pontiff should never have listened to Theognostus and should have accepted the verdict of the synod of 861. John VIII successfully defended his policy and was rewarded by Basil with military aid against the Arabs and with the surrender of Bulgaria to Roman jurisdiction, presumably on condition that the Greek clergy who had been working there should be allowed to stay.

If Rome was not finally successful in Bulgaria this was due to Boris himself, who profited by the competition between Rome and Constantinople to lay firm foundations for the first national Church in this part of Europe.

John VIII also tried vainly to save the rest of Illyricum for Rome by defending against East-Frankish bishops Hadrian's restoration of the metropolis of Sirmium to the Moravian missionary St Methodius. The grandiose plan to create on the confines of the Byzantine and Frankish-Latin worlds a new ecclesiastical structure with a Roman liturgy in the Slavic language, for which Hadrian II and John VIII fought so energetically, collapsed after the deaths of John and Methodius (884). The cultural inheritance of Moravia, planted there by Greek missionaries with Rome's approval, was saved by Boris' Bulgaria to be transmitted later to the Serbs, Russians and Rumanians. Only the Croatian part of the former Illyricum was definitely saved for Rome under John VIII and it is possible that the conclusion of peace between Rome and Constantinople in 879–80 contributed to this.

The Nicolaite party's strength in Rome was demonstrated when Marinus became Pope (882–4) after John's death. In spite of the reconciliation between the two sees, Marinus persisted in his hostile attitude to Photius and omitted to send the customary synodical letter to Constantinople. He died before a new conflict had developed and his successor Hadrian III (884–5) was a supporter of John's conciliatory policy. Stephen V (885–91), although a partisan of reconciliation with Photius, had to defend the memory of Marinus against a passionate attack from Constantinople. A small minority of the Byzantine clergy remained obdurate even after Photius' resignation (886) and refused to hold communion with Stephen, brother of the Emperor Leo VI (886–912), because he had been ordained deacon by Photius. This small group attempted under Stephen V and Formosus (891–6) to draw Rome to its side, but apparently in vain. The last vestiges of this small schism only vanished in about 898.

The consequences of this so-called Photian schism for the further relationship between Constantinople and Rome were not as disastrous as it is often believed. Although the Popes had often handled the affair badly, they gained considerably in the end, because of their interventions in Byzantine Church affairs. The right of appeal to Rome from the judgement of the Patriarch, which was practically sanctioned by the synod of 861, was made use of by the Emperor Leo VI in his struggle with the Patriarch Nicholas Mysticus (901–7, 912–25). The Patriarch refused to sanction the fourth marriage of the

Emperor, but Pope Sergius III (904–11) granted Leo the desired dispensation.

The unfortunate situation in Italy caused by the decadence of the Carolingian Empire and the growing influence of the Italian aristocracy both on the *patrimonium* of St Peter and in the elections to the Papacy, made of the Popes, however, willing instruments in the hand of the Emperor. This was illustrated in 920 when, in the presence of the legates of John X, a Byzantine synod summoned by the Emperor Romanus Lecapenus and Nicholas Mysticus condemned the practice of the fourth marriage. It was seen again in 933, when John XI sent legates to Constantinople at the request of Romanus I (920–44) to sanction the elevation of the Emperor's sixteen-year-old son Theophylact to the patriarchal throne.

The idea of apostolicity also triumphed at last in Constantinople in the ninth and tenth centuries when the legend of the foundation of the See of Byzantium by the apostle Andrew became popular. It is interesting to note that, although the legendary 'Acts of St Andrew' must have been known from the end of the third century on, and although the passage of the apostle through Thrace and Byzantium seems to have been mentioned in the primitive apocryphal Acts, no conclusion that the Bishopric of Byzantium was of apostolic origin is to be found anywhere before the beginning of the seventh century; and even then its apostolic character was derived from the fact that Constantinople became the heir of Ephesus (founded by St John) when jurisdiction over Asia was transferred from Ephesus to Constantinople (451). The fact that Byzantium was the imperial residence was regarded as a sufficient argument for Constantinople's claim to prominence in church organisation.

The stress which Rome had always laid on its apostolicity attracted the attention of some Byzantine clerics to the apocryphal Acts of Andrew and the tradition of the first Bishop Stachys, ordained by Andrew, which originally appeared in the 'Lists of Apostles and Disciples' and was further elaborated in Pseudo-Dorotheus' catalogue of Byzantine bishops. The idea of apostolicity seems to have been popular among the defenders of image-worship and was used by them against imperial interference in doctrinal matters. So it happened that in 861 Ignatius proudly declared in the presence of Roman legates that his see had been founded by St Andrew.

The spread of the idea of apostolicity in Byzantium coincides also with the origin of the doctrine that the Church is to be governed by five Patriarchs, a thesis which particularly predominates in the Acts of the Ignatian Council (869–70). From the Byzantine point of view this idea of a pentarchy—although not popular in Rome—marked an important step forward, because it stressed the principle that Church affairs should be regulated by the *sacerdotium* and therefore suggested a limitation of imperial intervention in ecclesiastical matters.

The sympathetic attitude towards Constantinople which left its traces in some Italian collections of canon law, which were willing to give Constantinople the second rank although Nicholas I had relegated it to the fourth, is easily explicable in the light of the situation in Italy in the tenth century. In face of the Arab menace to the whole of southern and central Italy, Byzantium was the only possible source of help. Basil I succeeded in reaffirming Byzantine authority throughout most of southern Italy, profiting by the decadence of the western imperial power. Constantinople did not take any official notice of the imperial titles of the last Carolingians and raised no objection to the presence in Italy of a puppet-king, Hugh of Provence, or Berengar, who could still be vaguely assumed to recognise Byzantine supremacy. Hugh was moreover a faithful ally and gave his daughter in marriage to Romanus II.

There was no reason for an open conflict between Rome and Constantinople prior to the restoration of the Western Empire by Otto I (962). That a Saxon king should come and take possession of Rome was an evident challenge to the rights of Byzantium. That the Popes should be willing or unwilling tools of the Roman aristocracy was a matter of indifference to Byzantines, but they drew the line at the nomination of Popes by so-called Western Emperors. It should be stressed that this direct intervention of the Ottonians and their successors in the elevation of Bishops of Rome contributed considerably to the growing estrangement between Constantinople and Rome.

Political complications aggravated the situation. Otto I, master of Rome and of the greater part of Italy, was anxious to annex the Byzantine part of the country. In 968, therefore, he sent Liutprand of Cremona to Constantinople to request for his son a Byzantine bride, who would bring the Byzantine provinces of Italy as her dowry. Nicephorus Phocas (963–9) received this offer with the greatest displeasure, and the chapters in which Liutprand describes the reaction of the Byzantines to this outrage illustrate better than anything else how wide the gap between East and West had grown. One detail mentioned by Liutprand[1] is particularly telling. Pope John XII, in a letter in which he recommended Otto I to Nicephorus, called the latter 'Emperor of the Greeks' and Otto 'august Emperor of the Romans'. The bearers of the letter were simply put into prison by the irate Byzantines and the Greek version of the transfer of

[1] *Legatio*, chs. 47–56.

imperial power to Constantinople by Constantine may be learned from Liutprand.

Fortunately John Tzimisces (969–76) ended this misunderstanding by consenting to the marriage of Theophano, most probably his niece, with Otto's son in 972. The Byzantines continued, however, to dislike the Popes selected by the German sovereigns. The restoration in 984 of the anti-Pope Boniface VII who had taken refuge in Constantinople was, most probably, achieved with the consent of Basil II (975–1025). The usurpation of Otto III's envoy to Constantinople, John Philagathus (997), in place of Gregory V seems to have been engineered by Crescentius. The imperial ambassador who came with John, however, is said to have participated in it, although he disliked John. The Byzantines kept their possessions and the death of Otto II in 983 eliminated the danger of an Ottonian conquest of southern Italy.

Although Otto III (983–1002) put an end to the rule of the pro-Byzantine Crescentius in Rome, and although he himself appointed a German and then a French Pope, and proclaimed a renovation of the Roman Empire, there was quite a chance that, had he lived longer, Constantinople and Rome would have been able to reach a new and enduring understanding. He was the son of a Byzantine princess, introduced Byzantine ceremonial at his court, and his second request for a Byzantine bride was received very favourably in Constantinople. The so-called Ottonian renaissance gave a foretaste of the advantages to western Europe had friendly contact with the cultured Byzantines been maintained.

Any such prospects were wrecked under Otto's successor Henry II (1002–24) who was more interested in German domestic affairs. His partner in Rome was Pope Benedict VIII (1012–24), of the family of Tusculum, known for its anti-Byzantine sentiments. There is no doubt that this Pope was in sympathy with the revolt organised by Melo with the help of Norman adventurers against the Byzantines, and this fact is the most probable explanation of vague rumours which were circulating among the Greeks that, under their Patriarch Sergius (1001–1019), there was a rupture between Constantinople and Rome.

This tension subsided under Conrad II (1024–39). The old Ottonian idea reappeared when Conrad turned again to Byzantium for a bride for his son the future Henry III. His embassy was better received than that of Liutprand, and although the negotiations were fruitless, the ambassador returned with many presents from the Emperor Romanus III Argyrus (1028–34).

In spite of the growing estrangement between the Byzantine East and the Latin West during the tenth and the first half of the eleventh centuries, there is no reliable indication that Rome and Constantinople were already in open schism. Through its possessions in southern Italy, Byzantium was still not far from the walls of Rome, although unwilling or unable to intervene in the city itself. Southern Italy was a bridge between East and West. The destruction of this bridge by the Norman conquest of Sicily and southern Italy in the eleventh century was therefore a major turning point in the relationship between East and West and contributed considerably to the rupture between Rome and Constantinople.

Especial responsibility for the growing estrangement attaches, however, to the far-reaching revolution in Western Church administration caused by the application of the Germanic notion of ownership to Church institutions. Unable to conceive the possibility of any property being vested in a society or organisation, the Germanic nations, after their christianisation, continued to regard churches as the property of their founders who claimed also the right of appointing the priests. This system of proprietary churches or 'Eigenkirchen' was also extended to abbeys and bishoprics, especially in France, and, combined with the feudal system, it helped the Ottos to make of the Church a 'Reichskirche' absolutely devoted to the King and Emperor.

The abuses which accompanied this practice—simony, investiture by laymen, marriage of priests—were responsible for the decadence of the Western Church in the tenth century and provoked a reform movement which began in Lorraine and Burgundy. This movement became particularly effective in Rome when Henry III (1039–56), who deposed three Popes, installed one of the reformers, his uncle, the Bishop of Toul, on the papal throne as Leo IX (1049–54). Leo chose his most intimate councillors—the monks Humbert and Hildebrand and the archdeacon Frederick of Lorraine—from amongst the most zealous reformers. These men saw the root of the abuses in the theocratic system of Priest-Kings with their 'Eigenkirchen'. They saw no other remedy than in strengthening the power of the Papacy and in giving the largest and fullest definition to the idea of the Roman primacy. The writings of Humbert already disclose the basis on which his friend Hildebrand was later to build, as Gregory VII, his hierocratic system of the superiority of the spiritual power over the temporal, and of the fullness of papal jurisdiction over the whole Church, defined so forcefully in his *Dictatus Papae*.

This reform successfully permeated the Western Church, but the fact that the leading reformers came from Lorraine and Burgundy had its effect on Rome's relations with Constantinople. The 'barbarian West', as the Byzantines called the region of Lombardy,

Germany and France, had little understanding of the exceptional position occupied in the Christian world by Byzantium and the East. The reformers were impervious to the distinction between theoretical primacy and practical autonomy to which the East had always adhered. Had the reform movement started in Italy it is possible that such a misunderstanding would not have developed, because the clergy of Rome and southern Italy were more prepared to appreciate the peculiar circumstances of the Byzantines.

One incident illustrates the reformers' feelings towards Byzantium. Raoul Glaber reports that they were scandalised by the news that the Byzantines had approached Pope John XIX (1024–33) with an offer to purchase their primacy. Although Raoul Glaber is not a reliable historian his report seems to have some basis of truth. He says that the Byzantines asked 'whether with the Roman Pontiff's consent the Church of Constantinople might be entitled, within its own limits, to be called, and treated as, universal, just as Rome was universal throughout the world'.[1] It is quite possible that the mighty Basil II (976–1025) made an attempt to terminate by a friendly agreement with the Pope the old quarrel with Rome about the oecumenical character of the Patriarchate of Constantinople in the East. If Glaber can be trusted this attempt was frustrated by the intervention of the reformers.

Such were the men who had to play the main role in the negotiations between Rome and Constantinople under Leo IX. The tragic drama seems to have started in southern Italy and was again complicated by the Normans. The Pope was determined to impose his reforms on the Latin communities under Byzantine rule, and as a firm believer in the authenticity of the Donation of Constantine, he extended his claims over the whole of Italy, also acting here as the Emperor Henry's ally. The reforming decrees—some of them directed against certain Greek usages adopted in Italy—were voted at an important synod at Siponto in 1050. After this date, the Latin clergy intensified their activity throughout southern Italy, much to the consternation of the Greeks. The Pope's friendly attitude at this time towards the Normans who had seized part of Byzantine Apulia, the occupation of Benevento by Leo IX (1051) and the appointment of an Archbishop of Sicily, though that island still ranked as Byzantine territory and was in the hands of the Arabs, afforded ground for apprehension.

The Patriarch Michael Cerularius (1043–58) was an ambitious and proud man. A former claimant to the imperial throne, he initiated an offensive against the Latins in reprisal for Latin activity in southern

[1] Raoul (Radulphus) Glaber, *Historiae sui temporis*, IV, i (*MGH, Script.* VII, p. 66).

Italy. All Latin establishments in Constantinople were told to adopt the Greek rite and rule and, as a warning to the Greeks in Apulia against the threatening danger, the Patriarch asked Leo, the Archbishop of Ochrida, to raise the alarm among the Greek and Latin clergy in Italy. Leo did so and sent to the Latin Bishop of Trani, a loyal supporter of the Byzantines, his notorious letter directing his main criticism against the use of unleavened bread in the liturgy and against other Latin customs, without however mentioning the *Filioque*.

The Patriarch's temper was not improved when he heard that the Emperor Constantine IX Monomachus (1042–54) intended to appoint as the commander-in-chief and governor of Apulia a Latin, Argyrus, whom he especially disliked. He strove to the utmost to prevent this appointment, but without success, and Argyrus, governor of Byzantine Apulia (1051), opened negotiations with the Pope for concerted action against the Normans. Leo IX, anxious to put a stop to the Norman devastations of papal territory, welcomed the offer. However, despite the Pope's blessing, Argyrus was defeated and the papal troops routed in June 1053, and the Pope was held prisoner by the Normans at Benevento for a year.

The circular letter of the Archbishop of Ochrida was sent off at a very inopportune moment, for it had stirred public animosity against the Latins. Cardinal Humbert prepared a lengthy refutation of Leo's attack, and composed the letter which still figures in the papal correspondence and is believed to have let loose the storm that sundered the two Churches. This opinion, however, needs correction. For before the letter had been dispatched from Benevento, Leo IX received another message from the Emperor. Alarmed by the Normans' progress the Emperor now invited the Pope to open fresh negotiations, and forwarded a short but friendly letter from the Patriarch. It seems then that a shorter script couched in more soothing terms was substituted for the original reply, though it was hardly likely to satisfy the Patriarch, since the persistent Humbert had again managed to slip in a summary of all that he had said in the longer letter. This cast unwarranted doubts on the legitimacy of the Patriarch's consecration and forbade him to use the title of Oecumenical Patriarch, as usurping the rights of the sees of Alexandria and Antioch which should precede those of Constantinople, and showing disrespect toward the See of Rome which is the mother of all sees.

This letter and another destined for the Emperor were to be delivered by their real author, Humbert, accompanied by his friend Frederick and the Bishop of Amalfi. A man less disposed to understand the Greek mentality—although he knew their language reasonably well—could hardly be imagined. The Patriarch expected a different missive in response to his letter and suspected an intrigue by his enemy Argyrus with whom the legates had had an interview before sailing for Constantinople. Offended by the arrogant behaviour of Humbert, Cerularius refused to receive the legates, declaring that they were envoys of Argyrus. Humbert then published as a pamphlet against the Patriarch the first and longer letter, which had remained undelivered. This was composed in a spirit which could only offend the Byzantines profoundly.

These letters and other pamphlets by Humbert first revealed to the East the claims of the western reformers. If the development of Byzantine ideas concerning the Papacy and its position in the Church is borne in mind, then it is easy to appreciate how hopelessly the dialectic of the western reformers seemed to be at variance with the old traditions known to the Byzantines.

The legates were anything but tactful. They evidently felt sure that they would find it easy, with the Emperor's assistance, to overthrow the Patriarch. In this they were disappointed, for the clergy rallied like one man to Cerularius out of exasperation at the legates' assumption of the superiority of the Pope and of western customs. The famous bull excommunicating the Patriarch, which the overzealous Cardinal placed on the altar in St Sophia, was of questionable validity since the Pope who had delegated Humbert was already dead. But it shows better than any document how the Western Church had recently developed on its own lines under the influence of the reformers, and how little understanding the latter had of the customs and usages of the Eastern Church. The contents of the bull shocked profoundly not only the Patriarch but also the Emperor. In view of the agitation which the news had provoked among the people, the Emperor was obliged, after a last attempt at mediation, to convoke the permanent synod. This condemned the bull and its author and a copy of the document was solemnly burned. At another meeting of the synod an official edict was composed condemning the action of the legates who were designated as envoys of Argyrus, not of the Pope.

Thus the edict did not attack Rome and left the door open for new negotiations. The letters in which Cerularius later described these events to Peter of Antioch reveal, however, the profundity of the rift between Constantinople and Rome and the degree to which Cerularius was personally responsible. The Patriarch of Antioch, anxious to preserve the unity of the Church, tried in vain to calm Cerularius. Although Peter of Antioch had sent his synodical letter to the Pope before the rupture of 1054, this correspondence shows how far the

East had drifted from the West and how low the prestige of the Pope had fallen during the tenth and eleventh centuries in the eyes of the Easterners. The Patriarch was still a firm believer in the pentarchy (the rule of the Church by the five great Patriarchs), but he regarded the Patriarch of Rome as the equal of the other four. This serves to explain how strange the theses of the reformers as interpreted by themselves, on the plenitude of the Roman primacy in all matters, appeared to the Easterners.

Despite all that had happened, the possibility of a rapprochement still remained as long as Constantinople and Rome were bound by an identity of political interests in southern Italy. Unfortunately, even this bond became loose under Leo's successors. Victor II (1055–7) is said to have sent a legate in 1055/6 to the Empress Theodora. The result of this embassy must have been unsatisfactory because the Pope started negotiations with the Normans. His successor, Stephen IX (1057–8), reverted to Leo's policy. His legates were on their way to Constantinople when they learned of Stephen's death. Nicholas II (1059–61) reversed the papal policy and at the Synod of Melfi he concluded an alliance with the Normans sanctioning their conquests.

During the contest for the papal throne between the reformer Alexander II (1061–73) and Honorius II (1061–72), the candidate of the German court and local nobility, the Emperor Constantine X Ducas (1059–67) made a last effort to conclude an anti-Norman alliance with the German court and Honorius II. The reformers, however, succeeded in winning over the German court to their candidate. But in spite of this, Honorius did not abandon all hope. In 1072 he is said to have sent Peter, Bishop of Anagni, to Byzantium in order to congratulate the new Emperor Michael VII Ducas (1071–8), but the opposition of Michael Psellus and the Patriarch John Xiphilinus (1064–75) is believed to have ended any hope of a rapprochement.

Peter Damian composed, with Alexander's encouragement, a treatise on Greek errors which he dedicated to a Patriarch who had asked for an explanation of the Latin position, and whose name cannot be established with certainty. The Patriarch Leichudes (1059–63) could hardly have made such a démarche, because until 1064 the Emperor Constantine Ducas was in touch with the anti-Pope Honorius II.

The initiative of Michael VII at the beginning of the reign of Gregory VII (1073–85) appeared more hopeful. After the disaster of Manzikert (1071) the Empire was in danger of being completely swallowed up by the Seljuq Turks who had overrun most of Asia Minor. A letter which the Pope sent to Constantinople in 1073 shows that the Emperor had approached Gregory with a request for military help and giving hope for reunion. The Pope's answer was cordial and Gregory expressed to Henry IV and others his satisfaction at this new approach. He cherished the idea of collecting an army to help the Christians of Constantinople and of accompanying it himself. Gregory's appeal to the western princes was, however, not answered and soon the violent conflict with the young Henry IV, who opposed the new papal political ideology, threw the Pope completely into the arms of the Normans. He remained faithful to Michael VII, however, and excommunicated Nicephorus III Botaneiates (1078–81) who had deposed Michael. Gregory even blessed the adventurous invasion of Greece by Robert Guiscard, when the astute Norman produced an impostor pretending to be Michael VII.

It is highly doubtful whether Gregory would have been any more successful than Leo IX. A perusal of his *Dictatus Papae* shows the enormous gulf in political and ecclesiastical ideologies which then separated Constantinople from Rome. Its terms would have been unacceptable to the Byzantines: for example, the Pope's pretension to the right to depose emperors and to dispense subjects from allegiance to bad rulers, or his claim to wear imperial insignia and that all rulers should salute him by kissing his feet. In fact, Gregory opened the archives to his collaborators in order to find better documentary support for his conception of papal primacy. So it came about that the correspondence of Nicholas I was rediscovered and became the basis of the new canon law. The discovery of the Ignatian council of 869–70 and its promotion to the rank of an Oecumenical council by the reformers contributed more than anything else to the rise of the Photian legend. This grew steadily during the middle ages, adding fresh fuel to the ardent polemics and placing new obstacles in the way of a reconciliation.

In spite of that, there is no doubt that Gregory VII was sincere in his desire for union and, although he welcomed the introduction of the Latin rite into the Greek territory conquered by the Normans, there is no indication that he was hostile to the Greek rite. In his desire for uniformity of ritual in the West, however, he forbade the use of Slavonic as a liturgical language in Bohemia. By this action he unwittingly cut off the route by which Latin theological works in Slavonic and the cult of western saints were penetrating into Kievan Russia from the West.

The letter which the Metropolitan of Kiev, John II (1080–9), who was a Greek by birth, had sent to the anti-Pope Clement III shows that all hope of an understanding between Constantinople and Rome had not yet been abandoned. The Metropolitan shows a very friendly attitude towards Rome, although deploring the introduction of bad customs into the Western Church. He advises Clement to communicate with the Patriarch of Constantinople and to work for the eradication of those 'abuses'. Clement III was already in touch with Constantinople when he received this letter. The Emperor Alexius I Comnenus (1081–1118) was forced to turn towards Gregory's enemy Henry IV with whom he had concluded an alliance in about 1081 against the Normans, and it seems that this gave Gregory VII the opportunity to pronounce another excommunication of a Byzantine Emperor.

Soon after securing his election, despite the opposition of the anti-Pope, Urban II (1088–99) sent legates to Constantinople. The details of these negotiations may be learned from the *acta* of a synod held in Constantinople in 1089. The Emperor, realising the usefulness of an alliance with the rightful Pope supported by the Normans, disclosed that Urban II had expressed his readiness to re-establish harmonious relations between Constantinople and Rome and had complained that his name had been uncanonically removed from the diptychs of Constantinople. The prelates replied that no official document attested a break with Rome or the suppression of the Pope's name in the diptychs. But, in view of the important differences between the two Churches, they considered it advisable to eliminate these before restoring the Pope's name in the diptychs. The Patriarch Nicholas III (1084–1111) therefore asked the Pope to send his profession of faith to Constantinople on the understanding that if it were found satisfactory, his name would be restored in the diptychs. Eighteen months after that a synod would be convoked in Constantinople, to which the Pope would be invited, and this would discuss and eliminate the difficulties existing between the two Churches.

In spite of some indications that the Pope was inclined to accept this compromise, no evidence is available to indicate that he sent his letter to the Patriarch and that his name was put back into the diptychs. The Patriarch was rather cautious and sent Basil, the expelled Greek Metropolitan of Reggio, who had served as his envoy to Clement III, to Rome to report on Urban's real intentions. Basil had previously met Urban at a synod in Melfi, which probably also revoked Alexius' excommunication, and his report to the Patriarch discloses the profound bitterness of the Greek clergy who were gradually being replaced in Italy by Latin bishops. Nicholas III also wrote to his colleague in Jerusalem, Symeon II, criticising the Pope's pretensions to the primacy and the use of unleavened bread at Mass by the Latins.

In spite of this, it seems that the negotiations made progress and that good relations between Constantinople and Rome were restored. It was again an Archbishop of Ochrida—Theophylact—who was chosen to give the official point of view on the controversial matters. In his treatise Theophylact declared that the differences in rite and in custom were not important and should not lead to schism. He was not alarmed by the papal claims to primacy and he also found an explanation for the most important point, the addition of the words *Filioque*, in the poverty of the Latin language in theological terminology. Other eastern theologians, especially Symeon II of Jerusalem, also showed remarkable restraint in discussing the differences.

Alexius also tried to exploit his good relations with the Pope for political ends. He had been able to stop the advance of the Seljuqs and also to avert the danger threatening the western boundary of his Empire, but he needed more western recruits for his wars with the Turks. He must have treated with the Pope on this matter, because Anna Comnena says that her father expected soldiers from Rome in 1091. Alexius revealed his plan in full in 1095 at the synod held by the Pope in Piacenza. There his envoys seem to have appealed to the sense of Christian duty of the Westerners for help for the Christians in the East in their fight against the infidel. It can be surmised that they also mentioned the Holy Places in Jerusalem, knowing the veneration which the Westerners had for them.

It seems that the Pope and the bishops were impressed by the address of the Greeks and that the initiative taken by the Pope a few months afterwards at Clermont was inspired in great part by Alexius' suggestions. It is thus most probable that Urban, in whose mind the reunion of the Churches was intimately connected with the idea of the crusade, had reached an agreement with Alexius that the union would be definitely concluded when the brotherly collaboration of western and eastern Christians had been publicly demonstrated on the battle-field against the infidels. Included in this agreement was the Emperor's requirement that all cities conquered by the crusaders which had previously belonged to the Empire would be given back to Alexius. The conclusion of special treaties required by Alexius of some leaders of the crusade indicates some previous convention between the Emperor and the Pope. Bishop Adhemar of Puy, who was to represent the Pope on the expeditions, was entrusted with supervising the fulfilment of all agreements.

Alexius took every precaution to prevent incidents between the crusaders and the Greeks, and generally took good care to provision the armies, while the crusaders on their side faithfully respected their commitments for over a year and a half. In this spirit, they reinstated the Greek Patriarch in Antioch when that city had been finally secured. The respect manifested by Adhemar towards the Patriarch of Jerusalem, Symeon II, also indicates that he acted in accord with a previous understanding between the Pope and the Emperor that there should be only one united Church.

Another indication in this respect is the convocation of a synod at Bari in 1098 where the question of reunion with the Greeks was to be discussed and where it was decided to continue the discussion in Rome. All this shows that Urban thought, at that time, that he was near the realisation of his aim and started preparations for the final act.

How then did it come about that the union was not realised and that, on the contrary, the crusade contributed to a greater estrangement between Rome and Constantinople? The main reason lies in the selfish behaviour of Bohemond who decided to build up Antioch as an independent domain for his family, thus breaking the agreement which the crusaders had made with Alexius. The latter regarded the possession of this city as so important that, from that time on, he directed all his forces to reconquering Antioch from the usurper. The second reason was the death of Adhemar which deprived the crusaders of their leader. The third was the premature death of the Pope, which prevented the appointment of another representative instead of Adhemar. Before his death the Pope saw clearly that his great hope was collapsing, and this may explain why, at the Synod of Rome in 1099, the question of union was not even mentioned.

Urban's plan was thus wrecked by the selfishness of a Norman adventurer. Bohemond was moreover the pioneer of the idea that the best way to assure the security of the crusaders and of the new Latin states in Syria and Palestine was to bring Constantinople under Latin rule. He almost won the approval of Paschal II (1099–1118), but his army, recruited in the West, got no further than Dyrrachium where it was defeated by Alexius. But the idea of the conquest of Constantinople had been launched and was nourished by accusations of bad faith against the Greeks.

Alexius, however, did not lose all hope. The crusaders had helped him to combat the Turkish danger and, feeling secure in the East, he turned his eyes towards the West, trying to exploit the conflict between the Papacy and the German Emperors. He approached Paschal II, humiliated by being forced to crown Henry V Emperor in 1111, with an offer of union of the Churches, if the Pope would acknowledge him as Roman Emperor. The Pope welcomed the idea, but made it clear that Alexius' imperial plan could be discussed only when the union had been accomplished. His successor Calixtus II

(1119–24), who needed help against Henry V, approached the Emperor John (1118–43) and received a favourable reply in 1124. Honorius II (1124–30) repeated his predecessor's gesture. John was willing, but stated his price clearly: recognition as the only Roman Emperor.

The best chance of realising these hopes arose under Manuel Comnenus (1143–80). He tried to reduce the differences between Latins and Greeks by adopting many western customs, by appointing Latins to important posts and by cultivating good relations with the Latin states in the East. He approached Alexander III (1159–81) when the latter was struggling with Frederick Barbarossa, and got a friendly answer. But when he presented a concrete plan for the realisation of his imperial idea, the Pope remained cold. The Papacy had become a great power aiming, in the spirit of the Gregorian conception of the supremacy of the spiritual over the temporal, at dominating both Eastern and Western Empires and not at establishing the supremacy of the Eastern, which was the logical aim of the Comneni.

On the other hand, any project of reunion encountered passionate opposition among the Byzantine clergy. Many of them rejected the Papal primacy in general, and the others who were ready to accept it objected to its absolutist nature as defined by the Latins. Nicetas of Nicomedia expressed this Greek point of view best in his disputation with Bishop Anselm of Havelberg, in Constantinople (1136).[1] Moreover, the Greek clergy criticised bitterly the political power over princes which the Popes claimed.

The possibilities which the plans of the Comneni seemed to open were definitively buried in 1182 when a popular revolution swept away the regency of Manuel's widow, replacing his young son Alexius II by Andronicus I Comnenus (1183–5), and the Latins resident in Constantinople were massacred by the irate populace. This bloody incident also revealed the true feeling of the Greeks towards the Latins and the unpopularity of the pro-western policy of the deceased Emperor.

This seemed to confirm the thesis launched by Bohemond[2] that the conquest of Constantinople was the only solution left. The attempt of the Norman King William II of Sicily in 1185 to avenge the massacre was not successful. Frederick Barbarossa was about to attack Constantinople when he got into difficulties with the Greeks during the Third Crusade (1189–90). The Bulgarians and Serbians who had revolted against Byzantium offered Frederick their troops for the enterprise, but the danger was averted by negotiations. His

---

[1] L. d'Achery, *Spicilegium sive collectio veterum aliquot scriptorum* (3rd ed., Paris, 1723), I, pp. 161 f.

[2] Cf. Anna Comnena, *Alexiad*, XI, 12 (ed. Reifferscheid, II, p. 142).

son, Henry VI, heir to the Normans in Sicily, might have become master of Byzantium if a premature death (1197) had not put an unexpected end to his grandiose schemes. The Papacy, alarmed by such a prospect, came to Byzantium's help by threatening to excommunicate the Emperor if he attacked a Christian nation.

The idea of conquest was so well embedded in western minds that not even the threats of excommunication launched by the greatest medieval Pope, Innocent III (1198–1216), could prevent its realisation in 1204 by the Fourth Crusade at the instigation of Venetian merchants and some feudal lords. However, the presence of a Latin Emperor in Constantinople and the division of the Byzantine Empire was less dangerous to the Papacy than would have been its conquest by Barbarossa or Henry VI. Thus Innocent III quickly reconciled himself to the new situation, hoping that a union of the Churches would now be an easy task.

In this respect, however, Innocent, who called himself 'the true vicar of Christ, successor of Peter, the anointed of the Lord, placed between God and man, standing under God, but above man, who has the right to judge anybody, but can be judged by nobody', was mistaken. Although he issued instructions that the Greek rite should be tolerated and the Greek prelates be won over by moderation, his first envoy Cardinal Benedict only succeeded in persuading a minority of the Greek clergy to promise obedience to the Pope. Even this success, however, was minimised by the harsh treatment of the Greeks by Cardinal Pelagius who had tried vainly to win over to union the Emperor and the Patriarch of Nicaea. The bitter words in which Nicetas Choniates described the horrible scenes enacted by the Latins in the conquered city and the desecration of Greek sanctuaries by the rough soldiery, explain more than anything why the cleft between Latins and Greeks became ever wider, and why, in spite of their co-existence in the same regions for several generations, the Greeks could never forget what had happened in their country in 1204.

In one respect Innocent thought that he had won a considerable victory. The prestige of the Papacy was so high in his time that the rulers of the newly created states of Bulgaria and Serbia, Kalojan and Stephen II Nemanja, requested him to send them royal crowns. Innocent could congratulate himself that now the greater part of the former Illyricum was again under Rome's direct jurisdiction.

Bulgaria might have become an important ally of the Latin Emperor against the Greeks. But Baldwin I offended the national consciousness of the Bulgarians by summoning their king to become his vassal. Baldwin's army was routed in battle and he died in Bulgarian captivity. The Latins understood too little the mentality of the

new uniates and so the Bulgarian Tsar John Asen II (1218–41),
offended by the refusal of the Latin clergy to consent to the marriage
of his daughter with the young Latin Emperor, although he was in
communion with Rome, made an alliance with Nicaea and bled the
Latin Empire to death. The Bulgarians returned to the Orthodox
Church and Nicaea consented to the restoration of a Bulgarian Patriarchate. Almost at the same time, Nicaea created an autonomous
Serbian Archbishopric for Sava, King Stephen's brother. It was useless for Stephen to explain to Rome that he wanted to be on friendly
terms with both Rome and the Greeks; he was regarded as an
apostate. Latin gains in the former Illyricum were thus of short
duration.

The negotiations of Innocent IV (1243–54) with John III Vatatzes
(1222–54) seemed more promising. The Emperor was willing to
induce his churchmen to accept the papal primacy and to reinstate
the Pope's name in the diptychs on condition that the Pope should
work for the restitution of Constantinople to the Greeks. Natural
distrust, however, hampered the conclusion of negotiations, and the
manner in which the Pope demanded the recognition of his supremacy
seemed too humiliating to the Greek clergy.

Only when Michael Palaeologus (1259–82) had reconquered Constantinople in 1261 did the cause of union make some real progress.
The Emperor, anxious to assure his possession of the city, started negotiations with the Papacy, and at last, under Gregory X (1271–6), a
Council met at Lyons in 1274 and proclaimed a union rather hastily,
without long theological discussions, because both sides remembered
the disastrous effects of such discussions in the past. Although concluded for political reasons, the union had some chance of enduring,
because its staunch defenders were the Patriarch John Beccus and his
supporters. Unfortunately, the memories of the Latin domination
were still too fresh in Greek minds and the Emperor compromised the
union by his harshness towards its adversaries. Moreover, the in-
temperate demands of Gregory's successors were hurtful to Greek
national feelings. The reaction against Palaeologus' religious policy
was so violent that after his death he was even denied decent burial.
His successor Andronicus II (1282–1328), seeking to curry favour with
his subjects, became the leader of the anti-Latin movement and was
excommunicated in 1307 by Clement V.

The Council of Lyons also ended any possibility of winning back
the Serbians and the Bulgarians to Rome. Because the Serbian king
Stephen Uroš and the Bulgarian Tsar Constantine Tich were giving
support to Charles of Anjou, Michael Palaeologus' most dangerous
enemy, the astute Emperor proposed the suppression of the Patri-

archate of Bulgaria and of the autonomous Archbishopric of Serbia on the grounds that both were created without the Pope's consent. The Latins were completely deceived by this move and the Popes lost all possibility of a new approach to Serbia and Bulgaria.

The growing Turkish danger, however, forced Andronicus II to enter into new negotiations with Rome in 1323, and these continued intermittently throughout the fourteenth century. The Popes insisted that failing a union with Rome the Greeks would obtain no military aid from the West. John V Palaeologus (1341–76) submitted in 1369, but his gesture was not followed by his subjects.

At the end of the century the danger grew to such an extent that Boniface IX ordered the preaching of a new crusade to help the Greeks without waiting for the union. But enthusiasm for such an enterprise had long ago died away in the West. The Emperor Manuel II Palaeologus (1391–1425) was bitterly disappointed when a personal plea to the different courts in the West only elicited vain promises.

In the meantime, important changes were taking place in the mentality of the Latins and Greeks. The West had discovered, at last, the treasures of the Greek classical age, and scholars, full of admiration for the glorious past of Greece, started to spread a knowledge of the Greek language and literature in western universities and schools. The Byzantines also became acquainted with the works of great Latin Fathers—Augustine, Anselm and Thomas Aquinas. The translation of St Thomas' *Summa Contra Gentiles* by Demetrius Cydones was particularly well received in Constantinople. And there were also the works of John Beccus and his unionists, favourable to the Latins. All this seemed to presage a new approach to a better understanding.

In this atmosphere the last Council for Union, that of Ferrara–Florence (1438–9) was convened in the presence of the Emperor John VIII Palaeologus.[1] The leading theologians of both sides then met for the first time in detailed and dignified discussions of the main issues: primacy, the procession of the Holy Ghost, the use of unleavened bread in the Sacrament, and purgatory. The Emperor still acted in the spirit of Christian Hellenism, while Pope Eugenius IV (1431–47) contented himself with a vague definition of his primacy, and the decree of union was signed by both sides.

But all was in vain. Although only one of the prominent Greek theologians—Mark of Ephesus—refused to sign the decree, most of the others recanted on their return to Constantinople, in face of the hostility of the great majority of the clergy. The union could only be

---

[1] For a full discussion of this Council see J. Gill, *The Council of Florence* (Cambridge, 1959).

proclaimed on Greek territory still in Latin hands and only in December 1452 in Constantinople itself. Even then, only a small minority of the clergy adhered to it. Neither the Turkish menace nor the Emperor's demands and threats could induce the masses to accept union with the Latins. The capture of Constantinople by the Turks (29 May 1453) was described by the Patriarch Gennadius II in 1454 as a punishment for the betrayal of the ancestral faith at Florence.

The only enduring result of the Council was the impulse given by the meeting of the Latins with prominent Greek scholars—Plethon, Scholarius, Bessarion and others—to the spread of the cultural renaissance over the whole West.

It is not surprising that this last attempt at reunion failed. The gulf had widened too much since the tenth and eleventh centuries: it was then that the real estrangement between Constantinople and Rome began.

CHAPTER XI

THE EMPIRE AND ITS NORTHERN NEIGHBOURS, 565–1018

The Empire's relations with the countries of the north during the four and a half centuries between the death of Justinian I and the conquest of the First Bulgarian Empire by Basil II are marked by three main characteristics. In the military annals of Byzantium this was an heroic age, during which, with few intermissions, the Empire fought to defend its frontiers—and sometimes its very life—against the ever-recurring thrust of the northern invader, of Avar and Slav, of Bulgar and Magyar, of Russian and Pecheneg.[1] Secondly, in these centuries was forged, in reply to the northern challenge, by steadfast faith and lucid thinking, by careful study and observation, by trial and error, that essential weapon of East Roman policy —the imperial diplomacy which remains one of Byzantium's lasting contributions to the history of Europe. Finally, it was in this period that the Byzantine statesmen became fully aware of the importance of the North in the Empire's system of security; and a study of the relevant sources—accounts of military missions, ambassadors' reports, handbooks of military strategy, confidential guides to foreign policy, academic histories and monastic chronicles—reveals their growing preoccupation with the area that lay immediately beyond the northern border of the Empire. This, broadly speaking, was the area limited in the west by the Hungarian plain and in the east by the Caspian Sea; it stretched over the Carpathian Mountains, the South Russian steppe, and the lowlands to the north of the Caucasus, and was bounded in the north by a semi-circle extending over the lower course of the great Russian rivers—the Dniester, the Dnieper and the Don—and whose tips came to rest on the middle Danube in the west and on the lower Volga in the east. It was from the periphery of this semi-circle that issued the never-ending flow of tribes and nations which, in war and in peace, were irresistibly drawn into the orbit of Byzantium, whose attacks and invasions fill the military records of the Empire, and whose fears, ambitions and lust for conquest taxed so severely the ingenuity of the statesmen in Constantinople. And within this semi-circle, the encounter of Byzantium with its northern neighbours was particularly felt in three sectors which served as the pivots of the Empire's policy in the north: the Danube, the Crimea and the Caucasus.

[1] The 'Patzinaks' of the Greek sources.

The importance of these three sectors had become fully apparent during the reign of Justinian; it was this Emperor above all who developed and bequeathed to his successors a conception of diplomacy as an intricate science and a fine art, in which military pressure, political intelligence, economic cajolery and religious propaganda were fused into a powerful weapon of defensive imperialism. A brief survey of the Empire's position along its northern frontier in the closing years of his reign is thus a fitting introduction to the policy of his successors.

The significance of the Caucasian sector for the Empire's security was a matter of political geography: for at the extremities of this great isthmus separating the Black Sea from the Caspian the Graeco-Roman civilisation of the Mediterranean met and clashed with the westward expansion of Asian cultures: in the north, with the nomads of Eurasia, moving to the Black Sea and the Danube; in the south, with the occupiers of the Iranian plateau, pushing towards Asia Minor and the Bosphorus. Both these westward movements spelled constant danger to Byzantium; and the effort of the imperial diplomacy in this sector was directed as much towards achieving a favourable balance of power in the lowlands north of the Caucasus, as to creating a bulwark against possible attacks of Persians and Arabs through Asia Minor towards Constantinople itself. The basic aim of Byzantine policy in this sector was always the same: to build up a chain of allied, or vassal, states from the lower Volga and the Sea of Azov to Lake Van in Armenia. Their peoples could render the Empire services consonant with their geographical position and military resources: on the eastern coast of the Black Sea, the Zikhi and the Abasgians could help the Byzantine fleet to operate in Caucasian waters and thus hold the left sector of the Empire's north-eastern front; further south, along the coast, the Lazi and the Tzani guarded the approaches to the northern coast of Asia Minor; the Georgians in the central Caucasus and the Alans further north on the Terek stood guard over the Pass of Darial and could prevent the Eurasian nomads from striking south at Byzantine Asia Minor. All these Caucasian tribes were successfully wooed by the diplomacy of Justinian; the first four were converted to Christianity in the sixth century by Byzantine missionaries, and the new ecclesiastical organisation set up in their lands was to prove, on the whole, an effective means of keeping them under the political influence of East Rome. And the roads and fortresses which the Byzantines built in these countries were the material counterpart of the flattering though less tangible links which their rulers were induced to form with the imperial court of Constantinople. The tribes which inhabited the steppe land between the lower Volga and the Sea of Azov, at the northern extremity of this sector, could, if they were friendly and sufficiently powerful, be counted upon to guard the eastern end of the European 'steppe corridor' and generally to help preserve the balance of power along the whole length of the Empire's northern front. Here too, by his alliance with the Sabiri on the western shores of the Caspian and with the Utigurs on the eastern coast of the Sea of Azov, Justinian pointed the way to his successors.

In the central segment of the semi-circle that marked in the sixth century the effective limit of Byzantium's sphere of interest in the north, half-way between its tips which rested on the middle Danube and on the lower Volga, lay the second pivot of the Empire's northern front. During the whole period covered by this chapter Byzantine possessions and dependencies in the Crimea—above all the city of Cherson (the ancient Χερσόνησος)—acted as the northern outpost of the Empire's diplomacy in the steppe; their importance was partly economic, for the Crimea provided Byzantium with the raw materials of the hinterland—fish from the rivers of South Russia, salt from the Azov region, furs and honey from the forests further north—and sold to the barbarians the manufactured articles of Byzantine industry. Politically, Cherson and its neighbouring region, subject or vassal of the Empire during the greater part of the period under review, was an invaluable observation post, a watch-tower planted on the very fringe of that barbarian world of South Russia which Byzantine diplomacy was ever anxious to influence and control. It was from the Crimea that Justinian's government could follow the moves of the Utigurs and the Kutrigurs, encamped on both sides of the Sea of Azov, and, by a timely bribe or by stirring up internal strife among them, divert their attacks from the Balkans. It was from Byzantine Crimea that his successors were able to pursue towards the northern barbarians the traditional Roman policy of 'divide and rule', or at least, when this proved impracticable, 'weaken and watch'. And, true again to the time-honoured methods of Roman diplomacy, Byzantium had secured in the mountains of southern Crimea, as a counterbalance to its enemies in the steppe, a useful satellite, half vassal and half ally, the Crimean Goths. The security of the Empire's Balkan provinces, as later events were so frequently to confirm, depended as much upon the watchfulness of its agents in the Crimea as upon the influence it wielded in the north Caucasian area.

The third sector of the Empire's northern front was on the lower and middle Danube; and this section of the *limes Romanus* was, in the military sense, much more of a 'front' than the Crimea or the northern Caucasus. This too was a matter of geography: for the lower

Danube lay near the terminus of the 'steppe corridor', that immemorial highway taken by nomadic invaders from Asia; and for many of them, who had succeeded in avoiding the entanglements and traps laid for them by the Byzantine diplomats in the Caucasian and Crimean sectors, the Danube proved no insuperable obstacle, and the road into the Balkans lay open. The contrast in the strategic position of Constantinople, admirably protected from attack by sea, but open to a chance invasion by land across the plains of Thrace—already observed by Polybius[1]—provides a constant and tragic background to the medieval history of the Balkans. Justinian had seen his Danubian frontier constantly threatened and frequently overrun by Kutrigurs and Slavs. The Slavs, whose incursions into the Balkans had started in the reign of his predecessor Justin I and increased in strength throughout the sixth century, had expanded from their European homes north of the Carpathians and were then divided into two main groups: the Sclaveni, north of the middle and lower Danube, and the Antes (or Antae), further east, between the Carpathians and the Donets.[2] The havoc wrought by the Slavs in the Balkans, described by Procopius,[3] was a harbinger of worse things to come. Justinian's fortifications and skilful diplomacy could not compensate for the lack of soldiers. It has been suggested that the Emperor's failure to protect adequately the Danube frontier can be partly explained by his obsession with classical reminiscences: his wars with Persia, which evoked memories of Marathon and Salamis, and his reconquest of Roman lands, offered more appeal than border warfare on the Danube against barbarians.[4] Whether this is so or not, his successors were certainly left to deal with the problem of the Balkans.

Justinian's death in 565 ushered in a new period in the history of the Empire's Danubian frontier: for the next sixty years Byzantine policy in this sector was conditioned by the Avar threat. The Avars, whose hordes included, it would seem, Mongol and Turkic tribes, had

[1] See the remarks of Polybius on the exposure of the ancient Byzantium to attacks by land, *Hist.* IV, 45 (ed. T. Büttner-Wobst, Leipzig, 1889, pp. 57–8).

[2] The origin, ethnic character and geographical distribution of the Antes still raise some puzzling questions. The main contemporary authorities are Jordanes, *Getica*, V, 32–7 (*MGH, Auct. ant.* V, 1, pp. 62 ff.) and Procopius, *History of the Wars*, VII, 14, 22–30 and VIII, 4, 9 (ed. J. Haury, Leipzig, 1905, pp. 354 ff.) who regard them as Slavs, ethnically and linguistically related to the Sclaveni. The former locates them along the Black Sea coast, between the Danube and the Dniester, and as far as the Dnieper; the latter mentions them in the region of the Donets, north of the Sea of Azov. Several different tribes were originally ruled by a non-Slav, possibly Iranian, minority, but slavicised, at least in Bessarabia, by the sixth century. See G. Vernadsky, *Ancient Russia* (New Haven, 1944), pp. 104–8, 155–60 and *passim*; F. Dvornik, *The Making of Central and Eastern Europe* (London, 1949), pp. 279–82.

[3] *Hist. of the Wars,* VII, 29, 1–3 (*op. cit.* p. 423).

[4] E. Stein, *Histoire du Bas-Empire,* II, p. 310.

arrived in the north Caucasian region at the close of Justinian's reign, in headlong flight from their erstwhile subjects, the Central Asian Turks.[1] Through the intermediary of the Alans they sought the Empire's protection, and in 558 concluded a *foedus* with East Rome, promising to submit to the Emperor and to fight his enemies. Justinian could not but welcome this chance of easing the pressure on the northern front, believing, as Menander saw it, that 'whether the Avars are victorious, or whether they are defeated, in either case the Romans will profit'.[2] The Avars played their part as imperial *foederati* only too thoroughly: by 561 they were on the lower Danube, having subjected in their westward advance the Sabiri, the Utigurs, the Kutrigurs and the Antes of Bessarabia. Their relations with the Empire now entered a new and more critical phase. Their requests to be allowed to cross the Danube and to settle in the Dobrudja were studiously ignored by Justinian: thus was created the first of the many bones of contention between Byzantium and the Avars.

Justin II inherited this increasingly tense situation. A few days after his accession he received an Avar embassy in the palace. The Emperor, determined to abandon Justinian's humiliating policy of buying off the northern barbarians,[3] haughtily rejected their request for tribute.[4] The Avars, meanwhile, had become entangled in the affairs of Central Europe: as allies of the Lombards they defeated the Gepids, seized their lands in Dacia and Eastern Pannonia (567) and, on the departure of the Lombards to Italy in the following year, occupied the whole of the Hungarian plain. The establishment of the Avars as the dominant power in Central Europe, lords of an empire that stretched from Bohemia to the lower Danube and from the

---

[1] A number of modern authorities identify the Avars who migrated to Europe with the Juan-juan of the Chinese: J. B. Bury, *History of the Later Roman Empire*, II (London, 1923), pp. 314–16; G. Vernadsky, *Ancient Russia*, pp. 178–9; E. Stein, *op. cit.* II, pp. 541–2. In the view of some scholars, the distinction made by Theophylactus Simocatta (*Hist.* VII, caps. 7–8, ed. C. de Boor, Leipzig, 1887, pp. 256 ff.) between the 'true Avars' (the Juan-juan) and the 'pseudo-Avars' (who alone migrated to Europe) rests on somewhat fragile foundations: see V. Minorsky, *Ḥudūd al-ʿĀlam* (London, 1937), pp. 447–8; R. Grousset, *L'empire des steppes* (Paris, 1939), pp. 226–7. For a different view, see E. Chavannes, 'Documents sur les Tou-Kiue occidentaux', *Sbornik Trudov Orkhonskoj Ekspeditsij*, VI (St Petersburg, 1903), 229–33; C. A. Macartney, 'On the Greek sources for the history of the Turks in the sixth century', *BSOAS*, XI (1943–6), 266–75; see also H. W. Haussig, 'Theophylakts Exkurs über die Skythischen Völker', *B*, XXIII (1953), 275–462; A. Kollautz, 'Die Awaren', *Saeculum*, V (1954), 129–78.

[2] *Excerpta de legationibus*, ed. C. de Boor, I (Berlin, 1903), p. 443.

[3] On Justin II's new policy towards the barbarians see E. Stein, *Studien zur Geschichte des byzantinischen Reiches, vornehmlich unter den Kaisern Justinus II und Tiberius Constantinus* (Stuttgart, 1919), pp. 3 ff.

[4] On the Avar embassy of 565 see Menander, *op. cit.* p. 446 and the vivid description of Corippus, *In laudem Iustini*, III, lines 231–407 (*MGH*, *Auct. ant.* III, 2, pp. 143–7). Cf. H. Howorth, 'The Avars', *JRAS*, XXI, 4 (1889), 732–4.

Alps to the steppes of South Russia and was centred in the Theiss (Tisza) valley, drastically altered the balance of power along Byzantium's northern frontier. It was not long before the supreme ruler of the Avars, the Khan Bajan, a ruthless conqueror and an able diplomatist, showed where his true ambitions lay. The city of Sirmium on the lower Sava, the key to the Byzantine fortifications in northern Illyricum, had, in the confusion of the Lombard–Gepid war, eluded his grasp. And now, with a clear perception of its strategic importance, combining force with diplomacy, Bajan concentrated on this objective. But Sirmium stood firm, and in 574 a treaty was concluded between Byzantium and the Avars, Justin II undertaking to pay a yearly tribute of 80,000 *nomismata*.[1]

At this stage Byzantium's relations with the Avars were suddenly entangled with the Empire's diplomatic activity on the North Caucasian front. In 568 there arrived in Constantinople an embassy from the Central Asian Turks (the T'ou Kiue of the Chinese), whose Empire stretched from Mongolia to Turkestan and was now expanding westwards towards the Northern Caucasus; the envoys brought Justin II peace proposals from Silzibul,[2] Khan of the western branch of the T'ou Kiue. The Turks, and their vassals, the Sogdians, controlled the eastern sector of the silk route from China to Europe; the western sector, leading to Byzantium, crossed Persian territory. The Turks were as interested in the silk trade as the Byzantines: the former, aspiring to the role of commercial intermediaries between China and Byzantium, sought an outlet to the south-west; the East Roman government now saw in the Turks a means of circumventing Persian control of the silk routes from China to the Black Sea, which had so often in the past threatened to make the Empire economically dependent on its traditional enemy. To the realisation of this joint plan the Sassanid Empire was the main obstacle; and it seems that the agreement concluded in Byzantium between Justin II and the Turks provided—next to a clause relating to the silk trade—for a military alliance against Persia. 'It was thus', Menander observes, 'that the Turkish nation became friends of the Romaioi.'[3]   A Byzantine em-

---

[1] *DR*, 34.

[2] On the different forms of this name, see J. B. Bury, 'The Turks in the Sixth Century', *EHR*, xii (1897), 418, n. 2.

[3] Menander, *op. cit.* i, p. 452. Some historians believe that the Byzantine government, while expressing 'benevolent interest' in the Turkish proposals, was unwilling to commit itself to a formal alliance in 568: N. H. Baynes, *CMH*, ii, pp. 269–70; S. Vailhé, 'Projet d'alliance turco-byzantine au VIe siècle', *EO*, xii (1909), 206–14; C. Diehl and G. Marçais, *Le monde oriental de 395 à 1081* (Paris, 1944), pp. 128–9. Yet Menander seems to imply that the Turkish offer of ὁμαιχμία was accepted by the Emperor; and an agreement about silk may be inferred both from the embassy's terms of reference and from the fact that ten porters carrying this commodity accompanied

bassy, headed by Zemarchus, journeyed to Silzibul's capital in the Ektag mountain in the Tekes valley, in the eastern Tien Shan.[1] During the next few years relations between Byzantium and the Turks were friendly and close, to judge at least from the numerous embassies that travelled between Constantinople and Central Asia. But in 576 the situation altered dramatically. When the Byzantine envoys, headed by Valentinus, presented their credentials to the Khan Tourxath,[2] Silzibul's son and successor, they were met with an explosion of rage. Placing his fingers in his mouth, the Turkish sovereign exclaimed: 'Are you not those Romans, who have ten tongues, and one deceit?...As my ten fingers are now in my mouth, so you have many tongues, using one to deceive me, another to deceive the Varchonites [i.e. the Avars], my slaves. You flatter and deceive all peoples with cunning words and treacherous intent, indifferent to those who fall headlong into misfortune, from which you yourselves derive benefit.' 'It is strange and unnatural', he added in stinging rebuke, 'for a Turk to lie.' Bitterly reproached with the alliance which their Emperor had concluded with the hated enemies of the Turks, the Avars, 'slaves that had fled from their masters', the Byzantine envoys barely escaped with their lives; the alliance between the Empire and the Turks, which had lasted for eight years, was abruptly terminated;[3] and in the same year (576) a Turkish army, moving westwards from the Caspian Sea, captured the Byzantine city of Bosporus in the Crimea and threatened the Empire's whole defensive system in the peninsula.

The collapse of the Turko-Byzantine alliance was probably due as much to the new turn the Empire's diplomacy was taking on its north-eastern front as to its activity on the Danube. Menander's frank reporting affords us a suggestive glimpse of the moral indignation which the methods of this diplomacy so often provoked among its victims in the Eurasian steppe. The Turks, it may be surmised, had come to realise that the Byzantine statesmen were losing interest in so distant an ally; and the agreement which the Empire, two years previously, had concluded with the Avars they chose to regard as a hostile act.

the Byzantine envoys on their return journey from Silzibul's capital to Constantinople. Cf. N. V. Pigulevskaja, 'Vizantijskaja diplomatija i torgovlja šelkom v V–VII vv.', *VV*, n.s. I (1947), 184–214.

[1] E. Chavannes, *Documents*, pp. 235–7.

[2] The form Τούρξαθος, which occurs in a sixteenth-century manuscript of Menander in the library of Trinity College, Cambridge (O. 3. 23: πρεσβεία ἐκ τοῦ ὀγδόου λόγου Μενάνδρου, ff. 3–5) is preferred by G. Moravcsik to the habitual Τούρξανθος: 'Zur Geschichte der Onoguren', *Ungarische Jahrbücher*, x (1930), 63; *Byzantinoturcica*, II, p. 328 (2nd ed.).

[3] Menander, *op. cit.* I, pp. 205–6.

Tiberius (578–82), whose realism led him to prefer negotiation to the intransigent imperialism of his predecessor, tried to use the Avars to check the Slavs whose raids across the Danube were causing grave concern in Constantinople.[1] But Bajan proved a treacherous ally: the Danubian frontier was continually sagging throughout Tiberius' reign, and between 578 and 586 Avar raids, alternating and frequently combining with invasions of Slavs, spread havoc in Thrace, Illyricum and Greece.[2] John of Ephesus describes a formidable invasion of the Balkans by the Slavs in 581; they reached the 'Long Wall' outside Constantinople and, having 'learnt to fight better than the Romans', were still at the time of writing (584) in possession of the conquered land.[3] Many of them remained on imperial territory, and the first important Slav settlements in Thrace, Macedonia and Northern Greece undoubtedly date from this time. The position was no less perilous in northern Illyricum, where the Avar threat to Sirmium was growing. To Bajan's demand to surrender the city Tiberius replied that he would sooner give one of his daughters to the Khan than abandon the fortress of his own free will. But Bajan, who knew that Tiberius was fully occupied with the Persian war, was not to be bluffed; and after a siege of two years Sirmium, inadequately defended and provisioned, was surrendered on the Emperor's orders to the Avars (582).[4]

With the key to the northern Balkans now in Avar hands, the Empire for the next ten years was forced on to the defensive. In vain did the Emperor Maurice attempt to buy off the Avars by agreeing to increase their annual subsidy (584);[5] Thrace, Macedonia, Greece, and it seems the Peloponnese itself, were raided and partly overrun during the next few years by the Avars and their subjects, the Slavs.[6] But Maurice's genius succeeded to some extent in restoring

---

[1] Cf. *DR*, 46.

[2] The contemporary sources and secondary authorities dealing with these invasions are listed by H. Grégoire, 'L'origine et le nom des Croates et des Serbes', *B*, XVII (1944–5), 104–10, and by A. Bon, *Le Péloponnèse byzantin* (Paris, 1951), pp. 31–2.

[3] *Hist. eccl.* VI, 25; Engl. trans. R. Payne Smith (Oxford, 1860), pp. 432–3.

[4] Menander, *op. cit.* I, pp. 220–1, I, p. 476; H. Howorth, 'The Avars', *JRAS*, XXI (1889), 744–9; L. Hauptmann, 'Les rapports des Byzantins avec les Slaves et les Avares pendant la seconde moitié du VIe siècle', *B*, IV (1927–8), 137–70; P. Lemerle, 'Invasions et migrations dans les Balkans depuis la fin de l'époque romaine jusqu'au VIIIe siècle', *RH*, CCXI (1954), 289–90.

[5] Theoph. Simocatta, I, caps. 5–6, ed. C. de Boor, pp. 48–52; Howorth, *op. cit.* pp. 749–52.

[6] Much learned controversy has been aroused by the statement in the *Chronicle of Monemvasia*, confirmed by a tenth-century scholium of Arethas of Caesarea and echoed in a letter of the Patriarch Nicholas III (1084–1111), that in 587 the Avars and the Slavs conquered and settled the Peloponnese, and that only Corinth, the Argolid and the eastern part of the peninsula remained in Byzantine hands after that date. The reliability of this evidence is strongly and convincingly supported by

the Empire's position on the Danube during the decade from 592 to 602. In 591 the successful completion of the Persian war enabled him to bring his seasoned troops back to Europe. Priscus, his greatest commander, was entrusted with the double task of maintaining the Danube as a frontier line against the Avars and stopping the incursions of the Slavs. The latter were still able to launch, under the auspices of the Khan, a massive attack against Thessalonica in 597.[1] But on the whole Priscus was remarkably successful, crossing the Danube to subdue the Slavs and recapturing Singidunum from the Avars. In 600 a treaty between Byzantium and the Avars fixed the Empire's frontier on the Danube, Maurice undertaking to increase the tribute.[2] But in 601 Priscus was across the Danube and, carrying the war into the enemy's territory, inflicted a crushing defeat on Bajan's forces on the Theiss. Not since the days of Justinian had the arms of Byzantium won such a triumph in Europe.[3]

But Maurice's successes on the Danube were soon undone. In 602 the Emperor's order that the troops were to winter beyond the Danube provoked a mutiny. The rebellious army marched on Constantinople, seized the city and proclaimed their leader Phocas Emperor. Phocas' disastrous reign (602–10) marks a turning point in the history of the Empire's northern frontier. The *limes* on the lower Danube and on the Sava, held—albeit imperfectly and precariously—by Justinian's three successors, now collapsed, and the barbarians surged over the Balkans. The three-pronged attacks of the Avaro-Slav hordes towards the Adriatic, the Aegean and the Bosphorus in the reigns of Phocas and Heraclius led to a permanent occupation by the Slavs of Illyria, Dalmatia, Macedonia and Thrace. Salona was sacked (*c.* 614), Thessalonica was attacked several times and then in 617 the Avars reached the suburbs of Constantinople itself.[4] It was then, in all probability, that the Slavs, spreading south irresistibly, settled in large numbers in Greece and the Peloponnese, forming indepen-

P. Charanis ('The Chronicle of Monemvasia and the Question of the Slavonic Settlements in Greece', *DOP*, v (1950), 139–66; 'On the Question of the Slavonic Settlements in Greece during the Middle Ages', *BS*, x (1949), 254–8). The source references and other works on this controversial topic are cited in A. Bon, *Le Péloponnèse byzantin*, pp. 32–5. See also P. Charanis, 'On the Slavic Settlement in the Peloponnesus', *BZ*, xlvi (1953), 91–103.

[1] *Miracula S. Demetrii*, *MPG*, cxvi, 1284–93; A. Tougard, *De l'histoire profane dans les Actes grecs des Bollandistes* (Paris, 1874), pp. 88 ff. The Avaro-Slav army is here said to have arrived before the city walls on Sunday 22 September, in the reign of Maurice. This gives two possible dates—586 and 597; opinion is divided as to which of these years is to be accepted. [2] *DR*, 131.

[3] The chronology of Maurice's Avaro-Slav wars of 592–602, as reconstructed from the evidence of Theophylactus Simocatta, remains confused and controversial. See the bibliography in Ostrogorsky, *History of the Byzantine State*, p. 75, n. 2.

[4] N. H. Baynes, 'The Date of the Avar Surprise', *BZ*, xxi (1912), 110–28.

dent communities (*Sclaviniae*) over which the Byzantine authorities were for nearly two centuries incapable of exercising effective control. In 623 they ravaged Crete. Without much exaggeration Isidore of Seville could write that at the beginning of Heraclius' reign 'the Slavs took away Greece from the Romans'.[1] The supreme crisis came in 626 when a vast Avar horde, supported by Slavs, other northern barbarians and—ineffectually—by a Persian army encamped on the Asian side of the Bosphorus, hurled itself for ten days at the defences of Constantinople. The courage of the garrison, inspired by the Patriarch Sergius, and the naval victory gained by the Byzantines over the Slavs, saved the city. The Khan abandoned the siege, and the Avars, badly defeated, withdrew to Pannonia.[2] Never again did they seriously threaten the Empire.

Though incapable of stemming the flow of Slavs into his Balkan provinces, Heraclius could at least, to prevent further Avar invasions, attempt to stabilise the northern frontier by diplomatic means. This policy was attended with a measure of success. About 623 the Slavs of Bohemia, Moravia and Slovakia were liberated from the yoke of the Avars by Samo, who founded a short-lived realm stretching from the upper Elbe to the middle Danube. Whether or not Samo's revolt was instigated by Heraclius' diplomacy, there is no doubt that the rise of his kingdom, by weakening the power of the Avars on the eve of their assault on Constantinople, served the interests of Byzantium. Of more lasting significance were the measures taken by Heraclius, probably soon after 626, to relieve the Avar pressure on the middle Danube and in Illyricum. Constantine Porphyrogenitus tells us that the Emperor called in the Croats against the Avars. The Croats, who came from 'White Croatia' north of the Carpathians, defeated the Avars, expelled them from Illyricum, and, together with the Serbs from 'White Serbia', were then settled by Heraclius as subjects of the Empire in their present homes in the Balkans. The Serbs and the Croats were subsequently converted to Christianity by missionaries sent from Rome on Heraclius' orders;[3] and these new subjects of

---

[1] *Chronicon, MPL*, LXXXIII, 1056.

[2] *Chronicon Paschale*, I, pp. 719 ff. (*CSHB*); Theophanes, *Chronographia*, I, pp. 315 ff. (ed. C. de Boor); George Pisides, *Bellum Avaricum*, pp. 47–68 (*CSHB*); and the account of an anonymous eye-witness of the siege: Περὶ τῶν ἀθέων 'Αβάρων (A. Mai, *Nova Patrum Bibliotheca*, Rome, 1853, VI, pp. 423 ff.; see also *Izvori za Bŭlgarskata Istorija = Fontes Historiae Bulgaricae*, VI, Sofia, 1960, pp. 41–55; and F. Barišić, 'Le siège de Constantinople par les Avares et les Slaves en 626', *B*, XXIV (1954), 371–95).

[3] *De administrando imperio*, caps. 31, 32, *DAI*, I, pp. 146–60. The reliability of Constantine's account of the southward migration of the Croats and the Serbs in the seventh century has been the subject of a long controversy which is still not finally resolved. However, scholars are increasingly inclined to accept this account as substantially true. See the discussions of this problem by G. Ostrogorsky (*History of the*

Byzantium must have provided some measure of stability in the chaos which the Avaro-Slav invasions had brought into the Balkans.

The desire to keep the Avars in check was also, it seems, a prime factor in Heraclius' diplomacy on the Empire's north-eastern, Caucasian, front. The collapse of the alliance with the T'ou Kiue and the Turkic threat to the Crimea in the eighth and ninth decades of the sixth century had, moreover, made it necessary for Byzantium to acquire a strong and reliable ally in this sector. In 619 Heraclius received in Constantinople the visit of a 'Hunnic' ruler, had him baptised at his own request together with his retinue, and before sending him home granted him the title of *patricius*.[1] His subjects were undoubtedly the Onogurs, a people of West Siberian origin, belonging to the Bulgaric (West Turkic) linguistic group, who had lived since the fifth century between the Sea of Azov and the Northern Caucasus.[2] About 635 Kovrat, ruler of the Onogurs, rose against the Avars and drove them out of his country; whereupon he concluded an alliance with the Emperor and was made a patrician in his turn.[3] Kovrat, John of Nikiu tells us, had been baptised as a child and brought up at the court of Constantinople where he became a life-long friend of Heraclius.[4] Kovrat's loyalty served the Empire in good stead. His kingdom, known to the Byzantines as 'Old Great Bulgaria' (ἡ παλαιὰ Βουλγαρία ἡ μεγάλη), which stretched from the Caucasus to the Don, and perhaps as far as the Dnieper, successfully withstanding the Avars in the west and the Turks in the east, acted until Kovrat's death in 642 as the guardian of the Empire's interests in the North Caucasian sector.[5]

Byzantine State, p. 94, n. 3), F. Dvornik (in *DAI*, II, pp. 94–101, 114–16), and B. Ferjančić (*Vizantijskij Izvorij za istoriju naroda Jugoslavije*, II, Belgrade, 1959, pp. 37–58).

[1] Nicephorus, *Opusc. hist.* p. 12 (ed. C. de Boor).

[2] G. Moravcsik, 'Zur Geschichte der Onoguren', *Ungar. Jahrbücher*, x (1930), 53–90, and the bibliography in *Byzantinoturcica*, I, pp. 65 ff. (2nd ed.).

[3] Nicephorus, *op. cit.* p. 24. The Onogur ruler who visited Heraclius in 619 was probably Kovrat's uncle Organa (Orchan).

[4] *The Chronicle of John, Bishop of Nikiu*, trans. R. H. Charles (London, 1916), p. 197. Kovrat is certainly identical with Kurt, who according to the eighth-century list of Old Bulgar rulers reigned for sixty years, i.e. according to V. Zlatarski (*Istorija na bŭlgarskata dŭržava prez srednite vekove* (Sofia, 1918), I, 1, pp. 84–96, 353–82) from 584 to 642. Cf. S. Runciman, *A History of the First Bulgarian Empire* (London, 1930), pp. 272–9.

[5] K. M. Setton has tried to prove that 'some time after 641–2' the Onogur Bulgars 'under, conceivably, one of the sons of Kovrat, or under some other lieutenant, attacked and captured Corinth' ('The Bulgars in the Balkans', *SP*, xxv (1950), 502–43; 'The Emperor Constans II and the capture of Corinth by the Onogur Bulgars', *ibid.* xxvII (1952), 351–62). His arguments have failed to convince the present writer. Cf. their criticism by P. Charanis, 'On the Capture of Corinth by the Onogurs', *SP*, xxvII (1952), 343–50.

Shortly after Kovrat's death 'Old Great Bulgaria' broke up under the blows of the Khazars who in the middle of the seventh century struck westward from the lower Volga to the Sea of Azov. In the scattering of tribes that followed, two branches of the Onogur people salvaged enough of their national heritage to play a significant part in the destinies of Eastern Europe. The one, it seems, migrated northward and, settling by the junction of the middle Volga and the Kama, built up a powerful trading state, the kingdom of the Volga Bulgars, which became in the tenth century a northern outpost of Islam.[1] The other group, led by Kovrat's son Asparuch (Isperich),[2] left their homes in the North Caucasus region, moved westwards across the Pontic steppes and appeared on the Danube delta. But southern Bessarabia proved only a temporary resting place: doubtless anxious, like the Avars a century earlier, to exchange the hazards of the steppe for the security of cis-Danubian Dobrudja, Asparuch's Bulgars began in the eighth decade of the seventh century to push further south. It was the traditional policy of Byzantium to welcome potential allies on the north bank of the Danube, but to oppose their crossing of the river by every means; so in 680 Constantine IV rushed his armies to the Danube. But the victorious Bulgars swept through Moesia and the Dobrudja, occupying the imperial lands between the Danube and the Balkan Mountains. Byzantium bowed to the *fait accompli*: in 681 Constantine IV concluded peace with the Bulgars and undertook to pay them an annual tribute, thus accepting perforce the existence of an independent barbarian state on imperial territory.[3] The collapse of the Empire's Danubian frontier, which the Slav invasions had already brought about in the first half of the century, was now at last acknowledged by the Byzantine government. Asparuch had carved himself a kingdom that stretched from the Dniester to the Haemus range, a limpet that was to cling to the Empire's flank for more than three hundred years and was to become in the ninth and tenth centuries one of the great powers of Europe. From his new capital of Pliska, at

[1] The origin of the Khazars, who in the late sixth and early seventh centuries were subject to the Western Turks, is still a matter for debate. Cf. D. M. Dunlop, *The History of the Jewish Khazars* (Princeton, 1954), pp. 3–40; W. B. Henning, 'A Farewell to the Khagan of the Aq-Aquatārān', *BSOAS*, xiv (1952), 501–2.

[2] The form 'Isperich' occurs in the List of Old Bulgar Rulers; the Greek form ’Ασπαρούχ ('Aspar-hruk' in Armenian: see H. Grégoire; *B*, xvii (1944–5), 115, n. 34) is used here, as the more familiar.

[3] Theophanes, pp. 356–9 (ed. C. de Boor); Nicephorus, *Opusc. hist.* pp. 33–5 (ed. C. de Boor). Theophanes places all these events, the Bulgar 'Landnahme' and the foundation of the First Bulgarian Empire, in A.M. 6171 = A.D. 679–80: so V. Zlatarski, *Istorija*, i, 1, pp. 146–8; S. Runciman, *op. cit.* p. 27; but J. Kulakovsky (*Istorija Vizantii*, iii, p. 249) had already drawn attention to a piece of evidence (Mansi, xi, 617) which shows that the war still continued during part of 681. Cf. G. Ostrogorsky, *History of the Byzantine State*, p. 113, n. 5.

the southern extremity of the Dobrudja plain, the Sublime Khan and his military aristocracy of Onogur Bulgar boyars ruled over a population of Slav immigrants who, in the course of time, assimilated their conquerors;[1] from this gradual fusion of Bulgars and Slavs the First Bulgarian Empire was born.

It was not long before this new Balkan state began to loom large in the policy and destinies of Byzantium. In the burst of diplomatic activity which took place along the Empire's northern front at the turn of the century, its three main sectors—the north Caucasian, the Crimean and the Balkan—linked within an intricate web of power politics, jointly affected the fate of Constantinople itself. In 695 Justinian II was dethroned and exiled to Cherson. A few years later, hoping to regain his throne and fearing the loyalty professed by the Chersonites to Tiberius III, he fled to Khazaria. The Khan received Justinian with honour and married him to his sister, the Khazar princess being baptised as Theodora, a name which, with its patent allusion to her more celebrated namesake, doubtless symbolised the Khan's ambitions for the restoration of his brother-in-law to the throne of the Romans. Soon, however, an embassy from Constantinople demanding Justinian's extradition made him change his mind. Warned by his wife of his imminent arrest, Justinian fled from Khazaria to the mouth of the Danube. The final scene of the drama was enacted in the Balkans. The exiled Emperor appealed for help to Tervel, Asparuch's successor; and in the autumn of 705 Tervel's army of Bulgars and Slavs appeared before the walls of Constantinople. The city fortifications proved impregnable, but Justinian slipped in unobserved, and in the panic that ensued regained his throne. The timely, though hardly disinterested, services of the Bulgar Khan were not forgotten: seated by the Emperor's side, Tervel was invested by him with the dignity of Caesar.[2] The event was a notable one, for next to the imperial dignity the rank of Caesar was the highest in the hierarchy of Byzantium. No barbarian ruler had ever risen so high, and the Bulgarians were not soon to forget that their Khan had received, as an associate of the imperial majesty, the homage of the people of East Rome.[3] But in Byzantine eyes the

---

[1] Contrary to V. Zlatarski, *op. cit.* i, 1, pp. 142–5, who argued that the Slavs entered into a contractual agreement with Asparuch, I. Dujčev has convincingly shown ('Protobulgares et Slaves', *Sem. Kond.* x (1938), 145–54) that they were actually subjugated by the Bulgars.

[2] There is some doubt as to where this ceremony took place. According to Nicephorus (p. 42) it was in Tervel's camp outside the city walls. The *Suda*, on the other hand, states that Tervel addressed the people of Byzantium in the palace of the Chrysotriclinus (more precisely, in the βασιλική: *Suidae Lexicon*, ed. A. Adler, i, p. 459).

[3] Nicephorus, *Opusc. hist.* p. 42 states that Justinian Τέρβελιν . . . προσκυνεῖσθαι σὺν αὐτῷ ὑπὸ τοῦ λαοῦ ἐκέλευε.

ceremony of 705 had a different significance: Tervel's title carried no power with it, and could indeed be regarded as a sign of his recognition of the Emperor's supreme and universal authority.[1]

Justinian's adventures on the northern shores of the Black Sea illustrate the struggle that took place in the late seventh and early eighth centuries between Byzantium and the Khazars for the control of the southern Crimea and of the straits of Kerch. The Turkic threat to the Crimea which led to the fall of Bosporus in 576 was removed by the dissensions that weakened the Empire of the T'ou Kiue and by the rise of the Old Great Bulgaria; by the end of the sixth century Byzantine authority had been restored in Bosporus. But the Empire's whole position in the peninsula was once again challenged by the westward expansion of the Khazars, who were in possession of the city by the end of the seventh century. The intrigues of Justinian II, and even more the three largely unsuccessful expeditions which, upon his restoration, he sent to the Crimea to punish the Greek cities for their former conspiracy against him, threw the Byzantine possessions in the peninsula into the hands of the Khazars: by about 705 Cherson as well was controlled by the Khan, and the revolution of 711 which led to the assassination of Justinian was organised in the Crimea with Khazar support.

The Khazar pressure on the Crimea relaxed about this time, and Cherson seems to have remained under Byzantine sovereignty after 711. Circumstances were drawing Byzantium and the Khazars closer together. The Byzantines had long since realised their usefulness in the Empire's strategy on the north Caucasian front. Heraclius, on the eve of his great offensive against the Persian Empire in 627, had concluded a military agreement with them. And in the first half of the eighth century the common threat of Islam cemented that alliance between Byzantium and the Khazars which was an essential factor in the Empire's diplomacy for the next two hundred years. During this period the Khazar Khanate, that most civilised and ordered of states created by the Turkic people in the early middle ages, centred on the territory between the lower Volga, the northern Caucasus and the Sea of Azov, remained Byzantium's most constant and valued ally in the north-east. It is probable that in the eighth century the Khazar alliance did much to save Byzantium from the Arab menace, for had the Khazars not halted in the Caucasus the northward thrust of Islam, the Arabs might well have invaded the Pontic steppes and, appearing on the lower Danube, have outflanked the Empire's whole defensive system in the north. At the same time

---

[1] This may be implied from the statement of Theophanes (ed. C. de Boor, p. 374) that Tervel in 705 undertook *vis-à-vis* Justinian πάντα ὑπακούειν καὶ συντρέχειν.

the Khazars played a not unimportant role in the foreign trade of Byzantium; for by supplying Constantinople with gold from the Urals and with raw silk from China, they helped the Empire to readjust its economy after the loss of Syria and Egypt to the Arabs.[1] In spite of occasional clashes in the Crimea, relations between Constantinople and the Khazar capital of Itil in the Volga delta were friendly and close. In 733 Leo III married his son, the future Emperor Constantine V, to the Khan's daughter; christened Irene, the Khazar princess introduced her national dress, the *tzitzakion*, into the court of Constantinople.[2]

The Byzantine statesmen would have been false to the time-honoured traditions of East Roman diplomacy if they had not attempted to sanctify and consolidate this political alliance by converting the Khazars to Christianity. It is, however, remarkable that their missionary efforts in Khazaria seem to have derived some impetus from the iconoclast movement. For on the one hand Constantine V's (741–75) persecutions of the iconophiles caused a mass exodus of Orthodox monks from Constantinople and the central provinces to the outlying regions of the Empire, notably to the Crimea, a fact which strengthened the influence of Byzantine culture in Cherson, Bosporus and Gothia and enhanced the role of the peninsula as a missionary outpost. On the other hand, the East Roman authorities, while persecuting the defenders of the images nearer home, appear to have used them in the Crimea to propagate Christianity among the peoples of the North.[3] Christianity certainly spread to Khazaria in the eighth century,[4] partly from the Crimea,[5] and the Byzantine authorities must have actively encouraged this development. And it is not unreasonable to suppose that the list of eight bishoprics subject to the Patriarchate of Constantinople, forming the 'Eparchy of Gothia' administered by the Metropolitan of Doros (the chief city of the Crimean Goths), and covering a territory that extended from the Crimea to the lower Volga and the Caucasus—a list contained in C. de Boor's *Notitia Episcopatuum*—embodies a project,

---

[1] See the remarks on the Khazaro-Byzantine trade by S. Runciman, in *Cambridge Economic History*, II, pp. 91–2.

[2] G. Moravcsik, 'Proischoždenie slova τζιτζάκιον', *Sem. Kond.* IV (1931), 69–76.

[3] F. Dvornik, *Les légendes de Constantin et de Méthode vues de Byzance* (*BS*, Suppl. I, 1933), pp. 159–60.

[4] The *Life of St Abo of Tiflis*, describing conditions in Khazaria in the second half of the eighth century, states: 'in terra illa...multae sunt urbes et pagi, qui secundum Christi legem secure vivant' (P. Peeters, 'Les Khazars dans la Passion de S. Abo de Tiflis', *AB*, LII (1934), 25 ff., cf. F. Dvornik, *op. cit.* pp. 158–9, 163–5).

[5] Cf. *Menologion Basilii II Imperatoris*, *MPG*, CXVII, 181; *Synaxarium ecclesiae Constantinopolitanae*, ed. H. Delehaye, *Propylaeum ad AASS Novembris* (Brussels, 1902), col. 263.

conceived by the Byzantine authorities in the middle of the eighth century, to set up a missionary Church over the length and breadth of the Khazar Empire.[1] There is no evidence, however, that this vast ecclesiastical network was ever put into operation. In the second half of the eighth century the progress of Christianity in Khazaria was curtailed by the rival propaganda of Judaism and Islam. The former especially was gaining ground; medieval Hebrew sources, whose reliability is still a matter of dispute, date the first success of Judaism in Khazaria about 730–40 when some of its tenets are said to have been adopted by the Khan Bulan.[2] While recognising the controversial nature of this problem, the present writer believes that the conversion of the ruling circles of Khazaria to Judaism took place in gradual stages and that their final acceptance of the Mosaic law was delayed until the ninth century.[3] The failure to convert the Khazars to Christianity did not, on the whole, affect the friendly relations between Byzantium and its northern ally. Meanwhile the attention of Byzantine statesmen was shifting increasingly to the Balkan sector.

In the century between 650 and 750 the situation in the Balkans had, from the standpoint of the Empire, much deteriorated. Almost the whole peninsula was occupied by the Slavs, the Greek population being temporarily either submerged or pushed back to the coastal regions along the Black Sea and the Aegean. Thus most of Greece, and practically the entire Peloponnese, were for nearly two centuries outside Byzantine control while to the north lay an endless expanse of Slav territory, stretching continuously from the Adriatic, the Aegean and the Black Sea to the Baltic.[4] And this vast barbarian world, pressing down on Byzantium from all sides, had been

---

[1] G. I. Konidares, '*Αἱ μητροπόλεις καὶ ἀρχιεπισκοπαὶ τοῦ οἰκουμενικοῦ πατριαρχείου καὶ ἡ τάξις αὐτῶν. Texte und Forschungen zur byzant.-neugriechischen Philologie*, no. 13 (1934), p. 100. This is the interpretation given to the 'Gothic Eparchy' by V. Mošin ('*Επαρχία Γοτθίας* v Khazarii v VIII-m veke', *Trudy IV-go Sjezda Russkich Akademičeskich Organizacij za granicej*, I, Belgrade, 1929, 149–56); Mošin's conclusions were accepted by G. Moravcsik (*Zur Gesch. der Onoguren*, pp. 64–5), A. Vasiliev (*The Goths in the Crimea*, pp. 97–104), and to a large extent by F. Dvornik (*Les légendes*, pp. 160–8). For different views see G. Vernadsky, 'The Eparchy of Gothia', *B*, xv (1940–1), 67–76, and V. Laurent, 'L'érection de la métropole d'Athènes et le statut ecclésiastique de l'Illyricum au VIIIe siècle', *EB*, I (1943–4), 59.

[2] See D. M. Dunlop, *The History of the Jewish Khazars*, pp. 116–70.

[3] See below: pp. 492–3.

[4] There are two classic texts showing the predominance of the Slavs in the Peloponnese in the eighth century: (1) Constantine Porphyrogenitus states that in 746–7 ἐσθλαβώθη δὲ πᾶσα ἡ χώρα, καὶ γέγονε βάρβαρος (*De thematibus*, p. 91, ed. A. Pertusi); for the term ἐσθλαβώθη see A. Bon, *Le Péloponnèse byzantin*, p. 29, n. 1; (2) between 723 and 728 Willibald, Bishop of Eichstätt, on his way to Palestine stopped at Monemvasia, a city he locates 'in Slawinia terra' (*Vita S. Willibaldi, MGH, Script.* xv, 1, p. 93).

reinforced by the creation on the borders of Thrace of the Bulgar kingdom which was showing, under Tervel and his successors, an assertiveness that augured ill for the future.

Yet in this dark period of Balkan history that extends from the death of Maurice (602) to Irene's accession to power (780) Byzantine influence did not vanish from the peninsula. In the cities of eastern Greece and on the rugged east coast of the Peloponnese the Greek population held on, and was indeed reinforced by emigration from the interior, and this, together with the cultural inferiority of the Slavs at that time and their inability to form strong political groups in this region, made possible the work of rehellenisation and reconquest.[1] This work began in the second half of the seventh century, with the campaigns of Constans II (in 658) and Justinian II (in 688–9) against the Slavs of Macedonia; the creation of the imperial themes of Thrace (between 680 and 687) and of Hellas (between 687 and 695)[2] marks the result of this first serious counter-offensive against the Slavs since the reign of Maurice. But its effects were limited, and it was not until the late eighth century that the tide in the southern part of the Balkans began to turn against the Slavs. In 783 Irene's chief minister Stauracius marched through Greece and the Peloponnese, subduing Slav tribes; the establishment of the Peloponnesian theme at the end of the century was possibly a result of this expedition.[3] The real turning point in the history of the Peloponnese, however, was under Nicephorus I (802–11) whose forces suppressed a large-scale revolt of the Slavs round Patras (805) and settled Christian communities in various parts of the peninsula. The process of absorption and hellenisation of the Slavs in Greece and in the Peloponnese was now well under way. By the middle of the ninth century Byzantine authority was restored throughout most of these

[1] Of the immense literature of unequal value that has accumulated since the days of Fallmerayer (d. 1861) on the controversial question of the Slav settlements in Greece the most important works are cited in A. Bon, *Le Péloponnèse byzantin*, p. 30, n. 1. Bon himself provides a cautious and balanced analysis of the problem (pp. 27 ff.). See also Lemerle, 'Invasions et migrations', *op. cit.* 301–4.

[2] As G. Ostrogorsky has convincingly shown ('Postanak tema Helada i Peloponez: Die Entstehung der Themen Hellas und Peloponnes', *Zbornik Radova Vizantološkog Instituta Srpske Akademije Nauka*, XXI, 1 (1952), 64–77), the theme of Hellas was limited to the eastern part of Central Greece.

[3] The Peloponnesian theme used to be considered to have been created after the Byzantine victory over the Slavs at Patras (805). But, as Ostrogorsky has pointed out (*loc. cit.* pp. 71–3; *History of the Byzantine State*, p. 172, n. 2), the existence of this theme before 805, restricted no doubt to the eastern part of the peninsula, can be clearly inferred both from the *De administrando imperio*, cap. 49, *DAI*, I, p. 228, 5), and from the *Chronicle of Monemvasia* (ed. N. Bees, Βυζαντίς, I (1909), 68 f.). For a more cautious interpretation of the evidence see R. J. H. Jenkins, in *DAI*, II, pp. 184–5.

lands, and what was left undone by the imperial *strategi* and tax-collectors was later completed by the East Roman missionaries.

Before this reconquest of Greece and the Peloponnese had begun the Empire made a desperate, and almost successful, effort to regain Moesia from the Bulgars and restore its northern frontier to the Danube. For some twenty years (756–75) Constantine V strove to conquer Bulgaria. He cleverly exploited the country's social weakness by fanning the constant antagonism between the boyar aristocracy and the Slavs, and in a series of nine campaigns, mostly successful, which usually combined—in the time-honoured fashion— land attacks through Thrace with naval expeditions to the Danube, he routed the Bulgarian armies again and again. But even his victory over the Khan Telets at Anchialus in 763—the greatest of his reign— did not subdue the country. Constantine's death on his last campaign (775) left the Empire stronger in the Balkans than it had been since the reign of Maurice; but Bulgaria, though crippled and exhausted, was still on the map, its ruling classes bitterly hostile to Byzantium.

The vitality of the Bulgarian state and its powers of recovery were demonstrated when Krum, the mightiest of its early rulers, became Sublime Khan in the opening years of the ninth century. The destruction of the Avar Empire by Charlemagne had enabled the Bulgarians to annex eastern Pannonia, and Krum became the sovereign of a realm that stretched from northern Thrace to the northern Carpathians and from the lower Sava to the Dniester and adjoined the Frankish Empire on the Theiss. He was long remembered with terror by the Byzantines. The aggressive policy of Nicephorus I towards Bulgaria set Krum on a campaign of devastation: in 809 he captured Sardica (the modern Sofia) and in July 811 gained his most celebrated triumph: the Byzantine army was trapped by the Bulgarians in a defile of the Balkan Mountains and slaughtered almost to a man. Nicephorus himself perished in the fray, and from his skull Krum made a goblet, lined with silver, out of which he drank with his boyars. This was a terrible blow to the Empire's prestige: not since the death of Valens on the field of Adrianople in 378 had an Emperor fallen in battle. The triumphant Khan swept into Thrace, captured Develtus and Mesembria (812) and in July 813, having routed another Byzantine army, arrived before the walls of Constantinople. But 'the new Sennacherib'[1] was impressed by the fortifications of the city and opened negotiations. In the meeting that followed with the Emperor Leo V on the shore of the Golden Horn Krum barely escaped a Byzantine plot to murder him; breathing vengeance he

---

[1] Theophanes, ed. C. de Boor (Leipzig, 1883), p. 503.

laid waste the environs of the city and stormed Adrianople, transporting its inhabitants, numbering, it was said, ten thousand, to his own dominions north of the Danube. But the following spring, as he was preparing a huge assault on Constantinople, Krum burst a blood-vessel and died (April 814).

The Empire had had a narrow escape. But the balance of power in the Balkans had radically altered. Bulgaria, a country which fifty years before had seemed on the verge of extinction, was now one of the great military powers of Europe. Byzantium's northern line of defence was seriously undermined, since the border fortresses in Thrace—Sardica, Develtus, Mesembria and Adrianople—had been either destroyed or crippled by Krum. But fortunately for the Empire, Krum's aggressive policy was abandoned by his successors. In 815–16 the Khan Omortag concluded a thirty years' peace with Byzantium: the frontier between the two realms was to run along the Great Fence of Thrace from Develtus to Macrolivada, and thence northward to the Balkan Mountains, thus coinciding with the boundary established exactly a century before by the treaty between Tervel and Theodosius III. Save for a few frontier clashes, the Empire and Bulgaria were to remain at peace with one another until the end of the century. The new policy could not fail to strengthen Byzantine influence in Bulgaria, and together with men and ideas from Constantinople, and partly through the thousands of Greek prisoners whom Krum had settled in his realm, Christianity was beginning to spread in the country. The authorities, and especially the boyars who regarded Christianity as an insidious form of Byzantine imperialism, were understandably alarmed. So Omortag, largely it seems for political motives, persecuted his Christian subjects. But the progress of the new ideas which, under the cloak of the thirty years' peace, were spreading from Byzantium to Bulgaria could not be arrested for very long by these reactionary measures.

Meanwhile, with peace restored in the Balkans, the East Roman government was free to devote its attention to the other sectors of the Empire's northern front. The emergence of Bulgaria as a major power, and the uncertain situation in the Pontic steppes, more than ever required a favourable balance of power in the Crimea and northern Caucasus; yet all was not well in these areas: Byzantine Crimea, and especially Cherson, was restive under imperial control, and if the Empire was not to lose its invaluable outpost in the north, the local traditions of Greek municipal autonomy had to be diverted into lawful channels. Khazaria, moreover, on whose friendship the Byzantine statesmen had so long depended, now threatened, owing to the progress of Judaism in the land, to elude their grasp. During the reign of Theophilus, however, the Empire's position in these sectors suddenly improved. About the year 833 the Khazar Khan sent an embassy to the Emperor, asking for engineers to build a fortress on the lower Don; whereupon the *spatharocandidatus* Petronas Camaterus, escorted by a squadron of the imperial navy, went on Theophilus' orders to Khazaria by way of Cherson. After building the fortress of Sarkel for the Khazars, he returned to report to the Emperor on the situation in the Crimea. On Petronas' advice, Theophilus raised Cherson and its surroundings into an imperial theme, directly subordinated to the central government, and appointed Petronas its *strategus*, with authority over the local magistrates.[1] It seems clear that the building of Sarkel and the establishment of the theme of Cherson were due to the same cause—the pressure of unidentified barbarians on the lower Don.[2] The Cherson–Sarkel axis, which may well have included a chain of fortifications up the Don,[3] thus served both as an inner line of defence for the Khazar Khanate, whose sphere of influence extended by then to the Dnieper and the Oka, and as a pivot of Byzantium's strategic position in the steppes between the lower Volga and the Danube. Common problems of military security had once again confirmed the traditional alliance between the Empire and the Khazars.

The role played by the Khazar alliance in the Empire's diplomacy became even more apparent in the reign of Michael III. Probably at the end of 860, a Byzantine embassy left Constantinople for Khazaria, headed by a young priest from Thessalonica, named Constantine, who was accompanied by his elder brother, the monk Methodius. Their route lay through Cherson, where Constantine spent the winter and prepared for his mission by learning Hebrew. At the Khan's residence, which seems to have been then at Samandar, on the lower

---

[1] Const. Porphyr., *De administrando imperio*, cap. 42, *DAI*, I, pp. 182–4, and II, pp. 154–5.

[2] The identity of the barbarians who threatened the Khazars and Byzantine Crimea in the fourth decade of the ninth century is a matter of considerable dispute. Scylitzes-Cedrenus (II, pp. 129–30, *CSHB*) states explicitly and Theophanes Continuatus (p. 122, *CSHB*) by implication that they were the Pechenegs. It has, however, been pointed out (J. Marquart, *Osteuropäische und ostasiatische Streifzüge* (Leipzig, 1903), p. 28) that in 833 the Pechenegs were still east of the Volga; furthermore, recent archeological work has shown that Sarkel was situated on the left bank of the Don (M. Artamonov, 'Sarkel', *Sovetskaja Archeologija*, VI (1940), 130–67); 'Khazarskaja Krepost Sarkel', *Acta Arch. Acad. Sc. Hungaricae*, VII (1956), 321–41), and this must mean that it was built against attacks from the West. Those scholars who reject the statement of Scylitzes-Cedrenus believe in the main that the barbarians in question were either the Magyars (C. A. Macartney, *The Magyars in the Ninth Century* (Cambridge, 1930), pp. 74–5) or the Russian Vikings (J. B. Bury, *A History of the Eastern Roman Empire*, pp. 414–18; F. Dvornik, *Les légendes*, pp. 172–4; A. Vasiliev, *The Goths in the Crimea*, pp. 109 ff.).

[3] Cf. J. Marquart, *loc. cit.*; J. B. Bury, *op. cit.* p. 416.

Terek, he engaged in theological disputations with Jewish rabbis who held a dominant position at the Khazar court. But Constantine's ninth-century biographer, while depicting the Khan and his subjects as monotheists and people of the Book, clearly implies, in the present writer's opinion, that their final conversion to Judaism had not yet taken place.[1] This inference could be reconciled with the earlier dates at which Hebrew and Islamic sources set the conversion of the Khazars to Judaism[2] by supposing that some of the Khans had adopted Jewish monotheism between 730 and 860, without, however, submitting to all the requirements of the Mosaic law.[3] It seems significant that the earliest reference to the Khazars practising circumcision and observing 'all the traditions of Judaism' dates from about 864–6,[4] and it is thus difficult to escape the conclusion that the ruling circles of Khazaria formally accepted the Mosaic law soon after Constantine's mission.[5]

But if Constantine's embassy was no great success on the religious plane—some two hundred conversions and an ambiguous declaration from the Khan of his sympathy for Christianity were the measure of his missionary achievement at Samandar—politically he seems to have secured his object. The alliance between Byzantium and Khazaria was reaffirmed, and the Khan wrote to Michael III, professing his readiness to serve the Empire whenever he was needed.[6] The exact nature of the 'services' which the Empire required from the Khazars in 860–1 is not known, but it is safe to assume that Con-

[1] The Khazar envoys to Constantinople about 860 openly professed monotheism: see *Vita Constantini*, cap. 8: *Constantinus et Methodius Thessalonicenses: Fontes*, ed. F. Grivec and T. Tomšič (Zagreb, 1960) (*Radovi Staroslavenskog Instituta*, IV), p. 109; F. Dvornik, *Les légendes*, p. 358. Moreover, the Khan himself told the Byzantine envoys: 'we differ from you on this point alone: you glorify the Trinity and we worship one God, having received the Books' (*Vita Constantini*, cap. 9, ed. Grivec and Tomšič, p. 112; Dvornik, *op. cit.* p. 361). Yet the same Khazar envoys said to the Emperor: 'the Jews exhort us to embrace their faith and their traditions, but the Saracens on the other hand...urge us to accept their beliefs' (*ibid.* cap. 8, ed. Grivec and Tomšič, p. 109: Dvornik, *op. cit.* p. 358).

[2] About 730–40 ('The Hebrew Correspondence'; see above: p. 488, n. 2); in the reign of Hārūn-ar-Rashīd (768–809) (Mas'udi, *Les prairies d'or*, trans. C. Barbier de Meynard, II, Paris, 1863, p. 8).

[3] This partial conversion to Judaism seems to be implied in a passage of the *Life of St Abo of Tiflis*, where the Khazars are described as being in the late eighth century 'agrestes homines...qui legem nullam habent, nisi quod unum Deum creatorem norunt' (P. Peeters, *op. cit.* p. 25).

[4] 'una gens...[Gazari] circumcisa est, et omnem Judaismum observat.' Druthmar, *Expositio in Matthaeum*, *MPL*, CVI, 1456.

[5] The present writer cannot hence, without the above qualifications, accept F. Dvornik's statement (*Les légendes*, p. 171) that the Khazars already professed Judaism at the time of Constantine's mission, and agrees, with the same qualifications, with the conclusions of G. Vernadsky ('The Date of the Conversion of the Khazars to Judaism', *B*, XV (1940–1), 76–86); for a different view see Dunlop, *op. cit.* pp. 195–6.

[6] *Vita Const.* cap. 11, trans. F. Dvornik, *Les légendes*, p. 370.

stantine's mission was connected with a new danger that threatened
Byzantium from the north and must be viewed in the light of the
Empire's policy in that region during the seventh decade of the ninth
century. The remarkable achievements of this policy, which were to
leave a permanent mark on the history of Europe, were perhaps due
to three main factors: to the vigour and initiative which, after the
barbarian invasions of the post-Justinian period and the iconoclast
crisis, Byzantine diplomacy was now able to display beyond the
Empire's northern frontier; to an unprecedented expansion of the
Church's missionary work, now linked closer than ever to the aims of
East Roman diplomacy, which made the seventh decade of this
century one of the greatest in the history of Byzantine missions; and
to the fact that in this period the religious and cultural influence of
the Empire was able to strike out beyond the traditional perimeter
of Byzantium's northern front and, thrusting deep into eastern and
central Europe, to gain the allegiance of a substantial part of the
vast Slav world.

The story of this achievement begins on 18 June 860, when a fleet
of two hundred Viking ships, coming from the Black Sea, sailed into
the Bosphorus and turned against Constantinople. The city's position was serious indeed: the Byzantine fleet was probably in the
Mediterranean, fighting the Arabs, the army and the Emperor were
campaigning in Asia Minor. The suburbs and the coastline were defenceless against the savage depredations of the barbarians. Inside the invested city the Patriarch Photius urged the people to faith and
repentance. The strong fortifications once again saved Constantinople;
and probably before the Emperor hastily brought his army back, the
invaders raised the siege and withdrew to their homes in the north.[1]
The violent emergence of these Vikings—known to the Byzantines as
'Ρῶς,[2] to the Slavs as Rus' and to the Arabs as Rūs[3]—on the horizon
of East Rome was the outcome of a century-long process of expansion
which led the Scandinavians, mostly Swedes from Upland, Södermanland and East Götland, to sail up the Baltic rivers over the great

[1] The two homilies preached by Photius on this occasion, for all their rhetorical
exaggeration, give a vivid impression of the city's anguish in the summer of 860:
Müller, *FHG*, v, 1, pp. 162–73; see the translation and commentary by C. Mango,
The Homilies of Photius (Cambridge, Mass., 1958, pp. 74–110). Cf. the brief but clear
analysis of the sources in G. Laehr, *Die Anfänge des russischen Reiches* (Hist. Stud. 189,
Berlin, 1930), pp. 91–5, and the very full account of A. A. Vasiliev, *The Russian
Attack on Constantinople in 860* (Cambridge, Mass., 1946).

[2] The presence in Constantinople of an embassy from the Swedish *Rhos* is attested
as early as 839: *Annales Bertiniani*, *MGH*, *Script.* i, p. 434. Cf. A. Vasiliev, *op. cit.*
pp. 6–13.

[3] For the Arabic sources on the Rūs see V. Minorsky, 'Rūs', *Encycl. of Islam*, iii,
1181–3.

watershed of the East European plain. In the second half of the eighth century, drawn by the extensive trade that flourished, through the intermediary of the Volga Bulgars and the Khazars, between the fur and slave dealers of the northern forests and the luxury markets of Baghdad, they began to go down the Volga to Itil, and over the Caspian to the lands of the Caliphate. Somewhat later, in search of fresh markets and easier plunder, the Vikings explored the shorter routes to the warm and rich countries of the South: probably by the early ninth century, sailing down the Don[1] and the Dniester, they reached the Black Sea. Towards the middle of the ninth century began the third and most significant stage in the southward expansion of the Swedes: by moving up the rivers of the eastern Baltic—the Neva, the western Dvina, and the Niemen—and by dragging their ships over portages that lay beyond, the Varangians (as the Russian Swedes came to be known in eastern Europe) discovered the Dnieper which flowed into the Black Sea; and the whole of this elaborate network of rivers, lakes, portages and seas which led from Scandinavia to the Bosphorus, the 'route from the Varangians to the Greeks' of the Russian Chronicle, became in the second half of the century the true Swedish *Austrvegr*, the classic highway for the great Eastern adventure.[2] Along this waterway, on territory inhabited by Finns and eastern Slavs, the Varangians founded their trading colonies and carved out their military kingdoms. By the middle of the century an important 'Russian' settlement, ruled by the Viking Ryurik, existed in Novgorod. Some time between 850 and 860 two Varangians from Novgorod, Askold and Dir, went down the Dnieper and captured the city of Kiev from the Khazars.[3] This was an event of considerable importance: for when the Vikings replaced the Khazars as overlords of the middle Dnieper valley, the strong oriental influences to which the eastern Slavs in this region had for centuries been subjected suffered a sharp setback; while the lure of Byzantium, the fabulous Mikligarðr, that deflected the Varangian ships from the Volga and the Caspian to the Dnieper and the

---

[1] The Viking colonisation of the lower Don and Azov areas raises some controversial problems. The present writer believes that Viking bands had very probably reached the Azov region by the early ninth century, but finds it hard to accept the view of Vernadsky (*Ancient Russia*, pp. 278–86) and Mošin that the Norsemen built an organised and powerful state in this area: see the full discussion in Mošin, 'Varjago-russkij vopros', *Slavia*, x (1931), 109–36, 343–79, 501–37; 'Načalo Rusi. Normany v vostočnoj Evrope', *BS*, iii (1931), 33–58, 285–307.

[2] On this route see D. Obolensky in *DAI*, ii, pp. 18–61 (with bibliography).

[3] *The Russian Primary Chronicle* (*Povest' Vremennych Let*), ed. D. Lichačev and V. Adrianova-Peretc (Moscow–Leningrad, 1950), i, pp. 18–19; English trans. by S. H. Cross and O. P. Sherbowitz-Wetzor (Cambridge, Mass., 1953), pp. 59–60. This will be subsequently cited as *The Russian Primary Chronicle* and the English translation of 1953 as 'Cross–Sherbowitz'.

Black Sea, was a premonition and a cause of that irresistible attraction which the city of Constantine was to exert on the minds of the Russians for many centuries to come. It was Askold and Dir who led the Russian campaign on Constantinople in 860, and it can scarcely be doubted that the expedition was launched from Kiev.[1]

The Byzantine response to the Russian attack, whose failure they ascribed to the protection of the Mother of God, was swift and characteristic. It is highly probable that the main political object of Constantine's mission to Khazaria in 860–1 was to concert with the Khan on a joint policy against the Russians, the common enemy of Constantinople and Itil. This diplomatic encirclement of Kiev was followed up by an attempt to convert the Russians to Christianity. Soon after 860 ambassadors from the Rhos were baptised in Constantinople,[2] and in 867 the Patriarch Photius was able to announce that the Russians, who formerly surpassed all peoples in cruelty, had now accepted Christianity and were living under the spiritual authority of a Byzantine bishop as 'subjects and friends' of the Empire.[3] Finally, in the reign of Basil I, possibly about 874, the Russians concluded a treaty with Byzantium and an archbishop was sent to them by the Patriarch Ignatius.[4] The scantiness of the sources does not allow us to follow the fate of this first Byzantine ecclesiastical organisation on Russian soil; it is natural to suppose that its centre was at Kiev and that it was engulfed in the pagan reaction that swept over South Russia later in the century. Yet the bridgehead which Byzantine Christianity had secured beyond the Pontic steppes was never completely destroyed.

It is an impressive sign of the vision and resourcefulness which the Empire's foreign policy had acquired by the seventh decade of the ninth century that while the missionaries of Photius and Ignatius were labouring to convert the Slavs and their Viking overlords on the middle Dnieper, the cultural and political influence of Byzantium was able to strike out equally far to another region of the North. In 862 there arrived in Constantinople an embassy from Rastislav, prince of the Moravian Slavs. Its purpose was twofold: the Moravians, whose realm stretched from Bohemia to the Theiss and from the Carpathians to the middle Danube, desired to form an alliance with Byzantium to counteract the coalition recently made against them by Louis the

---

[1] The much-debated question as to whether the Russian attack of 860 was launched from Kiev or from the Azov region is discussed by A. Vasiliev (*op. cit.* pp. 169–75), whose arguments in favour of Kiev seem to the present writer convincing.

[2] Theoph. Cont. cap. 33, p. 196 (*CSHB*).

[3] Photius, *Epistolae*, *MPG*, CII, 736–7 (τὸ Ῥῶς...ἐν ὑπηκόων ἑαυτοὺς καὶ προξένων τάξει...ἐγκαταστήσαντες).

[4] Theoph. Cont. cap. 97, pp. 342–3. Cf. *DR*, 493.

German and the Bulgarian Khan Boris. Rastislav also requested Michael III to send him a missionary capable of teaching Christianity to his people in their own Slavonic tongue. Hitherto the Christian preachers in Moravia had been German missionaries and servants of the Frankish Emperor; a Slav-speaking clergy dependent on Constantinople, Rastislav believed, would help him preserve his independence and ensure a more rapid progress of Christianity in his land. The Moravian proposals were favourably received in Byzantium: the Franko-Bulgarian pact, which threatened to bring Carolingian influence to the very doors of Constantinople, could not but alarm so experienced a diplomatist as the Emperor's chief minister, Bardas; while the Patriarch Photius must have foreseen that Byzantine influence in Moravia would provide a means of exerting pressure on the Bulgarians and of bringing them too into the Christian fold. The Moravo-Byzantine alliance was concluded, and early in 863 an East Roman embassy left for central Europe, headed by Constantine, accompanied once again by his brother Methodius.

The two brothers were natives of Greek Thessalonica and well acquainted with the Slavonic language of the hinterland. Constantine was also an unusually gifted philologist: before embarking on his new mission he invented an alphabet for the use of the Moravian Slavs. This first unequivocally attested Slavonic script, identified by most modern authorities as Glagolitic, was adapted to a dialect of southern Macedonia. By gradually translating into this dialect the Scriptures and liturgy of the Christian Church Constantine and Methodius created a new literary language, known as Old Church Slavonic, which became in the course of time the sacred idiom of a large section of the Slavs and the third international language of Europe. The two brothers began their work in Moravia by translating the liturgical offices into Slavonic: it seems that at first they used only the Byzantine rite, but in the course of time also adopted and translated the Roman mass.[1] Their activities, which included the training of the clergy of Rastislav's new Slav Church, were viewed with open hostility by the Frankish clergy in Moravia who regarded them not only as dangerous innovators in matters of faith—for the Roman Church, in whose jurisdiction Moravia lay, did not favour the use of vernacular liturgies—but also, no doubt, as agents of Byzantine imperialism. In the winter of 867–8 Constantine and Methodius travelled to Rome at the invitation of Pope Nicholas I, and were received by his successor

---

[1] For the probable coexistence, and possible blending, of the Byzantine and the Roman rites in Moravia, see F. Dvornik, *The Slavs, their early History and Civilization* (Boston, 1956), pp. 84–5, 166–7; F. Grivec, *Konstantin und Method, Lehrer der Slaven* (Wiesbaden, 1960), pp. 179–84.

Hadrian II. They could scarcely have chosen a more propitious moment to plead their cause before the Holy See: for the work of these Byzantine missionaries in Moravia had suddenly become a crucial factor in the ecclesiastical politics of Europe, owing to the remarkable change that had befallen the relations between the Empire and Bulgaria.

The peace that prevailed between Byzantium and Bulgaria during Omortag's reign was endangered after his death (831) by the assertiveness of the Bulgarians who occupied Sardica and Philippopolis and annexed central Macedonia,[1] and by the pro-Frankish policy followed by the Khan Boris (852–89) at the beginning of his reign. In 864, fearing that Boris would carry out his promise to accept Christianity from the German court, the Emperor moved his army to the frontier and sent his fleet along the Black Sea coast. The Khan was forced to capitulate: he undertook to renounce the Frankish alliance, to receive Christianity from Constantinople and—at least in the Byzantine reading of the facts—to submit himself and his people to the Emperor's authority.[2] In the same year Boris was baptised,[3] being christened Michael in honour of his imperial godfather. A revolt of the boyars against his decision to enforce baptism on all his subjects was ruthlessly suppressed, and the triumph of Byzantine Christianity in Bulgaria seemed assured. The Patriarch Photius wrote a long and carefully worded letter to Boris, explaining the doctrines of the Church and the duties of a Christian ruler.[4] The Khan, however, was not altogether satisfied by this learned disquisition: how was he to reconcile his recognition of Byzantine supremacy with his desire to remain master in his own country? A separate ecclesiastical hierarchy, under a Bulgarian Patriarch, or at least under a bishop owing allegiance to Constantinople, seemed to provide a solution to his dilemma; but on this matter Photius was ominously silent. And so, disappointed with the Greeks, Boris turned to his former ally, Louis the German, and in 866 requested him to send a bishop and priests to Bulgaria; at the same time he sent an embassy to Rome asking the

---

[1] According to P. Mutafčiev, *Istorija na bŭlgarskija narod*, I (3rd ed., Sofia, 1948), pp. 171–6, the country round Ochrida and Prespa was part of the Bulgarian realm by 842.

[2] Οἱ δὲ Βούλγαροι...καὶ Χριστιανοὶ γενέσθαι καὶ ὑποτάττεσθαι τῷ βασιλεῖ καὶ Ῥωμαίοις ᾐτήσαντο: Georgius Monachus, p. 824/19–20 (*CSHB*).

[3] The date of Boris' baptism—864, and not, as V. Zlatarski (*Istorija*, I, 2, pp. 27–31) and S. Runciman (*First Bulgarian Empire*, p. 104) believed, 865—was established by A. Vaillant and M. Lascaris ('La date de la conversion des Bulgares', *Revue des Etudes Slaves*, XIII (1933), 5 ff.).

[4] *MPG*, CII, 628–96; *Fontes Historiae Bulgaricae*, VIII (Sofia, 1961), 59–99. Cf. I. Dujčev, 'Au lendemain de la conversion du peuple bulgare, l'épître de Photius', *Mélanges de Science Religieuse*, VIII (1951), 211–26.

Pope for a Patriarch. Determined to make full use of this opportunity to subject the Bulgarian Church to the Holy See, Nicholas I at once sent two bishops to Bulgaria and composed a reply to a list of 106 questions which Boris had sent him.[1] This shrewd and sagacious document shows that Boris was concerned at the social effects of the clash between the new Christian and the old Bulgarian traditions in his realm, that his understanding of Christianity was still rudimentary, but that he was prepared to exploit the rivalry between the Eastern and Western Churches to gain as much independence and prestige as possible for his own Church. Boris' request for a Patriarch was, however, adroitly side-stepped by the Pope: for the time being, the Khan was told, he would have to content himself with an archbishop. But since Byzantium had grudged him even a bishop, Boris considered that he had got the better deal out of Rome and swore to remain for ever the faithful servant of St Peter.

Such was the situation when Constantine and Methodius arrived in Rome. The Papacy, after its triumph over the Byzantine Church in Bulgaria, now seemed in a good position to regain the whole of Illyricum from the Patriarch of Constantinople and to impose its spiritual authority over the Slav world. The Slavonic liturgy was no doubt a break with traditional Roman practice; yet as a means of evangelising the Slavs it commended itself, particularly as it was enthusiastically supported by two Slav rulers in central Europe, Rastislav of Moravia and Kocel of Pannonia. And so the new Pope Hadrian II gave his unqualified approval to the work of Constantine and Methodius and publicly authorised the use of the Slavonic liturgy. After Constantine's death in Rome in February 869 (he died as a monk under the name Cyril), Methodius was sent back by the Pope to central Europe to set up a new Slav Church in Pannonia and Moravia. A few months later, however, he was back in Rome. Again his visit to the Pope coincided with an event of European importance which was causing a great stir in Rome; and again the cause of this stir was the unaccountable behaviour of Boris of Bulgaria.

In the course of the past three years Boris had realised that the Pope had no intention of allowing him to manage his own ecclesiastical affairs. Meanwhile, the full resources of Byzantine diplomacy were being marshalled in an attempt to detach Bulgaria from Rome.[2]

---

[1] *Responsa ad Consulta Bulgarorum*, *MPL*, cxix, 978–1016; *Fontes Historiae Bulgaricae*, vii (1960), 60–125. Cf. I. Dujčev, 'Die Responsa Nicolai I. Papae ad Consulta Bulgarorum als Quelle für die bulgarische Geschichte', *Festschrift zur Feier des Haus-, Hof- und Staatsarchivs*, i (Vienna, 1949), pp. 349–62.

[2] 'Graeci...diversa requirunt ingenia, munera post munera numerosa mittentes, et sophistica ei argumenta creberrime proponentes': Anastasius Bibliothecarius, *MPL*, cxxviii, 20.

In February 870 the last session of the anti-Photian Council in Constantinople was attended by a Bulgarian embassy which asked the assembled Fathers on behalf of their ruler whether his Church should be subject to Rome or Constantinople. A special conference of the eastern Patriarchs' representatives, summoned under the Emperor's chairmanship to deal with this doubtless not unprepared intervention, and from which the protesting papal legates were excluded, decided that Bulgaria should return to the jurisdiction of the See of Constantinople. Boris naturally accepted this decision, the Roman clergy were expelled from his country, and an Archbishop consecrated by the Patriarch Ignatius was sent to Bulgaria.[1]

The news of Boris' defection, or at least a warning that it was impending, probably arrived in Rome while Methodius was still there; it seemed hardly calculated to inspire the Pope with confidence in the good faith of the Slavs. But once again Hadrian II proved himself a statesman: he appointed Methodius Archbishop of Pannonia and Legate of the Holy See to the Slavonic nations, extending his diocese to the Bulgarian frontier and thus hoping, with the help of the Slavonic liturgy, to link the Slavs of central Europe still closer to Rome. But Methodius' work in his new archdiocese was crippled by the continued opposition of the Frankish clergy who considered that his Slavonic policy impinged on their own rights. For two and a half years they kept the Archbishop a prisoner in Germany; and under their influence the Papacy, after the death of John VIII, lost interest in the Slavonic liturgy. About 882, at the invitation of the Emperor Basil I, Methodius journeyed to Constantinople, where he was received with honour and affection. Two of his disciples, armed with the sacred books in Slavonic, remained in Byzantium as an instrument of further missionary work among the Slavs and Methodius' last gift to his fatherland.

In 885 Methodius, powerless against the intrigues of the Frankish party, the hostility of the new Moravian ruler Svatopluk and the indifference of Rome, died in Moravia, his work among the Slavs of central Europe on the brink of ruin. His principal disciples, including his successor Gorazd, were sentenced to perpetual exile. Yet the Slavonic liturgy and the Slavo-Byzantine culture which St Cyril and St Methodius had implanted north of the Danube and on both sides of the northern Carpathians did not vanish from these lands for another two centuries. In Bohemia, and possibly in southern Poland, their influence can be traced well into the eleventh century,[2] a sure

---

[1] On Boris' dealings with Rome and Constantinople see F. Dvornik, *The Photian Schism* (Cambridge, 1948), pp. 91–131, 151–8, and see above: chs. IV and X.

[2] Cf. F. Dvornik, *The Making of Central and Eastern Europe*, pp. 18–22, 124–9, 249–53; *The Slavs, Their Early History and Civilisation*, pp. 170–4.

sign of the appeal which Byzantine Christianity, in its vernacular Slavonic form, retained in what had been in the ninth century a distant outpost of the East Roman missions.

It may be assumed that Methodius' work in Moravia and Pannonia enjoyed at least the moral support of his sovereign Basil I. The value of the Slavonic liturgy as a means of evangelising the Slavs and of attracting them into the political orbit of Byzantium was certainly appreciated by this Emperor,[1] whose policy towards the Balkan Slavs was marked by high statesmanship and crowned with remarkable success. Thus the Serbian tribes in the valleys of the Tara, the Lim and the Ibar, together with the piratical Narentani on the Adriatic coast, were forced to acknowledge the Emperor's sovereignty and to accept Christianity, but were left some political autonomy. In 878 through its agent, the Croatian prince Zdeslav, the Empire strengthened its hold over Dalmatia. And though in the following year the Croats accepted the ecclesiastical sovereignty of the Roman See, the political and cultural influence of East Rome, ably furthered by Basil I and clothed in the attractive garb of the Cyrillo-Methodian vernacular tradition, remained paramount in the Balkans.

It was in Bulgaria, however, that the legacy of Cyril and Methodius yielded its greatest dividends and was saved for Europe and the Slavs. The Byzantines were careful in 870 to avoid repeating the mistake that had thrown Boris into the arms of the Papacy, especially since Pope John VIII was making desperate attempts to regain his allegiance. The Archbishop of Bulgaria, though a suffragan of the See of Constantinople, was granted a measure of autonomy.[2] Yet, as Boris must have realised, it was only by acquiring a native clergy and the Slavonic liturgy and letters that his people could safely continue to assimilate Byzantine civilisation without prejudice to their cultural and political independence. And so, when the disciples of Methodius, on their expulsion from Moravia, travelled down the Danube valley and arrived in Bulgaria, they were enthusiastically received by Boris. Clement, one of their leaders, was sent to Macedonia about 886, where he laboured among Boris' Slav subjects for thirty years, converting the pagans, establishing the Slavonic liturgy of the Byzantine rite, building churches and training large numbers of Slav-speaking priests. On Clement's appointment as bishop in 893, his companion Naum, who had founded a school of Slavonic letters at Preslav in north-eastern Bulgaria, joined him in Macedonia. Thanks to St

[1] As his treatment of a group of Methodius' disciples who were sold into slavery by the Moravians and redeemed by a Byzantine envoy in Venice shows: see S. Runciman, *op. cit.* p. 125.

[2] V. Zlatarski, *Istorija*, I, 2, pp. 145–51; G. Ostrogorsky, *History of the Byzantine State*, p. 208, n. 1.

Clement and St Naum Macedonia became a renowned centre of Slavo-Byzantine culture, and its chief city of Ochrida became the metropolis of Slavonic Christianity. At Ochrida and Preslav, during the next few decades, much Byzantine literature was translated into Slavonic: liturgical hymns, Greek patristic works, Byzantine chronicles and encyclopaedias, stories of Troy and of Alexander the Great, were made accessible to the Slavs in the Cyrillic script.[1] The literary wealth that accumulated during this 'first golden age' of Bulgarian literature, which included some original creations, was to nourish throughout the middle ages the religious and intellectual life of the Russians, the Serbs and the Rumanians.[2]

This cultural work was further stimulated when Boris' third son Symeon succeeded to the throne (893) after his father had emerged from the monastery to which he had retired four years earlier, to depose his elder son Vladimir, whose pagan excesses had endangered the state. Symeon seemed peculiarly well fitted to continue his father's work: like Boris, he combined a devotion to Byzantine culture with an enthusiasm for Slavonic letters; much of his youth had been spent in Constantinople, where, so Liutprand was informed, he became proficient in 'the rhetoric of Demosthenes and the syllogisms of Aristotle', earning the nickname of *hemiargos*, the half-Greek;[3] and on his return to Bulgaria he actively sponsored the literary movement. His new capital of Preslav he intended to make a second Constantinople; the splendour of its churches and palaces, we are assured by a contemporary Bulgarian writer, defied description; and in the royal palace sat Symeon 'in a garment woven with gold, a golden chain round his neck, girt with a purple girdle covered with pearls, and wearing a golden sword'.[4]

The imperial diplomatists, in observing the progress of Byzantium's northern proselyte, could congratulate themselves on the dividends which the Slav policy, devised by Photius and Basil I and carried out by Cyril and Methodius and their disciples, was yielding in Bulgaria. But in 894 these achievements were compromised by the carelessness of the Emperor Leo VI. An intrigue at the imperial court enabled

[1] The Cyrillic script which, except in Croatia and Dalmatia, rapidly supplanted the Glagolitic, is considered by most present-day authorities to have resulted from an attempt by Methodius' disciples in Bulgaria to adapt Greek uncial writing to the Slavonic tongue. The question of the relative priority of Glagolitic and Cyrillic may, however, still be considered an open one. For an attempt to argue the priority of Cyrillic, see E. Georgiev, *Slavjanskaja pismennost do Kirilla i Mefodija* (Sofia, 1952).

[2] Cf. M. Murko, *Geschichte der älteren südslawischen Litteraturen* (Leipzig, 1908), pp. 57 ff.; B. Angelov and M. Genov, *Stara bŭlgarska literatura* (Sofia, 1922).

[3] *Antapodosis*, lib. III, cap. 29 (ed. I. Bekker, p. 87).

[4] John the Exarch, *Šestodnev*, ed. R. Aitzetmüller, *Das Hexaemeron des Exarchen Johannes*, I (Graz, 1958), p. 195.

two Byzantine merchants to secure the monopoly of the Bulgarian trade and to transfer the market to Thessalonica, where they imposed heavy taxes on Bulgarian goods.[1] Symeon thought this an outrage. He promptly invaded Thrace, defeated a Byzantine army and advanced towards Constantinople. The peace which, save for a few minor encounters, had reigned in the Balkans for the past eighty years was at an end. Leo VI, whose best troops were in Asia, resorted to the traditional method of imperial diplomacy: he sent an embassy to Bulgaria's northern neighbours the Magyars, who then inhabited the steppes between the lower Dnieper and the lower Danube, to persuade them to attack Symeon in the rear. This Finno-Ugrian people, considerably mixed with and influenced by Turkic elements, had in all probability formed part of Kovrat's Onoguric realm; they had remained east of the Maeotis as subjects of the Khazars and in the course of the ninth century had moved westward across the Don and the Dnieper. Ferried across the Danube by the Byzantine fleet, the Magyars raided north-eastern Bulgaria, inflicting several defeats on Symeon's armies (895). But Symeon was capable of outplaying the East Romans at their own game: he opened negotiations with the Empire, arrested the Byzantine ambassador Leo Choerosphactes and, entangling him in a semi-ironic correspondence in which both parties quibbled about words and punctuation,[2] called in the Magyars' eastern neighbours, the Pechenegs. This Turkic people had recently been driven westward from their homes between the Emba and the Volga by the Uzes and had reached the Dnieper. Doubtless bribed by Symeon, they now combined with the Bulgarians to plunder the lands of the Magyars. Finding on their return from Bulgaria their homes occupied by the fearsome Pechenegs, the Magyars had no option but to migrate further west: so they crossed the Carpathians and in 895 entered the Pannonian plain. By 906 they had destroyed the Moravian realm and founded the medieval kingdom of Hungary. Symeon, meanwhile, invaded Thrace and routed the Byzantines at Bulgarophygon (896). Peace was then concluded and the Empire undertook to pay Bulgaria a yearly subsidy.

The events of these three years had seriously undermined the Empire's position in the Balkans. A hostile and ambitious Symeon now stood at the gates of Thrace, and the Slavs of Serbia and of the coastal region of Dyrrachium were falling under his influence.

---

[1] See G. I. Bratianu, 'Le commerce bulgare dans l'Empire byzantin et le monopole de l'empereur Léon VI à Thessalonique', *Sbornik Nikov: Izvestija na Bŭlgarskoto Istoričesko Družestvo*, xvi–xviii (1940), 30–6.

[2] G. Kolias, *Léon Choerosphactès* (Athens, 1939 = *Texte und Forschungen zur byzant.-neugriechischen Philologie*, xxxi); *Fontes Historiae Bulgaricae*, viii (1961), 175–84; cf. V. Zlatarski, *Istorija*, i, 2, pp. 302–12.

Further north, between the Danube and the Don, the Pechenegs had emerged as a disturbing factor in the steppes. In one respect only did these new barbarian invasions offer some prospect of relief: hitherto Byzantium had been hemmed in by a solid mass of Slavs, stretching from Thrace and Macedonia to the Baltic Sea; the coming of the Magyars to Pannonia, the result of Symeon's diplomacy, had driven a wedge into the centre of the Slav world, for ever precluding the formation of a united Slav empire and decisively halting any further expansion of Bulgaria into central Europe.

Menacing clouds were gathering in Leo VI's reign in another sector of the north. The Christian missions planted in Russia by Photius and Ignatius had fallen upon evil days. About 882 the Varangian Oleg, sailing south from Novgorod, captured Kiev from Askold and Dir.[1] The whole of the waterway from the gulf of Finland to a point in the lower Dnieper some hundred miles north of the rapids[2] was now united for the first time under a single Viking ruler, round Kiev, the capital of the new Russian state. The notorious controversy between the 'Normanist' and the 'anti-Normanist' schools of historians as to whether the ninth-century Russian state was a Scandinavian creation or the product of earlier Slavonic or oriental traditions shows few signs of abating;[3] in the present writer's opinion, it can no longer be doubted that the Slavs in the Dnieper basin had been taking an active part in the political and commercial life of the Iranian and Turkic overlords of the steppe for centuries before the Viking era; and that a pre-existing Slav land-owning aristocracy and merchant class remained the mainstay of the country's territorial stability and economic growth under its Scandinavian overlords. But it is equally clear that it was the Vikings who united the scattered tribes of Eastern Slavs into a single state based on the Baltic–Black Sea waterway, to which they gave their 'Russian' name.[4] In this sense

[1] *The Russian Primary Chronicle*, ed. Lichačev, I, p. 20; trans. Cross–Sherbowitz, pp. 60–1. *The First Novgorod Chronicle*, on the other hand, attributes the capture of Kiev jointly to Igor, Ryurik's son, and to Oleg, Igor playing the leading role: *Novgorodskaja Pervaja Letopis*, ed. A. Nasonov (Moscow–Leningrad, 1950), p. 107.

[2] On the Dnieper rapids and their Scandinavian and Slav names cited in the *De administrando imperio* (cap. 9), see *DAI*, I, pp. 58–60, and D. Obolensky in *DAI*, II, pp. 38–52.

[3] For the history of this controversy, see V. Mošin, 'Varjago-russkij vopros', *Slavia*, x (1931), 109–36, 343–79, 501–37; A. Stender-Petersen, *Varangica* (Aarhus, 1953), pp. 5–20; H. Paszkiewicz, *The Origin of Russia* (London, 1954), pp. 109–32; *DAI*, II, pp. 20–3.

[4] For a classic exposition of the 'Normanist' view, see V. Thomsen, *The Relations between Ancient Russia and Scandinavia and the Origin of the Russian State* (Oxford, 1877). The 'anti-Normanist' theory is now chiefly championed by Soviet historians: see, in particular, B. D. Grekov, *Kievskaja Rus*, 4th ed. (Moscow–Leningrad, 1944), pp. 250 ff.; V. P. Šušarin, 'O suščnosti i formach sovremennogo normanizma', *Voprosy Istorii*, VIII (1960), 65–93.

Oleg was certainly the founder of the Kievan realm. A wave of paganism swept over the Dnieper region during his reign and the predatory lust of the Vikings revived. In 907, with an amphibious host of Varangians and Slavs, Oleg appeared before Constantinople; after laying waste the suburbs of the city, he retired, and in 911 a treaty was signed between the Russians and the Empire.[1] The preferential treatment it accorded the Russian merchants in Constantinople[2] seems to have ensured Byzantium against new attacks from Kiev for the next thirty years. The commercial relations established in 911 mark a further stage in the gradual assimilation of the Vikings into the East European world. But so long as the Varangian rulers of Kiev were pagan, and regarded their capital largely as a stepping-stone on the road to more alluring horizons, the Russians remained a potential threat to both Cherson and Byzantium.

Leo VI's diplomacy at least succeeded in keeping the peace with Bulgaria after 896. But the Emperor's death in 912 precipitated a war with Symeon which lasted for eleven years, brought the Empire's power in the Balkans to the brink of ruin, and presented the Byzantine statesmen with a challenge the like of which they had never yet experienced. Symeon, meanwhile, was waiting for a chance to further his ambitions at the expense of a weakened Empire. The Byzantines seemed to be playing into his hands: his envoys, sent to renew the treaty of 896, had been brutally insulted by the Emperor Alexander. And after Alexander's death in June 913, the Empire, nominally ruled by a delicate child, Constantine Porphyrogenitus, and precariously governed by a regency council under the Patriarch Nicholas Mysticus, was rent by a severe internal crisis. Symeon at the head of a large army invaded Thrace and appeared in August before Constantinople. Like Krum exactly a century before, he was daunted by the fortifications and resolved to negotiate.

The nature and result of these negotiations, concluded at a meeting between Symeon and the Patriarch Nicholas,[3] are obscure and con-

---

[1] The Old Russian text of the treaty is preserved in the *Russian Primary Chronicle*, ed. Lichačev, I, pp. 25–9; trans. Cross–Sherbowitz, pp. 65–8. The historicity of Oleg's raid on Constantinople, frequently denied in recent years, has been convincingly established by Ostrogorsky ('L'expédition du Prince Oleg contre Constantinople en 907', *Sem. Kond.* XI (1940), 47–62) and by A. Vasiliev ('The Second Russian Attack on Constantinople', *DOP*, VI (1951), 163–225, where the relevant literature is exhaustively reviewed).

[2] The Russians were granted total exemption from customs, were allotted a special residence in the suburban quarter of St Mamas, and received free board for six months, a period twice as long as the normal limit of residence allowed to foreign merchants in Constantinople.

[3] On the question of whether this meeting took place within or outside Constantinople the Byzantine tradition is as ambiguous as in the case of Tervel's investiture (see above: p. 485, n. 2); Georgius Monachus (pp. 877–8, *CSHB*) and Theophanes

troversial. It is practically certain, however, that Symeon was then promised that one of his daughters would marry the Emperor Constantine and it is possible that he obtained from the Byzantine government on the same occasion the title of 'Emperor of the Bulgarians' (βασιλεὺς Βουλγάρων).[1] It is probable in any case that Symeon's great ambition, which was to haunt him for the rest of his life, took shape as early as 913. The promised position of *Basileopator*, as the Emperor's father-in-law, offered power in Constantinople and seemed to point the way to the very throne of the Empire. The title of 'Emperor of the Bulgarians'—if it was ever granted—was at best a makeshift: for Symeon was too well grounded in the Byzantine doctrine of sovereignty to imagine for a moment that there could ever be two Empires in the Balkans; by its nature the Empire was universal and its only centre was Constantinople. It was not a national Bulgarian βασιλεία that Symeon desired, but the *imperium* of the Romans, the throne of the οἰκουμένη. And the Patriarch Nicholas, who for twelve years exerted all his diplomatic skill in an attempt to induce him to abandon this venture,[2] saw this very clearly: Symeon's bid for world domination he castigated as *tyrannis*, a rebellious usurpation of the imperial authority.[3] The Patriarch, who was prepared to go to almost any length to appease the Bulgarian ruler, significantly refused to concede this one vital point; against Symeon's claims to hegemony he solemnly reiterated the essential tenet of Byzantine political philosophy: the power of the Emperor, he wrote to Symeon, 'stands above all earthly authority and was alone on earth established by the Lord of all'.[4]

But Symeon's hopes proved vain. Hardly was he back in Preslav

---

Continuatus (p. 385, *CSHB*) imply that the Patriarch visited Symeon outside the city; but according to Scylitzes-Cedrenus (II, p. 282, *CSHB*) Symeon was entertained by the Emperor at a feast in the Blachernae Palace.

[1] This view is argued by Ostrogorsky ('Avtokrator i Samodržac', *Glas*, CLXIV (1935), 121 ff.; 'Die Krönung Symeons von Bulgarien durch den Patriarchen Nikolaos Mystikos', *Actes du IVe Congrès International des Etudes Byzantines*, Sofia, 1935, I, 275–86), and is accepted by P. Mutafčiev (*Istorija*, I, p. 240). For a different view, see F. Dölger, 'Der Bulgarenherrscher als geistlicher Sohn des byzant. Kaisers', *Sbornik Nikov, loc. cit.*, pp. 221, n. 1, and 228, n. 2 (= *Byzanz u. d. europäische Staatenwelt*, pp. 185, n. 7, and 193, n. 20).

[2] There are twenty-nine extant letters of Nicholas Mysticus concerned with Bulgarian affairs, all written during his second Patriarchate (912–25), twenty-six of which are addressed to Symeon: *MPG*, CXI, 40–196; *Fontes Historiae Bulgaricae*, VIII (1961), 185–297. Zlatarski provides a detailed commentary on them in *Sbornik za Narodni Umotvorenija, Nauka i Knižnina*, X (1894), 372–428; XI (1894), 3–54; XII (1895), 121–211. Cf. *GR*, nos. 614 ff.

[3] *Ep.* 5, *MPG*, CXI, 45–56. Cf. F. Dölger, 'Bulgarisches Zartum und byzantinisches Kaisertum', *Actes du IVe Congrès International des Etudes Byzantines*, I, 61–2 (= *Byzanz u. d. europäische Staatenwelt*, p. 147).

[4] *Ep.* 8, *MPG*, CXI, 64.

before the Empress Zoe seized control of the government in Constantinople; the Patriarch's influence declined and the plan of a marriage alliance was conveniently forgotten. Baulked in his immediate ambition, Symeon invaded Thrace and Macedonia. In vain did Nicholas urge him to desist from aggression: Symeon's retort was to demand that the Byzantines recognise him as their Emperor.[1] Zoe's government, determined to crush him, sent an army into Bulgaria. On 20 August 917, by the Achelous river near Anchialus, it was utterly routed by Symeon; the Bulgarians swept into Thrace, and at Catasyrtae, not far from Constantinople, gained another victory. Symeon, whose dominions now extended from the Black Sea to the Adriatic and from Sirmium to the neighbourhood of Thessalonica, was master of the Balkans.

In the dark days between 917 and 919, when the fate of the Empire hung in the balance, Byzantium was saved once again by its diplomacy and by its capacity for producing great leaders. Zoe gained a precious respite by entangling Symeon with Serbia; and while the regency government was sinking into disaffection and intrigue, the Admiral Romanus Lecapenus began his steady climb to power. In May 919, through the marriage of his daughter to Constantine VII, he became *Basileopator*; on 17 December 920 he was crowned co-Emperor. Symeon had lost the race for power: the son of an Armenian peasant had gained the throne by the very means the Bulgarian sovereign had planned to use. In vain did Nicholas try to appease his impotent fury by sending him conciliatory letters: Symeon now demanded the deposition of Romanus in favour of himself;[2] every year now he invaded the Empire, reaching the approaches of Constantinople in 921, 922 and 924, and retaking Adrianople in 923. But Romanus had a policy for dealing with the Bulgarians: he allowed Symeon to exhaust himself in fruitless attacks on the capital, while Byzantine diplomacy stirred up trouble against him in Serbia, negotiated for a grand anti-Bulgarian coalition of northern peoples—Magyars, Pechenegs, Russians and Alans—and successfully countered his attempt to secure the use of the Egyptian Fatimid navy against Byzantium.

In the autumn of 924 Symeon's army appeared for the last time before Constantinople. Realising no doubt that he could not hope to storm the city without a fleet, he opened negotiations. At Cosmidium, on a pier built out into the Golden Horn, Symeon and the Emperor Romanus met and conversed. Contemporary chroniclers, whose imagination was fired by this interview between the two most power-

---

[1] Leo the Deacon, p. 123 (*CSHB*): αὐτοκράτορα ἑαυτὸν ἀνακηρύττειν Ῥωμαίοις ἐκέλευεν.
[2] Nicholas Mysticus, *Ep.* 18, *MPG*, cxi, 125; *Ep.* 19, *MPG*, cxi, 128.

ful monarchs of Europe, give a dramatic picture of the Bulgarian ruler, at first mocking and flippant, gradually cowed by the majesty of imperial Rome and humbled by the Emperor's moral authority.[1] Be that as it may, the meeting with Romanus sounded the death-knell of Symeon's ambitions: Constantinople, he must have realised by then, would never be his. Back in his own country, however, his insolence revived: he spurned the last pathetic appeals of the Patriarch Nicholas;[2] defiantly entitled himself 'Emperor of the Bulgarians and of the Romans', to the indignation of Romanus who protested to Symeon in 925 not so much against his title of βασιλεύς, as against his 'tyrannical' claim to the throne of the Romaioi;[3] and, perhaps about 926, raised the Archbishop of Bulgaria to the rank of Patriarch.[4] But these constitutionally vacuous gestures could not conceal the fact that Symeon's bid for world hegemony had broken against the impregnable walls of Constantinople, the patient defensive policy of Romanus and the skill of Byzantine diplomacy. His armies were still able to subdue and devastate Serbia, where the Empire had been active against him; but in 926 a Bulgarian army which invaded Croatia was completely routed by the Emperor's ally, the Croatian king Tomislav. On 27 May 927 Symeon died.

The death of the Bulgarian tsar altered the whole balance of power in the Balkans. Exhausted and ruined by his wars, Bulgaria ceased for the next sixty years to play an active part in the politics of eastern Europe. In the autumn of 927 a peace treaty was signed between Byzantium and the Bulgarian government:[5] Peter, Symeon's son and successor, was married to Maria Lecapena, Romanus' grand-daughter, and was acknowledged by the Byzantine authorities as Emperor of Bulgaria (βασιλεὺς Βουλγαρίας); the autocephalous Bulgarian Patriarchate was also recognised. But these flattering concessions were but a cloak that barely concealed the extent of the Empire's diplomatic victory over Symeon's mild and saintly son. The Byzantine tsaritsa of Bulgaria ensured the dominance of Constantinople over the court

[1] Georgius Mon. pp. 900–1; Theoph. Cont. pp. 405–9; Scylitzes-Cedrenus, II, pp. 303–6 (*CSHB*). Cf. S. Runciman, *Romanus Lecapenus* (Cambridge, 1929), p. 92, who quotes Romanus' speech to Symeon.

[2] *Ep.* 31, *MPG*, CXI, 188–96.

[3] According to Romanus Lecapenus (*Epistolae*, ed. Sakkelion, D, I, 1883, 658–64, 665–6; *Fontes Historiae Bulgaricae*, VIII, 1961, 298), Symeon entitled himself βασιλεὺς Βουλγάρων καὶ 'Ρωμαίων. However, a leaden *bulla* has been discovered with the simple inscription: Συμεὼν ἐν Χρισ[τῷ] βασιλε[ὺς] 'Ρομεῶν [*sic*]: T. Gerassimov, *Bulletin de l'Institut Archéol. Bulgare*, VIII (1934), 350–6.

[4] The date of the foundation of the Bulgarian Patriarchate provides a difficult problem: it was probably established by Symeon, and doubtless after the death of Nicholas Mysticus (15 May 925); see S. Runciman, *First Bulgarian Empire*, pp. 163, n. 2, and 174.

[5] *DR*, 612.

of Preslav; while her husband, for all his imperial rank, sank to the level of a docile satellite of Byzantium, honoured and chastened at once by the title of 'spiritual son' of the Emperors of East Rome.[1]

The decline of Bulgarian power affected the Empire's northern policy in another sense: an effective buffer which had long prevented the trans-Danubian nations of the steppe from raiding Thrace was removed in 927, and the defence of the Empire's northern frontier now depended more and more on the skill of its diplomatists. Freed from the Bulgarian peril, and forced to meet a changing and complex situation between the middle Danube and the northern Caucasus, during the rest of Romanus' reign (i.e. 927 to 944) and the personal reign of Constantine VII (945–59) Byzantine diplomacy embarked upon one of its most successful periods.

In each of the three sectors of the Empire's northern front solid results were achieved. In the Balkans, next to an increasingly byzantinised Bulgaria, the Empire restored its sovereignty over the Serbs (c. 927); kept a somewhat nominal control over the coastal cities of Dalmatia, which since the seventies of the ninth century formed an imperial theme under a *strategus* resident at Zara,[2] and retained some political authority in Croatia. The only serious danger to its Balkan provinces in this period came from the Magyars who ravaged Thrace in 934 and 943. The imperial diplomatists were equal to the occasion: in or about the year 948 the Magyar chieftain Bulcsu came to Constantinople, was baptised in the city and, before returning home, was made a *patricius* by the Emperor. Soon afterwards another Hungarian leader named Gyula followed his example; and on his homeward journey Gyula was accompanied by the monk Hierotheus, whom the Patriarch had consecrated as 'Bishop of Hungary' (Turkia) (ἐπίσκοπος Τουρκίας) and who appears to have laboured successfully in his missionary diocese.[3] This new expansion of Byzantine Christianity to Pannonia, less than a century after the work of St Methodius in that land, did not prevent the Magyars from resuming their attacks on Thrace between 958 and 968; but at least it ensured a respite from their raids during the previous decade.

---

[1] Cf. F. Dölger, 'Der Bulgarenherrscher als geistlicher Sohn des byzant. Kaisers', *Sbornik Nikov* (1940), pp. 219–32 (= *Byz. u. d. europ. Staatenwelt*, pp. 183–96); G. Ostrogorsky, 'Die byzantinische Staatenhierarchie', *Sem. Kond.* VIII (1936), 41–53.

[2] See J. Ferluga, *Vizantiska Uprava u Dalmacii* (Belgrade, 1957), pp. 68–86.

[3] Scylitzes-Cedrenus (II, p. 328) refers to the two chieftains as Βουλοσουδής and Γυλᾶς: Constantine Porphyrogenitus calls the former Βουλτζοῦς (*De ad. imp.* c. 40, *DAI*, I, p. 178, l. 66); in the Hungarian tradition he is known as Bulcsu: cf. B. Hóman, *Gesch. des ungar. Mittelalters*, I (Berlin, 1940), pp. 127–32, 146–7. 'Gyula' was, according to Constantine (*loc. cit.* ll. 51–2), a title and not a proper name. Cf. C. A. Macartney, *The Magyars in the Ninth Century*, pp. 117–18.

At no time was the Crimean sector of more vital importance to the Empire than in the reigns of Romanus I and Constantine VII. Never was Byzantium's traditional policy of hanging on to Cherson more clearly vindicated. From here alone could the East Roman statesmen effectively adjust their northern policy to the changes that had taken place in the steppes since the end of the ninth century. For the past two hundred years they had relied for preserving order in that region mainly on the Khazars, but Khazar power was declining; so in the first half of the tenth century Byzantium turned to the Pechenegs, who were then encamped along the Black Sea coast between the Danube and the Don. By the middle of the century alliance with the Pechenegs had become the corner-stone of the Empire's diplomacy in the north. Of this new and urgent preoccupation the opening chapters of the *De administrando imperio* have preserved a striking memorial: for, as Constantine is at pains to explain to his son, if this alliance is kept, Byzantine Crimea is safe, trade with Russia can flourish, and the Empire's northern neighbours, Bulgarians and Magyars and Russians, who tremble with fear before the Pechenegs, will not dare to attack Byzantium. 'I conceive, then,' the Emperor writes, 'that it is always greatly to the advantage of the Emperor of the Romans to be minded to keep the peace with the nation of the Pechenegs and to conclude conventions and treaties of friendship with them and to send every year to them from our side a diplomatic agent with presents befitting and suitable to that nation.'[1] The responsibility for negotiating with the Pechenegs inevitably lay with the *strategus* of Cherson.

Another factor which enhanced the importance of Byzantine Crimea in this period was the continued growth of Kievan Russia. In 941 Igor, Oleg's successor, led a great sea-borne expedition against Byzantium. Repulsed from the northern entrance of the Bosphorus, the Russians landed on the coast of Bithynia and plundered the country from Heraclea to Nicomedia; but, as they were withdrawing, their ships were attacked by the imperial navy under the *proto-vestiarius* Theophanes: the Greek fire wrought terrible destruction, and the Russian armada was all but annihilated. In 944, at the head of a large army of Varangians and Slavs, Igor set off once more against Byzantium. An embassy from Romanus succeeded, however, in buying off the Russians and their Pecheneg allies on the Danube. Then, as in 941, the Byzantines were forewarned of the approaching danger by the intelligence bureau of the *strategus* of Cherson: the Emperor was informed by the Chersonites 'that the Russes were advancing with innumerable ships, and covered the sea with their

[1] *De admin. imp.* c. 1, ll. 16–20 and c. 2–8, *DAI*, i, pp. 48–56.

vessels'.[1] The desire to safeguard the security of Cherson is evident in the treaty concluded between Russia and the Empire in 944.[2] A comparison between the *pacta* of 911 and 944 suggests that the balance of power was shifting in favour of Byzantium: the trading privileges of the Russians were now considerably curtailed,[3] and, most significantly, a notable proportion of the envoys sent to Constantinople by Igor to ratify the treaty belonged to a Christian community in Kiev. Gradually, through trade and diplomacy, the Christian and imperial propaganda was breaking down the pagan isolation of the Viking rulers of Russia. In the autumn of 957 Igor's widow, Olga, regent of the realm, went on a mission of peace to Constantinople; there, amid splendid court receptions, she was baptised by the Byzantine Patriarch, adopting the name, symbolic by its past associations, of the reigning Empress Helena, wife of Constantine VII.[4] And though Olga was unwilling or unable to impose her religion on her subjects at large, and made an abortive attempt in 959 to obtain a German bishop from Otto I,[5] her relations with the Empire paved the way for the triumph of Byzantine Christianity in Russia in the reign of her grandson.

The diplomacy of Romanus I and Constantine VII was no less successful in the North Caucasian area. Relations with the Khazars had become cooler since the Khan's conversion to Judaism and the arrival of the Pechenegs in the Pontic steppes. It is true that in the Empire's diplomatic protocol the Khan still ranked, among non-Christian rulers, second only to the Caliph of Baghdad.[6] But Byzantium no longer really trusted the Khazars. And just as their task of

---

[1] *Russian Prim. Chron.*, ed. Lichačev, I, p. 34; II, p. 285; trans. by Cross–Sherbowitz, pp. 72–3.

[2] *Russian Prim. Chron.* I, pp. 34–9; Cross–Sherbowitz, pp. 73–7; *DR*, 647.

[3] Exemption from customs duties is no longer mentioned, and the Russians were forbidden to buy large silk fabrics higher in price than 50 *nomismata*; cf. R. Lopez, 'Silk Industry in the Byzantine Empire', *SP*, xx (1945), 34–5.

[4] The place of Olga's baptism provides a controversial problem, for while the *Russian Primary Chronicle* (I, pp. 44–5; Cross–Sherbowitz, pp. 82–3), Scylitzes-Cedrenus (II, p. 329) and Continuator Reginonis (*MGH, SGUS*, p. 170) state that she was baptised in Constantinople, Constantine Porphyrogenitus in his detailed account of Olga's reception in the capital in September and October 957 (*De cerimoniis*, pp. 594 ff., *CSHB*) does not mention her baptism. Accordingly, some historians believe that Olga was baptised in Kiev a few years before her journey to Constantinople (see G. Vernadsky, *Kievan Russia*, New Haven, 1948, p. 40; G. Ostrogorsky, *History of the Byzantine State*, p. 251, n. 2). The present writer does not accept this view and, together with G. Laehr (*Die Anfänge des russ. Reiches*, pp. 103–5) and F. Dvornik (*The Slavs, Their Early History and Civilisation*, pp. 200–1), is of the opinion that Olga's baptism took place in Constantinople.

[5] Continuator Reginonis, pp. 170, 172. Cf. G. Laehr, *op. cit.* pp. 105–6; F. Dvornik, *op. cit.* pp. 201–2.

[6] *De cerim.* pp. 686 ff.; cf. G. Ostrogorsky, 'Die byzantinische Staatenhierarchie', *Sem. Kond.* VIII (1936), 50–2.

policing the steppes in the interests of the Empire had recently devolved upon the Pechenegs, so the role they had formerly been
assigned by the Byzantine diplomatists of guarding the Northern
Caucasus was now transferred to the Alans, whose lands marched with
the Khanate in the south. Since the sixth century the Alans had been
the most loyal of the Empire's satellites in this area, for all their
strong attachment to paganism; it was not until the early years
of the tenth century that the ruler of Alania accepted Christianity
and an archbishop from the Patriarch Nicholas Mysticus. Despite
a subsequent and brief relapse into paganism, the Alans were held
in high esteem in Byzantium, and Constantine Porphyrogenitus
stressed their usefulness in checking possible Khazar encroachments on the Crimea.[1] Their ruler, who held the Byzantine title of
ἐξουσιαστής, was one of the three imperial satellites to glory in the
title of the Emperor's 'spiritual son'.[2] Of comparable importance was
the ἐξουσιαστής of Abasgia, who guarded Byzantium's interests in
the strategically vital area between Alania, Armenia and the Black
Sea coast.[3]

Thus within the semi-circle which, in the tenth as in the sixth
century, marked the effective limits of the Empire's influence in the
north, in the vast area that extended from the Hungarian Alföld, over
the steppes and rivers of South Russia to the lower Volga and the
North Caucasian lowlands, the diplomacy of Romanus and Constantine had built up by the middle of the century a chain of vassal and
allied states, satellites supposedly revolving in obedient harmony round
the throne of the universal Autocrat in Constantinople, barbarians
rendered quiescent by the power or the liberalities of the Emperor, or
proselytes attracted by the prestige and spiritual appeal of Byzantium's Christian culture. It was the work of these two emperors that
paved the way for the forces of expansion which in the next fifty years
were to carry the armies of East Rome to the Danube and the
influence of its civilisation to the confines of the Baltic Sea.

From the death of Romanus II (963) to the year 1018 the Empire's
northern policy was dominated by its relations with Bulgaria and
Russia.[4] Bulgaria in the reign of the Tsar Peter (927–69) was rent by
a social and economic crisis: the accumulation of power and wealth
in the hands of an oppressive aristocracy was undermining the authority of the state and, as in the Empire, was depriving the peasants of
their small holdings. Many of the latter, especially in Macedonia,

[1] *De admin. imp.* c. 10 and 11, *DAI*, I, p. 62/3–4 and p. 64.
[2] *De cerim.* pp. 688 f.; cf. G. Ostrogorsky, 'Staatenhierarchie', *op. cit.* p. 52.
[3] *De cerim.*, *ibid.*
[4] See also above: ch. IV, pp. 151 ff. and 187 ff.

were falling under the sway of Bogomilism, a new sectarian movement that combined neo-Manichaean dualism and an evangelical and anti-sacramental interpretation of Christianity with an attitude of revolt against the established authorities of Church and State, and which was soon to spread over the whole Balkan peninsula.[1] And, still worse, the Tsar Peter, shortly after his wife's death, committed an error which precipitated the gravest crisis his country had yet experienced. In the winter of 965–6 he sent an embassy to Constantinople to demand the former 'tribute'. This was more than the Emperor Nicephorus Phocas, fresh from his victories of Tarsus and Crete, could endure; Peter's envoys were whipped and dismissed, and Nicephorus moved his army to the Bulgarian border.[2] Reluctant, however, to campaign in that dangerous country, he confined himself to seizing a few frontier forts and sent the *patricius* Calocyras to Russia with instructions to bribe its ruler Svjatoslav to attack Bulgaria. The pagan and warlike son of Olga had the makings of an empire builder: he had recently inflicted a crushing defeat on the Khazars (*c.* 965). He was easily persuaded by the Byzantine ambassador: in 967[3] he crossed the Danube at the head of a large army and rapidly overran the Dobrudja, setting up his residence at Little Preslav (Perejaslavec), by the river delta. It soon became clear, however, that Svjatoslav had no intention of behaving as Byzantium's hireling; in 968, or early in 969 he returned home at the news that the Pechenegs were besieging Kiev:[4] it is difficult to avoid the surmise that the Emperor, mindful of the precepts of the *De administrando imperio,* had called them in. Before the middle of August 969, having defeated the Pechenegs, Svjatoslav was back in Bulgaria, intending—

---

[1] Cf. H.-C. Puech and A. Vaillant, *Le traité contre les Bogomiles de Cosmas le Prêtre* (Paris, 1945); D. Obolensky, *The Bogomils* (Cambridge, 1948).

[2] The chronology of the next three years is confused, as the sources give different dates. Thus Leo the Deacon (pp. 61–3) implies that Nicephorus invaded Southern Bulgaria in the spring of 966, while Scylitzes-Cedrenus (II, p. 372) states that the Emperor marched to the frontier in June 967. The present writer finds it hard to agree with Runciman (*First Bulgarian Empire,* pp. 303–5) that these were two separate expeditions: both Leo and Scylitzes assert that Nicephorus' campaign was immediately followed by the dispatch of Calocyras to Russia.

[3] The date of the first Russian invasion of Bulgaria is not easy to determine, in view of the conflicting evidence of the sources. While recognising the complexity of the problem, the present writer prefers the date 967 which is given by the *Russian Primary Chronicle* (I, p. 47; Cross–Sherbowitz, p. 84), and accepted by S. Runciman (*op. cit.* p. 304), M. Levčenko (*Očerki po istorii russko-vizantijskikh otnošeny,* Moscow, 1956, pp. 258–9), and A. D. Stokes ('The Background and Chronology of the Balkan Campaigns of Svyatoslav Igorevich', *SEER,* XL, 94, 1961, 50–7). The date August 968, supplied by Scylitzes-Cedrenus (II, p. 372), is accepted by P. Karyškovsky ('O chronologii russko-vizantijskoj vojny pri Svjatoslave', *VV,* v, 1952, 127–38) and G. Ostrogorsky (*History of the Byzantine State,* p. 259).

[4] *Russ. Prim. Chron.* I, pp. 47–8; Cross–Sherbowitz, pp. 85–6.

it seems—to make Little Preslav the capital of his realm.[1] Marching south, he captured Great Preslav, the Bulgarian capital, and stormed Philippopolis; by the end of the year the whole of eastern Bulgaria was in Russian hands. Svjatoslav's ambitions now centred on Constantinople itself: the Pechenegs, the Magyars and, it seems, the Bulgarians themselves had joined with him in a vast barbarian coalition against the Empire. Calocyras himself had turned traitor and was plotting, with the help of the Russians, to seize the Byzantine throne. Conscious of this serious danger, the new Emperor John Tzimisces began negotiations: Svjatoslav's reply was to demand that the Byzantines, if unwilling to pay him an enormous tribute, depart from Europe and cross over into Asia.[2] Not since the days of Symeon had a barbarian ruler dared to address the Emperor of Byzantium in such tones. In the summer of 970 the Russians invaded Thrace, but were defeated at Arcadiopolis by Bardas Sclerus.[3]

In the spring of 971,[4] at the head of a large and well-trained army, John Tzimisces set out on one of the greatest campaigns in the history of Byzantine arms. In April Great Preslav, furiously defended by Svjatoslav's men, was taken by storm. The Russians, fighting desperately, fell back on Silistria (Dristra, Dorystolum) where their prince had entrenched himself. For three months packed with heroic episodes, the city was besieged, until finally the Russians, overwhelmed by Tzimisces' iron-clad host, terrified by the fire-shooting ships of the imperial navy that had appeared on the Danube to cut off their retreat, and exhausted by famine, gave up in despair. Svjatoslav undertook to leave Bulgaria, begging only to be allowed to cross the river and to be given some food for the remnant of his army.[5] The Emperor accepted these terms; in July 971 a treaty was signed between the two rulers: the Russian prince pledged himself never again

[1] *Russ. Prim. Chron.* I, pp. 48–50; Cross–Sherbowitz, pp. 86–7. The Russian chronicler's dating of Svjatoslav's second invasion of Bulgaria (971) is, as all the authorities agree, unacceptable. Here again Scylitzes supplies the accurate date (Scylitzes-Cedrenus, II, p. 372).

[2] Leo the Deacon, p. 105.

[3] Leo the Deacon, pp. 108 ff.; Scylitzes-Cedrenus, II, pp. 384–8. The *Russian Primary Chronicle* (I, p. 50; Cross–Sherbowitz, pp. 87–8) falsely describes this battle as a Russian victory. Cf. G. Schlumberger, *L'épopée byzantine à la fin du Xe siècle*, I (Paris, 1896), pp. 46–52.

[4] The date of John Tzimisces' Russian campaign (April–July 971) has been conclusively established by F. Dölger ('Die Chronologie des grossen Feldzuges des Kaisers Johannes Tzimiskes gegen die Russen', *BZ*, XXXII (1932), 275–92); cf. C. Göllner, 'Les expéditions byzantines contre les Russes sous Jean Tzimiscès', *RHSE*, XIII (1936), 342–58; H. Grégoire, 'La dernière campagne de Jean Tzimiskès contre les Russes', *B*, XII (1937), 267–76.

[5] The *Russian Primary Chronicle* (I, p. 51; Cross–Sherbowitz, pp. 88–9) brazenly implies that the Russians won the war. Cf. the detailed account in G. Schlumberger, *op. cit.* chs. 1–3; and see above, ch. IV.

to attack the Empire, Bulgaria, or Cherson, and to fight the enemies of Byzantium;[1] the Emperor renewed the old trading privileges of the Russians.[2] After a brief meeting on the banks of the Danube,[3] the two monarchs started on their homeward journeys: Svjatoslav was ambushed by the Pechenegs near the Dnieper rapids and slain in battle (972); John Tzimisces returned in triumph to Constantinople, where the Bulgarian Tsar Boris II publicly abdicated his throne. Bulgaria was thus annexed to the Empire. In a single year John Tzimisces had restored the Empire's northern frontier to the Danube, from which Asparuch had evicted the East Romans three centuries earlier, and freed Byzantium from the Russian menace.

Once again, after three centuries, the Empire found itself, across the lower Danube, face to face with the steppes and its denizens. More than ever it needed now a strong and reliable satellite in the north: the Khazar Khanate could fulfil this role no more; it would never recover from the blow dealt to it by Svjatoslav; the Pechenegs had several times proved themselves treacherous allies; the Magyars were increasingly looking to Germany for their culture and religion. Only the prince of Kiev, who now ruled over a vast territory from the Carpathians to the lower Oka and from the gulf of Finland to the lower Dnieper, could stand between the Empire and the chaos of Eurasia. And it was by Christianity alone that Byzantium could hope to secure his abiding loyalty. For all his inveterate heathenism, Svjatoslav, it seems, had not the time or the inclination to undo his mother's work in Kiev; and all through the tenth century Christianity was slowly filtering into Russia—from Bulgaria especially, through the Slavonic translations of the disciples of Cyril and Methodius, from Bohemia perhaps, where the vernacular Slavonic culture still survived, and probably also from Germany and Rome. But it was left to the Emperor Basil II to ensure, with the help of his missionaries and diplomatists, the final triumph of Byzantine Christianity in Russia.

The story of Russia's conversion is told at great length by the *Russian Primary Chronicle*[4] and briefly by the eleventh-century Arab historian Yaḥyā of Antioch.[5] The former, if allowance is made for its peculiar blend of fact and fiction and for probable later interpolations, may be used to supplement the latter, and the following picture then emerges. In the spring of 988, at the most critical moment of his

---

[1] *Russ. Prim. Chron.* I, p. 52; Cross–Sherbowitz, pp. 89–90; *DR*, 739.
[2] Leo the Deacon, pp. 155–6.   [3] *Ibid.* pp. 156–7.
[4] I, pp. 59–83; Cross–Sherbowitz, pp. 96–119.
[5] Ed. I. Kračkovsky and A. Vasiliev (with a French trans.), *PO*, XXIII, 423. The other sources on Russia's conversion are cited in G. Laehr, *Die Anfänge des russischen Reiches*, pp. 110–15.

reign, when the troops of the usurper Bardas Phocas stood on the Asian side of the Bosphorus, Basil II was saved by the arrival in Constantinople of six thousand Varangian warriors. The timely assistance of these professional soldiers enabled the Emperor to defeat his rival at Chrysopolis. This expeditionary corps, which was to form the nucleus of the Emperor's celebrated Varangian guard, had been sent by Svjatoslav's son, Vladimir, the prince of Kiev, in fulfilment of an agreement he had contracted with the Empire in the previous winter.[1] For his military assistance Vladimir had been promised the hand of the Emperor's sister, the Porphyrogenita Anna, on condition that he and his people accepted Christianity. But now that the acute danger was past, Basil II seemed in no hurry to honour an obligation so incompatible with the honour and traditions of East Rome.[2] In the spring of 989, doubtless to compel Byzantium to send him his promised bride, Vladimir marched to the Crimea and invested Cherson; by the summer the city was his, and the unwilling princess, sacrificed to the interests of the Empire, was dispatched across the Black Sea. Whether Vladimir became a Christian in Russia on the conclusion of his agreement with Byzantium, as some Russian sources seem to imply, or whether, as the *Primary Chronicle* prolixly relates, he was baptised in Cherson by the local bishop before his marriage, is a question to which—in the present writer's view—no certain answer can at present be given without ignoring or maltreating part of the evidence. But whichever view is adopted, the role played by Cherson in the conversion of Russia will appear decisive, and this city, so long the focus of missionary work among the northern barbarians, took her captor captive: for after their marriage Vladimir and his imperial bride were escorted from the Crimea to Kiev by members of the local clergy, who began to implant Christianity throughout the Russian realm, while Cherson was returned by Vladimir to the Empire. The new Russian Church was subordinated to the Patriarchate of Constantinople;[3] Vladimir's act of faith and statesmanship linked Russia to Byzantine culture and to eastern Christianity; and the East Roman missionaries and diplomatists thus peacefully gained for the Byzan-

---

[1] *DR*, 771.

[2] On the Byzantine attitude to marriages of imperial, and particularly Porphyrogenitae, princesses to foreigners, see G. Ostrogorsky, 'Vladimir Svjatoj i Vizantija', *Vladimirskij Sbornik* (Belgrade, 1938), pp. 34 ff.

[3] The fact, impugned by several current theories, that Vladimir's Church was from the moment of its foundation placed under the authority of the Byzantine Patriarch has, in the present writer's view, been conclusively established by V. Laurent ('Aux origines de l'Eglise russe', *EO*, xxxviii (1939), 279–95), E. Honigmann ('The Foundation of the Russian Metropolitan Church according to Greek sources', *B*, xvii (1944–5), 128–62) and M. Levčenko ('Vzaimootnošenija Vizantii i Rusi pri Vladimire', *VV*, n.s. vii (1953), 194–223; *Očerki*, pp. 340–85).

tine οἰκουμένη and for Europe a territory which in size exceeded the Empire itself.

The Byzantine government had all the more reason to feel satisfied with the success of its Russian policy, as the situation in the Balkans was rapidly deteriorating. John Tzimisces' conquests, it seems, had been inadequately consolidated; outside the main cities of eastern Bulgaria, Byzantine domination was never secure, and in the west, amid the high lakes and valleys of Macedonia, seems not to have been felt at all. It was there that, on the Emperor's death in 976, the sons of a provincial Macedonian governor, the four Comitopuli, raised the standard of revolt.[1] The rebellion became a war of liberation. By 987 Samuel, the youngest of the four, was the sole ruler of a powerful kingdom, whose capital was first Prespa and later Ochrida, and which comprised by the end of the century most of the former Bulgarian lands between the Black Sea and the Adriatic, with the addition of Thessaly and Epirus, as well as Serbia. In 997 or 998 Samuel proclaimed himself Tsar, and this act, coupled with his restoration of the Bulgarian Patriarchate abolished by John Tzimisces, whose seat was eventually fixed at Ochrida, signified his deliberate assumption of the traditions of the First Bulgarian Empire.

Basil II's first attempt to deal with Samuel ended in disaster: in August 986, returning from an abortive siege of Sardica, his army was ambushed in a mountain pass and slaughtered by the Bulgarians. For the next three years, during which the Emperor was occupied in suppressing the revolts of Bardas Sclerus and Bardas Phocas, Samuel's expansion continued unchecked. By the spring of 991 Basil II was back in Macedonia, where he campaigned for three years with increasing, but still indecisive, success. He was handicapped by having to fight on two fronts, and his wars in Syria and the Caucasus (995–1001) enabled the Bulgarians to thrust at Thessalonica and to invade Greece down to the gulf of Corinth.

But in 1001 the Emperor had made peace with the Fatimids and was back in Constantinople, free to devote all his carefully nurtured powers of mind and body and his military and political genius to what he had come to regard as the main task of his reign. In a series of carefully planned and brilliantly executed campaigns he captured the cities of eastern Bulgaria, including Pliska and the two Preslavs, and advanced deep into Macedonia, seizing fortress after fortress. In four years of this ruthless and methodical strategy Samuel had lost half his Empire. Any hopes he might have had of saving the re-

---

[1] The much-debated problem of the origin and early stages of the Bulgarian revolt is admirably discussed by G. Ostrogorsky, *History of the Byzantine State*, p. 268, n. 1.

mainder were dashed in July 1014, when his army was routed in the mountain pass of Kleidion (Cimbalongus) near the Strymon valley. Basil had all the Bulgarian captives—numbering, it was said, fourteen thousand[1]—blinded, save for one in every hundred who was left with one eye to lead his comrades back to the Tsar. At the sight of this gruesome procession Samuel fell to the ground in a fit. Two days later, on 6 October 1014, he was dead.

The end was very near. It was hastened by the chaos that engulfed the remnant of Bulgaria. Samuel's son and successor, Gabriel Radomir, was murdered by his cousin John Vladislav (1015). In vain did the new Bulgarian Tsar, like his predecessor, promise obedience to the Byzantine Emperor; Basil pursued his systematic conquest of Macedonia. Early in 1018, when the news reached him in Constantinople that John Vladislav had been killed in a vain attack on Dyrrachium, the Emperor set out on his last campaign of the war. It was a bloodless and triumphant procession. At the gates of Ochrida he received the formal submission of the late Tsar's family. After a last tour of the conquered territory, his work completed, the 'Bulgar-Slayer' paid a visit to Athens, where, before the more splendid triumph that awaited him in Constantinople, he offered humble thanks to Our Lady of Athens in her church, the Parthenon.

For the first time since the Avaro-Slav attacks of the late sixth century the entire Balkan peninsula, from the middle and lower Danube to the southern tip of the Peloponnese, and from the Black Sea to the confines of Istria, now lay in the unchallenged possession, or under the sovereignty, of East Rome. In 1018 the three traditional sectors of the Empire's northern front—the Danube, the Crimea and the south-western approaches to the Caucasus—were more firmly than ever under its sway. In the steppes a favourable balance of power seemed assured for the future, and further north the boundless expanses of Russia had been brought within the orbit of the Byzantine οἰκουμένη.

---

[1] Cecaumenus (*Strategicon*, cap. 49, ed. B. Wassiliewsky and V. Jernstedt, St Petersburg, 1896, p. 18) puts the number at 14,000, Scylitzes-Cedrenus (II, p. 458) at 15,000. These figures are probably exaggerated; cf. G. Ostrogorsky, *op. cit.* p. 275, n. 1.

CHAPTER XII

THE BALKANS, 1018-1499

With the fall of Samuel's Empire, the whole Balkan peninsula came once again under the domination of Byzantium after a lapse of three and a half centuries. Yet Byzantium did not succeed in bringing all the lands of the Balkan Slavs under her immediate control and organising them as themes. In the western portion of the peninsula, earlier political entities were preserved, with their native rulers who reigned as Byzantine vassals—Serbia (Rascia) in the mountainous region of the upper Drina, the Lim and the Ibar;[1] Zeta (Dioclea) in the coastal region in the area of the Lake of Scutari; Hum, or Zachlumia, around the river Neretva. In the region lying between the rivers Neretva and Cetina, the 'Pagania' of Constantine Porphyrogenitus was still preserved, and its ruler, even in the middle of the eleventh century, still had the title of king.[2] Only the principal coastal towns, together with the hinterland and a few islands, came under the direct administration of Byzantium, as the theme of Dalmatia.

It was natural that these semi-independent lands, with their local dynasties and rulers, should attempt to free themselves completely from the Byzantine yoke. This struggle for independence was long and arduous. It was carried on for a century and a half, first by Zeta, later by Serbia (Rascia), and was finally crowned with success when, after the death of Manuel Comnenus in 1180, Byzantium had to abandon its claims to complete control of the Balkans.

The first indications of the weakness of Byzantium became apparent with the challenge to its authority in Zeta. Prince Stephen Vojislav staged an unsuccessful revolt in 1036. He was swiftly overthrown, and borne away as a hostage to Constantinople, and Zeta was included in the theme of Dyrrachium. But an insurrection in Macedonia, under Peter Deljan (1040–1), an attempt to reconstitute Samuel's former Empire, quickly provoked a fresh rising in Zeta. Stephen Vojislav succeeded in escaping from Constantinople, and placed himself at the head of a new liberation movement (1040). Byzantium, although it succeeded in subjecting Peter Deljan, entirely

---

[1] The present writer cannot agree with V. Laurent ('Le thème byzantin de Serbie', *Balcania*, VI, 1943, 35 ff., and 'Le thème byzantin de Serbie au XIe siècle', *REB*, xv, 1957, 185 ff.) who maintains that a theme of Serbia existed.

[2] M. Barada, *Vjesnik za arheologiju i historiju dalmatinsku*, L (1932), 177: Berigoy rex (1050).

failed to renew its authority over Zeta; and the independence of this region was ensured for a long period. Its territory was consolidated and extended by the descendants of Stephen Vojislav—his son Michael (c. 1050–82), and his grandson Constantine Bodin (c. 1082–1100). Michael bore indeed the title of king, obtained in all probability from Pope Gregory VII,[1] and the Bishopric of Bar was raised to the dignity of Archbishopric, owing allegiance to Rome. King Constantine Bodin conquered Rascia and Bosnia, and imposed on them his own nominees as rulers. Thus Zeta embraced practically all the lands which were peopled by Serbs.

But Bodin's state had no future. Internecine warfare for the throne among the numerous members of the dynasty quickly caused its decline. The neighbouring lands of Rascia, Bosnia and Zachlumia, which were only loosely united, easily broke away from the body of the state, so that it soon comprised only Zeta and Trebinje. The influence of Byzantium, which was enjoying a period of revival under the Comneni, again grew strong. Bodin's heirs had to acknowledge its suzerainty and only maintained their authority with its assistance.[2]

From the end of the eleventh century onwards, Rascia showed much greater energy in waging war to effect its deliverance from Byzantium; and in this struggle it discovered a natural ally in Hungary. Byzantino-Hungarian wars were a continual accompaniment to the Serbian risings against the Empire and took the form of attacks and raids on Byzantine territory. All three of the great Comnenian Emperors were obliged personally to undertake expeditions against Rascia, but always with doubtful and ephemeral results. Temporary successes might oblige the Serbs to make peace, to hand over hostages and to swear their submission, but at the first favourable opportunity they would once again renew the struggle. The Byzantine practice of deposing unreliable Grand Župans (*Veliki Župani*) and bringing others to power was of little avail. All immediately resumed the policy of their predecessors.[3] The stubborn struggle of the Serbs finally achieved their complete liberation from Byzantine hegemony during the reign of Stephen Nemanja (1169–96).[4]

Stephen Nemanja began his political career as the prince of eastern Serbia, whilst his eldest brother was Grand Župan and his other brothers ruled over various parts of the country. This was a system peculiar to Serbia and favoured by Byzantium in that it weakened the country's power to resist, and strengthened imperial influence.

---

[1] F. Rački, *Documenta historiae Chroaticae periodum antiquam illustrantia* (Zagreb, 1877), p. 211.

[2] F. Šišić, *Letopis popa Dukljanina* (Belgrade, 1928), pp. 360 ff.

[3] C. Jireček, *Geschichte der Serben* (Gotha, 1911), I, pp. 244 ff.

[4] For a different dating for Stephen Nemanja's accession, see above: ch. v, p. 233.

One particular fraternal conflict resulted in the elevation of Nemanja to the position of Grand Župan. The *status quo* in Serbia, established by Manuel Comnenus, was thus shattered, and war with Byzantium was inevitable. The time was not yet ripe, however, for Serbia's final emancipation from Byzantine rule. In the course of one successful expedition, Manuel Comnenus succeeded in reducing Nemanja to the position of a vassal (1172). But with Manuel's death in 1180, the last remaining link binding Serbia to Constantinople was broken, and Nemanja took immediate advantage of the decline in Byzantine power. The attacks of the Hungarians and Normans on Byzantium, the movement for independence in Bulgaria, and the crusade led by Frederick Barbarossa across the Balkans, gave him the opportunity of considerably expanding the boundaries of his state at the expense of the eastern Empire. The last remnants of the principality of Zeta together with the coastal towns (Scutari, Bar, Ulcinj, Kotor) fell to Rascia.

Byzantium made one last attempt to retain Serbia within the Empire. The Emperor Isaac Angelus defeated Nemanja in a battle on the river Morava in 1190 and forced him to make peace. But one failure on the battlefield was not sufficient to nullify all Serbia's previous gains. There was now no possibility of Serbia's continued subjection to Byzantium, or of any return to the old frontier or to the position which it had occupied under the Comneni; and a considerable area of the conquered districts remained to the Serbs. For the first time in the history of Serbo-Byzantine relations, Byzantium tried to win Serbia to the idea of a marriage alliance between the two countries, by the union of Eudocia, a daughter of Alexius Angelus, with Nemanja's son, Stephen.[1]

By the end of the twelfth century the Serbs had thus succeeded in gaining complete independence. By this time the eastward trend of their cultural and religious orientation was also clearly apparent. The mountainous regions far from the Adriatic Sea had always been under the influence of the Christian East. At Ras, near modern Novi Pazar, a bishopric had existed from the ninth century and its jurisdiction extended over the central areas of those lands where the Serbs had settled. Through Ras, and neighbouring bishoprics in the outlying districts (in Belgrade, Braničevo, Niš and Prizren), the Orthodox faith had become firmly established.[2] Though Serbia had escaped from the political suzerainty of Byzantium, the cultural influence of

---

[1] M. Laskaris, *Vizantiske princeze u srednjevekovnoj Srbiji* (Belgrade, 1926), pp. 7 ff.
[2] S. Novaković, 'Ohridska arhiepiskopija u početku XI v.', *Glas*, LXXVI (1908), 33 ff.

the Empire did not wane; on the contrary it gained in strength. Stephen Nemanja, the architect of Serbia's political independence, did much to carry this development still further by building monasteries and strengthening the influence of the Church. He himself entered the Serbian monastery of Studenica after his abdication in 1196, before retiring to Mt Athos. And through the medium of the Church, Serbian literature, fostered by the priesthood, was also completely subject to Byzantine influence. Moreover, the Church was the agent for the reception of Byzantine legal thought. Further conquests of imperial territory in the course of the thirteenth and the first half of the fourteenth centuries led to the adoption of various Byzantine offices and institutions. The culmination of this influence was seen when Stephen Dušan adopted the imperial title in 1345 and set up the Serbian Patriarchate.

The complete liberation of Serbia from the Eastern Empire was not the only result of the rapid disintegration of Byzantium following the death of Manuel Comnenus in 1180; the Bulgarian state also claimed its independence. The authority of Byzantium over Bulgaria was undermined by various factors, partly by the domestic conflicts which promoted its own weakness, and partly by the attacks of the Magyars and the Normans who penetrated deep into Byzantine territory. The Bulgarian liberation movement began near Trnovo in 1185. When the Emperor Isaac Angelus refused the request of two boyars, the brothers Theodore and Asen, that they should be granted certain lands in *pronoia*, they took advantage of the discontent of the people at increased taxation and raised a revolt.[1] Byzantium was unable to suppress this outbreak in time. The general Alexius Branas succeeded in crushing the Normans who had sacked Thessalonica and were already advancing on Constantinople, but when he was then ordered to move against the Bulgarian insurgents he proclaimed himself Emperor at Adrianople. Only after the usurper had been overthrown was Isaac Angelus able to undertake in person an attack on Bulgaria. But the success which attended his expedition was only transient. The Byzantine army crossed the Balkan range and dispersed the rebels, who were as yet unorganised. In the summer of 1186 Theodore and Asen fled with a small retinue across the Danube, and took refuge with the Cumans. The Emperor Isaac ravaged the country and then

[1] Contemporary sources refer to a revolt of the Bulgars and Vlachs (see later for further reference to these). The role of the Vlachs during the restoration of the Bulgarian state has been the subject of much discussion in modern times. Rumanian historians tend to over-estimate, Bulgarians to undervalue it (P. Mutafčiev, *Istorija na bŭlgarskija narod*, II (Sofia, 1944), p. 36; N. Jorga, *Histoire des Roumains et de la Romanité orientale*, Bucharest, 1937, III, p. 104).

returned in triumph to his capital. But he took no real security measures; and in the autumn of the same year, Theodore and Asen reappeared with a large Cuman army and quickly liberated northern Bulgaria, whilst their allies ravaged Thrace. All the efforts of Byzantium to reimpose her authority north of the Balkan Mountains were unavailing. An advance by Isaac across the Balkan range, and an ineffectual three-month siege of Loveč in the spring of 1187, finished with a truce. Byzantium's failure to put down the revolts, and more particularly the conclusion of the truce, meant, if not a formal, then certainly a *de facto*, recognition of the new Bulgarian state. Then, and perhaps even earlier, Theodore and Asen began to organise the government and administration of their state on the model of the First Bulgarian Empire. Two bishops and the Metropolitan of Vidin consecrated a certain Basil as Archbishop at Trnovo, the capital of the restored Bulgaria. The elder brother, Theodore, was crowned Tsar, and took the name of Peter, but he soon relinquished his authority if not his title to his more energetic brother Asen, contenting himself with the possession of Great Preslav and the eastern districts of the country. The 'Old' Asen was later regarded by the Bulgarians as the founder of the new state.[1] This establishment of the new Bulgarian Empire was to some extent assisted by the passage through the Balkans of the Third Crusade. But as soon as Isaac Angelus was freed from the embarrassment of the crusaders, he was able once again to consider an offensive against the Bulgarians, whose Cuman allies had ravaged Thrace. Whilst the Byzantine fleet sailed up the Danube with the aim of cutting off Bulgar from Cuman, the overland army from Mesembria advanced into northern Bulgaria. Isaac penetrated as far as Trnovo, but the city was strongly fortified; and when he received news that a large Cuman army had crossed the Danube and was advancing to the relief of the besieged Trnovo, Isaac ordered a withdrawal, across the Balkan range into Thrace. But his army was surprised in a mountain pass and the greater part of it annihilated. Thus, Byzantium's last endeavour to prevent the restoration of the Bulgarian state collapsed, and Bulgarian independence was assured for a long period.

Further developments inside Byzantium itself, as well as the Fourth Crusade, frustrated any effective intervention. The Bulgarians were now able to take the offensive. While the Emperor Isaac was engaged in a successful campaign against Stephen Nemanja of Serbia, the Bulgarians were able to extend the frontiers of their new state westward. It was at this time that Sardica (Sofia) came under Bul-

---

[1] V. N. Zlatarski, *Istorija na bŭlgarskata dŭržava prez srednite vekove*, II (Sofia, 1934), pp. 410 ff.

garian authority. The Bulgarian army also pressed southward across the Balkans, and inflicted a telling defeat on Byzantine forces at Arcadiopolis (Lüleburgaz). Isaac now determined to settle accounts with the Bulgars; and in the spring of 1195, he assembled a great Byzantine army near the town of Cypsela. But in the midst of his preparations a rebellion broke out. Isaac was thrown from power, and his place was usurped by his brother, Alexius III Angelus. The new Byzantine Emperor abandoned his brother's plans and tried to come to an agreement with the Bulgarians · they, however, stipulated unacceptable conditions and the war was continued. But the young Bulgarian state was unable to concentrate all its strength on the task of further expansion owing to the outbreak of internal disorder. A plot was hatched by some of the discontented boyars, who had only with misgiving tolerated the strengthening of a central government, and Asen was murdered. Peter again assumed power, succeeded in putting down the rising, and occupied Trnovo. But he too was murdered in 1197 and John (Kalojan, or Joanica) his youngest brother seized power.

Under the energetic guidance of Kalojan (1197–1207), the Bulgarians continued their campaigns, at first against Byzantium, and later against the Latin conquerors. Byzantium lost its last important defensive outpost north of the Balkan mountains, the city of Varna on the Black Sea. Bulgaria made remarkable territorial gains in the west, where the imperial authority was utterly eclipsed, although Hungary actively contested the Bulgarian claims in this area. Kalojan succeeded in temporarily capturing Braničevo and Niš, and possibly even Belgrade. A large part of Macedonia and the adjoining provinces was also occupied. Bulgarian bishops were installed at Prizren, Skoplje, Ochrida, and Verria (Ber), in place of Greeks. At the same time Bulgaria also obtained recognition of her independence from the papal curia. Kalojan entered into negotiations with Innocent III. Promising to recognise the spiritual power of the Pope, he sought both recognition and his coronation as Emperor (*Imperator*), and the elevation of the head of the Bulgarian Church to the rank of Patriarch. Working on the principle that there existed but one universal Empire, the Pope agreed to grant Kalojan only the title of king (*rex*) and to bestow on the chief prelate the dignity of Primate of Bulgaria. After lengthy negotiations, agreement was reached, and the papal legate, Cardinal Leo, crowned Kalojan king at Trnovo on 8 November 1204 with a crown brought from Rome; on the following day the Archbishop of Trnovo was consecrated Primate.[1] Meanwhile,

---

[1] A. Theiner, *Vetera monumenta Slavorum Meridionalium historiam sacram illustrantia* (Rome, 1863), i, pp. 15 ff.

in Bulgaria it was considered that precisely what had been demanded had in effect been achieved; Kalojan and all his successors were called Emperor, and the head of his Church bore the title of Patriarch. In this respect therefore the tradition of the First Bulgarian Empire was continued. These successes were realised at the price of the union of the Bulgarian with the Roman Church. But it was a union which could not endure for long: for Bulgaria still retained its attachment to Orthodoxy—an attachment so strongly fostered by religious traditions and by the geographical position of the country that not even the founding of the Latin Empire could effect a lasting conquest in the East for the Roman Church.

Byzantium could not reconcile itself to the fact that Bulgarian independence was a *fait accompli*, but her temporary eclipse assured to the young state an undisturbed development. The Latin conquerors of Constantinople naturally accepted the Greek view that Bulgaria was only a seditious province of the Empire. When Kalojan sent a deputation to Baldwin I, with the object of establishing friendly relations with the Latin Empire, he was ordered to lay down his arms and abandon his throne; the Latins threatened to lay waste and ravage with fire the whole of 'Moesia' since Kalojan had no legal right to rule the district, and had driven thence the 'Romaioi', its lawful rulers. The Latins paid dearly for their arrogance. Kalojan joined with the Greeks of Thrace, who had started a revolt, and massacred the Latins. In the spring of 1205 Baldwin I tried to put down the rising and laid siege to Adrianople. But Kalojan hastened with a large army of Bulgars and Cumans to the relief of the beleaguered city. The Latin army was destroyed in a bloody battle and Baldwin himself, with most of his knights, was taken prisoner and brought to Trnovo (14 April 1205). The Bulgarians and Cumans then swept over the whole country, up to Constantinople, and Kalojan took Serres and besieged Thessalonica. Boniface of Montferrat succeeded in keeping the Bulgarians out of Thessalonica but they occupied the remainder of Macedonia. These fierce recriminations between Bulgarians and Latins continued until the death of Kalojan, who died in a way as yet unexplained, whilst a new attack was being made on Thessalonica (8 October 1207).

The struggle of the three Asen brothers had, after twenty years, finally assured the independence of the new Bulgarian state: but its peaceful development had been disturbed by the various internal troubles which accompanied that struggle. The very fact that all three brothers, Peter, Asen, and Kalojan, met with violent ends indicates how difficult was the task of the internal consolidation of Bulgaria, the organisation of a stable government and the curbing of the power and independence of the boyars. After the death of Kalo-jan, Bulgaria had to face a serious crisis. His nephew, Boril (1207–18), gained the throne, but he was unable to unite the boyars in his support. His accession caused risings which seriously threatened the unity of the realm; and two of his relatives carved out principalities of their own. The Despot Alexius Slav established himself in the southern part of the land in the area of the Rhodope range, and created an independent province based on Melnik. In Macedonia, around the strong town of Prosek on the lower Vardar, the *sebasto-crator* Strez set himself up, with the help of the Grand Župan of Serbia, the son of Stephen Nemanja. Boril made a vain attempt to assert his authority by making war on the Latins; but his army was destroyed near Philippopolis in 1208. The Despot Alexius Slav there-upon became a vassal of the Latin Emperor Henry, married his daughter, and received the Emperor's promise that he would help him to gain the Bulgarian crown. South of the Balkan mountains the authority of the Bulgarian state had evaporated. In Macedonia the revolt of Strez was brought to an end with severe losses; but when Strez was murdered by his own men, his stronghold of Prosek came under the control of the Greeks of Epirus. Even on the Danube, Boril's power was not completely secure. In the district of Vidin, yet another insurrection broke out and was only crushed with the help of the Hungarian army. The disorganisation of the country gave fresh impetus to the Bogomil heresy, which began to spread swiftly. The Emperor Boril convened an ecclesiastical council (*Săbor*) at Trnovo at which the heresy was condemned. Its adherents, if they refused to recant, were harshly punished or exiled; but Bogomilism was too firmly rooted in Bulgaria to be destroyed by measures such as these.[1]

To consolidate his power Boril turned for support to Hungary and the Latin Empire. The Hungarian king, Andrew II, helped him to crush the revolt at Vidin: and in 1213 after many years of unavailing warfare, he concluded an alliance with the Latin Empire through the mediation of Pope Innocent III. But the alliance was not a happy one for Boril. A combined Latin–Bulgarian attack on Serbia proved a complete failure, and Boril's already insecure position was even more seriously undermined. The death of the Latin Emperor Henry (11 June 1216) and the absence of the Hungarian king Andrew II, who had gone on a crusade in 1217, left Boril with no outside support. In these circumstances John Asen, son of Asen I, who had been living in exile in Russia, had little difficulty in overthrowing Boril with Russian help, and seizing power. Boril was driven back and en-trenched himself in Trnovo; but the citizens opened the gates of the

[1] D. Angelov, *Bogomilstvoto v Bălgarija* (Sofia, 1947), p. 139.

capital to the pretender. Boril was blinded and John Asen II was recognised as Emperor (1218–41).

The reign of John Asen II represents the most brilliant epoch of the restored Bulgarian state. But some considerable time was needed for it to recover from the internal and external misfortunes it had suffered during the reign of Boril. For more than ten years Bulgaria had played no active part in the Balkans; the initiative had passed to Epirus whose ruler, Theodore Ducas, was now strong enough to expel the Latins from Serres and Thessalonica and the Greeks of Nicaea from Adrianople, and to extend his frontiers to the foothills of the Balkan mountains and to the suburbs of Constantinople. The Frankish barons on the Bosphorus in their distress sought the support of Bulgaria as a fellow-sufferer from this new Balkan power, and solicited the protection of John Asen. Theodore Ducas of Epirus had therefore also to reckon with Bulgaria in his plans for the conquest of Constantinople. In the spring of 1230 he advanced from Adrianople up the river Marica into Bulgaria, but near the village of Klokotnica John Asen inflicted a heavy defeat on him. Theodore himself was captured. Few battles in the history of the Balkans have had such immediate and far-reaching consequences. The might of Epirus was shattered in one stroke, and Bulgaria took her place as the leading Balkan power. The Bulgarian army marched unopposed through Thrace, Macedonia and Albania; and John Asen proudly recorded his conquests in an inscription at Trnovo: 'I waged war in "Romania", defeated the Greek army and captured the Emperor Lord Theodore Comnenus himself and all his boyars; and I occupied all the land from Adrianople to Dyrrachium, Greek, Serbian and Albanian alike. The Franks hold only the cities in the vicinity of Constantinople and Constantinople itself; but even they are under the authority of my Empire, since they have no other Emperor but me and only thanks to me do they survive, for thus God has decreed.'[1] The territorial extent of the Bulgaria of this time is revealed in a document granting the citizens of Ragusa (Dubrovnik) the right to trade freely as far as Vidin, Braničevo, Belgrade, the province of Karvuna (the modern Dobrudja), Adrianople and Didymotichus, and in the districts of Skoplje, Prilep and Devol.[2]

The sudden growth of the power of Bulgaria after the battle of Klokotnica transformed the very basis of her relations with the Latin Empire. The barons and clergy, relying upon the Pope, frustrated Asen's plans for the control of Constantinople, and introduced John of Brienne, titular King of Jerusalem, as regent of the Empire; he

---

[1] V. N. Zlatarski, *Istorija*, III, pp. 587 ff.
[2] L. Stojanović, *Stare srpske povelje i pisma* (Belgrade, 1934), I, 2, p. 205.

had himself crowned Emperor. A Magyar attack on Bulgaria in 1232, in which Belgrade and Braničevo were recaptured, may perhaps have some connection with these changes. Much embittered, John Asen repudiated the union with the Roman Church, a union which from the start had been but formal, and made an offer of alliance to John Vatatzes, Emperor of Nicaea. Among other items of the alliance, the Bulgarian Church was recognised as an independent Patriarchate[1] and Asen's daughter was married to the son of Vatatzes, Theodore Lascaris (1235).[2] The allied armies then marched on Constantinople and laid siege to the city, but without success. Pope Gregory IX was swift to give his protection to the Latin Empire; he invited Hungary to come to its aid, and excommunicated John Asen. Indeed Asen soon realised that in the event of victory Nicaea stood to profit more from his efforts than Bulgaria; for Constantinople and its surrounding districts were to go to Vatatzes by agreement. Furthermore, Bulgaria was in serious danger from the north, where the Mongols had already conquered South Russia. Asen's policy in these circumstances betrayed a certain hesitancy. In 1237 he suddenly betrayed his Greek allies and made a shortlived agreement with the Latins; but within the year he changed his plans yet again and renewed his treaty with John Vatatzes.

The founders of the new Bulgarian state based their actions on the traditions of Symeon's Bulgaria. From the very beginning the title 'Emperor' was used for the rulers, probably in the sense of 'Emperor of the Bulgars and the Greeks'. Ansbert holds, indeed, that Peter was called Emperor of Greece—'a suis dictus imperator Grecie'—and that he had sought Frederick Barbarossa's confirmation of this title: 'qui se imperatorem et coronam imperialem regni Grecie ab eo sibi imponi efflagitabat'.[3] The full title of the ruler as inscribed on native monuments is 'Emperor of the Bulgars and the Greeks' ('Car Bŭlgarom i Grŭkom').[4] As in Byzantium, the sovereign ruled 'by the grace of God', he was 'crowned by God' and was 'holy'. The outward marks of his authority were the same; the Church was organised on the same model. Kalojan, to be sure, succeeded in obtaining from Innocent III only the title of *Primas Bulgariae* for the head of the

---

[1] S. Stanojević's attempt, *Glas*, CLVI (1933), 171 ff., to show that the Serbian Archbishop Sava intervened with the Eastern Patriarchs to gain recognition for the Patriarchate of Trnovo is, in the opinion of the present writer, unconvincing; cf. N. Radojčić, 'St Sava and the Independence of the Serbian and Bulgarian Churches', *Glas*, CLXXIX (1939), 237 ff. (in Serbian). On the question as to whether the Bulgarian Church was dependent on Constantinople, see V. N. Zlatarski, *Istorija*, III, pp. 596 ff.

[2] *DR*, 1745.

[3] *Expeditio Friderici Imperatoris*, *MGH*, *Script.*, n.s. v, p. 58.

[4] G. Ostrogorsky, 'Avtokrator i Samodržac', *Glas*, CLXIV (1935), 138 ff.

Bulgarian Church instead of that of Patriarch which he had sought. But just as Kalojan himself, although only crowned King, considered that he had obtained the imperial dignity, so the new *Primas* sent thanks to the Pope that his legate had conferred on him 'universalem plenitudinem patriarchalis dignitatis';[1] and under John Asen II in 1235, the Eastern Churches recognised the Bulgarian Patriarchate, which was to endure until the fall of the medieval Bulgarian state in 1393.

The titles and functions at court were of Byzantine origin: *despotes*, *sebastocrator*, *logothetes*, *protovestiarius*, and so on. Besides stimulating national consciousness, one consequence of the long period of direct Byzantine rule in Bulgaria was the adoption of the Byzantine administrative and fiscal system. In Bulgarian charters are found the terms *praktor*, *sevast*, *duka*, *katepan*, amongst others; taxes and duties appear as *komod*, *mitat*, *ariko*. Ranks and titles which originated from the non-Slavonic Bulgars, and had been preserved in the time of the first Bulgarian Empire (such as *Kakvan*, *Tarkan*, *Bagaini*, *Bagaturi*, and others), no longer occur. The Slav inheritance, moreover, in the administrative field was noticeably much weaker than before, and the influence of Byzantium on the internal organisation of Bulgaria was undoubtedly far stronger than in Serbia.[2]

Though in theory his power was unrestrained, the ruler was to some extent limited by a powerful nobility, the boyars. They played an important role even under normal conditions, but even more so when the central power rested in feeble hands. The boyars, who often held extensive districts under their personal control, threatened the unity of the country and the frequent violent changes on the throne were usually due to them. In the long run it was the boyars who had the final word in the filling of the vacant throne.

There was a considerable number of towns in Bulgaria, but their citizens, particularly south of the Balkan range and on the shores of the Black Sea, were predominantly Greek. In the mining centres there were some Germans who, in Bulgaria as in Serbia and Bosnia, operated the mining industry. The Ragusans took an important part in trade, though not to the same extent as in the western regions of the Balkan peninsula.[3] The native element developed slowly, and, even down to the time of the fall of the medieval Bulgarian state, had

---

[1] A. Theiner, *Mon. Slav. Merid.* I, p. 39.

[2] P. Mutafčiev, *Istorija na bŭlgarskija narod*, II, pp. 118 ff., *BZ*, xxx (1930), 387 ff.; M. Laskaris, *Vatopedskata gramota na car Ivan Asenja II*, pp. 35 ff. (*Bŭlgarski starini*, xi, Sofia, 1930).

[3] C. Jireček, *Die Bedeutung von Ragusa in der Handelsgeschichte des Mittelalters* (Vienna, 1899), p. 45 and notes 77–9. I. Sakazov, *Bulgarische Wirtschaftsgeschichte* (Berlin and Leipzig, 1929).

not succeeded in attaining a predominant role in either the economic or political life of the country.

The tenant peasants (*paroikoi* in Greek terminology) formed the mass of the population on the lands of the nobles, the rulers and the Church. The paucity of sources makes it impossible to define their position more precisely, but there is no doubt that their status was humble and that it gradually deteriorated as a result of the internal development of Bulgaria and the growth of the Turkish danger. The nature of their position was evidenced by their attachment to the lord's estate, their duties, and the forced labour (*rabota*). In the villages there was a considerable body of tradesmen (*tehnitari*). In the mountainous areas lived the Vlach herdsmen, whose lot was rather more favourable than that of the *paroikoi*.

The great changes which occurred in the Balkans at the end of the twelfth and at the beginning of the thirteenth centuries made impossible any future reimposition of Byzantine control over Serbia. The formation of the new Bulgarian Empire not only considerably diminished the power of Byzantium and placed on her flank a powerful enemy, but it also meant that Serbia was no longer hedged in by the long Byzantine frontier which, running through Belgrade, Braničevo, Niš, Skoplje, and Prizren, had formerly enclosed it on three sides. Contact between the two countries was now possible only in the south, in Macedonia and Albania. And for several decades Byzantium itself was eclipsed as a result of the Fourth Crusade. When the Greek Empire was restored in 1261 it was no longer able to consider the reassertion of its political power over Serbia, and had in fact to go over to the defensive, gradually losing more and more territory.

When Stephen Nemanja abdicated the throne he gave orders to his assembly of nobles (*Sabor*) that his heir was to be his second son, Stephen (1196–1227), while his elder son, Vukan, had to content himself with the maritime provinces of Zeta and Trebinje, which he had ruled during his father's reign. This decision concerning the succession was probably dictated by the desire to maintain friendly relations with Byzantium, since Stephen was married to the daughter of Alexius III Angelus. But in fact it led to a war between the two brothers which threatened the very independence of the country. In 1202 Vukan called on the help of the Hungarians, drove out his brother and conquered the whole realm; but the very next year he was forced to withdraw to the maritime regions under pressure from the Bulgarians, who restored Stephen to the throne.[1] The brothers

[1] S. Stanojević, 'Hronologija borbe izmedju Stevana i Vukana', *Glas*, CLIII (1933), 91 f.

soon made their peace, however, and returned to the state of affairs which had prevailed at the time of Stephen Nemanja's abdication. Thus Hungary failed in its attempt to subject Rascia to its control and to introduce there the organisation of the Roman Church: but its claim to Rascia was not set aside, and was clearly manifested in the term *Rex Serbiae* which the Hungarian kings added to their titles.

Serbia quickly recovered from these disturbances and soon took a vigorous part in Balkan politics, waging successful wars against Bulgaria, Hungary and the Latin Empire. The Bulgarian renegade, Strez, found favour with the Grand Župan. A combined attack on Serbia by the Latin Emperor Henry of Flanders and the Bulgarian Emperor Boril was a complete disaster; an assault on Zeta made by the ruler of Epirus, Michael I, likewise failed; and Stephen succeeded in overcoming the danger from the anti-Serb alliance between Hungary and the Latin Empire.[1] Although all these successes brought no increase of territory, they demonstrated the real power of the country, and the personal authority of its ruler; and as a result Stephen was able to raise Serbia to the dignity of a kingdom, and its Church to the status of an autocephalous Orthodox community. He obtained a crown from Pope Honorius III whose legate performed his coronation as the 'First-Crowned' King of Serbia in 1217. The conditions which Stephen had to agree to and the promises he made to gain this concession are not clear.[2] But at all events it is evident from his efforts to organise the Orthodox Church in Serbia that his dealings with Rome had no lasting consequences. The Bishopric at Ras had hitherto been subject to the Archbishopric of Ochrida, which was now in the territory of Epirus. In order to free Serbia from this ecclesiastical subordination, Stephen appealed to Nicaea, sending as his ambassador his brother Sava, who as a young man had fled from his father's court to enter a monastery on Mt Athos. Sava succeeded in obtaining an independent archbishopric for Serbia (1219), being himself appointed the first archbishop, and it was arranged that his successors should be chosen and consecrated in Serbia itself, without the confirmation of the Patriarch.[3] The rivalry between Nicaea and Epirus, and the desire to see Orthodoxy firmly

---

[1] V. Ćorović, 'Žitije Simeona Nemanje' (with Old Slavonic text); *Svetosavski Zbornik II*, pp. 63 ff. (= *Srbska Kraljevska Akademija*, posebna izdanja cxxv, Društeni i Istoriski Spisi, 50, Belgrade, 1939).

[2] For the question of the contradictions of sources concerning the proclamation of the kingdom, and the attempt to prove that Stephen was crowned twice, once by the papal legate and then by his brother, Sava, compare D. Anastasijević, 'Je li Sv. Sava Ktrunisao Prvovenčanog', *Bogoslovlje*, x (1935), 211 ff.

[3] For the dispute as to whether the Serbian Church obtained all these concessions at one time or by instalments, see S. Stanojević, 'Sv. Sava i nezavisnost srpske crkve', *Glas*, clxi (1934), 199 ff. and N. Radojčić, *op. cit.*, *Glas*, clxxix (1939), 181 ff.

established in Serbia, caused the Emperor Theodore I Lascaris, and the Patriarch Manuel, to be willing to meet the Serbian requests. Despite bitter protests by Demetrius Chomatianus,[1] Archbishop of Ochrida, to both Serbia and Nicaea, Archbishop Sava continued to organise the Serbian Church by setting up a large number of new bishoprics. With the whole-hearted support of the monarchs, who founded many monasteries and endowed them with vast estates, the Church rapidly became an influential factor in feudal Serbia. The rulers found that the Church was a powerful instrument for strengthening their own authority and reducing that of the aristocracy. Side by side with the lords, the Church's representatives participated in the assembly of nobles. It was the Church also which made possible the development of a native literature in the national tongue, in the Serbian form of the old Slavonic language.

After the death of Stephen the First-Crowned, Serbia entered upon another epoch of internal troubles caused by the weakness of his immediate successors, and the subsequent strengthening of the influence of the nobles. The prevailing confusion was reflected in the swift and violent changes on the throne; and the situation did not improve until Uroš I (1243–76), the third son of Stephen, became ruler.

At this time the intensive exploitation of Serbia's rich mineral resources was begun, an event of considerable importance for its future development. Experienced German miners (*Sasi*) came to Serbia probably from Hungary, as a result of the Mongol invasion of that country, and they founded their own colonies which became the nuclei of a large number of new towns. In the middle of the thirteenth century the town of Brskovo, in the valley of the river Tara (in modern Montenegro), rapidly developed. A little later, the Germans founded Rudnik on the mountain of the same name where the Romans had had a mining settlement. But the most important mining area flourished on the Kopaonik and its spurs, where a whole series of settlements, large and small, sprang up, notably Novo Brdo (Novus Mons, Novomonte), Trepča, Plana, Janjevo and Koporići. The most important metal extracted from the Serbian mines was silver. Particularly valuable was the silver from Novo Brdo, *glama*, which contained a certain percentage of gold. Great quantities of lead, copper, and iron[2] were extracted from the majority of the mines.

---

[1] G. Ostrogorsky, 'Pismo Dimitrija Homatijana sv. Savi' (with Greek text); *Svetosavski Zbornik II* (*op. cit.*), pp. 96 ff.

[2] C. Jireček, *Staat und Gesellschaft im mittelalterlichen Serbien* (Vienna, 1912–19), II, 43 ff.; IV, 57 ff.

The opening up of the mines and the strengthening of commerce made the striking of a native currency essential, though only silver coins were minted (*denarii, grossi*). The mints were usually found in the mining centres (the most important were at Brskovo, Rudnik, and Novo Brdo).

The development of mining considerably increased Serbia's economic resources. Trade with the Adriatic coastal towns, particularly with Ragusa (Dubrovnik), was intensified. The rulers made an increasing use of currency in their dealings, a policy which was seen both in internal and foreign transactions. Whilst the monasteries which had been built by Stephen Nemanja and his immediate successors were on a fairly modest scale, the endowments of the later kings outstripped them in size, magnificence and splendour. The rulers could now pay for the upkeep of a regular mercenary army, composed of foreigners, with which they were able to keep the nobles in subjection, and to achieve a remarkable expansion of their territory. Later, when the Turkish conquest of the Balkans began, it was thanks to its economic strength that Serbia was able to offer a stiff and protracted resistance. The Burgundian knight Bertrandon de la Brocquière, was particularly impressed by the economic prosperity of the country when he travelled through the Serbia of George Branković in 1433: 'Et m'ont dit gens qui le sçavent bien que le dispot a une ville que l'on nomme Nyeuberghe qui est sur la rivyere de la Morave sur la marche de Vulgairie et de l'Esclavonie et d'Albanie et de Bossene. Et en ceste ville a mine d'or et d'argent tout ensamble, et en tire tous les ans plus de deux cent mille ducatz, et se n'estoit cela, je tiens qu'ils fust ores chacié hors de son pays de Rascie.'[1]

The results of Serbia's economic progress soon made themselves felt. From the reign of Uroš II Milutin (1282–1321), the second son of King Uroš I, Serbia vigorously expanded and within the space of a few generations became the greatest and most powerful state in the Balkans. An energetic, reckless man, Milutin, from the moment of his accession, took the offensive against Byzantium; and within a few years his army brought the whole of northern Macedonia under Serbian rule, including the towns of Skoplje, Tetovo, Štip, Veles, Kičevo and Debar. For a long time Byzantium was unable to reconcile herself to the loss of this province, but when her last attempts to drive out the Serbians completely failed, she was obliged to sue for peace. The negotiations and conditions showed the extent to which relations between Serbia and the eastern Empire had changed, to the latter's disadvantage. The Byzantine envoy, Theodore Meto-

---

[1] Bertrandon de la Brocquière, *Voyage d'Outremer*, p. 212 (ed. C. Schefer, Paris, 1892), p. 214.

chites, had to come five times to the Serbian court before an agreement was reached. By its terms the Emperor Andronicus II gave Milutin his five-year-old daughter Simonis in marriage, and recognised the occupied towns as dowry (1299). From now onwards, Milutin's relations with Byzantium remained friendly, and this period was characterised by the growth of Byzantine cultural influence in Serbia. The conquest of ancient provinces of the Empire and the arrival of Simonis at the Serbian court hastened this development; and it was at this time that the Byzantine system of granting land as *pronoia*[1] became established in Serbia.

Milutin's death in October 1321 led to fresh disturbances. A conflict within the dynasty had left the question of the succession unsettled. Three pretenders assumed the royal title, and fought amongst themselves for the country, until, after a long struggle, the victor was Stephen Uroš III (1321–31), Milutin's son, for whom the majority of the nobles had declared.[2] He overthrew his brother Constantine, whom his father, before his death, had nominated his successor, and handed over to him the government of Zeta. In the same way, Vladislav, son of Milutin's elder brother Dragutin, was excluded, after he had tried and failed to get recognition of his right to the throne which had been established by earlier agreements. The consequences of this civil war were not disastrous. Certain territorial losses were sustained (the Bosnians occupied Zachlumia); but Serbia was soon able successfully to resume its conquests in the south and to repair the damage done to its prestige.

During the subsequent civil war in Byzantium between Andronicus II and his grandson Andronicus III, Stephen Uroš III helped the elder Emperor with his army, at the same time extending the area of Serbian rule in Macedonia. Consequently, when Andronicus III had finally won the Byzantine throne, he concluded an anti-Serbian alliance with Bulgaria. Michael, the Bulgarian Emperor, opened the assault with an attack on Serbian territory, but his army was completely annihilated at Velbužd (modern Kjustendil in Bulgaria). Michael was killed in flight, and the Bulgarians had to conclude peace. After this defeat the Byzantine army, which in the meantime had begun to penetrate into Serbia from the south under the command of Andronicus III, was obliged to abandon the fight. Thus the battle of Velbužd (28 June 1330) frustrated the intentions of the anti-Serbian coalition formed by the two Empires, and ensured for Serbia a dominant role in the Balkans. But Stephen Uroš III was

---

[1] G. Ostrogorsky, *Pour l'histoire de la féodalité byzantine*, pp. 187 ff.

[2] Uroš III is generally known by the name of Stephen Dečanski, after the monastery of Dečani which he founded.

not to enjoy the fruits of this triumph for long. The nobles were discontented that he had not taken greater advantage of the victory, and they sided with his son, Stephen Dušan. Dušan had played a leading part in the battle and enjoyed the confidence of the war party, and it was by these nobles that he was brought to power. Uroš III was deposed and strangled in 1331.

In Bulgaria after the death of John Asen II a swift decline[1] set in as a consequence of internal conflicts and external dangers. Bulgaria not only declined as the possible successor of the Latin Empire, but her very sovereignty was brought into question. After the passage of the Mongols, who crossed from Hungary and swept through Bulgaria, she was obliged to pay tribute to the Mongol Khan.[2] John Vatatzes took the offensive against the young Michael II Asen and occupied the districts around Serres, Melnik, Adrianople, Velbužd (Kjustendil), Rhodope and the whole of Macedonia to the east of the river Vardar, while the Epirotes from the other flank occupied western Macedonia and Albania. Thus the greater part of the gains made in the time of John Asen II were lost. Bulgaria's attempts, after the death of John Vatatzes (1254), to recover the occupied districts in the south ended in severe defeats and new losses. The army of Michael VIII Palaeologus, after repelling fresh Bulgarian attacks, succeeded in extending the Byzantine frontier to the foothills of the Balkan Mountains: in 1263 the district around Philippopolis and the coastal towns of Sozopolis, Develtus, Anchialus and Mesembria were lost. Hungary, likewise, took advantage of Bulgaria's difficulties and once again occupied Belgrade and Braničevo. The Ban of the Mačva, Rostislav Mihailovič, the son-in-law of King Béla IV of Hungary, was for some time a very influential personality at the Bulgarian court. He had given his daughter in marriage to Michael II Asen; and after Michael's murder he tried to gain the Bulgarian throne, and proclaim himself Emperor ('Imperator Bulgariae'), but he was only able to maintain himself in the area around Vidin.[3] The conflict with Hungary lasted for several years, during which one Hungarian army penetrated to Trnovo itself. When peace was concluded in 1261, the Vidin province remained in the control of Hungary; and under Hun-

---

[1] The quick and violent changes of ruler demonstrate the extent of the crisis into which the country had fallen: Koloman I (1241–6), Michael II Asen (1246–57), and then the usurper Mico (1257), Constantine Tich (1257–77), Ivajlo (1277–9), John Asen III (1279–80). All met with violent deaths or were overthrown; most of them did not reign for more than five years.

[2] P. Nikov, *Tataro-bŭlgarskite otnošenija prez srednite vekove* (Sofia, 1920), gives an exhaustive account of the influence of the Tatars on Bulgarian history.

[3] V. G. Prokofjev, 'Rostislav Mihailovič', *Jubilejnij Sbornik russkago archeologičeskago obščestva* (Belgrade, 1936), pp. 149 ff.

garian patronage a separate province developed in western Bulgaria, which was ruled for some time by Jakov Svetoslav, a former Despot of that region, who now styled himself Emperor. After the death of the Hungarian King Stephen V in 1272, Svetoslav became independent. Thus Bulgaria had been virtually partitioned into two 'Empires', an eastern and a western. Internal decay and the arrogance of the boyars, which the central authority had been in no position to check, as well as the frequent assaults and ravages of the Tatars, finally led to risings in the lower ranks of society, which reveal the nature of all the divisions and antagonisms that were disturbing the peace of Bulgaria. A popular movement was inspired and led by a swineherd called Ivajlo, who was moved by mystical fanaticism and a belief that he was destined by providence to save the country. He succeeded in gathering around himself a large number of malcontents; and after repelling the Tatar hordes which were devastating Bulgaria, he advanced to Trnovo to seize supreme power. Constantine Tich, who had succeeded Mico as Emperor in 1257, tried to oppose him, but his army was overcome, and he himself was killed (1277). The whole of Bulgaria quickly succumbed to Ivajlo's authority, except for Trnovo, where the Empress Maria, Constantine's widow, held out with her followers. At this point Byzantium intervened. Michael VIII Palaeologus supported John, the son of the former Emperor Mico, as claimant to the Bulgarian throne, married him to one of his own daughters, and sent him with a large army into Bulgaria. In the face of this danger, the Empress Maria joined Ivajlo, handed over the capital to him, and married him. Ivajlo's success, however, was only temporary. His followers, who had supported him so long as they believed that he was fighting for an improvement of their condition, began to desert him, and the boyars were unable to work up any genuine enthusiasm for him. Whilst Ivajlo was repulsing fresh Tatar attacks on the Danube, the Byzantine army marched on Trnovo bringing its protégé John. The boyars and the Empress Maria came to an agreement with him and he occupied the Bulgarian throne as John Asen III (1279–80). But the new Emperor could only maintain himself with the help of a Byzantine army; and when this was defeated by Ivajlo, he was forced to fly from his capital and take refuge at Constantinople. The nobles then proclaimed George Terter, one of their own representatives, as Emperor (1280–92). Ivajlo enlisted the support of the Tatars to restore his fortunes, but was assassinated at a banquet on the orders of their leader Nogaj.

Bulgaria's position did not greatly improve with the accession of George Terter. The bitter internal conflicts were indeed momentarily assuaged, but pressure from the outside did not cease. In order to repel the influence of Byzantium, George Terter allied with Charles of Anjou, who was preparing the destruction of the Byzantine Empire; but the Sicilian Vespers wrecked his plans. Bulgaria was again invaded and ravaged by the Tatars with whom Michael VIII Palaeologus had struck up an alliance and Terter was forced to become a vassal of their leader Nogaj. External difficulties and the inability of the central government to curb the boyars contributed to the decline of Bulgaria. In the west an independent state, with its centre at Vidin, arose under the Despot Šišman, and quickly became dependent upon Serbia. In the rest of the country Terter lost more and more territory owing to the defection of individual boyars who invited the Tatars to assist them, until finally he had to leave Bulgaria and seek asylum in Byzantium. The Tatar Nogaj set up in his place a minor boyar, Smilec (1292–8). Anarchy thereupon became rife throughout the country, until the young and vigorous son of George Terter, Theodore Svetoslav (1298–1322), came to the throne. Svetoslav took drastic measures to restore order and re-establish the imperial power: even the Patriarch Joachim, accused of betraying the country to the Tatars, was ordered to throw himself from the ramparts of Trnovo. It was fortunate that Svetoslav's accession coincided with a relaxation of external pressure on his country. The Tatars, preoccupied with their own internecine conflicts, ceased to be a danger in the north; and Byzantium, occupied for many years by both the Turkish danger and the depredations of the Catalans, was no longer able to interfere in Bulgarian affairs. Svetoslav was thus able more easily to renew Bulgarian power south of the Balkan mountains, while the more settled conditions inside Bulgaria led to some sort of economic progress. Through the towns on the Black Sea trade flourished with Genoa and Venice, and native coins were minted in great numbers.

During the reign of Stephen Dušan (1331–55), the rise of Serbia, virtually uninterrupted from the time of Nemanja, reached its culmination; its obvious expression lay in the attempt, based on the earlier example of Bulgaria, to succeed to the Byzantine imperial position. The extension of Byzantine influence in Serbia had been great since the beginning of the fourteenth century; now it took the form of a systematic attempt to take over everything Byzantine.

After he had established himself on the throne and secured himself from the Bulgarian side by marrying the sister of the new Emperor John Alexander, Dušan commenced the conquest of Byzantium. Having taken Ochrida, Strumica, and certain other towns in Byzantine Macedonia, he penetrated, in the summer of 1334, to Thessalonica.

Andronicus III had to bring up an army with all speed to prevent the second town of the Empire falling into the enemy's hands. At a personal meeting between the two rulers an agreement was reached. Serbia retained most of the conquered districts. (Her southern border ran approximately along the present-day frontier of Jugoslavia.) Soon after the death of the Emperor Andronicus III in 1341 the civil war which broke out in Byzantium gave Serbia its opportunity for further conquest, first of all in alliance with the rival Emperor, John Cantacuzenus, and afterwards without him. A number of Byzantine towns fell to the Serbians in quick succession: Kroja, Bellagrada (Berat) and Avlona in Albania; Castoria, Verria, Serres, Drama, Philippi and Chrysopolis in Macedonia and Thrace. Mt Athos also fell into Serbian hands. Thessalonica and its surroundings were thus cut off from the other Byzantine provinces on the land side. By the end of 1345 (November or December) Dušan felt able to proclaim himself 'Emperor of the Serbs and the Greeks', βασιλεὺς τῶν Σέρβων καὶ 'Ρωμαίων, as his title appears in Greek archives. He was solemnly crowned at Skoplje on Easter Day, 16 April 1346, by the former Serbian Archbishop Joannicius who had been raised to the dignity of 'Patriarch of the Serbs and Greeks' by the Bulgarian Patriarch, the Archbishop of Ochrida and representatives from Athos; and by this act the autocephalous Patriarchate of Serbia was established as an indispensable corollary to the independent Empire. The court was organised on the Byzantine model whose ranks and titles, such as *despotes, sebastocrator,* or Caesar, and the like were systematically adopted. In strong emphasis of the pronouncement that he was 'the successor to the great and holy Emperors of the Greeks', Dušan formally partitioned his realm into 'Srblje and Romania'. His son, Uroš, who was crowned king at Skoplje, administered the old Serbian lands, and signed himself 'King of the whole of Serbia'. Dušan himself retained the newly subjected 'Romania', that is, the recently acquired Byzantine provinces. For this reason Byzantine titles were given only to that ruler who had authority in the provinces which composed 'Romania'; in the Serbian lands ('Srpska Zemlja') the Slav titles, such as župan, knez (prince), voivode, were retained.[1] The aim of this division was to win over the Greeks to the new Empire. In actual fact, it only had a token meaning, since the new 'King of the Serbs' was still a child under ten years of age, and Dušan ruled over the whole country.

The occupation of the extensive Byzantine provinces and the assumption of the imperial title made it essential to strengthen the

[1] A. V. Solovjev, *Zakonodavstvo Stefana Dušana cara Srba i Grke* (Skoplje, 1928), pp. 68 ff.

legal system and to make other adjustments to suit new circumstances. The *Syntagma* or legal manual of Matthew Blastares, which had been published in 1335, had been translated into Serbian from the Greek. But now Serbia received her own original law code. At a meeting of the assembly of nobles in Skoplje the 'Code (*Zakonik*) of the Blessed Emperor Stephen' was approved on 21 May 1349; five years later it was considerably expanded, and it is the most important legal monument of medieval Serbia, invaluable for its information about the country's feudal organisation.

Byzantium, since it still firmly held that there existed only one universal Empire, was unable to accept Dušan's new title, which clearly showed his intention of conquering Constantinople itself. But the civil war, which had facilitated Dušan's rise to power, prevented the Byzantines from taking energetic or united action against the Serbian usurper of the imperial title. While the Patriarch Callistus, under pressure from John Cantacuzenus, anathematised the Emperor Dušan and his new Patriarch, John V Palaeologus appeared to be ready to make certain concessions to Dušan with the object of getting his support against Cantacuzenus. In one document (July 1351) he calls him 'most illustrious Emperor of Serbia',[1] thereby recognising Dušan's claim but as applying to Serbia only, as Byzantium had done before in the case of the Bulgarian claimants to the imperial title.

The assumption of the imperial title represented for Dušan a programme rather than the realisation of a stated aim—the conquest of Constantinople. In January 1346, on the occasion of announcing to Venice his intention of being crowned Emperor 'in imperio Constantinopolitano', Dušan offered the republic an alliance in order to bring about the complete overthrow of Byzantium, 'pro acquisitione imperii Constantinopolitani'; Venice rejected this, as she did all subsequent offers, for she did not find that it was in her own interest to exchange a powerful Serbia for the 'sick man' on the Bosphorus. Unable to find an ally who would assist his programme by providing him with a fleet, Dušan was obliged to restrict himself to the conquest of the neighbouring Byzantine provinces, since Constantinople was impregnable by land alone. In a short time Epirus, Aetolia, Acarnania and Thessaly were occupied. Only Thessalonica, despite religious and social ferment within the city and the fact that one section of the population was favourably inclined towards the Serbs, remained in Byzantine hands to the end. Serbia now ruled over the extensive maritime provinces between Ragusa and the Gulf of Corinth in the west, and a large stretch of the shore of the Aegean;

---

[1] L. Petit, *Actes de Chilandar*, I: *Actes grecs*, *VV*, XVII (1911), p. 292.

Dušan therefore decided to convert his country into a sea power, and acquired from Venice four galleys which were to form the nucleus of the new Serbian fleet. But his premature death put an end to his plans.

The whole foreign policy of Serbia in the time of Stephen Dušan was focused on the conquest of Byzantium. With this end in view he had to keep in alliance with Bulgaria and maintain friendly relations with Venice, offering her many services which the Republic usually did not accept; Venice, indeed, desired to co-operate with Serbia, not against Byzantium, but against Hungary which was then her chief enemy. Dušan himself always remained on the defensive towards Hungary, repulsing her attacks on his northern frontiers (1335, 1354); but Hungary retained the Mačva and the towns of Belgrade and Golubac, south of the Sava and the Danube. Nor was Dušan able to devote sufficient attention to the question of the Bosnian frontier. He was never reconciled to the loss of Zachlumia which the Bosnians had taken during the reign of his father, and in 1350 he tried to repair the loss by force; but after an auspicious opening to his campaign he had to retire when he was informed that John Cantacuzenus, taking advantage of the situation, had begun to attack the towns in the south of Serbia.

Serbia's relations with the papal curia were conditioned by circumstances in the East. In Serbia itself Dušan showed not the least toleration towards the Roman Catholics. According to his Code every attempt to convert his Orthodox subjects to the 'Latin heresy' was severely punished. Even marriage between 'half-believers' (Catholics) and 'Christians' (Orthodox) was forbidden. Yet at times Dušan raised hopes in Avignon of the possibility that the Serbian Church would submit to the Papacy. At the beginning of 1347 the Catholic bishop at Scutari informed Pope Clement VI that the Serbian Emperor was ready to enter into a union. The offer, however, was not really sincere, and probably arose as a result of strained relations between Serbia and Byzantium after the proclamation of the Empire, and the negotiations were quickly broken off. One of Dušan's envoys made a similar offer to Pope Innocent VI in 1354, when the Serbian Emperor was asking the Pope to place him at the head of a Christian crusade against the Turks who had recently made their first appearance in the Balkans—'ab eadem ecclesia, matre tua, contra Turchos ipsos capitaneus ordinari'. But again the offer was scarcely disinterested, for its acceptance would merely have given Dušan a moral pretext for securing the road to Constantinople.[1]

When Stephen Dušan died on 20 December 1355 his Empire at

[1] M. Purković, *Avinjonske pape i srpske zemlje* (Požarevac, 1934), pp. 44 ff.

once began to fall apart and its greatness to decline. His son and heir, the Emperor Uroš (1355–71), was a feeble ruler and proved unable to prevent the collapse of the power of the central government and the subsequent division of the Empire into both large and small independent feudal units. During Dušan's reign, as a result of many wars and the remarkable territorial expansion of the country, the authority of individual lords had increased; already the first danger signs from this source had made themselves felt; the lord Hrelja (Chreles), whose estate was situated in eastern Macedonia (around Štip and Strumica), had separated from Dušan and for about two years remained independent between Serbia, Byzantium, and Bulgaria (1340–2).

The decline of the Empire was hastened by dynastic strife. Symeon, Dušan's half-brother and governor of Epirus, proclaimed himself Emperor of the Serbs and Greeks, and tried to usurp the power of his nephew. The attempt failed, but it brought about the secession of the southern provinces, Epirus and Thessaly, where Symeon retained the imperial title. A little later, even in those areas which still formally remained in the body politic, various feudal lords declared their independence. The chief personality in Macedonia was Vukašin, who was župan of Prilep during the Emperor Dušan's reign, and had received the title of Despot from Uroš. From 1365 Vukašin called himself 'King of the Serbs and Greeks' and held personal sway over the district around Prilep, Skoplje, Prizren and Ochrida. His relations with the Emperor Uroš are not clear. When he concluded an agreement with the Ragusans and allowed them freedom of trade he did not so much as mention the Emperor. But contemporary portraits of the two rulers together, and coins which bear on one side the inscription 'Urosius imperator' and on the other side 'king', show that a complete rupture between them did not occur. To the east of Vukašin's lands, around Kumanovo, Kratovo, Štip, Strumica and Velbužd, ruled the brothers Dragaš and Constantine Dejanović. The district around Serres was governed by Vukašin's brother, the Despot John Uglješa. Individual nobles also assumed power in Albania, of whom the strongest in the north was the 'princeps Albanie', Charles Topia. Such was the position in the Emperor Dušan's 'Romania'.

Circumstances were no better in the purely Serbian districts of the Empire. In Zeta the three brothers Stracimir, George, and Balša Balšić seized power. In the north the župan Nicholas Altomanović constructed a province which, towards the end of the reign of the Emperor Uroš, embraced the area from Rudnik to Ragusa. To the east of Altomanović, in the area of the river Morava, Prince Lazar was slowly building up his position. The disintegration of the central government was felt on all sides. From 1357 the assembly (*sabor*) was no longer convoked. The feudal lords warred amongst themselves and appropriated regal power; Nicholas Altomanović struck his own currency and ordered the Ragusans to pay him the two thousand *hyperpyra* which they had paid yearly to the Serbian monarch in return for freedom of trade; when they refused he declared war on them and mercilessly devastated their lands.[1]

With the death of the Emperor Uroš in 1371, the dynasty of the Nemanjids came to an end and the last vestiges of a unified government disappeared. When the Turks attacked their country the Serbians were unable to offer any united opposition; only individual magnates could take action. The Despot Uglješa and 'King' Vukašin attempted to destroy Turkish power in the Balkans with one attack on the new Turkish capital at Adrianople, but they were completely defeated on the river Marica at Črnomen (26 September 1371) and both of them were killed. After this victory the Turks extended their authority over Macedonia. Vukašin's son, Marko, and the brothers Dejanović became vassals, under the obligation to pay tribute and to give military aid. These semi-independent principalities were annexed in 1395 when Marko and Constantine Dejanović were killed whilst helping the Sultan Bāyezīd against the Vlachs in a battle near Rovine.

When the dynasty of George Terter became extinct on the death of Svetoslav in 1323, the boyars chose as Emperor of Bulgaria Michael, son of Šišman, Despot of Vidin. Michael Šišman reigned from 1323 to 1330, and his dynasty was to rule in Bulgaria until her final collapse. He had succeeded his father as Despot of Vidin, and his election as Emperor meant the peaceful reunion of that province with the Empire—an event of the greatest importance to Bulgaria. Michael attempted to reimpose Bulgarian power south of the Balkans in the area of the fortresses of Sliven and Kopsis, where the boyar Vojsil, brother of the late Emperor Smilec, had established himself under Byzantine patronage and set himself up as pretender to the Bulgarian throne. Michael succeeded in expelling Vojsil from his lands, but the Byzantines occupied Philippopolis and Sozopolis on the Black Sea.

Michael's assumption of the Bulgarian crown had significant consequences for Bulgaria's relationships with Serbia. At the end of the thirteenth century Vidin was under the political influence of Serbia, and Michael himself was married to the daughter of King Milutin.

[1] M. Dinić, *O Nikoli Altomanoviću* (Belgrade, 1932), pp. 11 ff.

The reunion of Vidin with the rest of Bulgaria under Michael completely removed that influence, and very soon relations between the two countries deteriorated. The Bulgars helped the pretender Vladislav against Stephen Uroš III in Serbia, and Michael divorced his Serbian wife Anna, Uroš III's sister, so that he could marry Theodora, the sister of Andronicus III. After the uncertain state of affairs in Byzantium had been resolved by the final accession of Andronicus III, an alliance was struck between Bulgaria and Byzantium, directed against Serbia, whose steady rise to power represented a danger for both Empires. But the Bulgarian attack on Serbia ended in the great defeat at Velbužd, and in the death of the Emperor Michael himself (28 June 1330).[1]

John Stephen, Michael Šišman's son by his Serbian wife, was then established as Emperor at Trnovo, but his reign was brief. He was unable to gain the support of the boyars, who disapproved of the way in which he had reached the throne and resented the resultant Serbian influence. The instability of the new regime also presented Byzantium with a pretext to interfere. When Andronicus III was informed of the Bulgarian defeat at Velbužd and its consequences, he broke off the war with the Serbs and attacked Bulgaria, using the excuse that his sister had been removed from the Bulgarian throne. John Stephen was able to survive only with Serbian support. As soon as this was withdrawn, the boyars, led by the *protovestiarius* Raksin and the Logothete Philip, overthrew him and in the spring of 1331 proclaimed John Alexander, nephew of Michael Šišman, Emperor.[2]

After the defeat at Velbužd, Bulgaria played a comparatively minor role in the Balkan peninsula, while Serbia, under Stephen Dušan, became the dominant power. Bulgaria was able however to take advantage of the civil war in Byzantium between Cantacuzenus and Palaeologus, though only to the extent of regaining the towns in the south which had been lost earlier, including Philippopolis (1344). Bulgaria's weakness was aggravated by internal dissensions which quickly brought about the dissolution of the state. The Emperor Alexander himself contributed to this end by introducing discord into his family relations. He abandoned his first wife and married Theodora, a converted Jewess. Under her influence he disinherited the sons of his first marriage, and proclaimed as heir John Šišman, his son by the 'newly enlightened Empress', Theodora. By way of compensation, he handed over the district of Vidin to his eldest son, Stracimir. Thus Vidin was once again separated from the

---

[1] A. Burmov, 'Istorija na Bǔlgarija prez vremeto na Šišmanovci', *Godišnik na Sofijskija Universitet, ist.-filolog. fakultet*, XLII, I (1946–7), 5 ff.

[2] *Ibid.* II, 3 ff.

Bulgarian Empire. Stracimir was dissatisfied; he assumed the imperial title, separated his province from the Bulgarian Patriarchate of Trnovo, and made his submission to the Patriarch of Constantinople. He emphasised his independence by minting his own currency. But he was not able to maintain that independence for long. In the spring of 1365 the Hungarian king, Louis I, attacked across the Danube, occupied Vidin, took Stracimir prisoner, and set up a 'Province of Bulgaria' ('banatus Bulgariae') where the newly arrived Franciscans began the conversion of the people to the Roman faith. Five years later, however, Louis was forced to return Vidin to Stracimir, though admittedly as his vassal.

At the same time the jurisdiction of the central government disappeared in north-eastern Bulgaria, in the Dobrudja, where the boyar Balik had defected; Balik was to be succeeded by his brother Dobrotica. Here also political separation from the main body of the state was followed by ecclesiastical recognition of the Byzantine Patriarchate.

The decline of Bulgaria continued during the reign of John Šišman (1371–93), the last Bulgarian Emperor. His first task was to suppress a rival claimant to the throne, Šišman, son of the late Michael III; the pretender made an appearance in Bulgaria, but was killed in a battle at Zlatica. John Stracimir attempted to conquer the whole of Bulgaria from Vidin, and occupied the district around Sofia (1371), but he was unable to hold his gains for long, and retired within the limits of his former province. The Despot Dobrotica also remained independent of the Bulgarian Emperor; he had contrived to construct a fleet and expended his energies in fighting Genoa, and intervening in the internal troubles of the Empire of Trebizond. His son and heir, Ivanko, abandoned his father's policy, concluded peace and made a commercial agreement with Genoa (1387).

The weakness of Bulgaria in the last years of her independence was accompanied by religious and social unrest within the country. From Byzantium the teaching of the hesychasts infiltrated into Bulgaria, where it found its most forceful protagonists in Theodosius of Trnovo and Romil of Vidin. Other sects also made their appearance, and the Bogomil movement, which had never completely disappeared, was again flourishing. The Emperor John Alexander's attempts to crush the various sects by convening ecclesiastical councils were comparatively unsuccessful. The religious disorder and the war waged by the official Church against heresy had at least one good result in that literary activity was stimulated. Since the era of the Emperor Symeon, literature in Bulgaria had never flourished so much as at this time. Besides works of a religious nature, either original or translations from the Greek, secular works, such as the chronicle of Constantine Manasses or the story of the Trojan war, were translated. At the head of this literary movement was the last Patriarch of Trnovo, Euthymius (1375–93), who wrote many works on varied subjects, including eulogies and letters. This enthusiasm for literature found its echo in Serbia, where many literary men took refuge after the fall of Bulgaria. Constantine the Philosopher, a disciple of the Patriarch Euthymius, who left behind him an excellent biography of the Despot Stephen Lazarević, was one of this number.

Whilst Bulgaria was passing through this phase of political and religious disintegration, the pressure of the Turks, who obtained their first permanent base in the Balkans in 1352, was becoming stronger and more direct. The Turks were rapidly making it clear that they aimed at having their political centre in Europe, for they moved the administrative centre of their new conquests, first to Didymotichus on the river Marica (1361) and a little later to Adrianople (about 1363).[1] By virtue of her geographical position, Bulgaria was the first of the Slav lands in the Balkans to be exposed to the blows of the Ottomans. One after the other the towns south of the Balkan mountains fell into the hands of the invaders. The Emperor John Šišman, soon after coming to the throne, had to recognise the authority of Murād I and deliver his own sister, Tamara, into Murād's harem, an act which did little to slow up the Turkish advance. Marauding raids and temporary conquests in Danubian Bulgaria preceded and foreshadowed the final settlement. In the spring of 1393, a large Turkish army laid siege to Trnovo, which had to capitulate (17 July) after a long resistance, and after Trnovo all the other cities fell. With the extinction of the medieval Bulgarian state, the Bulgarian national Church also ceased to exist. The Patriarch Euthymius was imprisoned in a monastery, and shortly afterwards a Metropolitan of the Byzantine Patriarchate was sent to Trnovo.

The provinces of the Dobrudja and Vidin suffered the same fate as the main body of the state which had its centre at Trnovo. The former lands of Prince Ivanko were ruled for a brief space (1390–1) by the Vlach *voivode* Mircea, before falling into the hands of the Turks. Stracimir reigned for a short time at Vidin as a Turkish vassal. But when the Hungarian king Sigismund advanced against the Turks in 1396 and passed through his province, Stracimir took the Christian

---

[1] A. Burmov, 'Koga e zavladen Odrin ot Turcite', *Izvestija na bŭlgarskoto istoričesko družestvo*, XXI (1945), 23 ff., has tried to prove that the Turks captured Adrianople in 1371, after the battle of the river Marica, but the reasons put forward are not entirely convincing. But see above, ch. VIII, p. 369 and below, ch. XIX, p. 763.

side. After the defeat of the crusaders at Nicopolis, Bāyezīd occupied Vidin and put an end to the independence of this last remnant of the medieval Bulgarian state.

While Serbia was degenerating temporarily into an era of feudal disorganisation, after the death of Stephen Dušan, and Bulgaria was approaching final dissolution, Bosnia was attaining the summit of her medieval development. The nucleus of an individual political entity in this area could already be perceived in the first half of the tenth century, when Constantine VII Porphyrogenitus described the region around the modern Sarajevo as a separate district within the framework of the Serbia of that time. The Bosnian state was gradually built up in this inaccessible locality. The association of Croatia with Hungary at the beginning of the twelfth century was of great significance for Bosnia's subsequent destiny. Hungary became Bosnia's immediate neighbour and always showed a desire to extend its authority in this direction. The struggle against its northern neighbour was to form one of the essential characteristics of the history of the Bosnian land down to the time of its fall and vitally affected the course of its internal development. From 1138 the Hungarian king made clear his claims to Bosnia in his title; a little later (c. 1154–62) the Ban Borić was a Hungarian vassal and gave Hungary military help in a war against Byzantium. When Manuel Comnenus was victorious over Hungary for a short time Bosnia was temporarily brought within the orbit of the Eastern Empire.

At the end of the twelfth century the first signs appeared of the religious movement which was to develop into a separate 'Bosnian Church', the *Ecclesia Bosnensis*. Bosnia was the religious frontier between the Catholic and the Orthodox Churches, and it was indeed formally within the Catholic province; in the second half of the eleventh century its bishopric was subordinated to the Catholic Archbishopric at Bar, and later to the Archbishopric of Ragusa; but ecclesiastical organisation in this primitive frontier area was not sufficiently developed for the Western Church to be able to secure a lasting supremacy. Accusations began to be received at Rome that the Ban Kulin (c. 1180–1204) had given refuge to the Patarenes (Bogomils) who had fled from the Dalmatian towns, and that he himself had adopted this heresy, together with his family and more than ten thousand Catholics. Pope Innocent III took vigorous measures for the protection of Catholicism, and he charged the Hungarian king to root out the heretics, and to spare not even the Ban himself if he refused to return to 'the true path'. In the face of this threat Kulin had to yield. In the presence of a papal legate, representatives of the Patarenes and Kulin guaranteed that in the future they would strenuously uphold the teachings of the Catholic Church (8 April 1203). An embassy then travelled to Hungary, where the guarantees were repeated in the presence of the king and representatives of the Roman Church.[1]

But such measures failed to root out the Bogomil heresy in Bosnia. Very soon reports again began to arrive at Rome that Bosnia was full of heretics. In 1221 the papal curia sent a legate to Bosnia, and at the same time urged the Hungarian king to assist in the annihilation of the heresy. The Dominicans, who had distinguished themselves by their zeal in the campaign against heresy in France, were introduced into the country. But as increasing pressure was brought to bear, so resistance in Bosnia grew. Hungary was not powerful enough to impose its authority on the Bosnians for long, or to secure a final victory for Catholicism, and its military assaults had only temporary success. It was obvious that the Catholic Church was steadily losing ground in Bosnia, for in the middle of the thirteenth century the Catholic bishop had to leave the country and transfer his see to Dyakovo, north of the river Sava, whence he never returned.

The 'Bosnian Church', which reigned supreme in Bosnia after the elimination of the Catholic bishopric, developed from that great heretical dualist movement which for several centuries smouldered in the countries of southern Europe from the Black Sea to the Pyrenees; in the Balkans its adherents were called Bogomils, in the west Patarenes, Cathari and Albigenses. The main features of the organisation of this Church are clear. At its head stood the 'Bishop of the Bosnian Church', usually called 'Djed'; under him were the 'Gosti', of whom there appear to have been twelve, and a larger number of 'Starci' (elders). The Djed, the Gosti and the Starci were drawn from the ranks of the 'Krstjani', who correspond to the 'accomplished ones' or 'the chosen' in the west (*perfecti*, *electi*). The Krstjani used to live in groups scattered over the whole country (*domus christianorum*, *domus patarenorum*).[2]

The victory of the 'Bosnian Church' was of supreme importance for the later history of Bosnia, the only medieval European state in

---

[1] T. Smičiklas, *Codex Diplomaticus regni Croatiae, Dalmatiae et Slavoniae*, III (Zagreb, 1905), p. 24; D. Kniewald, 'Vjerodostojnost latinskih izvora o bosanskim krstjanima', *Rad Jugoslavenske Akademije*, CCLXX (1949), 115 ff.

[2] In more recent times there have been mistaken attempts to deny the dualistic element in the philosophy of the 'Bosnian Church', and to demonstrate that it was either an individual Orthodox Church (V. Glušac) or a Church which had developed from a Bosnian Catholic bishopric which had broken away from authority and was for this reason charged as heretical on insufficient grounds (J. Šidak). An exhaustive survey of the newer literature on the subject of dualism in the Balkans is given by A. Schmaus, 'Der Neumanichäismus auf dem Balkan', *Saeculum*, II (1951), 271 ff.

which a heretical Church was pre-eminent and of long duration. This development was made possible partly by the geographical position of the country, and partly by the fact that the Roman Church used Hungary in attacking the Bosnian heretics, so that the conflict very easily became a part of Hungary's attempt to impose its authority on Bosnia. The 'Bosnian Church', whose existence largely depended on an independent Bosnian state, devoted all its resources to the maintenance of Bosnian freedom. Here the Church found a natural ally in the powerful nobility of Bosnia, which stubbornly repulsed the attacks both of Hungary and of the Roman Church. Church and nobility also gave each other mutual support in internal affairs. It was the alliance of these two forces which prevented the development of strong central government in Bosnia. This supremacy of Bogomilism also gave an individual character to Bosnian cultural development. The teaching and organisation of the 'Bosnian Church' prevented the building of monasteries, and thus retarded the development of architecture, painting and sculpture. Literature was able to emerge only in the service of the learning of the ruling Church.

Hungarian pressure on Bosnia continued during the second half of the thirteenth century. But it was temporarily abandoned right at the end of the century, when Hungary fell victim to fierce dynastic disputes which gave the great feudal lords their opportunity. Then the Šubići, Croatian magnates, whose power rapidly increased during this period of strife, ruled for some time over Bosnia (1299–1322). Liberation came only when the Hungarian king Charles Robert (1301–42), after restoring authority in his own country, destroyed the power of the Šubići. From this time onwards the strength of Bosnia began to grow. The Ban, Stephen II Kotromanić (1322–53), though his vassal status towards Hungary remained unchanged, succeeded in doubling the extent of his territory. A royal clerk (*dyak*) of his court, in a document issued towards the end of his reign, was able to boast not without justice that 'the Ban rules from the river Sava to the Adriatic sea, from the river Cetina to the Drina'.[1] This territorial expansion of Bosnia brought with it an increase in economic resources. The outlet to the sea made possible a more intensive import and export trade with the coastal towns, particularly with Ragusa. The exploitation of Bosnia's rich minerals, especially silver and lead, now began. As in Serbia, Germans helped to develop the mines. The abundant minting of native money (silver *grossi*) demonstrates the extent of the economic advance.

Stephen Kotromanić's successor, his nephew Tvrtko I (1353–91),

---

[1] L. Thallóczy, *Studien zur Geschichte Bosniens und Serbiens im Mittelalter* (Munich and Leipzig, 1914), pp. 15 ff.

experienced considerable difficulty at the beginning of his reign. Hungary, under Louis the Great, was at the height of its power, and the Hungarian king forced Tvrtko to abandon the coastal districts west of the river Neretva (1357), and to accept stringent obligations as his vassal. But as had happened earlier, increased pressure from Hungary provoked strong resistance. Louis attacked Bosnia in order to preserve his influence, but completely failed (1363). The reputation of the young Ban grew rapidly, but this provoked the feudal lords who always feared a strong ruler and at the beginning of 1366 they broke into open revolt. Tvrtko was overthrown and compelled to flee to Hungary; and his younger brother Vuk was chosen as Ban. Tvrtko contrived to restore his position with Hungarian military assistance and returned as Ban of Bosnia, but only, as he himself emphasises, 'by the grace of God and our master King Louis'.[1] Within a few years, however, he had eradicated the consequence of this revolt and had overcome his most stubborn antagonists in the ranks of the nobility.

With the passing of this internal crisis and the firm establishment of Tvrtko on the throne, Bosnia was able to continue to grow in strength and to take advantage of the decline of Serbia. In 1373 an alliance was concluded between Ban Tvrtko and Prince Lazar against the župan Nicholas Altomanović, which brought Bosnia considerable territorial gain at the expense of the former state of the Nemanjids. Having thus added to his possessions Tvrtko, as a descendant of the extinct dynasty of the Nemanjids by the female line, assumed the old Serbian royal title, and had himself crowned 'King of Serbia and Bosnia' at Mileševo—a title which flattered his self-esteem but gave him no authority whatsoever over those Serbian lands which remained outside his own boundaries.

The decline of Hungary after the death of Louis in 1382 not only freed Bosnia from pressure in the north, but also enabled Tvrtko to recover the districts lost at the beginning of his reign, and to extend his frontiers in the direction of Dalmatia and Croatia. Within a few years the Bosnians had taken Cattaro (Kotor) and the whole of Dalmatia down to Zara (Zadar) and that part of Croatia south of Velebit. Only Ragusa remained independent of Bosnian authority.

The dynasty of the Nemanjids came to an end when the Emperor Stephen Uroš died on 4 December 1371. With his death the last shreds of central authority in Serbia vanished and bitter strife began between the lords. The warlike župan Nicholas Altomanović tried to

---

[1] S. Ljubić, *Listine o odnošajih izmedju Južnoga Slavenstva i Mletačke Republike*, IV (*MHSM*, Zagreb, 1874), 84.

expand his territory at the expense of his neighbours: but he was overthrown by the combined effort of the Bosnian Tvrtko and Prince Lazar in 1373; he was captured and blinded, and his broad lands were partitioned between the allies, Prince Lazar obtaining the districts around Rudnik and Užice. With the removal of his dangerous rival, Prince Lazar was left the most powerful man in Serbia. Circumspect, but vigorous, he expanded his own territory and influence by eliminating the weaker, and allying with the stronger magnates, a policy in which he was assisted by his Church. On its own initiative the Serbian Church had made its peace with the Patriarch of Constantinople: and in 1375 the Serbian Patriarch was received back into communion and his patriarchal status was recognised at Byzantium.[1] Lazar allied with Vuk Branković, ruler of the district around Kossovo, giving him his daughter in marriage. He established a similar link with Zeta, when George II Balšić also became his son-in-law.

While Prince Lazar was infusing fresh vigour into the Serbian state, the danger from the Turks was becoming increasingly pressing. From small marauding raids, they progressed to more serious attacks, which were not always wholly successful, and finally to a full-scale campaign. A great assault on Serbia was organised by the Sultan Murād I. With Asian and European contingents and auxiliary formations supplied by vassal princes, he penetrated to the field of Kossovo. Prince Lazar did all that was in his power to oppose him. Besides an army from his own and Vuk Branković's lands, he received considerable help from his Bosnian ally, Tvrtko I. The two forces met at Kossovo on 15 June 1389. The course of the battle is little known. It appears that the Christians had a measure of success to begin with, and that some confusion was caused in the Turkish camp by the death of Murād I, who was killed by a Serbian noble, Miloš Kobilić, posing as a deserter. But the command was immediately assumed by Murād's son, Bāyezīd, and victory was assured for the Turks. Prince Lazar was taken prisoner and executed after the battle. The death of the Sultan and the withdrawal of the Turkish army immediately after their victory gave rise to a false rumour in the western world that the Serbs had been victorious. News of a great Turkish defeat, spread by Tvrtko, reached Paris, inspiring Philippe de Mézière, in a work which he had only just completed, to write of Murād: 'Il a este desconfit tout a desroy et malemecheance es parties d'Albanie; et lui et son

---

[1] M. Laskaris, 'Le patriarcat de Peć a-t-il été reconnu par l'église de Constantinople en 1375?', *Mélanges Charles Diehl*, i (Paris, 1930), 171 ff., considers that Constantinople confined itself merely to re-establishing relations with the Serbian Church, but did not concede the title of Patriarch to its head, although this latter continued to bear it. See also V. Laurent, 'L'archevêque de Peć et le titre de patriarche après l'union de 1375', *Balcania*, vii (1944), 303 ff.

filz mors en bataille et les plus vaillans de son ost.' But the illusion was soon shattered.[1]

The battle of Kossovo, one of the most decisive moments in the century-long struggle of the Serbs against the Turks, quickly became the subject of legend. In the national ballads it became the quintessence of that struggle; Prince Lazar and Miloš, with historical inaccuracy, were given pride of place in the war against the infidel, while Vuk Branković was characterised as the typical traitor.

The immediate consequence of the battle of Kossovo was that Serbia became a vassal state of the Turks. Lazar's successor, his son Stephen Lazarević (1389–1427), had to accept the obligation of paying tribute and supplying an auxiliary army under his personal command. Since it was no longer possible to think of offering serious resistance to the Turks, he concentrated on the careful fulfilment of his obligations; and he was to be seen participating in all the major Turkish attacks: in Bāyezīd's attack on Wallachia (1395), in the great conflict with the Christians at Nicopolis (1396) and finally in the fateful battle of Ankara (1402). He also took advantage of this dearly bought security from the Turks to break the resistance of the rebellious lords and to strengthen the central authority in his own state.

The Mongol victory over the Turks at Ankara gave temporary relief to the Serbs and the other Balkan lands. On his return from Asia Minor through Constantinople, where he received from the Emperor John the title of Despot, Stephen Lazarević looked to Hungary for support. After recognising Hungary's old claims to overlordship, Stephen, as the vassal of King Sigismund, was granted Belgrade and the Mačva. The Despot transformed Belgrade, which had been destroyed in earlier wars, into a powerful fortress which was later to become famous in the struggle against the Turks; he also made it his capital. He helped Sigismund both in the Balkans in his attacks on Bosnia, and in the north against the Hussites. For these services he was given extensive estates in Hungary itself, and the particularly rich mining town of Srebrnica in Bosnia from which he obtained a yearly income of about thirty thousand ducats, though it became a continual source of conflict between Serbia and Bosnia in the last years of their independence.

During the ten years of civil war which divided the Turks after the battle of Ankara when Bāyezīd's sons quarrelled amongst themselves for the throne, Serbia was unable to remain neutral. Her troops played a prominent part in the fighting in the Balkans, helping one

[1] M. Dinić, 'Hronika sen-deniskog kaludjera kao izvor za bojeve na Kosovu i Rovinama', *Prilozi za književnost, jezik, istoriju i folklor*, XVII (1937), 51 ff.; *Glas*, CLXXXII, 133 ff.

pretender against another. Serbia's position was complicated by dissension within the ruling family. Stephen's younger brother Vuk, with help from Sulaymān, forced his brother to cede to him in 1409 the southern portion of the state over which he then ruled as a Turkish vassal. Vuk was executed in the following year by Mūsa, Bāyezīd's second son, and the unity of the Serbian state was rapidly restored. But Mūsa did not for long remain the master of the Turks in Europe. Having roused the antagonism of both Turks and Christians he plunged into war against Bāyezīd's third son, Muḥammad; and beneath Mt Vitoš, in Bulgaria, a decisive battle between the brothers took place. Here Serbian, Bosnian and Hungarian detachments, under the command of Stephen's nephew, George Vuković, inflicted a heavy blow on the enemy and contributed to Muḥammad's triumph over all his rivals (1413). Stephen was rewarded for these services by the grant of the district around Niš.

This temporary peaceful interlude in its relations with the Turks was very welcome to Serbia, in that it was enabled to extend its power over Zeta, and to obtain once again an outlet to the sea. Ever since the fall of Dušan's Empire, Zeta had been ruled by the Balšići; they had also succeeded for a time in conquering a large area of Albania until they were expelled by the Turks. From the other side, Venice also brought pressure to bear on the Balšići and made them give up their principal city, Scutari (1396), and the territory which joined it to the sea. The last of the Balšići, Balša III (1403–21), made a vain effort to repulse the Venetians from the river Bojana, but his strength was insufficient and he died in the attempt. Since he had no direct descendant, he had appointed as his heir his uncle, the Despot Stephen Lazarević, who continued the war with Venice. But Stephen proved unable to fulfil his nephew's ambition, and he had to reconcile himself to the continued Venetian occupation of Scutari and Ulcinj, whilst he retained Zeta with the coastal towns of Bar and Budva (1423).

The swift recovery of the Turks after the civil war, and the growing evidence of renewed Turkish activity in the area of the Danube, drove Serbia and Hungary to strengthen their relationship, which had continued to be cordial since the battle of Ankara. In May 1426 Stephen and King Sigismund made a treaty at Tata by the terms of which Stephen's nephew, George Vuković (Branković), was to succeed him in Serbia as a Hungarian vassal. In order to secure the defence of its southern border against the Turks, Hungary was to receive the towns of Belgrade and Golubac, as well as the province of Mačva on the death of Stephen.[1]

---

[1] G. Fejér, *Codex diplomaticus Hungariae ecclesiasticus et civilis*, x, 6, pp. 809 ff.; J. Radonić, 'Sporazum u Tati 1426 i srpsko-ugarski odnosi od XIII–XVI veka', *Glas*, CLXXXVII (1941), 176 ff.

When Stephen died (19 July 1427) King Sigismund visited the southern frontier to superintend the fulfilment of the terms of the recently concluded treaty, but he was only partially successful. The new Despot, George, the son of Vuk Branković, handed over Belgrade to the Hungarians, and there swore an oath of fidelity to the Hungarian king. But the garrison commander of Golubac, the *voivode* Jeremiah, had already surrendered to the Turks, and Sigismund completely failed in his attempt to secure this important Danubian town for Hungary (1428). Moreover, the Turks had occupied the frontier towns of Niš and Kruševac, and had begun to penetrate into the interior of Serbia. Branković was forced to submit to the Sultan, to pay an annual tribute and to supply an auxiliary force. The loss of these important frontier towns was compensated by the construction of a mighty fortress in Smederevo, on the Danube; this became the last capital of medieval Serbia and the last outpost of her independence.

Serbia was unable to remain for long at peace in view of the Turkish advance. The main burden of the struggle against the onslaught of Islam had fallen on Hungary, but the rival armies fought their battles on Serbian territory. In the spring of 1439 the Sultan Murād II laid siege to Smederevo itself, and the fortress fell after a defence lasting three months. In order to secure an approach to Hungary, Murād II also tried to take Belgrade, but, well fortified and brilliantly defended, it withstood successfully a six months' siege (1440). Their defeat before Belgrade did not prevent the Turks from occupying those areas of Serbia which were still free: and after the fall of Novo Brdo (June 1441) the whole of Serbia, with the exception of Zeta, had passed into their hands.

The danger to Hungary was greatly increased by the completion of the Turkish occupation of Serbia. Though preoccupied with their domestic difficulties, the Hungarian kings put up a determined resistance to the infidel. It was in the course of this resistance that John Hunyadi came to the fore as a brilliant commander and a determined champion of the Christian cause against the Turks. His victories in Transylvania and Wallachia (1442) made possible the great assault on the Balkans which the papal legate, Cardinal Julian Cesarini, was trying to organise. The Despot George Branković pledged himself to attack with all his forces in the hope that by a decisive defeat of the Turks Serbia might once more be re-established. He placed at Hungary's disposal his great experience of Turkish affairs, considerable financial resources and some military aid. From Belgrade the allies travelled by the well-known road through Niš and Sofia, the road along which all great advances through the Balkans had been made;

and after a few victories over the Turks, they penetrated to the Balkan passes. But winter and the well-fortified positions of the enemy did not allow them access to the valley of the Marica, and they were forced to return by the same route. The Turks, who dogged their footsteps, suffered fresh defeats.

These events made Murād II willing to conclude peace, particularly since the Christians were striving to strengthen the coalition by the inclusion of Venice and Burgundy; moreover, war was imminent between the Turks and the Sultan of Karamania in Asia Minor. But the negotiations did not lead to any lasting settlement;[1] and a fresh assault by the Christian allies ended in a heavy defeat at the battle of Varna on 10 November 1444. The Despot George was not, on this occasion, on the Christian side, for he had already concluded an independent peace (15 August 1444) by which Serbia was reconstituted as a state. With the object of dividing him from the allies, the Turks were conciliatory and returned to him the towns of Golubac and Kruševac which he had lost at the very beginning of his reign.

But even with the connivance of the Turks Serbia was not able to survive for long. Devastated during the recent wars, it lacked its earlier unity, and the Despot Branković only partly succeeded in renewing his authority over Zeta. The Venetians kept the coastal towns of Bar and Budva which they had occupied during the period of Serbia's decline; and war against Venice, generally to the detriment of Serbia, dragged on for years. The noble family of the Crnojevići took over more and more the former role of the Balšići, and played off Serbia against Venice. Relationships with Hungary were damaged, and deteriorated still more when John Hunyadi advanced across Serbia in his attack on the Turks and was defeated at Kossovo (October 1448). Forced to fly northwards, Hunyadi was seized by the Despot and only allowed his liberty after he had promised compensation for the damage caused by the Hungarian army's advance.

After the fall of Constantinople, the Sultan Muḥammad II spared Serbia no longer. At the end of a two years' campaign, during which the country suffered dreadful devastation, southern Serbia was finally

---

[1] O. Halecki, *The Crusade of Varna* (New York, 1943), pp. 13 f., rejects the traditional view that peace was concluded at Szegedin, and that King Vladislav broke his pledge a few days later. He points to the recently ascertained fact that emissaries of Vladislav, the Despot George Branković and Hunyadi, came to Adrianople and there, in the middle of June, drafted the treaty with the Sultan for a ten-year truce, with the provision that it be ratified by the Hungarian king. A Turkish embassy came to Szegedin to perform this duty, but Vladislav refused to ratify. F. Pall, 'Autour de la croisade de Varna', *Bull. hist. de l'Acad. Roumaine*, XXII (1941), 144 ff., upholds the old view. See also F. Babinger, 'Von Amurath zu Amurath. Vor- und Nachspiel der Schlacht bei Varna', *Oriens*, III (1950), 229 ff. and G. Ostrogorsky, *History of the Byzantine State*, p. 503 and n. 1. See above, ch. VIII, p. 384 and below, ch. XIX, p. 771.

subjected to the Turks (1455). The Despotate of George Branković now embraced only the district north of Kruševac; Novo Brdo, Trepča, Priština, Prizren, Peć and other towns were lost to the Turks. The very next year a great Turkish army, under the Sultan's leadership, advanced up the valley of the Morava towards the Danube. Unable to take the well-fortified position of Smederevo quickly by siege, the Sultan moved on to Belgrade, his principal objective. Though hemmed in and attacked from all sides the town offered a bitter resistance, and the Sultan, himself wounded during a determined assault, had to raise the siege (July 1456). The resistance of Belgrade seemed a victory for the Christian cause, and it was hailed with great enthusiasm in the west; but it could not save Serbia. A swift decline set in after the death in 1456 of George Branković, who, by virtue of his great influence with both Hungary and the Turks, had succeeded in preserving himself for thirty years between the two. Dynastic strife broke out, and the influential magnates were divided in their allegiance between Turkey and Hungary. Meanwhile, in 1458, the Turks, with little difficulty, occupied the principal towns of the despotate (Resava, Višeslav, Žrnov, Bela Stena, Golubac). The question remained as to whether Smederevo was to fall to Hungary or to Turkey. There was an attempt under Hungarian patronage to unite what was left of the despotate with Bosnia, by placing on the Serbian throne the son of the Bosnian king, Stephen Tomašević, who was married to the daughter of the Despot Lazar: but this combination was frustrated by Muḥammad II, who took Smederevo without a struggle on 20 June 1459.

Bosnia's rise to power had been made possible by four factors: the strong personality of Tvrtko I, who temporarily curbed the independence of the Bosnian feudal lords; the decline of the Serbian state of the Nemanjids; the weakness of Hungary after the reign of King Louis; and, finally, the fact that the Turks had not yet begun seriously to encroach upon the country. It was not long, however, before internal weaknesses again began to undermine its security and hasten its decline. Not even Tvrtko I was able to secure the lasting supremacy of the ruler's authority over the nobility. The weakness of the Bosnian kings, as compared with the rulers of Serbia, lay in the fact that they were unable to organise a strong mercenary army with which to crush the power of the nobility, and that the system of *pronoia* did not take root in Bosnia.[1] Through the assembly of nobles, which in Bosnia was usually called the *stanak*, the lords exercised a very strong influence on state affairs. They did not even allow the

---

[1] G. Ostrogorsky, *Pour l'histoire de la féodalité byzantine*, pp. 189, 218 ff.

establishment of direct succession to the throne. It is true that the rights of the Kotromanići as a dynasty were respected to the end, but the lords in their own assembly selected their ruler from members of this extensive family. It was characteristic of the later history of Bosnia that Tvrtko I was not able to ensure the throne for his son. When he died in 1391 the magnates placed on the throne his old and incompetent cousin, Dabiša (1391–5); and after his death an era began in which rulers followed each other in rapid succession. Real power rested in the hands of prominent aristocratic families; and discord between these families often led to violent conflicts which promoted open anarchy.

While these domestic conflicts divided the country, Hungary was reviving its ambition to impose its authority on Bosnia, using as an excuse, not only the destruction of heresy, but also the need to prevent the establishment of the Turks there and to secure its southern frontier. King Sigismund had already compelled Dabiša to recognise him as his 'natural master', to agree to Sigismund's right after his (Dabiša's) death to dispose of the Bosnian throne, and finally to renounce his possession of Croatia and Dalmatia. The defeat at Nicopolis, however, and the long struggle which followed with the pretender to the Hungarian throne, Ladislas of Naples, prevented Sigismund from putting his plans for Bosnia into effect. Even after he had overthrown Ladislas, despite many attacks on Bosnia, he achieved only partial success. He had to give up his intention of having himself crowned king of Bosnia and to content himself with a vague reimposition of his imperial rights (1411). Such a compromise could not last for long. The powerful Hrvoje Vukčić-Hrvatinić of Bosnia, threatened with subjection to Sigismund, called the Turks to his assistance. A Hungarian army was annihilated in Bosnia and the results of many years of effort on Sigismund's part were destroyed (1415). After this victory, Turkish influence in Bosnia was established on a much firmer basis. King Ostoja was recognised by, and received the support of, the Sultan. Individual magnates called on the support of Turkish detachments in their internal conflicts, undertaking in return certain obligations to the Sultan. The Pavlovići became Turkish vassals in order to overthrow their opponents. Sandalj Hranić Kosača followed the same course. The Sultan disposed of Bosnian provinces, seizing and sharing them out as he thought fit, and setting up and supporting pretenders to the throne against the unreliable kings.

Bosnia was the last of the greater Balkan states to fall to the Turks, not because it was in a position to offer stronger resistance, but simply owing to its geographical position: its turn came after

Bulgaria, Byzantium and Serbia. All its attempts to preserve its freedom by enlisting the help of the West inevitably failed, generally because of the particular religious issues involved. The last Bosnian kings strove to secure the support of Hungary and the Catholic Church at the price of favouring Catholic propaganda and condoning the banishment of the Bogomils, but they had insufficient power to take any decisive step in this direction. The Bosnian nobility, always opposed to foreign authority, was in the main antagonistic to any such policy and supported the 'Bosnian Church'. King Stephen Tomašević (1461–3), who came to the throne when it was already transparently obvious that the *coup de grâce* might be expected from the Turks at any moment, immediately turned for help to Pope Pius II. His envoys explained the danger which in the event of Bosnia's downfall would threaten not only Hungary but also Dalmatia and even Italy. In order to strengthen his reputation both at home and abroad, he asked the Pope to send him a crown, so that he could be crowned by a papal legate. Pius II, himself eager for a large-scale war against the Turks, fulfilled the king's request. It seems that at the eleventh hour even most of the Bosnian nobles realised that the sovereignty of their country could be preserved only by dependence upon the West. But the hope that a Christian coalition might be formed was quickly shown to be unfounded. King Stephen Tomašević, who had already refused to pay tribute to the Turks, sent an embassy to Constantinople to request a fifteen year truce. This was promised, but as soon as the Bosnian envoys had left Constantinople, the Sultan Muḥammad II advanced into Bosnia with a great army. Taken by surprise Bosnia succumbed before help could arrive from outside. The influential nobles, across whose territory the Turks advanced, surrendered without a fight and were promptly executed. The king tried to save himself by fleeing from the country, but the Turkish cavalry caught him up in the town of Ključ on Sana, and he had to give himself up. After he had been forced to issue an order that all towns were to surrender to the Turks, he too was executed. Little more than a month later, in the summer of 1463, the Bosnian kingdom had ceased to exist.

With the fall of Serbia and Bosnia, the most important Balkan states of the middle ages disappeared. But the Turks still had to conquer certain mountainous regions in the western part of the Balkans. In northern Albania they met a stubborn resistance from George Castriota; his father, John Castriota, had had to send him to Constantinople as a hostage, and there he had been brought up as a Muslim and given the name of Iskender with the title of *bey*, which his countrymen corrupted into 'Skanderbeg'.[1] After his father's death he escaped from the Turks, became a Christian once more, and gathered round him the Albanian nobility and the tribes of northern Albania. The chief centre of his resistance was the strong town of Kroja, whose defence was to make him famous in the Christian world. In the summer of 1450, the Sultan Murād II laid siege to Kroja, but after several unsuccessful attacks, and despite the use of artillery, he had to withdraw. Kroja was again besieged in 1466 and 1467 by Muḥammad II the Conqueror, but with no greater success. The town remained in Skanderbeg's hands until his death in 1468, when it was temporarily occupied by the Venetians, who already held Scutari, Dyrrachium and several smaller towns in Albania. But Venice was unable to retain her isolated Albanian possessions for long. Muḥammad II finally captured Kroja in 1478, and from there advanced on Scutari; after a stiff resistance the Venetians were forced to yield in the following year. Venetian power in Albania was completely broken with the Turkish capture of Dyrrachium in 1501.

During the period of Bosnia's decline from the beginning of the fifteenth century onwards, her southern areas, ruled by the *voivode* Sandalj Hranić Kosača (d. 1435), had become more and more detached from the main principality. Sandalj's nephew and successor, Stephen Vukčić Kosača (1435–66), virtually broke the link with Bosnia, making himself mainly dependent on the Turks, and expanding his territory with their help. The Turks acknowledged his title of 'Herceg' (1448), for which reason his land became known as Hercegovina. Supported by the Turks, he came into conflict with all his neighbours, harming both himself and them by fruitless warfare which only benefited the infidels. Nevertheless, when the moment came, the Turks did not spare the Herceg's lands. When the last assault was made on Bosnia, they took several of his towns and had soon occupied the greater part of his state, so that at the time of his death in 1466 it was confined only to the coastal region, where for some time to come his sons, Vladislav and Vlatko, fought for power. But when the town of Novi, at the entrance of the Gulf of Cattaro (Kotor), was surrendered to the Turks in 1482, the last remnants of the Herceg's state disappeared.

In the neighbouring mountainous regions of Zeta a measure of independence was maintained. At the time of the first fall of Smederevo (1439), Zeta, where the Turks had not yet penetrated, passed into

---

[1] The most important material for the history of George Castriota has been published by J. Radonić, *Djuradj Kastriot Skenderbeg i Albanija u XV v.* (George Castriota Skanderbeg and Albania in the fifteenth century), *Spomenik srpske Akademije*, xcv (Belgrade, 1942). See also the bibliographical survey by G. C. Soulis, 'Αἱ νεώτεραι ἔρευναι περὶ Γεωργίου Καστριώτου Σκανδερμπέη', *EEBS*, xxviii (1958), 446–57.

the hands of the local noble family of the Crnojević. When George Branković restored the Despotate of Serbia in 1444, he tried, though without great success, to regain control over Zeta. Stephen Crnojević held his own, placing himself under Venetian protection. His son and heir, John Crnojević (1465–90), to a large extent continued the same policy. When the Turks were fighting the Venetians around Scutari, they occupied his territory, and John had to flee to Italy; but the disturbances in Anatolia following the death of Sultan Muḥammad II gave him an opportunity which he quickly exploited to return to Zeta in 1481 and to set up a capital in the mountains of Cetinje; and there he succeeded in keeping his position, though as a Turkish vassal. Conflicts between his sons, after his death, hastened annexation by the Turks (1499). Even in these dark moments, when the remains of the medieval Serbian state were destroyed in Zeta, it is remarkable that cultural developments still continued. John Crnojević built a monastery of modest proportions in his capital at Cetinje, and his successor George (1490–6) founded the first Serbian printing press, on which the monk Macarius printed beautifully executed ecclesiastical books, 'opera per tutto laudata et apreciata', as a contemporary wrote.[1]

Of all the medieval Balkan states, only the republic of Ragusa (Dubrovnik) escaped total destruction. Ragusa had developed into a small aristocratic state, first as a Byzantine town, and later under Venetian (1205–1358) and Hungarian (1358–1526) patronage, and it played a remarkably large part in the economic life of the Balkans, out of all proportion to its size. The Ragusans were the principal trading agents in medieval Bosnia and Serbia, and in a large area of Bulgaria. They imported into these countries products of their own and of western lands, and exported raw materials, particularly metals. When the Turks began to approach their frontiers, they were wise enough to regulate their relations with them in time. For an insignificant tribute—twelve thousand five hundred ducats annually —they preserved intact the internal organisation of the republic, and obtained the right to trade freely throughout the Turkish domains. In this way the little republic existed until the beginning of the nineteenth century, when it was dissolved (1808).

The disappearance of the Serbian and Bosnian states made Turkey the immediate neighbour of Hungary. King Matthew Corvinus made great efforts to create for the defence of Hungary a defensive belt south of the rivers Sava and Danube. In northern Bosnia, which he had wrested from the Turks, he set up two districts (banovine), based

[1] Dj. Radojičić, 'Die ersten serbischen Druckereien', *Gutenberg-Jahrbuch*, xv (1940), p. 249.

on the centres of Jajce and Srebrnica. The banovine of Šabac and Belgrade played a similar role in Serbia. For some years these outlying positions were held, exposed though they were to Turkish attacks; there were continual frontier incidents and marauding raids by both sides. The numerous emigrant Serbs who had moved into Hungary, bore the main burden of the defence of Hungary's southern border, still cherishing the hope that the Serbian state would eventually be restored. Members of the Branković dynasty and, after its extinction, prominent Serbian or Croatian magnates were actually given the title of Serbian Despot (*Rascie Despotus*) by the Hungarian kings. At one time there even existed a titular king of Bosnia, Nicholas Iločki (1471–7), who actually minted his own currency. The continued advance of the Turks and the weakness of Hungary, however, finally put an end to this struggle. The Turks first of all took Srebrnica (1512), then Šabac and Belgrade (1521), and finally, after the battle of Mohacs, Jajce (1528). The conquests of Sultan Sulaymān the Magnificent (1520–66), who occupied the greater part of Hungary, put an end to the last hopes that the Serbian people would be liberated from the Turks with Hungarian help.

After they had destroyed the Bulgarian state, the Turks came into contact with the Rumanians. The history of this people down to the later middle ages is obscure; and its origins are the subject of much discussion. Rumanian historians, with rare exceptions, resolutely defend the point of view that the Rumanians are the descendants of Roman settlers and ancient Dacians, who were romanised during imperial times. Outside Rumania, however, the more probable view is generally held that the origin of the Rumanian people is to be found south of the Danube, in the romanised population of the Balkan peninsula which, after the Slav settlement, took themselves to the mountains to become a race of herdsmen. Some of these 'Vlachs', as they were known from the end of the tenth century, remained in the Balkans, and they were gradually assimilated into the people amongst whom they were living. The last traces of them are the Cincari in Macedonia and northern Greece. They are frequently mentioned in medieval documents. In Serbian archives they are referred to as herdsmen, to differentiate them from the farming population; in the course of time the name 'Vlach' lost its ethnical significance and became a synonym for shepherd. We have already seen that the Vlachs played a part in the development of the second Bulgarian Empire. By virtue of their great numbers in Thessaly this province became known as Great Wallachia, whilst Epirus was known as Upper Wallachia. Others crossed the Danube and settled in the Carpathian region, and infiltrated slowly into the neighbouring plains. In the thirteenth century the first indications of political activity became apparent, and it was soon clear that attempts were being made to shake off Hungarian rule. At the beginning of the fourteenth century, in 1324, a large political unit developed south of the Carpathians under the leadership of the *voivode* Basaraba, a Hungarian vassal ('ad Basarab, Wayvodam nostrum transalpinum'); Basaraba soon began the struggle for emancipation from Hungarian control. King Charles Robert led an expedition against his mutinous vassal but the Hungarian army was surrounded and destroyed in the Carpathians in November 1330; and this victory assured the independence of Wallachia. Charles Robert's successor, Louis the Great, was also unable to impose his authority permanently on Wallachia; and the temporary successes that he achieved were quickly effaced by another Vlach victory over the Hungarian army in 1369.

Soon after the appearance of Wallachia, yet another principality, Moldavia, appeared on Rumanian soil. Moldavia originated in the Hungarian mark which Louis the Great established on the eastern slopes of the Carpathians for defence against the Tatars. The *voivode* Bogdan, who had freed himself from Hungarian hegemony (1365), played a similar role in Moldavia to that of Basaraba in Wallachia. King Louis' efforts to frustrate the formation of this Rumanian principality only resulted in Moldavia's recognition of Hungarian sovereign power and the paying of an annual tribute, an arrangement which was essentially of a temporary nature.

The emergence of these Rumanian principalities and their wars with Hungary had far-reaching consequences in the religious field. For Hungary's efforts to impose and preserve its authority over the Vlachs and Moldavians went hand in hand with its endeavours to organise the Catholic Church in the districts behind the Carpathians. Liberation from Hungarian rule virtually put an end to such efforts and ensured the establishment of the Orthodox Church. The *voivode* Nicholas Alexander, Basaraba's successor, turned to the Patriarch of Constantinople (1359) who appointed a Metropolitan for Wallachia, with his seat at Argeş (Curtea de Argeş). A little later Suceava, the principal town of Moldavia, at last obtained its Metropolitan (1401). In both principalities Slavonic was the official language in the national administration as well as in the Church. In Rumania, Slavonic played a role similar to that of the Latin language in the West, and in the middle ages it hindered the development of literature written in the national tongue.

Slav influence, particularly that of its nearest neighbours, the Bulgarians, is reflected in both the character and the nomenclature of Rumanian institutions. The ruler's court was organised on a model which had its origin much earlier on in the south, though there was some Hungarian influence. In so far as the titles were of Byzantine origin (such as *logothet*, *protovestiar*, *comis*), they did not come direct from Byzantium, but by way of the Slavs. The *dvornik* (lord steward) was the supreme judge at the court and in the country. The *posteljnik* (chamberlain), *peharnik* (cup-bearer) and the *stolnik* (table steward), were all known at the courts of the southern Slavs. The power of the ruler (*voivode*) was theoretically absolute. He was the supreme commander of the army and chief justice, he endowed nobility and Church with lands, had coins minted bearing his own likeness, and drew the revenue from taxes. Every act of public life was connected with his person. In practice, however, the nobility exercised a powerful influence upon national affairs. They determined in their own assembly who should occupy the throne, since no established line of succession existed. Such a system had obvious disadvantages and conflicts arose between pretenders and their supporters, usually complicated by outside intervention. All this inevitably diminished the authority of the ruler and hindered the consolidation of the state.

The peasants were mainly dependent on the feudal lords. They owned their land, and were not bound to the soil, but they had certain obligations, such as working on the land of their masters, or handing over one tenth of their produce. There were also completely free peasants, who were subject to no feudal lord: these appear to have been fairly numerous in Moldavia. Like the dependent peasants, they also had to pay a national tax (*bir*), for which individual villages were assessed as a taxable unit, the sum being again divided amongst the peasants according to the size of their holdings. As the needs of the boyars grew, the position of the peasants deteriorated, and by the sixteenth century they had lost their freedom and were bound to the soil.

The Rumanian principalities came to birth in the struggle against Hungary. Though Hungary could not prevent their development, it did not abandon its claim to them, and from time to time it succeeded in imposing various obligations upon their *voivodes*, and even on occasion brought its own candidate to the throne. Moldavia was also exposed to Polish pressure, and for some time had to recognise Polish authority. But the greatest danger to the independence and future of the principalities came from the south, where the Turks, after the fall of Bulgaria, had pushed their frontier to the Danube. By the reign of Mircea the Old (1386–1418), Wallachia had become a theatre of war in which the Turks played the leading part. One section of the boyars, who were discontented with Mircea, with the aid of the

Sultan Bāyezīd I, proclaimed Vlad *voivode*. Mircea had to seek refuge with the Hungarian king, Sigismund. An allied army advanced into Wallachia in the spring of 1395 and defeated the Turks at Rovine (17 May); this drove the usurper Vlad to place himself under Polish protection. Mircea, for his part, remained with Sigismund, and accompanied him on the expedition against the Turks which ended in the catastrophe at Nicopolis (1396). He succeeded in saving himself, and freed himself from his rival, Vlad, who was captured in 1397 by Stibor, *voivode* of Transylvania; he drove back fresh Turkish attacks and retained control of the Danubian crossings. The Turkish defeat at Ankara (1402) and the civil war between Bāyezīd's sons brought some relief to Wallachia. The *voivode* Mircea strengthened the defences of the southern frontier by occupying a belt of land on the right bank of the Danube, notably the town of Silistria: in his title he now held that he was 'lord and ruler of the land from beyond the Danube to the Black Sea and Silistria'. When Sultan Muḥammad I restored Turkish unity, Mircea was soon forced to pay tribute. The Turks, however, were still not sufficiently powerful to impose their authority on Wallachia. Hungary, which had taken the leading part in the Christian war, tried, as with Serbia and Bosnia, to draw the Vlachs into its camp. The attempts of both the Turks and Hungary to secure their supremacy over Wallachia and to bring their vassals to the throne, resulted in constant changes of ruler and fierce internal strife.[1] But as Hungary abandoned its offensive attitude towards Turkey and went over to the defensive, Ottoman control over Wallachia was gradually extended.

Moldavia was unable to avoid the same fate. In 1455 the Moldavians were forced to pay an annual tribute of two thousand ducats to the Sultan Muḥammad II the Conqueror. When Stephen the Great (1457–1504) came to the throne, Moldavia obtained a vigorous ruler, who was to lead his state in war against the Turks for an exceptionally long time. He made sure of his position with regard to Poland by swearing an oath of fealty to King Casimir; an attack made by Matthew Corvinus, with the object of restoring Hungarian supremacy and reinstating Stephen's dethroned predecessor, Peter Aron, failed. Stephen the Great's efforts to wrest Wallachia from the power of the Turks, and to make the line of the Danube his defensive frontier, were only temporarily successful. He succeeded in defeating a Turkish vassal, Radul 'the Handsome', and in setting up his own nominee in his place, but as soon as a Turkish army appeared the new *voivode*

---

[1] From the death of Mircea the Old (1418) to the end of the fifteenth century, Wallachia had fifteen *voivodes*. On the average each reign lasted barely five and a half years.

went over to the enemy. But the Turkish advance into Moldavia was halted in the wooded country round Vasluiu on the river Rakovica, where Stephen inflicted a heavy defeat on the enemy in 1475. Muḥammad II was obliged to undertake in person the task of settling accounts with Moldavia, whilst his allies the Tatars ravaged the eastern area of the country. The Turkish army was at its strongest in the open conflict at Valea Alba, and destroyed the Moldavian detachments (26 July 1476). The Sultan advanced as far as the capital, Suceava, and destroyed it with fire. But he was unable either to pacify the country or to overthrow the *voivode* Stephen, although he had with him a pretender to the throne in the person of Peter Aron's son; and the outbreak of an epidemic in his army, combined with the fierce resistance of the Moldavians, supply difficulties, and finally the danger of a Hungarian army from Transylvania cutting his line of retreat, obliged him to withdraw. Like Skanderbeg of Albania, the *voivode* Stephen was celebrated in the West as a fighter against the infidel and Pope Sixtus IV called him 'the athlete of Christ'. But the organisation of a large-scale campaign against the infidel was beyond the realms of possibility.

The death of the Sultan Muḥammad II in 1481, and the war which followed over the succession between his sons Bāyezīd and Dzem, enabled the Moldavian *voivode* to take the offensive again and to place his own nominee in Wallachia. But the lull on the Danube lasted only for a short time. As soon as Bāyezīd II had made sure of his position on the throne, the Turkish attacks on Moldavia were renewed. In the summer of 1484 the towns of Chilia on the mouth of the Danube and Cetatea Alba on the mouth of the Dniester, the principal Moldavian ports, were captured. In the following year, Turkish detachments penetrated to Suceava and again burned the town. Unable to count upon effective aid from the rest of Christendom, Moldavian resistance gradually diminished. Stephen the Great had to submit to the Sultan, pledging himself to pay an annual tribute of four thousand ducats, and agreeing to dispatch one of his sons to Constantinople. The old *voivode* was not easily reconciled to the new state of affairs, and deluded himself with the hope that an anti-Turkish alliance would finally be formed by the neighbouring countries; but this hope was not realised. He had to expend the last energies of his country in repelling Polish attacks. Immediately after his death Moldavia finally became a Turkish vassal state.

The consequences of Rumania's subjection to the Turks were not the same as in the other Balkan countries. Continuity with the past was not fundamentally shattered. Wallachia and Moldavia preserved their institutions, and *voivodes* remained at the head of the government. Their courts were very much the same as they had been before the arrival of the Turks. There were no radical changes in the social order. The boyars were not destroyed nor changed into Turkish spahis. Turkish colonisation was avoided, nor was there a partial conversion to Islam, as in Bosnia, Serbia, Bulgaria, Greece and Albania. When the decline of the Turkish Empire set in, it needed only the unification of the two principalities, and the repudiation of the Sultan's suzerainty, to bring about the creation of modern Rumania.

CHAPTER XIII

HUNGARY AND BYZANTIUM IN THE MIDDLE AGES

I. THE AGE OF MIGRATIONS

A solid foundation for our knowledge of the beginnings of Hungarian history is afforded by linguistics. These show that the basic stratum of the structure and vocabulary of the Magyar language is of Finno-Ugrian origin, and that the languages most nearly related to it are those of the Voguls (Man'shi) and Ostyaks (Chanti), who today inhabit Siberia. The Magyars must thus once have been in close connection with these two peoples, somewhere in the neighbourhood of the Ural Mountains. But it has also been shown that the Magyar language was at an early date enriched with Turkish elements, and also that the Magyar people, when first mentioned in the tenth-century sources, showed various Turkic characteristics, and that some of their oldest personal and tribal names and titles of dignitaries are of Turkic origin. All this suggests that the Finno-Ugrian Magyars were subjected to strong Turkish influences in the age of migration which preceded the conquest of Hungary. The same conclusion emerges from examination of the ethnic names under which the Magyar people figure in the Byzantine sources. Of these, the form Οὔγγροι, from which are derived the various names current to this day among the people of Europe (Old Church Slavonic, Ugri; Russian, Vengri; German, Ungarn; English, Hungarians; French, Hongrois; Italian, Ungheresi, and so on) comes from the Turkic ethnic name *onogur*, meaning 'ten Ogur'; Τοῦρκοι is the same as 'Turks', Οὖννοι as 'Huns'. Therefore in examining the early history of the Magyars it is necessary to take into account those Turkic peoples with whom the Magyar people may have come in contact in the course of their migrations and who may have played a part in their formation. The area over which those migrations took place was the region extending from the northern confines of the Urals to the Caucasus in the south and thence westward to the Carpathians. Up to the end of the twelfth century the southern part of this area fell within the sphere of influence of Byzantium, exerted through its possessions on the north coast of the Black Sea, and it is therefore understandable that during its formative period in the age of migration the Magyar people, or at least certain ethnic elements which contributed to their make-up, were touched by the far-reaching influences of Byzantine culture.

It is in fact known that Byzantine missionaries achieved big successes in the fifth and sixth centuries among the Huns, Bulgars and other Turkic peoples. The Magyars must have been among these: there are indeed indications that this was so. In about 463 the Onogurs, whose camping-grounds must at the time have lain between the Don and the Caucasus, were hard pressed by the Sabirs, and, together with other Ugrian peoples, sent ambassadors to Constantinople, obviously with the object of gaining Byzantium's goodwill and friendship and thus assuring for themselves safe possession of the country newly occupied by them near the northern frontiers of the Empire.[1] The price of this was obviously the usual 'alliance', that is, an undertaking to protect Byzantine interests. It is recorded that on one occasion the Onogurs—probably at the instigation of Byzantium—waged a campaign against the Lazi living south of the Caucasus, on the eastern shores of the Black Sea.[2] This is probably the first instance of contact between Byzantium and certain constituent elements of the Hungarian people, who, as already shown, derive their name from the Onogurs.

In 527–8, the first year of the Emperor Justinian's reign, a certain Gordas, Prince of the Huns living near the Crimean city of Bosporus, arrived in Constantinople. Here he received baptism, the Emperor himself standing as his godfather, and returned home laden with gifts and charged with the defence of Bosporus and of imperial interests in that city, which was then the centre of trade between Byzantium and the Huns. On returning home, Gordas melted down the Huns' silver idols, afterwards exchanging them in Bosporus for Byzantine money. The Huns' priests however joined forces with Gordas' brother, Mouageris, and stirred up an insurrection. The people killed Gordas and made his brother prince in his stead. The rebels then overpowered the Byzantine guards and took possession of the town, and Justinian had to send a punitive expedition before he succeeded in restoring order.[3] It is probable that these 'Huns' were Onogurs or some kindred people; but what is more important is the probability that the name Mouageris is related to the ethnic name Magyar. If so, this 'Hun' prince may be regarded as a prince of the Magyars, and it would follow that Byzantium was making attempts to convert the Magyars early in Justinian's reign, that is, that a part of the Magyar people, then in process of formation, was in touch with Byzantine Christianity as early as the sixth century. This is also supported by other evidence, for a list of Byzantine bishoprics,

---

[1] Priscus, fr. 14; *Excerpta de legationibus*, ed. C. de Boor, p. 586.
[2] Agathias, III, 5, p. 146 (*CSHB*).
[3] Malalas, pp. 431–2 (*CSHB*); Theophanes, pp. 175–6 (ed. C. de Boor).

probably dating from the mid-eighth century, gives among the episcopal sees subject to the Metropolitan of the Crimean Goths, the Bishop of the Huns, and with him, also the Bishop of the 'Onogurs'. Obviously these were missionary bishops whose task was that of converting the peoples in question. Moreover, Kovrat, Prince of the Onogur-Bulgars, who at the beginning of the seventh century founded 'Great Bulgaria' on the Maeotis, had spent his childhood in Constantinople at the imperial court, where he became a Christian and concluded an alliance with the Emperor Heraclius. The creation of the Onogur missionary see was thus probably a consequence of earlier developments.[1]

The acquaintance of certain elements of the Hungarian people with Byzantine Christianity can then be dated to the days when they were still inhabiting the northern shores of the Black Sea, long before the conquest of Hungary.[2] Such ecclesiastical evidence is also supported by archaeological remains and linguistic and literary sources. For instance, early contact with the cultural world of Byzantium is indicated both by the entry of the word *görög* (Greek) into the Hungarian language, *via* Slavonic, before the conquest, and by the presence of Greek letters in the old Hungarian runic alphabet. Byzantine influence may also be deduced from the fact that when Árpád was elected prince in the late ninth century he was raised on a shield, a counterpart of the Byzantine ceremony of coronation.[3] The oldest Hungarian bridles are also constructed after Byzantine models. There are therefore certain suggestions of Byzantine cultural influence which confirm what the written sources say about commercial connections. Mention has already been made of the fact that trade between Byzantium and the 'Huns' went through Bosporus. An Oriental source relates that the Magyars were accustomed to barter their Slav slaves against carpets and other objects in a Byzantine harbour.[4] A Byzantine source mentions that the Khazars and 'Turks' (that is, Magyars) often used to ask for imperial raiment and diadems as reward for their services.[5]

Presently the Magyars moved westwards from the Don region, their troops appearing at the mouth of the Danube as early as the thirties of the ninth century. In 837 the Bulgars, being hard pressed by the

[1] Gy. Moravcsik, 'Zur Geschichte der Onoguren', *Ungarische Jahrbücher*, x (1930), 53–90.

[2] Gy. Moravcsik, 'Byzantine Christianity and the Magyars in the Period of their Migration', *The American Slavic and East European Review*, v (1946), 29–45.

[3] Const. Porph., *De admin. imp.* c. 38, *DAI*, i, p. 172. Cf. O. Treitinger, *Die oströmische Kaiser- und Reichsidee nach ihrer Gestaltung im höfischen Zeremoniell* (Jena, 1938; repr. Darmstadt, 1956), pp. 20–3.

[4] Ibn Rusta, *A magyar honfoglalás kútfői*, p. 169.

[5] Const. Porph., *De admin. imp.* c. 13, *DAI*, i, p. 66.

revolt of Macedonian Byzantine prisoners of war, appealed for help to a people also described by the Byzantine source for the story as Οὖγγροι.[1] These were most certainly Magyars. They duly appeared at the mouth of the Danube and did battle with the rebels, but Byzantine ships, sent to help the latter, carried away the prisoners. This is the first historical mention of direct contact between Magyars and Greeks. By the end of the ninth century the Magyars were found in a region called Etelköz, the lowlands north of the Danube estuary and east of the Carpathians, whither they had migrated from their earlier home Levedia, probably between the Don and the Dnieper, under pressure from the Pechenegs. At this time the Byzantine Empire was being threatened by its northern neighbours, the Bulgarians, whose ruler Symeon had defeated the armies of the Emperor Leo VI in Macedonia (894). Byzantium, in its extremity, resorted to old and well-tried methods of diplomacy: it enlisted the Bulgars' eastern neighbours against them. At the beginning of 895 the Byzantine Emperor's envoys sought out the princes of the Magyars, Árpád and Kusan, at the mouth of the Danube and concluded an alliance with them against the Bulgars.[2] The Magyars gave hostages as pledges of their good faith. Byzantine ships arrived to fetch the Magyars, and although Symeon obstructed the river with wicker-work booms, they ferried their allies over to the south bank. The Magyar troops attacked the Bulgars from the north, and defeated them in several engagements. The Magyars sold their prisoners to the Greeks, as agreed. In 896 Symeon sued for peace. Leo had attained his objective, whereupon he threw over his allies, who were now left exposed to the Bulgars' vengeance. Symeon, following the Byzantine example, in turn stirred up the Pechenegs to attack the Magyars and while the bulk of the Magyar army was away on a distant campaign, their quarters in Etelköz were ravaged by their Pecheneg neighbours.[3] Thereupon the Magyars moved westward and occupied their present home in the Carpathian basin. Thus the conquest of 896 was, in the last instance, the indirect result of Byzantine policy.

II. THE CONQUEST AND THE ERA OF THE RAIDS

The territory occupied by the Hungarian people in the last years of the ninth century had once been an integral part of the Roman Empire, but then, after the disruption of the *pars occidentalis*, had come within Constantinople's sphere of influence. The conquering Hungarians found in their new homes not only relics of the old

[1] Georgius Cont., pp. 818–19 (*CSHB*).   [2] *DR*, 519–22.
[3] Const. Porph., *De admin. imp.* c. 40, *DAI*, I, p. 176.

Roman rule, but also Byzantine traditions which were transmitted to them through its former population, Avars, Slavs and Bulgars, who had come into contact with Christian Byzantine culture during earlier centuries. Byzantium moreover still preserved the tradition of the unity of the Roman Empire and maintained its claim to the territory which was now Hungary; when for instance the Ostrogoths, the Lombards, and later the Avars settled in this area, in each case the consent of the Byzantine Emperor was obtained. Memories of this tradition are also found in the work of the Hungarian chronicler known as the 'Anonymus' who tells how the chiefs of the Bulgarians and other peoples inhabiting the land met the newly arrived Hungarians with the claim that they held their lands by the grace of the Greek Emperor, and how they summoned Greek help against the Hungarians.[1] When, however, the Hungarians had established themselves in their new home by force of arms Byzantium had to recognise the *de facto* position, and at once concentrated on attracting the new people into its own sphere of influence and using them for its own ends. True to its traditional policy, it tried to enlist the help of the Hungarians against other peoples, such as the Bulgars and the Pechenegs. Byzantine embassies often sought out the Hungarian princes, and the memory of these diplomatic contacts is preserved in the formula of the imperial letters sent by Constantine VII Porphyrogenitus and his co-Emperor 'to the Princes of the Turks (*sc.* Magyars)'.[2] The 'Turks' mentioned as serving in the imperial bodyguard at Constantinople in the tenth century are probably Magyars, and 'Turks', that is, Magyars, are found in the Byzantine army sent to Lombardy in 935. There are also indications that fragments of the Hungarian people settled on Byzantine territory, where they are mentioned under the names of 'Turks' and 'Vardariotes'; the Hungarian national tradition remembers them under the name of 'Csaba's Magyars'. A hagiographical source mentions 'Turks' near Mt Athos at the end of the tenth century.[3]

Even after the conquest the Magyars continued to live by plunder. Magyar armies raided not only western Europe, but also territories of the Byzantine Empire, whence they returned home loaded with rich spoils. Alternatively, they extracted considerable sums from the imperial court as their price for refraining from raids. A contemporary Byzantine hagiographical source, the *Life of Basil the Younger*, describes the constant attacks by the Magyars as the punishment

[1] *Anonymi Gesta Hungarorum*, c. 12, 20 (*SRH*, ɪ, 51, 61).

[2] *De cerim.* p. 691 (*CSHB*): γράμματα Κωνσταντίνου καὶ Ῥωμανοῦ τῶν φιλοχρίστων βασιλέων Ῥωμαίων πρὸς τοὺς ἄρχοντας τῶν Τούρκων.

[3] *Vita Athanasii*, ed. L. Petit, *AB*, xxv (1906), 72.

inflicted by God on the Byzantines for their sins.[1] Raids into the Byzantine Empire, in which the tribes living in the south took the main part, were usually made by the Magyars in the spring. Their road led them through Bulgaria, and they often ravaged all Thrace and Macedonia; in 936 one band even penetrated as far as Attica. The memory of this may be enshrined in the Boeotian village name Ungria and the 'Ungrolimne', or Magyar Lake, in the same area.[2] The raids conducted by Hungarian armies into Byzantine territory in 934, 943, 959 and 961 were particularly devastating.[3] In 934 and 959 Hungarian armies were encamped under the walls of Constantinople. The Hungarian chronicles recall one of these raids in a story of the hero Botond, who overthrew a Greek giant in a wrestling match and with his battle-axe clave through the Golden Gate of Constantinople —an act equivalent to throwing down the gauntlet of war.[4] The raids seem to have been suspended during the reign of Constantine VII (944–59). But later on, in 967–8, the Emperor asked the ruler of Bulgaria to prevent the Hungarians from invading Byzantine territory.[5] Two years after this (969–70) Hungarians were found in the army with which the Russian Prince Svjatoslav attacked the Byzantine Empire.

There also exist concrete memorials of Byzantino-Hungarian contacts, some of them objects which must have been carried back to Hungary as spoils of war. Graves of the period have yielded Byzantine coins and objects such as ear-rings of Byzantine manufacture, or a silver button bearing a Christian inscription in Greek. The object known in Hungarian national tradition as 'Lehel's horn', which Botond is supposed to have brought back from Constantinople, is of Byzantine origin and was probably made originally for use in the circus.

Hungarians often appeared at the Byzantine court. When a peace was concluded in 943 noble Magyar hostages were left behind in Constantinople, and during the invasion of 961 many Magyars were taken prisoner. So the Magyars were enabled to make first-hand acquaintance with the splendid ceremony and brilliant culture of Byzantium. Hungarian ambassadors came several times to the imperial court, and it was even visited by some members of the reigning family and by certain tribal 'leaders'. In the struggle which went on between the prince and the tribal leaders, it looks as though some of the latter sought support in Byzantium. About 948 the

---

[1] *Vita Basilii iunioris*, ed. A. N. Veselovsky, *Sbornik otdelenija russkago jazyka i slovesnosti Imp. Akad. Nauk*, XLVI (1889), no. 6, Priloženije, pp. 64–5.

[2] *DR*, 1228.   [3] *DR*, 626, 640.

[4] *Anonymi Gesta Hungarorum*, c. 42 (*SRH*, I, p. 87). *Chronici Hungarici compositio saeculi XIV*, c. 62 (*ibid.* p. 310).   [5] *DR*, 710.

Greek sources record two consecutive Hungarian visits.[1] First the
'leader' Bulcsú and Árpád's great-grandson, Termács, visited Constantine VII's court, where Bulcsú accepted Christianity. A miniature in a Byzantine manuscript of Scylitzes has even depicted the
scene in which the Emperor is raising Bulcsú from the font. The
convert was presented with many gifts and the rank of patrician, but
after his return home he relapsed into paganism, and took up arms
against Byzantium. It is most likely that Termács, whom Constantine distinguished by the title of 'friend', was baptised at the same
time as Bulcsú. A little later a second Hungarian 'leader', Gyula,
visited the Byzantine court. He, too, was baptised, receiving the
name of Stephen and the rank of patrician. His conversion had,
however, more lasting consequences. He continued to maintain good
relations with Byzantium, ransomed and set free the Byzantine
prisoners, and—most important of all—took back with him to Hungary a monk named Hierotheus, whom Theophylact, then Patriarch
of Constantinople, had first ordained Bishop of 'Turkia', that is,
Hungary. The first Hungarian bishop carried through successful missionary work in the land of Gyula whose tribe had settled on the two
banks of the Maros. He was perhaps helped by the fact that there
were already some adherents of Christianity among the Magyars. The
new bishopric, which included the whole of Hungary, was obviously
missionary in character and its bishop similar to the one who had
worked among the Onogurs before the conquest. It is not impossible
that the Byzantine signet, on which the inscription 'Theophylact,
Bishop of the Turks' is still legible, also preserves the memory of the
first Hungarian bishopric.[2] It was thus the Byzantine Church that
first spread Christianity among the Hungarians by taking root in the
district east of the Theiss during the tenth century.

III. THE BYZANTINE ORIENTATION

Towards the end of the tenth century the Hungarians experienced
great changes. There were settled peoples living all around the natural
frontiers which guarded their new home and they had to adapt their
form of life to their new environment. The nomad pastoral society of
the earlier generations consequently underwent a radical transformation. Raids into foreign countries gradually ceased, the organisation
by clans and tribes was replaced by a strong central authority, and

---

[1] Const. Porph., *De admin. imp.* c. 60, *DAI*, I, p. 178; Seylitzes-Cedrenus, II, p. 328
(*CSHB*).

[2] V. Laurent, 'L'évêque des Turcs et le proèdre de Turquie', *Acad. Roumaine,
Bulletin de la section historique*, XXIII, 2 (1942), 147–58.

the Hungarians entered the community of Christian peoples. At the beginning of the eleventh century the Hungarian state and the Hungarian kingdom took shape.

The territory in which they had settled lay at the point of inter-section of the two cultural spheres of influence, the Western or Latino-Germanic, and the Eastern or Greco-Slav. Both geographical situa-tion and historical tradition raised the question as to whether the Hungarian people should attach themselves to the western cultural sphere or the eastern; should they turn to Rome, or to Constan-tinople? It was the Byzantine Church which had begun the work of conversion, well before the conquest. But in the seventies of the tenth century Rome also began proselytising. From now on there was in a very real sense competition between the two Churches for possession of the Hungarians. During the tenth century the Hun-garian tribes showed a tendency to waver in their political attitude, but Prince Géza's policy was already definitely westward in orienta-tion. St Stephen, Hungary's first king (1000–38), then took the decisive step when he chose the western form of Christianity for himself and his people, thus making the Hungarians members of the group which found its religious, cultural and political centre in Rome. As symbol thereof St Stephen received a crown from Pope Sylvester II; in other words, Rome sanctified his assumption of the royal dignity.

This association with Rome did not however necessarily break the ecclesiastical, cultural and political ties which linked Hungary to Byzantium. The very fact that Byzantium, by its conquest of Bulgaria at the beginning of the eleventh century, had become the immediate neighbour of the kingdom of Hungary, in itself made essential the maintenance of good relations. The eastern and western Empires were at that moment drawing closer to one another; and in the same spirit St Stephen concluded an alliance with Basil II, and gave him armed support in his wars against Bulgaria. In 1004 Hungarian troops took part in the capture of Skoplje, whence they brought back with them the relics of St George.[1]

Neither did the influence of the Byzantine Church die out in eastern Hungary. Traces of Byzantine Christianity are found here even in St Stephen's day. According to the *Life of St Gerard*, Ajtony, the ruler of the land between the Transylvanian mountains and the Theiss, had been baptised in Vidin according to the Eastern rite, and had built a monastery in Marosvár which he dedicated to St John the Baptist and peopled with Greek monks.[2] The foundations of the

---

[1] H. Bresslau, *Neues Arch.* VIII (1883), 592.
[2] *Legenda S. Gerhardi*, c. 8–9 (*SRH*, II, pp. 492–3).

Greek church and the font have been found there. Everything goes to suggest that Ajtony accepted baptism for political reasons, the act also constituting an act of homage to Basil II, who was then engaged on his Bulgarian campaigns. Ajtony's corpse, after his later defeat by St Stephen, was buried in this Greek monastery. Later St Gerard transplanted the monks from Marosvár to a new monastery, also dedicated to St John the Baptist, which was founded at Oroszlán south of the Maros. All these facts show that the Byzantine form of Christianity, brought to Hungary in the tenth century when Gyula was baptised in Constantinople, was stronger then ever in the south-east of the country fifty years later. As recent research suggests[1] that the Temes district fell within the competence of the Archbishopric of Ochrida, this provides further evidence to the same effect.

But the threads of the conversion of Gyula of Transylvania lead further still, to St Stephen's own court. The daughter of that elder Gyula who received baptism in Constantinople was Sarolta, wife of Prince Géza and mother of St Stephen, who was probably herself baptised by Bishop Hierotheus. It was thus no mere chance that the first Hungarian king received in baptism the same name as had been bestowed on his grandfather on the like occasion. The frequency with which Christian names of Byzantine origin occur in St Stephen's family is striking. But we also have written proof that the eastern form of Christianity penetrated into the western parts of Hungary. We possess a charter in Greek, transcribed in 1109, which describes how Stephen I, king of Hungary (1000–38), established in Veszprém a nunnery which he dedicated to the Theotokos (the Mother of God) and bestowed endowments and privileges on it.[2] The later Latin re-issue of the charter attributes the Greek original to St Stephen and notes that it was sealed with St Stephen's seal and that the original deed was written in Greek, conformably with the language of the founder of the nunnery. Who the founder was still remains unknown. Some have supposed it to be St Stephen's mother, the daughter of the Gyula baptised in Constantinople; others have guessed at St Stephen's wife, or his sister, the wife of a banished Bulgarian royalty. It has also been suggested that the founder may have been the wife of St Emeric, the son of St Stephen, who, according to certain late sources, was a daughter of the Byzantine Emperor. But whoever the founder was it was certainly some member of the royal family. This unique document, which is written in popular Greek and was obvi-

---

[1] M. Gyóni, 'L'église orientale dans la Hongrie du XIe siècle', *RHC*, xxv (1947), 42–9.

[2] Critical ed. by Gy. Czebe, *A veszprémvölgyi oklevél görög szövege* (Hung. Acad. of Sciences, 1916).

ously composed by a Greek priest, testifies to the Byzantine influence which was present at the Hungarian court as early as the beginning of the eleventh century. And there are also many other contemporary traces of it. Hungarian sources state that St Stephen built a magnificent church in Constantinople, and endowed it sumptuously.[1] His son, St Emeric, carried in his bosom a cross which contained a piece of the True Cross and had been presented to his father, St Stephen, by the Byzantine Emperor. The author of the *Life of St Emeric* also writes that when he visited Constantinople he heard that when Emeric prince of Hungary died, a Greek archbishop saw in a vision angels carrying St Emeric's soul up to heaven.[2] We read in the *Life of St Stephen* that a Greek bishop had a similar vision when the first king of Hungary died.[3] St Stephen's so-called *Admonitions*, written for his son, resemble the Byzantine Mirrors for Princes, and contain, amongst others, the following sentence: 'Quis Grecus regeret Latinos Grecis moribus, aut quis Latinus regeret Grecos Latinis moribus?'[4] This shows what importance was then generally attached to the difference between the Greek and Latin worlds.

The Hungarian chronicles several times mention Greeks among the foreigners who settled in Hungary in the days of St Stephen and later. The Greek etymologies found occasionally in Hungarian historical works testify to a certain knowledge of the Greek language, and medieval Hungarian contains several loan-words of Greek origin, though many of these do not appear until the fifteenth century. But Byzantine influence is unmistakably reflected in the use of such Greek names as Achilles, Duka, Kalianus, Katapan, Opos, and so on, in the Arpadian period (1000–1301). Of ecclesiastics conversant with Greek there is specific mention of Simon, bishop of Pécs, who in 1109 transcribed the Veszprém nunnery's Greek charter for King Koloman. He is probably identical with the Simon who signed the peace treaty of 1108, as plenipotentiary of the Hungarian king. Greek ecclesiastical works were certainly known in Hungary at the time. The library of the Abbey of Pannonhalma contained in the eleventh century a 'psalterium Graecum', and the library of the Abbey of Pásztó contained works by the Greek Fathers. The Venetian-born Bishop Gerard, who lived at the court of St Stephen, used Greek sources, among others, in his *Deliberatio*.

Byzantine influence was not confined to the Church and the language. There are, for instance, also indications that literary forms

---

[1] *Legenda S. Stephani regis*, c. 11 (*SRH*, II, p. 386).
[2] *Legenda S. Emerici ducis*, c. 6 (*ibid.* II, p. 456).
[3] *Legenda S. Stephani regis*, c. 19 (*ibid.* II, p. 428).
[4] *Libellus de institutione morum*, c. 8 (*ibid.* II, p. 626).

and motifs penetrated to Hungary. Certain motifs of the legends of St Ladislas, for example, are strongly reminiscent of the legends of various military saints which were so widely current in Byzantium. In particular there is a great similarity of motif in the legends attached to the name of St Demetrius. The cradle of the cult of St Demetrius was in Sirmium, then part of Hungary, where the place-names Szávaszentdemeter and Mitrovica preserve his memory. The punishment of blinding, so frequent among the Árpáds, came from Byzantium, derived in turn from the Sassanids. And some scholars see in the military organisation of frontier districts the influence of the corresponding Byzantine system.

Byzantine influence also left perceptible traces on early Hungarian art. Memorials in the Byzantine style are to be found everywhere in Hungary and there can be no doubt that Byzantine master-craftsmen worked there. The cathedrals of St Stephen's day, to judge by what remains of them, show Byzantine influence. The stone coffin in which, according to tradition, the remains of St Stephen once rested, is certainly Byzantine in style. Frescoes in the Byzantine style dating from the tenth and eleventh centuries—the oldest in Hungary—are still to be seen on the vaulting of the crypt in Feldebrö. The Corona-tion robe also copies a Byzantine model; the embroidery is probably the work of the Greek nuns of Veszprém. In addition there are many other objects which are indubitably of Byzantine origin, such as the famous reliquary of Esztergom; and coins and seals also show marked Byzantine traits.

The equilibrium which was preserved during St Stephen's reign between the eastern and western orientations of Hungarian policy was upset under his successors. The Hungarian kings who represented the national resistance to German interference sought, as certain tribal chiefs had done before them, the support of Byzantium. A reminder of this is the so-called Crown of Constantine Monomachus, which was found in Hungary by a peasant ploughing and is now in the Hungarian National Museum. The gold and enamel plaques of the crown represent the Byzantine Emperor Constantine IX, his wife Zoe, his sister-in-law the Empress Theodora, two female dancers, two allegorical female figures and the apostles St Andrew and St Peter. These plaques must have been made between 1042 and 1050. Al-though no record remains of how the crown got to Hungary, it must in all probability have been a gift from Byzantium to King Andrew I (1046–60).[1] As Andrew came to the throne after expelling the pro-German Peter, the Crown may indicate political advances made by

---

[1] M. Bárány-Oberschall, 'The Crown of the Emperor Constantine Monomachos', *Archaeologia Hungarica*, XXII (Budapest, 1937).

Andrew to Byzantium. Andrew had been baptised in Kiev and had married Anastasia, the daughter of Jaroslav, Prince of Kiev. He is known to have strengthened Byzantine influence in Church affairs. He founded near Visegrád a monastery of the Greek rite, which was dedicated to St Andrew, and, according to a papal document of 1221, Greek monks were still living in it then.[1] It was also Andrew who settled on the peninsula of Tihany the Greek monks who were then living in the caves still visible there. Recent excavations have shown remarkable resemblances between the situations and structure of the hermitages of both Tihany and Zebegény and those of the monasteries of Mt Athos and Russia (for instance, Kiev or Pskov).[2] It is known from later sources that there were a number of other Greek monasteries in Hungary, for example in Pásztó, in Szávaszentdemeter, and in Dunapentele (where Greek nuns were living). There is no record of the exact dates of foundation but there is reason to believe that they were in existence in the eleventh century. There must have been many more Greek monasteries on Hungarian soil, for in a letter from Pope Innocent III, dated 1204, it appears that there was then some idea of uniting the Greek monastic churches in Hungary under a Greek bishop.[3]

Modern research has then made it clear that the influence of the Byzantine Church in Hungary in the eleventh century was much more important than was realised by earlier historians; the influence of Greek ceremonial and rites is indeed clearly perceptible in Hungarian ecclesiastical affairs right up to the reign of King Koloman, that is, to the end of the eleventh century. More than one of the resolutions adopted by Hungarian synods correspond to the practice of the Greek Church. The saints revered by the Hungarian Church in the Árpád period include several of Byzantine origin, and the Byzantine calendar was followed in the commemoration of saints, including St Demetrius, St Nicholas and St John. In this and in other ways Hungarian liturgical books of the period reflect the strength of the Greek rite in their Church in the eleventh century.[4]

There appears to have been hardly any conflict between Hungary and Byzantium in the course of that century. Under Andrew I Magyar and Pecheneg forces raided Byzantine territory in 1059, but

---

[1] A. Theiner, *Vetera monumenta historica Hungariam sacram illustrantia*, I, no. 53, p. 29.

[2] J. Csemegi, 'The Hermit-caves of Tihany', *Archaeologiai Értesitő*, ser. III, vols. VII–IX (1946–8), 396–407.

[3] G. Fejér, *Codex diplomaticus Hungariae ecclesiasticus ac civilis*, II, pp. 429–30.

[4] P. Váczy, 'Les racines byzantines du christianisme hongrois', *Nouvelle Revue de Hongrie*, XXXIV (1941), 99–108; Gy. Moravcsik, 'The Role of the Byzantine Church in Medieval Hungary', *American Slavic and East European Review*, VI (1947), 134–52.

when Isaac I Comnenus collected an army and marched out against them, he had gone no further than Sardica (Sofia) before he met an embassy from the Hungarian king which sued for peace.[1] It looks as though it was only the Pechenegs settled on the frontier who had dragged the Hungarians into this war. Romanus IV Diogenes (1068–71), who before ascending the throne had been *strategus* at Sardica in Bulgaria (then subject to the Eastern Empire), certainly found it advantageous to ally himself with the Hungarians.

In 1071 there was another incident on the Hungaro-Byzantine frontier. Pechenegs settled in the northern part of Bulgaria after its conquest invaded Sirmium (then Hungarian) at the instigation of the governor of Belgrade. King Salomon of Hungary and the 'Dukes' his cousins thereupon besieged Nándorfehérvár (Belgrade), and the governor, Nicetas, was forced to surrender. Shortly after, King Salomon and Duke Géza marched against Niš, whence they carried off the hand of St Procopius the Martyr. This campaign was probably connected with the rising which broke out at the time in the conquered province of Bulgaria, in which the Pechenegs took part. The sources say that when Belgrade surrendered its governor made his subjection expressly to Duke Géza.[2] The Emperor Michael VII Ducas sent ambassadors to Duke Géza to confirm peace and friendship, whereupon Géza restored the Greek prisoners to him.[3] In spite of this treaty King Salomon led his armies against Niš. This shows clearly the conflicting policies of King Salomon and Duke Géza. Salomon had gained the crown in 1063 with German help, and later, in 1074, after his fall he turned for help to his brother-in-law, the German King Henry IV. Salomon was thus an exponent of the German orientation and hostile to Byzantium. As such, he afterwards took part in an attack directed against Byzantium by the Pechenegs in 1087; one source says that he fell in that campaign.[4] Duke Géza, on the other hand, was the friend and ally of Byzantium. His wife was the daughter of Theodore Synadenus and niece to the later Emperor Nicephorus III Botaneiates (1078–81); after the death of Géza in 1077 she went back to Constantinople. This marriage, which probably took place in 1075, was perhaps connected with the conclusion of a Hungaro-Byzantine treaty, and it is likely that it was on this occasion that Géza, who was by now king (Géza I, 1074–7), received the Byzantine crown which forms the lower half of the Hungarian royal crown. On the peak of this crown the Redeemer,

---

[1] *DR*, 942.
[2] *Chronici Hungarici compositio saeculi XIV*, c. 104 (*SRH*, i, pp. 369–70).
[3] *DR*, 990ª.
[4] Anna Comnena, vii, 1, ii, p. 87 (ed. B. Leib).

the Byzantine Pantocrator, is shown sitting in state; below him to the left, the Archangel Michael, St George and St Cosmas; to the right, the Archangel Gabriel, St Demetrius and St Damian, depicted in enamel. At the back of the crown, on the same level as the picture of the Redeemer, is an enamel portrait of a Byzantine Emperor, identified by a Greek inscription in red letters as Michael VII Ducas (1071–8); under him, to the left, is another imperial figure inscribed in red letters 'Constantine', who must be Michael Ducas' son or brother and co-Emperor, and to the right, another male figure, with a Greek inscription in blue letters reading 'Géza, the faithful King of Turkia', that is, Géza I.[1] This arrangement of the portraits on the crown, the insignia borne by the different figures, and the colouring of the inscriptions show unmistakably that according to Byzantine ideas the King of Hungary was inferior to the Emperor of Byzantium in rank and dignity; Hungary stood below the Empire in the hierarchy of states. It does not however follow from this, as some have supposed, that Hungary was in a position of political subjection to the Empire. There is no trace of such a suggestion in the Byzantine terminology. Indeed, the fact that the Emperor recognised Géza as king of 'Turkia' (Hungary) actually implied, in the circumstances, a guarantee of the independence of that kingdom. When King Géza came to the throne in 1074 he needed such recognition to ensure both his own rule and the independence of the country against Salomon, who had offered it as a fief to his German brother-in-law. But the Hungaro-Byzantine alliance was not entirely one-sided. Byzantium itself was threatened by risings among its Serb and Bulgarian subjects as well as by the Seljuq Turks, Pechenegs and Uzes, and it therefore had an interest in preserving good relations with Hungary. Géza's crown no less than Andrew's is thus a memorial of the Byzantine orientation of the Hungarian kingdom in the eleventh century.

The weight and authority of the Hungarian kingdom steadily grew as the century closed, and its attitude became an important factor in imperial calculations, particularly as the armies of the western crusaders marched eastwards across Hungarian soil.[2] The growing political importance of the kingdom, the lessons of the First Crusade and the danger threatening from the Normans of southern Italy, led Alexius I Comnenus to seek the help of Hungary. The marriage, in 1104, of a Hungarian princess, the orphaned daughter of St Ladislas,

[1] Γεωβιτζὰς πιστὸς κράλης Τουρκίας. On the title, see Gy. Moravcsik, *Byzantino-turcica*, II, p. 173. For a photograph of this crown, see A. Grabar, *L'empereur dans l'art byzantin* (Paris, 1936), pl. xvii; also *The Hungarian Quarterly*, IV (1938), 656–67.

[2] Gy. Moravcsik, 'Les relations entre la Hongrie et Byzance à l'époque des croisades', *Revue des Etudes Hongroises*, VIII–IX (1933), 301–8.

to John Comnenus, the heir to the Byzantine Empire, sealed this alliance, and made it possible for the King of Hungary to conquer Dalmatia in the following year. He also gave Alexius I effective help against the Normans. Hungarian troops took part as allies of the Byzantines in their campaigns, and the signatories of the peace treaty of 1108 include plenipotentiaries of King Koloman.[1] St Ladislas' daughter, who in Constantinople assumed the name of Irene, ascended the throne of Byzantium in 1118 as the wife of John II Comnenus. She presented her husband with eight children, one of whom was the later Emperor Manuel I. She died in 1134, having, as was customary in Byzantium, assumed the veil before her death, when she took the name of Xene (stranger). The Byzantine Church reckoned her among the blessed, and her memory is preserved in many contemporary sources, for her name is connected with the foundation of one of the most splendid of Constantinople's medieval monasteries, the Pantocrator Monastery, to which three churches, a hospital and a charitable institution were attached. The Empress Irene did not live to see the final completion of this work, but the foundation charter given by her husband in 1136 shows that it was constructed in accordance with the wishes of his dead wife. The three churches of this monastery, turned by the Turks into the Zeirek-Kilisse Djamii Mosque, still stand on one of the hills of Istanbul. In front of them is a huge sarcophagus, in which tradition says that the remains of the foundress rest.[2]

The court of the Emperor John and the Empress Irene was a refuge for the dukes of the House of Árpád and the Hungarian notables whom party vicissitudes forced to leave their native land. Here King Koloman's blinded brother, Álmos, found refuge in 1116; he took the name of Constantine and founded in Macedonia a town named after himself. With him was his son, also blinded, the later King Béla II (1131–41), who was kept there in secret until his return to Hungary. For a time the Byzantines afforded refuge to Boris, the pretender who claimed to be Koloman's son by his banished wife, known to the Byzantine chroniclers as Kalamanos; he married a Byzantine princess. His son, another Kalamanos, who figured in Byzantium under the name of Constantine, later became governor of Cilicia. It is thus clear that in the internal struggles which went on within the Árpád family the opposition regularly counted on the help of Byzantium against the party in power.

---

[1] Anna Comnena, XIII, 12, III, p. 139 (ed. B. Leib).
[2] Gy. Moravcsik, *Die Tochter Ladislaus des Heiligen und das Pantokrator-Kloster in Konstantinopel* (Budapest–Constantinople, 1923); *DR*, 1311.

IV. STRUGGLES WITH BYZANTIUM

It was this support given by the Byzantine Empire to Hungarian refugees which led to armed intervention from Hungary. King Stephen II, Koloman's son and successor, when the Byzantines refused a demand from him to extradite Álmos, took as pretext the alleged ill-treatment of Hungarian merchants in Barancs, and in 1127 invaded the territory of the Empire, captured Belgrade, Barancs, Niš and Sardica, and advanced with his armies as far as Philippopolis. The next year the Emperor John II Comnenus retaliated. He defeated Stephen II's armies near Haramvár and took Sirmium and Barancs. In 1129 the Hungarians attacked again, recovering Sirmium and Barancs; whereupon the two sovereigns met and concluded peace.[1] This war was the prelude to the embittered struggles which Hungary was to wage with the Empire in the second half of the twelfth century.

In 1143 the Emperor John Comnenus died. He was succeeded by his son Manuel I, who was also the grandson of the Hungarian King St Ladislas. The central objective of Manuel's political ambitions was to reconquer the western half of the old Roman Empire and thus restore imperial unity. There were two possible ways of realising this grandiose plan: the one, by attacking Italy, the other, by conquering Hungary and turning it into a base and hinterland for an attack on Germany. For two decades Manuel fought to achieve his objective, not only by arms, but also with the weapons of diplomacy. It was with this in view that he intervened in the party struggles in Hungary, supported the great feudal magnates and the pretenders to the throne, and finally tried to realise his ambitions by a dynastic union.

The struggle opened in 1150, when Manuel attacked the Serbs, who, with the agreement and support of the Hungarians, had allied themselves with the Normans in southern Italy. Manuel himself took part in the campaign and fought a duel with a Hungarian commander named Bakchinos near the river Tara.[2] In 1151 Manuel launched a direct attack on Hungary, across the 'water bastion', as contemporary sources call the Danube.[3] Byzantine forces captured Semlin, while the pretender Boris, whom Manuel had brought with him on the campaign, laid waste the Temes district. A few years later hostilities were renewed. Manuel's cousin, Prince Andronicus, later

---

[1] *DR*, 1306.

[2] *DR*, 1381; see R. Browning, 'A New Source on Byzantine–Hungarian Relations in the Twelfth Century', *Balkan Studies*, II (1961), 173–214.

[3] *DR*, 1383.

the Emperor Andronicus I (1183–5), who was governor of Barancs and Niš, had offered these two cities to the Hungarians in return for their support in his own effort to gain the imperial crown. Manuel, however, got news of the conspiracy in time and had Andronicus arrested. In 1155 Duke Stephen, King Géza II's younger brother, was found in Manuel's army: he had fled to Constantinople and Manuel hoped to use him for his own ends. He gave him his own niece, Princess Maria, in marriage. A few years later Géza's second brother, Duke Ladislas, was also in Constantinople. Meanwhile fighting broke out anew each year in the frontier districts, without bringing decisive advantage to either side.[1]

On Géza's death in 1162 his son, Stephen III, succeeded to the throne, but a party among the Hungarians proclaimed as king Ladislas II, who had now returned to Hungary, and after his death, rallied behind his younger brother, Stephen IV, who had also enjoyed Manuel's protection in Byzantium, where he was again forced to take refuge in 1163, after a reign of only a few months.[2] Having decided that Stephen IV's cause was hopeless, Manuel evolved a different plan. In 1163 he sent George Palaeologus on an embassy to the court of Stephen III, with whom he concluded an important agreement.[3] He undertook to marry his daughter Maria to Géza II's younger son, Béla, and to make him heir to the throne of Byzantium in return for Hungary's cession to himself of Béla's patrimony, Dalmatia. The Byzantine embassy carried Béla back to Constantinople, where he took the name of Alexius and had conferred on him the newly created title of *despotes*.[4] Soon after, Béla and his betrothed Maria were proclaimed heirs to the imperial throne.[5] Béla naturally accepted membership of the Eastern Church, and attended the Synod of 1166 in his capacity as the Emperor's son-in-law.

All this notwithstanding, Manuel continued his attacks on Hungary, first as the champion of Stephen IV and afterwards of Béla, alleging as pretext that Stephen III had not kept his agreement with the Byzantine court. In 1164, taking Béla with him, he led an army across the Sava, and when encamped on Hungarian soil sent a threatening letter to the Hungarian king.[6] The Greek troops then crossed the Danube and advanced northward as far as Bács. In the end peace was concluded. Stephen III handed over his patrimony to Béla, and Manuel promised to stop supporting Stephen IV. On the occasion of this campaign Manuel recovered the hand of St Procopius

---

[1] *DR*, 1386, 1404, 1405, 1410.
[2] *DR*, 1440, 1441, 1452.   [3] *DR*, 1455.
[4] G. Ostrogorsky, 'Urum-Despotes. Die Anfänge der Despoteswürde in Byzanz', *BZ*, xliv (1951), 448–60.
[5] *DR*, 1458.   [6] *DR*, 1462.

the Martyr which the Hungarians had carried away in 1071–2 and lodged in the Church of St Demetrius in Szávaszentdemeter, and he restored the relic to Niš. This was not, however, the end of the war. In 1165 there was further fighting in Sirmium, in the course of which Semlin changed hands several times. Finally peace was concluded again, Manuel receiving Sirmium and Dalmatia. In 1166 the Hungarians attacked once more. Manuel sent three armies against them; Duke Béla was in their ranks. On this occasion John Ducas, one of Manuel's generals, set up a gold cross on Hungarian territory, with an inscription extolling Manuel's exploits, while Kalamanos, the son of the Hungarian Duke Boris who had found refuge in Byzantium, presented Manuel with a golden dish on which his triumphs in Hungary were depicted. Manuel, as a document dating from 1166 shows,[1] was so proud of his triumphs that in token of them he added in Roman fashion to the various titles which he had already assumed that of Οὐγγρικός. In reality however all that happened was that the Byzantine armies ravaged part of Transylvania and returned laden with prisoners and booty.

In 1167 Manuel opened his last campaign against Hungary: but while the preparations for this were in progress, a miracle occurred. Two bronze statues, representing Hungary and Byzantium respectively, had been placed at the triumphal gate of the Forum of Constantine, and the statue Romaia, or 'Byzantine Woman', fell down. The superstitious Emperor ordered the statue to be re-erected and the Ungrissa, or 'Hungarian Woman', to be overthrown. This last campaign, which was conducted by the Emperor's nephew, Andronicus Contostephanus, ended in a glorious victory for Byzantine arms in Sirmium. The Hungarian general Dénes (Dionysius) was completely defeated. Manuel ordained a splendid triumph in his capital to celebrate the defeat of the 'invincible' Pannonians (that is, Hungarians).[2] The real truth was that the Emperor now saw that he could not realise his ends by force of arms.

In calling Béla to his court and designating him as his heir, Manuel had not regarded him simply as a political pawn, like Stephen IV and Ladislas II, but had had in his mind the idea of bringing about, through him, a personal union between Hungary and the Empire. Béla himself, who passed ten years in Constantinople, grew up in the belief that he would one day become ruler of both Empires. But in 1169 a son was born to Manuel of his second marriage, and this altered his plans. He broke off Béla's betrothal to his daughter and married him to his sister-in-law, the Princess Anne de Châtillon.

[1] P. Zepos, *Jus Graeco-romanum*, I, p. 410.
[2] *DR*, 1472, 1473, 1474, 1475.

After this Béla only enjoyed the inferior title of Caesar. In 1172 Manuel, following the usual Byzantine custom, took his son (who, like Béla, had been christened Alexius) as co-Emperor. In the spring of the same year Stephen III died, and an embassy came from Hungary to fetch the new king home to be crowned. Before leaving, Béla (as is proved by a recently discovered Byzantine document)[1] swore fealty to Manuel, declaring that he would always pay regard to the interests of the Emperor and his Empire. And as crowned King of Hungary he continued to maintain friendship and alliance with the Byzantines. Inter-dynastic connections were also strengthened. Béla III's sister married Isaac Comnenus, one of Manuel's grand-nephews, and his younger brother, Duke Géza, married a Byzantine princess.

On Manuel's death in 1180 his small son Alexius II inherited the throne, but two years later Manuel's cousin Andronicus seized the power. Béla saw the danger threatening Manuel's family from Andronicus I, who had also shown him personal hostility, being the only person to protest when Manuel had proclaimed him as his heir. Béla therefore allied himself with the Serbs and marched south with the object of ejecting the usurper and protecting the interests of Manuel's widow and child. But Andronicus had already had the little Alexius II, to whom he had sworn fealty only shortly before, strangled; this was followed by the execution of Manuel's widow on the pretext that she was in secret communication with the King of Hungary and was inciting him to war.

With Manuel's widow and his son dead, the task of overthrowing the tyrant Andronicus devolved on Béla, in virtue of his old oath to Manuel. He now put forward his personal claim to the throne, in accordance with Manuel's original plans. When his wife died in 1184 he tried to bring the Hungaro-Byzantine union about by asking for the hand of Manuel's elder sister, Theodora, the one surviving member of Manuel's family, whose second husband had also been assassinated by Andronicus; and with this end in view he entered into contact with Andronicus' enemies, the aristocratic Latin party, amongst whom he gained many adherents. But since Andronicus had shut up Theodora in a convent and forced her much against her will to take the veil, the permission of the Church was required for the marriage. As Béla's armies were waiting at Sardica for word to come from Constantinople, the position in the capital suddenly changed; on hearing of the successful Norman capture of Thessalonica, the people of Byzantium turned against Andronicus and on 12 September 1185 raised Isaac Angelus to the throne. This event put an end to

---

[1] Cinnamus, vi, 11, p. 287 (*CSHB*); V. Laurent, *RHSE*, xviii (1941), pp. 129–30.

Béla's proposed marriage to which in any case the Synod had refused consent.[1] It meant, too, a complete change in his other plans.

Béla now entered into an alliance with the new Emperor. He gave him in marriage his daughter Margaret, who took the name of Maria, and with her, as dowry, those lands which he had conquered in his campaign against Andronicus.[2] Dalmatia, which Béla had occupied on Manuel's death, remained in the possession of the Hungarians. The marriage, which set again a Hungarian princess on the throne of Byzantium, was celebrated with great pomp at the end of 1185. From this union sprang John Angelus (Kaloyan), who afterwards came to Hungary and was governor of Sirmium, Belgrade, and the districts of Barancs and Makó until 1254. Soon after the conclusion of the marriage Béla sent back to Sardica the relics of St John of Rila, which had been kept in Esztergom since 1183.

Of the two partners to the alliance, it was the Byzantine Empire that had the greater need of it. In 1185 the Bulgarians revolted and the Serbs also were in an uproar. In 1189 a crusading army—the third—again passed through Hungary, when Frederick Barbarossa stayed at the Hungarian court at Esztergom. On this occasion also Béla kept Byzantium's interests in view and his mediation was very useful to his son-in-law. In 1190 Isaac himself came to meet his father-in-law on the banks of the Sava; agreement was reached on the Serbian question. In spite of this, Béla's armies invaded Serbia in 1192–3, whereupon Isaac sent a Byzantine army to the help of the Serbian prince, Stephen Nemanja. Finally, the differences were settled peaceably.[3] In 1195 the two rulers agreed on a common action to be carried out against the Bulgars; but the plan was never realised, for Isaac lost his throne in the same year and in 1196 Béla himself died.

The foundation of the Second Bulgarian Empire and the growth of the Serbian kingdom at the end of the twelfth century cut Hungary off from Byzantium. The interests endangered by the southward expansion of the Hungarian state were now no longer those of the Empire, but of Bulgaria and Serbia. The armies of the Fourth Crusade did not pass through Hungary; they proceeded instead by sea and in the end captured Constantinople. At the outset of the thirteenth century one more attempt was made to set a Hungarian ruler on the throne of the Empire, or rather of its Latin successor: in 1216 one

[1] Gy. Moravcsik, 'Pour une alliance byzantino-hongroise (seconde moitié du XIIe siècle)', *B*, VIII (1933), 555–68.

[2] A. Theiner, *Vetera monumenta Slavorum meridionalium historiam illustrantia*, I, p. 36.

[3] V. Laurent, 'La Serbie entre Byzance et la Hongrie à la veille de la quatrième croisade', *RHSE*, XVIII (1941), 109–30.

party put forward Béla's son Andrew (King Andrew II, 1205–35) as candidate for the throne; but the plan came to nothing. Andrew took part in the Fifth Crusade, visiting Cyprus and the Holy Land, but even his family connections could not bring him the prize of Constantinople, and this was the last flickering attempt at realising Béla's and Manuel's dream of union.

Manuel's Hungarian plans were undoubtedly strongly influenced by the fact that Hungary was the westernmost state in which Byzantine Christianity had struck root; the ground was thus to some extent favourable for conquest from Byzantium. This is also proved by the fact that when in 1164 Manuel entered Sirmium, the ecclesiastical centre of which was in Bács, north of the Danube, the population received him ceremonially, the priests going ahead gospel in hand, while the people greeted him with Greek hymns. It cannot be doubted that in the twelfth century the Greek Church possessed many adherents in Hungary, particularly in the south of the country. This is also indicated by the fact that the Greek monastery of Szávaszentdemeter, whose abbot was directly under the Patriarch of Constantinople, remained, as shown by a letter of Pope Clement written in 1344, in the hands of monks of the Eastern rite up to the first years of the fourteenth century, when it was taken over by Benedictines.[1] Other Greek monasteries founded in the eleventh century, such as that of Visegrád, passed into the hands of western orders at the beginning of the thirteenth century—a consequence of the fate which had overtaken the Byzantine Empire. For after Constantinople was captured by the western crusaders in 1204, a Latin Patriarchate was established, and in 1215 the Fourth Lateran Council instructed its bishops to send Latin priests to churches following the Greek rite. Thus the Greek monasteries in Hungary, their Byzantine spiritual roots cut, isolated in a Latin environment, gradually became Latinised. But that the Greek element in Hungary was still considerable even in the fifteenth century is proved in interesting fashion by the advice given by Pope Pius II (1458–64) to King Ladislas V to learn Greek, since this would be of great advantage to him in governing Hungary, 'cui Greci complures sunt'.[2] How lively the connection between the Hungarian Church authorities and Byzantium was at the end of the twelfth century is also illustrated by a recently discovered Greek letter, which Demetrius Tornices wrote about 1190 for Isaac Angelus to Job, Archbishop of Esztergom, on a point of doc-

---

[1] A. Theiner, *Vetera monumenta historica Hungariam sacram illustrantia*, I, no. 1002, pp. 667–8; Gy. Györffy, 'Das Güterverzeichnis des griechischen Klosters zu Szávaszentdemeter (Sremska Mitrovica) aus dem 12. Jahrhundert', *Studia Slavica Acad. Scient. Hung.* V (1959), 9–74.

[2] *Fontes rerum Austriacarum, Diplomataria et Acta*, LXVII, p. 138.

trine; the letter shows that Job himself had been to Constantinople on an embassy and that he was in correspondence with the Emperor.[1] It is therefore no accident that the main porch of Esztergom Cathedral, which was constructed under the same Job, shows traces of the Byzantine style.[2] There is also interesting literary evidence of Byzantine influence, dating from about the middle of the twelfth century. A certain Cerbanus, a Venetian by origin, who had spent several years in Constantinople at the imperial court, translated into Latin for the benefit of Pannonhalma Abbey parts of the works of the Greek patristic writers Maximus the Confessor and John of Damascus, and dedicated his translation, which he made from a Greek manuscript in the possession of the Abbey of Pásztó, to David, Abbot of Pannonhalma (1131–50), in gratitude for the hospitality he had enjoyed there. This was the first translation into Latin of John of Damascus' works, and it exercised a great influence on later translations. Western theologians, such as Peter Lombard, made their first acquaintance with the great Greek Father through this translation.[3] Thus it is clear that the Greek monasteries of Hungary acted as a link between East and West. There are moreover traces of ecclesiastical connections with Byzantium at a still later date. A Greek charter of 1391 speaks of a Greek monastery near the village of Körtvélyes in Máramaros.[4] In the middle of the fifteenth century comes the foundation of the Greek bishopric of Munkács, which in all probability is connected with Cardinal Isidore's journey to Hungary in 1443. The Greek Church in Hungary always numbered Magyar adherents, as well as Slavs and Rumanians.

Besides the dynastic, diplomatic and ecclesiastical links which joined Hungary to Byzantium, there were also commercial ties. Hungarian merchants often visited Constantinople, as noted by a Jewish merchant who was at the Byzantine court during Manuel's reign. There were Hungarian trading communities not only in Barancs and Philippopolis (for these we have definite evidence) but also in other southern centres. Hungarian traders bought the products of the East in Constantinople, and sold them to Prague. The Byzantine merchants' trade-routes to the West also ran across Hungary. In Béla III's time the Byzantine gold coin was in general

---

[1] V. Laurent, 'Une lettre dogmatique de l'empereur Isaac l'Ange au primat de Hongrie', *EO*, xxxix (1940), 59–77.

[2] T. Bogyay, 'L'iconographie de la "Porta Speciosa" d'Esztergom et ses sources d'inspiration', *REB*, viii (1950), 85–129.

[3] *Translatio Latina Ioannis Damasceni* (*De orthodoxa fide*, i. iii, c. 1–8) *saeculo XII. in Hungaria confecta*, ed. R. L. Szigeti (Budapest, 1940); *Translatio Latina Sancti Maximi Confessoris* (*De caritate ad Elpidium*, i, i–iv) *saeculo XII. in Hungaria confecta*, ed. A. B. Terebessy (Budapest, 1944).

[4] Miklosich–Müller, *Acta et Diplomata*, ii, no. 426.

currency in Hungary. That Hungarian king, who had passed his youth at Manuel's court, had learnt many things there, and he utilised his experiences in his own country.

The double cross of the Hungarian coat of arms was introduced by Béla III. Up to his time the royal emblem of the Hungarian kings was the single Apostolic Cross. The double cross appears for the first time on Béla III's coinage about 1190, when he took it over from Byzantium, where it was the imperial emblem from the ninth to the thirteenth centuries, spreading thence to other countries. Bearing in mind Manuel's and Béla's plans of union, it is legitimate to conclude that Béla's purpose in adopting the double cross was to represent the dignity of the kingdom of Hungary as similar to that of the Byzantine Empire. It was probably also Béla who joined the Byzantine crown given by Michael Ducas to Géza I to that which Hungarian tradition regards as the Crown of St Stephen. Béla must have been well aware of the significance attached in the Comnenian period to the closed imperial crown. When the old Byzantine circle was welded together with the western upper crown, the resultant Hungarian royal crown became similar to the imperial emblem worn by the Comneni. In doing this Béla obviously had the same end in view as when he took over the double cross. The Hungarian Crown thus enshrines the memory of the prolonged struggles which Hungary waged with Byzantium, partly in defence of her national existence, partly in her effort to realise Manuel's daring dreams.

V. STRUGGLES FOR BYZANTIUM

After the Fourth Crusade a fundamental change took place in the relations between Hungary and Byzantium. The Eastern Empire, which in the twelfth century had been one of Europe's leading states, had broken into small fragments, and when the Palaeologi restored the Greek Empire, it was only a shadow of its old self. At the same time Hungary was extending its frontiers eastward and southward and in the fourteenth century was one of the important European powers. In consequence of the shift of geographical frontiers and the alteration in the balance of power there was little room for any clash of interests between Hungary and Byzantium, and Hungary was now too strong to need the support of the Empire, which was in any case no longer in a position to threaten it. On the contrary: Byzantium in its extremity more than once turned for help to Hungary, which now fought, not against Byzantium, but for it.

When King Andrew II journeyed eastward in 1217–18 in connection with the Fifth Crusade, he visited the court of Nicaea on his return journey and carried away with him the Emperor Theodore I Lascaris' daughter Maria, who in 1220 became the wife of his son, the later Béla IV (1235–70). This marriage, one of the fruits of which was the Hungarian princess St Margaret, was perhaps not unconnected with Andrew's hopes of securing the throne of the Latin Empire. But the court of Nicaea had also an interest in gaining Hungary's support. When Michael VIII Palaeologus, co-ruler with the minor John IV Lascaris, sent an embassy to the Hungarian court to ask King Béla for help, the result was a Hungarian–Byzantine alliance against the coalition of Epirus with the Franks. Hungarian and Cuman troops in fact took part at the battle of Pelagonia, in which Michael Palaeologus inflicted a decisive defeat on his enemies in 1259. Cumans from Hungary also played a part in the recapture of Constantinople in 1261. Thus the Hungarian kings had a share in the restoration of the Byzantine Empire.[1]

Shortly after this, in 1263, the armies of Hungary and Byzantium met once again, and for the last time, in battle. The Emperor had invaded the territory of western Bulgaria, which belonged to Hungary's sphere of influence and owed allegiance to the King of Hungary. The young king, Stephen V, Béla IV's son, sent a Hungarian force to the support of his vassal, Sphentislav, lord of the area in question. Together they drove the Byzantines back at Sardica and near Philippopolis, and that was the end of hostilities.

Byzantium's last dynasty, the Palaeologi, then sought to link themselves with the Árpáds. In 1271–2 ambassadors arrived at the court of Stephen V to ask the hand of his daughter, Anna, the granddaughter of Theodore I Lascaris, Emperor of Nicaea, for Michael VIII Palaeologus' son Andronicus.[2] The marriage was celebrated, but Anna, the third princess of the house of Árpád to be crowned in Constantinople, did not live to see her husband become sole ruler when his father Michael VIII died in 1282. Anna's eldest son, Michael, never himself mounted the throne, but from him sprang all the later rulers of the house of Palaeologus. Michael Palaeologus' object in seeking this dynastic alliance with the Árpáds was obviously the political one of gaining a free hand in Bulgaria and Serbia.

During the fourteenth century the expansion of the Ottoman Turks led Byzantium to seek help and support in the West. In the first days of 1366, while deep winter still reigned, a little party set out from Constantinople. They were not ambassadors: the Emperor himself, John V Palaeologus, was starting for Buda with his two sons,

---

[1] See E. Darkó, *Byzantinisch-ungarische Beziehungen in der zweiten Hälfte des XIII. Jahrhunderts* (Weimar, 1933).

[3] *DR*, 1982.

Manuel (afterwards Emperor) and Michael, together with his chancellor, George Manicaites, and a small escort. They could not go by land, along the old military road, since Adrianople and Philippopolis were already in Turkish hands. They travelled by boat across the tempestuous Black Sea to the mouth of the Danube, whence they made their way through snowstorms and across frozen rivers to the court of the King of Hungary, Louis the Great (1342–82).[1] The contemporary narrative tells that the King of Hungary received his imperial guests, whose bearing still betrayed the old pride of Byzantium, with great honour and splendour.[2] Yet it was the Emperor himself who was reduced to seeking out one of Europe's mightiest rulers to beg for the help of the western powers against the Turks. King Louis undertook to mediate in the matter, and opened negotiations with Pope Urban V, who made his help conditional on a union between the Churches. King Louis himself also demanded the rebaptism of the Greeks, but the Emperor rejected his request and, leaving his son Manuel as hostage, he returned to Constantinople. But his journey proved ineffectual, and the 'crusade of liberation' never materialised.[3]

The project of helping Byzantium was in the air again and again in subsequent years, and some campaigns, in all of which Hungary played a leading part, were undertaken for that purpose. For instance, a crusading army of western knights assembled on the invitation of the Hungarian king Sigismund (1387–1437) to attack the Turks, assisted by powerful support from Venice. The enterprise however ended in defeat at the battle of Nicopolis (1396), when Sigismund himself only succeeded with difficulty in making his way by ship to Constantinople, whence he returned home by a long detour. A year later the Patriarch of Constantinople called on the King of Poland to ally himself with the ruler of Hungary against the Turks.

In the spring of 1424 another member of the house of Palaeologus arrived in Buda. The later Emperor John VIII Palaeologus, at that time still only heir to the throne, was travelling round the western courts in search of help and called on Sigismund to present to the Hungarian king his personal request for help for Byzantium. He passed two months at Buda, where he painted in moving words the

[1] Zachariae von Lingenthal, *SPAW*, xxvii–xxix (Berlin, 1888), p. 1419; see O. Halecki, *Un empereur de Byzance à Rome* (Warsaw, 1930), pp. 111–37.

[2] Giovanni di Ravenna, ed. T. Kardos, *Archivum Philologicum*, lx (Budapest, 1936), 295–6.

[3] J. Meyendorff, 'Projets de Concile Œcuménique en 1367: Un dialogue entre Jean Cantacuzène et le légat Paul', *DOP*, xiv (1960), 147–77; Gy. Moravcsik, 'Vizantijskije imperatory i ich posly v g. Buda', *Acta Historica Acad. Scient. Hung.* viii (1961), 239–56.

siege which Constantinople had undergone in the previous year, emphasising the horrors of the war and the critical situation of the Byzantine Empire.[1]

In 1444 Byzantium was again expecting help from the Hungarian king, as is shown by a letter written by the Emperor John Palaeologus—the former visitor to Buda—from Mistra in the Peloponnese to Ulaszló I, King of Hungary (1440–4).[2] The battle of Varna was fought on 10 November of that year, but the Christian army was defeated, the Hungarian king himself being among the fallen. The Greek poem about the battle praises, however, not the king, but John Hunyadi, 'Governor' of the kingdom during the interregnum from 1446 to 1452, whom the imagination of the Byzantine people raised to an almost supernatural sphere, and around whom Byzantine tradition has spun a web of legend. One of the last of the Byzantine historians has noted an episode of Hunyadi's youth. When 'Jankó'—as the Greek sources call him—was hunting at the court of the prince of Serbia, he pursued a wolf so successfully that he caught it alive and killed it. When he brought the beast's pelt to the prince, the latter prophesied that the boy would one day come to great power.[3] The very fact that Byzantine popular tradition attached a myth of this kind—long current in Byzantium in connection with Basil I—to the person of Hunyadi, shows that popular opinion in Byzantium ranked him as the equal of the founder of the Macedonian dynasty and counted him amongst the great heroes of all time. Certain sources would even have it that Hunyadi's mother was a Greek and one of the Palaeologi.[4] In the eyes of the author of the popular Greek poem on the battle of Varna Hunyadi figures as 'a second Alexander the Great', 'the anointed of God', 'worthy of the imperial crown and a worthier heir than any', 'the Emperor of the Romans'.[5] This homage paid to the figure of Hunyadi is the highest which Byzantium could offer. And no wonder, for in his heroic campaigns lay the last hope of the dying Empire. Recent researches have demonstrated that John Hunyadi indeed offered to send to the last Emperor a Hungarian army to the port of Mesembria in Thrace as help against the Turks, but this plan was not to be realised. According to a trustworthy source, Constantine issued a chrysobull, a document bearing a golden

---

[1] Sphrantzes, I, 31, ed. Papadopoulos, p. 121; Sp. Lambros, Παλαιολόγεια καὶ Πελοποννησιακά, III (Athens, 1926), pp. 219–20.

[2] *Ioannis Dlugossi Historiae Polonicae libri XII*, ed. G. Groddeckius, I (Frankfurt, 1711), cols. 790–3.

[3] Laonicus Chalcocandyles, ed. E. Darkó, II, pp. 33–4.

[4] E. Margalits, *Szerb történelmi repertorium*, I (Budapest, 1918), p. 137.

[5] Ἑλληνικὸν ποίημα περὶ τῆς μάχης τῆς Βάρνης, ed. Gy. Moravcsik (Budapest, 1935), pp. 14–19; see M. Gyóni, 'Hunyadi, "empereur de Byzance"', *Nouvelle Revue de Hongrie*, XXXIII (1940), 499–504.

seal, in which he conferred on Hunyadi the ownership of Mesembria in gratitude for his services.[1] It is well known that when the Turks stormed Constantinople in May 1453 rumours were abroad that Hunyadi would appear with his armies to raise the siege. The threnodies which lament the fall of Constantinople recall in melancholy tones the memory of the Hungarian hero.

But even after the Byzantine polity had disintegrated its influence lived on, finding new heirs in the West. One of these was Matthew Corvinus, Hunyadi's son, and King of Hungary from 1458 to 1490. He personally was in contact with many Byzantine humanists, such as George Argyropulus and Bessarion, and his library, the Corvina, found room for manuscripts not only of classical but also of Byzantine writers, such as the historical works of Procopius, Theophanes and Zonaras, Nicephorus Callistus' ecclesiastical history and Constantine Porphyrogenitus' treatise on the *Ceremonies of the Byzantine Court*. It was in the Corvina that the only complete manuscript of the last-named work was preserved for posterity.

[1] Sphrantzes, p. 327 (*CSHB*); see Gy. Moravcsik, 'Ungarisch-byzantinische Beziehungen zur Zeit des Falles von Byzanz', *Acta Antiqua Academiae Scientiarum Hungaricae*, II (1954), 349–60.

CHAPTER XIV

ARMENIA AND GEORGIA

I. THE ABOLITION OF THE CAUCASIAN MONARCHIES

Cis-Caucasia, where the Armenian and Georgian states flourished, is
the north-easternmost region of the Mediterranean world. Protected
to the north by the Caucasian range and washed to the east and
west by the Caspian and the Black Sea, it opens out in a semi-circle
towards the south, linking up with Asia Minor, Syria, Mesopotamia
and Iran. In the late Roman epoch it contained four polities. The
chief of these was Armenia; the others, bordering it in the north
from sea to sea, were the two Georgian lands of Egrisi, on the Euxine,
and of K'art'li, east and south of it, as well as Caspian Albania
(Aḷuank'). To the classical world, K'art'li was always Iberia (Hiberia),
while Egrisi was at first known as Colchis and then as Lazica. Iberia
was the nucleus of Georgia, wherein the historical continuity of the
nation and its historical memory were preserved, in contrast to
Egrisi whose early history is obscured by foreign domination. Of
Albania, too, little is known at this early period; it stands in the
same relation to Armenia as West Georgia to Iberia: for the history
of either we have to rely on the occasional light shed by the historical
tradition of its more articulate neighbour and by the scattered data
of foreign sources.[1]

Belonging to the Mediterranean world and bordering on Iran, the
(cis-)Caucasian states were subjected to powerful influences from
both; they became involved in the struggle of two imperial expan-
sions, Roman and Iranian; and they owed the survival of their cultural and political individuality to the equipoise of the two rivals.
The civilisation of Caucasia (Armenia and Georgia) reached back,
uninterruptedly, to Hittite and Assyrian times; it has formed a part
of the patterns of civilised existence that succeeded and influenced
one another in the Mediterranean world: Aegean-Anatolian, Mesopotamian, Iranian, Hellenistic, Romano-Byzantine. The Caucasian
social structure, as will be seen, bears a striking resemblance to that
of the West: both arose from the blending of tribal conditions and
more advanced, especially Romano-Hellenistic, political forms. The

---

[1] The term 'Transcaucasia' for the regions south of the Caucasus range derives
from a geo-political conception wholly alien to the period covered in this chapter.
These regions are designated here as cis-Caucasia or, simply, Caucasia; cf. C. Toumanoff,
'Introduction to Christian Caucasian History: the Formative Centuries (IVth–
VIIIth)', *Trad.* xv (1959), 2, 6–7.

chief art of Caucasia, architecture, is in style akin to Romanesque and contains seeds of Gothic, the relationship between them being, as Focillon puts it, that of two different experiments conducted with the same media.[1] Last but not least, Caucasia became a part of Christendom, whence the similarity of its literatures—another important achievement—with those of the rest of the Christian world. But religious separation and barbarian invasions (which afflicted Caucasia much later than the West) prevented its sharing in the subsequent cultural development of Christendom: after the middle ages, its history is largely one of arrested growth.

It was in the clash of empires that the monarchies of Armenia, Iberia and Albania fell into abeyance. Both Rome and Iran claimed the overlordship of Caucasia: the latter from the days of the Achaemenids;[2] the former after its victory over Mithridates' Caucasian allies when Roman suzerainty was imposed upon Armenia, Iberia, Albania and Colchis.[3] Neither power could acquiesce in the other's hegemony in Caucasia, which was of supreme strategic importance to both: it controlled the frontier between them as well as the passes protecting the civilised world from hyperborean barbarians beyond the mountains; thence the heart of Iran could be struck at, and the Roman lake reached through the Euxine.

After intermittent wars, a compromise was reached as far as the most important Caucasian state was concerned, in the treaty of Rhandeia of 63. An Iranian Arsacid was placed on the Armenian throne as a vassal of Rome. How this settlement affected the other Caucasian kingdoms can only be surmised. The establishment of an Arsacid branch on the throne of Albania, within that century, and of another on that of Iberia, in the second century, may indicate similar arrangements with regard to these countries. Colchis had meantime passed to the kings of Bosporus, clients of Rome, and then was annexed in 64 to the Roman Empire.

The settlement of Rhandeia continued in force, in theory at least, until the political and religious events of the third and fourth centuries. The Hellenised Arsacids of Iran were overthrown by the nationalist Sassanids, and the new rulers of a renovated Iran could no longer accept a settlement that, in their eyes, infringed upon their imperial rights. At the same time, the dynastic condominium of the Arsacids—Iranian, Armenian, Iberian, Albanian—which, in guaranteeing the family ascendancy of the Great King over the Caucasian

---

[1] H. Focillon, preface to J. Baltrušaitis, *Etudes sur l'art médiéval en Géorgie et en Arménie* (Paris, 1929), p. viii.

[2] In the fourth century B.C.

[3] Pompey imposed Roman suzerainty upon these kingdoms in 66–64 B.C.

kings, had compensated him for the admission of Roman influence into Caucasia, came to an end. Instead, a family feud separated these kings from the usurping Sassanids. The latter, it is true, soon after, secured the throne of Iberia for a branch of the Mihranids, one of the 'seven great houses' of Iran, but the religious developments of the time frustrated this diplomatic move. These were the establishment of militant Zoroastrianism as the state creed of the Sassanid 'New Iran', and the conversion in the following century of both the Roman Empire and the Caucasian kingdoms to Christianity.[1] The conversion of Caucasia was not only of a great spiritual, but also of a profound political significance. The easy mingling of cultural and religious forms that had in part made Rhandeia possible existed no more than the Arsacid condominium. The convergence of religious and dynastic reasons enhanced, on the one hand, the suzerainty exercised in fact or in theory by the Roman Empire in Caucasia and, on the other, created a chasm between it and Iran.

Thus the strife between the empires was intensified. In 363 the defeat of Julian forced his successor to cede to Sapor II the overlordship of Armenia, Iberia and Albania: Iran regained what had been lost by the treaty of Nisibis.[2] Within that decade, however, Valens re-established Roman supremacy in Armenia. But he was able to recover only a half of Iberia: the country was split into two kingdoms, one, ephemeral, under Roman, the other under Iranian suzerainty. It had become obvious by the fourth century that two mutually exclusive political and religious influences could not exist within the same polity. Division appeared to be the only solution. It was tried in Iberia; then, at the end of the century, it was used as a basis for a renewed *modus vivendi* between Rome and Iran in Armenia.

The success of these imperial policies was guaranteed by internal complications resulting from the nature of Caucasian society.[3] Like

[1] The conversion of Armenia took place in 314, under Tiridates III; that of Iberia occurred, under Mirian I (III), in 337; cf. P. Ananian, 'La data e circostanze della consecrazione di S. Gregorio Illuminatore', *Le Muséon*, LXXIV (1961), xxx ff.; C. Toumanoff, 'Christian Caucasia between Byzantium and Iran: New Light from Old Sources', *Trad.* x (1954), 124 ff.

[2] By that treaty, in 298, the Great King ceded to Rome the suzerainty over Armenia and Iberia.

[3] For the genesis and structure of Caucasian society, see C. Toumanoff, 'Introduction to Christian Caucasian History', I and II, *Trad.* xv and xvII (1959–61). The situation was similar to that in the Holy Roman Empire after the Peace of Westphalia, except that the German princes, hardly any of whom was of dynastic origin, did indeed owe their rights to a concession of the Crown, whereas the rights of the Caucasian princes antedated those of the Crown and any concession on its part was a legal fiction. For the international status of the Armenian princes, placed under Roman suzerainty in 298 and 387 ('satrap' is the Roman bureaucratic misnomer, see

Caucasian civilisation, the social structure of Caucasia had its beginnings in Hittite and Assyrian times: in the Urartian phase of its history. The salient feature of that society was the survival of a whole class, a caste in fact, of dynastic princes, which had evolved from the tribal aristocracy of Urartian days. They were older than kingship, which derived from them. Their principalities were self-sufficient and self-determined, being territorialised tribes and clans of old. And their rights over these states were fully sovereign, including executive, judiciary, legislative and fiscal independence, control of their own armed forces, and, from the princes' point of view at least, the right to negotiate with foreign powers. On the international scale, they received the treatment accorded to minor kings. Armenia and Iberia were therefore largely federations of princely states presided over by the king. However, the Crown had from the start sought to increase its ascendancy over each federation. In this way, to the purely political dependence of one sovereign upon another, there were added certain feudal features. What the Crown could not reduce by force, it attempted to control by sanction; it admitted the princely rights, but tended to regard them as of its own delegation. All the Armenian dynastic princes were at the same time feudal dukes, ruling their principalities and commanding their armies in the service of the king. In Iberia, where the Crown was comparatively stronger, the ducal office was conferred on only a few of the princes. In both monarchies, many dynasts were enfeoffed of great Crown offices, often aulic in character. The lesser nobility was composed of the knights, vassals of the king and of the princes, who served in the cavalry of the realm.

The most prominent Armenian princes on the eve of the abolition of the monarchy were those invested with the hereditary control of the four marches of the kingdom, notably the margraves (*vitaxae*) of Gogarene in the north and of Arzanene in the south, as well as the Mamikonids (Mamikonian) of Tayk', Taraun, Bagravandene, and Acilisene, hereditary High Constables; the Bagratids (Bagratuni) of Syspiritis, Kogovit and Tamoritis, hereditary Coronants of the Kings

---

Procopius, *De aed.* III, 1, 18–23, where their ceremonial vestments are described). Sent to them by the Emperor, these insignia included the red boots, 'which only the Roman and the Iranian emperors have the right to wear'. They were more splendid than those sent to the vassal kings of Lazica.—The dynastic aspect of the princes was expressed by the Armenian terms *ishkhan, nahapet*, and (*tanu*)*tēr* and the Georgian terms *mt'avar* and *sep'etsul*; their feudal aspect, as dukes, by the Armenian *nakharar* and the Georgian *erist'av*. The margravial *vitaxae* went by the Armenian title of *bdeashkh* and the Georgian *pitiakhsh*. The differentiation of the Arab period between the greater princes and the lesser ones, their vassals, came to be expressed by the titles of *ishkhan* and *nakharar* respectively. Princely cadets had the title of *sepuh*. The lesser nobles were designated by the term *azat* in Armenian and *aznaur* in Georgian.

of Armenia; the Princes of Siunia; the Kamsarakans of Siracene and Arsharunik'; the Ŗshtuni ruling the southern shore of lake Van; and the Artsrunis connected with the margraviate of Adiabene. In the Syrian march of Armenia (once the kingdom of Sophene), which had passed by the treaty of Nisibis under dual Roman–Armenian control and been given the Roman appellation of *gentes*, there were the Princes of Ingilene and of Greater and Lesser Sophene.[1]

The balance between the Crown and the dynasts was one of tension, and thus delicate; and in the history of Armenia and Iberia it was frequently upset. The ensuing struggles often became involved in the vaster conflict of empires. While the Arsacids of Armenia and the Chosroids (Mihranids) of Iberia gravitated towards the autocratic and bureaucratic Roman state, their princely vassals, though Christians, were drawn to the aristocratic realm of the Sassanids. One of the internal Armenian crises led in 377/8 to the expulsion of King Varazdat by Manuel, Prince of the Mamikonids,[2] who then assumed the power. As the chief quarrel with Iran of the princely party whom Manuel represented was religious, Sapor II's guarantee of religious freedom and political autonomy to Armenia induced the Mamikonid government to recognise, in 378/9, the suzerainty of the Great King. At that moment, the Roman Empire was paralysed by the disaster of Adrianople; but soon the weakness of Sapor's successors and the rise of the great Theodosius decided Manuel to transfer Armenia's allegiance to the Empire. Restoring the throne to two Arsacid brothers, the co-kings Arsaces III and Valarsaces, Manuel continued to rule until his death in 385/6. Thereafter, the co-operation of Crown and dynasts came to an end. Some of the princes revolted against Arsaces III and appealed to Ctesiphon for another Arsacid king. Varazdat's son Chosroes was sent at the head of an Iranian army and occupied the greater part of the kingdom, reducing Arsaces to the western

---

[1] The political weight of these houses is best illustrated by the size of their cavalry contingents, placed at the service of their suzerain, the King of Armenia and, later, the Great King: Gogarene and Arzanene, 4500 and 4000 horse respectively; Ingilene, 3400; Artsruni, Bagratids, Mamikonids, Sophene, 1000 each; Kamsarakan, 600; Siunia, at a later period, 9400 horse; cf. C. Toumanoff, 'Introduction', II, table V. The number of the princely states varied at different epochs. There were some fifty states belonging to some thirty dynasties in the Arsacid monarchy; after its abolition, the number decreased to forty-two states and twenty-seven dynasties, *c.* 400; thirty-four states and twenty dynasties, *c.* 500; and to some twenty states and thirteen dynasties, *c.* 800; *ibid.* tables II and III.—Though of local provenance, many dynasties devised for themselves exotic antecedents: the Bagratids claimed Hebrew origin, which later evolved into the celebrated Davidic tradition, the Mamikonids deduced themselves from the Emperors of China, and the Artsrunis from the Kings of Assyria.

[2] Surnames in the genitive plural often figure in the princely nomenclature of Armenia; C. Toumanoff, 'Introduction', I, p. 73.

province of Upper Armenia. Thus it was Armenia itself which brought about its partition. And in 387 Theodosius I and Sapor III made peace on the basis of the *fait accompli*, recognising the existence of two Armenian kingdoms, one under Roman, the other under Iranian overlordship.[1] Faced with the barbarian pressure elsewhere and beset with internal troubles, the Christian Empire had to cede an important part of Christendom to its chief foe of the day. The whole of Iberia had by then been abandoned to Iran, as had also been Albania.

Division in Armenia was followed by political disintegration. It sealed the secessionist trend of many frontier principalities; thus the *Gentes* came under the sole aegis of the Empire and the *Vitaxae* of Gogarene passed to Iberia. Arsaces III died *c.* 390, and the Emperor allowed him no successor. His kingdom (*Armenia interior*, or *magna*) was placed under the *comes Armeniae*, residing at Theodosiopolis (Erzerum), and its princely states acquired the same status of sovereign vassals of the Empire as the *Gentes*.[2] Inner Armenia and the *Gentes* formed Roman Armenia. In Iranian Armenia, four times larger than the other, the Sassanids strove to strengthen their control, while the aristocracy kept quarrelling with the Crown. At the instance of the princes, Chosroes III was deposed by the Great King, replaced by his brother Vṛamshapuh, then reinstated. Finally, after the reign of Yazdgard I's son Sapor—a step towards the intended absorption of Armenia—Vṛamshapuh's son Artaxias IV was brought to the throne by the princes. But they had grown tired of any authority above their own in Armenia; and, despite the solemn warnings of the chief prelate of Armenia, St Isaac, last male descendant of St Gregory, the apostle of the country, they resolved upon a fatal step. They petitioned the Great King to abolish the very institution of the Armenian monarchy and to become their immediate suzerain. Vahrām V, who could hardly have hoped for such a fulfilment of

[1] This writer agrees entirely with N. H. Baynes, 'Rome and Armenia in the Fourth Century', *EHR*, xxv, 625–43, E. Stein, *Histoire du Bas-Empire*, i (Paris, 1959), 205–6, and S. Der Nersessian, *Armenia and the Byzantine Empire*, p. 6, regarding the date of the partition of Armenia. The date 384, proposed anew by J. Doise, 'Le partage de l'Arménie sous Théodose Ier', *Revue des Etudes Anciennes*, xlvii (1945), 274–7, is contradicted by the sequence of events in Faustus of Buzanda, 5. 37–44; 6. 1. Cf. C. Toumanoff, 'Iberia on the Eve of Bagratid Rule: An Enquiry into the Political History of Eastern Georgia between the VIth and the IXth Century', *Le Muséon*, lxv (1952), 1, n. 5; *Christian Caucasia*, p. 131, n. 80.—The recently discovered new version of the *Narratio de rebus Armeniae* attributes the founding of Theodosiopolis to Theodosius I, linking it to the partition of Armenia, whereas Procopius would assign both events to the reign of Theodosius II; cf. G. Garitte, *La Narratio de rebus Armeniae. Edition critique et commentaire* (Louvain, 1952), pp. 27, 67–9; C. Toumanoff, 'Christian Caucasia', p. 131.

[2] Among the princes of the former kingdom were the scions of the Arsacid dynasty, destined to play a considerable role in Byzantine history in the sixth and seventh centuries; C. Toumanoff, 'Introduction', ii, § 12.

the Armenian policy of his house, hastened to accede. In 428 he deposed Artaxias IV, deprived St Isaac of his office,[1] and showered favours upon the princes. The court of Ctesiphon was careful to respect their sovereign rights; its suzerainty was expressed in the presence of a viceroy (*marzpān*) at the old royal capital of Dvin, in the fealty of the princes and in their military aid (for which subsidies were now given). For the rest they remained sovereign oligarchs of Armenia.

Though respecting the social and political *status quo* of their new dependency, the Sassanids attempted to spread Iranian cultural and religious influences. In this they were not successful. The conversion of Armenia had already thwarted their programme; and now the invention of the Armenian alphabet, at the turn of the fifth century, by St Mesrop (Mashtots') ensured a more thorough Christianisation of the people and achieved Armenia's linguistic and cultural independence of its neighbours. Armenian literature was born and a school of translators arose who rendered into Armenian the Scriptures as well as Greek patristic, philosophical and historical works. Original writers made their appearance, especially in the field of history.[2] To counterbalance this spiritual independence, Iran at first encouraged Syrian influence in Armenia. Iranian Christianity was largely Syrian and was already then drifting away from the rest of Christendom (as was soon manifested in the Nestorian secession); thus it looked as though a link between Armenia and Iran might be forged, and Armenian ties with the Roman Empire weakened.

The next step was more radical. The politic Vahrām V was succeeded in 438/9 by the fanatical Yazdgard II, whose declared intention was to convert Caucasia to Zoroastrianism. Armenia sustained the first blow. Encouraged by the temporising of the princes, Yazdgard launched a terrible persecution of Armenian Christians. But before the year was over, a popular revolt broke out; the princes joined this and St Vardan II, Prince of the Mamikonids, took the

---

[1] With the deposition in 428 of St Isaac, in whose family the position of chief prelate of Armenia had become quasi-hereditary, and under the Iranian nominee who replaced him, the Church of Armenia, hitherto a dependency of Caesarea (in Cappadocia), broke with its mother-church. After that event, the chief bishops of Armenia began to style themselves *Katholikoi*. This was doubtless done in imitation of the *Katholikoi* of Seleucia-Ctesiphon who had, by 424, evolved from mere 'Representatives General' of Antioch to be the heads of national Syro-Iranian Christianity (soon to become Nestorian in doctrine); cf. G. Garitte, *Narratio*, pp. 56–7; C. Toumanoff, 'Christian Caucasia', § 21.

[2] The historians of this 'Golden Age' of Armenian literature included Agathangelus and Faustus of Buzanda (fifth century, though possibly translations of earlier works in Greek or Syriac), Lazarus of P'arpi and Eliseus (fifth–sixth centuries); to this age also belonged the hagiographer Koriun and the theologian Eznik of Kołb (fifth century) and possibly the philosopher David the Invincible.

command of what became a war of liberation. But it was doomed to failure. The Emperor Marcian was unable to aid the Christians; a group of princes, under Vasak of Siunia, viceroy of Armenia, withdrew from the struggle; and the insurgents were utterly crushed at Avarayr, on 2 June 451, when St Vardan lost his life. An understanding was thereupon reached by the conciliatory party and the Great King; but Yazdgard was obliged to give up his religious policy in Armenia. In Albania, this policy provoked the revolt of King Vachʻē II *c.* 460, the result of which was the dispossession of the Albanian Arsacids *c.* 461. In Iberia, the Sassanids appear to have been more cautious, and the anti-Iranian revolt occurred two decades later.

After the partition of Armenia, Roman power tended to weaken in West Georgia. One of the local dynasties, rulers of the Lazian people, spread its control to the whole of Colchis; and the war measures of the imperial government in 456 succeeded merely in imposing Roman suzerainty over these Lazic kings. About 468 the Iranians dared to attack Colchis or, as it was now called, Lazica. At the same time Iberia turned towards the Empire. King Vakhtang I Gorgasal (*c.* 440–522)[1] was a strong monarch and, while the high nobility inclined towards Iran, he ended by espousing a pro-Roman policy. In 482 he put to death his most powerful vassal, Varskʻen, *Vitaxa* of Gogarene, who had become Zoroastrian and martyred his Christian wife, St Susan, daughter of the Mamikonid Vardan II. By this act he placed himself in open revolt against his suzerain the Great King, who had induced Varskʻen to apostatise. Vakhtang appealed to the Armenian princes for co-operation and to the Huns north of the Caucasus for aid. After some hesitation, the Armenians, led by Vardan II's nephew Vahan, joined the insurrection. Some assistance, it seems, was obtained—unofficially—from the Emperor Zeno. This insurrection had no more military success than that of 451. The Iberians were routed and the Armenians took to guerrilla warfare. Then the unexpected happened. The Great King Pērōz fell in 484 fighting the Hephthalites, and his successor Valāsh was obliged, in view of the weakened state of his realm, to re-establish peace in Caucasia. In 485 he concluded an agreement with the Armenian princes: instead of an Iranian viceroy, the Mamikonid Vahan became a presiding prince (with the title of *marzpān*), Christianity was to be undisturbed, while Zoroastrianism was proscribed. Peace was also

---

[1] For the chronology of this monarch adopted here and his identification with the Gurgenes of Procopius (*Bell. pers.* 1. 12. 1–13; 2. 28. 20), see C. Toumanoff's review of E. Stein's *Histoire du Bas-Empire*, II, in *Trad.* VII (1949–51), and 'Iberia on the Eve of Bagratid Rule', *Le Muséon*, LXV (1952).

made with Vakhtang of Iberia; and this made possible his *rapproche-ment* with the Empire. Vakhtang adhered to Zeno's religious policy and, in recompense, his chief bishop was raised, in 486/8, to the rank of a *Katholikos*, dependent on Antioch.[1] In Albania, too, the Arsacids were temporarily restored, with Vach'agan III. The peace of Valāsh lasted until the following century.

When he broke the Hundred Years Peace with the Empire, the Great King Kavādh I also broke the peace of Valāsh in Caucasia. In Kavādh's Roman war of 502–6, Vakhtang of Iberia refused to participate; Kavādh must have resumed the Zoroastrianising policy towards Iberia after his restoration in 498/9 and thus again have turned Vakhtang against Iran. In 513/14 the Armenians unsuccessfully rose against the Great King, and lost their autonomy. The guarantee of religious freedom, thereupon conceded by Kavādh, may indicate that the revolt had been caused by his failure to observe the stipulations of 485. About that time, King Damnazes of Lazica professed Zoroastrianism and passed to Iranian allegiance. Thus the Sassanids now controlled the whole of Caucasia, except for Iberia where they seem to have met with considerable resistance. But by 517/18 an Iranian viceroy had been installed at Tiflis, the capital, and Vakhtang, apparently, reduced to a part of his realm; and this must have caused his appeal for protection to Justin I. Meantime, Damnazes' successor Tzathus I returned to Christianity and Roman allegiance, and an imperial army was dispatched to Lazica. But the aid to Vakhtang proved insufficient, and, unable to withstand the foe, the aged king fled to West Georgia. All these events led to the Persian war which Justinian inherited from Justin in 527 and terminated in the peace of 532. The *status quo* in Caucasia was then restored, with Armenia divided as before, Iberia in Iranian hands, and Lazica under Roman control.

The Empire's attempts to consolidate its position in Caucasia led to a reduction of local autonomies and to oppression by provincial officialdom. Zeno had already infringed the sovereign rights of the princes of the *Gentes*. In 532 Justinian suppressed these principalities altogether. Their military independence had already been destroyed by 528, with the creation of the *magister militum per Armeniam*, in command of five *duces*; and in 536 the newly annexed territories were organised as the provinces of First Armenia (the former kingdom) and Fourth Armenia (the *Gentes*). Finally, so as to crush the

---

[1] See C. Toumanoff, 'Christian Caucasia', §§ 31–5, and, for this ecclesiastical title, see above p. 599, n. 1. In choosing it, Iberia, like Albania later on, followed the example of Armenia. Later in the middle ages, Abasgia (West Georgia), following the East Georgian example, also had a *Katholikos* at the head of its ecclesiastical organisation.

economic independence of the now 'mediatised' dynasts of Roman Armenia, the Emperor, beginning in 535, strove to quash the local law of agnatic succession. All this and the behaviour of Roman officials caused Armenia to revolt in 539 and to appeal to the Great King. A similar picture was presented by Lazica: Roman representatives bullied the king and robbed the population until Gubazes II likewise appealed to Chosroes I for aid. The peace of 532 had meantime been broken and the second Persian war begun in Syria. Chosroes heeded the two appeals; in 541 Iranian forces occupied Lazica with its great fortress of Petra; and in 543 war was carried into Armenia. When a truce was concluded in 545, Lazica was not included in its provisions.

But Iranian control implied Zoroastrianising, and soon Gubazes II and his people again turned to the Empire. From 549 to 557 war was waged on Lazic territory and was complicated by the pro-Iranian sympathies of Lazica's vassal principalities of Abkhazia and Suania, and by the murder of Gubazes by an imperial official which nearly sent the kingdom back into the Great King's arms. This was averted by the Emperor's justice and the solemn installation of the slain king's brother Tzathus II. When the Lazic war ended in 561, Iran abandoned all claims to West Georgia, though the question of Suania was left undecided.

The Fifty Years Peace of 561 lasted three years longer than the 'Limitless Peace' of 532. In 572, with the assassination of the Iranian viceroy by the Mamikonid Vardan III, another insurrection flared up in Armenia which was joined by some Iberians. The insurgents appealed to the Empire, and Justin II decided to aid them. This, together with other events, led to another Persian war, which was to last till 591. The war was not at first propitious to the Christians. By 575 Iran regained control over Armenia and, undoubtedly, Iberia. There, the defeat in 522 of Vakhtang Gorgasal had spelt victory no less for his vassals than for his Iranian overlord. The powers of his successors were curtailed and they were relegated, with an empty royal title, to their demesne of Kakhetia, on the Albanian border, while an Iranian viceroy and the princes ruled at Tiflis. But soon the latter grew impatient of even the restricted Crown; and when, in 580, King Bacurius III died leaving young sons, the Iberian princes, exactly like their Armenian confrères, transferred their allegiance to the Great King. With this, the Iberian Crown went into abeyance.[1]

---

[1] For the facts and the chronology of the abolition of the Iberian monarchy, see C. Toumanoff, 'Iberia on the Eve of Bagratid Rule', I. The curtailment of the powers of Vakhtang Gorgasal's successors was mistaken by Procopius (*Bell. pers.* 2. 28. 20–1) for the abolition itself.

Of the Lazic kings, nothing is known after Tzathus II; probably the extinction of the dynasty led to the passing of the kingdom under direct Roman control. Thus by the end of the sixth century all the Christian Caucasian states had become kingless.

II. EPOCH OF THE PRINCIPATES

The Persian war inherited from Justin II by his successors entered a new phase in 582 with the counter-offensive of Maurice. Meanwhile, Hormizd IV's burdensome fiscal measures and, it seems, oppressive religious policy made the Iberian high nobility less pro-Iranian and, without a Romanophile Crown to oppose, more pro-Roman. Maurice's victories and the Turkish attack on Iran released Iberia from Sassanid control; in 588 the Iberian princes passed to imperial allegiance and requested the Emperor to give them a Chosroid as king. The former royal house was then composed of two branches: the elder, royal, branch having Kakhetia as its appanage, and the younger, the Guaramid, branch, ruling the south-western provinces of Cholarzene (Klarjet'i) and Javakhet'i. The Emperor's choice fell on Guaram of Cholarzene-Javakhet'i, who appears to have led the revolt of 572 in Iberia.[1] But instead of becoming a king, Guaram, who received the high dignity of Curopalate, was appointed to be a presiding prince of Iberia, combining the functions of High Constable with those of imperial viceroy. Thus the system of the principate, already adumbrated in Armenia in 485, was introduced into Caucasia. In the peace of 591,[2] which terminated the war, Chosroes II, son of Hormizd, recognised the *fait accompli* in Iberia, but retained the eastern part of the country.

In Armenia the peace of 591 pushed the Roman frontier roughly to the line between lakes Van and Sevan, with Dvin in the reduced Iranian part. But the Roman victory was not to the advantage of the Armenians who now had to endure all the rigours of centralisation and officialdom, foreign to their dynastic-feudal ideas. Like Justinian, Maurice resorted to mass deportation of Armenians to Europe. Iranian suzerainty appeared light in comparison, and the court of Ctesiphon was not slow in assuming the role of protector of the Armenian princes. These, however, dreamt of independence; there were revolts against both the Emperor and the Great King, which the two joined forces to quell. In this turmoil, the heroic Mamikonids lost their ascendancy over the other princes, while the star of the

---

[1] The principate of Iberia and its chronology, as well as the identity of Guaram of Cholarzene-Javakhet'i with the Gorgenes of Theophanes of Byzantium and John of Ephesus are discussed by C. Toumanoff in 'Iberia on the Eve of Bagratid Rule'.

[2] *DR*, 104.

cautious Bagratids began to rise: at the end of the sixth century, Smbat IV Bagratuni, *persona gratissima* at the courts of Ctesiphon and of Constantinople, was the most important dynast in Armenia.

During this period the solidarity of Caucasia was rent by the religious rupture between Armenia and Iberia. Zeno's *Henoticon*, which attempted to bridge the gap between Catholicism and Monophysitism, had been accepted by both countries, and also by Albania, at the Council of Dvin of 506. Fear of Nestorianism and of Syro-Iranian influence, once forced upon them by the Sassanids, made the Armenians, especially of the Iranian zone, together with the Monophysites, imagine that they saw a Nestorian tinge in Chalcedon. Added fear of absorption by the Empire, coupled with strong Monophysite influence, finally determined the Armenian reaction to Justin I's reunion with Rome in 519 and the Empire's return to the faith of Chalcedon. The Armenian bishops, at another Council of Dvin, in 555 officially adopted Monophysitism. With this, the national Armenian Church was born. In Roman Armenia, however, though Justin II's attempt at reunion in 572 had failed, Catholicism was maintained for a while by Maurice. Between 591 and 610/11 there were two Armenian *Katholikoi*: the Catholic in the Roman zone and the Monophysite in the Iranian. Lazica and Iberia followed the Emperor's religion; and Albania was long to waver between Catholic and national Armenian Christianity. It is against this background, complicated by the Armenian Church's desire to assert its ascendancy over the Iberian, that Cyrion I, *Katholikos* of Iberia, and the Monophysite Armenian *Katholikos* Abraham clashed in 607. At still another Council of Dvin in 608/9, the latter excommunicated Cyrion and the Iberians, and the seeds of discord were sown between the two nations.[1]

The overthrow of Maurice by Phocas gave rise to another, and final, Persian war, of 604–29. The initial success was Chosroes II's, who between 607 and 612 united the whole of Armenia under his aegis; in the late 590's Stephen I of Iberia, Guaram's son, had already accepted Iranian overlordship.[2] But the accession of Heraclius and the

---

[1] G. Garitte's critical edition of the *Narratio de rebus Armeniae* (see above p. 598, n. 1) and his commentary on this text make it necessary to revise some hitherto accepted notions of Armenian religious history down to the eighth century; cf. C. Toumanoff, 'Christian Caucasia'. The formation of the national Armenian (Monophysite) Church was connected with that of the national calendar.—See the following note.

[2] Cf. C. Toumanoff, 'Christian Caucasia', pp. 37–40. Anxious to separate its Christian vassals from the Empire, the Sassanid government tended, after 519, to patronise Monophysitism in Caucasia. Accordingly, Stephen I's Iranophile policy entailed the installation as *Katholikos* of a Monophysite: Cyrion (Kyrion) I. When, however, the latter gave up Monophysitism for Catholicism, he came into conflict with his former co-religionist, Abraham of Iranian Armenia.

opening of his counter-offensive in 622 turned the tide. The following year saw the Byzantines return to Armenia and Albania. When Heraclius came to Iberia in 626, Stephen I refused to abandon the Iranian alliance; but he was killed during the siege of Tiflis in 627, and the Emperor, departing for Iran, conferred the principate upon Adarnase of Kakhetia, son of the last king. With the aid of the Emperor's Khazar allies, Adarnase finally took Tiflis. Another Iberian ally of Iran, Vahrām-Arshusha V of Gogarene, was captured in December 627, when the Iranians were defeated by Heraclius. Chosroes was overthrown and in June 629 his successor accepted the Byzantine terms of peace. In Armenia, accordingly, the frontier of 591 was re-established. Each moiety was placed under a local prince: Varaz-Tirots' II Bagratuni as viceroy for the Great King and Mezezius Gnuni as commander-in-chief for the Emperor. In 635 the latter was overthrown by David Saharuni upon whom, in view of the princely support he had received, the Emperor had to confer the principate of Armenia and the dignity of Curopalate: the Iberian pattern was followed in Armenia. In Albania, too, the principate was introduced, during Heraclius' campaigns, in favour of Varaz-Gregory, the Mihranid Prince of Gardman. As trans-Cyran Albania was occupied about this time by the Khazars, the new arrangement chiefly concerned the cis-Cyran regions. The appearance, in that century, of two successive 'Patricians of Lazica' may indicate the setting up of a similar institution in West Georgia. Nearly the whole of Caucasia was now controlled by the Empire; and in 632/3 Heraclius secured Armenian adherence to Chalcedon.

The destruction of Sassanid power paved the way for a new foe. Within two decades, Roman overlordship in Caucasia was replaced by that of the Caliphate. The Saracens began raiding Armenia in 640–6. In spite of Constans II's attempts to regain Armenia in 647, the princes, aware of the uncertainty of the Byzantine position, of Byzantine bureaucratic high-handedness, and of their own religious separateness, turned, under the leadership of Theodore Ṛshtuni, to the invaders. A peace concluded by Theodore and the future Caliph Muʻāwiya I in 653/4 recognised Armenia as an autonomous tributary state. At the same time, Stephen II of Iberia accepted Saracen suzerainty, Tiflis becoming an Arab enclave, and so also Juansher of Albania. The three Caucasian states now formed one viceroyalty of the Caliphate (designated as *Armīniya*), Dvin being the seat of the viceroys. The following two centuries were marked, especially for Armenia, by a fierce tug-of-war between Byzantine interference and Saracen reprisal, with the presiding princes wavering between the two allegiances and national consolidation thwarted by ceaseless strife.

All imperial attempts to regain Caucasia proved abortive. In 654 Constans II launched his second offensive. Supported by the Mamikonids and the Bagratids, he overran a great part of Armenia, while the Princes of Iberia, Albania and Siunia sided with Theodore Ṛshtuni. The Emperor proceeded, somewhat forcibly, to re-establish religious unity; and appointed Musheḷ Mamikonian his viceroy, who, as soon as Constans departed, went over to the Arabs. Yet the latter were not compliant overlords. Ṛshtuni was deposed and replaced by his son-in-law, the Mamikonid Hamazasp II, who lost no time in bringing the country into Byzantine obedience and was made a Curopalate in recompense. His brother Gregory, to whom the Caliph, having again subdued Armenia, next gave the principate, revolted against his suzerain in 681/2, joined by Adarnase II of Iberia; and, in 684, together with him, perished in the Khazar raid on Caucasia.

The Caliph then transferred his favour from the Mamikonids to the Bagratids in Armenia and, in Iberia, from the Chosroids to the Guaramids. The principate of the Bagratid Ashot II coincided with another Byzantine offensive, undertaken by Justinian II. At first successful, the Emperor restored Byzantine suzerainty over the three Caucasian states (685). In Armenia, the Curopalate Nerseh Kamsarakan replaced Ashot II, and religious union with the Empire was momentarily re-established. This was ephemeral. The three countries had reverted to the Caliphate by 693; and in 696/7, even Lazica, under the Patrician Sergius, passed from Byzantine to Saracen control. The Arab successes and the devastation wrought in Caucasia in 693 by the Emperor's Khazar allies caused Smbat VI Bagratuni, whom Justinian had named to the principate of Armenia, to go over to the enemy and wage something of a family feud with the Emperor Tiberius III (II).

The independent spirit of the dynasts twice inspired the Saracens to attempt to suppress them. The first effort by the viceroy ʿAbd Allāh ibn-Ḥātim, it is true, was limited to arrests and confiscations (c. 695); and the good offices of the Armenian Church brought about an improvement of Armeno-Arab relations. So good, in fact, had these relations become that, when, in 702/704, Albania attempted to espouse Catholic, instead of Armenian, Christianity, the *Katholikos*, who regarded it as a dependency, did not hesitate to invoke the Caliph's aid in forcibly restoring that country to Armenian obedience. Meantime, outraged by ʿAbd Allāh's actions, Smbat VI passed back to the Empire, was made a Curopalate, and warred successfully on the Arabs, though in the end he could maintain himself only on the north-western confines of Armenia.

In 705, upon his defeat by the joint forces of Smbat VI and the Emperor, the viceroy Muḥammad ibn-Marwān decided to carry out the idea, reborn under the new Caliph, al-Walīd, of exterminating the Armenian high nobility. Several hundred Armenian lords with their families and retainers were inveigled into Nakhchevan and there were locked up in churches and burnt, or crucified after torture. This terrible holocaust sent many princes fleeing the country, and Smbat VI removed to Lazica, which had meantime reverted to the Empire. Armenia lay at the Caliph's mercy; yet he changed his policy. The constant menace of the Khazars, allies of Byzantium, made Armenia more desirable as a buffer state than as a province. The exiled princes were invited to return, their property and privileges guaranteed. It was then that the fickle Smbat VI, having quarrelled with the Byzantines, pillaged the city of Phasis, where he was residing, and returned to Saracen Armenia (711). At this time too, apparently, the Prince of Abkhazia became the Caliph's vassal.

The Khazar invasion of Caucasia in the 730's seems to have aided the Empire in recovering Abkhazia and retaining Lazica, but it also helped to bring about a collaboration of the rest of Caucasia with the Caliphate. In the principate of Smbat VI's cousin Ashot III, Armenians took part in Marwān ibn-Muḥammad's war on the Khazars, in the course of which West Georgia was attacked and trans-Cyran Albania wrested from the Khazars by the Arabs (736–7). Ashot was supported by the Caliph against insubordination at home; he in turn strove to aid the Umayyads against the Abbasids.

The civil war of 744–50 in the Caliphate coincided with a new Byzantine offensive of Constantine V. The anti-Arab elements in Caucasia stirred; and in 748 Ashot III was deposed and blinded by the Mamikonid princes, Gregory and David, the political differences between the two houses having become a family feud. Gregory seized the principate and turned to the Empire; after his death, the third brother Mushel continued to head the anti-Arab lords. At that time the Guaramids of Iberia were replaced in the principate by a new dynasty, represented by Adarnase III, whose title of Curopalate indicated a return to imperial allegiance. But the Empire proved once again to be a broken reed; its thrust into north-western Armenia failed; and the Abbasids, once in power, held Caucasia as firmly as the Umayyads. Though disliking the Bagratids for Ashot III's Umayyad loyalty, they disliked the Byzantinophile Mamikonids more. So Isaac III Bagratuni, Ashot's cousin, was named ruling High Constable of Armenia *c.* 755. By this time the Bagratids, no less than the Mamikonids, had been weakened; and a new power was rising in Armenia, the Artsrunis, who, having spread their rule to the south-eastern province of Vaspurakan (including Bagratid Kogovit and Tamoritis), were building up a strongly fortified princely state.

Abbasid rule proved heavier than Umayyad, especially fiscally. Caucasia was annually drained of ten million dirhams in taxes. The oppression of a series of viceroys made matters worse. New revolts flared up in Armenia. In 771 Artavazd Mamikonian led a popular uprising, but was defeated by the loyalist Smbat VII Bagratuni, Ashot III's son and Isaac III's successor as High Constable. Then another Mamikonid, Mushel, returned to the scene as leader of another insurrection. Soon other princes joined it, Samuel, head of the Mamikonid dynasty, and his son-in-law, Smbat VII himself, among them. The Artsrunis, however, tended to keep aloof. Like all other revolts, that of 771–2 was doomed. Constantine V did not heed the appeals of the princes, while al-Manṣūr poured troops into Armenia. In two great battles, of Archēsh on 15 April 772, and of Bagravandene on 25 April, the insurgents were utterly crushed. The flower of the nobility, including Smbat, Samuel and Mushel, fell in this war. For a time the principate was left vacant.

The immediate repercussion of this defeat was also felt in Iberia. Adarnase III's son Nerse[1] was carried off to Baghdad and Saracen suzerainty was reasserted. But, with the accession of al-Mahdī to the Caliphate (775), Nerse was allowed to return to Iberia. Armenia, too, was soon given a presiding prince. Tachat Andzevats'i, one of the lesser princes, having been *strategus* of the Bucellarians in imperial service and then fallen into disgrace under Irene, fled to the Arabs. Seizing this opportunity of counterbalancing both the Bagratids and the Artsrunis, the Caliph appointed him to be High Constable in 780. But he fell in a joint Armeno-Arab campaign against the Khazars *c.* 785.

Armenia groaned under Abbasid oppression; but it was chiefly the Georgians, backed by the Khazars, who now offered resistance. The centres of discontent were Iberia proper and the Chosroid princedom of Kakhetia. In reprisal, the viceroy Khuzaima ibn-Khāzim resorted to the same policy of extermination as had been seen in Armenia in 705. In 786 he caused the decapitation of many Caucasian dynasts, including Stephen III of Iberia, Nerse's nephew, and the Chosroid St Arch'il of Kakhetia. The Guaramids became extinct and the Chosroids neared extinction. After this, the Caliph appointed no presiding princes in either Armenia or Iberia; and these countries were administered directly by his representatives.

---

[1] Armenian and Georgian forms of the same *praenomina* differ occasionally, thus: Atrnerseh and Adarnase, Bagarat and Bagrat, Gurgēn and Gurgen, Smbat and Sumbat, Nerseh or Nersēs and Nerse.

Caucasia was devastated, its aristocracy reduced and decimated by wars and repression. Nobles and peasants began removing in large numbers to the Empire. And yet these disasters contained the seeds of future recovery. The Saracen insistence on collecting taxes and tribute in money, not in kind, led to an economic revival. The nobility and peasantry found themselves obliged to abandon their autarkic rural economy and to produce a surplus of raw and manufactured products for sale. Thus commerce and urban economy, stifled during the upheavals of the Sassanid and Saracen domination, recovered; the middle class revived; new cities, like Ani, Kars, Baḷēsh (Bitlis), Artanuji, rose beside the old, such as Artaxata, Dvin, Theodosiopolis, Tiflis, Partav (Bardha'a). Caucasia once again became the nexus of trade-routes connecting Europe and Asia, and the prosperity of the medieval period was founded.

Then, too, the ruin and extinction of many dynastic houses profited the few that remained intact. Instead of numerous principalities, a few larger ones arose, composed of a number of former princedoms; and a few great princes, suzerains of their once co-equal and now weakened confrères, held sway in Caucasia. The Bagratids at first (after 772) lost all their domains, save Syspiritis, whither Smbat VII's son Ashot IV fled after the disaster. But the silver mines he possessed there enabled him to purchase from the tottering Kamsarakans the principalities of Arsharunik' and Siracene. He wrested some Mamikonid territory from the Arab amir Jaḥḥāf the 'Qaysid' and, directly from the Mamikonids, Taraun and southern Tayk'. Other successes awaited his dynasty. His cousin Adarnase, son of Smbat VII's younger brother Vasak, removed to Iberia after 772. There he acquired the lands of Erushet'i and Artani (Ardahan), and, at the turn of the century, inherited the state of the Guaramids, comprising Cholarzene, Javakhet'i, and northern Tayk', or Tao, taken earlier from the Mamikonids. With the extermination of many Iberian princes in 786, this younger Bagratid branch became the leading house of Iberia.

Finally, the growth of local separatism in the Caliph's empire further contributed to Bagratid hegemony in Caucasia. The Arab Qaysids were entrenched in the fortress-town of Manazkert (Manzikert), north of Van, and defied the Caliph. In 792–3 there was a Muslim revolt in south-eastern Albania. In 809 the amir of Tiflis, Ismā'īl ibn-Shu'aib, proclaimed his independence. In 813–37 eastern Armenia was involved in the revolt of Bābak. In the 820's the Qaysids of Manazkert attacked Dvin, the seat of the viceroys having been transferred to Bardha'a. Another amirate was established, about this time, at Arzen. The Caliph's government was compelled to seek the support of a Caucasian dynasty. Distrustful of the growing Artsrunis and anxious to forestall an *entente* of the Empire and the Bagratids, whose state lay on the Byzantine frontier, it chose the latter. The Bagratids had the added advantage of being at once in Armenia and in Iberia. Accordingly, in 806 the principate was revived in the former country for Ashot IV the Brave and in 813 in the latter for Adarnase's son Ashot I the Great. Thenceforth the two principates became a Bagratid monopoly. In 813, too, the Emperor Leo V, himself an Armenian, possibly a Gnunid prince,[1] conferred the title of Curopalate upon Ashot of Iberia. The latter was happy to counterbalance Baghdad by Constantinople, while Leo V was eager to restore imperial influence in Caucasia. By then the Empire had lost its Lazic dependency: in the 790's, Leo II of Abkhazia subdued all of West Georgia, founding the kingdom of Abasgia virtually independent of Constantinople.[2]

Kakhetia had in the meantime, after the extinction of the Chosroids, seceded from Iberia under its own presiding princes. Southeast of it, cis-Cyran Albania (Arrān) was inherited in 821/2 from the House of Gardman by Atrnerseh, of Siunid lineage. So now Caucasia was divided into the following large states: the kingdom of Abasgia; Armenia with the Bagratid principalities of Bagaran (Arsharunik'-Siracene) and Taraun, Artsrunid Vaspurakan, Siunia, and the Muslim amirates; Iberia with the Bagratid principalities of Tao, Cholarzene, and Javakhet'i, the amirate of Tiflis, and Kakhetia; and Albania with lesser princedoms dependent on it.[3]

In the ninth century some of the larger states also weakened owing to a new development in the dynastic law. The system of patrilineal seniority had become modified through the granting of appanages and the occasional partition of states among brothers. When Ashot IV

---

[1] C. Toumanoff, 'Introduction', II, p. 12, no. 14 and n. 228.—The *comes Obsequii* Mezezius, who was proclaimed Emperor by the armies in Sicily upon the murder of Constans II in September 668 and was killed at the beginning of 669, belonged to the same princely family.

[2] 'Abkhazia' renders the narrow sense of *Ap'khazet'i*, that is, the north-western-most province of West Georgia; 'Abasgia' translates the same word in its broad sense of the medieval kingdom coextensive with West Georgia; cf. C. Toumanoff, 'Chronology of the Kings of Abasgia and Other Problems', *Le Muséon*, LXIX (1956), 73.

[3] Several Caucasian dynasties claimed the title of Albania: (1) the Mihranid princes of Gardman, set up by Heraclius as presiding princes of (cis-Cyran) Albania and, from 821/2, their Siunid successors, whom the expanding Shirvānshāhs, Muzāfarids of Azerbaijan, Bagratids of Loṛi, and Shaddādids reduced to the territory of P'aṛisos on the Albano-Siunian border; (2) the dynasty founded at the end of the ninth century in Shakki and Heret'i, in trans-Cyran Albania, which however was ultimately superseded by the rulers of Kakhetia; and (3) the Bagratids of Loṛi who, by virtue of holding some Albanian lands, regarded themselves as kings of Albania.

died in 826 Taraun passed to his eldest son Bagarat II, and Bagaran to another, Smbat VIII. The sons of Ashot of Iberia likewise divided his state: Adarnase II took Tao and Cholarzene, Bagrat I had the principate, with the dignity of Curopalate which had become attached to it, and Guaram Javakhet'i. Siunia and Vaspurakan became similarly divided.

Seeing in division the only guarantee of its hold on Caucasia, in 826 the Caliphate appointed Smbat VIII to be his father's successor as High Constable, while the title of 'Prince of Princes of Armenia' was given to Bagarat II, but not until 830. A quarrel between the brothers inevitably followed. Nevertheless, the Bagratids now enjoyed indisputable hegemony in Armenia and Iberia, and converting this into kingship was merely a matter of time. Meantime, Caucasia was to sustain another Byzantine offensive and another Saracen oppression.

As part of his Arab war, in 837 the Emperor Theophilus led two campaigns in Armenia: in the north-west and in the south-west. Faced with Byzantine devastations, the Princes of Taraun and of Vaspurakan sided with the Saracens, even participating, after the Emperor's defeat, in the Arab reprisal of 838. Theophilus' only success was to install an Armenian Bagratid in Syspiritis as a vassal of the Empire.

The Saracen oppression was far worse. The last energetic Abbasid, al-Mutawakkil, resolved to suppress the growing Christian and Muslim independencies of Caucasia. Three punitive expeditions were sent thither, of which the last, led by Bugha, was marked by a particular ferocity. By 855 Taraun had been reduced to ruins, Vaspurakan, Siunia, Albania, Tiflis subdued, the heads of all the princely states taken prisoner to Sāmarrā, including Smbat VIII, who had loyally co-operated with the Caliph's Turkish general. It was then that he earned his appellation of Confessor by rejecting liberation at the price of a feigned apostasy and dying in captivity between 862 and 867. Only Bagrat of Iberia, who, too, was loyal to the Caliph, remained on his throne, happy to see Bugha's reduction of the amirate of Tiflis. Once again Armenia was at the Caliph's mercy, and once again he changed his policy. The Paulician and the Arab war of Michael III in 856–9 and the growing impotence of the Caliphate itself after al-Mutawakkil's death in 861 made it imperative to cultivate the Caucasian princes. So most of the captives were allowed to return. In 856 Smbat VIII's son, Ashot V, had already been made High Constable; in 862 he was recognised as Prince of Princes: even the *divide et impera* policy was abandoned by the Caliphate, whose tutelage over Caucasia was visibly coming to an end.

III. BAGRATID RESTORATION AND THE PREDOMINANCE OF ARMENIA

Caucasia's historical existence hinged on its consolidation and on the equipoise between its imperial neighbours. In the second half of the ninth century, the Caliphate could no longer control it, and the Empire, faced with the Bulgar and the Saracen, seemed uninterested in dominating it. So, when the ascendancy of the Bagratids in Armenia was crowned by the predominance among them of one man —Ashot V the Great—its independence became a matter of mere formality. True enough, his endeavour to ensure the equipoise of empires by securing the support of Constantinople was hampered by the refusal of the Armenian Church to respond to Photius' advances (862).[1] But he achieved Armenia's consolidation, thanks both to his personality and to his policy. Dynastic alliances spread his influence to Vaspurakan, Siunia, and Iberia; his scrupulous loyalty towards the Caliph sanctioned his control over all the Caucasian rulers, Christian and Muslim; the national Church lent him its wholehearted support. Even the princely feuds, weakening others, enhanced his power. During his Saracen campaigns in the 870's the Emperor Basil I imposed Byzantine suzerainty on Taraun and, to oppose the Caliph's vassal, appointed another Ashot, Bagarat II of Taraun's son, to be Curopalate of Armenia; but the latter was at once captured by the Prince of Vaspurakan; Taraun passed to another brother, while Ashot the Great remained a satisfied observer. The Empire was clearly adopting the policy of division just abandoned by the Caliphate. Ashot, meantime, was enlarging his state: he acquired, somewhat violently, the Mamikonid principality of Bagravandene and inherited some border territory from Guaram of Javakhet'i.

It was historical justice that the Armenian princes, whose ancestors had demanded the abolition of the monarchy in 428, should in 885 have requested the Caliph to recognise Ashot as their king. Sanctioning what was beyond his control, al-Mu'tamid sent a crown and royal vestments to Ashot, who was solemnly crowned at his capital of Bagaran by the *Katholikos* George II. Basil I also hastened to send a crown to the new king and to conclude a treaty of friendship with him. Armenia was again independent, though still bound to pay tribute to the Caliph; this, however, was now complied with only

---

[1] The so-called 'Letter of Photius' to the *Katholikos* Zacharias regarding the union with the Byzantine Church is apocryphal, as has been shown by G. Garitte, *Narratio*, pp. 370–5; cf. C. Toumanoff, 'Caucasia and Byzantine Studies', *Trad.* XII (1956), 410 and n. 7. It exists only in Armenian and is based on the prototype of the Armenian text (now lost) of the *Narratio*. Another part of this document purports to be Photius' letter to Ashot V of Armenia.

occasionally and under duress. The Crown, replacing both the Caliph's viceroy and the presiding prince, was the guarantee of national autonomy and a symbol of unity; in assuming it, Bagratid suzerainty over the other dynasts was consecrated.

Ashot the Great inherited from the viceroys of old the claim to control Iberia and Albania. In Iberia the Empire and Abasgia were anxious to counter-balance that hegemony. In 881 the pro-Armenian Curopalate David I, son of Bagrat I, was murdered by his cousin, and a civil war followed. The murderer was supported by the Byzantines and the Abasgians, while David's son Adarnase IV was aided by the King of Armenia and the Liparitids, a Mamikonid branch established in Lower Iberia. True to the policy of division, the Emperor confirmed as Curopalate, not Adarnase, but his cousin Gurgēn I of Tao. Adarnase, however, was victorious in 888. Not being a Curopalate and having Armenia's example before him, he assumed the title of king. Thus, within three years, the Bagratids restored the two major monarchies of Caucasia. (It was, however, only in 899 that Armenia recognised Adarnase's royal status.) As in Armenia, the Emperor adapted himself to the circumstances and, upon Gurgēn of Tao's death in 891, recognised Adarnase IV as Curopalate.

The complexity of the Caucasian political system was increased by the fact that, parallel to the Armenian monarchy and its dependencies, there existed the supra-national, dynastic condominium of the Bagratids. The King of Armenia was its doyen and the King of Iberia second after him; then came the other Bagratid branches: Taraun, and later Kars and Lori, in Armenia, and Tao and Cholarzene-Artanuji in Iberia. Neither system was however to survive. The delicate fabric of Bagratid rule in Armenia was menaced from the outset by feudal insubordination and foreign pressure; and the condominium collapsed through a lack of family solidarity.

The Caliphate might grow weak, but not its Muslim vassals. The half-rebellious Sājids were building a powerful state in Azerbaijan, which Armenia found to be an implacable foe. Despite some successes against the amirs of Dvin and Manazkert, the reign of Ashot's son, Smbat I the Martyr (890–914), was made tragic by the recalcitrance of his uncle, the High Constable Abas, of Siunia and of Vaspurakan. He was also especially harassed by the repeated invasions of the Sājid amirs Afshīn and Yūsuf, with whom the Artsrunis treacherously threw in their lot. In 908 the Artsrunid Khach'ik-Gagik of Vaspurakan was proclaimed king by Yūsuf; and Armenia became divided into two monarchies. At the same time Smbat I's relations with the King of Abasgia, aimed at extending Armenian influence to West Georgia, brought about a break with Abasgia's enemy, Adarnase IV of Iberia. Thus weakened, Smbat was unable to withstand Yūsuf. He was finally captured and barbarously executed by the Sājid in 914.

The death of Smbat the Martyr brought about a change. Adarnase of Iberia and Khachʻik-Gagik of Vaspurakan hastened to make peace with his son Ashot II. Yūsuf had fallen temporarily into the Caliph's hands, and Ashot II, who came to be surnamed the Iron, organised guerrilla warfare and cleared much of Armenian territory of the invaders. But it was obvious that, unaided, the Bagratids were no match for the ferocious Sājids. At that moment, the Empire appeared as an ally. Armenia, and Caucasia in general, was indispensable to it in the impending struggle with the Muslims on its eastern frontier. In the years 918–20 negotiations went on between the two courts, carried on by the Patriarch Nicholas I and one of Ashot's close collaborators, the *Katholikos* John VI, with a view to organising an alliance of all the Caucasian princes against the Saracens. The journey of Ashot II to Constantinople in 921 and the conclusion of a Byzantine–Armenian alliance was the culmination of these efforts.[1] After a splendid reception, Ashot returned to Armenia accompanied by an imperial army. In reprisal for this alliance, Yūsuf, back in Azerbaijan, set up the king's first cousin, Ashot of Bagaran and Koḷb, as an anti-king; and a civil war began. Only at the price of a humiliating peace with his father's murderer was Ashot II able to stop the war. Triumphant in the end over this and other instances of insubordination, he directed his efforts to increasing the power and prestige of the Crown. The royal domain was enlarged with the annexation of northern border lands (Samshvilde, Gardman, Otene); and to assert his suzerainty over the other Caucasian kings he assumed, *c.* 922, the title of King of Kings.

The Iberian Bagratids also had their difficulties. In 904 Constantine III of Abasgia, competing with Adarnase IV for hegemony in Georgia, seized from him the Iberian throne: this, in part, prevented the latter from aiding Smbat the Martyr. Until the end of the Abasgian domination in 975 the lawful Iberian kings were relegated to their portion of the 'Hereditary Lands' in south-western Iberia. In 941 the line of Tao became extinct, with Gurgēn II, and his state passed to Adarnase's sons. The ex-royal line was then subdivided into two branches: the elder, of the Curopalates of Iberia, in Upper Tao and other domains; the younger, of the titular kings, in Lower Tao.

Armenia reached the apogee of power, prosperity and cultural achievement under Ashot II's successors: his brother Abas I (928–52), who set up his capital at Kars; the latter's son Ashot III the Merciful (952–77), who transferred the capital to Ani; and his sons, Smbat II

[1] *DR*, 596.

the Conqueror (977–89) and Gagik I (989–1020). The King of Kings commanded an army of 80,000 (twice the number that Ashot the Great had been able to muster). The carefully cultivated and irrigated soil of Caucasia was fertile. Its industries and commerce flourished through their association with two great economic systems: the Saracen (trans-Caspian) and the Byzantine (Black Sea region). Bardha'a was the great centre of the former; Artanuji, the connecting link between the two. Caucasia exported to the Empire, *via* Trebizond, and to the Caliphate, *via* Van–Bitlis–Mosul and Dvin–Nakhchevan–Tabrīz; it offered a great variety of products: its celebrated fabrics and textiles, metal work, armour, jewellery, horses and cattle, salt, cereals, wine, honey, timber, leather and furs.

The Bagratid period brought about a renaissance of the chief art of Armenia and Georgia—architecture. It was distinguished by originality and genius, and, according to some, its influence on Byzantium and the West has been decisive. There is but one Caucasian architecture, though the Armenian aspect of it is distinct from the Georgian. Whatever the constructions of antiquity, this art came into its own in the Christian period; and the largest number of extant monuments are churches. Perhaps the two salient features of these stone constructions are the existence of two different and intricately connected plans, internal and external, and the related tendency to subordinate structural and functional considerations to decorative (plastic and geometrical) effect. A good example of this is the conically or pyramidally roofed dome. Besides differences in ornamentation, the more extravagant ('baroque') treatment of the correlation of the two plans distinguishes the Georgian style from the Armenian. The first period of Caucasian architecture, from the conversion to the Saracen overlordship, showed two principal types of churches: the centralised domed edifice—like St Hrip'simē's at Vaḷarshapat (618) and the Holy Cross (Juari) near Mts'khet'a (588–650)—and the basilica (a Graeco-Syrian importation), later domed—like those of Ereruyk' and Bolnisi (fifth–sixth centuries). After an awakening inspired by the older models, the dormancy of the Abbasid epoch passed into Bagratid renaissance, when, between the tenth and the thirteenth century, the above two types were blended into a new, cruciform domed type—as in the cathedrals of Ani (988–1000) and Kutais (1003). Emulating the Mamikonids and the Guaramids of old, the Bagratids, Armenian and Georgian, the Artsrunis and the Siunis, the Pahlavids and the Zachariads, assisted by great architects, like Tiridates of Ani and Arsakidze, vied with one another in building castles and abbeys, and embellishing their cities of Ani, Kars, Kutais, Mts'khet'a, Ostan, Aḷt'amar, Tat'ev with palaces and shrines.

Armenian architects enjoyed an international reputation; thus Odo the Armenian took part in the construction of the Palatine chapel at Aix and Tiridates of Ani restored the church of Holy Wisdom at Constantinople after the earthquake of 989. Mention should also be made of Caucasian sculpture which, deriving from Hellenistic, Sassanid, and even Sumerian sources, remained ancillary to architecture, and of Caucasian painting of similar parentage, both mural and miniature, as well as enamels.

Armenia's literary tradition was, meantime, continued.[1] Monasteries, like Tat'ev, Sevan, Haḷpat and Sinahin, were centres of intellectual activity, containing great libraries, as was the city of Kars under its kings.

The Bagratid period coincided with the great Byzantine offensive against Islam captained by men of Caucasian origin, like the Curcuae and (perhaps) the Phocae. While the Byzantines were reducing the Muslims on Armenia's western frontier, the Bagratids and the Artsrunis performed the same task in their respective realms. Yet, in the east, the momentarily powerful state of the Daylamite Musāfarids of Azerbaijan succeeded in imposing heavy tribute on various Armenian and Albanian rulers, including the kings of Armenia and of Vaspurakan. Armenia nevertheless was given the opportunity of consolidating its strength for the future; instead, however, new divisions further weakened it. In 961/2 Ashot III ceded Kars-Vanand and the title of king to his younger brother Musheḷ. In 970 Smbat II of Siunia proclaimed himself king. The kingdom of Vaspurakan was split into several appanages. Disunion penetrated the Establishment: between 969 and 972, there were two rival *Katholikoi*. All the while Siunia and Albania tended to move away from Armenian political and religious obedience, towards the political sphere of Iberia and the doctrines of Chalcedon.

Their military successes in the tenth century reawakened in the Byzantine Emperors a taste for expansion over their Christian neighbours. Though the west of Armenia had been wrested from the Muslims, expansion continued. In 968 Bagratid Taraun, long a dependency, was annexed to the Empire, the Byzantine family of the Taronitae becoming its ruling house. Then, in 974, in the course of his Saracen war, John Tzimisces approached the frontiers of the Armenian monarchy. For once feudal Armenia made a show of

---

[1] This was the age of the historians like Sebēos (seventh century), Leontius (Levond, eighth century), Pseudo-Moses of Khoren (late eighth century), the *Katholikos* John VI (d. 931), Moses of Kaḷankaytuk' or of Daskhurēn and Thomas Artsruni (tenth century), Stephen Asoḷik of Taraun (eleventh century), Aristakēs of Lastivert (d. 1071). The 'Armenian Pindar' Gregory of Narek (d. 1010) and the polyhistor Gregory Pahlavuni (d. 1058) also flourished at that time.

unity. All the princes hastened to rally round Ashot III, and the impressed Emperor concluded a treaty of alliance with the King of Kings.[1]

In spite of all the achievement, the seeds of decay were apparent in the Armenian polity. Smbat II was faced with further division and feudal strife: the revolt of his uncle Musheḷ of Kars and the formation, in 982, by his younger brother Gurgēn of the kingdom of Loṛi (Tashir), on the Iberian border, as well as with the interference of a Georgian Bagratid, the *Magister* (from 990, Curopalate) David the Great of Upper Tao. The latter's role was a symptom of the changing times: emerging at the height of Armenian history, David was the precursor, indeed the founder, of Georgia's subsequent preponderance in Caucasia. His activity, however, was not limited to Caucasia; and the Empire benefited by his intervention. Byzantium also had to face the recalcitrance of nascent feudalism among the 'powerful' of Anatolia. There the revolt of Bardas Phocas (970) was followed in 976–9 by that of his adversary Bardas Sclerus. The sympathies of the Armenian princes were with the rebel; but Phocas, placed by the imperial government at the head of their forces, was an old friend of David's. To him, accordingly, appeals for military aid were sent, along with promises of recompense.[2] David dispatched 12,000 horse under the command of his vassal T῾ornik Ch῾orduaneli, who temporarily abandoned his cell on Mt Athos for the role of a general. On 24 March 979 Phocas, with Georgian aid, defeated Sclerus at Pancalia. David received, *ad personam*, a vast territory in western Armenia stretching from Tao towards lake Van and including Theodosiopolis; he became thus the most powerful prince in Caucasia. It was possibly to counterpoise this Georgian enclave in Armenia that Smbat II countenanced the rise of the kingdom of Loṛi, an Armenian enclave in Iberia.

It was largely due to David of Upper Tao that Iberia began to unite, while Armenia was disintegrating. Being childless, he adopted his young cousin Bagrat, of the 'royal' branch of Lower Tao. Bagrat was the son of Gurgēn and grandson of the titular King of Iberia, Bagrat II the Simple; his mother was Gurandukht, sister of Theodosius III, king of Abasgia and (*de facto*) of Iberia. The boy was thus the potential heir of three crowns. As Theodosius III was unpopular with the nobility, John Marushidze, viceroy of Iberia, came to an understanding with David and with Smbat II in 975, and ceded Iberia to David. Since Bagrat was under age and his grandfather in his dotage, it was the boy's father Gurgēn who became King of Iberia. In 978/9, again through Marushidze's efforts, Theodosius III was

---

[1] *DR*, 746, 749–53. [2] *DR*, 761.

deposed and Bagrat, now of age, proclaimed King of Abasgia. But the bright prospects of the Georgian Bagratids were soon somewhat darkened. Bagrat III of Abasgia and his adopted father quarrelled in 988; a war broke out, in which the Kings of Abasgia and Iberia fought David of Tao, the dotard Bagrat II and Smbat of Armenia, and were defeated. Meantime, in 987–9, another revolt shook the Empire; Bardas Phocas was the chief rebel now, and David chose to aid him by sending him 2000 horse. Upon Phocas' defeat, David, fearing Basil II's reprisals, sought to placate the Emperor by offering to make him heir of all his lands instead of Bagrat III (990). He was forgiven and confirmed as Curopalate;[1] but his action was to have important consequences. Meantime in 994 the Bagratid condominium in Caucasia came to an end with Gurgēn, who on his father's death assumed the title of King of Kings which marked his independence of Armenian tutelage.

The civil wars within the Empire encouraged Armenia's Muslim foes. The Sallārids of Azerbaijan succeeded in imposing a tribute upon Smbat II, and attacked Vaspurakan; a new Muslim dynasty, the Marwānids, held Archēsh and Khlat' (Khīlāṭ), Martyropolis (May-yāfāriqīn) and Amida, and finally acquired Manazkert. At the same time, in Byzantine Armenia, religious tension and the old policy of transplanting Armenians to other parts of the Empire caused friction. As yet another symptom of impending decay, great numbers of Armenians began to emigrate to Cilicia and northern Syria, whence the Macedonians had driven out the Saracens.

Faced with Muslim aggression, the Curopalate David, now the veritable doyen of the Bagratids, succeeded in organising a counter-offensive. In 992/4 he took Manazkert and then, with the assistance of other Bagratids, twice defeated Mamlān of Azerbaijan's retaliatory attacks on Armenia (997, 998). David's death on 31 March 1000 provided the Byzantines with another opportunity of despoiling Christian Caucasia, and Basil II hastened to collect his inheritance. David's hereditary state of Upper Tao and all his Armenian territories were annexed to the Empire. Bagrat III, David's former heir, and his father accepted the inevitable and were recompensed: Bagrat becoming a Curopalate (in this, indeed, David's successor) and Gurgēn a *Magister*. For a time, however, other things occupied the attention of the Georgian Bagratids. In 1008 Bagrat III succeeded his father in Iberia, and, for the first time in history, the two Georgias, eastern and western, were united. David's policy was bearing fruit. The king of united Georgia then imposed his suzerainty upon Kakhetia; defeated, with the aid of Gagik I of Armenia, still another rising Muslim

---

[1] *DR*, 780.

dynasty, the Kurdish Shaddādids of Ganja in Albania (Arrān); and wrested from his Bagratid cousins the state of Cholarzene, with Artanuji, in 1101. At his death, on 7 May 1014, Georgia was the most important Caucasian kingdom.

Armenia, on the other hand, was rapidly disintegrating. Gagik I achieved some success in his struggle with his insubordinate nephew of Lori, who, in carving out for himself a considerable state, had extended his control to the amirs of Tiflis and of Ganja. But Gagik's death in 1020 opened the final chapter of Armenian history. The royal domain, now only Siracene, and the royal dignity were divided between his two sons, the corpulent and phlegmatic John-Smbat III and the energetic and ambitious Ashot IV the Valiant. A drawn-out struggle between the brothers ensued, in which the Kings of Georgia and of Vaspurakan, and even the Caliph, took part. In the meantime, the Daylamites from Azerbaijan invaded Armenia in 1021 and, between 1018 and 1021, bands of Seljuq Turks made their appearance in Vaspurakan. All the enemies of Armenia had now entered the arena. They included the Empire, which, instead of aiding these weakened and divided Armenian buffer-states in the face of the common barbarian menace, proceeded to enlarge itself at their expense. Under Byzantine pressure, the harassed Sennacherib-John of Vaspurakan ceded in 1021 his kingdom, with its ten cities, seventy-two fortresses and some 4000 villages, to the Emperor, and, recompensed with the dignity of *Magister* and domains in Cappadocia, removed thither together with his vassals. Vaspurakan became the Byzantine province of Basparacania.[1]

The kingdom of Armenia (Ani and a part of Siracene) was next. John-Smbat III repeated the error of David of Tao. Having supported George I of Georgia in his unsuccessful wars with Basil II,[2] he now sought to appease the victor by proposing in 1022 to designate him as his heir.[3] He, too, was given the titles of *Magister* and of *Archon* of Ani and Great Armenia, as well as, later, the hand of the Emperor Romanus III's niece. When he died, childless, in 1040, having survived Ashot IV by a year, the Emperor Michael IV claimed the inheritance. Within the reduced kingdom, high personages, like the *Katholikos* Peter and the *Vestes* Sargis Siuni, sided with the Empire; but Vahrām (Kamsarakan-)Pahlavuni rallied the nobility and the troops round Ashot IV's son Gagik, who was proclaimed king. With the aid of Vahrām and his learned nephew Gregory, Gagik II was able to repel both the Byzantine attack and the incursions of the King of Lori and of the Shaddādid amir of Dovin, whom the

---

[1] *DR*, 809.   [2] See below: p. 621.
[3] *DR*, 813.

Emperor Constantine IX did not scruple to incite against the Christian King of Armenia. Soon, however, the Pahlavids were superseded at court by the treacherous Sargis Siuni. With his and the *Katholikos'* assistance, Gagik II was inveigled into Constantinople in 1045 and there bullied into abdication. He received the usual domains in Cappadocia and the dignity of *Magister*, and a palace in the imperial capital to boot. His kingdom was annexed and placed under the *dux* of Byzantine Iberia, that is, of the territories wrested from Georgia: the consequences of two foolish bequests thrown together. The Armenian nobility began to emigrate in great numbers to Georgia or, following the exiled kings, to the Empire, some, like the Pahlavids, exchanging their domains for imperial fiefs. If the annexation was a crime, the government of Constantine IX now committed an error that was *plus qu'un crime*. Needing money, they replaced the feudal levy-in-mass obligations by heavy taxation. Armenia was not only leaderless, but also disarmed.

The Empire did not long enjoy its spoils. Beginning in 1045/6 Armenia was subjected to repeated Seljuq attacks, and in 1064 Ani fell to Alp Arslan. In that year, the King of Kars, Gagik-Abas, ceded his state to the Empire on the usual conditions, but it was snatched by the Turks. A few sovereigns still remained in Armenia. The Kings of Loṛi and of Siunia, having accepted Seljuq suzerainty, survived until the 1090's; upon the extinction of the House of Siunia, its now reduced territories were inherited by the House of Gardman-Albania (P'aṛisos), which, in turn, became extinct in 1166, when its entire, but diminished, inheritance devolved upon the Princes of Khach'ēn. In the south, the Artsrunis held the principality of Moxoene and the Mamikonids reigned, at first under imperial suzerainty, in Sasun and Arsamosata until their dispossession in 1189/90 by the new Muslim power in Armenia, the Shāh-Arman dynasty. Later, in the twelfth and thirteenth centuries, the Armenian house of the Zachariads (Mkhargrdzeli) ruled in northern Armenia at Ani, Loṛi, Kars, and Dvin under the Georgian aegis.

Religious and ethnic animosities between the Armenian dynasts settled in Cappadocia and the Byzantines led to excesses such as the brutal murder, on Gagik II's orders, of the Metropolitan of Caesarea and, ultimately, to Gagik's own death and those of the remaining Armenian royalties, at the hands of the Byzantines, in 1079–80. Meanwhile, Alp Arslan captured Manazkert in 1070. And it was there that he inflicted, the following year, the momentous defeat upon the Emperor Romanus IV which deprived the Empire of Armenia and opened to the Turks the road to Anatolia.

IV. PREDOMINANCE OF GEORGIA

The Georgian Bagratids were more successful than their Armenian cousins in building a united national monarchy. Both, indeed, had to face feudal insubordination, division and Saracen enclaves at home; but in Georgia's case, geography rendered foreign aggression less deadly. With the decline and dismemberment of Iberia after 786, Tao and Cholarzene—the 'Hereditary' Lands of the Bagratids, soon to be free from the Caliph's control, yet still buttressed by imperial suzerainty—became the cultural and economic centre of Georgia. Thence the Bagratids embarked upon the unification of all the Georgian lands, supported by the Church, the lesser nobility and the burgesses. But they met with the resistance of the high nobility, apprehensive of a strong pan-Georgian Crown, and of the Kings of Abasgia, anxious to secure that crown for themselves. It has been seen how the political acumen of David of Tao exploited the initial Abasgian successes for the Bagratids.

Bagrat III of Georgia (Abasgia and Iberia) was followed by a line of capable rulers, successful in overcoming imperial, Seljuq and feudal hostility. Bagrat kept on good terms with the Empire, but his son George I (1014–27) quarrelled with Basil II over the Tao succession. In two devastating wars, of 1021 and 1022, George was defeated and constrained to cede to Basil important Iberian fortresses and his own son Bagrat as a hostage. Dying early, he was followed by the boy Bagrat IV, whose early years were guided by his mother Mary, daughter of Sennacherib-John of Vaspurakan. It was a troubled reign. From the start, the Empire sought, by invasion, by bribery, and by producing claimants to Cholarzene, to wreck the new power in Caucasia. Georgia was saved by the loyalty of its most powerful dynast, Liparit IV, duke of T'rialet'i and subsequently High Constable of the realm; and also by the death of Constantine VIII (1028). The new Emperor, Romanus III Argyrus, was alive to the changing times: the military prowess of the Empire had passed with Basil II; it was wiser to resort to diplomacy. In 1031/2, after the *Katholikos* of Iberia, Melchisedech, and the Queen-Mother had journeyed to Constantinople, peace was concluded, and Bagrat received the dignity of Curopalate (denied to his father) and the hand of the Emperor's niece Helena.[1] Yet the *entente* ended with her untimely death. In 1033 Bagrat's ambitious younger brother Demetrius fled to the Empire, ceding to it the fortress of Anakop'ia, another apple of discord between the two states.

The Georgian lands still outside Bagrat IV's realm were the king-

[1] *DR*, 833.

dom of Kakhetia and the amirate of Tiflis. In the former, the principate having become hereditary, Kvirike III (1010–29) proclaimed himself king. His daughter was married to David I of Lori and their younger son Gagik succeeded in 1029 to Kvirike's throne. The kings of Georgia tried repeatedly to reunite Kakhetia with Iberia; and they, no less than the Kakhetian rulers, made attempts to conquer Tiflis. Bagrat thrice took the city (1046, 1049, 1062), only to lose it again, for his strength was sapped. In 1038, moreover, he rashly fell foul of Liparit, and with that the latent tension between the Crown and the dynastic nobility passed into an armed conflict. With the Emperor's backing, Liparit twice induced Prince Demetrius to try for the crown; he openly fought Bagrat; and he finally wrested from him the south-western moiety of the realm (*c.* 1045/7). In this struggle Constantine IX acted as mediator: the despoiler of Armenia evidently had similar designs on Georgia. Liparit was indeed the chief Caucasian ally of the Empire; he was a *Magister* and in 1048 commanded imperial armies against the Seljuqs in Armenia (captured in battle, he was soon released by Alp Arslan). In 1054 Bagrat himself went to see the Emperor, who created him a *Nobilissimus*, yet detained him for three years at Constantinople. During this time, Liparit proclaimed Bagrat's son George king and himself regent of Georgia. Finally, in 1059, the princes in Liparit's following grew tired of his sway and, seizing him, delivered him to the king. Liparit was forced into a monastery and the Crown was saved.

Next, Alp Arslan's Seljuqs invaded Georgia in 1064 and 1068, devastating the south-western provinces, reducing Kakhetia, and installing the amir of Ganja at Tiflis. Before this common menace, a *rapprochement* was effected between the Empire and the only great Christian state east of it: in 1065, Bagrat IV, a *Sebastus* now, sent his daughter Martha to be the wife of Constantine X's son and co-Emperor Michael Ducas.[1] Before his death on 14 November 1072, Bagrat expelled the Shaddādid from Tiflis, but relinquished it to another Muslim ruler.

His son George II, who received the dignity of Caesar from his (second) brother-in-law, Nicephorus III (*c.* 1081), was the least fortunate of the kings of the period. He was confronted by the revolt led by the Liparitids and pacified them only at the price of new concessions. And, although he acquired at that time from the harassed Empire all its possessions in Georgia, he was attacked by the Turks of Malikshāh and forced to accept the Sultan's suzerainty.

---

[1] Martha of Georgia took the name of Mary on marrying Michael. She was known as Mary of Alania, her mother, Bagrat IV's second wife, having been a princess of Alania-Ossetia. Mary subsequently married Nicephorus III Botaneiates.

In 1089 he was reduced to the position of a co-king by his son David, and died in 1112.

In the 'Golden Age' of David III the Builder (1089–1125),[1] his son Demetrius I (1125–55), the latter's son George III (1156–84), and his daughter Thamar the Great (1184–1212), Georgia was transformed into a powerful military pan-Caucasian empire, stretching from sea to sea, commanding vassal kingdoms, and enjoying the zenith of culture and prosperity. This success was grounded in the predominance of the Crown over the dynasts weakened by further feudalisation. It was now that Georgian feudalism reached its highest development, showing all the complexity observable in the West: fiefs and sub-fiefs; *dominium directum* and *dominium utile*; allods, benefices, office-fiefs; vassalage, investiture, homage; feudal service and immunity. David III was fortunate in subduing the recalcitrance of the Liparitids or, as they were now called, Orbelis (Orbelianis); he combated the nobles' monopoly of high positions in the Church; and he made himself less dependent on the feudal levy by introducing mercenary troops, recruited from the trans-Caucasian Kipchak tribes. Nevertheless, complications in the royal house twice evoked feudal revolt. The successor of Demetrius I, who entered a monastery, was his elder son David IV, who reigned for six months in 1155. He was followed, during the minority of his son Demetrius, by his younger brother George III. In 1174–7 the young Demetrius, aided by two great houses, the Orbelianis—he married an Orbelid princess—and the T'orelis, attempted to reach the throne. George III's repression was ruthless: Demetrius was mutilated and thrown into prison, and the principal Orbelid line was in part exterminated and in part forced out of Georgia. In opposing the aristocracy, George raised men of lesser or of no birth to high offices, previously a monopoly of the great families. For a time the nobles were cowed; then came another opportunity of asserting themselves. George, in default of sons, was succeeded by his daughter Thamar.[2] In 1185, despite reluctance, the Queen was prevailed upon to marry the vicious and brutal George of Russia, son of the Grand Duke Andrew of Vladimir. But in 1187/8 this childless marriage was dissolved and in 1189 Thamar married her Bagratid cousin, David Soslan, a descendant of Bagrat IV's brother Demetrius. The expelled George of Russia made three attempts to seize the kingdom, and the nobility, especially of West Georgia, rose in great numbers on his behalf. Upon the whole, how-

---

[1] Georgian historiography has erroneously called David 'the Second', though he was the third of that name among the Bagratid sovereigns.

[2] Georgian knows no distinction of genders; accordingly, Thamar as a reigning sovereign was entitled *mep'e* (that is, king or queen regnant). This has sometimes been erroneously interpreted by modern historians as her having been proclaimed a 'king'.

ever, the tension between the Crown and the aristocracy resolved itself into an equipoise in the reign of Thamar. She was obliged to remove upstarts from high office-fiefs, but she counterpoised the local families by the Armenian Mkhargrdzelis (Zachariads); at the same time, the Crown had to accept limitations imposed upon it by the Council of State composed of lords temporal and spiritual—an embryonic parliament.

The strength of the Crown at home made expansion possible; it was enhanced by the break-up, after Malikshāh, of the Seljuq realm and by the Seljuq struggle with the Fatimids and the crusaders. David III, in fact, launched a 'Georgian crusade' which, together with those of the Franks, placed the Seljuq succession states within Christian pincers. In 1105 David annexed Kakhetia, a vassal state of the Turks. In 1110 he began clearing Georgia of Turkish raiders and 'pockets'; in the course of this, the former kingdom of Loṛi was acquired in 1118. From 1117 Georgian ascendancy was established over the Muslim kingdom of Shirvan, and, c. 1119, over Alania-Ossetia. The Islamic counter-offensive, captained by the Ortukid al-Ghāzī and the Seljuq Ṭughrïl of Arrān, was utterly routed by David in August 1121. In 1122 Tiflis, the last Muslim enclave, was captured, and replaced Kutais in Abasgia as the seat of court and government. Finally, in 1123/4 David wrested Ani from the Seljuqs' Shaddādid vassals, as well as territories in northern Armenia and the Acampsis valley, including Syspiritis, once a Bagratid princedom. The crusade was continued by George III who led victorious campaigns against the Shāh-Arman, the Shaddādids, the *Atābeg* of Azerbaijan, and other Muslim princes. Thamar, assisted by her High Constable Zacharias I Mkhargrdzeli and his brother John, in 1199 recovered Ani, which the Shaddādids had several times retaken and which, in 1201, she bestowed upon the Mkhargrdzelis; in 1203 she annexed Arrān, with Shamk'or and Ganja, and Dvin in Armenia; in 1209 she captured Kars; and she carried her victories into Azerbaijan, as far as Ardabīl and Tabrīz. In 1204 the Queen aided her Comnenian relatives Alexius and David, grandsons of her aunt, the first wife of Andronicus I, to found the Empire of Trebizond, which at first was a tributary of Georgia—as were various amirs of Armenia and Azerbaijan. Georgia's theoretical dependence on the Eastern Empire had meantime been terminated: David III was the last sovereign to bear a Byzantine title (*Panhypersebastus*).

Possessed of great commercial and industrial centres—Tiflis, Artanuji, Dmanisi, Samshvilde, Ani, Kars, Dvin, Ganja—Georgia succeeded to Armenia's prosperity. The tribute of her client states and war booty alone brought to the Crown the yearly revenue of 75 million dirhams. The wealth and luxury of the period gave rise to the saying that 'the peasants were like nobles, the nobles like princes, and the princes like kings'. The artistic aspect of Georgian civilisation has been mentioned above. In the Golden Age, letters also flourished. Arising soon after the conversion, Georgian literature had begun with translations and hagiography, then historiography followed.[1] While Armenian literature was mostly historical and philosophical or purely ecclesiastical, Georgian literature further developed a purely secular aspect, especially poetry, lyric and epic, and achieved a moment of splendour with Shot'a of Rust'avi (Rust'aveli)'s epic *The Man in the Panther's Skin*. As in the West, chivalric ideals flourished, being inherent in a Christian feudal society; but, under sufic-gnostic influences, they became adulterated with those of courtly and troubadour love, leaving a considerable imprint on secular literature. Still, as in Armenia, intellectual life was centred chiefly in the monasteries (some of which were abroad, in the Holy Land, or on Mt Athos). Further developing the pattern of earlier schools, abbeys like Gelat'i and Iqalt'o set up academies on the Byzantine model. Philosophy flourished in the academies of Georgia; the Aristotelian school was headed by Arsenius of Iqalt'o (d. *c.* 1130) and the neoplatonist by John Petritsi (d. *c.* 1125), a disciple of Psellus and Italus whose original works included commentaries on Proclus and Nemesius of Emesa, in addition to his numerous translations. Astronomy was cultivated at Tiflis where an observatory had been built by the Arabs. Throughout the Georgian crusade, cultural contacts with the Islamic world were maintained, no less than with the Byzantine, and the relations between the Christian and Muslim lords in Caucasia bore a distinctly chivalrous stamp.

This *grand siècle* was abruptly terminated by another barbarian invasion, that of the Mongols. Appearing in Georgia in 1220, they defeated Thamar's son George IV the Resplendent (1212–23) and his 90,000 horse; but they did not follow up the victory and, in 1222, passed beyond the Caucasus. George died in 1223, leaving the throne, during the minority of his son David, to his sister Rusudan (1223–45). While the Queen was considering the papal proposal to undertake a crusade—the break with Rome seems to have become definitive only during that century—her realm was invaded in 1225 by Jalāl-ad-Dīn of Khʷārizm, recently mauled by the Mongols. All of Iberia fell to

---

[1] The historians included: Gregory the Deacon (seventh century), Leontius of Ruisi (Leonti Mroveli, eighth century), Juansher (eighth–ninth century), Sumbat son of David (eleventh century), Arsenius the Monk (the biographer of David III), the two Historians of Thamar, the Historian of George IV, and the Meschian Chronographer (fourteenth century). The works of some of these, and of others, came to form the Georgian Royal Annals (*K'art'lis Ts'khovreba*).

the Turkomans, and their ferocity made the next Mongol wave in 1236 appear almost as a deliverance. The feudal army of the Bagratids was no match for the war machine of the invaders, when they came; all the princes of East Georgia accepted their suzerainty, and in 1243 Rusudan, who had taken refuge in Abasgia, was obliged to do the same.

The Mongols left Georgia autonomous, but exacted tribute and military aid. The new taxation, in addition to the old feudal dues, and the participation in long and distant Mongol wars proved ruinous to the peasantry. Their only escape—flight—was combated by legislative measures. The decline of the rural economy that ensued was followed by that of the towns, as industry and commerce dwindled. Further weakening came from dynastic complications. In 1234 Rusudan co-opted David (V), her son by her Seljuq Prince-Consort,[1] and put aside the lawful heir, George IV's son David. In 1250, however, the Great Khan recognised both the Seljuq David V and the Bagratid David VI as joint kings of Georgia. But in 1258 growing regional separatism enabled the former to secede in Abasgia, thenceforth called Imeretia (Imereti). Georgia was again divided, and the reduced Crown became a plaything of the great houses, the immediate vassals of the Mongols.[2]

David VI (1250–69) was succeeded in Iberia by his son Demetrius II the Devoted (1269–89), who, embroiled in the intrigues of the Il-khan's court, gave himself up to be executed by the Mongols in order to save his people from invasion. The adoption, after him, of the Byzantine system of collegial sovereignty led to the confusion of simultaneous kings: Vakhtang II, David V's son set up by the Mongols (1289–92); Demetrius' sons David VII (1292–1301; co-king, 1291–2, 1301–10), George (VI, co-king, 1299–1314), and Vakhtang III (1301–7); and David VII's son George V the Little (1307–c. 1314).[3]

---

[1] He was a son of the Prince of Erzerum. His conversion to Christianity, at his father's instance, and the subsequent founding of the Georgian line of the Seljuqs in Imeretia (West Georgia) bear witness to the spiritual and cultural influence of Georgia upon its Islamic neighbours—a peaceful counterpart of the Georgian Crusade. For the Imeretian Seljuqs, see C. Toumanoff, 'The Fifteenth-century Bagratids and the Institution of Collegial Sovereignty in Georgia', *Trad.* VII (1949–51), 181–3.

[2] The most important princely houses were at that time the Mkhargrdzeli-Zachariads of Loṛi, Jaqelis of Meschia (Samts'khe), Dadianis of Mingrelia, Sharvashidzes of Abkhazia, T'orelis of Javakhet'i, Orbeli-Kakhaberidzes of Racha, Orbelianis of Surami. The latter's cousins, exiled under George III, had come to reign, under the protection of the *Atābegs* of Azerbaijan and, later, the Mongols, in the Armenian principality of Siunia.

[3] The system of collegial sovereignty is to be distinguished from the universal practice of co-opting the heir. For this system and for the reasons for counting George the Illustrious as the Sixth, as well as for the order of succession followed here, see C. Toumanoff, *op. cit.*, *Trad.* VII (1949–51).

About 1314 George VI the Illustrious became the sole ruler. At first he kept on excellent terms with the declining Ilkhans: the Mongol tribute was decreased and Georgian control over Armenian territories recognised. Georgia enjoyed a great prestige in the world of Islam of the period.[1] Then in 1327 the fall of George's friend the regent Chūpān ended the Georgian–Muslim co-operation. George VI transferred his residence to Kutais and confined his activities to West Georgia, where he reduced the Seljuq kings to vassal dukes and enforced obedience on other princes. Georgia's international orientation also changed, as its relations with Trebizond and the West, especially the Papacy, were intensified. Economically, this seems to have been a moment of recovery, and commercial contacts with Iran, the Golden Horde, Anatolia, and the Italian republics flourished. George's son David VIII (1346–60) and grandson Bagrat V (1360–95) continued the policy of recovery, interrupted by the Black Death (1346–8) and the struggle over East Georgia between the Ilkhans' successors the Jalāirids and the Golden Horde. But in the late 1350's Mongol control had become tenuous; the court returned to Tiflis; and, even though the pan-Caucasian empire had been lost, it enjoyed a certain ascendancy over Shirvan, Arrān, and Trebizond.

Another barbarian wave ended this momentary consolidation. In 1386 Tiflis was sacked and Bagrat V and his queen Anna Comnena of Trebizond were led captive by Tamerlane. The Imeretian rulers regained independence, while the incursions of Tamerlane, his successors, and, later, the Aq-Qoyunlu Turks left Georgia utterly devastated. Bagrat V's sons, George VII (1395–1405) and Constantine I (1405–12),[2] fell fighting the invaders. The latter's son Alexander I the Great (1412–42) attempted with some success to stem the decline. He re-established political unity and undertook a series of measures to restore prosperity. His son and third successor, George VIII (1446–65), felt strong enough to attempt joining the defence of Christendom against the tide of Islam. In 1451 his daughter was betrothed to Constantine XI Palaeologus; and in 1458–60 he strove, together with the Emperor of Trebizond and other princes, to realise Pius II's abortive crusade. These new efforts at consolidation were wrecked, however, and from within. It would still have been possible to prepare for the coming Islamic onslaught of the Ottomans and the

[1] D. M. Lang, 'Georgia in the Reign of Giorgi the Brilliant', *BSOAS*, xvii (1955), 74–91. This study made it necessary to revise the traditional conception of that reign; cf. also W. E. D. Allen's review of Lang's *Studies in the Numismatic History of Georgia in Transcaucasia*, in *BSOAS*, xvii (1956), 379–81. Lang does not seem to accept the above order of succession and the implications of collegial sovereignty.

[2] For 1405 as the year of George VII's death and Constantine I's accession, see C. Toumanoff, 'Fifteenth-century Bagratids', p. 174.

Ṣafavids. But the dynasty which had made the country great now fatally weakened it. The system of collegial sovereignty reappeared among the descendants of Bagrat V's Comnenian queen. And, in conjunction with feudalism and regional separatism, enhanced by an economy now broken into local autarkies, this extraneous constitutional development brought about, in 1454–91, the partition of the realm between three lines of the royal house into three kingdoms: of Georgia proper (Iberia), Imeretia and Kakhetia. In the course of the struggles accompanying the partition, five western ducal houses, the Jaqelis of Meschia, Dadian-Gurielis of Guria, Dadianis of Mingrelia, Sharvashidzes of Abkhazia, and Gelovanis of Suania, seceded from Georgia forming five independent principalities. Except Meschia, all these states survived until the Russian annexations of the nineteenth century.

V. ARMENIA IN EXILE (LESSER ARMENIA)

The aftermath of the Seljuq conquest of Armenia was the deflection, unique in history, of its social and political *élite* to foreign lands, and the establishment of a New Armenia in exile: an artificial creation indeed, but less so than the Frankish states of the Levant most of which it outlived. When Cappadocia, where many of the Armenian royalties and dynasts had settled, fell to the Turks after 1074, the Armenian *émigrés* moved to the only region left unoccupied by the invaders: the south-eastern corner of Asia Minor and northern Syria. Thither immigrants from Armenia had been streaming after the tenth century, so that the new arrivals, including the *Katholikos* and his ecclesiastics, found these lands only half-foreign. Cut off from the Empire, this region was consolidated in the face of the Muslim menace by the warlike newcomers. The first organiser of this Armenia in exile was Philaretus Brachamius (Vahrām), commander of Melitene and Germanicea (Marʻash) under Romanus IV. He refused to recognise Michael VII, set up an independency in Germanicea and ruled Melitene through vassals, the most notable of whom was Gabriel. In 1077 another vassal of Philaretus took Edessa with its largely Armenian population, and in 1078 Philaretus was invited to rule in Antioch. His hegemony also extended to Cilicia, where the Artsrunis, established by the Empire at Tarsus, and the Hetʻumids of Lambron accepted his overlordship. Philaretus further strengthened his position by making peace with Nicephorus III and obtaining the title of Curopalate and, simultaneously, by becoming a vassal, for Antioch, of the Atābeg of Mosul. His state, however, was not to last. In 1085 Antioch fell to the Seljuqs and in 1098

Philaretus' successor in Edessa, the Curopalate Theodore (T'oros), was rather cavalierly superseded by his *condottiere* and adopted son, Baldwin of Boulogne, and his Franks. The rest of this first neo-Armenian polity fell into several units, including Melitene (annexed by the Dānishmends), Mar'ash and Kaysūn-Ra'bān (taken by the Franks in 1104 and 1116), and, not least, Cilicia of the Rubenids. The attempt of Theodore of Edessa to found an Armeno-Frankish condominium failed; thenceforth Syria was to be only Frankish and Cilicia the land of New Armenia.[1]

While other Armenian dynasts in these regions willingly enough submitted to imperial suzerainty (whenever asserted), Ruben, who established himself c. 1080 in the castle of Bardzrberd in the Cilician mountains, represented the anti-Byzantine faction once grouped round Gagik II. That he was that king's relative, as later historians claimed, seems doubtful; Rupenes, *strategus* of Larissa and Hellas in 1018/19, may have been his kinsman. The formation of Rubenid Armenia upon the foundation laid by Philaretus followed. This was aided by the same external factors as the greatness of Bagratid Georgia: the dismemberment of the Seljuq realm and its struggle with the Fatimids and the crusaders. The latter received, upon arrival, military aid, supplies, and guidance from the friendly Armenian lords of Cilicia and Syria, and the adherence of the Armenian population of great cities, like Antioch; their presence, in turn, enabled Ruben's son Constantine I (1095–9) to consolidate his princedom and to enlarge it at the expense of the Byzantines and the Muslims. Despite the initial Armeno-Frankish frictions in Syria and occasional subsequent conflicts, the Armeno-Latin *entente*, strengthened by numerous princely marriages and much cultural interpenetration, was to continue to the end in the face of the Byzantine and Muslim danger. Anti-Byzantine sentiments also induced the Armenian Church to be rather conciliatory towards Catholicism.

The period of Constantine's sons Theodore I (1100–29) and Leo I (1129–38), the latter's son Theodore II (1145–69), and of his son Ruben II (1169–70), his brother Mlēh (1170–5), and nephew Ruben III (1175–86) was one of steady, if interrupted, growth, and of struggle with foes from several quarters. Theodore I wrested from the Empire the upper valley of the Pyramus, with Sis and Anazarbus; Leo I, seizing Mopsuestia (Mamistra), Adana, and Tarsus (which the

---

[1] New Armenia has also been called Lesser or Little Armenia, Armeno-Cilicia, and Sisuan.—In transcribing Armenian names, the classical pronunciation of Armenian is followed throughout this study, although in New Armenia the language was affected by the phonetic development of western Armenian, whereby the surd consonants are pronounced as sonant and *vice versa*. For this reason, the Rubenids are sometimes referred to as 'Rupenids' or 'Rupenians'.

Byzantines had taken from the crusaders), by 1133 held the whole of eastern Cilicia. His seizure of a fortress on the Antiochene border, however, led to a war with the Prince of Antioch. The two sovereigns then came to terms before the common menace of the Emperor John II's offensive aimed at recovering both Cilicia and Antioch. In 1137 the Emperor overran and annexed Rubenid Cilicia, in 1138 taking captive Leo I and two of his sons; the Prince died in captivity (1141), his elder son expired after suffering blinding, but his younger son Theodore II escaped his gaolers after John II's death (1143). Returning to Cilicia, where Armenians groaned under Byzantine repression, he organised a struggle for independence. He defeated the punitive expedition sent by the Emperor Manuel under the command of Andronicus Comnenus and made himself master of the Cilician cities of Sis, Anazarbus, Adana, Tarsus and Mamistra. Neither the Seljuq attacks of 1153 and 1154, nor the war with Antioch in 1155—all prompted by imperial diplomacy—could dislodge the Rubenid. Finally, in 1158 Manuel took the field in person against not only Cilicia, but also Antioch. Nearly taken by surprise, Theodore II fled to the mountains while the imperial armies occupied lower Cilicia. In 1159 Baldwin III of Jerusalem, proponent of a crusader–Byzantine alliance, arranged a peace between Manuel and Theodore; accepting imperial suzerainty, the latter received upper Cilicia and the title of *Pansebastus*.[1] Yet Armeno-Byzantine relations worsened. In 1162 the Prince's younger brother Stephen, while attempting to expand over Muslim territory, was captured by the imperial governor of lower Cilicia and boiled alive. Theodore rose in revolt again and seized Mamistra and Anazarbus. A peace, upholding the *status quo*, was however again arranged by the king of Jerusalem, Baldwin's brother Amaury I.

Ruben II was under age at accession, and his uncle Mlēh, once a Templar and then a renegade to Islam, invaded his realm with the aid of Nūr-ad-Dīn, Atābeg of Aleppo and Damascus, and seized the throne. Ruben took refuge in the *Katholikos'* fortress of Hṛomkla, where he soon died. Reversing the policy of his dynasty, Mlēh allied himself with the Muslims against the crusaders; and it was only after Nūr-ad-Dīn's death that his own vassals slew Mlēh in 1175. His successor was Ruben III, son of the unfortunate Stephen. Taking advantage of the Empire's plight after Myriocephalum (1176), he achieved the consolidation of all Cilicia under his sceptre. But, while reducing to obedience the pro-Byzantine dynast of Lambron, Het'um II, he was treacherously captured by the latter's ally, Bohemond III of Antioch, who then marched into Cilicia. Bohemond,

[1] *DR*, 1431.

however, reckoned without Ruben's brother Leo. Leo beat off the Antiochene and forced Het'um of Lambron to obtain Ruben's release; Adana and Mamistra, a part of his ransom, were subsequently recovered. In 1186 Ruben III retired to a monastery leaving no son, and Leo became prince.

With Leo II the Great, or the Magnificent (1186–1219), and his son-in-law Het'um (Hayton) I (1226–69), Armenia in exile reached the summit of power and prosperity: it became a kingdom and played a decisive role in world politics and international commerce. All this was largely due to the administrative genius, military prowess, diplomatic skill, and above all grandiose political vision of these two monarchs. Yet the pressure of external foes did not diminish during this period; the eastern Empire, indeed, no longer mattered as an enemy, but the newly risen Ayyūbids infused fresh vigour into Islam by bringing Egypt within the Sunnite sphere, and organised a counter-offensive which in the end destroyed both the crusader states and New Armenia.

In his Antiochene policy, however, Leo was not successful. His attempt to annex Antioch in 1194, by seizing his brother's former captor Bohemond by a trick, failed when a hint at Armenian religious intolerance provoked the submissive city to reject its new master. Then, through the mediation of Henry of Champagne, king of Jerusalem, peace was made, Bohemond restored, Armenia's precedence over Antioch accepted, and Alice, Ruben III's daughter, married to Bohemond's son Raymond. This peace nevertheless held seeds of war—the war of the Antiochene succession. When in 1201 Bohemond III died, his throne was seized by his younger son Bohemond IV to the exclusion of the rightful heir, Raymond-Ruben, son of the lately deceased elder son Raymond. His great-uncle Leo of Armenia, the Latin clergy and most of the nobility of Antioch, and the Knights Hospitallers supported Raymond-Ruben; the usurper, on the other hand, sought the assistance of the Ayyūbids of Aleppo (whose attack on Armenia Leo had repulsed in 1189) and of the Iconian Seljuqs, and found support with the Antiochene Greeks and the Templars (who disputed Leo's possession of the castle of Gastim). In 1206 Leo defeated an army of Aleppo, but was unsuccessful against those of both Aleppo and Iconium in 1208. In 1211 the Templars gained from him Gastim. Though he seized Heraclea and Laranda in that year from the Seljuqs, he lost to them Isauria down to Seleucia in 1216. Thus, even in his great reign, the Rubenid realm had already suffered diminution. And when in that same year Leo definitively set up Raymond-Ruben in Antioch, the ungrateful young man quarrelled with his benefactor.

It was in his *Weltpolitik* that Leo achieved eminent success. Fearing the Ayyūbids, whose *jihād* was then reducing the Latin states, and distrusting Saladin's Byzantine allies, he decided on close collaboration with the West. Armenia, it so happened, fitted well into the Hohenstaufen dream of universal Empire. Hence the *rapprochement* of Leo with Frederick Barbarossa and, later, Henry VI. Pursuing his policy, Leo gave wholehearted support to Frederick's ill-starred crusade and worked for a reunion with Rome. His negotiations with Pope Celestine III and the Emperor Henry VI, begun in 1195, were culminated in 1198 (1199?), when, recognised by both as King of Armenia and recognising, together with the *Katholikos* Gregory VI Pahlavuni, the supremacy of the Holy See, Leo was solemnly crowned at Tarsus by Cardinal Conrad of Wittelsbach and by the *Katholikos*.[1]

King Leo II also applied his energies to reorganising his kingdom. In order further to enhance the powers of the Crown, he constitutionalised the change of the basically dynastic Caucasian structure of society into a Western, purely feudal, one. Various lesser sovereigns under his suzerainty were 'mediatised' as mere feudatories, holding fiefs on a contractual basis and bereft of many former rights. The fact that they had been uprooted from their native soil and that many of them were not originally dynastic, may account for the ease of the change. Yet resentment there must have been, as is attested by the revolt of the Prince of Lambron, before Leo's reign was over. Below these ex-dynastic 'great barons' were, as ever, the lesser nobles or arrière vassals, and then the burghers. Many of the Armenian peasant immigrants were freeholders, while the local Cilician peasants were serfs. The judicial system was organised on the western pattern. At Sis, the capital, there was the High Court, modelled on the Assizes of Antioch and alone endued with the right of 'high justice' once held by the great barons; and the Low Court, for the burgesses. There were also baronial and monastic courts, those of the Orders, like the Hospitallers established at Isaurian Seleucia, and the consular tribunals of the Genoese and the Venetians. Various aulic functions and titles were borrowed from the crusaders and the Byzantines (Bailiff, Marshal, Seneschal, *Basileopator*, *Porphyrogenitus*,

---

[1] The earlier title of the Rubenids was that of 'Prince', which was later interpreted in the peculiarly medieval-Armenian (as well as early-medieval Western) sense of 'Baron'. Some historians compute the ordinal numbers of the neo-Armenian sovereigns from the coronation of Leo, the Princes being given a different numeration. This, to be sure, has the sepulchral inscription of the last king in its favour; but the system adopted here helps to avoid confusion. The case of the Bagratid Kings of Armenia is different, because the ordinals of the earlier presiding princes are those of family heads.

Proximus); some Armenian offices assumed Latin names. The institution of chivalry was introduced. Latin and French, next to Armenian, were the official languages of the realm. Leo also paid attention to a better organisation of the armed forces and to the fortification of the frontiers.

The King promoted economic development. More important than industry and export was Armenia's position at the junction of several trade-routes—Syria–Iconium–Constantinople; Tabrīz–Mar'ash–the Mediterranean; the Persian Gulf–Syria–Cilicia—which converged towards its ports of Ayas (Lajazzo), Korikos, Tarsus, and were used especially for the spice trade. Aware of the urgency of Western aid, Leo strove to make his kingdom accessible and interesting. Extensive privileges were granted to the Genoese and the Venetians; and an Armenian fleet was built in order to facilitate trade with Italy. From the West came also scholastic philosophy, and works of St Thomas Aquinas were translated in the fourteenth century. This was a period of great literary endeavour, both in New and, under foreign rule, Old Armenia.[1]

Dying on 2 May 1219 without male heirs, Leo II had his daughter Isabel (Zabel) proclaimed queen the day before. The veritable ruler, however, was one of the two regents, the king-maker Constantine, Prince of Askura and Lemos, of the house of Lambron. He deposed, and disposed of, the Antiochene Raymond-Ruben, who claimed Armenia in 1221, and Isabel's husband, King Philip (1222–5), son of Bohemond IV of Antioch. Finally, he forced the queen to marry, in 1226, his own son Het'um. After age-long rivalry, the Het'umids of Lambron thus finally succeeded the Rubenids.

Het'um I was, naturally enough, faced with Antioch's enmity; and it was only in the 1250's that he and Bohemond V were reconciled by St Louis of France, then in the Levant. The marriage of Het'um's daughter Sibyl to Bohemond VI in 1254 sealed the alliance of the two Christian states—a *conditio sine qua non* of survival in the face of the Mamluks, now continuing the Egyptian *jihād* of the Ayyūbids. Secure in this quarter, Het'um I embarked upon his own *Weltpolitik*. The advent of the Mongols, ruining Georgia, saved Armenia. It lay outside the path of their conquests and shared with them a common foe in the Mamluks. Het'um's programme was, accordingly, to replace the Western by the Mongol alliance and to organise a Christian–

---

[1] This was the epoch of the historians like Matthew of Edessa and Samuel of Ani (twelfth century), Vardan the Great (d. 1271), Kirakos of Ganja (d. 1272), the Constable Smbat of Armenia (d. 1276), Stephen Orbelian of Siunia (d. 1304), Thomas of Metsop' (d. 1446) and others. Religious poetry reached great heights with the *Katholikos* Nersēs IV the Gracious (d. 1173), and theology in the works of Nersēs of Lambron (d. 1198). This epoch is known as the Silver Age.

Mongol offensive against Islam and its stronghold Egypt. Through his brother, the Constable Smbat, in 1247, and in 1254, when he journeyed in person to see the Great Khan, the king placed his realm under Mongol suzerainty. And it was this policy that was largely responsible for the Mongol invasion of Syria and Mesopotamia, in which Armenian, Georgian and Antiochene knights took part and which culminated in the capture of Baghdad in 1258. Simultaneously, Het'um waged an economic war on Egypt, which, in addition to religious and political considerations, was Armenia's rival in the spice trade.

The Mongol 'crusade', however, miscarried no less than Barbarossa's. The Franks of the Levant, lacking Het'um's vision, failed to co-operate. And in 1260 the Mamluks inflicted upon the Mongols their first defeat and restored Egyptian control of Syria. The Mongol Empire had itself meantime become dismembered; and Bereke, Khan of the Golden Horde, embraced Islam. Armenia's protectors, the Ilkhans, paralysed by the alliance of Bereke with Baybars of Egypt, could not retaliate for the defeat of 1260. Baybars, on his part, pursued the Mamluk victory. In 1266 he invaded Armenia, subjecting it to fire and sword, and led 40,000 captive, including the king's son Leo. In 1268 Antioch fell to the Mamluks. Het'um was constrained to sue for peace and to ransom his son at the price of territorial concessions. Nevertheless, upon Het'um's assuming the habit of a Franciscan, Leo III (1269–89) continued his father's Mongol policy, which found its Western proponent in Edward I of England. Surrounded by the sea of Islam and prompted by the Kings of Armenia and of England, the Ilkhans worked, for their part, towards a Christian–Mongol coalition. In 1281 the Ilkhan Abagha, assisted by Armenians, Georgians and Franks, took the field against the Mamluks, only to meet with a defeat at Homs (30 October).

The epoch of Leo III's successors was one of mortal disaster, speeded by internal disruption as much as by blows from the outside. The Crown weakened owing to the dynasty itself. Of the sons of Leo III, five reached the throne. The eldest, Het'um II, abdicated in his fourth year (1293) in favour of his next brother, Theodore III, but was recalled to the throne in 1294. In 1296 the third brother, Smbat I, seized the crown, strangling Theodore and blinding Het'um, but was overthrown in 1298 by the fourth brother, Constantine II. His power was ephemeral, for the barons presently restored Het'um II, whose sight had partially recovered; but in 1305 he abdicated in favour of Theodore III's young son, Leo IV (1305–8), yet continued to rule for him. The weakness of the Crown gave rein to baronial insubordination, and rebellious vassals did not hesitate to conspire with the country's enemies. Worse still, Armenian society became rent by internal strife between the small governing group, kings and *Katholikoi*, lords spiritual and temporal, clinging to the tenuous union with Rome and to Western alliances, and the anti-Western and anti-Catholic baronial and ecclesiastical faction.[1] In 1308 the latter stooped to organising the murder, by some Muslim Mongols, of King Leo IV, the old Het'um II, and a number of lords in their following. Political decay was accompanied by moral decadence. Leo III's fifth son, Oshin I (1308–20),[2] was succeeded by his son, the last Het'umid, Leo V (1320–41), under whom the court of Sis became a scene of bloody tragedies. The head of the council of regency in the king's minority was one of the milder nationalists, Oshin, Count of Koṟikos, who married Oshin I's widow, Joan of Anjou-Taranto, and who forced Leo V to marry his daughter by a previous marriage. To diminish Western influence at court, he caused the death of the king's aunt Isabel, widow of Amaury of Lusignan, Prince of Tyre, and of two of her sons. Later, in 1329, Leo V assumed power and put to death both his unloved wife and his father-in-law. Dying childless, Leo V bequeathed the Crown to his Lusignan cousins, sons of his aunt Isabel of Tyre.

While thus undermined internally, Armenia was incessantly battered by the Muslims. Between 1274 and 1305 this Christian bastion in the Near East was continually invaded, pillaged and laid waste by the Mamluks of Egypt and Syria and by the Seljuqs from the north. It is astonishing that Leo III and Het'um II were at all able to repulse the aggressors and to propitiate them, in lieu of conquest, with tribute and territorial concessions. But though Armenia's independence was preserved, its prosperity vanished during this struggle. The Ilkhans had ceased to offer protection and were themselves rapidly succumbing to Islamic influences. In 1299–1300 an attempt to resume the anti-Mamluk offensive, on the part of Ghazan-Khan, Het'um II and the King of Georgia, though at first successful, came to nought,[3] as did another attempt in 1303. And in 1304 the Ilkhans definitively espoused Islam: Armenia's protectors became its enemies, and the Muslim ring round it grew narrower. Armenia had now to sustain the added Mongol pressure, while treachery at home, as in 1308, incited the new foe to new attacks.

---

[1] The latter faction found support and sympathy in the clergy of Old Armenia, reconciled with foreign rule.

[2] Oshin I is considered by some to have been a brother of Leo IV.

[3] In the course of this campaign, the Mongols ceded Jerusalem to their Georgian allies, who kept the city for a year (1300) and who, for some time thereafter, enjoyed certain rights with regard to the Holy Sepulchre; see M. Tamarati, *L'Eglise géorgienne des origines jusqu'à nos jours* (Rome, 1910), pp. 436–7 (and the sources cited therein).

The West indeed remained the only hope; and Oshin I and his successors continued, despite nationalist opposition, the traditional policy of strengthening their blood ties with the Cypriot, Byzantine and West European courts. Appeals for aid were ceaselessly sent to the West and there reiterated by the Papacy, only to fall on deaf ears. Armenia had to go on fighting alone. More enemy attacks were repulsed between 1319 and 1323. In that year, the fierce Armenian resistance forced Nāṣir of Egypt to conclude a fifteen years' truce; Leo V promised, *inter alia*, to pay the annual tribute of 50,000 gold florins and half the customs revenues of Ayas, which the Sultan, having destroyed it in the war, undertook, on his part, to rebuild. When Philip V of France, in 1335 yielding at last to the Pope's incessant entreaties, decided to aid Armenia, the Muslims struck again. Leo V was compelled to conclude another treaty with Nāṣir, in 1337, wherein he pledged himself never again to associate with the West.

Under the Lusignans Armenia's death agony began. The internal strife grew more intense. King Guy, third son of Isabel of Armenia and Amaury of Tyre, ascended the throne in 1342, in accordance with Leo V's bequest, intending to fight with Western aid in defence of his country. But two years later (17 November 1344), he and 300 Western knights, who had come to that defence, were massacred by the fanatically nationalist and defeatist barons. These then raised to the throne men outside the royal line. Nevertheless, their creature, Constantine III (1344–63), son of Baldwin of Nigrinum, Marshal of Armenia, descendant through his mother of the Constable Smbat, and husband of the daughter of Oshin of Koṛikos by Joan of Anjou-Taranto, continued the same policy. He reaffirmed the union with Rome in 1345 and, with the aid of the King of Cyprus and the Hospitallers, defeated in 1356 the Mamluk invaders of Armenia. In 1359, however, lower Cilicia was overrun by the Muslims. The next king, Constantine IV (1365–73), a cousin of his predecessor, and son of Hetʻum, Chamberlain of Armenia, was slain by the barons who had set him up, while in 1368–9 a part of the country welcomed as king Peter I of Cyprus. Finally, the crown reverted in 1373 to the lawful line in the person of the last King of Armenia, Leo VI, son of King Guy's brother John[1] by a Georgian princess. The new king found his realm reduced to Sis and Anazarbus with adjoining regions and a few castles, and obviously incapable of withstanding another enemy blow. That blow was finally dealt in 1375 by the Mamluk viceroy of Aleppo,

---

[1] John de Lusignan, who was Regent of Armenia for his brother Guy, is regarded by some historians as King Constantine III, with the resulting change in the numeration of the subsequent rulers of that name.

and powerfully aided by baronial betrayal at home. On 13 April 1375 Sis fell to the Muslims, and the king, his wife Margaret of Soissons and their two children were taken into captivity. Upon refusing to regain his crown at the price of apostasy, Leo VI and his family were brought to Cairo, where the queen and the children died in prison. Only in 1382 was the last King of Armenia set at liberty through the mediation of the King of Castile; he came to Europe and finally settled in Paris, the recipient of the Papal Golden Rose, where he died on 29 November 1393. With him the political history of Armenia came to a close. Cilicia formed part of the Mamluk possessions until the sixteenth century, when it passed to the Ottomans. The title of King of Armenia was inherited by the Lusignans of Cyprus and, from them, by the House of Savoy. Only in Old Armenia could some vestiges of the once imposing structure of the Armenian polity be found in the houses of dynasts (*meliks*) in Qarabagh (Siunia and a part of cis-Cyran Albania), sovereign under Muslim suzerainty until the Russian annexation in the nineteenth century; while a number of houses of the Armenian dynastic aristocracy survived in the princely nobility of neighbouring Georgia.

NOTE ON TRANSLITERATION

Phonetic transcription of Armenian and Georgian words is used in this chapter and its notes. A more scientific transliteration is used in the Bibliography and List of Rulers: there each letter of the Armenian and Georgian alphabets corresponds to a single letter of the Latin alphabet, thus necessitating the use of diacritical marks. Names are indexed under the transcription found in this chapter and cross-references given to the transliteration used in the List of Rulers.

ADDENDUM

Some details of the genealogy and chronology in the section on *Armenia in Exile* need revision in the light of the study by W. H. Rüdt-Collenberg, *The Rupenides, Hethumides and Lusignans: the Structure of the Armeno-Cilician Dynasties* (Lisbon, 1963), which appeared after this chapter was ready for press.

CHAPTER XV

GOVERNMENT, SOCIETY AND ECONOMIC LIFE UNDER THE ABBASIDS AND FATIMIDS

On 25th Ramaḍān 129, corresponding to 9 June 747, Abū Muslim, the emissary of the Hāshimiyya sect, unfurled the black flags of revolt in the East Persian province of Khurasan. He and his predecessors had already done nearly thirty years' work in the province, preaching a doctrine of revolution against the Umayyad Caliphs, and the ground was well prepared. The Persian population, especially that part of it that was converted to Islam, was deeply resentful of the inequalities imposed by Umayyad rule. The Arab soldiers and settlers, half Persianised by long residence, were sharply divided among themselves, and even during the triumphal progress of the revolt diverted their own and the government's energies to Arab tribal conflict. With chiefly non-Arab, but with some important Arab support, Abū Muslim was soon able to seize all Khurasan from the tottering Umayyad power. From Khurasan, further victories opened the way across Persia to Iraq. In 749 his armies crossed the Euphrates and defeated another Umayyad force and, in the same year, Abu 'l-'Abbās, the leader of the sect, was hailed as Caliph by the troops in Kūfa with the title of as-Saffāḥ. Further defeats in 749 and 750 in Iraq and Syria sealed the fate of the Umayyads, and the authority of the new Caliph was soon recognised all over the Islamic Empire. The new dynasty were known as the sons of 'Abbās, after their ancestor, 'Abbās ibn 'Abd al-Muṭṭalib, the uncle of the Prophet Muḥammad.

The struggle which led to the replacement of the Umayyad by the Abbasid Caliphate was more than a simple change of dynasty. It was a revolution in the history of Islam, comparable with the French and Russian revolutions in the history of Europe. The new regime was established, not by a palace conspiracy or *coup d'état*, but by a secret revolutionary organisation, propagating a new doctrine that impugned the right to rule of the old regime. This body, built up over a long period of time, responded to the dissatisfactions of important elements of the population with the Arab Umayyad kingdom, and even commanded the support of certain groups among the Arabs themselves. Like most revolutionary movements, it was a coalition of different interests, held together by a common desire to overthrow the existing order, but doomed to break up into warring factions once victory was obtained.

This character of the Abbasid victory has long been recognised by both eastern and western historians, and the latter have devoted much effort to interpreting it. Many nineteenth-century European scholars, still influenced by the racial theories of Gobineau and his successors, saw in the revolution a revolt of Aryan Iran against the semitism of Arabia and Islam, and interpreted the accession of the Abbasids as a victory of Persians over Arabs—the destruction of the Arab kingdom of the Umayyads and the establishment of a new Iranian Empire under a veneer of Persianised Islam.[1]

At first sight there is much to support this view—the important role of Persians in the revolutionary movement, the prominence of Persian ministers and courtiers in the new regime, the strong Persian element in Abbasid culture. But subsequent research and experience have led historians to modify, in several important respects, their theories of Persian victory and Arab defeat. The Shī'ite heresy,[2] for long regarded by western scholars as an expression of an 'Iranian National Consciousness', has been shown to be in fact of Arab origin. It was strongest among the mixed population of southern Iraq and was taken into Persia by Arab colonists who for long provided its main support. The revolt of Abū Muslim was directed against Umayyad rule and Syrian predominance rather than against the Arabs as such. As well as Persians, the revolutionary movement had many Arab supporters, including several of its leaders and generals. Though racial antagonisms played some part, and though Persians were prominent among the victors, the movement served an Arab pretender, and established an Arab dynasty. After the victory, many of the high offices of government were reserved to Arabs, Arabic remained the sole language of government and culture, Arabian land remained fiscally privileged, and socially, at least, the doctrine of Arab superiority was maintained—at any rate to the extent of inducing some ambitious non-Arabs to provide themselves with ficti-

---

[1] The first critical modern studies of the Abbasid revolution were those of G. van Vloten, *De Opkomst der Abbasiden in Chorasan* (Leiden, 1890), *Recherches sur la domination arabe...* (Amsterdam, 1894), and J. Wellhausen, *Das arabische Reich und sein Sturz* (Berlin, 1902) (English translation Calcutta, 1927). For two recent evaluations of the revolutionary leader Abū Muslim see R. N. Frye, 'The Role of Abū Muslim in the Abbasid Revolt', *Moslem World*, xxxvii (1947), 28–38, and S. Moscati, 'Studi su Abū Muslim', i–iii, *Rendiconti Accademia Naz. Lincei* (1949), 323–5, 474–95; (1950), pp. 89–105. For some more general reflections by the same authors, see R. N. Frye, 'The Abbasid Conspiracy and Modern Revolutionary Theory', *Indo-Iranica*, v (Calcutta, 1952), pp. 9–14, and S. Moscati, *Oriente in Nuova Luce* (Florence, 1954), pp. 119–47 ('La crisi dell'impero arabo').

[2] On Shī'ism see also below: chapter xvi, pp. 647 ff. and 680 ff.

tious Arab pedigrees. What the Arabs had lost was not, as was once thought, the reality of power—this came later—but the exclusive right to the fruits of power, which they were now compelled to share with other peoples. Persians and others, as well as Arabs, rose at the Abbasid court, where the favour of the ruler, and not, as under the Umayyads, pure Arab descent, was the passport to power and prestige. If a term must be set to the Arab kingdom, it should be put later, with the decline of the Arab warriors from the status of a privileged caste, and the rise to power of the Turkish Guards in the capital, and of local autonomous dynasties in the provinces.

The real significance of the Abbasid victory may be seen in the effects of the change that followed it rather than in dubiously documented hypotheses on the movement that produced it. The first and most striking change was the transfer of the capital from Syria, from which the Umayyads had ruled for a century, to Iraq, the centre of gravity of the great cosmopolitan Empires of the ancient Middle East. The first Abbasid Caliph, as-Saffāḥ, set up a temporary capital by the Euphrates. His brother and successor, al-Manṣūr (754–75), the second Caliph and in many ways the real founder of the Abbasid Caliphate, established a permanent capital in a new city on the west bank of the Tigris. This new city was at an intersection of trade-routes; significantly, it was near the ruins of the old Sassanid Persian capital of Ctesiphon, which the Arabs called al-Madā'in—the cities. Ctesiphon was the first great metropolis conquered by Islam, and Persia the first great civilisation completely absorbed by it. Already in the early periods of Arab conquest, the artists and artisans, the scribes and gentlemen of the old imperial capital must have contributed much that was vital to the life of the new garrison cities founded by the conquerors, and to the new civilisation that was growing up in them. Not much more than a century later, Iraq once again became the centre of an imperial system and society, and its new capital the heart of Islamic civilisation. From the ruins of Ctesiphon many stones were taken, for use in the building of the new city.[1]

The official name of the new capital was Madīnat as-Salām—the City of Peace—but it is usually known by the name of the small town that previously occupied the site—Baghdad. From this city, or its neighbourhood, the Caliphs of the House of Abbas reigned as heads

[1] The importance of the capture of Ctesiphon to the new Muslim Empire, rather neglected by previous historians, was shown by M. Streck in his article 'Al-Madā'in', in the *Encyclopaedia of Islam* (1st ed.). The point was developed by Louis Massignon, *Salmân Pâk et les prémices spirituelles de l'Islam iranien* (Tours, 1934), pp. 3 ff., and *idem*, 'La "Futuwwa" ou "pacte d'honneur artisanal" entre les travailleurs musulmans au moyen âge', *La Nouvelle Clio*, IV (1952), pp. 176–7.

of most of the Islamic world for five centuries—at first as effective rulers of the Empire, later, after a period of rapid political decline, as nominal suzerains, while real power was exercised by secular, mostly military, rulers.

The Abbasids, like others before and after them who had won power by means of a revolutionary movement, soon found themselves forced to choose between the tenets and objectives of their supporters on the one hand, and the needs of government and empire on the other. The Abbasid Caliphs chose orthodoxy and continuity, and had to meet and suppress the angry resentment of some of their more radical followers. Abū Muslim himself, the architect of their victory, was put to death, as were several of his associates. This alienated the extremist wing, which thereafter found expression in a series of religio-political revolts in Iran, and later in the extremer forms of Shī'ism. At the same time, the change reassured the orthodox and helped al-Manṣūr to meet and overcome the dangers of foreign war and domestic rebellion, and, in a long and brilliant reign, to lay the foundations of Abbasid government. In this task, he was ably seconded by a family that was to play an outstanding role in the first half-century of Abbasid rule. The Barmakids are usually described as Persian. It would be more accurate to describe them as Central Asian Iranians, descended from the aristocratic Buddhist priesthood of the city of Balkh. Shortly after the foundation of Baghdad, Khālid al-Barmakī became the wazīr, or chief minister, of al-Manṣūr. Thereafter he and his descendants, as wazīrs, developed and directed the administration of the Empire until the dramatic and still unexplained destruction of the Barmakids by the Caliph Hārūn ar-Rashīd in 803.

The capital had been moved eastward, nearer to the old centres of Iranian civilisation. The Arab aristocratic monopoly of power had ended, and an Islamised Persian aristocracy was naturalised into the ruling class. The Persians, with their superior skills and experience, were becoming more numerous on all levels of the administration, and the Barmakids were firmly established as heads of the whole apparatus of the state under the supreme authority of the Caliph. It is not surprising that Persian influences became stronger and stronger. Sassanid traditions were revived and Sassanid Persian models followed both in court ceremonial and in the administration of government. This meant considerable departure from Arab tribal tradition, which indeed could offer little guidance in either respect. The formation for the first time in the Islamic state of a standing army on the Persian model reduced the dependence of the dynasty on the Arab tribal levies and thus further diminished the Arab influences at court. Under al-Manṣūr's successors, the process of Persianisation was accelerated and Persians played an increasingly important part in both political and cultural life.

In administration, the early Abbasid Caliphs followed along the lines of the late Umayyads, with far less break in continuity than was at one time believed. Certain changes, begun under the preceding dynasty, continued at an accelerated pace. From an Arab super-shaykh governing by the intermittent consent of the Arab aristocracy, the Caliph became an autocrat, claiming a divine origin for his authority, resting it on his armed forces, and exercising it through a vast and growing bureaucratic organisation. Stronger in this respect than the Umayyads, the Abbasids were nevertheless weaker than the old oriental despots, in that they lacked the support of an established feudal caste and a priestly hierarchy.

To compensate for this, and to replace the failing bond of Arab solidarity, the Caliphs laid increasing stress on Islamic piety and conformity, trying to impose on their cosmopolitan Empire the unity of a common creed and culture. Again following Sassanid precedent, they stressed the religious element in the authority and functions of the Caliphate, and, by the patronage and encouragement of orthodox theologians, tried to buttress the regime with a class of official exponents of religion—a priesthood in the sociological, although not in the sacerdotal, sense. In pursuance of this policy, the Caliphs rebuilt the holy cities of Mecca and Medina, organised the pilgrimage to them from Iraq on a regular basis, and began an inquisitorial persecution of various heretical movements and especially of Manichaeism, which became prominent in this period. The Caliph al-Ma'mūn (813–33) and his successors attempted to impose one doctrine, that of the Hellenising school known as the Muʿtazila, as the official doctrine of the state, and persecuted followers of other teachings. This attempt failed, and when al-Mutawakkil (847–61) needed popular support against the insubordinate Turkish soldiery, he was compelled to abandon and even to suppress the Muʿtazila and to adopt orthodox views. Islamic orthodoxy and the Islamic religious institution were already strong enough to resist and overcome the attempt by the state to impose its will on them in matters of doctrine, even when the state was that of the orthodox Caliph. This attempt at an Erastian Islam had failed and was not repeated. After al-Mutawakkil, the Abbasids adhered, formally at least, to the most rigid orthodoxy, nor did any other dynasty not openly heretical try to dictate doctrine to the Islamic religious institution.[1]

---

[1] On these points see the important observations of H. A. R. Gibb, 'An Interpretation of Islamic History', *Journal of World History*, i (1953), 46–7. For another

The Abbasid victory has been described, with some colour, as a 'bourgeois revolution'—as a political victory of the new bourgeois class which had been gaining in wealth and power since the beginnings of the Arab Empire. The conquests, and the upheavals and dispossessions that had inevitably accompanied and followed them, had resulted in a release and movement of capital on a vast scale. The accumulated treasures of state, Church, and aristocracy were returned, after centuries, to free economic circulation, and a plentiful supply of precious metals greased the wheels of commerce in the Islamic Empire and beyond. A new class of merchants, many of them non-Arab and even non-Muslim, arose to profit from this situation, and was soon able to build up great fortunes. The concentration of capital was paralleled by a concentration of labour, made readily and cheaply available through the flight of the peasants to the towns, the use of forced labour, and the ruination of the pre-Islamic privileged classes. The new Arab towns, with their garrisons and cantonments, their courts and administrations, provided a market and an opportunity for trade both in necessities and in the more profitable luxuries, for which a mixed and newly enriched imperial society quickly developed a taste. The rise of the new bourgeoisie, already noticeable under the Umayyads, advanced rapidly under the Abbasids, where conditions seem to have been much more favourable to their activities. Despite the hostility and resistance of the bureaucrats, still affected by older Persian aristocratic and feudal traditions, they found their way even to the seats of government, in which they began to play an increasingly active role. The flourishing trade and thriving traders of the time have their echoes also in religion and literature. Religious tradition, hostile to government and government service, heaps praise on buying and selling, and in the popular prototype the warrior-conqueror gives way, as an ethical and religious ideal, to the upright merchant.[1]

The Empire had rich resources. Wheat, barley and rice were the

view on the emergence at this time of a Persian-inspired state clericalism and the formation of a Muslim scribal (rather than clerical) class see I. Goldziher, 'Islamisme et Parsisme', *Revue de l'Histoire des Religions*, XLIII (1901), 1 ff. and C. H. Becker, *Islamstudien*, I (Leipzig, 1924), pp. 13 f. The use of the term 'religious institution' to denote the rather vaguely defined religious personnel and apparatus of Islam seems to date back to A. H. Lybyer's contrast of the 'Ruling Institution' and the 'Muslim Institution' in his *The Government of the Ottoman Empire in the Time of Suleiman the Magnificent* (Cambridge, Mass., 1913).

[1] For a recent discussion of these points see S. D. Goitein, 'The Rise of the Near-Eastern Bourgeoisie in early Islamic Times', *Journal of World History*, III (1957), 583–604. See also W. Björkman, 'Kapital-entstehung und -anlage im Islam', *Mitteilungen des Seminars für Orientalische Sprachen*, XXXII, 2 (1929), 80–98; and B. Lewis, *The Arabs in History* (London, 5th ed. 1960), pp. 91 ff.

main crops grown in the great irrigated river-valleys. Dates and olives were important secondary food crops. The Empire was rich in metals too—silver from the eastern provinces, especially from the Hindu Kush, copper from near Isfahan, iron from Persia and Central Asia, gold from Nubia and the Sudan, precious stones from many parts, pearls from the Persian Gulf. Timber was lacking in the western provinces but available in the east, and much more was imported from India and beyond.

The Abbasids are reported to have improved agriculture. They extended irrigation works and reorganised the land-tax in a form more equitable to the peasants, though the status of the peasants was still bad and was in time worsened by the speculations of wealthy merchants and landowners and by the introduction of slave labour on large estates. The most important industry was textiles, which were produced in great quantities all over the Empire, both for home consumption and for export—cloth, clothes, carpets, tapestries, etc. Linen was manufactured mainly in Egypt. Cotton was at first imported from India and then cultivated in eastern Persia, from which it spread westwards as far as Spain. Silk was made in Persia, carpets and cloth almost everywhere. After the capture in 751 of some Chinese papermakers in a battle east of the Jaxartes river, the use and then the manufacture of paper spread rapidly westwards across the Islamic world, bringing with it a cultural revolution comparable, albeit on a smaller scale, with that later brought by another Chinese discovery—printing.

These and other products were carried by a vast network of trade connections which linked the different provinces of the Empire with one another, and also with the outside world by the land and sea routes to Europe, Africa, India, south-east Asia and the Far East.

Economic changes of this magnitude brought with them important social consequences. The Arab warrior caste which had been the dominant element in the Umayyad state was in time replaced by a new, composite ruling class of landowners and bureaucrats, merchants and men of religion, professional soldiers and *literati*—often in conflict with one another. The Islamic town was transformed from a garrison city to a market and exchange and then in time to the centre of a flourishing and diversified urban civilisation. This was the classic age of Islam, when a new and rich civilisation, born of the mingling of many races and traditions, came to maturity.

The reign of Hārūn ar-Rashīd (786–809) is usually regarded as the 'golden prime' of Abbasid power, but it is from this time that the first portents of decline are seen. One of these is the collapse of the political authority of the Caliphate in the provinces, which advanced rapidly under his successors. In the west, after the loss first of Spain and then of North Africa (756–800), Egypt fell away in 868 when the governor, Aḥmad ibn Ṭūlūn, a Turkish pretorian sent from Baghdad, made himself independent and extended his rule to Syria. The fall of his dynasty was soon followed by the accession of another Turkish dynasty of similar origin, and thereafter Egypt was never again ruled from Baghdad. The rise of an independent centre in Egypt, often ruling Syria too, created a new no-man's-land between Syria and Iraq, and allowed the Bedouin Arab tribes of the desert fringes to recover the independence they had lost after the fall of the Umayyads. At times, during intervals of military weakness, they were even able to extend their power into the settled lands of Syria and Mesopotamia, to seize cities and establish transitory dynasties.

In the east, the process of disruption took a somewhat different form. The early Abbasids had maintained an alliance with the Persian aristocratic wing of the movement that had brought them to power. This alliance was badly shaken by an obscure internal convulsion during the reign of Hārūn, which culminated in the degradation and destruction of the Barmakids and the assumption by Hārūn of the reins of power in his own not too competent hands. After Hārūn's death, civil war broke out between his sons, al-Amīn and al-Ma'mūn. Al-Amīn's strength lay mainly in the capital and in Iraq, al-Ma'mūn's in Persia; and the civil war has been interpreted as a national conflict between Arabs and Persians, ending in a Persian victory. It was more probably a continuation of the social struggles of the immediately preceding period, complicated by a regional rather than national rivalry between Persia and Iraq. Al-Ma'mūn, relying upon eastern support, for a while projected the transfer of the capital from Baghdad to Merv, but in the face of the fierce resentment of Baghdad, and indeed of Iraq, decided to return to the imperial city. Thereafter, Persian aristocratic and regional aspirations found an outlet in local autonomous dynasties. In 820 Ṭāhir, al-Ma'mūn's Persian general, became virtually independent in Khurasan and founded a dynasty. In doing so, he set a precedent for many others who, while for the most part still recognising the suzerainty of the Caliphs, deprived them of all effective authority in the regions under their sway.

Perhaps even more ominous than the growth of provincial autonomy was the weakness of the defences of the Empire. By Abbasid times the territorial frontiers of Islam had been more or less stabilised. The great Arab conquests had ended; the only foreign wars of any importance were with the Byzantines, and even these seem to have been more for show than for effect. The inconclusive march of Hārūn ar-Rashīd to the Bosphorus in 782 was the last major offensive launched against Byzantium by Islam until the coming of the Turks. Till then, Islam was on the defensive. Byzantine armies sought out weak spots in Syria and Mesopotamia, while Khazar invaders from the steppe country entered Islamic territory in Armenia and the Caucasus.

While the power of the Caliphs in the provinces in both east and west was reduced to the granting of diplomas of investiture to the *de facto* rulers, their authority even in the metropolitan province of Iraq was rapidly diminishing. As long as Baghdad retained control of the vital trade-routes leading through it, the political fragmentation of the Empire did not impede, and in some respects actually helped, the expansion of economic and cultural life. But soon more dangerous developments appeared. A spendthrift court and an inflated bureaucracy produced chronic financial disorder, aggravated by the loss of provincial revenues and, subsequently, by the exhaustion or loss to invaders of gold and silver mines. From the time of al-Muʿtaṣim (833–42) and al-Wāthiq (842–7), the Caliphs became the puppets of their own generals, who were often able to appoint and depose them at will.

By the early years of the tenth century, the decay of the authority of the Caliphate was completed. The event that is usually taken to symbolise this process was the grant to the governor of Iraq, Ibn Rā'iq, of the title *amīr al-umarā'*—Commander of Commanders. This title, apparently intended to assert the primacy of the military commander of Baghdad over his colleagues elsewhere, served at the same time to give formal recognition to the existence of a supreme temporal authority, exercising effective political and military power, and leaving the Caliph only as formal head of the state and the faith and representative of the religious unity of Islam. Finally, on 17 January 946, came the ultimate degradation, when the Shīʿite Persian house of Buwayh, which had already established itself as a virtually independent dynasty in western Persia, invaded the capital and destroyed the last shreds of the Caliph's independence.

From this time until the conquest of the city by the Mongols in 1258, the Caliphate became a purely titular institution, representing the headship of orthodox Sunnī Islam and acting as a legitimating authority for the numerous secular rulers who exercised effective sovereignty. The Caliphs themselves, except for a brief period before the end, were at the mercy of these secular rulers.

The arrival of the Buwayhids in Baghdad was not only significant as a turning-point in the political evolution of the Caliphate—it also marks an important moment in what has been called the 'Iranian

Intermezzo' in Middle Eastern history.[1] Between the decline of Arab power in the ninth century and the final establishment of Turkish power in the eleventh century, there was an interval of Iranian revival, this time in an unmistakably national form, through Iranian dynasties resting on Iranian support, based on Iranian territory and, most important of all, fostering a revival of an Iranian national spirit and culture in a new Islamic form. As we have seen, the first Muslim Persian independent dynasty was that of the Tahirids in eastern Persia (821–73). It was followed by those of the Saffarids (867–903) and Samanids (875–999) in the east and by the Buwayhids (932–1055) and others in the north and west. The Buwayhid advance from Iran into Iraq was paralleled by the establishment of other Iranian dynasties, of both Persian and Kurdish stock, further north, in Azerbaijan, Armenia and beyond. All these dynasties were Muslim. Some of them were still imbued with Arab Islamic ideals and indifferent to Persian culture, but the course of events and the nature of their support made them willing or unwilling sponsors of a Persian renaissance. The most creative role was that of the Samanids, whose capital at Bukhara was a centre of Persian cultural revival. Under most of the Samanid rulers the official language was Persian. They encouraged Persian poets and scholars, and the tenth and eleventh centuries saw the birth of a new Persian literature, written in Arabic letters and profoundly influenced by the Muslim faith and tradition, but nevertheless distinctively and essentially Persian.

As well as the Iranian revival, Buwayhid supremacy also inaugurated a period of Shī'ite expansion, and indeed the two have often been erroneously identified. After the death of the Shī'ite pretender Ja'far aṣ-Ṣādiq in 765, his followers split into two main groups, supporting the claims to the succession of his sons Mūsā and Ismā'īl. The followers of the former recognised Mūsā and his descendants as rightful Imāms of Islam until the twelfth in line after the Caliph 'Alī. This twelfth descendant disappeared in obscure circumstances and his messianic return is awaited by the so-called Twelver Shī'a to this day. The Twelvers were generally moderate in their doctrines, which differed to a comparatively minor extent from those of Sunnī Islam.

The second group, however, known as the Ismā'īlīs from their support of Ismā'īl, inherited the extremist and revolutionary teachings and functions of earlier Shī'ism in the Umayyad period. The transformation of the Caliphate in the eighth and ninth centuries from an agrarian, military state to a cosmopolitan Empire with an intensive commercial and industrial life had subjected the loose social

[1] The term was first used by V. Minorsky; for an evaluation of the Buwayhids see his *La domination des Dailamites* (Paris, 1932).

structure of the Empire to grave strain, and engendered widespread discontent. The rapid growth of the intellectual life of Islam, and the clash of cultures and ideas resulting from outside influence and internal development, again helped to prepare the way for the spread of heretical movements which, in a theocratic society, were the only possible expression of dissent from the existing order. The endemic disorders and upheavals of the late ninth and early tenth centuries brought these strains to breaking-point, and the Caliphs were called upon to deal with a series of challenges ranging in form from the revolutionary violence of the Carmathians in Bahrain, Syria–Mesopotamia and Southern Arabia, to the more subtle and ultimately more effective criticism of peaceful moralists and mystics in Baghdad itself. In the late ninth and early tenth centuries, the Carmathian revolts in Syria and Mesopotamia were with difficulty suppressed by the Caliphs, and the rebels in Bahrain were isolated. In the Yemen, however, the Ismāʿīlīs won a more lasting victory and succeeded in establishing themselves in power.

From the Yemen, they sent emissaries to North Africa, where they succeeded so well that in 908 they were able to enthrone the Ismāʿīlī pretender, ʿUbayd Allāh, as the first Fatimid Caliph—so called because of his claim to be descended from the Prophet through his daughter Fāṭima. The first three Fatimid Caliphs ruled only in North Africa, but in 969 the Caliph al-Muʿizz conquered Egypt, where he built the new city of Cairo as his capital.

For the first time there ruled in the Middle East a powerful independent dynasty that did not recognise even the titular authority of the Abbasids, but on the contrary founded a Caliphate of its own, challenging the Abbasids for the headship of the whole Islamic world. The political and military power of the Fatimids was supported by an elaborate religious organisation, commanding a multitude of agents, propagandists and sympathisers in the Abbasid dominions, and also by a skilful economic policy aimed at diverting the eastern trade from the Persian Gulf to the Red Sea, and thus at the same time strengthening Egypt and weakening Iraq.[1] The Fatimids rapidly extended their sway into Palestine, Syria and Arabia, and for a while greatly surpassed in power and influence the orthodox Caliphs in Baghdad. The peak of the Fatimid period in Egypt was the reign of the Caliph al-Mustanṣir (1036–94), under whom the Fatimid Empire included the whole of North Africa, Sicily, Egypt, Syria and western Arabia.

[1] For the evidence in favour of this hypothesis see B. Lewis, 'The Fatimids and the Route to India', *Revue de la Faculté des Sciences économiques de l'Université d'Istanbul*, XI (1949–50), 50–4.

But the Fatimids failed to win the ultimate victory against the Abbasids. After the death of al-Mustanṣir in 1094 they declined rapidly, and were never again able to offer a serious challenge to Abbasid supremacy. One important cause of their failure was the dissipation of Shīʿite energies in the conflict between the Ismaʿīlī and Twelver Shīʿa. The latter also had an important following, including several of the local dynasties of Persia. It is ironic that at the moment of the great Fatimid challenge to Baghdad, the Abbasids themselves were under the dominion of the Twelver Shīʿite Buwayhid Amirs. Despite their Shīʿism, the Buwayhids made no attempt to instal an Alid as Caliph—the Twelfth Imām of the Twelvers had disappeared some seventy years earlier—but gave outward homage to the Abbasids, retaining them as an orthodox cover for their own power and as an instrument of their policies in the Sunnī world.

By the eleventh century, Islamic state and society show many signs of internal decay. The symptoms of decadence are discernible even earlier: in the fragmentation of the Empire into a series of autonomous regional sovereignties; the decline of the power and prestige of the Caliphs even in their own capital, where they fell under the rule of dynasties of alien and heretical Mayors of the Palace; the collapse of the whole political and administrative structure elaborated by the Islamic Empire on foundations inherited from Byzantium and Sassanid Iran. While the real power of the Caliphs and of the Islamic state was lost to a series of military autocrats ruling through their troops, even the religious status of the Caliph as head of orthodox Islam was dragged to the lowest level, as great sections of the population followed heretical sects, and most of the Empire from Persia to Egypt, even including the city of the Caliphs itself, fell under the rule of Shīʿite generals and princes.

In economic life signs of decay appear somewhat later. The Buwayhids restored for a while the order and prosperity of the central provinces. The Fatimids inaugurated the age of the greatest prosperity in medieval Egyptian history. But the signs of economic decay were increasing in the east and later also in Egypt. The once profitable trade with China dwindled and died away, partly for reasons arising out of internal conditions in that country. Trade with Russia and the Baltic countries, which had flourished during the eighth, ninth and tenth centuries, diminished and disappeared during the eleventh, while the growing shortage of precious metals helped to stifle commerce even inside the Empire and accelerated the development of a feudal type of economy.

Grants of land and revenues, of various kinds, had been known since the beginning of the Islamic Empire. By the tenth century, however, an entirely new kind of grant, differing in several important respects from the earlier forms, makes its appearance. The farming out of state revenues had already become a common practice, and soon the government found a precarious remedy for its shortage of ready money by leasing out state revenues to officers and high officials in lieu of pay. Unlike the grants of the early Caliphs, these were not of property rights in state lands, but were grants of the right to collect taxes from lands outside the state domain. Unlike both the earlier grantee and the tax-farmer, the holder of this kind of lease owed no money payment to the state. He was not a land-owner and did not reside on his grant, from which he merely drew revenues through a steward. The tax-farmers continued to function, but now farmed from the great lease-holders instead of from the treasury.[1]

Before long, provincial governors were given the tax-farms of the provinces they governed, with the obligation only of remitting an agreed sum to the central treasury after having met the cost of the provincial forces and administration. These farmer-governors thus became, in effect, vassals or tenants-in-chief of the central power. Soon they became the real rulers of the Empire, the more so when grants and governorships became the prerogative of the military caste, who alone had the strength and authority needed to enforce obedience.

In cultural life, the eighth, ninth and tenth centuries had seen a great intellectual expansion. The economic expansion of the time brought into existence a series of cities with a rich urban life and a population with leisure, taste and curiosity. The translation of Greek scientific and philosophic literature into Arabic initiated what has been called 'The Renaissance of Islam',[2] while even traditional and orthodox Islam, in reaction against Greek learning and Persian worldly wisdom, renewed and enriched the old Arabic humanities with which it became increasingly identified.[3] This Islamic Renaissance was, however, insecure and impermanent. It was a culture of cities, limited to the urban leisured classes and only to certain sections amongst them. Its relations with orthodoxy, and through orthodoxy

---

[1] Islamic 'feudalism' has formed the subject of an extensive and controversial literature. The most recent and most authoritative studies are those of Claude Cahen, notably his 'L'évolution de l'iqta' du IXe au XIIIe siècle', *Annales*, VIII (1953), 25–52. This should be read in conjunction with the same author's further observations in *Arabica*, I (1954), 346–53.

[2] By A. Mez in his book *Die Renaissance des Islams* (Heidelberg, 1922) (English translation, London, 1937). This book remains one of the best yet written on classical Islamic civilisation.

[3] See H. A. R. Gibb, 'The Social Significance of the Shuʻūbīya', *Studia Orientalia Ioanni Pedersen* (Copenhagen, 1953), pp. 105–14.

with the deeper strains of the Islamic religious movement, remained uncertain and tenuous.

During the eleventh and early twelfth centuries, the material weakness of the Empire was revealed by a series of almost simultaneous attacks by internal and external enemies on all sides. In Europe, the forces of Christendom advanced in both Sicily and Spain, wresting vast territories from Muslim rule in a wave of reconquest which culminated in the arrival of the crusaders in the Near East itself. In Africa, a new religious movement among the Berbers led to the rise of a new Berber Empire in Spain and North Africa. Further east, the two great Bedouin Arab tribes of Hilāl and Sulaym burst out of Upper Egypt, where they had lived hitherto, and swept across Libya and Tunisia, wreaking havoc and devastation from which Arab North Africa has not yet recovered. On the northern borders of the Caliphate, already weakened by Byzantine offensives and Khazar raids in the previous centuries, the Christian Georgians were able to restore a Georgian Empire stretching from the Black Sea to the foothills of Daghestan and thence to advance far into Muslim territory.

Most important of all in its permanent effect was the wave of invaders from the east—from the Altaic peoples of the great Asian steppes. The Muslims first met the Turks on the eastern borders of the Empire, and had for some time been importing them into the Muslim Empire as slaves, especially of the kind trained from childhood for military service and later known as Mamluks—an Arabic word meaning 'owned', distinguishing them from the humbler slaves, usually African, used for domestic and other purposes. Occasionally, Turkish slaves appear in the Middle East under the early Abbasids and even earlier, but the first to use them extensively was the Caliph al-Muʻtaṣim (833–42), who collected a large force of Turkish military slaves even before his accession, and later arranged to receive a large number annually as part of the tribute from the eastern provinces. From this time onwards, the Caliphs relied to an increasing extent on Turkish troops and commanders, who in time ousted the Arabs and Persians from military, and therefore from political, hegemony. As the military caste became predominantly Turkish, and as the regimes of Islam became predominantly military, the Turks established a domination in the Middle East that lasted for a thousand years. As early as 868, the first independent dynasty in Muslim Egypt was founded by a Turkish slave, and most subsequent regimes in Egypt were of similar origin. In Persia, national dynasties lasted for a while, but the most important and longest-lived—that of the Samanids—relied to an increasing extent on Turkish forces and was in due course supplanted by one of the most distinguished Turkish dynasties—that of the Ghaznavids (962–1186), founded by a Turkish slave in the Samanid service.

These were, however, single soldiers or groups of soldiers entering the service of Muslim states as slaves or mercenaries and then taking them over. In 960 an event of quite different significance took place —the conversion of the Karakhanids, a Turkish dynasty beyond the frontier of Islam, with their people. Hitherto, conversion to Islam had only been of individuals or groups of individuals. Now for the first time a whole free Turkish people, numbering, according to the Arab chronicler, 200,000 tents, were converted with their Khan and went over to Islam, forming the first Muslim Turkish kingdom in the lands beyond the Jaxartes. After their conversion, the Karakhanids seem to have forgotten their pre-Islamic Turkish past, and identified themselves to the full with Middle Eastern Islamic civilisation.

A distinguishing feature of Turkish Islam, from its very beginning, is the completeness with which the Turks surrendered themselves to their new religion. Partly because of the simple intensity of the faith as they encountered it on the frontiers of Islam and heathendom, partly because their conversion to Islam at once involved them in Holy War against their own heathen kinsmen, the converted Turks sank their national identity in Islam as the Arabs and Persians had never done. There is no Turkish equivalent to Arab memories of the heroic days of pagan Arabia, to Persian pride in the bygone glories of ancient Iran. Save for a few fragments of folk poetry and of genealogical legend, the civilisations, states, religions and literatures of the pre-Islamic Turkish past were blotted out and forgotten. Even the very name Turk came to be synonymous with Muslim, for Turks as well as for Westerners. In the earnestness and seriousness of their loyalty to Islam the Turks are equalled by no other people. It is therefore not surprising that in time a great orthodox revival began and spread under the aegis of Turkish dynasties.[1]

It may be useful to pause for a moment and survey the political situation in the Middle East at the beginning of the eleventh century. In Egypt, the Fatimid Caliphate was still a great power, with its rule extending into Western Arabia and into Syria, where, however, it was forced to share power with local desert-based Bedouin dynasties. In Iraq and Western Persia Iranian dynasties ruled, the most important of them, the Buwayhids, in the central provinces. In the east, the heritage of the Samanids was divided between two states—

---

[1] The encounter between the Turkish peoples and Islam, and its effects on both of them, were studied by P. Wittek in 'Türkentum und Islam', *Archiv für Sozialwissenschaft und Sozialpolitik*, LIX (1928), 489–525; the origins, nature, and effects of the orthodox revival were analysed by H. A. R. Gibb in 'An Interpretation of Islamic History', *loc. cit.* This interpretation has, in the main, been followed in this chapter.

the Ghaznavids south of the Oxus, and the Karakhanids north of the Oxus. Both of these were Turkish, but they were very different. The former was a classical Muslim state headed by a Turkish general with a Turkish Mamluk army; the latter was a Turkish state ruled by a Khan with his own free Turkish tribesmen.

At about this time, two great migrations of the Turkish peoples occurred that transformed the face of the Middle East and for a while of eastern Europe. Far to the north, in the lands beyond the Jaxartes, lived the Oghuz Turks, and beyond them, in the neighbourhood of the Irtish river, the Kipchaks. These last now advanced from the Irtish to the Jaxartes, displacing the Oghuz, and then moved westwards across South Russia into eastern Europe where they were variously known as Polovtsi and Cumans. The Oghuz, forced out of their homeland, migrated into Islamic territory. There were several waves of immigration, the most important being that known as the Seljuqs, after the family that led them. Seljuq and his family seem to have entered Islamic territory in the late tenth century, settled in the province of Bukhara, and were converted to Islam. With the armies which they assembled, the sons of the house of Seljuq served various Muslim dynasties, the last of whom were the Ghaznavids. From these they parted, and in the struggle against them swiftly won power. The grandsons of Seljuq, Tughrîl Bey and Chaghri Bey, led Turkish armies into Khurasan, crushing the Ghaznavids and seizing their chief cities.

It was not long before they began to act on their own behalf. In 1037 prayers were recited in their names in the mosques of Merv and Nishapur. They soon overran the rest of eastern Persia, and then marched westwards, leading a growing army of Turks to the conquest of western Persia. Finally, in 1055, Tughrîl Bey led his army into Baghdad, seizing the city from the last of the Buwayhid Amirs. A new Empire had arisen in Islam. By 1079 the Seljuqs had wrested Syria and Palestine from local rulers and from the declining Fatimids, and, succeeding where the Arabs and Persians alike had failed, they conquered from Byzantium the greater part of Anatolia, which became, and remained, a Muslim Turkish land.

In the second half of the eleventh century, the great Seljuq Sultans ruled over a united Empire, comprising almost the whole of the lands of the Caliphate in south-west Asia, with the addition of Anatolia. After the death of the third great Seljuq, Malikshāh, in 1092, civil war broke out between his sons, and the process of political fragmentation, which had been interrupted by the Seljuq conquest, was resumed, this time under different branches or officers of the Seljuq family. The most important were the Seljuq monarchies of Kirman, Iraq,

Syria and Anatolia, all owing a tenuous allegiance to the great Seljuq, who resided in Khurasan.

It was during this period of weakness and dissension that in 1096 the Latin crusaders arrived in the Near East. For the first thirty years the disunity of the Muslim world made things easy for the invaders, who advanced speedily down the coast of Syria into Palestine. But even in this first period of success the crusaders were limited in the main to the coastal plains and slopes facing the Mediterranean and the western world. In the interior, looking eastwards to the desert and Iraq, the reaction was preparing. The Seljuq princes who held Aleppo and Damascus were unable to accomplish very much, and the real strength of the movement came from further east. In 1127 Zangi, a Turkish officer in the Seljuq service, seized Mosul, and in the following years gradually built up a powerful Muslim state in northern Mesopotamia and Syria. His son, Nūr ad-Dīn, took Damascus in 1154, creating a single Muslim power in Syria and confronting the crusaders for the first time with a really formidable adversary. The issue before the two sides was now the control of Egypt, where the Fatimid Caliphate, in the last stages of decrepitude, was tottering towards final collapse. A Kurdish officer called Ṣalāḥ ad-Dīn—better known in the West as Saladin—was sent to Egypt, where he served at the same time as wāzir to the Fatimids and as representative of the interests of Nūr ad-Dīn. In 1171 he abolished the Fatimid Caliphate, restored the titular supremacy of the Abbasid Caliphs in Egypt, and established himself as effective ruler while professing a somewhat ambiguous allegiance to Nūr ad-Dīn. After Nūr ad-Dīn's death in 1174, Saladin seized Muslim Syria from his heirs as a preliminary to launching a Holy War against the crusaders in 1187. By 1193, the year of his death, he had recaptured Jerusalem and expelled the crusaders from all but a narrow coastal strip. It was only the break-up of Saladin's Syro-Egyptian Empire into a host of small states under his successors which permitted the crusading states to drag out an attenuated existence for another century, until the reconstitution of a Syro-Egyptian state under the Mamluks in the thirteenth century brought about their final extinction, along with that of the other states of Syria.

In Anatolia the Turkish occupation seems to have been accomplished by migrating tribes rather than by any deliberate action on the part of the great Seljuqs. After the conquest, however, the Seljuq prince Sulaymān ibn Kutlumîsh was sent to organise the new province, and by the end of the twelfth century his successors had built up a strong Turkish monarchy in Anatolia with its capital in Konya (the ancient Iconium). Under the rule of the Anatolian Seljuqs, which in various forms lasted until the beginning of the fourteenth century, central and eastern Anatolia gradually became a Turkish land. Masses of Turkish immigrants from further east entered the country and a Turkish Muslim civilisation replaced Greek Christianity.

Meanwhile the Seljuq states in the East, weakened by constant dissension and strife, faced new external and internal enemies. In the north-east a new steppe people, the Kara-Khitay, appeared on the frontiers of Islam. They were immigrants from China, of Mongol stock, forerunners of a deadlier enemy yet to come. Towards the middle of the twelfth century they conquered Transoxania from the Karakhanids and set up a vast Empire stretching from the Oxus to the Yenisei river and the borders of China. A Holy War declared against these infidel invaders failed with the defeat and flight of the Seljuq Sultan Sinjar in 1141, at the crucial battle of the Qatwān steppe. Revolts among the nomadic Turkish tribes accelerated the decline of Seljuq power, and after the death of Sinjar in 1157 his crumbling realm broke up into a number of small states, most of them ruled by former Seljuq officers. Even the Caliph in Baghdad for a while succeeded in reasserting his independence and in maintaining a sort of ephemeral ecclesiastical state in the ancient capital of Sunnī Islam, while further east the Turkish governor of Khʷārizm, the province south of the Aral Sea, created a new Empire which for a while seemed about to inherit the territories and powers of the great Seljuqs.

This period of Turkish immigration and of the establishment of Turkish political and military supremacy also saw certain significant changes in government, in economic and social life, in culture and in religion.

The Seljuq conquests established a new great Empire in the Middle East, the greater part of which was now united under a single authority for the first time since the early Abbasid Caliphate. The Seljuqs were Sunnī Muslims, and retained the Caliphs as nominal rulers, even strengthening their position in two important respects—first by extending the area under their suzerainty, and then by eliminating the heretical regimes that had denied their titular headship of Islam. But the real sovereigns of the Empire were the Seljuq Great Sultans, who had swept away the petty sovereignties into which it had been divided and had met and defeated both the Byzantine and the Fatimid enemies in the west. The title Sultan adopted by Ṭughrīl after his conquest of Baghdad in 1055 is often attributed by chroniclers to earlier rulers like the Buwayhids and Ghaznavids, who exercised a secular sovereignty. The Seljuq Sultans appear, however, to have been the first to have used the title officially and inscribed it on their

coins. In fact, the Seljuq Great Sultanate was the logical development of the office of *amīr al-umarā'*, and the title has remained in use
ever since for the holder of supreme secular power.

In their administration, the new rulers of the Empire relied largely
on Persians and on the well-entrenched Persian bureaucracy. One of
the most notable figures of the period was the great Persian minister
Niẓām al-Mulk, who developed and systematised the trend towards
feudalism that was already inherent in the tax-farming practices of
the immediately preceding period. The misuses of the previous era
now became the rules of a new social and adminstrative order, based
on land instead of money. In time the Seljuqs introduced a number
of innovations, notably the large-scale grant—of a city and district
or province, granted as a form of governorship or as an appanage of a
member of the reigning family. A new kind of grant seems to have
first appeared in border or steppe areas, where it was imposed by
conditions of insecurity. Its use became general as this insecurity
spread across the Seljuq dominions, largely as a result of the migrations of the Turkish tribes. In the new order, the grantee was given
firmer tenure and great discretion. In theory the grant carried a
right to the collection of taxes; it was a remuneration, granted for a
limited time, and could be revoked. This was in fact the case under
the first Seljuq Sultans. Later, however, the grants tended to become
permanent and even hereditary. The state was interested in military
service rather than in revenue, and this new form of grant was no
longer defined by its fiscal value but by the military service rendered
—that is, the number of soldiers maintained. By the late Seljuq
period the grant was no longer a lease of taxes but a hereditary
landed fief over which the grantee exercised seigneurial powers and
in return for which he rendered military service and maintained a
specified number of soldiers. These soldiers really became *his* men,
answerable and loyal to him, and paid by him either with money or
with smaller grants from within his own grant. It is at this point that
Islamic feudalism approximates most closely to the West European
pattern.[1] While the tendency to form a hereditary feudal class with
stable functions thus existed, until Ottoman times no regime was
immune from invasion and overthrow for a sufficiently long period
to allow the completion of this process.

Social upheaval in such a period of change was inevitable. The
Persian aristocracy found itself displaced and pauperised by the
emergence of a new Turkish military ruling class. Landowners were
hard hit by the appearance of new non-resident feudal lords. Trade
withered and declined; minted money became far less common, and

[1] C. Cahen, 'L'évolution de l'iqta'', *Annales*, VIII (1953), 43.

the merchants and artisans joined their resentments to those of the countryside.

The chief opposition movement was again the Ismā'īlī Shī'a, but in a new and radically altered form. After the death of the Fatimid Caliph al-Mustanṣir in 1094 the Ismā'īlīs split into two groups, one recognising his younger son and successor on the throne of Cairo, the other proclaiming its allegiance to an elder son who had been set aside and then put to death in Alexandria. The Persian Ismā'īlīs, led by Ḥasan-i-Ṣabbāḥ, rejected the new Fatimid Caliph and severed connections with the emasculated organisation in Cairo. At the same time they elaborated a revised form of their faith and embarked on a new campaign of intensive activity as a revolutionary movement in the Seljuq dominions. The name 'Assassins', by which they are known, is derived from the Arabic word *hashīsh*, which they are said to have used to induce ecstasy. The modern meaning of the word derives from their political tactics.

The activities of the Assassins were the last serious attempt by the Shī'a to overthrow the Sunnī Caliphate and the orthodox religious institution. For meanwhile a great orthodox revival had been taking place, which in time affected every aspect of Muslim life, thought and letters.[1] Its roots may be sought far back in the past. The religious institution had long since disentangled itself from the state and had jealously guarded its prerogatives in the fields of doctrine, law, education and social institutions, developing according to its own inner logic and only indirectly affected by the needs and pressures of state and government. Though this brought some advantages to the religious institution, it also involved a dangerous failure of co-ordination. The tension between religion and the state was much worsened when the victory of the army commanders in the multipartite struggle for supreme power reduced the connection between state and subject to one resting only on force and concerned only with taxation. The gulf was further widened when the military caste ceased to be of the same ethnic origin as the population and became separate and distinct, and when supreme political authority was held by heretics who denied the basic political precepts of orthodoxy. The removal of the last moral and personal links between ruler and ruled, in a theocratically conceived society, led to a profound crisis in the Islamic religion. Government was left to soldiers and heretics, administration to a secular educated literate class deriving its social and ethical ideals from pre-Islamic Greek and Persian sources. Even in the religious field itself, heresy offered seductive alternatives to orthodox teachings and gained wide support, especially in the cities.

[1] H. A. R. Gibb, 'An Interpretation of Islamic History', *op. cit.* pp. 54 ff.

The militant orthodox revival began in the early eleventh century in Khurasan, which under the Sunnī Turkish Ghaznavids was the only important area of the Muslim world not under Shī'ite rule. Determined but unsuccessful attempts were made by the Shī'ites to win over Maḥmūd of Ghazna (*reg.* 999–1030), who instead gave his support to the Karrāmī sect. These, though themselves accused of heresy, were the spearheads of an anti-Shī'ite Sunnī revival.[1] From the Ghaznavids the mission was taken over by the Seljuqs, who carried the orthodox revival westwards to Baghdad and beyond. Their capture of the city was regarded by the orthodox as a liberation from the heretical Buwayhids.[2]

The purposes of a Sunnī revival, conscious or unconscious, were, briefly, three: to overthrow the Shī'ite regimes and restore the Caliphate; to reformulate and disseminate the orthodox answer to the Shī'ite challenge of ideas; and, most difficult of all, to integrate the religious institution into the political life of Islam.[3]

The first of these was almost completely accomplished. In the east, the Buwayhids and other Shī'ite dynasties were overthrown and the political unity of Sunnī Islam restored. After the suppression of the Fatimid Caliphate by Saladin, a pious Sunnī, in 1171, prayers were recited in the name of the Sunnī Caliph of Baghdad over all the lands of Islam from Central Asia into Africa. Even the militant Assassins, though not overcome, were contained in their mountain fastnesses, and their attempt to overthrow the Sunnī order was defeated. The military strength, political tenacity, and religious seriousness of the Turks which had made these things possible also gave the Islamic world the strength to meet and defeat the infidel, to conquer Anatolia for Islam and to repel the attack of western Christendom in Syria and Palestine.

The struggle against the Shī'ite heresy was carried through with conspicuous success. It began in Khurasan, under the wing of the Sunnī political resurgence. In the early eleventh century, Sunnī divines and jurists began to organise orthodox colleges called *madrasa*,

---

[1] W. Barthold, *Turkestan down to the Mongol Invasion* (translated from the Russian, London, 1928), pp. 289–90; Barthold takes an unfavourable view of Maḥmūd's orthodoxy, attributing it not to 'true piety' but to an understanding of 'the link between political and religious conservatism'. For a more lenient judgement see B. Spuler, *Iran in frühislamischer Zeit* (Wiesbaden, 1952), pp. 111 ff.

[2] This opinion is, however, sharply contested by V. Minorsky in *Göttingische Gelehrte Anzeigen*, ccvii (1953), 196–7.

[3] On the third of these three points, see A. K. S. Lambton, 'Quis custodiet custodes: Some Reflections on the Persian Theory of Government, I', *Studia Islamica*, v (1956), 130 ff., where further evidence and arguments are brought to confirm Sir Hamilton Gibb's account of 'a renewed association of the ruling institution and the orthodox institution'.

in imitation of the Ismāʿīlī mission schools in Cairo and elsewhere, in which the Fatimids had trained the religious propagandists of their cause. After the Seljuq conquests Niẓām al-Mulk established a *madrasa* in Baghdad, and others soon appeared in cities all over the Empire. The *madrasa* system was extended by Saladin and his successors to Egypt. In these theological colleges, Sunnī teachers formulated and disseminated the orthodox reply to the doctrines that had come first from the colleges and missions of Fatimid Egypt, and later, in a more radical form, from the secret emissaries of the Assassins. The Sunnī victory was almost complete. Shīʿism, of both kinds, had been discredited by the weakness and misgovernment of the late Buwayhids and Fatimids. On the level of dogmatic theology, the final and authoritative Sunnī formulations of the Ashʿarī and Māturīdī schools ousted Shīʿī dogmatics among all but small minorities. On the level of popular piety, much of the emotional content of Shīʿism was transferred to Ṣūfism, which, while expressing the intuitive and mystical religion of the masses as against the cold dogmatism of the orthodox state and hierarchy, nevertheless remained within the orthodox fold.

In the course of time the religious institution not only recovered, but actually greatly improved on the position which it had held in the early Islamic state. A new orthodox bureaucracy, trained in the *madrasas*, replaced the secular secretarial class of earlier times, and the religious institution itself, with its own recognised hierarchy and its own jealously guarded preserves, acquired for the first time an established and authorised position as one of the pillars of the social and political order. The ancient dichotomy of religious and political authority, of faith and power, of law and opportunism, was retained, and indeed institutionalised, in the parallel sovereignties of Caliph and Sultan. But the religious institution had made significant gains.

Turkish Islam was dedicated from the start to the defence or advancement of the faith and power of Islam, and never lost this militant quality. It was born on the frontier against heathendom, was carried to the frontier against Christendom, and took control of the Caliphate at a time when Islam itself had to be defended against the threefold attack of the eastern heathen, the western infidel, and the internal heretic. This long, bitter and ultimately successful struggle could not fail to affect Islamic society and institutions in the age of Turkish dominance. Under Seljuq rule a high seriousness of religious purpose begins to inform the whole structure of government and administration. It is most obvious in the increased power and prestige and better organisation of the orthodox hierarchy, and in the growing stress laid on religious education and personal piety even for lay officials. The religious institution had codified its doctrines, increased its cohesion, extended its influence both with the people and the state. Its final integration into the structure of political authority was to follow under the Ottoman Sultans.

Meanwhile a new external threat to Islam, more deadly than any yet, was in preparation. Far away in the north-eastern corner of Asia, the Mongol prince Temujin had, after a bitter struggle, united the warring nomadic tribes and made himself master of Mongolia, with the title of Jenghiz Khan. In the spring of 1206 Jenghiz summoned all the Mongol tribes to a great assembly by the sources of the Onon river. There he unfurled before them the white banner with the nine horsetails, and they reaffirmed their loyalty to him as their Khan. The great Mongol Empire had begun.

During the following years the remaining Mongol and pagan Turkish peoples, even the forest tribes of southern Siberia, were forced or terrified into submission, and Jenghiz Khan was ready to launch the steppe peoples on a vast career of conquest. By 1218, with north-east Asia at his feet, he was ready to turn his attention westward. Under the command of his general Jebe Noyon, Mongol troops invaded the country of the Kara-Khitay, and, by occupying all the lands up to the Jaxartes, became the neighbours of the Muslim Turkish Shāh of Khʷārizm. In the same year, at the border town of Utrar on the Jaxartes, by order of the Khʷārizmian governor, a caravan from Mongolia was pillaged, and the merchants, some 450 in number, most or all of them Muslims, were put to the sword.

The vengeance of Jenghiz Khan was swift and overwhelming. In 1219 he led his armies across the Jaxartes into the lands of Islam—by 1220 the cities of Bukhara and Samarqand, and all Transoxania, were in their hands. Crossing the Oxus without difficulty, they swept on to the capture of Merv and Nishapur and the conquest of all eastern Iran.

The death of Jenghiz Khan in 1227 brought a brief respite, but soon the new Khan was ready to resume the attack. In 1230 a new offensive was launched against the broken remnants of the Khʷārizmian state and army. By 1240 the Mongols had conquered western Iran and invaded Georgia, Armenia and northern Mesopotamia—in 1243 they met and overwhelmed the forces of the Seljuq Sultan of Anatolia.

In the middle of the century a new move westward was planned and executed. The Mongol prince, Hülegü, a grandson of Jenghiz, crossed the Oxus with orders from the great Khan, now ruling from Peking, to conquer all the lands of Islam as far as Egypt. Within a few short months the long-haired Mongol horsemen thundered across Persia, overcoming all resistance and crushing even the Assassins, who in their castles had withstood all previous attackers.

Finally, in January 1258, the Mongol armies converged on the city of Baghdad. The last Caliph, al-Mustaʻṣim, after a brief and futile attempt at resistance, pleaded in vain for terms or for mercy. The city was stormed, looted and burnt, and on 20 February 1258 the Commander of the Faithful, together with as many members of his family as could be found, was put to death. The House of ʻAbbās, for almost exactly five centuries the Heads of orthodox Islam, had ceased to reign.

CHAPTER XVI

MUSLIM CIVILISATION IN THE ABBASID PERIOD

During the Caliphate of the Abbasid dynasty (750–1258) the political organisation of the Islamic domain changed from a national to a multi-national empire which was later to break up into a number of territorial states. Simultaneously the basis of Islamic unity shifted from the common descent of the ruling caste to the common faith of the full members of the community and a sense of that common civilisation into which the religious system had early been growing. At the same time the representation of the community passed into different hands. Where the Umayyad ruler had been the social as well as the political head of the Arab tribes, their affiliates and subjects, the Abbasid prince embodied the power that rendered possible the life of the faithful in the organised pursuit of godliness; but with the weakening of the community's political aspirations the ruler yielded his unifying function to the learned and the pious, the anonymous bearers of the essence of Islam as it had emerged during the course of some six hundred years.

The replacement of political by religious and cultural self-identification, and probably even the relatively short-lived rule of the Arabs over areas widely differing both ethnically and linguistically, would have been impossible but for the Hellenisation which those regions, Arabia proper not excluded, had previously undergone. Although this Hellenisation was for the most part somewhat ineffective politically, it had at least created one level of spiritual uniformity by accustoming the varied populations of what was to become the *dār al-Islām* (the land of Islam) to the scientific systematisation of thought, and to a certain readiness to accept religious experience in terms of theology rather than in the form of a myth. When Islam arrived in the former Persian and Byzantine territories, Gnosticism, the latest, and largely Hellenised, attempt at mythical world-interpretation, was on the wane, and Christian teaching in its several more or less unorthodox forms (and, to a certain extent, Zoroastrianism as reconstituted under the last Sassanids) had imposed yet another layer of Hellenisation. On a less representative, but perhaps more pervasive, level the Hellenistic heritage meant the welding and formalising of largely indigenous beliefs and practices, ranging from convivial etiquette to the conventions of letter-writing and from dream-interpretation to the use of specific techniques of magic and love-charms.

The Semitic populations of the Fertile Crescent and the Copts of Egypt had also been taught by the alien regimes which preceded the domination of the Arabs to keep aloof from government, and to view authority as intrinsically suspect, or even as outright evil. Without this indifference of the conquered to participation in rulership the Arab minority could never have established itself so rapidly and so firmly. Where the people had to be removed from control by the Arabs themselves, as in Iran proper, the conquerors were soon compelled to readmit the natives to an evergrowing share in the administration.

The loosely co-ordinated opposition to Umayyad rule on the part of the Islamised non-Arabs, the ethnically mixed middle class of the urban centres and its spokesmen, the pious of orthodoxy and dissent, flared into revolt in north-east Persia in 747, enabling the descendants of the Prophet's uncle 'Abbās to assume the Caliphate after a campaign of little more than two years. The Abbasids claimed the throne on the grounds of legitimacy. Their conspiratorial skill thrust aside the 'People of the House', the Alids, who traced their origin from Muḥammad's son-in-law and cousin, 'Alī ibn Abī Ṭālib (the fourth Caliph, assassinated in 661) and his daughter Fāṭima. Although an Arab dynasty, the Abbasids relied largely on the support of the non-Arabs and the merely Arabicised, except that for a time the highest political, and for somewhat longer the highest military, offices remained on the whole reserved for members of the Arab aristocracy which was now clustering about the court in Baghdad (refounded as the capital in 762). Iraq became the centre of gravity of the Empire, together with Iran its most important constituent. This reorientation away from the Mediterranean could not but promote the early crumbling of Abbasid possessions in the West. Spain broke loose as early as 756 and Idrisid Morocco in 788; twelve years later Aghlabid Tunisia attained *de facto* independence.

The situation of the Arab conquerors had been remarkably similar to that of the Germanic conquerors of western Roman territories. Like them, they found themselves compelled to utilise existing administrative machinery; and, as in the West, the principle of the personality of law facilitated the co-existence of culturally disparate populations, except that under Islam a man's religion rather than his ethnic affiliation would determine his legal position in society. Moreover, with the gradual Islamisation, not to say Arabisation, of the central sections of the Empire, the law of the Muslims, that is, in this context, canon law, together with law arising from executive ordinance, increasingly encroached on that of the other communities.

The crisis of the Umayyad state had in part been administrative. The Abbasids attempted centralisation as a remedy. The work of the government bureaux was improved by specialisation, and stabilised by location in the capital: the Umayyads had not had a permanent capital, but each ruler had chosen his own residence in accordance with personal preference and for the most part outside the big cities. Further, there was a resumption of that financial and administrative routine which had been the strength of the Roman state. But these promising beginnings did not result in consolidation for any length of time, partly by reason of insufficient technical means to overcome the separatist tendencies inherent in the vast and heterogeneous area ruled by the Caliphs, and partly because of the absence of a national group, or a sufficiently large and important social class, whose interests were bound up with the perpetuation of the Empire. The ruling house did not have retainers of adequate power and loyalty; the officials of the chancery, even when not of the disinterested non-Muslim groups, were technicians willing to take service with any prince. The army consisted increasingly of foreign mercenaries whose identification was primarily with their national group or their chieftains who now commanded them as the Caliph's generals, and who, in certain cases, were hostile to the dynasty on sectarian grounds. Turks, Daylamites, Berbers in varying degrees of Islamisation contended for effective power in the capital, while in the provinces the *amīr* would wrest the administration of taxation from the *'āmil* or, more rarely, the tax-farmer could aspire to administrative authority, in order to exercise his power under the Caliph as a preliminary to complete independence.

Even in its great days the Empire had not been concerned to enforce uniformity. Local tradition, legal and administrative, was never really uprooted. When attained, independence was disguised and protected by the recognition of the Caliph's suzerainty expressed through *khuṭba* and *sikka*, the mention of the Caliph's name in the 'bidding-prayer' of the Friday service and on the coinage. The local landowners had little reason to object when the drainage of funds to the capital ceased. Local independence often meant increased stability, as the frequent deposition of governors had soon become almost the only means whereby the central government could assert its authority. Disintegration was promoted by the private character of administrative loyalties; fealty was to the person of the ruler, not to the office or the State as such.

With due allowance for exaggeration, the state of the Caliphs might be described as a self-governing religious community with its executive powers vested in the absolute ruler. The Abbasids had ascended the throne in order to rid the Muslims of the impiousness and worldliness of the Umayyads. The faith was to be the mortar of the body politic and religion was to become a matter of public concern. Here, as in administration, Abbasid practice was rooted in that of its predecessors. Nevertheless, the gradual transformation of the king into a pontiff, of the vicegerent of (the earlier vicegerents of) the Prophet to the vicegerent and shadow of the Lord himself was to contemporaries a new departure in political style. The deliberate wedding of kingship or empire, *mulk* or *daula*, and religion, *din*, which from the eighth century to the end of the middle ages are frequently described as 'twin-brothers', resulted in a style of public life unheard of before. By proclaiming religion his first concern the Caliph grew to be the head of what might be called the invisible church of Islam. Less fortunate than Constantine and his successors, the Caliph could not depend on organised religion as part of his administrative machinery; less fortunate than the Sassanid kings, he could not even rely on an organised priestly caste; but as his territorial commitments decreased his office developed into a symbol of the continuity of the good life under the *sharī'a*, the canon law, and therewith into the fountain-head, not of political, but of legitimate, authority. An upstart dynast, especially among the peoples on the fringes of the Islamic domain, needed investiture by the Caliph to be considered the lawful ruler. The Caliph concerned himself the more readily with the purity of the faith as political opposition was inevitably articulated in terms of religious reform or sectarian dissent. This was all the more true as the opposition of the Alid rivals of the Abbasids never really subsided, and as a certain sympathy and reverence for this family permeated even such circles as were entirely devoted to the dynasty in power. Sentimentally even more than intellectually, *tashayyu' ḥasan*, moderate Shī'ism, was an integral element of the atmosphere in which the Abbasid Caliphate had to function.[1]

From al-Manṣūr (754–75), or in his full title al-Manṣūr billāh, that is, 'he that is assisted by the Lord', often called the real founder of Abbasid rule, every Caliph assumed on his accession a throne name of which Allāh, God, was one constituent. As protector of the faith the Caliph as the head of the government was primarily faced with three sets of tasks: to safeguard the Muslim community *vis-à-vis* the non-Muslim world—'to safeguard' usually being interpreted as meaning 'to expand', with the consequent obligation of prosecuting 'Holy War' or *jihād*; to protect the Muslim community against schism and heresy; and to enforce the stipulations of the good life as set forth

[1] On Shī'ism, see also above: ch. xv, pp. 647 ff.

in canon law on the basis of revelation and tradition in accordance
with accepted principles of interpretation. The Caliph was therefore
not free to add to, or abrogate, parts of the law, nor was he entitled
to interpret it according to his own lights. He was no more than the
guarantor of its execution. In theory he was elected, but election was
so defined as to cover appointment by his predecessor, provided that
the community would rally to him. The electoral fiction was reality
only in so far as it was true that the consensus of the people could
make, or unmake, the ruler. His relation to his subjects was viewed as
a contract, *bai'a*, which left open the possibility of his dethronement.

The vizier, at first the Caliph's chief adviser, soon became the
intermediary between the secluded Caliph and the community. When
Hārūn ar-Rashīd, in 803, disgraced the Barmakids the process was
slowed but not reversed. A hundred years later the vizier was the
actual ruler, and the Caliph exercised his supreme authority by appointing and dismissing him. In 936 the Caliph became in fact the
prisoner of his commander-in-chief whose surveillance he exchanged,
in 945, for that of the sectarian Buwayhids, a family of Daylamite
tribesmen who in turn were displaced, 110 years later, by the orthodox Seljuq Turks. But while the actual wielding of authority by the
Sultan was hardly contested, the Caliph and public opinion vigorously
rejected the Sultan's suggestion that the Caliph's function be defined
as merely spiritual. Thus al-Māwardī's (d. 1058) *Institutes of Rulership*
defined the Caliph's prerogatives in ideal terms, but at the same time
allowed for the deplored realities of the moment, including the possibility of a plurality of Caliphs.

It followed from the concept of an *umma Muḥammadiyya*, or
Muslim congregation, the Muhammadan counterpart to the political
and religious concept of *christianitas* in the medieval western world,
that non-Muslims could not be full members of the community of
true believers. So the non-Muslims were neutralised in largely self-
governing religious communities of their own, whose relations to the
ruling *umma* were settled by treaties that tended to degenerate into
unilateral contracts. It was in keeping with this view that the most
ostentatiously 'pious' of the Abbasid Caliphs, al-Mutawakkil, was
also the ruler who attempted most purposefully to depress the position of both Christians and Jews. Freed from military service the
non-Muslim, *dhimmī*, was excluded from sharing in executive power.
His tax burden was heavier than that of the Muslim and he laboured
under certain social disabilities. His indispensability in administration (where his presence was, strictly speaking, illegal), in commerce
and in finance was resented; his intellectual contribution was accepted more gracefully. On the whole, his enforced detachment from

state and society was probably more detrimental to his own than to the ruling community.

The littérateur al-Jāḥiẓ (d. 869) contrasts the state of the Abbasids as a Persian, with that of the Umayyads as an Arab, kingdom. In making this distinction his judgement may have been guided by the newly won political importance of the Iranian Muslims, by the progressive obliteration of the social disabilities of the *mawālī* (converted clients of non-Arab stock), by the infiltration of Persian blood into families of hitherto pure Arab descent (not excluding the caliphal house itself), or by the military superiority of the Iranian lands as it was exhibited once again during the ninth-century civil war between Hārūn's sons, when al-Ma'mūn's Khurasanians secured the unity of the Empire for another century by their victory over al-Amīn who controlled the Arabic-speaking areas. Persian revolts and heresies promoted by Iranians dominated the politics of the Empire throughout the essayist's life. But his observation may well have been induced by a realisation of the Persian character of the prevailing regime, the manners and mannerisms of the court, the autocrat's seclusion, his rare but dramatic interference with affairs of state, the aloofness of the world of the court from the people and the ceremonial designed to assure this separation, the secretiveness of the despot's palace with its refinement and its brutality, its singing-girls and its executioner, its pomp and circumstance disrupted by sudden bloodshed.

The tradition of Persian absolutism, Sassanid and older, had produced its system of ethics, a morality designed to assure survival in the whirl of intrigue that surrounded a ruler regarded with awe by virtue of his unpredictability. It was a thoroughly pragmatic system of rules of behaviour, *āyēn*; at its best it would be worthy of the ideal king and the ideal courtier, but by and large the precepts of the *āyēn* were attuned to such kings as are usually found on thrones and to such courtiers as are educated by the necessity to please them. The injunctions of the early Arabic *adab* books are largely translations and adaptations of the *āyēn*. The shrewd and disillusioned practical wisdom offered in a tone of professional buoyancy, which the Persians were wont to collect in the guise of Counsels, *andarz* (in form a close kin to the Hellenistic *diatheke*), handed down by a virtuous king, vizier, or priest, lived on in the Arabic *waṣiyya*. Fashion, reflecting the Persian emphasis on distinctions of status, the *mores* of conviviality, and, in general, the ceremonial of life in the capital and the eastern provinces, was being moulded more and more to accommodate Persian taste and style.

Persian national feeling asserted itself more crudely in merciless and often petty criticism of everything Arabic. The social leadership of the Arab aristocracy and the Arab assumption of cultural superiority, their arrogance based on their kinship with the Prophet and their imperial tradition, were contested by an intelligentsia of Persian descent with arguments that were all too often borrowed from the allegedly inferior antagonist. The racial purity of the Arab clans was impugned, their customs ridiculed as barbarous, the ancient glory of Iran vaunted above the upstart successes of the Arab Caliphs. This *shuʿūbiyya*, or nationalism, was not confined to the Persians, for the Copts, the Nabataeans (the agricultural Semites of Mesopotamia, not of Petra), and even the Abyssinians, also asserted their worth over against the pretensions of the Arabs who soon found themselves defensively wielding the primitive, yet deadly, weapons of their attackers.

But in spite of all this, Arabisation proceeded apace. In fact, it was under the Abbasids that Arabic won the battle of languages and that the Persians yielded to the joint prestige of *ʿarabiyya* and Islam to make henceforth their greatest contributions in the tongue of their conquerors and to become identified with them, at least externally, by the common system of Muslim nomenclature. The Arabisation of Persia deepened throughout the ninth century. Nor did the Samanid revival of the Iranian spirit in the tenth prevent a poet from characterising himself as of Persian blood but Arab song, declaring himself a Persian who had been Arabicised.[1] The ultimate blending of the two traditions is adumbrated when an Arab poet of the ninth century travelled to learn the language and study the literature of the Persians because, as he said, it was only in Persian books that real thought was to be found. The Arabs, he argued, possess eloquence and a classical language, the Persians, ideas.[2]

A more disturbing aspect of Persian influence was reflected in the word *zindīq* which was widely and somewhat loosely used to denote the religious freethinker, but more specifically the dualist, *thanawī*, or Manichaean. The Pahlavi term, *zandīk*, which might be rendered by 'interpretationist' or 'allegorist', originally refers to those innovators in religion who forsake the basic text of the Avesta for a new or wilful or allegorical interpretation. It is probable that his adversaries taunted Mani with being a *zandīk*, which would account for the specific accusation implied when the term is used in the early Abbasid era.[3] It is not altogether clear why Manichaeism attracted the

---

[1] For this poet, Abū Saʿīd ar-Rustamī, cf. I. Goldziher, *Muhammedanische Studien* (Halle a/S., 1888–90), I, pp. 162–3.

[2] For al-ʿAttābī's (d. 823) attitude cf. G. Richter, *Studien zur Geschichte der älteren arabischen Fürstenspiegel* (Leipzig, 1932), p. 84, n. 3.

[3] Cf. H. H. Schaeder, *Iranische Beiträge* (Halle a/S., 1930), I, pp. 82–3. *Zandaqa* was also used for the somewhat ostentatious libertinism that was the fashion in Baghdad literary circles between c. 770 and 820.

Muslim intellectual of the eighth century, unless it was that it could offer the maturity of an integrated philosophical and religious system which had coped neatly and consistently with the problems of good and evil in relation to God and the position of man in the universe, problems that had become burning during the preceding forty or fifty years, and that could not as yet be satisfactorily treated by means of the logical and philosophical equipment at hand in the genuine Islamic tradition. Dualism relieved God of responsibility for whatever evil tainted a world not his by creation; the cause and goal of man's degraded but aspiring existence was made evident by the commingling in him of elements spiritual and material. The appeal of its doctrine must have been enhanced by its esotericism, as well as by the liturgical and artistic beauty of its practice, in stark contrast to the sternness and aridity of Muhammadan ritual.

More than a century later, and at a time when there still existed a Manichaean community in Iraq, the fight against Manichaeism was to turn into a fight against 'allegorists' who arose inside the Islamic community itself. This is one symptom of that crisis of theological thinking which can be felt almost from the beginning of the eighth century and which reached its height in its second half. Viewed from the outside the crisis was brought on by the necessity to adjust the Arabian faith to the cultural milieu of Hellenised and Persianised Syria and Iraq, both as regards formulation and content. The believers were confronted with the doctrines of older and philosophically more subtly developed religions, principally Christianity in its Greek orthodox complexion, but they were also and perhaps even more urgently compelled to face up to the inner logic of the Islamic message itself. Thus problems were forced on them which could no longer be solved unambiguously from Scripture. Certain early thinkers attempted to reach a reasoned statement of their faith by condensing the descriptive language of the Koran into anthropomorphic tenets. These were soon to become offensive to many of their fellows, partly because of the traditionalist and literalist bent of mind of large sections of their public, but also partly because of the apprehensiveness of the dialectically unskilled that he would lose himself in the arbitrary suggestions of an undisciplined process of reasoning. It is at this time therefore that popular and educated religious thinking in Islam began to go their separate ways, and some of the differences between the thinkers themselves were mainly expressive of the greater or lesser distance separating them from the religious feeling of the people.

The crisis was accentuated by a gradual shift in the focusing of the theological interest which was to take some four or five centuries to complete; it was revealed in a preoccupation with human responsibility rather than divine omnipotence in the speculation of the *qadarī*, that is, those concerned with the *qadar* or eternal decree of Allāh. The ethical orientation of the *qadarī* was inherited by their intellectual successors, the Muʿtazilites,[1] who had to face the intense antagonism of the representatives of the prevailing and rigidly determinist attitude of the community. The Muʿtazilites endeavoured to cleanse the conception of God of all anthropomorphic dross, to define it in terms of the Lord's true oneness and to make his omnipotence subservient to his justice. The epistemological weakness of Muʿtazilite rationalism with its one-sided human orientation is strikingly characterised by a late theologian, who observes that their curtailment of divine omnipotence is due to 'their limited consideration of the various kinds of knowledge dealing with divine matters and because by temperament they are firmly intent on finding an analogy between the seen and the unseen'.[2] It is but consistent with the tenor of their thinking that the Muʿtazilites were out of sympathy with the strong popular interest in eschatological speculation, which in its craving for fanciful dramatisation of the Judgement and the Hereafter was apt to embarrass even the more conservative and anti-rationalist divines.

The Muslim heresiographers have always been aware of the interaction between religious and political motives in the formation of Islamic sects, that is, in so far as the distinction holds in a body that looks upon itself as a theocracy. The more readily the theologian would turn a dissenter out of Islam, the more hesitant appeared the community to ratify his verdict. Broadly speaking, the community never actually excluded a dissenting group unless its teachings articulated a religious theme or thought-motif that Revelation had expressly ruled out. Thus incarnationists and such doctrinaires as revered a particular personage as a divine manifestation were always outside the pale, as were those who denied the final character of the Koranic revelation; but the 'impious' Muʿtazilites remained within. In fact, it was as semi-political champions of Islam against Manichaeism that the Muʿtazilites acquired an importance beyond the field of dogma. As the only group within Islam that was possessed of an integrated epistemological and theological system, and as the only group that was schooled in disputation, the government encouraged their championing of the true faith against the dualists. With the Manichaean danger no longer acute the government of Hārūn ar-Rashīd (786–809) could afford a less favourable attitude, but the great

---

[1] On the name cf. C. A. Nallino, *Rivista degli studi orientali*, vii (1916–18), 429–54.
[2] Taftazānī (d. 1389), in E. E. Elder, *A Commentary on the Creed of Islam. Saʿd al-Dīn al-Taftazānī on the Creed of Najm al-Dīn al-Nasafī* (New York, 1950), p. 98.

period of Mu'tazilite ascendancy was to come when al-Ma'mūn embraced their view on the createdness of the Koran and placed the power of the executive at their disposal in an attempt to impose conformity with the official theology of the state. The Mu'tazilites maintained the createdness of the Book in order to avoid another entity appearing to be coeval with the Creator himself, in other words, to uphold monotheism uncontaminated, with a *logos* existing from eternity with, or in, the Lord. The battle was lost when al-Ma'mūn's third successor, al-Mutawakkil, rallied to orthodox opinion which had unflinchingly supported the passionate reverence of the believing masses for the Book to the point of declaring, not only its Heavenly Prototype, but the very copy of the Koran in the hand of the individual Muslim, as well as his actual recitation therefrom, to be uncreate.

When the Mu'tazilites were accused of being under foreign influence the charge was defensible from three points of view. Their aloofness from the religious needs of the majority of the faithful would justify the intended slight, as would the solution they proposed for controversial issues, such as the question of the divine attributes. The real justification of the accusation lies, however, in their readiness to make use of the Greek *art de penser* in their reasoning. It is doubtful at what moment the logical writings of Aristotle and Porphyry's *Eisagoge* became available to the Arabs.[1] It is, however, obvious from the structure of Mu'tazilite thought itself, and from evidence bearing on the state of mind of the intellectual strata of the community in general, that before about 800 considerable information on Greek philosophy was accessible to Muslim thinkers. It must be realised that familiarity with Aristotelian logic meant much more than the acquisition of a technique to organise and present abstract argument. For instance, to be introduced to the terms 'substance' and 'accident', 'form' and 'matter', implied introduction to the problems from which the terms first arose. Also, the early contact with a mature system of logic saved the Arab thinkers from having to go through a 'pre-Socratic' and 'pre-Aristotelian' stage of winning control of abstraction and operating with the abstracted concepts. This circumstance accounts for the relatively finished form in which Arab philosophy makes its appearance and also for the detachment which Muslim society as such preserved with regard to this lightly acquired and ambivalent gift.[2] Greek modes of thinking entered through translation, as most of the medical and philosophical know-

---

[1] Cf. Richter, *op. cit.* p. 103; F. Gabrieli, *Rivista degli studi orientali*, XIII (1931–2), 198, n. 1.

[2] The corresponding effect on Western scholastic thinking of acquaintance with Arabic Aristotelianism has been lucidly expounded by G. Théry, *Entretien sur la*

ledge became accessible, either directly from the Greek or through Syriac intermediaries.[1] In addition they were absorbed through the influence of Persian science, more specifically of alchemy, astronomy and mathematics, which, although constituting a development of Hellenistic work, had in the eighth century come to the Arabs from the cultural centres of northern and eastern Persia.[2]

The answer of the community to the growing complexities of the situation was traditionalism. It was during the second century of its existence when the disruptive pressure of both the Islamised national civilisations and of foreign cultural contributions made itself felt that the community began to consolidate its structure by stressing the authority of the Prophet's *sunna*, or tradition. It is not that the appeal to the Prophet's *sunna* had been an innovation. Less than a century after revelation had come to its close, the opinion had been held that in case of doubt the *sunna* would prevail over the Koran. Thus Islam supplemented the direct divine ordinance by the precept implied in the ways and words of the Seal of the Prophets. Actually, the practice of the community remained the basis of Muslim life as it was normally described by the learned in terms of the Prophetic

philosophie musulmane et la culture française (Oran, 1945), pp. 78–9. To a late observer (Tāj ad-Dīn Subkī [d. 1370], in Murtaḍā az-Zabīdī, *Itḥāf as-sāda 'l-muttaqīn* [Cairo, 1311], II, 87 middle, cited by H. Bauer, *Die Dogmatik al-Ghazālī's* [Halle a/S., 1912], p. 27, n. 1) it looked as though the Greeks accepted only reason, *'aql*, as a source of knowledge; the theologians who wished to remain within the Muslim framework did so by accepting, in addition, *naql*, tradition or authority. The intense irritation provoked by the foreign methods of discursive thinking is reflected in sayings like Shāfi'ī's (d. 820): 'When I hear someone say: The name is either identical with the thing named or it is not identical with it, I declare that he belongs to the speculative theologians and has no religion' (Ghazzālī, *Iḥyā' 'ulūm-ad-dīn* [Būlāq, 1289/1872], II, 93[26]; trans. Bauer, *op. cit.* p. 20).

[1] Direct translation from the Latin seems to have been confined to Orosius and perhaps Columella; cf. G. Levi Della Vida, *Miscellanea G. Galbiati*, III (1951), 186, n. 2 (*Fontes Ambrosiani*, XXVII).

[2] Cf. J. Ruska, *Tabula Smaragdina* (Heidelberg, 1926), pp. 167–76, and M. Plessner, *Der Islam*, XVI (1927), 103–5. The infiltration of Hellenism and its prestige are traceable in such disparate symptoms as the taking over of the Alexandrine *athetesis* of a doubtful word by putting dots or a line over it; cf. C. Rabin, *Ancient West Arabian* (London, 1951), p. 69; Qudāma ibn Ja'far's (c. 948) Aristotelianising translation of the Persian name of the First Man, Gayōmard (lit. 'mortal life') as 'the living, the speaking (i.e. the rational; *nāṭiq*), the mortal' (*Kitāb al-kharāj*, ed. M. J. de Goeje [Leiden, 1889], p. 234, text, and p. 178, translation); and the acceptance of astrology and at least the rudiments of its non-deistic world-view against the opposition of orthodoxy. In this controversy a kind of reconciliation with orthodoxy is effected by explaining that astrology had been a true science but lost its force with the advent of the Prophet; cf., for example, Muṭahhar b. Ṭāhir al-Maqdisī (fl. 966), *Kitāb bad 'al-khalq*, ed. C. Huart (Paris, 1899–1919), III, pp. 47–8 (of Arabic text). This appeal to the different texture of pre-Islamic and Islamic times also recurs in other contexts, cf. Goldziher, *op. cit.* I, p. 24. For the position of astrology cf. C. A. Nallino, *Raccolta di scritti editi e inediti* (Rome, 1939–48), V, 19–38; and Kai Kā'ūs ibn Iskandar, *Qābūs Nāma*, trans. R. Levy as *A Mirror for Princes* (London, 1951), p. 175.

tradition. And it was, so to speak, for the community to select between conflicting solutions of problems posed by everyday practice, solutions that had been articulated as *sunna* by diverse bodies of the learned on the basis of local custom, personal or group preference, or political interest. The *ijmā'*, the consensus, not of the community as such, but as reflected in that of its *prudentes*, was always, and still is, the supreme source of the Prophetic tradition.

The Abbasid government encouraged the intensification of loyalty to the *sunna*. Political and administrative measures were styled and justified in its spirit. Controversial points were settled by investigation of such precedent as was endorsed by the traditionalists of Medina, the city in which the Prophet had spent the years of his legislative activity. But the occasional archaisms and the apparent artificiality of the argumentation must not obscure the fact that, under the cover of an adjustment of the present to the conditions of the days of the Founder, Islam codified, as it were, its current situation, constantly and unobtrusively including an ever increasing number of verdicts pronounced and examples set by the Prophet. The individual traditions, or *ḥadīth* (a saying of, or about, the Prophet traced back to his time by a chain of witnesses), were often forged, as the Muslims themselves admitted. But by acknowledging any one *ḥadīth* as expressive of *sunna* no more was intended than the authentication of its content as in the spirit, and therefore as an indispensable part, of the Islamic tradition as it was, or at least as it ought to have been, and therefore should be in the future. This is, however, not to deny the earnest concern of the *muḥaddithūn*, the traditionalists, with the genuineness of the material they transmitted. During the ninth century the *'ilm ar-rijāl* was developed, the scrutiny of the moral and religious standing of the persons appearing in the *isnād's*, the chains of witnesses, a scrutiny which was made more subtle by the investigation of the historical or geographical possibility of the several witnesses ever having met or been taught one by the other. Considerations of material truth were not rejected *a limine* but their application was limited by a number of factors of which the most effective were the uncertainty of the historical sense and the miraculous foreknowledge of the Prophet.

The first of the great collections of *ḥadīth*, the *Muwaṭṭa'* of Mālik ibn Anas (d. 795), illustrates the reasons behind this expanding traditionalism. It is not a *corpus traditionum* but a *corpus juris*. The author does not propose to collect the sound *ḥadīth* current in the community. He is interested only in finding a basis in the *sunna* for such legal and ritual practice as is upheld by the *ijmā'* of Medina. The next phase in the development of *ḥadīth* collections is represented by the so-called *musnad* works, of which the most celebrated is that of Aḥmad ibn Ḥanbal (d. 855). Here the traditions (critically sifted) are arranged according to their original transmitter (short of the Prophet), that is, all the traditions ever reported from any 'companion' or 'successor' of the Prophet are lumped together regardless of subject-matter or such repetition as would be caused by the same tradition having been transmitted by two or more 'companions', and so on. The difficulty of using such a corpus as the *musnad* was overcome by the *muṣannaf* works. Here the *ḥadīth* is arranged according to subjects, mainly law and ritual, but in the so-called *jāmiʿ* there is also biography of the Prophet and the early companions, history, asceticism and ethics, and within those subjects was further subdivision into problems or events. The individual sections unite, with their variants, all the *ḥadīth* bearing on the particular topic. To the Muslims the most outstanding *muṣannaf* work (not a *jāmiʿ*), which yields in venerableness to the Koran alone, is the *Ṣaḥīḥ* of al-Bukhārī (d. 870), which may be characterised as a system of theology and law whose individual positions are, wherever possible, supported by traditions which have been subjected to very severe criticism. The work of his younger contemporary, Muslim ibn al-Ḥajjāj (d. 875), again classifies the *ḥadīth* according to the system of the law. But his *Ṣaḥīḥ* is less interested in supporting the law from the sources of tradition than in making available all the materials that would stand the rigid scrutiny of the *ʿilm al-jarḥ waʾt-taʿdīl*, the science of impugning and justifying (the witnesses of the *isnād*). Of the numerous collections of *ḥadīth* four more have attained to high authority, all of them originating towards the end of the ninth century: the *Sunan* (pl. of *sunna*)[1] of Abū Dāʾūd as-Sijistānī (d. 888), the *Jāmiʿ* of Abū ʿĪsà Muḥammad at-Tirmidhī (d. *c.* 892), and the *Sunan* of an-Nasāʾī (d. 915) and Ibn Māja (d. 886). As holds good generally for the treatment of *ḥadīth* involving matters of legal and ethical practice, the conditions of admission to these works are considerably less rigid than those applied in matters of doctrine and ritual: without such lowering of critical standards the *ijmāʿ* of legal practice could never have been consolidated into tradition.

Islam as a way of life is a legal system rather than a system of religious beliefs. The elaboration of the law is the principal task of the learned and as the law is 'like the *jurisprudentia* of the Romans, *rerum divinarum atque humanarum notitia*',[2] the lines between the

---

[1] A title used for collections exclusively concerned with the *sunna*, the law and the legal practice; cf. Goldziher, *op. cit.* II, p. 249.

[2] Goldziher, *Encyclopaedia of Islam*, II, 101 *a*. This definition of jurisprudence echoes the Stoic definition of philosophy, for which cf. K. Reinhardt, *Poseidonios* (Munich, 1921), p. 58.

faqīh, the jurist, and the theologian cannot be sharply drawn. The Muslims have defined jurisprudence as 'knowledge of the practical rules of religion', which body of rules is called *fiqh* (originally, 'knowledge'). Together with *kalām*, scholastic theology, *fiqh* builds the *sharī'a*, the 'straight path', the sacred or canon law, where 'sacred' relates to the source rather than the subject-matter of the regulations.[1] Thus 'the sacred law of Islam is an all-embracing body of religious duties rather than a legal system proper; it comprises on an equal footing ordinances regarding cult and ritual, as well as political and (in the narrow sense) legal rules'.[2] Structurally, therefore, Muslim law is a highly original achievement although somewhat akin in its aspiration to Talmudic law, and this in spite of the many and profound influences exercised on it in certain areas by Roman and Byzantine law.[3] The legists' need for support by tradition was responsible for a considerable body of forged *ḥadīth*; besides, it not infrequently gave rise to statements on persons and events of relatively 'modern' profane history that were, in fact, nothing but decisions on juridical problems provided with an alleged historical precedent.[4]

In Iraq 'Muhammadan legal science started in the later part of the Umayyad period, taking the legal practice of the time as its raw material'. The lack of uniformity in legal practice in the several parts of the Empire 'accounts for some of the original differences in doctrine between the ancient schools of law'.[5] It is essential to realise that norms developed from the Koran (apart from certain fields such as cult, ritual and family law) were generally made part of Islamic law only at a later stage. This Islamisation of the law is perhaps the most significant aspect of the consolidation of the community through tradition. In the process of lifting the law out of its popular and administrative basis, which was done in part by systematisation and, more importantly, by its incorporation into the body of duties incumbent on every Muslim, Medina, far removed from the immediate concerns of the government, seems to have gradually become the

---

[1] Cf. G. E. von Grunebaum, *Medieval Islam. A Study in Cultural Orientation* (2nd ed. Chicago, 1953), pp. 144–5.

[2] J. Schacht, *The Origins of Muhammadan Jurisprudence* (Oxford, 1950), p. v.

[3] On this subject cf. for example G. Bergsträsser, *Orientalistische Literaturzeitung*, XXXII (1929), 277–82; De L. O'Leary, *How Greek Science Passed to the Arabs* (London, 1949), pp. 139–40; Goldziher, *op. cit.* I, p. 188, n. 2, and II, pp. 75–6; M. Gaudefroy-Demombynes, *Les institutions musulmanes* (Paris, 1921), p. 156, and *Revue des Etudes Islamiques*, XIII (1939), 109–47. R. Strothmann, *Orientalistische Literaturzeitung*, XXV (1922), 462, has remarked on the influence of Talmudic law in the spheres of marriage and commercial law.

[4] Cf. R. Brunschvig, *Annales de l'Institut d'Etudes Orientales, Faculté des Lettres de l'Université d'Alger*, VI (1942–7), 108–55, esp. p. 153.

[5] Schacht, *op. cit.* p. 190; for some of the following statements cf. *ibid.* pp. 224 and 283.

principal seat of legal learning. The establishment of the Iraqian
school of Abū Ḥanīfa (d. 767), perhaps by his students rather than
himself, was followed by that of the Medinese schools of Mālik ibn
Anas and ash-Shāfi'ī (d. 820), both distinguished traditionalists, and,
as the last of the four surviving so-called orthodox 'rites', *madhāhib*,
that of the conservative theologian and *muḥaddith*, Aḥmad ibn Ḥanbal of Baghdad. To all of these schools the *ijmā'* was the true basis of
law although in the list of its *uṣūl*, or 'roots',[1] it is preceded by Koran
and *sunna*, an arrangement which clearly reflects the tendencies of
the great systematisers. It is followed by *qiyās*, analogy, that is, the
drawing of conclusions on the basis of the *'illa*, the ratio, of the
precedent formulated by Koran or *sunna*; this *aṣl* was slowest in
gaining theoretical recognition because of the subjectivism it was
feared to introduce. This charge prevented a fifth *aṣl*, *ra'y*, reasoning
or opinion, from obtaining universal acceptance. Nor was the
principle of giving room to considerations of the public interest,
istiṣlāḥ, to win general admission to legal theory. The deviations of
the several schools affect, on the whole, only minor points, but in
judging the significance of the areas of controversy between the
schools the feeling of contemporaries must be weighed, and at various
times down to the eighteenth century they found in their divergent
opinions a sufficient ground for violence and even bloodshed.

The victory of traditionalism in the second and third centuries A.H.
which gave Muslim civilisation its structural strength and relative
uniformity is responsible for the predominance of an attitude that
allows reform only in terms of a progression backwards, of a re-
establishment of the unpolluted Islam of the early generations. Pope
Stephen's (254–7) saying, *Nihil innovetur, nisi quod traditum*,[2] sums
up the approach to innovation in both East and West during the
middle ages. In the West, however, the authority of the old by virtue
of its being old weakens from the eleventh century onwards, whereas
owing to historical circumstances it is from just this period that it
becomes ever more firmly established in the world of Islam.

In the economic sphere, the superiority of the Muslim over the
Western world outlasted the dismemberment of the Caliphate through
the eleventh century, some two hundred and fifty years after the
Caliph had become the tool of his mercenaries. A short series of
energetic rulers at the end of the ninth century proved unable in the
long run to reverse that distribution of power which, in the tenth
century, left the Caliph with little executive authority. Agriculture

---

[1] The Arabic term *aṣl* translates both Pahlavi *bun* and Greek ἀρχή.
[2] Quoted by St Cyprian, *Epistula*, 74, 1, 2 in *CSEL*, III, 3, pp. 799, 800, ed. W.
Hartel (Vienna, 1871), cited by F. J. Dölger, *Antike und Christentum*, I, i (1929), p. 79.

suffered first. Civil disturbances in his area would at once affect the farmer. Less immediate yet more pernicious was the effect of the soldiery being paid increasingly through land grants in territories in which the individual grantees had no incentive or obligation to reside. Taxation hit the farmer hardest. The canon law combined with local tradition in making effective exploitation of agricultural income possible and usual, and tax-farming naturally affected only the rural sections. Also, the farmer profited much less than the industrialist or the merchant by the fact that he was the subject of a great power. The protection which the provinces derived from forming part of a large political unit lessened as the central government weakened and as domestic conflicts proved no less destructive than foreign attacks.[1]

Wealth gravitated toward the cities. The money which the absentee owner drew from his estates went into industry and trade which the underdeveloped tax machinery of the government could harass but not undermine. A very substantial proportion of revenue was spent in a few places, above all in Baghdad. Investments concentrated on a small number of favoured industries, largely textile and metallurgical, and on commerce, interprovincial as well as international. The idea of state credit being unknown, the government had no means of meeting an emergency except by levying extraordinary taxes. What the imposition of liturgies on the wealthy meant to the Greek *polis*, the enormous sums extracted from a few individuals meant for the Abbasid state. A special *dīwān*, or bureau, was set up in the capital to deal with *muṣādara*, that is, fines or *res repetundae*. For in most cases it was a fallen official who was made to disgorge, by persuasion or torture, the gains of his tenure of office. The distinction between state moneys and the privy purse of the Caliph was somewhat uncertain; caliphal contributions to public expenditures were loudly advertised; but to have to ask for them was apt to undermine a needy vizier's position. Between an unspecified year of the reign of Hārūn ar-Rashīd (786–809) and the year 918/19, the total revenue appears to have dropped from something like 59 million (pre-world-war II) dollars to 37 million.[2] In the intervening period large sections of Iran had regained their independence under the native dynasties of the Tahirids (820–72), Saffarids (868-903) and Samanids (874–999); the expansion of a money economy had helped

[1] Cf. the observation of Yāqūt, *Muʿjam al-buldān*, ed. F. Wüstenfeld (Leipzig and St Petersburg, 1866–73), IV, 264, lines 14–15: 'Any land whose wealth is spent on another will be ruined; countries will prosper only when the *sulṭān* resides in them.'

[2] For these figures cf. R. Levy, *An Introduction to the Sociology of Islam* (London, 1931–3), pp. 328, n. 1, 343–7, and A. von Kremer, 'Über das Einnahmebudget des Abbasiden-Reiches vom Jahre 306 H. (918–919)', *Denkschriften d. Wiener Akademie d. Wissenschaften, phil.-hist. Cl.* XXXVI (1888), 283–362.

to concentrate landed property in fewer hands; slave labour had gained in importance especially on the large estates; the contrast between rich and poor had sharpened; the state had exchanged the silver standard traditional in its eastern provinces for the gold standard of its erstwhile Byzantine provinces with some resultant loss in the wealth of the East;[1] the dynasty and the bureaucracy had emerged as the only stable elements of the Empire; and, both result and partial cause of these developments, public morality had reached rock-bottom. 'The viziers and governors [no longer] will attend to the concerns of the people and wear themselves out for them, except for the sake of perquisites accruing to themselves. It is not religion that induces them to look into people's affairs, for this [that is, religion] is far removed from them; and when they are barred from receiving those perquisites they leave the people to their troubles, so they will find no one to extend a helping hand to them and to settle their needs.'[2]

Thus the basic equalitarianism of a society devoted to the service of God, whose members acquired their status by reason of their piety alone, had become heavily overlaid by the social values that had developed from the conflict and amalgamation of the Arabic and the Persian traditions, and again from the emergence of dominating militant foreign groups of somewhat dubious social antecedents. The times were not yet when it had become a mark of social inferiority to speak Arabic as one's native tongue, but the prestige of the Arab aristocracy was on the wane; even the members of the ruling house could be found in every walk of life; only the Alids were, to a certain extent, protected from social disregard by the religious significance of their lineage. The government organised the Hashimids and Alids under a *naqīb*, or marshal, and paid them pensions, but their great numbers and the distress of the times only too frequently defeated the intention of keeping them all within the upper class. Purity of descent had been the watchword of the Arab nobility. Under the Abbasids, most of whom were themselves the sons of slave-girls, the maternal background came to count for less and less. In court society, it was official position and wealth, both usually owed to the favour of the ruler, which determined status. The scholar and the poet occupied a marginal, though often influential, position as instruments of the grandees' convivial and cultural needs and as spokes-

---

[1] On the other hand, it was the reliable value of its gold currency that secured the international position of the Muslim economy; cf. M. Lombard, 'Les bases monétaires d'une suprématie économique: L'or musulman du VIIe au XIe siècle', *Annales: économies, sociétés, civilisations*, II (1947), 143–60.

[2] Ibn al-Athīr, *al-Kāmil fī 't-ta'rikh*, ed. C. J. Tornberg (Leiden, 1851–76), VIII, pp. 166–7, *sub anno* 319/931; cf. Kremer, *loc. cit.* p. 341.

men for, and to, the community outside. This community, hardworking and conscious of material values as it was, showed considerable mobility, although the families whose members we can follow for generations in the same calling are rather numerous—merchants, traditionalists, and, hazardously but profitably involved with the life of the court, physicians and financiers, *kuttāb* (that is, virtually the professional administrators) and judges. Countless anecdotes told by its members, as well as a large section of the *Arabian Nights' Entertainments*, portrayed the life of a bourgeoisie of tradesmen and artisans with its upper layer of wealthy businessmen, corn-merchants, tax-farmers, importers and absentee gentlemen farmers. Court society vented its dislike of this (on the whole) industrious and God-fearing class by denying it refinement (*adab*)[1] and, in general, by reviving the classical prejudice against the technician.[2] The soldier was held in low repute. When the pious Aḥmad ibn Khiḍrūya (d. 854/5) wished to expose himself to public contempt he donned military garb.[3]

Class-consciousness was strong. The manners and customs of the several strata differed noticeably and were keenly observed.[4] In making diverse men's estate God had a special design. 'God had power, truth to tell, to make all men rich; but in His wisdom He decreed that some should be rich and others poor, that the rank and honour due to different men might be clearly shown and the more noble of them be distinguished.'[5] The hierarchy of men corresponded to the hierarchy of the constituent parts of man himself, and this hierarchy was in turn paralleled by the hierarchy of objects. In Islamic as in western medieval thought, the Aristotelian notion of the particular and natural *topos*, or place, which any object possessed within the closed system of the world, led to the idea of a graded participation in *being*; more perfect *being*, as indicated by higher rank in the creaturely hierarchy, bespoke a more elevated status in the hierarchy of moral perfections, until in God the *summum ens* and the *summum bonum* coincided—an unimpeachable justification of the given social structure from the standpoint of both the individual and the group. For in the last analysis, it is the higher *virtus* of the

---

[1] Cf. Tauḥīdī (d. 1023), *Kitāb al-imtāʿ wa 'l-muʾānasa* (Cairo, 1939–44), III, 60–1.

[2] Cf. Tauḥīdī, 'Risāla fī 'l-ʿulūm', in *Risālatāni* (Constantinople, 1301), pp. 205–6, with its strict distinction between the representative of theoretical and applied mathematics.

[3] Hujwīrī, *Kashf al-maḥjūb*, trans. R. A. Nicholson (Leiden and London, 1911), p. 119; the passage is quoted by R. Hartmann, *Der Islam*, VIII (1918), 198. Cf. also Ghazzālī in H. Bauer, *Islamische Ethik*, III (Halle a/S., 1922), pp. 94–5, 100, 101.

[4] Cf. *A Mirror for Princes*, pp. 55–6, on the eating habits of different social classes.

[5] *Ibid.* p. 18. The book was written in 1082/3.

Muslim as the sole possessor of ultimate truth that calls forth his higher honour, or *sharaf, vis-à-vis* the unbeliever in the polity.

The disintegration of the Empire furthered rather than impeded the efflorescence of its intellectual life. The comparative economic stability of the outgoing ninth and again of the second half of the tenth century, when the Buwayhids controlled Baghdad and the Caliph, may have assisted in the quickening of speculation and research, but there is no evidence of a lull in the intervening decades. The multiplicity of princely courts acted as a stimulant. The Arabism of the Hamdanids in Aleppo (from about 944 to the close of the century), the Iranism of the Samanids in Bukhara provided curious foils to the unbridled cosmopolitanism of the capital.[1] But the intellectual effort of those last hundred and fifty years of the first millennium, however diversified and original, appeared rather marginal, and in a sense irrelevant, when viewed from orthodox Islam as it was reconstituted during the eleventh and twelfth centuries. Of the most celebrated effort of the period, the reception and development of Hellenistic science, it must be admitted that its cultural significance was much more keenly felt through its subsequent effect on Western thought than through any permanent imprint it left on the Muslim idea of the meaning of man's life, and that where it did become truly acceptable to Islamic thinking this was due to the adoption of a characteristically theological approach to its subject.

Thus Hellenistic zoology might be integrated in the orthodox world view by being used as a means of answering the question 'How did all the creatures of God come into being?' in preference to, say, a biological examination of the animal kingdom. In this manner, the arrangement of 'objects of nature' in a progressive sequence from mineral to plant and on to animal and lastly man, could become a commonplace as an illumination of God's procedure in creating this world. But the concepts of an autonomous *physis* or an autonomous evolution, that is, a 'gradual transformation of one species into another' without supernatural intervention could not be assimilated or thought out. In other words, the achievements of tenth-century thought were never allowed to affect the core of the Muslim world view because they were inspired by interests not shared by the body of believers and because they were, in fact, offered as alternatives to Sunnite Islam.

---

[1] Cf. Goldziher, *ZDMG*, LXII (1908), 1–4; see specifically the governmental edict of 897 forbidding book-dealers to sell philosophical and dialectical works, Abū 'l-Maḥāsin Ibn Taghrī Birdī, *Annales*, ed. T. G. J. Juynboll and B. F. Matthes (Leiden, 1855–61), II, 87, and Ṭabarī, *Annales*, ed. M. J. de Goeje *et al.* (Leiden, 1879–1901), III, 2165, 12–13.

These alternatives were disquietingly attractive to contemporaries. Shī'ism, in its moderate form a modification of Sunnite Islam rather than an alternative, offered direction through the divinely guided, infallible and impeccable *imām* from the House of the Prophet. But it permitted itself to be frittered away in minor political movements and religious conventicles that broke off from the (never formally organised) main body in disputes over the person of the true *imām*. Only at the fringes of the Muslim domain, in the Yemen, in Ṭabaristān, in Morocco, did the moderate Shī'ites score more or less enduring political successes. Shī'ism did however consolidate, as it were, when on the death of the eleventh *imām*, the twelfth, a minor, disappeared, or went into concealment (*ghayba*) in 879, while the community of what came to be known as the Twelver Shī'ites found itself awaiting his return in charge first of deputies (*wakīl*), and then of the learned through whom the *Hidden Imām* would commune with the faithful.

The main dissenters from 'moderate' Shī'ism were the groups that declared the line of visible leaders to have ended with the seventh *imām*, Ismā'īl, who is not recognised by the Twelvers as having predeceased his father but who had, in the view of the Seveners or Ismā'īlīs, betimes bequeathed his offices to his son Muḥammad. From the existence of an authoritative doctrine withdrawn from and above human searching, which to them is a rational necessity, the Ismā'īlīs infer the necessary existence of its dispenser, the *imām*. With the Ismā'īlīs symbolic interpretation of the Koran and the *ḥadīth* of the *imām* sustains a Gnostic cosmology. God appears somewhat like the Plotinian One. He has contact with the universe through his emanations—Universal Reason, Universal Soul, Primeval Matter, Space, Time and the material world, the first two being instruments through which God created the last. To the seven phases of emanation will correspond seven cycles of Time that in turn will correspond to seven manifestations of the deity. Seven, again, are the prophets or speakers (from Adam to Muḥammad and, as the last, the Ismā'īlī *imām*), incarnations of Universal Reason, who are assisted by seven 'bases', incarnations of Universal Soul. Thus Aaron assisted Moses; Peter, Jesus; 'Alī, Muḥammad, in evolving by allegoresis, the inner, *bāṭin*, meaning of the 'speaker's' teaching. The advent of a new speaker introduces a new period of history which will possess the divine knowledge in a purer and more developed form; and it seems that manifestation in science was to be the specific content of the Ismā'īlī-Qarmaṭian message. Since the degrees of initiation were originally seven (later nine) the structural co-ordination of universe and Ismā'īlī organisation was complete. On the highest level of initiation religious truth was recognised as relative and *qua* truth contained in Ismā'īlism.

'...It befits our brothers that they should not show hostility to any kind of knowledge or reject any book. Nor should they be fanatical in any doctrine, for our opinion and our doctrine embrace all doctrines, and resume all knowledge.'[1] In the words of an adversary, 'their longed-for goal is the removal of all positive religion. They took counsel from Magians, Mazdakites, heretical dualists and many followers of the old philosophers, with whom they worked out a method, through which they would be able to free themselves from the rule of Islam.'[2]

Like the early Manichaeans, the Ismāʿīlī adjusted their message to the heritage of their audiences, but unlike them they drew strength from the pent-up revolutionary sentiment of the times. The great revolts in Iran, under Sunbād (755), Ustādhsīs (767–8), al-Muqannaʿ (776–89) and Bābak (816/17–837/8), had in fact, as well as in the eyes of the contemporaries, renewed the levelling programme of Mazdak (executed in 528 or 529). As leader of the Zanj, the negroslaves of the salt-marshes of southern Mesopotamia, an alleged Alid had been able to resist the Caliph's government from 869 to 883, until he was defeated as much by the superior resources of the Empire as by his own lack of a true programme of social reform. The Qarmatians, who in 899 possessed themselves of Baḥrain (now Laḥsā) where they developed an oligarchic welfare state, were charged with communism as well as anti-Islamism. They were accused of having abolished the Koran whose doctrine, in their own view, they were but developing in accordance with the Prophet's intentions. They horrified the Muslim world by massacring the pilgrims assembled in Mecca and by taking the Black Stone away from the Kaʿba in January 930, possibly in order to demonstrate the obsoleteness of the Islamic revelation through God's withdrawal of protection from his sanctuary; but they restored it, at Fatimid bidding, in 951, and withdrew into political passivity. Contemporaries had noted that the Qarmatians were usually recruited from the peasantry; they were likewise aware of the special appeal of Ismāʿīlism to the common people, more specifically the labourers and artisans in the formation of whose guilds they appear to have played an important part. The Ismāʿīlian 'conspiracy' led, in 909, to the Fatimids taking over Ifrīqiya whence they occupied Egypt in 969—a small Shīʿite oligarchy governing a country whose Sunnite allegiance they never tried to change. A curious sense of enthusiasm, of rejuvenation seems to have accompanied their conquests; it was from Abbasid decrepitude that

---

[1] *Rasāʾil Ikhwān aṣ-Ṣafāʾ* (Cairo, 1928), IV, 105.
[2] Goldziher, *Streitschrift des Ġazālī gegen die Bāṭinijjasekte* (Leiden, 1916), pp. 38–9. Cf. B. Lewis, *The Origins of Ismāʿīlism* (Cambridge, 1940), pp. 94 and 90.

they proposed to wrest the *dār al-Islām*, and but for the western crusaders, they might well have succeeded.

The conflict between the two sources of knowledge, revelation and reason, or *in concreto*, the Muslim tradition and speculative or scientific investigation, was the characteristic problem of scholastic philosophy East and West. Two methods of procedure were possible according to whether the datum of faith or the datum of reason was postulated as the primary principle to which the other had to be reconciled. It was here that the Mu'tazilites and the *falāsifa*, the philosophers of Islam, parted company. Their acceptance of the datum of reason as vantage-point put the *falāsifa eo ipso* outside the pale which the Mu'tazila, in spite of their antagonism to orthodoxy, had never left. The dispute over the eternity of the world, inadmissible from the Islamic, ineluctable from the Aristotelian, viewpoint, strikingly illustrated the contrasting points of view. Also shared by Western and Islamic philosophy was the problem of reconciling Plato and Aristotle, or more precisely, the original Aristotelian and neoplatonic elements of which the Arab Aristotle actually consisted, since the Muslims accepted the so-called *Theology of Aristotle*[1] as genuine. The three great philosophers of the period were the Arab polyhistor al-Kindī (d. 873) who was primarily a neoplatonist; the Turk al-Fārābī (d. 950), a logician and intellectual monist with wide interests in ethics and politics; and the Persian Ibn Sīnā (Avicenna; d. 1037), who was most lastingly effective as a medical encyclopedist. It was Ibn Sīnā who best harmonised the dominant currents and who thus represented, in a sense, the zenith of Arab philosophy.

With a keen understanding of the essentials of their own civilisation, the Muslims classified their sciences into two groups. First, the *'ulūm shar'iyya*, that is, studies concerned with the religious law, which is regarded as the core of their intellectual life; these were also described as the Arab sciences, and in addition to *fiqh* and *kalām* (scholastic philosophy) they comprised the necessary introductory disciplines to the study of the *shar'*, such as grammar, lexicography, rhetoric, poetics and history. Secondly, there were those 'intellectual' or 'philosophical' sciences, *'ulūm 'aqliyya* or *hikmiyya*, which by reason of their origin were often designated as the foreign sciences, *'ulūm al-'ajam*, or the ancient sciences, *'ulūm al-awā'il*. This second group, whose subdivision into metaphysics, natural sciences and

---

[1] This was the work of a Syriac writer of the sixth century who used extracts from Plotinus, *Enneads*, IV–VI, in Porphyry's recension. It was translated into Arabic c. 840–50; cf. P. Kraus, *Revue de l'histoire des religions*, CXIII (1936), 211–12. For evidence dating from the eleventh century that there existed in some quarters a certain hesitation with regard to Aristotle's authorship of the *Theology*, cf. S. Pines, *Archives d'histoire doctrinale et littéraire du moyen âge*, XIX (1952), 9, n. 1.

mathematical sciences followed the system established by the neo-platonic commentators of Aristotle,[1] was the glory of medieval Islam in Western and modern Muslim eyes, primarily because of its preser-vation and, in many instances, enrichment of the Hellenic heritage which from the twelfth century onward the Occident was to take over through retranslation from the Arabic. The productive span of Arabic science, that is, science propounded in Arabic by representatives of Muslim civilisation, Easterners for the most part, and many of them Christians or Jews, began in the ninth century when translation from the Greek (or the Syriac), already in vogue in Jundē Shāpūr *c.* 750, began on a large scale, and extended to the end of the eleventh century when creativeness had been sacrificed to consolidation. An overwhelming eagerness to learn and to apply directed the selection of subject-matter from Indian, (Hellenised) Persian and, for the most part, Greek, sources. Even the greatest among the Muslim physicians such as ar-Rāzī (d. 925 or 924) allowed the skeleton of Greek an-thropology to stand. Their contribution to the Corpus of Galen lay in the finesse of their observation, the precision with which a subtle terminology would convey its results, the indefatigable amassing of additional detail, on occasion also experimental modification of traditional prescription and cure.

In contrast to this great interest in sciences it is characteristic of the movement that it disregarded Greek belles-lettres. Patronised by circles who must have felt the need for 'westernisation', fashionable through the encouragement of the court, attractive through the multiplicity of information and techniques it conveyed, and reward-ing through the esoteric newness of its approach, Hellenised thinking and Hellenised science were fully assimilated only by little groups of researchers, who despite their small numbers established the un-contested leadership of Arabic science for approximately three cen-turies. This limited Hellenisation also set the intellectual style of high society as a whole. As might be expected the ethical roots of Greek thought in an anthropocentric universe of primarily political orienta-tion could not be transplanted. The *faqīh* (legist) and the *mutakallim* (scholastic) would admit the foreign element on the practical level or would make use of Greek dialectics in self-defence against the *falāsifa* (philosophers). But its intellectualism was felt to be irrecon-cilably opposed to the faith. 'Who deals with logic falls into heresy.'[2]

[1] Cf. Nallino, *Scritti*, v, pp. 2–3.

[2] Muh. Ben Cheneb, *Proverbes arabes de l'Algérie et du Maghrib*, II (Paris, 1906), 283: *man tamanṭaqa tazandaqa*. Cf. for example I. Goldziher, 'Die Stellung der alten islamischen Orthodoxie zu der antiken Wissenschaft', *SBAW, phil.-hist. Kl.* (1915–18), p. 24.

If alchemy and astrology, which were developed as part of the Ismāʿīlī world-view and used in its propaganda, attracted high-placed protectors and gave a powerful impulse to astronomical and chemical studies, this was one more reason for the theologian to combat the intruder. In the circumstances the great accomplishments of individuals in medicine and chemistry, mathematics and astronomy, are more surprising than is the failure of Hellenism to humanise and rationalise the ethos of Muslim civilisation. With all this, the intellectual taste of the ninth and tenth centuries retains much in common with Hellenistic and declining antiquity. The predilection for *mirabilia*, *ʿajāʾib*, was strong enough to silence scrutiny when curiosity was to be gratified by a tall story of venerable antiquity. Geography, including cartography, as well as history, in spite of their painstaking accuracy in the area of the directly observable, was loth to cut out those margins where legend and fancy were found. The mere fact that the present had grown out of an episode of 'sacred' history compelled a duplicity of critical standards. On the other hand it was from that very episode that a brilliant tradition of historiography developed. The life of the Prophet was its first subject; the history of the World its definitive major form. From creation through the incidents of biblical and pagan times to the greatest event of all, the call of the Prophet and its realisation, down to the writer's own day, aṭ-Ṭabarī (d. 923) would allow his narrative to stretch in conscientious and comfortable meanderings, placing source next to source, surveying in annalistic sequence the several sections of the *dār al-Islām*, careful of those princely obituaries from which in due course biographical encyclopedias were to develop. Throughout the middle ages the historiographical tradition was to remain alive in the form of biographical or genealogical manuals, of histories of individual regions, cities, reigns or events, as histories of the world (with emphasis on contemporary happenings), as panegyrics or as factual illustration of a philosophic thesis.[1] It was relatively little affected by that crisis which engulfed belles-lettres after the eleventh century and made Islamic civilisation of the later middle ages a civilisation of handbooks.

What was to become the definitive style and outlook in the sphere of literature developed during the first three centuries of the Abbasid period through the partial victory of a revolt against the 'classical' tradition that drew its strength from the linguistic and sentimental authority of pre-Islamic poetry. The rebels struck out for the admission of an urban locale, the displacement of the plaintive stereotypes of the *nasīb*, or the amatory prelude, of the conventional *qaṣīda*,

---

[1] E.g. Miskawayh (d. 1030), *Tajārib al-umam*, 'history as the instruction of the living'.

or ode, the recognition of both religious experience and minor descriptive plaisanteries as legitimate topics, and the acceptance of *ẓarf*, or elegant wit, as an accomplishment deserving of effort and applause. The several parts of the *qaṣīda* became independent; a certain dramatisation of love poetry took place; the use of shorter and lighter metres became the badge of the innovators; and, above all, the *muḥdath*, or Modern, indulged in *badīʿ*, a 'new-fangled' mode of pointed and largely trope-ridden expressions. A novel imagery often inspired by a sharpened response to colours and the elements of an idyllic scenery became popular, though it earned the derision of the critics who felt repelled by the exaggerated use of hyperbole and other ornaments of speech which they slowly learned to distinguish and to define in the very process of criticism. The gaiety and visual precision of Abū Nuwās (d. 810 or 813), the contrite simplicity of Abū 'l-ʿAtāhiya's (d. 828) religious poems, or *zuhdiyyāt*, the recherché grandeur of Abū Tammām (d. 846), the intricacies of whose richly configurated verse made him the prototype of the 'new' style, were characteristic of the varied aspirations of an age groping toward sophistication. Equally characteristic is the contrast between the frivolity and even smuttiness of Abū Nuwās and his followers, and the Platonising strain of the romantic conception of passion that is found in the delicate records of al-ʿAbbās ibn al-Aḥnaf's (d. 806) affection for his lady, where love appears as ennobling and as the prerogative of the noble, a strain that was to be transplanted to Spain and ultimately to inject itself into the *fin amors* of the troubadours.

The critics found fault with the unclassical language employed by the Moderns, with their reckless use of figurative speech and the artifices of their *concettismo*; but fundamentally they shared their opponents' aesthetic outlook. Poets and critics considered that a finer rendering of an inherited motif was the equivalent of originality in the western sense. They conceived of beauty as an element extraneous to the conceptual content; both concentrated on the individual verse rather than the composition as a whole; both were agreed that the author should aim at surprise, the extraordinary, and the paradoxical. The critics would plead for moderation, but be incapable of defining it except in terms of appropriateness. The tenth century witnessed the rise of literary theory as a science and saw the transition from the keen but disjointed observations of Ibn Qutayba (d. 889) to the purely formal analysis of the *badīʿ* by the poet Ibn al-Muʿtazz (wrote in 887/8; d. 908); and the *Criticism of Poetry* (*Naqd ash-shiʿr*) on the basis of Aristotelian categories by Qudāma ibn Jaʿfar (d. *c.* 948), and again the abandonment of the dialectical foundation of theory later in the century is an index of the influx and gradual neutralisation of Greek methods. The modernism of the tenth century was in large measure a mood of daring and youthfulness. Al-Mutanabbī's (d. 965) fresh perception of age-old experience, his unsurpassed mastery of language, the reckless rhetorisation of his odes made him the object of embittered critical controversy from which he emerged in Arab eyes as their greatest poet. But not only was he unsurpassed, he was unsurpassable. Style could not be refined any more without becoming tortured and dulled. The last great master,[1] Abū 'l-ʿAlāʾ al-Maʿarrī (d. 1058), unbearably mannered in much of his ornate prose, holds our interest because of the timelessness of his piercing pessimism and his Ismāʿīlī-tainted disgust with the hollowness of institutionalised religion. The Moderns had not produced an aesthetic theory; so modernism shrank to verbalism and irrelevancy when the spirit of the age sank in the eleventh century.

The Abbasid, as the Hellenistic, poet was a man of learning. Khalīl ibn Aḥmad (d. 791) had established the canon of prosody by working the available metres, classical and contemporary, into an ingeniously contrived system which he rendered all-inclusive by pruning such 'variations' of the standard metres as seemed too irregular to him whatever the pre-Islamic evidence for their occurrence. Older borrowings from Persian prosody were accommodated, more recent intrusions left aside. The interaction of Arabic and Persian poetry in the Abbasid period needs further investigation, but it is clear that a different type of imagery was beginning to develop in Persia and that Arabic was ahead, by perhaps two centuries, of Persian literature in its taste for the ornate and the mannered.

Largely based on evidence from poetry (and the *ḥadīth*) for its rules and observations, Arabic grammar began with Sībawayh (d. c. 796) as a comprehensive series of descriptive statements and developed into a system during the next centuries. The undertaking as such is hardly conceivable without classical inspiration, nor are basic notions such as the three kinds of words likely to have been developed without reference to the corresponding Aristotelian concepts. Grammar and lexicography chiefly catalogued and classified the Bedouin language. The effectiveness of the fight for linguistic correctness was, however, lessened by the gradual decline of that archaising romanticism that upheld Bedouin prestige, as well as an increasing

[1] Except for the mystic Ibn al-Fāriḍ (d. 1235), whose work, like that of the man who has achieved the perfection of the *maqāma*, al-Ḥarīrī (d. 1122), belongs to a later period than that with which this section is concerned.

awareness of language change as such and the working out of a philosophical basis for linguistics in general.[1]

True to the dominant Aristotelian strain in Muslim civilisation the Arabs created a theory of art rather than of beauty,[2] which is one reason why the theoretical discussion of the arts is strictly technical, unless it be conducted with a view to proving or disproving their religious admissibility. This controversy took architecture for granted, but discouraged music (without being able to overcome its popularity) and condemned the plastic arts. Practice adopted a compromise akin to the sentiment of the Greek Church by acquiescing in pictures in the flat (including flat relief) but rejecting them in the round, an attitude that excluded sculpture, but allowed for such painting as was to develop in the later middle ages.[3]

Two different conceptions of a Muslim existence had been evolved —Islam as a rule of life inspired by a sense of the golden mean, but tending toward merely formal correctness; and Islam as ascetic hostility to the world, gloomily continuing the austerity of Syriac monasticism. Now both were proving emotionally insufficient. This dissatisfaction of the heart led to a crisis more dangerous to the unity of the *umma* and more important in its influence on its future than any other disintegrating element of the times, be it political, social or intellectual, not even excluding the religious views to be met with in Ismā'īlī and also in certain 'enlightened' Sunnite circles.[4] It would seem that the movement toward a warmer and more personalised relationship towards the Lord started among the petty bourgeoisie of the *mawālī* population of the Iraqian towns; but it soon transcended these social and geographical boundaries, though in some important aspects it only revived and reinstated older motifs of religious experience which original Islam had more or less consciously essayed to sidestep. In contrast to the other faiths that had grown up against the background of Hellenism, Muḥammad had emphasised the essen-

---

[1] Cf. J. Fück, 'Arabīya. Untersuchungen zur arabischen Sprach- und Stilgeschichte', *Abh. Sächs. Akad. d. Wiss., philolog.-hist. Kl.* XLV, 1 (1950). Somewhat divergent views on the Kūfan and Baṣrain schools of grammarians will be found in R. Blachère, *Histoire de la littérature arabe des origines à la fin du XVᵉ siècle de J.-C.*, I (all published; Paris, 1952), p. 109, and C. Pellat, *Langue et littérature arabes* (Paris, 1952), p. 32.

[2] Cf. Ghazzālī, *Iḥyā'*, IV, 285–7 (and elsewhere in Book 36 of the *Iḥyā'*; cf. the Dutch translation of H. H. Dingemans, *Alghazali's Boek der Liefde* [Leiden, 1938], pp. 62–8), who describes God as the *summum pulchrum*. But despite the importance of beauty in his religious experience, Ghazzālī does not investigate its nature.

[3] L. Massignon, 'Les méthodes de réalisation artistique des peuples de l'Islam', *Syria*, II (1921), 47–53, 149–60, analyses the artistic aspiration of the Muslims in terms of its underlying theological and metaphysical assumptions. Cf. also G. Marçais, 'La question des images dans l'art musulman', *B*, VII (1932), 161–83.

[4] Cf. Tauḥīdī, *Imtā'*, III, 193 ff.

tial unbridgeableness of the gap separating Creator and creature. Now the *ṣūfī*, as the new type of seeker after God came to be called because of his white wool (*ṣūf*) garments, narrowed the abyss through the love of God reaching out to receive the self-effacing passion of the longing soul. Soon he came to close it entirely, if only for moments of semi-conscious ecstasy, by allowing for the union of the soul with its Lord in a mystical rapture that was fundamentally incompatible with the accepted notion of the Divine, although some of the formulae in which it was to be rationalised were less offensive than others to the dogmatists' conception of God.

The spread of Islam to erstwhile Christian populations and the more or less conscious competition with Jesus Christ into which the Muḥammad of the Muslim apologists and missionaries had to enter had early made a powerful thaumaturge of the human Messenger of Allāh. The Prophet became a mediator, the incarnation, as it were, of one more religious motif which the historical Muḥammad had laboured to eliminate. But simultaneously the Ṣūfī *shaykh*, adept himself and therefore spiritual guide of an informal circle of disciples, was accorded a veneration distasteful to the sobriety of the Koranic faith, and was elevated to sainthood upon his death or, at a somewhat later period, recognised as a saint while still walking this earth. The saints came to be regarded as members of a hierarchy presided over by the *quṭb*, or Pole, the true governor of the world, 'the old Demiurgos in an Islamic dress'.[1] The universe could not dispense with the spiritual functioning of the saints. 'Know that the principle and foundation of Ṣūfism and knowledge of God rests on Saintship.'[2] In a sense, the fight between theology and mysticism was conducted through the dispute about the relative superiority of prophet and saint. It was essential to orthodox doctrine to uphold the supremacy of the prophets, and its gradual sanctioning of an ever more intense cult of the prophet Muḥammad was in large measure to be explained as a kind of self-defence against the inroads of the saints on the devotion of the masses. The saints were recognised officially and their miracles accepted as a reality in the first half of the tenth century.[3] It took much longer for orthodoxy to accept gracefully the Ṣūfī style of life—the wandering *darvīsh* with his patched frock,[4] the spiritual

---

[1] H. A. R. Gibb, *Mohammedanism. An Historical Survey* (London, 1949), p. 138.

[2] Hujwīrī, *op. cit.* p. 210.

[3] The saints appear in Ṭaḥāwī's (d. 933) *'aqīda*; then in art. 16 of the *Fiqh Akbar II*, middle of the tenth century; cf. A. J. Wensinck, *The Muslim Creed. Its Genesis and Historical Development* (Cambridge, 1932), p. 225.

[4] This *muraqqa'a*, originally blue, has a venerable ancestry having been used by Syriac ascetics like St Ephraim, Jacob Barde'ānā and Mar Babai. Here an old mourning-rite, neglect of body and dress, has become an ascetic practice and finally

concert, or *samā'*, the exercise of the *dhikr*, or the repetition of a pious formula or the name of God to induce ecstatic experiences. The early connection of Ṣūfism and Shī'a, although the Ṣūfīs did not share the revolutionary tendencies of the Shī'ites and although Shī'ite legitimist authoritarianism soon discovered its incompatibility with the ecstatic's immediate access to God, did not contribute towards making the movement acceptable to orthodoxy. The conflict was deepened by the rejection of *'ilm*, intellectual and traditional knowledge, the epistemological basis of orthodoxy, in favour of *ma'rifa*, gnosis, the immediate insight conveyed by ecstatic intuition, which is attainable only through God's removing the veil of 'otherness' from between himself and his saints, who are those that 'behold God with their hearts'. The traditionalists, as the upholders of community organisation in earlier faiths, saw the whole structure of Islam endangered by the inspirational individualism of *illuminati*, who if not altogether averse to formal education were yet more often than not inimical to the study of law and theology.

Attacked from within and without, leaning on a Caliphate that had little strength independent of the prestige of the religion it was expected to protect, and feeling itself to be acutely threatened by Ismā'īlī aggression and Shī'ite obstruction, orthodox Islam in the eleventh century through the consensus of the doctors took the final step to safeguard itself from possible dangers inherent in any given political situation and to enable it to meet every intellectual and emotional challenge by a new (and as it turned out, definitive) integration. It was then that al-Ash'arī's (d. 935) doctrine obtained the sanction of the *ijmā'*. This doctrine was essentially a compromise between the ultra-rationalism of the Mu'tazila, and the anthropomorphic leanings of the Ḥanbalites, whose distrust of conceptual thought was characteristic of popular piety but obsolete in an age that had tasted of Hellenic dialectic. Al-Ash'arī's occasionalism saved the absoluteness of divine omnipotence by degrading the connection of cause and effect from a necessary to a habitual relationship. Allāh was free, bound neither by his own precedent nor by a moral law identical with or superior in order to his will. The insistence on the eternity of the divine attributes that had seemed incompatible with the logically more consistent *tauḥīd* or concept of divine oneness of the Mu'tazila was accompanied by careful negation of anthropomorphic implications. Predestination and justice were harmonised by allowing man the acquisition, or *kasb*, of his works, akin to the

grown into a symbol of a specific religious behaviour; cf. A. J. Wensinck, *Verhandelingen d. Kon. Akademie van Wetenschapen, Afd. Letterkunde,* n.s. xviii, i (1918), 54–5.

assent, or συγκατάθεσις, which was to the Stoic the hall-mark of man's freedom of choice.

At the same time that the Ash'arites emerged from popular disfavour and worse, leading Ṣūfīs like Hujwīrī (d. after 1072), Qushayrī (d. 1074) and Anṣārī Harawī (d. 1088/9) attempted to reconcile the mystic path with the recognition of the law and its obligatoriness. This was done by a conscious turn toward the ethical, rather than the doctrinal, aspect of religious experience. Ṣūfism as the expression of one constant relation to the supernatural was in itself compatible with adherence to each and any legal rite. Hujwīrī's solution was fairly representative. 'The Law without the Truth is ostentation, and the Truth without the Law is hypocrisy. Their mutual relation may be compared to that of body and spirit: when the spirit departs from the body, the living body becomes a corpse, and the spirit vanishes like wind. The Muslim profession of faith includes both: the words, 'There is no god but Allāh', are the Truth, and the words, 'Muḥammad is the apostle of Allāh', are the Law; any one who denies the Truth is an infidel, and any one who rejects the Law is a heretic'.[1] An ethical turn is again intended to take out the sting from the unitive experience, when the true meaning of *ittiḥād* is found in this, 'that when a man goes forth from his own qualities and enters into the qualities of God, he goes forth from his own will and enters into the will of God . . . so that he becomes entirely devoted to God . . .'.[2] Humanity as such cannot be sloughed off, but the inborn qualities of humanity may be changed by the radiance shed on it of the divine reality. Hujwīrī[3] explains 'union', *jam'*, as 'concentration of thought upon the desired object', a far cry indeed from the reckless expression of the experience of divinisation that had cost Ḥallāj his life barely a hundred and fifty years earlier.

But it was left to al-Ghazzālī (1058–1111), Ash'arite theologian and eloquent defender of Sunnism against the Bāṭinī, to assure Ṣūfism its rightful place within Islam by pointing out the autonomous character of the religious experience.[4] The law is binding but must not be confused with religion as such. Ghazzālī realised that even the most stringently structured doctrinal system, in the last analysis, owes its

---

[1] R. A. Nicholson, *The Mystics of Islam* (London, 1914), pp. 92–3 (combining Hujwīrī, *op. cit.* pp. 383–4 and 139–40).

[2] Abū Naṣr as-Sarrāj (d. 988), *Kitāb al-luma' fī 't-taṣawwuf*, ed. R. A. Nicholson (Leiden and London, 1914), p. 433; quoted in Nicholson, *Mystics*, p. 157.

[3] *Op. cit.* p. 258 (cf. *Mystics*, p. 159). Cf. also Hujwīrī, *op. cit.* p. 257: 'Sound union is that which God produces in man when he is in the state of rapture and ecstasy, and when God causes him to receive and fulfil His commandments and to mortify himself.'

[4] This autonomy of the religious experience had been more or less dimly realised by the orthodox in contradistinction to the Mu'tazilites; cf. the somewhat groping statement by the heresiographer Ibn Ḥazm (d. 1064) in T. Andrae, *Die Person Muhammads in Lehre und Glauben seiner Gemeinde* (Stockholm, 1918), p. 100.

conclusiveness to an act of faith that validates its premises. Being godlike, the soul knows God and knows him through his self-revelation in what subjectively appears as an experience of immediate, supernatural realisation of the Divine. The end of religion is moral perfection. Mind and will play their parts; reasoning articulates the experiential data and develops them in accordance with Koranic revelation on which Ghazzālī falls back somewhat after the manner in which the reformers turned to the Bible; the will guides man through the phases of the purgative life to the Beatific Vision. Although moved by fear of the wrath to come and opposed to the conciliatory softness of contemporary preaching, Ghazzālī with the other mystics exalted love as the basic motive of the Ṣūfī, disinterested love, evoked by that beauty which is in God and in God alone. The secrets of the heart are many and so are the degrees of religious insight. The simple are to be protected by the government against exposure to teachings that are beyond them and therefore apt to corrupt them. The theosophy of his esoteric writings allows a freer rein to the neoplatonist and Christian ideas which he had made his own, but neither contradicts nor supplants what he has to say to the general public, since religious truth is experienced in several superimposed frames of reference.

Popular opinion supported Ghazzālī's placing of Ṣūfic piety in the very centre of orthodox religion, even as it supported his broad acceptance into the fold of all who would assent to the basic beliefs and practices of Islam. It is in the spirit of these developments that from the end of the eleventh century the *ijmāʿ*, which had grown exceedingly careful of internal conflict, began to recognise the equal standing of the four leading law-schools whose disputes had made political history only a short while before. Sunnism, and in this respect also Ghazzālī stands out as one of its authoritative spokesmen, detached itself energetically from the vicissitudes to which any given government might be exposed. True, the body religious retained its identity with the body politic. Sunnite *ijmāʿ* had always held valid the prayer behind the unrighteous *imām*. Any government was to be accepted that would enable the *umma* to continue under the law, however unlawful its origin and however lawless its actions. The successful usurper would do as well as the legitimate ruler. The believers as such were to lead their lives in as definite a detachment from governmental affairs as the concern for the faith would permit. Simultaneously the picture of the ideal ruler was given more and more the features of the saint.[1] The unity of Islam was established

---

[1] Cf., for example, Niẓām al-Mulk's (d. 1092) idea of the one chosen ruler who appears every century, *Siyāsat Nāmah*, ed. trans. C. Schefer (Paris, 1891–3), p. 5

independent of the administrative organisation of its domain. For Islam had become a civilisation recognisable by its style of life.

This style was essentially conservative; the Ancients had definitely overcome the Moderns. Scientific progress continued at a modest pace, but the unsettling effect it might have on the religious and therewith on the social structure made the researcher uneasy in his own conscience and suspect to public opinion.[1] Materially, the Muslim style of life was marked by the final rejection of Greek *paideia* in favour of *adab*, that intellectually neutral combination of an education derived from literary manuals with the graceful and almost ritualistic manners of the man of the world, that would enjoin knowledge without pedantry, a keen sense of the proprieties of every station and every situation, and an articulateness at the same time witty and ceremonious. *Adab* as an upper-class accomplishment would filter down the social ladder; *futuwwa* as a group-forming ethos was taken up (at the end of the twelfth century) by the court after it had developed among the lower middle classes and during the tenth and eleventh centuries been impregnated with the spirit of Ṣūfism. Originally denoting the conduct of life becoming to an Arabic *fatà*, or *Junker*, then adopted by the Islamised nobility of Iran, *futuwwa* came under Ṣūfī influence to be understood as an ethic of altruism and self-denial. In terms of organisation the *fityān* were saved from irrelevancy by entering the fight against the unbelievers and bringing Ṣūfism to the border garrisons. In the cities they seem to have enforced a kind of justice after the manner of Robin Hood, combining depredation of the rich with mutual assistance within their own ranks. Their organisation opposed and obstructed the agents of the tyrannical government and their activities, part open, part conspiratorial, made them attractive to the lower and an irritant to the upper classes who had, however, long since become affected by the moral purpose of an association of whose disruptive practices they necessarily disapproved. The Caliph an-Nāṣir (1180–1225) reconstituted the *futuwwa* as an international courtly order and in this manner not only elimi-

of text, p. 5 of translation, with the concept of the *mujaddid* of Islam also expected to arise at the end of every hundred-year period. For an attempted analysis of the motivation, structure and scope of Muslim government cf. G. E. von Grunebaum, 'Government in Islam', in *Islam: Essays in the Nature and Growth of a Cultural Tradition* (2nd ed. London, 1961), pp. 127–40.

[1] Cf., for example, 'Umar Khayyām (d. 1123) in the Introduction to his *Algebra*, ed. trans. F. Woepcke (Paris, 1851), p. 2: 'We are being tried by the disappearance, *inqirād*, of men of learning of whom only a handful is left, small in number but large in tribulations....And most of those who assume the appearance of scholars in our time will but cloak truth with falsehood.' Cf. also the characteristic statement of as-Samau'al al-Maghribī, converted to Islam in 1163, translated by F. Rosenthal, *Osiris*, IX (1950), 563–4.

nated the disquieting social implications of the movement but made manifest the significance of the *futuwwa* ethos, hitherto but the chivalry of the little man, as an element in the supra-political unity of Islamic society.

This society had long been conscious of the heterogeneity of its cultural life. The division of the sciences into Arab and foreign is an early symptom of this realisation.[1] But along with an awareness of disparate origins went an insight into what constituted the principle of integration. According to the Pure Brethren of Baṣra, 'the ideal and morally perfect man should be of East Persian derivation, Arabic in faith, of Iraqi (that is, Babylonian) education, a Hebrew in astuteness, a disciple of Christ in conduct, as pious as a Syrian monk, a Greek in the individual sciences, an Indian in the interpretation of all mysteries, but lastly and especially, a Ṣūfī in his whole spiritual life'.[2]

In extensive writings on heresy (the earliest going back to the reign of Mahdī [775–85]),[3] the community took stock of its religious state, surveying and judging itself as in a mirror and providing for itself the opportunity to reformulate its *ijmāʿ*. Cultural self-consciousness came to consider analytically the nature of its accomplishment, and it is more than remarkable that al-Bērūnī (d. 1048), perhaps the greatest scholar of the Islamic world, and in any case its only outstanding student of India, drew the same conclusion about his own civilisation which modern research has come to affirm. 'Each people excels in some science or technical branch of work. Among the Greeks there were men, before Christendom, who excelled in the spirit of inquiry, promoting [scientific] things to their utmost possible degree and advancing them to perfection.... But now the West has obtained the success for itself'—al-Bērūnī is speaking specifically of *materia medica*—'and made us profit by its meritorious powers. On the contrary, in the East there is no people inclined towards the

---

[1] Cf. the clear-cut opposition of 'Greek' and 'Eastern' philosophy that is expressed in book-titles such as Avicenna's *al-Falsafa* (or: *al-Ḥikma*) *'l-mashriqiyya*, i.e. 'Eastern Philosophy' (the work is lost for the most part; the first section was published under the title *Manṭiq al-mashriqiyyīn*; on this title cf. Nallino, *Rivista degli studi orientali*, x [1923–5], 433–67, esp. 454 ff.) and Fakr ad-Dīn ar-Rāzī's (d. 1209) *al-Mabāḥith al-mashriqiyya*, 'Oriental Investigations', in which the author contrasts the 'Oriental' doctrines of the Muslim *mutakillimūn* with the Western or Greek methods and ideas of the Greek Aristotelians and their Arab followers. S. Pines, *op. cit.* pp. 10–11, has made a case for the view that Avicenna referred to his own philosophy as the 'Oriental philosophy' while designating his opponents, the Peripatetic thinkers of contemporary Baghdad, as the 'Westerners'. His arguments seem to have weakened the position of those scholars who interpret the 'Easterners' as the Baghdadi Peripatetics and identify the 'Occidentals' with the Greek commentators of Aristotle.

[2] T. J. de Boer, *The History of Philosophy in Islam* (London, 1903), p. 95.

[3] Cf. H. Ritter, *Der Islam*, xviii (1929), 34.

sciences except the Indians. But this branch particularly (viz. Medicine) is based by them upon principles which are opposite to the Western rules to which we are accustomed. Moreover, the contrast between them and ourselves concerning language, religion, manners and customs, and their excessive awe concerning purity and impurity prevents intercourse and cuts short scientific discussion.'[1] Their knowledge that their cultural affiliation was with the Hellenic West rather than the Indian East did not, however, disturb the proud sense of the *umma* of their separate identity which is incisively expressed by the eleventh-century Persian princeling who wrote these words: 'I propose to expound the rules of "nobility" [*juvān-mardī*; the Persian rendering of *futuwwa*] prevailing in this community, because no community endures such hardship as this in living its life sincerely and honourably, for the reason that its members regard themselves as superior to the rest of mankind.'[2]

[1] M. Meyerhof, *Islamic Culture*, xi (1937), 27, from Bērūnī's Introduction to his *Book of Drugs*. Cf. Bar Hebraeus' (d. 1286) verdict in his *Chronography*, ed. trans. E. A. W. Budge (London, 1932), I, p. 92: 'And there arose among them [i.e. the Arabs] philosophers, and mathematicians, and physicians, who surpassed the ancient [sages] in the exactness of their knowledge. The only foundations on which they set up their buildings were Greek houses; the wisdom-buildings which they erected were great by reason of their highly polished diction, and their greatly skilled researches. Thus it hath happened that we [Syrian Christians], from whom they [i.e. the Arabs] have acquired wisdom through translators, all of whom are Syrians, have been compelled to ask for wisdom from them.'

[2] *A Mirror for Princes*, p. 247. H. Corbin, *Eranos-Jahrbuch*, xx (1952), 215, n. 98, interprets the *juvān-mard* as a 'chevalier spirituel'.

CHAPTER XVII

BYZANTIUM AND THE MUSLIM WORLD TO THE MIDDLE OF THE ELEVENTH CENTURY

In theory there existed a permanent state of war between Byzantium and the Muslim world, since, in contrast to 'the territory of Islam', the Byzantine Empire was 'the territory of warfare', and it was one of the precepts of Muslim law that such territory should be conquered or brought into submission by Islam although it was not to be forcibly converted. The war against the Byzantine Empire was the Holy War, a religious duty; the idea (originally a Jewish conception) that warriors who fell in the struggle against the infidel went to heaven, acted as a powerful ally in securing the performance of this duty, as did the material enticements of pay and booty. The Muslims had everything to gain and nothing to lose in the Holy War, which would certainly reward them with the good things of either this world or the next. Certain other ideas, both political and religious, can also be adduced in explanation of this permanent state of war: belief in the inevitable fall of Constantinople, preached by the Prophet[1] and associated with the belief that 'the Hour would come', together with the conviction that the Islamic Empire, as the heir of the Sassanids, had in the Romano-Byzantine Empire a hereditary enemy.

Nevertheless, this permanent state of war did not prevent the existence of peaceful relations and commercial and cultural exchanges, since Muslim law allowed the conclusion of truces with the enemy, whether of long or short duration, during which more peaceful relations might be established between the representatives of the two Empires, always provided that this was in the interests of Islam. Moreover, even during periods of overt hostility, this was never general, and more amicable relations continued in the territories not affected.

At most periods, there were continual and quite independent military operations in progress on two fronts, the Eastern front being always more important than the Western. At the beginning of the Umayyad period (in Damascus, 661–750), Arab expeditions, which

---

[1] A *ḥadīth*, or saying of the Prophet, apparently foretold that Constantinople would be conquered by a Caliph bearing a prophet's name; cf. P. K. Hitti, *History of the Arabs* (London, 1956), p. 203.

were planned by the Caliph or Imām (that is to say, the head of the Muslim community), were frequently directed towards the capture of the Byzantine capital. However, once the full difficulty of achieving the capture of Constantinople and completely subduing the Byzantine Empire had been realised (and it was demonstrated with particular force by the failure of Maslama's expedition of 717), this objective was abandoned and activities were confined to holding the line of the Taurus, with occasional expeditions to secure bases for attack or to harass the Byzantines on the other side, for example in southern Cappadocia. By degrees, the practice of making two, or sometimes three, expeditions each year became established, following the example of the Prophet, who set out against the infidel at least once each year. In the ninth century officials were laying down a schedule for these operations. According to Qāduma (d. 948/9)

the first, or spring expedition, should take place after the horses have been given pasture, from 10 May to 10 June, the time when the grass in enemy country is most plentiful, the second, or summer expedition, begins on 10 July, when the horses have regained their strength, and lasts 60 days, until 8 September. The winter expedition, which is more unusual and occurs only in case of necessity, lasts only 20 days, from the end of February into March; campaigning at this time means that the horses must carry provisions for both themselves and their riders, but has the advantage of catching the enemy at a weak moment.

These rules, particularly those laying down the duration of the campaigns, were not always followed to the letter. But it now became much rarer than it had been in the preceding period for Muslim armies to winter in enemy territory. The effective strength of the forces sent into action by the Muslims varied; but it was never very great, and the numbers given by the chroniclers are often exaggerated.

The Greeks had a system of beacon signals to give warning of an invasion from the moment the Arabs set foot on Byzantine territory. Along and behind the Taurus mountains they built a series of fortresses and frontier posts, guarded by special detachments of *akritai*; the most forward districts of the frontier themes were formed into *kleisurarchai*, which possessed a degree of independence in the conduct of defence. Until such time as they could aim directly at a campaign of reconquest, the Byzantines were usually content to hold their strong places, making surprise attacks on the advancing or retiring enemy as occasion offered, either destroying them or making counter-incursions of their own. Over a long period the Byzantine frontier was organised on a defensive rather than an offensive basis, whereas it was only at a relatively late date, during the Abbasid era, that the Arab frontier was put on a defensive footing.

I. UMAYYADS AND ABBASIDS: THE EASTERN FRONT

At the accession on 25 March 717 of Leo III, the *strategus* of the Anatolikon theme, the Empire seemed to be in desperate straits. A large Arab army was encamped in western Asia Minor; Maslama, who was its leader, had already been in negotiation with Leo and was convinced that he could be brought to surrender.[1] In that spring, Maslama took Sardes and Pergamum; when he saw that no assistance could be expected from Leo he advanced to Abydus, crossed into Thrace, destroying fortified places as he went, and in July encamped before Constantinople. He was joined on 1 September by one fleet, and later by another. But while they were manœuvring into position to blockade the city, twenty of these vessels were separated from the rest and destroyed by fire-ships. Thenceforth the fleet remained inactive. Attempts were made to bribe Maslama to depart, but these were in vain and his army suffered heavy losses from cold and famine during the hard winter of 717–18. In the spring new ships arrived from Egypt and Africa with reinforcements, and an attack by Slavs was beaten off. However, the Bulgars, whom Leo summoned to his aid, defeated one Muslim army, while another was annihilated in Bithynia. Some Egyptian sailors who had deserted supplied information about the disposition of the shipping, so that Leo was able to destroy the recently arrived vessels with Greek fire. The naval blockade was thus more or less raised, and the Caliph 'Umar II, who had come to the throne in September 717, recalled his exhausted army, which departed on 15 August 718. During the retreat, many ships were either wrecked or captured, and only a few reached Syria. The Caliph also decided to abandon Daranda, as the place was too exposed, but ordered the reinforcement of Melitene (Malaṭya). The expedition of 717–18 was the last Arab attempt to take Constantinople.

The reign of Yazīd II (720–4) was quiet, marked only by a few attacking forays, but during that of Hishām (724–43) there was an energetic renewal of military activity, and his sons and brothers took part in campaigns which also brought fame to two Umayyad *mawālī* (or client princes), Baṭṭāl and 'Abd al-Wahhāb, who later acquired a striking legendary importance. It was unusual for the Byzantines to take the initiative in these operations; the Arabs seem to have acted on the plan of making each year a systematic and simultaneous attack on the north, south and centre of the Byzantine provinces, with the aim of converging on a point at the centre of the Empire. The most westerly provinces of Phrygia, Asia and Bithynia were

---

[1] These and subsequent events are described above in their Byzantine setting in chapters III, IV and V.

frequently laid waste. The Anatolikon provinces lived in a state of periodic insecurity, but thanks to the administrative and military organisation of the themes they continued to be a solid bastion in the defence of the Empire. The Byzantines retaliated by direct or indirect operations (through the medium of the Khazars) in the Caucasus and in Armenia. In 740 Leo achieved a great victory; two Muslim detachments under Baṭṭāl had broken through, one into Asia and the other into Phrygia; Baṭṭāl laid siege to Acroinon, but was defeated by Leo in person and killed. At this point, however, the force of the Arab offensive greatly diminished as a result of internal discords. The Arabs were therefore unable to profit from the troubled situation of the Empire immediately after the death of Leo in June 741 and the accession of Constantine V (741–75), since Hishām himself died in 743 and was replaced by the incapable al-Walīd II, who was assassinated in 744; the Umayyad Caliphate then fell into complete anarchy.

There were two Byzantine naval campaigns directed against Egypt during this period, in 736 and 739; in the second expedition Damietta was successfully attacked. In 743, however, the Arabs directed the naval war against Cyprus, where they made a landing; some of the native population emigrated to Byzantine territory, and the rest were deported to Syria. But in 747 the Greeks destroyed an Egyptian fleet off Cyprus and Egyptian naval power was reduced to impotence for the next hundred years.

When the Abbasids wrested the headship of the Muslim world from the Umayyads in 750, they entered into possession of an Empire stretching from the Indus to the Atlantic and from the southern shore of the Caspian Sea to the Indian Ocean. It had absorbed the whole of the Persian Empire of the Sassanids, and the rich provinces of the Roman Empire on the eastern and southern shores of the Mediterranean. But though Constantinople itself had been threatened more than once, and raids into Asia Minor had at certain periods become almost a yearly occurrence, the ranges of the Taurus and the Anti-Taurus still served as the eastern barrier of Byzantine territory against the spread of Arab domination. In Africa, however, all opposition to the westward advance of the Arabs had been broken down, and the whole of the peninsula of Spain, with the exception of Asturia, had passed under Muslim rule. For ninety years Damascus had been the capital of the Arab Empire, and the mainstay of the Umayyad forces at the time of their greatest power had been the Arab tribes domiciled in Syria from the days when that province still formed part of the Roman Empire. The Abbasids, on the contrary, had come into power mainly through support from Persia. They removed the capital to Baghdad, founded in 762 by al-Manṣūr, the second Caliph of the new dynasty, on a site only thirty miles from Ctesiphon, the capital of the Sassanid Shāhanshāh, thus marking their recognition of the shifting of the centre of power.

From this period Persian influence became predominant and the chief offices of state came to be held by men of Persian origin; the most noteworthy example is that of the family of the Barmecides (Barmakids), which for half a century exercised the predominant influence in the government until Hārūn destroyed them in 803. It was probably due to the influence of the old Persian ideal of kingship that under the Abbasids the person of the Caliph came to be surrounded with greater pomp and ceremony. The court of the Umayyads had retained something of the patriarchal simplicity of early Arab society, and they had been readily accessible to their subjects; but as methods of government became more centralised and the court of the Caliph more splendid and awe-inspiring, the ruler himself tended to be more difficult of access, and the presence of the executioner by the side of the throne became under the Abbasids a terrible symbol of the autocratic character of their rule.

A further feature of the new dynasty was the emphasis it attached to the religious character of the dignity of the Caliph. In their revolt against the Umayyads, the Abbasids had come forward in defence of the purity of Islam as against those survivals of the old Arab heathenism which were so striking a feature of the Umayyad court. The converts and descendants of converts, whose support had been most effective in the destruction of the Umayyads, were animated with a more zealous religious spirit than had ever found expression among large sections of the Arabs, who, in consequence of the superficial character of their conversion to Islam, and their aristocratic pride and tribal exclusiveness, so contrary to the spirit of Islamic brotherhood, had been reluctant to accord to the converts from other races the privileges of the new faith. The Abbasids raised the standard of revolt in the name of the family of the Prophet, and by taking advantage of the widespread sympathy felt for the descendants of 'Alī, they obtained the support of the various Shī'a factions. Though they took all the fruits of victory for themselves, they continued to lay emphasis on the religious character of their rule, and theologians and men of learning received a welcome at their court such as they had never enjoyed under the Umayyads. On ceremonial occasions the Abbasid Caliph appeared clad in the sacred mantle of the Prophet, and titles such as that of Khalīfa of Allāh (vicegerent of God) and Shadow of God upon earth came to be frequently applied to him. As the power of the central authority grew weaker, so the etiquette of the court tended to become more elaborate and servile, and the

Caliph made his subjects kiss the ground before him or would allow the higher officials to kiss his hand or his foot or the edge of his robe.

The vast Empire into the possession of which they had entered was too enormous and made up of elements too heterogeneous to be long held together under a system whose sole unifying principle was investiture of governors by, and payment of tribute to, the Caliph. A prince of the Umayyad family, 'Abd ar-Raḥmān, who had succeeded in escaping to Spain when practically all his relatives had been massacred, in 756 took advantage of tribal jealousies among the Arab chiefs in Spain to seize this country for himself and to detach it from the Empire. North Africa, which had been placed by Hārūn under the government of Ibrāhīm ibn al-Aghlab, became practically independent under this energetic governor, who established a dynasty that lasted for more than a century (800–909); though his successors contented themselves with the title of amir, the Caliph in Baghdad appears to have been powerless to interfere with their administration. Hārūn himself seems to have realised that the break-up of the Arab Empire was inevitable, since in 802 he made arrangements for dividing the administration of it between his sons al-Amīn and al-Ma'mūn. But on the death of their father in 809 civil war broke out between the two brothers. The Arabs lent their support to al-Amīn, and under his leadership made a last effort to regain for themselves the control of the Caliphate; but in 813 Ṭāhir, al-Ma'mūn's brilliant Persian general, defeated him, and as a reward for his successful siege of Baghdad was appointed by al-Ma'mūn to the government of Khurasan, where he and his descendants for half a century were practically independent. Egypt broke away from the Empire when a son of one of al-Ma'mūn's Turkish slaves, Aḥmad ibn Ṭūlūn, having been appointed deputy-governor of Egypt in 868, succeeded in making himself independent not only in Egypt but also in Syria, which he added to his dominions, and ceased paying tribute to Baghdad. This breaking away of the outlying provinces of the Empire was facilitated by the weakness of the central government. Al-Ma'mūn's brother and successor, al-Mu'taṣim (833–42), made the fatal mistake of creating an army composed almost entirely of Turkish mercenaries. Their excesses made life in Baghdad so intolerable that the Caliph, in order to be safe from the vengeance of the inhabitants of his own capital, moved to a site three days' journey up the Tigris to the north of Baghdad, and from 836 to 892 Samarra was the Abbasid capital where nine successive Caliphs lived, practically as prisoners of their own Turkish bodyguard. While the Turkish officers made and unmade Caliphs as they pleased, the country was ruined by constantly recurring disorders and insurrection.

In 865, while rival claimants were fighting for the crown, Baghdad was besieged for nearly a year, and the slave revolt for fourteen years (869–83) left the delta of the Euphrates at the mercy of undisciplined bands of marauders who terrorised the inhabitants and even sacked great cities, such as Baṣra, Ahwāz and Wāsiṭ, showing the weakness of the central power even in territories so close to the capital. A further disaster was soon to follow in the great Carmathian revolt, which takes its name from one of the propagandists of the Ismāʿīlī Shīʿa doctrine in Iraq during the latter part of the ninth century. His followers for nearly a century (890–985) spread terror throughout Mesopotamia, and even threatened Baghdad. They extended their ravages as far as Syria, murdering and pillaging wherever they went. In 930 they plundered the city of Mecca, put to death 30,000 Muslims there, and carried off the Black Stone together with immense booty.

These movements represent only a part of the risings and revolts that brought anarchy into the Caliph's dominions and cut off the sources of his revenue. In the midst of this period of disorder the Caliph al-Muʿtamid, shortly before his death in 892, transferred the capital once more to Baghdad, but the change did not bring the Caliphs deliverance from the tutelage of their Turkish troops, and they were as much at their mercy as before.

Deliverance came from Persia where the Buwayhids, who claimed descent from one of the Sassanid kings, had been extending their power from the Caspian Sea southward through Persia, until in 945 they entered Baghdad, nominally as deliverers of the Caliph from his rebellious Turkish troops. For nearly a century from this date the Caliphs were mere puppets in the hands of successive Buwayhid amirs, who set them upon the throne and deposed them as they pleased. The Caliph al-Mustakfī, whose deliverance from his mutinous Turkish soldiery had been the pretext for the Buwayhid occupation of Baghdad, was in the same year dragged from his throne and cruelly blinded. So low had the office of Caliph sunk by this period that there were still living two other Abbasid princes who like al-Mustakfī had sat upon the Abbasid throne, but blinded and robbed of all their wealth were now dependent upon charity or such meagre allowance as the new rulers cared to dole out to them. His cousin al-Muṭīʿ was set up to succeed him, but though he held the office of Caliph for twenty-eight years (946–74) he had no voice in the administration, and could not even nominate any of the ministers who carried on the business of the state in his name; helpless in the hands of his Buwayhid master, he lived upon a scanty allowance. He was compelled to abdicate in favour of his son aṭ-Ṭāʾiʿ, after a violent outburst of religious intolerance in Baghdad, and aṭ-Ṭā'i' for seventeen years (974–91) suffered similar humiliations. He was deposed at last in favour of his cousin al-Qādir (991–1031), of whose reign of forty years hardly any incident is recorded, because political events pursued their course without any regard to him.

Meanwhile in upper Mesopotamia an Arab family, the Hamdanids, at first governors of Mosul, extended their authority over the surrounding country, and one member of the family, Sayf ad-Dawla, made himself master of Aleppo and brought the whole of northern Syria under his rule in 944. In North Africa a rival Caliphate had arisen under the Shī'a Fatimids, who annexed Egypt in 969, and after more than one attempt occupied Syria in 988. By the beginning of the eleventh century the power of the Buwayhids was on the decline and they had to give way before the Ghaznavids and the Seljuqs, the latter a Turkish tribe which made its first appearance in history about the middle of the tenth century. In 1055 the Seljuq chief, Ṭughrīl Bey, having conquered the greater part of Persia, entered Baghdad and delivered the Caliph from subservience to the Buwayhids. From Baghdad Ṭughrīl Bey marched to the conquest of Mosul and upper Mesopotamia, and when he died in 1063 he left to his successor, Alp Arslan, an Empire which eight years later stretched from the Hindu Kush to the shores of the Mediterranean.

The fall of the Umayyad dynasty and the rise of the Abbasids (750) created a confused situation which proved favourable to Byzantium. In June 751 Constantine V embarked on a campaign which led successively to the capture and destruction of Melitene and the seizure of Claudias (Qalawdhiya), whose population was transported to Byzantine territory. The governor of Mesopotamia was unable to come to the assistance of these cities since the whole region was in a state of rebellion. The Emperor failed in his attempt to capture Arsamosata (Shimshāṭ), but Kūshān, an Armenian who had taken refuge with the Byzantines, and who had been sent by the Emperor against Camacha, succeeded in capturing both this place and Theodosiopolis (Qālīqalā), which he destroyed. Throughout these campaigns Constantine always behaved generously towards the peoples of the captured cities. There was no retaliatory action from the Muslims during the brief reign of the first Abbasid Caliph. In 754 'Abd Allāh ibn 'Alī, governor of Syria and uncle of the Caliph, was preparing an expedition starting from Dulūk, but was dissuaded from his enterprise by the death of the Caliph and his decision to seek the throne for himself.

The years between 756 and 863 represent one of the most successful periods of Muslim activity in the East. It can be subdivided into

four phases. In the first, from 756 to 775, the year in which both the
Emperor Constantine V and the Caliph al-Manṣūr died, there was
little action on a large scale. The second lasted from 775 to 809, and
covered the reigns of the Caliphs al-Mahdī and Hārūn ar-Rashīd
(786–809). Under al-Mahdī a number of important Arab enterprises
were initiated, to be continued on an even greater scale under Hārūn
ar-Rashīd. In all its strength, the Abbasid Empire often showed itself
superior in battle to the Byzantine Empire of Constantine VI and
Irene (780–802) and of Nicephorus (802–11). During the third phase,
from 809 to 842, once the interlude of the civil war between al-Amīn
and al-Ma'mūn was concluded with the victory of the latter, there was
continuous warfare between the two Empires. Al-Ma'mūn (809–33)
and al-Mu'taṣim (833–42) achieved some notable successes, particularly over Theophilus the Amorian (829–42). The final phase lasted
from 842 to 863. From 842 the decline of the Abbasid Caliphate set
in, becoming increasingly marked under al-Mutawakkil (847–61) and
his successors. With the Byzantine victory of 863 under Michael III
came the turning point in the struggle between the Byzantines and
the Arabs.

In 756 Ṣāliḥ ibn 'Alī, an Abbasid prince, tried to penetrate into
Cappadocia by the Ḥadath pass, but withdrew on learning that
Constantine was preparing to march against him. An exchange of
prisoners followed. The next three years were principally occupied
by the Muslims in the reconstruction of places formerly dismantled
by the Byzantines. Melitene, for example, was rebuilt by 'Abd
al-Wahhāb, governor of Mesopotamia, with the help of Ḥasan ibn
Qaḥṭaba, and provided with large barracks as quarters for the
Ghāzīs. Claudias was also restored. In 758 Constantine tried to
prevent the reconstruction of Melitene and Maṣṣīṣa (Mopsuestia,
Mamistra), but dared not attack the Arab army with its greater
strength. In 759 Constantine was engaged with the Slavonic tribes
of Thrace and Macedonia and was unable to prevent Ṣāliḥ from rebuilding and repopulating Adana and Maṣṣīṣa, both of which had been
damaged in an earthquake. In 760, whilst Constantine was fighting
the Bulgars, 'Abbās, the brother of the Caliph al-Manṣūr, defeated
the *strategus* of Armeniakon at a place on the Melas in the region of
Caesarea, and took forty-two important personages prisoner.

During the next five years al-Manṣūr had to deal with internal
revolts and Khazar invasions, probably provoked by Byzantium,
while Constantine was faced with the Bulgar danger. In 766 'Abbās
set out from Melitene with a powerful army to lay siege to Camacha;
but the city withstood all his attacks, and the Muslims retired at the
approach of winter. A detachment which had penetrated beyond

Caesarea was attacked during its withdrawal and ebbed away in disorder towards Melitene and Theodosiopolis.

In 768 Ṣāliḥ, governor of North Syria and the frontier marches, rebuilt and fortified Marʿash; ʿAbbās meanwhile undertook the restoration of Arsamosata, but was interrupted by the arrival of a Byzantine army in Armenia Quarta in 769. In the same year the native population of Marʿash and Samosata were deported to Palestine, on suspicion of having supplied spies to the Byzantines. Between 770 and 775, the Arabs took Laodicea Kekaumene (770), and in 770 or 771 reached Syke, marching along the coast of Isauria, flanked by a naval force. When this fleet was separated by the Cibyrraeots from the land army it sailed away to Cyprus and captured the governor ἐκ προσώπου. In 772 the Byzantine commander of Camacha was surprised and overcome by the Arabs whilst he was pursuing Kūshān and his Armenian troops, who departed to return to their own country. In this same year Constantine, who wished to have his hands free to deal with the Bulgars, made overtures of peace to al-Manṣūr, which were rejected.

Leo IV and the Caliph al-Mahdī came to their thrones at the same time (775). Leo IV was able to prosecute the war with more vigour than Constantine, who in his preoccupation with the Bulgars had been content merely to stave off Arab attacks; in 776 he made an expedition against Samosata. But the Caliph collected an army bigger than any seen since 740, and this force, under his uncle ʿAbbās, took Kasin in Cappadocia and then advanced to Ancyra. In 778, however, Michael Lachanodracon, the *strategus* of the Thrakesion theme, made a successful attack first on Ḥadath and then on Marʿash, where he took a number of prisoners, chiefly Syrian Jacobites. As a result the Caliph transferred the command to Ḥasan ibn Qaḥṭaba, who with a large army entered the Ḥadath pass and reached Dorylaeum without opposition, since the Emperor had given orders that combat should be refused and the population taken to safety in fortified positions. At the end of two weeks Ḥasan was forced by lack of supplies to beat a retreat. In March 780 the Caliph joined the campaign in person and reached Arabissos by way of Aleppo and Ḥadath. There he made over the command to his son Hārūn, the future Hārūn ar-Rashīd, who was to be assisted by Ḥasan ibn Qaḥṭaba. In the operations which followed, Ḥasan reached Asia but was defeated by Lachanodracon. Hārūn entered the theme of Armeniakon and took Sēmalouos (Samalū), deporting the population to Baghdad. On the advice of Ḥasan, the Caliph decided to rebuild Ḥadath and Tarsus. The rebuilding of Ḥadath was begun in 780 and not completed before 785. Tarsus was still in ruins at the accession of Hārūn.

Leo died in 780, and Irene became regent for her son Constantine. Her regency was a disastrous period. It is true that the expedition sent out by al-Mahdī in 781 was forced to retreat by Michael Lachanodracon and Tatzates, *strategus* of the Bucellarion theme; but in 782 an expedition under the command of Hārūn reached Chryso- polis (Scutari). On the advice of Tatzates (who had gone over to the Arabs on account of a personal feud with the Logothete Stauracius), Hārūn offered to make peace with Irene, who sent three emissaries, Stauracius among them. But Hārūn had them arrested and by this means coerced Irene into accepting the following conditions: the Byzantines were to pay tribute, free prisoners and provide guides and open markets for the Arabs on their return journey. Irene thus gained a three-year period of truce. After the return of the expedition Maṣṣīṣa (Mamistra) and the fort guarding the bridge of Adana were rebuilt.

The truce in fact only lasted for thirty-two months, for the Byzantines broke it before the death of al-Mahdī (which took place in April 785), and in 786 destroyed the walls surrounding Ḥadath and Zibaṭra (Sozopetra), which were none too strong. In September 786 Hārūn ar-Rashīd came to the throne, and with his accession began a period of warfare which was to last throughout his reign (he died in 809) and which was to bring considerable success to the Arabs who were able to profit from the embarrassments of the Empire (the conflict between Constantine and Irene, the arrest and blinding of Constantine, and the fall of Irene). The Abbasid Empire, then at its zenith, was served during this period by a whole galaxy of remarkable generals and administrators. Moreover, Hārūn did not pursue a purely offensive policy; he reinforced the defences of his territories, forming the frontier districts into autonomous units of government separate from the provinces of North Syria and Mesopotamia and divided into two zones: the forward zones were called the *Thughūr* and those in the rear, from Antioch to the Euphrates, the *'Awāṣim*. He rebuilt places on the frontiers: Ḥadath in 786–7, Tarsus in 787–8, Kafarbayyā on the Jayḥān (Pyramus) opposite Maṣṣīṣa (Mamistra), at about the same time, and Zibaṭra (Sozopetra). Later, in 796, he fortified Anazarbus ('Ayn Zarba) and in 799 built Hārūniya, to the south-west of Mar'ash. He also founded al-Kanīsat as-Sawdā' ('the black Church'), to the north of the gulf of Alexandretta.

Although Hārūn was not able to campaign in person until 796, his troops were successful both on land and sea: their victories included the battle of Podandus in the Isaurian mountains (788); the capture of the *strategus* of the theme of the Cibyrraeots in the bay of Attalia in 790; the capture in 793 of Camacha, betrayed by the rebellious troops of Armeniakon, and of Thebasa in Cappadocia; the expedition of 794 which, accompanied by Elpidius, a Byzantine deserter and formerly *strategus* of Sicily, reached Amisus on the Black Sea; and the expeditions of 795, which reached the region of Urgub,[1] and of 796, which penetrated as far as Amorium. During this same period Constantine launched two expeditions, in 791 and 795, neither of which met with much success; the Arabs in their turn, however, suffered heavy losses from a winter campaign of 791–2 in the theme of Chaldia.

In the summer of 796 Hārūn took up residence at Raqqa on the Euphrates, nearer the theatre of operations; in 797 he himself took aṣ-Ṣafṣāf in the extreme north of the Cilician Gates, while one of his lieutenants was marching on Ancyra. Constantine set out on campaign, but he was recalled by a conspiracy and in August deprived of his throne. Irene then made overtures of peace, which were rejected by the Caliph. In 798 there were two Arab advances: from one side against the imperial stud-farm at Malagina, where the horses of the Logothete were captured, and from the other against Ephesus and in the Opsikion theme. However, a Khazar invasion caused the Caliph to accept the peace proposals made by Irene together with tribute, and hostilities were interrupted.

But in 802 Irene was deposed and Nicephorus, Logothete τοῦ γενικοῦ, was proclaimed Emperor. He refused to continue paying tribute; the result was a resumption of the war in 803 whilst he was occupied with a rebellion by the *strategus* of the Anatolikon theme. The attack started with two expeditions, one into Cappadocia, led by al-Qāsim, son of the Caliph and Prefect of 'Awāṣim, and the other led by the Caliph himself against Heraclea, according to Ṭabarī. In the following year a lieutenant of al-Qāsim defeated the Emperor at Krasos in Phrygia. In 805 there was an exchange of prisoners. In April, however, the Caliph had to leave for Persia; after restoring the fortifications at Ancyra, Thebasa and Andrasos in Cappadocia, Nicephorus took the offensive. He pillaged Cilicia, but was made to surrender his booty by the garrison at Maṣṣīṣa (Mamistra). On his return from Persia at the end of the year, the Caliph prepared for a great expedition; in 806 he was able to take Heraclea after a month's siege, and to take up residence at Tyana, where he built a mosque: he also captured several places in southern Cappadocia. Nicephorus, threatened as he was by the Bulgars, had to sue for peace; he was forced to undertake the payment of an annual tribute, including an amount from his own purse for himself and his son, and to promise

---

[1] See H. Grégoire, 'Rapport sur un voyage d'exploration dans le Pont et en Cappadoce', *Bulletin de correspondance hellénique*, XXXIII (1909), 141–2.

not to restore the places dismantled by the Arabs, Heraclea being particularly mentioned. On his side Hārūn promised not to demolish certain of the places he had captured. But once the Arabs had departed the Emperor hastened to rebuild and fortify the forbidden places. On hearing of this breach of their agreement, the Caliph returned unexpectedly and recaptured one of the places, Thebasa.[1] But in the following year, 807, success smiled on the Greeks, who defeated one Arab contingent in the Cilician Gates and another before Marʿash: the Caliph did not go beyond the Ḥadath pass. Shortly afterwards Hārūn was obliged by Persian affairs to leave Raqqa. An exchange of prisoners was concluded in 808, and there was no further Arab expedition of importance up to the time of the death of the Caliph on 24 March 809.

Maritime expeditions made by the Arabs during the period 775–809 included operations against Cyprus, Rhodes and Crete. In 806, alleging that the Cypriots had violated the treaty of neutrality which since 698 had regulated their relations with both Byzantium and Islam, the Arabs landed in Cyprus, laid waste the island and brought back to Raqqa 16,000 prisoners, including the archbishop; once the treaty of neutrality had been renewed these were allowed to return. In 807 Rhodes was devastated, but the fortress proved impregnable. On their return journey the Arabs touched at Myra in Lycia, but lost several of their ships in a storm.

The successes of Hārūn against Irene, Constantine and Nicephorus, despite their immediate effects, did not weaken the Empire beyond hope of recovery. Moreover, the Caliph did not attempt to make any definite conquests beyond the Cilician Gates; his main preoccupation lay rather with the consolidation of the frontier marches. Al-Amīn, the successor of Hārūn, only continued his father's defensive policy in that he rebuilt and fortified Adana and the stronghold of Sayḥān, in 810. The civil war between al-Amīn and his brother al-Maʾmūn gave the Byzantines the opportunity of recapturing Camacha which was surrendered to them by the amir ʿUbayd Allāh ibn al-Aqṭaʿ, in exchange for the return of his son who had been taken prisoner and who is perhaps to be identified with the famous ʿAmr (Ambron) of Arab and Byzantine legend. But the Byzantines, occupied as they were with the Bulgars, could not take full advantage of the situation; they were, in any case, fortunate during the bad years between 811 and 814 to be attacked only by the amir of Tarsus, who on one occasion, in 812, was severely defeated.

---

[1] Theophanes, a.m. 6298, p. 123 (ed. C. de Boor). The Arab historians are ignorant of this breach of the treaty and the return of the Caliph in 806, but recount a similar tale for the year 803.

Leo V the Armenian (formerly *strategus* of the Anatolikon theme and victor over the amir of Tarsus) on his accession to the throne in 813 concluded a thirty years' truce with the Bulgars. But operations against the Arabs were not immediately resumed since both he and al-Ma'mūn, the new Caliph (since 813), had internal problems to deal with. Leo V did, indeed, try to take advantage of his enemies' difficult situation. About 817 he sent a fleet to attack Damietta; but although Naṣr, the rebellious Arab in North Syria, offered to conclude an alliance with the Emperor, no such agreement was reached, since Naṣr's own partisans were against it. The Caliph al-Ma'mūn in his turn made a pact with Thomas the Slav, a Byzantine officer who had fled to the Arabs in the time of Hārūn, making himself out to be Constantine VI; with the consent of the Caliph he was even crowned Emperor by the Patriarch of Antioch. By December 820, the date of the assassination of Leo V and the accession of the Amorian Michael II, Thomas, assisted by Muslim auxiliaries provided by the Caliph, had already passed through Armenia and reached the theme of Chaldia. Most of the themes of Asia Minor rallied to his side and he began his march on Constantinople, and it was not until 823 that Michael finally overcame him. As a result of these events the Muslims were able to recapture Camacha and make a number of maritime raids on the coasts and islands of Asia Minor. Further, the refugees from Cordova who had settled at Alexandria now began to make incursions into Crete. In 825, after the defeat of Thomas and the destruction of Zibaṭra (Sozopetra) by imperial troops, Michael sought a truce. The Caliph, who had recently been disembarrassed of Naṣr, refused, and ordered further attacks, although he did not himself undertake any expeditions until 830.

In 827 Byzantium lost Crete. The island was captured by the Cordovans who had settled in Alexandria, but who had now been expelled from Egypt. They met no resistance and proceeded to build the powerful fortress of Chandax. In 828 two expeditions were dispatched in the hope of dislodging them; both failed, and the second was a complete disaster: the *strategus* of the theme of the Cibyrraeots was taken by surprise, his troops massacred and his fleet annihilated, and although he himself escaped, he was overtaken at Cos and crucified. Crete became a nest of corsairs, who ravaged the islands and even terrorised the monks of Mt Athos and Mt Latros; in 829 they destroyed a Byzantine fleet before Thasos. The squadron of Ooryphas, however, succeeded in bringing their depredations temporarily to a halt.

The reign of Theophilus (829–42) was taken up with continuous warfare with the Caliph al-Ma'mūn. Al-Ma'mūn, despite the revolt of Bābak and of the Khurramites in Azerbaijan and Djabal, took the opportunity of the Emperor's preoccupation with Sicily to launch an expedition in 830. Under the command of ʿAbbās, the Caliph's son, accompanied by the *patricius* Manuel, who had fled to the Arabs in the time of Michael II, a section of the army set out from Melitene. The Caliph himself entered Cappadocia by way of the Cilician Gates, and after capturing several places in this region he returned to Syria. ʿAbbās made his way back through the Ḥadath pass, but Manuel turned traitor once more and, escaping from the Arabs at Geron, near Ḥadath, re-entered Byzantine territory and became reconciled to the Byzantine Emperor. At the beginning of the following year Theophilus made some successful penetrations into Cilicia and returned in triumph to Constantinople. Al-Maʾmūn replied with a new campaign in the region of Heraclea and in Cappadocia, putting the Emperor himself to flight. At this point Theophilus sent an embassy to the Caliph, led by John the Grammarian, but the letter he carried annoyed the Caliph by its form of address, and the Emperor had to send a second letter observing the protocol demanded. The Emperor's offer of 100,000 dinars and 7000 prisoners in exchange for the surrender of captured fortresses and a five years' truce was refused. In 832 the Arabs took Loulon (Luʾluʾa); the Emperor was unable to raise the siege and the defenders surrendered. The Muslims established a garrison in the fortress and thus acquired mastery of the northern end of the defile. A new embassy from Byzantium achieved no success, since the Caliph had conceived the grandiose idea of seizing Amorium and marching on Constantinople. With this in mind, in May 833 he sent his son ʿAbbās to establish a valuable foothold at Tyana, rejecting a further request from the Emperor for a truce. But before reaching Loulon the Caliph fell ill, and died at Podandus on 7 August 833. His brother al-Muʿtaṣim, who succeeded him, was disturbed by the extension of the Khurramite revolt and therefore gave the order to abandon Tyana, returning himself to Baghdad.

The only incident in the early part of al-Muʿtaṣim's reign was a raid by ʿAmr ibn ʿUbayd Allāh, amir of Melitene. Nor did Theophilus take any action, preoccupied as he was by the war in Sicily, although he had potential support in the band of Persian Khurramites who, with the Kurd Naṣr (known to the Byzantines as Theophobus), crossed into Byzantine territory after their defeat in the winter of 833–4. In 837, however, at the instigation of Bābak, who had started negotiations with him, Theophilus destroyed Zibaṭra (Sozopetra), pillaged the region of Melitene, besieged and took Arsamosata (Shimshāṭ), as well as several towns in Armenia, and returned to Melitene, which now opened its doors to him, surrendering its prisoners. The sack of Zibaṭra made a great impression on al-Muʻtaṣim, who, too late, sent two of his generals to pursue Theophilus. The Emperor celebrated his triumph at Constantinople with great magnificence.

In 838, however, after the capture of Bābak, al-Muʻtaṣim resolved to put into execution al-Maʼmūn's plan of taking Amorium and marching on Constantinople. He set out with a strong army divided into two: one section with Afshīn advanced by the Ḥadath defile and after joining the troops under ʻAmr from Melitene marched towards the north-east, while the other, with Ashinās, followed two days later by the Caliph, advanced by way of the Cilician Gates. The Emperor originally intended to await the enemy on the Halys; but on hearing that Afshīn had invaded the theme of Armeniakon he hurried to meet him, and was severely defeated on the Iris in the region of Dazimon, escaping only by a hair's breadth. He fled in the direction of Constantinople, giving orders to Aetius, the *strategus* of Anatolikon, to defend Amorium. The detachment under Ashinās reached Ankara by way of Nyssa and the left bank of the Halys, where it was met by the section commanded by Afshīn. They marched together on Amorium, beginning the siege on 1 August 838. The city was taken on 13 August after bitter resistance; an old man who was a Muslim prisoner revealed the existence of a weak spot in the walls, and the commander of that part of the defences, Boiditzes, surrendered. Aetius was the last to give himself up. Part of the population was massacred and the rest taken into captivity. The Emperor had already unsuccessfully tried to open negotiations after his own defeat; with the fall of Amorium his case was certainly not improved, and the Caliph now demanded from him the surrender of Naṣr and Manuel, although he abandoned his intention of marching on Constantinople and on 25 September left Amorium, moving in the direction of Tarsus. During his retreat he lost a large number of men while crossing the desert west of the Great Salt Lake, and had many prisoners put to death. At Samarra, Aetius was crucified: the forty-two martyrs of Amorium were not executed until seven years later, in 845. During the years between the capture of Amorium and the deaths in 842 of Theophilus and al-Muʻtaṣim, there was no activity apart from Arab raids made by Abū Saʻīd, governor of Syria and Mesopotamia, and his lieutenant, Bashīr, commander at Maṣṣīṣa. Naṣr, the renegade, was killed during one of these raids; in another, in 841, the Greeks were victorious, capturing Ḥadath and occupying part of the region around Melitene. The naval war was kept alive by a Byzantine attack on Seleucia Pieria, the port of Antioch.

Between 809 and 842, although they had scored some notable successes which had at least the negative effect of enfeebling the

Byzantine Empire, the Arabs had achieved no positive results. Moreover, they were themselves becoming weaker, which permitted the Byzantines to strengthen their own position in the succeeding period. During the reign of al-Wāthiq (842–7), the successor of al-Muʻtaṣim, the pace of the war on the Arab side slowed down. ʻAmr of Melitene, who in 844 thrust forward as far as Malagina, defeated Theoctistus, Logothete of the Drome, while Abū Saʻīd also made several expeditions. The Greeks, however, engaged in some naval activity. The defeat of the great naval expedition (initiated by al-Muʻtaṣim) directed against Constantinople encouraged the Byzantines to dispatch in the same year (843) a fleet against Crete, commanded by Theoctistus. But the Emperor abandoned his army and returned to Constantinople just when the action was meeting with complete success, and his men were cut to pieces.[1] After an exchange of prisoners in 845 the amir of Tarsus made a winter expedition which proved disastrous. The decline of the Abbasid Caliphate had now set in. The pretorian Turks (who took no part in the Byzantine wars except in 858 under Boghā) henceforth made and unmade Caliphs at will. Only the amirs of the frontier marches, ʻAlī the Armenian and ʻAmr of Melitene, made annual excursions into Byzantine territory: an expedition of ʻAlī in 853 nearly reached Constantinople. They were almost completely independent within their fiefs (ʻAmr governed Melitene for twenty-eight years and ʻAlī Tarsus for eleven), but could depend only on their local resources. The Empire was never in any danger from these attacks. On several occasions the Byzantines took over the offensive both by sea and land, preparing by degrees for their recovery, which reached its climax in the victory of 863.

In 855 the Byzantines unexpectedly attacked Anazarbus and captured the Zott (Tziganes)[2] who had been deported there in 835. The Caliph agreed to an exchange demanded by Theodora, which took place in 856. There followed operations directed against the Paulicians and their Arab allies at Melitene. The Paulicians, persecuted for their faith, had taken refuge on Muslim territory and were established in the mountainous region to the south of Sivas at Argaouth, Amara and Tephrice (Divrigi), their capital; their leader Carbeas, who had come there with 5,000 Paulicians in the time of Theophilus, took an active part in the operations of ʻAmr of Melitene against the Byzantines. In 856 Petronas, *strategus* of Thrakesion and brother of Bardas, Theodora's chief minister, set out from the region of Arsamosata, penetrated as far as Amida and returned, ravaging Paulician territory in the region of Tephrice as he went, without

[1] For a different interpretation, see above: ch. IV, p. 106.
[2] Or the Jats; cf. G. C. Soulis, *DOP*, XV (1961), 143 ff.

meeting any resistance from ʿAmr and Carbeas. But the most important of the Greek operations was a naval expedition of 853, directed against Egypt, which had been supplying Crete with arms and materials. In May 853 a fleet took and burned Damietta, killing some of the population and taking the rest captive, and seized the store of arms and supplies. Ushtūm, at the entry of the Tinnis lagoon, was also destroyed. In 854 the Byzantine fleet returned to Damietta, probably with the object of hindering the rebuilding of the Egyptian ships and the repair work ordered by the Caliph; they stayed for a month, looting all that could be found. There was a third expedition against the Egyptian coast (at Faramā or Pelusa) in 859.

In 856 Theodora was deprived of her powers as regent by her brother Bardas, who became all-powerful as the minister of Michael III and continued the offensive against the Arabs, also rebuilding the fortifications of Ancyra. Operations recommenced after an exchange of prisoners in May 860, which almost miscarried because of some negotiations which were taking place between the Byzantines and the insubordinate Arab garrison of Loulon. There were several Arab and Paulician attacks during the summer: ʿAmr advanced as far as Sinope and an Arab fleet took Attalia. The Emperor, who had set out on campaign, was suddenly recalled by the appearance of a Russian fleet and only with difficulty retained his capital city. After the assassination of al-Mutawakkil in 861 the Muslims suffered a heavy defeat and lost two of their most energetic *ghāzīs*, ʿAmr of Melitene and ʿAlī the Armenian. ʿAmr had been operating independently of the Caliph's army and had advanced first to the Black Sea and then to Amisus (Samsoun); on his return he was surrounded near the Halys by an army under Petronas, brother of Bardas, and was killed while trying to escape. This took place in September 863. In October ʿAlī, who for the past year had been governor of Armenia, was also killed, while hurrying from Mayyāfāriqīn to meet the Byzantines who were marching eastward. The victories of 863 avenged the defeat of Amorium. Byzantium had regained the upper hand: the turning point in the struggle had been reached.

These successes, however, did not arrest the Arab and Paulician attacks, which continued in 864 and 865. But while the decline of the Abbasid Caliphate was further accentuated by the civil war which broke out in 865, the Byzantines continued to prepare for offensive action. Bardas resolved to effect a landing on Crete, with the object of putting an end to the attacks the Cretans had been making, first in 860 in the Cyclades and the Proconnesus, and later, between 862 and 866, on Mt Athos. But when the expedition was already assembled for departure from bases in Asia Minor, Bardas was assassinated in

April 866. The campaign was postponed, and Michael III, who had acquiesced in the murder of Bardas, returned to Constantinople, only to be himself murdered in the following year. Crete was to remain a nest of pirates for nearly another hundred years.

The war with the Saracens was the chief problem confronting Basil I, the founder of the Macedonian dynasty, when he came to the throne in 867. Although the Arabs had taken the offensive in the West, circumstances favoured the adoption of constructive policy in the East: the Empire was at peace with its other neighbours, Bulgaria, Russia, Venice and Germany, and Egypt, thanks to the Abbasid decline, was from 868 in the hands of the Tulunids, a quasi-independent rebel dynasty. Basil continued, only more systematically, the offensive begun in the later years of the Amorian dynasty, aiming at mastery of the invasion routes and the extension of the frontier eastwards. His first concern was to deal with the Paulician problem; the death of Carbeas in 863 and the victory of Petronas had in no way diminished the force of their attacks, for one of their forays, led by Chrysocheir, the nephew and son-in-law of Carbeas, had reached as far as Ephesus. After the failure of an attempt at reaching agreement with Chrysocheir and an unsuccessful expedition in 871, Basil sent out in 872 the Domestic of the Schools, who razed Tephrice, the Paulician capital, and took several other places, including Daranda, to the west of Melitene. In the same year Chrysocheir was killed in the neighbourhood of Dazimon. In the course of a campaign in 873, Basil took Zibaṭra (Sozopetra), Samosata and places between Melitene and Tephrice, and sent troops into the district between the Euphrates and the Arsanas. He was defeated, however, before Melitene, and could not take possession of the region.[1]

During this period the Byzantine navy was engaged both with the Arab fleet from Crete, which was infesting the Aegean, and with the fleet from Tarsus, which ranged as far as Chalcis in Euboea; in 872 the Byzantine navy destroyed an enemy fleet off the Peloponnese and in about 874 captured Cyprus, which remained in Byzantine hands for seven years.

An appreciable success was achieved in 876 and 877 with the acquisition of Loulon, the key to the northern entrance of the Cilician Gates; the place was surrendered to the Byzantines by its badly paid garrison while the Caliph's forces were engaged in lower Mesopotamia against the rebellious Zanj. The Syrian frontier march, which was now isolated, was at that time under the Tulunid ruler of Egypt, who

---

[1] According to E. Honigmann, *Die Ostgrenze des byzantinischen Reiches von 363 bis 1071* (Brussels, 1935), pp. 58–9, Basil I besieged Melitene twice without success in 873.

could make his authority felt only with difficulty. Between 877 and 883 there were several successful Byzantine campaigns. The Arab sources mention Byzantine operations near Podandus in 878, before Adana in 879, and in 879 or 880 near Heraclea and in Mesopotamia. It is possible that the Cilician operations were conducted by Nicephorus Phocas the Elder, and that these victories are, in fact, those usually attributed to the year 900. The Byzantine sources describe in considerable detail an expedition undertaken by the Emperor himself; departing from Caesarea, in 878–9, the Emperor besieged first Mar'ash and later Ḥadath, in both cases unsuccessfully. A little later, in 881 or 882, the Emperor again made an expedition against Melitene, but failed to take it, since help arrived from the garrisons of Mar'ash and Ḥadath. Although they failed to achieve their main objective, these campaigns nevertheless were sufficiently successful to justify the triumph Basil claimed in his capital. The year 882, however, marked the emergence as amir of Tarsus of Yazman, a eunuch of considerable energy who inflicted a crushing defeat on the Greeks before Tarsus. Basil, who died in 886, was not destined to renew his eastern campaigns. However, he concluded a treaty of friendship with Ashot, king of Armenia, and recognised his royal title, as the Arabs had also done. Considered as a whole, it can be said that Basil I's policy had taken the best advantage possible of the internal difficulties troubling the Arabs at that time.

In the reign of Leo VI (886–912) conditions were less favourable for conducting the struggle against the Muslims, since the Emperor was confronted with both the Bulgar war, which only ended in 897, and the Russian threat to Constantinople. Moreover, the war in the East now became extended into the distant regions of northern Armenia. In Armenia, Smbat, the successor of Ashot, who had made an offensive alliance with Leo against the Arabs in 893, was rendered powerless by Afshīn, the governor of Azerbaijan, who took Kars and forced Smbat to accept a humiliating peace; Yūsuf, Afshīn's successor, between 908 and 910 ravaged Armenia with fire and sword. Byzantine troops in 900 or 901 had expelled the Arabs from the Phasiane and in 902 captured Theodosiopolis. But this was the most that Leo could do, and the plan he evolved on the eve of his death of bringing help to Smbat was abandoned by his successor. Smbat was taken and put to a cruel death in 914.

Leo VI made no real move against the eastern frontier until 900. Yazman, amir of Tarsus (who died in 891), and after him other amirs dependent on the Tulunids (and later on the Caliph al-Mu'taḍid), continued to make profitable forays, which were interrupted only by an exchange of prisoners in 896; one of the most successful of these attacks was a maritime expedition of 898. The end of the Bulgar war, in which the Empire had been forced to arm Arab prisoners in defence of Constantinople, gave Byzantium the opportunity of regaining the offensive in the East; from 900 onwards the Byzantines were able to make a series of successful campaigns in Cilicia and other expeditions by both sea and land.[1] Nevertheless, the Syrian fleets operating from Tarsus and Crete still presented a grave danger and achieved some striking victories, with the help of two Byzantine renegades, Damian and Leo of Tripoli, and this despite the fact that the naval power of Tarsus was weakened by the policy of al-Muʿtaḍid (892–902). In 902 an Arab fleet ravaged the islands, destroyed Demetrias on the coast of Thessaly and attempted a landing in Attica; in 903 Lemnos was sacked; finally, in 904 Leo of Tripoli took Thessalonica after a siege lasting three days, without any disturbance from the imperial fleet under Himerius, and seized a vast quantity of booty and many prisoners.

In 904, however, Byzantine troops reached Marʿash, and in 906 Cyrrhestice. A project was then formed of making a grand maritime expedition with the co-operation of Andronicus Ducas, the victor of Marʿash, who was to sail with the fleet commanded by Himerius. Andronicus, however, was seduced by the slanders of the eunuch Samonas (a Muslim by origin and perhaps still at heart a Muslim, although he was a favourite with Leo VI) into believing that once he had embarked, he would be arrested and blinded. Instead he therefore revolted, joined the amir of Tarsus and went to Baghdad, where he arrived in 906. Leo Choerosphactes was sent as an envoy to Baghdad, but failed to persuade him to return, although he succeeded in negotiating a fresh exchange of prisoners (the Byzantines had themselves broken off the exchange which had been begun at the end of September 905), and in arranging for representation of the oriental Patriarchs at a synod in 907. The exchange duly took place in 908; after it the Arab attacks began afresh. Meanwhile, however, Himerius had achieved a brilliant naval victory (apparently in October 906) which encouraged the Emperor to plan a new maritime expedition; preparations for it were made in great secrecy and were assisted by reports from secret agents. The *archon* of Cyprus having first been won over, the island was captured in the summer of 910 and made the base for a landing in northern Syria at Laodicea, where Himerius took a number of prisoners. In 911, however, Damian recaptured Cyprus and with Leo of Tripoli defeated the fleet of Himerius near Samos, or, more probably, near Chios. The inhabitants

---

[1] Cf. R. J. H. Jenkins, B. Laourdas and C. A. Mango, 'Nine Orations of Arethas from Cod. Marc. Gr. 524', *BZ*, XLVII (1954), 12–14 and 30 ff.

of Cyprus were deported by Damian but were later allowed to return home, thanks to an application made by their bishop to Baghdad and a letter from Nicholas Mysticus to the Caliph al-Muqtadir (908–32).[1] Taken as a whole, the reign of Leo VI was thus more remarkable for Arab than Byzantine successes, particularly at sea. But it is to his credit that Leo was responsible for bringing in the Armenians as permanent occupants of the regions east of Caesarea which had either been abandoned by the Paulicians or simply left defenceless; and it was Melias, one of the most celebrated of the Armenians, who built the powerful fortress of Tzamandus and laid the foundations of the future theme of Lycandus.

The following period (913–34) covers the brief reign of Alexander (912–13), the regency of Zoe, mother of Constantine VII Porphyrogenitus (913–19), and the first part of the rule of Romanus I Lecapenus (919–44). During the early years of this period the monotony of the annual forays of the frontier garrisons on either side was broken only by an exchange of prisoners in 917, the result of a Byzantine embassy received at Baghdad with much splendour. The outstanding figures were, on the Byzantine side, Melias (Malīh al-Armanī), particularly for the role played before Mar'ash in 915, and on the Arab side two eunuchs, Mu'nis, as a commander on land, and, at sea, Thamal, successor of Damian (who died in 913 or 914). The Byzantines achieved some successes during the revolt of Ḥusayn ibn Hamdān, and the Empire also gave some assistance to Ashot, the King of Armenia, in reconquering his kingdom from a rival enjoying Arab support; this alliance arose from a visit paid by Ashot to Constantinople in 914.[2]

Romanus Lecapenus, himself an Armenian by origin, had the liberation of Armenia very much at heart, but he failed in his attempt in 921 to secure Dvin, the capital of Arab Armenia. In 921 or 922 the imperial fleet almost captured Leo of Tripoli, but in 924 Thamal reached the Sea of Marmora and joined counsel with the Bulgars; no effective results followed, since the Bulgar offensive was halted soon after this, and in 925 the Caliph, who was now exposed to the attacks of the Carmathians, was forced to accept an exchange. Romanus Lecapenus took advantage of the Caliph's difficulties, and, thanks to the assistance of the Armenian John Curcuas (appointed Domestic of the Schools in 923), achieved some decisive successes. After an ultimatum to the inhabitants of the frontier marches, the territory

---

[1] R. J. H. Jenkins, 'The Mission of St Demetrianus of Cyprus to Baghdad', *Mélanges Grégoire*, I = *AIPHO*, IX (1949), 267–75.

[2] On this date see M. Canard, *Histoire de la dynastie des H'amdanides*, I (Algiers, 1951), p. 725, n. 15.

around Melitene and the suburbs of the city were devastated by Byzantine troops in 926; in the following years, after the end of the Bulgar war in 927, the eastern frontier was the object of systematic effort. Melitene was first captured in 931 and then lost again; it was finally taken in 934, after a long siege. Shortly after this the Byzantines took first Anzitena and Ḥiṣn Ziyād (Kharpūt) and then Shimshāṭ (Arsamosata), all beyond the Euphrates. Curcuas was also active against Arab Armenia and devastated the Phasiane. He was unable to capture Dvin, but secured the surrender of Arab Armenian places on Lake Van, sacking them as he went. Terror reigned on the Mesopotamian frontier, and the prestige of the Empire increased, as is proved by the surrender of the Arabs of Melitene and the migration into Byzantine territory of the Arab Mesopotamian tribe of the Banū Habīb after 935. The capture of Melitene marked a decisive stage in the advance of Byzantium, and the Muslim response in the next period was to prove inadequate to the task of recovering the ground already lost.

Between 934 and 955 there was a Muslim recovery, though this was briefly halted between 940 and 945; despite some Muslim defeats, the Byzantines were forced to slacken their offensive. The mainspring of the recovery was the Hamdanid amir ʿAli, surnamed Sayf ad-Dawla, 'the Sword of the Empire' (that is to say, of the Abbasid Empire); from 936 he acted as prefect in the northern province of Mesopotamia for his brother the amir of Mosul, and later became master of the whole of northern Syria and of the Syrian–Mesopotamian frontier. From 936 onwards Curcuas had to reckon with Sayf as a redoubtable enemy. In 938 Sayf defeated him in a brilliant victory at Anzitena, and in 939 forced the Byzantines to raise the siege of Qālīqalā (Theodosiopolis), which had reverted to Arab hands at a date unknown; in 940 he subjugated all Armenia to his authority and then pressed on to Colonea, inflicting a fresh defeat on Curcuas. Meanwhile, however, Romanus Lecapenus had been negotiating with the Ikhshīd amir of Syria and Egypt, in order to have his hands free to act on the Syrian frontier, and in 938 was conceded an exchange of prisoners. In 942–3, whilst the Hamdanid was in Baghdad, the Byzantines carried their depredations into both northern Syria and Mesopotamia. Having entered Mayyāfāriqīn, Arzen, Dara and Nisibis, they laid siege to Edessa, in 943; after lengthy negotiations, in which the powerless Caliph was himself consulted by the inhabitants, the Byzantines were rewarded by the surrender of the famous *mandylion* miraculously imprinted with the features of Christ himself, which in 944 was conveyed with due solemnity to Constantinople. The capture of this relic was regarded as equivalent to a territorial conquest and crowned the work of Curcuas and Romanus Lecapenus. Romanus fell from power in 944, but bequeathed to Constantine Porphyrogenitus an eastern frontier extending as far as Shimshāṭ and valuable additions to the theme of Mesopotamia, established under Leo VI.

In 944 Sayf ad-Dawla entered Aleppo, asserting his right to the city against that of the Ikhshīd, who was forced in 947 to recognise his claim to possession. From 946 Sayf's authority extended as far as the frontier march in Syria and was soon to include the entire frontier from Tarsus to Armenia. All his energies were henceforth devoted to the struggle with Byzantium, at this time represented by the Domestic Bardas Phocas and his three sons, Nicephorus, *strategus* of Anatolikon, Leo, *strategus* of Cappadocia, and Constantine, *strategus* of Seleucia. (Bardas' tenure of office as Domestic in fact covers the second part of this period of Arab recovery.) The war was first local, confined to the region of Mar'ash–Ḥadath, but it soon spread over the entire front; and the operations of Sayf ad-Dawla were far-ranging indeed, extending into Cappadocia and Charsianon. After an exchange of prisoners in 946 (originally negotiated by the Ikhshīd and preceded by some skirmishing on the Syrian frontier), the Byzantines, in an attempt at gaining mastery of the road from Ḥadath to Mar'ash, dismantled Ḥadath in 948 and took Mar'ash in the following year. But this was no permanent occupation. The capture of Qālīqalā, on the other hand, at the other extreme end of the frontier and outside Sayf's sphere of operations, was a lasting conquest. In 950 the Hamdanid took the offensive with a powerful army and made an audacious attack which took him to the Halys, by way of the region containing the sources of the Jayḥān (Pyramus); from the Halys he went to Kharshana (Charsianon Castron), thence to Ṣārikha on the upper Halys and then farther north to a point on the Iris where he defeated Bardas. On his return he was surprised in a defile before arriving at Ḥadath and was beaten. His raids in 951 were more fortunate. Now more prudent, the Hamdanid made it his first concern to restore the places on the frontiers. In 952 the Greeks entered Mesopotamia, took Sarūj in the west and ravaged the region between Amida and Nisibis, not without meeting a lively response from the amir.

Since 950 the Emperor had been seeking a truce, and between 953 and 956 he sent out several embassies, all of them encountering obstinate refusals from the Hamdanid. In 953 Sayf achieved one of his greatest successes; having penetrated first into the region of Melitene and thence into Anzitena, as he returned he heard that Bardas was in North Syria, and hurried to surprise him at Mar'ash

(Germanicea), where Bardas was heavily defeated, being himself wounded in the face, and his son Constantine taken prisoner, to die in captivity. Bardas was twice more defeated, in 954 and 955, before Ḥadath, attempting in vain to prevent its reconstruction.

The Byzantines were no more fortunate at sea, although here they were confronted only by the Arabs from Crete, since Egypt was neutral and the Syrian (or Tarsiot) fleet had fallen into neglect. In order to halt the depredations of the Cretan sailors, Constantine prepared an expedition on a grandiose scale (details of the forces are given in his *Book of Ceremonies*), under the command of Constantine Gongylas. But in 949 this expedition, like that under Himerius, met with complete disaster. Even the Tarsiots managed to make one naval expedition, in 951, though this was their sole effort at sea during the Hamdanid period.

The failures of the period 945–55 were in large measure due to the ineptitude of the elderly Bardas Phocas, who in 955 was replaced as Domestic by his son Nicephorus. The succeeding period, from 955 to 1001, was the most brilliant in the history of the Macedonian dynasty. The policy of the Empire was throughout remarkably consistent, showing a continuous urge to conquest, and a systematic direction in the extension and maintenance of its gains. Three phases may be noted. The first period, from 955 to 969, covers the conquests of Nicephorus and the treaty establishing a protectorate over the amirate of Aleppo. During the second, from 970 to 976, John Tzimisces was extending his campaigns into the heart of Mesopotamia and Syria. Finally, between 976 and 1001 Basil II triumphantly defended both his own conquests and the amirate of Aleppo against the jealous designs of the Fatimids, who stopped at nothing short of war.

Nicephorus Phocas found his principal aides in the struggle with the Muslims in his brother Leo and in John Tzimisces, *strategus* of Mesopotamia. Victory, however, was still some way off, since in 956 Sayf ad-Dawla achieved some successes in Anzitena and on the right bank of the Arsanas, defeating Tzimisces in the region north-east of Amida; in a further campaign he thrust as far as Kharshana and returned by way of Adana, although in the meantime the Byzantine fleet had made a raid on Tarsus. The balance was redressed in favour of Byzantium in 957. Nicephorus sacked Ḥadath and put the inhabitants to flight; Tzimisces, in 958, after a raid into upper Mesopotamia, took Samosata and with the help of Basil the *parakoimomenos* defeated the amir at Raʿbān, on the border of Syria. During the summer of 959 Tzimisces spread terror throughout Mesopotamia, and at the end of the year Leo Phocas made a victorious progress through the Muslim territories of Cilicia and upper Mesopotamia. Taking advantage of the successes already achieved in the East, Romanus II who had succeeded Constantine VII in 959 decided to send an expedition under Nicephorus against Crete, whilst Leo was to remain at his station on the eastern front. Nicephorus embarked in 960 and landed on Crete after a keen battle; he then besieged Chandax, which he took by storm in March 961. The amir of Crete had applied for help to the Fatimid al-Mu'izz, who broke the truce concluded in the West in 957–8 and who wrote in such terms to the Emperor; the Cretans, however, derived no assistance from his intervention. The reconquest of Crete was followed by the conversion, voluntary or otherwise, of the population. On his return, Nicephorus gathered an army at Caesarea and from thence carried the war into Cilicia and northern Syria, which he was anxious to reconquer. In January 962 he captured Anazarbus and other places, returning to spend Lent at Caesarea, whilst operations were continued with the capture of Dulūk, Ra'bān, Mar'ash, together with an important prisoner, Abū Firās, cousin to the amir, who was taken near Manbij. In December Nicephorus marched against Aleppo; after a siege he took and plundered the town, only the citadel holding out, and then returned. The amir had taken flight at the beginning of the engagement (December 962–January 963).

Romanus II died in March 963. In July Nicephorus Phocas was proclaimed Emperor by his troops at Caesarea, to be crowned at Constantinople the following April. After consolidating his position on the throne, he prepared to renew his contest with Sayf ad-Dawla, who, despite illness and the diminution of his resources by rebellion, had been able with the help of volunteers to take offensive action at two points in the autumn of 963. But at the end of the year Tzimisces, who was now Domestic of the Schools, invaded Cilicia. Although he was forced by widespread famine to withdraw again at the beginning of 964, he returned with Nicephorus at the end of the year. The year 965 saw the capture by force of Maṣṣīṣa (Mamistra), the refuge of the population of Adana after its abandonment, and of Tarsus, which the regent of Egypt tried in vain to prevent. Sayf ad-Dawla then negotiated an exchange, which took place in 966. Meanwhile, however, the Byzantine fleet had achieved the final conquest of Cyprus and the defeat of the Egyptian fleet, in August 965.

The way to Syria lay open. After the expiry of the truce of 966 Mesopotamia and Syria were invaded. At Manbij Nicephorus took possession of the *keramidion* (the brick stamped with Christ's image), then devastated the region around Aleppo and went up towards Antioch; he failed to take the city and was driven by lack of supplies

to return to Constantinople. After a long period on the defensive, the
Hamdanid died at Aleppo in February 967. Nicephorus was prevented by his preoccupation with the Bulgars and other problems
from profiting from the troubles which ensued over the succession.
It was not until October 968 that he reappeared on the scene, first in
Mesopotamia and later in Syria. Ignoring Antioch and Aleppo, he
advanced as far as Tripoli, passing as he went through Homs, where
he took from the church the head of St John the Baptist. He returned towards Antioch by way of the coast, ravaging the country,
burning mosques and indulging in a deliberate campaign of terror.
He then departed, leaving Michael Burtzes with the task of restoring
Baghras, at the passage over the Amanus. At the end of 969, while
the Emperor was at Constantinople, his lieutenants Michael Burtzes
and Peter Phocas the stratopedarch took advantage of the dissensions
reigning at Antioch and Aleppo and captured both these cities. In
December 969–70 Qarghuyah, the chamberlain of Aleppo, who had
expelled Sa'd ad-Dawla, the son of Sayf ad-Dawla, signed a treaty
with the stratopedarch by which the amirate of Aleppo in fact became
a Byzantine protectorate. The amirate was also deprived in the north
and west of a large tract of territory, west and north of a line starting
north of Tripoli, following the mountains to the west of the Orontes
and rejoining the Euphrates after crossing the Orontes north-east of
Antioch. Finally, the amirate of Aleppo was bound to pay tribute
to assist the Emperor in warfare against non-Muslims, to prohibit the
entry of a Muslim army hostile to the Emperor and to submit to
certain clauses covering legal matters, trading and customs regulations. In return the Empire promised to defend the amirate against
its enemies. At the moment of the signing of the treaty Nicephorus
was no longer alive, for he had been assassinated on the night of
10–11 December 969. Nevertheless, it was his work as *domesticus* and
Emperor which had been crowned by this treaty, reasonable and
skilful in its conception, but to Islam an unprecedented humiliation.

John I Tzimisces, the successor of Nicephorus II Phocas, was to
find himself confronted with a new situation in the East, since the
southward extension of the Byzantine frontier in Syria now brought
the Empire into contact with the Fatimids, who had become masters
of Palestine and central Syria at the end of 969 and were aiming at
fresh conquests. In the first years of his reign Tzimisces was prevented from making any intervention in the East by his wars with
the Bulgars and the Russian prince Svjatoslav and by the revolt of
Bardas Phocas. In 971 a Fatimid army attempted the capture of
Antioch. Once Tzimisces had his hands free, he concentrated his
efforts on Mesopotamia. In 972 he reached Nisibis, which he burnt

down, and then laid fruitless siege to Mayyāfāriqīn; after this he departed, having received tribute from the Hamdanid amir Abū Taghlib, leaving an army under Melias the *domesticus* in Anzitena. On 4 July in the following year, 973, Melias was defeated, wounded, and taken prisoner at a point beyond Amida; he died in captivity in March 974. Tzimisces was then engaged on a further attack, entering Mesopotamia by way of Amida, passing Edessa and advancing to the extreme limits of the territory held by Baghdad; according to Matthew of Edessa he took more than 300 places on this campaign. It is probable that as a result of this raid several fortresses in the region round the sources of the Tigris as far as Armenia fell under Byzantine domination. The Hamdanid amir, engaged in a struggle with the Buwayhid amir of Baghdad, could do nothing. In 975 Tzimisces conducted a campaign in the Hamdanid and Fatimid territories of Syria which, judging by the letter announcing his victory addressed to Ashot of Armenia, was aimed at the liberation of Jerusalem. He progressed through Homs, Baalbek (where Alptekin the Turk, the ruler of Damascus, did homage to him), Tiberias and Nazareth to Mt Tabor where he received a delegation from Ramleh and Jerusalem, and then turned towards the coast to subdue Caesarea. He made his return by Sidon, Beirut and Byblos. Before Tripoli he had a clash with a Fatimid army. He then went up to the north, taking various places including some which were subject to the amir of Aleppo, and in September returned to Antioch. The resistance shown by the Fatimids had made it impossible for him to press his advance as far as Jerusalem. This triumphal march, which considerably enhanced the prestige of the Empire, seems to have brought no increase of Byzantine territory in Syria, and soon afterwards, in January 976, the Emperor died at Constantinople.

For the first years of his reign the youthful Basil II, Emperor jointly with his brother Constantine VIII, was assisted by his great-uncle, Basil the *parakoimomenos*. The main event of these years was the rebellion of Bardas Sclerus, *strategus* of the theme of Mesopotamia, who was proclaimed Emperor by his army of Armenians and Melitene Arabs. He established his headquarters at Ḥiṣn Ziyād (Kharpūt) and concluded an alliance with the Hamdanid of Mosul, who furnished him with several contingents of troops. For a brief moment Bardas was master of almost the whole of Asia Minor and of Byzantine North Syria. In 979 he was beaten and took refuge at Baghdad with the Buwayhid, who had conquered Mesopotamia and was thus now a close neighbour of the Empire. There followed lengthy negotiations between the Emperor and the Buwayhid 'Aḍud ad-Dawla; the former was anxious to secure the surrender of Sclerus, while the latter was seeking the return of places in Mesopotamia which had fallen under Byzantine rule and the recognition of his suzerainty over the amirate of Aleppo. These negotiations failed and in 986 Sclerus was set at liberty by the Buwayhid, in order that he (Sclerus) might re-open his attack on the young Basil II; the rebellion was not finally crushed until 989.

The Byzantine possessions in Syria were also being threatened at this period, both by internal disaffection and by Fatimid forces operating from Tripoli. In 977 Saʿd ad-Dawla, who had returned to Aleppo, refused to pay tribute and in 981 Bardas Phocas was obliged to extract his contribution by force. Bardas intervened again in 983, this time to support the amir against one of his own subordinates, who was in alliance with the Fatimids; in 985, however, Bardas was forced to yet a further intervention, to put an end to the hostile actions of the amir himself, who had been driven thereto by the Fatimids. In 987, as a result of his defeat on the Bulgar front and internal revolts, Basil II was obliged to sign a treaty with the Fatimid al-ʿAzīz (975–96); by a clause in this treaty the Emperor was bound to hand over various precious objects and to allow the name of the Fatimid Caliph to be mentioned in prayers at the mosque in Constantinople.

After the rebellions of Bardas Phocas and Bardas Sclerus had come to an end, Basil II could once again turn his attention to the East. His immediate aim was to provide protection for the amirate of Aleppo against Fatimid attacks which were becoming frequent, being sometimes indirect, as in 991, when use was made of a pro-Fatimid rebel, and sometimes direct, as in 992 and 994, after the death of Saʿd ad-Dawla. Burtzes, responsible for the defence of the amirate, proved unequal to his task; in 992 he allowed the Fatimids to lay waste the region of Antioch, and in 994 was himself crushed on the banks of the Orontes. The Hamdanid, blockaded at Aleppo, appealed directly to the Emperor who reached him from the Bulgarian front in only sixteen days (spring 995) and forced the Fatimid army to raise the siege; he then occupied several places, restored Anṭarṭūs, handed over the tribute to the Hamdanid and replaced Burtzes by Dalassenus. The Caliph al-ʿAzīz, however, decided to intensify his struggle with Aleppo and Byzantium and in 996 set out on campaign, but died almost immediately. Under his successor al-Ḥākim (996–1021) Dalassenus again had to fight Fatimid troops, and in 998 achieved a victory near Apamea; but while pursuing the enemy to Baalbek he received a mortal wound and the victory was turned to defeat. In 999 the Emperor appeared in person, but after a victorious march through Shayzar, Homs and Baalbek he was repulsed before Tripoli. He retreated into Cilicia, where he spent the winter. In 1001, however, negotiations which had been started with al-Ḥākim in 998 ended in the conclusion of a ten years' peace, and there were no further open hostilities between the Empire and Egypt. During the reign of al-Ḥākim prayers for the Fatimid continued to be said in the mosque at Constantinople. Basil II, both by his military valour and by his diplomacy, had preserved intact the heritage left him in the East by his predecessors.

The latter part of the reign of Basil II (1001–25) and the reigns of the last Emperors of the Macedonian dynasty (1025–56) were marked in the East only by operations on a small scale. Relations with the Fatimid Caliphate continued untroubled until 1009, when al-Ḥākim began the persecution of Christians and destroyed the Church of the Holy Sepulchre. No warfare followed, however, and Basil II made no retaliation. This persecution ceased with the death of al-Ḥākim in 1021, and in 1023 the Patriarch of Jerusalem was dispatched to Constantinople to announce that the destroyed churches would be restored and that the Christians could henceforth live in safety.

In 1002 the chamberlain Lu'lu' deposed the last Hamdanids at Aleppo. But he was careful not to give offence to Byzantium and ordered the arrest of a Mesopotamian adventurer who was preaching the Holy War. His son, on the other hand, inclined towards the Fatimids. One of the sons of the Hamdanid amir, in exile at Cairo, fled to Constantinople and then attempted to bring about a Hamdanid restoration at Aleppo; but he received no support from the Emperor and after his attempt had failed returned to Constantinople. After 1016 Aleppo passed into the hands of the Mirdasids, a weak Arab dynasty, who were occasionally forced to appeal for Byzantine help against the Fatimids, as for example in 1024, when Fatimid troops had seized the citadel of Aleppo; Basil lost interest in the amirate of Aleppo and contented himself with maintaining the Byzantine possessions intact; the frontier to the north of Tripoli seems to have receded a little at this date. The weakness of Basil's successors encouraged the Mirdasids to indulge in open hostility; in 1029 the Arabs of Aleppo defeated Spondyles, the catepan of Antioch, who had attacked without orders from the Emperor. In 1030 the Emperor Romanus III Argyrus decided to take possession of Aleppo, and set out on campaign. But his troops were defeated north of Aleppo and he himself narrowly escaped capture. An agreement was reached with Aleppo in 1031 and with the Palestinian amir Ibn al-Jarrāḥ, who had detached himself from the Fatimids, in 1032. In 1032, however, George Maniaces, the brilliant Byzantine commander at Samosata, took Edessa from the Marwānids of Mesopotamia. This was the final addition made to the conquests achieved under the Amorian and Macedonian dynasties, and Edessa remained a Byzantine possession until the days of the crusades, despite an attack in 1036. There was no change in the position of the amirate of Aleppo, which in theory remained a vassal state, though in practice it was often hostile.

In considering Macedonian relations with the Fatimids, it should be noted that it is doubtful whether in fact any treaty was made with the Caliph az̧-Zāhir (1021–35) in 1027[1] providing for the rebuilding of the Church of the Holy Sepulchre as well as the mosque at Constantinople which the Caliph wished to see restored and provided with a muezzin. It is true that these questions were raised during the time of Romanus III Argyrus (1028–34), but the alliance between Byzantium and the amir Ibn al-Jarrāḥ led to a coolness in Byzantine relations with the Fatimid Caliphate. It was only in 1037 that negotiations led to a treaty with Michael IV, concluded in the name of the Caliph al-Mustanṣir by his mother and his regent. By this treaty the Emperor was permitted to restore the Church of the Holy Sepulchre at his own expense, and he also had the right to appoint the Patriarch of Jerusalem. But there is no reason for thinking that henceforth there was any kind of Byzantine 'protectorate' over the Holy Places. A fresh treaty was concluded in 1047–8, under Constantine Monomachus (1042–55) who on several occasions exchanged embassies with the Fatimid al-Mustanṣir (1035–94) and in 1051–2 brought about the arrest and dispatch to him of an emissary from Baghdad who was on his way to the rebel governor of North Africa. In 1054, when Egypt was suffering from famine, al-Mustanṣir sent requests for corn, and these negotiations were continued in 1055 with the Empress Theodora, who was anxious to secure an alliance in return for this help, probably against the Seljuqs. When the Caliph refused, the Empress likewise refused her corn. A further cause of discord in Byzantine–Fatimid relations was the negotiations which took place in 1049 between Byzantium and Ṭughrîl Bey: as a result, permission was given for prayers to be said in the mosque at Constantinople for Ṭughrîl Bey and the Abbasid Caliphate. The reason for this *rapprochement* lay in the new menace to Byzantium presented by the Seljuqs, whose first incursions started in 1048. In 1055 the Fatimid ambassador found himself in Constantinople at the same time as the Seljuq envoy who was authorised to say prayers there. As a reprisal al-Mustanṣir confiscated the treasures of the Holy Sepulchre.

The last Emperors of the Macedonian dynasty, despite their weakness, succeeded in preserving and even extending their possessions

[1] Magrīzī, *Khiṭaṭ*, I, p. 355, ed. M. K. Adawi (Būlāk, 1853).

in the East, thanks chiefly to the anarchy which prevailed there at the time.

Thus a survey of the opening years of the eighth century to the coming of the Turks reveals how Byzantine fortunes in the East had changed. Until 717 East Rome was fighting for its very existence, and from that date until 743 was still engaged in a grim defensive struggle. Between 744 and 754, however, there was a period of respite, occasioned by the growing anarchy of Islam and the eclipse of the still only feebly established Abbasid dynasty. But from 754 to 863 the re-established Abbasid Empire once again forced the Byzantines into a critical defensive position, until in 863 they secured a victory over two of the most famous Abbasid amirs. The Amorian Michael III's reign opened a period in which Byzantium took the offensive against the declining Abbasid Empire, though not without some vicissitudes. From 886 the Arabs regained their mastery on both land and sea, until they suffered a check with the capture of Melitene by the Byzantines in 934. But even after this, the Hamdanid Sayf ad-Dawla continued to present an effective obstacle to the Byzantine advance until 955. Between 955 and 1001, Nicephorus Phocas (first as *domesticus* and later as Emperor) and his successors conquered and retained Cilicia and a part of North Syria, despite the arrival on the scene of the Fatimids. Between 1001 and 1056 the war lost some of its former intensity and Byzantium was for the moment no longer confronted by any major enemies, and with the capture of Edessa in Mesopotamia (1032) its conquests were indeed extended. But in 1048 began the incursions of the Seljuqs into Armenia.

II. THE STRUGGLE IN THE WEST

The earliest attacks against Byzantine possessions in the West had come from the East, but from the eighth century onwards the chief danger was from the Arabs of North Africa, whose attacks were facilitated by the absence of a Byzantine fleet permanently based on Sicily. As early as 752–3 the governor of Ifrīqiya had dreamed of the subjugation of Sardinia (which was forced to pay tribute) and Sicily; but it was only after Ibrāhīm ibn al-Aghlab had founded his semi-independent dynasty in Africa in 800 that Sicily was directly threatened, and even then, in 805 the *patricius* Constantine managed to secure a ten years' truce. Despite this there were some attacks on the islands in 812. In 813 the Aghlabid was induced by the intervention of an imperial fleet, with assistance from Gaeta and Amalfi, to conclude a further truce for ten years. In 819, however, there was a fresh attack on Sicily, followed by another truce.

In 827 the Arabs gained a definite foothold in Sicily. Euphemius, commander of the Byzantine fleet, had rebelled and taken Syracuse; he was there proclaimed Emperor, but when Syracuse was retaken by one of his subordinates acting in the name of the Emperor, he took refuge in Africa, seeking the help of the Aghlabid Ziyādat Allāh. At first Ziyādat Allāh was hesitant, but sent an army which landed with Euphemius at Mazara in June 827 and proceeded to lay siege to Syracuse. But in 828, perturbed by the outbreak of an epidemic and the arrival of reinforcements in Sicily, the Arabs were anxious to retreat. They found their exit blocked by the Byzantine fleet, and they therefore burnt their boats and turned westward by land. They took Girgenti and besieged Enna (Castrogiovanni). Meanwhile Euphemius had been assassinated by the Sicilians. Byzantine reinforcements arrived to raise the siege of Enna and repulse the Arabs. Girgenti was abandoned, the Arabs retaining only Mineo and Mazara. In 830 they received help from Africa and Spain. Most of the reinforcements from Spain soon withdrew on account of an epidemic, but the Africans went on to besiege Palermo; Theophilus could send no help as he was occupied in the East, and the city fell in August/September 831, to become the capital of Arab Sicily.

For some time internal dissensions prevented the Arabs from following up their successes. After the arrival as governor of Abu 'l-Aghlab, cousin of Ziyādat Allāh, in 835, Enna was conquered, but not occupied (837). In 838 Cefalù, with help brought by Alexius Musele, the son-in-law of Theophilus, put up a resistance. But Alexius was recalled and in 840 and 841 several important places fell into Arab hands. Although the Emperor had the support of a Venetian fleet, the Arabs could not be prevented from penetrating South Italy and taking Taranto and Bari, ravaging the coasts of the Adriatic and reaching Rome itself, which they did in 846.

At the beginning of the reign of Michael III the Arabs seized Messina (end of 842 or 843), assisted by the Neapolitans with whom they had concluded an alliance in 836. After a truce in 845, an army sent out by Theodora was defeated, and in 846–7 Leontini, between Catana and Syracuse, was captured. In the decade following the death of Abu 'l-Aghlab in 851 Arab attacks multiplied, to culminate in the capture of Enna in January 859. The Emperor then dispatched a fleet of considerable size, but this was defeated near Syracuse, and the subject places which had been encouraged to revolt were submitted to a fresh subjugation. The Arabs then fortified Enna, which barred the route to the west, as a precaution against possible Byzantine attacks. In 861 the death took place of ʻAbbās, the successor of Abu 'l-Aghlab, and the real conqueror of Sicily, although the conquest was still incomplete. After his death and a period of dissension with the amir of Africa, a new governor, Khafāja, was sent from Africa, who continued the conquest. In 867, when the Amorian dynasty came to an end, Byzantium held practically nothing except Syracuse and Taormina, and Taormina had already treated with the enemy.

Basil I, at the beginning of his reign, sent a fleet to the West which put a stop to Arab activities in the Adriatic (868). Basil had also a wider plan of a combined operation by himself, the Western Emperor Louis II and the Pope against the Arabs in South Italy, and the imperial fleet helped Louis II to take Bari in 871. But the Arab attacks on south Italy continued, and in 873 Benevento, and then Apulia, appealed to Basil for aid, and after the death of Louis in 875 Basil gained a firm foothold in Italy and occupied Bari himself. But in 882 the Arabs took advantage of a dispute between Gaeta and the Pope to establish themselves permanently on the banks of the Garigliano.

The position of the Arabs in Sicily was reinforced in 870 by the capture of Malta. After a period of troubles, the new amir of Africa, Ibrāhīm (875–902), gave his support to an aggressive policy in Sicily and in August 877 Syracuse was besieged, to fall in May 878 without having received any help from the Emperor. The capture of the city was followed by a savage massacre; its loss was a severe blow to the Byzantines. They soon made retaliation. In 880 an Arab fleet was destroyed off the west coast of Greece and successful operations were conducted on the northern coast of Sicily and in southern Italy. Taranto was recaptured and the last years of the reign of Basil, from 885, were marked by important successes achieved in Italy by the energy of Nicephorus Phocas the Elder, who completely restored the situation there, expelling the Arabs from several places in Calabria.

In Sicily, however, the reign of the next Emperor, Leo VI, brought no improvement, despite the dissensions between the Sicilian and the African Arabs; nor was any benefit derived by Byzantium from a rebellion which only ended in 900, with the recapture of Palermo from the rebels by 'Abd Allāh, the son of the amir Ibrāhīm. In 901 'Abd Allāh took Reggio, despite the arrival of Byzantine reinforcements. In 902 Ibrāhīm campaigned in person; he captured Taormina, the last important Byzantine possession, and then advanced into Calabria with grandiose ambitions of pressing on to Constantinople. But in 902 he died while besieging Cosenza, and the siege was immediately raised. After his death new dissensions arose in Sicily, and Leo VI in 907 managed to establish relations with Ziyādat Allāh III, who was perhaps disturbed by the threat represented by the Fatimids. However, in 910 hostilities were resumed. But Sicily was

no longer of importance. As for Italy, Leo VI died without being able
to bring any help to the Italian principalities against the Arabs of the
Garigliano. In 915, however, during the regency of Zoe, Byzantium
helped the Lombard principalities to expel the Arabs from this district. But the Fatimid Caliph al-Mahdī secured recognition of his
authority at Palermo and in 918 the governor, his representative,
made a surprise landing at Reggio in south Italy and captured it.
Zoe was forced to pay tribute to the tune of 20,000 gold solidi for her
Italian possessions. In Sicily, Taormina, which had been reoccupied
by its former Greek inhabitants, concluded a truce with the Arabs.

The first part of the reign of Romanus I Lecapenus brought no
improvement, and the payment of tribute did not prevent the Arabs
from making incursions into Calabria. However, a chain of diplomatic events made for slightly more cordial relations. The Byzantines
had captured in Calabria some Bulgarian envoys who were returning
home from an embassy to the Fatimids, with whom the Bulgars were
now on friendly terms; the Bulgar envoys were accompanied by some
Arab ambassadors, who were also captured and accorded favourable
treatment by the Byzantines. For this the Caliph was grateful and
showed his gratitude by renouncing the Bulgar alliance and halving
the tribute to be paid to him. Despite all this the Arab raids in
Calabria continued, and Oria, Taranto and other places were taken.
The death of al-Mahdī was followed by a rebellion in Sicily which
lasted until 941. Romanus Lecapenus took advantage of the situation to intervene in Italy; he helped Hugh of Provence to expel the
Arab colony at Fraxinetum, supported Girgenti, which was in revolt,
and ceased to pay the tribute money. Al-Qā'im (934–46) and al-
Manṣūr (946–53) were both confronted with a formidable revolt in
Africa, which lasted until 947. Once al-Manṣūr had emerged from
this triumphant he again exacted the tribute money from Byzantium;
in 946 he had received a Byzantine embassy. Hostilities were resumed, and landings in Calabria in 951 and 952 forced the Byzantines
to seek a new agreement, an embassy being sent to al-Manṣūr in 953.
After the accession of al-Mu'izz (953–75) war broke out again, following the conclusion of an alliance between Byzantium and the Umayyad Caliph of Spain. Byzantium had always been on friendly terms
with the Umayyads, who had promised never to lend their support
to Byzantine enemies in the East, in Crete or in Africa; these terms
had been agreed on by ambassadorial exchanges in 839–40, 945–6 and
949–50, but no actual alliance had been concluded. But in 955–6,
the Umayyad had sought the help of Constantine VII against the Fatimids, his rivals in Africa. In 956–7, after an initial success against
the combined navies of Byzantium and Spain, the Fatimid fleet was

dispersed by a storm and beaten. However, this victory had no successors, and in 957–8 the Emperor was obliged to send an embassy to Africa; a new truce was obtained which endured until the Cretan expedition. Calabria, however, had already been depopulated as a result of the Arab incursions.

During the reign of Romanus II the Sicilian Arabs reoccupied Taormina, in 962. The Byzantines now held only Rametta, which was besieged by the Muslims. Nicephorus Phocas sent out an expedition under the *patricius* Manuel Phocas and the admiral Nicetas with the object of relieving Rametta. After capturing Messina, Manuel marched on Rametta, but in October 964 he was killed and his army thrown into disorder. A few months later the fleet was completely destroyed and Nicetas taken prisoner. Rametta was taken by storm in 965; with it the Byzantines lost their one remaining Sicilian possession. But in the face of the common danger presented by the German Emperor, Nicephorus and al-Muʿizz became reconciled, concluding a peace treaty in 967. During the reign of Basil II the Arabs continued their attacks on South Italy and defeated the Emperor Otto II in 982; and when as a consequence of this event Byzantine authority had been restored in Apulia, they supported revolts in this region against the Empire. But the Byzantines had some stout allies: the Venetians, who in 1004 relieved Bari from an Arab siege, and the Pisans, who in 1005 helped the Byzantines to destroy an Arab fleet before Reggio. Basil thus re-established his authority in Apulia, and at the end of his reign was preparing for the reconquest of Sicily. He sent an army to Italy which succeeded in taking Messina, but before he could join it he died, in December 1025. His plan was taken up again later at a time when dissensions in Sicily seemed likely to favour it. In 1037 Oropus, the catepan of Italy, landed in Sicily, but he could not gain a foothold. In 1038 George Maniaces at the head of an army composed of Normans and Varangians took Messina, defeated the Arabs at Rametta and in 1040 occupied Syracuse. But Maniaces was recalled on account of dissensions within the army and the Arabs recovered all his conquests, with the exception of Messina. Shortly afterwards the Normans began their slow progress into Byzantine Italy; and it was the Normans who were to liberate Sicily from the Arabs.

It would then appear that the Byzantines attached less importance to the western theatre of operations, since the territories there were remote from the capital and did not occupy a position of central importance as did Anatolia. In any case, they were at first less threatened. Arab attacks only began during the Abbasid period, when the Aghlabids, a lesser and semi-independent dynasty, who had to rely on their own resources, established themselves in North Africa. The Arabs of the Maghrib and of Spain played no part in these assaults, but it was otherwise with the Fatimids when they arrived on the scene.

The war in the West was preponderantly maritime in character. Its main stages may be summarised as follows. Until 827 Arab attacks merely took the form of naval assaults, without any important results. Between 827 and 861 Sicily, with the exception of Syracuse and Taormina, was conquered by stages. The years between 861 and 913 saw the fall of the last Sicilian strongholds, and subsequent attacks on South Italy. Between 913 and 959 Byzantium was forced to enter into humiliating agreements and to pay tribute for Calabria. However, the later period of the Macedonian dynasty (959–1057) was marked by two attempts to reconquer Sicily.

In conclusion, it is clear that warfare between Byzantium and the Muslim world was for the most part made up of innumerable raids and sorties broken only by the periodic dispatch of envoys and truces for the exchange of prisoners. Its story is only rarely spectacular, but its recital is essential: it enables the historian to reconstruct the vital struggle which was an integral part of both Byzantine and Muslim policy.

In the East Byzantium suffered many changes of fortune, and success here was not assured until Nicephorus Phocas by his achievements turned the balance decisively in favour of the Empire. The Caliphs had always the advantage of being confronted by only one enemy and on only one front, though they had their own internal enemies to contend with. Their resources of manpower were immense and their armies and practice of warfare less expensive for them than for Byzantium. But they lacked any central direction, their financial organisation was weak and they had no tradition of military discipline comparable with that of their enemies, though in compensation they could draw on all the reserves of spirit called forth by the waging of a Holy War, a spirit which Byzantium never possessed in quite the same sense. The Caliphate laboured under one great disadvantage; whereas the Byzantine Empire was continually improving its organisation and aimed increasingly at reconquest and territorial expansion, the Empire of the Caliphs was no longer ambitious for territorial conquest and was increasingly the prey of internal anarchy; in fact it was really the frontier provinces which were seriously engaged in the fight against Byzantium. In the West the Empire was confronted only by one relatively minor province of the Empire of the Caliphs, Africa (Ifrīqiya). But Sicily was so remote from the main resources of the Byzantine strength, and often so badly served by Emperors such as Basil I who employed his fleet to transport materials for building churches instead of using it in defence of Sicily, that it was soon lost; the Byzantine territories in South Italy, where the Empire had other enemies to reckon with as well, were only with difficulty preserved.

III. PEACEABLE RELATIONS BETWEEN BYZANTIUM AND THE MUSLIM WORLD

Relations between the two Empires were always tinged with hostility, but there was one part of the Muslim Empire, Umayyad Spain, which was never directly at war with Byzantium. If, according to the Muslim law, there existed a permanent state of war, nevertheless there was nothing to prevent peaceful interchanges during the various periods of truce. In theory it was even possible for a citizen of Byzantium to gain permission from the frontier authorities to take up residence in Muslim territory and engage in commerce, always provided that he did not traffic in articles forbidden by the religious law or the interests of national safety, such as arms or horses. The Byzantine Empire was perhaps less liberal in these matters than the Arabs. In the tenth century there were Muslims established at Trebizond, in some towns in Bithynia and, indeed, at Constantinople, where, however, the mosque was only for the use of prisoners. Trebizond had close relations with Armenia which, on account of its peculiar status, could freely trade with the Arabs, exporting Byzantine goods and importing Muslim merchandise. The same was true of Cyprus, which had a central position between the two Empires and where Muslims were also established. Clauses in the treaty made between the Empire and the amirate of Aleppo in 969 sanctioned commercial exchanges between caravans of merchants which must have already been taking place before the date of the treaty. A Persian traveller during the Fatimid period provides evidence of trade between Constantinople and Egypt at this date, and this trade must also have been taking place earlier. Egyptian cloth was as much sought after by the Byzantines as Byzantine cloth was by the Arabs. Byzantine manufactured articles, which are mentioned by Arab geographers and which were in current use, were not merely acquired as booty or produced on Muslim territory by captured Greek workmen but were also being regularly exported. There appears to be little information concerning private commercial transactions. But it is known that ambassadors who were sent, for example, to the Caliphs or to the amirs of Egypt were allowed to engage in commercial activities, as is shown by a letter from the amir of Egypt to Romanus Lecapenus in 936. It is also known that a governor of

Calabria sold corn to the Sicilian Arabs and that the Fatimid al-Mustanṣir asked for corn from the Emperor.

Non-commercial relations arose in a variety of circumstances: diplomatically, with the exchange of embassies; through the internment of prisoners of war on both sides; through the deportation of the populations of captured cities; through the movements of traitors and exiles from both camps; and through the attendance at councils by the oriental Patriarchs or their delegates and the visits to the Eastern Patriarchates made by the envoys of the Patriarch of Constantinople. Thus both sides were in a position to gather information on the situation in the other camp and the conditions of life there, as shown by the writings of the Arab geographers; this intelligence was of course additional to that gained by espionage. At Constantinople prisoners were used as sources of information: Nicephorus Phocas engaged in animated conversation with Abū Firās, cousin to the amir of Aleppo, who was captured in 962. On certain festival occasions Arab ambassadors were invited to the Emperor's table and admitted to the Hippodrome and St Sophia. An envoy of the Caliph al-Wāthiq (842–9) was allowed to visit the cave of the Seven Sleepers at Ephesus; an ambassador of Sayf ad-Dawla visited a pagan temple containing a large store of manuscripts, a three days' journey from Constantinople; while Byzantine ambassadors were admitted to Christian sanctuaries in Muslim territory.

Information concerning the life led by Greek prisoners in Muslim territory is sparse. Arab prisoners at Constantinople enjoyed a measure of freedom, they had a mosque and were not forced to eat food forbidden by Muslim law; in 912–13 envoys of the Caliph were allowed to visit the prisoners and report their impressions of the conditions in which they lived. Some of the prisoners were invited to the Emperor's table and to the games in the Circus on the occasion of certain festivals. Their life seems to have been tolerable, apart from the humiliations they had to endure in the Circus when an Emperor was celebrating a triumph. Abū Firās enjoyed privileged treatment. Prisoners were not excluded from cultural intercourse; al-Ma'mūn heard of Leo the Philosopher from a Greek prisoner.

These exchanges between the two camps were further assisted by the renegades, Muslims like Samonas who entered the service of Byzantium, and Greeks who went over to the Muslims, such as Leo of Tripoli, the eunuch Mu'nis, and the Chamberlain of al-Muqtadir, Naṣr, who also brought over his brother 'from the land of the Greeks'. The same can be said of the Greek women who filled the harems of the East, women such as Shaghab, the all-powerful mother of the Caliph al-Muqtadir, whose brother also held positions of high importance. According to a Persian traveller, in the Fatimid period many of the chief offices of the Caliphate were occupied by Greeks.

The capitals of the two Empires vied with each other in magnificence, artistic splendour and cultural refinement. The Caliphs, like the Emperors, loved to dazzle foreign ambassadors; the accounts of an Arab embassy of 946, and of a Byzantine embassy to Baghdad in 917 and of another to Cordova in 947 all bear witness to this. Both sides were anxious to receive important personages as envoys or precious objects as gifts. Al-Ma'mūn pestered Theophilus to send him Leo the Philosopher, but the Emperor refused him his wish, sending instead an assortment of Greek scientific works, chosen by a delegation of Muslim and Christian scholars. According to one Arab source, the Emperor asked Hārūn ar-Rashīd to send him the poet Abu 'l-'Atāhiya. Constantine Porphyrogenitus sent manuscripts of Dioscorides and Orosius to Cordova, together with a basin and columns of marble; the Fatimid al-'Azīz was presented with pillars for a pavilion. Palaces were built in mutual imitation, both in architecture and decoration; the impressive mechanical devices in the Audience Room at Baghdad seem to have been in the style of those of the Great Palace, while the Fatimid palace was probably an imitation of the palace at Constantinople. Theophilus' building projects were inspired by what he had heard of the splendours of the palace at Baghdad, which served as a model for the palace at Bryas. A recent study has shown that Muslim art exercised a distinct influence on the Byzantine court of the tenth and eleventh centuries.[1]

The inhabitants of the frontier regions were in frequent contact and the populations there were to some extent mixed. In 860 the garrison of Loulon were on the point of reverting to Christianity and the Byzantine fold. The amirs of Tarsus and Melitene on occasion concluded pacts of local application with the Empire, as is shown by the account of the embassy of Choerosphactes of 906.[2] Certain families, such as those of 'Abd al-Bāqī at Adana and of 'Amr of Melitene, had permanent connections with the Byzantines, by no means due to the exigencies of war; before its surrender in 934 the city of Melitene contained both a pro- and anti-Byzantine party. The mass movements of the Banū Habīb into Byzantine territory and of the Paulicians into Arab lands provide further instances of the interpenetrations which existed on the frontiers, and it is well known that the Byzantine and Arab epics (*Digenis Akritas*, and *Delhemma* and *Baṭṭāl*) influenced each other.

---

[1] A. Grabar, 'Le succès des arts orientaux à la cour byzantine sous les Macédoniens', *Münchener Jahrbuch der bildenden Kunst*, Dritte Folge, II (1951), 32–60.

[2] Cf. G. Kolias, *Léon Choerosphactès* (Athens, 1939), pp. 47 ff.

CHAPTER XVIII

THE TURKS AND THE BYZANTINE EMPIRE TO THE END OF THE THIRTEENTH CENTURY

I. THE GROWTH OF TURKISH SUPREMACY IN WESTERN ASIA

In the eleventh century there emerged in western Asia a new race destined to play a decisive part in the history of the Byzantine Empire—the Turks. The first to appear in history under this name, in the middle of the sixth century (552), were the so-called 'blue Turks' or Kökturks. They established an Empire in Mongolia, with its centre in the region of the rivers Orkhon and Selenga, to the south of Lake Baikal, but with its sphere of influence extending as far west as the shores of the Black Sea, where the Turks first came into contact with the Byzantines. When at the beginning of the seventh century war broke out between the Persian King Chosroes II and the Byzantine Emperor Heraclius, the latter sought to conclude an alliance with the Turkish Empire in order to attack Persia on two fronts, while Chosroes stirred up against Byzantium the Avars, a people who had formerly been expelled from Mongolia by the Turks and had subsequently penetrated into eastern Europe.

The seventh century saw the Arabs shake the old world to its foundations in the name of their new religion, Islam, conquering both the eastern provinces of the Roman Empire and the Persian Sassanid realm, while in the Far East the Chinese T'ang dynasty assumed increasing power. In consequence the Kökturkish Empire forfeited its dominant position, came for a time under Chinese suzerainty, and after a brief revival fell victim to a coalition of other Turkish tribes led by the Uighurs, who in their turn established an Empire in northern Mongolia. The Uighurs were, however, unable to retain the entire territory of the original Kökturkish Empire; it was overrun in the west, in the region of Lake Balkhash, by the Karluks (766), who were first the allies of the Uighurs and later their enemies. The Uighur Empire was itself overthrown in 840 by the Kirghiz. The Karluk Empire eventually extended its sphere of influence as far as the Tarim basin, the modern East Turkistan, and so bordered directly on a part of the Islamic world, the Persian Samanid kingdom in Transoxania, the modern West Turkistan. Here, since the middle of the ninth century, there had flourished a Persian renaissance which brought to full maturity a new Islamic-Persian national culture. Under the influence of their new neighbours the Karluks embraced the Islamic faith in the particular form current in the Samanid kingdom, namely Sunnitism with Hanifitish rites. The recent development of a Persian national culture in the Samanid kingdom also determined the nature of the Karluk culture. Historically these Karluk conquerors who underwent conversion to Islam are known as Karakhanids. When civil dissension broke out in the Samanid kingdom towards the end of the tenth century, the Karakhanids intervened and by 1003 had finally subjugated Transoxania, bringing it permanently under Turkish rule and infusing substantial Turkish elements into the language.

During the tenth and early eleventh centuries Islam spread from the Samanid kingdom to other Turkish tribes, notably the Oghuz, who had settled in the territory near the lower Jaxartes (Sir Daryā) and on the shores of the Aral Sea. Internal disorders caused a section of them, under the leadership of their princes of the house of Seljuq, to occupy Karakhanid territory in Transoxania, in the vicinity of Bukhara. Expelled from here, they drove on into Khurasan, the northern province of the Persian highlands, which formed part of the Ghaznavid kingdom in eastern Persia, the modern Afghanistan. In 1040, led by the two Seljuq brothers Ṭughrîl Bey Muḥammad and Chagri Bey Dā'ūd, the Oghuz gained a victory over the Ghaznavid Sultan, destroying the power of the Ghaznavid kingdom and forcing an entry into Persia. And these Turkish hordes now overran not merely Persia but the whole of western Asia. The regular armies of the Seljuq princes followed victorious in their wake; in 1055 Ṭughrîl Bey entered Baghdad, the seat of the Caliphate, where the Caliph proclaimed him Sultan, the legitimate holder of temporal power. Ṭughrîl Bey until his death in 1063, and later his nephew Alp Arslan, advanced their dominions until they extended right across western Asia to the confines of the Byzantine Empire in eastern Anatolia and of the Shī'ite Fatimid kingdom in Palestine. In 1070 the Seljuq general Atsîz captured Jerusalem, a disaster which is recognised as providing the initial impetus for the crusades in the West. The significance of these events in world history is the addition of a new race, the Turks, to the medley of peoples in the Middle East; they henceforward assumed the political leadership of this part of the old world and founded almost all the princely families in western Asia.

The new Turkish rulers of the Muslim world in western Asia felt themselves bound as Muslims to uphold the traditional values of that world. Far from attempting to undermine them, the Turks endeavoured, as soon as their wars of conquest were over, to defend and foster these values. The Seljuq conquerors were particularly anxious to protect Islamic orthodoxy, Sunnitism, against heretical tendencies. Thus the system of theological teaching with its schools of theology, the *madrasas*, may be traced back to its original encouragement by the Seljuqs and their nobles. The Seljuq overlords also felt an obligation to promote the Persian national culture, and its spread from eastern Persia to the entire country and subsequent dissemination over the whole of western Asia were the results of the encouragement afforded it by the Turkish princes.

On the other hand the main instrument of the Seljuq conquests, the Turkish soldiery, remained impervious to this Arabic–Persian culture spread by Islamic civilisation, and persisted in an extremely primitive cultural state of a nomadic character. What was most apparent to them as Muslims was the inherent dynamism of militant Islam which was represented in Muslim teaching by the doctrine of Holy War (*jihād*). This had been foreseen by the Seljuq rulers and their shrewd Persian advisers, particularly the great Niẓām al-Mulk, who served the Seljuq Sultans Alp Arslan and Malikshāh as vizier and was for almost thirty years (1063–92) responsible for the administration of the Empire. To restrain the Turkish troops, intent only on war and plunder, from laying waste the central provinces of the Islamic world, their rulers directed them to the frontiers of the Empire, where they might increase the dominions of Islam by waging Holy War against the infidels. The most important consequences of this policy were the subjugation of the Caucasus and the penetration of Azerbaijan, and the conquest of Anatolia, which took on a completely Turkish character. In 1080 the Christian kingdom of the Bagratids in Armenia, in the coastal regions of the Caucasus, fell to the Turkish warriors who had settled in Azerbaijan. The Bagratid Ruben with a band of loyal supporters founded a new kingdom in Cilicia, which became known as Lesser Armenia, and which persisted under his descendants, the Rubenians, until the fourteenth century (1375). But the conquest of Anatolia was to prove of even greater significance.

II. THE CONQUEST OF ANATOLIA

It was against Anatolia that the main weight of the Holy War had always been directed and the 'Roman Land', *bilād ar-Rūm*, as the Muslims called it, was stubbornly defended by the Byzantines. At this period Caliphs and other Muslim princes waged an annual campaign against it, in obedience to the demands of the Islamic faith for war on behalf of Allāh (*fī sabīl Allāh*). The frontier between the

Byzantine Empire and Islam, apart from occasional slight modifications, had for centuries run from the Black Sea, east of Trebizond, to a point on the Mediterranean coast of Cilicia, and was a permanent battle-ground. Frontier wars between Muslims and Christians were of constant occurrence and created similar conditions on both sides. The Muslim ranks were composed of warriors from every country in Islam, united in their devotion to the Holy War; they were honoured as heroes and holy warriors (*ghāzīs*) and gradually developed into a professional military force waging unceasing war against the infidel. On the Byzantine side a correspondingly professional frontier defence force, principally Armenian and called the *akritai* (border warriors), was arrayed against the Muslims. Though at first the Muslim *ghāzīs* were almost exclusively Arabs, or subjects of other Muslim countries who had undergone Arab influences, they were increasingly reinforced by Turks, long before the appearance of the Seljuqs in western Asia, until gradually the Turkish element preponderated and the conduct of the Holy War on the Byzantine frontier was almost entirely in its hands.

The fighting spirit of these professional soldiers, and consequently the situation on the frontier, depended largely on the way in which each side treated its frontier troops. When every attention was paid to the men's requirements, they would fight with good heart; the frontier would be adequately protected, and could occasionally be pushed back a considerable distance into enemy territory. But when supplies were short, or the frontiersmen harassed by taxation, then the defences were weakened and easily forced, and there were often desertions to the enemy.

It so happened that when the Turks, led by the Seljuq princes, had conquered western Asia, and the warlike Turkish troops were posted to the frontier, they found it insufficiently manned by the Byzantines; it was therefore a simple matter for them to cross into imperial territory. As a result there were, during the decade 1060–70, bands of nomadic Turks roaming at large throughout Asia Minor, endangering communications between the towns and terrorising the countryside. This was not the intentional policy of the Seljuq Sultans, who had established their Empire in the heart of the Islamic East, but rather a course of action pursued by the Turkish armies in complete independence of Seljuq political authority, led by frontier warriors of proved worth in battle.

Despite the purely local character of these Turkish attacks the Byzantine Emperor Romanus IV Diogenes judged it expedient to ward off the Turkish threat by embarking on a campaign against the Seljuq Alp Arslan at the head of a powerful army. At the battle of

Manzikert (Melazgerd) in 1071 he was defeated and taken prisoner by Alp Arslan, who however treated him well and released him with favourable terms of peace.[1] But the news of the Emperor's defeat had provoked a revolution in Constantinople and he returned to find that he had lost his throne to the ineffective Michael VII Ducas. The situation on the Byzantine frontier was thereby aggravated still further, so that the Turkish soldiery ranged the countryside with even greater freedom than before.

On the death of Alp Arslan in 1072, soon after his victory over the Byzantine Emperor, his son and successor, the young Sultan Malik-shāh, placed a Seljuq prince, Sulaymān ibn Kutlumîsh, in command of the Turkish armies in Anatolia, entrusting him with the prosecution of the war against the Byzantines. His task was considerably simplified by the struggles for the throne which were taking place in Byzantium. The Emperor Michael VII and, after his abdication (1078), Nicephorus III Botaneiates both sought his help.[2] This was granted in exchange for their recognition of his dominion over the territories occupied by the Turks, including the surrender of recently conquered cities such as Cyzicus and Nicaea (1081). This latter town (in Turkish Iznik) Sulaymān made his headquarters. Thanks to the Turkish soldiery scattered throughout the country, he was now almost complete master of Anatolia where the political power of Byzantium was practically at an end. After his successes in Anatolia, Sulaymān then turned eastwards in search of further conquests, and he succeeded in wresting Antioch (Antākiya) from the Byzantines; but when he advanced on Aleppo he encountered the Seljuq amirs, particularly Tutush the brother of Malikshāh, and was defeated and killed in battle (1086).

These events brought Malikshāh to Aleppo in person, to reorganise the affairs of the western provinces of the great Seljuq Empire; he then took back with him to Iraq Sulaymān's son Kîlîj Arslan. Anatolia was left to manage its own affairs under the Turkish army commanders, of whom the most powerful was Malik Dānishmend Aḥmed Ghāzī, a genuine holy warrior tracing his descent from Sayyid Baṭṭāl Ghāzī, the Arab leader who in 740 fell in battle against the Byzantines and was the prototype of the *ghāzī* on the Byzantine frontier. Not until after the death of Malikshāh (1092) did his son and successor, Barkiyāruq, allow Kîlîj Arslan to return to Anatolia. But Kîlîj Arslan found it difficult to assert his position against the Turkish princes, particularly Malik Dānishmend, who was himself bent on establishing control over Anatolia.

Meanwhile conditions in Byzantium became more stable when in

[1] *DR*, 972.   [2] *DR*, 1007.

1081 Alexius Comnenus overthrew the Emperor Nicephorus III and himself ascended the throne as Alexius I. In the interests of Byzantium he exploited the growing crusading spirit in the West, which had been further stimulated by the Turkish conquest of Asia Minor; he required the Frankish princes passing through Byzantine territory on the First Crusade in 1097 to take the oath of fealty with respect to any conquests of former Byzantine territory which they might make.

The Turks, led by Kîlîj Arslan I and Malik Dānishmend,[1] were then defeated at Nicaea by the combined forces of the crusaders and Byzantines, and their headquarters there were besieged and finally taken on 20 June 1097. On 1 July 1097 the crusaders won a victory at Dorylaeum, near the modern Eskishehir, thus determining the fate of western Anatolia and throwing open a path through further Turkish territory. They pushed on to Antioch which fell to them on 3 June 1098 after a protracted siege; here they established the first crusaders' state, the principality of Antioch, which nominally owed allegiance to Byzantium; the same year they founded the principality of Edessa (now Urfa) in Mesopotamia. These exploits of the crusaders rendered it comparatively easy for Alexius to expel the Turks from western Anatolia, to reincorporate this region into the Byzantine Empire, and to strengthen the fortifications along the boundary which ran through the middle of Anatolia and separated it from territory remaining in Turkish hands. A limit was thus set to Turkish expansion.

III. THE RISE AND HIGH-WATER MARK OF THE SELJUQ EMPIRE OF RŪM

The departure of the crusaders for Syria and Palestine brought a recrudescence of the rivalry between the two Turkish princes in Anatolia, the Seljuq Kîlîj Arslan, and Malik Dānishmend (or his son). The former was established in central Anatolia, with Konya, the ancient Iconium, as his headquarters; the latter occupied north-east Anatolia, with his headquarters at Sivas (Sebastea). A particularly violent struggle broke out for the possession of Malaṭiya (Melitene) in the anti-Taurus district; only after the death of Dānishmend (1104 or 1106)[2] did Kîlîj Arslan succeed in bringing the town under his sway. But the remaining territory held by Dānishmend was retained

---

[1] According to some sources Malik Dānishmend was already dead (*c.* 1084); in that case the soldier called by the Byzantines Τανισμὰν ὁ σουλτάν (Anna Comnena, *Alexiad*, XI, 3 (II, p. 111, ed. A. Reifferscheid), who fought against the crusaders, was his son Malik (or Amīr) Ghāzī Gümüshtigin.

[2] But see note 1 above.

by his descendants. In the following year Kîlîj Arslan sought to make further conquests in Upper Mesopotamia; marching on Mosul, he was defeated in battle on the banks of the Khabur by the combined armies of the Seljuq amirs, and perished in flight by drowning (3 June 1107).

Very little is known of the two sons of Kîlîj Arslan I, Malikshāh and Mas'ūd I, who reigned from 1107 to 1116 and from 1116 to 1155 respectively. The Seljuq state in Anatolia (Rūm) was still a nominal dependency of the greater Seljuq Empire based on Persia. The rapid decline of this Empire was accelerated by the crushing defeat sustained by the Sultan Sinjar in the Katvan steppe at Samarqand on 9 September 1141 at the hands of the Kara Khitay advancing out of eastern Asia; after the death of the Sultan in 1157 its fall seemed inevitable. Meanwhile the Seljuq state of Rūm, or, as the crusaders called it, the Sultanate of Iconium, had almost attained independence. Konya, the new capital of the Seljuq Sultans of Rūm, was gradually rebuilt in the style of the capital cities of the Muslim world. During the twelfth century this Seljuq state of Rūm, consisting merely of the steppes of central Anatolia, was of little importance. The more fertile land of western Anatolia, the Black Sea coast and the Mediterranean seaboard were all held by the Byzantines, now stubbornly defending their frontiers. Cilicia to the south had been absorbed by the Christian kingdom of Lesser Armenia, which itself adjoined two Christian crusader states, the principality of Antioch and the principality of Edessa. Thus the Seljuq state of Rūm was almost a Muslim enclave surrounded by Christian powers. The one remaining point of contact with the Muslim world was in the east; the mountainous region of north-east Anatolia was occupied by the Dānishmends, who also gave the name of bilād ar-Rūm ('Roman land') to their territory; in upper Mesopotamia (Amida-Diyār-Bakr, Mosul, etc.) were established the dependent Seljuq principalities of the Ortukids and the Zangids. This opening on to the Muslim world was eventually enlarged when in 1144 the Atabeg Zangī of Mosul and his great son Nūr ad-Dīn launched a powerful attack against the crusader states, and Nūr ad-Dīn captured Edessa. It was this event which led to the Second Crusade, during which an army of crusaders under the German king Conrad III attempted to follow the same route through Turkish-occupied central Anatolia as that taken by the armies of the First Crusade. But, owing to their defeat by the Turks at Dorylaeum on 26 October 1147, they had to take a coastal route through Byzantine territory.

Mas'ūd's son and successor Kîlîj Arslan II (1155–92) set himself to dispossess the rivals of the Seljuqs, the Dānishmends, in the hope of uniting under his sway the whole of central and eastern Anatolia. The Dānishmends applied for help to the powerful Nūr ad-Dīn, who did in fact send troops to assist them, and succeeded in thwarting Kīlīj Arslan's desire for expansion, at the same time reproving him for his non-Muslim attitude. It was not until the death of Nūr ad-Dīn (1174) that Kīlīj Arslan succeeded in attaining his object of incorporating the territory of the Dānishmends into the dominions of the Seljuqs of Rūm. The Byzantine Emperor Manuel I Comnenus, eager to prevent the union of the whole of eastern Anatolia under Seljuq rule, laid claim to the Dānishmend territory, marched against Kīlīj Arslan, and in 1176 was overwhelmingly defeated at Myriocephalum (Chardak Pass). Turkish control of eastern Anatolia was finally assured, but the imposing figure of the Egyptian Sultan Ṣalāḥ ad-Dīn (Saladin) proved an effective deterrent to further expansion eastward by Kīlīj Arslan.

As Kīlīj Arslan declined in years, he and his Empire suffered heavy misfortunes, first at the hands of the crusaders, who under the German Emperor Frederick Barbarossa marched through Turkish Anatolia on the Third Crusade and even for a time occupied its capital Konya, and also as a result of a quarrel between his sons, amongst whom Kīlīj Arslan, following Turkish practice, had divided his Empire. Throughout this quarrel the ageing Sultan was a mere plaything in the hands of his ambitious sons. Neither the fall of Konya to Frederick Barbarossa shortly before his death in the river Saleph (in ancient times Calycadnus, now Göksu) in Cilicia (10 June 1190), nor the death of Kīlīj Arslan II (1192), had any material effect on this Seljuq dispute. It continued for several years until at last in 1204 the youngest son, Ghiyāth ad-Dīn Kaykhusraw I, who had afforded the aged Kīlīj Arslan a final place of refuge in which to die, was able to ascend the throne in Konya and assume the reins of government.

The increased vigilance of the Byzantines in the twelfth century had held in check the incursions of the Muslim frontier forces and obliged the Turks to settle in the part of Anatolia they already possessed, and to adopt a fixed agricultural mode of life instead of a nomadic existence. The result was the Turkish colonisation of the Greek, or rather long-since Hellenised, area of Anatolia, and the introduction of Turkish manners and customs into considerable tracts of territory. But alongside this newly developing Turkish pastoral community there persisted in certain districts, particularly in the steppes of central Anatolia, Turkish nomads called Yürüks who may be found there to this day. This Turkish element in Anatolia has been matched, down to recent times, by the survival, almost intact,

of the Hellenic element. As was inevitable under Muslim rule, converts were made amongst the indigenous population, thereby creating
fresh Turkish subjects, so that the boundary between Islam and
Christendom constantly coincided with the frontier between Turks
and Greeks; the former, however, became to a considerable degree
racially assimilated to the indigenous population of Anatolia. But
the urban population was extremely varied; in addition to the Turks
attracted by the courts of the Sultan or his governors and the native
Greek population, there was an influx of foreign races from the older
dominions of the Islamic world, particularly that part of it under
Seljuq rule, Syria, Iraq, and Persia; some were there at the behest of the
Seljuq Sultans of Rūm, others had come of their own accord to help
in the construction of the new state, and the Christians were represented by traders from Armenia. Thus the whole character of the
country was gradually changed; from being an exclusively Christian
country with Byzantine civilisation and a Greek population, it became a Muslim country with a mainly Turkish population, even
though it still contained strong Greek elements. In fact during the
Seljuq period there may have been scattered areas where the Greeks
still outnumbered the Turks. Thus the Seljuqs, though their conquest
brought most of Anatolia under Turkish domination, succeeded at
first in effectually colonising only a small part of it. Complete
colonisation had to await a further influx of Turkish races into
Anatolia, and this followed the conquest of the Middle East by the
Mongols.

The *ghāzīs* who had achieved the subjugation of the country and
were still pre-eminent in rural districts formed a distinct element who
did not always maintain amicable relations with the Seljuq Sultans
in Konya and their followers or with the governors of the large
provincial cities. The rivalry between the Seljuqs in Konya and the
Dānishmends is the expression on the political level of the tension
between Seljuq administration with its adherence to orthodox Islam,
and the *ghāzīs* in whom the Turkish element predominated. These
Turkish warriors were rough soldiers who had scarcely come into
contact with the refinements of Islamic civilisation; all they asked
was to do battle for Islam. The increasing strength of Byzantium in
the twelfth century frustrated this desire, and so rendered them an
occasional source of danger within the structure of the Seljuq state
of Rūm. In religion they were far from orthodox, inclining rather to
sectarian tendencies to which they were predisposed by the popular
Turkish piety they had brought with them, which was now, through
contact with the population of Anatolia, combined with local religious
forms, both Christian (orthodox and heretical) and pre-Christian.

Thus the final shape assumed by this popular Turkish piety of the holy warriors, namely the Dervish order of the Baktashis, presents, alongside its main Shī'ite structure, Shamanistic elements from central Asia together with Christian and pre-Christian elements native to Anatolia.

A completely different spirit prevailed in the towns, the centres of the state administrative system emanating from the Sultan's court in Konya. The Sultans of Rūm, like the former Sultans at Isfahan, felt it their mission to promote Islamic culture, making their court its centre. The high artistic merit of the buildings in the towns throughout the country still bears witness to their efforts; artists were summoned from Syria and Persia to help in their construction, though, to judge by the inscriptions on the buildings, the work was sometimes done by native Greeks or Armenians. Learned scribes from the East were commissioned with the task of elaborating the machinery of government after the pattern of the greater Seljuq Empire; they helped to set up the administrative offices of the Sultan and his officials, employing Arabic and Persian as the official languages. Moreover, academies were established to foster Arab learning and Persian culture. The extent to which the Sultans themselves were imbued with Persian culture may be gauged by the fact that in the thirteenth century many of them bore names from Persian heroic saga, such as Kaykāwūs, Kayqubād and Kaykhusraw. The court of the Seljuq Sultans of Konya was entirely modelled on the royal courts of the older Islamic Persian territory, Iraq and Syria. In such an atmosphere there was naturally no room for sectarianism; instead Sunnite orthodoxy prevailed. Nor was there any great enthusiasm for the Holy War; on the contrary, relations with the Byzantine court usually remained cordial, even culminating in an occasional alliance by marriage between Konya and Constantinople. Each court constantly offered asylum to statesmen fleeing in disgrace from the other, or was used as a place of banishment for princes ousted from power by an opposing faction.

The capture of Constantinople by the Fourth Crusade in 1204 was a decisive event which not only left its mark on the history of southeastern Europe but also affected the fortunes of the Turks. The Byzantines who fled from the imperial city on the Bosphorus when the crusaders established their 'Latin Empire' founded another Byzantine Empire in western Anatolia, with Theodore Lascaris at its head and Nicaea as its capital. Further to the east the so-called 'Grand Comneni' ruled from Trebizond over the north-eastern coastline of Anatolia, and formed an important trading link between Persia and the Italian mercantile republics; while in northern Greece another separatist Byzantine state was set up in Epirus. The

Byzantine Empire, despite its partial restoration after the reconquest of Constantinople in 1261, never really recovered from this defeat at the hands of the West; it was unable thereafter to prevent the steady increase of Turkish power, which culminated in the erection of the Ottoman Empire on its ruins and in the sack of Constantinople by the Turks in 1453.

The immediate consequences of this weakening of the strength of Byzantium soon became evident. Theodore Lascaris and his successors concentrated primarily on the reconquest of Constantinople, and thus made it possible for the Seljuq Sultan Kaykhusraw of Rūm in 1207 to seize the port of Attalia (since called Antaliya or Adaliya), and thus to obtain access to the Mediterranean. He was later defeated by Theodore Lascaris at the battle of Antioch on the Meander in 1211, where he met his death (possibly in single combat with his adversary). His son and successor 'Izz ad-Dīn Kaykāwūs I (1210–19) obliged the Emperor of Trebizond Alexius in 1214 to cede Sinope (Sinop) and thereby obtained access to the Black Sea. The Seljuq Empire of Rūm was now thrown open to world trade; negotiations with the Italian mercantile republics brought a revival of commerce and an unexpected prosperity to the country.

The Seljuqs of Rūm appear to have remained content with these triumphs over the Greek world. The next few decades saw the establishment of a certain equilibrium between the two powers, and a mutual recognition of each other's possessions. Their interests lay in opposite directions: whereas the Greeks turned their attention to the west and aimed at retaking Constantinople, the Seljuqs looked east for means of consolidating their Empire more firmly in the Islamic world. Thus Kaykāwūs succeeded in advancing his dominions which lay near Lesser Armenia as far as the Cilician Gates (1216), though failing in his attempts to annex Ayyūbid possessions in North Syria (Aleppo and other towns). At his death (1219) the Empire of Rūm had emerged as a great power with a flourishing economy.

The death of Kaykāwūs I was followed by the reign of his brother Kayqubād, formerly held prisoner on account of his attempts to seize power; even now he encountered resistance before finally ascending the throne. Under 'Alā' ad-Dīn Kayqubād (1219–37) the Empire attained its richest prosperity and widest extent. He took advantage of civil disturbances in Lesser Armenia to enlarge his Mediterranean frontier, seizing the fort of Kalonoros (καλὸν ὄρος) and turning it into a considerable seaport which he called Alā'iyya (now Alaya or Alanya); he also used it as his winter quarters. He acquired territory towards the east in upper Mesopotamia from the Ortukids of Amida (Diyār-Bakr) and of Hiṣn Kayfā, obliging them to recognise his suzerainty.

The Emperors of Nicaea and Trebizond, like the Christian king of Lesser Armenia, were compelled to contribute troops to the Seljuq Sultan.

The reign of Kayqubād marked the supreme development not only of political power but also of material prosperity in the Empire of Rūm. Access to the Mediterranean and the Black Sea enabled the Sultan, with the help of the Italian mercantile republics, to throw open his realm to international trade which he fostered by every means in his power, so that great riches poured into the land. In the interests of Italian commerce Kayqubād also undertook an expedition to the Crimea. This accumulation of wealth favoured the flowering of a highly developed civilisation, evidence of which may be seen in the magnificent buildings erected by the Sultan and his nobles in the capital, Konya, and also in other cities such as Kaysarīya (now Kayseri) and Sivas. Many of these were mosques for Muslim worship or *madrasas* for theological instruction, but the physical well-being of the people was also cared for by building hospitals, and trade communications were secured by caravanserais.

The invasion of Persia by Jenghiz Khan occurred during the reign of Kayqubād. Great numbers of the refugees fleeing from the lands threatened by the Mongols turned westwards to seek a retreat in Anatolia. Amongst them came members of the Persian intellectual *élite* with their families, as well as swarms of Turkoman nomads. Against these Kayqubād had to fight many battles; but he soon managed to enlist them into his service to reinforce his troops. The representatives of Islamic cultural life who escaped to Rūm from Persia were warmly welcomed by the Sultan, who installed them in office and otherwise rewarded them. One of these refugees, a priest from Balkh called Bahā' ad-Dīn Muḥammad Veled, fled from Jenghiz Khan between 1220 and 1230, made his way to Konya with his son Jalāl ad-Dīn (born 1207), and was there appointed as a preacher by 'Alā' ad-Dīn Kayqubād. His son, a devotee of Ṣūfism, became the focus of a religious movement of a specifically visionary nature; and as leader of this group he bore the epithet 'Mevlānā', 'our lord'. Soon after his death in 1273 his adherents created the Dervish Order of the Mevleviye. Because of their religious practices, characterised by music and whirling dance (*samā*), they became renowned as 'whirling dervishes' and were the most highly esteemed of all the Turkish dervish orders. Moreover, Mevlānā Jalāl ad-Dīn, under the name of Rūmī, is found amongst the Persian classics on account of his great mystical poem written in Persian, the famous *Masnavī-i ma'navī*, a work which provided a powerful stimulus to the development of a poetic literature in the Turkish tongue of Rūm.

Jenghiz Khan's invasion of Persia also affected the Empire of Rūm in political and military spheres. Jalāl ad-Dīn Mengubirtī, the son of Khʷārizm Muḥammad who was defeated by Jenghiz Khan and perished when fleeing before the mighty conqueror, endeavoured after the departure of the Mongols (1223) to carve out a new Empire in western Persia and Kurdistan. He therefore came into conflict with Kayqubād, who was expanding eastwards. The Turkish princes of Erzinjān and Erzerum, the former of the race of the Mengüjukids, the latter descended from a collateral line of Seljuq, sought Jalāl ad-Dīn's protection against Kayqubād. In spite of this the prince of Erzinjān was forced to cede his territory to Kayqubād in 1225. Although Jalāl ad-Dīn did actually go to the help of the prince of Erzerum, he suffered an overwhelming defeat at Erzinjān (10 August 1230), and Kayqubād was also able to incorporate Erzerum into his Empire. When in the following year (1231) Jalāl ad-Dīn was murdered, Kayqubād occupied the city of Khilāt (now Ahlat), to which he had laid siege, thereby coming into conflict with his former allies, the Ayyūbids, to whom the city had originally belonged. But they were powerless against Kayqubād; in fact they were obliged to suffer even further losses at his hands. Thus the crowded reign of this energetic Sultan was devoted partly to military expeditions and partly to promoting trade and culture. In 1237, when preparing for another expedition, Kayqubād was poisoned at Kaysarīya, probably at his son's instigation.

It was after the accession of his son Ghiyāth ad-Dīn Kaykhusraw II (1237–45) that the first signs of decline became apparent. Kaykhusraw did indeed succeed in adding to his dominions the town of Amida (Diyār-Bakr), so long an objective of the Seljuqs of Rūm. But the luxurious existence of the new Sultan and the nobles, coupled with the tyranny of the amir Saʿd ad-Dīn who had carried through the accession of Kaykhusraw and to whom his indolent master had relinquished the cares of government, brought to a crisis the latent resentment felt for the Seljuq court and its adherents by the followers of the popular Turkish dervish religion so closely connected with the Muslim holy warriors. They organised a powerful revolt led by Baba Ishāk (or Baba Rasūl), a dervish revered as a prophet, whose disciples were known as Babaʿīya. His execution merely increased his following, so that the Sultan was obliged to deploy considerable military force before the revolt was suppressed in a bloody massacre in 1241.

In that same year the Mongol general Baydju Noyon reached the frontier of Rūm from the Caucasus and captured Erzerum. An attempt was made to raise a powerful army to meet this new danger;

but the Seljuq forces, depleted by the civil wars of recent years, were defeated at the battle of Köse Dagh in eastern Anatolia on 26 June 1243. The Mongols then advanced beyond Sivas to Kaysarīya, laying waste the countryside. Only the death of the Great Khan Ügedei in December 1241, which necessitated the return to Mongolia of the Mongol generals for the election of a successor, delayed until 1246, prevented the complete conquest of the Empire of Rūm. Nevertheless its power was broken, and its subsequent history was overshadowed by the new Mongolian world Empire; the Seljuq Sultans of Rūm became vassals of the Great Khan of the Mongols.

IV. DISSOLUTION OF THE SELJUQ EMPIRE OF RŪM AND THE RISE OF THE KARAMANS

After its defeat at the hands of the Mongols the Seljuq state of Rūm appears to have fallen into the utmost confusion and there was no attempt at a revival. On the contrary, this Empire, which had been so prosperous, was now rent by the struggles of ambitious viziers urging on their own claimants to the throne and engaged in futile struggles for supremacy. Each rival faction sought support from the new Mongol power in order to obtain for its own candidate a mandate to the throne (*yarligh*) which would dislodge its opponents. Thus even during the reign of Kaykhusraw II, Batu, the great conqueror of Russia and founder of the Empire of the Golden Horde, was involved in the internal affairs of Rūm. After the entry of Hülegü into Persia and the establishment of the Persian Mongol Empire of the Ilkhans, Rūm made overtures here in view of its very close proximity in Azerbaijan. This made it easy for the Mongols to gain a firm footing in Anatolia. They regarded the Seljuq Empire of Rūm as their vassal state, intervened in the quarrels between the claimants to the throne, and sent out raiding expeditions to pillage the country. In 1256 they installed an imperial administrator of their own choosing, Muʿīn ad-Dīn Sulaymān, giving him the title of Parwāna; in their name he exercised all real power in the realm.

One consequence of the protracted struggle between the Sultans and their viziers was that the son and successor of Kaykhusraw II, ʿIzz ad-Dīn Kaykāwūs II, was supplanted by his brother Rukn ad-Dīn Kîlîj Arslan IV, who had the support of the Parwāna Muʿīn ad-Dīn Sulaymān and was installed as Sultan by the Great Khan of the Mongols. He fled to Constantinople (1261), which had in the meantime been recaptured by the Greeks, and lived there in exile until the Khan of the Golden Horde, Mengu Tīmūr, took him to the Crimea (1269) where he eventually died (1280). Closer examination of the struggles for the throne in the Seljuq Empire of Rūm during the second half of the thirteenth century is unnecessary here. It is sufficient to mention that when the Parwāna foresaw that Ḳilij Arslan IV might be an embarrassment to him, he killed him (1266) and set on the throne his son Ghiyāth ad-Dīn Kaykhusraw III while still a minor.

Occasionally the Turkish amirs of Rūm were able to turn to good account the antagonism felt by the Khans of the Golden Horde in alliance with the Mamluk Sultans of Egypt (the successors of the Ayyūbids) towards the Mongol rulers of Persia, the Ilkhans, who had constituted themselves overlords of the Seljuqs of Rūm. Thus one party in Rūm attempted to win the support of Egypt in order to rid their country of the Mongol yoke. The Mamluk Sultan aẓ-Ẓāhir Baybars, in response to the pressure of one or two amirs who had emigrated to Egypt, marched to Rūm in 1277, towards the end of his eventful reign, defeated the Mongols in a fierce encounter at Elbistan (in the anti-Taurus district), and advanced to Kaysarīya (April 1277). But for lack of adequate support he was compelled to turn back without achieving his object, whereupon the Ilkhan Abagha, Hülegü's successor, descended on Rūm with an army and wrought terrible vengeance; even the Parwāna Muʿīn ad-Dīn Sulaymān was suspected of conspiring with the Egyptians and was executed (2 August 1277). The final result of this ineffective attempt at diverting the course of events was the further subservience of Rūm to the Ilkhan Empire of Persia.

The fall of the Parwāna also endangered the position of his Sultan, Kaykhusraw III; at the earliest opportunity, when he was implicated in the downfall of the Mongol pretender Kunkuratai, he was removed (1283). He was succeeded by his cousin, Ghiyāth ad-Dīn Masʿūd II, a son of Kaykāwūs II.

During these disturbances one of the Turkoman captains, Muḥammad ibn Karaman ibn Nūra Ṣūfī, succeeded in establishing control over territory on the foreshore of the Taurus range, on the boundary of the provinces of Lycaonia and Cilicia, around Ermenek (the old Germanicopolis). To judge from his grandfather's name he appeared to have come of a Dervish family and so belonged to those popular Turkish sectarian circles which so constantly fell foul of the rule of the Seljuq dynasty and its adherents. Taking advantage of the anarchy during Sultan Baybars' approach to Rūm, Muḥammad Bey put forward as pretender to the throne a certain Jimrī, giving out that he was the son of Kaykāwūs II who had fled to the Crimea; he captured Konya and installed him on the Seljuq throne as Sultan Siyāwush. It was characteristic of the Karaman Oghlu Muḥammad

Bey's attitude that he introduced Turkish instead of Persian as the official language of the Seljuq Empire of Rūm. However, after the departure of the Sultan Baybars, Konya was captured by Mongol troops in the course of the Ilkhan Abagha's punitive expedition and the Karamans were obliged to retire into their mountains; but Jimrī, escaping in a north-westerly direction, was defeated at Sakaria by Seljuq forces (June 1277), taken prisoner and put to death. So this further attempt at shaking off the Mongol yoke ended ignominiously. The Ilkhan sent his vizier Shams ad-Dīn Juvayni to Rūm to re-organise its affairs. Henceforth the country was virtually no more than an outlying province of the Mongol Ilkhan Empire in Persia; real power was exercised not by the Sultan of Rūm but by the com-mander (*amīr al-umarā*) of the Mongol garrison, whose function was really to govern in the name of the Ilkhan.

The antagonism dividing the two great oriental powers, the Ilkhan Empire in Persia and the Mamluk Empire in Egypt, during the latter part of the thirteenth century, did at times tempt the Mongol governor of the somewhat exposed province of Rūm to seek Egyptian aid in obtaining freedom from his overlord, the Ilkhan. Thus in 1297 the governor of Rūm, Sülamīsh, declared his independence of the reigning Ilkhan, Ghazan, and was invested with the territory of Rūm by the Mamluk Sultan an-Nāṣir. But early in 1299 Ghazan dispatched his general Qutlughshāh to Anatolia, where he defeated Sülamīsh at Eskishehir on 27 April 1299, took him prisoner and put him to death.

During this period of disintegration there grew up among the Turk-ish artisan town-dwellers, independently of the conflicting political forces, a semi-religious brotherhood or corporation, the *akhīs* (*ak̇ilik*), a counterpart of the Dervish movement. It derived partly from that specific form of gild associated with the holy warrior class of the *ghāzīs* and called the *futuwwa* (literally 'youth', 'young aristocracy', in Turkish *fütüvvet*), which was turned into a chivalrous organisation with mutual bonds between follower and lord by the Abbasid Caliph an-Nāṣir (1180–1225), counting amongst its Sultan members Kaykā-wūs I of Rūm (1210–19). But the form which it took in the towns, with its resemblance to the gild system, also points to the probable influence of native pre-Turkish and possibly Byzantine models, par-ticularly as the *akhīs* subsequently merged with the Turkish gild movement of a later period. The *akhīs* brotherhood, composed of associations in every town of young men, usually unmarried and organised under a leader, the *akhī*, avoided taking sides in the political struggle, to which they were hostile; it was said of them that they put to death tyrants and their henchmen. They devoted themselves to hospitality and good works, and thus in a period of disintegration acted as a unifying element which helped to stem the flood of misery inevitable at such times.

The Seljuq Empire of Rūm had only a nominal existence during the closing decades of the thirteenth century and by the end of the century it had fallen into complete dissolution. After the death of Mas'ūd II, the Ilkhan Ghazan installed in 1298 yet another Seljuq as Sultan of Rūm, a grandson of Kaykāwūs II named 'Alā' ad-Dīn Kayqubād III ibn Farāmarz, but his authority was negligible compared with that of the Mongol governor. The death of this puppet Sultan (the exact date is unknown, 1307 or 1308 being generally accepted) marks the inglorious end of the once famous Seljuq Empire of Rūm; henceforward it was openly recognised as a province of the Mongol Ilkhan Empire in Persia.

CHAPTER XIX

THE OTTOMAN TURKS TO 1453

I. THE SUCCESSORS OF THE SELJUQS OF RŪM IN EASTERN ANATOLIA

The jurisdiction of the Mongol governors residing at Sivas extended over the entire territory of the former Seljuq Empire of Rūm. This did not prevent the Karamans, who had settled in the south-east around Ermenek on the foreshore of the Taurus mountains, from attempting to extend their dominions, relying on the support of the enemies of the Ilkhans, the Mamluk Sultans of Egypt. The Karaman Badr ad-Dīn Muḥammad Bey was thus enabled to take Konya (c. 1308); shortly afterwards the Ilkhan generalissimo (amīr al-umarā) Chūpān, who had been sent to Anatolia by the Ilkhan Uljaitū to reorganise its affairs, expelled him from Konya (1315), obliging him to return to Ermenek. A second attempt to take Konya also failed (1320). Later the Karamans succeeded in capturing the town of Laranda (now Karaman), which they made their capital. In the 1320's, when Anatolia felt the impact of the disturbances in the Ilkhan Empire, the Karamans finally obtained possession of Konya, though retaining Laranda as their capital. In the course of the fourteenth century they extended their sway into western Anatolia, so coming into contact with the young Turkish principalities which were growing up there. Thus the Karaman state developed into a great power, rivalling the newly arisen amirate of the Ottomans in western Anatolia well into the fifteenth century.

The Ilkhan Empire, at the zenith of its power under Ghāzān (1294–1304) and Uljaitū Khodābanda (1304–16), had exercised complete control over Anatolia; their governor in Anatolia was Timūrtash, the son of the generalissimo Chūpān already mentioned. The disturbances which broke out in the Ilkhan Empire during the reign of Uljaitū's son Abū Saʿīd (1316–35) were not without their effect in Anatolia. Timurtash, who by his exploits in the west against the Turkish petty princes had added to the dominions of the Mongol Empire in Persia an occasional tract of frontier territory, and had also frustrated the renewed attempt by the Karamans to take possession of Konya (1320), secured the support of the Mamluk Sultan an-Nāṣir and rose against his overlord, the Ilkhan, investing himself with the halo of a Mahdī; but he was forced into submission. When his father the High Amir Chūpān was overthrown and executed (November

48

1327) as a result of palace intrigues at the Ilkhan court, Timurtash took refuge with the Egyptian Sultan. However, he was soon recognised as a source of danger by the Mamluk Sultan an-Nāṣir, who at the request of the Ilkhan Abū Saʿīd put him to death (August 1328). These events led to the final loss of Konya and southern Anatolia to the Karamans, and to the rise of Karaman power. During the lifetime of Abū Saʿīd, however, the more extensive northern half of the former Seljuq territory of Rūm remained under his control, as is shown by an inscription in Ankara dated 1330 which refers to the system of taxation in Anatolia. After the death of Abū Saʿīd (1335) the governor in Rūm (who was Eretna from 1328 onwards) at first acknowledged the suzerainty of the Mamluk Sultan an-Nāṣir, but the outbreak of disturbances in Egypt on the death of the Sultan (1340) enabled him to assert his independence and to reign as Sultan ʿAlāʾ ad-Dīn in Sivas. When he died in 1352 his authority descended to his sons.

With the decline of the Ilkhan Empire the governors in Sivas lost their hold over their western territories in Rūm, particularly the city of Ankara. Here, in default of any effective political rule, a rich *akhī* family had assumed the status of a royal house and exercised an authority which ultimately passed into the hands of the Ottoman prince Murād I, when he marched on Ankara at the outset of his reign (1361).

In the Eretnid state the vizier Qadi Burhān ad-Dīn Aḥmad of Kaysarīya (from 1365) assumed ever-increasing power, until he finally ascended the throne in Sivas as Sultan Aḥmad. His dominions lay between two new and expanding states: in the west the Ottomans were aiming at consolidating their newly won position as a great power by further gains in Anatolia; in the east the new Turkoman prince of western Persia, Kara-Yülük ʿUthmān, descended from the tribe of 'White Rams' (Aq-Qoyunlu), was endeavouring to gain a footing in eastern Anatolia. He ultimately defeated and killed Sultan Aḥmad (1397). But in that same year there appeared on the scene the mighty Ottoman conqueror, Sultan Bāyezīd I Yîldîrîm, who captured Sivas. This victory was the decisive step in the assimilation by the Ottoman Empire of the territory in north-east Anatolia ruled by the Ilkhan governors.

II. THE TURKISH PRINCIPALITIES OF WESTERN ANATOLIA AND THE RISE OF THE OTTOMANS

From the thirteenth century onwards there had been a considerable influx of Turkish races into Anatolia. The armies of the Mongol conquerors were largely composed of Turks whom they had pressed into service; and other bands of Turks, whom the Mongols had driven from their homes further east, fled westward from the oppressor. The situation in the west had also changed. When the fragment of the Byzantine Empire set up at Nicaea had acquired internal strength and stability, Michael VIII Palaeologus recovered Constantinople from the Latins in 1261 and restored the East Roman Empire. But its former power was never regained. The Palaeologian Emperors turned their attention increasingly to the Balkans, and neglected their eastern frontier. In fact their desire to strengthen their position led them to adopt unpopular measures such as the abolition of the privileges accorded to the frontier forces (*akritai*). In consequence a state of anarchy developed in western Anatolia, enabling the newly arrived Turkish hordes to take possession in the name of the Holy War (*jihād*) of regions where they were induced to establish themselves by the attraction of land more fertile than in the barren interior. In this way the Palaeologian Emperors were gradually obliged to abandon more and more of their possessions in Asia Minor, and by about 1300 almost the whole of western Anatolia was in Turkish hands. This second wave of Turks, which for the first time reached the shores of the Aegean, finally assured Turkish preponderance; from now onwards there was no part of Anatolia without a proportion of Turks amongst the remaining non-Turkish population.

This conquest of western Anatolia lacked central direction exactly as had that of the eleventh century, when the Turks first overran the country. It was pursued independently by bands of soldiers united under various leaders; its results were correspondingly diverse. On the newly conquered territory, formerly held by Byzantium, there sprang up a series of small Turkish principalities all of which owed their existence to the *jihād* against the Byzantine infidel. There is little detailed information about this development. But all indications suggest that the first Turkish princely family to establish its sway in western Anatolia, in what had been Phrygia, was that of Germiyān; indeed a certain 'Alī Shīr played a part in the many wars that marked the last decades of the Empire of Rūm, and also threatened Byzantine possessions in western Anatolia. The princes of Germiyān took up their residence at Kütahiya (formerly Cotyaeum); they also possessed Qara Ḥiṣar-i Ṣāḥib (now Afyon Karahisar), and according to an inscription dated 1299 they even held Ankara for a time, but were never able to take the Byzantine city of Philadelphia (the modern Alashehir). At the end of the thirteenth century and during the first half of the fourteenth this Germiyān principality was the most powerful of the western Anatolian states, some of whose rulers were under its overlordship.

Soon a number of other Turkish principalities grouped themselves
round Germiyān, where certain of their founders appear to have
originated. The most important, running from south to north, were
Ḥamīd in Pisidia, Tekke in Lycia (it is not clear whether Adalia
belonged to one of these two principalities), Menteshe in Caria, Aydîn
in southern Lydia in the hinterland of Smyrna (which for the time
being remained Byzantine), Ṣarukhān in northern Lydia including
Maghnisa (Magnesia) and Bergama (Pergamum), and finally Karasi
in Mysia. All these principalities had been established by Turkish
ghāzīs, who had first settled with their princes in the hilly districts of
their respective territories, and had then fought their way to the
coast. Some of them, for example the Menteshe, put to sea, where
they continued Holy War as redoubtable pirates.

These principalities on the Aegean coast were separated from the
Ottoman amirate in north Phrygia by Byzantine territory which
consisted of the Asian seaboard opposite the imperial capital together
with Brusa, Nicaea and Nicomedia. Further east in Paphlagonia on
the Black Sea coast lay the kingdom of the Jāndār with Kastamuni
(Castra Comnenon, the modern Kastamonu) as its capital. This kingdom apparently owed its origin to a Germiyān amir called Umur Bey,
and on his death (*c.* 1291) the Turkoman prince of Aflani, Timur
Jāndār, took possession of it. The principalities sharing a common
boundary with the territory of Rūm, such as Jāndār, Germiyān
and Ḥamīd, had all annexed portions of it. The Ilkhan governor
Timurtash did after 1316 recover a good deal of this land, but when
he fled in 1327 it once more passed out of the control of the Ilkhan
Empire.

In all these Turkish principalities which were the outcome of
Holy War there was at first an entirely popular Turkish culture
with no trace of Islamic influence. But once the princes had established themselves they sought cultural contacts with the East in so
far as their means permitted.

Thus from the beginning of the fourteenth century Anatolia was
split up into a varied assortment of small states: in the west the
principalities of the holy warriors already mentioned, in the south-
east the Karaman state, in the north-east the territory ruled by the
Mongol governors, who regarded themselves as independent sovereigns after the decline of the Persian Mongol Empire following the
death of the Ilkhan Abū Saʿīd (1335). The unifying element in this
collection of principalities was supplied by the gild system of the
akhīs already mentioned, which had developed according to the
principles of 'chivalry' (*futuwwa*), and which drew many of its members from the artisan town population. A vivid picture of this *akhīs*

system is given us by a Moorish traveller round the world, Ibn Baṭṭūṭa, who passed through Anatolia in the first half of the fourteenth century, a picture which is completed by surviving original manuscripts, and other documents of this gild system. Charity was the guiding principle of the *akhīs*, and was shown in generosity and hospitality. In every town he visited Ibn Baṭṭūṭa found a group of gild members with its leader, the *akhī*—in some towns there were several of these *akhīs* associations—and all of them extended to him the most generous hospitality. These associations also had a political and social bias; they supported the oppressed against tyrants and, as Ibn Baṭṭūṭa shows, did not scruple to murder tyrants or their associates; in one town where there was no municipal government—as may have often happened during this period of transition—they themselves were responsible for the administration. Thus they were a factor which made for the preservation of good order. There was a certain connection between the town-dwelling *akhīs* and the *ghāzīs*, the holy warriors, whose guiding principle was also the *futuwwa*.

The subsequent history of Asia Minor, and indeed of Byzantium, was however determined by what was originally the smallest of the Turkish amirates in western Anatolia, with the Ghāzī 'Uthmān ('Osmān) ibn Ertoghrul as its ruler; it was situated on the extreme north-west frontier of the country, near Eskishehir, adjoining the heart of the former Byzantine Empire and its capital, Constantinople, a region most stubbornly defended by the Emperors. The other Turkish principalities soon exhausted their possibilities of conquest, encountering an effective check to any further advance upon reaching the coast where their exploits came to an end, except for those amirs who turned pirate and continued to wage the Holy War by sea. The Ottomans on the other hand carried on war for generations, constantly discovering some new and profitable undertaking. So it was that the Ottoman principality finally became the centre of the Turkish *ghāzī* tradition, and the Ottomans were constantly being reinforced from the other Turkish states. It is thus easy to realise how the Ottoman principality constantly expanded at its neighbours' expense, until it completely absorbed the Turkish part of Anatolia and became the nucleus of a mighty Empire through which the Turkish races of Asia Minor were to become one of the decisive influences on the history of both East and West.

The origins of the Ottomans are lost in legend. The only ancestor of the Ghāzī 'Uthmān ('Osmān) mentioned in the oldest chronicles is his father Ertoghrul, who may therefore be accepted as a historical figure, although the relationship between 'Osmān and Ertoghrul may well be in doubt. Later on, in the fourteenth century, the house of 'Osmān was accredited with a most illustrious genealogy reaching back to Oghuz Khan, the eponymous hero of the Turkish tribe of the Oghuz, from which the great majority of all the Anatolian Turks were descended. The grandfather of 'Osmān was said to have borne the name of that celebrated Seljuq prince, Sulaymānshāh, who was held to be the first of the Seljuq line of the Sultans of Rūm. And finally, incidents taken from the history of the early Seljuqs were incorporated in his life story: his arrival in Anatolia from the East (which was even assigned a definite date, 1224), his march to Aleppo and his death by drowning in the Euphrates near the fortress of Ja'ber (Kîlîj Arslan I, as may be remembered, was drowned in the river Khabur, a tributary of the Euphrates). Even the exploits attributed to Ertoghrul, his intervention on the side of the Seljuqs of Rūm against the Mongols in the Pasin Ovasî (to the east of Sivas), and his subsequent enfeoffment with the north-west frontier region of the Empire of Rūm in the vicinity of Eskishehir by the famous Seljuq Sultan Kayqubād I, must be regarded as apocryphal; the sole purpose of the second tale was to establish a legitimate connection between the Ottomans and the Seljuqs who had preceded them. The same purpose must have inspired the story of the official conferment of the insignia of sovereignty, drum and banner, on Ertoghrul's son 'Osmān by the last of the Rūm Sultans 'Alā' ad-Dīn Kayqubād III, which the Ottoman chroniclers usually place in the year 1299. In addition, 1290 is given as the year that marked the beginning of 'Osmān's independence (with the reading aloud of his name during the Friday service).

In fact little is really known of the rise of the Ottomans. In all probability 'Osmān, or even Ertoghrul who was regarded as his father, was a successful holy warrior like other Turkish princes of the day—hence his epithet of *ghāzī*—who gathered to his banners ardent warriors in the cause of Islam, though it would be difficult to decide whether they were impelled primarily by enthusiasm for the fight for Islam or by the hope of booty. There were also under his command Christian soldiers who were either opposed to the Palaeologi or who merely recognised in 'Osmān a figure who was able to introduce order into the chaotic affairs of Anatolia during the later Byzantine era. All of them, whether Turks or Greeks—and the latter very soon adopted Islam and the Turkish way of life—took the name 'Osmānlî after their leader. The last feeble Sultans can scarcely have come into contact with 'Osmān, who was then little more than a successful commander, and it is in fact doubtful whether they had ever heard of him.

About the turn of the century 'Osmān made a stealthy advance from the barren land of north Phrygia around Dorylaeum (Eskishehir) into the more fertile plains of Bithynia, considerably extending this newly acquired territory at the expense of the Byzantines. Next he waged war on the Christian magnates of northern Phrygia and took possession of their castles without which any real control of his conquered territory was impossible. He must first have attracted the notice of the government at Constantinople with his victory over a Byzantine army on 27 July 1301 at Baphaeum (Koyunḥiṣār near Nicaea).[1]

He finally succeeded in occupying the important centre of Melangeia (Yenishehir), cutting off land communications between Brusa and Nicaea, so that Brusa and western Bithynia were now only accessible from Constantinople by sea. Yenishehir, lying in a fairly extensive plain, now became the base for the wars against the Byzantines; it remained an important centre for subsequent military operations on Asian soil. Further military exploits brought the Ottomans to the coast of the Black Sea and the Sea of Marmora and completed the encirclement of Brusa and Nicaea.

On 6 April 1326 'Osmān's son, Ghāzī Orkhan, at last succeeded in taking Brusa (Prusa, the Turkish Bursa), the most important town in Bithynia, which immediately became the capital of his kingdom. 'Osmān appears to have died that same year, and was succeeded by Orkhan. He now set about the conquest of Nicaea and Nicomedia, and annexed the Bithynian peninsula which juts out into the Bosphorus, giving it in fief to his general Aḳtshe Koja from whom it took the name of Koja eli; he also conquered the shores of the Gulf of Nicomedia, which severed the overland communication between Nicomedia and Constantinople. In 1329 the Emperor Andronicus III marched against the Turks in the hope of regaining Nicomedia, but was defeated at Philocrene (Tavshanjhil) and Pelecanum (Maltepe), and by 1330 was compelled to acknowledge the Turkish conquests. The following year (2 March 1331) saw the fall of Nicaea (Isnik). Nicaea was, after Brusa, the town most richly endowed by Orkhan, so that it developed into one of the most prosperous in the whole land during the early Ottoman period. It was the residence of Orkhan's consort Nīlūfer, where she received in audience the Moorish traveller, Ibn Baṭṭūṭa. At last, in 1337, came the fall of Nicomedia (Iznikomid, later Izmit).[2]

Orkhan's rule initiated the absorption of the remaining Turkish

---

[1] The identity of the battle of Baphaeum related by the Byzantine chronicler Pachymeres with the battle of Koyunḥiṣār in the ancient Ottoman chronicles (Ashikpashazade) is, however, uncertain and contestable.

[2] Sometimes dated to 1330 or 1338.

principalities in Anatolia, whose holy warriors in any event preferred to support the son of 'Osmān ('Osmān oghlu) who was still prosecuting the religious war, rather than to remain at home where there was no further opportunity for expansion. As early as 1336 Orkhan was thus able without bloodshed to incorporate into his own realm the principality of Karasi in Mysia when the succession was disputed; he now commanded the entire south coast of the Sea of Marmora with access to the Dardanelles, and the northernmost part of the Aegean coast (as far as Pergamum). The Ottoman kingdom now consisted of four provinces: Sultān üyügi, the original territory, including Eskishehir and Söğüt, Hudāvendkar eli, 'the Ruler's domain', which the prince retained for himself, including Brusa and Isnik, Koja eli, including Izmit, and Karasi eli, including Balikesir (Palaeocastro) and Bergama (Pergamum).

The extension of his sphere of influence and the possession of such important cities as Brusa, Nicaea and Nicomedia made it possible, in fact imperative, for Orkhan to give to his rule, hitherto loosely maintained by the sword alone, a more national character. He therefore created his brother 'Alā' ad-Dīn 'Alī Pasha (the first to bear this title) his adviser; he was responsible for the minting of coins and the introduction of a national headgear (a white felt cap with a flap that hung down at the back) resembling the one described by Ibn Baṭṭūṭa as that worn by the *akhīs* and probably that of the holy warriors; he also established a standing army which was fashioned into a powerful instrument in the hand of the sovereign and which abolished the previous haphazard, semi-nomadic methods of warfare. The new army organisation involved the recruitment of an infantry force (*yaya*) from the constant influx of holy warriors, which was later to form the basis of the janissary corps, and the setting up of a cavalry force (*sipāhī*) chosen from the sovereign's closest comrades-in-arms, who received in fee tracts of conquered territory; later a distinction was made, according to their extent, between large fiefs (*zi'āmet*) and small (*tīmār*). These two types of soldier, a standing infantry force and a cavalry of vassals, remained henceforward the two main pillars of the Ottoman army organisation. In addition the Greek inhabitants of the conquered cities, most of whom embraced Islam and the Turkish way of life, brought their administrative skill to bear on the task of organising the political structure of the semi-nomadic Ottoman kingdom. This young expanding Ottoman principality also attracted scribes from the East, from Karamania and particularly from Ilkhan Persia; some were summoned, some came of their own accord, bringing with them the basic principles of administrative practice in their own countries. Thus the two sources of Ottoman administration stemmed on the one hand from Byzantium and on the other from Rūm and the Īlkhan Empire.

Orkhan's relations with Byzantium were not entirely hostile. The conditions obtaining in Constantinople, when the Emperors John V Palaeologus and John VI Cantacuzenus were at war with each other, made it inevitable that both sides should regard the new Asiatic military power as a welcome ally, making frequent appeals to Orkhan for auxiliary troops. There was even an inter-marriage between the courts of Constantinople and Brusa: in 1345 Orkhan, though no longer young, married Theodora, a daughter of the Emperor John VI Cantacuzenus. Occasional unorganised raids by Turkish marauders on European soil, together with the infiltration of Turks into Europe brought about by the Byzantines themselves, paved the way for the subsequent conquest of the Balkan peninsula by the Turks. The Ottoman chroniclers cite as the first step in this direction the crossing of the Dardanelles at Tzympe (Chimenlik) in 1353 by a body of Turks led by Orkhan's eldest son Sulaymān Pasha, an event soon followed (1354) by the capture of the stronghold of Callipolis (Gallipoli, modern Turkish Gelibolu), when the town had been evacuated after an earthquake. Once in Turkish hands, Gallipoli became the base for further expeditions into Europe.

In 1359 Orkhan died, leaving to his second son Murād (the elder son Sulaymān had died the previous year) a domain which could already compare in size with the larger Anatolian principalities such as Germiyān and the Jāndār eli, but which differed from them by reason of its more highly developed administrative system, while the inherent possibilities of its geographical position and its organised standing army made it an easy task for an energetic ruler like the young prince Murād (Bey, not yet Sultan) to turn the mistakes of his opponents to his own account and to use such opportunities in order to develop his heritage into an imposing great power.

III. THE FIRST RISE TO POWER OF THE OTTOMAN EMPIRE AND ITS DOWNFALL

Orkhan was the first of a succession of outstandingly capable and shrewd rulers who conferred prominence on the house of 'Osmān in its infancy and whose skill enabled them to exploit the confusion of their Christian neighbours in order to expand their domain from its modest beginnings of an association of holy warriors on the Byzantine–Rūm frontier to a great power, and finally to a world-wide Empire, all within the relatively brief period of two and a half centuries, from the beginning of the thirteenth to the middle of the fifteenth century.

Orkhan had extended the dominions inherited from his father 'Osmān until they equalled and even surpassed the other Turkish principalities, stretching from the Dardanelles to the western coasts of the Black Sea and completely enclosing Byzantine territory in Asia. Moreover his reign had seen the creation, with Persian and Byzantine help, of an administration which, though continuing the tradition of the *ghāzīs*, transformed it by the reorganisation of the army into a different more rigidly disciplined system. It was, however, his son Murād I who really established the Empire; during the thirty years of his reign (1359–89) he devoted his skill and boundless energy to constructing an impressive power on the foundations laid by his father. This state, with its zeal for the Holy War and its urge to expand, became the terror of Christendom.

Murād's policy was twofold: he aimed primarily at prosecuting the Holy War and acquiring further territory for Islam on the European side of the straits; he already possessed an excellent base for attack in his occupation of the Thracian Chersonese, the Gallipoli peninsula. His second and equally important aim was to gain a firmer hold in Anatolia, the heart of his Empire and source of its power, whose development must keep pace with expansion in Europe. His first expedition was therefore directed towards the extension of his growing Empire in Anatolia; he marched against Ankara, wrested it from the control of the *akhīs* and incorporated it into his dominions. Later he acquired the principality of Ḥamīd by purchase, thus becoming master of a region on the Mediterranean coast in southern Anatolia possessing the important harbour of Adalia (formerly Attalia, now Antalya). His plans were furthered by alliances with Anatolian princes: Murād married his eldest son Bāyezīd to a daughter of the prince of Germiyān, and he gave his own daughter in marriage to the prince of Karaman 'Alā' ad-Dīn Bey, the successor of the Seljuqs of Rūm and the most powerful Anatolian prince apart from the Ottomans.

For his military expeditions against Byzantium and the Balkan Christian states Murād had at his disposal a number of admirable generals, among whom were his tutor Lala Shāhīn and a certain *ghāzī* Evrenos Bey who had made his name in the Holy War. Immediately upon his accession Murād dispatched an expedition to the Balkan peninsula (which the Turks called Rūm eli, 'the Roman land', Rumelia). In 1360 Demotika (Didymotichus, in Turkish Dimetoka) was captured, and Murād immediately erected a mighty fortress there; soon afterwards (early in 1361) he took Adrianople, the important city on the main highway from Constantinople to the Danube. This event, news of which reached Venice as early as 14 March 1361, created a powerful impression and drew the attention of the West for the first time to this new power emerging in the Levant. Some sources assign a different date to this epoch-making event, putting it in 1368–9, or even 1371, which would appear to indicate that firm possession of the town was not immediately established; however, Adrianople (Turkish Edirne) did in fact soon come permanently under Turkish rule, and by 1365 was being used by Murād as a court second only in importance to Brusa, replacing Demotika which had for a short time enjoyed this position.[1]

From Adrianople further expeditions were carried out in the eastern Balkans under the leadership either of Lala Shāhīn or the Sultan himself. Lala Shāhīn is alleged to have taken possession of the town of Philippopolis (Turkish Filibe) as early as 1363–4, where he took up his residence as the chief governor (Beylerbey) of Rumelia. The military operations which Murād directed against the south-east Balkan peninsula came to a conclusion in about 1370; a considerable portion of Thrace from the Aegean to the Black Sea was held by the Turks, and Constantinople, with its narrow hinterland in Europe, was henceforth completely encircled by Turkish territory and cut off from the rest of Christendom. Murād, who no longer styled himself Bey but Sultan, obliged both the Byzantine Emperor and the tsar of Bulgaria to acknowledge his suzerainty and contribute troops. His stature was now so considerable that the chroniclers usually refer to him merely as 'Ruler' (Hudāvendkār, abbreviated to Hunkār).

In 1371 the first attempt was made to meet the Turkish threat. Evrenos Bey penetrated so far into western Thrace that he soon reached the southern lands of the kingdom of Serbia, which was then the most important power in the Balkans. This Turkish menace provoked the Serbs to take the field against Murād with a powerful army, but they were defeated on 26 September 1371 at Črnomen on the Marica (in the Turkish chronicles the battle is called Sîrf sindîgî, 'Destruction of the Serbs', and this name was afterwards given to the site of the battle).

After successfully countering this attack Murād next addressed himself to organising the affairs of the conquered territories. He divided them (apparently about 1375–6) into great and small fiefs (*ziʿāmet* and *tīmār*) and gave them to his soldiers; larger tracts of land, 'special fiefs' (*khāṣṣ*), were allotted to his commanders. Apparently on the advice of his vizier Hayr ad-Dīn Pasha, he introduced an important innovation into his standing army, namely the reinforcement of the infantry established under Orkhan by prisoners of

[1] For the date of the capture of Adrianople see G. Ostrogorsky, *History of the Byzantine State*, p. 478 and n. 3.

war, one-fifth of whom were considered under Islamic law as the Sultan's property. This was the first stage in the transformation of these 'new troops' (*yeni cheri* or janissaries) into the slave army which was to become so familiar.

The defeat of the Serbs at Črnomen gave the Turks access to Serbian territory in both the north and south Balkans. In the north the Sultan's regular army operated under his personal leadership and captured Sofia (probably in 1385, at the earliest 1384), the environs of which had for some time been in the hands of the Turks; shortly after they took Niš (according to the Serbian chronicles, in 1386). In the same year, 1386, Murād marched against the Serbian prince Lazar, whom he compelled to acknowledge his suzerainty. In the south the campaign was carried out by the holy warriors led by Evrenos Bey and Hayr ad-Dīn Pasha. In 1387 they took Serres, and after a three years' siege Thessalonica also fell. Thessalonica did eventually pass from Turkish control, but Serres remained permanently in Turkish hands, becoming an important base for further Turkish expeditions in western and southern Rumelia.

The Karaman 'Alā' ad-Dīn Bey grew considerably alarmed at the increasing power of the Ottoman Bey, whose acquisition of Ankara and Ḥamīd had made them neighbours. Consequently, despite the fact that he was Murād's son-in-law, he seized the opportunity of Murād's absence in Rumelia to attempt an extension of his own lands at the expense of the Ottoman kingdom. Murād refused to countenance such an action and marched into Anatolia with a powerful army reinforced even then by Greek, Bulgarian and Serbian auxiliaries, vanquishing 'Alā' ad-Dīn at Konya and obliging him to sue for peace through his wife, Murād's daughter; it was accorded him in exchange for certain frontier districts such as Akshehir (1386). This moderation shown to a Muslim prince, from whom he did not exact an acknowledgement of his overlordship after victory as he did from Christian rulers, reveals Murād's attitude as a Muslim fighter; he regarded his task as consisting solely in the extension of the authority of Islam over the infidels; on the soil of Islam he only sought peaceful conquests. This encounter with the Karaman ruler was the first of a series which accompanied the rise of the Ottoman Empire. The Karamans, who were after the Ottomans the most powerful Turkish princes in Anatolia, proved to be their most dangerous rivals and were for almost a century a constant thorn in the flesh, until at last Muḥammad II absorbed Karamania into the Ottoman Empire.

Murād's absence in Anatolia was regarded by the Serbian prince Lazar, who had allied himself with Bulgaria and Bosnia, as an opportune moment to rise in revolt against Ottoman rule. Murād made war in person against the insurgents, forcing into submission Šišman, tsar of the Bulgars. Next he marched on Serbia, where on 15 June 1389 the Turks won a decisive victory at the Battle of the Field of the Blackbird (Kossovopolje, Turkish Kosova). During the battle, however, Sultan Murād I was murdered by a Serb, and Prince Lazar was taken prisoner and put to death.

The murdered Sultan was immediately succeeded by his eldest son Bāyezīd, who had no sooner assumed the reins of government than he ordered the death of his brother Ya'qūb. By this deed he finally broke with the ancient Turkish custom which vested sovereignty in the entire reigning house, the members of which held governorships in the provinces, and he introduced, along with the cruel act of fratricide for reasons of state, the rigid practice of undivided rule in the Ottoman Empire.

Bāyezīd I differed in other respects from the earliest Ottoman rulers whose origins went back to the Holy War. He resembled more closely the oriental type of despot whose court etiquette he introduced, a step which alienated him from the *ghāzīs*. He also diverged from the policy of his ancestors in his attitude to the Turkish principalities of Anatolia in that he did not hesitate to wage war on them as on the infidels in Rumelia; a pretext was in fact provided by the hostile behaviour of the Karaman 'Alā' ad-Dīn. Finally he dispossessed them all and extended his sway over the whole of Anatolia, an act which subsequently spelt his doom. He sought to give an air of legitimacy to his violence by requesting the Abbasid Caliph in Cairo, in 1394, to confer on him the title of 'Sultan of Rūm', which he readily obtained. His father, Murād I, had already adopted the title of Sultan, regarding his actual power as sufficient justification, but he was in fact only 'prince' (*bey*); it was Bāyezīd who first assumed the title of Sultan with all its implications according to Sunnite doctrine, as the legitimate wielder of power in his dominions.

His exploits in Anatolia by no means deflected Bāyezīd's attention from events in Rumelia; on the contrary he would often arrive on the spot with uncanny speed if his presence was necessary, earning for himself the nickname of 'Thunderbolt' (*yıldırım*). When the tsar of Bulgaria, John Šišman, tried during Bāyezīd's absence in Anatolia to shake off the Ottoman yoke, Yıldırım hastened to the spot. As a result of this revolt the Bulgarian tsar lost his capital, Trnovo, was himself taken prisoner in the fortress of Nicopolis where he had sought refuge, and was finally deprived of his throne. Bulgaria now became an integral part of the Ottoman Empire (1393). During another of Bāyezīd's absences in Anatolia the prince of Wallachia, Mircea, invaded Ottoman territory; he too was defeated (in the encounter known as the battle of Rovine, or Argeş, autumn 1393) and compelled to acknowledge Ottoman suzerainty and to pay a tribute (1394).[1]

After these exploits Yĭldĭrĭm continued to extend the scope of his activities so that the Turkish menace assumed gigantic proportions; in 1394 the Sultan embarked on further military expeditions in Rumelia (the reconquest of Thessalonica and campaigns in Greece which penetrated as far as the Peloponnese, and were probably directed by Evrenos Bey). The following year (1395) the Sultan made his preparations for a really considerable undertaking: he commenced the siege of Constantinople and resolved to attack Hungary. The Hungarians were well aware of his intentions, and the western world determined on a crusade against the Turks. The king of Hungary, Sigismund, who later became the German Emperor, took the field with a strong cavalry force containing contingents from every nation in Europe, but suffered an overwhelming defeat at the hands of Bāyezīd on 25 September 1396 at Nicopolis on the Danube. This was a victory won by the rigidly disciplined regular army of the Ottoman military machine over the undisciplined feudal army with its motley array of rival national contingents—a victory won by the unity of purpose inherent in a despotically governed oriental Empire over this multiplicity of western states, whose divergent aims rendered a united defensive front most difficult to achieve. The status of the Ottoman Empire as a first-class power was now firmly established and evident to all.

After Nicopolis Bāyezīd resumed the siege of Constantinople which had temporarily been raised in view of the approaching crusaders' army. But Byzantium was granted yet another period of respite, for in the East a storm was gathering which was to break over Bāyezīd's head. Timurlenk, the Tamerlane of the western chroniclers, a Turk originally of Mongol stock, had established an Empire beyond the Oxus intended as a basis for the revival of the Mongol Empire. Since 1380 he had subjugated the whole of Persia, and in 1400 had captured Baghdad. The dispossessed Turkish princes of Anatolia took refuge with him and incited him to declare war on Bāyezīd. After Bāyezīd had annexed what had once been the territory of the Mongol governors in north-eastern Anatolia Timur complied with the wishes of the Anatolian princes and marched from Baghdad against Rūm. As early as 1400 he took Sivas, where, following his usual practice, he organised a cruel massacre, particularly of the Christians in the city. He then turned his attention to Syria, conquering Aleppo and Damascus. After an interchange of messages, in which Timur sought to restrict Bāyezīd within his own confines, reminding him that his real

---

[1] For a different dating see above, pp. 375 and 563.

concern should be the prosecution of the Holy War against the infidels, and demanding restitution of the Anatolian principalities to their titular owners, the Mongol attack was launched in 1402. On 20 July, in the plain of Čibuq Ābād, to the north-east of Ankara, the two Emperors met in battle, from which Timur emerged victorious. The proud Bāyezīd was taken prisoner and compelled to accompany Timur on his passage through Anatolia carried in a litter (some accounts say in a cage); the following year (8 March 1403) he died while Timur's prisoner, probably by his own hand. In the autumn of 1402 Brusa, the Ottoman capital, was captured and pillaged; then Timur himself made a significant contribution to the Holy War by taking Smyrna (Turkish Izmir); next he re-established all the Turkish princes in their domains before his departure in 1404 and his return to his court at Samarqand; he died soon after on 19 February 1405. The Ottoman Empire had fallen headlong from its rapid rise to power. The West could breathe once more.

IV. THE REVIVAL OF THE OTTOMAN EMPIRE AS A GREAT POWER IN ASIA MINOR AND IN EUROPE

After the catastrophe inflicted by Timur at the battle of Ankara the young Ottoman Empire, which had been constructed with such rapidity and energy, collapsed and was left dismembered. True, the recently conquered portion of the Empire in Europe, Rumelia, remained more or less intact after the disaster, and in Adrianople Bāyezīd's eldest son, the amir Sulaymān, ascended the throne on the death of his father and ruled over a brilliant court. But the Ottoman possessions in Anatolia were severely reduced. All the Turkish princes were reinstated. In north-west Anatolia they only retained their original lands with Brusa, covering approximately the same area as when Orkhan bequeathed it to his son. To the north-east they still had the former domain of the Mongol governors, with Sivas and Amasea, and here Bāyezīd's youngest son, Muḥammad (Meḥmed) Chelebi, had established control. Two other sons, 'Īsā and Mūsā, disputed possession of the older territory. 'Īsā was soon defeated, and Mūsā then attempted to reunite the Empire under his sway by declaring war on his elder brother the amir Sulaymān, who himself aimed at annexing Anatolia, and did in fact succeed in temporarily occupying Brusa (1406), though he was soon driven out. Finally Mūsā defeated Sulaymān and reunited Rumelia with the older territory in Anatolia (1410); Sulaymān was put to death when escaping to Constantinople (17 February 1411).

It is a measure of the prestige which the Ottoman Empire as a power in its own right had already acquired in the eyes of its neighbours, and also of the lack of purpose displayed by the Christians, that no advantage was taken of the weakness of the divided Empire to launch a counter-attack. Sigismund of Hungary, who had since 1410 been German Emperor, did attempt to form a coalition against the Turks, but without success. The Ottomans were thus given time to recover.

Bāyezīd's elder sons, particularly the amir Sulaymān, had adapted themselves so completely to their new environment in Rumelia, which Murād I and Bāyezīd I had conquered, that they adopted many of the customs prevalent in neighbouring Christian states. By so doing, however, they lost the support of their ancestors' former adherents, the 'holy warriors'. In contrast, Muḥammad, the youngest son, who held court at Amasea in north-east Anatolia, was surrounded by a much more primitive society in which the old popular Turkish traditions of religious warfare still flourished vigorously. His attitude was therefore more in harmony with that of the *ghāzīs* who joined his ranks in considerable numbers. When it came to a decisive struggle between Mūsā and Muḥammad, the latter was victorious at Jamurlu in Serbia (July 1413) and was able to reunite the entire Empire under a single ruler. Mūsā perished in flight.

Muḥammad (Meḥmed) I had many obstacles to overcome before peaceful conditions prevailed in the reunited Empire. Scarcely had he ascended the throne when the Karaman ruler made a belated attempt to use the situation as an opportunity for an attack on the Ottomans. The Karaman army penetrated as far as Brusa and invested the Ottoman capital, but the garrison captain at Brusa, 'Ivaz Pasha, forced it to withdraw. Muḥammad then attacked the Karamans and besieged Konya; finally peace was made between the two (1414). Soon afterwards a dangerous dervish revolt broke out in western Anatolia in the neighbourhood of Smyrna; it coincided with a seditious movement in Rumelia (originating in Wallachia) led by a certain Badr ad-Dīn Maḥmud who was known as the 'Son of the Judge of Samavna'. Considerable military force was necessary to quell these disturbances. In the end the leader of both rebellions, Badr ad-Dīn Maḥmud, was seized and executed in Serres (1416). After a brief interval there appeared near Smyrna an adventurer called Junayd, and yet another who claimed to be Muṣṭafā, one of Sultan Bāyezīd's sons (known as Düzme Muṣṭafā), of whom nothing had been heard since the battle of Ankara. Both were completely unsuccessful and were obliged to flee to Constantinople, whereupon Muḥammad concluded an agreement with the Emperor Manuel II which assured the custody of these two disturbers of the peace (1421).

Muḥammad I was thus preoccupied throughout his reign with over-coming domestic difficulties; the prosecution of the Holy War was out of the question. He died of apoplexy on 4 May at Gallipoli.

His son and successor Murād II (1421–51) was also confronted with internal problems at the outset of his reign. The Emperor Manuel released both the false Muṣṭafā and Junayd. Muṣṭafā had some success to begin with, and the Greeks took advantage of the struggle to regain possession of Gallipoli for a time. But Muṣṭafā was ulti-mately reduced to submission. Murād then directed his attack against the Byzantine Emperor, determined to punish him for his unfriendly conduct, and he again laid siege to Constantinople (1422). But the machinations of Junayd and the appearance of the Sultan's younger brother, the young Muṣṭafā, who claimed the throne—though this design was soon frustrated by his capture and execution (1423)—obliged Murād to make peace again with the Emperor John VIII, Manuel's successor, and to raise the siege. In 1424 a treaty was made with Byzantium, which reduced the East Roman Empire to little more than the city of Constantinople. It was not until Junayd had been finally defeated and put to death in 1425, and a further attack by the Karamans had been repulsed (1426), that domestic tranquillity was restored and the way lay open for a resumption of the Holy War. Meanwhile, Murād had been trying to extend his principality in Anatolia by peaceful means. To this end he con-cluded a treaty in 1423 with Isfendiyār, the prince of Kastamuni, by which an area rich in mineral deposits was ceded to the Ottoman Empire; he also married the prince's daughter. Under his regime the Empire and the house of Ottoman so retrieved its position that the Anatolian princes regarded Murād as their overlord. The only dis-agreements that still persisted were between the Ottoman rulers and their old rivals the Karamans; the reign of Murād II saw three out-breaks of war between Ottoman and Karaman.

Meanwhile the aged Evrenos Bey had been richly rewarded with lands in western Thrace and Macedonia which he governed as Bey of the Frontier, and his son had been leading expeditions into Albania and Greece, going as far south as the Peloponnese. Murād himself now marched on Macedonia, completing its subjugation, and captured Thessalonica which the Venetians had recently purchased from the Byzantines (March 1430). The partial subjection of Albania was then carried out, mainly during the years 1435–6. There was also fighting on the Hungarian frontier; Transylvania was invaded from Wallachia, Hungary from Serbia; in 1439 Semendria (Smederevo) on the Danube fell to the Turks, and remained a base for their cam-paigns against Hungary.

This renewed activity on the part of the Muslims provoked a response from the Christians. The Byzantine Emperor John VIII Palaeologus tried to obtain the help of the West in an attempt to break the Turkish encirclement, by negotiating a union between the Byzantine and the Roman Churches. He journeyed in person to Italy, and at the Council of Ferrara–Florence in 1438–9 he agreed to the union with Rome. Nevertheless the Council's decisions were vigorously attacked in Constantinople, and formally condemned by the Patriarch in 1443; his action was no doubt influenced by the knowledge that the Turks would oppose a union of the Eastern and Western Churches. The Council was therefore a failure from the ecclesiastical point of view, but it did arouse in the West a renewed interest in Eastern affairs.

The campaigns of the Turkish holy warriors in Hungary and Albania called forth men who successfully championed the Christian cause within the means at their disposal. When the Turks under Evrenoszade 'Ali Bey besieged Belgrade by land and water (1440–1), the city was delivered at the end of six months by King Vladislav III of Poland, now also king of Hungary. But the real heart of Hungarian resistance to the Turks was the *voivode* of Transylvania, John Hunyadi, who in the same year won a victory over the Turks at Semendria and in the following year drove back Turkish attacks on Transylvania. At this point Pope Eugenius IV called for a crusade against the Turks. A Hungarian crusaders' army reinforced with Germans and Poles and led by King Vladislav and John Hunyadi invaded Rumelia in 1443, while the Sultan was absent in Anatolia engaged in repelling a Karaman attack. The Christians defeated the Turks at Niš, captured Sofia and achieved several further victories; but as they were crossing the mountains (Sredna Gora) into the plain of Philippopolis in the depth of winter, they encountered invincible Turkish resistance at Zlatica (Turkish Izladî), which compelled them to turn back (12 December 1443), though they did gain victories over the Turks during their retreat.

These Christian successes encouraged George Castriota, the Bey of Dibra in central Albania, to raise the standard of revolt; when a boy he had lived at the court of Murād II as a hostage, where he was brought up in the Muslim faith and bore the Muslim name of Iskender Bey (to the Western world he was known as Skanderbeg). He had subsequently been created Bey of the Frontier, receiving Dibra in fee. He now returned to the Christian fold and took possession of the town of Kroja (Turkish Akche-ḥiṣār, in the mountainous region between Durazzo and Alessio), where he concluded an alliance with the Albanian chiefs in the hope of throwing off the Turkish yoke.

By means of guerrilla warfare he successfully resisted Turkish attempts to suppress this revolt. Confronted with this difficult situation —reverses in Hungary, rebellions in Albania and Greece, above all the threatening attitude of the Karaman Ibrāhīm Bey in Anatolia— Murād II was reduced to concluding a ten-year truce with Hungary. It was signed by the Sultan in Adrianople on 12 June 1444, and is said to have been accepted on oath by King Vladislav at Szegedin[1] at the end of July (at the latest on 1 August 1444).

After the conclusion of the truce Murād departed into Anatolia with the intention of subduing his adversary, the Karaman oghlu Ibrāhīm Bey, leaving behind in Adrianople his son Muḥammad (Meḥmed) Chelebi, a twelve-year-old boy, who later succeeded him, to rule over the European portion of the Empire under the protection of his old advisers, more especially the vizier Halīl Pasha, grandson of the vizier of Murād I.

Meanwhile the crusading movement had gained ground, thanks to the encouragement of Pope Eugenius IV. As early as June 1444, before the conclusion of the truce, a crusaders' fleet had put to sea at Venice, and on 4 August, only a few days after the truce, King Vladislav committed himself on oath to carry through to the end the crusade which was to expel the Turks from Europe. The crusading army was soon on the move, crossed the Danube at Orsova and marched through Bulgaria in the direction of Varna, from which it was hoped to launch an attack upon the Turks by sea. On receiving the news Murād hastily concluded the Karaman campaign, made peace with Ibrāhīm Bey and hurried back to Europe, where he inflicted a crushing defeat on the Christians at Varna on 10 November 1444; the king of Hungary, Vladislav, fell in battle, and only fragments of the crusaders' army were able to make their way home.

Soon after the battle of Varna, in December 1444 or early in January 1445, Murād II, for reasons unknown, abdicated in favour of his son, Muḥammad (Meḥmed) Chelebi—an isolated case in oriental history—and retired to Maghnisa, formerly Magnesia (the modern Manisa). But certain difficulties which the janissaries caused the young Sultan, coupled with the news that Constantine, the Despot of Mistra in the Peloponnese, and also Hunyadi, were behaving in a hostile manner, caused the vizier Halīl Pasha to summon Murād back to the throne. Accordingly he became Sultan once again (August 1446) and sent his son to Maghnisa. His first campaign was directed

---

[1] The Polish historians deny that Vladislav took his oath to the truce at Szegedin, and allege that it was only a question of some kind of separate peace with George Branković, the king of Serbia, who in fact did not take part in the crusade that followed (compare the critical analysis of this question by F. Babinger, *Oriens*, III (1950), 239 ff.; and see above: ch. XII, p. 554, note 1).

against Constantine; he stormed and destroyed the Hexamilion, the wall across the Isthmus of Corinth which Constantine XI had erected, and imposed Ottoman rule on the despotate of Mistra. Next Hunyadi, eager to avenge the ignominy of Varna, made war on the Turks and invaded Serbia. Murād took the field with a mighty army and gained a decisive victory on 17–19 October 1448, on the Field of the Blackbirds (Kossovopolje) where in 1389 Serbia's fate had been decided. This victory finally restored Ottoman rule over the Balkans. It was only in Albania that the rebels held out under George Castriota (Skanderbeg); even so Murād succeeded in capturing one or two fortified places, but his siege against Kroja, Castriota's headquarters, was unavailing (1450). On 3 February 1451 Murād II died near Adrianople, from a fit of apoplexy during a meal, at the early age of forty-nine.

The reign of Murād II is important for the subsequent history of the Ottoman Empire by reason of his organisation of the army and his encouragement of intellectual interests at court. It is of decisive significance that under his regime the practice of the youth tribute (*devshirme*), whereby the janissary corps drew reinforcements, became an accepted procedure; it is reported by Bartholomaeus de Jano that Murād introduced it in 1438. The youth tribute required suitable boys between ten and fifteen years of age to be selected from the Christian populations in the Balkans at stated intervals, originally every five years, later more often; they were brought up as Muslims at court and by Turkish high dignitaries, and when they had completely assimilated the Turkish religion, language and culture, they joined the ranks of the janissaries, where a brilliant career awaited them, with the possibility of holding the highest offices of the Empire. This practice enabled the Turks to deprive their Christian subject races of the flower of their manhood, and at the same time strengthened the Turkish core of their Empire; hence the large number of generals and statesmen, grand viziers and other high officials of the Sublime Porte during the later fifteenth and sixteenth centuries who sprang from the ranks of the conquered Christian races; the older Ottoman nobility, whose help and advice Murād II himself had continued to draw on, were increasingly excluded from political life.

Another important aspect of Murād's reign was the interest displayed both by the Sultan himself and his dignitaries in every sphere of intellectual life. Here Murād II was continuing the trend which began under Bāyezīd I and was taken over by the Amir Sulaymān; under him the Ottoman court, like those of the great oriental rulers, became a centre of cultural life. Turkish literature, encouraged by the Sultan himself and by his nobles, received a powerful impetus, and in the imperial capitals, Brusa and Adrianople, there arose buildings of artistic worth whose style (*mutatis mutandis*) presents an undeniable spiritual affinity with contemporary renaissance art.

v. THE CONQUEST OF CONSTANTINOPLE

The young Sultan Muḥammad (Meḥmed) II, by now in his twenty-second year, and possessed of unusual vigour, had no sooner ascended the throne in Adrianople for the second time (18 February 1451) than he planned to crown the achievements of his ancestors by making an end of the miserable remnant of the Byzantine Empire, which now consisted merely of the imperial city on the Bosphorus. His vizier Halīl Pasha, who had served Murād II, was against the project, fearing a coalition of Western powers if Constantinople were seriously endangered. But Muḥammad was not to be put off. He embarked upon extensive preparations, amassed a great collection of artillery and in 1452 constructed a castle at the narrowest point of the Bosphorus on the European side, facing the similar fortress already built by Bāyezīd I on the Asian shore and called Boghaz Kesen (now Rūmeli-ḥiṣār). With these two strongholds he could blockade the straits. Under the pressure of this threat the Emperor Constantine XI Dragases tried to revive the union between the Churches of Byzantium and Rome (12 December 1452), hoping to ensure the support of the West; but even at the eleventh hour the populace refused to recognise the union, which was therefore completely fruitless. Only the Genoese Giovanni Giustiniani, with a body of his countrymen, came to reinforce the besieged Byzantines; and he indeed became the driving force of the defence.

When all his preparations were made, the Sultan Muḥammad began to close in on Constantinople by land and sea at the beginning of April 1453. The passage of ships into the city's harbour was blocked by a chain thrown across the mouth of the Golden Horn; but during the night of 21 to 22 April the Turks hauled a great number of their ships overland from the Bosphorus across the heights of Pera and launched them inside the Golden Horn before the terrified gaze of the besieged inhabitants.

After the first attacks on the city had been repulsed, a certain dervish shaykh, Ak Shams ad-Dīn, who was with the Turkish army, was told in a vision the site of the grave of Abū Ayūb Khālid ibn Zayd al-Anṣārī, one of the old Arab holy warriors who had died in battle at the gates of the city during the first long siege of Constantinople by the Muslims (c. 674–8) and had been buried there. This discovery of the grave of Abū Ayūb was an event comparable to the discovery of the Holy Lance made by the crusaders on the First Crusade during the siege of Antioch, and it fired the courage of the besieging army. On 24 May 1453 the assault on the city began, and on 29 May the Turks forced an entrance through the breaches made in the walls by the artillery. Constantine, the last of the East Roman Emperors, fell fighting courageously.

The conquered city was sacked and pillaged for three days. Then Sultan Muḥammad the Conqueror (Fātiḥ), as he was henceforth known, entered the city and performed the Friday prayers in St Sophia, the Church of the Holy Wisdom built by the Emperor Justinian. After supervising the more important arrangements and installing a provost (*subashi*), he returned to Adrianople. His first act there was to imprison and put to death his vizier Halīl Pasha, a member of the old vizier family of the Jandarlîzade against whom he nursed a grudge because of his behaviour on his father's abdication, and whose advice concerning the attack on Constantinople had been proved overcautious.

The Sultan then proceeded to regularise the situation in the conquered city, which he raised to the dignity of his new imperial capital. The Greek Christian inhabitants, whose numbers had already been greatly reduced in the last few years, were expelled and only some were allowed to return at a later period. The Sultan replaced them with Turks from Anatolia, thus converting the Greek Christian city of Constantinople into a city with a predominantly Turkish Muslim population and only a minority of Greek Christians. His relations with this minority, as indeed with all the Christians in the Empire, were governed by the good Muslim tradition of levying the poll tax (*jizyah*) which Islam required of non-Muslims, in exchange for the right of self-government. To this end a new Patriarch was elected, George Scholarius, known as Gennadius II, the head of the anti-unionist party; he became at the same time the political leader of the Orthodox Christians in the Ottoman Empire and acted as their representative in dealing with the Sultan. And as the Orthodox Christians looked up to the Oecumenical Patriarch of Constantinople not only as their ecclesiastical but also as their political head, so did the Gregorian Armenians regard their Patriarch, and the Jews their chief rabbi (Khakhambashî).

Muḥammad II adorned Constantinople, as befitted a new imperial capital, with civic and ecclesiastical buildings. In the centre of the city he erected his palace, and later on he built a second on the tongue of land projecting into the Golden Horn, the Bosphorus and the Sea of Marmora (completed in 1467). The former was called 'the Old Palace' (eski Saray); it was pulled down during the 1870's and replaced by the Ministry of War (Seraskerat), now converted into the university buildings. The latter was called 'the New Palace' (yeni

Saray, now Topkapî Sarayî). The Church of St Sophia (Aya Sofya) was no longer used for Christian services, but was turned into the main Friday mosque of the capital. In addition Muḥammad built at the highest point of the city a great mosque to replace the Church of the Holy Apostles put up by Constantine and now falling into decay; with it were connected eight *madrasas* which were regarded as the most celebrated schools of theology in the Empire, and to which the most eminent scholars were constantly appointed as professors. By such means Sultan Muḥammad sought to assure that the new imperial capital also held pre-eminence within the Empire on the religious plane.

The capture of Constantinople by Muḥammad II marked the conclusion of a development in the imperial capital on the Bosphorus which had begun two and a half centuries previously. The conquest by the Latins in 1204 had inflicted a blow from which it never recovered. The Palaeologi who recaptured it in 1261 had not the necessary resources to hold in check the decay that increasingly gained ground; the constantly growing Turkish menace also militated against effective recuperation. So it came about that when Muḥammad II captured Constantinople in 1453 he took over a city lying in ruins, except for one or two old and monumental buildings such as St Sophia, the Church of St Irene and a few more churches which were in a reasonable state of preservation; others, like Constantine's Church of the Holy Apostles, were in a dilapidated condition.

The racial composition of the city had also materially altered since 1204. There had been an increase of Latin elements, particularly members of the Italian mercantile republics most of whom were Genoese, who did not in fact inhabit the ancient city of Byzantium enclosed within the Theodosian wall, but were quartered in Galata on the farther shore of the Golden Horn, under their own political leaders. But from the fourteenth century onwards more and more Turks entered the city, and Bāyezīd I had obtained for these the allocation of a special quarter and the permission to build a mosque (*c.* 1400). They too were almost independent of the suzerainty of the weakened late Byzantine Empire, and came under the jurisdiction of a Qadi. All that was necessary to reorganise the captured city was for the Turks to take over the political control from the Greeks.

After the conquest of 1453 Constantinople experienced under the Sultans of the following century a new era of prosperity as a brilliant imperial capital, but now under the Muslim and not the Christian faith. For the Ottoman Empire as a whole the conquest of Constantinople did indeed represent the culmination of its development; it included both the peninsulas of Rumelia and Anatolia which projected from Europe and Asia to face each other across the straits, and the newly conquered city on the Bosphorus supplied its natural centre.

LISTS OF RULERS

These give some of the dynasties and rulers referred to in this work; fuller lists may be found in V. Grumel, *La chronologie*, and other authorities cited in the General Bibliography. Some dates are uncertain or controversial which may account for apparent inconsistencies.

1 Byzantine Emperors
2 Epirus and Thessalonica
3 The Morea
4 Venice (to 1205)
5 Bulgaria
6 Serbia
7 Armenia and Georgia
8 Caliphs
9 Seljuqs
   (A) Iran, Mesopotamia, Syria
   (B) Rūm
10 Ottomans (to 1481)

1. BYZANTINE EMPERORS

Constantine I	324–37	Philippicus Bardanes	711–13
Constantius II	337–61	Anastasius II	713–15
Julian	361–3	Theodosius III	715–17
Jovian	363–4	Leo III	717–41
Valens	364–78	Constantine V	741–75
Theodosius I	379–95	Leo IV	775–80
Arcadius	395–408	Constantine VI	780–97
Theodosius II	408–50	Irene	797–802
Marcian	450–7	Nicephorus I	802–11
Leo I	457–74	Stauracius	811
Leo II	474	Michael I Rangabe	811–13
Zeno	474–5	Leo V	813–20
Basiliscus	475–6	Michael II	820–9
Zeno (again)	476–91	Theophilus	829–42
Anastasius I	491–518	Michael III	842–67
Justin I	518–27	Basil I	867–86
Justinian I	527–65	Leo VI	886–912
Justin II	565–78	Alexander	912–13
Tiberius II Constantine	578–82	Constantine VII	913–59
Maurice	582–602	Romanus I Lecapenus	920–44
Phocas	602–10	Romanus II	959–63
Heraclius	610–41	Nicephorus II Phocas	963–9
Constantine III and Heraclonas	641	John I Tzimisces	969–76
		Basil II	976–1025
Constans II	641–68	Constantine VIII	1025–8
Constantine IV	668–85	Romanus III Argyrus	1028–34
Justinian II	685–95	Michael IV the Paphlagonian	1034–41
Leontius	695–8		
Tiberius III	698–705	Michael V Calaphates	1041–2
Justinian II (again)	705–11	Zoe and Theodora	1042

Constantine IX Monomachus	1042–55	(ruling from Nicaea, 1204–61)	
		Constantine (XI) Lascaris	1204
Theodora (again)	1055–6	Theodore I Lascaris	1204–22
Michael VI Stratioticus	1056–7	John III Ducas Vatatzes	1222–54
Isaac I Comnenus	1057–9		
Constantine X Ducas	1059–67	Theodore II Lascaris	1254–8
Eudocia	1067	John IV Lascaris	1258–61
Romanus IV Diogenes	1068–71	Michael VIII Palaeologus	1259–82
Eudocia (again)	1071		
Michael VII Ducas	1071–8	Andronicus II Palaeologus	1282–1328
Nicephorus III Botaneiates	1078–81		
		Andronicus III Palaeologus	1328–41
Alexius I Comnenus	1081–1118		
John II Comnenus	1118–43	Michael IX Palaeologus	1294–1320
Manuel I Comnenus	1143–80	John V Palaeologus	1341–91
Alexius II Comnenus	1180–3	John VI Cantacuzenus	1347–54
Andronicus I Comnenus	1183–5	Andronicus IV Palaeologus	1376–9
Isaac II Angelus	1185–95		
Alexius III Angelus	1195–1203	John VII Palaeologus	1390
Isaac II (again) and Alexius IV Angeli	1203–4	Manuel II Palaeologus	1391–1425
		John VIII Palaeologus	1425–48
Alexius V Murtzuphlus	1204	Constantine XI (XII) Palaeologus	1449–53

2. EPIRUS AND THESSALONICA

(i) *Rulers and Despots of Epirus*

Michael I (without the title of Despot)	1204–c. 1215	[conquered in 1339 by the Byzantine Emperor Andronicus III and then in 1348 by the Serbian Stephen Dušan]	
Theodore (probably without the title of Despot)	c. 1215–25		
[Constantine?	1225–c. 1230]	Symeon Uroš Palaeologus	1349–56
Michael II	c. 1230–?before 1268	Nicephorus II (again)	1356–9
Nicephorus I	? before 1268–c. 1290	[various Serbian, Albanian and Italian rulers in Arta and in Joannina 1359– 1460, followed by the Turkish conquest]	
Thomas	c. 1290–1318		
Nicholas Orsini	1318–23		
John Orsini	1323–35		
Nicephorus II	1335–9		

(ii) *Emperors and Despots of Thessalonica*

Theodore (Emperor)	1225–30	Demetrius (Despot)	1244–46
Manuel (Despot)	1230–37/40	[Conquered by John III Vatatzes of Nicaea in 1246]	
John (Emperor until 1242, then Despot)	1237/40–44		

3. THE MOREA (MISTRA)

Byzantine Despots of the Morea

Manuel Cantacuzenus, son of John VI	1348–80	Theodore II Palaeologus, son of Manuel II (alone) with his brothers Constantine and Thomas	1407–28 1428–43
Matthew Cantacuzenus, son of John VI	1380–3		
Demetrius Cantacuzenus, son of Matthew	1383	Constantine and Thomas (in 1449 Constantine became Emperor)	1443–9
Theodore I Palaeologus, son of John V	1383–1407	Thomas and his brother Demetrius	1449–60

4. VENICE (TO 1205)

(compiled by R. Cessi)

Paulicius patricius, exarch of Ravenna	723–7	Peter I Candiano	April– September 887
Marcellus magister militum	?–727	Peter Tribuno	April 888–
Ursus dux	727–38		May 912
Dominicus magister militum	739	Orso II Badoer Paureta	May 912–932
Felix Cornicula magister militum	740	Peter II Candiano	932–9
		Peter Badoer	939–42
Deusdedit, Ursi ducis filius, magister militum	741	Peter III Candiano	942–59
		Peter IV Candiano	959–11 June 976
Jovianus Ypatus magister militum	742		
		Peter I Orseolo	July 976– August 978
Johannes Fabricius magister militum	743	Vitale Candiano	September 978– October 979
Deusdedit, Ursi ducis filius, dux	744–56	Tribuno Menio	December 979–991
Galla Gaulus	756	Peter II Orseolo	991–September 1008
Domenicus Monegarius	756–65		
Maurice	765–87	Otto Orseolo	1008–26
John and Maurice II	787–802	Domenico Barbolano Centranico	1026–30
Obelerius	802–10		
Beatus	808–10	Orso Orseolo (also patriarch of Grado)	1030–2
Agnellus Partecipazio	810–27		
Justinian Partecipazio	819–29	Domenico Orseolo	1032
John Partecipazio	829–36	Domenico Flabianico	1032–43
Peter (vulgo Trasdominico)	836–15 March 864	Domenico Contarini	1043–70
		Domenico Silvo	1070–84
Orso I Badoer	864–81	Vitale Faliero	1084–96
John Badoer	881–8 April 888	Vitale I Michiel	1096–1101

Ordelaffo Faliero	1101–18	Sebastiano Ziani	27 May 1172–
Domenico Michiel	1118–29		12 April 1178
Peter Polani (ante Sept.)	1129–1148	Orio Malipiero	14 April 1178–
Domenico	1148–February 1155		21 June 1192
Morosini		Enrico Dandolo	21 June 1192–
Vitale II Michiel	February 1155–		1 June 1205
	27 May 1172		

5. BULGARIA

Early Period and First Bulgarian Empire

Early rulers

Asparuch (Isperich)	681–702
Tervel	702–18
(not known)	718–25
Sevar	725–40
Kormisoš	740–56
Vinech	756–62
Telec	762–5
Sabin	765–7
Umar	767
Toktu	767–72
Pagan	772
Telerig	c. 772–7
Kardam	777–803

Dynasty of Krum

Krum	803–14
Omortag	814–31

Malamir	831–6
Presijan	836–52
Boris I Michael (I)	852–89
Vladimir	889–93
Symeon	893–927
Peter	927–69
Boris II	969–72

Macedonian Empire (the Comitopuli)

The Comitopuli brothers, David, Moses, Aaron and Samuel (sons of the *Comes* Nicholas)	976–c. 987
Samuel (ruling alone)	c. 987–1014
Gabriel Radomir	1014–15
John Vladislav	1015–18

Second Bulgarian Empire

Dynasty of Asen

Asen I	1187–96
Peter, his brother	1196–7
Kalojan, his brother	1197–1207
Boril, nephew of Kalojan	1207–18
John Asen II, son of Asen I	1218–41
Koloman, son of John Asen II	1241–6
Michael II Asen, son of John Asen II	1246–57
Constantine Tich	1257–77

Ivajlo, married widow of Tich	1277–9
John Asen III, nephew of Michael II Asen	1279–80

Dynasty of Terter

George I Terter, married sister of John Asen III	1280–92
Smilec	1292–8
Čaka, son of Nogaj, married daughter of George I	1299

Dynasty of Terter (*cont.*)

Theodore Svetoslav,   1300–22
son of George I

George II Terter, son   1322–3
of Theodore Svetoslav

Dynasty of Šišman

Michael Šišman   1323–30

John Stephen, son of   1330–1
Michael Šišman

John Alexander,   1331–71
nephew of Michael
Šišman

John Šišman, son of   1371–93
John Alexander (at
Trnovo)

John Stracimir (at   *c.* 1360–96
Vidin)

6. SERBIA

Dynasty of Nemanja

Stephen Nemanja,   *c.* 1168–96
Grand Župan [abdi-
cated, and died in 1200
as the monk Symeon
on Mount Athos]

Stephen, Grand Župan   1196–1217
King, the First   1217–27/8
Crowned

Stephen Radoslav   1227/8–34

Stephen Vladislav   1234–43

Stephen Uroš I   1243–76

Stephen Dragutin   1276–82

Stephen Uroš II Milutin   1282–1321

Stephen Uroš III   1321–31
Dečanski

Stephen Uroš IV Dušan,
King   1331–45
Emperor   1345–55

Stephen Uroš V   1355–71

7. ARMENIA AND GEORGIA

(*compiled by C. Toumanoff*)

Armenian princes appointed to be Iranian viceroys (*marzpāns*)
of Armenia

Vasak I[1] of Siunia, *c.* 442–51

[Isaac II of the Bagratids, insurgent Viceroy, 482–3]

Vahan of the Mamikonids, autonomous Viceroy, 485–505/10

Vard Mamikonean, autonomous Viceroy, 505/10–509/14

Mezezius (Mžēž) I Gnuni, 518–48

Philip Siwni, 574–6

Mušeł II of the Mamikonids, 591 ?

Varaz-Tiroc' II of the Bagratids, 628–after 631

---

[1] The ordinal numbers of the viceroys and the presiding princes of Armenia are (save when in parentheses) those of heads of individual families. In some families, the surname of the head may differ from that of the other members; thus, 'of the Bagratids', 'of the Mamikonids', 'of Siunia' apply to the reigning heads of these princely dynasties, and 'Bagratuni', 'Mamikonean', 'Siwni' to cadets. The ordinal numbers of the kings continue those of the princes, their predecessors. The only exception is Armenia, its monarchy being in no sense a continuation of the Bagratid princely State, but the restoration of a vaster realm.

Presiding princes of Armenia[1]

Mezezius II Gnuni, Commander-in-chief of the Imperial troops, 628–35
David Saharuni, Curopalate, 635–8
Theodore Ṛštuni, High Constable and Patrician, 638–*c.* 645
Varaz-Tiroc' II of the Bagratids, Curopalate, *c.* 645–645
Theodore Ṛštuni, High Constable for the Emperor, 645–53; for the Caliph, 653/4–55
Mušeł II Mamikonean, Master of the Horse for the Emperor; passes to the Caliph, 654
Hamazasp II of the Mamikonids, for the Caliph, 655–7; Curopalate, for the Emperor, 657–8
Gregory (I) Mamikonean, for the Caliph, 662–84/5
Ašot II of the Bagratids, for the Caliph, 686–89/90
Nerseh Kamsarakan, Curopalate, for the Emperor, 689/90–1
Smbat VI of the Bagratids, Patrician, for the Emperor, 691–7; for the Caliph, 697–700; Curopalate, for the Emperor, 700–11
Ašot III of the Bagratids, for the Caliph, 732–48
Gregory (II) Mamikonean, for the Caliph, 748–50
[Mušeł Mamikonean, head of the insurgent Princes, *c.* 750]
Isaac (III) Bagratuni, High Constable, for the Caliph, *c.* 755–61
Smbat VII of the Bagratids, High Constable, for the Caliph, 761–72
Tačat Anjewac'i, for the Caliph, 780–82/5
Ašot IV of the Bagratids, for the Caliph, 806–26
Smbat VIII of the Bagratids, High Constable, for the Caliph, 826–55
Bagarat II Bagratuni of Tarawn, Prince of Princes, for the Caliph, 830–52
Ašot V of the Bagratids, High Constable, 856; Prince of Princes, for the Caliph, *c.* 862–85
Ašot I Bagratuni of Tarawn, Curopalate, for the Emperor, 877–8

Presiding princes of Iberia[2]

Guaram I the Guaramid, Curopalate, for the Emperor, 588–*c.* 590
Stephen I the Guaramid, passes to the Great King, *c.* 590–627
Adarnase I the Chosroid, Patrician, for the Emperor, 627–37/42
Stephen II the Chosroid, Patrician, for the Emperor, 637/42–645; for the Caliph, 645–*c.* 650 ?
Adarnase II the Chosroid, for the Caliph, *c.* 650 ?; Patrician, for the Emperor, *c.* 662–84/5
Guaram II the Guaramid, for the Caliph, 684/5–89; Curopalate, for the Emperor, 689–before 693
Guaram III the Guaramid, Curopalate, for the Emperor, before 693; for the Caliph, 693–*c.* 748

[1] Bearing the title of Prince (*išxan*), unless otherwise specified (as, High Constable, Master of the Horse, Prince of Princes). The Arabs applied to the presiding princes of Armenia, Iberia, and Albania the title of *baṭrīq*, i.e. 'Patrician'.

[2] This list is, with some modifications (in the case of Adarnase I, Stephen II, and Adarnase II), based on C. Toumanoff, *Iberia on the Eve of Bagratid Rule.*

Adarnase III Nersiani, Curopalate, for the Emperor, *c.* 748–60
Nerse Nersiani, for the Emperor, *c.* 760–72; for the Caliph, 775–79/80
Stephen III the Guaramid, for the Caliph, 779/780–6
Ašot I Bagrationi (Bagratuni), Curopalate, for the Emperor and the
    Caliph, 813–30
Bagrat I Bagrationi, Curopalate, for the same, 842/3–76
David I Bagrationi, Curopalate, for the same, 876–81
Gurgen I Bagrationi, Curopalate, for the Emperor, 881–91

Kings of Armenia (*Bagratid Dynasty*)

Ašot I (V) the Great, 885–90
Smbat I (IX) the Martyr (*son*), 890–914
Ašot II (VI) the Iron (*son*), King of Kings, 914–28
Abas I (*brother*), 928–52
Ašot III (VII) the Merciful (*son*), 952–77
Smbat II (X) the Conqueror (*son*), 977–89
Gagik I (*brother*), 989–1020
John-Smbat III (XI) (*son*), 1020–40
Ašot IV (VIII) the Valiant (*brother*), 1021–39
Gagik II (*son*), 1042–5 [cedes Armenia to the Empire]; † *c.* 1079

Kings and Curopalates of Iberia (*Bagratid Dynasty*)

Adarnase IV, King, 888–923, Curopalate, 891–923 [kings of Abasgia con-
    trol Iberia, 912–75]
David II (*son*), tit. King, 923–37
  Ašot II (*brother*), Curopalate, 923–54
  Sumbat I (*brother*), Curopalate, 954–8 (and tit. King, 937–58)
Bagrat II the Simple (*son*), tit. King, 958–94
  Adarnase (III) (*son of Bagrat, Sumbat's brother*), Curopalate, 958–61
  David II the Great (*son*), Curopalate, 990–1000
Gurgen I (*son of Bagrat II*), co-King, 975; King of Kings, 994–1008
Bagrat III (*son*), Curopalate, 1000; King of Kings, 1008

Kings of Abasgia[1] (*Ančʻabad Dynasty*)

Leo II, 767/8–811/12
Theodosius II (*son*), 811/12–837/8
Demetrius II (*brother*), 837/8–872/3
George I Ağcʻepʻeli (*brother*), 872/3–878/9
John Šavliani (*outsider*), 878/9–*c.* 880
Adarnase Šavliani (*son*), *c.* 880–887/8
Bagrat I (*son of Demetrius II*), 887/8–898/9
Constantine III (*son*), 898/9–916/17

---

[1] See C. Toumanoff, 'Chronology of the Kings of Abasgia', *Le Muséon*, LXIX
(1956).

George II (*son*), 916/17–960/1. Co-King: Bagrat II (*brother*)
Leo III (*son of George II*), 960/1–969/70
Demetrius III (*brother*), 969/70–976/7
Theodosius III (*brother*), 976/7–978/9
Bagrat III Bagrationi of Iberia (*nephew*), 978/9

Kings of Georgia (Abasgia and Iberia) (Bagratid Dynasty)

Bagrat III, 1008–14; Curopalate, 1000
George I (*son*), 1014–27
Bagrat IV (*son*), 1027–72; Curopalate, 1031/2; *Nobilissimus, c.* 1052;
　Sebastus, c. 1060
George II (*son*), 1072–89; Curopalate, *c.* 1060; Caesar, *c.* 1081
David III (II)[1] the Builder (*son*), 1089–1125 (*Panhypersebastus*). Co-
　Kings: George II, 1089–1112; Demetrius (I), 1125
Demetrius I (*son*), 1125–55, 1155–6
David IV (III) (*son*), 1155
George III (*brother*), 1156–84. Co-ruler: Thamar, 1179
Thamar the Great (*daughter*), 1184–1212. Co-Kings: David Soslan (*cousin
　and consort*), *c.* 1193–1207; George (IV), 1205
George IV the Resplendent (*son*), 1212–23
Rusudan (*sister*), 1223–45. Co-King: David (V), 1234
[Interregnum, 1245–50]
David V (IV) (*son*), 1250–8 [secedes in Abasgia, or Imeretia]
David VI (V) (*son of George IV*), 1250–69
[Interregnum, 1269–73]
Demetrius II the Devoted (*son*), 1273–89
Vaxtang II of Imeretia (*son of David V*), 1289–92. Co-King: David (VII),
　1291
David VII (VI) (*son of Demetrius II*), 1292–1301. Co-King: George (VI),
　1299
Vaxtang III (*brother*), 1301–7. Co-Kings: David (VII) and George (VI)
George V The Little[1] (*son of David VII*), 1307–14. Co-Kings: David
　(VII, † 1310), and George (VI), Regent
George VI the Illustrious[1] (*son of Demetrius II*), 1314–46 [Imeretia
　recovered]
David VIII (VII) (*son*), 1346–60. Co-King Bagrat (V), *c.* 1355
Bagrat V the Great (*son*), 1360–95. Co-King: George (VII), 1369 [Imeretia
　lost]
George VII (*son*), 1395–1405
Constantine I (*brother*), 1405–12. Co-Kings: Alexander (I), Bagrat,
　George (*sons*), *c.* 1408
Alexander I the Great (*son*), 1412–42 († 1446). Co-Kings: Vaxtang (IV),
　Demetrius (III), George (VIII) in Kakhetia, Zaal († *c.* 1438) (*sons*),
　1433 [Imeretia recovered]

---

[1] See above, chapter xiv, p. 627, note 1.

Vaxtang IV (*son*), 1442–6. Co-Kings: Demetrius (III) and George (VIII)
Demetrius III (*brother*), 1446–53 *de jure*
George VIII (*brother*), 1446–65 *de facto*. Co-King: Alexander (*son*),
   c. 1460 [secedes in Kakhetia as George I, 1466–76]
Bagrat VI (*son of George, Alexander I's brother*), 1465–78. Co-King:
   Constantine (II), *c.* 1465
Constantine II (*son of Demetrius III*), 1478–1505 [partition of Georgia:
   Alexander, son of George VIII, is recognised as King of Kakhetia
   in 1490 and Alexander, son of Bagrat VI, is recognised as King of
   Imeretia in 1491]

Kings of Kars (*Bagratid Dynasty*)

Mušeḷ (*son of Abas I of Armenia*), 962–84
Abas I (*son*), 984–1029
Gagik-Abas II (*son*), 1029–64 († 1080) [cedes Kars to the Empire]

Kings of Loṛi and Albania (*Bagratid Dynasty*)

Gurgēn I (*son of Ašot III of Armenia*), 982–9
David Lackland (*son*), 989–1046/8
Gurgēn II-Kvirike (*son*), 1046/8–1081/9 [Loṛi annexed by the Seljuqs]

Kings of Vaspurakan (*Arcruni Dynasty*)

Xač'ik-Gagik, 908–36/7
Derenik-Ašot (*son*), 936/7–53
Abusahl-Hamazasp (*brother*), 953–72
Ašot-Isaac (*son*), 972–83
Gurgēn-Xač'ik (*brother*), 983–1003
Sennacherib-John (*brother*), 1003–21, [cedes Vaspurakan to the Empire],
   † 1027

Kings of Siunia
A. Line of Siunia

Smbat II, 963–*c.* 998
Vasak VI (*son*), *c.* 998–1019
Smbat III (*cousin and nephew*), 1019–?
Gregory V (*brother*), ?–*c.* 1091

B. Line of Gardman-Albania

John-Sennacherib (*adopted son of Gregory V*), *c.* 1091–1105
Gregory VI (*son*), 1105–66

Kings of Kakhetia
A.

Kvirike III the Great, 1010–29

B. (*Bagratid Dynasty*)

Gagik of Loṛi (*son of David Lackland and nephew of Kvirike III*), 1029–58
Ağsart'an I (*son*), 1058–84
Kvirike IV (*son*), 1084–1102
Ağsart'an II (*nephew*), 1102–5 [Kakhetia annexed by Georgia]

Princes and kings of Little or Cilician Armenia (*Armenia in Exile*)
A. (*Rubenid Dynasty*)

Ruben I, 1080–95
Constantine I (*son*), 1095–9
Theodore I (*son*), 1100–29
Leo I (*brother*), 1129–38, †1141
[Cilicia occupied by the Byzantines, 1138–45]
Theodore II (*son*), 1145–69
Ruben II (*son*), 1169–70
Mlēh (*uncle*), 1170–5
Ruben III (*nephew*), 1175–86
Leo II (I) the Great (*brother*), 1186–98/9; King of Armenia, 1198/9–1219
Isabel (*daughter*), 1219–22
Philip of Antioch (*consort*), 1222–5

B. (*Het'umid Dynasty*)

Het'um I of Lambron (*second consort of Isabel*), 1226–69 (†1270)
Leo III (II) (*son*), 1269–89
Het'um II (*son*), 1289–93, 1294–6, 1299–1305 (†1308)
Theodore III (I) (*brother*), 1293–4 (†1299)
Smbat (*brother*), 1296–8
Constantine II (I) (*brother*), 1298–9
Leo IV (III) (*son of Theodore III*), 1305–8
Ōšin (*son of Leo III*), 1308–20
Leo V (IV) (*son*), 1320–41

C. (*Lusignan Dynasty*)

Guy I de Lusignan (*cousin of Leo V*), 1342–4; Regent: John de Lusignan[1]
    (*brother*), 1342
Constantine III (II) (*outsider*), 1344–63
Constantine IV (III) (*cousin*), 1365–73
Peter de Lusignan, King of Cyprus, invited, 1368–9
Leo VI (V) de Lusignan (*Guy's nephew*), 1373–5 [Mamluk conquest of
    Little Armenia]

[1] See above, chapter XIV, p. 636, note 1.

8. CALIPHS

(giving the year of the Hegira and of the Christian era)

A. Direct descendants of the Prophet

Abu Bakr	11/632	'Uthmān ('Osmān)	23/644
'Umar	13/634	'Alī	35/656

B. Umayyads

Mu'āwiya I	41/661	'Umar II	99/717
Yazīd I	60/680	Yazīd II	101/720
Mu'āwiya II	64/683	Hishām	105/724
Marwān I	64/684	al-Walīd II	125/743
'Abd-al-Malik	65/685	Yazīd III	126/744
al-Walīd I	86/705	Marwān II	127/744
Sulaymān	96/715		

C. Abbasids

as-Saffāḥ	132/750	al-Muttaqī	329/940
al-Manṣūr	136/754	al-Mustakfī	333/944
al-Mahdī	158/775	al-Mutī'	334/946
al-Hādī	169/785	aṭ-Ṭā'i'	363/974
Hārūn ar-Rashīd	170/786	al-Qādir	381/991
al-Amīn	193/809	al-Qā'im	422/1031
al-Ma'mūn	198/813	al-Muqtadī	467/1075
al-Mu'taṣim	218/833	al-Mustazhir	487/1094
al-Wāthiq	227/842	al-Mustarshid	512/1118
al-Mutawakkil	232/847	ar-Rāshid	529/1135
al-Muntaṣir	247/861	al-Muqtafī	530/1136
al-Musta'īn	248/862	al-Mustanjid	555/1160
al-Mu'tazz	252/866	al-Mustadī	566/1170
al-Muhtadī	255/869	an-Nāṣir	575/1180
al-Mu'tamid	256/870	az-Ẓāhir	622/1225
al-Mu'taḍid	279/892	al-Mustanṣir	623/1226
al-Muqtafi	289/902	al-Musta'ṣim	640/1258
al-Muqtadir	295/908	[Early 1258, Baghdad sacked by
al-Qāhir	320/932	the Mongols under Hülegü]
ar-Rāḍī	322/934		

9. SELJUQS

A. *Early Seljuqs of Iran, Mesopotamia, Syria*

Ṭughrîl Beg	1055–63	Malik-Shāh	1072–92
Alp Arslan	1063–72	Maḥmūd	1092–4

B. *Rūm*

Sulaymān ibn	*c.* 1077–86	Kaykāwūs I	1210–19
Kutlumish		Kayqubād I	1219–37
Kîlîj Arslan I	1092–1107	Kaykhusraw II	1236–45
Malik-Shāh	1107–16	Kaykāwūs II ('Izz ad-Dīn)	1246–59
Mas'ūd I	1116–55	Kîlîj Arslan IV	1248–64
Kîlîj Arslan II	1155–92	Kayqubād II	1249–57
Kaykhusraw I	1192–6	Kaykhusraw III	1264–82
Sulaymān II	1196–1204	Mas'ūd II	1282–1304
Kîlîj Arslan III	1203	Kayqubād III	1298–?1301
Kaykhusraw I (again)	1204–10	Mas'ūd III	1307–8

10. OTTOMANS (TO 1481)

'Osmān	1299–1326	Muḥammad (Meḥmed) I	1413–21
Orkhan	1326–60	(sole ruler)	
Murād I	1360–89	Murād II	1421–51
Bāyezīd I	1389–1402	Muḥammad (Meḥmed) II	1451–81
Struggle between Īsā,	1402–13	the Conqueror	
Muḥammad (Meḥmed),			
Sulaymān and Mūsā			

GENEALOGICAL TABLES

The names of Byzantine Emperors are given in capitals. These tables do not claim to be complete. Additional tables may be found in V. Grumel, *La chronologie*, and in other works of reference cited in the General Bibliography. Tables 9 and 10 were compiled by D. M. Nicol.

For reasons of space members of families in the tables are not always placed in order of birth; where practicable this is indicated on the trees.

1　Dynasty of Heraclius
2　North Syrian or Isaurian Dynasty
3　Amorian or Phrygian Dynasty
4　Macedonian Dynasty
5　Dynasty of Ducas
6　Dynasty of Comnenus
7　Dynasty of Angelus
8　Dynasty of Lascaris
9　Dynasty of Palaeologus
10　Greek, Italian and Serbian rulers of Epirus, Thessalonica and Thessaly

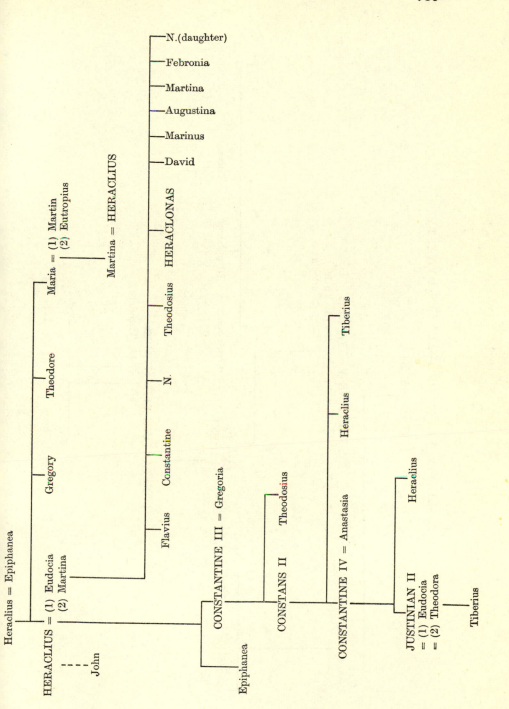

789

790

2. NORTH SYRIAN OR ISAURIAN DYNASTY

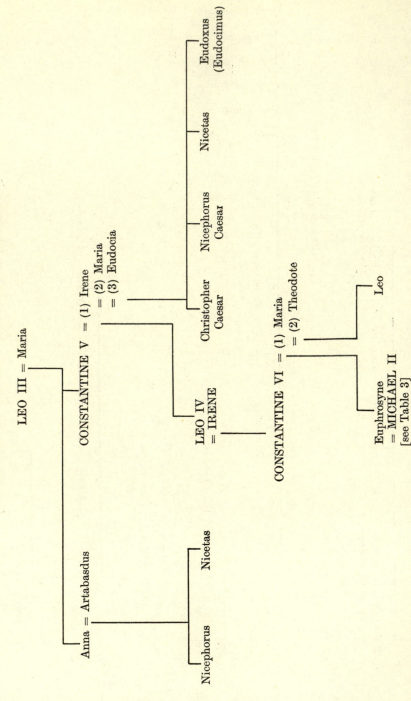

3. AMORIAN OR PHRYGIAN DYNASTY

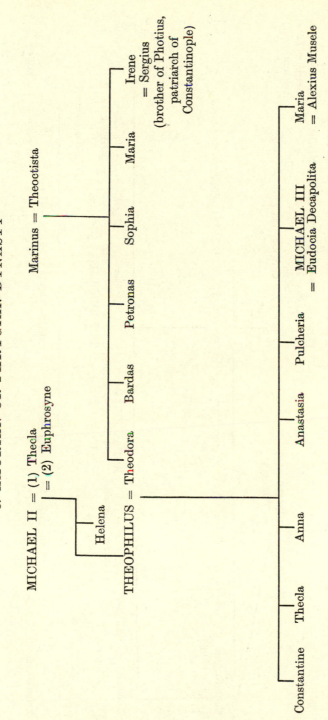

MICHAEL II = (1) Thecla
= (2) Euphrosyne

Marinus = Theoctista

Helena

THEOPHILUS = Theodora

Bardas   Petronas   Sophia   Maria   Irene
= Sergius
(brother of Photius,
patriarch of
Constantinople)

Constantine   Thecla   Anna   Anastasia   Pulcheria   MICHAEL III   Maria
= Eudocia Decapolita   = Alexius Musele

4. MACEDONIAN DYNASTY

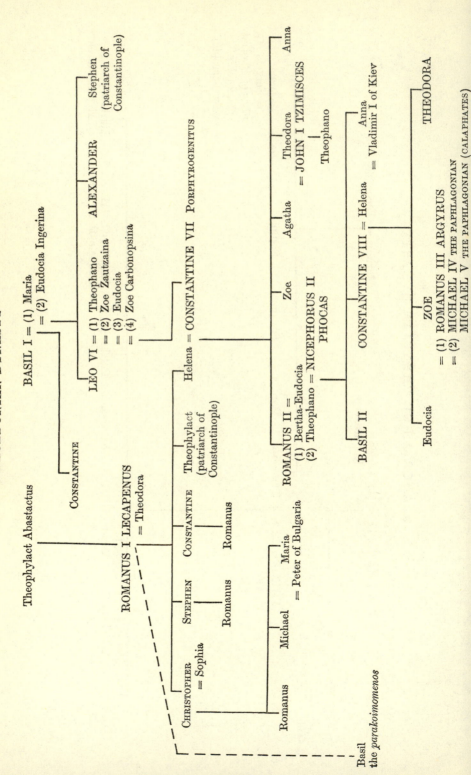

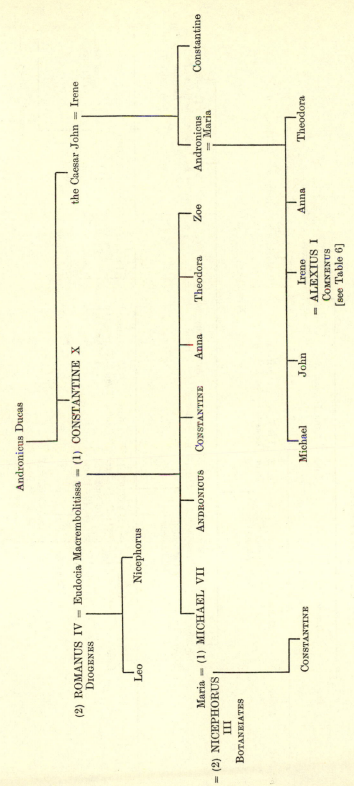

5. DYNASTY OF DUCAS

Andronicus Ducas

			the Caesar John = Irene

(2) ROMANUS IV = Eudocia Macrembolitissa = (1) CONSTANTINE X
DIOGENES

Leo   Nicephorus

Maria = (1) MICHAEL VII   ANDRONICUS   CONSTANTINE   Anna   Theodora   Zoe   Andronicus
= (2) NICEPHORUS   = Maria
III
BOTANEIATES

Constantine   Michael   John   Irene   Anna   Theodora   Constantine
                              = ALEXIUS I
                              COMNENUS
                              [see Table 6]

6. DYNASTY OF COMNENUS

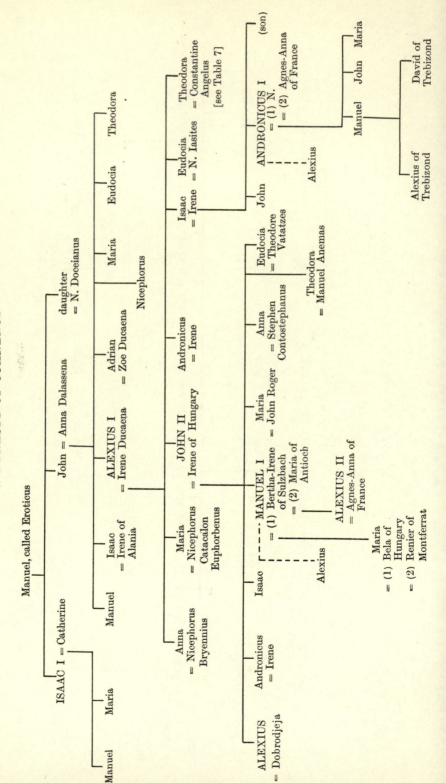

7. DYNASTY OF ANGELUS

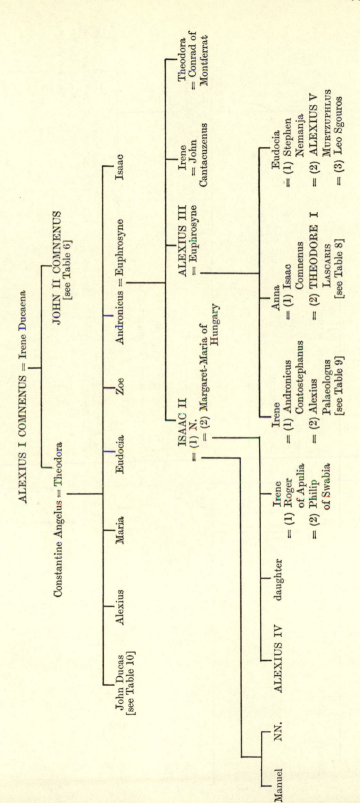

8 DYNASTY OF LASCARIS

N.

Manuel | Michael | CONSTANTINE (XI) | Alexius | Isaac

THEODORE I LASCARIS
= (1) Anna, d. of Alexius III
= (2) Philippa, niece of
Leo II of Armenia
= (3) Maria of Courtenay

Constantine

1.
Irene
= (1) Andronicus Palaeologus
= (2) JOHN III DUCAS VATATZES

2.
Maria
= Bela IV of Hungary

3.
Eudocia
= Anseau of Cahieu

4.
Nicholas

5.
John

THEODORE II LASCARIS
= Helena, d. of John Asen II

= (2) Anna (Constance) of Hohenstaufen

Irene
= Constantine Tich

Maria
= Nicephorus I of Epirus

JOHN IV LASCARIS

Theodora
= Matthew of Walincourt

Eudocia
= Count of Ventimiglia

N.

Isaac Ducas

John Ducas Vatatzes
= Eudocia, d. of John Angelus

d.
= Constantine, son of Alexius Strategopulus

Michael Strategopulus

Theodora
= MICHAEL VIII PALAEOLOGUS

N.

d.
= Alexius Raoul

ECCLESIASTICAL LISTS

1. POPES, 314–1455

Sylvester I	314–35	Honorius I	625–38
Mark	336	Severinus	640
Julius	337–52	John IV	640–2
Liberius	352–66	Theodore I	642–9
(Felix II	355–65)	Martin I	649–55
Damasus I	366–84	Eugenius I	654–7
(Ursinus	366–7)	Vitalian	657–72
Siricius	384–99	Deusdedit II	672–6
Anastasius I	399–401	Domnus	676–8
Innocent I	401–17	Agatho	678–81
Zosimus	417–18	Leo II	682–3
Boniface I	418–22	Benedict II	684–5
(Eulalius	418–19)	John V	685–6
Celestine I	422–32	Conon	686–7
Sixtus III	432–40	(Theodore	687)
Leo I the Great	440–61	(Pascal	687)
Hilary	461–8	Sergius I	687–701
Simplicius	468–83	John VI	701–5
Felix III (II)	483–92	John VII	705–7
Gelasius I	492–6	Sisinnius	708
Anastasius II	496–8	Constantine I	708–15
Symmachus	498–514	Gregory II	715–31
(Laurence	498, 501–5)	Gregory III	731–41
Hormisdas	514–23	Zacharias	741–52
John I	523–6	(Stephen II	752)
Felix IV (III)	526–30	Stephen III (II)	752–7
Boniface II	530–2	Paul I	757–67
(Dioscorus	530)	(Constantine	767–9)
John II	533–5	(Philip	768)
Agapetus I	535–6	Stephen IV	768–72
Silverius	536–7	Hadrian I	772–95
Vigilius	537–55	Leo III	795–816
Pelagius I	556–61	Stephen V	816–17
John III	561–74	Pascal I	817–24
Benedict I	575–79	Eugenius II	824–7
Pelagius II	579–90	Valentine	827
Gregory I the Great	590–604	Gregory IV	827–44
Sabinian	604–6	(John	844)
Boniface III	607	Sergius II	844–7
Boniface IV	608–15	Leo IV	847–55
Deusdedit I	615–18	Benedict III	855–8
Boniface V	619–25	(Anastasius	855, d. c. 880)

Nicholas I	858–67	Gregory VI	1045–6
Hadrian II	867–72	Clement II	1046–7
John VIII	872–82	Benedict IX (again)	1047–8
Marinus I	882–4	Damasus II	1048
Hadrian III	884–5	Leo IX	1049–54
Stephen VI	885–91	Victor II	1055–7
Formosus	891–6	Stephen X	1057–8
Boniface VI	896	(Benedict X	1058–9)
Stephen VII	896–7	Nicholas II	1059–61
Romanus	897	Alexander II	1061–73
Theodore II	897	(Honorius II	1061–72)
John IX	898–900	Gregory VII	1073–85
Benedict IV	900–3	(Clement III	1080–1100)
Leo V	903	Victor III	1086–7
(Christopher	903–4)	Urban II	1088–99
Sergius III	904–11	Pascal II	1099–1118
Anastasius III	911–13	(Theodoric	1100, d. 1102)
Lando	913–14	(Albert	1102)
John X	914–28	(Sylvester IV	1105–11)
Leo VI	928	Gelasius II	1118–19
Stephen VIII	928–31	(Gregory VIII	1118–21)
John XI	931–5	Calixtus II	1119–24
Leo VII	936–9	Honorius II	1124–30
Stephen IX	939–42	(Celestine II	1124)
Marinus II	942–6	Innocent II	1130–43
Agapetus II	946–55	(Anacletus II	1130–8)
John XII	955–64	(Victor IV	1138)
Leo VIII	963–5	Celestine II	1143–4
Benedict V	964–6	Lucius II	1144–5
John XIII	965–72	Eugenius III	1145–53
Benedict VI	973–4	Anastasius IV	1153–4
(Boniface VII	974, and 984–5)	Hadrian IV	1154–9
Benedict VII	974–83	Alexander III	1159–81
John XIV	983–4	(Victor IV	1159–64)
John XV	985–96	(Pascal III	1164–8)
Gregory V	996–9	(Calixtus III	1168–78)
(John XVI	997–8)	(Innocent III	1179–80)
Sylvester II	999–1003	Lucius III	1181–5
John XVII	1003	Urban III	1185–7
John XVIII	1004–9	Gregory VIII	1187
Sergius IV	1009–12	Clement III	1187–91
Benedict VIII	1012–24	Celestine III	1191–8
(Gregory	1012)	Innocent III	1198–1216
John XIX	1024–32	Honorius III	1216–27
Benedict IX	1032–44	Gregory IX	1227–41
Sylvester III	1045	Celestine IV	1241
Benedict IX (again)	1045	Innocent IV	1243–54

Alexander IV	1254–61	Benedict XII	1334–42
Urban IV	1261–4	Clement VI	1342–52
Clement IV	1265–8	Innocent VI	1352–62
Gregory X	1271–6	Urban V	1362–70
Innocent V	1276	Gregory XI	1370–8
Hadrian V	1276	Urban VI	1378–89
John XXI	1276–7	Boniface IX	1389–1404
Nicholas III	1277–80	Innocent VII	1404–6
Martin IV	1281–5	Gregory XII	1406–15
Honorius IV	1285–7	(Clement VII	1378–94)
Nicholas IV	1288–92	(Benedict XIII	1394–1423)
Celestine V	1294 (d. 1296)	(Alexander V	1409–10)
Boniface VIII	1294–1303	(John XXIII	1410–15)
Benedict XI	1303–4	Martin V	1417–31
Clement V	1305–14	Eugenius IV	1431–47
John XXII	1316–34	(Felix V	1439–49)
(Nicholas V	1328–30)	Nicholas V	1447–55

2. PATRIARCHS OF CONSTANTINOPLE, 381–1456

Nectarius	381–97	Sergius I	610–38
John I Chrysostom	398–404	Pyrrhus	638–41
Arsacius	404–5	Paul II	641–53
Atticus	406–25	Pyrrhus (again)	654
Sisinnius I	426–7	Peter	654–66
Nestorius	428–31	Thomas II	667–9
Maximian	431–4	John V	669–75
Proclus	434–46	Constantine I	675–7
Flavian	446–9	Theodore I	677–9
Anatolius	449–58	George I	679–86
Gennadius I	458–71	Theodore I (again)	686–7
Acacius	472–89	Paul III	688–94
Fravitas	489–90	Callinicus I	694–706
Euphemius	490–6	Cyrus	706–12
Macedonius II	496–511	John VI	712–15
Timothy I	511–18	Germanus I	715–30
John II Cappadox	518–20	Anastasius	730–54
Epiphanius	520–35	Constantine II	754–66
Anthimus I	535–6	Nicetas I	766–80
Menas	536–52	Paul IV	780–4
Eutychius	552–65	Tarasius	784–806
John III Scholasticus	565–77	Nicephorus I	806–15
Eutychius (again)	577–82	Theodotus Melissenus	815–21
John IV the Faster	582–95	Cassiteras	
Cyriacus	595–606	Antony I Cassimatas	821–37
Thomas I	607–10	John VII Grammaticus	837–43

Methodius I	843–7	Chariton Eugeniotes	1178–9
Ignatius	847–58	Theodosius Boradiotes	1179–83
Photius	858–67	Basil II Camaterus	1183–6
Ignatius (again)	867–77	Nicetas II Muntanes	1186–9
Photius (again)	877–86	Dositheus of	1189
Stephen I	886–93	Jerusalem	
Antony II Cauleas	893–901	Leontius Theotokites	1189
Nicholas I Mysticus	901–7	Dositheus of Jerusalem	1189–91
Euthymius I	907–12	(again)	
Nicholas I Mysticus	912–25	George II Xiphilinus	1191–8
(again)		John X Camaterus	1198–1206
Stephen II	925–7	Michael IV	1208–14
Tryphon	927–31	Autorianus	
Theophylact	933–56	Theodore II	1214–16
Polyeuctus	956–70	Irenicus	
Basil I Scamandrenus	970–4	Maximus II	1216
Antony III the	974–9	Manuel I Sarantenus	1217–22
Studite		Germanus II	1222–40
Nicholas II	979–91	Methodius	1240
Chrysoberges		Manuel II	1244–54
(unoccupied 991–6)		Arsenius Autorianus	1255–9
Sisinnius II	996–8	Nicephorus II	1260
Sergius II	1001–19	Arsenius Autorianus	1261–4
Eustathius	1019–25	(again)	
Alexius the Studite	1025–43	Germanus III	1265–6
Michael I Cerularius	1043–58	Joseph I	1266–75
Constantine III	1059–63	John XI Beccus	1275–82
Leichudes		Joseph I (again)	1282–3
John VIII	1064–75	Gregory III (George of	1283–9
Xiphilinus		Cyprus)	
Cosmas I	1075–81	Athanasius I	1289–93
Eustratius Garidas	1081–4	John XII Cosmas	1294–1303
Nicholas III Kyrdi-	1084–1111	Athanasius I (again)	1303–9
niates Grammaticus		Niphon I	1310–14
John IX Agapetus	1111–34	John XIII Glykys	1315–19
Leo Stypes	1134–43	Gerasimus I	1320–1
Michael II Curcuas	1143–6	Isaias	1323–32
(Oxeites)		John XIV Calecas	1334–47
Cosmas II Atticus	1146–7	Isidore I	1347–50
Nicholas IV Muzalon	1147–51	Callistus I	1350–3
Theodotus II	1151–4	Philotheus Coccinus	1353–4
(Neophytus I	1153–4)	Callistus I (again)	1355–63
Constantine IV	1154–7	Philotheus Coccinus	1364–76
Chliarenus		(again)	
Luke Chrysoberges	1157–70	Macarius	1376–9
Michael III of	1170–8	Nilus	1379–88
Anchialus		Antony IV	1389–90

Macarius (again)	1390–1	Gregory III Mamme	1443–50
Antony IV (again)	1391–7		(when he
Callistus II Xanthopulus	1397		left Constantinople;
Matthew I	1397–1410		d. 1459)
Euthymius II	1410–16	Gennadius II Scholarius (first term of	1454–6
Joseph II	1416–39	office)	
Metrophanes II	1440–3		

BIBLIOGRAPHIES

LIST OF ABBREVIATIONS

AASS	*Acta Sanctorum Bollandiana* (see Gen. Bibl. IV).
AB	*Analecta Bollandiana* (Paris and Brussels, 1882–).
AcadIBL	*Académie des Inscriptions et Belles-lettres.*
AcadIP	*Académie Impériale de St Pétersbourg.*
AHR	*American Historical Review* (New York and London, 1895–).
AIPHO	*Annales de l'Institut de Philologie et d'Histoire Orientales et Slaves de l'Université de Bruxelles* (Brussels, 1932–).
AJT	*American Journal of Theology* (Chicago, 1897–).
AKKR	*Archiv für katholisches Kirchenrecht* (Mainz, 1857–).
AMAP	*Atti e memorie dell'Accademia patavina di sc., lett. ed arti* (Padua).
AMur.	*Archivio Muratoriano, Rerum Italicarum Scriptores* (Milan, Bologna, etc., 1723–).
AOC	*Archives de l'Orient Chrétien* (Bucharest, 1948–).
Arch. Praed.	*Archivum Fratrum Praedicatorum* (Rome, 1930–).
Arch. Ven.	(and *N. Arch. Ven.*; *N. Arch. Ven. n.s.*; *Arch. Ven.-Tri.*; *Arch. Ven.* ser. 5). *Archivio Veneto*, 40 vols. (Venice, 1871–90); continued as *Nuovo Archivio Veneto*, 20 vols. (1891–1900); *Nuovo Archivio Veneto*, nuova serie, 42 vols. (1901–21); *Archivio Veneto-Tridentino* (1922–6); *Archivio Veneto*, quinta serie (1927–).
ASAK	*Anzeiger für schweizerische Alterthumskunde* (Zurich, 1869–1938).
ASBM	*Annales ordinis Sancti Basilii Magni* (Rome, 1949–).
ASI	*Archivio storico italiano* (Florence). Ser. I, 20 vols. and App. 9 vols. 1842–53. Index 1857. Ser. nuova, 18 vols. 1855–63. Ser. III, 26 vols. 1865–77. Indexes to II and III 1874. Supplt. 1877. Ser. IV, 20 vols. 1878–87. Index 1891. Ser. V, 49 vols. 1888–1912. Index 1900. Anni 71, etc. 1913– , in progress (Index to 1927 in *Catalogue of the London Library*, I, 1913 and Supplts., 1920, 1929).
ASL	*Archivio storico lombardo* (Milan, 1874–).
ASP	*Archiv für slavische Philologie* (Berlin, 1876–1929).
ASPN	*Archivio storico per le province napoletane* (Naples, 1876–).
ASRSP	*Archivio della società romana di storia patria* (Rome, 1878–).
Atti Ist. Ven. S.L.A.	*Atti. Istituto Veneto di Scienze, Lettere ed Arte* (Venice, 1841–).
AU	*Archiv für Urkundenforschung* (Berlin, 1907–).
B	*Byzantion. Revue Internationale des Etudes Byzantines* (Paris and Liège, 1924–9; Paris and Brussels, 1930; Brussels, etc., 1931–).
BA	*Byzantinisches Archiv* (at intervals; Leipzig and Munich, 1898–).
BBI	*Bulletin of the Byzantine Institute* (Paris, 1946–).
BEC	*Bibliothèque de l'Ecole des Chartes* (Paris, 1939–).
Beck	Beck, H.-G., *Kirche und theologische Literatur* (see Gen. Bibl. I).
Bess.	*Bessarione* (Rome, 1896–1923).

BHE	*Bibliothèque de l'Ecole des Hautes Etudes* (Paris, 1839–).
BHG	*Bibliotheca hagiographica graeca* (see Gen. Bibl. IV).
BIDR	*Bullettino dell'Istituto di diritto romano* (Rome, 1888–).
BISI	*Bullettino dell'Istituto storico italiano* (Rome, 1886–).
BM	*Byzantina Metabyzantina*, I (New York, 1946); II (1949).
BNJ	*Byzantinisch-neugriechische Jahrbücher* (Berlin, 1920–5; at intervals, Athens, 1926–).
BS	*Byzantinoslavica* (Prague, 1929–).
BSA	*British School (of Archaeology) at Athens. Annual* (London, 1895–).
BSOAS	*Bulletin of the School of Oriental and African Studies* (London, 1917–).
Budé	*Collection byzantine publiée sous le patronage de l'Association Guillaume Budé* (Paris).
BUniv.	*Biographie universelle* (see Gen. Bibl. I).
BZ	*Byzantinische Zeitschrift* (Leipzig, 1892–).
CAH	*Cambridge Ancient History* (Cambridge, 1923–39).
CH	Langlois, V., *Collection des historiens anciens et modernes de l'Arménie*, 2 vols. (Paris, 1868–9).
CHJ	*Cambridge Historical Journal* (Cambridge, 1924–57).
CHM	*Cahiers d'Histoire Mondiale* (Paris, 1953–).
CM	*Classica et Medievalia* (Copenhagen, 1938–).
CMH	*Cambridge Medieval History* (Cambridge, 1913–).
CR	*Classical Review* (London, 1887–).
CSCO	*Corpus scriptorum christianorum orientalium* (see Gen. Bibl. IV).
CSEL	*Corpus scriptorum ecclesiasticorum latinorum* (see Gen. Bibl. IV).
CSHB	*Corpus scriptorum historiae Byzantinae* (see Gen. Bibl. IV).
D	Δελτίον τῆς Ἱστορικῆς καὶ Ἐθνολογικῆς Ἑταιρείας τῆς Ἑλλάδος (Athens, 1883–).
DA	Δελτίον τῆς Πατριαρχικῆς Βιβλιοθήκης τῆς Ἀλεξανδρείας (Alexandria, 1948–).
DACL	*Dictionnaire d'archéologie chrétienne et de liturgie* (see Gen. Bibl. I).
DAI	Constantine Porphyrogenitus, *De administrando imperio*, ed. Gy. Moravcsik and R. J. H. Jenkins (see Gen. Bibl. IV).
DDC	*Dictionnaire de droit canonique* (see Gen. Bibl. I).
DHGE	*Dictionnaire d'histoire et de géographie ecclésiastique* (see Gen. Bibl. I).
DOP	*Dumbarton Oaks Papers* (Cambridge, Mass., 1941–).
DR	Dölger, F., *Regesten der Kaiserurkunden des oströmischen Reiches* (see Gen. Bibl. IV).
DS	*Dictionnaire de spiritualité* (see Gen. Bibl. I).
DTC	*Dictionnaire de théologie catholique* (see Gen. Bibl. I).
DZG	*Deutsche Zeitschrift für Geschichtswissenschaft* (Freiburg-im-Breisgau, 1889–98) (continued as *Historische Vierteljahrsschrift* [*HVJS*], q.v.).
DZKR	*Deutsche Zeitschrift für Kirchenrecht* (Tübingen, 1861–1917).
EB	*Etudes byzantines*, I–III (Bucharest, 1943–5) (continued as *Revue des études byzantines* [*REB*], q.v.).
EcfrAR	*Ecoles françaises d'Athènes et de Rome* (Paris).
ECQ	*Eastern Churches Quarterly* (Ramsgate, 1936–).
EEBS	Ἐπετηρὶς Ἑταιρείας Βυζαντινῶν Σπουδῶν (Athens, 1924–).

EHR	*English Historical Review* (London, 1886–).
EO	*Echos d'Orient* (Constantinople and Paris, 1897–1942) (continued as *Etudes Byzantines* [*EB*], q.v.).
Ersch–Gruber	Ersch, J. S. and Gruber, J. G., *Allgemeine Encyklopädie* (see Gen. Bibl. i).
FHG	Müller, C., *Fragmenta historicorum graecorum* (see Gen. Bibl. iv).
Fonti	*Fonti per la storia d'Italia* (see Gen. Bibl. iv).
GBL	K. Krumbacher, *Geschichte der byzantinischen Litteratur* (see Gen. Bibl. v).
Glas	*Glas Srpska Akademii Nauka* (Belgrade, 1949–) (continuation of *Glas Srpska Kraljevska Akad.*, Belgrade, 1888–1940).
Gn	*Gnomon*, i–xx (Berlin, 1925–44); xxi– (Munich, 1949–).
GOTR	*Greek Orthodox Theological Review* (Brookline, Mass., 1954–).
GR	Grumel, V., *Les Regestes des Actes du Patriarcat de Constantinople* (see Gen. Bibl. iv).
HJ	*Historisches Jahrbuch* (Görres-Gesellschaft) (Munich, 1880–).
HTR	*Harvard Theological Review* (Cambridge, Mass., 1908–).
HVJS	*Historische Vierteljahrsschrift* (continuation of *Deutsche Zeitschrift f. Geschichtswissenschaft* [*DZG*]) (Leipzig, 1898–).
HZ	*Historische Zeitschrift* (von Sybel) (Munich and Berlin, 1859–).
IRAIK	*Izvestija Russkago Archeologičeskago Instituta v Konstantinopole* [*Transactions of the Russian Archaeological Institute at Constantinople*] (Odessa, 1896–).
JA	*Journal Asiatique* (Paris, 1822–).
Jaffé	Jaffé, P., *Regesta Pontificum Romanorum* (see Gen. Bibl. iv).
JEH	*Journal of Ecclesiastical History* (London, 1950–).
JHS	*Journal of Hellenic Studies* (London, 1880–).
JOBG	*Jahrbuch der österreichischen byzantinischen Gesellschaft* (Vienna, 1951–).
JRAS	*Journal of the Royal Asiatic Society of Great Britain* (London, 1833–).
JRS	*Journal of Roman Studies* (London, 1911–).
JTS	*Journal of Theological Studies* (London, 1900–).
KAW	(*Kaiserliche*) *Akademie der Wissenschaften* (Vienna).
LTK	*Lexikon für Theologie und Kirche* (see Gen. Bibl. i).
MA	*Le moyen âge* (Paris, 1888–).
Mansi	Mansi, J. D., *Sacrorum conciliorum collectio* (see Gen. Bibl. iv).
MEC	*Mémoires et documents publ. par l'Ecole des Chartes* (see Gen. Bibl. iv).
Med. Hum.	*Medievalia et Humanistica* (Boulder: Colorado, 1943–).
Med. Stud.	*Medieval Studies* (Pontifical Academy of Toronto) (Toronto, 1939–).
Mém. Acad. IP.	*Mémoires de l'Académie impériale des sciences de St Pétersbourg.*
MGH	*Monumenta Germaniae Historica* (see Gen. Bibl. iv).
MGT	*Magyar-Görög Tamulmányok*, Οὐγγροελληνικαὶ Μελέται (Budapest, 1945–).
MHP	*Monumenta historiae patriae* (Turin) (see Gen. Bibl. iv).
MHSM	*Monumenta spectantia historiam Slavorum meridionalium* (see Gen. Bibl. iv).
MIOG	*Mittheilungen des Instituts für österreichische Geschichtsforschung* (Innsbruck, 1880–).

MM	F. Miklosich and J. Müller, *Acta et diplomata graeca medii aevi sacra et profana* (see Gen. Bibl. IV).
MPG	Migne, *Patrologiae cursus completus. Ser. graeco-latina* (see Gen. Bibl. IV).
MPL	Migne, *Patrologiae cursus completus. Ser. latina* (see Gen. Bibl. IV).
NE	Νέος Ἑλληνομνήμων (Athens, 1904–27).
Neu. Arch.	*Neues Archiv der Gesellschaft für ältere deutsche Geschichtskunde* (Hanover and Leipzig, 1876–).
NRDF	*Nouvelle revue historique du droit français* (Paris, 1921–).
OC	*Oriens Christianus* (Leipzig, 1901–).
OCA	*Orientalia Christiana Analecta* (Rome, 1923–).
OCP	*Orientalia Christiana Periodica* (Rome, 1935–).
ÖstCh	*Östliches Christentum* (Munich, 1923–).
Pauly–Wissowa	Pauly, A., Wissowa, G. and Kroll, W., *Real-Encyclopädie der classischen Alterthumswissenschaft* (see Gen. Bibl. I).
PAW	*Königliche preussische Akademie d. Wissenschaften* (Berlin).
PO	*Patrologia Orientalis* (Paris, 1907–).
PR	Potthast, A., *Regesta Pontificum Romanorum* (see Gen. Bibl. IV).
QFIA	*Quellen und Forschungen aus italienischen Archiven und Bibliotheken* (Rome, 1897–).
RA	*Revue archéologique* (Paris, 1844–).
RAAD	*Revue de l'Académie arabe (de Damas)* (Damascus, 1921–).
RAC	*Reallexikon für Antike und Christentum* (see Gen. Bibl. I).
RBén	*Revue bénédictine* (Maredsous, 1890–).
REB	*Revue des études byzantines* (Bucharest and Paris, 1946–).
Rec. hist. cr.	*Recueil des historiens des croisades* (see Gen. Bibl. IV).
REG	*Revue des études grecques* (Paris, 1888–).
RH	*Revue historique* (Paris, 1876–).
RHC	*Revue d'histoire comparée* (Budapest, Paris, 1943–8).
RHE	*Revue d'histoire ecclésiastique* (Louvain, 1900–).
RHSE	*Revue historique du sud-est européen* (Bucharest, 1924–).
RISS	See Muratori in Gen. Bibl. IV.
RN	*Revue numismatique* (Paris, 1836–).
ROC	*Revue de l'orient chrétien* (Paris, 1896–).
ROL	*Revue de l'orient latin* (Paris, 1893–).
RP	Rhalles, G. A. and Potles, M., Σύνταγμα τῶν θείων καὶ ἱερῶν κανόνων (see Gen. Bibl. IV).
RQCA	*Römische Quartalschrift für christliche Altertumskunde und Kirchengeschichte* (Rome, 1887–).
RQH	*Revue des questions historiques* (Paris, 1866–).
RSI	*Rivista storica italiana* (Turin, 1884–).
SBAW	*Sitzungsberichte der bayerischen Akademie der Wissenschaften* (formerly *Königlichen Akad. der Wiss.*) (Munich, 1860–70). Separate *Phil.-Hist. Klasse* (Munich, 1871–).
SBN	*Studi Bizantini e Neoellenici* (Rome, 1924–).
SEER	*Slavonic and East European Review* (London, 1922–).
Sem. Kond.	*Seminarium Kondakovianum* (Prague, I–IX, 1929–35). Continued as *Annales de l'Institut Kondakov* (Belgrade, 1936–40).
SGUS	*Scriptores rerum Germanicarum in usum scholarum* (see *Monumenta Germaniae Historica* in Gen. Bibl. IV).
SHF	*Société de l'Histoire de France* (Publications. Paris, 1833–).

SKAW	*Sitzungsberichte der (kaiserlichen) Akademie der Wissenschaften. Philosoph.-hist. Classe* (Vienna, 1848–).
SP	*Speculum* (Cambridge, Mass., 1925–).
SPAW	*Sitzungsberichte der königlichen preussischen* [after 1944 called *deutschen*] *Akademie der Wissenschaften* (Berlin, 1896–).
SRH	*Scriptores rerum Hungaricarum* (see Gen. Bibl. IV).
Trad.	*Traditio* (New York, 1943–).
TRHS	*Transactions of the Royal Historical Society* (London, 1869–).
VV	*Vizantijskij Vremennik* (Βυζαντινὰ Χρονικά), old series I–XXV (St Petersburg, 1894–1928); new series I (XXVI)– (Leningrad, 1947–).
WMBH	*Wissenschaftliche Mittheilungen aus Bosnien und der Hercegovina* (Vienna, 1893–1912).
ZCK	*Zeitschrift für christliche Kunst* (Düsseldorf, 1888–1921).
ZDMG	*Zeitschrift der deutschen morgenländischen Gesellschaft* (Leipzig, 1846–).
ZKG	*Zeitschrift für Kirchengeschichte* (Stuttgart, 1876–).
ZKT	*Zeitschrift für katholische Theologie* (Innsbruck, 1877–).
ZMNP	*Žurnal ministerstva narodnago prosveščenija* [*Journal of the Ministry of Public Instruction*] (St Petersburg, 1834–).
ZR	*Zeitschrift für Rechtsgeschichte* (Weimar, 1861–78) (continued as *ZSR*, below).
ZSR	*Zeitschrift der Savigny-Stiftung für Rechtswissenschaft* (Weimar, 1880–).
ZWT	*Zeitschrift für wissenschaftliche Theologie* (Jena, etc., Frankfurt-am-Main, 1858–1914).

Abh.	Abhandlungen.	n.d.	no date.
antiq.	antiquarian, antiquaire.	n.s.	new series.
app.	appendix.	publ.	published, publié.
coll.	collection.	R.⎫	reale.
diss.	dissertation.	r. ⎭	
Ge., Gé.	Georgia, Géorgie.	roy.	royal, royale.
hist.	history, historical, historique, historisch.	ser.	series.
		soc.	society, société, società.
Jahrb.	Jahrbuch.	subs.	subsidia.
k.	kaiserlich, königlich.	supplt.	supplement.
mem.	memoir.	*TU*	*Texte und Untersuchungen.*
mém.	mémoire.	Viert.	Vierteljahrsschrift.

GENERAL BIBLIOGRAPHY

A classified bibliography of works on Byzantine history and civilisation published from 1892 onwards may be found in the periodical *Byzantinische Zeitschrift.*

A number of works cited have been reprinted unaltered; such reprints are not generally noted here.

I. DICTIONARIES, BIBLIOGRAPHIES AND GENERAL WORKS OF REFERENCE

Altaner, B., *Patrologie*, 5th ed. (Freiburg, 1958); English transl. H. C. Graef (New York, 1960).

American Historical Association's Guide to Historical Literature, ed. by G. F. Howe and others (New York, 1961).

Beck, H.-G., *Kirche und theologische Literatur im byzantinischen Reich* (Munich, 1959). [Beck.]

Bernheim, E., *Lehrbuch der historischen Methode und der Geschichtsphilosophie* (5th and 6th enlarged eds., Leipzig, 1908).

Bibliografia storica nazionale [on works since 1939] (Giunta Centrale per gli Studi Storici: Rome, 1942–9; Bari, 1950–).

Biographie universelle, ancienne et moderne, 45 vols. (Paris, ed. L. G. Michaud and others, 1843–65). [Greatly improved ed. of earlier work, 1811–28, and its supplements, 1832–62.] [*BUniv.*]

Bresslau, H., *Handbuch der Urkundenlehre für Deutschland und Italien*, I and II, pt. 1, 3rd ed. (Leipzig, 1914); II, pt. 2, by H.-W. Klewitz, 2nd ed. (Leipzig, 1931); 2 vols. and Index vol. (Berlin, 1958–60).

Capasso, B., *Le fonti della storia delle provincie napoletane dal 568 al 1500*, ed. E. O. Mastrojanni (Naples, 1902).

Ceillier, R., *Histoire générale des auteurs sacrés et ecclésiastiques*, 23 vols. (Paris, 1729–63); new ed. 19 vols. (Paris, 1858–70).

Chevalier, C. U. J., *Répertoire des sources historiques du moyen âge. Biobibliographie* (Paris, 1883–8; rev. ed. 2 vols. 1905–7). *Topo-bibliographie* (Montbéliard, 1894–1903).

Colonna, M. E., *Gli storici bizantini dal IV al XV secolo. I. Storici profani* (Naples, 1956).

Cross, F. L. (ed.), *The Oxford Dictionary of the Christian Church* (Oxford, 1957).

Demetrakos, D. B., Μέγα λεξικὸν τῆς ἑλληνικῆς γλώσσης, 9 vols. (Athens, 1933–51).

Dictionnaire d'archéologie chrétienne et de liturgie, ed. F. Cabriol and H. Leclercq (Paris, 1907–1953). [*DACL.*]

Dictionnaire de droit canonique, ed. R. Naz (Paris, 1935 ff.). [*DDC.*]

Dictionnaire de spiritualité, ed. M. Villier, F. Cavallera and J. de Guibert (Paris, 1937 ff., in progress). [*DS.*]

Dictionnaire de théologie catholique, ed. A. Vacant, E. Mangeot and others, 15 vols. in 18 (Paris, 1905–50). [*DTC.*]

Dictionnaire d'histoire et de géographie ecclésiastiques, ed. A. Baudrillart, A. Vogt, U. Rouzies and others (Paris, 1912 ff., in progress). [*DHGE.*]

Dix années d'études byzantines. Bibliographie Internationale 1939–1948. Publ. by the Association Internationale des Etudes Byzantines (Paris, 1949).

Dölger, F. and Schneider, A. M., *Byzanz* (Berne, 1952).

Du Cange, C. du Fresne, *Glossarium ad scriptores mediae et infimae Latinitatis*, eds. of G. A. L. Henschel, 7 vols. (Paris, 1840–50); and L. Favre, 10 vols. (Niort, 1883–8).

Du Cange, C. du Fresne, *Glossarium ad scriptores mediae et infimae Graecitatis*, 2 vols. (Lyons, 1688).

Enciclopedia Italiana di scienze, lettere ed arti (Rome, 1929–36; and later supplementary volumes).

Encyclopaedia Britannica, 11th and later eds. (Cambridge, London and New York, 1910 ff.; new ed. in progress).

Encyclopedia of Islam. A Dictionary of the Geography, Ethnography, and Biography of the Muhammadan Peoples, 4 vols. and supplement (Leiden, 1913–48); 2nd ed. B. Lewis, C. Pellat and J. Schacht (Leiden and London, 1954 ff.). [In progress.]

Ersch, J. S. and Gruber, J. G., *Allgemeine Encyklopädie der Wissenschaften und Künste* (Berlin, 1818–90; incomplete). [Ersch–Gruber.]

Ghellinck, J. de, *Patristique et moyen-âge*, 3 vols. (Paris and Brussels, 1947–9).

Giry, A., *Manuel de diplomatique*, reprinted in 2 vols. (Paris, 1925).

Jugie, M., *Theologia dogmatica Christianorum orientalium ab ecclesia catholica dissidentium*, 5 vols. (Paris, 1926–35).

Krumbacher, K., *Geschichte der byzantinischen Litteratur.* [See below, v.]

Langford-James, R. L., *A Dictionary of the Eastern Orthodox Church* (London, n.d.).

Lexikon für Theologie und Kirche, ed. M. Buchberger; 2nd ed. J. Hofer and K. Rahner (Freiburg, 1957 ff.). [*LTK*.]

Λεξικὸν τῆς ἑλληνικῆς γλώσσης. Α'. Ἱστορικὸν λεξικὸν τῆς νέας ἑλληνικῆς τῆς τε κοινῆς ὁμιλουμένης καὶ τῶν ἰδιωμάτων (Athens, 1933–).

Maigne d'Arnis, W. H., *Lexicon manuale ad scriptores mediae et infimae Latinitatis* (publ. Migne) (Paris, 1866).

Meester, P. de, *De monachico statu iuxta disciplinam byzantinam. Statuta selectis fontibus et commentariis instructa* (Vatican City, 1942).

Milaš, N., *Das Kirchenrecht der morgenländischen Kirche*, 2nd ed. (Mostar, 1905).

Moravcsik, Gy., *Byzantinoturcica*, 2 vols., I: *Die byzantinischen Quellen der Geschichte der Türkvölker*; II: *Sprachreste der Türkvölker in den byzantinischen Quellen*, 2nd ed. (Berlin, 1958).

Oudin, Casimir, *Commentarius de scriptoribus ecclesiae antiquae illorumque scriptis tam impressis quam manuscriptis adhuc extantibus in celebrioribus Europae bibliothecis a Bellarmino, etc., omissis ad annum MCCCCLX* (Frankfurt and Leipzig, 1722).

Paetow, L. J., *Guide to the Study of Medieval History*, rev. ed. (London, 1931) [a supplement for the years 1930–60 is in preparation].

Patristic Greek Lexicon, ed. G. W. H. Lampe (Oxford, 1961 ff.). [In progress.]

Pauly, A. F. von, *Real-Encyclopädie der classischen Alterthumswissenschaft* (Vienna, 1837–52); new ed. G. Wissowa, W. Kroll and others (Stuttgart, 1893 ff.). [Pauly–Wissowa.]

Philips, C. H., ed., *Handbook of Oriental History* (London, 1951).

Potthast, A., *Bibliotheca historica medii aevi. Wegweiser durch die Geschichtswerke des europäischen Mittelalters bis 1500*, 2nd ed. 2 vols. (Berlin, 1896) (see below, *Repertorium*).

Quasten, J., *Patrology*, III (Westminster: Maryland, 1960).

Reallexikon für Antike und Christentum, ed. T. Klausner, F. Dölger, H. Lietzmann and others (Stuttgart, 1950 ff.). [In progress.] [*RAC*.]

Repertorium Fontium Historiae Medii Aevi, primum ab Augusto Potthast digestum, nunc de cura collegii historicorum e pluribus nationibus emendatum et auctum. I. *Series Collectionum* (Istituto Storico Italiano per il Medio Evo, Rome, 1962).

Sophocles, E. A., *Greek Lexicon of the Roman and Byzantine Periods* (B.C. 146 to A.D. 1100) (Boston, 1870); ed. J. H. Thayer (New York, 1887 and 1893).

Stephanus, H., *Thesaurus linguae graecae*, ed. C. B. Hase, G. Dindorf and L. Dindorf, I–VIII (Paris, 1831–65).

Überweg, F., *Grundriss der Geschichte der Philosophie*, I, 12th ed. by K. Praechter; II, 11th ed. by B. Geyer (Berlin, 1926, 1928).

II. ATLASES AND GEOGRAPHY

Anderson, J. G. C., *Map of Asia Minor* (Murray's Handy Classical Maps, ed. G. B. Grundy) (London, 1903); partially revised by W. M. Calder and G. E. Bean, *A Classical Map of Asia Minor* (London, 1958).

Banduri, A., *Imperium orientale sive antiquitates Constantinopolitanae*, 2 vols. (Paris, 1711).

Bischoff, H. T. and Möller, J. H., *Vergleichendes Wörterbuch der alten, mittleren, und neuen Geographie* (Gotha, 1829).

Deschamps, P., *Dictionnaire de géographie* [supplt. to Brunet, J. C., *Manuel du Libraire*] (Paris, 1870); 2nd ed. 2 vols. (1878–80).

Dictionnaire d'histoire et de géographie ecclésiastiques [see above, I].

Du Cange, C. du Fresne, *Constantinopolis Christiana* (*Historia Byzantina*, pts. II and III). [See below, V.]

Freeman, E. A., *Historical Geography of Europe* [with Atlas] (London, 1881); 3rd ed. rev. and ed. J. B. Bury, 2 vols. (London, 1903).

Grässe, J. G. T., *Orbis Latinus* (Dresden, 1861, with index of modern names); 2nd ed. F. Benedict (Berlin, 1909; reprinted Berlin, 1922).

Hazard, H. W. and Cooke, H. L., *Atlas of Islamic History*, 3rd ed. (Princeton, 1954).

Heussi, K. and Hermann, M., *Atlas zur Kirchengeschichte*, 2nd ed. (Tübingen, 1919).

Honigmann, E., *Die Ostgrenze des byzantinischen Reiches von 363 bis 1071* (see Gen. Bibl. V).

Janin, R., *Constantinople byzantine: développement urbain et répertoire topographique* (Paris, 1950).

Janin, R., *La géographie ecclésiastique de l'empire byzantin*, part I: *Le siège de Constantinople et le patriarcat oecuménique*, vol. 3: *Les églises et les monastères* (Paris, 1953).

Kiepert, H., Πίναξ τοῦ μεσαιωνικοῦ Ἑλληνισμοῦ κατὰ τὴν δεκάτην ἑκατονταετηρίδα. Published by the Athenian Σύλλογος πρὸς διάδοσιν τῶν Ἑλληνικῶν γραμμάτων (Berlin, 1883).

Le Strange, G., *Palestine under the Moslems* (Cambridge, 1890).

Le Strange, G., *The Lands of the Eastern Caliphate: Mesopotamia, Persia and Central Asia, from the Moslem Conquest to the Time of Timur* (Cambridge, 1905).

Le Strange, G., *Baghdad during the Abbasid Caliphate, from Contemporary Arab and Persian Sources* (London, 1900).

Meer, F. van der and Mohrmann, C., *Atlas of the Early Christian World*, transl. and ed. by M. H. Hedlund and H. H. Rowley (London, 1958).

Mordtmann, A., *Esquisse topographique de Constantinople* (Lille, 1892).

Philippson, A., *Das byzantinische Reich als geographische Erscheinung* (Leyden, 1939).

Philippson, A. and Kirsten, E., *Die griechischen Landschaften*, I–II in 4 pts. (Frankfurt, 1950–2, 1956–8).

Poole, R. L. (ed.), *Historical Atlas of Modern Europe* (Oxford, 1902).

Putzger, F. W., *Historischer Schul-Atlas*, ed. A. Baldamus and others (Bielefeld and Leipzig, various editions).

Ramsay, W. M., *Cities and Bishoprics of Phrygia*. 1 vol. in 2 (Oxford, 1895–7). [All publ.]

Ramsay, W. M., *Historical Geography of Asia Minor* (Roy. Geog. Soc., Suppl. papers, 4) (London, 1890).

Roolvink, R. and others, *Historical Atlas of the Muslim Peoples* (Amsterdam, 1957).

Setton, K. M., 'The Archaeology of medieval Athens', *Essays in Medieval Life and Thought presented in Honor of Austin Patterson Evans* (New York, 1955), 227–58.

Shepherd, W. R., *Historical Atlas*, 8th ed. (Pikesville: Maryland, 1956).

Spruner–Menke, *Hand-Atlas für die Geschichte des Mittelalters und der neueren Zeit* (Gotha, 1880) (3rd ed. of K. von Spruner's *Hand-Atlas*, etc., ed. T. Menke).

Tafrali, O., *Topographie de Thessalonique* (Paris, 1913).

Van Millingen, A., *Byzantine Constantinople: the Walls of the City and adjoining Historical Sites* (London, 1899).

Van Millingen, A., *Byzantine Churches in Constantinople* (London, 1912).

Vasmer, M., *Die Slaven in Griechenland*. (*Abh. d. Preuss. Akad. d. Wissensch., philos.-hist. Kl.*, 12) (Berlin, 1941).

Vivien de Saint-Martin, L., and others, *Nouveau dictionnaire de géographie universelle*, 7 vols. (Paris, 1879–95); supplt. by L. Rousselet, 2 vols. (1895–7). [Contains short bibliographies.]

III. CHRONOLOGY, EPIGRAPHY, NUMISMATICS, GENEALOGY AND DEMOGRAPHY

(A) CHRONOLOGY

L'art de vérifier les dates et les faits historiques, par un religieux de la congrégation de St Maur, 4th ed. by N. V. de St Allais and others, 44 vols. (Paris, 1818–44).

Cappelli, A., *Cronologia, cronografia, e calendario perpetuo dal principio dell'era cristiana ai giorni nostri*, 2nd ed. (Milan, 1930).

Chaine, M., *La chronologie des temps chrétiens en Égypte et en Éthiopie* (Paris, 1925).

Dulaurier, E., *Recherches sur la chronologie arménienne*. I: *Chronologie technique* (Paris, 1925).

Gams, P. B., *Series episcoporum ecclesiae Catholicae* [with supplt.] (Ratisbon, 1873, 1886); reprinted (Leipzig, 1931).

Ginzel, F. K., *Handbuch der mathematischen und technischen Chronologie*, 3 vols. (Leipzig, 1906–14).

Grotefend, H., *Taschenbuch der Zeitrechnung des deutschen Mittelalters und der Neuzeit*, 10th ed. by T. Ulrich (Hanover, 1960).

Grotefend, H., *Zeitrechnung des deutschen Mittelalters und der Neuzeit*, 2 vols. (Hanover, 1891–8).

Grumel, V., *La Chronologie* (*Traité d'études byzantines*, ed. P. Lemerle, I) (Paris, 1958).

Haig, T. W., *Comparative Tables of Muhammadan and Christian Dates* (London, 1932).

Ideler, C. L., *Handbuch der mathematischen und technischen Chronologie*, 2 vols. (Berlin, 1825–6); new ed. (Breslau, 1883).

Kubitschek, W., *Grundriss der antiken Zeitrechnung* (*Handbuch der Altertumswissenschaft*, I, 7) (Munich, 1928).

Lane-Poole, S., *The Mohammedan Dynasties: Chronological and Genealogical Tables with Historical Introductions* (London, 1894); see also the fuller Russian edition by V. Bartold (St Petersburg, 1899).

Lietzmann, H., *Zeitrechnung der römischen Kaiserzeit, des Mittelalters und der Neuzeit für die Jahre 1–2000 nach Christus*, 3rd ed. by D. K. Aland (Berlin, 1956).

Mas Latrie, J. M. J. L. de, *Trésor de chronologie, d'histoire, et de géographie pour l'étude et l'emploi des documents du moyen âge* (Paris, 1889).

Muralt, E. de, *Essai de chronographie byzantine* (*395–1057*) (St Petersburg, 1855).

Muralt, E. de, *Essai de chronographie byzantine* (*1057–1453*), 2 vols. (Basle and Geneva, 1871–3).

Neugebauer, P. V., *Hilfstafeln zur technischen Chronologie* [reprinted from *Astronomische Nachrichten*, Bd. 261] (Kiel, 1937).

Poole, R. L., *Medieval Reckonings of Time* (Helps for Students of History) (London, 1918).

Ruhl, F., *Chronologie des Mittelalters und der Neuzeit* (Berlin, 1897).

Schram, R., *Kalendariographische und chronologische Tafeln* (Leipzig, 1908).

Stokvis, A. M. H. J., *Manuel d'histoire de généalogie et de chronologie de tous les états du globe, depuis les temps les plus reculés jusqu'à nos jours*, 3 vols. (Leiden, 1888–93).

Wüstenfeld, H. F., *Wüstenfeld-Mahler'sche Vergleichungs-Tabellen zur muslimischen und iranischen Zeitrechnung mit Tafeln zur Umrechnung orient-christlicher Ären*, 3rd ed. by J. Mayr and B. Spuler (Wiesbaden, 1961).

Information may also be found in such works as Giry; and Philips [see I above]; and in Dölger, *Regesten*; Grumel; Gedeon; Le Quien; Ughelli [see IV below].

(B) EPIGRAPHY

Corpus der griechisch-christlichen Inschriften in Hellas, ed. N. A. Bees and others (Athens, 1941; in progress).

Grégoire, H., *Recueil des inscriptions grecques chrétiennes d'Asie Mineure*, I (Paris, 1922).

Jalabert, L. and Mouterde, R., *Inscriptions grecques et latines de la Syrie*, I–IV (Paris, 1929–55).

Michailov, G., *Inscriptiones graecae in Bulgaria repertae*, I: *Inscriptiones orae Ponti Euxini* (Sofia, 1956).

Millet, G., Pargoire, J. and Petit, L., *Recueil des inscriptions chrétiennes du Mont-Athos* (Bibliothèque des Ecoles françaises d'Athènes et de Rome, 91) (Paris, 1904).

See also the 'Bulletin épigraphique', in *REG* (e.g. J. and L. Robert, LVII (1944) and later vols.).

(c) NUMISMATICS

Adelson, H. L., *Lightweight Solidi and Byzantine Trade during the Sixth and Seventh Centuries* (*Num. Notes and Monographs*, 138) (New York, 1957); see the review by J. P. C. Kent, *Numismatic Chronicle*, XIX (1959), 237–40.

Bellinger, A. R., *The Anonymous Byzantine Bronze Coinage* (*Num. Notes and Monographs*, 35) (New York, 1928).

Bertelè, T., *L'imperatore alato nella numismatica bizantina* (Rome, 1951).

Breckenridge, J. D., *The Numismatic Iconography of Justinian II* (*Num. Notes and Monographs*, 144) (New York, 1959).

Codrington, O., *Manual of Musalman Numismatics* (Royal Asiatic Soc.) (London, 1904).

Corpus nummorum italicorum, vols. I–XV (Rome, 1910 ff., in progress).

Engel, A. and Serrure, R., *Traité de numismatique du moyen âge*, 2 vols. (Paris, 1891–4).

Goodacre, H., *A Handbook of the Coinage of the Byzantine Empire*, 3 vols. (London, 1928–33); new ed. (1957).

Grierson, P., *Coins and Medals; a Select Bibliography* (Historical Association, *Helps for Students of History*, 56) (London, 1954).

Grierson, P., 'Coinage and Money in the Byzantine Empire 498–c. 1090', *Settimane di studio del Centro italiano di studi sull'alto medioevo, Spoleto 1960*, VIII (1961), 411–53.

Konstantopoulos, K., Βυζαντιακὰ μολυβδόβουλλα (Athens, 1917).

Laurent, V., 'Bulletin de numismatique byzantine 1940–49', *REB*, IX (1951), 192–251.

Laurent, V., 'Bulletin de sigillographie byzantine', *B*, V (1929–30), 571–654; VI (1931), 771–829.

Laurent, V., *Documents de sigillographie byzantine; la collection C. Orghidan* (Bibliothèque byzantine, ed. P. Lemerle, Documents I) (Paris, 1952).

Longuet, H., *Introduction à la numismatique byzantine* (London, 1961).

Macdonald, G., *The Evolution of Coinage* (Cambridge, 1916).

Metcalf, D. M., 'The Byzantine Empire', *Congresso Internazionale di Numismatica*, I (Rome, 1961), 233–45.

Mosser, S. M., *A Bibliography of Byzantine Coin Hoards* (*Num. Notes and Monographs*, 67) (New York, 1935).

Pančenko, B. A., 'Katalog molivdovulov' ['Catalogue of lead seals'], *IRAIK*, VIII (1903), 199–246; IX (1904), 341–96; XIII (1908), 78–151.

Ratto, R., *Monnaies byzantines* (Lugano, 9 Dec. 1930; a sale catalogue, illustrated with a great deal of material; reprinted Amsterdam, 1959).

Sabatier, J., *Description générale des monnaies byzantines*, 2 vols. (Paris and London, 1862) (reprinted Leipzig, 1930 and Graz, 1955).

Schlumberger, G., *Numismatique de l'orient latin* (Société de l'Orient Latin), 2 vols. (Paris, 1878, 1882).

Schlumberger, G., *Sigillographie de l'empire byzantin* (Paris, 1884).

Schlumberger, G., Chalandon, F. and Blanchet, A., *Sigillographie de l'orient latin* (Paris, 1943).

Tolstoi, J., *Vizantijskie monety* [*Byzantine coins*], fasc. 1–7 (St Petersburg, 1912–14).

Wroth, W., *Catalogue of the Coins of the Vandals, Ostrogoths, and Lombards, and of the Empires of Thessalonica, Nicaea, and Trebizond in the British Museum* (London, 1911).

Wroth, W., *Catalogue of the Imperial Byzantine Coins in the British Museum,* 2 vols. (London, 1908).

(D) GENEALOGY

Argenti, P. P., *Libro d'Oro de la Noblesse de Chio:* I. *Notices historiques.* II. *Arbres généalogiques* (London, 1955).

Chatzes, A. C., Οἱ Ῥαούλ, Ῥάλ, Ῥάλαι (*1080–1800*) (Kirchain, 1908).

Du Cange, C. du Fresne, *Familiae Augustae Byzantinae. Familiae Dalmaticae, Sclavonicae, Turcicae.* (*Historia Byzantina*, pt. 1. See below, V.)

Du Cange, C. du Fresne, *Les familles d'outre-mer*, ed. E. Rey (Paris, 1869). (Collection de documents inédits sur l'histoire de France.)

George, H. B., *Genealogical Tables illustrative of Modern History* (Oxford, 1873); 5th ed. J. R. H. Weaver, revised and enlarged (1916).

Grote, H., *Stammtafeln mit Anhang calendarium medii aevi* (vol. IX of Münz-studien) (Leipzig, 1877).

Hopf, K., *Chroniques gréco-romanes* [see below, IV].

Papadopulos, A., *Versuch einer Genealogie der Palaiologen, 1259–1453* (Diss., Munich, 1938).

Zambaur, E. K. M. von, *Manuel de généalogie et de chronologie pour l'histoire de l'Islam* (Hanover, 1927).

[See also *L'art de vérifier les dates* and S. Lane-Poole, *Mohammadan Dynasties* (III (A) above) and other works under III (A), (B), (C) and (E).]

(E) DEMOGRAPHY

Cahen, C., 'Le problème ethnique en Anatolie', *CHM*, II (1954), 347–62.

Charanis, P., 'The Armenians in the Byzantine Empire', *BS*, XXII (1961), 196–240.

Kyriakides, S. P. *The Northern Ethnological Boundaries of Hellenism* (Thessalonica, 1955); see also Ἐτ. Μακ. Σπουδ., V (Thessalonica, 1946).

Lemerle, P., 'Invasions et migrations dans les Balkans depuis la fin de l'époque romaine jusqu'au VIIIᵉ siècle', *RH*, CXXI (1954), 265–308.

Mayer, R., *Byzantion-Konstantinopolis-Istanbul; eine genetische Stadtgeographie* (*Akademie der Wissenschaften, Wien, Philosoph.-Hist. Kl. Denkschriften,* 71) (Vienna, 1943).

Starr, J., *The Jews in the Byzantine Empire, 641–1204* (Athens, 1939).

Starr, J., *Romania: the Jewries of the Levant after the Fourth Crusade* (Paris, 1949).

Vryonis, S., Jr., 'Byzantium: the Social Basis of Decline in the Eleventh Century', *Greek, Roman and Byzantine Studies*, II (1959), 157–75.

See also Moravcsik (I above); Vasmer (and other works in II above); III (D) above; Barišič (IV below); and the bibliography on Anthropological and Demographic Studies by I. Ševčenko in the *American Historical Association's Guide* (I above).

IV. SOURCES AND COLLECTIONS OF SOURCES

Achéry, L. d', *Spicilegium sive collectio veterum aliquot scriptorum*, 13 vols. (Paris, 1655 (1665)–77); new ed. L. F. J. de la Barre, 3 vols. (Paris, 1723).

Acta Conciliorum Oecumenicorum, ed. E. Schwartz, 4 vols. in 12 (Berlin, 1914–40).

Acta Sanctorum Bollandiana (Brussels, 1643–1770; Paris and Rome, 1866, 1887; Brussels, 1894 ff., in progress). [*AASS*.]

Acts of Athos

    Chilandari: L. Petit and B. Korablev, *Actes de Chilandar*, ɪ: *Actes grecs*, *VV*, xvɪɪ (1911); ɪɪ: *Actes slaves*, *ib.* xɪx (1912). V. Mošin and A. Sovre, *Supplementa ad acta graeca Chilandarii* (Ljubljana, 1948).

    Esphigmenou: L. Petit and W. Regel, *Actes d'Esphigménou*, *VV*, xɪɪ (1906).

    Kutlumus: P. Lemerle, *Actes de Kutlumus* (Archives de l'Athos, ɪɪ) (Paris, 1937).

    Lavra: G. Rouillard and P. Collomp, *Actes de Lavra* (Archives de l'Athos, ɪ) (Paris, 1937).

    Panteleimon: *Akty russkogo na svjatom Afone monastyrja sv. velikomučenika i celitelja Pantelejmona* [*Acts of the Russian Monastery of the Great Martyr and Healer St Panteleimon on the Holy Mt Athos*] (Kiev, 1873).

    Pantocrator: L. Petit, *Actes de Pantocrator*, *VV*, x (1903).

    Philotheou: W. Regel, E. Kurtz and B. Korablev, *Actes de Philothée*, *VV*, xx (1913).

    Zographou: W. Regel, E. Kurtz and B. Korablev, *Actes de Zographou*, *VV*, xɪɪɪ (1907).

    See also V. Mošin, *Akti iz svetogorskih arhiva* [*Acts from the archives of the Holy Mountain*], Spomenik, xcɪ (Belgrade, 1939). T. Florinsky, *Afonskie akty* [*Acts of Athos*] (St Petersburg, 1880).

Amari, M., see under Muratori.

Archivio storico italiano. Cf. list of Abbreviations: *ASI*.

Barišič, F. and others (edd.), *Vizantiski izvori za istoriju narodna Jugoslavije* [*Byzantine sources for the history of the South Slavs*] (Belgrade, 1955 ff.).

Barker, E., *Social and Political Thought in Byzantium from Justinian I to the Last Palaeologus* (Oxford, 1957). [English transl. of passages from Byzantine writers and documents; see the review of this by R. J. H. Jenkins in *JTS*, n.s. x (1959), 418–21.]

Basilicorum libri LX, vols. ɪ–vɪ, ed. W. E. Heimbach (Leipzig, 1833–70). With 2 supplts.: 1, ed. K. E. Zachariae von Lingenthal (Leipzig, 1846) [containing books xv–xɪx]; and 2 (vol. vɪɪ), ed. E. C. Ferrini and J. Mercati (Leipzig, 1897); ed. H. J. Scheltema and others, series A: *Textus*; series B: *Scholia* (Groningen, 1953 ff., in progress).

Bataille, A., *Les Papyrus* (*Traité d'études byzantines*, ed. P. Lemerle, ɪɪ) (Paris, 1955).

Bibliotheca hagiographica graeca (Subsidia hagiographica, 8ᵃ), 3rd ed. by F. Halkin, 3 vols. (Brussels, 1957). [*BHG*.]

Boissonade, J. F., *Anecdota graeca*, 5 vols. (Paris, 1829–33).

Boissonade, J. F., *Anecdota nova* (Paris, 1844).

Brightman, F. E., *Liturgies Eastern and Western*. I. *Eastern Liturgies* (Oxford, 1896).

Byzantine Texts, ed. J. B. Bury, 5 vols. (London, 1898–1904).

Christ, W. and Paranikas, M., *Anthologia graeca carminum christianorum* (Leipzig, 1871).

Codex Theodosianus, ed. T. Mommsen, P. M. Meyer and others (Berlin, 1905); transl. C. Pharr (Princeton, 1952).

Comnena, Anna, *Alexiad*, ed. A. Reifferscheid, 2 vols. (Leipzig, 1884); also L. Schopen and A. Reifferscheid, 2 vols. *CSHB* (1839–78); *MPG*, cxxxi (1864); and B. Leib (Budé with French transl.), 3 vols. (Paris, 1937–45); English transl. by E. A. S. Dawes (London, 1928).

Constantine Porphyrogenitus, *De cerimoniis aulae byzantinae*, ed. J. J. Reiske, *CSHB* (1829–40); new ed. of book i, c. 1–83 by A. Vogt, *Constantin VII Porphyrogénète: Le Livre des Cérémonies* (Paris, 1935, 1939–40); *De thematibus* and *De administrando imperio*, ed. I. Bekker, 3 vols. *CSHB* (1829–40); and *MPG*, cxii–cxiii; *De thematibus*, new ed. A. Pertusi, *Costantino Porfirogenito De thematibus* (Vatican, 1952); *De administrando imperio*, ed. (with English transl.) Gy. Moravcsik and R. J. H. Jenkins, 2 vols. (Budapest, 1949, and London, 1962). [*DAI.*]

Corpus scriptorum christianorum orientalium, ed. J. B. Chabot and others (Paris, Rome, etc., 1903 ff.). [*CSCO.*]

Corpus scriptorum ecclesiasticorum latinorum (Vienna, 1866 ff., in progress). [*CSEL.*]

Corpus scriptorum historiae Byzantinae (Bonn, 1828–97). [*CSHB.*]

Dimitrievsky, A., *Opisanie liturgičeskich rukopisej, chranjaščichsja v bibliotekach pravoslavnago vostoka* [*The liturgical manuscripts in the libraries of the Orthodox East*]. i: *Typica*, pt. i (Kiev, 1895); ii: *Euchologia* (Kiev, 1901); iii: *Typica*, pt. ii (St Petersburg, 1917).

Dölger, F., *Aus den Schatzkammern des heiligen Berges*, 2 vols. (Munich, 1948).

Dölger, F., *Regesten der Kaiserurkunden des oströmischen Reiches* (*Corpus der griechischen Urkunden des Mittelalters und der neueren Zeit*, Reihe A, Abt. i), pt. i: 565–1025; ii: 1025–1204; iii: 1204–1282; iv: 1282–1341 (Munich–Berlin, 1924–60; in progress). [*DR.*]

Ehrhard, A., *Überlieferung und Bestand der hagiographischen und homiletischen Literatur der griechischen Kirche von den Anfängen bis zum Ende des 16. Jh.* (Texte und Untersuchungen zur Geschichte der altchristlichen Literatur, 50–2), 3 vols. (Leipzig, 1937–52).

Eparch, Book of the, ed. J. Nicole, Λέοντος τοῦ Σοφοῦ τὸ ἐπαρχικὸν βιβλίον (Geneva, 1893); reprinted in Zepos, *Jus graeco-romanum*, ii; French transl. J. Nicole (Geneva, 1894); English transl. E. H. Freshfield, *Roman Law in the Later Roman Empire* (Cambridge, 1938), and A. E. R. Boak, *J. Econ. Business History*, i (1929), 600–19.

Fejér, G., *Codex diplomaticus Hungariae ecclesiasticus ac civilis* (chronological table by F. Knauz, index by M. Czinár), 45 vols. (Budapest, 1829–66).

Fonti per la storia d'Italia. Publ. Istituto storico italiano (Genoa, Leghorn and Rome, 1887 ff., in progress). [*Fonti.*]

Gedeon, M. J., Πατριαρχικοὶ Πίνακες (Constantinople, 1890).

Goar, J., *Euchologion sive rituale graecorum complectens ritus et ordines divinae liturgiae, officiorum, sacramentorum* (Paris, 1647).

Graevius, J. G. and Burmannus, P., *Thesaurus antiquitatum et historiarum Italiae, Siciliae, Sardiniae, Corsicae, etc.*, 45 vols. (Leiden, 1704–25).

Grumel, V., *Les Regestes des Actes du Patriarcat de Constantinople*, i: *Les Actes des Patriarches*, i: 381–715; ii: 715–1043; iii: 1043–1206 (Socii Assumptionistae Chalcedonenses, 1932, 1936, 1947). [In progress.] [*GR.*]

Haller, J., *Die Quellen zur Gesch. der Entstehung des Kirchenstaates* (Leipzig and Berlin, 1907). (In *Quellensammlung zur deutschen Geschichte*, ed. E. Brandenburger and G. Seeliger.)

Hergenröther, J., *Monumenta graeca ad Photium eiusque historiam pertinentia* (Regensburg, 1869).

Historiae patriae monumenta, see *Monumenta historiae patriae.*

Hopf, C., *Chroniques gréco-romanes inédites ou peu connues* (Berlin, 1873).

Jaffé, P., *Regesta Pontificum Romanorum ab condita ecclesia ad annum post Christum natum 1198* (Berlin, 1851); 2nd ed. W. Wattenbach, S. Loewenfeld, F. Kaltenbrunner and P. Ewald (Leipzig, 1885–8), 2 vols. [Jaffé.]

Justinian, *Codex Justinianus*, ed. P. Krueger (Berlin, 1877); also ed. P. Krueger in *Corpus juris civilis*, II; 9th ed. (Berlin, 1915).

Justinian, *Novellae*, ed. K. E. Zachariae von Lingenthal, 2 pts. and appendix (Leipzig, 1881–4); ed. R. Schoell and W. Kroll, in *Corpus juris civilis*, III; 4th ed. (Berlin, 1912).

Kehr, P. F., *Regesta Pontificum Romanorum. Italia Pontificia*, ed. P. F. Kehr, vol. I: *Rome*; II: *Latium*; III: *Etruria*; IV: *Umbria, etc.*; V: *Aemilia*; VI: *Liguria* (*Lombardy, Piedmont, Genoa*); VII: *Venetiae et Histria*; VIII: *Regnum Normannorum*; *Campania* (Berlin, 1906–35).

Le Quien, M., *Oriens Christianus*, 3 vols. (Paris, 1740).

Liber Censuum de l'église romaine, I, ed. P. Fabre and L. Duchesne (*EcfrAR*) (Paris, 1889–1910) (II in progress).

Liber Pontificalis, 3 vols. (Rome, 1724–55); ed. L. Duchesne, 2 vols. (*EcfrAR*) (Paris, 1884–92); ed. T. Mommsen, *Gesta Pontif. Romanorum*, I (to 715), *MGH* (1898).

Mai, A., ed., *Scriptorum veterum nova collectio*, 10 vols. (Rome, 1825–38).

Mai, A., ed., *Spicilegium romanum*, 10 vols. (Rome, 1839–44).

Mansi, J. D., *Sacrorum conciliorum nova et amplissima collectio*, 31 vols. (Florence and Venice, 1759–98); reprinted J. B. Martin and L. Petit, with continuation, vols. XXXII–L. (Paris, 1901 ff., in progress.) [Mansi.]

Migne, J. P., *Patrologiae cursus completus. Series graeco-latina*, 161 vols. in 166 (Paris, 1857–66). [*MPG.*] Indices, F. Cavallera (Paris, 1912). [This is the series containing Greek texts with Latin translations in parallel columns. The so-called *Series graeca* (81 vols. in 85, 1856–67) contains the Latin translations only.]

Migne, J. P., *Patrologiae cursus completus. Series latina*, 221 vols. (Paris, 1844–55). Index, 4 vols. (1862–4). [*MPL.*]

Miklosich, F. and Müller, J., *Acta et diplomata graeca medii aevi sacra et profana*, 6 vols. (Vienna, 1860–90). [MM.]

    I, II. *Acta patriarchatus Constantinopolitani*, 2 vols. (1860, 1862).

    III. *Acta et diplomata res graecas italasque illustrantia* (1865).

    IV–VI. *Acta et diplomata monasteriorum et ecclesiarum*, 3 vols. (1870–90).

Mirbt, C., *Quellen zur Geschichte des Papsttums und des römischen Katholizismus*, 4th ed. (Tübingen, 1924).

Monumenta Germaniae historica, ed. G. H. Pertz, T. Mommsen and others (Hanover, 1826 ff.); new eds. in progress (Hanover and Berlin). [*MGH.*] [For a full list of this series to 1960 see *Repertorium Fontium Historiae Medii Aevi*, above, I; details to 1936 may be found in *CMH*, V and VIII, Gen. Bibl. IV.]

Monumenta historiae patriae, 19 vols. fol.; 2 vols. 4º (Turin, 1836 ff.). [*MHP.*]

Monumenta Hungariae historica (published by the Hungarian Academy). In four series, I: *Diplomataria*; II: *Scriptores*; III: *Monumenta comitialia*; IV: *Acta extera* (Budapest, 1857 ff.).

Monumenta musicae Byzantinae, ed. C. Höeg, H. J. W. Tillyard and E. Wellesz (Copenhagen, etc., 1935 ff.). [See bibliography to chapter XXIV.]

Monumenta spectantia historiam Slavorum meridionalium (Zagreb, 1868 ff.). [*MHSM.*]

Müller, C., *Fragmenta historicorum graecorum*, 5 vols. (Paris, 1841–83). [*FHG.*]

Muratori, L. A., *Rerum Italicarum scriptores*, 25 vols. (Milan, 1723–51). Supplements: J. M. Tartini, 2 vols. (Florence, 1748–70); and J. B. Mittarelli (Venice, 1771); and M. Amari, *Biblioteca arabo-sicula*, Italian transl. and Appendix (Turin, Rome, etc., 1880–1, 1889). *Indices chronolog.* (Turin, 1885). New enlarged ed. with the chronicles printed as separate parts by G. Carducci and others (Città di Castello and Bologna, 1900 ff., in progress). [*RISS.*]

Muratori, L. A., *Antiquitates italicae medii aevi*, 6 vols. (Milan, 1738–42). *Indices chronolog.* (Turin, 1885).

Nova Patrum Bibliotheca, vols. I–VII, ed. A. Mai (Rome, 1852–7); vols. VIII–X, ed. J. Cozza-Luzi (1871–1905).

Pauler, G. and Szilágyi, S., *A Magyar honfoglalás kútföi* [*Sources for the occupation of Hungary by the Magyars*] (Pest, 1900).

Pitra, J. B., *Juris ecclesiastici Graecorum historia et monumenta*, 2 vols. (Rome, 1864–8).

Pitra, J. B., *Analecta sacra et classica spicilegio Solesmensi parata*, 8 vols. (Paris, 1876–88).

Potthast, A., *Regesta Pontificum Romanorum inde ab anno 1198 ad annum 1304*, 2 vols. (Berlin, 1874–5). [*PR.*]

Prefect, Book of the, see above *Eparch, Book of the.*

Prochiron, ed. K. E. Zachariae von Lingenthal, Ὁ Πρόχειρος Νόμος. *Imperatorum Basilii, Constantini, et Leonis Prochiron, etc.* (Heidelberg, 1837); re-edited F. Brandileone (*Fonti*, 1895); Zepos, J. and P., *Jus graeco-romanum*, II (1931).

Recueil des historiens des croisades. AcadIBL (Paris, 1841 ff.). [*Rec.Hist.Cr.*]
  Documents arméniens, 2 vols. (1869, 1906).
  Historiens grecs, 2 vols. (1875, 1881).
  Historiens occidentaux, 5 vols. (1844–95).
  Historiens orientaux, 5 vols. (1872–1906).
  Lois, 2 vols. (1841, 1843).

Regesta chartarum Italiae, publ. by K. preuss. hist. Instit. and Istituto storico italiano (Rome, 1907 ff., in progress).

Rhalles, G. A. and Potles, M., Σύνταγμα τῶν θείων καὶ ἱερῶν κανόνων κτλ., 6 vols. (Athens, 1852–9). [RP.]

Sathas, K. N., Μεσαιωνικὴ βιβλιοθήκη. *Bibliotheca graeca medii aevi*, 7 vols. (Venice and Paris, 1872–94).

Sathas, K. N., Μνημεῖα Ἑλληνικῆς ἱστορίας. *Documents inédits relatifs à l'histoire de la Grèce au moyen âge*, 9 vols. (Paris, 1880–90).

Scriptores rerum Germanicarum in usum scholarum, see above, *Monumenta Germaniae Historica.* [*SGUS.*]

Scriptores rerum Hungaricarum tempore ducum regumque stirpis Arpadianae gestarum, ed. E. Szentpétery, I–II (Budapest, 1937). [*SRH.*]

Soloviev, A. and Mošin, V., *Grčke povelje srpskih vladara* [*Greek documents of the Serbian rulers*] (Belgrade, 1936).

Stritter, J. G., *Memoriae populorum olim ad Danubium, Pontum Euxinum, Paludem Maeotidem, Caucasum, Mare Caspium, et inde magis ad septentriones incolentium, e scriptoribus historiae Byzantinae erutae et digestae*, 4 vols. (St Petersburg, 1771–9).

Tafel, G. L. F. and Thomas, G. M., *Urkunden zur älteren Handels- und Staatsgeschichte der Republik Venedig*, pts. I–III (*Fontes Rerum Austriacarum*, Abt. II, vols. XII–XIV) (Vienna, 1856–7).

Thallóczy, L. de, Jireček, C. J. and Sufflay, E. de, *Acta et diplomata res Albaniae mediae aetatis illustrantia*, 2 vols. (Vienna, 1913–18).

Theiner, A., *Codex diplomaticus dominii temporalis S. Sedis*, 3 vols. (Rome, 1861–2).

Thiriet, F., *Régestes des délibérations du Sénat de Venise concernant la Romanie*, I–III (Paris, 1958–61).

Trinchera, F., *Syllabus Graecarum membranarum* (Naples, 1865).

Troya, C., *Codice diplomatico Longobardo dal 568 al 774* (Storia d'Italia del Medio-Evo, vol. IV, pts. 1–5), 5 vols. and index (Naples, 1852–9).

Ughelli, F., *Italia sacra*; 2nd ed. N. Coleti, 10 vols. (Venice, 1717–22).

Watterich, J. M., *Pontificum Romanorum qui fuerunt inde ab exeunte saeculo IX usque ad finem saeculi XII vitae*, 2 vols. (Leipzig, 1862).

Zachariae von Lingenthal, K. E., Ἀνέκδοτα (Leipzig, 1843).

A. *Breviarium Novellarum Theodori Hermopolitani.*
B. *Regulae Institutionum.*
C. *Codicis per Stephanum graece conversi fragmenta.*
D. *Fragmenta Epitomae graecae Novellarum ab Anonymo confectae.*
E. *Edicta Praefectorum Praetorio.*

Zachariae von Lingenthal, K. E., *Collectio librorum juris graeco-romani ineditorum*. Ecloga Leonis et Constantini. Epanagoge Basilii, Leonis, et Alexandri (Leipzig, 1852). [Continued in *Jus graeco-romanum* below.]

Zachariae von Lingenthal, K. E., *Jus graeco-romanum*, 7 vols. (Leipzig, 1856–84).

I. *Practica ex actis Eustathii Romani* (= *Pira*).
II. *Synopsis minor; Ecloga.*
III. *Novellae constitutiones Imperatorum post Justinianum.*
IV. *Ecloga privata aucta; Ecloga ad Prochiron mutata; Epanagoge aucta.*
V. *Synopsis maior.*
VI. *Prochiron auctum.*
VII. *Epitome legum.*

Zepos, J. and P., *Jus graeco-romanum*, 8 vols. (Athens, 1931). [Contains reprints of works edited by Zachariae von Lingenthal, Heimbach and others.]

I. *Novellae Imperatorum post Justinianum*, ed. Zachariae and including some constitutions published elsewhere.
II. *Ecloga*, ed. Zachariae; *Leges rusticae, militares, navales*, ed. Ashburner; *Prochiron, Epanagoge*, ed. Zachariae; *Eparchikon Leonis*, ed. Nicole.
III. *Paraphrasis Theophili*, ed. Ferrini; *Rhopae*, ed. Zachariae; *Tract. de peculiis, Tract. de actionibus*, ed. Heimbach.
IV. *Pira, Epitome*, ed. Zachariae.
V. *Synopsis maior*, ed. Zachariae.
VI. *Epanagoge aucta, Ecloga aucta, Ecloga ad Prochiron mutata, Synopsis minor*, ed. Zachariae.
VII. *Prochiron auctum*, ed. Zachariae; *Meditatio de nudis pactis*, ed. Monnier and Platon; *Pselli synopsis*, ed. Bosquet; *Attaliatae Ponema*, ed. Zachariae; *Chomatiani Decisiones*, ed. Battandier.
VIII. *Codices Moldaviae et Walachiae. Collectio consuetudinum.*

V. MODERN WORKS

Alexander, P. J., *The Patriarch Nicephorus of Constantinople: Ecclesiastical Policy and Image Worship in the Byzantine Empire* (Oxford, 1958).

Allen, W. E. D., *A History of the Georgian People* (London, 1932).

Amantos, K., Ἱστορία τοῦ Βυζαντινοῦ Κράτους, 2 vols. (Athens, 1939–47).

Amari, M., *Storia dei Musulmani di Sicilia*, 3 vols., 2nd ed. C. A. Nallino (Catania, 1933–9).

Ammann, A. M., *Abriss der ostslawischen Kirchengeschichte* (Vienna, 1950).

Arnold, T. W., *The Caliphate* (Oxford, 1924).

Atiya, A. S., *The Crusade in the Later Middle Ages* (London, 1938).

Atiya, A. S., *The Crusade of Nicopolis* (London, 1934).

Attwater, D., *The Christian Churches of the East*, 2 vols. (Milwaukee, 1948); new ed. (London, 1961).

Bank, A. V., *Iskusstvo Vizantii v sobranii gosudarstvennogo Ermitaža* [*Byzantine Art in the Hermitage Museum*] (Leningrad, 1960).

Baronius, C., *Annales Ecclesiastici una cum critica historico-chronologica P. A. Pagii, contin. O. Raynaldus*; ed. J. D. Mansi, 34 vols. (Lucca, 1738–46); Apparatus, 1 vol., Index, 4 vols. (1740, 1757–9); new ed. (Bar-le-Duc, 1864–83).

Baynes, N. H., *The Byzantine Empire* (London, 1925; revised ed. 1943).

Baynes, N. H., *Byzantine Studies and Other Essays* (London, 1955).

Beck, H.-G., *Kirche und theologische Literatur im byzantinischen Reich* (Munich, 1959). [Beck.]

Bertolini, O., *Roma di fronte a Bizanzio e ai Longobardi* (Rome, 1941).

Bon, A., *Le Péloponnèse byzantin jusqu'en 1204* (Paris, 1951).

Bratianu, G. I., *Etudes byzantines d'histoire économique et sociale* (Paris, 1938).

Bréhier, L., *L'Eglise et l'Orient au moyen âge. Les croisades*, 5th ed. (Paris, 1928).

Bréhier, L., *Le monde byzantin*, i: *Vie et mort de Byzance*; ii: *Les institutions de l'empire byzantin*; iii: *La civilisation byzantine* (Paris, 1947–50).

Bréhier, L., *La querelle des images* (*VIIIe–IXe siècles*) (Paris, 1904).

Bréhier, L., *Le schisme oriental du XIe siècle* (Paris, 1899).

Brockelmann, C., *Geschichte der arabischen Litteratur*, 2 vols. (Weimar and Berlin, 1898–1902).

Bryce, J., *The Holy Roman Empire*, enlarged ed. (London, 1907).

Bulgakov, S., *The Orthodox Church* (London, 1935).

Bury, J. B., *The Constitution of the Later Roman Empire* (Creighton Memorial Lecture) (Cambridge, 1910); reprinted in *Selected Essays* [see below].

Bury, J. B., *History of the Eastern Roman Empire from the Fall of Irene to the Accession of Basil I (802–867)* (London, 1912).

Bury, J. B., *History of the Later Roman Empire from Arcadius to Irene (395–800)*, 2 vols. (London, 1889); new ed. [395–565], 2 vols. (London, 1923).

Bury, J. B., *The Imperial Administrative System in the Ninth Century*. With revised text of the Kletorologion of Philotheos (British Academy. Supplemental papers, i) (London, 1911).

Bury, J. B., *Selected Essays of J. B. Bury*, ed. H. Temperley (Cambridge, 1930).

Bussell, F. W., *The Roman Empire: Essays on the Constitutional History . . . (81 A.D. to 1081 A.D.)*, 2 vols. (London, 1910).

Byzantium, ed. N. H. Baynes and H. St L. B. Moss (Oxford, 1948).

Caetani, L. C. (Duca di Sermoneta), *Annali dell'Islam*, 10 vols. in 12 (Milan, 1905–26).

Cahen, C., *La Syrie du nord à l'époque des croisades* (Paris, 1940).

Caspar, E., *Geschichte des Papsttums von den Anfängen bis zur Höhe der Welt-herrschaft*, 2 vols. (Tübingen, 1930–3).

Cessi, R., *Storia della Repubblica di Venezia*, 2 vols. (Milan, 1944–6).

Chalandon, F., *Histoire de la domination normande en Italie et en Sicilie*, 2 vols. (Paris, 1907).

Chalandon, F., *Les Comnènes. Etudes sur l'empire byzantin aux XIe et XIIe siècles*, I: *Essai sur le règne d'Alexis Comnène (1081–1118)*; II: *Jean II Comnène (1118–1143) et Manuel I Comnène (1143–1180)* (Paris, 1900–13).

Chapman, C., *Michel Paléologue, restaurateur de l'empire byzantin* (Paris, 1926).

Charanis, P., 'The Monastic Properties and the State in the Byzantine Empire', *DOP*, IV (1948), 51–119.

Dalton, O. M., *Byzantine Art and Archaeology* (Oxford, 1911).

Dalton, O. M., *East Christian Art* (Oxford, 1925).

Demus, O., *Byzantine Mosaic Decoration* (London, 1948).

Dennis, G. T., *The Reign of Manuel II Palaeologus in Thessalonica, 1382–1387 (OCA, 159)* (Rome, 1960).

Der Nersessian, S., *Armenia and the Byzantine Empire* (Cambridge, Mass., 1945).

Diehl, C., *Byzance: grandeur et décadence* (Paris, 1919); English transl. by N. Walford, ed. P. Charanis, *Byzantium: Greatness and Decline* (New Brunswick, 1957).

Diehl, C., *Etudes byzantines* (Paris, 1905).

Diehl, C., *Figures byzantines*, 2 series (Paris, 1906–8, and later editions); English transl. by H. Bell, *Byzantine Portraits* (New York, 1927).

Diehl, C., *Histoire de l'empire byzantin* (Paris, 1930).

Diehl, C., *Manuel d'art byzantin* (Paris, 1910); 2nd ed. (Paris, 1925–6).

Diehl, C., *Les grands problèmes de l'histoire byzantine* (Paris, 1943).

Diehl, C. and Marçais, G., *Le monde oriental de 395 à 1081*, 2nd ed. (Paris, 1944).

Diehl, C., Guilland, R., Oeconomos, L. and Grousset, R., *L'Europe orientale de 1081 à 1453* (Paris, 1945).

Dölger, F., *Beiträge zur Geschichte der byzantinischen Finanzverwaltung besonders des 10. und 11. Jahrhunderts (BA, IX)* (Leipzig–Berlin, 1927); reprinted (Hildesheim, 1960, with addenda and corrigenda).

Dölger, F., *Byzanz und die europäische Staatenwelt* (Ettal, 1953).

Dölger, F., *Byzantinische Diplomatik* (Ettal, 1956).

Dölger, F., ΠΑΡΑΣΠΟΡΑ: *30 Aufsätze zur Geschichte, Kultur und Sprache des byzantinischen Reiches* (Ettal, 1961).

Du Cange, C. du Fresne, *Histoire de l'empire de Constantinople sous les empereurs françois* (Paris, 1657); ed. J. A. Buchon, 2 vols. (Paris, 1826).

Du Cange, C. du Fresne, *Historia Byzantina duplici commentario illustrata*, 3 pts. (Paris, 1680).

Dvornik, F., *The Photian Schism* (Cambridge, 1948).

Dvornik, F., *Les Slaves, Byzance et Rome au IXe siècle* (Paris, 1926).

Dvornik, F., *The Making of Central and Eastern Europe* (London, 1949).

Ebersolt, J., *Orient et Occident. Recherches sur les influences byzantines et orientales en France avant et pendant les croisades*, 2nd ed. (Paris, 1954).

Every, G., *The Byzantine Patriarchate (451–1204)* (London, 1948); 2nd ed. (London, 1962).

Fallmerayer, J. P., *Geschichte des Kaiserthums von Trapezunt* (Munich, 1827).

Faris, Nabih Amin (ed.), *The Arab Heritage* (Princeton, 1946).

Finlay, G., *History of Greece*, B.C. *146 to* A.D. *1864*, ed. H. F. Tozer, 7 vols. (Oxford, 1877).

Fleury, Claude, *Histoire ecclésiastique*, 20 vols. (Paris, 1691–1720). [Continued to end of eighteenth century under O. Vidal. Many editions. (Orig. ed. to 1414). 4 additional vols. by Fleury to 1517, publ. Paris, 1836–7.]

Fliche, A. and Martin, V. (ed.), *Histoire de l'Eglise* (Paris, 1934 ff., in progress).

Fortescue, A. K., *The Orthodox Eastern Church* (London, 1927).

French, R. M., *The Eastern Orthodox Church* (London, 1951).

Gardner, A., *The Lascarids of Nicaea* (London, 1912).

Gaudefroy-Demombynes, M. and Platonov, S. F., *Le monde musulman et byzantin jusqu'aux croisades*, in E. Cavaignac, *Histoire du Monde*, VII, 1 (Paris, 1931).

Gay, J., *L'Italie méridionale et l'empire byzantin (867–1071)* (*EcfrAR*) (Paris, 1904).

Geanakoplos, D. J., *Emperor Michael Palaeologus and the West 1258–1282: a Study in Byzantine–Latin Relations* (Cambridge, Mass., 1959).

Gelzer, H., *Abriss der byzantinischen Kaisergeschichte*. In Krumbacher, K., *Geschichte d. byzant. Litteratur* [see below].

Gelzer, H., *Byzantinische Kulturgeschichte* (Tübingen, 1909).

Gelzer, H., *Ausgewählte kleine Schriften* (Leipzig, 1907).

Gerland, E., *Geschichte des lateinischen Kaiserreiches von Konstantinopel* (*Geschichte der Frankenherrschaft in Griechenland*, II, 1) (Homburg v.d. Höhe, 1905).

Gfrörer, A. F., *Byzantinische Geschichten*, ed. J. B. Weiss, 3 vols. (Graz, 1872–7).

Gibbon, E., *The History of the Decline and Fall of the Roman Empire* (London, 1776–81); ed. in 7 vols. by J. B. Bury (London, 1896–1900), and other editions. [Bury's notes essential, especially for bibliography.]

Gibbons, H. A., *The Foundation of the Ottoman Empire* (Oxford, 1916).

Gill, J., *The Council of Florence* (Cambridge, 1959).

Golubinsky, E. E., *Kratkij očerk istorii pravoslavnich cerkvi bolgarskij, serbskoj i ruminckoj ili moldo-valašskoj*. [*Short outline of the history of the Orthodox Churches of Bulgaria, Serbia and Rumania or Moldavia*] (Moscow, 1871).

Golubinsky, E. E., *Istorija russkoj cerkvi* [*History of the Russian Church*], 2 vols. in 4 (Moscow, 1900–11).

Goubert, P., *Byzance avant l'Islam*, I, II (1) (Paris, 1951, 1956).

Grabar, A., *L'empereur dans l'art byzantin. Recherches sur l'art officiel de l'Empire de l'Orient* (Paris, 1936).

Gregorovius, F., *Geschichte der Stadt Athen im Mittelalter*, 2 vols. (Stuttgart, 1889); Greek transl. with additions by S. P. Lampros, 3 vols. (Athens, 1904–6).

Gregorovius, F., *Geschichte der Stadt Rom im Mittelalter*, 8 vols. (Stuttgart, 1859–72). [Translated from 4th ed. by Mrs A. Hamilton (London, 1894–1902), 8 vols. in 13.]

Grousset, R., *L'empire du Levant. Histoire de la Question d'Orient* (Paris, 1949).

Grousset, R., *Histoire des croisades et du Royaume Franc de Jérusalem*, 3 vols. (Paris, 1934–6).

Grunebaum, G. E. von, *Medieval Islam. A Study in Cultural Orientation*, 2nd ed. (Chicago, 1953).

Guilland, R., *Etudes byzantines* (Paris, 1959).

Guilland, R., 'Etudes sur l'histoire administrative de l'empire byzantin'. [These articles are widely scattered in periodicals and a bibliography from 1938 to 1957 will be found in *B*, xxv–xxvii (1955–7, published 1957), 695–6.]

Hackett, J., *History of the Orthodox Church of Cyprus* (London, 1901).

Hammer Purgstall, J. von, *Geschichte des osmanischen Reiches*, 2 vols. (Pest, 1827–35) [with bibliography]; French transl. J. J. Hellert, 18 vols. and atlas (Paris, 1835–43).

Hartmann, L. M., *Geschichte Italiens im Mittelalter*, i–iv (Gotha, 1897–1915).

Hartmann, L. M., *Untersuchungen zur Geschichte der byzantinischen Verwaltung in Italien (540–750)* (Leipzig, 1889).

Hefele, C. J., contin. J. A. G. Hergenröther, *Conciliengeschichte*, 9 vols. (Freiburg-i.-B., 1855 ff.); revised in French transl. by H. Leclercq and others, *Histoire des Conciles* (Paris, 1907 ff.).

Hertzberg, G. F., *Geschichte der Byzantiner und des osmanischen Reiches bis gegen Ende des XVI^{en} Jahrhunderts* (Berlin, 1883). (Allgemeine Geschichte in Einzeldarstellungen.)

Hertzberg, G. F., *Geschichte Griechenlands seit dem Absterben des antiken Lebens bis zum Gegenwart*, 4 vols. (Gotha, 1876–9). (Geschichte der europäischen Staaten.)

Heyd, W., *Geschichte des Levantehandels im Mittelalter* (Stuttgart, 1879); French transl. F. Raynaud, *Histoire du commerce du Levant au moyen âge*, 2nd ed. (Leipzig, 1923); reprinted (1936).

Hill, Sir George, *A History of Cyprus*, vols. i–iii (Cambridge, 1940–8).

Hirsch, F., *Byzantinische Studien* (Leipzig, 1876).

Hitti, P. K., *History of the Arabs from the Earliest Times to the Present*, 6th ed. (London, 1956).

Hodgkin, T., *Italy and Her Invaders*, 8 vols. (Oxford, 1880–99), vols. vi (2nd ed. 1916) to viii.

Holl, K., *Gesammelte Aufsätze zur Kirchengeschichte. II. Der Osten* (Tübingen, 1928).

Honigmann, E., *Die Ostgrenze des byzantinischen Reiches von 363 bis 1071 nach griechischen, arabischen, syrischen und armenischen Quellen* (*Corpus Bruxellense Hist. Byz.* iii) (Brussels, 1935).

Hopf, K., *Geschichte Griechenlands vom Beginn des Mittelalters bis auf unsere Zeit* (Ersch–Gruber, vols. lxxxv and lxxxvi) (Leipzig, 1867, 1868).

Hussey, J. M., *Church and Learning in the Byzantine Empire 867–1185* (London, 1937).

Hussey, J. M., *The Byzantine World*, 2nd ed. (London, 1961).

Il Monachesimo Orientale: Atti del convegno di studi orientali che sul predetto tema si tenne a Roma, sotto la direzione del Pontifico Istituto Orientale, nei giorni 9–12 Aprile 1958. [*OCA*, 153.] (Rome, 1958.)

Jireček, C. J., *Geschichte der Bulgaren* (Prague, 1876).

Jireček, C. J., *Geschichte der Serben*, i, ii (all publ.) (Gotha, 1911–18).

Joannou, P., *Christliche Metaphysik in Byzanz. I. Die Illuminationslehre des Michael Psellos und Joannes Italos* (*Subsidia patristica et byzantina*, iii) (Ettal, 1956).

Jorga, N., *Brève histoire de la petite Arménie: l'Arménie cilicienne* (Paris, 1930).

Jorga, N., *Geschichte des osmanischen Reiches*, i–ii (Gotha, 1908–9).

Jorga, N., *Geschichte des rumänischen Volkes*, 2 vols. (Gotha, 1905).

Jorga, N., *Histoire de la vie byzantine. Empire et civilisation*, 3 vols. (Bucharest, 1934).

Jorga, N., *Histoire des Roumains et de la Romanité orientale*, I–IV in 5 vols. (Bucharest, 1937).

Jugie, M., *Le schisme byzantin. Aperçu historique et doctrinal* (Paris, 1941). [Cf. A. Michel's review in *BZ*, XLV (1952), 408–17, with important additions.]

Jugie, M., *Theologia dogmatica Christianorum orientalium ab ecclesia catholica dissidentium*, 5 vols. (Paris, 1926–35).

Kidd, B. J., *The Churches of Eastern Christendom* (London, 1927).

Köhler, G., *Die Entwicklung des Kriegswesen und der Kriegsführung in der Ritterzeit von der Mitte des 11. Jahrhunderts bis zu den Hussitenkriegen*, 3 vols. (Breslau, 1886–90).

Kondakoff (Kondakov), N. P., *Histoire de l'art byzantin*, French transl. F. Trawinski, 2 vols. (Paris, 1886–91).

Kornemann, E., *Doppelprinzipat und Reichsteilung in Imperium Romanum* (Leipzig and Berlin, 1930).

Kovačević, J., *Srednjovekovna nošnja balkanskich Slovena. Studija iz istorije srednjovekovne kulture Balkana* [*The Medieval Dress of the Balkan Slavs. A Study in the History of Medieval Culture in the Balkans*] (Belgrade, 1953).

Krekić, B., *Dubrovnik (Raguse) et le Levant au moyen-âge* (Paris, 1961).

Kretschmayr, H., *Geschichte von Venedig*, I–II (Gotha, 1905–20).

Krumbacher, K., *Geschichte der byzantinischen Litteratur (527–1453)*, 2nd ed. (*Handbuch d. klass. Altertums-Wissenschaft*, ed. I. von Müller, vol. IX, i) (Munich, 1897). [*GBL.*]

Kukules, Ph., Βυζαντινῶν Βίος καὶ Πολιτισμός, I–VI and supplts. in 8 vols. (Athens, 1947–57).

Kulakovsky, J., *Istorija Vizantii* [*History of Byzantium*], I–III (Kiev, 1913, 1912, 1915).

Lamma, P., *Comneni e Staufer: ricerche sui rapporti fra Bizanzio e l'Occidente nel secolo XII*, 2 vols. (Rome, 1955–7).

Lampros (Lambros), S. P., Ἱστορία τῆς Ἑλλάδος, I–VI (Athens, 1886–1908).

Lebeau, C., *Histoire du Bas-Empire*, ed. J. A. Saint-Martin and M. F. Brosset, 21 vols. (Paris, 1824–36).

Leib, B., *Rome, Kiev et Byzance à la fin du XIe siècle* (Paris, 1924).

Lemerle, P., *Philippes et la Macédoine orientale à l'époque chrétienne et byzantine* (*EcfrAR*, 158) (Paris, 1945).

Lemerle, P., 'Esquisse pour une histoire agraire de Byzance: les sources et les problèmes', *RH*, CCXIX (1958), 32–74, 254–84; CCXX (1958), 42–94.

Levčenko, M. V., *Istorija Vizantii* [*History of Byzantium*] (Moscow, Leningrad, 1940); French transl. *Byzance des origines à 1453* (Paris, 1949).

Lewis, B., *The Arabs in History*, 5th ed. (London, 1960).

Lombard, A., *Constantin V, empereur des Romains* (Paris, 1902).

Longnon, J., *L'empire latin de Constantinople et la principauté de Morée* (Paris, 1949).

Lot, F., *La fin du monde antique et le début du moyen âge* (Paris, 1927).

Lot, F., *L'art militaire et les armées au moyen âge en Europe et dans le Proche Orient*, 2 vols. (Paris, 1946).

Marquart, J., *Osteuropäische und ostasiatische Streifzüge* (Leipzig, 1903).

Martin, E. J., *History of the Iconoclastic Controversy* (London, n.d. [1930]).

Mathew, G., *Byzantine Aesthetics* (London, 1963).

Meliarakes, A., Ἱστορία τοῦ Βασιλείου τῆς Νικαίας καὶ τοῦ Δεσποτάτου τῆς Ἠπείρου (*1204–61*) (Athens, 1898).

Michel, A., *Die Kaisermacht in der Ostkirche (843–1204)* (Darmstadt, 1959). [A reprint of articles in *Ostkirch. Studien*, ii–v (1953–6).]

Miller, W., *Essays on the Latin Orient* (Cambridge, 1921).

Miller, W., *The Latins in the Levant: A History of Frankish Greece (1204–1566)* (London, 1908); enlarged Greek transl. Lampros (Lambros), S. P., Ἱστορία τῆς Φραγκοκρατίας ἐν Ἑλλάδι (Athens, 1909–10).

Miller, W., *Trebizond: the Last Greek Empire* (London, 1926).

Mosheim, J. L. von, *Institutionum historiae ecclesiasticae antiquae et recentioris libri* iv, 4 vols. (Helmstedt, 1755); transl. J. Murdock, ed. H. Soames, 4 vols. (London, 1841); 2nd rev. ed. (1850).

Moss, H. St L. B., *The Birth of the Middle Ages, 395–814* (Oxford, 1935).

Muir, W., *The Caliphate: its Rise, Decline, and Fall*, revised ed. T. H. Weir (Edinburgh, 1924).

Muratori, L. A., *Annali d'Italia*, 12 vols. (Milan, 1744–9). [Also other editions and reprints.]

Mutafčiev, P., *Istorija na bŭlgarskija narod* [*History of the Bulgarian Nation*], 2 vols., 3rd ed. (Sofia, 1948).

Neale, J. M., *History of the Holy Eastern Church*, pt. i: *General Introduction*, 2 vols. (London, 1850).

Neumann, C., *Die Weltstellung des byzantinischen Reiches vor den Kreuzzügen* (Leipzig, 1894); French transl. Renauld and Kozlowski (Paris, 1905); and in *ROC*, x (1903–4), 56–171.

Nicol, D. M., *The Despotate of Epiros* (Oxford, 1957).

Niederle, L., *Manuel de l'antiquité slave*, i: *L'histoire*; ii: *La civilisation* (Paris, 1923, 1926).

Norden, W., *Das Papsttum und Byzanz: die Trennung der beiden Mächte und das Problem ihrer Wiedervereinigung bis zum Untergange des byzantinischen Reichs (1453)* (Berlin, 1903); reprinted (1958).

Obolensky, D., *The Bogomils: a Study in Balkan Neomanichaeism* (Cambridge, 1948).

Ohnsorge, W., *Das Zweikaiserproblem im früheren Mittelalter* (Hildesheim, 1947).

Ohnsorge, W., *Abendland und Byzanz: Gesammelte Aufsätze zur Geschichte der byzantinisch-abendländischen Beziehungen und des Kaisertums* (Darmstadt, 1958).

Oman, C. W. C., *History of the Art of War in the Middle Ages* (London, 1898); 2nd ed., 2 vols. (London, 1924).

Ostrogorsky, G., *Studien zur Geschichte des byzantinischen Bilderstreites* (Breslau, 1929).

Ostrogorsky, G., 'Agrarian Conditions in the Byzantine Empire in the Middle Ages', *Cambridge Economic History of Europe*, i (1942), 194–223, 579–83.

Ostrogorsky, G., *Pour l'histoire de la féodalité byzantine* (*Corpus Bruxellense Hist. Byz.*, Subsidia i, Brussels, 1954).

Ostrogorsky, G., *Quelques problèmes d'histoire de la paysannerie byzantine* (*Corpus Bruxellense Hist. Byz.*, Subsidia ii, Brussels, 1956).

Ostrogorsky, G., *History of the Byzantine State* (Oxford, 1956).

Paparrhegopoulos, K., Ἱστορία τοῦ Ἑλληνικοῦ ἔθνους. 4th ed. P. Karolides, 5 vols. (Athens, 1903).

Pargoire, J., *L'église byzantine de 527 à 847* (Paris, 1905).

Pears, E., *The Destruction of the Greek Empire and the Story of the Capture of Constantinople by the Turks* (London, 1903).

Pears, E., *The Fall of Constantinople, being the Story of the Fourth Crusade* (London, 1885).

Pertile, A., *Storia del diritto italiano dalla caduta dell'impero Romano alla codificazione*, 2nd ed., 6 vols., P. Del Giudice (Turin, 1892–1902); Index, L. Eusebio (Turin, 1893).

Rambaud, A., *L'empire grec au dixième siècle: Constantin Porphyrogénète* (Paris, 1870).

Romano, G. and Solmi, A., *Le dominazioni barbariche in Italia (395–888)*, 3rd ed. (Milan, 1909).

Rouillard, G., *La vie rurale dans l'empire byzantin* (Paris, 1953).

Runciman, S., *The Emperor Romanus Lecapenus and his Reign. A Study of Tenth-Century Byzantium* (Cambridge, 1929).

Runciman, S., *A History of the First Bulgarian Empire* (London, 1930).

Runciman, S., *Byzantine Civilisation* (London, 1933).

Runciman, S., *A History of the Crusades*, 3 vols. (Cambridge, 1951–4).

Runciman, S., *The Eastern Schism: a Study of the Papacy and the Eastern Churches during the XIth and XIIth Centuries* (Oxford, 1955).

Runciman, S., *The Sicilian Vespers. A History of the Mediterranean World in the Late Thirteenth Century* (Cambridge, 1958).

Schaube, A., *Handelsgeschichte der romanischen Völker des Mittelmeergebiets bis zum Ende der Kreuzzüge* (Munich and Berlin, 1906).

Schenk, K., *Kaiser Leo III* (Halle, 1880).

Schlumberger, G., *Un empereur byzantin au X*^{e} *siècle: Nicéphore Phocas* (Paris, 1890).

Schlumberger, G., *L'épopée byzantine à la fin du X*^{e} *siècle.* I: *Jean Tzimiscès, Basile II (969–89)*; II: *Basile II (989–1025)*; III: *Les Porphyrogénètes, Zoé et Théodora (1025–57)* (Paris, 1896–1905).

Schupfer, F., *Manuale di storia del diritto italiano* (Città di Castello, 1904).

Schwarzlose, K., *Der Bilderstreit. Ein Kampf der griechischen Kirche um ihre Eigenart und um ihre Freiheit* (Gotha, 1890).

Setton, K. M. (editor-in-chief), *A History of the Crusades.* I: *The First Hundred Years*, ed. M. W. Baldwin; II: *The Later Crusades, 1189–1311*, ed. R. L. Wolff and H. W. Hazard (Philadelphia, 1955–62). [In progress.]

Setton, K. M., *Catalan Domination of Athens, 1311–1388* (Cambridge, Mass., 1948).

Šišić, F., *Geschichte der Kroaten* (Zagreb, 1917).

Skabalanovič, N., *Vizantijskoe gosudarstvo i cerkov' v XI v. [Byzantine State and Church in the Eleventh Century]* (St Petersburg, 1884).

Spinka, M., *A History of Christianity in the Balkans* (Chicago, 1933).

Stadtmüller, G., *Geschichte Südosteuropas* (Munich, 1950).

Stein, E., 'Untersuchungen zur spätbyzantinischen Verfassungs- und Wirtschaftsgeschichte', *Mitt. zur Osman. Gesch.* II (1923–5), 1–62; reprinted separately (Amsterdam, 1962).

Stein, E., *Geschichte des spätrömischen Reiches*, I: *Vom römischen zum byzantinischen Staate, 284–476* (Vienna, 1928); French ed. (Paris, 1959).

Stein, E., *Histoire du Bas-Empire*, II: *De la disparition de l'Empire d'Occident à la mort de Justinien, 476–565* (Paris, Brussels, Amsterdam, 1949).

Strzygowski, J., *Die Baukunst der Armenier und Europa*, 2 vols. (Vienna, 1919).

Tafrali, O., *Thessalonique au quatorzième siècle* (Paris, 1913).

Talbot Rice, D., *Byzantine Art* (Oxford, 1935); new ed. (London, 1954).

Talbot Rice, D., *The Beginnings of Christian Art* (London, 1957).

Talbot Rice, D., *The Art of Byzantium* (London, 1959).

Talbot Rice, D., *The Byzantines* (London, 1962).

Temperley, H. W. V., *History of Serbia* (London, 1917).

Thiriet, F., *La Romanie vénitienne au moyen âge. Le développement et l'exploitation du domaine colonial vénitien (XIIe–XVe siècles)* (*EcfrAR*, 193) (Paris, 1959).

Treitinger, O., *Die oströmische Kaiser- und Reichsidee nach ihrer Gestaltung im höfischen Zeremoniell* (Jena, 1938); reprinted (Darmstadt, 1956).

Uspensky, F. I., *Očerki po istorii vizantijskoj obrazovannosti* [*Studies in the History of Byzantine Civilisation*] (St Petersburg, 1891).

Uspensky, F. I., *Istorija vizantijskoj imperii* [*History of the Byzantine Empire*], I; II, 1; III (St Petersburg, 1913; Leningrad, 1927; Moscow, 1948).

Vasiliev, A. A., *History of the Byzantine Empire* (Madison, 1952).

Vasiliev, A. A., *Vizantija i Araby*, 2 vols. (St Petersburg, 1900–2) [the history from 813 with translation of passages from Arabic writers, but see now the French edition: *Byzance et les Arabes*, I: *La dynastie d'Amorium*, by H. Grégoire, M. Canard, etc. (Brussels, 1935); II: *La dynastie macédonienne*, by H. Grégoire and M. Canard, 2e partie: *Extraits des sources arabes*, by M. Canard (Brussels, 1950) covers the years 820–959, with translation of relevant passages from Arabic writers; the first part of vol. II has not yet appeared].

Vasilievsky, V. G., *Trudy* [*Works*], 4 vols. (St Petersburg and Leningrad, 1908–30).

Vinogradoff, P., *Roman Law in Mediaeval Europe* (London and New York, 1909).

Vogt, A., *Basile Ier, empereur de Byzance et la civilisation byzantine à la fin du IXe siècle* (Paris, 1908).

Weil, G., *Geschichte der Chalifen*, 3 vols. (Mannheim, 1846–51).

Weil, G., *Geschichte der islamitischen Völker von Mohammed bis zur Zeit des Sultans Selim* (Stuttgart, 1866).

Weitzmann, K., *Geistige Grundlagen und Wesen der Makedonischen Renaissance* (*Arbeitsgemeinschaft des Landes Nordrhein-Westfalen: Geisteswissenschaften*, Heft 107) (Cologne and Opladen, 1963).

Wellesz, E., *History of Byzantine Music and Hymnography*, 2nd ed. (Oxford, 1961).

Wittek, P., *The Rise of the Ottoman Empire* (*Royal Asiatic Soc. Monographs*, XXIII) (London, 1938).

Xénopol, A. D., *Histoire des Roumains de la Dacie Trajane . . . (513–1859)*, 2 vols. (Paris, 1896). [Abridged from the Rumanian edition.]

Xivrey, B. de, *Mémoire sur la vie et les ouvrages de l'empereur Manuel Paléologue* (Mém. de l'Inst. de France, *AcadIBL*, 19, 2) (Paris, 1853).

Zachariae von Lingenthal, K. E., *Geschichte des griechisch-römischen Rechts*, 3rd ed. (Berlin, 1892).

Zakythinos, D. A., *Le Despotat grec de Morée*, 2 vols. (Paris, 1932–53).

Zakythinos, D. A., *Crise monétaire et crise économique à Byzance du XIIIe au XVe siècle* (Athens, 1948).

Zernov, N., *Eastern Christendom: a Study of the Origin and Development of the Eastern Orthodox Church* (London, 1961).

Zlatarsky, V. N., *Istorija na bŭlgarskata dŭržava prez srednite vekove* [*History of the Bulgarian State in the Middle Ages*], 3 vols. (Sofia, 1918–40).

1054–1954. L'église et les églises, neuf siècles de douloureuse séparation entre l'orient et l'occident (Etudes et travaux offerts à Dom Lambert Beauduin), 2 vols. (Chevetogne, 1954–5).

CHAPTER I. THE FORMATION OF THE EAST ROMAN EMPIRE, 330–717

For the period with which this introductory chapter is concerned, the bibliographies to volumes I (1911) and II (1913) of the *Cambridge Medieval History* should be consulted. Supplementary lists of more recent publications would be out of place in the present volume; references to some periodical surveys may be found in G. Ostrogorsky's *History of the Byzantine State* (Oxford, 1956), pp. 1–2, and for publications during the years 1938–52 see also the critical study of F. Dölger and A. M. Schneider, *Byzanz* (Bern, 1952).

On the topics discussed in chapter I, a selection of books and articles is given below.

I. GENERAL

(For works covering the whole period of Byzantine History, see General Bibliography v)

Bury, J. B., *History of the Later Roman Empire (395–565)* [see Gen. Bibl. v].
Charanis, P., 'Ethnic Changes in the Byzantine Empire in the Seventh Century', *DOP*, XIII (1959), 23–44.
Lot, F., *La fin du monde antique et le début du moyen âge* [see Gen. Bibl. v].
Ostrogorsky, G., 'The Byzantine Empire in the World of the Seventh Century', *DOP*, XIII (1959), 1–21.
Piganiol, A., *L'empire chrétien 325–395* (*Histoire générale*, ed. G. Glotz: *Histoire romaine*, IV, 2 (Paris, 1947)).
Seeck, O., *Geschichte des Untergangs der antiken Welt*, 6 vols. (Stuttgart, 1920–1).
Stein, E., *Histoire du Bas-Empire*, I (*284–476*) (and in German); II (*476–565*) [see Gen. Bibl. v].

II. CONSTANTINE THE GREAT

The concluding chapters of the *Cambridge Ancient History*, volume XII (1939), should be consulted, together with the relevant bibliographies. See also J. Vogt and W. Seston, 'Die Konstantinische Frage', *Relazioni del X Congresso Internazionale di Scienze Storiche*, VI: *Relazioni Generali e Supplementi* (Florence, 1955), pp. 731–99 [a bibliographical study].

Alföldi, A., *The Conversion of Constantine and Pagan Rome*, transl. H. Mattingly (Oxford, 1948).
Baynes, N. H., 'Constantine the Great and the Christian Church', *Proceedings of the British Academy*, XV (1929), 341–442 [publ. separately, 107 pp.].
Dörries, H. D., *Das Selbstzeugnis Kaiser Konstantins. Abh. der Akad. d. Wissenschaften zu Göttingen*, Phil.-Hist. Klasse 3. F., no. 34 (Göttingen, 1954).
Franchi de' Cavalieri, P. P., *Constantiniana* (Studi e Testi, 171) (Rome, 1953).
Hönn, K., *Konstantin der Grosse. Leben einer Zeitenwende*, 2nd ed. (Leipzig, 1945).
Jones, A. H. M., *Constantine and the Conversion of Europe* (London, 1948).
Kraft, H., *Kaiser Konstantins religiöse Entwicklung* (Tübingen, 1955).

Schwartz, E., *Kaiser Constantin und die christliche Kirche*, 2nd ed. (Leipzig–Berlin, 1936).

Vogt, J., *Constantin der Grosse und sein Jahrhundert* (Munich, 1949).

Vogt, J., 'Constantinus der Grosse', *RAC*, III (Stuttgart, 1956), 306–79.

III. CONSTANTINOPLE

Diez, E. and Glück, H., *Alt-Konstantinopel* (Munich, 1920).

Janin, R., *Constantinople byzantine* [see Gen. Bibl. II].

Janin, R., *La géographie ecclésiastique de l'empire byzantin*, pt. I, vol. III: *Constantinople: les églises et les monastères* [see Gen. Bibl. II].

Krischen, F., *Die Landmauer von Konstantinopel*, 2 vols. (Berlin, 1938–43).

Van Millingen, A., *Byzantine Constantinople* [see Gen. Bibl. II].

IV. THE EMPEROR

Alföldi, A., 'Die Ausgestaltung des monarchischen Zeremoniells am römischen Kaiserhofe', *Mitt. d. Deutschen Archäol. Inst.*, Röm. Abt., XLIX (Munich, 1934), 1–118.

Baynes, N. H., 'Eusebius and the Christian Empire', *AIPHO*, II (1933–4). *Mélanges Bidez* (Brussels, 1933), pp. 13–18. Reprinted in *Byzantine Studies*, pp. 168–72 [see Gen. Bibl. V].

Baynes, N. H., 'The Byzantine State', *Byzantine Studies*, pp. 47–66 [see Gen. Bibl. V].

Bréhier, L., *Les institutions de l'empire byzantin*, pp. 1–88 [see Gen. Bibl. V].

Bréhier, L. and Batiffol, P., *Les survivances du culte impérial romain* (Paris, 1920).

Bury, J. B., *The Constitution of the Later Roman Empire* [see Gen. Bibl. V].

Charlesworth, M. P., 'The Virtues of a Roman Emperor', *Proceedings of the British Academy*, XXIII (1939), 105–33.

Deér, J., 'Der Ursprung der Kaiserkrone', *Schweitzer Beiträge zur allgemeinen Geschichte*, VIII (1950), 51–87.

Dölger, F., 'Rom in der Gedankenwelt der Byzantiner', *ZKG*, LVI (1937), 1–42. Reprinted in *Byzanz und die europäische Staatenwelt*, pp. 83 ff. [see Gen. Bibl. V].

Dölger, F., 'Die Kaiserurkunde der Byzantiner als Ausdruck ihrer politischen Anschauungen', *HZ*, CLIX (1938–9), 229–50. Reprinted in *Byzanz und die europäische Staatenwelt*, pp. 1–33.

Ensslin, W., 'The End of the Principate', *CAH*, XII (1939), 352–82 [with bibliography].

Ensslin, W., 'Das Gottesgnadentum des autokratorischen Kaisertums der frühbyzantinischen Zeit', *Atti del V Congresso internazionale di Studi bizantini*, I (Rome, 1939), 154–66.

Ensslin, W., 'Gottkaiser und Kaiser von Gottes Gnaden', *SBAW*, VI (1943).

Ensslin, W., 'Der Kaiser in der Spätantike', *HZ*, CLXXVII (1954), 449–68.

Grabar, A., *L'empereur dans l'art byzantin* [see Gen. Bibl. V].

Ostrogorsky, G., 'Die byzantinische Staatenhierarchie', *Sem. Kond.* VIII (1936), 41–61.

Setton, K. M., *Christian Attitude towards the Emperor in the Fourth Century* (New York, 1941).

Straub, J., *Vom Herrscherideal der Spätantike. Forschungen zur Kirchen- und Geistesgeschichte*, XVIII (Stuttgart, 1939).

Treitinger, O., *Die oströmische Kaiser- und Reichsidee* [see Gen. Bibl. V].

V. THE CHURCH

Baynes, N. H., 'Alexandria and Constantinople: a Study in Ecclesiastical Diplomacy', *Journal of Egyptian Archaeology*, XII (1926), 145–56. Reprinted in *Byzantine Studies*, pp. 97–115 [see Gen. Bibl. v].

Burn, A. E., *The Council of Nicaea* (London, 1925).

Caspar, E., *Geschichte des Papsttums*, II [see Gen. Bibl. v].

Duchesne, L., *Histoire ancienne de l'Eglise*, 3 vols. (Paris, 1906–8). English transl. from the 4th ed.: *Early History of the Christian Church* (London, 1909, 1912, 1924).

Duchesne, L., *L'Eglise au VIème siècle* (Paris, 1925).

Fliche, A. and Martin, V. (edd.), *Histoire de l'Eglise*, III: *De la paix constantinienne à la mort de Théodose*; IV: *De la mort de Théodose à l'élection de Grégoire le Grand*; V: *Grégoire le Grand, les états barbares et la conquête arabe, 590–737* [see Gen. Bibl. v].

Grillmeier, A. and Bacht, H. (edd.), *Das Konzil von Chalkedon*, II: *Entscheidung um Chalkedon* (Würzburg, 1953).

Hardy, E. R., *Christian Egypt: Church and People: Christianity and Nationalism in the Patriarchate of Alexandria* (New York, 1952).

Hefele, C. J. and Leclerq, H., *Histoire des Conciles* [see Gen. Bibl. v].

Honigmann, E., *Evêchés et évêques monophysites d'Asie antérieure au VIe siècle* (Louvain, 1951).

VI. DEFENCE OF THE FRONTIERS

Chapot, V., *La Frontière de l'Euphrate* (Paris, 1907).

Christensen, A. E., *L'Iran sous les Sassanides*, 2nd ed. (Copenhagen, 1944).

Demougeot, E., *De l'unité à la division de l'empire romain, 395–410* (Paris, 1951).

Diehl, C., *Justinien et la civilisation byzantine au VIème siècle* (Paris, 1901).

Ensslin, W., *Theoderich der Grosse* (Munich, 1947).

Honigmann, E., *Die Ostgrenze des byzantinischen Reiches von 363 bis 1071* [see Gen. Bibl. v].

Lemerle, P., 'Invasions et migrations dans les Balkans depuis la fin de l'époque romaine jusqu'au VIIIe siècle', *RH*, CCXI (1954), 265–308.

Pernice, A., *L'imperatore Eraclio. Saggio di storia bizantina* (Florence, 1905).

Rubin, B., *Das Zeitalter Justinians*, I (Berlin, 1960).

Schmidt, L., *Geschichte der Wandalen*, 2nd ed. (Munich, 1942).

Thompson, E. A., *A History of Attila and the Huns* (Oxford, 1948).

Vasiliev, A. A., *Justin the First. An Introduction to the Epoch of Justinian the Great* (Cambridge, Mass., 1950).

VII. ADMINISTRATION

Boak, A. E. R., 'The Roman *Magistri* in the Civil and Military Service of the Empire', *Harvard Studies in Classical Philology*, XXVI (1915), 73–164.

Boak, A. E. R., *The Master of the Offices in the Later Roman and Byzantine Empires* (New York, 1919).

Bréhier, L., *Les institutions de l'empire byzantin*, pp. 89 ff. [see Gen. Bibl. v].

Bury, J. B., *The Constitution of the Later Roman Empire* [see Gen. Bibl. v].

Bury, J. B., *The Imperial Administrative System in the Ninth Century* [see Gen. Bibl. v].

Dunlap, J. E., *The Office of the Grand Chamberlain in the Later Roman and Byzantine Empires* (New York, 1924) [also published with Boak's *Master of the Offices* as *Two Studies in Later Roman and Byzantine Administration* (New York and London, 1924)].

Ensslin, W., 'The Emperor and the Imperial Administration', *Byzantium*, ed. N. H. Baynes and H. St L. B. Moss, pp. 268–307 [see Gen. Bibl. v].

Guilland, R. [various studies of individual offices. A list may be found in *B*, XXV–XXVII (1955–7), 695–6].

Kolias, G., *Ämter- und Würdenkauf im früh- und mittelbyzantinischen Reich* (Athens, 1939).

Palanque, J. R., *Essai sur la préfecture du prétoire du Bas-Empire* (Paris, 1933).

Stein, E., *Untersuchungen über das Officium der Prätorianerpräfektur seit Diokletian* (Vienna, 1922).

A. THE PROVINCES

Bell, H. I., 'Egypt and the Byzantine Empire', *The Legacy of Egypt*, ed. S. R. K. Glanville (Oxford, 1942), pp. 332–47.

Diehl, C., *Etudes sur l'administration byzantine dans l'exarchat de Ravenne, 568–751* (Paris, 1888).

Diehl, C., *L'Afrique byzantine. Histoire de la domination byzantine en Afrique, 533–709* (Paris, 1896).

Gelzer, M., *Studien zur byzantinischen Verwaltung Ägyptens* (Leipzig, 1909).

Hartmann, L. M., *Untersuchungen zur Geschichte der byzantinischen Verwaltung in Italien (540–750)* [see Gen. Bibl. v].

Rouillard, G., *L'administration civile de l'Egypte byzantine*, 2nd ed. (Paris, 1928).

Warmington, B. H., *The North African Provinces from Diocletian to the Vandal Conquest* (Cambridge, 1954).

B. THE ARMY

Aussaresses, F., *L'armée byzantine à la fin du VIe siècle* (Paris, 1909).

Berchem, D. van, *L'armée de Dioclétien et la réforme constantinienne* (Paris, 1952).

Bréhier, L., *Les institutions de l'empire byzantin*, pp. 334 ff. [see Gen. Bibl. v].

Ensslin, W., 'Zum Heermeisteramt des spätrömischen Reiches', *Klio*, XXIII (1929), 306–25; XXIV (1930), 102–47, 467–502.

Grosse, R., *Römische Militärgeschichte von Gallienus bis zum Beginn der byzantinischen Themenverfassung* (Berlin, 1920).

C. THE THEME SYSTEM

Baynes, N. H., 'The Emperor Heraclius and the Military Theme System', *EHR*, LXVII (1952), 380 ff.

Diehl, C., 'L'origine du régime des thèmes dans l'empire byzantin', *Etudes byzantines* (Paris, 1905), pp. 276–92.

Dölger, F., 'Zur Ableitung des byzantinischen Verwaltungsterminus θέμα', *Historia*, IV (1955), 189–98.

Ensslin, W., 'Der Kaiser Herakleios und die Themenverfassung', *BZ*, XLVI (1953), 367 ff.

Gelzer, H., *Die Genesis der byzantinischen Themenverfassung* (Leipzig, 1899).

Haussig, H.-W., 'Anfänge der Themenordnung', in F. Altheim and R. Stiehl, *Finanzgeschichte der Spätantiken* (Frankfurt-am-Main, 1957), pp. 82–114.

Karayannopulos, J., 'Contribution au problème des thèmes byzantins', *L'Hellénisme Contemporain*, x (1946), 457–502.

Karayannopulos, J., *Die Entstehung der byzantinischen Themenordnung* (Byzantinisches Archiv, x) (Munich, 1959).

Ostrogorsky, G., 'Sur la date de la composition du livre des Thèmes', *B*, xxiii (1953), 31–66.

Pertusi, A., *Costantino Porfirogenito 'De Thematibus'* (Studi e Testi, 160) (Rome, 1952).

Pertusi, A., 'Nuova ipotesi sull'origine dei temi bizantini', *Aevum*, xxviii (1954), 126–50.

Stein, E., 'Zur Entstehung der Themenverfassung', *Studien zur Geschichte des byzantinischen Reiches* (Stuttgart, 1919), pp. 117–40.

Stein, E., 'Ein Kapitel vom persischen und vom byzantinischen Staat', *BNJ*, i (1920), 50–89.

See also A. Pertusi, 'La formation des thèmes byzantins', *Berichte zum XI. Internationalen Byzantinisten-Kongress*, i (Munich, 1958), 1–40, and G. Ostrogorsky, *ibid.* vii, 1–8.

VIII. TAXATION AND ECONOMIC LIFE

The following chapters of the *Cambridge Economic History of Europe* should be consulted, together with the relevant bibliographies. Volume i (1941), chapter i: 'Agrarian Conditions in the Byzantine Empire in the Middle Ages', by G. Ostrogorsky. Volume ii (1952), chapter ii: 'Trade and Industry under the Later Roman Empire in the West', by F. Walbank, and chapter iii: 'Byzantine Trade and Industry', by S. Runciman. See also the bibliographies to chapters vi and vii of N. H. Baynes, *The Byzantine Empire* (revised edition, Oxford, 1958).

Andréadès, A. M., 'Deux livres récents sur les finances byzantines', *BZ*, xxviii (1928), 287–323.

Andréadès, A. M., 'The Economic Life of the Byzantine Empire', and 'Public Finances', *Byzantium*, ed. Baynes and Moss, chaps. ii and iii, pp. 51–70, 71–85 [see Gen. Bibl. v].

Déléage, A., *La capitation du Bas-Empire* (Mâcon, 1945).

Dölger, F., *Beiträge zur Geschichte der byzantinischen Finanzverwaltung* [see Gen. Bibl. v].

Karayannopulos, J., *Das Finanzwesen des frühbyzantinischen Staates* (Munich, 1958).

Lopez, R. S., 'The Role of Trade in the Economic Readjustment of Byzantium in the Seventh Century', *DOP*, xiii (1959), 67–85.

Mazzarino, S., *Aspetti sociali del quarto secolo* (Rome, 1951).

Mickwitz, G., *Geld und Wirtschaft im römischen Reich des vierten Jahrhunderts nach Chr.* (Helsingfors, 1932).

Ostrogorsky, G., 'Löhne und Preise in Byzanz', *BZ*, xxxii (1932), 293–333.

Ostrogorsky, G., 'Byzantine Cities in the Early Middle Ages', *DOP*, xiii (1959), 45–66.

Teall, J. L., 'The Grain Supply of the Empire, 330–1025', *DOP*, xiii (1959), 87–139.

CHAPTER II. THE CHRISTIAN BACKGROUND

I. PRIMARY SOURCES

The Greek Christian sources referred to in this chapter are still most readily consulted in Migne's edition (*Patrologiae cursus completus, Series graeco-latina*, ed. J. P. Migne, 161 vols., Paris, 1857–66), which has a parallel Latin translation of the text: indices to the series by F. Cavallera (Paris, 1912).

For convenience a list of the principal writers mentioned, with the volumes of the *Patrologia* in which their works are to be found, is given here:

Athanasius of Alexandria (*c.* 295–373), *MPG*, xxv–xxviii.
Basil of Caesarea (*c.* 330–379), *MPG*, xxix–xxxii.
Cyril of Alexandria (d. 444), *MPG*, lxviii–lxxvii.
Pseudo-Dionysius the Areopagite (*c.* 500), *MPG*, iii–iv.
Gregory of Nazianzus (329/30–*c.* 390), *MPG*, xxxv–xxxviii.
Gregory of Nyssa (d. 394), *MPG*, xliv–xlvi.
John of Damascus (d. 750), *MPG*, xciv–xcvi.
John Chrysostom (344/54–407), *MPG*, xlvii–lxiv.
Maximus the Confessor (*c.* 580–662), *MPG*, xc–xci.
Methodius of Olympus (d. *c.* 311), *MPG*, xviii.
Nemesius of Emesa (4th–5th cent.), *MPG*, xl.
Procopius of Gaza (*c.* 475–538), *MPG*, lxxxvii.
Theodoret of Cyrrhus (*c.* 393–460), *MPG*, lxxx–lxxxiv.

Four other Christian sources utilised in this chapter will also be found in Migne: the *Iambi ad Seleucum* of Amphilochius of Iconium (*c.* 340–400) are printed among the *Carmina* attributed to Gregory of Nazianzus, and the characteristically seventh-century treatise *De Sacrosancta Trinitate* is printed as being by Cyril of Alexandria. Similarly, much of John Philoponus is printed under John of Damascus, whilst Leontius of Byzantium is elided with the Origenist Leontius of Jerusalem (*MPG*, lxxxvi).

The texts of Migne must be treated throughout with caution. Each has no more than the value of the earlier text of which it is a reprint, and the authority of these varies greatly. Again the great majority of the volumes so far cited contain either acknowledged spuria or treatises the authenticity of which has been questioned.

Critical bibliographies may be found in B. Altaner, *Patrologie*; J. Quasten, *Patrology*; and H.-G. Beck, *Kirche und theologische Literatur* (see Gen. Bibl. i and also the bibliography for chapters xxv, xxvi and xxvii).

II. MODERN WORKS

Alivisatos, H. S., *Die kirchliche Gesetzgebung Justinians* (Leipzig, 1913).
Altaner, B., *Patrologie* [see Gen. Bibl. i].
Baur, Chr., *Johannes Chrysostomus und seine Zeit*, 2 vols. (Munich, 1929–30).
Baynes, N. H., 'The Hellenistic Civilization and East Rome', *Byzantine Studies* [see Gen. Bibl. v].
Baynes, N. H., 'The Thought World of East Rome', *Byzantine Studies* [see Gen. Bibl. v].

Bell, H. I., *Egypt from Alexander the Great to the Arab Conquest: a Study in the Diffusion and Decay of Hellenism* (Oxford, 1948).
Biondi, B., *Giustiniano I, Principe e Legislatore* (Milan, 1936).
Bréhier, L. and Battifol, P., *Les survivances du culte impérial romain* (Paris, 1920).
Callahan, J. F., 'Greek Philosophy and the Cappadocian Cosmology', *DOP*, XII (1958), 29–57.
Chabot, J.-B., *Littérature syriaque* (Paris, 1934).
Cherniss, H. F., *The Platonism of Gregory of Nyssa* (Berkeley, 1930).
Clarke, W. L., *St Basil the Great, a Study in Monasticism* (Cambridge, 1913).
Cochrane, C. N., *Christianity and Classical Culture* (Oxford, 1940).
Daniélou, J., *Platonisme et théologie mystique* (Paris, 1944).
Delehaye, H., *Les légendes grecques des saints militaires* (Paris, 1909).
Delehaye, H., *Les saints stylites* (Brussels, 1923).
Dieterich, K., *Hellenism in Asia Minor* (New York, 1913).
Driver, G. R. and Hodgson, L., *The Bazaar of Heracleides* (Oxford, 1925).
Ensslin, W., 'Gottkaiser und Kaiser von Gottes Gnaden', *SBAW*, VI (1943).
Fleury, E., *Hellénisme et Christianisme* (Paris, 1930).
Gelzer, H., 'Das Verhältnis von Staat und Kirche in Byzanz', *HZ*, LXXXVI (1901), 193–252; reprinted in *Ausgewählte kleine Schriften* [see Gen. Bibl. v].
Ghellinck, J. de, *Patristique et moyen-âge* [see Gen. Bibl. I].
Grillmeier, A. and Bacht, H. (edd.), *Das Konzil von Chalkedon*, vols. I and II (Würzburg, 1951–3).
Guignet, M., *Saint Grégoire de Nazianze et la rhétorique* (Paris, 1911).
Hoeck, J. M., 'Stand und Aufgaben der Damaskenos-Forschung', *OCP*, XVII (1951), 5–60.
Holl, K., *Enthusiasmus und Bussgewalt beim griechischen Mönchtum* (Leipzig, 1898).
Hoppner, Th., *Über die Koptisch-Sahidischen Apophthegmata Patrum* (Vienna, 1918) [cf. *MPG*, LXV].
Humbertclaude, P., *La doctrine ascétique de Saint Basile de Césarée* (Paris, 1932).
Jacks, L. V., *Basil and Greek Literature* (Washington, 1936).
Jugie, M., *Theologia dogmatica*, v, *De theologia dogmatica Nestorianorum et Monophysitarum* [see Gen. Bibl. v].
Karst, J., *Littérature géorgienne chrétienne* (Paris, 1934).
Koch, H., *Pseudo-Dionysius Areopagita in seinen Beziehungen zum Neoplatonismus und Mysterienwesen* (Mainz, 1900).
Krumbacher, K., *Geschichte der byzantinischen Litteratur* [see Gen. Bibl. v].
Ladner, G. B., 'The Philosophical Anthropology of Saint Gregory of Nyssa', *DOP*, XII (1958), 59–94.
Ladner, G. B., *The Idea of Reform: its Impact on Christian Thought and Action in the Age of the Fathers* (Cambridge, Mass., 1959).
Lefort, L. Th., *Les Vies Coptes de Saint Pachome et de ses premiers successeurs* (Louvain, 1943).
Muckle, J., *The Doctrine of Gregory of Nyssa on Man as the Image of God* (Toronto, 1945).
Murphy, M. G., *St Basil and Monasticism* (Washington, 1930).
Otis, B., 'Cappadocian Thought as a Coherent System', *DOP*, XII (1958), 95–124.
Pargoire, J., *L'église byzantine de 527 à 847* [see Gen. Bibl. v].

Peeters, P., *Le tréfonds oriental de l'hagiographie byzantine* (Brussels, 1950).

Pinault, H., *Le Platonisme de Grégoire de Nazianze* (Paris, 1930).

Prestige, G. L., *God in Patristic Thought* (London, 1936).

Puech, A., *Histoire de la littérature grecque chrétienne* (Paris, 1930).

Quasten, J., *Patrology* [see Gen. Bibl. I].

Resch, P., *La doctrine ascétique des premiers maîtres égyptiens du IVᵉ siècle* (Paris, 1931).

Richard, M., 'Léonce de Jérusalem et Léonce de Byzance', *Mélanges de Science religieuse* (Lille, 1944), pp. 35–88.

Salaville, S., 'De la spiritualité patristique et byzantine à la théologie russe', *REB*, III (1945), 215–44 [bibliographical survey].

Voigt, K., *Staat und Kirche von Konstantin dem Grossen bis zum ende der Karolingerzeit* (Stuttgart, 1936).

Volker, W., *Das Vollkommenheits-ideal des Origenes* (Tübingen, 1932).

Wenger, A., 'Bulletin de spiritualité et de théologie byzantines', *REB*, XIII (1955), 140–96. [This is a survey of work published from July 1952 to December 1954 and includes sections on texts and manuscripts, Gregory of Nyssa and the pseudo-Macarius, Evagrius of Pontus, and the pseudo-Dionysius.]

Wolfson, H. A., *The Philosophy of the Church Fathers*, I (Cambridge, Mass., 1956).

Wolfson, H. A., 'Philosophical Implications of the Theology of Cyril of Alexandria', *DOP*, XI (1957), 1–19.

Wolfson, H. A., 'Philosophical Implications of Arianism and Apollinarianism', *DOP*, XII (1958), 3–28.

Zilliacus, H., *Zum Kampf der Weltsprachen im oströmischen Reich* (Helsingfors, 1936).

CHAPTER III. ICONOCLASM AND IMPERIAL RULE, 717–842

The list of works here cited should be supplemented by the bibliographies to other chapters (e.g. VI, X, XI, XIV, XV and XVII).

I. PRIMARY SOURCES

Fuller detail on hagiographical sources may be found in *Bibliotheca Hagiographica Graeca*, and on the historical writings in Gy. Moravcsik, *Byzantinoturcica* [see Gen. Bibl. I].

Abel, S. and Simson, B., *Jahrbücher des fränkischen Reiches unter Karl dem Grossen, 768–814* (Jahrbücher der deutschen Geschichte), vol. I, 2nd ed. (1888); vol. II (1883) (Leipzig).

Acta concilii 815, ed. D. Serruys. *Mélanges d'archéologie et d'histoire publiés par l'Ecole française de Rome*, XXIII (1903), 345–51; see also P. J. Alexander, 'The Iconoclastic Council of St Sophia (815) and its definition (*Horos*)', *DOP*, VII (1953), 37–66.

Anastasius Bibliothecarius, *Praefatio in Concilium Constantinopolitanum IV*, Mansi, vol. XVI [see Gen. Bibl. IV].

Andrew in Crisi (†766 or 767), *Vita, AASS,* 17 October, VIII (1853), 124–49.

Annales et chronica, ed. G. H. Pertz, *MGH, Script.* I and IV [see Gen. Bibl. IV].

Annales regni Francorum inde ab a. 741 usque ad a. 829, ed. F. Kurze (Hanover, 1895).

Anonymi Chronographia syntomos e codice Matritensi no. 121 (nunc 4701), ed. A. Bauer (Leipzig, 1909).

Anonymus, *Ad Constantinum Caballinum, MPG,* xcv, 309–44.

Athanasia heg. in Aegina insula saec. IX, *Vita, AASS,* 14 August, III (1737), 168–75.

Bacchus iunior mon. m. in Palaestina saec. VIII ex., *Vita,* ed. F. Combefis, *Christi martyrum lecta trias* (Paris, 1666), pp. 61–126.

Bees, N., '*Τὸ «περὶ τῆς κτίσεως τῆς Μονεμβασίας» χρονικόν',* Βυζαντίς, I (1909), 57–105.

Beltrani, G., *Documenti longobardi e greci per la storia dell'Italia meridionale nel medio evo* (Rome, 1877).

Böhmer, J. F. and others, *Regesta imperii,* I, new ed. (Graz, 1908)

Brunner, H. and Zeumer, K., *Die Constantinische Schenkungsurkunde,* I: *Das Constitutum Constantini;* II: *Der älteste Text* (Berlin, 1888) [published separately and in the Festgabe R. von Gneist].

Caspar, E., 'Papst Gregor II und der Bilderstreit', *ZKG,* LII (1933), 29–89.

Cedrenus, George, *Compendium historiarum,* ed. I. Bekker, 2 vols., *CSHB* (1838–9).

Codex Carolinus, ed. W. Gundlach, *MGH, Ep.,* III (1892), 469–657.

Coleman, C. B., *The Treatise of Lorenzo Valla on the Donation of Constantine* (New Haven, 1922). [Latin text with English translation.]

Concilia aevi Karolini, 1–2, *MGH, Legum Sectio* III; Concilia, II, 1–2, ed. A. Werminghoff (Hanover–Leipzig, 1906–8).

Constantine Porphyrogenitus, *De cerimoniis aulae byzantinae; De thematibus; De administrando imperio* [see Gen. Bibl. IV].

Costa-Louillet, G. da, 'Saints de Constantinople aux VIIIe, IXe et Xe siècles', *B,* XXIV (1954), 179–263, 453–511; XXV–XXVII (1955–7), 783–852.

Costa-Louillet, G. da, 'Saints de Grèce aux VIIIe, IXe et Xe siècles', *B,* XXXI (1961), 309–69.

Costa-Louillet, G. da, 'Saints de Sicile et d'Italie méridionale aux VIIIe, IXe et Xe siècles', *B,* XXIX–XXX (1959–60), 89–173.

David, Symeon and George. I. van den Gheyn, 'Acta graeca SS. Davidis, Symeonis et Georgii Mitylenae in insula Lesbo', *AB,* XVIII (1899), 209–59, 368.

Dölger, F., *Regesten der Kaiserurkunden des oströmischen Reiches* [see Gen. Bibl. IV].

Duchesne, L., 'L'iconographie byzantine dans un document grec du IXe siècle', *Roma e l'Oriente,* V (1912–13), 222–39, 273–85, 349–66. (Epistola ad Theophilum.)

Ecloga, ed. K. E. Zachariae von Lingenthal, *Collectio librorum juris graeco-romani ineditorum;* J. and P. Zepos, *Jus graeco-romanum,* II [see Gen. Bibl. IV]. Also ed. A. G. Monferratos (Athens, 1889). English transl. E. H. Freshfield, *A Manual of Roman Law, the Ecloga* (Cambridge, 1926). [See also bibliography for chapter XXI.]

Einhard, *Vita Karoli Magni,* ed. G. H. Pertz, G. Waitz and C. Holder-Egger, 6th ed., *SGUS* (Hanover–Leipzig, 1911); ed. L. Halphen, 3rd ed., with French translation (Paris, 1947).

Elias iunior m. Damasci saec. VIII, *Passio*, ed. F. Combefis, *Christi martyrum lecta trias* (Paris, 1666), pp. 155–206; ed. A. Papadopoulos-Kerameus, Συλλογὴ παλαιστινῆς καὶ συριακῆς ἁγιολογίας, I: *Pravoslavnyj Palestinskij Sbornik*, XIX, 3 (= fasc. 57) (St Petersburg, 1907), pp. 42–59.

Epistolae Merowingici et Karolini aevi, *MGH*, *Ep.*, III–VI.

Eudocimus iun. in Charsiano sub Theophilo. Loparev, C., 'Βίος τοῦ ἁγίου καὶ δικαίου Εὐδοκίμου', *Pamjatniki drevnej Pismennosti*, XCVI (St Petersburg, 1893).

Eustratius conf. sub Leone Armeno, *Vita*, ed. A. Papadopoulos-Kerameus, Ἀνάλεκτα ἱεροσολ. σταχνολογίας, IV (1897), 367–400; V (1898), 408–10.

Genesius, Joseph, *Regna*, ed. C. Lachmann, *CSHB* (1834).

George, bishop of Amastris (†c. 802–7). *Vita*, ed. V. Vasilievsky, *Russko-Vizantijskija Izsljedovanija*, II (St Petersburg, 1893), pp. I–CLI, 1–73.

George of Cyprus, Νουθεσία γέροντος περὶ τῶν ἁγίων εἰκόνων, ed. B. M. Melioransky, *Georgij Kiprijanin i Ioann Ierusalimljanin, dva maloizvestnych borca za pravoslavie v VIII v.* [*George of Cyprus and John of Jerusalem, two little known champions of Orthodoxy in the VIIIth century*] (St Petersburg, 1901).

George the Monk, *Chronicon*, ed. C. de Boor, 2 vols. (Leipzig, 1904).

Georgius Limniotes m. sub Leone Isauro, *Epitome*, *AASS*, 24 August, IV (1739), 842.

Gericke, W., 'Wann entstand die Konstantinische Schenkung?', *ZSR*, LXXXVII, Kan. Abt., XLIII (1957), 1–88 [includes the Latin text].

Germanus Patriarcha, *Opera*, *MPG*, XCVIII; *Vita Germani Patriarchae*, ed. A. Papadopoulos-Kerameus, Μαυρογορδάτειος βιβλιοθήκη, Ἀνέκδ. ἑλλην., suppl. to vol. XVII of the Ἑλληνικὸς Φιλολογικὸς Σύλλογος of Constantinople (1886), 1–17. Also ed. (*sub nom.* Theophanis) C. de Boor, see below, Theophanes. *Book of Dreams*, ed. F. Drexl, 'Das Traumbuch des Patriarchen Germanos', Λαογραφία, VII (1923), 428–48; 'Homélie de saint Germain sur la délivrance de Constantinople', ed. with French translation, V. Grumel, *REB*, XVI (1958), 183–205.

Grégoire, H., 'Saint Démétrianos, évêque de Chytri (île de Chypre)', *BZ*, XVI (1907), 204–40.

Grégoire, H., 'Un nouveau fragment du "Scriptor incertus de Leone Armenio"', *B*, XI (1936), 417–27.

Gregorius Decapolita (†842), 20 November, *Vita*, ed. Theophilos Ioannou, Ἁγιολογικὰ Μνημεῖα (Venice, 1884), pp. 129–64; F. Dvornik, *La Vie de Saint Grégoire le Décapolite et les Slaves macédoniens au IXᵉ siècle* (Paris, 1926), pp. 45–75.

Gregory II, Pope, *Epistolae*, *MPL*, LXXXIX; see also Caspar, E.

Grumel, V., *Les regestes des Actes du Patriarcat de Constantinople* [see Gen. Bibl. IV].

Haller, J., *Die Quellen zur Geschichte der Entstehung des Kirchenstaates* (Leipzig–Berlin, 1907).

Ioannicius mon. in Bithynia (†846), *Vita*, *AASS*, 4 November, II, I (1894), 311–435; *MPG*, CXVI, 35–92.

Jaffé, P., *Regesta Pontificum Romanorum* [see Gen. Bibl. IV].

John Bishop of Gotthia (†c. 800), *Vita*, *AASS*, 26 June, V (1709), 184–94; 3rd ed. VII, 162–72.

John of Damascus, Πρὸς τοὺς διαβάλλοντας τὰς ἁγίας εἰκόνας, *MPG*, XCIV; transl. M. H. Allies (London, 1892).

John of Damascus, Πηγὴ γνώσεως, *MPG*, XCIV. [See also bibliography for chapter XXVI.]

John Psichaita conf. sub Leone Armeno, *Vita*, ed. P. van den Ven, *Le Muséon*, n.s. III (1902), 103–25.

Josephus hymnographus (†886), *Vita*, ed. A. Papadopoulos-Kerameus, *Monumenta graeca et latina ad historiam Photii patriarchae pertinentia*, II (St Petersburg, 1901), 1–14; *MPG*, cv, 940–76.

Kehr, P. F., *Regesta Pontificum Romanorum. Italia Pontificia* [see Gen. Bibl. IV].

Leo Grammaticus, *Chronographia*, ed. I. Bekker, *CSHB* (1842).

Liber Pontificalis, ed. L. Duchesne [see Gen. Bibl. IV].

Libri Carolini, ed. H. Bastgen, *MGH*, *Legum Sectio* III. Concilia. 2, Supplementum (Hanover, 1924).

Loparev, C., 'Vizantijskija žitija svjatich VIII–IX v.' [Byzantine Lives of the saints of the 8th and 9th centuries], *VV*, XVII (1910), 1–224; XVIII (1911, publ. 1913), 1–147; XIX (1912, publ. 1915), 1–151.

Macarius heg. Pelectae in Bithynia conf. sub Leone Armeno et sub Theophilo, *Acta*, ed. I. van den Gheyn, *AB*, XVI (1897), 140–63.

Mansi, J. D., *Sacrorum conciliorum nova et amplissima collectio*, vols. XII–XIII [see Gen. Bibl. IV].

Martyres XX Sabaitae (†797), *Passio*, ed. A. Papadopoulos-Kerameus, Συλλογὴ παλαιστινῆς καὶ συριακῆς ἁγιολογίας, I, *Pravoslavnyj Palestinskij Sbornik*, XIX, 3 (= fasc. 57) (St Petersburg, 1907), 1–41; *AASS*, March, III (1668), App. 2, 2–14.

Martyres XLII Amorienses (†838), *Acta*, ed. A. Vasiliev, *Mém. AcadIP. Cl. hist.-philol.*, 8ᵉ série, III, no. 3 (1898), 9–17; V. Vasilievsky and P. Nikitin, 'Skazanija o 42 Amorijskich mučenikach' ['Acts of the 42 Amorian martyrs'], *Mém. AcadIP. Cl. hist.-philol.*, 8ᵉ série, VII, no. 2 (1905).

Martyres LX (vel LXIII) occisi Hierosolymis sub Leone Isauro, *Acta*, ed. A. Papadopoulos-Kerameus, *Pravoslavnyj Palestinskij Sbornik*, XII, 1 (= fasc. 34) (St Petersburg, 1892), pp. 1–7.

Melioransky, B. M., *Perečen vizantijskich gramot i pisem*. I. *Dokumenty 784–850 g. Neskol'ko slov o rukopisjach i izdanijach pisem prepodobnago Feodora Studita* [Catalogue of Byzantine documents and letters. I. Documents of the years 784–850. Remarks on the MSS. and editions of St Theodore the Studite], *Mém. AcadIP. Cl. hist.-philol.*, 8ᵉ série, IV, no. 5 (1899).

Mendham, J., *The Seventh General Council* (London, 1850).

Mercati, Giovanni, 'La lettera di Pasquale I a Leone V sul culto delle sacre immagini', *Studi e Testi*, V (Vatican, 1901), 227–35.

Methodius Patriarcha Cp. (†847), *Vita*, *AASS*, 14 June, II (1698), 960–73; 3rd ed. III, 439–47; *MPG*, c, 1244–72. *Opera*, ed. J. B. Pitra, *Juris ecclesiastici Graecorum historia et monumenta*, II [see Gen. Bibl. IV]; Gouillard, J., 'Une œuvre inédite du Patriarche Méthode: la vie d'Euthyme de Sardes', *BZ*, LIII (1960), 36–46.

Michael Syncellus Hierosol. (†Cp. 846), *Vita*, ed. T. I. Schmit, *IRAIK*, XI (1906), 227–79; Sophronius Eustratiades, Νέα Σιών, XXXI (1936), 329–38.

Nicephorus Patriarcha Cp. (†829), *Vita*, *AASS*, 13 March, II (1668), 704–27; 3rd ed. pp. 901–20; *MPG*, c, 41–160; ed. Theophilos Ioannou, Μνημεῖα Ἁγιολογικά (Venice, 1884), pp. 115–28; *Opuscula historica*, ed. C. de Boor (Leipzig, 1880); *Opera*, *MPG*, c, and also ed. J. B. Pitra, *Spicilegium Solesmense*, I and IV (Paris, 1852 and 1858); *Book of Dreams*, ed. F. Drexl, 'Das Traumbuch des Patriarchen Nikephoros', *Festgabe Ehrhard* (Bonn and Leipzig, 1922), pp. 94–118.

Nicephorus hegumenus Medicii in Bithynia (†813), *Vita*, ed. F. Halkin, *AB*, LXXVIII (1960), 396–430.

Nicephorus mon. conf. sub Leone Armeno, deinde hegumenus τῆς Σεβαζῆ in Bithynia, *Vita*, ed. F. Halkin, *B*, xxiii (1953), 18–30.

Nicetas Mediciensis (†824), *Vita*, *AASS*, 3 April, i (1675), 253–66, app. xxii–xxxii; 3rd ed. xviii–xxviii; K. C. Dukakis, Μέγας Συναξαριστής, April (Athens, 1892), pp. 36–51.

Nicholas the Studite (†868), *Vita*, *AASS*, 4 Febr. i (1658), 538–52; *MPG*, cv, 864–925; L. Clugnet, *Histoire de Saint Nicolas. Bibliothèque hagiographique orientale*, iii, no. 2 (Paris, 1902), 27–38.

Oelsner, L., *Jahrbücher des fränkischen Reiches unter König Pippin* (*Jahrbücher der deutschen Geschichte*) (Leipzig, 1871).

Orthodoxiae festum, see *Bibliotheca Hagiographica Graeca*, 3rd ed., App. v, pp. 183 ff. [see Gen. Bibl. iv].

Paul of Caiumas m. sub Constantino V, *Passio*, ed. A. Papadopoulos-Kerameus, ᾽Ανάλεκτα ἱεροσολ. σταχυολογίας, iv (1897), 247–51.

Paulus Diaconus, *Historia Langobardorum*, ed. L. Bethmann and G. Waitz, *SGUS* (Hanover, 1878).

Petrus hegumenus S. Zachariae Atroae in Bithynia (†837), *Vita*, ed. V. Laurent, *La vie merveilleuse de saint Pierre d'Atroa* (†837). (*Subsidia hagiographica*, xxix, Brussels, 1956); idem, *La via retractata et les miracles postumes de saint Pierre d'Atroa.* (*Subsidia hagiographica*, xxxi, Brussels, 1958).

Philaretus eleemosynarius (†792), *Vita*, ed. M. H. Fourmy and M. Leroy, *B*, ix (1934), 85–167 (with French transl.); cf. F. Dölger, *BZ*, xxxv (1935), 194–6; *Vita*, ed. A. A. Vasiliev, *IRAIK*, v (1900), 64–86.

Pitra, J. B., *Juris ecclesiastici Graecorum historia et monumenta*, ii (Rome, 1868), 295–365. (Texts of Patriarchs Germanus, Tarasius, Nicephorus, Methodius.)

Plato of Studios, abbot of Saccudion (†Cp. 814), *Funeral oration by Theodore the Studite*, *AASS*, 4 April, i (1675), *Synaxarion*, pp. xlviii–lv; *MPG*, xcix, 804–49.

Scriptor incertus de Leone Bardae Armenii filio, ed. I. Bekker (with Leo Grammaticus), *CSHB* (1842); *MPG*, cviii, 1009–37.

Scriptores rerum Langobardicarum et Italicarum saec. vi–ix, ed. L. Bethmann and G. Waitz (Hanover, 1878).

Simson, B., *Jahrbücher des fränkischen Reiches unter Ludwig dem Frommen 814–840* (*Jahrbücher der deutschen Geschichte*), 2 vols. (Leipzig, 1874–6).

Stephanus episcopus Suroziae saec. viii, *Vitae epitome*, ed. V. Vasilievsky, *op. cit.* under George of Amastris, pp. clii–ccv, 74–103.

Stephanus iun. conf. (vel m.) (†764), *Vita*, *MPG*, c, 1069–1186; J. Gill, *OCP*, vi (1940), 115–36.

Symeon Magister (or Logothetes), *Chronicle*, see Leo Grammaticus, ed. I. Bekker, *CSHB* (1842). Old Slavonic version ed. V. Sreznevsky (St Petersburg, 1905).

Tarasius Patriarcha Cp. (†806), *Vita* by Ignatius Diaconus, ed. I. A. Heikel, *Acta societatis scientiarum Fennicae*, xvii (Helsingfors, 1891), 395–423; *Opera*, *MPG*, xcviii, 1424–1500; *Narratio de sanctis Patriarchis Tarasio et Nicephoro*, *MPG*, xcix, 1849–53.

Theoctista Lesbia saec. ix, *Vita*, *AASS*, November, iv (1925), 224–33; ed. Theophilos Ioannou, Μνημεῖα ῾Αγιολογικά (Venice, 1884), pp. 1–39.

Theodora imperatrix (†867), *Vita* and *Narratio de Theophili imperatoris absolutione et de imaginum restitutione*, ed. W. Regel, *Analecta byzantino-russica* (St Petersburg, 1891), pp. 1–43.

Theodora of Thessalonica († 892), *Vita*, ed. E. Kurtz, *Des Klerikers Gregorios Bericht über Leben, Wunderthaten und Translation der hl. Theodora von Thessalonich nebst der Metaphrase des Joannes Staurakios, Mém. AcadIP, Cl. hist.-philol.*, 8ᵉ série, VI, no. 1 (1902).

Theodorus Studita († 826), *Opera, MPG*, XCIX; ed. A. Mai and G. Cozza-Luzi, *Nova Patrum Bibliotheca*, VIII, no. 1 (Rome, 1871); IX, nos. 1–2 (Rome, 1888); *Parva catechesis*, ed. E. Auvray (Paris, 1891); ed. A. Papadopoulos-Kerameus, Μεγάλη Κατήχησις (Βιβλίον δεύτερον ἐκδοθὲν ὑπὸ τῆς Αὐτοκρατορικῆς ᾽Αρχαιογραφικῆς ᾽Επιτροπῆς) (St Petersburg, 1904); R. Devreesse, 'Une lettre de S. Théodore Studite relative au Synode Moechien (809)' *AB*, LXVIII (1950), 44–57.

Theodosia m. Cp. sub Leone Isauro, *Laudatio, AASS*, 29 May, VII (1688), 69–87; 3rd ed. pp. 64–85; *MPG*, CXL, cols. 893–936.

Theodosius Melitenus, *Chronographia*, ed. G. L. F. Tafel (Munich, 1859).

Theophanes Confessor Chronographus († 817), *Vita, AASS*, 12 March, II (1668), 700–4; 3rd ed. pp. 898–901; ed. C. de Boor, *Theophanis Chronographia*, II, 3–30; *Vita a Methodio Patr. Cp.*, ed. V. Latyšev, *Mém. Acad. des sciences de Russie, Cl. Hist.-philol.*, 8ᵉ série, XIII, no. 4 (1918), 1–40; C. van der Vorst, 'Un panégyrique de S. Théophane le Chronographe par S. Théodore Studite', *AB*, XXXI (1912), 11–23; *Chronographia*, ed. C. de Boor, 2 vols. (Leipzig, 1883–5); L. Breyer, 'Bilderstreit und Arabersturm in Byzanz. Das 8. Jahrhundert (717–813) aus der Weltchronik des Theophanes', *Byzantinische Geschichtsschreiber*, VI (1957).

Theophanes continuatus, *Chronographia*, ed. I. Bekker, *CSHB* (1838).

Theophanes et Theodorus fratres grapti sub Theophilo, *Vita*, ed. A. Papadopoulos-Kerameus. ᾽Ανάλεκτα ἱεροσολ. σταχυολογίας, IV (1897), 185–223; V (1898), 397–9.

Theophylactus ep. Nicomediae conf. sub Leone Armeno († c. 840), *Vita*, ed. A. Vogt, *AB*, L (1932), 67–82.

Uspensky, F., *Sinodik v Nedelju Pravoslavija* [*Synodicon for Orthodoxy Week*] (Odessa, 1893).

Zachariae von Lingenthal, K. E., *Jus graeco-romanum*, pt. III. *Novellae Constitutiones* [see Gen. Bibl. IV].

Zepos, J. and P., *Jus graeco-romanum*, II [see Gen. Bibl. IV].

Zonaras, John, *Epitome historiarum*, ed. T. Büttner-Wobst, vol. III, *CSHB* (1897).

II. MODERN WORKS

Adelson, H. and Baker, R., 'The Oath of Purgation of Pope Leo III in 800', *Trad.* VIII (1952), 35–80.

Alexander, P. J., 'The Iconoclastic Council of St Sophia (815) and its Definition (*Horos*)', *DOP*, VII (1953), 35–66.

Alexander, P. J., *The Patriarch Nicephorus of Constantinople. Ecclesiastical Policy and Image Worship in the Byzantine Empire* (Oxford, 1958).

Amann, E., 'Théodore le Studite', *DTC*.

Amari, M., *Storia dei Musulmani di Sicilia* [see Gen. Bibl. v].

Anastasiu, I. E., Οἱ Παυλικιανοί (Athens, 1959).

Anastos, M. V., 'The Argument for Iconoclasm as presented by the Iconoclastic Council of 754', *Late Classical and Mediaeval Studies in Honor of A. M. Friend, Jr.* (Princeton, 1954), pp. 177–88.

Anastos, M. V., 'The Ethical Theory of Images Formulated by the Iconoclasts in 754 and 815', *DOP*, VIII (1954), 151–60.

Anastos, M. V., 'The Transfer of Illyricum, Calabria, and Sicily to the Jurisdiction of the Patriarchate of Constantinople in 732–33', *SBN*, ix (1957 = *Silloge Bizantina in onore di S. G. Mercati*), 14–31.

Andrejev, I., *German i Tarasij, Patriarchi Konstantinopol'skie* [*Germanus and Tarasius, Patriarchs of Constantinople*] (Sergiev Posad, 1907).

Bănescu, N., *L'ancien état bulgare et les pays roumains*, Inst. Roumain d'ét. byz., n.s., v (Bucharest, 1947).

Barišić, F., 'Les sources de Génésios et du Continuateur de Théophane pour l'histoire du règne de Michel II (820–829)', *B*, xxxi (1961), 257–71.

Baynes, N. H., 'Idolatry and the Early Church', *Byzantine Studies and Other Essays*, pp. 116–43 [see Gen. Bibl. v].

Baynes, N. H., 'The Icons before Iconoclasm', *HTR*, xliv (1951), 93–106; reprinted in *Byzantine Studies and Other Essays*, pp. 226–39 [see Gen. Bibl. v].

Beck, H.-G., *Kirche und theologische Literatur* [see Gen. Bibl. v].

Bertolini, O., 'I rapporti di Zaccaria con Costantino V e con Artavasdo nel racconto del biografo del Papa e nella probabile realtà storica', *Archivio della Società Rom. di Storia Patria*, 3 ser., ix (1955), 1–21.

Bognetti, G. P., 'I rapporti etico-politici fra Oriente e Occidente dal sec. v al sec. viii', *X Congresso internazionale di scienze storiche: Roma, 1955. Relazioni*, iii. *Storia del Medioevo* (Florence, 1956), pp. 3–65.

Bon, A., 'Le problème slave dans le Péloponnèse à la lumière de l'archéologie', *B*, xx (1950), 13–20.

Bon, A., *Le Péloponnèse byzantin* [see Gen. Bibl. v].

Bratianu, G. I., 'Empire et "Démocratie" à Byzance', *BZ*, xxxvii (1937), 86–111; reprinted in *Etudes byzantines* [see Gen. Bibl. v].

Bratianu, G. I., 'La politique fiscale de Nicéphore 1er (802–811) ou Ubu roi à Byzance', *Etudes byzantines*, pp. 183–216 [see Gen. Bibl. v].

Bréhier, L., *La querelle des images (VIIIe–IXe siècles)* (Paris, 1904).

Bréhier, L., *Le monde byzantin*, i [see Gen. Bibl. v].

Bréhier, L., 'La marine de Byzance du VIIIe au XIe siècle', *B*, xix (1949), 1–16.

Brooks, E. W., 'On the Date of the Death of Constantine, the Son of Irene', *BZ*, ix (1900), 654–7.

Brooks, E. W., 'On the Date of the First Four Books of the Continuator of Theophanes', *BZ*, x (1901), 416–17.

Brooks, E. W., 'The Marriage of the Emperor Theophilus', *BZ*, x (1901), 540–5.

Brooks, E. W., 'The Sources of Theophanes and the Syriac Chroniclers', *BZ*, xv (1906), 578–87.

Bury, J. B., *History of the Later Roman Empire*, ii (London, 1889) [see Gen. Bibl. v].

Bury, J. B., 'The Identity of Thomas the Slavonian', *BZ*, i (1892), 55–60.

Bury, J. B., 'The Bulgarian Treaty of A.D. 814 and the Great Fence of Thrace', *EHR*, xxv (1910), 276–87.

Bury, J. B., 'The Chronological Cycle of the Bulgarians', *BZ*, xix (1910), 127–44.

Bury, J. B., 'The Naval Policy of the Roman Empire in Relation to the Western Provinces from the 7th to the 9th Century', *Centenario della nascita di Michele Amari*, ii (Palermo, 1910), 21–34.

Bury, J. B., *History of the Eastern Roman Empire* [see Gen. Bibl. v].

Campenhausen, H. von, 'Die Bilderfrage als theologisches Problem der alten Kirche', *Zeitsch. Theol. u. Kirche*, xlix (1952), 33–60.

Canard, M., 'Les expéditions des Arabes contre Constantinople dans l'histoire et dans la légende', *JA*, ccviii (1926), 61–121.

Canard, M., 'Questions épiques, i: Delhemma, épopée arabe des guerres arabo-byzantines', *B*, x (1935), 283–300; ii: 'Delhemma, Sayyid Battāl et 'Omar al-No'mān', *B*, xii (1937), 183–6.

Caspar, E., *Geschichte des Papsttums*, ii [see Gen. Bibl. v].

Caspar, E., 'Das Papsttum unter fränkischer Herrschaft', *ZKG*, liv (1935), 132–264.

Cassimatis, G., 'La dixième "vexation" de l'empereur Nicéphore', *B*, vii (1932), 149–60.

Charanis, P., 'Nicephorus I, the Savior of Greece from the Slavs (810 A.D.)', *BM*, i (1946), 75–92.

Charanis, P., 'On the Question of the Slavonic Settlements in Greece during the Middle Ages', *BS*, x (1949), 254–8.

Charanis, P., 'The Chronicle of Monemvasia and the Question of the Slavonic Settlements in Greece', *DOP*, v (1950), 139–66.

Charanis, P., 'On the Capture of Corinth by the Onogurs and its Recapture by the Byzantines', *SP*, xxvii (1952), 343–50.

Charanis, P., 'The term *Helladikoi* in Byzantine Texts of the Sixth, Seventh and Eighth Centuries', *EEBS*, xxiii (1953), 615–20.

Charanis, P., 'Hellas in the Greek sources of the sixth, seventh and eighth centuries', *Late Classical and Mediaeval Studies in Honor of A. M. Friend, Jr.* (Princeton, 1954), pp. 161–76.

Christophilopulu, A. A., ''Η οἰκονομικὴ καὶ δημοσιονομικὴ πολιτικὴ τοῦ Αὐτοκράτορος Νικηφόρου Α'', Εἰς μνήμην Κ. 'Ι. 'Αμάντου (Athens, 1960), pp. 413–31.

Classen, P., 'Romanum gubernans imperium. Zur Vorgeschichte der Kaisertitulatur Karls des Grossen', *Deutsches Archiv für Erforschung des Mittelalters*, ix (1951–2), 103–21.

Delius, W., *Die Bilderfrage im Karolingerreich* (Halle, 1928).

Der Nersessian, S., 'Une Apologie des Images du Septième Siècle', *B*, xvii (1944–5), 58–87.

Der Nersessian, S., *Armenia and the Byzantine Empire* [see Gen. Bibl. v].

Der Nersessian, S., 'Image Worship in Armenia and its Opponents', *Armenian Quarterly*, i (1946), 67–81.

Diehl, C., *Etudes sur l'administration byzantine dans l'Exarchat de Ravenne (568–751)* (Paris, 1888).

Diehl, C., 'L'origine du régime des thèmes dans l'empire byzantin', *Etudes byzantines* (Paris, 1905), pp. 276–92.

Diehl, C., *Figures byzantines*, i [see Gen. Bibl. v].

Diehl, C., 'Une vie de Saint de l'époque des empereurs iconoclastes', *Comptes rendus AcadIBL* (1915), pp. 134–50.

Diehl, C., 'Le sénat et le peuple byzantin aux VIIᵉ et VIIIᵉ siècles', *B*, i (1924), 201–13.

Diehl, C., 'La légende de l'empereur Théophile', *Sem. Kond.* iv (1931), 33–7.

Dobroklonsky, A. P., *Prep. Feodor, ispovednik i igumen studijskij* [*Saint Theodore, confessor and Abbot of Studios*], 2 vols. (Odessa, 1913–14).

Dobschütz, E. von, *Christusbilder; Untersuchungen zur christlichen Legende* (Leipzig, 1899).

Dobschütz, E. von, 'Methodios und die Studiten', *BZ*, xviii (1909), 41–105.

Dölger, F., *Beiträge zur Geschichte der byzantinischen Finanzverwaltung* [see Gen. Bibl. v].

Dölger, F., 'Rom in der Gedankenwelt der Byzantiner', *ZKG*, LVI (1937), 1–42; reprinted in *Byzanz u. die europ. Staatenwelt*, pp. 70–115 [see Gen. Bibl. v].

Dölger, F., 'Europas Gestaltung im Spiegel der fränkisch-byzantinischen Auseinandersetzung des 9. Jahrhunderts', *Der Vertrag von Verdun 843*, ed. T. Mayer (Leipzig, 1943), pp. 203–72; reprinted in Dölger, *Byzanz und die europäische Staatenwelt*, pp. 282–369 [see Gen. Bibl. v].

Dölger, F., *Das Kaiserjahr der Byzantiner*, *SBAW*, Heft 1 (1949).

Dölger, F., 'Der Pariser Papyrus von St Denis als ältestes Kreuzzugsdokument', *Actes du Ier Congrès Intern. d'Et. Class. Paris, 1950* (Paris, 1951), pp. 93–102; reprinted in *Byzantinische Diplomatik*, pp. 204–14 [see Gen. Bibl. v].

Dölger, F., 'Byzanz und das Abendland vor den Kreuzzügen', *X Congresso internazionale di scienze storiche. Roma, 1955. Relazioni, III. Storia del Medioevo* (Florence, 1955), pp. 67–112; reprinted in ΠΑΡΑΣΠΟΡΑ (Ettal, 1961), pp. 73–106.

Dubler, César E., 'Sobre la crónica arábigo-bizantina de 741 y la influencia bizantina en la Península Ibérica', *Al-Andalus*, XI (1946), 283–349.

Duchesne, L., *Les premiers temps de l'état pontifical*, 3rd ed. (Paris, 1911).

Duchesne, L., *L'Illyricum ecclésiastique*, *BZ*, I (1892), 531–50.

Dujčev, I., 'San Teodoro Studita ed i Bulgari', *Bullettino dell'Istituto Storico Italiano per il Medio Evo e Archivio Muratoriano*, LXXIII (1961), 71–83.

Dvornik, F., 'La lutte entre Byzance et Rome à propos de l'Illyricum au IXe siècle', *Mélanges Charles Diehl*, I (Paris, 1930), 61–80.

Dvornik, F., *Les légendes de Constantin et de Méthode vues de Byzance*, *BS* suppl. I (Prague, 1933).

Dvornik, F., 'The Patriarch Photius and Iconoclasm', *DOP*, VII (1953), 67–97.

Eckhardt, T., 'Überlegungen zur Bilderverehrung und Stil ostkirchlicher Kunst', *Jahrbücher für Geschichte Osteuropas*, n.s. VIII (1960), 269–99.

Fahmy, A. M., *Muslim Sea-power in the Eastern Mediterranean from the Seventh to the Tenth Century A.D.* (London, 1950).

Fichtenau, H., *Das karolingische Imperium* (Zurich, 1949); translated in part by P. Munz (Oxford, 1957).

Fichtenau, H., 'Byzanz und die Pfalz zu Aachen', *MIOG*, LIX (1951), 1–54.

Fichtenau, H., 'Karl der Grosse und das Kaisertum', *MIOG*, LXI (1953), 257–334.

Fliche, A. and Martin, V. (edd.), *Histoire de l'église*, V–VI [see Gen. Bibl. v].

Fuhrmann, H., 'Konstantinische Schenkung und Silvesterlegende in neuer Sicht', *Deutsches Archiv für Erforschung des Mittelalters*, XV (1959), 523–40.

Ganshof, F. L., *The Imperial Coronation of Charlemagne* (Glasgow, 1949).

Ganshof, F. L., 'Note sur les origines byzantines du titre "Patricius Romanorum"', *AIPHO*, X (1950), 261–82.

Gardner, A., *Theodore of Studium, his Life and Times* (London, 1905).

Gasquet, A., *L'empire byzantin et la monarchie franque* (Paris, 1888).

Gay, J., *L'Italie méridionale* [see Gen. Bibl. v].

Gelzer, H., 'Die Genesis der byzantinischen Themenverfassung', *Abh. d. kg. Sächs. Ges. d. Wiss., Phil.-hist. Cl.*, XVIII, no. 5 (Leipzig, 1899).

Gelzer, H., 'Das Verhältnis von Staat und Kirche in Byzanz', *HZ*, LXXXVI (1901), 193–252; reprinted in *Ausgewählte kleine Schriften* [see Gen. Bibl. v].

Gericke, W., 'Das Constitutum Constantini und die Silvesterlegende', *ZSR*, LXXXVIII, Kan. Abt. XLIV (1958), 343–50.

Gericke, W., 'Das Glaubensbekenntnis der "Konstantinischen Schenkung"', *ZSR*, XCI, Kan. Abt. XLVII (1961), 1–76; *ibid.* 293–304.

Gibb, H. A. R., 'Arab–Byzantine Relations under the Umayyad Caliphate', *DOP*, XII (1958), 221–33.

Gill, J., 'A Note on the Life of St Stephen the Younger by Symeon Metaphrastes', *BZ*, XXXIX (1940), 382–6.

Gill, J., 'The Life of Stephen the Younger by Stephen the Deacon, Debts and Loans', *OCP*, VI (1940), 114–39.

Gouillard, J., 'Deux figures mal connues du second iconoclasme', *B*, XXXI (1961), 371–401.

Grabar, A., 'La représentation de l'intelligible dans l'art byzantin du moyen âge', *Actes du VIe Congrès international d'Etudes Byzantines. Paris, 1948*, II (Paris, 1951), 127–43.

Grabar, A., *L'iconoclasme byzantin. Dossier archéologique* (Paris, 1957).

Grégoire, H., 'Etudes sur l'épopée byzantine', *REG*, XLVI (1933), 29–69.

Grégoire, H., 'L'Empereur Nicéphore le Chauve et Kroum, "premier" de Boulgarie', *Bulletin de la Classe des Lettres* (Académie royale de Belgique, 5e série), XX (1934), 261–72.

Grégoire, H., 'An Armenian Dynasty on the Byzantine Throne', *Armenian Quarterly*, I (1946), 4–21.

Grégoire, H., 'Pour l'histoire des églises pauliciennes', *OCP*, XIII (1947), 509–14.

Grégoire, H., 'Cathares d'Asie Mineure, d'Italie et de France', *Mémorial L. Petit* (Bucharest, 1948), pp. 142–51.

Grondijs, L. H., 'Images de saints d'après la théologie byzantine du VIIIe siècle', *Actes du VIe Congrès international d'Etudes Byzantines. Paris, 1948*, II (Paris, 1951), 145–70.

Grumel, V., 'Cassia', *DHGE*.

Grumel, V., 'L'iconologie de saint Théodore Studite', *EO*, XX (1921), 257–68.

Grumel, V., 'L'iconologie de Saint Germain de Constantinople', *EO*, XXI (1922), 165–75.

Grumel, V., 'L'année du monde dans la chronographie de Théophane', *EO*, XXXIII (1934), 396–408.

Grumel, V., 'Chronologie des patriarches iconoclastes du IXe siècle', *EO*, XXXIV (1935), 162–6.

Grumel, V., 'L'année du monde dans l'ère byzantine', *EO*, XXXIV (1935), 319–26.

Grumel, V., 'La politique religieuse du patriarche Saint Méthode. Iconoclastes et Studites', *EO*, XXXIV (1935), 385–401.

Grumel, V., 'Notes d'histoire et de philologie byzantines, I: Les lettres de Léon III l'Isaurien au Pape Grégoire II', *EO*, XXXV (1936), 234–7.

Grumel, V., 'Jean Grammaticos et saint Théodore Studite', *EO*, XXXVI (1937), 181–9.

Grumel, V., 'L'annexion de l'Illyricum oriental et de la Sicile et de la Calabre au patriarcat de Constantinople', *Recherches de sciences religieuses*, XL. *Mélanges Jules Lebreton*, II (1952), 191–200.

Grumel, V., 'Le vicariat de Thessalonique et le premier rattachement de l'Illyricum oriental au patriarcat de Constantinople', *Annuaire de l'école des législations religieuses. Institut Catholique de Paris, 1950–1951* (1952), pp. 49–63.

Grumel, V., *La Chronologie* [see Gen. Bibl. III].

Grumel, V., 'Les "douze chapitres contre les iconomaques" de saint Nicéphore de Constantinople', *REB*, XVII (1959), 127–35.

Guilland, R., 'Le droit divin á Byzance', *Eos*, XLII (1947), 142–68; reprinted in *Etudes byzantines* [see Gen. Bibl. v].

Guilland, R., 'L'expédition de Maslama contre Constantinople (717–718)', *Al-Machriq*, XLIX (1955), 89–112; reprinted in *Etudes byzantines* [see Gen. Bibl. v].

Haendler, G., *Epochen karolingischer Theologie, eine Untersuchung über die karolingischen Gutachten zum byzantinischen Bilderstreit* (Berlin, 1958).

Halkin, F., 'La passion de saint Théoctiste', *AB*, LXXIII (1955), 55–65.

Halkin, F., 'Saint Théoctiste, moine sabaïte et martyr († 797)', *AB*, LXXIII (1955), 373–4.

Halkin, F., 'Y a-t-il trois saints Georges, évêques de Mytilène et "confesseurs" sous les iconoclastes?', *AB*, LXXVII (1959), 464–9.

Halphen, L., *Charlemagne et l'empire carolingien* (Paris, 1949).

Hartmann, L. M., *Untersuchungen zur Geschichte der byzantinischen Verwaltung in Italien (540–750)* (Leipzig, 1889).

Hartmann, L. M., *Geschichte Italiens im Mittelalter*, II, 2–III, 1 [see Gen. Bibl. v].

Hausherr, I., *Saint Théodore Studite, l'homme et l'ascète (d'après ses catéchèses)*, *OC*, VI, 1 (1926), 1–86.

Hefele, C. J. and Leclerq, H., *Histoire des conciles*, III, 2; IV, 1 [see Gen. Bibl. v].

Hirsch, F., *Byzantinische Studien* [see Gen. Bibl. v].

Hodgkin, T., *Italy and Her Invaders*, VI–VIII [see Gen. Bibl. v].

Hoeck, J. M., 'Johannes von Damaskus', *Lexikon für Theologie und Kirche*, v, 2nd ed. (1960).

Hofmann, G., 'Johannes Damaskenos, Rom und Byzanz (1054–1500)', *OCP*, XVI (1950), 177–90.

Honigmann, E., *Die Ostgrenze des byzantinischen Reiches von 363 bis 1071* [see Gen. Bibl. v].

Jerphanion, G. de, 'L'image de Jésus-Christ dans l'art chrétien', *La voix des monuments*, n.s. (1938), pp. 1–26.

Jireček, C. J., *Geschichte der Bulgaren* [see Gen. Bibl. v].

Jugie, M., 'Jean Damascène', *DTC*.

Kitzinger, E., 'On some Icons of the Seventh Century', *Late Classical and Mediaeval Studies in Honor of A. M. Friend, Jr.* (Princeton, 1954), pp. 132–50.

Kitzinger, E., 'The Cult of Images in the Age before Iconoclasm', *DOP*, VIII (1954), 83–150.

Kleinclausz, A., *Charlemagne* (Paris, 1934).

Kleinclausz, A., *L'empire carolingien, ses origines et ses transformations* (Paris. 1902).

Kollwitz, J., 'Zur Frühgeschichte der Bilderverehrung', *RQCA*, XLVIII (1953), 1–20.

Kollwitz, J., 'Bild (III, christlich)', *RAC*, II (Stuttgart, 1954), 318–41.

Kulakovsky, J., *Istorija Vizantii*, I–III (Kiev, 1913, 1912, 1915).

Kyriakides, S., Βούλγαροι καὶ Σλάβοι εἰς τὴν Ἑλληνικὴν ἱστορίαν. Ἐθνικὴ βιβλιοθήκη. Δημοσιεύματα τῆς Ἑταιρείας Μακεδονικῶν Σπουδῶν, v (Thessalonica, 1946).

Ladner, G. B., 'Origin and Significance of the Byzantine Iconoclastic Controversy', *Med. Stud.* II (1940), 127–49.

Ladner, G. B., 'The Concept of the Image in the Greek Fathers and the Byzantine Iconoclastic Controversy', *DOP*, VII (1953), 1–34.

Ladner, G. B., 'Eikon', *RAC*, IV (1959), 771–86.

Laurent, J., *L'Arménie entre Byzance et l'Islam depuis la conquête arabe jusqu'en 886 (EcfrAR, 117)* (Paris, 1919).

Laurent, V., 'L'érection de la métropole d'Athènes et le statut ecclésiastique de l'Illyricum au VIII⁰ siècle', *EB*, I (1943), 58–72.

Lemerle, P., 'Invasions et migrations dans les Balkans depuis la fin de l'époque romaine jusqu'au VIII⁰ siècle', *RH*, CCXI (1954), 265–308.

Lewis, A. R., *Naval Power and Trade in the Mediterranean, A.D. 500–1100* (Princeton, 1951).

Lipšic, E. E., 'O pochode Rusi na Vizantiju ranee 842 goda' ['Russian campaigns against Byzantium before 842'], *Istoričeskie zapiski*, XXVI (1948), 312–31.

Lipšic, E. E., 'Nikifor i ego istoričeskij trud' ['Nicephorus and his historical work'], *VV*, n.s. III (1950), 85–105.

Lipšic, E. E., *Byzanz und die Slaven, Beiträge zur byzantinischen Geschichte des 6.–9. Jahrhunderts* (Weimar, 1951).

Lipšic, E. E., 'Pavlikianskoe dviženie v Vizantii v VIII i pervoj polovine IX vv.' ['The Paulician Movement in Byzantium in the eighth and the first half of the ninth centuries'], *VV*, n.s. V (1952), 49–72.

Lipšic, E. E., *Očerki istorii vizantijskogo obščestva i kul'tury, VIII–pervaja polovina IX v.* [*Studies in Byzantine social and cultural history: the eighth century to the first half of the ninth*] (Moscow–Leningrad, 1961).

List, J., *Studien zur Homiletik Germanos I. von Konstantinopel und seiner Zeit* (Texte und Forschungen zur byz.-neugriechischen Philologie, XXIX, Athens, 1939).

Lombard, A., *Constantin V, empereur des Romains (740–775)* (Paris, 1902).

Loos, M., 'Deux contributions à l'histoire des Pauliciens', *BS*, XVII (1956), 19–57; XVIII (1957), 202–17.

Maricq, A., 'Notes sur les Slaves dans le Péloponnèse et en Bithynie et sur l'emploi de "Slave" comme appellatif', *B*, XXII (1952), 337–55.

Marin, E., *Saint Théodore (759–826)* (Paris, 1906).

Martin, E. J., *History of the Iconoclastic Controversy* (London, 1930).

Menges, H., *Die Bilderlehre des hl. Johannes von Damaskus* (Münster i. W., 1938).

Moravcsik, Gy., *Byzantinoturcica* [full bibliography] [see Gen. Bibl. I].

Munz, P., *The Origin of the Carolingian Empire* (Leicester–Otago, 1960).

Nasrallah, J., *Saint Jean de Damas, son époque, sa vie, son œuvre* (Harissa–Paris, 1950).

Obolensky, D., *The Bogomils* (Cambridge, 1948).

Ohnsorge, W., *Das Zweikaiserproblem im früheren Mittelalter* (Hildesheim, 1947).

Ohnsorge, W., 'Orthodoxus imperator. Vom religiösen Motiv für das Kaisertum Karls des Grossen', *Jahrb. der Gesellschaft für niedersächsische Kirchengeschichte*, XLVIII (1950), 17–28; reprinted in *Abendland und Byzanz* [see Gen. Bibl. v].

Ohnsorge, W., 'Das Mitkaisertum in der abendländischen Geschichte des früheren Mittelalters', *ZSR*, LXXX, Ger. Abt. LXVII (1950), 309–35; reprinted in *Abendland und Byzanz* [see Gen. Bibl. v].

Ohnsorge, W., 'Die Konstantinische Schenkung, Leo III und die Anfänge der kurialen römischen Kaiseridee', *ZSR*, LXXXI, Ger. Abt. LXVIII (1951), 78–109; reprinted in *Abendland und Byzanz* [see Gen. Bibl. v].

Ohnsorge, W., 'Byzanz und das Abendland im 9. und 10. Jahrhundert', *Saeculum,* v (1954), 194–220; reprinted in *Abendland und Byzanz* [see Gen. Bibl. v].

Ostrogorsky, G., 'Sojedinenie voprosa o sv. ikonach s christologičeskoj dogmatikoj' ['The Holy Icons and their connection with christological doctrine'], *Sem. Kond.* I (1927), 35–48.

Ostrogorsky, G., 'Gnoseologičeskija osnovy vizantijskago spora o sv. ikonach' ['Epistemological foundations of the Byzantine controversy on the Holy Images'], *Sem. Kond.* II (1928), 47–52.

Ostrogorsky, G., 'Die Chronologie des Theophanes im 7. und 8. Jahrhundert', *BNJ,* VII (1928–9, publ. 1930), 1–56.

Ostrogorsky, G., *Studien zur Geschichte des byzantinischen Bilderstreites* [see Gen. Bibl. v].

Ostrogorsky, G., 'Über die vermeintliche Reformtätigkeit der Isaurier', *BZ,* xxx (1929–30), 394–400.

Ostrogorsky, G., 'Les débuts de la querelle des images', *Mélanges Charles Diehl,* I (1930), 235–55.

Ostrogorsky, G., 'Rom und Byzanz in Kampfe um die Bilderverehrung', *Sem. Kond.* VI (1933), 73–87.

Ostrogorsky, G., 'Avtokrator i Samodržac' ['Autocrat and Samodržac'], *Glas,* LXXXIV, 3 (1935), 95–187.

Ostrogorsky, G., 'Postanak tema Helada i Peloponez' ['The Origin of the Themes of Hellas and the Peloponnese'], *Zbornik Radova Viz. Institut,* I (1952), 64–77.

Ostrogorsky, G., *History of the Byzantine State* [see Gen. Bibl. v].

Ostrogorsky, G., 'Theophanes', Pauly–Wissowa.

Papadopulos, J. B., Ἡ Κρήτη ὑπὸ τοὺς Σαρακηνούς (824–961)', *Texte und Forschungen zur byz.-neugriechischen Philologie,* XLIII (Athens, 1948).

Partington, J. R., *A History of Greek Fire and Gunpowder* (Cambridge, 1960).

Peeters, P., 'L'autobiographie de S. Antoine le néomartyr', *AB,* XXXIII (1914), 52–63.

Petit, L., 'Les évêques de Thessalonique', *EO,* IV (1900–1), 212–21.

Posedel, J., 'Pitanje dalmatinskog temata u prvoj polovici IX. stoljeća' ['The problem of the Theme of Dalmatia in the first half of the ninth century'], *Historijski Zbornik,* III (1950), 217–20.

Rajković, M., 'O poreklu Tome, vodje ustanka 821–823 g.' ['On the ancestry of Thomas, the leader of the revolt of 821–823'], *Zbornik Radova Viz. Inst.* II (1953), 33–8.

Regel, W., 'Récits sur l'empereur Théophile et l'impératrice Théodora concernant le rétablissement du culte des saintes images', *Analecta byzantino-russica* (St Petersburg, 1891), pp. iii–xix.

Runciman, S., *A History of the First Bulgarian Empire* (London, 1930).

Schade, H., 'Die *Libri Carolini* und ihre Stellung zum Bild', *ZKT,* LXXIX (1957), 69–78.

Scheidweiler, F., 'Paulikianer Probleme', *BZ,* XLIII (1950), 10–39, 366–84.

Schenk, K., *Kaiser Leon III* (Halle, 1880).

Schenk, K., 'Kaiser Leons III Walten im Inneren', *BZ,* v (1896), 257–301.

Schneider, G. A., *Der hl. Theodor von Studien. Sein Leben und Wirken* (Münster i. W., 1900).

Schramm, P. E., 'Das Versprechen Pippins und Karls des Grossen für die römische Kirche', *ZSR,* LVIII, Kan. Abt., XXVII (1938), 180–217.

Schramm, P. E., 'Die Anerkennung Karls des Grossen als Kaiser', *HZ*, CLXXII (1951), 449–515.

Schwarzlose, K., *Der Bilderstreit* (Gotha, 1890).

Starr, J., *The Jews in the Byzantine Empire 641–1204* (Texte und Forschungen zur byz.-neugriechischen Philologie, XXX, Athens, 1939).

Starr, J., 'An Eastern Christian Sect: the Athinganoi', *HTR*, XXIX (1936), 93–106.

Steinen, W. von den, 'Entstehungsgeschichte der Libri Carolini', *Quellen und Forschungen aus italienischen Archiven und Bibliotheken*, XXI (1929–30), 1–93.

Studer, B., *Die theologische Arbeitsweise des Johannes von Damaskus* (Studia Patristica et Byzantina, II, Ettal, 1956).

Thomas, C., *Theodor von Studion und sein Zeitalter* (Osnabrück, 1892).

Tougard, A., 'La persécution iconoclaste d'après la correspondance de Saint Théodore Studite', *RQH*, n.s. VI = L (1891), 80–118.

Ullmann, W., *The Growth of Papal Government in the Middle Ages* (London, 1955).

Uspensky, F. I., *Očerki po istorii vizantijskoj obrazovannosti* [see Gen. Bibl. v].

Uspensky, K. N., 'Očerki po istorii ikonoborčeskogo dviženija v vizantijskoj imperii v viii–ix vv. Feofan i ego chronografija' [Studies in the history of the Iconoclast Movement in the Byzantine Empire in the 8th and 9th centuries. Theophanes and his Chronicle], *VV*, n.s. III (1950), 393–438; IV (1951), 211–62.

Vasiliev, A. A., *Byzance et les Arabes*, I [see Gen. Bibl. v].

Vasiliev, A. A., *The Goths in the Crimea* (Cambridge, Mass., 1936).

Vasiliev, A. A., *History of the Byzantine Empire* [see Gen. Bibl. v].

Vasmer, Max, *Die Slaven in Griechenland. Abhandlungen der preussischen Akademie der Wissenschaften. Philos.-hist. Kl.*, no. 12 (1941).

Ven, P. van den, 'La patristique et l'hagiographie au concile de Nicée de 787', *B*, XXV–XXVII (1955–7), 325–62.

Visser, A. J., *Nikephoros und der Bilderstreit* (The Hague, 1952).

Visser, W. J. A., *Die Entwicklung des Christusbildes in Literatur und Kunst in der frühchristlichen und frühbyzantinischen Zeit* (Bonn, 1934).

Wallach, L., 'The Unknown Author of the *Libri Carolini*: Patristic Exegesis, Mozarabic Antiphons, and the *Vetus Latina*', *Didascaliae, Studies in Honor of Anselm M. Albareda* (New York, 1961), pp. 469–515.

Xanalatos, D., Οἱ Ἕλληνες καὶ οἱ Βούλγαροι εἰς τὴν Μακεδονίαν καὶ Θράκην (Athens, 1944).

Zakythinos, D. A., Οἱ Σλάβοι ἐν Ἑλλάδι. Συμβολαὶ εἰς τὴν ἱστορίαν τοῦ μεσαιωνικοῦ Ἑλληνισμοῦ (Athens, 1945).

Zlatarsky, V. N., *Istorija na bŭlgarskata dŭržava*, vol. I, pt. I (2nd ed. Sofia, 1938) [see Gen. Bibl. v].

CHAPTER IV. THE AMORIANS AND MACEDONIANS, 842–1025

I. PRIMARY SOURCES

Western, Slav and Oriental sources are too numerous to be generally cited here. Some of these may be found in the bibliographies for chapters VI and X–XVII. French translations of a number of passages from Arabic sources may be found in A. A. Vasiliev, *Byzance et les Arabes*, I and II pt. 2 (by M. Canard) [see Gen. Bibl. V].

Acts of Athos [see Gen. Bibl. IV].
Arethas, *9 Orations*, ed. R. J. H. Jenkins, B. Laourdas and C. A. Mango, *BZ*, XLVII (1954), 1–40.
Basilicorum libri LX [see Gen. Bibl. IV and bibliography for chapter XXI].
Benešević, V., 'Die byzantinischen Ranglisten', *BNJ*, V (1926–7), 97–167.
Cameniates, John, *De excidio Thessalonicensi*, ed. I. Bekker, *CSHB* (after Theophanes Continuatus) (1838).
Cedrenus, George, *Synopsis historiarum* [containing John Scylitzes and Scylitzes Continuatus; cf. Gy. Moravcsik, *Byzantinoturcica*, I, 335 ff.; see Gen. Bibl. I], ed. I. Bekker, 2 vols., *CSHB* (1838–9); *MPG*, CXXI–CXXII.
Constantine Porphyrogenitus, *Vita Basilii* = Theophanes Continuatus, bk V, see below.
Constantine Porphyrogenitus, *Opera* [see Gen. Bibl. IV].
Cosmas the Priest, *Treatise against the Bogomils*, ed. M. Popruženko (Sofia, 1936); French transl. and commentary by H. C. Puech and A. Vaillant (Paris, 1945).
Darrouzès, J., *Epistoliers byzantins du Xe siècle* (*AOC*, VI) (Paris, 1960).
Digenis Akrites, ed. with transl. and commentary by J. Mavrogordato (Oxford, 1956); ed. P. Kalonaros, Βασίλειος Διγενὴς Ἀκρίτας, 2 vols. (Athens, 1941).
Dölger, F., *Regesten der Kaiserurkunden* [see Gen. Bibl. IV].
Epanagoge [see Gen. Bibl. IV under Zepos, J. and P., and bibliography for chapter XXI].
Eparch, Book of the [see Gen. Bibl. IV].
Genesius, Joseph, *Regna*, ed. C. Lachmann, *CSHB* (1834); *MPG*, CIX.
Georgius Monachus (Hamartolus), *Chronicle*, ed. C. de Boor, 2 vols. (Leipzig, 1904); ed. E. Muralt [a later and interpolated version] (St Petersburg, 1859); *MPG*, CX.
Georgius Monachus Continuatus, *Chronicle*, ed. I. Bekker, *CSHB* (1838) [in Theophanes Continuatus].
Giovanni Diacono, *Cronaca Veneziana*, ed. G. Monticolo, *Cronache veneziane antichissime*, I, *Fonti* (Rome, 1890), pt. 4.
Glycas, Michael, *Chronicle*, ed. I. Bekker, *CSHB* (1836).
Grumel, V., *Les Regestes des Actes du Patriarcat*, II [see Gen. Bibl. IV].
Jaḥjā ibn-Saʿīd al-Anṭakī, *History*, ed. with French transl. I. Kratchkovsky and A. A. Vasiliev, *PO*, XVIII (1924); ed. in part with Russian transl. and notes V. R. Rosen, *Imperator Vasilij Bolgarobojca, Izvlečenija iz letopisi Jachji Antiochijskago* [*The Emperor Basil the Slayer of the Bulgars; extracts from the Chronicle of James of Antioch*], *AcadIP*, XLIV (St Petersburg, 1883); French transl. in part by M. Canard, in A. A. Vasiliev, *Byzance et les Arabes*, II, ii [see Gen. Bibl. V].

Joel, *Chronographia*, ed. I. Bekker, *CSHB* (1837).

John Geometres (Cyriotes), *Poems*, *MPG*, cvi.

Juris ecclesiastici Graecorum historia et monumenta, ed. J. B. Pitra [see Gen. Bibl. iv].

Jus graeco-romanum, iii, ed. K. E. Zachariae von Lingenthal; i–ii, ed. J. and P. Zepos (Athens, 1931) [see Gen. Bibl. iv].

Leo VI, *Opera*, *MPG*, cvii.

Leo VI, *Tactica*, ed. R. Vári, 2 vols. (Budapest, 1917–22); *MPG*, cvii.

Leo VI, *Panegyric of Basil I*, ed. A. Vogt and I. Hausherr, Oraison funèbre de Basile I par son fils Léon VI le Sage (text and transl.; *OC*, xxvi) (Rome, 1932).

Leo VI, *Problemata*, ed. A. Dain (Paris, 1935).

Leo VI, *Novels*, ed. with French transl. P. Noaille and A. Dain (Paris, 1944).

Leo Choerosphactes, *Letters*, ed. G. Kolias (Athens, 1939).

Leo the Deacon, *History*, ed. C. B. Hase, *CSHB* (1828); *MPG*, cxvii.

Leo Grammaticus, *Chronographia*, ed. I. Bekker, *CSHB* (1842); *MPG*, cviii.

Leunclavius, J., *Juris graeco-romani tam canonici quam civilis tomi II . . . cura M. Freheri . . .* (Frankfurt, 1596).

Liber Pontificalis, ed. L. Duchesne [see Gen. Bibl. iv].

Liutprand, Bishop of Cremona, *Antapodosis; Relatio de legatione Constantinopolitana*, ed. I. Bekker, *SGUS* (1915); English transl. F. A. Wright, *The Works of Liutprand of Cremona* (London, 1930).

Manasses, Constantine, *Synopsis historica*, ed. I. Bekker, *CSHB* (1837) [with Joel and George Acropolites]; *MPG*, cxxvii.

Mansi, J. D., *Sacrorum conciliorum nova et amplissima collectio*, xv–xix [see Gen. Bibl. iv].

Meyer, P., *Die Haupturkunden für die Geschichte der Athosklöster* (Leipzig, 1894).

Moravcsik, Gy., 'Sagen und Legenden über Kaiser Basileios I', *DOP*, xv (1961), 61–126.

Nicetas, David, *Vita Ignatii*, Mansi, xvi; *MPG*, cv.

Nicholas Mysticus, Patriarch of Constantinople, *Letters*, *MPG*, cxi.

Petit, L., 'Office inédit en l'honneur de Nicéphore Phocas', *BZ*, xiii (1904), 398–420.

Philopatris seu qui docetur dialogus, ed. C. B. Hase, *CSHB* (1828) [with Leo the Deacon].

Philotheus, *Kletorologion*, ed. J. B. Bury, *The Imperial Administrative System* [see Gen. Bibl. v].

Photius, Patriarch of Constantinople, *Opera*, *MPG*, ci–civ; see also J. A. G. Hergenröther, *Monumenta graeca ad Photium eiusque historiam pertinentia* (Ratisbon, 1869).

Photius, Patriarch of Constantinople, *Letters*, ed. A. Papadopoulos-Kerameus (St Petersburg, 1896).

Photius, Patriarch of Constantinople, *Homilies*, ed. S. Aristarches, 2 vols. (Constantinople, 1900); ed. with English transl. C. Mango (Cambridge, Mass., 1958).

Prochiron [see Gen. Bibl. iv and bibliography for chapter xxi].

Psellus, Michael, *Chronographia*, ed. K. N. Sathas, *Bibl. graeca med. aev.* iv [see Gen. Bibl. iv]; ed. J. B. Bury (London, 1899); ed. E. Renauld, 2 vols. (Budé) (Paris, 1926–8); English transl. E. R. A. Sewter (London, 1953).

Rhalles, G. A. and Potles, M., *Syntagma* [see Gen. Bibl. iv].

Russian Primary Chronicle. *Polnoe Sobranie Russk. Letopisej*, I (1926–8); English transl. S. H. Cross and O. P. Sherbowitz-Wetzor (Cambridge, Mass., 1953).

Schramm, P. E., 'Neun Briefe des byzantinischen Gesandten Leo von seiner Reise zu Otto aus den Jahren 997–998', *BZ*, xxv (1925), 89–105.

Scylitzes, John, see Cedrenus.

Stephen of Taron, *Armenische Geschichte*, German transl. H. Gelzer and A. Burckhardt (Leipzig, 1907), pp. 198–215.

Sylloge Tacticorum, quae olim 'Inedita Leonis Tactica' dicebatur, ed. A. Dain (Paris, 1938).

Symeon Logothetes, *Chronicle*. [This has survived in various versions: Leo Grammaticus, Georgius Monachus Continuatus, Theodosius Melitenus (q.v.), and in an Old Slavonic transl., ed. V. I. Sreznevsky (St Petersburg, 1905).]

Symeon, Pseudo- (Symeon Magister), *Chronicle*, ed. I. Bekker [with Theophanes Continuatus], *CSHB* (1838).

Symeon the New Theologian, *MPG*, cxx, *Orationes* (Latin only).
  Liber divinorum amorum (Latin only). German transl. K. Kirchhoff (Hellerau, 1930). The Greek text of four of these hymns is edited by P. Maas, 'Aus der Poesie des Mystikers Symeon', *Festgabe Albert Ehrhard*, ed. A. M. Königer (Bonn, 1927), pp. 327–41.
  Capita practica et theologica.
  De alterationibus animae et corporis (Latin only).
  Duae orationes.

Epistola de confessione, ed. K. Holl, *Enthusiasmus und Bussgewalt* (Leipzig, 1898), pp. 110–27. [Also *MPG*, xcv, where it is wrongly attributed to John of Damascus.]
  Letter to Stephen, Archbishop of Nicomedia, ed. I. Hausherr and G. Horn, *OC*, xii, 45 (July–August, 1928), lxiii–lxv.

Synodicon for Orthodoxy Week, ed. F. I. Uspensky, *Sinodik v Nedelju Pravoslavija* (*Zapiski imperatorskago novorossijskago universiteta*, LIX) (Odessa, 1893).

Theodosius the Deacon, *De expugnatione Cretae*, ed. C. B. Hase, *CSHB* [with Leo the Deacon] (1828); *MPG*, cxiii.

Theodosius Melitenus, *Chronicle*, ed. G. L. F. Tafel (Munich, 1859).

Theophanes Continuatus, *Chronographia*, ed. I. Bekker, *CSHB* (1838); *MPG*, cix.

Uspensky, F. I., 'Vizant. tabel' o rangach' ['The Byzantine List of Ranks'], *IRAIK*, iii (1898), 98–137.

Vita Sancti Euthymii (Patr. Cp., †917), ed. C. de Boor (Berlin, 1888).

Vita Sancti Pauli iunioris (†955), ed. H. Delehaye, *AB*, xi (1892), 19–74, 136–81.

Vita Sanctae Theodorae imperatricis (†867), ed. W. Regel (*Analecta Byzantino-Russica*) (St Petersburg, 1891).

Vita Sanctae Theophano (Empress, †893), ed. E. Kurtz (*Zwei griechische Texte über die hl. Theophano die Gemahlin Leo VI*), *Mém. AcadIP*, viii, sér. iii, 2 (1898).

Zonaras, John, *Epitome historiarum*, ed. M. Pinder and M. Büttner-Wobst, 3 vols., *CSHB* (1841–97); ed. L. Dindorf, 6 vols. (Leipzig, 1868–75); *MPG*, cxxxiv–cxxxv.

II. MODERN WORKS

Adontz, N., 'L'âge et l'origine de l'empereur Basile I', *B*, VIII (1933), 475–550; IX (1934), 223–60.

Adontz, N., 'Samuel l'Arménien, roi des Bulgares', *Mémoires de l'acad. roy. de Belgique, cl. des lettres*, XXXIX (1938), 1–63.

Alexander, P. J., 'Secular Biography at Byzantium', *SP*, XV (1940), 194–209.

Amann, E., *L'époque carolingienne* (Paris, 1947) [= Fliche et Martin, VI; see Gen. Bibl. V].

Amann, E. and Dumas, A., *L'église au pouvoir des laïques, 888–1057* (Paris, 1943) [= Fliche et Martin, VII; see Gen. Bibl. V].

Angelov, D., *Der Bogomilismus auf dem Gebiet des byzantinischen Reiches* (Sofia, 1948).

Bach, E., 'Les lois agraires byzantines du Xᵉ siècle', *Classica et Mediaevalia*, V (1942), 70–91.

Boak, A. E. R., 'Earliest Russian Moves against Constantinople', *Queen's Quarterly*, 55 (Queen's College, Kingston, Canada), pp. 308–17.

Bon, A., *Le Péloponnèse byzantin jusqu'en 1204* [see Gen. Bibl. V].

Bratianu, G. I., 'Le commerce bulgare dans l'empire byzantin et le monopole de l'empereur Léon VI à Thessalonique', *Sbornik P. Nikov = Izvestija, Bulg. Hist. Soc.* XVI–XVII (1939), 30–6.

Bréhier, L., *Le schisme oriental du XIᵉ siècle* (Paris, 1899).

Bury, J. B., *The Imperial Administrative System* [see Gen. Bibl. V].

Bury, J. B., *Eastern Roman Empire* [see Gen. Bibl. V].

Canard, M., 'La date des expéditions mésopotamiennes de Jean Tzimiscès', *Mélanges Grégoire*, II = *AIPHO*, X (1950), 99–108.

Canard, M., 'Histoire de la dynastie des H'amdanides de Jazīra et de la Syrie', *Publications de la faculté des lettres d'Alger*, sér. 2, XXI (Paris, 1953), 694–714, 844–59.

Canard, M., 'Une vie du patriarche melkite d'Antioche, Christophore (†967)', *B*, XXIII (1953, publ. 1954), 561–9.

Canard, M., 'Quelques "à côté" de l'histoire des relations entre Byzance et les Arabes', *Studi Orientalistici in onore di G. Levi Della Vida*, I (Rome, 1956), pp. 98–119.

Canard, M., 'Les aventures d'un prisonnier arabe et d'un patrice byzantin à l'époque des guerres bulgaro-byzantines', *DOP*, XI–X (1956) 49–72.

Charanis, P., 'The Monastic Properties and the State in the Byzantine Empire' [see Gen. Bibl. V].

Chatzepsaltes, K. C., 'Η Κύπρος κατὰ τὸ δεύτερον ἥμισυ τοῦ ἐνάτου καὶ τὰς ἀρχὰς τοῦ δεκάτου μ. Χ. αἰῶνος. Acts of the IXth Internat. Byz. Congress: Thessalonica, 1953 = Ἑλληνικά, παράρτ. IX (Athens, 1956), 327–41.

Dain, A., 'L'encyclopédisme de Constantin Porphyrogénète', *Lettres d'Humanité* XII = *Bull. Assoc. Budé, Supplément* III, 4 (1953), 64–81.

Diehl, C., *Figures byzantines I* [see Gen. Bibl. V].

Dikigoropoulos, A. I., 'The Political Status of Cyprus A.D. 648–965', *Report of the Department of Antiquities, Cyprus, 1940–48* (Nicosia, 1958), pp. 94–114.

Dölger, F., 'Die Chronologie des grossen Feldzuges des Kaisers Johannes Tzimiskes gegen die Russen', *BZ*, XXXII (1932), 275–92.

Dölger, F., 'Bulgarisches Zartum und byzantinisches Kaisertum', *Izvestija Bulgar. Archeolog. Inst.* IX (1935), 57–68; reprinted in *Byzanz und die europäische Staatenwelt* [see Gen. Bibl. V].

Dölger, F., 'Der Bulgarenherrscher als geistlicher Sohn des byzantinischen Kaisers', *Sbornik P. Nikov = Izv. Bulg. Hist. Soc.* 16/17 (1939), pp. 219–32; reprinted in *Byzanz und die europäische Staatenwelt* [see Gen. Bibl. v].

Dölger, F., 'Wer war Theophano?', *HJ*, LXII–LXIX (1949), 646–58.

Dölger, F., 'Byzanz und das Abendland vor den Kreuzzügen', *X Congresso internazionale di scienze storiche, Roma, 1955. Relazioni*, III. *Storia del Medioevo* (Florence, 1956), pp. 67–112; reprinted in ΠΑΡΑΣΠΟΡΑ (1961), pp. 73–106.

Dunlop, D. M., *The History of the Jewish Khazars* (Princeton, N.J., 1954).

Dvornik, F., *Les Slaves, Byzance et Rome au IXe siècle* (Paris, 1926).

Dvornik, F., *Les légendes de Constantin et de Méthode vues de Byzance* (*BS* supplementa, I) (Prague, 1933).

Dvornik, F., *The Photian Schism* [see Gen. Bibl. v].

Dvornik, F., 'Photius et la réorganisation de l'Académie patriarcale', *Mélanges Peeters*, II = *AB*, LXVIII (1950), 108–25.

Dvornik, F., 'The Patriarch Photius and Iconoclasm', *DOP*, VII (1953), 69–97.

Dvornik, F., 'Byzantine Political Ideas in Kievan Russia', *DOP*, IX–X (1956), 73–121.

Ebersolt, J., *Le grand Palais de Constantinople et le livre des Cérémonies* (Paris, 1910).

Every, G., *The Byzantine Patriarchate* [see Gen. Bibl. v].

Ferjančić, B., 'O upadu Sklavisijana na Peloponez za vreme Romana Lakapina' ['The Sklavesian Invasion of the Peloponnese under Romanus I Lecapenus'], *Zbornik Rad. Viz. Inst. Serb. Akad. Nauk.* III (1955), 37–48.

Ferluga, J., 'Niže vojno-administrativne jedinice tematskog uredjenja' ['The military and administrative theme units of lesser rank'], *Zbornik Radova Viz. Inst.* II (1953), 61–94.

Ferluga, J., 'Vreme postanka teme Dalmacije' ['The date of the establishment of the theme of Dalmatia'], *Univerzitetu Beogradu, Zbornik Filozofskog Fakulteta*, III (1955), 53–67.

Gay, J., *L'Italie méridionale et l'empire byzantin* [see Gen. Bibl. v].

Glykatzi-Ahrweiler, H., *Recherches sur l'administration de l'empire byzantin aux IXe–XIe siècles* (= *Bulletin de Correspondance hellénique*, LXXXIV) (Athens and Paris, 1960).

Gorjanov, B. T., 'Pozdnevizantijskij immunitet' ['Late Byzantine immunity'], *VV*, n.s. XI (1956), 177–99; XII (1957), 97–116.

Granić, B., 'Kirchenrechtliche Glossen zu den vom Kaiser Basileios II dem autokephalen Erzbistum von Achrida verliehenen Privilegien', *B*, XII (1937), 395–415.

Grégoire, H., 'Inscriptions historiques byzantines. Ancyre et les Arabes sous Michel l'Ivrogne', *B*, IV (1927/8), 437–68.

Grégoire, H., 'Michel III et Basile le Macédonien dans les inscriptions d'Ancyre', *B*, V (1929/30), 327–46.

Grégoire, H., 'La chronologie de la guerre russe de Tzimiscès', *B*, VI (1931), 337–42.

Grégoire, H., 'Etudes sur le neuvième siècle', *B*, VIII (1933), 515–50.

Grégoire, H., 'Etudes sur l'épopée byzantine', *REG*, XLVI (1933), 29–69.

Grégoire, H., 'L'histoire et la légende d'Oleg, prince de Kiev', *Nouv. Clio*, IV (1952), 281–7.

Grégoire, H., 'Le communiqué arabe sur la prise de Thessalonique (904)', *B*, XXII (1952), 373–8.

Grégoire, H., 'La carrière du premier Nicéphore Phocas', Προσφορὰ εἰς Στ. Κυριακίδην. = Ἑλληνικά, παράρτημα IV (Thessalonica, 1953), 232–54.

Grégoire, H. and Orgels, P., 'La guerre russo-byzantine de 941', *B*, XXIV (1954, publ. 1955), 155–6.

Grégoire, H. and Orgels, P., 'Les invasions russes dans le synaxaire de Constantinople', *B*, XXIV (1954, publ. 1955/6), 141–5.

Grierson, P., 'Coinage and Money in the Byzantine Empire 498–c. 1090' [see Gen. Bibl. III C].

Grierson, P., 'Nomisma, tetarteron et dinar: un plaidoyer pour Nicéphore Phocas', *Revue belge de numismatique*, C (1954), 75–84.

Grumel, V., *La Chronologie* [see Gen. Bibl. III A].

Grumel, V., 'La chronologie des événements du règne de Léon VI', *EO*, XXXV (1936), 5–42.

Grumel, V., 'Notes de chronologie byzantine', *EO*, XXXV (1936), 331–5.

Guilland, R., 'Etudes sur l'histoire administrative de l'empire byzantin' [see Gen. Bibl. V].

Guilland, R., 'Etudes sur Constantinople byzantine. Les Thomaïtes et le Patriarcat', *JOBG*, V (1956), 27–40.

Guilland, R., 'Les patrices byzantins sous le règne de Constantin VII Porphyrogénète (913–959). Contribution à l'histoire administrative et à la prosopographie de l'empire byzantin', *Silloge Bizantina in onore di S. G. Mercati*, *SBN*, IX (1957), 188–221.

Hefele, C. J., *Conciliengeschichte*, French transl. H. Leclercq [see Gen. Bibl. V].

Hergenröther, J. A. G., *Photius, Patriarch von Konstantinopel*, 3 vols. (Ratisbon, 1867–9).

Hirsch, F., *Byzantinische Studien* [see Gen. Bibl. V].

Hirsch, F., *Kaiser Konstantin VII Porphyrogennetos* (Berlin, 1873).

Honigmann, E., *Die Ostgrenze des byzantinischen Reiches von 363 bis 1071* [see Gen. Bibl. V].

Honigmann, E., 'Studies in Slavic Church History', *B*, XVII (1944–5), 128–82.

Hussey, J. M., *Church and Learning in the Byzantine Empire* [see Gen. Bibl. V].

Jenkins, R. J. H., 'Constantine VII's portrait of Michael III', *Bull. de l'Acad. de Belgique, Cl. d. Lettr.* V, XXXIV (1948), 71–7.

Jenkins, R. J. H., 'The Supposed Russian Attack on Constantinople in 907: Evidence of the Pseudo-Symeon', *SP*, XXIV (1949), 403–6.

Jenkins, R. J. H., 'Cyprus between Byzantium and Islam, 688–965', *Studies presented to D. M. Robinson*, II (St Louis, 1953), 1006–14.

Jenkins, R. J. H., 'The Date of Leo VI's Cretan Expedition', Προσφορὰ εἰς Στ. Κυριακίδην = Ἑλληνικά, παράρτημα IV (Thessalonica, 1953), 277–81.

Jenkins, R. J. H., 'The Classical Background of the Scriptores post Theophanem', *DOP*, VIII (1954), 13–30.

Jenkins, R. J. H., 'The Date of the Slav Revolt in the Peloponnese under Romanus I', *Late Classical and Mediaeval Studies in honor of A. M. Friend, Jr.* (Princeton, N.J., 1955), pp. 204–11.

Jerphanion, G. de, 'La date du couronnement de Romain II', *OCP*, I (1935), 490–5.

Jugie, M., *Le schisme byzantin* [see Gen. Bibl. V].

Jugie, M., 'Les origines romaines de l'église russe', *EO*, XXXVI (1937), 257–70.

Karayannopulos, J., *Die Entstehung der byzantinischen Themenordnung* (Byz. Archiv., Heft X) (Munich, 1959).

Karyškovsky, P. O., 'O chronologii russko-vizantijskoj vojny pri Svjato-slave' ['The chronology of the Russo-Byzantine War in the time of Svjatoslav'], *VV*, n.s. v (1952), 127–38.

Každan, A. P., 'Raby i mistii v Vizantii IX–XI vekov' ['Slaves and hire-lings in Byzantium from the 9th to the 11th centuries'], *Učenje Zapiski of the State Pedagogic Institute in Tula*, II (1951), 63–84.

Každan, A. P., 'Vizantijskie goroda v 7–11 vv.' ['Byzantine cities from the 7th to the 11th centuries'], *Sovetskaja Archeologija*, XXI (1954), 164–88.

Každan, A. P., 'K voprosu ob osobennostjach feodal'noj sobstvennosti v Vizantii VIII–X vv.' ['On the question of the distinctive characteristics of feudal property in Byzantium from the 8th to the 10th centuries'], *VV*, n.s. X (1956), 48–65.

Každan, A. P., 'Formirovanie feodal'nogo pomestja v Vizantii X v.' ['The development of feudal property in Byzantium in the 10th Century'], *VV*, n.s. XI (1956), 98–122.

Každan, A. P., 'Social'nij sostav naselenija vizantijskich gorodov v IX–X vv.' ['The social composition of the population of Byzantine cities in the 9th and 10th centuries'], *VV*, n.s. VIII (1956), 85–96.

Každan, A. P., 'Vizantijskaja obščina v IX–X vekach' ['Byzantine com-munities in the 9th and 10th centuries'], *Učenie Zapiski of the State Pedagogic Institute in Velikie Luki* (1956), pp. 77–102.

Každan, A. P., 'Osnovnye problemy istorii Vizantii' ['Fundamental problems of Byzantine history'], *Vestnik istorii mirovoj kul'tury*, II (1957), 64–80.

Kolias, G., *Léon Choerosphactès, magistre, proconsul et patrice* (Athens, 1939).

Krekić, B., *Dubrovnik* [see Gen. Bibl. v].

Krumbacher, K., *Geschichte der byzant. Litteratur* [see Gen. Bibl. v].

Lamma, P., 'Il problema dei due imperii dell'Italia meridionale nel giudizio delle fonti letterarie dei secoli IX e X', *Atti 3° Congresso internaz. di Studi sull'Alto Medioevo 1956* (Spoleto, 1959), pp. 155–253.

Laurent, J., *L'Arménie entre Byzance et l'Islam depuis la conquête arabe jusqu'en 886* (*EcfrAR*, CXVII) (Paris, 1919).

Laurent, V., 'Bulletin de numismatique byzantine' [see Gen. Bibl. III c].

Lemerle, P., 'Esquisse pour une histoire agraire de Byzance' [see Gen. Bibl. v].

Levčenko, M. V., *Očerki po istorii russko-vizantijskich otnošenij* [*Studies in the History of Russo-Byzantine Relations*] (Moscow, 1956).

Lipšic, E. E., 'Vizantijskij učenyj Lev Matematik' ['The Byzantine scholar Leo the Mathematician'], *VV*, n.s. II (1949), 106–49.

Litavrin, G. G., 'Voprosy obrazovanija drevnerusskogo gosudarstva' ['The problems of the origin of the Old Russian State'], *Srednie Veka*, VIII (1956), 386–95.

Litavrin, G. G., 'Nalogovaja politika Vizantii v Bolgarii v 1018–1185 gg.' ['Fiscal policy of Byzantium in Bulgaria from 1018 to 1185'], *VV*, n.s. X (1956), 81–110.

Loparev, C., 'Vizantijskija žitija svjatich VIII–IX v.' ['Byzantine lives of the saints of the 8th and 9th centuries'], *VV*, XVII (1910), 1–224; XVIII (1911, publ. 1913), 1–147; XIX (1912, publ. 1915), 1–151.

Lopez, R. S., 'East and West in the Early Middle Ages. Economic Relations', *X Congresso Internazionale di scienze storiche, Roma, 1955. Relazioni*, III. *Storia del Medioevo* (Florence, 1956), pp. 113–63.

Macartney, C. A., *The Magyars in the Ninth Century* (Cambridge, 1930).

Michel, A., *Die Kaisermacht in der Ostkirche (843–1204)* [see Gen. Bibl. v].

Mitard, M., 'Le pouvoir impérial au temps de Léon VI le Sage', *Mélanges Diehl*, I (Paris, 1930), pp. 217–23.

Moravcsik, Gy., *Byzantinoturcica* [see Gen. Bibl. I].

Mortreuil, J. A. B., *Histoire du droit byzantin*, 3 vols. (Paris, 1843–7).

Mutafčiev, P., 'Der Byzantinismus im mittelalterlichen Bulgarien', *BZ*, XXX (1929–30), 387–94.

Mutafčiev, P., 'Russko-bolgarskie otnošenija pri Svjatoslave' ['Russo-Bulgarian relations in the time of Svjatoslav'], *Sem. Kond.* IV (1931), 77–92.

Nasledova, P. A., 'Remeslo i torgovlija Fessaloniki konca IX–načala X v. po dannym Ioanna Kameniaty' ['Handicraft and trade in Thessalonica at the end of the ninth and the beginning of the tenth centuries from the data of John Cameniates'], *VV*, n.s. VIII (1956), 61–84.

Neumann, C., *Die Weltstellung des byzantinischen Reiches vor den Kreuzzügen* (Leipzig, 1894); French transl. *ROL*, X (1903–4), 56–171.

Obolensky, D., *The Bogomils* (Cambridge, 1948).

Obolensky, D., 'Byzance et la Russe de Kiev', *Messager de l'Exarch. Petr. Russe en Europe Occidentale*, XXIX (Paris, 1959), 20–35.

Ohnsorge, W., *Das Zweikaiserproblem* [see Gen. Bibl. v].

Ohnsorge, W., 'Die Legation des Kaisers Basileios II an Heinrich II', *HJ*, LXXIII (1954), 61–73; reprinted in *Abendland und Byzanz* [see Gen. Bibl. v].

Ohnsorge, W., 'Das Kaiserbündnis von 842–844 gegen die Sarazenen. Datum, Inhalt, und politische Bedeutung des "Kaiserbriefes aus St Denis"', *Archiv für Diplomatik, Schriftgesch., Siegel- und Wappenkunde*, I (1955), 88–131; reprinted in *Abendland und Byzanz* [see Gen. Bibl. v].

Ohnsorge, W., 'Sachsen und Byzanz. Ein Überblick', *Niedersächs. Jahrbuch für Land.-Geschichte*, XXVII (1955), 1–44; reprinted in *Abendland und Byzanz* [see Gen. Bibl. v].

Ohnsorge, W., *Abendland und Byzanz* [see Gen. Bibl. v].

Ohnsorge, W., 'Zur Frage der Töchter Kaiser Leons VI', *BZ*, LI (1958), 78–81.

Ohnsorge, W., 'Die Anerkennung des Kaisertums Ottos I durch Byzanz', *BZ*, LIV (1961), 28–52.

Ostrogorsky, G., 'Die ländliche Steuergemeinde des byzantinischen Reiches im 10. Jahrh.', *Vierteljahrsschr. f. Sozial- und Wirtschaftsg.* XX (1927), 1–108.

Ostrogorsky, G., 'Avtokrator i Samodržac' ['Autocrator and Samodržac'], *Glas*, CLXIV (1935), 95–187.

Ostrogorsky, G., 'Die Krönung Symeons von Bulgarien durch den Patriarchen Nikolaos', *Izvest. Bulg. Arch. Inst.* IX (1935), 275–80.

Ostrogorsky, G., 'Die byzantinische Staatenhierarchie', *Sem. Kond.* VIII (1936), 41–61.

Ostrogorsky, G., 'L'expédition du prince Oleg contre Constantinople en 907', *Annales de l'Inst. Kond.* XI (1939), 47–62, 296–8.

Ostrogorsky, G., 'The Peasant's Pre-emption Right: an Abortive Reform of the Macedonian Emperors', *JRS*, XXXVII (1947), 117–26.

Ostrogorsky, G., 'Une ambassade serbe auprès de l'empereur Basile II', *B*, XIX (1949), 187–94.

Ostrogorsky, G., 'Sur la date de la composition du Livre des Thèmes et sur l'époque de la constitution des premiers thèmes d'Asie Mineure', *B*, XXIII (1953, publ. 1954), 31–66.

Ostrogorsky, G., 'O vizantijskim državnim seljacima i vojnicima—dve povelje iz doba Jovana Cimiska' ['On Byzantine state farmers and soldiers—two documents from the period of John Tzimisces'], *Glas*, CCXIV (1954), 23–46.

Ostrogorsky, G., *Pour l'histoire de la féodalité byzantine* [see Gen. Bibl. v].

Ostrogorsky, G., 'Lav Ravduh i Lav Hirosfakt' ['Leo Rhabduchus and Leo Choerosphactes'], *Zbornik Rad. Viz. Inst. Serb. Akad. Nauk*, III (1955), 29–36.

Ostrogorsky, G., *History of the Byzantine State* [see Gen. Bibl. v].

Ostrogorsky, G., *Quelques problèmes d'histoire de la paysannerie byzantine* [see Gen. Bibl. v].

Ostrogorsky, G., 'Pour l'histoire de l'immunité à Byzance', *B*, XXVIII (1958, publ. 1959), 165–254.

Ostrogorsky, G. and Stein, E., 'Die Krönungsordnungen des Zerimonienbuches', *B*, VII (1932), 185–233.

Papadopulos, I., 'Ἡ Κρήτη ὑπὸ τοὺς Σαρακηνούς *(824–961)* (Athens, 1948).

Posedel, J., 'Pitanje dalmatinskog temata u prvoj polovici IX stoljeća' ['Problems connected with the Dalmatian Theme in the first half of the IXth century'], *Historijski Zbornik*, III (1950), 217–20.

Prokić, B., *Die Zusätze in der Hs. des J. Skylitzes cod. Vindob. hist. gr. LXXIV* (Munich, 1906).

Radojičić, G. S., 'La date de la conversion des Serbes', *B*, XXII (1952), 253–6.

Rambaud, A., *L'empire grec au Xe siècle* [see Gen. Bibl. v].

Rémondon, R., 'A propos de la menace byzantine sur Damiette sous le règne de Michel III', *B*, XXV (1953, publ. 1954), 245–50.

Runciman, S., *A History of the First Bulgarian Empire* (London, 1930).

Runciman, S., *The Emperor Romanus Lecapenus* [see Gen. Bibl. v].

Scharf, J., 'Photius und die Epanagoge', *BZ*, XLIX (1956), 385–400.

Schlumberger, G., *L'épopée byzantine à la fin du Xe siècle* [see Gen. Bibl. v].

Schlumberger, G., *Un empereur byzantin au Xe siècle: Nicéphore Phocas* [see Gen. Bibl. v].

Schramm, P. E., 'Kaiser, Basileus und Papst in der Zeit der Ottonen', *BZ*, CXXIX (1924), 424–75.

Setton, K. M., 'On the raids of the Moslems in the Aegean in the 9th and 10th centuries and their alleged occupation of Athens', *American Journal of Archaeology*, LVIII (1954), 311–18.

Šišić, F. von, *Geschichte der Kroaten*, I (Zagreb, 1917).

Spulber, C. A., *Les novelles de Léon le Sage* (Cernauţi, 1934).

Stender-Petersen, A., 'Das Problem der ältesten byzantinisch-russisch-nordischen Beziehungen', *X Congresso internazionale di scienze storiche, Roma, 1955. Relazioni*, III. *Storia del Medioevo* (Florence, 1956), pp. 165–88.

Taube, M. de, 'Nouvelles recherches sur l'histoire politique et religieuse de l'Europe orientale à l'époque de la formation de l'état russe', *Istina*, V (1957), 9–32, 265–78.

Teall, J. L., 'The Grain Supply of the Empire, 330–1025', *DOP*, XIII (1959), 87–139.

Treitinger, O., *Die oströmische Kaiser- und Reichsidee nach ihrer Gestaltung im höfischen Zeremoniell* [see Gen. Bibl. v].

Uspensky, F. I., 'Konstantinopol'skij sobor 842 goda i utverždenie pravoslavija' ['The Constantinopolitan synod of 842 and the confirmation of orthodoxy'], *ZMNP*, CCLXXIII (January 1891), 73–158.

Uspensky, F. I., *Očerki po istorii vizantijskoj obrazovannosti* [see Gen. Bibl. v].

Vasiliev, A. A., *Byzance et les Arabes* [see Gen. Bibl. v].

Vasiliev, A. A., 'The Emperor Michael III in Apocryphal Literature', *BM*, I, pt. I (1946), 237–48.

Vasiliev, A. A., *The Russian Attack on Constantinople in 860* (Cambridge, Mass., 1946).
Vasiliev, A. A., 'The Second Russian Attack on Constantinople', *DOP*, VI (1951), 161–225.
Vasiliev, A. A., *History of the Byzantine Empire* [see Gen. Bibl. v].
Vernadsky, G., *The Origins of Russia* (Oxford, 1959).
Vogt, A., *Basile I, empereur de Byzance et la civilisation byzantine à la fin du IX*e *siècle* (Paris, 1908).
Vogt, A., 'Note sur la chronologie des patriarches de Constantinople au IXe et au Xe siècles', *EO*, XXXII (1933), 275–8.
Vogt, A., 'La jeunesse de Léon VI le Sage', *RH*, CLXXIV (1934), 403 ff.
Zachariae von Lingenthal, K. E., *Geschichte des griechisch-römischen Rechts* [see Gen. Bibl. v].
Zakythinos, D. A., Οἱ Σλάβοι ἐν Ἑλλάδι (Athens, 1945).
Zlatarsky, V. N., *Istorija na bŭlgarskata dŭržava*, I, 2 [see Gen. Bibl. v].

CHAPTER V. THE LATER MACEDONIANS, THE COMNENI AND THE ANGELI, 1025–1204

I. SOURCES

Bibliography on the Crusades may be found in S. Runciman, *History of the Crusades*; and K. M. Setton (gen. ed.), *History of the Crusades* [see Gen. Bibl. v].

PRIMARY AUTHORITIES

Western, Slav and Oriental sources are too numerous to be generally cited here; some of these may be found in the bibliographies for chapters VI and X–XVII.

Acts of Athos [see Gen. Bibl. IV].
Allatius, L., *De ecclesiae occidentalis atque orientalis perpetua consensione* (Cologne, 1648). [This contains a report on the synod's action in the suppression of the Bogomil heresy in Manuel Comnenus' reign.]
Anonymus of Bari, *Chronicle*, ed. L. A. Muratori, *RISS*, v.
Anthologia Palatina, ed. H. Stadtmüller, 3 vols. (Leipzig, 1894–1906); for other editions see *GBL*, p. 728.
Attaleiates, Michael, *Historia*, ed. I. Bekker, *CSHB* (1853); French transl. by H. Grégoire, *B*, XXVIII (1958), 325–62 [in progress].
Attaliates, Michael, *Diataxis*, ed. MM, v and K. N. Sathas, *Bibliotheca graeca medii aevi*, I [see Gen Bibl. IV].
Balsamon, Theodore, *Canones SS. apostolorum, conciliorum, et in epistolas canonicas SS. patrum*, *MPG*, CXXXVII–CXXXVIII; and in *RP*.
Benjamin of Tudela, *Itinerary*, ed. and transl. by A. Asher, 2 vols. (London and Berlin, 1840–1); and by M. N. Adler (London, 1907).
Bryennius, Nicephorus, *Historiarum libri* IV, ed. A. Meineke, *CSHB* (1836); *MPG*, CXXVII; French transl. and notes by H. Grégoire, *B*, XXII (1953) and XXV–XXVII (1957).

Cecaumenus, *Strategicon*. *Cecaumeni strategicon et incerti scriptoris de officiis regiis libellus*, edd. B. Wassiliewsky and V. Jernstedt (St Petersburg, 1896); German transl. by H.-G. Beck (= Byzantinische Geschichtsschreiber, v, ed. E. von Ivánka, Graz, 1956).

Cedrenus, George, *Compendium historiarum* [containing John Scylitzes and Scylitzes Continuatus; cf. Gy. Moravcsik, *Byzantinoturcica*, i, pp. 335 ff.] [see Gen. Bibl. i], ed. I. Bekker, 2 vols, *CSHB* (1838–9); *MPG*, cxxi–cxxii.

Cerularius, Michael, *MPG*, cxx [one sermon and a ruling on adultery, otherwise concerned with the schism of 1054]. See below, A. Michel, *Humbert und Kerullarios*.

Christodulus, *Diataxis*, MM, vi, pp. 59–80 [see also below, *Milet*].

Christophorus Mytilenaeus, *Die Gedichte des Christophoros Mytilenaios*, ed. E. Kurtz (Leipzig, 1903).

Cinnamus, John, *Historia*, ed. A. Meineke, *CSHB* (1836); *MPG*, cxxxiii.

Comnena, Anna, *Alexiad* [see Gen. Bibl. iv].

Digenis Akrites, ed. with transl. and commentary J. Mavrogordato (Oxford, 1956); ed. P. Kalonaros, Βασίλειος Διγενὴς ᾿Ακρίτας, 2 vols. (Athens, 1941).

Dölger, F., *Regesten der Kaiserurkunden* [see Gen. Bibl. iv].

Eustathius Boilas, *Will*, ed. V. Benešević, ʻZavješčanie vizantijskago bojarina XI veka' [ʻThe will of a Byzantine magnate of the eleventh century'], *ZMNP*, xviii (1911), 107–15; English transl. S. Vryonis, *DOP*, xi (1957), 263–77.

Eustathius of Thessalonica, *Opuscula*, ed. G. L. F. Tafel (Frankfurt, 1832). [This contains various sermons, addresses and letters.]

Eustathius of Thessalonica, *Orationes*, ed. G. L. F. Tafel, *De Thessalonica eiusque agro* (Berlin, 1839), pp. 401–39; ed. W. Regel, *Fontes rerum Byzantinarum*, i, fasc. i (St Petersburg, 1892).

Eustathius of Thessalonica, *MPG*, cxxxv–cxxxvi contain nearly all Eustathius' writings, other than the commentaries, for which see Cohn's article in Pauly–Wissowa, vi, 1.

Eustathius of Thessalonica, *De capta Thessalonica*, ed. S. Kyriakidis (Ist. Sicil., Testi, v) (Palermo, 1961); ed. I. Bekker (after Leo Grammaticus), *CSHB* (1842); German transl. H. Hunger (= Byzantinische Geschichtsschreiber, iii, ed. E. von Ivánka, Graz, 1955).

Eustratius of Nicaea, ed. A. K. Demetracopoulos, *Bibliotheca ecclesiastica* (Leipzig, 1866) [writings on theological controversies]; ed. G. Heylbut, *Berliner Aristoteleskommentare*, xx (Berlin, 1892). [His commentaries on the *Ethics*.]

Euthymius Malaces, Metropolitan of Neae-Patrae, ed. T. L. F. Tafel, *De Thessalonica eiusque agro* (Berlin, 1839), pp. 394–400 [funeral oration on Eustathius]; ed. M. Treu, Δελτίον τῆς ῾Ιστορικῆς καὶ ᾿Εθνολογικῆς ῾Εταιρείας τῆς ῾Ελλάδος, v (1896–1900), 197–218; ed. A. Papadopoulos-Kerameus, *Noctes Petropolitanae* (St Petersburg, 1913), pp. 89–102, 115–25; ed. K. G. Bonis, Εὐθυμίου τοῦ Μαλάκη μητροπολίτου Νέων Πατρῶν (῾Υπάτης) τὰ σῳζόμενα, 2 vols. (Athens, 1937–49); see also Stadtmüller, *Michael Choniates…*, pp. 306 ff.

Euthymius Zigabenus, *Panoplia dogmatica*, and other theological works, *MPG*, cxxviii–cxxxi.

Falcandus, Hugo, *La Historia o Liber de regno Sicilie*, ed. G. B. Siragusa (*Fonti*) (Rome, 1897).

Glycas, Michael, *Annales*, ed. I. Bekker, *CSHB* (1836); *Letters and Annals*, *MPG*, CLVIII.

Gregorius Magister, see below, V. Langlois.

Gregory Parcourianus, *Typicon*, ed. L. Petit, *VV*, XI (1904), supplt. no. I, pp. i–xxxii, 1–63, *Typicon de Grégoire Parcourianos pour le monastère de Pétritzos (Bačkovo) en Bulgarie;* see also *CSCO*, CXLIII (1953) and CXLIV (1954).

Grumel, V., *Les Regestes des Actes du Patriarcat*, II–III [see Gen. Bibl. IV].

Guilelmus Apuliensis, *Gesta Roberti Wiscardi*, ed. R. Wilmans, *MGH*, *Script.*, IX, 240 ff.; ed. M. Mathieu (Ist. Sicil., Testi, IV) (Palermo, 1961).

Irene Ducaena, Empress, *Typicon*, ed. MM, V, pp. 327–91; also *MPG*, CXXVII.

Isaac Comnenus (brother of John II Comnenus), *Typicon*; ed. L. Petit, *IRAIK*, XIII (1908), 17–77.

Italus, John, *Opuscula selecta*, ed. G. Cereteli, 2 vols. (Tiflis, 1924–6).

Italus, John, *Quaestiones quodlibetales* ('Ἀπορίαι καὶ Λύσεις), ed. P. Joannou (Ettal, 1956).

Italus, John, *Trial of John Italus for Heresy*, ed. T. Uspensky, *IRAIK*, II (1897), 1–66.

John of Antioch, *Oratio de disciplina monastica et de monasteriis laicis non tradendis*, *MPG*, CXXXII.

John II Comnenus, *Typicon*, ed. A. Dimitrievsky, I: *Typica*, pt. I, pp. 656–702 [see Gen. Bibl. IV].

John Mauropous, Archbishop of Euchaita, *Constitution of the Law Faculty in the University of Constantinople* (with Latin transl.); ed. J. Cozza-Luzi, *Studi e documenti di storia e diritto*, V, 289–316 (Rome, 1884); ed. A. Salač (Latin transl.) (Prague, 1954). [On the authorship of this *Constitution*, see below, J. Cvetler.]

John Mauropous, Archbishop of Euchaita, *Poems, Sermons, Life of St Dorotheus*, ed. P. de Lagarde (Abh. d. Wiss. zu Göttingen, XXVIII) (Göttingen, 1882); also *MPG*, CXX. [The more complete edition is that of Lagarde; but see the review of K. Neumann, *Theol. Literaturzeitung* (1886), no. 24, cols. 565 ff., and no. 25, cols. 594 ff. See also L. Sternbach, *De Ioanne Psello*, concerning the authenticity of poems 13–17 in Lagarde.]

Kanellakes, K. N., Χιακὰ ἀνάλεκτα (Athens, 1890).

Lampros, S. P., *Collection de romans grecs en langue vulgaire et en vers* (Paris, 1880).

Langlois, V., 'Mémoire sur la vie et les écrits du Prince Grégoire Magistros', *JA*, 6me série, XIII (1869), 5–64.

Leunclavius, J., *Juris graeco-romani tam canonici quam civilis tomi II...cura M. Freheri...* (Frankfurt, 1596).

Lupus Protospatharius, *Chronicles*, ed. G. H. Pertz, *MGH*, *Script.*, V.

Malaterra, Gaufredus, *Historia Sicula*, ed. L. A. Muratori, *RISS*, V.

Manasses, Constantine, *Synopsis historica*, ed. I. Bekker, *CSHB* (1837) [with Joel and George Acropolites]; *MPG*, CXXVII.

Mansi, J. D., *Sacrorum conciliorum nova et amplissima collectio*, XV–XXII [see Gen. Bibl. IV].

Matthew of Edessa, *History*, ed. and transl. E. Dulaurier (Paris, 1858) (Bibliothèque historique arménienne).

Meyer, P., *Die Haupturkunden für die Geschichte der Athosklöster* (Leipzig, 1894).

Michael Choniates (Acominatus), *Opera*, ed. S. P. Lampros, 2 vols. (Athens, 1879–80); *MPG*, CXL [containing some letters, two sermons, the orations on Eustathius and Nicetas, and a poem on Athens].

Michael Italicus, *Letters*, ed. J. A. Cramer, *Anecdota graeca e codicibus manuscriptis bibliothecarum Oxoniensium*, III (Oxford, 1836), 158–203.

Michael the Syrian, *Chronicle*, ed. with French transl. J. B. Chabot (Paris, 1900–10).

Michel, A., *Humbert und Kerullarios. Quellen und Studien zum Schisma des XI. Jahrhunderts* (Quellen und Forschungen aus dem Gebiete der Geschichte der Görresgesellschaft, XXI and XXIII), 2 vols. (Paderborn, 1924–30).

Miklosich, F. and Müller, J., *Acta et diplomata graeca*, V–VI [see Gen. Bibl. IV].

Milet. Ergebnisse der Ausgrabungen und Untersuchungen seit dem Jahre 1899, ed. T. Wiegand (Königliche Museen zu Berlin), III, pt. i (Berlin, 1913): *Der Latmos*. See *Monumenta Latrensia Hagiographica*, ed. H. Delehaye, pp. 97 ff. [especially on Christodulus].

Nicetas Byzantinus, *Refutatio epistolae regis Armeniae. Refutatio Mohamedis*, *MPG*, CV.

Nicetas Choniates (Acominatus), *Chronicle*, ed. I. Bekker, *CSHB* (1835); *MPG*, CXXXIX; German transl. F. Grabler (= Byzantinische Geschichtsschreiber, VII–IX, ed. E. von Ivánka, Graz, 1958).

Nicetas Choniates (Acominatus), *Thesaurus orthodoxae fidei*, *MPG*, CXXXIX–CXL.

Nicetas Stethatus, *MPG*, CXX. *De salutatione manuale. Libellus contra Latinos* [Latin only; the Greek is given by A. Michel, *Humbert und Kerullarios*, II, 322 ff., see above].

Nicetas Stethatus, *Dialexis*, ed. A. Michel, *op. cit.* II, 320–1.

Nicetas Stethatus, *De azymis et sabbatorum jejuniis, et nuptiis sacerdotum* (*Antidialogue*), ed. A. Michel, *op. cit.* II, 322–42.

Nicetas Stethatus, *Altera synthesis contra Latinos de Filioque*, ed. A. Michel, *op. cit.* II, 371–409.

Nicetas Stethatus, *Tres centuriae asceticae*, *MPG*, CXX; ed. with French transl. M. Chalendard, *Le paradis spirituel et autres textes annexes* (Sources chrét. VIII) (Paris, 1943).

Nicetas Stethatus, *Vie de Syméon le nouveau théologien*, ed. with French transl. I. Hausherr and G. Horn (*OC*, XII) (Rome, 1928).

Nicetas Stethatus, Μυστικὰ συγγράμματα, ed. P. K. Chrestos, S. Sakkos and G. Mantzaridos (Thessalonica, 1957).

Nicoulitza, *De officiis regiis libellus*, edd. B. Wassiliewsky and V. Jernstedt (St Petersburg, 1896).

Parthey, G. F. C., *Hieroclis synecdemus et notitiae Graecae episcopatuum. Accedunt Nili Doxopatrii notitia patriarchatuum et locorum nomina immutata* (Berlin, 1866). [There is the later edition of E. Gerland, but only the first volume has been published. See *B*, VII (1932), 512–26.]

Petit, L., 'Le monastère de Notre Dame de Pitié en Macédoine', *IRAIK*, VI (1900). [Contains diplomas of the Comnenian rulers.]

Petit, L., 'Documents inédits sur le concile de 1166 et ses derniers adversaires', *VV*, XI (1904), 465–93.

Philippus Solitarius, *Dioptra*, *MPG*, CXXVII.

Prodromus, Theodorus, *MPG*, CXXXIII [poetry and letters]; ed. E. Miller and E. Legrand, *Trois poèmes vulgaires de Théodore Prodrome* (Paris, 1875); ed. E. Legrand, *Bibliothèque grecque vulgaire*, I (Paris, 1880) [six poems, including the three edited by Miller and Legrand]; ed. D.-C. Hesseling and H. Pernot, *Poèmes prodromiques en grec vulgaire* (Amsterdam, 1910). [See also Gy. Moravcsik, *Byzantinoturcica*, I, 522–6; Gen. Bibl. I.]

Psellus, Michael, *Chronographia*, ed. K. N. Sathas, *Bibl. graeca med. aev.* IV [see Gen. Bibl. IV]; ed. J. B. Bury (London, 1899); ed. E. Renauld, 2 vols. (Budé) (Paris, 1926–8); English transl. E. R. A. Sewter (London, 1953).

Psellus, Michael, Letters and orations, ed. K. N. Sathas, *op. cit.* IV–V; ed. E. Kurtz and F. Drexl, 2 vols. (Milan, 1936–41).

Psellus, Michael, Various works, *MPG*, CXXII. For fuller bibliography on Psellus' writings see Gy. Moravcsik, *Byzantinoturcica*, I, 437 ff. [see Gen. Bibl. I]; and J. M. Hussey, *Church and Learning in the Byzantine Empire*, pp. 236 ff. [see Gen. Bibl. V].

Romuald of Salerno, *Chronicle*, ed. W. Arndt, *MGH*, *Script.* XIX; ed. C. A. Garufi, *RISS*, VII.

Scylitzes, John, see Cedrenus.

Synodicon for Orthodoxy Week, ed. F. I. Uspensky, *Sinodik v nedelju pravoslavija* (*Zapiski imperatorskago novorossijskago universiteta*, LIX) (Odessa, 1893).

Syropulus, John, *Oratio*, ed. M. Bachmann, *Die Rede des Johannes Syropulos an den Kaiser Isaak II Angelos*. Diss. (Munich, 1935).

Tafel, G. L. F. and Thomas, G. M., *Urkunden zur älteren Handels- und Staatsgeschichte der Republik Venedig*, I [see Gen. Bibl. IV].

Theophylact of Ochrida, Archbishop of Bulgaria, *MPG*, CXXIII–CXXVI [letters and exegesis].

Timarion, ed. B. Hase, *Notices et extraits*, IX, 2 (1813), 163–246; ed. A. Ellissen, *Analekten der mittel- und neugriechischen Literatur*, pt. 4 (Leipzig, 1860) [with translation].

Will, C., *Acta et scripta quae de controversiis ecclesiae graecae et latinae saeculo undecimo composita extant* (Leipzig and Marburg, 1861).

Xiphilinus, John, *Orationes*, *MPG*, CXX.

Zachariae von Lingenthal, K. E., *Jus graeco-romanum* [see Gen. Bibl. IV].

Zonaras, John, *Epitome historiarum*, ed. M. Pinder and M. Büttner-Wobst, 3 vols., *CSHB* (1841–97); ed. L. Dindorf, 6 vols. (Leipzig, 1868–75); *MPG*, CXXXIV–CXXXV.

II. MODERN WORKS

Amann, E. and Dumas, A., *L'église au pouvoir des laïques, 888–1057* (Paris, 1943) [= Fliche et Martin, VII, see Gen. Bibl. V].

Angelov, D., *Der Bogomilismus auf dem Gebiet des byzantinischen Reiches* (Sofia, 1948).

Berndt, A., *Joannes Mauropus', Erzbischofs von Euchaita, Gedichte, ausgewählt und metrisch übersetzt* (Wissenschaftliche Beilage zu dem Programme des Gymnasiums und Realgymnasiums zu Plauen i. V., Ostern, 1887, Progr. Nr. 507) (Plauen, 1887).

Bezobrazov, P., *Materialy dlja istorii vizantijskoj imperii*.
    I. *ZMNP*, CCLIV (Nov. 1887), 65–78 [monastic records].
    II. *Ibid.* CCLXII (March 1889), 72–91 [Psellus' writings].
    III. *Ibid.* CCLXV (May 1889), 23–31 [Michael VII and Robert Guiscard].
    IV. *Ibid.* pp. 32–84 [Michael Cerularius].

Bibicou, H., 'Une page d'histoire diplomatique de Byzance au XIᵉ siècle: Michel VII Doukas, Robert Guiscard et la pension des dignitaires', *B*, XXIX–XXX (1959–60), 43–75.

Bidez, J., 'Psellus et le commentaire du Timée de Proclus', *RP*, XXIX (1905), 321–7.

Bidez, J., *Michel Psellus, Epître sur la Chrysopée. Opuscules et extraits sur l'alchimie, la météorologie et la démonologie. En appendice, Proclus, Sur l'art hiératique; Psellus, Choix de dissertations inédites* (Catalogue des manuscrits alchimiques grecs, VI) (Brussels, 1928). See review of H. Grégoire, *B*, IV (1927–8, publ. in 1929), 728–34.

Bon, A., *Le Péloponnèse byzantin* [see Gen. Bibl. v].

Bonis, K. G., Ἰωάννης ὁ Ξιφιλῖνος· ὁ νομοφύλαξ, ὁ μοναχός, ὁ πατριάρχης καὶ ἡ ἐποχὴ αὐτοῦ (Texte und Forsch. zur byz.-neugriech. Philologie, 24) (Athens, 1937).

Bratianu, G. I., 'Le monopole du blé au XIᵉ siècle', *Etudes byzantines*, pp. 141–57 [see Gen. Bibl. v].

Bréhier, L., *Le monde byzantin* [see Gen. Bibl. v].

Bréhier, L., *Le schisme oriental du XIᵉ siècle* [see Gen. Bibl. v].

Bréhier, L., 'L'enseignement supérieur à Constantinople dans la dernière moitié du XIᵉ siècle', *Revue internationale de l'enseignement*, XXXVIII, 8 (1899, Aug.), 97–112.

Bréhier, L., 'Notes sur l'histoire de l'enseignement supérieur à Constantinople', *B*, III (1926), 73–94; IV (1927–8), 13–28.

Brosset, M. F., *Les ruines d'Ani, capitale de l'Arménie sous les rois bagratides, aux Xᵉ et XIᵉ siècles. Histoire et description* (St Petersburg, 1860).

Browning, R., 'The Death of John II Comnenus', *B*, XXXI (1961), 229–35.

Browning, R., 'A New Source on Byzantine–Hungarian Relations in the Twelfth Century: the Inaugural Lecture of Michael ὁ τοῦ Ἀγχιάλου as ὕπατος τῶν φιλοσόφων', *Balkan Studies*, II (Thessalonica, 1961), 173–4.

Buckler, G. G., *Anna Comnena* (Oxford, 1929).

Bury, J. B., 'Roman Emperors from Basil II to Isaac Komnenos', *EHR*, IV (1889), 19, 41, 251 ff.; reprinted in *Selected Essays* [see Gen. Bibl. v].

Bussell, F. W., *The Roman Empire* [see Gen. Bibl. v].

Cahen, C., 'La première pénétration turque en Asie Mineure', *B*, XVIII (1948), 5–67.

Cessi, R., *Storia della Repubblica di Venezia* [see Gen. Bibl. v].

Chalandon, F., *Les Comnènes* [see Gen. Bibl. v].

Chalandon, F., *Histoire de la domination normande en Italie et en Sicilie* [see Gen. Bibl. v].

Charanis, P., 'The Monastic Properties and the State' [see Gen. Bibl. v].

Chrestos, P. K. with Sakkos, S. and Mantzaridos, G., Νικήτα Στηθάτου μυστικὰ συγγράμματα (Thessalonica, 1957).

Cognasso, F., *Partiti politici e lotte dinastiche in Bizanzio alla morte di Manuele Comneno* (Turin, 1912).

Cognasso, F., 'Un imperatore bizantino della decadenza: Isacco II Angelo', *Bess.* XIX (1915), 29–60.

Cvetler, J., 'The Authorship of the Novel on the Reform of Legislative Education at Constantinople (about 1045 A.D.)', *Eos*, XLVIII, II (= Symbolae R. Taubenschlag, II) (1957), 297–328.

Dawkins, R. M., *The Monks of Athos* (London, 1936).

Dawkins, R. M., 'The later history of the Varangian Guard: some notes', *JRS*, XXXVII (1947), 39–46.

Der Nersessian, S., *Armenia and the Byzantine Empire* [see Gen. Bibl. v].

Diehl, C., *Figures byzantines* [see Gen. Bibl. v].

Diehl, C., 'La société byzantine à l'époque des Comnènes', *RHSE*, VI (1929), 197–280; and printed separately (Bucharest, 1929).

Dölger, F., *Beiträge zur Geschichte der byzantinischen Finanzverwaltung* [see Gen. Bibl. v].

Dölger, F., *Byzanz und die europäische Staatenwelt* [see Gen. Bibl. v].

Dölger, F., 'Byzanz und das Abendland vor den Kreuzzügen', *X Congresso internazionale di scienze storiche, Roma, 1955. Relazioni*, III. *Storia del Medioevo* (Florence, 1955), pp. 67–112; reprinted in ΠΑΡΑΣΠΟΡΑ (Ettal, 1961), pp. 73–106.

Dölger, F., 'Finanzgeschichtliches aus der byzantinischen Kaiserkanzlei des 11. Jahrhunderts. Zum Tetarteron', *SBAW*, Phil.-Hist. Kl. (1956), pp. 3–33; reprinted in ΠΑΡΑΣΠΟΡΑ (Ettal, 1961), pp. 326–49.

Dölger, F. and Maas, P., 'Zu dem Abdankungsgedicht des Nikolaos Muzalon', *BZ*, XXXV (1935), 2–14.

Draeseke, J., 'Zu Michael Psellos', *ZWT*, XXXII (1889), 303–30.

Draeseke, J., 'Johannes Mauropus', *BZ*, II (1893), 461–93.

Draeseke, J., 'Zu Eustratios von Nikäa', *BZ*, V (1896), 319–36.

Draeseke, J., 'Michael Psellos im "Timarion"', *BZ*, VI (1897), 483–90.

Draeseke, J., 'Psellos und seine Anklageschrift gegen den Patriarchen Michael Kerullarios', *ZWT*, XLVIII (1905), 194–259, 362–409.

Dreves, G., 'Johannes Mauropus', *Stimmen aus Maria-Laach*, XXVI (1884), Heft II, 159–79.

Ebersolt, J., *Orient et Occident* [see Gen. Bibl. v].

Every, G., *The Byzantine Patriarchate* [see Gen. Bibl. v].

Ferluga, J., 'Niže vojno-administrativne jedinice tematskog uredjenja' ['The military and administrative theme units of lesser rank'], *Zbornik Radova Viz. Inst.* II (1953), 61–94.

Ficker, G., *Erlasse des Patriarchen von Konstantinopel Alexios Studites* (Kiel, 1911).

Fischer, W., *Studien zur byzantinischen Geschichte des elften Jahrhunderts* (Gym. Program. Nr. 495) (Plauen i. V., 1883).

Frolow, A., *Recherches sur la déviation de la IVᵉ Croisade vers Constantinople* (Paris, 1955).

Fuchs, F., *Die höheren Schulen von Konstantinopel im Mittelalter* (*BA*, VIII) (Leipzig, 1926).

Gay, J., *L'Italie méridionale et l'empire byzantin* [see Gen. Bibl. v].

Giunta, F., *Bizantini e Bizantinismo nella Sicilia Normanna* (Palermo, 1950).

Glykatzi-Ahrweiler, H., *Recherches sur l'administration de l'empire byzantin aux IXᵉ–XIᵉ siècles* (= *Bulletin de Correspondance hellénique*, LXXXIV) (Athens and Paris, 1960).

Gordlevsky, V., *Gosudarstvo Sel'džukidov Maloj Azii* [*The Seljuq State in Asia Minor*] (Moscow–Leningrad, 1941).

Grierson, P., 'The Debasement of the Bezant in the Eleventh Century', *BZ*, XLVII (1954), 379–94.

Grierson, P., 'Coinage and Money in the Byzantine Empire' [see Gen. Bibl. v].

Grierson, P., 'The Fineness of the Byzantine Solidus', *BZ*, LIV (1961), 91–7.

Grumel, V., 'Les préliminaires du schisme de Michel Cérulaire ou la question romaine avant 1054', *REG*, X (1953), 5–23.

Grumel, V., *La Chronologie* [see Gen. Bibl. III].

Guilland, G., *Etudes byzantines* (Paris, 1959).

Heilig, K. J., 'Ostrom und das Deutsche Reich um die Mitte des 12. Jahrhunderts', *Kaisertum und Herzogsgewalt im Zeitalter Friederichs I*, by T. Mayer, K. Heilig and C. Erdmann (Leipzig, 1944), pp. 3–371.

Heyd, W., *Histoire du commerce du Levant* [see Gen. Bibl. v].

Honigmann, E., *Die Ostgrenze des byzantinischen Reiches* [see Gen. Bibl. v].

Hussey, J. M., 'Michael Psellus, the Byzantine Historian', *SP*, x (1935), 81–90.

Hussey, J. M., *Church and Learning in the Byzantine Empire 867–1185* [see Gen. Bibl. v].

Hussey, J. M., 'The Byzantine Empire in the Eleventh Century', *Trans. Roy. Hist. Soc.* xxxii (1950), 71–85.

Hussey, J. M., 'The Writings of John Mauropous: a Bibliographical Note', *BZ*, xliv (1951), 278–82.

Hussey, J. M., *Ascetics and Humanists in Eleventh-Century Byzantium* (Annual Lecture to Friends of Dr Williams's Library) (London, 1960).

Jamison, E., *Admiral Eugenius of Sicily; His Life and Work and the Authorship of the Epistola ad Petrum and the Historia Hugonis Falcandi Siculi* (London, 1957).

Janin, R., 'Un Ministre byzantin: Jean l'Orphanotrophe', *EO*, xxx (Oct.–Dec. 1931), 431–43.

Joannou, P., 'Psellos et le Monastère τὰ Ναρσοῦ', *BZ*, xliv (1951), 283–90.

Joannou, P., *Christliche Metaphysik in Byzanz* [see Gen. Bibl. v].

Jorga, N., *Brève histoire de la petite Arménie* [see Gen. Bibl. v].

Jugie, M., *Le schisme byzantin* [see Gen. Bibl. v].

Kap-Herr, H. von, *Die abendländische Politik Kaiser Manuels mit besonderer Rücksicht auf Deutschland* (Strassbourg, 1881).

Karayannopulos, J., *Die Entstehung der byzantinischen Themenordnung* (*BA*, Heft x) (Munich, 1959).

Krekić, B., *Dubrovnik* [see Gen. Bibl. v].

Krumbacher, K., *Geschichte der byzantinischen Litteratur* [see Gen. Bibl. v].

Kurtz, E., 'Zu Michael Psellos', *BZ*, xv (1906), 590–8.

Lamma, P., *Comneni e Staufer* [see Gen. Bibl. v].

Le Barbier, E., *St Christodule et la réforme des couvents grecs* (Paris, 1863).

Lebedev, A. P., *Istorija razdelenija cerkvej v IX, X i XI veke* [*The history of the separation of the Churches in the ninth, tenth and eleventh centuries*] (Moscow, 1905).

Leib, B., 'Les patriarches de Byzance et la politique religieuse d'Alexis Ier Comnène (1081–1118)', *Mélanges J. Lebreton*, ii (= *Recherches sc. relig.* xl, 1952), 201–22.

Leib, B., *Rome, Kiev et Byzance à la fin du XIe siècle* [see Gen. Bibl. v].

Leib, B., 'Nicéphore III Botaneiates (1078–1081) et Marie d'Alanie', *VI Congr. Intern. d'Et. Byz., Paris, 1948*, i (1950), 129–40.

Leib, B., 'Jean Doukas, César et moine. Son jeu politique à Byzance de 1067 à 1081', *Mélanges Peeters*, ii (= *AB*, lxviii, 1950), 163–79.

Lemerle, P., 'Esquisse pour une histoire agraire de Byzance' [see Gen. Bibl. v].

Lemerle, P., 'Recherches sur le régime agraire à Byzance: la terre militaire à l'époque des Comnènes', *Cahiers de civilisation médiévale*, ii (1959), 265–81.

Lemerle, P., *Prolégomènes à une édition critique et commentée des 'Conseils et Récits' de Kékauménos* (Acad. Roy. Belgique, Mém. liv, fasc. 1) (Brussels, 1960).

Mädler, H., *Theodora, Michael Stratiotikos, Isaac Komnenos. Ein Stück byzantinischer Kaisergeschichte* (Wissensch. Beilage zu dem Progr. des königlichen Gymnasiums zu Plauen i. V., Progr. Nr. 545) (Plauen i. V., 1894).

Mayne, R., 'East and West in 1054', *CHJ*, xi (1954), 133–48.

Michel, A., 'Die römischen Angriffe auf Michael Kerullarios wegen Antiocheia (1053–54)', *BZ*, xliv (1951), 419–27.

Michel, A., 'Schisma und Kaiserhof im Jahre 1054. M. Psellos', *1054–1954.*
    L'église et les églises, ɪ, 351–440 [see Gen. Bibl. v].
Michel, A., *Die Kaisermacht in der Ostkirche (843–1204)* [see Gen. Bibl. v].
Moravcsik, Gy., *Byzantinoturcica* [see Gen. Bibl. ɪ].
Mortreuil, J. A. B., *Histoire du droit byzantin*, 3 vols. (Paris, 1843–7).
Neumann, K., 'Über die urkundlichen Quellen zur Geschichte der byzantin-
    isch-venetianischen Beziehung vornehmlich im Zeitalter der Komnenen',
    BZ, ɪ (1892), 366–78.
Neumann, K., *Die Weltstellung des byzantinischen Reiches vor den Kreuzzügen*;
    French transl. in *ROC* [see Gen. Bibl. v].
Nissen, W., *Die Diataxis des Michael Attaliates von 1077* (Jena, 1894).
Norden, W., *Der vierte Kreuzzug im Rahmen der Beziehungen des Abendlandes
    zu Byzanz* (Berlin, 1898).
Norden, W., *Das Papsttum und Byzanz* [see Gen. Bibl. v].
Obolensky, D., *The Bogomils* (Cambridge, 1948).
Oeconomos, L., *La vie religieuse dans l'empire byzantin au temps des Comnènes
    et des Anges* (Paris, 1918).
Ohnsorge, W., 'Ein Beitrag zur Geschichte Manuels I von Byzanz', *Festschrift
    A. Brackmann* (Weimar, 1931), pp. 371–93; reprinted in *Abendland und
    Byzanz* [see Gen. Bibl. v].
Ohnsorge, W., 'Die Bedeutung der deutsch-byzantinischen Beziehungen im
    12. Jahrhundert für den deutschen Ost.', *Deutsches Archiv für Landes-
    und Volksforschung*, v (1942), 249–59; reprinted in *Abendland und Byzanz*
    [see Gen. Bibl. v].
Ohnsorge, W., 'Zu den Aussenpolitischen Anfängen Friedrich Barbarossas',
    Quellen und Forsch. aus italienischen Arch. u. Bibl. xxxɪ (1942), 13–32;
    reprinted in *Abendland und Byzanz* [see Gen. Bibl. v].
Ohnsorge, W., 'Die Byzanzpolitik Friedrich Barbarossas und der "Lands-
    verrat" Heinrichs des Löwen', *Deutsch. Archiv. für Gesch. Mittelalters*, vɪ
    (1943), 118–49; reprinted in *Abendland und Byzanz* [see Gen. Bibl. v].
Ohnsorge, W., *Das Zweikaiserproblem* [see Gen. Bibl. v].
Ohnsorge, W., 'Sachsen und Byzanz. Ein Überblick', *Niedersächs. Jahrbuch
    für Land.-Geschichte*, xxvɪɪ (1955), 1–44; reprinted in *Abendland und
    Byzanz* [see Gen. Bibl. v].
Ohnsorge, W., *Abendland und Byzanz* [see Gen. Bibl. v].
Ostrogorsky, G., *Pour l'histoire de la féodalité byzantine* [see Gen. Bibl. v].
Ostrogorsky, G., *Quelques problèmes d'histoire de la paysannerie byzantine* [see
    Gen. Bibl. v].
Ostrogorsky, G., *History of the Byzantine State* [see Gen. Bibl. v].
Ostrogorsky, G., 'Pour l'histoire de l'immunité à Byzance', *B*, xxvɪɪɪ (1958,
    publ. 1959), 165–254.
Parker, J., 'The Attempted Byzantine Alliance with the Sicilian Norman
    Kingdom (1166–1167)', *Papers Brit. School at Rome*, xxɪv = n.s. xɪ
    (1956), 86–93.
Radojčić, N., *Dva posljednja Komnena na carigradskom prijestolu* [*The two
    last Comneni on the throne of Constantinople*] (Zagreb, 1907).
Rambaud, A., 'Michel Psellos', *RH*, ɪɪɪ (1877), 241–82; reprinted in *Etudes sur
    l'histoire byzantine* (Paris, 1912).
Runciman, S., *The Eastern Schism* [see Gen. Bibl. v].
Salaville, S., 'Philosophie et théologie ou épisodes scolastiques à Byzance de
    1059 à 1117', *EO*, xxɪx (1930), 132–56.
Schlumberger, G., *L'épopée byzantine* [see Gen. Bibl. v].

Skabalanovič, N., *Vizantijskoe gosudarstvo i cerkov' v XI v.* [see Gen. Bibl. v].

Sokolov, N. P., 'K voprosu o vzaimootnošenijach Vizantii i Venecii v poslednie gody pravlenija Komninov' ['On the question of the relations between Byzantium and Venice in the last years of the Comneni'], *VV*, n.s. v (1952), 139–51.

Stadtmüller, G. L., *Michael Choniates, Metropolit von Athen* (*OCA*, xxxiii, 2) (Rome, 1934).

Stephanou, P. E., 'Jean Italos: l'immortalité de l'âme et la résurrection', *EO*, xxxii (1933), 413–28.

Stephanou, P. E., *Jean Italos, philosophe et humaniste* (*OCA*, cxxxiv) (Rome, 1949).

Sternbach, L., 'De Ioanne Psello', *Eos*, ix (1903), 5–10.

Suvorov, N., *Vizantijskij papa* [*A Byzantine Pope*] (Moscow, 1902).

Svoronos, N. G., *Recherches sur le cadastre byzantin et la fiscalité aux XIe et XIIe siècles: le cadastre de Thèbes* (*EcfrAR*) (Paris, 1959) (= *Bulletin de Correspondance hellénique*, lxxxiii (1959), 1–145; 805–25).

Thiriet, F., *La Romanie vénitienne au moyen âge* [see Gen. Bibl. v].

Uspensky, F. I., 'Imperatory Aleksej II i Andronik Komneny', *ZMNP*, ccxii (1880), 95–130 and ccxiv (1881), 52–85.

Uspensky, F. I., 'Poslednie Komniny: Načalo reakcii' ['The last Comneni: the beginning of the reaction'], *VV*, xxv (1927–8), 1–23.

Vasiliev, A. A., 'Manuel Comnenus and Henry Plantagenet', *BZ*, xxix (1929–30), 237–40.

Vasiliev, A. A., *History of the Byzantine Empire* [see Gen. Bibl. v].

Vasiliev, A. A., 'The Opening Stages of the Anglo-Saxon Immigration to Byzantium in the Eleventh Century', *Annales de l'Inst. Kondakov*, ix (1937), 39–70.

Vasilievsky, V., 'Vizantija i Pečenegi' ['Byzantium and the Patzinaks'], *ZMNP*, clxiv (1872), 116 ff.

Vernadsky, G., 'The Byzantine–Russian War of 1043', *Südostforschung*, xii (1953), 47–67.

Vernadsky, G., 'The Russo-Byzantine War of 1043', *BNJ*, xviii (1945–9, publ. 1960), 123–43.

Vryonis, S., Jr., 'The Will of a Provincial Magnate, Eustathius Boilas (1059)', *DOP*, xi (1957), 263–77.

Vryonis, S., Jr., 'Byzantium: the Social Basis of Decline in the Eleventh Century', *Greek, Roman and Byzantine Studies*, ii (1959), 157–75.

Wittek, P., 'Deux chapitres de l'histoire des Turcs de Roum', *B*, xi (1936), 285–319.

Wittek, P., *The Rise of the Ottoman Empire* [see Gen. Bibl. v].

Xanalatos, A. D., *Beiträge zur Wirtschafts- und Sozialgeschichte Makedoniens im Mittelalter, hauptsächlich auf Grund der Briefe des Erzbischofs Theophylaktos von Achrida*. Diss. (Munich, 1937).

Zachariae von Lingenthal, K. E., *Geschichte der griechisch-römischen Rechts* [see Gen. Bibl. v].

Zervos, C., *Un philosophe néoplatonicien du XIe siècle: Michel Psellos* (Paris, 1919).

CHAPTER VI. VENICE TO THE EVE
OF THE FOURTH CRUSADE

Further bibliography may be found in chapters ɪ–v and vɪɪ. For the Crusades see also S. Runciman, *History of the Crusades*, and K. M. Setton (gen. ed.), *History of the Crusades* [see Gen. Bibl. v].

I (*a*). COLLECTIONS OF SOURCES

On the Venetian archives see:

Thiriet, F., *Les archives vénitiennes et leur utilisation pour l'étude de l'Orient gréco-latin jusqu'à la conquête turque* (Mémoire de l'Ecole pratique des Hautes-Etudes) (Paris, 1949–50).

Baschet, A., *Histoire de la Chancellerie Secrète* (Paris, 1870).

Mosto, A. da, *L'Archivio di Stato di Venezia*, 2 vols. (Venice, 1937–40).

Archivio storico italiano (*ASI*) [see List of Abbreviations].

Archivio Veneto (*Arch. Ven.*; *N. Arch. Ven.*; *N. Arch. Ven.* n.s.; *Arch. Ven.-Tri.*; *Arch. Ven.* ser. 5):

Archivio Veneto, 40 vols. (Venice, 1871–90).

Nuovo Archivio Veneto, 20 vols. (1891–1900).

Nuovo Archivio Veneto, nuova serie, 42 vols. (1901–21).

Archivio Veneto-Tridentino (1922–6).

Archivio Veneto, quinta serie (1927 ff).

See List of Abbreviations.

Atti. Istituto Veneto di Scienze, Lettere ed Arte (*Atti Ist. Ven. S.L.A.*). See List of Abbreviations.

Deputazione Veneta di Storia Patria. Continued as *Deputazione Storia Patria per le Venezie* (*Deput. Stor. Patr.*). *Monumenti storici*.

    ɪ. *Documenti*.

    ɪɪ. *Statuti*.

    ɪɪɪ. *Cronache*.

    ɪv. *Miscellanea*: (i) *Miscellanea di Studi e Memorie*; (ii) *Monumenti storici*, n.s. (Venice, 1876 ff.).

Fonti per la storia d'Italia (*Fonti*) [see Gen. Bibl. ɪv].

I (*b*). SPECIAL BIBLIOGRAPHIES

Bertoldi, A., 'Bollettino di bibliografia veneta', *Arch. Ven.* xxxɪɪɪ (1887), 1–34; xxxɪv (1887), 3–68; xxxv (1888), 1–37; xxxvɪ (1888), 39–67; xxxvɪɪ (1889), 1–23. [These bulletins are numbered separately at the back of each volume.]

Cecchetti, B., *Di alcune fonti della storia veneziana fino al sec. XIII* (Venice, 1867).

Cicogna, E. A., *Saggio di bibliografia veneziana* (Venice, 1847).

Fulin, R., 'Bollettino bibliografico dell'Archivio Veneto, 1872–84', *Arch. Ven.* ɪv–xxvɪɪɪ (1872–84).

Giomo, G., 'Indici per nome d'autore e per materia delle pubblicazioni sulla storia medioevale italiana (1890–98), raccolte e recensite da C. Cipolla nel N. Arch. Ven.', *Deput. Stor. Patr.* (Venice, 1903).

Kretschmayr, H., *Geschichte von Venedig* [see Gen. Bibl. v].

Manfroni, C., 'Gli studi storici in Venezia dal Romania ad oggi', *N. Arch. Ven.* n.s. xvi (1908), 352–72.

Monticolo, G., see bibliography in new edition of Sanudo, *Le Vite dei Dogi, RISS* [see below ii, under Sanudo].

Pastorello, E., 'Indici per nome d'autore e per materia delle pubblicazioni sulla storia medioevale italiana (1899–1910), raccolte e recensite da C. Cipolla', *Deput. Ven. Stor. Patr.* (Venice, 1916).

Segarizzi, A., 'Bollettino bibliografico della regione veneta (1901–1905)', *N. Arch. Ven.* n.s. v–xiii (1903–7).

Soranzo, G., *Bibliografia veneziana in aggiunta e continuazione del saggio di E. A. Cicogna* (Venice, 1885).

Tinazzo, G., 'Bibliografia degli scritti di Roberto Cessi', *Miscellaneo in onore di Roberto Cessi,* i (Rome, 1958), pp. xlv–lxxvii.

II. SOURCES

Annales Regni Francorum, ed. F. Kurze, *SGUS* (1895).

Annales Venetici breves, MGH, Script. xiv (1883); R. Fulin, *Arch. Ven.* xii (1876), 335–49.

Baracchi, A., 'Le carte del mille e del millecento, che si conservano nel R. Archivio notarile di Venezia', *Arch. Ven.* vi (1873), 293–321; vii (1874), 80–98, 352–69; viii (1874), 134–53; ix (1875), 99–115; x (1875), 332–51; xx (1880), 51–80, 314–30; xxi (1881), 106–20; xxii (1881), 313–32.

Bertaldo, J., *Splendor consuetudinum civitatis Venetiarum,* ed. F. Schupfer (Bologna, 1896).

Besta, E., *Bilanci generali,* i. In *Commissione documenti finanziari Rep. Veneta,* i (Venice, 1907).

Böhmer, J. F. and others, *Regesta imperii,* 2nd ed. (Graz, (1908–   ).

Cassiodorus, *Variae,* ed. T. Mommsen, *MGH, Auct. ant.* xii (1894).

Cessi, R., *Documenti relativi alla storia di Venezia anteriori al mille,* 2 vols. (Padua, 1942).

Cessi, R., *Le deliberazioni del Maggior Consiglio di Venezia* [Accad. Lincei. Atti delle Assemblee Costit. Italiane. Ser. 3, Sez. i], ii–iii (Bologna, 1931–4).

Cessi, R., Sambin, P. and Brunetti, M., *Deliberazione del Consiglio dei Rogati,* i–ii. *Deput. Stor. Patr., Monumenti,* xv–xvi (1960–1).

Chronicon gradense, ed. H. Simonsfeld, *MGH,* xiv; ed. G. Monticolo, *Cronache veneziane antichissime,* i, *Fonti* (1890), pt. 2, pp. 19–51; ed. R. Cessi, *Origo civitatum Italiae, Fonti* (1933).

Chronicon venetum quod vulgo dicunt Altinate, ed. A. Rossi, *ASI,* ser. 1, viii (1845), 1–228; ed. H. Simonsfeld, *MGH,* xiv; ed. R. Cessi, *Origo civitatum Italiae, Fonti* (1933).

Cicogna, E. A., *Delle iscrizioni veneziane,* 6 vols. (Venice, 1824–53).

Cipolla, C., 'Pubblicazioni straniere sulla storia medioevale d'Italia, a. 1906–1910', *N. Arch. Ven.* i, iii, iv, vi–xx (1891–1900) and n.s. xv–xx (1908–10; Appendices).

Cipolla, C., 'Fonti edite della storia della regione veneta dalla caduta dell'impero Romano sino alla fine del secolo x', *Monumenti storici pubb. dalla R. Deputazione Veneta di Storia Patria,* viii. Serie 4, Misc. ser. i, vol. 2, no. 1 (Venice, 1882/3).

Cipolla, C., 'Fonti edite della storia della regione veneta dalla caduta dell'impero romano sino alla fine del sec. x', *Monumenti storici pubb. R. Deput. Veneta di Storia Patria,* viii. Serie 4, Misc. ser. i, vol. 3 (Venice, 1884).

Cipolla, C., 'Fonti per la storia della regione veneta al tempo della dominazione Longobarda (568–774)', *Atti della R. Deputazione Veneta di Storia Patria* in *Arch. Ven.* XIX (1880), 404–55.

Cipolla, C., 'Note di storia veronese. VIII. Trattati commerciali e politici del sec. XII inediti o imperfettamente noti', *N. Arch. Ven.* XV (1898), 288–352.

Codice diplomatico padovano, ed. A. Gloria, I: *Dal sec. VI a tutto l'undecimo*; II: *Dall'anno 1101 alla pace di Costanza, 1183. Deput. Ven. Stor. Patr. Documenti*, II, IV, VI (Venice, 1877–81).

Comnena, Anna, *Alexiad* [see Gen. Bibl. IV].

Constantine Porphyrogenitus, *De administrando imperio* [see Gen. Bibl. IV].

Corpus nummorum italicorum VII. Veneto (Venezia, pt. 1, Dalle origini a Marin Grimani), Accad. Lincei (Rome, 1915).

Cronaca brevissima di Grado, ed. G. Monticolo, *Cronache veneziane antichissime*, I, *Fonti* (1890), pt. 3, pp. 55–6.

Cronache veneziane antichissime, I, ed. G. Monticolo, *Fonti* (1890).

Cronica de singulis patriarchis Nove Aquileie, ed. G. Monticolo, *Cronache veneziane antichissime*, I, *Fonti* (1890), pt. 1, pp. 5–16.

Dandolo, Andrea, *Chronicon Venetum*, ed. L. A. Muratori, *RISS*, XII; E. Pastorello, *ibid.* new ed. (Bologna, 1938–42).

Documenti per la storia dell'augusta basilica di S. Marco in Venezia dal nono secolo alla fine del XVIII (Venice, 1886).

Einhard, *Annales, MGH, Script.* I, see *Annales Regni Francorum*.

Einhard, *Vita Caroli, MGH, Script.* I; *SGUS*, IX.

Galliciolli, G., *Memorie venete antiche*, 8 vols. (Venice, 1795).

Ghetti, B., *I patti tra Venezia e Ferrara dal 1191 al 1313 esaminati nel loro testo* (Rome, 1907).

Giovanni, Diacono, *Cronaca veneziana*, ed. G. Monticolo, *Cronache veneziane antichissime*, I, *Fonti* (1890), pt. 4, pp. 59–171.

Historia Ducum Venetorum, MGH, Script. XIV.

Jaffé, P., *Regesta Pontificum Romanorum* [see Gen. Bibl. IV].

Judicia a probis iudicibus promulgata, ed. B. Pitzorno, *Riv. Ital. Sc. Giur.* XLIV (1908), 269–92.

Justiniani Chronicon, MGH, Script. XIV; *Venetiarum Historia vulgo Petro Iustiniano adiudicata*, ed. R. Cessi and F. Bennato, *Dep. Stor. Patr., Monumenti*, n.s. XVIII (1964).

Kandler, P., *Codice diplomatico istriano* (Trieste, 1853–64).

Kehr, P. F., *Regesta Pontificum Romanorum. Italia Pontificia VII.* 1: *Provincia Aquileiensis.* 2: *Respublica Venetiarum—Provincia Gradensis—Histria* (Berlin, 1923–5) [see Gen. Bibl. IV].

Lanfranchi, L., 'S. Lorenzo di Ammiana', *Fonti Storia Venezia*, ser. II. Diocesi Torcellana (1947).

Lenel, W., 'Un trattato di commercio tra Venezia e Imola del 1099', *N. Arch. Ven.* n.s. XVI (1908), 62–7.

Lorenzo de Monacis. *Chron. de rebus venetis*, ed. F. Cornelius (Venice, 1758); *RISS*, VIII, App., 1–320.

Marco, *Chronica* (extracts), ed. A. Zon, *ASI*, ser. 1, VIII (1845), 257–67.

Martin da Canale, *Chron. des Veniciens*, ed. F. L. Polidori, *ASI*, ser. I, VIII (1845), 231–56, 268–707.

Monticolo, G., 'Il testo del patto giurato dal doge Domenico Michiel al comune di Bari', *N. Arch. Ven.* XVIII (1889), 90–140.

Monticolo, G., 'L'"inventio" e la "translatio" dei santi Ermagora e Fortunato', *N. Arch. Ven.* III (1892), 117–56.

Monticolo, G., 'L'apparitio S. Marci ed i suoi manoscritti', *N. Arch. Ven.* IX(1895), 111–77.

Morozzo della Rocca, R. and Lombardo, A., *Documenti del commercio veneziano nei sec. XI–XIII* (Documenti e studi stor. comm. e diritto comm. XIX–XX), 2 vols. (Turin, 1940).

Morozzo della Rocca, R. and Lombardo, A., *Nuovi documenti del commercio veneto nei sec. XI–XIII.* Deput. Stor. Patr., *Monumenti*, VII (1953).

Pacta and *Praecepta* relating to the Western Empire are printed in *MGH, Leges*, sect. II, *Capitularia* II; *Leges*, sect. IV, *Constitutiones* I; *Diplomata* I–V [see Gen. Bibl. IV].

Paul the Deacon, *Historia Langobardorum, MGH, Script. rerum Langobardorum* (1878).

Procopius, *De Bello Gothico*, ed. D. Comparetti (Rome, 1895) (*Fonti*); ed. J. Haury (Leipzig, 1905); transl. H. B. Dewing (London, 1914).

Ratio de lege romana, ed. B. Pitzorno, *Riv. Ital. Sc. Giur.* XLIII (1907), 125–36.

Relatio de pace veneta, ed. U. Balzani, *BISI*, X (1890), 7–16.

Romuald of Salerno, *Chronicle*, ed. W. Arndt, *MGH, Script.* XIX; ed. C. A. Garufi, *RISS*, VII.

Sanudo, Marino, *Le vite dei Dogi di Venezia*, ed. L. A. Muratori, *RISS*, new ed. by G. Monticolo, *RISS*, XXII (1900).

Sanudo Torsello, Marino, *Liber secretorum fidelium S. Crucis*, ed. J. Bongars, *Gesta Dei per Francos*, II (Hanover, 1611).

Sauerland, N. H., 'Annales Veneti sec. XII', *N. Arch. Ven.* VII (1894), 5–8.

Simonsfeld, H. and Bellemo, V., 'Documenti del secolo XI relativi a Brondolo e a Chioggia', *Arch. Ven.* XXXII (1886), 111–31.

Statutum parvum Henrici Danduli, ed. E. Besta and R. Predelli. *N. Arch. Ven.* n.s. I (1901), 205–300.

Strabo, *Geographica*, bks. IV–V, ed. and transl. H. L. Jones, II (London, 1923).

Tafel, G. L. F. and Thomas, G. M., *Urkunden zur älteren Handels- und Staatsgeschichte der Republik Venedig* [see Gen. Bibl. IV].

Tafel, G. L. F. and Thomas, G. M., *Der Doge Andreas Dandolo und die von demselben angelegten Urkundensammlungen zur Staats- und Handelsgeschichte Venedigs* (Munich, 1855).

Thomas, G. M., 'Acta et Diplomata res venetas graecas atque levantis illustrantia', *Arch. Ven.* XVII (1879), 188–91.

Translatio magnifici martyris Isidori a Chio insula, Junii 1125, auct. Cerbano Cerbani, Rec. Hist. Cr. V, 321–34.

Translatio S. Nicolai; auct. monachus anonimus littorensis. Rec. Hist. Cr., Hist. occident. V (1895), 253–92.

Ughelli, F., *Italia Sacra*, V [see Gen. Bibl. IV].

Villehardouin, Geoffrey of, *La conquête de Constantinople*, ed. N. de Wailly (Paris, 1872); ed. with transl. E. Faral, 2 vols. (Paris, 1938–9).

William of Apulia, *Gesta Roberti Wiscardi, MGH, Script.* IX; also ed. M. Mathieu (Ist. Sicil., Testi, IV) (Palermo, 1961).

III. CRITICISM OF SOURCES

Bersi, R., *Le fonti della prima decade della 'Historia rerum Venetiarum' di Marcantonio Sabellico, N. Arch. Ven.* n.s. XIX (1910), 422–60, XX (1910), 115–62.

Besta, E., 'I trucchi della cosidetta Chronica Altinate', *Atti Ist. Ven. S.L.A.* LXXIV (1914–15), pt. II, 1275–1330.

Besta, E., 'Nuove ricerche sul Chronicon Altinate', *N. Arch. Ven.* n.s. XV (1908), 5–71.

Besta, E., 'La genesi del cosidetto patto venetico di Lotario I', *Studi in Memoria di A. Albertoni*, III (Padua, 1938), 591–618.

Besta, E., 'Sulla composizione della cronaca veneziana attribuita al diacono Giovanni', *Atti Ist. Ven. S.L.A.* LXXIII (1914), pt. II, 775–802.

Besta, E., 'Tomaso Diplovataccio e l'opera sua', *N. Arch. Ven.* n.s. VI (1903), 261–361.

Besta, E., 'Una parola ancora sulla raccolta e la trascrizione di antichi documenti veneziani per opera di Tomaso Diplovataccio', *N. Arch. Ven.* n.s. XXVII (1914), 425–44.

Bethmann, L., 'Nachrichten über die von ihm für die MGH benutzten Sammlungen von Handschriften und Urkunden Italiens aus dem Jahre 1854', *Arch. d. Gesell. f. ält. deutsche Geschichtskunde*, XII (1874), 201–758

Bresslau, H., 'Karls des Grossen Urkunde für das Bistum Torcello', *Neu. Arch.* XXXVIII (1913), 527–34.

Cessi, R., 'Il *pactum Lotharii* del 840', *Atti Ist. Ven. S.L.A.* XCIX (1939–40), 1111–49.

Cessi, R., 'Studi sopra la composizione del cosidetto *Chronicon Altinate*', *BISI*, XLIX (1933), 1–116.

Cessi, R., 'Pacta veneta. I: Pacta carolina; *Arch. Ven.* ser. 5, III (1928), 118–84; II: Dal *pactum Lotharii* al *foedus Ottonis*', *ibid.*, V (1929), 1–77; and in R. Cessi, *Le origini del ducato veneziano* (Naples, 1951), pp. 245–321.

Cessi, R., 'Pactum Clugiae', *Atti Ist. Ven. S.L.A.* LXXXVII (1927–8), pt. II, 991–1023.

Cipolla, C., 'Annales veteres: annales breves, necrologium S. Firmi de Leonico', *Arch. Ven.* IX, 2 (1875), 77–98.

Cipolla, C., 'Ricerche sulle tradizioni intorno alle antiche immigrazioni nella laguna', *Arch. Ven.* XXVII (1884), 338–73; XXVIII (1884), 104–31, 297–334; XXIX (1885), 331–53; XXXI (1886), 129–46, 423–42.

Cipolla, C., 'Ricerche sulle tradizioni intorno alle antiche immigrazioni nella laguna. Il Chronicon Altinate in confronto col Chronicon Gradense', *N. Arch. Ven.* n.s. XXVI (1913), 275–301.

Fulin, R., 'Di una versione del *Liber secretorum fidelium crucis* frammento conservato da Marin Sanuto', *Arch. Ven.* XXII (1881), 49–51.

Galli, R., 'La storia di Venezia dal principio del VI alla fine del XII secolo rinnovata', *Atti Ist. Ven. S.L.A.* ser. 6, IV (1885–6), 769–71.

Galli, R., 'Venezia e Roma in una cronaca del secolo VI', *N. Arch. Ven.* n.s. III (1902), 259–372.

Lenel, W., 'Zur älteren Geschichte Venedigs', *HZ*, ser. 3, III (1907), 473–514.

Lenel, W., *Die Entstehung der Vorherrschaft Venedigs an der Adria mit Beiträgen zur Verfassungsgeschichte* (Strasbourg, 1897).

Lenel, W., *Venetianisch-Istrische Studien* (Strasbourg, 1911).

Magnocavallo, A., 'Di alcuni codici del "Liber secretorum fidelium crucis" di Marin Sanudo il vecchio', *N. Arch. Ven.* n.s. VI (1903), 174–80.

Monticolo, G., 'I manoscritti e le fonti della cronaca del diacono Giovanni', *BISI*, IX (1890), 37–328.

Monticolo, G., 'La costituzione del doge Pietro Polani febbraio 1143 (1142 m.v.) circa la "Processio scholarum"', *Rend. Accad. Lincei*, IX (1900), 91–133.

Monticolo, G., 'La cronaca del diacono Giovanni e la politica di Venezia sino al 1009', *Arch. Ven.* xxv (1883), 1–22; and in *Ann. Liceo Forteguerri* (Pistoia, 1882).

Monticolo, G., 'Intorno agli studi fatti sulla cronaca del diacono Giovanni', *Arch. Ven.* xv (1878), 1–45; xvii (1879), 35–73.

Monticolo, G., 'Per l'edizione critica del poema di Castellano da Bassano sulla pace di Venezia del 1177', *Bull. Soc. Fil. Rom.* vi (Rome, 1904), 29–54.

Monticolo, G., 'Spigolature d'Archivio: V. Dell'uso dei documenti nella cronaca veneziana di Giovanni Diacono; VI. Intorno al significato del nome "Venetia" nella cronaca veneziana di Giovanni diacono', *N. Arch. Ven.* iii (1892); subsection v, 351–86; subsection vi, 365–86.

Monticolo, G., 'I cognomi dei tre canonici autori di una relazione sincrona della pace di Venezia (1177)', *Boll. Soc. Fil. Rom.* vi (Rome, 1904), 55–8.

Schmeidler, B., 'Zum Chronicon Venetum', *Neu. Arch.* xxxi (1906), 457–67.

Simonsfeld, H., *Andreas Dandolo und seine Geschichtswerke* (Munich, 1876); and *Arch. Ven.* xiv (1887), 49–149.

Simonsfeld, H., *Das Chronicon Altinate* (Munich, 1878).

Simonsfeld, H., 'Intorno a Marin Sanuto il vecchio. Studi', *Arch. Ven.* xxiv (1882), 251–79.

Simonsfeld, H., 'Notizie sui codici del "Secreta fidelium Crucis"', *Arch. Ven.* xx (1880), 401–2.

Simonsfeld, H., 'Sugli Annali Veneti', *N. Arch. Ven.* vii (1894), 493.

Simonsfeld, H., 'Sulle scoperte del dott. R. Galli sulla cronaca altinate', *Arch. Ven.* xxv (1888), 117–34.

Simonsfeld, H., *Venetianische Studien. I. Das Chronicon Altinate* (Munich, 1878); and *Arch. Ven.* xviii (1879), 235–73; xix (1880), 54–71, 294–326; xxi (1881), 167–202; xxiv (1882), 111–31.

Tafel, G. L. F. and Thomas, G. M., *Der Doge Andreas Dandolo und die von demselben angelegten Urkundensammlungen zur Staats- und Handels-geschichte Venedigs* (Munich, 1855).

Waitz, G., 'Reise nach Italien im Frühjahr 1876', *Neu. Arch.* ii (1877), 325–81 (see p. 350 on the *Chronicon Gradense*).

IV. WORKS FROM THE FIFTEENTH CENTURY ONWARDS

Amelot de la Houssaie, A. N., *Histoire du gouvernement de Venise*, 2 vols. (Paris, 1677).

Armingaud, J., *Venise et le Bas-Empire* (Paris, 1867).

Averone, A., *Sull'antica idrografia veneta* (Mantua, 1911).

Baer, A., *Die Beziehungen Venedigs zum Kaiserreichz in der staufischen Zeit* (Innsbruck, 1888).

Bailly, A., *La république de Venise* (Paris, 1946).

Barozzi, N., 'Un trittico bizantino in avorio del sec. xi', *N. Arch. Ven.* x (1885), 387–8.

Battistella, A., 'Contributo alla storia delle relazioni fra Venezia e Bologna dall'undecimo al sedicesimo secolo', *Atti Ist. Ven. S.L.A.*, lxxv (1915–16), pt. ii, 1733–1881.

Battistella, A., *La Repubblica di Venezia negli undici secoli della sua storia* (Venice, 1912).

Bellemo, V., *Il territorio di Chioggia* (Chioggia, 1893).

Bellemo, V., *Questioni di storia veneziana*. I: *I 'tribuni maritimorum' di Cassiodoro*; II: *Il duce o condottiere nelle Venezie nel sec. VI*; III: *Lo Scisma dei Tre Capitoli con altre eresie e l'indipendenza delle isole veneziane dall'impero d'Oriente*; IV: *Toponomastica antica nell'agro di Cluza* (Venice, 1914).

Bertaldo, J., *Splendor consuetudinum civitatis Venetiarum*, ed. F. Schupfer (Bologna, 1896).

Besta, E., 'Intorno a due opere recenti sulla costituzione e sulla politica veneziana nel medioevo', *N. Arch. Ven.* XIV (1897), 195–245.

Besta, E., 'Jacopo Bertaldo e lo "Splendor consuetudinum civitatis Venetiarum"', *N. Arch. Ven.* XIII (1897), 109–33.

Besta, E., *Il diritto e le leggi civili di Venezia fino al dogado di Enrico Dandolo* (Venice, 1900).

Besta, E., 'Il senato veneziano', *Dep. Ven. Stor. Patr.*, Miscell. ser. 2, V (1899), 1–290.

Besta, E., 'La cattura dei Veneziani in Oriente per ordine dell'imperatore Emanuele Comneno e le sue conseguenze nella politica interna ed esterna del Comune di Venezia', *Antologia Veneta*, I (Feltre, 1900).

Besta, E. and Predelli, R., 'Gli Statuti civili anteriori al 1242 editi per la prima volta', *N. Arch. Ven.* n.s. I (1901), 5–117, 205–300.

Bistort, G., *La Repubblica di Venezia dalle trasmigrazioni nella laguna fino alla caduta di Costantinopoli, 1453* (Venice, 1916).

Blondus, F., *Italia illustrata* (Verona, 1481); and in J. G. Graevius, *Thesaurus...Italiae*, I [see Gen. Bibl. IV].

Boni, G., 'Antiche murature veneziane', *Arch. Ven.* XXXII (1886), 435–7.

Botteon, V., *Un documento prezioso riguardo alle origini del vescovado di Ceneda e la serie dei vescovi cenedesi* (Conegliano, 1907).

Bresslau, H., *Jahrbücher d. deutschen Reiches unter Konrad II*, 2 vols. (Leipzig, 1879–84).

Bresslau, H., 'Venetianische Studien', *Festgabe für G. Meyer von Kronau* (Zürich, 1913).

Brunelli, V., *Storia della città di Zara dai tempi più remoti. I: Dall'origine al 1409* (Venice, 1913).

Brunetti, M., 'Torcello nella sua storia', *Torcello* (Venice, 1940).

Carabellese, F., 'Il patto barese-veneziano del 1122', *Rassegna Pugliese*, XVII (Trani, 1900).

Carabellese, F. and Zambler, A., *Le relazioni commerciali tra la Puglia e la Repubblica di Venezia dal sec. X al XV* (Trani, 1897–8).

Cecchetti, B., 'Appunti sulle finanze antiche della Repubblica di Venezia', *Arch. Ven.* XXXV (1888), 29–56; XXXVI (1888), 71–98.

Cecchetti, B., *Il doge di Venezia* (Venice, 1864).

Cecchetti, B., 'I nobili e il popolo di Venezia', *Arch. Ven.* III (1872), 421–48.

Cecchetti, B., 'La vita dei Veneziani fino al sec. XIII', *Arch. Ven.* II (1871), 63–123.

Cecchetti, B., *La vita dei Veneziani fino al 1200* (Venice, 1870).

Cecchetti, B., 'Le industrie in Venezia nel sec. XII', *Arch. Ven.* IV (1872), 211–57.

Cessi, R., 'La *curia forinsecorum* e la sua prima costituzione', *N. Arch. Ven.* n.s. XXVIII (1914), 202–7.

Cessi, B., 'Il diritto penale in Venezia prima del mille', *N. Arch. Ven.* n.s. XXXIII (1917), 5–23.

Cessi, R., 'La diversione del Brenta ed il delta ilariano nel sec. XII', *Atti Ist. Ven. S.L.A.* LXXX (1920–1), pt. II, 1225–43.

Cessi, R., *Le origini del ducato veneziano* (Naples, 1951).

Cessi, R., 'Problemi monetari veneziani', in *Commiss. documenti finanz. Republl. Venezia*, ser. 4, I (Padua, 1937).

Cessi, R., *Storia della Repubblica di Venezia*, 2 vols. (Milan, 1944–6).

Cessi, R., 'Un falso diploma di Lotario (839) ed il delta di S. Ilario', *AMAP*, n.s. XXXVII (1920–1), 133–47.

Cessi, R., 'Il diploma carolino per la chiesa altinate e la sua falsificazione', *AMAP*, n.s. LVIII (1941–2), 139–45.

Cessi, R., 'Un patto fra Venezia e Padova e la *Curia forinsecorum* al principio del sec. XIII', *AMAP*, n.s. XXX (1913–14), 263–75.

Cessi, R., *Venezia Ducale I : Duca e popolo* (Venice, 1940).

Cessi, R., 'Il problema della Brenta dal secolo XII al secolo XV' and 'Lo sviluppo dell'interramento nella laguna settentrionale e il problema della Piave e del Sile fino al secolo XV', in *La laguna di Venezia*, ed. G. Brunelli, G. Magrini and P. Orsi, vol. II, pt. IV, tom. VII, fasc. i (Venice, 1943) (Delegazione italiana della Commissione per l'esplorazione scientifica del Mediterraneo), pp. 1–77 and 79–108.

Cessi, R., *Storia della Repubblica di Venezia*, I–II (Venice, 1944–6).

Cessi, R., 'Da Roma a Bisanzio', *Storia di Venezia*, ed. P. Marinotti, I (Venice, 1957), 179–401.

Cessi, R., 'Bizantinismo veneziano', *Arch. Ven.* ser. 5, LXIX (1961), 3–22.

Cessi, R., 'L'eredità di Enrico Dandolo', *Arch. Ven.* ser. 5, LXVII (1960), 1–25.

Cipolla, C., 'Annales veneti', *N. Arch. Ven.* VII (1894), 494.

Cipolla, C., 'Della giurisdizione metropolitana della sede milanese nella regione X — Venetia et Histria', *Ambrosiano* (Milan, 1897).

Cipolla, C., 'Storia veneta in antichi documenti ravennati di recente pubblicazione', *Arch. Ven.* XXVI (1883), 57–76, 307–29.

Cipolla, C., 'Le origini di Venezia', *ASI*, ser. 6, LXXIII (1915), I, 5–36 (Florence, 1915).

Conton, L., *Torcello, il suo estuario e i suoi monumenti* (Venice, 1927).

Cornaro, A., *Scritture sopra la laguna veneta*, ed. R. Cessi. *Antichi Scrittori d'Idraulica Veneta*, II, 2. Ufficio idrografico (Venice, 1930).

Cornaro, M., *Scritture sopra la laguna veneta*, ed. G. Pavanello. *Antichi Scrittori d'Idraulica Veneta*, I. Ufficio idrografico (Venice, 1919).

Cornelius (Corner), F., *Ecclesiae venetae et torcellanae*, VIII, X (Venice, 1749).

Diehl, C., *Etudes byzantines* (Paris, 1905).

Diehl, C., *Etudes sur l'administration byzantine dans l'exarchat de Ravenne, 568–751* (Paris, 1888).

Diehl, C., *Une république patricienne : Venise* (Paris, 1915).

Errera, C., 'I crociati veneziani in Terra Santa: dal concilio di Clermont alla morte di Ordelafo Falier', *Arch. Ven.* n.s. XXXVIII (1889), 237–77.

Fanta, A., *Die Verträge der Kaiser mit Venedig bis 984. MIOG* Ergänzungsbd. I (Innsbruck, 1885).

Fiastri, G., 'L'assemblea del popolo a Venezia come organo costituzionale della stato', *N. Arch. Ven.* n.s. XXV (1913), 5–48, 349–80.

Ficker, J., *Forschungen für Reichs- und Rechtsgeschichte Italiens* (Innsbruck, 1868–74).

Filiasi, G., *Memorie storiche de' Veneti primi e secondi*, 9 vols. (Venice, 1796).

Fiocco, G., 'Bisanzio, Ravenna e Venezia', *Rivista di Venezia*, IX (1930).

Fotheringham, J. K., *Marco Sanudo, Conqueror of the Archipelago* (Oxford, 1915).

Fulin, R., *Breve riassunto della storia di Venezia* (Venice, 1876).
Gfrörer, A. F., *Geschichte Venedigs bis zum Jahre 1048* (Graz, 1872); and *Arch. Ven.* XII (1876), 5–28, 274–93; XIII (1877), 79–103, 291–349; XIV (1877), 251–328; XV (1878), 46–148, 287–371.
Giustinian, B., *Historia de origine urbis Venetiarum* (Venice, 1492).
Hain, A., *Der Doge von Venedig seit dem Sturze der Orseoler bis zur Ermordung Vitale Michiel* (Leipzig, 1893).
Harnach, O., *Das Karolingische und byzantinische Reich in ihren Wechselbeziehungen* (Göttingen, 1880).
Hartmann, L. M., *Geschichte Italiens im Mittelalter* [see Gen. Bibl. v].
Hartmann, L. M., *Untersuchungen zur Geschichte der byzantinischen Verwaltung in Italien (450–750)* (Leipzig, 1889).
Hartmann, L. M., 'Die wirtschaftlichen Anfänge Venedigs', *Vierteljahrsschrift f. Sozial- und Wirtschaftsgeschichte*, II (1904), 434–42.
Heyd, W., *Histoire du commerce du Levant au moyen âge* [see Gen. Bibl. v].
Heynen, R., *Zur Entstehung des Kapitalismus in Venedig* (Stuttgart–Berlin, 1905).
Hodgson, F. C., *The Early History of Venice from the Foundation to the Conquest of Constantinople* (London, 1901).
Jéhan de Johannis, A., 'La storia idraulica della laguna di Venezia', *Arch. Ven.* VIII (1874), 81–101; IX (1875), 46–76.
Kehr, P., 'Papsturkunden in Venezien und Friaul', *Nachrichten d. Kön. Gesell. d. Wiss.* (Göttingen, 1892).
Kehr, P. F., 'Rom und Venedig bis ins XII. Jahrhundert', *QFIA*, XIX (1927), 1–180.
Kohlschütter, O., *Venedig unter dem Herzog Peter II Orseolo* (Göttingen, 1868).
Kretschmayr, H., 'Die Beschreibung der venezianischen Inseln bei Konstantin Porphyrogennetos', *BZ*, XIII (1904), 482–9.
Kretschmayr, H., *Geschichte von Venedig*, I–II [see Gen. Bibl. v].
Laigne, R. de, *Les Doges Sébastien et Pierre Ziani* (Paris, 1906).
Lazari, V., *Del traffico e delle condizioni degli schiavi a Venezia nel tempo di mezzo*. Misc. Storia Ital., ser. 1, I (Turin, 1862).
Lazzarini, V., 'I titoli dei dogi di Venezia', *N. Arch. Ven.* n.s. V (1903), 271–313.
Lazzarini, V., 'Il preteso documento della fondazione di Venezia e la cronaca del medico Jacopo Dondi', *Atti Ist. Ven. S.L.A.* LXXV (1915–16), pt. II, 1263–81.
Lazzarini, V., 'Malipiero e Mastropiero', *N. Arch. Ven.* n.s. XLII (1921), 242–7.
Lazzarini, V., 'Originali antichissimi della cancelleria veneziana', *N. Arch. Ven.* n.s. VIII (1904), 199–229.
Lazzarini, V., 'Un iscrizione torcellana del sec. VII', *Atti Ist. Ven. S.L.A.* LXXIII (1913–14), pt. II, 387–97.
Lazzarini, V., 'Un privilegio del doge Pietro Tribuno per la badia di S. Stefano d'Altino', *Atti Ist. Ven. S.L.A.* LXVIII (1908–9), pt. II, 975–93.
Lazzarini, V., 'Una donazione di Naimerio Polani alla dogaressa Michiel (1155)', *Arch. Ven.* ser. 5, I (1927), 181–5.
Le Bret, J. F., *Staatsgeschichte der Republik Venedigs*, 3 vols. (Leipzig and Riga, 1769–77).
Lenel, W., *Die Entstehung der Vorherrschaft Venedigs an der Adria* (Strassburg, 1897).
Lenel, W., 'Die Epochen der älteren venezianischen Geschichte', *HZ*, ser. 3, VIII (1909–10), 237–77.

Lenel, W., 'Zur älteren Geschichte Venedigs', *HZ*, ser. 3, III (1907), 473–514.

Lentz, E., *Das Verhältniss Venedigs zu Byzanz nach dem Fall des Exarchats bis zum Ausgang des 9. Jahrhunderts* (Berlin, 1891).

Lentz, E., 'Der allmähliche Uebergang Venedigs von faktischer zu nomineller Abhängigkeit von Byzanz', *BZ*, III (1894), 64–115.

Luzzatto, G., *Studi di storia economica veneziana* (Padua, 1955) [reprints articles written from 1924 onwards].

Luzzatto, G., 'I più antichi trattati tra Venezia e le città Marchigiane 1141–1345', *N. Arch. Ven.* n.s. XI (1906), 5–91.

Luzzatto, G., *I prestiti della Repubblica di Venezia. R. Accad. dei Lincei.* Docum. Finanzari della Rep. di Venezia, ser. 3, I, pt. 1 (Padua, 1929).

Luzzatto, G., *Storia economica di Venezia dall' XI al XVI secolo* (Venice, 1961).

Luzzatto, G., *Storia del commercio. I : Dall'antichità al Rinascimento* (Florence, 1914).

Magnocavallo, A., 'La carta "De mari Mediterraneo" di Marin Sanudo il vecchio', *Boll. Soc. Geogr. Ital.* ser. 4, III (1902), 438–49.

Magnocavallo, A., *Marin Sanudo il vecchio e il suo progetto di crociata* (Bergamo, 1901).

Malagola, C., *Le Lido de Venise* (Venice, 1909).

Manfrin, P., *I Veneti salvatori di Roma* (Rome, 1884).

Manfroni, C., *Storia della marina italiana dalle invasioni barbariche alla caduta di Costantinopoli*, I (Rome, 1892).

Maranini, G., *La costituzione di Venezia dalle origini alla Serrata del Maggior Consiglio* (Venice, 1927).

Marin, C. A., *Storia civile e politica del commercio de' Veneziani*, 8 vols. (Venice, 1796–1808).

Marzemin, G., 'Le abbazie veneziane dei SS. Ilario e Benedetto e di S. Gregorio', *N. Arch. Ven.* n.s. XXIII (1912), 96–162, 351–407.

Marzemin, G., *Le origini romane di Venezia* (Venice, 1938).

Merores, M., 'Der grosse Rat von Venedig und die sogenannte Serrata vom Jahre 1297', *Viert. f. Soz.- und Wirtsch.-geschichte*, XXI (1928), 33–113.

Merores, M., 'Der Venetianische Adel', *Vierteljahrsschrift f. Soz.- und Wirtschaftsgeschichte*, XIX (1926), 193–237.

Merores, M., 'Die ältesten venetianischen Staatsanleihen und ihre Entstehung', *Vierteljahrsschrift f. Soz.- und Wirtschaftsgeschichte*, XV (1920), 381–98.

Merores, M., 'Die venetianischen Salinen der alteren Zeit in ihrer wirtschaftlichen und sozialen Bedeutung', *Vierteljahrsschrift f. Soz.- und Wirtschaftsgeschichte*, XIII (1915), 71–107.

Meyer, W., *Die Spaltung des Patriarchates Aquileia. Königliche Gesellschaft der Wissenschaften* (Göttingen, 1898).

Miari, F. L. 'Bolla ducale inedita del doge Pietro Ziani', *Arch. Ven.* n.s. XXXIV (1887), 393–6.

Michieli, A. A., 'Il fiume Piave', *Boll. Soc. Geogr. Ital.* ser. 5, VII (1918), 855–70.

Michieli, A. A., 'Il fiume Sile', *Boll. Soc. Geogr. Ital.* ser. 5, VIII (1919), 27–41.

Michieli, A. A., *Il porto di Venezia e il suo avvenire* (Venice, 1918).

Michieli, A. A., *La laguna di Venezia ed i suoi caratteri economici* (Novara, 1919).

Molmenti, P., *La dogaressa di Venezia* (Turin, 1887).

Molmenti, P., *La storia di Venezia nella vita privata*, 6th ed., 3 vols. (Bergamo, 1923); English transl. H. F. Brown, 6 vols. (London, 1906–8).

Molmenti, P., *Venezia* (Florence, 1897).

Monticolo, G., 'L'ufficio della giustizia vecchia a Venezia dalle origini sino al 1330', *Deput. Ven. Stor. Patr.* ser. 4, Miscell. ser. 1, XII, no. 2 (1892).

Monticolo, G., 'Due documenti veneziani del sec. XII', *N. Arch. Ven.* XIX (1900), 56–75.

Musatti, C., *Storia della promissione ducale* (Padua, 1888).

Musatti, E., *Storia di Venezia*, 3rd ed., 2 vols. (Milan, 1936).

Musatti, E., *Storia di un lembo di terra, ossia Venezia ed i Veneziani*, 2nd ed. (Padua, 1888).

Neumann, C., 'Über die urkundlichen Quellen zur Geschichte der byzantinisch-venetianischen Beziehungen vornehmlich im Zeitalter der Komnenen', *BZ*, I (1892), 366–78.

Nissen, H., *Italienische Landeskunde*, 2 vols. (Berlin, 1883–1902).

Ottenthall, E., 'Das Brondolo Privilegio Leo's IX', *MIOG*, XXXVI (1915), 288–311, 404 [with a plate at p. 404].

Papadopoli, N., *Le monete di Venezia descritte. I: Dalle origini a Cristoforo Moro* (Venice, 1893).

Papadopoli, N., *Sulle origini della Veneta zecca e sulle antiche relazioni dei Veneziani cogli Imperatori* (Venice, 1882).

Papadopoli, N., 'Sul valore della moneta veneziane', *Atti Ist. Ven. S.L.A.* (1884–5), 671–709.

Pasolini, D., *Delle antiche relazioni fra Venezia e Ravenna* (Florence, 1874).

Pauli, C., *Die Veneter und ihre Schicksale* (Leipzig, 1891).

Pavanello, G., 'Di un'antica laguna scomparsa', *Arch. Ven.-Tri.* III (1923), 263–307.

Pavanello, G., *La città di Altino e l'agro altinate orientale* (Treviso, 1900).

Pavanello, G., 'San Marco nella leggenda e nella storia', *Rivista di Venezia*, VII (1928).

Pavanello, G., 'La storia della laguna fino al 1140' in *La laguna di Venezia*, ed. G. Brunelli, G. Magrini and P. Orsi, II, pt. III, VI (Venice, 1935) (Delegazione italiana della Commissione per l'esplorazione scientifica del Mediterraneo), 1–73.

Pinton, P., 'Della origine della sede vescovile di Caorle nell'estuario veneto', *Arch. Ven.* XXVII (1884), 283–92.

Pinton, P., 'La storia di Venezia di A. F. Gfrörer', *Arch. Ven.* XXV (1883), 23–63, 288–313; XXVI (1883), 330–65; XXVII (1884), 75–90; XXIX (1885), 305–16.

Pinton, P., 'Veneziani e Longobardi a Ravenna', *Arch. Ven.* XXXVIII (1889), 369–84.

Pitzorno, B., *Gli statuti civili attribuiti ad Enrico Dandolo* (Perugia, 1913).

Pitzorno, B., 'I consoli veneziani di Sardegna e di Maiorca', *N. Arch. Ven.* n.s. XI, 1 (1906), 92–106.

Pitzorno, B., 'Il "Liber romanae legis" della "Ratio de lege romana". Per la storia della c.d. Codi in Italia', *Rivista Ital. Scien. Giurid.* XLIII (1907), 101–36.

Pitzorno, B., 'La "carta mater" e la "carta filia". Studi storico-giuridici', *N. Arch. Ven.* n.s. XVII (1909), 385–432; XVIII (1909), 94–130.

Pitzorno, B., 'Il "Liber romanae legis" degli "Iudicia a probis iudicibus promulgata". Nota II per la storia della c.d. Codi in Italia', *Rivista Ital. Scien. Giurid.* XLIV (1908), 269–92.

Pitzorno, B., 'Le consuetudini giudiziarie veneziane anteriori al 1229', *Deput. Ven. Stor. Patr. Miscell.*, ser. 3, II (1910), 293–348.

Pitzorno, B., 'Le magistrature giudiziarie veneziane e i loro capitolari fino al 1300', *ASI*, ser. 6, LXXI (1913), I, 156–84 [review of M. Roberti, *Le magistrature...*, see below].

Praga, G., 'Zaratini e Veneziani nel 1190: la battaglia di Trani', *Rivista Dalmatica*, VIII (1925).

Predelli, R., 'Bolla grande di papa Alessandro III 3 agosto 1177 inedita', *N. Arch. Ven.* XII (1896), 159–70.

Predelli, R., 'Nota sui prestiti pubblici dei Veneziani', *Arch. Ven.* XXXVI (1888), 74–9.

Predelli, R., 'Notizia a due recenti pubblicazioni (P. Kehr, *Papsturkunden in Venedig...*)', *N. Arch. Ven.* XIV (1897), 186–94.

Predelli, R. and Sacerdoti, A., 'Gli statuti marittimi fino al 1255', *N. Arch. Ven.* n.s. IV (1902), 113–61, 267–91.

Roberti, M., 'Dei giudici veneziani prima del 1220', *N. Arch. Ven.* n.s. VIII (1904), 230–45.

Roberti, M., *Le magistrature giudiziarie veneziane e i loro capitolari fino al 1300*, I (Padua, 1906); II–III, *Mon. Stor. pub. Deput. Ven. Stor. Patr.* 17–18, ser. 2 (*Statuti*), vols. 2–3 (Venice, 1909–11).

Roberti, M., 'Studi e documenti di storia veneziana. I. La "Racio lombardo seu francisci"; II. I trattati fra Venezia e Padova anteriori al dominio ezzeliniano', *N. Arch. Ven.* n.s. XVI (1908), 5–61.

Romanin, S., *Storia documentata della Repubblica di Venezia*, 2nd ed., 10 vols. (Venice, 1912–21).

Rossi, A., *Studi di storica politico-ecclesiastica veneziana anteriore al mille* (Bologna, 1901).

Roth, C., *Venice* (Philadelphia, 1930).

Sabalich, G., *La Dalmazia nei commerci della Serenissima* (Zara, 1892).

Sabellico, M. A., *Historia Venetiana* (Venice, 1487); also in *Istorici d. cose veneziane*, I (Venice, 1718).

Sandi, V., *Principi di storia civile della Repubblica di Venezia*, 10 vols. (Venice, 1700–67).

Schaube, A., *Storia del commercio dei popoli latini del Mediterraneo sino alla fine delle crociate*. Bibl. dell'Economista, ser. 5, XI (Turin, 1915).

Schlumberger, G., *L'épopée byzantine à la fin du Xe siècle* [see Gen. Bibl. v].

Schmeidler, B., *Der dux und das comune Venetiarum von 1141–1229* (*Historische Studien*, ed. E. Ebering) (Berlin, 1902).

Schmeidler, B., 'Venedig und das deutsche Reich vom Jahre 983–1024', *MIOG*, XXV (1904), 545–75.

Schulte, A., *Geschichte des Levantehandels und Verkehrs zwischen Westdeutschland und Italien mit Ausschluss von Venedig* (Leipzig, 1900).

Streit, L., *Venedig und die Wendung des vierten Kreuzzuges gegen Konstantinopel* (Anklam, 1877); see R. Fulin, 'Venezia e la quarta crociata, dissertazione del dottore Lodovico Streit', *Arch. Ven.* XVI (1878), 46–9, 239–71.

Tassini, G., *Lido. Cenni storici* (Venice, 1869).

Tentori, C., *Saggio sulla storia della Repubblica di Venezia*, 12 vols. (Venice, 1785–90).

Thiriet, F., *La Romanie vénitienne au moyen âge: le développement et l'exploitation du domaine colonial vénitien (XIIe–XVe siècles)* [see Gen. Bibl. v].

Urbani de Gheltoff, D., 'Leggenda veneziana di Alessandro III', *Arch. Ven.* XIII (1877), 361–9.

Uzielli, G., *Osservazioni sopra alcuni principi dell'idraulica in relazione alle condizioni dei fiumi dell'alta Italia. La laguna veneta* (Florence, 1885).

Vaccani, C., *Delle lagune di Venezia e dei fiumi nelle attigue provincie* (Florence, 1867).

Verdi, A., *Da Anagni a Venezia. Saggio storico (1176–1177)* (Este, 1886).

Wüstenfeld, T., *Venetorum historia ab antiquissimis temporibus usque ad ducum sedem Rivoalti fixam deducta* (Göttingen, 1846).

Zendrini, B., *Memorie storiche dello stato antico e moderno delle lagune di Venezia*, 2 vols. (Padua, 1811).

Zwiedineck-Südenhorst, H., *Venedig als Weltmacht und Weltstadt* (Bielefeld and Leipzig, 1899).

CHAPTER VII. THE FOURTH CRUSADE AND THE GREEK AND LATIN EMPIRES, 1204–61

I. ORIGINAL SOURCES

1. COLLECTIONS OF SOURCES

(a) Greek

Dölger, F., *Regesten der Kaiserurkunden*, III [see Gen. Bibl. IV].

Gelzer, H., 'Ungedruckte und wenig bekannte Bistümerverzeichnisse der orientalischen Kirche', *BZ*, I (1892), 245–82; II (1893), 22–72.

Gelzer, H., 'Ungedruckte und ungenügend veröffentlichte Texte der Notitiae Episcopatuum', *Abh. der K. Bayerischen Akademie der Wissenschaften, I. Klasse*, XXI, 3 (1901), 529–641.

Grumel, V., *Les Regestes des Actes du Patriarcat de Constantinople* [see Gen. Bibl. IV].

Marković, M., 'Vizantiske povelje Dubrovačkog arhiva' ['Byzantine documents in the archives of Dubrovnik'], *Sbornik Radova, Vizantološki Institut*, I (1952), 206–58.

Meyer, P., *Die Haupturkunden für die Geschichte der Athosklöster* (Leipzig, 1894).

Miklosich, F. and Müller, J., *Acta et Diplomata* [see Gen. Bibl. IV].

Parthey, G., *Hieroclis Synecdemus et Notitiae Graecae Episcopatuum* (Berlin, 1866).

Sathas, K. N., Μεσαιωνικὴ Βιβλιοθήκη [see Gen. Bibl. IV].

Sathas, K. N., Μνημεῖα Ἑλληνικῆς Ἱστορίας. [see Gen. Bibl. IV].

(b) Latin

Acta Honorii III (1216–1227) et Gregorii IX (1227–1241), ed. A. L. Tăutu, Pontificia commissio...juris canonici orientalis, Fontes, 3 ser., III (Vatican, 1950).

Acta Innocentii III (1198–1216), ed. P. T. Haluščynskyj, Pontificia commissio...juris canonici orientalis, Fontes, 3 ser., II (Vatican, 1944).

Auvray, L., *Les Registres de Grégoire IX*, Bibliothèque *EcfrAR*, 3 vols. (Paris, 1890–1910).

Berger, E., *Les Registres d'Innocent IV*, Bibliothèque *EcfrAR*, 4 vols. (Paris, 1884–1921).

Bertolotto, G., 'Nuova serie di Documenti sulle relazioni di Genova coll'Impero Bizantino', *Atti della Soc. Ligure di Storia Patria*, xxviii (1898), 339–573.

Böhmer, J. F., *Regesta Imperii*, v, *Regesten des Kaiserreichs*, ed. J. B. Ficker and E. Winkelmann, 3 vols. (Innsbruck, 1881–1901).

Bourel de la Roncière, C., *Les Registres d'Alexandre IV*, Bibliothèque *EcfrAR*, 2 vols. (Paris, 1895–1902).

Buchon, J. A., *Recherches historiques sur la principauté française de Morée et ses hautes baronnies*, 2 vols. (Paris, 1845).

Devillers, L., *Chartes du Comte de Hainaut*, Publication extraordinaire du Cercle archéologique de Mons (Mons, 1898); also *MGH*, *Script.* xxi, 619–21.

du Bouchet, J., *Histoire généalogique de la maison royale de Courtenay* (Paris, 1661).

Dujčev, I., *Prepiskata na Papa Innokentija s bŭlgarite* (*Innocentii III epistolae ad Bulgariae historiam spectantes*). *Godišnik na Sofijskija Universitet, ist.-filol. fakultet*, xxxvii, 3 (1942).

Duvivier, C., *Actes et Documents anciens intéressants la Belgique, Nouvelle Série* (Brussels, 1903).

Galesloot, L., 'Cinq chartes inédits de l'Empereur de Constantinople', *Compte rendu de la Commission royale d'Histoire ou recueil de ses bulletins*, 4 ser. iii (1876), 139–54.

Golubovich, G., *Biblioteca bio-bibliografica della Terra Santa e dell'Oriente francescano*, 5 vols. (Quaracchi, 1906–27).

Hampe, K., 'Aus verlorenen Registerbänden der Päpste Innozenz III und Innozenz IV', *MIOG*, xxiii (1902), 545–67; xxiv (1903), 198–237.

Honorii III Romani Pontificis Opera Omnia, ed. C. A. Horoy, Medii Aevi Bibliotheca Patristica, 4 vols. (Paris, 1879–83).

Huillard-Bréholles, J. L. A., *Historia Diplomatica Friderici Secundi*, 6 vols. (Paris, 1852–61).

Innocentii III Romani Pontificis Opera Omnia, 4 vols., *MPL*, ccxiv–ccxvii.

Martène, E. and Durand, U., *Thesaurus Novus Anecdotorum*, i (Paris, 1717).

Morozzo della Rocca, R. and Lombardo, A., *Documenti del Commercio Veneziano nei secoli XI–XIII*. Documenti e Studi per la Storia del Commercio e del Diritto commerciale italiano, xix–xx. 2 vols. (Turin, 1940).

Potthast, A., *Regesta Pontificum Romanorum* [see Gen. Bibl. iv].

Predelli, R., *Il Liber Communis detto anche Plegiorum*. Arch. *Ven.* ii, supplement (1872).

Predelli, R. and Sacerdoti, A., 'Gli statuti marittimi Veneziani fino al 1255', *N. Arch. Ven.* n.s. iv (1902), 113–61.

Pressutti, P., *Regesta Honorii Papae III*, 2 vols. (Rome, 1888, 1895).

Raynaldus, O., *Annales Ecclesiastici*, ed. A. Theiner, xx–xxii (Bar-le-Duc, 1870).

Reiffenberg, F. A. de, *Monuments pour servir à l'histoire de Namur, de Hainaut, et de Luxembourg*, i (Brussels, 1844).

Riant, P., *Exuviae Sacrae Constantinopolitanae*, 2 vols. (Geneva, 1877–8).

Ricotti, E., *Liber Jurium Reipublicae Genuensis*, i. Historiae Patriae Monumenta, 7 (Turin, 1854).

Sbaralea, J., *Bullarium Franciscanum*, ɪ (Rome, 1759).

Table chronologique des chartes et diplômes imprimés concernant l'histoire de Belgique, ɪɪɪ, ɪᴠ, ᴠɪɪ, 1, 2, ed. A. Wauters; xɪ, 1, ed. S. Bormans and J. Halkin (Brussels, 1871–1907).

Tafel, G. L. F. and Thomas, G. M., *Urkunden zur älteren Handels- und Staats- geschichte der Republik Venedig* [see Gen. Bibl. ɪᴠ].

Teulet, A., *Layettes du Trésor des Chartes*, ɪɪ, ɪɪɪ, Archives de l'Empire, Inven- taires et Documents publiés par l'ordre de l'Empereur (Paris, 1866).

Thallóczy, L. de, Jireček, C. and Sufflay, E. de, *Acta et Diplomata res Albaniae . . . illustrantia*, ɪ [see Gen. Bibl. ɪᴠ].

Theiner, A., *Vetera Monumenta Historica Hungariam Sacram illustrantia*, 2 vols. (Rome, 1859–60).

Theiner, A., *Vetera Monumenta Slavorum Meridionalium Historiam illus- trantia*, ɪ (Rome, 1863).

2. INDIVIDUAL SOURCES

(a) *Greek*

Acropolites, Constantine, Λόγος εἰς τὸν μεγαλομάρτυρα καὶ μυροβλήτην Δημήτριον, ed. A. Papadopoulos-Kerameus, Ἀνάλεκτα Ἱεροσολυμιτικῆς Σταχνολογίας, ɪ (St Petersburg, 1891), 160–215.

Acropolites, George, *Opera*, ed. A. Heisenberg, ɪ: *Historia, Breviarium historiae, Theodori Scutariotae additamenta*; ɪɪ: *Scripta minora* (Leipzig, 1903).

Andréeva, M. A., 'A propos de l'éloge de l'Empereur Jean III Vatatzes par son fils Théodore II Lascaris', *Annales de l'Institut Kondakov* (*Sem. Kond.*), x (1938), 133–45.

Apocaucus, John, Metropolitan of Naupactus, *Works*, ed. V. G. Vasilievsky, 'Epirotica Saeculi XIII', *VV*, ɪɪɪ (1896), 233–99 (published separately, St Petersburg, 1903); A. Papadopoulos-Kerameus, *Noctes Petropolitanae* (St Petersburg, 1913), pp. 249–94; and bibliography in D. M. Nicol, *Despotate of Epiros*, Appendix ɪɪ [see Gen. Bibl. v].

Bachmann, L., *Theodori Ducae Lascaris imperatoris in laudem Nicaeae urbis oratio* (Rostock, 1847).

Bachmann, M., *Die Rede Johannes Syropoulos an den Kaiser Isaak II Angelos (1185–1195)* (Munich, Diss. 1935).

Bardanes, George, Metropolitan of Corfu, *Works*, ed. A. Mustoxidi, *Delle Cose Corciresi*, App., pp. l–lvii; A. Papadopoulos-Kerameus, 'Κερκυραϊκά', *VV*, xɪɪɪ (1906), 334–51, and 'Κανονικαὶ πράξεις Γεωργίου Βαρδάνη καὶ Ἰωάννου Ἀποκαύκου', Ἐκκλησιαστικὸς Φάρος, ɪᴠ (Alexandria, 1909), 62–7; E. Kurtz, *BZ*, xᴠ (1906), 603–13; xᴠɪ (1907), 134–6, 139–40.

Blemmydes, Nicephorus, *Curriculum Vitae et Carmina*, ed. A. Heisenberg (Leipzig, 1896).

Chomatianus, Demetrius, Archbishop of Ochrida, *Works*, ed. J. B. Pitra, *Analecta Sacra et Classica Spicilegio Solesmensi parata*, ᴠɪɪ (ᴠɪ) (Rome, 1891).

Choniates, Michael (Acominatus), *Works*, ed. Sp. Lambros, Μιχαὴλ Ἀκομινάτου τοῦ Χωνιάτου τὰ σωζόμενα, 2 vols. (Athens, 1879–80).

Choniates, Michael (Acominatus), Ὑπομνηστικὸν εἰς τὸν βασιλέα κῦρ Ἀλέξιον τὸν Κομνηνόν, ed. G. Stadtmüller, *Michael Choniates, Metropolit von Athen* (Rome, 1933) pp. 161–4.

Choniates, Nicetas, *Historia*, ed. I. Bekker, *CSHB* (Bonn, 1835).

Chronicle of Galaxidi. Τὸ Χρονικὸν τοῦ Γαλαξειδίου, ed. K. N. Sathas (Athens, 1865); ed. G. Valetas (Athens, 1944).

Chronicle of the Morea. Τὸ Χρονικὸν τοῦ Μορέως, ed. J. Schmittt (London, 1904); ed. P. Kalonaros (Athens, 1940). See also *Cronaca di Morea, Libro de los Fechos, Livre de la Conqueste* under (c) below.

Cotelerius, J. B., *Ecclesiae Graecae Monumenta*, III (Paris, 1686), 510–14. [Letter from the Greeks of Constantinople to Innocent III.]

Dragoumis, S., 'Θεοδώρου Δούκα Λασκάρεως Ἐπιτάφιος εἰς Φρεδερίκον Β′ Βασιλέα τῶν ᾿Αλαμάνων', Βυζαντίς, II (1911), 404–13.

Drinov, M., 'O nekotorych trudach Dimitrija Chomatiana kak istoričeskom materiale' ['On some works of Demetrius Chomatianus as historical material'], *VV*, I (1894), 319–40; II (1895), 1–23.

Emminger, E., *Studien zu den griechischen Fürstenspiegeln I. Zum ἀνδριὰς βασιλικὸς des Nikephoros Blemmydes*, Gymnasialprogramm (Munich, 1906).

Ephraem, ed. I. Bekker, *CSHB* (Bonn, 1840).

Festa, N., 'Le lettere greche di Federigo II', *ASI*, ser. 5, XIII (1894), 1–34.

Gregoras, Nicephorus, *Byzantina Historia*, ed. L. Schopen, I. Bekker, 3 vols., *CSHB* (Bonn, 1829–55).

Grumel, V., 'L'authenticité de la lettre de Jean Vatatzès, Empereur de Nicée, au Pape Grégoire IX', *EO*, XXIX (1930), 450–8.

Heisenberg, A., 'Studien zu Georgios Akropolites', *SBAW*, II, 4 (1899), 463–558.

Heisenberg, A., *Analecta. Mitteilungen aus italienischen Handschriften byzantinischer Chronographen* (Munich, 1901).

Heisenberg, A., *Aus der Geschichte und Literatur der Palaiologenzeit*, *SBAW*, Abh. X (Munich, 1920).

Heisenberg, A., *Neue Quellen zur Geschichte des lateinischen Kaisertums und der Kirchenunion*. I: *Der Epitaphios des Nikolaos Mesarites auf seinen Bruder Johannes*; II: *Die Unionsverhandlungen vom 30. August 1206*; III: *Der Bericht des Nikolaos Mesarites über die politischen und kirchlichen Ereignisse des Jahres 1214. SBAW*, phil.-hist. Klasse (Munich, 1922), Abh. V; (1923), Abh. II and III.

Job monachus, *Life of Theodora of Arta*, ed. A. Mustoxidi, Ἑλληνομνήμων (1843), pp. 42–59; J. A. Buchon, *Nouvelles recherches historiques sur la principauté française de Morée*, II (Paris, 1843), pp. 401–6; *MPG*, CXXVII, 901–6.

Krekić, B., 'Dva dokumenta o Krfu u XIII veku' ['Two documents concerning Corfu in the thirteenth century'], *Godišnjak Filoz. Fakulteta u Novom Sadu*, III (1958), 45–53.

Kurtz, E., 'Georgios Bardanes, Metropolit von Kerkyra', *BZ*, XV (1906), 603–13.

Lappa-Zizicas, E., 'Un traité inédit de Théodore II Lascaris', *Actes du VIe Congr. Intern. d'Et. Byz.* I (1950), 119–26.

Laurent, V., 'Charisticariat et commende à Byzance (Deux fondations patriarcales en Epire aux XIIe et XIIIe siècles)', *REB*, XII (1954), 101–13.

Lemerle, P., 'Le privilège du Despote d'Epire Thomas I pour le Vénitien Jacques Contareno', *BZ*, XLIV (1951) (= *Festschrift F. Dölger*), 389–96.

Lemerle, P., 'Trois actes du Despote d'Epire Michel II concernant Corfou', Ἑλληνικά, IV (1953) (= Προσφορὰ εἰς Στ. Π. Κυριακίδην), 405–26.

Manousakas, M. I., 'Τὸ ἑλληνικὸ δημοτικὸ τραγούδι γιὰ τὸ βασιλιὰ Ἑρρῖκο τῆς Φλάντρας', Λαογραφία, XIV (1952), 1–52 and XVI, (1954), 366–70.

Meyer, P., 'Bruchstücke zweier τυπικὰ κτητορικά', *BZ*, IV (1895), 45–58.
Michael VIII Palaeologus, ed. J. Troitsky, *Imperatoris Michaelis Palaeologi de
vita sua opusculum necnon regulae quam ipse monasterio S. Demetrii
praescripsit fragmentum* (St Petersburg, 1885); new edition by H. Grégoire, 'Imperatoris Michaelis Palaeologi de Vita Sua', *B*, XXIX–XXX
(1959–60), 447–75.
Murnu, G., 'Din Nichita Acominatos Honiatul', *Analele Academiei Române*,
2 ser., XXVIII (1905–6), *Memoriile Sectiunii Istorice*, 357–467.
Nicole, J., 'Bref inédit de Germain II Patriarche de Constantinople avec une
recension nouvelle de l'empereur Jean Ducas Vatatzes, *REG*, VII (1894),
68–80.
Ostrogorsky, G., 'Pismo Dimitrija Homatijana sv. Save' ['Demetrius Choma-
tianus' letter to St Sava'], *Svetosavski Zbornik*, II (1939), 91–113
(*Srpska Kraljevska Akademija, posebna izdanja*, CXXV, *Drustveni i
Istoriski Spisi*, 50).
Pachymeres, George, *De Michaele et Andronico Palaeologis*, 2 vols., ed. I.
Bekker, *CSHB* (Bonn, 1835).
Panaretos, Michael, *Chronicle*. Τραπεζουντιακὸν Χρονικόν, ed. S. Lambros, *NE*,
IV (1907), 257–95.
Pétridès, S., 'Jean Apokaukos, lettres et autres documents inédits', *IRAIK*,
XIV, 2–3 (Sofia, 1909), 1–32.
Scutariotes, Theodore, *Chronicle*, in K. N. Sathas, Μεσαιωνικὴ βιβλιοθήκη, VII;
see Acropolites, ed. Heisenberg, I, 275–302.
Theodore II Lascaris, *Theodori Ducae Lascaris Epistolae CCXVII*, ed. N.
Festa (Florence, 1898).

(b) *Latin*

Albericus Trium Fontium, *Chronica, MGH, Script.* XXIII, 631–950.
Annales Colonienses Maximi, MGH, Script. XVII.
Annales Cremonenses, MGH, Script. XXXI.
Annales Placentini Gibellini, MGH, Script. XVIII.
Annales S. Iustinae Patavini, MGH, Script. XIX; also known as *Chronicon
Marchiae Tarvisinae et Lombardiae*, ed. L. Botteghi, *RISS*, VIII, 3 (1916).
Annali Genovesi di Caffaro e de' suoi Continuatori (= *Annales Ianuenses*), ed.
L. Belgrano and C. I. de Sant'Angelo, 5 vols., *Fonti*, XI–XIV *bis* (Genoa and
Rome, 1890–1929).
Assizes of Romania, ed. G. Recoura, *Les Assises de Romanie* (Paris, 1930);
transl. with commentary by P. W. Topping, *Feudal Institutions as revealed
in the Assizes of Romania* (Philadelphia, 1949).
Benvenuto di San Giorgio, *Historia Montisferrati, RISS*, XXIII.
Chronica Regia Coloniensis, Continuatio IV, ed. G. Waitz, *SGUS* (Hanover,
1880).
Chronicle of Novgorod. Chronista Novgorodensis, ed. C. Hopf, *Chroniques
gréco-romanes* (Berlin, 1873), pp. 93–8; *Novgorodskaja Pervaja Letopis'*,
ed. A. Nasonov (Moscow–Leningrad, 1950).
Chronicon Generalium Ministrorum Ordinis Fratrum Minorum, Analecta
Franciscana, III (Quaracchi, 1897), pp. 1–575.
Chronicon Hanoniense quod dicitur Balduini Avennensis, MGH, Script. XXV.
Dandolo, Andrea, *Chronica, RISS*, XII (Bologna, 1941–9).
Devastatio Constantinopolitana, ed. C. Hopf, *Chroniques gréco-romanes* (Berlin,
1873), pp. 86–92.
Gesta Episcoporum Halberstadensium, MGH, Script. XXIII.

Gesta Pontificum Autissiodorensium, ed. L.-M. Duru, *Bibliothèque historique de l'Yonne*, 2 vols. (Paris and Auxerre, 1850).

Golubovich, G., 'Disputatio Latinorum et Grecorum', *Archivum Francisca-num Historicum*, XII (1919), 418–70.

Gunther of Pairis, *Historia Constantinopolitana*, ed. P. Riant, *Exuviae Sacrae*, I (Geneva, 1875); German transl. and commentary by E. Assmann, *Gunther von Pairis, Die Geschichte der Eroberung von Konstantinopel* (Köln–Graz, 1956).

Historia Ducum Venetorum, MGH, Script. XIV.

Lauer, P., 'Une lettre inédite d'Henri Ier d'Angre, Empereur de Constanti-nople aux prélats italiens (1213?)', *Mélanges offerts à G. Schlumberger*, I (Paris, 1924), 191–201.

Lazzarini, V., 'Il Testamento di P. Giustiniani, Patriarca di Costantinopoli', *Arch. Ven.* LXX (1940), 80–8.

Liber Pontificalis, ed. L. Duchesne [see Gen. Bibl. IV].

Ljetopis Popa Dukljanina [The Chronicle of the Priest of Dioclea], ed. F. Šišić, Srpska Kraljevska Akademija, Posebna Izdanja, 18 (Belgrade, 1928) (Latin text); new ed. by V. Mošin (Zagreb, 1950).

Lorenzo de Monacis, *Chronicon de rebus Venetis*, ed. F. Cornelius (Venice, 1758).

Matthew Paris, *Chronica Majora*, ed. H. R. Luard, Rolls Series, II–V (London, 1874).

Navagero, Andrea, *Andreae Naugerii Patritii Veneti Historia Veneta*, RISS, XXIII.

Riant, P., 'Une lettre de l'impératrice Marie de Constantinople', *Archives de l'Orient latin*, II, 2 (Paris, 1884), 256–7.

Richard of San Germano, *Ryccardi de Sancto Germano notarii Chronica, a. 1189–1243*, MGH, Script. XIX; *Chronica Regni Sicilie*, ed. L. Garufi, RISS, VII, 2.

Robert of Auxerre, *Roberti Altissiodorensis Chronici Continuatio II*, MGH, Script. XXVI.

Salimbene de Adam, *Chronica*, MGH, Script. XXXII; new ed. by F. Bernini, 2 vols. (Bari, 1942).

Sanudo Torsello, Marino, *Fragmentum*, ed. C. Hopf, *Chroniques gréco-romanes* (Berlin, 1873), pp. 171–4; ed. R. L. Wolff, 'Hopf's so-called "Fragmen-tum" of Marino Sanudo Torsello', *Joshua Starr Memorial Volume*, Jewish Social Studies Publication, 5 (New York, 1953), pp. 149–59.

Sanudo Torsello, Marino, *Liber Secretorum Fidelium Crucis*, ed. J. Bongars, *Gesta Dei per Francos*, II (Hanover, 1611).

Schillmann, F., 'Zur byzantinischen Politik Alexanders IV', *RQCA*, XXII (1908), 108–31. [Contains letters not in the registers.]

Sicard of Cremona, *Sicardi Episcopi Cremonensis Cronica*, RISS, VII; MGH, Script. XXXI.

Thomas Tuscus, *Gesta Imperatorum et Pontificum*, MGH, Script. XXII.

Van den Gheyn, J., 'Lettre de Grégoire IX concernant l'Empire latin de Constantinople', *ROC*, IX (1902), 230–4.

Wadding, Luke, *Annales Minorum*, 27 vols. (Quaracchi, 1931–4).

William of Nangis, *Chronique latine de Guillelmo de Nangiaco*, ed. H. Géraud, *SHF*, I (Paris, 1843).

William of Rubruck, *Itinerarium Willelmi de Rubruc*, ed. A. van den Wyngaert, *Sinica Franciscana*, I (Quaracchi, 1929), 147–332; transl. by W. W. Rock-hill, *The Journey of William of Rubruck*, Hakluyt Society, 2nd ser., IV (London, 1900).

Wolff, R. L., 'A New Document from the Period of the Latin Empire of Constantinople: the Oath of the Venetian Podestà', *AIPHO*, XII (1952) (= *Mélanges H. Grégoire*, IV), 539–73.

(c) *Western sources, vernacular*

Chronique de Flandre et des Croisades, ed. J. J. de Smet, Collection de Chroniques Belges inédites, III (Brussels, 1856).

Cronaca di Morea [Italian version of the *Chronicle of the Morea*], ed. C. Hopf, *Chroniques gréco-romanes* (Berlin, 1873), pp. 414–68.

Ernoul, *Chronique d'Ernoul et de Bernard le Trésorier*, ed. L. de Mas-Latrie, *SHF* (Paris, 1871).

L'Estoire d'Eracles Empereur, *Rec. Hist. Cr. Occ.* II [see Gen. Bibl. IV].

Henri de Valenciennes, *Histoire de l'Empereur Henri de Constantinople*, ed. J. Longnon, *Documents relatifs à l'histoire des croisades*, publiés par l'Académie des Inscriptions et Belles-Lettres, II (Paris, 1948).

Joinville, J. de, *Histoire de Saint Louis*, ed. N. de Wailly (Paris, 1874); English transl. by F. Marzials (London, 1908) and J. Evans (London, 1938).

Libro de los Fechos et Conquistas del Principado de la Morea [Aragonese version of the *Chronicle of the Morea*], ed. A. Morel-Fatio (Geneva, 1885).

Le Livre de Baudoyn Conte de Flandre, ed. C. P. Serrure and A. Voisin (Brussels, 1836).

Livre de la Conqueste de la Princée de l'Amorée, Chronique de Morée, 1204–1305, ed. J. Longnon, *SHF* (Paris, 1911).

Martin da Canale, *La Cronique des Veniciens de maistre Martin da Canal*, ed. F.-L. Polidori and G. Galvani, *ASI*, ser. I, VIII (1845), 229–798.

Mouskes, Philip, *Chronique rimée de Philippe Mouskès*, ed. F. A. de Reiffenberg, Collection de Chroniques Belges inédites, II (Brussels, 1838).

Robert of Clari, *La Conquête de Constantinople*, ed. P. Lauer (Paris, 1924); English transl. by E. H. McNeal (New York, 1936).

Sanudo, Marino Torsello, *Istoria del Regno di Romania*, ed. C. Hopf, *Chroniques gréco-romanes* (Berlin, 1873), pp. 99–170.

Villehardouin, Geoffrey of, *La Conquête de Constantinople*, ed. N. de Wailly (Paris, 1874); ed. E. Faral, 2 vols. (Paris, 1938, 1939); English transl. by F. Marzials (London, 1908).

Wallensköld, A., *Chansons de Conon de Béthune* (Helsingfors, 1891); new ed. (Paris, 1921).

(d) *Slavonic and Oriental*

Bar Hebraeus, *The Chronography of Gregory Abû'l Faraj...Bar Hebraeus*, transl. from the Syriac by E. A. W. Budge (London, 1932).

Duda, H. W., *Die Seltschukengeschichte des Ibn Bībī* (Copenhagen, 1959).

Dujčev, I., *Iz Starata Bŭlgarska Knižnina* [*From Old Bulgarian Literature*], 2 vols. (Sofia, 1943–4).

Gošev, I., 'Novootkritata Vatopedska Gramota na car Ivan Asen II' ['The newly discovered document of Tsar John Asen II at Vatopedi'], *Bŭlgarski Pregled*, II, 1 (1933), 65–90.

Houtsma, T., 'Über eine türkische Chronik zur Geschichte der Selguqen Klein-Asiens', *Actes du VIe Congr. Intern. des Orientalistes*, II (Leyden, 1885), 369–84.

Ilinsky, G., 'Gramota carja Ioanna Asenja II' ['A document of Tsar John Asen II'], *IRAIK*, VII (1901), 25–39.

Jakubovsky, A. J., 'Rasskaz Ibn-al-Bibi o pochode maloazijskich turok na Sudak, polovcev i russich v načale XIII v.' ['Ibn-al-Bibi's account of the expedition of the Asia Minor Turks against Sudak, the Polovci and the Russians at the beginning of the thirteenth century'], *VV*, xxv (1927), 53–76.

Laskaris, M., *Vatopedskata Gramota na car Ivan Asienija II* [*A Vatopedi Document of Tsar John Asen II*], *Bŭlgarski Starini*, xi (Sofia, 1930).

Melioransky, P., 'Seldžuk-name kak istočnik dlja istorii Vizantii v XII i XIII vekach' ['The work of the Seljuq-Nameh as a source for the history of Byzantium in the twelfth and thirteenth centuries'], *VV*, i (1894), 613–40.

Pavlov, A., 'Sinodal'naja gramota 1213 goda o brake grečeskago imperatora s dočerju armjanskago knjazja' ['A synodal letter of 1213 on the marriage of a Greek Emperor with the daughter of an Armenian prince'], *VV*, iv (1897), 160–6.

Seljuq-Nameh (Ibn Bibi), ed. C. Schéfer, 'Quelques chapitres de l'abrégé de Seljouq Nameh composé par l'Emir Nassir Eddin Yahia', *Recueil de textes et de traductions publié par les professeurs de l'Ecole des Langues Orientales Vivantes*, i (Paris, 1889), 1–102.

Uspensky, F. I., 'O drevnostjach goroda Tyrnova' ['On the antiquities of the city of Trnovo'], *IRAIK*, vii (1902), 1–24.

Zlatarski, V. N., 'Asenovjat nadpis pri Stanimeka' ['The inscription of Asen near Stenimachus'], *Izvestija na Bŭlgarskoto archeologičeskoto Družestvo*, ii (1912), 230–47.

Zlatarski, V. N., 'Tŭrnovskijat nadpis na Ivan Asenja II' ['Inscription from Trnovo on John Asen II'], *Bŭlg. Ist. Bibl.* iii, 3 (1930), 56–64.

II. MODERN WORKS

Alphandéry, P. and Dupont, A., *La Chrétienté et l'idée de Croisade*, ii. *L'Evolution de l'humanité*, 38 *bis* (Paris, 1959).

Altaner, B., *Die Dominikanermissionen des 13. Jahrhunderts* (Habelschwerdt, 1924).

Andreeva, M., *Očerki po kul'ture vizantijskogo dvora v XIII v.* [*Studies in the culture of the Byzantine court in the thirteenth century*] (Prague, 1927).

Andreeva, M., 'Priem tatarskich poslov pri nikejskom dvore' ['The reception of the Tatar ambassadors at the court of Nicaea'], *Recueil d'études dédiées à la mémoire de N. P. Kondakov* (Prague, 1926), pp. 187–200.

Angelov, D., 'Prinos kŭm narodnostnite i pozemelni otnošenija v Makedonija (Epirskaja despotat) prez pŭrvata četvŭrt na XIII vek.' ['A contribution to the study of racial and agrarian conditions in Macedonia (Despotate of Epirus) in the first quarter of the thirteenth century'], *Izvestija na Kamarata narod. Kultura*, iv, 3 (1947), 1–46.

Angelov, D., 'K voprosu o praviteljach fem v epirskom despotate i nikejskoj imperii' ['On the question of the governors of the Themes in the Despotate of Epirus and in the Empire of Nicaea'], *BS*, xii (1951), 56–74.

Aravantinos, P., Χρονογραφία τῆς Ἠπείρου, 2 vols. (Athens, 1856).

Banescu, N., *Un problème d'histoire médiévale. Création et caractère du Second Empire Bulgare* (Bucharest, 1943).

Bertelè, T., 'Monete di Giovanni Comneno Duca imperatore di Salonicco 1237–1244', *Numismatica* (Rome, 1950), 19 pp.

Bertelè, T., *L'Imperatore alato nella Numismatica bizantina* (Rome, 1951).

Bertelè, T., 'Una moneta dei Despoti di Epiro', *BZ*, XLIV (1951), 25–6.

Böhm, L., *Johann von Brienne, König von Jerusalem, Kaiser von Konstantinopel* (Heidelberg, 1938).

Bon, A., 'La prise de Calamata par les Francs en 1205', *Mélanges C. Picard*, I (1949) (= *RA*, 6 ser., XXIX), 98–104.

Borchgrave, E. de, 'Henri de Flandre, empereur de Constantinople (1206–1216) et le roi Etienne Ier Némanié de Serbie', *Compte-rendu des séances de la Commission royale d'Histoire*, 5 ser., V (Brussels, 1895), 360–72.

Borsari, S., 'Federigo II e l'Oriente bizantino', *RSI*, LXIII (1951), 279–91.

Brown, E. A. R., 'The Cistercians in the Latin Empire of Constantinople and Greece 1204–1276', *Trad.* XIV (1958), 63–120.

Bury, J. B., 'The Lombards and Venetians in Euboea', *JHS*, VII (1886), 301–52.

Cahen, C., 'Quelques textes négligés concernant les Turcomans de Rūm au moment de l'invasion Mongole', *B*, XIV (1939), 131–9.

Cahen, C., 'Seldjukides de Rūm, Byzantins et Francs d'après le *Seljuknāmeh* anonyme', *AIPHO*, XI (1951) (= *Mélanges H. Grégoire*, III), 97–106.

Canart, P., 'Nicéphore Blemmyde et le mémoire adressé aux envoyés de Grégoire IX (Nicée, 1234)', *OCP*, XXV (1959), 310–26.

Cerone, F., 'Il Papa ed i Veneziani nella quarta crociata', *Arch. Ven.* XXXVI (1888), 57–70, 287–97.

Cervellini, V., 'Come i Veneziani acquistarono Creta', *N. Arch. Ven.* n.s., XVI (1908), 262–78.

Cessi, R., 'Venezia e la quarta crociata', *Arch. Ven.* 5 ser., XLVIII–XLIX (1951), 1–52.

Chapman, C., *Michel Paléologue, restaurateur de l'Empire byzantin* (Paris, 1926).

Charanis, P., 'On the Asiatic frontiers of the Empire of Nicaea', *OCP*, XIII (1947), 58–62.

Charanis, P., 'The aristocracy of Byzantium in the thirteenth century', *Studies in honor of A. C. Johnson* (Princeton, 1951), pp. 336–55.

Chatzepsaltes, K., 'Σχέσεις τῆς Κύπρου πρὸς τὸ ἐν Νικαίᾳ Βυζαντινὸν Κράτος', Κυπριακαὶ Σπουδαί, XV (1951), 65–82.

Cognasso, F., 'Un imperatore bizantino della decadenza, Isacco II Angelo', *Bess.* XIX (1915), 29–60, 247–89.

Končev, D. and Stoilov, S., 'La forteresse d'Asên', *BS*, XXII (1961), 20–54.

Crescini, V., 'Ancora delle lettere di Rambaut de Vaqueiras', Accademia di Scienze, Lettere, ed Arti in Padova, *Atti e Memorie*, XV (1899), 79–103.

Crescini, V., 'Rambaldo di Vaqueiras a Baldoino Imperatore', *Atti del real istituto Veneto*, LX (1900–1), 871–913.

Crescini, V., *Rambaut de Vaqueiras et le Marquis Boniface I de Montferrat* (Toulouse, 1901).

Czebe, G., 'Studien zum Hochverratsprozesse des M. Paläologos im Jahr 1252', *BNJ*, VIII (1931), 59–98.

Dade, E., *Versuche zur Wiedererrichtung der lateinischen Herrschaft in Konstantinopel* (Jena, 1938).

Dalleggio d'Alessio, E., 'Les sanctuaires urbains et suburbains de Byzance sous la domination latine, 1204–1261', *REB*, XII (1953), 50–61.

Darkó, J., *Byzantinisch-ungarische Beziehungen in der zweiten Hälfte des 13. Jahrhunderts* (Weimar, 1933).

Dawkins, R., 'The Later History of the Varangian Guard: Some Notes', *JRS*, XXXVII (1947), 39–46.

De Bartholomaeis, V., 'Un Sirventès historique d'Elias Cairel', *Annales du Midi*, XVI (1904), 468–94.

de Mundo Lo, S., 'La cuarta cruzada según el cronista novgorodense', *Anales de Historia Antigua y Medieval* (Buenos Aires, 1950), pp. 135–42.

de Mundo Lo, S., *Cruzados en Bizancio. La cuarta Cruzada a la luz de las fuentes latinas y orientales* (University of Buenos Aires, 1957).

Demus, O., 'A Renaissance of Early Christian Art in Thirteenth Century Venice', *Late Classical and Medieval Studies in honor of Albert Mathias Friend jr.* (Princeton, 1955), pp. 348–62.

Dendias, M., ''Ελένη 'Αγγελίνα Δούκαινα, Βασίλισσα Σικελίας καὶ Νεαπόλεως', 'Ηπειρωτικὰ Χρονικά, I (1926), 219–94.

Dendias, M., 'Le roi Manfred de Sicile et la bataille de Pélagonie', *Mélanges C. Diehl*, I (Paris, 1930), 55–60.

Diehl, C., 'Constance de Hohenstaufen, impératrice de Nicée', *Figures Byzantines*, II (Paris, 1908), 207 ff.; reprinted in *Impératrices de Byzance* (Paris, 1959), pp. 249–64.

Diehl, C., 'L'Empire latin de Constantinople', *Dans l'Orient Byzantin* (Paris, 1917), pp. 167–202.

Dölger, F., 'Die dynastische Familienpolitik des Kaisers Michael VIII. Palaiologos (1258–1282)', *Festschrift E. Eichmann* (Paderborn, 1940), pp. 179–90; reprinted in ΠΑΡΑΣΠΟΡΑ (Ettal, 1961), pp. 178–88.

Dölger, F., 'Zwei byzantinische Reiterheroen erobern die Festung Melnik', *Sbornik G. Katsarov* (= *Izvestija Bulg. Arch. Inst.* XVI, Sofia, 1950), pp. 275–9; reprinted in ΠΑΡΑΣΠΟΡΑ (Ettal, 1961), pp. 299–305.

Dräseke, J., 'Theodoros Laskaris', *BZ*, III (1894), 498–515.

Du Cange, C. du F., *Histoire de l'empire de Constantinople sous les empereurs françois* [see Gen. Bibl. v].

Fallmerayer, J. P., *Geschichte des Kaiserthums von Trapezunt* (Munich, 1827).

Faral, E., 'Geoffroi de Villehardouin. La question de sa sincérité', *RH*, CLXXVII (1936), 530–82.

Ferjančić, B., *Despoti u Vizantiji i južnoslovenskim zemljama* [*Despots in Byzantium and the South Slav lands*]. Posebna Izdanja Srpsk. Akad. Nauk., 336, Vizantološki Institut, VIII (Belgrade, 1960).

Finlay, G., *A History of Greece*, ed. H. F. Tozer, IV (London, 1877).

Fotheringham, J. K., 'Genoa and the Fourth Crusade', *EHR*, XXV (1910), 20–57.

Fotheringham, J. K., *Marco Sanudo, Conqueror of the Archipelago* (Oxford, 1915).

Frances, E., 'Sur la conquête de Constantinople par les Latins', *BS*, XV (1954), 22–6.

Frolow, A., *Recherches sur la déviation de la IVe Croisade vers Constantinople* (Paris, 1955).

Gardner, A., *The Lascarids of Nicaea: The Story of an Empire in Exile* (London, 1912).

Geanakoplos, D. J., 'Greco-Latin relations on the eve of the Byzantine Restoration: The Battle of Pelagonia—1259', *DOP*, VII (1953), 99–141.

Geanakoplos, D. J., 'The Nicene Revolution of 1258 and the Usurpation of Michael VIII Palaeologus', *Trad.* IX (1953), 420–30.

Geanakoplos, D. J., *Emperor Michael Palaeologus and the West* (Cambridge, Mass., 1959).

Gelzer, H., *Der Patriarcat von Achrida. Abh. der K. Sächsischen Gesellschaft der Wissenschaften*, XX, 5 (Leipzig, 1902).

Gerassimov, T., 'Pŭrvata zlatna moneta na car Ivan Asen II' ['The first gold coin of John Asen II'], *Izvestija Bŭlg. Arch. Inst.* VIII (1934), 361–8.

Gerland, E., *Neue Quellen zur Geschichte des lateinischen Erzbistums Patras* (Leipzig, 1903).

Gerland, E., 'Der vierte Kreuzzug und seine Probleme', *Neue Jahrb. für das klassische Altertum*, XIII (1904), 505–14.

Gerland, E., *Geschichte des lateinischen Kaiserreiches von Konstantinopel*, I: *Geschichte der Kaiser Balduin I und Heinrich 1204–1216* (Homburg v. d. Höhe, 1905).

Gerola, G., 'Giovanni e Gualtero di Brienne in S. Francesco di Assissi', *Archivum Franciscanum Historicum*, XXIV (1931), 330–40.

Glykatzi-Ahrweiler, H., 'La politique agraire des empereurs de Nicée', *B*, XXVIII (1958) (= *Mélanges R. Guilland*, 1960), 51–66.

Gordlevsky, V., *Gosudarstvo Seldžukidov Maloj Ažii [The Seljuq State in Asia Minor]* (Moscow and Leningrad, 1941).

Grégoire, H., 'The Question of the Diversion of the Fourth Crusade', *B*, XV (1940–1), 158–66.

Grousset, R., *L'Empire du Levant* (Paris, 1946).

Güldner, J., *Über die Versuche Papst Innocenz III eine Union zwischen der abendländischen und morgenländischen Kirche herbeizuführen* (Tübingen, 1893).

Halphen, L., 'Le rôle des "Latins" dans l'histoire intérieure de Constantinople à la fin du XIIe siècle', *Mélanges C. Diehl*, I (Paris, 1940), 141–5.

Hanotaux, G., 'Les Vénitiens ont-ils trahi la chrétienté en 1202?', *RH*, IV (1877), 74–102.

Heisenberg, A., 'Kaiser Johannes Batatzes der Barmherzige', *BZ*, XIV (1905), 160–233.

Heisenberg, A., 'Zu den armenisch-byzantinischen Beziehungen am Anfang des 13. Jahrhunderts', *SBAW, phil.-hist. Klasse*, Abh. VI (Munich, 1929).

Heyd, W., *Histoire du Commerce du Levant* [see Gen. Bibl. v].

Hodgman, A. W., 'The Fourth Crusade: A Latin Document written in 1208', *Classical Journal*, XLIII (1948), 225–8.

Hopf, K., 'Veneto-byzantinische Analekten', *SKAW*, XXXII (1859), 365–528.

Hopf, K., *Geschichte Griechenlands vom Beginn des Mittelalters bis auf unsere Zeit* [see Gen. Bibl. v].

Hopf, K., *Bonifaz von Montferrat und der Troubadour Rambaud von Vaqueiras*, ed. L. Streit (Berlin, 1877).

Houtsma, T., 'Over de Geschiedenis der Seldjuken van Klein-Azië', *Verslagen en Mededeelingen der K. Akademie van Wetenschapen, Afdeeling Letterkunde*, 3 ser. (Amsterdam, 1892), pp. 133–52.

Iorga, N., 'France de Constantinople et de Morée', *RHSE*, XII (1935), 81–105, 177–217, 324–56.

Iucov, B., 'Ivan Asen II kato obraz nacionalno sŭznanie prez vreme na robstvoto' ['John Asen II as an example of national consciousness during the time of oppression'], *Bŭlg. Ist. Bibl.* III, 3 (1930), 187–227.

Janin, R., 'Au lendemain de la conquête de Constantinople. Les tentatives d'union des Eglises, 1204–1214', *EO*, XXXII (1933), 5–21, 195–202.

Janin, R., 'Les sanctuaires de Byzance sous la domination latine', *EB*, II (1944; Bucharest, 1945), 134–84.

Janin, R., 'Les sanctuaires des colonies latines à Constantinople', *REB*, IV (1946), 163–77.

Jerphanion, G. de, 'Les inscriptions Cappadociens et l'histoire de l'Empire Grec de Nicée', *OCP*, I (1935), 239–56.

Jerphanion, G. de, 'Σαμψὼν et Ἄμισος, une ville à déplacer de neuf cent kilomètres', *OCP*, I (1935), 257–67.

Jireček, K., *Geschichte der Bulgaren* (Prague, 1876).

Jireček, K., *Geschichte der Serben*, I (Gotha, 1911).

John, E., 'A Note on the Preliminaries of the Fourth Crusade', *B*, XXVIII (1958) (= *Mélanges R. Guilland*, 1960), 95–103.

Juglev, K. I., 'Prinos kŭm istorijata na srednovekovna Bŭlgarija vŭz osnova na chronikata na Chenrich do Valancien' ['A contribution to medieval Bulgarian history from the chronicle of Henry of Valenciennes'], *Godišnik na Sofijskija Universitet, ist.-fil. fak.* XLVI (1949–50), 119.

Kalligas, P., Μελέται Βυζαντινῆς Ἱστορίας ἀπὸ τῆς πρώτης μέχρι τῆς τελευταίας ἁλώσεως (Athens, 1894).

Kantorowicz, E., *Kaiser Friederich II*, 2 vols. (Berlin, 1927).

Klimke, C., *Die Quellen zur Geschichte des vierten Kreuzzuges* (Breslau, 1875).

Krause, J., *Die Eroberungen von Constantinopel im dreizehnten und fünfzehnten Jahrhundert* (Halle, 1870).

Krekić, B., *Dubrovnik* [see Gen. Bibl. v].

Kretschmayr, H., *Geschichte von Venedig* [see Gen. Bibl. v].

Kurtz, E., 'Christophoros von Ankyra als Exarch des Patriarchen Germanos', *BZ*, XVI (1907), 120–42.

Lagopatis, S., Γερμανὸς ὁ Β′ πατριάρχης Κωνσταντινουπόλεως-Νικαίας (1222–1240) (Tripoli, 1913).

Lah, V., 'De unione Bulgarorum cum Ecclesia Romana ab anno 1204–1234', *AKKR*, XLIV (1880), 193–261.

Laskaris, M., *Vizantiske princeze u srednjevekovnoj Srbiji* [*Byzantine Princesses in medieval Serbia*], Diss. (Belgrade, 1926).

Laskaris, M., 'Vagenitia', *RHSE*, XIX (1942), 423–37.

Lathoud, D. and Bertelè, T., 'Les clefs de S. Pierre sur une monnaie de Jean Doucas Vatatzès, empereur de Nicée (1222–1245)', *Unitas*, I (1948), 189–96.

Laurent, V., 'Héraclée du Pont. La métropole et ses titulaires (1232/50–1387)', *EO*, XXXI (1932), 316–26.

Laurent, V., 'La généalogie des premiers Paléologues', *B*, VIII (1933), 125–48.

Laurent, V., 'Le Pape Alexandre IV (1254–1261) et l'Empire de Nicée', *EO*, XXXIV (1935), 26–55.

Laurent, V., 'La date du premier couronnement de Michel VIII Paléologue', *EO*, XXXVI (1937), 165–9.

Laurent, V., 'Notes de chronographie et d'histoire byzantine', *EO*, XXXVI (1937), 162–5.

Laurent, V., 'Bulle et monnaies inédites de Jean Ducas Comnène, empereur de Thessalonique (1240–1244)', *Cronica numismatică și arheologică*, XVII (1943), 83–94.

Lazzarini, V., 'I Titoli dei Dogi di Venezia', *N. Arch. Ven.* n.s. V (1903), 271–313.

Lehmann, B., *Die Nachrichten des Niketas Choniates, G. Akropolites und Pachymeres über die Selčuqen in der Zeit von 1180 bis 1280* (Leipzig, 1939).

L'Huillier, P., 'La nature des relations ecclésiastiques gréco-latines après la prise de Constantinople par les Croisés', *Akten des XI. Intern. Byzantinisten-Kongresses* (Munich, 1960), pp. 314–20.

Longnon, J., *Recherches sur la vie de Geoffroi de Villehardouin, suivies du Catalogue des Actes des Villehardouin* (Paris, 1939).

Longnon, J., 'Le patriarcat latin de Constantinople', *Journal des Savants* (1941), pp. 174 ff.

Longnon, J., 'La campagne de Henri de Hainaut en Asie Mineure en 1211', Académie Royale de Belgique, *Bulletin de la Classe des lettres*, 5 ser. XXXIV (1948), 442–52.

Longnon, J., 'Domination franque et civilisation grecque', *Mélanges C. Picard*, II (1949) (= *RA*, 6 ser. XXX), 657–67.

Longnon, J., 'Notes sur la diplomatique de l'Empire latin de Constantinople', *Mélanges F. Grat*, II (1949), 3–18.

Longnon, J. *L'empire latin de Constantinople et la principauté de Morée* (Paris, 1949).

Longnon, J., 'La reprise de Salonique par les Grecs en 1224', *Actes du VIe Congr. Intern. d'Et. Byz.* I (Paris, 1950), 141–6.

Longnon, J., 'L'empereur Baudouin II et l'ordre de St Jacques', *B*, XXII (1952), 297–9.

Luchaire, A., *Innocent III. La Question d'Orient* (Paris, 1907).

Magnocavallo, A., *Marin Sanudo il Vecchio e il suo progetto di Crociata* (Bergamo, 1901).

Manfroni, C., 'Le relazioni fra Genova, l'impero bizantino e i Turchi', *Atti della Soc. Ligure di Storia Patria*, XXVIII (1886), fasc. 3.

Marinesco, C., 'Du nouveau sur Constance de Hohenstaufen', *B*, I (1924), 451–68.

Marquardt, J., 'Über das Volkstum der Kumanen', *Abh. der K. Gesellschaft der Wissenschaften zu Göttingen, phil.-hist. Klasse*, Neue Folge, XIII (1914), 25–236.

Mas Latrie, L. de, 'Les Patriarches latins de Constantinople', *ROL*, III (1895), 435–56.

Mayer, H. E., *Bibliographie zur Geschichte der Kreuzzüge* (Hanover, 1960).

Meliarakes, A., Ἱστορία τοῦ Βασιλείου τῆς Νικαίας καὶ τοῦ Δεσποτάτου τῆς Ἠπείρου (Athens, 1898).

Meščersky, N. A., 'Drevnerusskaja povest' o vzjatii Cargrada frjagami kak istočnik po istorii Vizantii' ['The old Russian accounts of the capture of Constantinople by the Franks as sources for the history of Byzantium'], *VV*, n.s. IX (1956), 170–85.

Miller, W., *The Latins in the Levant* (London, 1908).

Miller, W., 'Salonika', *EHR*, XXXII (1917), 161–74.

Miller, W., *Essays on the Latin Orient* (Cambridge, 1921).

Miller, W., *Trebizond, the Last Greek Empire* (London, 1926).

Mitrofanov, P., 'Izmenenie napravlenii četvertago krestovago pochoda' ['The diversion of the goal of the Fourth Crusade'], *VV*, IV (1897), 461–523.

Mušmov, N. A., 'Monetitě na Ivan Asenja II i na negovoto semejstvo' ['The currency of John Asen II and his family'], *Bŭlg. Ist. Bibl.* III, 4 (1930), 81–93.

Mušmov, N. A., 'Un sceau en plomb du Tsar Kaloyan (1196–1207)', *BS*, IV (1932), 135–8.

Mustoxidi, A., *Delle Cose Corciresi* (Corfu, 1848).

Mutafčiev, P., *Istorija na bŭlgarskija narod* [*History of the Bulgarian Nation*], 2 vols. (Sofia, 1943).

Mutafčiev, P., 'Vladitelotě na Prosek' ['The affair at Prosek'], *Sbornik Bŭlg. Akad. Nauk.* I (1913), 1–85.

Nicol, D. M., 'Ecclesiastical Relations between the Despotate of Epirus and the Kingdom of Nicaea in the Years 1215–1230', *B*, XXII (1952), 207–28.

Nicol, D. M., 'The Date of the Battle of Pelagonia', *BZ*, XLIX (1956), 68–71.

Nicol, D. M., *The Despotate of Epiros* [see Gen. Bibl. v].

Nikov, P., 'Cŭrkovnata politika na Ivan Asenja II' ['The ecclesiastical policy of John Asen II'], *Bŭlg. Ist. Bibl.* III, 3 (1930), 65–111.

Nikov, P., 'Die Stellung der bulgarischen Kirche zum Patriarchat von Konstantinopel um das Jahr 1235', *Actes du IIIe Congr. Intern. des Et. Byz.* (Athens, 1932), pp. 34–5.

Norden, W., *Der Vierte Kreuzzug im Rahmen der Beziehungen des Abendlandes zu Byzanz* (Berlin, 1898).

Norden, W., *Das Papsttum und Byzanz* [see Gen. Bibl. v].

Orgels, P., 'Sabas Asidénos, dynaste de Sampson', *B*, x (1935), 67–77.

Ostrogorsky, G., 'Vozvyšenie roda Angelov' ['The rise of the Angelus family'], *Jubilejnij Sbornik Russkago Archeologičeskago Obščestva v Belgrade* (1936), pp. 111–29.

Ostrogorsky, G., *History of the Byzantine State* [see Gen. Bibl. v].

Ostrogorsky, G., *Quelques problèmes d'histoire de la paysannerie byzantine* [see Gen. Bibl. v].

Ostrogorsky, G., 'Pismo Dimitrija Homatijana sv. Save' ['Demetrius Chomatianus' letter to St Sava'], *Svetosavski Zbornik*, II (Belgrade, 1939) (*Srpska Kraljevska Akademija, posebna izdanja*, CXXV, *Drustveni i Istoriski Spisi*, 50).

Palmieri, A., 'I vicarii patriarcali di Costantinopoli', *Bess.* VII (1904), 41–53.

Papadopoulos-Kerameus, A., 'Théodore Eirenicos, patriarche œcuménique de Nicée', *BZ*, x (1901), 182–92.

Pappadopoulos, J. B., *Théodore II Lascaris, Empereur de Nicée* (Paris, 1908).

Paris, G., 'Henri de Valenciennes', *Romania*, XIX (1890), 63–72.

Pears, E., *The Fall of Constantinople: The Story of the Fourth Crusade* (London, 1885).

Pelliot, P., 'A propos des Coumains', *JA*, 11 ser. xv (1920), 125–85.

Popov, V., *700 Godini ot Klokotniškata Bitka* [*700 years after the Battle of Klokotnica*] (Sofia, 1930).

Popov, V., 'Bitkata pri Klokotnica v 1230 godina' ['The Battle of Klokotnica in 1230'], *Voenno-Istorič. Sbornik*, XXVI, 3 (1957), 78–85.

Primov, B., 'Robert de Clari i otnošenijata meždu Bulgarija i Latinskata imperija' ['Robert of Clari and relations between the Bulgarian and Latin Empires'], *Godišnik na Sofijskija Universitet, Ist.-Fil. Fak.* XLIII (1946, 1947), 6–22.

Primov, B., 'Grŭcko-Bŭlgarski sŭjuz v načalo na XIII vek' ['The Greco-Bulgarian alliance at the beginning of the thirteenth century'], *Istoričeski Pregled*, IV (1947–8), 22–39.

Primov, B., 'Bulgaren, Griechen und Lateiner in Plovdiv, 1204–1205', *Izvestija na Bŭlgarskoto Istoričesko Družestvo*, XXII–XXIII (1948), 145–58.

Primov, B., 'Vŭrchu njakoi vŭprosi ot obštata i bŭlgarska srednovekovna istorija vŭv vrŭzka četvŭrtija krŭstonoden pochod' ['Various problems of general and of Bulgarian medieval history connected with the Fourth Crusade'], *Izvestija Inst. Bulg. Ist.* (Sofia, 1951), pp. 427–40.

Prinet, M., 'Les armoires des Empereurs latins de Constantinople', *RN*, ser. IV, xv (1911), 250–6.

Radojčić, N., 'O nekim gospodarima grada Proseka na Vardaru' ['On certain Lords of the town of Prosek on the Vardar'], *Letopis Matiće Srpske*, LXXXV, fasc. CCLIX (1909), pp. 1–19; fasc. CCLX (1909), pp. 32–40.

Ramnusius, Paulus, *De Bello Constantinopolitano et Imperatoribus Comnenis per Gallos et Venetos restitutis Historia* (Venice, 1634).

Rasovsky, D. A., 'Die Polovcer und Byzanz', *Actes du IVe Congr. Intern. d'Et. Byz.* (Sofia, 1934). *Izvestija Bulg. Arch. Inst.* IX (1935), 346–54.

Rasovsky, D. A., 'Polovci' ['The Polovci or Cumans'], *Sem. Kond.* VII (1935), 245–62; VIII (1936), 161–82; IX (1937), 71–85; X (1938), 155–78; XI (Belgrade, 1940), 86–128.

Rasovsky, D. A., 'Rol Polovcev v vojnach Asenej vizantijskoj i latinskoj imperijami v 1186–1207 g.' ['The role of the Polovci in the wars of the Asenids with the Byzantine and Latin Empires'], *Spisanie na Bŭlg. Akad.* (1939), pp. 203 ff.

Riant, P., 'Les dépouilles religieuses enlevées à Constantinople au XIIIe siècle', *Mémoires de la Soc. Nationale des Antiquaires de France*, IV ser., VI (1875), 1–214.

Riant, P., 'Innocent III, Philippe de Souabe, et Boniface de Montferrat', *RQH*, XVII (1875), 321–74; XVIII (1875), 5–75.

Riant, P., 'Le changement de direction de la IVe Croisade', *RQH*, XXIII (1878), 71–114.

Roberti, M., 'Ricerche intorno alla colonia Veneziana in Costantinopoli', *Scritti storici in onore di C. Manfroni* (Padua, 1925), pp. 138–47.

Romanin, S., *Storia documentata di Venezia*, 10 vols., 2nd ed. (Venice, 1912–21).

Romanos, J. A., Περὶ τοῦ Δεσποτάτου τῆς Ἠπείρου ἱστορικὴ πραγματεία (Corfu, 1895); reprinted in Ἰωάννου τοῦ Ῥωμανοῦ ἱστορικὰ ἔργα, ed. K. Daphnes (Kerkyra, 1959), pp. 3–87.

Roncaglia, M., *Georges Bardanès, métropolite de Corfou, et Barthélémy de l'Ordre des Franciscains*, Studi e Testi Francescani, IV (Rome, 1953).

Roncaglia, M., *Les Franciscains (Frères Mineurs) et l'Eglise grecque orthodoxe au XIIIe siècle* (1231–74), Biblioteca bio-bibliografica della Terra Santa e dell'Oriente Francescano, 4 ser. II (Cairo, 1954).

Runciman, S., *A History of the Crusades*, III [see Gen. Bibl. v].

Runciman, S., *The Sicilian Vespers* (Cambridge, 1958).

Santifaller, L., *Beiträge zur Geschichte des lateinischen Patriarchats von Konstantinopel, 1204–1261* (Weimar, 1938).

Schaube, A., 'Eine bisher unbekannte Regentin des lateinischen Kaiserreiches', *MIOG*, VIII (1887), 587–94.

Schlumberger, G., *Numismatique de l'orient latin* (Paris, 1878).

Schlumberger, G., Chalandon, F. and Blanchet, A., *Sigillographie de l'orient latin* (Paris, 1943).

Schlumberger, G., 'Sceaux et Bulles des Empereurs latins de Constantinople', *Bulletin Monumental*, LVI, 6 ser. VI (1890), 5–29.

Schlumberger, G., 'Un nouveau sceau de l'Empereur latin Henri Ier d'Angre de Constantinople', *RN*, ser. IV, V (1901), 396–7.

Schlumberger, G., 'Le tombeau d'une impératrice byzantine à Valence en Espagne', *Byzance et Croisades* (Paris, 1927), pp. 57–86.

Schmitt, L., 'Der falsche Balduin von Flandern', *Stimmen aus Maria Laach*, XLV (1893), 247–57, 363–72, 482–95.

Sinogowitz, B., 'Über das byzantinische Kaisertum nach dem vierten Kreuzzuge (1204–1205)', *BZ*, XLV (1952), 345–56.

Sinogowitz, B., 'Zur Eroberung Thessalonikes im Herbst 1224', *BZ*, XLV (1952), 28.

Smet, J. J. de, 'Mémoire sur Baudouin IX, Comte de Flandre et de Hainaut et sur les chevaliers Belges à la cinquième Croisade', *Mémoires de l'Académie Royale de Belgique*, n.s. XXXI (1859), 79.

Stadtmüller, G., *Michael Choniates, Metropolit von Athen, OCA*, XXXIII (1934).

Stanojević, S., 'Sv. Sava i proglas bŭlgarske patriaršije' ['St Sava and the establishment of the Bulgarian patriarchate'], *Glas*, CLVI (1933), 173 ff.

Stanojević, S., 'Sveti Sava i nezavisnost srpske crkve' ['St Sava and the independence of the Serbian Church'], *Glas*, CLXI (1934), 199–251.

Stiernon, L., 'Les origines du Despotat d'Epire', *REB*, XVII (1959), 90–126.

Streit, L., *Venedig und die Wendung des vierten Kreuzzugs gegen Konstantinopel* (Anklam, 1877).

Swift, E. H., 'The Latins at Hagia Sophia', *American Journal of Archaeology*, 2 ser. XXXIX (1935), 458–74.

Tafel, G. L. F., *De Thessalonica eiusque agro dissertatio geographica* (Berlin, 1839).

Tafel, G. L. F., *Symbolarum criticarum, geographiam Byzantinam spectantium, partes duae. Abh. der hist. Klasse der K. bayerischen Akademie der Wissenschaften*, V (1849), Abt. II, III.

Tessier, J., *La Quatrième Croisade. La Diversion sur Zara et Constantinople* (Paris, 1884).

Thil-Lorrain, M., *Baudouin de Constantinople, Fondateur de l'Empire latin de Constantinople* (Brussels, n.d.).

Thiriet, F., 'Les chroniques vénitiennes de la Marcienne et leur importance pour l'histoire de la Romanie gréco-vénitienne', *Mélanges d'Archéol. et d'Hist.* LXVI (1954), pp. 241–92.

Thiriet, F., *La Romanie vénitienne au moyen âge* [see Gen. Bibl. v].

Tomadakis, N. B., 'Οἱ λόγιοι τοῦ δεσποτάτου τῆς Ἠπείρου', *EEBS*, XXVII (1957), 3–62.

Topping, P. W., 'The Formation of the Assizes of Romania', *B*, XVII (1944–5), 304–19.

Toumanoff, C., 'On the Relationship between the Founder of the Empire of Trebizond and the Georgian Queen Thamar', *SP*, XV (1940), 299–312.

Uspensky, F. I., *Vizantijskij pisatel, Nikita Akominat iz Chon* [*A Byzantine author, Nicetas Acominatus from Chonae*] (St Petersburg, 1874).

Uspensky, F. I., *Obrazovanie vtorago bolgarskago carstva* [*The formation of the Second Bulgarian Empire*] (Odessa, 1879); cf. V. G. Vasilievsky, *ZMNP*, CCIV (1879), 114–217, 318–48.

Uspensky, F. I., 'Vydelenie Trapezunta iz sostava vizantijskoj imperii' ['The secession of Trebizond from the main body of the Byzantine Empire'], *Sem. Kond.* I (Prague, 1927), 21–34.

Uspensky, F. I., *Očerki iz istorii trapezuntskoj imperii* [*Studies in the history of the Empire of Trebizond*] (Leningrad, 1929).

Usseglio, L., *I Marchesi di Monferrato in Italia ed in Oriente durante i secoli XII e XIII*, 2 vols., Biblioteca della Soc. Storica Subalpina, n.s. VI and VII (Turin, 1926).

Vasiliev, A. A., 'The Foundation of the Empire of Trebizond', *SP*, XI (1936), 3–37.

Vasiliev, A. A., 'Mesarites as a Source', *SP*, XIII (1938), 180–2.

Vasiliev, A. A., 'The Empire of Trebizond in History and Literature', *B*, XV (1940–41), 316–77.

Vasiliev, A. A., *History of the Byzantine Empire* [see Gen. Bibl. v].

Vasilievsky, V. G., 'Obnovlenie bolgarskago patriaršestva pri care Ioanne Asene II v 1235 godu' ['The restoration of the Bulgarian patriarchate under the Tsar John Asen II in 1235'], *ZMNP*, CCXXXVIII (1885), 1–56, 206–24.

Verlinden, C., *Les Empereurs Belges de Constantinople* (Brussels, 1945).

Verlinden, C., 'Boudewijn van Henegouwen, een onbekend reiziger door Azie uit de XIII eeuw', *Tijdschrift voor Geschiednis*, LXV (1952), 122–9.

Vriens, H., 'De Kwestie van den vierden Kruistocht', *Tijdschrift voor Geschiednis*, XXXV (1922), 50–82.

Weitzmann, K., 'Constantinopolitan Book Illumination in the period of the Latin Conquest', *Gazette des Beaux Arts*, XXV (1944), 193–214.

Wellnhofer, M., *Johannes Apokaukos, Metropolit von Naupaktos in Aetolien (c. 1155–1233): sein Leben und seine Stellung im Despotate von Epirus unter Michael Doukas und Theodoros Komnenos* (Munich Diss., Freising, 1913).

Wertner, M., 'Margarethe von Ungarn, Kaiserin von Griechenland und Königin von Thessalonich', *Vierteljahrsschrift für Siegel-, Wappen- und Familienkunde*, XVII (1890), 219–55.

Winkelmann, E., *Philipp von Schwaben und Otto IV von Braunschweig* (Leipzig, 1873–8).

Wirth, P., 'Von der Schlacht von Pelagonia bis Wiedereroberung Konstantinopels. Zur äusseren Geschichte der Jahre 1259–1261', *BZ*, LV (1962), 30–7.

Wittek, P., 'Von der byzantinischen zu türkischen Toponomie', *B*, X (1935), 11–64.

Wittek, P., 'L'Epitaphe d'un Comnène à Konia', *B*, X (1935), 505–15.

Wittek, P., 'Encore l'Epitaphe d'un Comnène à Konia', *B*, XII (1937), 206–11.

Wittek, P., 'Deux chapitres de l'histoire des Turcs de Roum', *B*, XI (1936), 285–302.

Wittek, P., 'Le Sultan de Roum', *AIPHO*, VI (1938), 361–90.

Wolff, R. L., 'The Latin Empire of Constantinople and the Franciscans', *Trad.* II (1944), 213–37.

Wolff, R. L., 'The Organisation of the Latin Patriarchate of Constantinople, 1204–1261. Social and Administrative Consequences of the Latin Conquest', *Trad.* VI (1948), 33–60.

Wolff, R. L., 'Romania: The Latin Empire of Constantinople', *SP*, XXIII (1948), 1–34.

Wolff, R. L., 'Footnote to an Incident of the Latin Occupation of Constantinople: The Church and the Icon of the Hodegetria', *Trad.* VI (1948), 319–28.

Wolff, R. L., 'The "Second Bulgarian Empire": Its Origin and History to 1204', *SP*, XXIV (1949), 167–206.

Wolff, R. L., 'The Lascarids' Asiatic Frontiers Once More', *OCP*, XV (1949), 194–7.

Wolff, R. L., 'Baldwin of Flanders and Hainaut, First Latin Emperor of Constantinople. His Life, Death, and Resurrection, 1172–1225', *SP*, XXVII (1952), 281–322.

Wolff, R. L., 'Mortgage and Redemption of an Emperor's Son. Castile and the Latin Empire of Constantinople', *SP*, XXIX (1954), 45–84.

Wolff, R. L., 'Politics in the Latin Patriarchate of Constantinople, 1204–1261', *DOP*, VIII (1954), 225–303.

Wolff, R. L. (ed.), *A History of the Crusades*, II (Philadelphia, 1962).

Xanalatos, D., 'Wirtschaftliche Aufbau- und Autarkie-Massnahmen im 13. Jahrhundert (Nikänisches Reich 1204–61)', *Leipziger Viert. für Südosteuropa*, III (1939), 129 ff.

Zaborov, M. A., 'Papstvo i zachvat Konstantinopolja krestonoscami v načale XIII veka' ['The Papacy and the capture of Constantinople by the crusaders at the beginning of the thirteenth century'], *VV*, n.s. v (1952), 152–77.

Zaborov, M. A., 'K voprosu o predistorii četvertogo krestovogo pochoda' ['On the question of the preliminaries to the Fourth Crusade'], *VV*, n.s. VI (1953), 233–5.

Zakythinos, D., *Le Despotat grec de Morée*, I (Paris, 1932).

Zakythinos, D., 'Μελέται περὶ τῆς διοικητικῆς διαιρέσεως καὶ τῆς ἐπαρχιακῆς διοικήσεως ἐν τῷ Βυζαντινῷ κράτει', *EEBS*, XXI (1951), 179–217; XXII (1952), 159–82.

Zlatarsky, V. N., 'Grŭcko-bŭlgarski sŭjuz prez 1204–5 god' ['The Greco-Bulgarian alliance during the years 1204–5'], *Godišnik na Sofijskija Universitet, ist.-fil. fak.*, VIII–IX (1911–13), 1–23.

Zlatarsky, V. N., *Geschichte der Bulgaren*, I. *Von der Gründung des Bulgarischen Reiches bis zu Türkenzeit, 679–1396* (Leipzig, 1918).

Zlatarsky, V. N., *Istorija na bŭlgarskata dŭržava* [*History of the Bulgarian State*], 3 vols. in 4 (Sofia, 1918–40).

Zlatarsky, V. N., 'Ivan Asen II, 1218–1241', *Bŭlg. Ist. Bibl.* III, 3 (1930), 1–55.

CHAPTER VIII. THE PALAEOLOGI, 1261–1453

See also the bibliographies for chapters IX, X and XII.

I. ORIGINAL AUTHORITIES

(A) LITERARY SOURCES

Acropolites, George, *Opera*, ed. A. Heisenberg, 2 vols. (Leipzig, 1903).

Anagnostes, John, ed. I. Bekker, *CSHB* (after George Sphrantzes; pp. 481–528).

Barbaro, Nicolo, *Giornale dell'assedio di Constantinopli 1453*, ed. E. Cornet (Vienna, 1856). [Bibliography on the source material for the capture of Constantinople may be found in J. B. Bury's edition of E. Gibbon, *The Decline and Fall of the Roman Empire*, VII, in A. A. Vasiliev, *History of the Byzantine Empire* and G. Ostrogorsky, *History of the Byzantine State*. See Gen. Bibl. v.]

Boissonade, J. F., *Anecdota graeca* [see Gen. Bibl. IV].

Cananus, John, ed. I. Bekker, *CSHB* (after George Sphrantzes; pp. 457–79).

Cantacuzenus, John, *Historiarum libri* IV, ed. L. Schopen, 3 vols., *CSHB* (1828–32).

Chalcocondyles, Laonicus, *Historiarum demonstrationes*, ed. E. Darkó, 2 vols. (Budapest, 1922–7); ed. I. Bekker, *CSHB* (1843).

Chronicle of the Morea, ed. J. Schmitt (London, 1904); ed. P. Kalonaros (Athens, 1940).

Codinus (Pseudo-), George, *De officialibus palatii Constantinopolitani et de officiis magnae ecclesiae liber*, ed. I. Bekker, *CSHB* (1839).

Critobulus, Michael, *De rebus gestis Mahumetis II*, ed. C. Müller, *Fragm. hist. graec.* V (1883), 52–164; ed. V. Grecu (Bucharest, 1963).

Cydones, Demetrius, *Letters*, ed. J. F. Boissonade, *Anecdota Nova* (Paris, 1844); ed. G. Cammelli, *Démétrius Cydonès, Correspondance* (Budé, with French transl.) (Paris, 1930); ed. R.-J. Loenertz (Studi e Testi, 186 and 208), 2 vols. (Vatican, 1956–60). See also G. Mercati, *Notizie di Procoro e Demetrio Cidone, Manuele Caleca e Teodoro Meliteniota* (Studi e Testi, 56) (Vatican, 1931).

Συμβουλευτικοί. Μονῳδία ἐπὶ τοῖς ἐν Θεσσαλονίκῃ πεσοῦσιν, *MPG*, CLIV.

Orations, ed. G. Cammelli, *BNJ*, III (1922), 67–76; IV (1923–4), 77–83, 282–95; ed. R.-J. Loenertz (in vol. I of the *Letters*).

Sententiae variae, ed. G. Cammelli, *BNJ*, V (1927), 48–57.

Prooemien zu Chrysobullen, ed. K. E. Zachariae von Lingenthal, *SPAW* (1888), II, 1409 ff.

Ducas, *Historia byzantina*, ed. I. Bekker, *CSHB* (1834); ed. V. Grecu, *Istorija turco-bizantină 1341–1462* (Bucharest, 1958).

Enveri, *Düstūrnāme*, ed. with transl. and notes by I. Mélikoff-Sayar, *Le Destan d'Umūr Pacha* (*Düstūrnāme-i-Enveri*) (Paris, 1953).

Epirotica, ed. I. Bekker, *CSHB* (1849); new ed. with commentary, Cirac Estopañan, *Bizancio y España*, I, 61–200; II, 35–54 (text) [see below, II].

Gorjanov, B. T. (ed.), 'Neizdannyj anonimnyj vizantijskij chronograf XIV veka' ['An unedited anonymous Byzantine chronicle of the 14th century'], *VV*, n.s. II (1949), 276–89.

Gregoras, Nicephorus, *Byzantina historia*, ed. L. Schopen–I. Bekker, 3 vols., *CSHB* (1829–55); letters, ed. S. Bezdeki, *Nicephori Gregorae epistolae XC, Ephemeris Dacoromana*, II (1924), 239–377; ed. R. Guilland, *Correspondance de Nicéphore Grégoras* (Budé, with French transl.) (Paris, 1927).

Hopf, C., *Chroniques gréco-romanes inédites ou peu connues* (Berlin, 1873).

Lampros, S., Παλαιολόγεια καὶ Πελοποννησιακά, I–IV (Athens, 1912–30).

Lampros, S. and Amantos, K., Βραχέα Χρονικά (Athens, 1932).

Legrand, E., *Lettres de l'empereur Manuel Paléologue* (Paris, 1893).

Martini, A., *Manuelis Philae carmina inedita* (*Atti della R. Accad.* XX, Suppl., Naples, 1900).

Meyendorff, J., 'Projets de concile œcuménique en 1367. Un dialogue inédit entre Jean Cantacuzène et le légat Paul', *DOP*, XIV (1960), 149–77.

Miller, E., *Manuelis Philae carmina*, 2 vols. (Paris, 1855–7).

Moravcsik, Gy., Ἑλληνικὸν ποίημα περὶ τῆς μάχης τῆς Βάρνης (Οὐγγροελληνικαὶ Μελέται, Budapest, 1935).

Müller, J., 'Byzantinische Analekten', *SBAW*, IX (1852), 336–420.

Muntaner, Ramón, *Chronik des edlen En Ramon Muntaner*, ed. K. Lanz (Stuttgart, 1844); English trans. by Lady Goodenough, 2 vols. (Hakluyt Soc., London, 1920–1).

Pachymeres, George, *De Michaele et Andronico Palaeologis libri XIII*, ed. I. Bekker, 2 vols., *CSHB* (1835).

Phrantzes, see Sphrantzes.

Previale, L., 'Un panegirico inedito per Michele VIII Paleologo', *BZ*, XLII (1942), 1–49.

Sathas, K. N., Μεσαιωνικὴ Βιβλιοθήκη, 7 vols. [see Gen. Bibl. IV].

Scholarius, Gennadius, *Œuvres complètes*, ed. L. Petit, X. A. Sidéridès and M. Jugie, 8 vols. (Paris, 1928–36).

Sphrantzes, George, *Chronicon*: '*Chronicon Minus*', *MPG*, CXLVI, 1025–80; '*Chronicon Maius*', ed. I. Bekker, *CSHB* (1838); ed. J. B. Papadopulos, I (Leipzig, 1935) [still incomplete].

Treu, M., *Maximi monachi Planudis epistulae* (Breslau, 1890).
Treu, M., *Dichtungen des Grosslogotheten Theodoros Metochites* (Potsdam Gymnasium Programme, 1895).
Treu, M., 'Manuel Holobolos', *BZ*, v (1896), 538–59.

(B) DOCUMENTARY SOURCES

Acts of Athos [see Gen. Bibl. IV].
Dölger, F., *Facsimiles byzantinischer Kaiserurkunden* (Munich, 1931).
Dölger, F., *Aus den Schatzkammern des Heiligen Berges* (Munich, 1948).
Dölger, F., *Sechs byzantinische Praktika des 14. Jahrhunderts für das Athoskloster Iberon, Abh. d. Bayer. Akad. d. Wiss., phil.-hist. Kl.*, N.F. XXVIII (Munich, 1949).
Gudas, M., Βυζαντιακὰ ἔγγραφα τῆς ἐν ῎Αθῳ ἱερᾶς μονῆς τοῦ Βατοπεδίου, *EEBS*, III (1926), 113–34; IV (1927), 211–48.
Jorga, N., *Notes et extraits pour servir à l'histoire des croisades au XVe siècle*, I–VI (Paris, 1899–1916).
Každan, A. P., 'Dva pozdnevizantijskich akta iz sobranija P. I. Sevastjanova' ['Two late Byzantine documents from the collection of P. I. Sevastjanov'], *VV*, n.s. II (1949), 313–21.
Ktenas, C., Χρυσόβουλλοι λόγοι τῆς ἐν ῎Αθῳ ἱερᾶς βασιλικῆς, πατριαρχικῆς καὶ σταυροπηγιακῆς μονῆς τοῦ Δοχειαρίου, *EEBS*, IV (1927), 285–311.
Miklosich, F. and Müller, J., *Acta et diplomata graeca medii aevi* [see Gen. Bibl. IV].
Regel, W., Χρυσόβουλλα καὶ γράμματα τῆς ἐν τῷ ἁγίῳ ὄρει ῎Αθῳ ἱερᾶς καὶ σεβασμίας μεγίστης μονῆς τοῦ Βατοπεδίου (St Petersburg, 1898).
Salaville, S., 'Deux documents inédits sur les dissensions religieuses byzantines entre 1275 et 1310', *REB*, v (1947), 116–36.
Soloviev, A. and Mošin, V., *Grčke povelje srpskih vladara* [*Greek documents of the Serbian rulers*] (Belgrade, 1936).
Tafel, G. L. F. and Thomas, G. M., *Urkunden zur älteren Handels- und Staatsgeschichte der Republik Venedig*, II, III [see Gen. Bibl. IV].
Thiriet, F., *Régestes des délibérations du Sénat de Venise*, I–III [see Gen. Bibl. IV].
Thomas, G. M., *Diplomatarium Veneto-Levantinum sive Acta et diplomata res Venetas, Graecas atque Levantis illustrantia (1300–1454)*, 2 vols. (Venice, 1880–99).
Uspensky, F. I. and Beneševič, V., *Actes de Vazélon* (Leningrad, 1927).
Zepos, J. and P., *Jus graeco-romanum*, I–VIII [see Gen. Bibl. IV].

II. MODERN WORKS

Anastasijević, D., 'Jedina vizantijska carica Srpkinja' ['A Byzantine Empress of Serbian descent'], *Brastvo*, XXX (1939), 26–49.
Anastos, M. V., 'Pletho's Calendar and Liturgy', *DOP*, IV (1948), 183–305.
Andreeva, M. A., 'Zur Reise Manuels II. Palaiologos nach Westeuropa', *BZ*, XXXIV (1934), 37–47.
Andreeva, M. A., 'Torgovyj dogovor Vizantii i Dubrovnika 1451 g. i istorija ego podgotovki' ['The commercial treaty between Byzantium and Dubrovnik in 1451 and its background'], *BS*, VI (1934/5), 110–65; reprinted in part in *B*, x (1935), 117–27.
Atiya, A. S., *The Crusade of Nicopolis* [see Gen. Bibl. V].

Atiya, A. S., *The Crusade in the Later Middle Ages* [see Gen. Bibl. v].

Babinger, F., *Beiträge zur Frühgeschichte der Türkenherrschaft in Rumelien* (Südosteuropäische Arbeiten 34) (Brünn–Munich–Vienna, 1944).

Babinger, F., 'Von Amurath zu Amurath. Vor- und Nachspiel der Schlacht bei Varna', *Oriens*, III (1950), 229–65.

Babinger, F., 'La date de la prise de Trébizonde par les Turcs', *REB*, VII (1950), 205–7.

Banescu, N., 'Le patriarche Athanase Iᵉʳ et Andronic II Paléologue: état religieux, politique et social de l'empire', *Acad. Roumaine, Bull. sect. hist.* XXIII (1942), 28–56.

Beck, H.-G., *Theodoros Metochites. Die Krise des byzantinischen Weltbildes im 14. Jahrhundert* (Munich, 1952).

Bertelè, T., *Monete e sigilli di Anna di Savoia, imperatrice di Bisanzio* (Roma, 1937).

Binon, S., 'L'histoire et la légende de deux chrysobulles d'Andronic II en faveur de Monembasie', *EO*, XXXVII (1938), 274–331.

Binon, S., *Les origines légendaires et l'histoire de Xéropotamou et de St Paul de l'Athos* (Louvain, 1942).

Blanchet, A., 'Les dernières monnaies d'or des empereurs byzantins', *RN*, XIV (1910), 78–90.

Bois, J., 'Grégoire le Sinaite et l'Hésychasme à l'Athos au XIVᵉ siècle', *EO*, v (1901), 65–73.

Bois, J., 'Le synode hésychaste de 1341', *EO*, VI (1903), 50–60.

Bratianu, G. I., 'Notes sur le projet de mariage entre l'empereur Michel IX Paléologue et Cathérine de Courtenay', *RHSE*, I (1924), 59–63.

Bratianu, G. I., *Recherches sur le commerce génois dans la Mer Noire au XIIIᵉ siècle* (Paris, 1929).

Bratianu, G. I., *Recherches sur Vicina et Cetatea Albă* (Bucarest, 1935).

Bratianu, G. I., *Privilèges et franchises municipales dans l'Empire byzantin* (Paris–Bucharest, 1936).

Bratianu, G. I., *Etudes byzantines d'histoire économique et sociale* [see Gen. Bibl. v].

Canard, M., 'Un traité entre Byzance et l'Egypte au XIIIᵉ siècle et les relations diplomatiques de Michel VIII Paléologue avec les Sultans Mamlūks Baibars et Qualā'ūn', *Mélanges Gaudefroy-Demombynes* (Cairo, 1937), pp. 197–224.

Chapman, C., *Michel Paléologue* [see Gen. Bibl. v].

Charanis, P., 'An Important Short Chronicle of the Fourteenth Century', *B*, XIII (1938), 335–62.

Charanis, P., 'Internal Strife in Byzantium during the Fourteenth Century', *B*, XV (1940/1), 208–30.

Charanis, P., 'The Strife among the Palaeologi and the Ottoman Turks, 1370–1402', *B*, XVI (1942/3), 286–314.

Charanis, P., 'The Monastic Properties and the State in the Byzantine Empire' [see Gen. Bibl. v].

Charanis, P., 'On the Social Structure and Economic Organisation of the Byzantine Empire in the Thirteenth Century and Later', *BS*, XII (1951), 94–153.

Charanis, P., 'Economic Factors in the Decline of the Byzantine Empire', *Journ. Econ. Hist.* XIII (1953), 412–24.

Černousov, E., 'Duka, odin iz istorikov konca Vizantii' ['Ducas, one of the historians of the downfall of Byzantium'], *VV*, XXI (1914), 171–221.

Cirac Estopañan, S., *Bizancio y España. El legado de la basilissa María y de los déspotas Thomas y Esaú de Joannina*, 2 vols. (Barcelona, 1943).

Dade, E., *Versuche zur Wiedererrichtung der lateinischen Herrschaft in Konstantinopel im Rahmen der abendländischen Politik, 1261 bis etwa 1310* (Jena, 1938).

Darkó, J., 'Zum Leben des Laonikos Chalkokondyles', *BZ*, xxiv (1923/4), 29–39.

Darkó, E., 'Neue Beiträge zur Biographie des Laonikos Chalkokondyles', *BZ*, xxvii (1927), 276–85.

Darkó, E., 'Neue Emendationsvorschläge zu Laonikos Chalkokondyles', *BZ*, xxxii (1932), 2–12.

Delaville le Roulx, J., *La France en Orient au XIVᵉ siècle*, 2 vols. (Paris, 1886).

Dennis, G. T., *The Reign of Manuel II Palaeologus in Thessalonica* [see Gen. Bibl. v].

Destunis, G., 'Opyt biografii Georgija Frandzija' ['An essay on the life of George Phrantzes'], *ZMNP*, cclxxxvii (1893), 427–97.

Diehl, C., 'L'empire byzantin sous les Paléologues', *Etudes byzantines* [see Gen. Bibl. v].

Diehl, C., 'La colonie vénitienne à Constantinople à la fin du XIVᵉ siècle', *Etudes byzantines* [see Gen. Bibl. v].

Diehl, C., *Une république patricienne: Venise* (Paris, 1915).

Dölger, F., *Regesten der Kaiserurkunden des oströmischen Reiches* [see Gen. Bibl. iv].

Dölger, F., 'Johannes VII., Kaiser der Rhomäer', *BZ*, xxxi (1931), 21–36.

Dölger, F., 'Die Frage des Grundeigentums in Byzanz', *Bull. of the Intern. Committee of Hist. Sciences*, v (1933), 5–15.

Dölger, F., 'Die Krönung Johannes VIII. zum Mitkaiser', *BZ*, xxxvi (1936), 318–19.

Dölger, F., 'Ein literarischer und diplomatischer Fälscher des 16. Jahrhunderts: Metropolit Makarios von Monembasia', *O. Glauning Festschrift* (Leipzig, 1936), pp. 25–35; reprinted in *Byzantinische Diplomatik*, pp. 371–83 [see Gen. Bibl. v].

Dölger, F., 'Johannes VI. Kantakuzenos als dynastischer Legitimist', *Annales de l'Inst. Kondakov*, x (1938), 19–30; reprinted in ΠΑΡΑΣΠΟΡΑ, pp. 194–207 [see Gen. Bibl. v].

Dölger, F., 'Die dynastische Familienpolitik des Kaisers Michael VIII. Palaiologos', *Festschrift Eichmann* (1940), pp. 179–90; reprinted in ΠΑΡΑΣΠΟΡΑ, pp. 178–88.

Dölger, F., 'Einiges über Theodora, die Griechin, Zarin der Bulgaren (1308–1330)', *Mélanges H. Grégoire*, i = *AIPHO*, ix (1949), 211–21; reprinted in ΠΑΡΑΣΠΟΡΑ, pp. 222–30.

Dölger, F., 'Der Vertrag des Sultans Quālā'ūn von Ägypten mit dem Kaiser Michael VIII. Palaiologos (1281)', *Serta Monacensia, Festschrift Babinger* (Leiden, 1952), pp. 60–79; reprinted in *Byzantinische Diplomatik*, pp. 225–44 [see Gen. Bib. v].

Dräseke, J., 'Zu Johannes Kantakuzenos', *BZ*, ix (1900), 73–84.

Dräseke, J., 'Plethons und Bessarions Denkschriften über die Angelegenheiten im Peloponnes', *Neue Jahrb. f. d. klass. Altertum*, xxvii (1911), 102–19.

Dräseke, J., 'Der Übergang der Osmanen nach Europa im 14. Jahrhundert', *ibid.* xxxi (1913), 476–504.

Engelhardt, J. G. V., 'Die Arsenianer und Hesychasten', *Zeit. f. d. Gesch. Theologie*, viii (1838), 48 ff.

Fallmerayer, J. P., *Geschichte des Kaiserthums von Trapezunt* (Munich, 1827).

Fallmerayer, J. P., *Geschichte der Halbinsel Morea*, II (Stuttgart, 1836).

Florinsky, T., *Južnye Slavjane i Vizantija vo vtoroj četverti XIV veka* [*The South Slavs and Byzantium in the second quarter of the 14th century*] (St Petersburg, 1882).

Florinsky, T., 'Andronik Mladšij i Ioann Kantakuzin' ['Andronicus the Younger and John Cantacuzenus'], *ZMNP*, CCIV (1879), 87–143, 219–51; CCV (1879), 1–48.

Gatto, I. *Il Pontificato di Gregorio X (1271–1276)* (Rome, 1959).

Gay, J., *Le pape Clément VI et les affaires d'Orient (1342–1352)* (Paris, 1904).

Gay, J., 'Notes sur le second royaume français de Sicile et la papauté d'Urbain IV à Boniface VIII (1261–1302)', *Mélanges N. Jorga* (1933), pp. 309–29.

Geanakoplos, D. J., *Emperor Michael Palaeologus* [see Gen. Bibl. v].

Geanakoplos, D. J., 'Greco-Latin relations on the eve of the Byzantine Restoration: the Battle of Pelagonia—1259', *DOP*, VII (1953), 99–141.

Gill, J., *The Council of Florence* [see Gen. Bibl. v].

Gorjanov, B. T., 'Vosstanie žilotov v Vizantii (1342–1349)' ['The revolt of the Zealots in Byzantium'], *Izvestija Akad. Nauk SSSR*, III (1946), 92–6.

Grecu, V., 'Pour une meilleure connaissance de l'historien Doukas', *Mémorial L. Petit* (Bucharest, 1948), pp. 128–41.

Grumel, V., *La Chronologie* [see Gen. Bibl. III].

Grumel, V., 'En Orient après le IIᵉ concile de Lyon', *EO*, XXIV (1925), 321–5.

Güterbock, K., 'Laonikos Chalkondyles', *Zeit. f. Völkerrecht und Bundesstaatsrecht*, IV (1909), 72–102.

Guilland, R., 'Le Palais de Métochite', *REG*, XXXV (1922), 82–95.

Guilland, R., *Essai sur Nicéphore Grégoras* (Paris, 1926).

Guilland, R., 'Les poésies inédites de Théodore Métochite', *B*, III (1926), 265–302.

Guilland, R., 'La correspondance inédite de Nicolas Cabasilas', *BZ*, XXX (1930), 96–102.

Guilland, R., 'La correspondance inédite d'Athanase, Patriarche de Constantinople (1289–1293; 1304–1310)', *Mélanges Ch. Diehl*, I (1930), 121–40; reprinted in *Etudes byzantines*, pp. 53–79 [see Gen. Bibl. v].

Halecki, O., *Un empereur de Byzance à Rome. Vingt ans de travail pour l'union des églises et pour la défense de l'Empire d'Orient: 1355–1375* (Warsaw, 1930).

Halecki, O., *The Crusade of Varna* (New York, 1943).

Halecki, O., 'Two Palaeologi in Venice, 1370–1371', *B*, XVII (1944/5), 331–5.

Hart, T. A., 'Nicephorus Gregoras: Historian of the Hesychast Controversy', *JEH*, II (1951), 169–80.

Heisenberg, A., *Aus der Geschichte und Literatur der Palaiologenzeit*, *SBAW* (1920), Abh. x (Munich, 1920).

Heyd, W., *Histoire du commerce du Levant au moyen âge* [see Gen. Bibl. v].

Hofmann, G., 'Die Konzilsarbeit in Ferrara', *OCP*, III (1937), 110–40, 403–55.

Hofmann, G., 'Die Konzilsarbeit in Florenz', *OCP*, IV (1938), 157–88, 372–422.

Hofmann, G., 'Rodrigo, Dekan von Braga; Kaiser Johann VIII. Palaiologos. Zwei Briefe aus Konstantinopel, 13. Oktober und 18. November 1437, zur Vorgeschichte des Konzils von Florenz', *OCP*, IX (1943), 171–87.

Hofmann, G., 'Ein Brief des Kardinals Isidor von Kiew an Kardinal Bessarion', *OCP*, XIV (1948), 405–14.

Hopf, K., *Geschichte Griechenlands vom Beginn des Mittelalters bis auf unsere Zeit* [see Gen. Bibl. v].

Inalcik, H., 'Mehmed the Conqueror (1432–1481) and his time', *SP*, xxv (1960), 408–27.

Jakovenko, P. A., *K istorii immuniteta v Vizantii [On the history of the immunity in Byzantium]* (Jurjev, 1908).

Jorga, N., *Philippe de Mézières et la croisade au XIVe siècle* (Paris, 1896).

Jorga, N., 'Latins et Grecs d'Orient et l'établissement des Turcs en Europe, 1342–62', *BZ*, xv (1906), 179–222.

Jorga, N., *Geschichte des osmanischen Reiches*, 2 vols. (Gotha, 1908, 1909).

Jugie, M., 'Le voyage de l'empereur Manuel Paléologue en Occident (1399–1403)', *EO*, xv (1912), 322–32.

Jugie, M., 'Démétrius Cydonès et la théologie latine à Byzance aux XIVe et XVe siècles', *EO*, xxvii (1928), 385 ff.

Kampuroglu, D. G., Οἱ Χαλκοκονδύλαι (Athens, 1926).

Každan, A. P., 'Vizantijskoe sel'skoe poselenie' ['The Byzantine village settlement'], *VV*, n.s. ii (1949), 215–44.

Kling, G., *Die Schlacht bei Nikopolis im Jahre 1396*, Diss. (Berlin, 1906).

Kretschmayr, H., *Geschichte von Venedig* [see Gen. Bibl. v].

Krivochein, (Archbishop) Basil, 'The Ascetic and Theological Teachings of Gregory Palamas', *ECQ*, iii (1938) = Mönch Wassilij, 'Die asketische und theologische Lehre des hl. Gregorius Palamas', *Das Östl. Christentum*, viii (1939).

Lameere, W., *La tradition manuscrite de la correspondance de Grégoire de Chypre* (Brussels–Rome, 1937).

Laurent, V., 'La correspondance de Démétrius Cydonès', *EO*, xxx (1931), 339–54.

Laurent, V., 'Un nouveau témoin de la correspondance de Démétrius Cydonès', Ἑλληνικά, ix (1936), 185–205.

Laurent, V., 'Notes de chronographie et d'histoire byzantine', *EO*, xxxvi (1937), 157–74.

Laurent, V., 'Grégoire X (1271–1276) et un projet de ligue antiturque', *EO*, xxxvii (1938), 257–73.

Laurent, V., 'La croisade et la question d'Orient sous le pontificat de Grégoire X (1272–1276)', *RHSE*, xxii (1945), 105–37.

Laurent, V., 'Le dernier gouverneur byzantin de Constantinople: Démétrius Paléologue Métochite, Grand Stratopédarque (†1453)', *REB* xv (1957), 196–206.

Laurent, V., 'Le rapport de Georges le Métochite, apocrisiaire de Michel VIII Paléologue auprès du pape Grégoire X, 1275/76', *RHSE*, xxiii (1946), 233–47.

Laurent, V., 'La chronologie des patriarches de Constantinople de la première moitié du XIVe siècle (1294–1350)', *REB*, vii (1950), 145–55.

Laurent, V., 'La chronique anonyme du cod. Mosquensis gr. 426 et la pénétration turque en Bithynie au début du XIVe siècle', *REB*, vii (1950), 207–12.

Lebedev, A. P., *Istoričeskie očerki položenija vizantijskoj vostočnoj cerkvi s konca XI do serediny XV veka [Historical studies on the state of the Byzantine Eastern Church from the end of the 11th century to the middle of the 15th century]* (Moscow, 1902).

Lemerle, P., *Philippes et la Macédonie orientale à l'époque chrétienne et byzantine* (Paris, 1945).

Lemerle, P., 'Le juge général des Grecs et la réforme judiciaire d'Andronic III', *Mémorial L. Petit* (Bucharest, 1948), pp. 292–316.

Lemerle, P., 'Recherches sur les institutions judiciaires à l'époque des Paléologues I: le tribunal impérial', *Mélanges H. Grégoire*, I = *AIPHO*, IX (1949), 369–84.

Lemerle, P., 'Recherches sur les institutions judiciaires à l'époque des Paléologues II: le tribunal du patriarcat ou tribunal synodal', *Mélanges P. Peeters*, II = *AB*, LXVIII (1950), 318–33.

Lemerle, P., *L'émirat d'Aydin, Byzance et l'Occident: recherches sur 'La geste d'Umur Pacha'* (Paris, 1957).

Loenertz, R.-J., 'Manuel Paléologue et Démétrius Cydonès. Remarques sur leurs correspondances', *EO*, XXXVI (1937), 271–87, 474–87; XXXVII (1938), 107–24.

Loenertz, R.-J., 'Démétrius Cydonès citoyen de Venise', *EO*, XXXVII (1938), 125–6.

Loenertz, R.-J., 'La première insurrection d'Andronic IV Paléologue (1373)', *EO*, XXXVIII (1939), 334–45.

Loenertz, R.-J., 'La date de la lettre de Manuel Paléologue et l'inauthenticité du "Chronicon maius" de Georges Phrantzès', *EO*, XXXIX (1940), 91–9.

Loenertz, R.-J., 'Pour l'histoire du Péloponnèse au XIVe siècle (1382–1404)', *EB*, I (1943), 152–96.

Loenertz, R.-J., 'Pour la biographie du cardinal Bessarion', *OCP*, X (1944), 116–49.

Loenertz, R.-J., 'Autour du Chronicon maius attribué à Georges Phrantzès', *Miscellanea G. Mercati*, III (Studi e Testi, 123) (Vatican, 1946), 273–311.

Loenertz, R.-J., *Les recueils des lettres de Démétrius Cydonès* (Studi e Testi, 131) (Vatican, 1947).

Loenertz, R.-J., 'Jean V Paléologue à Venise (1370–1371)', *REB*, XVI (1958), 217–32.

Longnon, J., *L'empire latin de Constantinople et la principauté de Morée* [see Gen. Bibl. v].

Marinescu, C., 'Le pape Nicolas V (1447–1455) et son attitude envers l'Empire byzantin', *Izvestija Bŭlg. Arch. Inst.* IX (1935), 331–42.

Mercati, A., 'Il decreto d'unione del 6 luglio 1439 nell'Archivio Segreto Vaticano', *OCP*, XI (1945), 5–44.

Mercati, G., *Notizie di Procoro e Demetrio Cidone, Manuele Caleca e Teodoro Meliteniota, ed altri appunti per la storia della teologia e della litteratura bizantina del secolo XIV* (Studi e Testi, 56) (Vatican, 1931).

Mercati, G., 'Per l'epistolario di Demetrio Cidone', *SBN*, III (1931), 201–30.

Mertzios, K., Μνημεῖα Μακεδονικῆς Ἱστορίας (Thessalonica, 1947).

Meyendorff, J., 'Jean-Joasaph Cantacuzène et le projet de concile œcuménique en 1367', *Akten des XI. Internat. Byz.-Kongresses: Munich, 1958* (Munich, 1960), pp. 363–9.

Meyendorff, J., *Introduction à l'étude de Grégoire Palamas* (Patristica Sorbonensia, 3) (Paris, 1959).

Miller, W., *The Latins in the Levant. A History of Frankish Greece (1204–1566)* (London, 1908).

Miller, W., *Essays on the Latin Orient* (Cambridge, 1921).

Miller, W., *Trebizond, the Last Greek Empire* (London, 1926).

Miller, W., 'The Historians Doukas and Phrantzes', *JHS*, XLVI (1926), 63–71.

Miller, W., 'The Last Athenian Historian: Laonikos Chalkokondyles', *JHS*, XLII (1922), 36–50.

Mompherratos, A., Διπλωματικαὶ ἐνέργειαι Μανουὴλ Β′ τοῦ Παλαιολόγου ἐν Εὐρώπῃ καὶ Ἀσίᾳ (Athens, 1913).

Mordtmann, J. H., 'Die erste Eroberung von Athen durch die Türken zu Ende des 14. Jahrhunderts', *BNJ*, IV (1923), 346–50.

Muratore, D., *Una principessa Sabauda sul trono di Bizanzio — Giovanna di Savoia imperatrice Anna Paleologina* (Chambéry, 1905).

Mutafčiev, P., 'Vojniški zemi i vojnici v Vizantija prez XIII–XIV v.' ['Military holdings and soldiers in Byzantium during the XIII and XIV centuries'], *Spisanie na Bŭlg. Akad. na naukite*, XXVII (Sofia, 1923), 1–113.

Nicol, D. M., 'The Date of the Battle of Pelagonia', *BZ*, XLIX (1956), 68–71.

Nicol, D. M., *The Despotate of Epiros* [see Gen. Bibl. v].

Nicolau d'Olwer, L., *L'Expansió de Catalunya en la Mediterrània oriental* (Barcelona, 1926).

Nimet, A., *Die türkische Prosopographie bei Laonikos Chalkokandyles*, Diss. (Hamburg, 1933).

Norden, W., *Das Papsttum und Byzanz* [see Gen. Bibl. v].

Oberhummer, E., *Die Türken und das osmanische Reich* (Leipzig–Berlin, 1917).

Obolensky, D., 'Byzantium, Kiev and Moscow: a Study in Ecclesiastical Relations', *DOP*, XI (1957), 21–78.

Ostrogorsky, G., 'Afonskie isichasty i ich protivniki' ['The Hesychasts of Athos and their opponents'], *Zapiski Russk. Naučn. Inst. v Belgrade*, V (1931), 349–70.

Ostrogorsky, G., 'Agrarian Conditions in the Byzantine Empire in the Middle Ages' [see Gen. Bibl. v].

Ostrogorsky, G., 'Vizantijskie piscovye knigi' ['The Byzantine Court rolls—practica'], *BS*, IX (1947–8), 203–306; French transl. in *Pour l'histoire de la féodalité byzantine* [see below].

Ostrogorsky, G., 'Le grand domaine dans l'Empire byzantin', *Recueils de la Société Jean Bodin IV : Le Domaine* (Wetteren, 1949), pp. 35–50.

Ostrogorsky, G., *Pronija, Prilog istoriji feudalizma u Vizantiji i u južnosloven-skim zemljama* (Belgrade, 1951); French transl. *Pour l'histoire de la féodalité byzantine* [see Gen Bibl. v].

Ostrogorsky, G., 'Byzance, état tributaire de l'Empire turc', *Zbornik radova Vizantološkog instituta*, V (1958), 49–58.

Ostrogorsky, G., 'Pour l'histoire de l'immunité à Byzance', *B*, XXVIII (1958, publ. 1959), 165–254.

Pall, F., 'Ciriaco d'Ancona e la crociata contro i Turchi', *Bull. hist. de l'Acad. Roumaine*, XX (1937), 9–60.

Pall, F., 'Autour de la croisade de Varna: la question de la paix de Szeged et de sa rupture (1444)', *ibid.* XXII (1941), 144–58.

Pall, F., 'Un moment décisif de l'histoire du Sud-Est européen: la croisade de Varna', *Balcania*, VII (1944), 102–20.

Pančenko, B. A., 'Krest'janskaja sobstvennost' v Vizantii' ['Peasant ownership in Byzantium'], *IRAIK*, IX (1904), 1–234.

Papadopulos, A., *Versuch einer Genealogie der Palaiologen, 1259–1453*, Diss. (Munich, 1938).

Papadopulos, J. B., 'Ἰωάννης Ζ' ὁ Παλαιολόγος καὶ τὸ Χρονικὸν τοῦ Φραντζῆ', *BZ*, XXXII (1932), 257–62.

Papadopulos, J. B., 'Phrantzès est-il réellement l'auteur de la grande chronique qui porte son nom?', *Izvestija Bŭlg. Arch. Inst.* IX (1935), 177–89.

Papadopulos, J. B., 'Über "Maius" und "Minus" des Georgios Phrantzes und über die Randnoten des angeblichen Pachomios', *BZ*, XXXVIII (1938), 323–31.

Papamichael, G., Ὁ ἅγιος Γρηγόριος ὁ Παλαμᾶς ἀρχιεπίσκοπος Θεσσαλονίκης (St Petersburg and Alexandria, 1911).
Parisot, V., *Cantacuzène homme d'état et historien* (Paris, 1845).
Pears, E., *The Destruction of the Greek Empire* [see Gen. Bibl. v].
Petit, L., 'La réforme judiciaire d'Andronic Paléologue (1329)', *EO*, IX (1906), 134–8.
Radonić, J., *Zapadna Evropa i balkanski narodi prema Turcima u prvoj polovini XV veka* [*Western Europe and the Balkan peoples before the Turks in the first half of the 15th century*] (Novi Sad, 1905).
Radonić, J., 'Kritovul, vizantijski istorik XV veka' ['Critobulus, the Byzantine historian of the 15th century'], *Glas*, CXXXVIII (1930), 59–83.
Radonić, J., *Djuradj Kastriot Skenderbeg i Arbanija u XV veku* [*George Castriota Scanderbeg and Albania in the XVth century*] (Spomenik 90) (Belgrade, 1942).
Rouillard, G., 'La politique de Michel VIII Paléologue à l'égard des monastères', *EB*, I (1943), 73–84.
Rubió y Lluch, A., *La Expedición y Dominación de los Catalanes en Oriente* (Barcelona, 1883).
Rubió y Lluch, A., *Los Navarros en Grecia y el Ducado catalán de Atenas en la Época de su Invasión* (Barcelona, 1886).
Rubió y Lluch, A., 'Atenes en temps dels Catalans', *Anuari de l'Inst. d'Estudis Catal.* I (1907), 225–54. [For the other works of this author see K. M. Setton, *Catalan Domination of Athens*, pp. 286 ff. and Bibliography for chapter IX.]
Runciman, S., *The Sicilian Vespers* [see Gen. Bibl. v].
Schlumberger, G., *Expéditions des 'Almugavares' ou routiers catalans en Orient* (Paris, 1902).
Schlumberger, G., *Un empereur de Byzance à Paris et à Londres* (Paris, 1916).
Setton, K. M., *Catalan Domination of Athens 1311–1388* [see Gen. Bibl. v].
Ševčenko, I., 'Nicolas Cabasilas' "Anti-Zealot" Discourse: a Reinterpretation', *DOP*, XI (1957), 81–171.
Silberschmidt, M., *Das orientalische Problem zur Zeit der Entstehung des türkischen Reiches nach venezianischen Quellen. Ein Beitrag zur Geschichte der Beziehungen Venedigs zu Byzanz, Ungarn und Genua und zum Reich von Kiptschak (1381–1400)* (Leipzig–Berlin, 1923).
Skržinskaja, E. C., 'Genuezcy v Konstantinopole v XIV veke' ['The Genoese in Constantinople in the 14th century'], *VV*, n.s. I (1947), 213–34.
Skržinskaja, E. C., 'Petrarka o genuezcach na Levante' ['Petrarch on the Genoese in the Levant'], *VV*, n.s. II (1949), 245–66.
Sokolov, J., 'Krupnye i melkie vlasteli v Fessalii v epochu Paleologov' ['Great and lesser magnates in Thessaly'], *VV*, XXIV (1923–6), 35–44.
Sokolov, N. P., 'Venecija i Vizantija pri pervych Paleologach (1263–1328)' ['Venice and Byzantium under the first Palaeologi'], *VV*, n.s. XII (1957), 75–96.
Solovjev, A., 'Fessalijskie archonty v XIV veke' ['Thessalian Archons in the XIVth century'], *BS*, IV (1932), 159–74.
Stein, E., 'Untersuchungen zur spätbyzantinischen Verfassungs- und Wirtschaftsgeschichte' [see Gen. Bibl. v].
Tafrali, O., *Thessalonique au XIVᵉ siècle* [see Gen. Bibl. v].
Thiriet, F., 'Les chroniques vénitiennes de la Marcienne et leur importance pour l'histoire de la Romanie gréco-vénitienne', *Mélanges d'Archéol. et d'Hist.* LXVI (1954), 241–92.

Tozer, H. F., 'A Byzantine Reformer', *JHS*, VII (1886), 353–80.

Udalcova, Z. V., 'Bor'ba partij v Vizantii XV v. i dejatel'nost Vissariona Nikejskogo' ['Party struggles in Byzantium in the 15th century and the activity of Bessarion of Nicaea'], *VV*, n.s. II (1949), 294–307.

Uspensky, F. I., 'Značenie vizantijskoj i južnoslavjanskoj pronii' ['The significance of the Byzantine and South-Slav pronoia'], *Sbornik statej po slavjanovedeniju sostavlennyj i izdannyj učenikami V. I. Lamanskago* (1883), pp. 1–32.

Uspensky, F. I., *Očerki po istorii vizantijskoj obrazovannosti* [*Studies in the History of Byzantine Civilisation*] (St Petersburg, 1891).

Uspensky, F. I., 'Bolgarskie Asenoviči na vizantijskoj službe v XIII–XIV v.' ['The Bulgarian Asenoviči in the service of Byzantium in the 13th and 14th centuries'], *IRAIK*, XIII (1908), 1–16.

Uspensky, F. I., 'Social'naja evoljucija i feodalizacija Vizantii' ['Social evolution and feudalisation of Byzantium'], *Annaly*, II (1923), 95–114.

Uspensky, F. I., 'Vizantijskie istoriki o mongolach i egipetskich mamljukach' ['Byzantine historians on the Mongols and Egyptian Mamluks'], *VV*, XXIV (1923/6), 1–36.

Uspensky, F. I., *Očerki po istorii Trapezuntskoj imperii* [*Studies in the history of the Empire of Trebizond*] (Leningrad, 1929).

Uspensky, F. I., 'Morskoe i suchoputnoe dviženie iz central'noj Azii v Evropu i obratno v XIII–XIV vv.' ['Traffic by sea and land from Central Asia to Europe and back in the 13th–14th centuries'], *VV*, n.s. II (1949), 267–75.

Vakalopoulos, A., 'Les limites de l'empire byzantin depuis la fin du XIVe siècle jusqu'à sa chute (1453)', *BZ*, LV (1962), 56–65.

Vasiliev, A. A., 'Putešestvie vizantijskogo imperatora Manuila II Paleologa po zapadnoj Evrope' ['The journey of the Byzantine Emperor Manuel II Palaeologus in Western Europe'], *ZMNP*, n.s. XXXIX (1912), 41–78, 260–304.

Vasiliev, A. A., 'Il viaggio dell'imperatore bizantino Giovanni V Paleologo in Italia (1369–1371) e l'Unione di Roma del 1369', *SBN*, III (1931), 151–93.

Vasilievsky, V. G., 'Materialy dlja vnutrennej istorii vizantijskago gosudarstva' ['Materials for the internal history of the Byzantine state'], *ZMNP*, CCII (1879), 160–232 (= *Trudy*, IV, 250–331), 368–438; CCX (1880), 98–170, 355–440.

Vernadsky, G. V., 'Zolotaja Orda, Egipet i Vizantija v ich vzaimootnošenijach v carstvovanie Michaila Paleologa' ['The Golden Horde, Egypt and Byzantium and their relationships during the reign of Michael Palaeologus'], *Sem. Kond.* I (1927), 73–84.

Verpeaux, J., *Nicéphore Choumnos, homme d'état et humaniste byzantin (c. 1250/1255–1327)* (Paris, 1959).

Viller, M., 'La question de l'Union des églises entre Grecs et Latins depuis le concile de Lyon jusqu'à celui de Florence', *RHE*, XVI (1921), 260–305, 515–32; XVIII (1922), 20–60.

Wittek, P., *Das Fürstentum Mentesche. Studie zur Geschichte Westkleinasiens im 13.–15. Jh.* (Istanbul, 1934).

Wittek, P., *The Rise of the Ottoman Empire* [see Gen. Bibl. v].

Wittek, P., 'Chroniques mineures byzantines', *B*, XII (1937), 309–23.

Xivrey, Berger de, *Mémoire sur la vie et les ouvrages de l'empereur Manuel Paléologue* [see Gen. Bibl. v].

Zachariae von Lingenthal, K. E., *Geschichte des griechisch-römischen Rechts* (Berlin, 1892).
Zakythinos, D. A., *Le despotat grec de Morée* [see Gen. Bibl. v].
Zakythinos, D. A., *Crise monétaire et crise économique à Byzance du XIIIᵉ au XVᵉ siècle* [see Gen. Bibl. v].

CHAPTER IX. THE LATINS IN GREECE AND THE AEGEAN FROM THE FOURTH CRUSADE TO THE END OF THE MIDDLE AGES

See also the bibliographies for chapters VIII, X and XII.

I. SPECIAL BIBLIOGRAPHIES

American Historical Association's Guide to Historical Literature (New York, 1961), esp. pp. 186–232.
Argenti, P. P., *Bibliography of Chios from Classical Times to 1936* (Oxford, 1940).
Atiya, A. S., *The Crusade in the Later Middle Ages* (London, 1938), pp. 490–509, 537–69.
Cobham, C. D., *Excerpta Cypria. Materials for a History of Cyprus* (Cambridge, 1908).
Cobham, C. D., *An Attempt at a Bibliography of Cyprus*, new ed. G. Jeffery (Cyprus, 1929).
Dix Années d'Etudes byzantines: Bibliographie Internationale, 1939–1948 [see Gen. Bibl. ɪ].
Gibbons, H. A., *The Foundation of the Ottoman Empire*, pp. 319–68 [contains some inaccuracies] [see Gen. Bibl. v].
Hellwald, F. de, *Bibliographie méthodique de l'ordre souverain de St Jean de Jérusalem, rédigée et publiée sous les auspices du grand maître* (Rome, 1885).
Hill, Sir George, *A History of Cyprus*, ɪɪ, pp. xiii–xl [see Gen. Bibl. v].
Legrand, E. and Pernot, H., *Bibliographie ionienne*, 2 vols. (Paris, 1910).
Miller, W., *The Latins in the Levant* (London, 1908); Greek transl. S. P. Lampros, Ἱστορία τῆς Φραγκοκρατίας ἐν Ἑλλάδι, ɪɪ (Athens, 1909–10), pp. 445–58.
Moravcsik, Gy., *Byzantinoturcica* [see Gen. Bibl. ɪ].
Setton, K. M., *Catalan Domination of Athens*, pp. 261–301 [see Gen. Bibl. v].
Zakythinos, D. A., *Le despotat grec de Morée*, ɪ, 303–16 [see Gen. Bibl. v].

II. PRIMARY AUTHORITIES

(A) VENETIAN DOCUMENTS

Archivio di Stato di Venezia, Deliberazioni Miste. Registers: vols. ɪ [1300–1302], xv–lx [4 March 1332 to 28 September 1440]. Rubrics: vols. ɪ–ɪv [1293–1440]. [For the period covered by the present volume complete microfilms of the *Deliberazioni Miste, Segrete, Mar*, and *Terra* exist in the Henry C. Lea Library of Medieval History, University of Pennsylvania.]

Giomo, G., 'Le Rubriche dei Libri *Misti* del Senato perduti', *Arch. Ven.* XVII, 126–40, 251–73; XVIII, 40–69, 315–38; XIX, 90–117; XX, 81–95, 293–313; XXIII, 66–83, 406–24; XXIV, 82–110, 309–28; XXVII, 91–105, 374–94 (Venice, 1879–84).

Giomo, G., 'Regesto di alcune deliberazioni del Senato *Misti*', *ibid.* XXIX, 403–10; XXX, 153–62; XXXI, 179–200 (Venice, 1885–6).

Giomo, G., *Lettere di Collegio, rectius Minor Consiglio 1308–10* (Venice, 1910).

Jorga, N., *Notes et extraits pour servir à l'histoire des Croisades au XVᵉ siècle*, 6 vols. (Paris and Bucharest, 1899–1916).

Jorga, N., 'Nouveaux documents sur l'Orient vénitien, d'après des registres de notaires aux Archives de Venise', Acad. Roum., *Bull. sect. hist.* XII (1935), 217–25.

Lamansky, V., *Secrets d'état de Venise* (St Petersburg, 1884).

Lampros, S. P., ''Έγγραφα ἐκ τοῦ Archivio di Stato in Venezia', *NE*, XXI (1927), 142–58. [Concerning the Catalan Grand Company, 1305–25; documents carelessly transcribed.]

Lampros, S. P., 'Συνθήκη μεταξὺ Ἰωάννου Η' Παλαιολόγου καὶ τοῦ δουκὸς τῆς Βενετίας Φραγκίσκου Φόσκαρη', *NE*, XII (1915), 153–97. [New edition of the document in MM, III, 216–24.]

Ljubić, S., *Monumenta spectantia historiam Slavorum meridionalium* (*MHSM*), III, IV, IX, XXII (1872–91).

Manousakas, M. I., 'Νέα ἀνέκδοτα βενετικὰ ἔγγραφα (1386–1420) περὶ τοῦ Κρητὸς ποιητοῦ Λεονάρδου Ντελλαπόρτα', Κρητικὰ Χρονικά, XII (1958–9), 387–434.

Manousakas, M. I., 'Μέτρα τῆς Βενετίας ἔναντι τῆς ἐν Κρήτῃ ἐπιρροῆς τοῦ Πατριαρχείου Κωνσταντινουπόλεως κατ' ἀνέκδοτα βενετικὰ ἔγγραφα (1418–1419)', *EEBS*, XXX (1960), 85–144.

Manousakas, M. I., 'Βενετικὰ ἔγγραφα ἀναφερόμενα εἰς τὴν ἐκκλησιαστικὴν ἱστορίαν τῆς Κρήτης τοῦ 14ᵒᵘ–16ᵒᵘ αἰῶνος', *D*, XV (1960–1), 149–233.

Mas Latrie, L. de, *Documents concernant divers pays de l'Orient latin, 1382–1413* (Paris, 1897). (*Extrait de la B. de l'Ecole des Chartes*, LVIII, 78–125.)

Miller, W. and Giomo, G., 'Le Rubriche dei Misti del Senato, Libri XV–XLIV', *D*, VII (1910), 69–119.

Morozzo della Rocca, R. and Lombardo, A., *Documenti del commercio veneziano nei secoli XI–XIII*, 2 vols. (Turin, 1940).

Mosto, Andrea da, *L'Archivio di Stato di Venezia*, 2 vols. (Rome, 1937–40). [A descriptive and historical survey of the Venetian State Archives, publ. as vol. V of *Bibliothèque des 'Annales Institutorum'*.]

Noiret, H., *Documents inédits pour servir à l'histoire de la domination vénitienne en Crète de 1380 à 1485* (Paris, 1892).

Predelli, R., 'Il Liber Communis detto anche Plegiorum', *Arch. Ven.* III ff. (Venice, 1872 ff.).

Predelli, R., *I Libri Commemoriali della Repubblica di Venezia, regesti*, 8 vols. (Venice, 1876–1914).

Relazioni degli Ambasciatori Veneti, I–IV (Florence, 1840–63).

Sathas, K. N., Μνημεῖα Ἑλληνικῆς Ἱστορίας [see Gen. Bibl. IV].

Tafel, G. L. F. and Thomas, G. M., *Urkunden zur älteren Handels- und Staatsgeschichte der Republik Venedig* [see Gen. Bibl. IV].

Theotokes, S. M., ''Η δῆθεν ἀφορμὴ τῆς ἀποστασίας τῆς Κρήτης τοῦ 1363', *EEBS*, VIII (1931), 206–13.

Theotokes, S. M., 'Πρεσβεία Ρογήρου de Lluria πρὸς τὴν βενετικὴν γερουσίαν 25. Ἰουλίου 1365 γ' Ἰνδικτιῶνος', *EEBS*, VIII (1931), 200–5.

Theotokes, S. M., Ἱστορικὰ Κρητικὰ ἔγγραφα ἐκδιδόμενα ἐκ τοῦ Ἀρχείου τῆς Βενετίας · Ἀποφάσεις Μείζονος Συμβουλίου Βενετίας (Maggior Consiglio, 1255–1669). Μνημεῖα τῆς Ἑλληνικῆς Ἱστορίας, I, i (Athens, 1933).

Thiriet, F., *Regestes des délibérations du Sénat de Venise concernant la Romanie* [see Gen. Bibl. IV].

Thomas, G. M., *Der Doge Andreas Dandolo...mit dem Original-Register des Liber Albus, des Liber Blancus, und der Libri Pactorum* (Munich, 1855).

Thomas, G. M. and Predelli, R., *Diplomatarium Veneto-Levantinum (1300–1454)*, 2 vols. (Venice, 1880–99).

(B) NEAPOLITAN DOCUMENTS

Barone, N., 'Notizie storiche di Re Carlo III di Durazzo', *ASPN*, XII (Naples, 1887), 5–30, 185–208, and cf. *ibid.* pp. 493–512, 725–39, for 'Notizie storiche' of Ladislas of Durazzo.

Del Giudice, G., *Codice diplomatico del regno di Carlo I e II d'Angiò (1265–70)*, 3 vols. (Naples, 1863–1902).

Del Giudice, G., *La famiglia di Re Manfredi*, 2nd ed. (Naples, 1896).

Minieri-Riccio, C., *Studi storici su' fascicoli angioini* (Naples, 1863).

Minieri-Riccio, C., *Alcuni fatti riguardanti Carlo I di Angiò dal 6 di Agosto 1252 al 30 di Dicembre 1270* (Naples, 1874).

Minieri-Riccio, C., *Il regno di Carlo I di Angiò negli anni 1271 e 1272* (Naples, 1875).

Minieri-Riccio, C., 'Il regno di Carlo I di Angiò, dal 2 Gennaio 1273 al 31 Dicembre 1283', *ASI*, ser. 3, XXII–ser. 4, V (Florence, 1875–80).

Minieri-Riccio, C., *Della dominazione angioina nel reame di Sicilia* (Naples, 1876).

Minieri-Riccio, C., *Nuovi studi riguardanti la dominazione angioina nel regno di Sicilia* (Naples, 1876).

Minieri-Riccio, C., *Studi storici fatti sopra 84 registri angioini* (Naples, 1876).

Minieri-Riccio, C., *Notizie storiche tratte da 62 registri angioini* (Naples, 1877).

Minieri-Riccio, C., *Saggio di codice diplomatico*, 2 vols. with supplt. (Naples, 1878–83).

Minieri-Riccio, C., 'Il regno di Carlo I d'Angiò, dal 4 Gennaio 1284 al 7 Gennaio 1285', *ASI*, ser. 4, VII (Florence, 1881).

(C) PAPAL DOCUMENTS

Epistolarum Innocentii III libri XVI, ed. E. Baluze, 2 vols. (Paris, 1682). Also *MPL*, CCXIV–CCXVII.

Honorii III Opera, ed. C. A. Horoy, 4 vols. (Paris, 1879–82).

Regesta Honorii Papae III, ed. P. Pressutti, 2 vols. (Rome, 1885–95).

Les registres de Grégoire IX (1227–1241), ed. L. Auvray, I, II and III, pts. 1 and 2, *EcfrAR* (Paris, 1896–1910).

Les registres d'Innocent IV (1243–1254), ed. E. Berger, I–IV, *EcfrAR* (Paris, 1884–1919).

Les registres d'Alexandre IV (1254–1261), ed. C. Bourel de la Roncière, J. de Loye and A. Coulon, 2 vols. [6 fascicules; 7th now in preparation], *EcfrAR* (Paris, 1895 ff.).

Les registres d'Urbain IV (1261–1264), ed. J. Guiraud, 4 vols. (12 fascs.), *EcfrAR* (Paris, 1901 ff.).

Les registres de Clément IV (1265–1268), ed. E. Jordan, *EcfrAR* (Paris, 1893 ff.).

Les registres de Grégoire X et Jean XXI (1271–1277), ed. J. Guiraud and L. Cadier, *EcfrAR* (Paris, 1892 ff.).

Les registres de Nicolas III (1277–1280), ed. J. Gay, *EcfrAR* (Paris, 1898 ff.).

Les registres de Martin IV (1281–1285), ed. Ecole française de Rome, I, pts. 1, 2 and 3, *EcfrAR* (Paris, 1901 ff.).

Les registres d'Honorius IV (1285–1287), ed. M. Prou, I (4 fascs.), *EcfrAR* (Paris, 1888 ff.).

Les registres de Nicolas IV (1288–1292), ed. E. Langlois, 2 vols. (9 fascs.), *EcfrAR* (Paris, 1886 ff.).

Les registres de Boniface VIII (1294–1303), ed. G. Digard, M. Faucon and A. Thomas, 4 vols. (17 fascs.), *EcfrAR* (Paris, 1884 ff.).

Les registres de Benoît XI (1303–1304), ed. C. Grandjean, I, pts. 1–5, *EcfrAR* (Paris, 1905).

Clément V (1305–14), *Regestum Clementis Papae V*, Benedictine edition, 9 vols. (Rome, 1885–92).

Jean XXII (1316–34), *Lettres secrètes et curiales relatives à la France*, ed. A. Coulon, I, II, *EcfrAR* (Paris, 1900–6).

Jean XXII (1316–34), *Lettres communes*, ed. G. Mollat, I–XVI, *EcfrAR* (Paris, 1904–47).

Jean XXII (1316–34), *Lettres de*, ed. A. Fayen, I, II. Analecta vaticano-belgica, II, III (Rome, 1908–9).

Benoît XII (1334–42), *Lettres closes, patentes et curiales se rapportant à la France*, ed. G. Daumet, I, pts. 1, 2 and 3, *EcfrAR* (Paris, 1899–1902).

Benoît XII (1334–42), *Lettres communes*, ed. J. M. Vidal, I–III, *EcfrAR* (Paris, 1903–11).

Benoît XII (1334–1342), *Lettres closes et patentes intéressant les pays autres que la France*, ed. J. M. Vidal, I (6 fascs.), *EcfrAR* (Paris, 1913 ff.).

Clément VI (1342–52), *Lettres closes, patentes et curiales se rapportant à la France*, ed. E. Déprez, I, pts. 1 and 2, *EcfrAR* (Paris, 1901–25).

Clément VI (1342–52), *Lettres de*, ed. P. van Isacker, Analecta vaticano-belgica, VI (Rome, 1924).

Innocent VI (1352–62), *Lettres closes, patentes et curiales se rapportant à la France*, ed. E. Déprez, I, pt. 1, *EcfrAR* (Paris, 1909).

Urbain V (1362–70), *Les registres d'Urbain V*, ed. H. Dubrulle, I, *EcfrAR* (Paris, 1926).

Urbain V (1362–70), *Lettres secrètes et curiales se rapportant à la France*, ed. P. Lacacheux, I, pts. 1 and 2, *EcfrAR* (Paris, 1902–6).

(D) VARIOUS DOCUMENTS

Acta Aragonensia. Quellen zur deutschen, italienischen, französischen, spanischen, zur Kirchen- und Kulturgeschichte aus der diplomatischen Korrespondenz Jaymes II (1291–1327), ed. H. Finke, 3 vols. (Berlin and Leipzig, 1908–22).

Archives de l'Orient latin, 2 vols. (Paris, 1881–4).

Argenti, P. P., *Diplomatic Archive of Chios, 1577–1841*, 2 vols. (Cambridge, 1954).

Atti della Società ligure di storia patria (Genoa, 1859 ff., in progress).

Barbaro, C., *Legislazione veneta. I capitolari di Candia* (Venice, 1940).

Canciani, P., *Barbarorum leges antiquae*, III (Venice, 1785).

Cosentino, G., 'Cessione del Regno di Sicilia alla casa di Aragona fatta dal Re Federico III', *Archivio storico Siciliano*, ser. nuova, VII (1883), 184–202. [Docs. on pp. 196–202.]

Delaville le Roulx, J., *Cartulaire général de l'ordre des Hospitaliers de S. Jean de Jérusalem*, 4 vols. (Paris, 1894–1906).

Dennis, G. T., 'The Correspondence of Rodolfo de Sanctis, Canon of Patras, 1386', *Trad.* xvii (1961), 285–321.

'Documenti riguardanti alcuni dinasti dell'Arcipelago', *Giornale Ligústico di Archeologia, Storia, e Belle Arti*, i, 84–90, 217–21; ii, 86–93, 292–7; iii, 313–16; v, 345–72 (Genoa, 1874–8).

Guardione, F., *Sul dominio dei ducati di Atene e Neopatras* (Palermo, 1895).

Lampros S. P., Ἔγγραφα ἀναφερόμενα εἰς τὴν μεσαιωνικὴν ἱστορίαν τῶν Ἀθηνῶν. [This is the third volume of Lampros's Greek transl. of F. Gregorovius, *Gesch. d. Stadt Athen im Mittelalter*, 2nd ed., 2 vols. (Stuttgart, 1889); none of these documents is in Gregorovius.] (Athens, 1906).

Lauer, P., 'Une lettre inédite d'Henri Ier d'Angre, empereur de Constantinople, aux prélats italiens (1213?)', *Mélanges G. Schlumberger*, i (Paris, 1924), 191–201.

Léonard, E. G., 'La Nomination de Giovanni Acciaiuoli à l'archevêché de Patras', *Mélanges N. Jorga* (Paris, 1933), pp. 513–35. [Contains three documents concerning Giovanni Acciaiuoli.]

Liber Jurium Reipublicae Genuensis, 2 vols., *MHP*, vii and ix (1854–7).

Loenertz, R.-J., 'Athènes et Néopatras: Regestes et notices pour servir à l'histoire des duchés catalans (1311–1394)', *Arch. Praed.* xxv (1955), 100–212, 428–31.

Loenertz, R.-J., 'Athènes et Néopatras: Regestes et documents pour servir à l'histoire ecclésiastique des duchés catalans (1311–1395)', *Arch. Praed.* xxviii (1958), 5–91.

Loenertz, R.-J., 'Hospitaliers et Navarrais en Grèce (1376–1383): Regestes et documents', *OCP*, xxii (1956), 319–60.

Loenertz, R.-J., 'Epître de Manuel II Paléologue aux moines David et Damien (1416)', *Silloge Bizantina, in onore di Silvio Giuseppe Mercati* (= *SBN*, ix, Rome, 1957), pp. 294–304.

Longnon, J., 'Le Traité de Viterbe entre Charles Ier d'Anjou et Guillaume de Villehardouin, prince de Morée (24 mai 1267)', *Studi in onore di Riccardo Filangieri*, i (Naples, 1959), pp. 307–14.

Makučev [Makushev], V., *Monumenta historica Slavorum meridionalium vicinorumque populorum*, 2 vols. (Warsaw and Belgrade, 1874–82).

Mango, A., 'Relazioni tra Federico III di Sicilia e Giovanna I di Napoli: Documenti degli Archivi del Vaticano', *Documenti per Servire alla Storia di Sicilia*, prima serie. Diplomatica, xxii, fasc. 1 (Palermo, 1915).

Mas Latrie, L. de, *Documents et mémoires servant de preuves à l'histoire de l'île de Chypre sous les Lusignans* [vols. ii and iii of his *Histoire de l'île de Chypre*] (Paris, 1852–5).

Mas Latrie, L. de, 'Nouvelles preuves de l'histoire de Chypre sous le règne des princes de la maison de Lusignan', *BEC*, xxxiii–xxxiv, and separately (Paris, 1873–4).

Mas Latrie, L. de, 'Commerce et expéditions militaires de la France et de Venise au moyen âge', *Mélanges historiques*, Choix de Documents, iii (Paris, 1880), 1–240.

Mas Latrie, L. de, 'Documents nouveaux servant de preuves à l'histoire de l'île de Chypre sous le règne des princes de la maison de Lusignan', *Mélanges historiques*, iv (Paris, 1882), 337–619.

Miklosich, F. and Müller, J., *Acta et diplomata graeca medii aevi* [see Gen. Bibl. iv].

Müller, G., *Documenti sulle relazioni delle città toscane coll'Oriente cristiano e coi Turchi fino all'anno MDXXXI* (Florence, 1879).

Pauli, S., *Codice diplomatico del sacro militare Ordine Gerosolimitano*, 2 vols. (Lucca, 1733–7).

Riant, P., *Exuviae sacrae Constantinopolitanae*, 2 vols. (Geneva, 1877–8).

Ross, L. and Schmeller, J. A., 'Urkunden zur Geschichte Griechenlands im Mittelalter', *Abhandlungen der philos.-philol. Classe der K. bayer. Akademie*, II (Munich, 1837).

Rubió y Lluch, A. [also Rubió i Lluch], 'Documentos inéditos relativos á la expedición navarra y el Ducado catalán de Atenas', *Memorias de la R. Acad. de Buenas Letras de Barcelona*, IV (Barcelona, 1887), 425–92. Also in Rubió's *Los Navarros en Grecia y el ducado catalán de Atenas en la Época de su Invasión* (Barcelona, 1886).

Rubió y Lluch, A., *Documents per l'Història de la Cultura catalana mig-eval*, 2 vols. (Barcelona, 1908–21).

Rubió y Lluch, A., 'Collection de documents relatifs à l'histoire de la ville d'Athènes pendant la domination catalane', Βυζαντίς, II (1912), 297–328.

Rubió y Lluch, A., *Diplomatari de l'Orient català (1301–1409)* (Barcelona, 1947).

(E) GREEK SOURCES

Acropolites, George, ed. A. Heisenberg, 2 vols. (Leipzig, 1903).

Bessarion, *MPG*, CLXI (1866).

Βραχέα Χρονικά, ed. S. Lampros and K. I. Amantos (Μνημεῖα τῆς Ἑλληνικῆς Ἱστορίας) (Athens, 1932).

Canabutzes, John, *Ad principem Aeni et Samothraces in Dionysium Halicarnassensem Commentarius* (Leipzig, 1890).

Cantacuzenus, John, *Historiarum libri* IV, ed. L. Schopen, 3 vols., *CSHB* (1828–32).

Chalcocondyles, Laonicus, *Historiarum demonstrationes*, ed. E. Darkó, 2 vols. (Budapest, 1922–7); ed. I. Bekker, *CSHB* (1843).

Chomatianus, Demetrius, Archbishop of Ochrida, *Works*, ed. J. B. Pitra (*Analecta sacra et classica spicilegio Solesmensi parata*, VII) (Paris and Rome, 1891).

Choniates, Michael (Acominatus), Τὰ σωζόμενα, ed. S. P. Lampros, 2 vols. (Athens, 1879–80).

Choniates, Nicetas, *Historia*, ed. I. Bekker, *CSHB* (1835).

Chronicle of the Morea, ed. J. Schmitt (London, 1904); ed. P. P. Kalonaros [in Greek] (Athens, 1940).

Chronicon breve, ed. I. Bekker, *CSHB* (1834).

Χρονικὸν περὶ τῆς Μυτιλήνης, ed. S. P. Lampros, 'Συμβολὴ εἰς τὴν ἱστορίαν τῶν ἐν Λέσβῳ δυναστευόντων Γατελούζων', *NE*, VI (1909), 257–95.

Χρονογράφοι Βασιλείου Κύπρου, ed. K. N. Sathas (Μεσαιωνικὴ Βιβλιοθήκη, II) [see Gen. Bibl. IV].

Critobulus, Michael, *De rebus gestis Mahumetis II*, ed. C. Müller (*FHG*, V) (1870); ed. V. Grecu (Bucharest, 1963).

Cydones, Demetrius, *Letters*, ed. J. F. Boissonade, *Anecdota Nova* (Paris, 1844); ed. G. Cammelli, *Démétrius Cydonès, Correspondance* (Budé, with French transl.) (Paris, 1930); ed. R.-J. Loenertz (Studi e Testi, 186 and 208), 2 vols. (Vatican, 1956–60). See also G. Mercati, *Notizie di Procoro e Demetrio Cidone, Manuele Caleca e Teodoro Meliteniota* (Studi e Testi, 56) (Vatican, 1931).

Dölger, F., *Regesten der Kaiserurkunden* [see Gen. Bibl. IV].

Dorotheus of Monemvasia, Βιβλίον Ἱστορικόν (Venice, 1805). [Pseudo-Dorotheus.]

Ducas, *Historia byzantina*, ed. I. Bekker, *CSHB* (1834); ed. V. Grecu (Bucharest, 1958).

Ecthesis chronica and *Chronicon Athenarum*, ed. S. P. Lampros (London, 1902).

Ephraim, *Chronicle*, ed. A. Mai, *CSHB* (1840).

Epirotica, ed. I. Bekker, *CSHB* (1849); *MPG*, CXLIII; ed. S. Cirac Estopañan, *Bizancio y España* [see below, III].

Gemistus (Plethon), George, *MPG*, CLX (1866); also ed. A. Ellissen, *Analekten der mittel- und neugriechischen Litteratur*, IV (Leipzig, 1860).

Gregoras, Nicephorus, *Historia byzantina*, ed. L. Schopen and I. Bekker, *CSHB*, 3 vols. (1829–55).

Gregoras, Nicephorus, *Epistolae XC*, ed. S. Bezdeki, *Ephemeris Dacoromana*, II (1924), 239–377; ed. R. Guilland (Budé, with French transl.) (Paris, 1927).

Historia politica et patriarchica Constantinopoleos, ed. I. Bekker, *CSHB* (1849).

John Apocaucus, Metropolitan of Naupactus, *Works*, ed. V. G. Vasilievsky, 'Epirotica saeculi XIII', *VV*, III (1896), 233–99; and bibliography in D. M. Nicol, *Despotate of Epiros*, appendix II [see Gen. Bibl. V].

Κυπριακοὶ Νόμοι, ed. K. N. Sathas (Μεσαιωνικὴ Βιβλιοθήκη) [see Gen. Bibl. IV].

Laurent, V., 'La liste épiscopale de la métropole d'Athènes d'après le synodicon d'une de ses églises suffragantes', *Mémorial Louis Petit* (Bucharest, 1948), pp. 272–91.

Lemerle, P., 'Trois actes du despote d'Epire Michel II concernant Corfou connus en traduction latine', Προσφορὰ εἰς Στ. Κυριακίδην (= Ἑλληνικά, Παράρτημα IV) (Thessalonica, 1953), pp. 405–26.

Lemerle, P., 'Le Privilège du despote d'Epire Thomas I pour le vénitien Jacques Contareno (1303)', *BZ*, XLIV (1951), 389–96.

Mazaris, Ἐπιδημία ἐν Ἅδου, ed. J. F. Boissonade, *Anecdota Graeca*, III (Paris, 1831); also ed. A. Ellissen, *Analekten der mittel- und neugriechischen Litteratur*, IV (Leipzig, 1860).

Noukios, Andronicus, Ἀποδημιῶν Βιβλία, ed. A. Mustoxidi, Ἱστορικὰ καὶ Φιλολογικὰ Ἀνέκδοτα (Corfù, 1872).

Ostrogorsky, G., 'Pismo Dimitrija Homatijana sv. Savi' ['Demetrius Chomatianus' letter to St Sava'], *Sveto-Savski Zbornik*, II (1938), 91–113.

Pachymeres, George, *De Michaele et Andronico Palaeologis libri XIII*, ed. I. Bekker, 2 vols., *CSHB* (1835).

Palaeologus, Manuel II, *MPG*, CLVI (1866); letters, ed. E. Legrand (Paris, 1893).

Palaeologus, Michael VIII, *De vita sua*, ed. J. G. Troitsky, *Christ. Čtenie*, II (1885), 529–79 and publ. separately (St Petersburg, 1885); ed. H. Grégoire, *B*, XXIX–XXX (1959–60), 447–75.

Sphrantzes, George, *Chronicon: 'Chronicon Minus'*, *MPG*, CXLVI, 1025–80; *'Chronicon Maius'*, ed. I. Bekker, *CSHB* (1838); ed. J. B. Papadopulos, I (Leipzig, 1935) [still incomplete]. It is now known that only the *Chronicon minus* was written by Sphrantzes, the *Chronicon maius* being an expansion of the *Minus* by Macarius Melissenus in the later sixteenth century.

Theodulus Rhetor, Πρεσβευτικὸς πρὸς τὸν Βασιλέα Ἀνδρόνικον τὸν Παλαιολόγον, and Περὶ τῶν ἐν τῇ Ἰταλῶν καὶ Περσῶν ἐφόδῳ γεγενημένων, ed. J. F. Boissonade, *Anecdota Graeca*, II (Paris, 1830).

Threnos, Θρῆνος τῆς Κωνσταντινουπόλεως, ed. W. Wagner, *Medieval Greek Texts...The Earliest Compositions in Vulgar Greek, prior to the Year 1500*, pt. I (London, 1870), 141–70.

Wagner, W. (Guilelmus), *Carmina Graeca Medii Aevi* (Leipzig, 1874).

Zoras, G. Th., Χρονικὸν περὶ τῶν τούρκων σουλτάνων (κατὰ τὸν Βαρβερινὸν ἑλληνικὸν κώδικα 111), Athens, 1958. This *Chronicle of the Turkish Sultans* was actually composed about 1600 from Francesco Sansovino's *Annali Turcheschi* (2nd ed. Venice, 1573), as shown by E. A. Zachariadou, Τὸ χρονικὸ τῶν τούρκων σουλτάνων (τοῦ Βαρβερινοῦ ἑλληνικοῦ κώδικα 111) καὶ τὸ ἰταλικό του πρότυπο, Society of Macedonian Studies (Thessalonica, 1960).

(F) MISCELLANEOUS

Adam, G., 'De modo Saracenos extirpandi', *Rec. hist. Cr., Documents arméniens*, II, 519–55 [see Gen. Bibl. IV].

Aeneas Sylvius (Pius II), 'Europa', *Opera* (Basle, 1571).

Aeneas Sylvius (Pius II), *Commentarii rerum memorabilium, quae temporibus suis contigerunt* (Frankfurt, 1614).

Albricus Monachus Trium Fontium, *Chronicon, MGH*, Script. XXIII (1874).

Amadi and Stambaldi, *Chroniques (615–1458)*, ed. L. de Mas Latrie, *Collection de documents inédits sur l'histoire de la France*, 2 vols. (Paris, 1891–3).

Bembo, P., *Rerum Venetarum historia* (Paris, 1551).

Benedict of Peterborough, *Gesta Regis Ricardi*, ed. W. Stubbs, *Gesta Henrici II*, II (*Rolls*) (1867).

Benjamin of Tudela, *The Itinerary of*, ed. M. Adler (Oxford, 1907).

Boucicaut, Messire Jean le Maingre dit, *Le livre des faicts du bon* (Paris, 1825).

Breuning von und zu Buochenbach, H. J., *Orientalische Reyss* (Strasbourg, 1612).

Brocquière, B. de la, *Voyage d'Outremer*, ed. C. Schefer (Recueil de voyages et de documents, XII) (Paris, 1892).

Buondelmonti, C., *Liber insularum Archipelagi*, ed. G. R. L. de Sinner (Berlin, 1824); also *Version grecque par un anonyme*, ed. E. Legrand (Paris, 1897).

Bustron, Florio, *Chronique de l'île de Chypre*, ed. L. de Mas Latrie, *Mélanges historiques*, V (Paris, 1886), 1–532.

Campofulgosus, B., *Exemplorum, hoc est, dictorum factorumque memorabilium ...lib.* IX (Basle, n.d.).

Canale, Martin da, 'La Chronique des Veniciens', *ASI*, VIII (Florence, 1845).

Caroldo, Gian Giacopo, *Cronica*, in Codex Marcianus Italicus VII, 128 *a*.

Casola, P., *Viaggio a Gerusalemme*, ed. G. Porro (Milan, 1855).

Cippico (Cepio), C., *Petri Mocenici imperatoris gesta*. Appended to P. Justiniani, *Rerum Venetarum historia* (Strasbourg, 1611).

Clavijo, Ruy Gonzalez de, *Itinéraire de l'ambassade espagnole à Samarkande en 1402–6*. English transl., C. R. Markham (Hakluyt Society, London, 1859). Better English transl. *Clavijo: Embassy to Tamerlane (1403–6)*, by G. Le Strange (Broadway Travellers) (New York and London, 1928).

Colucci, G., *Delle antichità picene*, XV (Fermo, 1792–6).

Contarini, G. P., *Historia delle cose successe dal principio della guerra mossa da Selim Ottomano a Venetiani* (Venice, 1572).

Conti, N., *Delle historie de' suoi tempi*, 2 vols. (Venice, 1589).

Cronaca di Morea (Italian version), ed. C. Hopf, *Chroniques gréco-romanes*, pp. 414–68 [see Gen. Bibl. IV].

Crusius (Kraus), M., *Turcograecia* (Basle, 1584).

Cyriacus Anconitanus, *Epigrammata reperta per Illyricum* (n.d.).

Cyriacus Anconitanus, *Itinerarium*, ed. L. Mehus (Florence, 1742).

Daniele di Chinazzo, *Cronica de la guerra da Veniciani a Zenovesi*, ed. V. Lazzarini, *Deput. Stor. Patr. Ven.*, *Monumenti Storici*, n.s. xi (Venice, 1958); also ed. *RISS*, xv (Milan, 1729), 695–804, but confused with the work of Andrea Gatari, on which see Lazzarini, and cf. *RISS*, new ed., xvii (1909–31), *passim*.

Edrisi, *Géographie de*, transl. A. Jaubert, ii (Paris, 1840).

Enveri, *Düstūrnāme*, ed. with transl. and notes by I. Mélikoff-Sayar, *Le Destan d'Umūr Pacha* (*Düstūrnāme-i Enveri*) (Paris, 1953).

Faber (Fabri), F., *Evagatorium*, 3 vols. (Stuttgart, 1843–9).

Fabricius, J. A., *Bibliotheca latina mediae et infimae aetatis*, vi (Padua, 1754).

Feyerabend, *Reyssbuch des Heyligen Lands* (Frankfurt, 1584).

Foglietta (Folieta), U., *Clarorum Ligurum Elogia* (Rome, 1573).

Foglietta (Folieta), U., *Historiae Genuensium libri XII* (Genoa, 1585).

Froissart, *Chroniques de*, ed. Kervyn de Lettenhove, xv, xvi (Brussels, 1870–7).

Gerlach, *Türkisches Tagebuch* (Frankfurt, 1674).

Golubovich, Girolamo (and others), *Biblioteca bio-bibliografica della Terra Santa e dell'oriente francescano*, 1st ser. *Annali*. 2nd ser. *Documenti*. 4th ser. *Studi* (Quaracchi, 1906 ff.; Cairo, 1954 ff.).

Guazzo, M., *Historie* (*1524–49*) (Venice, 1549).

Henri de Valenciennes, *Histoire de l'empereur Henri de Constantinople*, ed. J. Longnon, *Docs. rel. à l'hist. des Croisades, publ. par l'Acad. des Inscrs. et B.-L.* ii (Paris, 1948).

Jordanus, Friar, *Mirabilia descripta*, transl. H. Yule (London, 1863).

Joseph Ben Joshua, Rabbi, The Chronicles of, transl. C. H. F. Bialloblotzky, 2 vols. (London, 1836).

Jovius, P., *Historiae sui temporis* (Venice, 1553).

Les Gestes des Chyprois, ed. G. Raynaud (Geneva, 1887).

Libro de los Fechos et Conquistas del Principado de la Morea [Aragonese version of the *Chronicle of the Morea*], ed. and transl. A. Morel-Fatio (Geneva, 1885).

Livre de la Conqueste de la Princée de l'Amorée. Chronique de Morée (*1204–1305*), ed. J. Longnon (Paris, 1911).

Ludolph von Suchem, *De Itinere Terrae Sanctae*, ed. F. Deycks (Stuttgart, 1851).

Machaut, Guillaume de, *La Prise d'Alexandrie, ou chronique du Roi Pierre de Lusignan*, ed. L. de Mas Latrie (Geneva, 1877).

Martène, E. and Durand, U., *Thesaurus novus Anecdotorum*, 6 vols. (Paris, 1717).

Marthono, Nicolaus de, notarius, *Liber Peregrinationis ad Loca Sancta*, ed. Léon Legrand, *ROL*, iii (1895), 566–669.

Maurocenus (Morosini), Andreas, *Historia Veneta ab anno MDXXI usque ad annum MDCXV* (Venice, 1623).

Monacis, Laurentius de, *Chronicon de rebus Venetis ab u. c. ad annum MCCCLIV* (Venice, 1758).

Morosini, Antonio, *Chronique*, ed. L. Dorez, 4 vols. (Paris, 1848–52).

Mouskes, Philippe, *Chronique rimée*, ii, *Collection de chroniques belges inédites* (Brussels, 1838).

Muntaner, Ramón, *Chronica*, ed. K. Lanz (Stuttgart, 1844). Also *Cronache catalane del secolo XIII e XIV*, i, transl. F. Moisé (Florence, 1844). English transl. Lady Goodenough, 2 vols. (Hakluyt Society, London, 1920–1).

Muratori, L. A., *Antiquitates italicae medii aevi*, 6 vols. (Milan, 1738–42). *Indices chronolog.* (Turin, 1885).

Navagero (Navagiero), Andrea, *Storia della Repubblica Veneziana*, ed. L. A. Muratori, *RISS*, XXIII (Milan, 1733), 919–1216.

Nigropontis, De Captione, in Basle ed. of *Chalcocondyles* (Basle, 1556).

Pagnini, G. F., *Della Decima e di varie altre gravezze imposte dal comune di Firenze*, 4 vols. (Lisbon and Lucca, 1765–6).

Paris, Matthew, *Chronica Majora*, ed. H. R. Luard, 7 vols. (*Rolls*) (1872–83).

Paris, Matthew, *Historia Minor*, ed. F. Madden, 3 vols., *ibid.* (1866–9).

Paruta, P., *Historia Venetiana* (Venice, 1703).

Pegolotti, F. B., *La pratica della mercatura*, ed. A. Evans (Medieval Academy of America Publications, no. 24) (Cambridge, Mass., 1936).

Rizzardo, G., *La Presa di Negroponte*, ed. E. A. Cicogna (Venice, 1844).

Sabellico, M. A., *Historia Rerum Venetarum* (Basle, 1556).

Sa'd-ad-Dîn, *Chronica dell'origine e progressi di casa ottomana*, transl. V. Bratutti, 2 vols. (Vienna and Madrid, 1649–52).

Sansovino, Francesco, *Gl'Annali Turcheschi...* (Venice, 1571, 1573).

Sansovino, F., *Historia universale dell'origine et imperio de' Turchi* (Venice, 1560, and later editions).

Sanudo, Marino, *Vite de' duchi di Venezia*, ed. L. A. Muratori, *RISS*, XXII (Milan, 1733), 405–1252.

Sanudo, M., *Diarii*, 58 vols. (Venice, 1879–1903).

Sanudo Torsello, Marino, *Istoria del Regno di Romania*, in Hopf, *Chroniques gréco-romanes*, pp. 99–170.

Sanudo Torsello, Marino, *Secreta Fidelium Crucis*, ed. J. Bongars (*Gesta Dei per Francos*, II) (Hanover, 1611).

Smet, Joachim, *The Life of Saint Peter Thomas by Philippe de Mézières* (Textus et Studia historica Carmelitana, II) (Rome, 1954).

Spandugino, Th., *I Commentari di Theodoro Spandugino dell'origine de' Principi Turchi* (Florence, 1551).

Starrabba, R., 'Documenti riguardanti l'abdicazione di Giacomo II di Aragona al trono di Sicilia (1295) [comunicati da Don Manuel de Bofarull]', *Archivio storico Siciliano*, ser. nuova VII (1883), 275–93. [Docs. on pp. 283–93.]

Symon Simeonis, *Itinerarium*, ed. J. Nasmith (Cambridge, 1778).

Thiriet, F., 'Les Chroniques vénitiennes de la Marcienne et leur importance pour l'histoire de la Romanie gréco-vénitienne', *Mélanges d'archéologie et d'histoire*, LXVI (1954), 241–92.

Tozzetti, G. Targioni, *Relazioni di alcuni viaggi fatti in diverse parti della Toscana*, 2nd ed., 6 vols. (Florence, 1777).

Villehardouin, Geoffrey of, *La conquête de Constantinople. Avec la continuation de Henri de Valenciennes*, ed. N. de Wailly (Paris, 1874); ed. E. Faral, 2 vols. (Paris, 1938–9).

III. SECONDARY AUTHORITIES

Albanas, Ph., Περὶ τῶν ἐν Κερκύρᾳ τίτλων εὐγενείας καὶ περὶ τῶν τιμαρίων (Corfù, 1894).

Altaner, B., *Die Dominikanermissionen des 13. Jahrhunderts* (Habelschwerdt, 1924).

Andreades, A. M., Περὶ τῆς οἰκονομικῆς διοικήσεως τῆς Ἑπτανήσου ἐπὶ Βενετοκρατίας, 2 vols. (Athens, 1914).

Andrews, K., *Castles of the Morea* (Gennadeion Monographs, IV, Princeton, 1953).

Anonymous, *Historia del Regno di Negroponte e sue isole adjacenti* (Venice, 1695).

Anonymous [Delês, J.], Οἱ Γατελοῦζοι ἐν Λέσβῳ, *1355–1462* (Athens, 1901).

Aravantinos, P. A., Χρονογραφία τῆς Ἠπείρου, 2 vols. (Athens, 1856–7).

Argenti, P., *The Expedition of the Florentines to Chios, 1599* (London, 1934).

Argenti, P., *The Occupation of Chios by the Venetians, 1694* (London, 1935).

Argenti, P., *Chius Vincta* (Cambridge, 1941).

Argenti, P., *Hieronimo Giustiniani's History of Chios* (Cambridge, 1943).

Argenti, P., *The Occupation of Chios by the Genoese and their Administration of the Island, 1346–1566*, 3 vols. (Cambridge, 1958).

Argenti, P. and Kyriakides, S. P., Ἡ Χίος παρὰ τοῖς γεωγράφοις καὶ περιηγηταῖς ἀπὸ τοῦ ὀγδόου μέχρι τοῦ εἰκοστοῦ αἰῶνος, 3 vols. (Athens, 1946).

Arnakes, G. Georgiades, Οἱ πρῶτοι Ὀθωμανοί. Συμβολὴ εἰς τὸ πρόβλημα τῆς πτώσεως τοῦ Ἑλληνισμοῦ τῆς Μικρᾶς Ἀσίας *(1282–1337)* (Texte und Forschungen zur byz.-neugr. Philologie, 41) (Athens, 1947).

Atiya, A. S., *The Crusade of Nicopolis* [see Gen. Bibl. v].

Atiya, A. S., *The Crusade in the Later Middle Ages* [see Gen. Bibl. v].

Babinger, F., *Geschichtsschreiber der Osmanen und ihre Werke* (Leipzig, 1927).

Babinger, F., *Mehmed der Eroberer und seine Zeit* (2nd ed. Munich, 1959; French trans. of 1st ed., 1954; Italian trans. of 1st ed., 1957).

Babinger, F., 'Johannes Darius (1414–1494), Sachwalter Venedigs im Morgenland, und sein griechischer Umkreis', *SBAW*, Philos-.Hist. Kl., Heft 5 of Jahrgang 1961.

Babinger, F., 'Le Vicende veneziane nella lotta contro i Turchi durante il secolo XV', in *Civiltà veneziana del Quattrocento* (Florence, 1957), pp. 51–73.

Bakalopoulos, A. E., Ἱστορία τοῦ νέου ἑλληνισμοῦ, I (Thessalonica, 1961).

Bakalopoulos, A. E., 'Συμβολὴ στὴν ἱστορία τῆς Θεσσαλονίκης ἐπὶ Βενετοκρατίας (1423–1430)', Τόμος Κωνσταντίνου Ἀρμενοπούλου ['Ἐπιστημονικὴ Ἐπετηρίς, VI] (Thessalonica, 1952), pp. 127–49.

Bakalopoulos, A. E., *Thasos. Son histoire, son administration, de 1453 à 1912* (Paris, 1953) [with documents].

Bănescu, N., *Le déclin de Famagouste: fin du royaume de Chypre. Notes et documents* [Institut Roumain d'Etudes Byzantines, n.s. 4] (Bucharest, 1946).

Banús y Comas, C., *Expedición de Catalanes y Aragoneses en Oriente en principio del siglo XIV* (Madrid, 1929).

Bees, N. A., 'Βυζαντιναὶ ἐπιγραφαὶ Γορτυνίας' and 'Προσθῆκαι', *VV*, XI (1904), 63–72, 384–5.

Bees, N. A., 'Μνεῖαι τοῦ Ἄστρους κατὰ τοὺς μέσους αἰῶνας καὶ τὰ παρ' αὐτὸ κάστρα', *BZ*, XVII (1908), 92–107.

Bees, N. A., 'Bambacoratius, ein Beiname des Kaisers Alexios III. Angelos (1195–1203)', *BNJ*, III (1922), 285–6.

Bees, N. A.. *Der französisch-mittelgriechische Ritterroman 'Imberios und Margarone' und die Gründungssage des Daphniklosters bei Athen* (Texte u. Forsch. zur byz.-neugriech. Philol., Heft 4) (Berlin, 1924).

Bees, N. A., 'Zum Bericht des L. Chalkokondylis über den Feldzug Murads II. gegen Morea', *BNJ*, XVII (1944), 234–41.

Belabre, Baron de, *Rhodes of the Knights* (Oxford, 1908).

Bertelè, T., 'Una moneta dei Despoti di Epiro', *BZ*, XLIV (1951), 25–6.

Besta, E., *La cattura dei Veneziani in Oriente* (Feltre, 1920).

Beving, Ch. A., *La Principauté d'Achaïe et de Morée, 1204–1430* (Brussels, 1879).

Bires [Μπίρης], Κ., Αἱ Ἐκκλησίαι τῶν παλαιῶν Ἀθηνῶν (Athens, 1940).

Blantês, S. A., Ἡ Λευκὰς ὑπὸ τοὺς Φράγκους, τοὺς Τούρκους, καὶ τοὺς Ἐνετούς (*1204–1797*) (Levkas, 1902).

Blastos, A. M., Χιακά, 2 vols. (Hermoupolis, 1840); English transl. A. P. Ralli (London, 1913).

Bodnar, E. W., *Cyriacus of Ancona and Athens* (Collection Latomus, XLIII) (Brussels, 1960).

Bogiatzides, I. K., ''Ὁ Λακεδαιμόνιος Βιβλιογράφος Στρατηγόπουλος' [in Andros, 1538–9], *BZ*, XIX (1910), 122–6.

Bogiatzides, I. K., Τὸ Χρονικὸν τῶν Μετεώρων, *EEBS*, I (1924), 139–75; II (1925), 149–82.

Bon, A., *Karytaina et la baronnie dite de la Skortá* (Comptes-Rendus de l'Académie des Inscriptions et Belles-Lettres) (1928), pp. 127–8.

Bon, A., *The Medieval Fortifications of Acrocorinth* (Cambridge, Mass., 1936).

Bon, A., 'Forteresses médiévales de la Grèce centrale', *Bull. Corr. Hell.* LXI (1937), 136–208.

Bon, A., 'A propos de quelques châteaux francs de Grèce', *RA*, ser. 6, XI (1938), 80–5.

Bon, A., 'La prise de Kalamata par les Francs en 1205', *Mélanges Charles Picard*, I (Paris, 1949), 98–104.

Bon, A., *Le Péloponnèse byzantin jusqu'en 1204* [see Gen. Bibl. v].

Bonis [Μπόνης], Κ. G., Εὐθυμίου τοῦ Μαλάκη, μητροπολίτου Νέων Πατρῶν (Ὑπάτης), τὰ σωζόμενα (Θεολογικὴ Βιβλιοθήκη, 2) (Athens, 1937).

Bonis, K. G., 'Εὐθυμίου τοῦ Μαλάκη, μητροπολίτου Νέων Πατρῶν [Ὑπάτης], δύο ἐγκωμιαστικοὶ λόγοι', Θεολογία, XIX (1941–8), 513–58; XX (1949).

Borchgrave, E. de, *Croquis d'Orient* (Brussels, 1908).

Borsari, S., 'La politica bizantina di Carlo I d'Angiò dal 1266 al 1271', *ASPN*, n.s. XXXV (1956), 319–49.

Boschini, M., *L'Arcipelago* (Venice, 1658).

Bosio, G., *Dell'Istoria della sacra Religione et ill*[ma] *Militia di S. Gio. Gierosol*[mo], I and II (Rome, 1594); 2nd ed. (Rome, 1621–9).

Botta, C., *Storia naturale e medica dell'isola di Corfù* (Milan, 1823).

Bottarelli, G. and Monterisi, M., *Storia politica e militare del Sovrano Ordine di S. Giovanni di Gerusalemme detto di Malta*, 2 vols. (Milan, 1940).

Bozzo, S. V., *Notizie storiche siciliane del secolo XIV* (Palermo, 1882).

Brătianu, G. I., 'Notes sur un projet de mariage entre l'empereur Michel IX Paléologue et Cathérine de Courtenay (1288–1295)', *RHSE*, I (1924), 59–63.

Brătianu, G. I., *Recherches sur le commerce génois dans la Mer Noire au XIII*[e] *siècle* (Paris, 1929).

Brokines, L. S., Περὶ τῶν ἐτησίως τελουμένων ἐν Κερκύρᾳ λιτανειῶν τοῦ Θ. λειψάνου τοῦ Ἁγίου Σπυρίδωνος, 2nd ed. (Corfù, 1894); English transl. Mrs Dawes (Bonn, n.d.).

Brokines, L. S., Ἡ περὶ τὰ μέσα τοῦ ΙΣ´ αἰῶνος ἐν Κερκύρᾳ ἀποίκησις τῶν Ναυπλιέων καὶ τῶν Μονεμβασιέων (Corfù, 1905).

Brown, E. A. R., 'The Cistercians in the Latin Empire of Constantinople and Greece, 1204–1276', *Trad.* XIV (1958), 63–120.

Buchon, J. A., *Recherches et matériaux pour servir à une histoire de la domination française, etc.*, 2 vols. (Paris, 1840).

Buchon, J. A., *La Grèce continentale et la Morée* (Paris, 1843).

Buchon, J. A., *Nouvelles recherches historiques sur la Principauté française de Morée*, 2 vols. (Paris, 1845).

Buchon, J. A., *Recherches historiques sur la Principauté française de Morée*, 2 vols. (Paris, 1845).

Buchon, J. A., *Histoire des conquêtes et de l'établissement des français dans les états de l'ancienne Grèce* (Paris, 1846).

Buchon, J. A., *Atlas des nouvelles recherches historiques* (Paris, n.d.).

Buchon, J. A., *Voyage dans l'Eubée, les Îles Ioniennes, et les Cyclades en 1841.* Publié...par J. Longnon. Préface de M. Barrès (Paris, 1911).

Burns, R. I., 'The Catalan Company and the European Powers 1305–1311', *SP*, XXIX (1954), 751–71.

Bury, J. B., 'The Lombards and Venetians in Euboia (1205–1470)', *JHS*, VII (1886), 309–52; VIII (1887), 194–213; IX (1888), 91–117.

Calonaros, P., 'A travers le Magne: Les châteaux francs de Passava et du Grand Magne', *L'Hellénisme contemp.* III (1938), 375–80.

Camariano, N., 'La Chronique de la Morée sur les combats de Jean Assen avec les Latins', *Balcania*, VII (1944), 349–62.

Carabellese, Fr., *Carlo d'Angiò nei rapporti politici e commerciali con Venezia e l'Oriente* (Bari, 1919).

Carmoly, E., *Don Joseph Nassy, Duc de Naxos*, 2nd ed. (Frankfurt, 1868).

Caron, 'Trouvailles de monnaies du moyen-âge à Delphes', *Bull. de correspondance hellénique*, XXI (1897), 26–39.

Cerone, F., 'Il Papa ed i Veneziani nella quarta crociata', *Arch. Ven.* XXXVI (1888), 57–70, 287–97.

Cerone, F., 'La Politica orientale di Alfonso d'Aragona', *ASPN*, XXVII (1902); XXVIII (1903).

Cessi, R., 'Venezia e l'acquisto di Nauplia ed Argo', *N. Arch. Ven.* XXX (1915), 147–73.

Cessi, R., 'Amadeo di Acaia e la rivendicazione dei domini sabaudi in Oriente', *N. Arch. Ven.* XXXVII (1919), 5–64.

Cessi, R., *Storia della Repubblica di Venezia*, 2 vols. (Milan and Messina, 1944–6).

Chiotes, P., Ἱστορικὰ Ἀπομνημονεύματα Ἑπτανήσου, II, III (Corfù, 1858–63).

Cirac Estopañan, S., *Bizancio y España: la unión, Manuel II Paleologo y sus recuerdos en España* (Barcelona, 1952).

Cirac Estopañan, S., 'I tesori bizantini passati in Spagna attraverso l'Italia: Il reliquiario della basilissa Maria e del despota Tommaso d'Epiro', *Atti V. Congr. Int. St. Biz.* (Rome, 1936); *SBN*, VI (1940), 73–7.

Cirac Estopañan, S., *Bizancio y España: El legado de la basilissa Maria y de los déspotas Thomas y Esaú de Joannina*, 2 vols. (Barcelona, 1943).

Cognasso, F., *Il Conte Verde, 1334–1383* (Turin, 1930).

Cohn, Willy, *Die Geschichte der sizilischen Flotte unter der Regierung Konrads IV. und Manfreds (1250–1266)* (Berlin, 1920).

Conze, A., *Reise auf den Inseln des Thrakischen Meeres* (Hanover, 1860).

Conze, A., *Reise auf der Insel Lesbos* (Hanover, 1865).

Conze, A., Hauser, A. and Niemann, G. (Benndorf, O. in vol. II), *Archäologische Untersuchungen auf Samothrake*, 2 vols. (Vienna, 1875–80).

Cornelius (Corner), F., *Ecclesiae Venetae*, VIII (Venice, 1749).

Cornelius (Corner), F., *Creta Sacra*, 2 vols. (Venice, 1755).

Coronelli, V. M. and Parisotti, *Isola di Rodi geografica-storica, antica, e moderna, coll'altre adjacenti* (Venice, 1688).

Coronelli, V. M., *Memorie Istoriografiche de' Regni della Morea, Negroponte e Littorali fin'a Salonichi*, 2nd ed. (Venice, n.d.).

Creta Christiana, 2 vols. (Candia, 1912–15), in Χριστιανικὴ Κρήτη.

Çurita (Zurita), G., *Anales de la Corona de Aragón*, 7 vols. (Saragossa, 1610–21).

Curtius, E., *Naxos* (Berlin, 1846).

Dade, E., *Versuche zur Wiedererrichtung der lateinischen Herrschaft in Konstantinopel im Rahmen der abendländischen Politik 1261 bis etwa 1310* (Jena, 1938).

Daru, P., *Histoire de la République de Venise*, 3rd ed., 8 vols. (Paris, 1826).

Datta, P. L., *Spedizione in Oriente di Amadeo VI* (Turin, 1826).

Datta, P. L., *Storia dei Principi di Savoia del ramo d'Acaja*, 2 vols. (Turin, 1832).

Delaville le Roulx, J., *La France en Orient au XIVe siècle*, 2 vols. (Paris, 1886).

Delaville le Roulx, J., *Les Hospitaliers en Terre Sainte et en Chypre* (Paris, 1904).

Delaville le Roulx, J., *Mélanges sur l'Ordre de S. Jean de Jérusalem* (Paris, 1910).

Dendias, M., 'Le Roi Manfred de Sicile et la bataille de Pélagonie', *Mélanges Ch. Diehl*, I (1930), 55–60.

Dennis, G. T., *The Reign of Manuel II Palaeologus in Thessalonica, 1382–1387* (*OCA*, 159) (Rome, 1960).

Dennis, G. T., 'The Capture of Thebes by the Navarrese', *OCP*, XXVI (1960), 42–50.

Desimoni, C., 'Actes passés à Famagouste, de 1299 à 1301, par devant le notaire Lamberto di Sambuceto', *ROL*, I (1893), 58–139, 275–312, 321–53.

Desimoni, C., 'Notes et observations sur les actes du notaire génois Lamberto di Sambuceto', *ROL*, II (1894), 1–34, 216–34.

Desimoni, C., 'Observations sur les monnaies, les poids, et les mesures cités dans les actes du notaire génois Lamberto di Sambuceto', *ROL*, III (1895), 1–26.

De Stefano, A., *Federigo III d'Aragon re di Sicilia, 1296–1337* (Palermo, 1937).

Diehl, Ch., *L'église et les mosaïques du couvent de Saint Luc en Phocide* (Paris, 1889).

Dölger, F., 'Die Urkunden des byzantinischen Kaisers Andronikos II. für Aragon unter König Jakob II', *Estudis Universitaris Catalans*, XVIII (1933), 300–8; reprinted in *Byzanz und die europäische Staatenwelt*, pp. 128–39 [see Gen. Bibl. v].

Dragoumes, S., Χρονικῶν Μορέως τοπωνυμικά, τοπογραφικά, ἱστορικά (Athens, 1921).

Dräseke, J., 'Aus dem Athen der Acciaiuoli', *BZ*, XIV (1905), 239–53.

Dräseke, J., 'Plethons und Bessarions Denkschriften über die Angelegenheiten im Peloponnes', *Neue Jahrbücher für das klassische Altertum*, XXVII (1911), 102–19.

Du Cange, C. du Fresne, *Histoire de l'Empire de Constantinople* [see Gen. Bibl. v].

Dudan, B., *Il dominio veneziano di Levante* (Bologna, 1938).

Dugit, M. E., 'Naxos et les établissements latins de l'Archipel', *Bulletin de l'Académie Delphinale*, ser. 3, X (Grenoble, 1875).

Dyobouniotes, K. J., Θεοδόσιος Ζυγομαλᾶς; reprinted from Θεολογία, I (Athens, 1923), 18 ff.

Ebersolt, J., *Orient et Occident* [see Gen. Bibl. v].

Egidi, P., 'Di un'iscrizione medievale italo-greca sulle mura di Rodi', *Atti della reale Accademia delle Scienze di Torino, Classe di Scienze Morali, Storiche e Filologiche*, LXIII (1928), 61–9.

Eubel, C., *Hierarchia Catholica Medii Aevi (1198–1600)*, 3 vols. (Münster, 1898–1910).

Fallmerayer, J. P., *Geschichte der Halbinsel Morea während des Mittelalters*, 2 vols. (Stuttgart and Tübingen, 1830–6).

Fallmerayer, J. P., *Hagion-Oros oder der heilige Berg Athos. Mit einem Nachwort von Franz Dölger* (Vienna, 1949).

Fanelli, F., *Atene Attica* (Venice, 1707).

Faure, M. C., 'Le Dauphin Humbert II à Venise et en Orient (1345–47)', *Mélanges de l'Ecole française de Rome*, XXVII (1907), 509–62.

Finlay, G., *History of Greece*, III, IV [see Gen. Bibl. v].

Foerster, R., 'Eine Monodie auf Theodoros Palaiologos', *BZ*, IX (1900), 641–8.

Fotheringham, J. K., 'Genoa and the Fourth Crusade', *EHR*, XXV (1910), 26–57.

Fotheringham, J. K., *Marco Sanudo, Conqueror of the Archipelago* (Oxford, 1915).

Frederich, E., 'Aus Samothrake', *Mitteilungen des k. deutschen Archäologischen Instituts* (Athenische Abtheilung), XXXIV (1909), 23–8.

Gabriel, A., *La Cité de Rhodes (1310–1522)*, 2 vols. (Paris, 1921–3).

Gaddi, G., *Corollarium poeticum* (Florence, 1636).

Gaddi, G., *Elogiographus* (Florence, 1638).

Gauthier, J., 'Othon de la Roche, conquérant d'Athènes et sa famille (1217–1335)', *Académie des Sciences, Belles-Lettres, et Arts de Besançon. Année 1880*, pp. 139–55.

Geanakoplos, D. J., *Emperor Michael Palaeologus and the West (1258–1282)* (Cambridge, Mass., 1959).

Geanakoplos, D. J., *Greek Scholars in Venice* (Cambridge, Mass., 1962).

Gerakares, N. S., Κερκυραϊκαὶ Σελίδες, *1204–1386* (Corfù, 1906).

Gerland, E., 'Bericht über Carl Hopfs litterarischen Nachlass und die darin vorhandene fränkisch-griechische Regestensammlung', *BZ*, VIII (1899), 347–86.

Gerland, E., 'Noch einmal der litterarische Nachlass Carl Hopfs', *BZ*, XI (1902), 321–32.

Gerland, E., *Neue Quellen zur Geschichte des lateinischen Erzbisthums Patras* (Leipzig, 1903).

Gerland, E., *Geschichte des lateinischen Kaiserreiches von Konstantinopel* [see Gen. Bibl. v].

Gerland, E., *Histoire de la Noblesse crétoise au moyen âge* (extrait de la *ROL*, X, XI) (Paris, 1907).

Gerola, G., *La Dominazione genovese in Creta*; reprinted from *Atti dell'I. R. Accademia di Scienze…in Rovereto*, ser. 3, VIII (Rovereto, 1902).

Gerola, G., *L'arte Veneta a Creta* (Rome, 1905).

Gerola, G., 'I francescani di Creta al tempo del dominio veneziano', *Collectanea Franciscana*, II (1932), 301–61.

Gerola, G., *Monumenti Veneti nell'Isola di Creta*, 4 vols. (Venice, 1905–32).

Gerola, G., *Un piccolo feudo napoletano nell'Egeo* (L'isoletta di Castelrosso, ora Kastellòrizo); reprinted from *Ausonia* (Rome, 1913).

Gerola, G., *Per la cronotassi dei vescovi cretesi all'epoca Veneta*; reprinted from *Miscellanea di Storia Veneta*, ser. 3, VII (Venice, 1914).

Gerola, G., *I Monumenti Medioevali delle Tredici Sporadi*, 2 vols. (Bergamo, 1914–15).

Gerola, G., *Topografia delle chiese della città di Candia*; reprinted from *Bess.* (Rome, 1918).

Gerola, G., 'Le Fortificazioni di Napoli di Romania', *Annuario R. Scuola archeol. Atene*, XIII–XIV (1934), 347–410.

Gerola, G., 'Elenco topografico delle chiese affrescate di Creta', *Atti Ist. Ven. S.L.A.* (1934–5), pp. 139–216.

Gheyn, J. van den, 'Le siège épiscopal de Diaulia en Phocide', *BZ*, VI (1897), 92–5.

Giannopoulos, N. I., 'Χριστιανικαὶ ἐπιγραφαὶ Θεσσαλίας', *Bull. de correspondance hellénique*, XXIII (1899), 396–416.

Giannopoulos, N. I., Οἱ δύο μεσαιωνικοὶ Ἁλμυροὶ καὶ ὁ νῦν (Athens, 1904).

Giannopoulos, N. I., 'Μολυβδόβουλλα προερχόμενα ἐκ τοῦ Νοτίου μεσαιωνικοῦ Ἁλμυροῦ', *BZ*, XVII (1908), 131–40.

Giannopoulos, N. I., 'Χριστιανικαὶ ἐπιγραφαὶ Θεσσαλίας', *BZ*, XXI (1912), 150–68.

Giannopoulos, N. I., ''Επισκοπικοὶ κατάλογοι Θεσσαλίας', 'Επετηρὶς τοῦ Παρνασσοῦ, X (1914), 253–312.

Giannopoulos, N. I., 'Συμβολαὶ εἰς τὴν ἱστορίαν τῶν ἰουδαϊκῶν παροικιῶν ἐν τῇ ἀνατολικῇ ἠπειρωτικῇ Ἑλλάδι', *EEBS*, X (1933), 187–91.

Giry, A., 'Les Châtelains de Saint-Omer (1042–1386)', *BEC*, XXXV (1874), 325–55; XXXVI (1875), 91–117.

Gittio, A. G., *Lo Scettro del Despota* (Naples, 1697).

Gkikas, Giannes, 'Η ἅλωση τῆς Χαλκίδας ἀπὸ τοὺς Τούρκους στὰ 1470 (Athens, 1959).

Gkion, K. I., 'Ιστορία τῆς νήσου Σίφνου (Syra, 1876).

Grandi, Jacopo, *Risposta di...sopra alcune richieste intorno S. Maura, e la Prevesa* (Venice, 1686).

Gregorio, Rosario, *Considerazioni sopra la storia di Sicilia*, II (Palermo, 1833).

Gregorovius, F., *Geschichte der Stadt Athen im Mittelalter* [see Gen. Bibl. V].

Grousset, R., *L'Empire du Levant* (Paris, 1946).

Grumel, V., *La Chronologie* [see Gen. Bibl. III].

Grumel, V., 'Les Ambassades pontificales à Byzance après le IIᵉ Concile de Lyon (1274–80)', *EO*, XXIII (1924), 437–47.

Grumel, V., 'En Orient après le IIᵉ concile de Lyon', *EO*, XXIV (1925), 321–5.

Guglielmotti, A., *Storia della Marina pontificia nel medio evo, dal 728 al 1499*, 2nd ed., I and II (Rome, 1886).

Guichenon, S., *Histoire généalogique de la royale maison de Savoye*, 2 vols. (Lyons, 1660).

Guillaume, Abbé, *Histoire généalogique des Sires de Salins*, 2 vols. (Besançon, n.d.).

Guldencrone, Baronne Diane de, *L'Achaïe féodale* (Paris, 1886).

Gunnis, R., *Historic Cyprus: a Guide to its Towns and Villages, Monasteries and Castles* (London, 1936).

Haberkorn, E., *Der Kampf um Sizilien in den Jahren 1302–1337* (Berlin and Leipzig, 1921). [*Abhandl. z. mittl. u. neuer. Gesch.*, Heft 67.]

Hājjī Khalīfah, *Cronologia historica*, transl. G. R. Carli (Venice, 1697).

Hājjī Khalīfah, *The History of the Maritime Wars of the Turks*, transl. J. Mitchell (London, 1831).

Halecki, O., *Un Empereur de Byzance à Rome* (Warsaw, 1930).

Halecki, O., *The Crusade of Varna* (New York, 1943).

Halecki, O., 'Two Palaeologi in Venice, 1370–1371', *B*, XVII (1944–5), 331–5.

Hammer-Purgstall, J. von, *Geschichte des osmanischen Reiches*, I, II [see Gen. Bibl. V].

Hanotaux, G., 'Les Vénitiens ont-ils trahi la chrétienté en 1202?', *RH*, IV (1887), 74–102.

Hasluck, F. W., 'Depopulation in the Aegean Islands and the Turkish Conquest', *Annual of the British School at Athens*, XVII (1910–11), 151–81.

Hasluck, F. W., 'Heraldry of the Rhodian Knights, formerly in Smyrna Castle', *Annual of the British School at Athens*, XVII (1910–11), 145–50.

Hasluck, F. W., 'A French Inscription at Adalia', *Annual of the British School at Athens*, XVI (1909–10), 185–6.

Hasluck, F. W., 'The Latin Monuments of Chios', *Annual of the British School at Athens*, XVI (1909–10), 137–84.

Hasluck, F. W., 'Frankish Remains at Adalia', *Annual of the British School at Athens*, XV (1908–9), 270–3.

Hasluck, F. W., 'Monuments of the Gattelusi', *Annual of the British School at Athens*, XV (1908–9), 248–69.

Hasluck, F. W., 'Albanian Settlements in the Aegean Islands', *Annual of the British School at Athens*, XV (1908–9), 223–8.

Hasluck, F. W., 'Note on a Greek Inscription of the Knights at Budrum', *Annual of the British School at Athens*, XVIII (1911–12), 215.

Hasluck, F. W., 'On Imitations of the Venetian Sequin Struck for the Levant', *Annual of the British School at Athens*, XVIII (1911–12), 261–4.

Hasluck, F. W., 'Contributions to the History of Levant Currencies', *Annual of the British School at Athens*, XIX (1912–13), 174–81.

Hatzidakis (Chadzidakis), M., Μυστράς (Athens, 1948).

Hatzidakis, G. N., 'Μυζήθρα, Μυζηθράς, Μυστράς', *VV*, II (1895), 58–77.

Hatzidakis, G. N., ''Ο Μορέας oder τὸ Μόρεον', *BZ*, V (1896), 341–6.

Haviarâs, D., 'Μελέται περὶ τῆς νήσου Σύμης', *VV*, XIV (1906–9), 237–45.

Heisenberg, A., *Aus der Geschichte und Literatur der Palaiologenzeit* (Munich, 1920) (also in *SBAW, Philos.-philol. u. hist. Kl.*, X, 1920).

Heisenberg, A., *Neue Quellen zur Geschichte des lateinischen Kaisertums und der Kirchenunion*: I: 'Der Epitaphios des Nikolaos Mesarites auf seinen Bruder Johannes'; II: 'Die Unionsverhandlungen vom 30. August 1206. Patriarchenwahl und Kaiserkrönung in Nikaia 1208'; III: 'Der Bericht des Nikolaos Mesarites über die politischen und kirchlichen Ereignisse des Jahres 1214', *SBAW, Philos.-philol. u. hist. Kl.* (Munich, 1922–3).

Hertzberg, G. F., *Geschichte Griechenlands seit dem Absterben des antiken Lebens bis zur Gegenwart*, II, III (Gotha, 1876–9).

Herzog, R., 'Ein türkisches Werk über das ägäische Meer aus dem Jahre 1520', *Mitteilungen des k. deutschen Archäologischen Instituts* (Athenische Abtheilung), XXVII (1902), 417–30.

Heyd, W., *Histoire du Commerce du Levant au moyen âge* [see Gen. Bibl. V].

Hidromenos, A. M., Συνοπτικὴ Ἱστορία τῆς Κερκύρας (Corfù, 1895).

Hill, Sir George, *History of Cyprus*, II, III [see Gen. Bibl. V].

Hofmann, G., 'Wie stand es mit der Frage der Kircheneinheit auf Kreta im XV. Jahrhundert?', *OCP*, X (1944), 91–115.

Hofmann, G., 'Papst Pius II und die Kircheneinheit des Ostens', *OCP*, XII (1946), 217–37.

Hopf, K., *De Historiae Ducatus Atheniensis fontibus* (Bonn, 1852).

Hopf, K., 'Geschichtlicher Überblick über die Schicksale von Karystos', *SKAW*, XI (Vienna, 1853); Italian transl. G. B. Sardagna, with author's additions, *Dissertazione documentata sulla storia di Karystos* (Venice, 1856); Greek transl. E. Galanes (Athens, 1867).

Hopf, K., *Walther VI. von Brienne, Herzog von Athen und Graf von Lecce*, in F. V. Raumer, *Historisches Taschenbuch*, III, pt. 5 (Leipzig, 1854).

Hopf, K., 'Geschichte der Insel Andros und ihrer Beherrscher', *SKAW*, XVI (Vienna, 1855).

Hopf, K., 'Urkunden und Zusätze zur Geschichte der Insel Andros', *SKAW*, XXI (Vienna, 1856); Italian transl. of both by G. B. Sardagna, *Dissertazione documentata sulla storia dell'Isola di Andros* (Venice, 1859); Greek transl. Z. Delagrammatika (Andros, 1886).

Hopf, K., 'Ghisi', Ersch–Gruber, LXVI (Leipzig, 1857) [see Gen. Bibl. I].

Hopf, K., 'Giorgi', Ersch–Gruber, LXVII (Leipzig, 1858) [see Gen. Bibl. I].

Hopf, K., 'Giustiniani', Ersch–Gruber, LXVIII (Leipzig, 1859) [see Gen. Bibl. I]; French transl. E. A. Vlasto, *Les Giustiniani, dynastes de Chios* (Paris, 1888); Italian transl. G. B. Sardagna, 'Di alcune dinastie latine nella Grecia', *Arch. Ven.* XXXI (Venice, 1886), and by A. Wolf, *Storia dei Giustiniani di Genova, Giornale Ligustico*, VII–IX (Genoa, 1881–2).

Hopf, K., 'Veneto-byzantinische Analekten', *SKAW*, XXXII (Vienna, 1859).

Hopf, K., 'Gozzadini', Ersch–Gruber, LXXVI (Leipzig, 1863) [see Gen. Bibl. I].

Hopf, K., *Geschichte Griechenlands vom Beginn des Mittelalters bis auf unsere Zeit* [see Gen. Bibl. V].

Hopf, K., *Chroniques gréco-romanes inédites ou peu connues* [see Gen. Bibl. IV].

Jacobs, E., 'Die Thasiaca des Cyriacus von Ancona im Codex Vaticanus 5250', *Mitteilungen des k. deutschen Archäologischen Instituts* (Athenische Abtheilung), XXII (1897), 113–38.

Jegerlehner, J., 'Der Aufstand der kandiotischen Ritterschaft gegen das Mutterland Venedig, 1363–1365', *BZ*, XII (1903), 78–125.

Jegerlehner, J., 'Beiträge zur Verwaltungsgeschichte Kandias im XIV. Jahrhundert', *BZ*, XIII (1904), 435–79.

Jireček, C., 'Eine Urkunde von 1238–40 zur Geschichte von Korfù', *BZ*, I (1892), 336–7.

Jireček, C., 'Die Witwe und die Söhne des Despoten Esau von Epirus', *BNJ*, I (1920), 1–16.

Jordan, E., *Les origines de la domination angevine en Italie* (Paris, 1909).

Jorga, N., 'Latins et Grecs d'Orient et l'établissement des Turcs en Europe (1342–1362)', *BZ*, XV (1906), 179–222.

Jorga, N., 'Ramón Muntaner et l'empire byzantin', *RHSE*, IV (1927), 325–55.

Jorga, N., 'Rapports italo-orientaux dans l'art du moyen âge', *Mélanges Diehl*, II (1930), pp. 59–69.

Jorga, N., *Les commencements de Venise*, I: 'Les Venises populaires'; II: 'Les débuts de Venise et Byzance'; III: 'Venise et Italie', *Acad. Roum., Bull. sect. hist.*, XVIII (1931), 101–43.

Jorga, N., 'Les grandes familles byzantines et l'idée byzantine en Roumanie', *Acad. Roum., Bull. sect. hist.*, XVIII (1931), 1–21.

Jorga, N., *France de Chypre* (Paris, 1931).

Jorga, N., *Une ville 'romane' devenue slave: Raguse. Trois conférences données en Sorbonne*, I: 'Origines. Rapports avec Venise'; II: 'Raguse et les Slaves'; III: 'Raguse et les Turcs', *Acad. Roum., Bull. sect. hist.*, XVIII (1931), 32–100.

Jorga, N., 'Deux siècles d'histoire de Venise. Conférences données en Sorbonne', *RHSE*, IX (1932), 1–59.

Jorga, N., 'France de Constantinople et de Morée. "Déviation" de la quatrième croisade. Participation de l'élément français', *RHSE*, XII (1935), 81–105, 177–217, 324–56.

Jorga, N., 'Les voyageurs français dans l'Orient européen', *Revue des Cours et Conférences*, 27th year, 2nd ser. (Paris, 1926), pp. 2–17, 481–508 and ff.

Jubainville, H. d'Arbois de, *Voyage paléographique dans le département de l'Aube* (Troyes, 1855).

Judeich, W., 'Athen im Jahre 1395 nach der Beschreibung des Niccolò da Martoni', *Mitteilungen des k. deutschen Archäologischen Instituts* (Athenische Abtheilung), XXII (1897), 423–38.

Kampouroglous, D. G., Ἱστορία τῶν Ἀθηναίων, 3 vols. (Athens, 1889–96).

Kampouroglous, D. G., Μνημεῖα τῆς Ἱστορίας τῶν Ἀθηναίων, 3 vols., 2nd ed. (Athens, 1891–2).

Kampouroglous, D. G., Οἱ Χαλκοκονδύλαι (Athens, 1926).

Karavias, G. N., Ἱστορία τῆς νήσου Ἰθάκης (Athens, 1849).

Kohler, C., 'Documents chypriotes du début du XIVᵉ siècle', *ROL*, XI (1908), 440–52.

Kolias, G., Σιδερόκαστρον', *EEBS*, X (1933), 72–82.

Kolias, G., 'Das Lehngut von Gravia', *BZ*, XXXVI (1936), 330–6.

Konstantinides, G., Ἱστορία τῶν Ἀθηνῶν ἀπὸ Χριστοῦ γεννήσεως μέχρι τοῦ ἔτους 1821, 2nd ed. (Athens, 1894).

Köprülü, M. F., *Les origines de l'empire Ottoman* (Paris, 1935).

Kougeas, S., 'Notizbuch eines Beamten der Metropolis in Thessalonike aus dem Anfang des XV. Jahrhunderts', *BZ*, XXIII (1914), 144–63.

Krekić, B., *Dubrovnik* [see Gen. Bibl. v].

Kurtz, E., 'Georgios Bardanes, Metropolit von Kerkyra', *BZ*, XV (1906), 603–13.

Kurtz, E., 'Christophoros von Ankyra als Exarch des Patriarchen Germanos II', *BZ*, XVI (1907), 120–42.

Kyrou, A., Βησσαρίων ὁ Ἕλλην, 2 vols. (Athens, 1947).

Laborde, Ctᵉ de, *Athènes aux XVᵉ, XVIᵉ, et XVIIᵉ siècles*, 2 vols. (Paris, 1854).

Lami, G., *Deliciae eruditorum*, V, IX (Florence, 1738–40).

La Monte, John L., 'Chronology of the Latin Orient', *Bull. of the International Committee of Historical Sciences*, XII, pt. II, no. 47 (1943), 140–202.

Lampakes, G., Χριστιανικὴ Ἀρχαιολογία τῆς Μονῆς Δαφνίου (Athens, 1889).

Lampros, P., *Monete inedite dei Gran maestri dell'Ordine di S. Giovanni di Gerusalemme in Rodi*, transl. C. Kunz (Venice, 1865); *Primo supplemento* (Venice, 1866); originals in Πανδώρα, IX, XVI (Athens, 1859–65).

Lampros, P., *Illustrazione di due monete inedite battute dai Conti di Salona*, transl. (Athens, 1866).

Lampros, P., *Unedirte Münzen und Bleibullen der Despoten von Epirus* (Vienna, 1873).

Lampros, P., Ἀνέκδοτα νομίσματα τοῦ μεσαιωνικοῦ Βασιλείου τῆς Κύπρου (with French transl.) (Athens, 1876).

Lampros, P., Ἀνέκδοτα νομίσματα κοπέντα ἐν Γλαρέντσᾳ κατὰ μίμησιν τῶν Ἐνετικῶν ὑπὸ Ῥοβέρτου τοῦ ἐξ Ἀνδηγαυῶν, Ἡγεμόνος τῆς Πελοποννήσου (1346–1364) (Athens, 1876).

Lampros, P., *Monnaies inédites de Chio* (Paris, 1877).

Lampros, P., *Monnaies inédites des Grands Maîtres de Rhodes de l'Ordre de Saint-Jean de Jérusalem* (Paris, 1877).

Lampros, P., *Monnaies inédites de Pierre-Raymond Zacosta* (Athens, 1877).

Lampros, P., Ἀνέκδοτα νομίσματα καὶ μολυβδόβουλλα τῶν κατὰ τοὺς μέσους αἰῶνας Δυναστῶν τῆς Ἑλλάδος (Athens, 1880).

Lampros, P., Νομίσματα τῶν ἀδελφῶν Μαρτίνου καὶ Βενεδίκτου Βʹ Ζαχαριῶν Δυναστῶν τῆς Χίου (Athens, 1884).

Lampros, P., Μεσαιωνικὰ νομίσματα τῶν Δυναστῶν τῆς Χίου (Athens, 1886).

Lampros, Sp. P., Αἱ ᾿Αθῆναι περὶ τὰ τέλη τοῦ δωδεκάτου αἰῶνος (Athens, 1878).

Lampros Sp. P., ᾿Ιστορία τῆς ῾Ελλάδος, v–vi [see Gen. Bibl. v].

Lampros, Sp. P., 'Die erste Erwähnung von Astros, Leonidion, und Areia', *BZ*, ii (1893), 73–5.

Lampros, Sp. P., 'Mazaris und seine Werke', *BZ*, v (1896), 63–73.

Lampros, Sp. P., 'Tavia, eine verkannte mittelgriechische Stadt', *BZ*, vii (1898), 309–15.

Lampros, Sp. P., Μικταὶ Σελίδες (Athens, 1905).

Lampros, Sp. P., Παλαιολόγεια καὶ Πελοποννησιακά, 4 vols. (Athens, 1912–30).

Lampros, Sp. P., ῎Ελεγχος ἱστορικῶν ἐγγράφων περὶ διαφόρων ἑλληνικῶν χωρῶν ἐν τῷ δημοσίῳ ἀρχείῳ τῆς Βενετίας' [from 16th to 18th century], *NE*, xi (1914), 449–64.

Lampros, Sp. P., ῾Κωνσταντῖνος Παλαιολόγος Γραίτζας ὁ ἀμύντωρ τοῦ Σαλμενίκου', *NE*, xi (1914), 260–88.

Lampros, Sp. P., ῾Σφραγῖδες ᾿Ατζαϊώλων καὶ Παλαιολόγων', *NE*, xviii (1924), 45–7.

Lamprynides, M. G., ῾Η Ναυπλία (Athens, 1898).

Laurent, V., 'Grégoire X (1271–76) et le projet d'une ligue anti-turque', *EO*, xxxvii (1938), 257–73.

Lemerle, P., *L'Emirat d'Aydin, Byzance et l'Occident: Recherches sur 'La geste d'Umur Pacha'* (Paris, 1957).

Léonard, E. G., *La Jeunesse de Jeanne Première, Reine de Naples, Comtesse de Provence*, 3 vols. (Monaco and Paris, 1932–7).

Léonard, E. G., *Les Angevins de Naples* (Paris, 1954).

Le Quien, M., *Oriens Christianus*, ii [see Gen. Bibl. iv].

Levy, M. A., *Don Joseph Nasi, Herzog von Naxos* (Breslau, 1859).

Litta, P. and others, *Le famiglie celebri italiane* (Milan, etc., 1819–   ).

Loenertz, R.-J., 'Manuel Paléologue et Démétrius Cydonès. Remarques sur leurs correspondances', *EO*, xxxvi (1937), 271–87, 474–87; xxxvii (1938), 107–24.

Loenertz, R.-J., *La Société des Frères Pérégrinants: Etude sur l'Orient domini-cain* (Institut. hist. FF. PP., Dissert. hist., fasc. vii) (Rome, 1937).

Loenertz, R.-J., 'Pour l'histoire du Péloponnèse au XIVᵉ siècle 1382–1404', *EB*, i (1943), 152–96.

Loenertz, R.-J., 'Une Page de Jérôme Zurita relative aux duchés catalans de Grèce (1386)', *REB*, xiv (1956), 158–68.

Loenertz, R.-J., 'Jean V Paléologue à Venise (1370–1371)', *REB*, xvi (1958), 217–32.

Loenertz, R.-J., 'Marino Dandolo, seigneur d'Andros et son conflit avec l'évêque Jean (1225–1238)', *OCP*, xxv (1959), 165–81.

Loenertz, R.-J., 'Généalogie des Ghisi, dynastes vénitiens dans l'Archipel, 1207–1390', *OCP*, xxviii (1962), 121–68.

Longnon, J., 'Le Rattachement de la principauté de Morée au royaume de Sicile en 1267', *Journ. des Savants* (1942), pp. 134–43.

Longnon, J., 'Le Chroniqueur Henri de Valenciennes', *Journ. des Savants* (1945), pp. 134–50.

Longnon, J., 'La reprise de Salonique par les Grecs (1224)', *Actes VIᵉ Congr. internat. d'études byzantines: Paris, 1948*, i (Paris, 1950), 141–6.

Longnon, J., 'Problèmes de l'histoire de la principauté de Morée', *Journ. des Savants* (1946), pp. 77–100, 147–61.

Longnon, J., 'L'Organisation de l'église d'Athènes sous Innocent III', *Mémorial Louis Petit* (Bucharest, 1948), pp. 336–46.

Longnon, J., 'Domination franque et civilisation grecque', *Mélanges Charles Picard*, II (Paris, 1949), 659–67.

Longnon, J., *L'Empire latin de Constantinople et la principauté de Morée* [see Gen. Bibl. v].

Lopez, R., *Genova Marinara nel duecento. Benedetto Zaccaria, ammiraglio e mercante* (Messina and Milan, 1933).

Lopez, R., 'L'attività economica di Genova nel marzo 1253 secondo gli atti notarili del tempo', *Atti Soc. Ligure di St. Patria*, LXIV (1935), 163–269.

Lopez, R., *Storia delle colonie genovesi nel Mediterraneo* (Bologna, 1938).

[Loredano, Gio. Fr.], *Historie de' Rè Lusignani publicate da Henrico Giblet* (Venice, 1667).

Lountzes (Lunzi), E., Περὶ τῆς πολιτικῆς καταστάσεως τῆς Ἑπτανήσου ἐπὶ Ἐνετῶν (Athens, 1856); enlarged Italian version, *Della condizione politica delle Isole Ionie sotto il dominio veneto* (Venice, 1858).

Loverdos, J. P. K., Ἱστορία τῆς νήσου Κεφαλληνίας; Greek transl. from the Italian MS. by P. K. Gratsiatos (Cephalonia, 1888).

Luce, S. B., 'Modon, A Venetian Station in Mediaeval Greece', *Classical and Mediaeval Studies in honor of E. Kennard Rand* (New York, 1938), pp. 195–208.

Luttrell, A. T., 'Venice and the Knights Hospitallers of Rhodes in the Fourteenth Century', *Papers Brit. School at Rome*, XXVI = n.s. XIII (1958), 195–212.

Luttrell, A., 'Interessi fiorentini nell'economia e nella politica dei Cavalieri Ospedalieri di Rodi nel Trecento', *Annali della Scuola Normale Superiore di Pisa: Lettere, Storia, e Filosofia*, 2nd ser., XXVIII (1959), 317–26.

Luttrell, A., 'Greek Histories Translated and Compiled for Juan Fernández de Heredia, 1377–1396', *SP*, XXXV (1960), 401–7.

Magni, Cornelio, *Relazione della città di Atene* (Parma, 1688).

Magni, Cornelio, *Quanto di più curioso e vago ha potuto raccorre Cornelio Magni in viaggi e dimore per la Turchia* (Parma, 1692).

Mai, A., *Spicilegium Romanum*, 10 vols. (Rome, 1839–44).

Mamalakes, I. P., Γεώργιος Γέμιστος Πλήθων (Texte u. Forschungen zur byz.-neugriech. Philologie, 32) (Athens, 1939).

Manousakas, M. I., 'La littérature crétoise à l'époque vénitienne', *L'Hellénisme contemp.*, 2nd ser., IX (1955), 95–120.

Manousakas, M. I., ''Αρχιερεῖς Μεθώνης, Κορώνης καὶ Μονεμβασίας γύρω στὰ 1500', Πελοποννησιακά, III (1959) 95–147.

Manousakas, M. I., Ἡ ἐν Κρήτῃ συνωμοσία τοῦ Σήφη Βλαστοῦ (*1453–1454*) καὶ ἡ νέα συνωμοτικὴ κίνησις τοῦ *1460–1462* (Athens, 1960).

Marinescu, C., 'Alphonse V, roi d'Aragon et de Naples, et l'Albanie de Scanderbeg', *Mélanges de l'Ecole Roumaine en France* (Paris, 1923), pp. 1–135.

Marinescu, C., 'Notes sur les Catalans dans l'empire byzantin pendant le règne de Jacques II (1291–1327)', *Mélanges F. Lot* (Paris, 1946), pp. 501–13.

Marinescu, C., 'Tentatives de mariage de deux fils d'Andronic II Paléologue avec des princesses latines', *RHSE*, I (1924), 139–40.

Marinescu, C., 'Manuel II Paléologue et les rois d'Aragon. Commentaire sur quatre lettres inédites en latin, expédiées par la chancellerie byzantine', *Acad. Roumaine, Bull. de la section historique*, XI (1924), 192–206.

Marinescu, C., 'Le pape Nicolas V (1447–1455) et son attitude envers l'Empire byzantin', *Izvestija Bŭlg. Arch. Inst.* IX (1935), 331–42.

Marinescu, C., 'Le pape Calixte III (1455–1458), Alfonse d'Aragon, roi de Naples, et l'offensive contre les Turcs', *Bull. Acad. Roum., Sect. Hist.* XIX (1935), publ. separately, 23 pp.

Marinescu, C., 'Contribution à l'histoire des relations économiques entre l'Empire byzantin, la Sicile et le royaume de Naples de 1419 à 1453', *Atti V Congr. Intern. Studi Biz: Rome, 1936, SBN,* V (1939), 209–19.

Marmora, A., *Historia di Corfù* (Venice, 1672).

Mas Latrie, L. de, *Histoire de l'île de Chypre sous le règne des Princes de la Maison de Lusignan,* 3 vols. (Paris, 1852–61).

Mas Latrie, L. de, 'Généalogie des rois de Chypre de la famille de Lusignan', *Arch. Ven.* XXI (Venice, 1881), 309–59.

Mas Latrie, L. de, *Histoire des archevêques latins de l'île de Chypre* (Genoa, 1882).

Mas Latrie, L. de, 'Les seigneurs terciers de Négrepont', *ROL,* I (1893), 413–32.

Meliarakes, A., Ἄνδρος, Κέως (Athens, 1880).

Meliarakes, A., ' Ἀμοργός', *D,* I (1884), 569–656.

Meliarakes, A., Γεωγραφία πολιτικὴ νέα καὶ ἀρχαία τοῦ νομοῦ Ἀργολίδος καὶ Κορινθίας (Athens, 1886).

Meliarakes, A., Γεωγραφία πολιτικὴ νέα καὶ ἀρχαία τοῦ νομοῦ Κεφαλληνίας (Athens, 1890).

Meliarakes, A., Ἱστορία τοῦ Βασιλείου τῆς Νικαίας καὶ τοῦ Δεσποτάτου τῆς Ἠπείρου [see Gen. Bibl. V].

Meliarakes, A., 'Κίμωλος', *D,* VI (1902), 3–43.

Meliarakes, A., Οἰκογένεια Μαμωνᾶ (Athens, 1902).

Mercati, G., *Scritti d'Isidoro il cardinale Ruteno e codici a lui appartenuti che si conservano nella Biblioteca Vaticana* (Studi e Testi, 46) (Vatican, 1926).

Mercati, G., *Se la versione dall'ebraico del Codice Veneto Greco VII sia di Simone Atumano* (Studi e Testi, 30) (Vatican, 1916).

Mercati, S. G., 'Venezia e la poesia neogreca', *Italia e Grecia* (volume a cura dell'Istituto Nazionale per le Relazioni Culturali con l'Estero) (Florence, 1939), pp. 309–39.

Metcalf, D. M., 'The Currency of Deniers Tournois in Frankish Greece', *Annual of the British School at Athens,* LV (1960), 38–59.

Meyer, E., *Peloponnesische Wanderungen* (Zürich and Leipzig, 1939).

Michel, K. and Struck, A., 'Die mittelbyzantinischen Kirchen Athens', *Mitteilungen des k. deutschen Archäologischen Instituts* (Athenische Abtheilung), XXXI (1906), 279–324.

Miller, W., 'The Name of Santa Maura', *EHR,* XVIII (1903), 513–14.

Miller, W., 'Ithake under the Franks', *EHR,* XXI (1906), 513–17; reprinted in *Essays on the Latin Orient* [see Gen. Bibl. V].

Miller, W., 'The Mad Duke of Naxos', *EHR,* XXI (1906), 737–9; reprinted in *Essays on the Latin Orient.*

Miller, W., 'The Name of Navarino', *EHR,* XX (1905), 307–9; XXI (1906), 106; reprinted in *Essays on the Latin Orient.*

Miller, W., 'Der älteste Stammbaum der Herzöge von Naxos', *BZ,* XVI (1907), 258–61.

Miller, W., 'The Last Venetian Islands in the Aegean', *EHR,* XXII (1907), 304–8; reprinted in *Essays on the Latin Orient.*

Miller, W., 'Monemvasia', *JHS,* XXVII (1907), 229–41, 300–1; reprinted in *Essays on the Latin Orient.*

Miller, W., 'Notes on Athens under the Franks', *EHR*, XXII (1907), 518–22; reprinted in *Essays on the Latin Orient*.

Miller, W., *The Latins in the Levant* [see Gen. Bibl. v].

Miller, W., 'The Marquisate of Boudonitza (1204–1414)', *JHS*, XXVIII (1908), 234–49; reprinted in *Essays on the Latin Orient*.

Miller, W., 'The Turkish Capture of Athens', *EHR*, XXIII (1908), 529–30; reprinted in *Essays on the Latin Orient*.

Miller, W., 'Two Letters of Giovanni IV, Duke of the Archipelago', *BZ*, XVII (1908), 463–70.

Miller, W., 'The Frankish Inscription at Karditza', *JHS*, XXIX (1909), 198–201; reprinted in *Essays on the Latin Orient*.

Miller, W., 'The Zaccaria of Phocaea and Chios', *JHS*, XXXI (1911), 42–55; reprinted in *Essays on the Latin Orient*.

Miller, W., 'The Gattilusi of Lesbos (1355–1462)', *BZ*, XXII (1913), 406–47; reprinted in *Essays on the Latin Orient*.

Miller, W., 'The Genoese in Chios, 1346–1566', *EHR*, XXX (1915), 418–32; reprinted in *Essays on the Latin Orient*.

Miller, W., 'Salonika', *EHR*, XXXII (1917), 161–74; reprinted in *Essays on the Latin Orient*.

Miller, W., *Essays on the Latin Orient* [see Gen. Bibl. v].

Miller, W., 'The Last Athenian Historian: Laonikos Chalkokondyles', *JHS*, XLII (1922), 36–49.

Miller, W., 'The Historians Doukas and Phrantzes', *JHS*, XLVI (1926), 63–71.

Millet, G., 'Rapport sur une mission à Mistra', *Bull. de correspondance hellénique*, XIX (1895), 268–72.

Millet, G., *Le monastère de Daphni* (Paris, 1899).

Millet, G., 'Inscriptions byzantines de Mistra', *Bull. de correspondance hellénique*, XXIII (1899), 97–156.

Millet, G., 'Inscriptions inédites de Mistra', *Bull. de correspondance hellénique*, XXX (1906), 453–66.

Millet, G., *Monuments byzantins de Mistrâ*. Album (Paris, 1910).

Mohler, L., *Kardinal Bessarion als Theologe, Humanist und Staatsmann* (Quellen und Forschungen, herausgegeben von der Görres-Gesellschaft, XX) (Paderborn, 1923).

Mommsen, A., *Athenae Christianae* (Leipzig, 1868).

Mompherratos, A. G., Οἱ Παλαιολόγοι ἐν Πελοποννήσῳ (*1383–1458*) (Athens, 1913).

Mompherratos, A. G., Μεθώνη καὶ Κορώνη ἐπὶ Ἐνετοκρατίας ἀπὸ κοινωνικήν, πολιτικὴν καὶ δημοσιονομικὴν ἔποψιν (Athens, 1914).

Moncada, F. de, *Expedición de los Catalanes y Aragoneses contra Turcos y Griegos* (Biblioteca de Autores Españoles, XXI) (Madrid, 1868).

Monnier, P., *Le Quattrocento. Essai sur l'histoire littéraire du XVᵉ siècle italien*, 2 vols. (Paris, 1924).

Monti, G. M., *Il Mezzogiorno d'Italia nel Medioevo* (Bari, 1930).

Monti, G. M., *Nuovi studi Angioini* (R. Deput. St. patr. per le Puglie: Documenti e Monografie, n.s. XXI) (Trani, 1937).

Monti, G. M., 'Il Mezzogiorno d'Italia e gli Stati Balcanici dai Normanni agli Aragonesi', *Atti V Congr. Intern. Studi Biz.: Roma, 1936, SBN*, V (1939), 220–4.

Monti, G. M., 'La dominazione napoletana in Albania: Carlo I d'Angiò, primo re degli Albanesi', *Rivista d'Albania*, I (1941), 50–8.

Moravcsik, Gy., 'Zur Quellenfrage der Helenaepisode in Goethes Faust', *BNJ*, VIII (1931), 41–56.

Mordtmann, J. H., 'Die erste Eroberung von Athen durch die Türken zu Ende des 14. Jahrhunderts', *BNJ*, IV (1923), 346–50.

Morisini, A., *Corsi di penna e catena di materie sopra l'Isola della Ceffalonia* (Venice, 1628).

Moschides, A., 'Η Λῆμνος, I [to 1770] (Alexandria, 1907).

Moutsopoulos, N., 'Le Monastère franc de Notre-Dame d'Isova (Gortynie)', *Bulletin de correspondance hellénique*, LXXX (1956), 76–94.

Mustoxidi, A., *Illustrazioni Corciresi*, 2 vols. (Milan, 1811–14).

Mustoxidi, A., *Delle cose Corciresi*, I (Corfù, 1848). [Incomplete.]

Mustoxidi [Μουστοξύδης], M. A., 'Ἱστορικὰ καὶ φιλολογικὰ Ἀνάλεκτα (Corfù, 1872).

Nicolau d'Olwer, Ll., *L'Expansió de Catalunya en la Mediterrània oriental* (Barcelona, 1926).

Nicolau d'Olwer, Ll., 'Les Seigneurs catalans d'Egine', Εἰς Μνήμην Σπ. Π. Λάμπρου (Athens, 1935), pp. 389–92.

Nitti di Vito, F., *Le Pergamene di S. Nicola di Bari: Periodo angioino, 1309–1343* (R. Deput. St. patr. per le Puglie: Codice diplomatico barese, XVI, nuova serie) (Trani, 1941).

Norden, W., *Der vierte Kreuzzug im Rahmen der Beziehungen des Abendlandes zu Byzanz* (Berlin, 1898).

Norden, W., *Das Papsttum und Byzanz* [see Gen. Bibl. v].

Omont, H., 'Un nouvel évêque latin de Milo, Etienne Gatalusio (1563)', *ROL*, I (1893), 537–9.

Origo, Iris, 'The Domestic Enemy: The Eastern Slaves in Tuscany in the Fourteenth and Fifteenth Centuries', *SP*, XXX (1955), 321–66.

Orlandos, A. K., 'Μεσαιωνικὰ Μνημεῖα τῆς πεδιάδος τῶν Ἀθηνῶν καὶ τῶν κλιτύων Ὑμηττοῦ-Πεντελικοῦ, Πάρνηθος καὶ Αἰγάλεω', Εὑρετήριον τῶν Μνημείων τῆς Ἑλλάδος (Athens, 1933), pp. 123–231.

Orlandos, A. K., 'Η Παρηγορήτισσα τῆς Ἄρτης (Athens, 1921). [For numerous other publications on Arta by Orlandos, see *BZ*, XXXVII (1937), 562–5.]

Ostrogorsky, G., *History of the Byzantine State* [see Gen. Bibl. v].

Pagano, C., *Delle Imprese e del Dominio dei Genovesi nella Grecia* (Genoa, 1846).

Pall, Fr., 'Ciriaco d'Ancona e la crociata contro i Turchi', *Acad. Roum., Bull. sect. hist.*, XX (1937), 9–60.

Pall, Fr., 'Autour de la croisade de Varna: La question de la paix de Szeged et de sa rupture (1444)', *Acad. Roum., Bull. sect. hist.*, XXII (1941), 144–58.

Pall, Fr., 'Les Croisades en Orient au Moyen Age: Observations critiques sur l'ouvrage de M. Atiya', *RHSE*, XIX (1942), 527–83.

Pall, Fr., 'Un moment décisif du Sud-Est européen: la croisade de Varna', *Balcania*, VII (1944), 102–20.

Panvinius, O., *Antiquitatum Veronensium libri VIII* (Verona, 1648).

Papadopulos, A. Th., *Versuch einer Genealogie der Palaiologen, 1259–1453* (Munich, 1938).

Papadopoulos, Chr. [Archbishop of Athens], 'Ἀπόπειραι ἑνώσεως τῶν Ἐκκλησιῶν κατὰ τὸν χρόνον τῆς Φραγκοκρατίας ἐν Κπόλει (1204–1261)', Θεολογία, XIV (1936), 5–23.

Papadopoulos, T. H., *Studies and Documents Relating to the History of the Greek Church and People under Turkish Domination* (Brussels, 1952).

Papadopoulos-Kerameus, A., 'Περὶ τῆς ἐπισκοπῆς Διαυλείας', *BZ*, VII (1898), 50–6.

Papadopoulos-Kerameus, A., ''Αθηναϊκὰ ἐκ τοῦ ΙΒ' καὶ ΙΓ' αἰῶνος', 'Αρμονία, III (1902), 209–24, 273–93.

Papadopoulos-Kerameus, A., 'Παρατηρήσεις εἰς τὰ Epirotica saeculi XIII', *VV*, XI (1904), 849–66.

Papadopoulos-Kerameus, A., 'Δυρραχηνά', *BZ*, XIV (1905), 568–74.

Papadopoulos-Kerameus, A., 'Κερκυραϊκά. 'Ιωάννης 'Απόκαυκος καὶ Γεώργιος Βαρδάνης', *VV*, XIII (1906), 334–51.

Paparrhegopoulos, K., 'Ιστορία τοῦ 'Ελληνικοῦ ''Εθνους, 4th ed., ed. P. Karolides, 5 vols. (Athens, 1903).

Paschales, D. P., Νομισματικὴ τῆς νήσου ''Ανδρου (Athens, 1892).

Paschales, D. P., 'Η ''Ανδρος, 2 vols. (Athens, 1925–7).

Paschales, D. P., Λατῖνοι 'Επίσκοποι ''Ανδρου (*1208–1716*) (Athens, 1927).

Paschales, D. P., 'Δώδεκα ἐν ''Ανδρῳ Βυζαντινὰ μοναστήρια', *EEBS*, XII (1936), 19–45.

Pasch di Krienen, Conte, *Breve descrizione dell'Arcipelago* (Leghorn, 1773).

Pègues, Abbé, *Histoire et phénomènes du volcan et des îles volcaniques de Santorin* (Paris, 1842).

Perrhaibos, Ch., 'Ιστορία σύντομος τοῦ Σουλίου καὶ Πάργας (Athens, 1857).

Petritzopoulos, D., *Saggio storico sull'età di Leucadia* (Venice, 1824).

Philadelpheus, Th. N., 'Ιστορία τῶν 'Αθηνῶν ἐπὶ Τουρκοκρατίας, 2 vols. (Athens, 1902).

Piacenza, F., *L'Egeo redivivo* (Modena, 1688).

Pouqueville, F. C. H. L., *Voyage dans la Grèce*, 5 vols. (Paris, 1820–1).

Promis, D., *La Zecca di Scio durante il dominio dei Genovesi* (Turin, 1865).

P[runni], G., 'Due Senesi governatori a Corfù', *Bull. Senese Storia patria*, XLVII (1940), 327–8.

Psilakes, B., 'Ιστορία τῆς Κρήτης ἀπὸ τῆς ἀπωτάτης ἀρχαιότητος μέχρι τῶν καθ' ἡμᾶς χρόνων, 3 vols. (Canea, 1901–10).

Puig i Cadafalch, J., 'Les iconostases et les retables catalans', Εἰς Μνήμην Σπ. Π. Λάμπρου (Athens, 1935), pp. 385–8.

Put, A. van de, 'Note on the Armorial Insignia in the Church of St George, Geraki', *Annual of the British School at Athens*, XIII (1906–7), 281–4.

Ramsay, W. M., 'A Romaic Ballad', *JHS*, I (1880), 293–300.

Raynaldus, O., *Annales ecclesiastici* (1198–1565) [see Gen. Bibl. V under C. Baronius].

Reinhard, J. P., *Vollständige Geschichte des Königreichs Cypern*, 2 vols. (Erlangen, 1766–8).

Remondini, B. M., *De Zacynthi antiquitatibus et fortuna* (Venice, 1756).

Rhomaios, K. A., 'Τοπογραφικὰ τῆς Φραγκοκρατίας', Πελοποννησιακά, II (1957), 1–26.

Rodd, Sir Rennell, *The Princes of Achaia and the Chronicles of Morea*, 2 vols. (London, 1907).

Rodokanakes, Prince de, 'Ιουστινιᾶναι—Χίος (Syra, 1900).

Romanin, S., *Storia documentata di Venezia*, II–VI (Venice, 1854–7).

Romanos, J. A., Γρατιανὸς Ζώρζης, 'Αυθέντης Λευκάδος (Corfù, 1870).

Romanos, J. A., Δημοσία Κερκυραϊκὴ Πρᾶξις (Corfù, 1882).

Romanos, J. A., 'Η 'Εβραϊκὴ Κοινότης τῆς Κερκύρας; reprint from the 'Εστία (Athens, 1891).

Romanos, J. A., Περὶ τοῦ Δεσποτάτου τῆς 'Ηπείρου (Corfù, 1895).

Rubió y Lluch, Antonio, for a critical appraisal of his numerous writings, see K. M. Setton, *Catalan Domination of Athens*, pp. 285–91 [see Gen. Bibl. V].

Rubió y Lluch, Antonio [Antoni Rubió i Lluch], 'Estudios sobre los historiadores griegos acerca de las expediciones catalanas a Oriente', *Revista de Ciencias históricas*, III (1881), 57–70.

Rubió y Lluch, A., 'Nicéforo Gregoras y la expedición de los Catalanes a Oriente', *Museo Balear de Historia y Literatura, Ciencias y Artes*, II (1885).

Rubió y Lluch, A., 'Συμβολαὶ εἰς τὴν Ἱστορίαν τῶν Καταλωνίων ἐν Ἑλλάδι', *D*, II (1887), 458–66.

Rubió y Lluch, A., 'La Expedición y Dominación de los Catalanes en Oriente, juzgadas por los Griegos', *Memorias de la Real Academia de Buenas Letras de Barcelona*, IV (1883).

Rubió y Lluch, A., *Los Navarros en Grecia, y el Ducado catalán de Atenas en la Época de su Invasión* (Barcelona, 1886); *Memorias de la Real Academia de Buenas Letras de Barcelona*, IV (1887).

Rubió y Lluch, A., 'Noticia geográfica del Oriente segons en Muntaner', *Butl-letí del Centre Excursionista de Catalunya* (1891, 1892).

Rubió y Lluch, A., 'De la época en que 'ls Catalans perderen a Athenas', *Butl-letí del Centre Excursionista de Catalunya* (1892).

Rubió y Lluch, A., 'Περὶ τῆς ἐποχῆς καθ' ἣν οἱ Καταλάνοι ἀπώλεσαν τὰς Ἀθήνας' (Greek transl. G. N. Mavrakis), *D*, V (1893), 535–46.

Rubió y Lluch, A., 'El ducat català d'Atenes en el regnat de D. Joan I', *Revista de Catalunya* (November, 1896), pp. 33–43.

Rubió y Lluch, A., 'La lengua y la cultura catalanas en Grecia en el siglo XIV', *Homenaje a Menéndez y Pelayo*, II (Madrid, 1899).

Rubió y Lluch, A., 'Ὁ πολιτισμὸς καὶ ἡ γλῶσσα τῶν Καταλανῶν ἐν Ἑλλάδι κατὰ τὴν ΙΔ' ἑκατονταετηρίδα' (Greek transl. by G. N. Mavrakis), Ἁρμονία, I (1900), 273–88, 337–46.

Rubió y Lluch, A., *Catalunya a Grecia: Estudis històrics i literaris* (Biblioteca Popular de 'L'Avenç', 49) (Barcelona, 1906).

Rubió y Lluch, A., 'Atenes en temps dels Catalans', *Anuari de l'Institut d'Estudis Catalans*, I (1907), 225–54.

Rubió y Lluch, A., *La Acrópolis de Atenas en la Época catalana* (Academia Provincial de Bellas Artes de Barcelona (Barcelona, 1908), 34 pp.

Rubió y Lluch, A., 'Els Castells catalans en la Grècia continental', *Anuari de l'Institut d'Estudis Catalans*, II (1908), 364–425.

Rubió y Lluch, A., 'La llengua catalana a Grècia', *Primer Congrés Internacional de la Llengua Catalana* (1908), pp. 235–48.

Rubió y Lluch, A., 'La Llengua catalana a Grècia', *Lectura Popular*, XVI, no. 262.

Rubió y Lluch, A., 'La Població dels ducats catalans de Grècia', *Boletín de la Real Academia de Buenas Letras de Barcelona*, IV (1908), 489–503.

Rubió y Lluch, A., 'Tradicions sobre la caiguda del comtat català de Salona', *Butl-letí del Centre Excursionista de Catalunya*, XX (1910), 117–20, 144–50.

Rubió y Lluch, A., 'Els Governs de Matheu de Moncada i Roger de Lluria en la Grècia catalana, 1359–1370', *Anuari de l'Institut d'Estudis Catalans*, IV (1911–12), 3–58.

Rubió y Lluch, A., Περὶ τῶν Καταλανικῶν φρουρίων τῆς ἠπειρωτικῆς Ἑλλάδος, transl. G. N. Mavrakis, in the Greek periodical Ἑστία (Athens, 1912).

Rubió y Lluch, A., 'La Grècia catalana des de la mort de Roger de Lluria fins a la de Frederic III de Sicilia, 1370–1377', *Anuari de l'Institut d'Estudis Catalans*, V (1913–14), 393–485.

Rubió y Lluch, A., 'La Grècia catalana des de la mort de Frederic III fins a la Invasió Navarresa, 1377–1379', *Anuari de l'Institut d'Estudis Catalans*, VI (1915–20), 127–99.

Rubió y Lluch, A., 'Joan I humanista i el primer període de l'humanisme català', *Estudis Universitaris Catalans*, x (1917–18), 1–117.

Rubió y Lluch, A., 'La Companyía catalana sota 'l comandament de Teobald de Cepoy: Campanyes de Macedònia i de Tesàlia, 1307–1310', *Miscel. lània Prat de la Riba*, i (1923), 219–70; trans. G. P. Cicellis, *L'Hellénisme contemporain*, ser. 2, viii (1954), 394–406, 499–521; ix (1955), 43–65.

Rubió y Lluch, A., 'Conquista de Tebas en 1379 por Juan de Urtubia: Episódio de la Historia de los Navarros en Grecia', *Bulletin de la section historique de l'Académie Roumaine*, xi (Bucharest, 1924), 170–91. [The same article, in somewhat more extended form and with completer notes, was also publ. in the *Homenaje a D. Carmelo de Echegaray: Miscelánea de Estudios referentes al País Vasco* (San Sebastian, 1928).]

Rubió y Lluch, A., 'Els darrers prohoms d'Atenes de la època catalana (1382–1388)', *Abhandlungen aus dem Gebiete der mittleren u. neueren Geschichte u. ihrer Hilfswissenschaften: Eine Festgabe zum siebzigsten Geburtstag Geh. Rat Prof. Dr. Heinrich Finke gewidmet* (Münster, 1925), pp. 209–32.

Rubió y Lluch, A., 'Significació de l'elogi de l'Acròpolis d'Atenes pel Rei Pere 'l Ceremoniós', *Homenaje ofrecido a D. Ramón Menéndez Pidal: Miscelánea de Estudios lingüisticos, literarios, e históricos*, iii (Madrid, 1925).

Rubió y Lluch, A., 'Une figure athénienne de l'époque de la domination catalane: Dimitri Rendi', *B*, ii (1925); 'Un personatge atenès de la època catalana: Dimitrio Rendi', in *Estudios eruditos...en homenaje...a D. Adolfo Bonilla y San Martin*, i (Madrid, 1927); also Περὶ τῆς καταστάσεως τῶν Ἑλλήνων ἐπὶ Καταλανοκρατίας καὶ περὶ τοῦ Ἀθηναίου Δημήτρη Ρέντη, transl. G. N. Mavrakis, *D*, i (1928).

Rubió y Lluch, A., *Paquimeres i Muntaner* (Barcelona, 1927).

Rubió y Lluch, A., 'Per què donem el nom de Catalana a la dominació de la Corona d'Aragó a Grècia', *Estudis Universitaris Catalans*, xii (1927), 1–12.

Rubió y Lluch, A., *Los Catalanes en Grecia: Últimos años de su Dominación: Cuadros históricos* (Editorial Voluntad, Manuales Hispania: series F, vol. i) (Madrid, 1927).

Rubió y Lluch, A., 'Mitteilungen zur Geschichte der griechischen Sklaven in Katalonien im XIV. Jahrhundert', *BZ*, xxx (1929–30), 462–8.

Rubió y Lluch, A., 'Nuevos aspectos de Roger de Flor en la historia de Paquimeres', *Boletín de la Real Academia de Buenas Letras de Barcelona*, xiv (1929–30), 40–7.

Rubió y Lluch, A., 'Setge i conquesta de l'Acròpolis d'Atenes per Rainer Acciajuoli (1387–1388)', *Miscel. lània Crexells* (Publicacions de la Fundació Bernat Metge, i) (Barcelona, 1929), 191–204.

Rubió y Lluch, A., *La Població de la Grècia catalana en el XIV^{en} segle* (Barcelona, 1933).

Rubió y Lluch, A., 'Chanceliers et notaires dans la Grèce catalane', Εἰς Μνήμην Σπ. Π. Λάμπρου (Athens, 1935), pp. 150–5.

Runciman, S., *History of the Crusades*, iii [see Gen. Bibl. v].

St Genois, Comte J. de, *Droits primitifs des anciennes terres et seigneuries du pays et comté de Haynaut*, i (Paris, 1782).

Saint-Sauveur, A. G., *Voyage historique, littéraire, et pittoresque dans les îles et possessions ci-devant vénitiennes du Levant*, 4 vols. (Paris, An viii [1799–1800]).

Sakazov, I., *Bulgarische Wirtschaftsgeschichte* (*Grundriss der slavischen Philologie und Kulturgeschichte*, ed. R. Trautmann and M. Vasmer, 5) (Berlin, Leipzig, 1929).

S[alapantas], P. A., Ἡ Πάργα (Athens, 1861).

[Salvator, Archduke Ludwig], *Paxos und Antipaxos*, 2nd ed. (Würzburg and Vienna, 1889).

[Salvator, Archduke Ludwig], *Zante*, Allgemeiner Teil (Prague, 1904).

[Salvator, Archduke Ludwig], *Zante*, Specieller Teil (Prague, 1904).

[Salvator, Archduke Ludwig], *Parga* (Prague, 1907).

[Salvator, Archduke Ludwig], *Anmerkungen über Leukas* (Prague, 1908).

[Salvator, Archduke Ludwig], *Versuch einer Geschichte von Parga* (Prague, 1908).

Santifaller, L., *Beiträge zur Geschichte des lateinischen Patriarchats von Kpel., 1204–1261, und der venezianischen Urkunde* (Historisch-diplomatische Forschungen, 3) (Weimar, 1938).

Sassenay, Cte F. de, *Les Brienne de Lecce et d'Athènes* (Paris, 1869).

Sathas, K. N., Χρονικὸν ἀνέκδοτον Γαλαξειδίου (Athens, 1865); reprinted (1914); ed. G. Valetas (Athens, 1944).

Sathas, K. N., Τουρκοκρατουμένη Ἑλλάς (Athens, 1869).

Sauger, Robert, *Histoire nouvelle des anciens ducs et autres souverains de l'Archipel* (Paris, 1699); Greek transl. A. Karales (Hermoupolis, 1878).

Sauli, L., *Della colonia dei Genovesi in Galata*, 2 vols. (Turin, 1831).

Schlumberger, G., *Les Principautés franques du Levant* (Paris, 1877).

Schlumberger, G., *Numismatique de l'Orient latin* [see Gen. Bibl. III].

Schlumberger, G., *Expédition des 'Almugavares' ou routiers catalans en Orient de l'an 1302 à l'an 1311* (Paris, 1902).

Schlumberger, G., Chalandon, F. and Blanchet, A., *Sigillographie de l'Orient latin* (Haut Commissariat de l'Etat Français en Syrie et au Liban. Service des Antiquités. Bibliothèque archéologique et historique, 37) (Paris, 1943).

Schreiner, H., 'Neue Quellen zur Komposition und Entstehungsgeschichte des mittelgriechischen Romans Imberios und Margarona', *BZ*, xxx (1929–30), 121–30.

Schultz, R. W. and Barnsley, S. H., *The Monastery of St Luke of Stiris, in Phocis* (London, 1901).

Schultz-Gora, O., *Le epistole del trovatore Rambaldo di Vaqueiras* (Florence, 1898).

Servion, J., *Gestez et chroniques de la Mayson de Savoye*, ed. F. E. Bollati, 2 vols. (Turin, 1879).

Setton, K. M., 'The Archbishop Simon Atumano and the Fall of Thebes to the Navarrese in 1379', *BNJ*, xviii (1945–9, publ. 1960), 105–22.

Setton, K. M., 'The Avignonese Papacy and the Catalan Duchy of Athens', *B*, xvii (1944–5), 281–303.

Setton, K. M., *Catalan Domination of Athens* [see Gen. Bibl. v].

Setton, K. M., 'The Archbishop Pierre d'Ameil in Naples and the Affair of Aimon III of Geneva (1363–64)', *SP*, xxviii (1953), 643–91.

Setton, K. M., 'The Archaeology of Medieval Athens', *Essays in Medieval Life and Thought Presented in Honor of Austin Patterson Evans* (New York, 1955), pp. 227–58.

Setton, K. M. (gen. ed.), *A History of the Crusades* [see Gen. Bibl. v].

Setton, K. M., 'The Byzantine Background to the Italian Renaissance', *Proceedings of the American Philosophical Society*, c, no. 1 (1956), pp. 1–76.

Ševčenko, I., 'The Zealot Revolution and the Supposed Genoese Colony in Thessalonica', Προσφορὰ εἰς Στ. Κυριακίδην (= Ἑλληνικά, Παράρτημα 4) (1953), pp. 603–17.

Sguros, K. A., Ἱστορία τῆς νήσου Χίου ἀπὸ τῶν ἀρχαιοτάτων χρόνων μέχρι τοῦ 1700 μ. Χ., ed. P. P. Argenti (Athens, 1937).

Silberschmidt, M., *Das orientalische Problem zur Zeit der Entstehung des türkischen Reiches nach venezianischen Quellen. Ein Beitrag zur Geschichte der Beziehungen Venedigs zu Sultan Bajezid I, etc. (1381–1400)* (Leipzig–Berlin, 1923).

Sinogowitz, B., 'Zur Eroberung Thessalonikes im Herbst 1224', *BZ*, XLV (1952), 28.

Soranzo, G., 'Venezia e le repubbliche marinare italiane nella storia delle Crociate', *Società Italiana per il Progresso delle Scienze: Atti della XXVI Riunione*, III, 1 and 2 (1938), 47–53.

Soteriou, G. A., 'Le Château fort de Chloumoutzi et son atelier monétaire de Tournois de Clarencia', *Journ. intern. d'arch. numism.* XIX (1918–19), 9 pp.

Soteriou, G. A., ''Ελληνικαὶ ἀνασκαφαὶ Χριστιανικῶν μνημείων', *BZ*, XXVI (1926), 244–7.

Soteriou, G. A. and Xyngopulos, A., Εὑρετήριον τῶν μεσαιωνικῶν μνημείων τῆς Ἑλλάδος. Μέρος Α´. ι. Μεσαιωνικὰ Μνημεῖα Ἀττικῆς. Α. Ἀθηνῶν, pts. ι–ιι (Athens, 1927–9), in K. Kuruniotis and G. A. Soteriou (edd.), Εὑρετήριον τῶν Μνημείων τῆς Ἑλλάδος (1927 ff.).

Sourmeles, D., Κατάστασις συνοπτικὴ τῆς πόλεως Ἀθηνῶν, 3rd ed. (Athens, 1846).

Spon, J. and Wheler, G., *Voyage d'Italie, de Dalmatie, de Grèce, et du Levant*, 3 vols. (Lyons, 1678).

Stadtmüller, G., *Michael Choniates, Metropolit von Athen* (ca. 1138–ca. 1222), *OCA*, XXXIII (Rome, 1934).

Stai, N., *Raccolta di antiche autorità…riguardanti l'Isola di Citera oggidì Cerigo* (Pisa, 1847).

Stamatelos, I., Φιλολογικαὶ διατριβαὶ περὶ Λευκάδος (Athens, 1851).

Stamatiades, E., Οἱ Καταλάνοι ἐν τῇ Ἀνατολῇ (Athens, 1869).

Stamatiades, E., Ἰκαριακά, ἤτοι Ἱστορία καὶ περιγραφὴ τῆς νήσου Ἰκαρίας (Samos, 1893).

Starr, J., *Romania. The Jewries of the Levant after the Fourth Crusade* (Paris, 1949).

Stein, E., 'Untersuchungen zur spätbyzantinischen Verfassungs- und Wirtschaftsgeschichte', *Mitteilungen zur Osmanischen Geschichte*, II (1923/5), 1–62.

Stiernon, L., 'Les Origines du despotat d'Epire', *REB*, XVII (1959), 90–126.

Storrs, R., *A Chronology of Cyprus* (Nicosia, 1930).

Struck, A., 'Vier byzantinische Kirchen der Argolis', *Mitteilungen des k. deutschen Archäologischen Instituts* (Athenische Abtheilung), XXXIV (1909), 189–236.

Struck, A., *Mistra. Eine mittelalterliche Ruinenstadt* (Vienna and Leipzig, 1910).

Stubbs, W., 'The Mediaeval Kingdoms of Cyprus and Armenia', *Seventeen Lectures on the Study of Mediaeval and Modern History*, 3rd ed. (Oxford, 1900), pp. 179–239.

Terrier de Loray, Marquis, 'Un Parlement de dames au XIIIᵉ siècle', *Académie des Sciences, Belles-Lettres, et Arts de Besançon* (1880), pp. 205–21.

Thallon, I. C., 'A Mediaeval Humanist: Michael Akominatos', *Vassar Mediaeval Studies* (New Haven, 1923), pp. 275–314.

Theotokes, Sp. M., 'Τὸ ἀρχεῖον τοῦ δουκὸς τῆς Κρήτης', Ἡμερολόγιον τῆς Μεγάλης Ἑλλάδος (1922), pp. 315–403.

Theotokes, Sp. M., 'Οἱ Σκλάβοι εἰς τὸ Βενετικὸν Κράτος', Ἑλληνικά, VI (1933), 145–8.

Thiriet, F., 'Venise et l'occupation de Ténédos au XIVe siècle', *Mélanges d'archéologie et d'histoire*, LXV (1953), 219–45.

Thiriet, F., 'Les Vénitiens à Thessalonique dans la première moitié du XIVe siècle', *B*, XXII (1952–3), 323–32.

Thiriet, F., *La Romanie vénitienne au moyen âge* [see Gen. Bibl. v].

Tipaldou, G. E., 'Εἷς ἄγνωστος σύγγαμβρος Κωνσταντίνου τοῦ Παλαιολόγου', *D*, IX (1926), 525–33.

Tipaldou, G. E., Τὰ Φραγκικὰ οἰκόσημα τῆς Χαλκίδος, *EEBS*, IV (1927), 352–64.

Topping, P., 'Le régime agraire dans le Péloponnèse latin au XIVe siècle', *L'Hellénisme Contemp.* 2nd series, X (1956), 255–95.

Torr, C., *Rhodes in Modern Times* (Cambridge, 1887).

Tournefort, P. de, *Relation d'un voyage du Levant*, 2 vols. (Amsterdam, 1718).

Tozer, H. F., 'Byzantine Satire', *JHS*, II (1881), 233–70.

Tozer, H. F., 'The Franks in the Peloponnese', *JHS*, IV (1883), 165–236.

Tozer, H. F., 'A Byzantine Reformer [Gemistus Plethon]', *JHS*, VII (1886), 353–80.

Traquair, R., 'Laconia: The Mediaeval Fortresses', *Annual of the British School at Athens*, XII (1905–6), 258–76.

Traquair, R., 'Mediaeval Fortresses of the Northwestern Peloponnesus', *Annual of the British School at Athens*, XIII (1906–7), 268–81.

Traquair, R., 'The Churches of Western Mani', *Annual of the British School at Athens*, XV (1908–9), 177–213.

Ubaldini, G. B., *Origine della famiglia delli Acciaioli* (Florence, 1638).

Usseglio, Leopoldo, *I Marchesi di Monferrato in Italia ed in Oriente durante i secoli XII e XIII*, 2 vols. (Turin, 1926).

Vasiliev, A. A., *History of the Byzantine Empire* [see Gen. Bibl. v].

Vasiliev, A. A., 'Il Viaggio dell'imperatore bizantino Giovanni V Paleologo in Italia (1369–1371) e l'Unione di Roma del 1369', *SBN*, III (1931), 151–93.

Vasiliev, A. A., 'Pero Tafur, a Spanish Traveller of the Fifteenth Century and His Visit to Constantinople, Trebizond and Italy', *B*, VII (1932), 75–122.

Vasilievsky, V., ''Ηπειρωτικὰ κατὰ τὴν ιγ' ἑκατονταετηρίδα', *VV*, III (1896), 233–99.

Viller, M., 'La question de l'union des églises entre Grecs et Latins depuis le concile de Lyon jusqu'à celui de Florence (1274–1438)', *RHE*, XVI (1921), 260–305, 515–32; XVIII (1922), 20–60.

Vitale, V., 'Statuti e ordinamenti sul governo del banco di San Giorgio a Famagosta', *Atti Soc. Ligure di St. patria*, LXIV (1935), 390–454.

Volonakes, M. D., *The Island of Roses and Her Eleven Sisters, or the Dodecanese* (London, 1922).

Wace, A. J. B., 'Frankish Sculptures at Parori and Geraki', *Annual of the British School at Athens*, XI (1904–5), 139–45.

Wadding, L. and others, *Annales minorum*, 2nd ed., 25 vols. (Rome, etc., 1740–1886).

Wellnhofer, M., *Johannes Apokaukos, Metropolit von Naupaktos in Aetolien (ca. 1155–1233)* (Munich, 1913).

Wittek, P., *Das Fürstentum Mentesche. Studie zur Geschichte Westkleinasiens im 13.–15. Jh.* (Istanbul, 1934).

Wittek, P., *The Rise of the Ottoman Empire* (London, 1938).

Wittek, P., 'The Castle of Violets: from Greek Monemvasia to Turkish Menekshe', *BSOAS*, xx (1957), 601–13.

Works of Art in Greece, the Greek Islands and the Dodecanese: Losses and Survivals in the War (London, H.M. Stationery Office, 1946).

Xanthoudides, S., Ἡ Ἐνετοκρατία ἐν Κρήτῃ καὶ οἱ κατὰ τῶν Ἐνετῶν ἀγῶνες τῶν Κρητῶν (Texte und Forschungen zur byzantinisch-neugriechischen Philologie, 34) (Athens, 1939).

Xivrey, B. de, *Mémoire sur la vie et les ouvrages de l'empereur Manuel Paléologue* (Mémoires de l'Institut de France. Académie des inscriptions et belles-lettres, xix, 2) (Paris, 1853).

Xyngopulos, A., Τὰ Βυζαντινὰ καὶ Τουρκικὰ Μνημεῖα τῶν Ἀθηνῶν, Εὑρετήριον τῶν Μνημείων τῆς Ἑλλάδος', ed. K. Kuruniotes and G. A. Soteriou, i, 1 (Athens, 1929), 59–122.

Zakythinos, D. A., Ὁ ἀρχιεπίσκοπος Ἄντελμος καὶ τὰ πρῶτα ἔτη τῆς λατινικῆς ἐκκλησίας Πατρῶν', *EEBS*, x (1933), 401–17.

Zakythinos, D. A., 'Une princesse française à la cour de Mistra au XIVe siècle. Isabelle de Lusignan Cantacuzène', *REG*, xlix (1936), 62–76.

Zakythinos, D. A., Οἱ Σλάβοι ἐν Ἑλλάδι (Athens, 1945).

Zakythinos, D. A., *Crise monétaire* [see Gen. Bibl. v].

Zakythinos, D. A., *Le despotat grec de Morée*. [Vol. ii on 'Vie et Institutions' combines articles published in *L'Hellénisme contemporain* (1949–52); see Gen. Bibl. v].

Zepos, P. I., Τὸ δίκαιον εἰς τὸ Χρονικὸν τοῦ Μορέως', *EEBS*, xviii (1948), 202–20.

Zerlentes, P. G., Ναξία, νῆσος καὶ πόλις', *BZ*, xi (1902), 491–9.

Zerlentes, P. G., Γράμματα Φράγκων δουκῶν τοῦ Αἰγαίου πελάγους (͵αυλγ'— ͵αφξδ')', *BZ*, xiii (1904), 136–57.

Zerlentes, P. G., Ἡ ἐν Πελοποννήσῳ ἑλληνικὴ ἐκκλησία ἐπὶ Ἐνετῶν (Athens, 1921).

Zerlentes, P. G., Μηλιγγοὶ καὶ Ἐζερῖται ἐν Πελοποννήσῳ (Hermoupolis, 1921).

Zerlentes, P. G., Γράμματα τῶν τελευταίων Φράγκων δουκῶν τοῦ Αἰγαίου Πελάγους (*1438–1565*) (Hermoupolis, 1924).

Ziebarth, E., 'Ein griechischer Reisebericht des fünfzehnten Jahrhunderts', *Mitteilungen des k. deutschen Archäologischen Instituts* (Athenische Abtheilung), xxiv (1899), 72–88.

Zolotas, G. J. *et al.*, Ἱστορία τῆς Χίου, iii, 1 (Athens, 1926): Τουρκοκρατία.

CHAPTER X. CONSTANTINOPLE AND ROME

I. SOURCES

It is only possible to cite here some of the many Greek and Latin writings on ecclesiastical union in the middle ages. See also chapters i–ix, xi–xiv and xxiii–xxvi.

The Byzantine and other historians and chroniclers may be found in the bibliographies to chapters i–ix.

Acta Conciliorum Oecumenicorum, ed. E. Schwartz [see Gen. Bibl. iv].

Anselm, Bishop of Havelberg, *Dialogi*, *MPL*, clxxxviii, 1139–1248.

Anselm of Lucca, *Collectio Canonum*, ed. F. Thaner (Oeniponte, 1906).

Anselm, St (1033–1109), *Refutation of the Greeks on the procession of the Holy Ghost*, *MPL*, CLVIII, 285–326.

Aquinas, St Thomas, *Treatise against the Errors of the Greeks addressed to Urban IV*, ed. S. E. Fretté in *Opera*, XXIX, 344–73 (Paris, 1876); ed. P. Glorieux (Monumenta christiana selecta, Tournai, 1957).

Basil, Archbishop of Ochrida (Achrida), *Dialogues with Anselm of Havelberg, 1155*, ed. J. Schmidt, *Des Basilius aus Achrida bisher unedierte Dialoge* (Munich, 1901); cf. also *MPG*, CLXXXVIII, 1139–1248. Letter to Pope Hadrian IV, Mansi, XXXI, 799.

Beccus, John, *Writings on the Union of the Churches*, *MPG*, CXLI.

Bessarion, Cardinal, *Encyclica ad Graecos*, *MPG*, CLXI; *Oratio dogmatica de unione*, ed. E. Candal (Rome, 1958).

Calecas, Manuel, *Adversus Graecos*, *MPG*, CLII, 11–258.

Camaterus, Andronicus, Ἱερὰ ὁπλοθήκη, *Dialogues of the Emperor Manuel Comnenus and the cardinals, 1166–7*, *MPG*, CXLI, 396–613 [incomplete]. See J. A. G. Hergenröther, *Photius*, III (Ratisbon, 1869), pp. 811–14.

Cerularius, Michael, *Letters and Synodal Edict*, *MPG*, CXX; see also below C. Will, *Acta*; A. Michel, *Humbert und Kerullarios*.

Chrysolanus, Peter, Archbishop of Milan, Papal legate to Constantinople, 1113, *Oration on the Holy Ghost*, *MPL*, CXXVII, 912–20.

Council of Lyons, 1274, Mansi, XXIV, 38–136. See also L. Delisle, *Recueils épist. de Bérard de Naples* (*Notices et extr. des MSS de la Bibl. Nationale*), XXVII, 2 (Paris, 1879), pp. 87–167, Appendix, pp. 150–67. [Latin transl. of documents laid before the Council of Lyons by the Greek ambassadors.]

Council of Basle, 1431–9, Mansi, XXX–XXXI*a*, 1–247.

Councils of Ferrara and Florence, 1438–9, Mansi, XXXI*a*–XXXI*b*; *Concilium Florentinum. Documenta et scriptores*, ed. G. Hofmann, E. Candal, B. Schulze and J. Gill, 7 vols. (Rome, 1944–58).

Council of St Sophia, Constantinople, 1450, Mansi, new ed. XXXII (Paris, 1912), 99–114.

Creyghton, R., *Vera historia unionis non verae inter Graecos et Latinos* (Hague, 1660).

Deusdedit, Cardinal, *Canonical Collection*, ed. V. Wolf von Glanvell, *Die Kanonensammlung des Kardinals Deusdedit* (Paderborn, 1905).

Diplomas of patriarchs of Constantinople, Miklosich, F. and Müller, J., *Acta et diplomata graeca*, I and II [see Gen. Bibl. IV].

Dölger, F., *Regesten der Kaiserurkunden* [see Gen. Bibl. IV].

Epistolae imperatorum et pontificum (*Collectio Avellana*), ed. O. Günther, *CSEL*, XXXV (Vienna, 1898).

Eustratius, Archbishop of Nicaea, *Speech on the Holy Ghost* (*c. 1115*), ed. A. Demetrakopoulos, Ἐκκλησιαστικὴ βιβλιοθήκη, I (Leipzig, 1866), 84–198.

Formosus, Pope, *Letters to Stylion*, Mansi, XVI, 439, 456–8.

Friedberg, E. A., *Corpus Juris Canonici*, 2 vols. (Leipzig, 1879); also *MPL*, CLXXXVII.

Gennadius, Patriarch of Constantinople (1453–68), *Oration on the Union and treatises against the Latins*, *MPG*, CLX, 320–73.

George of Cyprus, Patriarch of Constantinople (1241–89), *Treatises against Beccus and the Latins*, *MPG*, CXLII, 233–45.

Germanus II, Patriarch at Nicaea (1222–40), *Against the Latins*, *MPG*, CXL, 621–757.

Gregory I, Pope, *Registrum Epistolarum*, ed. P. Ewald and L. Hartmann (Berlin, 1887, 1891); *MGH, Ep.* I.

Gregory VII, Pope, *Registrum*, ed. E. Caspar, *Das Register Gregors VII*; *MGH, Ep. Selectae*, II, 2 vols. (1920, 1923).

Grumel, V., *Les Regestes des Actes du Patriarcat de Constantinople* [see Gen. Bibl. IV].

Hadrian II, Pope, *Epistolae, MGH, Ep.* VI, 691–765.

Hugo Etherianus of Pisa, *De haeresibus quas Graeci in Latinos devolvunt, MPL*, CCII, 232–3.

Humbert, Cardinal, *Contra Graecorum calumnias, MPL*, CXLIII, 930–74; *De gestis legatorum, ibid.* 1001–4; see also below C. Will, *Acta*.

Humbert, Cardinal, *Contra simoniacos, MGH, Lib. de lite*, I, 100–254; *MPL*, CXLIII, 1005–1210.

Humbert de Romanis, 'De his quae tractanda videbantur in concilio generali Lugduni, opus tripartitum', in Mansi, XXIV, 109–36. [Important contemporary Dominican source for problems of union, especially Council of Lyons.]

Innocent III, Pope, *Opera, MPL*, CCXIV–CCXVII.

Jaffé, P. and Wattenbach, W., *Regesta pontificum Romanorum* [see Gen. Bibl. IV].

John VIII, Pope, *Epistolae, MPL*, CXXVI, 651–967; *MGH, Ep.* VII, ed. E. Caspar.

Jorga, N., *Notes et extraits pour servir à l'hist. des croisades au XVᵉ siècle*, 6 vols. (Paris and Bucharest, 1899–1916).

Joseph, Bishop of Methone, see Plusiadenus, John.

Justinian, *Novellae* [see Gen. Bibl. IV].

Justinian, *Corpus Juris Civilis* [see Gen. Bibl. IV].

Kalojan, tsar of Bulgaria, *Letters to Innocent III, MPL*, CCXIV, 1112 ff.; *ibid.* CCXV, 287–92.

Lampros, S. P., 'Αὐτοκρατόρων τοῦ Βυζαντίου χρυσόβουλλα καὶ χρυσᾶ γράμματα ἀναφερόμενα εἰς τὴν ἔνωσιν τῶν Ἐκκλησιῶν', *NE*, XI (1914), 94–128, 241–54 [with facsimiles].

Leo, Archbishop of Ochrida, *Epistola de azymis, MPG*, CXX, 835–44; and see below, C. Will, *Acta*.

Leo IX, Pope, *Epistolae et decreta pontificia, MPL*, CXLIII, 592–838; Mansi, XIX; C. Will, *Acta* [see below].

Liber Diurnus, ed. T. E. Sickel (Vienna, 1889); ed. H. Foerster (Bern, 1958).

Liber Pontificalis, ed. L. Duchesne [see Gen. Bibl. IV].

Liutprand, Bishop of Cremona, *Antapodosis; relatio de legatione Constantinopolitana*, ed. I. Bekker, *SGUS* (1915); English transl. F. A. Wright, *The Works of Liutprand of Cremona* (London, 1930).

Mansi, J. D., *Sacrorum conciliorum amplissima collectio* [see Gen. Bibl. IV].

Manuel II Palaeologus, *Letters*, ed. E. Legrand (Paris, 1893).

Manuel Rhetor, *De Marco Ephesio deque rebus in Synodo Florentino gestis*, ed. L. Petit, *PO*, XVII (1923), 491–522.

Mark Eugenicus, Archbishop of Ephesus, *Dialogus. Epistola Encyclica*, ed. L. Petit, *PO*, XVII (1923), 415–59; *Treatises against the Latins and encyclicals against the Council of Florence, MPG*, CLX, 1071–1100.

Metochites, George, *Historiae dogmaticae lib. I et II*, ed. A. Mai, *Nova patrum bibl.* VIII (Rome, 1871).

Meyendorff, J., 'Projets de concile œcuménique en 1367. Un dialogue inédit entre Jean Cantacuzène et le légat Paul', *DOP*, XIV (1960), 149–77.

Nicephorus, Patriarch of Constantinople, *Epistola ad Leonem III*, *MPG*, c, 169–200.

Nicephorus Blemmydes, Patriarch at Nicaea (1260), *On the Procession of the Holy Ghost*, *MPG*, cxlii, 533–84.

Nicetas, Chartophylax (under Manuel Comnenus), *Dialogues on the Holy Ghost* (favouring the Latins), *MPG*, cxxxix, 169–221.

Nicetas-David, *Vita Ignatii*, *MPG*, cv, 487–574.

Nicetas Nicenus, *De schismate Graecorum*, *MPG*, cxx, 713–29.

Nicetas Stethatus, *Libellus contra Latinos*, *MPG*, cxx, 1011–22.

Nicholas I, Pope, *Epistolae*, *MGH*, *Ep.* vi, pp. 257–690; *MPL*, cxix; Mansi, xv.

Nicholas Mysticus, *Epistolae*, *MPG*, cxi, 27–392.

Nicholas of Otranto, Abbot of Casole, *Treatises on the Procession of the Holy Ghost and on the Azymites*. Greek text ed. Bishop Arsenij from the Moscow MS. Synod. 240 (Novgorod, 1896) [a Greek version of Latin views at the disputations held at Constantinople, 1205, under the auspices of Benedict, Cardinal of Santa Susanna; see W. Norden, *Das Papsttum und Byzanz*, p. 184; see Gen. Bibl. v].

Petit, L. (ed.), *Documents relatifs au Concile de Florence*, *PO*, xv, xvii (Paris, 1920–3).

Photius, Patriarch of Constantinople, *Collationes*, *MPG*, civ, 1220–32.

Photius, Patriarch of Constantinople, *Mystagogia*, *MPG*, cii, 279–400.

Photius, Patriarch of Constantinople, *Ad Amphilochium*, *MPG*, ci; ed. S. Oeconomos (Athens, 1858).

Photius, Patriarch of Constantinople, *Epistolae*, *MPG*, cii, cols. 585–990; ed. J. N. Valettas (London, 1864).

Photius, Patriarch of Constantinople, *Monumenta Graeca ad Photium pertinentia*, ed. J. Hergenröther (Ratisbon, 1869).

Photius, Patriarch of Constantinople, *Epistolae XLV*, ed. A. Papadopoulos-Kerameus (St Petersburg, 1896).

Photius, Patriarch of Constantinople, *Photiaca*, ed. A. Papadopoulos-Kerameus (St Petersburg, 1897).

Photius, Patriarch of Constantinople, *Monumenta Graeca et Latina ad historiam Photii patriarchae pertinentia*, ed. A. Papadopoulos-Kerameus, 2 vols. (St Petersburg, 1899–1901).

Photius, Patriarch of Constantinople, *Orationes et Homiliae*, ed. S. Aristarches (Constantinople, 1900); trans. C. Mango (Cambridge, Mass., 1958).

Plusiadenus, John (Joseph, Bishop of Methone), *Apology for the Council of Florence*, *MPG*, clix, 959–1394.

Prophetarum vitae fabulosae, Indices apostolorum discipulorumque Domini. Dorotheo, Epiphano, Hippolyto aliisque vindicata, ed. T. Schermann (Leipzig, 1907).

Psellus, Michael, *Letters and Speeches*, ed. K. N. Sathas, *Bibliotheca graeca medii aevi*, iv and v. [See Gen. Bibl. iv. See esp. *Funeral oration on Michael Cerularius*, iv, 303–87.]

Psellus, Michael, *Accusation of Patriarch Michael Cerularius before the Synod* (*1059*), ed. L. Bréhier, 'Un discours inédit de Psellos', *REG*, xvi (1903), 375–416; *ibid.* xvii (1904), 35–76; also ed. E. Kurtz and F. Drexl, ii, 233–328 (see below).

Psellus, Michael, *Scripta minora*, ed. E. Kurtz and F. Drexl, 2 vols. (Milan, 1936–48).

Scholarius, George, *Works*, ed. L. Petit, X. A. Sidéridès and M. Jugie, 8 vols. (Paris, 1928–36); see also Gennadius (above).

Stephen V, Pope, *Fragmenta et Epistolae*, *MGH*, *Ep.* VII, 334–65; Mansi, XVIII, 11–13 (letter to Basil I).
Stylianus of Neo-Caesarea, *Letter to Pope Stephen V*, *MGH*, *Ep.* VII, 375–82; Mansi, XVI, 426–35.
Syropoulus, Silvester, *Memoirs*, ed. R. Creyghton, see above.
Theiner, A. and Miklosich, F., *Monumenta spectantia ad unionem ecclesiarum Graecae et Romanae* (Vienna, 1872).
Theodore Irenicus, Patriarch of Constantinople, *Encyclical to the Orthodox still under Latin Rule (1214)*, ed. A. Papadopoulos-Kerameus, *BZ*, x (1901), 187–92.
Theodore II Lascaris, *De processione S. Spiritus*, ed. H. B. Swete (London, 1875).
Theophylact, Archbishop of Ochrida, *Liber de iis quorum Latini incusantur*, *MPG*, CXXVI, 221–49.
Thiel, A. (ed.), *Epistolae Romanorum Pontificum*, 2 vols. (Brumergae, 1868).
Turner, C. H., *Ecclesiae occidentalis monumenta iuris antiquissima* (Oxford, 1899).
Will, C., *Acta et Scripta quae de controversiis eccl. Graecae et Latinae s. XI extant* (Leipzig, 1861).

II. MODERN WORKS

Alexander, P. J., *The Patriarch Nicephorus* [see Gen. Bibl. v].
Alföldi, A., *The Conversion of Constantine and Pagan Rome* (Oxford, 1948).
Alivisatos, H. S., *Die kirchliche Gesetzgebung des Kaisers Justinian I* (Berlin, 1913).
Allatius, L., *De ecclesiae occidentalis atque orientalis perpetua consensione* (Cologne, 1648) [Allatius is important as representing the Uniate tradition of the Council of Florence; see 'Allatius', *DHGE*].
Allatius, L., *De utriusque ecclesiae occidentalis et orientalis perpetua in dogmate de purgatorio consensione* (Rome, 1655).
Allatius, L., *De libris et rebus ecclesiasticis graecorum* (Paris, 1646).
Allatius, L., *Graeciae Orthodoxae tomus primus et secundus* (Rome, 1652, 1659).
Allatius, L., *De Octava Synodo Photiana* (Rome, 1662).
Allatius, L., *In Roberti Creyghtoni Apparatum, Versionem et Notas ad historiam Concilii Florentini* (Rome, 1665).
Amann, E., 'Photius', *DTC*, XII (1935), 1536–1604.
Amann, E., 'Jean VIII', *DTC*, VIII (1924), 602–13.
Arquillière, H. X., 'Sur la formation de la "Théocratie" pontificale', *Mélanges F. Lot* (Paris, 1925), pp. 1–24.
Arquillière, H. X., *Saint Grégoire VII: essai sur sa conception du pouvoir pontifical* (Paris, 1934).
Bach, E., 'Imperium Romanum, Etude sur l'idéologie politique du XIIᵉ siècle', *CM*, VII (1945), 138–45.
Batiffol, P., *L'Eglise naissante et le Catholicisme* (Paris, 1909).
Batiffol, P., *Le Siège apostolique*, 3rd ed. (Paris, 1924).
Batiffol, P., 'Papa, sedes apostolica, apostolatus', *Rivista Archeologica Cristiana*, II (1925), 99–116.
Batiffol, P., 'L'Empereur Justinien et le siège apostolique', *Recherches de science religieuse*, XVI (1925), 193–264.
Batiffol, P., *Saint Grégoire le Grand*, 3rd ed. (Paris, 1928).

Batiffol, P., *Cathedra Petri* (Paris, 1938).

Bauer, J. Chr., 'Die Anfänge des byzantinischen Cäsaropapismus', *AKKR*, III (1931), 99–113.

Baynes, N. H., *Constantine the Great and the Christian Church* (Proc. Brit. Acad. xv) (London, 1931).

Baynes, N. H., *The Hellenistic Civilization and East Rome* (Oxford, 1945); reprinted in *Byzantine Studies and Other Essays* [see Gen. Bibl. v].

Baynes, N. H., *The Thought-World of East Rome* (Oxford, 1947); reprinted in *Byzantine Studies and Other Essays* [see Gen. Bibl. v].

Berkhof, H., *Kirche und Kaiser. Eine Untersuchung zur Entstehung der byzantinischen und der theokratischen Staatsauffassung im vierten Jahrhundert* (Zollikon–Zurich, 1947).

Bernheim, E., 'Mittelalterliche Zeitanschauungen in ihrem Einfluss auf Politik und Geschichtsschreibung', *Anschauungen über das Verhältnis von Regnum und Sacerdotium*, I, 110–233 (Tübingen, 1918).

Bertolini, O., *Roma di fronte a Bisanzio e ai Langobardi* (Storia di Roma, IX) (Bologna, 1941).

Biondi, B., *Giustiniano primo, principe e legislatore cattolico* (Pubblicazioni della Univ. Catt. del S. Cuore, ser. II, XLVIII) (Milan, 1936).

Brackmann, A., 'Die Erneuerung der Kaiserwürde im Jahre 800', *Geschichtliche Studien für A. Hauck* (Leipzig, 1916).

Brackmann, A., *Der römische Erneuerungsgedanke und seine Bedeutung für die Reichspolitik der deutschen Kaiser*, Sitzungsber. der Preuss. Akad., Hist. Phil. Kl. (1932).

Bréhier, L., *Le schisme oriental du XIᵉ siècle* (Paris, 1899).

Bréhier, L., 'Normal Relations between Rome and the Churches of the East before the Schism of the XIth Century', *The Constructive Quarterly* (New York, 1916), IV, 645–72. [Cf. A. Michel's review in *BNJ*, III (1922), 406 ff.]

Bréhier, L., *L'Eglise et l'Orient. Les Croisades* [see Gen. Bibl. v].

Bréhier, L., 'L'investiture des patriarches de Constantinople au moyen âge', *Miscellanea G. Mercati*, III (Studi e Testi, CXXIII) (Vatican, 1946), pp. 368–72.

Bréhier, L., *Le Monde Byzantin* [see Gen. Bibl. v].

Bréhier, L., 'Ἱερεὺς καὶ βασιλεύς', *Mémorial L. Petit* (Bucharest, 1948), pp. 41–5.

Bury, J. B., *History of the Later Roman Empire from Arcadius to Irene* [see Gen. Bibl. v].

Bury, J. B., *History of the Eastern Roman Empire* [see Gen. Bibl. v].

Carlyle, R. W. and A. J., *A History of Medieval Political Theory in the West*, (London–Edinburgh, 1903–1936), 5 vols.

Cartellieri, A., 'Otto III, Kaiser der Römer', *Festschr. W. Judeich* (Weimar, 1929), pp. 173–205.

Caspar, E., *Pippin und die römische Kirche* (Berlin, 1914).

Caspar, E., *Geschichte des Papsttums*, 2 vols. (Tübingen, 1930, 1933).

Caspar, E., 'Papst Gregor II und der Bilderstreit', *ZKG*, LII (1933), 29–89.

Caspar, E., 'Das Papsttum unter fränkischer Herrschaft', *ZKG*, LIV (1935), 132–264.

Chalandon, F., *Essai sur le règne d'Alexis Comnène* [see Gen. Bibl. v].

Chalandon, F., *Les Comnène. Jean II et Manuel Comnène* [see Gen. Bibl. v].

Chalandon, F., *Histoire de la domination normande en Italie et en Sicilie* [see Gen. Bibl. v].

Charanis, P., *Church and State in the later Roman Empire (491–518)*. *The Religious Policy of Anastasius the First* (Madison, 1939).

Darrouzès, J., 'Conférence sur la primauté du pape à Constantinople en 1357', *REB*, XIX (= *Mélanges R. Janin*) (1961), 76–109.

Denpf, A., *Sacrum Imperium. Geschichts- und Staatsphilosophie des Mittelalters und der polit. Renaissance* (Munich, 1929).

Devreesse, R., 'Le cinquième concile et l'œcuménicité byzantine', *Miscellanea G. Mercati*, III (Studi e Testi, 123) (Vatican, 1946), pp. 1–15.

Diehl, Ch., *Justinien et la civilisation byzantine au VIᵉ s.* (Paris, 1901).

Dölger, F., 'Rom in der Gedankenwelt der Byzantiner', *ZKG*, LVI (1937), 1–42; reprinted in *Byzanz und die europäische Staatenwelt*, pp. 70–115 [see Gen. Bibl. v].

Dölger, F., 'Die Kaiserurkunde der Byzantiner als Ausdruck ihrer politischen Anschauungen', *HZ*, CLIX (1938–9), 229–50; reprinted in *Byzanz und die europäische Staatenwelt*, pp. 1–33 [see Gen. Bibl. v].

Dölger, F., 'Europas Gestaltung im Spiegel der fränkisch-byzantinischen Auseinandersetzung des 9. Jahrhunderts', *Der Vertrag von Verdun 843*, ed. by Th. Mayer (Leipzig, 1943), pp. 203–73; reprinted in *Byzanz und die europäische Staatenwelt*, pp. 282–369 [see Gen. Bibl. v].

Dräseke, J., 'Bischof Anselm von Havelberg', *ZKG*, XXI (1900), 160–85.

Dräseke, J., 'Der Kircheneinigungsversuch des Kaisers Michael VIII. Paläologos', *ZWT*, XXXIV (1891), 325–55.

Dräseke, J., 'Nikolaos von Methone', *BZ*, I (1892), 438–78.

Dräseke, J., 'Zum Kircheneinigungsversuch des Jahres 1439', *BZ*, V (1896), 572–86.

Dräseke, J., 'Zu Eustratios von Nikäa', *BZ*, V (1896), 319–36.

Duchesne, L., *Les premiers temps de l'Etat pontifical* (Paris, 1898).

Duchesne, L., *Les Eglises séparées, l'Illyricum ecclésiastique* (Paris, 1905).

Duchesne, L., *L'Eglise au VIᵉ siècle* (Paris, 1928).

Dvornik, F., *Les légendes de Constantin et de Méthode* (Prague, 1933).

Dvornik, F., 'Rome and Constantinople in the Ninth Century', *ECQ*, III (1939), 409–16.

Dvornik, F., *National Churches and the Church Universal* (London, 1944).

Dvornik, F., 'The Study of Church History and Christian Reunion', *ECQ*, VI (1945), 17–36.

Dvornik, F., 'The Photian Schism in Western and Eastern Tradition', *The Review of Politics*, X (1948), 310–31.

Dvornik, F., *The Photian Schism* [see Gen. Bibl. v].

Dvornik, F., 'Photius et la réorganisation de l'Académie patriarcale', *AB*, LXVIII (1950), 108–25.

Dvornik, F., 'Emperors, Popes and General Councils', *DOP*, VI (1951), 1–23.

Dvornik, F., 'The Patriarch Photius and Iconoclasm', *DOP*, VII (1953), 67–97.

Dvornik, F., *The Idea of Apostolicity in Byzantium and the Legend of the Apostle Andrew* (Cambridge, Mass., 1958).

Dvornik, F., 'The Patriarch Photius in the Light of Recent Research', *Berichte z. XI. Internat. Byz.-Kongress: Munich, 1958*, III (2), 56 pp.

Dvornik, F., 'Patriarch Photius, Scholar and Statesman', *Classical Folia*, XIII (1959), 3–18; XIV (1960), 3–22.

Dvornik, F., 'Byzantium and the Roman Primacy', *American Ecclesiastical Review*, CXLIV (1961), 289–312.

Dvornik, F., *The Ecumenical Councils* (New York, 1961); *The General Councils of the Church* (London, 1961); *Histoire des Conciles* (Paris, 1962).

Ensslin, W., 'Valentinianus III. Novellen XVII u. XVIII von 445. Ein Beitrag zur Stellung von Kirche und Staat', *ZSR*, röm. Abt., LVII (1937), 367–78.

Ensslin, W., 'Gottkaiser und Kaiser von Gottes Gnaden', *SBAW*, VI (1943).

Erdmann, C., *Die Entstehung des Kreuzzugsgedankens* (Stuttgart, 1935).

Evert-Kappesowa, H.,'Une page de l'histoire des relations byzantino-latines. Le clergé byzantin et l'union de Lyon (1274–1282)', *BS*, XIII (1952–3), 68–92.

Evert-Kappesowa, H., 'La société byzantine et l'union de Lyon' *BS*, X, (Prague, 1949), 28–41.

Evert-Kappesowa, H., 'Une page de l'histoire des relations byzantino-latines. Byzance et le Saint Siège à l'époque de l'union de Lyon', *BS*, XVI (1955), 297–317.

Evert-Kappesowa, H., 'Une page de l'histoire des relations byzantino-latines. La fin de l'union de Lyon', *BS*, XVII (1956), 1–18.

Every, G., *The Byzantine Patriarchate* [see Gen. Bibl. v].

Fischer, E. H., 'Gregor der Grosse und Byzanz. Ein Beitrag zur Geschichte der päpstlichen Politik', *ZSR*, Kanon. Abt. XXXVI (1950), 15–144.

Fliche, A. and Martin, V. (edd.), *Histoire de l'Eglise*, I–X [see Gen. Bibl. v].

Fliche, A., 'Les origines de l'action de la Papauté en vue de Croisade', *RHE*, XXXIV (1938), 265–775.

Fliche, A., *La réforme Grégorienne*, 3 vols. (Louvain, 1952).

Fournier, P. and Le Bras, G., *Histoire des collections canoniques en occident*, 2 vols. (Paris, 1931–2).

Fuhrmann, H., 'Studien zur Geschichte mittelalterlicher Patriarchate', *ZSR*, XXXIX (1953), 147–76.

Ganshof, F. L., 'Note sur "Patricius Romanorum"', *AIPHO*, X (1950), 261–82. [Cf. F. Dölger's review in *BZ*, XLV (1952), 187–190.]

Ganshof, F. L., *The Imperial Coronation of Charlemagne* (Glasgow, 1949).

Gasquet, A., *De l'autorité impériale en matière religieuse à Byzance* (Paris, 1879).

Gauss, J., 'Die Dictatus-Thesen Gregors VII als Unionsforderungen', *ZSR*, XXIX (1940), 1–15.

Gay, J., *L'Italie méridionale et l'Empire byzantin (867–1071)* [see Gen. Bibl. v].

Gay, J., *Le Pape Clément VI et les affaires d'Orient* (Paris, 1904).

Gay, J., *Les Papes du XIe siècle et la Chrétienté* (Paris, 1926).

Geanakoplos, D. J., *Emperor Michael Palaeologus and the West* [see Gen. Bibl. v].

Geanakoplos, D. J., 'Michael VIII Palaeologus and the Union of Lyons (1274)', *HTR*, XLVI (1953), 79–89.

Geanakoplos, D. J., 'On the Schism of the Greek and Roman Churches. A Confidential Papal Directive for the Implementation of Union (1278)', *GOTR*, I (1954), 16–24.

Geanakoplos, D. J., 'The Council of Florence (1438–1439) and the Problem of Union between the Greek and Latin Churches', *Church History*, XXIV (1955), 324–46 [contains bibliography on unionist negotiations of later middle ages].

Gelzer, H., 'Der Streit über den Titel des ökumenischen Patriarchen', *Jahrb. für protestant. Theologie*, XIII (1887), 549–84.

Gelzer, H., 'Das Verhältnis von Staat und Kirche in Byzanz', *HZ*, LXXXVI (1901), 193–252; reprinted in *Ausgewählte kleine Schriften* (Leipzig, 1907), pp. 57–141.

Gill, J., *The Council of Florence* [see Gen. Bibl. v].

Gill, J., 'The Sources of the "Acta" of the Council of Florence', *OCP*, XIV (1948), 43–79.

Gill, J., 'The "Acta" and the Memoirs of Syropoulus as History', *OCP*, XIV (1948), 303–55.

Gill, J., 'Greeks and Latins in a Common Council. The Council of Florence (1438–1439)', *OCP*, XXV (1959), 265–87.

Gmelin, U., *Auctoritas. Römischer Princeps und päpstlicher Primat*, in *Geistige Grundlagen römischer Kirchenpolitik* (Forschungen zur Kirchen- und Geistesgesch. II) (Stuttgart, 1937).

Gordillo, M., 'Photius et Primatus Romanus', *OCP*, VI (Rome, 1940), 5–39.

Grégoire, H., 'Notules II: Patriarche œcuménique', *B*, VIII (1933), 570–1.

Gregorovius, F., *Geschichte der Stadt Rom im Mittelalter* [see Gen. Bibl. V].

Greinacher, A., *Die Anschauungen des Papstes Nikolaus I über das Verhältnis von Staat und Kirche* (Berlin, 1909).

Gren, E., 'Zu den Legenden von der Gründung Konstantinopels', *Serta Kazaroviana*, I (Serdicae, 1950), 151–7. [Cf. *Eranos*, XLV (1947), 153–64.]

Grisar, H., 'Der römische Primat nach der Lehre und der Regierungspraxis Gregors des Grossen', *ZKT*, III (1879), 655–93.

Grisar, H., 'Ökumenischer Patriarch und Diener der Diener Gottes', *ZKT*, IV (1880), 468–523.

Grumel, V., 'Le IIe concile de Lyon et la réunion de l'église grecque', *DTC*, IX, pt. 1, cols. 1391–1410.

Grumel, V., 'Les ambassades pontificales à Byzance après le IIe concile de Lyon (1274–1280)', *EO*, XXIII (1924), 437–47.

Grumel, V., 'En Orient après le IIe concile de Lyon', *EO*, XXIV (1925), 321–5.

Grumel, V., 'Saint Thomas et la doctrine des Grecs sur la procession du Saint-Esprit', *EO*, XXV (1926), 257–80.

Grumel, V., 'Y eut-il un second Schisme de Photius?', *Revue des Sciences phil. et théol.* XII (1933), 432–57.

Grumel, V., 'La liquidation de la querelle Photienne', *EO*, XXXIII (1934), 257–88.

Grumel, V., 'L'encyclique de Photius aux Orientaux', *EO*, XXXIV (1935), 128–38.

Grumel, V., 'Les lettres de Jean VIII pour le rétablissement de Photius', *EO*, XXXIX (1940), 138–56.

Grumel, V., 'Les préliminaires du schisme de Michel Cérulaire ou la question romaine avant 1054', *REB*, X (1952), 5–23.

Grumel, V., 'Les relations politico-religieuses entre Byzance et Rome sous le règne de Léon V l'Arménien', *REB*, XVIII (1960), 19–44.

Guberina, A., 'De conceptu petrae ecclesiae apud ecclesiologiam byzantinam usque ad Photium', *Bogoslovska Smotra*, XVII (Zagreb, 1929), 345–76; XVIII (1930), 145–74, 307–17.

Guggisberg, K., 'Matth. 16, 18 und 19 in der Kirchengeschichte', *ZKG*, LIV (1935), 276–300.

Haacke, R. M., 'Die kaiserliche Politik um Chalkedon (451–553)', *Das Konzil von Chalkedon*, ed. A. Grillmeier, H. Bacht (Würzburg, 1953), II, 95–177.

Haacke, W., 'Die Glaubensformel des Papstes Hormisdas,' *Analecta Gregoriana*, XX (1939), 349–63.

Halecki, O., *Un Empereur de Byzance à Rome, 1355–1375* (Warsaw, 1930).

Haller, J., 'Die Karolinger und das Papsttum', *HZ*, CVIII (1912), 38–76.

Haller, J., *Das altdeutsche Kaisertum* (Stuttgart, 1934).

Haller, J., *Nikolaus I. und Pseudo-Isidor* (Stuttgart, 1936).

Halphen, L., 'La cour d'Otton III à Rome', *Mélanges d'Archéol. et d'Histoire*, XXV (1905), 513–33.

Hammer, W., 'The Concept of the New and Second Rome in the Middle Ages', *SP*, xix (1944), 50–62.

Hampe, K., 'Kaiser Otto III und Rom', *HZ*, cxl (1929), 513–33.

Harapin, Th., *Primatus Pontificis Romani in Concilio Chalcedonensi et Ecclesiae dissidenti* (Quaracchi, 1923).

Hartmann, L. M., *Geschichte Italiens im Mittelalter* [see Gen. Bibl. v].

Hauck, A., *Der Gedanke der päpstlichen Weltherrschaft bis auf Bonifaz VIII* (Leipzig, 1904).

Hefele, C. J. and Leclerq, H., *Histoire des Conciles* [see Gen. Bibl. v].

Heiler, F., *Altkirchliche Autonomie und päpstlicher Zentralismus* (Munich, 1941).

Heisenberg, A., *Die Unionsverhandlungen vom 30. August, 1206, Patriarchenwahl und Kaiserkrönung in Nikaia, 1208, SBAW*, ii (Munich, 1923).

Heldmann, K., *Das Kaisertum Karls des Grossen. Theorien und Wirklichkeit* (Quellen und Studien für Verfassungsgesch. des Deutschen Reiches im Mittelalter und Neuzeit, vi, Heft 2) (Weimar, 1928).

Henze, W., 'Über den Brief Kaiser Ludwigs II an den Kaiser Basilius I', *Neu. Arch.* xxxv (1909/10), 663–76.

Hergenröther, J., *Photius, Patriarch von Konstantinopel*, 3 vols. (Regensburg, 1867–9).

Herman, E., 'Chalkedon und die Ausgestaltung des konstantinopolitanischen Primats', *Das Konzil von Chalkedon*, ed. A. Grillmeier and H. Bacht, i (Würzburg, 1953), 459–90.

Hill, J. H., 'Raymond of Saint Gilles in Urban's Plan of Greek and Latin Friendship', *SP*, xxvi (1951), 265–76.

Hofmann, G., 'Die Konzilsarbeit in Ferrara', *OCP*, iii (1937), 110–40, 403–55.

Hofmann, G., 'Die Konzilsarbeit in Florenz 26. Febr. 1439–26. Febr. 1443', *OCP*, iv (1938), 157–88, 372–422.

Hofmann, G., 'Papst Kalixt III und die Frage der Kircheneinheit im Osten', *Miscellanea G. Mercati*, iii (Studi e Testi, 123) (Vatican, 1946), 209–37.

Hofmann, G., 'Der Kampf der Päpste um Konzil und Dogma von Chalkedon von Leo dem Grossen bis Hormisdas (451–519)', *Das Konzil von Chalkedon*, ed. A. Grillmeier and H. Bacht, ii (Würzburg, 1953), 13–94.

Hofmann, G., 'Patriarch von Nikaia Manuel II an Papst Innozenz IV', *OCP*, xix (1953), 59–70.

Holtzmann, W., 'Studien zur Orientpolitik des Reformpapsttums und zur Entstehung des ersten Kreuzzuges', *HVJS*, xxii (1924), 167–99.

Holtzmann, W., 'Unionsverhandlungen zwischen Kaiser Alexios I und Papst Urban II im Jahre 1089', *BZ*, xxviii (1928), 38–67.

Hubert, H., 'Etude sur la formation des Etats de l'Eglise. Les papes Grégoire II, Grégoire III, Zacharie et Etienne II et leurs relations avec les empereurs iconoclastes 726–756', *RH*, lxix (1899), 1–39, 242–71.

Jäntere, Kaarb, *Die römische Weltreichsidee und die Entstehung der weltlichen Macht des Papstes* (Annales Univ. Turkuensis, ser. B, xxi) (Turku, 1936).

Jorga, N., 'Der lateinische Westen und der griechische Osten während des Mittelalters', *Studium Lipsiense, Ehrensgabe für K. Lamprecht* (Berlin, 1909), pp. 89–99.

Jugie, M., 'Le Culte de Photius dans l'Eglise Byzantine', *ROC*, iii, 3rd ser. (1922–3), pp. 105–122.

Jugie, M., *Theologia dogmatica* [see Gen. Bibl. v].

Jugie, M., *Le Schisme byzantin* [see Gen. Bibl. v].

Jugie, M., 'Schisme', *DTC*.

Jugie, M., 'L'unionisme de Georges Scholarios', *EO*, xxxvi (1937), 65–86.

Jugie, M., 'Georges Scholarios, professeur de philosophie', *Atti del V Congresso intern. di studi biz.*, *Rome 1936, SBN*, v (1939), 482–94.

Karmires, J. N., 'The Schism of the Roman Church', English transl. Θεολογία, xxi (1950), 37–67.

Karmires, J. N., 'Δύο βυζαντινοὶ ἱεράρχαι καὶ τὸ σχίσμα τῆς Ῥωμαϊκῆς Ἐκκλησίας', Ἐκκλησία (Athens, 1950), 119 pp. [printed separately].

Kissling, W., *Das Verhältnis zwischen Sacerdotium und Imperium nach den Anschauungen der Päpste von Leo d. Gr. bis Gelatius*, i (Görres-Gesellschaft, Veröffentl. der Sektion f. Rechts- und Sozialwiss., xxxviii) (Paderborn, 1920).

Klinkenberg, H. M., 'Papsttum und Reichskirche bei Leo dem Grossen', *ZSR*, lxix, Kan. Abt. xxxviii (1952), 37–112.

Knabe, L., *Die gelasianische Zweigewaltentheorie bis zum Ende des Investitur-streites* (Histor. Studien, Heft 292) (Berlin, 1936).

Kneller, C. A., 'Papst u. Konzil im ersten Jahrtausend', *ZKT*, xxviii (1904), 58–91; 519–44; 699–722.

Koch, H., 'Gelasius im kirchenpolitischen Dienste seiner Vorgänger; Ein Beitrag zur Sprache des Papstes Gelasius I', *SBAW, philos.-hist. Kl.*, vi (1935).

Kölmel, W., *Rom und der Kirchenstaat im 10. u. 11. Jhdt. bis in die Anfänge der Reform* (Abhandlungen zur mittl. u. neueren Geschichte, 78. Heft) (Berlin, 1935).

Krumbacher, K., *Geschichte der byzantinischen Litteratur* (with bibliography to 1897) [see Gen. Bibl. v].

Ladner, G. B., 'Origin and Significance of the Byzantine Iconoclastic Controversy', *Med. Stud.* ii (1940), 127–99.

Laehr, G., *Die Konstantinische Schenkung* (E. Ebering, Hist. Studien, 166) (Berlin, 1926).

Lämmer, H., *Papst Nikolaus I und die byzantinische Staatskirche* (Berlin, 1857).

Lapôtre, A., *L'Europe et le Saint Siège* (Paris, 1895).

Laurent, V., 'Le serment anti-latin du Patriarche Joseph Ier (juin 1273)', *EO*, xxvi (1927), 396–407.

Laurent, V., 'Le cas de Photius dans l'apologétique du patriarche Jean XI Beccos (1275–1282) au lendemain du IIe concile de Lyon', *EO*, xxix (1930), 396–415.

Laurent, V., 'Le Pape Alexandre IV (1254–1261) et l'Empire de Nicée', *EO*, xxxiv (1935), 26–55.

Laurent, V., 'Le titre du patriarche œcuménique et Michel Cérulaire', *Miscellanea G. Mercati*, iii (Studi e Testi, 123) (Vatican, 1946), pp. 373–96.

Laurent, V., 'Les grandes crises religieuses à Byzance. La fin du schisme arsénite', *Acad. Roum., Bull. Sect. Hist.*, xxvi (1945), 225–313.

Laurent, V., 'La croisade et la question d'Orient sous le pontificat de Grégoire X (1272–1276)', *RHSE*, xxii (1945), 105–37; xxiii (1946), 233–47.

Laurent, V., 'Le titre du patriarche œcuménique et la signature patriarcale', *REB*, vi (1948), 5–26.

Lebedev, A. P., *Rimskie papy v otnošenijach k cerkvi vizantijskoj v IX–X v.* [*Roman Popes and their relations with the Byzantine Church in the IX–Xth centuries*] (Moscow, 1875).

Lebedev, A. P., *Istorija konst. soborov IX. v.* [*History of the Constantinopolitan Councils in the IXth century*] (Moscow, 1880).

Lebedev, A. P., *Istorija razdelenija cerkvej v IX, X i XI veke* [The history of the separation of the Churches in the ninth, tenth and eleventh centuries] (Moscow, 1905).

Leib, B., *Rome, Kiev et Byzance à la fin du XI*e *siècle* (Paris, 1924).

Leib, B., 'Les idées et les faits à Byzance au XIe siècle', *OCP*, ɪ (1935), 164–203.

Lintzel, M., 'Das abendländische Kaisertum im neunten und zehnten Jahrhundert', *Die Welt als Geschichte*, ɪᴠ (1938), 423–47.

Loenertz, R.-J., 'Les dominicains byzantins Théodore et André Chrysobergès et les négociations pour l'union des Eglises grecque et latine de 1415–1430', *Arch. Praed.* ɪx (1939), 5–61; 128–83.

Loenertz, R.-J., 'Pour la biographie du Cardinal Bessarion', *OCP*, x (1944), 116–49.

Loenertz, R.-J., 'Ambassadeurs grecs auprès du pape Clément VI (1348)', *OCP*, xɪx (1953), 178–96.

Luchaire, A., *Innocent III, Rome et l'Italie* (Paris, 1905).

Luchaire, A., *Innocent III et la question d'Orient* (Paris, 1907).

Maccarone, M., *Vicarius Christi, Storia del titolo papale* (Rome, 1952).

Manoussakas, M., 'Recherches sur la vie de Jean Plousiadénos (Joseph de Méthone) (1429?–1500)', *REB*, xᴠɪɪ (1959), 28–51.

Martin, E. J., *History of the Iconoclastic Controversy* [see Gen. Bibl. v].

Mayne, R., 'East and West in 1054', *CHJ*, xɪ (1954), 133–48.

Mercati, A., 'Il decreto d'unione del 6 luglio 1439 nell'Archivio Segreto Vaticano', *OCP*, xɪ (1945), 5–44.

Meyendorff, J., 'Jean-Joasaph Cantacuzène et le projet de concile œcuménique en 1367', *Akten XI. Internat. Byz.-Kongress: Munich, 1958* (Munich, 1960), pp. 363–9.

Meyendorff, J., 'Der heilige Petrus, sein Primat und seine Sukzession in der byzantinischen Theologie', *Der Primat des Petrus in der orthodoxen Kirche* (Zurich, 1961), pp. 95–117.

Michel, A., *Humbert und Kerullarios* (Quellen u. Forschungen aus dem Gebiete der Geschichte, xxɪ, xxɪɪɪ), 2 vols. (Paderborn, 1925, 1930). [Cf. V. Laurent's review in *EO*, xxxɪ (1932), 96–110.]

Michel, A., 'Verstreute Kerullarios- und Humberttexte', *RQCA*, xxxɪx (1931), 353–76.

Michel, A., 'Von Photius zu Kerullarios', *RQCA*, xLɪ (1933), 1–38.

Michel, A., 'Die Botschaft Petros III von Antiochien an seine Stadt über seine Ernennung', *BZ*, xxxᴠɪɪɪ (1938), 111–18.

Michel, A., *Amalfi und Jerusalem im griechischen Kirchenstreit, 1054–1090*, *OCA*, cxxɪ (1939).

Michel, A., 'Die Echtkeit der Panoplia des Michael Kerullarios', *OC*, xxxᴠɪ (1941), 168–204.

Michel, A., 'Die Rechtsgültigkeit des römischen Bannes gegen Michael Kerullarios', *BZ*, xLɪɪ (1942), 193–205.

Michel, A., 'Die byzantinische und römische Werbung um Symeon II. von Jerusalem', *ZKG*, Lxɪɪ (1943–4), 164–77.

Michel, A., 'Die folgenschweren Ideen des Kardinals Humbert und ihr Einfluss auf Gregor VII', *Studi Gregoriani*, ɪ (1947), 65–92.

Michel, A., 'Die Friedensbotschaft Grados an Antiocheia im Schisma des Kerullarios (1053–1054) und ihr Widerhall', *Studi Gregoriani*, ɪɪ (1947), 163–88.

Michel, A., 'Sprache und Schisma', *Festschrift Kardinal M. Faulhaber* (Munich, 1949), pp. 37–69.

Michel, A., 'Die Anfänge des Kardinals Humbert bei Bischof Bruno von Toul (Leo IX)', *Studi Gregoriani*, III (1948), 299–319.

Michel, A., 'Die Weltreichs- und Kirchenteilung bei Rudolf Glaber', *HJ*, LXX (1951), 53–64.

Michel, A., 'Die römischen Angriffe auf Michael Kerullarios wegen Antiocheia (1053–1054)', *BZ*, XLIV (1951), 419–27.

Michel, A., 'Der Kampf um das politische oder petrinische Prinzip der Kirchenführung', *Das Konzil von Chalkedon*, ed. A. Grillmeier–H. Bacht, II (Würzburg, 1953), 491–562.

Michel, A., 'Schisma und Kaiserhof im Jahre 1054. Michael Psellos', *1054–1954. L'église et les églises*, I, 351–440. [See Gen. Bibl. v *ad fin.*]

Michel, A., *Die Kaisermacht in der Ostkirche (843–1204)* [see Gen. Bibl. v].

Möhler, L., *Kardinal Bessarion als Theologe, Humanist und Staatsman* (Paderborn, 1923).

Moravcsik, Gy., *Byzantinoturcica* (with bibliography to 1958) [see Gen. Bibl. I].

Morin, G., 'Le discours d'ouverture du concile générale de Latran (1179) et l'œuvre littéraire de Maître Rufia, évêque d'Assise', *Atti d. Pont. Acad. Rom. di Archeol.*, Mem. II (1928), 122–32.

Neumann, C., *Die Weltstellung des byzantinischen Reiches vor den Kreuzzügen* [see Gen. Bibl. v].

Nicol, D. M., 'The Greeks and the Union of the Churches: The Preliminaries to the Second Council of Lyons, 1261–1274', *Medieval Studies presented to A. Gwynn* (Dublin, 1961), pp. 454–80.

Nicol, D. M., 'Byzantium and the Papacy in the Eleventh Century', *JEH*, XIII (1962), 1–20.

Norden, W., *Das Papsttum und Byzanz* [see Gen. Bibl. v].

Ohnsorge, W., *Das Zweikaiserproblem im früheren Mittelalter* (Hildesheim, 1947).

Ohnsorge, W., 'Orthodoxus imperator. Vom religiösen Motiv für das Kaisertum Karls des Grossen', *Jahrbücher der Gesellschaft f. niedersächs. Kirchengesch.* XLVIII (1950), 17–28.

Ohnsorge, W., 'Die Konstantinische Schenkung, Leo III und die Anfänge der kurialen römischen Kaiseridee', *ZSR*, Germ. Abt., LXVIII (1951), 78–109.

Ostrogorsky, G., *History of the Byzantine State* [see Gen. Bibl. v].

Ostrogorsky, G., 'Les débuts de la querelle des Images', *Mélanges Charles Diehl* (Paris, 1930), I, 235–55.

Ostrogorsky, G., *Studien zur Geschichte des byzantinischen Bilderstreites* [see Gen. Bibl. v].

Pargoire, J., *L'Eglise byzantine* [see Gen. Bibl. v].

Perels, E., *Papst Nikolaus I. und Anastasius Bibliothecarius* (Berlin, 1920).

Pewesin, W., *Imperium, Ecclesia universalis, Rom* (Forschungen zur Kirchen- und Geistesgesch. II) (Stuttgart, 1937).

Popov, N. A., *Imperator Lev VI Mudryj i ego pravlenie v cerkovnom otnošenii [The Emperor Leo VI the Wise and his rule in relation to ecclesiastical policy]* (Moscow, 1892).

Roncaglia, M., *Les frères mineurs et l'église grecque orthodoxe au XIIIᵉ siècle (1221–1274)* (Cairo, 1954).

Rowe, J. G., 'The Papacy and the Greeks (1122–1153)', *Church History*, XXVIII (1959), 115–30, 310–27.

Runciman, S., *The Eastern Schism* [see Gen. Bibl. v].

Sägmüller, J. B., 'Die Idee Gregor's VII vom Primat in der päpstlichen Kanzlei', *Theol. Quartalschr.* LXXVIII (Tübingen, 1896), 577–613.

Sägmüller, J. B., *Zur Geschichte der Entwicklung des päpstlichen Gesetz-gebungsrechtes* (Rottenburg d. N., 1937).

Salaville, S., 'Un thomiste à Byzance au XVᵉ siècle: Gennade Scholarios', *EO*, XXIII (1924), 129–36.

Salin, E., *Civitas Dei* (Tübingen, 1926).

Scharnagel, A., 'Die kanonistische Sammlung der Handschrift von Freising', *Festgabe z. Jub. d. hl. Korbinian* (Munich, 1924), pp. 126–46.

Schmidt, K. D., 'Papa Petrus ipse', *ZKG*, LIV, (1935), 267–75.

Schneider, T., *Rom und Romgedanke im Mittelalter* (Munich, 1926).

Schoeman, E., *Die Idee der Volkessouveränität im mittelalterlichen Rom* (Diss.) (Frankfurt a. M., 1919).

Schramm, P., 'Kaiser, Basileus und Papst in der Zeit der Ottonen', *HZ*, CXXIX (1929), 424–75.

Schramm, P., *Kaiser, Rom und Renovatio* (Studien der Bibliothek Warburg, XVII) (Berlin, 1929).

Schramm, P., 'Die Anerkennung Karls des Grossen als Kaiser. Ein Kapitel aus der Geschichte der mittelalterlichen "Staatssymbolik"', *HZ*, CLXXII/CLXXIII (1951), 449–515.

Schubert, H., *Der Kampf des geistlichen und weltlichen Rechts, Sitzungsber. der Akad. Heidelberg, hist. phil. Kl.* (1927).

Schultze, B., 'Das letzte ökumenische Einigungskonzil theologisch gesehen', *OCP*, XXV (1959), 288–309.

Schwartz, E., 'Über Reichskonzilien von Theodosius bis Justinian', *ZSR*, XLII, Kanon. Abt., II (1921), 208–53.

Schwartz, E., 'Der sechste nicäische Kanon auf der Synode von Chalkedon', *Sitzungsberichte Berl. Ak., phil.-hist. Kl.*, XXVII (1930), 611–40.

Seppelt, F. X., *Der Aufstieg des Papsttums. Geschichte der Päpste von den Anfängen bis zum Regierungsantritt Gregors des Grossen* (Leipzig, 1921).

Seppelt, F. X., *Das Papsttum im Frühmittelalter. Geschichte der Päpste vom Regierungsantritt Gregors des Grossen bis zur Mitte des 11. Jahrhunderts* (Leipzig, 1934).

Ševčenko, I., 'Intellectual Repercussions of the Council of Florence', *Church History*, XXIV (1955), 291–323.

Sherrard, P., *The Greek East and the Latin West. A Study in the Christian Tradition* (Oxford, 1959).

Stein, E., *Histoire du Bas-Empire I–II* [see Gen. Bibl. v].

Stengel, E. E., 'Kaisertitel und Souveränitätsidee,' *Deutsches Archiv f. Geschichte des Mittelalters*, III (1939), 1–56.

Stephanou, P., 'Korreferat zu F. Dvornik, The Patriarch Photius in the Light of Recent Research', *Berichte zum XI. Internat. Byz. Kongress, München, 1958*, VII, 17–23.

Symonds, H. E., *The Church Universal and the See of Rome* (London, 1939).

Tanssi, A., *Le Ve Centenaire du Concile Œcuménique de Florence et l'Unité dans l'Église du Christ* (Istanbul, 1938).

Treitinger, O., *Die oströmische Kaiser- und Reichsidee* [see Gen. Bibl. v].

Treitinger, O., 'Vom oströmischen Staats- und Reichsgedanken', *Leipziger Vierteljahrsschrift für Südosteuropa*, IV (1940), 1–26.

Uhlirz, M., 'Die italienische Kirchenpolitik der Ottonen', *MIOG*, XLVIII (1934), 202–321.

Ullmann, W., *The Growth of Papal Government in the Middle Ages: a Study in the Ideological Relation of Clerical to Lay Power* (London, 1955).

Van Moé, E., 'L'envoi de nonces à Constantinople par les papes Innocent V et Jean XXI', *Mélanges d'archéologie et d'histoire*, XLVII (1930), 39–62.

Vasiliev, A. A., *History of the Byzantine Empire* [see Gen. Bibl. v].

Vast, H., *Le Cardinal Bessarion: étude sur la chrétienté et la renaissance vers le milieu du XVe siècle* (Paris, 1878).

Viller, M., 'La question de l'union des églises entre Grecs et Latins depuis le concile de Lyon jusqu'à celui de Florence (1274–1438)', *RHE*, XVI (1921), 260–305, 515–32 and XVIII (1922), 20–60, and issued separately (Louvain, 1922).

Vogelstein, M., *Kaiseridee—Romidee und das Verhältnis von Staat und Kirche seit Konstantin* (Historische Untersuchungen, VII) (Breslau, 1930).

Vogt, A., *Basile Ier* (Paris, 1908).

Voigt, K., *Staat und Kirche von Konstantin dem Grossen bis zum Ende der Karolingerzeit* (Stuttgart, 1936).

Voigt, K., 'Das Problem "Staat und Kirche" im Hoch- und Spätmittelalter', *Die Welt als Geschichte*, v (1939), 59–86.

Wuyts, A., 'Le 28-ième canon de Chalcédone et le fondement du primat romain', *OCP*, XVII (1951), 165–282.

Zhishman, J., *Die Unionsverhandlungen zwischen der orientalischen und römischen Kirche seit dem Anfange des XV. Jhts. bis zum Conzil von Ferrara* (Vienna, 1859).

Zoepffel, R., *Die Papstwahlen und die mit ihnen im nächsten Zusammenhang stehenden Ceremonien in ihrer Entwicklung vom 11. bis zum 14. Jh.* (Göttingen, 1871).

CHAPTER XI. THE EMPIRE AND ITS NORTHERN NEIGHBOURS, 565–1018

I. SOURCES

Reference to the more important passages in the sources is given from time to time in the footnotes. More detailed references will be found in the following:

Constantine Porphyrogenitus, *DAI*, II [see Gen. Bibl. IV].

Dieterich, K., *Byzantinische Quellen zur Länder- und Völkerkunde (5.–15. Jht.).* (Quellen und Forschungen zur Erd- und Kulturkunde, v) (Leipzig, 1912).

Dölger, F., *Regesten der Kaiserurkunden des oströmischen Reiches* [see Gen. Bibl. IV].

Grumel, V., *Les Regestes des Actes du Patriarcat de Constantinople*, I, fascs. 1, 2 [see Gen. Bibl. IV].

Izvori za bŭlgarskata istorija [*Fontes historiae bulgaricae*], I (Sofia, 1954); II (Sofia, 1958); III (Sofia, 1958); VI (Sofia, 1960); VII (Sofia, 1960); VIII (Sofia, 1961) (Bŭlgarska Akademija na Naukite: Institut za Bŭlgarska Istorija).

Moravcsik, Gy., *Byzantinoturcica*, I, II [includes a bibliography of modern works] [see Gen. Bibl. I].

Vizantiski izvori za istoriju naroda Jugoslavije [*Fontes byzantini historiam populorum Jugoslaviae spectantes*], I, ed. F. Barišić and others (Belgrade, 1955); II, ed. B. Ferjančić (Belgrade, 1959) (Srpska Akademija Nauka, poseb. izd., CCXLI, CCCXXIII).

II. GENERAL WORKS

(A) RELEVANT TO THE WHOLE PERIOD

Bachrušin, S. and Kosminsky, E., *Les états barbares et Byzance*, in *Histoire de la Diplomatie*, ed. V. Potemkin, I (Paris, 1946), 82–105.

Dölger, F., *Byzanz und die europäische Staatenwelt* (Ettal, 1953).

Marquart, J., *Osteuropäische und ostasiatische Streifzüge* (Leipzig, 1903).

Ostrogorsky, G., 'Avtokrator i Samodržac', *Glas Srpske Akademije*, CLXIV (1935), 95–187.

Ostrogorsky, G., 'Die byzantinische Staatenhierarchie', *Sem. Kond.* VIII (1936), 41–61.

Ostrogorsky, G., 'The Byzantine Emperor and the Hierarchical World Order', *SEER*, XXXV (1956–7), 1–14.

Spinka, M., *A History of Christianity in the Balkans* (Chicago, 1933).

Stadtmüller, G., *Geschichte Südosteuropas* (Munich, 1950).

Vernadsky, G., *Ancient Russia* (New Haven, 1944).

(B) DEALING WITH PARTICULAR REIGNS

Diehl, C., *Justinien et la civilisation byzantine au VIe siècle* (Paris, 1901). (Chapter VIII, pp. 367–413: 'L'œuvre diplomatique'.)

Rambaud, A., *L'Empire Grec au Xe siècle. Constantin Porphyrogénète* (Paris, 1870).

Runciman, S., *The Emperor Romanus Lecapenus and his Reign* (Cambridge, 1929).

III. SPECIAL TOPICS

(A) AVARS

Alföldi, A., 'Zur historischen Bestimmung der Avarenfunde', *Eurasia Septentrionalis Antiqua*, IX (1934), 285–307.

Barišić, F., 'Le siège de Constantinople par les Avares et les Slaves en 626', *B*, XXIV (1954), 371–95.

Barišić, F., 'Car Foka (602–610) i podunavski Avaro-Sloveni' ['De Avaro-Slavis in Phocae imperatoris aetate'], *Zbornik Radova Srpske Akad. Nauka*, XLIX (Belgrade, 1956), 73–88 (Vizantološki Institut, IV). [With a summary in Latin.]

Baynes, N. H., 'The Date of the Avar Surprise', *BZ*, XXI (1912), 110–28.

Csallány, D., *Archäologische Denkmäler der Awarenzeit in Mitteleuropa. Schrifttum und Fundorte* (Budapest, 1956).

Eisner, J., 'Pour dater la civilisation "Avare"', *BS*, IX (1947–8), 45–54.

Hauptmann, L., 'Les rapports des Byzantins avec les Slaves et les Avares pendant la seconde moitié du VIe siècle', *B*, IV (1927–8), 137–70.

Haussig, H. W., 'Theophylakts Exkurs über die Skythischen Völker', *B*, XXIII (1953), 275–462.

Howorth, H. H., 'The Avars', *JRAS*, XXI (1889), 721–810.

Kollautz, A., 'Die Awaren. Die Schichtung in einer Nomadenherrschaft', *Saeculum*, V (1954), 129–78.

Labuda, G., 'Chronologie des guerres de Byzance contre les Avars et les Slaves à la fin du VIe siècle', *BS*, XI (1950), 167–73.

László, G., 'Etudes archéologiques sur l'histoire de la société des Avars', *Archaeologia Hungarica*, XXXIV (1955).

(B) TURKS (TOU KIUE)

Bury, J. B., 'The Turks in the Sixth Century', *EHR*, XII (1897), 417–26.

Cahun, L., *Introduction à l'histoire de l'Asie. Turcs et Mongols des origines à 1405* (Paris, 1896), pp. 108–18.

Chavannes, E., 'Documents sur les Tou-Kiue (Turcs) Occidentaux', *Sbornik Trudov Orchonskoj Ekspedicij*, VI (St Petersburg, 1903).

Macartney, C. A., 'On the Greek Sources for the History of the Turks in the Sixth Century', *BSOAS*, XI (1943–6), 266–75.

Parker, E. H., 'The Origin of the Turks', *EHR*, XI (1896), 431–45.

Pigulevskaja, N. V., 'Vizantijskaja diplomatija i torgovlja šelkom v V–VII vv.' ['Byzantine diplomacy and the silk trade in the Vth–VIIth Centuries'], *VV*, n.s. I (1947), 184–214.

Sinor, D., 'The Historical Role of the Turk Empire', *CHM*, I (1953), 427–34.

Vailhé, S., 'Projet d'alliance turco-byzantine au VIe siècle', *EO*, XII (1909), 206–14.

(C) THE SLAVS AND THEIR INVASIONS OF THE EMPIRE

Barišić, F., *Čuda Dimitrija Solunskog kao istoriski izvori* [*Les Miracles de St. Démétrius comme source historique*] (Belgrade, 1953) (Srpska Akademija Nauka, poseb. izd., CCXIX, Vizantološki Institut, 2). [With a summary in French.]

Bon, A., *Le Péloponnèse byzantin jusqu'en 1204* (Paris, 1951).

Brajčevsky, M. J., 'Ob "Antach" Psevdomavrikija' ['On the "Antes" of Pseudo-Maurice'], *Sovetskaja Etnografija* (1953), 2, pp. 21–36.

Burmov, A., 'Slavjanskite napadenija srešču Solun v "Čudesata na sv. Dimitra" i tjachnata chronologija' ['Les sièges de Thessalonique par les Slaves dans "Miracula Sancti Demetrii Martyris" et leur chronologie'], *Godišnik na Sofijskija Universitet, filos.-ist. fak.*, XLVII, 2 (1952), 167–215. [With a summary in French.]

Charanis, P., 'Nicephorus I, the Savior of Greece from the Slavs (810 A.D.)', *BM*, I (1946), 75–92.

Charanis, P., 'The Chronicle of Monemvasia and the Question of the Slavonic Settlements in Greece', *DOP*, V (1950), 139–66.

Charanis, P., 'On the Slavic Settlement in the Peloponnesus', *BZ*, XLVI (1953), 91–103.

Charanis, P., 'Ethnic Changes in the Byzantine Empire in the Seventh Century', *DOP*, XIII (1959), 23–44.

Diomedes, A. N., Βυζαντιναὶ Μελέται, II: Αἱ σλαβικαὶ ἐπιδρομαὶ εἰς τὴν Ἑλλάδα καὶ ἡ πολιτικὴ τοῦ Βυζαντίου (Athens, 1946).

Djakonov, A., 'Izvestija Ioanna Efesskogo i sirijskich chronik o slavjanach VI–VII vekov' ['The evidence of John of Ephesus and of the Syrian Chronicles on the Slavs in the VIth and VIIth centuries'], *Vestnik Drevnej Istorii* (1946), 1 (15), pp. 20–34.

Dvornik, F., *Les Slaves, Byzance et Rome au IXe siècle* (Paris, 1926).

Dvornik, F., *The Slavs: their Early History and Civilization* (Boston, 1956).

Grafenauer, B., 'Nekaj vprašanj iz dobe naseljevanja južnih Slovanov
[Quelques problèmes relatifs à l'époque de l'immigration des Slaves du
Sud]', *Zgodovinski Časopis*, IV (Ljubljana, 1950), 23–126 [with a summary
in French].

Grafenauer, B., 'Kronološka vprašanja selitve južnih slovanov ob podatkih
spisa Miracula S. Demetrii' ['Questions chronologiques concernant les
migrations des Slaves méridionaux sur la base des Miracula S. Demetrii'],
Zbornik Filozofske Fakultete, Univerza v Ljubljani, II (1955), 21–54. [With
a summary in French.]

Jażdżewski, K., *Atlas to the Prehistory of the Slavs*, 2 parts (Lodz,
1948–9).

Kyriakides, S., Βυζαντιναὶ Μελέται, VI: Οἱ Σλάβοι ἐν Πελοποννήσῳ (Thessalonica, 1947).

Lemerle, P., 'La composition et la chronologie des deux premiers livres des
Miracula S. Demetrii', *BZ*, XLVI (1953), 349–61.

Lemerle, P., 'Invasions et migrations dans les Balkans depuis la fin de
l'époque romaine jusqu'au VIIIe siècle', *RH*, CCXI (1954), 265–308.

Levčenko, M. V., 'Vizantija i Slavjane v VI–VII vv.' ['Byzantium and the
Slavs in the VIth and VIIth centuries'], *Vestnik Drevnej Istorii* (1938),
1 (5), 23–48.

Lipšic (Lipshits), E. E., *Byzanz und die Slaven* (Weimar, 1951).

Niederle, L., *Slovanské starožitnosti* [*Slavonic Antiquities*], I (Prague, 1902–4);
II (Prague, 1906–10).

Niederle, L., *Manuel de l'Antiquité slave*, I (Paris, 1923).

Rybakov, B. A., 'Anty i Kievskaja Rus'' ['The Antes and Kievan Russia'],
Vestnik Drevnej Istorii (1939), 1 (6), pp. 319–37.

Vasiliev, A. A., 'Slavjane v Grecij' ['The Slavs in Greece'], *VV*, V (1898),
404–38, 626–70.

Vasmer, M., *Die Slaven in Griechenland* (*Abhandlungen der Preussischen
Akademie der Wissenschaften, philos.-hist. Kl.*, XII (1941)).

Vernadsky, G., 'On the Origins of the Antae', *Journ. American Oriental Soc.*
LIX (1939), 56–66.

Zakythinos, D., Οἱ Σλάβοι ἐν Ἑλλάδι (Athens, 1945).

(D) SAMO

Grafenauer, B., 'Novejša literatura o Samu i njeni problemi' ['The most
recent literature on Samo and its problems'], *Zgodovinski Časopis*, IV
(1950), 151–69. [With a summary in French.]

Labuda, G., *Pierwsze państwo słowiańskie* [*The First Slavonic State*] (Poznań,
1949) [with a summary in French]. [Reviewed by V. Chaloupecký in *BS*,
XI (1950), 223–39.]

Mikkola, J., 'Samo und sein Reich', *Archiv für slavische Philologie*, XLII
(1929), 77–97.

Vernadsky, G., 'The Beginnings of the Czech State', *B*, XVII (1944–5), 315–28.

(E) SERBS AND CROATS

Ferluga, J., *Vizantiska uprava u Dalmacii* [*L'Administration byzantine en
Dalmatie*] (Belgrade, 1957) (Srpska Akademija Nauka, poseb. izd.,
CCXCI, Vizantološki Institut, 6). [With a summary in French.]

Grafenauer, B., 'Prilog kritici izvještaja Konstantina Porfirogenita o doseljenju Hrvata' ['Ein Beitrag zur Kritik des Berichtes Konstantin Porphyrogennetos über die Einwanderung der Kroaten'], *Historijski Zbornik*, v (Zagreb, 1952), 1–56. [With a summary in German.]

Grégoire, H., 'L'origine et le nom des Croates et des Serbes', B, xvii (1944–5), 88–118.

Hauptmann, L., 'Seoba Hrvata i Srba' ['The Migration of the Croats and the Serbs'], *Jugoslovenski Istoriski Časopis*, iii (1937), 30–61.

Hauptmann, L., 'Podrijetlo hrvatskog plemstva' ['The origin of the Croat nobility'], *Rad Jugoslavenske Akademije Znanosti i Umjetnosti*, cclxxiii (1942), 79–112.

Jireček, C. J., *Geschichte der Serben*, i (Gotha, 1911). [In the revised Serbian version of this standard work (*Istorija Srba*, i, 2nd ed. (Belgrade, 1952)) the bibliographical references have been brought up to date by the translator, J. Radonić.]

Novak, G., *Prošlost Dalmacije* [*Dalmatia's Past*], i (Zagreb, 1944).

Ostrogorsky, G., 'Serbskoje posol'stvo k imperatoru Vasiliju II' ['A Serbian Embassy to the Emperor Basil II'], *Glas*, cxciii (1949), 15–29.

Ostrogorsky, G., 'Une ambassade serbe auprès de l'empereur Basile II', B, xix (1949), 187–94.

Radonić, I., 'O političeskich otnošenijach Dalmatinskich gorodov k Vizantii v X veke' ['On the Political Relationships between the Dalmatian Cities and Byzantium in the Xth Century'], *IRAIK*, vi, 2–3 (1901), 408–17.

Šišić, F., *Geschichte der Kroaten*, i (Zagreb, 1917).

Šišić, F., *Povijest Hrvata u vrijeme narodnih vladara* [*A History of the Croats in the Period of their National Rulers*] (Zagreb, 1925).

Stanojević, S., *Vizantija i Srbi* [*Byzantium and the Serbs*], i (Novi Sad, 1903).

Temperley, H. W. V., *History of Serbia* (London, 1917).

(F) KHAZARS

A comprehensive bibliography of sources and modern works relating to the Khazars was compiled by the Slavonic Division of the New York Public Library: 'The Khazars', *Bulletin of the New York Public Library*, xlii, no. 9 (1938); lxiii, no. 5 (1959).

Artamonov, M. I., 'Sarkel i nekotorie drugie ukreplenija v Severo-Zapadnoj Khazarii' ['Sarkel and some other fortifications in North-western Khazaria'], *Sovetskaja Archeologija*, vi (1940), 130–67. [With a summary in French.]

Artamonov, M. I., 'Khazarskaja krepost' Sarkel' ['The Khazar fortress of Sarkel'], *Acta Archaeologica Academiae Scientiarum Hungaricae*, vii (1956), 321–41.

Brutzkus, J. D., *Pis'mo khazarskogo evreja ot X veka* [*A Tenth-Century Letter of a Khazar Jew*] (Berlin, 1924).

Brutzkus, J. D., 'Chasaren', *Encyclopaedia Judaica* (Berlin, 1930), v, cols. 337–50.

Brutzkus, J. D., 'The Khazar Origin of Ancient Kiev', *SEER*, xxii (1944), 108–24.

Dunlop, D. M., *The History of the Jewish Khazars* (Princeton, 1954).

Dvornik, F., *Les Légendes de Constantin et de Méthode vues de Byzance* (Prague, 1933) (chapter v, pp. 148–211: 'Byzance et les Khazars vers 861').

Gorjanov, B. T. 'Vizantija i Khazary' ['Byzantium and the Khazars'], *Istoričeskie Zapiski*, xv (Moscow, 1945), 262–77.

Grégoire, H., 'Le "Glozel" Khazare', *B*, xii (1937), 225–66, 739–40.

Kokovcov, P. K. (ed.), *Evrejsko-khazarskaja perepiska v X veke* [*The Jewish–Khazar Correspondence of the Xth Century*] (Leningrad, 1932).

Kudrjašov, K. V., 'O mestonachoždenii Khazarskogo goroda Sarkela' ['On the Location of the Khazar City of Sarkel'], *Izvestija Akademii Nauk S.S.S.R., serija ist. i filos.*, iv, no. 6 (1947), 536–56.

Landau, M., *Beiträge zum Chazarenproblem* (Breslau, 1938) (Schriften der Gesellschaft zur Förderung der Wissenschaft des Judentums, xliii).

Moravcsik, Gy., 'Proischoždenie slova Tzitzakion' ['The Origin of the Word *Τζιτζάκιον*'], *Sem. Kond.* iv (1931), 69–76. [With a summary in German.]

Mošin, V., 'Les Khazares et les Byzantins d'après l'anonyme de Cambridge', *B*, vi (1931), 309–25.

Mošin, V., 'Chel'gu khazarskogo dokumenta' ['Chel'gu of the Khazar Document'], *Slavia*, xv (1938), 191–200.

Peeters, P., 'Les Khazars dans la Passion de S. Abo de Tiflis', *AB*, lii (1934), 21–56. [Reviewed by H. Grégoire in *B*, ix (1934), 484–8.]

Rybakov, B. A., 'Rus' i Khazarija (K istoričeskoj geografii Khazarii)' ['Russia and Khazaria (A contribution to the historical geography of Khazaria)'], *Akademiku B. D. Grekovu ko dnju semidesjatiletija: Sbornik statej* (Moscow, 1952), pp. 76–88.

Schechter, S., 'An Unknown Khazar Document', *Jewish Quart. Rev.* iii, 2 (1912), 181–219.

Togan, A. Zeki Velidi, 'Völkerschaften des Chazarenreiches im neunten Jahrhundert', *Kőrősi Csoma-Archivum*, iii, 1 (Budapest–Leipzig, 1940), 40–76.

Vernadsky, G., 'The Date of the Conversion of the Khazars to Judaism', *B*, xv (1940–1), 76–86.

Zajaczkowski, A., *Ze studiów nad zagadnieniem chazarskim* [*Etudes sur le problème des Khazars*] (Cracow, 1947) (Polska Akademia Umiejętności. Prace Komisji Orientalistycznej, xxxvi) [with a summary in French]. [Reviewed by O. Pritsak in *Der Islam*, xxix (1949), 96–103.]

(G) THE CRIMEA AND THE NORTHERN COAST OF THE BLACK SEA

Jakobson, A. L., 'Srednevekovij Chersones (XII–XIV vv.)' ['Medieval Chersonesus (XIIth to XIVth centuries)'], *Materialy i Issledovanija po archeologii S.S.S.R.* xvii (1950).

Jakobson, A. L., 'Vizantija v istorii rannesrednevekovoj Tavriki' ['Byzantium in the Early Medieval History of the Crimea'], *Sovetskaja Archeologija*, xxi (1954), 148–63.

Kulakovsky, J., 'K istorii Bospora Kimmerijskogo v konce VI veka' ['A contribution to the history of the Cimmerian Bosporus at the end of the sixth century'], *VV*, iii (1896), 1–17.

Latyšev, V., 'K istorii Christianstva na Kavkaze' ['A contribution to the history of Christianity in the Caucasus'], *Sbornik archeologičeskich statej, podnesennij gr. A. A. Bobrinskomu* (St Petersburg, 1911), pp. 169–98.

Minns, E. H., *Scythians and Greeks* (Cambridge, 1913).

Mošin, V., ''Επαρχία Γοτθίας v Khazarii v VIII veke' ['The 'Επαρχία Γοτθίας in Khazaria in the eighth century'], *Trudy IV-go Sjezda Russkich Akademičeskich Organizacij za granicej*, i (Belgrade, 1929), 149–56.

Rostovtzeff, M., *Iranians and Greeks in South Russia* (Oxford, 1922).

Šestakov, S. P., *Očerki po istorii Chersonesa v VI–X vekach po R. Chr. [An outline of the history of Chersonesus in the VIth–Xth centuries of the Christian era*'] (Pamjatniki Christianskogo Chersonesa, iii) (Moscow, 1908).

Stratonov, I., 'Die Krim und ihre Bedeutung für die Christianisierung der Ostslaven', *Kyrios*, i (Königsberg, 1936), 381–95.

Talis, D. L., 'Iz istorii russko-korsunskich političeskich otnošenij v IX–X vv.' ['Political relations between Russia and Cherson in the ninth and tenth centuries'], *VV*, xiv (1958), 103–15.

Vasiliev, A. A., *The Goths in the Crimea* (Monographs of the Mediaeval Academy of America, no. 11) (Cambridge, Mass., 1936).

Vernadsky, G., 'The Eparchy of Gothia', *B*, xv (1940–1), 67–76.

Zagorovsky, E. A., *Očerk istorii severnogo Pričernomor'ja [An Outline of the History of the Northern Coast of the Black Sea*], i (Odessa, 1922).

(H) ST CYRIL AND ST METHODIUS

The sources and the very considerable bibliography of modern works relating to St Cyril and St Methodius are listed in G. A. Iljinsky, *Opyt sistematičeskoj Kirillo-Mefodjevskoj bibliografii [An attempt at a systematic bibliography of works on Cyril and Methodius*] (Sofia, 1934), and in the sequel to this work: M. Popruženko and S. Romanski, *Kirilometodijevska bibliografija za 1934–1940 god. [A bibliography of works on Cyril and Methodius published between 1934 and 1940*] (Sofia, 1942).

Alexander, P. J., 'The Papacy, the Bavarian Clergy, and the Slavonic Apostles', *SEER*, xx (1941), 266–93.

Dvornik, F., *Les Slaves, Byzance et Rome au IXe siècle* (Paris, 1926).

Dvornik, F., *Les Légendes de Constantin et de Méthode vues de Byzance* (Prague, 1933).

Georgiev, E., *Slavjanskaja pis'mennost' do Kirilla i Mefodija [The Slavonic written language before Cyril and Methodius*] (Sofia, 1952).

Georgiev, E., *Kiril i Metodij, osnovopoložnitsi na slavjanskite literaturi* [Cyril and Methodius, founders of Slavonic literatures] (Sofia, 1956).

Grivec, F., *Konstantin und Method, Lehrer der Slaven* (Wiesbaden, 1960).

Grivec, F. and Tomšič, F., *Constantinus et Methodius Thessalonicenses: Fontes* (Zagreb, 1960) (Radovi Staroslavenskog Instituta, iv).

Onasch, K., 'Der cyrillo-methodianische Gedanke in der Kirchengeschichte des Mittelalters', *Wissenschaftliche Zeitschrift der Martin-Luther-Universität Halle-Wittenberg, gesellschafts- und sprachwissenschaftliche Reihe*, vi (1956–7), 27–39.

Poulík, J., 'The latest archaeological discoveries from the period of the Great Moravian Empire', *Historica*, i (Prague, 1959), 7–70.

(I) THE BULGARS AND THE FIRST BULGARIAN EMPIRE

Adontz, N., 'Samuel l'Arménien, roi des Bulgares', *Mémoires de l'Académie Royale de Belgique, cl. des lettres*, xxxix, i (1938).

Angelov, B. and Genov, M., *Stara bŭlgarska literatura [Old Bulgarian Literature*], ii (Sofia, 1922).

Angelov, D., 'Vizantijski vlijanija vŭrchu srednovekovna Bŭlgarija' ['Byzantine influences on medieval Bulgaria'], *Istoričeski Pregled*, IV, 4–5 (Sofia, 1948), 401–16; V, 5 (1949), 587–601.

Beševliev, V., 'Pŭrvobŭlgarski nadpisi' ['Proto-Bulgarian Inscriptions'], *Godišnik na Sofijskija Universitet, ist.-filol. fak.* XXXI, 1 (1934).

Beševliev, V., 'K voprosu o nagrade, polučennoj Tervelem ot Justiniana II v 705 g.' ['A contribution to the problem of the reward received by Tervel from Justinian II in 705'], *VV*, XVI (1959), 8–13.

Beševliev, V. and Irmscher, J. (edd.), *Antike und Mittelalter in Bulgarien* (Berlin, 1960) (Berliner Byzantinistische Arbeiten, XXI).

Bratianu, G. I., 'Le commerce bulgare dans l'Empire byzantin et le monopole de l'empereur Léon VI à Thessalonique', *Sbornik v pamet' na P. Nikov: Izvestija na Bŭlgarskoto Istoričesko Družestvo*, XVI–XVIII (Sofia, 1940), 30–6.

Burmov, A., 'Kŭm vŭprosa za proizchoda na prabŭlgarite' ['A contribution to the problem of the origin of the Proto-Bulgarians'], *ibid.* XXII–XXIV (1948), 298–337. [With a summary in French.]

Bury, J. B., 'The Bulgarian Treaty of A.D. 814, and the Great Fence of Thrace', *EHR*, XXV (1910), 276–87.

Cuchlev, D., *Istorija na bŭlgarskata cŭrkva* [*A History of the Bulgarian Church*], I (Sofia, 1910).

Dölger, F., 'Bulgarisches Zartum und byzantinisches Kaisertum', *Actes du IVe Congrès International des Etudes Byzantines*, I (Sofia, 1935), 57–68; reprinted in *Byzanz und die europäische Staatenwelt* (Ettal, 1953), pp. 140–58.

Dölger, F., 'Der Bulgarenherrscher als geistlicher Sohn des byzantinischen Kaisers', *Sbornik v pamet' na P. Nikov: Izvestija na Bŭlgarskoto Istoričesko Družestvo*, XVI–XVIII (1940), 219–32; reprinted in *Byzanz und die europäische Staatenwelt*, pp. 183–96.

Dujčev, I., 'Protobulgares et Slaves [Sur le problème de la formation de l'Etat bulgare]', *Sem. Kond.* X (1938), 145–54.

Dujčev, I., 'Die Responsa Nicolai I. Papae ad Consulta Bulgarorum als Quelle für die bulgarische Geschichte', *Festschrift zur Feier des Zweihundertjährigen Bestandes des Haus-, Hof- und Staatsarchivs*, I (Vienna, 1949), pp. 349–62.

Dujčev, I., 'Au lendemain de la conversion du peuple bulgare. L'épître de Photius', *Mélanges de Science Religieuse*, VIII (1951), 211–26.

Georgiev, E., *Razcvetŭt na bŭlgarskata literatura v IX–X v.* [*The Golden Age of Bulgarian Literature in the ninth and tenth centuries*] (Sofia, 1962).

Grégoire, H., 'Les sources épigraphiques de l'histoire bulgare', *B*, IX (1934), 745–86.

Istorija Bolgarii [*A History of Bulgaria*], ed. P. N. Tretjakov and others, I (Moscow, 1954).

Istorija na Bŭlgarija [*A History of Bulgaria*], ed. D. Kosev and others, I (Sofia, 1954).

Ivanov, I., *Bŭlgarski Starini iz Makedonija* [*Bulgarian Antiquities from Macedonia*], 2nd ed. (Sofia, 1931).

Kolias, G., *Léon Choerosphactès* (Texte und Forschungen zur byzant.-neugriechischen Philologie, XXXI) (Athens, 1939).

Kusseff, M., 'St Clement of Ochrida', *SEER*, XXVII (1948), 193–215.

Moravcsik, Gy., 'Zur Geschichte der Onoguren', *Ungarische Jahrbücher*, X (1930), 53–90.

Murko, M., *Geschichte der älteren südslawischen Litteraturen* (Leipzig, 1908).

Mutafčiev, P., 'Der Byzantinismus im mittelalterlichen Bulgarien', *BZ*, xxx (1929–30), 387–94.

Mutafčiev., P., *Istorija na bŭlgarskija narod* [*A History of the Bulgarian People*], I, 3rd ed. (Sofia, 1948).

Obolensky, D., *The Bogomils* [see Gen. Bibl. v].

Ostrogorsky, G., 'Die Krönung Symeons von Bulgarien durch den Patriarchen Nikolaos Mystikos', *Actes du IVe Congrès International des Etudes Byzantines*, I (Sofia, 1935), 275–86.

Puech, H.-C. and Vaillant, A., *Le traité contre les Bogomiles de Cosmas le prêtre* (Paris, 1945).

Runciman, S., *A History of the First Bulgarian Empire* (London, 1930).

Runciman, S., *The Medieval Manichee*, 2nd ed. (Cambridge, 1955).

Sakŭzov, I., *Bulgarische Wirtschaftsgeschichte* (Berlin and Leipzig, 1929).

Schlumberger, G., *L'Epopée byzantine à la fin du Xe siècle*, I, II [see Gen. Bibl. v].

Sergheraert, G. (Ch. Gérard), *Les Bulgares de la Volga et les Slaves du Danube* (Paris, 1939).

Sergheraert, G. (Ch. Gérard), *Syméon le Grand* (Paris, 1960).

Setton, K. M., 'The Bulgars in the Balkans and the Occupation of Corinth in the Seventh Century', *SP*, xxv (1950), 502–43. [Cf. P. Charanis in *SP*, xxvii (1952), 343–50, and Setton's reply *ibid.* pp. 351–62.]

Snegarov, I., *Kratka istorija na sŭvremennite pravoslavni cŭrkvi* (*Bŭlgarska, Ruska i Srbska*) [*A brief history of the present Orthodox Churches* (*the Bulgarian, the Russian and the Serbian*)], II (Sofia, 1946).

Tunicky, N. L., *Sv. Kliment, episkop slovenskij* [*St Clement, Bishop of the Slavs*] (Sergiev Posad, 1913).

Vaillant, A. and Lascaris, M., 'La date de la conversion des Bulgares', *Revue des Etudes Slaves*, xiii (1933), 5–15.

Voinov, M. I., 'Za pervija dopir na Asparuchovite bŭlgari sŭs slavjanite i za datata na osnovavaneto na bŭlgarskata dŭržava.' ['The first contact of Asparukh's Bulgars with the Slavs and the date of the foundation of the Bulgarian State'], *Izvestija na Instituta za Bŭlgarska Istorija*, VI (1956), 453–80. [With summaries in Russian and French.]

Zlatarsky, V. N., 'Pismata na carigradskija patriarch Nikolaja Mistika do bŭlgarskija tsar Simeona' [The Letters of the Patriarch Nicholas Mysticus to the Bulgarian car Symeon'], *Sbornik za Narodni Umotvorenija, Nauka i Knižnina*, x (1894), 372–428; xi (1894), 3–54; xii (1895), 121–211.

Zlatarsky, V. N., *Istorija na bŭlgarskata dŭržava prez srednite vekove* [*A history of the Bulgarian State in the middle ages*], I, 1, 2 (Sofia, 1918, 1927).

(J) VOLGA BULGARS

Canard, M., 'La relation du voyage d'Ibn Fadlân chez les Bulgares de la Volga', *Annales de l'Institut d'Etudes Orientales, Faculté des Lettres de l'Université d'Alger*, xvi (1958), 41–146.

Grekov, B. D., 'Volžskie Bolgary v IX–X vekach' ['The Volga Bulgars in the IXth and Xth centuries'], *Istoričeskie Zapiski*, xiv (Moscow, 1945), 3–37.

Hrbek, I., 'Bulghār', *Encyclopaedia of Islam*, 2nd ed., I (Leiden and London, 1960), 1304–8.

Kračkovsky, I. J. (ed.), *Putešestvie Ibn-Fadlana na Volgu* [*Ibn-Fadlan's journey to the Volga*] (Moscow, Leningrad, 1939).

Macartney, C. A., 'On the Black Bulgars', *BNJ*, VIII (1931), 150–8.
Smirnov, A. P., *Volžskie bulgary* [*The Volga Bulgars*] (Trudy Gosudarstven-nogo Istoričeskogo Museja, XIX) (Moscow, 1951).
Togan, A. Zeki Velidi, *Ibn Fadlans Reisebericht* (Leipzig, 1939) (Abhandlungen für die Kunde des Morgenlandes, XXIV, 3).

(K) RUSSIANS

Reference to the most important sources is made in the footnotes; the following, however, deserve special mention:

The Russian Primary Chronicle (*Povest' Vremennych Let*), ed. D. S. Lichačev and V. P. Adrianova-Peretc, I–II (Moscow–Leningrad, 1950). [The English transl. by S. H. Cross and O. P. Sherbowitz-Wetzor, *The Russian Primary Chronicle: Laurentian Text* (Cambridge, Mass., 1953), is useful, but at times inaccurate.]
Constantine Porphyrogenitus, *DAI*, I, cap. 9, pp. 56–62 [see Gen. Bibl. IV].

(a) General

Arne, T. J., *La Suède et l'Orient. Etudes archéologiques sur les relations de la Suède et de l'Orient pendant l'âge des Vikings* (Uppsala, 1914).
Barsov, N. P., *Očerki istoričeskoj geografii. Geografija Načal'noj Letopisi* [*Studies in historical geography: the geography of the Primary Chronicle*] (Warsaw, 1873).
Bernštejn-Kogan, S. V., 'Put' iz Varjag v Greki' ['The Way from the Varan-gians to the Greeks'], *Voprosy Geografii*, XX (1950), 239–70.
Brim, V. A., 'Put' iz Varjag v Greki' ['The Way from the Varangians to the Greeks'], *Bulletin de l'Académie des Sciences de l'U.R.S.S., 7e série, cl. des sciences sociales* (1931), 2, pp. 201–47.
Chadwick, N. K., *The Beginnings of Russian History* (Cambridge, 1946).
Dvornik, F., *The Making of Central and Eastern Europe* (London, 1949).
Falk, K.-O., *Dneprforsarnas namn i Kejsar Konstantin VII Porfyrogennetos' De Administrando Imperio.* [*Lunds Universitets Årsskrift*, N.F., Avd. 1, Bd. 46, nr. 4 (1951); with a summary in German.]
Grekov, B. D., *Kievskaja Rus'* [*Kievan Russia*], 4th ed. (Moscow–Leningrad, 1944).
Istorija kul'tury drevnej Rusi [*The history of the culture of ancient Russia*], ed. B. D. Grekov and M. I. Artamonov, I–II (Moscow–Leningrad, 1948, 1951).
Laehr, G., *Die Anfänge des russischen Reiches* (Historische Studien, 189) (Berlin, 1930).
Levčenko, M. V., *Očerki po istorii russko-vizantijskich otnošenij* [*An Outline of the History of Russo-Byzantine Relations*] (Moscow, 1956).
Minorsky, V., 'Rūs', *Encyclopaedia of Islam*, III (1936), 1181–3.
Mošin, V., 'Načalo Rusi. Normany v vostočnoj Evrope' ['The beginnings of Russia. The Northmen in Eastern Europe'], *BS*, III (1931), 33–58; 285–307.
Mošin, V., 'Varjago-russkij vopros' ['The Varangian–Russian problem'], *Slavia*, X (1931), 109–36, 343–79, 501–37.
Mošin, V., 'Rus' i Khazarija pri Svjatoslave' ['Russia and Khazaria in the reign of Svjatoslav'], *Sem. Kond.* VI (1933), 187–208.
Nasonov, A. N., '*Russkaja Zemlja' i obrazovanie territorii drevnerusskogo gosudarstva* [*The 'Land of Russia' and the territorial growth of the ancient Russian state*] (Moscow, 1951).

Očerki istorii S.S.S.R. [*Studies in the history of the U.S.S.R.*]: *Krizis rabovladel'-českoj sistemy i zaroždenie feodalizma, III–IX vv.*, ed. B. A. Rybakov (Moscow, 1958); *Period feodalizma, IX–XV vv.*, I, ed. B. D. Grekov (Moscow, 1953).

Odinec, D. M., *Vozniknovenie gosudarstvennogo stroja u vostočnych slavjan* [*The Rise of Political Life among the Eastern Slavs*] (Paris, 1935).

Paszkiewicz, H., *The Origin of Russia* (London, 1954).

Presnjakov, A. E., *Lekcii po russkoj istorii* [*Lectures on Russian History*], I, (Moscow, 1938).

Rybakov, B. A., *Remeslo drevnej Rusi* [*Handicrafts in ancient Russia*] (Moscow, 1948).

Seredonin, S. M., *Istoričeskaja geografija* [*Historical geography*] (Petrograd, 1916).

Smirnov, P., *Volž'ky šljach i starodavni Rusi* [*The Volga Route and the Ancient Russians*] (Kiev, 1928) (Ukraïns'ka Akad. Nauk, Zbirnik ist.-filol. vid., LXXV).

Stender-Petersen, A., *Die Varägersage als Quelle der altrussischen Chronik* (Aarhus, 1934) (Acta Jutlandica, VI, 1).

Stender-Petersen, A., *Varangica* (Aarhus, 1953).

Stender-Petersen, A., 'Das Problem der ältesten byzantinisch–russisch–nordischen Beziehungen', *X Congresso Internazionale di Scienze Storiche* [Rome]: *Relazioni*, III (Florence, 1955), 165–88.

Thomsen, V., *The Relations between Ancient Russia and Scandinavia and the Origin of the Russian State* (Oxford, 1877). [Revised ed. in V. Thomsen's *Samlede Afhandlinger*, I (Copenhagen, 1919), 231–449.]

Tretjakov, P. N., *Vostočnoslavjanskie plemena* [*The East Slavonic Tribes*], 2nd ed. (Moscow, 1953).

Vasiliev, A. A., 'Economic Relations between Byzantium and Old Russia', *Journ. Economic and Business History*, IV (1932), 314–34.

Vasilevsky, V. G., *Varjago-russkaja i varjago-anglijskaja družina v Konstantinopole XI i XII vv.* [*The Russian Varangian and the English Varangian Guard in Constantinople in the Eleventh and Twelfth Centuries*], in his *Trudy*, I (St Petersburg, 1908), pp. 176–377.

Vernadsky, G., *Kievan Russia* (New Haven, 1948).

(b) *War, Trade and Diplomacy*

Da Costa-Louillet, G., 'Y eut-il des invasions russes dans l'Empire byzantin avant 860?', *B*, XV (1940–1), 231–48.

Istrin, V., 'Dogovory russkich s grekami X veka' ['The Russian–Byzantine treaties of the Xth century'], *Izvestija Otdel. Russk. Jazyka i Slovesnosti Rossijskoj Akademii Nauk*, XXIX (1924), 383–93.

Lipšic, E. E., 'O pochode Rusi na Vizantiju ranee 842 goda' ['On the campaign of the Russians against Byzantium before 842'], *Istoričeskie Zapiski*, XXVI (1948), 312–31.

Mikucki, S., 'Etudes sur la diplomatique russe la plus ancienne', *Bulletin International de l'Académie Polonaise des Sciences et des Lettres, classes de philologie et d'histoire et de la philosophie*, no. supplémentaire VII (Cracow, 1953), 1–40.

Pamjatniki prava Kievskogo gosudarstva, X–XII vv. [*Legal Documents of the Kievan State, X–XII centuries*], ed. A. A. Zimin (Moscow, 1952) (Pamjatniki Russkogo Prava, I).

Pargoire, J., 'Saint-Mamas, le quartier des Russes à Constantinople', *EO*, XI (1908), 203–10.

Vasilevsky, V. G., *Žitie sv. Georgija Amastridskogo* [*The Life of St George of Amastris*], in his *Trudy*, III (St Petersburg, 1915).

(i) *The attack of 860*

Vasiliev, A. A., *The Russian Attack on Constantinople in 860* (Mediaeval Academy of America. Publication no. 46) (Cambridge, Mass., 1946).

(ii) *Oleg's attack of 907*

Dolley, R. H., 'Oleg's Mythical Campaign against Constantinople', *Bulletin de l'Académie Royale de Belgique, cl. des lettres et des sciences morales et politiques*, XXXV (1949), 106–30.

Grégoire, H., 'La légende d'Oleg et l'expédition d'Igor', *ibid.* XXIII (1937), 80–94.

Jenkins, R. J. H., 'The Supposed Russian Attack on Constantinople in 907: Evidence of the Pseudo-Symeon', *SP*, XXIV (1949), 403–6.

Levčenko, M. V., 'Russko-vizantijskie dogovory 907 i 911 gg.' ['The Russo-Byzantine Treaties of 907 and 911'], *VV*, V (1952), 105–26; reprinted in his *Očerki*, pp. 91–127.

Ostrogorsky, G., 'L'expédition du prince Oleg contre Constantinople en 907', *Sem. Kond.* XI (1940), 47–62.

Vasiliev, A. A., 'The Second Russian Attack on Constantinople', *DOP*, VI (1951), 161–225.

(iii) *Igor's attack of 941*

Bártová, K., 'Igorova výprava na Cařihrad r. 941' ['Igor's expedition against Byzantium in 941'], *BS*, VIII (1939–46), 87–108.

Grégoire, H., 'Saint Théodore le Stratélate et les Russes d'Igor', *B*, XIII (1938), 291–300.

(iv) *John Tzimisces' war against Svjatoslav (970–1)*

Dölger, F., 'Die Chronologie des grossen Feldzuges des Kaisers Johannes Tzimiskes gegen die Russen', *BZ*, XXXII (1932), 275–92.

Göllner, C., 'Les expéditions byzantines contre les Russes sous Jean Tzimiscès (970–1)', *RHSE*, XIII (1936), 342–58.

Grégoire, H., 'La dernière campagne de Jean Tzimiskès contre les Russes', *B*, XII (1937), 267–76.

Karyškovsky, P. O., 'O chronologii russko-vizantijskoj vojny pri Svjatoslave' ['On the chronology of the Russo-Byzantine war in the reign of Svjatoslav'], *VV*, V (1952), 127–38.

Karyškovsky, P. O., 'Balkanskie vojny Svjatoslava v vizantijskoj istoričeskoj literature' ['Svjatoslav's Balkan wars in Byzantine historical literature'], *VV*, VI (1953), 36–71.

Karyškovsky, P. O., 'K istorii balkanskich vojn Svjatoslava' ['A contribution to the history of Svjatoslav's Balkan Wars'], *VV*, VII (1953), 224–43.

Mutafčiev, P., 'Russko-bolgarskie otnošenija pri Svjatoslave' ['Russo-Bulgarian relations in the reign of Svjatoslav'], *Sem. Kond.* IV (1931), 77–94. [With a summary in French.]

Schlumberger, G., *L'Epopée byzantine à la fin du Xe siècle*, I (Paris, 1896).

Stokes, A. D., 'The background and chronology of the Balkan campaigns of Svyatoslav Igorevich', *SEER*, XL (1961), 44–57.
Stokes, A. D., 'The Balkan campaigns of Svyatoslav Igorevich', *ibid.* XL (1962), 466–96.
Znojko, N. D., 'O posol'stve Kalokira v Kiev' ['Calocyras's embassy to Kiev'], *ZMNP* (April 1907), 229–72.

(c) *Russia's conversion to Christianity*

Baumgarten, N. de, 'Saint Vladimir et la Conversion de la Russie', *OC*, XXVII, I (1932).
Golubinsky, E. E., *Istorija russkoj cerkvi* [*A History of the Russian Church*], I, 1, 2nd ed. (Moscow, 1901).
Honigmann, E., 'The Foundation of the Russian Metropolitan Church according to Greek Sources', *B*, XVII (1944–5), 128–62.
Kartašev, A. V., *Očerki po istorii russkoj cerkvi* [*Studies in the history of the Russian Church*], I (Paris, 1959).
Koch, H., 'Byzanz, Ochrid und Kiev, 987–1037', *Kyrios*, III (1938), 253–92.
Laurent, V., 'Aux origines de l'Eglise russe. L'établissement de la hiérarchie byzantine', *EO*, XXXVIII (1939), 279–95.
Levčenko, M. V., 'Vzaimootnošenija Vizantii i Rusi pri Vladimire' ['The Relations between Byzantium and Russia in the Reign of Vladimir'] *VV*, VII (1953), 194–223.
Müller, L., *Zum Problem des hierarchischen Status und der jurisdiktionellen Abhängigkeit der russischen Kirche vor 1039* (Cologne–Braunsfeld, 1959) (Osteuropa und der deutsche Osten, III, 6).
Nikolaev, V., *Slavjanobŭlgarskijat faktor v christijanizacijata na Kievska Rusija* [*The Slavo-Bulgarian factor in the Christianisation of Kievan Russia*] (Sofia, 1949). [With a summary in French.] [Reviewed by B. Zástěrová in *BS*, XI (1950), 240–54].
Obolensky, D., 'Byzantium, Kiev and Moscow: A Study in Ecclesiastical Relations', *DOP*, XI (1957), 21–78.
Ostrogorsky, G., 'Vladimir Svjatoj i Vizantija' ['St Vladimir and Byzantium'], *Vladimirskij Sbornik* (Belgrade, 1938), pp. 31–40.
Priselkov, M. D., *Očerki po cerkovno-političeskoj istorii Kievskoj Rusi X–XII vv.* [*An outline of ecclesiastical and political history of Kievan Russia in the Xth–XIIth centuries*] (Zapiski ist.-filol. fakulteta Imperat. Sankt-Peterburgskago Universiteta, CXVI) (St Petersburg, 1913).
Šachmatov, A., 'Korsunskaja Legenda o kreščenii Vladimira' ['The Cherson legend of Vladimir's baptism'], *Sbornik statej, posvjaščennych V. I. Lamanskomu*, II (St Petersburg, 1908), 1029–1153.
Stokes, A. D., 'The Status of the Russian Church, 988–1037', *SEER*, XXXVII (1958–9), 430–42.
Vernadsky, G., 'The Status of the Russian Church during the First Half-century following Vladimir's Conversion', *SEER*, XX (1941), 294–314.

(L) MAGYARS

Darkó, J., 'Die auf die Ungarn bezüglichen Volksnamen bei den Byzantinern', *BZ*, XXI (1912), 472–87.
Dölger, F., 'Ungarn in der byzantinischen Reichspolitik', *Archivum Europae Centro-Orientalis*, VIII (Budapest–Leipzig, 1942), 315–42.

Grégoire, H., 'Le nom et l'origine des Hongrois', *ZDMG*, XCI (1937), 630–42.

Hóman, B., *Geschichte des ungarischen Mittelalters*, I (Berlin, 1940).

Ivánka, E. von, 'Griechische Kirche und griechisches Mönchtum im mittelalterlichen Ungarn', *OCP*, VIII (1942), 183–94.

Macartney, C. A., *The Magyars in the Ninth Century* (Cambridge, 1930).

Moravcsik, Gy., 'Die archaisierenden Namen der Ungarn in Byzanz', *BZ*, XXX (1929–30), 247–53.

Moravcsik, Gy., 'Zur Geschichte der Onoguren', *Ungarische Jahrbücher*, X (1930), 53–90.

Moravcsik, Gy., 'Byzantine Christianity and the Magyars in the Period of their Migration', *The American Slavic and East European Rev.* V, 14–15 (1946), 29–45.

Moravcsik, Gy., 'The Role of the Byzantine Church in Medieval Hungary', *ibid.* VI, 18–19 (1947), 134–51.

Moravcsik, Gy., *Bizánc és a magyarság* [*Byzantium and the Magyars*] (Budapest, 1953).

Moravcsik, Gy., 'Die byzantinische Kultur und das mittelalterliche Ungarn', *Sitzungsberichte der Deutschen Akademie der Wissenschaften zu Berlin, philos.-hist. Kl.* (1955), no. 4.

Mutafčiev, P., 'Madžarite i bŭlgaro-vizantijskite otnošenija prez tretjata četvŭrt na X v.' ['The Magyars and the relations between Bulgaria and Byzantium in the third quarter of the tenth century'], *Godišnik na Sofijskija Universitet, ist.-filol. fak.*, XXXI, 8 (1935).

(M) PECHENEGS (PATZINAKS)

Bajraktarević, F., 'Pečenegs', *Encyclopaedia of Islam*, III (1936), 1036–7.

Kurat, A. N., *Peçenek Tarihi* [*A History of the Pechenegs*] (Istanbul, 1937).

Macartney, C. A., 'The Petchenegs', *SEER*, VIII (1929), 342–55.

Menges, K. H., 'Etymological Notes on some Päčänäg Names', *B*, XVII (1944–5), 256–80.

Parchomenko, V., 'Rus' i Pečenegi' ['Russia and the Pechenegs'], *Slavia*, VIII (1929), 138–44.

Rasovsky, D. A., 'Pečenegi, Torki i Berendei na Rusi i v Ugrii', ['The Pechenegs, the Uzes and the Berendei in Russia and Hungary'], *Sem Kond.* VI (1933), 1–66. [With a summary in French.]

Vasilievsky, V. G., *Vizantija i Pečenegi* [*Byzantium and the Pechenegs*], in his *Trudy*, I (St Petersburg, 1908), 1–175.

(N) ALANS

Grumel, V., 'La date de la conversion des Alains et l'archevêché d'Alanie', *EO*, XXXIII (1934), 57–8.

Kulakovsky, J., 'Alany po svedenijam klassičeskich i vizantijskich pisatelej' ['The Alans according to the Evidence of Classical and Byzantine Writers'], *Čtenija v Istoričeskom Obščestve Nestora Letopisca*, XIII, 2 (Kiev, 1899), 94–168.

Kulakovsky, J., 'Christianstvo u Alan' ['Christianity among the Alans'], *VV*, V (1898), 1–18.

CHAPTER XII. THE BALKANS, 1018–1499

See also the bibliographies for chapters IV–XI, and XIII–XIX.

I. SPECIAL BIBLIOGRAPHIES

Angelov, D. and Dimitrov, D., 'Bulletin des publications sur les travaux bulgares dans le domaine de la byzantinologie pendant les années 1939–1945', *B*, IX (1947–8), 355–78.

Bianu, J. and Hodos, N., *Bibliografia Românéscă veche 1508–1830*, vol. I and 3 parts (to 1784) (Bucharest, 1903–7).

Bulletin de l'Institut pour l'étude de l'Europe sud-orientale, 9 vols. (Bucharest, 1914–22).

Ćorović, V., 'Histoire yougoslave', *RH*, CLV (1927), 112–62.

Dix années d'études byzantines. Bibliographie internationale des Etudes byzantines (Paris, 1949).

Dujčev, I., 'Pregled na bŭlgarskata istoriografija' ['Survey of Bulgarian historical Writings'], *Jugoslovenski Istoriski Časopis*, IV (1938), 40–74.

Dujčev, I., 'Die bulgarische Geschichtsforschung während des letzten Vierteljahrhunderts (1918–1942)', *Südostforschungen*, VII (1942), 546–73.

Hammer-Purgstall, J. von, *Geschichte des osmanischen Reiches*, vol. I, pp. xxix–xlii [see Gen. Bibl. V; contains a bibliography of the Oriental sources down to 1453].

Ivanov, D. D., *Istorija Bolgarii do 9 sentjabra 1944* [Bulgarian history to 9 September 1944], *Ukazatel' literatury 1945–1958* (Moscow, 1962).

Kersopoulos, J. G., *Albanie. Ouvrages et articles de revues parus de 1555 à 1934* (Athens, 1934).

Legrand, E., *Bibliographie albanaise. Description rais. des ouvrages publ. en albanais ou relat. à l'Albanie du xve siècle jusqu'à 1900*, complétée par H. Guys (Paris, 1912).

Manek, F., Pekmezi, G. and Stoltz, A., *Albanesische Bibliographie* (Vienna, 1909).

Moravcsik, Gy., *Byzantinoturcica* (includes a bibliography of modern works) [see Gen. Bibl. I].

Nopcsa, F., *Az Albániárol szóló legujabb irodalom* (Budapest, 1918).

Petrović, N. S., *Essai de bibliographie française sur les Serbes et les Croates (1554–1900)* (Belgrade, 1900).

Šoć, P., *Ogled bibliografije o Crnoj Gori na stranim jezikima* [*Review of Bibliography on Montenegro in Foreign Languages*] (Belgrade, 1948).

Tadić, J., *Ten Years of Jugoslav Historiography (1945–1955)* (Belgrade, 1955).

Tenneroni, A., *Per la bibliografia del Montenegro*, 2nd ed. (Rome, 1896).

Veress, A., *Bibliografia română-ungară*, I–III (Bucharest, 1931–5).

II. ORIGINAL AUTHORITIES

Byzantine historians and other Greek sources are not generally cited here; for these see chapters IV–X.

Acts of Chilandari [see Gen. Bibl. IV, under *Acts of Athos*].

Adam, G., *Directorium ad passagium faciendum. Rec. hist. cr., Doc. arméniens*, II, 365–517 (the part about Bulgaria and Serbia is pp. 422–85) [see Gen. Bibl. IV].

Albericus Monachus Trium Fontium, *Chronicon, MGH, Script.* XXIII (1874).

Annales Senenses, MGH, Script., XIX (1866).

Bogdan, D. P., *Acte moldoveneşti dinainte de Ştefan cel Mare* (Bucharest, 1938).

Bonfinius, A., *Rerum Hungaricarum decades quatuor cum dimidia*, 3rd ed. (Hanover, 1606).

Brocquière, B. de la, *Voyage d'Outremer, Recueil de voyages et de documents*, XII, ed. C. Schefer (Paris, 1892). [Pp. 582–92 refer to the Near East.]

Callimachus, P., *De Rebus gestis a Vladislao Polonorum atque Hungarorum Rege ad Casimirum Regem*, ed. J. G. Schwandtner, *SRH*, I, 433–518 (Vienna, 1746); or II, 40–142 (Vienna, 1768).

Chomatianus, Demetrius, Πονήματα διάφορα, ed. J. B. Pitra, *Analecta sacra et classica*, VII (Paris and Rome, 1891).

Chronique du Religieux de Saint-Denis, ed. M. L. Bellaguet, II (Paris, 1840), 386–91. [Contains accounts of the battles of Rovine and Nicopolis.]

Ćorović, V., *Spisi sv. Save* [*The Writings of St Sava*] (Belgrade, 1928).

Čremošnik, G., *Kancelariski i notarski spisi* [*Acta cancellariae et notariae annorum 1278–1301*], Archivi Ragusini (Belgrade, 1932).

Danilo (Serbian Archbishop), *Životi kraljeva i arhiepiskopa srpskih* [*Lives of Serbian kings and archbishops*], ed. G. Daničić (Zagreb, 1866).

Dinić, M., *Odluke veća dubrovačke republike* [*Acta consiliorum Reipublicae Ragusinae*] (Belgrade, 1951).

Długosz, J., *Historia Polonica*, II–V (= *Opera Omnia*. XI–XIV) (Cracow, 1873–8).

Documenta historiam Valachorum in Hungaria illustrantia usque ad annum 1400 p. Chr. Curante E. Lukinich et adiuvante L. Galdi ediderunt A. Fekete-Nagy et L. Mákkai (Budapest, 1941).

Domentijan, *Život Svetoga Simeuna i Svetoga Save* [*Life of St Simeon and St Sava*], ed. G. Daničić (Belgrade, 1865); French transl. of C. Živković's abridgement (made in 1794) of this biography by A. Chodźko, *Légendes slaves du moyen âge, 1169–1237. Les Nemania, vie de St Syméon et de St Sabba* (Paris, 1858).

Dujčev, I., 'Prepiskata na papa Innokentij s bŭlgarite' [Correspondence of Pope Innocent with the Bulgarians], *Godišnik na Sofijskija Universitet, ist.-filol. fak.*, XXXVII, 3 (1942).

Dujčev, I., *Knižovni i istoričeski pametnici ot vtoroto bŭlgarsko carstvo* [*Literary and historical documents of the Second Bulgarian Empire*] (Sofia, 1944).

Fejér, G., *Codex diplomaticus Hungariae ecclesiasticus ac civilis*, III–XI [see Gen. Bibl. IV].

Fermendžin, E., *Acta Bosnae, potissimum ecclesiastica, MHSM*, XXIII (Zagreb, 1892).

Froissart, *Chroniques*, ed. Kervyn de Lettenhove, XV, XVI (Brussels, 1870–7).

Gelcich, J. and Thallóczy, L. von, *Diplomatarium Relationum Reipublicae Ragusanae cum Regno Hungariae* (Budapest, 1887).

Górka, O., *Anonymi descriptio Europae Orientalis*, '*Imperium Constantino-politanum, Albania, Serbia, Ruthenia, Ungaria, Polonia, Bohemia*', *anno MCCCVIII exarata* (Cracow, 1916).

Hafner, S., *Serbisches Mittelalter. Altserbische Herrscherbiographien I. Stefan Nemanja nach den Viten des hl. Sava und Stefans des Erstgekrönten.* (Graz–Vienna–Cologne, 1962).

Hasdeu, B. P., *Arhiva istorică a României*, I (Bucharest, 1865).

Histoire de Charles VI, Roy de France, par un autheur contemporain, Religieux de l'Abbaye de St Denis, I (Paris, 1663).

Hurmuzaki, E. de, *Documente privitóre la Istoria Românilor*, I, II (pts. i and ii), XIV (Bucharest, 1887–1915).

Ilinsky, G. A., *Gramoty bolgarskich carej* [*Documents of the Bulgarian Tsars*] (Moscow, 1911).

Innocent III, *Opera, MPL*, CCXIV–CCXV.

Jorga, N., *Notes et extraits pour servir à l'histoire des croisades au XVe siècle*, I–VI (Paris–Bucharest, 1899–1916).

Kukuljević, I., *Codex diplomaticus Regni Croatiae, Dalmatiae, et Slavoniae*, II (Zagreb, 1875).

Kukuljević, I., *Jura Regni Croatiae, Dalmatiae, et Slavoniae*, I (Zagreb, 1862).

Laskaris, M., *Vatopedskata gramota na car Ivan Asenja II* [*Document of Tsar John Asen II for Vatopedi*] (Bŭlgarski starini, XI) (Sofia, 1930).

Laskaris, M., 'Actes serbes de Vatopédi', *BS*, VI (1935–6), 166–84.

Letopis popa Dukljanina [*The Chronicle of the Priest of Dioclea*], ed. F. Šišić (Belgrade, 1928); ed. V. Mošin (Zagreb, 1950).

Ljubić, S., *Commissiones et Relationes Venetae*, I (1433–1527), *MHSM*, VI (Zagreb, 1876).

Ljubić, S., *Listine*, 11 vols., *MHSM*, I–V, IX, XII, XVII, XXI, XXII, XXIV (Zagreb, 1868–93). [Venetian documents concerning the South Slavs, 960–1469.]

Makuscev (Makušev), V., *Monumenta historica Slavorum Meridionalium vicinorumque populorum*, 2 vols. (Warsaw and Belgrade, 1874–82).

Mayer, A., *Kotorski spomenici*, I (1326–1335), *Monumenta Catarensia*, I (Zagreb, 1951).

Mazzerius (= Maizières, P. de), *Vita S. Petri Thomasii, AASS*, 29 Jan., II (1643). [Pp. 997–9 give a description of Dušan and his court in 1355.]

Miklosich, F., *Monumenta Serbica spectantia historiam Serbiae, Bosnae, Ragusii* (Vienna, 1858).

Miklosich, F. and Müller, J., *Acta et diplomata graeca medii aevi*, I, II [see Gen. Bibl. IV].

Monumenta Hungariae historica. Acta extera, I–VIII (1874–8) [see Gen. Bibl. IV].

Monumenta Hungariae historica. Codex diplomaticus partium Regno Hungariae adnexarum (1198–1526) (1907) [see Gen. Bibl. IV].

Monumenta Vaticana Hungariae, ser. I, vols. I–VI (Budapest, 1885–91).

Nandriş, G., *Documente româneşti în limba slavă din mănăstirile Muntelui Athos (1372–1658)* (Bucharest, 1937).

Novaković, S., *Zakonski spomenici srpskih država srednjega veka* [*Legislative memorials of the Serbian principalities in the middle ages*] (Belgrade, 1912).

Ostrogorsky, G., 'Pismo Dimitrija Homatijana sv. Savi' ['Demetrius Choma-tianus' Letter to St Sava'], *Svetosavski Zbornik*, II (Srpska Kraljevska Akademija, posebna izdanja, CXXV, Društveni i Istoriski Spisi, 50) (Belgrade, 1939), 91–113.

Panaitescu, P. P., *Documentele ţării româneşti. Documente interne (1369–1490)* (Bucharest, 1938).

Popruženko, M. J., *Sinodik carja Borila* [*Synodicon of Tsar Boril*] (Sofia, 1928).

Pucić, Count Medo, *Spomenici srpski iz dubrovačke Arhive*, I–II [*Serbian memorials from the archives of Dubrovnik*] (Belgrade, 1858–62).

Rački, F., *Documenta historiae Chroaticae periodum antiquam illustrantia* (Zagreb, 1877).

Rački, F. and Gelcich, J., *Monumenta Ragusina, Libri Reformationum*, 5 vols. (1301–96), *MHSM*, x, xii, xxvii–xxix (Zagreb, 1879–97).

Radojčić, N., *Zakon o rudnicima despota Stefana Lazarevića* [*Jus metallicum despotae Stephani Lazarević*] (Belgrade, 1962).

Radonić, J., *Dubrovačka akta i povelje* [*Acta et diplomata Ragusina*], I, 1–2 (Belgrade, 1934).

Reisen des Johannes Schiltberger aus München, ed. K. F. Neumann (Munich, 1859); English transl. *The Bondage and Travels of Johann Schiltberger* (London, 1879).

Sa'd-ad-Din, *Chronica dell'origine e progressi di casa ottomana*, transl. V. Bratutti, 2 vols. (Vienna and Madrid, 1649–52).

Šafařík, P. J., *Památky dřevního pismenictví Jihoslovanův* (Prague, 1851; new ed. 1873).

Servion, J., *Gestez et chroniques de la Mayson de Savoye*, II, ed. F. E. Bollati (Turin, 1879).

Smičiklas, T., *Diplomatički zbornik kraljevine Hrvatske, Dalmacije i Slavonije* [*Codex diplomaticus regni Croatiae, Dalmatiae et Slavoniae*], II–xv (Zagreb, 1904–34).

Soloviev, A. and Mošin, V., *Grčke povelje srpskih vladara* [*Diplomata Graeca regum et imperatorum Serbiae*] (Belgrade, 1936).

Srpske narodne pjesme (Belgrade, 1895) [the national edition of Vuk Karadžić's collection of Serbian ballads]. French selection and transl. A. Dozon, *Poésies populaires serbes* (Paris, 1877); English transl. Sir J. Bowring, *Servian Popular Poetry* (London, 1827); and O. Meredith, *Serbski Pesme; or, National Songs of Servia* (London, 1861); and D. H. Low, *The Ballads of Marko Kraljević* (Cambridge, 1922); Italian transl. P. Kasandrić, *Canti popolari serbi e croati* (Milan, 1914).

Stojanović, Lj., *Stari srpski zapisi i natpisi* [*Old Serbian Documents and Inscriptions*], I–vi (Belgrade, 1902–26).

Stojanović, Lj., *Stari srpski rodoslovi i letopisi* [*Old Serbian Genealogies and Chronicles*] (Belgrade, 1927).

Stojanović, Lj., *Stare srpske povelje i pisma* [*Old Serbian Documents and Letters*], I, 1–2 (Belgrade, 1929–34).

Tadić, G., *Pisma i uputstva Dubrovačke republike* [*Litterae et commissiones Ragusinae*], I (Belgrade, 1935).

Thallóczy, L. de, Jireček, C. and Sufflay, E. de, *Acta et diplomata res Albaniae mediae aetatis illustrantia*, I, II (344–1406) (contains a bibliography) [see Gen. Bibl. iv].

Theiner, A., *Vetera monumenta historica Hungariam sacram illustrantia*, 2 vols. (Rome, 1859–60).

Theiner, A., *Vetera monumenta Slavorum Meridionalium historiam sacram illustrantia*, I (Rome, 1863).

Thomas Archidiaconus Spalatensis, *Historia Salonitanorum Pontificum atque Spalatensium*, *MHSM*, xxvi (Zagreb, 1894).

Thurócz, J. de, *Chronica Hungarorum*, ed. J. G. Schwandtner, *Scriptores Rerum Hungaricarum*, I, 39–291 (Vienna, 1746); or I, 47–366 (Vienna, 1766).

Vanich, V. and Hankey, C. P., *Lives of the Serbian Saints* (London, 1921).

Vechile cronice moldovenesci pana la Urechia, ed. J. Bogdan (Bucharest, 1891).
Zakonik Stefana Dušana, cara Srpskog, 1349–1354 [*The Legal Code of Stephen Dušan, Serbian Tsar*], ed. S. Novaković (Belgrade, 1898); other editions are those of P. J. Šafařik (Prague, 1851); H. Jireček, *Svod žakonův slovanských* [*Codex legum Slavonicarum*] (Prague, 1880); M. Zigel, *Zakonik Stefana Dušana* (St Petersburg, 1872); A. Boué, *La Turquie d'Europe* (Paris, 1840), IV, pp. 426 ff. (contains a French transl. of articles 1–105); English transl. M. Burr, 'The Code of Stephen Dušan, Tzar and Autocrat of the Serbs and Greeks, translated from the Old Serbian with Notes', *SEER*, XXVIII (1949), 198–217; *ibid.* (1950), 516–39; N. Radojčić (Belgrade, 1960).

III. MODERN WORKS

Angelov, D., *Bogomilstvoto v Bŭlgarija* [*Bogomilism in Bulgaria*] (Sofia, 1947; new ed. 1961); and *Der Bogomilismus auf dem Gebiete des byzantinischen Reiches*, 2 pts. (Sofia, 1948–51).

Angelov, D., 'Zur Frage des Feudalismus auf dem Balkan im XIII. bis zum XIV. Jahrhundert', *Acad. Sc. Bulg., Inst. Hist., Recueil ét. hist. XIᵉ Congr. Internat. Sc. Hist. Stockholm, 1960* (Sofia, 1960), pp. 107–28.

Angyal, D., 'Le traité de paix de Szeged avec les Turcs (1444)', *Revue de Hongrie*, XX (15 March, 15 April 1911), and separately (Budapest, 1911).

Atiya, A. S., *The Crusade of Nicopolis* [see Gen. Bibl. v].

Atiya, A. S., *The Crusade in the Later Middle Ages* [see Gen. Bibl. v].

Babinger, F., *Beiträge zur Frühgeschichte der Türkenherrschaft in Rumelien* (*14.–15. Jahrhundert*) (Munich, 1944).

Bain, R. N., 'The Siege of Belgrade by Muhammad II, July 1–23, 1456', *EHR*, VII (1892), 235–52.

Bănescu, N., *Un problème d'histoire médiévale: création et caractère du second empire bulgare* (Bucharest, 1943).

Bogdan, J., 'Ein Beitrag zur bulgarischen und serbischen Geschichtsschreibung', *ASP*, XIII (1891), 481–543.

Borchgrave, E. de, *L'empereur Etienne Douchan et la péninsule balcanique au XIVᵉ siècle* (Brussels, 1884).

Božić, I., *Dubrovnik i Turska u XIV i XV veku* [*Dubrovnik and the Turks in the 14th and 15th centuries*] (Belgrade, 1952).

Bratianu, G. I., *Traditie istorică despre întemeirea statelor românești* (Bucharest, 1945).

Braun, M. *Kosovo. Die Schlacht auf dem Amselfelde in geschichtlicher und epischer Überlieferung* (Leipzig, 1937).

Braun, M., *Die Slawen auf dem Balkan bis zur Befreiung von der türkischen Herrschaft* (Leipzig, 1941).

Burmov, A., 'Istorija na Bŭlgarija prez vremeto na Šišmanovci (1323–1396)' ['A History of Bulgaria under the Šišmanovs'], *Godišnik na Sofijskija Universitet, istoriko-filologičeski fakultet*, XLII (1946–7), fasc. I, 1–58, fasc. II, 1–22.

Burmov, A., 'Koga e zavladen Odrin ot Turcite' ['The date of the capture of Adrianople by the Turks'], *Izvestija na Bŭlgarskoto Istoričesko Družestvo*, XXI (1945), 23–32.

Cecchetti, B., 'Intorno agli stabilimenti politici della Repubblica Veneta nell'Albania', *Atti del Istituto Veneto*, III, ser. 4 (Venice, 1873–4), 977–98.

Čekrezi, C. A., *Albania Past and Present* (New York, 1919).

Coquelle, P., *Histoire du Monténégro et de la Bosnie* (Paris, 1895).

Ćorović, V., *Istorija Jugoslavije* [*History of Jugoslavia*] (Belgrade, 1933).

Ćorović, V., 'Serbische Volkslieder über den Abgang des heiligen Sava zu den Mönchen', *ASP*, xxviii (1908), 629–33.

Ćorović, V., *Historija Bosne* [*History of Bosnia*] (Belgrade, 1940).

Ćorović, V., 'Ban Borić i njegovo potomstvo' ['Ban Borić and his descendants'], *Glas*, clxxxii (1940), 63–83.

Deér, J., 'Die dalmatinische Munizipalverfassung unter der ungarischen Herrschaft bis zur Mitte des 12. Jahrhunderts', *Ungarische Jahrbücher*, xi (1931), 377–87.

Deér, J., 'Die Anfänge der ungarisch-kroatischen Staatsgemeinschaft', *Archivum Europae Centro-orientalis*, ii (1936), 5–45.

Dinić, M., *O Nikoli Altomanoviću* [*Concerning Nikola Altomanović*] (Belgrade, 1932).

Dinić, M., 'Hronika sen-deniskog kaludjera kao izvor za bojeve na Kosovu i Rovinama' ['The Chronicle of the Monk of St Denis as a Source for the Battles of Kosovo and Rovine'], *Prilozi za književnost, jezik, istoriju i folklor*, xvii (1937), 51–66.

Dinić, M., 'Dva savremenika o boju na Kosovu' ['Two contemporaries on the Battle of Kosovo'], *Glas*, clxxxii (1940), 131–48.

Dinić, M., 'Zemlje hercega Svetoga Save' ['The lands of Herceg St Sava'], *Glas*, clxxxii (1940), 149–57.

Dinić, M., *Državni sabor srednjevekovne Bosne* [*The State Council of Medieval Bosnia*] (Belgrade, 1955).

Dinić, M., *Za istoriju rudarstva u srednjevekovnoj Srbiji i Bosni*, i–ii [*The Industry in Medieval Serbia and Bosnia*] (Belgrade, 1955–62).

Dölger, F., *Regesten der Kaiserurkunden* [see Gen. Bibl. iv].

Drăganu, N., *Românii în veacurile IX–XIV pe baza toponîmiei şi a onomasticei* (Bucharest, 1933).

Ducange, C. du Fresne, *Illyricum vetus et novum* (Pressburg, 1749).

Dujčev, I., 'Il francescanesimo in Bulgaria nei sec. XIII e XIV', *Miscell. Francescana*, xxxiv (1934).

Dujčev, I., *Proučvanija vürhu bŭlgarskoto srednovekovnie* [*Investigations about Medieval Bulgaria*] (Sofia, 1945).

Elekes, L., 'Die Anfänge der rumänischen Gesellschaft. Versuch einer rumänischen Entwicklungsgeschichte im XIII.–XVI. Jh.', *Archivum Europae Centro-orientalis*, vii (1941), 461–88.

Erber, T., *La Contea di Poglizza: studio storico* (Zara, 1886).

Farlati, D., *Illyricum Sacrum*, i–viii (Venice, 1751–1819).

Franić, D., 'Die Lage auf der Balkanhalbinsel zu Beginn des 13. Jahrhunderts', *WMBH*, v (1897), 304–36.

Gamillscheg, E., 'Zur Herkunftsfrage der Rumänen', *Südost-Forschungen*, v (1940), 1–21.

Gegaj, A., *L'Albanie et l'invasion turque au XVᵉ siècle* (Louvain, 1937).

Gelcich, G., *La Zedda e la Dinastia dei Balšidi* (Spalato, 1899).

Giurescu, C. C., *Contribuţiuni la studiul marilor dregătorii în secolele XIV şi XV* (Vălenii-de-Munte, 1926).

Giurescu, C. C., *Noi contribuţiuni la studiul marilor dregătorii în secolele XIV şi XV* (Bucharest, 1926).

Giurescu, C. C., *Istoria Românilor*, i, 4th ed. (Bucharest, 1942).

Glušac, V., *Istina o bogumilima* [*The Truth about Bogomilism*] (Belgrade, 1945).

Gopčević, Sp., *Geschichte von Montenegro und Albanien* (Gotha, 1914).

Grumel, V., *Les regestes des actes du patriarcat de Constantinople* [see Gen. Bibl. IV].

Halecki, O., *The Crusade of Varna. A Discussion of Controversial Problems* (New York, 1943).

Hammer Purgstall, J. von, *Geschichte des osmanischen Reiches*, I, II [see Gen. Bibl. V].

Hecquard, H., *Histoire et description de la Haute Albanie ou Guégarie* (Paris, n.d. (1858–64)).

Hýbl, Fr., *Dějiny národa bulharského*, I (Prague, 1930).

Iucov, B., 'Ivan Asen II kato obraz na nacionalno sŭznanie prez vreme na robstvoto' ['John Asen II as an example of national consciousness during the time of oppression'], *Bŭlg. Ist. Bibl.* III, 3 (1930), 187–227.

Ivić, A., *Istorija Srba u Vojvodini. Od najstarijih vremena do osnivanja potisko-pomoriške granice (1703)* [*The history of the Serbs in Voivodina from the earliest times to 1703*] (Novi Sad, 1929).

Jireček, C., *Geschichte der Serben*, I–II [see Gen. Bibl. V].

Jireček, C., *Geschichte der Bulgaren* [see Gen. Bibl. V].

Jireček, C., 'Die Beziehungen der Ragusaner zu Serbien unter Car Uroš und König Vlkašin (1355–71)', *Sitzungsberichte der k. böhmischen Gesellschaft der Wissenschaften, 1885* (Prague, 1885), pp. 114–41.

Jireček, C., 'Zur Würdigung der neuentdeckten bulgarischen Chronik', *ASP*, XIV (1892), 255–77.

Jireček, C., 'Das Gesetzbuch des serbischen Caren Stephan Dušan', *ASP*, XXII (1900), 144–214.

Jireček, C., *Istorija na Bŭlgarite. Popravki i dobavki ot samija avtor* [*History of the Bulgarians: the Author's Corrigenda and Addenda*] (Sofia, 1939).

Jireček, C., *Staat und Gesellschaft im mittelalterlichen Serbien. Studien zur Kulturgeschichte des 13.–15. Jahrhunderts*, 1–4 Teil. *Denkschriften der KAW*, LVI and LVIII (Vienna, 1912–19).

Jireček, C., *Die Bedeutung von Ragusa in der Handelsgeschichte des Mittelalters* (Vienna, 1899).

Jorga, N., *Geschichte des osmanischen Reiches*, I, II [see Gen. Bibl. V].

Jorga, N., *Geschichte des rumänischen Volkes*, I [see Gen. Bibl. V].

Jorga, N., *Brève histoire de l'Albanie et du peuple albanais* (Bucharest, 1919).

Jorga, N., *Histoire des Roumains* [see Gen. Bibl. V].

Jorga, N. and others, *Istorija naroda Jugoslavije* [*History of the Jugoslav Peoples*], I (Belgrade, 1953).

Jorga, N., *Histoire des états balcaniques jusqu'à 1924* (Paris, 1925).

Jorga, N., *Istoria Rominilor din Peninsula Balcanica* (Bucharest, 1919).

Kadlec, K., *Valaši a valašké pravo v zemich slovanských a uherských* (Prague, 1916).

Kiselkov, V. S., *Patriarch Evtimij* [*The Patriarch Euthymius*] (Sofia, 1938).

Klaić, V., *Geschichte Bosniens*. German transl. by I. von Bojnčić (Leipzig, 1885).

Kniewald, D., 'Vjerodostojnost latinskih izvora o bosanskim krstjanima' ['The Reliability of Latin Sources about Bosnian Christians'], *Rad Jugoslavenske Akademije znanosti i umjetnosti*, CCLXX (1949), 115–276.

Kniezsa, I., 'Pseudorumänen in Pannonien und in den Nordkarpathen', *Archivum Europae Centro-orientalis*, I (1935), 97–220; II (1936), 84–178.

Kovačević, J., *Srednjovekovna nošnja balkanskich Slovena* [see Gen. Bibl. V].

Krekić, B., *Dubrovnik* [see Gen. Bibl. V].

Laskaris, M., 'A propos d'un épitaphios du monastère de Putna', *RHSE*, II (1925), 356–61.

Laskaris, M., *Vizantiske princeze u srednjevekovnoj Srbiji* [*Byzantine Princesses in Medieval Serbia*] (Belgrade, 1926).

Laskaris, M., 'Joachim métropolite de Moldavie et les relations de l'Eglise moldave avec le patriarcat de Peć et l'archevêché d'Achrid au XVe siècle', *Bulletin de la sect. hist. de l'Acad. Roumaine*, XIII (1927), 129–59.

Laskaris, M., 'Deux chartes de Jean Uroš, dernier Némanide (Novembre 1372, indiction XI)', *B*, XXV–XXVII (1955–7), 277–323.

Laurent, V., 'Le thème byzantin de Serbie', *Balcania*, VI (1943), 35–47.

Laurent, V., 'Le thème byzantin de Serbie au XIe siècle', *REB*, XV (1957), 185–95.

Lilek, E., 'Die Schatzkammer der Familie Hranići (Košaca)', *WMBH*, II (1894), 125–51.

Marguliés, A., 'Bulgarien und Byzanz in ihren kulturellen Beziehungen', *ZDMG*, LXXX (1926), 172–88.

Marich, D., *Papstbriefe an serbische Fürsten im Mittelalter* (Sremski Karlovci, 1933).

Marković, G., *Gli Slavi ed i Papi*, II (Zagreb, 1897).

Mijatović, C., *Despot Gjuragj Branković*, 2 vols. (Belgrade, 1880–2); I, 2nd ed. (Belgrade, 1907).

Miklosich, F., *Die serbischen Dynasten Crnojević. Ein Beitrag zur Geschichte von Montenegro* (Vienna, 1886).

Miller, W., 'Bosnia before the Turkish Conquest', *EHR*, XIII (1898), 643–6; republished in *Essays on the Latin Orient* [see Gen. Bibl. v].

Miller, W., 'The Founder of Montenegro', *EHR*, XXV (1910), 308; republished in *Essays on the Latin Orient* [see Gen. Bibl. v].

Miller, W., 'Balkan Exiles in Rome', *Journ. British and American Archaeological Society of Rome*, IV, 5 (1912), 479–97; republished in *Essays on the Latin Orient* [see Gen. Bibl. v].

Miller, W., 'The Mediaeval Serbian Empire', *Quarterly Rev.* 226, no. 449 (1916), 488–507; republished in *Essays on the Latin Orient* [see Gen. Bibl. v].

Miller, W., 'Valona', *JHS*, XXXVII (1917), 184–94; republished in *Essays on the Latin Orient* [see Gen. Bibl. v].

Mladenović, M., *L'Etat serbe au moyen âge* (Paris, 1931).

Mušmov, N. A., *Monetite i pečatite na bŭlgarskite care* [*Currency and seals under the Bulgarian Tsars*] (Sofia, 1924).

Mutafčiev, P., *Bulgares et Roumains dans l'histoire des pays danubiens* (Sofia, 1932).

Mutafčiev, P., *Istorija na bŭlgarskija narod* [*History of the Bulgarian Nation*], I, 2nd ed. (Sofia, 1943); II (1944).

Nandriş, G., 'The Beginnings of Slavonic Culture in the Roumanian Countries', *SEER*, XXIV (1946), 160–71.

Nikov, P., *Bŭlgarsko-ungarski otnošenija ot 1257–1277* [*Bulgaro-Hungarian relations from 1257 to 1277*] (Sofia, 1920).

Nikov, P., *Tataro-bŭlgarskite otnošenija prez srednite vekove s ogled kŭm caruvaneto na Smileca* [*Tatar–Bulgarian relations in the Middle Ages with reference to the rule of Smilec*] (Sofia, 1920).

Nikov, P., *Istorija na Vidinskoto knjažestvo do 1323 g.* [*History of the Principality of Vidin to 1323*] (Sofia, 1922).

Nikov, P., *Vtoro bŭlgarsko carstvo 1186–1396* [*The Second Bulgarian Empire 1186–1396*] (Sofia, 1937).

Nistor, I., 'Temeiurile româno-bizantine ale începuturilor organizaţiei noastre de Stat', *Memoriile secţiei istorice a Academiei Române*, XXV (1943).

Nistor, J., *Die auswärtigen Handelsbeziehungen der Moldau im 14., 15. und 16. Jh.* (Gotha, 1911).

Nony, A. B. and others, *Poviest hrvatskih zemalja Bosne i Hercegovine od najstarijih vremena do 1463 godine* [*History of the Croatian lands Bosnia and Hercegovina from the earliest times to 1463*] (Sarajevo, 1942).

Novak, G., *Prošlost Dalmacije* [*Dalmatia's Past*], I–II (Zagreb, 1944).

Novaković, S., *Srbi i Turci XIV i XV veka* (Belgrade, 1893); German transl. K. Jezdimirović, *Die Serben und Türken in XIV. und XV. Jahrhundert. Geschichtliche Studie über die ersten Kämpfe mit dem türkischen Eindringen vor und nach der Schlacht auf dem Amselfelde* (Semlin, 1897); ed. S. Ćirković with addenda and corrigenda (Belgrade, 1960).

Novaković, S., 'Ohridska arhiepiskopija u početku XI veka' ['The Archbishopric of Ochrida in the early XIth century'], *Glas*, LXXVI (1908), 1–62.

Novaković, S., 'Les problèmes serbes', *ASP*, XXXIII (1911), 438–66; XXXIV (1912), 203–33.

Orbini, M., *Il regno degli Slavi hoggi corrottamente detti Schiavoni* (Pesaro, 1601).

Ostrogorsky, G., *History of the Byzantine State* [see Gen. Bibl. v].

Ostrogorsky, G., 'Avtokrator i Samodržac', *Glas*, CLXIV (1935), 95–188.

Ostrogorsky, G., *Pour l'histoire de la féodalité byzantine* [see Gen. Bibl. v].

Pall, Fr., 'Autour de la croisade de Varna. La question de la paix de Szeged et de sa rupture', *Bulletin de la section historique de l'Académie Roumaine*, XXII (1941), 144–79.

Pall, Fr., 'Les croisades en Orient au moyen âge. Observations critiques sur l'ouvrage de M. Atiya', *RHSE*, XIX (1942), 527–83.

Pall, Fr., 'Die Geschichte Skanderbeg im Lichte der neueren Forschung', *Leipziger Vierteljahrsschrift für Südosteuropa*, VI (1942), 85–98.

Pall, Fr., 'Un moment décisif du Sud-Est européen: la croisade de Varna', *Balcania*, VII (1944), 102–20.

Pavich von Pfauenthal, A., Matić, T. and Rešetar, M., 'Statut der Poljica', *WMBH*, XII (1912), 324–40.

Pavich von Pfauenthal, A., 'Beiträge zur Geschichte der Republik Poljica bei Spalato', *WMBH*, X (1910), 156–344.

Philippide, A., *Originea Românilor*, I (Jaşi, 1923); II (1927).

Praga, G., *Storia di Dalmatia. I. Dall'Impero di Roma alla Signoria di Venezia* (Zara, 1941).

Prokofjev, V. G., 'Rostislav Michailovič, russkij knjaz XIII veka' ['Rostislav Mihailovič, a Russian prince of the XIIIth century'], *Jubilejnij Sbornik Russkago Archeologičeskago Obščestva* (Belgrade, 1936), pp. 131–59.

Purković, M., *Avinjonske pape i srpske zemlje* [*The Avignon Popes and Serbia*] (Požarevac, 1934).

Radojčić, N., 'Sveti Sava i autokefalnost srpske i bugarske crkve' ['St Sava and the independence of the Serbian and Bulgarian Churches'], *Glas*, CLXXIX (1939), 177–259.

Radojčić, N., *Srpski državni sabori u srednjem veku* [*The Serbian State Council in the middle ages*] (Belgrade, 1940).

Radonić, J., 'Sporazum u Tati 1426 i srpsko-ugarski odnosi od XIII–XVI veka' ['The Treaty at Tata (1426) and Serbo-Magyar relations in the XIII–XVI centuries'], *Glas*, CLXXXVII (1941), 117–232.

Radonić, J., 'Der Grossvojvode von Bosnien Sandalj Hranić-Kosača', *ASP*, XIX (1897), 380–465.

Radonić, J., *Zapadna Evropa i balkanski narodi prema Turcima u prvoj polovini XV veka* [*The Relations of Western Europe and the Balkan Peoples with the Turks in the First Half of the 15th Century*] (Novi Sad, 1905).

Radonić, J., *Djuradj Kastriot Skenderbeg i Albania u XV v.* [*George Castriota Scanderbeg and Albania in the XVth century*] (Belgrade, 1942).

Rupčić, B., *Entstehung der Franziskanerpfarreien in Bosnien, der Herzegovina und ihre Entwicklung bis zum Jahre 1878* (Breslau, 1937).

Ruvarac, H., 'Die Regierung des Banus Tvrtko (1353–77)', *WMBH*, IV (1896), 324–42.

Šafařík, P. J., *Slavische Alterthümer*, II, German transl. (Leipzig, 1844).

Šafařík, P. J., *Geschichte der südslavischen Literatur*, III, ed. J. Jireček (Prague, 1865).

Sakăzov, I., *Bulgarische Wirtschaftsgeschichte* (Berlin and Leipzig, 1929).

Saria, B., 'Die Entwicklung des altserbischen Münzwesens', *Südost-Forschungen*, XIII (1954), 22–61.

Schmaus, A., 'Der Neumanichäismus auf dem Balkan', *Saeculum*, II (1951), 271–99.

Seliščev, A. M., *Slavjanskoe naselenie v Albanii* [*The Slav Population of Albania*] (Sofia, 1931).

Seton-Watson, R. W., *A History of the Roumanians from Roman Times to the Completion of Unity* (Cambridge, 1934); *Histoire des Roumains. De l'époque romaine à l'achèvement de l'unité* (Paris, 1937).

Šidak, J., 'Problem "bosanske crkve" u našoj historiografiji od Petranovića do Glušca' [*'The Problem of the "Bosnian church" in our Historiography from Petranović to Glušac'*], *Rad Jugosl. Akademije*, CCLIX (Zagreb, 1937), 37–182.

Šidak, J., *'Crkva bosanska' i problem bogumilstva u Bosni* [*The 'Bosnian Church' and the Problem of Bogomilism in Bosnia*] (Zagreb, 1940).

Šišić, F., *Geschichte der Kroaten I* (to 1102) (Zagreb, 1917).

Šišić, F., *Poviest Hrvata u vrijeme narodnih vladara* [*A History of the Croats under their National Rulers*] (Zagreb, 1925).

Šišić, F., *Poviest Hrvata* (1102–1205) [*A History of the Croats 1102–1205*] (Zagreb, 1944).

Šišić, F., 'Die Schlacht bei Nikopolis (25 September, 1396)', *WMBH*, VI (1898), 291–327.

Snegrov, I., *Istorija na ochridskata archiepiskopija ot osnovaneto do zavladevaneto na Balkanskija poluostrov ot turcite* [*The history of the Archbishopric of Ochrida from its establishment to the conquest of the Balkans by the Turks*] (Sofia, 1924).

Soloviev, A. V., *Zakonodavstvo Stefana Dušana cara Srba i Grka* [*The Legislation of Stephen Dušan Tsar of the Serbs and Greeks*] (Skoplje, 1928).

Stadtmüller, G., 'Forschungen zur albanischen Frühgeschichte', *Archivum Europae Centro-orientalis*, VII (1941), 1–196.

Stadtmüller, G., *Geschichte Südosteuropas* (Munich, 1950).

Stanojević, S., 'Die Biographie Stefan Lazarević's von Konstantin dem Philosophen als Geschichtsquelle', *ASP*, XVIII (1896), 409–72.

Stanojević, S., *Istorija srpskoga naroda* [*History of the Serbian People*], 3rd ed. (Belgrade, 1926), with full bibliography.

Stanojević, S., 'Sveti Sava i proglas bŭlgarske patriaršije' ['St Sava and the Establishment of the Bulgarian Patriarchate'], *Glas*, CLVI (1933), 171–88.

Stanojević, S., 'Hronologija borbe izmedju Stevana i Vukana' ['The Chronology of the War Between Stephen and Vukan'], *Glas*, CLIII (1933), 91–102.

Stanojević, S., 'Sveti Sava i nezavisnost srpske crkve' ['St Sava and the Independence of the Serbian Church'], *Glas*, CLXI (1934), 198–251.

Stanojević, S., *Istorija srpskoga naroda u srednjem veku* [*History of the Serbian People in the Middle Ages*], I (Belgrade, 1937).

Stevenson, F. S., *A History of Montenegro* (London, n.d. (1913)).

Šufflay, M., *Städte und Burgen Albaniens hauptsächlich während des Mittelalters* (Vienna, 1924).

Šufflay, M., *Srbi i Arbanasi. Njihova simbioza u srednjem veku* [*Serbs and Albanians: Symbiosis in the Middle Ages*] (Belgrade, 1925).

Taranovski, T., *Istorija srpskog prava u Nemanjićkoj državi* [*The History of Serbian Law under the Nemanići*], I–IV (Belgrade, 1931–5).

Temperley, H. W. V., *History of Serbia* [see Gen. Bibl. v].

Thallóczy, L. v., *Studien zur Geschichte Bosniens und Serbiens im Mittelalter*. German transl. F. Eckhart (Munich and Leipzig, 1914).

Thallóczy, L. v., 'Bruchstücke aus der Geschichte der nordwestlichen Balkan-länder', *WMBH*, III (1894), 298–371.

Thallóczy, L. v., 'Herzog Hervoja und sein Wappen', *WMBH*, II (1894), 108–24; cf. his *Studien*, pp. 303–6; see above.

Thallóczy, L. v., 'Wie und wann wurde Hervoja Grossvojvode von Bosnien?', *WMBH*, VI (1898), 284–90.

Thallóczy, L. v., 'Untersuchungen über Ursprung des bosnischen Banates mit besonderer Berücksichtigung der Urkunden im Körmender Archive', *WMBH*, XI (1909), 237–85; reprinted in his *Studien*, pp. 1–75; see above.

Thallóczy, L. v., *Illyrisch-Albanische Forschungen*, 2 vols. (Munich and Leipzig, 1916).

Truhelka, C., 'Verzeichniss der bosnischen, serbischen, und bulgarischen Münzen des Landesmuseums in Sarajevo', *WMBH*, IV (1896), 303–23.

Truhelka, C., 'Eine handschriftliche Chronik aus Sarandapor', *WMBH*, IV (1896), 363–80.

Truhelka, C., 'Das mittelalterliche Staats- und Gerichtswesen in Bosnien', *WMBH*, X (1907), 71–155.

Truhelka, C., 'Der bosnische Münzenfund von Ribiči', *WMBH*, XI (1908), 184–236.

Truhelka, C., 'Die Klosterchronik von Fojinica', *WMBH*, XII (1909), 301–23. [Important document of 1461.]

Villari, L., *The Republic of Ragusa* (London, 1904).

Voinovich, L. de, *Histoire de Dalmatie*, I–II (Paris 1934).

Vuletić-Vukasović, V., 'Bündnissvertrag Herzog Hervojes und der Republik Ragusa gegen König Ostoja von Bosnien', *WMBH*, IV (1896), 390–3.

Wolff, R. L., 'The "Second Bulgarian Empire". Its origin and history to 1204', *SP*, XXIV (1949), 167–206.

Xénopol, A. D., *Histoire des Roumains de la Dacie Trajane* [see Gen. Bibl. v].

Zinkeisen, J. W., *Geschichte des osmanischen Reiches in Europa*, I, II (Gotha, 1840–54).

Zlatarsky, V. N., *Istorija na bŭlgarskata dŭržava prez srednite vekove* [*A History of the Bulgarian State during the Middle Ages*], II, 1–2 (Sofia, 1934, 1940).

Zlatarsky, V. N., *Geschichte der Bulgaren, I (679–1396)* (Leipzig, 1918).

CHAPTER XIII. HUNGARY AND BYZANTIUM IN THE MIDDLE AGES

I. ORIGINAL SOURCES

(A) BYZANTINE SOURCES

Bíborbanszületett Konstantín, *A birodalom kormányzása*. A görög szöveget kiadta és magyarra fordította Moravcsik, Gy. (Constantine Porphyrogenitus, *De administrando imperio*. Greek text and Hungarian transl. Gy. Moravcsik) (Budapest, 1950).

Constantine Porphyrogenitus, *De Administrando Imperio* [see Gen. Bibl. IV].

Moravcsik, Gy., *A magyar történet bizánci forrásai* [*Byzantine Sources for Hungarian History*] (Budapest, 1934).

Moravcsik, Gy., 'Les sources byzantines de l'histoire hongroise', *B*, IX (1934), 663–73.

Moravcsik, Gy., 'Αἱ βυζαντιναὶ πηγαὶ τῆς οὐγγρικῆς ἱστορίας', Ἑλληνικά, VIII (1935), 19–27.

Moravcsik, Gy., *Byzantinoturcica*, I: *Die byzantinischen Quellen der Geschichte der Türkvölker*, 2nd ed. (Berlin, 1958) [see Gen. Bibl. I].

Schönebaum, H., *Die Kenntnis der byzantinischen Geschichtsschreiber von der ältesten Geschichte der Ungarn vor der Landnahme* (Ungarische Bibliothek, Reihe I, 5, Berlin–Leipzig, 1922).

(B) HUNGARIAN SOURCES

Macartney, C. A., *Studies on the Earliest Hungarian Historical Sources*, I–II (Etudes sur l'Europe Centro-Orientale, 18) (Budapest, 1938).

Macartney, C. A., *Studies on the Early Hungarian Historical Sources* (Etudes sur l'Europe Centro-Orientale, 21) (Budapest, 1940).

Macartney, C. A., *The Medieval Hungarian Historians : a Critical and Analytical Guide* (Cambridge, 1953).

Macartney, C. A., 'Dlugosz et le Chronicon Budense', *RHC*, XXIV (1946), 301–18.

Macartney, C. A., *Studies on the Earliest Hungarian Historical Sources*, VI–VII (Oxford, 1951).

Scriptores rerum Hungaricarum tempore ducum regumque stirpis Arpadianae gestarum. Edendo operi praefuit E. Szentpétery, I–II (Budapest, 1937–8).

(C) SLAVONIC SOURCES

Az orosz évkönyvek magyar vonatkozásai. 'Az orosz évkönyek teljes gyűjteménye' (*Polnoe sobranie russkich letopisej*) köteteiből A. M. Tud. Akadémia történelmi bizottságának megbízásából fordította Hodinka A. [Hungarian references in the *Russian Chronicle*. From the *Polnoe sobranie russkich letopisej*, transl. A. Hodinka] (Budapest, 1916).

(D) COLLECTIONS OF SOURCES

A magyar honfoglalás kutfői [*Sources for the conquest of Hungary*]. Szerkesztette Pauler Gy., Szilágyi S. (Budapest, 1900). [Texts with Hungarian translations.]

A magyar történet kútfőinek kézikönyve [*Enchiridion Fontium Historiae Hungarorum*]. Angyal D. közreműködésével szerkesztette Marczali H. (Budapest, 1902). [Texts with Hungarian translations.]

Catalogus fontium historiae Hungaricae aevo ducum et regum ex stirpe Arpad descendentium ab anno Christi DCCC usque ad annum MCCCI...collegit, ex veteribus iam fugientibus editionibus revocavit,...illustravit A. Fr. Gombos, I–IV (Budapest, 1937–43).

Macartney, C. A., *The Magyars in the Ninth Century* (Cambridge, 1930).

Marczali, H., *Ungarns Geschichtsquellen im Zeitalter der Árpáden* (Berlin, 1882).

II. MODERN WORKS

(A) GENERAL

Many of the works in Hungarian have a résumé in English, French or German.

A Companion to Hungarian Studies, ed. The Society of the Hungarian Quarterly (Budapest, 1943).

Balanyi, G., *The History of Hungary*, 2nd ed. (Budapest, 1933).

Divéky, A., *Ungarns Geschichte* (Budapest, 1942).

Domanovszky, A., *Die Geschichte Ungarns* (Munich–Leipzig, 1923).

Eckhart, F., *A Short History of the Hungarian People* (London, 1931).

Elekes, L., Lederer, E. and Székely, Gy., *Magyarország története a korai és virágzó feudalizmus korában (a honfoglalástól 1526-ig)* [*A History of Hungary in the Period of the Early and Flourishing Feudalism (from the Conquest of Hungary to 1526)*] (Budapest, 1957). [In Hungarian.]

Hóman, B., *Geschichte des ungarischen Mittelalters*, I–II (Berlin, 1940–3).

Hóman, B. and Szekfü, G., *Magyar történet* [*A History of Hungary*], I–VIII (Budapest, 1928–34); 3rd ed. I–V (Budapest, 1941).

Kosáry, D. G., *A History of Hungary* (Cleveland–New York, 1941).

Lukács, G. (ed.), *La Hongrie et la civilisation. Histoire, géographie, ethnographie, constitution et rapports internationaux*, I–III (Paris, 1928–9).

Lukinich, I., *A History of Hungary in Biographical Sketches*, transl. C. Dallas (London–Budapest, 1937).

Macartney, C. A., *Hungary* (London, 1934).

Mályusz, E., *Geschichte des ungarischen Volkstums von derLandnahme bis zum Ausgang des Mittelalters* (Budapest, 1940).

Molnár, E., *A magyar társadalom története az őskortól az Árpádkorig* [*A History of Hungarian Society from the Prehistoric Age to the Arpadian period*], 2nd ed. (Budapest, 1949).

Molnár, E., *A magyar társadalom története az Árpádkortól Mohácsig* [*A History of Hungarian Society from the Arpadian Period to Mohács*] (Budapest, 1949).

Szabó, S., *Ungarisches Volk. Geschichte und Wandlungen* (Budapest–Leipzig, 1944).

Szekfü, F., *Der Staat Ungarn* (Stuttgart–Berlin, 1922).

Teleki, P., *The Evolution of Hungary and its Place in European History*. With a bibliography of the Hungarian literature in English and other foreign languages (New York–London, 1923).

Török, P., *Ungarische Geschichte* (Budapest, 1944).

Yoland, A. B., *The History of Hungary* (Budapest, 1928).

(B) SPECIAL

Bárány-Oberschall, M., 'Konstantinos Monomachos császár koronája' ['The Crown of the Emperor Constantine Monomachos'], *Archaeologia Hungarica*, XXII (Budapest, 1937).

Bárány-Oberschall, M., 'Byzantinische Pastoralkreuze aus ungarischen Funden', *Forschungen zur Kunstgeschichte und christlichen Archäologie*. II: *Wandlungen christlicher Kunst im Mittelalter* (Baden-Baden, 1953), pp. 207–51.

Bödey, J., 'Rilai Szent Iván legendájának magyar vonatkozásai' ['Die ungarischen Beziehungen der Legende des hlg. Ivan von Rila'], *Archivum Philologicum*, LXIV (1940), 217–21.

Bogyav, T., 'L'iconographie de la "Porta Speciosa" d'Esztergom et ses sources d'inspiration', *REB*, VIII (1950), 85–129.

Bratianu, G. I., 'Byzance et la Hongrie', *RHSE*, XXII (1945), 147–57.

Browning, R., 'A New Source on Byzantine–Hungarian Relations in the Twelfth Century', *Balkan Studies*, II (1961), 173–214.

Buytaert, E. M., 'The Earliest Latin Translation of Damascene's *De orthodoxa fide* iii. 1–8', *Franciscan Studies*, XI, 3–4 (1951), 49–67.

Csemegi, J., 'A tihanyi barlanglakások' ['The Hermit-caves of Tihany'], *Archaeologiai Értesitö*, ser. 3, VII–IX (1946–8), 396–407.

Czeglédy, K., ΤΕΡΜΑΤΖΟΥΣ, *Acta Antiqua Academiae Scientiarum Hungaricae*, X (1962), 79–84.

Darkó, E., 'Ἑλληνοουγγρικαὶ σχέσεις κατὰ τοὺς βυζαντινοὺς καὶ κατὰ τοὺς μετὰ τὴν ἅλωσιν χρόνους', Νέα Ἑστία, V (1931), 120–5, 195–8.

Darkó, E., 'Zu den byzantinisch-ungarischen Beziehungen', *Ungarische Jahrbücher*, XIII (1933), 1–18.

Darkó, E., *Byzantinisch-ungarische Beziehungen in der zweiten Hälfte des XIII. Jahrhunderts* (Weimar, 1933).

Darkó, E., 'Die ursprüngliche Bedeutung des unteren Teiles der ungarischen Heiligen Krone', *Sem. Kond.* VIII (1936), 63–77.

Decker-Hauff, H., 'A legkorábbi magyar-bizánci házassági kapcsolatok' ['Les plus anciennes relations familiales byzantino-hongroises'], *Századok*, LXXXI (1947), 95–108, 367–8.

Deér, J., 'A IX. századi magyar történet időrendjéhez' ['Contributions à la chronologie de l'histoire hongroise du IXe siècle'], *Századok*, LXXIX–LXXX (1945–6), 3–20, 318.

Deér, J., 'Le problème du chapitre 38 du De administrando imperio', *AIPHO*, XII (1952) (*Mélanges Henri Grégoire*, III), 93–121.

Dölger, F., 'Ungarn in der byzantinischen Reichspolitik', *Archivum Europae Centro-Orientalis*, VIII (1942), 315–42 (Ostmitteleuropäische Bibliothek, 42), reprinted in ΠΑΡΑΣΠΟΡΑ (Ettal, 1961), pp. 153–77.

Fasoli, G., *Le incursioni ungare in Europa nel secolo X* (Bibl. storica Sansoni, n.s. 12, Florence, 1945).

Fehér, G., *Bulgarisch-ungarische Beziehungen in den V.–XI. Jahrhunderten* (Keleti Szemle, XIX, 2, Pécs, 1921).

Fehér, G., 'Ungarns Gebietsgrenzen in der Mitte des 10. Jahrhunderts. Nach dem De administrando imperio des Konstantinos Porphyrogennetos', *Ungarische Jahrbücher*, II (1922), 37–69.

Fehér, G., 'Vlijanie na bulgarskata čerkva na Madžarsko' ['Influence of the Bulgarian Church on Hungary'], *Sbornik v česta na V. N. Zlatarski* (Sofia, 1925), pp. 485–98.

Fehér, G., 'A nagyszentmiklósi kincs-rejtély megfejtésének útja. A görög-nyelvű feliratok megfejtése' ['Pour dévoiler le mystère du trésor de Nagyszentmiklós. Le déchiffrement des inscriptions grecs'], *Archaeologiai Értesitö*, LXXVII (1950), 34–49.

Graf, A., 'Újabb adalékok a Szent László leányára vonatkozó bizánci szöve-gekhez' ['Nouvelles contributions aux textes byzantins relatifs à la fille de Saint Ladislas'], *Archivum Philologicum*, LXV (1939), 74–6.

Grégoire, H. and Orgels, P., 'L'invasion hongroise dans la "Vie de Saint Basile le Jeune"', *B*, XXIV (1954), 147–54.

Gyóni, M., *Magyarország és a magyarság a bizánci források tükrében [Ungarn und das Ungartum im Spiegel der byzantinischen Quellen]* (Οὐγγροελληνικαὶ Μελέται, 7) (Budapest, 1938).

Gyóni, M., 'Hunyadi, empereur de Byzance', *Nouvelle Revue de Hongrie*, LXIII (33rd year, pt. 2, 1940), 499–505.

Gyóni, M., *A magyar nyelv görög feljegyzéses szórványemlékei [Die Streudenk-mäler der ungarischen Sprache in griechischen Texten]* (Οὐγγροελληνικαὶ Μελέται, 24) (Budapest, 1943).

Gyóni, M., 'L'église orientale dans la Hongrie du XIe siècle', *RHC*, XXV (1947), 42–9.

Gyóni, M., 'A legkorábbi magyar-bizánci házassági kapcsolatok kérdéséhez' ['Contributions au problème des plus anciennes relations familiales byzantino-hongroises'], *Századok*, LXXXI (1947), 212–19, 370.

Györffy, Gy., 'Kurszán és Kurszán vára. A magyar fejedelemség kialakulása és Óbuda honfoglaláskori története' ['Kurzan und Kurzans Burg. Angaben zur Frage des Doppelkönigtums und zur Geschichte von Óbuda zur Zeit der Landnahme'], *Budapest Régiségei*, XVI (1955), 9–40.

Györffy, Gy., 'Das Güterverzeichnis des griechischen Klosters zu Szávaszent-demeter (Sremska Mitrovica) aus dem 12. Jahrhundert', *Studia Slavica Academiae Scientiarum Hungaricae*, V (1959), 9–74.

Halecki, O., 'Un empereur de Byzance à Buda', *Un Empereur de Byzance à Rome* (Warsaw, 1930), pp. 111–37.

Haring, N. M., 'The First Traces of the so-called Cerbanus Translation of St John Damascene, De fide orthodoxa iii. 1–8', *Medieval Studies*, XII (1950), 214–16.

Heisenberg, A., *Ungarn und Byzanz. A Debreceni Tisza István Tudományos Társaság. I. Osztályának Kiadványai*, IV, 3 (Debrecen, 1928).

Ivánka, E., 'Görög hatások a XII. századbeli Nyugat szellemi életére' ['Griechische Einflüsse im westlichen Geistesleben des XII. Jahrhunderts'], *Archivum Philologicum*, LXIV (1940), 211–17.

Ivánka, E., 'Griechische Kirche und griechisches Mönchtum im mittel-alterlichen Ungarn', *OCP*, VIII, 1–2 (1942), 183–94.

Kádár, Z., 'Byzantinische Denkmäler in Ungarn', *Archäologische Funde in Ungarn* (Budapest, 1956), pp. 389–417.

Každan, A. P., 'Iz istorii vizantino-vengerskich svjazej vo vtoroj polovine XI v.' ['From the History of Byzantine–Hungarian Relations in the Second Half of the Eleventh Century'], *Acta Antiqua Academiae Scientia-rum Hungaricae*, X (1962), 163–6.

Kelleher, P. J., *The Holy Crown of Hungary. Papers and Monographs of the American Academy in Rome*, XII (Rome, 1951).

Kolias, G. T., ''Η παρὰ τὸ Βουλγαρόφυγον μάχη καὶ ἡ δῆθεν πολιορκία τῆς Κωνσταντινουπόλεως (896)', ᾿Αρχεῖον τοῦ Θρακικοῦ Λαογραφικοῦ καὶ Γλωσσικοῦ Θησαυροῦ, VII (1940–1), 341–62.

Kolias, G. T., ''Η πρώτη ἑλληνοουγγρικὴ συμμαχία (895)', Νέα ῾Εστία, LXI (1957), 204–8.

Komjáthy, M., 'Quelques problèmes concernant la charte de fondation de l'Abbaye de Tihany', *Etudes historiques publiées par la Commission Nationale des Historiens Hongrois*, I (Budapest, 1960), 219–52.

Kumorowitz, L. B., 'A magyar címer kettőskeresztje' ['Das Doppelkreuz des ungarischen Wappens'], *Turul*, LV (1941), 45–62.

László, Gy., 'Die Reiternomaden der Völkerwanderungszeit und das Christentum in Ungarn', *ZKG*, LIX (1940), 125–46.

László, Gy., 'Die Anfänge der ungarischen Münzprägung', *Annales Universitatis Scientiarum Budapestinensis de Roland Eötvös nominatae*, Sectio Historica, IV (Budapest, 1962), 27–53.

Laurent, V., ''Ο Βαρδαριωτῶν ἤτοι Τούρκων. Perses, Turcs asiatiques ou Turcs hongrois?', *Bulletin de la Société Historique Bulgare*, XVI–XVIII (1940), 275–89.

Laurent, V., 'Une lettre dogmatique de l'empereur Isaac l'Ange au primat de Hongrie', *EO*, XXXIX (1940), 59–77.

Laurent, V., 'La Serbie entre Byzance et la Hongrie à la veille de la quatrième croisade', *RHSE*, XVIII (1941), 109–30.

Laurent, V., 'L'évêque des Turcs et le proèdre de Turquie', *Académie Roumaine, Bulletin de la section historique*, XXIII, 2 (Bucharest, 1942).

Macartney, C. A., *The Magyars in the Ninth Century* (Cambridge, 1930).

Moravcsik, Gy., *Szent László leánya és a bizánci Pantokrator-monostor* [Die Tochter Ladislaus des Heiligen und das Pantokrator-Kloster in Konstantinopel]. *Mitteilungen des Ungarischen Wissenschaftlichen Instituts in Konstantinopel*, VII–VIII (Budapest–Constantinople, 1923).

Moravcsik, Gy., 'Zur Geschichte der Onoguren', *Ungarische Jahrbücher*, X (1930), 53–90, 363.

Moravcsik, Gy., 'Die archaisierenden Namen der Ungarn in Byzanz', *BZ*, XXX (1929–30), 247–53.

Moravcsik, Gy., 'Les relations entre la Hongrie et Byzance à l'époque des croisades', *Revue des Etudes Hongroises*, VIII–IX (1933), 301–8.

Moravcsik, Gy., 'Pour une alliance byzantino-hongroise (seconde moitié du XIIᵉ siècle', *B*, VIII (1933), 555–68.

Moravcsik, Gy., *Görög költemény a várnai csatáról* = ῾Ελληνικὸν ποίημα περὶ τῆς μάχης τῆς Βάρνης (Οὐγγροελληνικαὶ Μελέται, 1) (Budapest, 1935).

Moravcsik, Gy., 'Inscription grecque sur le triptyque de Grenoble', *Revue des Etudes Hongroises*, XIII (1935), 193–203.

Moravcsik, Gy., 'A magyar Szent Korona görög feliratai' ['Les inscriptions grecques de la Sainte Couronne hongroise'], *Archivum Philologicum*, LIX (1935), 113–62.

Moravcsik, Gy., 'A magyar Szent Korona görög feliratainak olvasásához és magyarázatához' ['Comment lire et expliquer les inscriptions grecques de la Sainte Couronne hongroise'], *Archivum Philologicum*, LX (1936), 152–8.

Moravcsik, Gy., 'The Holy Crown of Hungary', *The Hungarian Quarterly*, IV (1938–9), 656–67.

Moravcsik, Gy., 'Byzanz und die Ungarn vor der Landnahme', *VIe Congrès International d'Etudes Byzantines, Alger, Résumés des rapports et communications* (Paris, 1940), pp. 4–6.

Moravcsik, Gy., 'Byzantine Christianity and the Magyars in the Period of their Migration', *American Slavic and East European Rev.* v (1946), 29–45.

Moravcsik, Gy., 'The Role of the Byzantine Church in Medieval Hungary', *American Slavic and East European Rev.* VI (1947), 134–52.

Moravcsik, Gy. 'La Tactique de Léon le Sage comme source historique hongroise', *Acta Historica Academiae Scientiarum Hungaricae*, I (1952), 161–84.

Moravcsik, Gy., *Bizánc és a magyarság [Byzantium and the Hungarians]* (Budapest, 1953), 120 pp. with XVI plates [in Hungarian].

Moravcsik, Gy., *Ungarisch-byzantinische Beziehungen zur Zeit des Falles von Byzanz* (Acta Antiqua Academiae Scientiarum Hungaricae, 2) (1954), 349–60.

Moravcsik, Gy., *Die byzantinische Kultur und das mittelalterliche Ungarn* [Sitzungsberichte der Deutschen Akademie der Wissenschaften zu Berlin, Klasse für Philosophie, Geschichte, Staats-, Rechts- und Wirtschaftswissenschaften, Jahrgang 1955. Nr. 4] (Berlin, 1956).

Moravcsik, Gy., 'Bizánci krónikák a honfoglalás elötti magyarságról' ['Byzantine Chronicles about the Magyars before the Conquest of Hungary'], *Antik Tanulmányok-Studia Antiqua*, IV (1957), 275–88. [In Hungarian with Greek texts.]

Moravcsik, Gy., *Byzantinoturcica* [see above I (A), and Gen. Bibl. I].

Moravcsik, Gy., 'Die Problematik der byzantinisch-ungarischen Beziehungen', *BS*, XIX (1958), 206–11.

Moravcsik, Gy., 'Sagen und Legenden über Kaiser Basileios I', *DOP*, xv (1961), 59–126.

Moravcsik, Gy., 'Vizantijskije imperatory i ich posly v g. Buda' ['Les empereurs de Byzance et leurs ambassadeurs à Buda'], *Acta Historica Academiae Scientiarum Hungaricae*, VIII (1961), 239–56. [In Russian with a French résumé.]

Muráti, F., 'Μανουὴλ ὁ Κομνηνὸς καὶ αἱ σχέσεις αὐτοῦ πρὸς Βέλαν τὸν Γ΄ καὶ τοὺς προκατόχους του', *EEBS*, XI (1935), 283–90.

Mutafčiev, P., 'Madžarite i bŭlgaro-vizantijskite otnošenija prez tretijata četvert na X. v.' ['Magyar and Bulgaro-Byzantine Relations in the Third Quarter of the Tenth Century'], *Godišnik na Sofijskija Universitet, Ist.-Filol. Fakultet*, XXX, 8 (Sofia, 1935), 1–35.

Ostrogorsky, G., 'Urum-Despotes. Die Anfänge der Despoteswürde in Byzanz', *BZ*, XLIV (1951), 448–60.

Papp, G., 'I monaci dell'ordine di San Basilio in Ungheria nel secolo XIII', *ASBM*, ser. II, sect. II, I (VII), fasc. 1 (1949), 39–56.

Rácz, I., *Bizánci költemények Mánuel császár magyar hadjáratairól =* Βυζαντινὰ ποιήματα περὶ τῶν οὐγγρικῶν ἐκστρατειῶν τοῦ αὐτοκράτορος Μανουήλ (Οὐγγροελληνικαὶ Μελέται, 16) (Budapest, 1941).

Sicilianos, D., 'Rapports gréco-hongrois à l'époque byzantine', *Parthenon*, VIII (1934), 10–12.

Somogyi, Á., 'Nouvelles données sur la staurothèque byzantine d'Esztergom', *Az Iparmüvészeti Múzeum Évkönyvei*, III–IV (1959), 81–99.

Székely, G., 'Ungarns Stellung zwischen Kaiser, Papst und Byzanz zur Zeit der Kluniazenserreform', *Atti del II Convegno del Centro di Studi sulla spiritualità medievale* (Todi, 1960), pp. 311–25.

Székely, Gy., 'Gemeinsame Züge der ungarischen und polnischen Kirchen-
    geschichte des XI. Jahrhunderts', *Annales Universitatis Scientiarum
    Budapestinensis de Rolando Eötvös nominatae,* Sectio Historica, IV (Buda-
    pest, 1962), 55–80.
Szigeti, R. L., *Translatio Latina Ioannis Damasceni (De orthodoxa fide,* III,
    c. 1–8) saeculo XII. in Hungaria confecta (Οὐγγροελληνικαὶ Μελέται, 13)
    (Budapest, 1940).
Terebessy, A. B., *Translatio latina Sancti Maximi Confessoris (De caritate ad
    Elpidium,* I–IV) *saeculo XII. in Hungaria confecta* (Οὐγγροελληνικαὶ
    Μελέται, 25) (Budapest, 1944).
Váczy, P., 'Les racines byzantines du christianisme hongrois', *Nouvelle Revue
    de Hongrie,* XXXIV (1941), 99–108.
Váczy, P., 'Deutschlands Anteil an der Begründung des ungarischen König-
    tums', *Ungarn,* I (1941), 12–42.
Wirth, P., 'Das bislang erste literarische Zeugnis für die Stefanskrone aus der
    Zeit zwischen dem X. und XIII. Jahrhundert', *BZ,* LIII (1960), 79–82.
Zlatarsky, V. N., 'Wer war Peter Deljan?', *Annales Academiae Scientiarum
    Fennicae,* XXVII (1927), 354–63.

For a detailed bibliography of works written in Hungarian see Gy. Moravcsik,
    Byzantinoturcica [see above I(A)], I, 134–45 and under the sources cited.

For recent Hungarian research, see:

Gyóni, M., 'Ein Jahrzehnt ungarischer Byzantinologie', *Donaueuropa,* II,
    (1942), 226–32.
Gyóni, M., 'Les études byzantines en Hongrie pendant la guerre 1939–1945',
    REB, V (1947), 240–56.
Harmatta, J., 'Les études grecques et latines en Hongrie de 1939 à 1946',
    Bulletin de l'Association Guillaume Budé, n.s. V (1948), 126–50.
Moravcsik, Gy., 'Les récentes études byzantines en Hongrie', *Revue des
    Etudes Hongroises et Finno-Ougriennes,* I (1923), 61–70.
Moravcsik, Gy., 'Bulletin hongrois (1922–38)', *B,* VI (1931), 657–702, XIV
    (1939), 459–96.
Moravcsik, Gy., 'Byzantine Studies in Hungary 1939–1945', *BS,* IX (1948),
    379–92.

The most recent Hungarian work will be found in the specialised bibliographies
    regularly appearing in *BZ* (contributed by Gy. Moravcsik from 1950–)
    and *BS* (contributed by M. Gyóni from 1949 to 1955 and by Gy. Moravcsik
    from 1956–).

CHAPTER XIV. ARMENIA AND GEORGIA

I. BIBLIOGRAPHICAL GUIDES

*Academies, Book Palace of Georgia. The Book Chronicle. Government Biblio-
    graphical Organ of the USSR* [in Georg.], 11 vols. (Tiflis, 1926–35).
Anasyan, H. S., *Armenian Bibliology* [in Arm.] (Erevan, 1959).
C'agareli, A., *Information on the Monuments of Georgian Literature* [in Russ.],
    3 vols. (St Petersburg, 1886–94).

Finck, F., 'Abriss der armenischen Literatur', *Amelang's Literatur des Ostens*, 7 (Leipzig, 1907).

Kiknaje, G. (ed.), *The Georgian Book, a Bibliography* [in Georg.], 2 vols. (Tiflis, 1941, 1950–4).

Lang, D. M., *Catalogue of Georgian and Other Caucasian Printed Books in the British Museum* (London, 1962).

Lazikean, A., *New Armenian Bibliography and Encyclopaedia of Armenian Life, 1512–1905* [in Arm.], 2 vols. (Venice, 1909–12).

Melik'set-Begi, L., *Publications of the Written Sources of Georgian History* [in Georg.], Catalogue 1 (Tiflis, 1949).

Miansarov, M., *Bibliographia caucasica et transcaucasica* (St Petersburg, 1874–6).

Patkanov, K., *Bibliographical Survey of Armenian Literature* [in Russ.] (St Petersburg, 1880).

P'eratean, P., *Armenian Bibliography* [in Arm.] (Vienna, 1919).

Salmaslian, A., *Bibliographie de l'Arménie* (Paris, 1946).

Tichomirov, M., *Study of Sources for the History of USSR* [in Russ.], I (Moscow, 1940).

Zarphanalean, G., *Armenian Bibliography* [in Arm.] (Venice, 1883).

II. COLLECTIONS OF SOURCES

Akinean (Akinian), N., *Texte und Untersuchungen der altarmenischen Literatur* [in Arm.] (Vienna, 1952ff.) [*TU*].

Ališan, Ł., *Armeniaca* [Haypatum; in Arm.], 2 vols. (Venice, 1901–2).

Ališan, Ł., *Armenian Writings* [in Arm.], 24 vols. (Venice, 1853–1934).

Brosset, M. F., *Collection d'historiens arméniens*, 2 vols. (St Petersburg, 1874–6) [*CHA*].

The Georgian Royal Annals, see below, III (B), *ad init.*

Imniašvili, I., *Historical Chrestomathy of the Georgian Language* [in Georg.] (Tiflis, 1949, 1953).

Kekelije, K., *Monumenta hagiographica georgica*, 2 vols. (Tiflis, 1918, 1946).

Langlois, V., *Collection des historiens anciens et modernes de l'Arménie*, 2 vols. (Paris, 1868–9) [*CH*].

Melik'set-Begi (-Begov), L., *Georgian Sources Regarding Armenia and the Armenians* [in Arm.], 3 vols. (Erevan, 1934–55).

Monumenta georgica, publ. Universitatis Tphilisensis (Tiflis, 1920).

Peeters, P., *Histoires monastiques géorgiennes* [in Latin], *AB*, XXXVI–XXXVII (1917–19).

Qubaneišvili, S., *Chrestomathy of Old Georgian Literature* [in Georg.], 2 vols. (Tiflis, 1946, 1949).

Rec. Hist. Cr. [see Gen. Bibl. IV]. Documents arméniens: 1 [Armenian texts and French transl.], publ. E. Dulaurier (Paris, 1869); 2 [Latin and French sources], publ. C. Kohler (Paris, 1906).

Sabinini, M., *The Paradise of Georgia* [in Georg.] (St Petersburg, 1882).

Šahnazarean, G. (Chahnazarian, K.), *Armenian Historical Gallery, or Selected Armenian Historians* [in Arm.], 8 vols. (Paris, 1859–60).

T'aqaišvili, E., *Three Historical Chronicles* [in Georg.] (Tiflis, 1890); Russian transl. *Sbornik materialov…Kavkaza*, XXVIII (1900).

Weber, S., *Ausgewählte Schriften der armenischen Kirchenväter*, 2 vols. (Munich, 1927) (Bibl. der Kirchenväter, 54–5).

Žordania, T'., *Chronicles and Other Materials for the History of Georgia* [in Georg.], 2 vols. (Tiflis, 1892–7).

III. LITERARY SOURCES

A. ARMENIAN

Agathangelus (Agatʻangeḷos; fifth cent.), *History of the Conversion of Armenia* (Constantinople, 1709, 1824; Venice, 1835, 1862, 1930; Tiflis, 1882; G. Tēr-Mkrtčʻean and S. Kanayeancʻ, 1909, 1914); Italian transl. N. Tommaseo (Venice, 1843); French transl. V. Langlois, *CH*, I; German transl. P. de Lagarde (Göttingen, 1887).

Ananias of Moxoene (Mokacʻi), *Katholikos* of Armenia (†967), *On the Defection of the Albanians*, publ. G. Tēr-Mkrtčʻean, *Ararat*, XXX–XXXI (1897).

Ananias of Siracene (Širakacʻi; seventh cent.), *Works*, publ. Kʻ. P[atkanean] (St Petersburg, 1877).

Ananias of Siracene, *Geography* [formerly ascribed to Ps. Moses of Xoren or Chorene] (Amsterdam, 1668; Venice, 1752, 1843, 1862); publ. and French transl. J. Saint-Martin, *Mém. hist. géogr. Arm.* II (Paris, 1819); A. Soukry (Venice, 1881); publ. and Russian transl. K. Patkanov (St Petersburg, 1877); publ. and German transl. J. Marquart, *Ērānšahr nach d. Geogr. d. Ps. Moses Xor.* (Berlin, 1901).

Ananias of Siracene, *Cosmography and the Theory of the Calendar*, publ. A. Abrahamyan (Erevan, 1940).

Ananias of Siracene, *Problems and Solutions*, publ. G. Tēr-Mkrtčʻean, *Ararat*, XXIX–XXX (1896); publ. and Russian transl. I. Orbeli (Petrograd, 1918).

Anonymous Chronicle (seventh cent.?), publ. B. Sargisean (Venice, 1904).

Aristaces of Lastivert (Aristakēs Lastivertcʻi), *Vardapet** (†1071), *History of Armenia* [from *c.* 1000 to *c.* 1070] (Venice, 1844, 1901; Tiflis, 1912); French transl. (extracts) M. F. Brosset, *Additions et éclairc. à l'Hist. de la Gé.*, XI (St Petersburg, 1851); and E. Dulaurier, *Recherches chron. armén.* (Paris, 1859); French transl. E. Prud'homme (Paris, 1864). [**Vardapet* is the Armenian ecclesiastical title borne by priests distinguished for their learning.]

Armenian Martyrdom of St Susan [Sušanik of Gogarene, daughter of the Prince of the Mamikonids] (seventh cent.?) (Venice, 1853, 1901); Latin transl. P. Peeters, *AB*, LIII (1935).

Basil the Doctor (†1162/3), 'Funeral Oration on Baldwin, Count of Marʻaš and Kaysūn', publ. and French transl. *Rec. Hist. Cr.*, Docs. arm., 1.

The Book of Letters [coll. of docs. of the fifth, sixth, seventh, and later cent., some translations from the Greek, relative to the religious history of Armenia and of Caucasia in general], publ. Y. Ismireancʻ (Tiflis, 1901); French transl. M. Tallon (Beirut, 1955–).

Canons attributed to St Isaac [Sahak] (seventh cent.) (Venice, 1853); English transl. F. C. Conybeare, *AJT*, II (1898).

Canons of the Synod of Manazkert (726), publ. A. Tēr-Mikʻēlean [together with Samuel of Ani] (Vaḷaršapat, 1893).

Canons of the Synod of Šahapivan (444), publ. N. Akinean (Akinian), *Handes Amsorya*, LXIII (1949); and *TU*, I, 2 (Vienna, 1953).

Chosroes the Great, Bishop of Anjewacʻikʻ (†965), *Works* (Venice, 1869); Latin transl. P. Vetter (Freiburg/B., 1880).

Chronique arménienne, see below, III (B) (under *Georgian Royal Annals*).

Cyriacus of Ganja (Kirakos Ganjakec'i; †1272), *History of Armenia* [from the fourth cent. to 1265] (Moscow, 1858; Venice, 1860, 1865; Tiflis, 1909); extract and French transl. *Rec. Hist. Cr.*, Docs. arm., 1; French transl. (extracts), M. F. Brosset, *Additions et éclairc. à l'Hist. de la Gé.*, XXIV (St Petersburg, 1851); (extract) E. Dulaurier, *Les Mongols d'après les historiens arm.* (Paris, 1858); M. F. Brosset, *Deux hist. arm.* I (St Petersburg, 1870); Germ. transl. (extracts) (Berlin, 1870).

David the Philosopher, or the Invincible (sixth cent.?), *Works* (Constantinople, 1731; Venice, 1833).

Eliseus (Eḷišē), *Vardapet* (fifth cent.?, beginning of the seventh cent.?), *History of Vardan* [*II of the Mamikonids*] *and of the Armenian War* (Constantinople, 1764, 1813, 1823, 1866; St Petersburg, 1787; Naxčevan, 1787; Calcutta, 1816; Venice, 1825, 1828, 1832, 1838, 1852, 1859, 1864, 1903, 1950; Feodosija, 1861; Moscow, 1861, 1893; Jerusalem, 1865; Smyrna, 1879; Tiflis, 1879, 1913); English transl. C. Neumann (London, 1830, reprinted in an abridged form, New York, 1952); Italian transl. G. Cappelletti (Venice, 1840); French transl. G. Kabaragy (Paris, 1844); V. Langlois, *CH*, II; Russian transl. P. Sansiev (Tiflis, 1853); E. Dillen (Kharkov, 1884); German transl. S. Weber, *Ausgewählte Schriften*, II.

Eznik of Koḷb (Koḷbac'i), probably Bishop of Bagravandene [wrote c. 445/448], *Against the Sects* (publ. Constantinople, 1763; Smyrna, 1772; Venice, 1826, 1850, 1863, 1914, 1926; Tiflis, 1914); French transl. P. Levaillant de Florival (Paris, 1853); anonym., in *CH*, II (extract); German transl. J. Schmid (Vienna, 1900); S. Weber, *Ausgewählte Schriften*, I.

Eznik the Priest (fifth or sixth cent.?), *Register of Successions* [of the Kings and chief Bishops of Armenia to the fifth cent.; continued to the eighth], publ. A. Tēr-Mik'ēlean (Vaḷaršapat, 1893); N. Akinean (Akinian), *Handes Amsorya*, LI (1937); N. Adontz, *Sion*, XII (Jerusalem, 1938).

Faustus of Buzanda (P'avstos Buzandac'i; fifth cent.), *History of Armenia* [from the conversion to 387; a transl., according to some, from either the Syriac or the Greek] (Constantinople, 1730; Venice, 1832, 1889, 1914, 1933; St Petersburg, 1883); French transl. J. B. Emine, *CH*, I; German transl. W. Lauer (Cologne, 1879).

Galanus Chronicle (fourteenth cent.), publ. G. Galanus, *Conciliat. Eccl. Arm. cum Rom.* (Rome, 1650–61).

Gregory of Akner or Akanc' (thirteenth cent.), *History of the Nation of the Archers* [*scil.* the Mongols; to 1272] (hitherto ascribed to Malachias [Maḷak'ia] the Monk) (St Petersburg, 1870; Jerusalem, 1870); publ. (under the new name) and English transl. R. P. Blake and R. Frye, *Harvard Journ. Asiatic Studies*, XII (1949), also another ed. in 1954; Russian transl. K. Patkanov (St Petersburg, 1871); French transl. M. F. Brosset, *Additions et éclairc. à l'Hist. de la Gé.*, XXV (St Petersburg, 1851).

Gregory VII of Anazarbus, *Katholikos* of Armenia (†1307), *Letter to Het'um II, King of Armenia*, publ. C. Galanus, *Conciliat. Eccl. Arm. cum Rom.* (Rome, 1650–61).

Gregory, Abbot of Narek (†1010), *Works* (Venice, 1827, 1840).

Gregory II, Prince Pahlavuni, *Magister* and *Dux* of Mesopotamia (†1058), *Correspondence*, publ. K. Kostaneanc' (Alexandropol, 1910).

Gregory IV Pahlavuni, the Child (Tḷa), *Katholikos* of Armenia (†1190), *Dogmatic Letters* (Venice, 1838).

Gregory IV Pahlavuni, the Child (Tḷa), *Elegy on the Capture of Jerusalem* [in 1187], publ. and French transl. *Rec. Hist. Cr.*, Docs. arm., 1.

Het'um II, King of Armenia († 1308), *Historical Poem* (Amsterdam, 1666; Constantinople, 1705; Venice, 1733); publ. and French transl. *Rec. Hist. Cr.*, Docs. arm., 1.

Het'um, Count of Korikos (Monk Haythonus, † 1340), *Chronological Table* [1076–1307; attributed to him] (Venice, 1842); publ. and French transl. *Rec. Hist. Cr.*, Docs. arm., 1.

John VI of Drasxanakert (Drasxanakertc'i), *Katholikos* of Armenia (John the *Katholikos*; † 931), *History of Armenia* [to 925] (Jerusalem, 1843, 1867; Moscow, 1853; Tiflis, 1912); French transl. J. Saint-Martin [ed. Lajard] (Paris, 1841).

John, Patriarch of Jerusalem, *Letter* [574/577] to Abas, *Katholikos* of Albania, publ. G. Tēr-Mkrtč'ean, *Ararat*, xxix–xxx (1896); Latin transl. A. Vardanian, *OC*, N.F. ii (1912); and partially *ZKT*, i (1910); French transl. S. Salaville (extract), *EO*, xiii (1910).

Pseudo-John Mamikonean (eighth cent.?), *History of Taraun* [latter part of Pseudo-Zenobius of Glak] (Constantinople, 1708, 1719; Venice, 1832, 1843, 1889); A. Abrahamyan (Erevan, 1941); French transl. J. B. Emine, *CH*, i.

John I Mandakuni, *Katholikos* of Armenia († 490), *Works* (Venice, 1836, 1860); Germ. transl. J. M. Schmid (Regensburg, 1871).

John IV of Ōjun (Ōjnec'i), the Philosopher, *Katholikos* of Armenia († 729), *Works* (Venice, 1833, 1953); publ. and Latin transl. J. B. Aucher (Venice, 1834).

John IV of Ōjun (Ōjnec'i), *Against the Phantasiasts*, publ. J. B. Aucher (Venice, 1816); also in *The Book of Letters*.

John IV of Ōjun (Ōjnec'i), *History of the Armenian Councils* [attributed to John IV] in *The Book of Letters*.

John I Tzimisces, Eastern Emperor († 976), *Letter to Ašot III, King of Armenia*, *apud* Matthew of Edessa.

Koriun the Admirable (fifth cent.?), *Life of the Blessed Mesrōp* (Venice, 1833, 1864, 1894; Smyrna, 1847; Tiflis, 1913; Jerusalem, 1930); M. Abelyan (Erevan, 1941 and Cairo, 1954; Boston, 1951); N. Akinean (Akinian), *Handes Amsorya*, lxiii (1949); and *TU*, i, 1 (Vienna, 1952); German transl. B. Welte (Tübingen, 1841); S. Weber, *Ausgewählte Schriften*, i.

Koriun the Admirable, *Brief Version of the same* (ninth to tenth cent.?) (Venice, 1854, 1894); French transl. J. B. Emine, *CH*, ii.

Lazarus of P'arpi (Lazar P'arpec'i), the Rhetor [wrote c. 504], *History of Armenia* [387–485] (Venice, 1793, 1807, 1873, 1891, 1933); G. Tēr-Mkrtč'ean and S. Malxasean (Tiflis, 1904, 1907, 1917); French transl. G. Kabaragy (extract) (Paris, 1843); S. Ghésarian, *CH*, ii.

Lazarus of P'arpi (Lazar P'arpec'i), *Letter to Prince Vahan Mamikonean* (Moscow, 1853; Venice, 1873); G. Tēr-Mkrtč'ean and S. Malxasean (Tiflis, 1904, 1907).

Leontius (Levond) the Priest, *Vardapet* (eighth cent.), *History of Armenia* [contin. of Sebēos to 788] (Paris, 1854); K. Ezeanc' (St Petersburg, 1887); French transl. G. Chahnazarian (Šahnazarean), *Histoire…par…Ghévond* (Paris, 1856); Russian transl. K. Patkanov (St Petersburg, 1862).

Lesser Chronicles (thirteenth to eighteenth cent.), publ. V. Hakobyan, 2 vols. (Erevan, 1951–6).

Letter to Prince Isaac Arcruni attributed to Pseudo-Moses of Chorene (eleventh cent.?) (Venice, 1865).

Letters of Photius (ninth cent.?) [purporting to be from Photius of Constantinople to Zacharias I, *Katholikos* of Armenia, and to Ašot V Bagratuni,

Prince of Armenia] *and the Armenian Replies*, publ. and Russian transl. A. Papadopoulos-Kerameus and N. Marr, *Pravoslavnyj Palestinskij Sbornik*, xxxi (1892); publ. partially in the *Book of Letters*; abridged version in Vardan; partial Latin transl. A. Mai, *Spicilegium rom.* x (Rome, 1844 = *MPG*, cii).

Martyrdom of Vahan of Colthene (Goḷt'nac'i; eighth cent.) (Venice, 1854).

Maštoc', later *Katholikos* of Armenia, *Letter* [in the 890's] to the *Katholikos* George II, publ. Y. Giuḷxandanean, *Ararat*, xxxv–xxxvi (1902).

Matthew of Edessa (Matteos Uṛhayec'i; twelfth cent.), *Chronicle* [952–1136; contin. by Gregory the Priest to 1168] (Jerusalem, 1869; Vaḷaršapat, 1898); extracts and French transl. *Rec. Hist. Cr.*, Docs. arm., 1; French transl. J. Saint-Martin (Paris, 1811); Ch. de Cirbiet (Paris, 1812) [both partial]; M. F. Brosset (extract), *Additions et éclairc. à l'Hist. de la Gé.*, xiii (St Petersburg, 1851); French transl. E. Dulaurier (Paris, 1858) (Bibliothèque hist. arm., 1).

Mesrōp-Maštoc' (fifth cent.), *Stromata* [attributed to St Gregory the Illuminator of Armenia] (Venice, 1838, 1954); A. Tēr-Mik'elean (Vaḷaršapat, 1894–6).

Mesrōp the Priest (in 967), *Genealogy of the House of St Gregory and Life of St Nersēs* (Venice, 1853); French transl. J. R. Emine, *CH*, ii.

Michael the Syrian, Jacobite Patriarch of Antioch († 1199), *Chronicle* [to 1196]; Armenian transl. from the Syriac and contin. by Išōx (1248) (Jerusalem, 1871); publ. and French transl. (extract), *Rec. Hist. Cr.*, Docs. arm., 1; French transl. (extract), E. Dulaurier, *JA*, 4th ser. xii; V. Langlois (Venice, 1868).

Pseudo-Moses of Chorene (Xorenac'i; mid-eighth cent.), *History of Armenia* [to c. 450] (Amsterdam, 1695; Venice, 1752, 1827, 1843, 1862, 1865; Tiflis, 1858, 1903), M. Abeḷean and S. Yarut'iunean (1913). Latin transl. H. Brenner (Stockholm, 1733); Gu. [W.] and G. Whiston (London, 1736); French transl. P. Levaillant de Florival (Paris, 1836, 1845; Venice, 1841); V. Langlois, *CH*, ii; Italian transl. G. Cappelletti (Venice, 1841); N. Tommaseo (Venice, 1841, 1850); Russian transl. J. Ioanesov (St Petersburg, 1809); N. Emin (Moscow, 1858, 1893); German transl. M. Lauer (Regensburg, 1869).

Moses of Kaḷankaytuk' (Kaḷankatuac'i) or of Dasxurēn (Dasxuranc'i) (tenth cent.), *History of Albania* [to the end of the tenth cent. contin. to the twelfth]; publ. K. Šahnazarean (Paris, 1860); J. B. Emin (Moscow, 1860; Tiflis, 1912); French transl. E. Boré (extract), *Institut sci. hist.* cxxxvi (1847) and *Nouv. annales des voyages*, ii (1848); reproduced, K. (C.) Neumann, *Beiträge z. arm. Lit.* (Munich, 1849); French résumé M. F. Brosset, *Additions et éclairc. à l'Hist. de la Gé.* (St Petersburg, 1851); Russian transl. K. Patkanov (St Petersburg, 1861); English transl. C. J. F. Dowsett (London, 1961) (London Oriental Series, 8).

Mxit'ar of Ani (Anec'i; end of the twelfth cent.), *Universal History*, publ. [extant fragment] K. Patkanov (St Petersburg, 1879).

Mxit'ar of Ayrivank' (Ayrivanec'i), *Vardapet* (thirteenth cent.), *Chronological History* [to 1289] (Moscow, 1860; St Petersburg, 1867); Russian transl. K. Patkanov (St Petersburg, 1869); French transl. M. F. Brosset (St Petersburg, 1869).

Mxit'ar Goš († 1213), *Book of the Tribunals, or Legal Code* (Vaḷaršapat, 1880).

Mxit'ar of Tašir, *Relation of the Conference held with the Papal Legate in 1262*, publ. and French transl. *Rec. Hist. Cr.*, Docs. arm., 1.

Nersēs of Lambron (Lambronac'i), Archbishop of Tarsus († 1198), *Synodal Discourse*, publ. and Italian transl. J. B. Aucher (Venice, 1812, 1865); German transl. C. Neumann (Leipzig, 1834); French transl. Ch. B. Mercier (Venice, 1948).

Nersēs of Lambron (Lambronac'i), *Letters and Panegyrics* (Venice, 1838) [together with the *Letters* of Gregory IV].

Nersēs of Lambron (Lambronac'i), *Meditation on the Institution of the Church and the Mystery of the Mass* (Venice, 1847); extracts and French transl. *Rec. Hist. Cr.*, Docs. arm., 1.

Nersēs of Lambron (Lambronac'i), *Letter to Leo II, King of Armenia*, publ. and French transl. *Rec. Hist. Cr.*, Docs. arm., 1.

Nersēs of Lambron (Lambronac'i), *Political Laws*, English transl. K. Basmadjian (Paris, 1907).

Nersēs of Lambron (Lambronac'i), *Commentary on the Books of Solomon*, publ. and German transl., 3 vols., Max of Saxony (Leipzig, 1919–26).

Nersēs of Lambron (Lambronac'i), *Commentary on Ecclesiastes*, publ. and German transl. Max of Saxony (Leipzig, 1929).

Nersēs IV Pahlavuni, the Gracious or of Hṛomkla (Klayec'i), *Katholikos* of Armenia († 1173), *Works* [including the rhymed *History of Armenia*, to 1045] (Venice, 1830); Latin transl. G. Cappelletti (Venice, 1833).

Nersēs IV Pahlavuni, the Gracious or of Hṛomkla, *Eulogy on the Capture of Edessa* [1144] (Madras, 1810; J. Zohrab, Paris, 1823; Calcutta, 1832); publ. and French transl. *Rec. Hist. Cr.*, Docs. arm., 1.

Nersēs IV Pahlavuni, the Gracious or of Hṛomkla, *Pastoral Letter to the Clergy and the Faithful* (St Petersburg, 1788; Constantinople, 1825; Jerusalem, 1871); publ. and Latin transl. G. Cappelletti (Venice, 1829).

Peter, Bishop of Siunia († 558), *Works*, publ. G. Tēr-Mkrtč'ean, *Ararat*, xxxv (1902).

Primary History of Armenia (fourth to fifth cent.?) [*apud* Sebēos; hence 'Pseudo-Sebēos'] (Constantinople, 1851, etc.); French transl. V. Langlois [as 'Pseudo-Agathangelus'], *CH*, i.

Samuel of Ani (Anec'i) the Priest (twelfth cent.), *Chronology* [to 1179; anonym. contin. to 1358], publ. (extracts) and French transl. *Rec. Hist. Cr.*, Docs. arm., 1; publ. A. Tēr-Mik'ēlean (Vaḷaršapat, 1893); Latin transl. J. Zohrab and A. Mai (Milan, 1818, Rome, 1839); in *MPG*, xix; French transl. M. F. Brosset, *CHA*, ii.

Pseudo-Šapuh Bagratuni (ninth cent.), Prince of Syspiritis, *History of Armenia*, publ. G. Tēr-Mkrtč'ean and Bishop Mesrōp Tēr-Movsēsean (Vaḷaršapat, 1921) [its authenticity is contested by A. Ačarean, *Bazmavēp* (Venice, 1922), and N. Akinean (Akinian), *Handes Amsorya* (Vienna, 1922)].

The Seal of the Faith (seventh cent.), publ. G. Tēr-Mkrtč'ean (Vaḷaršapat, 1914).

Sebēos, Bishop of the Bagratid Princedom, or Xosrovik (seventh cent.), *History of Heraclius* [mid-fifth to mid-seventh cent.] (Constantinople, 1851; St Petersburg, 1879; Tiflis, 1913); S. Malxazyanc' (Erevan, 1939); Russian transl. K. Patkanov (St Petersburg, 1862); German transl. (extracts), J. Hübschmann, *Zur Geschichte Armeniens* (Diss. Leipzig, 1875); French transl. F. Macler (Paris, 1904).

Smbat of Lambron, Prince of Paperon, High Constable of Armenia († 1277), *Chronicle* [952–1274; contin. to 1335] (Moscow, 1856; Paris, 1859; Venice, 1956); partially and French transl. *Rec. Hist. Cr.*, Docs. arm., 1; French transl. (partial), V. Langlois (St Petersburg, 1862).

Smbat of Lambron, Prince of Paperon, *Legal Code* (Vaḷaršapat, 1918); publ. and German transl. J. Karst, *Armenisches Rechtsbuch* (I. Sempad'scher Kodex oder mittelarm. Rechtsbuch; II. Kommentar, a. u. d. T.: Sempad'-scher Kodex a. d. 13. Jahrh. in Verbindung mit dem gross-arm. Rb. des Mechithar Gosch a. d. 12. Jahrh.), 2 vols. (Strasbourg–Venice, 1905–6).

Smbat of Lambron, Prince of Paperon, *Translation of the Assizes of Antioch*, publ. and French transl. Ḷ. Ališan (Venice, 1876).

Stephen Asoḷik, or Asoḷnik, of Taraun, *Vardapet* [wrote in 1004], *Universal History* [to 1004] (Paris, 1854); S. Malxazeanc' (St Petersburg, 1885); Russian transl. N. Emin (Moscow, 1864); French transl. [pt. 1], E. Dulaurier (Paris, 1883); [pt. 2], F. Macler (Paris, 1917); German transl. H. Gelzer and A. Burckhardt (Leipzig, 1907).

Stephen Orbelian (Ōrpēlean) of Siunia, Archbishop of Siunia [wrote in 1297, † 1304], *History of the House and of the Land of Sisakan* [= *Siunia*], publ. (extract) (Madras, 1775); (extract) and French transl. J. Saint-Martin, *Mém. hist. géogr. Arm.* II (Paris, 1819); publ. (Paris, 1859; Moscow, 1861; Tiflis, 1910); Latin transl. (extract), V. Lacroze (Berlin, 1717); reproduced J. v. Klaproth, *Archiv f. asiat. Lit.* I (St Petersburg, 1810); French transl. (extracts), M. F. Brosset, *Additions et éclairc. à l'Hist. de la Gé.*, XVI, XVIII (St Petersburg, 1851); French transl. M. F. Brosset (St Petersburg, 1864).

Stephen the Philosopher, Bishop of Siunia († 735), *On the Incorruptibility of the Flesh*, publ. G. Tēr-Mkrtč'ean, *Ararat*, XXXV (1902) (Vaḷaršapat, 1902).

Thomas Arcruni, *Vardapet* (tenth cent.), *History of the House of Arcruni* [to 936; anonym. contin. to 1226] (Constantinople, 1852); K'. P[artkanean] (St Petersburg, 1887); idem (Tiflis, 1917); French transl. M. F. Brosset, *CHA*, I.

Thomas, Abbot of Mecop' († 1446), *History of Tamerlane*, publ. K. Šahna-zarean (Paris, 1860); publ. and Georgian transl. L. Melik'set-Begi (Tiflis, 1937); French transl. F. Nève, *Exposé des guerres de Tamerlan..d'après... Thomas de Médzoph* (Brussels, 1860).

Pseudo-Uxtanēs (eleventh cent.?), *History of Armenia* [from the beginning, and of the religious break between Armenia and Iberia] (Vaḷaršapat, 1871); French transl. M. F. Brosset, *Deux hist. arm.* II (St Petersburg, 1871).

Vahram the Doctor, of Edessa (thirteenth cent.), *Rhymed Chronicle of the Rubenids, or of the Kingdom of Little Armenia* [to 1280] (Madras, 1810; Calcutta, 1832; Paris, 1859); publ. and French transl. *Rec. Hist. Cr.*, Docs. arm., 1; English transl. (partial), C. Neumann (London, 1831); French transl. S. Pétrossian, *Revue de l'Orient* (1864).

Vardan the Great, *Vardapet* († 1271), *Universal History* [to 1268] (Moscow, 1861; Venice, 1862); extract and French transl. *Rec. Hist. Cr.*, Docs. arm., 1; publ. and French transl. (partial), J. Muyldermans, *La domination arabe en Arm.* (Louvain–Paris, 1927); French transl. (extracts), M. F. Brosset, *Additions et éclairc. à l'Hist. de la Gé.*, XI, XII, XIV, XVI, XVII, XVIII (St Petersburg, 1851); French transl. (extract), E. Dulaurier, *Les Mongoles d'après les hist. arm.* (Paris, 1861); Russian transl. N. Enim (Moscow, 1861); German transl. (extract), J. Marquart, *Osteuropäische u. ostasiat. Streifzüge*, see below, Modern Works, A.

Vardan the Great, *Geography of Armenia* [attributed to Vardan] (thirteenth/fourteenth cent.) (Constantinople, 1728); publ. and French transl. J.Saint-Martin, *Mém. hist. géogr. Arm.* II (Paris, 1819).

Xosrovik the Translator (seventh or eighth cent.), *Works*, publ. G. Yovsep'ean (Vaḷaršapat, 1899–1903).

Pseudo-Zenobius of Glak (eighth cent.?), *History of Taraun* [opening part of Pseudo-John Mamikonean, purporting to belong to the fourth cent.] (Constantinople, 1719; Venice, 1832, 1843, 1889); French transl. E. Prud'-homme, *JA* (1863); V. Langlois, *CH*, I.

B. GEORGIAN

The Georgian Royal Annals (K'art'lis C'xovreba). I: *Chronique arménienne* [twelfth to thirteenth cent. Armenian adaptation of the then extant parts of the *Annals*] (Venice [as 'Juanšer, History of Iberia'], 1884; Tiflis, 1953); French transl. M. F. Brosset, *Additions et éclairc. à l'Hist. de la Gé.*, I (St Petersburg, 1851); II: (*A* =) *Queen Anne Codex* (1479/95), publ. S. Qauxč'išvili (Tiflis, 1942); III: (*M* =) *Queen Mary Variant* (1638/45), publ. E. T'aqaišvili (Tiflis, 1906); IV: (*V* =) *King Vaxtang VI Redaction* (1703/61), publ. M. F. Brosset, *Histoire de la Géorgie, depuis l'Antiquité jusqu'au XIXᵉ siècle, publiée en géorgien*, I, 1–2 (St Petersburg, 1849–50); D. Č'ubinašvili, *Hist. de la Gé.*, II (St Petersburg, 1854); reprinted Z. Čičinaje (Tiflis, 1897); N. Marr, Petrograd, 1923 (partially); French transl. M. F. Brosset, *Hist. de la Gé....traduite du géorgien*, 2 vols., 4 *livraisons* (St Petersburg, 1849–50), 56–7; V: (*Q* =) collated ed. S. Qauxč'išvili, *K'art'lis C'xovreba*, 2 vols. (Tiflis, 1955, 1959).

Abuserije, Bishop of Tbet'i (Tbeli; thirteenth cent.), *Khwārazmian Invasion of Georgia*, publ. T'. Žordania, *Chronicles*, II.

Abuserije, Bishop of Tbet'i, *Treatise on the Calendar*; publ. and French transl. M. F. Brosset, *Mém. Acad. IP.*, 7th ser., II.

Arsenius I of Sap'ara (Sap'areli), *Katholikos* of Iberia (†815), *Religious Separation of Iberia and Armenia*, publ. T'. Žordania, *Chronicles*, I, Annex 1; extracts and French transl. G. Garitte, *La Narratio de rebus Arm.* (*CSCO*, CXXXII, Subs. 4) (Louvain, 1952).

Arsenius II, *Katholikos* of Iberia (†980), *Lives of the Thirteen Syrian Fathers*. I: *Long Version*, publ. M. Sabinini, *Paradise of Georgia*; II: *Brief Version*, publ. S. Kakabaje (Tiflis, 1928).

Arsenius the Monk (twelfth cent.), *History of King David III (II)* [1072–1125; part of the *Georgian Annals*], publ. *A, M, V, Q*; French transl. M. F. Brosset, *Hist. de la Gé.*, I, 1; German transl. M. v. Tseretheli, *Bedi Karthlisa*, XXVI–XXVII (1957).

Arsenius the Monk, *Testament of the Holy King David the Builder* [*III (II)*], publ. M. Sabinini, *Paradise of Georgia*.

Arsenius the Monk, *Testament of David for the Šio-Mǧvime Monastery*, publ. T'. Žordania (Tiflis, 1895).

Bagrat III, King of Georgia (†1014), *Divan of the Kings* [chronol. list of the sovereigns of Abasgia to the author], publ. E. T'aqaišvili, *L'Ancienne Géorgie*, II (1911–13); French transl. idem (Takaïchvili), *JA*, CCX (1927).

Bagrat III (†1014) and David III (II) (†1125), Kings of Georgia, *Statutes*, *apud* the *Code* of Bek'a II and Aǧbuǧa I.

Basil, Master of the Court (thirteenth cent.), *History of Queen Thamar*, publ. *Q* II; Russian transl. V. Dondua, *Monuments of the Epoch of Rust'aveli* (Leningrad, 1938).

Basil of Zarzma (Zarzmeli; tenth cent.), *Life of St Serapion of Zarzma*, publ. M. Janašvili, *Georg. Literature* [in Georg.], II (Tiflis, 1909); K. Kekelije, *Early-Feudal Literature of Georgia* (Tiflis, 1935); Latin transl. P. Peeters, *Hist. mon. gé.*, III.

Bek'a II Ĵaqeli († 1391) and Aǧbuǧa I Ĵaqeli († 1451), Princes of Meschia (Samc'xe), *Code of Laws*, publ. D. Č'ubinašvili, *Georgian Chrestomathy*, ɪ (St Petersburg, 1863); Russian transl. A. Fraenkel and D. Bak'raje, apud *Collection of the Laws of King Vaxtang VI of Georgia* (Tiflis, 1887); French transl. J. Karst, *Corpus juris ibero-caucasici*, ɪv (Strasbourg, 1938).

Canons of the Synod of Ruisi-Urbnisi (1103), publ. M. Sabinini, *Paradise of Georgia*; T'. Žordania, *Chronicles*, ɪɪ.

Č'axruxaje (= Šot'a Rust'aveli?) (1192/1195), *Thamariad*, publ. P. Ioseliani (Tiflis, 1838); D. Č'ubinašvili, *Georgian Chrestomathy* (St Petersburg, 1863); Z. Čičinaje (Tiflis, 1882), N. Marr, *Teksty i razyskanija po arm.-gruz. filol.* ɪv (1902).

Chronicle of Iberia [786–1072; part of the *Georgian Annals*], publ. *A, M, V, Q*; French transl. M. F. Brosset, *Hist. de la Gé.*, ɪ, 1.

Chronicle of the Kings of Abasgia (thirteenth cent.), publ. (extracts) T'. Žordania, *Chronicles*, ɪ.

Chronique géorgienne, or the *Paris Chronicle* [1373–1703], publ. M. F. Brosset (Paris, 1829); French transl. idem (Paris, 1831); *Mém. Acad. IP.*, 6th ser., v (1841).

Egnatašvili the Monk (eighteenth cent.), *Chronicle* [continuing the *Georgian Annals*: fourteenth to eighteenth cent.], publ. I. Ĵavaxišvili (Tiflis, 1940); *Q* ɪɪ.

Ephrem (Karičije) Minor (eleventh cent.), *Narration of the Conversion of Iberia*, publ. T. Bregaje (Tiflis, 1959).

First Continuation of the Georgian Annals (eighteenth cent.) [1346–1453], publ. *M* (Annex 2); *V* (partially); *Q*, ɪɪ; French transl. M. F. Brosset, *Additions et éclairc. à l'Hist. de la Gé.*, xx, and *Hist. de la Gé.*, ɪ, 2 (see below under vA).

First Historian of Queen Thamar (thirteenth cent.), *Histories and Eulogies of the Sovereigns* [1156–1212; part of the *Georgian Annals*], publ. *M, V, Q,* ɪɪ; French transl. M. F. Brosset, *Hist. de la Gé.*, ɪ, 1; Russian transl. K. Kekelije (Tiflis, 1954).

George VI (V) the Illustrious, King of Georgia († 1346), *Code of Laws*, publ. S. Kakabaje (Tiflis, 1913–14); J. Karst, *Corpus juris ibero-caucasici*, vɪ (Strasbourg, 1940); Russian transl. A. Fraenkel and D. Bak'raje, apud *Collection of the Laws of King Vaxtang VI of Georgia* (Tiflis, 1887); English transl. O. Wardrop, *JRAS* (July 1914); French transl. J. Karst, *Corpus juris ibero-caucasici*, v (Strasbourg, 1939).

George the Hagiorite (Mt'acmindeli, † 1065), *Life of Sts John and Euthymius* [written c. 1045], publ. M. Sabinini, *Paradise of Georgia*; A. Xaxanašvili and M. Ĵanašvili, *The Manuscript of 1074* (Tiflis, 1901); I. Ĵavaxišvili and A. Šanije (Tiflis, 1946) (Monumenta linguae georgicae); S. Qubaneišvili, *Chrestomathy*, ɪ; Latin transl. P. Peeters, *Hist. mon. gé.*, ɪ; English transl. (extracts), D. Lang, *Lives and Legends of the Georgian Saints* (London, 1956).

George the Hieromonk, or Minor (eleventh cent.), *Life of St George the Hagiorite* [written c. 1070], publ. M. Sabinini, *Paradise of Georgia*; A. Xaxanašvili and M. Ĵanašvili, *The Manuscript of 1074* (Tiflis, 1901); Latin transl. P. Peeters, *Hist. mon. gé.*, ɪɪ; English transl. (extract), D. Lang, *Lives and Legends of the Georgian Saints* (London, 1956).

George Merč'uli, or Merč'ule, *Life of St Gregory of Xanjt'a* (written in 950/1), publ. N. Marr, *Teksty i razyskanija po arm.-gruz. filol.* vɪɪ (1911);

S. Qubaneišvili, *Chrestomathy*, I; P. Ingoroqva (Tiflis, 1949); Latin transl. P. Peeters, *Hist. mon. gé.*, IV; English transl. (extracts), D. Lang, *Lives and Legends of the Georgian Saints* (London, 1956).

Georgian Agathangelus, I [fragments of an eleventh/twelfth-cent. transl. of the Armen. Agathangelus], publ. G. Garitte, 'Sur un fragment géorgien d'Agathange', *Le Muséon*, LXI (1948); II [eleventh-cent. transl. of the Armen. metaphrastic Life of St Gregory], publ. L. Melik'set-Bek, *Monumenta georgica*, I.

Gregory the Deacon (seventh cent.), *Conversion of Iberia*, publ. E. T'aqaišvili, *Three Hist. Chron.*; T'. Žordania, *Chronicles*, I; E. T'aqaišvili, *Sbornik Materialov...Kavkaza*, XLI–XLII (1910, 1912); I. Qip'šije, *Chrestomathy of Anc. Georg. Lit.* [in Georg.] (Tiflis, 1918); N. Marr and M. Brière, *La Langue géorgienne* (Paris, 1931) [both partially]; Russian transl. E. T'aqaišvili, *Sbornik materialov...Kavkaza*, XXVIII (1900).

Gregory Pacurianus (Bakurianije), Grand Domestic of the West (†1086), *Typikon* for the Petritzos Monastery, publ. M. Tarchnišvili, *CSCO*, CXLIII (1954); Latin transl. idem, *CSCO*, CXLIV (1954).

Historian of King George IV (*c.* 1223), *History of Five Reigns* [1125–1223; part of the *Georgian Annals*], publ. *A*, (partially) *V*, *Q*; partial French transl. (of *K*), M. F. Brosset, *Hist. de la Gé.*, I, 1.

History of the Invasions of Timur (written *c.* 1424/50?), publ. in the *First Continuation of the Georgian Annals*.

History of the Mameluke War of King Vaxtang III (fourteenth cent.?) [interpolated into the *History of the Mongol Invasions* by the Meschian Chronographer].

Institution of the Sovereign's Court (thirteenth/fourteenth cent.), publ. E. T'aqaišvili, *Monumenta georgica*, IV (1920).

James the Priest, or of C'urtavi (C'urtveli; fifth cent.), *Martyrdom of St Susan (Šušanik) the Princess* [of Gogarene, daughter of the Prince of the Mamikonids, †17 Oct. 475], publ. M. Sabinini, *Paradise of Georgia*; S. Gorgaje (Kutais, 1917); I. Abulaje (Tiflis, 1938); S. Qubaneišvili, *Chrestomathy*, I; Latin transl. P. Peeters, 'Ste Sousanik, martyre en Arm.-Géorgie', *AB*, LIII (1935); English transl. (extracts), D. Lang, *Lives and Legends of the Georgian Saints* (London, 1956).

John Petrici (†*c.* 1125), *Works*, publ. S. Qauxč'išvili, *Joannis Petritzii opera*, 2 vols. (Tiflis, 1937–40).

John Sabanije (eighth cent.), *Martyrdom of St Abo of Tiflis*, publ. M. Sabinini, *Paradise of Georgia*; K. Korbelašvili (Tiflis, 1899); K. Kekelije, *Early-Feudal Literature of Georgia* (Tiflis, 1935); S. Qubaneišvili, *Chrestomathy*, I; German transl. K. Schultze, *Texte u. Untersuchungen*, N.F. XIV (1905); Latin transl. (extract), P. Peeters, *AB*, LII (1934); English transl. D. Lang, *Lives and Legends of the Georgian Saints* (London, 1956).

John Šavt'eli (twelfth cent.), *Abdulmesia* [Ode to King David III (II)], publ. P. Ioseliani (Tiflis, 1838); D. Č'ubinašvili, *Georgian Chrestomathy* (St Petersburg, 1863); Z. Čičinaje (Tiflis, 1883); N. Marr, *Teksty i razyskanija po arm.-gruz. filol.* IV (1902).

Ĵuanšer Ĵuanšeriani, *History of King Vaxtang I Gorgasal* (written *c.* 790/800) [fifth to end of the eighth cent.; part of the *Georgian Annals*], publ. *A*, *M*, *V*, *Q*; French transl. M. F. Brosset, *Hist. de la Gé.*, I, 1.

Leontius, Bishop of Ruisi (Leonti Mroveli; eighth cent.), *History of the Kings of Iberia* [to the fifth cent.; part of the *Georgian Annals*], publ. *A*, *M*, *V*, *Q*; French transl. M. F. Brosset, *Hist. de la Gé.*, I, 1.

Life of St Nino [the Illuminatrix of Iberia] (tenth cent.?), publ. E. T'aqaišvili, *Three Hist. Chron.*; idem (Tiflis, 1891); idem, *Sbornik Materialov… Kavkaza*, XLI, XLII (1910, 1912); J. Qip'šije (extract), *Chrestomathy of Anc. Georg. Lit.* (Tiflis, 1918); T'. Žordania, *Chronicles*, I; N. Marr and M. Brière, *La Langue géorgienne* (Paris, 1931) (extract); Russian transl. E. T'aqaišvili, *Sbornik Materialov…Kavkaza*, XXVIII (1900); English transl. M. and O. Wardrop (Oxford, 1900) (Studia biblica et ecclesiastica, 5); (extracts), D. Lang, *Lives and Legends of the Georgian Saints* (London, 1956).

Life of Peter the Iberian [adaptation of the Syriac of Zacharias Rhetor (fifth cent.) by Macarius, rewritten by the Protopope Paul (thirteenth/fourteenth cent.)], publ. and Russian transl. N. Marr, *Pravoslavnyj Palestinskij Sbornik*, XVI, 2 (1896).

List of the *Katholikoi* and Sovereigns of Armenia and Extracts from the *Narratio de rebus Armeniae*, publ. T'. Žordania, *Chronicles*, I, Annex 2; G. Garitte, *La Narratio de rebus Armeniae* (*CSCO*, CXXXII, Subs. 4) (1952).

Martyrdom of St Arč'il (written in the tenth cent.?) [wrongly attributed to Leontius of Ruisi; part of the *Georgian Annals*], publ. *A, M, V, Q*; French transl. M. F. Brosset, *Hist. de la Gé.*, I, 1.

Martyrdom of Constantine-Kaxay (written in the ninth cent.), publ. M. Sabinini, *Paradise of Georgia*; P. Peeters, *Acta Sanctorum Novembris*, IV (1925).

Martyrdom of St Eustace of Mc'xet'a (Evst'ati Mc'xet'eli) (written in the sixth cent.), publ. M. Sabinini, *Paradise of Georgia*; S. Kakabaje, *Bulletin hist.* III (Tiflis, 1928); S. Qubaneišvili, *Chrestomathy*, I; I. Imniašvili, *Hist. Chrestomathy*; German transl. I. Dschawakhoff (Javaxišvili) and A. v. Harnack, 'Das Mart. d. hl. Eusthatius v. Mzchetha', *SPAW*, XXXVIII (1901); English transl. D. Lang, *Lives and Legends of the Georgian Saints* (London, 1956).

Martyrdom of the Nine Infants of Kola (written in the eighth cent.?), publ. and Russian transl. N. Marr, *Teksty i razyskanija po arm.-gruz. Filol.* V (1903); English transl. D. Lang, *Lives and Legends of the Georgian Saints* (London, 1956).

Meschian Chronographer (fourteenth cent.), *History of the Mongol Invasions* [1222–1318; part of the *Georgian Annals*], publ. *M, V, Q*, II; French transl. M. F. Brosset, *Hist. de la Gé.*, I, 1.

Monument of the Dukes [of K'sani] (fifteenth cent.) [sixth to fifteenth cent.], publ. T'. Žordania, *Chronicles*, II; French transl. M. F. Brosset, *Additions et éclairc. à l'Hist. de la Gé.*, XXI (St Petersburg, 1851).

Primary History of Iberia, or *History of Alexander's Invasion* [found together with the *Conversion of Iberia* of Gregory the Deacon].

Royal List: I [fourth cent. B.C.–fourth cent.]; II [fourth–seventh cent.]; III [seventh–ninth cent.]. [Found together with the *Conversion of Iberia* of Gregory the Deacon.]

Statutes of the Royal Coronation (beginning of the thirteenth cent.), publ. S. Kakabaje (Tiflis, 1913).

Stephen, Bishop of Tbet'i (Mtbevari), *Martyrdom of St Gobron* (written in 914/18), publ. M. Sabinini, *Paradise of Georgia*.

Sumbat Davit'ije, *History of the Bagratids* (written *c.* 1030), publ. E. T'aqaišvili, *Three Hist. Chron.*; *M, Q*; Russian transl. E. T'aqaišvili, *Sbornik materialov…Kavkaza*, XXVIII (1900).

C. SOURCES IN LANGUAGES OTHER THAN ARMENIAN AND GEORGIAN

Arabic Life of St Gregory [the Illuminator of Armenia] [transl. from the Greek, ninth cent.?], publ. and Russian transl. N. Marr, *Zapiski vostočn. otd. Imp. Russ. Archeol. Obšč.* XVI (1905); Latin transl. G. Garitte, *Documents pour l'étude du livre d'Agathange* (Vatican City, 1946) (Studi e Testi, 127).

Constantine VII Porphyrogenitus, *De administrando imperio* (chaps. 43, 45, 46) [see Gen. Bibl. IV].

Daniel de Thaurisio, *Responsio ad errores impositos Hermenis* (written c. 1341), publ. *Rec. Hist. Cr.*, Docs. arm., 2.

Διήγησις or *Narratio de rebus Armeniae* [Greek transl. of an Arm. work now lost, of c. 700], publ. F. Combefis, *Novum Auctarium*, II (Paris, 1648); reproduced A. Gallandi, *Biblioth. vet. patrum*, XIV (Venice, 1781); in *MPG*, CXXVII and CXXXII; publ. G. Garitte, *La Narratio de rebus Armeniae* (Louvain, 1952) (*CSCO*, CXXXII, Subs. 4). [Found in one of its MSS together with a Greek List of the *Katholikoi* (to the end of the seventh cent.) and Sovereigns (to c. 700) of Armenia, transl. from the Arm. There exist also a Georg. transl. of this List and an abridged Georg. transl. of the *Narratio*.]

Dositheus, Greek Patriarch of Jerusalem (†1707), Ἱστορία περὶ τῶν ἐν Ἱεροσο-λύμοις πατριαρχευσάντων [contains a Greek version of the Georg. Divan of the Kings of Bagrat III] (Bucharest, 1715).

George VIII, King of Georgia (†1476), *Letter* (of 5 Nov. 1459) to Philip the Good, Duke of Burgundy [in connection with the proposed Crusade of Pope Pius II]; Latin text, Aeneas Sylvius, *Epist.* lib. I.

Greek Agathangelus [transl. from the Armenian c. 464/8], publ. and Latin transl. J. Stiltingh, *Acta sanctorum* (Antwerp, 1762); reproduced (partially) V. Langlois, *Coll. hist. anc. mod. Arm.* I; publ. P. de Lagarde, *Abhandlungen* (Göttingen, 1888); see above III A.

Greek Life of St Gregory [the Illuminator of Armenia] [transl. from the Arm., in the seventh cent.?], publ. G. Garitte, *Documents pour l'étude du livre d'Agathange* (Vatican City, 1946) (Studi e Testi, 127). Its abbreviated Ethiopian transl. [fourteenth/fifteenth cent.] publ. F. M. Esteves Pereira, *Boletim da Soc. de Geogr. de Lisboa*, IX (1901).

Gregory I the Great, Pope (†604), *Letter* (of June/July 601) to Quiricus [Cyrion], Bishop [*Katholikos*] of Hiberia [Iberia], publ. *MGH, Epist.*, II; *MPL*, LXXVII; French transl. M. Tamarati, *L'Eglise gé.* (Rome, 1910); P. Goubert, *Byzance avant l'Islam* (Paris, 1951).

Gregory Pacurianus (Bakurianije), Grand Domestic of the West (†1086), *Typikon for the Petritzos Monastery*; Greek text publ. L. Petit, *VV* (1904).

Het'um, Count of Korikos (Monk Haythonus, †1340), *La flor des estoires de la terre d'Orient* [dictated to Nicole Falcon; contains a *History of the Tatars*] (Paris, 1517; Lyons, 1585, 1595; Paris, 1877); *Rec. Hist. Cr.*, Docs. arm., II; Latin transl. N. Falcon, *Flos historiarum terre orientis* (Haguenau, 1529; Basel, 1532, 1555; Helmstedt, 1585, 1602; Berlin, 1671); *Rec. Hist. Cr.*, Docs. arm., II; mod. French version (The Hague, 1735); English transl. A. Barclay (London, 1520–30); S. Purchas (London, 1625); (extracts) Yule, *Cathay and the Way thither* (London, 1866); German transl. M. Herr

(Strasbourg, 1534); Italian transl. Ramusio, *Delle navig. et viaggi*, II (Venice, 1559); Horologgi, *Hist. degli imp. greci* (Venice, 1562); Sansovino (?), *La hist. de gli imp. greci* (Venice, 1562); Dutch transl. C. Ablijn (Antwerp, 1563); (from Purchas) (Amsterdam, 1655); J. Glazemaker (Amsterdam, 1664); Spanish transl. A. Centeno (Cordoba, 1597); Armenian transl. J. B. Aucher, *Hist. of the Tatars* (Venice, 1842).

Jean Dardel (†1384), *Chronique d'Arménie*, publ. *Rec. Hist. Cr.*, Docs. arm., II.

John I, Prince Mxargrjeli, *Atabeg (Comestabulus)* of Georgia (†1227), *Letter* (1224) to Pope Honorius III; Latin text publ. Raynaldus, *Annal. eccles.*

Macarius III Za'in, Melkite Patriarch of Antioch (†1672), *History of the Conversion of the Georgians*; French transl. from the Arabic, O. de Lebedew (Rome, 1905).

Papal Documents Relative to Armenia and Georgia [including letters to Kings, *Katholikoi*, etc., of Popes Gregory VII, Innocent III, Honorius III, Gregory IX, Innocent IV, Clement IV, Gregory X, Nicholas IV, Clement V, John XXII, Benedict XII, Clement VI, Innocent VI, Urban V, Gregory XI, Clement VII, Callixtus III, Pius II, and Alexander VI], publ. Baronius and Raynaldus, *Annal. eccles.*; *Bullarium francisc.*; Mansi; *MPL*; E. Caspar, *Das Regest. Gregors VII*; Wadding, *Annal. Minorum*; also Balgy, *Hist. doctr. cath.*; Galanus, *Conciliatio*; Tamarati, *L'Eglise gé.*; see below, Modern Works, A.

Qvarqvare III Jaqeli, Duke of Meschia (Samc'xe) and *Atabeg* of Georgia (†1466), *Letter* (Nov. 1459) to Philip the Good, Duke of Burgundy [in connection with the proposed Crusade of Pope Pius II]; Latin text, Aeneas Sylvius, *Epist.* lib. I.

Rusudan, Queen of Georgia (†1245), *Letter* (1224) to Pope Honorius III; Latin text publ. Raynaldus, *Annal. eccles.*

Smbat of Lambron, Prince of Paperon, High Constable of Armenia (†1277), *Letter* (d. Samarkand, 7 Feb. 1248, in French) to Henry I, King of Cyprus, publ. *Recueil des historiens de la France*, XX.

D. COLLECTIONS OF FOREIGN SOURCES RELATIVE TO CAUCASIA

Brosset, M. F., *Additions et éclaircissements à l'Hist. de la Gé.* [extracts from Arabic and Persian authors], XIII, XVIII, XXII, XXIII (St Petersburg, 1851).

Defrémery, C., 'Fragments de géographes et d'historiens arabes et persans inédits, relatifs aux anciens peuples du Caucase et de la Russie méridionale, traduits et accompagnés de notes critiques', *JA*, 4th ser., XIII–XVII (1849–51).

Dietrich, K., *Byzantinische Quellen zur Länder- und Völkerkunde* (Leipzig, 1912).

Karaulov, N., Notices of Arab authors about Caucasia, Armenia, and Azerbaijan [in Russ.], *Sbornik materialov…Kavkaza*, XXIX, XXXI, XXXII.

Latyšev, V., *Scythica et Caucasica e veteribus scriptoribus grecis et latinis*, 2 vols. (St Petersburg, 1902, 1906); Russian transl. (Greek authors), *Izdanija Imp. Russ. Archeol. Obšč.* (St Petersburg, 1900); (Latin authors), *Zapiski klass. otd. Imp. Russ. Archeol. Obšč.* II (St Petersburg, 1904–6).

Latyšev, V., Notices of ancient writers about Scythia and Caucasia [in Russ.], *Vestnik drevnej istorii* (Moscow, 1947–9).

Qauxč'išvili, S., *Georgia. Scriptorum byzantinorum excerpta ad Georgiam pertinentia*, 3 vols. (Tiflis, 1934–6).

Stritter, J. G. von, *Memoriae populorum olim ad Danubium, Pontum Euxinum, Paludem Maeotidem, Caucasum, Mare Caspium et inde magis ad septentrionem incolentium e scriptoribus historiae byzantinae erutae et digestae* (St Petersburg, 1779); Russian transl. (partial) K. Hahn, *Sbornik materialov...Kavkaza*, IX.

Xalat'eanc', B., *Armenia in Arab Historians* [in Arm.] (Vienna, 1919).

IV. OTHER SOURCES

A. DIPLOMATA AND MANUSCRIPTS

Adjarian (Ačarean), H., *Catalog der armenischen Handschriften in der Bibliothek des Sanassarian-Institutes zu Erzerum* (Vienna, 1900).

Adjarian (Ačarean), H., *Katalog der armenischen Handschriften in Täbris* (Vienna, 1910).

Adjarian (Ačarean), H., *Katalog der armenischen Handschriften in Novo-Bayazet* (Vienna, 1924).

Babgēn, *Katholikos* (Kiulēsēryan), *Catalogue of the Armenian Manuscripts at the Red Monastery of Ankara and Environs* [in Arm.] (Antilias, 1957).

Baronian, S. and Conybeare, F. M., *Catalogue of the Armenian Manuscripts in the Bodleian Library* (Oxford, 1918).

Blake, R. P., 'Catalogue des manuscrits géorgiens de la bibliothèque patriarcale grecque à Jérusalem', *ROC*, XXIII–XXV (1922–6).

Blake, R. P., 'Catalogue of the Georgian Manuscripts in the Cambridge University Library', *HTR*, XXV (1932).

Blake, R. P., 'Catalogue des manuscrits géorgiens de la bibliothèque de la Laure d'Iviron au Mont Athos', *ROC*, XXVIII–XXIX (1931–4).

Buchthal, H. and Kurz, O., *A Handlist of Illuminated Oriental Christian Manuscripts* (London, 1942).

C'agareli, A., 'Monuments of Georgian Antiquity in the Holy Land and on Mount Sinai' [in Russ.; Georg. texts], *Pravoslavnyj Palestinskij Sbornik*, IV (1888).

Conybeare, F. C. and Wardrop, J. O., *A Catalogue of the Armenian Manuscripts in the British Museum...to which is appended a Caaalogue of the Georgian Manuscripts in the British Museum* (London, 1913).

Dashian (Tašean), J., *Catalog der armenischen Handschriften in der K. K. Hofbibliothek zu Wien* (Vienna, 1891).

Dashian (Tašean), J., *Catalog der armenischen Handschriften in der Mechitharisten-Bibliothek zu Wien* (Vienna, 1895–6).

Der Nersessian, S., *The Chester Beatty Library. Catalogue of the Armenian Manuscripts*, 2 vols. (Dublin, 1958).

Documents (Akty) collected by the Caucasian Archaeographical Commission [in Russ.; Georg. texts], I (Tiflis, 1866).

Finck, E. and Gjandschezian, L., *Verzeichniss der armenischen Handschriften der königlichen Universitätsbibliothek zu Tübingen* (Tübingen, 1907).

Garegin, *Katholikos* (Yovsep'ean), *Colophons of Armenian Manuscripts* [in Arm.], I (fifth cent.–1250) (Antilias, 1951).

Garitte, G., *Catalogue des manuscrits géorgiens littéraires du Mont Sinaï* (Louvain, 1956) (*CSCO*, CLXV).

Janašvili, M., *Description of the Manuscripts in the Church Museum of Tiflis* [in Russ.] (Tiflis, 1908).

Javaxišvili (Džavaxov), I., 'Hagiographical Materials of the Iviron Manuscripts' [in Russ.; Georg. texts], *Zapiski vost. otd. Imp. Russ. Archeol. Obšč.* XIII (1901).

Javaxišvili (Džavaxov), I., *Description of the Georgian Manuscripts of Mount Sinaï* [in Georg.] (Tiflis, 1947).

Kakabaje, S., *Historical Documents* [in Georg.], 4 vols. (Tiflis, 1913).

Kakabaje, S., *Church Documents of West Georgia* [in Georg.] (Tiflis, 1921).

Kakabaje, S., 'On the Blood Charters' [in Georg.], *Bull. hist.* II (1924).

Kalemk'ear, G., *Catalogue of the Armenian Manuscripts of the Munich Library* [in Arm.] (Vienna, 1892).

Karamianz, N., *Verzeichniss der armenischen Handschriften der königlichen Bibliothek zu Berlin* (Berlin, 1888).

Kareneanc', Y., *General Catalogue of the Manuscripts in the Library of Eǰmiacin* [in Arm.] (Tiflis, 1863).

Karičašvili, D., *Description of the Manuscripts in the Library of the Society for the Propagation of Georgian Education* [in Georg.] (Tiflis, 1905).

Lalayean, E., *Catalogue of the Armenian Manuscripts of Vaspurakan* [in Arm.] (Tiflis, 1915).

Langlois, V., *Le Trésor des chartes d'Arménie, ou Cartulaire de la chancellerie royale des Roupéniens* (Venice, 1863).

Macler, F., *Catalogue des manuscrits arméniens et géorgiens de la Bibliothèque Nationale* (Paris, 1908).

Macler, F., *Rapport sur une mission scientifique en Arménie russe et en Arménie turque (juillet–octobre 1909)* (Paris, 1911) (Nouv. Archives des Missions sci. et litt., n.s. II).

Macler, F., 'Notices de manuscrits arméniens vus dans quelques bibliothèques de l'Europe Centrale', *JA*, 11th ser., II (1913).

Macler, F., 'Notices de manuscrits arméniens ou relatifs aux Arméniens vus dans quelques bibliothèques de la Péninsule Ibérique et du Sud-Est de la France', *Revue des Etudes arm.* I–II (1920–2).

Marr, N., *The Synodikon of the Holy Cross Monastery in Jerusalem* [in Georg.] (St Petersburg, 1914) (Bibliotheca armeno-georgica, 3).

Marr, N., *Description of the Georgian Manuscripts in the Sinai Monastery* [in Russ.] (Moscow–Leningrad, 1940).

Orbeli, R., 'The Collection of the Georgian Manuscripts in the Oriental Institute of the Academy of Sciences of the USSR' [in Russ.], *Učenye zapiski Inst. Vostokovedenija*, VIII (1954).

Orbeli, R., *Catalogue of the Georgian Manuscripts in the Oriental Institute of the Academy of Sciences of the USSR* [in Russian] (Moscow–Leningrad, 1956).

Peeters, P., 'De codice hiberico Bibliothecae Bodleianae Oxoniensis', *AB*, XXXI (1912).

Peradze (P'eraje), G., 'Georgian Manuscripts in England', *Georgica*, I (1935).

Peradze (P'eraje), G., 'Über die georgischen Handschriften in Österreich', *Wiener Zeitschrift f. d. Kunde d. Morgenlandes*, XLVII (1940).

Polish Academy of Sciences, *Catalogue des manuscrits arméniens et géorgiens. Manuscrits arméniens décrits par K. Roszko sous la direction d'E. Sluszkiewicz. Manuscrits géorgiens décrits par J. Braun* (Warsaw, 1958).

Rec. Hist. Cr., Docs. arm., I. *Chartes*, ed. E. Dulaurier [see Gen. Bibl. IV].

Šanije, A., 'The Georgian Manuscripts in Gratz' [in Georg.], *Bull. de l'Univ. de Tiflis*, IX (1929).

Šarašije, K., *Description of the Manuscripts of the Georgian Historico-Ethnographical Society* [in Georg.] (Tiflis, 1948).

Sargisean, B., *Grand catalogue des manuscrits arméniens de la bibliothèque des PP. Mékhitharistes de Saint-Lazare* [in Arm.] (Venice, 1914, 1924).

Simon, J., 'Répertoire des bibliothèques publiques et privées d'Europe contenant des manuscrits arméniens', *Orientalia*, n.s. II (1933).

Simon, J., 'Répertoire des bibliothèques publiques et privées d'Europe contenant des manuscrits géorgiens', *Orientalia*, n.s. III (1934).

State Historical Museum of Kutais, *Description of the Manuscripts* [in Georg.], I (Tiflis, 1953).

State Museum of Georgia, Tiflis, *Description of the Georgian Manuscripts of the State Museum of Georgia* [in Georg.] (Tiflis, 1946–).

State Museum of Georgia, Tiflis, *Guide to the Ancient Manuscript Collections of the State Museum of Georgia* [in Georg.] (Tiflis, 1951).

Surmeyan, A., *Catalogue des manuscrits arméniens se trouvant à Alep à l'Eglise des Quatre Martyrs ainsi qu'auprès des particuliers* [in Arm.], 2 vols. (Jerusalem, 1935; Aleppo, 1936).

Surmeyan, A., *Grand catalogue des manuscrits arméniens des collections particulières d'Europe* (Paris, 1950).

Surmeyan, A., *Catalogue of the Armenian Manuscripts of the Monastery of St James in Jerusalem* [in Arm.], I (Venice, 1948); II–V [continued by N. Bolarean] (Jerusalem, 1953–60).

T'aqaišvili, E. (ed.), *Les antiquités géorgiennes* [in Georg.], 3 vols. (Tiflis, 1899–1900), supplt. to vol. III (Tiflis, 1926).

T'aqaišvili, E., 'Description of the Manuscripts of the Library of the Society for the Propagation of Georgian Education' [in Russ.], *Sbornik Materialov...Kavkaza*, XXXI–XLI (1903–10).

T'aqaišvili, E. (Takaïchvili), *Les manuscrits géorgiens de la Bibliothèque Nationale de Paris et les vingt alphabets secrets géorgiens* (Paris, 1933).

Tarchnišvili, M., 'Georgian Manuscripts and Old Books in Roman Libraries' [in Georg.], *Bedi Karthlisa*, XIII–XIV (1952–3).

Tisserant, E., *Codices armeni Bibliothecae Vaticanae* (Rome, 1927).

Xač'ikean, L., *Colophons of Armenian Manuscripts of the Fourteenth Century* [in Arm.] (Erevan, 1950).

Xač'ikean, L., *Colophons of Armenian Manuscripts of the Fifteenth Century* [in Arm.], I, 1400–1450 (Erevan, 1955); II, 1451–1480 (Erevan, 1958).

Žordania, T'., *Chronicles*, see above, II.

Žordania, T'., *Historical Documents of the Šio-Mǧvime Monastery* [in Georg.] (Tiflis, 1895).

Žordania, T'., *Historical Documents of the Monasteries and Churches of Iberia and Kakhetia* [in Georg.] (Poti, 1903).

Žordania, T'., *Description of the Manuscripts of the Church Museum of Tiflis* [in Russ.], 2 vols. (Tiflis, 1902–3).

B. EPIGRAPHIC

Bak'raje, D., *Archaeological Journey through Guria and Ačara* [in Russ.] (St Petersburg, 1873).

Basmadjian, K., 'Les inscriptions arméniennes d'Ani, de Bagnaïr et de Marmachêne', *ROC*, XXII–XXVII (Paris, 1920–30).

Brosset, M. F., *Rapports sur un voyage archéologique dans la Géorgie et dans l'Arménie* (St Petersburg, 1849–51).

C'agareli, A., *Monuments*, see above, I.

Ceret'eli, G., 'Complete Collection of the Inscriptions on the Walls and of the Postils of the MSS in the Monastery of Gelat'i' [in Russ.; Georg. texts], *Drevnosti vostočnyja*, ɪ (Moscow, 1895).

Jean de la Crimée, *Description des monastères arméniens d'Haghpat et de Sanahin* (St Petersburg, 1863).

Kostaneanc', K., *The Lapidary Chronicle* (in Arm. = Bibliotheca armeno-georgica, 2) (St Petersburg, 1913).

Langlois, V., *Inscriptions grecques, romaines, byzantines et arméniennes de la Cilicie* (Paris, 1854).

C. NUMISMATIC AND SPHRAGISTIC

Basmadjian (Basmajean), K., *The Numismatics of Armenia* [in Arm.] (Venice, 1936).

Javaxišvili, I., *Georgian Numismatics and Metrology* (Aims, Sources, and Methods of History, Formerly and at Present, 3, 1) [in Georg.] (Tiflis, 1925).

Kapanaje, D., *Georgian Numismatics* [in Georg.] (Tiflis, 1950); [in Russ.] (Moscow, 1955).

Lang, D. M., *Studies in the Numismatic History of Georgia in Transcaucasia* (New York, 1955) (Numismatic Notes and Monographs, 130).

Langlois, V., *Numismatique générale de l'Arménie* (Paris, 1859).

Langlois, V., *Essai de classification des suites monétaires de la Géorgie* (Paris, 1860).

Morgan, J. de, *Manuel de numismatique orientale de l'antiquité et du moyen âge*, ɪ (Paris, 1923–36).

Paxomov, E., 'Georgian Coins' [in Russ.], *Zapiski numizmat. otd. Imp. Russ. Archeol. Obšč.* ɪ (St Petersburg, 1910).

Schlumberger, G., 'Les monnaies médiévales des rois de la Petite Arménie', *Revue des études arm.* ɪ (1920).

Sibilean, C., 'Numismatique arménienne', *Revue de l'Orient*, xɪɪ (Paris, 1860).

Sibilean, C., *Classification of the Rubenid Coins* [in Arm.] (Vienna, 1892).

V. MODERN WORKS

[A selective list, exclusive of the *biblica* and the *liturgica*.]

A. HISTORY AND RELIGION

Ačaṛyan, H., *Armenian Prosopographic Dictionary* [in Arm.], 4 vols. (Erevan, 1942–).

Adontz (Adonc'), N., *Armenia in the Epoch of Justinian* [in Russ.] (St Petersburg, 1908).

Adontz (Adonc'), N., 'Notes arméno-byzantines, 4: L'aïeul des Roubéniens', *B*, x (1935).

Adontz (Adonc'), N., 'Les Taronites en Arménie et à Byzance' and 'Les Taronites à Byzance', *B*, ɪx, x, xɪ (1934–6).

Adontz (Adonc'), N., 'La généalogie des Taronites', *B*, xɪv (1939).

Akinean (Akinian), N., *Cyrion, Katholikos of Iberia* [in Arm.] (Vienna, 1910).

Akulian, A., *Einverleibung armenischer Territorien durch Byzanz im XI. Jahrhundert* (Zurich, 1912).

Ališan (Alischan, Alishan), Ḷ., *Description of Great Armenia* [in Arm.] (Venice, 1855); French transl. E. Dulaurier, 'Topogr. de la Gr. Arménie', *JA*, 6th ser., xɪɪɪ (1869).

Ališan (Alischan, Alishan), Ł., *Nersēs the Gracious and His Family* [in Arm.] (Venice, 1873).

Ališan (Alischan, Alishan), Ł., *Geography of the Land of Siracene* [in Arm.] (Venice, 1881).

Ališan (Alischan, Alishan), Ł., *Léon le Magnifique, roi de Sissouan ou de l'Arméno-Cilicie* (Venice, 1888).

Ališan (Alischan, Alishan), Ł., *Ayrarat* [in Arm.] (Venice, 1890).

Ališan (Alischan, Alishan), Ł., *Sisakan* [in Arm.] (Venice, 1893).

Ališan (Alischan, Alishan), Ł., *Susuan or Armeno-Cilica* [in Arm.] (Venice, 1885); French version (Venice, 1899).

Allen, W. E. D., *A History of the Georgian People* [see Gen. Bibl. v].

Altunian, D., *Die Mongolen und ihre Eroberung im kaukasischen und klein-armenischen Ländern, XIII. Jahrhundert* (Berlin, 1911).

Amaduni, G., *Testi vari di diritto canonico armeno (secoli IV–XVIII)* (Vatican City, 1952).

Asdourian, P., *Die politischen Beziehungen zwischen Armenien und Rom vom 190 v. Chr. bis 428 n. Chr.* (Venice, 1911).

Avalichvili, Z., 'La succession du curopalate David d'Ibérie, dynaste de Tao', *B*, VIII (1933).

Azarian, E., *Ecclesiae armenae traditio de Romani Pontificis primatu juris-dictionis et inerrabili magisterio* (Rome, 1870).

Balgy (Palčean), A., *Historia doctrinae catholicae inter Armenos unionisque eorum cum Ecclesia romana in concilio Florentino* (Vienna, 1878).

Basmadjian, K., *Le Droit arménien depuis l'origine jusqu'à nos jours* (Mâcon, 1901).

Berjenišvili, N., *Essay on the Development of Feudal Relations in Georgia, in the 13th–14th Centuries* [in Russ.] (Tiflis, 1938).

Berjenišvili, N., Javaxišvili, I. and Janašia, S., *History of Georgia* [in Georg.] (Tiflis, 1943); [in Russ.] (Tiflis, 1946, 1950).

Brosset, M. F., *Additions et éclaircissements à l'histoire de la Géorgie* [still useful are Add. 1, 4, 9, 11–26] (St Petersburg, 1851).

Brosset, M. F., *Histoire de la Géorgie, depuis l'antiquité jusqu'au XIXᵉ siècle, traduite du géorgien*, 2 vols. (St Petersburg, 1849–50, 1856–7).

Brosset, M. F., *Introduction à l'Histoire de la Géorgie* (St Petersburg, 1858).

Caraci, G. *et al.*, 'Armenia', *Enciclopedia Cattolica.*

Caraci, G. and Tarchišvili, M., 'Georgia', *Enciclopedia Cattolica.*

Conybeare, F. C., *Rituale Armenorum* (Oxford, 1905).

Daghbaschean, H., *Gründung des Bagratidenreiches durch Aschot Bagratuni* (Berlin, 1893).

Der Nersessian, S., 'Une apologie arménienne des images du septième siècle', *B*, XVII (1944).

Der Nersessian, S., *Armenia and the Byzantine Empire* [see Gen. Bibl. v].

Der Nersessian, S., 'Image Worship in Armenia and Its Opponents', *Armenian Quart.* I (1946).

Devreesse, R., 'Négotiations ecclésiastiques arméno-byzantines au XIIIᵉ siècle', *Atti V Congr. intern. di studi bizantini*, I (1939).

Dulaurier, E., *Recherches sur la chronologie arménienne, technique et historique* (Paris, 1859).

Dulaurier, E., 'Etude sur l'organisation politique, religieuse et administrative du royaume de la Petite-Arménie', *JA*, 5th ser., XVII, XVIII (1861).

Dulaurier, E., 'Le royaume de la Petite-Arménie ou la Cilicie au temps des Croisades' [introduction to], *Rec. Hist. Cr.*, Docs. arm.

Eremyan, S., 'The Trade-routes of Transcaucasia in the Epoch of the Sassanids, according to the Tabula Peutingeriana' [in Russ.], *Vestik Drevnej Istorii*, ɪ, 6 (1939).

Gelzer, H., *Die Anfänge der armenischen Kirche* (Leipzig, 1895).

Grousset, R., *Histoire des Croisades et du royaume franc de Jérusalem*, 3 vols. (Paris, 1934–6).

Grousset, R., *L'Empire du Levant. Histoire de la question d'Orient* (Paris, 1946).

Grousset, R., *Histoire de l'Arménie des origines à 1071* (Paris, 1947).

Gugushvili, A., 'Ethnographical and Historical Division of Georgia, *Georgica*, ɪ, 2–3 (1936).

Gugushvili, A., 'The Chronological–Genealogical Table of the Kings of Georgia', *Georgica*, ɪ, 2–3 (1936).

Güterbock, K., *Römisch-Armenien und die römischen Satrapien im 4. bis 6. Jahrhundert* (Königsberg, 1900).

Gvritišvili, D., *From the History of Social Relations in Feudal Georgia: the Iberian Princedoms* [in Georg.] (Tiflis, 1955); Russ. version (Tiflis, 1961).

Hatzuni, V., 'Disciplina armena', *Studi storici sulle fonti del diritto canonico orientale* (Vatican City, 1932).

Heyd, W., *Histoire du commerce du Levant au moyen-âge* [see Gen. Bibl. v].

Higgins, M., 'International Relations at the Close of the Sixth Century', *Cath. Hist. Rev.* xxvɪɪ (1941).

Honigmann, E., *Die Ostgrenze des byzantininschen Reiches von 363 bis 1071, nach griechischen, arabischen, syrischen und armenischen Quellen* (Brussels, 1945) (Corpus Bruxellense historiae byzantinae, 3).

Hübschmann, J., *Die altarmenischen Ortsnamen. Mit Beiträgen zur historischen Topographie Armeniens* (Strasbourg, 1904).

Inglisian, V., 'Chalkedon und die armenische Kirche', A. Grillmeier and H. Bacht, *Das Konzil von Chalkedon*, ɪɪ (Würzburg, 1953).

Janašia, S., *Works* [in Georg.], 2 vols. (Tiflis, 1949–52).

Janin, R., 'Géorgie', *DTC*.

Javaxišvili (Džavaxov), I., 'The Apostolate of St Andrew and of St Nino in Georgia' [in Russ.], *ZMNP*, cccxxxɪɪɪ (1901).

Javaxišvili (Džavaxov), I., 'The Polity of Ancient Georgia and Ancient Armenia' [in Russ.], *Teksty i razyskanija po arm.-gruz. filol.* vɪɪɪ (1905).

Javaxišvili (Džavaxov), I., 'History of the Religious Break between Georgia and Armenia at the Beginning of the VIIth Century' [in Russ.], *Bull. de l'Acad. I.P.*, 6th ser. (1908).

Javaxišvili (Džavaxov), I., *History of the Georgian People* [in Georg.] (Tiflis, 1908, 1913, 1928, 1941, 1948, 1951).

Javaxišvili (Džavaxov), I., *History of Georgian Law* [in Georg.], 3 vols. (Tiflis, 1928–9).

Javaxišvili (Džavaxov), I., *Economic History of Georgia* [in Georg.], 2 vols. (1930, 1934).

Justi, F., *Iranisches Namenbuch* (Marburg, 1895).

Kakabaje, S., *Historical Researches* [in Georg.] (Tiflis, 1924).

Karbelašvili, K., *The Hierarchy of the Georgian Church* [in Georg.] (Tiflis, 1904).

Karst, J., 'Grundriss der Geschichte des armenischen Rechts', *Zeitschrft. f. vergleichende Rechtswiss.* xx (1907).

Karst, J., *Corpus juris ibero-caucasici*, 6 vols. (Strasbourg, 1935–40).

Kekelije, K., 'On the Question of the Hierosolymite origin of the Georgian Church' [in Russ.], *Soobščenija Imp. Pravosl. Palest. Obšč.* xxv (1914).

Kekelije, K., 'On the Question of the Arrival of the Syrian Fathers in Iberia' [in Georg.], *Bull. de l'Université de Tiflis*, VI (1925).

Kekelije, K., 'Chief Historico-Chronological Problems in Connection with the Conversion of the Georgians' [in Georg.], *Mimoxilveli*, I (1926).

Kekelije, K., 'Die Bekehrung Georgiens zum Christentum', *Morgenland, Darstell. aus Gesch. u. Kultur d. Ostens*, XVIII (1928).

Kherumian, R., 'Esquisse d'une féodalité oubliée', *Vostan*, I (1948–9).

Kogean, S., *The Kamsarakans, Princes of Siracene and Aršarunik'* [in Arm.] (Vienna, 1926).

Kohler, C., *Lettres pontificales concernant l'histoire de la Petite-Arménie* (Paris, 1909).

Krymskij, A., 'Pages from the History of Northern or Caucasian Azerbaijan (Classical Albania)' [in Russ.], *Collection of Articles for S. F. Oldenburg* (Leningrad, 1934).

La Monte, J., 'Chronology of the Latin Orient: Lords and Kings of Lesser Armenia (Cilicia)', *Bull. of the International Comm. of Hist. Sciences*, 47, XII, 2 (1943).

Lang, D. M., 'Georgia in the Reign of Giorgi the Brilliant', *BSOAS*, XVII (1955).

Langlois, V., 'Documents pour servir à l'histoire des Lusignan de la Petite–Arménie (1342–94)', *RA*, XVI (1859).

Langlois, V., 'Essai historique sur la constitution sociale et politique de l'Arménie sous les rois de la dynastie roupénienne', *Mém. Acad. IP.*, 7th ser., VIII, 3 (1860).

Laurent, J., *Byzance et les Turcs seldjoucides dans l'Asie occidentale jusqu'en 1081* (Nancy, 1913).

Laurent, J., *L'Arménie entre Byzance et l'Islam depuis la conquête arabe jusqu'en 886* (Paris, 1919).

Laurent, J., 'Des Grecs aux Croisés, étude sur l'histoire d'Edesse de 1071 à 1098', *B*, I (1924).

Laurent, J., 'Byzance et Antioche sous le curopalate Philarète', *Revue des Etudes arm.* IX (1929).

Laurent, V., 'Alliances et filiation des premiers Taronites, princes arméniens médiatisés', *EO*, XXXVII (1938).

Macler, F., 'Les couvents arméniens', *Revue de l'hist. relig.* LXXIII (1916).

Macler, F., 'Le Liber pontificalis des Catholicos d'Athamar', *JA*, CCXXII (1923).

Manandyan (Manandean, Manandian), Y. (H.), *Note on the Position of the Šinakans in Ancient Armenia, in the Epoch of the Marzpans* [in Arm.] (Erevan, 1925).

Manandyan, Y. (H.), *On the Trade and Cities of Armenia, in Connection with the World Commerce of Antiquity* [in Russ.] (Erevan, 1930, 1954).

Manandyan, Y. (H.), *Notes on the Fief and the Feudal Army of Parthia and Arsacid Armenia* [in Russ.] (Tiflis, 1932).

Manandyan, Y. (H.), *Arab Invasions of Armenia (Chronological Notes)* [in Arm.] (Erevan, 1932); French transl. H. Berberian, *B*, XVIII (1948).

Manandyan, Y. (H.), *Feudalism in Ancient Armenia* [in Arm.] (Erevan, 1934).

Manandyan, Y. (H.), 'The Itinerary of the Persian Campaigns of the Emperor Heraclius' [in Russ.], *VV*, III (1950).

Manandyan, Y. (H.), *Critical Survey of the History of the Armenian People* [in Arm.], 3 vols. (Erevan, 1944, 1957–60, 1952).

Manandyan, Y. (H.), *Beiträge zur albanischen Geschichte* (Leipzig, 1897).

Markwart (Marquart), J., *Osteuropäische and ostasiatische Streifzüge* (Leipzig, 1903).

Markwart (Marquart), J., *Skizzen zur historischen Topographie und Geschichte von Kaukasien* (Vienna, 1927).

Markwart (Marquart), J., 'Die Genealogie der Bagratiden und das Zeitalter des Mar Abas und Ps. Moses Xorenac'i', *Caucasica*, VI (1930).

Markwart (Marquart), J., *Südarmenien und die Tigrisquellen nach griechischen und arabischen Geographen* (Vienna, 1930).

Markwart (Marquart), J., 'Enstehung der armenischen Bistümer', *Orientalia Christiana*, XXVII (1932).

Marr, N., 'Ark'aun, the Mongol Name for Christians in Connection with the Problem of the Chalcedonian Armenians' [in Russ.], *VV*, XII (1906).

Maxaraje, T., Javaxišvili, I. *et al.*, 'Georgia' [in Russ.], *The Great Soviet Encyclopaedia*.

Mécérian, J., 'Bilan des relations arméno-iraniennes au Ve siècle après J.C.', *Bulletin Arménologique*, II (Beirut, 1953).

Melikset-Bekov, L., *Introduction to the History of the Political Formations of Southern Caucasia* [in Russ.] (Tiflis, 1924).

Mikaelyan, G., *History of the Armeno-Cilician State* [in Russ.] (Erevan, 1952).

Minorsky, V., 'Tiflis', *Encyclopaedia of Islam*.

Minorsky, V., 'Transcaucasica', *JA*, CCXVII (1930).

Minorsky, V., 'Caucasica II', *BSOAS*, XIII (1951).

Minorsky, V., 'Roman and Byzantine Campaigns in Atropatene', *BSOAS*, XI (1944).

Minorsky, V., *Studies in Caucasian History* (London, 1953) (Cambridge Oriental Series, 6).

Minorsky, V., 'Caucasica IV', *BSOAS*, XV (1953).

Mlaker, K., 'Die Herkunft der Mamikonier und der Titel Cenbakur', *Wien. Zeitschrift f. d. Kunde d. Morgenlandes*, XXIX (1932).

Movsêsian, L., 'Histoire des rois Kurikian de Lori, traduite de l'arm. par F. Macler', *Revue des Etudes arm.* VII (1927).

Muyldermans, J., 'Le dernier prince Mamikonien de Bagrévand', *Handes Amsorya*, XL (1926).

Orbeli, I. (gen. ed.), *Monuments of the Epoch of Rustaveli* [in Russ.] (Leningrad, 1938).

Ormanian, M., *The Church of Armenia* (London, 1955).

Oskean, H., 'The Princedom of the Gnunis' [in Arm.], *Handes Amsorya*, LXV (1951).

Peeters, P., 'L'intervention politique de Constance II dans la Grande Arménie en 338', *Bull. de la cl. des lettr., Acad. roy. de Belgique*, 5th ser., XVII (1931).

Peeters, P., 'Les débuts du christianisme en Géorgie d'après les sources hagiographiques', *AB*, L (1932).

Peeters, P., 'Les Khazars dans la Passion de S. Abo de Tiflis', *AB*, LII (1934).

Peeters, P., 'Sainte Sousanik, martyre en Arméno-Géorgie', *AB*, LIII (1935).

Peeters, P., 'S. Grégoire l'Illuminateur dans le calendrier lapidaire de Naples', *AB*, LX (1942).

Peradze, G., 'Die Anfänge des Mönchtums in Georgien', *ZKG*, XLVI (1927).

Peradze, G., 'Les monuments liturgiques prébyzantins en langue géorgienne', *Le Muséon*, XLV (1932).

Sköld, H., 'L'origine des Mamikoniens, d'après Moïse de Khorène', *Revue des Etudes arm.* V (1925).

Tamarati, M., *L'Eglise géorgienne des origines jusqu'à nos jours* (Rome, 1910).

T'aqaishvili, E., 'Georgian Chronology and the Beginning of Bagratid Rule in Georgia', *Georgica*, I (1935).

Tarchnišvili, M., 'Die Legende der hl. Nino und die Geschichte des georgischen Nationalbewusstseins', *BZ*, XL (1940).

Tarchnišvili, M., 'Die Enstehung und Entwicklung der kirchlichen Autokephalie Georgiens', *Kyrios*, V (1940–1); *Le Muséon*, LXXIII (1960).

Tarchnišvili, M., 'Sources arméno-géorgienennes de l'histoire ancienne de l'Eglise de Géorgie', *Le Muséon*, LX (1947).

Tarchnišvili, M., 'Die heilige Nino, Bekehrerin von Georgien', *ASBM* (Rome, 1953).

Ter-Mikelian, A., *Die armenische Kirche in ihren Beziehungen zu den byzantinischen (vom IV. bis zum XIII. Jahrhundert)* (Leipzig, 1891).

Ter-Minassiantz, E., *Die armenische Kirche in ihren Beziehungen zu den syrischen Kirchen bis zum Ende des 13. Jahrhunderts nach den armenischen und syrischen Quellen* (Leipzig, 1904).

Ter-Mkrttschian, K., *Die Paulikianer im byzantinischen Kaiserreiche und verwandte ketzerische Erscheinungen in Armenien* (Leipzig, 1893).

Thopdschian, H., *Die innere Zustände von Armenien unter Asot I* (Berlin, 1904).

Thopdschian, H., *Politische und Kirchengeschichte Armeniens unter Asot I. und Smbat I., nach armenischen, arabischen, syrischen, und byzantinischen Quellen bearbeitet* (Berlin, 1905).

Toumanoff, C., 'On the Relationship between the Founder of the Empire of Trebizond and the Georgian Queen Thamar', *SP*, XV (1940).

Toumanoff, C., 'The Fifteenth-century Bagratids and the Institution of Collegial Sovereignty in Georgia', *Trad.* VII (1949–51).

Toumanoff, C., 'The Early Bagratids: Remarks in Connexion with Recent Publications', *Le Muséon*, LXII (1949).

Toumanoff, C., 'Iberia on the Eve of Bagratid Rule: an Enquiry into the Political History of Eastern Georgia between the VIth and the IXth Century', *Le Muséon*, LXV (1952).

Toumanoff, C., 'Christian Caucasia between Byzantium and Iran: New Light from Old Sources', *Trad.* X (1954).

Toumanoff, C., 'Chronology of the Kings of Abasgia and Other Problems', *Le Muséon*, LXIX (1956).

Toumanoff, C., 'A Note on the Orontids', *Le Muséon*, LXXII–LXXIII (1959–60).

Toumanoff, C., 'Introduction to Christian Caucasian History', *Trad.* XV (1959); XVII (1961).

Tournebize, F., *Histoire politique et religieuse de l'Arménie* (Paris, 1910).

Tournebize, F., 'Aghovanie (Albanie du Caucase)', *DHGE*.

Tournebize, F., 'Arménie', *DHGE*.

Trever, K., *Studies in the History and Culture of Caucasian Albania* [in Russ.] (Moscow/Leningrad, 1959).

Vasmer, R., *Chronologie der arabischen Statthalter von Armenien unter den Abbasiden, von as-Saffach bis zum Krönung Aschots I., 750–887* (Vienna, 1931).

Vaxušt of Georgia, *Geographical Description of Georgia*, Georgian text and French transl. M. F. Brosset, *Description géogr. de la Gé. par le Tsarévitch Wakhoucht* (St Petersburg, 1842); publ. and Russian transl. M. J̌anašvili (Tiflis, 1904); publ. Tʻ. Lomouri and N. Berjenišvili (Tiflis, 1941).

Weber, S., *Die katholische Kirche in Armenien. Ihre Begründung und Entwicklung vor der Trennung* (Freiburg i. B., 1903).

Yovsepean (Hovsepian), G., *Xaḷbakids or Pṛošids* [in Arm.], I (Vaḷaršapat, 1928); II (Jerusalem, 1944).

B. ARTS AND LETTERS

Abelyan, M., *History of Ancient Armenian Literature* [in Arm.], 2 vols. (Erevan, 1944, 1946; Beirut, 1955, 1959); Russian transl. (Erevan, 1948).

Agababyan, E., *The Composition of the Domed Structures of Georgia and Armenia* [in Russ.] (Erevan, 1950).

Akinean, N., 'Armenian Translations of Holy Scripture' [in Arm.], *Handes Amsorya*, XLIX (1935).

Alpoyačean, A., *History of the Armenian Schools* [in Arm.], I (Cairo, 1947).

Amiranašvili, Š., *History of Georgian Art* [in Russ.], I (Moscow, 1950).

Ancient Armenian Miniature Painting [in Russ.], Arm. SSR. (Erevan, 1952).

Ap'ak'ije *et al.*, *Mcxeta: Results of the Archaeological Investigations*, I (*Archaeological Monuments of Armazis-Xevi in the Light of the Excavations of 1937–1946*) [in Russ.] (Tiflis, 1958).

Ars georgica: Works of the Institute of the History of Georgian Art [in Georg. and Russ.] (Tiflis, 1955 ff.).

Bak'raje, D., *Archaeological Journey through Guria and Ačara* [in Russ.] (St Petersburg, 1873).

Baltrušaitis, J., *Etudes sur l'art médiéval en Géorgie et en Arménie* (Paris, 1929).

Baltrušaitis, J., *Le problème de l'ogive en Arménie* (Paris, 1936).

Basmajean, K., *Masters of Ancient Armenian Art* [in Arm.] (Paris, 1926).

Blake, R. P., 'Georgian Theological Literature', *JTS*, XXVI (1924).

Blake, R. P., 'Ancient Georgian Versions of the Old Testament', *HTR*, XIX (1926).

Blake, R. P., 'Georgian Secular Literature, Epic, Romantic, and Lyric (1100–1800)', *Harvard Studies and Notes in Philology and Literature*, XV (1933).

Brosset, M. F., *Les ruines d'Ani, capitale de l'Arménie sous les rois Bagratides aux X⁰ et XI⁰ siècles* (St Petersburg, 1860–1).

Buniatov, N. and Jaralov, Ju., *The Architecture of Armenia* [in Russ.] (Moscow, 1950).

Buxton, D., *Transcaucasia* (Cambridge, 1934) (Russian Mediaeval Architecture, II).

Č'ubinašvili (Tschubinaschwili), G., 'Die christliche Kunst im Kaukasus und ihr Verhältnis zur allgemeinen Kunstgeschichte', *Monatshefte f. Kunstwiss.* XV (1922), 217–37. A critical evaluation of J. Strzygowski, *Die Baukunst der Armenier und Europa*, see below.

Č'ubinašvili, G., *Die georgische Kunst und die Probleme ihrer Entwicklung* (Berlin, 1930).

Č'ubinašvili, G., *History of Georgian Art* [in Georg.], I (Tiflis, 1936).

Č'ubinašvili, G., *The Georgian Gold and Silver Repoussé Work (ok'romčedloba): Researches in the History of Medieval Georgian Art* [in Georg.] (Tiflis, 1959).

Č'ubinašvili, G. and Severov, N., *Development of Georgian Architecture* [in Russ.] (Tiflis, 1936).

Dashian (Tašean), J., *Outline of Armenian Palaeography* [in Arm.] (Vienna, 1898).

Der Nersessian, S., *Manuscrits arméniens illustrés des XII⁰, XIII⁰ et XIV⁰ siècles*, 2 vols. (Paris, 1936, 1937).

Der Nersessian, S., 'The Armenian Chronicle of the Constable Smpad or of the "Royal Historian"', *DOP*, XIII (1959).

Frasson, G., *L'architettura armena et quella di Bisanzio* (Rome, 1939).

Garitte, G., *Documents pour l'étude du livre d'Agathange* (Vatican City, 1946) (Studi e Testi, 127).

Garitte, G., *La Narratio de rebus Armeniae. Edition critique et commentaire* (Louvain, 1952) (*CSCO*, cxxxii, Subs. 4).

Gordeev, D., *Historical Monuments of Soviet Armenia* [in Arm.] (Erevan, 1937–47).

Gordeev, D., 'Georgian Art' [in Russ.], *Great Soviet Encyclopaedia.*

Historical Monuments of Soviet Armenia [in Arm.] (Erevan, 1937–47).

Inglisian, V., *Das armenische Schrifttum* (Linz, 1929).

Ingoroqva, P., *Old-Georgian Ecclesiastical Poetry* [in Georg.] (Tiflis, 1913).

Ingoroqva, P., *George Merč'ule, a Georgian Author of the Tenth Century* [in Georg.] (Tiflis, 1954).

Javaxišvili, I., *Ancient Georgian Historical Writing* [in Georg.] (Tiflis, 1921) (The Aims, Sources, and Methods of History, 1).

Javaxišvili, I., *Georgian Palaeography* [in Georg.] (Tiflis, 1926) (The Aims, Sources, and Methods of History, 3); 2nd ed. (Tiflis, 1949).

Javaxišvili, I., *Ancient Armenian Historiography* [in Georg.] (Tiflis, 1935).

Javaxišvili, I., *Basic Problems of the History of Georgian Music* [in Georg.] (Tiflis, 1938).

Kakabaje, K. and Baramije, A., *History of Georgian Literature* [in Georg.] (Tiflis, 1954).

Karst, J., *Littérature géorgienne chrétienne* (Paris, 1934).

Karst, J., *La littérature arménienne* (Paris, 1937).

Kekelije, K., *Early-Feudal Literature of Georgia* [in Georg.] (Tiflis, 1935).

Kekelije, K., *Periods of Feudal Georgian Literature* [in Georg.] (Tiflis, 1939).

Kekelije, K., *Survey of the History of Old-Georgian Literature* [in Russ.] (Tiflis, 1939).

Kekelije, K., *History of Georgian Literature* [in Georg.], 2 vols. (Tiflis, 1923–4, 1941–3, 1951).

Kekelije, K., *Monumenta hagiographica georgica* (Tiflis, 1918, 1946).

Khatchatrian, A., 'L'architecture arménienne. Essai analytique', *Vostan*, i (1948–9).

Lang, D. M., *The Wisdom of Balahvar. A Christian Legend of the Buddha* (London, 1957).

Lang, D. M., 'Recent Work on the Georgian New Testament', *BSOAS*, xix (1957).

Lyonnet, S., *Les versions arménienne et géorgienne* (Paris, 1935) (M. Lagrange, 'Introduction à l'étude du Nouveau Testament', chap. 10).

Lyonnet, S., *Les origines de la version arménienne et le Diatessaron* (Rome, 1950) (Biblica et Orientalia, 13).

Macler, F., *Miniatures arméniennes* (Paris, 1913).

Macler, F., 'L'architecture arménienne et ses rapports avec l'art syrien', *Syria*, i (1920).

Macler, F., *Documents d'art arménien* (Paris, 1924).

Macler, F., *L'enluminure arménienne profane* (Paris, 1928).

Manandyan, Y., *The Hellenistic School and the Phases of its Development* [in Arm.] (Vienna, 1928).

Mariès, L., *Le De Deo d'Eznik de Kolb connu sous le nom de Contre les sectes* (Paris, 1924).

Marr, N., 'John Petrici, Georgian Neoplatonist of the 11th–12th Century' [in Russ.], *Zapiski vostočn. otd. Imp. Russ. Archeol. Obšč.* xii (1900).

Marr, N., *Monuments of Armenian Architecture. Ani, the Palatine Church* [in Russ.] (Petrograd, 1915).

Marr, N., *Description of the Palatine Church of Ani* [in Russ.] (Petrograd, 1916).

Marr, N., 'Ani, la ville arménienne en ruines, d'après les fouilles de 1892–1893 et de 1904–1917', *Revue des Etudes arm.* I (1921).

Marr, N., *Ani* [in Russ.] (Leningrad/Moscow, 1934).

Merk, A., *Die Miniaturen des armenischen Evangeliar no. 697 der Wiener Mechtharisten-Bibliothek* (Vienna, 1927).

Molitor, J., *Monumenta iberica antiquiora* (Louvain, 1956) (*CSCO*, CLXVI, Subs. 10).

Orbeli, I., *The Ruins of Ani* [in Russ.] (St Petersburg, 1913).

Orbeli, I., 'Armenian Art', 'Georgian Art' [in Russ.], *Novyj Enciklopedičeskij Slovar'*.

Peeters, P., 'Pour l'histoire des origines de l'alphabet arménien', *Revue des Etudes arm.* IX (1919).

Peradze, G., 'Die altgeorgische Literatur und ihre Probleme', *OC*, 3rd ser., II (1927).

Peradze, G., 'Die alt-christliche Literatur in der georgischen Überlieferung', *OC*, 3rd ser., III–VIII/IX (1928–34).

Pope, A. U., 'Iranian and Armenian Contributions to the Beginnings of Gothic Architecture', *Armenian Quart.* I, 2 (1948).

Rice, T., 'The Role of Georgia in Mediaeval Art', *Asiatic Rev.* (Jan. 1930).

Sakissian, A., *Tissus royaux arméniens des X*, *XI* et *XIII* siècles* (Paris, 1935).

Sakissian, A., *Pages d'art arménien* (Paris, 1940).

Sakissian, A., 'Notes on the Sculpture of the Church of Akhtamar', *The Art Bull.* XXV (1943).

Saruxan, A., 'The City of Ani' [in Arm.], *Handes Amsorya*, LIV (1940).

Severov, N., *Monuments of Georgian Architecture* [in Russ.] (Moscow, 1947).

Strzygowski, J. v., *Das Edjmiadzin Evangeliar* (Vienna, 1891).

Strzygowski, J. v., *Kleinarmenische Miniaturmalerei* (Tübingen, 1907).

Strzygowski, J. v., *Ein zweites Etschmiadzin Evangeliar* (Vienna, 1911).

Strzygowski, J. v., *Die Baukunst der Armenier und Europa*, 2 vols. (Vienna, 1918).

Svirin, A., *The Miniature in Ancient Armenia* [in Russ.] (Moscow/Leningrad, 1939).

T'aqaišvili, E., *Archaeological Excursions, Researches, and Notes* [in Georg.], 2 vols. (Tiflis, 1897, 1914); [in Russ.], 5 vols. (Tiflis, 1905–15).

T'aqaišvili, E., *Album d'architecture géorgienne* (Tiflis, 1924).

Tarchnišvili, M., 'Zwei georgische Lektionarfragmente aus dem 5. und 8. Jahrhundert', *Kyrios*, VI (1942).

Tarchnišvili, M., 'Les récentes découvertes épigraphiques et littéraires en géorgien', *Le Muséon*, LXIII (1950).

Tarchnišvili, M., 'Kurzer Überblick über den Stand der georgischen Literaturforschung', *OC*, XXXVII (1953).

Tarchnišvili, M., 'Die Anfänge der schriftstellerischen Tätigkeit des hl. Euthymius und der Aufstand von Bardas Skleros', *OC*, XXXVIII (1954).

Tarchnišvili, M., *Geschichte der kirchlichen georgischen Literatur* (Vatican City, 1955) (Studi e Testi, 185).

Thorossian, H., *Histoire de la littérature arménienne* (Paris, 1951).

Tokarsky, N., *Architecture in Ancient Armenia* [in Russ.] (Erevan, 1946).

Tolmačevskaja, N., *Frescoes of Ancient Georgia* [in Russ.] (Tiflis, 1931).

Tolmačevskaja, N., *The Decorative Heritage of the Georgian Frescoes* [in Russ.] (Tiflis, 1939).

T'oramanyan, T., *Materials for the History of Armenian Architecture* [in Arm.], 2 vols. (Erevan, 1942, 1948).

Toumanoff, C., 'Medieval Georgian Historical Literature (VIIth–XVth Centuries)', *Trad.* I (1943).

Toumanoff, C., 'The Oldest Manuscript of the Georgian Annals', *Trad.* V (1947).

Toumanoff, C., 'Caucasia and Byzantine Studies', *Trad.*, XII (1956).

Toumanoff, C. 'On the Date of Pseudo-Moses of Chorene', *Handes Amsorya* LXXV (1961).

Van den Oudenrijn, M.-A., 'Eine armenische Übersetzung der Summa Theologica des hl. Thomas im 14. Jahrhundert', *Divus Thomas* (1930).

Weitzmann, K., 'Die altarmenische Buchmalerei des 10. und beginnenden 11. Jahrhunderts', *Istanbul. Forschungen*, IV (1933).

Yarut'yunyan (Arutjunjan), V., *Zvart'noc'* [in Arm. and Russ.] (Erevan, 1947).

Yarut'yunyan (Arutjunjan), V., *Architectural Monuments of Dvin* [in Russ.] (Izvestija Akad. Nauk Arm. SSR. 1947).

Yarut'yunyan (Arutjunjan), V., 'Architecture of the Patriarchal Palace in Dvin' [in Russ.], *Collection of Learned Works of the Polytechnical Institute of Erevan*, III (1948).

Yarut'yunyan (Arutjunjan), V., *Architectural Monuments of Dvin of the 5th to the 7th Centuries* [in Arm.] (Erevan, 1950).

(Y)arut'yunyan, V. and Safaryan, S., *Monuments of Armenian Architecture* [in Russ.] (Moscow, 1951).

Yovsepean (Hovsepian), G., *Materials for the Study of Armenian Art and Culture* [in Arm.], 3 vols. (Jerusalem, 1935; New York, 1943, 1944).

Zarphanalean, K., *Catalogue of Ancient Armenian Translations* [in Arm.] (Venice, 1889).

Zarphanalean, K., *Literary History of Ancient Armenia* [in Arm.], 4th ed. (Venice, 1932).

Addenda: see below, p. 1041.

CHAPTER XV. GOVERNMENT, SOCIETY AND ECONOMIC LIFE UNDER THE ABBASIDS AND FATIMIDS

I. BIBLIOGRAPHIES

American Historical Association, *Guide to Historical Literature* (New York, 1961), section M, 'The Muslim World', pp. 218–32.

Brockelmann, C., *Geschichte der arabischen Litteratur*, 5 vols. (Weimar and Leiden, 1898–1942).

Ettinghausen, R. (ed.), *A selected and annotated bibliography of books and periodicals in western languages dealing with the Near and Middle East, with special emphasis on mediaeval and modern times* (Washington, 1952) (supplt., 1954).

Gabrieli, F., 'Studi di storia musulmana, 1940–1950', *RSI*, LXII (1950), 99–111.

Gabrieli, G., *Manuale di bibliografia musulmana* (Rome, 1916).

Gamal el-Din el-Shayyal, 'A sketch of Arabic historical works published in Egypt and the Near East during the last five years (1940–1945)', *Royal Society of Historical Studies, Proceedings*, ɪ (Cairo, 1951), 143–74.

Mayer, L. A., *Bibliography of Moslem Numismatics, India excepted*, 2nd ed. (London, 1954).

Minorsky, V., 'Les études historiques et géographiques sur la Perse', *Acta orientalia*, x (1932), 278–93; xvɪ (1937), 49–58; xxɪ (1951), 108–23.

Pearson, J. D., *Index Islamicus* (Cambridge, 1958); supplt. (1962).

Pfannmüller, G., *Handbuch der Islam-Literatur* (Berlin and Leipzig, 1923).

Rizzitano, U., 'Studi di storia islamica in Egitto (1940–1952)', *Oriente moderno*, xxxɪɪɪ (Nov. 1953), 442–56.

Sauvaget, J., *Introduction à l'histoire de l'orient musulman*, revised by C. Cahen (Paris, 1961).

Spuler, B. and Forrer, L., *Der Vordere Orient in islamischer Zeit* (Bern, 1954).

Storey, C. A., *Persian Literature: a Bio-bibliographical Survey*, 1 vol. in 3 (London, 1927–53).

II. WORKS ON HISTORIANS

Gibb, H. A. R., 'Ta'rīkh', *Encyclopedia of Islam*, Supplt. [see Gen. Bibl. ɪ].

Lewis, B. and Holt, P. M. (eds.), *Historians of the Middle East* (London, 1962).

Margoliouth, D. S., *Lectures on Arabic Historians* (Calcutta, 1930).

Rosenthal, F., *A History of Muslim Historiography* (Leiden, 1952).

III. WORKS OF REFERENCE

Encyclopedia of Islam [see Gen. Bibl. ɪ].

Hazard, H. W. and Cooke, H. L., *Atlas of Islamic History*, 3rd ed. (Princeton, 1954).

Hinz, W., *Islamische Masse und Gewichte: umgerechnet ins metrische System* (Leiden, 1955).

Lane-Poole, S., *The Mohammedan Dynasties* [see Gen. Bibl. ɪɪɪ A].

Pareja, F. M., *Islamologia*, Italian version (Rome, 1951); Spanish version (Madrid, 1952–4).

Roolvink, R. and others, *Historical Atlas of the Muslim Peoples* (Amsterdam, 1957).

Zambaur, E. de, *Manuel de Généalogie et de Chronologie pour l'histoire de l'Islam* (Hanover, 1927).

IV. GENERAL WORKS

Cahen, C. (ed.), *L'Elaboration de l'Islam* (Paris, 1961).

Diehl, C. and Marçais, G., *Le monde oriental de 395 à 1081* [see Gen. Bibl. v].

Gabrieli, F., *Gli Arabi* (Florence, 1957).

Gaudefroy-Demombynes, M. and Platonov, S. F., *Le monde musulman et byzantin jusqu'aux croisades* [see Gen. Bibl. v].

Grunebaum, G. E. von, *Medieval Islam* [see Gen. Bibl. v].

Grunebaum, G. E. von, *Islam, Essays in the Nature and Growth of a Cultural Tradition* (London, 1955).

Hitti, P. K., *History of the Arabs* [see Gen. Bibl. v].

Kremer, A., *Culturgeschichte des Orients unter den Chalifen*, 2 vols. (Vienna, 1875–7); partial translation, *The Orient under the Caliphs* (Calcutta, 1920).

Levy, R., *The Social Structure of Islam*; being the second edition of the *Sociology of Islam* (Cambridge, 1957).

Lewis, B., *The Arabs in History* [see Gen. Bibl. v].

Muir, Sir William, *The Caliphate, its Rise, Decline, and Fall*, new and rev. ed. by T. H. Weir (Edinburgh, 1915).

Müller, F. A., *Der Islam im Morgen*, 2 vols. (Berlin, 1885–7).

Perroy, E. and others, *Le Moyen Age*, 2nd ed. (Paris, 1957) [see particularly pt. I, chs. IV and VI; pt. II, ch. II].

Setton, K. M. (editor-in-chief), *A History of the Crusades*, I, chs. III–V, XIV, XVI and XVIII; II, chs. XIX–XXII [see Gen. Bibl. v].

Weil, G., *Geschichte der Chalifen*, 5 vols. (Stuttgart, 1846–62).

V. WORKS ON SPECIAL PERIODS, AREAS, OR TOPICS

(A) ABBASID CALIPHATE

Abbott, N., *Two Queens of Baghdad* (Chicago, 1946).

Ayalon, D., 'Studies on the Transfer of the ʿAbbāsid Caliphate from Bagdād to Cairo', *Arabica*, VII (1960), 41–59.

Bowen, H., *The Life and Times of ʿAlī ibn ʿĪsà* (Cambridge, 1928).

Cahen, C., 'Fiscalité, propriété, antagonismes sociaux en Haute-Mésopotamie au temps des premiers Abbasides d'après Denys de Tell-Mahre', *Arabica*, I (1954), 136–52.

Dietrich, A., 'Das politische Testament des zweiten Abbasiden-khalifen al-Mansur', *Der Islam*, XXX (1952), 133–65.

Frye, R. N., 'The Role of Abu Muslim in the Abbasid Revolt', *Moslem World*, XXXVII (1947), pp. 28–38.

Gabrieli, F., *Al Maʾmūn e gli Alidi* (Leipzig, 1929).

Gabrieli, F., 'La Successione di Hārūn al-Rašid', *Rivista degli Studi Orientali*, XI (1928), 341–97.

Goitein, S. D., 'The Rise of the Near Eastern Bourgeoisie in Early Islamic Times', *J. World History*, III (1957), 583–604.

Mez, A., *Die Renaissance des Islāms* (Heidelberg, 1922); English transl. by Salahuddin Khuda Bukhsh and D. S. Margoliouth (London, 1937).

Minorsky, V., *La domination des Dailamites* (Paris, 1932).

Moscati, S., 'Le Califat d'al-Hadi', *Studia orientalia*, 13/IV (Helsinki, 1946), pp. 1–28

Moscati, S., 'Studi sul califfato di al-Mahdi', *Orientalia*, n.s. XIV (1945), 300–54; n.s. XV (1946), 155–79.

Moscati, S., 'Studi su Abū Muslim', *Rendiconti della Classe di Scienze morali, storiche, e filologiche, Acc. Naz. dei Lincei*, ser. 8, IV (1949), 323–35, 474–95; V (1950), 89–105.

Moscati, S., 'La Crisi dell'Impero arabo', *Oriente in Nuova Luce* (Florence, 1954), pp. 119–47.

Noeldeke, T., *Orientalistische Skizzen* (Berlin, 1892); transl. J. S. Black, *Sketches from Eastern History* (London, 1892).

Sourdel, D., 'La politique religieuse des successeurs d'al-Mutawakkil', *Studia Islamica*, XIII (1961), 5–21.

Vloten, G. van, *De opkomst der Abbasiden in Chorasan* (Leiden, 1890).

(B) EGYPT AND SYRIA

Becker, C. H., *Beiträge zur Geschichte Ägyptens* (Strasbourg, 1902–3).
Cahen, C., *La Syrie du nord à l'époque des croisades et la principauté franque d'Antioche* (Paris, 1940).
Canard, M., 'L'impérialisme des Fatimides et leur propagande', *Annales de l'Institut d'Etudes Orientales d'Alger*, VI (1942–7), 156–93.
Canard, M., *Histoire de la dynastie des Hamdanides* (Algiers, 1951).
Hassan, Z. M., *Les Tulunides: étude de l'Egypte musulmane à la fin du IXe siècle, 868–905* (Paris, 1933).
Hitti, P. K., *History of Syria* (London, 1951).
Hrbek, I., 'Die Slawen im Dienste der Fatimiden', *Archiv Orientální*, XXI (1953), 543–81.
Lammens, H., *La Syrie, précis historique* (Beirut, 1921).
Lane-Poole, S., *History of Egypt in the Middle Ages* (London, 1925).
Munier, H. and Wiet, G., *L'Egypte byzantine et musulmane* (Cairo, 1932).
O'Leary, De Lacy, *A Short History of the Fatimid Caliphate* (London, 1923).
Wiet, G., *L'Egypte arabe*, ed. G. Hanotaux, *Histoire de la Nation égyptienne*, IV (Paris, 1937).
Wüstenfeld, F., *Geschichte der Fatimiden Chalifen* (Göttingen, 1881).

(C) PERSIA AND CENTRAL ASIA

Barthold, V. V., *Histoire des Turcs d'Asie centrale*, transl. by M. Donskis (Paris, 1945).
Barthold, W., *Turkestan down to the Mongol Invasion* (London, 1928).
Bosworth, C. E., 'Ghaznavid Military Organization', *Der Islam*, XXXVI (1960), 37–77.
Dunlop, D. M., *The History of the Jewish Khazars* (Princeton, 1954).
Frye, R. N. and Sayili, A. M., 'Turks in the Middle East before the Saljuqs', *J. Amer. Oriental Soc.* LXIII (July–September 1943), 194–207.
Nazim, M., *The Life and Times of Sultan Mahmud of Ghazna* (Cambridge, 1931).
Pritsak, O., 'Die Karakhaniden', *Der Islam*, XXXI (1953), 17–68.
Pritsak, O., 'Karachanidische Streitfragen 1–4', *Oriens*, III (Leiden, 1950), 209–28.
Sadighi, G. H., *Les mouvements religieux iraniens* (Paris, 1938).
Spuler, B., *Iran in früh-islamischer Zeit* (Wiesbaden, 1952).

(D) ANATOLIA AND THE CAUCASUS

Cahen, C., 'La première pénétration turque en Asie-Mineure', *B*, XVIII (1948), 5–67.
Gordlevsky, V. A., *Gosudarstvo Sel'džukidov Maloi Azii* [*The Seljuq State in Asia Minor*] (Moscow and Leningrad, 1941).
Minorsky, V., *Studies in Caucasian History* (London, 1953).
Wittek, P., 'Deux chapitres de l'histoire des Turcs de Roum', *B*, XI (1936), 285–319.

(E) ECONOMIC AND SOCIAL

Ashtor, E., 'Le coût de la vie dans l'Egypte médiévale', *J. Econ. Social Hist. Orient*, III (1960), 56–77.

Ashtor, E., 'Essai sur les prix et les salaires dans l'empire califien', *Rivista degli Studi orientali*, XXXVI (1961), 19–69.

Brunschvig, R., 'Urbanisme médiéval et droit musulman', *Revue des études islamiques*, XV (1947), 127–55.

Cahen, C., 'L'évolution de l'iqta' du IXᵉ au XIIIᵉ siècle: contributions à une histoire comparée des sociétés médiévales', *Annales: économies, sociétés, civilisations*, VIII (1953), 25–52.

Cahen, C., 'Zur Geschichte der städtischen Gesellschaft im islamischen Orient des Mittelalters', *Saeculum*, IX (1958), 59–76.

Cahen, C., 'Mouvements populaires et autonomisme urbain dans l'Asie musulmane du moyen âge', *Arabica*, V (1958), 225–50; VI (1959), 25–56, 223–65.

Dennett, D. C., *Conversion and the Poll Tax in Early Islam* (Cambridge, Mass., 1950).

Grunebaum, G. E. von, 'Die islamische Stadt', *Saeculum*, VI (1955), 138–53.

Heyd, W., *Histoire du commerce du Levant au moyen âge* [see Gen. Bibl. v].

Hourani, G. F., *Arab Seafaring in the Indian Ocean in Ancient and Early Medieval Times* (Princeton, 1951).

Lewis, A. R., *Naval Power and Trade in the Mediterranean, A.D. 500–1100* (Princeton, 1951).

Løkkegaard, F., *Islamic Taxation in the Classic Period, with Special Reference to Circumstances in Iraq* (Copenhagen, 1950).

Massignon, L., 'La "Futuwwa" ou "pacte d'honneur artisanal" entre les travailleurs musulmans au moyen âge', *La nouvelle Clio*, IV (May 1952), 171–98.

Poliak, A. N., 'La féodalité islamique', *Revue des études islamiques*, X (1936), 247–65.

(F) GOVERNMENT AND LAW

Arnold, T. W., *The Caliphate* (Oxford, 1924).

Becker, C. H., 'Barthold's Studien über Kalif und Sultans', *Der Islam*, VI (1915–16), 350–412.

Gaudefroy-Demombynes, M., 'Notes sur l'histoire de l'organisation judiciaire en pays d'Islam', *Revue des études islamiques*, XIII (1939), 109–47.

Goldziher, I., *Vorlesungen über den Islam* (Heidelberg, 1910); French translation, *Le dogme et la loi de l'Islam: histoire du développement dogmatique et juridique de la religion musulmane* (Paris, 1920); 2nd ed. (1958).

Macdonald, D. B., *Development of Muslim Theology, Jurisprudence and Constitutional Theory* (New York, 1903).

Santillana, D., *Istituzioni di diritto musulmano malichita, con riguardo anche al sistema sciafiita*, 2nd ed., 2 vols. (1938).

Schacht, J., *The Origins of Muhammadan Jurisprudence* (Oxford, 1950).

Sourdel, D., *Le vizirat 'abbāside de 749 à 936*, 2 vols. (Damascus, 1959–60).

Tyan, E., *Histoire de l'organisation judiciaire en pays de l'Islam*, 2 vols. (Paris, 1938–43).

Tyan, E., *Institutions du droit public musulman*, 2 vols. (Paris, 1954–6).

CHAPTER XVI. MUSLIM CIVILISATION IN THE ABBASID PERIOD

See also the bibliography for chapter xv.

I. WORKS OF REFERENCE

Bibliographies may be found in *Der Islam* and *Revue des études islamiques*.

Chauvin, V., *Bibliographie des ouvrages arabes ou relatifs aux Arabes publiés dans l'Europe chrétienne de 1810–1903* (Liège, 1892–1903).

Khalil Edhem, *Düvel-i islamiye* [revised edition of S. Lane-Poole, *Mohammedan Dynasties*] (Istanbul, 1927).

Miller, K., *Mappae Arabicae. Arabische Welt- und Länderkarten*, 6 vols. (Stuttgart, 1926–31).

Pfannmüller, G., *Handbuch der Islam-Literatur* (Berlin and Leipzig, 1923).

Sauvaget, J., *Introduction à l'histoire de l'Orient musulman : éléments de bibliographie* (Paris, 1943); 2nd ed., rev. by C. Cahen (Paris, 1961); English ed. in preparation.

Schwarz, P., *Iran im Mittelalter nach den arabischen Geographen* (Leipzig, 1896–1936).

And see the works cited under i–iv in the bibliography for chapter xv.

II. AUTHORITIES

(A) MUSLIM

(i) *Arabic*

Abdalqāhir al-Jurjānī, *Asrār al-balāgha*, ed. H. Ritter (Istanbul, 1954); transl. H. Ritter, *Die Geheimnisse der Wortkunst* (Wiesbaden, 1959).

Abu'l Faraj Iṣfahānī, *Kitāb al-aghānī* (Cairo, 1867–8; 1905); vol. xxi, ed. R. Brünnow (Leyden, 1888); new ed. of the whole work begun (Cairo, 1927 ff.).

Abu'l-Muṭahhar, *Ḥikāyah Abi'l-Qāsim al-Baghdādī*, ed. A. Mez (Heidelberg, 1902).

Abū Yūsuf Ya'qūb ibn Ibrāhīm, *Kitāb al-Kharāj* (Cairo, 1885); transl. E. Fagnan, *Le livre de l'impôt foncier* (Paris, 1921).

Aḥmad ibn abī Ṭāhir Ṭaifūr, *Sechster Band des Kitāb Baġdād*, ed. and transl. H. Keller (Leipzig, 1908).

Alf Laila wa-laila, ed. W. H. Macnaghten, 4 vols. (Calcutta, 1839–42). [Numerous edd.]

Anūshirwān ibn Khālid, *Histoire des Seldjoucides de l'Irâq par al-Bondari, d'après Imâd addin al-Kâtib al-Isfahāni*, ed. M. T. Houtsma (Leyden, 1889).

Ash'arī, *Maqālāt al-islāmiyyīn*, ed. H. Ritter, 2 vols. and index vol. (Istanbul, 1929–30).

Averroes, *Commentary on Plato's Republic*, ed. and transl. E. I. J. Rosenthal (Cambridge, 1956).

Averroes, *Kitāb faṣl al-maqāl*, ed. G. F. Hourani (Leiden, 1959); transl. G. F. Hourani (Gibb Memorial, n.s. xxi) (London, 1961).

Averroes, *Tahāfut at-tahāfut*, transl. S. van den Bergh (Gibb Memorial, n.s. XIX), 2 vols. (London, 1954).

Bāqillānī, *Kitāb al-bayān 'an al-farq bain al-mu'jizāt wa'l-karāmāt*, ed. R. J. McCarthy (Beirut, 1958).

Baqillānī, *I'jāz al-Qur'ān* (Cairo, 1349); and other edd.; transl. in part: *A Tenth-century Document of Arabic Literary Theory and Criticism. The sections on poetry of al-Bāqillānī's I'jāz al Qur'ān transl. and annotated* by G. E. von Grunebaum (Chicago, 1950).

Bāqillānī, *Kitāb al-luma'* and *Risālat istiḥsān al-khauḍ fī 'ilm al-kalām*, ed. and transl. R. J. McCarthy, *The Theology of al-Ash'ari* (Beirut, 1953).

Bāqillānī, *Kitāb at-tamhīd*, ed. Khudairī and A. H. Abū Rīda (Cairo, 1947); ed. R. J. McCarthy (Beirut, 1957).

Dīnawarī, *Kitāb al-Akhbār aṭ-ṭiwāl*, ed. V. Guirgass (Leyden, 1888).

Fragmenta Historicorum Arabicorum, ed. M. J. de Goeje, 2 vols. (Leyden, 1869, 1871).

Ghazzālī, *Iḥyā' 'ulūm ad-dīn*, 16 vols. (Cairo, 1356–7); *Analyse et index*, by G. H. Bousquet (Paris, 1955).

Ghazzālī, *Al-Iqtiṣād fī'l-i'tiqād* (Cairo, 1327); transl. M. Asín Palacios, *El justo medio en la creëncia* (Madrid, 1929).

Ghazzālī, *Al Munqiḍ min aḍ-ḍalāl* [many edd.]; transl. C. Barbier de Meynard, *JA*, ser. 7, IX (1873), 1–93; C. Field (London, 1909); W. M. Watt, *The Faith and Practice of al-Ghazali* (London and New York, 1953).

Ghazzālī, *Kīmiyā' as-sa'āda*, transl. in part H. Ritter, *Das Elixir der Glückseligkeit*... (Jena, 1923; Cologne, 1959).

Ghazzālī, *Persian Letters*, ed. A. Eghbal (Teheran, 1959).

Ghazzālī, *Tahāfut al-falāsifa*, ed. M. Bouyges (Beirut, 1927); S. Dunyā (Cairo, 1955); transl. S. A. Kamali (Lahore, 1958).

Hilāl ibn Muḥassin, *Kitāb al-Wuzarā*, ed. H. F. Amedroz (Beirut, 1904).

Hilāl b. Muḥassin, *Kitāb al-wuzarā'*. *Some Lost Fragments Collected and Edited by M. Awad* (Baghdad, 1948).

Hujwirī, *Kashf al-maḥjūb*, ed. V. A. Žukovskij (Leningrad, 1928); transl. R. A. Nicholson (Leyden and London, 1911).

Ibn abī Uṣaibi'a, '*Uyūn al-anbā*', ed. A. Müller (Cairo, 1882).

Ibn al-Athīr, *Chronicon*, ed. C. J. Tornberg, 14 vols. (Leyden, 1862–76).

Ibn Baṭṭa al-'Ukbarī, *Šarḥ al-ibāna*, ed. with French transl. H. Laoust (Damascus, 1958).

Ibn Ḥazm, *Kitāb al-faṣl fī'l-milal*, 5 vols. (Cairo, 1317–21); M. Asín Palacios, *Abenhazam de Córdoba y su Historia crítica de las ideas religiosas*, 5 vols. (Madrid, 1927–32).

Ibn Khaldūn, *Kitāb al-'Ibār*, 7 vols. (Cairo, 1867); *Prolégomènes*, ed. E. M. Quatremère, 3 vols. (Paris, 1858), *Notices et extraits des manuscrits*, XVI, 1; XVII, 1; XVIII, 1. French transl. G. de Slane, 3 vols. (Paris, 1862–8), *Notices et extraits des manuscrits*, XIX, 1; XX, 1; XXI, 1. English transl. F. Rosenthal (New York, 1958).

Ibn Khallikān, *Kitāb wafayāt al-a'yān*, 2 vols. (Cairo, 1882); ed. F. Wüstenfeld (Göttingen, 1835–43); English transl. G. de Slane, *Biographical Dictionary*, 4 vols. (Paris, 1843–71).

Ibn al-Qalānisī, *History of Damascus 363–555 A.H.*, ed. H. F. Amedroz (Beirut, 1908).

Ibn Qutaiba, *Kitāb al-Ma'ārif*, ed. F. Wüstenfeld (Göttingen, 1850).

Ibn Qutaiba, '*Uyūn al-akhbār* (Cairo, 1343–9, 1929–30).

Ibn aṭ-Ṭiqṭaqa, *Al-Fakhrī. Histoire du Khilafat et du Vizarat*, ed. H. Dérenbourg (Paris, 1895); French transl. E. Amar (Paris, 1910); English transl. C. E. J. Whitting (London, 1947).

Ikhwān aṣ-Ṣafā, *Rasā'il* (Bombay, 1887–8; Cairo, 1928; Beirut, 1957).

Jāḥiz, *Kitāb al-bayān wa't-tabyīn* (Cairo, 1313); ed. H. as-Sandūbī (Cairo, 1927).

Jāḥiz, *Kitāb al-bukhalā'*, ed. G. van Vloten (Leyden, 1900); (Cairo, 1948); French transl. C. Pellat (Paris, 1951).

Jāḥiz, *Kitāb al-ḥayawān* (Cairo, 1323–5/1905–7; 1357–64/1938–45).

Jāḥiz, *Kitāb at-tāj*, ed. Aḥmad Zakī Pasha (Cairo, 1914); French transl. C. Pellat, *Le livre de la couronne* (Paris, 1954).

Jahshiyārī, *Kitāb al-wuzarā'*, ed. H. von Mžik (Leipzig, 1926).

Kalabādī, *Kitāb at-ta'arruf li-madhab at-taṣawwuf*, ed. A. J. Arberry (London, 1934); transl. A. J. Arberry (Cambridge, 1935).

Kharrāz, *The Book of Truthfulness*, ed. and transl. A. J. Arberry (London, 1937).

Khayyāṭ, *Le livre du triomphe et de la réfutation d'Ibn ar-Rāwandī*, ed. H. S. Nyberg (Cairo, 1925).

Malatī, *Die Widerlegung der Irrgläubigen und Neuerer*, ed. S. Dedering (Istanbul, 1936).

Mas'ūdī, *Kitāb at-tanbīh wa'l-ishrāf*, ed. M. J. de Goeje (Leyden, 1894); French transl. A. Carra de Vaux (Paris, 1897).

Mas'ūdī, *Murūj adh-Dhahab*, ed. and transl. C. Barbier de Meynard and Pavet de Courteille, 9 vols. (Paris, 1861–77).

Māwardī, *Kitāb al-aḥkām as-sulṭāniyyah* (Cairo, 1881); French transl. E. Fagnan (Algiers, 1915).

Miskawaihi, Abū Shujā' Rūdhrāwarī and Hilāl ibn Muḥassin, *The Eclipse of the Abbasid Caliphate*, ed. and transl. H. F. Amedroz and D. S. Margoliouth, 7 vols. (Oxford, 1920–1).

Miskawaihi, *Al-Ḥikma al-khālida*, ed. 'A. Badawī (Cairo, 1952).

Muḥammad ibn Isḥāq an-Nadīm, *Kitāb al-Fihrist*, ed. G. Flügel, J. Roediger and A. Müller, 2 vols. (Leipzig, 1871–2).

Muḥāsibī, *Kitāb ar-ri'āya li-ḥuqūq Allāh*, ed. M. Smith (London, 1940).

Naubakhtī, *Firaq ash-Shī'a*, ed. H. Ritter (Istanbul, 1931).

Niffarī, *The Mawāqif and Mukhāṭabāt*, ed. A. J. Arberry (Gibb Memorial, n.s. ix). (London, 1935).

Niẓām al-Mulk, *Siyāsat-Nāmah*, ed. with French transl. C. Schefer (Paris, 1891–3); English transl. H. Darke (London, 1960).

al-Qāsim b. Ibrāhīm, *La lotta tra l'Islam e il Manicheismo: un libro di Ibn al-Muqaffa' contro il Corano, confutato da al-Q. b. I.*, ed. and transl. M. Guidi (Rome, 1927). [Cf. H. S. Nyberg, 'Zum Kampf zwischen Islam und Manichäismus', *Orient. Literatur-Zeitung*, xxxii (1929), 425–41.]

Qifṭī, *Ta'rīkh al-ḥukamā'*, ed. J. Lippert (Leipzig, 1903).

Qushairī, *ar-Risāla fī 'ilm at-taṣawwuf* [many edd.].

Rāzī, *Al-Razi's Buch der Geheimnisse*, transl. J. Ruska (Berlin, 1937).

Rāzī, *Opera philosophica fragmentaque quae supersunt*, ed. P. Kraus, pt. i (all published) (Cairo, 1939).

Sarakhsī, ed. F. Rosenthal, *Aḥmad b. aṭ-Ṭayyib as-Sarahsī* (New Haven, Conn., 1943) [a collection of his fragments].

Sarrāj, *Kitāb al-lumā, fi't-taṣawwuf*, ed. R. A. Nicholson (London and Leyden, 1914; A. J. Arberry, *Pages from the Kitāb al-Luma*...being the lacuna in the edition of R.A.N. (London, 1947).

Shahrastānī, *Kitāb al-milal wa'n-niḥal*, ed. W. Cureton (London, 1846); transl. T. Haarbrücker (Halle, 1850–1).

Sibṭ ibn al-Jauzī, *Mir'āt az-Zamān*, ed. J. Jewett (Chicago, 1907).

Sulamī, ʿAbd ar-Raḥmān, *Ṭabaqāt aṣ-Ṣūfiyya*, ed. N. Sharība (Cairo, 1953); ed. J. Pedersen (Leiden, 1960).

Suyūṭī, *Ta'rīkh al-Khulafā'* (Cairo, 1888); transl. H. S. Jarrett (Bibliotheca Indica) (Calcutta, 1880).

Ṭabarī, ʿAlī b. Rabban, *Firdaus al-ḥikma*, ed. M. Z. Siddiqi (Berlin, 1928).

Ṭabarī, ʿAlī b. Rabban, *Kitāb ad-dīn wa'd-daula*, ed. A. Mingana (Manchester, 1923); transl. M. Z. Siddiqi (Manchester, 1922).

Ṭabarī, Muḥammad b. Jarīr, *The Reign of al-Muʿtaṣim (833–842)*, transl. E. Marin (New Haven, Conn., 1951).

Ṭabarī, Muḥammad b. Jarīr, *Annales*, ed. M. J. de Goeje, 15 vols. (Leyden, 1879–1901).

Tanūkhī, Muḥassin, *Nishwār al-muḥāḍara*, pt. 1, ed. and transl. D. S. Margoliouth, *The Tabletalk of a Mesopotamian Judge* (London, 1921–2); pt. 2, *RAAD* x, xII; pt. 8, printed Damascus (1348/1930); pts. 2 and 8 transl. D. S. Margoliouth, *Islamic Culture* (1932 ff.).

Tauḥidī and Miskawaihi, *Kitāb al-hawāmil*, ed. A. Amīn and A. Ṣaqr (Cairo, 1951).

Tauḥidī, Abū Ḥayyān, *Kitāb al-imʾāʿ wa'l-muʾānasa*, ed. A. Amīn and A. Ṣaqr (Cairo, 1939–44).

Tauḥidī, Abū Ḥayyān, *Kitāb al-Ishārāt al-ilāhiyya*, ed. ʿA. Badawī (Cairo, 1950).

Tauḥidī, Abū Ḥayyān, *Kitāb al-Muqābasāt* (Cairo, 1929).

Yaḥyā b. ʿAdī, *Petits traités apologétiques*, ed. and transl. A. Périer (Paris, 1920).

Yaḥyā ibn Ādam, *Kitāb al-Kharāj*, ed. T. W. Juynboll (Leyden, 1896).

Yāqūt, *Dictionary of Learned Men*, ed. D. S. Margoliouth, 4 vols. (Leyden and London, 1907–13).

(ii) *Persian*

Baihaqī, Abu'l-Faḍl (d. 1077), *Ta'rīkh-i Baihaqī*, ed. Fayyāḍ and Ghanī (Teheran, 1945); ed. S. Nafīsī (Teheran, 1940–53).

Baihaqī, Abu'l-Faḍl, *Ta'rīkh-i-āl-i-Subuktigīn*, ed. W. H. Morley (Bibliotheca Indica) (Calcutta, 1862).

Gardīzī, *Zain al-Akhbār*, ed. M. Nazim (Berlin and London, 1928).

Ḥamdullāh Mustaufī, *Ta'rīkh-i-Guzīda*, ed. and transl. E. G. Browne (Gibb Memorial Series) (London, 1911, 1914).

Ibn Isfandiyār, *History of Ṭabaristān*, abridged transl. E. G. Browne (Gibb Memorial Series) (London, 1905).

Juwainī, *Ta'rīkh-i-Jahān-Gushā*, ed. Mīrzā Muḥammad, 2 vols. (Gibb Memorial Series) (London, 1912, 1916); ed. and transl. J. A. Boyle, 2 vols. (Manchester, 1958).

Minhāj-i-Sirāj al-Jūzjānī, *Ṭabaqāt-i-Nāṣirī: a General History of the Mohammedan Dynasties of Asia*, transl. H. G. Raverty (Bibliotheca Indica) (London, 1873–81).

Mirkhwānd, *Rauḍat uṣ-Ṣafā'* (Bombay, 1854–5; Lucknow, 1883). *Mirchond's Geschichte der Sultane aus dem Geschlechte Bujeh*, ed. and transl. F. Wilken (Berlin, 1835).

Rāwandī, *Rāḥat uṣ-Ṣudūr wa Āyat us-Surūr*, being a History of the Saljūqs, ed. Muḥammad Iqbāl (Gibb Memorial, n.s. II) (London, 1921).

(B) CHRISTIAN

(i) *Syriac*

Barhebraeus, *Chronicon Ecclesiasticum*, ed. and transl. J. B. Abbeloos and T. J. Lamy (Louvain, 1872–7).

Barhebraeus, *Chronicon Syriacum*, ed. P. Bedjan (Paris, 1890).

Dionysius of Tall Maḥray, *Chronique de Denys de Tell Mahré, quatrième partie*, ed. and transl. J. B. Chabot (Paris, 1895). [Review by F. Nau, *Bull. Critique de Littérature* (Paris), 15 June, 1896.]

Elias bar Shīnāyā, *Eliae Metropolitae Nisibeni opus chronologicum*, ed. E. W. Brooks and J. B. Chabot, *CSCO*, ser. III, vols. VII–VIII (Paris, 1909–10).

Elias bar Shīnāyā, *Fragmente syrischer und arabischer Historiker*, ed. F. Baethgen (Leipzig, 1884).

Michael the Syrian, *Chronique de Michel le Syrien, patriarche jacobite d'Antioche (1166–99)*, ed. and transl. J. B. Chabot (Paris, 1899–1911).

Thomas of Margā, *The Book of Governors: the Historia Monastica*, ed. and transl. E. A. W. Budge (London, 1893).

(ii) *Arabic*

Barhebraeus (Abu'l Faraj), *Ta'rīkh mukhtaṣar ad-duwal*, ed. A. Ṣāliḥānī (Beirut, 1890).

Eutychius (Sa'īd ibn Batrīq), *Annales*, ed. L. Cheikho, A. Carra de Vaux and H. Zayyat, *CSCO*, Script. Arabici, ser. III, vols. VI and VII (Paris, 1906–9).

Mārī ibn Sulaimān, 'Amr ibn Mattai and Ṣalībā ibn Yuḥannā, *Maris, Amri et Slibae De Patriarchis Nestorianorum Commentaria*, ed. H. Gismondi (Rome, 1896–9).

III. MODERN WORKS

Abbott, N., *Two Queens of Baghdad, Mother and Wife of Hārūn al-Rashīd* (Chicago, 1946).

Abd-el-Jalil, J., *Aspects intérieurs de l'Islam* (Paris, 1949).

The American Historical Association's Guide to Historical Literature (New York, 1961); esp. sections D, M and S.

Anawati, G. C. and Gardet, L., *Mistica musulmana* (Turin, 1960); French ed. (original), *Mystique musulmane* (Paris, 1961).

Andrae, T., *Islamische Mystiker* (Stuttgart, 1960) [Swedish original: 1947].

Annuaire du monde musulman, ed. L. Massignon, 4th ed. (Paris, 1954).

Arberry, A. J., *An Introduction to the History of Ṣūfism* (London, 1943).

Arberry, A. J., *Classical Persian Literature* (London, 1958).

Arberry, A. J., *Revelation and Reason in Islam* (London, 1957).

Arberry, A. J., *Sufism: an Account of the Mystics of Islam* (London, 1950).

Arnaldez, R., *Grammaire et théologie chez Ibn Ḥazm de Cordoue. Essai sur la structure et les conditions de la pensée musulmane* (Paris, 1956).

Arnold, T. W., *The Preaching of Islam: a History of the Propagation of the Muslim Faith*, 2nd ed. (London, 1913).

Arnold, T. W., *The Caliphate* (Oxford, 1924).

Arnold, T. W., *Painting in Islam: a Study of the Place of Pictorial Art in Muslim Culture* (Oxford, 1928).

Arnold, T. W. and Guillaume, A. (eds.), *The Legacy of Islam* (Oxford, 1931).

Asín Palacios, M., *Aben Masarra y su escuela, Orígenes de la filosofía hispano-musulmana* (Madrid, 1914).

Asín Palacios, M., 'La mystique d'al-Gazzali', *Mélanges de la faculté orientale de Beyrouth*, VII (1914–21), 67–104.

Atlas of the Arab World and the Middle East, with a Foreword by C. F. Beckingham (London and New York, 1960).

Barthold, W., 'Barthold's Studien über Kalif und Sultan. Besprochen und im Auszuge mitgeteilt von C. H. Becker', *Der Islam*, VI (1916), 350–412.

Barthold, W., *Histoire des Turcs d'Asie Centrale* (Paris, 1945).

Barthold, W., *Turkestan Down to the Mongol Invasion* (London, 1928).

Baumstark, A., *Geschichte der syrischen Literatur* (Bonn, 1922).

Becker, C. H., *Das Erbe der Antike im Orient und Okzident* (Leipzig, 1931).

Becker, C. H., *Christenthum und Islam* (Tübingen, 1907); transl. H. J. Chaytor (London, 1909).

Becker, C. H., *Vom Wesen und Werden der islamischen Welt. Islamstudien* (Leipzig, 1924–32).

Ben Shemesh, A., *Taxation in Islam*. I: *Yaḥyā ben Adam's Kitāb al Kharāj* (Leiden, 1958).

Berchem, M. van, *La propriété territoriale et l'impôt foncier sous les premiers califes. Etude sur l'impôt du Kharāg* (Geneva, 1886).

Bergsträsser, G., *Grundzüge des islamischen Rechts*, ed. J. Schacht (Berlin and Leipzig, 1935).

Bergsträsser, G., *Neue Materialien zu Ḥunain ibn Isḥāq's Galen-Bibliographie* (Leipzig, 1932).

Björkmann, W., 'Kapitalentstehung und Anlage im Islam', *Berlin. Univ. Mitt. d. Sem. f. orient. Sprachen*, Westasiat. Stu. XXXII (1929), 80–98.

Blachère, R., *Un poète arabe du IVe siècle de l'hégire (Xe siècle de J.-C.): Abou ṭ-Ṭayyib al-Motanabbi (Essai d'histoire littéraire)* (Paris, 1935).

Brockelmann, C., *Geschichte der islamischen Völker und Staaten* (Munich and Berlin, 1939); English transl. J. Carmichael and M. Perlmann (New York, 1947).

Brockelmann, C., *Geschichte der arabischen Litteratur* [see Gen. Bibl. v].

Browne, E. G., *Arabian Medicine* (Cambridge, 1921).

Browne, E. G., *A Literary History of Persia*, 2 vols. (London, 1902–6); 4 vols. (Cambridge, (1928–9).

Brunschvig, R. and Grunebaum, G. E. von (edd.), *Classicisme et déclin culturel dans l'histoire de l'Islam* (Paris, 1957); also G. E. von Grunebaum and W. Hartner, *Klassizismus und Kulturfall* (Frankfurt, 1960).

Buckler, F. W., *Harunu 'l-Rashid and Charles the Great* (Cambridge, Mass., 1931).

Caetani, L. (Duca di Sermoneta), *Annali dell'Islam* (Milan, 1905). [In progress.]

Canard, M., 'La guerre sainte dans le monde islamique et dans le monde chrétien', *Revue Africaine*, LXXIX (1936), 605–23.

Cantor, M., *Vorlesungen über Geschichte der Mathematik*, 2nd ed., I (Leipzig, 1894).

Carra de Vaux, A., *Les grands philosophes. Avicenne* (Paris, 1900).

Carra de Vaux, A., *Les grands philosophes. Gazali* (Paris, 1902).

Carra de Vaux, A., *Les penseurs de l'Islam*, 5 vols. (Paris, 1921–6).

Castro, A., *The Structure of Spanish History* (Princeton, 1954).

Cattenoz, H.-G., *Tables de Concordance des ères chrétienne et hégirienne*, 2nd ed. (Rabat, 1954).

Corbin, H., *Avicenne et le récit visionnaire*, 2 vols. (Bibliothèque iranienne, IV and V) (Paris, 1954); English transl. W. R. Trask (New York, 1960).

Cresswell, K. A. C., *A Short Account of Early Muslim Architecture* (Harmondsworth, Middlesex, 1958).

Creswell, K. A. C., *Early Muslim Architecture. Umayyads, Early Abbasids, and Tulunids* (Oxford, 1932–40).

Daniel, N., *Islam and the West* (Edinburgh, 1960).

Dennett, Jr., D. C., *Conversion and the Poll Tax in Early Islam* (Cambridge, Mass., 1950).

Diehl, C. and Marçais, G., *Le Monde Oriental de 395 à 1081* [see Gen. Bibl. V].

Diercks, G., *Die Araber im Mittelalter und ihr Einfluss auf die Cultur Europas*, 2nd ed. (Leipzig, 1882).

Dozy, R., *Histoire des Musulmans d'Espagne*, ed. E. Lévi-Provençal, 3 vols. (Leiden, 1932).

Drague, G., *Esquisse d'histoire religieuse du Maroc* (Paris, 1951).

Duval, R., *La littérature syriaque*, 3rd ed. (Paris, 1907).

Ess, J. van, *Die Gedankenwelt des Ḥārit al-Muḥāsibī* (Bonn, 1961).

Ettinghausen, R., *Arab Painting* (n.p., 1962).

Fahmy, A. M., *Muslim Sea-Power in the Eastern Mediterranean from the 7th to the 10th Century A.D.* (n.p., 1950).

Faris, Nabih Amin (ed.), *The Arab Heritage* (Princeton, 1946).

Farmer, H. G., *A History of Arabic Music to the 19th Century* (London, 1929).

Fattal, A., *Le statut légal des non-musulmans en pays d'Islam* (Beirut, 1958).

Fischel, W., *Jews in the Economic and Political Life of Mediaeval Islam* (London, 1937).

Fischel, W., 'The Origin of Banking in Mediaeval Islam', *JRAS* (1933), pp. 339–52.

Fries, N., *Das Heerwesen der Araber zur Zeit der Omaijaden nach Tabari*. Diss., Kiel (Tübingen, 1921).

Fritsch, E., *Islam und Christentum im Mittelalter* (Breslau, 1930).

Fück, J., 'Arabiya. Untersuchungen zur arabischen Sprach- und Stilgeschichte', *Abh. Sächs. Akad. d. Wiss.*, Philologisch.-histor. Kl. XLV/1 (1950); now slightly expanded French transl. J. Cantineau (Paris, 1955).

Fyzee, A. A. A., *An Introduction to the Study of Mahomedan Law* (London, 1931).

Fyzee, A. A. A., *Outlines of Muhammadan Law* (London, 1949).

Gabrieli, F., *Al-Ma'mūn e gli Alidi* (Leipzig, 1929).

Gabrieli, F., 'Ibn al-Muqaffa'', *Rivista degli studi orientali*, XIII (1931–2), 197–247.

Gabrieli, F., *Storici arabi delle crociate* (Turin, 1957).

Gabrieli, F., *Storia della letteratura araba* (Milan, 1951).

Gardet, L., *La cité musulmane* (Paris, 1954).

Gardet, L. and Anawati, M. M., *Introduction à la théologie musulmane. Essai de théologie comparée* (Paris, 1948).

Gaudefroy-Demombynes, M., *Les institutions musulmanes* (Paris, 1921); 2nd ed. (Paris, 1954); English transl. J. P. MacGregor (London, 1950); 2nd ed. (London, 1958).

Gaudefroy-Demombynes, M. and Platonov, S. F., *Le monde musulman et byzantin jusqu'aux croisades* [see Gen. Bibl. V].

Gauthier, L., 'Scolastique musulmane et scolastique chrétienne', *Revue de l'Histoire de la philosophie*, II (1928), 221–53, 333–65.

Gautier, E. F., *Les siècles obscurs du Maghreb. L'Islamisation de l'Afrique du Nord* (Paris, 1927).

Gibb, H. A. R., *Arabic Literature. An Introduction* (London, 1926).

Gibb, H. A. R., *Mohammedanism. An Historical Survey* (revised ed., London, 1961).

Gibb, H. A. R., *Studies on the Civilization of Islam* (Boston, 1962).

Goeje, M. J. de, *Mémoire sur les Carmathes du Bahrain et les Fatimides*, 2nd ed. (Leiden, 1886).

Goeje, M. J. de, 'International handelsverkeer in de middeleeuwen', *Verslagen en Mededeelingen der K. Akad. van Wet., afd. Letterkunde*, 4th ser., IX, 245 ff. (Amsterdam, 1908).

Goldziher, I., 'Muhammedanisches Recht in Theorie und Wirklichkeit', *Zeit. vergleichende Rechtswissenschaft*, VIII (Stuttgart, 1888).

Goldziher, I., *Muhammedanische Studien*, 2 vols. (Halle, 1888–90).

Goldziher, I., 'Die islamische und die jüdische Philosophie des Mittelalters', *Die Kultur der Gegenwart*, ed. P. Hinneberg, Teil I, Abt. II, pp. 45–77; 2nd ed. (Leipzig, 1913).

Goldziher, I., *Die Richtungen der islamischen Koranauslegung. De Goeje-Stiftung*, VI (Leiden, 1920).

Goldziher, I., *Vorlesungen über den Islam*, 2nd ed. F. Babinger (Heidelberg, 1925).

Gottschalk, H. L., *al-Malik al-Kāmil und seine Zeit* (Wiesbaden, 1958).

Gottschalk, H., *Die Mādarā'ijjūn, ein Beitrag zur Geschichte Ägyptens unter dem Islām* (Berlin and Leipzig, 1931).

Graf, A., *Geschichte der christlichen arabischen Literatur*, 5 vols. (Vatican City, 1944–53).

Grégoire, H. and Goossens, R., 'Byzantinisches Epos und arabischer Ritter-roman', *ZDMG*, LXXXVIII (1934), 213–32 (with bibliography).

Grohmann, A. and Arnold, T. W., *The Islamic Book* (Paris and New York, 1929).

Grunebaum, G. E. von, 'The Aesthetic Foundations of Arabic Literature', *Comparative Literature*, IV (1952), 323–40.

Grunebaum, G. E. von, *Islam: Essays in the Nature and Growth of a Cultural Tradition*, 2nd ed. (London, 1961).

Grunebaum, G. E. von, *Kritik und Dichtkunst. Studien zur arabischen Literatur-geschichte* (Wiesbaden, 1955).

Grunebaum, G. E. von, *Medieval Islam*, 2nd ed. (Chicago, 1953); Phoenix Book: 1961; enlarged German ed. (Zurich, 1963).

Grunebaum, G. E. von, *Muhammadan Festivals* (New York, 1951).

Grunebaum, G. E. von (ed., contr.), *Unity and Variety in Muslim Civilization* (Chicago, 1955).

Grunebaum, G. E. von, 'The World of Islam in the Twelfth Century', in M. Clagett, G. Post and R. Reynolds (edd.), *Twelfth-century Europe and the Foundations of Modern Society* (Madison, Wis., 1961), pp. 189–211.

Gruner, O. C., *A Treatise on the Canon of Medicine of Avicenna incorporating a translation of the First Book* (London, 1930).

Guidi, M., 'Trois conférences sur quelques problèmes généraux de l'Orien-talisme', *AIPHO*, III (1938), 167–216.

Guillaume, A., *The Traditions of Islam. An Introduction to the Study of the Hadith Literature* (Oxford, 1924).

Hamidullah, M., *The Muslim Conduct of State*, 3rd ed. revised (Lahore, 1953).

Handbook of Oriental History, ed. C. H. Philips (London, 1951).

Hariz, J., *La part de la médecine arabe dans l'évolution de la médecine française* (Paris, 1922).

Hartmann, M., 'Die islamische Verfassung und Verwaltung', *Die Kultur der Gegenwart*, ed. P. Hinneberg, Teil II, Abt. II, 1, pp. 49–86 (Leipzig, 1911).

Hassan, Z. M., *Les Tulunides* (Paris, 1933).

Hell, J., *Von Mohammed bis Ghazālī* (Jena, 1923).

Heller, B., *Die Bedeutung des arabischen 'Antar-Romans für die vergleichende Literaturkunde* (Leipzig, 1931).

Hellige, W., *Die Regentschaft al-Muwaffaqs* (Berlin, 1936).

Heyd, W. von, *Histoire du commerce du Levant au moyen âge* [see Gen. Bibl. v].

Historia Mundi, vol. VI: *Hohes und spätes Mittelalter* (Bern, 1958).

Hitti, P. K., *History of the Arabs*, 6th ed. (1956).

Hitti, P. K., *Lebanon in History* (London and New York, 1957).

Hitti, P. K., *The Origins of the Druze People and Religion* (New York, 1928).

Hitti, P. K., *History of Syria including Lebanon and Palestine* (New York, 1951).

Hodgson, M. G., *The Order of Assassins* ('s-Gravenhage, 1955).

Hoenerbach, W., 'Zur Heeresverwaltung der 'Abbāsiden', *Der Islam*, XXIX (1950), 257–90.

Hopkins, J. F. P., *Medieval Muslim Government in Barbary until the Sixth Century of the Hijra* (London, 1958).

Horovitz, S., 'Über den Einfluss der griechischen Philosophie auf die Entwicklung des Kalam', *Jahresbericht des jüdisch-theologischen Seminars zu Breslau* (1909).

Horovitz, S., *Der Einfluss der griechischon Skepsis auf die Entwicklung der Philosophie bei den Arabern* (Breslau, 1915).

Horten, M., *Die philosophischen Systeme der spekulativen Theologen im Islam* (Bonn, 1912).

Horten, M., *Die Philosophie des Islam* (Munich, 1924).

Hourani, G. F., *Arab Seafaring in the Indian Ocean in Ancient and Early Medieval Times* (Princeton, 1951).

Jacob, G., *Arabische Berichte von Gesandten an germanische Fürstenhöfe aus dem 9. und 10. Jahrhundert* (Berlin, 1927).

Jockel, R., *Islamische Geisteswelt von Mohammed bis zur Gegenwart* (Darmstadt and Geneva, 1954).

Julien, C.-A., *Histoire de l'Afrique du Nord*, 2nd ed., revised by C. Courtois and R. Le Tourneau, 2 vols. (Paris, 1956).

Juynboll, T. W., *Handbuch des islamischen Gesetzes* (Leiden, 1910).

Khadduri, M., *War and Peace in Islam* (Baltimore, Md., 1955).

Kraemer, J., *Das Problem der islamischen Kulturgeschichte* (Tübingen, 1959).

Kraus, P., 'Jābir ibn Ḥayyān. Contribution à l'histoire des idées scientifiques dans l'Islam', *Mémoires de l'Institut d'Egypte*, XLIV–XLV (Cairo, 1942–3).

Kremer, A. von, *Culturgeschichte des Orients unter den Chalifen*, 2 vols. (Vienna, 1875–7); transl. S. Khuda Bukhsh (Calcutta, 1920).

Kremer, A. von, *Culturgeschichtliche Streifzüge auf dem Gebiete des Islams* (Leipzig, 1873); transl. S. Khuda Bukhsh, *Contributions to the History of Islamic Civilization* (Calcutta, 1905).

Kremer, A. von, *Geschichte der herrschenden Ideen des Islams* (Leipzig, 1868).

Kremer, A. von, 'Über das Einnahmebudget des Abbasiden-Reichs vom Jahre 306 H. (918–19)', *Denkschriften der KAW.*, Philos.-hist. Classe, XXXVI (Vienna, 1888), 283 ff.

Kremer, A. von, 'Über das Budget der Einnahmen unter der Regierung des Hārūn alraśíd', *Verh. d. VII. internat. Orientalisten-Congresses*. Semit. Section (Vienna, 1888), pp. 1 ff.

Lambton, A. K. S., *Landlord and Peasant in Persia* (Oxford, 1953).

Lammens, H., *La Syrie*, 2 vols. (Beirut, 1921).

Lammens, H., *L'Islam, croyances et institutions*, 2nd ed. (Beirut, 1941); English transl. E. Ross, *Islam: Beliefs and Institutions* (London, 1929).

Leclerc, L., *Histoire de la médecine arabe*, 2 vols. (Paris, 1876).

The Legacy of Persia, ed. A. J. Arberry (Oxford, 1953).

Le Strange, G., *Baghdad during the Abbasid Caliphate* (London, 1900).

Le Strange, G., *Palestine under the Moslems. A description of Syria and the Holy Land from A.D. 650 to 1500. Translated from the Works of the Mediaeval Arab Geographers* (London, 1890).

Le Strange, G., *The Lands of the Eastern Caliphate* [see Gen. Bibl. II].

Lévi-Provençal, E., *La civilisation arabe en Espagne: vue générale* (Cairo, 1938).

Lévi-Provençal, E., *Histoire de l'Espagne musulmane*, 3 vols. reaching to 1031 (Paris, 1950–3).

Lévi-Provençal, E., *Islam d'Occident: études d'histoire médiévale* (Paris, 1948).

Levy, R. A., *A Baghdad Chronicle* (Cambridge, 1939).

Levy, R. A., *An Introduction to the Sociology of Islam*, 2 vols. (London, 1931–3); reissued as *The Social Structure of Islam* (Cambridge, 1957).

Lewin, B., 'L'idéal antique du philosophe dans la tradition arabe. Un traité d'éthique du philosophe Bagdadien Ibn Suwār', *Lychnos* (1954–5), 267–84.

Lewis, A. R., *Naval Power and Trade in the Mediterranean, A.D. 500–1100* (Princeton, 1951).

Lewis, B., *The Arabs in History* [see Gen. Bibl. V].

Lewis, B., *The Origins of Ismāʿīlism: a Study of the Historical Background of the Fāṭimid Caliphate* (Cambridge, 1940).

Løkkegaard, F., *Islamic Taxation in the Classic Period with Special Reference to Circumstances in Iraq* (Copenhagen, 1950).

Lombard, M., 'Les bases monétaires d'une suprématie économique: l'or musulman du VIIe au XIe siècle', *Annales: économies, sociétés, civilisations*, II (1947), 143–60.

Lopez Ortiz, J., *Derecho musulmán* (Barcelona, 1932).

Macdonald, D. B., *Development of Muslim Theology, Jurisprudence, and Constitutional Theory* (London, 1903).

Macdonald, D. B., 'The Development of the Idea of Spirit in Islam', *Acta orientalia*, IX (1931), 307–51; *Muslim World*, XXII (1932), 25–42, 153–68.

Madkour, I., *L'Organon d'Aristote dans le monde arabe. Ses traductions, son étude et ses applications* (Paris, 1934).

Madkour, I., *La place d'al-Fārābī dans l'école philosophique musulmane* (Paris, 1934).

Malvezzi, A., *L'Islamismo e la cultura europea* (Florence, 1956).

Marçais, G., *L'Architecture musulmane d'Occident* (Paris, 1954).

Marçais, G., *La Berbérie musulmane et l'Orient au moyen âge* (Paris, 1946).

Massé, H., *L'Islam* (Paris, 1930); English transl. by Halide Edib (New York, 1938).

Massignon, L., *Essai sur les origines du lexique technique de la mystique musulmane* (Paris, 1922); 2nd ed. (Paris, 1954).

Massignon, L., *Recueil de textes inédits concernant l'histoire de la mystique en pays d'Islam* (Paris, 1929).

Massignon, L., 'L'influence de l'Islam au moyen âge sur la fondation et l'essor des banques juives', *Bull. d'études orientales* (Institut Français de Damas), I (1931), 3–12.

Mayer, H. E., *Bibliographie zur Geschichte der Kreuzzüge* (Hanover, 1960).

Meier, F., *Die Fawā'iḥ al-ǧamāl wa-fawātiḥ al-ǧalāl des Naǧm ad-Dīn al-Kubrā. Eine Darstellung mystischer Erfahrungen im Islam aus der Zeit um 1200 n. Chr.* (Wiesbaden, 1957).

Meyerhof, M., 'Von Alexandrien nach Bagdad. Ein Beitrag zur Geschichte des philosophischen und medizinischen Unterrichts bei den Arabern', *SBAW*, phil. hist. Kl. (1930), pp. 389–429.

Mez, A., *Die Renaissance des Islams* (Heidelberg, 1922); English transl. S. Khuda-Bukhsh and D. S. Margoliouth (London, 1937).

Mieli, A., *La science arabe et son rôle dans l'évolution scientifique mondial* (Leiden, 1939).

Minorsky, V., *La domination des Dailamites* (Paris, 1932).

Moreno, M. M., *Antologia della mistica arabo-persiana* (Bari, 1951).

Moreno, M. M., *L'Islamismo e l'educazione* (Biblioteca dell'educazione, xcviii) (Milan, 1951).

Moreno, M. M., 'Mistica musulmana e mistica indiana', *Annali Lateranensi*, x (1946), 103–212.

Mubarak, Z., *La prose arabe au IVᵉ siècle de l'Hégire (Xᵉ s.)* (Paris, 1931).

Muir, W., *The Caliphate: its Rise, Decline, and Fall*, revised ed. T. H. Weir (Edinburgh, 1924).

Müller, A., *Der Islam im Morgen- und Abendland*, 2 vols. (Berlin, 1885–7).

Nader, A. N., *Le système philosophique des Mu'tazila* (Beirut, 1956).

Nazim, M., *The Life and Times of Sultan Maḥmūd of Ghazna* (London, 1931).

Neuburger, M., *Geschichte der Medizin* (Stuttgart, 1908).

Nicholson, R. A., *Studies in Islamic Poetry* (Cambridge, 1921).

Nicholson, R. A., *Studies in Islamic Mysticism* (Cambridge, 1921).

Nicholson, R. A., *The Idea of Personality in Sufism* (Cambridge, 1923).

Nicholson, R. A., *A Literary History of the Arabs*, 2nd ed. (Cambridge, 1930).

Nöldeke, T., *Orientalische Skizzen* (Berlin, 1892); transl. J. S. Black, *Sketches from Eastern History* (London, 1892).

Obermann, J. J., *Der philosophische und religiöse Subjektivismus Ghazalis* (Vienna, 1921).

O'Leary, De Lacy, *Arabic Thought and its Place in History* (London, 1922).

Oxford Regional Economic Atlas. The Middle East and North Africa (Oxford, 1960).

Padwick, C. E., *Muslim Devotions. A Study of Prayer-Manuals in Common Use* (London, 1961).

Pagliaro, A. and Bausani, A., *Storia della letteratura persiana* (Milan, 1960).

Pareja, F. M., *Islamologia* (Rome, 1951).

Patzelt, E., *Die fränkische Kultur und der Islam* (Brunn, 1932).

Pawlikowski-Cholewa, A. von, *Die Heere des Morgenlandes* (Berlin, 1940).

Pearson, J. D. and Ashton, J. F., *Index Islamicus. 1906–1955* (Cambridge, 1958); supplt., 1956–60 (Cambridge, 1962).

Périer, A., *Yahya ben Adi. Un philosophe arabe chrétien du Xᵉ siècle* (Paris, 1920).

Perroy, E. with J. Auboyer, C. Cahen *et al.*, *Le moyen âge. Histoire générale des civilisations*, ed. M. Crouzet, vol. iii (Paris, 1957).

Pines, S., *Beiträge zur islamischen Atomenlehre* (Berlin, 1936).

Pirenne, H., *Mohammed and Charlemagne* (New York, 1939).

Plessner, M., *Die Geschichte der Wissenschaften im Islam als Aufgabe der modernen Islamwissenschaft. Ein Versuch* (Tübingen, 1931).

Plessner, M., *Der Οἰκονομικός des Neupythagoreers 'Bryson' und sein Einfluss auf die islamische Wissenschaft* (Heidelberg, 1928).

Poliak, A. N., 'L'Arabisation de l'Orient sémitique', *Revue des Etudes Islamiques*, XII (1938), 35–63.

Pritsch, E., 'Die islamische Staatsidee', *Zeit. vergleichende Rechtswissenschaft*, LIII (1939), 33–72.

Rahman, F., *Prophecy in Islam* (London, 1958).

Rescher, O., *Abriss der arabischen Litteraturgeschichte* (Stuttgart, 1925–33).

Richter, G., *Das Geschichtsbild der arabischen Historiker des Mittelalters* (Tübingen, 1933).

Richter, G., *Studien zur Geschichte der älteren arabischen Fürstenspiegel* (Leipzig, 1932).

Ritter, H., *Das Meer der Seele* (Leiden, 1955).

Ritter, H., 'Muhammedanische Häresiographen', *Der Islam*, XVIII (1929), 34–55.

Ritter, H., 'Studien zur Geschichte der islamischen Frömmigkeit', *Der Islam*, XXI (1933), 1–83.

Ritter, H., *Über die Bildersprache Niẓāmās* (Berlin and Leipzig, 1927).

Roolvink, R. et al., *Historical Atlas of the Muslim Peoples* (Cambridge, Mass., 1957).

Rosenthal, E. I. J., *Political Thought in Medieval Islam* (Cambridge, 1958).

Rosenthal, F., *A History of Muslim Historiography* (Leiden, 1952).

Rosenthal, F., *Humor in Early Islam* (Philadelphia, 1956).

Rosenthal, F., *The Muslim Concept of Freedom Prior to the Nineteenth Century* (Leiden, 1960).

Rosenthal, F., *The Technique and Approach of Muslim Scholarship* (Rome, 1947).

Ruska, J., *Arabische Alchemisten*, 2 pts. (Heidelberg, 1924).

Ruska, J., *Tabula Smaragdina: ein Beitrag zur Geschichte der hermetischen Literatur* (Heidelberg, 1926).

Ruska, J., 'Über das Fortleben der antiken Wissenschaft im Orient', *Archiv für Geschichte der Mathematik, der Naturwissenschaften und der Technik*, X (N.F. I, 1927/8), 112–35.

Rypka, J., *Iranische Literaturgeschichte* (Leipzig, 1959).

Sadighi, G. H., *Les mouvements religieux iraniens au II*[e] *siècle et au III*[e] *siècle de l'hégire* (Paris, 1938).

Sadruddin, M., *Saifuddaulah and His Times* (Lahore, 1930).

Santillana, D., *Istituzioni di diritto musulmano malichita*, I (Rome, 1926).

Sarton, G., *Introduction to the History of Science*, 4 vols. (Baltimore, 1927–47).

Sauvaget, J., *Introduction à l'histoire musulmane*, 2nd ed. revised by C. Cahen (Paris, 1961); English transl. ed. in preparation.

Schacht, J., *Der Islam mit Ausschluss des Qor'ans* (Tübingen, 1931).

Schacht, J., *Esquisse d'une histoire du droit musulman* (Paris, 1952).

Schacht, J., *The Origins of Muhammadan Jurisprudence* (Oxford, 1950).

Schacht, J., 'Zur soziologischen Betrachtung des islamischen Rechts', *Der Islam*, XXII (1935), 207–38.

Schacht, J. and Meyerhof, M., *The Medico-Philosophical Controversy Between Ibn Butlan of Baghdad and Ibn Ridwan of Cairo* (Cairo, 1937).

Schaeder, H. H., 'Die islamische Lehre vom Vollkommenen Menschen, ihre Herkunft und ihre dichterische Gestaltung', *ZDMG*, LXXIX (1925), 192–268.

Schaeder, H. H., 'Die Orientforschung und das abendländische Geschichtsbild', *Die Welt als Geschichte*, II (1936), 377–96.

Schaeder, H. H., 'Der Orient und das griechische Erbe', *Die Antike*, IV (1938), 226–65.

Schroeder, E., *Muhammad's People. An Anthology of Muslim Civilization* (Portland, Me., 1955).

Setton, K. M. (editor-in-chief), *A History of the Crusades* [see Gen. Bibl. V].

Smith, M., *An Early Mystic of Baghdad: A Study of the Life and Teachings of Hārith b. Asad al-Muḥāsibī, 781–857* (London, 1935).

Smith, M., *Al-Ghazālī, the Mystic* (London, 1944).

Smith, M., *Rābi'a the Mystic and Her Fellow-Saints in Islām* (Cambridge, 1928).

Smith, M., *Readings from the Mystics of Islām* (London, 1950).

Smith, M., *Studies in Early Mysticism in the Near and Middle East* (London, 1931).

Sourdel, D., *Le Vizirat 'abbāside de 749 à 936* (Damascus, 1959–60).

Spuler, B., 'Der Verlauf der Islamisierung Persiens. Eine Skizze', *Der Islam*, XXIX (1950), 63–76.

Spuler, B., *Iran in früh-islamischer Zeit (633–1055)* (Wiesbaden, 1952).

Spuler, B., *The Muslim World*, transl. F. R. C. Bagley. I: *The Age of the Caliphs*. II: *The Mongol Period* (Leiden, 1960).

Stegemann, V., *Beiträge zur Geschichte der Astrologie* (Heidelberg, 1935).

Steinschneider, M., 'Alfarabi, des arabischen Philosophen, Leben und Schriften, mit besonderer Rücksicht auf die Geschichte der griechischen Wissenschaft unter den Arabern', *Mém. Acad. IP.* ser. VII, vol. XIII, no. 4 (St Petersburg, 1869).

Steinschneider, M., *Die arabischen Übersetzungen aus dem Griechischen.*
   I. *Philosophie* (in *Beihefte zum Centralblatt für Bibliothekswesen*, VII, 51 ff.; XII, 129 ff., Leipzig, 1889, 1893).
   II. *Mathematik* (in *ZDMG*, L (1896), pp. 161 ff.).
   III. *Medicin* (in Virchow's *Archiv für Pathologie*, CXXVI, Berlin, 1891).

Steinschneider, M., 'Die europäischen Übersetzungen aus dem Arabischen', *SKAW*, CXLIX and CLI (Vienna, 1904, 1905).

Strothmann, R., 'Islamische Konfessionskunde und das Sektenbuch des Asari', *Der Islam*, XIX (1931), 193–242.

Strothmann, R., *Die Zwölfer-Schi'a* (Leipzig, 1926).

Suter, H., *Die Araber als Vermittler der Wissenschaften in ihrem Übergang vom Orient in den Occident*, 2nd ed. (Aarau, 1897).

Suter, H., *Die Mathematiker und Astronomen der Araber und ihre Werke* (Leipzig, 1900).

Sweetman, J. W., *Islamic and Christian Theology: a Study of the Interpretation of Theological Ideas in the Two Religions* (London, 1945 ff.).

Taeschner, F., 'Der Anteil des Sufismus an der Formung des Futuwwaideals', *Der Islam*, XXIV (1937), 43–74.

Taeschner, F., 'Das Futuwwa-Rittertum des islamischen Mittelalters', *Beiträge zur Arabistik, Semitistik und Islamwissenschaft*, ed. R. Hartmann and H. Scheel (Leipzig, 1944), pp. 230–385.

Taeschner, F., 'Die islamischen Futuwwebünde', *ZDMG*, LXXXVII (1934), 6–49.

Taeschner, F., 'Das islamische Rittertum im Mittelalter. Der Orient in deutscher Forschung', *Vorträge der Berliner Orientalistentagung* (autumn, 1942); ed. H. H. Schaeder (Leipzig, 1944), pp. 94–104 [with bibliography].

Taeschner, F., 'Futuwwa, eine gemeinschaftsbildende Idee im mittelalterlichen Orient und ihre verschiedenen Erscheinungsformen', *Schweizerisches Archiv für Volkskunde*, LII (1956), 122–58.

Terrasse, H., *Histoire du Maroc* (Casablanca, 1949–50).

Terrasse, H., *Islam d'Espagne* (Paris, 1958).

Tkatsch, J., *Die arabische Übersetzung der Poetik des Aristoteles* (Vienna, 1922–32).

Trabulsi, A., *La critique poétique des Arabes jusqu'au Ve siècle de l'Hégire (XIe siècle de J.C.)* (Damascus, 1956).

Tritton, A. S., *The Caliphs and their Non-Muslim Subjects: a Critical Study of the Covenant of Umar* (London, 1930).

Tritton, A. S., *Islam: Belief and Practices* (London, 1951).

Tritton, A. S., *Materials on Muslim Education in the Middle Ages* (London, 1957).

Tritton, A. S., *Muslim Theology* (London, 1947).

Tyan, E., *Institutions du droit public musulman*. I: *Le Califat*. II: *Sultanat et Califat* (Paris, 1954–7).

Vasiliev, A. A., *Byzance et les Arabes* (Brussels, 1935–50) [see Gen. Bibl. v].

Vatikiotis, P. J., *The Fatimid Theory of State* (Lahore, 1957).

Vesey-Fitzgerald, S. G., *Muhammadan Law: an Abridgment according to its Various Schools* (London, 1931).

Vonderheyden, M., *La Berbérie orientale sous la dynastie des Benou 'l-Arlab 800–909* (Paris, 1927).

Watt, W. M., *Free Will and Predestination in Early Islam* (London, 1948).

Weil, G., *Geschichte der Chalifen* [see Gen. Bibl. v].

Weil, G., *Die grammatischen Schulen von Kufa und Basra* (Leiden, 1913).

Wensinck, A. J., *Concordance et indices de la tradition musulmane* (Leiden, 1938 ff.).

Wensinck, A. J., 'Genèse et évolution de la culture musulmane', *Semietische Studien uit de Nalatenschap* (Leiden, 1941), pp. 127–53.

Wensinck, A. J., *A Handbook of Early Muhammadan Tradition* (Leiden, 1927).

Wensinck, A. J., *The Muslim Creed. Its Genesis and Historical Development* (Cambridge, 1932).

Wensinck, A. J., *La pensée de Ghazzālī* (Paris, 1940).

Wiedemann, E., articles in *Beiträge zur Geschichte der Naturwissenschaften*, X–XXXII [and numerous other contributions to the history of Arabic science] (Erlangen, 1906–13).

Wüstenfeld, F., *Die Übersetzungen arabischer Werke in das Lateinische seit dem XI. Jahrhundert*. Abh. Gött. Gesellschaft d. Wiss. XXII (Göttingen, 1877).

Wüstenfeld-Mahler'sche Vergleichungs-Tabellen zur muslimischen und iranischen Zeitrechnung mit Tafeln zur Umrechnung orient-christlicher Ären. Revised by B. Spuler with the collaboration of J. Mayr (Wiesbaden, 1961).

Young, T. C. (ed.), *Near Eastern Culture and Society* (Princeton, 1951) [see the chapters on Islamic Art and Archaeology, Arabic and Persian Literatures, by R. Ettinghausen, G. E. von Grunebaum, and A. J. Arberry respectively].

Zambaur, E. K. M. von, *Manuel de généalogie et de chronologie pour l'histoire de l'Islam* (Bad Pyrmont, 1955).

CHAPTER XVII. BYZANTIUM AND THE MUSLIM WORLD TO THE MIDDLE OF THE ELEVENTH CENTURY

See also the bibliographies for chapters III–V, XIV–XVI and XXVIII (for military and naval science).

I. PRIMARY AUTHORITIES

The Greek and Latin sources are not generally cited here: see the bibliographies for chapters III–V.

French translations of a number of relevant passages from Arabic sources may be found in A. A. Vasiliev, *Byzance et les Arabes*, I and II, pt. 2 (by M. Canard) [see Gen. Bibl. v].

Abu'l Faraj, see Bar Hebraeus.

Abu'l Fidā, *Annales Muslemici* [Arab.], ed. with Latin transl. J. J. Reiske and I. G. C. Adler, 5 vols. (Copenhagen, 1789–94); ed. Anon. 4 vols. (Constantinople, 1870); another ed. (Cairo, 1325 A.H.).

Abu'l Maḥāsin, *Annales* [Arab.], ed. with Latin transl. J. D. Carlyle, 2 pts. (Cambridge, 1792) (from 971); ed. T. G. J. Juynboll and B. F. Matthes, 2 vols. (Leiden, 1852–61). Continued by W. Popper (Univ. of California Publications in Semitic Philology, II) (Berkeley, 1909, etc.; in progress). New ed. 12 vols. (Cairo, 1929 ff.; in progress). Relevant parts to 959 transl. A. A. Vasiliev, *Vizantija i Araby*, and French edition, II, pt. 2 [see Gen. Bibl. v].

Agapius, see Maḥbūb.

'Ainī, *Monile Margaritarum* [Arab.], unpublished. Extract ed. with French transl. E. Fagnan, 'Nouveaux textes historiques', *Centenario della nascita di M. Amari*, II, 86 (Palermo, 1910). Relevant parts to 959 transl. A. A. Vasiliev, *Byzance et les Arabes*, II, pt. 2 [see Gen. Bibl. v].

Amari, M., *Biblioteca Arabo-Sicula*, vers. ital., 2 vols. and app. 8vo ed. (Turin, Florence, and Rome, 1881, 1889). [Introduction on authors dealing with Sicily.] Notices of the Arabic authorities are also given in the Appendix to A. A. Vasiliev, *Byzance et les Arabes* [see Gen. Bibl. v].

'Arīb, *Chronicon* [Arab.], ed. M. J. de Goeje (Leiden, 1897). Relevant parts transl. A. A. Vasiliev, *Byzance et les Arabes*, II, pt. 2 [see Gen. Bibl. v]. [Continuation of Ṭabarī.]

Aristaces Lastivertensis, *Historia Armeniae* [Arm.], ed. Anon. [Mkhitharists] (Venice, 1844); French transl. E. Prud'homme, *Revue de l'Orient*, XV (1863), 343; XVI (1864), 41, 159, 268, 289; XVII (1865), 5 (Soc. Orientale de France).

Asoghik (Asolik), see Stephanus Taronensis.

Balādhuri, *Liber expugnationis regionum* [Arab.], ed. M. J. de Goeje (Leiden, 1863); English transl. P. K. Hitti (Columbia University Studies in History, Economics and Public Law, LXVIII, 163) (New York, 1916) and part II, F. C. Murgotten (New York, 1924); German transl. O. Rescher (Leipzig, 1917). [Balādhuri died in 892, but his work contains nothing relevant after 838 except one Sicilian notice.]

Bar Hebraeus, *Gregorii Abulpharagii sive Bar-hebraei chronicon syriacum*, ed. with Latin transl. P. J. Bruns and G. C. Kirsch, 2 vols. (Leipzig, 1789).

Bar Hebraeus, *Chronicon ecclesiasticum*, ed. with Latin transl. J. B. Abbeloos and T. J. Lamy, 3 vols. (Paris–Louvain, 1872–7).

Bar Hebraeus, *The Chronography of Gregory Abūl Faraj*..., ed. with English transl. E. A. W. Budge (London, 1932).

Chronicon anni 846 [Syr.], ed. E. W. Brooks, with Latin transl. by J. B. Chabot, *CSCO*, Chronica Minora, II (1904). [Contains nothing relevant after 726.]

Chronicon ad ann. 1234 pertinens [Syr.], ed. J. B. Chabot, 2 vols. (*CSCO*, 81, 82) (Paris, 1917–20).

Chronicon Cantabrigiense, ed. G. Cozza-Luzi (Documenti per servire alla storia di Sicilia, ser. 4, II), (Soc. Siciliana per la storia patria) (Palermo, 1890); ed. P. Batiffol, *Comptes Rendus*, *AcadIBL*, ser. 4, XVIII (1890). (From the Paris MS. only.) [This chronicle was first discovered in an Arabic version at Cambridge, which is published with the Greek text with Italian transl. in Cozza-Luzi's ed. The Greek text is reprinted with a transl. of the Arabic in A. A. Vasiliev, *Byzance et les Arabes*, II, pt. 2; see Gen. Bibl. v.]

Dhahabī, *Historia Islamica* [Arab.], unpublished. Relevant parts to 959 transl. A. A. Vasiliev, *Byzance et les Arabes*, II, pt. 2 [see Gen. Bibl. v]; extracts in M. Canard, *Sayf al Daula, Recueil de textes*..., Bibl. arab. publ. par la Fac. des Lettres d'Alger, VIII (Algiers, 1934).

Dionysius (so-called) of Tellmahré, *Chronicon* [Syr.], ed. with French transl. J. B. Chabot, *BHE*, CII (1895). [A work of the year 775, probably by Joshua the Stylite of Zuqnin.]

Elias Nisibenus, *Opus chronologicum* [Syr. and Arab.], ed. with Latin transl. E. W. Brooks and J. B. Chabot, *CSCO*, SS Syri ser. 3, VII–VIII (1909–10); ed. and German transl. F. Baethgen, *Fragmente syrischer und arabischer Historiker*, Abh. f. die K. d. Morg. VIII, 3 (Leipzig, 1884); French transl. L. P. Delaporte, *BHE*, CLXXXI (1910).

Eutychius, *Annales* [Arab.], ed. P. L. Cheikho and others (*CSCO*), 2 vols. (Beirut and Paris, 1909–12); Latin transl. E. Pocock, *MPG*, CXI.

Hamidullah, Muhammad, *Corpus des traités et lettres diplomatiques de l'Islam à l'époque du Prophète et des Khalifes Orthodoxes* (Paris, 1935).

Ibn 'Adhārī ('Idhārī), *Notitiae Occidentis* [Arab.], ed. R. P. A. Dozy, 2 vols. (Leiden, 1848–51); French transl. by E. Fagnan, 2 vols. (Algiers, 1901–4); new ed. G. S. Colin and E. Lévi-Provençal (Leiden, 1948, 1950); oriental ed. 2 vols. (Beirut, 1950).

Ibn al-Athīr, *Chronicon perfectissimum* [Arab.], ed. C. J. Tornberg, 14 vols. (Leiden, 1851–76); passages relating to Asia Minor for period 717–813 transl. E. W. Brooks, *JHS*, XVIII (1898), 162–205 [see below, II]; relevant passages to 959 transl. A. A. Vasiliev, *Byzance et les Arabes*, II, pt. 2 [see Gen. Bibl. v]; passages relating to Sicily transl. M. Amari, *Biblioteca Arabo-Sicula*, vers. ital. I, 353 [see above].

Ibn al-Azraq, *Historia Mayyāfāriqīn*, unpublished. Extracts in H. F. Amedroz, *JRAS* (1902), 785 ff.; J. Markwart, *Südarmenien* [see below, II]; M. Canard, *Sayf al Daula*...; relevant parts to 959 transl. in A. A. Vasiliev, *Byzance et les Arabes*, II, pt. 2 [see Gen. Bibl. v].

Ibn al-Jauzī, Sibṭ, *Liber speculi temporum* [Arab.], unpublished. Relevant parts to 959 transl. A. A. Vasiliev, *Byzance et les Arabes*, II, pt. 2 [see Gen. Bibl. v].

Ibn Ḥauqal, *Opus Geographicum*. *Bibliotheca Geographorum Arabicorum*, II (Leiden, 1875); new ed. J. H. Kramers, 2 vols. (Leiden, 1938–9); relevant parts transl. A. A. Vasiliev, *Byzance et les Arabes*, II, pt. 2 [see Gen. Bibl. v].

Ibn ʿIdhārī, *see* Ibn ʿAdhārī.

Ibn Kathīr, *Historia universalis* [Arab.], 14 vols. (Cairo, 1932–9). Relevant parts to 959 transl. A. A. Vasiliev, *Byzance et les Arabes*, II, pt. 2 [see Gen. Bibl. v].

Ibn Khaldun, *Historia Islamica* [Arab.], ed. Anon. 7 vols. (Būlāḳ, 1867); new ed. J. A. Dagher (Beirut, 1956–9). Relevant parts relating to Sicily transl. M. Amari [see above], II, 161 ff. [The Eastern portions are taken from existing sources.]

Ibn al-Khaṭīb (Lisān-ad-Dīn), *Gesta regum clarorum* [Arab.], ed. H. H. Abdul-Wahab, 'Contributions à l'histoire de l'Afrique du nord et de la Sicile', *Centenario della nascita di M. Amari*, II (Palermo, 1910), pp. 427 ff.; ed. E. Lévi-Provençal, *Extraits relatifs à l'histoire de l'Espagne musulmane* (Rabat, 1934); relevant parts transl. A. A. Vasiliev, *Byzance et les Arabes*, II, pt. 2 [see Gen. Bibl. v].

Ibn Khurdādhbih, *Liber viarum et provinciarum* [Arab.], ed. with French transl. M. J. de Goeje (Bibliotheca Geographorum Arabicorum, VI) (Leiden, 1889). [With extracts from Qudāma: see below.]

Ibn Ḳutaiba, *Manuale Historiae* [Arab.], ed. F. Wüstenfeld (Göttingen, 1850). Relevant passages from 813 transl. A. A. Vasiliev, *Byzance et les Arabes*, II, pt. 2 [see Gen. Bibl. v]. [The author lived 828–88, but records nothing relevant after 838.]

Ibn al-Qalānisī, *History of Damascus 363–555 A.H.* [Arab.], ed. H. F. Amedroz (Leiden, 1908). [No transl. for the part concerning the end of the tenth century except extracts transl. M. Canard, *REB*, XIX (1961).]

Ibn Rosteh, *Bibliotheca Geographorum Arabicorum*, VII (1892). [Contains the relation of Harūn ibn Yaḥyā.]

Ibn Shaddād, *Liber pretiosarum margaritarum* [Arab.], unpublished except parts concerning the 'Awāṣim by C. Ledit (Mashrik, 1934), Aleppo by D. Sourdel (Damascus, 1953) and Damascus by S. Dahan (Damascus, 1956). Extracts transl. A. A. Vasiliev, *Byzance et les Arabes*, II, pt. 2 [see Gen. Bibl. v].

Ibn Ẓāfir, *Liber de dynastiis praeteritis* [Arab.], unpublished except extracts in M. Canard, *Sayf al Daula* (see above under Dhahabī). Relevant parts transl. A. A. Vasiliev, *Byzance et les Arabes*, II, pt. 2 [see Gen. Bibl. v].

Johannes Catholicus, *Historia Armeniae* [Arm.], ed. Anon. (Jerusalem, 1867); French transl. J. Saint-Martin (Paris, 1841).

Kamāl ad-Dīn, *Selecta ex historia Halebi* [Arab.]. Full text unpublished. Portions ed. with Latin transl. G. Freytag:
(i) *Sel. ex hist. Hal.* (637–947) (Paris, 1819);
(ii) *Regnum Saahd-Aldaulae* (968–991) (Bonn, 1820);
(iii) *Locmani fabulae et plura loca ex codd....historicis* (991–1002) (Bonn, 1823).
Latin transl. (extracts) J. J. Müller, *Historia Merdasidarum* (1002–79) (Bonn, 1829); relevant parts from 945 to 957 ed. M. Canard, *Sayf al Daula* (see above under Dhahabī), and transl. A. A. Vasiliev, *Byzance et les Arabes*, II, pt. 2 [see Gen. Bibl. v]; new ed. S. Dahan, *Histoire d'Alep*, I (1–457 A.H.) (Damascus, 1951).

al-Khaṭīb al-Baghdādī, *Historia Baghdad*, 14 vols. (Cairo, 1941). (Part concerning the embassy of 917 transl. A. A. Vasiliev, *Byzance et les Arabes*, II, pt. 2 [see Gen. Bibl. v]; cf. below, G. Le Strange and G. Salmon.)

Kindī, *Liber rectorum* [Arab.], ed. R. Guest (Gibb Memorial Series, 19) (Leiden and London, 1912). Relevant passages transl. E. W. Brooks, *BZ*, XXII (1913) and A. A. Vasiliev, *Byzance et les Arabes*, II, pt. 2 [see Gen. Bibl. v].

Leontius (Ghevond), *Historia Chalifarum* [Arm.], ed. K. Ezean (St Petersburg, 1887); French transl. V. Chahnazarian (Paris, 1856); Russian transl. K. Patkanian (St Petersburg, 1862); Latin transl. (of extracts with commentary) E. Filler [see below].

Liber fontium (*Kitāb al-ʾuyūn*) [Arab.], ed. M. J. de Goeje. (Fragm. Historicorum Arabicorum, I) (Leiden, 1871). Relevant passages transl. E. W. Brooks, *JHS*, XIX (1899), 19–33, and A. A. Vasiliev, *Byzance et les Arabes*, II, pt. 2 [see Gen. Bibl. v].

Maḥbūb (Agapius) of Manbij (Hierapolis), *Liber tituli* [Arab.], ed. with French transl. A. A. Vasiliev, *PO*, v, 561 ff.; VII, 458 ff.; VIII, 396 ff., 3 pts. (Paris and Freiburg, 1910–12). (In part unpublished. Extracts in Russian transl. V. R. Rosen, *ZMNP*, CCXXXVII (1884), 47 ff.)

Makīn, *Historia Saracenica* [Arab.], ed. with Latin transl. T. Erpenius (Leiden, 1625). French transl. P. Vattier (Paris, 1657).

Malikī, *Horti animarum* [Arab.]; analysis by H. R. Idris, *Rev. Et. Islam.* IX (1935), 105–77, 273–305 and X (1936), 45–104. Vol. I ed. H. Monés (Cairo, 1951). Parts relating to Sicily transl. M. Amari, *Biblioteca Arabo-Sicula*, I (Turin and Rome, 1889), 294–324 (ch. XXVIII, Rīad ʾan Nufūs) and *Appendice* (Turin, Florence and Rome, 1889), 75–82; Russian transl. A. A. Vasiliev, *Vizantija i Araby* [see Gen. Bibl. v].

Maqdisī, *Descriptio imperii moslemici*, ed. M. J. de Goeje (Bibl. Geogr. Arab. III) (Leiden, 1876–7); new ed. (1906). Extracts transl. A. A. Vasiliev, *Byzance et les Arabes*, II, pt. 2 [see Gen. Bibl. v].

Maqrīzī, *Liber admonitionis et considerationis* [Arab.], ed. M. K. Adawi, 2 vols. (Būlāḳ, 1853); ed. G. Wiet, *Mém. de l'Institut français d'Archéologie Orientale*, XXX ff. (Cairo, 1911 ff.; in progress); French transl. U. Bouriant, *Mém. de la Mission Archéologique du Caire*, XVII, 2 pts. (Paris, 1895–1900); continued by P. Casanova, *Mém. de l'Institut français d'Archéologie Orientale*, III (Cairo, 1906; in progress). Passage on Muʿizz's restoration of the Egyptian fleet transl. V. R. Rosen, *Imp. Vasilij Bolgarobojca*, 274–6 [see below]; see also A. A. Vasiliev, *Byzance et les Arabes*, II, pt. 2 [see Gen. Bibl. v].

Masʿūdī, *Liber commonitionis et recognitionis* [Arab.], ed. M. J. de Goeje (Bibl. Geogr. Arab. VIII) (Leiden, 1894); French transl. B. Carra de Vaux (Paris, Société Asiatique, 1896).

Masʿūdī, *Prata aurea*, ed. with French transl. C. A. C. Barbier de Meynard, 9 vols. (Paris, 1861–77); new ed. C. Pellat (Paris, 1962, in progress).

Matthew of Edessa, *Chronicon* [Arm.]. Full text unpublished. Parts relating to period 963–74 ed. with French transl. J. P. L. F. E. Dulaurier, *Rec. hist. Cr.*, *Doc. armén.* I (1869). Complete French transl. Dulaurier, *Bibl. Hist. Arm.* pt. II (Paris, 1858).

Michael, Syrus, *Chronicon* [Syr.], ed. with French transl. J. B. Chabot, 3 vols. (*AcadIBL*) (Paris, 1899–1910); Arm. version (epitome with additions relating to Armenia) ed. Anon. (Jerusalem, 1870–1), French transl. V. Langlois (Venice, 1868).

Miskawaihī, *Probationes gentium* [Arab.], ed. with English transl. H. F. Amedroz and D. S. Margoliouth, *The Eclipse of the 'Abbasid Caliphate*, I, II, IV, V (Oxford, 1920, 1921). Relevant parts transl. A. A. Vasiliev, *Byzance et les Arabes*, II, pt. 2 [see Gen. Bibl. v].

Narratio de imagine Edessena, ed. E. Dobschütz, in *Texte und Untersuchungen*, N.F. III (Leipzig, 1899), 39**.

Nāṣir i-Khusraw, *Sefer Nāmeh* (*Liber Itineris*), ed. and French transl. C. Schefer (Paris, 1881).

Nāṣir i-Khusraw, *A Diary of a Journey through Syria and Palestine*, transl. G. Le Strange (Palestine Pilgrims' Text Society, IV) (London, 1896).

an-Noʿmān ibn Moḥammed (Abū Ḥanīfa), *Liber conventorum et colloquiorum*, unpublished. Extract with English transl. S. M. Stern, *B*, XX (1950), 239–58; extracts in H. I. Hassan and T. A. Sharaf, *Al-Muʿizz li-dīn-i'llah* (Cairo, 1948); French transl. M. Canard, *REB*, XIX (1961).

Nuwairī, *Encyclopaedia* [Arab.], 18 vols. (Cairo, 1924–49). Parts relating to Sicily ed. with transl. M. Amari, *Bibl. Arabo-Sicula*, pp. 423 ff. [see above]; transl. A. A. Vasiliev, *Byzance et les Arabes*, II, pt. 2 [see Gen. Bibl. v].

Qudāma, *Liber tributi* [Arab.], see Ibn Khurdādhbih, above. [Important for Arab military organisation.]

Risālat Abī'r-Rabīʿ Mohammed ben al-Laith ilā Qustanṭīn malik ar-Rūm, ed. Asad Lutfī Hasan (Cairo, 1936). [From Hārūn ar-Rashīd.]

Rosen, V. R., *Imperator Vasilij Bolgarobojca, Izvlečenija iz letopisi Jachji Antiochijskago* [*The Emperor Basil the Slayer of the Bulgarians, Extracts from the Chronicle of Yaḥyā of Antioch*] (*Mém. Acad. IP.* 44) (St Petersburg, 1883).

Rudhrāwarī Abū Shujāʾ, *Historia Islamica* [Arab.], ed. and transl. H. F. Amedroz and D. S. Margoliouth, *The Eclipse of the 'Abbasid Caliphate*, III, VI (Oxford, 1920–1) [continuation of Miskawaihī].

Stephanus Taronensis, *Historia Armeniae* [Arm.], ed. S. Malkhasian (St Petersburg, 1885); German transl. H. Gelzer and A. Burckhardt (Leipzig, 1907); French transl. I, J. Dulaurier (Paris, 1883); II, F. Macler (Paris, 1917).

Ṭabarī, *Historia populorum et regum* [Arab.], ed. M. J. de Goeje and others, 15 vols. (Leiden, 1879–1901). Relevant parts transl. E. W. Brooks, *JHS*, XVIII–XIX (1898–9), *EHR*, XV (1900), and A. A. Vasiliev, *Byzance et les Arabes*, II, pt. 2 [see Gen. Bibl. v].

Ṭaifūr, Ahmed ibn abī Ṭāhir, *Sechster Band des Kitāb Baghdād*, ed. and German transl. H. Keller (Leipzig, 1908). Relevant part transl. A. A. Vasiliev, *Byzance et les Arabes*, I [see Gen. Bibl. v].

Tanūkhī, *The Table-talk of a Mesopotamian Judge*, ed. and transl. D. S. Margoliouth (London, 1921, 1922); extracts transl. A. A. Vasiliev, *Byzance et les Arabes*, II, pt. 2 [see Gen. Bibl. v].

Theodosius Monachus, *Ep. ad Leonem diaconum de expugnatione Syracusarum*, Greek text (imperfect), ed. C. O. Zuretti, Ἰταλοελληνικά. *Centenario della nascita di M. Amari*, I (Palermo, 1910), 165 ff.; Latin version (complete) Josaphat of Messina, *RISS* (1st ed.), I, ii, 256 ff. (Milan, 1725).

Vie du patriarche melkite d'Antioche Christophore († 967) *par le protospathaire Ibrāhīm ibn Yuhannā*. Document inédit du Xe siècle, publ. par H. Zayat. Proche-Orient Chrétien, II (Jerusalem, 1952).

Vita Sancti Eliae Siculi mon. in Calabria († 903), *AASS*, 17 Aug. III (1737), 489–507 (Latin).

Vita Sancti Pauli iunioris († 955), ed. H. Delehaye, *AB*, XI (1892), 19–74, 136–81.

Yaḥjā of Antioch, *Annales* [Arab.], ed. P. L. Cheikho and others (*CSCO*) (Beirut and Paris, 1909) [with Eutychius]. Extracts relating to reign of Basil II ed. with Russian transl. and commentary, V. R. Rosen [see above]. Relevant parts to 959 transl. A. A. Vasiliev, *Byzance et les Arabes*, II, pt. 2 [see Gen. Bibl. v].

Ya'qūbi ibn Wādīh, *Historiae* [Arab.], ed. M. T. Houtsma, 2 vols. (Leiden, 1883). Relevant parts for period 717–813 transl. E. W. Brooks, 'The Arabs in Asia Minor from Arabic Sources', *JHS*, XVIII (1898); *EHR*, XV (1900). See also A. A. Vasiliev, *Vizantija i Araby*, I (for period 813–67) and *Byzance et les Arabes*, II, pt. 2 [see Gen. Bibl. v].

II. MODERN WORKS

Amari, M., *Biblioteca Arabo-Sicula*, vers. ital. 2 vols. and app. 8vo ed. (Turin, Florence and Rome, 1881, 1889). [Introduction on authors dealing with Sicily.] Notices of the Arabic authorities are also given in A. A. Vasiliev, *Byzance et les Arabes* [see Gen. Bibl. v].

Amari, M., *Storia dei Musulmani di Sicilia*, 4 vols. (Florence, 1854–68); 2nd ed. revised by C. A. Nallino, 3 vols. (Catania, 1933, 1935, 1937).

Amedroz, H. F., 'An Embassy from Baghdad to the Emperor Basil II', *JRAS* (1914), 915–42.

Anderson, J. G. C., 'The Campaign of Basil I against the Paulicians in 872', *CR*, X (1896), 136.

Anderson, J. G. C., 'The Road-system of Eastern Asia Minor', *JHS*, XVII (1897), 22–44 (with map).

Bartikian, R. M., *Istočniki dlja izučenija istorii povlikianskovo dvizenija* (*Sources for a study of the Paulician movement*). Acad. of Sc. of the S.S.R. of Armenia (Erevan, 1961).

Boor, C. de, 'Der Angriff der Rhôs auf Byzanz', *BZ*, IV (1895), 445–66. [For the chronology of the campaigns of 859–63.]

Bréhier, L., 'La marine de Byzance du VIIIe au XIe siècle', *B*, XIX (1949), 1–16.

Brockelmann, C., *Geschichte der arabischen Literatur*, 2 vols. (Weimar and Berlin, 1897–1902). *Supplementbände*, 3 vols. (Leiden, 1937–42). And in another form in *Die Litteraturen des Ostens*, VI (Leipzig, 1901).

Brooks, E. W., 'The Arabs in Asia Minor (641–750) from Arabic sources', *JHS*, XVIII (1898), 182–208 [translation of relevant passages with notes].

Brooks, E. W., 'The Campaign of 716–18 from Arabic Sources', *JHS*, XIX (1899), 19. [Translation of passages from the *Kitāb al-'uyūn* and Ṭabarī with notes.]

Brooks, E. W., 'Byzantines and Arabs in the time of the early Abbasids', *EHR*, XV (1900), 728; XVI (1901), 84. [Translation of relevant passages with notes and map.]

Brooks, E. W., 'The Arab Occupation of Crete', *EHR*, XXVIII (1913), 431.

Brooks, E. W., 'The Relations between the Empire and Egypt from a New Arabic Source', *BZ*, XXII (1913), 381–91. [With translation of extracts from Kindi.]

Brooks, E. W., 'The Sources of Theophanes and the Syriac chroniclers', *BZ*, XV (1906), 578–87.

Bury, J. B., 'The Identity of Thomas the Slavonian', *BZ*, I (1892), 55 ff.

Bury, J. B., 'Mutasim's March through Cappadocia', *JHS*, XXIX (1909), 120.

Bury, J. B., 'The Embassy of John the Grammarian', *EHR*, XXIV (1909), 296.

Bury, J. B., 'The Naval Policy of the Roman Empire in Relation to the Western Provinces from the 7th to the 9th Century', *Centenario della nascita di M. Amari*, II (Palermo, 1910), 23 ff.

Bury, J. B., *History of the Eastern Roman Empire* [see Gen. Bibl. v].

Bussell, F. W., *The Roman Empire* [see Gen. Bibl. v; specialises on Armenian relations].

Cahen, C., 'La première pénétration turque en Asie Mineure (seconde moitié du XIe siècle)', *B*, XVIII (1948), 5–67.

Canard, M., 'La guerre sainte dans le monde islamique', *2e Congrès de la Fédération des Sociétés savantes de l'Afrique du Nord, avril 1936*, II, 2 (Algiers, 1936), 605–23.

Canard, M., 'Un personnage de roman arabo-byzantin', *2e Congrès national des Sc. Hist. Alger, avril 1930* (Algiers, 1932), 87–100.

Canard, M., 'Les expéditions des Arabes contre Constantinople dans l'histoire et dans la légende', *JA*, CCVIII (1926), 61–121.

Canard, M., 'Le cérémonial fatimite et le cérémonial byzantin. Essai de comparaison', *B*, XXI (1951), 355–420.

Canard, M., 'Deux documents arabes sur Bardas Skléros', *Atti del V Congresso Internazionale degli Studi Bizantini* (Rome, 1936), *SBN*, v (1939), 55–69.

Canard, M., 'Deux épisodes des relations diplomatiques arabo-byzantines au Xe siècle', *Bull. d'Et. Or. de l'Inst. fr. de Damas*, XIII (1949–50), 51–69.

Canard, M., 'La date des expéditions mésopotamiennes de Jean Tzimiscès' (= *Mélanges H. Grégoire*, II), *AIPHO*, X (1950), 99–108.

Canard, M., *Histoire de la dynastie des Hamdanides de Jazira et de Syrie*, I (Algiers, 1951) (Publ. de la Fac. des Lettres d'Alger, IIe série, XXI).

Canard, M., 'Les Hamdanides et l'Arménie', *Ann. Inst. d'Et. Or. Alger*, VII (1948), 77–94.

Canard, M., 'L'impérialisme des Fatimides et leur propagande', *Ann. Inst. d'Et. Or. Alger*, VI (1942–7), 156–93.

Canard, M., 'Mutanabbi et la guerre byzantino-arabe. Intérêt historique de ses poésies', *Mém. de l'Inst. fr. de Damas: Al-Mutanabbi* (Beirut, 1936), pp. 99–114.

Canard, M., 'Arabes et Bulgares au début du Xe siècle', *B*, XI (1936), 213–23.

Canard, M., 'Une lettre de Muhammed Ibn Tugj al-Ihsīd, émir d'Egypte à l'empereur Romain Lécapène', *Annales de l'Inst. d'Et. Or. de la Fac. des Lettres d'Alger*, II (1936), 189–209.

Canard, M., 'Quelques "à côté" de l'histoire des relations entre Byzance et les Arabes', *Studi orientalistici in onore di Giorgio Levi Della Vida*, I (Rome, 1956), 98–119.

Canard, M., 'Quelques observations sur l'Introduction géographique de la Bughyat at-Talab de Kamal ad-din Ibn al-Adim d'Alep', *Ann. Inst. d'Et. Or. Alger*, XV (1957), 41–53. [On the ribāt of Tarsus.]

Canard, M., 'Les sources arabes de l'histoire byzantine aux confins des Xe et XIe siècles', *REB*, XIX (1961), 284–314.

Canard, M. et Adontz, N., 'Quelques noms de personnages byzantins dans une pièce du poète arabe Abū Firās (Xe siècle)', *B*, XI (1936), 451–60.

Cipolla, C., 'Testi greci della cronaca arabo-sicula di Cambridge', *Atti della R. Accad. delle scienze di Torino*, XXVII (1892), 830 ff.

Cozza-Luzi, G., *Sulla scoperta di due cronache greche siculo-saraceniche e loro correlazione coll'arabico di Cambridge* (Rome, 1893).

Diehl, C. et Marçais, G., *Le Monde Oriental de 395 à 1081* [see Gen. Bibl. v].

Dölger, F., *Regesten der Kaiserurkunden des oströmischen Reiches* [see Gen. Bibl. IV].

Dolley, R. H., 'A Forgotten Byzantine Conquest of Kypros', *Acad. Roy. de Belg. Bull. de la Classe des Lettres*, XXXIV (1948), 209–24.

Dolley, R. H., 'The Lord High Admiral Eustathios Argyros and the Betrayal of Taormina to the African Arabs in 902', *Atti dello VIII Congresso Internaz. di Stud. Biz.* (Palermo, 1951), *SBN*, VII (1953), 340–53.

Dolley, R. H., 'Naval Tactics in the Heyday of the Byzantine Thalassocraty', *Atti dello VIII Congresso Internaz. di Studi Biz.* (Palermo, 1951), *SBN*, VII (1953), 324–39.

Dozy, R., *Histoire des Musulmans d'Espagne*, new ed. revised by E. Lévi-Provençal, 3 vols. (Leiden, 1931).

Dubler, C. E., 'Los asedios musulmanes de Constantinople en la "Primera Cronica General" de Alfonso lo Sabio', *Al-Andalus*, IX (1944), 141–55.

Dujčev, I., 'Odna iz osobennostej rannevizantijskich mirnych dogovorov' ['A peculiarity of early Byzantine peace treaties'], *VV*, XV (1959), 64–70.

Dulaurier, J. P. L. F. E., *Recherches sur la chronologie arménienne*. Bibl. Hist. Arm. pt. I (Paris, 1859).

Duval, R., *La Littérature Syriaque* (Bibliothèque de l'enseignement de l'histoire ecclésiastique) (Paris, 1899); 3rd ed. (1907).

Eickhoff, E., 'Byzantinische Wachtflottillen in Unteritalien im 10. Jahrhundert', *BZ*, XLV (1952), 340–4.

Fahmy, Aly Mohammed, *Muslim Sea-Power in the Eastern Mediterranean from the Seventh to the Tenth Century A.D.* (London, 1950).

Filler, E., *Quaestiones de Leontii Armenii historia* (Commentationes philologicae Jenenses 7, fasc. 1) (Jena, 1903).

Freytag, G., 'Geschichte der Dynastie der Hamdaniden in Mosul und Aleppo', *ZDMG*, X–XI (1856–7), 178 ff. and 441 ff.

Gabotto, F., *Eufemio e il movimento separatista nell'Italia bizantina* (Turin, 1890).

Gabrieli, F., *Il califfato di Hishâm. Studi di storia omayyade* (Alexandria, 1935) (Mém. de la Soc. Roy. d'Arch. d'Alexandrie, VII, 2).

Gabrieli, F., 'L'eroe omayyade Maslamah ibn 'Abd al-Malik', *Rend. Acc. Lincei*, VIII, 5 (1950), 22–39.

Gaudefroy-Demombynes, J. and Platonov, S. F., *Le Monde musulman et byzantin jusqu'aux Croisades* [see Gen. Bibl. v].

Gay, J., *L'Italie méridionale et l'Empire byzantin (867–1071)* [see Gen. Bibl. v].

Ghazarian, M., 'Armenien unter der arabischen Herrschaft bis zur Entstehung des Bagratidenreiches', *Zeit. f. armenische Philologie*, II (1903), 149–225; printed separately (Marburg, 1903).

Gibb, H. A. R., 'Arab–Byzantine Relations under the Umayyad Caliphate', *DOP*, XII (1958), 221–33.

Grabar, A., 'Le succès des arts orientaux à la cour byzantine sous les Macédoniens', *Münchener Jahrbuch der bildenden Kunst*, III, 2 (1951), 32–50.

Graf, G., *Geschichte der christlichen arabischen Literatur*, 2 vols. (Vatican City, 1944, 1947).

Grégoire, H., 'Héros épiques méconnus', *La Nouv. Clio*, IV (1952), 378–84.

Grégoire, H., 'Le communiqué arabe sur la prise de Thessalonique (904)', *B*, XXII (1952), 373–8.

Grégoire, H., 'La carrière du premier Nicéphore Phocas', *Mélanges Kyriakidès* (Thessalonica, 1953), 238–54 (= Ἑλληνικά, παράρτημα IV).

Grégoire, H., 'Manuel et Théophobe ou la concurrence de deux monastères', *B*, IX (1934), 183–204.

Grégoire, H., 'Etudes sur l'épopée byzantine', *REG*, XLVI (1933), 29–69.

Grégoire, H., 'Etudes sur le IXe siècle', *B*, VIII (1933), 515–50.

Grégoire, H., 'Michel III et Basile le Macédonien dans les inscriptions d'Ancyre', *B*, V (1929), 327–46.

Grégoire, H., 'Inscriptions historiques byzantines. Ancyre et les Arabes sous Michel l'Ivrogne', *B*, IV (1927–8), 437–68.

Grégoire, H., 'Le tombeau et la date de Digenis Akritas', *B*, VI (1931), 481–508.

Grégoire, H., 'Saint-Démétrianos, évêque de Chytre (île de Chypre)', *BZ*, XVI (1907), 204–40.

Grumel, V., *La Chronologie* [see Gen. Bibl. III].

Grumel, V., 'La révolte d'Andronic Doux sous Léon VI. La victoire navale d'Himérios', *EO*, XXXVI (1937), 202–7.

Grumel, V., 'Chronologie des événements du règne de Léon VI', *EO*, XXXV (1936), 5–42.

Guilland, R., 'Les Patrices stratèges byzantins en Italie méridionale de l'avènement de Basile Ier à la mort de Léon VI (867–912). Contribution à la prosopographie de l'empire byzantin', *Atti dello VIII Congresso Internaz. di Studi Biz.* (Palermo, 1951), *SBN*, VII (1953), 377–86.

Güterbock, C., *Der Islam im Lichte der byzantinischen Polemik* (Berlin, 1912).

Halkin, F., 'Saint-Antoine le Jeune et Petronas le vainqueur des Arabes en 863 (d'après un texte inédit)', *AB*, LXII (1944), 187–225.

Hartmann, L. M., *Geschichte Italiens im Mittelalter*, III, IV [see Gen. Bibl. V].

Hill, G. F., *A History of Cyprus*, I [see Gen. Bibl. V].

Hitti, P. K., *History of the Arabs* [see Gen. Bibl. V].

Hitti, P. K., *History of Syria, including Lebanon and Palestine* (London, 1951).

Holm, A., *Geschichte Siciliens im Alterthum*, III (Leipzig, 1898).

Honigmann, E., 'Charsianon Kastron', *B*, X (1935), 129–60.

Honigmann, E., *Die Ostgrenze des byzantinischen Reiches von 363 bis 1071* [see Gen. Bibl. V].

Huart, C., *Histoire des Arabes*, 2 vols. (Paris, 1912).

Ibrāhīm Ahmed al-'Adawī, *The Byzantine Empire and the Islamic Empire* [in Arabic] (Cairo, 1951).

Izeddin, M. and Therriat, P., 'Un prisonnier arabe à Byzance au IXe siècle, Hāroun ibn Yahya', *Rev. des Et. Isl.*, 1941–7 (Paris, 1947), 41–62.

Janin, R., 'Un Arabe ministre à Byzance: Samonas (IXe–Xe siècle)', *EO*, XXXIV (1935), 307–18.

Jeffery, A., 'Ghevond's Text of the Correspondence between Umar II and Leo III', *HTR*, XXXVII (1944), 269–332.

Jenkins, R. J. H., 'Cyprus between Byzantium and Islam A.D. 688–965', *Studies presented to D. M. Robinson*, II (1953), 1006–14.

Jenkins, R. J. H., 'The Emperor Alexander and the Saracen prisoners', *Atti dello VIII Congresso Internaz. di Studi Biz.* (Palermo, 1951), *SBN*, VII (1953), 389–93.

Jenkins, R. J. H., 'The Flight of Samonas', *SP*, XXIII (1948), 217–35.

Jenkins, R. J. H., 'The Mission of St Demetrianos of Cyprus to Bagdad', *AIPHO*, IX (1949) (= Mélanges H. Grégoire, I), 267–75.

Jenkins, R. J. H., 'The Date of Leo VI's Cretan Expedition', Προσφορὰ εἰς Στ. Κυριακίδην = Ἑλληνικά, Παράρτημα IV (Thessalonica, 1953), 277–81.

Jenkins, R. J. H., Laourdas, B. and Mango, C. A., 'Nine Orations of Arethas', *BZ*, IV (1954), 1–40.

Kutschuk-Ioannesov, C., 'La lettre de l'empereur Jean Tzimiscès au roi Arménien Ashot III', *VV*, x (1903), 91–101 [in Russian].

Laurent, J., *Byzance et les Turcs Seljoucides dans l'Asie occidentale jusqu'en 1081* (Ann. de l'Est, publ. par la Fac. des Lettres de l'Univ. de Nancy, XXVII–XXVIII) (Paris, 1913–14).

Laurent, J., *L'Arménie entre Byzance et l'Islam depuis la conquête arabe jusqu'en 886* (*EcfrAR*, 117) (Paris, 1919). [Bibliography and useful map.]

Lavagnini, B., 'Siracusa occupata dagli Arabi (Teodosio Monaco narra)', *La Giara*, I (1952), 69–74.

Lebeau, C., *Histoire du Bas-Empire* [see Gen. Bibl. v].

Lemerle, P., *Histoire de Byzance* (Paris, 1948).

Leonhardt, K., *Kaiser Nicephorus II Phokas und die Hamdaniden* (Halle, 1887).

Le Strange, G., *Baghdad during the Abbasid Caliphate* (Cambridge, 1900).

Le Strange, G., 'A Greek Embassy to Baghdad', *JRAS* (1897), 35–45.

Le Strange, G., *The Lands of the Eastern Caliphate* [see Gen. Bibl. II].

Levčenko, M. V., *Istorija Vizantii*, and French translation [see Gen. Bibl. v].

Levi Della Vida, G., 'A Papyrus Reference to the Damietta Raid of 853 A.D.', *B*, XVII (1944–5), 212–21.

Levi Della Vida, G., 'Costantinopoli nella tradizione islamica', *Acc. Naz. dei Lincei. Rendiconti dell'adunanze solenni*, vol. v, fasc. 8 (Rome, 1953), pp. 363–73.

Lévi-Provençal, E., 'Un échange d'ambassades entre Cordoue et Byzance au IXe siècle', *B*, XII (1937), 1–24.

Lévi-Provençal, E., *Histoire de l'Espagne musulmane*, 3 vols. (Paris–Leiden, 1950–3).

Lewis, A. R., *Naval Power and Trade in the Mediterranean A.D. 500–1100* (Princeton, 1951).

Lewis, B., 'An Arabic Account of a Byzantine Palace Revolution', *B*, XIV (1939), 383–6.

Markwart, J., *Osteuropäische und ostasiatische Streifzüge* (Leipzig, 1903).

Markwart, J., *Südarmenien und die Tigrisquellen nach griechischen und arabischen Geographen* (Vienna, 1930).

Mercier, E., *Histoire de l'Afrique septentrionale* (Paris, 1888).

Nau, F., 'Les auteurs des chroniques attribuées à Denys de Tellmahré et à Josué le Stylite', *Bull. crit. de litt., hist. et théol.*, ser. 2, III (1897), 54–8.

Nau, F., 'La 4me partie de la chronique de Denys de Tellmahré' [review of Chabot's ed.], *Bull. crit. de litt., hist. et théol.*, ser. 2, II (1896), 321–7.

Nau, F., 'Nouvelle étude sur la chronique attribuée à Denys de Tellmahré', *Bull. crit. de litt., hist. et théol.*, ser. 2, II (1896), 464–79.

Nau, F., 'Etude sur les parties inédites de la Chronique ecclésiastique attribuée à Denys de Tell Mahré, *ROC*, II (1897), 41 ff.

Nöldeke, T., 'La chronique de Denys de Tellmahré' [review of Chabot's ed.], *Vienna Oriental Journal*, x (1896), 160–70.

Obolensky, D., *The Bogomils* [see Gen. Bibl. v].

Ostrogorsky, G., *History of the Byzantine State* [see Gen. Bibl. v].

Rambaud, A. N., *L'empire grec au Xe siècle* [see Gen. Bibl. v].

Ramsay, W. M., *The Historical Geography of Asia Minor* [see Gen. Bibl. II].

Rémondon, R., 'A propos de la menace byzantine sur Damiette sous le règne de Michel III', *B*, XXIII (1953), 243–50.

Runciman, S., *The Emperor Romanus Lecapenus* [see Gen. Bibl. v].

Runciman, S., *The Medieval Manichee. A Study of the Christian Dualist Heresy* (Cambridge, 1947).

Runciman, S., 'Le "protectorat" byzantin sur la Terre Sainte au XIe siècle', *B*, XVIII (1948), 207–15.

Salmon, G., *Introduction topographique à l'Histoire de Bagdad* (Bibl. de l'Ec. des Hautes Etudes, no. 180) (Paris, 1904). [The embassy of 917.]

Schlumberger, G., *Un empereur byzantin au Xe siècle* [see Gen. Bibl. v].

Schlumberger, G., *L'épopée byzantine* [see Gen. Bibl. v].

Shangin, M. A., 'Vizantijskie meroprijatija po ochrane granic' ('Mesures byzantines pour la défense des frontières'), *Istorik Marksist*, vol. 92, no. 4 (1941), 89–92.

Stern, S. M., 'An Embassy of the Byzantine Emperor to the Fatimid Caliph Al-Mu'izz', *B*, XX (1950), 239–58.

Strück, A., 'Die Eroberung Thessalonikes durch die Sarazenen im Jahre 904', *BZ*, XIV (1905), 532–62.

Tomaschek, W., 'Historisch-topographisches vom oberen Euphrat und aus Ost-Kappadokien', *Kiepert-Festschrift* (Berlin, 1898), pp. 137–49.

Tomaschek, W., 'Zur historischer Topographie v. Kleinasien im Mittelalter', *SKAW*, CXXIV (1891), Abh. 8, 106 ff.

Tomaschek, W., 'Sasun und das Quellgebiet des Tigris', *SKAW*, CXXXIII (1895), Abh. 4, 14 ff.

Vasiliev, A. A., 'Harun-ibn-Yahya and His Description of Constantinople', *Sem. Kond.* v (1932), 149–63.

Vasiliev, A. A., *History of the Byzantine Empire* [see Gen. Bibl. v].

Vasiliev, A. A., *Vizantija i Araby*; and French edition *Byzance et les Arabes*. [Critical history from 813 with translation of relevant passages from Arabic writers [see Gen. Bibl. v].]

Vasiliev, A. A., 'The "Life" of St Peter of Argos and its historical significance', *Trad.* v (1947), 163–91.

Vogt, A., *Basile I* [see Gen. Bibl. v].

Weil, G., *Geschichte der Chalifen*, I–II [see Gen. Bibl. v].

Wellhausen, J., *Das arabische Reich und sein Sturz* (Berlin, 1902).

Wellhausen, J., 'Die Kämpfe d. Araber mit den Romäern in d. Zeit d. Umaijiden', *Nachrichten d. K. Gesellschaft d. Wissenschaften zu Göttingen*, Philol.-hist. Cl. (1901), Heft 4, pp. 414 ff. [Detailed criticism of the records and reconstruction.]

Wüstenfeld, F., 'Die Geschichtsschreiber der Araber und ihre Werke', *Abh. d. Kön. Gesellschaft d. Wissenschaften zu Göttingen*, Hist.-phil. Cl. XXVIII, no. 2, 3; XXIX, no. 1 (1881–2).

CHAPTER XVIII. THE TURKS AND THE BYZANTINE EMPIRE

Only works in European languages are given; original sources are included only if they are available in translation or arrangement in a European language.

I. THE SELJUQS OF RŪM

Duda, H. W., *Die Seltschukengeschichte des Ibn Bībī* (Copenhagen, 1959).

Gordlevsky, V., *Gosudarstvo Seldžukidov Maloj Azii* [*The Seljuq State in Asia Minor*], Akademija Nauk SSSR: Institut Vostokovedenija, Moscow (Leningrad, 1941).

Isiltan, E., *Die Seltschuken-Geschichte des Askerayi* (Collection of Oriental Studies published by Otto Harrassowitz, XII) (Leipzig, 1943).

Lehmann, B., *Die Nachrichten des Niketas Choniates, Georgios Akropolites und Pachymeres über die Selčuqen in der Zeit von 1180 bis 1280 n. Chr.* Leipzig Thesis (Gräfenhainichen, 1939).

Mordmann, A. D., 'Die Dynastie der Danischmende', *ZDMG*, xxx (1870), 467–86.

Talbot Rice, T., *The Seljuks* (London, 1961).

II. THE ANATOLIAN PRINCIPALITIES

Giesecke, H. H., *Das Werk des ʿAzīz ibn Ārdašīr Astarābādī. Eine Quelle zur Geschichte des Spätmittelalters in Kleinasien* (Collection of Oriental Studies published by Otto Harrassowitz, II) (Leipzig, 1940).

Ibn Baṭṭūṭa, *Travels*, ed. and transl. C. Defrémery and B. R. Sanguinetti, 4 vols. (Paris, 1853–8); transl. H. A. R. Gibb, 2 vols. (Cambridge, 1958–62).

Quatremère, M., 'Notice de l'ouvrage qui a pour titre: Mesalek alabsar fi memalek alamsar. Voyages des yeux dans les royaumes des différentes contrées. (Manuscrit arabe de la Bibliothèque du Roi. No. 583)', *Notices et extraits des manuscrits de la Bibliothèque du Roi et autres Bibliothèques*, XIII (Paris, 1838), 151–384.

Wittek, P., *Das Fürstentum Mentesche. Studien zur Geschichte Westkleinasiens im 13.–15. Jh.* (Istanbuler Mitteilungen, II) (Istanbul, 1934).

Wittek, P., 'Deux chapitres de l'histoire des Turcs de Roum', *B*, XI (1936), 285–319.

CHAPTER XIX. THE OTTOMAN TURKS TO 1453

Babinger, F., 'Schejch Bedr ed-din. Der Sohn des Richters von Simaw', *Der Islam*, XI (1921), 1–106.

Babinger, F., 'Der Islam in Kleinasien', *ZDMG*, LXXVI (1922), 126–52.

Babinger, F., *Beiträge zur Frühgeschichte der Türkenherrschaft in Rumelien (14.–15. Jahrhundert)* (Southern European Studies, commissioned by the German Institute of Foreign Studies [Berlin], the South-east Institute [Munich], and the South-east Society of Viennese Universities, 34) (Munich, 1944).

Babinger, F., 'Von Amurath zu Amurath. Vor- und Nachspiel der Schlacht bei Varna (1444)', *Oriens*, III (1950), 229–65; and IV (1951), 80.

Babinger, F., *Mehmed der Eroberer und seine Zeit* (Munich, 1963) [also translations in French and Italian].

Die altosmanischen anonymen Chroniken (Tevārih-i āl-i ʿOsmān). Text and transl. F. Giese, Teil II. Translation (*Abhandlungen für die Kunde des Morgenlandes, Deutsche Morgenländische Gesellschaft*, XVII,1)(Leipzig,1925).

Draeseke, J., 'Der Übergang der Osmanen nach Europa im XIV. Jahrhundert', *Neue Jahrbücher für das klassische Altertum*, XXXI (1913), 476–504.

Duda, H. W., *Balkantürkische Studien*. Österreichische Akademie der Wissenschaften. Philos.-histor. Kl., Sitzungsberichte, Bd. 226, Abh. I (Vienna, 1949).

Georgiades Arnakes, G., Οἱ πρῶτοι Ὀθωμανοί. Συμβολὴ εἰς τὸ πρόβλημα τῆς πτώσεως τοῦ Ἑλληνισμοῦ τῆς Μικρᾶς Ἀσίας *(1282–1337)* (Texte und Forschungen zur byzantinisch-neugriechischen Philologie, 41) (Athens, 1947).

Gibb, H. A. R., and Bowen, H., *Islamic Society and the West*, I, pts. 1 and 2 (London, 1950–7).

Gibbons, H. A., *The Foundation of the Ottoman Empire. A History of the Osmanlis up to the death of Bayezid I, 1300–1403* (Oxford, 1916).

Giese, F., 'Das Problem der Entstehung des osmanischen Reiches', *Zeit. Semitistik*, II (1923), 246–71.

Hammer-Purgstall, J., *Geschichte des osmanischen Reiches*, I. *Von der Gründung des osmanischen Reiches bis zur Eroberung Constantinopels, 1300–1453* (Pest, 1827); reprinted (1962).

Hartmann, R., 'Das "älteste" uns erhaltene "osmanische Geschichte enthaltende Werk"', *Mitteilungen zur osmanischen Geschichte*, II (1923–6), 306–8.

Hertzberg, G. F., *Geschichte der Byzantiner und des osmanischen Reiches bis gegen Ende des sechzehnten Jahrhunderts* (Berlin, 1883).

Huart, C., 'Les origines de l'Empire Ottoman', *Journ. Savants*, n.s. XV (1917), 157–66.

Jorga, N., *Geschichte des osmanischen Reiches, nach den Quellen dargestellt*, I (to 1451) (Gotha, 1908).

Kissling, H. J., 'Das Menaqybname Scheich Bedr ed-Din's, des Sohnes des Richters von Samavna', *ZDMG*, C (1950), 112–76.

Köprülü, Mehmed Fuad, *Les Origines de l'Empire Ottoman* (Etudes Orientales, publiées par l'Institut Français d'Archéologie de Stamboul, sous la direction de M. Albert Gabriel, III) (Paris, 1935).

Kraelitz, F. von, 'Das osmanische Herrscherhaus und die Gründung des osmanischen Reiches', *Österreichische Monatsschrift für den Orient*, XL (1914), 8–40.

Kramers, J. H., 'Wer war Osman?', *Acta orientalia*, VI (1927), 242–54.

Kreutel, R. F., *Vom Hirtenzelt zur Hohen Pforte* (Graz, 1959).

[Kurat], Akdes Nimet, *Die türkische Prosopographie bei Laonikos Chalkokondyles*. Diss. (Hamburg, 1933).

Langer, W. L. and Black, R. P., 'The Rise of the Ottoman Turks and its historical background', *AHR*, XXXVII (1932), 468–505.

Leunclavius, Johannes, *Annales Sultanorum Othmanidarum, a Turcis sua lingua scripti* (Frankfurt am Main, 1588).

Leunclavius, Johannes, *Historiae Musulmanae Turcorum de monumentis ipsorum exscriptae*, libri XVIII (Frankfurt, 1591).

Lewenklaw von Amelsbüren, Hans, *Neuwe Chronica Türckischer Nation, von Türcken selbst beschrieben* (Frankfurt am Main, 1590).

Lewenklaw von Amelsbüren, Hans, *Neuwer Musulmanischer Histori Türckischer Nation, von ihrem Herkommen, Geschichten und Thaten, drey Bücher die ersten unter dreyssigen* (Frankfurt am Main, 1590).

Marquart, J., *Über die Herkunft der Osmanen* (Über das Volkstum der Komanen, Anhang II). Abhandlungen der Kgl. Gesellschaft der Wissenschaft zu Göttingen. Phil.-hist. Kl. N.F. XIII (1914), 25–240.

Nöldeke, T., 'Auszüge aus Nésrî's Geschichte des osmanischen Hauses', *ZDMG*, XIII (1859), 176–218 (History of 'Osmān); and XV (1861), 333–71 (History of Bāyezīd I).

Seif, T., 'Der Abschnitt über die Osmanen in Šükrullahs persischer Universalgeschichte', *Mitteilungen zur osmanischen Geschichte*, II (1923–6), 63–128.

Silberschmidt, M., *Das orientalische Problem zur Zeit der Entstehung des türkischen Reiches nach venezianischen Quellen. Ein Beitrag zur Geschichte der Beziehungen Venedigs zu Sultan Bajezid I., zu Byzanz, Ungarn und Genua und zum Reiche von Kiptschak, 1381–1400* (Contributions to a Cultural History of the Middle Ages and the Renaissance, published by W. Goetz, XXVII) (Leipzig–Berlin, 1923).

Taeschner, F., 'Der Weg des osmanischen Staates von Glaubenskämpferbund zum islamischen Weltreich', *Die Welt als Geschichte*, VI (1940), 206–15.

Taeschner, F. and Wittek, P., 'Die Vezirfamilie der Ğandarlyzāde (14./15. Jhdt.) und ihre Denkmäler', *Der Islam*, XVIII (1929), 40–75.

Wittek, P., 'De la défaite d'Ankara à la prise de Constantinople (un demi-siècle d'histoire ottomane)', *Revue des Etudes Islamiques*, (1938), 1–34.

Wittek, P., 'Der Stammbaum der Osmanen', *Der Islam*, XIV (1925). 94–100.

Wittek, P., *The Rise of the Ottoman Empire* (Royal Asiatic Society Monographs, XXIII) (London, 1938).

Wittek, P., 'Le Sultan de Rūm', *Mélanges Emile Boisacq = AIPHO*, VI (1938), (1)–(30).

Zinkeisen, J. W., *Geschichte des osmanischen Reiches in Europa. I: Urgeschichte und Wachsthum des Reiches bis zum Jahre 1453* (Hamburg, 1840).

ADDENDA TO CHAPTER XIV

Bedoukian, P. Z., *Coinage of Cilician Armenia* (*Num. Notes and Mon.* 147) (New York, 1962).

Rüdt-Collenberg, W. H., *The Rupenids, Hethumides and Lusignans: the Structure of the Armeno-Cilician Dynasties* (Lisborn, 1963).

Toumanoff, C., *Studies in Christian Caucasian History* (Georgetown University, 1963).

INDEX

Bold figures denote a major entry.

Aachen (Aix-la-Chapelle), 97, 228, 260, 272, 448
  Palatine chapel at, 616
Aaron Comitopulus of Bulgaria, 178
Abagha, Il-Khan leader, 634, 750–1
Abas I, king of Armenia, 614
Abas, High Constable under Smbat I of Armenia, 613
Abasgia, Georgian kingdom, 610 and n. 2, 613, 617–18, 621, 624, 626
  and Basil II, 189
  strategic importance to Byzantium, 474, 512
  the Church in, 601 n. 1
  renamed Imeretia, q.v. (1258), 626
  rulers, *see* List of Rulers 7
Abastactus, Theophylact, father of Romanus Lecapenus, 137 n. 1
'Abbās, uncle of the Prophet Muḥammad, 638, 663
'Abbās, brother of al-Manṣūr, wars with Byzantium, 704–5
'Abbās, son of al-Ma'mūn, wars with Byzantium, 710
'Abbās, Arab governor of Sicily, 728–9
al-'Abbās ibn al-Aḥnaf, poet of Irak, 686
Abbasid Caliphate, *see* List of Rulers 8c *and* Baghdad; **638–61, 662–95**
  ancestry of Caliphs, 638
  overthrow of Umayyads, 607, 638–40, 663, 699, 703
  Persian influence, 641–3, 645, 649, 657, 667–9, 678, 680, 700
  Turkish influence, 651–2, 655, 659–60, 664, 701–2, 712
  religious policy, 641–2, *and see* Sunnitism
  religious status of Caliphs, 646, 649, 655, 657, 659, 661, 664–6, 690, 700–1
  court ceremonial, 641, 700–1, 735
  political theory, 665–6, 700–1
  and social structure, 643–4, 647–8, 651, 656–7, 664, 666–8, 678–80, 693–4
  administration, 642, 649, 656–7, 659, 664, 700
  and agriculture, 643–4, 676–7
  and industry, 644
  and economic life, 646, 649–50, 656, 676–8

army, 641–2, 649, 651, 664, 701–2
  revolts against, 609, 641–2, 645–9, 655, 657, 667, 682, 701–2, 704, 709–10, 714, 717
  decline, 139–40, 644–6, 649, 702–4, 712–14, 727
  under Buwayhids, 649, 655, 659, 666, 680, 702–3, 723
  and Seljuq sultans, 653–60, 737–41
  treatment of non-Muslims, 666–7, 680
  treatment of Bardas Sclerus, 177–8
  loss of Spain, North Africa, Egypt and Syria, 645, 663, 701
  and Caucasia, 607–13
  wars with Byzantium, 645–6, 651, **703–18**, 727
  challenge of Fatimids, 648–9
  Khazar raids on, 651, 707
  destruction by Mongols, 660–1
Abbasid Caliphs in Egypt, 654, 765
abbeys
  in Greece, 397, 411
  in Hungary, 575, 587
  in Caucasia, 615, 625
  in the West, 266, 409, 459
'Abd al-Bāqī, Muslim family in Adana, 735
'Abd Allāh, Arab commander in Sicily, 729
'Abd Allāh ibn 'Alī, Abbasid governor of Syria, 703
'Abd Allāh ibn-Hātim, Arab viceroy in Caucasia, 606
'Abd al-Wahhāb, Umayyad prince, 698 governor of Mesopotamia, 704
'Abd ar-Raḥmān I, Umayyad ruler of Spain, 701
'Abd ar-Raḥmān II, Umayyad ruler of Spain, appealed to for help by Theophilus (839), 103
Abgar, king of Edessa, and the μανδήλιον, 141
Abkhazia, north-west province of Georgian Abasgia (q.v.), 602, 607, 610 and n. 2, 626 n. 2, 628
Abraham, monophysite *Katholikos* of Armenia, 604 and n. 1
Abū Ayūb Khālid ibn Zayd al-Anṣārī, grave of, 773–4
Abū Dā'ūd as-Sijistānī, Muslim jurist, 674

Abū Firās, cousin of Sayf ad-Dawla, prisoner of Nicephorus II Phocas, 721, 734

Abū Hafs, amir of Melitene, 139

Abū Ḥanīfa, Muslim jurist, 676

Abū 'Īsà Muḥammad at-Tirmidhī, Muslim jurist, 674

Abu 'l-'Abbās, *see* as-Saffāḥ

Abu 'l-Aghlab, Arab governor of Sicily, 728

Abu 'l-'Alā' al-Ma'arrī, Arabic poet and philosopher, 687

Abu 'l-'Atāhiya, Arabic religious poet, 686, 735

Abū Muslim, leader of Abbasid revolt against the Umayyads, 638, 639 and n. 1, 641

Abū Nuwās, Arabic poet, 686

Abū Sa'īd, governor of Syria and Mesopotamia for the Abbasids, 711–12

Abū Sa'īd, Il-Khan leader, 753–4, 756

Abū Sa'īd ar-Rustamī, Muslim poet, 668 n. 1

Abū Taghlib, Hamdanid amir of Mosul
and John Tzimisces' campaigns, 164–5, 167, 723
ally of Bardas Sclerus, 177

Abū Tammām, Arabic poet, 686

Abydus, town in Asia Minor on the Hellespont, 63, 89, 93, 179, 698
battle (989), 179
and the Fourth Crusade, 281

Acacian schism (484–519), 71, 434–5

Acacius, Patriarch of Constantinople
and the *Henoticon* of Zeno, 434–5
and the title Oecumenical Patriarch, 439

Acamer of Belzetia, Slav official, 89

Acampsis valley, in Caucasia, 624

Acarnania, district of Greece
claimed by the Venetians in 1204, 289, 392
under the rulers of Epirus, 296 n. 1, 299, 392
subject to Andronicus III, 355
under John Angelus, 359
conquered by Stephen Dušan, 362, 539

Acciajuoli, Florentine banking family in Greece, 406

Acciajuoli, Angelo, son of Niccolò, 407

Acciajuoli, Antonio I, duke of Athens, 421, 423–4

Acciajuoli, Donato, brother of Nerio I, 424

Acciajuoli, Francesco I, duke of Athens, 424

Acciajuoli, Franco, duke of Athens, 424

Acciajuoli, Franco (Francesco), son of Donato, 424

Acciajuoli, Nerio I, duke of Athens, 375, 407, 419, 420 and n. 1, 421, 422–3

Acciajuoli, Nerio II, duke of Athens, 383, 424

Acciajuoli, Niccolò, 406–7

Achaea, Latin principality of, 380, 391 and n. 2, 392–408, 410–11, 419, 423, 429–30
High Court of, 409, 411

Achaemenids, Persian dynasty, 26, 30, 594 and n. 2

Achelous, river in the Balkans, 507

Acilisene, district in Armenia, 596

acolouthia composed in honour of Nicephorus II, 155

Acre (Ptolemais, 'Akkā), town in Palestine
captured by John Tzimisces, 170
naval force sent by Manuel I, 239
Genoese expelled from, 326

Acrocorinth, citadel of Corinth, 388, 389, 408

Acroinon, town in Phrygia, battle (740), 64, 699

Acropolis at Athens, 284, 389, 418, 421–4, 429

Acropolites, George, historian and statesman
view of the Empire of Nicaea, 321
praetor of the western provinces, 322
captured at fall of Prilep, 323
at the Second Council of Lyons, 337

Acts of St Andrew, 456

Adalgisus (Theodotus), son of the last Lombard king
marriage to Pepin III's daughter, 77
at Constantinople, 82
supported by Irene, 88

Adalia, Adaliya, *see* Attalia

Adana, town in Cilicia
Byzantine campaigns against Arabs, 120–1, 149–50, 715, 720–1
rebuilt by Arabs, 704, 706, 708
and Romanus IV, 210
and Lesser Armenia, 629–31
friendly relations with Byzantium, 735

Adarnase I, prince of Iberia, 605

Adarnase II, prince of Iberia, 606

Adarnase III, prince of Iberia, 607–8

Adarnase IV, king of Iberia, 613–14

Adarnase II, Bagratid ruler of Tao and Cholarzene, 611

Adarnase, cousin of Ashot IV of Armenia, 609

Adata (Hadath, Ḥadath), town and pass in Taurus mountains
on route of Arab invasions, 63, 704–5, 708, 710, 719
occupied by Byzantine troops, 103, 146, 711
rebuilt by Arabs, 705, 706, 720
Adela of Vohburg, first wife of Frederick I, marriage annulled, 229
Adhemar, bishop of Puy, and the First Crusade, 466–7
Adiabene, district of Armenia, 597
administration, Byzantine, **32–7**; *see also* civil service
influence on Ottoman administration, 760–1
Adramyttium, town in N.-W. Asia Minor
victory of Henry of Flanders (1205), 291
limit of the Latin Empire, 300
Adrian, Byzantine admiral under Basil I, 121
Adrianople (Edirne), town in Thrace
battle of (378), 26, 94, 490, 597
captured by Bulgars (813), 98, 491
capital of the theme of Macedonia, 116
taken by Symeon of Bulgaria, 136, 507
proclamation of pretenders as Emperors, 203, 522
reached by Nicephorus Bryennius, 211
treaty of (1190), 246
under the Latin Empire, 288, 289
and Kalojan of Bulgaria, 293, 294, 525
clash between John Vatatzes and Theodore Ducas, 309, 527
under John Asen II, 310, 527
taken by John Vatatzes, 535
rising of the populace against the aristocracy, 358
coronation of John VI Cantacuzenus, 361
and Matthew Cantacuzenus, 365
plundered by John VI's Turkish troops, 365–6
capture by Turks, 369, 545 n. 1, 762–3
Turkish capital, 369, 542, 545, 554 n. 1, 763, 767, 771, 773
agreement between the Christian powers and the Turks, 383 and n. 1, 384, 771, *and see also* Szegedin
Adriatic Sea
Slav pirates, 25
Byzantine fleets in, 71, 129, 132, 187, 258–9, 729
Venetian trade in, 182, 271–2
Venetian navy in control of, 187

limit of Byzantine Empire under Basil II, 190
Arab raids, 728–9
'Aḍud ad-Dawla, Buwayhid amir of Baghdad, 723–4
Aegean islands
opposition to iconoclasm, 70, 73
repopulation of Constantinople from, 73
under the Latin Emperor of Constantinople, 289, 309
naval operations of Michael VIII, 337
Latin dominion in, 425–7
Venetians in, 425 and n. 1, 426
tributaries of the Turks, 426
Aegean Sea
cities of, 40
trade, 41
wreck of Arab fleet, 63
drungariate of, 64
Byzantine fleets in, 107, 114, 337
Arab fleet in, 129
theme of, 64, 145
Venetian trade in, 271
reached by the Turks, 755, 760
Aegina, Greek island, 289
Aegium, *see* Vostitza
Aetius, eunuch, Irene's minister, 89–90
Aetius, *strategus* of the Anatolikon theme, and the fall of Amorium (838), 711
Aetolia, district of Greece
claimed by the Venetians in 1204, 289, 392
under Michael I of Epirus as vassal of Venetians, 299, 392
under John Angelus, 359
conquered by Stephen Dušan, 362, 539
Afghanistan, 737
Africa, Central, 41
Africa, North
and Justinian, 21, 28, 437
part of Roman Empire, 25
under influence of See of Rome, 432
trade with Europe, 25
in German hands, 27
and Vandals, 28
under Heraclius, 29, 30
Arab conquest, 31, 35, 41, 699
Elpidius welcomed by Arabs (782), 83
Muslim help for Slavs in the Peloponnese, 92
Byzantine prisoners in, 153 and n. 1
Arab army at siege of Antioch (970–1), 163
Arab army in Syria, 170
and crusade of 1270, 335

Africa, North (*cont.*)
independent amirate in ninth century, 645, 701, 727–9, 731–2
and the Ismāʿīlīs, 648
under Fatimids, 648, 682, 703, 726
Berber Empire in, 651
invasion by Bedouins from Egypt, 651
Arab attacks on western Byzantine possessions, 100–1, 121, 153, 727–32
see also Egypt
Afshīn, military commander under al-Muʿtaṣim, 711
Afshīn, Sājid amir in Azerbaijan, 613, 715
Aftakīn, governor of Damascus, 169–70
Afyon Karahisar, *see* Qara Ḥiṣar-i Ṣāḥib
Agapetus I, Pope, 436–7
Agathangelus, Armenian historian, 599 n. 2
Agatho, Pope, and Sixth General Council, 441
Agathon, archbishop, and See of Moravia, 124 n. 1
Agathopolis, town in Thrace on Black Sea, 289
Aghlabid dynasty in North Africa, 663, 727–9, 731–2
conquest of Sicily, 728–9
Agnes (Agnes-Anna) of France, daughter of Louis VII, wife of Alexius II and Andronicus I, 238, 244
Agnes, daughter of Boniface of Montferrat, wife of Henry of Flanders, 294
agriculture, 94
agrarian policy of Comneni, 212
decline in Thrace, 363
in Aegean islands, 426
in Seljuq Sultanate of Rūm, 743
Ahlat, modern name of Khilāt, q.v.
Aḥmad, sultan at Sebastea (Sivas), 754
Aḥmad ibn Ḥanbal, Muslim jurist, 674, 676
Aḥmad ibn Ṭūlūn, independent ruler of Egypt and Syria, 645, 701
Ahwāz, city in Euphrates delta, 702
Aimery, Latin Patriarch of Antioch, reinstated, 235
Aistulf, Lombard king
capture of Ravenna (751), 75, 445
and Pope Stephen II, 76
relations with Venice, 254
Aix (Aix-la-Chapelle), *see* Aachen
Ajtony, Hungarian leader, 573–4
Akche-ḥiṣār, *see* Kroja
akhīs, Turkish semi-religious brotherhoods, 751–2, 756–7, 760
and Murād I, 754, 762

Akova, town in Peloponnese, taken by Turks (1395), 375
akritai, Byzantine frontier troops, 697, 739, 755
akrostichon, Byzantine land-tax, *see* land-tax
Ak Shams ad-Dīn, dervish shaykh at siege of Constantinople (1453), 773–4
Akshehir, frontier district between Ottomans and Karamans, 764
Aḳtshe Koja, Ottoman general, 759
al-: names beginning thus are indexed under the capital letter immediately following
ʿAlāʾ ad-Dīn, name taken by Eretna as sultan in Sebastea (Sivas), 754
ʿAlāʾ ad-Dīn ʿAlī Pasha, brother and adviser of Orkhan, 760
ʿAlāʾ ad-Dīn Bey, prince of Karaman, 762, 764–5
ʿAlāʾ ad-Dīn Kayqubād, *see* Kayqubād I *and* III
Alāʾīyya, *see* Kalonoros
Alania and Alans
and defence of Byzantine frontier, 474, 477, 512
Alans used against Bulgaria, 507
Christianity in, 512
Alania-Ossetia, district in Caucasia, 622 n. 1, 624
Alanya, *see* Kalonoros
Alaric, leader of Visigoths
in Balkans, 26–7
capture of Rome (410), 27
Alashehir, *see* Philadelphia
Alaya, *see* Kalonoros
Albania
invaded by Robert Guiscard, 271
invaded by John Asen II, 527
relations with rulers of Epirus, 305, 322, 535
relations with Empire of Nicaea, 319
relations with Angevins of Sicily, 337
insurrection under Andronicus III, 355
conquests of Stephen Dušan, 356, 362, 538
independent rulers, 541
and the Balšići of Zeta, 552
and Navarrese Company, 419
revolt of Skanderbeg against Turks, 383, 557–8, 770–2
Turkish conquest, 558, 769, 772
Albania, Caspian (Aḷuankʿ), 593–4, 598, 600, 601, 605–6, 609, 610 and n. 3, 611, 613, 616, 620

Albania, Caspian (*cont.*)
  cis-Cyran (Arrān), 605, 610 and n. 3,
    619, 624, 627, 637
  trans-Cyran, 605, 610 n. 3
  Church in, 601 n. 1, 604, 606
Albertino of Canossa, 389
Albigenses, heretical dualist sect in West,
    547
alchemy, and the Arabs, 672, 685
Alcuin, 87–8
Aleaume, brother of Robert of Clari, and
    capture of Constantinople (1204), 285
Aleppo (Turkish Haleb), town in Syria
  and Hamdanids, 146, 149, 680, 703,
    719, 722, 724, 725
  captured by the Byzantines, 148, 721,
    722
  Byzantine protectorate, 150, 182, 720,
    722, 724, 726
  trade with Byzantium, 733
  amirs of, 169, 224, 721
  and Fatimids, 182, 197, 720, 725
  and Latins, 223–4
  and Seljuqs, 654, 740
  and Mirdasids, 725
  and Ayyūbids, 631, 746
  and Mamluks, 636–7
  taken by Timur, 766
  see also Sayf ad-Dawla *and* Nūr-ad-Dīn
Alexander, Emperor
  and council of 879–80, 123
  and Nicholas Mysticus, 132, 134
  appointment of regents for Constan-
    tine VII, 134
  war with Bulgaria, 134, 505
  relations with Zoe, 134, 136
  referred to in epic poem, 137 n. 1
  Arab frontier raids, 717
  death, 130
Alexander the Great, 502
  Hellenistic successors, 2, 24
  conquests in Asia, 24
Alexander II, Pope, 463
Alexander III, Pope, 230, 242–3, 468
Alexander IV, Pope
  relations with Empire of Nicaea, 323
  relations with Baldwin II, 326
Alexander I the Great, king of Georgia,
    627
Alexander, *see* John Alexander, Bul-
    garian tsar
Alexandria
  traditions, 4
  libraries, 4
  centre of learning, 48, 58
  school of theology, 55
  threat from Vandals, 25

affinities with Levant, 54
centre of Christianity, 19, 54
loss to Empire, 36, 39
circus parties, 40
base for Arab attacks, 74, 709
trade, 427
settlement of Arab refugees from
    Cordova, 709
Alexandria, Patriarchs of
  status, 18–19, 433–5, 461
  jurisdiction, 19
  and Arian heresy, 20
  and Church Councils, 66, 84, 113, 118,
    131–2, 434, 716
  political influence, 19
Alexius I Comnenus, Emperor, 193, 194,
    205, **212–19**, 221
  general under Michael VII, 210
  marriage to Irene Ducas, 210–12
  accession, 212, 741
  relations with Seljuqs, 212–14, 466,
    741
  invasion of Greece by Normans, 212–13,
    215–16, 219, 221, 271, 467, 579–80
  attacks from north, 212–14, 221
  trial of John Italus for heresy, 213, 217
  relations with the Papacy, 213–14,
    465–7
  campaigns in Asia Minor, 214–16, 219
  and First Crusade, 214–16, 227, 466–7,
    741
  extent of frontiers, 216
  ecclesiastical policy and Bogomil
    heresy, 217–18
  financial policy, 218
  military policy and grants of land in
    pronoia, 218–19
  relations with Hungary, 579–80
Alexius II Comnenus, Emperor
  birth, 231, 234, 583–4
  marriage to Agnes of France, 238
  under regency, 243–4
  supplanted by Andronicus I and
    strangled, 244, 584
Alexius III Angelus, Emperor, **247–9**,
    281–2
  character, 247
  deposition of Isaac II, 247, 275, 524
  enmity of Henry VI, 247–8, 275
  loss of influence in Balkans, 248, 275,
    524–5
  relations with Pope Innocent III over
    reunion of Churches, 248, 280
  hostility of Latins under leadership of
    Venice, 248–9, 274, 275
  commercial agreement with Venice,
    289

Alexius III (*cont.*)
  and Alexius IV, 278
  and crusaders' attack on Constantinople (1203), 281–2
  in hiding, 283, 286, 288
  connection with Theodore I Lascaris, 291
  in Thessaly with Leo Sgouros, 292, 296, 389
  at Seljuq court at Iconium, 296
  in monastery at Nicaea, 296
Alexius IV Angelus, Emperor
  appeal to West for help against Alexius III, 278
  and Fourth Crusade, 279–84
  co-Emperor with Isaac II, 283–4
  murdered, 284
Alexius V Murtzuphlus, Emperor
  overthrow of Alexius IV, 284
  opposition to Latins of Fourth Crusade, 284
  crusaders' attack on Constantinople (1204), 285–6
  in hiding in Thrace, 286
  capture and death, 291
Alexius the Studite, Patriarch of Constantinople
  and marriage of Zoe to Romanus Argyrus, 195
  hostility of the Paphlagonian Emperors and family, 198–9
Alexius Slav, kinsman of Boril of Bulgaria, and independent principality at Melnik, 299, 526
Alexius Strategopulus, Caesar, general under Michael VIII, 325–8
Alexius, *protostrator* under Manuel I, 230
Alfonso V, king of Aragon and Naples, abortive attempt to restore the Latin Empire, 385–6
'Alī, Caliph, descendant of the Prophet Muḥammad, 647, 663, 681
  Alids, his descendants, 649, 663, 665, 678, 682, 700
Alice, daughter of Ruben III of Lesser Armenia, 631
'Alī ibn Yaḥyā, amir of Tarsus, later governor of Armenia
  campaigns against Byzantium, 712
  defeated and killed at Mayyāfāriqīn (863), 111, 713
'Alī Shīr, Turk powerful in Asia Minor, 755
allelengyon, tax liability, 93, 184
  abolished by Romanus III, 195
Almaric, king of Jerusalem, treaty with Manuel I over Egypt, 236

Álmos, brother of Koloman, king of Hungary, 580, 581
Alp Arslan, Seljuq sultan
  aims, 209
  treatment of Romanus IV, 209–10, 739–40
  attacks on Armenia, 620, 622
  attacks on Georgia, 622
  extent of his Empire, 703, 737
Alpheus, river in the Peloponnese, 394, 405
Alps, 76, 478
Alptekin the Turk, ruler of Damascus, homage to John Tzimisces, 723
Altaic peoples of Central Asia, 651
Alṭ'amar, town in Caucasia, 615
Altino, town in Italy, and Lombard invasion, 250
Altomanović, Nicholas, independent Serbian ruler, 541–2, 549–50
Alūank', *see* Albania, Caspian
Amadeo Buffa, Constable of the Latin Empire, captured and killed by Michael I of Epirus, 299
Amadeo V, count of Savoy, 404
Amadeo VI, count of Savoy
  and crusades against Turks, 370, 429
  acquisition of Tenedos, 373
  prince of Achaea, 423
Amalfi, Italian port
  growth of independence, 77
  envoy at Constantinople, 143
  overshadowed by Venice, 268
  aid for Byzantine fleet against Arabs, 727
  bishop, and schism of 1054, 461–2
Amantea, town in Calabria, and Arab occupation of South Italy, 121
Amanus, mountain range in northern Syria, 195, 722
Amara, town south of Sebastea in Asia Minor, home of Paulicians, 712
Amasea, town in Armeniakon theme in Asia Minor, 157, 767–8
Amastris, town in Asia Minor on Black Sea, 300
Amaury I, king of Jerusalem, 630
Amaury of Lusignan, prince of Tyre, 635–6
Ambron, *see* 'Amr
Ami, Norman count, expelled from Dalmatia by Venetians, 271
Amida (Diyār-Bakr), town in Mesopotamia, Byzantine armies at, 110, 140, 164, 167, 712, 719–20, 723
  battle (973), 165
  under Marwānids, 618

Amida (*cont.*)
  under Ortukids, 742, 746
  under Seljuqs of Rūm, 748
al-Amīn, Abbasid Caliph of Baghdad,
    civil war with al-Ma'mūn, 645, 667,
    701, 704, 708
Amisus (Samsoun), town in Pontus on
    Black Sea, 707, 713
Amorgos, Aegean island, under Venetian
    rule, 425
Amorian (Phrygian) dynasty, 100, **105–
    16**, 127
Amorium, town in Phrygia
  birthplace of Michael II, 100, 103
  and Byzantine–Arab wars, 62–3, 103,
    109–10, 707, **710–11**
  battle of Pancalia (978), 177
  Seljuq attacks, 209
  home of Ibn Bagrat, 115
  forty-two martyrs of, 711
Amphilochius, bishop of Iconium, 50–1
Amphissa, town in Greece, 389, 400
'Amr Alaqta', *see* 'Amr ibn 'Ubayd Allāh
'Amr (Ambron), figure in Byzantine and
    Arab legend, 708
'Amr ibn 'Ubayd Allāh, amir of Melitene,
    735
  son of 'Ubayd Allāh ibn al-Aqṭa', 708
  grandfather of Abū Hafs, 139 and n. 2
  campaigns against Byzantium, 110,
    710–13
  killed in battle (863), 110, 111 n. 1, 713
Amyclae, town in Peloponnese, Latin
    See of, 396
an-: names beginning thus are indexed
    under the capital letter immediately
    following
Ἀνακάθαρσις τῶν παλαιῶν νόμων, legal work
    commissioned by Basil I, 133
Anakop'ia, fortress in Georgia, 621
Anaphe (Namfio), Aegean island, under
    Latin rule, 425
Anargyri (St Cosmas and St Damian),
    monastery of, 197
Anastasia, daughter of Jaroslav of Kiev,
    wife of Andrew I of Hungary, 577
Anastasius I, Emperor
  and Long Wall, 9
  ecclesiastical appointments, 56
  religious policy, 435
  financial measures, 27
  death, 28
Anastasius II, Emperor
  and Leo III, 62
  preparations for an Arab attack, 63
  involved in revolt of Nicetas Xylinites,
    64

Anastasius, Patriarch of Constantinople
  excommunicated by Pope Gregory II,
    71
  support for Artavasdus' revolt against
    Constantine V, 73
  death, 78
Anastasius of Sinai, on Cyril of Alexan-
    dria, 52
Anastasius, papal librarian, 118
Anatolia, *see* Asia Minor
Anatolikon theme
  subdivision by Leo III, 64
  loyal to Constantine V, 73
  Arab attacks, 699
  strategi, 62, 98, 211, 698, 707, 709, 711,
    719
Anatolius, Patriarch of Constantinople,
    and Council of Chalcedon, 434
Anatolius, deacon, and Pope Gregory the
    Great, 439
Anazarbus ('Ayn Zarba), town in Cilicia,
    148, 172, 629–30, 636, 706, 712,
    721
Anchialus, town on west coast of Black
    Sea, 97
  battle (763), 74, 490; (917), 137, 507
  attacked by Latins (1206), 294
  held by Byzantines, 333, 336, 353,
    369, 535
  recovered by Bulgaria, 348, 353
Ancona, town in Italy
  and Manuel I's attempt on South
    Italy, 229
  rivalry with Venice, 272
  arrival of Alexius Angelus, 278
  silk trade with Peloponnese, 428
Ancyra (Angora, Ankara), town in Asia
    Minor
  and wars of Byzantines against Arabs,
    103, 120, 705, 707, 713
  attacked by Danishmends, 223
  taken by Ottomans (1361), 754, 762
  and princes of Germiyān, 755
  battle (1402), 377–9, 551, 563, 767
  inscriptions from, 110, 117, 754
Andrasos, town in Cappadocia, 707
Andravida, town in Peloponnese, 390
  parliament at, 393–4
  seat of bishop of Olena, 396
Andrés Zavall, Catalan captain of
    Neopatras, 422–3
Andrew I, king of Hungary, 576–8
Andrew II, king of Hungary
  relations with Latin Empire of Con-
    stantinople, 301, 307, 586, 589
  relations with Boril of Bulgaria, 526
  relations with Empire of Nicaea, 588–9

Andrew the Scythian, Domestic of the Schools under Basil I, 120

Andronicus I Comnenus, Emperor, **244–5**
plot against Manuel I, 229, 581–2
relations with Venice, 232, 245, 273–4
governor of Cilicia, 235, 630
governor of Pontus, 244
murder of Alexius II and seizure of throne, 244, 468, 584
character, 244
attempt to reform civil service and control landowners, 244
attacked by Hungary, Serbia and Sicily, 245, 584
treaty with Saladin, 245
murdered by populace, 245, 584

Andronicus II Palaeologus, Emperor, **340–52**
marriages, 336, 345, 589
as co-Emperor, 340–1
and the armed forces, 342–4
financial policy, 343–4, 350
ecclesiastical policy, 344, 470
foreign policy, 344–6
policy of dynastic marriages, 345, 534
hostility of France and Naples, 345, 349
Serbian invasions, 345, 533–4
involved in struggle between Genoa and Venice, 345–6
Turkish invasions in Asia Minor, 346–7, 351
relations with the Papacy, 470–1
relations with Roger de Flor and Catalan Company, 347–8
loss of Anchialus and Mesembria to Bulgaria, 348
treaty with Venice, 349
civil war with Andronicus III, 350–2, 534
abdication, 352
reform of judiciary, 352

Andronicus III Palaeologus, Emperor, **350–6**
civil war with Andronicus II, 350–2
relations with Bulgaria, 351–2, 353, 543
reform of judiciary, 352–3
relations with Serbia, 354, 534, 538, 543
losses to Ottomans, 354, 759
collaboration with Turkish amirates in Asia Minor, 354–5
attacks on Genoese in Aegean, 354–5
subjugation of northern half of Thessaly, 355
subjugation of Epirus and Acarnania, 355–6
death, 356

Andronicus IV Palaeologus, Emperor
regent for John V during his visit to Italy, 371
revolt against John V, 372–3
relations with Ottoman Sultan, 373

Andros, island in the Aegean
bishopric of, 409
under Venetian rule, 425

Angeli, imperial family, **245–9**
and Fourth Crusade, 274, 388
rulers of Epirus, 296 n. 1, 304 n. 1, 349
rulers of Thessaly, 349
and Michael VIII, 324

Angelus, Constantine, grandfather of Michael I of Epirus, 296 n. 1

Angelus, John (Kaloyan), son of Isaac II, 585

Angelus, John, nephew of John VI Cantacuzenus
governor of Epirus, 356
governor of Thessaly, 359

Angevins, in Sicily, *see* Charles of Anjou
attempt to restore the Despot of Epirus, 355–6, 416
interest in the Peloponnese, 402–7, 410, 423
struggle for Sicily after the Sicilian Vespers, 404
attempt to overthrow the Catalan duchy of Athens, 415–16

Anglo-Saxons, conversion of, 439

Angora (Ankara), *see* Ancyra

Ani, town and district in Armenia, 609, 614, 619–20, 624
lands bequeathed to Byzantium by John Smbat III, 189, 197, 619
cathedral of, 615

Ankara, *see* Ancyra

Anna Comnena, daughter of Alexius I, wife of Nicephorus Bryennius, 212, 216–18, 220, 466

Anna Comnena Ducaena, daughter of Michael II of Epirus, wife of William of Villehardouin, prince of Achaea, 324, 400, 402

Anna Comnena of Trebizond, wife of Bagrat V of Georgia, 627

Anna Dalassena, mother of Alexius I, 211, 217

Anna Palaeologina, daughter of Michael IX, wife of Thomas of Epirus and of Nicholas Orsini of Epirus, 349

Anna Palaeologina, wife of John Orsini, 355

Anna of Savoy, wife of Andronicus III
regent for John V, 357, 360, 361

Anna of Savoy (*cont.*)
  opposition to hesychasts, 357–8
  pawning of crown jewels, 363–4
Anna, daughter of Alexius III, wife of
  Theodore I Lascaris, 291
Anna, daughter of Leo III, wife of
  Artavasdus, 62
Anna, sister of Michael I of Epirus, wife
  of Matthew Orsini, 297
Anna, daughter of Milutin, first wife of
  Michael Šišman, 353, 542–3
Anna, daughter of Romanus II, wife of
  Vladimir of Kiev, 179, 180, 516
Anna, daughter of Stephen V of Hungary,
  wife of Andronicus II, 589
Anna, *see* Zoe Carbonopsina
Annals of Lorsch, 448
Anne of Châtillon, daughter of Constance
  of Antioch, wife of Béla III of
  Hungary, 234, 583
Anne of Hungary, first wife of Androni-
  cus II, 336, 345
Annesi, in Asia Minor, site of community
  founded by Basil of Caesarea, 58
annona
  levied by the praetorian prefects, 34
  extension under Diocletian, 38
  commuted for money payments, 38
Anonymus, the, Hungarian chronicler,
  570
Anṣārī Harawī, Ṣūfī leader, 691
Ansbert, Austrian chronicler, 528
Anseau of Toucy, possible identification
  as traitor to Baldwin II at Con-
  stantinople, 326
Anselm (*c.* 1033–1109), Latin theologian
  and archbishop of Canterbury,
  studied by Byzantines, 471
Anselm, bishop of Havelberg, 241, 468
Antae, see Antes
Antākiya, *see* Antioch
Antalya, *see* Attalia
Anṭarṭūs (Tortosa), port in Syria, 182, 724
Antes (Antae), tribe from east of the
  Carpathians, 476 and n. 2, 477
Anthimus I, Patriarch of Constantinople,
  condemnation under Justinian I, 436
Anthimus, *nobilissimus*, son of Con-
  stantine V, half-brother of Leo IV,
  82 and n. 2, 83, 88–9, 97
anthypatus, title, 139
Antioch, town on the Meander in Asia
  Minor, battle (1211), 296, 746
Antioch (Antākiya), city on the Orontes
  in Syria
  contrasted with Constantinople, 4
  centre of learning, 20, 50

  trade, 26
  taken by Persians (611), 30
  and Greek culture, 54
  city proletariate, 55
  school of theology, 19, 55
  loss to the Empire, 36
  birthplace of John Chrysostom, 51
  circus parties, 40
  and Nicephorus II's campaigns, 721–2
  taken by Byzantines (969), 150, 151,
    156 and n. 2, 158, 179, 722
  besieged by Muslims (970–1), 163, 168,
    722
  John Tzimisces at, 168–9, 171–2, 723
  Byzantine governors of, 175, 178, 180,
    182, 186, 724
  Basil II's campaigns, 182, 186, 724
  under Constantine VIII, 195
  under Romanus III, 195
  and Lesser Armenia, 628
  Seljuq attacks, 209, 628, 740
  claimed by Alp Arslan, 210
  Latin principality of, 215–16, 221, 223,
    467, 741–2
  held by Bohemond as an imperial fief,
    216
  Normans defeated by Danishmends,
    223
  and Roger II of Sicily, 224
  struggle for control between Byzan-
    tines and Latins, 223–5, 226–7, 231,
    234–5
  captured by Mamluks of Egypt (1268),
    634
Antioch, Patriarchs of
  status, 18–19, 433–5, 461
  jurisdiction, 19
  and Church councils, 66, 84, 113, 118,
    131–2, 434, 716
  and Thomas the Slavonian, 709
  and Basil II, 190
  and First Crusade, 467
  struggle between Latins and Greeks
    over appointment, 216, 222–5, 234–5
  and Church in Iberia, 601
Antiparos, Aegean island, under Venetian rule, 425
anti-semitism in Byzantium, 122
anti-Taurus range, barrier between
  Byzantines and Arabs, 699
Antony I Cassimatas, Patriarch of
  Constantinople, 101
Antony II Cauleas, Patriarch of Constantinople, 126, 127 and n. 1
Anzitena, town in Mesopotamia, 719, 720,
  723
  battle (938), 718

Apachounis, district in Caucasia, 181
Apalire, Greek fortress on Naxos, 425
Apamea, town in Syria, 169, 186, 724
Aphusia, Proconnesian island in the Sea of Marmora, place of exile of Constantine V's sons, 97
Apocaucus, Alexius, *megas dux*
  supporter of Andronicus III in the civil war, 350
  enemy of John Cantacuzenus, 357–8
  in control of Constantinople, 357
  murdered, 360–1
Apocaucus, John, *megas primicerius*, son of Alexius, 360
Apocaucus, John, metropolitan of Naupactus
  championship of Theodore of Epirus, 306–8
  literary work, 321
Apollonius of Tyana, Life of, 57
apostolicity in the Church, 18–19, 432–5, 440, 446–7, 449–50, 456–7
Aprus, fortress in Thrace, battle (1305), 348
Apulia, district in South Italy
  and Nicephorus Phocas the Elder, 128
  and Arabs, 729, 731
  and Normans, 197, 201, 208, 460–1
  campaigns of Manuel I, 229–30, 232–3
  rivalry with Venice, 268
Aq-Qoyunlu Turks, 627, 754
Aquae Saravenae, in the theme of Charsianon, battle (979), 177
  see also Pancalia
Aquileia, port on the north Adriatic coast
  metropolitan See, 252–3, 262, 269–71
  trade, 26
Aquinas, Thomas
  studied by Byzantines, 471
  translated into Armenian, 633
ar-: names beginning thus are indexed under the capital letter immediately following
Arab sources for Byzantine history, 106, 109–10, 111 n. 1, 121, 139, 146, 149, 156 n. 2, 164–5, 170, 171, 172, 707, 708 n. 1, 715
Arabia
  and Bedouin tribes, 645
  and Carmathians, 648
  under Egyptian control, 648, 652
Arabian Nights' Entertainments, 679
Arabic language, literature and culture
  theological writings, 68
  translations of Greek works, 650, 671–2, 684
  translations of Latin works, 672 n. 1

translations from Syriac, 672, 683 n. 1, 684, 695 n. 1
retranslations of Greek works for West, 684
script used for Persian, 647
Persian superseded by, 668
grammar, 683, 687, 688 and n. 1
official language under Seljuqs of Rūm, 745
study of philosophy, 671 and n. 2, 680 n. 1, 683–4, 694 n. 1, 695 n. 1
study of science, 671, 672 and n. 2, 680, 683–5, 693 and n. 1, 694–5
geographers, 733–4
peaceful contacts with Byzantines, 733–5
Arabic scholars in Byzantium, 150
literature, 157 n. 1, 667–8, 679, 683, 685–7
art and architecture, 688 and n. 3, 735
Arab iconoclasm, 66, 67, 68
Arabissos, town in the anti-Taurus range, 705
Arabs (Saracens)
  attacks on Byzantine Empire and Persia in seventh century, 22, 30, 31, 39, 41, 438, 605
  wars with the Byzantines, **696–733**
  campaigns against Leo III, 62–4, 698–9
  siege of Constantinople (717–18), 63, 698
  attacked by Khazars in Caucasus, 64, 606–7, 699
  invasion of Phrygia (742), 73, 698–9
  defeated by Constantine V, 73–4, 78, 607–8, 703
  campaigns of Leo IV (777–80), 82, 705
  campaigns against Constantine VI and Irene, 83, 84, 88, 706–7
  campaigns against Nicephorus I, 91, 707–8
  quiescent under Leo V, 98, 709
  capture of Crete (*c.* 828), 100, 709
  campaigns against Theophilus, 103, 611, 709–12, 728
  defeats in eighth century, 104
  loss of Cyprus, 107 n. 1, 716
  defeats under Michael III, 109–11, 115, 119, 611, 713–14, 727
  helped by Paulicians, 109, 111, 120, 137 n. 1, 712–14
  defeated in Calabria by Nicephorus Phocas the Elder, 121, 129 n. 1, 729
  siege of Ragusa (866–8), 122
  and Himerius, 129–30, 716
  and Andronicus Ducas, 130, 131
  defeat at the Garigliano (915), 136, 730

Arabs (*cont.*)
  threat to Italy in tenth century, 457, 730–1
  in Provence, 140, 730
  wars of Constantine VII, 146, 719–21, 730–1
  Byzantine attacks on Crete under Romanus II, 147, 721
  serving in Byzantine army, 176, 716
  support for Bardas Sclerus, 176, 177, 178, 180, 723–4
  raids under Romanus III, 195, 725–6
  in Sicily under Michael IV, 197, 731
  amirates in Caucasia, 609–11, 613
  see also Africa, Egypt, Italy, Persia, Sicily, Fatimid Caliphate, Umayyad Caliphate and the Emperors Basil I, Leo VI, Romanus I, Nicephorus II, John I and Basil II
Aragon, kingdom of
  appealed to by Manuel II for help against Turks, 376
  Aragonese in Catalan Company, 411, 417
Aral Sea, 737
Aramæan culture in Syria and Mesopotamia, 55
Arbe (Rab), island off Dalmatian coast, 268
Arcadia, district in Peloponnese, under Latin rule, 292
Arcadia (Kyparissia), fortress in Peloponnese, 390
  Latin barony, 394 and n. 1
Arcadiopolis (Lüleburgaz), town in Thrace
  battle (970), 158, 175, 514 and n. 3
  defeat of Isaac II by Bulgaria, 524
Arcadius, Emperor
  criticised by Synesius, 16
  and the Church, 20
  rivalry with Honorius, 26
  death, 43
Archêsh, town in Armenia, 618
  battle (772), 608
Arch'il of Kakhetia, St, 608
Archipelago, the
  Venetian colonies in, 346
  duchy of, 425–7
architecture
  Byzantine influence in Hungary, 587
  Caucasian, 594, 615–16
  Arab, 688, 735
archons, local rulers in Greece, 292, 399
  of Crete, 106
  of Cyprus, 716
  title of John Smbat III, 619

Ardabīl, town in Azerbaijan, 624
Ardahan (Artani), district in Iberia, 609
Arethas, archbishop of Caesarea, 130, 136 and n. 1, 480 n. 6
Argaouth, town in anti-Taurus region, home of Paulicians, 712
Argeş (Curtea de Argeş), town in Wallachia
  metropolitan See, 561
  battle (Rovine, q.v.), 766
Argolid, district of Greece
  and partition of Empire under Baldwin I, 289
  and Leo Sgouros, 292
  and Navarrese Company, 419
  and Avars and Slavs, 480 n. 6
Argos, town in Peloponnese
  held against Latins, 297, 389
  under Latin rule, 399, 400, 408–11, 416
  under Venetians from 1388, 376, 380
  besieged by Ottomans, 376
  Latin See of, 396
Argyri, Byzantine family, under Basil II, 192
Argyrus, son of Melo of Bari, Lombard leader, in Byzantine service, 197, 202, 461–2
Arians and Arianism, 20, 47
Aristakēs of Lastivert, Armenian historian, 616 n. 1
aristocracy, Bulgarian, 485, 490, 512
aristocracy, Byzantine
  struggle for power between the civil and military aristocracy in the eleventh century, 199–219 *passim*
  antagonism to Manuel I, 243
  antagonism to Andronicus I, 584
  under Latin Empire, 290
  under Empire of Nicaea, 319–20, 321, 324
  under the Palaeologi, 341–2, 358–9
  support for Andronicus III, 350
  support for John Cantacuzenus, 357, 358–9
  attacked by the Zealots, 358–9
  see also landowners
aristocracy, Italian, influence over the Papacy, 456–7
aristocracy, Serbian, 532
  support for Stephen Dušan, 535
  independent rulers, 541–2
aristocracy, Slav, on northern shores of Black Sea, 504
Aristotle and Aristotelianism, 46, 49
  studied in eleventh century, 201
  and Symeon of Bulgaria, 502
  in Georgia, 625

Aristotle (*cont.*)
  and Arabs, 671 and n. 2, 672 n. 2, 679, 683–4, 686–8, 694 n. 1
  Theology of Aristotle, 683 and n. 1
Arles, town in Gaul, 18
Armenia and the Armenians, **593–637**
    and see List of Rulers 7
  struggle for control between Rome (later Byzantium) and Persia, 593–5, 597–605
  conversion to Christianity, 595 and n. 1, 599
  partition, 27, 598 and n. 1
  breakdown of the monarchy, 598–9
  Syrian influence, 599, 604
  revolts against Persia, 599–602
  under Justinian I, 601–2, 603
  deportations, 603, 618
  under Umayyad Caliphs, 605–7, 699
  under Abbasids, 607–12, 646–7
  restoration of monarchy, 612–13
  secession of Vaspurakan, 613
  Armenia Quarta, 601, 705
  recruiting of troops by Byzantines, 29, 35, 739
  and iconoclasm, 66, 68, 73
  and monophysitism, 68, 604
  and Paulicians, 73
  and murder of Michael III, 115
  and Basil I, 116, 612
  captives settled in Bulgaria by Krum (813), 116
  restoration of Ashot II, 136, 614, 717
  and campaigns of John Curcuas, 139, 717–18
  peasant-soldiers under Romanus I, 142; under Nicephorus II, 154
  and Hamdanids, 146, 149, 718
  cause of panic in Constantinople under Nicephorus II, 152 and nn. 1 and 2
  and John I Tzimisces' Russian campaign, 160 and n. 3
  and John I Tzimisces' eastern campaigns, 165–7, 616–17
  support for Bardas Sclerus, 176, 177, 179, 180, 617
  origin of Comitopuli, 178
  relations with Basil II, 186, 189, 190, 203, 618
  relations with Constantine IX, 203–4, 620
  Bagratid lands ceded to Byzantium (1045), 189, 197, 204, 620
  Seljuq attacks, 204, 206, 209, 619–20, 727
  lost to Empire under Romanus IV, 209, 210, 620

  Mongol invasions, 660
  commercial colony in Thebes, 414
  trade relations with Trebizond, 733
  merchants in Sultanate of Rūm, 744
  see also Armenian Church, Armenian language, Armenian literature, Lesser Armenia, Rupenians
Armenia, theme of, 204
Armeniakon theme
  support for Leo III, 62
  support for Artavasdus' revolt, 73
  rebellion against Constantine VI, 88–9, 707
  loyal to Michael II, 100
  subdivided by Theophilus, 102–3
  and campaigns against Arabs, 704–5, 707, 711
Armenian Church, 20, 242, 599 and n. 1, 600, 604 and n. 1, 605–6, 612, 616, 635 n. 1
  in Lesser Armenia, 628–9, 632, 635
  Patriarch of Gregorian Armenians as political leader, 774
Armenian language
  forms of foreign names, 484 n. 2
  alphabet, 599
  translations of the Scriptures, 599
  translations of Greek authors, 599
  spelling of names, 608 n. 1, 629 n. 1, in New Armenia, 629 n. 1
Armenian literature, 55, 594, 599 and n. 2, 616 and n. 1, 625, 633 and n. 1
Armoroupoulos, epic hero, and Michael III, 110, 117
army, **34–6**
  as political factor, 12, 14, 16, 82, 148, 156, 201, 205, 226, 481, 721
  pay, 37, 38, 218
  equipment, 37
  paganism in, 3
  use of Latin in, 23
  mutiny, 481
  reorganised by Irene, 84, 88
  reforms of Nicephorus I, 92–3
  and ownership of land, 153–4, 190, 218–19, 220
  organisation under Basil II, 181
  rivalry between European and Asian troops, 203, 205, 211
  Pechenegs in, 203, 208, 218
  neglected by Constantine X, 207
  use of mercenaries by Alexius I, 218
  and John II, 220
  Seljuq contingent in, 236–7, 239, 333
  contingent from Rascia, 233, 239
  contingent from Serbia, 324
  contingent from Hungary, 324

army (*cont.*)
    under the Palaeologi, 342
    see also mercenaries, Varangian guard
Árpád, ninth-century Magyar prince, 568–9
Arpadian dynasty in Hungary, 575–7, 580, 589
Arrān, cis-Cyran Albania, *see under* Albania, Caspian
Arsaber, claimant to throne under Nicephorus I, 91
Arsaces III, co-king of Armenia with Valarsaces, 597–8
Arsacids, Persian rulers in Caucasia, 594–5, 597 and n. 1, 598 n. 2, 600–1
Arsafius the *spatharius*, Byzantine representative in Venice, relations with Charlemagne, 260–1
Arsakidze, Caucasian architect, 615
Arsamosata (Shimshāṭ), town on upper Euphrates, 703, 705, 712, 718–19
    captured from Arabs (837), 103, 710
    under Mamikonids, 620
Arsanas, river in Mesopotamia, 714, 720
Arsenites, supporters of the Patriarch Arsenius against Michael VIII, 338, 344
    see also Zealots
Arsenius Autorianus, Patriarch of Constantinople
    in Nicaea, 321, 324
    in Constantinople, 328
    excommunication of Michael VIII, 338
    death, 344
Arsenius of Iqaltʻo, Georgian philosopher, 625
Arsenius the Monk, Georgian historian, 625 n. 1
Arsharunikʻ, principality in Armenia, 597, 609–10
art, Byzantine
    influenced by classical paganism, 2–3
    and iconoclasm, 60, 81, 87
    influence of dogma, 88
    in Trebizond, 328–9
    in Hungary, 576
    plastic arts, 688
    encouraged under John Vatatzes, 321
    under the Palaeologi, 340
    destruction of works of art in Constantinople by crusaders (1204) and Turks (1453), 286–7, 387
Arta, town and district in Epirus
    and rulers and despots of Epirus, 292, 296, 314, 321, 325–6, 329, 355
    Alexius III a refugee in, 296

centre of Byzantine tradition, 321
churches and monasteries, 321, 329
pro-Byzantine party in, 355
taken by Walter II of Brienne, 416
Artani, *see* Ardahan
Artanuji, town in Caucasia, 609, 613, 615, 619, 624
Artavasdus, general of Armeniakon theme
    support for Leo III, 62
    revolt against Constantine V, 73
    honoured in Rome, 75
Artavazd Mamikonian, leader of Armenian revolt against Abbasids, 608
Artaxata, town in Caucasia, 609
Artaxias IV, king of Armenia, 598–9
Articles of Athens, Catalan document, 421
artillery, Turkish, at siege of Constantinople (1453), 386, 773–4
Artsrunis, Armenian dynasty, 597 and n. 1, 607–8, 610, 613, 615–16, 620
    in Lesser Armenia, 628
Arzanene, district in southern Armenia, 596, 597 n. 1
Arzen, in Mesopotamia
    amirate, 609
    taken by the Byzantines, 718
as-, aṣ-: names beginning thus are indexed under the capital letter immediately following
Ascetica, attributed to Basil of Caesarea, 58
asceticism, 45, 50, 58, 218, 357, 689 n. 4
Asen I, Bulgarian tsar
    founding of the Second Bulgarian Empire, 245, **522–4**
    murdered (1196), 248, 524–5
al-Ashʻarī, Arab theologian, 690–1
Ashʻarī school of Sunnī theology, 659, 691
Ashinās, military commander under al-Muʻtaṣim, 711
Ashot (Ašot) II, Bagratid prince of Armenia, 606
Ashot III, Bagratid prince of Armenia, 607
Ashot IV the Brave, Bagratid prince of Armenia, 609, 610–11
Ashot V, prince of princes of Armenia, *see* Ashot I (V) the Great, king of Armenia
Ashot I (V) the Great, king of Armenia, 611, 612 and n. 1, 613, 615, 715
Ashot II the Iron, king of Armenia, 614
    restored to his throne with Byzantine help (915), 136 and n. 2, 717

Ashot III the Merciful, king of Armenia, 614, 616
  relations with John Tzimisces, 165–70, 616–17, 723
Ashot IV the Valiant, king of Armenia, brother of John Smbat III, 197, 203, 619
Ashot I the Great, Bagratid prince of Iberia, 610–11
Ashot of Bagaran and Koḷb, pretender to throne of Armenia, 614
Ashot of Taraun, curopalate of Armenia, 612
Ashot, son of Gregory Taronites, captured by Samuel of Bulgaria, 184
Asia, Central, and the Mongols, 377
Asia, province in Asia Minor
  Arab attacks, 698–9
  diocese of, 434, 456
Asia Minor (Anatolia)
  part of Roman Empire, 24
  within See of Constantinople, 19
  invaded by Persia in seventh century, 29, 30
  campaign of Heraclius, 30
  Arab raids in seventh and eighth centuries, 30, 39, 63, 64, 74
  military and economic resources, 31
  settlement of soldier-farmers, 39
  Slavs transferred to, 32, 39
  defence of, 35
  road system, 41
  Christianity in, 42, 55
  Hellenism in, 51
  landed aristocracy, 15, 39, 55, 144, 172, 182–4, 199, 201, 202, 209, 319–20, 617
  stronghold of monophysites and Paulicians, 66, 714, 717
  support of themes for iconoclasm, 70, 98
  and Constantine V's Arab campaign, 74, 704–5
  and Leo IV's Arab campaigns, 82, 705
  support of themes for Constantine VI, 88
  invasions under Hārūn ar-Rashīd, 83, 91, 705–8
  troops from, 94
  civil war under Leo V and Michael II, 100, 709
  exposed to Arab attacks from Crete, 101
  invaded by al-Ma'mūn and al-Mu'taṣim, 710–11
  Arab campaign of Michael III, 117, 713
  unpopularity of Basil I, 117
  attacks of Paulicians against Basil I, 119–20, 714

  campaign of Nicephorus Phocas the Elder, 120–1, 129, 715
  invaded by Sayf ad-Dawla, 719, 720
  rising of Bardas Sclerus, 176–7, 723
  rising of Bardas Phocas, 179
  hostile to the Paphlagonian Emperors, 199
  proclamation of Isaac I Comnenus as Emperor, 205
  Seljuq attacks in eleventh century, 15, 206, 207–8, 737–40
  defections to Seljuqs, 207
  surrender of Romanus IV to John Ducas' sons, 210
  support for Nicephorus Botaneiates against Michael VII, 211
  establishment of Sultanate of Rūm (q.v.), 210, 211–12, 653–5, 740–2
  campaign of Alexius I, 214, 215, 216
  and First Crusade, 215, 741
  campaigns of John II, 223
  and Manuel I, 226–7, 234–9, 743
  and Second Crusade, 227, 742
  Bogomils in, 242
  and Third Crusade, 246
  under Latin Empire, 287–9, 290–1, 300, 304
  under Byzantine Emperor at Nicaea, 295, 300–1, 304, 319–20
  loss of territory by Latins, 308
  Turkish invasions after 1200, 754–6
  lost to Turks, 346–7, 354
  Turkish amirates and principalities in, 354–5, 383, 753–7, 759–60, 765–7, 769
  Mongol invasions, *see under* Mongols
Askold, Varangian leader
  capture of Kiev, 495
  attack on Constantinople (860), 496
  loss of Kiev to Oleg, 504
Ašot, *see* Ashot
Aspar, Alan general, 27
Asparuch (Isperich), Bulgar khan
  and the settlement south of the Danube, 484–5
  relations with Slavs in Bulgaria, 485 and n. 1
aspron, unit of coinage under the Palaeologi, 380
Assassins, Ismā'īlī sect, 657–9, 661
Assizes and Customs of Romania, 414
Assizes of Romania, 401–2, 405
Assyrian civilisation and Caucasia, 593, 596, 597 n. 1
astrology
  in fourth century, 43
  Manuel I's belief in, 243
  and Arabs, 672 n. 2, 685

astronomy
  studied at university of Constantinople, 200
  studied in Georgia, 625
  studied by the Arabs, 672, 685
Asturia, district in Spain not under Muslim rule, 699
Astypalaea (Stampalia), Aegean island, under Venetian rule, 425
aṭ-: names beginning thus are indexed under the capital letter immediately following
atābeg, title of rulers
  of Azerbaijan, 624, 626 n. 2
  of Mosul, 628, 742
  of Aleppo and Damascus, 630
Atel Kuzu, Magyar territory, 128
Athanasius of Alexandria, Church Father
  and Arianism, 20
  life and work, 47–8
  influence on Cyril of Alexandria, 52
  encyclicals, 54
Athanasius I, Patriarch of Constantinople, letters of, 343 n. 2
Athanasius II, Greek Patriarch of Antioch, 235
Athanasius, founder of monastery of the Lavra on Mt Athos, 155
Athena Promachos, statue by Phidias, torn down in Constantinople in 1204, 284
Athens
  university of, 4, 23, 48
  place of exile, 89
  visit of Basil II, 518
  under Latin rule, 292, 298, 309, 389, **408–24**
  attacked by Leo Sgouros, 389
  sacked by Catalan Company, 411
  French duchy of, 300, 348–9, 389, **408–11**
  Catalan duchy of, *see under* Catalan
  Florentine duchy of, 375, 383, **422–4**
  and Navarrese Company, 421
  parliament at, 421–2
  population in fourteenth century, 422 n. 1
  Venetians in temporary control, 423–4
  occupied by Ottomans (1397), 376, 423; (1456), 387, 424
  occupied by Constantine XI, 383
  see also Acropolis, Parthenon
Athingani, heretical sect in Asia Minor
  relations with Nicephorus I, 95
  under Michael I, 96
Athos, Mount, and its monasteries
  under Nicephorus II, 154, 155

Iviron monastery, 177
  under Alexius I, 218
  under protection of the Papacy, 303
  encouraged under Andronicus II, 344
  raided by Catalan Company, 348, 411
  and hesychasts, 357
  retreat of Stephen Nemanja, 522
  retreat of St Sava, 531
  taken by Stephen Dušan, 538
  and Patriarchate of Serbia, 538
  and Hungarians, 570
  hermitages, 577
  and Armenians, 617
  and Georgians, 177, 625
  raided by Arabs from Crete, 709, 713
Atlas mountains in Africa, barrier to migration, 26
Atrnerseh, ruler in Caspian Albania, 610; *and see* 608 n. 1
Atsîz, Seljuq general, capture of Jerusalem, 737
Attaleiates, Michael, historian
  on Constantine IX, 200
  on Pecheneg threat to Constantinople (1064), 208
Attalia (Antalya, Adalia, Adaliya), town in Pamphylia in Asia Minor, 224, 756
  naval battle in bay of (790), 706
  taken by Arab fleet (860), 713
  seized by Seljuqs (1207), 746
  under Ottomans, 762
Attica, district of Greece
  and partition of the Empire under Baldwin I, 289
  invaded by Leo Sgouros, 389
  under Latin rule, 389, **408–24**
  cultivation of olives and vines, 428
  threatened by Arab fleet (902), 716
Attila, leader of the Huns, 9, 27
Auctoritas of Emperor, 45
Augusta, imperial title, 7, 131–2, 135–7
Augustine of Hippo, Latin Church Father
  influence on Charlemagne, 448
  studied by Byzantines, 471
Augustus, Roman Emperor
  founder of the Empire, 2–3
  comparison with Constantine, 3
  basis of his power, 10
  and hereditary succession, 14
  and history of Venice, 250
Aulon, town in Greece, bishopric of, 409
Austria, duke of, *see* Henry of Babenburg
Autocrator, imperial title
  and Michael III, 117
  under the Palaeologi, 341 n. 1, 380

Autun, bishop of, 439
Auxentius, monastery of, 80
Avarayr, town in Armenia, battle (451), 600
Avars
  origins, 476, 477 and n. 1, 736
  attacks on Constantinople, 10, 29, 481–2
  in central Europe, 29, 477–8, 482
  attacks on Balkans, 29–30, 32, 39, 480–3
  attacks on Greece, 29, 480–2
  attacks on Illyricum, 438, 478, 480–2
  relations with Justinian I, 476–7
  relations with Justin II, 477–9
  and Onogurs, 483
  destruction by Charlemagne, 490
Aversa, town in South Italy, 202
  count of, *see* Rainulf
Avesta, 668
Avicenna (Ibn Sīnā), Muslim philosopher and physician, 683, 694 n. 1
Avignon, residence of the Popes, 368, 369, 371, 415, 540
Avkhat, *see* Euchaïta
Avlona, town on Albanian coast, 215, 325, 337, 538
'Awāṣim, *see* al-Qāsim
Axuch, *see* John Axuch
Ayas (Lajazzo), port in Cilicia, 633, 636
Aydîn, Turkish principality in the region of Smyrna, 756
'Ayn Zarba, *see* Anazarbus
Ayyūbids, Muslim dynasty, 631–3, 746, 748
aẓ-: names beginning thus are indexed under the capital letter immediately following
Azerbaijan, region of north-west Persia
  limit of Byzantine Empire under Basil II, 190
  relations with Armenia, 613–14, 616, 618–19, 715
  relations with Georgia, 624
  and the Turks, 738
  and the Mongols, 749
  atābegs of, 624, 626 n. 2
  dynasties of, 610 n. 3, 613, 616, 618–19, 647, 710
al-'Azīz, Fatimid Caliph
  threat to Syria under Basil II, 182, 724
  gift from Byzantine Emperor, 735
Azov, Sea of (the Maeotis), 474–5, 495 n. 1, 503, 568
azymes, unleavened bread, 283, 312, 394, 461, 465, 471

Baalbek, *see* Heliopolis
Baba Ishāk *or* Baba Rasūl, dervish leader, 748
Baba'īya, followers of Baba Ishāk, 748
Bābak, leader of revolt against Abbasids, 609, 682, 710–11
Babylonia, 169
Bács, town in Hungary, 582, 586
Bacurius III, king of Iberia, 602
Badoer, Venetian family, 262, 263
Badr ad-Dīn Maḥmud, leader of revolts against Muḥammad I, 768
Badr ad-Dīn Muḥammad Bey, Karaman leader, 753
Bagaran, principality in Armenia, 610–11
Bagarat II of Taraun, prince of princes of Armenia, 611–12
Baghdad
  capital of Abbasid Caliphs, 73, 640–1, 645–6, 648, 663, 677, 699–702, 735
  besieged during civil disorders, 702
  and Andronicus Ducas, 131, 716
  Byzantine embassies to, 131, 716–17, 735
  Abbasid Caliphate of, 139–40, 163, 511, **640–61, 662–95**
  and John Tzimisces' Mesopotamian campaigns, 164, 167, 169, 170
  captivity of Bardas Sclerus in, 177–8, 723–4
  trade, 495, 646
  captured by Buwayhids (945), 646, 702
  captured by Seljuqs (1055), 653, 655, 658, 703, 737
  captured by Mongols (1258), 634, 646, 661
  captured by Mongols under Timur (1400), 766
Baghras, town in Syria, 722
Bagrat I, prince of Iberia, 611, 613
Bagrat II the Simple, titular king of Iberia, 617–18
Bagrat III, king of Georgia (Abasgia and Iberia), 186, 189, 617–19, 621
Bagrat IV, king of Georgia, 621–2
Bagrat V the Great, king of Georgia, 627
Bagrat, king of Abasgia and prince of Karthli, *see* Bagrat III, king of Georgia
Bagratids (Bagratuni), Armenian dynasty, 166, 203–4, 596, 597 n. 1, 604, **606–20**, 632 n. 1, 738
  rulers of Georgia, **621–8**
  and see List of Rulers 7
Bagravandene, principality in Armenia, 596, 612
  battle (772), 608

Bahā' ad-Dīn Muḥammad Veled, Muslim priest, refugee in Iconium, 747
Bahrain (Baḥrain, Laḥsā), district in Arabia on Persian Gulf, 648, 682
Baichu, Mongol general, defeat of Kaykhusraw II, 315
Baikal, lake in Central Asia, 736
bailies
  of Euboea, 393, 400, 418
  of Achaea and the Morea, 403, 410–11
  of duchy of Athens, 410
Bajan, Avar khan, 478, 480–2
Bakchinos, Hungarian commander, and Manuel I Comnenus, 581
Baktashis, Dervish order, 745
Balamea, town in Syria, taken by John Tzimisces, 171
Balaton, lake in central Europe, 124
Baldwin I, Latin Emperor of Constantinople, **285–93**
  and Fourth Crusade, 276, 285–6
  election as Emperor, 287–8
  relations with Innocent III, 288
  partition of Byzantine Empire, 288–9
  relations with Seljuqs, 290
  relations with Kalojan of Bulgaria, 290, 292–3, 469, 525
  relations with Greeks, 290
  invasion of Asia Minor, 290–1
  capture and presumed death, 293, 391, 469, 525
Baldwin II, Latin Emperor of Constantinople
  birth, 305
  under regency, 309–10, 398
  plans for marriage, 310–11
  appeals for help to the Pope, 312–13, 317, 326
  return to Constantinople, 314–15
  relations with Frederick II, 314, 316–17
  financial difficulties, 317–18
  protected by Venetian fleet, 326–7
  flight from Constantinople (1261), 327
  aided by kings of Sicily, 328, 334
  death, 339
Baldwin I (of Boulogne), king of Jerusalem, 629
Baldwin III, king of Jerusalem, and Manuel I, 234–5, 630
Baldwin IX of Hainault, count of Flanders, *see* Baldwin I, Latin Emperor of Constantinople
Baldwin of Nigrinum, marshal of Armenia, 636
Balěsh, *see* Bitlis

Balik, independent boyar ruler of the Dobrudja, 544
Balikesir, *see* Palaeocastro
Balkan War of 1912–13, 9
Balkans
  part of See of Rome, 19
  landowners in, 39
  attacks by Visigoths, 26
  exposed to Arab attacks, 101
  under Byzantine hegemony, 122, 217
  danger to Empire in eleventh century, 193, 194
  Pecheneg raids, 196, 203, 208, 213–14
  Hungarian ambitions in north-west, 212, 221
  support for Ducas family against Alexius I, 213
  waning of Byzantine influence under John II, 221
  importance to Manuel I, 233
  extension of papal authority under Alexius III, 248
  Turkish conquest, 369, 371, 373–4, 375–6, 387, 762–6
  Byzantine diplomacy in, 485–6, 488–91, 498–504, 505–9
  military road through, 553, 590, 762
  Slav invasions, *see* Slavs
  Avar attacks, *see* Avars
Balkh, city in Central Asia, 641, 747
Balkhash, lake in Central Asia, 736
Balšić, Balša, George and Stracimir, brothers in power in Zeta, 541
Balšić, Balša III, ruler of Zeta, 552
Balšić, George II, ruler of Zeta, 550
Baltic Sea and Baltic countries
  and Slavs, 488
  and Vikings, 494–5
  trade with Islam, 649
Bambyke, *see* Hierapolis (Manbij)
ban, title of the rulers of Bosnia, *see* Borić, Kulin, Stephen II Kotromanić, Tvrtko I, Vuk
banovine, Hungarian districts, 559–60
Banū Habīb, Arab Mesopotamian tribe, migration into Byzantine territory, 718, 735
Baphaeum (Koyunḥiṣār), near Nicaea in Asia Minor, battle (1301), 759 and n. 1
Bar, town in Zeta
  archbishopric of, 520, 546
  taken by Rascia, 521
  under Stephen Lazarević, 552
  under Venice, 554
Baradaeus, *see* Jacob

Barancs, town and district in Balkans, 581–2, 585, 587

Bardanes, George, metropolitan of Corfu
overtures to the Patriarch in Nicaea, 309
literary work, 321

Bardanes Turcus, claimant to the throne under Nicephorus I, 91, 95, 99

Bardas, Caesar, uncle of Michael III
hostility to Theodora and Theoctistus, 105, 107
murder of Theoctistus, 108
adviser to Michael III, 108, 450–1, 497, 713
correspondence with Pope Nicholas I, 113
and Photius, 117
and the university of Constantinople, 133
popularity, 117
murder, 114–15, 117, 120, 453, 713–14

Bardas Phocas, *see* Phocas

Bardas Sclerus, *see* Sclerus

Bardha'a, *see* Partav

Bardzrberd, castle in Cilicia, 629

Bari, town in Apulia
taken by Arabs, 728
recaptured by Emperor Louis II and Byzantine fleet (871), 729
occupied by Basil I, 729
attacked by Otto I, 151
besieged by Arabs (1004), 731
taken by Lombards and retaken by Normans (1040, 1051, 1052), 197, 202
under Norman control, 208
taken by Manuel I, 229
synod of (1098), 467

Barkiyāruq, Seljuq leader, 740

Barlaam of Calabria, monk, views on division in Church, 330

Barmakids (Barmecides), Central Asian Iranians, under Abbasids, 641, 645, 666, 700

Barozzi, Jacopo, lord of Thera, 425

Bartolomea, daughter of Nerio I Acciajuoli, wife of Theodore I Palaeologus, 423

Basaraba, *voivode*, and independence of Wallachia, 561

Bashīr, commander at Maṣṣiṣa (Mopsuestia) for the Abbasids, 711

Basil I, Emperor, **116–25**
origins, 116
founder of Macedonian dynasty, 116
early history, 116–17
marriage to Eudocia Ingerina, 117

praised by Leo VI, 116, 126; and by Constantine Porphyrogenitus, 116, 120, 122
unpopularity with army, 117
and recapture of Cyprus, 107 n. 1
as adviser and favourite of Michael III, 108, 115, 117
and murder of Michael III, 114, 115–16, 453
rivalry with and murder of Bardas, 115, 453
and conflict between Photius and Ignatius, 117–19, 122–3, 126, 453
and father of Romanus Lecapenus, 137 and n. 1
policy towards Balkan Slavs, 501
and Caucasia, 612–13, 715
eastern campaigns, 119–21, 128, 129 n.1, 132, 137 n. 1, 147, 714 and n. 1, 715, 729
and council of 867, 117–18
and council of 869–70, 118, 453
and council of 879–80, 123, 454
relations with Bulgaria, 118–19, 127
relations with Rome, 118–19, 122, 454, 729
relations with his son Leo VI, 125, 130
legislative work, 132–3
Basilica, 133
Procheiron, 133
Epanagoge, 133, 134
interest in West, 132, 448, 457, 729
missionary zeal, 121–2, 132–3, 500–1
building of churches, 733
death, 121, 125

Basil II, Emperor, **175–92**
infancy, 148
and the great landowners, 144 n. 1, 173, 182–4, 190, 193–5, 212
eastern campaigns, 149, 173, 182, 186–7, 517, 720, 724–5
and the Phocas family, 156, 176–7, 192
relationship to Theodora, wife of John I, 159
comparison with Nicephorus Phocas and John Tzimisces, 172
and Basil the *parakoimomenos*, 174, 177–8, 723
plot against life, 174, 178
accession, 175
relations with Georgia and Armenia, 177, 179, 181, 186, 189, 190, 192, 197, 203, 618–19, 621
and Bardas Phocas, 176–9, 516, 517, 618, 724
negotiations with Baghdad, 177–8

Basil II (*cont.*)
  relations with Vladimir of Kiev, 179–
    80, 191, 515–17
  civil wars, 176–7, 178–9, 180–1, 723–4
  relations with Bardas Sclerus, 175–81,
    517, 723–4
  revolt of Bulgaria and Bulgarian
    campaigns, 178–82, 184–9, 192,
    517–18
  military tactics and strategy, 181,
    185–6, 191
  alliance with Venice, 182, 187, 731
  agreement with Serbs, 182
  agreement with Hungary, 573
  relations with the Papacy and West,
    184, 187, 190, 192, 195, 458, 460
  use of Russian troops, 179, 186, 190,
    516
  relations with Fatimid Caliphate, 187,
    517, 724–5
  blinding of Bulgarian prisoners, 188,
    518 and n. 1
  taxation of Slav provinces, 189, 196–7
  extent of Empire, 189–90, 518
  use of Slav troops, 190
  Lombard revolt in South Italy, 190, 731
  treatment of Church, 190–1
  attitude to learning and arts, 191
  death, 192, 193, 195
  assessment of reign, 190–2, 193
Basil II, Grand Duke of Moscow, opposition to union with Roman Church,
  382
Basil the Great of Caesarea, Church
  Father, 48–51
  and the religious life, 58
Basil the *parakoimomenos*
  and Nicephorus II, 148 and n. 1,
    153 n. 3, 156, 174
  hostility to Phocas family, 157–8
  under John Tzimisces, 157–8, 161 n. 1,
    172–5, 720
  and Basil the *rector*, 161 n. 1
  and Romanus of Bulgaria, 162 n. 3
  under Basil II, 174–8, 723
  banished to Crimea, 178
  issue of deeds of grant for land, 183
Basil Pediadites, metropolitan of Corfu,
  and Lateran Council of 1215, 304
Basil the *protospatharius* ὁ ἐπὶ τῶν
  δεήσεων, under Nicephorus II, 153
  n. 3
Basil the *rector*, 161 and n. 1
Basil, metropolitan of Reggio, 465
Basil, archbishop of Trnovo
  consecration, 523
  coronation of Kalojan, 248

Basilacius, Nicephorus, *dux* of Dyrrachium, pretender under Nicephorus
  III, 211
βασιλεοπάτωρ, *basileopator*
  title of Stylianus Zautzes, 127 n. 2,
    133
  title hoped for by Leo Phocas, 137;
    and by Symeon of Bulgaria, 506
  title of Romanus Lecapenus, 137–8,
    144, 507
βασιλεύς, Basileus, imperial title
  prerogative of Byzantine Emperor,
    225, 227
  and Basil I, 115, 117
  under the Palaeologi, 341 n. 1, 380
  and Charlemagne, 90, 96–7, 448
  and Symeon of Bulgaria, 135, 138,
    506, 508 and n. 3
Basilica, legal code of Leo VI
  debt to the *Ecloga*, 65
  and Basil I, 133
Basilica Therma, battle (978), 177
basilicas
  in Constantinople, 8
  of the Virgin at Torcello or Cittanova,
    251
  of St Euphemia at Grado, 252
  in Caucasia, 615
basilikos, imperial commissioner, 171
Basiliscianus, favourite of Michael III,
  115
Basparacania, province of, Byzantine
  name for Vaspurakan, q.v.
Baṣra, town on the Euphrates delta, 702
  Baṣrain school of Arabic grammarians,
    688 n 1.
  Pure Brethren of, 694
Bāṭinī, opponents of Sunnism, 691
Batn Hanzith, town in Mesopotamia, 164
Baṭṭāl, Umayyad general and epic hero,
  698–9, 735, 740
Batu, leader of the Golden Horde, 749
Baybars, Mamluk Sultan of Egypt and
  Syria, 634, 750–1
Baydju Noyon, Mongol general, capture
  of Erzurum (1241), 748
Bāyezīd I Ylîdîrîm, Ottoman Sultan,
  765–7
  marriage, 762
  control of Byzantine policy, 374–5, 377
  at battle of Kossovo, 550
  invasion of Turkish principalities of
    Asia Minor, 754, 765
  conquest of Bulgaria, 546, 765
  attack on Wallachia and the battle of
    Rovine (1395), 542, 551, 563, 765–6
  campaigns in Greece, 423, 766

Bāyezīd I (*cont.*)
  siege of Constantinople, 766
  defeat of Sigismund of Hungary, 766
  defeat by Timur and the Mongols, 377, 767
  fort built on the Bosphorus, 773
  and the Turkish colony in Constantinople, 775
  and Turkish culture, 772
Bāyezīd II, Ottoman Sultan
  war with his brother Dzem, 564
  conquest of Moldavia, 564
Beatrice, daughter of Charles of Anjou, king of Sicily, 334
Beatrice of Burgundy, second wife of Frederick I, 229
Beatus, leader of a faction in Venice, later doge, 256–7, 259
Beaufort (Levtro), castle in the Peloponnese, 399
Bedouin tribes
  incursions into Syria and Mesopotamia, 645, 652
  in North Africa, 651
  language, 687–8
Beirut, town in Syria
  law school, 4, 23
  miraculous representation of Christ, 85
  captured by Fatimid troops (975), 169
  captured by John Tzimisces, 170, 723
Béla II the Blind, king of Hungary
  understanding with Conrad III and Rascia, 221
  Bosnia given to his son, 221
  helped by Byzantium, 580
Béla III, king of Hungary, 582–5
  proposed marriage to Manuel I's daughter, 231, 234, 239, 582, 583
  for a time heir to Manuel I, 231, 234, 239, 582–3
  marriage to Manuel I's sister-in-law, 234, 583
  marriage alliance with Isaac II, 245, 247, 585
  reconquest of Dalmatia, Croatia and Sirmium, 245, 585
  Byzantine influence on his coinage, 587–8
Béla IV, king of Hungary, 313, 535, 589
Béla-Alexius, *see* Béla III
Belasica, in the Balkan range, 188
Bela Stena, town in the Balkans, 555
Belgrade (Singidunum, q.v., Nándorfehérvár), town on Danube, 524, 527–8, 530, 581, 585
  bishopric of, 521
  under Hungary, 535, 540, 553, 578
  under Stephen Lazarević, 551, 552
  attacked by Turks, 553, 555, 560, 770
  taken by Turks (1521), 560
Bellagrada, *see* Berat
Bellevaux, Cistercian abbey in Burgundy, 409
Benedict VIII, Pope, 458
Benedict XII, Pope, 330
Benedict, cardinal of Santa Susanna, papal legate in Constantinople in 1205, 302 and n. 2, 394, 469
Benedictines, in Hungary, 586
Benevento, town in South Italy
  ceded to Charlemagne (798), 88
  and Arab attacks, 729
  and Pope Leo IX, 460, 461
  campaign of Manuel I, 229
  battle (1266), 334, 402
Benevento, prince of, alliance with Otto I, 151
Benjamin, tribe of, 171
Benjamin of Tudela, traveller, on Thebes, 428
Ber, *see* Berroea
Bérard, Latin archbishop of Athens, 395, 408–9
Berat (Bellagrada), town in Albania, 325, 337, 538
Berbers, North African people
  under Abbasids, 664
  empire in Spain and North Africa, 651
Bereke, khan of Golden Horde, conversion to Islam, 634
Berengar, *see* Hugh of Provence
Berenguer Estañol of Ampurias, vicar-general of the duchy of Athens, 412
Bergama, *see* Pergamum
Bernard of Clairvaux, St
  views on Sicily, 222
  and Second Crusade, 227
Bernini, architect of Piazza di San Pietro, Rome, 7
Berroea (Verria, Ber), town in Macedonia
  taken and retaken in Basil II's Bulgarian campaigns, 179, 181, 187
  taken by Stephen Dušan, 538
  bishops of, 524
Bertha (Eudocia), first wife of Romanus II, 147
Bertha of Sulzbach (Irene), sister-in-law of Conrad III, first wife of Manuel I, 222, 224, 226–8
Bertrand, cardinal bishop of Ostia and Velletri, 429
Bertrandon de la Brocquière, Burgundian knight, description of Serbia, 533

Bertranet Mota, Gascon in Navarrese Company, 421
al-Bērūnī, Islamic scholar, 694–5
Besançon, town in France, 230
Bessarabia
  and Antes, 476 n. 2, 477
  and migration of Onogur Bulgars, 484
Bessarion, archbishop of Nicaea, later cardinal
  and union of Florence, 382, 472
billeting, 218
bir, Rumanian national tax, 562
Bithynia, district in Asia Minor
  and Leo III's Arab campaigns, 63, 698–9
  settlement of Slavs from Bulgaria, 74
  visited by John Tzimisces, 172
  exile of Caesar John Ducas, 210
  penetration by Seljuqs, 212
  exclusion from Sultanate of Rūm (1081), 213
  held by Ottomans, 347, 354, 759
  plundered by Russians under Igor, 510
  Muslim traders in, 733
Bitlis (Balēsh), town in Caucasia, 609, 615
Black Sea (Euxine)
  importance for trade, 39, 41, 478
  Genoese and Venetian trade in, 326–7, 345, 365, 537
  ports on west coast, 97, 333, *and see* Anchialus, Develtus, Mesembria, Sozopolis
  themes bordering on, 102–3
  arrival of Vikings, 495
  loss of Byzantine possessions on north coast, 180
  Danishmend attacks, 223
  Seljuqs at, 746–7
  reached by Ottoman Turks, 759
  Byzantine fleets in, *see* navy, Byzantine
Blastares, Matthew, jurist, his *Syntagma* translated into Serbian, 539
Blemmydes, Nicholas, scholar, tutor of Theodore II Lascaris, 321
Bodin, *see* Constantine Bodin
Boeotia, district of Greece
  and partition of Empire under Baldwin I, 289
  under Latin rule, 292, 389, 408–24
  and Navarrese Company, 419
  lost to duchy of Athens, 422
  cultivation of olives and vines, 428
Bogdan, *voivode* of Moldavia, 561
Boghā, *see* Bugha
Boghaz Kesen (Rūmeli ḥiṣār), Turkish fort on European side of the Bosphorus, 385, 773

Bogomils and Bogomilism, dualist heresy
  description of, 513
  connection with Paulicianism, 120
  alliance with the Pechenegs, 213
  in the Balkans till the fifteenth century, 217
  and Constantine Chrysomalus, 220
  in Bulgaria, 213, 217, 242, 513, 526, 544
  in Macedonia, 242, 512–13
  in Cappadocia, 242
  in Bosnia, 546–8
  in western Europe, 547
  see also Albigenses, Cathari, Patarenes
Bohemia
  trade with Bulgaria, 159
  Gregory VII's ban on Slavonic liturgy, 464
  and Avars, 477, 482
  and Moravians, 496
  influence of St Cyril and St Methodius, 500–1
  and conversion of Russia, 515
Bohemond I of Antioch, son of Robert Guiscard
  campaigns in Greece, 213, 215–16, 467
  prince of Antioch, 215–16, 467
  recognition of Alexius I and his son as overlords, 216
  death, 216
Bohemond II of Antioch, death (1130), 224
Bohemond III of Antioch, relations with Lesser Armenia, 630–1
Bohemond IV of Antioch, 631, 633
Bohemond V of Antioch, 633
Bohemond VI of Antioch, 633
Boiannes, Basil, catepan of South Italy under Basil II, 190, 192
Boiditzes, Byzantine commander, and fall of Amorium (838), 711
Boilas, Romanus, plot against Constantine IX, 203
Bojana, river in Balkans, 552
Bolnisi, in Armenia, church at, 615
Boniface III, Pope, 440
Boniface VII, anti-Pope, 458
Boniface VIII, Pope, 404, 450
Boniface IX, Pope, 471
Boniface, marquis of Montferrat
  leader of Fourth Crusade, 277–9, 281, 283, 285–7
  marriage to Isaac II's widow, 287–8
  king of Thessalonica, 288, 294, 389, 525
  sale of Crete to Venice, 289, 427
  and Alexius III, 296

Boniface (*cont.*)
 operations in Greece, 291–2, 389–90, 392
 killed on campaign against Kalojan, 294, 297, 391
Boniface of Verona, triarch of Euboea, 412
Bonne, sister of Guy I de la Roche, 408
Book of ceremonies, see *De cerimoniis* s.v. Constantine VIII Porphyrogenitus
Boor, C. de, *Notitia Episcopatuum*, 487
Borić, ban of Bosnia, 546
Boril, Bulgarian tsar
 usurpation of throne, 299, 526
 attacks on Latin Empire, 300, 526
 alliance with Henry of Flanders, 301
 struggle with John Asen II, 305, 307, 526–7
 political alliances, 526, 531
 condemnation of Bogomil heresy, 526
Boris I Michael, Bulgarian khan
 negotiations with Franks, 112, 113, 452, 497–8
 capitulation to Michael III (864), 113, 498
 relations with Rome, 112–13, 118–19, 124, 452–3, 455, 498–500
 relations with Patriarchate of Constantinople, 118–19, 452, 498–501
 baptism, 113, 124, 127, 452, 498
 abdication, 127, 502
 encouragement of use of Slavonic, 501–2
Boris II, Bulgarian tsar
 and Nicephorus II, 151
 captured by Svjatoslav, 151
 taken prisoner by John I Tzimisces, 160
 deposition, 162 and nn. 2 and 3, 515
 death, 178
Boris (Kalamanos), Hungarian pretender, 580–1, 583
Βορζῶ, *see* Burzuya
Bosnia, Serbian state, **546–9, 555–7**
 invaded by Samuel of Bulgaria, 185
 self-governing under Basil II, 189
 under Constantine Bodin of Zeta, 520
 within orbit of Hungary, 221, 546–9, 555–7, 559–60
 under Manuel I, 234, 546
 battle of Kossovo (1389), 374, 764–5
 occupation of Zachlumia, 534, 540
 cultural development, 548
 expansion in fourteenth century, 548–9
 mineral resources, 548, 551
 trade, 548
 minting of coins, 548, 560

organisation and administration, 555–6
 Turkish influence, 556
 appeal to the Pope, 557
 destroyed by the Turks, 557–8
 rulers of, *see under* ban, *and* Šubići, Stephen Tomašević, Dabiša, Hrvoje Vukčić-Hrvatinić, Ostoja, Iločki
Bosnian Church, 546–8, 557
 acknowledgement of papal authority, 248, 546–7
 Bogomilism, 546–8, 557
 independence of Rome, 547–8, 557
 organisation, 547
Boso, cardinal, author of life of Pope Alexander III, 242 and n. 4, 243
Bosphorus, the
 Arab fleet in, 63
 reached by Hārūn ar-Rashīd (782), 83, 645–6
 Russian fleet in, 203
 Venetian fleet in, 326
 naval battle between Venice and Genoa (1352), 365
 Turkish forts on, 385, 773
Bosporus, in the Crimea
 place of exile, 178
 captured by Central Asian Turks (576), 479, 486
 under Khazars, 486
 Christianity in, 487, 567–8
 centre of trade, 567–8
 early kings of, 594
Botaneiates, *see* Nicephorus III
Botaneiates, Theophylact, governor of Thessalonica under Basil II, 188
Botond, Hungarian hero, 571
Boucicaut, French marshal, and defence of Constantinople against Turks, 376–7, 429
Boudonitza (Mendenitza), town near Thermopylae in Greece
 under Latin rule, 389, 399, 410
 Venetian house of, 424
Branas, Alexius, general under Isaac II, 522
Branas, Theodore, and Kalojan's attacks on Adrianople, 293–4
Braničevo, town in the Balkans, 524, 527–8, 530, 535
 bishopric of, 521
Branković, Serbian dynasty, 560
 see also George *and* Vuk Branković
Briel, de, *see* Geoffrey of Bruyères
Brienne, *see* John of, Walter of
Brindisi, Italian port on Adriatic, 197, 416
 captured by Robert Guiscard, 208
 battle (1156), 229–30

Bringas, Joseph, favourite of Theophano, 147–8, 161 n. 1, 162 n. 3
Britain
part of Roman Empire, 25
lost to Roman Empire, 27
prosperity of, 40
Brskovo, mining town in Serbia, 532–3
Bruges, town in Flanders, and Fourth Crusade, 276
Brunhilda, Frankish queen, and Pope Gregory the Great, 439
Brusa (Prusa, Bursa), town in Bithynia in Asia Minor
and Theodore I Lascaris, 291
held against Turks, 347, 756, 759
capital of Ottoman Sultans, 351, 759–60, 763, 773
Manuel II Palaeologus at, 374
taken by Timur, 767
besieged by Karamans, 768
Bryennius, Nicephorus, *dux* of Dyrrachium
general under Constantine IX, 203
claimant to throne, 204, 211
husband of Anna Comnena, 220
buccellarii, retainers attached to a military commander, 35
Bucellarion theme
created by Constantine V, 73
defection of general, 83, 608, 706
subdivided by Theophilus, 102
Buda, town in Hungary, 589–91
Buddhism in Central Asia, 641
Budva, town on coast of Zeta in Balkans, 552, 554
Bugha (Boghā), amir of Tiflis, army commander under al-Mutawakkil, 611, 712
Bukhara in Transoxania, capital of Samanids, 647, 680
and Seljuq Turks, 653, 737
captured by Jenghiz Khan, 660
al-Bukhārī, Muslim jurist, 674
Bulan, Khazar khan, 488
Bulcsu, Magyar chieftain, *patricius*, visit to Constantinople, 509 and n. 3, 572
Bulgaria, Bulgarian Empire and the Bulgars, **483–6, 490–1, 501–4, 505–9, 512–15, 517–18, 522–30, 535–7, 542–6**, *and see* List of Rulers 5
Old Great Bulgaria in south Russia, 483–4, 486, 568
Volga Bulgars, 484, 495
Bulgars in Hungary, 570
foundation of Bulgarian state in Dobrudja (First Bulgarian Empire), 32, 484 and n. 3, 485
attacks on Constantinople, 10, 98, 138, 485
and Arab siege of Constantinople (717–18), 63, 698
Constantine V's successes against, 74–5
treaty of 716, 74
exodus of Slavs to escape conscription, 74
campaigns against Constantine VI and Irene, 88
annexation of Pannonia, 490
invasions by Nicephorus I, 92, 94, 490
attacks against Michael I, 97–8
settlement of Armenian prisoners (813), 116
threatened by Franks, 98
definition of Bulgaro-Byzantine frontier, 98, 129, 491
help for Michael II against Thomas the Slavonian, 100
and Michael III, 111, 113, 114, 498
dealings with Franks, 112, 114, 452, 497, 498
wars against Byzantium under Symeon, 127–9, 134–9, 502–3, 505–8, 717–18
extent of Symeon's empire, 507
buffer state between Magyars and Thrace, 146, 509, 571
relations with Nicephorus II, 149, 151 and n. 1, 167, 513 and n. 2
Russian invasions and occupation under Svjatoslav, 151, 156, 158–62, 513 and n. 3, 514 and n. 1
Byzantine province, 163, 189, 208, 212, 515
revolt under the Comitopuli, 178, 179, 517–18
Basil II's campaigns, 178, 181–2, 184–6, 187–9, 517–18
settlements in Vaspurakan, 190
support of Ducas family against Alexius I, 213
expeditions of Isaac II, 245, 247, 522–4
establishment of Second Bulgarian Empire, 245, 246, 275, 388, 523, 585
waning of Byzantine influence under Alexius III, 248, 275, 524–5
extent of Empire under John Asen II, 310, 527
relations with Frederick Barbarossa, 468
relations with Latin Empire of Constantinople, 469–70, 525–8
relations with Michael VIII, 326, 333, 336, 338, 339, 470–1, 535–7

Bulgaria (*cont.*)
and the Mongol invasion, 336, 535
and the Tatars, 535 n. 2, 536–7
partition into eastern and western empires, 536
and Charles of Anjou, 337, 339, 470, 537
decline under Šišman dynasty, 542–5
defeat by Serbs at Velbužd (1330), 353, 534, 543
economic distress, 369
losses to Amadeo of Savoy, 370
Turkish conquest, 371, 375, 545–6, 763, 765
invaded by a Christian army, 383, 545–6
relations with Hungary, 524, 526, 528, 535–6, 544
relations with Fatimid Caliphate, 507, 730
relations with Serbia, 245–6, 248, 542–3, 764
and Magyars, 128, 503, 568–9
and Pechenegs, 128, 162, 203, 503, 510, 578
and Cumans, 522–3
disaffection and power of boyars, 524, 526, 529, 536–7, 542–4
influence of Byzantine institutions, 528–9
conversion to Christianity, 112, 122, 127, 491, 498
and conversion of Russia, 515
administrative system, 529
industry, 529, *and see* trade
see also Bulgarian Church, Bulgarian literature
Bulgarian Church
under an archbishop, 119, 122, 190–1, 248, 499, 500, 501, 523
demand for separate Patriarchate, 113, 118, 452, 470, 498–9
under a Patriarch, 508 and n. 4, 517, 525, 528 and n. 1, 529
Primate of All Bulgaria, 290, 306, 524, 528–9
autonomy and patriarchal status recognised by John Vatatzes, 311, 528
extinction of Bulgarian Patriarchate by Turks, 545
relations with Rome, 112, 114, 118–19, 123, 248, 311, 452–3, 454–5, 469, 470–1, 498–500, 524–5
relations with Byzantine Church, 113, 118–19, 122, 452–4, 498–502, 528 n.1, 529

under Byzantine Patriarchate from fifteenth century, 545
defection of Bulgarian provinces, 544
and council of 869–70, 118, 500
use of Slavonic in liturgy, 124, 455, 501
and Paulicianism, 120
and Bogomilism, 120, 213, 217, 242, 526, 544
and hesychasts, 544
influence of St Cyril and St Methodius, 501–2
and Patriarchate of Serbia, 538
Bulgarian literature, 501–2, 544–5
Bulgaric linguistic group, 483
Bulgarophygon, near Adrianople, battle (896), 128, 129 n. 1, 503
bulls
papal, 462
imperial, *see* chrysobulls
Burgas, gulf on Black Sea, 97
Burgundy
and Frederick Barbarossa, 230
movement for reform of Western Church, 459–60
and anti-Turkish coalition under Hunyadi, 554
Bursa, *see* Brusa
Burtzes, Michael
capture of Antioch (969), 150, 156 n. 2, 722
murder of Nicephorus II, 156
governor of Antioch, 175–6, 182, 724
and Bardas Sclerus, 176
Bury, J. B., 36, 105
Burzuya (Βορζῶ), castle in the Lebanon, taken by John Tzimisces, 171
Butrinto, town in Greece opposite Corfu, 337–8
Buwayhids, Persian dynasty
threat to Hamdanids, 149, 723
capture of Baghdad from Abbasid Caliph, 646, 702
advance into Mesopotamia, 647 and n. 1, 723
virtually control Abbasids, 649, 655, 659, 666, 680, 702–3, 723–4
defeated by Seljuqs, 653, 658
supporters of Shī'ism, 646–7, 649, 658–9
Byblos (Arab. Jubail, mod. Gibelet), town in Syria, 170, 723
Byzantine Empire
frontiers before 717, 22–32, 33, 35, 37, 41
defence of frontiers under Constantine V, 73, 74, 75
loss of Italy, 71, 75, 76, 77

Byzantine Empire (*cont.*)
　relations with Charlemagne, 90, 96–7
　Bulgaro-Byzantine frontier defined, 98, 129, 491
　defences of Arab frontiers under Theophilus, 103
　separation from West, 104
　expansion of frontiers under Basil II, 189–90, 216–17, 518
　contraction under the later Macedonians, 194
　breakdown of defence system under Constantine X, 207–8
　disagreement with Latins on alliances with Muslims, 214
　frontiers under Alexius I, 216–17
　weakening of central authority under the Comneni, 240, 519–22
　partition after Fourth Crusade, 288–9
　capital transferred to Nicaea in Bithynia, 295
　achievements of Empire of Nicaea, 319–21
　state of Empire in 1261, 328–9
　loss of Asia Minor to Turks, 346–7
　extent of Empire under John VI Cantacuzenus, 363
　Ottoman Turks established in Europe, 366
　a tributary state of Ottoman Empire, 371
　reduced to Constantinople and its suburbs in fifteenth century, 380
　fall of Constantinople to Turks, 386–7
　end of the Byzantine Empire, 387
　see also diplomacy
Byzantium, *see* Constantinople
Byzantium, ancient, 476 n. 1
Byzantium, See of, legendary foundation by St Andrew, 456

Cabasilas, Nicholas, the so-called 'Anti-Zealot Discourse', 219 and n. 2, 358 n. 1
Cadmea, citadel of Thebes, 391, 400, 408, 416, 424, 429
Caesar, imperial title
　of Nicephorus and Christopher, half-brothers of Leo IV, 82 n. 2
　of Bardas, uncle of Michael III, 108
　of Bardas Phocas, father of Nicephorus II, 148
　of John Ducas, brother of Constantine X, 208
　given to Renier of Montferrat, 277
　given to Leo Gabalas, 311
　given to Alexius Strategopulus, 326

　given to Roger de Flor, 347
　given to the *panhypersebastus* John Palaeologus, 351
　given to Tervel of Bulgaria, 485 and nn. 2 and 3, 486
　given to Béla III of Hungary, 584
　given to George II of Georgia, 622
　used in Serbia, 538
Caesar-worship, *see* ruler-worship
Caesarea (Kaysarīya, Kayseri), city in Cappadocia
　centre of Christianity, 20
　birthplace of St Basil, 48, 209
　and the Armenian Church, 599 n. 1
　metropolitan of, 620
　buildings, 747
　proclamation of Nicephorus II as Emperor, 148, 721
　and Arab campaigns, 64, 704–5, 721
　sacked by Seljuq Turks (1067), 209
　reached by Mongols, 749
　reached by Mamluks, 750
Caesarea in Palestine, taken by John Tzimisces, 170–1, 723
Caesaropapism, 133–4
Cairo
　Fatimid capital, 648, 657, 659
　under Mamluks, 637
　Hamdanids in exile in, 725
　Abbasid Caliph in, 765
Calabria, district of South Italy
　taxation under Leo III, 65, 71, 444
　transfer to See of Constantinople, 71, 87–8
　under Byzantine control in eighth century, 75
　Arab invasions, 103, 729–32
　campaigns of Nicephorus Phocas the Elder, 121–2, 128, 179, 729
　home of John Philagathus, 184
　under Norman control, 208
　sale of corn to Sicilian Arabs, 734
Calabria, theme of, 121
Calixtus II, Pope, 222 n. 2, 467–8
Callipolis (Gallipoli, Gelibolu), in Thrace on the Hellespont
　attacked by John Vatatzes, 309, 398
　Catalan Company at, 347, 411
　in Turkish hands (1354), 366 and n. 1, 369, 761
　retaken by Amadeo of Savoy, 370, 372
　handed over to Turks by Andronicus IV, 372
　death of Muḥammad I, 769
Callistus I, Patriarch of Constantinople
　opposition to John VI, 366
　relations with Serbia, 369, 539

Callistus, Nicephorus, manuscript of his ecclesiastical history, 592

Calocyras, *patricius* under Nicephorus II, 513 and n. 2, 514

Calonymus (Calolimno), island in Sea of Marmora off Asia Minor coast, place of exile, 161

Caltabellotta, peace of (1302), 347, 404
counts of, 418

Calycadnus (Saleph, Göksu), river in Cilicia, 743

Camacha (Kamacha), town on upper Euphrates, between Tephrice and Theodosiopolis
and wars between Byzantium and Abbasids, 83, 703–9

Camaterus, *see* John X Camaterus, Patriarch

Camaterus, Petronas, *strategus* of theme of Cherson under Theophilus, 492

Campania, part of Byzantine Italy, 75

Câmpulungu (Long Plain), in Strymon valley, 188

Camytzes, Manuel, in rebellion against Alexius III, 278

Canabus, Nicholas, proclaimed Emperor by the mob in 1204, 284

Candia (Chandax), town in Crete, 147, 427, 709, 721
Venetian dukes of, 427

Candiano, Venetian family, 265–6

Candiano, Peter I, doge of Venice, 264, 268

Candiano, Peter II, doge of Venice, 268

Candiano, Peter III, doge of Venice, 268

Candiano, Peter IV, doge of Venice, 265–6

Candiano, Vitale, doge of Venice, 266–7

Candiano, Vitale, Patriarch of Grado, 266

Candidianus, metropolitan of Grado, 252

Cannae, in Italy, battle of, 190

canon law
on marriage, 131, 307
western, 439, 457, 464
Collectio canonum of Deusdedit, 451
Islamic, 663, 665–6, 677

Cantacuzenus, John, *see* John VI Cantacuzenus

Cantacuzenus, Manuel, Despot of Mistra, 363, 367, 403, 429

Cantacuzenus, Matthew, son of John VI
granted principality in Thrace, 363, 365, 367
crowned co-Emperor, 366
Despot of the Morea, 367

cantilenas of Andronicus and Constantine Ducas, 135 n. 1

Caorle, bishopric of, 264

Capitula (Statutes) of Catalan Company, 413–14

Cappadocia, district in Asia Minor
invaded by Persians, 30
and wars with Arabs, 74, 83, 111, 697, 704–5, 707, 710, 719
conflict between Aetius and Stauracius, 90
visited by John Tzimisces, 172
invaded by Bardas Sclerus, 176
large estates in, 182–3
Caucasian rulers settled in, 204, 619–20, 628
home of Romanus IV, 209
cities recaptured by Kilij Arslan II, 237
Bogomils in, 242
invaded by Seljuqs, 209, 628

Cappadocia, theme of, 103, 121, 719

Cappadocian fathers, **48–51**
and John Chrysostom, 52
and monasticism, 58
see also Basil the Great of Caesarea, Gregory of Nazianzus *and* Gregory of Nyssa

Capua, prince of, alliance with Otto I, 151

Carabisiani, theme of, subdivision in eighth century, 64

Carantenus, Constantine, duke of Antioch under Romanus III, 195

Carbeas, Paulician leader in ninth century, 119, 150, 712–14

Carintana dalle Carceri, second wife of William of Villehardouin, 400

Carloman, son of Pepin III, *patricius Romanorum*, 76

Carmania, desert district of Persia, 168

Carmathians (Qarmaṭians), Muslim sect
invasion of Syria, 163, 169
and Ismāʿīlis, 681–2, 702
revolt against Abbasid Caliphs, 648, 682, 702, 717

Carolingian Empire, 104
and the Papacy, 449–50
decadence, 449, 450, 456, 457
see also Charlemagne

Carpathians, mountains in Central Europe, 128, 476, 490, 496, 503, 515, 560–1

Carthage
defeated by Rome, 25
exarchate, 29
and Heraclius, 30

cartography, Arab, 685

Carystus, town in Euboea
bishopric of, 409
seized by Alfonso Fadrique, 412–13

Casimir, king of Poland, 563
Časlav, prince of Serbia, 139
Caspar, E., 443
Caspian Albania, *see* Albania
Caspian Sea, and Vikings, 495
Cassandrea, town and peninsula south of Thessalonica, Catalan Company in, 348
Castel Tornese, *see* Chloumoutsi
Castile, king of, and Leo VI of Lesser Armenia, 637
castles
  of Latins in Greece and the Aegean, 388–9, 392–3, 397, 399, 401–2, 405–8, 412–13, 416–17
  in Caucasia, 615
  in Cilicia, 629, 636
  in Syria and the Lebanon, 171
  of the Assassins, 661
  in Phrygia, 759
Castoria, town in Macedonia, 325, 538
Castra Comnenon (Kastamuni, Kastamonu), Turkish capital in Paphlagonia, 756, 769
Castriota, George, *see* Skanderbeg
Castriota, John, father of George (Skanderbeg), 557
Castrogiovanni, *see* Enna
Castrum Ennae, *see* Enna
Catalan Company
  in Byzantine service, 347, 411
  attacks on Empire, 347–8, 411
  in Frankish Greece, 348–9, **411–22**
Catalan duchy of Athens, 348–9, 359, 375, 406, **411–22**
  deed of allegiance, 412
  organisation and statutes, 413–14
  agreement with Venetians of Euboea, 415–16
  relations with the Papacy, 415–16
  relations with Turks, 418
  under Aragonese rule, 417, 419–22
Catalan duchy of Neopatras, 412, 414, 417–18, 421–3
Catasyrtae, near Constantinople, battle (917 or 918), 137, 507
catepan, 190, 198, 529, 725, 731
Cathari, heretical dualist sect in West, 547
Catherine of Courtenay, titular Latin Empress of Constantinople, wife of Charles of Valois, 345, 349, 355, 406
catholicus, see *Katholikos*
Cattaro (Kotor), town on Dalmatian coast, 521, 549
Caucasia
  civilisation, 593–4

political system, 595 and n. 3, 596–7, 613, 632, 637
struggle for control between Rome (later Byzantium) and Persia, 594–5, 597–605
and the Holy War, 738
under Umayyads, 605–7
under Abbasids, 607–13
taxation under Abbasids, 608–9
see also Armenia, Georgia, Iberia, Lazica, Caspian Albania
Caucasus
source of recruits for army, 10, 35
part of See of Constantinople, 20
Khazar raids on, 64, 646, 699
unrest under Constantine VIII, 195
local feuds, 197
Byzantine diplomacy in, 473–5, 478–9, 483, 486–8, 511–12, 518, 567
cavalry
in Byzantine army, 154, 218
Caucasian, 597 n. 1, 617–18, 625
French and Frankish, 292, 325, 389
German, 325, 401
Turkish, 557, 760
Cavarzere, town in Italy, and the Lombard invasion, 250
Cecaumenus, author of the *Strategicon*
on Michael IV, 197
on taxes in Georgia and Mesopotamia, 204
Cedrenus, George, chronicler, on Nicephorus II, 152
Cefalù, town in Sicily, and Arab conquest of Sicily, 728
Čelebi, *see* Saudži Čelebi
Celestine III, Pope, and Leo II of Lesser Armenia, 632
Celts, 23
Ceos (Zia), island in Cyclades
bishopric of, 409
under Venetian rule, 425
Cephalonia, Ionian island
under Matthew Orsini, 297, 299, 388
refuge of Michael II of Epirus, 325
Latin bishopric of, 396
Cephalonia, theme of, 92, 121
Cephissus, river in Boeotia, battle (1311), 348, 411–12, 415
Cerbanus, Venetian in Constantinople, translations of Greek Fathers into Latin, 587
Cerigo, *see* Cythera
Cerigotto, Aegean island, under Latin rule, 426
Cerularius, *see* Michael I Cerularius, Patriarch

Cesarini, Julian, cardinal
and union of Florence, 382
and crusade of Vladislav III, 384, 553
Cetatea Alba, Moldavian port at mouth
of Dniester, 564
Cetina, river in Balkans, 519, 548
Cetinje, capital of Zeta under John
Crnojević, 559
Chaghri Bey, early Seljuq leader, 653,
737
Chalandritza, Latin barony in the
Peloponnese, 394, 405
Chalcedon, town in Asia Minor on the
Bosphorus
attacked by Persians, 10, 30
Council of, *see under* councils and
synods
formula of, 20, 21, 56, 604–5, 616
supporters of the formula (Chalcedonians), 55
and Andronicus I's march on capital,
244
and Fourth Crusade, 281
Chalcedon, archbishop of, guarantee for
safety of Romanus IV, 210
Chalcis in Euboea, Arab raids on, 714
Chaldia, theme of, 102, 157, 177, 707,
709
Chandax, *see* Candia
Chanti, language of Ostyaks of Siberia,
566
Chardak Pass, *see* Myriocephalum
charisticarius, 219
charisticium, grant of care of monastic
property, 219
charitable institutions
taxed by Nicephorus I, 93
under Nicephorus II, 154–5
under John Vatatzes, 320
and Irene, wife of John II, 580
see also hospitals
Charlemagne
relations with the Papacy, 72, 446–9
titles, 76, 90, 96, 447–8
defeat of Lombards (774), 77, 446
betrothal of his daughter to Constantine VI, 83, 87
in Italy, 83, 88, 446
and Seventh General Council, 87, 88,
449
coronation by Pope Leo III (800), 90,
257, 447
relations with Byzantine Empire, 90,
96–7, 260–1, 447–8, 449
destruction of Avar Empire, 490
Charles VI, king of France, help for
Byzantium against Turks, 376

Charles of Anjou, king of Sicily and
Naples, **334–40**
hostility to Byzantium, 328, 334–9,
402, 470, 537
relations with the Papacy, 334–7, 339
treaty with Baldwin II, 334, 402
treaty with Baldwin's son Philip, 339
relations with St Louis of France, 335
relations with Bulgaria and Serbia,
337, 339, 470, 537
relations with Albania, 337
relations with the principality of
Achaea, 334, 337–8, 402–4
relations with Nicephorus I of Epirus,
338
relations with Venice, 339
relations with John I of Thessaly, 339
overthrown by Peter III, king of
Aragon, 339–40
Charles II, king of Naples, 345, 404, 410
Charles II, king of Navarre, 419
Charles Martel
defeat of Muslims at Poitiers (732), 63
pact with Lombards, 444
Charles Robert, king of Hungary, 548,
561
Charles Topia, Albanian lord, 419, 541
Charles of Valois, brother of Philip IV of
France, hostility to Byzantium, 345,
349
Charsianon
theme of, 103, 120–1, 177
province of, 182, 719
Charsianon Castron (Kharshana), in
Charsianon theme in Asia Minor,
719–20
charters of monasteries, 574–5, 580, 587;
see also *typicon*
chartophylax, office of John Beccus, 338
cheese, exported from Crete, 428
chemistry, studied by Arabs, 685
Cherson, town in Crimea
missionary work in, 111–12, 487, 492
and relics of Pope Clement I, 112, 124
captured by Vladimir of Kiev, 180,
516
importance in Byzantine diplomacy,
475, 491–2, 510
under Khazars, 486
Russian threat, 505, 515
and conversion of Russia, 516
Cherson, theme of, in south Russia, 102–
3, 492, 510
Chersonese, Thracian, 398
Χερσόνησος, *see* Cherson
Chiara Zorzi (Giorgio), duchess of
Athens, 424

Chilia, Moldavian port at mouth of Danube, 564

Chimenlik, *see* Tzympe

China
death of Timur, leader of Mongols, 377
Chinese names of Central Asian tribes, 477 n. 1, 478
silk trade with Europe, 478, 487
and the Mamikonids of Armenia, 597 n. 1
paper and invention of printing, 644
trade with Islam, 649
home of Kara-Khitay, 655
T'ang dynasty in, 736

Chios, island in Aegean
taken by Arabs, 30
defeat of Byzantine fleet under Himerius, 130, 716
Bardas Phocas transported to, 158, 176
under Latin Empire, 289
seized by Genoese (1304), 346
under Byzantine sovereignty (1329), 354–5
recaptured by Genoese (1346), 364
taken by Turks (1566), 427

Chloumoutsi (Clermont, Castel Tornese), castle in the Peloponnese, 397

Choerosphactes, Leo, Byzantine diplomat under Leo VI, 129, 131, 503, 716, 735

Cholarzene (Klarjet'i), province of Iberia, 603, 609–11, 613, 619, 621

Chomatianus, Demetrius, archbishop of Ochrida
championship of Theodore Ducas of Epirus, 306–7
coronation of Theodore Ducas by, 308
literary work, 321
and Serbian Church, 532

Chonae (Colossae), town in Phrygia in Asia Minor, sacked by Turks, 209

Choniates, Michael, metropolitan of Athens, 302, 395, 408, 425, 428, 430

Choniates, Nicetas, historian
on John II, 220
on Manuel I, 232, 237, 240–2
on sack of Constantinople in 1204, 286–7, 469
on Empire under the Angeli, 388
on Leo Sgouros, 388–9

Chortaitou, monastery near Thessalonica, 304

Chosroes I, king of Persia, 602

Chosroes II, king of Persia, 29, 603–5, 736

Chosroes III, king of Armenia, 597–8

Chosroids, royal dynasty in Iberia, 597, 603, 606, 608, 610
see also Mihranids

Chreles, *see* Hrelja

Christian of Mainz, chancellor under Frederick Barbarossa, embassy to Manuel I, 231

Christians
status under Abbasids, 666–7
and Arabic science, 684
in Turkish army, 758
see also persecution

Christodulus, abbot of monastic house on Patmos, 218

Christological controversies, 20, 47, 49, 55–6, 68, 79 and n. 3, 86–7

Christopher, Caesar, half-brother of Leo IV, 82 and n. 2, 83, 88–9, 97

Christopher, son-in-law of Basil I, 120

Christopher, eldest son of Romanus Lecapenus, 143

Christopher, bishop of Olivolo, 256

Christopolis, town in western Thrace, 363

chronicles
Byzantine, translated into Slavonic, 502
Turkish, 758, 759 n. 1, 761, 763
Serbian, 764
see also Arab sources, *and under* Hungary, Russia

chrysobulls, 228, 241, 244, 271, 304 n. 1, 308 n. 1, 314, 317, 591–2

Chrysocheir, Paulician leader, campaigns against Basil I, 119–20, 714

Chrysomalus, Constantine, twelfth-century heretic, 220

Chrysopolis (Scutari), town on Asia Minor side of Bosphorus opposite Constantinople
monastery in, 58
reached by Hārūn ar-Rashīd, 83, 706
reached by Bardas Phocas, 179
battle (988), 179, 516
and Fourth Crusade, 281

Chrysopolis, town in Thrace, 538

Chūpān, Il-Khan general, 627, 753–4

Church administration and organisation, 18, 432, 433, 438, 456–7, 459, 474
under Ottomans, 774
see also Greek Church

church buildings
in Bulgaria, 501–2
in Hungary, 574, 576–7
in Caucasia, 615
see also following entries and under Constantinople

Church of the Holy Sepulchre in Jerusalem, 287, 725–6

Church of the Holy Wisdom in Nicaea, 84
Church of St Denis in Paris, 76
Church of St John at Ephesus, 119
Čibuq Ābād, plain to north-east of Ankara, 767
Cibyrraeot theme
  created between 710 and 732, 64
  loyal to Constantine V, 73
  legislation regarding property, 145
  and campaigns against Arabs, 705–6, 709
Cicero on education, 46
Cilicia, district in Asia Minor
  part of See of Antioch, 19
  invaded by Byzantine troops, 120, 148, 149, 707, 710, 715–16, 721
  frontier with Arabs, 128
  Peter Phocas in, 150
  reconquest under Nicephorus II, 150, 154, 156
  visited by John Tzimisces, 172
  Seljuq attacks, 209, 630, 635
  campaigns of Alexius I, 215
  invaded by Danishmends, 223
  campaigns of John II, 224, 234, 630
  and Manuel I, 226, 234–5, 630
  Armenians in, 618, 628
  creation of Lesser Armenia (q.v.), 629, 742
  under Mamluks, 637
  under Ottomans, 637
Cilician Gates, pass in Taurus range in Asia Minor, 707–8, 710, 714, 746
Cimbalongus, *see* Kleidion
Cincari, remnant of Vlachs in Macedonia and northern Greece, 560
Cinnamus, John, historian
  on John II, 220, 224
  on Manuel I, 226, 228, 231, 241–2
  on the Papacy and its claims, 242–3
circus parties
  in Antioch and Alexandria, 40
  see also Greens
cis-Caucasia, 593 and n. 1
Cistercians
  occupation of Greek monastery of Chortaitou, 304
  given monastery of Daphni, 409
Cittanova, part of Venice, 251, 254–6, 259
  bishopric of, 264
city prefect, 36–7, 195, 198
civil service
  as check on Emperor, 15
  pay, 38, 211, 244
  organisation, 13, 33
  and taxation, 37

and Christianity, 42, 43, 44
educational standard, 46, 55
and Nestorius, 56
and paganism, 44
under Constantine IX, 200
opposed to Isaac I Comnenus, 205
under Constantine X, 207
Andronicus I's attempt at reform, 244
abuses under Isaac II, 245
Civitate, town in Apulia in Italy, battle (1053), 202
Claudias (Qalawdhiya), on Euphrates east of Melitene, 703, 704
Cleanthes hymn, 45
Clement I, Pope, discovery of relics near Cherson, 112, 124
Clement III, anti-Pope, 464–5
Clement IV, Pope, 335
Clement V, Pope, 470
Clement VI, Pope, 415, 540, 586
Clement of Alexandria, Church Father, political theory, 431
Clement, disciple of St Methodius, work among Slavs in Macedonia, 501–2
Clermont, town in France, and First Crusade, 466
Clermont, *see* Chloumoutsi
Codex of Justinian, 133, 141
co-Emperor
  change in status under the Palaeologi, 341 and n. 1
  and Charlemagne, 448
coinage
  representation of Emperor on, 3, 16, 446
  debasement in third century, 32
  and *Virtus Augusti*, 45
  representation of Rome and Constantinople on, 24 n. 1
  bearing image of Christ, 67 and n. 2
  under Nicephorus II, 151, 155
  debasement under Michael IV, 196, 200
  debasement under Constantine IX, 200
  under Alexius I, 218
  of Theodore Ducas, 304 n. 1
  debasement under the Palaeologi, 342–3
  minting of coins under Manuel II and John VIII, 380
  Venetian, 273
  gold coins of Italian republics, 342
  of duchy of Athens, 410
  minting of coins at Rome in eighth century, 446
  Serbian, 533, 541, 542
  Bulgarian, 537

coinage (*cont.*)
of Vidin, 544
Bosnian, 548, 560
Rumanian, 562
Hungarian, 576, 587–8
under Abbasids, 656, 664, 678
minting of coins by Ottomans, 760
see also *aspron, denarii,* dinar, dirham,
ducat, florin, *grossi, hyperpyron,
keration,* mark, *miliaresion, nomisma,
solidus, tetarteron*
Colchis, *see* Lazica
Colonea, in Asia Minor south-west of
Trebizond, 718
Colonea, archbishop of, guarantee of
safety for Romanus IV, 210
Colonea, theme of, 157
coloni, 38, 173; and see *paroikoi*
Colopini, Venetian family, 267
Columella, Latin author, translated into
Arabic, 672 n. 1
Comacchio, port on the Adriatic, Frankish naval base, 258–9
comes
Bulgar governor, 116
title used in Rumania (*comis*), 562
comitatenses, 34
Comitopuli, Bulgarian leaders, 178, 517;
see also Aaron, David, Moses and
Samuel
Comneni, Byzantine family
under Basil II, 192
Grand Comneni, *see under* Trebizond
and Michael VIII, 324
Comnenian line of Emperors, **212–45,**
331
and the Church, 60
established by Alexius I, 205
control of nomad invaders, 208
Comnenus, Alexius, eldest son of John II,
death (1142), 224–5
Comnenus, Alexius, *protosebastus,* nephew
of Manuel I, 244
Comnenus, Alexius, grandson of Andronicus I, Emperor of Trebizond,
291, 624
vassal of Seljuq ruler of Rūm, 301
Comnenus, Andronicus, second son of
John II, 224
death, 225
Comnenus, David, grandson of Andronicus I, and Empire of Trebizond, 291,
624
vassal of Latin Emperor, 295
killed in battle, 301
Comnenus, Isaac, Sebastocrator, brother
of Alexius I, 213, 229

Comnenus, Isaac, third son of John II,
224
passed over in favour of Manuel I,
225–6
suggestion of heresy, 242
Comnenus, Isaac, grandnephew of Manuel I, independent ruler of Cyprus,
245, 246
marriage to Béla III's sister, 584
Comnenus, John, brother of Isaac I, 207
Comnenus, Manuel, Emperor of Trebizond, vassal of the Mongols, 315–16
Comnenus, Manuel, military commander
under Basil II, 176, 180
Comune, political status of Venice, 272
Conrad II, Western Emperor, 269, 458
Conrad III, German king
and John II, 221, 222, 224, 227
ally and friend of Manuel I, 227–8, 233
and Second Crusade, 227–8, 742
Conrad, brother of Boniface of Montferrat, 277
Conrad of Wittelsbach, cardinal, and
Leo II of Lesser Armenia, 632
Consilium sapientium of Venice, 272–3
consonantia of Church and State, 17
Constable (Grand Constable), Latin
title, 299
title of Michael VIII Palaeologus, 322
Constance
treaty of (1153), 228–9
council of (1153), 229
Constance of Sicily, wife of Henry VI,
232, 246
Constance, Norman princess of Antioch,
wife of Raymond of Poitiers and
Reynald of Châtillon, 223, 225–6,
234–5
Constance-Anna of Hohenstaufen, second
wife of John III Vatatzes, 316, 323
Constans II Pogonatus, Emperor
and Muslim advance, 31, 32, 605–6
plans for West, 31
Typus, 440
campaigns against Slavs in Macedonia,
489
murder, 610 n. 1
Constantine I the Great, Emperor
representation on coinage, 3
as new Moses, 3
law and administration, 4, 23, 32, 36,
37
wall of Constantinople, 8, 9
relations with the Church, 17–18,
42–3, 47, 432
and army, 34
as defender of the faith, 4, 62

Constantine I (*cont.*)
the *Donation of Constantine*, 76, 445–8, 460
funeral, 1, 2
Constantine IV, Emperor
and Sixth General Council, 21, 31, 441
and Bulgar migration, 484
Constantine V, Emperor, **72–81**
marriage to Irene, Khazar princess, 64, 487
co-Emperor with Leo III, 64, 72
and the *Ecloga*, 65
iconoclastic policy, 68, 73, 78–81, 97, 99
relations with the Papacy and West, 75–8, 82, 445
and themes, 73
Arab wars, 73–4, 607–8, 699, 703–5
and Bulgaria, 74–5, 97, 490, 704–5
popularity, 72, 84, 97
five sons, half-brothers of Leo IV, 82 and n. 2, 83, 88–9, 97
Constantine VI, Emperor, **82–9**
co-Emperor with Leo IV, 81–2
joint sovereign with Irene, 82
betrothal to Charlemagne's daughter, 83, 87 and n. 1
proclaimed sole Emperor, 88
conflict with Irene, 88–9, 706
marriages, 89, 95
supporter of the images, 99
impersonated by Thomas the Slavonian, 100, 709
correspondence with Pope Hadrian I, 72 n. 2, 446–7
Arab campaigns, 83, 645–6, 707
Constantine VII Porphyrogenitus, Emperor, **144–6, 509–12**
historian, 105, 482 and n. 3, 488 n. 4, 510, 519, 546
legal commentaries, 133
biographer of Basil I, 116, 120, 122
Vita Basilii, 122
De cerimoniis, 130, 592, 720
De administrando imperio, 144, 510, 513
coronation, 130, 132 and n. 1
baptism and legitimisation, 131–2, 138
under council of regency, 134, 505
marriage plans, 135, 137
agrarian policy, 142, 145–6, 148 n. 1, 173
rebellion of Romanus I's sons, 143
support of western envoys, 143
opinion of Romanus I, 144–5
and Bulgaria, 146
Arab wars, 146, 718–20, 730–1

influence on Romanus II, 147
and Basil the *parakoimomenos*, 148 n. 1
his daughter married to John I Tzimisces, 159
diplomacy on the northern frontiers, 509–12
and Hungary, 570–2
gifts to Muslim rulers, 735
Constantine VIII, Emperor, **193–5**
infancy, 148
character as portrayed by Psellus, 193
relationship to Theodora, wife of John I, 159
accession, 175
negotiations with Bardas Sclerus, 180
sole Emperor, 193, 195
taxation, 195
death, 621
Constantine IX Monomachus, Emperor, **199–204**
and Zoe, his wife, 194, 199
imprisoned by Michael IV, 199
Psellus on, 199–200
debasement of the coinage, 200
advisers, 200
reorganisation of university, 200–1
relations with the Papacy and West, 201–2, 461–2
rebellions against, 201–3
attacks by Russians and Pechenegs, 203
and crown of Hungary, 576–7
relations with Armenia, 203–4, 620
and Georgia, 204, 622
Seljuq raids, 203–4
concern about heresy, 217
relations with Fatimid Caliphs, 726
Constantine X Ducas, Emperor, **207–8**
Psellus on, 207
anti-military policy, 207
support of the Church, 207
break-up of the Empire, 207–8
loss of South Italy, 208
relations with the Papacy, 463
relations with Georgia, 622
death, 208
Constantine (XI) Lascaris, brother of Theodore, proclaimed Emperor, 286 and n. 1, 291, 295
in Asia Minor, 291
death, 295
Constantine XI (XII) Palaeologus (Dragases), Emperor, **383–7**
Despot of the Morea (Mistra), 380, 771
campaigns against Turks in Greece, 383, 384–5, 771–2
accession on death of John VIII, 385

Constantine XI (*cont.*)
attempt at union with Roman Church, 385, 773
and John Hunyadi, 591–2
connection with Georgia, 627
killed fighting at fall of Constantinople (1453), 387, 774
Constantine I, Pope, visit to Constantinople, 442
Constantine II, Patriarch of Constantinople, deposed and executed by Constantine V, 80
Constantine III Leichudes, Patriarch of Constantinople, 200, 206, 463
Constantine III, king of Abasgia, 614
Constantine I, king of Georgia, 627
Constantine I of Lesser Armenia, 629
Constantine II of Lesser Armenia, 634
Constantine III of Lesser Armenia, 636
Constantine IV of Lesser Armenia, 636
Constantine, prince of Aksura and Lemos, king-maker in Lesser Armenia, 633
Constantine Bodin, prince of Zeta, 520
Constantine (Cyril) of Thessalonica, apostle to the Slavs
and Theoctistus, 107
work at Cherson and among Khazars, 111–12, 492–4, 496
and the conversion of Moravia and the Slavs, 112, 119, 497–9
relations with Rome and Constantinople, 124, 497–9
and relics of Pope Clement I, 112, 124
and the Slavonic liturgy, 124, 497, 499
influence, 500–2, 515
death in Rome, 111 n. 2, 124, 499
Constantine, Despot of Mistra, *see* Constantine XI (XII)
Constantine, Despot, brother of Theodore, Emperor of Thessalonica, 309, 313
Constantine, bishop of Nacolea, 66
Constantine the *parakoimomenos*, minister under Zoe, 136
Constantine, *patricius*, and Arab raids on Sicily in ninth century, 727
Constantine the Philosopher, biographer of Stephen Lazarević, 545
Constantine Phocas, *see* Phocas
Constantine Tich, Bulgarian tsar
marriage to Theodore II Lascaris' daughter, 322
alliance with Michael VIII, 326
marriage to Michael VIII's niece Maria, 336
relations with Charles of Anjou, 470
defeat and death (1277), 535 n. 1, 536

Constantine, eldest son of Basil I, 117, 125, 133
Constantine, uncle of Michael V, *nobilissimus*, 198
Constantine, son of Michael I of Epirus, 314 n. 1
Constantine, son of Stephen Uroš II Milutin, 534
Constantine, *see* Symbatius, Kalamanos
Constantinople, city of, **6–10**
foundation by Constantine the Great, 431
comparison with Rome, 2, 4, 12, 18, 23, 24, 36, 431
Hellenistic tradition, 431
importance of site, 4, 5, 10, 476
centre of culture and learning, 4, 48, 340, *and see* Constantinople, university, *below*
destruction of pagan temples, 8
building of churches and monasteries, 8, *and see* Constantinople, churches *and* monasteries, *below*
Councils, *see* councils and synods
triumphs of Byzantine Emperors, 162 and n. 2, 164, 169, 515, 583, 711
and iconoclasm, 66, 67, 84
anti-German movement, 27
state visits, 159, 228, 236, 241, 511
visit of papal legates (907), 127 n. 1
political parties and city proletariate, 55
communications, 8, 26, 337, 438, *and see* Via Egnatia
trade, 41, 128, *and see* corn supplies
foreign colonies in, 222, 232, 244, 272–4, 275–6, 283, 326, 327, 334, 345–6, 363–4, 372, 468, 505 and n. 2, 587, 745, 775
Muslims in, 733–4
foreign languages spoken in, 429
position in the fifth century, 28
population augmented from Greece and the islands, 73
attacked by Avars, 10, 29, 480–2; by Slavs, 480; by Arabs, 10, 25, 31, 63, 64, 698, 773–4; by Pechenegs and Uzes, 208; by Hungarians, 571; by pretenders to throne, 100, 203; by Bulgars, 74, 98, 138, 293, 398–9, 485, 490–1, 528; by Russians, 111, 130 n. 4, 140, 159, 494 and n. 1, 496 and n. 1, 505 and n. 1, 510–11, 713, 715–16
objective of Crusades, 215, 467, 468–9
on route of Second Crusade, 227

Constantinople, city of (*cont.*)
proposal to transfer seat of Empire back to Rome, 231, 243
threatened by Frederick Barbarossa and Third Crusade, 246, 468–9
and Fourth Crusade, 274, 278–87
captured and sacked by crusaders (1204), 5, 9, 286–7
under Latin rule, 287–328, 388
threatened by Theodore Ducas, 309, 527
besieged by Nicaea and Bulgarians in 1235 and 1236, 312, 398–9, 528
recapture by Michael VIII Palaeologus (1261), 325–8, 746
threatened by Ottoman Turks, 369, 375, 376–7, 378, 379, 385, 763, 766, 769
saved by Mongols under Timur, 377
final capture by Turks (1453), 10, 386–7, 472, 746, 773–4
capital of Ottoman Empire, 774–6
Constantinople, buildings, streets, etc.
Acropolis, 6, 7
Baths of Zeuxippus, 7
Circus, 734
column of Theodosius, 291
Great Theatre, 198
harbours, 7, 9
Mese, main street, 7, 8
Milliarium (Milion), triumphal arch, 8
Praetorium, 9
Senate House, 4, 8
statues, 8, 9, 284, 583
Tetrastoön (Fourfold Portico), 7
under the Ottoman Empire, 774–5
see also Hippodrome
Constantinople, churches
Holy Apostles, 1, 7, 84, 116, 125, 248, 775
St Irene, 109, 775
of the Blachernae, 366
oratory of Christ of the Chalke, 173
one built by Stephen I of Hungary, 575
three attached to the Pantocrator monastery, 580
all reopened by the Latin Emperor Henry, 304
see also St Sophia
Constantinople, districts
Blachernae, 6, 9
Cosmidium, 507–8
Pera, 8, 773
St Mamas, 505 n. 2
Seraglio Point, 6, 7
see also Chrysopolis, Galata, Golden Horn

Constantinople, fora
Augusteum, 7, 8, 162 n. 2
of Constantine, 7, 162 n. 2, 583
Tauri, 7
Constantinople, gates
Adrianople, 7
Chalce (Bronze or Brazen), 8, 68
of the Fountain, 327
Golden, 8, 328, 571
Pempton, 386
Constantinople, monasteries
Chora, 6
foundation of Irene, wife of Alexius I, 218
Pantocrator, 220, 580
Petrion, 199
see also Chrysopolis, Studites
Constantinople, mosques, 283, 580, 724–6, 733–4, 775
Constantinople, palaces
Blachernae, 6, 281–2, 284, 362, 550 n. 3
Bryas (on Asian Bosphorus), 735
Bucoleon, 285, 287, 314
Chrysotriclinus, 485 n. 2
Eleutherius, 88, 91
Great Palace (Βασιλική), 4, 7, 8, 9, 13, 68, 364, 485 n. 3, 735
Magnaura, 91 n. 1
St Mamas, 115
Ottoman palaces, 774–5
see also Hieria
Constantinople, university, 23, 68, 133, 200–1, 453
Constantinople, walls and fortifications
legend of invincibility, 5
Constantine's wall, 6, 9
Long Wall, 9, 480
Theodosian wall, 6, 8, 9, 775
Chatalja Lines (modern), 9
rebuilt by Leo III, 65
added to by Theophilus, 102
during Fourth Crusade, 281, 282, 285
under John V, 374
in 1453, 386–7, 774
Constantinople, Patriarchate of
status, 4, 5, 18, 302, 433–5, 437, 439–40, 447, 453, 457, 460
jurisdiction, 19–20, 71, 72, 434, 444, 447, 454, 456
schism with Rome, 21, 60, 104, 201–2, 246, 434–5, 455
reconciliation with Rome under Justin I, 21, 28, 604
attempts at reunion after 1054, *see under* Roman Church

Constantinople, Patriarchate of (*cont.*)
  rivalry with Rome over Bulgarian Church, 109, 118–19, 123, 452–3, 454, 498–500, 528–9
  dispute with Rome over Illyricum, 109, 112, 113, 124 n. 1, 447, 452, 455, 469–70, 499
  and Moravian Church, 124 and n. 1, 455
  recognition of status of Rome, 435–7
  relations with Rome under Leo VI, 126–7
  authority over Bulgarian bishops, 163, 544, 545
  subservience to Basil II, 190–1
  appointment of Patriarchs of Antioch, 216, 234–5
  Latin Patriarchs of Constantinople, 285, 293, 297, 301–4, 307, 317, 391, 586
  Patriarchs in Nicaea, 295, 302–4, 306–7, 309, 312, 318, 321, 324
  restoration of Greek Patriarchate (1261), 328
  ecclesiastical court of justice, 353
  the title Oecumenical Patriarch, 439–40, 447, 460, 461
  apostolicity and legend of St Andrew, 456
  and Russian Church, 516 and n. 3
  relations with Serbian Church, 531 and n. 3, 550 and n. 1
  relations with the Church in Rumania, 561
  relations with the Church in Hungary, 573, 586
  political leadership after fall of Constantinople, 774
Constantius II, Emperor
  at Constantine's funeral, 1
  visit to Rome, 12
  religious policy, 42–3
  and civil service, 46
Constitutions of Catalonia, 413
consul, honorary title in Venice, 261
consulate, 12–13
Contarini, Bartolomeo, and Duchess Chiara Zorzi in Athens, 424
Continuator of Theophanes, *see under* Theophanes, chronicler
Contostephanus, Andronicus, *megas dux*, admiral
  supporter of Andronicus I, 244
  service under Manuel I, 583
copper mining, 532, 644
Copts, 663, 668
  Coptic Christian literature, 54

Cordova, town in Spain
  Arab refugees from, 709
  Arab capital, 735
Corfu, island off coast of Epirus
  seized by Normans (1081), 212
  Norman defeat off, 213, 271
  attacks by the Normans of Sicily in twelfth century, 227–8, 232, 239, 245
  and Fourth Crusade, 281
  claimed by Venetians in 1204, 289
  taken by Venetians (1207), 297
  occupied by Michael I of Epirus, 300
  and Theodore Ducas, 308 n. 1
  and Michael II of Epirus, 314
  ceded to Manfred of Sicily, 323
  on Venetian trade-route to East, 427
Corinth, town in the Peloponnese
  and invasion of Greece by Roger II of Sicily, 227–8
  under Latin rule, 292, 297, 390, 406
  defeat of Theodore I Palaeologus by Ottomans, 375
  Latin See of, 396
  held by Nerio I Acciajuoli, 419, 421
  held by Theodore I Palaeologus, 423
  centre of silk manufacture, 428
  and Avars and Slavs, 480 n. 6
  and Onogur Bulgars, 483 n. 5
Corinth, gulf of, 517
Corinth, isthmus of, 184, 376, 379, *and see* Hexamilion
Cormons, actual seat of metropolitans of Aquileia, 252
corn supplies, 19, 25, 39, 152 n. 2, 734
  proposed state monopoly under Michael VII, 211
  exports from Caucasia, 615
  for Egypt, 726, 734
  see also wheat
Coron, port in Peloponnese
  under Venetian control, 289, 380, 391–2, 427
  Latin bishopric of, 396
Coronea, bishopric of, 409
Corpus Dionysiacum of the Pseudo-Dionysius, 59–60
Corpus Iuris Civilis, basis of Leo III's *Ecloga*, 65
Corvina, library of Matthew Corvinus of Hungary, 592
Cos, Aegean island, 709
Cosenza, town in Calabria, besieged by the Arabs (902), 729
Cosmas and Damian, Sts
  miracle attributed to, 85
  monastery of the Anargyri, 197

Cosmas II Atticus, Patriarch of Constantinople, 242

Cotyaeum (Kütahiya), in Asia Minor, seat of princes of Germiyān, 755

Coueln, *see* Gabala

councils and synods

oecumenical: I Nicaea (325), 18, 20, 432, 434; II Constantinople (381), 18, 302, 433; III Ephesus (431), 20, 56, 87, 433; IV Chalcedon (451), 18, 19, 20, 52, 433–4; V Constantinople (553), 87, 252, 438; VI Constantinople (680–1), 21, 31, 56, 87, 441; VII Nicaea (787), 66, 72 and n. 2, 78, 84–8, 94, 99, 101, 102, 104, 113, 446, 449

Rome (382), 433

'robber' council of Ephesus (449), 20, 56

Marano (591), 252

in Trullo (Quinisextum) (692), 22, 67, 441

Pavia (695), 252

Rome (731), 71

palace of Hieria (iconoclast) (754), 78–80, 84, 99, 101, 104

Gentilly (Frankish) (767), 77

Rome (769), 77

Frankfurt (794), 72, 87, 102

Constantinople (806), 94–5, 96

Constantinople (809), 95, 96

Constantinople (iconoclast) (815), 99, 101, 104

Paris (825), 102

Mantua (827), 262

Constantinople (843), 104, 112

Constantinople (861), 112, 113, 451, 454, 455

Rome (863), 113, 452

Constantinople (Photian) (867), 113–14, 117, 453

Constantinople (Ignatian) (869–70), 118, 123, 126, 453, 454, 456, 464, 500

Regensburg (870), 124

Constantinople (879–80), 123, 126, 454, 455

Constantinople (907), 131–2

Constantinople (920), 137–8, 456

Siponto (1050), 460

to try Cerularius, 206

Melfi (1059), 463, 465

to try John Italus (1082), 217

Constantinople (1089), 465

Piacenza (1095), 466

Clermont (1095), 466

Bari (1098), 467

Rome (1099), 467

against Constantine Chrysomalus (1140), 220

Constance (1153), 229

Constantinople (1166), 582

third Lateran (1179), 238

fourth Lateran (1215), 304, 397, 586

Lyons (1245), 317

Lyons (1274), 337, 344, 382, 470

summoned by John of Thessaly (1277), 338

in palace of the Blachernae (hesychast controversy) (1351), 362

Ferrara–Florence (1438–9), 381–2, 471–2, 770

in Hungary, 577

in Armenia, 604

procedure, 432

Count of the Private Estates, 33

Count of the Sacred Largesse, 33

court ceremonial, 13, 17, 37, 191, 232

see also under Abbasid Caliphate

Crescentius, patrician of Rome, and the Papacy, 184, 458

Crete

transfer to See of Constantinople, 71, 87–8

attacked by Slavs (623), 482

Arab attacks, 100–2, 114–15, 708–9

base for Arab raids, 101, 709, 713–14, 716, 720

Byzantine expeditions against, 101, 106, 107, 114–15, 146–8, 152, 155, 179, 712–14, 721

and prisoners from Thessalonica, 129

revolt against Alexius I, 214

purchased by Venice (1204), 289

under Venetian rule, 427–8

on trade-route to East, 427

exports, 427–8

Crimea

part of See of Constantinople, 20

Byzantine diplomacy in, 111, 473–4, 475, 479, 483, 485–8, 491–4, 510–11, 515–17, 567

place of exile, 178, 441, 485

Crimean Goths, *see* Goths

and Khazars, 486–7, 492, 512

Christianity in, 487, 516

and Pechenegs, 510

and Huns, 567–8

Seljuq expedition to, 747

and Mongols, 749

Crispi, Italian family in Aegean islands, 425–7

Crispo, Jacopo IV, duke of the Archipelago, 426

Crnojević, George, ruler of Zeta, 559

Crnojević, John, ruler of Zeta, 559
Crnojević, Stephen, ruler of Zeta, 559
Crnojevići, ruling family in Zeta, 554, 559
Črnomen, battle (1371), *see under* Marica
Croatia, Croats
  settled in Balkans by Heraclius, 482 and n. 3, 483
  coastal cities ceded to Byzantium by Franks, 96
  missionary work among, 122, 482
  attacked by Symeon of Bulgaria, 138–9, 508
  Byzantine political authority in, 509
  self-governing dependency under Basil II, 189
  link with Byzantium weakened in later eleventh century, 208
  Hungarian influence, 216, 233, 546
  and Béla III of Hungary, 234, 245
  under See of Rome, 501
  relations with Bosnia, 548, 549
  see also Liburnia
Crusades
  capture of Jerusalem by Seljuqs (1070), 737
  First Crusade, **214–16**, 220, 271, **466–7**, 579, 654, 741, 774
  Second Crusade, **226–8**, 236, 742
  Third Crusade, **246–7**, 468–9, 521, 523, 585, 632
  Fourth Crusade and capture of Constantinople (1204), 5, 9, 228, 233, 249, 274, **276–88**, 329–30, 469, 523, 530, 585, 745
  later Crusades, 310, 317, 335, 369–70, 383–4, 416, 429, 471, 526, 546, 553–4, 586, 588, 590, 627, 766, 770, 771 and n. 1
  Georgian Crusade, 624–5
crustica (*akrostichon*), Byzantine land-tax, *see* land-tax
Csaba's Magyars, settled on Byzantine territory, 570
Ctesiphon, capital of Sassanid Empire, 597, 599, 603–4, 640 and n. 1, 700
Cumans
  origins, 653
  pressure on Uzes, 208
  threat to Empire under Alexius I, 212, 213
  used by Alexius I, 213–14
  mercenaries in Byzantine army, 218, 324–5, 401, 589
  attack under Manuel I, 228
  and grants in *pronoia*, 240, 320
  allies of Bulgaria, 522–3

  invasion of Thrace, 523
  incorporated in Second Bulgarian Empire, 245
  under Kalojan, 293, 525
  in service of Latins, 313, 314–15
Curcuae, Byzantine family, 616
Curcuas, John, general under Romanus I and Constantine VII
  eastern campaigns, 139 and nn. 1 and 2, 140–1, 146, 158, 717–18
  defence of Constantinople, 140 and n. 1, 160
  fall from power, 143–4
curia in Constantinople, 134
curiales, 39–40
curopalates, curopalate
  title of Leo Phocas, 148, 149, 152 n. 2, 176
  title of David, prince of Tao, 177, 181, 186
  title of Bagrat, king of Abasgia, 186
  title of presiding princes of Iberia and Armenia, 603, 605, *and see* List of Rulers 7
Curtea de Argeş, *see* Argeş
Curzola, *see* Korčula
customs dues, 89, 93, 240, 261, 363–4, 505 n. 2, 511 n. 3, 636, 722
Customs of Barcelona, 413–14, 418
customs of Notre Dame of Paris, 408
Cuwalhide, amir of Baghdad, 167
Cyclades, islands in Aegean
  revolt against iconoclasm, 70
  under Latin rule, 426, 429
  on trade-route to East, 427
  raids by Cretan corsairs, 713
Cydones, Demetrius, writer and statesman under the Palaeologi, 369, 471
Cynics, 12
Cyprian, St, bishop of Carthage, 432
Cyprus
  captured by Arabs, 25, 30
  destruction of Egyptian fleet off (747), 74, 699
  iconophile monks deported to, 81
  raided by Arabs, 91, 705, 708, 716–17
  Muslims settled in, 733
  in Byzantine hands, 107 and n. 1, 714, 716
  final conquest under Nicephorus II, 150, 179, 721
  revolt against Constantine IX, 202–3
  revolt against Alexius I, 214
  on trade-route to East, 427, 733
  and John II's plans, 224
  Venice granted trading privileges in, 228

Cyprus (*cont.*)
  attacked by Reynald of Châtillon (1156), 234, 235
  lost to Empire (1185), 245
  taken by Richard I of England, 246–7
  given to Templars, 247
  given to Lusignan house (1192), 247
  recognition of overlordship of Henry VI, 248
  visited by Andrew II of Hungary, 586
  archbishop taken prisoner by Arabs, 708
  bishop of, 717
Cyriacus of Ancona, humanist, historical source for year 1444, 383 n. 1
Cyril, Patriarch of Alexandria, **52–3**
  and Third General Council, 20
  writings appealed to in later controversies, 21
  influence on the monk Leontius, 58
Cyril, St, apostle of the Slavs, *see* Constantine (Cyril)
Cyrillic script, 502 and n. 1
Cyrion (Kyrion) I, *Katholikos* of Iberia, 604 and n. 2
Cyrrhestice, in North Syria, 716
Cythera (Cerigo), Aegean island, under Latin rule, 425
Cythnos (Thermia), Aegean island, under Latin rule, 425–6
Cyzicus, city on Asian side of Sea of Marmora
  taken by Turks, 740
  retaken from Turks by Alexius I, 214

Dabiša, Bosnian ruler, 556
Dacia, Roman province
  diocese of, 71
  Avars in, 477
  and Rumanians, 560
Dadian-Gurielis, Caucasian dynasty, 628
Dadianis, Caucasian dynasty, 626 n. 2, 628
Daghestan, district of eastern Caucasus, 651
Dalassenus, family of, 191–2; *and see* Anna Dalassena
Dalassenus, Constantine, and Michael V, 198
Dalassenus, Damian, governor of Antioch under Basil II, 182, 186, 724
Dalmatia
  Slav invasions in seventh century, 32, 481
  lost to Franks, 92, 257
  returned to Byzantium (812), 96
  relations with Slavs, 268

under rulers of Croatia, 138, 185, 501
invaded by Samuel of Bulgaria, 185
relations with Venice, 185, 268–9, 271
Byzantine province, 189
link with Byzantium weakened in later eleventh century, 208
Hungarian interest in, 212, 216, 221, 233, 580
opposition to Alexius I, 213
rivalry between Hungary and Venice, 221, 233, 234
rivalry between Venice and Byzantium, 232, 233
and Béla III of Hungary, 234, 245, 582–3, 585
and Normans, 271
and expansion of Bosnia, 549
Dalmatia, theme of, 132, 509, 519
Damala, town in Peloponnese near Troezen
  Latin See of, 396
  under William de la Roche, 400
Damascus, city in Syria
  betrayal to Arabs in 635, 67
  Arab capital under Umayyads, 73, 696, 699
  Egyptian army at, 163
  Syrian campaigns of John Tzimisces, 169–70
  Syrian campaigns of Basil II, 182
  attacked by Zengi of Mosul, 224
  under Seljuq rule, 654
  taken by Nūr-ad-Dīn, 654
  taken by Timur, 766
Damasus, Pope, 43, 433
Damian (Ibn Qatuna), Byzantine chamberlain under Michael III, 106 n. 1
Damian, Byzantine renegade, Arab admiral in tenth century, 106 n. 1, 130, 716–17
Damian, St, *see* Cosmas
Damietta, port in Egypt
  attacked by Byzantines, 106 and n. 1, 107 and n. 1, 110, 699, 709, 713
  siege of (1169), 236
Damnazes, king of Lazica, 601
Dandolo, Enrico, doge of Venice
  and Fourth Crusade, 249, **276–85**, **287–8**
  economic reforms, 273
  statutum parvum, 273
  partition of Byzantine Empire, 288–9
  death at Constantinople, 293, 294
Dandolo, Marino, enfeoffed with island of Andros, 425
Danielis, wealthy widow, friend of Basil I, 117

Dānishmends, Seljuq dynasty of north-
east Anatolia
defeat of Bohemond of Antioch (1100),
215
attacks against John II, 223
relations with Manuel I, 226, 236–7,
743
relations with Nūr-ad-Dīn, 236–7, 743
struggle for Melitene, 223, 629, 741
absorbed by Seljuqs of Rūm, 742–3
see also Ghāzī III, Muḥammad, Malik
Danube region
devasted by Huns, 27
invaded by Slavs, 29, 480
settlement of Armenian prisoners
(813), 116
importance in Byzantine diplomacy,
473–4, 475–8, 480–3, 490, 518
Danube, river
frontier of Roman Empire, 25, 26, 29,
35
frontier of Byzantine Empire, 163, 217,
475–7, 480–1, 515
crossed by Bulgars in seventh century,
32, 484
naval expeditions to, *see under* navy,
Byzantine
and Magyars, 128, 503, 568–9
and Hungarians, 221, 544, 581, 582
Russian advance stopped at, 140
and Basil II's campaigns, 185–7, 189,
190
and Pechenegs, 196, 203, 212–13
and Cumans, 212, 523
crossed by crusaders of 1443–4, 383,
771
crossed by Russians, 513
Tatar attacks, 536
reached by Ottomans, 376, 555, 562,
766
Daphni, monastery near Athens, 409, 411
Daphnusia, town on an island in Black
Sea off Bithynia, Venetian fleet at
(1261), 327
Dara, town in Mesopotamia, 718
Daranda, in Asia Minor west of Melitene
abandoned by Umayyads, 698
captured by Byzantines (872), 714
Dardanelles, strait
Venetian fleet in, 376
and Ottoman Turks, 760–1
Darial, pass in Caucasus, 474
Daulia, town in Greece, bishopric of, 409
David Comitopulus of Bulgaria, 178
David, abbot of Pannonhalma, 587
David, prince of Taik (David II the Great
of Iberia), *curopalates*, **617–18**, 621

and Bardas Phocas, 177, 181, 617–18
and Basil II, 181, 189, 618
murder, 186, 618
David I, prince of Iberia, 613
David II the Great of Iberia, *see* David,
prince of Taik
David III (II) the Builder, king of
Georgia, 623 and n. 1, 624, 625 n. 1
David IV (III), king of Georgia, 623
David V (IV), king of Georgia, 626
David VI (V), king of Georgia, 625–6
David VII (VI), king of Georgia, 626
David VIII (VII), king of Georgia, 627
David the Invincible, Armenian philo-
sopher, 599 n. 2
David (I) Lackland, king of Loṛi, 622
David Saharuni, prince of Armenia, 605
David Soslan, second husband of Tha-
mar, queen of Georgia, 623
David, brother of Gregory (II) Mami-
konean, 607
Davidic tradition in Armenia, 597 n. 1
Daylamites in Azerbaijan, 616, 619
under Abbasids, 664, 666
Dazimon, town in Asia Minor, south-east
of Amasea, 714
battle (838), 711
Debar (Dibra), town in Albania, 533, 770
Dejanović, Constantine, Serbian ruler,
541–2
Dejanović, Dragaš, Serbian ruler, 541–2
Delhemma, Arab epic hero, 735
Deljan, *see* Peter
Demetrias, town on coast of Thessaly,
129, 716
Demetrius of Montferrat, king of Thes-
salonica
threatened by rebellion under Hubert
of Biandrate, 298, 391
under regency, 298, 306
attempt to regain Thessalonica with
Latin help, 308, 398
Demetrius I, king of Georgia, 623
Demetrius II the Devoted, king of
Georgia, 626
Demetrius, Despot of Thessalonica, 317,
398
Demetrius, brother of Bagrat IV of
Georgia, 621–3
Demetrius, son of David IV of Georgia,
623
demosiakoi, δημοσιάριοι, tenants with
obligations to imperial fisc, 173, 241
Demosthenes, Greek orator, and Symeon
of Bulgaria, 502
Demotika, *see* Didymotichus
denarii, Serbian silver coins, 533

Dénes (Dionysius), Hungarian general, 583

dervishes, 745, **747**, 748, 750–1, 768, 773

Desiderius, last Lombard king, 77, 82, 253, 446

despot, *despotes*, Byzantine title
given to Theodore I Lascaris by Alexius III, 291
of rulers of Epirus, 296 n. 1
given to Alexius Slav, 299
of rulers of Thessalonica, 315, 317, 379
of Michael VIII Palaeologus, 324
of John Palaeologus, 326
of Stephen Lazarević, 378, 551
of rulers of the Morea (Mistra), *see* List of Rulers 3
used in Serbia, 371, 383, 538, 541, 555, 559, 560
used in Bulgaria, 529, 536–7, 542, 544
given to Béla III of Hungary, 582

Deusdedit, *Collectio canonum*, 451

Deusdedit, leader of faction in Venice, 255

Develtus, town in Balkans on Black Sea, 97, 98, 333, 490–1, 535

Devol, town in Balkans west of Ochrida
treaty of (1108), 216, 223
under John Asen II, 527

Dhū'n-Nūn, Danishmend leader, relations with Manuel I, 237

Diadochi, successors of Alexander the Great, 2; *see also* Ptolemies, Seleucids

Dibra, *see* Debar

Didymotichus (Demotika, Dimetoka), town in Thrace on the Marica, 360, 363
attacked by Kalojan of Bulgaria, 293
refuge of John Camaterus after 1204, 295
under John Asen II, 310, 527
proclamation of John VI Cantacuzenus as Emperor (1341), 357, 361
captured by Ottoman Turks, 369, 762
Turkish court at, 545, 763

Digenis Akritas, epic hero, 141–2, 145, 735

Digest of Justian, 133

dikerata, tax, 65

Dimetoka, *see* Didymotichus

Dimitzana, modern town near Matagrifon, 393, 405

dinar, unit of coinage, 83, 710

Dioclea, Serbian state, 182, 185, 189; *see also* Zeta

Diocletian, Emperor
conception of imperial office, 4

reform of law and administration, 4, 32, 36
restoration of order, 23
fiscal system, 37–8
social regime, 39

Diogenes Laertius, definition of philosophy, 46

Dionysius (Pseudo-) the Areopagite, *see* Pseudo-Dionysius

Dionysius Exiguus, 439

Dionysius, *see* Dénes

Dioscorides, manuscript of, 735

Dioscorus, Patriarch of Alexandria, condemned at Council of Chalcedon, 20, 21

diplomacy, Byzantine science of, 473–518 *passim*

diptychs, 465, 470

Dir, Varangian leader
capture of Kiev, 495
attack on Constantinople (860), 496
loss of Kiev to Oleg, 504

dirham, unit of coinage in Caucasia, 608, 625

Divrigi, *see* Tephrice

Diyār-Bakr, *see* Amida

Djabal, revolt of Khurramites in, 710

Dmanisi, town in Caucasia, 624

Dnieper, river in Russia, 128, 503, 569
eastern limit of Asparuch's kingdom, 484
western limit of Khazar influence, 492
and Vikings, 504 and n. 2
defeat of Svjatoslav by Pechenegs, 162, 515

Dniester, river in Russia
limit of Krum's Bulgarian Empire, 490
on route of Vikings, 495

Dobrotica, independent despot of the Dobrudja, 544

Dobrudja (Karvuna), district south of Danube delta
under Justinian I, 477
settled by Bulgarians, 32, 484
invaded by Russians under Svjatoslav, 513
overrun by Basil II's troops, 186
under John Asen II, 527
separation from Bulgaria, 544
under Turkish rule, 376

Doctors of the Church, 52

Doiran, town in Macedonia, 188

Doliche (Dulūk), town in North Syria, 703
home of monophysites, 73
captured from Muslims, 74, 721

Domenico Barbolano Centranico, doge of Venice, 270
Domenico Contarini, doge of Venice, 270
Domenico Flabianico, doge of Venice, 270
Domenico Michiel, doge of Venice, 271–2
Domenico Silvo, doge of Venice, 271
Domenico Tino, writer on Venice, 270
Domestic of the East
   under Romanus II, 147
   John Tzimisces as, 149, 156
   under John Tzimisces, 164–5
   and Bardas Sclerus, 175
Domestic of the Schools, 108, 120, 134, 140 n. 1
   division of office under Romanus II, 147
   title of John Curcuas, 717
   title of Bardas Phocas, father of Nicephorus II, 148
   title of Nicephorus II, 720
   title of John Tzimisces, 156–7
   title of Bardas Phocas under Basil II, 177–8
Dominate, the, 12
Dominator, title of Venetian rulers, 294
Dominican friars
   intermediaries between the Pope and John Vatatzes, 312
   campaign against heresy in Bosnia, 547
Domokos, town in Greece, 413, 417
Don, river in Russia, 103, 492 and n. 2, 495 and n. 1, 503, 568–9
Donation of Constantine, 76, 445–8, 460
Donatist controversy, 432
Donets, river in Russia, 476 and n. 2
Doros, chief city of Crimean Goths, metropolitan of, 487
Dorotheus, *see* Pseudo-Dorotheus
Dorylaeum (Eskishehir), town in Asia Minor south-east of Nicaea, rebuilt by Manuel I, 237
   and wars against Arabs, 705
   battle (1097) (First Crusade), 741
   battle (1147) (Second Crusade), 742
   battle (1299), 751
   and Ottoman Turks, 757–60
Dorystolum (Durostorum, Dristra, Silistria, Theodoropolis), town in Bulgaria on Danube
   siege of (971), 160–1, 514
   change of name, 161 and n. 3
   occupied by Mircea the Old, 563
Dovin, Shaddādid amir of, 619–20
Dracon, river in Asia Minor, boundary of Sultanate of Rūm in 1081, 213

Dragaš, Constantine, grandfather of Constantine XI, 385
   see also Dejanović, Dragaš
Dragases, family name of Constantine XI, 385
Dragutin, brother of Stephen Uroš II Milutin, 534
Drama, town in Macedonia, 538
Drina, river in Balkans, 519, 548
Dristra, *see* Dorystolum
drungariate of Aegean Sea, 64
drungarius, 161 and n. 1
družina, Russian military contingent, 179
Držislav, *see* Stephen
Dubrovnik, *see* Ragusa
Ducas family
   in tenth century, 130
   and Michael Psellus, 207 n. 1
   hostility to Romanus IV, 209, 210
   placated by Alexius I, 212
   opposition to him, 213–14, 217
   and Michael VIII, 324
   as Emperors, 331
   see also Constantine X, Michael VII, Michael and Theodore of Epirus, John III Vatatzes
Ducas, Andronicus, general under Leo VI
   victory over Arabs (904), 130 and n. 2, 716
   desertion to Arabs, 131, 716
   and Nicholas Mysticus, 131, 135
   in epic poetry, 135 n. 1
Ducas, Andronicus, son of Constantine X, 208
Ducas, Andronicus, son of John Ducas, Caesar, 209–10
Ducas, Constantine, Domestic of the Schools under Constantine VII, 134, 135 and n. 1
Ducas, Constantine, son of Constantine X, 208
Ducas, Constantine, son of Michael VII, 211
   proposed marriage to Robert Guiscard's daughter, 212
Ducas, John, Caesar, brother of Constantine X, 208–11
Ducas, John, *sebastocrator*, father of Michael I of Epirus, 292 and n. 1
Ducas, John, lord of Neopatras, son of Michael II of Epirus, 325, 326, 401, 410
Ducas, John, general under Manuel I, 583
Ducas, Michael, *see* Michael I of Epirus
Ducas Murtzuphlus, Alexius, *see* Alexius V

Ducas, Theodore, of Epirus, *see* Theodore
  Ducas, Emperor of Thessalonica
ducat, Venetian unit of coinage, 363,
  365, 370–1, 380 n. 1, 407, 423–4, 551,
  559, 563–4
duke, title of lords of Athens, 409–10
  used in Hungary, 578
Dulūk, *see* Doliche
Dunapentele, in Hungary, monastery of,
  577
δυνατοί, the 'powerful'
  under Constantine VII, 145
  under Basil II, 173, 184
  in Asia Minor, 617
  see also landowners
Durazzo, *see* Dyrrachium
Dušan, *see* Stephen Uroš IV
dux
  title of commander in the provinces,
    34
  title of governor of a theme, 175, 292
  title of governor of Antioch, 175, 178
  title of governor of Dyrrachium, 211
  title of governor of Venice, 250–1,
    253–4
  title of rulers of Athens, 410
  title of rulers of Byzantine Iberia, 620
dux Dalmatiae, title taken by doge of
  Venice, 268, 271
Dvin, town in Armenia, 603, 609, 615,
  620, 624, 717–18
  councils, 604
  seat of viceroys of the Caliph, 605, 717
  amirs of, 613
Dvina, river in northern Europe, 495
Dvornik, F., 114
Dyakovo, town north of river Sava,
  bishopric of, 547
dye, manufacture of, 428
Dyrrachium (Durazzo), port on Adriatic
  terminus of Via Egnatia, 8, 26
  province of, 189
  and Symeon of Bulgaria, 503
  seized by Samuel of Bulgaria, 185
  surrendered to Byzantium (1005), 187
  attacked by John Vladislav, 518
  and George Maniaces, 201
  and Nicephorus Basilacius, 211
  taken by the Normans (1081) and
    retaken, 213, 271, 467
  Alexius IV accepted as Emperor, 281
  acquired by Venetians, 289, 297, 299
  captured by Michael I of Epirus, 300
  besieged by Peter of Courtenay, 305
  taken by John Asen II, 310
  claimed by Theodore II Lascaris, 322
  attacked by Manfred of Sicily, 323

  attacked by Michael VIII, 337
  under Angevins, 355
  taken by Charles Topia, 419
  on Venetian trade-route to East, 427
  captured by Turks (1501), 558
Dyrrachium, theme of, 92, 211, 519
Dzem, brother of Bāyezīd II, 564

earthquakes, 8–9, 15, 65, 120, 235, 241,
  366, 616, 704
Ecbatana, town in Persia, 164, 167
Ecloga, legal code of Leo III, 61, 65, 133,
  443 n. 2, 447
Ecthesis of Heraclius, 56, 440
Edessa (Urfa), city in Mesopotamia
  besieged by Curcuas, 140–1, 718
  capture by George Maniaces, 140, 196,
    725–7
  transfer of *mandylion* to Constanti-
    nople, 141, 143, 149, 718
  claimed by Alp Arslan, 210
  Latin county, 215, 741–2
  captured by Zengi of Mosul and Nūr-
    ad-Dīn (1144), 225, 227, 742
  and Lesser Armenia, 628–9
Edessa, town in Balkans, *see* Vodena
Edict of Union, see *Henoticon*
Edirne, *see* Adrianople
education, Graeco-Roman, 44, 46–51
Edward I, king of England, and the Il-
  Khans, 634
Egrisi, *see* Lazica
Egypt
  administration, 33
  landowners in, 38, 39
  economic condition before Arab con-
    quest, 39
  industry and commerce, 40–1, 427, 644
  source of corn supplies, 19, 39
  conversion to Christianity, 42, 54
  and monophysitism, 20, 21, 56
  and Hellenism, 54
  source of wonder tales, 55
  conquered by Persia in seventh
    century, 21, 30
  conquered by Arabs (641–2), 5, 20, 21,
    30, 35
  Byzantine expeditions against, 114,
    699, 713
  Egyptian deserters from Arab fleet, 63,
    698
  lost by Abbasids (868), 645, 701
  Ikhshīdid dynasty in, 140, 149
  peace with Isaac I, 206
  aimed at by Alp Arslan, 209
  controlled by Nūr-ad-Dīn and Saladin,
    236, 654

Egypt (*cont.*)
objective of Crusades, 248, 276–7, 279, 283, 369
and Ayyūbids, 631
and Mamluks, 633–4, 651, 654, 750–1
in control of Syria, 634, 645, 648, 652, 703, 714–15, 718, 722
Bedouin tribes, 651
and Tulunids, 714–15
Fatimid dynasty in, *see* Fatimid Caliphate
Eigenkirchen, proprietary churches, 459
Einhard, biographer of Charlemagne, 447
Ektag, mountain in Tien Shan, 479
Elbe, river, boundary of Samo's realm, 482
Elbistan, in anti-Taurus district, battle (1277), 750
Eleanora, wife of Pedro IV of Aragon, 419
Elias, bishop of Aquileia in sixth century, 252
Elijah the prophet, 125
Elis, district in Peloponnese
called the Morea, 390
and Navarrese Company, 419
Eliseus, Armenian historian, 599 n. 2
Elpidius, commander in Sicily
revolt against Constantine VI and Irene (781), 83
deserter to Arabs, 707
Emba, river in Central Asia, 503
Emeric, St, son of Stephen I of Hungary, 574–5
Emesa (Homs), town in Syria, 51
relic of St John the Baptist, 722
and John Tzimisces, 169, 723
and Basil II, 182, 724
battle (1281), 634
Emperor, **10–17, 45–6,** *and see* List of Rulers 1
as Pontifex Maximus, 3
as God's vicegerent, 3, 15, 45, 431, 432, 437, 506
as defender of orthodoxy, 4, 17, 43, 44, 62, 78, 134, 217, 432, 437
election of, 12, 14, 447
as source of law, 13, 16, 134
hereditary principle, 14, 81–2, 135, 136, 148, 199
limitations on power, 14–15
obligations, 15–16, 17, 37, 62, 133, 134
'theology of the imperial victory', 16–17
as supreme commander of army, 16–17, 34, 134, 190
as head of administration, 33, 34, 36, 190
as head of ecclesiastical affairs, 71, 78, 95, 104, 126, 134, 190, 436–8
conflict with the Church, 95, 101, 134
and Charlemagne's claims, 90, 96–7
relations with the Patriarch, 70–1, 80, 133, 134, 190–1, 361
changes under the Palaeologi, 341 and n. 1, 363
intervention in religious affairs, 435, 437–8, 440–1, 443–4, 456–7; see also *imperium*
Hellenistic titles, 431, 432; *and see* ruler-worship
and procedure of Church Councils, 432
Western conception of, 448–9, 524
title of rulers of Second Bulgarian Empire, 525, 527, 528, 535–6
title of Stephen Uroš IV Dušan of Serbia, 538–9
title of other Serbian rulers, 541
enamel, 576, 579, 616
encyclopaedias
Byzantine, translated into Slavonic, 502
Arabic, 683, 685
Engelberga, wife of Louis II, 114
England and the English
mercenaries in Byzantine army, 218
appealed to by Manuel II for help against Turks, 376–7
Enna (Castrogiovanni, Castrum Ennae), town in Sicily
murder of Euphemius (828), 100
and Arab conquest of Sicily, 728
ἔννομος ἀρχή, 16
Epanagoge, law book of Basil I, 133–4
Ephesus, city in Asia Minor
displaced by See of Constantinople, 19, 456
Council (431), 20, 56, 87, 433
'Robber' Council (449), 20, 56
city proletariate, 55
attacked by Arabs (797–8), 83, 707
taken by Paulicians, 119, 714
cave of Seven Sleepers, 734
Ephraim, St, Syriac ascetic, 689 n. 4
epic poetry
as historical source, 110, 111 n. 1, 135 n. 1, 137 n. 1, 139 n. 2, 146, 150, 179
poem on battle of Varna, 591
Georgian, 625
Arab and Byzantine, 735
Epictetus, Stoic philosopher, 45
epigraphy, 15, 54; *see also* inscriptions
ἐπιλωρικοφόροι, armed cavalrymen under Nicephorus II, 154

Epiphanius, Patriarch of Constantinople, 436

Epirus
part of Samuel of Bulgaria's Empire, 517
invaded by Robert Guiscard, 213, 271
Normans expelled by Isaac II, 245
claimed by Venetians in 1204, 289, 297, 392
and Michael I of Epirus, 296–300, 392
despotate, 296 n. 1, 388, 745, *and see* List of Rulers 2 (i)
Orthodox Church in, 312
invaded by Manfred of Sicily, 323
invaded by Michael VIII's troops, 325
opposition to Constantinople after 1261, 329, 332, 333
end of dynasty of the Angeli (Ducae) (1318), 349, 415
subjugated by Andronicus III, 355–6
under John Angelus, 356, 359
conquered by Stephen Dušan, 362, 539
independent province, 541
and Vlachs, 560

Equilo, near Venice, 259
bishopric of, 264

Erastianism in Islam, 642
Ereruyk', in Armenia, church at, 615
Eretna, governor of Rūm under Il-Khans, 754
Eretnid state, 754
Erez, in Mesopotamia, 186
Ermenek, *see* Germanicopolis
Ertoghrul, relationship with 'Osmān, Ottoman Sultan, 757–8
Erushet'i, district in Iberia, 609
Erythro, *see* Rotrud
Erzerum, *see* Theodosiopolis
Erzinjān, town on upper Euphrates west of Theodosiopolis, battle (1230), 748
Erzurum (Erzerum), *see* Theodosiopolis
Eskishehir, *see* Dorylaeum
Esztergom, town on Danube in Hungary
reliquary of, 576
relics of St John of Rila, 585
Frederick Barbarossa at, 585
cathedral of, 587

Etelköz, region north of Danube estuary, and Magyars, 569

Euboea (Negroponte), island off east coast of Greece
Arab raids on, 714
and partition of Empire under Baldwin I, 289, 392
under Latin rule, 292, 313, 389, 399, 400, 429

refuge of Baldwin II in 1261, 327
occupied by Michael VIII's fleet, 337
Venetians in, 392–3, 400, 412–13, 423
and Catalan duchy of Athens, 412–13
captured by Turks (1470), 393
bishopric of, 409
export trade, 428

Euchaïta (Avkhat), city in Paphlagonia in Asia Minor, 161 n. 3, 162 n. 1
Euchaneia, town in Pontus, 161 n. 3
Eudocia Baiana, third wife of Leo VI, 130–1
Eudocia (Bertha), first wife of Romanus II, 147
Eudocia Decapolita, wife of Michael III, 108, 113
Eudocia Ingerina
mistress of Michael III, 108
wife of Basil I, 117
Eudocia Macrembolitissa, niece of Michael Cerularius, wife of Constantine X and of Romanus IV Diogenes, 207–10
Eudocia, daughter of Constantine VIII, Psellus on, 193
Eudocia, daughter of Alexius III, wife of Stephen the First Crowned, Alexius V, and Leo Sgouros, 247–8, 389, 521, 530
Eudocia, daughter of Theodore I Lascaris, 307
Eudocimus, *nobilissimus*, son of Constantine V, half-brother of Leo IV, 82 n. 2, 83, 88–9, 97
Eugenius III, Pope
truce with Roger II of Sicily, 228
and treaty of Constance (1153), 228–9
death, 229
Eugenius IV, Pope
and council of Florence, 471
crusades against Turks, 770–1
Eulogia, sister of Michael VIII Palaeologus, 328, 338
Euphemius, renegade Byzantine admiral, and Arab attacks on Sicily, 100, 728
Euphrates, river, 638, 640, 702, 758
frontier of Roman Empire, 25
Byzantine armies at, 110–11, 114, 139, 142, 164, 714, 718
home of Paulicians, 139 n. 2
cities under control of George Maniaces, 195–6
Euphrosyne, wife of Alexius III, 296
Euphrosyne, illegitimate daughter of Michael VIII, wife of Nogaj, leader of Golden Horde, 336

Euripides
  Hippolytus, 47
  quoted by Athanasius, 47
  quoted by Cyril of Alexandria, 53
Europe
  trade with Africa, 25
  silk trade with China, 478
Eusebius, bishop of Caesarea, historian
  Vita Constantini, 1 n. 1
  description of Constantine the Great's
    funeral, 1, 2
  political theory, 3, 14, 431
Eustace, brother of Henry of Flanders,
  guardian to Demetrius of Thessa-
  lonica, 298–9
Eustathius, archbishop of Thessalonica,
  views on *charisticium*, 219
Euthymius I, Patriarch of Constantinople, 132, 135, 136 and n. 1
Euthymius, Patriarch of Trnovo
  literary work, 545
  imprisonment, 545
Eutyches, condemned for heresy under
  Justinian I, 436
Eutychius, last exarch of Ravenna, 70, 444
Euxine, *see* Black Sea
Evrenos Bey, Ottoman general, 762–4,
  766, 769
Evrenoszade 'Alī Bey, Ottoman general,
  770
Exarch, *see* Ravenna *and* Carthage
Exarch of All Asia, title of metropolitan
  of Ephesus, 303
Exarch of the Orthodox Church in
  Epirus, 312
excavations
  at Athens, 389
  in Hungary, 577
excommunication
  of Byzantine Emperors by the Pope,
    464, 465, 470; by the Patriarch of
    Constantinople, 338
  of Patriarchs of Constantinople by the
    Pope, 71, 462
  of John Asen II by the Pope, 528
ἐξουσιαστής, Byzantine title
  of rulers of Alania, 512
  of rulers of Abasgia, 512
Eznik of Koḷb, Armenian theologian,
  599 n. 2

Facundus, African bishop, and Justinian
  I, 437
Fadrique, Aragonese family in Greece,
  413, 417
Fadrique, Alfonso, vicar-general of duchy
  of Athens, count of Salona, 412–17

Fadrique, James, vicar-general of duchies of Athens and Neopatras,
  417–18
Fadrique, Luis, vicar-general of duchies
  of Athens and Neopatras, 418, 421–2
Fallmerayer, J. P., 92, 489 n. 1
al-Fārābī, Turkish philosopher, 683
Faramā, on coast of Egypt, 713
Farmer's Law, 39, 61
Fāṭima, daughter of the Prophet Muḥammad, 648, 663
Fatimid Caliphate in North Africa and
  Egypt
  and Ismā'īlīs, 648, 659
  establishment in North Africa and
    Egypt, 648, 682, 703, 729
  relations with Byzantium, 187, 204,
    517, 725–6, 730–3
  challenge to Abbasid Caliphate, 648–9
  threat to Hamdanids, 149
  and Syria, 163, 168, 169, 171, 197,
    652–3, 703, 720, 722–5, 727
  and Seljuqs, 624, 629, 653, 726, 737
  and Carmathians, 682
  rebellion in North Africa, 726, 730
  operations in Sicily and South Italy,
    730–2
  relations with Bulgaria, 507, 730
  and Umayyads of Spain, 730–1
  in Palestine, 725–6, 737
  abolished by Saladin, 654, 658
Faustus of Buzanda, Armenian historian,
  598 n. 1, 599 n. 2
Fayum, district of Egypt, hellenisation
  of, 54
Feldebrö, in Hungary, frescoes of, 576
Ferrara, council of, 381, 471–2, 770
Fertile Crescent
  Byzantine trade with, 41
  Semitic population of, 663
feudalism
  in Byzantine Empire, 142, 241, 243,
    244, 290, 341–2
  under Latin Empire, 287, 289, 290,
    395, 426
  in Thessaly, 348
  in Achaea, 401–2, 405
  in Western Europe, 265, 459
  in Hungary, 581
  in Serbia, 532, 539, 541–2
  in Bosnia, 549, 555
  in Rumania, 562
  in Asia Minor, 617
  in Caucasia, 595 and n. 3, 596, 603,
    613, 616–17, 621, 623, 625–6, 628
  in Lesser Armenia, 632–3
  in Persia, 643

feudalism (*cont.*)
    under Islam, 649, 650 and n. 1, 656
    see also fief, homage, suzerain, vassals
feudum, comparison with *pronoia*, 240
fief, 579, 620, 656
    status of Antioch (1108), 216
    under Latins, 285, 289, 389, 392–3,
        394, 399, 402, 406, 409, 410, 423,
        425, 427
    and *pronoia*, 319, 341–2, 426
    status of Thessaly under Andronicus
        II, 349
    under Ottomans, 760, 763
Filibe, *see* Philippopolis
Filioque clause in Nicene Creed, 113–14,
    283, 302, 312, 394, 449, 453, 461,
    466, 471
Finland, gulf of, 504, 515
Finno-Ugrians, 503, 566
Finns, 495
fish imported from the Crimea, 475
Flavian, Patriarch of Constantinople,
    condemned for Nestorianism, 20, 56
Florence, council of, 381–2, 471–2, 770
    union of, 381–2, 471–2
Florent of Hainault, second husband of
    Isabella, princess of Achaea, 404,
    410
florin, unit of coinage, 376, 419
    gold florins, 636
Focillon, H., quoted, 594
foederati, 26–8, 35, 477
Forcalquier, county of, 404
forced labour in Bulgaria, 530
Formosus, Pope, and Photian schism,
    455
Fortunatus, bishop of Grado, 256–7, 262
Foscolo, Leonardo, lord of Anaphe, 425
France
    and Second Crusade, 227
    support for Pope Alexander III, 230
    appealed to by Hungary for help
        against Turks, 376
    appealed to by Manuel II, 376–7
    trade with East, 427
    French language used in Lesser
        Armenia, 633
Francesca, daughter of Nerio I Accia-
    juoli, wife of Carlo Tocco, 423
Franciscans
    intermediaries between John Vatatzes
        and the Pope, 311–12
    missionaries in Vidin, 544
    and Het'um I, 634
Frankfurt, council of (794), 72, 87, 102
Franks
    rise of Frankish kingdom, 76–7

defeat of Lombards (774), 77, 253
    version of cause of war of 788, 87 n. 1
    gains in Italy and on Adriatic coast,
        92, 257–8
    negotiations with Michael I, 96
    and Bulgaria, 98, 112, 452, 496–7
    and Michael III, 113
    doctrinal questions, 113, 449, 453
    and First Crusade (q.v.), 741
    in Syria after First Crusade, 223–5
    dissatisfaction with Manuel I over
        Second Crusade, 227
    relations with Venice, 255–61, 262
    partition of Byzantine Empire in 1204,
        285
    in Greece, 332
    Frankish Church, 449–50, 497, 500
Fraxinetum, fortress in Provence
    in Arab hands, 140
    retaken by Hugh of Provence, 730
Frederick I Barbarossa, Western Em-
    peror
    and treaty of Constance (1153), 228–9
    marriage negotiations, 229
    plans for Italy, 229, 230, 231
    hostility to Byzantium, 229–32, 238,
        246, 468
    rift with the Papacy, 230, 242, 468
    leader of Third Crusade, 246, 468, 585,
        743
    treaty of Adrianople (1190), 246
    relations with Sultanate of Rūm, 237,
        246, 743
    relations with Venice, 273
    relations with Bulgaria, 528
    relations with Lesser Armenia, 632
    death, 246
Frederick II, Western Emperor
    and John of Brienne, 310
    and Baldwin II, 314, 316–17
    and John Vatatzes, 316
    and the Papacy, 316–17
Frederick III, king of Aragon, *see*
    Frederick II, king of Sicily
Frederick II, king of Sicily, and Catalan
    Company, 347, 411–12
Frederick III, king of Sicily
    duke of Athens, 413, 417 and n. 1,
        418–19
Frederick of Lorraine, archdeacon
    and reform of Western Church, 459–
        60
    and schism of 1054, 461–2
frescoes
    in Trebizond, 328–9
    in Thebes, 416
    at Feldebrö in Hungary, 576

fruit growing and trade
  in Greece, 159, 428
  in Abbasid Empire, 644
Fulk of Anjou, king of Jerusalem
  relief of Damascus (1139), 224
  relations with John II over Antioch,
    225
Fulk of Neuilly, preacher of Fourth
    Crusade, 276–7
fur and skin trade, 159, 475, 495, 615
futuwwa, system of Muslim ethic, 693–5,
    751, 756–7

Gabala (Coueln, Gabauon), town in
    Syria, taken by John Tzimisces, 171
Gabalas, John, brother of Leo, governor
    of Rhodes, 318
Gabalas, Leo, Caesar, vassal of Nicaea in
    Rhodes, 311
Gabauon, *see* Gabala
Gabriel, ruler of Melitene, 628
Gabriel Radomir, Bulgarian tsar
  marriage, 185
  opposition to Basil II, 188, 518
Gabrielopulus, Stephen, ruler of Thessaly,
    355
Gaeta, Italian port
  growth of independence, 77
  envoy at Constantinople, 143
  aid for Byzantine fleet against Arabs,
    727
  dispute with Pope, 729
  see also John, duke of Gaeta
Gagik I, king of Armenia, 615, 618–19
Gagik II, king of Armenia, 629
  in revolt against Michael IV, 197, 619
  relations with Constantine IX, 203–4,
    620
  retirement to Cappadocia, 204, 620
Gagik of Lori, king of Kakhetia, 622
Gagik-Abas II, king of Kars, 620
Gainas, Gothic general, 27
Galata, suburb of Constantinople, 8, 115
  landing by Fourth Crusade, 281
  attacked by Greeks in 1260, 326
  Genoese colony in, 334, 345–6, 363–4,
    372, 775
  fortified by Genoese, 346
Galatia, district of Asia Minor, invaded
    by Arabs (797–8), 83
Galcerán de Peralta, service in Catalan
    duchy of Athens, 418, 421
Galen, Corpus of, and Arabs, 684
Galeran d'Ivry, bailie and vicar-general
    of Achaea, 403
Galilee, 170
Gallipoli, *see* Callipolis

Ganja in Caspian Albania, 624
  amirs of, 619, 622
Gardiki, town in Greece, and duchy of
    Athens, 410, 413, 417
Gardman, district in Caucasia, 610 and
    n. 3, 614, 620
Garigliano, river in Italy
  Arabs established at, 729–30
  battle (915), 136
Garro *or* Guarro, leader of Navarrese
    Company, 419
Gascons in Navarrese Company, 420–1
Gastim, fortress in Syria, 631
Gattilusio, Francesco, Genoese corsair in
    service of John V, 366–7
Gaul
  government, 18
  part of Roman Empire, 25
  in German hands, 27, 28
  and See of Rome, 432
Gaza, town in south Palestine, Syriac
    spoken at, 55
Gegnesius, Paulician leader, visit to
    Constantinople before 726, 67
Gelasius I, Pope, and independence of
    Church and State, 435, 439, 444, 450
Gelat'i, abbey in Georgia, 625
Gelibolu, *see* Callipolis
Gelovanis, Caucasian dynasty, 628
Gelzer, H., 134
General Justices of the Romans, under
    the Palaeologi, 352–3
Gennadius II, George Scholarius,
    Patriarch of Constantinople
  and union of Florence, 472
  under Ottoman Empire, 774
Genoa, Italian port, and Genoese
  rivalry with Venice, 212, 221, 232, 249,
    271, 272–3, 276, 326–7, 333–4, 371,
    400
  threat to Empire under Alexius I, 216
  negotiations with John II, 222
  relations with Manuel I, 229, 232, 240
  Genoese in Constantinople, 232, 273,
    326, 334, 345–6, 363–4, 372–3, 775
  attack on Rhodes, 318
  alliance with Michael VIII, 326–7,
    333–4
  colonies and trade in Black Sea, 345,
    365, 537, 544
  wars with Venice, 345–6, 365, 372–3,
    417, 427
  rivalry with Pisa, 345
  occupation of Phocaea and Chios, 346,
    354–5, 364
  relations with Ottomans, 365, 378
  relations with John V, 366

Genoa (*cont.*)
  relations with Andronicus IV, 372–3
  help for Constantinople in 1453, 386, 773
  community in Athens, 409
  community in Thebes, 409
  trade with East, 427
  relations with despots of the Dobrudja, 544
  in Lesser Armenia, 632–3
gentes in Roman Armenia, 597, 598, 601
Gentilly, Frankish council of (767), 77
Geoffrey of Bruyères (de Briel), lord of Karytaina, 400, 401
Geoffrey of Villehardouin, Marshal of Champagne, chronicler
  and Fourth Crusade, 276, 277, 279, 287
  and Latins in Greece, 390
Geoffrey I of Villehardouin, nephew of the above, **392–8**
  and conquest of Peloponnese, 292, 390, 408
  prince of Achaea, 298, 392
  treaty with Venice (1209), 392
  and parliament at Andravida, 393–4
  absent from second parliament of Ravennika, 395–6
  dealings with Latin Church and the Papacy, 397–8
Geoffrey II of Villehardouin, prince of Achaea, 312, 393 and n. 1, 398–9
George I Terter, Bulgarian tsar, 339, 536–7
George I, king of Georgia (Abasgia and Iberia)
  alliance with Armenia against Basil II, 189, 619
  defeat by Basil II, 621
George II, king of Georgia, 622–3
George III, king of Georgia, 623–4, 626 n. 2
George IV the Resplendent, king of Georgia, 625 and n. 1
George V the Little, king of Georgia, 626
George VI the Illustrious, king of Georgia, 626 and n. 3, 627 and n. 1
George VII, king of Georgia, 627
George VIII, king of Georgia, 627
George of Russia, son of Grand Duke Andrew of Vladimir, first husband of Thamar, queen of Georgia, 623
George II, *Katholikos* of Armenia, 612
George Brancović (Vuković), Serbian Despot, **552–5**
  economic prosperity under, 533
  ally of Muḥammad I, 552
  relations with Hungary, 552–3

and crusade against Turks in Europe, 383, 553–4
and treaty of Szegedin, 384 and n. 1, 554 and n. 1, 771 n. 1
death, 555
George Gemistus Plethon, fifteenth-century philosopher, 378–9, 381, 472
George Vuković, *see* George Branković
Georgia and Georgians, **593–628** *and see* List of Rulers 7
  Christianity in, 55, 626 n. 1
  Armenian Georgia, 139
  Iviron monastery on Mt Athos, 177
  relations with Basil II, 177, 179, 181, 186, 619, 621
  relations with Bardas Phocas, 179, 617
  relations with Michael IV, 197
  relations with Constantine IX, 204, 622
  taxation and defections to the Muslims, 204
  Seljuq attacks, 204, 622, 624
  relations with Seljuqs, 626–7
  and defence of Byzantine frontier, 474
  Arab attacks, 607
  under Abbasids, 608
  union under Bagrat III, 618–19, 621
  the Church in, 621, 623
  under Bagratid kings, 621–8, 651
  partition of, 628
  spelling of names, 608 n. 1
  Mongol invasions, 625–7, 660
  relations with the Papacy, 625, 627
  monarchical system, 624, 626 and n. 3, 627 n. 1
  relations with Trebizond, 291, 624, 627–8
  Turkish raids, 627
  alliance with Mongols, 634, 635 and n. 3
  see also Iberia
Georgian literature, 594, 625 and n. 1
Georgian Royal Annals, 625 n. 1
Gepids, 10, 477
Geraki, *see* Hierakion
Gerard, St, bishop in Hungary, 574
  author of *Deliberatio*, 575
German Church
  and Moravia, 112, 124–5, 497
  and Russia, 511, 515
'German' tax, exacted from Alexius III, 247–8
Germanic peoples
  and Roman Empire, 26
  raids on Italy, 435

Germanicea (Mar'ash, Marash), city in North Syria
connection with Leo III, 62 n. 1
home of monophysites, 73
and establishment of Lesser Armenia, 628–9
deportation of native population, 705
and Byzantine campaigns against Arabs, 74, 103, 146, 148, 705, 708, 715–17, 719–21
Germanicopolis (Ermenek), in southeast Anatolia, 750, 753
Germanus I, Patriarch of Constantinople and Leo III, 62
against iconoclasm, 66, 67
forced to resign by Leo III, 70, 71
Germanus II, Patriarch of Constantinople in Nicaea, 309, 312
Germany and Germans
relations with John II, 222, 227
and Second Crusade, 227
under Frederick Barbarossa (q.v.), 229–30
interest in Serbian states, 233
and Third Crusade, 246
theory of property ownership and the Church, 459
influence in Hungary, 515, 576, 578, 579
and mining industry in Balkans, 529, 532, 548
and Hungarian crusade against Turks, 770
Germiyān, Turkish principality in Phrygia, 755–6, 762
γηροκομεῖα, 154
Geron, town near Ḥadath in North Syria, 710
Gervase, Latin Patriarch of Constantinople, 397
Géza I, king of Hungary, 578–9, 588
Géza II, king of Hungary, struggle with Manuel I, 233, 582
Géza, prince of Hungary, father of St Stephen, 573, 574
Géza, Hungarian duke, brother of Béla III, 584
Ghazan-Khan, Ilkhan leader, 635, 751–2, 753
Ghāzī III, Danishmend amir, 223
al-Ghāzī, Ortukid leader, 624
ghāzīs, Muslim holy warriors, 704, 713, 739–40, 744–5, 748, 751, 756–8, 760–2, 764–5, 768, 770
Ghaznavids, Turkish dynasty in Persia, 652–3, 655, 658, 703, 737
al-Ghazzālī, Muslim theologian, 688 n. 2, 691–2

Ghibellines, 404
Ghisi, Andrea and Geremia, in control of certain Aegean islands, 425
Ghiyāth ad-Dīn Kaykhusraw, see Kaykhusraw I, II and III
Ghiyāth ad-Dīn Mas'ūd, see Mas'ūd II
Gilas, see Helos
gilds, see guilds
Gimenes, see Zemena
Girgenti (Agrigento), town in Sicily, and Arab conquest of Sicily, 728, 730
Gisela, daughter of Pepin III, marriage to Adalgisus, 77
Giustiniani, Genoese family in Chios, 364
Giustiniani, Giovanni, leader of Genoese troops at defence of Constantinople in 1453, 386, 773
Glaber, Raoul, western historian, 460
Glagolitic script, 497, 502 n. 1
glama, silver from Novo Brdo, 532
Glarentza, port in Elis in Peloponnese, and silk trade, 428
gnosticism
influence on Georgian literature, 625
in Persia, 662
and Shī'ism, 681
Gnunid dynasty in Armenia, 610 and n. 1
Gobarus, Stephen, lay theologian at Alexandria, 58
Gobineau, racial theories of, 639
Gogarene, district in northern Armenia, 596, 597 n. 1, 598
Göksu, see Calycadnus
gold
government loans, 93
trade in, 159, 487
uses of, 238, 286, 576, 583
and Manuel I's foreign policy, 232, 240
gold plate given to finance Fourth Crusade, 278
mines, 532–3, 644, 646
currency, 71, 342, 380, 587–8, 636, 678 and n. 1; and see solidus, hyperpyron
Golden Horde, Mongol army
relations with Michael VIII, 336
alliance with Venice against Genoese in Pontus, 345
in south Russia, 377
in Caucasia, 627
and Seljuq Empire of Rūm, 749–50
Golden Horn, inlet of sea at Constantinople, 6, 7, 8, 115, 281, 283, 285, 346, 386–7, 490, 773–4
Golubac, town in Balkans on Danube
under Hungary, 540
under Serbia, 552, 554
occupied by Turks, 553, 555

Gongylas, Constantine, naval commander under Constantine VII, 720

Gorazd, successor to Methodius, apostle of the Slavs, 500

Gordas, prince of the Huns in Crimea, 567

Gorgenes of Iberia, 603 n. 1

Gothia in Crimea, ecclesiastical eparchy of, 487, 488 and n. 1

Goths
  defeat of Valens at Adrianople, 26
  in Italy, 27
  defence of Danube area, 35
  Crimean Goths, 475, 487, 568

Götland, East, home of Vikings, 494

Gozzadini, Italian family in Aegean islands, 425, 426

Gradenigo, Marco, Podestà of Venetians in Constantinople, 327

Gradenigo, Pietro, Venetian bailie of Negroponte, 418

Grado, port on the northern Adriatic, 256, 259
  metropolitan See (Patriarchate), 252–3, 256–7, 262, 264, 269–71

Grand Comneni, *see under* Trebizond

Grand Domestic, title
  of John Axuch, 220
  of George Muzalon, 321
  of John Palaeologus, 324
  of William of Villehardouin, 332
  of John Cantacuzenus, 351

Grand Duke, title of Michael VIII Palaeologus, 324

Grand Logothete, title
  of George Acropolites, 337
  of Theodore Metochites, 351

Grand Magne, *see under* Maina

Grand Seneschal
  of Sicily, 403, 417
  of Naples, 406

graptoi, 103

Gravia, town in Greece, in duchy of Athens, 410

Great Fence of Thrace, frontier with Bulgaria, 98, 491

Greece
  part of See of Rome, 19
  Avar attacks, 480
  attacked by Slavs, 29, 480
  Slav settlements in, 83, 92, 480–2, 488, 489 and n. 1, 490
  and Vlachs, 560
  opposition to iconoclasm, 70, 73
  repopulation of Constantinople from, 73
  invaded by Samuel of Bulgaria, 517
  trade with Bulgaria, 159
  laid waste by Pechenegs and Uzes (1064), 208
  invaded by Normans of Sicily, 212–13, 215–16, 219, 227–8, 245
  partition under Latin Empire, 289
  Ottoman attacks, *see under* Ottoman Turks
  see also Greek Church, Greek city-states, Greek language, Greek literature

Greek Church, *see also* Constantinople, Patriarchate of
  general relations with State, 3, 17, 22, 94–5, 104, 133, 206, 431–2, 436–7
  independence of the civil power, 45, 47 and n. 2
  and monophysites, 56
  taxation under Nicephorus I, 93
  property laws of Basil II, 183–4, 191
  objections to imperial marriages, 127, 131–2, 137–8, 195, 307, 455–6
  opposition to Isaac I, 205–6
  as owner of property, 211, 218, 219, 241, 395
  exaction of forced loan under Alexius I, 213, 217
  and the *charisticium*, 219
  opposition to Manuel I's pro-Latin policy, 241
  under Latin rule, 285, 288, 301–4, 394–6
  centre transferred to Nicaea, 295
  opposition of Church in Greece to Church in Nicaea, 306–7
  Greek clergy in South Italy, 460–1, 464–5
  relations with the Papacy, *see* Roman Church
  attempts at reunion with Rome after 1054, *see under* Roman Church

Greek city-states, 22, 24, 677

Greek fire, 25, 63, 98, 282, 510, 514, 698

Greek language
  spoken in West, 23
  language of the Church, 23
  and education, 46
  knowledge of in West, 471
  translations of Latin works, 471
  knowledge of in Hungary, 574–5

Greek literature
  studied in West, 471
  influence on Hungarian literature, 575–6

Green Count, *see* Amadeo VI, count of Savoy

Greens, political party, 55

Gregorovius, F., 422

Gregory I the Great, Pope
　on images, 87
　and schismatics in North Italy, 252
　relations with Byzantine Empire and
　　Church, 438–9, 440
Gregory II, Pope, conflict with iconoclast
　Emperor Leo III, 68, 70 and n. 1,
　71–2, 442–4
Gregory III, Pope, conflict with
　iconoclast Emperor Leo III, 71, 444
Gregory V, Pope, 184, 458
Gregory VII, Pope (Hildebrand)
　relations with Venice, 270–1
　and medieval theory of the Papacy,
　　450, 468
　and reform of Western Church, 270–1,
　　459–60
　Dictatus Papae, 459, 464
　relations with Constantinople, 463–5
　relations with principality of Zeta, 520
Gregory IX, Pope
　and John Asen II, 311, 528
　and John Vatatzes, 311–12
　and Latin Emperors of Constantinople,
　　309–10, 312–14, 528
　death, 315
Gregory X, Pope, 335 and n. 2, 336, 337,
　470
Gregory, St, apostle of Armenia, 598
Gregory, bishop of Syracuse, and Pope
　Gregory the Great, 439, 440
Gregory Asbestas, bishop of Syracuse,
　and the Patriarch Ignatius, 108,
　450, 451
Gregory the Deacon, Georgian historian,
　625 n. 1
Gregory (I) Mamikonean, prince of
　Armenia, 606
Gregory (II) Mamikonean, prince of
　Armenia, 607
Gregory, duke of Naples, 136
Gregory of Narek, Armenian poet,
　616 n. 1
Gregory of Nazianzus, **48–51**
　and monasticism, 58
　influence on Cyril of Alexandria, 52
Gregory of Nyssa, **48–51**
　and ascetic theory, 45
Gregory VI Pahlavuni, *Katholikos* of
　Armenia, 632
Gregory Pahlavuni, Armenian polyhistor,
　616 n. 1
Gregory, Armenian scholar, 619–20
Gritzena, Latin barony in Peloponnese,
　394
grossi, Serbian silver coins, 533
　in Bosnia, 548

Guaimar V of Salerno
　and Michael IV's Sicilian campaign,
　　197
　relations with Henry III, 202
Guaram I, prince of Iberia, 603 and n. 1
Guaram, son of Ashot I of Iberia, ruler
　of Javakhet'i, 611, 612
Guaramid dynasty of Iberia, 603, 606–9,
　615
Guarro, *see* Garro
Gubazes II, king of Lazica, 602
Guelfs, 415
guilds, 37, 39, 682, 751–2, 756–7
Guiscard, *see* Robert
Gurandukht, mother of Bagrat III of
　Iberia, 617
Gurgēn (Gurgen) I, king of Iberia, 617–18
Gurgēn I, king of Loṛi, 617
Gurgēn (Gurgen) I of Tao, 613
Gurgēn (Gurgen) II of Tao, 614
Gurgenes of Iberia, 600 n. 1
Guria, district in Caucasia, 628
Guy I de Lusignan of Lesser Armenia,
　636
Guy I de la Roche, lord of Athens and
　Thebes, 389, 399, 400, 402, 408,
　409–10
Guy II de la Roche, duke of Athens,
　410–11
Guyot, *see* Guy II de la Roche
Gyula, Stephen, Hungarian leader, visit
　to Constantinople, 509 and n. 3,
　572, 574

Hadath, Ḥadath, *see* Adata
ḥadīth, sayings of or about Muḥammad,
　673–5
Hadrian I, Pope
　relations with Charlemagne, 72, 446
　correspondence with Constantine VI
　　and Irene, 72 n. 2, 446–7
　dating of papal documents, 77, 446
　and Seventh General Council, 87, 449
　criticised by synod of Paris (825), 102
Hadrian II, Pope
　relations with Constantine (Cyril) and
　　Methodius, 112, 124, 498–500
　attitude towards Photius, 114, 453
　and conflict between Photius and
　　Ignatius, 118–19, 453
　eastern policy, 123, 453, 498–500
　approval of Slavonic liturgy, 124, 455,
　　499, 500
Hadrian III, Pope, 455
Hadrian IV, Pope
　policy regarding Sicily and Manuel I,
　　229–30

Hadrian IV (*cont.*)
  hope of union of Roman and Greek churches, 229
  rift with Frederick Barbarossa, 230
Haemus, mountain range in Balkans
  limit of Great Fence, 98
  limit of Asparuch's kingdom, 484
Hafjij, fortress on river Phasis, south-west of Erzurum (Theodosiopolis), 186
hagiography, 42, 47, 54, 57, 111 n. 1, 129, 140 and n. 1, 144, 570–1, 625
al-Ḥakam, Umayyad ruler of Spain, 100
al-Ḥākim, Fatimid Caliph, and Basil II, 724–5
Halīl Pasha, vizier under Murād II and Muḥammad II, 771, 773–4
Halmyros, port on gulf of Volos in Thessaly
  and trade with West, 291–2
  export of wheat, 428
Ḥalpat in Armenia, monastery of, 616
Halys, river in Asia Minor, 177, 711, 713, 719
Hamam, founder of dynasty in Caspian Albania, 610 n. 3
Hamazasp II of the Mamikonids, prince of Armenia, 606
Hamdanids, Arab dynasty in Syria and Mesopotamia
  rise of, 139, 703
  threatened by Buwayhids and Fatimids, 149, 723
  loss of Aleppo, 150, 722
  amirs of Mosul, 163, 164, 723
  and Basil II, 182, 723–4
  cultural life, 680
  fall of dynasty in Aleppo, 725
  see also Aleppo, Sayf ad-Dawla
Ḥamīd, Turkish principality in Pisidia in Asia Minor, 756, 762, 764
Ḥanbalites, Muslim sect, 690
Ḥanifitish rites of the Sunnites, 737
Hanzith, district in Mesopotamia, 165, 186
Haramvár, town in the Balkans, battle (1128), 581
harems, 545, 734
al-Ḥarīrī, Arabic author, 687 n. 1
Harold Hardraga, Norwegian warrior and hero, in Sicily with George Maniaces, 197
Harq, district of Armenia, 165, 181
Hārūn ar-Rashīd, Abbasid Caliph of Baghdad, 735
  destruction of Barmakids, 641, 666, 700
  contraction of Abbasid Empire, 644–6, 677, 701
  religious policy, 670
  campaigns against Byzantium, 83, 91, 645–6, **704–8**
  frontier defences, 706
  and Thomas the Slavonian, 709
Hārūniya, town in North Syria, 706
Ḥasan ibn Qaḥṭaba
  and rebuilding of Melitene, 704
  campaigns against Byzantium, 705
Ḥasan-i-Ṣabbāḥ, leader of Persian Ismā'īlīs, 657
Hashimids, Hāshimiyya, Muslim house and sect, 638, 678
Hayr ad-Dīn Pasha, vizier of Murād I, 763–4, 771
Hayton, *see* Het'um
Hebrew
  learnt by Constantine (Cyril), 111, 492
  sources for history of Khazaria, 488, 493 and n. 2
Helen, daughter of Béla II of Hungary, marriage to Uroš of Rascia, 221
Helen, daughter of John Asen II, wife of Theodore II Lascaris, 310, 311, 312
Helena Comnena Ducaena, daughter of John Ducas of Neopatras, wife of William de la Roche and Hugh of Brienne, 410
Helena Lecapena, wife of Constantine VII, 137, 147, 511
Helena, mother of Constantine the Great, 7
Helena, wife of Manuel II, 385
Helena, daughter of Michael II of Epirus, wife of Manfred, king of Sicily, 323, 325, 401
Helena, niece of Romanus III, wife of Bagrat IV of Georgia, 196, 621
Heliopolis (Baalbek), town in Syria, 169, 723–4
Hellas, province of, invaded by Samuel of Bulgaria, 184
Hellas, theme of
  creation, 489 and n. 2
  revolt against iconoclasm, 70
  strategus, 629
Hellenism
  in fourth and fifth centuries, 42, 45
  in fifteenth century, 378–9
  and Christianity, 431
  Christian Hellenism, 431–2, 435, 436, 443, 444, 447
  under Justinian I, 436, 437
  under Abbasids, 642, 662–3, 669, 672 and n. 2, 680, 684–5, 690

Hellenism (*cont.*)
Hellenistic theory of kingship, 431–2, *and see* ruler-worship
in Egypt, 54
in Asia Minor, 51, 743
in Syria, 54
hellenisation of Slavs in Greece, 489–90
Helos (Gilas), town in Laconia in Peloponnese, Latin See of, 396
Henoticon, Zeno's doctrinal edict, *see under* Zeno
Henry of Flanders, Latin Emperor of Constantinople
and Fourth Crusade, 276, 285
and invasion of Asia Minor, 290–1, 295, 300
crowned Emperor, 293, 391
relations with the Comneni of Trebizond, 295, 300
alliance with Seljuqs, 295
relations with kingdom of Thessalonica, 298, 391
relations with Michael I of Epirus, 298–9, 300
relations with Latin principalities in Greece, 391, 408
treaty with Theodore I Lascaris, 300 and n. 1, 303–4
relations with Bulgaria, 293, 294, 300, 301, 526
relations with Hungary, 301
relations with Serbia, 301, 531
relations with Greek Church, 302–4
assessment of his work, 301
Henry II, German Emperor, 190, 458
Henry III, German Emperor, 202, 458, 459, 460
Henry IV, German Emperor
relations with Alexius I, 213, 465
and Venice, 271
relations with Pope Gregory VII, 464
relations with Hungary, 578
Henry V, German Emperor, 467, 468
Henry VI, German Emperor
plans for marriage, 231–2
marriage to Constance of Sicily, 232, 246
and Third Crusade, 246
claim to Sicilian lands, 247
relations with Cyprus, 248
relations with Lesser Armenia, 248, 632
hostility to Byzantium, 247–8, 275, 469
Henry III, king of England, and Baldwin II, 317

Henry of Babenburg, first duke of Austria, marriage to Manuel I's niece Theodora, 228
Henry of Champagne, king of Jerusalem, 631
Henry the Lion, nephew of Welf VI, 228
Hephthalites (Huns), attack on Persia, 600
Heraclea (Cybistra), town in southern Cappadocia in Asia Minor, 631, 707–8, 710, 715
taken by Arabs (806), 91, 707
Heraclea Pontica, town in Asia Minor on Black Sea
and Theodore I, 295, 300, 303–4
held against Turks, 347, 354
Russian attack under Igor, 510
Heraclea (Propontic), town in Thrace on Sea of Marmora, 373
See of, and suffragan See of Byzantium, 18
Heraclea (in Greece), *see* Siderocastron
Heraclius, Emperor
Slav and Avar invasions, 10, 481–3
Persian campaigns, 10, 21, 29, 30, 486, 604–5, 736
policy in the Caucasus, 483, 610 n. 3
Ecthesis, 56, 440
military agreement with Khazars, 486
and defences of Constantinople, 9, 482
and Arab conquests, 30
and Africa, 29, 30
dynastic claims of family, 67
and missionary work among Serbs and Croats, 122, 482
connection with Venice, 251
death, 25
Heraklion, modern port in Crete, 427
herceg, title, 558
Hercegovina, in Balkans, 558
Heredia, *see* Juan Fernández de Heredia
Heret'i, district in Caucasia, 610 n. 3
hermitages, 577
Hervé Francopulus, Norman soldier in service of Turks, 205
hesychasts, hesychasm
teaching, 357
opposed by the Patriarch John Calecas, 357–8
alliance with John Cantacuzenus, 358
orthodoxy established (1351), 362
in Bulgaria, 544
hetaireia, 148 n. 1
Het'um (Hayton) I of Lesser Armenia, 631, 633–4
Het'um II of Lesser Armenia, 634–5
Het'um II of Lambron, and Rubenids of Lesser Armenia, 630–1

Het'um, chamberlain of Armenia, 636
Het'umids of Lambron, dynasty in Lesser Armenia, 628, 630–1, 633–6
Hexabiblos, another name for the *Basilica*, 133
Hexamilion, wall across isthmus of Corinth, 379, 383, 384–5, 772
Hibāt Allāh, brother of Abū Taghlib, 165
Hiera, island in Aegean, volcanic eruption in 726, 68
Hierakion (Geraki), town in Peloponnese
   ceded to Michael VIII by Franks, 332 and n. 2, 401 n. 1
   Latin barony, 394, 403
Hierapolis (Manbij), town in North Syria
   Christian relic at, 149, 721
   capture by Byzantines, 169
Hieria, palace of, on Asian coast of Sea of Marmora, iconoclast council at (754), 78
Hierotheus, first bishop of Hungary, 509, 572, 574
Hierus, customs post for Constantinople, 89
Hilāl, Bedouin tribe, and devastation of North Africa, 651
Hildebrand, *see* Gregory VII, Pope
Himera, town in Sicily, 152
Himerius, Byzantine admiral, 129–30, 131, 716, 720
Himerius, teacher of Basil the Great, 48
Hincmar, archbishop of Reims, leader of Frankish Church, 450
Hindu Kush, mountain range in Central Asia
   source of silver, 644
   limit of Alp Arslan's Empire, 703
Hippodrome in Constantinople
   building, 4, 7
   politics, 12
   ritual, 17
   humiliation of iconophiles, 80
   panic of crowd under Nicephorus II, 152
   celebrations in, 74, 238, 734
Hippolytus of Euripides, 47
Hishām, Umayyad Caliph
   and iconoclasm, 66
   wars with Byzantium, 698–9
Hiṣn Kayfā, town in Mesopotamia, 746
Hiṣn Ziyād, *see* Kharput
Histria, *see* Istria
Hittite civilisation, and Caucasia, 593, 596
Hodegetria, icon of the, 328

Hohenstaufen, imperial dynasty in Germany and Italy in twelfth century, 217, 233, 239, 247
   overthrown in Italy by Charles of Anjou, 334
   see also Frederick I Barbarossa, Henry VI, Frederick II
Holobolus, Manuel, Byzantine poet, 321
Holy Land, *see* Palestine
Holy Places, 19, 170, 214, 225, 466, 726
Holy War, Muslim, 149, 665, 696–7, 725, 732, 738–9, 745, 755–7, 760, 762, 765, 767, 769
   holy warriors, see *ghāzīs*
homage
   of Dalmatians to Venice, 268
   among Latins, 287, 294, 298, 409, 410, 425
   of ruler of Damascus to John Tzimisces, 723
Homer, and Greek Church Fathers, 48, 50, 53
Homs, *see* Emesa
honey, trade in, 159, 428, 475, 615
Honigmann, E., 124 and n. 1
Honorius, Emperor of western half of Roman Empire, 26
Honorius I, Pope, and monothelete heresy, 440, 441
Honorius II, Pope, 222 n. 2, 468
Honorius III, Pope
   and Stephen of Serbia, 305, 531
   and Peter of Courtenay, 305
   and Demetrius of Montferrat, 308
   and the Latin Patriarch Gervase, 397
Honorius II, anti-Pope, 463
Hormizd IV, king of Persia, 603
Horos of iconoclast council of 754, 78–80
   refuted by Seventh General Council (787), 85
horses, trade in, 159, 615, 733
   stud-farm at Malagina, 707
Hospitallers, order of, 396, 405 n. 1, 407, 420, 631–2
hospitals, 220, 320, 580, 747
Hrelja (Chreles), independent lord in Macedonia, 541
Hṛomkla, fortress in Lesser Armenia on Euphrates, 630
Hrvoje Vukčić-Hrvatinić, ruler of Bosnia, 556
Hubert, count of Biandrate, in revolt against Henry of Flanders, 298, 391
Hugh of Brienne, count of Lecce, bailie of duchy of Athens, 410
Hugh I, count of Champagne, grandfather of William of Champlitte, 390

Hugh of Provence (Berengar), father of Bertha, first wife of Romanus II, 147, 457
attack on Arabs, 730
Hujwīrī, Ṣūfī leader, 691
Hülegü, Mongol khan
relations with Michael VIII, 336
attack on Islamic lands, 660–1, 749
Hum, *see* Zachlumia
Humbert, cardinal
and schism of 1054, 201–2, 461–2
and reform of Western Church, 459
Hundred Years War in Europe, 406
Hungarian (Magyar) language, 566, 575
runic alphabet, 568
Hungary and the Hungarians, **566–92**
earlier inhabitants of Hungary, 29, 570
foundation of Hungarian kingdom by Magyars (q.v.), 128, 503, 569–70
and Byzantine diplomacy, 570
settlements on Byzantine territory, 570
contacts with Byzantium and spread of Byzantine influence, 571–2, 573–7
friendly relations with Byzantium, 576–7, 578–80, 588–92
wars with Byzantium, 570–1, 577–8, 581–3, 584, 589
treaties with Byzantium, 245, 578
attacks on Constantinople, 571
and Basil II, 186, 573–4
expedition of Isaac I, 206, 577–8
gain from weakness of Byzantium in later eleventh century, 208
interest in western Balkans and Dalmatia, 212, 221, 245, 556, 580
marriage alliance with the Comneni, 216, 580
rivalry with Venice, 221, 233, 234, 271
relations with Manuel I, 229–30, 231, 233–4, 581–4, 586
relations with Normans of Sicily, 233
connections with Kiev, 233, 571, 577
relations with Isaac II, 245, 247, 584–5
and Third Crusade, 585
and Fourth Crusade, 279, 280, 585
relations with Michael VIII, 324, 336, 589
visit of John V, 370, 589–90
visit of John VIII, 590–1
opposition to Turks, 375–6, 383, 553–4, 559–60, 590–2, 766, 770–1
invasion of kingdom of Naples, 406
trade, 159, 581, 587
relations with Second Bulgarian Empire, 524, 526, 528, 535–6
relations with Rome, 528

relations with Serbia (Rascia), 221, 228, 233, 248, 520, 530–1, 540, 551, 552–5, 560, 584, 585
relations with Bosnia, 221, 234, 546–9, 551, 555, 556, 559–60
relations with Croatia, 216, 233–4, 245, 546, 556
Hussites, 551
Turkish conquests, 560, 769
relations with Wallachia and Moldavia, 561, 562–4
German influence, 515, 576, 578, 579
crowns of the kings of Hungary, 573, 576–7, 578–9, 588
coat of arms, 588
chronicles, 570, 571, 575
Hungary, Church in
first bishop, 572
relations with Constantinople, 573, 586
Byzantine influence, 573–5, 577, 586–7
relations with Rome, 573, 577, 586
synods, 577
Hunkār, Hudāvendkār, appellation of Murād I, 763
Huns
raids in fifth century, 9, 27, 435
and Magyars, 567–8
bishop of the Huns, 568
and Iberia, 600
Hunyadi, John Corvinus, Voivode of Transylvania
victories over Turks, 383, 553–4, 770
armistice and treaty of Szegedin, 383 and n. 1, 384 and n. 1, 554 n. 1
defeat at Kossovo (1448), 554, 771–2
Byzantine legends of, 591–2
and Mesembria in Thrace, 591–2
Ḥusayn ibn Hamdān, leader of revolt against Abbasids, 717
Hussites, 551
Huyastan, district of Armenia, 167
Hylilas, *see* John VII Grammaticus
hymnography
influence of Syriac, 55
translations into Slavonic, 502
Hypate, *see* Neopatras
hypatos, head of faculty of philosophy in university of Constantinople, 201
hyperpyron, Byzantine gold coin, 397, 398, 417, 542
debasement under the Palaeologi, 342–3, 363

Iamblichus, neoplatonist studied in eleventh century, 201
Ibar, river in Balkans, 501, 519

Ibas of Edessa, condemned under Justinian I, 56
Iberia (Kʻartʻli, Karthli), Iberians
monks, 55
Iviron monastery on Mt Athos, 177
Bardas Phocas in, 177
troops in service of Basil II, 186
invaded by Basil II, 189
struggle for control between Rome and Persia, 593–5, 597–8, 600–2
conversion to Christianity, 595 and n. 1
revolt against Persia, 600
Church in, 600, 601 and n. 1, 604
abolition of monarchy, 602 and n. 1
break with Persia, 603
under Umayyad Caliphs, 605–7
under Abbasids, 607–12
rise of Bagratids, 609–13
restoration of monarchy, 613
under kings of Georgia, 621
rulers of, *see* List of Rulers 7
see also Georgia
Iberian peninsula, 97
Iberians in western Empire, 23
see also Spain
Ibn al-Fāriḍ, Arabic author and mystic, 687 n. 1
Ibn al-Jarrāḥ, Palestinian amir, agreement with Romanus III, 725–6
Ibn al-Muʻtazz, Arabic poet, 686
Ibn Bagrat from Amorium, revolt under Michael III, 115
Ibn Baṭṭūṭa, Moorish visitor to Asia Minor in fourteenth century, 757, 759–60
Ibn Ḥazm, Muslim heresiographer, 691 n. 4
Ibn Māja, Muslim jurist, 674
Ibn Qatuna, Arabic name for Byzantine admiral, 106 n. 1
Ibn Qutayba, Arab author, 686
Ibn Rāʼiq, governor of Iraq under Abbasids, 646
Ibn Sīnā, *see* Avicenna
Ibrāhīm, amir of North Africa, and capture of Syracuse (878), 729
Ibrāhīm Bey, Karaman leader, 771
Ibrāhīm ibn al-Aghlab, governor of North Africa under Hārūn ar-Rashīd, 701, 727
and see Aghlabid dynasty
Iconium (Konya), city in Asia Minor
sacked by Turks, 209
seat of Seljuq rulers of Rūm (q.v.), 213, 214, 216, 223, 224, 226, 290, 654, 741–2, 747, 750
threatened by Manuel I, 226
occupied by Frederick Barbarossa, 743
captured by Mongols, 751
Karaman campaigns, 753–4, 764, 768
iconoclasm and iconoclasts, 19, 31, 60, **61–104**
under Leo III, 61–2, 65–72
under Leo V, 68, 98–9
under Constantine V, 72, 78–81, 97, 487
denounced by Roman synod of 769, 77
one cause of rift between Italy and Empire, 77, 254
theology, 78–80, 86–7, 99
under Leo IV, 81
under Irene, 83–4
refuted by Seventh General Council, 84–8
economic policy, 93 n. 2, 94
under Nicephorus I, 95
under Leo V, 98–9
under Michael II, 101–2
and synod of Paris (825), 102
condemnation at council of 861, 112, 450–1
and council of 867, 113–14
influence on spread of Christianity in Khazaria, 487
iconophiles
chroniclers hostile to Leo III, 61
not mentioned in Leo III's *Ecloga*, 65
in Italy, Greece and Aegean islands, 70
arrests under Constantine V, 78
persecutions, 80–1, 102, 103–4, 487
theology, 86, 87, 99
economic policy, 93 n. 2, 94
and synod of Paris (825), 102
restoration of images, 84–7, 104, 106
and idea of apostolicity, 456
Idrisid dynasty in Morocco, 663
Ifrīqiya, North Africa (*see under* Africa), 682, 727, 732
Ignatius, Patriarch of Constantinople
appointment, 107, 108
attitude to Michael III, 108
extremist policy, 108–9, 127, 132
deposition, 108 n. 2
conflict with Photius, 109, 112, 113, 117–19, 138, 451–4
policy regarding Bulgaria, 114, 122, 123, 453, 500
reinstated under Basil I, 114
and Church in Moravia, 124 n. 1; and in Russia, 496
and Pope Nicholas I, 450–2
and idea of apostolicity, 456
death, 123, 454
see also Stylianus *and* Theognostus

Ignatius of Smolensk, chronicler, 374 n. 1

Igor, prince of Kiev
attacks on Constantinople, 140, 159, 510–11
commercial treaty with Byzantium (944), 140, 511

Igor, son of Ryurik, Viking leader, and capture of Kiev, 504 n. 1

Ikhshīd, amir of Syria and Egypt, 718–19

Ikhshīdid dynasty in Egypt, 140, 149

Ilario, town in Italy, and Lombard invasion, 250

Ilkhans (Il-Khans), Mongol dynasty, 626–7, 634–5, **749–52, 753–4**

Illyricum
prefecture, 27
and See of Rome, 432
transfer to See of Constantinople, 71, 87–8, 444
disputes between Rome and Constantinople over, 109, 112, 113, 124 n. 1, 447, 452, 455, 469–70, 499
invasion by Avars and Slavs, 438, 478, 480
Slav settlements in, 481

Iločki, Nicholas, titular king of Bosnia, 560

Imbros, island in Aegean, under Latin rule, 289

Imeretia (Imereti), new name of Abasgia (q.v.), 626 and n. 1, 627–8

imperator, 14, 16, 101, 524

imperator Graecorum, 309

Imperator Romanorum, and Charlemagne, 90, 447

imperium, 436, 438, 446, 450, 506
see also *regnum*

India
and Timur, 377
export of timber and cotton, 644
scientific works studied by Arabs, 684, 694–5

industry, 5, 37, 40–1, 475
under Abbasids, 644
in Caucasia, 609, 615, 624
see also mines and minerals, silk

Ingilene, district of Armenia, 597 and n. 1

Innocent II, Pope, 222 and n. 2, 223–4

Innocent III, Pope
extension of influence in Balkans, 248, 469, 524–5
correspondence with Alexius III on reunion, 248, 280
and Fourth Crusade, 248, 276–81, 469
account of sack of Constantinople, 287

relations with Baldwin I, 288
relations with Theodore I Lascaris, 295
relations with Greek Church, 301–4, 394–5, 469
relations with Latins in Greece, 391 and n. 2, 393, 408–9
relations with Bulgaria, 524–5, 526, 528–9
relations with Bosnia, 546–7
relations with Hungary, 577

Innocent IV, Pope, 316, 317, 318, 323, 470

Innocent VI, Pope
relations with John V Palaeologus, 368–9
relations with Stephen Dušan, 540

inscriptions
as historical source, 110, 117, 177, 251, 527, 754, 755
co-Emperors cited on, 143 n. 1
see also epigraphy

Ionian islands, 92, 289, 297, 388

Ios (Nio), Aegean island, under Venetian rule, 425

Iqalt'o, abbey in Georgia, 625

Iran, *see* Persia

Iranians
and Antes, 476 n. 2
and Slavs, 504
see also Barmakids

Iraq, *see* Mesopotamia

Irene, Empress, wife of Leo IV, **82–91**
and restoration of images, 81, 82, 83, 84–8, 99, 106
joint sovereign with Constantine VI, 82
policy in West, 83, 88
Elpidius' revolt, 83
payment of tribute to Arabs, 83
Arab campaigns, 83, 88, 704, 706–7
Bulgar campaigns, 88
reorganisation of army, 84, 88
conflict with Constantine VI, 88–9
correspondence with Pope Hadrian I, 72 n. 2, 446–7
as sole ruler, 89
taxation, 89, 93
proposed marriage with Charlemagne, 90
exile and death, 91

Irene Ducas (or Ducaena), wife of Alexius I, 210–11, 212, 220
Typicon of, 218

Irene, Khazar princess, wife of Constantine V, 64, 487

Irene of Montferrat, second wife of Andronicus II, 345

Irene, daughter of Alexius III Angelus, 282

Irene, daughter of Isaac II Angelus, wife of Philip of Swabia, 247, 278

Irene, daughter of St Ladislas of Hungary, wife of John II, 216, 220, 579–80

Irene, wife of Manuel I, *see* Bertha of Sulzbach

Irene, daughter of Michael VIII, wife of John Asen III, 338

Irene, daughter of Theodore I Lascaris, wife of John III Vatatzes, 307, 320

Irene, daughter of Theodore II Lascaris, wife of Constantine Tich, 322, 336

Irene, daughter of Theodore Ducas, wife of John Asen II, 313

Iris, river in Asia Minor, 58, 711
  battle (950), 719

iron mines, 532, 644

irrigation, 615, 644

Irtish, river in Central Asia, 653

'Īsā, son of Bāyezīd I, struggle for power with brothers, 767–8

Isaac I Comnenus, Emperor, 205–7
  and attacks on Empire, 194, 206, 578
  deprived of command by Theodora, 204
  proclaimed Emperor by army in Asia Minor, 205
  schemes for economy, 205, 206, 207
  conflict with Church, 205–6
  foreign policy, 206
  Psellus one of his supporters, 207 n. 1
  abdication and death, 206–7

Isaac II Angelus, Emperor, 245–7, 282–4
  compared with Andronicus I, 245
  administrative abuses, 245
  landowners unchecked, 245
  foreign policy, 245–7
  loss of Cyprus, 245, 246–7
  relations with Hungary, 245, 247, 584–5, 586–7
  Normans expelled from Greece, 245
  loss of Bulgaria, 245, 247, 522–4
  hostility of Serbia, 245–6, 247, 521, 523
  hostility of Frederick Barbarossa, 246
  hostility of Henry VI, 247
  renewal of alliance with Saladin, 246
  Third Crusade, 246–7, 523
  treaty of Adrianople (1190), 246
  deposed and blinded by Alexius III, 247, 275, 524
  Emperor again during Fourth Crusade, 282–4

Isaac III Bagratuni, High Constable of Armenia, 607

Isaac, Exarch of Ravenna, 251

Isaac, St, chief prelate of Armenia, 598, 599 and n. 1

Isabel, wife of Amaury of Lusignan, 635–6

Isabel (Zabel), queen of Lesser Armenia, 633

Isabella de la Roche, first wife of Hugh of Brienne, 410

Isabella, princess of Achaea, daughter of William of Villehardouin, wife of Philip of Anjou, Florent of Hainault and Philip of Savoy, 334, 402, 403, 404–5, 410

Isauria, district of Asia Minor
  connection with Leo III, 62 n. 1
  lost to Seljuqs, 631

Isaurians
  mercenaries, 27
  Emperors, 36, *and see* Leo III, Constantine V, Leo IV, Constantine VI and Irene

Isfahan, town in Persia, 644, 745

Isfendiyār, prince of Castamuni, and Murād II, 769

Isidore, Greek metropolitan of Russia, later cardinal, supporter of union of Churches, 382
  papal legate to Constantinople in 1452, 385
  visit to Hungary (1443), 587

Isidore of Seville, scholar, on Slav invasions of Greece, 482

Isidore, *see* Pseudo-Isidore

Iskender Bey, *see* Skanderbeg

Islam
  expansion, 30, 41
  check to, 31
  crusading attitude of Byzantium, 149–50, 214
  among Volga Bulgars, 484
  in the Caucasus, 486
  in Khazaria, 488
  Islamic sources on Judaism in Khazaria, 493 and n. 2
  in Greece and Balkans, 565
  among Mongols, 634–5
  among Turks, 652–3, 655, 658–60, 737–8
  religious institution and relationship with state under Abbasids, 642 and n. 1, 657, 658 and nn. 1 and 3, 659–60, 692–3
  theological colleges (*madrasas*), 659, 738, 747, 775
  theology, 669–71, 688–93
  traditionalism, 672–6, 690

Islam (*cont.*)
  influence of Christian ideas, 692, 694
  Christian converts to, 204, 224, 689, 758, 760
  Muslim converts to Christianity, 241, 721
Ismāʻīl ibn-Shuʻaīb, amir of Tiflis under Abbasids, 609
Ismāʻīl, Shīʻite imām, and Ismāʻīlīs, 647, 681
Ismāʻīlīs, Shīʻite Muslim sect, 647–9, 657, 659, 681–3, 685, 688, 690, 702
  Seveners, 681
  see also Assassins
Isnik, *see* Nicaea
Isperich, *see* Asparuch (*and* 484 n. 2 *on spelling*)
Istria
  ceded to Charlemagne (798), 88, 253
  returned to Byzantium (812), 96, 448
  separated from Venetia, 250, 252–3
  Lombard invasions, 253, 255
  under Franks, 258
  threat from Slavs, 268
  bishops of, 252–3
Italian cities
  growth of independence, 77
  activity in east Mediterranean, 216
  relations with Manuel I, 229, 232–3, 239, 240
  trade relations with Muslims, 745–7
  trade relations with Georgia, 627
  and see Amalfi, Gaeta, Genoa, Naples, Pisa, Venice
Italicus, Michael, theologian, on Fulk of Jerusalem, 225
Italus, John, eleventh-century philosopher, 201, 213, 217
Italy
  overrun by Odoacer, 21, 28, 435
  decline and depopulation, 24
  invaded by Ostrogoths, 27, 28, 435
  reconquest by Justinian, 21, 28
  Lombard invasion, 29, 250, 438–9
  exarchate, 31
  administration, 33
  impoverishment in fifth century, 40
  taxation, 71, 442, 444
  opposition to iconoclasm, 70
  support for Pope against Emperor, 441, 444
  split with East, 72, 77
  and Constantine V, 75, 76, 77
  and Leo IV, 82
  and Charlemagne, 83, 88, 446, 448
  and Irene, 88
  Arab attacks, 101, 457, 728–32

  defeat of Arabs at the Garigliano (915), 136
  naval expeditions under Basil I and Leo VI, 129, 729–30
  Lombard revolt under Basil II, 190, 731
  contraction of Byzantine rule in eleventh century, 194, 197, 459, 460
  George Maniaces as catepan and magister, 198, 201
  attacks on south by Normans and Lombards, 202, 731
  Normans established in south, 206, 208, 212, 215, 217, 221, 459, 460, 463
  South Italy united with Sicily under Roger II, 222
  Manuel I's plans, 227, 229–30, 232, 233, 234
  and treaty of Thessalonica, 228
  and Frederick Barbarossa, 229, 230, 231
  defeat of Hohenstaufen by Angevins (1266), 334
  Italians in Byzantine service, 337
  Italians in Navarrese Company, 420
  see also Italian cities
Ithaca, Ionian island, under Venetian suzerainty, 297
Itil, town in Volga delta
  Khazar capital, 487, 496
  and Vikings, 495
Itsh Kaleh, harbour fortress at Nauplia, 410
ius terragii, see land-tax
Ivajlo, Bulgarian tsar, 535 n. 1, 536
Ivanko, prince of the Dobrudja, 544, 545
ʻIvaz Pasha, Ottoman commander at Brusa, 768
Iviron, Georgian monastery on Mt Athos, 177
Izladî, *see* Zlatica
Izmir, *see* Smyrna
Izmit, Iznikomid, *see* Nicomedia
Iznik, *see* Nicaea
ʻIzz ad-Dīn Kaykāwūs, *see* Kaykāwūs I and II

Jaballah of Ghassan, Arabian king, ancestor of Nicephorus I, 91
Jaʻber, fortress on Euphrates, 758
Jacob Baradaeus, monophysite bishop, 21
Jacobites, Syrian monophysites, 705
Jacques des Baux, prince of Achaea, last titular Latin Emperor, 407, 420
Jaʻfar aṣ-Ṣādiq, Shīʻite pretender, 647
Jaḥḥāf the Qaysid, Arab amir in Caucasia, 609

al-Jāḥiẓ, Muslim essayist, 667
Jajce, town in northern Bosnia, 560
Jalāīrids, successors of Il-Khans, 627
Jalāl ad-Dīn, *see* Mevlānā Jalāl ad-Dīn
Jalāl-ad-Dīn of Khʷārizm, Turkoman leader, 625–6, 748
James of Avesnes, in Euboea, 389, 392
James II of Majorca, and Latins in Morea, 406
Jamurlu, in Serbia, defeat of Mūsa by Muḥammad I (1413), 768
Jāndār, Turkish kingdom on Black Sea in northern Asia Minor, 756, 761
Jandarlîzade, vizier family under Ottomans, 774
janissaries in Turkish army, 760, 764, 771, **772**
  at capture of Constantinople (1453), 387
Janko, Greek name for John Hunyadi, q.v.
Jaqelis, Caucasian dynasty, 626 n. 2, 628
Jaroslav, prince of Kiev, 577
Jats, *see* the Zott
Javakhetʻi, province of Iberia, 603, 609–11, 626 n. 2
Jaxartes (Sir Daryā), river in Central Asia, 644, 652–3, 660, 737
Jayḥān, *see* Pyramus
Jazira, region of upper Mesopotamia, 169
Jebe Noyon, general under Jenghiz Khan, 660
Jenghiz Khan (Temujin), Mongol leader, 377, 660, 747–8
Jeremiah, *voivode*, and surrender of Golubac to Turks, 553
Jerusalem
  pilgrimages to, 19
  taken by Persians (614), 30
  Laura near, 58
  Syriac spoken, 55
  and Nicephorus II, 149
  and John Tzimisces, 170, 723
  captured by Seljuqs (1070), 737
  objective of Crusades, 214, 246, 276, 279–80, 429, 466, 737
  Latin kingdom of, 215, 223, 277, 310, 403
  and Manuel I, 236, 238
  captured by Saladin, 246, 654
  treatment of Christians in, 287, 725
  and Mongols, 635 n. 3
Jerusalem, Patriarchs of
  jurisdiction, 19
  appointment, 726
  and Church Councils, 66, 84, 113, 118, 131–2, 716

and Basil II, 190, 725
  coronation of John Cantacuzenus at Adrianople, 361
  see also Symeon II
Jews
  treatment under Leo III, 68
  conversions at Beirut, 85
  influence on Khazars, 111
  Basil I's attempt to convert, 122
  Jewish merchants in Greece, 291–2, 428
  in Constantinople, 587
  status under Abbasids, 666–7
  and Arabic science, 684
  chief rabbi as political leader, 774
  see also Judaism
Jeyhan, *see* Pyramus
Jimrī (Sultan Siyāwush), Seljuq pretender, 750–1
Joachim, Patriarch of Bulgaria, accused of treason by Svetoslav, 537
Joan of Anjou-Taranto, wife of Oshin I of Lesser Armenia and of Oshin of Ḳoṛikos, 635–6
Joanica, *see* Kalojan
Joanna I of Naples, 407
Joanna, duchess of Durazzo, 419
Joannicius, Patriarch of Serbia, 538
Joannina (Ioannina), fortress in Epirus
  in Byzantine hands in early fourteenth century, 349
  taken by Stephen Dušan, 356
Joasaph, monastic name of John VI Cantacuzenus, 367
Job, archbishop of Esztergom, correspondence with Isaac II, 586–7
Job, monk, biographer of St Theodora of Arta, 314 n. 1
John I Tzimisces, Emperor, **156–75**
  ancestry, 158
  marriages, 159
  favourite of Theophano, 147, 156, 157
  capture of Samosata (958), 146, 148 n. 1, 149, 720
  campaigns against Arabs in Mesopotamia, Syria and Palestine, 149, 154, 163–5, 167–72, 720–3
  victory at Mount of Blood (963–4), 149, 157 n. 1
  and murder of Nicephorus II, 156
  career under Nicephorus II, 156–7 and nn., 721
  exile of Theophano, 157
  and Phocas family, 157–8
  invasion of Cilicia, 721
  Russian campaign, 158–62 and nn., 163, 164, 175, 179, 514 and n. 4, 722

John I (*cont.*)
revolt of Bardas Phocas, 158, 176, 722
revolt of Leo and Nicephorus Phocas, 160–1
embassy to Pechenegs, 162 and n. 1
triumph over Bulgaria, 162 and nn. 2 and 3, 514–15, 517, 722
relations with West, 163, 458
relations with Armenians, 165–70, 172, 616–17
legislation against landowners, 173–4
accounts of his death, 172–5
John II Comnenus, Emperor, **219–26**
character, 220
marriage to Irene, a Hungarian princess, 216, 220, 221, 579–80
accession, 219–20
care for orthodoxy and the Church, 220
agrarian policy, 220
foreign policy, 220–5, 227
policy in Balkans, 221, 581
and Bohemond of Antioch, 216
relations with Venice and West, 221–2, 223–4, 227
relations with the Papacy, 222 and n. 2, 223–4, 468
campaigns in Asia Minor and Syria, 223–5, 630
choice of successor, 225–6
John III Ducas Vatatzes, Emperor of Nicaea, **307–9, 311–21**
dispute over accession, 307–8
gains in Asia Minor, 308, 309
clash with Theodore Ducas, 309
relations with Bulgaria, 311, 312, 313, 398–9, 528, 535
relations with the Papacy, 311–12, 318, 470
attacks on Latin Empire, 309, 312, 398–9, 528
conquest of Rhodes, 311, 318
relations with Thessalonica, 313, 315
truce with Baldwin II, 315, 316
friendship with Frederick II, 316
relations with Michael II of Epirus, 315, 317, 318–19
invasion of Bulgaria, 316–17
capture of Thessalonica (1246), 317, 398
relations with Albanians, 319, 320
relations with Mongols, 320
relations with Seljuqs, 315, 320
agrarian and economic policy, 319–20
charitable endowments, 320
encouragement of arts, 321
death, 319, 401
canonisation, 321 n. 1

John IV Lascaris, Emperor of Nicaea
under regency, 324, 589
deserted in Nicaea, blinded and imprisoned by Michael VIII, 328, 338
John V Palaeologus, Emperor, **356–74**
civil war on death of Andronicus III, 356–61
under regency, 356–7
relations with Serbia, 359, 365, 366, 369, 539
relations with Bulgaria, 360, 366, 370
in Thessalonica, 362
negotiations with Venice, 365, 369, 370–1 and n. 1, 372–3
civil war with John VI, 365–7
negotiations with Genoese, 366–7, 369
attempt at reunion with Roman Church, 368–9, 370–1, 471
visit to Hungary, 370, 589–90
helped by Amadeo of Savoy, 370
relations with Ottoman Sultans, 372–3, 374, 761
rebellion of his son Andronicus IV, 372–3
visits to western powers, 370–1
death, 374
John VI Cantacuzenus, Emperor, **356–67**
quoted, 296 n. 1
support for Andronicus III in civil war, 350–2
service as Grand Domestic under Andronicus III, 352, 354–6, 406
civil war after Andronicus III's death, 356–61
at Didymotichus, 357, 360, 361
supported by aristocracy, 357–9
supported by hesychasts, 358
relations with Stephen Dušan, 359–60, 362–3, 538–40
relations with Turks, 354, 359–60, 361, 366, 761
coronation, 361, 364
relationship to John V, 361
financial straits, 363–4
trouble with Genoese, 364–5
civil war with John V, 365–7
abdication and retirement as monk Joasaph, 367
John VII Palaeologus, Emperor
childhood, 372
claim to throne, 374–5
negotiations with Charles VI of France, 376
Emperor during Manuel II's absence abroad, 377

John VIII Palaeologus, Emperor, **379–82, 384–5**
in Peloponnese, 379, 591
extent of Empire, 380, 769
negotiations for union with Roman Church, 381–2, 471, 770
subservience to Turks, 384
visit to Hungary, 590–1
death and succession, 385
John II, Pope, 436–7
John VI, Pope, 441
John VII, Pope, 442
John VIII, Pope
eastern policy, 119, 123, 126
and Byzantine attack on Arabs in Calabria, 121, 454
and Bulgarian Church, 122, 123, 454–5, 501
and Photius, 123, 126, 454
and Slavonic liturgy, 123–5, 455, 500
and Germans, 123, 125
and Church in Moravia, 123, 124 and n. 1, 125, 455
John X, Pope, 136, 456
John XI, Pope, 456
John XII, Pope, 457
John XIX, Pope, 269, 460
John XXII, Pope, 416
John I Chrysostom, Patriarch of Constantinople, Church Father, **51–2**
banished from Constantinople, 20
John IV the Faster, Patriarch of Constantinople, and title Oecumenical Patriarch, 439–40
John VII Grammaticus (John the Grammarian, Hylilas), Patriarch of Constantinople
iconoclastic zeal, 99
tutor of the Emperor Theophilus, 102
sent on embassy to Abbasid Caliph, 710
Patriarch, 103
deposed, 104
John VIII Xiphilinus, Patriarch of Constantinople, jurist
nomophylax of university of Constantinople, 200
opposition to Pope Alexander II, 463
John X Camaterus, Patriarch of Constantinople, refusal to crown Theodore I Lascaris, 295
relations with Pope Innocent III, 302 and n. 2
John XI Beccus, Patriarch of Constantinople, 338, 470, 471
John XIV Calecas, Patriarch of Constantinople

opposition to John Cantacuzenus, 357
regent for John V, 357
opposition to hesychasts, 357–8
John Alexander, Bulgarian tsar
territorial gains from Byzantium, 353, 360, 543
marriage of his sister to Stephen Dušan, 353, 537
troubles of reign, 543–4
John I Angelus of Thessaly, *sebastocrator*, 335–6, 337, 338, 339
John II Angelus of Thessaly, grandson of the above, 348, 349
John, metropolitan of Aquileia, 252
John I, king of Aragon, duke of Athens, 422
John VI, *Katholikos* of Armenia, 614, 616 n. 1
John Asen II, Bulgarian tsar, **526–8**
usurpation of throne by Boril, 299
civil war, 305, 526–7
relations with Latin Empire of Constantinople, 307, 309–11, 314, 398–9, 470, 527–8
relations with Theodore Ducas, 309, 310, 313, 527
invasion of Empire of Thessalonica, 310–11, 398, 527
relations with John Vatatzes, 311, 312, 313, 315, 398–9, 470, 528
attacks on Constantinople, 312, 528
relations with the Papacy, 311, 313, 528
death, 315
extent of his realm, 527
John Asen III, Bulgarian tsar, 338, 339, 535 n. 1, 536
John Axuch, Grand Domestic under John II and Manuel I, 220, 225, 226
John of Brienne, regent for Latin Empire of Constantinople
previous career, 310
crowned Emperor, 527–8
attack on Lampsacus, 311
defence of Constantinople (1235–6), 312, 398–9
death, 312
John of Cappadocia, officer under Justinian I, 44
John of Chaldia, general of Basil II, 181, 184
John Colonna, papal legate, detained by Theodore Ducas of Epirus, 305
John Curcuas, *see* Curcuas
John of Damascus, Church Father
parentage, 67
codification of Greek patristic theology, 58

John of Damascus (*cont.*)
De Fide Orthodoxa, 52
service under Umayyads, 67–8
at monastery of St Sabas, 58, 68
condemnation of Leo III, 70
works translated into Latin, 587
John the Deacon, chronicler, on history of Venice, 253, 269
John of Ephesus, historian, 480, 603 n. 1
John, duke of Gaeta, 136
John Geometres, on Nicephorus II, 151
John the Grammarian, *see* John VII Grammaticus
John of Gravina, prince of Achaea, 405–6, 419
John II, metropolitan of Kiev, and the anti-Pope Clement III, 464–5
John de Lusignan, regent of Lesser Armenia, 636 and n. 1
John, count of Nevers, 429
John, bishop of Nikiu, chronicler, on Kovrat, 483
John the Orphanotrophus, eunuch, brother of Michael IV, 196, 197–8
John Petritsi, Georgian philosopher, 625
John XVI Philagathus, bishop and anti-Pope, 184, 458
John the Presbyter and Seventh Oecumenical Council (787), 66
John of Procida, adventurer in service of Michael VIII, 339
John de la Roche, lord of Athens, 409–10
John the Silentiary, and Pope Stephen II's visit to Pepin III, 76
John Šišman, Bulgarian tsar
disintegration of Bulgaria, 544–5
capitulation to Turks, 545, 765
John Smbat III, Bagratid king of Armenia
and Basil II, 189, 203, 619
marriage to Romanus III's niece, 196, 619
death (1040), 197
John Stephen, Bulgarian tsar, 353, 543
John Stracimir, Bulgarian tsar at Vidin, 543–4, 545–6
John, Emperor (afterwards Despot) of Thessalonica, 313, 315, 317, 398
John Tornik (Tornicius, T'ornik Ch'orduaneli), Iberian general and monk, 177, 617
John, bishop of Trani, 202, 461
John de Urtubia, captain of Navarrese Company in Greece, 419–21
John, doge of Venice, 264
John Vladimir, prince of Dioclea
and Basil II, 182

taken prisoner by Samuel of Bulgaria, 185
John Vladislav, Bulgarian tsar, relations with Basil II, 188, 518
John, Bulgar ambassador to Rome, 113
John Asen, *see* Kalojan
Joscelin, count of Edessa, and John II, 224
Joseph I, Patriarch of Constantinople, opposition to union with Rome, 338
Joseph II, Patriarch of Constantinople, 381
Joseph, archbishop of Thessalonica, nephew of the abbot Plato, 89, 96
Joseph Bringas, *see* Bringas
Joseph, priest at marriage of Constantine VI and Theodote, 89, 94–5, 96
Juan Fernández de Heredia, grand master of the Hospitallers, 405 n. 1, 407
Juan-juan of Chinese, and Avars, 477 n. 1
Juansher, Georgian historian, 625 n. 1
Juansher, ruler of Caspian Albania, 605
Judaism, 2, 49
in Khazaria, 488, 491, 493 and nn. 1–5, 511
judicial system
reforms under the Palaeologi, 352–3
exemptions from feudal jurisdiction, 395, 397
in Lesser Armenia, 632
see also Achaea, High Court of; *Assizes of Romania*; *Customs of Barcelona*
Jugoslavia, 538
Julian the Apostate, Emperor
building of harbour at Constantinople, 9
comparison of Constantinople with Rome, 24
religious reaction under, 43, 431
on education, 46
and Caucasia, 595
Julius Caesar, 17
Junayd, Ottoman pretender, 768–9
Jundē Shāpūr, centre of learning in southwest Persia, 684
Justin I, Emperor, 21, 435, 476, 601, 604
Justin II, Emperor
restoration of harbour at Constantinople, 9
relations with Avars, 477–8
relations with Turks of Central Asia, 478 and n. 3, 479
war with Persia over Caucasia, 602
and Church, 604
Justinian I, Emperor
methods of warfare, 35

Justinian I (*cont.*)
frontier policy, 29, **474–7**, 567
defeat of Vandals (532), 25, 435
reconquest of western Empire, 21, 22,
28, 29, 41, 435–6, 476
Persian wars, 476, 601
treatment of Armenia, 601–2
and Huns of Crimea, 567
legislation and Roman law, 19, 65,
132, 133, 436
Novels, 23, 57, 133, 436–7
Codex, 133, 141
study of Latin in East, 23
as a theologian, 436–8
survival of paganism in his reign, 44, 65
condemnation of Nestorians, 56, 436–7
defence of the Church, 62
theory of Church and Emperor, 436–8,
446
attitude towards Rome and the Papacy,
435–8
building programme, 8, 37, 40
encouragement of silk industry, 41
position at end of reign, 10, 28
Justinian II, Emperor
relations with the Papacy, 31, 441
military campaigns, 32, 489, 606
and Leo III, 62 and n. 1, 67
coinage bearing image of Christ, 67
exile, 485
relations with Bulgarians, 485–6
loss of territory to Khazars, 486

Kafarbayyā, Arab frontier post on river
Pyramus in Cilicia, 706
Kaffa, Genoese colony on Black Sea, 365
Kaisariane, monastery near Athens, 409
Kakhaberidzes, Caucasian family, 626
n. 2
Kakhetia, district of Georgia, 602–3, 605,
608, 610 and n. 3, 618, 622, 624, 628
Kalamanos (Constantine), Hungarian in
service of Manuel I, 580, 583
see also Boris (Kalamanos)
Kalamata, town in Peloponnese, 391, 393,
399, 420
Latin barony, 394
Kalavryta, Latin barony in Peloponnese,
394, 403
Kalojan, Bulgarian tsar, **524–5**
ambitions, 275
title, 524–5, 529
recognition of papal supremacy, 248,
469, 524
and Bulgarian Church, 524–5, 528–9
relations with Baldwin I, 290, 292–3,
391, 525

attack on Latin Empire, 293, 294, 525
alliance with Theodore I Lascaris, 295
territorial gains, 524–5
death, 294, 299, 525
Kalonoros (Alā'īyya, Alaya, Alanya),
fort on south coast of Asia Minor,
746
Kaloyan, *see* Angelus, John
Kama, tributary of Volga, 484
Kamacha, *see* Camacha
Kamāl ad-Dīn, Arab historian
on Nicephorus II, 149
on capture of Antioch, 156 n. 2
Kamsarakans, Armenian dynasty, 597
and n. 1, 609, 619
al-Kanīsat as-Sawdā, Abbasid stronghold north of gulf of Alexandretta,
706
καπνικόν, hearth-tax, 93 and n. 2
Karakhanids (Karluks), Turkish dynasty
of Asia
in Central Asia, 736
conversion to Islam, 652, 737
established in Transoxania, 653, 737
defeated by Kara-Khitay, 655
Kara-Khitay, Mongol people from China
attack on Seljuq Empire, 655, 742
attacked by Jenghiz Khan, 660
Karalis, lake in Asia Minor, 224
Karaman, *see* Laranda
Karamania, Turkish state in Asia Minor,
and Karamans
establishment, 750–1, 756
expansion of, 753–4
conflict with Ottomans, 383, 554,
764–5, 768, 769, 770, 771
scribes from, 760
Karasi, Turkish principality in Mysia in
Asia Minor, 756, 760
Kara-Yülük 'Uthmān, Turkoman prince
of western Persia, 754
Karbeas, *see* Carbeas
Karguyah (Karois, Qarghuyah), gover-
nor of Aleppo, surrender to Byzan-
tium (969–70), 150, 722
Karluks, *see* Karakhanids
Karrāmī, Muslim sect, 658
Kars, town and district in Armenia, 609,
613–16, 620, 624, 715
Karthli, K'art'li, *see* Iberia
Karvuna, province of Bulgaria, *see*
Dobrudja
Karydi, Mt, between Megara and Thebes,
battle (1258), 400, 409
Karytaina, Latin barony and castle in
Peloponnese, 393–4, 405
Kasin, town in Cappadocia, 705

Kastamonu, Kastamuni, *see* Castra Comnenon
Katakolo, cape in Peloponnese, 390
Katakylas, general of Opsikion theme under Michael II, 100
Katholikos, catholicus, title of chief bishops of certain eastern churches of Armenia, 599 n. 1
　of Iberia, 601 and n. 1
　of Caspian Albania, 601 n. 1
　of Abasgia, 601 n. 1
Katvan, *see* Qatwān
Kavādh I, king of Persia, 601
Kavalla, town in Macedonia, 131
Kaykāwūs I, Seljuq sultan of Rūm
　relations with Theodore I Lascaris, 296
　acquisition of Sinope, 746
　expeditions in East, 746
　and *futuwwa*, 751
Kaykāwūs II, Seljuq sultan of Rūm
　alliance with Theodore II Lascaris, 322
　alliance with Michael VIII, 326
　in Constantinople, 749
Kaykhusraw I, Seljuq sultan of Rūm
　accession, 743
　relations with Baldwin I, 290
　marriage of his daughter to a Greek, 291
　alliance with Henry of Flanders against Nicaea, 295–6
　and Alexius III, 296
　seizure of Attalia on Mediterranean, 746
Kaykhusraw II, Seljuq sultan of Rūm
　treaty with Latin Empire, 314
　Mongol invasion, 315–16, 748–9
　alliance with John Vatatzes, 315
　dervish revolt against, 748
Kaykhusraw III, Seljuq sultan of Rūm, 750
Kayqubād I, Seljuq sultan of Rūm, 746–8, 758
Kayqubād III, Seljuq sultan of Rūm, 752, 758
Kaysarīya, Kayseri, *see* Caesarea
Keduktos, town in Thrace, battle (823), 100
κεφαλή, title of Byzantine governor of Mistra, 404
keramidion, sacred relic of Manbij, 721
keration, silver coin, 93
Kerch, straits of, 486
kermes, scarlet dye, 428
Khabur, tributary of Euphrates, defeat and death of Kīlij Arslan I, 742, 758
Khach'ēn in Armenia, princes of, 620

Khach'ik-Gagik (Xač'ik-Gagik), king of Vaspurakan, 613–14
Khafāja, Arab governor of Sicily, 729
Khakhambashî, Turkish name for Jewish chief rabbi, 774
Khālid al-Barmakī, wazīr of al-Manṣūr, 641
Khalīl ibn Aḥmad, Arabic grammarian, 687
Kharpūt (Ḥiṣn Ziyād), in Mesopotamia, 718, 723
Kharshana, *see* Charsianon Castron
Khazars, Khazaria, 486–8
　origin, 484 n. 1
　trade, 487, 495
　pressure on Onogur Bulgars in South Russia, 484
　and Justinian II, 485–6
　pressure on Crimea, 486, 512
　allies of Byzantium, 64, 486–7, 491–4, 496, 510, 511–12, 568, 605, 607, 699
　and building of Sarkel, 103, 492 and n. 2
　capture of Kiev by Varangians, 495
　under pressure from Kiev, 111
　ports on Black Sea, 189
　missionary work among, 111–12, 487 and n. 4, 488, 492–4
　and Judaism, 488, 491, 493 and nn. 1–5, 511
　and Islam, 488
　raids on Islamic Empire, 651, 707
　and Magyars, 503
　defeated by Svjatoslav (c. 965), 513, 515
　in Caucasia, 64, 605, 606–8, 646, 699
Khilāt (Khīlāṭ, Khlat', Ahlat), town in Armenia on Lake Van
　under Marwānids, 618
　taken by Seljuqs (1231), 748
Khozan, in Armenia, and birthplace of John Tzimisces, 158
Khurasan, district east of Caspian Sea
　province of Persia, 638
　support for al-Ma'mūn, 667
　under Tahirids, 645, 701
　under Ghaznavids, 653, 658, 737
　under Seljuqs, 653–4, 737
Khurramites of Azerbaijan and Djabal, revolt against al-Ma'mūn, 710
Khuzaima ibn-Khāzim, Abbasid viceroy in Caucasia, 608
Khʷārizm, province south of Aral Sea, 625, 655, 660
Khʷārizm Muḥammad, defeated by Jenghiz Khan, 748
Kičevo, town in northern Macedonia, 533
Kiersey, national assembly of Franks (754), 445

Kiev, town in Russia on Dnieper
  Scandinavian rulers of, 111
  and Svjatoslav, 159
  marriage alliance with rulers of Hungary, 233
  contact with West, 464
  captured by Varangians from Khazars, 495, 496 and n. 1
  captured by Oleg, 504 and n. 1
  hermitages of, 577
  see also Igor, Jaroslav, Oleg, Olga, Svjatoslav, Vladimir
Kĭlĭj Arslan I, Seljuq sultan of Rūm, 214, 740–2, 758
Kĭlĭj Arslan II, Seljuq sultan of Rūm
  relations with Manuel I, 236–7, 241, 743
  and Nūr-ad-Dīn, 236–7, 743
  relations with Frederick Barbarossa, 237, 246, 743
  and Danishmends, 742–3
Kĭlĭj Arslan IV, Seljuq sultan of Rūm, 749–50
al-Kindī, Arab philosopher and polyhistor, 683
King of Kings, title of kings of Armenia, 165, 166, 614, 617–18
Kipchak tribes of Central Asia
  mercenaries in army of Georgia, 623
  migration into eastern Europe, 653
  see also Cumans
Kirakos of Ganja, Armenian historian, 633 n. 1
Kirghiz, Turkish tribe in Central Asia, 736
Kirman, district in south of Persia, Seljuq rulers of, 653–4
Kjustendil in Bulgaria, *see* Velbužd
Klarjet'i, *see* Cholarzene
Kleidion (Ključ, Cimbalongus), pass near Strymon valley, battle (1014), 188, 518
κλεισοῦραι, military frontier districts under *kleisurarchai*, 102–3, 697
κλιβανοφόροι, armed cavalrymen under Nicephorus II, 154
klimata, themes around Black Sea, 103
Ključ, *see* Kleidion
Ključ on the Sana, town in Balkans, capture of king of Bosnia by Turks, 557
Klokotnica, on river Marica in Balkans, battle (1230), 310, 398, 527
knez (prince), Serbian title, 538
knights' fees, 393–4
Kocel, Slav prince of Pannonia, and Methodius, 124, 499
Kogovit, district in Armenia, 596, 608

κοιτωνίτης (chamberlain), 106 n. 1
Koja eli, Turkish name for Bithynian peninsula, 759–60
Kökturks (blue Turks), Empire in Mongolia and Central Asia, 736
Koloman, king of Hungary, 575
  Greek influence, 577
  allies with Alexius I, 580
Koloman I, Bulgarian tsar, 15, 3316, 535 n. 1
Konya, *see* Iconium
Kopaonik, mountain in Serbia, mining area, 532
Kopsis, fortress south of Balkan range, 542
Koran, 669–72, 674–6, 681–2, 689, 692
Korčula (Curzola), island off Dalmatian coast, 268
  naval battle (1298), 346
Korikos, port in Cilicia, 633
Koriun, Armenian hagiographer, 599 n. 2
Kormisoš, Bulgarian khan
  war with Constantine V, 74
  father-in-law of Sabinus, 75
  treaty with Constantine V, 97
Körtvélyes, village in Máramaros in Hungary, monastery near, 587
Kosača, Sandalj Hranić, Bosnian *voivode*, 556, 558
Kosača, Stephen Vukčić, herceg in southern Bosnia, 558
Kosara, wife of John Vladimir of Dioclea, 185
Köse Dagh, in eastern Anatolia, battle (1243), 749
Kossovo (Kossovopolje, Kosova), in Balkans
  battle (1389), 373–4, 550–1, 765
  battle (1448), 554, 772
Kotor, *see* Cattaro
Kotromanići, Bosnian dynasty, 556
Koundoura in Messenia in Peloponnese
  battle between Michael I of Epirus and Latins, 292, 390
Kovrat, ruler of Onogurs
  ally and friend of Heraclius, 483 and nn. 3 and 4, 568
  and Magyars, 503
Koyunhişār, *see* Baphaeum
Krasos in Phrygia, battle (804), 707
Kratovo, town in Balkans, 541
Kroja (Akche-ḥiṣār), town in Albania
  taken by Stephen Dušan, 538
  and revolt of Skanderbeg, 558, 770, 772
Krum, Bulgarian khan, 92, 94, 96, 97, 98, 114, 116, 490–1

Kruševac, town in Balkans, 553, 554, 555

Kūfa, town on Euphrates, 638
Kūfan school of grammarians, 688 n. 1

Kulayb, renegade Muslim, made *patricius* and *basilikos* of Antioch, 171

Kulin, ban of Bosnia, 546–7

Kumanovo, town in Balkans, 541

Kunkuratai, Mongol pretender, 750

Kunovica, mountain in Balkans, battle (1444), 383

Kurdistan, 748

Kurds, 619, 654, 710; see also Shaddādids

K'urercs (Λιθοπρόσωπον), defile in Syria, 170

Kurt, Old Bulgar ruler, 483 n. 4; see Kovrat

Kurya, Pecheneg prince, 162

Kusan, ninth-century Magyar prince, 569

Kūshān, Armenian in service of Constantine V
campaigns against Arabs, 703
return to Armenia, 705

Kütahiya, see Cotyaeum

Kutais, town in Abasgia, 624, 627
cathedral of, 615

Kutrigurs, tribe in region of Sea of Azov, 475, 476, 477

Kvirike III the Great, king of Kakhetia, 622

Kyminas, in Bithynia in Asia Minor, and Michael Maleinus, 155

Kyparissia, see Arcadia

Kyrion, see Cyrion

labarum, 17

Lacedaemonia, in Peloponnese, 390
castle of La Crémonie, 393
Latin See of, 396

Lachanodracon, Michael, *strategus* of Thracesion theme in eighth century, 80–1, 705–6

Laconians, see Tzakones

La Crémonie, see Lacedaemonia

Ladislas, St, king of Hungary, 576, 579–80, 581

Ladislas II, king of Hungary, brother of Géza II, 582, 583

Ladislas V, king of Hungary, recommended to learn Greek, 586

Ladislas, king of Naples
and duchy of Athens, 423
claim to throne of Hungary, 556

Lagosta (Lastova), island off Dalmatian coast, 268

Laḥsā, see Bahrain

Lajazzo, see Ayas

Lakape (Laqabin), town between Melitene and Samosata, birthplace of Romanus Lecapenus, 137 n. 1, 139

Lala Shāhīn, general under Murād I, 762–3

La Mandria, town in north-west Peloponnese, 406

Lambron, near Tarsus in Cilicia
princes of, 628, 632–3
see also Het'umids

Lamia (Zeitounion), town in Thessaly
taken by Theodore Ducas of Epirus, 306
parliament of Latin barons, 391
part of duchy of Athens, 410, 413
in duchy of Neopatras, 414

Lampsacus, town in Asia Minor on Hellespont
celebration of Theodore II Lascaris' wedding, 311
attacked by John of Brienne, 311
Michael VIII at, 401

Lancia, Nicholas, vicar-general of Catalan Company, 416

landowners
in Asia Minor, see under Asia Minor
in Egypt, 38, 39
in Syria, 39
in Balkans, 39
in West, 40
in Bulgaria, 530
Slav, 504
land tenure under Islam, 649–50, 656, 677
as collectors of taxes, 38, 341
represented by senate, 12
control over peasants, 61
taxation of, 93 n. 2
and *pronoia*, 219, 290
restrained under Romanus I, 141–2, 195
and Constantine VII, 145
and Nicephorus II, 153–4
and John Tzimisces, 172–4
and Basil II, 173, 182–4, 190, 194, 195, 212
under Macedonian Emperors, 194
concession to, under Romanus III, 195
alienated by Michael VII, 211
called on for levies of troops by Alexius I, 218
under Manuel I, 239, 241
alienated by Andronicus I, 244
unchecked by Isaac II, 245
under Latin Empire, 290, 291
under Empire of Nicaea, 319–20
under the Palaeologi, 341, 358–9
expropriated by Zealots, 358

land-tax, 343
  akrostichon, crustica, 395, 397, 408
  ius terragii, 414
  under Abbasids, 644
Landulph, prince of Benevento and
  Capua, 136
Langobardia, north Italian region conquered by Lombards, 250
Laodicea, port in Syria opposite Cyprus,
  attacked by Byzantine fleet (910),
  716
Laodicea Katakekaumene (Kekaumene),
  town in Asia Minor, Byzantine
  troops defeated by Arabs (770), 74,
  705
Lapara-Lycandus in Cilicia, battle (976),
  176
Laqabin, *see* Lakape
Laranda (Karaman), town in south of
  Asia Minor
  captured by Leo II of Lesser Armenia
  (1211), 631
  capital of Karamania, q.v., 753
Larissa, town in Thessaly
  refuge of Alexius III, 292
  taken by Michael I of Epirus, 299–300
  held by Theodore Ducas, 306
  cultivation of figs and vines, 428
  strategus of, 629
Larissa of Argos, the, 410
Larmena, castle in Euboea, seized by
  Alfonso Fadrique, 412–13
Lascaris family
  desertion to Latins, 308
  see also Constantine (XI), Theodore I,
  Theodore II, Eudocia
latifundia, 39
Latin Church in Greece and the islands,
  394–5, 396–8, 406, 408–9, 426
Latin Empire of Constantinople, **287–330**
  election of Emperor, 285, 287–8
  partition of Byzantine Empire, 288–9
  loss of Asia Minor, 308, 309
  extent of Empire in 1225, 309
  decline, 317–18, 323, 527–8
  loss of Constantinople to Michael VIII,
  325–8
  see also Baldwin I, Henry of Flanders,
  Peter of Courtenay, Yolanda, Robert
  of Courtenay, John of Brienne, Baldwin II
Latin language
  official use in Eastern Empire, 23
  despised by Greeks, 452
  and theological terminology, 87, 466
  translations of Greek Church Fathers,
  587

official language in Lesser Armenia,
  633
  translations into Arabic, 672 n. 1; into
  Slavonic, 464
Latin Patriarchs, *see under* Constantinople *and* Antioch
Latins
  and First Crusade, 214–16
  principalities in east Mediterranean
  region, 215, 216, 221, 223, 234–5,
  236, 467
  under the Comneni, 226, 239, 240,
  388
  and Second Crusade, 227
  jealousy of Byzantium, 246
  and Third Crusade, 246–7
  and Fourth Crusade, **276–88**
  soldiers serving under Michael I of
  Epirus, 299
  mercenaries in Byzantine army of
  Nicaea, 320, 322, 324
  principalities in Greece and the Aegean,
  373, 376, 380, **388–430**; *see also*
  William of Villehardouin
  attacked by Turks, 354–5, 406, 407,
  423–4
Latros, Mt, in western Asia Minor,
  monasteries on, 709
Laura (Lavra), monastic settlement near
  Jerusalem, 58
Lavra, monastic house of St Athanasius
  on Mt Athos, 155
law, Byzantine, 65, 133
  in Serbia, 522, 539
  influence on Muslim law, 675
  faculty of law in university of Constantinople, 200
law, Muslim, 663, 665–6, 673–6, 691–2,
  733–4, 764
law, Roman, 65, 133, 436, 674 and n. 2,
  675
law, Serbian, 539, 540
law, Talmudic, 675 and n. 3
Lazar, Serbian prince, 541–2, 549, 550,
  764
  at battle of Kossovo, 374, 550–1, 765
Lazarus, monk and icon-painter, 104
Lazarus of P'arpi, Armenian historian,
  599 n. 2
Lazi, Caucasian people, and Byzantine
  frontier, 474, 567
Lazica (Colchis, Egrisi), part of Georgia,
  593–4, 600–3, 605–7, 610
  Church in, 604
lead mining, 532, 548
league of Christian powers against
  Turkish pirates, 355, 368

Lebanon, mountain range, 171
Lecapenid family, 143–4, 148; *and see* Romanus I Lecapenus
Lecapenus, Constantine
  revolt against Romanus I, 143
  unpopularity, 144
Lecapenus, Stephen
  revolt against Romanus I, 143
  unpopularity, 144
Lechena, town in north-west Peloponnese, 406
Leichudes, *see* Constantine III Leichudes, Patriarch
Lembos, monastery of, rebuilt by John Vatatzes, 319
Lemnos, island in the Aegean
  sacked by Arabs (903), 716
  under Latin rule, 426
  judicial system under the Palaeologi, 353
Leo I, Emperor, and Gothic troops, 27
Leo III the Isaurian (or North Syrian), Emperor, **612–7**
  iconoclastic policy, 61–2, 65–72, 99, 443
  legal reforms, 61, 62, 65; see also *Ecloga*
  taxation, 64–5, 442, 444
  repulse of Arab attacks, 62–4, 698–9
  defence of Constantinople, 10, 63, 442, 698
  relations with Khazars, 64, 487
  reorganisation of themes, 64
  relations with the Papacy and West, 65, 68–72, 442–4
  imitated by Leo V, 98
Leo IV the Khazar, Emperor, **81–2**
  proposed marriage to Pepin III's daughter, 77
  popularity, 81–2
  iconoclastic policy, 81
  interest in Italy, 82
  campaigns against Arabs, 82, 705
  asylum given to Telerig, 82
Leo V the Armenian, Emperor, **98–100**
  and iconoclasm, 68, 98–9, 101, 103
  treaty with Louis the Pious, 97 n. 1
  general of Anatolikon theme under Michael I, 98, 709
  civil war in Asia Minor, 100, 709
  relations with Bulgaria, 98, 490–1, 709
  and Ashot I of Iberia, 610
  murder, 99–100, 102, 105, 709
Leo VI the Wise, Emperor, **125–34**
  birth (866), 117
  accession, 121, 125

marriages, 127 and n. 2, 130–2, 137–8, 455–6
  and council of 879–80, 123
  and union with Roman Church, 126, 127 and n. 1
  and Nicholas Mysticus, 127
  and Magyars, 128, 503, 569
  and peasant soldiers, 137
  relations with Basil I, 125
  relations with Photius, 125–7
  relations with Armenia, 715, 717
  relations with Arabs of North Africa and Sicily, 729
  and Russian attack on Constantinople, 130 n. 4, 505 n. 1, 715
  war with Bulgaria, 127–9, 134, 502–3, 505, 569, 715–16
  naval warfare against Arabs, 129–30, 146, 147, 716–17
  legislative work, 127, **132–4**, 141–2
  Novels, 133–4
  Basilica, 133
  Strategicon, 35
  Tactica, 141
  and funeral of Michael III, 116, 125
  funeral oration on Basil I, 116, 126
  death, 134
Leo I the Great, Pope, and Council of Chalcedon, 18, 20–1, 434
Leo III, Pope
  appealed to by Studites, 95
  relations with Charlemagne, 90, 447–9
  relations with Greek Church, 96
Leo IX, Pope, 202, 459–63
Leo II, king of Abasgia, 610
Leo I of Lesser Armenia, 223, 629–30
Leo II the Great of Lesser Armenia, 631–3
  relations with Theodore I Lascaris, 320 and n. 1
Leo III of Lesser Armenia, 634–5
Leo IV of Lesser Armenia, 634, 635 and n. 2
Leo V of Lesser Armenia, 635–6
Leo VI of Lesser Armenia, 636–7
Leo, archbishop of Ochrida, and Michael Cerularius, 202, 461
Leo, cardinal, papal legate
  consecration of Primate of Bulgaria, 248, 524
  coronation of Kalojan, 524
Leo Choerosphactes, *see* Choerosphactes
Leo the Deacon, historian
  on Nicephorus II, 152 and n. 2, 153
  on siege of Tarsus (965), 157 n. 1
  on Theodora, wife of John I, 159
  on Svjatoslav, 159 and n. 2

Leo the Deacon (*cont.*)
  on John Tzimisces' eastern campaigns, 164, 165, 167–9, 171
  on John Tzimisces' death, 172–3, 174, 175
Leo the *drungarius*, under John Tzimisces, 160 n. 2, 161 and n. 1
Leo the Philosopher or the Mathematician and al-Ma'mūn, 734–5
Leo Phocas, *see* Phocas
Leo of Tripoli, Byzantine renegade, Muslim admiral, 717, 734
  and capture of Thessalonica (904), 129, 716
  battle off Chios (912), 130, 716
Leo, brother of the eunuch Aetius, 90, 91
Leontarion, town in Peloponnese, taken by Turks (1395), 375
Leonti Mroveli, *see* Leontius of Ruisi
Leontini, town in Sicily
  taken by Arabs (846–7), 728
  retaken by Byzantines, 152
Leontius, sixth-century monk, 58
Leontius (Ļevond), Armenian historian, 616 n. 1
Leontius of Ruisi (Leonti Mroveli), Georgian historian, 625 n. 1
Lesbos, Aegean island
  used as place of exile, 91
  under Latins, 289, 355
  promised by John V to Francesco Gattilusio, 367
Lesser (Little, Cilician) Armenia, **628–37**, 742
  under Rubenids, 629–33, 738
  occupied by Byzantines, 223, 630
  under Het'umids, 631, 633–6
  under Lusignan dynasty, 636–7
  under Mamluks, 637
  under Ottomans, 637
  political system, 632–3
  relations with Byzantium, 223, 234, 628–30, 636
  relations with the Papacy, 629, 632, 635–7
  relations with Western powers, 632–7
  relations with Latins in the East, 629–30, 633–4
  relations with Antioch, 628–31, 633
  relations with Seljuqs, 628–31, 635, 746–7
  relations with Muslims of Egypt, 631, 633–7
  relations with Mongols, 633–5
Leucas (Santa Maura), Ionian island
  taken by Walter II of Brienne, 416

Levedia, region probably between Don and Dnieper, and Magyars, 569
Ļevond, *see* Leontius
Levtro, *see* Beaufort
Levunium, Mt, in Balkans, battle (1091), 214
Libanius, teacher of rhetoric, 50
Liber Diurnus, 441
Liber Pontificalis, 440, 442
libraries
  in Hungary, 575, 592
  in Armenia, 616
Libri Carolini, attributed to Alcuin, 87
Liburnia (Croatia, q.v.)
  lost to Franks (810), 92
  returned to Byzantium (812), 96
Libya, in North Africa, invasion by Bedouin tribes, 651
Licario, *megas dux* under Michael VIII, naval operations in Aegean, 337, 410
Liconia, town in Greece, 413, 417
Life of Basil the Younger, 140 and n. 1, 570–1
Life of St Abo of Tiflis, 487 n. 4, 493 n. 3
Life of St Emeric, 575
Life of St Gerard, 573
Life of St Michael Maleinus by Theophanes, 144
Life of St Nicephorus, bishop of Miletus, 153 n. 1
Life of St Stephen, 575
Lim, river in Balkans, 501, 519
limes, 475, 481
limitanei, frontier troops, 34, 36
Lipari islands, off north coast of Sicily, naval battle (880), 121
Liparit IV, duke of T'rialet'i, supporter of Bagrat IV of Georgia, 621–2
Liparitids, branch of Mamikonids in Iberia, 613, 622–3; *see also* Orbelis
Lists of Apostles and Disciples, 456
literature
  studied at university of Constantinople, 200
  encouraged by John Vatatzes, 321
  translations from Greek into Slavonic, 502
  Persian, 647, 668, 683, 747
  Arabic, 667–8, 679, 683, 685–7
  Serbian, 522, 532, 545
  Turkish, 652, 747, 773
  Bulgarian, 501–2, 544–5
  Caucasian, 594
  Armenian, 55, 599 and n. 2, 616 and n. 1, 625, 633 and n. 1
  Georgian, 625 and n. 1
Λιθοπρόσωπον, *see* K'urercs

Lithosoria, battle (773), 75
Little Armenia, *see* Lesser Armenia
liturgy
  Slavonic, 123–5, 126, 455, 464, 497, 499, 500, 501
  in Moravia, 497 n. 1
Liutprand, Lombard king
  relations with Popes, 70, 75, 444
  connection with Venice, 253–4
  campaigns in Italy, 444
Liutprand, bishop of Cremona, ambassador in Constantinople
  Antapodosis, 140
  and revolt of Romanus I's sons, 143
  and Basil the *parakoimomenos*, 148 n. 1
  date of arrival in Constantinople, 150, 151 n. 1, 153
  attitude to Bulgars, 151 n. 1
  and Nicephorus II, 153 and n. 2, 457–8
  and Symeon the *protoasecretis*, 153 n. 3
  and marriage of Otto II, 163
  on Symeon of Bulgaria, 502
Livadia, town in Attica
  and Catalan Company, 411, 414
  taken by Navarrese Company, 420 n. 1, 421
  under the Acciajuoli, 421, 423
Livadostro, Theban port on gulf of Corinth, 415
livestock
  regulation on sales of, 93
  included in system of *pronoia*, 240
  breeding encouraged by John Vatatzes, 320
  in Caucasia, 615
  see also horses
logothete, *logothetes*, official, 90, 211, 706
  in Bulgaria, 529, 543
  in Rumania, 562
  see also Grand Logothete
Logothete of the Drome, 105, 115, 127 n. 2, 157 n. 1
  τοῦ γενικοῦ, 707
Loidoriki, town in Greece, 413, 417
Lombard League, 231
Lombards
  in Italy, 29, 31, 250, 251, 252, 253, 438–9, 441, 443, 444–5, 477
  relations with Byzantium, 88
  Louis the Pious entitled king of the Lombards, 101
  war with Gepids, 477–8
  in Hungary, 570
  defeated by Franks, 77, 88, 445, 446
  attacks on Arabs in Italy, 730
  revolt against Basil II, 190
  alliance with Normans in Italy, 202

in Greece under Latin Empire, 298, 299–300, 391, 392, 429
London
  visit of Baldwin II, 317
  visit of Manuel II Palaeologus, 377
Longobardia, Byzantine theme of, in South Italy, 121, 136
Long Plain, *see* Câmpulungu
Lord Chamberlain, 33
Lori (Tashir) in Caucasia, Bagratid dynasty of, 610 n. 3, 613, 617, 619–20, 622
  acquired by Georgia, 624
  under Zachariads, 620, 626 n. 2
Lorraine (Lotharingia), and movement for reform of Western Church, 459–60
Lorsch, see *Annals of Lorsch*
Lothair I, Western Emperor, and Venice, 262
Lothair II, and Pope Nicholas I, 450
Lothair III, Western Emperor, and John II, 222, 224, 227
Louis I the Pious, Western Emperor
  treaty with Leo V, 97 n. 1
  and negotiations between Michael II and Rome, 101–2
  failure to help Theophilus against Arabs, 103
  titles, 449
Louis II, Western Emperor
  use of imperial title, 448
  and council of 867, 114
  and meeting of German bishops at Regensburg, 124
  and Pope Nicholas I, 450, 453
  relations with Bulgaria, 496–7
  and capture of Bari from Arabs, 729
Louis VII, king of France
  and Second Crusade, 227
  desire for crusade against Constantinople, 228
  withdrawal from alliance against Frederick Barbarossa, 230
Louis IX, king of France, 314, 317, 335, 409, 633
Louis the German, *see* Louis II, German Emperor
Louis I the Great, king of Hungary
  appealed to by John V, 370 and n. 1, 590
  and province of Vidin, 544
  and Bosnia, 549
  and Wallachia and Moldavia, 561
Louis, count of Blois
  and Fourth Crusade, 276
  and invasion of Asia Minor, 290
  killed in battle (1205), 293

Louis of Evreux, brother of Charles II of Navarre, and Navarrese Company, 419

Louis, brother of William of Champlitte, 392

Loulon (Lu'lu'a), at northern entrance of Cilician Gates, 710, 713, 714, 735

Loveč, town in Balkans, siege of (1187), 523

Lüleburgaz, *see* Arcadiopolis

Lu'lu', chamberlain of Aleppo, and deposition of Hamdanids, 725

Lu'lu'a, *see* Loulon

Lusignan family
in Cyprus from 1192, 247, 637
rulers of Lesser Armenia, 635–7

Lycandus, theme of, 142, 717

Lycaonia, district in Asia Minor, 96, 750

Lyons, councils of, *see* councils and synods

Macarius, monk, and first Serbian printing press, 559

Macedonia
ancient diocese, 71
centre of Slavo-Byzantine culture, 502
Slav penetration, 32, 480–1, 489
Avar attacks, 480
and Bulgarians, 97, 99, 116, 310, 322, 498, 501, 507, 526–7
and revolt of Comitopuli, 185, 517–18
Magyar attacks, 571
support for Leo Tornicius, 203
laid waste by Pechenegs and Uzes (1064), 208
invaded by Robert Guiscard, 213
Bogomils in, 242, 512–13
Normans expelled by Isaac II, 245
occupation by Kalojan, 524–5
rise of small principalities, 248, 299, 526, 541
under Latin Empire, 289, 306
under John Vatatzes, 317, 535
invaded by Michael II of Epirus, 322–3, 535
invaded by Serbia, 339, 345, 533, 537–8
invaded by John I of Thessaly, 339
invaded by Catalan Company, 411
and revolt of Andronicus III, 350
under Serbian domination, 353–4, 537–8
loss of independence to Turks, 371, 542, 769
and Vlachs, 560

Macedonia, theme of, 92, 116, 121

Macedonian Emperors, 116–92, 193–205
legitimist principle, 14, 199
and Church, 60

and *Basilica*, 65
debt to Amorian Emperors, 100, 105
return to direct line in 976, 175
contrast between Basil II and Constantine VIII, 193
Theodora last of line, 204–5
general review, 194, 331, 720

Macrolivada, town in Thrace on Great Fence, 98, 491

Mačva, district to south of Danube and Sava
ruled by Rostislav, 535
under Hungary, 540
under Stephen Lazarević, 551, 552

al-Madā'in, Arab name of Ctesiphon, 640

Madīnat as-Salām, official name of Baghdad, 640

madrasas, see under Islam

Madytus, town in Thrace on Hellespont, 206

Maeotis, *see* Azov, Sea of

Maghnisa, *see* Magnesia

Maghrib Arabs of Africa, 168, 732

Magians, 682

magister militum
title of Byzantine governor of Venice, 250–2, 253–4
see also Master of Soldiers

magister militum orientis, 51

magister officiorum, μάγιστρος τῶν θείων ὀφφικίων, 127 n. 2; *see also* Master of Offices

Magnesia (Maghnisa, Manisa), town in western Asia Minor
and John Vatatzes, 321 n. 1
held against Turks, 347
attacked by Catalan Company, 347
under Turkish rule, 756, 771–2

Magyars, 566–9
origins, 566
early history, 503, 567–9
used by Byzantium against Bulgaria, 128, 503, 507, 569
migration to Hungary (q.v.), 128 503, 504, 569
attacks on Thrace, 146, 509
and Khazars, 492 n. 2, 503
and Pechenegs, 510, 569
and Russians, 514
relations with Germany, 515
and Onogurs, 566–7
and Huns, 566–8
and Bulgarians, 568–9
migrations, 566–9
contact with Byzantine Christianity, 567–8
and Greek Church in Hungary, 587

Magyars (*cont.*)
    contact with Byzantine culture, 568, 569–70
    trade, 568
al-Mahdī, Abbasid Caliph of Baghdad, 694
    father of Hārūn ar-Rashīd, 83
    and Caucasia, 608
    wars against Byzantium, 704–6
al-Mahdī, Fatimid Caliph, operations in South Italy, 730
Mahiot de Coquerel, leader of Navarrese Company, 419–20
Maḥmūd of Ghazna, and orthodox revival in Islam, 658 and n. 1
maiestas, 14 n. 1, 45
Maina, Old Maina, fortress in south of Peloponnese
    ceded to Michael VIII by Franks, 332, 401–2, 403
    Latin See of, 396
    castle of Old Maina (le Grand Magne), 399–400
Makó, district in Hungary, 585
Makry-Plagi, pass in Peloponnese, battle (1264), 333
Malagina, town in Bithynia in Asia Minor, 84, 707, 712
Malakopia, town in Cappadocia in Asia Minor, near site of battle (863), 111 n. 1
Malamocco, part of Venice, 254–5, 256, 259–60, 261, 262
    bishopric of, 264
Malaṭiya, Malatya, *see* Melitene
Malea, cape in Peloponnese, 289
Maleini, Byzantine family, 144 n. 1, 176
Maleinus, Eustathius, landowner under Basil II, 173, 176, 182–3
Maleinus, Michael, monk of Kyminas in Bithynia
    Life of St Michael Maleinus by Theophanes, 144
    uncle of Nicephorus II, 155
Malīḥ al-Armanī, *see* Mleh
Malik Dānishmend Aḥmed Ghāzī, Turkish leader in Asia Minor, 740, 741 and n. 1
Malīk (or Amīr) Ghāzī Gümüshtigin, son of the above, 741 n. 1
Mālik ibn Anas, Muslim jurist, 673, 676
Malik-Shāh, Seljuq sultan, 624, 653, 740
    relations with Alexius I, 214
    attack on Georgia, 622
Malik-Shāh, Seljuq of Rūm, 216, 742
Malmsey wine, 428
Malta, taken by Arabs (870), 729
Malta and Gozo, counts of, 413, 427

Maltepe, *see* Pelecanum
Mamikonean, Mamikonian, *see* Mamikonids
Mamikonids (Mamikonean, Mamikonian), Armenian dynasty, 596, 597 and n. 1, 603, 606–7, 609, 612, 615, 620
Mamistra, *see* Mopsuestia
Mamlān of Azerbaijan, and David of Tao, 618
Mamluks
    Turkish slaves of Muslims, 651–2
    in power in Egypt, 633, 635, 654, 750–1, 753
    victories over Mongols, 634, 750
    in Syria, 634–5, 654
    conquest of Cilicia (Lesser Armenia), 635–7
al-Ma'mūn, Abbasid Caliph of Baghdad
    religious policy, 642, 671
    alliance with Thomas the Slavonian, 100, 709
    civil war with al-Amīn, 645, 667, 701, 704, 708
    wars with Byzantium, 704, 709–10
    and Leo the Philosopher, 734–5
Manasses, Constantine, chronicler, 545
Manazkert, *see* Manzikert
Manbij, *see* Hierapolis
Mancaphas, Theodore, landowner in Asia Minor, resistance to Latin Empire, 291, 295
μανδήλιον, *mandylion*, miraculous picture of Christ at Edessa, 141, 143, 149, 718
Manes, general of Cibyrraeot theme under Leo III, 71
Manfred, king of Sicily
    relations with Michael II of Epirus, 323, 324–5, 326, 401
    and Baldwin II, 328
    and the Papacy, 334, 402
Manfred, duke of Athens, 412
manglavites, office, 120
Maniaces, George, general
    and Constantine IX, 194
    under Romanus III, 195–6
    capture of Edessa, 140, 196, 725–6
    Sicilian campaign, 197, 731
    catepan and magister of Italian provinces, 198, 201
    rebellion against Constantine IX, 201–2, 203
    Psellus on, 202
Manicaites, George, chancellor of John V, 590
Manicheans and Manichaeism, 43, 65, 513, 642, 668–70, 682

Manisa, *see* Magnesia

Manjūtakīn, Fatimid commander in time of Basil II, 182

Man'shi, language of Voguls of Siberia, 566

al-Manṣūr, Abbasid Caliph of Baghdad, 608, **640–1**, 665, 699–700, **704–5**

al-Manṣūr, Fatimid Caliph, 730

Mantua, synod of (827), 262

Manuel I Comnenus, Emperor, **225–43**
character and family connections, 226
marriage to Bertha of Sulzbach, 222, 224, 226, 227, 228
Mary of Antioch, second wife, 226, 235
accession, 225–6
friendly attitude to Latins, 226, 235, 238, 239, 240–1, 243
foreign policy, 226–39, 243, 581
in Asia Minor, 226–7, 234–9, 240, 243, 630, 743
on campaign in Asia Minor and Syria with John II, 224
and Second Crusade, 227–8
negotiations with Roger II of Sicily, 227
German alliance, 227, 228, 233
plans for Italy, 227, 228
in Syria, 231, 234–5, 243, 630
Norman attack on Corfu and Greece, 227–8
extension of Venice's trading privileges, 228
Cuman attack, 228
treaty of Constance (1153), 228–9
attempt on South Italy, 229–30, 233, 234, 243
relations with Frederick Barbarossa, 228–32, 238
relations with Hungary, 228, 229–30, 231, 233–4, 239, 581–4, 586
relations with Sicily, 230, 231, 232, 234, 239
relations with the Papacy, 228–30, 231, 232, 239, 242–3, 468
relations with France, 230, 232
relations with Italian cities, 229, 232–3, 239, 240
relations with kings of Jerusalem, 234–5, 236, 238
relations with Iconium, 236–8
relations with Serbia, 233, 521, 581
state of armed forces, 239
economic policy, 239–40
ownership of property and grants in *pronoia*, 239–41
interest in Church and theology, 241–3

trials of heretics, 242
desire for union of Churches, 230, 242–3
death and succession, 243–4

Manuel II Palaeologus, Emperor, **371–80**
childhood, 368
visit to Hungary with John V, 590
ruler of Thessalonica, 371–2, 373
co-Emperor with John V, 372–3
struggle for power with John VII, 374–5
vassal of Ottoman Sultan, 374–5
appeal to West for help, 376–7, 471
and Ottoman dynastic struggles, 378
and Ottoman pretenders, 768–9
defence of Peloponnese, 378–9
retirement as monk Matthew, 380

Manuel I Sarantenus, Patriarch of Constantinople in Nicaea, 307, 532

Manuel, prince of the Mamikonids, 597

Manuel, Despot of Thessalonica, 309–11, 313–16, 398

Manuel, commander of cavalry under Nicephorus II, *see* Phocas, Manuel

Manuel, *patricius*, in service of Arabs and of Byzantines, 710–11

manuscripts, 81, 757
of Scylitzes, 572
of Maximus the Confessor and John of Damascus, 587
in the Corvina library, 592
in pagan temple near Constantinople, 734
of Dioscorides and Orosius, 735

Manzikert (Manazkert, Melazgerd), town in Armenia, north of lake Van
battle (1071), 209, 210, 463, 620, 740
Qaysids of, 609
amirs of, 613
acquired by Marwānids, 618

Mar Babai, Syriac ascetic, 689 n. 4

Marano, synod of (591), 252

Marash, Mar'ash, *see* Germanicea

Marcellus, *magister militum* of Venice, 253–4

Marcian, Emperor
and Council of Chalcedon, 20
and persecution of Armenian Christians, 600

Marcus Aurelius, Emperor, 26

Mardasān, Muslim general, defeated in Bithynia under Leo III, 63

Margaret of Soissons, wife of Leo VI of Lesser Armenia, 637

Margaret (Maria), daughter of Béla III, wife of Isaac II and of Boniface of Montferrat, 245, 287, 292, 585

Margaret (Maria) (*cont.*)
  regent for her son Demetrius in Thessalonica, 298, 306
  flight to Hungary, 308
Margaret, St, daughter of Béla IV of Hungary, 589
Margaret, second daughter of William of Villehardouin, 406
Maria Argyrou, wife of John Urseolo, 187, 191
Maria of Bourbon, wife of Robert of Taranto, claim to principality of Achaea, 406–7
Maria Lecapena, wife of Peter of Bulgaria, 139, 508–9
Maria Palaeologina, niece of Michael VIII, second wife of Constantine Tich, wife of Ivajlo, 336, 338, 536
Maria of Paphlagonia, first wife of Constantine VI, 89
Maria, wife of Boniface of Montferrat, *see* Margaret (Maria)
Maria, illegitimate daughter of John Asen II, wife of Manuel, Despot of Thessalonica, 309
Maria, daughter of John of Brienne, 310
Maria, niece of Manuel I, wife of Stephen IV of Hungary, 582
Maria, daughter of Theodore I Lascaris, wife of Béla IV of Hungary, 589
Maria, daughter of Theodore II Lascaris, wife of Nicephorus I of Epirus, 318–19, 322
Marica, river in Balkans, 316, 322, 360, 398, 554
  battle (1371), 371, 542, 545 n. 1, 763
Marinus I, Pope, 455
  papal legate during Photian controversy, 453, 454
Marj al Usquf, in southern Cappadocia in Asia Minor, probable site of battle (863), 111 n. 1
Mark the Deacon, author of life of St Porphyry, 55
Mark Eugenicus, metropolitan of Ephesus, opposition to union with Rome, 381, 471
mark, unit of coinage in West, 277, 278, 287
Marko, son of Vukašin, vassal of Turks, 542
Marmora, Sea of
  and site of Constantinople, 6, 7, 8, 9
  and Alexius I's campaigns against Seljuqs, 214, 216
  Norman fleet in, 245
  Arab fleet in, 31, 717
  Venetian trade in, 271

coastal cities in Thrace under Andronicus IV, 373; under Manuel II, 378
  reached by Ottoman Turks, 759–60
Maros, river in Hungary, 572
Marosvár, town in Hungary, monastery at, 573–4
Martha, daughter of Bagrat IV of Georgia, *see* Mary the Alan
Martin I, Pope, and Constans II, 31, 440–1, 442
Martin IV, Pope, 339, 344
Martin, abbot of Pairis, and Fourth Crusade, 276
Martin, Bulgar ambassador to Rome, 113
Martyropolis (Mayyāfāriqīn), town in Mesopotamia
  battle (863), 110–11, 713
  taken by Curcuas, 140, 718
  John Tzimisces' campaigns, 156 n. 1, 164, 167, 723
  under Marwānids, 618
Marulla (Maria), wife of Alfonso Fadrique, 412–13
Marushidze, John, viceroy of Iberia, 617–18
Marwān II, Umayyad Caliph, and Constantine V's Arab campaigns, 73
Marwān ibn-Muḥammad, leader of Arab attack on Khazars, 607
Marwānids, Muslim dynasty, 618, 725
Mary the Alan, wife of Michael VII and Nicephorus III, 211, 622 and n. 1
Mary of Antioch, daughter of Constance of Antioch, second wife of Manuel I, 226, 235, 243–4, 245, 584
Mary, wife of George I of Georgia, 621
Mary, daughter of the Sebastocrator Isaac Comnenus, 229
Mary, daughter of Manuel I
  proposals for her marriage, 230–2, 234, 239, 582, 583
  marriage to Renier of Montferrat, 232, 238
  executed by Andronicus I, 244
Mashtots', *see* Mesrop
Maslama, Arab general, campaigns against Leo III, 62–4, 697, 698
Massalian heresy, 220, 242
Maṣṣīṣa, *see* Mopsuestia
Master of Offices, 33, 36; see also *magister officiorum*
Master of Soldiers, 34, 36; see also *magister militum*
Mas'ūd I, Seljuq ruler of Rūm, 226, 742
Mas'ūd II, Seljuq ruler of Rūm, 750, 752
Mas'ūdī, Arab historian, and reign of Michael III, 115

Matagrifon, Latin barony and castle in Arcadia, 393, 405

Matapan, cape in south of Peloponnese, 399

mathematics
studied at university of Constantinople, 200
studied by Arabs, 672, 679 n. 2, 684–5, 695 n. 1

Matilda of Hainault, princess of Achaea, wife of Guy II de la Roche, 405, 410

Matteo de Peralta, vicar-general of the duchies of Athens and Neopatras, 418

Matthew, Latin Patriarch of Constantinople, 307

Matthew Corvinus, king of Hungary, son of Hunyadi
defence against Turks, 559–60
relations with Moldavia, 563
encouragement of learning, 592

Matthew of Edessa, Armenian chronicler, 633 n. 1
on John Tzimisces' eastern campaigns, 164–8, 170, 723
on John Tzimisces' death, 172

Matthew of Moncada, vicar-general of duchies of Athens and Neopatras, 417

Matthew of Montona, Venetian castellan of Athens, 423

Matthew, monastic name of Manuel II Palaeologus, 380

Māturīdī school of Sunnī theology, 659

Maurice, Emperor
building of new Praetorium, 9
use of mercenaries, 35
events of reign, 29
relations with Pope Gregory the Great, 439
policy on northern frontier, 480, 481 and nn. 1 and 3
and Caucasia, 603–4
death, 40

Maurice, eighth-century *dux* of Venice, his family, 255–6, 257, 261

Mauropous, John, archbishop of Euchaïta in Asia Minor, poet, scholar and monk, 200

Mavrozomes, Manuel, landowner in Asia Minor, resistance to Baldwin I, 291

al-Māwardī, Muslim author of *Institutes of Rulership*, 666

Maxentius, Stephen, *strategus* under Basil I, 121

Maximus the Confessor, Greek Church Father

scholia on Pseudo-Dionysius, 58
studied by laity, 60
translated into Latin, 587

Mayyāfāriqīn, *see* Martyropolis

Mazara, town in Sicily, held by Arabs, 100, 728

Mazdak, leader of revolt in Persia, and Mazdakites, 682

Meander, river in western Asia Minor, 115
and Manuel I's campaigns against Iconium, 236, 237, 238
Greek resistance to Baldwin I, 291
settlements of Cumans in thirteenth century, 320

Mecca, holy city of Islam
rebuilt by Abbasids, 642
theft of Black Stone, 682, 702

medicine and the Arabs, 671–2, 683–5, 694, 695 and n. 1

Medina, holy city of Islam
rebuilt by Abbasids, 642
seat of legal learning, 673, 675–6

megadux, title of Latin ruler of Lemnos, 426

Megara, town in Greece
bishopric of, 409
taken by Nerio I Acciajuoli, 419

megas dux, 244, 337, 347, 351, 357

megas primicerius, 360

Meḥmed, *see* Muḥammad

Melangeia (Yenishehir), south of Nicaea in Asia Minor, taken by Ottomans, 759

Melas, river in Asia Minor, Byzantine troops defeated by Arabs (759–60), 74, 704

Melazgerd, *see* Manzikert

Melchisedech, *Katholikos* of Iberia, 621

Melfi, town in South Italy
under Norman rule in eleventh century, 197, 202
synod of, 463, 465

Melias, *see* Mleh

Melings, Slav tribe in Peloponnese, under Latin rule, 390, 400

Melisseni, Byzantine family
under Basil II, 192
landowners in Thessaly in fourteenth century, 349

Melissenus, Leo, and plot against Basil II, 174, 178

Melissenus, Nicephorus, pretender under Nicephorus III, 211–12

Melitene (Malaṭiya, Malatya), town in Mesopotamia
home of Paulicians, 73
fortified by Umayyads, 698

Melitene (*cont.*)
  razed to ground by Constantine V, 74,
    703
  rebuilt by Abbasids, 704
  captured from Arabs (837), 103, 710
  occupation by Byzantine troops (841),
    103
  Michael III's campaign of 860, 111, 120
  in Arab hands, 120, 704–5, 710–12
  and Basil I's campaigns, 714 and n. 1,
    715
  taken by John Curcuas (934), 139,
    142, 717–18, 727, 735
  and Sayf ad-Dawla, 719
  John Tzimisces' campaigns, 164
  and Basil II, 186
  Romanus IV's campaign against
    Seljuqs, 209
  struggle for possession between Seljuqs
    and Danishmends, 223, 236, 629, 741
  and establishment of Lesser Armenia,
    628–9
  local pacts with Byzantines, 735
Melnik, fortress above Strymon valley in
    Macedonia, 299, 317, 351, 526, 535
Melo of Bari, Lombard leader, father of
    Argyrus, 202, 458
Melon, in Asia Minor, Arab defeat at
    (781), 83
Melos, Aegean island
  under Venetian rule, 425
  bishopric of, 426
Μέμπετζε, *see* Hierapolis (Manbij)
Menae, *see* Mineo
Menander Protector, historian
  on Avars, 477 and n. 4
  on Central Asian Turks, 478 and n. 3,
    479 and n. 2
Mendenitza, *see* Boudonitza
Mengüjukids, Turkish family, 748
Mengu Tīmūr, khan of Golden Horde,
    749
Menteshe, Turkish principality in south-
    western Asia Minor, 756
mercenaries in imperial army
  in early Byzantine period, 27, 35, 37
  in Italy, 40
  Normans, 197, 210, 214, 731
  Turks, 209, 213, 214, 324–5, 355, 364,
    401
  Latins, 214, 299, 320, 322, 324
  Pechenegs and Uzes, 203, 208, 218
  Cumans, 218, 324–5, 401, 589
  English, 218
  Bulgars, 401
  Serbs, 401
  Hungarians, 401, 570

  Varangians, 731
  Germans, 401
  recruited from neighbouring peoples
    by Isaac I, 206; and by Constantine
    X, 208
  commonly used by John II, 220
  used by Manuel I, 228, 239
  used by Alexius III, 281
  used by Michael I of Epirus, 299
  under the Palaeologi, 342, 347, 355, 364
  see also Catalan Company, Varangian
    guard
Merv, town between Caspian Sea and
    Oxus, 645, 653, 660
Mesarites, John, brother of Nicholas,
    support of Greek Church against
    Latins, 302 and n. 2
Mesarites, Nicholas, metropolitan of
    Ephesus, scholar
  spokesman for Greek Church, 302 and
    n. 2, 303–4
Meschia (Samts'khe), district in Cau-
    casia, 626 n. 2, 628
Meschian Chronographer, 625 n. 1
Mesembria, town in Thrace on west
    coast of Black Sea, 97, 98, 333, 336,
    348, 353, 370, 490, 491, 523, 535,
    591–2
Mesopotamia
  part of See of Antioch, 19
  part of Roman Empire, 24
  and Aramæan culture, 55
  attacked by Persia, 29
  attacked by Arabs, 30
  invasions under Romanus I, 139–40
  and Sayf ad-Dawla, 149, 718–20
  strategus of, and relief of Antioch, 163
  campaigns of John Tzimisces, 164–5,
    167–9, 720–3
  under Michael IV, 197
  and Seljuq Turks, 204, 209–10, 653–4,
    703, 742, 746
  Mongol invasions, 377, 634, 660
  and Carmathians, 648
  under Abbasid Caliphate, 638–61,
    662–95 *passim*
  and Buwayhids (q.v.), 647, 723–4
Mesopotamia, theme of
  Bardas Sclerus as *dux*, 175, 723
  taxation under Constantine IX, 204
  John Tzimisces as *strategus*, 720
Mesopotamites, Constantine, metro-
    politan of Thessalonica, 308
Mesrop, St, and Armenian alphabet, 599
Messenia, district in Peloponnese
  and Geoffrey of Villehardouin, 292, 390
  and Navarrese Company, 419

Messina, town in Sicily
captured by Arabs (842/3), 728
retaken by Byzantines, 197, 731
metaphysics, 220
Meteorium, camp of Michael VIII in Asia Minor, 327–8
Methodius I, Patriarch of Constantinople
elected Patriarch, 104
harshly treated by Michael II, 101
toleration of iconoclasts, 107
restoration of icons, 108
Methodius, apostle of the Slavs, archbishop of Pannonia
brother of Constantine (Cyril), 107
mission to Moravia and the Slavs, 119, 122, **124** and n. 1, **125**, 455, **497–500**
mission to Khazars, 492
and Slavonic liturgy, 124–5, 497, 499
relations with Rome and Constantinople, 124, 497–500
relations with Franks, 500
influence of his work, **500–2**, 515
Methodius of Olympus in Lycia, 47
Dialogues, 47
Banquet of the Ten Virgins, 47
Metochites, Alexius, governor of Thessalonica, 362
Metochites, Theodore, statesman and scholar under Andronicus II, 5–6, 351, 533–4
Mevlānā Jalāl ad-Dīn, religious leader under Seljuqs of Rūm, 747
Mevlevīye, Dervish order, 747
Mezezius, pretender under Constantine IV, 610 n. 1
Mezezius II Gnuni, prince of Armenia, 605
Michael I Rangabe, Emperor, **95–8**
support of the images, 97, 99
father of the Patriarch Ignatius, 107
relations with Charlemagne, 96–7, 448, 449
subservience to the Patriarch, 96, 97
attacked by Krum, 97–8
Michael II, Emperor, **100–2**
birthplace, 100, 103
convicted of treason by Leo V, 99
and iconoclasm, 100, 101, 102
negotiations with Rome through Louis the Pious, 101–2
treatment of Methodius, 101, 104
served by Theoctistus, 105, 106
and revolt of Thomas the Slavonian, 100–1, 709
and Arab attacks on Crete and Sicily, 100–1
Michael III, Emperor
grandson of Michael II, 100

under regency, 104, 105–8
marriage plans, 108
personal rule, **108–16**
proclamation as sole Emperor, 108 and n. 2
campaigns against Arabs, 109–11, 117, 119, 120, 147, 611, 704, 713–14, 727
and Bulgaria, 111–14, 498
and first Russian attack on Constantinople, 111, 713
relations with Khazaria, 492–4
and conflict between Ignatius and Photius, 113, 450–2
and council of 867, 114, 117–18
relations with the Papacy, 109, 113, 114
and Slavonic Churches, 112, 497–8
and condemnation of iconoclasm, 112, 113
future Basil I his favourite, 115, 117
popularity with army, 110, 117
troubles at close of reign, 115
murder, 114, 115–16, 118, 453, 714
funeral, 116, 125
Michael IV the Paphlagonian, Emperor, **196–8**
marriage to and treatment of Zoe, 196, 198
attacks on Empire, 194, 196–7
debasement of coinage, 196, 200
losses in South Italy, 197
trouble in east, 197
and Michael V, 198
and Caucasia, 197, 619
treaty with Fatimid Caliph, 726
retirement and death, 197–8
Michael V Calaphates, Emperor
popular rising against, 198–9
and George Maniaces, 198, 201
blinded and exiled, 199
Michael VI Stratioticus the Aged, Emperor, 205
Michael VII Ducas, Emperor, **210–11**
death of Constantine X and accession of Romanus IV, 208–9
sole ruler, 210
under influence of Nicephoritzes, 210–11
rival Emperors, 211
concern about heresy, 217
relations with the Papacy, 463–4
relations with Hungary, 578–9, 588
relations with Seljuqs, 740
abdication, 211, 212
marriage of his wife to Nicephorus III, 211, 622 n. 1
his name taken by pretender to throne, 213, 464

Michael VIII Palaeologus, Emperor, **322–30, 331–40**
service under John Vatatzes, 319, 322
service under Theodore II Lascaris, 322–3
regent and co-Emperor with John IV, 324
campaigns against Michael II of Epirus, 324–5, 326, 333, 401
campaigns against John I of Thessaly, 337
recapture of Constantinople from Latins, 325–8, 755
alliance with Seljuqs, 326
alliance with Mongols, 326, 336, 537
relations with Genoese, 326–7, 333, 402
relations with Bulgaria, 326, 333, 336, 338, 339, 470–1, 535–7
treatment of John IV, 328, 338
operations against Franks in Greece, 332–3, 337–8, 401–2, 410, 589
relations with West, 332 and n. 1
relations with Venetians, 333–4, 336, 337, 402
relations with Sicily, 334–5, 336–7, 339–40, 470
relations with the Papacy, 335, 336–7, 339, 470–1
relations with St Louis of France, 335
relations with Serbia, 336, 339, 470–1
relations with Hungary, 336, 589
policy of dynastic marriages, 333, 335–6, 589
and union of Churches, 329, 335, 336–7, 338–9, 402, 470
opposition of Greek Church over union with Rome, 338–9, 470
results of reign, 340
Michael IX Palaeologus, co-Emperor with Andronicus II, 340–1, 589
marriage to Armenian princess, 345
opposition to Catalan Company, 348
friend of Theodore Synadenus, 350
Michael I Cerularius, Patriarch of Constantinople, 191, 201–2, 204, 205, 206, 207 and n. 1, 460–3
Michael IV Autorianus, Patriarch of Constantinople in Nicaea, 295, 302
Michael II Asen, Bulgarian tsar
loss of territory to John Vatatzes, 316, 535
treaty with Theodore II Lascaris, 322
relations with Hungary, 535
murder, 535 and n. 1
Michael Burtzes, *see* Burtzes

Michael I, ruler of Epirus, **296–300**
conflict with Latins, 292, 296–7, 303, 390–1, 392
payment of ransom for Alexius III, 296
relations with Venetians, 297, 298–9, 300, 314 n. 1, 392
relations with Matthew Orsini, 297
relations with Henry of Flanders, 298, 299, 300, 392
relations with kingdom of Thessalonica, 298, 299, 392
relations with Bulgarians, 299
relations with the Pope, 297, 299
relations with Church, 303, 304
use of Latin mercenaries, 299
murdered, 300
Michael II, Despot of Epirus, **314–19, 322–5**
early history, 314 and n. 1
invasion of Thessaly, 315
relations with Frederick II, 316
territorial gains in northern Greece, 317
relations with John Vatatzes, 318–19
relations with Theodore II Lascaris, 322
revolt against Nicaea, 322–5, 400–1
relations with Manfred of Sicily, 323, 324–5, 401
relations with William of Villehardouin, 323–4, 324–5, 399, 400–1
defeated by Michael VIII, 324–5, 333, 401
recapture of Arta (1260), 326
death, 335
Michael Ducas Angelus Comnenus, *see* Michael I, ruler of Epirus
Michael III Šišman, Bulgarian tsar, **542–3**
and civil war between Andronicus II and III, 351–2
defeated and killed at battle of Velbužd (1330), 353, 534, 543
Michael the Syrian, monophysite Patriarch of Antioch, on Constantine V, 68
Michael, king of Zeta, 520
Michiel, *see* Domenico *and* Vitale
Mico, Bulgarian tsar, 535 n. 1, 536
Mihranids, ruling family in Iberia and Caspian Albania, 595, 597, 610 n. 3
see also Chosroids
Mikligarŏr, Scandinavian name for Byzantium, 495
Milan
loss of prestige to Ravenna, 18
residence of western co-Emperors, 432
Mileševo, town in Bosnia, coronation of Tvrtko I, 549
miliaresion, Byzantine silver coin, 65, 93

military code, see *Strategicon*

Miloš Kobilić, Serbian noble at battle of Kossovo, 550–1

Milutin, Serbian king, *see* Stephen Uroš II Milutin

Mineo (Menae), town in Sicily, held by Arabs, 100, 728

mines and minerals, 37
  alum in Phocaea, 346
  exports from Crete, 428
  in Bulgaria, 529
  in Serbia, 529, 532–3
  in Bosnia, 529, 548, 551
  in the Caucasus, 609
  in Abbasid Empire, 644, 646
  in Asia Minor, 769
  gold (q.v.), 532–3, 644, 646
  silver, 532–3, 548, 609, 644, 646
  lead, 532, 548
  copper, 532
  iron, 532

Mingrelia, district in Caucasia, 626 n. 2, 628

Mircea the Old, Wallachian prince
  opposition to Turks, 375–6, 562–3, 765–6
  in control of Dobrudja, 545

Mirdasids, Arab dynasty in Aleppo, 725

Mirian I (III) of Iberia, 595 n. 1

'Mirrors for Princes', 15, 575

Misis, *see* Mopsuestia

missionary work
  among Slavs, 111–12, 455, 490, 496, 499–502
  among Germanic nations, 443
  among Bulgars, 452, 497, 498, 501–2, 567
  among Caucasian tribes, 474
  among Serbs and Croats, 122, 482
  among Khazars, 111–12, 487 and n. 4, 488, 492–4
  among Russians, 122, 496, 504, 515–17
  in Moravia, 112–13, 119, 124, 455, 497–501
  in Pannonia, 124, 499–501, 509
  among Huns, 567–8
  among Turkic peoples, 567
  among Magyars, 567–8
  in Hungary, 572

Mistra, town in Peloponnese
  Byzantine Despotate of, *see* List of Rulers 3; 394, 403, 404, 405, 406, 771–2
  under Latin rule, 399
  ceded to Michael VIII by Franks, 332, 401–2, 403
  John VIII at, 591

  overrun by Turks, 387, 772
  home of George Gemistus Plethon, 378
  and manufacture of silk, 428
  see also the Morea

Mithridates, and Caucasia, 594

Mitrovica, place in Hungary, 576

Mkhargrdzeli, *see* Zachariads

Mleh (Melias, Malīh al-Armanī), Armenian soldier, *strategus* of theme of Lycandus, 142, 717

Mleh the Armenian (Melias), army commander under John Tzimisces, 164–5, 167, 723

Mleh (Mlēh), ruler of Lesser Armenia, 235, 629–30

modios, unit of dry measure, 343

Modon, port in Peloponnese
  under Venetian control, 289, 380, 390, 392, 427
  Latin bishopric of, 396

moechian controversy, 89

Moesia
  overrun by Asparuch's Bulgars, 484
  campaigns of Constantine V, 490
  under Kalojan, 525

Mohacs, battle (1528), 560

Moldavia, Rumanian principality
  Church in, 561
  relations with Hungary, 561
  relations with Poland, 562, 563, 564
  Turkish conquest, 563–5

Momčilo, Hajduk, adventurer in Balkans, 360

monasteries, monks and monasticism
  influence of, 60, 94–5
  early Byzantine monachism, 54, **57–9**
  monastic property, 61, 81, 93, 94, 154–5, 219, 241, 344, 358 n. 1, 371–2 and n. 1
  monastic libraries, 52
  attitude to Emperor, 12, 95
  opposition to Nestorius, 56
  persecuted by iconoclasts, 80, 81, 487
  iconoclastic monasteries, 81
  under Leo IV, 81
  and Seventh General Council, 84
  under Irene, 89
  under Nicephorus I, 93–5
  under Nicephorus II, 154–5
  under Alexius I, 218
  under Latins, 303, 409
  endowments under John Vatatzes, 320
  encouragement under Andronicus II, 344
  in Serbia, 522, 559
  in Hungary, 573–5, 577, 586–7
  in Russia, 577

monasteries (*cont.*)
 in Caucasia, 55, 616, 625
 in Palestine, 58, 68, 625
 in Syria, 58, 688
 in Egypt, 19, 54
 see also Athos, Constantinople (monasteries), Studites, Benedictines, Cistercians, Dominican friars, Franciscans
Monegarius, Domenicus, *dux* of Venice in eighth century, 255
Monemvasia, town in Peloponnese
 and the Latins, 292, 399, 400
 ceded to Michael VIII, 332, 401–2, 403
 sea-route to, 337
 Chronicle of, 92, 480 n. 6
 Latin See of, 396
 export of wine, 428
money-lending, 93
Mongolia, 478, 660, 736, 749
Mongols
 and Avars, 476
 invasion of Europe in thirteenth century, 313
 invasion of Asia Minor, 315–16, 320, 660, 748–9, 754, 756
 in south Russia, 528, 749
 in Caucasia, 625, 626 and n. 2, 627, 660
 invasion of Persia, 660–1, 747–8, 766
 invasion of Syria and Mesopotamia, 633–4, 660, 744
 and Jerusalem, 635 n. 3
 destruction of Abbasid Caliphate of Baghdad, 660–1
 alliances with Byzantium, 320, 326
 and Mamluks of Egypt, 634, 750–1
 conversion to Islam, 634–5
 pressure on Turks, 346, 755
 defeat of Turks at battle of Ankara (1402), *see under* Ancyra
 see also Bereke, Golden Horde, Il-Khans, Jenghiz Khan, Kara-Khitay, Nogaj, Tatars, Timur
Monobatae, monastery on Bosphorus, 198–9
monophysitism and monophysites
 in Asia Minor, 66
 in Syria, 56, 66, 73, 440
 in Egypt, 56, 440
 in Armenia, 68, 604
 in Thrace, 73
 within Greek Church, 56
 theology of, 79 and n. 3
 opposed to use of images, 66, 68, 73
 and *Henoticon* of Zeno, 435, 604
 monophysite Emperor, 28
 and Greens, 55

 and Council of Chalcedon, 20, 21
 and Seventh General Council, 86, 87
monopolies
 in Catalan duchy of Athens, 414
 of Bulgarian trade, 128, 503
 under Michael VII, 211
monostrategus, 121
monotheletism, 440–1, 442
monoxyla, ships of Russian fleet, 111
Montanism and Montanists, treatment under Leo III, 65, 68
Montferrat, house of, *see* Boniface, Demetrius, Renier, William, Irene
 renunciation of claim to kingdom of Thessalonica, 345
Mopsuestia (Mamistra, Maṣṣīṣa, Misis), town in south-east Asia Minor, 629–31, 704, 706–7
 taken by Nicephorus II (965), 149, 721
 attacked by John Tzimisces, 157 n. 1
 John II at, 225
 and Manuel I, 234, 630
Morava, river in Balkans, tributary of Danube
 battle (1190), 521
 and Prince Lazar, 541–2
Moravians, Moravia
 conversion, 112, 113, 119, 124, 497–501
 and See of Rome, 123–5, 126, 455
 archbishop of, 122, 124, 125
 work of Methodius, 124–5, 455, 499–501
 death of Methodius and expulsion of archbishop, 122
 and German Church, 124–5
 and Slavonic liturgy, 126, 455, 497, 499
 liberated from Avars, 482
 under leadership of Rastislav, 496–8, 499
 invasion by Magyars, 128, 503
Morea, the
 Byzantine Despots of, *see* List of Rulers 3
 judicial system under the Palaeologi, 353
 recovery from the Cantacuzeni by the Palaeologi, 373
 invaded by Turks, 375, 376, 379, 380, 385
 overrun by Ottomans (1460), 387
 centre of Byzantine culture in fifteenth century, 378–9, 403
 Chronicle of the Morea, 393, 397, 399, 405 and n. 1, 409
 name for Elis, 390
 name used for Achaea, 391 n. 2
 see also Peloponnese *and* Mistra

Morocco, 663, 681
Morosini, Venetian family, 267; *see also* Thomas
mortmain, 155, 183
mosaics, 13, 80, 194
Moscow, Grand Dukes of
gift to church of St Sophia, 364
appealed to by Manuel II, 376
opposition to union with Roman Church, 382
Moses Comitopulus of Bulgaria, 178
Moses of Kaḷankaytuk' or of Daskhurēn, Armenian historian, 616 n. 1
mosques
in Constantinople, 283, 580, 724–6, 733–4, 775
in Tyana, 91, 707
in Athens (the Parthenon), 387
in Asia, 653
in Tarsus, 149
in Syria, 722
in Sultanate of Rūm, 747
Mosul, 163, 164, 226, 628, 703, 718, 723, 742
trade, 615
rulers of, *see* Sayf ad-Dawla, Abū Taghlib, Zengi
Mosynopolis, town in Thrace, 289, 294, 309
Mouageris, prince of the Huns in Crimea, and name Magyar, 567
Mount of Blood, battle before Tarsus (963–4), 149, 157 n. 1
Moxoene, Armenian principality, 620
Mts'khet'a in Caucasia, church at, 615
Mu'āwiya I, Umayyad Caliph, 605
Mu'āwiya, Muslim general, campaigns against Leo III, 64
Muḥammad the Prophet, 30, 241, 638, 648, 663, 672–4, 681–2, 685, 688–9, 691, 696 and n. 1, 697, 700
Muḥammad ibn Karaman ibn Nūra Ṣūfī (Muḥammad Bey), Turkoman leader, 750–1
Muḥammad ibn-Marwān, Caliph al-Walīd's viceroy, attempts extermination of Armenian nobility, 607
Muḥammad (Meḥmed) I, Ottoman Sultan, **767–9**
struggle for power with his brothers, 378, 552, 767–8
friendly relations with Byzantium, 378, 768
and Wallachia, 563, 768
and Karamans, 768
internal revolts, 768–9
death, 379, 769

Muḥammad (Meḥmed) II the Conqueror, Ottoman Sultan, **771–6**
and capture of Constantinople (1453), 385–7, 773–6
conquest of Peloponnese, 387, 408
and the Acciajuoli of Athens, 424
conquest of Serbia, 554–5
conquest of Bosnia, 557
conquest of Albania, 558
and Moldavia, 563–4
and Karamania, 764
relations with his father Murād II, 771–2
death, 564
Muḥammad (Meḥmed) Chelebi, *see* Muḥammad I and II
Muḥammad, Dānishmend amir, campaign of John II against, 223, 224
Muḥammad, son of Ismā'īl, 681
Mu'īn ad-Dīn Sulaymān, Parwāna of Seljuqs of Rūm, 749–50
al-Mu'izz, Fatimid Caliph, 168, 169, 648, 721, 730–1
al-Mumenin, *see* al-Mu'izz
municipia, status of Italian cities, 432
Mu'nis, eunuch, Arab military commander, 717, 734
Munkács in Hungary, bishopric of, 587
al-Muqanna', leader of revolt against Abbasids, 682
al-Muqtadir, Abbasid Caliph of Baghdad, 717, 734
Murād I, Ottoman Sultan, **762–5**
accession, 761
marriage alliances, 762
titles, 761, 763, 765
in Adrianople, 369, 762–3
relations with John V, 372–3, 763
relations with Bulgaria, 545, 763, 765
relations with Karamans, 764
attack on Serbia and battle of Kossovo (1389), 550–1, 763–5
capture of Ankara, 754, 762
Murād II, Ottoman Sultan, **769–73**
siege of Constantinople (1422), 379, 769
in Peloponnese, 379
and councils of Ferrara and Florence, 382
and crusade of Hunyadi, 383–4, 553–4, 770
trouble in Asia Minor, 383, 384, 554, 769–71
subjection of Greece and Peloponnese, 384–5, 769, 772
conquest of Serbia, 553, 772
attacks on Albania, 558, 769, 772
revolt in Albania, 770–1

Murād II (*cont.*)
attacks on Transylvania and Hungary, 769
truce with Hungary, 771, *and see* Szegedin
and battle of Varna (1444), 771
and janissaries, 772
encouragement of arts, 772–3
succeeded by Muḥammad II, 385, 771, 773
Mus, town in Armenian province of Taron, 167
Mūsa, son of Bāyezīd I, struggle for power with brothers, 378, 552, 767–8
Mūsā, son of pretender Ja'far aṣ-Ṣādiq, Shī'ite imām, and Twelver Shī'a, 647
Muscovite Empire, *see* Moscow, Grand Dukes of, *and* Russia
Mušeḷ, *see* Mushel
Musele family, landowners under Basil II, 183
Musele, Alexius, commander of Armeniakon theme under Constantine VI, 88
Musele, Alexius, son-in-law of the Emperor Theophilus, and Arab attack on Sicily, 728
Mushel, king of Kars, 616–17
Mushel (Mušeḷ) II Mamikonian of Armenia, 606
Mushel, brother of Gregory (II) Mamikonean, 607–8
music
studied at university of Constantinople, 200
and Arabs, 688
Muslim ibn al-Ḥajjāj, Muslim jurist, 674
Muslims, *see* Arabs, Abbasid, Fatimid and Umayyad Caliphates, Islam, navy, trade
Muṣṭafā, brother of Murād II
in rebellion against him, 379, 769
name taken by pretender, 768–9
al-Mustakfī, Abbasid Caliph of Baghdad, 702
al-Mustanṣir, Fatimid Caliph, 648–9, 657, 726, 734
al-Musta'ṣim, last Abbasid Caliph of Baghdad, 661
al-Mu'taḍid, Abbasid Caliph of Baghdad, 715–16
al-Mu'tamid, Abbasid Caliph
and Armenia, 612
capital moved back to Baghdad, 702
al-Mutanabbi', Arab poet, 157 n. 1, 687

al-Mu'taṣim, Abbasid Caliph of Baghdad
and decline of Caliphate, 646, 701
wars with Byzantium, 103, 704, 710–12
use of Turkish slaves (Mamluks) in army, 651, 701
al-Mutawakkil, Abbasid Caliph of Baghdad
policy in Caucasia, 611
religious policy, 642, 666, 671
decline of Caliphate, 704
assassination, 713
Mu'tazila, Hellenising school of Islam 642, 670–1, 683, 690, 691 n. 4
al-Muṭī', Abbasid Caliph, 150, 702–3
Muẓāfarids of Azerbaijan, 610 n. 3, 616
Muzalon, George, Grand Domestic under Theodore II Lascaris, 321, 324
Mykonos, Aegean island, under Venetian rule, 425
Myra, port in Lycia, 708
Myriocephalum (Chardak Pass), pass in Asia Minor, defeat of Manuel I by Kīlīj Arslan (1176), 237–9, 630, 743
mysticism in Islam, 648, 659, 687 n. 1, 689, 691 and n. 3, 692, 747

Nabataeans of Mesopotamia, 668
Nakhchevan, town in Armenia, 607, 615
Namfio, *see* Anaphe
Nándorfehérvár, *see* Belgrade
Naples, city in Italy
growth of independence, 77
alliance with Arabs of Sicily, 728
kingdom of and the Morea, 403–4, 405
invaded by Hungary, 406
Narentani, *see* Narentians
Narentians, mountain-dwellers of Croatia, 122, 501
τὰ Ναρσοῦ, monastery in Constantinople, 207 n. 1
Narzotto dalle Carceri, triarch of Euboea, 400
an-Nasā'ī, Muslim jurist, 674
Nasar, Byzantine admiral under Basil I, 121
Nasi, Joseph, last duke of the Archipelago, 426
an-Nāṣir, Abbasid Caliph of Baghdad, 693–4, 751
Nāṣir, an-Nāṣir, Mamluk Sultan of Egypt, 636, 751, 753–4
Naṣr, Byzantine renegade, chamberlain of al-Muqtadir, 734
Naṣr (Theophobus), rebellious Arab in North Syria, 709
renegade to Byzantines, 710–11

Naum, St, disciple of St Methodius, work in Bulgaria and Macedonia, 501–2

Naupactus, port in Aetolia, 289, 297, 299
metropolis of, 308 n. 1

Nauplia, town in Peloponnese, 380, 389, 390, 399, 400, 408, 409, 410, 411, 416

Navarino, town in Peloponnese, 392, 420

Navarrese Company in Greece
capture of Thebes, 375, 420 and n. 1, 421
in Peloponnese, 375, 379, 407–8, 419–20
in Albania, 419
relations with Nerio I Acciajuoli, 420 and n. 1

Navigaioso, Filocalo, *megadux* of Lemnos, 426

navy, Aragonese, ally of Venice, 365

navy, Armenian, 633

navy, Byzantine
in Black Sea, 189, 345, 474, 492, 498
in Adriatic, 71, 129, 132, 187, 258–9, 729
operations against Arabs, 106 n. 1, 107, 110, 121–3, 129–30, 494, 699, 709, 711–14, 716–17, 720–1, 727–33
operations against Bulgarians, 113
expeditions to Danube, 116, 128, 160, 490, 503, 514, 523, 569
defeat of Vandal fleet, 25
defence of Constantinople, 25, 63, 100, 482, 698
under Manuel I, 239
under Emperors of Nicaea, 307, 311
alliance with Genoese against Franks and Venice, 333–4
operations in Aegean under Michael VIII, 337
reduced under Andronicus II, 342, 343
rebuilt under Andronicus III, 354
destroyed by Genoese under John VI, 364
at fall of Constantinople (1453), 386
described in *De cerimoniis*, 130, 720
weakness, 25, 101, 218
loss of supremacy, 331–2

navy, Frankish, flotilla in Adriatic (807), 258

navy, Genoese
attack on Rhodes, 318
help promised to Michael VIII, 326–7
defeated by Venetians, 333
relied on by Andronicus II, 342
in control of Black Sea, 345
at war with Venice, 345–6

navy, Muslim (Arab, Egyptian, Fatimid)
capture of Cyprus, Rhodes and Chios in seventh century, 25, 30–1

blockade of Constantinople (674–8), 25, 31
and Maslama's attack on Constantinople (717–18), 63, 698
destroyed off Cyprus (747), 74, 699
at Cyprus, 705
capture of Thessalonica (904), 129, 716
defeated by Himerius and Andronicus Ducas, 130, 716
victory over Himerius (912), 130, 716
defeat under Nicephorus II (965), 149, 721
operations based on Crete, Syria and Egypt, 25, 706, 708–9, 712–14, 716–17, 720
operations based on North Africa and Sicily, 727–32
and Symeon of Bulgaria, 507
see also piracy

navy, Norman, in Sea of Marmora, 245

navy, Russian
attacks on Constantinople, 111, 140, 494, 505, 510–11, 713
in Black Sea, 495–6, 510
in Bosphorus, 203

navy, Serbian, 540

navy, Turkish, 213, 386–7, 773

navy, Venetian
defeated by Arabs (840), 103, 728
check to Samuel of Bulgaria on Adriatic coast, 187
control of Adriatic, 187, 189
help for Alexius I against Normans, 213, 218
and Fourth Crusade, 276–85 *passim*
attacks on Dyrrachium and Corfu, 297
transport for Peter of Courtenay, 305
maintenance of communications for Latin Empire, 309
protection of Constantinople under Latins, 312, 326, 399
flight from Constantinople to Euboea, 327
defeat of Genoese in 1263 and 1266, 333
lent to Charles of Anjou, 339
at war with Genoa, 345–6
in Dardanelles to fight Turks, 376
and crusade of Vladislav III, 384, 771

navy of Geoffrey II of Villehardouin, 399

Naxos, Aegean island
duchy of, 399, 425, 426–7
buildings on, 426
archbishopric of, 426

Nazareth, 170, 723

Nazianzen, *see* Gregory of Nazianzus

Nazianzus, town in Cappadocia
near site of battle (863), 111 n. 1
see also Gregory of Nazianzus
N*εαραί, see* Novels
Negroponte, *see* Euboea
Nemanja, *see* Stephen
Nemesius, bishop of Emesa, philosopher,
51
commentary on, 625
Neocaesarea, town in Pontus in Asia
Minor, attacked by Manuel I's
forces, 237
Neopatras (Hypate), town in Thessaly
taken by Theodore Ducas of Epirus, 306
seized by Catalan duchy of Athens
(1319), 349, 412–13, 415
and Nerio I Acciajuoli, 422–3
captured by Turks (1393–4), 423
neoplatonism
link with Cappadocians, 58
and *Corpus Dionysiacum*, 60
religious doctrines, 44–5, 48
in Georgia, 625
and Arabs, 683–4, 692
Neretva, river in Balkans, 519, 549
Nerse Nersiani, prince of Iberia, 608
Nerseh Kamsarakan, prince of Armenia,
606
Nersēs IV the Gracious, *Katholikos* of
Armenia, poet, 633 n. 1
Nersēs of Lambron, Armenian theologian,
633 n. 1
Nestongus, Andronicus, conspiracy
against John III Vatatzes, 320
Nestorian Chronicle, 162 n. 1
Nestorianism and Nestorians, 21, 55–6,
79 and n. 3, 86, 599 and n. 1, 604
Nestorius, Patriarch of Constantinople,
20, 56, 79 and n. 3, 436
Nestos, river in Macedonia, 362
Neva, river in northern Europe, 495
Nicaea (Isnik, Iznik), town in Bithynia
in Asia Minor
Nicene Creed, 449; see also *Filioque*
inscription from, 110
Arab attack (726), 64
taken by Paulicians, 119
defended by Manuel Comnenus against
Bardas Sclerus, 176, 180
proclamation of Nicephorus III as
Emperor, 211
Nicephorus Melissenus in, 211
taken by Seljuqs (1081), 740
taken by Latins (1097), 215, 741
and Theodore I Lascaris, 291, 295
capital of Byzantine Empire, 295,
320–1, 388, 745

Patriarchs of Constantinople in, *see*
Constantinople, Patriarchate of
discussions between Greek and Roman
Churches (1234), 312
relations with Seljuqs, 747
capital moved back to Constantinople
(1261), 328
held against Turks, 347, 756, 759
occupied by Turks (1331), 354, 759, 760
Councils of, *see* councils and synods
Nicephoritzes or Nicephorus, logothete
under Michael VII, 210–11
Nicephorus I, Emperor, **91–5**
logothete under Irene, 90
fiscal and military reforms, 92–4
ecclesiastical questions, 94–5
support of the images, 99
relations with Charlemagne, 96, 448
revolts against, 91, 99
loss of territory in West, 92
settlement of Sclavinia, 92, 97
defeat of Slavs in Peloponnese, 92, 489
and n. 3
Bulgarian campaigns, 92, 94, 96, 490
Arab campaigns, 91, 704, 707–8
Nicephorus II Phocas, Emperor, **147–56**
son of Bardas Phocas, 143, 144, 146
capture of Ḥadath (957), 146, 720
expedition against Crete (960–1), 147,
152, 721, 731
eastern campaigns, 147–8, 149, 150,
157 n. 1, 163, 169, 720–2, 727, 732
and Theophano, 148, 156
proclaimed emperor by army, 148, 721
capture of Tarsus, 149, 721
and Otto I, 150–1, 457–8
and Svjatoslav, 151, 159, 513 and n. 2
and 'Armenian frenzy', 152 and nn. 1
and 2
expedition against Sicily, 152, 153 and
nn. 1 and 2, 731
and John Tzimisces, 156–7, 172, 720–1
strategus of Anatolikon, 719
relations with Bulgaria, 512–13, 722
relations with West, 163
legislation concerning army, 153–4
legislation concerning ecclesiastical
property, 154–5, 157
novels, 148 n. 1, 153 and n. 3, 154
agrarian policy, 148 n. 1, 153–4
attitude to Islam, 149–50
taxation, 151, 152 n. 2, 155
debasement of coinage, 155
and Mt Athos, 154, 155
unpopularity, 151–3, 155–6
murder, 151, 156, 174
service to Empire, 175, 179

Nicephorus III Botaneiates, Emperor, **211–12**
proclaimed Emperor in Constantinople and Nicaea, 211
marriage to Mary the Alan, wife of Michael VII, 211, 622 n. 1
pretenders to throne, 211–12
abdication, 212, 741
excommunicated by Pope, 464
connection with Hungary, 578
connection with Lesser Armenia, 628
relations with Seljuqs, 740
Nicephorus I, Patriarch of Constantinople
historian, 68, 72
Patriarch, 94, 95, 96, 97, 99, 136 n. 1, 449
theologian, 99
deposed, 99
recalled from exile, 101
Nicephorus, Caesar, son of Constantine V, half-brother of Leo IV
revolt against Leo IV (776), 82
revolts against Constantine VI and Irene, 82 and n. 2, 83, 88, 89, 97
Nicephorus I, Despot of Epirus
marriage plans, 318–19, 322, 333
at battle of Pelagonia, 325
visit to Italy, 326
in control of Epirus, 335, 338
Nicephorus II, Despot of Epirus, 355–6
Nicephorus, bishop of Miletus in Asia Minor, and Sicilian expedition of Nicephorus II, 153 n. 1
Nicephorus Phocas the Elder, *see under* Phocas
Nicephorus Uranus, *vestes* under Basil II, 178, 184–5, 186
Nicephorus, *see* Nicephoritzes
Nicetas I, Patriarch of Constantinople
appointed by Constantine V, 80
death, 81
Nicetas, archbishop of Nicomedia, and Anselm of Havelberg, 468
Nicetas, admiral under Basil I, 121
Nicetas, admiral under Nicephorus I, expedition to Venice, 258
Nicetas, governor of Belgrade in 1071, 578
Nicetas, *nobilissimus*, son of Constantine V, half-brother of Leo IV, 82 n. 2, 83, 88, 89, 97
Nicetas, *patricius* and admiral under Nicephorus II, 152, 153 n. 1, 731
Nicetas, friend of Michael Psellus, 200
Nicholas I, Pope
and conflict between Ignatius and Photius, 109, 112, 113, 124, 450–2, 454

relations with Bulgaria, 112, 113, 122, 452–3, 499
and theory of papal supremacy, 449–50, 457
and Constantine and Methodius, 497
correspondence, 113, 452, 464
condemned by council of 867, 114, 453
death, 114, 453
Nicholas II, Pope, 463
Nicholas V, Pope, 386
Nicholas I Mysticus, Patriarch of Constantinople
and Leo VI, 127, 131, 132, 455–6
and the Emperor Alexander, 132, 134
president of council of regency for Constantine VII, 134–5, 505
and Symeon of Bulgaria, 135, 505–8
under Zoe, 136, 137
and Romanus Lecapenus, 137, 138, 456
and Alans, 512
and Armenia, 614
letters, 506 n. 2, 717
Nicholas III Kyrdiniates Grammaticus, Patriarch of Constantinople, 465, 480 n. 6
Nicholas Alexander, *voivode* of Wallachia, 561
Nicholas, *patricius* and eunuch under John Tzimisces, 163
Nicomedia (Iznikomid, Izmit), town in Bithynia in Asia Minor
and death of Constantine the Great, 1
the Patriarch Methodius banished to, 101
taken by Paulicians, 119
Russian attack under Igor, 510
defeat of Peter of Amiens by Seljuqs, 215
under Latin Empire, 308
held against Turks, 347, 756
taken by Ottomans, 354, 759 and n. 2
under Ottomans, 760
Nicopolis, town on Danube, 765
battle (1396), 376, 384, 546, 551, 556, 563, 590, 766
Nicopolis, town in Epirus, 292
Niemen, river in northern Europe, 495
Nika riot (532), 8
Nikli, town in Laconia in Peloponnese, 390
Latin barony, 394
parliament of dames, 402
High Court of Achaea, 409
Nile valley
part of Roman Empire, 24
survival of ancient culture, 54
tribes of upper Nile, 26

Nīlüfer, consort of Orkhan, Ottoman Sultan, 759
Ninfa, imperial estate south of Rome, granted to Pope Zacharias by Constantine V, 75
Nio, *see* Ios
Niphon, monk, condemned for heresy (1143), 242
Niš (Naissus), town in Balkans, 301, 524, 530, 552, 553, 578, 581, 582, 583
  battle (1443), 383, 770
  taken by Ottomans, 764
  bishopric of, 521
Nishapur, town in Khurasan, 653, 660
Nisibis, town in Mesopotamia, 164, 167, 718–19, 722–3
  treaty of (298), 595 and n. 2, 597
Niẓām al-Mulk, Persian minister under Seljuqs, 656, 659, 692 n. 1, 738
nobilissimus, title, 82 n. 2, 198, 622
Nogaj, leader of the Golden Horde
  marriage to Michael VIII's daughter Euphrosyne, 336
  attacks on Bulgaria, 536–7
nomisma, Byzantine gold coin, 65, 91, 93, 200, 218, 478, 511 n. 3
nomophylax, head of faculty of law in university of Constantinople, 200
νόμος ἔμψυχος, 16
Norma, imperial estate south of Rome, granted to Pope Zacharias by Constantine V, 75
Normans
  in Italy in eleventh century, 190, 192, 193, 197, 201–2, 206, 208, 212, 215, 458–61, 463, 731
  mercenaries in Byzantine army, 197, 210, 214, 731
  alliance with Lombards, 202
  invasion of Greece under Robert Guiscard, 212–13, 218, 219, 271
  ambitions in east Mediterranean, 213
  and First Crusade, 215
  in Italy in twelfth century, 217, 221, 222, 579–80
  in Sicily, 221, 222, 233, 468–9, 731
  struggle for control of Antioch, 221–7
  attacks on Corfu and Greece in twelfth century, 227–8, 232, 245, 247
  approached by Manuel I's agents, 229
  relations with Hungary, 233
  driven out of Greece by Isaac II, 245, 522
  relations with the Papacy, 206, 208, 463, 464–5
Norsemen, 495 n. 1

Novels
  of Justinian I, 23, 57, 133, 436–7
  of Leo VI, 133
  of Romanus I, 142, 143 n. 1, 145
  of Romanus II, 145, 153 n. 3
  of Nicephorus II, 148 n. 1, 153 and n. 3, 154
Novgorod, town in Russia, Vikings in, 495, 504
Novi, town on gulf of Cattaro, 558
Novi Pazar, *see* Ras
Novo Brdo (Novus Mons, Novomonte) mining settlement in Serbia, 532–3
  taken by Turks, 553, 555
Novomonte, Novus Mons, *see* Novo Brdo
Nubia in Africa, source of gold, 644
numen, denoting imperial majesty, 14 and n. 1, 45
Nūr-ad-Dīn, ruler of Aleppo and Damascus
  treaty with Manuel I, 235, 236
  interest in Egypt, 236, 654
  and Seljuqs, 236–7, 743
  and Lesser Armenia, 630
  and capture of Edessa (1144), 742
Nymphaeum, town in Asia Minor
  taken by Latins, 300
  discussions between Greek and Roman Churches, 312
  death of John Vatatzes, 319, 321 n. 1
  treaty between Michael VIII and Genoese (1261), 326

Obelerii, Venetian family, 261–2
Obelerius, leader of a faction in Venice, later doge, 256–7, 259, 262
Ochrida, town in Balkans
  capital of Samuel of Bulgaria's empire, 186, 517
  submission to Basil II, 518
  taken by Theodore of Epirus, 305
  taken by John Asen II, 310
  retaken by Greeks, 317
  and defeat of Michael II of Epirus, 325
  on Byzantine frontier with Serbia, 345
  taken by Stephen Dušan, 537
  under Vukašin, 541
  centre of culture, 502
  archbishopric of, 306, 308, 502, 524, 531–2, 538, 574
  seat of Bulgarian Patriarchate, 517
Oderzo, town in Italy, and Lombard invasion, 250, 251
Odo the Armenian, architect, 616
Odoacer, German leader in Italy, 21, 28, 435
oeconomus of St Sophia, 195

Oecumenical Councils
  Eighth Oecumenical Council, 123
  see also under councils and synods
Oecumenical Patriarch, *see* Constanti-
    nople, Patriarchate of
offices and institutions, Byzantine
  adopted by Serbia, 522, 538
  adopted by Bulgaria, 528–9
  adopted by Rumania from the Slavs,
    562
  sale of offices under Constantine X,
    207
Oghuz, Central Asian Turkish tribe, 653,
    737, 758
Ogražden, mountain in Balkans, 188
Oka, tributary of the Volga, 492, 515
Olbianus, general of Armeniakon theme
    under Michael II, 100
Old Maina, *see* Maina
Oleg, prince of Kiev
  founder of Russian state, 504–5
  attack on Constantinople, 130 n. 4,
    505 and n. 1
  capture of Kiev, 504 and n. 1
Olena, town in Peloponnese, Latin See
    of, 396
Olga, princess of Kiev, mother of
    Svjatoslav, 151, 159, 511 and n. 4,
    515
Olivolo, in lagoon of Venice, bishopric of,
    256–7, 260
Olympius, leader of insurrection against
    Constans II, 441
Omar, Turkish pasha, and occupation of
    Acropolis of Athens, 424
Omortag, Bulgarian khan, 98, 100, 491,
    498
Omur, Seljuq amir, ally of John Canta-
    cuzenus, 359–60, 361
Onogurs, **483–5**
  in south Russia, 483–4, 503, 567
  on middle Volga, 484
  and founding of First Bulgarian
    Empire, 484 and n. 3, 485
  and Corinth, 483 n. 5
  and Magyars, 566–7
  bishop of, 568
Onon, river in north-east Asia, 660
Ooryphas, Byzantine admiral, 111, 709
Opsikion theme
  support for Artavasdus' revolt, 73
  subdivided, 73
  loyal to Michael II, 100
  and wars with Arabs, 707
Orbelis (Orbelianis), later name of the
    Liparitids (q.v.), 623, 626 n. 2
Orchan, *see* Organa

Orchomenus, town in Arcadia in Pelo-
    ponnese, 388
Ordelaffo Faliero, doge of Venice, 271–2
Oreos, Latin barony in Euboea, 400
  bishopric of (Zorconensis), 409
Organa (Orchan), Onogur ruler, 483 n. 3
Oria, town in Calabria in South Italy, 730
Origenism, 47
Orkhan, Ottoman Sultan, **759–62**
  capture of Brusa (1326), 351, 759
  capture of Nicaea (1331), 354, 759
  agreement with Genoese, 365
  relations with Byzantium, 361, 366,
    759, 761
  extent of realm, 759–60, 762, 767
  administration and military organisa-
    tion, 760–1, 762
Orkhon, river in Mongolia, 736
Orontes, river in Syria, 169, 182, 223,
    722, 724
Oropus, catepan of Italy, unsuccessful
    landing in Sicily, 731
Orosius, Latin author
  translated into Arabic, 672 n. 1
  manuscript, 735
Oroszlán in Hungary, monastery at, 574
Orphanotrophus (guardian of the
    orphans), title of John, brother of
    Michael IV, 196
Orseoli, Venetian family, 265, 270
Orseolo, John, son of Peter II
  negotiations with Basil II, 185
  marriage to Maria Argyrou, 187, 191
Orseolo, Orso, doge of Venice and Pat-
    riarch of Grado, 270
Orseolo, Otto, doge of Venice, 269
Orseolo, Peter I, doge of Venice, 266,
    267
Orseolo, Peter II, doge of Venice, 267–9
Orsini family of Cephalonia, 415, *and see
    individual entries and* Nicephorus II,
    Despot of Epirus
Orsini, John II, Count of Cephalonia,
    Despot of Epirus, 355, 416
Orsini, Matthew, Count of Cephalonia,
    Italian adventurer in Ionian islands,
    297, 299, 325, 388, 399
Orsini, Nicholas, of Cephalonia, Despot
    of Epirus, 349
Orso (Ursus), *dux* of Venice, 254
Orso I, doge of Venice, 263–4, 268
Orso II, doge of Venice, 265, 268
Orsova, on Danube, 771
Orthodoxy, Feast of, 104, 106
Ortukids, dynasty in Mesopotamia, 624,
    742, 746
Orvieto, treaty of (1281), 339

Oshin (Ōšin) I of Lesser Armenia, 635
and n. 2, 636
Oshin, count of Koṛikos, 635–6
Ōšin, *see* Oshin
'Osmān ('Uthmān), Ottoman Sultan
early history and origins, 757–8
in control of Bithynia, 347, 759
military exploits in Asia Minor, 758–9
Osmanli dynasty, founded by 'Osmān,
347; *and see* Ottoman Turks
'Osmānlis, Ottoman troops, 758
Ossero, city on island of Cherso (Cres) off
Dalmatian coast, 268
Ostan, town in Caucasia, 615
Ostoja, Bosnian king, 556
Ostrogoths
in Hungary, 570
in Italy, 27
see also Theodoric
Ostrovo, town in upper Macedonia,
battle (1043), 202
Otene, district in Caucasia, 614
Otho de la Roche, lord of Athens and
Thebes, 389, 396, 397, 408–9
Otranto, town in Apulia in South Italy,
208
Otto I the Great, Western Emperor
relations with Nicephorus II, 150–1,
457–8
marriage of his son to Byzantine
princess Theophano, 163, 457–8
in Rome and Italy, 457
and Olga, princess of Kiev, 511
Otto II, Western Emperor
relations with Venice, 266–7
marriage to Theophano, 458
defeated by Arabs in South Italy (982),
731
Otto III, Western Emperor
marriage plans, 184, 187, 191
relations with Venice, 269
relations with the Papacy, 458
Otto IV of Brunswick, German Emperor,
rivalry with Philip of Swabia, 275,
276
Ottoman Turks, **757–76** *and see* List of
Rulers 10
rise, 757–8
conquest of Asia Minor, 347, 351, 353–
4, 637, 753–4, 757, 759–60, 762, 765
attacks on Europe, 354, 366, 369, 761–6
conquest of Balkans, 369, 371, 373–6,
545, 761–3, 772
conquest of Albania, 558, 769, 772
conquest of Bosnia, 557–8
conquest of Bulgaria, 371, 375, 545–6,
763, 765

conquest of Rumania, 562–5
conquest of Serbia, 374, 550–5, 763–5,
772
capture of Thessalonica, 375, 380, 764,
766, 769
conquest of central and southern
Greece, 375–6, 408, 423–4, 766, 769,
772
defeated by Timur and Mongols, 377–
8, 551, 766–7
Byzantium tributary state of Ottoman
Empire, 371
threats to Constantinople, and final
capture (1453), *see under* Constantinople
conquest of whole Byzantine Empire,
387
theory of sovereignty, 765
culture, 772–3
treatment of non-Muslims, 774
organisation of army, 760–4, 766, 772
land tenure, 760, 763
administration, 760–2
Oxus, river in Central Asia, 653, 655,
660, 766

Pachymeres, George, historian, 321,
759 n. 1
Padua, town in Italy, and Lombard
invasion, 250
Pagania, Constantine VII's name for
district in Balkans, 519
paganism
at time of Constantine the Great, 2–3,
13, 17
and Christianity, 42–4, 48, 50, 57
and legislation, 65
and iconoclasm, 79
in West, 12, 18, 431
in Asia Minor, 55
in south Russia, 496, 505, 511
in Bulgaria, 114, 127, 501, 502
among Alans, 512
in Hungary, 572
Pahlavi language, 668, 676 n. 1
Pahlavids, Caucasian dynasty, 615, 619–
20
painting
Caucasian, 616
and Arabs, 688
Palaeocastro (Balikesir), town in Bithynia in Asia Minor, 760
Palaeologi, imperial family, **324–87**
reforms of judicial system, 352–3
civil wars, 350–2, 356–61, 365–7
class conflict, 358–9
economic distress, 363–4

Palaeologi (*cont.*)
  frontier policy, 755
  loss of the Morea to the Cantacuzeni, 367
  recovery of the Morea, 373, 403
Palaeologus, Andrew, leader of Zealot party, 360–1, 362
Palaeologus, Andronicus, son of Manuel II, governor of Thessalonica, 379, 380 n. 1
Palaeologus, Constantine, Despot of the Morea, *see* Constantine XI (XII)
Palaeologus, Demetrius, brother of John VIII, Despot of the Morea, 381, 387, 408, 424
Palaeologus, George, envoy of Manuel I in Hungary, 582
Palaeologus, John, *panhypersebastus*, nephew of Andronicus II, in revolt, 351
Palaeologus, John, Grand Domestic, brother of Michael VIII, 324–5, 326, 401
Palaeologus, Manuel, son of John V, *see* Manuel II
Palaeologus, Michael, cousin of Manuel I, 229
Palaeologus, Michael, son of John V, 590
Palaeologus, Michael, leader of Zealot party, 359, 360
Palaeologus, Theodore I, Despot of Mistra, 373, 375, 377, 407, 423
Palaeologus, Theodore II, Despot of Mistra, 379, 380, 385
Palaeologus, Thomas, Despot of the Morea, 380, 387, 408, 424
Palakatzio, lake in Iberia, 189
Palamas, Gregory, theologian, leader of hesychasts, 358, 362
Palermo, *see* Panormus
Palestine
  part of Roman Empire, 26
  invaded by Persia, 29, 30
  conquered by Arabs, 30
  under Arab rule, 68, 648, 705, 725–6, 737
  Byzantine desire for reconquest, 151
  campaigns of John Tzimisces, 169, 170, 723
  and Seljuqs, 653
  and First Crusade (q.v.), 654
  Latin ambitions in, 214
  Latin principalities in, 215, 221, 467
  John II's proposed visit, 225
  and Third Crusade, 246–7
  visited by Andrew II of Hungary, 586
  Georgian monasteries in, 625

Pallavicini, Guy, marquis of Boudonitza, 389
Pallavicini, Hubert, marquis of Boudonitza, 400
Pancalia, plain in Phrygia in Asia Minor
  battle (978), 177
  battle (979), 617, *and see* Aquae Saravenae
panhypersebastus, title
  of John Palaeologus, 351
  of Nicephorus II of Epirus, 356
  of David III (II) of Georgia, 624
Panidus, town in Thrace on Sea of Marmora, 373
Pannonhalma, abbey in Hungary, 575, 587
Pannonia, Roman province
  and work of St Methodius, 124, 499–501
  later missionary work, 509
  and Avars, 477, 482
  annexed by Bulgaria, 490
  archbishop of, 500
  occupied by Magyars, 503, 504
Panormus (Palermo), town in Sicily
  captured by Arabs (831), 103, 728
  revolt against Arabs, 729
  acknowledgement of Fatimid Caliphs, 730
  revolt against Charles of Anjou (1282), 339–40
  importation of silk workers from Greece, 428
Panormus (Antigoni), one of the Princes Islands in Sea of Marmora, 97
pansebastus, Byzantine title given to Theodore II of Lesser Armenia, 630
Panther or Pantherius, Domestic of the Schools, 140 n. 1, 143, 146
Papacy, *see* Roman Church *and* Ecclesiastical List 1
Paphlagonia, theme of, 102
Paphlagonian Emperors and their family, 196–9
papyri, 39, 54, 106
parakoimomenos, office, *see* Basil, Constantine, Joseph Bringas, Theophanes (*protovestiarius*)
Paraspondylus, Leo, *syncellus*, Theodora's minister, 204
Paris
  visits of Manuel II Palaeologus, 377
  visit of Guy I de la Roche, 409
  news of battle of Kossovo, 550
  and Leo VI of Lesser Armenia, 637
P'arisos, district in Caucasia, 610 n. 3, 620

Paristrium, Byzantine province on lower Danube, 189

parliament, *parliamentum*
at Constantinople, 288
at Ravennika, 391, 392, 395–6
at Andravida, 393–4
of dames, 402
in Paris, 409
on isthmus of Corinth, 411
in Athens, 421–2
and political system in Georgia, 624

Parnon, Mt, in Peloponnese, and the Tzakones, 399

paroikoi (*coloni*), πάροικοι, 173, 219, 239, 240, 241
in Bulgaria, 530

Paros, Aegean island, under Venetian rule, 425

Partav (Bardha'a), town in Caucasia, 609, 615
seat of Abbasid viceroys, 609

Partecipazi, Venetian family, 261, 262, 263

Partecipazio, Agnellus, doge of Venice, 262

Partecipazio, John, doge of Venice, 262

Partecipazio, Justinian, doge of Venice, 262

Parthenon at Athens
church of Our Lady of Athens, 423, 518
conversion from church into mosque, 387

Parwāna, title of Seljuq administrator appointed by Mongols, 749–50

Paschal II, Pope, 467

pasha, Turkish title under Ottomans, 760

Pasin Ovasï, to east of Sebastea, 758

Pasman, island off Dalmatian coast, 268

Passau, centre of Christianity, 112

Passavá (Passavant), Latin barony on gulf of Laconia in Peloponnese, 394, 403

Pastillas, iconoclast bishop of Perga in Asia Minor, 78

Pásztó in Hungary
abbey of, 575, 587
monastery of, 577

Patarenes, Bogomils in Bosnia, 546–7

Patmos, island in Aegean, monastery of Christodulus on, 218

Patras, town in Peloponnese
defeat of Slavs (805), 92, 489 and n. 3
under Latin rule, 390
See of, 391 n. 2, 394, 396, 406
Latin barony, 394, 405, 406
taken by Constantine Palaeologus from Latins (1430), 380
silk factory at, 117, 428

Patriarchates, *see* Alexandria, Antioch, Constantinople, Jerusalem, Bulgarian Church, Serbian Church, Grado
pentarchy of Patriarchs, 456–7, 463
Pope as first Patriarch, 450, 451
Oecumenical Patriarch, *see under* Constantinople

patricius, Byzantine title, 145, 152, 513, 727, 731
of prince of Zachlumia, 139
of Kulayb, renegade Muslim, 171
of rulers of Onogurs, 483
of Hungarian leaders, 509, 572

patricius Romanorum, title conferred on Pepin III and his sons, 76, 445

patrimonia, patrimonies, papal, *see under* Roman Church

patristic writings
canon, 52, 58
quoted for and against images, 85–6
translated into Slavonic, 502

Patzinakia, home of Pechenegs, 186

Patzinaks, Byzantine name for Pechenegs, q.v.

Paul I, Pope, 446

Paul IV of Cyprus, Patriarch of Constantinople, 81, 83–4

Paul, patrician and admiral under Nicephorus I, 259

Paulicians
in Asia Minor, 66, 96, 111, 119–20
in Syria, 66, 73
in Armenia, 73
in Thrace, 73, 120
in Bulgaria, 120
under Michael I, 96
under Manuel I, 242
relations with Nicephorus I, 95
support for Thomas the Slavonian, 100
and Arabs, 109, 111, 137 n. 1, 611, 712–13, 717, 735
attacks against Basil I, 119–20, 714
in Byzantine army in ninth century, 121, 122
opposed to use of images, 66–7, 73
conversion of, 120, 121, 139 n. 2
and Bogomilism, 120

Paulicius, Exarch of Ravenna, 70, 253–4, 443

Paulinus, bishop of Aquileia in sixth century, 252

Pavia, town in North Italy, 76, 255, 260, 445
synod of (695), 252

Pavlovići, Bosnian magnates, 556

pearls, 644

Peć, town in Balkans, 555

Pechenegs
alliance with Symeon of Bulgaria, 128, 503–4
and Svjatoslav, 158, 162, 513–14, 515
and John Tzimisces, 162
threat to Empire in eleventh century, 193, 195, 196, 203, 208, 212, 213–14, 577–8, 579
settlements in Bulgarian provinces, 203
enlisted in Byzantine army, 203, 208, 218
expedition of Isaac I, 206, 577–8
prisoners of war given land by John II, 220
allies of Byzantium, 507, 510, 511–12, 515
and Khazars, 492 n. 2
allies of Russians, 510, 514
and Magyars, 510, 569, 577–8

Pedro IV, king of Aragon, 365, 417
annexation of Catalan duchy of Athens, 419, 421–2
loss of Thebes to Navarrese Company, 420 n. 1

Pedro Bordo de San Superano, leader of Navarrese Company, prince of Achaea, 407–8

Pedro de Pau, service to Catalan duchy of Athens, 422

Pedro de Pou, Catalan vicar-general of duchies of Athens and Neopatras, 417–18

Pedro de la Saga, leader of Navarrese Company, 419

Peganes, friend of Symbatius, Logothete of the Drome, 115, 117

Peking in China, capital of Mongol Empire, 660

Pelagius, Spanish cardinal, papal legate in Constantinople in 1213, 303, 304, 469

Pelagonia, town in northern Greece, 316
battle (1259), 325 and n. 1, 332, 401, 589

Pelecanum (Maltepe), in Asia Minor on Sea of Marmora, battle (1329), 759

Peloponnese
Slav invasions and settlements, 32, 92, 480 and n. 6, 481–2, 488 and n. 4, 489 and n. 3
Avar invasions, 480 and n. 6
visited by the future Basil I, 116–17
ceded to Boniface of Montferrat by Baldwin I 287–8

Venetian claims in 1204, 289
under Latin rule, 292, 297, 309, 313, 388–94, 395–408
Latin Church in, 396, 397–8
Turkish attacks, 375, 376, 406, 407, 766, 769
and Navarrese Company, 419–20
export trade, 428
see also the Morea

Peloponnese, theme of, 92, 489 and n. 3

Pelusa, on coast of Egypt, 713

πένητες ('the poor'), πένητες στρατιῶται
under Romanus I, 141–3
under Nicephorus II, 153, 154

Pentapolis, region in Italy
support for Pope against Emperor, 441
presented to Popes by Charlemagne, 76, 446

pentarchy of Patriarchs, 456–7, 463

Pepin III, king of the Franks
consecration by Pope Stephen II, 76
relations with the Papacy, 76–7, 78, 445
relations with Constantine V, 76–7
opposition of Venice, 255
defeat of Lombards, 445

Pepin, son of Charlemagne, king of Italy, 88
agreement with Byzantium at Ravenna, 258–9
attack on Venice, 259, 260 n. 1
death, 260

Peralta, Catalan–Sicilian family, *see* Galcerán, Matteo

Percri, town on Armenian frontier, recaptured from Seljuqs (1037), 197

Peregrinatio Etheriae, 55

Perejaslavec (Little Preslav), on Danube delta
occupied by Svjatoslav, 159, 513, 514
taken by Basil II, 517

Pergamum (Bergama), town in Asia Minor
seized by Arabs under Maslama, 63, 698
seized by Latins, 300
under Turkish rule, 756, 760

Pernik, town in Bulgaria, 185

Pērōz, king of Persia, 600

Persarmenia, 203

persecution
of Christians before Constantine the Great, 3
of Christians in Bulgaria, 491
of Christians in Armenia, 599–600
of Christians by Fatimids, 725
of iconophiles under Constantine V, 80–1, 487

persecution (*cont.*)
  of Arabs under al-Ḥakam in Spain,
    100
  of the Patriarch Methodius by Michael
    II, 101
  of iconophiles under Leo V and
    Theophilus, 103–4
  of Manichaeism under Abbasids, 642
Persia and Persians
  struggle with Rome and Byzantium
    over Caucasia, 20, 27, 593–5, 597–
    605
  threat to See of Antioch, 19
  conquest of Syria and Egypt, 21
  wars with Byzantine Empire, 10, 21,
    29, 39, 438, 480–1, 603
  and Avar attack on Constantinople
    (626), 482
  conquered by Arabs, 30, 605, 640
  relations with Arabs and Arabisation,
    638–41, 663, 668
  under Umayyad rule, 638
  under Abbasids, **638–61, 662–95** *passim*,
    699–700
  revival of Persian dynasties, 646–7,
    652, 677
  overrun by Seljuqs, 653–4, 703, 737–8
  Mongol invasions, 377, 660–1, 747–8,
    766
  Turkish dynasties, 748
  under Ilkhans, 749–52, 753–4, 760
  and silk route from China, 478
  see also Achaemenids, Sassanids,
    Samanids
Persian Gulf
  source of pearls, 644
  trade-routes, 648
Persian language and literature, 647,
    668, 683, 687, 745, 747, 751
Pescatore, Enrico, count of Malta and
    Gozo, attempt to win Crete for
    Genoese, 427
Petasius, pretender to throne under
    Leo III, 70
Peter of Courtenay, Latin Emperor of
    Constantinople
  disappearance of, 305
  and William of Montferrat, 306
Peter III, king of Aragon, overthrow of
    Charles of Anjou, king of Sicily,
    339–40
Peter IV, king of Aragon, *see* Pedro IV
Peter I, king of Cyprus, and Lesser
    Armenia, 636
  and crusade, 369–70,
Peter, king of Hungary, 576
Peter, bishop of Alexandria, 43

Peter of Amiens (Peter the Hermit), and
    First Crusade, 215
Peter, bishop of Anagni in Italy, mission
    to Michael VII, 463
Peter, Patriarch of Antioch, and schism
    of 1054, 462–3
Peter, *Katholikos* of Armenia, 619–20
Peter Aron, *voivode* of Moldavia, 563, 564
Peter, Bulgarian tsar, son of Symeon,
    139, 146, 151, 178, 188, 508–9, **512–
    13**
Peter (Theodore), Bulgarian tsar, brother
    of Asen I
  title, 528
  founding of Second Bulgarian Empire,
    245, 522–3
  murdered (1197), 248, 524, 525
Peter Damian, treatise on errors of
    Greek Church, 463
Peter Deljan, leader of Slav revolt of
    1040, 197, 519–20
Peter the Hermit, *see* Peter of Amiens
Peter the Iberian, and Pseudo-Diony-
    sius, 59 n. 1
Peter Lombard, Western theologian, and
    works of John of Damascus, 587
Peter, doge of Venice, 263
  and the Slavs, 268
Peter, Bulgar ambassador to Rome, 113
Peter, name of two representatives of
    Rome at Seventh General Council,
    84
Petra, fortress in Lazica, 602
Petronas, *strategus* of Thracesion theme,
    uncle of Michael III
  as adviser to Michael III, 108
  campaigns against Arabs and Pauli-
    cians, 109–11, 147, 712–14
Phaedrus of Plato, 47
Pharsalus, town in Greece, 413, 417
Phasiane, district round Theodosiopolis,
    181, 189, 715, 718
Phasis, city in Lazica on Black Sea, 607
Phasis, river in Caucasus, 186
  battle (1022), 189
Philadelphia (Alashehir), town in Asia
    Minor
  Manuel I at, 237
  resistance to Baldwin I, 291
  held against Turks, 347, 354, 755
  captured by Turks with Byzantine
    help, 374 and n. 2
Philaretus Brachamius (Vahrām) of
    Lesser Armenia, 628–9
Philip, son of Charles of Anjou, marriage
    to William of Villehardouin's daugh-
    ter Isabella, 334, 402–3

Philip of Antioch, king-consort of Lesser Armenia, 633

Philip of Courtenay, son of Baldwin II, titular Latin Emperor, 318 and n. 1, 334, 339, 340

Philip Dalmau, viscount of Rocaberti, vicar-general of duchy of Athens, 422

Philip, count of Flanders, 238

Philip IV the Fair, king of France, 345, 404

Philip V, king of France, 636

Philip of Namur, son of Peter of Courtenay, 305

Philip of Savoy, count of Piedmont, third husband of Isabella, princess of Achaea, 404

Philip of Swabia, German king
marriage to Irene, daughter of Isaac II, 247, 275
civil war with Otto of Brunswick, 276
and Fourth Crusade, 278–9

Philip (I) of Taranto, son of Charles II, king of Naples
hostility to Byzantium, 345, 349
prince of Achaea, 404, 411

Philip (II) of Taranto, claim to principality of Achaea, 407

Philip, logothete, Bulgarian boyar, 543

Philippa, niece of Leo II of Lesser Armenia, second wife of Theodore I Lascaris, 320 n. 1

Philippe de Mézière, chancellor of Cyprus, on Murād I, 550–1

Philippi, town in Macedonia, 538

Philippicus Bardanes, Emperor, 21, 442

Philippopolis (Filibe), town on the Marica in Balkans, 98, 185, 498, 542, 581, 587, 589, 770
taken by Svjatoslav, 514
taken by Frederick Barbarossa on Third Crusade, 246
battle (1208), 526
surrendered by Bulgaria to Michael VIII, 333, 535
returned to Bulgaria under John V, 360, 543
captured by Turks (1363), 369, 763

Philocrene (Tavshanjhil), town in Asia Minor, battle (1329), 354, 759

Philokales, *protovestiarius* under Basil II, 183

Philoponus, John, grammarian and theologian at Alexandria, 58

philosophy
faculty of, in university of Constantinople, 200–1, 217

studied in Lesser Armenia, 633
see also Plato, Aristotle, Stoic philosophy, neoplatonism, metaphysics, Arabic language

Philotheus Coccinus, Patriarch of Constantinople, coronation of Matthew Cantacuzenus as co-Emperor, 366

Philotheus, author of *Cletorologion*, 127 n. 1

Philotheus or Theophilus, bishop of Euchaïta, 161 n. 3, 162 n. 1

Phocaea, town in Asia Minor north of Smyrna
occupied by Genoese, 346
held against Turks, 347
under Byzantine sovereignty, 355

Phocas, Emperor
disorders of reign, 10, 29, 30, 481
and Church, 440
Persian war, 604

Phocas, Byzantine family, 175, 176, 179, 183, 192, 616

Phocas, Bardas, Domestic of the Schools and Caesar, general, father of Nicephorus II, 136, 143, 144, 146, 148, 719–20

Phocas, Bardas, Domestic of the Schools, son of Leo the *curopalates*
under John I, 157, 176
rival Emperor, 158, 159, 179, 618, 724
plot against Basil II, 174, 178, 516
commander-in-chief under Basil II, 176–8, 724
and Bardas Sclerus, 179, 617
death, 179, 180, 181

Phocas, Constantine, brother of Nicephorus II, 146, 720
strategus of Seleucia, 719

Phocas, Leo, general, uncle of Nicephorus II, 136, 137, 144

Phocas, Leo, *curopalates*, brother of Nicephorus II, 146, 147
Domestic of the East, 147
curopalates, 148
strategus of Cappadocia, 719
campaign in Cilicia, 149, 157 n. 1, 720–1
engrossing of corn, 152 n. 2
exile under John I, 157
conspiracy against John I, 160, 161 and n. 1

Phocas, Leo, son of Bardas, Domestic of the Schools, 180

Phocas, Manuel, *patricius*, defeated and killed by Arabs of Sicily, 152–3, 731

Phocas, Nicephorus, the Elder, general under Basil I and Leo VI

Phocas, Nicephorus, the Elder (*cont.*)
military exploits in Asia Minor and Calabria, 120–1, 129 and n. 1, 150, 715, 729
Bulgar war, 121, 128
Domestic of the Schools, 121
comparison with Theophylact Abastactus, 137 n. 1
popularity, 156
Phocas, Nicephorus, son of Leo the *curopalates*
exiled, 157
conspiracy against John I Tzimisces, 160, 161 and n. 1
Phocas, Nicephorus, 'the wry-necked', son of Bardas, Domestic of the Schools, 179, 180
Phocas, Nicephorus, *see* Nicephorus II
Phocas, Peter, *stratopedarches* under Nicephorus II, John Tzimisces and Basil I, 150, 158 and n. 2, 175–6, 722
Phoenicia, and campaigns of John Tzimisces, 171
Photian schism, 455
Photius, Patriarch of Constantinople
on Athanasius, 47
as adviser to Michael III, 108, 112–14
conflict with Ignatius, 109, 112, 113, 117–19, 122–3, 126, 138, 451–4
relations with Rome, 109, 112, 113, 114, 122–3, 124, 451–5
and first Russian attack on Constantinople, 111, 494 and n. 1
and Bulgarian Church, 113, 452, 454, 498
and council of 861, 112
and council of 867, 113–14, 117–18
and council of 879–80, 123, 126, 454
and Constantine (Cyril) and Methodius, 124
relations with Leo VI, 125–7
and university of Constantinople, 133, 453
and Slavonic Churches, 112, 122, 146, 496–8
and Armenian Church, 136, 612 and n. 1
persecution by Emperor, 136 n. 1
Photian schism, 455
and conversion of Russians, 496
theological and literary work, 126
and *Epanagoge*, 133
homilies and letters, 111, 494 n. 1
Phrantzes, *see* Sphrantzes
Phrygia, district in Asia Minor
invaded by Arabs, 73, 698–9
home of Paulicians and Athingani, 96
in hands of Turks, 755–6, 759

Phrygian (Amorian) dynasty, 100, **105–16**, 127
Piacenza, synod at (1095), 466
Picingli, Nicholas, *strategus* of Longobardia, 136
Pindar, quoted by Cyril of Alexandria, 53
Pindus mountains in Greece, 384
boundary between Venetians and crusaders, 289
piracy
in Adriatic, 25, 501
in Aegean, 426, 709, 713–14
Turkish pirates, 355, 406, 756–7
Piraeus, port of Athens, 423
Pisa, city in Italy
rivalry with Venice, 212, 221, 232, 249, 271, 273, 276
trading concessions from Alexius I, 216 and John II, 222
relations with Manuel I, 229, 232, 240
Pisans in Constantinople, 232, 273
rivalry with Genoa, 345
trade with East, 427
ally of Basil II against Arabs, 731
Pius II, Pope, 557, 586, 627
Plana, mining settlement in Serbia, 532
Platamona, fortress in Thessaly, taken by Theodore Ducas of Epirus, 306
Plato and Platonism, 46, 49
Phaedrus, 47
Republic, 47, 378
Symposium, 47
Theaetetus, 47
studied in eleventh century, 201
and Arabs, 683, 686
Plato, abbot of Saccudium monastery in Asia Minor, 89, 96
Pliska, first capital of Bulgaria, 92, 94, 484–5, 517
Plotinus, neoplatonist
Enneads, 45
quoted by Cyril of Alexandria, 53
studied in eleventh century, 201
πλούσιοι καὶ εὐγενεῖς, privileged class, 142
Plutarch, quoted by Cyril of Alexandria, 53
Podandus, town in south-east Asia Minor
battles at, 120, 706, 715
estates of Basil the *parakoimomenos* at, 172
death of al-Ma'mūn, 710
Podestà, leader of the Venetians in Constantinople
relationship to doge of Venice, 293–4, 297

Podestà (*cont.*)
  relations with Empire of Nicaea, 307
  and recapture of Constantinople in
    1261, 327
poetry and poets
  Armenian, 616 n. 1
  Georgian, 625
  Persian, 647, 687, 747
  Turkish, 652, 747
  Arabic, 157 n. 1, 668, 685–7, 735
  pre-Islamic, 652, 685
  see also epic poetry
Poimanenon, town in Asia Minor
  defeat of Theodore I (1204), 291
  victory of John III (1225), 308
Poitiers, town in France, battle (732), 63
Poland
  influence of Constantine (Cyril) and
    Methodius, 500–1
  relations with Moldavia and Wallachia,
    562–3
  appealed to for help against Turks, 590
  and Hunyadi's campaigns, 770
Polani, Peter, doge of Venice, 272
police
  secret, 33
  urban, 36
  in Egypt, 38
Polovtsi, nomad people from Central Asia,
  653
Polybius, historian, on ancient Byzantium, 476 and n. 1
Polyeuctus, Patriarch of Constantinople,
  148, 157, 191
Pompey, and Caucasia, 594 n. 3
Ponthion, meeting-place of Pepin III
  and Pope Stephen II, 445
Pontic steppes
  importance in Byzantine diplomacy,
    486, 491–2, 496, 511–12
  and migration of Onogur Bulgars, 484
  Pechenegs in, 511–12
Pontifex Maximus, title of Christian
  Emperors, 3
Pontikocastro, *see* Pundico Castro
Pontus, district of Asia Minor on Black Sea
  trade rivalry between Venice and
    Genoa, 345
  diocese of, 434
Poppo of Treffen, Patriarch of Aquileia,
  269–70
Porphyrogenitus, *see* Constantine VII
Porphyry, neoplatonist
  quoted by Cyril of Alexandria, 53
  studied in eleventh century, 201
  and Arabs, 671
  Eisagoge, 671

Porphyry, St
  Mark the Deacon's life of, 54–5
postal system
  Byzantine, 33
  in Egypt, 38
Potamides, harbour in Naxos, 425
potentes, 38; *and see* δυνατοί
Pothus Argyrus, general under Constantine VII, 146
powerful, the, *see* δυνατοί
praetor, title of George Acropolites, 322
praetorian guard, at Rome, 12
praetorian prefect, 33–4, 36
Prague, market for Hungarian merchants, 587
prefectures, 33
Preslav (Great Preslav), Bulgarian capital, 160, 506, 509, 523
  school of Slavonic letters, 501–2
  development under Symeon, 502
  captured by Svjatoslav, 514
  captured by Basil II, 517
Preslav (Little Preslav), *see* Perejaslavec
Prespa, town in Macedonia, first capital
  of Samuel of Bulgaria, 517
Prespa, lake in Macedonia, 289
priest-kings, 448, 459
Prilep, town in Balkans, 188
  taken by Theodore of Epirus, 305
  under John Asen II, 310, 527
  and John Vatatzes, 316, 317, 319
  and Michael II of Epirus, 319, 322,
    323
  on Byzantine frontier with Serbia, 345
  under Vukašin, 541
Prince of Princes, Armenian title, 611
Princes Islands in Sea of Marmora, 97
Principo, one of the Princes Islands, used
  as place of exile, 91, 198
printing
  invented in China, 644
  of Greek texts in West, 428
  in Serbia in fifteenth century, 559
Prisca, Latin collection of canon law, 439
Priscus, general under the Emperor
  Maurice, 481
Priština, town in Balkans, 555
Prizren, town in Balkans, 530, 541, 555
  bishopric of, 521, 524
Procession of the Holy Ghost, *see*
  Filioque clause
Procheiron, πρόχειρος νόμος, law book of
  Basil I, 133
Proclus, neoplatonist
  and Pseudo-Dionysius, 59
  studied in eleventh century, 201
  commentary on, 625

Proconnesus, island in Sea of Marmora, raids by Cretan corsairs, 713

Procopia, wife of Michael I, 96

Procopius of Caesarea, historian, 44, 476 and n. 2, 592, 595 n. 3, 598 n. 1, 602 n. 1

Procopius, saint and martyr, relic of, 578, 582–3

Prohaeresius, teacher of Basil the Great, 48

pronoia, system of grants
 under Alexius I, 218–19
 under John II, 220
 under Manuel I, 239, 240, 241
 under Latin Empire, 290
 under Empire of Nicaea, 319–20
 under the Palaeologi, 341–2, 358 n. 1, 371–2
 in Aegean islands, 426
 introduced into Serbia, 534
 and Bosnia, 555
 comparison with Latin *feudum*, 240
 and monastic property, 371–2 and 372 n. 1
 grants refused to Theodore and Asen of Bulgaria, 522

pronoiars, *pronoiarii*, recipients of grant in *pronoia* (q.v.); see also *stratiotes*

Prosek, fortress in Vardar valley, 299, 526

proskynesis (obeisance)
 of Emperor, 1, 13, 485 n. 3
 of images, 80, 86

prostagma of Manuel II, 372 n. 1

Prote, one of the Princes Islands in Sea of Marmora, as place of exile, 143, 161 n. 2, 210

protoasecretis, see Symeon

protoedrus, title, 261

protosebastus, title, 244

protospatharius, title, 153 n. 3, 261

protostrator, official, 116, 120, 230, 355

protovestiarius, official, 140 and n. 1, 161 n. 1, 183, 284, 510
 title used in Bulgaria, 529, 543
 title used in Rumania, 562

Provence, in south of France
 Arabs in, 140
 ambassador at Constantinople, 143
 county of, 404
 see also Hugh of Provence

provinces
 size and number, 33
 administration, 34, 36
 government under the Palaeologi, 341
 judicial system, 352–3
 city life, 40

Prudentius quoted, 55

Prusa, *see* Brusa

Psellus, Michael (Constantine), scholar and statesman, quoted, 15, 195
 Chronographia, 193, 195, 200, 201, 207
 on Constantine VIII and his daughters, 193–4, 198, 199
 on Romanus III, 195, 196
 on Michael V, 198–9
 on Constantine IX, 199–200, 202
 on George Maniaces, 202
 on Romanus Boilas, 203
 on Michael VI, 205
 advice to Michael VI, 205
 on Isaac I, 205–6
 Accusation against Cerularius, 206, 207 n. 1
 oration in praise of Cerularius, 206
 on Constantine X, 207 and n. 1
 on Romanus IV, 209
 on Michael VII, 211
 in service of Michael V, 198
 in service of Constantine IX, 199–200
 opposition to Romanus IV, 209, 210
 doubts as to his orthodoxy, 217
 opposition to Pope Alexander II, 463
 and faculty of philosophy at university of Constantinople, 200–1, 217

Pseudo-Dionysius, **58–60**
 Corpus Dionysiacum, 59–60

Pseudo-Dorotheus, catalogue of Byzantine bishops, 456

Pseudo-Isidore, decretals of, 450

Pseudo-Moses of Khoren, Armenian historian, 616 n. 1

Pskov in Russia, hermitages of, 577

Pteleum, port in Thessaly
 under Venetians, 349
 export of wine, 428

Ptolemais, *see* Acre

Ptolemies, successors of Alexander the Great, 54

Pulcheria, Empress, grand-daughter of Theodosius I, 20

Pundico Castro (Pontikocastro), in Peloponnese, 390

purgatory, 471

Pyramus (Jayḥān, Jeyhan), river in Cilicia, 176, 629, 706, 719

Pyrrhus, 12

Qadi, title of head of Turkish colony in Constantinople, 775

Qadi Burhān ad-Dīn Aḥmad, vizier, *see* Aḥmad, Sultan at Sebastea

al-Qādir, Abbasid Caliph of Baghdad, 703

Qāduma, Muslim author, quoted, 697
al-Qā'im, Fatimid Caliph, 730
Qalawdhiya, *see* Claudias
Qālīqalā, *see* Theodosiopolis
Qara Ḥiṣar-i Ṣāḥib (Afyon Karahisar), town in Germiyān in Asia Minor, 755
Qarabagh, district in Caucasia, 637
Qarghuyah, *see* Karguyah
Qarmaṭians, *see* Carmathians
al-Qāsim, son of Hārūn ar-Rashīd, prefect of 'Awāṣim, 707
Qatwān (Katvan) steppe in Central Asia, battle (1141), 655, 742
Qaysids, Arabs in Caucasia, 609
quaestor, 145
Qudāma ibn Ja'far, Arab author of *Criticism of Poetry*, 686
Quinisextum Council (692), *see under* councils and synods (*in Trullo*)
Quirini, Giovanni, in control of Astypalaea (Stampalia), 425
Quirini-Stampalia, family name given to some buildings in Venice, 425
Quo Warranto, 183
Qushayrī, Ṣūfī leader, 691
Qutlughshāh, Il-Khan general, 751

Ra'bān, on border of Syria and Mesopotamia, 720–1
Racha, district in Caucasia, 626 n. 2
Radoald, papal legate, and conflict between Ignatius and Photius, 109, 451, 454
Radomir, town in Balkans, 185
Radul the Handsome, Turkish vassal in Wallachia, 563
Rafaniya, town in Syria, 182
Ragusa (Dubrovnik), port in Dalmatia
  history of, 559
  archbishopric of, 546
  besieged by Arabs (866–8), 122, 132
  support of Ducas family against Alexius I, 213
  attacked by Stephen Nemanja, 233
  attacked by Altomanović, 542
  silk trade with Peloponnese, 428
  trade with Bulgaria, 527, 529, 559
  trade with Serbia, 533, 541, 542, 559
  trade with Bosnia, 548, 559
  independence, 549, 559
Rainulf, Norman count of Aversa, 202
Rakovica, river in Moldavia, 564
Raksin, *protovestiarius*, Bulgarian boyar, 543
Rametta, town in Sicily, and Arabs, 731
Ramleh, town in Palestine, 170, 723

Ramón de Vilanova, service in the duchy of Athens, 422
Raqqa, town on Euphrates, 707–8
Ras, town in Serbia near Novi Pazar, bishopric of, 521, 531
Rascia, Serbian state
  under Basil II, 189
  vassal of Byzantium, 239, 519
  relations with Zeta, 216, 520, 521
  ally of Hungary, 221, 520
  claimed by Hungary, 531
  accession of Stephen Nemanja (q.v.), 233, 520
  see also Serbia
Rastislav, prince of the Moravians, 124, 496–7, 499
Ratchis, Lombard king, relations with Pope Zacharias, 75, 444–5
Ravano dalle Carceri, lord of Euboea, agreement with Venice, 392–3
Ravenna, town in Italy
  mosaics, 13
  site of imperial residence, 18, 432
  support for Pope against Emperor, 441
  held against Lombards, 29
  occupied by Lombards, 75, 444
  finally lost to Empire, 76
  Franco-Byzantine agreement of 807, 258–9
Ravenna, Exarchate of
  instituted by the Emperor Maurice, 29
  ended by Lombards (751), 75, 254–5, 444–5
  Irene's hope of recovery, 88
  presented to Popes by Franks, 76, 445–6
  relations with Venice, 251, 254–5
  relations with Rome, 441
Ravennika, town in Greece on Cephissus
  parliament of Latin barons, 391, 392
  second parliament of Ravennika, 395–6, 397, 408
Raymond, son of Bohemond III of Antioch, 631
Raymond of Poitiers, prince of Antioch
  struggle with John II, 223, 224–5
  and Manuel I, 226
Raymond of Toulouse, crusader, 215
Raymond-Ruben of Antioch, 631, 633
ar-Rāzī, Muslim physician, 684
rector, 161 and n. 1
Red Sea, 648
Regensburg, town in Germany
  meeting of German bishops at (870), 124 and n. 1
  Byzantine embassy at (1174), 232

Reggio, town in Calabria in South Italy
captured by Arabs, 729–30
Arab fleet destroyed off (1005), 731
captured by Robert Guiscard, 208
regnum, secular supremacy, 222, 224
see also *imperium*
relics, 5, 30, 81, 112, 124, 149, 246, 262,
280, 314, 573, 575, 578, 582–3, 585,
718, 721–2, 774
Renaissance
influence of Manuel II's visit to
Europe, 377
influence of scholars from Crete, 428
Islamic, 650 and n. 2, 651
Renier of Montferrat
marriage to Manuel I's daughter Mary,
232, 238
grant of property in Thessalonica, 277
Republic of Plato, 47, 378
Resava, town in Balkans, 555
responsa prudentium, 13
retsina, Attic wine, 428
rex, title granted by Pope to Kalojan, 524
Reynald of Châtillon, husband of Constance of Antioch, surrender to
Manuel I, 234–5
Rhaedestus (Rodosto), port in Thrace
on Sea of Marmora, 373, 428
Rhageas in Cappadocia in Asia Minor,
battle (977), 176
Rhandeia, treaty of (A.D. 63), 594–5
Rhine, river, frontier of Roman Empire,
25, 26, 27
Rhodes
attacked by Arabs, 25, 30, 708
Venice granted trading privileges in,
228
under Emperor of Nicaea, 311
attacked by Genoese, 318
relations with Ottomans, 378
taken by Turks (1523), 426–7
and order of Hospitallers of St John,
420
on trade-route to East, 427
Rhodian Sea Law, 61
Rhodope mountains in northern Greece
and Catalan Company, 348
and Hajduk Momčilo, 360
and John V, 365
and Alexius Slav, 526
occupied by John Vatatzes, 535
Rhos, ʿΡῶς, Byzantine name for Vikings,
494 and n. 2, 496
Rhyndacus, river in Asia Minor (Sea of
Marmora), battle (1211), 300
Rialto, part of Venice, seat of government, 259–60, 261, 262, 272

Richard I, king of England, and capture
of Cyprus on Third Crusade, 246–7
roads, 16, 25, 37, 41, 474, 553, 590, 719,
762; see also Via Egnatia
Robert of Courtenay, Latin Emperor of
Constantinople
relations with Empire of Nicaea, 307–8
attacked by rival Greek Empires, 309
relations with John Asen II of Bulgaria, 309
flight to Italy and death, 309, 398
Robert the Wise, king of Naples, 405–6,
416
Robert of Clari, historian of Fourth
Crusade, 285
Robert Guiscard, duke of Apulia
conquest of South Italy, 202, 208
attack on Corfu and Greek mainland,
212–13, 271, 464
trouble in Italy, 213
Robert of Taranto, prince of Achaea,
titular Latin Emperor, 406
Robert, cousin and heir of William of
Champlitte, 393
Rodosto, *see* Rhaedestus
roga magistratus, salary paid by Byzantium to doges of Venice, 261
Roger II, king of Sicily, 222, 224
negotiations with Manuel I, 227
and Second Crusade, 227
attack on Corfu and Greece (1147),
227–8, 428
treaty of Thessalonica directed against
him, 228
subsidy for Welf VI, 228
death, 229
Roger de Flor, leader of Catalan Company, 347–8, 411
Roger de Lluria, marshal of Catalan
Company, 417–18
Rolandino of Canossa, 389
Romaioi, synonym for Byzantines, 222
Roman Church
jurisdiction, 19, 71, 72, 109, 112, 432
apostolic and Petrine principle, 432–5,
440, 446–7, 449–50
claim to primacy over whole Church,
18, 76, 101, 109, 113, 123, 131, 242–3,
279, 283–4, 302, 318, 337, 338, 381–2,
395, **432–71** *passim*
claims of Pope Gregory VII, 464
loss of provinces to Constantinople, 71,
88
recognition of status of Constantinople,
435, 439, 447
relations with Emperor, 22, 31, 76–7,
434–47

Roman Church (*cont.*)
freedom from imperial control, 432, 435
appealed to by Emperors, 131–2, 455–6
break with Byzantine Empire under Pope Leo III, 447
in schism with Constantinople, 21, 60, 104, 201–2, 246, 434–5, 455
reconciliation with Constantinople, 21, 28
rivalry with Constantinople over Bulgarian Church, 109, 112, 118–19, 452–3, 454, 498–500, 528–9
dispute with Constantinople over Illyricum, 109, 112, 113, 124 n. 1, 447, 452, 455, 469–70, 499
relations with Constantinople under Leo VI, 126–7
appealed to by Greek Church, 95
attempts at reunion with Greek Church after 1054, 222, 229, 230, 242–3, 248, 279–81, 283, 306, 311–12, 318, 329–30, 335, 336–7, 338–9, 368–9, 370, 381–2, 385, 402, 463–72, 590, 770, 773
relations with Greek Church and clergy under Latin Empire, 301–4, 307, 394–5, 396, 397–8, 469
relations with Latin Church in Greece, 406, 408–9
and Russian Church, 515
papal patrimonies, 65, 71, 119, 439, 444, 456
beginnings of papal state, 76–7, 82, 445–6
claim to political primacy, 459–60, 464, 468
papal titles, 440, 469
election of Popes, 441, 442, 445, 456
influence of Italian aristocracy, 456, 457
movement for reform in eleventh century, 270–1, 459–60, 462–4
papal schism of 1159, 230
and Arian heresy, 20
and formula of Chalcedon, 20, 21
and synods of 731 and 769, 71, 77
and Seventh General Council, 84
and Studites, 95, 96, 101
approached by Michael II, 101–2
mediation between Bulgaria and Croatia, 139
relations with Constantine (Cyril), 112, 497–8
dispute over Photius and Ignatius, 109, 112–14, 117–19, 132, 450–4

and Moravia, 123, 497–8
subjugation by Otto I, 151
and Crusades, 193, 246, 329, 383, *and see* Innocent III, Urban II
recognition of Normans in South Italy, 206, 208
and Basil II, 184
relations with Alexius I, 213
relations with John II, 222 and n. 2, 223–4
and Patriarch of Antioch, 222–4, 225
and Henry VI, 248, 469
relations with Bulgaria, 248, 469, 524
relations with Hungary, 573
relations with Serbia, 248, 469, 470, 531, 540
relations with Bosnia, 248, 546–8
relations with Venice, 254, 269–71
relations with Lombards, 75–6, 444–5, 446
relations with Franks, 72, 76–8, 90, 257, 445–6, 447–50
relations with Latin rulers in Greece, 333, 397–8, 402, 408, 415–16
relations with German Emperors, 457–60, 463–4, 465, 467–9
dating of papal documents, 77, 446
minting of coins, 446
Roman Empire, western half
decline in fourth century, 4
invasions in fifth century, 40
Justinian's attempt at revival, 435–8
last Emperor, 28
Romania, Latin Empire of Constantinople, 294 and n. 1, 409
the Byzantine provinces acquired by Serbia, 538, 541
Romans, king of the, title given to Elpidius by Arabs (782), 83
Romanus I Lecapenus, Emperor, **137–44, 507–12**
rise to power, 137–8, 507
and Symeon of Bulgaria, 137, 138, 139, 507–8
relations with Rome, 139, 456
campaigns against Arabs, 139–40, 147, 717–19, 730
relations with Fatimids in Africa, 730, 733
diplomacy on northern frontiers, 509–12
and Constantine VII, 143, 144–5
and the Maleini, 144 n. 1
and Armenia, 717
his supporters and Nicephorus II, 148
father of Basil the *parakoimomenos*, 157, 175

Romanus I (*cont.*)
  relationship to Romanus III and Zoe,
    195
  ecclesiastical policy, 126
  agrarian policy, 141–3, 145, 148 n. 1,
    153, 173, 195
  referred to in epic poetry, 139 n. 2, 141
  appreciation by Theophanes, 144
  arrest and death, 143
Romanus II, Emperor, **147–8**
  marriages, 147, 457
  and Phocas family, 143, 147–8, 721,
    731
  and laws of property, 145, 153 n. 3
  and army, 147
  death, 148
  his sons, 175
Romanus III Argyrus, Emperor, **195–6**
  marriage to Zoe, daughter of Con-
    stantine VIII, 195
  Psellus on, 195
  abolition of *allelengyon*, 195
  eastern campaigns, 195–6, 725–6
  relations with Caucasian countries,
    196, 619, 621
  relations with Conrad II, 458
  relations with Fatimids of Egypt, 726
  death, 196
  comparison with the Paphlagonian
    Emperors, 199
Romanus IV Diogenes, Emperor, **209–10**
  and attacks on Empire, 194
  reliance on army, 205
  marriage to widow of Constantine X,
    209
  relations with Hungary, 578
  loss of Armenia, 209–10, 620
  campaign against Seljuqs, 209–10,
    739–40
  appeal to Seljuqs for help, 210
  deposition, exile and death, 210, 211
  referred to by Anna Comnena, 216
Romanus, brother of Boris II of Bulgaria,
    162 n. 3, 178
Rome
  Palatine, 4
  Circus Maximus, 4
  Piazza di San Pietro, 7
  Appian Way, 8
  unification of ancient world, 22, 23
  pagan tradition, 431
  education, 23
  transfer of capital of Empire to Con-
    stantinople, 432
  comparison with Constantinople, 2, 4,
    12, 18, 24, 36, 431
  Justinian I's conception of, 435–8

  capture by Visigoths (410), 9, 27
  and Armenia, 20
  position at end of sixth century, 29
  used as synonym for Byzantine em-
    pire, 31
  political split with East, 71, 76
  and creation of a papal state, *see under*
    Roman Church
  death of Constantine (Cyril), 111 n. 2
  coronation of Frederick I Barbarossa,
    229
  proposal to transfer seat of Empire
    back to, 231, 243
  difficulty of communication with Con-
    stantinople in seventh century, 438
  support for Pope Sergius I against
    Emperor, 441
  reached by Arabs of Sicily (846), 728
Rome, duchy of
  and Lombards, 444
  ceded to Popes by Franks, 76, 445–6
Romil of Vidin, supporter of hesychasm,
    544
Romulus Augustulus, Emperor of western
    half of Roman Empire, 28
Rostislav Mihailovič, Ban of the Mačva,
    relations with Bulgaria, 535
Rotrud (Erythro), daughter of Charle-
    magne, betrothal to Constantine VI,
    83, 87 and n. 1
Roussel of Bailleul, Norman mercenary,
    in revolt against Michael VII, 210
Rovine, town in Wallachia, battle (1395),
    375–6, 542, 563, 766
Ṛshtuni, Armenian dynasty, 597
Ṛshtuni, *see* Theodore Ṛshtuni (Ṛštuni)
Ruben I of Lesser Armenia, 629, 738
Ruben II of Lesser Armenia, 235, 629–30
Ruben III of Lesser Armenia, 629–31
Rubenians, Rubenids, *see* Rupenians
Rubió i Lluch, 421, 422
Rudnik, mining town in Serbia, 532–3,
    541, 550
Rukn ad-Dīn Kĭlĭj Arslan, *see* Kĭlĭj
    Arslan IV
ruler-worship, 2, 3, 13, 45
Rum, synonym for Byzantium, 167
Rūm, Seljuq Sultanate of (Sultanate of
    Iconium), **740–52**, *and see* List of
    Rulers 9 B
  establishment, 210–12, 654–5, 740–2
  relations with Byzantines, 210, 211,
    212–14, 216, 226, 227, 235, 236–8,
    313, 359–60, 740, 743, 745
  supply of troops for Byzantine army,
    236–7, 239, 333
  and First Crusade, 215

Rūm (*cont.*)

relations with Latin Emperors of Constantinople, 290, 295

relations with Emperors at Nicaea, 295–6, 315, 320, 322

relations with Empire of Trebizond, 300–1

invasion and conquest by Mongols, 315, 320, 660, 748–52, 753

attacked by Ottomans and Byzantines, 374

relations with Seljuq Empire based on Persia, 742

rivalry with Danishmends, 740–4

trouble with the Turkish *ghāzīs*, 744–5, 750

influx of refugees from Persia, 747

relations with Mamluks of Egypt, 750–1

change from nomadic to pastoral life, 743

mixture of population, 743–4

administration, religion and culture, 744–5, 747–8, 751–2

trade, 746–8

Rumania and the Rumanians

debt to Moravian culture, 455

debt to Bulgaria, 502, 561–2

early history, 560–1

organisation and administration, 561–2, 564–5

relations with Hungary, 561, 562–3

Turkish attacks, 562–4

under Turkish rule, 564–5

and Greek Church in Hungary, 587

see also Wallachia, Moldavia, Vlachs

Rumania, Church in

subject to Patriarch of Constantinople, 561

relation to *voivode*, 562

use of Slavonic in liturgy, 561

Rümeli-ḥiṣār, *see* Boghaz Kesen

Rumelia, Turkish name for Balkan peninsula, 762–8, 770

governor defeated at Niš (1443), 383

Rūmī, Persian name for Mevlānā Jalāl ad-Dīn, 747

runic alphabet, Hungarian, 568

Rupel, pass in Macedonia, 188

Rupen, *see* Ruben

Rupenes, *strategus* of Larissa and Hellas, 629

Rupenians (Rubenians, Rubenids), ruling dynasty of Lesser Armenia, **629** and n. 1, 630–3, 738

payment of tribute to Danishmends, 223

Rus', Rūs, Slav and Arab names for Vikings, 494 and n. 3

Russia and the Russians

creation of Russian state, 504 and n. 4, 505

attacks on Constantinople, 111, 130 n. 4, 140, 159, 494 and n. 1, 496 and n. 1, 505 and n. 1, 510–11

commercial colony in Constantinople, 505 and n. 2

and Byzantine diplomacy, 507, 515–17

and Pechenegs, 510

and Khazars, 513

highway for tribes moving westwards, 29, 653

theme of Cherson created by Theophilus, 102, 492 and n. 2

masters of Bulgaria, 158

defeat at Arcadiopolis, 158, 175

military support for Basil II, 179, 186, 190, 516

and Mongols, 377, 528, 749

treaties with Byzantium, 130 n. 4, 140, 162 n. 1, 179, 496, 505 and n. 2, 511, 514–15, 516

chronicles, 158, 159 and n. 2, 495, 515–16

influence of Bulgarian literature, 502

see also Vikings, Kiev, navy, paganism, trade

Russian Church

arrival of first bishop, 112, 496

arrival of archbishop, 496

establishment of Christianity, 122, 146, 190, 511, 515–17

under Patriarchate of Constantinople, 516 and n. 3

independent of Byzantium, 382

debt to Moravian culture, 455

contact with West, 464, 511

Rusudan, queen of Georgia, 625–6

Ruytash, Mamluk leader, 171

Ryurik, Viking leader in Novgorod, 495

Šabac, town in Serbia, 560

Sabas Asidenus, landowner in Asia Minor, resistance to Baldwin I, 291

Sabinus, Bulgarian khan, 75

Sabiri, Sabirs, tribe on western shores of Caspian, 475, 477, 567

sacerdotium, authority of, 222, 224, 436, 438, 450, 457

Sa'd ad-Dawla, son of Sayf ad-Dawla

expelled from Aleppo, 722

and Bardas Phocas, 724

Sa'd ad-Dīn, Seljuq amir under Kaykhusraw II, 748

Safavids, Islamic dynasty, 628
as-Saffāḥ (Abu 'l-'Abbās), Abbasid Caliph, 638, 640
Saffarids, Persian dynasty, 647, 677
aṣ-Ṣafṣāf, at extreme north of Cilician Gates, 707
Sahara desert, bar to migration, 26
Sahidic translation of Athanasius' encyclicals, 54
Saḥyūn, castle near Antioch in Syria, taken by John Tzimisces, 171
St Adrian, invoked by Macedonian captives from Bulgaria, 116
St Andrew, apostle
  said to have founded See of Byzantium, 456
  and crown of Hungary, 576
  monastery dedicated to, 577
St Demetrius, patron saint of Thessalonica, 294
  connection with Hungary, 576, 577, 583
St Euphemia, shrine of, desecrated by Constantine V, 80
St George, patron saint of Catalonia, 413
  relics of, 573
St John, apostle
  connection with Ephesus, 456
  in Hungarian liturgy, 577
St John the Baptist
  and monastic ideal, 57
  monasteries dedicated to, 573–4
  relic of at Homs, 722
St John the Hunter, monastery, 409
St John of Rila, relics of, 585
St Louis of France, *see* Louis IX
St Mark
  traditional founder of See of Alexandria, 19
  patron saint of Venice, 262, 264, 282
  cathedral in Venice, 364
St Michael of Cusa in Aquitaine, abbot of, and Peter I Orseolo, 266
St Nicholas, monastery of, 220
  in Hungarian liturgy, 577
St Omer, Flemish family
  interest in Thebes, 408
  castle in Thebes, 408, 416
St Paul, apostle, and Pseudo-Dionysius, 58
St Peter and apostolic See of Rome, 432–3
  and crown of Hungary, 576
  Byzantine Emperors' claim to succession, 65
St Sabas, monastery of, in Palestine, and John of Damascus, 58, 68
St Sophia, Church of, in Constantinople
  first church, 7

Justinian's church, 8
and Tiridates of Ani, architect, 616
scene of second iconoclast council (815), 99
barred to Leo VI, 131
coronation of Nicephorus II, 148
arrest of Leo and Nicephorus Phocas, 161 and n. 1
mosaic of Zoe, daughter of Constantine VIII, 194
grants increased by Romanus III, 195
and Cardinal Humbert, 462
proclamation of Emperors in, 199, 211, 284, 286
administration of property, 204
admission of Muslims, 734
and appointment of Patriarchs of Antioch, 216
Kīlij Arslan II refused admission, 241
and Fourth Crusade, 285, 286, 301
coronation of Latin Emperors, 287, 293
coronation of Michael VIII Palaeologus, 328
gift from Moscow for renovation, 364
celebration of Roman Mass by Cardinal Isidore (1452), 385
turned into mosque, 774–5
saints, Muslim, 689 and n. 3, 690, 692
Sājids, Muslim rulers in Azerbaijan, 613–14
Sakaria, in Asia Minor, 751
Saladin, Ṣalāḥ ad-Dīn, Sultan of Egypt and Syria
  in control of Egypt, 236, 654, 659
  capture of Jerusalem, 246, 654
  abolition of Fatimid Caliphate, 654, 658
  alliances with Byzantines, 245, 246, 632
  check to Seljuqs, 743
Salamis, island off Athens, 289
Saleph, *see* Calycadnus
Salerno, town in Italy, 197
  ruler of, *see* Guaimar
  archbishop of, on Manuel I, 230–1
Ṣāliḥ ibn 'Alī, Abbasid governor of North Syria, and wars against Byzantium, 704–5
Sallārids of Azerbaijan, 618
Salomon, king of Hungary, 578, 579
Salona, castle at Amphissa in Greece, 389, 417
  sacked by Avars and Slavs (c. 614), 481
  counts of, 413, 417, 418, 421
  captured by Turks (1393–4), 423

salt
imported from Crimea, 475
exported from Caucasia, 615
Salzburg, town in Austria, centre of Christianity, 112
Samalū, *see* Sēmalouos
Samandar, on river Terek (Caspian Sea), residence of Khazar khans, 492–3
Samanids, Persian dynasty in Transoxania, 647, 651–2, 668, 677, 680, 736–7
Samarqand, town in Transoxania, 660, 742, 767
Samarra, Sāmarrā, town on Tigris, temporary capital of Abbasid Caliphs, 611, 701, 711
Samo, leader of Slav revolt against Avars, 482
Samonas, Muslim eunuch, favourite of Leo VI, 716, 734
Samos, island in Aegean, 716
under Latin Empire, 289
Samos, theme of, 145
Samosata, town on Euphrates, 110, 120, 139 n. 2, 146, 148 n. 1, 195, 705, 714, 720, 725
Sampson, town in Asia Minor near Miletus, resistance to Baldwin I, 291
Samshvilde, district in Caucasia, 614, 624
Samsoun, *see* Amisus
Samts'khe, *see* Meschia
Samuel of Ani, Armenian historian, 633 n. 1
Samuel, head of Mamikonid dynasty, in revolt against Abbasids, 608
Samuel Comitopulus, Bulgarian tsar
proclamation as tsar, 185, 517
leader in wars against Byzantium, 178, 184–5, 187–8, 517–18
and Vladimir of Kiev, 180
relationship to Peter Deljan, 197
San Lorenzo, church at Rome, 305
Santa Maria de Zonklon (Navarino), 420
Santa Maura, *see* Leucas
Santameri Tower on Cadmea, 408
Santa Severina, in Calabria in South Italy, 121
Santorin (St Irene), *see* Thera
Sanudi, Venetian family, in Aegean islands, 425–7
Sanudo, Angelo, duke of the Archipelago, 399
Sanudo, Marco I, duke of Naxos, *or* of the Archipelago, 425, 426
Sanudo, Marino, the Elder, historian
on William of Villehardouin, 400
on Catalan Company, 411
on attitude of Greeks to Latins, 429
Sapor II, king of Persia, overlord of Armenia, Iberia and Caspian Albania, 595, 597
Sapor III, king of Persia, and partition of Armenia, 598
Sapor, son of Yazdgard I, king of Persia, 598
'Saracen-minded', term of reproach, 67
Saracens, *see* Arabs
Sarajevo, town in Balkans, 546
Sardica (Sofia), town in Bulgaria
destroyed by Krum (809), 92, 490, 491
occupied by Bulgarians, 498
and Basil II's campaigns, 178, 181, 185, 186, 517
and Isaac I's attack on Hungary, 578
captured by Stephen II of Hungary (1127), 581
and Béla III of Hungary, 584, 585
under Bulgarian authority, 523–4, 544
Byzantine defeat at (1263), 589
captured by Turks, 764
occupied by Hunyadi (1443), 383, 770
Sardinia, island in Mediterranean, payment of tribute to Arabs, 727
Sardis (Sardes), town in Asia Minor
seized by Arabs under Maslama, 63, 698
held against Turks, 347
Sargis Siuni, *vestes*, of Armenia, 619–20
Sargun ibn Manṣūr, official at Umayyad court, father of John of Damascus, 67
Ṣārikha, in Asia Minor on upper Halys, 719
Sarkel, fortress near mouth of Don, 103, 492 and n. 2
Sarolta, daughter of Gyula, wife of Géza, prince of Hungary, 574
Sarūj, town in Mesopotamia, 719
Ṣarukhān, Turkish principality in northern Lydia, 756
Sassanids, Sassanid Empire in Persia, 26, 699, 702, 736
and silk routes from China, 478
and punishment of blinding, 576
survival of traditions under the Muslims, 641–2, 662, 667
and Caucasia, 594–5, 597–603, 604 and n. 2, 605, 609, 616
Sasun, town in Armenia, 620
Saudži Čelebi, Ottoman prince in Thrace, 372
Sava, river, tributary of Danube, 478, 481, 490, 548, 559, 582, 585

Sava, St, autonomous archbishop of Serbia, 470, 528 n. 1, 531 and n. 2, 532

Savoy, house of, 637

Saxons, 457

Sayf ad-Dawla, Hamdanid amir of Aleppo, 139–40, 146, 147–8, 149, 703, **718–22**, 727

Sayḥān, frontier fortress rebuilt by al-Amīn, 708

Sayyid Baṭṭāl Ghāzī, *see* Baṭṭāl

Scandinavians
    rulers of Kiev (q.v.), 111
    migration to south, 494–6
    and creation of Russian Kievan state, 504 and n. 4

Schlumberger, G., on John Tzimisces, 170–1, 174

Scholarius, *see* Gennadius II, George Scholarius, Patriarch

schools, in West, 471

science
    Persian, 672
    Arab, 671, 672 and n. 2, 680, 683–4
    Greek, 735

Sclaveni, Slavs from region north of Danube, 476 and n. 2

Sclavinia ('the Sclavinias', Sclaviniae), Slav settlements in Balkans and Greece
    transfer of population to, 92
    evacuated by colonists, 97
    settlements in seventh century, 482

Sclerus, Bardas, general, brother-in-law of John Tzimisces, 158 and n. 2, 159, 161 n. 1, 174–5, 514
    under Basil II, 175–6
    rival Emperor, 176–7, 178–9, 180–1, 723–4
    in captivity at Baghdad, 177–8, 723–4
    and Bardas Phocas, 179, 617

Sclerus, Romanus, enemy of George Maniaces, 201

Scodra, *see* Scutari

sculpture
    Caucasian, 616
    and Muslims, 688

Scutari in Asia Minor, *see* Chrysopolis

Scutari (Scodra), town in southern Dalmatia on Lake Scutari (Scodra), 521, 552, 558, 559
    bishop of, 540

Scutari (Scodra), lake in southern Dalmatia, 519

Scylitzes, John, chronicler
    on reign of Romanus I, 143
    on Nicephorus II, 152

on John Tzimisces, 157 and n. 1, 172–3, 174
    on Bardas Sclerus, 177
    on Romanus III, 196
    on Michael V, 198
    on Isaac I and Cerularius, 206
    manuscript of, 572

Scythians, athletic champion defeated by Basil I, 117

seals
    of Catalan Company, 413
    Hungarian, 576

Sebastea (Sivas), in Asia Minor on upper Halys
    and Seljuqs, 741, 747
    and Mongols, 749, 753–4, 766
    and Ottomans, 754, 767

sebastocrator, title
    of Isaac Comnenus, 213
    of Stephen the First Crowned, 247
    of John Ducas, 292
    of John I of Thessaly, 335
    of Dobromir Strez, 526
    used in Bulgaria, 529
    used in Serbia, 538

Sebēos, Armenian historian, 616 n. 1

Selenga, river in Mongolia, 736

Seleucia, town in southern Asia Minor, 631, 632

Seleucia, theme of, 103, 719

Seleucia Pieria, port of Antioch in Syria, 711

Seleucids, successors of Alexander the Great, 54

Selim II, Sultan of Constantinople, 426

Seljuq Turks
    origins, 653, 703, 737
    conversion to Islam, 653
    and Abbasid Empire, **653–6, 658–60**, 666, 703, 737–40, 742
    amirs in Mesopotamia, 742
    struggle with Fatimids, 624, 629, 653
    in Caucasia, 206, 620, 622, 624, 626–8, 727, 738
    invasion of Asia Minor, 15, 206, 209, 210, 463, 620, 628, 653, **737–40**
    threat to Byzantine Empire in eleventh century, 189, 192, 193, 194, 197, 203–4, 206, 207–8, 209–10, 619–20, 622, 628, 726
    establishment in Asia Minor of Sultanate of Rūm, *see under* Rūm

Selymbria, town in Thrace on Sea of Marmora, 327, 373

Sēmalouos (Samalū), town in theme of Armeniakon, 705

Semendria (Smederevo), fortress on the Danube
building of, 553
first capture by Ottoman Turks, 558, 769
and campaigns of John Hunyadi, 383, 770
final capture by Ottomans (1459), 555
Semitic peoples, 663, 668
Semlin, town in province of Sirmium, 581, 583
Senacherim, governor of Nicopolis in Epirus, and Michael I of Epirus, 292
Senate
at Rome, 10, 12, 432
at Constantinople, 12, 14, 36, 82, 108, 134, 205, 207
Sennacherib-John, king of Vaspurakan, 621
lands ceded to Byzantium (1021–2), 189, 619
Septimius Severus, Emperor, 6
Septuagint, vocabulary of, 2
Serbia and Serbs, 520–2, 530–5, 537–42, 549–55; *see also* Bosnia, Rascia, Zeta and List of Rulers 6
settled in Balkans by Heraclius, 482 and n. 3
missionary work among, 122, 482–3
debt to Moravian culture, 455
debt to Bulgarian literature, 502
and Symeon of Bulgaria, 137–8, 507–8
under Byzantine sovereignty, 139, 501, 509
part of Samuel of Bulgaria's Empire, 517
agreement with Basil II, 182, 189
weakening of Byzantine influence, 208
in rebellion against Alexius I, 213, 214
prisoners of war given land by John II, 220
disturbances in twelfth century, 228, 520, 585
politically independent of Byzantium, 245–6, 247, 521–2
creation of the Serbian kingdom, 531 and n. 2
allies of Michael II of Epirus, 322
military aid for Michael VIII, 324
and Angevins of Sicily, 336, 337, 339
capture of Skoplje (1282), 345, 533
and civil wars under Andronicus II, 351, 534
expansion in thirteenth and fourteenth centuries, 353–4, 533–4, 537–40
extent of Serbian Empire under Stephen Dušan, 362–3, 539–40
collapse after death of Stephen, 369, 540–2
breakdown of central authority, 541, 549–50
Turkish attacks, 542, 550–1, 553–5, 763–5
defeated by Turks at the battle of Kossovo (1389), 373–4, 550–1, 765, 772
relations with Venice, 539–40, 552
campaigns of John Hunyadi, 383, 553–4
conquest by Muḥammad II, 554–5
relations with Bulgaria, 542–3
relations with Frederick Barbarossa, 468
relations with the Papacy, 248, 469, 470, 531, 540
mining industry, 529, 532–3
legal system, 538–9
relations with Hungary, *see under* Hungary
Serbian Church
monasteries, 522, 532, 533
Primate of Serbia, 306
autonomous archbishopric, 470–1, 531–2
Patriarchate, 522, 538, 550 and n. 1
bishoprics, 521, 531–2
and Byzantine law, 522
relations with the Byzantine Church, 531 and n. 3, 550 and n. 1
and Serbian literature, 522, 532
Serbian literature, 522, 532, 545
Serenus, bishop of Marseilles, 87
serfdom
of Greek priests, 397
in Aegean islands, 426
Sergius I, Pope, and council *in Trullo*, 441
Sergius III, Pope, and Leo VI, 131–2, 456
Sergius I, Patriarch of Constantinople
and defence of Constantinople, 10, 482
and monotheletism, 440
Sergius II, Patriarch of Constantinople, 184, 458
Sergius, ruler of Lazica, 606
Sergius, general of theme of Sicily, leader of revolt against Leo III, 64
Sergius Nicetiates, *magister* under Theodora, 106 and n. 1, 107, 115
Seriphos, Aegean island, under Venetian rule, 425
Serres, town in Macedonia, 188, 369, 371, 768
captured by Kalojan of Bulgaria, 293, 525

Serres (*cont.*)
  and rising of Lombard barons against
    Henry of Flanders, 298
  captured by Theodore Ducas of
    Epirus, 308, 527
  captured by John Asen II, 310
  captured by John Vatatzes, 316, 535
  attacked by John Cantacuzenus and
    Stephen Dušan, 359
  taken by Dušan (1345), 362, 538
  under John Uglješa, 541
  captured by the Ottomans (1387), 764
Servia, town in Macedonia, 187, 306, 322
Settepozzi, in gulf of Nauplia in Pelo-
    ponnese, naval battle (1263), 333
Sevan, lake in Armenia, 603
  monastery of, 616
Seveners, *see* Ismāʿīlīs
Severus of Antioch, reference to Pseudo-
    Dionysius, 58
Severus, schismatic metropolitan of
    Grado, 252
Sforza, Francesco, lord of Milan, and
    Franco Acciajuoli, duke of Athens,
    424
Sgouros, Leo, archon of Nauplia, Corinth
    and the Argolid
  conflict with Latins, 292, 297, 388–9
  relations with Alexius III, 292, 296,
    389
Shaddādids, Kurdish Muslim dynasty,
    610 n. 3, 619–20, 622, 624
Shaghab, Greek mother of al-Muqtadir,
    734–5
Shāhanshāh, title of Sassanid rulers, 700
Shāh-Arman, Muslim dynasty in Ar-
    menia, 620, 624
Shahinshah, brother of Kīlīj Arslan II,
    relations with Manuel I, 237
Shaizar (Shayzar), city in Syria on
    Orontes
  John II and amir of, 223
  Basil II at, 724
Shakki, district in Caucasia, 610 n. 3
Shamanistic influence on popular Turkish
    piety, 745
Shamkʿor (Shamkhor), town in Caspian
    Albania, 624
Shams ad-Dīn Juvayni, vizier under
    Ilkhans, 751
Sharvashidzes, Caucasian dynasty, 626
    n. 2, 628
Shayzar, *see* Shaizar
Shīʿism, Shīʿites, 639, 641, 646, **647–9**,
    657–9, 665, **681–3**, 690, 700, 702–3,
    737, 745
  Twelver Shīʿa, Twelvers, 647, 649, 681

Shimshāṭ, *see* Arsamosata
shipowners, restrictions imposed by
    Nicephorus I, 93
Shirkuh, Muslim general under Nur-ed-
    Din, 236
Shirvan, Muslim kingdom in Caucasia,
    624, 627
Shirvānshāhs, Caucasian dynasty, 610 n. 3
Shotʿa of Rustʿavi (Rustʿaveli), Georgian
    poet, author of *The Man in the
    Panther's Skin*, 625
Sībawayh, Arabic grammarian, 687
Siberia
  original home of Onogurs, 483
  and Jenghiz Khan, 660
Sibyl, daughter of Hetʿum I, wife of
    Bohemond VI of Antioch, 633
Sicilian Vespers, 339, 344, 404, 537
Sicily
  under Constans II, 31
  taxation under Leo III, 65, 71, 444
  transfer to See of Constantinople, 71,
    87–8
  under Byzantine control in eighth
    century, 75
  revolt of Elpidius (781), 83
  and Charlemagne, 90
  Arab attacks from Africa, 100–1,
    727–8
  lost to Arabs, 101, 102, 103, 121, 129,
    460, 728–9
  base for Arab raids, 101, 728–32
  under Fatimid Caliphate of Egypt,
    648, 730
  under Basil I, 121, 128, 129, 729, 733
  expedition of Nicephorus II, 152–3, 731
  proposed expedition of Basil II, 192,
    731
  expedition of George Maniaces, 197,
    731
  and Normans, 208, 221, 731
  united with South Italy under Roger
    II, 222
  under William I, 229
  support for Pope Alexander III, 230
  lands claimed by Henry VI, 247
  establishment of Aragon rule, 347, 404
  see also Roger II; Manfred; Charles of
    Anjou; Peter III, king of Aragon;
    Frederick II and III of Sicily
Sicily, See of, archbishop appointed by
    Pope, 460
Sicily, theme of, 64, 121, 707
Siderocastron, town in Greece, part of
    duchy of Athens, 410, 413, 414
Sidon, town in Syria, captured by John
    Tzimisces, 170, 723

Siegfried, bishop, ambassador from Provence at Constantinople, and Liutprand of Cremona, 143

Sifanto, *see* Siphnos

Sigismund, king of Hungary, later German Emperor
resistance to Turks, 376, 429, 545–6, 590, 766, 768
relations with Serbia, 551–3
relations with Bosnia, 556
relations with Wallachia, 563

signorie, 265

silentium, summoned by Leo III, 70

Silistria, *see* Dorystolum

silk trade and industry
in Greece, 41, 117, 409, 428
in Crete, 428
trade with China *via* Central Asia, 478 and n. 3, 487
Byzantine restrictions on Russian purchases, 511 n. 3
in Persia, 644

silver trade, 159
mining, 532–3, 548, 609, 644, 646
coinage, 380, 533, 548, 678

Silzibul, khan of western branch of T'ou Kiue, agreement with Justin II, 478 and n. 3, 479

Simon, bishop of Pécs, 575

Simonis, daughter of Andronicus II, wife of Milutin, Serbian king, 345, 534

simony, 459

Sinahin in Armenia, monastery of, 616

Singidunum, town on Danube, retaken from Avars, 481; *see also* Belgrade

Sinjar, Seljuq sultan, 655, 742

Sinope (Sinop), port on Black Sea in Asia Minor
Arab troops at (860), 713
incorporated into Empire of Trebizond, 291
taken by Seljuqs, 300–1, 746

Siphnos (Sifanto), Aegean island, under Latin rule, 425, 426

Siponto, synod of (1050), 460

Sir Daryā, *see* Jaxartes

Siracene, principality in Armenia, 597, 609–10, 619

Sîrf sîndîgî, Turkish name for site of battle of Marica (q.v.), 763

Sirmium, province and city on the river Sava
Byzantine province, 189
struggle for control between Byzantium and Hungary, 234, 245, 581, 583, 585
metropolitan See of, 455, 586

attacked by Avars, 478; taken (582), 480
attacked by Pechenegs, 578
and Bulgarian Empire under Symeon, 507
and St Demetrius, 576

Sis, town in Cilicia, capital of Lesser Armenia, 629–30, 632, 635–7

Sisinnius II, Patriarch of Constantinople, 184

Šišman, despot of Vidin, 537, 542; *see also* Michael Šišman, John Šišman

Šišman, son of Michael, Bulgarian pretender, 544

Sisuan, name for Lesser Armenia, q.v., 629 n. 1

σιτόκριθον, tax on grain payable in kind under Andronicus II, 343

Siunia, district in Armenia, 597 and n. 1, 606, 610–13, 616, 620, 626 n. 2, 637

Siunid dynasty in Caucasia, 610 and n. 3, 615, 620

Sivas, *see* Sebastea

Sixtus IV, Pope, and Stephen the Great of Moldavia, 564

Siyāwush, *see* Jimri

Skadar (Scodra), *see* Scutari

Skanderbeg (George Castriota, Iskender Bey), Albanian leader against the Turks, 383, 557–8, 564, 770–1, 772

Skiathos, Aegean island, under Venetian rule, 425

Skopelos, Aegean island, under Venetian rule, 425

Skoplje (Scupi), town in Macedonia, 185, 186, 187, 316, 530, 573
under Bulgaria, 524, 527
captured by Serbs (1282), 345, 533
coronation of Stephen Dušan as Emperor, 362, 538
coronation of Uroš V as king, 538
bishops of, 524
assembly to approve new legal code (1349), 539
under Vukašin, 541

Skortá, district round Karytaina in Peloponnese, 393

Skyros, island in Aegean
bishopric of, 409
under Venetian rule, 425

Slav Churches
and philological work of Byzantines, 112, 497
liturgy in Slavonic approved by Rome, 123, 124, 125, 455, 499

slavery and slaves, 93, 94, 159, 369, 495, 501 n. 1, 568, 644, 651–2, 678, 682, 702

Slavonic language
  used in liturgy, 123–5, 126, 455, 464,
    497, 499–501, 561
  Old Church Slavonic, 497
  used in missionary work, 497
  scripts, 497, 502 and n. 1
  literature and translations, 501–2, 515
  and Serbian, 532
  official language in Rumania, 561
Slavs
  attacks on Constantinople, 10, 480, 482
  and Avars, 10, 32, 480–3
  piracy in Adriatic, 25
  attacks on Balkans, 29, 30, 31, 32, 35,
    476, 480–3
  attacks on Illyricum, 438, 480–1
  and Bulgars, 32, 74, 485 and n. 1
  incursions in Danube region, 29, 476,
    480
  penetration into Greece, 29, 480–2,
    488, 489 and n. 1
  settlements in Asia Minor, 32, 39, 74
  settlements in Thrace and Macedonia,
    74, 480, 481, 489
  settlements in Dalmatia, 481
  defeated in Greece by Stauracius (783),
    83, 489
  pressure on Venice and Istria, 257,
    258, 262–3, 268
  and Dalmatia, 268, 271
  subjects of rulers of Kiev, 111, 504–5,
    510
  payment of tribute to Khazars, 111
  of Lake Balaton, 124
  Northern and Southern, separated by
    Magyars, 128, 504
  attacks on Empire in eleventh century,
    194, 196–7
  help for George Maniaces' rebellion,
    201–2
  independent policy of principalities,
    212
  in Peloponnese, 32, 92, 390, 399, 480
    and n. 6, 481–2, 488 and n. 4, 489
    and n. 3
  missionary work among, 111–12, 455,
    490, 496, 499–502
  and Viking migrations, 495, 504–5
  and Greek Church in Hungary, 587
Sliven, fortress south of Balkan range, 542
Slovakia, liberated from Avars (c. 623),
  482
smallholders, 36, 38
Smbat VI Bagratuni, prince of Armenia,
  606–7
Smbat VII Bagratuni, High Constable of
  Armenia, 608

Smbat VIII, High Constable of Armenia,
  611
Smbat I (IX) the Martyr, king of
  Armenia, 136, 613–14, 715
Smbat II the Conqueror, king of Armenia,
  614–15, 617–18
Smbat I of Lesser Armenia, 634
Smbat II, king of Siunia, 616
Smbat, constable of Armenia, historian,
  633 n. 1, 634, 636
Smederevo, *see* Semendria
Smilec, Bulgarian tsar, 537
Smyrna (Izmir), town in Asia Minor,
  under Empire of Nicaea, 319
  held against Turks, 347, 756
  taken by Timur, 767
  revolts against Ottomans, 768
Smyrna, amir of, *see* Tzachas
soap manufacture, 428
Södermanland, home of Vikings, 494
Sofia, *see* Sardica
Sogdians, Central Asian tribe, 478
Söğüt, town in Bithynia in Asia Minor,
  760
Soissons, town in France, and Fourth
  Crusade, 277
solidus, gold coin, 145, 410, 730
Sommaripa, Italian family, in Aegean
  islands, 425
Sophene, district of Armenia, 597 and
  n. 1
Sophocles, quoted by Cyril of Alexan-
  dria, 53
Sozopetra (Zapetra, Zibaṭra), town in
  northern Syria, 706, 709–11, 714
  captured by Theophilus (837), 103, 710
Sozopolis, town on west coast of Black
  Sea, 333, 370, 535, 542
Sozopolis, town in Asia Minor, 224
Spain
  part of Roman Empire, 25
  in German hands, 27, 28
  reconquest of south-east by Justinian,
    28
  Arab conquest, 41, 699
  and Arabic poetry, 686
  Umayyad rulers in, 100, 103, 701, 730
  and Arabs in Sicily, 728, 732
  lost by the Abbasids, 645, 663, 701
  Berber Empire in, 651
  prosperity, 40
  cultivation of cotton, 644
spatharius, title, 260
spatharocandidatus, title, 117, 492
Spercheius, river in Greece, battle (997),
  184, 187
Sphentislav, *see* Svetoslav, Jakov

Sphrantzes, George, historian, *Chronicon Maius*, 380 n. 1
spice trade, 41, 633–4
Σπογγάριος, 140 n. 1
Spoleto, duchy of, and Lombards, 444
Spondyles, catepan of Antioch under Romanus III, 725
Sporades, Aegean islands, under Latin rule, 425, 429
Σπωρακίον, τὰ, 140 n. 1
Srebrnica (Srebrnik), mining town in Bosnia, 551, 560
Sredna Gora, mountains in Balkans, 770
Stachys, bishop traditionally ordained by St Andrew, 456
Stampalia, *see* Astypalaea *and* Quirini-Stampalia
Stauracius, Emperor, 91, 96
Stauracius, eunuch, statesman under Irene
    victory over Slavs in Greece (783), 83, 489
    de facto ruler of Empire, 88
    rivalry with Aetius, 89–90
    Arab campaigns, 83, 706
Stenimachus, town in Thrace, 293, 333, 360
Stephen I, Pope, quoted, 676
Stephen II, Pope
    and eastern Illyricum, 72
    and Lombards, 75, 446
    relations with Pepin III, 76, 78, 445
Stephen III, Pope
    denunciation of iconoclasts at Roman synod of 769, 77
    and minting of coins, 446
Stephen V, Pope
    and Moravia, 124, 125, 126
    and Photius, 126, 455
Stephen IX, Pope, 463
Stephen I, Patriarch of Constantinople, brother of Leo VI, 126, 133, 138, 455
Stephen I, king of Hungary
    marriage of daughter, 185
    ecclesiastical policy, 573
    relations with Byzantium, 573, 575
    defeat of Ajtony, 574
    and the nunnery of Veszprém, 574–5
    Admonitions, 575
Stephen II, king of Hungary, war with Byzantium, 221, 581
Stephen III, king of Hungary, son Géza II
    relations with Manuel I, 233–4, 582
    death, 584
Stephen IV, king of Hungary, brother of Géza II, supported by Manuel I, 233, 582, 583

Stephen V, king of Hungary and Bulgaria, 536, 589
    relations with Michael VIII, 589
Stephen I, prince of Iberia, 604 and n. 2, 605
Stephen II, prince of Iberia, 605
Stephen III, prince of Iberia, 608
Stephen Nemanja, Grand Župan of Serbia, 520–2
    accession, 233, 520
    struggle against Manuel I, 233, 521
    allegiance to Andronicus I renounced, 245
    defeated by Isaac II, 247, 521, 523
    marriage of son Stephen to Alexius III's daughter Eudocia, 247, 248, 521, 530
    attacked by Hungary, 585
    encouragement of Orthodox Church, 522
    abdication, 248, 522, 530–1
Stephen the First Crowned, Serbian king, 530–2
    marriage to Alexius III's daughter Eudocia, 247, 248, 275, 521, 530
    struggle for the throne with his brother Vukan, 248, 530
    relations with Latin Empire, 301, 531
    relations with Theodore of Epirus, 305
    relations with the Papacy, 469, 470, 531
    relations with Dobromir Strez, 526, 531
    relations with Emperor in Nicaea, 531–2
    and Church in Serbia, 531–2
    coronation, 469, 531 and n. 2
Stephen Uroš I, Serbian king
    and Charles of Anjou, 470
    exploitation of mineral resources, 532
Stephen Uroš II Milutin, Serbian king
    invasion of Byzantine territory, 339, 345, 533–4
    relations with Andronicus II, 345, 349, 534
    relations with Michael Šišman, 542
Stephen Uroš III Dečanski, Serbian king, 534–5
    appealed to by *panhypersebastus* John Palaeologus, 351
    victory over Bulgaria (1330), 353, 534, 543
    civil war, 534
    help for Andronicus II, 534
    deposition and death, 535
Stephen Uroš IV Dušan, Serbian king and Emperor, 537–40
    deposition of Stephen Uroš III, 535

Stephen Uroš IV (*cont.*)
  gains in Macedonia, 354, 360, 362, 537–8
  relations with Bulgaria, 353, 537
  treaty with Byzantium (1334), 354, 538
  gains in Albania, 356, 362, 538
  gains in central Greece, 356, 362, 539
  relations with John VI Cantacuzenus, 359, 538–40
  relations with regency for John V, 359
  relations with Zealots, 362
  crowned Emperor, 362, 522, 538
  relations with John V, 365, 539
  relations with Venice, 539–40
  relations with the Papacy, 540
  relations with Hungary, 540
  law code, 538–9, 540
  extent of Empire, 362–3, 539–40
  collapse of Serbian Empire after his death, 369
Stephen Uroš V, Serbian Emperor, 538, **541–2**, 549
Stephen the Admiral, relative of Michael IV, 197
Stephen Asoḷik (Asoḷik) of Taron (Taraun), Armenian historian, author of a *Universal History*, 160 n. 3, 616 n. 1
Stephen Držislav, king of Croatia, 185
Stephen Dušan, *see* Stephen Uroš IV
Stephen the Great, *voivode* of Moldavia, 563–4
Stephen II Kotromanić, ban of Bosnia, 548
Stephen Lazarević, Serbian prince, **551–3**
  biography, 545
  relations with Ottomans, 378, 551–2
  relations with Venice, 552
  relations with Hungary, 551, 552–3
Stephen Orbelian of Siunia, Armenian historian, 633 n. 1
Stephen, brother of Theodore II of Lesser Armenia, 630
Stephen Tomašević, Bosnian king, 555, 557
Stephen Vojislav, prince of Zeta, 197, **519–20**
Stephen the Young, monk from monastery of Auxentius, murdered by iconoclasts, 80
Stibor, *voivode* of Transylvania, 563
Štip, town in Balkans, 345, 533, 541
Stoic philosophy
  and ruler-worship, 2
  Hellenistic tradition, 45
  and education, 46
  and Muslim theology, 691
  influence on Cappadocians, 49
  influence on John Chrysostom, 51
Stracimir, *see* John Stracimir
Strategicon, military manual, 35, 61
strategus, governor of theme, *see under* theme system *for list of themes*
stratiotes (στρατιώτης), name given to pronoiar, 219
stratopedarches, 150, 158, 175
Strez, Dobromir, Bulgarian chieftain
  independent principality at Prosek, 299, 526
  ally for a time of Michael I of Epirus, 299
  relations with Latin Empire, 299–301
  relations with Serbia, 526, 531
Stromoncourt, *see* Thomas I d'Autremencourt
Strumica, town in Balkans, 351, 537, 541
Strymon (Struma), river in Balkans, 32, 97, 188, 316
Studenica, monastery in Serbia, 522
Studites, and the monastery of Studius in south-west Constantinople
  power of, 94
  opposition to imperial intervention in Church affairs, 95
  under Michael I, 95
  interference in politics, 97–8
  support of the images, 100, 101, 102
  refuge of Michael V, 199
  entered by Isaac I, 206
  see also Theodore the Studite
Stylianus, leader of Ignatian party, 126
Stylianus Zautzes, Logothete of the Drome under Leo VI, *basileopator*, 127 and n. 2, 128, 130, 133–4
Suania, Georgian principality, 602, 628
Šubići, Croatian rulers of Bosnia, 548
Sublaeum, town in Asia Minor, fortifications of, 237
Sublime Porte, 426
Suceava, town in Moldavia
  metropolitan See, 561
  Turkish attacks, 564
Sudan, in Africa, source of gold, 644
Ṣūfism
  influence on Georgian literature, 625
  within Islam, 659, 688–94, 747
sugar
  exported from Crete, 428
  produced in Peloponnese, 428
Sülamîsh, governor of Rūm, in revolt against Mongols, 751
Sulaym, Bedouin tribe, and devastation of North Africa, 651

Sulaymān, son of Bāyezīd I
  struggle for power with brothers, 378, 552, 767–8
  and Turkish culture, 772
Sulaymān the Magnificent, Ottoman Sultan, conquests in Hungary, 560
Sulaymān, son of Orkhan, capture of Callipolis, 366 and n. 1, 761
Sulaymān ibn Kutlumîsh (Sulaymān-shāh), Seljuq of Rūm, 211, 213, 654, 740, 758
Sulaymān, Umayyad Caliph, 62, 63
Sulaymān, Umayyad general, 64
Sultan, Muslim title of secular head of state, 655–6, 659, 666, 737, 761, 763, 765
Sumbat son of David, Georgian historian, 625 n. 1
Summa Contra Gentiles of Thomas Aquinas, translated into Greek, 471
Sunbād, leader of revolt against Abbasids, 682
Sunnism, Sunnites, orthodox Muslim sect, 631, 646, 647, 649, 655, **657–9**, **672–3**, 680–2, 688, 691–2, 737–8, 745, 765
Surami, district in Caucasia, 626 n. 2
Susan, St, martyr, daughter of Vardan II, 600
suzerain, suzerainty, 290, 315, 333, 334, 391, 396, 406, 410, 416, 423
Svatopluk, nephew of Rastislav, ruler of Moravia, 124–5, 500
Svetoslav (Sphentislav), Jakov, ruler of western Bulgaria, 536, 589
Svetoslav, Theodore, Bulgarian tsar, territorial gains from Byzantium, 348, 537
Svjatoslav, prince of Kiev, **158–62, 513–15**
  invasion and occupation of Bulgaria, 151, 156, 158–62, 513 and n. 3, 514 and n. 1, 571
  defeat by John Tzimisces, 159–62, 164, 175, 514
  treaty with Byzantium, 161–2, 179, 514–15
  and Christianity, 515
Swedes, migration to south, 494 and n. 2, 495–6; *see also* Varangians
Syke, port in Cilicia, Byzantine troops defeated by Arabs (771), 74, 705
Sylvester I, Pope, and *Donation of Constantine*, 76
Sylvester II, Pope, and Stephen I of Hungary, 573
Symbatius (Constantine), eldest son of Leo V, 98

Symbatius, Logothete of the Drome under Michael III, 115, 117
Symeon II, Patriarch of Jerusalem, and negotiations for reunion of Rome and Constantinople in eleventh century, 465–7
Symeon, Bulgarian tsar, **502–4, 505–8**
  education, 127, 135
  wars against Byzantium, 127–9, 134–9, 502–3, 505–8, 569
  claim to imperial throne, 135, 137, 138, **505–8**
  and Magyars, 504
  attack on Serbia, 138, 507–8
  attack on Croatia, 138–9, 508
  and John Vladislav, 188
  encouragement of Slavonic letters and Byzantine culture, 502
  death, 139, 508
Symeon the New Theologian, writings widely read, 60
Symeon, *protoasecretis* under Romanus II and Nicephorus II, 148 n. 1, 153 n. 3
Symeon Uroš, Serbian ruler of Epirus and Thessaly, 541
Symmachus, Pope, 435, 444, 450
Symposium of Plato, 47
Synadenus, Theodore, father of the wife of Géza I of Hungary, 578
Synadenus, Theodore, *protostrator*
  supporter of Andronicus III in civil war, 350
  imperial governor of Epirus, 355
  governor of Thessalonica, 356, 358
Synaxarion of Constantinople, 105, 106, 108, 152 n. 1, 155
syncellus, official, 162 n. 1, 204
Synesius, rhetorician, criticism of the Emperor Arcadius, 16
Synodicon, official statement against heresies, 217
Syra, Aegean island, bishopric of, 426
Syracuse, port in Sicily
  the renegade Euphemius and Arab attacks, 728
  taken by Arabs (878), 121, 729
  retaken under Nicephorus II, 152
  taken by George Maniaces, 197, 731
Syrgiannes, *megas dux*
  in civil war between Andronicus II and III, 350–1
  in service of Stephen Dušan, 354
Syria
  part of Roman Empire, 24, 26, 699
  large landowners in, 39
  industry and commerce, 41, 427
  Venetian trade with, 272

Syria (*cont.*)
conquered by Persia, 21, 29, 30
conquered by Heraclius, 21
conquered by Muslims, 5, 20, 21, 30, 35
centre of Umayyad Empire, 699
ports used by Muslim navy, 25, 63
campaigns of Leo IV, 82
Byzantine fleets off, 107
under Hamdanids, 146, 703, 718–19
campaigns of Nicephorus II, 147–50,
154, 156, 721–2
invaded by the Carmathians, 163, 648
campaigns of John Tzimisces, 168,
169, 720
invaded by Fatimids (974), 169
campaigns of Basil II, 149, 173, 182
campaigns of Romanus III, 195–6
campaigns of Michael IV, 197
Romanus IV's campaigns against
Seljuqs, 209
Latin ambitions in, 214
Latin principality, 215, 221, 467
campaigns of Alexius I, 215, 216
campaigns of John II, 223–5
plans of Manuel I, 227
refuge of Conrad of Montferrat, 277
and First Crusade (q.v.), 654
Christian position in before Third
Crusade, 246
and Fourth Crusade, 279, 390
and Crusade of St Louis of France, 317
Mongol invasions, 377, 634, 766
and Seljuqs, 209, 653–4, 746
Armenians in, 618
under Egyptian control, 634, 645, 648,
652, 703, 714–15, 718, 722
under Abbasids, 638
and Saladin, 654
and Mamluks, 634–5, 654
and Ayyūbids, 746
Syriac
common language of Palestine, 55
Christian literature in, 55, 68
learnt by Constantine (Cyril), 112
translations of Greek works, 672
Syrian Church and culture
conversion to Christianity, 42
part of See of Antioch, 19
home of monophysites, 20, 21, 56, 66, 73
and Paulicians, 66, 73
and Hellenism, 54
and Aramæan culture, 55
source of wonder-tales, 55
monasteries and monasticism, 58, 688
influence in Armenia, 599
and Nestorianism, 599 and n. 1
Syrian dynasty, *see* Isaurians, Emperors

Syspiritis, district in Armenia, 596, 609,
611, 624
Szávaszentdemeter in Hungary, 576
monastery of, 577, 586
church of St Demetrius, 583
Szegedin, treaty of (1444), 384 and n. 1,
554 n. 1, 771 and n. 1

Ṭabarī, aṭ-Ṭabarī, Arabic historian, 109–
10, 685, 707
Ṭabaristān, region on southern shore of
Caspian Sea, 681
Tabor, Mt, in Palestine, 170, 723
Tabrīz, town in Azerbaijan, 615, 624
Tachat Andzevats'i (Tačat Anjewac'i),
see Tatzates
Tactica of Leo VI, 141
Ṭāhir, Persian general under al-Ma'mūn,
founder of dynasty in Khurasan,
645, 701
Tahirids, Persian dynasty, 647, 677
aṭ-Ṭā'i', Abbasid Caliph of Baghdad,
702–3
Taïk, *see* Tayk'
Tamara, sister of John Šišman of Bul-
garia, in Turkish harem, 545
Tamerlane, *see* Timur
Tamoritis, district in Armenia, 596, 608
Tancred, Norman crusader from South
Italy, 215, 216
T'ang dynasty in China, 736
Τανισμὰν ὁ σουλτάν, 741 n. 1
tanning, 428
Tao, northern Tayk' (q.v.), 181, 189,
609–11, 613–14, 617–18, 621
see also David, prince of Tao
Taormina, town in Sicily, 121, 129, 152,
729–32
Tara, river in Balkans, 501, 532, 581
Taranto, town in South Italy
taken by Arabs, 103, 728, 730
retaken by Byzantines under Basil I,
729
in Byzantine hands in eleventh century, 197, 201
captured by Robert Guiscard, 208
Tarasius, Patriarch of Constantinople
against iconoclasm, 66
appointment, 84, 109
and Seventh General Council, 85, 447
and Constantine VI's second marriage,
89, 95
death, 94
Taraun (Tarawn, Taron), principality in
Armenia, 165–7, 596, 609–13, 616
Tarchaniotes, Andronicus, nephew of
Michael VIII, 336

Tarim basin in Central Asia, 736

Taron, *see* Taraun

Taronitae, Byzantine family in Taraun, 616

Taronites, Gregory, *magister*, general, governor of Thessalonica under Basil II, 179, 184; *see also* Ashot (his son)

Tarsus, city in Cilicia in Asia Minor
  on route of Arab invasions, 63
  refortified by Arabs, 83, 705–6
  Tarsites defeated under Basil I, 120
  Arab defeat off (904), 130
  raided by Byzantine fleet, 720
  battle of Mount of Blood (963–4), 149
  taken by Nicephorus II, 149, 156, 157 n. 1, 721
  Basil II at, 186
  murder of Thoros' brother, 235
  and Armenians, 628–30, 632–3
  Arab naval base, 714, 716, 720

Tarsus, amirs of, 140, 708–9, 712, 715–16, 735

Tashir, *see* Loṛi

Tata, treaty (1426), 552–3

Tatars, Mongol tribe
  and Bulgaria, 535 n. 2, 536–7
  and Hungary, 561
  allies of Turks, 564
  pressure on Bulgaria, 336
  sent by Michael Šišman to help Andronicus II, 352
  see also Golden Horde

Tatʻev, town in Armenia, 615
  monastery of, 616

Tatzates (Tachat Andzevatsʻi), general of Bucellarion theme
  desertion to Arabs, 83, 706
  High Constable of Armenia, 608

Taurus, mountain range in Asia Minor, 22, 63, 139, 195, 216, 223, 225, 235, 750
  frontier against Arabs, 697, 699

Tavshanjhil, *see* Philocrene

taxation
  before 717, 37–40
  under Leo III, 64–5, 71, 442, 444
  under Irene, 89, 93
  reforms of Nicephorus I, 92–4
  under Romanus I, 141
  under Constantine VII, 145
  under Nicephorus II, 151, 152 n. 2
  under Basil II, 184, 190
  of Slav provinces under Basil II, 189, 196–7
  of Georgia and theme of Mesopotamia, 204, 209
  poorest classes liable under Alexius I, 218
  on Bulgarian goods, 503
  abuses under Isaac II, 245
  under Alexius IV, 283
  in Greece under the Latins, 292
  of the clergy under the Latin Empire, 303, 395
  under the Palaeologi, 341, 343, 350, 363
  in Catalan duchy of Athens, 414
  in Bulgaria, 522, 529
  in Rumania, 562
  of Caucasia under Abbasids, 608
  of Armenia under Constantine IX, 620
  of Georgia under Mongols, 626
  under Islam, 649–50, 656–7, 664, 666, 677, 774
  in Asia Minor under Il-Khans, 754
  farming of, 207, 218
  pronoiars' right of collection, 219, 239, 240
  see also *akrostichon, allelengyon, annona, bir, crustica, dikerata,* 'German' tax, καπνικόν, land-tax, σιτόκριθον

Taygetus, mountain range in Peloponnese, Slav settlement at, 390, 399, 400

Taykʻ (Taïk), district in Armenia, 177, 186, 189, 596, 609; *see also* Tao

Tchorlu, *see* Tzurulum

Tekes valley in Tien Shan, 479

Tekke, Turkish principality in Lycia, 756

Telerig, Bulgarian khan
  and war with Constantine V, 75
  given asylum by Leo IV, 82

Telets, Bulgarian khan, and war with Constantine V, 74–5, 490

Teluch, theme of, 195

Temes, district of Hungary, 574, 581

Templars, order of, 247, 396, 630, 631

Temujin, Mongol prince, *see* Jenghiz Khan

Tenedos, Aegean island
  promised to Venice by John V, 365, 370–1, 372
  under Amadeo of Savoy, 373

Tenos, Aegean island
  under Venetian rule, 425, 426
  bishopric of, 426

Tephrice (Divrigi), town in east of Asia Minor, home of Paulicians, 111, 120, 137 n. 1, 712, 714

terciers, see triarchs

Terek, river in Caucasus, 493

Termács, great-grandson of Árpád, visit to Constantinople, 572

Tervel, Bulgarian khan, 489, 491
  help for Justinian II, 485 and nn. 2 and 3, 486
  and revolt of Nicetas Xylinites against Leo III, 64

terzieri, *see* triarchs

Tessarakontapechys, a Jew of Tiberias, and Arab iconoclasm, 66

tetarteron, coin, 151 n. 2, 155

Tetovo, town in northern Macedonia, 533

Teutonic Knights, order of, in Peloponnese, 396

textile industry and trade, 159, 428, 568, 615, 644, 733; *see also* silk

Thamal, eunuch, Arab naval commander, 717

Thamar the Great, queen of Georgia, 623–4, 625 n. 1
  support for Comneni of Trebizond, 291, 624

Thasos, Aegean island, Byzantine fleet destroyed off (829), 709

Theaetetus of Plato, 47

Thebasa, town in Cappadocia, 707–8

Thebes, city in Greece
  under Latin rule, 292, 298, 309, 391, 408
  occupied by Leo Sgouros, 389
  French duchy of, 300, 389, 408
  capital of duchy of Athens, 410, 413
  sacked by Catalan Company, 411
  taken by Navarrese Company, 375, 419, 420 and n. 1, 421
  taken by Constantine XI, 383
  under the Acciajuoli, 421, 422, 423–4
  manufacture of silk and purple cloth, 428

Theiss (Tisza), river in central Europe, tributary of Danube, 478, 481, 490, 496, 572, 573

thelematarioi, Greek farmers under Latin Empire, 327

thema, *see* theme system

theme system
  development from exarchates, 29
  in Asia Minor in seventh century, 35–6
  subdivision of larger themes, 64, 73, 102
  support for iconoclasm in Asia Minor, 70, 98
  loyalty to Emperor, 82, 88
  new themes created by Nicephorus I, 92
  new themes created by Theophilus, 102–3, 492
  imperial themes, 489, 492, 509
  legislation about soldiers' property, 141–2, 145
  frontier themes, 697
  support for Thomas the Slavonian, 100, 709
  see also Aegean Sea, Anatolikon, Armenia, Armeniakon, Bucellarion, Cappadocia, Carabisiani, Cephalonia, Chaldia, Charsianon, Cherson, Cibyrraeot, Colonea, Dalmatia, Dyrrachium, Hellas, Longobardia, Lycandus, Macedonia, Mesopotamia, Opsikion, Paphlagonia, Peloponnese, Samos, Seleucia, Sicily, Teluch, Thessalonica, Thrace, Thracesion

Theoctistus, Logothete of the Drome under Theodora
  career, **105–8**
  restoration of icons, 106, 112
  military expeditions, 106–7, 115, 147, 712
  military plans, 109
  interest in learning, 107
  conflict with Bardas, 107–8
  comparison with Joseph Bringas, 147
  murder, 108 and n. 2

Theodatus, Gothic king, 436

Theodora, Empress, daughter of Constantine VIII
  Psellus on, 193, 199
  sent to nunnery by Zoe, 196
  co-Empress with Zoe, 199, 201
  sole Empress on death of Constantine IX, 204–5
  relations with the Papacy, 463
  relations with Fatimids, 726
  and crown of Hungary, 576

Theodora, wife of Theophilus
  regent for Michael III, 104, **105–8**
  restoration of icons, 106, 112
  naval and military operations, 106–7, 147, 712–13, 728
  dethroned by Michael III, 108 and n. 2, 450
  and letter from Pope Nicholas I, 113

Theodora, converted Jewess, second wife of John Alexander of Bulgaria, 543

Theodora, Khazar princess, wife of Justinian II, 485

Theodora Palaeologina, sister of Andronicus III, second wife of Michael Šišman of Bulgaria, 351, 353, 543

Theodora Petraliphina of Arta, wife of Michael II of Epirus, 314 n. 1, 318, 321, 322, 329

Theodora, daughter of Constantine VII, wife of John I Tzimisces, 159

Theodora, daughter of John VI Cantacuzenus, wife of Orkhan, Ottoman Sultan, 761

Theodora, grand-niece of John Vatatzes, wife of Michael VIII Palaeologus, 324

Theodora, niece of Manuel I
marriage to Henry of Babenburg, 228
wife of Baldwin III of Jerusalem, 235

Theodora, sister of Manuel I, 584

Theodore I Lascaris, Emperor of Nicaea
flight from Constantinople, 286, 291
resistance to Latins in Asia Minor, 291, 295, 300
alliance with Kalojan of Bulgaria, 295
relations with Pope Innocent III, 295
crowned Emperor at Nicaea, 295
war with Seljuqs, 295–6, 746
treaty with Latin Emperor, 300 and n. 1, 304, 307
relations with Empire of Trebizond, 295, 300–1, 303
marriage to Yolanda's daughter, 305, 307
and Theodore of Epirus, 296–7, 305–7
opposition of Greek clergy, 306–7
relations with Venetian Podestà of Constantinople, 307
relations with Leo II of Lesser Armenia, 320 and n. 1
and Church in Serbia, 532
marriage of his daughter to Béla IV of Hungary, 589
death, 307

Theodore II Lascaris, Emperor of Nicaea, **321–4**
character, 321
marriage to John Asen II's daughter Helen, 311, 312, 528
relations with Seljuqs, 322
relations with Bulgaria, 322
relations with Michael II of Epirus, 322–3
relations with the Papacy, 323
relations with Michael VIII Palaeologus, 322–3, 324
death, 324, 401

Theodore II Irenicus, Patriarch of Constantinople in Nicaea, 304

Theodore Ducas, Emperor of Thessalonica, half-brother of Michael I of Epirus, **304–10**
resistance to Latins, 296–7, 527
campaigns in Greece as ruler of Epirus, 304–6

treaty with Venetians, 305
and Theodore I Lascaris, 296–7, 305–7
support of Greek clergy, 306–7, 308–9
capture of Thessalonica, 308, 321, 398, 527
coronation as Emperor, 308 and n. 1, 309, 398
clash with Empire of Nicaea, 309, 527
relations with Bulgaria, 309, 310, 313, 527
threat to Constantinople, 309, 310, 527
taken prisoner, 310, 398
restored to Thessalonica, 313, 315
relations with Frederick II, 316
in retirement at Vodena, 317, 318–19
arrested by John Vatatzes, 315, 319

Theodore I of Lesser Armenia, 629

Theodore (Thoros) II of Lesser Armenia, 234–5, 629–30

Theodore III of Lesser Armenia, 634

Theodore Abū Qurra, bishop of Harran, 68

Theodore Decapolites, *patricius* and *quaestor* under Constantine VII and Romanus II, 145

Theodore (Tʻoros) of Edessa, curopalate, supplanted by Franks, 629

Theodore of Epirus, *see* Theodore Ducas, Emperor of Thessalonica

Theodore, bishop of Euboea, acceptance of papal supremacy, 395

Theodore Graptus, iconophile branded by Theophilus, 103

Theodore of Mopsuestia, theologian, condemned under Justinian I, 56

Theodore Rshtuni (Ṙštuni), High Constable of Armenia, 605–6

Theodore the Stratelates, St, 140 n. 1, 161 and n. 3

Theodore the Studite, monk
exiled by Constantine VI, 89
opposition to Nicephorus I, 94
recalled from exile by Michael I, 96
interference in politics, 97–8
protest against imperial intervention in Church affairs, 99, 101

Theodore, brother of Asen I of Bulgaria, *see* Peter (Theodore), Bulgarian tsar

Theodoret of Cyrrhus, church historian and theologian, condemned under Justinian I, 56

Theodoric, leader of Ostrogoths, 27, 28, 435

Theodorocanus, army commander under Basil II, 186

Theodoropolis, new name for Dorystolum or Euchaneia, 161 and n. 3
Theodosiopolis Erzerum, (Erzurum,
Qālīqalā), town in Armenia
founding, 598 n. 1
in Roman Armenia, 598
home of Paulicians, 73
razed to ground by Constantine V, 74,
703
and Byzantine–Arab wars in tenth
century, 715, 718, 719
Basil II at, 186
under Abbasids, 609, 705
given to David of Tao, 617
sacked by Seljuqs, 204
Turkish princes of, 626 n. 1, 748
captured by Mongols (1241), 748
Theodosius I the Great, Emperor
and Constantinople, 6
grandfather of Pulcheria, 20
settlement with Goths, 26, 35
peace with Persia, 27
and Armenia, 597, 598 and n. 1
comparison with Empire at end of
fifth century, 28
religious policy, 42, 43–4, 47, 50, 431
Theodosius II, Emperor
and land-walls of Constantinople, 6, 8,
9, 10
and Armenia, 598 n. 1
death, 20
Theodosius III, Emperor
ousted by Leo III, 62
treaty with Tervel of Bulgaria, 491
Theodosius III, king of Abasgia, 617–
18
Theodosius, iconoclast archbishop of
Ephesus, 66, 78
Theodosius of Trnovo, supporter of
hesychasm, 544
Theodote, second wife of Constantine VI,
89, 95
Theodotus Melissenus Cassiteras, Patriarch of Constantinople, 99, 101
Theodotus, *see* Adalgisus
Theognostus, supporter of the Patriarch
Ignatius, in Rome, 109, 112, 113,
117, 452, 454
Theophanes, author of *Life of St Michael
Maleinus*, 144
Theophanes, chronicler
on Constantine V's reign, 75, 80
on Charlemagne, 90, 447
on Irene and Nicephorus I, 91 and n. 1
reference to Caucasia, 603 n. 1
Continuator of, 109, 137 n. 1
manuscript in Corvina library, 592

Theophanes Graptus, iconophile branded
by Theophilus, 103
Theophanes, *protovestiarius* and *parakoimomenos* under Romanus I, 140
and n. 1, 510
Theophano, niece of John Tzimisces,
wife of Otto II, 163 and n. 1, 184, 458
Theophano, first wife of Leo VI, 130
Theophano, wife of Romanus II and
Nicephorus II
favourites, 147
regent, 148
marriage to Nicephorus II, 148
and John Tzimisces, 156, 157
and accession of Nicephorus II, 156
exile, 157
and Basil the *parakoimomenos*, 161 n. 1
Theophano, wife of Stauracius, son of
Nicephorus I, 91
Theophilitzes, favourite of Michael III,
116, 117
Theophilus, Emperor, **102–4**
co-Emperor with Michael II (821), 102
persecution of iconophiles, 102, 103–4
mentioned in *Timarion*, 102
and walls of Constantinople, 102
building projects, 735
new themes and defence districts,
102–3, 492
served by Theoctistus, 105, 106
interest in learning, 107, 735
interest in Arab culture, 103
Arab campaigns, 103, 110, 147, 611,
704, 709–12
and Arab attacks on Sicily and South
Italy, 103, 728
naval expedition up Danube, 116
Theophilus, Patriarch of Alexandria,
and John Chrysostom, 20
Theophilus Eroticus, in revolt against
Constantine IX, 202–3
Theophilus or Philotheus, bishop of
Euchaïta, 161 n. 3, 162 n. 1
Theophilus, *patricius* and *quaestor* under
Constantine VII, 145
Theophilus, *syncellus*, 162 n. 1
Theophilus, brother of John Curcuas,
grandfather of John Tzimisces, 158
Theophobus, *see* Naṣr
Theophylact, co-Emperor, son of Michael
I, 96
Theophylact, Patriarch of Constanti-
nople, son of Romanus I, 138, 144,
456, 572
Theophylact, archbishop of Ochrida, 466
Theophylact, archdeacon, leader of pro-
Byzantine party in Rome, 446

Theophylact Simocattes, historian, on Avars, 477 n. 1, 481 n. 3

theosis, 48

Thera (Santorin), Aegean island
under Latin rule, 425
bishopric of, 426

Thermia, *see* Cythnos

Thermopylae, pass in Thessaly, 292, 389, 400
bishopric of, 409

Thessalonica
edict of Theodosius I, 43
as place of exile, 89
and trade with Bulgaria, 128, 503
Slav attacks, 32, 481 and n. 1
captured by the Arabs (904), 129, 716
threatened by Samuel of Bulgaria, 179, 184, 517
and Basil II's Bulgarian campaigns, 181, 188
threatened by the Normans under Robert Guiscard, 213
treaty between Manuel I and Conrad III, 228
sacked by the Normans of Sicily (1185), 245, 522, 584
grant of property to Renier of Montferrat, 277
Latin kingdom of, 288–9, 294, 298, 299, 300, 306, 345, 389, 391, 392, 398, 429
campaigns of Kalojan of Bulgaria, 293–4, 525
attacked by Theodore of Epirus, 305; and captured (1224), 308–9, 321, 398, 527
Greek Empire of, 308–11, 312, 313, 315, 398
Despotate of, under Nicaea, 315
captured by John III Vatatzes (1246), 317, 398
threatened by Michael II of Epirus, 323
John Palaeologus at, 324–5, 326
attacked by Catalan Company, 348, 411
recognition of Andronicus III, 352
and conquests of Stephen Dušan, 537–9
judicial system under the Palaeologi, 353
under governorship of Synadenus, 356
conflict between popular party (Zealots) and aristocracy, 358–9, 360–1
resistance to John Cantacuzenus, 360, 361–2
held by John Cantacuzenus against Serbia, 362

under Manuel II Palaeologus, 371, 373
captured by Turks (1387 and 1394), 375, 764, 766
restored to Byzantium by Sulaymān, 378
ceded to Venetians (1423), 379–80 and n. 1, 769
captured by Turks (1430), 380, 769

Thessalonica, theme of, 92

Thessaly
abortive Bulgar invasion under Telerig, 75
part of Samuel of Bulgaria's empire, 517
Bulgarian garrisons uprooted by Basil II, 187
invaded by Normans, 213
and partition of Empire under Baldwin I, 289
under Latin Empire, 291–2, 298, 299
and Theodore of Epirus, 306
recovered by Michael VIII's troops, 325
opposition to Constantinople after 1261, 329, 332, 336
Catalan Company in, 348, 411
divided between Byzantine Empire and Catalan duchy of Athens, 349, 355
under John Angelus, 359
conquered by Stephen Dušan, 362, 539
independent province, 541
occupied by Turks, 375
and Vlachs, 560
export trade, 428

Thomas Morosini, Latin Patriarch of Constantinople, 293, 297, 301–3, 394

Thomas Artsruni, Armenian historian, 616 n. 1

Thomas I d'Autremencourt (Stromoncourt), lord of Salona, 389

Thomas II d'Autremencourt, lord of Salona, 400

Thomas, bishop of Claudiopolis in Asia Minor, 66, 67

Thomas, Despot of Epirus, 349

Thomas of Metsop', Armenian historian, 633 n. 1

Thomas the Slavonian (*or* Slav), leader of revolt (820–3), 100, 101, 709

Thoros, *see* Theodore II of Lesser Armenia

Thrace
source of corn supplies, 39, 428
subject to See of Constantinople, 20, 434

Thrace (*cont.*)
Slavs in, 32, 480–1
Avar attacks, 480
connection with Leo III, 62 n. 1
iconoclasts transplanted to, 73
building of forts by Constantine V, 74
invaded by Bulgars (763), 74
soldiers' support of icons, 84
troops from, 94
Arab invasions, 698
invaded by Krum, 97, 490–1
cities rebuilt by Leo V, 99
support for Thomas the Slavonian, 101
settlement of prisoners rescued from Bulgaria, 116
Paulicianism, 120
Bogomilism, 120
invaded by Symeon of Bulgaria, 136, 503, 505, 507
Magyar attacks, 146, 509, 571
Russian troops in, 158, 514
support for Leo Tornicius, 203
laid waste by Pechenegs and Uzes (1064), 208
occupied by Frederick Barbarossa on Third Crusade, 246
and Isaac II's Bulgarian campaigns, 523
refuge of Alexius III and Alexius V, 283, 286, 288
under Latin Empire, 289, 293
invaded by Kalojan of Bulgaria, 293, 294, 525
occupied by Theodore of Epirus, 309
invaded by John Asen II, 310, 527
settlements of Cumans in thirteenth century, 320
invaded by Michael Asen of Bulgaria, 322
Michael VIII's troops in, 324–7
Catalan Company in, 347–8, 411
and revolt of Andronicus III, 350–1
support for John Cantacuzenus, 357, 360
invaded by Stephen Dušan, 538
Matthew Cantacuzenus in, 363
decline of agriculture, 363
Turkish conquests in, 366, 369, 762–3, 769
invaded by Christian army under Vladislav III, 383
Thrace, theme of
creation of, 489
support for Artavasdus' revolt, 73
and Nicephorus Phocas the Elder, 121
Thracesion theme
created by Leo III (*c.* 741), 64

loyal to Constantine V, 73
strategi of, 80, 109, 129 n. 1, 705, 712
Thracian Chersonese, 762; *see also* Callipolis
Three Chapters and Justinian I, 437–8
Tibald, count of Champagne, original leader of Fourth Crusade, 276–7
Tiberias, town in Palestine, 170, 723
Tiberius II Constantine, Emperor, Avar and Slav attacks on Empire, 480
Tiberius III Apsimar, Emperor, 66, 441, 485, 606
Tiberius, pretender to throne under Leo III, 64
Tiberius, name taken by Petasius, 70
Tien Shan, 479
Tiepolo, Giacomo, Venetian duke of Candia, 427
Tiflis, capital of Iberia, 601–2
siege of (627), 605
Arab enclave, 605, 624
under Abbasids, 609, 611
amirate of, 609–11, 619, 622
seat of Georgian government, 624, 627
observatory at, 625
Tigris, river, 640, 723
Tihany, hermitages of, 577
Timarion, a twelfth-century satire, 102
timber trade, 615, 644
Timothy, bishop of Alexandria, and Council of Chalcedon, 434
Timur (Tamerlane, Tīmūr, Timūrlenk), Mongol ruler, conquests, 377–8, 627, 766–7
Timur Jāndār, Turkoman prince of Aflani, ruler of Jāndār, 756
Timurtash, Ilkhan governor of Asia Minor, 753–4, 756
Tipoukeitos, index to *Basilica*, 133
Tiridates III of Armenia, 595 n. 1
Tiridates of Ani, Armenian architect, 615–16
Tisza, *see* Theiss
titles, Armenian, 595 n. 3, 596, 598–9, 600, 601, 611, 614, 617, 619, 632 and n. 1, 633
titles, Byzantine
used in Bulgaria, 529
in Rumania, 562
titles, Georgian, 595 n. 3, 603, 622
Tocco, Carlo, count of Cephalonia, 375, 380, 423
Tocco, Leonardo III, of Cephalonia, 424
Tomislav, king of Croatia, 138, 508
τόμος ἑνώσεως, issued by council of 920, 137

Torcello, island in Venetian lagoon, 251
  bishopric of, 264
T'orelis, Caucasian family, 623, 626 n. 2
Tornices, Demetrius, and Isaac II's
  correspondence, 586–7
Tornicius, John, *see* John Tornik
Tornicius, Leo, Armenian in revolt
  against Constantine IX, 203
T'ornik Ch'orduaneli, *see* John Tornik
T'oros, *see* Theodore of Edessa
Tortosa (Anṭarṭūs), port in Syria, 182, 724
T'ou Kiue, Chinese name of Central
  Asian Turks, 478, 483, 486
Toul, bishop of, *see* Leo IX, Pope
Tourxath, khan of T'ou Kiue, rejection of
  Byzantine friendship, 479 and n. 2
Tovin, Muslim amir of, ally of Constantine IX, 203–4
trade, Bulgarian, 128, 159, 503, 527, 529,
  537, 559
trade, Byzantine
  with Bulgaria, 128, 503
  with Russia, 130 n. 4, 140, 162, 475,
    505 and n. 2, 510, 511 and n. 3, 515
  under Manuel I, 240
  trading concessions to Italian cities,
    232, 239; *see also* Genoa, Pisa, Venice
  exports, 428, 733
  decline under the Palaeologi, 363
  with Khazars, 487
  with Huns, 567, 568
  with Magyars, 568
  with China, 478
  with Muslims, 733
  with Turks, 320
trade, Catalan, 415, 427
trade, Caucasian, 609, 615, 624, 627, 733
trade, Egyptian, 40, 277, 634, 648–9, 733
trade, French, 427
trade, Khazar, 487, 495
trade, Lesser Armenian, 631, 633–4
trade, Muslim
  under Abbasids, 643–4, 649, 656–7,
    733, 745
  under Fatimids, 648–9, 733
trade, Russian, 130 n. 4, 140, 159, 162, 474,
    505 and n. 2, 511 and n. 3, 515, 649
trade, Serbian, 533, 559
trade, Slav, in the Dnieper basin, 504
trade of Volga Bulgars, 484, 495
trade as motive for war, 127–8, 233, 345,
    427, 502–3, 634
trade-routes, 5, 26, 41, 289, 427, 478,
    495, 587, 609, 615, 633, 640, 644,
    646, 648
Trajan's Gate, in Balkans, defeat of
  Basil II (986), 178, 181

Trani, port in Apulia in South Italy, 325
  taken by Manuel I, 229
  bishop of, *see* John, bishop of Trani
Transcaucasia, 593 n. 1
Transoxania, 655, 660, 736–7
Transylvania, 564, 583, 769
  victories of John Hunyadi, 553, 770
Trapani, port in Sicily, 412
Traù (Trogir), city on Dalmatian coast,
  268
Trebinje, Serbian province, 520, 530
Trebizond, city in Asia Minor on Black
  Sea
  trade, 615, 733, 745
  defeat of Taronites (988), 179
  allotted to Baldwin I, 290–1
  establishment of Empire of Trebizond
    under the Grand Comneni, 291, 388,
    624, 745
  subject to Seljuq Sultanate of Rūm,
    300–1, 746–7
  subject to Mongols, 315–16
  independent of Constantinople, 328–9
  internal troubles, 544
  overrun by Ottoman Turks (1461),
    329, 387
  relations with Georgia, 291, 624, 627
  relations with Armenia, 733
  churches, 328–9
  Muslims in, 733
Trepča, mining settlement in Serbia, 532,
  555
triarchs (*terzieri*, *terciers*), in Euboea,
  392–3, 399, 400, 412
tribuni (tribunes), civil officials in Venice,
  251–2, 253, 263
Tribuno Menio, doge of Venice, 266–7
Tribuno, Peter, doge of Venice, 264–5
Tridentine province, under metropolitan
  of Aquileia, 253
Trinacria, name for Sicily, q.v.
Tripoli, city in Syria
  and Nicephorus II, 722
  captured by Fatimid troops (974), 169
  and John Tzimisces, 170–1, 723
  and Basil II, 182, 186, 725
  Latin county of, 215
Trnovo, capital of Second Bulgarian
  Empire
  and liberation of Bulgaria, 247, 522–4
  Cathedral of Forty Martyrs in, 311
  ecclesiastical council to condemn
    Bogomilism, 526
  Baldwin I prisoner at, 525
  attacked by Hungarians, 535
  capitulation to Turks (1393), 375, 545,
    765

Trnovo, archbishop of
consecration of Basil, 523
and coronation of Asen I, 245
and coronation of Kalojan, 248
Primate of All Bulgaria, 290, 524, 528–
9
and Patriarchate, 528 n. 1, 529, 545
metropolitan under Patriarch of Constantinople, 545
Troezen, *see* Damala
troubadours, 686
Tshmishkatzak, *see* Khozan
Tudela, *see* Benjamin of Tudela
Ṭughrîl of Arrān, Seljuq leader, 624
Ṭughrîl Bey, early Seljuq leader, 204,
653, 655, 703, 726, 737
Tulunid dynasty in Egypt, 714–15
Tunis, town in North Africa, objective
of crusade of St Louis of France, 335
Tunisia in North Africa
under Aghlabids, 663
invasion by Bedouin tribes, 651
Turin, peace of (1382), 373
Turkestan, 478, 736
Turkia, Byzantine name for Hungary,
509, 572, 579
Turkic peoples
linguistic group, 483
Khazars (q.v.), 111, 484 n. 1, 486
attacks on Empire in eleventh century,
193, 203, 208, 213–14
and Avars, 476–7
and Magyars, 503, 566
and Slavs, 504
see also Pechenegs, Uzes
Turkish Guards in Baghdad, 640, 712
Turkish language, literature and art, 652,
747, 751, 773
Turkomans, nomad tribes driven west by
Mongols, 626, 747
prince of western Persia, 754
Turks, **736–52, 753–76** *and see* Seljuq
Turks, Ottoman Turks *and* List of
Rulers 9 and 10
in Central Asia, 477, 478–9, 483,
484 n. 1, 603, 651, 653, 660, 736–7
infiltration into Byzantine Empire in
twelfth century, 217
mercenaries in Byzantine army, 209,
213, 214, 324–5, 355, 364, 365–6,
401
conquest of Asia Minor, 346–7
amirates and principalities in Asia
Minor, 213–14, 354–5, 383, 753–7,
759–60, 765–7, 769
establishment of colonies in Europe,
366, 369

Mongol invasions, 660, 766–7
adoption of Islam, 652–3, 655, 658–60,
737–8
slaves under Abbasids, 651–2
in Muslim army, 651, 701–2, 738–9
in Mongol armies, 754–5
Turks, Byzantine name for Magyars, 566,
568, 570, 572
Tutush, Seljuq amir, 740
Tvrtko I, ban of Bosnia, 548–9, 550, 555,
556
Twelvers, *see under* Shī'ism
Tyana, town in south-east Asia Minor,
and Byzantine–Arab wars, 91, 707,
710
typicon for the monastic house (the
Lavra) of St Athanasius on Mt
Athos, 155
of Irene, wife of Alexius I, 218
Typus, religious edict of Constans II,
440
Tyropoion, stronghold of Bardas Phocas,
179
Tzachas, Turkish amir of Smyrna,
alliance with Pechenegs, 213–14
Tzakones, Laconian Greeks of Mt Parnon,
399
Tzamandus, fortress to east of Caesarea
in Cappadocia, 717
Tzani, Caucasian people, and Byzantine
frontier, 474
Tzathus I, king of Lazica, 601
Tzathus II, king of Lazica, 602–3
Tziganes (gypsies), *see* the Zott
Tzimisces, John, *see* John I Tzimisces
tzitzakion, Khazar national dress, 487
Tzurulum (Tchorlu), town in Thrace, 289,
313, 314, 317, 398
Tzympe (Chimenlik), fortress near Gal-
lipoli, Ottoman Turks at, 366, 761

'Ubayd Allāh, first Fatimid Caliph, 648
'Ubayd Allāh ibn al-Aqṭa', Arab amir,
708
Ugain, Bulgarian dynasty, 74
Ügedei, Great Khan of Mongols, 749
Uglješa, John, Serbian despot, brother of
Vukašin, 371, 541–2
Uighurs, Turkish tribe in Mongolia, 736
Ukil, Bulgarian dynasty, 74, 75
Ulaszló I, king of Hungary, 591
Ulcinj, town on Dalmatian coast, 521,
552
Uljaitū Khodābanda, Il-Khan leader,
753
'Umar II, Umayyad Caliph, and cam-
paigns against Leo III, 63, 698

Umayyad Caliphate in Damascus
  legal practice, 675
  wars with Byzantium, 696–9
  in Caucasia, 605–7
  comparison with Abbasids, 640, 642–3,
    647, 662, 664–5, 667, 699–700
  fall of, 73, 607, **638–40**, 663, 699, 703
Umayyad Caliphate in Spain, *see under*
  Spain
Umur Bey, Germiyān amir, 756
uncial script, Greek, 502 n. 1
Ungria and Ungrolimne in Boeotia, 571
universities
  in West, 471
  see also Athens *and* Constantinople
unleavened bread, see *azymes*
Upland, home of Vikings, 494
Ural mountains
  source of gold, 487
  and Magyars, 566
Urban II, Pope
  and First Crusade, 214, 271, 466–7
  relations with Constantinople, 465–7
Urban IV, Pope, 335, 402
Urban V, Pope, 370 n. 1, 590
Urfa, *see* Edessa
Urgub, in Cappadocia in Asia Minor, 707
Uroš, Župan of Rascia, marriage to
  Helen, daughter of Béla II, 221
Uroš, *see* Stephen Uroš, Symeon Uroš
Urseolo, *see* Orseolo
Ursus, *see* Orso
Ushtūm in Egypt, on Tinnis lagoon, 713
Ustādhsīs, leader of revolt against
  Abbasids, 682
'Uthmān ibn Ertoghrul, *see* 'Osmān,
  Ottoman Sultan
Utigurs, tribe on east coast of Sea of
  Azov, 475, 477
Utrar, town on Jaxartes, 660
Uzes, nomad tribe
  enemies of Pechenegs, 203, 503
  alliance with Pechenegs against Con-
    stantine X, 208
  attacks on Byzantine Empire, 579
Užice, town in Serbia, 550

Vachʻagan III, king of Caspian Albania,
  601
Vachʻē II, king of Caspian Albania, 600
Vahan, prince of the Mamikonids, 600
Vahan, *Katholikos* of Armenia, 166
Vahrām V, king of Persia, and Armenia,
  598–9
Vahrām-Arshusha III of Gogarene, 605
Vahrām (Kamsarakan-) Pahlavuni, sup-
  porter of Gagik II of Armenia, 619–20

Vahrām, *see* Philaretus Brachamius
Vakhtang I Gorgasal, king of Iberia,
  revolt against Persia, 600 and n. 1,
  601, 602
Vakhtang (Vaxtang) II, king of Georgia,
  626
Vakhtang (Vaxtang) III, king of Georgia,
  626
Valarsaces, co-king of Armenia with
  Arsaces III, 597
Vaḷarshapat in Caucasia, church at, 615
Valāsh, king of Persia, 600–1
Valea Alba, town in Rumania, battle
  (1476), 564
Valens, Emperor
  defeat at battle of Adrianople (378),
    26, 94, 490
  religious policy, 43
Valentinian I, Emperor, religious policy,
  43, 431
Valentinus, Byzantine envoy to
  Tourxath, 479
Van, lake in Armenia, 186, 189, 474, 597,
  603, 615, 617, 718
Vanand, district in Armenia, 616
Vandals
  sea-power, 25
  invasions in 406–7, 27
  in Africa, 28
Varangians, Russian Swedes
  migration to Black Sea, 495
  under Oleg, prince of Kiev, 505
  under Igor, 510
  in Byzantine army, 731, *and see*
    Varangian guard
Varangian guard in Byzantine army, 282,
  286, 516
Varazdat, king of Armenia, 597
Varaz-Gregory, Mihranid prince of Gard-
  man, 605
Varaz-Tirotsʻ II Bagratuni (Varaz-Tirocʻ
  II of the Bagratids), prince of
  Armenia, 605
Varchonites (Avars), 479
Vardan II, prince of the Mamikonids,
  revolt against Persia, 599–600
Vardan III, prince of the Mamikonids,
  602
Vardan the Great, Armenian historian,
  633 n. 1
Vardar, river in Macedonia, 32, 187, 289,
  319, 323, 401, 535
Vardariotes, Hungarians settled on
  Byzantine territory, 570
Varna, town in Bulgaria on Black Sea
  taken by Kalojan, 524
  battle (1444), 384, 554, 591, 771

Varsk'en, *vitaxa* of Gogarene, 600
Vasak, prince of Siunia, 600
Vasak, brother of Smbat VII of Armenia, 609
Vasluiu, town in Moldavia on Rakovica, battle (1475), 564
Vaspurakan, Armenian principality and kingdom, 166, 186, 608, 610–13, 616, 618–19
  ceded to Byzantium, 189, 619
  Bulgarians settled in, 190
vassals
  of Byzantine Emperor, 216, 233, 239, 311, 402, 519, 521, 726
  of Latin Emperor of Constantinople, 290, 295, 402, 426, 526
  in Aegean islands, 426
  of Villehardouin princes of Achaea, 399, 400, 426
  of Angevins of Naples and Taranto, 426
  of Venice, 293, 299, 392, 426
  of Mongols, 316, 537, 626, 749
  of Turks, 301, 315, 372–5, 383, 542, 545, 550, 551, 552, 556, 559, 563, 564
  of Hungary, 544, 546, 551, 552, 561, 589
  of kingdom of Sicily, 297
Vatatzes, Andronicus, general under Manuel I, defeated at Neocaesarea (1176), 237
Vatatzes, John
  in revolt against Constantine IX, 203
  see also John III Vatatzes
Vaxtang, *see* Vakhtang
Veglia (Krk), island off Dalmatian coast, 268
Velbužd (Kjustendil), town in Balkans
  taken by John Vatatzes, 535
  battle (1330), 353, 534, 543
  under the brothers Dejanović, 541
Velebit, town in Croatia, 549
Veles, town in Macedonia, 533
Veligosti, castle and barony in Peloponnese, 390, 394, 400
  Latin See of, 396
Venetia, region in North Italy, 250, 253, 260–1
Venice, **250–74**, *and see* navy *and* List of Rulers 4
  history up to end of twelfth century, 250–74
  under Augustus, 250
  and Lombards, 250–4
  Byzantine province, 75, 77, 250–64
  churches at, 251, 279
  persistence of Roman traditions, 251

civil government, 250–2, 260, 261, 263–4, 270, 272–3
ecclesiastical government, 251–3, 262, 263–4, 269–70
codification of law, 273
beginnings of independent dogeship, 77, 253–5
a sovereign power, 264, 267
civil strife, 254–5, 256–7, 262–3, 265–7
relations with Exarchate of Ravenna, 251, 254–5
relations with Istria, 250, 252–3, 255, 268
relations with Franks, 255–61, 262
pressure from Slavs, 257, 258, 262–3, 264, 268
and Franco-Byzantine agreements, 92, 96, 258–9, 260–1, 262, 448
position of doge in ninth and tenth centuries, 261, 263–5, 268
gain from weakness of Byzantium in later eleventh century, 208
relations with Alexius I, 213, 216, 271
economic policy in twelfth century, 217, 272–3
rivalry with Hungary, 221, 233, 234, 271, 540
attacks on Byzantine islands (1122–6), 222
relations with Manuel I, 228, 229, 232, 240, 272
Arab raids, 263, 268
relations with German Emperors, 266–8, 269, 272–3
relations with Dalmatia, 185, 221, 232–3, 268–9, 271–2
relations with the Papacy, 269–71, 288
relations with Normans, 271, 272
and First Crusade, 271
attack on all Venetians in Empire (1171), 232, 273
and Fourth Crusade, 233, 249, **276–87**
territorial gains in Aegean, Adriatic and Greece after Fourth Crusade, 288–9, 297, 425–7, 429
interest in Epirus and Ionian islands, 297
relations with Michael I and Theodore Ducas of Epirus, 298–9, 300, 305
and Greek Church in Constantinople, 288, 301–2
Constantine (Cyril) and Methodius at, 124
treaties with Byzantium, 182, 187, 267, 333–4, 336, 337, 340, 346, 349, 731
relations with Serbia, 539–40, 552

Venice (*cont.*)
  relations with Sicily, 229, 339, 340
  alliance with Golden Horde, 345
  acquisition of Pteleum in Thessaly, 349
  loans to the Palaeologi, 363–4, 365, 370–1
  and anti-Turkish coalitions, 376, 554, 590
  and fall of Adrianople, 762–3
  appealed to by Manuel II, 376–7
  relations with Ottomans, 378
  defeated by Turks in Albania, 558
  in Peloponnese, 379, 392, 396
  in control of Thessalonica (1423–30), 379–80, 769
  in Euboea, 392–3, 400, 412–13, 415, 416, 418, 423
  help for John of Brienne, 398–9
  in Athens, 409, 423–4
  in Thebes, 409
  in Lesser Armenia, 632–3
  in Crete, 427–8
  maritime power and trade, 261, 262–3, 267–8, 271–3, 289, 291, 320, 326–7, 331, 537
  trade in eastern Mediterranean, 212, 232, 271–3, 277, 326–7, 427
  rivalry with other Italian cities, 212, 221, 232, 249, 271, 272–3, 276, 326–7, 333–4
  wars with Genoa, 333, 345–6, 365, 372–3, 417, 427
  Venetians in Constantinople, 232, 272–3, 288, 293–4, 326–7, 346; *see also* Podestà
  commercial privileges, 182, 216, 221–2, 228, 232, 249, 267–8, 271–3, 275, 307, 326, 333–4
Venier, Marco, in control of Cythera, 425
Veregava, battle (759), 74
Verona, town in Italy, 278
Verria, *see* Berroea
Versinicia, town near Adrianople in Thrace, battle (813), 98
vestes, title, 178, 619
Veszprém in Hungary, nunnery at, 574–5, 576
Veteranitza, castle in Greece, 417
Via Egnatia, road from Dyrrachium to Constantinople, 8, 25–6, 201–2
Viaro, Jacopo, in control of island of Cerigotto, 425–6
vicar-general
  of the principality of Achaea, 403, 410
  of Catalan duchy of Athens, 412–14, 416, 417, 418, 422
vicarii, 33, 34

Victor II, Pope, 463
Victor IV, anti-Pope, 230
Victoria Augusti, 17
Vidin, fortress on Danube in Balkans, 185, 187, 370, 526, 527, 573
  metropolitan of, 523
  under Hungary, 535–6, 544
  independent state under Serbia, 537, 542
  reunited with Bulgaria, 542–3
  under Stracimir, son of John Alexander, 543–4
  occupied by Turks under Bāyezīd I, 546
Vigilius, Pope, 437–8
Vikings
  and Khazars, 492 n. 2
  attack on Constantinople (860), 494, 496
  account of migration from north, 494–6
  and creation of Russian state, 504–5
  fleet, *see* navy, Russian
Villehardouin, *see* Geoffrey, William
Virtus Augusti, 45
Visegrád, monastery in Hungary, 577, 586
Višeslav, town in Balkans, 555
Visigoths
  capture of Rome (410), 9
  attacks on Balkan provinces, 26
  see also Alaric
Vita Basilii of Constantine Porphyrogenitus, 122
Vita Constantini, 1 n. 1
Vitale Michiel, doge of Venice, 271, 273
vitaxa (margrave), Armenian title, 595 n. 3, 596
Viterbo, treaty of (1267), 334, 402–3, 404
Vitoš, mountain in Bulgaria, battle between Bāyezīd I's sons, 552
vizier (wazīr), Muslim official, 236, 641, 654, 666–7, 677–8, 738, 749, 751, 754, 763, 771–4
Vizya, town in Thrace, 317
Vlachs
  and liberation of Bulgaria, 522 n. 1
  incorporated in Second Bulgarian Empire, 245, 530
  under Kalojan, 290, 293
  in army of Michael II of Epirus, 325
  battle with Turks (1395), 542
  in Greece, 560
  and Rumania, 560–1
Vlad, Wallachian pretender, 563
Vladimir, Bulgarian ruler, 127, 502

Vladimir, prince of Kiev
  support for Basil II, 179, 516
  seizure of Cherson, 180, 516
  baptism and marriage, 180, 191, 516
  naval attack on Constantinople (1043), 203
Vladislav III, king of Poland and Hungary
  and relief of Belgrade, 770
  and crusade against Turks in Europe, 383, 770
  and treaty of Szegedin, 384 and n. 1, 554 n. 1, 771 and n. 1
  killed at battle of Varna (1444), 384, 771
Vladislav, son of Dragutin, 534, 543
Vladislav, son of Stephen Vukčić Kosača, 558
Vlatko, son of Stephen Vukčić Kosača, 558
Vodena (Edessa), town in Balkans, 178, 185, 317, 318, 319
voivode, Slav title, 383, 538, 545, 561, 562, 563 and n. 1, 564
Vojislav, *see* Stephen
Vojsil, brother of Smilec, Bulgarian pretender, 542
Volga, river, 111, 474–5, 492, 495, 503
  kingdom of Volga Bulgars, 484, 495
Volos, gulf of, in Thessaly, and trade with West, 291–2
Volos, town in Thessaly, 129
voluntaries, see *thelematarioi*
Vonitza, town in western Greece, taken by Walter II of Brienne, 416
Vostitza (Aegium), Latin barony on gulf of Corinth, 394, 405
Vṛamshapuh, king of Armenia, 598
Vuk, ban of Bosnia, 549
Vuk Branković, Serbian ruler, 550–1
Vuk Lazarević, brother of Stephen, 552
Vukan, eldest brother of Stephen the First Crowned of Serbia, struggle for throne, 248, 530
Vukašin, Serbian king in Macedonia, 371, 541, 542

Waldrada, wife of Peter IV Candiano of Venice, 265
al-Walīd I, Umayyad Caliph, policy in Armenia, 607
al-Walīd II, Umayyad Caliph
  and Constantine V's Arab campaigns, 73
  assassinated, 699
Wallachia, Rumanian principality, **560–5**
  expedition of Isaac II, 245

victories of John Hunyadi, 383, 553
  attacked by Bāyezīd I, 551, 563
  Great and Upper Wallachia, 560
  independent principality, 561
  metropolitan of, 561
  under Turkish control, 563–5, 769
  see also Mircea the Old
Walter I (V) of Brienne, duke of Athens, defeated and killed at battle of the Cephissus, 348, 411
Walter II (VI) of Brienne, 411, 415–16 and n. 2
Wāsiṭ, town in Mesopotamia on Tigris, 702
al-Wāthiq, Abbasid Caliph of Baghdad, 646, 712, 734
wax
  ground rents paid in, 414
  trade in, 159, 428
wazīr, *see* vizier
Welf VI, duke of Bavaria, revolt against Conrad III (1150), 228
wheat
  exported from Crete, 427
  exported from Greece, 428
  in Abbasid Empire, 643–4
  see also corn supplies
Wiching, German bishop in Moravia, 125
William I, king of Sicily
  and Manuel I, 229–30, 233, 234
  relations with Pope Hadrian IV, 229–30
  relations with Venice, 232
  death, 230
William II, king of Sicily
  proposals for marriage, 230–1, 239
  invasion of Greek territory, 247, 468
William of Champlitte, prince of Achaea, 292, 390, 391 and n. 2, 392, 393
William of Montferrat, claimant to kingdom of Thessalonica, 298, 306, 308, 391, 398
William de la Roche, brother of Guy I, 400
William de la Roche, duke of Athens, 410
William of Tyre, chronicler, on Manuel I, 238
William of Verona, triarch of Euboea, 400
William of Villehardouin, prince of Achaea
  birth, 393, 399
  marriages, 324, 400–1
  ally of Michael II of Epirus, 323–5, 399, 400–1
  taken prisoner after the battle of Pelagonia, 325, 401

William of Villehardouin (*cont.*)
rule in Peloponnese, **399–400, 401–3**
relations with Genoese, 318, 400
relations with Michael VIII, 332–3, 401
relations with Venice, 333
relations with the Papacy, 333, 402
relations with kingdom of Sicily, 334, 337, 402–3
relations with other Latin powers in Greece, 399–400
death, 337, 394, 403
William, duke of Athens, 412
Willibald, bishop of Eichstätt, visit to Monemvasia, 488 n. 4
wines, trade in, 159, 428, 615

Xač'ik, *see* Khach'ik
Xene, religious name of Irene, wife of John II Comnenus, 580
ξενῶνες, 154
Xenophon, quoted by Cyril of Alexandria, 53
Xeres, Basil, Manuel I's ambassador to Sicily, 227
Xiphias, general under Basil II
operations against Bulgaria, 186
revolt against Basil II, 189
Xiphilinus, *see* John VIII Xiphilinus, Patriarch
Xylinites, Nicetas, leader of revolt against Leo III, 64

Yaḥyā of Antioch, Arab chronicler
on John Tzimisces, 164, 175
on Basil the *parakoimomenos*, 174
on Basil II, 181
on conversion of Russia, 515–17
Yazdgard I, king of Persia, 598
Yazdgard II, king of Persia, and persecution of Christians in Armenia, 599–600
Yazīd II, Umayyad Caliph
and iconoclasm, 66
raids against Byzantium, 698
Yazman, amir of Tarsus, victory over Byzantines (882), 715
Yemen, district in south-west Arabia
and Ismā'īlīs, 648
and Shī'ism, 681
Yenisei, river in Siberia, 655
Yenishehir, *see* Melangeia
Yĭldĭrĭm, *see* Bāyezīd I
Yolanda, Empress, regent of Latin Empire, 305–6
death, 307

Yürüks, Turkish nomads in Asia Minor, 743
Yūsuf, Sājid amir in Azerbaijan, 613–14, 715

Zabel, *see* Isabel
Zaccaria, Genoese family, in Chios and Phocaea, 346, 354–5
Zaccaria, Benedetto, lord of Phocaea and Chios, 346
Zaccaria, Centurione II, prince of Achaea, 379, 408
Zachariads (Mkhargrdzeli), Caucasian dynasty, 615, 620, 624, 626 n. 2
Zacharias, Pope
relations with Constantine V, 75
relations with Lombards, 75, 444–5
Zacharias, *Katholikos* of Armenia, 612 n. 1
Zacharias I Mkhargrdzeli, High Constable under Queen Thamar of Georgia, 624
Zacharias, papal legate, and conflict between Ignatius and Photius, 109, 451
Zachlumia (Hum), Balkan principality, 139, 519, 520, 534, 540
Zacynthus (Zante), Ionian island
under Matthew Orsini, 297, 388
Latin See of, 396
Zadar, *see* Zara
aẓ-Ẓāhir, Fatimid Caliph, and Romanus III, 726
aẓ-Ẓāhir Baybars, *see* Baybars
Zangī, *see* Zengi
Zangids, Seljuq dynasty in Mesopotamia, 742
Zanj, negro slaves in southern Mesopotamia, 682, 714
Zante, *see* Zacynthus
Zapetra, *see* Sozopetra
Zara (Zadar), town in Dalmatia, 268, 549
captured for Venice by Fourth Crusade, 279, 280, 281
headquarters of *strategus* of theme of Dalmatia, 509
Zarzma, Georgian inscription at, 177
Zdeslav, Croatian prince, and Dalmatia, 501
Zealots, ecclesiastical party under the Palaeologi, 344
popular political party in Thessalonica, 358 and n. 1, 359, 360, 361, 362
Zebegény in Hungary, hermitages of, 577
Zeitounion, *see* Lamia
Zemarchus, Byzantine envoy to Silzibul, 479
Zemena (Gimenes), town near Corinth, Latin See of, 396

Zengi, ruler of Mosul, 223, 224, 225, 227, 654, 742
Zeno, Emperor
  Henoticon, 21, 56, 435, 604
  and Gothic troops, 27
  and Caucasia, 600–1
Zeno, Marino, Podestà of the Venetians in Constantinople, 293–4
Zeta, Serbian principality
  relations with Alexius I, 216
  relations with Stephen Nemanja, 233
  relations with Rome, 520
  in eleventh century, 519–20
  assimilated by Rascia, 521
  attacked by Michael I of Epirus, 531
  under Vukan, 530
  under Constantine, son of Milutin, 534
  independent of Serbia under Balšići, 541, 550, 552
  ceded to Stephen Lazarević, 552
  under Crnojevići, 554, 558–9
  captured by Turks, 559
  centre of culture, 559
  rulers of, *see* Stephen Vojislav, Michael, Constantine Bodin
  see also Dioclea
zeugarion, unit of land measurement, 343
Zia, *see* Ceos
Ziani, Pietro, doge of Venice
  control of Venetians in Constantinople, 294
  agreement with Michael I of Epirus, 299
Ziani, Sebastiano, doge of Venice, 273
Zibaṭra, *see* Sozopetra
Zichi, tribe on east coast of Black Sea, 474
Ziyādat Allāh, Aghlabid ruler in North Africa, 728
Ziyādat Allāh III, relations with Leo VI, 729

Zlatica (Izladî), town in Bulgaria
  defeat of pretender Šišman, 544
  check to John Hunyadi, 770
Zoe, Empress, daughter of Constantine VIII
  Psellus on, 193–4, 196, 198, 199
  proposed marriage to Otto III, 184, 187, 191
  husbands of, 194
  marriage to Romanus Argyrus, later Emperor, 195
  marriage to Michael the Paphlagonian, 196
  marriage to Constantine IX Monomachus, 199
  adoption of Michael IV's nephew and successor, 198
  exile to Principo, 198
  co-Empress with Theodora, 199, 201
  and crown of Hungary, 576
Zoe, second wife of Leo VI, 127 n. 2, 130
Zoe Carbonopsina (in religion Anna), fourth wife of Leo VI
  controversy over marriage, 131–2
  treatment by Alexander, 132, 134
  and Nicholas Mysticus, 135, 507
  personal rule, **135–7**, 137 n. 2, 507
  co-operation with West against Arabs, 136, 730
  help for Ashot II of Armenia, 136 and n. 2, 717
Zonaras, John, chronicler
  on Nicephorus II, 152
  on John Tzimisces' death, 172–3
  manuscript in Corvina library, 592
zoology and Arabs, 680
Zorconensis, *see* Oreos
Zoroastrianism, 595, 599, 600–2, 662
Zott, the, 712 and n. 2
Žrnov, town in Balkans, 555
Župan, Serbian title, 520–1, 538, 541